quicksi
icef

TOP EXPERIENCES MAP | NEXT PAGE

Lille, Flanders & the Somme p153

Around Paris p134

Normandy p191

Paris p42

Champagne p278

Alsace & Lorraine p301

Brittany p232

The Loire Valley p349

Burgundy p390

Atlantic Coast p594

Massif Central p521

French Alps & the Jura Mountains p461

Limousin, the Dordogne & the Lot p546

Lyon & the Rhône Valley p434

French Basque Country p632

Toulouse Area p681

Languedoc-Roussillon p704

Provence p752

The Pyrenees p659

The French Riviera & Monaco p817

Corsica p867

PAGE
953
SURVIVAL
GUIDE

YOUR AT-A-GLANCE REFERENCE
How to get around, get a room,
stay safe, say hello

Transport

GETTING THERE & AWAY

THIS EDITION WRITTEN AND RESEARCHED BY

Nicola Williams,

Alexis Averbuck, Oliver Berry, Stuart Butler, Jean-Bernard Carillet,
Kerry Christiani, Steve Fallon, Emilie Filou, Catherine Le Nevez, Tom Masters,
Daniel Robinson, Miles Roddis, John A Vlahides

France

Top Experiences >

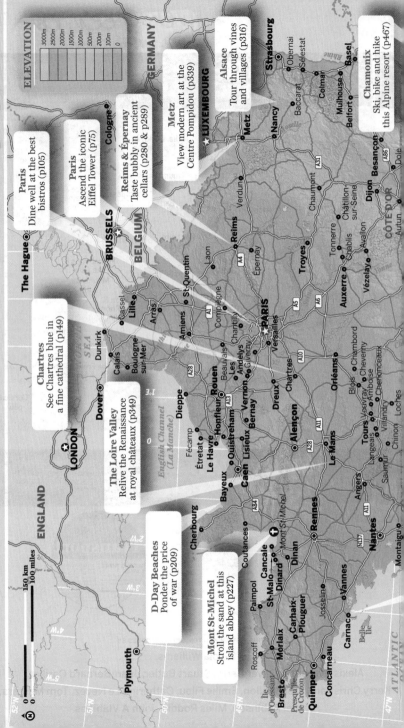

Paris
Dine well at the best bistros (p105)

Paris
Ascend the iconic Eiffel Tower (p75)

Reims & Épernay
Taste bubbly in ancient cellars (p280 & p289)

Metz
View modern art at the Centre Pompidou (p339)

Alsace
Tour through vines and villages (p316)

Chamonix
Ski, bike and hike this Alpine resort (p467)

Chartres
See Chartres blue in a fine cathedral (p149)

The Loire Valley
Relive the Renaissance at royal châteaux (p349)

D-Day Beaches
Ponder the price of war (p209)

Mont St-Michel
Stroll the sand at this island abbey (p227)

ELEVATION

3000m	
2500m	
2000m	
1500m	
1000m	
500m	
200m	
100m	
0	

0   150 km
0   100 miles

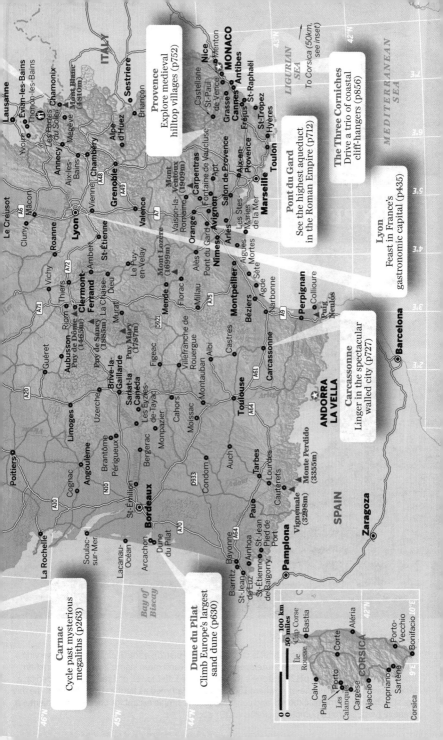

Carnac
Cycle past mysterious megaliths (p263)

Dune du Pilat
Climb Europe's largest sand dune (p630)

Provence
Explore medieval hilltop villages (p752)

Pont du Gard
See the highest aqueduct in the Roman Empire (p712)

The Three Corniches
Drive a trio of coastal cliff-hangers (p856)

Lyon
Feast in France's gastronomic capital (p435)

Carcassonne
Linger in the spectacular walled city (p727)

ITALY

Lausanne
Évian-les-Bains
Thonon-les-Bains
Yvoire
Mont Blanc (4810m)
Chamonix
Les Portes du Soleil
Megève
Sestriere
Briançon
Annecy
Aix-les-Bains
Chambéry
Alpe d'Huez
Grenoble
Vienne
A48
A49
Valence
A7
Le Creusot
A6
Mâcon
Cluny
Roanne
Vichy
A72
Lyon
St-Étienne
Le Puy-en-Velay
Ambert
La Chaise-Dieu
Thiers
Clermont-Ferrand
Riom
A71
Aubusson
Puy de Dôme (1465m)
Puy de Sancy (1885m)
Murat
Puy Mary (1787m)
Mont Lozère (1699m)
Mende
Florac
Millau
A75
Alès
Pont du Gard
Nîmes
Orange
Carpentras
Mont Ventoux (1909m)
Vaison-la-Romaine
Fontaine de Vaucluse
Apt
Avignon
Salon de Provence
Aix-en-Provence
Arles
Les Stes Maries de la Mer
Aigues Mortes
Sète
Agde
Béziers
Narbonne
A9
Montpellier
Castres
Villefranche de Rouergue
Figeac
Albi
Montauban
Cahors
Moissac
Toulouse
A61
Carcassonne
A64
A62
Auch
Condom
D933
Tarbes
Lourdes
Cauterets
Vignemale (3298m)
Monte Perdido (3355m)
ANDORRA LA VELLA
Puig Neulós
Perpignan
Collioure

Castellane
Grasse
St-Paul de Vence
Nice
Menton
MONACO
Antibes
Cannes
St-Raphaël
Fréjus
St-Tropez
Hyères
Toulon
Marseille

LIGURIAN SEA

To Corsica (50km, see inset)

MEDITERRANEAN SEA

43°N
42°N

Poitiers
La Rochelle
Soulac-sur-Mer
Lacanau-Océan
Arcachon
Dune du Pilat
Bordeaux
St-Émilion
Cognac
Angoulême
Guéret
Limoges
Uzerche
Brantôme
Périgueux
Bergerac
Brive-la-Gaillarde
Sarlat-la-Canéda
Les Eyzies-de-Tayac
Monpazier
Villeneuve-sur-Lot
A20
A10
A89
Ainhoa
Biarritz
Bayonne
St-Jean-de-Luz
St-Étienne-de-Baïgorry
St-Jean-Pied-de-Port
Pau
A64
Pamplona
Zaragoza

SPAIN

Bay of Biscay

46°N
45°N
44°N

Barcelona

Corsica

Île Rousse
Calvi
Piana
Porto
Les Calanques
Cargèse
Ajaccio
Propriano
Sartène
Bonifacio
Porto-Vecchio
Corte
Aléria
Bastia
Cap Corse

CORSICA

42°N
9°E
10°E

0   100 km
0   50 miles

Bistro Dining, Paris

1 The latest buzzword in the capital is *néo-bistro* (new bistro), a small, casual address serving outstanding cuisine under the tutelage of a talented (and often 'name') chef. Take Christian Constant's Les Cocottes (p112), a stone's throw from the Eiffel Tower, or Jadis (p111), hidden on a little-known street in middle-of-nowhere 15e. Tables are jammed as tight as ever, dishes of the day are still chalked on the blackboard, and cuisine is just as simple except for one new ingredient – a creative twist. Bistro Le Comptoir du Relais (p110), above

Eiffel Tower

2 Seven million people visit it annually but few disagree each visit is unique. From an evening ascent amid twinkling lights to lunch at 58 Tour Eiffel (p112) in the company of a staggering city panorama, there are 101 ways to 'do' it. Pedal beneath it, skip the lift and hike up, buy a crêpe from a stand here or a key ring from the street, snap yourself in front of it, visit it at night or – our favourite – on the odd special occasion when all 324m of the tower glows a different colour.

Mont St-Michel

3 The dramatic play of tides on this abbey-island in Normandy is magical and mysterious. Said by Celtic mythology to be a sea tomb to which souls of the dead were sent, Mont St-Michel (p227) is rich in legend and history, keenly felt as you make your way barefoot across rippled sand to the stunning architectural ensemble. Walk around it alone or, better still, hook up with a guide in nearby Genêts for a dramatic day hike across the bay.

Champagne

4 Name-brand Champagne houses like Mumm, Mercier and Moët & Chandon in the main towns of Reims and Épernay, are known the world over. But – our tip – much of Champagne's best liquid gold is made by almost 5000 small-scale *vignerons* (winegrowers) in 320-odd villages. Dozens of *maisons* (Champagne houses) welcome visitors for a taste, tipple and shopping at producer prices, rendering the region's scenic driving routes (p286) the best way to taste fine bubbly amid rolling vineyards and drop-dead-gorgeous villages. Our favourite: tasting in Le Mesnil-sur-Oger and lunch at Le Mesnil (p289).

Loire Valley Châteaux

5 If it's aristocratic pomp and architectural splendour you're after, this regal valley is the place to linger. Flowing for over 1000km into the Atlantic Ocean, the Loire is one of France's last *fleuves sauvages* (wild rivers) and its banks are a 1000-year snapshot of French high society. The valley is riddled with beautiful châteaux sporting glittering turrets and ballrooms, lavish cupolas and chapels. If you're a hopeless romantic seeking the perfect fairy-tale castle, head for moat-ringed Azay-le-Rideau (p376), Villandry and its gardens (left; p374), and less-visited Beauregard (p364).

Adrenalin Kick, Chamonix

6 Sure, 007 did it, but so can you: the Vallée Blanche (p469) is a once-in-a-lifetime experience. You won't regret the €70-odd it costs to do the more than 20km off-piste descent from the spike of the Aiguille du Midi to mountaineering mecca Chamonix – every minute of the five hours it takes to get down will pump more adrenalin in your body than anything else you've ever done. Craving more? Hurl yourself down Europe's longest black run, La Sarenne, at Alpe d'Huez (p504).

Ste-Chapelle & Chartres

7 This is a top experience reserved strictly for sunny days and those who like looking at the world through rose-coloured glass. Be stunned and inspired by the sublime stained glass in Paris' Ste-Chapelle (p65), one of Christendom's most beautiful places of worship. Then head out of town to Chartres, where you can't get bluer blue than the awesome stained-glass windows of Cathédrale Notre Dame de Chartres (below; p149). Leave with the true blue of so-called 'Chartres blue' firmly imprinted in your mind.

Dune du Pilat

8 The Dune du Pilat (p630) is a 'mountain' that just has to be climbed. Not only is the coastal panorama from the top of Europe's largest sand dune a stunner – it takes in the Banc d'Arguin bird reserve and Cap Ferret across the bay – but the nearby beaches have some of the Atlantic Coast's best surf. Cycle here from Arcachon and top off the heady trip with a dozen oysters, shucked before your very eyes and accompanied by *crepinettes* (local sausages).

DAVID TOMLINSON

The Three Corniches, Nice

9 It is impossible to drive this dramatic trio of coastal roads (p856), each one higher and more hairpin bend–riddled than the next, without conjuring up cinematic images of Grace Kelly, Hitchcock, the glitz of Monaco high life, and scandalous royals – all to the standing ovation of big view after big view of sweeping blue sea fringing Europe's most mythical coastline. To make a perfect day out of it, before leaving Nice, shop for a picnic at the morning market on Cours Saleya (p821).

Carcassonne at Dusk

GLENN BEANLAND

10 That first glimpse of La Cité's sturdy, stone, witch's-hat turrets above Carcassonne (p727) in the Languedoc is enough to make your hair stand on end. To properly savour this fairy-tale walled city, linger at dusk after the crowds have left, when the old town belongs to its 100 or so inhabitants and the few visitors staying at the handful of lovely hotels within its ramparts. Don't forget to look back when you leave to view the old city, beautifully illuminated, glowing in the warm night.

D-Day Beaches

DENNIS JOHNSON

11 This is one of France's most emotional journeys. The broad stretches of fine sand and breeze-blown bluffs are quiet now, but early on 6 June 1944 the beaches of northern Normandy (p209) were a cacophony of gunfire and explosions, the bodies of Allied soldiers lying in the sand as their comrades-in-arms charged inland. Just up the hill from Omaha Beach, the long rows of symmetrical gravestones at the Normandy American Cemetery & Memorial bear solemn, silent testimony to the horrible price paid for France's liberation from Nazi tyranny.

Gun bunker, Omaha Beach, left

Pont du Gard

12 This Unesco World Heritage Site (p712) near Nîmes in southern France is gargantuan: 35 arches straddle the Roman aqueduct's 275m-long upper tier, containing a watercourse that was designed to carry 20,000 cu metres of water per day. View it from afloat a canoe on the River Gard or pay extra to jig across its top tier. Oh, and don't forget your swimming gear for a spot of post-Pont, daredevil dives and high jumps from the rocks nearby – a plunge that will entice the most reluctant of young historians.

GLENN BEANLAND

Provençal Markets

13 No region is more of a market-must than this one. Be it fresh fish by the port in seafaring Marseille, early summer's strings of pink garlic, melons from Cavaillon all summer long or wintertime's earthy 'black diamond' truffles, Provence thrives on a bounty of fresh produce – grown locally and piled high each morning at the market. Every town and village has one, but those in Carpentras and Aix-en-Provence (left) are the best known. While you're here, stock up on dried herbs, green and black olives marinated a dozen different ways, courgette flowers and oils.

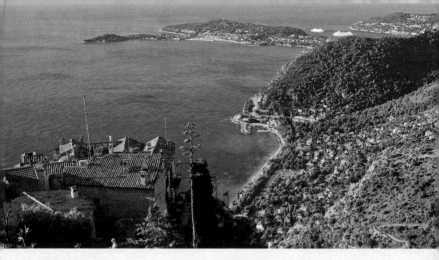

Hilltop Villages

14 Impossibly perched on a rocky peak above the Mediterranean, gloriously lost in back country, fortified or château-topped... southern France's portfolio of *villages perchés* is vast, impressive and calls for go-slow touring – on foot, by bicycle or car. Most villages are medieval, built from gold stone and riddled with cobbled lanes, flower-filled alleys and hidden squares silent but for the glug of a fountain. Combine a village visit with lunch alfresco – La Table de Ventabren (p776) and Les Deux Frères (p857) are two dreamy addresses – and you'll never want to leave.

View from Èze hilltop village, above

Lyonnais Bouchons

15 The red-and-white checked tablecloths, closely packed tables and decades-old bistro decor could be anywhere in France. It's the local cuisine that makes *bouchons* in Lyon (p448) unique, plus the quaint culinary customs, like totting up the bill on the paper tablecloth, or serving wine in a glass bottle wrapped with an elastic band to stop drips, or the 'shut weekends' opening hours. Various piggy parts drive Lyonnais cuisine but, have faith, this French city is said to be the gastronomic capital of France. Dine and decide. Chez Paul *bouchon*, above

Centre Pompidou-Metz

16 Bright white by day, all aglow after dark, this new star of the northern France art scene is on the tip of everyone's tongue. A provincial cousin to the well-known Centre Pompidou in Paris, this modern art museum (p339) was designed by a world-class, Japanese–French duo of architects and is as much architectural gem as exhibition powerhouse, easily on a par with Bilbao's Guggenheim and London's Tate. Part of the experience is a designer lunch, aka edible art on a plate, at the museum's La Voile Blanche (p343).

Carnac Megaliths

17 Pedalling past open fields dotted with the world's greatest concentration of mysterious megaliths gives a poignant reminder of Brittany's ancient human inhabitation. No one knows for sure what inspired these gigantic menhirs, dolmens, cromlechs, tumuli and cairns to be built – a sun god? Some phallic fertility cult? You decide. To top off the Breton experience, stop for crêpes and cider at Crêperie au Pressoir (p265), a traditional long house in Carnac set amid a circle of menhirs.

Alsatian Wine Route

18 It is one of France's most popular drives – and for good reason. Motoring in this far northeast corner of France takes you through a kaleidoscope of lush green vines, perched castles and gentle mist-covered mountains. The only pit stops en route are half-timbered villages and roadside wine cellars, where fruity Alsace vintages can be swirled, tasted and bought. To be truly wooed, drive the Route des Vins d'Alsace (p316) in autumn, when vines are heavy with grapes waiting to be harvested and colours are at their vibrant best.

welcome to France

... a country that seduces travellers with its unfalteringly familiar culture woven around café terraces, village-square markets and lace-curtained bistros with their plat du jour (dish of the day) chalked on the board

Cultural Savoir-Faire

France is all about world-class art and architecture, Roman temples and Renaissance châteaux, iconic landmarks known the world over, and rising stars few yet know. Stroll the lily-clad gardens Monet painted and savour *un café* at the Parisian café where Sartre and Simone de Beauvoir met to philosophise. See glorious pasts blaze forth and imagine the life of a French king at bourgeois Versailles. View tomorrow's art starts in squats secreted in abandoned 19th-century Haussmann mansions in Paris, or at new headline-grabbing museums up north. Drink cocktails in a shabby-chic Nantes warehouse. Listen to Marseille rap and Parisian jazz. Sense the subtle infusion of language, music and mythology in Brittany, brought by 5th-century Celtic invaders. Yes, French culture offers never-ending possibilities to fill any stay in France.

Gastronomic Art de Vivre

Or perhaps it is the French feast of fine food and wine that woos so many travellers. (This is, after all, the country that entices more than any other: more than 80 million visitors a year, ranking it the world's top tourist destination. But know that gastronomic France goes far deeper than Parisian bistro dining, long lunches outside, shopping for fruit and veg at the market and wolfing down croissants hot from the *boulangerie* (bakery) for breakfast. Learn how to make petits fours with the kids in Paris or flip crêpes in Brittany; taste wine with one of the world's top sommeliers in Bordeaux; visit an Atlantic Coast oyster farm; drink Champagne in ancient cellars in Reims; tour a Provençal melon farm; harvest olives, peaches and cherries in the hot south... and understand that food is as much an *art de vivre* (art of living) for the French as an essential to survive.

Lyrical Landscape

Then there is the *terroir* (land) and the startlingly varied journey it weaves from northern France's cliffs and sand dunes to the bright-blue sea of the French Riviera and Corsica's green oak forests. Outdoor action is what this lyrical landscape calls for, be it fast-paced and pulse-racing, slow and relaxed, solo or *en famille*. Walk barefoot across wave-rippled sand to Mont St-Michel; ride the cable car to mind-blowing glacial panoramas above mountaineering mecca Chamonix; cartwheel down Europe's highest sand dune; surf in Biarritz; ski the Alps; hike from one extinct volcano to another in the Massif Central; float between locks or pedal the towpath along the Canal du Midi. The action is endless and the next adventure just begging to be had.

need to know

Currency
» Euro (€)

Language
» French

When to Go

Brittany & Normandy •
GO Apr–Sep

Paris
• GO May & Jun

• French Alps
GO late Dec–early Apr (skiing)
or Jun & Jul (hiking)

French Riviera •
GO Apr–Jun, Sep & Oct

Corsica •
GO Apr–Jun, Sep & Oct

Warm to hot summers, mild winters
Warm to hot summers, cold winters
Mild year-round
Mild summers, cold winters
Polar climate

High Season
(Jul & Aug)

» Queues at big sights and on the road, especially August

» Christmas, New Year and Easter equally busy

» Late December to March is high season in French Alpine ski resorts

Shoulder
(Apr–Jun & Sep)

» Accommodation rates drop in southern France and other hot spots

» Spring: warm weather, flowers, local produce

» The *vendange* (grape harvest) is reason to visit in Autumn

Low Season
(Oct-Mar)

» Prices up to 50% less than high season

» Sights, attractions and restaurants open fewer days and shorter hours

Your Daily Budget

Budget up to
€100

» Dorm bed: €15–€40

» Double room in a budget hotel: €50–€70

» Free admission to many attractions first Sunday of month

» Set lunches: €10–€15

Midrange
€100-€200

» Double room in a midrange hotel: €70–€175

» Lunch *menus* (set meals) in gourmet restaurants: €20–€40

Top end over
€200

» Double room in a top-end hotel: €70–€175

» Lower weekend rates in business hotels

» Top restaurant dinner: *menu* €50, à la carte €100–€150

Money

» ATMs at every airport, most train stations and every second street corner in towns and cities. Visa, MasterCard and Amex widely accepted.

Visas

» Generally not required for stays of up to 90 days (or at all for EU nationals); some nationalities need a Schengen visa (p969).

Mobile Phones

» European and Australian phones work. Slip in a French SIM card to call with a cheaper French number.

Driving

» Drive on the right; steering wheel is on the left side of the car. Be aware of the potentially hazardous 'priority to the right' rule (p979).

Websites

» **France Guide** (www. franceguide.com) French government tourist office website

» **French Word-a-Day** (http://french-word-a-day.typepad.com) Fun language learning

» **Lonely Planet** (www.lonelyplanet.com/france) Destination information, hotel bookings, traveller forum and more

» **Voyages SNCF** (www.voyages-sncf.com) French railways

» **France.fr** (www.france.fr) The definitive portal on France

Exchange Rates

Australia	A$1	€0.71
Canada	C$1	€0.72
Japan	¥100	€0.88
NZ	NZ$1	€0.55
UK	UK£1	€1.17
US	US$1	€0.75

For current exchange rates see www.xe.com

Important Numbers

France country code	☏33
International access code	☏00
Europe-wide emergency	☏112
Ambulance (SAMU)	☏15
Police	☏17

Arriving in France

» **Aéroport Roissy Charles de Gaulle** (p130)

Trains, buses and RER – to Paris centre every 15 to 30 minutes, 5.30am to midnight. Night bus – hourly, 12.30am to 5.30am. Taxis – €45–€60; 30 minutes to Paris centre.

» **Aéroport d'Orly** (p130)

Buses and Orlyval rail – at least every 15 minutes, 6am to 11.30pm. Night bus – hourly, 12.30am to 5.30am. Taxis – €35–€50; 25 minutes to Paris centre.

In France to Shop!

OK, so Paris is the bees knees for luxury goods like haute-couture, high-quality fashion accessories (a Hermès silk scarf, Madame?), lingerie, perfume and cosmetics. Lovely as they are, they most probably aren't any cheaper to buy in France than at home.

Time your trip right and pick up designer and street fashion for a snip of the usual price at France's sales *(soldes),* by law held twice a year for three weeks in January and again in July. Other times look for the words *degriffés* (name-brand products with the labels cut out), *bonnes affaires* (cut-price deals) and *dépôt-vente* (secondhand). Find fab factory-outlet shops in Troyes (p298) and Calais (p167).

what's new

For this new edition of France, our authors have hunted down the fresh, the revamped, the transformed, the hot and the happening. Here are a few of our favourites. For up-to-the-minute reviews and recommendations, see lonelyplanet.com/france.

Supper Clubs

1 The trend of dining *à la maison* (at home) has swept Paris gourmets and socialites off their feet – the crème de la crème take you out to dinner at the latest 'in' addresses (p42).

Canal St-Martin, Paris

2 The shaded towpaths of this tranquil canal in Paris' eastern suburbs have undergone a real urban renaissance – enter one of the capital's hippest areas to drink, dine, stroll and picnic (p88 and p115)

Jadis, L'Agrume & Derrière, Paris

3 This hot trio is among a flurry of top-drawer, casually understated dining spaces to recently woo the capital. Even big-name chefs like Christian Constant and William Ledeuil are at it (p105).

Centre Pompidou-Metz

4 The space-age curves of Metz' gleaming white modern-art museum, sudden architectural star of the provincial north, is as much a show-stopper as its Parisian big brother (p339).

L'Aventure Michelin, Clermont-Ferrand

5 Now this is apt: the French tyre company that does so much more than rings of rubber finally tells its tale at this museum – travel has always been a big theme (p524).

Rue Le Bec, Lyon

6 Lyon's most creative chef proves he's still on top with his latest ground-breaking venture – a wholly affordable, market-style dining space on the Confluence aka rejuvenated industrial wasteland (p447).

Brive-Vallée de la Dordogne Airport

7 Our authors have all bases covered, including France's latest regional airport to open with budget flights between the Dordogne, Paris and London (p560).

Jean Nouvel in Sarlat-la-Canéda

8 Architect of Paris' Arab World Institute and Musée du Quai Branly is at it again, this time with a panoramic lift inside a village-church-turned-market in the Dordogne (p569).

Gorge Floating

9 Squeeze into a wetsuit, strap a buoyancy bag to your back and float between rocks on green water – this is *the* new big thrill of Provence's Gorges du Verdon (p814).

French Riviera Glamour

10 Hôtel Ermitage is the latest hip hotel to swing onto the scene in St-Tropez. It's hot, it's edgy, it's a 1950s-design must-stay that the celebs love (p850).

Mesdames Messieurs, Montpellier

11 Natural and organic wines are increasingly popular in France, as are Languedoc's sun-blessed vintages. Taste both at this brand new wine bar in the south's snappiest student city (p720).

Cité Internationale de la Dentelle et de la Mode, Calais

12 Victorian-era machinery clatters and clanks in Calais to turn thread into lace at this port city's newest museum – lace is what made Calais a big name in textiles (p165).

if you like...

Fabulous Food

Gourmet appetites know no bounds in France, paradise for food lovers with its varied cuisine, markets and local gusto for dining well. Go to Burgundy for hearty wine-based cooking, Brittany and the Atlantic Coast for seafood and Basque Country for a slice of Spanish spice.

Parisian bistros Capital dining embraces everything from checked-tablecloth tradition to contemporary minimalism (p105)

Lyon Eating local in France's gastronomic heart means piggy cuisine in a *bouchon* (p448)

Truffles Go to Provence (p753) and the Dordogne (p568) to try this earthy, ink-black delicacy

Oyster farms Sink oysters fresh from their beds around Arcachon (p628) and Bordeaux (p621) or Breton oyster capital Cancale (p242)

Basque tapas Proof of just how wildly varied French cuisine is – taste it in Bayonne (p640) or on the seashore (p648)

Bouillabaisse Marseille's mighty meal of fish stew (p767)

Munster Tasting, dairy tours and farmstays around this pungent, creamy cheese (p329)

Gorgeous Villages

There is no simpler French pleasure than meandering around quaint villages of gold stone, pink granite, or whitewashed Basque-style. Cobbled lanes twist and turn to sculpted fountains, hidden squares and shuttered houses strung with purple wisteria, vines or drying peppers.

Pérouges Day trip it from Lyon for cider and sugar-crusted *galettes* between yellow-gold medieval stone (p456)

St-Émilion A medieval village perched dramatically above a sea of vines in Bordeaux (p624)

St-Jean Pied de Port An ancient pilgrim outpost en route to Santiago de Compostela, Spain (p655)

Yvoire Château-clad on the southern shore of Lake Geneva, this flowery Savoy village is a privileged address (p480)

The Luberon This part of Provence is lavishly strewn with drop-dead gorgeous hilltop villages (p805)

Èze Fuses a stunning hilltop village with a sweeping Riviera panorama – wow! (p857)

The Dordogne Beautiful *bastides* (fortified towns) at every turn (p563)

Wine Tasting

Be it by tasting in cellars, watching grape harvests or sleeping *au château,* France's wine culture requires immediate road-testing.

Bistrot du Sommelier Food and wine are matched by one of the world's foremost sommeliers at this Parisian bistro (p113)

Bordeaux The Medoc, St-Émilion and Cognac set connoisseurs' hearts a-flutter in this wine-rich region (p619)

Burgundy Sample renowned vintages in Beaune (p404) and the Côte d'Or (p401)

Châteauneuf-du-Pape Vines planted by 14th-century popes yield southern France's most illustrious red (p796)

Alsace wine route Driving trails in northern France (p316)

Vin Jaune Something different: liquid gold in the Jura (p515 and p514)

Bandol and Cassis Wine tasting in these two Riviera villages is as much about the majestic Med setting as the wonderful wine (p855 and p771)

Musée de la Vigne et du Vin Champagne-making traditions are the focus of this essential-stop museum (and great lunch address) in Le Mesnil-sur-Oger (p289)

» Bread for sale at a marketplace in Ajaccio, Corsica

VERONICA GARBUTT

Castles

The Loire Valley is the first stop for anyone with a penchant for French châteaux dripping in period gold leaf. But venture elsewhere and you'll be surprised what other delights lie behind lumbering stone walls.

Versailles It has to be done: the country's largest, grandest château and palace, a stone's throw from Paris (p145)

Chambord A treasure of a Renaissance country-getaway castle, where French kings and queens played, hunted and had a ball (p361)

Azay-le-Rideau Conjure up a classic French château with moat, turrets and sweeping staircase and voila, it's Azay (p376)

Villandry The formal French gardens framing this Renaissance Loire Valley château are glorious (p374)

Château des Ducs de Bretagne Enter Nantes and one of the finest collections of French paintings outside Paris (p597)

Château Grimaldi Bijou 12th-century sea-facing castle-turned-studio and former home of artist Picasso (p835)

Cathar Fortresses Now ruined, these dramatic hilltop castles sizzling in the heat evoke 13th-century persecution (p748)

Coastal Paths

From pearly white cliff to fiery red rock, tiny pebble-strewn fishing cove to seemingly endless paradise sand, France's coastline has it all. Get up close with one of France's many *sentiers du littoral* (coastal footpaths) – often times windswept, other times scented with salty air and wild herbal scrub.

St-Tropez This *sentier du littoral* leads from mythical fishing cove to celebrity-laced sands (p855)

Bandol Stride the coast between inland vines and waterfront rock formations (p855)

Chemin de Nietzsche Spectacular and steep rocky footpath near Nice, place of reflection for the German philosopher to whom it pays homage (p857)

Corsica Hike from Italianate Bonifacio to a lighthouse (p889), or past Genoese watchtowers along Cap Corse's rugged Customs Officers' Trail (p874)

GR21 Trace the Norman coast to Le Havre (p200), or see opal blues along northern France's **GR120** (p168)

Belle Île and Île d'Ouessant A Breton island twinset with coastal walking trails (p267 and p254)

Markets

Art nouveau hangar, stall-packed street, plane-tree-shaded village square... French markets spill across an enticing mix of public spaces. Every town, village and hamlet has one – usually mornings and at least once or twice a week. Take your own bag or basket.

Lyonnais markets Les Halles and Croix Rousse are Lyon's two buxom market divas, endowed with stalls selling fruit, veg, meat, charcuterie and runny St Marcellin cheese (p450)

Place des Lices No town square is as celebrity-famous or jam-packed with Provençal market stalls as St-Tropez's (p850)

Marché des Capucins Enjoy oysters and white wine at this Saturday-morning market in Bordeaux (p622)

Marché Couvert Once a bishop's palace, now a temple to fresh local produce in Metz (p343)

Uzès Languedoc's most splendid farmers market fills colonnaded, cobbled place aux Herbes (p713)

If you like... dramatic driving, the trio of hairpin-laced corniches (coastal roads) near Nice are sure to thrill (p856)

Islands & Beaches

The country's 3200km-long coastline morphs from white chalk cliffs (Normandy) to treacherous promontories (Brittany) to broad expanses of fine sand (Atlantic Coast) and pebbly or sandy beaches (Mediterranean Coast).

Île de Porquerolles and Île de Port Cros France's only marine national park and a pedestrian paradise fringed with near-tropical beaches (p853)

Plage de Pampelonne Stars love this hip beach in St-Tropez, darling, and for good reason – it's glam and golden (p861)

Île de Ré This Paris-chic favourite is criss-crossed with cycling trails (p613)

Belle Île Its name means 'Beautiful Island' and that is just what this island off the coast of Brittany is (p267)

Corsica Plage de Palombaggia and Plage de Santa Giulia near Porto Vecchio are to die for (p891)

Les Landes Find this surfer's secret, backed by dunes, on the Atlantic Coast (p644)

Côte d'Opale Ramble along rousing, wind-buffeted beaches across from the white cliffs of Dover (p168)

Incredible Train Journeys

There is nothing quite like watching France's kaleidoscope of soaring mountains, rolling valleys, wild gorges and meandering rivers jog past from aboard an old-fashioned steam train or mountain railway.

Tramway du Mont Blanc Travel in the shade of Europe's biggest mountain by hopping aboard France's highest train, in Megève (p477)

Chemin de Fer de la Mure Spot marmots between tunnels and viaducts in France's largest national park (p502)

The Trembler Few coastal train journeys are as fabulous as Corsica's Tramway de la Balagne (p879)

The Canary Take in mind-blowing Pyrenean scenery from aboard a mountain train in Roussillon (p749)

Pine Cone Train Provençal hilltop villages peep down at passengers aboard this narrow-gauge railway from Nice (p826)

Chemin de Fer du Touristique du Haut-Quercy See the Lot by steam train (p593)

La Vapeur du Trieux Journey riverside from Breton harbour to an artists' village (p246)

Great Outdoors

With six wildlife-rich national parks and many more protected areas, the French landscape begs outdoor action. Mountainous areas like the Alps and Pyrenees offer a gamut of activities, but countrywide there's plenty more to choose from. *Allez!*

White-water sports Favourite gorges to ride wild waters: Gorges de l'Ardèche (p459), Gorges de l'Allier (p544) and Gorges du Verdon (p813)

Corsica Bonifacio diving, Porto hiking, boat trips everywhere – this island is one big outdoor fest (p867)

The Stevenson trail Hike with or without a donkey through Languedoc's hot, wild Cévennes (p735)

Gliding Float above the most staggering landscapes in the Auvergne (extinct volcanoes; p531), Chamonix (French Alps; p471), Brittany (p255) and Massif des Vosges (p329)

Vallée Blanche Chamonix's world-class, off-piste ski trail (p469)

Mountain biking Knuckle-whitening descents in Morzine (p478), Alpe d'Huez (p504) and Cauterets (p674) keep bikers on their toes

month by month

January

With New Year festivities done and dusted, it's time to play snow bunnies in the Alps. Crowds on the slopes thin out once school's back, but this is still a busy month. On the Mediterranean, mild winters cast a wonderful serenity over a part of France that's mad busy the rest of the year.

Vive le Ski!

Grab your skis or board and hit the slopes. Resorts in the Alps, Pyrenees and Jura open mid- to late December, but January is the start of the French ski season in earnest. Whether a vast purpose-built station or a lost Alpine village, France has a resort to match every mood and moment. Pick from our pick of the *pistes* on p466.

Hunting Black Diamonds

No culinary product is more aromatic or decadent than black truffles. Snout them out in the Dordogne (southeastern France; see p568) and Provence (southwestern France; see p753) – the truffle-hunting season runs late December to March but January is the prime month.

February

Crisp cold weather in the mountains – lots of china-blue skies now – translates as the ski season in top gear. Alpine resorts get mobbed by families during the February school holidays and accommodation is at its priciest; don't turn up without a reservation.

Nice Carnival

While northern France shivers, Nice makes the most of its mild Mediterranean climate with this crazy street carnival (www.nicecarnaval.com), France's largest. As well as the usual parade and costume shenanigans, merrymakers pelt each other with blooms during Carnaval de Nice's legendary flower battles.

Citrus Celebrations

No surprise that Menton on the French Riviera was once Europe's biggest lemon producer, given its exotic Fête du Citron (p858). These days it ships in a zillion and one lemons from Spain to sculpt into gargantuan carnival characters.

March

The tail end of the ski season stays busy thanks to ongoing school holidays (until mid-March) and temperatures that no longer turn lips purple. Down south, the first buds of spring herald the start of the bullfighting season and, depending on the year, *Pâques* (Easter).

Féria Pascale

No fest sets passions in France's hot south blazing more than this, held each Easter in Arles to open the bullfighting season (www.feriaarles.com, in French). Four days of street dancing, music, concerts al fresco and bullfighting is what this exuberant event is all about. Not all bulls die (see p782).

April

Dedicated ski fiends can carve glaciers in the highest French ski

resorts until mid-April. Otherwise, it's off with the ski boots, and on with the hiking gear as peach and almond trees flower pink against a backdrop of snow-capped peaks.

★ Counting Sheep

During the centuries-old Fête de la Transhumance in late April or May, shepherds across France walk their flocks of sheep up to lush green summer pastures; St-Rémy de Provence's fest is among the best known. Or head to villages in the Pyrenees (p670) and Massif Central (p536) to see this transit.

May

As the first melons ripen in Provence and outdoor markets burst forth with new-found colour, there is no lovelier month to travel. Spring is in.

★ May Day

No one works on 1 May, a national holiday that incites a real summer buzz with its *muguets* (lilies of the valley) sold at roadside stalls and given to friends as good-luck charms. In Arles, Camargue cowboys show off their bull-herding and equestrian skills at the Fête des Gardians (p782).

★ Pèlerinage des Gitans

Roma from all over Europe flock to the Camargue on 24 and 25 May and again in October (nearest Sunday to 22 October) for a flamboyant fiesta of street music, dancing and dipping their toes in the sea (p786; www. gitans.fr, in French).

★ Starring at Cannes

In mid-May film stars and celebrities walk the red carpet at Cannes, the biggest of Europe's cinema extravaganzas (p839; www. festival-cannes.com).

★ Monaco Grand Prix

How fitting that the most glamorous race of the Formula One season rips around the streets of one of the world's most glam countries (p861; www.formula1monaco.com).

June

With the onset of midsummer, France's festival pace quickens alongside a rising temperature gauge, which tempts the first bathers into the sea. Looking north, nesting white storks shower bags of good luck on farmsteads in Alsace.

★ Fête de la Musique

Orchestras, crooners, buskers and bands fill streets and squares with music during France's vibrant nationwide celebration of music on 21 June (www. fetedelamusique.culture. fr, in French). Free and fab concerts are particularly abundant in Paris, Lyon, Marseille and other big towns and cities.

July

If lavender's your French love, this is the month to catch it in flower in Provence. But you won't be the only one. School's out for the summer, showering the country with teems of tourists, traffic and too many *complet* (full) signs strung in hotel windows.

★ Tour de France

The world's most prestigious cycling race ends on av des Champs-Élysées in Paris on the third or fourth Sunday of July, but you can catch it for two weeks before all over France – the route changes each year but the French Alps are a hot spot (www.letour.fr).

★ Bastille Day

You can join the French in celebrating the storming of the Bastille, 14 July 1789, anywhere really – countrywide there are firework displays, balls, processions, parades and lots of hoo-ha all round.

★ Festival d'Avignon

Rouse your inner thespian with Avignon's legendary performing-arts festivals (p791; www.festival-avignon.com). Street acts in its fringe fest are as inspired as those on official stages.

★ Nice Jazz Festival

Jive between Roman ruins to jazz cats at this soulful music fest in Nice (www. nicejazzfest.fr).

August

It's that mad summer month when the French join everyone else on holiday. Paris, Lyon and other big cities empty; traffic jams at motorway toll booths test the patience of a saint; and temperatures soar. Avoid. Or don your party hat and join the mad crowd!

Proud to be Breton

The Fêtes d'Arvor is a passionate celebration of Breton culture. Think street parades, concerts and dozens of authentic *festoù-noz* (night festivals) spilling across the half-timbered, cobbled Vannes (p269; www.fetes-arvor.org, in French).

Celts Unite!

Celtic culture is the focus of the Festival Interceltique de Lorient (p265; www.festival-interceltique.com), when hundreds of thousands of Celts from Brittany and abroad flock to Lorient to celebrate just that.

September

As sun-plump grapes hang heavy on darkened vines and that August madness drops off as abruptly as it began, a welcome tranquillity falls across autumnal France. This is the start of France's *vendange* (grape harvest).

The Rutting Season

Nothing beats getting up at dawn to watch mating stags, boar and red deer at play. Observatory towers are hidden in woods around Château de Chambord (p361) but when a valley like the Loire is so choc-a-bloc with Renaissance hunting pads, who cares which one?

Braderie de Lille

The mountains of empty mussel shells engulfing the streets after three days of mussel-munching have to be seen to be believed. Then there's the real reason for visiting Lille the first weekend in September – its huge flea market (p159) is Europe's largest.

November

It's nippy now, especially in northern France, where winter is well under way. *Toussaint* (All Saints' Day) on 1 November ushers in the switch to shorter, winter opening hours for many sights and monuments. Lots of restaurants close two nights a week now, making dining out on Monday a real challenge in some towns.

Beaujolais Nouveau

At precisely the stroke of midnight on the third Thursday in November the first bottles of cherry-red Beaujolais *nouveau* wine are cracked open – and what a party it can be in Beaujolais, Lyon and other places nearby!

December

Days are short and it is cold everywhere bar the south of France. But there are Christmas school holidays and festive celebrations to bolster sun-deprived souls, not to mention some season-opening winter skiing in the highest-altitude Alpine resorts from mid-December.

Alsatian Christmas Markets

Meandering between fairy-light-lit craft stalls, mug of *vin chaud* (warm mulled wine) in gloved hand, at Alsace's traditional pre-Christmas markets, exudes cinematic romance.

Fête des Lumières

France's biggest and best light show, on 8 December, transforms the streets and squares of Lyon into an open stage (p444; www.lumieres.lyon.fr).

itineraries

Whether you've got five days or 50, these itineraries provide a starting point for the trip of a lifetime. Want more inspiration? Head online to lonelyplanet. com/thorntree to chat with other travellers.

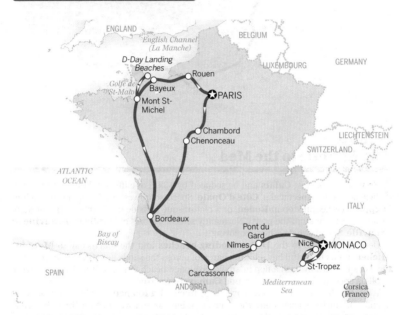

10 Days
Essential France

❯ No place screams 'France!' more than **Paris**. Spend two days in the capital, allowing for plenty of time between iconic sights to lounge on café terraces, dine in Parisian bistros and take romantic strolls along the Seine and Canal St-Martin (see Paris in Two Days, p46). Day three, enjoy Renaissance royalty at **Château de Chambord** and **Château de Chenonceau** in the Loire. Or skip this fabled valley, which gives such a fabulous nod to French architecture, and spend two days in Normandy instead, marvelling at **Rouen's** Notre Dame cathedral, the **Bayeux Tapestry**, sea-splashed **Mont St-Michel** and – should modern history be your love – the **D-Day landing beaches**.

Day five venture south through the **Bordeaux** wine region, staying overnight in an ecofriendly *chambre d'hôte* in Bordeaux's old wine-merchant quarter and perhaps enrolling in a wine-tasting course at the Maison du Vin de Bordeaux. Then it's a three-hour drive to the walled city of **Carcassonne**, Roman **Nîmes** and the **Pont du Gard**. Finish on the French Riviera with a casino flutter in Grace Kelly's **Monaco**, a portside aperitif in Brigitte Bardot's **St-Tropez** and a stroll around Matisse's **Nice**.

Two Weeks
The Atlantic to the Med

❯ Step off the boat in **Calais** and be seduced by 40km of cliffs, sand dunes and windy beaches on the spectacular **Côte d'Opale**. Speed southwest, taking in a fish lunch in **Dieppe**, a cathedral stop in **Rouen**, or a picturesque cliffside picnic in **Étretat** en route to your overnight stop: the pretty Normandy seaside resorts of **Honfleur**, **Deauville** or **Trouville**. Spend two days here exploring.

Devote day three to the **D-Day landing beaches** and the fourth day to **Mont St-Michel** and its beautiful bay – hiking barefoot across the sands here is exhilarating. End the week in Brittany with a flop in an old-fashioned beach tent in **Dinard** and a bracing stroll on spectacular headlands around **Camaret-sur-Mer**.

Week two begins with a long drive south to chic **La Rochelle** for its lavish seafood. Spend a night here, continuing the gourmet theme as you wend south through Médoc wine country to **Bordeaux**. Next morning, stop in **Toulouse** and/or **Carcassonne** before hitting the Med. **The Camargue** – a wetland of flamingos, horses and incredible bird life – is a unique patch of coast to explore and Van Gogh thought so too. Follow in his footsteps around **Arles**, breaking for a gastronomic lunch at L'Atelier or La Chassagnette before continuing on to gritty **Marseille**.

Three Weeks
Tour de France

❭ Get set in **Strasbourg**, ambling around its cathedral and canal-clad Petite France and dining in a traditional *winstub* (tavern). Then move onto greener climes, picking up the **Route des Vins d'Alsace** (Alsace Wine Route) to tipple your way around the **Massif des Vosges** foothills. But keep a clear head for art nouveau architecture in **Nancy**, where at least one night is obligatory to enjoy romantic place Stanislas lit after dark. End the week in the Champagne cellars of **Épernay**.

Week two features the pick of Normandy and Brittany: **Bayeux** and its tapestry, the **D-Day landing beaches**, **Mont St-Michel** and **Carnac** in France's Celtic land of legends. Then zoom south for more prehistory in the **Vézère Valley**.

The pace hots up in the third week. From the Dordogne, wiggle through Haut-Languedoc (Upper Languedoc) – through the spectacular **Gorges du Tarn** – to **Avignon** and its vibrant café culture. Slog like a Tour de France cyclist up **Mont Ventoux** then speed north to the majestic city of **Lyon**, from where, should you have another week at hand, a mountain adventure in the **Alps** is a dandy idea.

The last leg takes in wine-rich Burgundy: **Beaune**, **Dijon** and **Vézelay** are the obvious desirable places to stop en route to **Paris**.

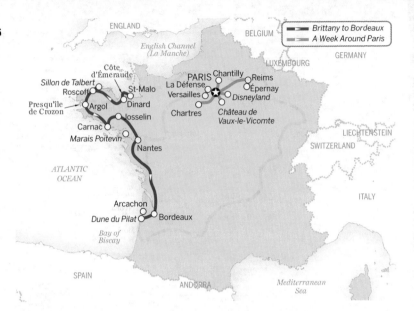

One Week
Brittany to Bordeaux

❯ This trip starts fresh off the boat in **St-Malo**, a walled city with sturdy Vauban ramparts that beg exploration at sunset. Linger at least a day in this gritty port. Walk across at low tide to Île du Grand Bé and lap up great views atop a 14th-century tower in pretty St-Servan. Motor along the **Côte d'Émeraude** the next day, stopping in **Dinard** en route to **Roscoff** 200km west – try to spot local seaweed harvesters around **Sillon de Talbert**. Devote day four to discovering Brittany's famous cider in **Argol** on the **Presqu'île de Crozon**, megaliths around **Carnac**, and a turreted medieval castle in **Josselin**. Push south next along the Atlantic coast, stopping in **Nantes** if you like big cities (and riding mechanical elephants), or continuing to the peaceful waterways of Green Venice, aka the **Marais Poitevin**. **Bordeaux** is your final destination for day six, from where a bevy of Bordeaux wine-tasting trips tempt. End the journey on a high atop Europe's highest sand dune, **Dune du Pilat**, near oyster-famed **Arcachon**.

One Week
A Week Around Paris

❯ Start in **Paris** (see p46 for more days), from where a journey of magnificent French icons, Renaissance châteaux and sparkling wine unfurls. Day one has to be France's grandest castle, **Château de Versailles**, and its vast gardens. The second day, feast on France's best-preserved medieval basilica and dazzling blue stained glass in **Chartres**, an easy train ride away. Small-town **Chantilly** is a good spot to combine a laid-back lunch with Renaissance château, formal French gardens and – if you snagged tickets in advance – an enchanting equestrian performance. Fourth day, catch the train to elegant **Reims** in the heart of the Champagne region. Scale its cathedral for dazzling views before tucking into the serious business of Champagne tasting. Dedicated bubbly aficionados can hop the next day to **Épernay**, France's other great Champagne city. On day six enjoy a lazy start then catch an afternoon fountain show at less crowded **Château de Vaux-le-Vicomte**, followed by a candlelit tour of the château. End the week with a look at futuristic **La Défense** or, for those with kids, **Disneyland**.

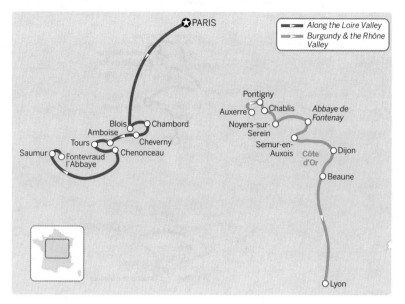

Five Days
Along the Loire Valley

❯ From France's soulful capital **Paris** head west to its regal surrounds. First up is the Unesco-hallmarked city of **Blois**, where you can make the most of the limited time you have by hooking up, day two, with an organised châteaux tour: queen of all castles **Château de Chambord** and the charmingly classical **Château de Cheverny**, with its hound-packed kennels, make a great combo. On the third day, continue southwest along France's longest river, the Loire, to **Amboise**, final home of Leonardo da Vinci, and solidly bourgeois **Tours**, from where **Château de Chenonceau**, beautifully strung across the River Cher 34km east, is an easy hop the next morning. End your trip with France's elite riding school in **Saumur** and the movingly simple abbey church **Fontevraud l'Abbaye**. Château de Verrières is a fabulous overnight address in this château-rich neck of the woods.

Five Days
Burgundy & Beyond

❯ Red-wine lovers can enjoy the fruits of Burgundy in this itinerary that begins in the Roman river-port of **Auxerre**, 170km southeast of Paris. Explore its ancient abbey, Gothic cathedral and cycle along towpaths in the afternoon. On day two consider an easy bike ride to Burgundy's last surviving example of Cistercian architecture in pretty **Pontigny**, 25km north. Stay overnight or push on to nearby **Chablis**, where bags more bike rides and gentle hikes between Burgundy vineyards await – allow plenty of time here to taste the seven *grands crus* of this well-known winemaking town. Day four, meander south to the picture-postcard village of **Noyers-sur-Serein**, then head east to the breathtaking, Unesco-listed **Abbaye de Fontenay**, before winding up for the night in **Semur-en-Auxois**, 25km south. On the last day discover **Dijon** and its beautiful medieval and Renaissance buildings. From here, should you have more time, take a road trip through the wine-making area of **Côte d'Or** to **Beaune**, or south to **Lyon** in the Rhône Valley.

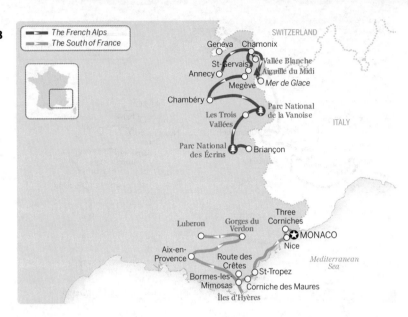

Five Days
The French Alps

❱ Warm up with some gentle old-town ambling, lakeside strolling and swimming (in summer) in fairy-tale **Annecy** (just 45km from Geneva, Switzerland). On day two move on to **Chamonix** at the foot of Mont Blanc, Western Europe's highest peak: ride a cable car to the **Aiguille du Midi** or a train to the **Mer de Glace** glacier, or (in winter) ski the legendary **Vallée Blanche**, off-piste all the way. Yet more unforgettable views of the Mont Blanc massif are cooked up on the ski slopes and hiking trails of **St-Gervais** and **Megève**, chic, picturesque Alpine villages. Let the adrenalin rip or push on via **Chambéry** to the **Parc National de la Vanoise**, where spectacular skiing and hiking in **Les Trois Vallées** easily pleases outdoor junkies. A fitting finale to your Alpine foray is the dizzying and staggeringly beautiful drive through **Parc National des Écrins** to **Briançon**, the loveliest of all the medieval villages in the French Alps and famous for its well-preserved Vauban fortifications.

10 Days
The South of France

❱ Hit the country's hot south in **Nice**, star of the coastline that unfurls in an extravagant pageant of belle époque palaces and celebrity sands. Drive along the French Riviera's trio of legendary **corniches** – the coastal views are mind-blowing – and day three take the train to glitzy **Monaco**. Then move on to the fishing port of **St-Tropez**, where millionaire yachts jostle for space with peddling street artists. Rise early the next morning for the Place des Lices market and frolic away the afternoon on the sand at Plage de Pampelonne. Day six is a toss-up between a dramatic drive along the **Corniche des Maures** to **Bormes-les-Mimosas** and the staggering **Route des Crêtes** mountain pass, or a boat trip to the *très belle* **Îles d'Hyères**. Head inland next to **Aix-en-Provence**, a canvas of graceful 19th-century architecture, stylish cafés and hidden squares. Devote your last two days to the wild **Gorges du Verdon**, Europe's largest canyon, two hour's drive northeast, or the gentler **Luberon** with its bounty of photogenic hilltop villages.

Travel with Children

Which Region?

Not sure which bit of France to visit? Here's our pick of regions and their main appeal.

Sun, Sand & Sea

French Riviera, Côte Vermeille in Roussillon, Corsica, the Atlantic Coast (beware of strong undertows), Brittany or Normandy

Hiking & Biking

The French Alps, French Basque Country, the Pyrenees, Massif Central, Corsica

History Lessons

Dordogne (prehistory), Loire Valley (Renaissance), Lille, Flanders and the Somme (WWI), Normandy (WWII)

Modern Art

Provence, the French Riviera, Côte Vermeille in Roussillon

Canal Cruising

Languedoc, Burgundy, Loire Valley, the Camargue

Be it kid-friendly extraordinaire capital or rural hinterland, France spoils families with its rich mix of cultural sights, activities and entertainment – some paid-for, many free. To get the most out of travelling *en famille,* plan ahead.

France for Kids

Once in situ there is no stopping the most zealous of sightseeing, activity-driven families from exploring. France has plenty to suit every age and interest.

Museums & Monuments

It pays to pick the right one. Most Paris museums organise imaginative *ateliers* (workshops) for children and/or families. Workshops are themed, require advance booking, last 1½ to two hours, and cost €5 to €10 per child. French children have no school Wednesday, meaning most workshops happen Wednesday, weekends and daily during school holidays. Most cater for kids aged seven to 14 years, although in Paris art tours at the Louvre start at four years and at the Musée d'Orsay, five years. Countrywide, check what activity sheets museums and monuments have when buying admission tickets – most have something to keep kids interested. Another winner is to arm your gadget-mad child (aged from six years) with an audioguide.

Savvy parents can find kid appeal in every sight in France, must-sees included. Skip the formal guided tour of Mont St-Michel, for example, and hook up with a walking guide to take you and the kids barefoot across the sand to the abbey; trade the daytime queues at the Eiffel Tower for a tour after dark with teens; don't dismiss wine tasting in Provence or Burgundy outright – rent bicycles and turn it into a family bike ride instead.

Outdoor Activities

Once the kids are out of nappies, skiing in the French Alps is the obvious family choice. Ski school École du Ski Français (www.esf.net) initiates kids in the art of snow plough (group or private lessons, half- or full day) from four years old, and many resorts open their fun-driven *jardins de neige* (snow gardens) to kids from three years old. Families with kids aged under 10 will find smaller resorts like Les Gets, Avoriaz (car-free), La Clusaz, Chamrousse and Le Grand Bornand easier to navigate and better value than larger ski stations. Then, of course, there is all the fun of the fair offpiste: ice skating, sledging, snowshoeing and mushing.

The French Alps and Pyrenees are prime walking areas. Tourist offices have information on easy, well-signposted family walks – or get in touch with a local guide. In Chamonix the cable-car ride and two-hour hike to Lac Blanc followed by a dip in the Alpine lake (p470) is a DIY family favourite; as are the mountain-discovery half-days for ages three to seven, and outdoor-adventure days for ages eight to 12 run by Cham' Aventure (www.cham-aventure.com). As with skiing, smaller places like the Parc Naturel Régional du Massif des Bauges (essentially set up for a local French audience) cater much better to young families than the big names everyone knows.

ADMISSION PRICES

There is no rule on how much and from what age children pay – many museums and monuments are free to under 18 years. Throughout this guide we note the paying price for a child – usually applicable to those aged six years, but in some cases from 12 years and over. In general, you can safely assume kids aged five years and under don't pay (a noteworthy exception is Paris' must-do Cité des Sciences et de l'Industrie which costs from two years).

White-water sports and canoeing are doable for children aged seven and older; the French Alps, Provence and Massif Central are key areas. Mountain biking is an outdoor thrill that teens can share – try Morzine.

Entertainment

France's repertoire is impressive: puppet shows al fresco, children's theatres, children's films at cinemas Wednesday afternoon and weekends, street buskers, illuminated monuments after dark, an abundance of music festivals and so on. A sure winner are the *son et lumière* (sound-and-light) shows projected onto Renaissance châteaux in the Loire Valley and cathedral facades in Rouen, Chartres and Amiens. In Paris, weekly entertainment magazine *L'Officiel des Spectacles* is the key to what's on – or ask at tourist offices.

Dining Out

French children, accustomed to threecourse lunches at school, expect a starter *(entrée)*, main course and dessert as their main meal of the day. They know the difference between brie and camembert, and are quite accustomed to eating salad as *entrée*. Main meals tend to be meat 'n' veg or pasta, followed by dessert and/or a slice of cheese; many families end with a square of *chocolate noir* (dark chocolate). Classic French mains loved by children include *gratin dauphinois* (sliced potatoes oven-baked in cream), *escalope de veau* (breaded panfried veal) and *boeuf bourguignon* (beef stew). Fondue and *raclette* (melted cheese served with potatoes and cold meats) become favourites from about five years, and *moules frites* (mussels and fries) a couple of years later.

Across the board, children's *menus* (fixed meal at a set price) are common, although anyone in France for more than a few days will soon tire of the ubiquitous spaghetti bolognaise or *saucisse* (sausage), or *steak haché* (beef burger) and *frites* (fries) followed by ice cream that most *menus* feature. Don't be shy in asking for a half-portion of an adult main – most restaurants, top-end places included, usually oblige. Ditto in budget and midrange places to ask for a plate of *pâtes au beurre* (pasta with butter) for fussy or very young eaters.

Bread, specifically slices of baguette, accompanies every meal and in restaurants is brought to the table before or immediately

Throughout this guide places to eat of particular interest to families are flagged with the icon 👶. This might mean the recommendation has a great children's menu and/or it provides high chairs, changing facilities or paper tablemats for kids to colour in. Or it might have none of these but simply be a great interest grabber for children (like the chefs that hand-pull noodles in front of you at Paris' Les Pâtes Vivantes, or the Jurassien and Alpine farm kitchens where kids collect the eggs that end up on their plate), or pique their culinary curiosity (frogs' legs in Paris, pink nail-sized *tellines* in the Camargue, *moules frites* in Lille).

after you've ordered – to the glee of children who wolf it down while they wait. Watch for the fight to ensue over who gets the *trognon* (the knobbly end bit, equally a hit with teething babies!).

It is perfectly acceptable to dine *en famille* after dark providing the kids don't run wild. Few restaurants open their doors, however, before 7.30pm or 8pm, making brasseries and cafés – many serve food continuously from 7am or 8am until midnight – more appealing for families with younger children. Many restaurants have high chairs.

France is fabulous snack-attack terrain. Parisian pavements are rife with crêpe stands and wintertime stalls selling hot chestnuts. Sweet and savoury *galettes* (crêpes) make for an easy light lunch, as does France's signature *croque monsieur* (toasted cheese and ham sandwich) served by most cafés and brasseries. *Goûter* (afternoon snack) is golden for every French child and *salons de thé* (tea rooms) serve a mouth-watering array of cakes, pastries and biscuits. Or go local: buy a baguette, rip off a chunk and pop a slab of chocolate inside!

Baby requirements are easily met. The choice of infant formula, soy and cow's milk, nappies (diapers) and jarred baby food in supermarkets and pharmacies is similar to any developed country, although opening hours are more limited (few shops open Sunday). Organic *(bio)* baby food is hard to find.

Drinks

Buy a fizzy drink for every child sitting at the table and the bill swiftly soars. Opt instead for a free *carafe d'eau* (jug of tap water) with meals and *un sirop* (syrup) in between. Every self-respecting café and bar in France has dozens of flavours to choose from: pomegranate-fuelled grenadine and

pea-green *menthe* (mint) are French-kid favourites, but there's peach, raspberry, cherry, lemon and a rainbow of others to pick from. Syrup is served diluted with water and, best up, costs a good €2 less than a coke. Expect to pay around €1.50 a glass.

Children's Highlights
Gastronomic Moments

» Fondue and *raclette* in the French Alps

» Breton crêpes served in a traditional long house encircled by 70 menhirs, Brittany

» Berthillon ice cream, Île St-Louis, Paris

» Oysters on an oyster farm, Gujan Mestras, near Bordeaux

» Grape-juice tasting (while parents taste the alcoholic equivalent), La Balance Mets et Vins, Arbois

» Snails for breakfast on a snail-farm B&B, Escargot Comtois, the Jura

» Frogs' legs and a lakeside bike ride, La Bicyclette Bleue, La Dombes

» Chocolate soup sprinkled with gingerbread croutons, Bistrot et Chocolat, Strasbourg

Energy Burners

» Skiing, snowboarding, sledging and dog-mushing (over four years), French Alps and the Pyrenees

» Scaling Aiguille du Midi by gondola and crossing glaciers into Italy (over four years), Chamonix

» Around an island by bike (over five years) or parent-pulled bike trailer (over one year), Île de Ré and Île de Porquerolles

» White-water sports (over seven years), Gorges du Verdon, Gorges du Tarn and Gorges de l'Ardèche

» Canoeing (over seven years) beneath the Pont du Gard, near Nîmes

» Donkey treks (over 10 years), like Robert Louis Stevenson in the wild Cévennes

Watching Wildlife

» Vultures in Parc National des Pyrénées

» Wolves in Parc National du Mercantour and Parc Animalier des Monts de Guéret

» Whistling marmots in Chamonix

» Sharks at Musée Océanographique, Monaco

» Dancing horses in Saumur, Versailles and Chantilly

» Bulls and flamingos in the Camargue

» Storks and kingfishers at Le Teich Parc Ornithologique, near Arcachon

» Fish (through a snorkelling mask), Île de Porquerolles and Corsica's Porto and Calvi

Rainy Days

» Build a house, Bob-style (over three years), Cité des Sciences et de l'Industrie, Paris

» Go Roman (over five years) at Ludo, Pont du Gard, near Nîmes

» Ride a house-sized, mechanical elephant (any age), Les Machines de l'Île de Nantes, Nantes

» Learn how planes are built (over six years), Jean Luc Lagardère factory, Toulouse

» Ogle at skulls (teens), Les Catacombes, Paris

» Discover V2 rocket technology in a subterranean bunker (teens), La Coupole, St-Omer

» Play cavemen (any age) in caves riddled with prehistoric art, Vézère Valley

» Enter wannabe-mechanic heaven (any age), Cité de l'Automobile and Cité du Train, Mulhouse

Theme Parks

» Cité de l'Espace (outer space), Toulouse

» Disneyland, Paris

» Vulcania (volcanoes), Massif Central

Planning
When to Go

Consider the season and what you want to do/see: teen travel is a year-round affair (there's always something to entertain, regardless of the weather), but parents travelling with younger kids will find the dry, pleasantly warm days of spring and early summer best suited to kidding around the park – every town has at least one *terrain de jeux* (playground) – and indulging in other energy-burning, outdoor pursuits.

France's fabulous festival repertoire is another planning consideration (see p20 for a month-by-month listing). Kids of all ages will be particularly enchanted by Avignon's fringe Festival Off, Lyon's Fête des Lumières and Nice Carnival – three freebie events worth planning a trip around.

Accommodation

In Paris and larger towns and cities, serviced apartments equipped with washing machine and kitchen are suited to families with younger children. Countrywide, hotels with family or four-person rooms can be hard to find – in this guide we flag them with a family-friendly icon (🐾) – and need booking in advance. Functional if soul-less chain hotels like Formule 1, found on the

---

TOP WEBSITES

» **Familiscope** (www.familiscope.fr, in French) Definitive family-holiday planner: endless activity, outing and entertainment listings.

» **Bienvenue à la Ferme** (www.bienvenue-a-la-ferme.com/en) Cooking courses, animals, nature activities and accommodation on farms France-wide.

» **Tots2France** (www.tots2france.co.uk) Self-catering properties vetted by a team of trained mums.

» **Baby-friendly Boltholes** (www.babyfriendlyboltholes.co.uk) 'Stylish escapes – perfect for pre-schoolers' is the strapline of this London-based enterprise specialising in sourcing charming and unique family accommodation.

» **Baby Goes 2** (www.babygoes2.com) Why, where, how-to-go travel guide aimed squarely at families.

» **Mumsnet** (www.mumsnet.com) No question is unanswerable for this UK-based gang of mothers: online discussion, advice, tips, open forum and so on, much of it France-related.

Babies & Toddlers

☐ A front or back sling for baby and toddler: France's cobbled streets, metro stairs and hilltop villages were not built with pushchairs (strollers) in mind. Several must-see museums, moreover, notably Château de Versailles, don't let pushchairs in.

☐ A portable changing mat, handwash gel etc (baby-changing facilities are a rarity)

☐ A canvas screw-on seat for toddlers (not many restaurants have high chairs)

☐ Kids' car seats: rental companies rent them but at proportionately extortionate rates. In France children under 10 years or less than 1.40m in height must, by law, be strapped in an appropriate car seat.

Six to 12 Years

☐ Binoculars for young explorers to zoom in on wildlife, sculpted cathedral facades, stained-glass windows etc

☐ A pocket video camera (such as Flip) to inject fun into 'boring' grown-up activities

☐ Activity books, sketchpad and pens, travel journal and kid-sized day pack

☐ Fold-away microscooter and/or rollerblades if you're doing lots of city walking

☐ Kite (for beaches)

Teens

☐ France-related iPhone apps

☐ French phrasebook

☐ Mask, snorkel and flippers

outskirts of most large towns, always have a generous quota of family rooms and make convenient overnight stops for motorists driving from continental Europe or the UK (Troyes is a popular stopover for Brits en route to the Alps). Parents with just one child and/or a baby in tow will have no problem finding hotel accommodation – most midrange hotels have baby cots and are happy to put a child's bed in a double room for a minimal extra cost.

In rural France, family-friendly B&Bs and *fermes auberges*, some of which cook up tasty evening meals, are the way to go. Bring a baby monitor so little children can sleep sweet upstairs while mum and dad wine and dine in peace downstairs. Or

what about a hip baby-and-toddler house party in a château in Burgundy or a chalet retreat in the French Alps? For older children, tree houses decked out with bunk beds and Mongolian yurts create a real family adventure. Dozens of family-friendly places are recommended throughout this guide – look for the 🖪 icon.

Camping is huge with French families: check into a self-catering mobile home, wooden chalet or family tent; sit back on the verandah with glass of wine in hand and watch as your kids – wonderfully oblivious to any barriers language might pose – run around with new-found French friends. Campgrounds require booking well in advance, especially during high season.

regions at a glance

Paris

Food ✓✓✓
Art ✓✓✓
Shopping ✓✓✓

Gourmet Paradise
Monsieur A Boulanger opened the city's first restaurant, near rue Rivoli, in 1765. Contemporary Parisian dining is an exuberant feast of neighbourhood bistros, old-time brasseries, zinc-bar cafés and starred restaurants.

Museums & Galleries
All the great masters star in Paris' extraordinary portfolio of museums. Not all the booty is stashed inside: buildings, metro stations, parks and other public art give *Mona* a good run for her money.

Fashion & Flea Markets
Luxury fashion houses, edgy boutiques, Left Bank designer-vintage and Europe's largest flea market: Paris really is the last word in fabulous shopping.

p42

Around Paris

Châteaux ✓✓✓
Cathedrals ✓✓
Green Spaces ✓

A Taste of Royalty
Château de Versailles – vast, opulent and *very* shimmery – has to be seen to be believed. Fontainebleau, Chantilly and Vaux-le-Vicomte are other fabled addresses in French royalty's little black book.

Sacred Architecture
The other heavyweight near Paris is Chartres cathedral, one of Western architecture's greatest achievements, with stained glass in awesome blue.

Paris' Lungs
Parisians take air in thick forests outside the city: Forêt de Fontainebleau, old royal hunting ground, is a hot spot for rock climbing and family walks. Chantilly means manicured French gardens and upper-class horse racing.

p134

Lille, Flanders & the Somme

Architecture ✓✓
History ✓✓✓
Coastline ✓✓✓

Flemish Style
Breaking for a glass of strong local beer between old-town meanders around extravagant Flemish Renaissance buildings is a highlight of northern France. Lille and Arras are the cities to target.

Gothic to WWI
Amiens evokes serene contemplation inside one of France's most awe-inspiring Gothic cathedrals, and emotional encounters in WWI cemeteries.

Coastal Capers
Hiking along the Côte d'Opale – a wind-buffeted area of white cliff, gold sand and ever-changing sea and sky – is dramatic and beautiful, as is a Baie de Somme bicycle ride past lounging seals.

p153

Normandy

Food ✓✓
Coastline ✓✓✓
Battlefields ✓✓✓

Calvados & Camembert
This coastal chunk of northern France is a pastoral land of butter and soft cheeses. Its exotic fruits: camembert, cider, fiery apple brandy and super-fresh seafood.

Cliffs & Coves
Chalk-white cliff to dune-lined beach, rock spire to pebble cove, coastal path to tide-splashed island-abbey Mont St-Michel: few coastlines are as inspiring.

D-Day Beaches
Normandy has long played a pivotal role in European history. But it was during WWII's D-Day landings that Normandy leaped to global importance. Museums, memorials, cemeteries and endless stretches of soft golden sand evoke that dramatic day in 1944.

p191

Brittany

Food ✓✓
Walking ✓✓✓
Islands ✓✓

Crêpes & Cider
These two Breton culinary staples are no secret but who cares? Devouring caramel-doused buckwheat pancakes in the company of homemade cider is a big reason to visit Brittany.

Wild Hikes
With its wild dramatic coastline, islands, medieval towns and thick Celtic forests laced in local lore and legend, this proud and fiercely independent region promises exhilarating walks.

Breton Beauties
Brittany's much-loved islands, dotted in black sheep and crossed with craggy coastal paths and windswept cycling tracks, are big draws. Don't miss dramatic Île d'Ouessant or the very aptly named Belle Île.

p232

Champagne

Champagne ✓✓✓
Walking ✓✓
Drives ✓✓✓

Bubbly Tasting
Gawp at a Champagne panorama from atop Rheims' cathedral then zoom in close with serious tasting at the world's most prestigious Champagne houses in Rheims and Épernay.

Vineyard Trails
Nothing quite fulfils the French dream like easy day hikes through neat rows of vineyards, exquisite picture-postcard villages bedecked in flowers and a gold-stone riverside hamlet right out of a Renoir painting.

Majestic Motoring
No routes are more geared to motorists and cyclists than the Champagne Routes, fabulously picturesque and well-signposted driving itineraries taking in the region's wealthy winemaking villages, hillside vines and traditional cellars.

p278

Alsace & Lorraine

Battlefields ✓✓✓
City Life ✓✓
Villages ✓✓✓

Emotional Journeys
Surveying the dazzling symmetry of crosses on the Verdun battlefields is painful. Memorials, museums, cemeteries, forts and an ossuary mark out the emotional journey.

Urban Icons
With the sublime (Strasbourg's cathedral) to the space-age (the new Centre Pompidou in Metz), this northeast chunk of France steals urbanite hearts with its city squares, architecture, museums and Alsatian dining.

Chocolate-box Villages
There is no lovelier way of acquainting oneself with this part of France than travelling from hilltop castles to stork-nest-blessed farms, to half-timbered villages framed by vines.

p301

The Loire Valley

Châteaux ✓✓✓
History ✓✓✓
Cycling ✓✓

Burgundy

Wine ✓✓✓
History ✓✓✓
Activities ✓✓

Lyon & the Rhône Valley

Food ✓✓✓
Roman Sites ✓✓
Cycling ✓

French Alps & the Jura Mountains

Food ✓✓
Outdoors ✓✓✓
Farmstays ✓✓✓

Royal Architecture

Endowed with dazzling structural and decorative gems from medieval to Renaissance and beyond, the Loire's lavish châteaux sweep most visitors off their feet.

Tempestuous Tales

This region is a dramatic story teller: through spectacular castles, fortresses, apocalyptic tapestries and court paintings, the gore and glory, political intrigue and sex scandals of medieval and Renaissance France fabulously unfolds.

Riverside Trails

The River Loire is France's longest, best-decorated river. Pedalling riverside along the flat from château to château is one of the valley's great joys.

p349

Reds & Whites

Mooch between vines and old-stone villages along Burgundy's *grand cru* wine route. But this region is not just about Côte d'Or reds. Taste whites in Chablis and Mâcon.

Medieval History

Nowhere is Burgundy's past as one of medieval Europe's mightiest states evoked more keenly than in the dashingly handsome capital Dijon. Complete the medieval history tour with abbeys Cluny and Cîteaux.

Great Outdoors

Hiking and biking past vineyards or cruising in a canal boat is the good life. Pedal the towpath to gloriously medieval Abbaye de Fontenay, open a bottle of Chablis and savour the best of Burgundy.

p390

Famous Flavours

No city in France excites taste buds more than Lyon. Savour local specialities in a checked-tableclothed *bouchon* (Lyonnais bistro).

Roman Remains

Not content with lavishing two majestic amphitheatres on Lyon (catch a concert alfresco after dark during Les Nuits de Fourvière – magical!), the Romans gifted the Rhône Valley with a third in jazz-famed Vienne.

Two-wheel Touring

Pedalling between vineyards in Beaujolais country or around frog-filled lakes swamped with bird life in Les Dombes is one of life's simple pleasures.

p434

Culture & Cuisine

Fondue is the tip of the culinary iceberg in this Alpine region, where cow's milk flavours dozens of cheeses. Around chic Lake Annecy chefs woo with wild herbs and lake perch.

Adrenalin Rush

Crowned by Mont Blanc (4810m), the French Alps show no mercy in their insanely challenging ski trails, mountain-bike descents and bike rides. Did we mention Europe's longest black downhill piste?

Back to Nature

Feel the humble rhythm of the land with an overnight stay on a farm. Bottle-feed calves, collect the eggs, have breakfast in a fragrant garden or before a wood-burning stove, and feel right at home.

p461

Massif Central

Volcanoes ✓✓✓
Architecture ✓
Activities ✓✓

Limousin, the Dordogne & the Lot

Food ✓✓✓
Hilltop Towns ✓✓
Cruises ✓✓✓

Atlantic Coast

Port Towns ✓✓
Wine ✓✓✓
Activities ✓✓✓

French Basque Country

Food ✓✓
Activities ✓✓✓
Culture ✓✓✓

Volcanoes

The last one erupted in 5000 BC but their presence remains felt: mineral waters bubble up from volcanic springs in Vichy and Volvic; volcanic stone paints Clermont-Ferrand black and there's the razzmatazz of Vulcania.

Belle Époque

A string of early 20th-century spa towns including Vichy add a string of understated elegance to this region's otherwise deeply provincial bow.

Hiking & Skiing

Walking is the best way to explore this unique landscape – an uncanny, grass-green moonscape of giant molehills crossed with trails. Then there are the little-known ski slopes of Le Mont-Dore.

p521

Mouth-watering Markets

Black truffles, foie gras and walnuts... Gourmets, eat your heart out in this fertile part of central and southwest France, where the fruits of the land are piled high at a bevy of atmospheric weekly markets.

Mighty Bastides

Not only is Dordogne's prized collection of fortified 13th-century towns and villages a joy to explore, valley views from the top of these cliff-top *bastides* are uplifting. Start with Monpazier and Domme.

Meandering Waterways

Be it aboard a canoe, raft or traditional flat-bottomed *gabarre,* cruising quietly along the region's rivers is an invitation to see *la belle France* at her most serene.

p546

Sea View

Hip dining rendezvous in an old banana-ripening warehouse in Nantes, limestone arcades and islands in La Rochelle, and brilliant art museums in wine-rich Bordeaux.

Wonderful Wines

France's largest winegrowing region, Bordeaux encompasses the Médoc with its magnificent châteaux and medieval hamlet of St-Émilion. The wine is wonderful (not to mention the Cognac).

Rural Retreats

Paddling emerald-green waterways in the Marais Poitevin, pedalling sun-baked Île de Re and wandering between weathered, wooden oyster shacks in Arcachon Bay is what this tranquil region is all about – slowing the pace right down.

p594

Culture & Cuisine

Independent and Catalan in soul, this exuberant region beneath the mist-soaked Pyrenees evokes Spain with its fiestas, bullfights, traditional *pelota* (ball games), tapas and famous Bayonne ham.

Surf's Up

Riding waves in the glitzy beach resort of Biarritz or on surfer beaches in Les Landes is good reason to visit this sun-slicked coastal region, snug in France's most southwest corner.

A Timeless Pilgrimage

For centuries pilgrims have made their way across France to the quaint walled town of St-Jean Pied de Port, just across the border from Santiago de Compostela in Spain. Do the same, on foot or by bicycle.

p632

The Pyrenees

Outdoors ✓✓✓
Scenery ✓✓✓
History ✓✓

Adrenalin Rush
Make Parc National des Pyrénées your playground. Vigorous hikes to lofty heights, good-value downhill skiing and racy white-water sports will leave you wanting more.

Jaw-dropping Views
France's last wilderness has rare flora and fauna, snow-kissed peaks, vulture-specked skies, waterfalls and lakes. Top views include those from Pic du Jer, Pic du Midi, Lescun, Cirque de Gavarnie, Lac de Gaube and pretty much every valley going.

Rare & Holy Cities
That same elegance that saw well-to-do 19th-century English and Americans winter in Pau still attracts guests today. Then there is sacred Lourdes, a provincial pilgrim city.

p659

Toulouse Area

Food ✓✓
History ✓✓✓
Cruises ✓✓

Cassoulet & Armagnac
Try Emile restaurant for Toulouse's best *cassoulet*, though this classic bean-stew dish simmers on the stove in most kitchens. Begin the experience with an aperitif and end with an Armagnac brandy.

Towns with Tales
Red-brick Toulouse's historic mansions, quintessential fortified town Montauban, Gothic Albi, Moissac's Romanesque abbey: this compact region is packed with historical tales and historic architecture.

Canal du Midi
Pop a cork out of a bottle of Vin de Pays d'Oc and savour the go-slow, lush-green loveliness of the Canal du Midi. Stroll or pedal its towpaths, soak in a spa or simply rent a canal boat and drift.

p681

Languedoc-Roussillon

Culture ✓✓
Roman Sites ✓✓
Activities ✓✓

So Near Spain
Roussillon is a hot, dusty, lively region, long part of Catalonia at the eastern end of the Pyrenees. Celebrate a Catalan fiesta in Perpignan, and modern art and *sardane* folk dances in Céret.

Aqueducts & Amphitheatres
Nîmes amphitheatre and the gracefully arched Pont du Gard are two of the Roman Empire's best-preserved sites.

Footpaths & Waterways
Try canoeing beneath the Pont du Gard, biking towpaths to Carcassonne, boating the Canal du Midi, climbing up to Cathar fortresses, donkey trekking in the Cévennes or hiking gorges in Haut-Languedoc.

p704

Provence

Food ✓✓✓
Villages ✓✓✓
Modern Art ✓✓✓

Eating & Drinking
Sip pastis over *pétanque*, spend all evening savouring *bouillabaisse* (fish stew), mingle over buckets of herbs and marinated olives at the market, hunt truffles, and taste Bandol reds and Côtes de Provence rosé.

Sensual Sauntering
Travelling *à la Provençal* is a sensual journey past scented lavender fields and chestnut forests, through apple-green vineyards and silvery olive groves, around markets, chapels, and medieval villages perched on rocky crags.

Avant-garde
Provence is an art museum and has the roll-call to prove it: Matisse, Renoir, Picasso, Cézanne, Van Gogh and Signac all painted and lived here.

p752

The French Riviera & Monaco

Resorts ✓✓✓
Glamour ✓✓✓
Coastline ✓✓✓

Coastal Queen

Urban grit, old-world opulence, art that moves and a seaside promenade everyone loves – Nice, queen of the French Riviera, will always be belle of the seaside ball.

Party Time

Enjoy the Riviera high life: trail film stars in Cannes, see Formula One meet high society in Monaco, guzzle champers in St-Tropez, frolic in famous footsteps on sandy beaches, dine between priceless art, dance til dawn...

Magnificent Scenery

With its glistening sea, idyllic beaches and coastal paths, this part of the Med coast begs wonderful walks. Cicadas sing on Cap Ferrat, while the sun turns the Massif de l'Estérel brilliant red.

p817

Corsica

Coastal Towns ✓✓
Hiking ✓✓✓
Boat Trips ✓✓✓

Postcard Home

Corsican coastal towns are impossibly picturesque: alley-woven Bastia, Italianate Bonifacio, celeb-loved Île Rousse, chichi Calvi... every one calls for a postcard home.

Great Outdoors

Hiking high-altitude mountain trails once the preserve of bandits and *bergers* (shepherds) is a trail-junkie favourite, as are the cliffhanging Gorges de Spelunca and beautiful pink, ochre and ginger Les Calanques.

The Big Blue

Nowhere does the Med seem bluer. Hop on deck in Porto, Bonifacio, Calvi or Porto-Vecchio for a boat excursion or view sapphire waters through a mask while diving and snorkelling.

p867

Look out for these icons:

 TOP CHOICE Our author's recommendation

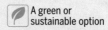 A green or sustainable option

FREE No payment required

See the Index for a full list of destinations covered in this book.

On the Road

Paris

POP: 2.2 MILLION

Best Places to Eat

» Chez Janou (p106)
» La Gazzetta (p106)
» Chez Michel (p114)
» L'Office (p114)
» Café Constant (p111)

Best Places to Stay

» Le Relais du Louvre (p94)
» Hôtel du Petit Moulin (p94)
» Hôtel Eldorado (p101)
» Hôtel Amour (p104)
» L'Apostrophe (p99)

Why Go

Paris has all but exhausted the superlatives that can reasonably be applied to any city. Notre Dame, the Eiffel Tower, the Seine – at sunrise, sunset, at night – and Left–Right Bank differences have been described countless times. But what writers haven't quite captured is the grandness and magic of strolling the city's broad avenues past impressive public buildings and exceptional museums to parks, gardens and esplanades.

With more famous landmarks than any other city, the French capital evokes all sorts of expectations: of grand vistas, of intellectuals discussing weighty matters in cafés, of Seine-side romance, of naughty nightclub revues. Look hard enough and you'll find them all. Or set aside those preconceptions of Paris that are so much a part of English-speaking culture, and explore the city's avenues and backstreets as though the tip of the Eiffel Tower or the spire of Notre Dame weren't about to pop into view at any moment.

When to Go

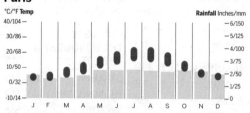

June Music ushers in the summer solstice with France's Fête de la Musique.

Mid-July to mid-August The Seine riverbank is a sandy beach with sunbeds, parasols and palm trees.

October Nuit Blanche when the city and its museums, bars etc stay awake all night.

Supper Clubs

Jim Haynes' Sunday dinner in a belle époque atelier in the 14e is the original, but these days, as in so many other world-class cities, supper clubs are popping up like toadstools after rain in the French capital. While *dîner chez Jim* is less about the food and more about socialising and perhaps even pulling, many of the newer clubs focus on multicourse gastronomic meals or visiting the 'in' *adresse* (restaurant) of the moment with a local foodie – meaning an excellent meal alongside the chance to meet people. Expect to pay from €80 per person and book well in advance. If you don't snag a spot, check Twitter a few days before your visit: many clubs tweet cancellations and last-minute available places. For our favourite five, see p110.

FOR FIRST TIMERS

You can't say you've been to Paris until you have at least gazed at Madame Eiffel, aka the Eiffel Tower, and strutted the length of av des Champs-Élysées: for an alternative perspective stand below the Arc de Triomphe, in front of the eternal flame, as night falls and watch the traffic surreally rush past. Notre Dame, Christendom's most beautiful house of worship, can be a mob of picture-snapping infidels much of the time but attending Mass or a Sunday-afternoon organ concert ensures a moment of peace. Monet's Water Lilies and *Decorations des Nymphéas* in the Musée de l'Orangerie provide a great alternative to the busy Louvre. And then there's the city's food markets (p107), all fabulous (although our favourite is Marché Bastille).

Top 5 Signature Splurges

» Sip a cocktail – ideally a Bloody Mary, its own invention – at Harry's New York Bar (p118)

» Tuck into a slice of *baiser Ladurée* (layered almond cake with strawberries and cream) at Ladurée (p113), Paris' most famous pâtisserie on the Champs-Élysées

» Select your open CD compilations at the musically renowned Buddha Bar (p118)

» Have your own personal scent mixed at the renowned *parfumerie* Fragonard (p112)

» Cruise around town on a vintage Vespa from Left Bank Scooters (p131)

PARIS

ARRONDISSEMENTS

Paris is spit into 20 *arrondissements* (districts) and addresses always include the *arrondissement* number – 1er for *premier* (1st), 2e for *deuxième* (2nd), 3e for *troisième* (3rd) etc.

Need to Know

» Most Paris museums close Monday, but a dozen-odd including the Louvre and Centre Pompidou close Tuesday instead.

Advance Planning

» Book accommodation and reserve tables at fine-dines, modish gastrobistros and supper clubs

» Surf Fnac and Virgin Megastore (p119) for big-ticket concerts, musicals and theatrical performances

» Buy e-tickets for the Eiffel Tower, Louvre and blockbuster exhibitions at the Grand Palais and Centre Pompidou

Resources

» Mairie de Paris: www. paris.fr

» Paris by Mouth: www. parisbymouth.com

» Paris Convention & Visitors Bureau: www. parisinfo.com

» My Little Paris: www. mylittleparis.com

Paris Highlights

1 Have a ball at one of Paris' best new museums: the architecturally stunning **Musée du Quai Branly** (p76) or **Cité de l'Architecture et du Patrimoine** (p75)

2 Be stunned and inspired by sublime stained glass in **Ste-Chapelle** (p65), one of Christendom's most beautiful houses of worship

3 Gawp at stately *hôtels particuliers* (private mansions) in the **Marais** (p54) by day, pulsating bars and clubs after dark

4 Enjoy the striking collections and spectacular rooftop views at the **Centre Pompidou** (p55), the world's most successful art and culture centre

5 Marvel at the incomparable collection of Impressionist and post-Impressionist art inside waterfront **Musée d'Orsay** (p73)

6 Enjoy the views and romance of the timeless **Seine** from its banks or afloat an evening cruise (p90)

7 Relive the *ooh-là-là* Paris of cancan and windmills on a **Montmartre** walking tour (p86)

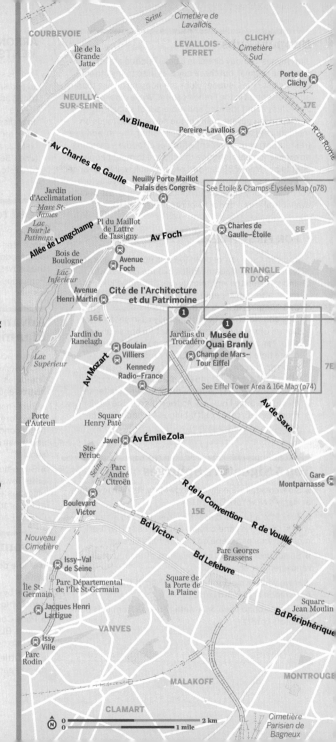

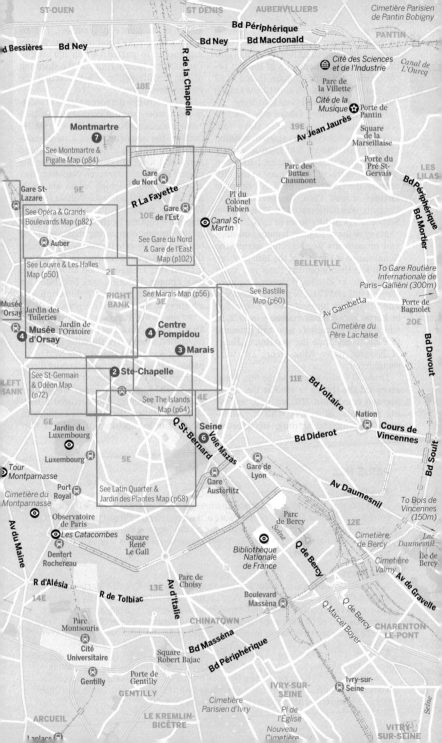

History

In the 3rd century BC a tribe of Celtic Gauls known as the Parisii settled on what is now the Île de la Cité. Centuries of conflict between the Gauls and Romans ended in 52 BC, and in 508 Frankish king Clovis I made Paris seat of his united Gaul kingdom.

In the 9th century France was beset by Scandinavian Vikings; within three centuries these 'Norsemen' started pushing towards Paris, which had risen so rapidly in importance that construction had begun on the cathedral of Notre Dame in the 12th century, the Louvre was built as a riverside fortress around 1200, the beautiful Ste-Chapelle was consecrated in 1248 and the Sorbonne opened its doors in 1253.

Many of the city's most famous buildings and monuments were erected during the Renaissance at the end of the 15th century. But in less than a century Paris was again in turmoil, as clashes between Huguenot (Protestant) and Catholic groups increased. The worst such incident was the so-called St Bartholomew's Day massacre in 1572, in which 3000 Huguenots who had gathered in Paris to celebrate the wedding of Henri of Navarre (later King Henri IV) were slaughtered.

Louis XIV, also known as the Sun King, ascended the throne in 1643 at the age of five and ruled until 1715, virtually emptying the national coffers with his ambitious building and battling. His greatest legacy is the palace at Versailles. The excesses of Louis XVI and his queen, Marie-Antoinette, in part led to an uprising of Parisians on 14 July 1789 and the storming of the Bastille prison – kick-starting the French Revolution.

France struggled under a string of mostly inept rulers until a coup d'état in 1851 brought Emperor Napoleon III to power. He oversaw the construction of a more modern Paris, with wide boulevards, sculpted parks and modern sewer system. Like his pugnacious uncle, however, Napoleon had a taste for blood, which led to his costly and unsuccessful war with Prussia in 1870. When the masses in Paris heard of their emperor's capture by the enemy, they took to the streets, demanding that a republic be declared. Despite its bloody beginnings, the Third Republic ushered in the glittering and very creative period known as the belle époque (beautiful age), celebrated for its graceful art nouveau architecture and advances in the arts and sciences.

By the 1930s, Paris was a centre for the artistic avant-garde and had established its reputation among free-thinking intellectuals. This was all cut short by the Nazi occupation of 1940; Paris remained under direct German rule until 25 August 1944.

After the war, Paris regained its position as a creative centre and nurtured a revitalised liberalism that reached a climax in the student-led uprisings of 1968. The Sor-

---

PARIS IN...

Two Days

Join a morning tour then concentrate on those great Parisian icons: Notre Dame, the Eiffel Tower and the Arc de Triomphe. Late afternoon have a coffee or pastis on av des Champs-Élysées then mooch to Montmartre for dinner. Next day enjoy the Musée d'Orsay, Ste-Chapelle and the Musée Rodin. Brunch on place des Vosges and enjoy a night of mirth and gaiety in the Marais.

Four Days

With another two days, consider a cruise along the Seine or Canal St-Martin and meander further afield to Cimetière du Père Lachaise or Parc de la Villette. By night take in a concert or opera at the Palais Garnier or Opéra Bastille, or a play at the Comédie Française, and go on a bar and club crawl along Ménilmontant's rue Oberkampf. The Bastille area also translates as another great night out.

A Week

Seven days allows you to see a good many of the major sights listed in this chapter, visit places around Paris such as La Défense and St-Denis, and leave Paris proper for a day or two: Vaux-le-Vicomte can be combined with Fontainebleau, Senlis with Chantilly and, if you travel hard and fast, Chartres with Versailles.

THE LOUVRE: TICKETS & TOURS

Buy your tickets in advance from the ticket machines in the Carrousel du Louvre or from the *billetteries* (ticket offices) of Fnac or Virgin Megastores (see p119) for an extra €1 to €1.60, and walk straight in without queuing. Tickets are valid for the whole day, so you can come and go as you please.

Free English-language *plans* (maps) of the labyrinthine Louvre can be obtained from the circular information desk in the centre of the Hall Napoléon. Excellent publications to self-guide include the *Louvre Visitors' Guide* (€8), *Louvre Masterpieces* (€10), *Louvre: The 300 Masterpieces* (€12) and the hefty, 485-page *A Guide to the Louvre* (€17). All are available from the museum bookshop.

English-language **guided tours** (☎01 40 20 52 63) lasting 1½ hours depart from the area under the Grande Pyramide, marked *Acceuil des Groupes* (Groups Reception), at 11am, 2pm and (sometimes) 3.45pm Monday and Wednesday to Saturday. Tickets cost €5 in addition to the cost of admission. Sign up at least 30 minutes before departure time.

Self-paced audioguides in six languages, with 1½ hours of commentary, can be rented for €6 under the pyramid at the entrance to each wing.

bonne was occupied, barricades were set up in the Latin Quarter and some nine million people nationwide were inspired to join in a general strike that paralysed the country.

During the 1980s President François Mitterrand initiated several costly *grands projets,* a series of building projects that garnered widespread approval even when the results were popular failures. In 2001, Bertrand Delanoë, a socialist with support from the Green Party, became Paris' – and a European capital's – first openly gay mayor. He was returned to power in the second round of voting in the 2008 elections.

◉ Sights

Paris' major sights are distributed more or less equally on the Right and Left Banks of the Seine. We start in the heart of the Right Bank in the area around the Louvre and Les Halles, which largely takes in the 1er and follows, more or less, the order of the *arrondissements.*

LOUVRE & LES HALLES

The area around the Louvre in the 1er contains some of the most important sights for visitors in Paris. To the northeast, the mostly pedestrian zone between the Centre Pompidou and the Forum des Halles, with rue Étienne Marcel to the north and rue de Rivoli to the south, is filled with people by day and by night, just as it was for the 850-odd years when part of it served as Paris' main marketplace, known as Les Halles.

Musée du Louvre   ART MUSEUM

(Map p50; www.louvre.fr; permanent collections/ permanent collections & temporary exhibitions €9.50/14, after 6pm Wed & Fri €6/12; ◷9am-6pm Mon, Thu, Sat & Sun, 9am-10pm Wed & Fri; Ⓜ Palais Royal-Musée du Louvre) The vast Palais du Louvre was constructed as a fortress by Philippe-Auguste in the early 13th century and rebuilt in the mid-16th century for use as a royal residence. In 1793 the Revolutionary Convention turned it into the nation's first national museum.

The paintings, sculptures and artefacts on display in the Louvre Museum have been assembled by French governments over the past five centuries. Among them are works of art and artisanship from all over Europe and important collections of Assyrian, Etruscan, Greek, Coptic and Islamic art and antiquities. Traditionally the Louvre's raison d'être is to present Western art from the Middle Ages to about the year 1848 (at which point the Musée d'Orsay takes over), as well as the works of ancient civilisations that informed Western art.

When the museum opened in the late 18th century, it contained 2500 paintings and objets d'art; today some 35,000 are on display. The 'Grand Louvre' project, inaugurated by the late President Mitterrand in 1989, doubled the museum's exhibition space, and new and renovated galleries have opened in recent years devoted to objets d'art such as Sèvres porcelain and the crown jewels of Louis XV (room 66, 1st floor, Apollo Gallery, Denon Wing).

The Louvre

A HALF-DAY TOUR

Successfully visiting the Louvre is a fine art. Its complex labyrinth of galleries and staircases spiralling three wings and four floors renders discovery a snakes-and-ladders experience. Initiate yourself with this three-hour itinerary – a playful mix of *Mona Lisa* obvious and up-to-the-minute unexpected.

Arriving by the stunning main entrance, pick up colour-coded floor plans at the lower-ground-floor information desk **1** beneath IM Pei's glass pyramid, ride the escalator up to the Sully Wing and swap passport for multimedia guide (there are limited descriptions in the galleries) at the wing entrance.

The Louvre is as much about spectacular architecture as masterly art. To appreciate this zip up and down Sully's Escalier Henri II to admire *Venus de Milo* **2**, then up parallel Escalier Henri IV to the palatial displays in Cour Khorsabad **3**. Cross room 1 to find the escalator up to the 1st floor and staircase-as-art *L'Esprit d'Escalier* **4**. Next traverse 25 consecutive galleries (thank you, floor plan!) to flip conventional contemplation on its head with Cy Twombly's *The Ceiling* **5**, and the hypnotic *Winged Victory of Samothrace* sculpture **6** – just two rooms away – which brazenly insists on being admired from all angles. End with the impossibly famous *Liberty Leading the People* **7**, *Mona Lisa* **8** and *Virgin & Child* **9**.

Mission Mona Lisa

If you just want to venerate the Louvre's most famous lady, use the Porte des Lions entrance, from where it's a five-minute walk. Go up one flight of stairs and through rooms 26, 14 and 13 to the Grande Galerie and adjoining room 6.

L'Esprit d'Escalier
Escalier Lefuel, Richelieu
Discover the 'Spirit of the Staircase' through François Morellet's contemporary stained glass, which casts new light on old stone. DETOUR» Napoleon III's gorgeous gilt apartments.

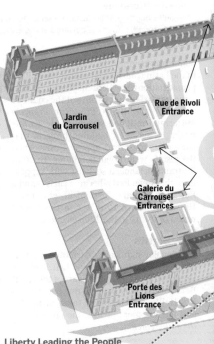

Rue de Rivoli Entrance

Jardin du Carrousel

Galerie du Carrousel Entrances

Porte des Lions Entrance

Liberty Leading the People
Room 77, 1st Floor, Denon
Decipher the politics behind French romanticism in Eugène Delacroix's rousing early 19th-century canvas and Théodore Géricault's *The Raft of the Medusa*.

BILL BACHMANN/ALAMY

TOP TIPS

» **Cent saver** Visit after 3pm or in the evening when tickets are cheaper

» **Crowd dodgers** The Denon Wing is always packed; visit on late nights Wednesday or Friday or trade Denon in for the notably quieter Richelieu Wing

» **2nd floor** Not for first-timers: save its more specialist works for subsequent visits

» **Multimedia guide** Worth it, if only to press the 'Where am I?' button when lost

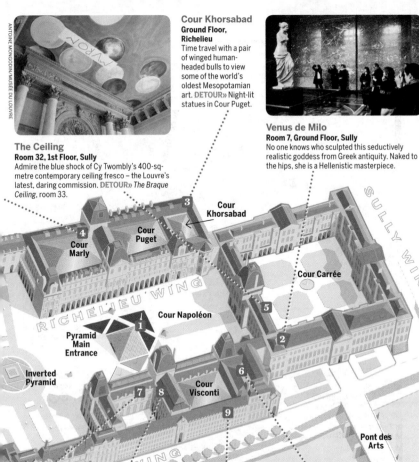

Cour Khorsabad
Ground Floor, Richelieu
Time travel with a pair of winged human-headed bulls to view some of the world's oldest Mesopotamian art. **DETOUR»** Night-lit statues in Cour Puget.

Venus de Milo
Room 7, Ground Floor, Sully
No one knows who sculpted this seductively realistic goddess from Greek antiquity. Naked to the hips, she is a Hellenistic masterpiece.

The Ceiling
Room 32, 1st Floor, Sully
Admire the blue shock of Cy Twombly's 400-sq-metre contemporary ceiling fresco – the Louvre's latest, daring commission. **DETOUR»** *The Braque Ceiling*, room 33.

ANTOINE MONGODIN/MUSÉE DU LOUVRE

WITOLD SKRYPCZAK

Cour Khorsabad 3

Cour Puget

Cour Marly 4

Cour Carrée

SULLY WING

RICHELIEU WING

Cour Napoléon 1

Pyramid Main Entrance

5

2

Inverted Pyramid

6

7 8 **Cour Visconti**

9

Pont des Arts

DENON WING

Pont du Carrousel

Virgin & Child
Room 5, Grande Galerie, 1st Floor, Denon
In the spirit of artistic devotion save the Louvre's most famous gallery for last: a feast of Virgin-and-child paintings by Raphael, Domenico Ghirlandaio, Giovanni Bellini and Francesco Botticini.

TERRY SMITH/ALAMY

Mona Lisa
Room 6, 1st Floor, Denon
No smile is as enigmatic or bewitching as hers. Da Vinci's diminutive *La Joconde* hangs opposite the largest painting in the Louvre – sumptuous, fellow Italian Renaissance artwork *The Wedding at Cana.*

Winged Victory of Samothrace
Escalier Daru, 1st Floor, Sully
Draw breath at the aggressive dynamism of this headless, handless Hellenistic goddess. **DETOUR»** The razzle-dazzle of the Apollo Gallery's crown jewels.

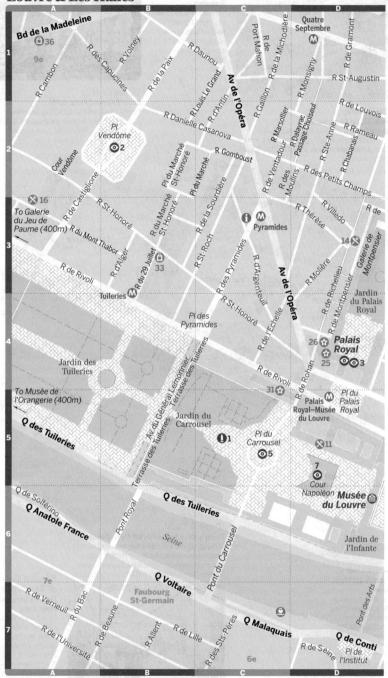

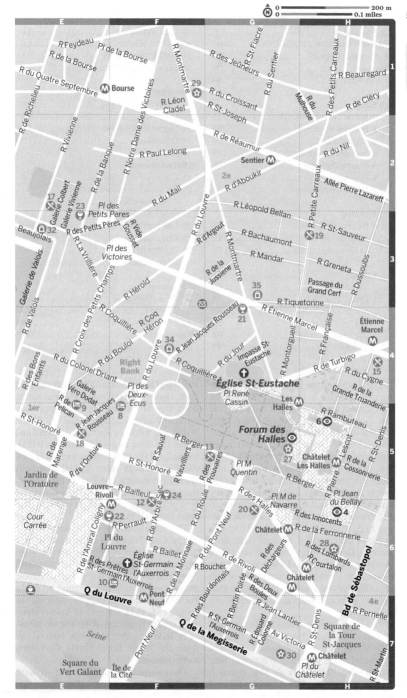

0   200 m
0   0.1 miles

R Feydeau
Pl de la Bourse
R de la Bourse
R du Quatre Septembre
M Bourse
R Montmartre
R des Jeuneurs
R St-Fiacre
R du Sentier
R des Petits Carreaux
R Beauregard
R de Richelieu
R de la Banque
Notre Dame des Victoires
R Léon Cladel
R du Croissant
R St-Joseph
R du Mulhouse
R de Cléry
R Vivienne
R Paul Lelong
R de Réaumur
R du Nil
17
Galerie Colbert
Galerie Vivienne
23
Pl des Petits Pères
R du Mail
Sentier **M**
R d'Aboukir
R Petite Carreaux
R St-Sauveur
Allée Pierre Lazareff
2e
32
Beaujolais
R des Petits Pères
R Vide Gousset
R du Louvre
R Léopold Bellan
R d'Argout
R Bachaumont
19
R La Vrillière
Pl des Victoires
R de la Jussienne
R Mandar
R Greneta
R Dussoubs
Galerie de Valois
R Hérold
R Montmartre
Passage du Grand Cerf
R de Valois
R Coquillière
R Coq Héron
R Jean Jacques Rousseau
35
R Tiquetonne
Étienne Marcel **M**
R des Bons Enfants
R Croix des Petits Champs
R du Bouloi
34
21
R Étienne Marcel
R Française
R du Colonel Driant
R du Louvre
R Jean Jacques Rousseau
R du Jour
Impasse St-Eustache
R Montorgueil
R de Turbigo
15
Right Bank
R Coquillière
Église St-Eustache
R du Cygne
R de la Grande Truanderie
Galerie Véro Dodat
R de Pelican
9
Pl des Deux-Écus
Pl René Cassin
Les Halles **M**
R Rambuteau
6
1er
R Jean-Jacques Rousseau
8
Forum des Halles
R des Lombards
R St-Denis
18
R St-Honoré
R Sauval
R Berger
13
27
Châtelet Les Halles **M**
R Lescot
R de la Cossonnerie
R de Marengo
R de l'Oratoire
R St-Honoré
R Vauvilliers
R des Prouvaires
Pl M Quentin
R Berger
Pl Jean du Bellay
Jardin de l'Oratoire
Louvre-Rivoli **M**
R Bailleul
24
12
R de l'Arbre Sec
R du Roule
R des Halles
20
Pl M de Navarre
R des Innocents
4
Cour Carrée
22
R Perrault
Pl du Louvre
Église St-Germain l'Auxerrois
R Baillet
R de la Monnaie
R du Pont Neuf
R de Rivoli
Châtelet **M**
R de la Ferronnerie
R des Déchargeurs
28
R des Lombards
R Courtalon
Bd de Sébastopol
R des Prêtres St-Germain l'Auxerrois
10
Pont Neuf
R Boucher
R des Bourdonnais
R Bertin Porée
R des Deux Boules
Châtelet
4e
R Pernelle
Q du Louvre
Pont Neuf
R St-Germain l'Auxerrois
R Jean Lantier
R Édouard Colonne
Av Victoria
R St-Denis
Square de la Tour St-Jacques
R St-Martin
Seine
Q de la Megisserie
30
Châtelet **M**
Pl du Châtelet
Square du Vert Galant
Île de la Cité

The Louvre may be the most actively avoided museum in the world. Daunted by the richness and sheer size of the place (the side facing the Seine is some 700m long, and it is said that it would take nine months just to glance at every piece of art here), both local people and visitors often find the prospect of an afternoon at a smaller museum far more inviting. Eventually, most people do their duty and come, but many leave overwhelmed, unfulfilled, exhausted and frustrated at having got lost on their way to da Vinci's *La Joconde,* better known as *Mona Lisa* (room 6, 1st floor, Salle de la Joconde, Denon Wing). Your best bet – after checking out a few works you really want to see – is to choose a particular period or section of the Louvre and pretend that the rest is in another museum somewhere across town.

The most famous works from antiquity include the *Seated Scribe* (room 22, 1st floor, Sully Wing), the *Code of Hammurabi* (room 3, ground floor, Richelieu Wing) and that armless duo, the *Venus de Milo* (room 7, ground floor, Denon Wing) and the *Winged Victory of Samothrace* (opposite room 1, 1st floor, Denon Wing). From the Renaissance, don't miss Michelangelo's *The Dying Slave* (ground floor, Michelangelo Gallery, Denon Wing) and works by Raphael, Botticelli and Titian (1st floor, Denon Wing). French masterpieces of the 19th century include Ingres' *The Turkish Bath* (room 60, 2nd floor, Sully Wing), Géricault's *The Raft of the Medusa* (room 77, 1st floor, Denon Wing) and works by Corot, Delacroix and Fragonard (2nd floor, Denon Wing).

The main entrance and ticket windows in the Cour Napoléon are covered by the 21m-high Pyramide du Louvre, a glass pyramid designed by the Chinese-born American architect IM Pei. You can avoid the queues outside the pyramid or at the Porte des Lions entrance by entering the complex via the Carrousel du Louvre shopping centre entrance, at 99 rue de Rivoli, or by following the 'Musée du Louvre' exit from the Palais Royal–Musée du Louvre metro station.

The Louvre is divided into four sections: the Sully, Denon and Richelieu Wings and the Hall Napoléon. The split-level public area under the glass pyramid is known as the Hall Napoléon (⊙9am-10pm Wed-Mon; temporary exhibition galleries ⊙9am-6pm Mon, Thu & Sun, 9am-10pm Wed, 9am-8pm Sat). The hall has temporary exhibition halls, bookshop and souvenir store, a café and auditoriums for lectures and films. The centrepiece of the Carrousel du Louvre, the shopping centre that runs underground from the pyramid to the Arc de Triomphe du Carrousel, is the pyramide inversée (inverted glass pyramid), also by Pei.

Jardin des Tuileries GARDEN
(Map p50; ⊙7am-7.30, 9 or 11pm; Ⓜ Tuileries or Concorde) Beginning just west of the Jardin du Carrousel, the formal, 28-hectare garden was laid out in its present form – more or less – in the mid-17th century by André Le Nôtre, who also created the gardens at Vaux-le-Vicomte (p150) and Versailles (p145). The Tuileries soon became the most fashionable spot in Paris for parading about in one's finery; today it is a favourite of joggers. It forms part of the banks of the Seine World Heritage Site listed in 1991.

The Voie Triomphale (Triumphal Way), also called the Axe Historique (Historic Axis), the western continuation of the Tuileries' east–west axis, follows the av des Champs-Élysées to the Arc de Triomphe and, ultimately, to the Grande Arche in the skyscraper district of La Défense (p135).

Galerie du Jeu de Paume GALLERY
(www.jeudepaume.org; 1 place de la Concorde, 1er; adult/child €7/5; ⊙noon-9pm Tue, noon-7pm Wed-Fri, 10am-7pm Sat & Sun; Ⓜ Concorde) Housed in an erstwhile *jeu de paume* (real, or royal, tennis) court built in 1861 during the reign of Napoleon III in the northwestern corner of the Jardin des Tuileries, the two-storey Jeu de Paume stages innovative exhibitions of contemporary art.

Musée de l'Orangerie ART MUSEUM
(www.musee-orangerie.fr; Jardin des Tuileries, 1er; adult/child €7.50/5.50; ⊙12.30-7pm Wed, Thu & Sat-Mon, to 9pm Fri; Ⓜ Concorde) Located in the southwestern corner of the Jardin des Tuileries, this museum, with the Jeu de Paume, is all that remains of the once palatial Palais des Tuileries, which was razed during the Paris Commune in 1871. It exhibits important Impressionist works, including a series of Monet's *Decorations des Nymphéas* (Water Lilies) in two huge oval rooms purpose-built in 1927 on the artist's

instructions, as well as works by Cézanne, Matisse, Picasso, Renoir, Sisley, Soutine and Utrillo. An audioguide costs €5.

Place Vendôme CITY SQUARE
(Map p50; Ⓜ Tuileries or Opéra) Octagonal place Vendôme and the arcaded and colonnaded buildings around it were constructed between 1687 and 1721. In March 1796 Napoleon married Josephine, Viscountess Beauharnais, in the building at No 3. Today, the buildings surrounding the square house the posh Hôtel Ritz Paris and some of the city's most fashionable boutiques. The 43.5m-tall Colonne Vendôme (Vendôme Column) in the centre of the square consists of a stone core wrapped in a 160m-long bronze spiral made from hundreds of Austrian and Russian cannons captured by Napoleon at the Battle of Austerlitz in 1805. The statue on top depicts Napoleon in classical Roman dress.

Palais Royal PALACE
(Map p50; place du Palais Royal, 1er; Ⓜ Palais Royal–Musée du Louvre) North of place du Palais Royal and the Louvre lies the Palais Royal, which briefly housed a young Louis XIV in the 1640s. Construction was begun in 1624 by Cardinal Richelieu, though most of the present neoclassical complex dates from the latter part of the 18th century. It now contains the governmental **Conseil d'État** (State Council) and is closed to the public.

MUSEUM PASS

The Paris Museum Pass (www.paris museumpass.fr; 2/4/6 days €32/48/64) is valid for entry to some 38 venues in Paris – including the Louvre, Centre Pompidou, Musée d'Orsay and new Musée du Quai Branly and Cité de l'Architecture et du Patrimoine. Outside the city limits but still within the Île de France region, it will get you into another 22 places, including the basilica at St-Denis (p143) and parts of the châteaux at Versailles (p145) and Fontainebleau (p147). Buy the pass online, at participating venues, branches of the Paris Convention & Visitors Bureau (p129), Fnac outlets (p119), RATP (Régie Autonome des Transports Parisians) information desks and major metro stations.

ℹ️ IT'S FREE

Permanent collections at most city-run museums are free, including the Maison de Victor Hugo, Musée Carnavalet and the Musée des Beaux-Arts de la Ville de Paris in Petit Palais. Temporary exhibitions usually command a fee.

National museums yield an even better bargain: admission is reduced for those aged over 60 and 18 to 25, and completely free for **EU residents under 26** years of age, **anyone under 18** years, and **everyone on the first Sunday of each month**. These include: the Louvre, the Musée National d'Art Moderne in the Pompidou, Musée de l'Orangerie, Musée du Quai Branly, Musée d'Orsay, Musée Guimet des Arts Asiatiques, Musée Rodin, Musée National du Moyen Âge, Cité de l'Architecture et du Patrimoine, Cité Nationale de l'Histoire de l'Immigration and Musée des Arts et Métiers.

Ditto for the following with the exception that they are only free the first Sunday of the month November to March: Arc de Triomphe, Conciergerie, Panthéon, Ste-Chapelle and the Tours de Notre Dame.

The colonnaded building facing place André Malraux is the Comédie Française (p123), the world's oldest national theatre founded in 1680.

Just north of the palace is the **Jardin du Palais Royal**, a lovely, 21-hectare park surrounded by two arcades, namely **Galerie de Valois** with its designer fashion shops, art galleries and jewellers, and **Galerie de Montpensier** with a few old shops remaining. At the southern end are the black-and-white striped columns of various heights by Daniel Buren, started in 1986, interrupted by irate Parisians and finished – following the intervention of the Ministry of Culture and Communication – in 1995. Toss a coin and if it lands on one of the columns, your wish will come true.

Forum des Halles   MARKET
(Map p50; www.forum-des-halles.com; 1 rue Pierre Lescot, 1er; ⊙shops 10am-7.30pm; MLes Halles or Châtelet Les Halles) Les Halles, the city's main wholesale food market, occupied the area just south of the Église St-Eustache from the early 12th century until 1969, when it was moved to the southern suburb of Rungis. In its place, the unspeakably ugly Forum des Halles, a huge underground shopping centre, was constructed in the glass-and-chrome style of the early 1970s. At last it's slated to be gutted and rebuilt by 2012, and topped with an architecturally stunning 'canopy'.

Atop the Forum des Halles is a popular rooftop garden. During the warmer months, street musicians, fire-eaters and other performers display their talents throughout the area, especially at place du Jean du Bellay, whose centre is adorned by a multitiered Renaissance fountain, the

Fontaine des Innocents, erected in 1549. It is named after the Cimetière des Innocents, a cemetery on this site from which two million skeletons were disinterred and transferred to the Catacombes (p71) in the 14e after the Revolution.

TOP CHOICE **Église St-Eustache**   CHURCH
(Map p50; www.st-eustache.org, in French; 2 impasse St-Eustache, 1er; ⊙9.30am-7pm Mon-Fri, 10am-7pm Sat, 9am-7.15pm Sun; MLes Halles) One of the most beautiful churches in Paris and consecrated to an early Roman martyr who is the patron saint of hunters, this majestic church is just north of the gardens above the Forum des Halles. Constructed between 1532 and 1637, St-Eustache is primarily Gothic, though a neoclassical facade was added on the western side in the mid-18th century. Inside, there are some exceptional Flamboyant Gothic arches holding up the ceiling of the chancel, although most of the interior ornamentation is Renaissance and even classical. The gargantuan organ above the west entrance, with 101 stops and 8000 pipes, is used for concerts (long a tradition here) and during Sunday Mass (11am and 6pm).

MARAIS & BASTILLE

The Marais, the area of the Right Bank north of Île St-Louis in the 3e and 4e, was exactly what its name implies – 'marsh' or 'swamp' – until the 13th century, when it was converted to farmland. In the early 17th century, Henri IV built the place Royale (today's place des Vosges), turning the area into Paris' most fashionable residential district and attracting wealthy aristocrats who then erected their own luxurious *hôtels particulier*. Today many of them are house museums and government institutions.

When the aristocracy moved from Paris to Versailles and Faubourg St-Germain during the late 17th and 18th centuries, the Marais and its townhouses passed into the hands of ordinary Parisians. The 110-hectare area was given a major facelift in the late 1960s and early 1970s. The Marais has become a much desired address in recent years, while remaining the centre of Paris' gay life and home to a long-established Jewish neighbourhood called the Pletzl.

After years as a run-down immigrant neighbourhood notorious for its high crime rate, the contiguous Bastille district (11e and 12e) has undergone a fair degree of gentrification, largely due to the opening of the Opéra Bastille almost two decades ago. Though the area is not the hip nightlife centre it was through most of the 1990s, it still has quite a bit to offer after dark, with numerous pubs, bars and clubs lining rue de Lappe and rue de la Roquette.

Centre Pompidou   MODERN ART MUSEUM

(Map p56; www.centrepompidou.fr; place Georges Pompidou, 4e; ⓂRambuteau) This centre has amazed and delighted visitors since it was inaugurated in 1977, not just for its outstanding collection of modern art, but also for its radical architectural statement.

The open space at ground level has temporary exhibitions and information desks, while the 4th and 5th floors house the Musée National d'Art Moderne (MNAM; National Museum of Modern Art; adult/child €10-12/free; Ⓢll am-9pm Wed-Mon), France's national collection of art dating from 1905 onwards. About a third of the 50,000-plus works, including the work of the surrealists and cubists, as well as pop art and contemporary works, are on display.

West of the Pompidou, place Georges Pompidou and nearby pedestrian streets attract buskers, musicians, jugglers and mime artists, and can be a lot of fun. South of the centre on place Igor Stravinsky, the fanciful mechanical fountains of skeletons, hearts, treble clefs and a big pair of ruby-red lips are a delight.

Atelier Brancusi   ART MUSEUM

(Map p56; Centre Pompidou; 55 rue Rambuteau, 4e; admission free; Ⓢ2-6pm Wed-Mon; ⓂRambuteau) West of the Centre Pompidou main building, this reconstruction of the studio of Romanian-born sculptor Constantin

Brancusi (1876–1957) designed by Renzo Piano contains some 160 examples of the sculptor's work.

Musée Picasso   ART MUSEUM

(Map p56; www.musee-picasso.fr, in French; 5 rue de Thorigny, 3e; Ⓢ9.30am-6pm Wed-Mon; ⓂSt-Paul or Chemin Vert) One of Paris' best-loved art museums, the Musée Picasso, housed in the mid-17th-century Hôtel Salé, includes more than 3500 of the *grand maître*'s engravings, paintings, ceramic works, drawings and sculptures. You can also see part of Picasso's personal art collection, which includes works by Braque, Cézanne, Matisse, Modigliani, Degas and Rousseau. It will reopen after extensive renovations in 2012.

Hôtel de Ville   CITY HALL

(Map p56; www.paris.fr; place de l'Hôtel de Ville, 4e; ⓂHôtel de Ville) After having been gutted during the Paris Commune of 1871, Paris' Hôtel de Ville was rebuilt in the neo-Renaissance style (1874–82). The ornate facade is decorated with 108 statues of noteworthy Parisians. There's a Salon d'Accueil (Reception Hall; 29 rue de Rivoli, 4e; Ⓢ10am-7pm Mon-Sat), which dispenses copious amounts of information and brochures and is used for temporary exhibitions, usually with a Paris theme.

Place des Vosges   CITY SQUARE

(Map p56; ⓂSt-Paul or Bastille) Inaugurated in 1612 as place Royale, Place des Vosges is an ensemble of three dozen symmetrical houses with ground-floor arcades, steep slate roofs and large dormer windows arranged around a large square. Only the earliest houses were built of brick; to save time and money, the rest were given timber frames and faced with plaster, which was then painted to resemble brick.

The author Victor Hugo lived at the square's Hôtel de Rohan-Guémenée from 1832 to 1848, moving here a year after the publication of *Notre Dame de Paris* (The Hunchback of Notre Dame). His former house, the Maison de Victor Hugo (www.musee-hugo.paris.fr, in French; admission adult/child €7/free; Ⓢ10am-6pm Tue-Sun), is now a municipal museum devoted to the life and times of the celebrated novelist and poet, with an impressive collection of his own drawings and portraits.

TOP CHOICE Hôtel de Sully   HISTORIC MANSION

(Map p56; 62 rue St-Antoine, 4e; Ⓢ9am-12.45pm & 2-6pm Mon-Thu, to 5pm Fri; ⓂSt-Paul)

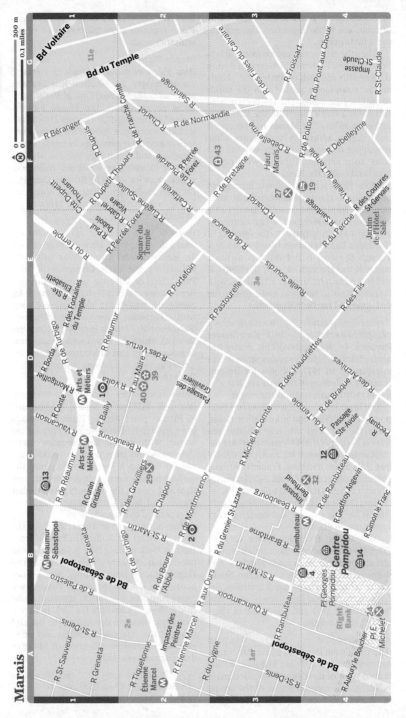

PARIS

Marais

0 0
200 m
0.1 miles

Bd Voltaire

Bd du Temple

11e

Bd du Temple

R des Filles du Calvaire

R du Pont aux Choux

Impasse St-Claude

R St-Claude

R Béranger

R Dupuis

R de Franche Comté

R Charlot

R de Normandie

R Saintonge

R Debelleyme

R de Poitou

R Debelleyme

Cité Dupetit Thouars

R Dupetit Thouars

R Gabriel Vicaire

R Eugène Spuller

R de Picardie

R Perrée

R de Forez

R de Bretagne

Haut Marais

R Vieille du Temple

R Froissart

R Paul Dubois

R Perrée Forez

Square du Temple

R Caffarelli

🏛️ 43

27 ✕

🍴 19

R de Beauce

R Charlot

R du Perche

R des Coutures St-Gervais

Jardin de l'Hôtel Salé

R du Temple

R Ste-Elisabeth

R des Fontaines du Temple

R Portefoin

R Pastourelle

3e

Ruelle Sourdis

R des Fils

R Borda

R de Turbigo

R Montgolfier

R Réaumur

R des Vertus

R des Haudriettes

R des Archives

Arts et Métiers Ⓜ

1 ⊙

R Volta

R au Maire

39 ☆

40 ⊙

Passage des Gravilliers

R Michel le Comte

R de Braque

R du Temple

Passage Ste-Avoie

R Pecquay

R Conte

R Vaucanson

R Beaubourg

R Bailly

Arts et Métiers Ⓜ

13 🏛️

R de Réaumur

R Cunin Gridaine

R des Gravilliers

29 ✕

R Chapon

R de Montmorency

12 🏛️

Impasse Berthaud

32 ✕

R Geoffroy Angevin

R Simon le Franc

Ⓜ Réaumur Sébastopol

Bd de Sébastopol

R Greneta

R de Turbigo

R St-Martin

R du Bourg l'Abbé

R du Grenier St-Lazare

Rambuteau Ⓜ

R Brantôme

R Beaubourg

R de Rambuteau

Centre Pompidou 🏛️

14 🏛️

R de Palestro

2e

R St-Denis

R Tiquetonne

Impasse des Peintres

R Étienne Marcel

Étienne Marcel Ⓜ

R aux Ours

R Quincampoix

Pl Georges Pompidou

4 🏛️

Right Bank

Pl E. Michelet

24 ✕

R St-Sauveur

R Greneta

R du Cygne

1er

R St-Denis

R Rambuteau

R Aubry le Boucher

Bd de Sébastopol

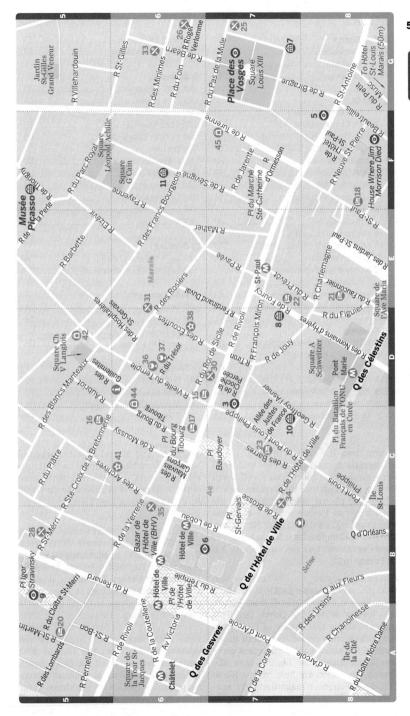

Dating from the early 17th century, this aristocratic mansion has two wonderful Renaissance-style courtyards – well worth the trip here. Combine them with a look at a first-class photographic exhibition at the house's **Jeu de Paume – Site Sully** (www.jeudepaume.org; adult/child €5/2.50; ⊙noon-7pm Tue-Fri, 10am-7pm Sat & Sun), a branch of the more famous Galerie Nationale du Jeu de Paume (p53).

Musée Carnavalet   HISTORY MUSEUM
(Map p56; www.carnavalet.paris.fr, in French; 23 rue de Sévigné, 3e; adult/child €7/free; ⊙10am-6pm Tue-Sun; MSt-Paul or Chemin Vert) This museum charts the history of Paris from the Gallo-Roman period to modern times. Some of the nation's most important documents, paintings and objects from the French Revolution are here (rooms 101 to 113), as is Fouquet's magnificent art nouveau jewellery shop from the rue Royale

(room 142) and Marcel Proust's cork-lined bedroom from his apartment on bd Haussmann (room 147), in which he wrote most of the 7350-page *À la Recherche du Temps Perdu* (In Search of Lost Time).

Musée des Arts et Métiers
SCIENCE & TECHNOLOGY MUSEUM
(Map p56; www.arts-et-metiers.net, in French; 60 rue de Réaumur, 3e; adult/child €6.50/free; ⊙10am-6pm Tue, Wed & Fri-Sun, to 9.30pm Thu; MArts et Métiers) The oldest museum of science and technology in Europe, this is a must for anyone with an interest in how things work. Housed in the 18th-century priory of St-Martin des Champs, some 3000 instruments, machines and working models from the 18th to 20th centuries are displayed on three floors. Taking pride of place is Foucault's original pendulum, which he introduced to the world in 1855.

Musée d'Art et d'Histoire du Judaïsme
JUDAISM MUSEUM

(Map p56; www.mahj.org; 71 rue du Temple, 3e; adult/child €6.80/free; ⊘11am-6pm Mon-Fri, 10am-6pm Sun; ⓂRambuteau) Housed in the sumptuous, 17th-century Hôtel de St-Aignan, this museum traces the evolution of Jewish communities from the Middle Ages to the present, with particular emphasis on the history of the Jews in France but also communities in other parts of Europe and North Africa. Exhibits include documents relating to the Dreyfus Affair (1894–1900) and works by Paris-based Jewish artists Chagall, Modigliani and Soutine. Temporary exhibitions cost an extra €7.50 and a combined ticket is €9.50.

Mémorial de la Shoah
MEMORIAL

(Map p56; www.memorialdelashoah.org; 17 rue Geoffroy l'Asnier, 4e; admission free; ⊘10am-6pm Sun-Wed & Fri, 10am-10pm Thu; ⓂSt-Paul) Established in 1956, the Memorial to the Unknown Jewish Martyr has metamorphosed into the Mémorial de la Shoah and documentation centre. The permanent collection and temporary exhibitions relate to the Holocaust and the German occupation of parts of France and Paris during WWII; the film clips of contemporary footage and interviews are heart-rending and the displays instructive and easy to follow. The actual memorial to the victims of the Shoah, a Hebrew word meaning 'catastrophe' and synonymous with the Holocaust, stands at the entrance, and there is a wall inscribed with the names of 76,000 men, women and children deported from France to Nazi extermination camps.

[TOP CHOICE] **Maison Européenne de la Photographie** PHOTOGRAPHY MUSEUM

(European House of Photography; Map p56; www. mep-fr.org, in French; 5-7 rue de Fourcy, 4e; adult/ child €6.50/3.50; ⊘11am-8pm Wed-Sun; ⓂSt-Paul or Pont Marie) Housed in the overly renovated Hôtel Hénault de Cantorbe, dating from the early 18th century, the European House of Photography hosts cutting-edge temporary exhibitions (usually retrospectives of single photographers) and a huge permanent collection on the history of photography and its connections with France. Frequent weekend-afternoon screenings of short films and documentaries.

Place de la Bastille
CITY SQUARE

(Map p60; ⓂBastille) The Bastille, built during the 14th century as a fortified royal residence, is probably the most famous monument in Paris that no longer exists; the notorious prison – the quintessential symbol of royal despotism – was demolished by a Revolutionary mob on 14 July 1789 and all seven prisoners were freed. Place de la Bastille in the 11e and 12e, where the prison once stood, is now a very busy traffic roundabout.

In the centre of the square is the 52m-high Colonne de Juillet (July Column), whose shaft of greenish bronze is topped by a gilded and winged figure of Liberty. It was erected in 1833 as a memorial to those killed in the street battles that accompanied the July Revolution of 1830; they are buried in vaults under the column. It was later consecrated as a memorial to the victims of the February Revolution of 1848.

Opéra Bastille
OPERA HOUSE

(Map p60; www.opera-de-paris.fr, in French; 2-6 place de la Bastille, 12e; ⓂBastille) Paris' giant 'second' opera house, the Opéra Bastille, designed by the Canadian architect Carlos Ott, was inaugurated on 14 July 1989, the 200th anniversary of the storming of the Bastille. It has three theatres, including the 2700-seat main auditorium; check the website for departure times of 1¼-hour **guided tours** (☏01 40 01 19 70; adult/child €11/6).

DON'T MISS

IF WALLS COULD TALK

Centuries of history are inscribed on the facades and pediments of the 4e *arrondissement* and in the narrow streets, alleys, porches and courtyards: the Marais is one of the few Parisian neighbourhoods that still has much of its pre-Revolutionary architecture intact. These include the house at 3 rue Volta (Map p56) in the 3e *arrondissement*, parts of which date back to 1292; the one at 51 rue de Montmorency (Map p56), also in the 3e and dating back to 1407 which is now a restaurant called Auberge Nicolas Flamel; and the half-timbered 16th-century building at 11 & 13 rue François Miron (Map p56).

Tickets go on sale 10 minutes before departure at the box office (130 rue de Lyon, 12e; ☺10.30am-6.30pm Mon-Sat).

THE ISLANDS

Paris' twinset of islands could not be more different. Île de la Cité is bigger, full of sights and very touristed (though very few people actually live here). Île St-Louis is residential and much quieter, with just enough boutiques and restaurants – and legendary ice-cream maker Berthillon (p108) – to attract visitors.

ÎLE DE LA CITÉ

The site of the first settlement in Paris, around the 3rd century BC, and later the Roman town of Lutèce (Lutetia), the Île de la Cité remained the centre of royal and ecclesiastical power even after the city spread to both banks of the Seine during the Middle Ages. The buildings on the middle part of the island were demolished and rebuilt during Baron Haussmann's great urban renewal scheme of the late 19th century.

Cathédrale de Notre Dame de Paris
CATHEDRAL

(Map p64; www.cathedraledeparis.com; 6 place du Parvis Notre Dame, 4e; audioguide €5; ☺8am-6.45pm Mon-Fri, 8am-7.15pm Sat & Sun; Ⓜ Cité) Cathédrale de Notre Dame de Paris is the true heart of Paris; in fact, distances from Paris to all parts of metropolitan France

are measured from place du Parvis Notre Dame, the square in front of Notre Dame. A bronze star, set in the pavement across from the main entrance, marks the exact location of **point zéro des routes de France** (point zero of French roads).

Notre Dame, the most visited site in Paris, with 10 million people crossing its threshold each year, is not just a masterpiece of French Gothic architecture but has also been the focus of Catholic Paris for seven centuries. Constructed on a site occupied by earlier churches – and, a millennium before that, a Gallo-Roman temple – it was begun in 1163 and largely completed by the mid-14th century. Architect Eugène Emmanuel Viollet-le-Duc carried out extensive renovations in the mid-19th century. The cathedral is on a very grand scale; the interior alone is 130m long, 48m wide and 35m high and can accommodate more than 6000 worshippers.

Notre Dame is known for its sublime balance, although if you look closely you'll see many minor asymmetrical elements introduced to avoid monotony, in accordance with standard Gothic practice. These include the slightly different shapes of each of the three main portals, whose statues were once brightly coloured to make them more effective as a *Biblia pauperum* – a 'Bible of the poor' to help the illiterate understand the Old Testament stories, the Passion of

Notre Dame

A TIMELINE

1160 Maurice de Sully becomes bishop of Paris. Mission: to grace growing Paris with a lofty new cathedral.

1182–90 The choir with double ambulatory **1** is finished and work starts on the nave and side chapels.

1200–50 The west facade **2**, with rose window, three portals and two soaring towers, goes up. Everyone is stunned.

1345 Some 180 years after the foundation stone was laid, the Cathédrale de Notre Dame is complete. It is dedicated to *notre dame* (our lady), the Virgin Mary.

1789 Revolutionaries smash the original Gallery of Kings **3**, pillage the cathedral and melt all its bells except the great bell Emmanuel. The cathedral becomes a Temple of Reason then a warehouse.

1831 Victor Hugo's novel *The Hunchback of Notre Dame* inspires new interest in the half-ruined Gothic cathedral.

1845–50 Architect Viollet-le-Duc undertakes its restoration. Twenty-eight new kings are sculpted for the west facade. The heavily decorated portals **4** and spire **5** are reconstructed. The neo-Gothic treasury **6** is built.

1860 The area in front of Notre Dame is cleared to create the *parvis*, an alfresco classroom where Parisians can learn a catechism illustrated on sculpted stone portals.

1935 A rooster bearing part of the relics of the Crown of Thorns, St Denis and St Geneviève is put on top of the cathedral spire to protect those who pray inside.

1991 The architectural masterpiece of Notre Dame and its Seine-side riverbanks become a Unesco World Heritage Site.

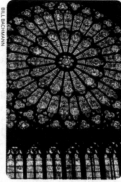

BILL BACHMANN

Virgin & Child
Spot all 37 artworks representing the Virgin Mary. Pilgrims have revered the pearly-cream sculpture of her in the sanctuary since the 14th century. Light a devotional candle and write some words to the *Livre de Vie* (Book of Life).

North Rose Window
See prophets, judges, kings and priests venerate Mary in vivid blue and violet glass, one of three beautiful rose blooms (1225–1270), each almost 10m in diameter.

Flying Buttresses

Choir Screen
No part of the cathedral weaves biblical tales more evocatively than these ornate wooden panels, carved in the 14th century after the Black Death killed half the country's population. The faintly gaudy colours were restored in the 1960s.

SIR/IMAGEBROKER

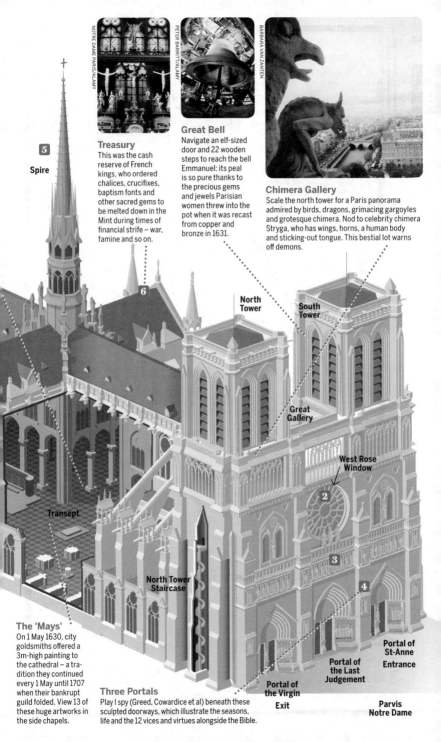

Treasury

This was the cash reserve of French kings, who ordered chalices, crucifixes, baptism fonts and other sacred gems to be melted down in the Mint during times of financial strife – war, famine and so on.

Great Bell

Navigate an elf-sized door and 22 wooden steps to reach the bell Emmanuel: its peal is so pure thanks to the precious gems and jewels Parisian women threw into the pot when it was recast from copper and bronze in 1631.

Chimera Gallery

Scale the north tower for a Paris panorama admired by birds, dragons, grimacing gargoyles and grotesque chimera. Nod to celebrity chimera Stryga, who has wings, horns, a human body and sticking-out tongue. This bestial lot warns off demons.

5 Spire

6

North Tower

South Tower

Great Gallery

West Rose Window

2

Transept

North Tower Staircase

3

4

The 'Mays'

On 1 May 1630, city goldsmiths offered a 3m-high painting to the cathedral – a tradition they continued every 1 May until 1707 when their bankrupt guild folded. View 13 of these huge artworks in the side chapels.

Three Portals

Play I spy (Greed, Cowardice et al) beneath these sculpted doorways, which illustrate the seasons, life and the 12 vices and virtues alongside the Bible.

Portal of the Virgin

Exit

Portal of the Last Judgement

Portal of St-Anne

Entrance

Parvis Notre Dame

NOTRE DAME PARIS/ALAMY

PETER BARRITT/ALAMY

BARBARA VAN ZANTEN

The Islands

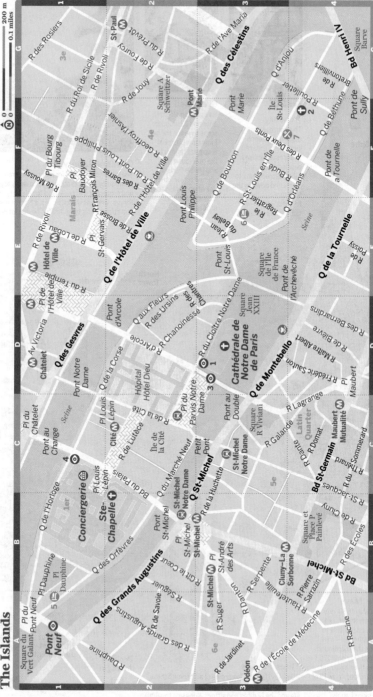

0 m 200 m
0 0.1 miles

The Islands

the Christ and the lives of the saints. One of the best views of Notre Dame is from square Jean XXIII, the lovely little park behind the cathedral, where you can see the mass of ornate **flying buttresses** that encircle the chancel and support its walls and roof.

Inside, exceptional features include three spectacular **rose windows**, the most renowned of which is the 10m-wide one over the western facade above the 7800-pipe organ, and the window on the northern side of the transept, which has remained virtually unchanged since the 13th century. The central choir, with its carved wooden stalls and statues representing the Passion of the Christ, is also noteworthy. There are free 1½-hour guided tours of the cathedral in English at noon on Wednesday, at 2pm on Thursday and at 2.30pm on Saturday.

The trésor (treasury; adult/child €3/1; ⊙9.30am-6pm Mon-Fri, 9.30am-6.30pm Sat, 1.30-6.30pm Sun), in the southeastern transept, contains artwork, liturgical objects, church plate and first-class relics – some of them of questionable origin. Among these is the Ste-Couronne, the 'Holy Crown' – purportedly the wreath of thorns placed on Jesus' head before he was crucified – which was brought here in the mid-13th century. It is exhibited between 3pm and 4pm on the first Friday of each month, 3pm to 4pm every Friday during Lent and 10am to 5pm on Good Friday.

The entrance to the **Tours de Notre Dame** (Notre Dame towers; rue du Cloître Notre Dame; adult/child €8/free; ⊙10am-6.30pm Apr-Jun & Sep, 9am-7.30pm Mon-Fri, 9am-11pm Sat & Sun Jul & Aug, 10am-5.30pm Oct-Mar), which can be climbed, is from the North Tower, to the right and around the corner as you walk out of the cathedral's main doorway. The 422 spiralling steps bring you to the top of the west facade, where you'll find yourself face to face with many of the cathedral's most frightening gargoyles, the 13-tonne bell Emmanuel (all the cathedral's bells are named) in the South Tower, and an absolutely spectacular view over the city.

⬛TOP CHOICE **Ste-Chapelle**   CHAPEL
(Map p64; 4 bd du Palais, 1er; adult/child €8/free; ⊙9.30am-5 or 6pm; Ⓜ Cité) The most exquisite of Paris' Gothic monuments, Ste-Chapelle is tucked away within the walls of the Palais de Justice (Law Courts). The 'walls' of the **upper chapel** are sheer curtains of richly coloured and finely detailed **stained glass**, which bathe the chapel in extraordinary coloured light on a sunny day. Built in just under three years (compared with nearly 200 years for Notre Dame), Ste-Chapelle was consecrated in 1248. The chapel was conceived by Louis IX to house his personal collection of holy relics (now kept in the treasury of Notre Dame).

A joint ticket with the Conciergerie (p65) costs €11.

Conciergerie   MONUMENT
(Map p64; 2 bd du Palais, 1er; adult/child €7/free; ⊙9.30am-5 or 6pm; Ⓜ Cité) Built as a royal palace in the 14th century for the concierge of the Palais de la Cité, the Conciergerie was the main prison during the Reign of Terror (1793–94) and was used to incarcerate alleged enemies of the Revolution before they were brought before the Revolutionary Tribunal in the Palais de Justice next door. Among the 2700 prisoners held in the *cachots* (dungeons) here before being sent in tumbrels to the guillotine were Queen Marie-Antoinette (see a reproduction of her cell) and, as the Revolution began to turn on its own, the radicals Danton, Robespierre and, finally, the judges of the Tribunal themselves.

The Gothic 14th-century **Salle des Gens d'Armes** (Cavalrymen's Hall) is a fine example of the Rayonnant Gothic style. It is the largest surviving medieval hall in Europe. The **Tour de l'Horloge** (cnr bd du Palais & quai de l'Horloge) has held a public clock aloft since 1370.

A joint ticket with Ste-Chapelle (p65) costs €11.

Pont Neuf   BRIDGE

(Map p64; Ⓜ Pont Neuf) The sparkling-white stone spans of Paris' oldest bridge, Pont Neuf – literally 'New Bridge' – have linked the western end of the Île de la Cité with both banks of the Seine since 1607, when King Henri IV inaugurated it by crossing the bridge on a white stallion. The seven arches, best seen from the river, are decorated with humorous and grotesque figures of barbers, dentists, pickpockets, loiterers etc.

ÎLE ST-LOUIS

The smaller of the Seine's two islands, Île St-Louis is just downstream from the Île de la Cité. In the early 17th century, when it was actually two uninhabited islets called Île Notre Dame (Our Lady Isle) and Île aux Vaches (Cows Island), a building contractor and two financiers worked out a deal with Louis XIII to create one island out of the two and build two stone bridges to the mainland. In exchange they would receive the right to subdivide and sell the newly created real estate. This they did with great success, and by 1664 the entire island was covered with fine new and airy houses facing the quays and the river.

Today, the island's 17th-century, grey-stone houses and the shops that line the streets and quays impart a village-like, provincial calm. The only sight as such, French baroque **Église St-Louis en l'Île** (19bis rue St-Louis en l'Île, 4e; ⊙9am-1pm & 2-7.30pm Tue-Sat, to 7pm Sun; Ⓜ Pont Marie), was built between 1664 and 1726.

LATIN QUARTER & JARDIN DES PLANTES

The centre of Parisian higher education since the Middle Ages, the Latin Quarter is so called because conversation between students and professors until the Revolution was in Latin. It still has a large population of students and academics affiliated with the Sorbonne (now part of the University of Paris system), the Collège de France, the École Normale Supérieure and other institutions of higher learning, though its near monopoly on Parisian academic life is not what it was. To the southeast, the Jardin des Plantes, with its tropical green-

houses and Musée National d'Histoire Naturelle, offers a bucolic alternative to the chalkboards and cobblestones.

Musée National du Moyen Âge

HISTORY MUSEUM

(Map p68; www.musee-moyenage.fr; 6 place Paul Painlevé, 5e; adult/child €8.50/free; ⊙9.15am-5.45pm Wed-Mon; Ⓜ Cluny–La Sorbonne or St-Michel) The National Museum of the Middle Ages is housed in two structures: the **frigidarium** (cooling room) and other remains of Gallo-Roman baths dating from around AD 200, and the late-15th-century **Hôtel de Cluny**, considered the finest example of medieval civil architecture in Paris.

The spectacular displays at the museum include statuary, illuminated manuscripts, weapons, furnishings, and objets d'art made of gold, ivory and enamel. But nothing compares with *La Dame à la Licorne* (The Lady with the Unicorn), a sublime series of late-15th-century tapestries from the southern Netherlands now hung in circular room 13 on the 1st floor. Five of them are devoted to the senses, while the sixth is the enigmatic *À Mon Seul Désir* (To My Sole Desire), a reflection on vanity.

Sorbonne   MONUMENT

(Map p68; 12 rue de la Sorbonne, 5e; Ⓜ Luxembourg or Cluny–La Sorbonne) Paris' most renowned seat of learning, the Sorbonne was founded in 1253 by Robert de Sorbon, confessor to Louis IX, as a college for 16 impoverished theology students. Today, the Sorbonne's main complex (bounded by rue de la Sorbonne, rue des Écoles, rue St-Jacques and rue Cujas) and other buildings in the vicinity house most of the 13 autonomous universities that were created when the University of Paris was reorganised after violent student protests in 1968. Parts of the complex are undergoing extensive renovation, scheduled to be completed in 2015.

Panthéon   MONUMENT

(Map p68; place du Panthéon, 5e; adult/child €8/free; ⊙10am-6.30pm Apr-Sep, to 6pm Oct-Mar; Ⓜ Luxembourg) The domed landmark now known simply as the Panthéon was commissioned around 1750 as an abbey church dedicated to Ste Geneviève, but because of financial and structural problems it wasn't completed until 1789 – not a good year for churches to open in France. Two years later, the Constituent Assembly converted it into a secular mausoleum for the *grands hommes de l'époque de la liberté française* (great men of the era of French liberty).

The Panthéon is a superb example of 18th-century neoclassicism, but its ornate marble interior is gloomy in the extreme. The 80-odd permanent residents of the crypt include Voltaire, Jean-Jacques Rousseau, Victor Hugo, Émile Zola, Jean Moulin and Nobel Prize winner Marie Curie, whose remains were moved here in 1995 – the first woman to be interred here.

Jardin des Plantes
BOTANICAL GARDEN

(Map p68; 57 rue Cuvier & 3 quai St-Bernard, 5e; ⊙7.30am-7pm; Ⓜ Gare d'Austerlitz, Censier Daubenton or Jussieu) Paris' 24-hectare Jardin des Plantes was founded in 1626 as a medicinal herb garden for Louis XIII. Here you'll find the Eden-like Jardin d'Hiver (Winter Garden), also called the Serres Tropicales (Tropical Greenhouses); the Jardin Alpin (Alpine Garden; weekend admission adult/child €1/0.50; ⊙8am-4.40pm Mon-Fri, 1.30-6pm Sat, 1.30-6.30pm Sun) with 2000 mountain plants; and the gardens of the École de Botanique (admission free; ⊙8am-5pm Mon-Fri) where students of Paris' Botany School 'practise'.

The Ménagerie du Jardin des Plantes (adult/child €8/6; ⊙9am-6 or 6.30pm), a medium-size (5.5 hectare, 1000 animals) zoo in the northern section of the garden, was founded in 1794. During the Prussian siege of Paris in 1870, most of the animals were eaten by starving Parisians.

A two-day combined ticket covering all the Jardin des Plantes sights, including all the sections of the Musée National d'Histoire Naturelle, costs €20/15.

Wedged between the Jardin des Plants and the Seine is the riverside Musée de la Sculpture en Plein Air (Open-Air Sculpture Museum; square Tino Rossi, 5e; admission free; ⊙24hr; Ⓜ Quai de la Rapée).

Musée National d'Histoire Naturelle
NATURAL HISTORY MUSEUM

(Map p68; www.mnhn.fr, in French; 57 rue Cuvier, 5e; Ⓜ Censier Daubenton or Gare d'Austerlitz) Created by a decree of the Revolutionary Convention in 1793, the Musée National d'Histoire Naturelle was the site of important scientific research during the 19th century. Housed in three buildings on the southern fringe of Jardin des Plantes, its highlight for kids is the Grande Galerie de l'Évolution (Great Gallery of Evolution; 36 rue Geoffroy St-Hilaire, 5e; adult/child €7/free; ⊙10am-6pm Wed-Mon) with imaginative ex-

hibits on evolution and humankind's effect on the global ecosystem. Rare specimens of endangered and extinct species dominate the **Salle des Espèces Menacées et des Espèces Disparues** (Hall of Threatened and Extinct Species) on level 2, while the **Salle de Découverte** (Room of Discovery) on level 1 houses kid-friendly interactive exhibits.

To the south, the Galerie de Minéralogie et de Géologie (Mineralogy & Geology Gallery; 36 rue Geoffroy St-Hilaire; adult/child €8/6; ⊙10am-6pm Wed-Mon) has an amazing exhibition of giant natural crystals and a basement display of jewellery and other objects made from minerals. Displays on comparative anatomy and palaeontology (the study of fossils) fill the Galerie d'Anatomie Comparée et de Paléontologie (2 rue Buffon; adult/child €7/free; ⊙10am-5 or 6pm Wed-Mon).

Institut du Monde Arabe
ARCHITECTURE, MUSEUM

(Institute of the Arab World; Map p68; ☑01 40 51 38 38; www.imarabe.org, in French; 1 place Mohammed V, 5e; Ⓜ Cardinal Lemoine or Jussieu) Set up by France and 20 Arab countries to promote cultural contacts between the Arab world and the West, the Institute of the Arab World is housed in a critically praised building (1987) that successfully mixes modern and traditional Arab and Western elements.

The institute hosts some fascinating temporary exhibitions (enter at 1 rue des Fossés St-Bernard; adult/child €7/4, parent accompanying child €5; ⊙10am-6pm Tue-Sun). Its permanent museum, closed for renovation since April 2010, will focus on painting a global vision of the Arab world through 19th-century to contemporary art and artisanship, instruments from astronomy and other fields of scientific endeavour in which Arab technology once led the world.

Mosquée de Paris
MOSQUE

(Map p68; www.mosquee-de-paris.org; 2bis place du Puits de l'Ermite, 5e; adult/child €3/2; ⊙9am-noon & 2-6pm Sat-Thu; Ⓜ Censier Daubenton or Place Monge) Paris' central mosque with striking 26m-high minaret was built in 1926 in an ornate Moorish style. Visitors must be modestly dressed and remove their shoes at the entrance to the prayer hall. The complex includes a North African–style *salon de thé* (tearoom) and restaurant (p110) and a **hammam**, a traditional Turkish-style bathhouse.

Latin Quarter & Jardin des Plantes

0 — 200 m
0 — 0.1 miles

Q des Célestins

Bd Henri IV

Square Barve

Q St-Bernard

Q d'Anjou

R de Bretonvilliers

St-Louis en l'Île

Pont de Sully

Institut du Monde Arabe

Pl Mohammed V

R Cuvier

R des Chantiers

19

Universités Paris VI & VII

Q de Béthune

Q de Bourbon

Île St-Louis

R des Deux Ponts

R Budé

Q d'Orléans

4e

Pont de la Tournelle

Pont Marie

R le Régrattier

R Boutarel

Seine

Pont St-Louis

Square de l'Île de France

Pont de l'Archevêché

Q de la Tournelle

21

R Cochin

R de Pontoise

R de Poissy

R du Cardinal Lemoine

R des Fossés St-Bernard

R Jussieu

Pl Jussieu

Jussieu

Square Jean XXIII

R des Bernardins

Bd St-Germain

R St-Victor

R des Écoles

14

R d'Arras

Cardinal Lemoine

R des Boulangers

R de Bièvre

R Maître Albert

23

10

Pl Maubert Market

R Monge

Square Paul Langevin

Jardin Carré

6

Cardinal Lemoine

Pont de l'Archevêché

R Frédéric Sauton

R de la Bûcherie

Pl Maubert

R de la Montagne Ste-Geneviève

R Descartes

Q de Montebello

Square R Viviani

R Lagrange

R Galande

R Dante

R des Grands

R Domat

Anglais

R des Carmes

R de l'École

R Laplace

R Clovis

Pont du Double

Maubert Mutualité

R des Écoles

R Valette

Pl de l'Abbé Basset

25

R St-Julien le Pauvre

12

St-Michel Notre Dame

R du Petit Pont

R St-Jacques

R du Sommerard

R de Latran

Jean de Beauvais

R de Lanneau

Impasse Chartière

Pl Ste-Geneviève

Panthéon

Eurolines

20

R Thénard

R d'Écosse

Pl Marcelin Berthelot

R du Cimetière St-Benoît

R Cujas

Pl du Panthéon

R Clotaire

R de Cluny

R de la Harpe

R de la Harpe

R Boutebrie

R Pierre Sarrazin

Cluny-La Sorbonne

Musée National du Moyen Âge

24

R St-Jacques

R Soufflot

R des Fossés St-Jacques

Bd St-Michel

8

Sorbonne (Universités Paris III & IV)

R Toullier

R Victor Cousin

R Malebranche

R Danton

R Serpente

6e

R Hautefeuille

R Champollion

R de la Sorbonne

Pl de la Sorbonne

R Racine

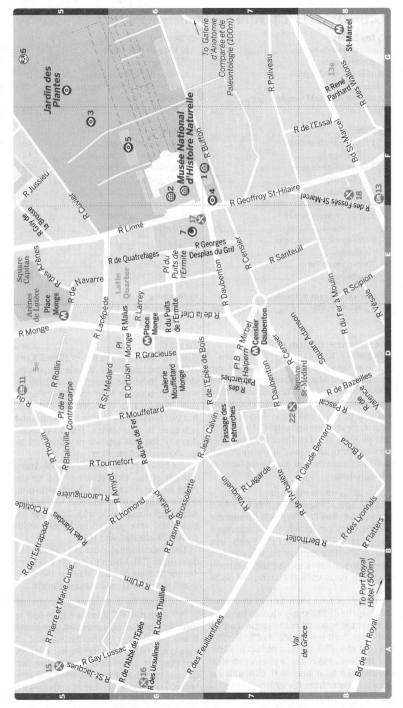

Jardin des Plantes

6

3

5

Musée National d'Histoire Naturelle

2

1

4

17

7

To Galerie d'Anatomie Comparée et de Paléontologie (100m)

R Buffon

R Poliveau

R René Panhard

R des Wallons

St-Marcel

13e

R de l'Essai

Bd St-Marcel

R Marcel

R Geoffroy St-Hilaire

R des Fossés St-Marcel

18

13

R Linné

R de Quatrefages

R Georges Desplas

R du Gril

R Censier

R Santeuil

Pl du Puits de l'Ermite

R Daubenton

R du Fer à Moulin

R Scipion

R Vésale

R Jussieu

R Guy de la Brosse

R Cuvier

Square Capitan

R des Arènes

R de Navarre

Latin Quarter

R Larrey

R de la Clef

Mirbel

Censier Daubenton

Square Adanson

Arènes de Lutèce

Place Monge

R Monge

R Lacépède

Pl Monge

R Malus

Place Monge

R du Puits de l'Ermite

R de l'Epée de Bois

Pl B Halpern

R Censier

R Daubenton

R de Bazeilles

R de Valence

R Pascal

5e

R St-Médard

R Ortolan

Galerie Mouffetard Monge

R Gracieuse

R des Patriarches

Square St-Médard

22

R Broca

11

R du

Pl de la Contrescarpe

R Rollin

R Mouffetard

R du Pot de Fer

R Jean Calvin

Passage des Patriarches

R Lagarde

R Claude Bernard

R des Lyonnais

R Thouin

R Blainville

R Tournefort

R Vauquelin

R de l'Arbalète

R Flatters

R Laromiguière

R Amyot

R Lhomond

R Erasme Brossolette

R Rataud

R Berthollet

R des Irlandais

R de l'Estrapade

R Clotilde

R d'Ulm

To Port Royal Hôtel (500m)

Val de Grâce

15

R St-Jacques

R Gay Lussac

16

R des Ursulines

R de l'Abbé de l'Epée

R Louis Thuillier

R Pierre et Marie Curie

R des Feuillantines

Bd de Port Royal

ST-GERMAIN, ODÉON & LUXEMBOURG

Centuries ago the Église St-Germain des Prés and its affiliated abbey owned most of today's 6e and 7e. The neighbourhood around the church began to develop in the late 17th century, and these days it is celebrated for its heterogeneity. Cafés such as Café de Flore and Les Deux Magots (p118) were favourite hang-outs of post-war Left Bank intellectuals and the birthplaces of existentialism.

Église St-Germain des Prés   CHURCH

(Map p72; 3 place St-Germain des Prés, 6e; ⊗8am-7pm Mon-Sat, 9am-8pm Sun; Ⓜ St-Germain des Prés) Paris' oldest church, the Romanesque Church of St-Germanus of the Fields, was built in the 11th century on the site of a 6th-century abbey and was the dominant church in Paris until the arrival of Notre Dame.

It has since been altered many times, but the Chapelle de St-Symphorien, to the right as you enter, was part of the original abbey and is the final resting place of St Germanus (AD 496–576), the first bishop of Paris. The bell tower over the western entrance has changed little since 990, although the spire only dates from the 19th century.

Église St-Sulpice   CHURCH

(Map p72; place St-Sulpice, 6e; ⊗7.30am-7.30pm; Ⓜ St-Sulpice) Lined with 21 side chapels inside, the Italianate Church of St-Sulpicius was built between 1646 and 1780. The facade, designed by a Florentine architect, has two rows of superimposed columns and is topped by two towers. The neoclassical décor of the vast interior is influenced by the Counter-Reformation.

The frescos in the Chapelle des Sts-Anges (Chapel of the Holy Angels), first to the right as you enter, depict Jacob wrestling with the angel (to the left) and Michael the Archangel doing battle with Satan (to the right) and were painted by Eugène Delacroix between 1855 and 1861.

The monumental 20m-tall organ loft dates from 1781. Listen to it in its full glory during 10.30am Sunday Mass or the occasional Sunday afternoon organ concert.

⟦TOP CHOICE⟧ Jardin du Luxembourg   CITY PARK

(Map p44; ⊗7.30am to 8.15am-5pm to 10pm according to the season; Ⓜ Luxembourg) When the weather is fine, Parisians of all ages come flocking to the formal terraces and chestnut groves of the 23-hectare Jardin du Luxembourg to read, relax and sunbathe. There are a number of activities for children here, and in the southern part of the garden you'll find urban orchards as well as the honey-producing Rucher du Luxembourg (Luxembourg Apiary).

The **Palais du Luxembourg** (rue de Vaugirard, 6e), at the northern end of the garden, was built for Marie de Médicis, Henri IV's consort; it has housed the **Sénat** (Senate), the upper house of the French parliament, since 1958. There are **guided tours** (☑reservations 01 44 54 19 49; www.senat.fr; adult/child €8/free) of the interior, usually at 10.30am one Saturday a month; advance reservations obligatory.

Top spot for sun-soaking – there are always loads of chairs here – is the southern side of the palace's 19th-century, 57m-long Orangery (1834) where lemon and orange trees, palms, grenadiers and oleanders shelter from the cold.

MONTPARNASSE

After WWI, writers, poets and artists of the avant-garde abandoned Montmartre on the Right Bank and crossed the Seine, shifting the centre of artistic ferment to the area around bd du Montparnasse. Chagall, Modigliani, Léger, Soutine, Miró, Kandinsky, Picasso, Stravinsky, Hemingway, Ezra Pound and Cocteau, as well as such political exiles as Lenin and Trotsky, all used to hang out in the cafés and brasseries for which the quarter became famous. Montparnasse remained a creative centre until the mid-1930s. Today, especially since the construction of the Gare Montparnasse complex, there is little to remind visitors of the area's bohemian past except the now very touristed restaurants and cafés.

Tour Montparnasse   PANORAMIC TOWER
(Map p44; www.tourmontparnasse56.com; rue de l'Arrivée, 14e; adult/child €11/8; ☺9.30am-11.30pm Apr-Sep, to 10.30pm Sun-Thu, 11pm Fri & Sat Oct-Mar; Ⓜ Montparnasse Bienvenüe) A steel-and-smoked-glass eyesore built in 1974, the 210m-high Tour Montparnasse affords spectacular views over the city – a view, we might add, that does not take in this ghastly oversized lipstick tube. A lift takes you up to the 56th-floor enclosed **observatory**, with exhibition centre, video clips, multimedia terminals and Paris' highest café. Finish with a hike up the stairs to the **open-air terrace** on the 59th floor, but arm yourself with the multilingual guide *Paris Vu d'En Haut* (Paris Seen from the

Top; €3), available from the ticket office, to know what you're looking at.

Cimetière du Montparnasse   CEMETERY
(Map p44; bd Edgar Quinet & rue Froidevaux, 14e; ☺8am-5.30 or 6pm Mon-Fri, 8.30am-6pm Sat, 9am-6pm Sun; Ⓜ Edgar Quinet or Raspail) Montparnasse Cemetery received its first 'lodger' in 1824. It contains the tombs of such illustrious personages as the poet Charles Baudelaire, writer Guy de Maupassant, playwright Samuel Beckett, sculptor Constantin Brancusi, painter Chaim Soutine, photographer Man Ray, industrialist André Citroën, Captain Alfred Dreyfus of the infamous Dreyfus Affair, actor Jean Seberg, philosopher Jean-Paul Sartre, writer Simone de Beauvoir and the crooner Serge Gainsbourg.

Les Catacombes   OSSUARY
(Map p44; www.catacombes.paris.fr, in French; 1 av Colonel Henri Roi-Tanguy, 14e; adult/child €8/4; ☺10am-5pm Tue-Sun; Ⓜ Denfert Rochereau) In 1785 it was decided to solve the hygiene and aesthetic problems posed by Paris' overflowing cemeteries by exhuming the bones and storing them in the tunnels of three disused quarries. One ossuary created in 1810 is now known as the Catacombes, which can be visited. After descending 20m (130 steps) from street level, visitors follow 1.7km of underground corridors in which the bones and skulls of millions of former Parisians are neatly stacked along the walls. During WWII these tunnels were used as a headquarters by the Resistance.

The route through the Catacombes begins at a small, dark-green belle-époque-style building in the centre of a grassy area of av Colonel Henri Roi-Tanguy. The exit is at the top of 83 steps on rue Remy Dumoncel (Ⓜ Mouton Duvernet), 700m to the southwest.

FAUBOURG ST-GERMAIN & INVALIDES

Paris' most fashionable neighbourhood during the 18th century was Faubourg St-Germain in the 7e, the area between the Seine and rue de Babylone 1km south. Some of the most interesting mansions, many of which now serve as embassies, cultural centres and government ministries, are along three streets running east to west: rue de Lille, rue de Grenelle and rue de Varenne. **Hôtel Matignon** (57 rue de Varenne, 7e) has been the official residence of the French prime minister since the start of the Fifth Republic in 1958.

St-Germain & Odéon

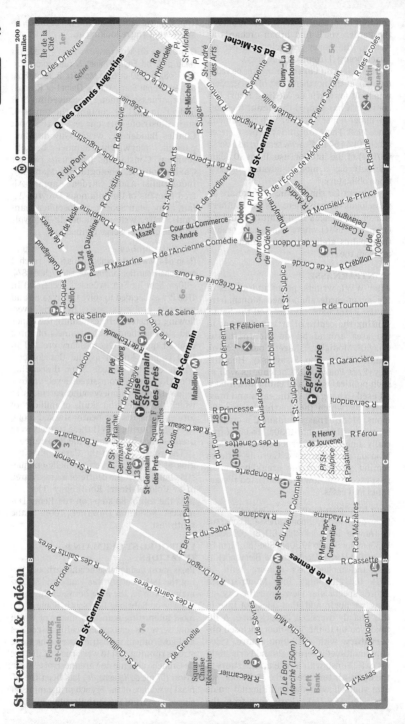

Musée d'Orsay ART MUSEUM
(Map p44; www.musee-orsay.fr; 62 rue de Lille, 7e; adult/child €8/free; ☺9.30am-6pm Tue, Wed & Fri-Sun, 9.30am-9.45pm Thu; ⓜMusée d'Orsay or Solférino) Facing the Seine from quai Anatole France, the Musée d'Orsay is housed in a former train station (1900). It displays France's national collection of paintings, sculptures, objets d'art and other works produced between the 1840s and 1914, including the fruits of the Impressionist, post-Impressionist and art nouveau movements.

Many visitors to the museum go straight to the upper level (lit by a skylight) to see the famous Impressionist paintings by Monet, Pissarro, Renoir, Sisley, Degas and Manet and the post-Impressionist works by Cézanne, Van Gogh, Seurat and Matisse, but there's also lots to see on the ground floor, including some early works by Manet, Monet, Renoir and Pissarro. The middle level has some superb art nouveau rooms.

English-language tours (☏information 01 40 49 48 48; €6 plus admission fee), lasting 1½ hours, include the 'Masterpieces of the Musée d'Orsay' tour. **Audioguide tours** (€5) point out around 80 major works. Tickets are valid all day, so you can leave and re-enter the museum as you please. The reduced entrance fee of €5.50 (€7 including temporary exhibition) applies to everyone after 4.15pm (6pm on Thursday). Those visiting the Musée Rodin on the same day save €2 with a combined €12 ticket.

TOP CHOICE **Musée Rodin** GARDEN, MUSEUM
(Map p74; www.musee-rodin.fr; 79 rue de Varenne, 7e; adult/child incl garden €7-10/free, garden only €1; ☺10am-5.45pm Tue-Sun; ♿; ⓜVarenne) One of our favourite cultural attractions, the Rodin Museum is both a sublime museum and one of the city's most relaxing green spots with its lovely **garden** sprinkled with sculptures and shade trees. Rooms on two floors of this 18th-century residence display extraordinarily vital bronze and marble sculptures by Rodin, including casts of some of his most celebrated works: *The Hand of God, The Burghers of Calais (Les Bourgeois de Calais), Cathedral,* that perennial crowd-pleaser *The Thinker (Le Penseur)* and the incomparable *The Kiss (Le Baiser).* There are also some 15 works by Camille Claudel (1864–1943), sister of the writer Paul Claudel and Rodin's mistress.

Hôtel des Invalides MONUMENT, MUSUEM
(Map p74; ⓜVarenne or La Tour Maubourg) A 500m-long expanse of lawn known as the Esplanade des Invalides separates Faubourg St-Germain from the Eiffel Tower area. At the southern end of the esplanade, laid out between 1704 and 1720, is the final resting place of Napoleon, the man many French people consider to be the nation's greatest hero.

Hôtel des Invalides was built in the 1670s by Louis XIV to provide housing for some 4000 *invalides* (disabled war veterans). On 14 July 1789 a mob forced its way into the building and, after some fierce fighting, seized 32,000 rifles before heading on to the prison at Bastille and the start of the French Revolution.

North of the main courtyard, in the **Cour d'Honneur**, is the Musée de l'Armée (Army Museum; www.invalides.org; 129 rue de Grenelle, 7e; adult/child €9/free; ☺10am-6pm Mon & Wed-Sat, to 9pm Tue, closed 1st Mon of month), which holds the nation's largest collection on the history of the French military.

South are the Église St-Louis des Invalides, once used by soldiers, and the Église

Eiffel Tower Area & 16e

N

0   400 m
0   0.2 miles

Map labels

Trocadéro M
Pl du Trocadéro et du 11 Novembre
6
Cité de l'Architecture et du Patrimoine
1
Jardins du Trocadéro
Pl de Varsovie
R le Tasse
R Benjamin Franklin
16e
Av des Nations Unies
Av de New York
Bd Delessert
R le Nâtre
R Beethoven
R Jardin
12
Passerelle Debilly
Pont de la Bourdonnais
Av de New York
R Fresnel
Av de New York
Seine
Pont d'Iéna
Batobus Stop
11
Eiffel Tower
7
Champ de Mars-Tour Eiffel
Allée Léon Bourgeois
Stade Émile Anthoine
R Jean Rey
Bir Hakeim M
Pont de Bir Hakeim
Pont de Bir Hakeim
Passy M
Q de Grenelle
R Nélaton
Pl des Martyrs Juifs du Vélodrome d'Hiver
15e
Bd de Grenelle
R St-Saëns
Av de Suffren
R de la Fédération
R Dessaix
R Edgar Faure
Pl A Sauvy
École Supérieure
Av Émile Acollas
Av Pierre Loti
Allée Thomy Thierry
Av Anatole France
Allée Adrienne Lecouvreur
Av Émile Deschanel
Av de la Bourdonnais
Av Charles Floquet
R Champfleury
Pl Jacques Rueff
Parc du Champ de Mars
Av Joseph Bouvard
R du Général Camou
R de Monttessuy
Av Élisée Reclus
R du Champ de Mars
École Militaire M
Passage de l'Union
R Valadon
R Cler
R Duvivier
R Ernest Psichari
Av de la Motte-Picquet
14
9
8
R Bosquet
Av Bosquet
Passage Landrieu
R Sédillot
R Augereau
13
R Marinoni
R Jean Nicot
R Malar
R Cognacq-Jay
Q d'Orsay
Seine
Pont de l'Alma
Pl de la Résistance
Pont de l'Alma M
5
Av Rapp
Cité de l'Alma
R E Valentin
R Dupont des Loges
R du l'Exposition
Av Franco Russe
R de l'université
Av de New York
Musée du Quai Branly
Q Branly M
Pont de l'Alma
Pont des Invalides
Pl de Finlande
R Surcouf
R Amélie
R de la Comète
R de Grenelle
R Ste-Dominique
Av Robert Schuman
7e
Bd de la Tour Maubourg
La Tour Maubourg M
Pl Santiago du Chili
R Santiago du Chili
Square Santiago du Chili
Esplanade des Invalides
Pl des Invalides
R Fabert
Av du Maréchal Galliéni
Invalides M
Invalides M
To: Musée d'Orsay & (800m)
Q de Solférino
Q d'Orsay
R de Constantine
R de Grenelle
R de Grenelle
Square d'Ajaccio
Varenne M
Musée Rodin
R de Varenne
Left Bank
Bd des Invalides
Hôtel des Invalides
4
3
2
Jardin de l'Intendant
Pl Vauban
Esplanade du Souvenir Français
R Bixio
R Louis Codet
10
R Chevert
Av de Lowendal
Av de Tourville
Av Duquesne
École Militaire M
Av Émile Deschanel
R du Champ de Mars

du Dôme whose sparkling dome (1677–1735) is visible throughout the city. The church received the remains of Napoleon in 1840: the very extravagant **Tombeau de Napoléon 1er** (Napoleon I's Tomb; ☉10am-5 or 6pm, closed 1st Mon of month), in its centre, consists of six coffins that fit into one another rather like a Russian stacking doll.

EIFFEL TOWER AREA & 16E

The very symbol of Paris, the Eiffel Tower, is surrounded by open areas on both banks of the Seine, which take in both the 7e and 16e, the most chichi (and snobby) part of the capital. While most of the area today won't send the same frisson of excitement down your spine as taking the lift up to the top of the Tower, it is nonetheless home to some outstanding museums to keep culture vultures busy.

Eiffel Tower   FAMOUS LANDMARK
(Map p74; ☎01 44 11 23 23; www.tour-eiffel.fr; to 2nd fl adult/child €8.10/4, to 3rd fl €13.10/9, stairs to 2nd fl €4.50/3; ☉lifts & stairs 9am-midnight

When it was built for the 1889 Exposition Universelle (World Fair), marking the centenary of the Revolution, the Tour Eiffel faced massive opposition from Paris' artistic and literary elite. The 'metal asparagus', as some Parisians snidely called it, was almost torn down in 1909 but was spared because it proved an ideal platform for the transmitting antennas needed for the new science of radiotelegraphy. Named after its designer, Gustave Eiffel, the tower is 324m high, including the TV antenna at the tip. This figure can vary by as much as 15cm, however, as the tower's 7300 tonnes of iron, held together by 2.5 million rivets, expand in warm weather and contract when it's cold.

The three levels are open to the public (entrance to the 1st level is included in all admission tickets), though the top level closes in heavy wind. You can either take the lifts (east, west and north pillars), or, if you're feeling fit, the stairs in the south pillar up to the 2nd platform. Buy tickets in advance online to avoid monumental queues at the ticket office.

Palais de Chaillot   ARCHITECTURE MUSEUM
(Map p74; 17 place du Trocadéro et du 11 Novembre, 16e; MTrocadéro) The two curved, colonnaded wings of the Palais de Chaillot, built for the 1937 Exposition Universelle held in Paris, and the terrace in between them afford an exceptional panorama of the Jardins du Trocadéro (named after a Spanish stronghold near Cádiz captured by the French in 1823), the Seine and the Eiffel Tower.

TOP CHOICE **Cité de l'Architecture et du Patrimoine** (www.citechaillot.fr, in French; 1 place du Trocadéro et du 11 Novembre, 16e; adult/child €8/free; ☉11am-7pm Mon, Wed & Fri-Sun, to 9pm Thu), in the palace's eastern wing, is the standout, a mammoth 23,000 sq metres spread over three floors devoted to French architecture and heritage. Exhibits include 350 wood and plaster casts of cathedral portals, columns and altars originally created for the 1878 Exposition Universelle. The highlight is the light-filled ground floor, which contains a beautiful collection of 350 plaster and wood casts *(moulages)* of cathedral portals, columns and gargoyles, and replicas of murals and stained glass originally created for the 1878 Exposition Universelle. The views of the

Eiffel Tower from the windows are equally monumental.

Cinéaqua
AQUARIUM

(Map p74; www.cineaqua.com; av des Nations Unies, 16e; adult/child €19.50/12.50; ⊙10am-6 or 7pm; ⓂTrocadéro) On the eastern side of the Trocadéro Gardens is one of Europe's most ambitious aquariums, with 500 species 'tanked' in more than 3500 sq metres of space. The shark tank and enormous tank forming the backdrop to the café-restaurant are phenomenal.

Musée du Quai Branly
ART MUSEUM

(Map p74; www.quaibranly.fr; 37 quai Branly, 7e; adult/child €8.50/free; ⊙11am-7pm Tue, Wed & Sun, to 9pm Thu-Sat; ⓂPont de l'Alma or Alma-Marceau) The architecturally impressive but unimaginatively named Quai Branly Museum introduces the art and cultures of Africa, Oceania, Asia and the Americas through innovative displays, film and musical recordings. With *Là où dialoguent les cultures* (Where cultures communicate) as its motto, the museum is one of the most dynamic and forward-thinking in the world. The anthropological explanations are kept to a minimum; what is displayed here is meant to be viewed as art. A day pass allowing entry to the temporary exhibits as well as the permanent collection costs adult/concession €10/7; an audioguide is €5. Don't miss the views from the 5th-floor restaurant Les Ombres (p112).

Musée des Égouts de Paris
SEWERS

(Map p74; place de la Résistance, 7e; adult/child €4.20/3.40; ⊙11am-5pm Sat-Wed May-Sep, 11am-4pm Sat-Wed Oct-Dec & Feb-Apr; ⓂPont de l'Alma) Paris' Sewers Museum is a working museum whose entrance – a rectangular

PARIS' WINE MUSEUM

The Musée du Vin (www.museeduvin paris.com; 5 square Charles Dickens, 16e; adult/child €11.90/free; ⊙10am-6pm Tue-Sun; ⓂPassy), headquarters of the prestigious International Federation of Wine Brotherhoods, introduces visitors to the fine art of viticulture with various mock-ups and displays of tools. Admission includes a glass of wine at the end of the visit. Entry is free if you have lunch at the attached **Restaurant Musée du Vin.**

maintenance hole topped with a kiosk – is across the street from 93 quai d'Orsay, 7e. Raw sewage flows beneath your feet as you walk through 480m of odoriferous tunnels, passing artefacts illustrating the development of Paris' waste-water disposal system. It'll take your breath away, it will.

ÉTOILE & CHAMPS-ÉLYSÉES

A dozen avenues radiate out from place de l'Étoile – officially called place Charles de Gaulle – and first among them is av des Champs-Élysées. This broad boulevard, whose name refers to the 'Elysian Fields' where happy souls dwelt after death, according to the ancient Greeks, links the cobblestone expanses of 18th-century place de la Concorde with the Arc de Triomphe. Symbolising the style and *joie de vivre* of Paris since the mid-19th century, the avenue is scuzzy in parts but remains a popular tourist destination.

Some 400m north of av des Champs-Élysées is rue du Faubourg St-Honoré (8e), the western extension of rue St-Honoré. It is home to some of Paris' most renowned couture houses, jewellers, antique shops and the 18th-century Palais de l'Élysée, official residence of the French president.

Arc de Triomphe
FAMOUS LANDMARK

(Map p78; viewing platform adult/child €9/free; ⊙10am-10.30 or 11pm; ⓂCharles de Gaulle–Étoile) Located 2km northwest of place de la Concorde in the middle of place Charles de Gaulle (or place de l'Étoile), Paris' Triumphal Arch is the world's largest traffic roundabout. It was commissioned by Napoléon in 1806 to commemorate his imperial victories but remained unfinished when he started losing battles and then entire wars. It was not completed until 1836. Since 1920, the body of an **Unknown Soldier** from WWI, taken from Verdun in Lorraine, has lain beneath the arch; his fate and that of countless others is commemorated by a **memorial flame** that is rekindled each evening around 6.30pm.

From the **viewing platform** atop the arch (50m up via 284 steps and well worth the climb) you can see the dozen broad avenues – many of them named after Napoleonic victories and illustrious generals (including the ultra-exclusive av Foch, which is Paris' widest boulevard) – radiating towards every part of the city. Tickets to the viewing platform of the Arc de Triomphe are sold in the underground passageway that surfaces on the even-numbered side of av des Champs-Élysées. It is the only sane way to get to the base of the arch and is not linked to nearby metro tunnels.

Grand Palais
EXHIBITION HALL

(Map p78; reservations ☑08 92 70 08 40; www. grandpalais.fr; 3 av du Général Eisenhower, 8e; with/without booking adult €12/11, child free; ☺10am-10pm Fri-Mon & Wed, to 8pm Thu; ⓂChamps-Élysées Clemenceau) Erected for the 1900 World Exposition, the Grand Palais now houses the Galeries Nationales du Grand Palais beneath its huge art nouveau glass roof. Special exhibitions, among the biggest the city stages, last for three or four months here.

Petit Palais
FINE ARTS MUSEUM

(Map p78; www.petitpalais.paris.fr; av Winston Churchill, 8e; permanent collections admission free, temporary exhibitions adult/child €9/free; ☺10am-6pm Wed-Sun, 10am-8pm Tue (temp exhibition only); ⓂChamps-Élysées Clemenceau) The Petit Palais, which was also built for the 1900 fair, is home to the Musée des Beaux-Arts de la Ville de Paris, the Paris municipality's Museum of Fine Arts, which contains medieval and Renaissance objets d'art, tapestries, drawings and 19th-century French painting and sculpture.

Palais de la Découverte
SCIENCE MUSEUM

(Map p78; ☑01 56 43 20 21; www.palais-decou verte.fr, in French; av Franklin D Roosevelt, 8e; adult/senior, student & 5-18yr/under 5yr €7/4.50/ free; ☺9.30am-6pm Tue-Sat, 10am-7pm Sun; ⓂChamps-Élysées Clemenceau) Inaugurated during the 1937 Exposition Universelle and thus the world's first interactive museum, this children's science museum has excellent temporary exhibits (eg moving life-like dinosaurs) as well as a hands-on, interactive permanent collection focussing on astronomy, biology, physics and the like. The planetarium (admission €3.50) has four shows a day; there are also hourly science demonstrations (both in French).

Palais de Tokyo
GALLERY

(Map p78; www.palaisdetokyo.com; 13 av du Pré-sident Wilson, 16e; adult/child €6/free; ☺noon-midnight Tue-Sun; ⓂTrocadéro) The Tokyo Palace, created for the 1937 Exposition Universelle and now a contemporary art space, has no permanent collection. Instead its shell-like interior of polished concrete and steel is the stark backdrop for rotating, interactive art installations (the rooftop, for example, has been the setting for attention-

getting projects like the transient Hotel Everland and the transparent-walled restaurant Nomiya). There's a great lunch deal called 'Formule Palais' (€16), which includes admission and lunch at Tokyo Eat (☺noon-11.30pm), the museum's trendy café. It's one of the better creative spaces in western Paris; DJs often hit the decks at night.

Musée Guimet des Arts Asiatiques
ART MUSEUM

(Map p78; www.museeguimet.fr; 6 place d'Iéna; adult/child €7.50/free; ☺10am-6pm Wed-Mon) ⓂIéna) France's foremost repository for Asian art, the Guimet Museum of Asian Art has sculptures, paintings, objets d'art and religious articles from Afghanistan, India, Nepal, Pakistan, Tibet, Cambodia, China, Japan and Korea. Part of the original collection – Buddhist paintings and sculptures brought to Paris in 1876 by collector Émile Guimet – is housed in the Galeries du Panthéon Bouddhique du Japon et de la Chine (Buddhist Pantheon Galleries of Japan & China; 19 av d'Iéna; ⓂIéna; admission free; ☺9.45am-5.45pm Wed-Mon) in the sumptuous Hôtel Heidelbach. Don't miss its wonderful Japanese garden (☺1-5pm Wed-Mon).

Place de la Concorde
CITY SQUARE

(Map p78; ⓂConcorde) The 3300-year-old pink granite obelisk with the gilded top in the middle of Place de la Concorde once stood in the Temple of Ramses at Thebes (today's Luxor) and was given to France in 1831 by Muhammad Ali, viceroy and pasha of Egypt. The **female statues** adorning the four corners of the square represent France's eight largest cities.

In 1793 Louis XVI's head was lopped off by a guillotine set up in the northwest corner of the square, near the statue representing Brest. During the next two years, a guillotine built near the entrance to the Jardin des Tuileries was used to behead 1343 more people, including Marie-Antoinette and, six months later, the Revolutionary leaders Danton and Robespierre. The square, laid out between 1755 and 1775, was given its present name after the Reign of Terror in the hope that it would be a place of peace and harmony.

Place de la Madeleine
CITY SQUARE

(Map p78; ⓂMadeleine) Ringed by fine-food shops, this square is named after the 19th-century neoclassical church in its centre, Église de Ste-Marie Madeleine (Church of St Mary Magdalene; www.eglise-lama deleine.com, in French; place de la Madeleine, 8e;

PARIS

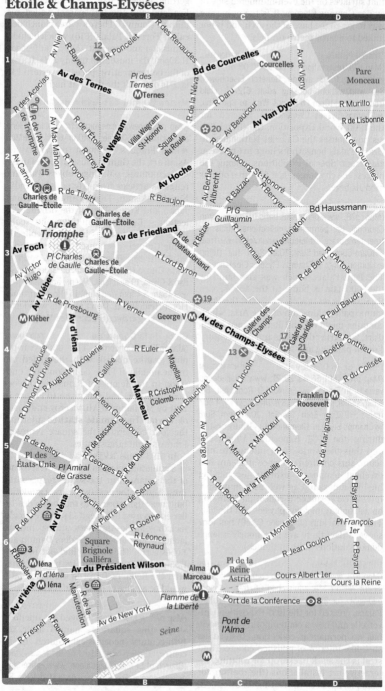

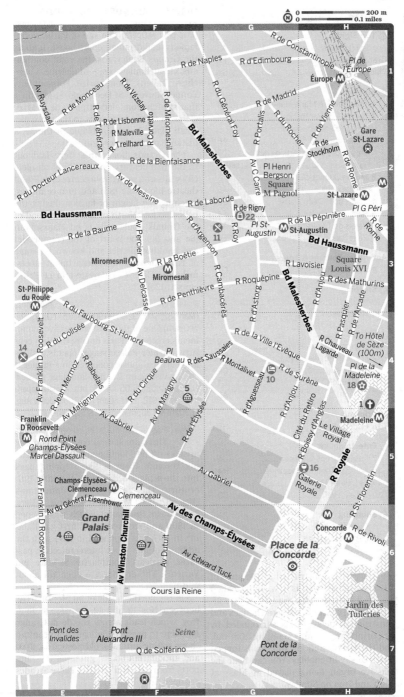

▲ N
0 ━━━━━━━━ 200 m
0 ━━━━━━━━ 0.1 miles

R de Constantinople

R de Naples
R d'Edimbourg
Pl de l'Europe

Av Ruysdael
R de Monceau
R de Vézelay
R de Miromesnil
R du Général Foy
R de Madrid
Europe M
R de Vienne

R de Téhéran
R de Lisbonne
R Corvetto
Bd Malesherbes
R Portalis
R du Rocher
R de Stockholm
Gare St-Lazare

R Maleville
R Treilhard
R de la Bienfaisance
Av C Caire
R de Rome
St-Lazare M

R du Docteur Lancereaux
Av de Messine
Pl Henri Bergson
Square M Pagnol
St-Augustin M

Bd Haussmann
R de Laborde
R de Rigny
22
Pl St-Augustin
R de la Pépinière
Pl G Péri

R de la Baume
Av Percier
R d'Argenson
R Roy
11
St-Augustin
R de la Pépinière
Bd Haussmann
R de Rome

Miromesnil M
R La Boétie
Av Delcassé
R Cambacérès
R Roquépine
Bd Malesherbes
R Lavoisier
Square Louis XVI
R des Mathurins

St-Philippe du Roule M
R du Faubourg-St-Honoré
R de Penthièvre
R d'Astorg
R d'Anjou
R Pasquier
R de l'Arcade

14
Av Franklin D Roosevelt
R du Colisée
Pl Beauvau
R des Saussaies
R de la Ville l'Evêque
R Chauveau Lagarde
To Hôtel de Sèze (100m)

R Jean Mermoz
R Rabelais
R du Cirque
R Montalivet
10
R de Surène
Pl de la Madeleine
18

R Matignon
Av Gabriel
R de Marigny
R de l'Elysée
R d'Aguesseau
R d'Anjou
Cité du Retiro
1

Franklin D Roosevelt M
Rond Point Champs-Élysées Marcel Dassault
5
Madeleine M

Av Franklin D Roosevelt
Av Gabriel
16
Galerie Royale
R Royale
R St-Florentin

Champs-Élysées Clemenceau M
Pl Clemenceau
R Boissy d'Anglas
Le Village Royal

Av du Général Eisenhower
Av des Champs-Élysées
Concorde M
R de Rivoli

Grand Palais
4
Av Winston Churchill
7
Av Dutuit
Av Edward Tuck
Place de la Concorde

Cours la Reine
Jardin des Tuileries

Pont des Invalides
Pont Alexandre III
Seine
Q de Solférino
Pont de la Concorde

Étoile & Champs-Élysées

⊙9.30am-7pm). Constructed in the style of a Greek temple, what is now simply called 'La Madeleine' was consecrated in 1842 after almost a century of design changes and construction delays. It is surrounded by 52 Corinthian columns standing 20m tall, and the marble and gilt interior is topped by three sky-lit cupolas. You can hear the massive organ being played at Mass at 11am and 7pm on Sunday.

OPÉRA & GRANDS BOULEVARDS

Place de l'Opéra
CITY SQUARE

(Map p82; Ⓜ Opéra) The site of Paris' world-famous (and original) opera house. It abuts the Grands Boulevards, the eight contiguous 'Great Boulevards' – Madeleine, Capucines, Italiens, Montmartre, Poissonnière, Bonne Nouvelle, St-Denis and St-Martin – that stretch from elegant place de la Madeleine in the 8e eastwards to the more plebeian place de la République in the 3e, a distance of just under 3km.

The Grands Boulevards were laid out in the 17th century on the site of obsolete city walls and served as a centre of café and theatre life in the 18th and 19th centuries, reaching the height of fashion during the belle époque. North of the western end of the Grands Boulevards is bd Haussmann (8e and 9e), the heart of the commercial and banking district and known for some of Paris' most famous department stores, including Galeries Lafayette and Le Printemps (p123).

Palais Garnier
OPERA HOUSE

(Map p82; ☎08 92 89 90 90; place de l'Opéra, 9e; Ⓜ Opéra) One of the most impressive monuments erected in Paris during the 19th century, Garnier Palace stages operas, ballets and classical-music concerts. In summer it can be visited on English-language guided tours (☎08 25 05 44 05; http://visites.opera deparis.fr; €12; ⊙11.30am & 2.30pm Jul & Aug, 11.30am & 2.30pm Wed, Sat & Sun Sep-Jun).

TOP
CHOICE **Passage Couverts** SHOPPPING ARCADES
There are several covered shopping arcades off bd Montmartre (9e), and walking through them is like stepping back into the sepia-toned Paris of the early 19th century. The passage des Panoramas (Map p82; 11 bd Montmartre & 10 rue St-Marc, 2e; Ⓜ Grands Boulevards), which was opened in 1800 and received Paris' first gas lighting in 1817, was expanded in 1834 with the addition of four other interconnecting passages: Feydeau, Montmartre, St-Marc and Variétés. The arcades are open till about midnight.

On the northern side of bd Montmartre, between Nos 10 and 12, is passage Jouffroy, which leads across rue de la Grange Batelière to passage Verdeau. Both contain shops selling antiques, old postcards, used and antiquarian books, gifts, pet toys, imports from Asia and the like. These arcades are open until 10pm.

Musée Grévin
WAX MUSEUM

(Map p82; www.grevin.com; 10 bd Montmartre, 9e; adult/child €20/12; ☉10am-6.30pm Mon-Fri, to 7pm Sat & Sun; MGrands Boulevards) Inside passage Jouffroy, the Musée Grévin has some 300 wax figures that look more like caricatures than characters, but where else do you get to see Marilyn Monroe, Charles de Gaulle and Spiderman face to face, or the real death masks of French Revolutionary leaders? The admission charge is positively outrageous and just keeps a-growin' every year.

MÉNILMONTANT & BELLEVILLE
A solidly working-class *quartier* (neighbourhood) with little to recommend it until just a few years ago, Ménilmontant in the 11e now boasts a surfeit of restaurants, bars and clubs.

On the other hand, Belleville (20e), home to large numbers of immigrants, especially Muslims and Jews from North Africa and Vietnamese and ethnic Chinese from Indochina, remains for the most part unpretentious and working-class. Parc de Belleville (MCouronnes), which opened in 1992 a few blocks east of bd de Belleville, occupies a hill almost 200m above sea level amid 4.5 hectares of greenery and offers superb views of the city. Paris' most famous necropolis lies just to the south of the park.

TOP CHOICE Cimetière du Père Lachaise
CEMETERY

(Map p44; www.pere-lachaise.com; ☉8am-6pm Mon-Fri, from 8.30am Sat, from 9am Sun; MPhilippe Auguste, Gambetta or Père Lachaise) The world's most visited graveyard, the Père Lachaise Cemetery opened its one-way doors in 1804. Its 69,000 ornate, even ostentatious, tombs form a verdant, 44-hectare open-air sculpture garden.

Among the 800,000 people buried here are the composer Chopin, the playwright Molière, the poet Apollinaire; the writers Balzac, Proust, Gertrude Stein and Colette; the actors Simone Signoret, Sarah Bernhardt and Yves Montand; the painters Pissarro, Seurat, Modigliani and Delacroix; the chanteuse Edith Piaf; the dancer Isadora Duncan; and even those immortal 12th-century lovers, Abélard and Héloïse, whose remains were disinterred and reburied here together in 1817 beneath a neo-Gothic tombstone.

Particularly frequented graves are those of **Oscar Wilde**, interred in division 89 in 1900, and 1960s rock star **Jim Morrison**, who died in an apartment at 17-19 rue Beautreillis, 4e, in the Marais in 1971 and is buried in division 6.

Père Lachaise has five entrances, two of which are on bd de Ménilmontant. Free maps indicating the location of noteworthy graves are available from the conservation office (16 rue du Repos, 20e) in the southwestern corner of the cemetery.

13E ARRONDISSEMENT & CHINATOWN
The 13e begins a few blocks south of the Jardin des Plantes in the 5e and has undergone a true renaissance with the advent of the Bibliothèque Nationale de France (BNF), the high-speed Météor metro line (No 14) and the ZAC Paris Rive Gauche project, the massive redevelopment of the old industrial quarter along the Seine. Add to that the stunning new footbridge, Passerelle Simone de Beauvoir, linking the BNF with Parc de Bercy and Docks en Seine, a 20,000-sq-metre riverside warehouse transformed into a state-of-the-art cultural and design centre, and you've got a district on the upswing. The stylishness of the neighbouring 5e extends to the av des Gobelins, while further south, between av d'Italie and av de Choisy, the succession of Asian restaurants, stalls and shops in the capital's Chinatown gives passers-by the illusion of having imperceptibly changed continents.

Bibliothèque Nationale de France
LIBRARY

(Map p44; www.bnf.fr; 11 quai François Mauriac, 13e; temporary exhibitions adult/child €7/free; ☉10am-7pm Tue-Sat, 1-7pm Sun ; MBibliothèque) Rising up from the banks of the Seine are the four glass towers of the controversial, €2 billion National Library of France, conceived by the late president François Mitterrand as a 'wonder of the modern world' and opened in 1988.

No expense was spared to carry out a plan that many said defied logic. While many of the books and historical documents were shelved in the sun-drenched, 23-storey, 79m-high towers – shaped like half-open books – readers sat in artificially lit basement halls built around a light well 'courtyard' of 140 50-year-old pines, trucked in from the countryside. The towers have since been fitted with a complex (and expensive) shutter system, but the basement is prone to flooding from the Seine. The national library

PARIS

Opéra & Grands Boulevards

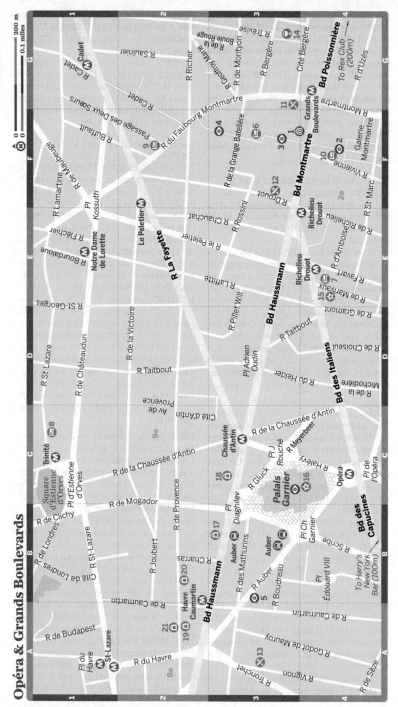

PARIS

SIGHTS

contains around 12 million tomes stored on some 420km of shelves and can accommodate 2000 readers and 2000 researchers. Temporary exhibitions (use Entrance E) revolve around 'the word', focusing on everything from storytelling to bookbinding.

MONTMARTRE & PIGALLE

During the late 19th and early 20th centuries the bohemian lifestyle of Montmartre in the 18e attracted a number of important writers and artists, including Picasso, who lived at the studio called **Bateau Lavoir** (11bis Émile Goudeau; Ⓜ Abbesses) from 1908 to 1912. Although the activity shifted to Montparnasse after WWI, Montmartre retains an upbeat ambience that all the tourists in the world couldn't spoil.

Only a few blocks southwest of the tranquil residential streets of Montmartre is lively, neon-lit Pigalle (9e and 18e), one of Paris' two main sex districts (the other, which is *much* more low-rent, is along rue St-Denis and its side streets north of Forum des Halles in the 1er). But Pigalle is more than just a sleazy red-light district; there are plenty of trendy nightspots, including clubs and cabarets, here as well. South of Pigalle, the district known as Nouvelle Athènes (New Athens), with its beautiful Greco-Roman architecture and private gardens, has long been favoured by artists.

The easiest way to reach the top of the Butte de Montmartre (Montmartre Hill) is via the RATP's sleek funicular (p132).

Basilique du Sacré Cœur   BASILICA
(Map p84; www.sacre-coeur-montmartre.com; place du Parvis du Sacré Cœur, 18e; ☉6am-10.30pm; Ⓜ Anvers) Perched at the very top of the Butte de Montmartre, the Basilica of the Sacred Heart was built from contributions pledged by Parisian Catholics as an act of contrition after the humiliating Franco-Prussian War of 1870–71. Construction began in 1873, but the basilica was not consecrated until 1919.

Some 234 spiralling steps lead you to the **basilica's dome** (admission €5, cash only; ☉9am-6 or 7pm), which affords one of Paris' most spectacular panoramas; they say you can see for 30km on a clear day.

Place du Tertre   CITY SQUARE
(Ⓜ Abbesses) Half a block west of the Église St-Pierre de Montmartre which once formed part of a 12th-century Benedictine abbey, is place du Tertre, once the main square of the village of Montmartre. These days it's filled with cafés, restaurants, tourists and rather obstinate portrait artists and caricaturists who will gladly do your likeness. Whether it looks even remotely like you is another matter.

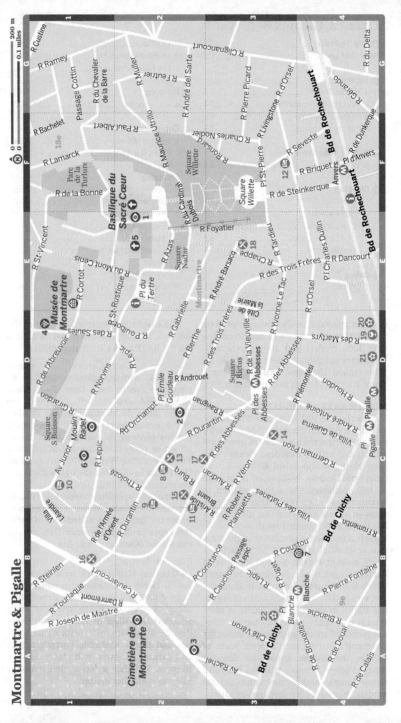

Montmartre & Pigalle

Cimetière de Montmartre

Basilique du Sacré Cœur

Musée de Montmartre

Parc de la Turlure

Square Willette

Square Nadar

Square J Rictus

Square S Buisson

Moulin Radet

Pl du Tertre

Pl Émile Goudeau

Pl des Abbesses

Pl Pigalle

Pl d'Anvers

Pl Blanche

Pl de Clichy

Cité de la Mairie

Cité Véron

Villa Léandre

Villa de Guelma

Villa des Platanes

Montmartre

18e

9e

Anvers

Abbesses

Pigalle

Blanche

Bd de Rochechouart

Bd de Clichy

R Custine

R Ramey

Passage Cottin

R du Chevalier de la Barre

R Muller

R Feutrier

R Clignancourt

R du Delta

R Bachelet

R Paul Albert

R Maurice Utrillo

R André del Sarte

R Pierre Picard

R Livingstone

R d'Orsel

R de Dunkerque

R Gérando

R Lamarck

R de la Bonne

R St-Vincent

R Cortot

R du Mont Cenis

R St-Rustique

R des Saules

R de l'Abreuvoir

R Norvins

R Poulbot

R Gabrielle

R Berthe

R Ronsard

R Charles Nodier

Pl St-Pierre

R Seveste

R Briquet

R de Steinkerque

R Tardieu

R Chappe

R André-Barsacq

R des Trois Frères

R Yvonne Le Tac

R Charles Dullin

Pl Charles Dullin

R Dancourt

R d'Orsel

R Azas

R Cardinal Dubois

R Foyatier

R des Trois Frères

R de la Vieuville

R des Abbesses

R des Martyrs

R Giradon

Av Junot

R Lepic

R Tholoze

R Androuet

R d'Orchampt

R Ravignan

R Durantin

R des Abbesses

R Audran

R Véron

R Germain Pilon

R André Antoine

R Piémontési

R Houdon

R Aristide Bruant

R Burq

R Robert Planquette

R de l'Armée d'Orient

R Durantin

R Constance

R Coustou

R Puget

R Lepic

Passage Lepic

R Cauchois

R Caulaincourt

R Steinlen

R Tourlaque

R Joseph de Maistre

R Darmremont

R Pierre Fontaine

R Fromentin

R Blanche

R de Bruxelles

R de Douai

R de Calais

Av Rachel

4

6

10

16

2

13

17

8

15

11

9

3

22

7

14

21

20

19

18

12

5

1

200 m
0.1 miles

PARIS SIGHTS

Cimetière de Montmartre CEMETERY
(Map p84; ☉8am-5.30 or 6pm Mon-Fri, from 8.30am Sat, from 9am Sun; Ⓜ Place de Clichy) The most famous cemetery in Paris after Père Lachaise, Cimetière de Montmartre was established in 1798. It contains the graves of writers Émile Zola, Alexandre Dumas and Stendhal; composer Jacques Offenbach; artist Edgar Degas; film director François Truffaut; and dancer Vaslav Nijinsky – among others. The entrance closest to the Butte de Montmartre is at the end of av Rachel, just off bd de Clichy or down the stairs from 10 rue Caulaincourt. Maps showing the location of the tombs are available free at that entrance.

Musée de Montmartre ART MUSEUM
(Map p84; www.museedemontmartre.fr; 12 rue Cortot, 18e; adult/child €7/free; ☉11am-6pm Tue-Sun; Ⓜ Lamarck Caulaincourt) One-time home to painters Renoir, Utrillo and Raoul Dufy, the Musée de Montmartre displays paintings, lithographs and documents, mostly relating to the area's rebellious and bohemian/artistic past, in a 17th-century manor house, which is the oldest structure in the quarter. It also stages exhibitions of artists still living in the *quartier*. There's an excellent bookshop here that also sells bottles of the wine produced from grapes grown in the Clos Montmartre, a small vineyard in the Montmartre area.

Musée de l'Érotisme ART MUSEUM
(Map p84; 72 bd de Clichy, 18e; adult/student €9/6; ☉10am-2am; Ⓜ Blanche) The Museum of Erotic Art tries to put some 2000 titillating statues and stimulating sexual aids and fetishist items from days gone by on a loftier plane, with erotic art – both antique and modern – from four continents spread over seven floors. But most of the punters know why they are here.

LA VILLETTE

The Buttes Chaumont, the Canal de l'Ourcq and especially the Parc de la Villette, with its wonderful museums and other attractions, create the winning trifecta of the 19e *arrondissement*. One new development that will bring in the crowds like never before is the **Philharmonie de Paris**, the ambitious new home of the Orchestre de Paris designed by Jean Nouvel, scheduled to open in 2012.

Parc de la Villette PARK
(Map p44; www.villette.com; Ⓜ Porte de la Villette or Porte de Pantin) The whimsical, 35-hectare Parc de la Villette, which opened in 1993 in the city's far northeastern corner, stretches from the Cité des Sciences et de l'Industrie south to the Cité de la Musique. Split into two sections by the Canal de l'Ourcq, the park is enlivened by shaded walkways, imaginative street furniture, a series of themed gardens for kids and fan-

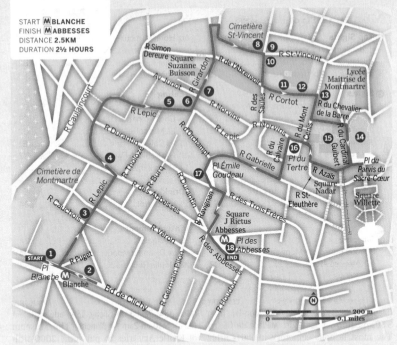

Walking Tour
Montmartre Art Attack

❯ Montmartre, from the French words for hill (*mont*) and martyr, has been a place of legend ever since St Denis was executed here in about AD 250 and began his headless journey on foot to the village north of Paris that still bears his name (p143). In recent times the Montmartre of myth has been resurrected by music, books and especially films like *Le Fabuleux Destin d'Amélie Poulain* (*Amélie*; 2002), which presented the district in various shades of rose, and *Moulin Rouge* (2001), which also made it pretty but gave it a bit more edge.

For centuries Montmartre was a simple country village filled with the *moulins* (mills) that supplied Paris with its flour. When it was incorporated into the capital in 1860, its picturesque charm and low rents attracted painters and writers – especially after the Communard uprising of 1871, which began here. The late 19th and early 20th centuries were Montmartre's heyday, when Toulouse-Lautrec drew his favourite cancan dancers and Picasso, Braque and others introduced cubism to the world.

After WWI such creative activity shifted to Montparnasse, but Montmartre retained an upbeat ambience. The real attractions here, apart from the great views from the Butte de Montmartre (Montmartre Hill), are the area's little parks and steep, winding cobblestone streets, many of whose houses seem about to be engulfed by creeping vines and ivy.

Begin the walk outside the Blanche metro station on place Blanche, whose name ('White Square') derives from the plaster (made from the locally mined gypsum) that was carted through the area. To the northwest is the legendary ❶ **Moulin Rouge** beneath its trademark red windmill. To the right is the ❷ **Musée de l'Érotisme**, an institution that portrays itself as educational rather than titillating. Yeah, right.

Walk up rue Lepic, lined with food shops, and halfway up on the left you'll find ❸ **Café des Deux Moulins** where heroine Amélie worked in the eponymous film. Follow the curve to the west: Théo van Gogh owned the ❹ **house at No 54**, and his brother, the artist Vincent, stayed with him on the 3rd floor from 1886 to 1888.

Further along rue Lepic are Montmartre's famous twinned windmills. The better-known ❺ **Moulin de la Galette** was a popular open-air dance hall in the late 19th century and was immortalised by Pierre-Auguste Renoir in his 1876 tableau *Le Bal du Moulin de la Galette* (Dance at the Moulin de la Galette). About 100m to the east, at the corner of rue Girardon is the ❻ **Moulin Radet** (now a restaurant confusingly called Le Moulin de la Galette).

Crossing through place Marcel Aymé you'll see a curious sculpture of a man emerging from a stone wall, the ❼ **Passe-Muraille statue**. It portrays Dutilleul, the hero of Marcel Aymé's short story *Le Passe-Muraille* (The Walker through Walls) who awakes one fine morning to discover he can do just what he's shown doing here. Aymé lived in the adjacent apartment building from 1902 to 1967.

Cross the street to leafy square Suzanne Buisson, turn left (north) onto rue Girardon, and pass Allée des Brouillards (Fog Alley), named after the adjacent 'Fog Castle' where several artists squatted in the late 19th century – Renoir lived at No 8 from 1890 to 1897. Descend the stairs from place Dalida into rue St-Vincent: on the other side of the wall is ❽ **Cimetière St-Vincent**, final resting place of Maurice Utrillo (1883–1955), the 'painter of Montmartre'.

Just over rue des Saules is the celebrated cabaret ❾ **Au Lapin Agile**, whose name seems to suggest a 'nimble rabbit' but actually comes from *Le Lapin à Gill*, a mural of a rabbit jumping out of a cooking pot by caricaturist André Gill, which can still be seen on the western exterior wall.

Turn right (south) onto rue des Saules. Just opposite is ❿ **Clos Montmartre**, a small vineyard dating from 1933 whose 2000 vines produce an average 800 bottles of wine each October, which is then auctioned off for charity. The ⓫ **Musée de Montmartre** is at 12-14 rue Cortot, the first street on the left after the vineyard. The museum is housed in Montmartre's oldest building, a manor house built in the 17th century, and was the one-time home

to painters Renoir, Utrillo and Raoul Dufy. Further along at No 6 is the ⓬ **house of Eric Satie** where the celebrated composer lived from 1892 to 1898.

At the end of rue Cortot turn right (south) onto rue du Mont Cenis – the attractive ⓭ **water tower** just opposite dates from the early 20th century – then left onto rue de Chevalier de la Barre and right onto rue du Cardinal Guibert. The entrance to the ⓮ **Basilique du Sacré Cœur**, and the stunning vista over Paris from the steps are just to the south.

From the basilica follow rue Azaïs west, then turn north to ⓯ **Église St-Pierre de Montmartre**. This church was built on the site of a Roman temple to Mars (or Mercury) – some say that the name Montmartre is derived from 'Mons Martis' (Latin for Mount of Mars), others prefer the Christian 'Mont Martyr' (Mount of the Martyr).

Across from the church is ⓰ **place du Tertre**, arguably Paris' most touristy place but buzzy and fun nonetheless. Cossack soldiers allegedly first introduced the term *bistro* (Russian for 'quickly') into French at No 6 (La Mère Catherine) in 1814. On Christmas Eve, 1898, Louis Renault's first car was driven up the Butte to place du Tertre, marking the start of the French auto industry.

From place du Calvaire take the steps onto rue Gabrielle, turning right (west) to reach place Émile Goudeau. At No 11b is the ⓱ **Bateau Lavoir** where Kees Van Dongen, Max Jacob, Amedeo Modigliani and Pablo Picasso once lived in an old piano factory later used as a laundry. It was dubbed the 'Laundry Boat' because of the way it swayed in a strong breeze. Picasso painted his seminal *Les Demoiselles d'Avignon* (1907) here. Originally at No 13, the real Bateau Lavoir burned down in 1970 and was rebuilt in 1978.

Take the steps down from place Émile Goudeau and follow rue des Abbesses south into place des Abbesses, where you can't miss the ⓲ **metro station** entrance designed by Hector Guimard. In the 18th-century gypsum miners excavated significant amounts of the Butte, which is why the Abbesses metro station was dug so deeply.

DON'T MISS

CANAL ST-MARTIN

The shaded towpaths of the tranquil, 4.5km-long St-Martin Canal (Map p44; MRépublique, Jaurès or Jacques Bonsergent) are a wonderful place for a romantic stroll or a bike ride past nine locks, metal bridges and ordinary Parisian neighbourhoods. The waterbanks here have undergone a real urban renaissance in recent years, and the southern stretch in particular is an ideal spot for café lounging, quay-side summer picnics and late-night drinks. Hip new bistros have moved into the area (most closed Sunday and often Monday) and if you're in Paris to tempt your tastebuds, you'll wind up in these eastern suburbs sooner rather than later.

Linking the 10e *arrondissement* with Parc de la Villette in the 19e via the Bassin de la Villette and Canal de l'Ourcq, the canal makes its famous dogleg turn in the 10e. Parts of the waterway – built between 1806 and 1825 to link the Seine with the 108km-long Canal de l'Ourcq – are higher than the surrounding land. Take a tour on a **canal boat** (see p90) to savour the real flavour.

ciful, bright-red pavilions known as *folies*. It is the largest open green space in central Paris and has been called 'the prototype urban park of the 21st century'.

TOP CHOICE **Cité des Sciences et de l'Industrie** SCIENCE MUSEUM
(Map p44; reservations ✆08 92 69 70 72; www. cite-sciences.fr; 30 av Corentin Cariou, 19e; ◷10am-6pm Tue-Sat, to 7pm Sun; MPorte de la Villette) At the northern end of Parc de la Villette, the huge City of Science & Industry has all sorts of high-tech exhibits. Bring a picnic and spend the day here.

There are two main exhibit areas inside, in addition to a **planetarium** (level 1; admission €3; ◷10am-6pm Tue-Sat, to 7pm Sun), two cinemas, a tiny **aquarium** (level 2; admission free; ◷10am-6pm Tue-Sat, to 7pm Sun) and a 1950s French Navy submarine (€3; ◷10am-5.30pm Tue-Sat, to 7pm Sun) that can be visited.

On the ground floor is the brilliant **Cité des Enfants** (€6), with imaginative, hands-on demonstrations of basic scientific principles in two sections: for 2- to 7-year-olds, and for 5- to 12-year-olds. In the first, kids can explore, among other things, the conduct of water (waterproof ponchos provided), a building site and a maze. The second lets children build toy houses with industrial robots and stage news broadcasts in a TV studio. Visits to both last 1½ hours and are scheduled five times a day (seven on weekends), beginning at 10am. Reserve several days in advance.

The huge **Explora** (levels 1 & 2; adult/child €8/6), the heart of the exhibitions at the Cité des Sciences et de l'Industrie, looks at everything from space exploration and automobile technology to genetics and sound. Tickets are valid for a full day and allow you to enter and exit at will. Access to some temporary exhibits costs an extra €2.

The giant mirrorlike sphere known as the **Géode** (✆08 92 68 45 40; www.lageode.fr in French; adult/child €10.50/9, 3D films €12.50/11; ◷10.30am-8.30pm) shows hi-res 3D and Imax films (40 minutes each) projected onto a 180-degree screen to surround you with the action. Free headsets for an English soundtrack are available.

The **Cinaxe** (€4.80; ◷10.30am-5pm), a cinema with hydraulic seating for 60 people, moves in synchronisation with the action on the screen. Shows begin every 15 minutes.

Cité de la Musique CONCERT HALL
(Map p44; www.cite-musique.fr; 221 av Jean Jaurès, 19e; ◷noon-6pm Tue-Sat, 10am-6pm Sun; MPorte de Pantin) On the southern edge of Parc de la Villette, the City of Music is a striking triangular-shaped concert hall whose brief is to bring non-elitist music from around the world to Paris' multiethnic masses. In the same complex, the **Musée de la Musique** (Music Museum; adult/child €8/free) displays some 900 rare musical instruments out of a collection of 4500 warehoused, and you can hear many of them being played through the earphones included in the admission cost.

OUTSIDE THE WALLS: BEYOND CENTRAL PARIS

Two of the city's most important recreational areas lie just 'outside the walls' of central Paris. To the southeast and the southwest are the 'lungs' of Paris, the Bois de Vincennes and the Bois de Boulogne.

Bois de Vincennes
WOOD

(bd Poniatowski, 12e; MPorte de Charenton or Porte Dorée) In the southeastern corner of Paris, Vincennes Wood encompasses some 995 hectares. On its northern edge, Château de Vincennes (www.chateau-vincennes.fr; av de Paris, 12e; ☺10am-5 or 6pm; MChâteau de Vincennes) is a bona fide royal château with massive fortifications and a moat. The château grounds can be strolled for free, but the 52m-high dungeon (1369), a prison during the 17th and 18th centuries, and the Gothic Chapelle Royale (Royal Chapel) can be visited only by **guided tour** (adult/child €8/free); call ahead for times.

TOP CHOICE Parc Floral de Paris (Paris Floral Park; www.parcfloraldeparis.com, in French; rte du Champ de Manoeuvre, 12e; adult/child €3/1.50; ☺9.30am-5pm, to 8pm summer; MChâteau de Vincennes), south of the château, is a vast green space with a butterfly garden, nature library, kids' play areas and open-air concerts in summer. The well-managed Parc Zoologique de Paris (Paris Zoological Park; www.mnhn.fr; 53 av de St-Maurice, 12e; ☺9am-5 or 6.30pm seasonal; MPorte Dorée), home to 600 animals, was undergoing a major renovation at the time of writing.

Fish and other sea creatures from around the globe make their home at the Aquarium Tropical (www.acquarium-portedoree.fr; Palais de la Porte Dorée, 293 av Daumesnil, 12e; adult/child €6.50/5; ☺10am-5.30pm Tue-Fri, to 7pm Sat & Sun; MPorte Dorée) on the wood's western edge. In the same building is the compelling Cité Nationale de l'Histoire de l'Immigration (National City of the History of Immigration; www.histoire-immigration.fr; adult/child during exhibition periods €5/free, non-exhibition periods €3/free; ☺10am-5.30pm Tue-Fri, to 7pm Sat & Sun; MPorte Dorée), which documents immigration to France through a series of informative historical displays.

Bois de Boulogne
WOOD

(Map p44; bd Maillot, 16e; MPorte Maillot) On the western edge of Paris just beyond the 16e, the 845-hectare Bois de Boulogne owes its informal layout to Baron Haussmann, who was inspired by Hyde Park in London. Be warned that the Bois de Boulogne becomes a distinctly adult playground after dark, especially along the allée de Longchamp, where male, female and transvestite prostitutes cruise for clients.

Families will be most interested in the Jardin d'Acclimatation (www.jardindaccli

matation.fr; av du Mahatma Gandhi; admission €2.90, under 3yr free; ☺10am-7pm Apr-Sep, to 6pm Oct-Mar; MLes Sablons), a great amusement park for kids with puppet shows, boat rides, a small water park, art exhibits and sometimes special movies. Just south of here will be the Fondation Louis Vuitton pour la Création (www.fondationlouisvuitton.fr), a fine arts centre designed by Frank Gehry, expected to open near the end of 2012.

The wood's enclosed Parc de Bagatelle (adult/child €5/free; ☺9.30am-5pm, to 8pm in summer), in the northwestern corner, is renowned for its beautiful gardens surrounding the 1775 Château de Bagatelle (route de Sèvres à Neuilly, 16e; adult/child €6/free; ☺tour 3pm Sat & Sun Apr-Oct). There are areas dedicated to irises (May), roses (June to October) and water lilies (August). The Pré Catalan (Catalan Meadow; ☺9.30am-5 or 8pm seasonal) to the southeast includes the Jardin Shakespeare in which plants, flowers and trees mentioned in Shakespeare's plays are cultivated.

The southern part of the wood has two horse-racing tracks, the Hippodrome de Longchamp for flat races and the Hippodrome d'Auteuil for steeplechases. The Stade Roland Garros, home of the French Open tennis tournament, is also the Tenniseum-Musée de Roland Garros (2 av Gordon Bennett, 16e; adult/child €7.50/4, with stadium visit €15/10; ☺10am-6pm Tue-Sun; MPorte d'Auteuil), the world's most extravagant tennis museum, tracing the sport's 500-year history. Stadium tours depart at 11am and 3pm (English) and at 2pm and 5pm in French; reservations required.

Rowing boats (per hr €15; ☺10am-6pm mid-Mar–mid-Oct) can be hired at Lac Inférieur (MAv Henri Martin), the largest of the wood's lakes and ponds. Paris Cycles (per hr €5; ☺10am-7pm mid-Apr–mid-Oct) rents bicycles on av du Mahatma Gandhi (MLes Sablons), across from the Porte Sablons entrance to the Jardin d'Acclimatation, and near the Pavillon Royal (MAv Foch) at the northern end of Lac Inférieur.

🏃 Activities

Paris now counts some 370km of cycling lanes in the city, plus many sections of road are shut to motorised traffic on Sunday and holidays. Pick up wheels with Vélib (see p130), join an organised bike tour (p90) or rent your own wheels and DIY with the following:

PARIS BREATHES

'Paris Respire' (Paris Breathes) kicks motorised traffic off certain streets at certain times to let pedestrians, cyclists, in-line skaters and other nonmotorised cruisers take over and, well, breathe – making Sundays particularly pedal-pleasurable.

The following tracks are off limits to cars on Sunday and public holidays. For exact routes and detailed maps see www.velo.paris.fr.

» **By the Seine** From quai des Tuileries, 1e, to Pont Charles de Gaulle, 12e, on the Right Bank; and on the Left Bank from the eastern end of quai Branly near Pont d'Alma, 7e, to quai Anatole France, 7e (9am to 5pm Sunday).

» **Latin Quarter, 5e** Rue de Cluny and from place Marcelin Berthelot by the Sorbonne to the rue Mouffetard market via rue de Lanneau, rue de l'École Polytechnique and rue des Descartes (10am to 6pm Sunday).

» **Bastille, 11e** Rue de la Roquette and surrounding streets (10am to 6pm Sunday July to August).

» **Montmartre & Pigalle** All the streets in Montmartre, 18e, encircled by rue Caulaincourt, rue de Clignancourt, bd de Rochechouart and bd de Clichy (11am to 7pm April to August, 11am to 6pm September to March), as well as rue des Martyrs, 9e (10am to 1pm Sunday).

» **Canal St-Martin, 10e** The area around quai de Valmy and quai de Jemmapes, 10e (10am to 6pm Sunday winter, 8pm summer); in July and August yet more streets running south from quai de Jemmapes become car-free.

» **Bois de Boulogne** (9am to 6pm Saturday and Sunday) and **Bois de Vincennes** (9am to 6pm Sunday).

» **Jardin du Luxembourg, 6e** Immediate surrounding streets, including parts of rue Auguste Compte, rue d'Assas, bd St-Michel and rue des Chartreux (10am to 6pm Sunday March to November).

Gepetto et Vélos   CYCLING
(Map p68; ☑01 43 54 19 95; www.gepetto-et
-velos.com, in French; 59 rue du Cardinal
Lemoine, 5e; per half-day/day/weekend/week
€9/15/25/60; ⊙9am-1pm & 2-7.30pm Tue-Sat;
Ⓜ Cardinal Lemoine)

Paris à Vélo, C'est Sympa!   CYCLING
(Map p60; ☑01 48 87 60 01; www.parisvelo
sympa.com; 22 rue Alphonse Baudin, 11e; per
half-day/day/weekend/week €12/15/25/60;
⊙9.30am-1pm & 2-6pm Mon-Fri, 9am-1pm &
2-7pm Sat & Sun, shorter hours winter; Ⓜ St-
Sébastien Froissart)

☞ Tours
Bicycle

Fat Tire Bike Tours   BICYCLE TOURS
(Map p74; ☑01 56 58 10 54; www.fattirebiketours
.com; 24 rue Edgar Faure, 15e; Ⓜ La Motte Pic-
quet Grenelle) Bike tours by day (€28; four
hours) and night; to Versailles, Monet's
garden (Giverny) and the Normandy
beaches. Participants generally meet
opposite the Eiffel Tower's South Pillar
at the start of the Champ de Mars. Costs

include the bicycle and rain gear. Reserve
in advance.

Boat

Bateaux Mouches   BOAT TOURS
(Map p78; ☑01 42 25 96 10; www.bateauxmou
ches.com; Port de la Conférence, 8e; adult/child
€10/5; ⊙Mar-Nov; Ⓜ Alma Marceau) Based
on the Right Bank just east of Pont de
l'Alma, Paris's most famous riverboat
company runs 1000-seat tour boats, the
biggest on the Seine. Cruises (70 minutes)
run regularly from 10.15am to 11pm April
to September and 13 times a day between 11am and 9pm the rest of the year.
French-English commentary.

Paris Canal Croisières   CANAL CRUISES
(☑01 42 40 96 97; www.pariscanal.com; Bassin
de la Villette, 19-21 quai de la Loire, 19e; adult/
child €17/10; ⊙Mar-Nov; Ⓜ Jaurès or Musée
d'Orsay) This company runs daily 2½-hour
cruises departing from near the Musée
d'Orsay (quai Anatole France, 7e) for
Bassin de la Villette, 19e, via the charming Canal St-Martin and Canal de l'Ourcq.

Bus

L'Open Tour BUS TOURS
(Map p82; 01 42 66 56 56; www.pariscityrama.com; 13 rue Auber, 9e; 1 day adult/child €29/15; Havre Caumartin or Opéra) This company runs open-deck buses along four circuits and you can jump on/off at more than 50 stops. Buy tickets from the driver.

Walking

Ça Se Visite ARTISAN TOURS
(www.ca-se-visite.fr, in French; €12) Meet local artists and craftspeople on resident-led 'urban discovery tours' of the northeast *arrondissements* (10e, 11e, 18e, 19e, 20e).

Eye Prefer Paris WALKING TOURS
(www.eyepreferparistours.com; €195 for 3 people) New Yorker turned Parisian leads offbeat tours of the city; cooking classes too.

Paris Go THEMED WALKS
(www.parisgo.fr; €20) Two-hour thematic tours followed by drinks in a local café or bar.

Paris Greeter WALKING TOURS
(www.parisiendunjour.fr; donation) See Paris through local eyes with these two- to three-hour city tours. Volunteers lead groups (maximum six people) to their favourite spots in the city. Minimum two week's advance notice needed.

Paris Walks THEMED WALKS
(www.paris-walks.com; adult/child €12/8) Long established and highly rated by our readers, Paris Walks offers thematic tours (fashion, chocolate, the French Revolution) in English.

✦ Festivals & Events

Innumerable festivals, cultural and sporting events and trade shows take place in Paris throughout the year; find them listed under 'What's On' on the website of the Paris Convention & Visitors Bureau (www.parisinfo.com).

January & February

Grande Parade de Paris NEW YEAR
(www.parisparade.com) The Great Paris Parade with marching and carnival bands, dance acts and so on, takes place on the afternoon of New Year's Day. It used to be held in the small backstreets of Montmartre but has become so popular that it has spread to the Grand Boulevards, from rue du Faubourg St-Denis at bd Bonne Nouvelle in the 10e to place de la Madeleine in the 8e.

Louis XVI Commemorative Mass
HISTORICAL EVENT
(www.monuments-nationaux.fr) On the Sunday closest to 21 January, royalists and right-wingers attend a Mass at the Chapelle Expiatoire marking the execution by guillotine of King Louis XVI in 1793.

Fashion Week FASHION
(www.pretparis.com) Prêt-à-Porter, the ready-to-wear fashion salon that is held twice a year in late January and again in September, is a must for fashion buffs and is held at the Parc des Expositions at Porte de Versailles, 15e (Porte de Versailles).

Chinese New Year NEW YEAR
(www.paris.fr) Dragon parades and other festivities are held in late January or early February in Paris' two Chinatowns: the smaller, more authentic in the 3e (rue du Temple, rue au Maire and rue de Turbigo); the larger flashier one in the 13e (between porte de Choisy, porte d'Ivry and bd Masséna).

March & April

Foire du Trône FUN FAIR
(www.foiredutrone.com, in French) Huge funfair with 350 attractions is held on the Pelouse de Reuilly of the Bois de Vincennes (Porte Dorée) for eight weeks early April to late May.

Marathon International de Paris SPORT
(www.parismarathon.com) The Paris International Marathon, on the first or second Sunday in April, starts on the av des Champs-Élysées, 8e, and finishes on av Foch, 16e.

May & June

French Tennis Open SPORT
(www.rolandgarros.com) The glitzy Internationaux de France de Tennis – the Grand Slam – is a two-week affair from late May to mid-June at Stade Roland Garros on the southern edge of the Bois de Boulogne.

Gay Pride March GAY
(www.gaypride.fr, in French) A colourful, Saturday-afternoon parade in late June through the Marais to Bastille celebrates Gay Pride Day, with bars and clubs sponsoring floats, and participants dressing outrageously.

PARIS FOR CHILDREN

Paris is extraordinarily kid-friendly and children are welcome participants in most aspects of social life in France. If you're on a family trip, you'll find no shortage of things to do, from playing tag around Daniel Buren's black-and-white columns at Palais Royal, laughing with puppets in the Jardin du Luxembourg, sailing down the Seine or resting younger legs with a DIY city sightseeing tour aboard one of Paris' two above-ground metro lines (2 and 6).

If museums are not free (lots are free for under-18s), they'll have cheaper child's rates; ages of eligibility vary though those aged seven years and upwards usually have to pay. Many organise fun-fuelled educational *ateliers enfants* (kids' workshops) for children aged four or six and upwards.

Many restaurants serve a *menu enfant* (set children's menu), usually for children under 12, though starters or the savoury crêpes served in brasseries can feel more imaginative *(steak haché* aka a hamburger patty without the bun and fries gets tiresome after a couple of days). Picnics by the Seine or in a park are a sunny option.

As for accommodation, families should consider renting an apartment – particularly convenient if you have young children and generally less expensive than staying in a hotel. Be aware that most hotel rooms are small and while many will happily put in a travel cot or a folding bed for one child, families of four or more will struggle for choice: few hotels have quads or connecting doubles.

On the metro, bizarrely you cannot buy a *carnet* (book of 10) of children's metro tickets (aged four to 11 years); they are only sold individually.

For the lowdown on current exhibitions and events with kids in mind, check the *What's On* directory of www.parisinfo.com. *Pariscope* and *L'Officiel des Spectacles* (p123) both have decent 'Enfants' sections; French daily newspaper *Libération* publishes a bimonthly supplement *Paris Mômes* (www.parismomes.fr, in French), occasionally translated into English; and many shops distribute the free twice-monthly listing magazine, *Bubble Mag* (www.bubblemay.fr, in French). If you understand French there is no better resource than Michelin's green-jacketed *Paris Enfants* guide.

Top 10 Sights & Activities

» **Bois de Vincennes** Tucked within these Parisian woods is one of Europe's best aquariums; there are tip-top climbing frames for older children as well as little 'uns in the Parc Floral de Paris.

» **Cinéaqua** Two words: shark tank.

» **Cité des Sciences et de l'Industrie** Hands-on science exhibits for kids aged two years and up, plus two special-effects cinemas, a planetarium and retired 1950s submarine. *And* there are great themed playgrounds.

» **Cité de la Musique** Music discovery workshops and concerts for children aged three years and upwards.

» **Eiffel Tower** Who doesn't enjoy scaling a giant Mechano/Erector set? Give kids a Flip camera to experiment with perspectives on the way up and down.

» **Jardin d'Acclimatation** Amusement park with puppet shows, boat rides and a small water park – a great small-scale alternative to Disneyland!

» **Jardin du Luxembourg** Sail a toy sailing boat from the 1920s, laugh with the puppets, ride a pony, then sail the boats again.

» **Musée National d'Histoire Naturelle** Life-size stuffed elephants and giraffes in one building, dinosaur skeletons in the other.

» **Palais de la Découverte** Riveting, hands-on science exhibitions off the Champs Élysées.

» **Ménagerie du Jardin des Plantes** Wildlife observation in the centre of Paris, plus a great maze to lose 'em in in surrounding Jardin des Plantes.

Paris Jazz Festival — JAZZ
(www.parcfloraldeparis.com; www.paris.fr) Free jazz concerts every Saturday and Sunday afternoon in June and July in Parc Floral de Paris.

July & August

Paris Plages — BEACH
(www.paris.fr) 'Paris Beaches' sees three waterfront areas transformed into sand-and-pebble 'beaches', complete with sun beds, beach umbrellas, atomisers, lounge chairs and palm trees, for four weeks from mid-July to mid-August.

September & October

Jazz à la Villette — JAZZ
(www.villette.com, in French) 10-day jazz festival in early September has sessions in Parc de la Villette, at the Cité de la Musique and in surrounding bars.

Nuit Blanche — EVENT
(www.paris.fr) 'White Night' is when Paris becomes 'the city that doesn't sleep', with museums across town joining bars and clubs and staying open till the very wee hours on the first Saturday and Sunday of October.

Fete des Vendanges de Montmartre — HARVEST
(www.fetedesvendangesdemontmartre.com, in French) This five-day festival during the second weekend in October celebrates Montmartre's grape harvest with costumes, speeches and a parade.

November & December

Christmas Eve Mass — CHRISTMAS
Celebrated at midnight on Christmas Eve at many Paris churches, including Notre Dame.

New Year's Eve — NEW YEAR
Bd St-Michel (5e), place de la Bastille (11e), the Eiffel Tower (7e) and especially av des Champs-Élysées (8e) are *the* Parisian hot spots to welcome in the new year.

🛏 Sleeping

Paris has a very wide choice of accommodation options that caters for all budgets. The city may not be able to boast the number of budget hotels (up to €80 for a double) it did a decade or so ago, but the choice remains ample, especially in the Marais, around the Bastille, and near the major train stations. Midrange hotels offer some of the best value for money of any European capital, charging between €80 and €175 for a double. Top-end places run the gamut from tasteful and discreet boutique hotels to palaces with more than 100 rooms.

The Paris Convention & Visitors Bureau (p129), particularly the Gare du Nord branch, can find you a place to stay for the night of the day you stop by and will make the booking for free. The only catch is that you have to use a credit card to reserve a room. Queues can be very long in high season.

For B&B accommodation in the city try Alcôve & Agapes (www.bed-and-breakfast-in-paris.com), Good Morning Paris (www.goodmorningparis.fr) or B&B Paris (www.2binparis.com).

LOUVRE & LES HALLES
The area encompassing the Musée du Louvre and the Forum des Halles, effectively the 1er and a small slice of the 2e, is very central but don't expect to find tranquillity or many bargains here. While it is more disposed to welcoming top-end travellers, there are some decent midrange places to choose from and the main branch of a popular hostel can also be found here.

RENTING APARTMENTS

Be it for one night or one month, this is increasingly the modish way to stay in Paris. Go to one-bedroom Consult agencies listed on the Paris Convention & Visitors Bureau (www.parisinfo.com) website or try:

» Haven in Paris (http://haveninparis.com) Luxury apartments starting at €575/week

» Paris Accommodation Service (www.paris-accommodation-service.com) Over 500 properties; studios from €520/week

» Paris Apartments Services (www.paris-apts.com) Mostly studios and one-bedroom flats, from €100/day

» Paris Attitude (www.parisattitude.com) 3000 properties, studios from €325/week

» Paris Stay (www.paristay.com) Over 200 vacation flats (ie convenient locations), with studios starting at €300.

TOP CHOICE Le Relais du Louvre

BOUTIQUE HOTEL €€

(Map p50; ☑01 40 41 96 42; www.relaisdulouvre. com; 19 rue des Prêtres St-Germain l'Auxerrois, 1er; s €125, d €170-215, tr €215; ❄☎; ⓜPont Neuf) If you're someone who likes style in a traditional sense, pick this lovely 21-room hotel just west of the Louvre and south of Église St-Germain l'Auxerrois. The nine rooms facing the street and the church are on the petite side; if you are looking for something more spacious, ask for one of the five rooms ending in a '2' (eg 52). Room 2 itself has access to the garden. The apartment on the top floor sleeps five, boasts a fully equipped kitchen and has memorable views over the rooftops.

BVJ Paris-Louvre

HOSTEL €

(Map p50; ☑01 53 00 90 90; www.bvjhotel. com; 20 rue Jean-Jacques Rousseau, 1er; dm/d €29/70; @☎⃰; ⓜLouvre-Rivoli) This modern, 200-bed hostel has doubles and bunks in a single-sex room for four to 10 people with showers down the corridor. Guests should be aged 18 to 35. Rooms are accessible from 2.30pm on the day you arrive and all day after that. There are no kitchen facilities.

Hôtel de Lille

BUDGET HOTEL €

(Map p50; ☑01 42 33 33 42; 8 rue de Pélican, 1er; s €39-43, d €50-55, tr €85; ⓜPalais Royal–Musée du Louvre) This old-fashioned but spotlessly clean 13-room hotel is down a quiet side street from the Louvre in a 17th-century building.

MARAIS & BASTILLE

Despite widespread gentrification in recent years, there are some fine hostels here and the choice of lower-priced hotels remains excellent. East of Bastille, the relatively untouristed 11e is generally made up of unpretentious, working-class areas and is a good way to see the 'real' Paris up close.

TOP CHOICE Hôtel du Petit Moulin

BOUTIQUE HOTEL €€€

(Map p56; ☑01 42 74 10 10; www.hoteldupetit moulin.com; 29-31 rue de Poitou, 3e; r €190-290; ❄@☎; ⓜFilles du Calvaire) This scrumptious boutique hotel (OK, we're impressed that it was a bakery at the time of Henri IV) was designed from top to bottom by Christian Lacroix and features 17 completely different rooms. You can choose from medieval and rococo Marais sporting exposed beams and dressed in toile de Jouy wall-

paper, to more modern surrounds with contemporary murals and heart-shaped mirrors just this side of kitsch. 'The Little Mill' is still one of our favourite hostelries in the Marais.

TOP CHOICE Hôtel St-Merry

HISTORIC HOTEL €€

(Map p56; ☑01 42 78 14 15; www.hotel-marais.com; 78 rue de la Verrerie, 4e; r €135-230, tr €205-275; ❄☎; ⓜChâtelet) The interior of this 12-room hostelry, with beamed ceilings, church pews and wrought-iron candelabra, is a neogoth's wet dream; you have to see the architectural elements of room 9 (flying buttress over the bed) and the furnishings of 12 (choir-stall bed board) to believe them. On the downside there is no lift connecting the postage-stamp lobby with the four upper floors, and only some of the rooms have air conditioning.

Hôtel Les Jardins du Marais

HOTEL €€€

(Map p60; ☑01 40 21 20 00; www.lesjardins dumarais.com; 74 rue Amelot, 11e; r €350-455; ❄@☎; ⓜChemin Vert) You'd never know you were in Paris after walking through the door of this 263-room hotel housed in nine separate buildings designed by Gustave Eiffel and surrounding an enormous courtyard of cobblestones and gardens. Rooms have an art deco feel – lots of blacks, whites, purples and straight lines – and the outlets are always bursting at the seams. It's a delight but way too big to call itself a boutique hotel.

Le Géneral Hôtel

DESIGN HOTEL €€

(Map p60; ☑01 47 00 41 57; www.legeneralhotel. com; 5-7 rue Rampon, 11e; s €155-175, d €190-220, tr €220-250; ❄☎; ⓜRépublique) This hotel is whiter than pale on the outside and a bonbon box of cherry and chocolate tones within. The décor at 'The General' is fresh and fun, and the 47 rooms are beautifully furnished. The cheery bar off the lobby is memorable – the gumdrops are a nice touch – and amenities include a small but well-equipped fitness centre and sauna.

BLC Design Hotel

DESIGN HOTEL €€€

(☑01 40 09 60 16; www.blcdesign-hotel-paris. com; 4 rue Richard Lenoir, 11e; s €95-180, d €180-230; ❄☎; ⓜCharonne) Cobbled from what was a very ordinary hotel, this 'symphony in white' has raised the bar on hotel standards east of the Bastille. Its 29 rooms, as comfortable as they are 'Zen' stylish, are spread over six floors and we love the intimate little bar in the lobby. More rock star than royal, maybe, but they're on a roll.

Hôtel Daval
BUDGET HOTEL €

(Map p60; ☎01 47 00 51 23; www.hoteldaval.com; 21 rue Daval, 11e; s €81, d €89-98, tr/q €109/127; ❉🖵; Ⓜ️Bastille) Always a favourite, this 23-room property is a very central option if you're looking for almost budget accommodation just off place de la Bastille. What's more, a refit has brought it well into the 21st century. Rooms and bathrooms are on the small side and if you're looking for some peace and quiet choose a back room (eg room 13).

Hôtel Candide
HOTEL €€

(☎01 43 79 02 33; www.new-hotel.com; 3 rue Pétion, 11e; s/d/tr €115/160/190; @; Ⓜ️Voltaire) This 48-room hotel within easy striking distance of the Bastille and the Marais offers relatively good value and is very convenient to the Marché Bastille on bd Richard Lenoir. It's on a very quiet street and we've always been impressed by the friendly, helpful service.

Hôtel de la Bretonnerie
HOTEL €€

(Map p56; ☎01 48 87 77 63; www.bretonnerie.com; 22 rue Ste-Croix de la Bretonnerie, 4e; r €135-165, tr/q €190; 🖵; Ⓜ️Hôtel de Ville) This is a very charming midrange hotel in the heart of the Marais nightlife area and dating from the 17th century. The décor of each of the 29 rooms and suites is unique, and some rooms have four-poster and canopy beds.

Hôtel de Nice
BUDGET HOTEL €

(Map p56; ☎01 42 78 55 29; www.hoteldenice.com; 42bis rue de Rivoli, 4e; s/d/tr €80/110/135; 🖵; Ⓜ️Hôtel de Ville) This is an especially warm, family-run place with 23 comfy rooms full of Second Empire–style furniture, Oriental carpets and lamps with fringed shades. Some have balconies high above busy rue de Rivoli.

Le Quartier Bastille Le Faubourg
FAMILY HOTEL €€

(☎01 43 70 04 04; www.lequartierhotelbf.com; 9 rue de Reuilly, 12e; s €113-168, d €133-163; ❉🖵; Ⓜ️Gare de Lyon) A short walk east from Gare de Lyon, this warm and welcoming boutique hotel has 42 generously sized rooms with all the comforts and then some; big-screen TVs may be *de rigueur* these days but are apples on the bed and free liquorice at reception? Rooms are paired and share an internal hallway.

Hôtel St-Louis Marais
HISTORIC HOTEL €€

(Off Map p56; ☎01 48 87 87 04; www.saintlouis-marais.com; 1 rue Charles V, 4e; s €99, d & tw €115-140, tr €150; 🖵Ⓜ️Sully Morland) This especially charming hotel in a converted 17th-century convent sports lots of wooden beams, terra-cotta tiles and heavy brocade drapes. Four floors but no lift; wi-fi costs €5.

Hôtel du 7e Art
THEMED HOTEL €€

(Map p56; ☎01 44 54 85 00; www.paris-hotel-7art.com; 20 rue St-Paul, 4e; s €75-150, d €95-155; 🖵; Ⓜ️St-Paul) Film buffs, this fun 23-room place with black-and-white-movie theme is for you.

Hôtel Caron de Beaumarchais
BOUTIQUE HOTEL €€

(Map p56; ☎01 42 72 34 12; www.carondebeaumarchais.com; 12 rue Vieille du Temple, 4e; r €125-162; ❉🖵; Ⓜ️St-Paul) Decorated like an 18th-century private house, this themed hotel has to be seen to be believed. A unique experience.

Maison Internationale de la Jeunesse et des Étudiants
HOSTEL €

(Map p56; ☎01 42 74 23 45; www.mije.com; dm/s/d/tr per person €30/49/36/32; @) The MIJE runs three hostels in attractively renovated 17th- and 18th-century *hôtels particuliers* in the heart of the Marais, and it's difficult to think of a better budget deal in Paris. Rooms are closed from noon to 3pm, and the curfew is 1am to 7am. Annual membership €2.50.

MIJE Le Fourcy (6 rue de Fourcy, 4e; Ⓜ️St-Paul), with 200 beds, is the largest of the three. There's a cheap eatery here called Le Restaurant, which offers a three-course fixed-price *menu* including a drink for €10.50.

MIJE Le Fauconnier (11 rue du Fauconnier, 4e; Ⓜ️St-Paul or Pont Marie) has 125 beds and is two blocks south of MIJE Le Fourcy.

MIJE Maubuisson (12 rue des Barres, 4e; Ⓜ️Hôtel de Ville or Pont Marie) – the pick of the three – is half a block south of the *mairie* (town hall) of the 4e and has 99 beds.

THE ISLANDS

The smaller of the two islands in the middle of the Seine, Île St-Louis, is the more romantic and has a string of excellent top-end hotels. Oddly enough, the only hotel on Île de la Cité is a budget one – for now.

Hôtel Henri IV
BUDGET HOTEL €

(Map p64; ☎01 43 54 44 53; www.henri4hotel.fr; 25 place Dauphine, 1er; r €42-69, tr €77-81; 🖵; Ⓜ️Pont Neuf or Cité) This place, known for its

The Seine

Dividing Paris neatly in two, the River Seine only adds to the fun and romance of the city. And never more so than in July and August, when sand is dumped on 5km of its riverbanks to create Paris Plages – yes, a riverside beach with water fountains, sprays, sun loungers and parasols.

Year-round, the Seine riverbanks are where Parisians come for cycling, jogging and taking a simple stroll to savour a river sufficiently precious to be in Unesco's World Heritage treasure trove. Stand on one of the bridges leading to the Seine's two elegant islands and watch lovers mingle with cello-playing buskers and teenaged skateboarders.

After dark, watch the river dance with the watery reflections of street lights, headlamps, stop signals, the dim glow of curtained windows and – occasionally – the superbright flood lamps of a tourist boat. You are in Paris.

BEST SEINE-SIDE PICNIC SPOTS

» **Musée de la Sculpture en Plein Air** (p67) A baguette beside a Brancusi at the Open-Air Sculpture Museum is picnic class

» **Square du Vert Gallant** Bijou park at the tip of Île de la Cité (p61)

» **Square Jean XXIII** Flowery park beneath the magnificent flying buttresses of Notre Dame (p61)

» **Pont St-Louis** Picnic on this pedestrian bridge linking Paris' two islands (p61) and be entertained by buskers, bands and street performers

» **Pont au Double** The other bridge, linking Notre Dame with the Left Bank, that guarantees a free show while you picnic

» **Jardin des Tuileries** (p53) Formal 17th-century gardens near the Louvre

Clockwise from top left
1. Relaxing near Pont Neuf 2. Cruising the Seine at sunset 3. Ferry at Square du Vert Gallant 4. The sun shines on Paris Plages.

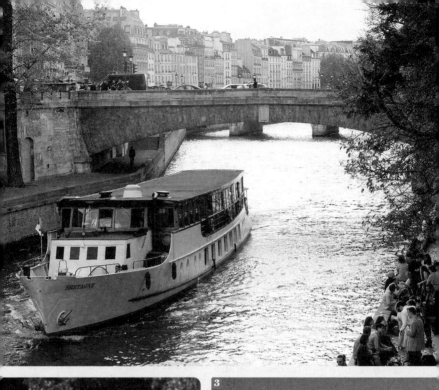

15 worn and very cheap rooms, has always been popular for its location. What we long expected has happened – under new management the hotel is cleaning up its act, refitting its rooms (check out room 4 with its ancient stone wall and wooden floor), and all but one room now has a shower. Views over the square are wonderful. Book well in advance.

Hôtel St-Louis HOTEL €€
(Map p64; ☑01 46 34 04 80; www.hotel-saint -louis.com; 75 rue St-Louis en l'Île, 4e; r €140-220, tr €270; ❋@☎; Ⓜ Pont Marie) The welcome has always been nothing short of passionate at this 19-room hotel on posh rue St-Louis en l'Île. Check out room 52 at the top with its beams and balcony.

LATIN QUARTER & JARDIN DES PLANTES

The northern section of the 5e close to the Seine has been popular with students and young people since the Middle Ages, though there is relatively little budget accommodation left in the area.

There are dozens of attractive midrange hotels in the Latin Quarter, including a cluster near the Sorbonne and another group along the lively rue des Écoles. Midrange hotels in the area are very popular with visiting academics, so rooms are hardest to find when conferences and seminars are scheduled (usually from March to June and in October).

Port Royal Hôtel BUDGET HOTEL €
(Off Map p68; ☑01 43 31 70 06; www.hotelpor-troyal.fr; 8 bd de Port Royal, 5e; s €41-89, d €52.50-89; ❋; Ⓜ Les Gobelins) This 46-room hotel, owned and managed by the same family since 1931, is one of those refreshingly unassuming budget hotels that really don't yearn for any more stars. Its six floors are served by a lift, but the cheapest (washbasin-clad) rooms share a toilet and shower (buy a token for €2.50 at reception). Rooms are spotless and very quiet, especially those that peep down on a small glassed-in courtyard. Predictably, this value-for-money place is no secret, so book ahead. No credit cards.

Hôtel La Demeure BOUTIQUE HOTEL €€
(Map p68; ☑01 43 37 81 25; www.hotella demeureparis.com; 51 bd St-Marcel, 13e; s/d €165/202; ❋@☎; Ⓜ Gobelins) This elegant little number at the bottom of the 5e is the domain of a charming father-son team (a former professional lawyer and a doctor no

less) who speak perfect English and are always at hand. Warm red and orange tones lend a real 'clubby' feel to public areas; wraparound balconies add extra appeal to corner rooms; and then there's those extra little touches – an iPod dock in every room, wine glasses for guests who like to BYO, art to buy on the walls...

Oops DESIGN HOSTEL €
(☑01 47 07 47 00; www.oops-paris.com; 50 av des Gobelins, 13e; dm €28-35; @☎❋; Ⓜ Gobelins) It might be discretely wedged between café terraces and shop fronts but once inside there is nothing discrete about this address aka Paris' first 'design hostel', a five-minute walk north from place d'Italie. A lurid candyfloss-pink lift scales its six floors, each spotlessly clean and painted a different bold colour. Doubles (which can be booked in advance) are well-sized and stylishly modern dorms max out at four to six beds, making it a superb choice for families. Breakfast is a particularly generous affair and in keeping with that true hostel spirit, guests must evacuate their room between 11am and 5pm. Reserve online.

Hôtel de Notre Maître Albert HOTEL €€
(Map p68; ☑01 43 26 79 00; www.hotel-paris -notredame.com; 19 rue Maître Albert, 5e; d €170-280; ❋@☎; Ⓜ Maubert Mutualité) A lovely little number hidden down a quiet street paces from the Seine, this quaint hotel is something of a labyrinth with its long corridors bedecked in striking cobbled-stone patterned carpet and rooms with low beamed ceilings; occasionally sloping. Bedrooms are brightly painted and modern, and marry perfectly with the soft muted colours of the beautiful tapestries covering the walls in reception.

Hôtel Henri IV Rive Gauche HOTEL €€€
(Map p68; ☑01 46 33 20 20; www.henri-paris -hotel.com; 9-11 rue St-Jacques, 5e; s/d/tr €159/185/210; ❋@☎; Ⓜ St-Michel Notre Dame or Cluny–La Sorbonne) This 'country chic' hotel with 23 rooms awash with antiques, old prints and fresh flowers is just steps from Notre Dame and the Seine – think manor house in Normandy. Front rooms have stunning views of the Église St-Séverin and its buttresses. Rates are cheapest online.

Hôtel des Grandes Écoles GARDEN HOTEL €€
(Map p68; ☑01 43 26 79 23; www.hotel-grandes -ecoles.com; 75 rue du Cardinal Lemoine, 5e; d €115-140; @☎; Ⓜ Cardinal Lemoine or Place Monge) This wonderful, very welcoming 51-

room hotel is tucked away in a courtyard off a medieval street with its own garden. Choose a room in one of three buildings: our favourites are the five with direct access to the garden (rooms 29 to 33).

Hôtel Minerve
HOTEL €€

(Map p68; 01 43 26 26 04; www.parishotel minerve.com; 13 rue des Écoles, 5e; s €96-126, d €126-142, tr €162; ✴@☎; Ⓜ Cardinal Lemoine) Housed in two Haussman buildings and owned by the same family who run the Familia Hôtel next door, the Minerve has a reception area kitted out in Oriental carpets and antique books. Some rooms have balconies and two have tiny, swooningly romantic courtyards.

ST-GERMAIN, ODÉON & LUXEMBOURG

Staying in the chic Left Bank neighbourhoods of St-Germain des Prés (6e) and the quieter 7e *arrondissement* next door is a delight, especially for those mad about boutique shopping. Excellent midrange hotels reign supreme.

TOP CHOICE L'Apostrophe
DESIGN HOTEL €€

(01 56 54 31 31; www.apostrophe-hotel. com; 3 rue de Chevreuse, 6e; d €150-350; ✴@☎; Ⓜ Vavin) As much a street work-of-art with its stencilled facade featuring the shadowy grey imprint of a leafy tree by French artist Catherine Feff, this art hotel, on a side street off bd du Montparnasse, is style. Its 16 themed rooms, each dramatically different in décor, pay homage to the written word: spray-painted graffiti tags cover one wall of room U (for 'urbain') which has a ceiling shaped like a skateboard ramp, while room P (for 'Paris parody') sits in the clouds overlooking Paris' rooftops. Clever design features like double sets of imprinted curtains (one for day, one for night) or the 'bar table' on wheels that slots over the bed top off the design-driven ensemble.

TOP CHOICE Hôtel Relais St-Germain
HOTEL €€€

(Map p72; 01 43 29 12 05; www.hotel -paris-relais-saint-germain.com; 9 Carrefour de l'Odéon, 7e; s/d €220/285; ✴@☎; Ⓜ Odéon) What rave reports this elegant top-end hotel with flowerboxes and baby-pink awning gets, and for good reason. Ceilings are beamed, furniture is antique and fabrics are floral (and very fine indeed) inside this 17th-century townhouse. Mix this with a chic contemporary air, ample art work to admire and one of Paris' most talked-about

bistros Le Comptoir as next-door neighbour. Absolutely delicious, darling!

Hôtel de l'Abbaye Saint Germain
PATIO HOTEL €€€

(Map p72; 01 45 44 38 11; www.hotelabbaye paris.com; 10 rue Cassette, 6e; d €260-380; ✴@☎; Ⓜ St-Sulpice) It's its delightfully romantic outside areas that set this elegant abode apart from the crowd. Swing through the wrought-iron gates and enjoy a moment in the front courtyard, bedecked with bench to enjoy its potted plants and flowers. Next morning linger over breakfast served beneath ivy-clad walls on one of the city's prettiest patios.

Hôtel La Sainte-Beuve
HOTEL €€

(01 45 48 20 07; www.parishotelcharme.com; 9 rue Ste-Beuve, 6e; d €159-365; ✴@☎; Ⓜ Notre Dame des Champs) 'Home away from home' is the motto of this 22-room *hôtel-maison* southwest of the Jardin du Luxembourg. Rooms are a riot of colour: take your pick from fuchsia-pink stylishly mixed with lime green and taupe, or racing green wed with oyster grey and burgundy.

MONTPARNASSE

Just east of mammoth train station Gare Montparnasse there are several budget and lower-end midrange places on rue Vandamme and rue de la Gaîté – though the latter street is rife with sex shops and peep shows.

TOP CHOICE Hôtel de la Paix
HOTEL €€

(01 43 20 35 82; www.paris-mont parnasse-hotel.com; 225 bd Raspail, 14e; d €93-165; ✴@☎; Ⓜ Montparnasse Bienvenüe) Stunningly good-value, this recently restyled hotel stacked on seven floors of a 1970s building (the facade still needs to be renovated), a short walk from Gare de Montparnasse, is a real charm. A hip mix of industrial workshop and *côte maison* (home-like), its 39 rooms are light, modern and have at least one vintage feature in each – old pegs to hang coats on, old-fashioned school desk, wooden-slat house shutters recycled as bed head. Cheaper rooms are simply smaller than dearer ones. Oh, and the circular contraption in the reception lounge used to clock factory workers in and out...

Aloha Hostel
HOSTEL €

(01 42 73 03 03; www.aloha.fr; 1 rue Borromée, 15e; per person dm/d €25/28 inc breakfast; ✴@☎Ⓜ Volontaires) A line-up of flags flutter outside this laid-back crash pad with a rainbow of colours as paint job – love the bright violet staircase – and opera music adding a touch of funk to the hybrid reception-lounge. Dorms have four to eight beds and the cream of the crop is its rooms for two (which cannot be reserved in advance). Rooms are locked from 11am to 5pm, curfew is at 2am, kitchen facilities are available and reception lends guests umbrellas and hairdryers. Located west of Gare de Montparnasse.

Hôtel Carladez Cambronne HOTEL €€
(☎01 47 34 07 12; www.hotelcarladez.com; 3 place du Général Beuret, 15e; s/d/tr/q €92/95/167/180; ✳@⊛⊕; ⓜVaugirard) This small dynamic hotel sits aplomb a quintessential neighbourhood square, bench-clad beneath trees in the middle and framed with cafés. Room No 11 opens onto a tiny courtyard with table for two. Rent coffee- and tea-making facilities from reception (€6) and make yourself at home. From Vaugirard metro station, walk east along rue de Vaugirard and take the first left along rue du Général Beuret to place du Général Beuret.

FAUBOURG ST-GERMAIN & INVALIDES
The 7e is a lovely *arrondissement* in which to stay, but apart from the northeastern section – the area east of Invalides and opposite the Louvre – it's fairly quiet and away from all the action.

Hôtel Cadran BOUTIQUE HOTEL €€
(Map p74; ☎01 40 62 67 00; www.paris-hotel -cadran.com; 10 rue du Champ de Mars, 7e; d €144-225; ✳⊛; ⓜÉcole Militaire) An address for gourmets, this concept hotel seduces guests with a designer tick-tock clock theme and a bold open-plan reception spilling into Bar à Chocolat (Chocolate Bar). Admire, taste and buy Christophe Roussel's colourful seasonal-flavoured *macarons* and chocolates (www.roussel-chocolatier.com), then retire to one of 41 futuristic rooms with all the mod cons. If bold colour is not your thing, go for one on the white-and-beige 2nd floor; the 3rd is orange and the pink 4th is *très fille* (very girly).

Hôtel Muguet FAMILY HOTEL €€
(Map p74; ☎01 47 05 05 93; www.hotelmuguet. com; 11 rue Chevert, 7e; s/d/tr €110/145/195; ✳⊛⊕; ⓜLa Tour Maubourg) Functional décor and generous-sized triples with armchair-bed converting separate lounge area into kid's bedroom make this a great family choice. From the 4th floor on, the Eiffel Tower starts to sneak into view and several rooms stare at the equally arresting Église du Dôme. Back down on ground level, a trio of rooms open onto a delightful courtyard garden.

Hôtel du Champ-de-Mars BUDGET HOTEL €
(Map p74; ☎01 45 51 52 30; www.hotelduchamp demars.com; 7 rue du Champ de Mars, 7e; s/d/ tr €91/98/128; @⊛⊕; ⓜÉcole Militaire) This charming 25-room hotel in the shadow of the Eiffel Tower is on everyone's wish list – book a month or two ahead.

ÉTOILE & CHAMPS-ÉLYSÉES
This area has some of Paris' finest palace hotels and trendsetters.

TOP CHOICE Hidden Hotel BOUTIQUE HOTEL €€€
(Map p78; ☎01 40 55 03 57; www.hidden -hotel.com; 28 rue de l'Arc de Triomphe, 17e; s €245, d €285-485; ✳@⊛; ⓜCharles de Gaulle–Étoile) The Hidden is one of the Champs-Élysées' best secrets: an ecofriendly boutique hotel, it's serene, stylish, reasonably spacious, and it even sports green credentials. The earth-coloured tones are the result of natural pigments (there's no paint), and all rooms feature handmade wooden furniture, stone basins for sinks, and linen curtains surrounding Coco-mat beds. The Emotion rooms, which have a terrace, are among the most popular. Need we say that the breakfast is almost 100% organic?

Hôtel de Sèze HOTEL €€
(Off Map p78; ☎01 47 42 69 12; www.hoteldeseze. com; 16 rue de Sèze, 9e; s €120-150, d €130-150, tr €160; ✳@⊛; ⓜMadeleine) This simple but stylish establishment is excellent value for its location – so close to place de la Madeleine. For a real treat, ask for the double with jacuzzi. Wi-fi costs €5.

Hôtel Alison HOTEL €€
(Map p78; ☎01 42 65 54 00; www.hotelalison. com; 21 rue de Surène, 8e; s €86-98, d €120-194, tr €192; ✳@⊛; ⓜMadeleine) This excellent-value 34-room midrange hotel attracts with bold colours and modern art.

CLICHY & GARE ST-LAZARE
These areas have some excellent midrange hotels. The better deals are away from Gare St-Lazare, but there are several places along rue d'Amsterdam beside the station worth checking out.

TOP CHOICE **Hôtel Eldorado** QUIRKY HOTEL €

(☏01 45 22 35 21; www.eldoradohotel. fr; 18 rue des Dames, 17e; s €35-60, d €70-80, tr €80-90; ☏☐; MPlace de Clichy) This bohemian place is one of Paris' greatest finds: a welcoming, reasonably well-run place with 23 colourfully decorated and (often) ethnically themed rooms in a main building on a quiet street and in an annexe with a private garden at the back. We love rooms 1 and 2 in the garden annexe; the choicest rooms in the main building are Nos 16 and 17 with their own terraces leading out into the garden. Cheaper-category singles have washbasin only. The hotel's excellent Bistro des Dames is a bonus. From the metro, head north along av de Clichy and take the first left onto rue des Dames.

OPÉRA & GRANDS BOULEVARDS

The avenues around bd Montmartre are popular for their nightlife area and it's a lively area in which to stay. It's very convenient for shopping as this is where you'll find Paris' premium department stores.

Hôtel Monte Carlo BUDGET HOTEL €

(Map p82; ☏01 47 70 36 75; www.hotelmonte carlo.fr; 44 rue du Faubourg Montmartre, 9e; s €55-105, d €69-129, tr €119-149; ☏☐; MLe Peletier) A unique budget hotel, the Monte Carlo is a steal, with colourful, personalised rooms and a great neighbourhood location. The owners go the extra mile and even provide a partly organic breakfast. The cheaper rooms come without bathroom or shower, but overall it outclasses many of the other choices in its price range. Rates vary with the season.

Hôtel Langlois HISTORIC HOTEL €€

(Map p82; ☏01 48 74 78 24; www.hotel-langlois. com; 63 rue St-Lazare, 9e; s €110-120, d €140-150; ☀@☏; MTrinité) If you're looking for a bit of belle époque Paris, the Langlois won't let you down. Built in 1870, this 27-room hotel has kept its charm, from the tiny caged elevator to sandstone fireplaces in many rooms (sadly decommissioned) as well as original bathroom fixtures and tiles. Room 64 has wonderful views of Montmartre's rooftops.

Hôtel Chopin HISTORIC HOTEL €€

(Map p82; ☏01 47 70 58 10; www.hotelchopin.fr; 46 passage Jouffroy & 10 bd Montmartre, 9e; s €68-84, d €92-106, tr €125; ☏; MGrands Boulevards) Dating to 1846, the 36-room Chopin is down one of Paris' most delightful 19th-century arcades. It may be a little faded around the edges, but it's enormously evocative of the fabulous belle époque.

Hôtel Favart HISTORIC HOTEL €€

(Map p82; ☏01 42 97 59 83; www.hotel-paris -favart.com; 5 rue Marivaux, 2e; s €105-130, d €135-160, tr €145-180, q €155-200; ☀☏; MRichelieu Drouot) With 37 rooms facing the Opéra Comique, the Favart is a stylish art nouveau hotel that feels like it never let go of the belle époque.

Hôtel Vivienne BUDGET HOTEL €

(Map p82; ☏01 42 33 13 26; www.hotel-vivienne. com; 40 rue Vivienne, 2e; s €64-118, d €79-118; @☏; MGrands Boulevards) This stylish 45-room hotel is amazingly good value for Paris.

GARE DU NORD, GARE DE L'EST & RÉPUBLIQUE

The areas east and northeast of the Gare du Nord and Gare de l'Est have always had a more than ample selection of accommodation: the budget- to midrange hotels around the train stations in the 10e are convenient for early birds to London or those wanting to crash on arrival. Place de la République is handy for Ménilmontant nightlife.

TOP CHOICE **St Christopher's Inn** HOSTEL €

(☏01 40 34 34 40; www.st-christophers. co.uk; 68-74 quai de la Seine, 19e; dm €15-38, d from €35; @☏☐; MRiquet or Jaurès) This is certainly one of Paris' best, biggest (300 beds) and most up-to-date hostels. It features a modern design, three types of dorms (10-bed, eight-bed, six-bed) as well as doubles with or without bathrooms. Other perks include a canal-side café, free wi-fi (temperamental) and breakfast, internet café, a female-only floor and bar. Seasonal prices vary wildly; check the website for an accurate quote. No kitchen.

Kube Hôtel BOUTIQUE HOTEL €€€

(☏01 42 05 20 00; www.muranoresort.com; 1-5 passage Ruelle, 18e; s €250, d €300-400; ☀@☏; MLa Chapelle) The easternmost edge of the 18e, virtually on the lap of Gare du Nord, is the last place in Paris you'd expect to find an uber-trendy boutique hotel, but this 41-room hostelry pulls it off. The theme is, of course, three dimensional square – from the glassed-in reception box in the entrance courtyard to the cube-shaped furnishings in the 41 guestrooms to the ice in the cocktails at the celebrated Ice Kube bar.

Gare du Nord & Gare de l'Est

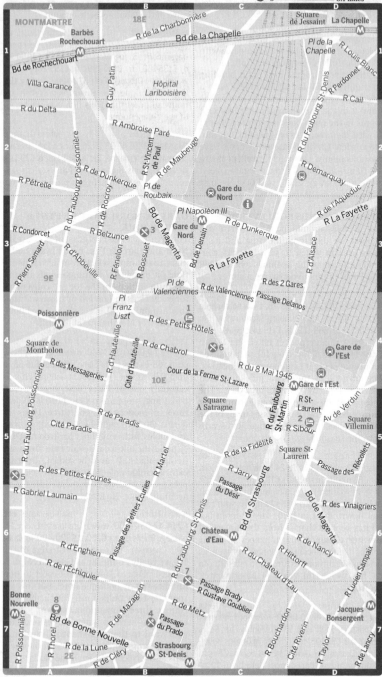

Hôtel du Nord
HOTEL €

(✆01 42 01 66 00; www.hoteldunord-leparivelo.com; 47 rue Albert Thomas, 10e; r/q €69/105; 🛜; Ⓜ République) A cosy place with 23 personalised rooms decorated with flea-market antiques, Hôtel du Nord's other winning attribute is its prized location near place République. Borrow a bike from reception.

République Hôtel
THEMED HOTEL €€

(✆01 42 39 19 03; www.republiquehotel.com; 31 rue Albert Thomas, 10e; s/d/tr/q €75/88/108/159; 🛜; Ⓜ République) This hip spot is heavy on the pop art and UK paraphernalia – the Union Jack and the Beatles turn up an awful lot – but you won't be able to fault the inexpensive rates and fantastic location off place République.

Sibour Hôtel
HOTEL €

(Map p102; ✆01 46 07 20 74; www.hotel-sibour.com; 4 rue Sibour, 10e; s €40-55, d €45-65, tr/q €80/110; 🛜🚻; Ⓜ Gare de l'Est) This friendly place has 45 well-kept rooms, some a tad old-fashioned, and a breakfast room with a *trompe l'œil* mural.

GARE DE LYON, NATION & BERCY
The neighbourhood around the Gare de Lyon has a few budget hotels as well as an independent hostel.

Hôtel Le Cosy
BUDGET HOTEL €

(✆01 43 43 10 02; www.hotel-cosy.com; 50 av de St-Mandé, 12e; s €45-65, d €55-110; ✳🛜; Ⓜ Picpus) This slightly eccentric budget hotel, immediately southeast of place de la Nation, oozes charm. The 28 rooms, though basic, are all decorated in warm pastels with hardwood floors. If feeling flush, choose one of four air-conditioned 'VIP' double rooms in the courtyard annexe, especially room 3 or 4 on the 1st floor. There's a decent café-restaurant with the same name next door.

Hôtel du Printemps
HOTEL €

(✆01 43 43 62 31; www.hotel-paris-printemps.com; 80 bd de Picpus, 12e; s €68-75, d €76-105, tr €98-120; 🛜🚻Ⓜ Picpus) It may not be in the centre of the action, but the 38-room 'Spring Hotel' offers excellent value for its standard and location just steps from place de la Nation. What's more, there's an in-house bar open day and night.

Hostel Blue Planet
HOSTEL €

(✆01 43 42 06 18; www.hostelblueplanet.com; 5 rue Hector Malot, 12e; dm €25; @; Ⓜ Gare de Lyon) This 43-room hostel is very close to Gare de Lyon – convenient if you're heading south or west at the crack of dawn or arriving in the wee hours. Dorm beds are in rooms for two to four people and the hostel closes between 11am and 3pm. No curfew.

MÉNILMONTANT & BELLEVILLE
The Ménilmontant nightlife district is an excellent area in which to spend the evening, but the selection of accommodation in all price ranges is a tad limited, particularly so for travellers on a tight budget.

Mama Shelter
DESIGN HOSTEL €

(✆01 43 48 47 40; www.mamashelter.com; 109 rue de Bagnolet, 20e; s €89-99, d €99-109; ✳🛜🚻; Ⓜ Alexandre Dumas or Gambetta) Coaxed into its zany new incarnation by uber-designer Philippe Starck, this former car park southeast of Cimetière du Père Lachaise boasts 170 super-comfortable (though smallish) rooms, trademark Starck details like a chocolate and fuchsia colour scheme, rough concrete walls and *bons mots* ('sweet nothings', for lack of a better translation) illuminated on the carpets. We love the open terrace on the 7th floor and the fabulous candle-lit pizzeria. Only drawback: Mama Shelter is a hike to the nearest metro stop.

Hôtel Beaumarchais
BOUTIQUE HOTEL €€

(Map p60; ✆01 53 36 86 86; www.hotelbeaumarchais.com; 3 rue Oberkampf, 11e; s €75-90, d €110-130, tr €170-190; ✳🛜; Ⓜ Filles du Calvaire) This brighter-than-bright 31-room boutique hotel, with its emphasis on sunbursts and bold primary colours, is just this side of kitsch. But it makes for a different Paris experience. There are monthly art exhibitions and guests are invited to the *vernissage* (opening night). Rooms are decent sized and bright.

Hôtel Croix de Malte
BUDGET HOTEL €

(Map p60; ✆01 48 05 09 36; www.hotelcroix demalte-paris.com; 5 rue de Malte, 11e; s €60-90, d €65-97; ⚇; ⓜOberkampf) With its glassed-in courtyard sporting a giant jungle mural, this cheery hotel will have you thinking you're in the tropics, not Paris. The 40 rooms are in two little buildings, only one of which has a lift.

MONTMARTRE & PIGALLE
Montmartre, encompassing the 18e and the northern part of the 9e, is one of Paris' most charming neighbourhoods with loads of variety, from boutique to bohemian and hostel to *hôtel particulier*. Many have views of some kind – whether of the streets of Montmartre and Sacré Cœur or the Paris skyline stretching away to the south – and top-floor availability is a good factor to take into account when choosing your room.

The flat area around the base of the Butte Montmartre has some surprisingly good budget deals. The lively, ethnically mixed area east of Sacré Cœur can be a bit rough; some say it's prudent to avoid Château Rouge metro station at night.

TOP CHOICE Hôtel Amour
BOUTIQUE HOTEL €€

(✆01 48 78 31 80; www.hotelamour-paris.fr; 8 rue Navarin, 9e; s €100, d €150-280; ⚇; ⓜSt-Georges or Pigalle) Planning a romantic escapade to Paris? Say no more. One of the 'in' hotels of the moment, the inimitable black-clad Amour (formerly a love hotel by the hour) features original design and artwork in each of the rooms and is very much worthy of the hype – you won't find a more original place to lay your head in Paris at these prices. Of course, you have to be willing to forgo television (none), but who needs TV when you're in love? The hotel is a five-minute walk from the metro.

Hôtel Particulier Montmartre
BOUTIQUE HOTEL €€€

(Map p84; ✆0153418140; http://hotel-particulier -montmartre.com; 23 av Junot, 18e; ❄⚇; ⓜLa-marck Caulaincourt) An 18th-century mansion hidden down a private alleyway, this *bijou* (jewel) sparkles from every angle. Much more than an exclusive hotel, it's the equivalent of staying in a modern art collector's

personal residence, with rotating exhibitions from around the world, five imaginative suites designed by top French artists (Philippe Mayaux, Natacha Lesueur), and a lush garden landscaped by Louis Benech of Jardin des Tuileries fame.

Hôtel des Arts
HOTEL €€

(Map p84; ✆01 46 06 30 52; www.arts-hotel-paris.com; 5 rue Tholozé, 18e; s/d €95/140; ⚇⚇; ⓜAbbesses or Blanche) The Hôtel des Arts is a friendly, attractive 50-room hotel, convenient to both place Pigalle and Montmartre. It has comfortable midrange rooms done up in a traditional style (lots of floral motifs); consider spending an extra €25 for the superior rooms, which have nicer views and are a tad larger. Just up the street is the old-style windmill Moulin de la Galette – how's that for location?

Hôtel Bonséjour Montmartre
BUDGET HOTEL €

(Map p84; ✆01 42 54 22 53; www.hotel-bon sejour-montmartre.fr; 11 rue Burq, 18e; s €33-69 d €56-69; ⚇; ⓜAbbesses) At the top of a quiet street, the 'Good Stay' is a perennial favourite. It's simple but welcoming, comfortable and very clean. Some rooms have balconies attached and No 55 glimpses Sacré Cœur. Hall showers cost €2.

Le Village Hostel
HOSTEL €

(Map p84; ✆01 42 64 22 02; www.villagehostel. fr; 20 rue d'Orsel, 18e; per person dm €28-38, d €70-90, tr €96-115, q €112-140; ⚇⚇⚇; ⓜAnvers) A fine 25-room address with beamed ceilings, lovely terrace and Sacré Cœur views. Kitchen facilities are available, and there's a popular bar too. Rooms are closed between 11am and 4pm; no curfew.

Plug-inn Hostel
HOSTEL €

(Map p84; ✆01 42 58 42 58; www.plug-inn.fr; 7 rue Aristide Bruant, 18e; dm €20-30, d €60-80, tr €90; ⚇⚇; ⓜAbbesses or Blanche) This 2010 hostel has several things going for it, central Montmartre location for starters. Lockout by day; no curfew by night.

Hotel Caulaincourt Square
BUDGET HOTEL €

(✆01 46 06 46 06; www.caulaincourt.com; 2 square Caulaincourt, 18e; dm €25, s €50-60, d & tw €63-76, tr €89; ⚇⚇⚇; ⓜLamarck Caulaincourt) This hotel with dorm rooms is perched on the backside of Montmartre, beyond the tourist hoopla in a real Parisian neighbourhood.

Eating

When it comes to food, Paris has everything...and nothing. As the culinary centre of the most aggressively gastronomic country in the world, the city has more 'generic French', regional, and ethnic restaurants than any other place in France. But *la cuisine parisienne* (Parisian cuisine) is a poor relation of that extended family known as *la cuisine des provinces* (provincial cuisine). That's because those greedy country cousins have consumed most of what was once on Paris' own plate, claiming it as their own. Today very few French dishes except maybe vol-au-vent (light pastry shell filled with chicken or fish in a creamy sauce), *potage St-Germain* (thick green pea soup), onion soup, the humble pig's trotters and *gâteau Paris-Brest*, a ring-shaped cake filled with praline and topped with flaked almonds and icing sugar, are associated with the capital.

That said, over the years certain foreign dishes have become as Parisian as pig's trotters. The *nems* and *pâtés impérials* (spring or egg rolls) and *pho* (soup noodles with beef) of Vietnam, the couscous and *tajines* of North Africa, the *boudin antillais* (West Indian blood pudding) from the Caribbean and the *yassa* (meat or fish grilled in onion and lemon sauce) of Senegal are all eaten with relish throughout the capital. Indian, Chinese and Japanese food are also very popular non-French cuisines in Paris. In fact, foreign food is what Paris does better than any other city in the country.

One of Paris' largest concentrations of foreign restaurants is squeezed into a labyrinth of narrow streets in the 5e *arrondissement* across the Seine from Notre Dame. The Greek, North African and Middle Eastern restaurants between rue St-Jacques, bd St-Germain and bd St-Michel, including rue de la Huchette, attract mainly foreigners, often under the mistaken impression that this little maze is the whole of the famous 'Latin Quarter'. But you'd be far better off looking elsewhere for ethnic food: bd de Belleville in the 20e for Middle Eastern; nearby rue de Belleville in the 19e for Asian (especially Thai and Vietnamese); rue du Faubourg St-Denis in the 10e for Indian, Pakistani and Bangladeshi; and Chinatown in the 13e for Chinese, especially av de Choisy, av d'Ivry and rue Baudricourt.

> **Av de Choisy, av d'Ivry and rue Baudricourt** Cheap Chinese and Southeast Asian (especially Vietnamese) eateries.

> **Bd de Belleville** Middle Eastern (Algerian, Tunisian) food, especially couscous.

> **Passage Brady** (Map p102) Magnet for Indian, Pakistani and Bangladeshi dishes.

> **Rue Cadet, rue Richer and rue Geoffroy Marie** (Map p82) Triangle of streets with Jewish (mostly Sephardic) and kosher food.

> **Rue Montorgueil** (Map p50) Pedestrian market street packed with tiptop quality, quick eats.

> **Rue Ste-Anne** (Map p50) The heart of Paris' Japantown.

> **Rue Rosiers** (Map p56) Hunting ground for Ashkenazic Jewish kosher food, especially felafel.

LOUVRE & LES HALLES

The area between Forum des Halles (1er) and the Centre Pompidou (4e) is filled with trendy restaurants, though few are particularly good – most cater to tourists. Streets lined with places to eat include rue des Lombards, the narrow streets north and east of Forum des Halles, and food streets rue Montorgueil and rue Ste-Anne (see p105).

Chez La Vieille
FRENCH €€€

(Map p50; ☏01 42 60 15 78; 1 rue Bailleul & 37 rue de l'Arbre Sec, 1er; lunch menu €26; ⊙lunch Mon-Fri, dinner to 9.45pm Mon, Tue, Thu & Fri; ⓂLouvre-Rivoli) 'At the Old Lady's', a favourite little restaurant south of Bourse, dining is on two floors but don't expect a slot on the more rustic ground floor; that's reserved for regulars. The small menu reflects the size of the place but is universally sublime.

L'Ardoise
BISTRO €€

(Map p50; ☏01 42 96 28 18; www.lardoise-paris.com; 28 rue du Mont Thabor, 1er; menu €34; ⊙Tue-Sat, dinner Tue-Sun; ⓂConcorde or Tuileries) This is a lovely little bistro with no menu as such (*ardoise* means 'blackboard', which is all there is), but who cares? The food prepared dextrously by chef Pierre Jay (ex-Tour d'Argent) is superb.

Le Grand Colbert
FRENCH €€€

(Map p50; ☎01 42 86 87 88; www.legrandcolbert.
fr; 2-4 rue Vivienne, 2e; lunch menus €22.50 &
€29.50; ⊗noon-1am; MPyramides) This former workers' *cafétéria* transformed into a
fin-de-siècle showcase is more relaxed than
many similarly restored restaurants and a
convenient spot for lunch if visiting the *passages couverts* or cruising the streets late at
night (last orders: 1am).

Café Marly
CAFÉ €€€

(Map p50; ☎01 46 26 06 60; cour Napoléon
du Louvre, 93 rue de Rivoli, 1er; mains €20-30;
⊗8am-2am; MPalais Royal–Musée du Louvre)
This classic venue facing the Louvre's inner courtyard serves contemporary French
fare throughout the day under the palace
colonnades. Views of the glass pyramid are
priceless and depending on how *au courant*
(familiar) you are with French starlets and
people who appear in *Match,* you should get
an eyeful.

Saveurs Végét'Halles
VEGAN €

(Map p50; ☎01 40 41 93 95; www.saveursveget
halles.fr; 41 rue des Bourdonnais, 1er; menus €10-
19; ⊗Mon-Sat; MChâtelet) This strictly vegan
eatery is egg-free and serves a fair few
mock-meat dishes such as *poulet végétal
aux champignons* ('chicken' with mushrooms) and *escalope de seitan* (wheat glu-
ten 'escalope'). No alcohol.

Le Petit Mâchon
LYONNAIS €€

(Map p50; ☎01 42 60 08 06; 158 rue St-Honoré,
1er; starters €7-12.50, mains €14-22; ⊗Tue-Sun;
MPalais Royal–Musée du Louvre) Close to the
Louvre, this upbeat bistro serves some of
the best Lyonnais specialities in town.

Joe Allen
AMERICAN €€

(Map p50; ☎01 42 36 70 13; 30 rue Pierre Lescot, 1er; lunch menu €14, dinner menu €18.10 &
€22.50; ⊗noon-1am; ⊛; MÉtienne Marcel) An
institution since 1972, Joe Allen is a little
bit of New York in Paris. The ribs are particularly recommended.

Franprix Les Halles
SUPERMARKET €€

(Map p50; 35 rue Berger, 1er; MChâtelet) One of
several supermarkets around Forum des
Halles.

MARAIS & BASTILLE

The Marais, filled with small restaurants of
every imaginable type, is one of Paris' premier neighbourhoods for eating out. Make
sure to book ahead for weekend dining.
Towards République is a decent selection
of ethnic cuisines: small Chinese noodle

shops and restaurants along rue Au Maire,
3e (MArts et Métiers); and Jewish restaurants (some Ashkenazic, some Sephardic,
not all kosher) cooking up specialities from
Central Europe, North Africa and Israel
along rue des Rosiers, 4e (MSt-Paul). Many
are closed on Friday evening, Saturday and
Jewish holidays. Takeaway falafel and *sha-
warma* (kebabs) are available at several
places along the street.

Bastille is equally chock-a-block with
restaurants, some of which have added a
star or two to their epaulets in recent years.
Then, of course, there is its fabulous open-
air market Marché Bastille (p107).

TOP CHOICE | Chez Janou
PROVENÇAL €€

(Map p56; ☎01 42 72 28 41; www.chez
janou.com; 2 rue Roger Verlomme, 3e; mains
€14.50-19, lunch menu €12.50; MChemin Vert)
This lovely little spot just east of place
des Vosges attracts celebs (last seen: John
Malkovich) and hangers on with its inspired Provençal cooking from the south
of France, 80 types of pastis and excellent
service. Try the superb ratatouille with anchovy and black olive dips and the spelt risotto with scallops.

TOP CHOICE | Le Hangar
BISTRO €€

(Map p56; ☎01 42 74 55 44; 12 impasse
Berthaud, 3e; mains €16-20; ⊗Tue-Sat; MLes
Halles) Unusual for big mouths like us, we almost balk at revealing details of this perfect
little restaurant. It serves all the bistro favourites – rillettes, foie gras, steak tartare –
in relaxing, very quiet surrounds. The terrace is a delight in fine weather and the service both professional and personal.

La Gazzetta
BRASSERIE €€€

(☎01 43 47 47 05; www.lagazzetta.fr; 29 rue de
Cotte, 12e; lunch menu €16, dinner menu €38 &
€50; ⊗lunch Tue-Sat, dinner Mon-Sat; MLedru
Rollin) This *néo-brasserie* has gained a substantial (and international) following under
the tutelage of Swedish chef Peter Nilsson
who is as comfortable producing dishes like
scallops with cress and milk-fed lamb confit
and ice Bleu d'Auvergne cheese as he is mini
anchovy pizzas. His lunchtime *menu* is excellent value; dinner *menus* involve five or
seven courses!

Derrière
FRENCH €€€

(Map p56; ☎01 44 61 91 95; 69 rue des Gravilliers,
3e; starters €12-15, mains €18-26; ⊗lunch Tue-Fri,
dinner to 11pm; MArts et Métiers) So secretive
it's almost a speakeasy, Behind is just that –
set in a lovely courtyard between (and be-

Based on the variety of fresh produce, ethnicity and neighbourhood, our favourite of Paris' 70-odd *marchés découverts* (open-air markets) that pop up in public squares two or three mornings a week are:

» **Marché Bastille** (Map p60; bd Richard Lenoir, 11e; ⊘7am-2.30pm Thu & Sun; Ⓜ Bastille or Richard Lenoir) Arguably the best open-air market in Paris with more different ethnic food stalls than ever before.

» **Marché Couvert Beauvau** (place d'Aligre, 12e; ⊘8am-1pm & 4-7.30pm Tue-Sat, 8am-1pm Sun; Ⓜ Ledru Rollin) Colourful Arab and North African enclave not far from Bastille.

» **Marché Belleville** (bd de Belleville btwn rue Jean-Pierre Timbaud & rue du Faubourg du Temple, 11e & 20e; ⊘7am-2.30pm Tue & Fri; Ⓜ Belleville or Couronne) Fascinating entry into the large, vibrant communities of the eastern neighbourhoods, home to artists, students and immigrants from Africa, Asia and the Middle East.

» **Marché Couvert St-Quentin** (Map p102; 85 bd de Magenta, 10e; ⊘8am-1pm & 3.30-7.30pm Tue-Sat, 8.30am-1pm Sun; Ⓜ Gare de l'Est) Iron-and-glass covered market built in 1866; lots of gourmet and upmarket food stalls.

» **Rue Cler** (Map p74; rue Cler, 7e; ⊘8am-7pm Tue-Sat, 8am-noon Sun; Ⓜ École Militaire) Fabulous street market that almost feels like a party on weekends when the whole neighbourhood seemingly shops en masse.

» **Rue Montorgueil** (Map p50; rue Montorgueil btwn rue de Turbigo & rue Réaumur, 2e; ⊘8am-7.30pm Tue-Sat, 8am-noon Sun; Ⓜ Les Halles or Sentier) This buzzy market is the closest market to Paris' 700-year-old wholesale market, Les Halles, which was moved from this area to the southern suburb of Rungis in 1969.

» **Rue Mouffetard** (Map p68; rue Mouffetard; ⊘8am-7.30pm Tue-Sat, 8am-noon Sun; Ⓜ Censier Daubenton) Paris' most photogenic market street: the place where Parisians send tourists (travellers go to Marché Bastille or rue Montorgueil).

hind) the North African 404 restaurant and Andy Walhoo bar and club. Chilled in a 'shoes-off' kind of way, this place is a lot more serious behind the scenes, serving both classic bistro and more inventive dishes. Vegetarians: more than half of the starts are meatless. Smokers: there's a *fumoir* behind the closet door upstairs.

Café Beaubourg FRENCH, INTERNATIONAL €€
(Map p56; ☑ 01 48 87 63 96; 100 rue St-Martin, 4e; mains €15-21; ⊘8am-1am Sun-Wed, to 2am Thu-Sat; Ⓜ Châtelet–Les Halles) This upbeat minimalist café across from the Centre Pompidou has been drawing a well-heeled crowd for breakfast and brunch (€13 to €24) on its terrace some two dozen years now. The leather chairs and books on shelves give the main room a clubby feel and there's always free entertainment on the *parvis* (large square) in front.

L'Écailler du Bistrot SEAFOOD €€€
(☑ 01 43 72 76 77; 22 rue Paul Bert, 11e; mains €22-36; ⊘Tue-Sat; Ⓜ Faidherbe Chaligny) Oyster lovers will luurvvv The Bistro Shucker, a

neighbourhood resto owned by the daughter of a famous Breton oyster culturist that serves up to a dozen varieties of fresh bivalves, freshly shucked and accompanied by a little lemon juice. Make sure you sample a half-dozen *oursins* (sea urchins) in March.

Ma Cantine SEAFOOD €€€
(Map p56; 5th fl, BHV, 14 rue du Temple, 4e; menus €11-15.60; ⊘11.15am-6pm Mon, Tue, Thu-Sat, to 8.30pm Wed; Ⓜ Hôtel de Ville) Peckish while shopping? This top-floor restaurant at the BHV department store offers three good-value *menus* and views to die for.

Chez Nénesse BISTRO €
(Map p56; ☑ 01 42 78 46 49; 17 rue Saintonge, 3e; starters €8-16, mains €18; ⊘Mon-Fri; Ⓜ Filles du Calvaire) The atmosphere here is charmingly 'old Parisian' and unpretentious. Dishes are prepared with fresh, high-quality ingredients and pose good value for money.

Le Trumilou BISTRO €€
(Map p56; ☑ 01 42 77 63 98; www.letrumilou.com; 84 quai de l'Hôtel de Ville, 4e; menus €16.50 & €19.50; Ⓜ Hôtel de Ville) This no-frills bistro

is a Parisian institution in situ for over a century. If you're looking for an authentic menu from the early 20th century and prices (well, almost) to match, you won't do better than this. *Confit aux pruneaux* (duck with prunes) and *ris de veau grand-mère* (veal sweetbreads) are specialities.

L'Alivi
CORSICAN €€€

(Map p56; ☎01 48 87 90 20; 27 rue du Roi de Sicile, 4e; starters €9-16, mains €15-23, lunch menus €17-29, dinner menus €25-29; ⓜSt-Paul or Bastille) The ingredients at this rather fashionable Corsican restaurant are always fresh and refined; brocciu cheese, *charcuterie* and basil are key ingredients in the kitchen.

Le Petit Marché
BISTRO €€

(Map p56; ☎01 42 72 06 67; 9 rue de Béarn, 3e; mains €16-24, lunch menu €12.50; ⓜChemin Vert) This great little bistro just up from place des Vosges fills up at lunch and dinner with a mixed crowd who come to enjoy its hearty cooking and friendly service.

Bofinger
HISTORIC BRASSERIE €€€

(Map p60; ☎01 42 72 87 82; www.bofingerparis.com; 5-7 rue de la Bastille, 4e; menus €20 & €30; ⓢlunch & dinner to midnight or 12.30am; ⓜBastille) Founded in 1864, Bofinger is reputedly Paris' oldest brasserie and its polished art nouveau medley of mirror, brass and glass is stunning.

Curieux Spaghetti
INTERNATIONAL €€

(Map p56; ☎01 42 72 75 97; www.curieuxspag.com; 14 rue St-Mérri, 4e; mains from €12; ⓢnoon-2am Sun-Wed, to 4am Thu-Sat; ⓦ; ⓜRambuteau) This upbeat restaurant-cum-hip hangout lures a young crowd with its mountain-sized pasta portions, test-tube shots of unusually flavoured vodka, great canned music and weekend brunch (€26).

TOP CHOICE Café Hugo
CAFÉ €€

(Map p56; ☎01 42 72 64 04; 22 place des Vosges, 4e; mains €10.70-13.30; ⓢ8am-2am; ⓜChemin Vert) Go for the *plat du jour* (dish of the day) with a glass of wine (€12.50) or brunch (€16.20) at our favourite affordable eatery on Paris' most beautiful square – and you'll love Paris forever.

Marche ou Crêpe
BRETON €

(Map p60; ☎01 43 57 04 78; www.marcheoucrepe.com; 88 rue Oberkampf, 11e; crepes & galettes €2.20-7.80; ⓢ6pm-midnight Tue-Thu, 6pm-2am Fri & Sat, 5pm-midnight Sun; ⓦ; ⓜParmentier) This little outlet near nightlife-busy rue Jean-Pierre Timbaud serves delicious

HIPPY GROOVE CUISINE

Tiny but almost perfect, Le Mouton Noir (Map p60; ☎01 48 07 05 45; www.lemoutonnoir.fr; 65 rue de Charonne, 11e; menu €29; ⓢdinner Tue-Sat, lunch Sat & Sun; ⓜCharonne) is no *mouton noir* (black sheep). Fabulously unique, this dining address with a mere two-dozen covers west of Bastille is a neighbourhood secret which we've just gone and blown. The idea is to use unusual products in traditional French cooking – *cuisine hippy groove* the chef calls it. Try crab bisque with red curry and lentils, sea bass with La Vache qui Rit cheese or eggplant with thyme. Brunch (€19) is a fine weekend tradition.

savoury galettes, sweet crêpes, homemade soups and salads – until late, very late.

L'As de Felafel
JEWISH, KOSHER €

(Map p56; 34 rue des Rosiers, 4e; dishes €5-7; ⓢnoon-midnight Sun-Thu, noon-5pm Fri; ⓜSt-Paul) This has always been our favourite place for deep-fried balls of chickpeas and herbs (€5). It's always packed, particularly at weekday lunch.

Grand Apétit
VEGETARIAN €

(Map p60; ☎01 40 27 04 95; 9 rue de la Cerisaie, 4e; soups €3-4, dishes €5-11; ⓢlunch Mon-Fri, dinner to 9pm Mon-Wed; ⓜBastille or Sully Morland) The menu here features filling dishes served with 100% organic cereals, vegetables and seaweed. Next door is an excellent organic-macrobiotic grocery store.

THE ISLANDS

Famed more for its ice cream than dining options, Île St-Louis is a pricey place to eat, although there are a couple of fine places worth a brunch or lunchtime munch. As for Île de la Cité, forget it – eating spots are almost nonexistent.

TOP CHOICE Berthillon
ICE-CREAM €

(Map p64; 31 rue St-Louis en l'Île, 4e; ice cream €2.10-5.40; ⓢ10am-8pm Wed-Sun; ⓜPont Marie) Berthillon is to ice cream what Château Lafite Rothschild is to wine. While the fruit flavours (eg cassis) produced by this celebrated *glacier* (ice-cream maker) are justifiably renowned, the chocolate, coffee, *marrons glacés* (candied chestnuts),

Agenaise (Armagnac and prunes), *noisette* (hazelnut) and *nougat au miel* (honey nougat) are even richer. Choose from among 70 flavours.

LATIN QUARTER & JARDIN DES PLANTES

From cheap-eat student haunts to chandelier-lit palaces loaded with history, the 5e has something to suit every budget and culinary taste. Rue Mouffetard is famed for its food market and food shops; while its side streets, especially pedestrianised rue du Pot au Fer, cook up some fine budget dining. Les Pâtes Vivantes (p113) is an excellent address for dining with kids.

TOP CHOICE **Bistroy Les Papilles** BISTRO €€
(Map p68; ☑01 43 25 20 79; www.lespap illesparis.com, in French; 30 rue Gay Lussac, 5e; 2-course menu Tue-Fri €22 & €24.50, 4-course menu €31; ⊗Tue-Sat; Ⓜ Luxembourg) This hybrid bistro, wine cellar and *épicerie* with sunflower-yellow facade is one of those fabulous dining experiences that packs out the place (reserve a few days in advance to guarantee a table). Dining is at simply dressed tables wedged beneath bottle-lined walls, and fare is market-driven: each weekday cooks up a different *marmite du marché* (€16). But what really sets it apart is its exceptional wine list. Taste over lunch then stock your own *cave* (wine cellar) at Les Papilles' *cave à vin*.

TOP CHOICE **L'Agrume** BISTRO €€
(Map p68; ☑01 43 31 86 48; 15 rue des Fossés St-Marcel, 5e; starters/mains €14/30,

menu lunch €14 & €16, dinner €35; ⊗Tue-Sat; Ⓜ Censier Daubenton) Lunching at this much vaunted, pocket-sized contemporary bistro on an unknown street on the Latin Quarter's southern fringe is magnificent value and a real gourmet experience. Watch chefs work with seasonal products in the open kitchen while you dine – at table, bar-stool seating or *comptoir* (counter). Evening dining is an exquisite, no-choice *dégustation* (tasting) melody of five courses, different every day. Snagging a table at L'Agrume – meaning 'Citrus Fruit' is tough; reserve several days ahead.

L'AOC TRADITIONAL FRENCH €€
(Map p68; ☑01 43 54 22 52; www.restoaoc.com; 14 rue des Fossés St-Bernard, 5e; 2-/3-course menu €21/29; ⊗Tue-Sat; Ⓜ Cardinal Lemoine) *'Bistrot carnivore'* is the strapline of this tasty little number concocted around France's most respected culinary products. The concept is AOC (Appellation d'Origine Contrôlée), meaning everything has been reared or made according to strict guidelines designed to protect a product unique to a particular village, town or area. The result? Only the best! Rare is the chance to taste *porc noir de Bigorre,* a type of black piggie bred in the Pyrénées.

Le Pré Verre BISTRO €€
(Map p68; ☑01 43 54 59 47; 25 rue Thénard, 5e; 2-/3-course menu €13.50/28; ⊗Tue-Sat; 🖰; Ⓜ Maubert Mutualité) Noisy, busy and buzzing, this jovial bistro plunges diners into the heart of a Parisian's Paris. At lunchtime join the flock and go for the fabulous-value

---

DON'T MISS

DINING WITH A VIEW

» **Café Beaubourg** (p107) The terrace at this café offers front-row seats to the Centre Pompidou and the entertainers performing in front of it.

» **Café Marly** (p106) Priceless views of the Louvre, its glass pyramids and the Tuileries.

» **Ma Cantine** (p107) A bird's-eye view of the Marais from the BHV department store's top-floor restaurant.

» **Café Hugo** (p108) Its terrace under the arcades of the place des Vosges looks onto what is arguably the most beautiful square in Paris.

» **Les Ombres** (p112) A rooftop restaurant whose name evokes the patterns cast by the Eiffel Tower's webbed ironwork.

» **Lafayette Café** (p126) Once you've finished shopping, head up to the top floor of the Galeries Lafayette for a well-deserved break.

» **58 Tour Eiffel** (p112) This Eiffel Tower restaurant serves lunch, dinner and a classic Parisian panorama.

formule dejeuner (€13). The wine list features France's small independent *vignerons* (wine producers).

La Mosquée de Paris NORTH AFRICAN €€
(Map p68; ☎01 43 31 38 20; 39 rue Geoffroy St-Hilaire, 5e; mains €15-20; ⊕ⓂCensier Daubenton or Place Monge) Dig into a couscous, *tajine* or meaty grill within the walls of the city's central mosque. Or spoil yourself with a peppermint tea and oriental pastry in its tearoom (☺9am-11.30pm) or lunch, body scrub and massage in its *hammam* (Turkish bath).

ST-GERMAIN, ODÉON & LUXEMBOURG

There's far more to this fabled pocket of Paris than the literary cafés (p118) of Sartre or the picnicking turf of the Jardin de Luxembourg. Rue St-André des Arts (ⓂSt-Michel or Odéon) is lined with places to dine as lightly or lavishly as your heart desires, as is the stretch between Église St-Sulpice and Église St-Germain des Prés (especially rue des Canettes, rue Princesse and rue Guisarde).

Build the king of picnics at the Harrods food hall of Paris (p127) or the food shops on pedestrian rue Cler. For afternoon tea, legendary Ladurée (p113) is sweet.

TOP CHOICE **Le Comptoir du Relais** BISTRO €€€
(Map p72; ☎01 44 27 07 97; 9 Carrefour de l'Odéon, 6e; dinner menu €50; ⓂOdéon) Simply known as Le Comptoir (The Counter), this gourmet bistro has provoked a real stir ever since it opened. The culinary handiwork of top chef Yves Camdeborde, it serves seasonal bistro dishes with a creative twist –

asparagus and foie gras salad anyone? Bagging a table without an advance reservation at lunchtime is just about doable providing you arrive sharp at 12.30pm, but forget more gastronomic evening dining without a reservation (weeks in advance for weekends).

TOP CHOICE **Quatrehommes** CHEESE SHOP €
(62 rue de Sèvres, 6e; ⓂVanneau) Buy the best of every French cheese, many with an original take (eg Epoisses boxed in chestnut leaves, Mont d'Or flavoured with black truffles, spiced honey and Roquefort bread etc) at this king of *fromageries*. The smell alone upon entering is heavenly. Find the cheese shop a two-second walk south of the metro station.

KGB FUSION €€
(Map p72; ☎01 46 33 00 85; http://zekitchen-galerie.fr, in French; 25 rue des Grands Augustins, 6e; lunch menus €27 & €34; ☺Tue-Sat; ⓂSt-Michel) KGB (as in 'Kitchen Galerie Bis') is the latest creation of William Ledeuil of Ze Kitchen Galerie (4 rue des Grands Augustins, 6e; lunch/dinner menu €26.50/65; ☺lunch & dinner Mon-Fri, dinner Sat; ⓂSt-Michel) fame. Overtly art gallery in feel, this small dining space plays to a hip crowd with its casual platters of Asian-influenced *zors d'œvres*, creative pastas and marmite-cooked meats. Roast pigeon with ginger and cranberry condiment anyone?

Au Pied de Fouet BISTRO €
(Map p72; ☎01 43 54 87 83; 50 rue St-Benoît, 6e; starters €3-5, mains €10; ☺Mon-Sat; ⓂSt-Germain des Prés) This busy address with Bordeaux facade, tightly packed tables and

TOP 5 SUPPER CLUBS

» **Jim Haynes** (☎01 43 27 17 67; www.jim-haynes.com; Atelier A2, 83 rue de la Tombe Issoire, 14e; ⓂAlésia) Dinner every Sunday (since 1978) with charismatic Louisianan Jim and 60-odd other guests; suggested donation €25.

» **Hidden Kitchen** (Map p50; www.hkmenus.com; 28 rue de Richelieu, 1er; ⓂPalais Royal–Musée du Louvre) One for gourmets, Laura and Braden cook up a 10-course seasonal meal to 16 guests four weekend evenings a month September to December and February to June.

» **Paris Supper Club** (www.thepariskitchen.com/paris-supper-club) Just fabulous! Dine with newfound friends at the latest 'in' restaurant or bistro; book well ahead.

» **Talk Time** (☎01 43 25 86 55, 06 20 87 76 69; www.meetup.com/TalkTime) Michael Muszlak's Saturday night food-and-bilingual-chat in the Latin Quarter, organised through the New York–based group Meetup.

» **Paris Soirees** (☎06 43 79 35 15; www.parissoirees.com) Twice-weekly Paris events hosted on Île de la Cité by Patricia Laplante-Collins.

devout crowd of regulars is an authentic bistro choice. Its classic dishes are astonishingly good value. Finish with a quintessential *tarte tatin* (upside-down apple pie), wine-soaked prunes or a simple bowl of *fromage blanc* (a cross between yoghurt, sour cream and cream cheese).

Bouillon Racine   TRADITIONAL FRENCH €€
(Map p72; ☑01 44 32 15 60; 3 rue Racine, 6e; lunch/dinner menu €14.90/29.50; MCluny–La Sorbonne) This 'soup kitchen' built in 1906 to feed city workers is an art nouveau palace. Age-old recipes such as roast snails, *caille confite* (preserved quail) and lamb shank with liquorice inspire the menu. End your foray into gastronomic history with an old-fashioned sherbet.

Cosi   SANDWICH BAR €
(Map p72; 54 rue de Seine, 6e; sandwich menus €10-15; ⊙noon-11pm; 🚻; MOdéon) With sandwich names like Stonker, Tom Dooley and Naked Willi, Cosi (which, incidentally, is of New Zealand origin) could easily run for Paris' most imaginative sandwich maker. Classical music and homemade Italian bread, still warm from the oven, adds to Cosi's natural sex appeal.

Marché St-Germain   MARKET €
(Map p72; 4-8 rue Lobineau, 6e; ⊙8.30am-1pm & 4-7.30pm Tue-Sat, 8.30am-1pm Sun; MMabillon) Covered food market with fresh veg, fruit and other seasonal goodies.

MONTPARNASSE

Since the 1920s, the area around bd du Montparnasse has been one of Paris' premier avenues for enjoying café life, though younger Parisians deem the quarter somewhat *démodé* and touristy these days. Glam it's not. But it does boast a handful of legendary brasseries and cafés warranting a culinary visit.

TOP CHOICE **Jadis**   BISTRO €€€
(☑01 45 57 73 20; www.bistrot-jadis. com, in French; 202 rue de la Croix Nivert, 15e; lunch menus €25 & €32, dinner menus €45 & €65; ⊙Mon-Fri; MBoucicaut) This upmarket *néo-bistro* with sober Bordeaux facade and white lace curtains on the corner of a very unassuming street in the 15e is one of Paris' most raved about (reserve in advance to avoid disappointment). Traditional French dishes pack a modern punch thanks to rising-star chef Guillaume Delage who dares to do things like braise pork cheeks in beer and use black rice instead of white. The

lunch *menu* is extraordinary good value and the chocolate soufflé – order it at the start of your meal – is nothing other than to-die-for heavenly. From the metro station, walk south along rue de la Convention and take the first right onto rue de la Croix Nivert.

TOP CHOICE **La Cabane à Huîtres**   OYSTERS €
(☑01 45 49 47 27; 4 rue Antoine Bourdelle, 14e; menu €18; ⊙Wed-Sat; MMontparnasse Bienvenüe) One of Paris' best oyster addresses; this earthy wooden-styled *cabane* (cabin) with just nine sought-after tables is the pride and joy of fifth-generation oyster farmer Françis Dubourg who splits his week between the capital and his oyster farm in Arcachon on the Atlantic Coast. Geared totally towards dedicated gourmets, the fixed menu features a dozen oysters, foie gras de Landes (from Gascony in southwest France) or *magret de canard fumé* (smoked duck breast) followed by Pyreneen *brebis* cheese or sweet *canelé* (a rum, vanilla and cinnamon-spiced cake). From Gare de Montparnasse, walk north along av du Maine and take the first left onto rue Antoine Bourdelle.

Le Dôme   HISTORIC BRASSERIE €€€
(☑01 43 35 25 81; 108 bd du Montparnasse, 14e; starters/mains €20/40; MVavin) A 1930s art deco extravaganza, Le Dôme is a monumental place for a meal service of the formal white-tablecloth and bow-tied waiter variety. Stick with the basics at this historical venue, opting perhaps for an impressive shellfish platter piled high with fresh oysters, king prawns, crab claws and so on, followed by creamy homemade *millefeuille* (pastry layered with cream). Wheeled in on a trolley and cut in front of you, the traditional French dessert is a deliciously decadent extravaganza not to be missed.

EIFFEL TOWER AREA & 16E

The museum- and monument-rich 16e *arrondissement* has some fine dines too. Around Mademoiselle Eiffel grab picnic supplies on foodie street rue Cler or pick from several restaurants on rue de Montessuy.

TOP CHOICE **Café Constant**   MODERN FRENCH €€
(Map p74; ☑01 47 53 73 34; www.cafe constant.com, in French; 139 rue Ste-Dominique, 7e; starters/mains/desserts €11/16/7; ⊙lunch & dinner to 10.30pm Tue-Sun; MÉcole Militaire or Port de l'Alma) Take a former Michelin-starred chef, a dead-simple corner café and

PATRICIA WELLS: COOKERY WRITER & TEACHER

The only American to have captured the soul of French cuisine, Patricia Wells (www.patriciawells.com) has lived, cooked and shopped in Paris since 1980. 'Only the best' is her label on the fresh fish, meat, cheese, breads and other market produce she works with. So just where does she shop for...

Weekly groceries

All over: The Sunday organic market (bd Raspail, 7e; M Rennes); Poilâne (www.poilane.fr; 8 rue du Cherche Midi, 6e; M Sèvres Babylone) for bread; Quatrehommes (p110) for cheese; Poissonnerie du Bac (69 rue du Bac, 7e; M Rue du Bac) for fish.

Gourmet meals

I shop regularly at Le Bon Marché (p127) because it is right down the street from me. But for special meals I always order things in advance and go from shop to shop. That is the fun of Paris and of France.

Creative culinary souvenir

Parisian perfume maker Fragonard (Map p56; www.fragonard.com; 51 rue des Francs Bourgeois, 4e; M St-Paul; 196 bd St-Germain, 6e; M St-Germain des Prés) has a changing litany of *great* things for the home, such as fabulous vases with an Eiffel Tower theme, lovely embroidered napkins with a fish or vegetable theme, great little spoons with a cake or pastry theme. Nothing is very expensive and the offerings change every few months, so you have to pounce when you find something you love. The gift wrapping in gorgeous Fragonard bags is worth it alone!

what do you get? Another Christian Constant hit with original mosaic floor, worn wooden tables and a massive queue out the door every meal time. The café doesn't take reservations but you can enjoy a drink at the bar while you wait. Cuisine is creative bistro, mixing grandma favourites like *purée de mon enfance* (mashed potato from my childhood) with Sunday treats such as foie gras-stuffed quail and herb-roasted chicken.

L'Astrance GASTRONOMIC €€€
(Map p74; ☑01 40 50 84 40; 4 rue Beethoven, 16e; menus €70-190; ⊙Tue-Fri; M Passy) It's been over a decade now since Pascal Barbot's dazzling cuisine at the three-star L'Astrance made its debut, but it has shown no signs of losing its cutting edge. Look beyond the complicated descriptions on the menu – what you should expect are teasers of taste that you never even knew existed, and a presentation that is an art unto itself. A culinary experience unique to Paris, reserve one/two months ahead for lunch/dinner.

Les Cocottes MODERN FRENCH €€
(Map p74; www.leviolondingres.com; 135 rue Ste-Dominique, 7e; starters/mains/desserts €11/16/7; ⊙Mon-Sat; M École Militaire or Port de l'Alma)

Cocottes are casseroles and that is precisely what Christian Constant's chic space is about. Day in day out, its contemporary interior is jam-packed with a buoyant crowd feasting on inventive seasonal creations cooked to perfection in little black enamel, oven-to-table *cocottes* (casserole dishes). Seating is on bar stools around high tables and the place doesn't take reservations. Get here at noon sharp or 7.15pm (or before) to get a table. If the queue's out the door, nip two doors down for a drink at Café Constant (p111).

Les Ombres MODERN FRENCH €€€
(☑01 47 53 68 00; www.lesombres-restaurant.com; 27 quai Branly, 7e; menus €26-95; ⊙Sun-Thu; M Pont de l'Alma or Alma Marceau) This sexy, glass-enclosed rooftop restaurant atop the Musée de Quai Branly (Map p74) is named The Shadows after the patterns cast by the Eiffel Tower's webbed ironwork. Dramatic views are complemented by Sébastien Tasset's elegant creations. We love his roasted turbot and cantal cheese with a buckwheat crêpe, or chicken stuffed with lemon confit.

58 Tour Eiffel MODERN FRENCH €€
(Map p74; ☑01 45 55 20 04; www.restaurants-toureiffel.com; 1st level, Champ de Mars, 7e;

lunch menu €17.50 & €22.50, dinner menu €65; ⊙11.30am-5.30pm & 6.30-11pm; Ⓜ Champ de Mars–Tour Eiffel or Bir Hakeim) If you're intrigued by the idea of a meal in the Tower, this is a pretty good choice. It may not be the caviar and black truffles of Jules Verne (on the 2nd level), but Alain Ducasse did sign off on the menu, making it far more than just another tourist cafeteria. For lunch, go first to the restaurant's outside kiosk (near the north pillar); for dinner, reserve online or by telephone.

ÉTOILE & CHAMPS-ÉLYSÉES

The 8e *arrondissement* around the Champs-Élysées is known for its big-name chefs (Alain Ducasse, Pierre Gagnaire, Guy Savoy) and culinary icons (Taillevent), but there are all sorts of under-the-radar restaurants scattered in the back streets where Parisians who live and work in the area dine. City square place de la Madeleine (Map p78) is the luxury food centre of one of the world's food capitals.

Bistrot du Sommelier   FRENCH, BISTRO €€€
(Map p78; ☑01 42 65 24 85; www.bistrotdusommelier.com; 97 bd Haussmann, 8e; lunch menu €33, incl wine €43, dinner menus €65-110; ⊙Mon-Fri; Ⓜ St-Augustin) If you're as serious about wine as you are about food, dine here. Indeed the whole point of this attractive eatery is to match wine with food, aided by one of the world's foremost sommeliers Philippe Faure-Brac. Sample his wine-food pairings on Friday when a three-course tasting

lunch with wine is €50 and a five-course dinner with wine is €75. The food, prepared by chef Jean-André Lallican, is hearty bistro fare and, surprisingly, not all the wines are French.

Le Boudoir   MODERN FRENCH €€€
(Map p78; ☑01 43 59 25 29; www.brasserieleboudoir.com; 25 rue du Colisée, 8e; lunch/dinner menu €19/50; ⊙lunch Mon-Fri, dinner Tue-Sat; Ⓜ St-Philippe du Roule or Franklin D Roosevelt) Spread across two floors, the quirky salons here – Marie Antoinette, Palme d'Or and the Red Room – are individual works of art with a style befitting the name. The menu runs from upscale bistro to more adventurous creations such as grilled tandoori scallops and saffron rice with mango. In a move towards yesteryear decadence, a private smoking room is hidden on the premises. The *prix fixe* lunch is an excellent deal.

Le Hide   FRENCH, BISTRO €€
(Map p78; ☑01 45 74 15 81; www.lehide.fr; 10 rue du Général Lanrezac, 17e; menus €22 & €29; ⊙lunch Mon-Fri, dinner Mon-Sat; Ⓜ Charles de Gaulle–Étoile) A reader favourite, Le Hide is a tiny neighbourhood bistro (seating 33 people) serving scrumptious traditional French fare: snails, baked shoulder of lamb, monkfish in lemon butter. The chef is Japanese – an indication of top quality in Paris – and the place fills up faster than you can scurry down the steps at the nearby Arc de Triomphe. Reserve well in advance.

TOP 5 PÂTISSERIES

» **Ladurée** (Map p78; www.laduree.fr, in French; 75 av des Champs-Élysées, 8e; Ⓜ George V) Specialities at this most famous and decadent of Parisian *pâtisseries* include its own invention, *macarons* (especially the chocolate and pistachio variety) and *le baiser Ladurée* (layered almond cake with strawberries and cream).

» **Le Nôtre** (Map p60; www.lenotre.fr, in French; 10 rue St-Antoine, 4e; Ⓜ Bastille) Famous *traiteur* (caterer) chain known for some of Paris' most delectable pastries and chocolate; 10 more outlets across the capital.

» **La Pâtisserie des Rêves** (www.lapatisseriedesreves.com; 93 rue du Bac, 7e; Ⓜ Rue du Bac) Extraordinary cakes and seasonal fruit tarts, far too beautiful to eat, showcased beneath glass domes at the oh-so-chic 'art' gallery of big-name *pâtissier* Philippe Conticini. Find it a two-minute walk south of the rue du Bac metro station.

» **Boulangerie Bruno Solques** (Map p68; 143 rue St-Jacques, 5e; Ⓜ Luxembourg) Arguably Paris' most inventive pâtissier, Bruno Solques excels at oddly shaped flat tarts with mashed fruit and fruit-filled brioches.

» **Dalloyau** (Map p60; www.dalloyau.fr; 5 bd Beaumarchais, 4e; Ⓜ Bastille) Specialities include *pain aux raisins* (raisin bread), *millefeuille* (pastry layered with cream), *tarte au citron* (lemon tart) and *opéra* (coffee-flavoured almond cake and chocolate).

Fromagerie Alléosse   CHEESE SHOP €
(Map p78; 13 rue Poncelet, 17e; MTernes) To our minds and taste buds, this is the best cheese shop in Paris and well worth a trip across town. Cheeses are sold as they should be: grouped and displayed in five main categories.

OPÉRA & GRANDS BOULEVARDS

L'Opéra marks the start of the Grands Boulevards and the 9e *arrondissement* where shoppers break for coffee between shops at Galeries Lafayette (p126). Just north of here the area becomes more residential, and the diversity increases: kosher delis, handmade Chinese noodles, organic cafés and Michelin-starred chefs are among the culinary riches.

TOP CHOICE **Les Pâtes Vivantes**   CHINESE €
(Map p82; 46 du Faubourg Montmartre, 9e; noodles €9.50-12; ⊙Mon-Sat; ✦; MLe Peletier) This is one of the few spots in Paris for hand-pulled noodles (*là miàn*) made to order in the age-old northern Chinese tradition. Latin Quarter **branch** (Map p68; ✆01 40 46 84 33; 22 bd St-Germain, 5e; MCardinal Lemoine)

Chartier   BISTRO €
(Map p82; ✆01 47 70 86 29; www.restaurant -chartier.com; 7 rue du Faubourg Montmartre, 9e; menu with wine €19.40; MGrands Boulevards) Chartier started life as a *bouillon* (soup kitchen) in 1896 and is a real gem because of its justifiably famous, 330-seat belle époque dining room. It's no longer the deal as it once was, but for a taste of old-fashioned Paris, it's unbeatable. Reservations are not accepted and some readers have been turned away at the last minute on busy nights – if there's a long queue, head elsewhere.

Le J'Go   SOUTHWEST FRENCH €€
(Map p82; ✆01 40 22 09 09; www.lejgo.com; 4 rue Drouot, 9e; menus €15-20; ⊙lunch Mon-Fri, dinner Mon-Sat; ✦; MRichelieu Drouot) This contemporary, Toulouse-style bistro magics diners away to southwestern France. Flavourful regional cooking revolves around a *rôtissoire* (meat on a spit), not to mention other Gascogne standards like cassoulet and foie gras. Roasting takes a minimum of 20 minutes.

Le Roi du Pot au Feu   BISTRO €€
(Map p82; 34 rue Vignon, 9e; menus €24-29; ⊙noon-10.30pm Mon-Sat; MHavre Caumartin) The typical Parisian bistro atmosphere adds to the charm of the 'King of Hotpots', but what you really come here for is its *pot au feu*, a stockpot of beef, root vegetables and herbs stewed together, with the stock served as starter and the meat and veg as main course. No bookings.

GARE DU NORD, GARE DE L'EST & RÉPUBLIQUE

These areas offer all types of food but most notably Indian and Pakistani, concentrated in Passage Brady (p105). Traditional brasseries and bistros cluster around Gare du Nord and great things await along Canal St-Martin's creative cobbled banks.

Self-caterers can shop at the extravagant covered market Marché Couvert St-Quentin (p107), or on **Rue du Faubourg St-Denis** (Map p102; 10e; MStrasbourg St-Denis or Château d'Eau), one of Paris' cheapest streets to buy food.

Chez Michel   FRENCH, BRETON €€
(Map p102; ✆01 44 53 06 20; 10 rue de Belzunce, 10e; menu €32; ⊙lunch Tue-Fri, dinner Mon-Fri; MGare du Nord) If all you know about Breton cuisine is crêpes and cider, come here. The formula is simple: order the three-course menu and replace an item should you fancy it with one of 25 specialities chalked on the blackboard (€5 to €30 extra). If you can't book a table, don't despair; Michel also prepares four-course picnic hampers (€43 including wine for two people) if you order ahead.

L'Office   MODERN FRENCH €€
(Map p102; ✆01 47 70 67 31; 3 rue Richer, 9e; lunch menus €17 & €21, dinner €30-35; ⊙lunch Thu & Fri, dinner Tue-Sat; MPoissonière or Bonne Nouvelle) Don't be misled by The Office's name. All part of its underground charm, this is more a place for creative types than white-collar workers. Its market-inspired menu is short – just two choices at lunchtime but often outstanding (seafood ragout with red rice and blood oranges, gnocchi with braised lamb and smoked ricotta).

Hôtel du Nord   MODERN FRENCH €€
(✆01 40 40 78 78; www.hoteldunord.org; 102 quai de Jemmapes, 10e; lunch menu €13.50, mains €15-23; ⊙9am-2.30am; ☎; MJacques Bonsergent) The setting for the eponymous 1938 film starring Louis Jouvet and Arletty, the interior of this vintage café feels as if it was stuck in a time warp with its zinc counter, red velvet curtains and old piano. Food is definitely modernist though. From the met-

CANAL ST-MARTIN: A PARISIAN-PERFECT PICNIC

Pink Flamingo (☑01 42 02 31 70; www.pinkflamingopizza.com; 67 rue Bichat, 10e; pizzas €10.50-16; ⊙lunch & dinner till 11pm Tue-Sat, 1-11pm Sun; ☑; Ⓜ Jacques Bonsergent) is not just another pizza place. *Mais non, chérie!* Once the weather warms up, the Flamingo unveils its secret weapon – pink helium balloons that the delivery guy uses to locate you and your perfect canal-side picnic spot (no GPS required). Nip into the canal-side pizzeria to order Paris' most inventive pizza (duck, apple and chèvre perhaps or what about gorgonzola, figs and cured ham?), grab a balloon, and stroll off along the canal to your perfect picnic spot.

To make your picnic Parisian perfect, buy a bottle of wine from nearby Le Verre Volé (☑01 48 03 17 34; 67 rue de Lancry, 10e; mains €12; ⊙lunch & dinner to 11pm; Ⓜ Jacques Bonsergent), a wine shop with a few tables, excellent wines (€5 to €60 per bottle, €4.50 per glass) and expert advice.

ro station walk five minutes east along rue de Lancry until you hit the water and quai de Jemmapes (the other side of the bridge).

La Marine FRENCH, BISTRO €€
(☑01 42 39 69 81; 55bis quai de Valmy, 10e; mains €14.50-21, lunch menus €14-16; ⊙8am-midnight Mon-Fri, from 9am Sat & Sun; ☎; Ⓜ République) This large, airy canal-side bistro is a favourite, especially in the warmer months, among *les branchés du quartier* (neighbourhood trendies).

MÉNILMONTANT & BELLEVILLE

In the northern section of the 11e and into the 19e and 20e *arrondissements,* rue Oberkampf and its extension, rue de Ménilmontant are popular with diners and denizens of the night, though rue Jean-Pierre Timbaud, running parallel to the north, has been giving them a bit of competition. Rue de Belleville and the streets off it are dotted with Chinese, Southeast Asian and Middle Eastern addresses; bd de Belleville has couscous restaurants.

Le Clown Bar FRENCH, THEMED €€
(Map p60; ☑01 43 55 87 35; 114 rue Amelot, 11e; menu €25; ⊙lunch & dinner to 1am Mon-Sat; Ⓜ Filles du Calvaire) A wonderful wine bar-cum-bistro next to the Cirque d'Hiver, the Clown Bar is like a museum, with its painted ceilings, mosaics on the wall, lovely zinc bar and circus memorabilia that touches on one of our favourite themes: the evil clown. The food is simple and unpretentious traditional French.

Le Tire Bouchon FRENCH, BISTRO €€
(Map p60; ☑01 47 00 43 50; 5 rue Guillaume Bertrand, 11e; lunch menu €12, dinner menu €15 & €26.50; ⊙Mon-Sat; Ⓜ St-Maur) 'The Cork-

screw' is a mock old-style bistro close to the flashy rue Oberkampf with a dozen gingham-clad tables arranged around a polished wooden bar. The *cassoulet confit* (casserole or stew with beans and meat) and *millefeuille de dorade* (sea bream in flaky pastry) will tickle your taste buds. Book in advance.

Au Trou Normand TRADITIONAL FRENCH €€
(Map p60; ☑01 48 05 80 23; 9 rue Jean-Pierre Timbaud, 11e; mains €12.50-18, lunch menus €13.50 & €15.50; Ⓜ Oberkampf) The Norman Hole remains the bargain-basement *cafétéria* of the trendy 11e *arrondissement.* In keeping with its surrounds, dishes served are simple and of hearty proportion.

Le Baratin BISTRO €€€
(☑01 43 49 39 70; 3 rue Jouye-Rouve, 20e; mains €18-24, lunch menu €16; ⊙lunch Tue-Fri, dinner to midnight Tue-Sat; Ⓜ Pyrénées or Belleville) *Baratin* (chatter) rhymes with *bar à vin* (wine bar) in French and this animated place, just a step away from the lively Belleville quarter, does both awfully well.

13E ARRONDISSEMENT & CHINATOWN

Foodies hot-foot it to Paris' Chinatown in search of authentic Asian food: av de Choisy, av d'Ivry and rue Baudricourt are the streets. Another wonderful district is the Butte aux Cailles, chock-a-block with interesting addresses.

Le Temps des Cérises TRADITIONAL FRENCH €
(☑01 45 89 69 48; 18-20 rue de la Butte aux Cailles, 13e; starters/mains €7/13; ⊙lunch Mon-Fri, dinner Mon-Sat; Ⓜ Corvisart or Place d'Italie) 'The Time of Cherries' (ie 'days of wine and roses' to English speakers), an easygoing restaurant

ONE-MAN SHOW

Chef Michelangelo (Map p84; ☑01 42 23 10 77; 3 rue André-Barsacq, 18e; menu around €25; ⊙dinner Tue-Sat; ⊛⋈Anvers or Abbesses) takes the meaning of one-man show to new extremes. The shopping, the chopping, the table-waiting, the cooking, the sitting down with guests for a glass of wine while the pasta is boiling... Michelangelo does it all. Dining here in fact is tantamount to being invited to a Sicilian chef's house for dinner. There are things to know, of course: 1) there are only 14 chairs (everyone eats at a long table in front of the open kitchen) so reservations are mandatory; 2) Michelangelo chooses the menu (three courses, about €25, cash only), so be prepared to eat anything; and 3) all the products – the olive oil, the wine (from €28 per bottle), the cheese – come from Sicily, so if there's no more oregano the restaurant may suddenly close for a week while he goes to stock up.

run by a workers' cooperative for three decades, offers faithfully solid fare in a quintessentially Parisian atmosphere. From place d'Italie head south along rue Bobillot then right onto rue de la Butte aux Cailles.

Chez Gladines
FRENCH BASQUE €

(☑01 45 80 70 10; 30 rue des Cinq Diamants, 13e; starters/mains from €5/6; ⊙lunch & dinner to midnight Sun-Tue, to 1am Wed-Sat; ⊛; ⋈Corvisart) This lively bistro in the heart of Buttes aux Cailles serves enormous 'meal-in-a-bowl' salads and traditional Basque specialities.

Les Cailloux
ITALIAN, CONTEMPORARY €€

(☑01 45 80 15 08; www.lescailloux.fr; 58 rue des Cinq Diamants, 13e; pasta/mains €15/20; ⋈Corvisart or Place d'Italie) It is pricey, chic and its pavement terrace smart in the heart of Butte aux Cailles is without question the spot to sit and be seen.

MONTMARTRE & PIGALLE

The 18e *arrondissement*, home to Montmartre and northern Pigalle, thrives on crowds and little else. When you've got Sacré Cœur, place du Tertre and Paris literally at your feet, who needs decent restaurants? But that's not to say that everything is a write-off in this well-trodden tourist area. You just have to pick and choose a bit more carefully than elsewhere in Paris. Many Montmartre restaurants only open for dinner.

La Mascotte
SEAFOOD €€

(Map p84; ☑01 46 06 28 15; www.la-mascotte-montmartre.com; 52 rue des Abbesses, 18e; lunch/dinner menu €20/38; ⊙lunch & dinner to midnight; ⋈Abbesses) The Mascot is a small, unassuming spot much frequented by regulars who can't get enough of its seafood and regional cuisine. In winter, sample shellfish. In summer sit on the terrace and savour delicious *fricassée de pétoncles* (queen scallops fricassee). Meat lovers, Troyes *andouillette* (veal tripe sausage) is for you.

Chez Toinette
TRADITIONAL FRENCH €€

(Map p84; ☑01 42 54 44 36; 20 rue Germain Pilon, 18e; mains €17-22; ⊙dinner Mon-Sat; ⋈Abbesses) In the heart of one of the capital's most touristy neighbourhoods, Chez Toinette has kept alive the tradition of old Montmartre with its simplicity and culinary expertise. *Perdreau* (partridge), *biche* (doe), *chevreuil* (roebuck) and the famous *filet de canard à la sauge et au miel* (fillet of duck with sage and honey) are house specialities.

Café Burq
BISTRO €€

(Map p84; ☑01 42 52 81 27; 6 rue Burq, 18e; menus €26 & €30; ⊙7pm-2am Tue-Sat; ⋈Abbesses) This convivial, retro bistro is always buzzing; book ahead – especially at weekends. Don't come for the décor or the space, though; both are nonexistent.

Le Café qui Parle
MODERN FRENCH €€

(Map p84; ☑01 46 06 06 88; 24 rue Caulaincourt, 18e; menus €12.50 & €17; ⊙lunch & dinner Mon-Sat, lunch Sun; ☎; ⋈Lamarck Caulaincourt or Blanche) We love The Talking Café's wall art and ancient safes below (the building was once a bank), but not as much as we love its weekend brunch (€17).

L'Épicerie
GOURMET FOOD €

(www.fuxia.fr, in French; 51 rue des Martyrs, 9e; dishes €10-18; ⊙10am-10pm; ⋈Pigalle) Serves all sorts of delicacies for the perfect picnic.

Le Grenier à Pain
BAKERY €

(Map p84; 38 rue des Abbesses, 18e; ⊙7.30am-8pm Thu-Mon; ⋈Abbesses) Delicious *fougasses* and *baguettes à la tradition* that won 'Best Baguette in Paris' contest in 2010.

🍷 Drinking

In a country where eating and drinking are as inseparable as cheese and wine, it's inevitable that the line between bars, cafés and bistros is blurred at best.

Drinking in Paris essentially means paying the rent for the space you take up, meaning it costs more sitting at tables than standing at the counter, more on a fancy square than a backstreet, more in the 8e than in the 18e. Come 10pm many cafés apply a pricier *tarif de nuit* (night rate).

Expect to pay at least €3 or €4 for a glass of wine or *demi* (half-pint) of beer, €10 to €15 for a cocktail and substantially more in chic bars and clubs.

LOUVRE & LES HALLES

Le Fumoir
COCKTAIL BAR

(Map p50; 6 rue de l'Amiral Coligny, 1er; ⊗11am-2am; ⓂLouvre-Rivoli) This colonial-style bar-restaurant opposite the Louvre's eastern flank is a fine place to sip top-notch gin from quality glassware while nibbling on olives at the vintage mahogany bar. Happy Hour (6pm to 8pm) sees cocktails, usually €8.50 to €11, drop to €7.

Le Cochon à l'Oreille
BAR, CAFÉ

(Map p50; 15 rue Montmartre, 1er; ⊗10am-11pm Tue-Sat; ⓂLes Halles or Étienne Marcel) A Parisian *bijou*, this heritage-listed hole-in-the-wall retains its belle époque tiles with market scenes of Les Halles and just eight tiny tables.

MARAIS & BASTILLE

Le Pure Café
CAFÉ

(14 rue Jean Macé, 11e; ⊗7am-2am; ⓂCharonne) This old café moonlights as a restaurant, but we like it as it was intended to be, espe-

cially over a *grand crème* (large white coffee) and the papers on Sunday morning. It has appeared as Central Casting's 'typical French café' in a number of films, including the 2004 British film *Before Sunset*. From the metro walk west along rue de Charonne, left onto rue Faidherbe then immediately left again onto rue Jean Macé.

Le Bistrot du Peintre
WINE BAR

(Map p60; 116 av Ledru-Rollin, 11e; ⊗8am-2am; 🔊; ⓂBastille) This lovely belle-époque address with its 1902 art nouveau bar, elegant terrace and spot-on service, is on our aperitif A-list – and that of local artists, *bobos* (bourgeois bohemians) and local celebs too.

Au Petit Fer à Cheval
BAR

(Map p56; 30 rue Vieille du Temple, 4e; ⊗8am-2am; ⓂHôtel de Ville or St-Paul) The original horseshoe-shaped zinc counter (1903) leaves little room for much else here, but nobody seems to mind at this genial place. It overflows with friendly regulars enjoying a drink or a sandwich (simple meals are served from noon to 1am).

La Chaise Au Plafond
BAR

(Map p56; 10 rue du Trésor, 4e; ⊗10am-2am; ⊗Hôtel de Ville or St-Paul) The Chair on the Ceiling is a peaceful, warm place with terrace – a real oasis from the frenzy of the Marais and worth knowing about in summer.

LATIN QUARTER & JARDIN DES PLANTES

Curio Parlor Cocktail Club
COCKTAIL BAR

(Map p68; 16 rue des Bernardins, 5e; ⊗7pm-2am Tue-Thu, 7pm-4am Fri & Sat; ⓂMaubert Mutualité) This hybrid bar-club looks to the inter-war *années folles* (crazy years) of 1920s Paris,

BAR-HOPPING STREETS

Prime Parisian drinking spots, perfect for evening meandering to soak up the scene:

» Rue Vieille du Temple and surrounding streets, 4e (Map p56) – Marais cocktail of gay bars and chic cafés.

» Rue Oberkampf and rue Jean-Pierre Timbaud, 11e (Map p60) – Hip bars, bohemian hang-outs and atmospheric cafés.

» Rue de la Roquette, rue Keller and rue de Lappe, 11e (Map p60) – Whatever you fancy; Bastille has the lot.

» Rue Montmartre, 2e (Map p50) – Modern, slick bars and pubs.

» Canal St-Martin, 10e (Map p44) – Heady summer nights in casual canal-side cafés.

» Rue Princesse and rue des Canettes, 6e (Map p72) – Pedestrian duo of student, sports 'n' tapas bars and pubs on the Left Bank.

London and New York for inspiration. Go to its Facebook page to find out what party's when.

Le Pub St-Hilaire   PUB
(Map p68; www.pubsthilaire.com; 2 rue Valette, 5e; ⊙11am-2am Mon-Thu, to 4am Fri, 4pm-4am Sat, 3pm-midnight Sun; MMaubert Mutualité) Generous happy hours, pool tables, board games, music and various gimmicks to rev up the party crowd (a metre of cocktails, 'be your own barman', etc) pack out this student favourite.

ST-GERMAIN, ODÉON & LUXEMBOURG

TOP CHOICE **Au Sauvignon**   WINE BAR
(Map p72; 80 rue des Saintes Pères, 7e; ⊙8am-midnight; MSèvres-Babylone) Grab a table in the evening sun or at a tightly packed table inside, overlooking the original zinc bar and painted ceiling celebrating French viticultural tradition. To savour the full flavour of this 1950s wine bar, order a plate of *casse-croûtes au pain Poilâne* – sandwiches made with the city's most famous bread.

Prescription Cocktail Club   COCKTAIL BAR
(Map p72; 23 rue Mazarine, 6e; ⊙7pm-2am Mon-Thu, 7pm-4am Fri & Sat; MOdéon) With bowler and flat-top hats as lampshades and a 1930s speakeasy New York air to the place, this cocktail club is Parisian-cool. Getting past the doorman can be tough, but once in it's friendliness and old-fashioned cocktails all round. Watch its Facebook page for events.

Le 10   CELLAR PUB
(Map p72; 10 rue de l'Odéon, 6e; ⊙5.30pm-2am; MOdéon) Plot the next revolution or conquer a lonely heart at this local institution that groans with students, smoky ambience and cheap sangria.

Café La Palette   HISTORIC CAFÉ
(Map p72; 43 rue de Seine, 6e; ⊙8am-2am Mon-Sat; MMabillon) In the heart of gallery land, this café where Cézanne and Braque drank, attracts fashionable people and art dealers. Its summer terrace is as beautiful.

Les Deux Magots   HISTORIC CAFÉ
(Map p72; www.lesdeuxmagots.fr; 170 bd St-Germain, 6e; ⊙7am-1am; MSt-Germain des Prés) St-Germain's most famous where Sartre, Hemingway and Picasso hung out.

ÉTOILE & CHAMPS-ÉLYSÉES

Buddha Bar   COCKTAIL BAR
(Map p78; 8-12 rue Boissy d'Anglas, 8e; ⊙noon-2am Sun-Thu, 4pm-3am Fri & Sat; MConcorde)

The décor is simply spectacular, with a two-storey golden Buddha and millions of candles, at this A-list cocktail bar, known for its Zen lounge music.

OPÉRA & GRANDS BOULEVARDS

Harry's New York Bar   COCKTAIL BAR
(Off Map p82; 5 rue Daunou, 2e; ⊙10.30am-4am; MOpéra) One of the most popular American-style bars in the pre-war years, Harry's once welcomed such habitués as writers F Scott Fitzgerald and Ernest Hemingway, who no doubt sampled the bar's unique cocktail and creation: the Bloody Mary (€12.50). The Cuban mahogany interior dates from the mid-19th century and was brought over from a Manhattan bar in 1911. There's a basement piano bar where Gershwin supposedly composed *An American in Paris* and, for the peckish, old-school hot dogs (€6) and generous club sandwiches. The advertisement for Harry's that occasionally appears in the papers still reads 'Tell the Taxi Driver Sank Roo Doe Noo' and is copyrighted.

TOP CHOICE **Au Limonaire**   WINE BAR
(Map p82; ☎01 45 23 33 33; http://limonaire.free.fr; 18 cité Bergère, 9e; ⊙7pm-midnight Mon, 6pm-midnight Tue-Sun; MGrands Boulevards) This little wine bar is one of the best places to listen to traditional French *chansons* and local singer-songwriters. Reservations are recommended.

GARE DU NORD, GARE DE L'EST & RÉPUBLIQUE

De La Ville Café   BAR, CAFÉ
(Map p102; 34 bd de Bonne Nouvelle, 10e; ⊙11am-2.30am; ☎; MBonne Nouvelle) This erstwhile brothel fuses history (original mosaic tiles, distressed walls) with industrial chic. Its terrace is among the best along the *grands boulevards* and DJs play Thursday to Saturday, making it a hot 'before' venue for the nearby Rex Club (p122).

MÉNILMONTANT & BELLEVILLE

Café Chéri(e)   BAR, CAFÉ
(44 bd de la Villette, 19e; ⊙noon-1am; ☎; MBelleville) An imaginative, colourful bar with its signature red lighting, infamous *mojitos* and *caiparinhas* and commitment to quality tunes, this is everyone's *chéri(e)* (darling) in this part of town. Lively, gritty, art-chic crowd and electro DJs Thursday to Saturday.

La Sardine   BAR, CAFÉ
(www.barlasardine.com; 32 place Ste-Marthe, 10e; ⊙9am-2am Apr-Sep, 9am-2am Tue-Sun Oct-Mar;

Sorting the good wines from the inferior ones when it comes to serious wine-tasting in Paris is no mean feat. Dozens of courses exist, but few come recommended.

One capital man who really knows his stuff is sommelier Juan Sánchez, who holds talks and *dégustations* (tastings) most Saturday evenings with independent French winegrowers (his suppliers) at his wine shop La Derniere Goutte (Map p72; www. ladernieregoutte.net; 6 rue du Bourbon le Château, 6e; MMabillon) in St-Germain des Prés. Legrand Filles & Fils (Map p50; www.caves-legrand.com; 1 rue de la Banque, 2e; MPyramides) is another well-informed wine shop with tasting room and all the accoutrements. Le Pré Verre (p109) and Au Sauvignon (p118) are atmospheric places on the Left Bank to taste interesting wines by small producers over a *casse-croûte* (quick light snack).

Oenophiles aspiring to headier heights should aim for a Saturday tasting with French winemakers held in Paris' oldest wine shop, Les Caves Augé (Map p78; 116 bd Haussmann, 8e; MSt-Augustin), in business since 1850. On the same street, one of the world's foremost sommeliers, Philippe Faure-Brac, pairs food and wine to perfection for a price at Bistrot du Sommelier (p113). Cellar tastings with winegrowers preempt Friday's brilliantly matched three-/five-course lunch/dinner (€50/75).

To learn how to sort the wheat from the chaff, embark on a one-day tasting course at the highly esteemed Centre de Dégustation Jacques Vivet (www.ecolededegustation.fr, in French; 48 rue de Vaugirard, 6e; MLuxembourg).

Then there's Ô Chateau (Map p50; www.o-chateau.com; 52 rue de l'Arbre Sec, 1er; MLouvre Rivoli), a young fun-charged company run by bilingual sommelier Olivier Magny that offers the full range of tastings and experiences in a 17th-century vaulted stone cellar near the Louvre: wine-tasting over dinner (€130) or a cheese lunch (€75), with chocolate (€65), *grands crus* master classes (€95) and so on. It also organises day trips to Champagne to taste you know what (€150), Champagne-fuelled river cruises (€45) and, by night, Champagne bus parties (€60) with music which include, hmm, learning how to open a bottle of champers with a sword in front of the Eiffel Tower.

For an updated and comprehensive monthly calendar of wine tastings in the city there's no better source than Paris by Mouth (www.parisbymouth.com).

🔊M Belleville) Out in the western flanks of Belleville, it's easy to miss rue Ste-Marthe and its colourful restaurants and bars exerting a dilapidated, funky charm. At the top, literally and figuratively, is this splendid and convivial café-wine bar, a bit of Marseille in Paris – brilliant for warm afternoons, tapas and organic wine.

MONTMARTRE & PIGALLE

La Fourmi   BAR
(Map p84; 74 rue des Martyrs, 18e; ⊙8am-2am Mon-Thu, to 4am Fri & Sat, 10am-2am Sun; MPigalle) A Pigalle stayer, 'The Ant' hits the mark with its lively yet unpretentious atmosphere. Décor is hip but not overwhelming, the zinc bar is long and inviting, the people laid-back, and the music mostly rock.

⭐ Entertainment

A night out in Paris can mean anything from swilling Champagne on the Champs-Élysées to opening unmarked doorways in search of a new club in the *banlieues* (suburbs) or dancing on tables till dawn in a mad-loud DJ bar. From jazz cellar to comic theatre, garage beat to go-go dancer, world-class art gallery to avant-garde artist squat, this is *the* capital of *savoir-vivre,* with spectacular entertainment to suit every budget, every taste.

Buy tickets for concerts, theatre performances and other cultural events at *billetteries* (box offices) in Fnac (☎08 92 68 36 22; www.fnacspectacles.com, in French) or Virgin Megastores (☎0825 129 139; www.virgin-mega.fr, in French). Both accept reservations by phone and the internet, and take most credit cards. Tickets generally cannot be returned or exchanged unless a performance is cancelled. Or try Paris' oldest ticket agency, Agence Marivaux (Map p82; ☎01 42 97 46 70; 7 rue de Marivaux, 2e; ⊙11am-7.30pm Mon-Fri, noon-4pm Sat; MRichelieu Drouot), just opposite the Opéra Comique.

Cabaret

Parisians don't tend to watch the city's risqué cabaret revues – tourists do. Times and prices for the dazzling, pseudo-bohemian productions starring women in two beads and a feather vary: first shows often begin between 8.15pm and 9.30pm, second shows between 10.45pm and 11.30pm. They all have lunch specials and additional evening shows on the weekend. Tickets cost anything from €55 to €100 per person (€140 to €280 with swish dinner and Champagne). All venues sell tickets online.

Moulin Rouge CABARET
(Map p84; ☎01 53 09 82 82; www.moulinrouge.fr; 82 bd de Clichy, 18e; ⓜBlanche) Ooh la la... Paris' most celebrated cabaret was founded in 1889 and its dancers appeared in the flamboyant posters by Toulouse-Lautrec. It sits under its trademark red windmill (a 1925 replica of the 19th-century original) and attracts viewers/voyeurs by the coachload.

Le Lido de Paris CABARET
(Map p78; ☎01 40 76 56 10; www.lido.fr; 116bis av des Champs-Élysées, 8e; ⓜGeorge V) Founded at the close of WWII, this gets top marks for its ambitious sets and lavish costumes, including the famed Bluebell Girls and Lido Boy Dancers.

Live Music

Music thrives in cosmopolitan Paris, a first-class stage for classical music and big-name rock, pop and independent acts, not to mention world-renowned jazz. A musical culture deeply influenced by rich immigration, vibrant subcultures and an open-minded public make it a fervent breeding ground for experimental music: Paris-bred world music, especially from Africa and South America, is renowned. As with the hybrid drinking-clubbing scene, bars are as much a space to revel in these sounds as specific music venues.

Palais Omnisports de Paris-Bercy (www.bercy.fr, in French); **Le Zénith** (www.le-zenith.com, in French) and **Stade de France** (www.stadefrance.com) are Paris' big-name venues. But it is the smaller concert halls loaded with history and charm that most fans favour.

Salle Pleyel CLASSICAL
(Map p78; ☎01 42 56 13 13; www.salle pleyel.fr; 252 rue du Faubourg St-Honoré, 8e; concert tickets €10-85; ⓦbox office noon-7pm Mon-Sat, to 8pm on day of performance; ⓜTernes) Dating from the 1920s, this highly regarded hall hosts many of Paris' finest classical music recitals and concerts, including those by the Orchestre de Paris (www.orchestre deparis.com, in French).

Point Éphemère ROCK, INDIE
(☎01 40 34 02 48; www.pointephemere.org; 200 quai de Valmy, 10e; admission free-€21; ⓦbar noon-2am Mon-Sat, 1pm-9pm Sun; ⓜLouis Blanc) This self-proclaimed 'centre for dynamic artists' has a great location by the Canal St-Martin, with indie concerts and the odd electro dance night. There's also a bar, restaurant and exhibit area on the scene.

FREE Le Vieux Belleville FRENCH CHANSONS
(☎01 44 62 92 66; www.le-vieux-belleville.com; 12 rue des Envierges, 20e; admission free; ⓦperformances 8pm Thu-Sat; ⓜPyrénées) This old-fashioned bistro at the top of Parc de Belleville is an atmospheric venue for performances of *chansons* featuring accordions and an organ grinder three times a week. It's a lively favourite with locals, though, so booking ahead is advised.

Cabaret Sauvage WORLD, LATINO
(☎01 42 09 03 09; www.cabaretsauvage.com; Parc de la Villette, 221 av Jean Jaurès, 19e; tickets €8-34; ⓦ7pm-2am Tue-Sun; ⓜPorte de la Villette) This super cool space (it looks like a gigantic yurt) hosts African, reggae and *rai* concerts as well as DJ nights that last till dawn; occasional hip-hop and indie acts pass through.

FREE L'Attirail WORLD, LATINO
(Map p56; ☎01 42 72 44 42; www.lattirail.com; 9 rue au Maire, 3e; ⓦ10.30am-1.30am Mon-Sat, 3pm-1.30am Sun; ⓜArts et Métiers) There are free concerts of *chansons françaises* and world music (Hungarian and Balkan

❶ HALF-PRICE TICKETS

Come the day of a performance, snag a half-price ticket (plus €3 commission) for ballet, theatre, opera etc at discount-ticket outlet **Kiosque Théâtre Madeleine** (Map p78; www.kiosquetheatre.com; opp 15 place de la Madeleine, 8e; ⓦ12.30-8pm Tue-Sat, to 4pm Sun; ⓜMadeleine).

Online, French-language websites www.billetreduc.com, www.ticketac.com and www.webguichet.com all sell discounted tickets.

DON'T MISS

FREE SHOWS

Paris' eclectic gaggle of clowns, mime artists, living statues, acrobats, roller-bladers, buskers and other street entertainers can be bags of fun and costs substantially less than a theatre ticket (a few coins in the hat is a sweet gesture). Some excellent musicians perform in the long echo-filled corridors of the metro, a highly prized privilege that artists do audition for. Outside, you can be sure of a good show at the following spots:

» **Place Georges Pompidou, 4e** The huge square in front of the Centre Pompidou.

» **Pont St-Louis, 4e** The bridge linking Paris' two islands (best enjoyed with Berthillon ice-cream).

» **Pont au Double, 4e** The pedestrian bridge linking Notre Dame with the Left Bank (ditto; p108).

» **Place Jean du Bellay, 1er** Musicians and fire-eaters near the Fontaine des Innocents.

» **Parc de la Villette, 19e** African drummers on the weekend.

» **Place du Tertre, Montmartre, 18e** Montmartre's original main square wins hands down as Paris' busiest busker stage.

Gypsy music, Irish folk, klezmer, southern Italian folk) almost daily at 9.30pm at this cosmopolitan enclave. Manic but friendly customers crowd the Formica bar with its cheap *pots* (460mL bottle) of wine.

Le Baiser Salé   JAZZ
(Map p50; ☎01 42 33 37 71; www.lebaisersale. com, in French; 58 rue des Lombards, 1er; admission free-€20; ⊗5pm-6am; ⓜChâtelet) One of several jazz clubs located on this street, this relaxed venue hosts concerts of jazz, Afro and Latin jazz and jazz fusion, and is known for discovering new talents. Sets start at 7.30pm and 10pm. Monday's jam session is free.

La Cigale   ROCK, JAZZ
(Map p84; ☎01 49 25 81 75; www.lacigale.fr; 120 bd de Rochechouart, 18e; admission €25-60; ⓜAnvers or Pigalle) Now classed as a historical monument, this music hall dates from 1887 but was redecorated 100 years later by Philippe Starck.

Clubbing

Paris is *not* London, Berlin or New York when it comes to clubbing, and hardcore clubbers from other European capitals might be surprised by the pick of Paris clubs. Lacking a mainstream scene, clubbing here tends to be underground and mobile, making blogs, forums and websites the savviest means of keeping apace with what's happening. The scene's hippest *soirées clubbing* (clubbing events) float

between a clutch of venues, including the city's many dance-driven bars (see p117).

But the beat is strong. Electronic music is of high quality, with excellent local house and techno. Funk and groove have given the whimsical predominance of dark minimal sounds a good pounding, and the Latin scene is huge; salsa dancing and Latino music nights pack out plenty of clubs.

Club admission costs anything from nothing to €20; admission is usually cheaper before 1am and men can't always get in if they're not with a woman.

TOP CHOICE **La Scène Bastille**   CLUB
(Map p60; www.scenebastille.com; admission €12-15; 2bis rue des Taillandiers, 11e; ⊗concerts from 7.30pm, club nights midnight-6am Mon-Sat; ⓜBastille or Ledru-Rollin) The unpretentious Bastille Scène puts on a mixed bag of concerts but focuses on electro, funk and hip hop Thursday to Saturday – the kind of place where local DJs go to relax and listen to music.

TOP CHOICE **Le Batofar**   BOAT CLUB
(www.batofar.org, in French; opp 11 quai François Mauriac, 13e; admission free-€15; ⊗9pm-midnight Mon & Tue, to 4am or later Wed-Sun; ⓜQuai de la Gare or Bibliothèque) This incongruous, much-loved, red-metal tugboat has a rooftop bar that's great in summer, while the club underneath provides memorable underwater acoustics between its metal walls and portholes.

Le Divan du Monde
CULTURAL CENTRE

(Map p84; www.divandumonde.com; 75 rue des Martyrs, 18e; admission €10-15; ☺11pm-5am Fri & Sat, sometimes open for events Mon-Fri; ⓜPigalle) Take some cinematographic events, Gypsy gatherings, *nouvelles chansons françaises* (new French songs). Add in soul/funk fiestas, air-guitar face-offs and rock parties of the Arctic Monkeys/Killers/Libertines persuasion and stir with an Amy Winehouse swizzle stick. You may now be getting some idea of the inventive, open-minded approach at this excellent cross-cultural venue in Pigalle.

Le Balajo
HISTORIC BALLROOM

(Map p60; www.balajo.fr; 9 rue de Lappe, 11e; admission from €12; ☺10pm-2am Tue & Thu, 11pm-5am Fri & Sat, 3-7.30pm Sun; ⓜBastille) A mainstay of Parisian nightlife since 1936, this ancient ballroom is devoted to salsa classes and Latino music weekdays. Weekends, DJs spin a very mixed bag of rock, disco, funk, R 'n' B and house. Its old-fashioned *musette* (accordion music) gigs on Sunday – waltz, tango and cha-cha for aficionados of retro tea-dancing – are jolly good fun.

Le Nouveau Casino
CLUB

(Map p60; www.nouveaucasino.net, in French; 109 rue Oberkampf, 11e; admission €5-10; ☺7.30pm or midnight to 2am or 5am Tue-Sun; ⓜParmentier) This club has a name for itself amid the Oberkampf bars for its live music concerts and lively weekend club nights. The programme is eclectic, underground and always up to the minute.

Le Rex Club
CLUB

(www.rexclub.com; 5 bd Poissonnière, 2e; admission free-€12; ☺11.30pm-6am Wed-Sat; ⓜBonne Nouvelle) The Rex reigns majestic in the House and techno scene, always has and probably always will.

Gay & Lesbian Venues

The Marais (4e), especially those areas around the intersection of rue Ste-Croix de la Bretonnerie and rue des Archives, and eastwards to rue Vieille du Temple, has been Paris' main centre of gay nightlife for over two decades. There are also a few bars and clubs within walking distance of bd de Sébastopol. Other venues are scattered throughout the city.

The lesbian scene is less public than its gay counterpart, and centres around a few cafés and bars in the Marais, especially along rue des Écouffes.

For more info contact **Centre Gai et Lesbien de Paris** (☏01 43 57 21 47; http://cglparis. org, in French; 61-63 rue Beaubourg, 3e; ☺6-8pm Mon, 3-8pm Tue & Thu, 2-8pm Wed, 12.30-8pm Fri & Sat, 4-7pm Sun; ⓜRambuteau or Arts et Métiers), just north of the Centre Pompidou.

3w Kafé
BAR, PUB

(Map p56; ☏01 48 87 39 26; 8 rue des Écouffes, 4e; ☺5.30pm-2am; ⓜSt-Paul) The name of this flagship cocktail venue on a street with several lesbian bars means 'Women with Women' so it can't be any clearer. It's relaxed and there's no ban on (girl-accompanied) men. Weekend dancing downstairs with a DJ and theme evenings.

Les Marronniers
BAR, CAFÉ

(Map p56; 18 rue des Archives, 4e; ☺9am-2am daily; ⓜHôtel de Ville) Strictly speaking not gay, but in this part of town how do you tell? What this place has got cubed is location, and its enormous pavement terrace is *the* place in the Marais for hunters and the hunted.

Le Tango
CLUB

(Map p56; ☏01 42 72 17 78; www.boite-a-frissons. fr; 13 rue au Maire, 3e; admission €8; ☺10.30pm-6am Fri & Sat, 5-11pm Sun; ⓜArts et Métiers) Billing itself as a *boîte à frissons* (club of thills), Le Tango ushers in a cosmopolitan gay and lesbian crowd. Housed in a historic 1930s dancehall, its atmosphere and style is retro and festive. Dancing gets going when it opens at 10.30pm with waltzing, salsa and tango. From 12.30am DJs play. Sunday's gay tea dance is legendary.

Cinema

Both *Pariscope* and *L'Officiel des Spectacles* list the full crop of Paris' cinematic pickings and screening times; online see http://cinema.leparisien.fr. Expect to pay around €10 for a first-run film. English-language films with French subtitles are labelled 'VO' (*version originale*).

Cinémathèque Française
CINEMA

(☏01 71 19 33 33; www.cinemathequefrancaise.com, in French; 51 rue de Bercy, 12e; adult/child €6.50/3.50; ☺box office noon-7pm Mon, Wed, Fri & Sat, noon-10pm Thu, 10am-8pm Sun; ⓜBercy) A two-minute walk south from the metro along rue de Bercy, this national institution is a temple to the 'seventh art' and always leaves its foreign offerings – often rarely screened classics – in their original language.

Theatre

Most theatre productions, including those originally written in other languages, are performed in French in Paris naturally enough. Very occasionally the odd itinerant English-speaking troupe plays at smaller venues around town.

Comédie Française
THEATRE

(Map p50; ☎08 25 10 16 80; www.comedie -francaise.fr; place Colette, 1er; tickets €8-47; box office ⊙11am-6pm; Ⓜ Palais Royal–Musée du Louvre) Founded in 1680 under Louis XIV, 'The French Comedy' theatre bases its repertoire around works of the classic French playwrights such as Molière, Racine and Corneille, though in recent years contemporary and even non-French works have been staged. There are three venues within the Comédie Française: Salle Richelieu, the main venue just west of the Palais Royal on place Colette; Studio Théâtre (Galerie du Carrousel du Louvre, 99 rue de Rivoli, 1er; Ⓜ Palais Royal–Musée du Louvre) and the Théâtre du Vieux Colombier (21 rue du Vieux Colombier, 6e; Ⓜ St-Sulpice)

Opera

The Opéra National de Paris (ONP) splits its performance schedule between the Palais Garnier, its original home completed in 1875, and the modern Opéra Bastille, which opened in 1989. Both opera houses also stage ballets and classical-music concerts performed by the ONP's affiliated orchestra and ballet companies. The season runs September to July.

Opéra Bastille
OPERA HOUSE

(Map p60; ☎08 92 89 90 90; www.opera-de-par is.fr, in French; 2-6 place de la Bastille, 12e; opera €5-172, ballet €5-87, concerts €5-49; Ⓜ Bastille) Despite some initial resistance to this 3400-seat venue, the main opera house in the capital, it's now performing superbly. While less alluring than Palais Garnier, seats in the main hall have an unrestricted view of the stage. Ticket sales begin at a precise date prior to each performance, with different opening dates for bookings by telephone, online or from the box office (130 rue de Lyon, 11e; ⊙10.30am-6.30pm Mon-Sat). Note: on the first day they are released, box office tickets can be bought only from the opera house at which the performance is to be held. At Bastille, standing-only tickets for €5 are available 1½ hours before performances begin.

WHAT'S ON

123

Savvy up on what's on when with Pariscope (€0.40), the capital's primary weekly listings guide published every Wednesday, or **L'Officiel des Spectacles** (€0.35; www.offi.fr, in French), the city's other weekly entertainment bible, out on Wednesday too and possibly easier to handle. Buy both (in French only) at newsstands.

Of the surfeit of French-language freebies (great for a gander between metro stops), **A Nous Paris** (www.anous.fr/paris, in French) is among the most informed; its contents are online. Pocket-sized booklet **LYLO**, free at bars and cafés, is a fortnightly lowdown on live music, concerts and clubs, and runs an information line (☎08 92 68 59 56; www.lylo.fr, in French). Flyers, schedules and programmes for cultural events float around box office areas in Fnac (see p119).

Palais Garnier
OPERA HOUSE

(Map p82; ☎08 92 89 90 90; www.opera-de-paris. fr; place de l'Opéra, 9e; Ⓜ Opéra) The city's original opera house is more intimate and glam than its Bastille counterpart, but some seats have limited (or no!) view. Ticket prices and conditions (including last-minute discounts) at the box office (⊙11am-6.30pm Mon-Sat, at the corner of rues Scribe and Auber) are identical to those at Opéra Bastille.

🛍 Shopping

Paris is a wonderful place to shop, whether you're in the market for a diamond-encrusted original Cartier bracelet or you're an impoverished *lèche-vitrine* (literally, 'window-licker') who just enjoys what you see from the outside looking in. From the ultrachic couture houses of av Montaigne and the cubby-hole boutiques of the Marais to the vast underground shopping centre at Les Halles and the flea-market bargains at St-Ouen, Paris is a city that knows how to make it, how to display it and how to charge for it.

Fashion is a big reason to shop in Paris. The Right Bank, especially the so-called Triangle d'Or (Ⓜ Franklin D Roosevelt or Alma Marceau, 1er & 8e) formed by av Montaigne and av Georges V; rue du Faubourg St-Honoré (Ⓜ Madeleine or Concorde, 8e) and

Shopping

Paris has it all: large boulevards with international chains, luxury avenues with designer fashion, famous *grands magasins* (department stores) and fabulous markets (p126). But the real charm resides in a peripatetic stroll along side streets where tiny speciality shops and cutting-edge boutiques, selling everything from strawberry-scented Wellington boots to candles scented like heaven, mingle with cafés, galleries and churches.

If you're after what the French do best – fashion – tread the haute-couture, luxury jewellery and designer perfume boardwalks in the Étoile and Champs-Élysées. For original fashion, street and vintage, head for the Marais and St-Germain des Prés.

But it's not just fashion. Paris is an exquisite treasure chest of fine food, wine, tea, books, beautiful stationery, fine art, antiques and original collectables. You won't be stuck for gifts and souvenirs to take home.

For practical tips on how to shop, see p127.

SHOP LIKE A PARISIAN FOR...

» **A rainbow of macaroons** from Left Bank *chocolatier* Pierre Hermé (p127)

» **Designer fashion** from an edgy boutique or concept store in the Marais or an haute-couture label in the Triangle d'Or (p123)

» **Perfume** from Fragonard (p112) or Guerlain (p126)

» **Postcards of Old Paris** from the *bouquinistes* (antiquarian-book sellers) who've set up stalls on the quays near Notre Dame since the 16th century

» **Parisian curios** from Marché aux Puces de la Porte de Vanves (p126), the most intimate of Paris' made-for-Sunday-mooching flea markets

Clockwise from top left
1. Fashion boutique in the Marais **2.** Inside *grand magasin* Galeries Lafayette **3.** A bright display of macaroons

DON'T MISS

FLEA MARKETS

» **Marché aux Puces de Montreuil** (av du Professeur André Lemière, 20e; ◷8am-7.30pm Sat-Mon; ⓜPorte de Montreuil) 19th century, 500-stall *marché aux puces* (flea market) particularly known for its second-hand clothing, designer seconds, engravings, jewellery, linen, crockery, old furniture and appliances.

» **Marché aux Puces de St-Ouen** (rue des Rosiers, av Michelet, rue Voltaire, rue Paul Bert & rue Jean-Henri Fabre, 18e; ◷9am-6pm Sat, 10am-6pm Sun, 11am-5pm Mon; ⓜPorte de Clignancourt) Founded in the late 19th century and said to be Europe's largest.

» **Marché aux Puces de la Porte de Vanves** (av Georges Lafenestre & av Marc Sangnier, 14e; ◷7am-6pm or later Sat & Sun; ⓜPorte de Vanves) The smallest and, some say, friendliest of the big three. Av Georges Lafenestre has lots of 'curios' that aren't quite old (or curious) enough to qualify as antiques.

its eastern extension, **rue St-Honoré** (ⓜTuileries); **place des Victoires** (ⓜBourse or Sentier, 1er & 2e) and the Marais' **rue des Rosiers** (ⓜSt-Paul, 4e), is traditionally the epicentre of Parisian fashion, though **St-Germain** (ⓜSt-Sulpice or St-Germain des Prés) on the Left Bank can also claim a share of boutiques.

Galeries Lafayette   DEPARTMENT STORE
(Map p82; 40 bd Haussmann, 9e; ◷9.30am-7.30pm Mon-Wed, Fri & Sat, 9.30am-9pm Thu; ⓜAuber or Chaussée d'Antin) Paris' famous *grand magasin* is a vast sight in itself, straddling two adjacent buildings and packed with fashion, accessories and the world's largest lingerie department. A fashion show (☎01 42 82 30 25 to book a seat) takes place at 3pm on Friday.

Colette   CONCEPT STORE
(Map p50; www.colette.fr; 213 rue St-Honoré, 1er; ⓜTuileries) This Japanese-inspired concept store has clothes and accessories as well as books, art, music and beauty products. Limited-edition sneakers, candles that smell like sex (so say staff, anyway), cutting-edge clocks – it's worth a look even if you're not buying. Colette's famous sales see huge reductions on the designer stock, including Comme des Garçons, Marc Jacobs and far more. The Water Bar café-restaurant in the basement features still and sparkling waters from around the world.

Ivoire   ART & ANTIQUES
(Map p72; 57 rue Bonaparte, 6e; ◷9am-noon & 2-6pm Tue-Fri; ⓜSt-Germain des Prés) This family-run business dating to 1913 is a two-man team comprising father Pierre Heckmann (in his mid-80s) and son Jean-Pierre (apprenticed at age 14 and not far off retirement himself). Sculpting and restoring ivory, bone and nacre is their trade and their art is extraordinary. The workshop interior, last refitted in 1937, is original.

Lavinia   WINE
(Map p50; www.lavinia.com, in French; 3 bd de la Madeleine, 1er; ⓜMadeleine) Among the largest (and certainly most exclusive) drinks shops is this bastion of booze near Madeleine. To be sure, come here for the fruit of the vine but we usually visit to top our collection of exclusive *eaux-de-vie* (fruit brandies).

E Dehillerin   KITCHEN WARES
(Map p50; www.dehillerin.com; 18-20 rue Coquillière, 1er; ⓜLes Halles) Founded in 1820, this two-level shop carries an incredible selection of professional-quality *matériel de cuisine* (kitchenware). You're sure to find something you desperately need, such as a *coupe volaille* (poultry scissors) or even a *turbotiére* (turbot poacher).

Shakespeare & Company   BOOKS
(Map p68; 37 rue de la Bûcherie, 5e; ◷10am-11pm Mon-Fri, 11am-11pm Sat & Sun; ⓜSt-Michel) Paris' most famous English-language bookshop sells new and used books and is a charm to browse (grab a read and sink into one of the two cinema chairs near the stairs out back); the staff's picks are worth noting and there's a dusty old library on the 1st floor. This isn't the original Shakespeare & Company owned by Sylvia Beach, who published James Joyce's *Ulysses;* that was closed down by the Nazis.

Guerlain   PERFUME
(Map p78; www.guerlain.com; 68 av des Champs-Élysées, 8e; ◷10.30am-8pm Mon-Sat, noon-7pm Sun; ⓜFranklin D Roosevelt) Guerlain is Paris' most famous *parfumerie,* and its shop

(around since 1912) is one of the city's most beautiful. With its shimmering mirror and marble art deco interior, it's a reminder of the former glory of the Champs-Élysées. For total indulgence, make an appointment at its decadent spa (☎01 45 62 11 21).

Merci CONCEPT STORE
(Map p60; www.merci-merci.com, in French; 111 bd Beaumarchais, 3e; MSt-Sébastien Froissart) The landmark pink Fiat Cinquecento in the courtyard marks the entrance to this unique multistorey concept store whose rallying cry is one-stop shopping. All the proceeds go to a children's charity in Madagascar.

Isabel Marant FASHION
(Map p60; www.isabelmarant.tm.fr; 16 rue de Charonne, 11e; MBastille) Great cardigans and trousers, interesting accessories, ethnic influences and beautiful fabrics: just a few reasons why Isabel Marant has become the *chouchou* (darling) of Paris fashion. Bohemian and stylish, these are clothes that people look good in.

Pierre Hermé CAKES & CHOCOLATES
(Map p72; www.pierreherme.com; 72 rue Bonaparte, 6e; ☻10am-7pm Sun-Fri, to 7.30pm Sat; MOdéon or Luxembourg) It's the size of a chocolate box, but once in your tastebuds will go wild. Pierre Hermé is one of Paris' top *chocolatiers* and his boutique is a veritable feast of perfectly presented petits fours, cakes, chocolate, nougats, macaroons and jam.

Le Bon Marché DEPARTMENT STORE
(24 rue de Sèvres, 7e; ☻10am-8pm Mon-Wed & Fri, 10am-9pm Thu & Sat; MSèvres Babylone)

Opened by Gustave Eiffel as Paris' first department store in 1852, The Good Market (which also means 'bargain' in French) is the Left Bank's chic one-stop shop. The icing on the cake is its glorious **food hall**.

Le Printemps DEPARTMENT STORE
(Map p82; www.printemps.com; 64 bd Haussmann, 9e; ☻9.35am-8pm Mon-Wed, Fri & Sat, to 10pm Thu; MHavre Caumartin) This is actually three separate stores – Le Printemps de la Mode (women's fashion), Le Printemps de l'Homme (for men) and Le Printemps de la Beauté et Maison (for beauty and household goods) – offering a staggering display of perfume, cosmetics and accessories, as well as established and up-and-coming designer wear.

Village Voice BOOKS
(Map p72; www.villagevoicebookshop.com; 6 rue Princesse, 6e; ☻2-7.30pm Mon, 10am-7.30pm Tue-Sat, noon-6pm Sun; MMabillon) With an excellent selection of contemporary North American fiction and European literature, lots of readings and helpful staff, the Village Voice is a favourite.

Kiliwatch FASHION
(Map p50; 64 rue Tiquetonne, 2e; ☻11am-7.30pm Tue-Sat; MÉtienne Marcel) A Parisian institution, Kiliwatch is always packed with hip guys and gals rummaging through rack after rack of new and used street wear and designs. There's a startling range of vintage goods including hats and boots, plus art/photography books, eyewear and the latest trainers.

SAVVY SHOPPING

» Start with an overview of Paris fashion at department stores like Le Bon Marché, Galeries Lafayette or Printemps.

» The most exclusive designer boutiques require customers to buzz to get in – don't be shy about ringing that bell.

» Clothes shopping in France is 'look but don't touch' style, meaning no disturbing perfectly folded piles of T-shirts or trying on shades without asking.

» Returning or exchanging a purchase without the *ticket de caisse* (receipt) is impossible. Keep the receipt safe and know you have one month to change the item.

» Buying a present for someone or simply fancy your purchase exquisitely gift-wrapped? Ask for *un paquet cadeau* (gift-wrapping). It costs nothing and is something practically every shop does – and very beautifully too.

» Winter *soldes* (sales) start mid-January; summer ones, the second week of June.

» Don't want to DIY? Invest in a personalised shopping tour by foot or chauffeur: www.secretsofparis.com and www.chicshoppingparis.com are two of many.

ℹ OPENING HOURS

Opening hours for Paris shops are generally 10am to 7pm Monday to Saturday. Smaller shops often shut all day Monday; other days, their proprietors may simply close from noon to around 2pm for a long lunch. Many larger stores hold *nocturnes* (late nights) on Thursday, remaining open until around 10pm. For Sunday shopping, the Champs-Élysées, Montmartre, the Marais and Bastille areas are the liveliest.

Huilerie J Leblanc et Fils CULINARY OILS
(Map p72; www.huile-leblanc.com; 6 rue Jacob, 6e; MSt-Germain des Près) The Leblanc family has made the smoothest of culinary oils (almonds, pistachios, sesame seeds, pine kernels, peanuts etc) at its stone mill in Burgundy since 1878. Taste and buy.

Tumbleweed TOYS
(Map p56; www.tumbleweedparis.com; 19 rue de Turenne, 4e; ⊙11am-7pm Mon-Sat, 2-7pm Sun; MSt-Paul or Chemin Vert) This gorgeous little shop specialises in *l'artisanat d'art ludique* (crafts of the playing art): think wonderful handmade wooden toys, many too nice to play with. The brain teasers, puzzles and 'secret' boxes that defy entry (for adults) are exquisitely made.

Deyrolle HOME & GARDEN
(46 rue du Bac, 7e; MRue du Bac) This shop, born in 1831, has to be seen to be believed. It stocks every stuffed animal species legally allowed.

Julien Caviste WINE
(Map p56; 50 rue Charlot, 3e; MFilles du Calvaire) This independent wine store on hip rue Charlot focuses on small, independent producers and organic wines.

Anna Joliet MUSIC BOXES
(Map p50; passage du Perron, 9 rue de Beaujolais, 1er; MPyramides) Magical music boxes, old and new.

Mariage Frères TEA
(Map p56; www.mariagefreres.com; 30, 32 & 35 rue du Bourg Tibourg, 4e; ⊙shop 10.30am-7.30pm, tearooms noon-7pm; MHôtel de Ville) Founded in 1854, this is Paris' first and arguably its finest teashop. Choose from more than 500 varieties of tea sourced from some 35 countries.

ℹ Information

Dangers & Annoyances

Paris is generally a safe city. Metro stations probably best avoided late at night include: Châtelet-Les Halles and its seemingly endless corridors; Château Rouge in Montmartre; Gare du Nord; Strasbourg St-Denis; Réaumur Sébastopol; and Montparnasse Bienvenüe. *Bornes d'alarme* (alarm boxes) are located in the centre of each metro/RER platform and in some station corridors.

Pickpocketing and thefts from handbags and packs is a problem wherever there are crowds (especially of tourists). Be particularly careful around Montmartre's Sacré Cœur; Pigalle; the areas around Forum des Halles and Centre Pompidou; the Latin Quarter (especially the rectangle bounded by rue St-Jacques, bd St-Germain, bd St-Michel and quai St-Michel); below the Eiffel Tower; and on the metro during rush hour.

Emergency

The numbers below are to be dialled in an emergency. See p129 for hospitals with 24-hour emergency departments. For nationwide emergency numbers, see p14.

SOS Helpline (☑01 46 21 46 46, in English; ⊙3-11pm daily)

SOS Médecins (☑01 47 07 77 77, 24hr house calls ☑3624; www.sosmedecins-france.fr)

Urgences Médicales de Paris (Paris Medical Emergencies; ☑01 53 94 94 94; www.ump.fr, in French)

Internet Access

Wi-fi is widely available at midrange and top-end hotels in Paris and usually free. For a list of almost 100 free-access wi-fi cafés in Paris, visit www.cafes-wifi.com, in French.

For those without a laptop and/or wi-fi access, Paris is awash with internet cafés, including:

Hitel (147 rue Lafayette, 10e; per 15/30/60min €1/1.50/2; ⊙9am-midnight; MGare du Nord) Just around the corner from the Gare du Nord. Also sells French SIM cards.

WANT MORE?

For in-depth information, reviews and recommendations at your fingertips, head to the Apple App Store to purchase Lonely Planet's *Paris City Guide* iPhone app.

Alternatively, head to Lonely Planet (www.lonelyplanet.com/france/paris) for planning advice, author recommendations, traveller reviews and insider tips.

Internet Café (place des Abbesses, 18e; per 10/60min €1/4; ⊙9am-7.45pm Mon-Fri, 10am-7pm Sat & Sun; ⓂAbbesses) In the heart of Montmartre.

Milk (www.milklub.com; 17 rue Soufflot, 5e; per 15/30/60min €2/3/4; ⊙24hr; ⓂLuxembourg) One of seven locations; including **Les Halles** (31 bd de Sébastopol, 1er; ⊙24hr; ⓂLes Halles).

Medical Services
American Hospital of Paris (☑01 46 41 25 25; www.american-hospital.org; 63 bd Victor Hugo, 92200 Neuilly-sur-Seine; ⓂPont de Levallois Bécon) Private hospital; emergency 24-hour medical and dental care.

Hôpital Hôtel Dieu (☑01 42 34 82 34; www.aphp.fr, in French; 1 place du Parvis Notre Dame, 4e; ⓂCité) One of the city's government -run public hospitals; after 8pm use emergency entrance on rue de la Cité, 4e.

SOS Dentaire (☑01 43 37 51 00; 87 bd de Port Royal, 14e; ⓂPort Royal) Private dental office open when most other dentists aren't (8pm to 11pm Monday to Friday, 9.45am to 11pm Saturday and Sunday).

Pharmacie Les Champs (☑01 45 62 02 41; Galerie des Champs, 84 av des Champs-Élysées, 8e; ⊙24hr; ⓂGeorge V)

Pharmacie des Halles (☑01 42 72 03 23; 10 bd de Sébastopol, 4e; ⊙9am-midnight Mon-Sat, 9am-10pm Sun; ⓂChâtelet)

Post
Main post office (Map p50; 52 rue du Louvre, 1er; ⊙24hr; ⓂSentier or Les Halles) Open round the clock (closed 6.20am to 7.20am Monday to Saturday, 6am to 7am Sunday), but currency exchange only during regular opening hours.

Tourist Information
Paris Convention & Visitors Bureau (Map p50; www.parisinfo.com; 25-27 rue des Pyramides, 1er; ⓂPyramides; ⊙9am-7pm Jun-Oct, 10am-7pm Mon-Sat & 11am-7pm Sun Nov-May) Main tourist office with a clutch of smaller centres elsewhere in the city.

❶ Getting There & Away
Air
Aéroport d'Orly (ORY; ☑39 50, 01 70 36 39 50; www.aeroportsdeparis.fr) Older and smaller of Paris' two major airports, 18km south of the city.

Aéroport Roissy Charles de Gaulle (CDG; ☑39 50, 01 70 36 39 50; www.aeroportsdeparis.fr) Three terminal complexes – Aérogare 1, 2 and 3 – 30km northeast of Paris in the suburb of Roissy.

Aéroport Beauvais (BVA; ☑08 92 68 20 66; www.aeroportbeauvais.com) 80km north of Paris, used by charter companies and budget airlines

For tips, recommendations and reviews, head to shop.lonelyplanet. com to purchase a downloadable PDF of the London chapter from Lonely Planet's *England* guide.

Bus
Eurolines (Map p68; ☑01 43 54 11 99; www.eurolines.fr; 55 rue St-Jacques, 5e; ⓂCluny–La Sorbonne) Reservations and tickets for international buses to Western and Central Europe, Scandinavia and Morocco.

Gare Routière Internationale de Paris-Galliéni (Off Map p44; ☑08 92 89 90 91; 28 av du Général de Gaulle; ⓂGalliéni) Paris' international bus terminal in the eastern suburb of Bagnolet.

Train
Paris has six major train stations. For mainline train information available round the clock contact **SNCF** (☑08 91 36 20 20, for timetables 08 91 67 68 69; www.sncf.fr).

Gare d'Austerlitz (Map p44; bd de l'Hôpital, 13e; ⓂGare d'Austerlitz) Trains to/from Spain and Portugal; Loire Valley and non-TGV trains to southwestern France (eg Bordeaux and Basque Country).

Gare de l'Est (Map p102; bd de Strasbourg, 10e; ⓂGare de l'Est) Luxembourg, parts of Switzerland (Basel, Lucerne, Zurich), southern Germany (Frankfurt, Munich) and points further east; regular and TGV Est trains to areas of France east of Paris (Champagne, Alsace and Lorraine).

Gare de Lyon (Map p44; bd Diderot, 12e; ⓂGare de Lyon) Parts of Switzerland (eg Bern, Geneva, Lausanne), Italy and points beyond; regular and TGV Sud-Est and TGV Midi-Méditerranée trains to areas southeast of Paris, including Dijon, Lyon, Provence, the Côte d'Azur and the Alps.

Gare Montparnasse (Map p44; av du Maine & bd de Vaugirard, 15e; ⓂMontparnasse Bienvenüe) Brittany and places en route from Paris (eg Chartres, Angers, Nantes); TGV Atlantique Ouest and TGV Atlantique Sud-Ouest trains to Tours, Nantes, Bordeaux and other destinations in southwestern France.

Gare du Nord (Map p102; rue de Dunkerque, 10e; ⓂGare du Nord) UK, Belgium, northern Germany, Scandinavia, Moscow etc (terminus of the high-speed Thalys trains to/from Amsterdam, Brussels, Cologne and Geneva and Eurostar to London); trains to the northern suburbs of Paris and northern France, including TGV Nord trains to Lille and Calais.

Gare St-Lazare (Map p44; rue St-Lazare & rue d'Amsterdam, 8e; MSt-Lazare) Normandy (eg Dieppe, Le Havre, Cherbourg).

❶ Getting Around

To/From the Airports

Getting into town is straightforward and inexpensive thanks to a fleet of public-transport options. Bus drivers sell tickets. Children aged four to nine years pay half price on most of the services.

AÉROPORT D'ORLY

Air France bus 1 (☑08 92 35 08 20; http://videocdn.airfrance.com/cars-airfrance; single/return €11.50/18.50; ☺6.15am-11.15pm from Orly, 6am-11.30pm from Invalides) This *navette* (shuttle bus) runs every 30 minutes to/from Gare Montparnasse (rue du Commandant René Mouchotte, 15e; MMontparnasse Bienvenüe) and Aérogare des Invalides (MInvalides) in the 7e.

Noctilien bus 31 (☑32 46; www.noctilien.fr; adult €6.40 or 4 metro tickets; ☺12.30am-5.30pm) Part of the RATP night service, Noctilien hourly bus 31 links Orly-Sud with Gare de Lyon, Place d'Italie and Gare d'Austerlitz (45 mins).

Orlybus (☑32 46; www.ratp.fr; adult €6.40; ☺6am-11.20pm from Orly, 5.35am-11.05pm from Paris) RATP bus every 15 to 20 minutes to/from metro Denfert Rochereau (20 to 30 minutes) in the 14e.

Orlyval (☑32 46; www.ratp.fr; adult €9.85; ☺6am-11pm) This RATP service links Orly with the city centre via a shuttle train and the RER (p132). Automatic rail (€7.60) to the RER B station Antony, then RER B4 north (€2.25; 35 to 40 minutes to Châtelet, every four to 12 minutes). Orlyval tickets are valid for the subsequent RER and metro journey.

RATP bus 183 (☑32 46; www.ratp.fr; adult €1.60 or 1 metro/bus ticket; 1hr; every 35min ☺5.35am-8.35pm) Cheapest way of getting to/from Orly Sud: very slow public bus linking only Orly-Sud (one hour) with metro Porte de Choisy every 30 minutes.

RATP bus 285 (☑32 46; www.ratp.fr; adult €6.40 or 4 metro tickets; ☺5.05am-midnight from Orly, 5am-12.40am from Paris) Every 10 to 30 minutes to/from metro Villejuif Louis Aragon (55 minutes).

RER C & shuttle (☑32 46; www.ratp.fr; adult €6.20; ☺5.30am-11.30pm) Shuttle bus every 15 to 30 minutes to RER line C station, Pont de Rungis-Aéroport d'Orly RER station, then RER C2 train to Paris' Gare d'Austerlitz (50 minutes).

AÉROPORT ROISSY CHARLES DE GAULLE

Air France bus 2 (☑08 92 35 08 20; http://videocdn.airfrance.com/cars-airfrance; single/return €15/24; ☺5.45am-11pm) Links airport every 30 mins with the Arc de Triomphe outside 1 av Carnot, 17e, and Porte Maillot metro station, 17e.

Air France bus 4 (☑08 92 35 08 20; http://videocdn.airfrance.com/cars-airfrance; adult single/return €16.50/27; 45-55min; every 30min; ☺7am-9pm from Roissy Charles de Gaulle, 6.30am-9.30pm from Paris) Links airport every 30 minutes with Gare de Lyon (20bis bd Diderot, 12e; MGare de Lyon) and Gare Montparnasse (rue du Commandant René Mouchotte, 15e; MMontparnasse Bienvenüe).

Noctilien buses 140 & 143 (☑32 46; www.noctilien.fr; adult €4.80 or 3 metro tickets; ☺12.30am-5.30am) Hourly night buses to/from Gare de l'Est (140 & 143) and Gare de Nord (143).

RATP bus 350 (☑32 46; www.ratp.fr; adult €4.80 or 3 metro tickets; ☺5.30am-11pm) Every 30 minutes to/from Gare de l'Est and Gare du Nord (both one hour).

RER B (☑32 46; www.ratp.fr; adult €8.50; ☺5.20am-midnight) Under extensive renovation at the time of research, with replacement buses on duty; RER line B3 usually links CDG1 and CDG2 with the city every 30 minutes (10 to 15 minutes).

Roissybus (☑32 46; www.ratp.fr; adult €9.10; ☺5.30am-11pm) Direct bus every 15 minutes to/from Opéra (corner of rue Scribe and rue Auber, 9e).

BETWEEN ORLY & CHARLES DE GAULLE

Air France shuttle bus 3 (www.cars-airfrance.com, in French; adult €19; ☺6am-10.30pm) Every 30 minutes; free for connecting Air France passengers; journey time one hour.

Orlyval (☑32 46; www.ratp.fr; adult €17.60; ☺6am-11pm) RER line B3 from Charles de Gaulle to the Antony station, then Orlyval automatic metro to Orly.

AÉROPORT PARIS-BEAUVAIS

Navette Officielle (Official Shuttle Bus; ☑08 92 68 20 64, airport ☑08 92 68 20 66; adult €14) Leaves Parking Pershing, west of the Palais des Congrès de Paris, 3¼ hours before flight departures (board 15 minutes before) and leaves the airport 20 minutes after arrivals, dropping passengers south of the Palais des Congrès on place de la Porte Maillot. Journey time 1¼ hours; buy tickets at sales point just outside the terminal and from a kiosk in the car park.

Bicycle

Two-wheeling has never been so good in the city of romance thanks to Vélib' (a crunching of *vélo*, meaning bike, and *liberté*, meaning freedom), a self-service bike scheme whereby you pick up a pearly-grey bike for peanuts from one roadside

Vélib' station, pedal wherever you're going, and park it right outside at another.

Vélib' (01 30 79 79 30; www.velib.paris. fr; day/week/year subscription €1/5/29, bike hire per 1st/2nd/additional half-hr free/€2/4) has revolutionised how Parisians get around. Its almost 1500 stations across the city – one every 300m – sport 20-odd bike stands a head (at the last count there were 23,500 bicycles in all flitting around Paris) and are accessible around-the-clock. iPhone users can download the Vélib' application.

To get a bike, open a Vélib' account: One- and seven-day subscriptions can be done at any station with any credit card that has a microchip; as deposit pre-authorise a direct debit of €150, all of which is debited if your bike is not returned/reported as stolen). If the station you want to return your bike to is full, swipe your card across the multilingual terminal to get 15 minutes for free to find another station. Bikes are geared to cyclists aged 14 and over, and are fitted with gears, antitheft lock with key, reflective strips and front/rear lights. Bring your own helmet.

Boat

Batobus (08 25 05 01 01; www.batobus.com; adult 1-/2-/3-day pass €13/17/20; every 15-30min; ◷10am-9.30pm May-Aug, shorter hrs rest of the year) Fleet of glassed-in trimarans dock at eight small piers along the Seine; buy tickets at each stop or tourist offices and jump on and off as you like.

Car & Motorcycle

The swiftest way to turn your stay in Paris into an uninterrupted series of hassles is to drive. If driving the car doesn't destroy your holiday sense of spontaneity, parking will. If you must drive, the fastest way to get across the city is usually via the bd Périphérique, the ring road that encircles the city.

Major car-rental companies (p977) have offices at airports and train stations. Street parking in central Paris is limited to two hours and costs €1.50-3 per hour; to pay buy a Paris Carte worth €10 or €30 at *tabacs* (tobacconists). Municipal

car parks cost €2-3.50 per hour or around €25 per 24 hours.

Got the urge to look like you've just stepped into (or out of) a 1950s French film? Grab a pastel-coloured Vespa XLV 50cc scooter from **Left Bank Scooters** (www.leftbankscooters. com). They'll deliver/pick up from your hotel and arrange tours (from €130) as far as Versailles. Renters must be at least 30 years old and hold a motorcycle license. Credit-card deposit is €1000.

Public Transport

Paris' public transit system, mostly operated by the **RATP** (32 46; www.ratp.fr) is one of Europe's cheapest and most efficient. View and download transport maps from RATP's website.

BUS

Paris' bus system runs from 5.30am and 8.30pm Monday to Saturday; after that certain *service en soirée* (evening service) lines continue until between midnight and 12.30am, after which some 42 Noctilien (www.noctilien.fr) night buses kick in, departing hourly until 5.30am. Night buses serve the main train stations and cross the major arteries of the city before leading out to the suburbs; many go through Châtelet (rue de Rivoli and bd Sébastopol). Look for blue *N* or 'Noctilien' signs at bus stops. There are two circular lines within Paris (the N01 and N02) that link four main train stations, St-Lazare, Gare de l'Est, Gare de Lyon, Montparnasse (but not Châtelet), as well as popular nightspots such as Bastille, the Champs-Élysées, Pigalle and St-Germain.

Noctilien services are included on your Mobilis or Paris Visite pass (p133) for the zones in which you are travelling. Otherwise pay a certain number of standard €1.60 metro tickets, depending on the length of your journey. Drivers sell tickets for €1.70 and can tell you how many you need for your destination.

All services are drastically reduced on Sunday and public holidays.

Short bus rides (ie rides in one or two bus zones) cost one metro/bus ticket. Transfer to

---

ⓘ WHEELS FOR A COUPLE OF HOURS

A godsend for those who need a car for just a couple of hours or half-day is self-service, pay-as-you-go scheme Connect by Hertz (08 00 45 04 00; www.connectby hertz.com), a carbon-copy of London's popular Streetcar service. Register online and pay €120 annual membership; locate via the internet the closest available vehicle to you; unlock the car with your membership card, release the key with a PIN and off you drive! Prices start at €4/32 per hour/day plus €0.35/km. Rates include insurance and petrol.

The Mairie de Paris hope to have a fleet of 3000-odd electric rental cars parked to go around the city by 2012 – a car equivalent of Vélib', hence the name Autolib'.

other buses – but not the metro – are allowed on the same ticket. Travel to the suburbs costs up to three tickets. Drivers sell special bus-only tickets.

You must punch single-journey tickets in the *composteur* (cancelling machine) next to the driver. If you have a Mobilis or Paris Visite pass flash it as you board. Do not cancel the magnetic coupon that accompanies your pass.

METRO & RER

Paris' underground network, also run by the RATP, consists of two separate but linked systems: the Métropolitain, or *métro*, with 16 lines and 384 stops; and the RER (Réseau Express Régional), a network of suburban lines, designated A to E and then numbered, that pass through the city centre.

Each **metro** train is known by the name of its terminus. On maps and plans each line has a different colour and number (from 1 to 14). Signs in stations indicate the way to the platform for your line. The *direction* signs on each platform indicate the terminus. On lines that split into several branches (such as lines 3, 7 and 13), the terminus served by each train is indicated with backlit panels on the cars, and electronic signs on each platform give the number of minutes until the next train.

Signs marked *correspondance* (transfer) show how to reach connecting trains. At stations with many intersecting lines, such as Châtelet and Montparnasse Bienvenüe, the connection can seem interminable.

Each metro line has its own schedule, but trains usually start at around 5.30am, with the last train beginning its run between 12.35am and 1.15am (2.15am on Friday and Saturday).

The same RATP tickets are valid on the metro, RER (for travel within the city limits), buses, trams and the Montmartre funicular. A single ticket – white in colour and called *un ticket t+* – costs €1.60 (half-price for children aged four to nine years) and a *carnet* of 10 is €11.60 (no carnets for kids). Ticket windows and vending machines accept most credit cards.

One ticket lets you travel between any two metro stations – no return journeys – for a period of 1½ hours, no matter how many transfers are required. You can also use it on the RER for travel within zone 1. A single ticket can be used to transfer between daytime buses and trams, but not from the metro to bus or vice versa.

Always keep your ticket until you exit from your station; you may be stopped by a *contrôleur* (ticket inspector) and will have to pay a fine (€25 to €50 on the spot) if you don't have a valid ticket.

METRO STOP TOUR *BY JUMPBEAN*

Abbesses (Line 12) Brightly painted murals may ease your journey up the lengthy staircase to the heights of Montmartre.

Arts Et Métiers (Line 11) Exposed oversize metal piping turns this station into a Jules Verne submarine.

Bastille (Line 1) Though the ancient prison no longer exists, the tumult of the uprising it sparked lives on in the unfinished mural depicting scenes from the French Revolution.

Concorde (Line 12) Here under the infamous location of the guillotine, lettered tiles on the wall spell out the French translation of the Universal Declaration of Human Rights.

Liège (Line 13) Mosaic tiles evoke the pastoral ambience of the old Flemish city.

Line 14 Paris' newest metro line, the Météor, is a journey of its own. Sit in the front car of the fully automated train to watch the eerie depths of the Paris subway system whiz by.

Louvre-Rivoli (Line 1) The museum experience starts from the subway station. Step out of the subway car into the belly of the Louvre. Egyptian artefacts greet you in the yellow gloom of a pyramid's interior.

Palais Royal–Musee Du Louvre (Line 7) The street-level entrance is decorated with bulbous coloured shapes that shine gaudily at the Louvre's northern wall.

Tuilleries (Line 1) Bright murals display the varied history of the city's central park.

Varenne (Line 13) The romance of Rodin's statues graces the platforms at the station closest to his former atelier.

TOURIST PASSES

Mobilis and Paris Visite passes are valid on the metro, RER, SNCF's suburban lines (p133), buses, night buses, trams and the Montmartre funicular. They do not require a photo but you should write your card number on the ticket. Passes are sold at larger metro and RER stations, SNCF offices in Paris, and the airports.

The Mobilis card coupon allows unlimited travel for one day in two to six zones (€5.60 to €15.90; €4.55 to €13.70 for children aged four to 11 years). Buy it at any metro, RER or SNCF station in the region. Depending how many times you plan to hop on/off the metro in a day, a *carnet* might work out to be cheaper.

The Paris Visite pass covers unlimited travel (including to/from airports) and discounted entry to certain museums and activities. They are valid for one, two, three or five consecutive days of travel in three or six zones. The version covering one to three zones costs €8.80/14.40/19.60/28.30 for one/two/three/five days. Children four to 11 years pay half-price.

TRAVEL PASSES

If you're staying in Paris longer than a few days, the cheapest and easiest way to use public transport is with a combined travel pass that allows travel on the metro, RER and buses for a week, month or year. You can get passes for travel in two to eight zones; for most tourists the basic ticket valid for zones 1 and 2 is sufficient.

Navigo (www.navigo.fr, in French) provides you with a refillable weekly, monthly or yearly pass that you can recharge at Navigo machines in most metro stations; swipe the card across the electronic panel as you go through the turnstiles. Standard Navigo passes, available to anyone with an address in Île de France, are free, but take up to three weeks to be issued; ask at the ticket counter for a form or go online. Otherwise pay €5 for a Navigo Découverte, issued on the spot but – unlike the Navigo pass – not replaceable if lost or stolen. Both passes require a passport photo and can be recharged for periods of one week or more.

Weekly tickets (*coupons hebdomadaires*) cost €17.20 for zones 1 and 2, valid Monday to Sunday. Even if you're in Paris for three or four days, it may work out to be cheaper than buying *carnets* and will certainly cost less than buying a daily Mobilis or Paris Visite pass (see above).

Suburban Train

The RER and **SNCF commuter lines** (☎08 91 36 20 20; www.sncf.fr) serve suburban destinations outside the city limits. Buy your ticket *before* you board the train or you won't be able to get out of the station when you arrive. You are not allowed to pay the additional fare when you get there.

If you are issued with a full-size SNCF ticket for travel to the suburbs, validate it in a time-stamp pillar *before* you board the train. You may also be given a *contremarque magnétique* (magnetic ticket) to get through any metro/RER-type turnstiles on the way to/from the platform. If you are travelling on a Paris Visite or Mobilis pass, do *not* punch the magnetic coupon in one of SNCF's time-stamp machines. Most – but not all – RER/SNCF tickets purchased in the suburbs for travel to the city allow you to continue your journey by metro. For some destinations, a ticket can be purchased at any metro ticket window; for others you'll have to go to an RER station on the line you need in order to buy a ticket.

Taxi

Prise en charge (flag fall) in a Parisian taxi is €2.20. Within city limits, it costs €0.89/km between 10am and 5pm Monday to Saturday (*Tarif A*; white light on meter), and €1.14/km at 'night' (5pm to 10am), all day Sunday, and on public holidays (*Tarif B*; orange light on meter). Travel in the suburbs (*Tarif C*; blue light) costs €1.33 per kilometre.

There's a surcharge of €2.75 for taking a fourth passenger. The first piece of baggage is free; additional pieces over 5kg cost €1 extra.

Flagging down a taxi can be hard. To order a taxi, call Paris' **central taxi switchboard** (☎01 45 30 30 30; passengers with reduced mobility ☎01 47 39 00 91; ☺24hr). You can also call or book online through the following radio-dispatched taxi companies, on call 24 hours.

Alpha Taxis (☎01 45 85 85 85; www.alpha taxis.com, in French)

Taxis Bleus (☎01 49 36 29 48; www.taxis -bleus.com, in French)

Taxis G7 (☎01 47 39 47 39; www.taxisg7.fr, in French)

Around Paris

Includes »

Best Places to Eat

» Côté Sud (p146)
» La Capitainerie (p148)
» La Chocolaterie (p152)

Best Tours

Pressed for time? Hop on an air-conditioned coach:

» **Cityrama** (☑01 44 55 60 00; www.pariscityrama.com) Half-day trips to Versailles (€54 to €74) or Chartres (€63) and various other full-day options

» **Paris Vision** (☑01 42 60 30 01; www.parisvision.com) Half-day trips to Versailles/ Giverny (€67/70), or full day to both; other options include Fontainebleau, Barbizon and Vaux-le-Vicomte, and Disneyland

Why Go?

The French capital is encircled by the Île de France, the 12,000-sq-km 'Island of France' shaped by five rivers. This was the 'seed' from which the kingdom of France grew from about AD 1100.

The Île de France counts some of the most extravagant châteaux in the land. At the top of the list is the palace at Versailles, whose opulence and extravagance partly spurred the Revolutionary mob to storm the Bastille in July 1789. It also boasts many of the nation's most beautiful and ambitious cathedrals, including that mother of all basilicas, the cathedral at Chartres, with its breathtaking stained glass and intricately carved stone portals.

But the Île de France is not stuck in the past. The modern cityscape of La Défense stands in contrast to the Paris of legend. And then there's every kid's favourite, Disneyland, which now has more attractions than ever.

When to Go

Chartres

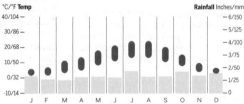

March/April	Mid-June to August	December
St-Denis and the northern suburbs host the Banlieues Bleues jazz festival.	Watch the magic fountains dance at the Château of Versailles.	Midnight Mass on Christmas Eve at Chartres Cathedral.

La Défense

POP 21,000

The ultramodern architecture of La Défense, the skyscraper district 3km west of the capital, is so strikingly different from the rest of centuries-old Paris that it's worth a visit in itself. When development of the 160-hectare site began in the late 1950s, it was one of the world's most ambitious civil-engineering projects. Its first major structure was the vaulted, largely triangular Centre des Nouvelles Industries et Technologies (CNIT; Centre for New Industries and Technologies), a giant 'pregnant oyster' inaugurated in 1958, extensively rebuilt three decades later and then reborn as a shopping and conference centre in 2008. Like many of its contemporaries, the centre is architecturally uninspiring. But later generations' structures still excite, including the Cœur Défense (Défense Heart; 2001), the Tour T1 and Tour Granite (2008) and, still to come, the record-breaking Tour Phare (p135).

Today La Défense counts more than 100 buildings, is home to three-quarters of France's 20 largest corporations and showcases extraordinary monumental art. A total of 1500 companies of all sizes employ some 150,000 people, transforming the nocturnal ghost town into a hive of high-flying commercial activity by day.

◉ Sights

Grande Arche de la Défense

MONUMENTAL ARCH

(www.grandearche.com; 1 parvis de la Défense; adult/child €10/8.50, Tue €5; ⊙10am-8pm; ⓂLa Défense Grande Arche) The most important sight is the remarkable cube-shaped 'Great Arch'. Housing government and business offices, it is made of white Carrara marble, grey granite and glass, and measures exactly 110m along each side. Inaugurated on 14 July 1989, the arch marks the western end of the 8km-long **Axe Historique** (Historic Axis) stretching from the Louvre's glass pyramid. Glass-enclosed lifts whisk you up to the 35th floor for views, a film, scale models and the new (and more interesting than it sounds) Musée de l'Informatique (Computer Museum; www.museeinformatique.fr), with 200 items dating back 100 years. Entry is included in the admission price.

FREE Musée de la Défense   MUSEUM
(www.ladefense.fr; 15 place de la Défense; ⊙10am-6pm Sun-Fri, to 7pm Sat; ⓂLa Défense

Grande Arche) Below the Espace Info-Défense, this museum traces the development of La Défense through the decades with drawings, architectural plans and scale models. Especially interesting are the projects that were never built, including the Tour sans Fin, a 'Never-Ending Tower' that would have been 425m high but just 39m in diameter.

Gardens & Monuments   GARDENS

Le Parvis, place de la Défense and Esplanade du Général de Gaulle, which together form a pleasant 1km-long pedestrian walkway, comprise a **garden of contemporary art**. More than five dozen sculptures and murals along the **Voie des Sculptures** (Sculpture Way) here include colourful and imaginative works by Calder, Miró, César and Moretti, among others.

In the southeastern corner of place de la Défense and across from the Info-Défense office is a much older monument – **La Défense de Paris**, which commemorates the defence of Paris during the Franco-Prussian War of 1870–71 and from which the district's name is derived. Behind is the **Bassin Agam**, a pool with fountains and Venetian mosaics.

✖ Eating

La Défense is mostly fast-food territory. The shopping centre Les Quatre Temps (www.les4temps.com, in French; 15 parvis de la Défense; ⊙10am-8pm, restaurants to 11pm) is loaded with places to eat quickly, be it pizza or pancakes, ice cream, soup and juice or even budget Japanese at K10 (15 parvis de la Défense; dishes €2.80-14; ⊙noon-10.30pm; ⓂLa Défense Grande Arche).

LIGHTHOUSE TOWER

Sky-high future architectural creations in the Parisian business district of La Défense promise to throw caution to the wind, but outranking them all in size, beauty and sustainability will be **Tour Phare** (Lighthouse Tower; 2014), a 300m-tall double office and retail tower that will torque like a human torso and, through awnings that will raise and lower when the sun hits them, use light as a building material. Some 30 wind turbines on the roof will feed the ventilation system when it opens in 2014.

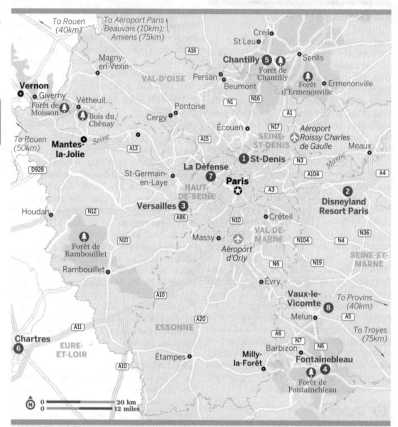

Around Paris Highlights

1 Admire Europe's most important collection of funerary sculpture in the crypt of the **Basilique de St-Denis** (p137)

2 Get behind the scenes – literally – at **Walt Disney Studios Park** (p139)

3 Relive the glory that was the kingdom of France in the 17th and 18th centuries at the **Château de Versailles** (p139)

4 Go for a walk, a cycle or even a climb in the Île de France's loveliest wood, the **Forêt de Fontainebleau** (p147)

5 Wonder at the colour and richness of the 15th-century *Très Riches Heures du Duc de Berry* illuminated manuscript at the **Château de Chantilly** (p147)

6 Get bluer than blue or look at the world through rose-coloured glass under

one of the awesome stained-glass windows at the **Cathédrale Notre Dame de Chartres** (p149)

7 Marvel at the France of the future amidst the forest of glass and steel skyscrapers in La Défense (p135)

8 See the interior of the **Château de Vaux-le-Vicomte** (p146) as our ancestors did after dark – by candlelight.

Globetrotter   INTERNATIONAL €€

(☎01 55 91 96 96; www.globetrottercafe.com; 16 place de la Défense; mains €15-33; ☺lunch Mon-Fri; Ⓜ La Défense Grande Arche) This attractive restaurant next to the Espace Info-Défense attempts to take diners on a culinary tour of the world's islands. Tables on the wooden decking terrace face La Grande Arche and those inside woo diners with first-row seats of the Bassin Agam. Lunchtime sandwich menus are €7 to €12.

Bistrot de l'Arche   BISTRO €€

(☑01 40 81 08 16; 38 parvis de la Défense; menus €21-24.50; Ⓜ La Défense Grande Arche) Expect no surprises at this all-day place serving standard bistro fare. But with its huge terrace at the foot of the steps leading up to the Grande Arche, this is a choice of location over substance. It does sandwiches (€4 to €6.60) and salads too.

❶ Information

Espace Info-Défense (☑01 47 74 84 24; www.ladefense.fr; 15 place de la Défense; ◷10am-6pm Sun-Fri, to 7pm Sat; Ⓜ La Défense Grande Arche) The local tourist office has reams of free information, including the useful *La Défense Short Guide* and three excellent brochures on the district's history, architecture and public art.

Post office (CNIT Bldg, ground floor, 2 place de la Défense; Ⓜ La Défense Grande Arche)

❶ Getting There & Away

La Défense Grande Arche metro station is the western terminus of metro line 1; the ride from the Louvre takes about 15 to 20 minutes. If you take the faster RER line A, remember that La Défense is in zone 3 and you must buy a ticket (€2.25) if you are carrying a travel pass for zones 1 and 2 only. Beware: the area is patrolled regularly by inspectors.

St-Denis

POP 102,000

For 1200 years the hallowed burial place of French royalty, St-Denis today is little more than a suburb with a very mixed population, a short metro ride above Paris' 18e *arrondissement*. The ornate royal tombs, adorned with some truly remarkable statuary, and the Basilique de St-Denis containing them are well worth the trip, as is the Stade de France, the futuristic stadium just south of Canal de St-Denis.

⦿ Sights

Basilique de St-Denis   CATHEDRAL

(www.monuments-nationaux.fr; 1 rue de la Légion d'Honneur; admission free; ◷10am-6pm Mon-Sat, noon-6pm Sun; Ⓜ Basilique de St-Denis) Serving as the burial place for all but a handful of France's kings and queens from Dagobert I (r 629–39) to Louis XVIII (r 1814–24), the basilica and its tombs and mausoleums constitute one of Europe's most important collections of funerary sculpture.

The single-towered structure, begun around 1136, was the first major building to be erected in the Gothic style and served as a model for many other 12th-century French cathedrals, including the one at Chartres (p149). Features illustrating the transition from Romanesque to Gothic can be seen here in the **choir** and the **ambulatory**, which are adorned with a number of 12th-century **stained-glass windows**.

During the Revolution and the ensuing Reign of Terror, the basilica was badly damaged and skeletal remains from the royal tombs were dumped into two pits outside. The mausoleums themselves, however, were put into storage in Paris and survived. They were brought back in 1816, and the royal bones were reburied in the crypt a year later. Restoration of the structure was initially begun under Napoléon Bonaparte, but most of the work was carried out by the Gothic Revivalist architect Eugène Viollet-le-Duc from 1858 until his death in 1879.

The royal tombs (adult/child €7/free) are decorated with life-size figures of the deceased. Those built before the Renaissance are adorned with *gisants* (recumbent figures). Those made after 1285 were carved from death masks and are thus fairly, er, lifelike; the 14 figures commissioned under Louis IX (St Louis; r 1214–70) are depictions of how earlier rulers may have looked. The oldest tombs (from around 1230) are those of Clovis I (d 511) and his son Childebert I (d 558). Don't miss the white marble **catafalque tomb** (1597) of Louis XII and Anne of Bretagne. The graffiti etched on the arms of the seated figures dates from the early 17th century.

Self-paced 1¼-hour audioguide tours of the basilica and the tombs cost €4.50 (€6 for two sharing).

ON YOUR WAY

The official **Paris Île de France** (www.nouveau-paris-ile-de-france.fr) website is a treasure trove of information on the area. If you're visiting the Île de France under your own steam, pick up a copy of IGN's *Île de France* (1:250,000; €5.70) or its larger-scale *Paris et Ses Environs* (1:100,000; €4.30), both available from the **Espace IGN** (p963) just off the av des Champs-Élysées in Paris.

Stade de France   STADIUM
(www.stadefrance.com; rue Francis de Pressensé; adult/child €12/8; ☺tours in French hourly 10am-5pm, in English 10.30am & 2.30pm; ⓜSt-Denis-Porte de Paris) Just south of central St-Denis, the 80,000-seat Stade de France was built in time for the 1998 World Cup, which France won by miraculously defeating favourite Brazil 3–0. The futuristic and quite beautiful structure, with a roof the size of place de la Concorde, is now used for football and rugby matches, and big-ticket music concerts. Visits by guided tour only.

✖ Eating

There is a **Franprix supermarket** (34 rue de la République; ☺8.30am-8.30pm Mon-Sat, to 1.30pm Sun) in the centre of town close to the post office.

Les Arts   NORTH AFRICAN €€
(☎01 42 43 22 40; 6 rue de la Boulangerie; menu €22; ⓜBasilique de St-Denis) This central restaurant has mostly Maghreb cuisine (couscous, *tajines,* 'Moroccan stews' etc, €12 to €18) plus a few traditional French dishes. It's just across from the basilica, so a handy pit stop throughout the day.

Le Petit Breton   TRADITIONAL FRENCH €
(☎01 48 20 11 58; 18 rue de la Légion d'Honneur; menus €12 & €15; ☺lunch Mon-Sat; ⓜSt-Denis-Porte de Paris) 'The Little Breton' is a decent spot for a lunch. It's name notwithstanding, this convivial place doesn't serve galettes (buckwheat pancakes) or crêpes, but traditional French fare. The plat du jour is a snip at €8.

ℹ Information

Office de Tourisme de St-Denis Plaine Commune (☎01 55 87 08 70; www.saint -denis-tourisme.com; 1 rue de la République; ☺9.30am-1pm & 2-6pm Mon-Sat, 10am-1pm & 2-4pm Sun; ⓜBasilique de St-Denis)

Post office (59 rue de la République; ⓜBasilique de St-Denis)

ℹ Getting There & Away

You can reach St-Denis in 20 minutes on metro line 13: take it to Basilique de St-Denis station for the basilica and tourist office, and to St-Denis-Porte de Paris station for the Stade de France (the latter can also be reached via RER line B; alight at La Plaine Stade de France station). Make sure to board a metro heading for St-Denis Université and *not* for Asnières-Gennevilliers Les Courtilles, as the line splits at La Fourche station.

Disneyland Resort Paris

Disneyland Resort Paris, 32km east of Paris, consists of three main areas: Disney Village, with its seven hotels, shops, restaurants and clubs; Disneyland Park, with its five theme *pays* (lands); and Walt Disney Studios Park, which brings film, animation and TV production to life. The first two are separated by the RER and TGV train stations; the studios are next to Disneyland Park. Moving walkways whisk visitors to the sights from the car park.

◉ Sights

One-day admission fees at **Disneyland Resort Paris** (☎01 60 30 60 53; www.disneyland paris.com; adult/child €52/44) include unlimited access to all rides and activities in *either* Walt Disney Studios Park or Disneyland Park. Multiple-day passes are also available: a **one-day pass** (adult/child €65/57) allows entry to both parks for a day; the multiday equivalents – **two-day pass** (€111/94) and **three-day pass** (€138/117) – allow you to enter and leave both parks as often as you like over nonconsecutive days within one year. Admission fees change season to season and a multitude of special offers and accommodation/transport packages are always available.

Disneyland Park   THEME PARK
(☺9am-11pm, to 8pm in winter) **Main Street USA** is a spotless avenue just inside the

---

HEADS UP

The basilica here is named in honour of St Denis, the patron saint of France (also known as Dionysius of Paris), who introduced Christianity to the city and was beheaded by the Romans in Montmartre for his pains. Legend has it that after said decapitation he then walked with his head under his arm to the very spot where the basilica was subsequently built. You can see a likeness of him – carrying his unfortunate head – on the carved western portal of Notre Dame Cathedral (p61) in Paris.

park's main entrance, reminiscent of Norman Rockwell's idealised small-town America circa 1910. Adjoining **Frontierland** is a re-creation of the 'rugged, untamed American West' with the legendary Big Thunder Mountain ride. **Adventureland**, meant to evoke the Arabian Nights, the wilds of Africa and other exotic lands portrayed in Disney films, is home to the Pirates of the Caribbean and the spiralling 360-degrees rollercoaster, Indiana Jones and the Temple of Peril. Pinocchio, Snow White and other fairy-tale characters come to life in **Fantasyland**, while **Discoveryland** is the spot for high-tech attractions and massive-queue rides like Space Mountain: Mission 2, Star Tours and the Toy Story 2–inspired Buzz Lightyear Laser Blast, apparently still the hottest thing since sliced bread here.

Walt Disney Studios Park THEME PARK
(☉9am-6pm) The sound stage, production back lot and animation studios provide an up-close illustration of how films, TV programs and cartoons are produced.

✕ Eating

You are not allowed to picnic on resort grounds, but there's an ample number of themed restaurants to choose from, be it Buzz Lightyear's Pizza Planet (Discoveryland); Planet Hollywood or the *Happy Days*–inspired Annette's Diner (Disney Village); the meaty Silver Spur Steakhouse or Mexican Fuente del Oro (Frontierland); and the seafaring Blue Lagoon restaurant (Adventureland) for wannabe pirates. Most have *menus* and meal coupons for adults/children (€24/10). Opening hours vary. To avoid yet another queue, pick your place online and reserve a table in advance (☎01 60 30 40 50).

ℹ Information

Espace du Tourisme d'Île de France et de Seine et Marne (☎01 60 43 33 33; www.pidf.com; place François Truffaut; ☉9.20am-8.45pm) The Île de France tourist office branch, near the RER and TCV train stations and facing Disney Village, shares space with an office dispensing information on the *département* of Seine et Marne.

ℹ Getting There & Away

Marne-la-Vallée/Chessy, Disneyland's RER station, is served by line A4; trains run every 15 minutes or so from central Paris (€6.50), with the last train back to Paris just after midnight.

If driving, follow route A4 from Porte de Bercy (direction Metz-Nancy) and take exit 14.

Versailles

POP 88,930

The prosperous and leafy suburb of Versailles, 28km southwest of Paris, is the site of the grandest and most famous château in France. It served as the kingdom's political capital and the seat of the royal court for more than a century, from 1682 to 1789 – the year Revolutionary mobs massacred the palace guard and dragged Louis XVI and Marie-Antoinette back to Paris, where they eventually were executed by guillotine.

◉ Sights

Château de Versailles PALACE
(☎01 30 83 78 00; www.chateauversailles.fr; palace adult/child €15/free, grounds & tours €18, on music days €25; ☉9am-6.30pm Tue-Sun) This splendid and enormous palace was built in the mid-17th century during the reign of Louis XIV – the Roi Soleil (Sun King) – to project the absolute power of the French monarchy, which was then at the height of its glory. Its scale and decor also reflect Louis XIV's taste for profligate luxury and his boundless appetite for self-glorification. Some 30,000 workers and soldiers toiled on the structure, the bills for which all but emptied the kingdom's coffers. The château has undergone relatively few alterations since its construction, though almost all the interior furnishings disappeared during the Revolution and many of the rooms were rebuilt by Louis-Philippe (r 1830–48). The current €400 million restoration program is the most ambitious yet and until it's completed in 2020 at least a part of the palace is likely to be clad in scaffolding when you visit.

Work began in 1661 under the guidance of three supremely talented men: the architect Louis Le Vau (Jules Hardouin-Mansart took over from Le Vau in the mid-1670s); the painter and interior designer Charles Le Brun; and the landscape artist André Le Nôtre, whose workers flattened hills, drained marshes and relocated forests as they laid out the seemingly endless gardens, ponds and fountains.

Le Brun and his hundreds of artisans decorated every moulding, cornice, ceiling and door of the interior with the most luxurious and ostentatious of appointments:

Versailles

A DAY IN COURT

Visiting Versailles – even just the State Apartments – may seem overwhelming at first, but think of it as a house where people ate, drank, worked, slept and conspired and you'll be on the right path.

Some two decades into his long reign, Louis XIV began turning his father's hunting lodge into a palace large enough to house his entire court (to keep closer tabs on the 6000-strong army of courtiers). Sparing no expense, the Sun King employed the greatest artists and craftspeople of the day and by 1682 he'd created the most extravagant dormitory in history.

The royal schedule was as accurate and predictable as a Swiss watch. By following this itinerary of rooms you can recreate the king's day, starting with the King's Bedchamber **1** and the Queen's Bedchamber **2**, where the royal couple were roused at about the same time. The royal procession then leads through the Hall of Mirrors **3** to the Royal Chapel **4** for morning Mass and returns to the Council Chamber **5** for late-morning meetings with ministers. After lunch the king might ride or hunt or visit the King's Library **6**. Later he could join courtesans for an 'apartment evening' starting from the Hercules Drawing Room **7** or play billiards in the Diana Drawing Room **8** before supping at 10pm.

VERSAILLES BY NUMBERS

- » **Rooms** 700 (11 hectares of roof)
- » **Windows** 2153
- » **Staircases** 67
- » **Gardens and parks** 800 hectares
- » **Trees** 200,000
- » **Fountains** 50 (with 620 nozzles)
- » **Paintings** 6300 (measuring 11km laid end to end)
- » **Statues and sculptures** 2100
- » **Objets d'art and furnishings** 5000
- » **Visitors** 5.3 million per year

CHRISTOPHE LEHENAFF/PHOTOLIBRARY

Queen's Bedchamber
Chambre de la Reine
The queen's life was on constant public display and even the births of her children were watched by crowds of spectators in her own bedchamber. DETOUR » The Guardroom, with a dozen armed men at the ready.

Lunch Break
Diner-style food at Sister's Café, crêpes at Le Phare St-Louis or picnic in the park.

Guardroom

South Wing

King's Library
Bibliothèque du Roi
The last resident, bibliophile Louis XVI, loved geography and his copy of *The Travels of James Cook* (in English, which he read fluently) is still on the shelf here.

RADIUS IMAGES/ALAMY

Savvy Sightseeing
Avoid Versailles on Monday (closed), Tuesday (Paris' museums close, so visitors flock here) and Sunday, the busiest day. Also, book tickets online so you don't have to queue.

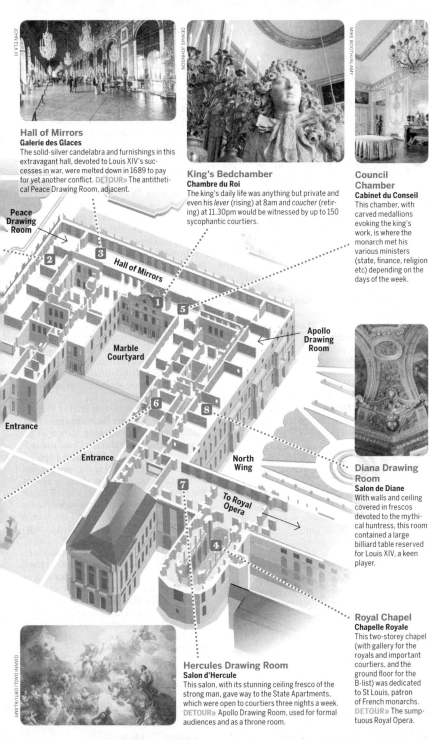

Hall of Mirrors
Galerie des Glaces
The solid-silver candelabra and furnishings in this extravagant hall, devoted to Louis XIV's successes in war, were melted down in 1689 to pay for yet another conflict. DETOUR» The antithetical Peace Drawing Room, adjacent.

King's Bedchamber
Chambre du Roi
The king's daily life was anything but private and even his *lever* (rising) at 8am and *coucher* (retiring) at 11.30pm would be witnessed by up to 150 sycophantic courtiers.

Council Chamber
Cabinet du Conseil
This chamber, with carved medallions evoking the king's work, is where the monarch met his various ministers (state, finance, religion etc) depending on the days of the week.

Peace Drawing Room

Hall of Mirrors

Marble Courtyard

Apollo Drawing Room

Entrance

Entrance

North Wing

To Royal Opera

Diana Drawing Room
Salon de Diane
With walls and ceiling covered in frescos devoted to the mythical huntress, this room contained a large billiard table reserved for Louis XIV, a keen player.

Royal Chapel
Chapelle Royale
This two-storey chapel (with gallery for the royals and important courtiers, and the ground floor for the B-list) was dedicated to St Louis, patron of French monarchs. DETOUR» The sumptuous Royal Opera.

Hercules Drawing Room
Salon d'Hercule
This salon, with its stunning ceiling fresco of the strong man, gave way to the State Apartments, which were open to courtiers three nights a week. DETOUR» Apollo Drawing Room, used for formal audiences and as a throne room.

frescos, marble, gilt and woodcarvings, many with themes and symbols drawn from Greek and Roman mythology. The King's Suite of the **Grands Appartements du Roi et de la Reine** (King's and Queen's State Apartments), for example, includes rooms dedicated to Hercules, Venus, Diana, Mars and Mercury. The opulence reaches its peak in the recently restored **Galerie des Glaces** (Hall of Mirrors), a 75m-long ballroom with 17 huge mirrors on one side and, on the other, an equal number of windows looking out over the gardens and the setting sun.

The Château

The château complex comprises four main sections: the **palais** (palace building), a 580m-long structure with multiple wings, grand halls, sumptuous bedchambers and the Grands Appartements du Roi et de la Reine; the vast gardens, canals and pools to the west of the palace; two much smaller palaces, the **Grand Trianon** and, a few hundred metres to the east, the **Petit Trianon**; and the **Hameau de la Reine** (Queen's Hamlet).

The basic palace ticket and more elaborate Passeport both include an English-language audioguide and allow visitors to freely visit the King's and Queen's State Apartments, Royal Chapel, the **Appartements du Dauphin et de la Dauphine** (Dauphin's and Dauphine's Apartments) and various galleries. The so-called Passe-

---

VERSAILLES TIPS

Many visitors to France consider Versailles a must-see destination and so they should. But in order to avoid disappointment, plan carefully in advance.

Monday is out for obvious reasons (it's closed). The best way to avoid the queues on other days is to arrive first thing in the morning; if you're interested in just the Grands Appartements, another good time to get here is about 4pm. The queues are longest on Tuesday, when many of Paris' museums are closed, and on Sunday. Most importantly, buy your château ticket in advance online (www.chateauversailles.fr) or from a branch of Fnac.

---

port additionally gets you into the two Trianons and, in high season, the Hameau de la Reine and the Grandes Eaux Musicales fountain displays.

Château Gardens

The section of the vast gardens (☉8.30am-8.30pm) nearest the palace, laid out between 1661 and 1700 in the formal French style, is famed for its geometrically aligned terraces, flowerbeds, tree-lined paths, ponds and fountains. The 400-odd statues of marble, bronze and lead were made by the most talented sculptors of the era. The English-style **Jardins du Petit Trianon** are more pastoral and have meandering, sheltered paths. Admission to the gardens is free, except on Tuesday and at weekends during the Grandes Eaux Musicales season.

The **Grand Canal**, 1.6km long and 62m wide, is oriented to reflect the setting sun. It is traversed by the 1km-long **Petit Canal**, creating a cross-shaped body of water with a perimeter of more than 5.5km. Louis XIV used to hold boating parties here. In season, you too can paddle around the Grand Canal in four-person **rowing boats**; the dock is at the canal's eastern end. The **Orangerie**, built under the Parterre du Midi (Southern Flowerbed) on the southwestern side of the palace, shelters tropical plants in winter.

The gardens' largest fountains are the 17th-century **Bassin de Neptune** (Neptune's Fountain), a dazzling mirage of 99 spouting gushers 300m north of the palace, and the **Bassin d'Apollon** (Apollo's Fountain) built in 1688 at the eastern end of the Grand Canal. The straight side of the Bassin de Neptune abuts a small round pond graced by a winged dragon. Emerging from the water in the centre of the Bassin d'Apollon is Apollo's chariot, pulled by rearing horses.

Try to time your visit for the Grandes Eaux Musicales (adult/child €8/6; ☉11am-noon & 3.30-5pm Tues, Sat & Sun Apr-Sep) or the after-dark Grandes Eaux Nocturnes (adult/child €21/17; ☉9-11.30pm Sat & Sun mid-Jun–Aug), truly magical 'dancing water' displays – set to music composed by baroque- and classical-era composers – throughout the grounds in summer.

In the middle of the vast 90-hectare park, about 1.5km northwest of the main palace, is the Domaine de Marie-Antoinette (Marie-Antoinette's Estate; adult/child €10/free; ☉noon-6.30pm). The pink-colonnaded **Grand Tri-**

anon was built in 1687 for Louis XIV and his family as a place of escape from the rigid etiquette of the court. Napoléon I had it redone in the Empire style and it was restored again in the 1960s. The much smaller, ochre-coloured **Petit Trianon**, built in the 1760s, was redecorated in 1867 by Empress Eugénie, the consort of Napoléon III, who added Louis XVI–style furnishings.

TOP CHOICE **Hameau de la Reine** is further north – a mock village of thatched cottages, a pond and photogenic mill constructed from 1775 to 1784 for the amusement of Marie-Antoinette, who liked to play milkmaid here.

Be advised that high-season tickets cover admission to the Grand and Petit Trianon, the Hameau de la Reine, Marie-Antoinette's dairy, the theatre, the English garden and so on; low-season tickets, which cost €6 for adults, only cover the Grand Trianon, Petit Trianon and gardens.

History and/or art buffs keen to delve deeper into life at court, music, Louis XV and Louis XVI's private apartments and so on can sign up for an informative lecture tour (☑01 30 83 78 00; adult with/without palace ticket €7.50/14.50, child €5.50; ☻9am-3.15pm Tue-Sun), some in English, at the main ticket office.

✕ Eating

Rue Satory is lined with restaurants serving cuisines from all over the world, including Indian, Chinese, Lebanese, Tunisian and Japanese. If you're headed for the outdoor Marché Notre Dame (place du Marché Notre Dame; ☻7.30am-2pm Tue, Fri & Sun) food market from the tourist office, enter via passage Saladin at 33 av de St-Cloud. There are also food halls (☻7am-1pm & 3.30-7.30pm Tue-Sat, 7.30am-1pm Sun) surrounding the marketplace. Monoprix (9 rue Georges Clemenceau; ☻8.30am-9.30pm Mon-Sat) department store, north of av de Paris, has a large supermarket section.

À la Ferme   SOUTHWEST FRENCH €€
(☑01 39 53 10 81; www.alaferme-versailles.com; 3 rue du Maréchal Joffre; menus €18 & €22.50; ☻Wed-Sun) Cowhide seats and rustic garlands strung from old wood beams add a country air to 'At the Farm', a temple to grilled meats and cuisine from southwest France.

Sister's Café   AMERICAN €€
(☑01 30 21 21 22; 15 rue des Réservoirs; menus €15.50-21) For a break with French tradi-

tion, try this relaxed 1950s-style American diner with club sandwiches, chicken fajitas, spinach salads and great weekend brunches. Mustard and ketchup are table standards.

Le Phare St-Louis   CRÊPERIE €
(☑01 39 53 40 12; 33 rue du Vieux Versailles; menus €11-18) This cosy Breton place heaves. Pick from 15 savoury galettes (buckwheat pancakes; €3.60 to €9) and 40-odd sweet crêpes (€3.60 to €7.50), including the Vieux Versailles (€5.50) topped with redcurrant jelly, pear and ice cream then set ablaze with Grand Marnier.

ⓘ Information

Office de Tourisme de Versailles (☑01 39 24 88 88; www.versailles-tourisme.com; 2bis av de Paris; ☻10am-6pm Mon, 9am-7pm Tue-Sun) Sells the Passeport to the château, as well as a detailed visitors guide (small €8.50, large €15) and a useful IGN walking map of the area (€10.50).

Post office (av de Paris)

ⓘ Getting There & Away

BUS RATP bus 171 (€1.60 or one metro/bus ticket, 35 minutes) links Pont de Sèvres metro station (15e) in Paris with the place d'Armes every six to nine minutes from between 5am and 6.30am to 1am.

CAR Visitors who are headed for Versailles *en voiture* (by car) should follow the A13 from Porte d'Auteuil and take the exit marked 'Versailles Château'.

TRAIN RER line C5 (€2.95) goes from Paris' Left Bank RER stations to Versailles-Rive Gauche station, 700m southeast of the château and close to the tourist office. Trains run every 15 minutes until shortly before midnight. Less convenient, RER line C8 links Paris with Versailles-Chantiers station, a 1.3km walk from the château.

SNCF operates up to 70 trains a day from Paris' Gare St-Lazare (€3.70) to Versailles-Rive Droite, 1.2km from the château. The last train to Paris leaves just after midnight. Versailles-Chantiers is served by half-hourly SNCF trains daily from Gare Montparnasse (€2.95); trains on this line continue to Chartres (€11.50, 30 to 60 minutes).

Fontainebleau

POP 21.800

The well-heeled town of Fontainebleau, 69km southeast of Paris, is renowned for its elegant Renaissance château, one of

France's largest royal residences. Bonus: it's much less crowded and pressured than Versailles. The town itself has a number of fine restaurants, swish cafés and cultural happenings, and is surrounded by the beautiful Forêt de Fontainebleau, a favourite hunting ground of many French kings and today rich in walking, cycling, rock-climbing and horse-riding opportunities.

⊙ Sights

Château de Fontainebleau PALACE
(☏01 60 71 50 70; www.musee-chateau-fontaine bleau.fr, in French; adult/child €8/free, admission free 1st Sun of month; ⊘9.30am-6pm Wed-Mon) The enormous, 1900-room Château de Fontainebleau, whose list of former tenants and their guests reads like a who's who of French royalty and aristocrats, is one of the most beautifully decorated and furnished châteaux in France. Every square centimetre of wall and ceiling space is richly adorned with wood panelling, gilded carv-

ings, frescos, tapestries and paintings. The parquet floors are of the finest woods, the fireplaces are ornamented with exceptional carvings, and many pieces of furniture date back to the Renaissance era.

The first château on this site was built in the early 12th century and enlarged by Louis IX a century later. Only a single medieval tower survived the energetic Renaissance-style reconstruction undertaken by François I (r 1515–47), whose superb artisans, many of them brought from Italy, blended Italian and French styles to create what is known as the First School of Fontainebleau. The *Mona Lisa* once hung here amid other fine works of art in the royal collection.

During the latter half of the 16th century, the château was further enlarged by Henri II (r 1547–59), Catherine de Médicis and Henri IV (r 1589–1610), whose Flemish and French artists created the Second School of Fontainebleau. Even Louis XIV got in on the act: it was he who hired landscape art-

Fontainebleau

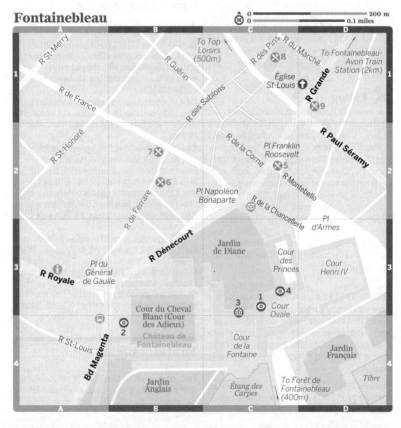

ist André Le Nôtre, celebrated for his work at Versailles, to redesign the gardens.

Fontainebleau, which was not damaged during the Revolution (though its furniture was stolen or destroyed), was beloved by Napoléon Bonaparte, who had a fair bit of restoration work carried out. Napoléon III was another frequent visitor. During WWII the château was turned into a German headquarters. After it was liberated by Allied forces under US General George Patton in 1944, part of the complex served as the Allied and then NATO headquarters from 1945 to 1965.

The Château

Visits take in the **Grands Appartements** (State Apartments), which contain several outstanding rooms. An informative 1½-hour audioguide (included in the price) leads visitors around the main areas.

The spectacular **Chapelle de la Trinité** (Trinity Chapel), whose ornamentation dates from the first half of the 17th century, is where Louis XV married Marie Leczinska in 1725 and where the future Napoléon III was christened in 1810. **Galerie François 1er**, a jewel of Renaissance architecture, was decorated from 1533 to 1540 by Il Rosso, a Florentine follower of Michelangelo. In the wood panelling, François I's monogram appears repeatedly along with his emblem, a dragon-like salamander. The **Musée Chinois de l'Impératice Eugénie** (Chinese Museum of Empress Eugénie) consists of four drawing rooms created in 1863 for the oriental art and curios collected by Napoléon III's wife.

The **Salle de Bal**, a 30m-long ballroom dating from the mid-16th century that was also used for receptions and banquets, is renowned for its mythological frescos, marquetry floor and Italian-inspired coffered ceiling. The large windows afford views of the Cour Ovale (Oval Courtyard) and the gardens. The gilded bed in the 17th- and 18th-century **Chambre de l'Impératrice** (Empress' Bedroom) was never used by Marie-Antoinette, for whom it was built in 1787. The gilding in the **Salle du Trône** (Throne Room), which was the royal bedroom before the Napoléonic period, is decorated in golds, greens and yellows.

Two 1¼-hour *guided tours* (adult/18-25yr €12.50/11) take visitors through the **Petits Appartements** (at 10.15am), the private rooms of the emperor and empress, and the **Musée Napoléon 1er** (2.30pm), which contains uniforms, hats, coats, ornamental swords and bric-a-brac that belonged to Napoléon and his relatives.

As successive monarchs added their own wings to the château, five irregularly shaped courtyards were created. The oldest and most interesting is the **Cour Ovale** (Oval Courtyard), no longer oval but U-shaped due to Henri IV's construction work. It incorporates the keep, the sole remnant of the medieval château. The largest courtyard is the **Cour du Cheval Blanc** (Courtyard of the White Horse), from where you enter the château. Napoléon, about to be exiled to Elba in 1814, bade farewell to his guards from the magnificent 17th-century **double-horseshoe staircase** here. For that reason the courtyard is also called the Cour des Adieux (Farewell Courtyard).

Château Gardens

The *gardens* (admission free; ☉9am-6pm) are quite extraordinary. On the northern side of the château is the **Jardin de Diane**, a formal garden created by Catherine de Médicis. Le Nôtre's formal, 17th-century **Jardin Français** (French Garden), also known as the Grand Parterre, is east of the **Cour de la Fontaine** (Fountain Courtyard) and the **Étang des Carpes** (Carp Pond). The informal **Jardin Anglais** (English Garden), laid out in 1812, is west of the pond. The **Grand Canal** was excavated in 1609 and predates the canals at Versailles by more than half a century. The **palace park** is open 24 hours.

Fontainebleau

✕ Eating

A plus for self-caterers is Fontainebleau's food market, *Marché République* (rue des Pins; ☉8am-2pm Tue, Fri & Sun), north of the central pedestrian area. The *Monoprix* (58 rue Grande; ☉8.45am-7.45pm Mon-Sat, 9am-1pm Sun) department store has a supermarket section on the 1st floor.

TOP CHOICE Côté Sud

SOUTHWEST FRENCH, PROVENÇAL €€

(☎01 64 22 00 33; 1 rue Montebello; menus €23-29) Our new favourite eatery in 'Bleau is this sunny restaurant with dishes that have a southern accent like *daube de sanglier* (wild boar stew) and *salade landoise* (an enormous salad of fresh and cooked vegetables, goose liver and *gésiers confits*, or preserved gizzards), offering one of the warmest welcomes in town. Bring your appetite.

Le Ferrare AUVERGNE €

(☎01 60 72 37 04; 23 rue de France; menus €11-12.50; ⏰7.30am-4pm Mon, to 10.30pm Tue-Thu, to 1am Fri & Sat) If you want to know where locals lunch, pile into this quintessential bar/brasserie with typical fare and a blackboard full of Auvergne specialities. The *plat du jour* (daily special) is a snip at €9.

La Rose de l'Orient MIDDLE EASTERN €

(☎06 08 88 36 49; 20 rue de Ferrare; dishes €4-7.50; ⏰10.30am-8pm Tue-Sat) This Lebanese eatery and *traiteur* (caterer) is the spot for a fast cheap lunch courtesy of two sisters, one of whom cooked for diplomats in Paris before launching her own business. Sit at one of five plastic tables inside or take away a picnic of meze (€1 to €3) and pita bread.

ℹ️ Information

Office de Tourisme de Pays de Fontainebleau (☎01 60 74 99 99; www.fontainebleau-tourisme.com; 4 rue Royale; ⏰10am-6pm Mon-Sat, 10am-1pm & 2-5.30pm Sun) The tourist office sells walking guides and maps, and hires out bicycles (per hour/half-day/full day €5/15/19).

Post office (2 rue de la Chancellerie)

ℹ️ Getting There & Around

Up to 40 daily SNCF commuter trains link Paris' Gare de Lyon hourly with Fontainebleau-Avon station (€8, 35 to 60 minutes); the last train back to Paris leaves Fontainebleau just before midnight daily.

Local bus line A links the train station with the château (€1.70), which is 2km southwest, every 10 minutes from 5.30am to 10.30pm (9.30pm Saturday, 11.30pm Sunday). The stop is opposite the main entrance.

Vaux-le-Vicomte

The privately owned Château de Vaux-le-Vicomte (☎01 64 14 41 90; www.vaux-le-vicomte.com; adult/child €14/11; ⏰10am-6pm Thu-Tue, closed early Nov–mid-Mar) and its magnificent **formal gardens**, 20km north of Fontaine-

bleau and 61km southeast of Paris, were designed and built by Le Brun, Le Vau and Le Nôtre between 1656 and 1661 as a precursor to their more ambitious work at Versailles.

TOP CHOICE Candlelight visits (adult/child €17/15) of the château, lasting four hours, take place at 8pm on Saturday from May to early October. During the same period there are elaborate **jeux d'eau** (fountain displays) in the gardens from 3pm to 6pm on the second and last Saturday of the month.

The beauty of Vaux-le-Vicomte turned out to be the undoing of its original owner, Nicolas Fouquet, Louis XIV's minister of finance. It seems that Louis, seething with jealousy that he had been upstaged at the château's official opening, had Fouquet thrown into prison, where the unfortunate *ministre* died in 1680.

Today visitors swoon over the château's beautifully furnished interior, including its fabulous dome. In the vaulted **cellars** an exhibition looks at Le Nôtre's landscaping of the formal gardens. A collection of 18th- and 19th-century carriages in the château stables forms the **Musée des Équipages** (Carriage Museum), entry to which is included in the château admission.

ℹ️ Getting There & Away

Vaux-le-Vicomte is not an easy place to reach by public transport. The château is 6km northeast of Melun, which is served by RER line D2 from Paris (€7.50, 45 minutes). The **Châteaubus shuttle** (€3.50 each way) links Melun station with the château four to six times daily at weekends from early April to early November; at other times you'll have to take a **taxi** (☎01 64 52 51 50; €15-20).

By car, follow the A6 from Paris and then the A5 (direction Melun), and take the 'St-Germain Laxis' exit. From Fontainebleau take the N6 and N36.

Chantilly

POP 11,350

The elegant old town of Chantilly, 50km north of Paris, is small, select and spoiled. Its château sits in a sea of greenery – parkland, gardens and the Forêt de Chantilly, which is packed with walking opportunities. Chantilly's racetrack is one of the most prestigious hat-and-frock addresses in Europe, and that deliciously sweetened thick *crème* called Chantilly was created here (see p148). Whatever you do, though, don't

FORÊT DE FONTAINEBLEAU

Beginning just 500m south of the château and surrounding the town, the 200-sq-km Forêt de Fontainebleau (Fontainebleau Forest) is one of the prettiest woods in the region. The many trails – including parts of the GR1 and GR11 – are excellent for jogging, walking, cycling and horse riding. The area is covered by IGN's 1:25,000-scale *Forêt de Fontainebleau* map (number 2417OT; €10.50). The tourist office sells the *Guide des Sentiers de Promenades dans le Massif Forestier de Fontainebleau* (€12), whose maps in French cover 19 forest walks, and *À Pied en Famille – Autour de Fontainebleau* (€8.50), which maps 18 family walks from 2.5km to 5km long. It also stocks a two-hour French-language DVD called *La Forêt de Fontainebleau* (€15).

Rock-climbing enthusiasts have long come to the forest's sandstone ridges, rich in cliffs and overhangs, to hone their skills before setting off for the Alps. There are different grades marked by colours, starting with white ones, which are suitable for children, and going up to death-defying black boulders.

A website called Bleau (http://bleau.info) has stacks of information in English on climbing in Fontainebleau. Two gorges worth visiting are the Gorges d'Apremont, 7km northwest near Barbizon, and the Gorges de Franchard, a few kilometres south of Gorges d'Apremont. If you want to give it a go, contact Top Loisirs (☑01 60 74 08 50; www.toploisirs.fr, in French; 16 rue Sylvain Collinet) about equipment hire and instruction. The tourist office also sells the comprehensive *Fontainebleau Climbs: The Finest Bouldering and Circuits* (€25).

come on Tuesday, when the imposing but heavily restored château is closed.

⊙ Sights

Château de Chantilly PALACE
(☑03 44 27 31 80; www.chateaudechantilly.com; adult/child €12/free; ⊙10am-6pm Wed-Mon) Left in a shambles after the Revolution, the Château de Chantilly is of interest mainly because of its superb paintings and gardens. The château consists of two attached buildings, the Petit and Grand Châteaux, which are entered through the same vestibule.

Containing the **Appartements des Princes** (Princes' Suites), the Petit Château was built around 1560 for Anne de Montmorency (1492–1567), who served six French kings as *connétable* (high constable), diplomat and warrior, and died doing battle with Protestants in the Counter-Reformation. The highlight here is the **Cabinet des Livres**, a repository of 700 manuscripts and more than 30,000 volumes, including a Gutenberg Bible and a facsimile of the *Très Riches Heures du Duc de Berry,* an illuminated manuscript dating from the 15th century that illustrates the calendar year for both the peasantry and the nobility. The **chapel**, to the left as you walk into the vestibule, has woodwork and stained-glass windows dating from the mid-16th century.

The attached Renaissance-style Grand Château, completely demolished during the Revolution, was rebuilt by the Duke of Aumale, son of King Louis-Philippe, from 1875 to 1885. It contains the **Musée Condé**, a series of unremarkable 19th-century rooms adorned with paintings and sculptures haphazardly arranged according to the whims of the duke – he donated the château to the Institut de France on the condition the exhibits were not reorganised and would remain open to the public. The most remarkable works, hidden in the **Sanctuaire** (Sanctuary), include paintings by Filippino Lippi, Jean Fouquet and Raphael, though the authenticity of the last is now disputed.

The château's excellent gardens (adult/child €5/free; ⊙10am-8pm Wed-Mon) were once among the most spectacular in France. The formal **Jardin Français** (French Garden), with flowerbeds, lakes and a Grand Canal all laid out by Le Nôtre in the mid-17th century, is northeast of the main building. To the west, the 'wilder' **Jardin Anglais** (English Garden) was begun in 1817. East of the Jardin Français is the rustic **Jardin Anglo-Chinois** (Anglo-Chinese Garden), created in the 1770s. Its foliage and silted-up waterways surround the **hameau**, a mock village dating from 1774, whose mill and half-timbered buildings inspired the

Hameau de la Reine at Versailles. *Crème Chantilly* was born here.

The château's **Grandes Écuries** (Grand Stables), built between 1719 and 1740 to house 240 horses and more than 400 hounds, stand apart from the château to the west and close to Chantilly's famous hippodrome (racecourse), inaugurated in 1834. Today the stables house the Musée Vivant du Cheval (Living Horse Museum; ✆03 44 27 31 80; www.museevivantducheval.fr; adult/child €10/8; ◷10am-5pm Wed-Mon), whose 30 pampered equines live in luxurious wooden stalls built by Louis-Henri de Bourbon, the seventh Prince de Condé, who was convinced he would be reincarnated as a horse (hence the extraordinary grandeur!). Displays include everything from riding equipment to rocking horses and portraits, drawings and sculptures of famous nags from the past.

Every visitor, big and small, will be mesmerised by the one-hour Chevaux en Fête Animation Équestre (Horses on Holiday Show; Pass Domaine adult/child €19/8, Pass Spectacle €28.50/15.50; ◷2.30pm Wed-Mon), a Chantilly must-do. Even more magical and highly sought-after are the handful of special **equestrian shows** performed in the stables year-round; tickets are like gold dust and can be reserved online. The Pass Domaine allows entry to the château and Grandes Écuries, including the Horses on Holiday Show, while the Pass Spectacle also includes one of the special shows.

Forêt de Chantilly   FOREST

South of the château is the 63-sq-km Forêt de Chantilly (Chantilly Forest), once a royal hunting estate and now crisscrossed by a variety of walking and riding trails. Long-distance trails here include the **GR11**, which links the château with the town of Senlis (p149) and its wonderful cathedral; the **GR1**, which goes from **Luzarches** (famed for its cathedral, parts of which date from the 12th century) to Ermenonville; and the **GR12**, which heads northeast from four lakes known as the Étangs de Commelles to the Forêt d'Halatte.

The area is covered by IGN's 1:25,000-scale *Forêts de Chantilly, d'Halatte and d'Ermenonville* map (number 2412OT; €10), available from the tourist office.

🍴 Eating

The large Simply Market (5 place Omer Vallon; ◷8.30am-8.30pm Mon-Fri, 8.30am-8pm Sat, 9am-12.45pm Sun) is midway between the train station and the château. Place Omer Vallon is also the location of the twice-weekly market (◷8.30am-12.30pm Wed & Sat).

TOP CHOICE Le Goutillon   BISTRO €€

(✆03 44 58 01 00; 61 rue du Connétable; menus €15-25) With its red-and-white checked tablecloths, simple wooden tables and classic bistro fare, Le Goutillon is a cosy, very friendly French affair much loved by local expats. It's as much wine bar as munch place.

La Capitainerie   TRADITIONAL FRENCH €€

(✆03 44 57 15 89; www.restaurantfp-chantilly.com; Château de Chantilly; lunch menus €15-31; ◷lunch Wed-Mon) Enviably nestled beneath the vaulted stone ceiling of the château kitchens, La Capitainerie captures history's grandeur and romance. Fare is traditional and includes *crème Chantilly* at every opportunity. Its weekend *formule buffet à volonté* (help-yourself buffet deal; €24) allows unlimited starters and a *plat du jour* or the latter plus unlimited desserts. The lot costs €31.

CHÂTEAU DE WHIPPED CREAM

Like every self-respecting French château three centuries ago, the palace at Chantilly had its own *hameau* (hamlet) complete with *laitier* (dairy), where the lady of the household and her guests could play at being milkmaids. But the cows at the Chantilly dairy took their job rather more seriously than their fellow bovines at other faux *crèmeries* (dairy shops), and the *crème Chantilly* (sweetened whipped cream) served at the hamlet's teas became the talk (and envy) of aristocratic 18th-century Europe. Indeed, even the future Habsburg emperor Joseph II paid a clandestine visit to this '*temple de marbre*' (marble temple), as he called it, to taste the white stuff in 1777. Chantilly (or more properly *crème Chantilly*) is whipped unpasteurised cream with a twist. It's beaten with icing and vanilla sugars to the consistency of a mousse and dolloped on berries. Sample it in any café or restaurant in town.

Le Vertugadin TRADITIONAL FRENCH €€
(☎03 44 57 03 19; www.restaurantlevertugadin.
fr; 44 rue du Connétable; menu €28; ☺lunch daily,
dinner Mon-Sat) Old-style and elegant, this
ode to regional cuisine – think meat, game
and terrines accompanied by sweet onion chutney – fills a white-shuttered town
house. A warming fire roars in the hearth
in winter, and summer welcomes diners to
its walled garden.

ℹ Information

Office de Tourisme de Chantilly (☎03 44
67 37 37; www.chantilly-tourisme.com; 60
av du Maréchal Joffre; ☺9.30am-12.30pm &
1.30-5.30pm Mon-Sat, 10am-1pm Sun) Ample
information on Chantilly, including accommodation lists and a trio of *promenades* leaflets
outlining walks through town, along Chantilly's
two canals and around the racecourse. It also
has information on walks and mountain-bike
trails in the forest.

ℹ Getting There & Away

The château is just over 2km northeast of the
train and bus stations; the most direct route
from there is to walk along av de la Plaine des
Aigles through a section of the Forêt de Chantilly. You will get a better sense of the town,
however, by following av du Maréchal Joffre and
rue de Paris, so you can connect with rue du
Connétable, Chantilly's principal thoroughfare.

Paris Gare du Nord links with Chantilly-
Gouvieux train station (€7.50, 25 to 40 minutes)
by SNCF commuter trains departing at least
hourly between 6.30am and 10.30pm.

If driving from Paris, the fastest way is via the
Autoroute du Nord (A1/E19); use exit 7 ('Survil-
liers-Chantilly'). The N1 then N16 from Porte de
la Chapelle/St-Denis is cheaper.

Senlis

POP 21,000

Just 10km northeast of Chantilly (53km
north of Paris), Senlis is an attractive medieval town of winding cobblestone streets,
Gallo-Roman ramparts and towers. It was a
royal seat from the time of Clovis in the 5th
and 6th centuries to Henri IV (r 1589–1610),
and contains four small but well-formed
museums (adult/child €2/free) devoted to
subjects as diverse as art and archaeology,
local history, hunting and the French cavalry in North Africa.

The real reason to come is to see the
Gothic Cathédrale de Notre Dame (place du
Parvis Notre Dame; admission free; ☺8am-6pm),

built between 1150 and 1191. The cathedral
is unusually bright, but the stained glass,
though original, is unexceptional. The magnificent carved-stone **Grand Portal** (1176),
on the western side facing place du Parvis
Notre Dame, has statues and a central relief
relating to the life of the Virgin Mary. It is
believed to have been the inspiration for the
portal at the cathedral in Chartres.

The Office de Tourisme de Senlis (☎03
44 53 06 40; www.senlis-tourisme.fr; place du
Parvis Notre Dame; ☺10am-12.30pm & 2-6.15pm
Mon-Sat, 10.30am-1pm & 2-6.15pm Sun) is just
opposite the cathedral.

Buses (€3.25, 25 minutes) link Senlis with
Chantilly's bus station, just next to its train
station, about every half-hour on weekdays
and hourly on Saturday, with about a half-
dozen departures on Sunday. The last bus
returns to Chantilly at 8pm on weekdays (at
7.30pm on Saturday and 7.15pm on Sunday).

Chartres

POP 45,600

The magnificent 13th-century cathedral at
Chartres, crowned by two very different
spires – one Gothic, the other Romanesque –
rises from rich farmland 91km southwest
of Paris and dominates the medieval town
around its base. The cathedral's varied
collection of relics, particularly the Sainte
Voile, attracted multitudes of pilgrims
during the Middle Ages, who contributed
to the building and extensions of the cathedral. With its astonishing blue stained
glass and other treasures, France's best-
preserved medieval basilica is a must-see
for any visitor.

◉ Sights

TOP CHOICE Cathédrale Notre Dame de
Chartres CATHEDRAL
(www.diocese-chartres.com, in French; place de la
Cathédrale; ☺8.30am-7.30pm, to 10pm Tue, Fri &
Sun) The 130m-long Cathédrale Notre Dame
de Chartres, one of the crowning architectural achievements of Western civilisation,
was built in the Gothic style during the first
quarter of the 13th century to replace a Romanesque cathedral that had been devastated by fire – along with much of the town –
in 1194. Because of effective fund-raising
and donated labour, construction took only
30 years, resulting in a high degree of architectural unity. It is France's best-preserved
medieval cathedral, having been spared

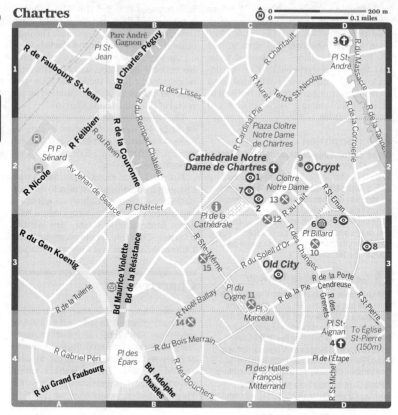

postmedieval modifications, the ravages of war and the Reign of Terror.

The cathedral's west, north and south entrances have superbly ornamented triple portals, but the west entrance, known as the **Portail Royal**, is the only one that predates the fire. Carved from 1145 to 1155, its superb statues, whose features are elongated in the Romanesque style, represent the glory of Christ in the centre, and the Nativity and the Ascension to the right and left, respectively. The structure's other main Romanesque feature is the 105m-high **Clocher Vieux** (Old Bell Tower; also called the Tour Sud or 'South Tower'), which was begun in the 1140s. It is the tallest Romanesque steeple still standing anywhere.

A visit to the 112m-high **Clocher Neuf** (New Bell Tower; adult/child €7/free; ⊗9.30am-12.30pm & 2-6pm Mon-Sat, 2-6pm Sun), also known as the Tour Nord (North Tower), is worth the ticket price and the climb up

the long spiral stairway (350 steps). Access is just behind the cathedral bookshop. A 70m-high platform on the lacy **Flamboyant Gothic spire**, built from 1507 to 1513 by Jehan de Beauce after an earlier wooden spire burned down, affords superb views of the three-tiered flying buttresses and the 19th-century copper roof, turned green by verdigris.

The cathedral's 172 extraordinary **stained-glass windows**, almost all of which date back to the 13th century, form one of the most important ensembles of medieval stained glass in the world. The three most exquisite windows, dating from the mid-12th century, are in the wall above the west entrance and below the rose window. Survivors of the fire of 1194 (they were made some four decades before), the windows are renowned for the depth and intensity of their blue tones, famously called 'Chartres blue'.

The cathedral's 110m crypt (adult/child €2.70/2.10; ⊗tours 11am Mon-Sat, daily 2.15pm, 3.30pm, 4.30pm & 5.15pm), a tombless Romanesque structure built in 1024 around a 9th-century predecessor, is the largest in France. Tours in French (with a written English translation) lasting 30 minutes start at La Crypte (⌨02 37 21 56 33; 18 Cloître Notre Dame), the cathedral-run shop selling souvenirs, from April to October. At other times they begin at the shop below the Clocher Neuf in the cathedral.

The shop also rents informative English-language audioguide tours (25/45/70min €3.20/4.20/6.20) – you'll need to leave your passport or other ID as a deposit. Guided tours in English (⌨02 37 28 15 58; millerchar tres@aol.com; €10; ⊗noon & 2.45pm Mon-Sat Apr-Oct) with the incomparable Malcolm Miller depart from the shop.

Old City
HISTORIC CENTRE

Chartres' meticulously preserved old city is northeast and east of the cathedral along the narrow western channel of the River Eure, which is spanned by a number of footbridges. From rue Cardinal Pie, the stairways called Tertre St-Nicolas and rue Chantault – the latter lined with medieval houses (number 29 is the oldest house in Chartres) – lead down to the empty shell of the 12th-century Collégiale St-André, a Romanesque collegiate church closed in 1791 and severely damaged in the early 19th century and again in 1944. It is now an exhibition centre.

Along the river's eastern bank, rue de la Tannerie and its extension rue de la Foulerie are lined with flower gardens, millraces and the restored remnants of riverside trades: wash houses, tanneries and the like.

Rue aux Juifs (Street of the Jews), on the west bank, has been extensively renovated. **Rue des Écuyers** has many structures dating from around the 16th century, including a half-timbered, prow-shaped house at number 26, with its upper section supported by beams. Escalier de la Reine Berthe (Queen Bertha's Staircase; 35 rue des Écuyers) is a towerlike covered stairwell clinging to a half-timbered house that dates back to the early 16th century.

There are some lovely **half-timbered houses** north of here on rue du Bourg and to the west on rue de la Poissonnerie; look for the magnificent 16th-century Maison du Saumon (Salmon House; 8-10 rue de la Poissonnerie; admission free), with its carved consoles of the eponymous salmon, the Archangel Gabriel, Mary, and Archangel Michael slaying the dragon. It now houses a branch of the tourist office and a multimedia exhibition on Chartres and its history.

From place St-Pierre you get a good view of the flying buttresses holding up the 12th- and 13th-century Église St-Pierre. Part of a Benedictine monastery in the 7th century, it was outside the city walls and vulnerable to attack; the fortresslike, pre-Romanesque **bell tower** attached to it was used as a refuge by monks and dates from around 1000. The fine, brightly coloured **clerestory windows** in the nave, the choir and the apse date from the early 14th century.

Église St-Aignan, first built in the early 16th century, is interesting for its wooden barrel-vault roof (1625), arcaded nave and painted interior of faded blue-and-gold floral motifs (c 1870). The stained glass and the Renaissance **Chapelle de St-Michel** date from the 16th and 17th centuries.

HOLY COVER-UP

The most venerated object in Chartres cathedral is the Sainte Voile, the 'Holy Veil' said to have been worn by the Virgin Mary when she gave birth to Jesus. It originally formed part of the imperial treasury of Constantinople but was offered to Charlemagne by the Empress Irene when the Holy Roman Emperor proposed marriage to her in 802. It has been in Chartres since 876, when Charles the Bald presented it to the town. The cathedral was built because the veil survived the 1194 fire; it is contained in a cathedral-shaped reliquary displayed in a side chapel at the end of the north aisle behind the choir. It doesn't look like much – a yellowish bolt of silk draped over a support – but as the focus of veneration for millions of the faithful for two millennia, it is priceless. But just how do they clean it?

Eating

There are a lot of food shops surrounding the covered market (place Billard; ☺7am-1pm Wed & Sat), just off rue des Changes south of the cathedral. The Monoprix (21 rue Noël Ballay & 10 rue du Bois Merrain; ☺9am-7.30pm Mon-Sat) department store with two entrances has a supermarket on the ground floor.

Le Bistro de la Cathédrale BISTRO €€
(☎02 37 36 59 60; 1 Cloître Notre Dame; menus €21-22; ☺Thu-Tue) Our favourite in the shadow of the cathedral, this stylish bistro/wine bar is the place for a long lazy lunch over a glass or three of wine. Tasty morsels to soak it up are chalked on the boards inside and out.

Punjab INDIAN €
(☎02 37 21 31 36; 13 rue Ste-Même; mains €4-9.50; ☑) If like us you need a fix of curry and/or biryani even in the midst of medieval Gothic splendour, head for this cheap and cheerful Pakistani eatery southwest of the cathedral. No alcohol is served and there is a decent selection of vegetarian selections.

Le Serpente BISTRO €€
(☎02 37 21 68 81; 2 Cloître Notre Dame; mains €16-21.50; ☺10am-11pm) Its location bangslap opposite the cathedral ensures that this atmospheric brasserie and *salon de thé* (tearoom) is always full. Cuisine is traditional, and its chef also constructs well-filled sandwiches (€3.90 to €6) and meal-sized salads (€12.50).

La Chocolaterie CAFÉ €
(☎02 37 21 86 92; 14 place du Cygne; ☺8am-7.30pm Tue-Sat, 10am-7.30pm Mon & Sun) Revel in local life at this bar-cum-chocolate-shop overlooking the open-air flower market in place du Cygne. Its coloured macaroons – flavoured with orange, apricot, pistachio, peanut, pineapple and so – are to die for, as are its sweet homemade crêpes, brownies and tiny madeleine sponge cakes.

Information

Office de Tourisme de Chartres (☎02 37 18 26 26; www.chartres-tourisme.com; place de la Cathédrale; ☺9am-7pm Mon-Sat, 9.30am-5.30pm Sun) The tourist office, across the square from the cathedral's main entrance, rents self-paced 1½-hour English-language audioguide tours of the medieval city (one/two people €5.50/8.50), as well as binoculars (€2), fabulous for seeing details of the cathedral up close. There's a branch office with an exhibition on Chartres' history in the historic **Maison du Saumon** (8-10 rue de la Poissonnerie; ☺9am-1pm & 2-6pm Mon-Fri, 10am-1pm & 4-6pm Sat)

Post office (3 bd Maurice Violette)

Getting There & Away

Some three dozen SNCF trains a day (20 on Sunday) link Paris' Gare Montparnasse (€13.50, 55 to 70 minutes) with Chartres, all of which pass through Versailles-Chantiers (€11.50, 45 minutes to one hour). The last train to Paris leaves Chartres just after 10.30pm Sunday to Friday and at 8.40pm on Saturday.

If you're driving from Paris, follow the A6 from Porte d'Orléans (direction Bordeaux–Nantes), then the A10 and A11 (direction Nantes). Take the 'Chartres' exit.

Lille, Flanders & the Somme

Includes »

Best Places to Eat

» À l'Huîtrière (p161)
» Chez la Vieille (p160)
» Le Tigzirt (p177)

Best Places to Stay

» L'Hermitage Gantois (p159)
» Grand Hôtel de l'Univers (p176)
» Maison St-Vaast (p179)

Why Go?

True, a tan is easier to come by along the Mediterranean, but when it comes to culture, cuisine, beer, shopping and dramatic views of land and sea – not to mention good old-fashioned friendliness – the Ch'tis (residents of France's northern tip) and their region compete with the best France has to offer. In Lille and French Flanders, the down-to-earth Flemish vibe mixes easily with French sophistication and savoir faire. And in the Somme, although WWI has been over for almost a century, the British, Canadians and Australians who perished in the trenches of the Western Front have not been forgotten. The moving memorials and cemeteries marking the front lines of 1916 remain places of pilgrimage and reflection.

If you snag a promotional fare on the Eurostar, Lille, Flanders and the Somme make for a superb short trip from London – with a much smaller carbon footprint than flying.

When to Go

Lille

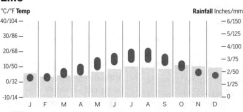

February and March Pre-Lenten carnivals bring out marching bands and costumed revellers.

1 July Remembrance ceremonies at Thiepval on the anniversary of the Battle of the Somme.

September (1st weekend) The world's largest flea market, the Braderie, takes over Lille.

Lille, Flanders & the Somme Highlights

1 Stroll around Lille's chic **old city** (p155) and sample the city's world-renowned **museums** (p157) and first-rate **restaurants** (p160)

2 Marvel at Amiens' breathtaking **Gothic cathedral** (p175) both inside and out

3 Ramble along the spectacular, windswept **Côte d'Opale** (p168), facing the white cliffs of Dover

4 Ponder the sacrifices and horror of WWI in **Vimy** (p187)

5 Reflect on a New York regiment's fallen at the **Somme American Cemetery** (p185)

6 Stroll around – and under – the **Flemish-style centre** (p178) of Arras

7 Watch clacking, Victorian-era machinery turn thread into lace at the new **Cité Internationale de la Dentelle et de la Mode** (p165) in Calais

8 Commune with sea creatures at **Nausicaä** (p169) in Boulogne-sur-Mer

History & Geography

In the Middle Ages, the Nord *département* (the sliver of France along the Belgian border; www.cdt-nord.fr), together with much of Belgium and part of the Netherlands, belonged to a feudal principality known as Flanders (Flandre or Flandres in French, Vlaanderen in Flemish), which has absolutely nothing to do with Homer Simpson's sanctimonious next-door neighbour Ned and everything to do with John McCrae's famous WWI poem 'In Flanders Fields'. Today, many people in the area still speak Flemish – essentially Dutch with some variation in pronunciation and vocabulary – and are very proud of their *flamand* culture and cuisine. Along with the neighbouring *département* of Pas-de-Calais (www.pas-de-calais.com), which runs inland from the Pas de Calais (Strait of Dover), the Nord forms the *région* of Nord-Pas de Calais (www.tourisme-nordpasdecalais.fr).

The area south of the Somme estuary and Albert forms the *région* of Picardy (Picardie; www.cr-picardie.fr), historically centred on the Somme *département* (www.somme-tourisme.com), which saw some of the bloodiest fighting of WWI. The popular British WWI love song 'Roses of Picardy' (www.firstworldwar.com/audio/rosesof picardy.htm) was penned here in 1916 by Frederick E Weatherley.

ⓘ Getting There & Away

Lille, Flanders and the Somme are a hop, skip and a jump from southwest England. By train on the **Eurostar** (www.eurostar.com; p973) pricey unless you've got a promotional fare (London–Lille starts at just UK£55 return) – Lille is just 70 minutes from London's St Pancras International train station. **Eurotunnel** (www.eurotunnel.com) can get you and your car from Folkestone to Calais, via the Channel Tunnel, in a mere 35 minutes (p972). For those with sturdy sea legs, car ferries (p973) link Dover with Calais, Boulogne-sur-Mer and Dunkirk. At present, the only sailings open to foot pas-

sengers are those run by P&O Ferries, during daylight hours, between Dover and Calais.

On the Continent, superfast Eurostar and TGV trains link Lille with Brussels (35 minutes), and TGVs make travel from Lille to Paris' Gare du Nord (one hour) and Charles de Gaulle Airport (one hour) a breeze. Compiègne is close enough to Paris to be visited on a day trip.

Lille

POP 232,000

Lille (Rijsel in Flemish) may be France's most underrated major city. In recent decades this once-grimy industrial metropolis, its economy based on declining industries, has transformed itself – with generous government help – into a glittering and self-confident cultural and commercial hub. Highlights for the visitor include an attractive old town with a strong Flemish accent, three renowned art museums, stylish shopping, some excellent dining options and a cutting-edge, student-driven nightlife scene. The Lillois have a well-deserved reputation for friendliness – and are so proud of being friendly that they often mention it!

Thanks to the Eurostar and the TGV, Lille makes an easy, environmentally sustainable weekend destination from London, Paris or Brussels.

History

Lille owes its name – once spelled L'Isle – to the fact that it was founded, back in the 11th century, on an island in the River Deûle. In 1667 the city was captured by French forces led personally by Louis XIV, who promptly set about fortifying his prize, creating the Lille Citadelle. In the 1850s the miserable conditions in which Lille's 'labouring classes' lived – the city was long the centre of France's textile industry – were exposed by Victor Hugo.

Lille has shown renewed vigour and self-confidence since the TGV came to town in 1993, followed a year later by the Eurostar from London.

◉ Sights & Activities

Exploring the City Centre   WALKING TOUR

The best place to begin a discovery stroll through the Flemish heart of the city centre is the **Vieille Bourse** (Old Stock Exchange; place du Général de Gaulle; Ⓜ Rihour), a Flemish Renaissance extravaganza ornately decorated with caryatids and cornucopia. Built in 1653, it consists of 24 separate houses set around a richly ornamented interior courtyard that hosts a **used-book market** (⊙1pm-7pm Tue-Sun); old postcards, comic books and CDs are also on sale. In the warm months locals often gather here to play *échecs* (chess).

Just west of the Vieille Bourse is **place du Général de Gaulle**, where you can admire the 1932 art deco home of **La Voix du Nord** (the leading regional newspaper), crowned by a gilded sculpture of the Three Graces. The goddess-topped **victory column** (1845) in the fountain commemorates

Lille

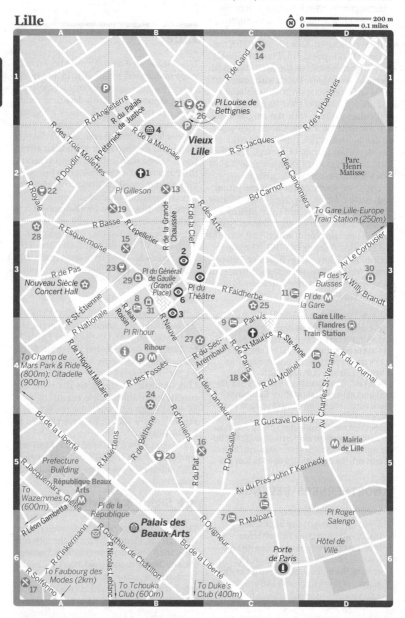

the city's successful resistance to the Austrian siege of 1792. On long, warm evenings in the spring and summer, Lillois come here by the thousands to stroll, take in the atmosphere and – somewhere nearby – stop for a strong local beer (p162).

Just east of the Vieille Bourse, impressive place du Théâtre is dominated by the

Louis XVI-style Opéra, its steps a favourite hang-out for young Lillois, and the neo-Flemish Chambre de Commerce, topped by a 76m-high spire that sports a gilded clock. Both were built in the early 20th century. Look east along rue Faidherbe and you can see Gare Lille-Flandres way at the other end.

Vieux Lille (Old Lille), justly proud of its restored 17th- and 18th-century brick houses, begins just north of here. Hard to believe, but in the late 1970s this quarter was a half-abandoned slum dominated by empty, dilapidated buildings, their windows breeze-blocked-up to keep out vandals and squatters. Head north along rue de la Grande Chaussée, lined with Lille's chic-est shops, and take a peek at À l'Huîtrière restaurant, an art deco masterpiece. Continue north along rue de la Monnaie (named after a mint constructed here in 1685), whose old brick residences now house boutiques and the Musée de l'Hospice Comtesse.

Turning left (west) on tiny rue Péter-inck and then left again will take you to the 19th-century, neo-Gothic Cathédrale Notre-Dame-de-la-Treille (⊙10am-12.30pm & 2-6pm or 6.30pm Mon-Sat, 10am-1pm & 3-6pm or 7pm Sun), which has a strikingly modern (some would say 'jarring') west facade (1999) that looks better from inside the nave, where you can admire some decent 19th-century stained glass and mosaics.

Lille

Palais des Beaux-Arts   ART MUSEUM
(www.pba-lille.fr; place de la République; adult €5.50; ⊙2-6pm Mon, 10am-6pm Wed-Sun; Ⓜ République Beaux Arts) Lille's world-renowned Fine Arts Museum displays a truly first-rate collection of 15th- to 20th-century paintings, including works by Rubens, Van Dyck and Manet. Exquisite porcelain and faience (pottery), much of it of local provenance, is on the ground floor, while in the basement you'll find classical archaeology, medieval statuary and 18th-century scale models of the fortified cities of northern France and Belgium. Tickets are valid for the whole day. Information sheets in French, English and Dutch are available in each hall.

Musée d'Art Moderne Lille-Métropole
    ART MUSEUM
(☎03 20 19 68 68; www.musee-lam.fr; 1 allée du Musée, Villeneuve-d'Ascq; adult €7, incl temporary exhibits €10; ⊙10am-6pm, closed Mon) Colourful, playful and just plain weird works of modern and contemporary art by masters such as Braque, Calder, Léger,

Miró, Modigliani and Picasso are the big draw at the renowned Museum of Modern Art, reopened in late 2010 after extensive renovations. A brand new wing features Art Brut (outsider art). Situated in the Lille suburb of Villeneuve-d'Ascq, in a sculpture park 9km east of Gare Lille-Europe. To get there, take metro line 1 to Pont de Bois and then bus 41 to Parc Urbain-Musée.

La Piscine Musée d'Art et d'Industrie

ART MUSEUM

(www.roubaix-lapiscine.com; 23 rue de l'Espérance, Roubaix; Ⓜ Gare Jean Lebas; adult €4.50; ◷ 11am-6pm Tue-Thu, 11am-8pm Fri, 1-6pm Sat & Sun) If Paris can turn a disused train station into a world-class museum (the Musée d'Orsay), why not take an art deco municipal swimming pool (built 1927–32) – an architectural masterpiece inspired by a combination of civic pride and hygienic high-mindedness – and transform it into a temple of the arts? This innovative museum, 12km northeast of Gare Lille-Europe, showcases fine arts, applied arts and sculpture in a delightfully watery environment.

Wazemmes

NEIGHBOURHOOD

(Ⓜ Gambetta) For an authentic taste of grass-roots Lille, head to the ethnically mixed, family-friendly *quartier populaire* (working-class quarter) of Wazemmes, 1.7km southwest of place du Général de Gaulle, where African immigrants and old-time proletarians live harmoniously alongside penurious students and trendy *bobos* (bourgeois bohemians).

The neighbourhood's focal point is the cavernous Marché de Wazemmes, Lille's favourite food market. The adjacent outdoor market (place de la Nouvelle Aventure; ◷ 7am-1.30pm or 2pm Tue, Thu & Sun) is *the* place to be on Sunday morning – it's a real carnival scene! Rue des Sarrazins and rue Jules Guesde are lined with shops, restaurants and Tunisian pastry places, many owned by, and catering to, the area's North African residents; they intersect in the southeastern corner of place de la Nouvelle Aventure, whose periphery is sprinkled with cafés.

Wazemmes is famed for its many outdoor concerts and street festivals, including **La Louche d'Or** (Golden Ladle; 1 May), a soup festival that has spread to cities across Europe.

Maison Natale de Charles de Gaulle

HOUSE MUSEUM

(www.maison-natale-de-gaulle.com; 9 rue Princesse; adult incl audioguide €6; ◷ 10am-1pm & 2-6pm Wed-Sat, 1.30-5.30pm Sun, last admission 1hr earlier) The upper-middle-class house in which Charles André Marie Joseph de Gaulle – WWII Resistance leader, architect of the Fifth Republic and ferocious defender of French interests – was born in 1890 is now a museum presenting the French leader in the context of his times, with an emphasis on his connection to French Flanders. Displays include de Gaulle's dainty baptismal robe and some evocative newsreels. The museum is 700m northwest of Musée de l'Hospice Comtesse along rue de la Monnaie and its northward continuation.

Musée de l'Hospice Comtesse ART MUSEUM

(32 rue de la Monnaie; adult €3.50; ◷ 10am-12.30pm & 2-6pm, closed Mon morning & Tue) Housed in a remarkably attractive 15th- and 17th-century poorhouse, the Hospice Comtesse Museum features ceramics, earthenware wall tiles, religious art and 17th- and 18th-century paintings and furniture. A rood screen separates the Salle des Malades (Hospital Hall) from a mid-17th century chapel (look up to see a mid-19th century painted ceiling).

Citadelle

FORTRESS

The greatest military architect of the 17th century, Sébastien le Prestre de Vauban (p944), designed this massive fortress, shaped like a five-pointed star, after the capture of Lille by France in 1667. Made of some 60 million bricks, it still functions as a French and NATO military base (for tour details see p159). It stands at the northeastern end of bd de la Liberté. Outside the 2.2km-long outer ramparts is the city centre's largest park.

LILLE CITY PASS

Available in one-/two-/three-day versions (€20/30/45), the **Lille Métropole** pass gets you into almost all the museums in greater Lille (www.destination-lille-metropole.eu) and affords unlimited use of public transport. The three-day version throws in sites in six cities in the Nord-Pas de Calais *région* and free use of regional TER trains. Available at the Lille tourist office.

BRADERIE DE LILLE

On the first weekend in September Lille's entire city centre – 200km of footpaths – is transformed into the Braderie de Lille, billed as the world's largest **flea market**. The extravaganza – with stands selling antiques, local delicacies, handicrafts and more – dates from the Middle Ages, when Lillois servants were permitted to hawk their employers' old garments for some extra cash.

The city's biggest annual event, the Braderie runs nonstop – yes, all night long – from 2pm on Saturday to 11pm on Sunday, when street sweepers emerge to tackle the mounds of mussel shells and old *frites* (French fries) left behind by the merrymakers. Before the festivities you can make room for all those extra calories by joining in the semi-marathon (www.semimarathon-lille.fr, in French) that begins at 9am on Saturday, or a 10km run at 11am; both set off from place de la République. Lille's tourist office can supply you with a free map of the festivities.

Children will love the amusement park, playground and small municipal zoo (admission free; ⏰10am- 6pm, closed mid-Dec–mid-Feb), all on the Citadelle's southeastern flank. Served by the Citadine shuttle bus.

🕝 Tours

The tourist office (☏08 91 56 20 04; www.lilletourism.com; place Rihour; ⏰9.30am-6.30pm Mon-Sat, 10am-noon & 2-5pm Sun & holidays; Ⓜ Rihour) runs various guided tours.

Citadelle GUIDED TOUR
(adult €7; ⏰3pm & 4pm Thu-Sun) This is the only way to see the inside of the Citadelle, usually a closed military zone. Sign up for the tour (in French) at least 24 hours ahead and bring a passport or national ID card.

Vieux Lille GUIDED TOUR
(adult €7; ⏰in English 10.15am Sat) Departs from the tourist office.

Battle of the Somme sites GUIDED TOUR
(half-day per person €44) Tailor-made itineraries with a private guide.

✵ Festivals & Events

The **Braderie**, a flea market extraordinaire, is held on the first weekend in September. Christmas decorations and edible goodies are sold at the Marché de Noël (Christmas market; place Rihour; ⏰late Nov-30 Dec). The varied art exhibitions associated with Lille 3000 (www.lille3000.com) 'explore the richness and complexities of the world of tomorrow'.

🛏 Sleeping

Many Lille hotels are at their fullest, and priciest, from Monday to Thursday. Several hotels face Gare Lille-Flandres.

TOP CHOICE **L'Hermitage Gantois**
DESIGN HOTEL **€€€**
(☏03 20 85 30 30; www.hotelhermitagegantois.com; 224 rue de Paris; d €215-325, ste €455; @🛜; Ⓜ Mairie de Lille) This luxury hotel creates enchanting, harmonious spaces by complimenting its rich architectural heritage – such as a Flemish-Gothic facade – with refined ultramodernism. We love the highly civilised atrium, and the 67 rooms are huge and sumptuous, with Starck accessories next to Louis XV-style chairs and bathrooms that sparkle with Carrara marble. One of the four courtyards is home to a 220-year-old wisteria that's been declared a historic monument. The still-consecrated chapel was built in 1637.

Grand Hôtel Bellevue HISTORIC HOTEL **€€**
(☏03 20 57 45 64; www.grandhotelbellevue.com; 5 rue Jean Roisin; d €145-175; ❄🛜; Ⓜ Rihour) Grandly built in the early 20th century, this Best Western–affiliated establishment has a charmingly creaky belle époque lift that trundles guests up to 60 spacious rooms equipped with marble bathrooms, gilded picture frames and flat-screen TVs. Rooms with views of place du Général de Gaulle start at €160. In 1765 the young Mozart stayed on this site (in an earlier building).

Hôtel Brueghel HOTEL **€€**
(☏03 20 06 06 69; www.hotel-brueghel.com; 5 parvis St-Maurice; d Mon-Thu €89, Fri-Sun €79; 🛜; Ⓜ Gare Lille-Flandres) The 65 rooms here mix vaguely antique furnishings with modern styling (eg the bathrooms), though they don't have nearly as much Flemish charm as the lobby. The tiny wood-and-wrought-iron lift and its shiny brass buttons date from the 1930s. Some south-facing rooms have sunny views of the adjacent church.

Hôtel du Moulin d'Or
HOTEL €€

(☎03 20 06 12 67; www.hotelmoulindor.com, in French; 15 rue du Molinel; d/tr Mon-Thu €87/98, Fri-Sun €61/71; ✳; ☎ⓂGare Lille-Flandres) Rich yellow and blue tones welcome you warmly to this family-run establishment. The 14 rooms – some flowery, others striped – come with bright colours, soundproofing and showers separate from the toilets. The cute little breakfast room feels like a B&B. No lift.

Hôtel Flandre-Angleterre
HOTEL €€

(☎03 20 06 04 12; www.hotel-flandreangleterre -lille.com; 13 place de la Gare; s/d Mon-Thu from €66/80, Fri-Sun from €60/69, q €95; ☎; ⓂGare Lille-Flandres) Forty-four comfortable, clean and quiet rooms, many with red or blue carpeting, await at this practical establishment. The best rooms have views of the bustling Lille-Flanders train station. Lift-equipped.

Auberge de Jeunesse
HOSTEL €

(☎03 20 57 08 94; www.hihostels.com; 12 rue Malpart; dm incl breakfast €18, d €37; ☺closed 23 Dec-late Jan; @☎; ⓂMairie de Lille) This central but Spartan former maternity hospital has 163 beds in rooms for two to eight, kitchen facilities and free car and bicycle parking. Toilets and showers are down the hall for most rooms; a few doubles have en-suite showers. The building is locked from 11am to 3pm (until 4pm from Friday to Sunday).

✖ Eating

Lille (especially Vieux Lille) has a flourishing culinary scene, with great new places opening up all the time. Keep an eye out for *estaminets* (traditional Flemish eateries, with antique knick-knacks on the walls and plain wooden tables) serving Flemish specialities such as *carbonade* (braised beef stewed with Flemish beer, spice bread and brown sugar) and *potjevleesch* (jellied chicken, pork, veal and rabbit).

Dining hot spots in Vieux Lille include: **rue de Gand** (northeast of Café Oz) – home to a dozen small, moderately-priced French and Flemish restaurants; **rue de la Monnaie** and its side streets (around Musée de l'Hospice Comtesse) – a good place to look for quirky, moderately priced restaurants; and **rue Royale** (just northwest of L'Illustration Café) – *the* place to come for ethnic cuisine (couscous, Japanese etc).

There are heaps of cheap eats along lively, student-dominated **rue Solférino** and **rue Masséna**, about 600m west of the Palais des Beaux-Arts. Good-value *restaurants populaires* can be found in Wazemmes.

Chez la Vieille
ESTAMINET €

(☎03 28 36 40 06; 60 rue de Gand; mains €9.50-12; ☺closed Sun & Mon) One of the best places in Lille to tuck into Flemish specialities. Old-time prints, antiques and fresh hops hanging from the rafters create the ambi-

---

THE GIANTS

In far northern France and nearby Belgium, *géants* (giants) – wickerwork body masks up to 8.5m tall animated by someone (or several someones) inside – emerge for local carnivals and on feast days to dance and add to the general merriment. Each has a name and a personality, usually based on the Bible, legends or local history. Giants are born, baptised, grow up, marry and have children, creating, over the years, complicated family relationships. They serve as important symbols of town, neighbourhood and village identity. For snapshots check out http://utan.lille.free.fr/geants_1.htm.

Medieval in origin – and also found in places such as the UK (www.giants.org.uk), Catalonia, the Austrian Tyrol, Mexico, Brazil and India – giants have been a tradition in northern France since the 16th century. More than 300 of the creatures, also known as *reuze* (in Flemish) and *gayants* (in Picard), now 'live' in French towns, including Arras, Boulogne, Calais, Cassel, Dunkirk and Lille. Local associations cater to their every need, while transnational groups such as the International Circle of Friends of the Giant Puppets (www.ciag.org) promote the creatures worldwide. France and Belgium's giants were recognised by Unesco as 'masterpieces of the oral and intangible heritage of humanity' in 2005.

Giants make appearances year-round but your best chance to see them is at pre-Lenten carnivals, during Easter and at festivals held from May to September, often on weekends. Dates and places – as well as the latest marriage and birth announcements – appear in the free, annual, French-language brochure *Le Calendrier des Géants*, available at tourist offices and online at www.geants-carnaval.org, in French.

ence of a Flemish village circa 1900. The vibe is informal but it's a good idea to call ahead.

À l'Huîtrière SEAFOOD €€
(☑03 20 55 43 41; www.huitriere.fr, in French; 3 rue des Chats Bossus; Mon-Sat lunch menus €45, other menus €120; ⊙closed dinner Sun & late Jul-late Aug) In 1928 the great-grandfather of the present owners turned to the nascent art deco movement – first exhibited (and named) in Paris just three years earlier – to find suitably elegant decoration for his fish shop on 'Street of the Hunchback Cats'. The sea-themed mosaics and stained glass are worth a look-in even if you're not in the mood to dine on super-fresh seafood – accompanied, perhaps, by a wine or two from the 40,000-bottle cellar. Book ahead for Friday dinner and Saturday.

La Source ORGANIC, VEGETARIAN €
(☑03 20 57 53 07; www.denislasource.com, in French; 13 rue du Plat; menus €9.50-16; ⊙11.30am-2pm Mon-Sat, 7-9pm Fri; ☑; MRépublique Beaux Arts) This Lille institution, founded way back in 1979, serves delicious vegetarian, fowl and fish *plats du jour*, each accompanied by five hot veggie side dishes. The light, airy ambience and the diners exude health, well-being and cheer.

Tous Les Jours Dimanche CAFÉ €
(☑03 28 36 05 92; 13 rue Masurel; menus €13.50-16; ⊙restaurant noon-2.30pm, salon de thé 2.30-6.30pm, closed Mon, also closed Sun May-Sep) Having tea or a light lunch here, surrounded by a motley assemblage of antique furniture and well-chosen objets d'art, is like hanging out in an arty friend's living room. Specialities include salads, sandwiches (€10) and quiche-like *tartes* (€10). On Sunday from October to April, you can have a *brunch anglais* (English brunch; €21) starting at 11.30am.

Self-Catering

TOP CHOICE **Marché de Wazemmes** FOOD MARKET€
(place de la Nouvelle Aventure; ⊙8am-2pm Tue-Thu, 8am-8pm Fri & Sat, 8am-3pm Sun & holidays; MGambetta) Lille's most beloved foodie space, situated 1.7km southwest of the tourist office in Wazemmes.

Marché Sébastopol FOOD MARKET €
(place Sébastopol; ⊙7am-2pm Wed & Sat; MRépublique Beaux Arts)

Fromagerie Philippe Olivier CHEESE SHOP €
(3 rue du Curé St-Étienne; ⊙9.30am-7.15pm Tue-Sat, 2.30-7.15pm Mon; MRihour)

Monoprix SUPERMARKET €
(112 rue de Paris; ⊙9am-10pm) Picnic supplies in the city centre.

Carrefour SUPERMARKET €
(Euralille shopping mall; ⊙9am-10pm Mon-Sat; MGare Lille-Europe) Vast, with no fewer than 62 checkout counters! Stocks more than two dozen different beers brewed right here in French Flanders.

Drinking
Lille has several drinking and nightlife areas. In Vieux Lille the small, stylish bars and cafés along streets such as rue Royale, rue de la Barre and rue de Gand are a big hit with chic 30-somethings. Especially on Friday and Saturday nights, in the rue Masséna student zone (MRépublique Beaux Arts) a university-age crowd descends on dozens of high-decibel bars along rue Masséna (750m southwest of the tourist office) and almost-perpendicular rue Solférino (as far southeast as Marché Sébastopol). London-style excess is not unknown here.

A number of edgy (and undercapitalised) cafés are tucked away around the periphery of place de la Nouvelle Aventure in Wazemmes (MGambetta), site of the Wazemmes food market.

In the warm season, sidewalk cafés make the square in front of the Opéra, the place du Théâtre (MRihour), a fine spot to sip beer and soak up the Flemish atmosphere.

TOP CHOICE **Meert** TEAROOM
(pronounced mehr; www.meert.fr; 27 rue Esquermoise; waffles €2.30; ⊙9.30am-7.30pm Tue-Fri, 9am-7.30pm Sat, 9am-1pm & 3-7pm Sun; MRihour) *Gaufres* (waffles) made in a hinged iron griddle with Madagascar vanilla are the speciality at this luxury tearoom-cum-pastry-and-sweets-shop, which has served kings, viceroys and generals (including Charles de Gaulle, a life-long fan) since 1761. Next door, Meert's chocolate shop (per kg €89) has a wrought-iron balcony, coffered ceiling and painted wood panels that will transport you back to 1839.

Café Le Relax CAFÉ
(48 place de la Nouvelle Aventure, Wazemmes; espresso €1.30, beer €2.20; ⊙7.30am or 8am-midnight Sun-Thu, to 1am Fri, to 2am Sat; MGambetta) Wazemmes denizens young and old drop by this ungentrified *café de quartier* (neighbourhood café) for an espresso or a strong Belgian beer – and to run into friends. A great place to get a feel for this

ethnically mixed, working-class part of town. Feel free to buy edibles at the nearby Wazemmes market and eat them here with a beer. Local groups perform live from about 9pm to midnight on Friday and Saturday and 7.30pm to 10.30pm on Sunday.

Café Citoyen   CAFÉ
(http://cafecitoyen.org, in French; 7 place du Vieux Marché aux Chevaux; coffee €1.50, glass of wine €3.30; ◎noon-midnight Mon-Fri, 2-8pm Sat; @⊛✐; MRépublique Beaux Arts) A friendly, informal bar, run as a cooperative, with a social, ideological and environmental mission. Internet access is free if you order an organic microbrewed beer (€2.90), a glass of wine or a cup of fair-trade coffee from the friendly fellow in the Trotsky-style glasses. Also serves light meals (salads, soup, sandwiches), including vegetarian and vegan options; all products are organic and most are sourced directly from local producers.

L'Illustration Café   BAR-CAFÉ
(www.bar-lillustration.com, in French; 18 rue Royale; ◎12.30pm-3am Mon-Fri, 2pm-3am Sat, 3pm-3am Sun) Adorned with art nouveau woodwork and changing exhibits by local painters, this laid-back bar attracts artists, musicians, budding intellectuals and teachers in the mood to read, exchange weighty ideas – or just shoot the breeze. The sound track is mellow, ranging from Western classical to jazz, French chansons and African. Very French in the best sense of the word.

Café Oz   PUB
(33 place Louise de Bettignies; ◎4pm-3am Mon-Fri, noon-3am Sat & Sun) Footy and rugby on a wide screen, Australiana on the walls

---

DON'T MISS

NORTHERN BREWS

French Flanders brews some truly excellent *bière blonde* (lager) and *bière ambrée* (amber beer) with an alcohol content of up to 8.5%. While in the area, beer lovers should be sure to try some of these brands, which give the Belgian brewers a run for their money: 3 Monts, Amadeus, Ambre des Flandres, Brasserie des 2 Caps, Ch'ti, Enfants de Gayant, Grain d'Orge, Hellemus, Jenlain, L'Angellus, La Wambrechies, Moulins d'Ascq, Raoul, Septante 5, St-Landelin, Triple Secret des Moines and Vieux Lille.

---

and cold bottles of Toohey's Extra Dry – what more could you ask for? Popular with English-speakers, including students, this place is packed when DJs do their thing from 9pm to 3am on Thursday, Friday and Saturday nights. Opens at noon daily in nice weather and has a great warm-season terrace. Happy hour 6pm to 9pm Monday to Saturday.

☆ Entertainment

Lille's free French-language entertainment guide, *Sortir* (www.lille.sortir.eu, in French), comes out each Wednesday and is available at the tourist office, cinemas, event venues and bookshops.

Tickets for Lille's rich cultural offerings can be bought at the **Fnac Billetterie** (www.fnacspectacles.com, in French; 16 rue du Sec-Arembault; ◎10am-7.30pm Mon-Sat; MRihour). Events details are posted by category on the walls and on flat screens.

Cinemas

Cinéma Majestic   CINEMA
(✆08 36 68 00 73; www.cinemaslumieres.com, in French; 56 rue de Béthune; MRihour) Non-dubbed films on six screens.

Cinéma Métropole   CINEMA
(✆08 36 68 00 73; www.cinemaslumieres.com, in French; 26 rue des Ponts de Comines; MGare Lille-Flandres) An art-house cinema with nondubbed films on four screens.

Gay & Lesbian

Tchouka Club   GAY DISCO
(80 rue Barthélemy Delespaul; admission free, beer €4, Champagne €10; ◎11pm-7am Fri, Sat & holiday eves) A till-dawn gay and lesbian disco that's got Lille's clubbing classes chattering. Has photo-montage wall murals, plenty of flashing lights, buff barmen in tank tops and a soundtrack that's heavy on electro, house and techno. So packed after 1am that you may have trouble getting in. Relaxed dress code. Has a Facebook page. Situated 700m due south of the Palais des Beaux-Arts.

Vice & Versa   GAY BAR
(3 rue de la Barre; ◎3pm-3am Mon-Sat, 4pm-3am Sun) The rainbow flies proudly at this well-heeled, sophisticated bar, which is as gay as it is popular (and it's very popular). Decor includes brick walls, a camp crystal chandelier and lots of red and green laser dots. Has 80s-themed nights from 10pm every Tuesday, a house-and-electro DJ from 10pm

on Friday and Saturday, and a *soirée* from 9pm on Sunday.

Coming Out
GAY BAR

(www.comingout-lille.eu, in French; 11 rue de Gand; ☺5pm-midnight, until 1am Fri & 2am Sat) Popular with thirty-somethings, this relaxed bolthole welcomes punters – most of them gay and lesbian – with dancing laser dots, three Belgian beers on tap (€2.90) and a lounge area with coffee tables and low stools. The eclectic soundtrack ranges from French chansons and 80s to techno, trending to house and dance on Friday and Saturday. A good source of information on the local gay scene.

Nightclubs

Although you no longer have to cross the Belgian frontier (eg to Gand) to dance past 4am, some locals still do because, they say, the techno is edgier, the prices lower, substances more available and the closing time even later (1pm!).

TOP CHOICE Network Café
DISCO

(www.network-cafe.net, in French; 15 rue du Faisan; admission free, beer €4; ☺10.30pm-5.30am Tue & Wed, 9.30pm-5.30am Thu, 10.30pm-7am Fri & Sat, 7pm-5am Sun; MRépublique Beaux Arts) At Lille's hottest discotheque, you can sip beer and boogie in the main hall, presided over by two 5m-high statues from faraway lands, or in the baroque Venetian room, decked out with velvet settees and crystal chandeliers. A magnet for guest DJs, Network is hugely popular with students (especially on Tuesday and Wednesday) and the 20-to-40 crowd. On Sunday salsa/R & B dominate before/after midnight. From 9.30pm to 11.30pm on Thursday you can learn the proper way to dance to rock music (€5). The door policy is pretty strict – locals dress up – but tends to be a bit more relaxed for tourists. Situated 600m northwest of the Palais des Beaux-Arts.

Duke's Club
DISCO

(www.dukesclub.fr, in French; 6-8 rue Gosselin; admission free, coat check €1.50, beer €5; ☺9pm-dawn Wed-Sat) A traditional disco with three bars and three dance spaces on three levels (used simultaneously only on Saturday night), theme nights (see the website), and black light that makes white shirts glow a radioactive purple. Most of the bouncing bods in the 30-to-50 age range. To learn the 'correct' way to dance to rock music, drop by from 9.30pm to 11pm on Friday for a pro-

fessional lesson (€6, including two drinks). Situated 600m southeast of the Palais des Beaux-Arts.

Shopping

Lille's snazziest clothing and housewares boutiques are in Vieux Lille, in the area bounded by rue de la Monnaie, rue Esquermoise, rue de la Grande Chausée (a window shopper's paradise!) and rue d'Angleterre. Keep an eye out for shops (eg at 23 rue Masurel) specialising in French Flemish edibles, including cheeses. For mid-range prices, locals often head to the hugely popular pedestrians-only zone south of place du Général de Gaulle (all near Rihour metro), including rue Neuve, rue de Béthune, rue des Tanneurs and rue du Sec-Arembault.

TOP CHOICE Maisons de Mode
FASHION

(www.maisonsdemode.com) Cool, cutting-edge couture by promising young designers can be found in two clusters of studio-boutiques, **Faubourg des Modes** (Nos 31, 51 & 58-60 rue du Faubourg des Postes, Lille Sud; MPorte des Postes), about 2.5km southwest of the Palais des Beaux-Arts, and around **La Piscine Musée d'Art et d'Industrie** (rue de l'Espérance & av Jean Lebas, Roubaix; MGare Jean Lebas), 12km northeast of Gare Lille-Europe.

Le Furet du Nord
BOOKSHOP

(15 place du Général de Gaulle; MRihour) One of Europe's largest bookshops. Has a good selection of English-language books, including LP guides and titles on Flanders and France.

Alice Délice
KITCHEN SUPPLIES

(5 Rue Esquermoise; MRihour) Almost every utensil and gadget a French kitchen might need – great for gifts!

Euralille
SHOPPING MALL

(www.euralille.com, in French; cnr av Le Corbusier & av Willy Brandt; ☺10am-8pm Mon-Sat; MGare Lille-Flandres or Gare Lille-Europe) A vast shopping mall with 120 popularly priced shops.

Information

Commercial banks (along rue National; MRihour)

Hobby Max (9 rue Maertens; per hr €3; ☺9am-9pm; MRépublique Beaux Arts) Internet access on 16 machines.

Hôpital Roger Salengro (☎03 20 44 61 40/41; rue du Professeur Émile Laine; ☺24hr; MCHR B Calmette) The *accueil urgences* (emergency room/casualty ward) of Lille's vast, 15-hospital Cité Hospitalière is 4km southwest of the city centre.

International Currency Exchange (☺7.30am-8pm Mon-Sat, 10am-8pm Sun; Ⓜ Gare Lille-Europe) Currency exchange in Gare Lille-Europe, next to *accès* (track access) H.

Net Arena (10 rue des Bouchers; per hr €3; ☺10am-10pm Mon-Sat, 2-8pm Sun) Internet access on about 30 computers. Situated half a block south of the bar Vice & Versa.

SOS Médecins (🗐03 20 29 91 91; 3 av Louise Michel; ☺24hr; Ⓜ Porte de Douai) Round-the-clock medical clinic (call ahead from 11pm to 9am) and house calls by doctors.

Tourist office (🗐from abroad 03 59 57 94 00, in France 08 91 56 20 04; www.lilletourism. com; place Rihour; ☺9.30am-6.30pm Mon-Sat, 10am-noon & 2-5pm Sun & holidays; Ⓜ Rihour) Occupies what's left of the Flamboyant Gothic-style Palais Rihour, built in the mid-1400s for Philip the Good, Duke of Burgundy; a war memorial forms the structure's eastern side. Has free maps and an excellent map-brochure (€2) outlining walking tours of five city *quartiers*. Can exchange small amounts of foreign currency but the rate is poor.

Travelex exchange bureau (☺8am-6.30pm Mon-Fri, 10am-5pm Sat, 10am-4pm Sun & holidays; Ⓜ Gare Lille-Flandres) Currency exchange in Gare Lille-Flandres, next to ticket counter N.

❶ Getting There & Away
Bus

Eurolines (🗐08 92 89 90 91; www.eurolines.fr; 23 parvis St-Maurice; ☺9.30am-6pm Mon-Fri, 10am-1pm & 2-6pm Sat; Ⓜ Gare Lille-Flandres) serves cities such as Brussels (€17, 1½ hours), Amsterdam (€42, five hours) and London (€35, 5½ hours; by day via the Channel Tunnel, at night by ferry). Buses depart from bd de Leeds, to the left as you arrive at Gare Lille-Europe from the city centre (look for the 'Eurolines' sign behind the taxi rank).

Car

Driving into Lille is incredibly confusing, even with a good map. To get to the city centre, the best thing to do is to suspend your sense of direction and blindly follow the 'Centre Ville' signs.

Parking at the **Champ de Mars** (bd de la Liberté), a P+R (park-and-ride) car park 1.2km northwest of the tourist office (next to the Citadelle), costs €3.20 a day, including return travel (for up to five people) to central Lille on the Citadine bus line (just show the driver the card issued at the entrance barrier). If you arrive between 8pm and 7am or on a Sunday or holiday, parking is free – but you don't get a free bus ticket into the centre.

Parking is free along some of the streets southwest of rue Solférino and up around the Maison Natale de Charles de Gaulle.

Avis, **Europcar**, **Hertz** and **National-Citer** have car-hire offices in Gare Lille-Europe. Domestic rental companies:

DLM (🗐03 20 06 18 80; www.dlm.fr, in French; 32 place de la Gare; Ⓜ Gare Lille-Flandres)

Locauto (🗐03 20 57 02 25; www.locauto.fr; 2 rue Gustave Delory; Ⓜ Mairie de Lille)

Rent-a-Car Système (🗐03 20 40 20 20; www.rentacar.fr, in French; 113 rue du Molinel; Ⓜ Rihour)

Train

Lille's two main train stations, old-fashioned Gare Lille-Flandres and ultramodern Gare Lille-Europe, are 400m apart on the eastern edge of the city centre. They are one stop apart on metro line 2 (in the Gare Lille-Europe metro station, look for the fabulous mural). Lille has been linked to Paris by rail since 1846.

For details on getting to/from Amiens, Arras, Boulogne, Calais and Dunkirk, see those sections.

Gare Lille-Flandres (Ⓜ Gare Lille-Flandres) Used by almost all intra-regional services and almost all TGVs to Paris' Gare du Nord (€40 to €55, one hour, 14 to 18 daily).

Gare Lille-Europe (Ⓜ Gare Lille-Europe) Topped by what looks like a 20-storey ski boot, this ultramodern station handles province-to-province TGVs, including services to Charles de Gaulle Airport (€40 to €55, one hour, at least hourly), Nice (€117 to €138, 7½ hours, two direct daily) and Strasbourg (€84 to €106, 3¼ to four hours, three direct daily); Eurostar trains (p973) to London (departures are from the station's far northern end); TGVs/Eurostars to Brussels-Nord (Monday to Friday €26, weekend & holidays €18, 35 minutes, a dozen daily).

❶ Getting Around
Bicycle & Segway

Station Oxygène (🗐03 20 81 44 02; team-segway@transpole.fr; Segway per 30 minutes/half-/full day €4/15/20, with bus ticket stamped within the hour €3.50/12/18, electric bicycle €1.50/7/10) Cruising around Lille by Segway – it's so noughties but still really cool! First-time riders (minimum age 18; if accompanied by an adult, 16) must take an intro lesson (€4) to get a Segway licence (we're not kidding). Credit card deposit of €500 required. Run by Transpole (the public transport company), which has two rental locations:

Champ de Mars (bd de la Liberté; ☺10am-6pm or 7pm, closed Sat & Sun Sep or Oct-Mar) A shiny glass structure that resembles a hovering flying saucer, next to the Citadelle.

Transpole information office (Gare Lille-Flandres; ☉7.30am-6.30pm Mon-Fri; Ⓜ Gare Lille-Flandres) On the track level at the station's place des Buisses exit.

Bus, Tram & Metro

Lille's two speedy metro lines (1 and 2), two tramways (R and T), two Citadine shuttles (C1, which circles the city centre in a clockwise direction, and C2, which goes the other way) and many urban and suburban bus lines – several of which cross into Belgium – are run by **Transpole** (☑08 20 42 40 40; www.transpole.fr). In the city centre, metros run every two to four minutes until about 12.30am. Useful metro stops include those at the train stations, Rihour (next to the tourist office), République Beaux Arts (near the Palais des Beaux-Arts), Gambetta (near the Wazemmes food market) and Gare Jean Lebas (near La Piscine). In this chapter, places with a metro stop within 500m have the name of the stop noted next to the street address.

Tickets (€1.30; valid for transfers for up to one hour) are sold on buses but must be purchased (and validated in the orange posts) *before* boarding a metro or tram. A pack *(carnet)* of 10 tickets costs €10.60. A Pass' Journée (all-day pass) costs €3.60 and needs to be time-stamped just once. A Pass Soirée, good for unlimited travel after 7pm, costs €1.60.

Taxi

Taxi Gare Lille (☑03 20 06 64 00; ☉24hr)
Taxi Rihour (☑03 20 55 20 56; ☉24hr)

Calais

POP 76,200

As Churchill might have put it, 'never in the field of human tourism have so many travellers passed through a place and so few stopped to visit'. There would seem to be few compelling reasons for the 15 million people who travel by way of Calais each year to stop and explore – pity the local tourist office, whose job it is to snag a few of the Britons racing south to warmer climes – but in fact the town *is* worth at least a brief stopover.

The city, a mere 34km from the English town of Dover (Douvres in French), makes a convenient base for exploring the majestic Côte d'Opale by car or public transport.

◉ Sights & Activities

TOP
CHOICE **Cité Internationale de la Dentelle et de la Mode**   LACE MUSEUM
(International Centre of Lace & Fashion; ☑03 21 00 42 30; www.cite-dentelle.fr; 135 quai du Commerce; adult €5; ☉10am-5pm or 6pm, closed Tue) Walk past the bizarre topiary and you'll enter the intricate world of lace-making, the industry that once made Calais a textile powerhouse. Opened in 2009, the informative, cutting-edge exhibits trace the history of lace from the early centuries of hand-knotting (some stunning samples are on display). The highlight is watching a century-old mechanical loom with 3500 vertical threads and 11,000 horizontal ones bang, clatter and clunk according to instructions given by perforated Jacquard cards. Signs are in French, English and Dutch. Situated 500m southeast of the Hôtel de Ville.

Burghers of Calais   STATUE
Rodin sculpted *Les Bourgeois de Calais* in 1895 to honour six local citizens who, in 1347, after eight months of holding off the besieging English forces, surrendered themselves and the keys to the starving city to Edward III. Their hope: that by sacrificing themselves they might save the town and its people. Moved by the entreaties of his consort, Philippa, Edward eventually spared both the Calaisiens and their six brave leaders.

Calais' cast of this world-famous work can be found in the formal garden in front of the Flemish Renaissance–style **Hôtel de Ville** (built 1911–25), whose Unesco World Heritage–listed **belfry** is being renovated; by the time you read this, it should be possible to take a lift up to the top.

Musée Mémoire 1939–1945   WAR MUSEUM
(☑03 21 34 21 57; http://museeguerrecalais.free.fr; adult incl audioguide €6; ☉10am-6pm) Housed in a concrete bunker built as a German naval headquarters, this WWII museum displays thousands of period artefacts, including weapons, uniforms and proclamations. Situated incongruously in flowery **Parc St-Pierre**, next to a boules ground and a **children's playground**.

Beachfront   BEACH
The unique attraction at Calais' cabin-lined **beach**, which begins 1km northwest of place d'Armes, is watching huge car ferries as they sail majestically to and from Dover. The sand continues westward along 8km-long, dune-lined **Blériot Plage**, named after the pioneer aviator Louis Blériot, who began the first ever trans-Channel flight from here in 1909. Both beaches are served by buses 3, 5 and 9.

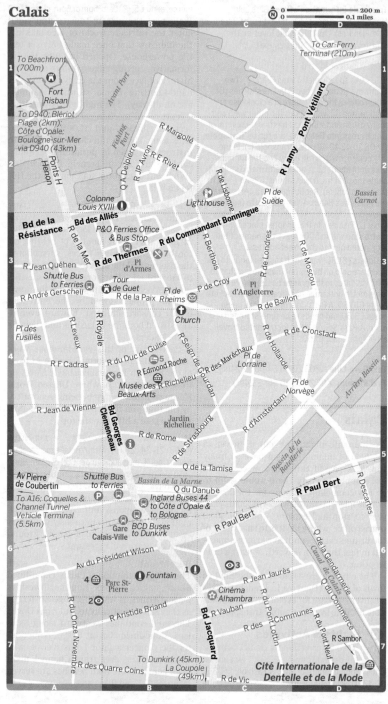

🛌 Sleeping

Lots of budget hotels can be found along, and just east of, rue Royale.

TOP CHOICE Hôtel Meurice TRADITIONAL HOTEL €€
(☎03 21 34 57 03; www.hotel-meurice.fr; 5-7 rue Edmond Roche; d €85-150; @🖥) A veteran hotel with 39 rooms and plenty of atmosphere thanks to the grand lobby staircase, antiques furnishings, a Hemingwayesque bar and a breakfast room with garden views.

Auberge de Jeunesse HOSTEL €
(☎03 21 34 70 20; www.auberge-jeunesse-calais.com; av Maréchal de Lattre de Tassigny; s incl breakfast €26, 2-bed dm per person €19; ⊘24hr; 🖥) Modern, well equipped and just 200m from the beach, with 162 beds. Served by buses 3, 5 and 9.

The following are in Coquelles, near the Channel Tunnel vehicle-loading area.

Hôtel Ibis CHAIN HOTEL €€
(☎03 21 46 37 00; www.ibishotel.com; place de Cantorbéry; d Mon-Thu €71, Fri-Sun €77)

Etap Hôtel CHAIN HOTEL €
(☎08 92 68 30 59; www.etaphotel.com; place de Cantorbéry; s/tr from €39/45)

🍴 Eating

Restaurants ring place d'Armes and are plentiful just south of there along rue Royale.

Histoire Ancienne BISTRO €
(☎03 21 34 11 20; www.histoire-ancienne.com; 20 rue Royale; weekday lunch menus €13-16, other menus €19-37; ⊘closed Sun & dinner Mon) A 1930s Paris-style bistro specialising in French and regional meat, fish and vegetarian mains, some grilled over an open wood fire.

Calais

🔘 **Top Sights**

Cité Internationale de la Dentelle et
de la Mode D7

🔘 **Sights**
1 Burghers of Calais Statue....................B6
2 Children's Playground.........................A7
3 Hôtel de Ville......................................C6
4 Musée Mémoire 1939–1945...............A6

🛏 **Sleeping**
5 Hôtel Meurice....................................B4

🍴 **Eating**
6 Histoire Ancienne..............................B4
7 Match Supermarket............................B3

Match SUPERMARKET €
(place d'Armes; ⊘8.30am-7.30pm Mon-Sat, 9am-12.30 Sun) For picnic supplies.

🛍 Shopping

Cité Europe SHOPPING MALL
(www.cite-europe.com; 1001 bd du Kent, Coquelles; ⊘10am-8pm Mon-Thu & Sat, 10am-9pm Fri) Has 20 restaurants, 12 cinema screens and 140 shops, including a vast **Carrefour hypermarket** (⊘8.30am-9pm Mon-Wed, 8.30am-10pm Thu-Sat). Situated next to the vehicle-loading area for the Channel Tunnel; from the A16, take exits 41 or 43.

L'Usine Côte d'Opale FACTORY OUTLETS
(www.usinecotedopale.fr, in French; bd du Parc, Coquelles; ⊘10am-7pm Mon-Sat) Discount clothing and accessories from 80 name brands. From the A16, take exit 41.

ℹ Information

Exchange rates aboard car ferries are inferior. Inexplicably, the car-ferry terminal lacks an ATM.

Bureau de Change (1 rue Royale; ⊘9-11am & 3.30-6pm Mon-Fri, 10am-noon & 2-4.30pm Sat) Currency exchange at atrocious rates.

Ferry Terminal Exchange Bureau (⊘9.30am-3.30pm Mon-Fri, 9.30am-2.30pm Sat)

Tourist office (☎03 21 96 62 40; www.calais-cotedopale.com; 12 bd Georges Clemenceau; ⊘10am-6pm) Situated two blocks southwest of place du Général de Gaulle.

ℹ Getting There & Away

For details crossing the English Channel by ferry and rail, see p973 and p972.

Boat

Each day, about 38 car ferries from Dover dock at Calais' bustling car-ferry terminal, situated about 1.5km northeast of place d'Armes (by car the distance is double that). Ferry company offices:

P&O Ferries (www.poferries.com) Calais town centre (41 place d'Armes); car-ferry parking lot (⊘24hr); car-ferry terminal (⊘6am-10pm) P&O is the only ferry company that still takes foot passengers across the Strait of Dover.

SeaFrance (www.seafrance.com) Calais town centre (2 place d'Armes); car-ferry parking lot (⊘24hr) No longer takes foot passengers.

Shuttle buses (€2, roughly hourly from 11am to 6pm or 7pm) link Gare Calais-Ville (the train station) and place d'Armes (the stop is in front of Café de la Tour) with the car-ferry terminal. Departure times are posted at the stops.

Bus

Bus 44, run by **Inglard** (☏03 21 96 49 54; www.colvert-littoral.com, in French; office in car-ferry terminal), follows the breathtaking Côte d'Opale coastal road (D940) to Sangatte, Wissant (€3.20), Ambleteuse, Wimereux and Boulogne-sur-Mer (€5.50, 1¼ hours, three daily Mon-Sat except holidays), where the stops are at Nausicaä and place de France (quai V, in front of the post office).

Ligne BCD (☏08 00 62 00 59; www.ligne-bcd.com, in French) links Calais' train station (hours posted) with Dunkirk (€8, 50 minutes, 11 daily Monday to Friday, three on Saturday).

Car & Motorcycle

To reach the Channel Tunnel's vehicle-loading area at Coquelles, about 6km southwest of Calais' town centre, follow the road signs on the A16 to 'Tunnel Sous La Manche' (Tunnel under the Channel) and get off at exit 42.

ADA (☏03 21 96 49 54), **Avis**, **Budget**, **Europcar**, **Hertz** and **National-Citer** have offices inside the car-ferry terminal but they're not always staffed.

Train

Calais has two train stations, linked by trains and a *navette* (shuttle bus; €2, free with train ticket).

Gare Calais-Ville, in the city centre, has direct services to Amiens (€24, 2½ to 3½ hours, six or seven daily), Boulogne (€7.50, 30 minutes, 19 daily Monday to Friday, 11 on Saturday, six on Sunday), Dunkirk (€8, 50 minutes, four to six daily Monday to Friday, two or three on Saturday) and Lille-Flandres (€16, 1¼ hours, 19 daily Monday to Friday, eight to 10 daily on weekend).

Gare Calais-Fréthun, a TGV station 10km southwest of town near the Channel Tunnel entrance, is served by TGVs to Paris' Gare du Nord (€41 to €62, 1½ hours, six daily Monday to Saturday, three on Sunday) as well as Eurostars to London St Pancras (€149, one hour, three daily).

Côte d'Opale

For a dramatic and beautiful introduction to France, head to the 40km of cliffs, sand dunes and beaches between Calais and Boulogne, known as the Côte d'Opale (Opal Coast) because of the ever-changing interplay of greys and blues in the sea and sky. The coastal peaks (frequently buffeted by gale-force winds), wide beaches and rolling farmland are dotted with the remains of Nazi Germany's Atlantic Wall, a chain of fortifications and gun emplacements built to prevent the Allied invasion that in the end took place in Normandy. The seashore

has been attracting British beach-lovers since the Victorian era.

Part of the **Parc Naturel Régional des Caps et Marais d'Opale** (Opal Coast Headlands & Marshes Regional Park; www.parc-opale.fr), the Côte d'Opale area is criss-crossed by hiking paths, including the **GR120 trail** (red-and-white trail markings) that hugs the coast – except where the cliffs are in danger of collapse. Some routes are also suitable for mountain biking and horse riding. Each village along the Côte d'Opale has at least one campground, and most have places to eat.

By car, D940 offers some truly spectacular vistas. For details on Inglard's bus 44, which links all the villages mentioned below with Calais and Boulogne, see left.

The Channel Tunnel slips under the Strait of Dover 8km west of Calais at the village of **Sangatte**, known for its white beach. Southwest of there, the coastal dunes give way to cliffs that culminate in windswept, 134m-high **Cap Blanc-Nez**, which affords breathtaking views of the Bay of Wissant, the port of Calais, the Flemish countryside (pock-marked by Allied bomb craters) and

---

WORTH A TRIP

LA COUPOLE

A top-secret subterranean V2 launch site just five minutes' flying time from London – almost (but not quite) put into operation in 1944 – now houses **La Coupole** (☏03 21 12 27 27; www.lacoupole.com; adult/family incl audioguide €9/19.50; ◎9am-6pm, closed 2 weeks around Christmas), an innovative museum that presents information using film and images:

» Nazi Germany's secret programs to build V1 and V2 rockets, which could fly at 650km/h and an astounding 5780km/h respectively

» Life in northern France during the Nazi occupation

» The postwar conquest of space with the help of V2 rocket technology – and seconded V2 engineers

La Coupole is 49km southeast of Calais just outside the town of Wizernes, near the intersection of D928 and D210. From A26, take exit 3 or 4.

the distant cliffs of Kent. The grey **obelisk** (erected 1922), a short walk up the hill from the parking area, honours the WWI Dover Patrol. Paths lead to a number of massive, concrete German bunkers and gun emplacements.

The tidy and very French seaside resort of Wissant is a good base for walks in the rolling countryside and along the beach between Cap Blanc-Nez to Cap Gris-Nez; check the tides at the tourist office (☎08 20 20 76 00; ⊙9.30am-noon & 2-6pm Mon-Fri, 9.30am-noon Sat) before setting out or you may get trapped between a rock and a wet place. Wissant boasts a vast fine-sand beach where you can admire England from afar – in 55 BC Julius Caesar launched his invasion of Britain from here.

Hôtel Le Vivier (☎03 21 35 93 61; www.levivier.com; place de l'Église, Wissant; d incl breakfast €60-90), across the street from the church and next to a millpond, has 39 nicely appointed rooms and a homey, nautically themed restaurant (menus €15-30; ⊙closed Tue & Wed low season) specialising in fresh local fish and seafood. There are several other hotels right nearby.

Topped by a lighthouse and a radar station serving the 600 ships that pass by each day, the 45m-high cliffs of Cap Gris-Nez are only 28km from the white cliffs of the English coast. The name – Grey Nose – is a corruption of the archaic English 'craig ness', meaning 'rocky promontory'. The area is a stopping-off point for millions of migrating birds.

Oodles of WWII hardware, including a massive, rail-borne German artillery piece with a range of 86km, are on display at the Musée du Mur de l'Atlantique (Atlantic Wall Museum; ☎03 21 32 97 33; www.batterietodt.com, in French; adult/child €6/3; ⊙10am-noon & 2-5pm Mon-Fri, to 6pm Sat & Sun, closed Dec & Jan), housed in a Brobdingnagian German pillbox. It is just southwest of Audinghen, 500m off D940.

The village of Ambleteuse, on the northern side of the mouth of the River Slack, is blessed with a lovely beach that was once defended from attack by the 17th-century Fort d'Ambleteuse, designed by Vauban (that's why it's also known as Fort Vauban). Just south of town is a protected area of grass-covered dunes known as Dunes de la Slack.

The neatly organised Musée 39-45 (☎03 21 87 33 01; www.musee3945.com; adult/

child €6.50/4.50; ⊙10am-6pm, closed Dec-Feb), at the northern edge of Ambleteuse, features realistic tableaux of WWII military and civilian life, and a 25-minute film. The dashing but wildly impractical French officers' dress uniforms of 1931 hint at why France fared so badly on the battlefield in 1940. Popular wartime songs accompany your visit. You can buy picnic supplies next door at the Shop supermarket (⊙closed Sun afternoon).

Boulogne-sur-Mer

POP 44,600

The most interesting of France's Channel ports, Boulogne makes a pretty good first stop in France, especially if combined with a swing north through the Côte d'Opale. The Basse Ville (Lower City) is an uninspiring assemblage of postwar structures but the attractive Ville Haute (Upper City), perched high above the rest of town, is girded by a 13th-century wall. The biggest draw is Nausicaä, one of Europe's premier aquariums.

Auguste Mariette (1821–81), the archaeologist who founded Cairo's Egyptian Museum, was born here, which is why Boulogne has a number of sculptures and artefacts related to the Pharaohs.

⊙ Sights

Nausicaä   AQUARIUM
(French Sea Experience Centre; ☎03 21 30 99 99; www.nausicaa.fr; bd Ste-Beuve; adult/student/child €17.50/12/11.50, audioguide €3.20; ⊙9.30am-6.30pm, closed 3 weeks in Jan) This superb aquarium complex, a few hundred metres north of the fishing port along quai Gambetta, lets you get up close and personal with see-through jellyfish, 250kg adult sharks (compare them to the shark eggs and hatchlings housed in a tiny tank), toothy speckled caimans (in the **Submerged Forest**), North Sea fish you usually see *au beurre* or *au gratin*, and arawanas, fish that can hop out of the water to pluck birds from overhanging branches (wearers of fancy feathered hats, beware!). Kid-friendly activities include feeding sessions and fish petting. Also a hit with younger visitors: California sea lions and African penguins, including young 'uns hatched right here. Details on the day's activities appear on

Boulogne-sur-Mer

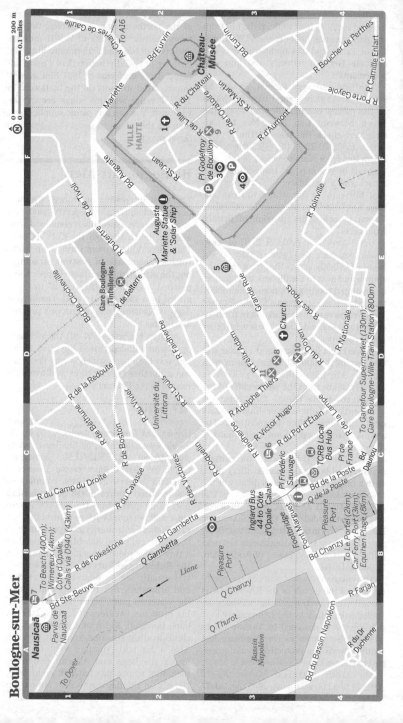

flat-screen bulletin boards. All signs are in French and English.

Ville Haute
HISTORIC QUARTER

You can walk all the way around the Upper City – a hilltop island of centuries-old buildings and cobblestone streets – atop the rectangular, tree-shaded ramparts, a distance of just under 1.5km. Among the impressive buildings around place Godefroy de Bouillon are the neoclassical Hôtel Desandrouin, built in the 1780s and later used by Napoléon, and the brick hôtel de ville (1735), with its square medieval **belfry** (ground floor accessible through the lobby).

Basilique Notre Dame (rue de Lille; ◔10am-noon & 2-5pm or 6pm), its towering, Italianate dome visible from all over town (and best admired from the ramparts), is an odd structure built from 1827 to 1866 with little input from trained architects. The partly Romanesque crypt and treasury (admission €2; ◔2-5pm Tue-Sun) are eminently skippable.

The cultures of the world mix and mingle inside the Château-Musée (Castle Museum; ☑03 21 10 02 20; adult/student €3/free; ◔museum 10am-12.30pm & 2-5.30pm, closed Tue, courtyard 7am-7pm daily), one of the few places on earth where you can admire Egyptian antiquities (including a mummy) next to 19th-century Inuit masks and compare Andean ceramics with Grecian urns, with an in-situ 4th-century Roman wall thrown in for good measure – all inside a 13th-century fortified castle.

Boulogne-sur-Mer

(113 Grande Rue; www.ambassadeargentine. net, in French; ◔10am-noon & 2-6pm Tue-Sat, closed Jan & 2 weeks Jul) Boulogne's most unexpected sight is the house where José de San Martín, the exiled hero of Argentine, Chilean and Peruvian independence, died in 1850. Ring the bell to visit an expatriated slice of 19th-century South America, complete with memorabilia related to San Martín's life and lots of gaudy military uniforms. Owned by the Argentine government, it is staffed by Argentine army personnel.

Basse Ville
PORT

At the fishing port (quai Gambetta), hungry seagulls dive and squawk overhead as they survey the fishing boats and the *poissonniers* (fishmongers) selling freshly landed *cabillaud* (Atlantic cod), *carrelet* (plaice) and sole – Boulogne's most important commercial fish – as well as *bar* (sea bass), mullet, *raie* (skate) and turbot. Take a good look so you know what you're getting next time you order *poisson* (fish).

Boulogne's lively shopping precinct is centred on rue Victor Hugo and rue Adolphe Thiers.

Seashore
BEACHES

Boulogne's beach begins just north of Nausica[], across the mouth of the Liane from a whirring wind farm on the one-time site of a steelworks.

There are other fine beaches 4km north of town at Wimereux (served two to four times per hour by buses 1 and 2 from place de France), a partly belle époque–style resort founded by Napoléon in 1806; 2.5km southwest at Le Portel (bus 23 from place de France); and 5km south at Equihen Plage (bus Ea or Eb from the train station or place de France). Note: Sunday bus numbers end in 'd'.

🛏 Sleeping

Hôtel La Matelote
HOTEL €€

(☑03 21 30 33 33; www.la-matelote.com; 70 bd Ste-Beuve; d Sun-Thu €100-160, Fri, Sat & holidays €115-185; ❄🛜♨) Boulogne's plushest hotel has a luxurious jacuzzi, *hammam* (Turkish sauna) and dry sauna. The 35 spacious rooms, many decorated in rich shades of red and gold, have ultramodern bathrooms and classic wood furnishings, and some come with balconies. Wheelchair access available. Situated a few hundred metres north of the fishing port along quai Gambetta.

Hôtel Faidherbe
HOTEL €

(☑03 21 31 60 93; www.hotelfaidherbe.fr; 12 rue Faidherbe; d/q €66/99; 🛜) Every guest elicits some sort of response from the house mascot, a myna bird named Victor – his repertoire includes laughing throatily, coughing and squawking *'bonjour'*, *'au revoir'* and 'bye-bye'. The 33 rooms are smallish but modern, flowery and practical.

Auberge de Jeunesse
HOSTEL €

(☑03 21 99 15 30; www.hihostels.com; place Rouget de Lisle; dm incl breakfast & sheets €19, s €25; ⊙closed 22 Dec-Jan; @🛜) This 137-bed outfit has a bar, a lounge area and spacious rooms with a timer-activated shower, toilet and two to five beds. Kitchen facilities are available. Situated about 1km south of the Basse Ville, facing the train station.

✖ Eating & Drinking

Thanks to its ready supply, Boulogne is an excellent place for fresh fish (everything except the salmon is likely to have been landed locally). In the Ville Haute, rue de Lille is lined with intimate restaurants (eg L'îlot Vert at No 36). In the Basse Ville, there's a selection of eateries in the area around place Dalton and rue du Doyen.

La Matelote
FRENCH €€

(☑03 21 30 17 97; 80 bd Ste-Beuve; menus €29-74; ⊙lunch Thu) A stylish establishment with white tablecloths, paper-thin wine glasses, fine porcelain and one Michelin star. Serves *cuisine de saveurs* (cuisine that 'mixes savours and flavours', or something like that) with a focus on fish and seafood. La Matelote also runs the excellent beach-view bistro (⊙closed dinner Sun, also closed dinner Mon Sep-May) inside Nausica[].

Self-Catering

Fromagerie
CHEESE SHOP €

(23 Grande Rue; ⊙closed morning Mon) For an excellent selection of local cheeses.

Trésor de Vin
WINE SHOP €

(12 rue Adolphe Thiers; ⊙closed Sun & Mon) A wine shop by and for people who are passionate about wine.

Marché
FOOD MARKET €

(place Dalton; ⊙morning Wed & Sat)

Carrefour Market
SUPERMARKET €

(53 bd Daunou)

ℹ Information

Several commercial banks can be found on or near rue Victor Hugo. Money can be changed aboard LP Ferries' trans-Channel car ferries.

Art et Image (87 rue Victor Hugo; ⊙9.30am-6.45pm Tue-Sat, also open Mon Jun-Aug; per hr €4) Has an internet computer where you can print out ferry tickets.

Tourist office (☑03 21 10 88 10; www.tour isme-boulognesurmer.com; parvis de Nauticaâ; ⊙10am-noon & 1.30-6pm or 7pm Mon-Sat, 10.30am-1pm & 2.30-5pm Sun) Has useful English brochures.

Tourist office annexe (forum Jean Noël; ⊙9.30am-12.30pm & 2-6pm Mon-Sat, 10am-1pm Sun & holiday) Located in an octagonal pavilion.

ℹ Getting There & Around

BOAT For information on **LD Lines** (☑03 21 22 34 77; www.ldlines.co.uk) car ferries to Dover (foot passengers not permitted), see p973. The new ferry port is 3km west of the city centre.

BUS For details on buses to Calais via the gorgeous Côte d'Opale, see p168.

TAXI To order a cab, call ☑03 21 91 25 00.

TRAIN The main train station, **Gare Boulogne-Ville**, is 1.2km southeast of the centre. Destinations include Amiens (€18.50, 1½ hours, seven to nine daily), Calais-Ville (€7.50, 30 minutes, 19 daily Monday to Friday, 11 on Saturday, six on Sunday), Gare Lille-Flandres or Gare Lille-Europe (€19.50, one to two hours, nine to 12 daily) and Paris' Gare du Nord (€33, 2¾ hours, four or five direct daily).

Dunkirk

POP 69,500

In 1940, Dunkirk (Dunkerque) – the name means 'church of the dunes' in Flemish – became world famous, and was flattened, almost simultaneously (p173). Rebuilt during one of the most uninspired periods in the entire history of Western architecture, the modern city has precious little charm but does offer visitors worthwhile museums, a family-popular beach and colourful pre-Lent carnivals.

⊙ Sights & Activities

The Musée Portuaire (Harbour Museum; www.museeportuaire.com; 9 quai de la Citadelle; adult/family €5/13; ⊙10am-12.45pm & 1.30-6pm, closed Tue), housed in a one-time tobacco warehouse, will delight fans of maritime history and, especially, of model ships. Guided tours (adult/family incl museum

EVACUATION OF DUNKIRK

In late May of 1940, as Nazi armies closed in, 1400 naval vessels and 'little ships' – fishing boats and pleasure craft crewed by civilian volunteers – braved intense German artillery and air attacks to ferry 340,000 Allied soldiers to the safety of England. Conducted in the difficult first year of WWII, this unplanned and chaotic evacuation – dubbed Operation Dynamo – failed to save any heavy equipment but was nevertheless seen as a heroic demonstration of Britain's resourcefulness and determination.

€10/25) take visitors aboard a lighthouse ship, a *peniche* (barge) and the *Duchesse Anne,* a three-masted training ship built for the German merchant marine in 1901 and acquired by France as WWII reparations. Some signs are in English. Situated 500m northwest of the tourist office.

To get a feel for the 1940 evacuation, drop by the not-for-profit Mémorial du Souvenir (☑03 28 26 27 81; www.dynamo-dunkerque. com; rue des Chantiers de France; adult/under 12yr €3.50/free; ☺10am-noon & 2-5pm Apr-Sep), a museum whose highlights include a 12-minute film, scale models and evocative period uniforms, weapons and photos.

The Dunkirk British Memorial (D601), honouring over 4500 British and Commonwealth soldiers 'with no known grave', is next to a Commonwealth military cemetery 1.5km southeast of the tourist office.

Malo-les-Bains, 2km northeast of Dunkirk's city centre, is a faded turn-of-the-20th-century seaside resort whose broad, sandy beach, Plage des Alliés, is named in honour of the Allied troops evacuated to England during Operation Dynamo. A bit to the northeast, off Zuydecoote, the wrecks of vessels sunk in 1940 can be visited on scuba dives, and a handful are accessible on foot during especially low tides (the tourist office has details of guided tours).

Stretching east from Malo-les-Bains to the Belgian border, the Dunes Flamandes (Flemish Dunes) represent a unique ecosystem harbouring hundreds of plant species, including rare orchids. Tides permitting, you can walk or cycle along the wet sand or the GR path from Malo-les-Bains to Leffrinckoucke, Zuydcoote and Bray-Dunes.

Eating

Restaurants can be found near the Musée Portuaire (along quai de la Citadelle) and facing the beach in Malo-les-Bains (along digue des Alliés and digue de Mer). Five blocks east of the tourist office, Dunkirk's first organic restaurant, La Demi-Lune (☑03 28 61 42 77; www.dunkerque-bio.com, in French; 65 bd Ste-Barbe; mains €10-13; ☺lunch only), serves light, healthy lunches at reasonable prices.

❶ Information

Tourist office (☑03 28 66 79 21; www.ot-dunkerque.fr; ☺9.30am-12.30pm & 1.30-6.30pm Mon-Sat, 10am-noon & 2-4pm Sun & holidays) Has a free brochure, *Dunkirk Wartime Memories*, on WWI and WWII sites and sells the **Pass Tourisme** (€12) discounts card. Situated in the base of a 58m-high **belfry** (adult €2.90; ☺tours 9 daily Mon-Sat), erected around 1440, with spectacular views and a 50-bell carillon (renovated in 2009) that sounds every quarter-hour.

❶ Getting There & Away

For details about getting from Dover to Dunkirk's car-ferry port, about 15km west of the town centre at Loon Plage (A16 exit 53), see p973.

BUS For details on buses to Calais, see p167.

TRAIN Dunkirk's train station is 1km southwest of the tourist office. Rail destinations include Lille (mainly to Gare Lille-Flandres; €13, 32 to 78 minutes, 20 direct daily Monday to Friday, 10 to 13 daily weekends) and Calais (€8, 50 minutes, four to six daily Monday to Friday, two or three on Saturday).

Cassel

POP 2430

At the summit of French Flanders' highest hill (though at 176m it's hardly Mont Blanc), the fortified, quintessentially Flemish village of Cassel offers panoramic views of the verdant Flanders plain.

Thanks to its elevated position, Cassel served as Maréchal Ferdinand Foch's headquarters at the beginning of WWI. In 1940 it was the site of intensive rearguard resistance by British troops defending Dunkirk during the evacuation.

Its citizens are enormously proud of Reuze Papa and Reuze Maman, the resident giants (p160), who are feted on Easter Monday. A bagpipe festival is held in Cassel on a weekend in mid-June.

The main square, fringed by austere brick buildings with steep slate roofs, is where you'll find the tourist office (☎03 28 40 52 55; www.cassel-horizons.com; 20 Grand' Place; ⏲8.30am-noon & 1.30-5.30pm Mon-Sat & 2-6pm Sun) and the brand new Musée Départemental de Flandre (22 Grand' Place), opened in late 2010, which spotlights Flanders' rich heritage and showcases Flemish art both old and new.

Ten generations ago, wheat flour was milled and linseed oil pressed just as it is today at the wooden moulin (windmill; adult/child €3/2.50; ⏲2-6pm Mon-Sat, 10am-12.30pm & 1.30-6.30pm Sun, closed Dec-early Jan, last tour 1hr before closing), perched on the highest point in town to catch the wind. The 45-minute hands-on tour is noisy but interesting. During the 19th century, the skyline of French Flanders was dotted with 2000 such windmills. Nearby, you can peer into Belgium from a flowery park; two orientation tables point to cities near and far.

Le Foch (☎03 28 42 47 73; www.hotel-foch. net, in French; 41 Grand' Place; d €67) has six spacious rooms with antique-style beds, some with views of the square. The elegant restaurant (menus €13-25; ⏲closed Fri & dinner Sun) serves French and regional cuisine, made with fresh local ingredients, amid carved woodwork and sparkling crystal. Other restaurants and cafés around the Grand' Place include the Taverne Flamande (☎03 28 42 42 59; 34 Grand' Place; menus €16-18, Sun menus €26; ⏲closed Wed & dinner Tue), whose classic 1933 dining room has red banquettes, red-and-white checked tablecloths and, on cold days, a crackling fire.

Cassel is 57km southeast of Calais. Cassel's train station, 3km down the hill from the centre, has direct services to Dunkirk (€6, 25 minutes, nine daily Monday to Friday, two or three daily on weekends).

Baie de Somme

The Somme Estuary (www.baiedesomme. org, in French, www.baiedesomme.fr) affords delightfully watery views as the cycle of the tides alternately hides and reveals vast expanses of sand. Le Crotoy (population 2340), a modest beach resort on the northern bank, makes a good base for exploring the area. From there, across the estuary, you can see Pointe du Hourdel, famed for its colony of sandbank-lounging seals and linked to Le Crotoy by a bike path (www. baiecyclette.com); lots of duck-hunting huts; and St-Valery-sur-Somme, which can be reached on foot (with a bit of knee-deep slogging) at low tide year-round, though only with a guide (the area is notorious for strong currents and galloping tides) – contact Promenade en Baie (☎03 22 27 47 36; www.promenade-en-baie.com, in French; 5 allée des Soupirs, Le Crotoy; ⏲9.30am-12.30pm & 2-6pm).

Le Crotoy's tourist office (☎03 22 27 05 25; www.tourisme-crotoy.com; 1 rue Carnot; ⏲9.30am-12.30pm & 2-5.30pm or 6pm) can supply you with an horaire des marées (tide schedule).

Les Tourelles (☎03 22 27 16 33; www. lestourelles.com; 2-4 rue Pierre Guerlain; d €79; @🖶), a sprawling family-run hotel overlooking the beach, has a bracing Victorian feel. Kids aged four to 14 can stay in a room with 14 bunk beds (€25 per child including breakfast). The attached restaurant (menus €23-34) serves French cuisine with Channel Coast touches and offers veggie and locavore options.

CROSS-DRESSING & AIRBORNE HERRINGS DANIEL ROBINSON

Dunkirk's carnivals, held both before and (mischievously) after the beginning of Lent, originated as a final fling for the town's cod fishermen before they set out for months in the frigid waters off Iceland. The biggest celebration is the bande (parade) held on the Sunday before Mardi Gras, when men traditionally dress up as women, costumed citizens of all genders march around town behind fife-and-drum bands, and general merriment reigns. At the climax of the festivities, the mayor and other dignitaries stand on the hôtel de ville balcony and pelt the assembled locals with dried salted herrings.

Once, in the Dunkirk suburb of St-Pol-sur-Mer, I caught one of Hizzoner's flying herrings. I was so very pleased with myself that, while I repeatedly deemed the fish unsuitable for lunch, I couldn't quite bring myself to throw it out either. So there it stayed, on the floor of my car, for weeks on end, with predictably unpleasant results...

PARC ORNITHOLOGIQUE DU MARQUENTERRE

An astonishing 360 species of bird have been sighted at the 2.6-sq-km Marquenterre Ornithological Park (☑03 22 25 68 99; www.parcdumarquenterre.com; adult/child €10/8, binoculars €4; ◎10am-7.30pm, last entry 2hr before closing), an important migratory stopover between the UK, Iceland, Scandinavia and Siberia and the warmer climes of West Africa. Three marked **walking circuits** (2km to 6km) take you to marshes, dunes, meadows, freshwater ponds, a brackish lagoon and 14 observation posts. Intro walks begin daily at 10.30am and 2pm. The park is in St-Quentin-en-Tourmont, a circuitous 10km northwest of Le Crotoy.

Amiens

POP 137,800

One of France's most awe-inspiring Gothic cathedrals is reason enough to spend time in Amiens, the comfy, if reserved, former capital of Picardy, where Jules Verne spent the last two decades of his life. The clean-lined, mostly pedestrianised city centre, rebuilt after the war, has aged remarkably well. Some 25,000 students give the town a youthful feel.

Amiens is an excellent base for visits to the Battle of the Somme Memorials.

◎ Sights & Activities

Place Gambetta, the city's commercial hub, is three blocks southwest of the cathedral.

TOP CHOICE Cathédrale Notre Dame   CATHEDRAL
(place Notre Dame; ◎8.30am-6.15pm)
The largest Gothic cathedral in France (it's 145m long) and a Unesco World Heritage Site since 1981, this magnificent structure was begun in 1220 to house the skull of St John the Baptist (◎on display approx Apr-Oct), shown – framed in gold and jewels – in the northern outer wall of the ambulatory. Connoisseurs rave about the soaring Gothic arches (42.3m high over the transept), unity of style and immense interior, but for locals, the 17th-century statue known as the **Ange Pleureur** (Crying Angel), in the ambulatory directly behind the over-the-top baroque (18th century) high altar, remains a favourite.

The octagonal, 234m-long **labyrinth** on the black-and-white floor of the nave is easy to miss as the soaring vaults draw the eye upward. **Plaques** in the south transept arm honour American, Australian, British, Canadian and New Zealand soldiers who perished in WWI.

To get a sense of what you're seeing, it's worth hiring a one-hour audioguide (1st/2nd person €4/3), available in six languages, at the tourist office (across the street). Weather permitting, it's possible to climb the north tower (☑03 22 92 03 32; ◎afternoon, closed Tue); tickets are sold in the boutique to the left as you approach the west facade.

A free 45-minute **light show** bathes the cathedral's facade in vivid medieval colours nightly from mid-June to mid-September and December to 1 January; the photons start flying at 7pm in winter and sometime between 9.45pm (September) and 10.45pm (June) in summer.

Hortillonnages   BOAT TOUR
(☑03 22 92 12 18; 54 bd de Beauvillé; adult/child €6/4.70; ◎1.30-4.30pm) Amien's market gardens – some 3 sq km in extent – have supplied the city with vegetables and flowers since the Middle Ages. Today, their peaceful *rieux* (waterways), home to 10 working farms and countless water birds, can be visited on 12-person boats whose raised prows make them look a bit like gondolas. Available later (to 6.30pm) if weather and demand allow.

Maison de Jules Verne   HOUSE MUSEUM
(Home of Jules Verne; ☑03 22 45 45 75; www.jules-verne.net; 2 rue Charles Dubois; adult €7, audioguide €2; ◎10am-12.30pm & 2-6.30pm Mon & Wed-Fri, 2-6.30pm Tue, 11am-6.30pm Sat & Sun) Jules Verne (1828–1905) wrote many of his best-known works of brain-tingling – and eerily prescient – science fiction while living in his turreted Amiens home. The models, prints, posters and other items inspired by Verne's fecund imagination afford a fascinating opportunity to check out the future as he envisioned it over a century ago, when going around the world in 80 days sounded utterly fantastic – and before WWI dashed Europeans' belief in a world destined to improve thanks to 'progress'. Signs are in French and English.

Musée de Picardie   MUSEUM
(☑03 22 97 14 00; www.amiens.fr/musees, in French; 48 rue de la République; adult €5; ◎10am-12.30pm & 2-6pm Tue-Sat, until 9pm Thu, 2-7pm Sun) Housed in a dashing Second Empire

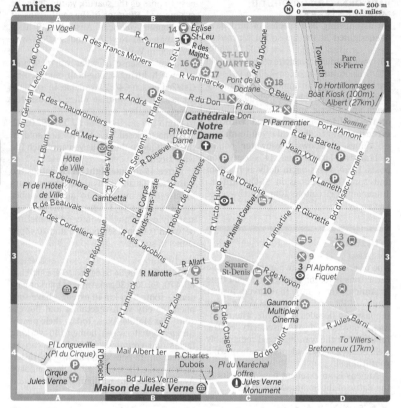

structure (1855–67), the Picardy Museum is surprisingly well endowed with archaeological exhibits, medieval art and Revolution-era ceramics.

Galerie du Vitrail Claude Barre
STAINED GLASS

(☎03 22 91 81 18; 40 rue Victor Hugo; adult €5; ⊙tours 3pm Mon-Sat) Ever wonder how stained glass is designed and put together? You can see firsthand at this workshop, whose artisans fill commissions from churches and private collectors.

Tour Perret
ARCHITECTURE

(place Alphonse Fiquet) Long the tallest building in Western Europe, the reinforced concrete Perret Tower (110m), facing the train station, was designed by the Belgian architect Auguste Perret (who also planned postwar Le Havre) and completed in 1954. Not open to visitors.

🛏 Sleeping

Amiens' hotels offer excellent value for money but often fill up with businesspeople from Monday to Thursday.

Grand Hôtel de l'Univers
HOTEL €€

(☎03 22 91 52 51; www.hotel-univers-amiens.com; 2 rue de Noyon; d €75-150; @🕸) Offering all the bourgeois comforts, this venerable, Best Western–affiliated hostelry is convenient to both the train station and the city's pedestrianised heart. The 41 rooms, set around a four-storey atrium, are immaculate and very comfortable; some on the 4th floor even come with views of the cathedral.

Hôtel Le St-Louis
HOTEL €

(☎03 22 91 76 03; www.le-saintlouis.com; in French; 24 rue des Otages; d/q from €60/97; 🕸) All the mod cons combined with more than a dash of 19th-century French class. The 24 rooms, some off a deck-like inner courtyard, are spacious and tasteful.

Hôtel Victor Hugo   HOTEL €

(☎03 22 91 57 91; www.hotel-a-amiens.com; 2 rue de l'Oratoire; d €44-55, q €59-67; 🛜) Just a block from the cathedral, this charming, family-run hostelry has two stars and 10 quiet, charming rooms with the pleasing ambience of days gone by. Good value, though the hallways may smell of smoke.

Hôtel Central & Anzac   HOTEL €

(☎03 22 91 34 08; www.hotelcentralanzac.com, in French; 17 rue Alexandre Fatton; s/d from €49/55; 🛜) Founded decades ago by an Australian ex-serviceman, this place has 26 clean, well-maintained rooms. Many have old-time touches but some are a bit on the small side.

✕ Eating

The **St-Leu Quarter** (quai Bélu) – not quite the 'northern Venice' it's touted to be – is lined with neon-lit riverside restaurants and pubs, many with warm-season terraces. There are more places to eat across the river at place du Don.

TOP CHOICE **Le Tigzirt**   COUSCOUS €

(☎03 22 91 42 55; 60 rue Vanmarcke, on weekends via 7 place du Don; mains €11-22; ⊗closed Mon, dinner Sun & lunch Sat) The welcome is as warm as the Algerian Berber-style couscous and *tajines* (stews), which are steamed, boiled, grilled and baked to perfection.

Le Bouchon   FRENCH €€

(☎03 22 92 14 32; www.lebouchon.fr, in French; 10 rue Alexandre Fatton; lunch menus Mon-Fri €18, other menus €24-42; ⊗closed dinner Sun)

The decor is a bit sparse but the traditional French cuisine is good value. The mouth-watering dessert list encompasses the French classics, including *Forêt Noire* (Black Forest chocolate cake; €9).

Le T'chiot Zinc   BISTRO €

(☎03 22 91 43 79; 18 rue de Noyon; menus €12-26; ⊗closed Sun, also closed Mon Jul & Aug) Inviting, bistro-style decor reminiscent of the belle époque provides a fine backdrop for the tasty French and Picard cuisine, including fish dishes and *caqhuse* (pork in a cream, wine vinegar and onion sauce). The proper, Picard pronunciation of the name is 'shtyoh-zang'.

Self-Catering

Covered market   FOOD MARKET €

(rue de Metz; ⊗9am-1pm & 3-7pm Tue-Thu, 9am-7pm Fri & Sat, 8.30am-12.30pm Sun)

Marché sur l'eau   FOOD MARKET €

(place Parmentier; ⊗to 12.30pm Sat, to 1pm in summer) Fruit and vegetables grown in the Hortillonnages are sold at this one-time floating market, now held on dry land (except once a year).

Match   SUPERMARKET €

(Centre Commercial Amiens 2; ⊗8.30am-8pm Mon-Sat)

◉ Drinking

TOP CHOICE **Café Bissap**   CAFÉ-BAR

(☎03 22 92 36 41; 50 rue St-Leu; ⊗noon-3am Tue-Sat, noon-1am Sun & Mon) An ethnically mixed crowd, including students, sips rum cocktails and West African beers (eg

Guinness Foreign Extra, brewed in Cameroon) amid decor from the Senegalese-born proprietor's native land. The soundtrack is African, Caribbean and Latin American. Super-friendly. Opens at 6pm during school holidays, including July and August.

Marott' Street WINE BAR
(☎03 22 91 14 93; 1 rue Marotte; ☉11am-1am, closed Sun) Designed by Gustave Eiffel's architectural firm in 1892, this exquisite ex-insurance office now attracts chic, well-off, thirty-somethings who sip Champagne (€11) while suspended – on clear-glass tiles – over the wine cellar.

☆ Entertainment

La Lune des Pirates CONCERT VENUE
(☎03 22 97 88 01; www.lalune.net, in French; 17 quai Bélu) Hosts cutting-edge concerts a dozen times a month.

Chés Cabotans d'Amiens MARIONETTES
(☎03 22 22 30 90; www.ches-cabotans-damiens .com, in French; 31 rue Édouard-David) A theatre whose stars are all traditional Picard marionettes. Great fun even if you don't speak Picard or French.

Ciné St-Leu CINEMA
(☎03 22 91 61 23; www.cine-st-leu.com, in French; 33 rue Vanmarcke) An art-house cinema with nondubbed films, some in English.

ⓘ Information

Banks can be found around place René Goblet and rue des Trois Cailloux.

Bibliothèque (☎03 22 97 10 00; 50 rue de la République; ☉2-7pm Mon, 9.30am-7pm Tue-Fri, 9.30am-6pm Sat) Free internet access in a grand public library built in the 1820s.

Tourist office (☎03 22 71 60 50; www. amiens-tourisme.com; 40 place Notre Dame; ☉9.30am-6pm or 6.30pm Mon-Sat, 10am-noon & 2-5pm Sun) Can supply details on the Somme memorials (including minibus tours) and cultural events. Sells the **City Pass** (€8), which offers various discounts.

ⓘ Getting There & Around

For details on public transport links to Villers-Bretonneux and Vimy Ridge Canadian National Historic Site, see p186 and p187.

Bicycle
Vélo Service (Buscyclette; ☎03 22 72 55 13; http://amiensveloservice.fubicy.org, in French; per hr/day/weekend €1/6/8, tandems per hr/day €2/8; ☉9am-7pm Mon-Sat) A nonprofit organisation that rents bikes from the courtyard of Tour Perret, behind the main entrance.

Car
There's free parking one or two blocks north of the Victor Hugo and Central & Anzac hotels, along rue Lameth, rue Cardon, rue Jean XXIII and rue de la Barette.

To hire a car to tour the memorials, try **Hertz** (☎03 22 91 26 24; 5 Boulevard d'Alsace-Lorraine).

Train
Amiens is an important rail hub. Accessed through a dramatic modern entrance, the train station offers direct services to Arras (€11, 50 minutes, six to 12 daily), Boulogne (€18.50, 1½ hours, seven to nine daily), Calais-Ville (€24, 2½ hours to 3½ hours, six or seven daily), Compiègne (€12.10, 1¼ hours, eight to 12 daily), Laon (€16, 1½ hours, four to nine daily), Lille-Flandres (€19, 1½ hours, six to 12 daily), Paris' Gare du Nord (€19, 1¼ to 1¾ hours, 14 to 30 daily) and Rouen (€18, 1¼ hours, four daily). SNCF buses go to the Haute Picardie TGV station (40 minutes, 15 to 20 daily), 42km east of the city.

Arras
POP 44,300

Arras (the final *s* is pronounced), former capital of Artois and *préfecture* (capital) of the *département* of Pas-de-Calais, is worth seeing mainly for its harmonious ensemble of Flemish-style arcaded buildings and two subterranean WWI sites.

The city makes a good base for visits to the Battle of the Somme Memorials.

⊙ Sights & Activities

Grand' Place & Petite Place ARCHITECTURE
Arras' two ancient market squares, the **Grand' Place** and the almost-adjacent, smaller **Petite Place** (officially known as place des Héros), are surrounded by 17th- and 18th-century Flemish-baroque houses topped by curvaceous 'Dutch' gables. Although the structures vary in decorative detail, their 345 sandstone columns form a common arcade unique in France. The squares, especially handsome at night, are about 600m northwest of the train station.

Hôtel de Ville BELFRY, CELLARS
Arras' Flemish-Gothic city hall (Petite Place) dates from the 16th century but was completely rebuilt after WWI. Three giants (p160) – Colas, Jacqueline and their son Dédé – make their home in the lobby.

The basement of the Hôtel de Ville is a veritable hub of activity. If you're in the mood for a panoramic view, this is the place to hop on a lift to the top of the Unesco World Heritage–listed, 75m-high belfry (adult €2.70; ☉same as tourist office). But for a truly unique perspective on Arras head into the slimy souterrains (tunnels). Also known as *boves* (cellars), they run under the Petite Place and were turned into British command posts, hospitals and barracks during WWI. Each spring, in a brilliant juxtaposition of underground gloom and horticultural exuberance, plants and flowers turn the tunnels into the lush, creative, life-affirming Jardin des Boves (Cellar Gardens; ☉20 Mar-20 Jun). Tours (adult €5) lasting 45 minutes (in English upon request), focusing on the gardens when they're there, generally begin at about 11am and runs at least twice in the afternoon from Monday to Friday, and every 30 minutes on Saturday and Sunday.

TOP CHOICE **Wellington Quarry** MEMORIAL, MUSEUM
The staging ground for the spring 1917 offensive in which the poet Siegfried Sassoon was wounded, Carrière Wellington (✉Arras tourist office 03 21 51 26 95; www.carriere-wellington.com; rue Delétoile; adult €6.50; ☉tours begin 10am-12.30pm or 1pm & 2.30-5pm, closed Christmas–mid-Jan) is a 20m-deep network of old chalk quarries expanded during WWI by tunnellers from New Zealand. Hour-long guided tours in French and English combine imaginative audiovisuals, evocative photos and period artefacts. It's easy to tell who wrote which graffiti when: signs painted in black are British and from WWI, those in red are French from WWII, when the site was used as a bomb shelter. Opened to the public in 2008, the quarry is about 1km south of the train station; by car, follow the 'Carrière' signs from the northeast corner of the Grand' Place (bd Faidherbe). Served by buses 1 and 4.

🛏 Sleeping

Place du Maréchal Foch, in front of the train station, has a number of hotels.

Hôtel de l'Univers HOTEL €€
(✉03 21 71 34 01; www.hotel-univers-arras.com; 3-5 place de la Croix Rouge; d €105-160; ❋☎) Ensconced in a 16th-century former Jesuit monastery, this Best Western–affiliated hostelry is arrayed in a U around a quiet neoclassical courtyard. Classic draperies and bedspreads give each of the 38 rooms a touch of French class – civilised comfort at reasonable prices. Situated four blocks southwest of the Hôtel de Ville and 50m south of No 29 on bustling rue Ernestale;

by car, take one-way rue Baudimont from the west and follow the orange hotel signs.

Maison St-Vaast HOSTEL €
(✉03 21 21 40 38; http://arras.catholique.fr/page-15065.html, in French; 103 rue d'Amiens; per person €21; ☉reception 7am-7pm Mon-Fri, closed holidays; ☎) Arras' Catholic diocese welcomes visitors to its dorm facilities, whose 43 rooms (91 beds), for one to four people, are Spartan (the floors are pine planks) but clean and practical. Constructed as a convent in the 1600s and rebuilt after WWI, the atmospheric building has a fine cloister and a 1920s chapel with lovely stained glass and an organ that's frequently played for practice. Disabled access. If you'll be checking in after 7pm or on a weekend or holiday, call or write ahead to arrange for the watchman to let you in.

Hôtel Moderne HOTEL €€
(✉03 21 23 39 57; www.hotel-moderne-arras.com; 2 place Maréchal Foch; d €80-90; ☎) Facing the train station, with five floors and 50 old-time rooms, each with a decommissioned fireplace. 'Comfort' doubles (€90) offer more space and fine views; some boast French windows and small balconies.

Ostel Les 3 Luppars HOTEL €€
(✉03 21 60 02 03; www.ostel-les-3luppars.com, in French; 47 Grand' Place; s/d/q from €60/75/90; ☎⟐) Occupying the Grand' Place's only non-Flemish-style building (it's Gothic and dates from the 1400s), this hotel has a private courtyard and 42 rooms, including 10 with fine views of the square and two fitted out for families. The decor is uninspired but the atmosphere is homey. Has a sauna (per person for a half-hour €5).

🍴 Eating

Places to eat are tucked away under the arches of the Grand' Place and along adjacent rue de la Taillerie, which leads to the

MCDONALD'S HAS BRANCHES – SOON THE LOUVRE WILL TOO

A local branch of the Louvre is coming to a depressed former coal-mining town near you – at least if you live in French Flanders. That's right, come 2012, when the Lou-vre-Lens (www.louvrelens.fr) is set to open in Lens, you'll no longer have to go to Paris to check out the world's most-visited museum.

We may as well be blunt: Lens (☏ tourist office 03 21 67 66 66; www.tourisme-lenslievin. fr), 18km northeast of Arras and 37km south of Lille, is known for absolutely nothing, at least as far as tourism is concerned. But thanks to a high-minded effort to 'democ-ratise' the Louvre by bringing its riches to the people, the town's 37,000 residents are hoping that the Louvre-Lens will do for them what the Guggenheim Museum did for Bilbao. Incidentally, the decision to situate this ultraprestigious project in Lens was apparently helped along by a municipal PR piece that juxtaposed IM Pei's Louvre pyra-mid with one of Lens' very own pyramidlike slag heaps!

Petite Place. There are more dining options around semicircular place du Maréchal Foch, facing the train station.

Café Georget
CAFÉ €

(☏ 03 21 71 13 07; 42 place des Héros, ie Petite Place; plat du jour €8; ☽ lunch Mon-Sat) An authentic neighbourhood café. Madame Delforge, who speaks English with a charmingly thick French accent, has been serving hearty, home-style French dishes to people who work in the neighbourhood since 1985. Situated 100m west of the Hô-tel de Ville.

Le Mamounia
NORTH AFRICAN €€

(☏ 03 21 07 99 99; 9 rue des Balances; mains €12.50-24; ☽ closed Mon, lunch Sat & dinner Sun) The elegant, brightly coloured decor mixes the Maghreb with Provence but the cous-cous and *tajines* are 100% Moroccan.

La Cave aux Saveurs
FRENCH €

(☏ 03 21 59 75 24; 36 Grand' Place; lunch menus €13; other menus €18-33; ☽ closed Sun) In a vaulted brick cellar that served as a brew-ery before WWII, this popular new res-taurant serves traditional French dishes as well as an innovative, low-fat *bien-être* (well-being) menu (€18). Flemish specialties include *potjevleesch* (€11).

Self-Catering

Open-Air Market
FOOD MARKET €

(place des Héros, Grand' Place & place de la Vacquerie; ☽ 7am-1pm Wed & Sat) Around the Hôtel de Ville. The Saturday market is really huge.

Monoprix
SUPERMARKET €

(30 rue Gambetta & 28 rue Ronville; ☽ 8.30am-7.50pm Mon-Sat) Four short blocks south of the Petite Place.

Spar
GROCERY €

(9 rue de la Taillerie; ☽ 8.30am-1pm & 3.30-8pm Tue-Sat, 9.30am-1pm & 5.30-8pm Sun) At the southwestern corner of the Grand' Place.

ℹ Information

Banks can be found along rue Gambetta and its continuation, rue Ernestale.

Cybercafé Citoyen (2 rue du Commandant Dumetz; per hr €2; ☽ 9am-8pm Mon-Fri, 10.30am-7pm Sat) Internet access four blocks east of the train station's back entrance.

Tourist office (☏ 03 21 51 26 95; www.ot -arras.fr, in French; place des Héros; ☽ 9am or 10am-noon & 2-6pm or 6.30pm Mon-Sat, 10am-12.30pm or 1pm & 2.30-6.30pm Sun & holidays) Inside the Hôtel de Ville.

ℹ Getting There & Around

Bicycle

Base Nautique de St-Laurent-Blangy
(☽ 03 21 73 74 93; http://eauxvivesslb.free. fr in French; rue Laurent Gers, Saint-Laurent-Blangy; half-/full day €11/17) Rents out bikes 2.5km northeast of the city centre.

Car

Avis (☏ 03 21 51 69 03; 8 rue Gambetta) Half a block northwest of the train station.

Europcar (☏ 03 21 07 29 54; 5 rue de Douai) Half a block to the right as you exit the train station.

France Cars (☏ 03 21 50 22 22; 31 bd Faid-herbe) Two blocks north of the train station.

Taxi

Alliance Arras Taxis (☏ 03 21 23 69 69; ☽ 24hr) Can take you to Somme battlefield sites (eg Vimy).

Train

Arras is linked to the following:

Amiens €11, 50 minutes, six to 12 daily

Calais-Ville €20, two hours, 13 daily Monday to Friday, seven on Saturday, four on Sunday

Lens €3.90, 20 minutes, 13 daily Monday to Friday, seven on Saturday, four on Sunday

Lille-Flandres €10, 40 to 70 minutes, nine to 16 daily

Paris Gare du Nord TGV €32 or €46, 50 minutes, 11 to 15 daily

Battle of the Somme Memorials

Almost 750,000 soldiers, airmen and sailors from Great Britain, Australia, Canada, the Indian subcontinent, Ireland, New Zealand, South Africa, the West Indies and other parts of the British Empire died during WWI on the Western Front, two-thirds of them in France. They were buried where they fell, in more than 1000 military cemeteries and 2000 civilian cemeteries that dot the landscape along a wide swathe of territory – 'Flanders Fields' – running roughly from Amiens and Cambrai north via Arras and Béthune to Armentières and Ypres (Ieper) in Belgium.

The focal point of each Commonwealth cemetery, now tended by the Commonwealth War Graves Commission (www.

cwgc.org), is the Cross of Sacrifice. Many of the headstones, made of Portland limestone, bear moving personal inscriptions composed by family members. Most cemeteries have a bronze **Cemetery Register** box that contains a visitors book, in which you can record your impressions, and a booklet with biographical details on each of the identified dead (Americans who died fighting with British forces can be spotted by their addresses). Some larger cemeteries also have a bronze plaque with historical information.

American war dead of the world wars were either repatriated (61%) or reburied in large cemeteries near where they fell (39%).

The sites in this section, listed in alphabetical order, are situated in the triangle defined by Lille, Amiens and St-Quentin. Except where noted, they are always open.

Area tourist offices can supply you with some really excellent English-language brochures, including *The Vistor's Guide to the Battlefields* and *Australians in the Somme*. For online information, see www.somme-battlefields.com and www.somme14-18.com.

☞ Tours

Tourist offices (including those in Lille, Amiens, Arras and Péronne) can help book tours of battlefield sites and memorials.

Battle of the Somme Memorials

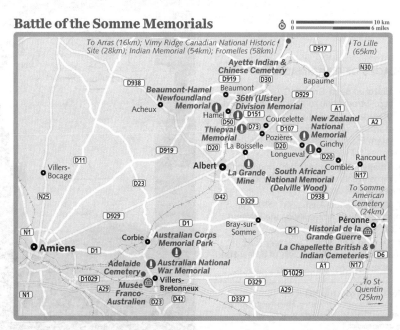

Battle of the Somme

The First Battle of the Somme, a WWI Allied offensive waged in the villages and woodlands northeast of Amiens, was designed to relieve pressure on the beleaguered French troops at Verdun. On 1 July 1916, British, Commonwealth and French troops 'went over the top' in a massive assault along a 34km front. However, German positions proved virtually unbreachable, and on the first day of the battle – the bloodiest day in the history of the British army – an astounding 21,392 Allied troops were killed and another 35,492 were wounded. Most casualties were infantrymen mown down by German machine guns.

By the time the offensive was called off in mid-November, a total of 1.2 million lives had been lost on both sides. The British had advanced 12km, the French 8km. The Battle of the Somme has become a symbol of the meaningless slaughter of war, and its killing fields remain sites of pilgrimage.

PLACES OF PILGRIMAGE

» **Historial de la Grande Guerre** (p185), a superb introduction to WWI and its context

» **Vimy Ridge Canadian National Historic Site** (p187), a cratered slice of the Western Front undisturbed since the day the guns fell silent

» **Thiepval Memorial** (p186), honouring Commonwealth soldiers who rest in unknown graves

» **Musée Franco-Australien** (p186), an intimate look at Anzac life on the Western Front

» **Somme American Cemetery** (p185), final resting place for soldiers of a New York regiment

Clockwise from top left
1. Somme American Cemetery 2. Flags flying over the Australian Corps Memorial Park 3. Headstone of an Australian soldier

Respected tour companies include Battlefield Experience (☎03 22 76 29 60; www.the battleofthesomme.co.uk) and Western Front Tours (www.westernfronttours.com.au; ⊙mid-Mar–mid-Nov).

ⓘ Getting There & Away

Visiting the Somme memorials is easiest by car but several sites can be reached by train from Amiens and/or Arras; details appear under Villers-Bretonneux and Vimy Ridge Canadian National Historic Site. Cycling on secondary roads is also an option.

AUSTRALIAN CORPS MEMORIAL PARK

This memorial (⊙vehicle access 9am-6pm, pedestrians 24hr) stands on the hilltop site of the Battle of Le Hamel (4 July 1918), fought by Australian and American troops under the command of Australian Lieutenant General John Monash. The German air ace Baron Manfred von Richthofen, aka the Red Baron, was shot down a bit northwest of here – Australian ground forces claimed credit but so did a Canadian pilot.

Inaugurated in 2008, the Australian Corps Memorial is 7km northeast of Villers-Bretonneux (and just east of Le Hamel); follow the signs to 'Mémorial Australien'.

AYETTE INDIAN & CHINESE CEMETERY

Towards the end of WWI, tens of thousands of Chinese labourers were recruited by the British government to perform noncombat jobs in Europe, including the gruesome task of recovering and burying Allied war dead. Some of these *travailleurs chinois* (Chinese labourers) died in the Spanish flu epidemic of 1918–19 and are buried in this Commonwealth cemetery beneath gravestones inscribed in Chinese and English with inscriptions such as 'a good reputation endures forever', 'a noble duty bravely done' and 'faithful unto death'. Nearby are the graves of Indians who served with British forces, marked in Hindi or Arabic, and the tomb of a single German.

The cemetery is 29km northeast of Albert, just off D919 at the southern edge of the village of Ayette.

BEAUMONT-HAMEL NEWFOUNDLAND MEMORIAL

Like Vimy, the evocative Mémorial Terre-Neuvien de Beaumont-Hamel preserves part of the Western Front in the state it was in at fighting's end. The zigzag trench system, which still fills with mud in winter, is clearly visible, as are countless shell craters and the remains of barbed-wire barriers.

On 1 July 1916 the volunteer Royal Newfoundland Regiment stormed entrenched German positions and was nearly wiped out; until recently, a plaque at the entrance noted bluntly that 'strategic and tactical miscalculations led to a great slaughter'. You can survey the battlefield from the bronze **caribou statue**, surrounded by plants native to Newfoundland. Canadian students based at the Welcome Centre (☎03 22 76 70 87; www.vac-acc.gc.ca; ⊙9am or 10am-5pm or 6pm), which resembles a Newfoundland fisher's house, give free guided tours (except from mid-December to mid-January).

Beaumont-Hamel is 9km north of Albert, mostly along D50.

FROMELLES

'The worst 24 hours in Australia's entire history' – in the words of Ross McMullin, writing for the Australian War Memorial (www.awm.gov.au) – took place at Fromelles on 19 and 20 July 1916, when a poorly planned offensive across a 3.6km-wide front, intended to divert German forces from the Battle of the Somme, turned into a disastrous rout: 1917 men of the Australian Imperial Force and 519 British soldiers were killed and another 3146 Australians and 977 British were wounded. It seems likely that one of the soldiers on the victorious German side was a 27-year-old corporal in the 16th Bavarian Reserve Infantry Regiment named Adolf Hitler.

After the battle, the Germans buried many of the Australian and British dead in mass graves behind their lines. Most were reburied after the war, but eight pits containing the remains of 250 men were not found until 2008. To provide them with a dignified final resting place, the hexagonal Fromelles (Pheasant Wood) Military Cemetery (www.cwgc.org/fromelles, www.fromellesdiscussiongroup.com) – the first new Commonwealth cemetery in half a century – was dedicated on 19 July 2010, the 94th anniversary of the catastrophic and pointless assault. At the time of writing, DNA testing had established the identity of 109 Australians.

After the surviving Australians retreated to their pre-battle front lines, hundreds of their comrades-in-arms lay wounded in no-man's land. For three days the survivors made heroic efforts to rescue them, acts of bravery commemorated by the sculpture *Cobbers* in the Fromelles Memorial Park. Inaugurated in 1998, it is situated atop a row of German blockhouses 2km northwest of the new cemetery; to get there, follow the signs to the 'Mémorial Australien'.

Nearby, in what was once no-man's land between the Australian and German front lines, is the VC Corner Australian Cemetery. There are no headstones because not a single one of the 410 corpses buried here was identified.

Fromelles is 22km southwest of Lille, mostly along A25 and N41.

INDIAN MEMORIAL

The evocative Mémorial Indien (Neuve-Chapelle Memorial), vaguely Moghul in architecture, records the names of 4700 soldiers of the Indian Army who 'have no known grave'. The units (31st Punjabis, 11th Rajputs, 2nd King Edward's Own Gurkha Rifles) and the ranks of the fallen – *sowar* (cavalry trooper), *havildar* (sergeant), *naik* (chief), *sepoy* (infantry private), labourer, follower – engraved on the walls evoke the pride, pomp and exploitation on which the British Empire was built. The 15m-high **column**, flanked by two tigers, is topped by a lotus capital, the Imperial Crown and the Star of India.

This seldom-visited – and poorly signposted – memorial is 20km southwest of Lille. To get there from La Bassée, head north along D947 for 5km.

LA GRANDE MINE

Just outside the hamlet of La Boisselle, this enormous crater looks like the site of a meteor impact. Some 100m across and 30m deep, the Lochnagar Crater Memorial (as it's officially known) was created on the morning of the first day of the First Battle of the Somme (1 July 1916) by about 25 tonnes of ammonal laid by British sappers in order to create a breach in the German lines – and is a testament to the boundless ingenuity human beings can muster when determined to kill their fellow creatures.

La Grande Mine is 4km northeast of Albert along D929.

PÉRONNE

The best place to begin a visit to the Somme battlefields – especially if you're interested in WWI's historical and cultural context – is the outstanding Historial de la Grande Guerre (Museum of the Great War; ☎03 22 83 14 18; www.historial.org; Château de Péronne; adult/child incl audioguide €7.50/3.80; ☺10am-6pm, closed mid-Dec–mid-Jan). Tucked inside Péronne's massively fortified château, this award-winning museum tells the story of the war chronologically, with equal space given to the German, French and British perspectives on what happened, how and why. A great deal of visually engaging material, including period films and the bone-chilling engravings by Otto Dix, capture the aesthetic sensibilities, enthusiasm, naive patriotism and unimaginable violence of the time. The proud uniforms of various units and armies are shown laid out on the ground, as if on freshly – though bloodlessly – dead soldiers. Not much glory here. The lake behind the museum is a fine place for a stroll or picnic.

Excellent English brochures on the battlefields can be picked up at Péronne's tourist office (☎03 22 84 42 38; www.haute somme-tourisme.com; 18 place André Audinot; ☺10am-noon & 2-5pm or 6.30pm, closed Sun), 100m from the museum entrance.

On D1017 at the southern edge of town (towards St-Quentin), La Chapellette British & Indian Cemeteries have multifaith, multilingual headstones, with a section for the fallen of units such as the 38th King George's Own Central India Horse.

Péronne (pop 8700) is about 60km east of Amiens, mostly along D1029 or A29.

SOMME AMERICAN CEMETERY

In late September 1918, just six weeks before the end of WWI, American units – flanked by their British, Canadian and Australian allies – launched an assault on the Germans' heavily fortified Hindenburg Line. One regiment of the 27th Infantry Division, a National Guard unit from New York, suffered 337 dead and 658 wounded on a single day.

Some of the fiercest fighting took place near the village of Bony, on the sloping site now occupied by the 1844 Latin Crosses and Stars of David of the Somme American Cemetery (www.abmc.gov; ☺9am-5pm). The names of 333 men whose remains were never recovered are inscribed on the walls of the **Memorial Chapel**, reached through massive bronze doors. The small **Visitors' Building** (turn left at the flagpole) has information on the battle.

The cemetery is 24km northeast of Péronne, mostly along D6, and 18km north of St-Quentin along D1044. From A26, take exit 9 and follow the signs for 17km.

SOUTH AFRICAN NATIONAL MEMORIAL

The Mémorial Sud-Africain stands in the middle of shell-pocked Delville Wood, which was almost captured by a South African brigade in the third week of July 1916. The avenues through the trees are named after streets in London and Edinburgh. The star-shaped museum (www.delvillewood.com; ☺10am-5.30pm, closed Mon, holidays, Dec & Feb) is a replica of Cape Town's Castle of Good Hope.

The memorial is 13km east-northeast of Albert, mostly along D20.

The New Zealand National Memorial is also in this area, 1.5km due north of Longueval.

THIEPVAL MEMORIAL

Dedicated to 'the Missing of the Somme', this Commonwealth memorial – its distinctive outline visible for many kilometres in all directions – is the region's most visited place of pilgrimage. Situated on the site of a German stronghold that was stormed on 1 July 1916 with unimaginable casualties, it was designed by Sir Edwin Lutyens and dedicated in 1932. The columns of the arches are inscribed with the names of 73,367 British and South African soldiers whose remains were never recovered or identified. The glass-walled visitors centre (☎03 22 74 60 47; admission free; ☺10am-6pm, closed 2 weeks around New Year) is discreetly below ground level.

Thiepval is 7.5km northeast of Albert, partly along D50 and D151.

THIRTY-SIXTH (ULSTER) DIVISION MEMORIAL

Built on a German frontline position assaulted by the overwhelmingly Protestant 36th (Ulster) Division on 1 July 1916, the Ulster Tower Memorial (☎03 22 74 87 14; ☺museum 10am-5pm, to 6pm May-Aug, closed Mon & Dec-Feb) is an exact replica of Helen's Tower at Clanboye, County Down, where the unit did its training. Dedicated in 1921, it has long been a Unionist pilgrimage site; a black obelisk known as the **Orange Memorial to Fallen Brethren** (1993) stands in an enclosure behind the tower. In a sign that historic wounds are finally healing, in 2006 the Irish Republic issued a €0.75 postage stamp showing the 36th Division in ac-

tion on this site, to commemorate the 90th anniversary of the Battle of the Somme.

Virtually untouched since the war, nearby Thiepval Wood can be visited on a guided tour (donation requested) at 11am and/or 3pm; call ahead for dates of scheduled group tours.

The monument is on D73 between Beaumont-Hamel and Thiepval; follow the signs to the 'Mémorial Irlandais'.

VILLERS-BRETONNEUX

For Aussies, Villers-Bretonneux (pop 4160) is a heart warming place. Billing itself as *l'Australie en Picardie,* the town religiously commemorates **Anzac Day** (25 April; www.anzac-france.com) and is home to the Musée Franco-Australien (Franco-Australian Museum; ☎03 22 96 80 79; www.museeaustralien.com; École Victoria, 9 rue Victoria; adult/student €4/2.50; ☺9.30am-5.30pm, closed Sun), whose displays of highly personal WWI Australiana include letters and photographs that evoke life on the Western Front. It is housed in a primary school that was built with funds donated by schoolchildren in the Australian state of Victoria. In 1993 the unidentified remains of an Australian soldier were transferred from Adelaide Cemetery, on D1029 at the western edge of town, to the Australian War Memorial in Canberra.

During WWI 313,000 Australians (out of a total population of 4.5 million) volunteered for overseas military service; 46,000 met their deaths on the Western Front (14,000 others perished elsewhere; www.wwIwesternfront.gov.au). The names of 10,982 Australian soldiers whose remains were never found are engraved on the base of the 32m-high Australian National War Memorial (D23), dedicated in 1938; two years later its stone walls were scarred by the guns of Hitler's invading armies. The views from the top of the tower are breathtaking; when the gardeners aren't present to open it, the keys can be picked up at the Gendarmerie in Villers-Bretonneux, on D1029 towards Amiens. The memorial is about 2km north of Villers-Bretonneux along D23.

Villers-Bretonneux is 17km east of Amiens, mostly along D1029 (formerly N29). The **train station**, well served from Amiens (€3.40, 13 minutes, 11 daily Monday to Friday, four to six daily weekends), is 700m south of the museum (take rue de Melbourne) and a walkable 3km south of the

Australian National War Memorial. A taxi (☑03 22 48 49 49) from Villers-Bretonneux to the memorial and back (at the time of your choosing) costs €18 to €20 return.

VIMY RIDGE CANADIAN NATIONAL HISTORIC SITE

Whereas the French, right after the war, attempted to erase all signs of battle and return the Somme region to agriculture and normalcy, the Canadians decided that the most evocative way to remember their fallen was to preserve part of the crater-pocked battlefield exactly the way it looked when the guns fell silent. As a result, the best place to get some sense of the hell known as the Western Front is the chilling, eerie moonscape of Vimy.

Of the 66,655 Canadians who died in WWI, 3598 lost their lives in April 1917 taking 14km-long Vimy Ridge (Crête de Vimy). Its highest point – site of a heavily fortified German position – was later chosen as the site of Canada's WWI memorial, designed by Walter Seymour Allward and built from 1925 to 1936. The 20 allegorical figures, carved from huge blocks of white Croatian limestone, include a cloaked, downcast female figure representing a young Canada grieving for her fallen. The two striking columns represent Canada and France. The names of 11,285 Canadians who 'died in France but have no known graves', listed alphabetically and within each letter by rank, are inscribed around the base. The peaceful, 1-sq-km park also includes two Canadian cemeteries and, at the vehicle entrance to the main memorial, a monument to France's Moroccan Division (in French and Arabic).

The rust-coloured Welcome Centre (☑03 21 50 68 68; www.vac-acc.gc.ca; ⊙9am or 10am-5pm or 6pm) and its modest exhibits are staffed by bilingual Canadian students. Nearby, visitors can see mine craters, visit infantry supply tunnels (☑03 22 76 70 86; ⊙tours depart hourly 9am or 10am-5pm or 6pm, closed mid-Dec–mid-Jan) and peer from reconstructed trenches (⊙9am or 10am-5pm or 6pm) towards the German front line, a mere 25m away. Herds of sheep – tended by the only two shepherds employed by Canada's federal government – keep the grass trimmed. Because countless bodies still lie buried among the trees and craters, the entire site is treated like a graveyard.

Vimy Ridge is 11km north of Arras (towards Lens), partly along N17. **Trains** link

Arras with the town of Vimy (€2.90, 12 minutes, seven daily Monday to Friday, two on Saturday), 6km east of the memorial. A **taxi** from Arras costs about €23 one-way (€28 on Sunday).

Compiègne

POP 43,360

The *cité imperiale* (imperial city) of Compiègne reached its glittering zenith under Emperor Napoléon III (r 1852-70), whose legacy is alive and well in the château – the star attraction – and its park. A forest clearing near the city was the site of the armistice that ended WWI and the French surrender in 1940.

On 23 May 1430 Joan of Arc (Jeanne d'Arc) – honoured by two statues in the city centre – was captured at Compiègne by the Burgundians, who later sold her to their English allies.

⊙ Sights

Château de Compiègne   PALACE, MUSEUMS
(☑03 44 38 47 00; www.musee-chateau-compiegne.fr, in French; place du Général de Gaulle; adult/under 26yr €6.50/free) Napoléon III's dazzling hunting parties drew aristocrats and wannabes from all around Europe to his 1337-room palace, built around eight courtyards. The sumptuous Grands Appartements (Imperial Apartments; ⊙10am-12.30pm & 1.30-5.45pm Wed-Mon, last admission 30min before closing), including the empress's bedroom and a ballroom lit by 15 chandeliers, can be visited with an audioguide (available in French, English, German and Japanese).

You have to join a French-language guided tour (included in the ticket price) to see the Musée du Second Empire, which illustrates the lives of Napoléon III and his family, and the Musée de la Voiture, which features vehicles that pre-date the internal combustion engine as well as early motorcars such as the Jamais Contente, a torpedo-shaped contraption from 1899. The Musée de l'Impératrice, which stars Eugénie and includes mementos of her dashing, exiled son, 'killed by the Zulus, in Zululand, Africa' in 1879 – he was serving, with Queen Victoria's express permission, in the British army – was closed for renovations at the time of writing.

Stretching east from the château, the 20-hectare, English-style Petit Parc links up with the Grand Parc and the Forêt de

WORTH A TRIP

WHEN BENNY MET LOUIE

From the American Revolution (when French generals led American patriots, and Benjamin Franklin lobbied Louis XVI) through WWI (when American volunteers carried out humanitarian work long before the doughboys arrived) and WWII (when the Parisians didn't exactly liberate themselves, whatever de Gaulle might have proclaimed), the USA and France have had a prickly but ardent love affair. All this and more is presented through art and artefacts at the Musée Franco-Américain (Franco-American Museum; ☏03 23 39 60 16; www.museefrancoamericain.fr; ⊘closed for renovations until late 2011), 30km northeast of Compiègne in the early 17th-century Château de Bléran-court. The Jardins du Nouveau Monde (New World Gardens; ⊘8am-7pm), open while the museum is being renovated, showcase 'exotic' flowers (in bloom from May to September or October), shrubs and trees (eg sequoias) native to the Americas.

Compiègne, a forest that surrounds Compiègne on the east and south and is crisscrossed by rectilinear paths. The area is a favourite venue for hiking and cycling (maps available at the tourist office) as well as horse riding. Napoléon I had the 4.5km Allée des Beaux-Monts laid out so that Empress Marie-Louise wouldn't miss Vienna's Schönbrunn palace quite so much.

Clairière de l'Armistice   HISTORIC SITE

(Armistice Clearing; ☏03 44 85 14 18; www.musee-armistice-14-18.fr; adult €4; ⊘10am-6pm, closed Tue Oct-Mar) The armistice that came into force on the 11th hour of the 11th day of the 11th month – the year was 1918 – and finally put an end to WWI was signed 7km northeast of Compiègne (towards Soissons) inside the railway carriage of the Allied supreme commander, Maréchal Ferdinand Foch.

On 22 June 1940, in the same railway car, the French – with Hitler looking on smugly – were forced to sign the armistice that recognised Nazi Germany's domination of France. Taken for exhibition to Berlin, the carriage was destroyed in April 1945 on the Führer's personal orders lest it be used for a third surrender – his own.

In the middle of a thick forest, Clairière de l'Armistice – staffed by volunteers (mainly French army veterans) – commemorates these events with monuments and a museum whose 700 stereoscopic (3-D) photos give you an eerie feeling of being right there in the mud, muck and misery of WWI. The wooden rail wagon now on display is of the same type as the original; the furnishings, hidden away during WWII, were the ones actually used in 1918.

Mémorial de l'Internement et de la Déportation   NAZI CAMP

(Internment & Deportation Memorial; ☏03 44 96 37 00; http://memorial.compiegne.fr, in French; 2bis av des Martyrs de la Liberté; adult incl English audioguide €3; ⊘10am-6pm, closed Tue) The French military base of Royallieu was used as a Nazi transit camp from 1941 to 1944; several of the original buildings have housed a memorial museum since 2008. Of the more than 53,000 men, women and children held here – Resistance fighters, political prisoners, prisoners of war, Jews (kept in a special section) and American civilians arrested after Pearl Harbour – 48,000 were marched through town to the train station for the trip east to concentration and extermination camps, including Auschwitz.

The memorial is 2.5km southwest of the city centre. To get there, take rue de Harlay southwest along the river, turn left (south) onto bd Gambetta, then right onto rue de Paris; or hop aboard bus 5.

🛏 Sleeping

There are several hotels near the train station and just across the River Oise.

Hôtel de Harlay   HOTEL €€

(☏03 44 23 01 50; www.hotel-compiegne.net; 3 rue de Harlay; d €74; ❉@🛜) Facing the river, this family-run establishment has 20 well-kept, comfortable rooms fitted out with colourful wallpaper, old-time tile bathrooms and rich carpeting.

🍴 Eating

Restaurants and cafés are sprinkled around the city centre, including rue Magenta, rue de l'Étoile and narrow, ancient rue des Lombards, which form a triangle two blocks south of the tourist office.

Bistrot des Arts BISTRO €€
(35 cours Guynemer; menus €14-28; ⊘closed Sun & lunch Sat) An old-time bistro with traditional French meat dishes and a selection of fresh fish (consult the blackboard). Midway between the tourist office and the train station, facing the river.

Monoprix SUPERMARKET €
(37 rue Solférino; ⊘8.30am-8.30pm Mon-Sat, 9am-1pm Sun) Two blocks northwest of the tourist office.

ℹ Information

Cyber Café l'Evasion (7 rue Jean Legende; per hr €3.50; ⊘10am-7pm Tue-Sat, 12.30-7pm Mon) Internet access inside the gallery next to the tourist office.

Tourist Office (☏03 44 40 01 00; www.compiegne-tourisme.fr, in French; place de l'Hôtel de Ville; ⊘9.15am-12.15pm & 1.45-6.15pm Mon-Sat) Has English brochures. Situated in a building attached to the Flamboyant Gothic Hôtel de Ville (dating from c 1500), facing a square with lots of tulips and a statue of (who else?) Joan of Arc.

ℹ Getting There & Away

Compiègne, 65km northeast of Paris, can be easily visited on a day trip from the capital.

TRAIN Compiègne is linked by train to Paris' Gare du Nord (€13, 41 to 77 minutes, 13 to 26 daily) and Amiens (€12.10, 1¼ hours, eight to 12 daily). As you walk from the station building out to the tracks, turn right and after about 80m you'll come to the **deportation memorial**, which includes two train carriages of the type used during WWII to ship Royallieu prisoners to concentration camps.

ℹ Getting Around

The tourist office, in the heart of the city centre, is 600m southwest of the château (served by buses 1 and 2, which are free Monday to Saturday, except holidays) and 1km southeast of the train station.

There's free parking in front of the château (place du Général de Gaulle), southeast of there along av Royale and av de la Résistance, and along the river (cours Guynemer).

Laon

POP 27,500

The walled, hilltop Ville Haute (Upper City) – an architectural gem – boasts a magnificent Gothic cathedral and commands fantastic views of the surrounding plains. About 100 vertical metres below sits the Ville Basse (Lower City), completely rebuilt after being flattened in WWII. Laon (the name, as pronounced locally, has one syllable and rhymes with *enfant*) makes a great spot for a romantic getaway.

Laon served as the capital of the Carolingian empire until it was brought to an end in 987 by Hugh Capet, who for some reason preferred ruling from Paris.

◉ Sights & Activities

The claw-shaped Ville Haute has no less than 84 listed historic monuments, the densest concentration in France. Laon's narrow streets, alleyways (some less than 1m wide) and courtyards are particularly rewarding territory for keen-eyed wandering.

Cathédrale Notre Dame CATHEDRAL
(⊘9am- 8pm) A model for a number of its more famous Gothic sisters – Chartres, Reims and Dijon among them – this medieval jewel was built (1150-1230) in the transitional Gothic style on Romanesque foundations. The 110m-long interior, remarkably well lit, has three levels of columns and arches and a gilded wrought-iron choir screen; some of the stained glass dates from the 12th century. A memorial plaque for Commonwealth WWI dead hangs just inside the west facade. The structure is best appreciated with an **audioguide**, available next door at the tourist office, which is also the place to sign up for a guided tour of the **south tower** (adult €4; ⊘2.30pm Wed-Sun, daily during school holidays, also at 4pm early Jul-early Sep).

TOP CHOICE **City Ramparts** WALK
To get a sense of the city and its commanding position, take a walk around the Ville Haute's 7km-long wall, pierced by three fortified gates. For some of the finest panoramic views, head to the 13th-century **Porte d'Ardon** (one of the gates); circular

CHICAGO'S FIRST

Laon-born Jesuit missionary **Jacques Marquette** (1637–75), a pioneer explorer of the Mississippi River and, in 1674, the first non-Native American to live in what is now Chicago, is commemorated by an haut-relief statue at square du Père Marquette, at the bottom of rue Franklin Roosevelt (below the Ville Haute Poma station).

Batterie Morlot, a one-time optical telegraph station; and rue du Rempart St-Rémi. Over 80 paths, known as *grimpettes,* take you down the steep forested slopes in every direction.

Sleeping & Eating

The pedestrianised, northwestern section of Rue Châtelaine (linking the cathedral with place du Général Leclerc) is home to several food shops selling nutritional basics such as bread (at No 54) and chocolate (at No 27).

Hôtel Les Chevaliers HOTEL €
(☏03 23 27 17 50; hotelchevaliers@aol.com; 3-5 rue Sérurier; d €57; ☏) Parts of this 13-room hostelry, right around the corner from the Haute Ville's *hôtel de ville,* date from the Middle Ages. Some rooms have ancient stone and brick walls. Renovated in 2010.

Hôtel des Arts HOTEL €
(☏03 23 79 57 16; www.hoteldesarts02.com, in French; 11 place de la Gare; d/tr/q €52/78/96; ☏) Facing the train station, this welcoming hotel has 24 simple, bright, cheery rooms. To get there by car, follow the signs to 'Gares'.

❶ Information

The **Tourist office** (☏03 23 20 28 62; www. tourisme-paysdelaon.com, in French; place de la Cathédrale, Ville Haute; ⊗9.30am-1pm & 2-6.30pm; @) can supply you with a free town map and excellent English brochures on Laon and the surrounds. Also offers **audioguides** (€4) for excellent one- to three-hour walking tours of the Ville Haute and the cathedral, guided tours (in French, with guides who speak English) and free internet access. Situated next to the cathedral in a 12th-century hospital decorated with 14th-century frescos.

❶ Getting There & Around

Laon is only 67km northwest of Reims (in Champagne).

CAR The Ville Haute's one-way streets circle round and round – if they don't drive you crazy they'll at least make you dizzy. Parking is available at the eastern end of the Ville Haute, around the Citadelle.

TRAIN The train station, in the Ville Basse, is linked to Amiens (€16, 1½ hours, four to nine daily), Paris' Gare du Nord (€21, 1½ hours, 14 daily Monday to Friday, nine on Saturday and Sunday) and Reims (€9, 40 minutes, eight daily Monday to Friday, four Saturday, three Sunday).

The Ville Haute is a steep 20-minute walk from the train station – the stairs begin at the upper end of av Carnot – but it's more fun to take the automated, elevated **Poma funicular railway** (return €1.10; ⊗every 4min 7am-8pm Mon-Sat, closed holidays, closed 2 wks late Jul-early Aug), which links the train station with the upper city in 3½ minutes flat.

Normandy

Best Places to Eat

» Le Bouchon (p218)

» Gill (p197)

» Les Nymphéas (p197)

» Restaurant de la Chaine d'Or (p205)

Best Places to Stay

» Hôtel de la Chaine d'Or (p205)

» Château de Bellefontaine (p208)

» La Maison de Lucie (p223)

» Hôtel de Bourgtheroulde (p196)

Why Go?

Ever since the armies of William the Conqueror set sail from its shores in 1066, Normandy has played a pivotal role in European history, from the Norman invasion of England to the Hundred Years War and the D-Day beach landings of 1944. This rich and often brutal past is what draws travellers to the region today, though the pastoral landscapes, small fishing ports, dramatic coastline and waistline-expanding cuisine are all equally good reasons to include this accessible and beautiful chunk of France on any trip.

The standout highlights of Normandy are world-renowned sights such as the Bayeux Tapestry, the D-Day beaches, Monet's garden at Giverny and the spectacular Mont St-Michel, but the region's lesser-known charms include a variety of stunning beaches and coastal landscapes, some excellent and little-known art museums, and architectural gems ranging from classic beauty Honfleur to postwar oddball Le Havre.

When to Go

Rouen

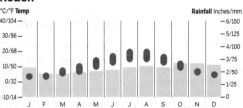

March Honfleur's Vieux Bassin comes alive with colourful fishing boats on Whit Sunday.

July Head to Rouen for the Tombée de la Nuit street festival in the first week of July.

September Deauville's American Film Festival is the accessible cousin of Cannes.

DRIVING NORMANDY

Though public transport in Normandy is good, driving here is highly recommended if you plan to visit the D-Day beaches independently or explore some of the region's lesser-known areas.

Must-Try Dishes

» *coquilles St-Jacques* (fresh scallops)

» *huîtres creuses* (literally, 'hollow oysters'; oysters on the half shell)

» *tripes á la mode de Caen* (tripe and vegetables slow cooked in cider)

» *sole dieppoise* (Dieppe sole)

Top 5 Quirky Sights

» Âitre St-Maclou (p196), Rouen

» Église St-Joseph (p202), Le Havre

» Les Maisons Satie (p222), Honfleur

» Palais Bénédictine (p201), Fécamp

» Le Volcan (p202), Le Havre

Resources

» Tourism and travel links: www.normandie-tourisme.fr and www.normandie-qualite-tourisme.com

» *Calvados* facts: vimoutiers.net/AppleCiderCalvados.htm

» Camembert fan? www.camembert-aoc.org

Itineraries

ONE WEEK

Coming from Paris, **Giverny** will be your first stop for Monet's Garden, with perhaps a side trip to gorgeous **Les Andelys** before continuing to **Rouen**, **Honfleur**, **Bayeux** and the **D-Day beaches**, ending at **Mont St-Michel**.

TWO WEEKS

With an extra week, follow the same route but take more time to explore places on the way. **Fécamp**, **Étretat** and **Le Havre** are all well worth detouring for, as are pretty **Trouville** and **Deauville**, interesting **Caen** and **Coutances** for its charming cathedral and unhurried pace of life.

ROUTE DU CIDRE

Normandy's signposted 40km Route du Cidre (Cider Route; routeducidre.free.fr), about 20km east of Caen, wends its way through the Pays d'Auge, a rural area of orchards, pastures, hedgerows, half-timbered farmhouses and stud farms, through picturesque villages such as Cambremer and Beuvron-en-Auge. Signs reading Cru de Cambremer indicate the way to about 20 small-scale, traditional producers who are happy to show you their facilities and sell you their home-grown cider (€3 a bottle) and *calvados*.

Traditional Normandy cider takes about six months to make. The apples are shaken off the trees or gathered from the ground between early October and early December. After being stored for two or three weeks, they are pressed, purified, slow-fermented, bottled and naturally carbonated, just like Champagne.

Normandy's AOC cider is made with a blend of apple varieties and is known for being fruity, tangy and slightly bitter – nothing like the mass-produced, pasteurised 'cidre' sold in French supermarkets. The good news is that you'll be able to enjoy it in any crêperie or restaurant throughout Normandy.

Top 5 Museums

» Musée Malraux (p202), Le Havre

» Musée des Impressionismes (p205), Giverny

» Musée de la Tapisserie de Bayeux (p206), Bayeux

» Musée Eugène Boudin (p222), Honfleur

» Musée des Beaux-Arts (p218), Caen

History

The Vikings invaded present-day Normandy in the 9th century, and some of invaders established settlements and adopted Christianity. In 911 French king Charles the Simple, of the Carolingian dynasty, and Viking chief Hrólfr agreed that the area around Rouen should be handed over to these Norsemen – or Normans, as they came to be known.

Throughout the Hundred Years War (1337–1453), the duchy seesawed between French and English rule. England dominated Normandy for some 30 years until France gained permanent control in 1450. In the 16th century, Normandy, a Protes-

NORMANDY

Normandy Highlights

❶ Admire the architecture, art and antiques of **Rouen's old town** (p194)

❷ Dive into an Impressionist masterpiece by visiting **Monet's garden** (p205) at Giverny

❸ Travel back a thousand years with the world's oldest comic strip, the **Bayeux Tapestry** (p206)

❹ See Normandy's historic D-Day beaches and the moving **war cemeteries** (p212)

❺ Watch the tide come in from the summit of the extraordinary abbey of **Mont St-Michel** (p227)

❻ Savour superfresh seafood at the harbourside restaurants of beautiful

Honfleur (p225) and glamorous **Trouville** (p221)

❼ Wander the spectacular coastline and marvel at the famous cliffs at **Étretat** (p201)

❽ Enjoy some rich **Norman cuisine**, from creamy Camembert and fresh oysters to cider and *calvados*

tant stronghold, was the scene of much fighting between Catholics and Huguenots.

For details on D-Day, see p211.

ⓘ Getting There & Around

Ferries to and from England and Ireland dock at Cherbourg, Dieppe, Le Havre and Ouistreham (Caen). The Channel Islands (Jersey and Guernsey) are most accessible from the Breton port of St-Malo but from April to September there are passenger services from the Normandy towns of Granville, Carteret and Diélette. For more information on ferries, see p973.

Normandy is easily accessible by train from Paris – Rouen is just 70 minutes from Paris Gare St-Lazare. Most major towns are accessible by rail, and with the **Carte Sillage Loisirs**, travel around the Basse Normandie region is remarkably cheap on weekends and holidays. However, bus services between smaller towns and villages are infrequent at best. To really explore Normandy's rural areas you need either two or four wheels.

SEINE-MARITIME

The Seine-Maritime *département* stretches along the chalk-white cliffs of the Côte d'Albâtre (Alabaster Coast) from Le Tréport via Dieppe to Le Havre, the fifth-busiest port in France. It's a region whose history is firmly bound up with the sea, and is ideal for coastal exploring and clifftop walks. When you fancy a break from the bracing sea air, head inland to the lively, lovely metropolis of Rouen, a favourite haunt of Monet and Simone de Beauvoir, and one of the most intriguing cities in France's northeastern corner.

Rouen

POP 119,927

With its elegant spires, beautifully restored medieval quarter and soaring Gothic cathedral, the ancient city of Rouen is one of Normandy's highlights. Rouen has had a turbulent history – it was devastated several times during the Middle Ages by fire and plague, and was occupied by the English during the Hundred Years War. The young French heroine Joan of Arc (Jeanne d'Arc) was tried for heresy and burned at the stake in the central square in 1431. During WWII Allied bombing raids laid waste to large parts of the city, especially the area south of the cathedral, but over the last six decades the city has been meticulously rebuilt.

◉ Sights & Activities

The old city, the heart of which is rue du Gros Horloge, lies north of the city centre's main east–west thoroughfare, rue Général Leclerc.

Place du Vieux Marché　　　　SQUARE
Rue du Gros Horloge runs from the cathedral west to this square, where 19-year-old Joan of Arc was executed for heresy in 1431. Dedicated in 1979, the thrillingly bizarre **Église Jeanne d'Arc** (☉10am-noon & 2-6pm Apr-Oct), with its fish-scale exterior, marks the spot where Joan was burned at the stake. The church's soaring modernist interior, lit by some marvellous 16th-century stained glass, is well worth a look.

Gros Horloge　　　　CLOCK TOWER
(rue du Gros Horloge; adult/child €6/3; ☉10am-1pm & 2-7pm Tue-Sun) Rue du Gros Horloge is spanned by this impressive structure, a Gothic belfry with one-handed medieval clocks on each side. On the west side, check out the gilded Latin inscription dedicated to Ludovico XV (Louis XV) in 1732 – see if you can count how many times the suffix -*issimo* appears.

Palais de Justice　　　　COURTS
(place Maréchal Foch) The ornately Gothic Law Courts, little more than a shell at the end of WWII, have been restored to their early-16th-century Gothic glory, though the 19th-century western facade is still pockmarked by bullet holes. The courtyard, with its impossibly delicate spires, gargoyles and statuary, is accessible via a metal detector from rue aux Juifs; this is also the entrance to use if you'd like to sit in on a trial.

Under the staircase at the courtyard's eastern end is the **Monument Juif** (Jewish Monument), the oldest Jewish communal structure in France and the only reminder of Rouen's medieval Jewish community, expelled by Philippe le Bel in 1306.

Cathédrale Notre Dame　　　　CATHEDRAL
(place de la Cathédrale; ☉7.30am-7pm Tue-Sat, 8am-6pm Sun, 2-7pm Mon) On a site occupied by churches since the 4th century, Rouen's magnificent cathedral was painted repeatedly by Claude Monet, who was fascinated by the subtle changes of light and colour on the cathedral's towering French Gothic facade. Built between 1201 and 1514, the building was damaged by time, WWII and a 1999 storm, and is still undergoing renovation. Monet would hardly recognise its recently cleaned facade, now almost white.

Rouen

The Romanesque crypt (☉tours 2.30pm Sat & Sun, daily Jul & Aug) was part of a cathedral completed in 1062 and destroyed by a conflagration that flattened much of the city at Easter in the year 1200. The free tours to the crypt, ambulatory and Chapel of the Virgin are in French, but some guides are happy to add English commentary. The Flamboyant Gothic late-1400s **Tour de Beurre** (Butter Tower), 75m high, was financed by local faithful who made donations to the cathedral in return for being allowed to eat butter during Lent – or so they say (some historians believe the name simply refers to the colour of the stone).

Musée des Beaux-Arts   ART MUSEUM

(☎02 35 52 00 62; esplanade Marcel Duchamp; adult/child €5/3; ☉10am-6pm Wed-Mon) This impressive museum is housed in a grand structure erected in 1870 and features a captivating collection of 15th- to 20th-century paintings. Artists include Caravaggio, Rubens, Modigliani, Pissarro, Renoir, Sisley (lots) and (of course) several works by Monet, including a study of Rouen's cathedral (in room 2.33). Some rooms have laminated art history sheets in English.

Musée Le Secq des Tournelles

BLACKSMITH MUSEUM

(☎02 35 88 42 92; 2 rue Jacques Villon; adult/child €3/2; ☉10am-1pm & 2-6pm Wed-Mon) Inside a desanctified Flamboyant Gothic church built in the early 1500s, this excellent museum is devoted to the blacksmith's craft. Displays include some 5000 wrought-iron items made between the 3rd and 19th centuries, including hanging shop signs, lots of locks and keys, and an elaborate choir grille from 1202.

Musée de la Céramique   PORCELAIN MUSEUM

(☎02 35 07 31 74; 1 rue du Faucon; adult/child €3/2; ☉10am-1pm & 2-6pm Wed-Sat) Housed in a 17th-century building with a fine courtyard, the Ceramics Museum was closed for renovations during our last visit, but will be open by the time you read this. It's known for its 16th- to 19th-century faience (decorated earthenware) and porcelain.

Église St-Maclou   CHURCH

(place Barthelemy; ☉10am-noon & 2-6pm Fri-Mon) This Flamboyant Gothic church was built between 1437 and 1521 but much of the decoration dates from the Renaissance. It is partly surrounded by half-timbered houses inclined at curious angles. The entrance is half a block east of 56 rue de la République.

Abbatiale St-Ouen   CHURCH

(place du Général de Gaulle; ☉10am-noon & 2-6pm Tue-Thu, Sat & Sun) This 14th-century abbey is a marvellous example of the Rayonnant Gothic style. The entrance is through a lovely garden along rue des Faulx.

Aître St-Maclou   HISTORIC QUARTER

(186 rue Martainville; admission free; ☉8am-8pm Apr-Oct) For a macabre thrill, check out the courtyard of this curious ensemble of half-timbered buildings built between 1526 and 1533. Decorated with lurid woodcarvings of skulls, crossbones, gravediggers' tools and hourglasses, it was used as a burial ground for plague victims as recently as 1781. Aître St-Maclou now houses the regional École des Beaux-Arts (School of Fine Arts).

🛏 Sleeping

TOP CHOICE **Hôtel de Bourgtheroulde** HOTEL €€€
(☎02 35 14 50 50; www.hotelsparouen.com; 15 place de la Pucelle; r €215-380; ❄🛜⊛) This stunning conversion of an old private mansion is a worthwhile treat, bringing a dash of glamour and luxury to Rouen's hotel scene. The rooms are large, gorgeously designed and feature beautiful bathrooms. There's a pool (you can see through the lobby bar's glass floor down into it), a sauna and spa in the basement, two restaurants and a sumptuous lobby bar.

Hôtel de la Cathédrale   HOTEL €

(☎02 35 71 57 95; www.hotel-de-la-cathedrale.fr; 12 rue St-Romain; s €56-79, d €66-96, tr & q €119; 🛜🛠) Hiding behind a 17th-century half-timbered facade, this atmospheric hotel has 27 stylishly refitted but quiet rooms with flat-screen TVs, mostly overlooking a tiny, plant-filled courtyard. Bathrooms are not quite as up to date, but the place remains a pleasant combination of modern and traditional.

Hôtel Dandy   HOTEL €€

(☎02 35 07 32 00; www.hotels-rouen.net; 93 rue Cauchoise; d €80-105; 🛜) Decorated in a grand Louis XV style, this charming place has individually designed rooms brimming with character (though bathrooms are rather less than exciting) and is passionately run by a friendly family.

Hôtel Andersen   HOTEL €

(☎02 35 71 88 51; www.hotelandersen.com; 4 rue Pouchet; s €45-56, d €56-63; 🛜) Ensconced in an early-19th-century mansion, this quietly stylish hotel has an old-world atmosphere, classical music wafting through the lobby and 15 spare but imaginative rooms with Laura Ashley wallpaper. One of half a dozen hotels right around the train station.

Hôtel des Carmes
HOTEL €

(02 35 71 92 31; www.hoteldescarmes.com, in French; 33 place des Carmes; d €49-65, tr €67-77; @ 🛜) This sweet little hotel has 12 rooms decked out with quirky decor and vibrant colours; some even have cerulean-blue cloudscapes painted on the ceilings. You can burn off some Camembert calories by taking one of the less pricey 4th-floor rooms.

Le Vieux Carré
HOTEL €

(02 35 71 67 70; www.vieux-carre.fr; 34 rue Ganterie; r €58-65; 🛜) Set around a cute little garden courtyard, this quiet half-timbered hotel has a delightfully old-fashioned *salon de thé* (tearoom) and 13 smallish rooms eclectically decorated with old postcard blowups and slightly threadbare rugs.

Hôtel le Cardinal
HOTEL €

(02 35 70 24 42; www.cardinal-hotel.fr; 1 place de la Cathédrale; s €56-72, d €66-89; 🛜) In a super central spot facing the cathedral, this hotel has 18 simple and unremarkable rooms with lots of natural light and spacious showers. The 4th-floor rooms have fantastic private terraces overlooking the square.

Auberge de Jeunesse Robec
HOSTEL €

(02 35 08 18 50; www.fuaj.org; 3 rue de la Tour; dm/s/d €19/30/50; 🛜) The rooms at this brand-new hostel are comfortable and have private bathrooms. Sadly, it's some way from the centre of town, off route de Darnétal – take bus T2 or T3 from Rouen's city centre and get off at the 'Auberge de Jeunesse' stop. Check in is from 5pm to 10pm only.

✖️ Eating

Little eateries crowd the north side of rue Martainville, facing Église St-Maclou; for ethnic cuisine, head two blocks south to rue des Augustins. More restaurants can be found along rue de Fontenelle (a block west of Église Jeanne d'Arc), and a few blocks east along rue Ecuyère.

TOP CHOICE **Les Nymphéas** TRADITIONAL FRENCH €€
(02 35 89 26 69; www.lesnympheas -rouen.com, in French; 7-9 rue de la Pie; menus €30-70; 12.15-1.45pm & 7.30-9.30pm Tue-Sat) Its formal table settings arrayed under 16th-century beams, this fine restaurant serves cuisine based on fresh local ingredients (including cider and *calvados*), giving a rich Norman twist to dishes such as farm-raised wild duck, scallops and lobster.

Gill
GASTRONOMIC €€

(02 35 71 16 14; www.gill.fr; 8-9 quai de la Bourse; menus €35-92; Tue-Sat) *The* place to go in Rouen for *gastronomique* French cuisine of the highest order, served in an ultrachic, ultramodern dining room. Specialities including fresh Breton lobster, scallops with truffles, Rouen-style pigeon and, for dessert, *millefeuille à la vanille*.

Thé Majuscule
TEAROOM €

(02 35 71 15 66; 8 place de la Calende; menus €13.50-16; restaurant noon-2pm Mon-Sat, salon de thé 2-6.30pm Mon-Sat) Downstairs it's a typically chaotic French secondhand bookshop; upstairs it's a classy tearoom with a warm-season terrace, homemade *tartes* (including one vegetarian pie), salads (in summer), plat du jour (€9.50), cakes and exotic teas (€3.30).

Le P'tit Bec
BISTRO €

(02 35 07 63 33; www.leptitbec.com, in French; 182 rue Eau de Robec; lunch menus €13-15.50; lunch Mon-Sat, dinner Tue-Sat) The down-to-earth menu is stuffed with pasta, salads, *œufs cocottes* (eggs with grated cheese baked in cream), several vegetarian options and homemade desserts. There's also a terrace for the summer months on one of Rouen's most picturesque side streets.

Pascaline
BISTRO €

(02 35 89 67 44; 5 rue de la Poterne; lunch menu €13, mains €10-20) A top spot for a great-value *formule midi* (lunchtime fixed-price *menu*), this bustling bistro serves up traditional French cuisine in typically Parisian surroundings – think net curtains, white tablecloths and chuffing coffee machines. There's live piano nightly, and jazz nights are held on Thursdays.

Les Maraîchers
BISTRO €€

(02 35 71 57 73; www.les-maraichers.fr; 37 place du Vieux Marché; menu from €16, mains €11.50-32) All gleaming mirrors, polished wood and colourful floor tiles, this bistro – established in 1912 and classified a *café historique d'Europe* – has a genuine zinc bar and a warm and very French ambience. Specialities include Normandy-raised beef.

Self-Catering

Halles du Vieux Marché
MARKET €

(place du Vieux Marché; 7am-7pm Tue-Sat, 7am-1pm Sun) A small covered market with an excellent *fromagerie* (cheese shop).

Léon Déant Fromager CHEESE €
(18 rue Rollin; ⊙9am-12.45pm & 3-7.30pm
Tue-Fri, 9am-12.45pm Sat) Normandy cheeses
are a speciality.

Drinking

The old town has no shortage of bars and
cafés that buzz with students from mid-day until the early hours. Rouen is also the
centre of Normandy's gay life – there are a
couple of bars around rue St-Etienne des
Tonneliers, south of rue Général Leclerc.

La Boîte à Bières BAR
(www.laboiteabieres.fr, in French; 35 rue Cau-choise; ⊙5pm-2am Tue-Sat) Affectionately
known as BAB, this lively, half-timbered
corner bar is a good place to down a few
local *bières artisanales* (microbrews) in
the company of a loyal student following.
Sometimes has karaoke, disco and concert
nights.

Le Bateau Ivre LIVE MUSIC
(http://bateauivre.rouen.free.fr, in French; 17 rue
des Sapins; ⊙9pm or 10pm-4am Wed-Sat, closed
Wed in summer) A longstanding live venue
with a varied program of concerts (French
chansons, blues, rock reggae etc) except on
Thursday, when anyone can join in the jam
session.

☆ Entertainment

The tourist office sells tickets to cultural
events, as does the Fnac Billetterie (⊅08
92 68 36 22; www.fnacspectacles.com, in French;
cnr rue St-Lô & rue de la Poterne; ⊙10am-7pm
Mon-Sat).

Cinéma le Melville CINEMA
(⊅02 35 07 18 48; 75 rue Général Leclerc)
Screens only nondubbed films, many of
them in English, in its four halls.

Théâtre des Arts OPERA, BALLET
(⊅02 35 71 41 36; www.operaderouen.com, in
French; place des Arts) Home to the Opéra

de Rouen, the city's premier concert
venue also stages ballets.

ℹ Information

Café Chéri (79 rue Ecuyère; ⊙9am-5.30pm
Mon-Sat) This friendly café has free wi-fi and
terminals upstairs.

CompuDream (37 rue de la République; per hr
€3; ⊙11am-11pm Tue-Sat, 2-11pm Sun-Mon)

Post office (45 rue Jeanne d'Arc) Changes
foreign currency.

Tourist office (⊅02 32 08 32 40; www.rouen
tourisme.com; 25 place de la Cathédrale;
⊙9am-7pm Mon-Sat, 9.30am-12.30pm &
2-6pm Sun & holidays) Inside a Renaissance
building from the 1500s. Hotel reservations
cost €3, and audioguides (€5) are available in
seven languages.

ℹ Getting There & Away

BUS Rouen is not very well served by buses,
though there's a useful service to Le Havre (€2,
2½ hours, six to seven daily) from the bus sta-tion on rue du Général Giraud.

CAR For car rental:

ADA (⊅02 35 72 25 88; 34 av Jean Rondeaux)

Avis (⊅02 35 88 60 94) In the train station
above track 4.

Europcar (⊅03 32 08 39 09) In the train
station.

Hertz (⊅02 35 70 70 71; 130 rue Jeanne d'Arc)

TRAIN In the city centre, train tickets are
sold at the **Boutique SNCF** (20 rue aux Juifs;
⊙10am-7pm Mon-Sat).

Amiens €18.50, 1¼ hours, four or five daily

Caen €23.50, 1½ hours, eight to 10 daily

Dieppe €10.50, 45 minutes, 10 to 16 daily
Monday to Saturday, five Sunday

Le Havre €13.50, 50 minutes, 18 daily Monday
to Saturday, 10 Sunday

Paris St-Lazare €20.50, 1¼ hours, 25 daily
Monday to Friday, 14 to 19 Saturday and
Sunday

NORMAN CUISINE

Normandy may be the largest region of France not to contain a single vineyard, but
its culinary wealth more than makes up for what it lacks in the wine department –
besides, any self-respecting Norman would far rather partake in a locally produced
cider or *calvados*. This is a land of soft cheeses, apples, cream and an astonishingly
rich range of seafood and fish. You simply shouldn't leave Normandy without trying
classics like *coquilles St-Jacques* (scallops) and *sole dieppoise* (Dieppe sole). And
whatever you do, don't forget your *trou normand* ('Norman hole') – the traditional
break between courses of a meal for a glass of *calvados* to cleanse the palate and
improve the appetite for the next course!

ℹ️ Getting Around

BICYCLE Cy'clic (☑08 00 08 78 00; cyclic.rouen.fr), Rouen's version of Paris' Vélib', lets you rent a city bike from 14 locations around town. Credit card registration for one/seven days costs €1/5. Use is free for the first 30 minutes; the 2nd/3rd/4th and subsequent half-hours cost €1/2/4 each.

BUS Rouen's bus lines are operated by **TCAR** (☑02 35 52 52 52; www.tcar.fr, in French) and provide service throughout the city.

CAR Free parking is available across the Seine from the city centre, along and below quai Jean Moulin.

METRO Rouen's **metro** (☑02 35 52 52 52; www.tcar.fr, in French) runs from 5am (6am on Sunday) to about 11pm and is useful for getting from the train station to the centre of town. One ticket costs €1.40 (10 tickets €11) and is valid for an hour. There are Espace Métrobus ticket offices inside the train station and at 9 rue Jeanne d'Arc.

TAXI For a taxi, call ☑02 35 88 50 50.

Dieppe

POP 34,450

Sandwiched between limestone cliffs, Dieppe – a seaside resort since 1824 – is salty and a bit shabby but authentic, the kind of place where leather-skinned herring fishermen rub shoulders with British day trippers and summertime tourists licking oversized ice creams. It's an excellent spot to try some Norman seafood – the harbour is chock-full of restaurants serving local specialities such as scallops, mussels and sole, though it's frankly not worth going out of your way to see otherwise.

History

Privateers from Dieppe pillaged Southampton in 1338 and blockaded Lisbon two centuries later. Explorers based here include Florence-born Giovanni da Verrazano, who in 1524 became the first European to enter New York Harbour. The early European settlers in Canada included many Dieppois and the town was one of France's most important ports during the 16th century, when ships regularly sailed to West Africa and Brazil.

On 19 August 1942 a mainly Canadian force of over 6000 landed on the Dieppe beaches, in part to help the Soviets by drawing Nazi military power away from the Eastern Front. The results were nothing short of catastrophic but lessons learned here proved useful in planning the Normandy landings two years later.

⊙ Sights

Les Bains Dieppe   SEAWATER BATHS
(☑02 35 82 80 90; www.lesbainsdieppe.com, in French; 101 bd de Verdun; adult/under 11yr €6/4.85; ⊙10am-8pm) Established in the 1800s and completely renovated in 2007, the baths have several seawater pools heated to 28°C, including a 50m outdoor pool, and plenty of facilities for kids. Also boasts a fitness centre (adult €12) with a *hammam* (Turkish baths), sauna and a beauty centre.

Château-Musée   MUSEUM
(☑02 35 06 61 99; rue de Chastes; adult/child under 12yr €3.50/free; ⊙10am-noon & 2-6pm, closed Tue Oct-May) High above the city on the western cliff, this 15th-century château is Dieppe's most imposing landmark. The museum inside is devoted to the city's maritime and artistic history, which often involved separating West African elephants from their tusks and shipping the ivory back to Dieppe. The craft of ivory carving reached extraordinary heights here during the 17th century and the results are on display.

Cité de la Mer   MARITIME MUSEUM
(☑02 35 06 93 20; estrancitedelamer.free.fr; 37 rue de l'Asile Thomas; adult/child under 16yr €6/3.50; ⊙10am-noon & 2-6pm) Exhibits on fishing, shipbuilding, the tides, Dieppe's cliffs and the Channel's sea and seaside habitats. Five large aquariums let you admire some especially large specimens of crustaceans and fish most often seen on French plates. An English-language brochure is available at the ticket desk.

Dieppe Port   HISTORIC QUARTER
Still used by fishing vessels but dominated by pleasure craft, the port makes for a bracing sea-air stroll.

Église St-Jacques   CHURCH
(place St-Jacques) Two blocks west of the port, this Norman Gothic church has been reconstructed several times since the early 13th century.

Beach   BEACH
Dieppe's often-windy, 1.8km-long beach is ideal if you hate sand – or love smooth, round pebbles far too big to make their way into your shoes or undies. The vast **lawns** were laid out in the 1860s by that seashore-loving imperial duo, Napoléon III and his wife, Eugénie. Kids will have a

ball at the ship-shaped jungle gym in the **playground** next to the **mini-golf**.

Canadian military cemetery CEMETERY
To visit the Canadian military cemetery 4km towards Rouen, take av des Canadiens (the continuation of av Gambetta) south and follow the signs, or hop on bus 22 (eight to 10 daily Monday to Saturday).

Sleeping

Les Arcades HOTEL €
(☎02 35 84 14 12; www.lesarcades.fr, in French; 1-3 arcades de la Bourse; d €63-79; 🛜) Perched above a colonnaded arcade, this 21-room Logis de France hotel has lovely port views, a tiny lift and quiet, spacious rooms with flat-screen TVs.

Au Grand Duquesne HOTEL €
(☎02 32 14 61 10; augrandduquesne.free.fr; 15 place St-Jacques; d €40-63; 🛜) Central but without harbour views, the 12 blue-themed bedrooms aren't anything special but they're quiet and have floodlit bathrooms.

Hôtel de la Plage HOTEL €€
(☎02 35 84 18 28; plagehotel.fr.st; 20 bd de Verdun; r €55-110, q €90-170; 🛜) One of several somewhat faded places along the seafront, this hotel has 40 modern, mod-con rooms – three with jacuzzi bathtubs – decorated in pale tones of blue, green and red. Seaview rooms come at a premium.

Eating & Drinking

Au Grand Duquesne TRADITIONAL FRENCH €
(☎02 32 14 61 10; 15 place St-Jacques; menus €14-35) A good bet for cuisine that's both *traditionelle* and *créative,* including fish and seafood. Specialities include *crêpiau deippois* (a thick, pear-filled crêpe). The veggie menu costs €18.50.

Au Goût du Jour MODERN FRENCH €€
(☎02 35 84 27 18; 16 rue Duquesne; menus €25-32; ⊙lunch Mon-Fri, dinner daily) At this jazzy restaurant, the reception is as warm and welcoming as the inventive French cuisine is fresh and tasty. Specialities include super-fresh fish, couscous with bass, and home-smoked salmon.

Le New Haven SEAFOOD €€
(☎02 35 84 89 72; 53 quai Henri IV; menus €18-30; ⊙closed dinner Mon, lunch & dinner Wed, open daily Jul & Aug) The harbour front is lined with flashy restaurants but this elegant, though unpretentious fish place is one of the best. Freshly landed specialities include

fish, prawns and *foie de lotte* (monkfish liver). The huge seafood selection for two, *le duo* (€75), will defeat even the biggest seafood lovers!

ℹ Information

Post office (2 bd Maréchal Joffre) Changes foreign currency.

Tourist office (☎02 32 14 40 60; www.dieppe-tourisme.com; 56 Quai Duquesne; ⊙9am-1pm & 2-7pm Mon-Sat, 10am-1pm & 2-5pm Sun) Has useful English brochures on Dieppe and nearby parts of the Côte d'Albâtre.

ℹ Getting There & Away

BOAT For information on car ferries from the ferry terminal to Newhaven, see p973.

CAR Dieppe is 65km north of Rouen, 108km northeast of Le Havre and 118km west of Amiens. Car rental companies:

Europcar (☎02 35 04 97 10; 33 rue Thiers)
Hertz (☎02 32 14 01 70; 5 rue d'Écosse)
TRAIN Trains running from Dieppe:

Le Havre €18.50, two to four hours, four to seven daily

Paris St-Lazare €27.50, two to three hours, six to 11 daily

Rouen €10.50, 45 minutes, 10 to 16 daily

Côte d'Albâtre

Stretching 130km from Le Tréport southwest to Étretat, the bone-white cliffs of the Côte d'Albâtre (Alabaster Coast) are strikingly reminiscent of the limestone cliffs of Dover, just across the Channel. The dramatic coastline is dotted with small villages and hamlets, lovely gardens, several fine beaches and two nuclear power plants (Paluel and Penly). The only towns of any note – in addition to Dieppe – are Fécamp, St-Valery-en-Caux and Étretat.

Without a car, the Côte d'Albâtre is pretty inaccessible, though walkers can take the coastal GR21 hiking trail, which follows the Côte d'Albâtre all the way from Le Tréport to Le Havre. If you're driving west from Dieppe, take the coastal roads (D75, D68 and D79) rather than the inland D925.

FÉCAMP
POP 19,630

Fécamp was an ordinary fishing village until the 6th century, when a few drops of Christ's blood miraculously found their way here and attracted hordes of pilgrims. Benedictine monks soon established a monastery, and the fiery 'medicinal elixir' that a Venetian monk concocted in 1510 (using East Asian herbs) helped keep Fécamp on the map. The recipe, lost during the Revolution, was rediscovered in an old book in the 19th century. Today, Bénédictine is one of the most widely marketed *digestifs* in the world.

◉ Sights & Activities

The port, still used by fishing craft, is connected to the sea by the narrow *avant port* (outer harbour). North of the port rises Cap Fagnet (110m), which offers fantastic views of the town and the coastline, while to the south is the beach, where you can rent catamarans, kayaks and windsurfers in summer.

Palais Bénédictine   LIQUEUR FACTORY

(☑02 35 10 26 10; www.benedictine.fr; 110 rue Alexandre Le Grand; adult/child €7/3.50; ☺tickets sold 10am-noon & 2-5.30pm, closed Jan) Opened in 1900, this unusually ornate factory is where all the Bénédictine liqueur in the world is made. Tours take you to a surprisingly interesting collection of 13th- to 19th-century religious art and paintings assembled by the company's visionary founder, Alexandre Le Grand. They continue to the production facilities, where you can admire copper alembics and touch and smell the natural ingredients used to make Bénédictine – the coriander seeds are the most fun to play with. As is only proper, adults end the visit with a shot of liqueur.

Abbatiale de la Ste-Trinité   ABBEY

(place des Ducs Richard; ☺9am-5pm) Built from 1175 to 1220 by Richard the Lionheart, this attractive abbey, 1.5km east of the beach (and a few blocks southeast of Fécamp's commercial centre), was the most important pilgrimage site in Normandy until the construction of Mont St-Michel, thanks to the drops of holy blood that miraculously floated to Fécamp in the trunk of a fig tree. Across from the abbey are the remains of the fortified château built by the earliest dukes of Normandy in the 10th and 11th centuries.

🛏 Sleeping & Eating

Quite a few restaurants are situated on the south side of the port, along quai de la Vicomté and nearby parts of quai Bérigny.

La Ferme de la Chapelle   FARMSTAY €€

(☑02 35 10 12 12; www.fermedelachapelle.fr; Côte de la Vierge; d/q €95/140, apt €145-220;

📶 🖤 🛜) High above town near Cap Fagnet, the 17 modern rooms and five kitchenette-equipped apartments overlook a grassy central courtyard, so there's no sea view – for that you'll have to step outside the compound. Guests are often greeted by four vociferous geese. Rates are cheaper from October to mid-February.

Hôtel Normandy   HOTEL €

(☑02 35 29 55 11; www.normandy-fecamp.com; 4 av Gambetta; s/d €56/64; 🛜) In a smart fin-de-siècle building just up the hill from the train station, this quiet place has 32 newly refurbished rooms – some quite spacious – with rather bland furnishings and lots of light. Rooms are often cheaper October to June.

Camping de Renéville   CAMPGROUND €

(☑02 35 28 20 97; www.campingdereneville.com; chemin de Nesmond; tent & 2 adults from €11.50; ☺Apr–mid-Nov) Dramatically situated on the western cliffs overlooking the beach, this campground also rents out two- and six-people chalets (€130 to €645 per week). In July and August the tent rate goes up to €15.

Le Maupassant   BRASSERIE €€

(☑02 35 29 55 11; 4 av Gambetta; menu €16) On the ground floor of the Hôtel Normandy, this very popular brasserie – charmingly decorated with glassware suspended from on high – serves French and Norman cuisine, with a few exotic dishes thrown in for good measure.

❶ Information

Tourist office (☑02 35 28 51 01; www.fecamp tourisme.com, in French; quai Sadi Carnot; ☺10am-6pm, closed Sun Sep-Mar) Situated at the southern end of the pleasure port, across the parking lot from the train station, the tourist office has useful English-language brochures. A beachfront annexe opens in July and August.

❶ Getting There & Away

BUS Bus 24, operated by **Cars Perier** (☑08 00 80 87 03; www.cars-perier.com), goes to Le Havre (€2, 1½ hours, eight to 10 daily) via Étretat.

TRAIN Rail destinations:

Le Havre €8, 45 to 75 minutes, seven to 11 daily

Rouen €13, 1¼ hours, seven to 10 daily

ÉTRETAT
POP 1550

The small village of Étretat, 20km southwest of Fécamp, is known for its twin cliffs, the Falaise d'Aval and the Falaise d'Amont, positioned on either side of the pebbly beach.

The Falaise d'Aval is renowned for its free-standing arch – compared by French writer Maupassant to an elephant dipping its trunk in the sea – and the adjacent Aiguille, a 70m-high spire of chalk-white rock rising from the surface of the waves. Further along the cliff is a second impressive arch, known as La Manneporte, reached by a steep path up the cliff from the western end of Étretat's beach. On the Falaise d'Amont, a memorial marks the spot where two aviators were last seen before their attempt to cross the Atlantic in 1927.

The tourist office (02 35 27 05 21; www. etretat.net; place Maurice Guillard; 10am-noon & 2-6pm Mon-Sat) has accommodation lists for the area (also available on the website) and a map of the cliff trails.

Bus 24, operated by Cars Perier (08 00 00 80 87 03; www.cars-perier.com), goes to Le Havre (€2, one hour, eight to 10 daily) and Fécamp (€2, 30 minutes, eight to 10 daily).

Le Havre

POP 182,400

All but obliterated in September 1944 by Allied bombing raids that killed 3000 civilians, Le Havre's city centre was totally rebuilt after the war by Belgian architect Auguste Perret. What emerged from the rubble is a most unexpected love letter to modernism, and an evocative portrait of France's postwar energy and optimism. It's a love-it or hate-it kind of place, but even if vast municipal squares and architectural quirks such as Oscar Niemeyer's Le Volcan aren't your thing, it's not hard to see why Unesco listed Le Havre as a World Heritage Site in 2005. The tourist office can supply you with an English map/brochure for a two-hour self-guided walking tour of the city centre's architectural highlights. With its fantastic Musée Malraux and friendly, progressive feel, Le Havre is far more than just another ferry port.

◉ Sights & Activities

TOP CHOICE **Musée Malraux** ART MUSEUM

(02 35 19 62 62; 2 bd Clemenceau; adult/child €5/free; 11am-6pm Mon-Fri, 11am-7pm Sat & Sun) At the city centre's southwestern tip, this fantastic modern space houses a truly fabulous collection of Impressionist

works – the finest in France outside of Paris – by luminaries such as Degas, Monet, Pissarro, Renoir, Sisley and Le Havre native Eugène Boudin. A section is devoted to Fauvist Raoul Dufy, also born in Le Havre. The temporary exhibits here are often of very high quality too.

Église St-Joseph CHURCH

(bd François 1er) The city is dominated by Perret's centrepiece, the magnificent 107m-high Église St-Joseph, which was begun in 1951 and inaugurated in 1959. Its 13,000 panels of coloured glass make the interior particularly striking when it's sunny.

Appartement Témoin SHOW APARTMENT

(adult/child €3/free; tours 2pm, 3pm, 4pm & 5pm Wed, Sat & Sun) Furnished in impeccable 1950s style, this perfectly preserved apartment within an ensemble of six striking Perret-designed residential buildings facing the town hall can be visited on a one-hour guided tour that starts at 1 place de l'Hôtel de Ville (in front of the Caron shoe shop).

Le Volcan CULTURAL CENTRE

(The Volcano; www.unvolcandanslaville.com, in French; espace Oscar Niemeyer) Although it's been compared to a truncated cooling tower or, even worse, a toilet bowl, Le Havre's most famous landmark is also its premier cultural venue and boasts concert halls and an excellent **art cinema**, L'Eden. One look and you'll understand how it got its name. It was conceived by Brazilian architect Oscar Niemeyer, who also designed the Brazilian capital.

Jardins Suspendus HANGING GARDENS

(rue du Fort; admission free; 10.30am-12.30pm & 1.45-6pm Mon-Fri, 10.30am-8pm Sat & Sun) An old hilltop fortress a bit over 1km north of the tourist office has been transformed into a beautiful set of gardens, whose hothouses (adult/under 12yr €1/free) and outdoor spaces feature rare plants and cacti from five continents.

Les Docks Vauban SHOPPING & ENTERTAINMENT CENTRE

(www.docksvauban.com, in French; 70 quai Frissard; 10am-8pm) Le Havre's avant-garde architectural ambitions continue to shape the city, as this formerly run-down docklands area on the far side of Bassin Vauban proves. A cutting-edge magnet for shopping, eating and the arts, designed by Jean Nouvel, it's well worth checking out. As well

Everyone discusses my art and pretends to understand, as if it were necessary to understand, when it is simply necessary to love.

Claude Monet

The undisputed leader of the Impressionists, Claude Monet was born in Paris in 1840 and grew up in Le Havre, where he found an early affinity with the outdoors. Monet disliked school and spent much of his time sketching his professors in the margins of his exercise books. By 15 his skills as a caricaturist were known throughout Le Havre, but Eugène Boudin, his first mentor, convinced him to turn his attention away from portraiture towards the study of colour, light and landscape.

In 1860 military service interrupted Monet's studies at the Académie Suisse in Paris and took him to Algiers, where the intense light and colours further fuelled his imagination. The young painter became fascinated with capturing a specific moment in time, the immediate impression of the scene before him, rather than the precise detail.

From 1867 Monet's distinctive style began to emerge, focusing on the effects of light and colour and using the quick, undisguised broken brushstrokes that would characterise the Impressionist period. His contemporaries were Pissarro, Renoir, Sisley, Cézanne and Degas. The young painters left the studio to work outdoors, experimenting with the shades and hues of nature, and arguing and sharing ideas. Their work was far from welcomed by critics; one of them condemned it as 'impressionism', in reference to Monet's *Impression: Sunrise* (1874). Much to the critic's chagrin, the name stuck.

From the late 1870s Monet concentrated on painting in series, seeking to re-create a landscape by showing its transformation under different conditions of light and atmosphere. *Haystacks* (1890–91) and *Rouen Cathedral* (1891–95) are some of the best-known works of this period. In 1883 Monet moved to Giverny, planting his property with a variety of flowers around an artificial pond, the Jardin d'Eau, in order to paint the subtle effects of sunlight on natural forms. It was here that he painted the *Nymphéas* (Water Lilies) series. The huge dimensions of some of these works, together with the fact that the pond's surface takes up the entire canvas, meant the abandonment of composition in the traditional sense and the virtual disintegration of form. A *Nymphéas* canvas from 1919, likely to be the last ever to come up for auction, sold in June 2008 for an astounding US$80 million.

For more info on Monet and his work, visit www.giverny.org.

---

as lots of big-brand shopping, there's also a large number of restaurants and a multiplex cinema.

🛏 Sleeping

Hôtel Vent d'Ouest　　　　HOTEL €€

(☎02 35 42 50 69; www.ventdouest.fr; 4 rue de Caligny; r €105-135, ste €155-165; 🛜) The 38-room West Wind, around the corner from Église St-Joseph, is decorated in maritime fashion, with nautical memorabilia downstairs and a range of stylish cream-walled rooms upstairs.

Hôtel Le Richelieu　　　FAMILY HOTEL €

(☎02 35 42 38 71; www.hotellerichelieu.com; 132 rue de Paris; s €47-58, d €50-65, apt €70; 🛜👶) Inside one of the architecturally interesting buildings along the rue de Paris, Le

Richelieu offers spotless, bright and often bizarrely decorated rooms that are great value for their comfort and location.

Le Petit Vatel　　　　　FAMILY HOTEL €

(☎02 35 41 72 07; www.lepetitvatel.com; 86 rue Louis Brindeau; s €49-60, d €60-73, tr €81; 🛜👶) Situated two blocks east of Église St-Joseph, this family-run hotel, renovated in 2008, has 25 well-kept, space-efficient rooms with straightforward decor.

Hôtel Voltaire　　　　　　HOTEL €

(☎02 35 19 35 35; hotel.voltaire@free.fr; 14 rue Voltaire; r €40/44, q €60-66) Le Havre's cheapest hotel has cheery orange hallways and 20 unsurprising rooms with period-appropriate linoleum floors. It's in a Perret building one block south and around the corner from Église St-Joseph.

✕ Eating

In Quartier St-François, rue du Général Faidherbe and perpendicular rue Jean de la Fontaine are lined with eateries. There are several more restaurants around the periphery of Le Volcan. There's also a great selection at the Docks Vauban.

La Petite Auberge   TRADITIONAL FRENCH **€€**
(☑02 35 46 27 32; 32 rue de Ste Adresse; menus €18-45; ☺lunch & dinner Tue & Thu-Sat, dinner Wed, lunch Sun) This absolute gem of a place is possibly Le Havre's most charming dining option. Its low-beamed dining room whispers of romance, even if you're dining alone. Seafood dominates the inventive yet traditional menu.

Crêperie Soizic   CRÊPERIE **€**
(☑02 35 43 27 88; www.creperie-soizic.fr; 17 rue de la Fontaine; menu €10; ☺lunch Mon-Fri, dinner daily) Our personal favourite of the many crêperies vying for your business on this busy block, the Soizic is always bustling with a loyal crowd of galette- and cider-loving locals.

☆ Entertainment

Le Cabaret Electric   CONCERT HALL
(☑02 35 19 91 32; www.cabaretelectric.fr, in French; espace Oscar Niemeyer; ☺bar 6-11pm Tue, Thu & Fri, 2-11pm Wed, 2-8pm Sat, during concerts) Not only do you get to see the inside of Le Havre's most striking building, but this funky bar is also the city's best venue for live gigs.

❶ Information

Change Collections (41 chaussée Kennedy; ☺9am-12.30pm & 2-6.30pm Mon-Fri, to 5pm Sat) An exchange bureau half a block west of the southern end of rue de Paris.

Microminute (☑02 35 22 10 15; 7 rue Casimir Periér; per hr €3.60; ☺2-7pm Mon, 10am-7pm Tue-Sat) Internet access a block east of the Hôtel de Ville.

Post office (place des Halles Centrales)

Tourist office (☑02 32 74 04 04; www. lehavretourisme.com; 186 bd Clemenceau; ☺9am-6.45pm Mon-Sat, 10am-12.30pm & 2.30-5.45pm Sun & holidays) A bit south of the western end of av Foch, there's free internet access here and very helpful staff.

❶ Getting There & Away

For details on ferry services to Portsmouth and Newhaven, see p973.

BUS Bus 20, run by **Bus Verts** (☑08 10 21 42 14; www.busverts.fr), runs from the bus sta-tion (next to the train station) to Caen (€10.50, 2½ hours), Deauville and Trouville (€6.50, one hour) and Honfleur (€4.25, 35 minutes). Express buses also run to Caen (€15, 1½ hours, four daily Monday to Saturday, two Sunday) via Honfleur. Bus 24, operated by **Cars Perier** (☑08 00 80 87 03; www.cars-perier.com), goes to Fécamp (€2, 1½ hours, eight to 10 daily) via Étretat.

CAR Avis (☑02 35 53 17 20; 87 quai Southampton)

France Cars (☑02 35 22 77 73; 36 rue des Magasins Généraux)

National/Citer (☑02 35 21 30 81; 91 quai de Southampton)

TRAIN Le Havre's **train station** (cours de la République) is 2km east of the Hôtel de Ville at the eastern end of bd de Strasbourg.

Fécamp €8, 45 to 75 minutes, seven to 11 daily

Paris St-Lazare €30, 2¼ hours, at least hourly

Rouen €13.50, 50 minutes, 18 daily Monday to Saturday, 10 Sunday

❶ Getting Around

Year-round, **Vélocéane bicycles** (per 2hr/half-day/full day €2/3/5) can be hired at five sites (seven in summer), including the tourist office (which has bike path maps) and the train station. Tandems and kids' bikes are also on offer.

EURE

Lovely day trips can be made from Rouen, particularly in the landlocked Eure (www. cdt-eure.fr) *département*. The beautiful gardens of Claude Monet are at Giverny, while the 12th-century Château Gaillard in Les Andelys affords a breathtaking panorama of the Seine.

Les Andelys

POP 8440

Some 40km southeast of Rouen, on a hairpin curve in the Seine, lies Les Andelys (the 's' is silent), crowned by the ruins of Château Gaillard, the 12th-century hilltop fastness of Richard the Lionheart.

◉ Sights

Built from 1196 to 1197, **Château Gaillard** (☑02 32 54 41 93; adult/child €3.15/2.60; ☺10am-1pm & 2-6pm Wed-Mon mid-Mar–mid-Nov) secured the western border of English territory along the Seine until Henry IV ordered its destruction in 1603. Fantastic views of the Seine's white cliffs can be enjoyed from the platform a few hundred metres up the one-lane road from the castle. The tourist office has details on tours (€5.50, in French with English-speaking guides). Entry to the château grounds is free.

From Petit Andely, the château is a 500m climb along a narrow road you can pick up 50m north of the tourist office. By car, take the turn-off opposite Église Notre Dame in Grand Andely and follow the signs.

🛏 Sleeping & Eating

Hôtel & Restaurant de la Chaine d'Or
TRADITIONAL HOTEL €€

(☎02 32 54 00 31; www.hotel-lachainedor.com; 27 rue Grande, Petit Andely; r €85-242, lunch menus €18.50-74; ⊗closed Jan, restaurant closed dinner Sun & all day Mon Nov-Mar; 🛜) Right on the Seine, this little rural hideaway, packed with character, is rustically stylish without being twee. The 12 rooms are spacious, tasteful and romantic, with antique wood furnishings and plush rugs; some are so close to the river you could almost fish out the window. The classy French restaurant is one of the best for miles around – specialities include lobster, escargots and cider sorbet.

ℹ Information

Tourist office (☎02 32 54 41 93; http://office-tourisme.ville-andelys.fr, in French; 24 rue Philippe Auguste; ⊗10am-noon & 2-6pm Mon-Sat, 10am-noon & 2-5pm Sun) In Petit Andely below the château.

Giverny

POP 530

The tiny country village of Giverny, 15km south of Les Andelys, is a place of pilgrimage for devotees of Impressionism, and can feel swamped by the tour-bus crowd in the summer months. Monet lived here from 1883 until his death in 1926, in a rambling house – surrounded by flower-filled gardens – that's now the immensely popular Maison et Jardins de Claude Monet.

⊙ Sights

Maison et Jardins de Claude Monet
ART MUSEUM

(☎02 32 51 28 21; www.fondation-monet.com; adult/child under 12yr €6/3.50; ⊗9.30am-6pm Apr-Oct) Monet's home for the last 43 years of his life is now a delightful house-museum. His pastel-pink house and Water

Lily studio stand on the periphery of the Clos Normand, with its symmetrically laid-out gardens bursting with flowers. Monet bought the Jardin d'Eau (Water Garden) in 1895 and set about creating his trademark lily pond, as well as the famous Japanese bridge (since rebuilt).

Draped with purple wisteria, the bridge blends into the asymmetrical foreground and background, creating the intimate atmosphere for which the 'painter of light' was renowned.

Seasons have an enormous effect on Giverny. From early to late spring, daffodils, tulips, rhododendrons, wisteria and irises appear, followed by poppies and lilies. By June, nasturtiums, roses and sweet peas are in flower. Around September, there are dahlias, sunflowers and hollyhocks.

Musée des Impressionismes Giverny
ART MUSEUM

(☎02 32 51 94 65; www.museedesimpressionnismesgiverny.com; 99 rue Claude Monet; adult/child under 12yr €6.50/3, free 1st Sun of the month; ⊗10am-6pm Apr-Oct) Until recently known as the Musée d'Art Américain, Giverny's other highly recommended attraction has been purchased by the local authorities and its name changed to focus more on the style than the nationality of the painters it presents. Surrounded by beautiful gardens, the museum displays works by American Impressionists who flocked to France in the late 19th and early 20th centuries. It's 100m down the road from the Maison de Claude Monet.

ℹ Getting There & Away

BICYCLE Facing the train station, you can rent a bike at the **Café de Chemin de Fer** (L'Arrivée de Giverny; ☎02 32 21 16 01; per day €12; ⊗7am-11.30pm).

BUS Shuttle buses (€4 round trip; seven daily Tuesday to Sunday April to October) run by **Veolia** (☎08 25 07 60 27; www.mobiregion.net, in French) meet most trains to and from Paris.

TRAIN From Paris Gare St-Lazare there are seven direct daily trains to Vernon (€12.50, 50 minutes), 7km to the west of Giverny. The last train back to Paris leaves Vernon at 20.53pm. From Rouen (€10.50, 40 minutes), several trains leave for Vernon before noon; to get back to Rouen, there's about one train every hour between 5pm and 10pm (till 9pm on Saturday).

CALVADOS

The *département* of Calvados (www.cal vados-tourisme.com) stretches from Honfleur in the east to Isigny-sur-Mer in the west and includes Caen, Bayeux – world-renowned for its tapestry – and the D-Day beaches. The area is famed for its rich pastures and farm products, including butter, cheese, cider and the distinctive apple brandy *calvados,* which bears the name of the *département.*

Bayeux

POP 14,350

Bayeux has become famous throughout the English-speaking world thanks to a 68m-long piece of painstakingly embroidered cloth: the 11th-century Bayeux Tapestry, whose 58 scenes vividly tell the story of the Norman invasion of England in 1066. But there's more to Bayeux than this unparal-

leled piece of needlework. The first town to be liberated after D-Day (on the morning of 7 June 1944), it is one of the few in Calvados to have survived WWII practically unscathed. A great place to soak up the Norman atmosphere, Bayeux' delightful city centre is crammed with 13th- to 18th-century buildings, including lots of wood-framed Norman-style houses, and a fine Gothic cathedral. Bayeux also makes an ideal launch pad for exploring the D-Day beaches just to the north.

◉ Sights

Bayeux Tapestry   MUSEUM

(☎02 31 51 25 50; www.tapisserie-bayeux.fr; rue de Nesmond; adult/child incl audioguide €8/3.80; ◎9am-6.15pm) Undoubtedly the world's most celebrated embroidery, the misnamed Bayeux Tapestry (it's actually wool thread embroidered onto linen cloth) vividly recounts the story of the Norman conquest of England in 1066. Divided into 58 scenes

Bayeux

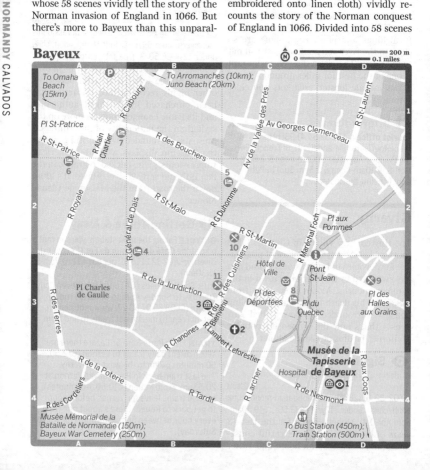

briefly captioned in almost-readable Latin, the main narrative – told from an unashamedly Norman perspective – fills up the centre of the canvas, while religious allegories and depictions of daily life in the 11th century unfold along the borders. The final showdown at the Battle of Hastings is depicted in truly graphic fashion, complete with severed limbs and decapitated heads (along the bottom of scene 52). Halley's Comet, which blazed across the sky in 1066, makes an appearance at the top of scene 32, while at the bottom of scene 15 there's – no, it can't be! – an 11th-century 'full Monty'.

Most scholars believe that the 68.3m-long tapestry was commissioned by Bishop Odo of Bayeux, William the Conqueror's half-brother, in southern England (probably Canterbury) for the opening of Bayeux' cathedral in 1077, although there are others who argue the tapestry was indeed produced in France.

The tapestry is housed in the **Musée de la Tapisserie de Bayeux**, where the extraordinarily well-preserved embroidery doubles back on itself on display behind glass. Upstairs is an excellent exhibition on the tapestry's creation, its remarkable history and its conservation, as well as a 15-minute film screened alternately in English and French.

For an animated version of the Bayeux Tapestry, check out David Newton's very creative short film on YouTube.

Cathédrale Notre Dame   CATHEDRAL
(rue du Bienvenu; ⊘8.30am-6pm) Most of Bayeux' spectacular Norman Gothic cathedral dates from the 13th century, though the crypt (accessible from the north side of the choir), the arches of the nave and the lower portions of the entrance towers are 11th-century Romanesque. The central tower was added in the 15th century; the copper dome dates from the 1860s. First prize for tackiness has got to go to 'Litanies de la Sainte Vierge', a 17th-century retable in the first chapel on the left as you enter the cathedral.

FREE **Conservatoire de la Dentelle**
LACE WORKSHOP
(Lace Conservatory; ☑02 31 92 73 80; http:// dentelledebayeux.free.fr; 6 rue du Bienvenu; ⊘9.30am-12.30pm & 2.30-6pm Mon-Sat) This workshop is dedicated to the preservation of traditional Norman lacemaking, and you can watch some of France's most celebrated lacemakers create intricate designs using dozens of bobbins and hundreds of pins. At its height, the local lace industry employed 5000 lacemakers.

Musée Mémorial de la Bataille de Normandie   MUSEUM
(Battle of Normandy Memorial Museum; ☑02 31 51 46 90; bd Fabien Ware; adult/child €6.50/2.80; ⊘9.30am-6.30pm) Using well-chosen photos (some in original colour), personal accounts, dioramas and wartime objects, this first-rate museum offers an excellent introduction to WWII in Normandy. Signs are in French and English. A new 25-minute film on the Battle of Normandy is screened in English three to five times a day.

Bayeux War Cemetery   CEMETERY
(bd Fabien Ware) This peaceful cemetery, a few hundred metres west of the Musée Mémorial, is the largest of the 18 Commonwealth military cemeteries in Normandy. It contains 4848 graves of soldiers from the UK and 10 other countries, including, rather surprisingly, Germany. Across the road is a memorial for 1807 Commonwealth soldiers whose remains were never found; the Latin inscription across the top reads: 'We, whom William once conquered, have now set free the conqueror's native land'. See p212 for details on the American war cemetery.

Mémorial des Reporters   MEMORIAL
Just beyond the cemetery and easily missed (the entrance is not on bd Fabien Ware itself), a landscaped promenade lists the names of nearly 2000 journalists killed in the line of duty around the world since

1944. A project of Reporters Without Borders (www.rsf.org) and the City of Bayeux, it was inaugurated in 2006.

🛏 Sleeping

The tourist office has a list of *chambres d'hôte* (B&Bs; €40 to €80) around Bayeux.

Château de Bellefontaine   HISTORIC HOTEL €€

(☑02 31 22 00 10; www.hotel-bellefontaine.com; 49 rue Bellefontaine; d €125-150, ste €150-230; ☜) Swans and a bubbling brook welcome you to this majestic 18th-century château, which is surrounded by a 2-hectare private park and has 20 enormous rooms, many of which have grand fireplaces and period mouldings. The suites in the converted barn beyond the main house are far more modern and rather less than charming – though they're a good deal if you're travelling in a small group. The hotel is 1.5km southeast of the tourist office.

Hôtel d'Argouges   TRADITIONAL HOTEL €€

(☑02 31 92 88 86; www.hotel-dargouges.com; 21 rue St-Patrice; d €90-120, q €280; ☜) This graceful hotel, in a stately 18th-century residence, has an elegant breakfast room overlooking a private garden, squeaky parquet floors and 28 rooms, some with period features such as marble chimneys.

Grand Hôtel du Luxembourg

TRADITIONAL HOTEL €€

(☑02 31 92 00 04; www.hotels-bayeux-14.com; 25 rue des Bouchers; r €100-145, ste & apt €200; ☜) With its grand 17th-century facade, this pleasant hotel has 27 comfortable rooms with old-time touches. There are 34 less-expensive rooms, smallish and rather nondescript, in the adjacent Hôtel de Brunville.

Hôtel Reine Mathilde   HOTEL €

(☑02 31 92 08 13; www.hotel-bayeux-reinemathilde.fr; 23 rue Larcher; d €60-63, tr/q €73/85; ☜) Above a bustling local café of the same name, this charming little hotel is an excellent bet, right in the centre of town, with smallish but comfortable rooms all named after Norman folk of yore.

Family Home   HOSTEL €

(☑02 31 92 15 22; 39 rue Général de Dais; dm/s €23/33) One of France's most charming youth hostels, this place – in a mainly 18th-century neighbourhood – sports a 17th-century dining room, a delightful 16th-century courtyard and 80 beds in rooms for one to four people. Check-in is possible all day – if reception isn't staffed, phone and someone will pop by.

Hôtel Mogador   FAMILY HOTEL €

(☑02 31 92 24 58; www.hotel-mogador-bayeux.fr; 20 rue Alain Chartier; d €46-56; 🐾) Situated on the main market square, this friendly, family-run hotel has 14 rooms with pastel curtains and lots of old wood beams. The small patio is a lovely spot for breakfast. Annoyingly, there's no wireless.

🍴 Eating

Local specialities to keep an eye out for include *cochon de Bayeux* (Bayeux-style pork). Rue St-Jean and rue St-Martin are home to a variety of cheap eateries and food shops. Appropriately, rue des Cuisiniers (north of the cathedral) also has some restaurants.

La Reine Mathilde   PATISSERIE €€

(☑02 31 92 00 59; 47 rue St-Martin; cakes from €2.50; ⊙8.30am-7.30pm Tue-Sun) A sumptuous, c 1900-style *pâtisserie* and *salon de thé* that's ideal if you've got a hankering for something soft and sweet. There's seating here, making it a great spot for breakfast or afternoon tea.

Le Pommier   TRADITIONAL FRENCH €

(☑02 31 21 52 10; www.restaurantlepommier.com; 38-40 rue des Cuisiniers; menus €14-35; ⊙closed Sun Nov-Mar & mid-Dec–mid-Jan) Specialities at this smart restaurant include fillet of roast duck, *filet mignon de porc* and a varied selection of imaginative French dishes made with fresh Norman products, including rare heirloom vegetables.

La Rapière   NORMAN CUISINE €€

(☑02 31 21 05 45; 53 rue St-Jean; lunch menu €15, dinner menus €27.50-33.50; ⊙closed Wed & Thu) Housed in a late-1400s mansion held together by its original oak beams, this restaurant specialises in hearty home cooking – the *timbale de pêcheur* (fisherman's stew) is served up piping hot in a cast-iron pan. For dessert, an excellent option is *trou normand* (apple sorbet with a dash of *calvados*).

ℹ Information

La Paillote (☑02 31 10 08 73; 25 rue Montfiquet; ⊙5pm-2am Sun-Thu, to 3am Fri & Sat, closed Sun & Mon in winter) A laid-back pub with a tropical vibe and internet access.

Post office (14 rue Larcher) Changes foreign currency.

Pub Fiction (☑02 31 10 17 41; 14 rue du Petit Rouen; per 15min €1; ⊙8.30pm-2am Sun-Thu, to 3am Fri & Sat) A popular, saloon-style pub with three internet computers.

Tourist office (☑02 31 51 28 28; www.bayeux -bessin-tourism.com; pont St-Jean; ◷9.30am-12.30pm & 2-6pm) Covers both Bayeux and the surrounding Bessin region, including the D-Day beaches. Has a walking tour map of town, English books on the D-Day landings and the Bayeux Tapestry, and bus and train schedules. Charges €2 to book hotels and B&Bs.

ⓘ Getting There & Away

BUS Bus Verts (☑08 10 21 42 14; www.busverts .fr) bus 30 links the train station and place St-Patrice with Caen (€4.25, one hour, three or four daily Monday to Friday except holidays). Travellers under 25 get a 15% discount. Bus Verts also runs regular buses to the D-Day beaches (see p219).

TRAIN To get to Deauville, change at Lisieux. For Paris Gare St-Lazare and Rouen, change at Caen.

Destinations from Bayeux:

Caen €6, 20 minutes, hourly Monday to Saturday, eight Sunday

Cherbourg €15.50, one hour, 14 daily Monday to Friday, three to five on weekends

Coutances €12, 50 minutes, eight daily Monday to Saturday, four Sunday

Pontorson Mont St-Michel €21, 1¾ hours, two or three direct daily

ⓘ Getting Around

Taxi (☑02 31 92 92 40) Can take you around Bayeux or out to the D-Day sites.

Vélos Location (Le Verger de l'Aure; ☑02 31 92 89 16; 5 rue Larcher; per half-/full day €10/15; ◷8am-8pm) Offers year-round bike rental in a grocery store near the tourist office.

D-Day Beaches

Code-named 'Operation Overlord', the D-Day landings were the largest military operation in history. On the morning of 6 June 1944, swarms of landing craft – part of an armada of over 6000 ships and boats – hit the northern Normandy beaches and tens of thousands of soldiers from the USA, the UK, Canada and elsewhere began pouring onto French soil.

The majority of the 135,000 Allied troops stormed ashore along 80km of beaches north of Bayeux code-named (from west to east) Utah, Omaha, Gold, Juno and Sword. The landings on D-Day – known as 'Jour J' in French – were followed by the 76-day Battle of Normandy, during which the Al-

lies suffered 210,000 casualties, including 37,000 troops killed. German casualties are believed to have been around 200,000; another 200,000 German soldiers were taken prisoner. About 14,000 French civilians also died.

Caen's Mémorial (p216) and Bayeux' Musée Mémorial (p207) provide a comprehensive overview of the events of D-Day, and many of the villages near the landing beaches (eg Arromanches) have local museums with insightful exhibits.

If you've got wheels, you can follow the D514 along the D-Day coast or several signposted circuits around the battle sites – look for signs for 'D-Day-Le Choc' in the American sectors and 'Overlord-L'Assaut' in the British and Canadian sectors. The area is also sometimes called the Côte de Nacre (Mother-of-Pearl Coast). A free booklet called *The D-Day Landings and the Battle of Normandy*, available from tourist offices, has details on the eight major visitors' routes.

Maps of the D-Day beaches are available at *tabacs* (tobacconists), newsagents and bookshops in Bayeux and elsewhere. All the towns along the coast have plenty of small hotels.

For more details on D-Day and its context, see www.normandiememoire.com and www .6juin1944.com.

☞ Tours

An organised minibus tour is an excellent way to get a sense of the D-Day beaches and their place in history. The Bayeux tourist office can handle reservations.

Normandy Sightseeing Tours D-DAY TOURS (☑02 31 51 70 52; www.normandywebguide. com) From May to October (and on request the rest of the year), this experienced outfit offers morning (adult/child under 10 years €40/20) and afternoon (€55/35) tours of various beaches and cemeteries. These can be combined into an all-day excursion (€85/45).

Normandy Tours D-DAY TOURS (☑02 31 92 10 70; 26 place de la Gare; adult/child €47/40) This local operator offers five-hour tours of the main sites from 1pm to 6pm most days, as well as personally tailored trips. Based at Bayeux' Hotel de la Gare.

Mémorial D-DAY TOURS (☑02 31 06 06 45; www.memorial-caen.fr; adult/child €75/59) Conducts excellent four-to five-hour minibus tours around the

THE BATTLE OF NORMANDY

In early 1944 an Allied invasion of Continental Europe seemed inevitable. Hitler's disastrous campaign on the Russian front and the Luftwaffe's inability to control the skies over Europe had left Germany vulnerable. Both sides knew a landing was coming – the only questions were where and, of course, when.

Several sites were considered. After long deliberations, it was decided that the beaches along Normandy's northern coast – rather than the even more heavily fortified coastline further north around Calais, where Hitler was expecting an attack – would serve as a surprise spearhead into Europe.

Code-named 'Operation Overlord', the invasion began on the night of 5 June 1944 when three paratroop divisions were dropped behind enemy lines. At about 6.30 on the morning of 6 June, six amphibious divisions stormed ashore at five beaches, backed up by an unimaginable 6000 sea craft and 13,000 aeroplanes. The initial landing force involved some 45,000 troops; 15 more divisions were to follow once successful beachheads had been established.

The narrow Straits of Dover had seemed the most likely invasion spot to the Germans, who'd set about heavily reinforcing the area around Calais and the other Channel ports. Allied intelligence went to extraordinary lengths to encourage the German belief that the invasion would be launched north of Normandy: double agents, leaked documents and fake radio traffic, buttressed by phoney airfields and an entirely fictitious American army group, supposedly stationed in the southeast of England, all suggested the invasion would centre on the Pas de Calais.

Because of the tides and unpredictable weather patterns, Allied planners had only a few dates available each month in which to launch the invasion. On 5 June, the date chosen, the worst storm in 20 years set in, delaying the operation. The weather had only marginally improved the next day, but General Dwight D Eisenhower, Allied commander-in-chief, gave the go-ahead: 6 June would be D-Day.

In the hours leading up to D-Day, teams of the French Resistance set about disrupting German communications. Just after midnight on 6 June, the first Allied troops were on French soil. British commandos and glider units captured key bridges and destroyed German gun emplacements, and the American 82nd and 101st Airborne Divisions landed west of the invasion site. Although the paratroops' tactical victories were few, they caused confusion in German ranks and, because of their relatively small numbers, the German high command was convinced that the real invasion had not yet begun.

Omaha & Utah Beaches

The assault by the US 1st and 29th Infantry Divisions on **Omaha Beach** (Vierville-sur-Mer, St-Laurent-sur-Mer and Colleville-sur-Mer) was by far the bloodiest of the day. From the outset, the Allies' best-laid plans were thrown into chaos. The beach was heavily defended by three battalions of heavily armed, highly trained Germans supported by mines, underwater obstacles and an extensive trench system. Strong winds blew many of the landing craft far from their carefully planned landing sectors. Many troops, overloaded with equipment, disembarked in deep water and simply drowned; others were cut to pieces by machine-gun and mortar fire from the cliffs. Only two of the 29 Sherman tanks expected to support the troops made it to shore and it proved almost impossible to advance up the beach as planned.

By noon the situation was so serious that General Omar Bradley, in charge of the Omaha Beach forces, considered abandoning the attack; but eventually, metre by metre, the GIs gained a precarious toehold on the beach. Assisted by naval bombardment, the US troops blew through a key German strongpoint and at last began to move off the beach. But of 2500 American casualties sustained there on D-Day, over 1000 were fatalities, most of them killed within the first hour of the landings.

The soldiers of the US 4th and 8th Infantry Divisions who landed at **Utah Beach** fared much better than their comrades at Omaha. Most of the landing craft came ashore in a relatively lightly protected sector, and by noon the beach had been cleared and soldiers of the 4th Infantry had linked with paratroopers from the 101st Airborne. By nightfall, some 20,000 men and 1700 vehicles had arrived on French soil via Utah Beach. However, during the three weeks it took to get from this sector to Cherbourg, US forces suffered one casualty for every 10m they advanced.

Sword, Juno & Gold Beaches

These beaches, stretching for about 35km from Ouistreham to Arromanches, were attacked by the British 2nd Army, which included significant Canadian units and smaller groups of Commonwealth, Free French and Polish forces.

At **Sword Beach**, initial German resistance was quickly overcome and the beach was secured within hours. Infantry pushed inland from Ouistreham to link up with paratroops around Ranville, but they suffered heavy casualties as their supporting armour fell behind, trapped in a massive traffic jam on the narrow coastal roads. Nevertheless, they were within 5km of Caen by 4pm, but a heavy German counterattack forced them to dig in and Caen was not taken on the first day as planned.

At **Juno Beach**, Canadian battalions landed quickly but had to clear the Germans trench by trench before moving inland. Mines took a heavy toll on the infantry, but by noon they were south and east of Creuilly.

At **Gold Beach**, the attack by the British forces was at first chaotic, as unexpectedly high waters obscured German underwater obstacles. By 9am, though, Allied armoured divisions were on the beach and several brigades pushed inland. By afternoon they'd linked up with the Juno forces and were only 3km from Bayeux.

The Beginning of the End

By the fourth day after D-Day, the Allies held a coastal strip about 100km long and 10km deep. British Field Marshal Montgomery's plan successfully drew the German armour towards Caen, where fierce fighting continued for more than a month and reduced the city to rubble. The US Army, stationed further west, pushed northwards through the fields and *bocage* (hedgerows) of the Cotentin Peninsula.

The prized port of Cherbourg fell to the Allies on 27 June after a series of fierce battles. However, its valuable facilities were sabotaged by the retreating Germans and it remained out of service until autumn. Having foreseen such logistical problems, the Allies had devised the remarkable Mulberry Harbours (see p212), two huge temporary ports set up off the Norman coast.

By the end of July, US army units had smashed through to the border of Brittany. By mid-August, two German armies had been surrounded and destroyed near Argentan and Falaise (the so-called 'Falaise Pocket'), and on 20 August US forces crossed the Seine at several points, around 40km north and south of Paris. Led by General Charles de Gaulle, France's leader-in-exile, both Allied and Free French troops arrived on the streets of the capital on 25 August and by that afternoon the city had been liberated.

landing beaches. The price includes entry to the Mémorial. You can book online or by telephone.

ⓘ Getting There & Away

BUS Bus Verts (☏08 10 21 42 14; www.bus verts.fr, in French) runs bus 70 (two or three daily Monday to Saturday, more frequently and on Sunday and holidays in summer), which goes northwest from Bayeux to Colleville-sur-Mer (Omaha Beach and the American Cemetery; €2.15, 35 minutes), Pointe du Hoc (€4.25) and Grandcamp-Maisy. Bus 74 (bus 75 in summer; three or four daily Monday to Saturday, more frequently and on Sunday and holidays in summer) links Bayeux with Arromanches (€2.15, 30 minutes), Gold and Juno Beaches, and Courseulles (€3.20, one hour).

ARROMANCHES

In order to unload the vast quantities of cargo needed by the invasion forces without having to capture – intact! – one of the heavily defended Channel ports (a lesson of the 1942 Dieppe Raid; see p199), the Allies set up prefabricated marinas, code-named **Mulberry Harbour**, off two of the landing beaches. These consisted of 146 massive cement caissons towed over from England and sunk to form a semicircular breakwater in which floating bridge spans were moored. In the three months after D-Day, the Mulberries facilitated the unloading of a mind-boggling 2.5 million men, four million tonnes of equipment and 500,000 vehicles.

The harbour established at Omaha was completely destroyed by a ferocious gale just two weeks after D-Day, but the remains of the second, Port Winston (named after Churchill), can still be seen near Arromanches, 10km northeast of Bayeux. At low tide you can walk out to one of the caissons from the beach. The best view of Port Winston and nearby Gold Beach is from the hill east of town, marked with a statue of the Virgin Mary.

Down in Arromanches itself and right on the beach, the Musée du Débarquement (Landing Museum; ☏02 31 22 34 31; www.normandy1944.com; place du 6 Juin; adult/child €6.50/4.50; ☉9am-7pm, closed Jan), redesigned in 2004 for the 60th anniversary of D-Day, makes an informative stop before visiting the beaches. Dioramas, models and two films explain the logistics and importance of Port Winston. Written material is available in 18 languages.

JUNO BEACH

Dune-lined Juno Beach, 12km east of Arromanches, was stormed by Canadian troops on D-Day. A Cross of Lorraine marks the spot where General Charles de Gaulle came ashore shortly after the landings. He was followed by Winston Churchill on 12 June and King George VI on 16 June.

The area's only Canadian museum, Centre Juno Beach (☏02 31 37 32 17; www.juno beach.org; adult/child €6.50/5; ☉9.30am-7pm Apr-Sep, reduced hours out of season, closed Jan) has multimedia exhibits on Canada's role in the war effort and the landings. Guided tours of Juno Beach (€5) are available from April to October.

LONGUES-SUR-MER

Part of the Nazis' Atlantic Wall, the massive casemates and 150mm German guns near Longues-sur-Mer, 6km west of Arromanches, were designed to hit targets some 20km away, including both Gold Beach (to the east) and Omaha Beach (to the west). Over six decades later, the mammoth artillery pieces are still in their colossal concrete emplacements – the only in situ large-calibre weapons in Normandy. For details on the tours available from April to October, contact the Longues tourist office (☏02 31 21 46 87).

Parts of the classic D-Day film, *The Longest Day* (1962), were filmed both here and at Pointe du Hoc. On clear days, Bayeux' cathedral, 8km away, is visible to the south.

OMAHA BEACH

The most brutal fighting on D-Day took place on the 7km stretch of coastline around Vierville-sur-Mer, St-Laurent-sur-Mer and Colleville-sur-Mer, 15km northwest of Bayeux, known as 'Bloody Omaha' to US veterans. Sixty years on, little evidence of the carnage unleashed here on 6 June 1944 remains except for concrete German bunkers, though at very low tide you can see a few remnants of the Mulberry Harbour.

These days Omaha is a peaceful place, a glorious stretch of fine golden sand partly lined with sand dunes and summer homes. Near the car park in St-Laurent-sur-Mer, a **memorial** marks the site of the first US military cemetery on French soil. There's also a sculpture on the beach called *Les Braves*, by the French sculptor Anilore Banon, commissioned to commemorate the 60th anniversary of the landings in 2004. Circuit de la Plage d'Omaha, trail-marked

The Battle of Normandy

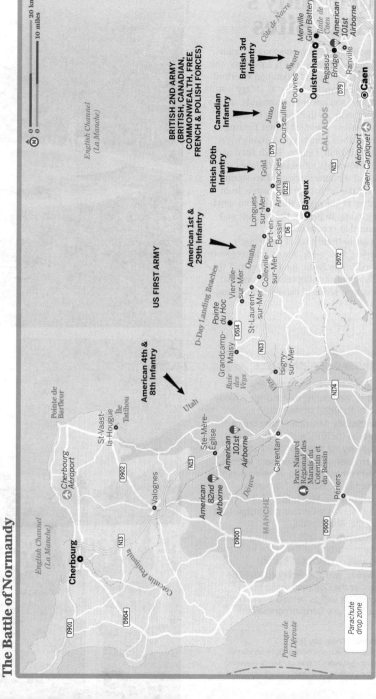

Normandy's D-Day Sites

Unimaginable danger, enormous human sacrifice and bravery that is legendary, the June 1944 landings of Operation Overlord – forever known to history as D-Day – still cast a long shadow over Normandy, and nowhere more so than on the beautiful beaches where the most brutal fighting occurred, their names synonymous with bloodshed: Utah, Omaha, Gold, Juno and Sword. Nowadays, of course, it takes some stretch of the imagination, when staring out over the brilliant golden sands from the edges of the green cliffs or from quiet fishing ports, to picture the carnage and heroism that occurred here.

A visit to these sites is particularly rewarding for anyone whose relatives were involved in the Battle for Europe, and the horrific events are impressively put into context by a series of excellent museums.

UNMISSABLE D-DAY SITES

» **Omaha Beach** (p212) The site of the worst fighting during the landings, 'bloody Omaha' shouldn't be missed

» **Normandy American Cemetery & Memorial** (p216) The sheer size of this vast graveyard is extraordinarily moving

» **Mémorial – Un Musée pour la Paix** (p216) Perhaps the best single museum devoted to the Battle of Normandy

» **Longues-sur-Mer** (p212) Visit some of the few surviving German gun installations along the 'Atlantic Wall'

» **Arromanches** (p212) See the incredible Mulberry Harbour at the beach here, and even walk out onto it at low tide

» **Bayeux War Cemetery** (p207) The largest of the Commonwealth burial grounds, as well as being the final resting place for many German combatants

Clockwise from top left
1. Remnants of gun emplacements, Pointe du Hoc
2. German gun near Longues-sur-Mer 3. Normandy American Cemetery & Memorial, overlooking Omaha Beach.

with a yellow stripe, is a self-guided tour all along Omaha Beach.

On a bluff above the beach, the huge Normandy American Cemetery & Memorial (Cimetière Militaire Américain; ☎02 31 51 62 00; www.abmc.gov; Colleville-sur-Mer; ⊙9am-5pm), 17km northwest of Bayeux, is the largest American cemetery in Europe. Featured in the opening scenes of Steven Spielberg's *Saving Private Ryan*, it contains the graves of 9387 American soldiers, including 41 pairs of brothers, and a memorial to 1557 others whose remains were never found. White marble crosses and Stars of David stretch off in seemingly endless rows, surrounded by an immaculately tended expanse of lawn. The cemetery is overlooked by a large colonnaded memorial, centred on a statue dedicated to the spirit of American youth. Nearby is a reflective pond and a small chapel.

Opened in 2007, the visitor center, mostly underground so as not to detract from the site, has an excellent free multimedia presentation on the D-Day landings, told in part through the stories of individuals. Be prepared for airport-type security. Visitor centre **tours** of the cemetery (one in the afternoon year-round, a second in the morning in summer) focus on personal stories.

POINTE DU HOC RANGER MEMORIAL
At 7.10am on 6 June 1944, 225 US Army Rangers commanded by Lt Col James Earl Rudder scaled the 30m cliffs at Pointe du Hoc, where the Germans had a battery of huge artillery guns perfectly placed to rain shells onto the beaches of Utah and Omaha. Unbeknown to Rudder and his team, the guns had already been transferred inland, and they spent the next two days repelling fierce German counterattacks. By the time they were finally relieved on 8 June, 81 of the rangers had been killed and 58 more had been wounded.

Today the site (☎02 31 51 90 70; admission free; ⊙9am-5pm), which France turned over to the US government in 1979, looks much as it did more than half a century ago. The ground is pockmarked with bomb craters, and the German command post (no longer open to the public because it's too close to the eroding cliff) and several of the concrete gun emplacements are still standing, scarred by bullet holes and blackened by flame-throwers.

As you face the sea, Utah Beach is 14km to the left.

UTAH BEACH
This beach is marked by memorials to the various divisions that landed here and the Musée du Débarquement (Landing Museum; ☎02 33 71 53 35; www.utah-beach.com; Ste-Marie du Mont; adult/6-14yr €6/2.50; ⊙9.30am-7pm).

Caen
POP 112,500

Founded in the 11th century by William the Conqueror, Caen – capital of the Basse Normandie region – was 80% destroyed during the 1944 Battle of Normandy. Rebuilt in the 1950s and '60s in a typically utilitarian style, modern-day Caen nevertheless offers visitors a walled medieval château, two ancient abbeys, several very attractive 19th-century areas and a clutch of excellent museums, including a groundbreaking museum of war and peace.

◉ Sights

Mémorial – Un Musée pour la Paix
MEMORIAL
(Memorial – A Museum for Peace; ☎02 31 06 06 45; www.memorial-caen.fr; esplanade Général Eisenhower; adult/child under 10yr €17.50/free; ⊙9am-7pm, closed Mon Nov-Feb) Situated 3km northwest of the city centre, this innovative memorial-museum provides an insightful and vivid account of the Battle of Normandy. Tickets bought after 1pm can be used to re-enter until 1pm the next day. All signs are in French, English and German.

The visit begins with a whistle-stop overview of Europe's descent into total war, tracing events from the end of WWI and the Treaty of Versailles, through the rise of fascism in Europe and the German occupation of France, right up through the Battle of Normandy. It's a hugely impressive affair, using sound, lighting, film, animation and audio testimony, as well as a range of artefacts and exhibits, to graphically evoke the realities of war, the trials of occupation and the joy of liberation.

A second section focuses on the Cold War. There's also an underground gallery dedicated to winners of the Nobel Peace Prize, located in bunkers used by the Germans in 1944.

To get here, take bus 2 from place Courtonne. By car, follow the signs marked 'Mémorial'.

FREE Château de Guillaume le
Conquérant   CASTLE

(Château of William the Conqueror; www.chateau.
caen.fr) Looming above the centre of the city
and surrounded by a dry moat and massive
battlements, the castle was established by
William the Conqueror, Duke of Normandy,
in 1060 and extended by his son Henry I.
Visitors can walk around the ramparts, and

visit the 12th-century Église St-Georges
(open during temporary exhibitions) and
the Échiquier (Exchequer), which dates
from about 1100 and is one of the oldest civic buildings in Normandy. The Jardin des
Simples is a garden of medicinal and aromatic herbs cultivated during the Middle
Ages – some of them poisonous.

NORMANDY CAEN

Caen

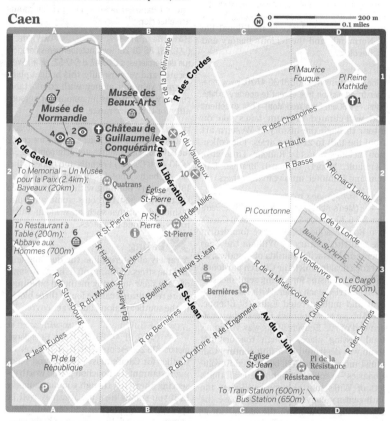

Caen

Near the château are two of the only prewar buildings left in the city centre: the half-timbered, 16th-century **Musée de la Poste** (Postal Museum; 52 rue St-Pierre) and the 15th-century **Maison des Quatrans** (25 rue de Geôle).

Musée de Normandie

(☎02 31 30 47 60; www.musee-de-normandie. caen.fr; admission free except temporary exhibitions; ◷9.30am-6pm, closed Tue Oct-May) This two-part museum looks at traditional life in Normandy and the region's history and archaeology.

Musée des Beaux-Arts

(Fine Arts Museum; ☎02 31 30 47 70; www.mba. caen.fr; admission free except temporary exhibitions; ◷9.30am-6pm Wed-Mon) This excellent and well-curated museum takes you on a tour through the history of Western art from the 15th to 21st centuries. The collection includes works by Rubens, Tintoretto, Géricault, Monet, Bonnard, Braque, Balthus and Dubuffet, among many others.

FREE **Abbaye aux Hommes**   ABBEY
(Men's Abbey; ☎02 31 30 42 81; ◷9am-1pm & 2-6.30pm Mon-Sat, 2-6.30pm Sun) Caen's two Romanesque abbeys were founded in the mid-11th century by William the Conqueror and his wife, Matilda of Flanders, as part of a deal in which the Church pardoned these fifth cousins for having semi-incestuously married each other. With its magnificent and multiturreted Église St-Étienne, the Abbaye aux Hommes is near the western end of rue Écuyère. This was William's final resting place, though the original tomb was destroyed by a 16th-century Calvinist mob and, in 1793, by fevered Revolutionaries – a solitary thighbone is all that's left of Will's mortal remains. Today, the 18th-century convent buildings house the town hall, and tours of the abbey run at 9.30am, 11am, 2.30pm and 4pm.

Abbaye aux Dames   ABBEY
(Women's Abbey; ☎02 31 06 98 98; tours free; ◷tours 2.30pm & 4pm) The counterpoint of the Abbaye aux Hommes is the Abbaye aux Dames at the eastern end of rue des Chanoines. The complex includes the **Église de la Trinité**. Look for Matilda's tomb behind the main altar and for the striking pink stained-glass windows beyond. Free twice-daily tours take you through the interior in some detail, though you can snoop around yourself at other times outside of Mass.

🛏 Sleeping

Hôtel Le Dauphin   TRADITIONAL HOTEL €€
(☎02 31 86 22 26; www.le-dauphin-normandie. com; 29 rue Gémare; s €75-185, d €85-190; 🛜) Although this Best Western–affiliated hotel is partly housed in a former priory, the facilities – including a sauna and fitness room – are thoroughly modern. Some of the 35 rooms have antique furniture and ancient exposed beams. The pricier rooms are cheerier.

Hôtel Bernières   FAMILY HOTEL €
(☎02 31 86 01 26; www.hotelbernieres.com; 50 rue de Bernières; s €40-47, d €47-52; 🛜👪) Well located and very friendly, this budget place is great value for money, with comfortable rooms with a surprising amount of personality for this price range.

Hôtel St-Étienne   HOTEL €
(☎02 31 86 35 82; www.hotel-saint-etienne.com; 2 rue de l'Académie; r with shared bathroom €29-38, r €40-48, tr €58; 🛜) Friendly and upbeat, this classic budget hotel – in a charming late-18th-century building with creaky wooden stairs – has just 11 rooms, some with old-fashioned features such as wooden wardrobes and stone fireplaces.

🍴 Eating

A variety of eateries line rue du Vaugueux and the streets running off it, home to some of Caen's few surviving medieval buildings. More restaurants can be found three blocks to the southeast along quai Vandeuvre.

TOP CHOICE **Le Bouchon**   NORMAN CUISINE €€
(☎02 31 44 26 26; 4 rue Graindorge; menus €18-26; ◷closed Sun & Mon) Look no further for Caen's most popular and buzzing restaurant. Le Bouchon is well worth reserving ahead for, though you may squeeze in if you simply turn up. You may well be the only foreigners here and certainly don't expect a translation of the chalk-board menu – but if your French is up to it, come and savour some spectacular modern Norman cooking and enjoy a wonderful choice of well-priced wines, which the manager will very passionately help you choose.

Le P'tit B   MODERN FRENCH €€
(☎02 31 93 50 76; 15 rue du Vaugueux; menu €18-25) This classy little stone-walled eatery gives traditional flavours a contemporary twist – the *wok de trois poissons* (three-fish stew) and beef fillet are a treat for the tastebuds. The menu changes four times a year.

Restaurant à Table   TRADITIONAL FRENCH €
(☎02 31 86 57 75; 43 rue St-Sauveur; menus €15-20; ☺closed Sun & Mon) An excellent option for traditional French cuisine – including four fish and four meat mains – at reasonable prices. Specialities include home-smoked salmon and some scrumptious desserts.

Drinking & Entertainment

Le Cargö   LIVE MUSIC
(☎02 31 86 79 31; www.lecargo.fr, in French; 9 cours Caffarelli) At the far end of the pleasure port, this *scène de musique actuelle* (venue for contemporary music) presents cutting-edge local bands as well as more-established groups.

❶ Information

L'Espace (☎02 31 93 37 14; 1 rue Basse; per hr €3.80; ☺10am-9pm Mon-Sat, 11am-1.30pm & 3.30-9pm Sun) Internet café.

Tourist office (☎02 31 27 14 14; www.tourisme.caen.fr; place St-Pierre; ☺9.30am-6.30pm Mon-Sat, 10am-1pm Sun)

❶ Getting There & Away

BUS Run by Caen-based **Bus Verts** (☎08 10 21 42 14; www.busverts.fr, in French; place Courtonne; ☺7.30am-7pm Mon-Fri, 9am-7pm Sat), bus 20 goes to Le Havre (€11, 2½ hours) via Deauville, Trouville and Honfleur. The Caen–Le Havre route is also served by an express bus (€15, 1½ hours, four daily Monday to Saturday, two Sunday) via Honfleur.

Bus 30 goes to Bayeux (€4.25, one hour, three or four daily Monday to Friday except holidays); bus 1 serves the ferry port at Ouistreham; and bus 3 will get you to Courseulles.

In Caen, most buses stop at the bus station and place Courtonne. When arriving or departing, your Bus Verts ticket is valid for an hour on Caen's buses and trams.

CAR Rental agencies:

ADA (☎02 31 34 88 89; 34 rue d'Auge)

Avis (☎08 20 61 16 81; 44 place de la Gare)

Europcar (☎02 31 84 61 61; 36 place de la Gare)

Hertz (☎02 31 84 64 50; 34 place de la Gare)

FERRY For details on Brittany Ferries' services from Portsmouth to Ouistreham, 14km northeast of Caen, see p973.

WILLIAM CONQUERS ENGLAND

Born out of wedlock to Robert the Magnificent, future Duke of Normandy, and Arlette, daughter of a furrier, William the Bastard (1027–87) – better known to posterity as William the Conqueror – became Duke of Normandy at the tender age of eight when his father died while on the way back from Jerusalem. Having survived several assassination attempts by rivals, including members of his own family, William assumed full control of the province at age 15 and set about regaining his lost territory and quashing rebellious vassals.

One of several pretenders to the English throne on the death of Edward the Confessor, William crossed the Channel with an army of about 6000 men to claim the throne from Harold Godwinson, Edward the Confessor's apparent death-bed choice of successor. William's forces landed at Pevensey before marching to Hastings, where, on 13 October 1066, Harold faced off against William with about 7000 men from a strong defensive position. The battle began the next day.

Although William's archers scored many hits, the Saxon army's ferocious defence ended a charge by the Norman cavalry and drove them back in disarray. Summoning the experience and tactical ability he had gained in numerous campaigns against rivals back in Normandy, William used the cavalry's rout to draw the Saxon infantry out of their defensive positions, whereupon the Norman infantry turned and caused heavy casualties among the undisciplined Saxon troops. Late in the afternoon the battle started to turn against Harold, who was slain – by an arrow through the eye, according to the Bayeux Tapestry. The embattled Saxons fought on until sunset and then fled. William immediately marched to London, ruthlessly quelled the opposition, and was crowned king of England on Christmas Day.

William thus became the ruler of two kingdoms, bringing England's feudal system of government under the control of Norman nobles. Ongoing unrest among the Saxon peasantry soured William's opinion of the country and, after 1072, he spent the rest of his life in Normandy, only going to England when compelled to do so. William left most of the governance of the country to the bishops. In 1087 William was injured during an attack on Mantes. He died at Rouen a few weeks later and was buried in Caen.

TRAIN In the city centre, tickets are sold at the **SNCF Boutique** (8 rue St-Pierre; ⏰9.15am-7pm Mon-Fri, 10am-7pm Sat). Train services:

Bayeux €6, 20 minutes, hourly Monday to Saturday, eight Sunday

Cherbourg €20, 1¼ hours, seven to 15 daily

Deauville €12.50, one hour, eight to 12 daily

Dieppe €30, 2¾ hours, via Rouen, seven daily

Paris Gare St-Lazare €31.50, two hours, 12 daily

Pontorson (Mont St-Michel) €24.50, two hours, two daily

Rouen €23, 1½ hours, eight to 14 daily

ℹ Getting Around

BIKE V'eol (☑08 00 20 03 06; www.veol.caen. fr, in French; 1st 30min free), Caen's answer to Paris' Velib', has 350 bicycles available at 40 automatic stations. The only problem is you need to sign up (one week/year €1/15).

BUS Twisto (www.twisto.fr, in French) runs the city's buses and the two tram lines, A and B, which link the train station with the city centre. A single/24-hour ticket costs €1.20/3.55.

TAXI For a taxi, call **Abbeilles Taxi** (☑02 31 52 17 89).

Trouville & Deauville

The twin seaside towns of Trouville (population 5075) and Deauville (population 4100), 15km southwest of Honfleur, are hugely popular with Parisians, who flock here year-round on weekends and all week long from April to September.

Chic Deauville – once a swamp, as Trouvillians are quick to point out – has been a playground of the wealthy ever since it was founded by Napoléon III's half-brother, the Duke of Morny, in 1861. Exclusive, expensive and brash, it's packed with designer boutiques, deluxe hotels and public gardens of impossible neatness, and is home to two racetracks and a high-profile American film festival.

Trouville, another veteran beach resort, is also a working fishing port and, in many ways, a much more attractive place to visit. The town was frequented by painters and writers during the 19th century, including Mozin and Flaubert, and many French celebrities have holiday homes here, lured by the 2km-long sandy beach and the laid-back seaside ambience.

The towns are linked by pont des Belges, just east of Deauville's train and bus stations, and by a low-tide footpath near the river's mouth (replaced at high tide by a boat that runs from mid-March to September, and on weekends and during school holidays the rest of the year).

◉ Sights & Activities

In Deauville, the rich and beautiful strut their stuff along the beachside **Promenade des Planches**, a 643m-long boardwalk lined with cabins named after famous Americans (mainly film stars), before swimming in the nearby 50m covered **Piscine Olympique** (Olympic swimming pool; ⏰closed 3 weeks in Jan & 2 weeks in Jun) or losing a wad at the **casino** 200m inland.

Trouville, too, has a **casino**, and a 583m **boardwalk** where you can swim in freshwater swimming pools, rent sailboats, windsurf and even surf. Nearby are lots of imposing **19th-century villas**.

Musée de Trouville   MUSEUM

(☑02 31 88 16 26; 64 rue du Général Leclerc; adult/child €2/1.50; ⏰11am-1pm & 2pm-5.30pm Wed-Mon Easter–mid-Nov) In the fine Villa Montebello, Trouville's museum is 1km to the northeast of the town's tourist office. With a panoramic view over the beach, the museum recounts Trouville's history and features works by Charles Mozin and Eugène Boudin.

Natur' Aquarium   AQUARIUM

(☑02 31 88 46 04; www.natur-aquarium.com, in French; 17 rue de Paris; adult/3-14yr €7.50/5.50; ⏰10am-noon & 2-6.30pm) Trouville's beach is home to an aquarium packed with multicoloured fish, fearsome reptiles and weird insects.

⚜ Festivals & Events

Deauville is renowned for its **horse racing** in July, August and October – with a few winter races – at two *hippodromes* (racetracks; see www.hippodromesdedeauville. com, in French): La Touques for flat races; and Clairefontaine (see www.hippodrome -deauville-clairefontaine.com) for flat, trotting and jumping races (steeplechases and hurdles).

Asian Film Festival   FILM FESTIVAL

(www.deauvilleasia.com) Deauville's Asian film festival runs for five days in mid-March.

American Film Festival   FILM FESTIVAL

(www.festival-deauville.com) Deauville's 10-day film festival is an altogether more welcoming affair than its better-known

OYSTER PICNIC

The **Poissonnerie** (fish market; cnr bd Fernand Moureaux & rue des Bains, Trouville; ⊙9am-7pm) is *the* place in Trouville to head for a waterfront picnic of fresh oysters with lemon (just €6.50 to €8.50 a dozen) – or for locally caught raw fish. Everything is fresh, so no energy is wasted on freezing, and since there are almost no middlemen you pay reasonable prices and the fishermen get a fair share of the proceeds. It's housed in temporary stalls while the market building – which burned down in 2006 – is being rebuilt.

cousin at Cannes. Tickets for most screenings are on sale to the public, and you're bound to catch glimpses of a few Hollywood stars when the festival's in full swing in early September.

🛏 Sleeping

Trouville offers much better accommodation value than Deauville. Prices are highest in July and August and on weekends, and lowest from October to Easter except during Paris' school holidays.

Le Trouville   FAMILY HOTEL €€
(☏02 31 98 45 48; www.hotelletrouville.com; 1 rue Thiers, Trouville; s €43, d €65-90; 🛜🍴) This family-run hotel may be small and simple but the rates are great, especially considering its proximity to the beach. The colourful bedcovers and wallpaper add a hint of much-needed character to the 15 smallish rooms.

La Maison Normande   HOTEL €
(☏02 31 88 12 25; www.maisonnormande.com, in French; 4 place de Lattre de Tassigny, Trouville; r €48-68, apt €90; 🛜) Stay in this late-17th-century Norman house and you'll feel like you're visiting your new Norman grandma. The 17 rooms are decorated in warm colours and some have views of the church opposite on rue Victor Hugo.

Le Fer à Cheval   HOTEL €€
(☏02 31 98 30 20; www.hotel-trouville.com; 11 rue Victor Hugo, Trouville; s/d/tr €94/99/104; 🛜) Occupying three beautiful turn-of-the-20th-century buildings, this modern hotel has 34 comfortable rooms with big

windows, horse-themed decor and bright bathrooms. Owned by a retired *boulanger* (baker) who loves to bake fresh croissants,. the prices outside July and August are very generously reduced.

🍴 Eating

In Trouville, there are lots of restaurants along bd Fernand Moureaux and perpendicular rue des Bains. Our two favourite eateries are next to each other opposite the former Poissonnerie.

Brasserie Le Central   BRASSERIE €€
(☏02 31 88 13 68; 158 bd Fernand Moureaux, Trouville; menus €20-35; ⊙7.30am-midnight) This buzzing brasserie adds a touch of Parisian class to the Trouville waterfront. The menu offers few surprises – fresh fish (all of it wild except for the salmon), mussels and seafood are the mainstays – but the atmosphere is fantastic on a summer evening.

Les Vapeurs   BRASSERIE €€
(☏02 21 88 45 85; 160 bd Fernand Moureaux, Trouville; mains €10-30; ⊙9am-11.30pm) Trouville's most famous restaurant is a home from home for sunglasses-class Parisian weekenders and even the odd movie star during the film festival. Unusually, the menu is à la carte only, with a divine selection of fresh fish and seafood dishes served up in grand brasserie style.

⭐ Entertainment

Nightlife is centred on Deauville.

Bar Le Zoo   BAR
(www.lezoo.fr, in French; 53 rue Désiré-le-Hoc, Deauville; ⊙6pm-3am) A sleek and sophisticated urban-style hang-out, tailor-made for cocktails (€8.50) and checking out the beautiful people. Has a DJ from 10pm on Friday and Saturday, when you can dance in the cellar. The website has details on theme nights.

🛍 Shopping

Shopping in Deauville (for instance right around the casino and along rue Eugène Colas) tends towards well-known Parisian brand names, while Trouville features less-glitzy wares along its main commercial street, rue des Bains.

ℹ Information

Deauville post office (rue Robert Fossorier) Exchanges currency.

NORMANDY TROUVILLE & DEAUVILLE

Deauville tourist office (☎02 31 14 40 00; www.deauville.org; place de la Mairie; ☺10am-6pm Mon-Sat, 10am-1pm & 2-5pm Sun) Situated about 400m west of the train station, Deauville's tourist office can supply you with an English-language walking tour brochure and a Deauville map (from which Trouville is completely missing).

Trouville tourist office (☎02 31 14 60 70; www.trouvillesurmer.org; 32 bd Fernand Moureaux; ☺9.30am-6.30pm Mon-Sat & 10am-1pm Sun) Situated about 200m north of pont des Belges, Trouville's tourist office has a free (Deauville-less) map of Trouville and sells maps for a self-guided architectural tour and two rural walks (7km and 11km). Internet access is €1 per 15 minutes.

❶ Getting There & Around

AIR A useful new **CityJet** (www.cityjet.com) service was introduced in mid-2010, linking Deauville's tiny airport to London City Airport four days a week.

BUS From next to Deauville's train station, **Bus Verts** (☎08 10 21 42 14; www.busverts.fr, in French) has hourly services:

Caen €5.50, 1¼ hours

Honfleur €2.15, 40 minutes

Le Havre €6.50, 1¼ hours

TRAIN Rail travel to and from Deauville and Trouville requires a change at Lisieux (€6, 20 minutes, eight to 12 daily). There is, however, a handful of direct trains to Paris Gare St-Lazare (€29.50, 2¼ hours, six to nine daily). Destinations from Lisieux:

Caen €8.50, 30 minutes, at least hourly

Rouen €17.50, 1¼ hours, hourly

TAXI For a cab, call **Central Taxis** (☎02 31 87 11 11).

Honfleur

POP 8350

Long a favourite with painters but now more popular with the Parisian jet set, Honfleur is arguably Normandy's most charming seaside town. Even though it can be overrun with tourists in the summer months, it's hard not to love its graceful beauty.

Its heart is the Vieux Bassin (Old Harbour), from where explorers once set sail for the New World. Now filled with pleasure vessels, this part of the port is surrounded by a jumble of brightly coloured buildings that evoke maritime Normandy of centuries past.

History

Honfleur's seafaring tradition dates back over a millennium. After the Norman invasion of England in 1066, goods bound for the conquered isle were shipped across the Channel from here.

Samuel de Champlain set sail from Honfleur in 1608, on his way to found Quebec City. In 1681 Cavelier de La Salle set out from here to explore the New World, reaching the mouth of the Mississippi and naming the area Louisiana in honour of Louis XIV.

During the 17th and 18th centuries, Honfleur achieved a degree of prosperity through maritime trade – including the slave trade – with the west coast of Africa, the West Indies and the Azores.

◉ Sights

Église Ste-Catherine　　　　　　　CHURCH
(place Ste-Catherine; ☺9am-6pm) Initially intended as a temporary structure, this extraordinary church has been standing in the square for over 500 years. Built by the people of Honfleur during the late 15th and early 16th centuries, after its stone predecessor had been destroyed during the Hundred Years War, wood was used in an effort to save funds for strengthening the fortifications around the walled Enclos. The structure is particularly notable for its double-vaulted roof and its twin naves, which from the inside resemble a couple of overturned ships' hulls.

Across the square is the church's freestanding wooden bell tower, **Clocher Ste-Catherine**, supposedly built away from the church in order to avoid lightning strikes and damage to the clock's clanging bells.

Museum Eugène Boudin　　　　ART MUSEUM
(☎02 31 89 54 00; opposite 50 rue de l'Homme de Bois; adult/child €5/3.20, Jul-Sep €6.50/5; ☺10am-noon & 2-6pm Wed-Mon) Named in honour of Eugène Boudin, an early Impressionist painter born here in 1824, this museum is three blocks northwest of the Lieutenance. It features a collection of Impressionist paintings from Normandy, including works by Dubourg, Dufy and Monet. One room is devoted to Boudin, whom Baudelaire called the 'king of skies' for his luscious skyscapes.

Les Maisons Satie　　　　　　　　MUSEUM
(☎02 31 89 11 11; 67 bd Charles V; adult/child under 10yr €5.50/free; ☺10am-7pm Wed-Mon) The

PONT DE NORMANDIE

Opened in 1995, this futuristic bridge (€5 each way per car) stretches in a soaring 2km arch over the Seine between Le Havre and Honfleur. It's a typically French affair, as much sophisticated architecture as engineering, with two huge V-shaped columns – somewhat reminiscent of giant toast tongs – holding aloft a delicate net of cables. Crossing is quite a thrill – and the views of the Seine are magnificent. In each direction there's a narrow footpath and a bike lane.

quirky Maisons Satie capture the spirit of the eccentric, avant-garde composer Erik Satie (1866–1925), who lived and worked in Honfleur and was born in the half-timbered house that now contains the museum. 'Esoteric' Satie was known for his surrealistic wit as much as for his starkly beautiful piano compositions. Visitors wander through the museum with a headset playing Satie's music and excerpts from his writings (in French or English). Each room is a surreal surprise – winged pears and self-pedalling carousels are just the start.

Musée de la Marine   MARITIME MUSEUM
(☎02 31 89 14 12; quai St-Etienne; adult/child €3.50/2.30; ◎10am-noon & 2-6.30pm Tue-Sun, closed mid-Nov–mid-Feb) Located in the Enclos quarter, the Maritime Museum has nautically themed displays of model ships, carpenters' tools and engravings. It is inside the deconsecrated 13th- and 14th-century Église St-Étienne.

Musée d'Ethnographie et d'Art Populaire Normand   MUSEUM
(rue de la Prison; adult/child €3.50/2.30; ◎10am-noon & 2-6.30pm Tue-Sun, closed mid-Nov–mid-Feb) Next to the Musée de la Marine, this museum occupies a couple of period houses and a former prison. Its nine rooms recreate the world of Honfleur during the 16th to 19th centuries, using a mix of costumes, furniture and artefacts. A combined ticket with the Musée de la Marine costs €4.70 for adults, or €3.10 for children.

Old Harbour   HISTORIC QUARTER
On the west side of the Vieux Bassin, with its many pleasure boats, quai Ste-Catherine is lined with tall, taper-thin houses – many

protected from the elements by slate tiles – dating from the 16th to 18th centuries. The Lieutenance, at the mouth of the old harbour, was once the residence of the town's royal governor. The Avant Port, just northeast of the Lieutenance, is home to Honfleur's 30 or so fishing vessels, which moor in the area northeast of quai de la Quarantaine.

Galleries   GALLERIES
There are quite a few art galleries around Église Ste-Catherine (for instance on the narrow cobblestone streets northwest of place Hamelin) and in the Enclos quarter.

Scenic Walks   WALKS
Honfleur is superb for aimless ambling. One option is to head north from the Lieutenance along quai des Passagers to Jetée de l'Ouest (Western Jetty), which forms the west side of the Avant Port, out to the broad mouth of the Seine. Possible stops include the Jardin des Personalités, a park featuring figures from Honfleur history; Naturospace (☎02 31 81 77 00; www.naturospace.com; bd Charles V; adult/under 15yr €8/6.50; ◎10am-1pm & 2-7pm), a tropical greenhouse filled with 60 different species of free-flying butterflies; and the beach.

Chapelle Notre Dame de Grâce   CHURCH
Built between 1600 and 1613, Chapelle Notre Dame de Grâce is at the top of the Plateau de Grâce, a wooded, 100m-high hill about 2km west of the Vieux Bassin. There's a great view of the town and port.

☞ Tours

Walking Tours   WALKING TOUR
(€6 to €7) Some of the tourist office's 1½- to two-hour walking tours of Honfleur are in English, including one that leaves at 3pm every Tuesday and Wednesday in May and June and from September to mid-October. Atmospheric night-time tours begin at 9pm Saturday from May to October.

Boat Tours   BOAT TOUR
(adult/concessions €7.50/5) From about March to mid-October, you can take a boat tour from the Avant Port (across the street from the Lieutenance) out to the Seine Estuary and the Pont de Normandie – look for the *Cap Christian, L'Évasion III* or the larger *Jolie France.*

🛏 Sleeping

TOP CHOICE La Maison de Lucie   BOUTIQUE HOTEL €€
(☎02 31 14 40 40; www.lamaisondelucie.com; 44 rue des Capucins; d €150-220, ste €315;

NORMANDY HONFLEUR

☎) Former home of the novelist Lucie Delarue Mardrus (1874–1945), this marvellous little hideaway has just 10 rooms and two suites, the latter decorated with a mixture of antiques and contemporary objets d'art from far-off lands. Some of the bedrooms, panelled in oak, have Moroccan-tile bathrooms and boast fantastic views across the harbour to the Pont de Normandie. The shady terrace is a glorious place for a summer breakfast. There's a chic jacuzzi in the old brick-vaulted cellar. Situated five short blocks west of the Lieutenance.

Hôtel du Dauphin   TRADITIONAL HOTEL €

(☎02 31 89 15 53; www.hoteldudauphin.com; 10 place Pierre-Berthelot; r €69-165; ☎) Right in the heart of Honfleur behind a 17th-century slate and half-timbered facade, this very well-run hotel has 34 modern, stylish rooms, most of which have been recently redecorated. The rooms in the nearby annexe do not have wi-fi, and there's no lift in either building.

Hôtel L'Écrin   HISTORIC HOTEL €€

(☎02 31 14 43 45; www.honfleur.com/default-ecrin.htm; 19 rue Eugène Boudin; d €100-180, ste €250; ☎🅿) This ridiculously lavish Norman manor house is stuffed with porcelain, oil paintings and antique furniture, re-creating the opulence of times long past. The 30 rooms, which come with thoroughly modern bathrooms, retain touches of the 1800s – alongside flat-screen TVs hung on the walls like oil paintings. To get here from Église Ste-Catherine, go southwest along rue Brûlée and turn right.

Les Maisons de Léa   TRADITIONAL HOTEL €€

(☎02 31 14 49 49; www.lesmaisonsdelea.com; place Ste-Catherine; d €165-205, ste €215; ☎) This beautiful old ivy-clad mansion right on Honfleur's main square and facing the church has been converted into a very sleek 30-room hotel. The style is decidedly French, with lots of floral patterns, but there's also a *hammam* (wet sauna) that's free to guests, as well as a small spa for pampering yourself.

Hôtel L'Absinthe   TRADITIONAL HOTEL €€

(☎02 31 89 23 22; www.absinthe.fr; 1 rue de la Ville; r €115-185; ☎) Another charming place right in the heart of town, the Absinthe has cosy rooms sporting exposed beams and plenty of charming old furniture in its individually designed rooms.

Hôtel Belvédère   FAMILY HOTEL €

(☎02 31 89 08 13; www.hotel-belvedere-honfleur.com; 36 rue Emile Renouf; s/d/tr €66/67/82; ☎🅿) Offering the best value in town, this cosy, welcoming hotel has nine well-kept rooms, some with views of the Pont de Normandie, others of the delightful, grassy back garden. Situated 1km southeast of the tourist office.

Etap Hôtel   HOTEL €

(☎08 92 68 07 81; rue des Vases; www.etaphotel.com; d €39.50-48) This almost comi-

---

CAMEMBERT COUNTRY

Some of the most enduring names in the pungent world of French *fromage* come from Normandy, including Pont L'Évêque, Livarot and, most famous of all, Camembert, all of which are named after towns south of Honfleur, on or near the D579.

It's thought that monks first began experimenting with cheesemaking in the Pays d'Auge sometime in the 11th century, but the present-day varieties didn't emerge until around the 17th century. The invention of Camembert is generally credited to Marie Harel, who was supposedly given the secret of soft cheesemaking by an abbot from Brie on the run from Revolutionary mobs in 1790. Whatever the truth of the legend, the cheese was a huge success at the local market in Vimoutiers, and production of Camembert quickly grew from a cottage industry into an international operation – it even received the imperial seal of approval from Napoléon III at the World Fair in 1855. The distinctive round wooden boxes in which Camembert is wrapped have been around since 1890; they were designed by a local engineer by the name of Monsieur Ridel to protect the soft disc during long-distance travel.

If you're interested in seeing how the cheese is made, you can take a guided tour of the President Farm (☎02 33 36 06 60; www.fermepresident.com; adult/child €5/2; ☺10am-noon & 2-6pm Jun-Aug, by reservation Mar-May, Sep & Oct), an early-19th-century farm restored by Président, one of the region's largest Camembert producers. It's in the centre of the town of Camembert, which is about 60km south of Honfleur.

cally anonymous chain hotel has 63 cheap, charmless rooms with bunk beds and functional bathrooms. It's included here as, in the absence of a youth hostel, it's the cheapest bed in town.

✖ Eating

L'Hippocampe MODERN FRENCH €€
(☎02 31 89 98 36; 46 quai Ste-Catherine; menus €18-34) This spot is equally great for al fresco dining in the warmer months and dining inside in the cosy interior, a melange of old and new. The food is of very high quality and the evening dinner menus are surprisingly affordable.

L'Absinthe TRADITIONAL FRENCH €€
(☎02 31 89 39 00; 10 quai de la Quarantaine; menus €28-64) Facing the Vieux Port, this well-regarded restaurant serves up sumptuous, sophisticated French cuisine – made with seasonally fresh produce – in the finest *gastronomique* tradition. Specialities include sole meunière, roasted pigeon and blue Breton lobster. It's a good idea to reserve ahead for Saturday dinner and Sunday lunch.

La Tortue TRADITIONAL FRENCH €
(☎02 31 81 24 60; www.restaurantlatortue.fr, in French; 36 rue de l'Homme de Bois; lunch menu €13, dinner menus €18-36; ⊗closed Tue & Wed) This traditionally styled eatery housed in a low-slung dining room with a charming beamed ceiling serves up French cuisine with Norman touches, offering four meat and six fish mains. Starters include oysters in aniseed sauce (€9). Situated two blocks northwest of the Lieutenance.

Travel's Coffee Shop CAFÉ €
(☎06 72 20 72 98; 6 place du Puits; mains €7-9; ⊗7.30am-7pm) A great spot to get away from the formality of the Quai Ste-Catherine and enjoy a good breakfast or a light lunch of quiches, sandwiches or salads, this café is run by a British ex-pat who also offers charming *chambre d'hôte* accommodation (€75 to €95).

🍷 Drinking

Café L'Albatros CAFÉ-BAR
(32 quai Ste-Catherine; ⊗8am-2am) Sailors, students, philosophers and layabouts are all at home at this café-bar, from breakfast (€5 to €13) through sandwiches and beer and on to nightcaps. Serves light meals till 10pm.

Le Perroquet Vert BAR
(52 quai Ste-Catherine; ⊗8am-2am) The brick-vaulted 'green parrot' has an excellent selection of beers and a fine terrace for people-watching. Serves breakfast, afternoon sandwiches and evening tapas (€5 to €8).

ℹ Information

Médiathèque (quai Lepaulmier; per 30min €2.50; ⊗2.30-6pm Tue-Fri, plus 10am-12.30pm Wed, 10am-12.30pm & 2.30-5.30pm Sat) The public library has several internet computers available.

Post office (7 cours Albert Manuel) On the southwestern continuation of rue de la République. Changes foreign currency.

Tourist office (☎02 31 89 23 30; www.ot-honfleur.fr; quai Lepaulmier; ⊗9.30am-12.30pm & 2pm-6pm Mon-Sat) Situated inside the Médiathèque (library) building. Has a free map detailing a 2km walking circuit. Internet access costs €1 for 15 minutes.

ℹ Getting There & Around

BUS The **bus station** (☎02 31 89 28 41) is two blocks east of the tourist office. **Bus Verts** (☎08 10 21 42 14; www.busverts.fr, in French) services include an express bus to Caen (€10.50, one hour):

Caen €7.50, two hours, 12 daily Monday to Saturday, six Sunday

Deauville & Trouville €2.15, 30 minutes

Le Havre €4.25, 35 minutes, eight daily Monday to Saturday, four Sunday

CAR Free parking is available next to Naturospace, which is 600m from the Avant Port on bd Charles V. There's also a small free car park by one of the roundabouts beyond the bus station as you head out of town towards the Pont de Normandie.

TRAIN To catch the train (eg to Paris), take the bus to Deauville, Le Havre or Lisieux (€4.25, 50 minutes, four or five daily).

MANCHE

The Manche *département* (www.manche tourisme.com) encompasses the entire Cotentin Peninsula, stretching from Utah Beach (see p216) northwest to Cherbourg and southwest to the magnificent Mont St-Michel. The peninsula's northwest corner is especially captivating, with unspoiled stretches of rocky coastline sheltering tranquil bays and villages. The fertile inland areas, criss-crossed with hedgerows, produce an abundance of cattle, dairy products and apples. The British crown dependencies of Jersey and Guernsey lie 22km and 48km offshore, respectively.

Manche is also known for its nuclear facilities, including an electricity-generating complex at Flamanville, a reprocessing facility at Cap de la Hague and a shipyard for building nuclear submarines at Cherbourg.

Cherbourg

POP 41,560

At the top of the Cotentin Peninsula sits Cherbourg, the largest – but hardly the most appealing – town in this part of Normandy. Transatlantic cargo ships, passenger ferries from Britain and Ireland, yachts and warships pass in and out of Cherbourg's monumental port. During WWII, most of the petrol used by the Allied armies during the Normandy campaign was supplied by an underwater pipeline laid from England to Cherbourg shortly after D-Day.

Modern-day Cherbourg – now united with adjacent Octeville – is a far cry from the romantic city portrayed in Jacques Demy's 1964 film *Les Parapluies de Cherbourg* (The Umbrellas of Cherbourg) but you may pass through if you're crossing the Channel by ferry.

◉ Sights & Activities

Cité de la Mer   AQUARIUM
(☏02 33 20 26 26; www.citedelamer.com; Gare Maritime Transatlantique; adult/child €18/13; ☺9.30am-6pm) Housed in Cherbourg's art deco transatlantic ferry terminal, this fascinating place was built in the 1930s and is both an aquarium – the deepest in Europe – and a showcase for French submarine prowess. This may be your only chance to go inside a French nuclear submarine, *Le Redoubtable*, in service from 1967 to 1991.

REGIONAL PARK

Inland from Utah Beach, to the south and southwest, is the 1450-sq-km Parc Naturel Régional des Marais du Cotentin et du Bessin (www.parc -cotentin-bessin.fr), with its waterways, marshes, moors and hedgerows. For details on hiking and cycling in the park and elsewhere in the Manche *département*, see www.mancheran donnee.com (in French).

⬚ Sleeping

La Régence   HOTEL €
(☏02 33 43 05 16; www.laregence.com; 42-44 quai de Caligny; d €66-110; ☎) Right on the seafront, this Logis de France establishment offers 21 tasteful, well-kept rooms with brass light fittings. The pricier rooms have great harbour views.

Hôtel Napoléon   HOTEL €
(☏02 33 93 32 32; www.hotel-napoleon.fr; 14 place de la République; s €25-42, d €36-55; ☎) Located on the area's main square and in one of the area's few surviving 19th-century buildings, the Napoléon offers 14 upbeat, pastel bedrooms, some with a limited view of the port. Cheaper rooms have shared facilities.

Auberge de Jeunesse   HOSTEL €
(☏02 33 78 15 15; www.fuaj.org; 55 rue de l'Abbaye; dm €18; ☎) Situated 1km northwest of the tourist office, this 99-bed hostel is housed in the French navy's old archives buildings and has a small kitchen for self-caterers. Rooms have two to five beds. Take bus 3 or 5 to the Hôtel de Ville stop. Check-in is 9am to 1pm and 6pm to 11pm.

✗ Eating & Entertainment

La Cale   SEAFOOD €
(☏02 33 93 11 23; 2 place de la République; menus €11.50-23) Ropes, oars and other maritime paraphernalia deck the timber walls of this popular and central seafood restaurant. There's a great terrace for eating on the square in the summer months.

La Régence   BISTRO €€
(☏02 33 43 05 16; 42-44 quai de Caligny; menus €20-35) An old-time French bistro right on the harbour with traditional fish, seafood and meat mains. Specialities include mussels, fish soup and *tartiflette au Camembert*.

Le Solier   PUB €
(☏02 33 94 76 63; 52 rue Grande Rue; ☺6pm-2am Tue-Sat) Opened in 1982, this convivial place is a cross between an English pub and a French bar. Hosts live traditional Irish music on the second Thursday of the month and jazz the last Thursday.

ⓘ Information

Arobase-Cherbourg (place de la Revolution, cnr rue Tour Carée; per hr €3.25; ☺10am-6.30pm Tue-Wed, 10am-9pm Thu-Sat) Internet access.

Post office (1 rue de l'Ancien Quai) Exchanges currency.

Tourist office (02 33 93 52 02; www.
ot-cherbourg-cotentin.fr; 2 quai Alexandre III;
⊘10am-7pm, closed Sun mid-Sep–mid-June)
Has useful information on visiting the city, the
Cotentin Peninsula and D-Day sites.

❶ Getting There & Away

FERRY For details on car ferry services from
Cherbourg's **ferry terminal** (www.port-cher
bourg.com) to Poole, Portsmouth and Rosslare
(Ireland), see p973.

TRAIN Direct trains:

Bayeux €15.50, one hour, 14 daily Monday to
Friday, three to five on weekends

Caen €19.50, 1¼ hours, seven to 15 daily

Coutances €18, 1½ hours, five to 10 daily,
change at Lisson

Paris St-Lazare €44.50, three hours, two to
six direct daily

Pontorson €26, three hours, two to three daily,
change at Lisson

❶ Getting Around

BUS In the warm months, a shuttle-bus service
links the ferry terminal with the town centre and
train station.

TAXI For a taxi, call 02 33 53 36 38. A daytime trip between the train station and ferry
terminal costs about €10.

Mont St-Michel

POP 43

It's one of France's most iconic images: the
slender towers and sky-scraping turrets of
the abbey of Mont St-Michel rising from
stout ramparts and battlements, the whole
ensemble connected to the mainland by a
narrow causeway. Fortunately, although it's
visited by huge numbers of tourists, both
French and foreign, the Mont still manages
to whisk you back to the Middle Ages, its
fantastic architecture set against the backdrop of the area's extraordinary tides.

The bay around Mont St-Michel is famed
for having Europe's highest tidal variations. Depending on the gravitational pull
of the moon and the sun (greatest 36 to 48
hours after the full and new moon, when
both bodies are lined up with the earth),
the difference between low and high tides
can reach an astonishing 15m. The Mont is
only completely surrounded by the sea every month or two, when the tidal coefficient
is above 100 and high tide is above 14m.
Regardless of the time of year, the waters
sweep in at an astonishing clip, said to be

as fast as a galloping horse. At low tide the
Mont is surrounded by bare sand for kilometres around, but at high tide, barely six
hours later, the whole bay – including some
of the nearby car parks – can be submerged.
The entire site is currently the focus of an
enormous project to build a new dam that
will flush out the sediment from the bay
and restore Mont St-Michel to its original
state, free of the surrounding salt marshes.
A new pedestrian bridge to replace the existing causeway is also planned. See www.
projetmontsaintmichel.fr for more information on the huge changes that will soon be
under way.

Be prepared for lots of steps, some of
them spiral – alas, the Mont is one of the
least wheelchair-accessible sites in France.
Be prepared also for big crowds; come early
in the morning to miss the worst of them,
though the Mont is never entirely free of
visitors.

Pontorson (population 4200), the nearest real town to Mont St-Michel, is 9km to
the south. It's the transport hub for travellers without their own wheels, but there's
no need to stay here really – Mont St-Michel
is a great day trip, but it doesn't usually call
for an overnight stay.

History

According to Celtic mythology, Mont St-
Michel was one of the sea tombs to which
the souls of the dead were sent. Bishop
Aubert of Avranches is said to have built
a devotional chapel on the summit of the
island in 708, following his vision of the
Archangel Michael, whose gilded figure,
perched on the vanquished dragon, crowns
the tip of the abbey's spire. In 966 Richard
I, Duke of Normandy, gave Mont St-Michel
to the Benedictines, who turned it into a
centre of learning and, in the 11th century,
into something of an ecclesiastical fortress,
with a military garrison at the disposal of
the abbot and the king.

In the 15th century, during the Hundred
Years War, the English blockaded and besieged Mont St-Michel three times. The fortified abbey withstood these assaults and
was the only place in western and northern
France not to fall into English hands. After
the Revolution, Mont St-Michel was turned
into a prison. In 1966 the abbey was sym-
bolically returned to the Benedictines as
part of the celebrations marking its millennium. Mont St-Michel and the bay became a
Unesco World Heritage Site in 1979.

Mont St-Michel

A TIMELINE

708 Inspired by a vision from St Michael **1**, Bishop Aubert is compelled to 'build here and build high'.

966 Richard I, Duke of Normandy, gives the Mont to the Benedictines. The three levels of the abbey **2** reflect their monastic hierarchy.

1017 Development of the abbey begins. Pilgrims arrive to honour the cult of St Michael. They walk barefoot across the mudflats and up the Grande Rue **3** to be received in the almonry (now the bookshop).

1203 The monastery is burnt by the troops of Philip Augustus, who later donates money for its restoration and the Gothic 'miracle', La Merveille **4**, is constructed.

1434 The Mont's ramparts **5** and fortifications ensure it withstands the English assault during the Hundred Years War. It is the only place in northern France not to fall.

1789 After the Revolution, Monasticism is abolished and the Mont is turned into a prison. During this period the treadmill **6** is built to lift up supplies.

1878 The causeway **7** is created. It allows modern-day pilgrims to visit without hip-high boots, but it cuts off the flow of water and the bay silts up.

1979 The Mont is declared a Unesco World Heritage Site.

TOP TIPS

» Bring a packed lunch from Pontorson to avoid the poor lunch selection on the Mont

» Leave the car – it's a pleasant walk from Pontorson, with spectacular views

» Pay attention to the tides – they are dangerous

» Take the excellent audioguide – it tells some great stories

Îlot de Tombelaine
Occupied by the English during the Hundred Years War, this islet is now a bird reserve. From April to July it teems with exceptional birdlife.

JOHN ELK III

Treadmill
The giant treadmill was powered hamsterlike by half a dozen prisoners, who, marching two abreast, raised stone and supplies up the Mont.

The West Terrace

Chapelle St-Aubert

Tour Gabriel

5

Les Fanils

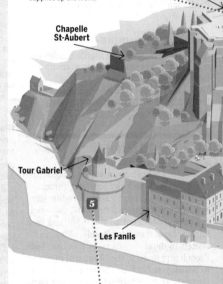

Ramparts
The Mont was also a military garrison surrounded by machicolated and turreted walls, dating from the 13th to 15th centuries. The single entrance, Porte de l'Avancée, ensured its security in the Hundred Years War. Tip: Tour du Nord (North Tower) has the best views.

ROCCO FASANO

Abbey

The abbey's three levels reflect the monastic order: monks lived isolated in church and cloister, the abbot entertained noble guests at the middle level, and lowly pilgrims were received in the basement. Tip: night visits run in July and August.

HUGHES HERVE/PHOTOLIBRARY

St Michael Statue & Bell Tower

A golden statue of the winged St Michael looks ready to leap heavenward from the bell tower. He is the patron of the Mont, having inspired St Aubert's original devotional chapel.

1

IZZET KERIBAR

La Merveille

The highlights of La Merveille are the vast refectory hall lit through embrasured windows, the Knights Hall with its elegant ribbed vaulting, and the cloister (above), which is one of the purest examples of 13th-century architecture to survive here.

The Gardens

2

4

6

Église St-Pierre

Cemetery

3

Toilets

Tour de l'Arcade

Tour du Roi

Tourist Office

Porte de l'Avancée (Entrance)

7

Grande Rue

The main thoroughfare of the small village below the abbey, Grande Rue has its charm despite its rampant commercialism. Don't miss the famous Mère Poulard shop here, for souvenir cookies.

DAVID TOMLINSON

Causeway

In 2014 the causeway will be replaced by a new bridge, which will allow the water to circulate and will return the Mont to an island. Tip: join a barefoot walking tour and see the Mont as pilgrims would.

JOHN ELK III

Best Views

The view from the Jardin des Plantes in nearby Avranches is unique, as are the panoramas from Pointe du Grouin du Sud near the village of St-Léonard.

COUTANCES

The lovely old Norman town of Coutances makes for a good detour when travelling between the D-Day beaches and Mont St-Michel. At the town's heart is its Gothic Cathédrale de Coutances (admission free; ⊙9am-7pm). Interior highlights include several 13th-century windows, a 14th-century fresco of St Michael skewering the dragon, and an organ and high altar from the mid-1700s. You can climb the lantern tower on a tour (adult/child €6.50/5.50; ⊙in French 11am & 3pm Mon-Fri, 3pm Sun Jul & Aug, in English 11.45am Tue Jul & Aug).

Across the square, is the splendid Jardin des Plantes (⊙9am-5pm Oct-Mar, to 8pm Apr-Sep, to 11.30pm Jul & Aug), a grand garden laid out in the 1850s that mixes French, Italian and English style in its terraces, flower beds, fountains, statues and maze.

⊙ Sights

Abbaye du Mont St-Michel   ABBEY
(⊘02 33 89 80 00; www.monuments-nationaux.fr; adult/child incl guided tour €8.50/free; ⊙9am-7pm, last entry 1hr before closing) The Mont's major attraction is the stunning architectural ensemble of the Abbaye du Mont St-Michel, towards which you'll be swept by a human tide ascending the Grande Rue and a steep stairway. From Monday to Saturday in July and August, there are illuminated *nocturnes* (night-time visits) with music from 7pm to 10pm.

Most rooms can be visited without a guide but it's worth taking the one-hour tour, included in the ticket price. The frequency of English tours ranges from twice a day (11am and 3pm) in the dead of winter to hourly in summer; the last leaves at least 1½ hours before closing time. Audioguides (one for €4.50, two for €6) are available in six languages. Don't forget to pick up the excellent free brochure-guide, available in 10 languages.

Église Abbatiale
The Église Abbatiale (Abbey Church) was built on the rocky tip of the mountain cone. The transept rests on solid rock, while the nave, choir and transept arms are supported by the rooms below. The church is famous for its mix of architectural styles: the nave and south transept (11th and 12th centuries) are solid Norman Romanesque, while the choir (late 15th century) is Flamboyant Gothic. Mass is held at 12.15pm from Tuesday to Sunday and at 11.30am on Sunday.

La Merveille
The buildings on the northern side of the Mont are known as La Merveille (The Marvel). The famous cloître (cloister) is surrounded by a double row of delicately carved arches resting on granite pillars. The early-13th-century, barrel-roofed réfectoire (dining hall) is illuminated by a wall of recessed windows – remarkable, given that the sheer drop precluded the use of flying buttresses. The Gothic Salle des Hôtes (Guest Hall), dating from 1213, has two enormous fireplaces. Look out for the promenoire (ambulatory), with one of the oldest ribbed vaulted ceilings in Europe, and the Chapelle de Notre Dame sous Terre (Underground Chapel of Our Lady), one of the abbey's oldest rooms, rediscovered in 1903.

The masonry used to build the abbey was brought to the Mont by boat and pulled up the hillside using ropes. The contraption that looks like a treadmill for gargantuan gerbils was in fact powered in the 19th century by half a dozen prisoners who, by turning the wheel, hoisted the supply sledge up the side of the abbey.

⊂╤ Tours

When the tide is out, you can walk all the way around Mont St-Michel, a distance of about 1km. Straying too far from the Mont can be very risky: you might get stuck in wet sand – from which Norman soldiers are depicted being rescued in one scene of the Bayeux Tapestry – or be overtaken by the incoming tide, providing your next-of-kin with a great cocktail party story.

Guided Walks   WALKING TOUR
Experienced outfits offering guided walks (€6.50) into – or even across – the bay include Découverte de la Baie du Mont-Saint-Michel (⊘02 33 70 83 49; www.decouvertebaie.com, in French) and Chemins de la Baie (⊘02 33 89 80 88; www.cheminsdelabaie.com, in French), both based across the bay

from Mont St-Michel in Genêts. Local tourist offices have details.

📭 Sleeping

There are eight rather pricey hotels on the Mont itself but most people choose to stay in one of the chain-style hotels in Beauvoir, on the mainland, or in the rather ordinary town of Pontorson, 9km due south of the Mont.

Auberge de Jeunesse　　　HOSTEL €
(Centre Duguesclin; ✆02 33 60 18 65; www.fuaj. org; 21 bd du Général Patton, Pontorson; dm €12; ☺mid-Apr–Sep) Situated 1km west of the train station near the new Gendarmerie building, this modern, 62-bed hostel has four- to six-bed rooms and kitchen facilities. Reception closes from noon to 5pm (except from mid-July to late August) but there's no curfew.

Hôtel La Tour Brette　　　HOTEL €
(✆02 33 60 10 69; www.latourbrette.com; 8 rue du Couesnon, Pontorson; d €37-43; ✆) A family-run place with 10 unsurprising, good-value en suite rooms. Sadly, wireless is not provided free by the hotel; you can pick it up from Orange only at a price.

Hôtel Montgomery　　　HOTEL €
(✆02 33 60 00 09; www.hotel-montgomery.com; 13 rue du Couesnon, Pontorson; d €93-117, ste €180-225; ✆) In a 16th-century mansion, this Best Western–affiliated hotel has a vine-covered Renaissance facade and, inside, creaky wood-panelled corridors and 32 rooms. One room comes with hefty Renaissance furniture and a four-poster bed just 135cm wide!

🍴 Eating

It's a good idea to bring your lunch with you to Mont St-Michel – all options on the Mont are massively overpriced. The Grande Rue is jammed with sandwich shops and crêperies, however, so while you may go bankrupt, you won't go hungry. There's little variety in the pickings available. In Pontorson, there are plenty of fast-food outlets and supermarkets, but for a good meal, try any of the larger hotels. Below are a couple of passable options on Mont St-Michel itself.

Crêperie La Sirène　　　CRÊPERIE €
(Grande Rue; crêpes €3.50-10; ☺9am-10.30pm) Not a bad budget option, with a good selection of sweet crêpes and savoury galettes and salads. Up an ancient spiral staircase from a souvenir shop.

Le Tripot　　　SANDWICH SHOP €
(Grande Rue; sandwiches from €2.80; ☺9am-8pm) Located a little further up the hill from Crêperie La Sirène, Le Tripot has the cheapest sandwiches we were able to find on the mount.

ℹ Information

Post office (Grande Rue, Mont St-Michel) Changes currency and has an ATM.

Tourist office – Mont St-Michel (✆02 33 60 14 30; www.ot-montsaintmichel.com; ☺9am-12.30pm & 2-6.30pm Mon-Sat, 9am-noon & 2-6pm Sun) Just inside Porte de l'Avancée, up the stairs to the left. An *horaire des marées* (tide table) is posted just inside the door and you can also change money here. A detailed map of the Mont costs €3. Just next door are toilets (€0.40) and an ATM. Internet access per 30 minutes/hour costs €4.50/8.

Tourist office – Pontorson (✆02 33 60 20 65; www.mont-saint-michel-baie.com, in French; place de l'Hôtel de Ville; ☺9am-12.30pm & 2-6.30pm Mon-Sat, 9am-noon & 2-6pm Sun) Has details on traversing the Bay of Mont St-Michel on foot and on local events. Situated on rue St-Michel half a block south of rue Couesnon. Internet access per 30 minutes/ hour costs €4.50/8.

ℹ Getting There & Around

BUS Mont St-Michel is linked to Beauvoir (eight minutes) and Pontorson (€2, 13 minutes) by bus 6, operated by **Manéo** (✆08 00 15 00 50; www. mobi50.com, in French), six to eight times daily (more frequently in July and August). Times are coordinated with the arrival in Pontorson of some trains from Caen and Rennes. **Les Couriers Bretons** (✆02 99 19 70 80) links Pontorson with St-Malo (1¼ hours, one round trip daily); times are coordinated with bus 6.

TRAIN Destinations from Pontorson:

Bayeux €21, 1¾ hours, two or three direct daily

Cherbourg €26, three hours, two to three daily

Coutances €11.50, 40 minutes, three or four daily

Rennes €12.50, 50 minutes, two to four daily.

Brittany

Best Places to Eat

» Le Chalut (p238)

» Restaurant Delaunay (p238)

» Le Coquillage (p244)

» L'Ambroisie (p260)

» Villa Margot (p266)

Best Places to Stay

» Hôtel Printania (p241)

» Hôtel du Centre (p250)

» Grand Hôtel Barrière (p241)

» Hôtel de Nemours (p273)

» Hôtel Manoir des Indes (p259)

Why Go?

Brittany is for explorers. Its wild, dramatic coastline, medieval towns and thick forests make an excursion here well worth the detour from the beaten track. This is a land of prehistoric mysticism, proud tradition and culinary wealth, where locals still remain fiercely independent, where Breton culture is celebrated and where Paris feels a very long way away indeed.

The entire region is wonderfully undiscovered once you go beyond its world-famous sights such as stunning St-Malo, regal Dinard and charming Dinan. Unexpected Breton gems – including the little-known towns of Roscoff, Quimper and Vannes, the megaliths of Carnac, the rugged coastlines of Finistère, the Presqu'île de Crozon and the Morbihan Coast – all quickly demonstrate that there's far more to Brittany than just delicious crêpes and homemade cider. Brittany's much-loved islands are also big draws – don't miss its two real stars, dramatic Île d'Ouessant and the very aptly named Belle Île.

When to Go

Brest

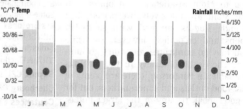

| June and early July Enjoy the beaches, outdoor adventures and sunshine before the crowds. | Late July Head to Quimper for traditional Celtic music at the Festival de Cornouaille. | Late November In winter, join the crowds in Rennes for the Yaouank night festival. |

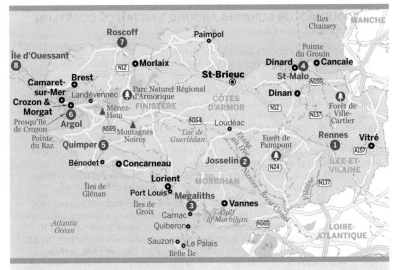

Brittany Highlights

❶ Enjoy crêpes, cider and student life in the charming old town of **Rennes** (p272)

❷ Tour the turreted medieval castle over the fairy-tale forest village of **Josselin** (p271)

❸ Cycle past fields full of prehistoric **megaliths** (p266) around Carnac

❹ Stroll along the **ramparts** (p235) at sunset for panoramic views over St-Malo

❺ Explore the often overlooked Breton city of **Quimper** (p257), with its wonderful cathedral and old town

❻ Sip Breton cider and learn about its production at the **Musée du Cidre** (p255) at Argol

❼ Take in the relaxed Breton atmosphere and unusual church of **Roscoff** (p247), a charming port town

❽ Hike around the barren coastline of the dramatic **Île d'Ouessant** (p254), home to some of Finistère's most appealing scenery

BRITTANY

History

Brittany's earliest known Neolithic tribes left a legacy of menhirs and dolmens that continue to baffle historians. Celts arrived in the 6th century BC, naming their new homeland Armor ('the land beside the sea'). The region was conquered by Julius Caesar in 56 BC. Following the withdrawal of the Romans in the 5th century AD, Celts driven from what is now Britain and Ireland by the Anglo-Saxon invasions settled in Brittany, bringing Christianity with them.

In the 9th century, Brittany's national hero Nominoë revolted against French rule. Wedged between two more-powerful kingdoms, the duchy of Brittany was continuously contested by France and England until a series of strategic royal weddings finally saw the region become part of France in 1532.

Brittany has retained a separate regional identity. Now there's a drive for cultural and linguistic renewal, and a consciousness of Brittany's place within a wider Celtic culture embracing Ireland, Wales, Scotland, Cornwall and Galicia in Spain.

❶ Getting There & Around

Ferries link St-Malo with the Channel Islands and the English ports of Portsmouth, Poole and Weymouth. From Roscoff there are ferries to Plymouth (UK) and Cork (Ireland). Alternatively, airports in Brest, Dinard, Lorient and, to the south, Nantes (p603) serve the UK and Ireland as well as other European and domestic destinations.

Brittany's major towns and cities have rail connections but routes leave the interior poorly served. The bus network is extensive, if generally infrequent, meaning that your own wheels are the best way to see the area, particularly out-of-the-way destinations.

With gently undulating, well-maintained roads, an absence of tolls and relatively little traffic outside the major towns, driving in Brittany is a

Sillon de Talbert Brittany's best coastal drives let you see long-standing traditions in action. West of Paimpol on the north coast, you may spot the local seaweed harvesters tossing strands of kelp into their carts.

Côte de Granit Rose The otter-inhabited coastline known as the Pink Granite Coast glows with pink granite cliffs, outcrops and boulders sculpted over the millennia by wind and waves. Their fiery colours are even more impressive when you're scaling them while following the 5km walking path, *sentier des douaniers* (custom officers' trail), just near the area's main town, the seaside resort of Perros-Guirec. Local fishermen sell their catch each morning at Peros' Marché des Pêcheurs on place du Marché. Offshore, head out on a boat trip to the Sept-Îles (Seven Islands), home to more than 20,000 marine birds including puffins, razorbills and fulmars. Check out www.armor-de couverte.fr for boat info.

Pays Bigouden If you're lucky enough to catch one of the cultural celebrations here in Finistère's southwestern corner, you might see women wearing the *coiffe bigoudène,* the area's traditional lace headdress that's up to 30cm tall. And if you're brave enough, you might want to join the hard-core surfers riding 'the lift' – a death-defying break off Pointe de la Torche. Near the car park, surf shops rent gear and offer advice; otherwise you can experience it vicariously listening to surfers recounting their survival at one of the point's cafés.

Côte Sauvage On the western edge of the peninsula en route to Quiberon, the aptly named 'wild coast' swoops between barren headlands and sheer cliffs. Bonus: you'll avoid the choked main-road traffic here – partly because the coast road (the D186a) isn't well signed. Heading south, turn off just before you reach St-Pierre-Quiberon, in the direction of Kemiscob and Kervozès.

Golfe du Morbihan (Morbihan Coast) Most people visiting Morbihan's megaliths never make it to this part of the gulf. But swinging southwest from Vannes to Port Navalo rewards you with stupendous views over the gulf and its islands. Picnic benches perch at Port Navalo's tip – bring a hamper and a bottle of Breton cider.

real pleasure. Cycling is also extremely popular, and bike-rental places are never hard to find.

NORTH COAST

Enveloped by belle époque beach resorts, fishing villages and curled headlands, Brittany's central north coast spans the *départements* of Ille-et-Vilaine and Côtes d'Armor. Green shallows give rise to the name Côte d'Émeraude (Emerald Coast) to the east; westwards, boulders blush along the Côte de Granit Rose.

St-Malo

POP 50,200

The mast-filled port of St-Malo has a cinematically changing landscape. With one of the world's highest tidal ranges, brewing storms under blackened skies see waves lash over the top of the ramparts ringing its walled city. Hours later, the blue sky merges with the deep marine-blue sea, exposing beaches as wide and flat as the clear skies above and creating land bridges to the granite outcrop islands.

Construction of the walled city's fortifications began in the 12th century. The town became a key port during the 17th and 18th centuries as a base for both merchant ships and government-sanctioned privateers (pirates, basically) against the constant threat of the English. These days English arrivals are tourists, for whom St-Malo, a short ferry hop from the Channel Islands, is a summer haven.

◉ Sights & Activities
INTRA MUROS
St-Malo's first inhabitants originally lived in St-Servan but later moved to this former island, which became linked to the mainland by the sandy isthmus of Le Sillon in the 13th century. For the best views of the

walled city, stroll along the top of the **ramparts**, constructed at the end of the 17th century under military architect Vauban, and measuring 1.8km.

Though you'd never guess it from the cobblestone streets and reconstructed monuments in 17th- and 18th-century style, during August 1944 the battle to drive German forces out of St-Malo destroyed around 80% of the old city, lovingly restored since then.

Cathédrale St-Vincent   CATHEDRAL

(Map p236; place Jean de Châtillon; ⊙9.30am-6pm except during Mass) The town's centrepiece was constructed between the 12th and 18th centuries, but damage during WWII was severe. A mosaic plaque on the floor of the nave marks the spot where Jacques Cartier received the blessing of the bishop of St-Malo before his 'voyage of discovery' to Canada in 1535. Cartier's tomb – all that remains of it post-1944 is his entombed head – is in a chapel on the north side of the choir.

Musée du Château   CITY MUSEUM

(Map p236; ☑02 99 40 71 57; adult/child €5/2.80; ⊙10am-noon & 2-6pm, closed Mon Oct-Mar) Within the Château de St-Malo, built by the dukes of Brittany in the 15th and 16th centuries, is the Musée du Château, also known as the Musée d'Histoire de la Ville (city history museum). The museum's most interesting exhibits – the history of cod fishing on the Grand Banks and photos of St-Malo after WWII – are in the **Tour Générale**.

La Maison de Corsaire   HISTORIC MANSION

(Map p236; ☑02 99 56 09 40; www.demeure-de-corsaire.com; 5 rue d'Asfeld; adult/child €5.50/4; ⊙10am-noon & 2-6pm, closed Mon in winter) You can visit this 18th-century mansion and historic monument, once owned by corsair (privateer) François Auguste Magon. Guided tours are in French; descriptions are available in English.

ÎLE DU GRAND BÉ

At low tide, cross the beach to walk out via the Porte des Bés to the rocky islet of Île du Grand Bé (www.petit-be.com, in French), where

St-Malo & St-Servan

▲ 0   200 m
Ⓝ 0   0.08 miles

English Channel
(La Manche)

Le Sillon
Isthmus

INTRA MUROS

Bassin
Duguay
Trouin

Esplanade
St-Vincent

Q St-Vincent

Bassin
Intérieur

Bassin
Vauban

See Intra Muros Map (p236)

Chaussée des Corsaires

R Georges Clemenceau

Gare
Maritime
du Naye

Ferries to UK

Port de Plaisance
(Pleasure Marina)

Plage des Bas Sablons

Corniche d'Aleth

Mémorial 39–45

Pl St-Pierre

Allée Gaston Guy

Esplanade du Commandant Yves Menguy

Q Solidor

R des Bas Sablons

ST-SERVAN

Port-Solidor

the great St-Malo-born 18th-century writer Chateaubriand is buried. Once the tide rushes in, the causeway remains impassable for about six hours; check tide times with the tourist office. Depths can be deceptive; if you get caught out, stay on the islet until the tide subsides.

About 100m beyond the Île du Grand Bé is the Vauban-built 17th-century **Fort du Petit Bé** (☎06 08 27 51 20), also accessible at low tide.

BEYOND THE WALLS
The pretty fishing port of St-Servan sits south of the walled city.

Fort National   FORT
(Map p235; www.fortnational.com; adult/child €5/3; ☉Easter & Jun–mid-Sep) The ramparts' northern stretch looks across to the remains of this former prison, built by Vauban in 1689. Standing atop a rocky outcrop, the fort can only be accessed at low tide.

Ask at the tourist office for times of tours during your stay.

Mémorial 39–45   MEMORIAL
(Map p235; ☎02 99 82 41 74; adult/child €5.50/2.80; ☉guided visits 2pm, 3.15pm & 4.30pm Tue-Sun, daily Jul & Aug) Constructed in the mid-18th century, **Fort de la Cité** was used as a German base during WWII. One of the bunkers now houses the Mémorial 39–45, which depicts St-Malo's violent WWII history and liberation, and includes a 45-minute film in French. Some guided visits are conducted in English; call ahead to confirm times.

Musée International du Long Cours Cap-Hornier   MARITIME MUSEUM
(Map p235; Museum of the Cape Horn Route; ☎02 99 40 71 58; adult/child €6/2.80; ☉10am-noon & 2-6pm, closed Mon Oct-Mar) Housed in the 14th-century **Tour Solidor**, this museum presents the life of the hardy sailors who followed the dangerous Cape Horn route

Intra Muros

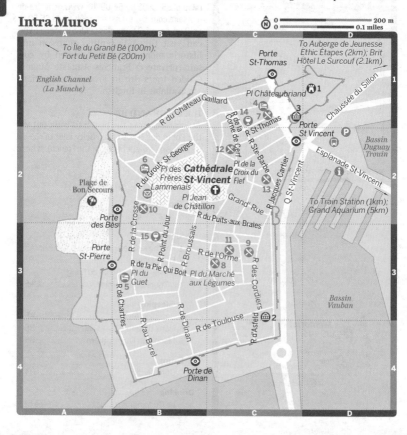

around the southern tip of South America. It also offers superb views from the top of the tower.

Grand Aquarium
AQUARIUM

(☑02 99 21 19 00; www.aquarium-st-malo.com; av Général Patton; adult/child €15.50/10; ☺10am-6pm; ☀) Allow around two hours to see St-Malo's excellent aquarium. About 4km south of the city centre, it's a great wet-weather alternative for kids, with a minisubmarine descent and a *bassin tactile* (touch pool), where you can fondle rays, turbot – even a baby shark. Bus C1 from the train station passes by every half-hour.

🏃 Activities

Ferries & Boat Excursions Compagnie Corsaire (☑08 25 13 80 35; www.compagnie corsaire.com) can take you *pêche en mer* (deep-sea fishing) for about four hours (€39, Monday, Wednesday and Friday July and August), and runs ferries from just outside Porte de Dinan to the following: **Bay of St-Malo** (adult/child €19/11, 1½ hours), **Cancale/Pointe du Grouin** (adult/child €8/16.50, 2½ hours), **Dinan** (adult/child return €30/18, April to September), **Île Cézembre** (adult/child return €14/8.50, two to seven departures per week daily April to September) and **Îles Chausey** (adult/child return €30/18, two to five departures per week April to September).

Vedettes de St-Malo (☑02 23 18 02 04; www.vedettes-saint-malo.com) also runs boat excursions.

🍴 Courses

To learn how to windsurf (lessons from €35 for one hour) or sail a catamaran (lessons from €50 for one hour), contact **Surf School** (☑02 99 40 07 47; www.surfschool.org, in French).

🛏 Sleeping

St-Malo has plenty of hotels, but accommodation books up quickly in summer – the tourist office website has continuous updates of availability. For *chambres d'hôte* (B&Bs), try the nearby towns of Cancale, Dinan and their surrounds.

INTRA MUROS

Hôtel San Pedro
HOTEL €

(Map p236; ☑02 99 40 88 57; www.sanpedro-hotel.com; 1 rue Ste-Anne; s €52-54, d €63-73; ☎) Tucked away at the back of the old city, the San Pedro has cool, crisp, neutral-toned decor with subtle splashes of colour, friendly service and superb sea views. Breakfast is an €8 feast.

Hôtel de l'Univers
TRADITIONAL HOTEL €

(Map p236; ☑02 99 40 89 52; www.hotel-univers-saintmalo.com; pl Chateaubriand; s/d/tr €77/89/103; ☎) Right by the most frequently used gateway to the old city (Porte St-Vincent), this cream-coloured place with 63 rooms is perfectly poised for all of St-Malo's attractions. Rooms are compact, in dark tones and with crisp linens. The whole place has a very club-like country

MONUMENT COMBO

A **combined ticket** (€13/6.50 per adult/child) gives you access to St-Malo's three major monuments: the Musée du Château, Musée International du Long Cours Cap-Hornier and Mémorial 39–45. It can be purchased at any of the three participating museums and is valid for the duration of your stay in St-Malo.

hotel feel, especially in the all-wood maritime bar.

Hôtel les Chiens du Guet
HOTEL €

(Map p236; ☑02 99 40 87 29; 4 place du Guet; r €52-57, tw €63-68; ☎) A narrow stone staircase next to this welcoming hotel pops you directly up on top of the ramparts; adjacent Porte St-Pierre opens directly to the beach. The 12 simple, sunlit rooms are homey if somewhat snug. There's a convivial on-site restaurant; *menus* start at €9.50.

BEYOND THE WALLS

Manoir du Cunningham
TRADITIONAL HOTEL €€

(Map p235; ☑02 99 21 33 33; www.st-malo-hotel -cunningham.com; 9 place Monseigneur Duchesne; r €110-190; ☎) The rather Disneyesque exterior of this hotel belies its very pleasant interior, a 13-room, mahogany-rich guesthouse a stroll from the ferry, with views out to sea. A great spot to be comfortable away from the crowds.

Brit Hôtel Le Surcouf
FAMILY HOTEL €

(☑02 99 56 30 19; www.surcoufhotel.com; 17 rue du Révérend Père Umbricht; s €45-75, d €55-75; ☎⚙) In a peaceful residential quarter 1km from the walled town and five minutes' walk from the beach, this charming and friendly hotel is ideal if you're driving, with free street parking out front. The classy aubergine-toned rooms are spacious, immaculate and contemporary. Breakfast (€7.50) is also superb.

Hôtel d'Aleth
HOTEL €

(Map p235; ☑02 99 81 48 08; www.st-malo -hotel-cunningham.com; 2 rue des Hauts Sablons;

ST-MALO & ST-SERVAN BEACHES

You can splash in the protected tidal pool west of the city walls at Plage de Bon Secours (Map p236) or climb its ladder to jump off into the sea.

St-Servan's Plage des Bas Sablons (Map p235) has a cement wall to keep the sea from receding completely at low tide.

The much larger Grande Plage stretches northeast along the isthmus of Le Sillon. Spectacular sunsets can be seen along the stretch from Grande Plage to Plage des Bas Sablons. Less-crowded Plage de Rochebonne is another 1km to the northeast.

---

r €50-65; ☎) Just a short stumble upstairs from the nautical pub, Le Cunningham, it's well worth paying a few extra euros for a sea view. Light sleepers beware: it's noisy to say the least. Frills are few: no lift, no in-room phones and no reception desk – check in at Manoir du Cunningham, a short walk up the road. The free wireless is very limited and can only be picked up in certain rooms.

Auberge de Jeunesse Éthic Étapes
HOSTEL €

(☑02 99 40 29 80; www.centrevarangot.com; 37 av du Père Umbricht; dm incl breakfast €17.50-20; ⚙) This efficient place has a self-catering kitchen (and supermarket two minutes' walk away) as well as free sports facilities. Take bus C1 from the train station.

Camping Aleth
CAMPGROUND €

(Map p235; ☑06 78 96 10 62; www.camping-aleth. com; allée Gaston Buy; tent/caravan per 2 people €13.50/18; ☺May-Sep) Perched on top of a peninsula next to Fort de la Cité, Camping Aleth (also spelt Alet) has panoramic 360-degree views and is close to beaches. It's also close but not *too* close to some lively bars.

✗ Eating

Browse the menus of the plethora of restaurants between Porte St-Vincent, the cathedral and the Grande Porte.

Le Chalut
SEAFOOD €€

(Map p236; ☑02 99 56 71 58; 8 rue de la Corne de Cerf; menus €25-68; ☺Wed-Sun) This unremarkable-looking establishment is in fact St-Malo's most celebrated restaurant and a must for any self-respecting seafood lover. The kitchen overflows with the best the Breton coastline has to offer – buttered turbot, line-caught sea bass and scallops in Champagne sauce. Reservations for dinner are advised.

La Bouche en Folie
MODERN FRENCH €

(Map p236; ☑06 72 49 08 89; 14 rue du Boyer; menus €13-29; ☺closed Mon & Tue) Hidden away from the tourist trail, this sleek joint oozes Gallic gorgeousness from every nook and cranny. The menu gives a modern spin to French staples – lamb is fricasséed with garlic and artichokes, while monkfish is partnered by peas, black olives and asparagus. Sumptuous.

TOP CHOICE Restaurant Delaunay
GASTRONOMIC €€

(Map p236; ☑02 99 40 92 46; www.restaurant -delaunay.com; 6 rue Ste-Barbe; menus €28-65;

⊗dinner Mon-Sat, closed Mon in winter) This superb yet unassuming-looking restaurant is where Chef Didier Delaunay creates standout gastronomic cuisine within aubergine-painted walls. The menu features succulent dishes both from the surf (Breton lobster is a speciality) and turf (tender lamb). The restaurant is fully wheelchair accessible.

Crêperie Margaux
CRÊPERIE €

(Map p236; ☑02 99 20 26 02; www.creperie-margaux.com; 3 place du Marché aux Légumes; crêpes €2.50-10; ⊗closed Tue & Wed, open daily Jul-Aug) Watch the owner of this wonderful little crêperie on violet-filled Marché aux Légumes making traditional crêpes by hand (her motto: 'if you're in a hurry, don't come here'). The aromas wafting through the timber-lined dining room, and the scads of happy diners, prove it's well worth the wait.

Côté Jardin
BRETON CUISINE €

(Map p235; ☑02 99 81 63 11; 36 rue Dauphine, St-Servan; menus €13-33; ⊗lunch Tue-Sun, dinner Tue & Thu-Sun) The charming, friendly Côté Jardin presents regional and traditional French cuisine, with a scenic terrace overlooking the marina and St-Malo's walled city. Doodlers can draw on the table with coloured pencils provided.

Café Licorne
BISTRO €

(Map p236; ☑02 99 40 05 18; www.cafe-licorne.com; 6 place Chateaubriand; mains €2.80-15; ⊗8am-11pm) This popular and relatively good-value place for a sit-down lunch within the walls has a buzzing terrace and a funky feel. Crêpes, omelettes, salads, a decent club sandwich and fresh *moules* (mussels) dominate the menu.

Self-Catering

Cheeses and butters handmade by Jean-Yves Bordier's La Maison du Beurre (Map p236; 9 rue de l'Orme; ⊗Tue-Sat, closed Wed afternoon) are shipped to famous restaurants all over the world. Just down the street is the covered market, Halle au Blé (Map p236; rue de la Herse; ⊗8am-noon Tue & Fri).

Drinking

L'Alchimiste
BAR

(Map p236; 7 rue St-Thomas; ⊗5pm-2am, closed Mon Oct-Apr) Ben Harper–type music creates a mellow backdrop at this magical place filled with old books and a toy flying fox. Take a seat at the bar draped with a red tasselled theatre curtain, on the carved timber

mezzanine (including a pulpit), or in the wood-heated basement.

L'Aviso
LIVE MUSIC BAR

(Map p236; 12 rue Point du Jour; ⊗6pm-3am) Regular live music features at this cosy place, which has more than 300 beers on offer (and over 10 – including Breton beer – on tap). If you can't decide, ask the friendly owner/connoisseur.

Le Cunningham
BAR

(Map p235; 2 rue des Hauts Sablons; ⊗6pm-3am Tue-Sat, to 2am Sun) Sail away at this curved wood bar with a wall of timber-framed windows looking out over water. Year-round live entertainment includes jazz, soul and Brazilian beats.

Entertainment

In summer, classical music concerts are held in Cathédrale St-Vincent and elsewhere in the city, and the pubs, bars and cafés have lots of live music – check the 'what's on' section of the tourist office's website (www.saint-malo-tourisme.com).

❶ Information

Main post office (1 bd de la République) Outside the walls.

Mokamalo (5 rue de l'Orme; ⊗9am-8pm) Internet access inside the walls.

Post office (place des Frères Lamennais) Inside the walls.

Tourist office (☑08 25 13 52 00, 02 99 56 64 43; www.saint-malo-tourisme.com; esplanade St-Vincent; ⊗9am-7.30pm Mon-Sat, 10am-6pm Sun) Just outside the walls.

❶ Getting There & Away

AIR See p268 for flight details.

BOAT **Brittany Ferries** (☑reservations in France 08 25 82 88 28, in UK 0871 244 0744; www.brittany-ferries.com) sails between St-Malo and Portsmouth, and **Condor Ferries** (☑in France 08 25 16 54 63, in UK 01202 207 216; www.condorferries.co.uk) runs to/from Poole and Weymouth via Jersey or Guernsey. Car ferries leave from the Gare Maritime du Naye.

From April to September, **Compagnie Corsaire** (☑08 25 13 80 35; www.compagniecorsaire.com) and **Vedettes de St-Malo** (☑02 23 18 41 08; www.vedettes-saint-malo.com) run a **Bus de Mer** (Sea Bus; adult/child return €7/4.30) shuttle service (10 minutes, at least hourly) between St-Malo and Dinard.

BUS All intercity buses stop by the train station. **Keolis Emeraude** (☑02 99 19 70 80; www.keolis-emeraude.com) has services to Cancale

COUNTING THE BEAT

Celtic culture is synonymous with music, and Brittany is no exception. Its wealth of indoor and outdoor festivals and concerts feature traditional instruments through to electronica (and everything in between), including big-name international acts. Keep your finger on the pulse by picking up the free monthly zine **Ty Zicos** (www.tyzicos. com, in French) in cafés and bars.

In addition to the festivals and events listed throughout this chapter, tune in to the region's top musical trio each year.

Les Vieilles Charrues de Carhaix (www.vieillescharrues.asso.fr) Old-school crooners, electronic beats and much more attract crowds of 300,000-plus to Carhaix in mid-July.

Astropolis (www.astropolis.org, in French) Brest's electronic music fest in early August, with the main event atmospherically set in a castle.

Les Transmusicales de Rennes (www.lestrans.com) Groundbreaking indie bands in Rennes, in early December.

(€2, 30 minutes) and Mont St-Michel (€3.30, 1½ hours, three to four daily). **Illenno** (☑02 99 82 26 26; www.illenoo-services.fr) services run to Dinard (€1.70, 30 minutes, hourly) and Rennes (€3, one to 1½ hours, three to six daily). **Tibus** (☑08 10 22 22 22; www.tibus.fr) buses go to Dinan (€2, 50 minutes, three to eight daily).

CAR Avis (☑02 99 40 18 54) and **Europcar** (☑02 99 56 75 17) have offices at the train station. Avis also has a desk at the Gare Maritime du Naye.

TRAIN TGV trains run from St-Malo:

Dinan €9, one hour, 10 daily (requiring a change in Dol de Bretagne)

Paris Montparnasse €63, three hours, up to 10 daily

Rennes €13, one hour, roughly hourly

❶ Getting Around

BUS St-Malo city buses (single journey €1.05, 24-hour pass €3) operate until about 8pm, with some lines extending until around midnight in summer. Between esplanade St-Vincent and the train station, take buses C1 or C2.

TAXI Call ☑02 99 81 30 30.

Dinard

POP 11,180

Visiting Dinard 'in season' is a little like stepping into one of the canvases Picasso painted here in the 1920s. Belle époque mansions built into the cliffs form a timeless backdrop to the beach dotted with blue-and-white striped bathing tents and the beachside carnival. Out of season, when holidaymakers have packed up their buckets and spades, the town is decidedly dor-

mant, but wintry walks along the coastal paths are spectacular.

◉ Sights & Activities

Scenic Walks WALKS

The romantically named **promenade du Clair de Lune** (moonlight promenade) has views across the Rance River estuary to St-Malo's walled city, and nightly sound-and-light spectacles in summer.

Two-hour **guided walks** (⊘2.30pm) explaining the town's history, art and architecture in English and French depart from the tourist office.

Beautiful **seaside trails** extend along the coast in both directions. Walkers can follow the shoreline from Plage du Prieuré to Plage de St-Énogat via Pointe du Moulinet, while cyclists can shadow the coastline on the road. Pack the Institut National Géographique (IGN) 1:50,000 map *Ille-et-Vilaine: Randonnées en Haute Bretagne*, which highlights walking trails throughout the *département*.

Barrage de la Rance BRIDGE

This 750m bridge over the Rance estuary carries the D168 between St-Malo and Dinard, lopping a good 30km off the journey. A feat of hydroelectrics, the **Usine Marémotrice de la Rance** (below the bridge) generates electricity by harnessing the lower estuary's extraordinarily high tidal range – a difference of 13.5m between high and low tide.

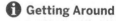 **Espace Découverte** (⊘10am-6pm May-Sep), on the Dinard bank, is good for the mechanically minded. It illustrates the power station's construction

and environmental impact, with a film in English.

Beaches & Swimming BEACHES

Framed by fashionable hotels, a casino and neo-Gothic villas, Plage de l'Écluse is the perfect place to shade yourself in style by renting one of Dinard's trademark blue-and-white striped bathing tents (☑02 99 46 18 12; per half-day €7.50-12, per day €8.50-15.50); you can also hire parasols and deckchairs. Reproductions of Picasso's paintings are often planted in the sand here in high summer.

Filled with heated seawater, the Olympic-sized indoor pool Piscine Municipale (☑02 99 46 22 77; promenade des Alliés; adult/child €4.50/3.50) is beside the beach.

Less chic (and less crowded) than the Plage de l'Écluse is Plage du Prieuré, 1km to the south. Plage de St-Énogat is 1km west of Plage de l'Écluse, on the far side of Pointe de la Malouine.

Water Sports WATER SPORTS

At Plage de l'Écluse, Wishbone Club (☑02 99 88 15 20; www.wishbone-club-dinard.com; ☺9am-9pm Jun-Sep) rents out windsurfing boards from €15 per hour, and can arrange lessons. The company also organises catamarans and kayak rental.

Dive trips are run by CSD (Club Subaquatique Dinardais; ☑02 99 46 25 18; from €18).

🛌 Sleeping

Dinard's prices match its cachet: budget travellers may want to consider staying in St-Malo and catching the ferry or strolling across.

TOP CHOICE Hôtel Printania TRADITIONAL HOTEL €
(☑02 99 46 13 07; www.printaniahotel.com, in French; 5 av George V; s €67, d €73-104; ☑mid-Mar–mid-Nov; ☎) This is a charming Breton-style hotel, complete with wood-and-leather furniture, which has a superb location overlooking the Baie du Prieuré. Guest rooms with a sea view cost more; otherwise get your fill of the grand views across the water to St-Servan at breakfast (€8.50). There's an annexe of the hotel on the road that you may come to before you get to the main building – there's no reception here, so keep on going until you see the hotel proper.

Grand Hôtel Barrière LUXURY HOTEL €€
(☑02 99 88 26 26; www.lucienbarriere.com; 3 bd Féart; s €165-200, d €180-300; ❄☎♨♿) Dinard's most fabulous address is this old-timer that has been given a very smart facelift and has prices to match. The rooms are spacious, many with balconies and magnificent sea views, though the style is very much anonymous chic. There's a large swimming pool (covered most of the year) and a glamorous lawn area for taking an evening cocktail. Wireless access is charged.

Hôtel de la Plage HOTEL €
(☑02 99 46 14 87; www.hoteldelaplage-dinard.com; 3 bd Féart; s €55-75, d €69-125; ☎) Refreshingly unpretentious, with warm staff and solid stone-walled rooms renovated with red-and-gold furnishings and heavy timber furniture, including sleigh beds. A handful of the 18 rooms here have huge timber decks looking out to the sea, a few footsteps away.

Camping Municipal du Port Blanc
CAMPGROUND €
(☑02 99 46 10 74; camping.municipal@ville-dinard.fr; rue du Sergeant Boulanger; site per 2 adults from €19; ☺Apr-Sep) You'll find this campground close to the beach, about 2km west of Plage de l'Écluse. There are some excellent views and direct access to the sand.

✗ Eating

Some of Dinard's best restaurants are attached to hotels, such as Hôtel Printania (menus €25-38), which serves top-notch fish and seafood.

Chez Ma Pomme BRETON CUISINE €€
(☑02 99 46 81 90; 6 rue Yves Verney; menus €20-26; ☺closed Mon, dinner Sun & Thu Sep-Jun) Codfish roasted in bacon and parmesan is among the innovative twists on local ocean-caught fish, while rich Breton caramel features in the tempting array of desserts. The team in the kitchen is hip and young, and the colourful interior equally bright.

L'Abri des Flots SEAFOOD €€
(☑02 99 16 99 48; 3 place de la République; lunch/dinner menus €23-35) Effortlessly chic, this modern temple to seafood does not disappoint. Its cavernous interior is usually filled to capacity every day when the morning's catch is lovingly transformed into classic French dishes. Highly recommended.

Crêperie Côté Mer CRÊPERIE €
(☑02 99 16 80 30; 29 bd Wilson; menus from €12.50; ☺closed Mon Sep-Jun) A crisp little crêperie with pine tables on a pretty pedestrianised street, the Côté Mer serves grilled

meat, salads, oysters and *moules frites* (mussels and fries) as well as (naturally) crêpes, galettes and ice cream year-round.

Self-Catering

Beach-picnic supplies abound at Dinard's large covered market (place Rochaid; ⊘7am-1.30pm Tue, Thu & Sat).

ℹ Information

Cyberspot (6 rue Winston Churchill; per hr €6; ⊘10am-7pm Wed-Sat, 2.30-7pm Sun & Mon)

Tourist office (✆02 99 46 94 12; www.ot-dinard.com; 2 bd Féart; ⊘9.30am-12.15pm & 2-6pm Mon-Sat) Staff book accommodation for free.

ℹ Getting There & Away

AIR Ryanair (www.ryanair.com) has daily flights to and from London Stansted. There's no public transport from Dinard airport (5km from Dinard) to town (or to neighbouring St-Malo); a daytime/evening taxi from Dinard to the airport costs around €15/22.

BOAT From April to September, **Compagnie Corsaire** (✆08 25 13 80 35; www.compagnie corsaire.com) and **Vedettes de St-Malo** (✆02 23 18 41 08; www.vedettes-saint-malo.com) run a **Bus de Mer** (Sea Bus; adult/child return €7/4.30) shuttle service (10 minutes) between St-Malo and Dinard, operating at least hourly.

BUS Illenoo (www.illenoo-services.fr) buses connect Dinard and the train station in St-Malo (€1.70, 30 minutes, hourly). Le Gallic bus stop, outside the tourist office, is the most convenient. Several buses travel to Rennes (€3.90, two hours).

ℹ Getting Around

BICYCLE To nip around you can hire bicycles (from €9 per day) and motor scooters (from €38 per day) from **Breiz Cycles** (✆02 99 46 27 25; 8 rue St-Énogat).

TAXI Call ✆06 64 98 59 59.

Cancale

POP 5440

The idyllic little fishing port of Cancale, 14km east of St-Malo, is famed for its offshore *parcs à huîtres* (oyster beds).

◉ Sights

Ferme Marine   OYSTER MUSEUM

(Marine Farm; www.ferme-marine.com; corniche de l'Aurore; adult/child €7/3.60; ⊘mid-Feb–Oct) This small museum dedicated to oyster farming and shellfish runs guided tours in English at 2pm from July to mid-September.

🛏 Sleeping & Eating

It's an easy day trip to Cancale from St-Malo or Dinard, but there are some appealing places if you want to spend the night.

La Pastourelle   B&B €

(✆02 99 89 10 09; www.baie-saintmichel.com, in French; Les Nielles, St-Méloir des Ondes; s €56-64, d €62-74; 🐾) The countryside around Cancale shelters some really lovely *chambres d'hôte* (ask the tourist office for a complete list). One of the most delightful is this vine-covered traditional Breton *longère* (long house) looking out to sea. Rooms are crisp and countrified, and convivial *tables d'hôte* (€27 per person) are available by reservation. It's on the D155.

Hôtel La Mère Champlain   HOTEL €

(✆02 99 89 60 04; www.lamerechamplain.com; 1 quai Thomas; d €69-149; 🐾) Reached by a newly installed lift (making it wheelchair accessible), the 15 delightfully renovated rooms at this quayside hotel have a relaxed ambience and pretty-as-a-picture port views. The nautical-style restaurant (*menus* €16 to €40), complete with crisp linen, specialises in grilled lobster and has amazing desserts.

Le Continental   HOTEL €€

(✆02 99 89 60 16; www.hotel-cancale.com, in French; 4 quai Thomas; d €88-148; ⊘mid-Feb–early Jan; 🐾) Above its portside, red-awning-shaded restaurant (*menus* €19 to €42), this *hôtel de charme* with good wheelchair access has beautiful timber-rich rooms. Sea-facing rooms are at a premium but the views, especially on the higher floors, are worth it.

Auberge de Jeunesse   HOSTEL €

(✆02 99 89 62 62; www.fuaj.org; Port Pican; dm from €19; ⊘Feb-Nov) Right by the seaside, Cancale's HI-affiliated youth hostel at Port Pican is 3km northeast of the town – take the bus (July and August only) to the Cancale Église or Port Pican stop and walk 500m towards the seafront. Campers can pitch up here for €6 per night.

Camping Municipal Le Grouin

    CAMPGROUND €

(✆02 99 89 63 79; Pointe du Grouin; site €15; ⊘Mar-Oct) Overlooking a fine-sand beach 6km north of Cancale near Pointe du Grouin, this place has 200 well-spaced sites, and facilities for wheelchairs.

Throughout Brittany you'll see bilingual Breton street and transport signs, and many other occurrences of the language popping up. Even though all Breton speakers also speak French, this is seen as an important gesture to normalising the use of a language that has been stigmatised and even banned throughout much of the early and mid-20th century.

Historically speaking, Breton is a Celtic language related to Cornish and Welsh, and more distantly to Irish and Scottish Gaelic. Following on from the French Revolution, the government banned the teaching of Breton in schools, punishing children who spoke their mother tongue. As happened with other marginalised Celtic cultures, speakers of all ages were stigmatised. For the next century and a half it remained a language spoken in the sanctum of private homes. Education, post-WWII economics, mass media and, most of all, fluid transportation between Brittany and the rest of the country also saw French rapidly gain ground. Between 1950 and 1990 there was an 80% reduction in Breton usage.

But what constitutes 'Breton' these days is trickier to pin down. The seeds of the language's revival were planted in the 1960s, particularly after France's May 1968 protests, driven by the younger generation rebelling against their oppressed cultural heritage. Bringing about the rebirth of the language, no longer passed on generationally, wasn't straightforward. More often spoken than written (and both spoken and written with regional differences), settling on a standardised Breton for teaching in schools is still complex.

There's also a distinct difference between the Breton of first-generation speakers and 'neo-Breton', particularly as the new incarnation often replaces French words long intermingled with Breton with completely Breton ones. Case in point: *Aotrou* and *Itron* are now used for the French *Monsieur* and *Madame*. Traditionally, though, they denote someone of exceedingly high rank (*Itron* is the respectful term of address for the Virgin Mary) – creating another generational language gap. (Bizarrely, it would be like being greeted by a stranger, without irony, as, 'Hello, Exalted One.') Some older Breton speakers also find it hard to shake the ostracism inflicted on them for their language, and aren't comfortable conversing in it openly.

Breton now also extends beyond its historic boundaries. Originally, Basse Bretagne (Lower Brittany, in the west) spoke variants of the Breton language, while Haute Bretagne (Upper Brittany, in the east, including areas such as St-Malo) spoke Gallo, a language similar to French. But today you'll find Breton signage in Rennes' metro stations and in many other parts of the east, emblemising Brittany's culture across the entire region.

When today's students integrate their school-taught Breton into society, Breton will evolve yet again, just as France's mosaic of cultures also continues to evolve. For now as the language regenerates, so does the sense of Breton identity.

Marché aux Huîtres   OYSTER MARKET   €

(⊙9am-6pm) Clustered by the Pointe des Crolles lighthouse, stalls sell oysters from €3.50 per dozen for small *huîtres creuses* to upwards of €20 for saucer-sized *plates de Cancale*.

ℹ Information

Tourist office (☑02 99 89 63 72; www.cancale
-tourisme.fr; ⊙9am-1pm & 2.30-6pm) At the top of rue du Port. In July and August there's an annexe in the wooden house where the fish auction takes place on quai Gambetta.

ℹ Getting There & Around

BICYCLE A variety of bikes can be hired at **Les 2 Roues de Cancale** (☑02 99 89 80 16; 7 rue de L'Industrie; per day from €13). It's a stunning 35km ride or walk along the coast from Cancale to St-Malo.

BUS Buses stop behind the church on place Lucidas and at Port de la Houle, next to the pungent fish market. **Keolis Emeraude** (www. keolis-emeraude.com) has year-round services to and from St-Malo (€2, 30 minutes). In summer, at least three daily Keolis Emeraude buses continue to Port Pican and Port Mer, near Pointe du Grouin.

Pointe du Grouin

At the northern tip of the wild coast between Cancale and St-Malo, this nature reserve juts out on a windblown headland. Just east offshore, Île des Landes is home to a colony of giant black cormorants whose wingspans can reach 170cm.

Via the GR34 coastal hiking trail, Pointe du Grouin is a stunning 7km hike from Cancale and 28km from St-Malo. By the D201 road, it's 4km from Cancale. Cancale tourist office's free map covers the local coastline.

Dinan

POP 11.600

Set high above the fast-flowing River Rance, the narrow cobblestone streets and squares lined with crooked half-timbered houses making up Dinan's old town are straight out of the Middle Ages – something that's not lost on the deluge of summer tourists.

◉ Sights

Tour de l'Horloge　　　　　　　　TOWER
(☑02 96 87 02 26; rue de l'Horloge; adult/child €2.95/1.90; ☺10am-6.30pm Jun-Sep) The half-timbered houses overhanging place des Cordeliers and place des Merciers mark the heart of the old town. A few paces south, climb up to the little balcony of this 15th-century clock tower whose chimes ring every quarter hour.

Basilique St-Sauveur　　　　　　CHURCH
(place St-Sauveur; ☺9am-6pm) With its soaring Gothic chancel, the Basilique St-Sauveur contains a 14th-century grave slab in its north transept reputed to contain the heart of **Bertrand du Guesclin**, a 14th-century knight noted for his hatred of the English and his fierce battles to ex-

pel them. Ironically, Dinan today has one of the largest English expat communities in Brittany!

Château de Dinan　　　　TEXTILE MUSEUM
(☑02 96 39 45 20; rue du Château; adult/child €4.40/1.75; ☺10am-6.30pm, closed Jan) The town's museum is atmospherically housed in the keep of Dinan's ruined 14th-century château. It showcases the town's textile industry, with a fine collection of *coiffes* (traditional Breton lace headdresses).

Just east of the church, beyond the tiny Jardin Anglais (English Garden), a former cemetery and nowadays a pleasant little park, is the 13th-century Tour Ste-Catherine, with great views down over the viaduct and port.

Vieux Pont　　　　　　HISTORIC QUARTER
Rue du Jerzual and its continuation, the steep (and slippery when wet) stone rue du Petit Fort, both lined with art galleries, antiques shops and restaurants, lead down to the Vieux Pont (Old Bridge). From here the little port extends northwards, while the 19th-century Viaduc de Dinan soars high above to the south.

🏃 Activities

Compagnie Corsaire　　　　BOAT TRIPS
(www.compagniecorsaire.com) Between May and September, boats sail along the River Rance to Dinard and St-Malo (return trip €30, 2½ hours). Sailing schedules vary according to the tides. From Dinard or St-Malo you can easily return to Dinan by bus (and, from St-Malo, by train too).

Self-Guided Walks　　　　　　WALKS
Ask at the tourist office for its free leaflet *Discovery Tours,* available in several languages including English, which plots three walking itineraries around town.

DON'T MISS

LE COQUILLAGE

Super chef Olivier Roellinger's latest project is his sumptuous restaurant Le Coquillage (☑02 99 89 64 76; www.maisons-de-bricourt.com; 1 rue Duguesclin; menus €26-90; ☺closed Jan & Feb) and hotel housed in the extremely impressive Château Richeux, 4km to the south of Cancale. Roellinger's creations have earned him three Michelin stars and you won't have trouble seeing why if you're lucky enough to get a table here. The Maritime Adventure *menu* (€90) takes in many culinary highlights of both Brittany and Normandy, from fresh scallops to the region's dishes, all beautifully cooked and imaginatively served. Booking well ahead is essential. As well as offering rooms at Château Richeux, Roellinger offers a range of cottages and other deluxe accommodation around Cancale. See the website for details.

✦✦ Festivals & Events

Festival des Ramparts MEDIEVAL FESTIVAL
(www.fete-remparts-dinan.com) No fewer than 100,000 visitors turn up to join Dinannais townsfolk dressed in medieval garb for the two-day Fête des Remparts, held every even-numbered year in late July.

🛏 Sleeping

In summer, advance reservations are recommended. Ask the tourist office for a list of *chambres d'hôte* in the surrounding area.

La Villa Côté Cour B&B €€
(☑02 96 39 30 07; www.villa-cote-cour-dinan. com; 10 rue Lord Kitchener; s €89-159, d incl breakfast €99-229; 🔊) Live the dream... opening onto a delightful garden, this exquisite *chambre d'hôte* has just four countrified rooms with checked fabrics, scrubbed floorboards and a decadent sauna (€9.50). Many rooms also have their own jacuzzis.

Hôtel de la Tour de l'Horloge
TRADITIONAL HOTEL €
(☑02 96 39 96 92; www.hotel-dinan.com; 5 rue de la Chaux; s/d €55/69; 🔊) In the centre of the old town, the 12-room Horloge occupies a charming 18th-century house on a cobbled, car-free lane, which contrasts with its brand-new renovations in colourful North African style. Head to the top floor, where rooms have exposed wooden beams and a lofty view of the hotel's namesake clock tower.

Hôtel Les Grandes Tours HISTORIC HOTEL €
(☑02 96 85 16 20; www.hotel-dinan-grandes -tours.com; 6 rue du Château; s €40-56, d €40-60, tr €73; ☺Feb-mid-Dec; 🔊) In its former life as the Hôtel des Messageries, this hotel was fabled as the place Victor Hugo stayed with his very good friend Juliette Drouet in 1836. Blue-shaded rooms (especially those on the sloped-ceilinged top floor) are snug but conducive to snuggling up, and there's lock-up parking (€8).

Auberge de Jeunesse Moulin de Méen
HOSTEL €
(☑02 96 39 10 83; www.fuaj.org; Vallée de la Fontaine des Eaux; camping €6, dm incl breakfast €13.50; ☺closed late Dec-early Feb; @) Dinan's HI-affiliated youth hostel is in a lovely vine-covered old water mill about 750m north of the port. Reception is open 9am to noon and 5pm to 9pm.

Camping Municipal Châteaubriand
CAMPGROUND €
(☑in summer 02 96 39 11 96, rest of yr 02 96 39 22 43; 103 rue Chateaubriand; per adult/tent/car €2.70/3/2.50; ☺late May-late Sep) This campground at the foot of the ramparts is the closest to the old town.

✕ Eating & Drinking

The old city has some really charming (and surprisingly good-value) eateries and bars, with more along the river at the old port.

Le Cantorbery TRADITIONAL FRENCH €€
(☑02 96 39 02 52; 6 rue Ste-Claire; menus €26-37; ☺closed Wed) Occupying a magnificent 17th-century house, this elegant, intimate restaurant is perfect for wining and dining your beloved over a romantic lunch or dinner. Its traditional menu – based on beef, grilled fish and seafood, including *coquilles St-Jacques* (scallops) from St-Brieuc – changes tempo in accordance with the seasons.

Chez La Mère Pourcel TRADITIONAL FRENCH €€
(☑02 96 39 03 80; 3 place des Merciers; menus €22-35; ☺lunch & dinner Tue-Sat & lunch Sun) The beamed dining room of this Dinan institution hasn't changed (much) since it was built in the 15th century. Stellar staples include regional salt-marsh lamb.

Le Chat Botté TRADITIONAL FRENCH €€
(☑02 96 85 31 58; 18 passage de la Tour de l'Horloge; menus €10-17.50; ☺closed Mon) 'Puss in Boots' is a local old-town favourite for fragrant grilled fish and crêpes.

Le Patio INTERNATIONAL CUISINE €
(☑02 96 39 84 87; 9 place du Champ Clos; menus €11-13; ☺noon-late, closed Mon & lunch Sun; 🔊) Set around a leafy garden, this contemporary spot is great for international cuisine, tapas or just a drink. The kitchen closes at midnight.

ℹ Information

Post office (7 place Duclos)

Tourist office (☑02 96 87 69 76; www.dinan -tourisme.com; 9 rue du Château; ☺9am-12.30pm & 2-6pm Mon-Sat) Offers internet access at €1 per hour.

ℹ Getting There & Around

BICYCLE Cycles Gauthier (☑02 96 85 07 60; 15 rue Déroyer; ☺9am-noon & 2-7pm Tue-Sat) rents out bikes for €15 per day from its ship near the train station.

BUS Buses leave from place Duclos and the bus station. **Illenoo** (☏02 99 26 16 00) runs several daily services:

Dinard €2.40, 40 minutes

Rennes €3.90, 1¼ hours

TAXI Call ☏06 08 00 80 90.

TRAIN Change in Dol de Bretagne:

Rennes €13.50, one hour

St-Malo €8.50, one hour, five daily

Paimpol

POP 8170

Set around a working fishing harbour and ringed by half-timbered buildings, Paimpol (Pempoull in Breton) is rich in history. It was the one-time home port of the Icelandic fishery, when the town's fishermen would set sail to the seas around Iceland for seven months and more at a stretch. And it's rich in legends – the fishermen lost at sea are recalled in folk tales and *chants de marins* (sea shanties).

South of the two harbours, Paimpol's town centre clusters around the market square of place du Martray. The bus and train stations are 100m south of this square.

◉ Sights & Activities

Enquire at the tourist office about canoeing and kayaking operators.

TOP / La Vapeur du Trieux   STEAM TRAIN
CHOICE
(☏08 92 39 14 27; www.vapeurdutrieux. com; adult/child return €22/11; ☺May-Sep) Between May and September, the 1922 steam train chuffs along the riverbank on a beautiful journey from Paimpol's station to the artists' town of Pontrieux, where there's time for a pleasant meal and a stroll before the return journey. Reserve at least one day ahead.

Abbaye de Beauport   ABBEY
(☏02 96 55 18 58; www.abbaye-beauport.com, in French; adult/child €5.50/2.5; ☺10am-7pm) If you have wheels (or you're up for a glorious 1½-hour walk along the seashore from the town harbour), head 3.5km east to the romantic abbey. En route, stop at the Pointe de Guilben for beautiful bay views. The tourist office has a free map.

Musée de la Mer   MARITIME MUSEUM
(Sea Museum; ☏02 96 22 02 19; rue Labenne; adult/child €4.70/2; ☺10.30am-12.30pm & 2.30-6.30pm) This splendid little museum charts the Paimpol region's maritime history and

is, rather appropriately, set in a former cod-drying factory.

Musée du Costume Breton   CLOTHING MUSEUM
(☏02 96 22 02 19; rue Raymond Pellier; adult/ child €2.80/1.20; ☺3-7pm Tue-Sun Jul & Aug) For land-bound history, in the summer months you can visit this rather curious museum containing traditional clothing items.

Île de Bréhat   ISLAND
Paimpol is the closest port to Île de Bréhat (Enez Vriad in Breton), a tiny, car-free island 8km offshore to the north. With a population of 350, it stretches just 5km from north to south. The most idyllic time to visit is in spring, when Mediterranean wildflowers bloom in its gentle microclimate. In the citadel on the southwestern edge you can visit the glass-making factory (☏02 96 20 09 09; www.verreriesdebrehat.com; admission €1). There is a seasonal municipal campground; contact Paimpol's tourist office for information.

Vedettes de Bréhat (☏02 96 55 79 50; www.vedettesdebrehat.com) operates ferries (adult/child return €8.50/7, 15 minutes, at least eight sailings daily) to Île de Bréhat from Pointe L'Arcouest, 6km north of Paimpol. Bikes cost an extra €15 return to transport, which is only possible on certain in- and out-bound journeys. It's cheaper to rent a bike on the island; shops line the right-hand side of the road when you get off the boat. The best way to protect the fragile environment, however, is to walk.

✲ Festivals & Events

Festival de Chant de Marin
CULTURAL FESTIVAL
(www.paimpol-festival.com) Traditional Breton dancing takes place on the quays in August every even-numbered year.

🛌 Sleeping & Eating

Hôtel Le Terre-Neuvas   HOTEL €
(☏02 96 55 14 14; www.le-terre-neuvas.com; 16 quai Duguay Trouin; d €34-48; ☺mid-Jan–mid-Dec; ☎) Perched right beside the harbour, and a few steps from the historic town centre as well as the seafront, the Terre-Neuvas has comfortable, incredibly inexpensive rooms, some with views out to sea. Its excellent restaurant (*menus* €20 to €30) is a popular port of call for guests and nonguests.

K' Loys   TRADITIONAL HOTEL €
(☏02 96 20 40 01; www.k-loys.com; 21 quai Morand; d €55-110; ☎) Each of the 15 rooms

at the cosy 'Chez Louise', a former ship-owner's mansion with good wheelchair access, is individually decorated with striped walls and paisley-pattern prints. There are lovely private lounges with richly upholstered booths to relax in over a drink.

Camping Municipal de Cruckin
CAMPGROUND €

(☎02 96 20 78 47; www.camping-paimpol.com; rue de Cruckin; site/per person €7.50/3.50; ☺Apr-Sep) Near the Abbaye de Beauport, this eco-campground runs an environmentally conscious program of energy, water and waste management. It's beautifully sited on the Baie de Kérity, 3.5km southeast of town off the road to Plouha.

Ty Krampoux
CRÊPERIE €

(☎02 96 20 86 34; 11 place du Martray; crêpes & galettes €2-10) Over two timber-balustraded levels *packed* with Paimpolaises (who wait outside for the doors to open), this cornerstone of the community on Paimpol's pretty main square prepares perfectly buttered Breton crêpes, as well as scrumptious fillings such as chocolate-laced chestnut cream. In summer more laden tables spill onto a pavement terrace. Order a pitcher of cider and settle back for an authentic slice of Breton life.

L'Islandais
SEAFOOD €€

(☎02 96 20 93 00; http://creperie-restaurant.l-islandais.com; 19 quai Morand; menus €18-35) You'll find a clutch of laid-back, quality seafood restaurants along the western side of the harbour, including this popular spot where the seafood platters are large enough to share between two.

Self-Catering
Paimpol's Tuesday-morning market spreads over place Gambetta and place du Martray. On weekends, vendors sell freshly shucked oysters at quai Duguay Trouin.

ⓘ Information
Tourist office (☎02 96 20 83 16; www.paimpol-goelo.com; place de la République; ☺9.30am-7.30pm Mon-Sat, 10am-12.30pm & 4.30-6.30pm Sun) Sells local rambling guides (€3).

ⓘ Getting There & Around
BICYCLE Intersport Paimpol (☎02 96 20 59 46; zone de Kerpuns), near the massive Carrefour supermarket complex, rents a wide variety of bikes and kayaks.

BUS Tibus (☎08 10 22 22 22) runs buses to and from St-Brieuc (€2.40, 1½ hours). In summer most continue to Pointe L'Arcouest.

TRAIN There are several trains or SNCF buses daily between Paimpol and Guingamp (€7, 45 minutes), where you can pick up connections to Brest, St-Brieuc and Rennes.

FINISTÈRE

The country's westernmost *département,* Finistère has a wind-whipped coastline scattered with lighthouses and beacons lashed by waves. Finistère's southern prow, Cornouaille, takes its name from early Celts who sailed from Cornwall and other parts of Britain to settle here, and today it harbours the Breton language, customs and culture.

Roscoff
POP 3780

Unlike many of its industrial and less-than-beautiful sister Channel ports, Roscoff (Rosko in Breton) provides a captivating first glimpse of Brittany. Granite houses dating from the 16th century wreathe the pretty docks, which are surrounded by emerald-green fields producing cauliflowers, onions, tomatoes, new potatoes and artichokes.

Once upon a time, Roscoff farmers known as 'Johnnies', wearing distinctive horizontally striped tops, loaded up their boats with plaited strings of locally grown small pink onions and crossed the Channel to the UK, then peddled – and pedalled – with their onions hanging from their bikes' handlebars, creating the traditional British stereotype of the French today. This trade began in the early 19th century, reaching its peak in the 1920s. Today, Johnnies have a near mythical status in the area, with a number still continuing the trade and a new wave of younger-generation Johnnies ensuring the survival of this iconic tradition.

Roscoff's waters conceal beds of *goémon* (algae), harvested for foodstuffs as well as *thalassothérapie* health and beauty treatments.

◉ Sights & Activities
Église Notre Dame de Kroaz-Batz CHURCH (place Lacaze-Duthiers; ☺9am-noon & 2-6pm) The most obvious sight in Roscoff is this unusual church at the heart of the old town.

The Breton Coast

Brittany's rugged coastline is one of the region's best-kept secrets. With brilliant sand beaches framing traditional fishing villages, rocky cliffs towering above the churning swell of the North Atlantic, and lots of activities to keep you occupied, there's plenty to discover.

Superb Stretches of Sand

1 Don't associate Brittany with beaches? Think again... Yes the water may be freezing, but the sand is spectacular and the backing sublime at St-Malo (p234), or Quiberon (p265). Alternatively, find your own patch of sand on the beaches of Belle Île (p267).

Hiking the Coasts

2 Get out into nature on the coastal hiking trail (p244) from Cancale to St-Malo, or from Morgat to Cap de la Chèvre (p256). For a challenge, walk the 45km coastal path on Île d'Ouessant (p254) or the 95km path around Belle Île (p267).

Coastal Villages

3 Find your own quiet bliss in the village life of the fishing port of Roscoff (p247), charming Camaret-sur-Mer (p257) and our personal favourite, chic hideaway Cancale (p242).

Island Life

4 Take the ferry to Île d'Ouessant (p254), with its rugged coastal path and great activities, or head out of season to Belle Île (p267), the southern coast's standout star. To get off the beaten track, head to Île de Batz (p250).

Get Active!

5 You can dive, windsurf and hire catamarans in Dinard (p240), canoe or kayak in Paimpol (p246), and hire bikes pretty much anywhere, though we recommend Presqu'Île de Crozon (p255) and any of Brittany's islands.

Clockwise from top left

1. The beach at St-Malo **2.** Brittany's rugged coastline
3. Boats in the harbour of Camaret-sur-Mer

With its Renaissance belfry rising above the flat landscape, the 16th-century Flamboyant Gothic structure is one of Brittany's most impressive churches.

Maison des Johnnies HISTORY MUSEUM
(02 98 61 25 48; 48 rue Brizeux; adult/child €4/2.50) Photographs trace Roscoff's roaming onion farmers from the early 19th century at this popular museum. Tours at 5pm on Tuesdays between mid-June and mid-September include a free hour-long meeting with Johnnies from 6pm to 7pm. Call ahead for tour times, as they change frequently.

Le Jardin Exotique de Roscoff GARDEN
(02 98 61 29 19; www.jardinexotiqueroscoff. com; adult/child €5/2; 10am-7pm, closed Dec-Feb) Wander through 3000 species of exotic plants, many from the southern hemisphere, at this impressive exotic garden.

Centre de Découverte des Algues MUSEUM
(02 98 69 77 05; www.decouvertedesalgues. com, in French; 5 rue Victor Hugo; admission free, walks per adult/child €5/3.50; 10am-7pm) You can learn about local seaweed harvesting at this enthusiastically run museum, which also organises guided walks and gives regular free lectures (often in English and German).

Thalasso Roscoff SEAWATER BATHS
(08 25 00 20 99; www.thalasso.com, in French; rue Victor Hugo; closed Dec) The perfect way to follow a visit to the Centre de Découverte des Algues is to immerse yourself in the stuff at this bathing complex, which offers health-inducing activities including a heated seawater pool, a *hammam* (Turkish bath) and a jacuzzi (€11 for all three).

Île de Batz ISLAND
Bordering what is basically a 4-sq-km vegetable garden fertilised by seaweed, the beaches on the Île de Batz (pronounced 'ba, Enez Vaz' in Breton; www.iledebatz.com) are a peaceful place to bask. The mild island climate supports the luxuriant Jardins Georges Delaselle (02 98 61 75 65; www .jardin-georgesdelaselle.fr; adult/child €4.60/2; 2-6pm Wed-Mon Apr-Oct, daily Jul & Aug), founded in the 19th century, with over 1500 plants from all five continents.

Ferries (adult/child return €7.50/4, bike €7, 15 minutes each way) between Roscoff and Île de Batz run every 30 minutes between 8am and 8pm from late June to mid-September; there are about eight sailings daily during the rest of the year.

On the island, Le Saout (02 98 61 77 65) and Roulez Jeunesse (02 98 61 76 91) rent bicycles for around €10 per day.

Sleeping & Eating

Roscoff's hotels are home to some first-rate restaurants.

TOP CHOICE **Hôtel du Centre** BOUTIQUE HOTEL €
(02 98 61 24 25; www.chezjanie.com; r €69-99; mid-Feb–mid-Nov;) Minimal and sleek rooms at this boutique hotel look like they've been lifted out of a magazine, and indeed they've featured in many. For a sea-view room looking out over the postcard-pretty old port, add a further €25. But it's perhaps best known for its restaurant, Chez Janie (menu €24), serving Breton classics like *kig ha farz* – a farmers' family meal based around the Breton cake *far,* cooked in a linen bag within a boiling bacon and vegetable stew.

Le Temps de Vivre BOUTIQUE HOTEL €€
(02 98 19 33 19; www.tycoz.com/letemps devivre; 19 place Lacaze Duthiers; d €140-268;) This glamorous place is hidden away in a lovely stone mansion complete with its own tower just opposite the church. With fantastic sea views from some rooms, decor that is a great blend of modernity and tradition, plus friendly staff, this is one of Roscoff's very best options. Internet access is free through cables in each room.

Hôtel Les Arcades TRADITIONAL HOTEL €
(02 98 69 70 45; www.en.hotel-les-arcades -roscoff.com; 15 rue Amiral Réveillère; r €46-62;) Perched right above the rocks on the waterfront in the town's heart, this cosy hotel, run by the same family for nearly a century, has 24 light-filled, light-coloured rooms and a glass-paned restaurant (mains around €15) serving up seafood and spectacular views.

Hôtel Les Chardons Bleus TRADITIONAL HOTEL €
(02 98 69 72 03; www.roscoffhotel.com, in French; 4 rue Amiral Réveillère; d €70-95; mid-Mar–Jan;) Set back just 100m from the port, in the town centre, the 'Thistles', a Logis de France, has 10 comfortable rooms, and an old-fashioned formal restaurant (*menus* €10 to €40) specialising in seafood.

Camping Aux Quatre Saisons
CAMPGROUND €

(☏02 98 69 70 86; www.camping-aux4saisons. fr; Le Ruguel; sites €9-11; ☺Easter-Sep) Close to a sandy beach in the grounds of a lovely 19th-century mansion, this campground is approximately 3km southwest of Roscoff.

La P'tite Fabrik
CRÊPERIE €

(☏02 98 69 92 69; 18 rue Jules Ferry) Watch artisan crêpes being handmade in the open kitchen of this crêpe shop in the old town, and perhaps pick some up for a beach picnic.

Le Surcouf
BRASSERIE €

(☏02 98 69 71 89; 14 rue Amiral Réveillère; menus €11-55) A reliable year-round opener, this brasserie-restaurant is unsurprisingly popular with locals. Opening hours and days can vary.

ⓘ Information

Post office (19 rue Gambetta)

Tourist office (☏02 98 61 12 13; www.roscoff -tourisme.com; quai d'Auxerre; ☺9.15am-noon & 2-6pm Mon-Sat, open Sun Jul-Aug) The new tourist office is next to the lighthouse. There's free internet access from the public computer here.

ⓘ Getting There & Away

BUS The combined bus and train station is on rue Ropartz Morvan. **Cars Bihan** (☏02 98 83 45 80) operates buses departing from the ferry terminal (Port de Bloscon) and passing by the town centre:

Brest €2, 1½ to two hours, up to four daily

Morlaix €2, 40 minutes, several daily

FERRY Brittany Ferries (☏reservations in France 08 25 82 88 28, in UK 0871 244 0744; www.brittany-ferries.com) links Roscoff to Plymouth in England (five to nine hours, one to three daily year-round) and Cork in Ireland (14 hours, once-weekly June to September). Boats leave from Port de Bloscon, about 2km east of the town centre.

TRAIN There are regular trains and SNCF buses to Morlaix (€5.50, 35 minutes), where you can make connections to Brest, Quimper and St-Brieuc.

Morlaix

POP 16.600

At the bottom of a deep valley sluicing through northeastern Finistère, Morlaix is an engaging and easily accessed city that's also a good gateway to the coast and the

enclos paroissiaux (enclosed parishes), the rich sculptures surrounding many of the parish churches fanning out to the south (such as the 16th-century masterpiece in the village of Pleyben).

Towering above the town, the arched 58m-high railway viaduct was built in 1863.

◉ Sights & Activities

Église St-Melaine
CHURCH

(☺9am-noon & 2-6pm) The late-15th-century Flamboyant Gothic Église St-Melaine bears a star-studded barrel-vault roof and polychrome wooden statues, including St Peter and the eponymous St Melaine.

Le Musée de Morlaix
MUSEUM

(☏02 98 88 07 75; www.musee.ville.morlaix.fr; place des Jacobins; ☺10am-noon & 2-5pm Wed-Sat & Mon, daily in summer) The area's history, archaeology and art are showcased at Le Musée de Morlaix. The museum also incorporates the beautifully preserved half-timbered house nearby, **La Maison à Pondalez** (☏02 98 88 68 88; 9 Grand' Rue). Tickets per adult/child cost €4/2.50 for both the museum and the house.

Le Léon à Fer et à Flots
BOAT TRIP

(☏02 98 62 07 52; www.aferaflots.org, in French; adult/child €25/13; ☺Apr-Sep) A great way to see the area by land and sea combines a boat trip through the islands of the Baie de Morlaix and a picturesque train trip between Roscoff and Morlaix with Le Léon à Fer et à Flots.

🛏 Sleeping & Eating

Rue Ange de Guernisac has several enticing restaurants.

Ty Pierre
B&B €

(☏06 80 01 37 75; 1bis place de Viarmes; s/d/tr with shared bathroom €34/50/65; ☜) Artworks and artefacts Pierre-Yves Jacquet picked up on his Asian travels now decorate his *chambre d'hôte*'s 10 spacious rooms. At this price there's no lift (count on climbing three or four floors), and most rooms don't have their own bathroom (they're just along the wide corridors), but bikes are available for rent from €15 per day. Bonus: the B&B's just across from the cosy Breton bar, La Chope (closed Monday), with French football on the telly and cider on tap.

Hôtel de l'Europe
TRADITIONAL HOTEL €

(☏02 98 62 11 99; www.hotel-europe-com.fr; 1 rue d'Aiguillon; r €60-88, ste €120; ☜) Regal, refined, yet still relaxed, the Hôtel de l'Europe occupies an elegant 19th-century building. Moulded ceilings, carved panelling and sculpted woodwork fill the sweeping public areas; the romantic guestrooms have rich apricot and rose tones, and mod cons including free broadband.

Grand Café de la Terrasse BRASSERIE €
(📞02 98 88 20 25; 31 place des Otages; mains €12.50-16.50; ⏰8am-midnight Mon-Sat) In the heart of town, Morlaix' showpiece is this stunning 1872-established brasserie with an original central spiral staircase. Sip tea, coffee or something stronger, or sup on classical brasserie fare like rabbit and leek crumble.

ℹ Information

Café de l'Aurore (📞02 98 88 03 05; 17 rue Traverse; ⏰Mon-Sat) Has a free internet terminal for bar customers.

Tourist office (📞02 98 62 14 94; www.tourisme .morlaix.fr; place des Otages; ⏰10am-2.30pm & 2-7pm Mon-Sat, 10am-12.30pm Sun). A few steps southwest below the railway viaduct. From the train station, take rue de Léon south, then turn left and descend the stairs of rue Courte.

ℹ Getting There & Away

Morlaix has frequent train services:
Brest €10, 45 minutes
Paris Montparnasse €66, four hours
Roscoff €5.50, 30 minutes

Brest

POP 146,500

A major port and military base that doesn't feel as remote from the rest of the country as it looks on the map, Brest is big, bold and dynamic, capping the department of Finistère and looking towards the Atlantic. Destroyed by Allied air attacks during WWII, modern Brest is a postwar creation, which, while enjoying its scenic moments, has none of the Breton charm of the nearby port of Roscoff. You'll see French sailors' blue uniforms with gold epaulettes throughout the town, as well as plenty of students from Brest's university, though most people come here on the way through to the sea-swept Île d'Ouessant.

◉ Sights & Activities

Océanopolis AQUARIUM
(📞02 98 34 40 40; www.oceanopolis.com; port de Plaisance; adult/child €16.50/11; ⏰9am-6pm)

With 50 tanks in three thematic pavilions – polar, tropical and temperate – the gleaming modern aquarium is great, especially on (not uncommon) rainy days. Tip: buying your ticket online for the same price allows you to skip the queues and head straight in to view the kelp forests, seals, crabs, anemones, penguins, sharks and more. It's about 3km east of the city centre; take bus 15 from place de la Liberté.

Musée de la Marine MARITIME MUSEUM
(Naval Museum; 📞02 98 22 12 39; www.musee -marine.fr; adult/child €5.50/free; ⏰10am-6.30pm, closed Tue mid-Sep–Mar) Learn about Brest's maritime military history at this excellent museum, housed within the fortified 13th-century Château de Brest, which was built to defend the harbour on the River Penfeld. Following the 1532 union of Brittany and France, both the castle and its harbour became a royal fortress. From its ramparts there are striking views of the harbour and the naval base. Museum tickets cost €4 and are available from the town's tourist office.

FREE Tour Tanguy TOWER
(📞02 98 00 88 60; place Pierre Péron; ⏰10am-noon & 2-7pm, closed Mon, Tue & Fri Oct-May) A sobering reminder of what Brest looked like on the eve of WWII can be seen at this 14th-century tower. Other exhibits on the town's history include the documented visit of three Siamese ambassadors in 1686, who presented gifts to the court of Louis XIV; rue de Siam was renamed in their honour.

La Société Maritime Azenor CRUISES
(📞02 98 41 46 23; www.azenor.fr, in French; adult/ child €15.50/11; ⏰Apr-Sep) This well-regarded cruise operator offers 1½-hour cruises around the harbour and the naval base two or three times daily from both the Port de Commerce (which is near the castle) and the Port de Plaisance (which is opposite Océanopolis).

✯ Festivals & Events

Les Jeudis du Port MUSIC FESTIVAL
(Harbour Thursdays; ⏰7.30pm-midnight Thu mid-Jul–late Aug) Plan to be in Brest on a Thursday night during summer when Les Jeudis du Port fill the port with live rock, reggae and world music, as well as street performances and children's events.

Sleeping

TOP CHOICE Hôtel St Louis BOUTIQUE HOTEL €
(☑02 98 44 23 91; www.brest-hotel.com, in French; 6 rue Algésiras; d €30-55; ☎) This sassy hotel has a 'boutique-on-a-budget' feel. The spartan rooms are livened by eccentric flourishes such as pop art prints, brightly painted walls and retro bathrooms tucked away within cupboards. Simple and cheap, but remarkably cool – reserve ahead.

Hôtel de la Rade HOTEL €
(☑02 98 44 47 76; www.hoteldelarade.com; 6 rue de Siam; s €52-62, d €51-66; ☎) Right in the centre of town, this good-value place has small but smart and stylishly simple rooms with tiny, yet functional bathrooms. Some rooms have good views onto the harbour.

Hôtel Continental HOTEL €€
(☑02 98 80 50 40; www.oceaniahotels.com; rue Émile Zola; s €120-150, d €170-190; ❖☎) With sleek, streamlined rooms and crisp white bathrooms finished off with tiled friezes, the classy Continental has a much more lavish, art deco–styled interior than its plain exterior lets on. All 73 soundproofed rooms are equipped with mod cons including satellite flatscreen TV. Considerable reductions on room rates on weekends.

Auberge de Jeunesse Éthic Étapes HOSTEL €
(☑02 98 41 90 41; brest.aj.cis@wanadoo.fr; rue de Kerbriant; dm incl sheets & breakfast €17.50; ☎) Near Océanopolis and a stone's throw from the artificial beach at Moulin Blanc, this bright, modern 118-bed hostel has bike storage and good wheelchair access. To stay here you'll need to be a member of Hostelling International – membership can be bought on arrival (under/over 26 €11/17). Take bus 15 from the train station, or the more regular bus 3 from place de la Liberté to the Port de Plaisance.

Camping du Goulet CAMPGROUND €
(☑02 98 45 86 84; www.campingdugoulet.com, in French; Ste-Anne du Portzic; sites €13-23; ☎☳) This huge, hilly campground is in Ste-Anne du Portzic, 6km southwest of Brest and 400m from the sea. Take bus 28 from rue Georges Clemenceau (near the tourist office) to the Le Cosquer stop.

Eating

Ma Petite Folie SEAFOOD €€
(☑02 98 42 44 42; Port de Plaisance; menus €20-40; ☺Mon-Sat) Aboard an old green-and-white lobster-fishing boat strung with buoys and forever beached at Moulin Blanc, this character-filled restaurant has exceptional crab, prawns and fresh fish in butter sauce, ideally finished off with pear tart for dessert and washed down with crisp white wine.

St Ex MODERN FRENCH €
(☑02 98 46 33 53; 4 rue de Siam; menus €10-40) This rightly popular crêpe specialist is not your run-of-the-mill café, but a smart and buzzing restaurant where the menu extends to more elaborate seafood and meat dishes. That said, the crêpes here are some of the best we have tasted.

Self-catering

Head to **Les Halles St-Louis** (☺9am-1pm & 4-7pm Mon-Sat, 9am-1pm Sun), Brest's covered market, for self-catering supplies. An **open-air market** takes place out front on Sunday mornings.

ℹ Information

Post office (place Général Leclerc)
Tourist office (☑02 98 44 24 96; www.brest -metropole-tourisme.fr; place de la Liberté; ☺9.30am-7pm Mon-Sat & 10am-noon Sun)

ℹ Getting There & Away

AIR Brest's newly expanded **airport** (www. brest.aeroport.fr) has regular Ryanair flights to/ from London (Luton), Dublin and Marseille; Flybe flights to/from Birmingham, Manchester and Southampton; and Air France flights to Paris, Lyon and Nice.

BOAT Ferries to Île d'Ouessant leave from the Port de Commerce. In summer, **Azénor** (☑02 98 41 46 23; www.azenor.com, in French) connects Brest with Camaret-sur-Mer on the Crozon Peninsula (one way adult/child €9/7, one hour, twice daily except Saturday during July and August).

BUS Brest's **bus station** (☑02 98 44 46 73) is beside the train station.

Le Conquet €2, 45 minutes, six daily

Roscoff €2, 1½ hours, four daily

CAR & MOTORCYCLE Hire companies:

ADA (☑02 98 44 44 88; 9 av Georges Clemenceau)

Europcar (☑02 98 44 66 88; rue Voltaire)

TRAIN For Roscoff, change trains at Morlaix.

Morlaix €10, 45 minutes

Paris Montparnasse from €69, 4½ hours, around 15 daily

Quimper €15.50, 1¼ hours

Rennes €32, two hours

❶ Getting Around

BUS Shuttle buses (one way €4.60) connect the bus station and airport approximately hourly; you can buy tickets on the bus. The local bus network **Bibus** (📞02 98 80 30 30) sells tickets good for two hours for €1.25 and day passes for €3.40. There's an information kiosk on place de la Liberté.

TAXI Call 📞02 98 80 18 01 or 📞02 98 80 68 06. A taxi for the 10km airport trip costs around €15.

Île d'Ouessant

POP 878

Although it's frequented by summer visitors by the ferryload, free-roaming little black sheep and traditional houses give an ends-of-the-earth feel to the windswept Île d'Ouessant (Enez Eusa in Breton, meaning 'Island of Terror'; Ushant in English) – best experienced by hiking its 45km craggy coastal path.

❂ Sights & Activities

Musée des Phares et des Balises

LIGHTHOUSE MUSEUM

(Lighthouse & Beacon Museum; 📞02 98 48 80 70; adult/child €4.30/3; ⏱11am-6pm) The black-and-white-striped Phare de Créac'h is the world's most powerful lighthouse. Beaming two white flashes every 10 seconds and visible for over 50km, it serves as a beacon for over 50,000 ships entering the Channel each year. Beneath is the island's main museum, which tells the story of these vital navigation aids; more interesting is the section on shipwrecks and underwater archaeology.

Écomusée d'Ouessant ECOMUSEUM

(📞02 98 48 86 37; Maison du Niou; adult/child €3.50/2.40; ⏱10.30am-6.30pm, closed Mon Oct-Mar) Two typical local houses make up this small 'ecomuseum'. One re-creates a traditional homestead, furnished like a ship's cabin, with furniture fashioned from driftwood and painted in bright colours to mask its imperfections; the other explores the island's history and customs. A combined ticket for both the lighthouse museum and the ecomuseum cost costs €7/4.50 for an adult/child. Check ahead as schedules are liable to change.

🛏 Sleeping & Eating

Hôtel Roc'h Ar Mor TRADITIONAL HOTEL €

(📞02 98 48 80 19; pagesperso-orange.fr/rocharmor; Lampaul; r €55-87; ⏱mid-Feb–mid-Nov; 🖥) In a superb location next to the Baie de Lampaul, this appealing 15-room hotel with sunlit blue-and-white rooms and good wheelchair access also boasts a good restaurant (half-board is recommended here), with a terrace overlooking the ocean. Thanks to the hotel's very own smokehouse, excellent smoked fish and meats regularly appear on the imaginative evening menu.

Auberge de Jeunesse HOSTEL €

(📞02 98 48 84 53; auberge-ouessant.com; La Croix-Rouge, Lampaul; dm incl breakfast €17.50; ⏱closed Dec-Jan) This friendly hostel, on the hill above Lampaul, has two- to six-person rooms. It's popular with school and walking groups; reservations are essential. Under 26s and students stay for €16.

Camping Municipal CAMPGROUND €

(📞02 98 48 84 65; fax 02 98 48 83 99; Stang Ar Glan, Lampaul; per person €3.05, plus per tent €3.05; ⏱Apr-Sep) About 500m east of Lampaul, this sprawling 100-pitch place looks more like a football field than a campground.

Crêperie Ti A Dreuz CRÊPERIE €

(📞02 98 48 83 01; Lampaul; crêpes around €3-9; ⏱Sat-Thu Easter-Sep) You could be forgiven for thinking you'd been at sea too long, or knocked back too much Breton cider, but 'the slanting house' is so-named for its wonky walls. This quaint island crêperie serves delicious galettes: try the *ouessantine,* with creamy potato, cheese and sausage.

Ty Korn SEAFOOD €€

(📞02 98 48 87 33; Lampaul; lunch/dinner menus €15/31; ⏱closed Sun & Mon) The ground floor of this hyperfriendly place is a bar, serving Breton black-wheat beers (made from the same *blé noire* as Breton galettes); upstairs there's an excellent restaurant where seafood is a speciality. Opening hours can vary, though the bar stays open until 1am.

ÎLE D'OUESSANT BEACHES

Plage de Corz, 600m south of Lampaul, is the island's best beach. Other good spots to stretch out are Plage du Prat, Plage de Yuzin and Plage Ar Lan. All are easily accessible by bike from Lampaul or Port du Stiff.

ℹ Information

Tourist office (☎02 98 48 85 83; www.ot
-ouessant.fr; place de l'Église, Lampaul;
☉9am-1pm & 1.30-7pm Mon-Sat, 9.30am-1pm
Sun) Sells walking brochures and can hook you
up with operators offering horse riding, sailing
and other activities.

ℹ Getting There & Away

AIR Finist'air (☎02 98 84 64 87; www.finistair.
fr) flies from Brest's airport to Ouessant in a
mere 15 minutes. There are two flights daily
(one way adult/child under 13yr €65/38, return
adult/child under 13yr €93/57).

BOAT Ferries depart from Brest and the tiny
town (and Brittany's most westerly point) of Le
Conquet (Konk Leon in Breton). Buses operated
by **Les Cars St-Mathieu** (☎02 98 89 12 02)
link Brest with Le Conquet (€2, 45 minutes, six
daily). In high summer it's a good idea to reserve
at least two days in advance and to check in
30 minutes before departure. Transporting a
bicycle costs €14.

Penn Ar Bed (☎02 98 80 80 80; www.penn
arbed.fr) sails from the Port de Commerce in
Brest (adult/child return €30/18.50, 2½ hours)
and from Le Conquet (€30/18.50, 1½ hours).
Boats run between each port and the island two
to five times daily from May to September and
once daily between October and April. There are
great savings to be made if you travel to Ouessant out of season – the return fare from both
Brest and Le Conquet is just €18 from November
to May (weekdays only).

ℹ Getting Around

BICYCLE Bike-hire operators have kiosks at the
Port du Stiff ferry terminal and compounds just
up the hill, as well as outlets in Lampaul. The going rate for town/mountain bikes is €10/14. You
can save by booking and prepaying for a mountain bike (€10) at the Brest tourist office. Cycling
on the coastal footpath is forbidden – the fragile
turf is strictly reserved for walkers.

MINIBUS Islander-run minibus services such
as **Ouessant Voyage** (☎06 07 90 07 43)
meet the ferry at Port du Stiff and will shuttle
you to Lampaul or your accommodation for a
flat fare of €2 (to guarantee a seat in July and
August, book ahead at the island tourist office
or at the tourist office in Brest). For the return
journey, the pick-up point is the car park beside
Lampaul's church. Minibus owners also offer
two-hour guided tours (€15 per person) of the
island, in French.

Presqu'île de Crozon

The anchor-shaped Crozon Peninsula
is part of the Parc Naturel Régional

d'Armorique, and one of the most scenic spots in Brittany. The partly forested
peninsula is criss-crossed by some 145km
of signed walking trails and excellent biking terrain, with crêperies in traditional
stone buildings tucked in and around the
hinterland.

MÉNEZ-HOM

To feel Brittany's wind beneath your wings,
the Club Celtic de Vol Libre (☎02 98 81
50 27; www.vol-libre-menez-hom.com, in French;
hang-gliding & paragliding from €70) offers
three-hour hang-gliding and paragliding
sessions off the rounded, 330m-high, heath-
er- and grass-clad hump of Ménez-Hom.
Situated at the peninsula's eastern end, a
surfaced road leads to the top of the summit, which has sublime views over the Baie
de Douarnenez.

LANDÉVENNEC
POP 358

To the north of Ménez-Hom, the River Aulne
flows into the Rade de Brest beside the pretty village of Landévennec, home to the ruined Benedictine Abbaye St-Guenolé. The
abbey museum (☎02 98 27 35 90; adult/child
€4/3; ☉10am-7pm, closed Sat May-Jun & late
Sep) records the history of the settlement,
founded by St Guenolé in 485 and the oldest Christian site in Brittany. Nearby, a new
abbey is home to a contemporary community of monks, who run a little shop selling
homemade fruit jellies.

ARGOL
POP 833

Argol is a quaint village in its own right,
but its main draw is the Musée du Cidre
du Bretagne (Breton Cider Museum; ☎02 98
17 21 87; www.musee-cidre-bretagne.com; adult/
child €5/free; ☉2-7pm Apr-Sep). This former
dairy's old stone buildings have been transformed into a working *cidrerie* producing
over 300,000 bottles annually. A visit (allow around an hour, including a French-
language but very visual film) takes you
through the history of cider in Brittany and
present-day production. And, of course, you
get to taste it too. In July and August, one
of the barns is used as a crêperie (crêpes
€4.50-7.50; ☉noon-10pm).

CROZON & MORGAT
POP 7950

The area's largest town, Crozon, is the engine room for the peninsula. On the water
2km south, Morgat was built in the 1930s

ECOBUZZ

Tucked away on the road to Crozon, 8km west of Le Faou, Ferme Apicole de Terenez (☎02 98 81 06 90; www.ferme-apicole-de-terenez.com; Rosnoën; s incl breakfast €30-39, d €37-43) is abuzz with live bees that you can view in its honey museum (admission free; ☺9am-7pm). Depending on the season, you might also see *apiculteurs* (beekeepers) Irène and Stéphane Brindeau using environmentally friendly cold-extraction methods to extract the all-natural honey from giant combs in the workshop here, produced with the pollen of flowers and trees. You can buy honey, nougat and other homemade honey products like *hydromel* (*chouchen* in Breton; a fermented alcoholic drink made from honey and water).

But this little haven is more than just a hive of honeymaking. The grounds extend to a private forest and even a private island (accessible by foot at low tide; you can walk around it in about 30 minutes), which guests can explore while staying in one of the farm's six timber-lined *chambre d'hôte* rooms. Rates include the sweetest of breakfasts, with the farm's honey baked into cakes, biscuits and more. The Brindeau family (who describe their work here as 'not a job, a passion') can also help organise kayak rental to paddle around the property and beyond. You can cook up a feast on the barbecue, or head just 200m down the road to the postcard-perfect waterfront restaurant L'Ermitage (☎02 98 81 93 61; menus €17-37; ☺lunch & dinner Wed-Sun, lunch Tue, closed Mar), serving fish caught right outside the door.

by the Peugeot brothers (of motor-vehicle fame) as a summer resort.

🏃 Activities

Coastal Hike WALK

Beyond the marina at the southern end of Morgat's fine sandy beach, the coastal path offers an excellent 13km hike (part of the GR34) along the sea cliffs to Cap de la Chèvre.

Boat Tours BOAT TOURS

Morgat-based companies Vedettes Rosmeur (☎06 85 95 55 49; www.rosmeur.fr) and Vedettes Sirènes (☎02 98 26 20 10) operate 45-minute boat trips to the colourful sea caves along the coast. Tours (adult/child €11/8) depart from Morgat harbour several times daily from April to September.

🎉 Festivals & Events

Every Tuesday during July and August, free concerts take place on place d'Ys.

Festival du Bout du Monde MUSIC FESTIVAL

(Festival of the End of the World; www.festivalduboutdumonde.com, in French) The place d'Ys area hosts the Festival du Bout du Monde festival in mid-August, featuring world music.

🛏 Sleeping & Eating

Morgat's seafront and place d'Ys are good spots to trawl for seafood restaurants.

Hôtel de la Baie FAMILY HOTEL €

(☎02 98 27 07 51; hotel.delabaie@presquile-crozon.com; 46 bd de la Plage, Morgat; s from €27, d €45-72; 🕸📶) One of the *very* few places to remain open year-round, this simple, friendly, family-run spot on Morgat's promenade has views over the ocean and is one of the best deals around – even better value if you take a room with shower only.

Camping Les Pieds Dans l'Eau CAMPGROUND €

(☎02 98 27 62 43; http://lespiedsdansleau.free.fr; St-Fiacre; per person/tent/car from €4/4/2.30; ☺mid-Jun–mid-Sep) 'Camping feet in the water' (almost literally, at high tide) is one of 16 campgrounds along the peninsula.

Saveurs et Marées SEAFOOD €

(☎02 98 26 23 18; 52 bd Plage, Morgat; menus €14-45; ☺closed Feb) Our pick of Morgat's clutch of restaurants is this lemon-yellow cottage overlooking the sea for its breezy dining room, sunny terrace and consistently good, locally caught seafood (including succulent lobster).

ℹ Information

Crozon tourist office (☎02 98 27 07 92; www.crozon.com, in French; bd Pralognan; ☺9.15am-12.30pm & 2-7pm Mon-Sat, 10am-noon Sun) Housed in the former railway station, on the main road to Camaret.

Morgat tourist office (☎02 98 27 29 49; www.officedetourisme-crozon-morgat.fr;

9.15am-12.30pm & 2-7pm Mon-Sat, 10am-noon Sun) Overlooks the promenade at the corner of bd de la Plage and doubles as the town's post office.

CAMARET-SUR-MER
POP 2600

At the western extremity of the Crozon Peninsula, Camaret (unusually in French, the final 't' is pronounced) is a classic fishing village – or at least it was until early last century, when it was France's then-biggest crayfish port. Abandoned fishing-boat carcasses now decay in its harbour, but it remains an enchanting place that lures artists. There's an ever-increasing number of galleries dotted around town, particularly along rue de la Marne and around place St-Thomas, one block north of the waterfront.

⊙ Sights

Chapelle Notre-Dame-de-Rocamadour
CHURCH

(⊙school holidays only) Its timber roof like an inverted ship's hull, the Chapelle Notre-Dame-de-Rocamadour is dedicated to the sailors of Camaret, who have adorned it with votive offerings of oars, lifebuoys and model ships.

Pointe de Pen-Hir
MEMORIALS

Three kilometres south of Camaret, this is a spectacular headland bounded by steep, sheer sea cliffs, with two WWII memorials.

🛏 Sleeping & Eating

Hôtel Vauban
HOTEL €

(☑02 98 27 91 36; 4 quai du Styvel; d €41-51; ⊙Feb-Nov) Its airy rooms are contemporary but the Vauban's old-fashioned hospitality extends to its large rear garden, with a barbecue to grill your own fish and a piano to play. Its bar remains a favourite with Camaret's old-timers too.

Crêperie Rocamadour
CRÊPERIE €

(☑02 98 27 93 17; quai Kléber; mains €10-14; ⊙closed Mon & Tue Sep-Jun) Close to the tourist office, this beamed-ceilinged place turns out carefully prepared galettes as well as mains such as citrus-infused salmon. Finish off with a flaming flambéed crêpe or one smothered in melted chocolate.

Del Mare
SEAFOOD €

(☑02 98 27 97 22; 16 quai Gustave Toudouze; menus €13.50-26.50; ⊙closed Tue & Wed early Apr-Jun & Sep–mid-Nov) Seafood is the order of the day at this marine-styled place on the main stretch of waterfront, with a clutch of tables on its little timber terrace. Service is prompt and friendly.

ℹ Information

Tourist office (☑02 98 27 93 60; www.camaret-sur-mer.com, in French; 15 quai Kléber; ⊙9.15am-noon & 2-6pm, closed Sun Sep-Jun) On the waterfront.

ℹ Getting There & Around

BICYCLE To rent a bike, contact **Point Bleu** (☑02 98 27 09 04; quai Kador, Morgat) or, in summer, the open-air stall in front of Morgat's tourist office. The daily rate is €10.

BOAT Azénor (☑02 98 41 46 23; www.azenor.com, in French) runs seasonal ferries between Brest and the Presqu'île de Crozon.

From mid-April to mid-September, **Penn Ar Bed** (☑02 98 80 80 80; www.pennarbed.fr) sails between Camaret and Île d'Ouessant (adult/child return from €18/15.50 September to June, €30/17 July to August).

BUS Five buses daily run from Quimper to Crozon (€2, 1¼ hours), continuing to Camaret (€2), and up to four go from Camaret and Crozon to Brest (€2, 1¼ hours, daily). Buses also run between Morgat, Crozon and Camaret several times daily (€2, 10 minutes).

Quimper
POP 67,250

Small enough to feel like a village, with its slanted half-timbered houses and narrow cobbled streets, and large enough to buzz as the troubadour of Breton culture and arts, Quimper (pronounced 'kam-pair') is Finistère's thriving capital. Derived from the Breton word *kemper,* meaning 'confluence', Quimper sits at the juncture of the small Rivers Odet and Steïr, criss-crossed by footbridges with cascading flowers. Despite being one of Brittany's most charming towns, it is nevertheless often overlooked by visitors.

⊙ Sights & Activities

Cathedral St-Corentin
CATHEDRAL

(place St-Corentin; ⊙9.30am-noon & 1.30-6.30pm) At the centre of the city stands this impressive cathedral, the distinctive kink built into its soaring light-filled interior said by some to symbolise Christ's head inclined on one shoulder as he was dying on the cross. Begun in 1239, the cathedral wasn't completed until the 1850s, with the seamless addition of its dramatic twin spires. Between them, high on the west facade, is an equestrian statue of King Gradlon, the city's mythical 5th-century founder.

BRITTANY QUIMPER

Musée des Beaux-Arts ART MUSEUM

(☎02 98 95 45 20; 40 place St-Corentin; adult/
child €4.50/2.50; ☉10am-7pm) The ground-
floor halls are home to some fairly morbid
16th- to 20th-century European paintings,
but things lighten up on the upper levels of
the town's main art museum. A room dedicated to Quimper-born poet Max Jacob includes sketches by Picasso.

Musée Départemental Breton

BRETON MUSEUM

(☎02 98 95 21 60; 1 rue du Roi Gradlon; adult/
child €4/free; ☉9am-6pm) Recessed behind
a magnificent stone courtyard beside the
cathedral, this museum is housed in the
former bishop's palace. Superb exhibits
showcase Breton history, furniture, costumes, crafts and archaeology. Adjoining
the museum is the Jardin de l'Évêché
(Bishop's Palace Garden; admission free; ☉9am-
5pm or 6pm).

For even more serenity, pop into the
hidden, flower-filled Jardin de la Retraite
(☉9am-7.15pm), secluded behind high walls.

Following the switchback path just
east of the tourist office up the 72m-high
Mont Frugy rewards with captivating city
views.

⚑ Tours

Vedettes de l'Odet BOAT TOURS

(☎08 25 80 08 01, 02 98 57 00 58) From June
to September, Vedettes de l'Odet runs boat
trips (adult/child €25/15, 1¼ hours) from
Quimper along the serene Odet estuary to
Bénodet, departing from quai Neuf.

✷ Festivals & Events

Festival de Cornouaille CELTIC FESTIVAL

(www.festival-cornouaille.com, in French) A
celebration of traditional Celtic music,
costumes and culture takes place between the third Saturday and fourth
Sunday of July. After the traditional

Quimper

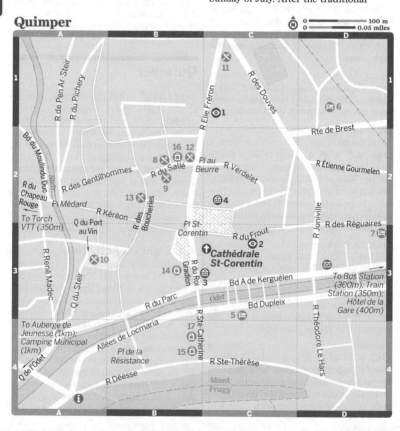

festival, classical-music concerts are held at different venues around town.

🛌 Sleeping

Unfortunately, Quimper has a chronic shortage of inexpensive accommodation, and none in the old city.

Hôtel Gradlon   TRADITIONAL HOTEL €€
(🖉02 98 95 04 39; www.hotel-gradlon.com; 30 rue de Brest; s €101-119, d €109-135; ⊘closed mid-Dec–mid-Jan; 🛜) This place may not look like much from the street, but its rather bland and modern facade belies a charming country manor interior. The smallish but well-furnished rooms all have plenty of character and individual touches. It's a short walk from the old town and secure parking is available.

Hôtel Kregenn   DESIGN HOTEL €€
(🖉02 98 95 08 70; www.hotel-kregenn.fr; 13 rue des Réguaires; s €105, d from €120, ste €150; 🌂🛜) A Zen timber-decked courtyard and a guest lounge with outsized mirrors and white leather sofas give you the initial impression that Quimper's coolest hotel is

contemporary in style, but the plush rooms (in pistachio green, ocean blue or chocolate) evoke a traditional feel, as does the warm-hearted welcome. Higher-priced rooms have air-con; two rooms are equipped for wheelchairs and free internet access by cable is available in each room.

TOP CHOICE Hôtel Manoir des Indes   DESIGN HOTEL €€
(🖉02 98 55 48 40; www.manoir-hoteldesindes. com; 1 Allée de Prad ar C'hras; s €105-150, d €150-170, ste €180-260; 🛜🌂) This stunning hotel conversion just west of Quimper is a hugely impressive labour of love for a couple who have brought an old manor house back to life as a hotel with Indian decor, an homage to the original owner, one René Madec, who travelled the world before retiring here. The 10 rooms and four suites are all exquisitely furnished in a minimal and modern style, with Asian objets d'art and lots of exposed wood. The hotel is set within its own lovely 2-hectare grounds and is just a short drive from the centre of Quimper.

Hôtel de la Gare   HOTEL €
(🖉02 98 90 00 81; www.hoteldelagarequimper. com; 17 av de la Gare; s/d €49/54; 🛜) This cheap and friendly place opposite the station is the best deal in town. The rooms are simple (those in the slightly older rooms in the annexe are even cheaper) and there's a very pleasant café feel to the lobby, plus free parking and a small courtyard garden to relax in.

Hôtel Dupleix   HOTEL €
(🖉02 98 90 53 35; www.hotel-dupleix.com; 34 bd Dupleix; s €66-112, d €79-112; ⊘closed Christmas period; 🛜) Rather overpriced given its unrefurbished '70s style and ugly business complex building, the Dupleix is nevertheless enviably located right on the river and has free secure parking, which can be a godsend in Quimper's crowded streets.

Camping Municipal   CAMPGROUND €
(🖉02 98 98 89 24; av des Oiseaux; sites from €4.60; ⊘tents Apr-Sep, campervans year-round) This wooded park is 1km west of the old city and 3km from the train station. From quai de l'Odet, follow rue Pont l'Abbé northwestwards and continue straight ahead where it veers left. Alternatively, take bus 1 from the train station to the Chaptal stop.

Auberge de Jeunesse   HOSTEL €
(🖉02 98 64 97 97; www.fuaj.org/quimper; 6 av des Oiseaux; camping €6, dm incl breakfast from €13, sheets €3; ⊘Apr-Sep) Quimper's seasonal youth hostel has self-catering facilities.

✗ Eating & Drinking

As a bastion of Breton culture, Quimper has some exceptional crêperies. Rue du Frout near the cathedral has a couple of small pubs that attract a Breton-speaking clientele.

TOP CHOICE **Le Cosy Restaurant** BRETON CUISINE €
(☎02 98 95 23 65; 2 rue du Sallé; mains €10-14.50; ⊙lunch Tue-Sat, dinner Wed, Fri & Sat) *Pas de crêpes!* (No crêpes!) the blackboard menu on the street proclaims. Inside, make your way through the *épicerie* (specialist grocer) crammed with locally canned sardines, ciders and other Breton produce and up the narrow staircase to the eclectic, artistic dining room, where you can tuck in to specialities like gratins and *tartines* (open sandwiches) made from market ingredients. It's important to reserve for evening dining, as this place is fearfully popular.

L'Ambroisie GASTRONOMIC €€
(☎02 98 95 00 02; www.ambroisie-quimper.com; 49 rue Elie Fréron; menus €22-63; ⊙lunch & dinner Tue-Sat, lunch Sun) Quimper's most celebrated gastronomic restaurant is sumptuously decorated with contemporary art and elegant china on snow-white tablecloths. Regional produce provided by chef Gilbert Guyon's friends is used in the creation of house specials like sole with new potatoes and caramelised onions. Cooking classes are available by request.

Le Petit Gaveau BISTRO €
(☎02 98 64 29 86; 16 rue des Boucheries; mains €8-15 ⊙lunch Mon-Sat, dinner Wed-Sat) This charming find is a sleek conversion of an old stone-walled house that plays host to simple yet excellent food (the gourmet burger is superb), and is a world away from the fussy gastronomy and crêpes you'll find elsewhere in town. There's live jazz Thursday to Saturday (€3 supplement per diner). It's worth reserving in the evenings.

Crêperie la Krampouzerie CRÊPERIE €
(9 rue du Sallé; galettes €2-7; ⊙closed Mon and lunch Sun) In an atmospheric space with blue-and-white-tiled wooden tables, crêpes and galettes are made from organic flours and regional ingredients like *algues d'Ouessant* (seaweed from the Île d'Ouessant), Roscoff onions and homemade ginger caramel. Tables fill the square outside in fine weather, giving it a street-party atmosphere.

Crêperie du Sucré-Salé CRÊPERIE €
(6 rue du Sallé; galettes €1.90-8; ⊙Tue-Sat) For a quarter of a century, locals have crowded into this crêperie decorated with lace curtains, wooden dressers and painted plates on the walls. Breton specialities include *saucisse fumée* (smoked sausage) and the house speciality *forestière*, made with mushrooms, smoked lard (fatty bacon) and cheese.

Self-Catering

The covered market **Halles St-François** in the old town has a slew of salad and sandwich options. One of the best, with a clutch of outdoor terrace tables, is **Ti Cass' de'Halles** (3 Halles St-François; dishes from €3.30; ⊙10am-3pm Mon-Thu, 10am-7pm Fri & Sat).

☆ Entertainment

From mid-June to mid-September traditional Breton music and dance takes place in the **Jardin de l'Évêché** (admission €5; ⊙9pm Thu).

Check posters and leaflets pasted up around town or ask the tourist office for times and venues of a local *fest-noz* (night festival). On average there's one in or near Quimper every couple of weeks.

🔒 Shopping

François Le Villec POTTERY
(4 rue du Roi Gradlon) Several shops in the old town sell Quimper's traditional faience pottery, including this one.

Keltia Musique MUSIC & BOOKS
(1 place au Beurre) Breton and Celtic music and art are available at Keltia Musique, which carries an excellent range of books and CDs.

Ar Bed Keltiek BOOKS
(Celtic World; 2 rue du Roi Gradlon) A great range of books on everything Breton.

Ty Blurt Records MUSIC
(7 rue Ste-Catherine; ⊙2-7pm Mon-Sat) For a total change of tune, flip through '70s pop, French punk and rock vinyl.

Galerie Ste-Catherine ART
(13 rue Ste-Catherine; ⊙11am-12.30pm & 2.30-7pm Tue-Sat) A few doors up from Ty Blurt Records, you can check out traditional and contemporary art on sale here.

ℹ Information

Main post office (bd Amiral de Kerguélen)

Mediathèque des Ursulines (10 rue de Falkirk; ⊙12.30-7pm Tue-Sat, 2-5pm Sun) One hour's daily free use of the internet is available to all comers at this swanky new media centre.

Tourist office (☑02 98 53 04 05; www.quimper-tourisme.com; place de la Résistance; ◷9.30am-12.30pm & 1.30-6.30pm) Runs weekly 1½-hour guided city tours in English (€5.20) in July and August, and sells the Pass' Quimper (€10) whereby two people can access four attractions or tours of their choosing (from a list of participating organisations).

ℹ Getting There & Away

BUS CAT/Viaoo (www.viaoo29.fr) has regular buses to Brest (€6.50, 1¼ hours). **Le Coeur** (☑02 98 54 40 15) runs buses to Concarneau (€2, 45 minutes, seven to 10 daily); three buses that depart daily continue to Quimperlé (€2, 1½ hours).

CAR Rental agencies have offices outside the train station:

ADA (☑02 98 52 10 65)

Avis (☑02 98 90 31 34)

Europcar (☑02 98 90 00 68)

TRAIN Frequent services:

Brest €15.50, 1¼ hours, up to 10 daily

Paris Montparnasse €75, 4¾ hours, hourly

Rennes €32, 2½ hours, hourly

Vannes €18, 1½ hours, hourly

ℹ Getting Around

BICYCLE Torch VTT (☑02 98 53 84 41; www.torchvttquimper.com; 58 rue de la Providence) rents out mountain bikes for €18 per day. The friendly owner is a fount of information about local cycle routes.

BUS QUB (www.qub.fr; 2 quai de l'Odet), the Quimper bus network, has an information office opposite the tourist office; a single/day ticket costs €1/3.

TAXI Call ☑02 98 90 21 21.

Concarneau

POP 21,000

The sheltered harbour of Concarneau (Konk-Kerne in Breton), 24km southeast of Quimper, radiates out from its trawler port, which brings in close to 200,000 tonnes of *thon* (tuna) from the Indian Ocean and off the African coast (the adjacent Atlantic's too cold). Jutting out into the port, the old town, Ville Close, is circled by medieval walls.

◉ Sights

The walled town, fortified in the 14th century and modified by Vauban two centuries

later, huddles on a small island linked to place Jean Jaurès by a footbridge.

Maison du Patrimoine   CITY MUSEUM
(☑02 98 60 76 06; admission €1) Between 15 June and 15 September, the walled town can also be accessed through this old house, which has exhibits on the town's history – ask for an English-language brochure. Once you're within the walls, rue Vauban and place St-Guénolé outside are enchanting for their old stone houses converted into shops, restaurants and galleries.

Musée de la Pêche   MARITIME MUSEUM
(Fisheries Museum; ☑02 98 97 10 20; www.musee delapeche.eu; 3 rue Vauban; adult/child €6/4; ◷9.30am-8pm, closed Jan) Concarneau's seafaring traditions, offshore fishing trawlers, model ships and fishing exhibits feature at the ever-popular Musée de la Pêche, in the middle of the walled town.

Marinarium   AQUARIUM
(☑02 98 50 81 64; www.mnhn.fr/concarneau; place de la Croix; adult/child €5/3; ◷10am-noon & 2-6pm) Founded in 1859, the Concarneau Marinarium is the world's oldest institute of marine biology. Alongside its 10 aquariums are exhibits on oceanography and marine flora and fauna.

Château de Keriolet   CHÂTEAU
(☑02 98 97 36 50; www.chateaudekeriolet.com; adult/child €5/3; ◷10.30am-1pm & 2-6pm Sun-Fri, 10.30am-1pm Sat Jun-Sep, by reservation Easter-May) This impressive building is an exquisite example of 19th-century architecture. Its intriguing Russian connections are revealed during a guided tour. The castle is a well-signed five-minute drive from town (turn right just before the large Leclerc supermarket).

⚞ Activities

Walking & Cycling   WALKING & CYCLING
The tourist office sells two excellent guides: *Balades au Pays des Portes de Cornouaille* (€2.50; in French), describing 18 walks around Concarneau; and *VTT de Cornouaille* (€3.50), outlining 39 cycling circuits.

Vedettes Glenn   BOAT TRIPS
(☑02 98 97 10 31; www.vedettes-glenn.fr; 17 av du Dr Nicolas) In July and August four-hour river trips (adult/child €27/13, sailing 2.15pm Tuesday to Friday and Sunday) sail from Concarneau along the gorgeously scenic estuary of the River Odet. Boat trips also

Plage des Sables Blancs is on Baie de la Forêt, 1.5km northwest of the town centre; take bus 2, northbound, from the tourist office. For **Plage du Cabellou**, 5km south of town, take bus 2, southbound.

operate to the Îles de Glénan – a cluster of nine little islands about 20km south of Concarneau – starting at €26/13.

🛏 Sleeping

Hôtel des Halles
FAMILY HOTEL €

(✆02 98 97 11 41; www.hoteldeshalles.com; place de l'Hôtel de Ville; s €49-84, d €64-80; ☎🖶) A few steps from Ville Close, this 22-room hotel looks plain on the outside but its renovated rooms come in a rainbow of colour combinations like pistachio green and hot pink, with lavender trimmings throughout the public areas (even the lift doors). The all-organic breakfast (€9) includes homemade jams and bread straight from the oven. Broadband internet's free through cables in each room and the family owners are ultrahelpful.

Les Sables Blancs
BOUTIQUE HOTEL €€

(✆02 98 50 10 12; www.hotel-les-sables-blancs. com; place des Sables Blancs; s €115-160, d €130-195, ste €260-370; ☎) Right on the 'white sands' of the beach from which it takes its name, this ultrachic hotel has spacious rooms and an excellent restaurant, with good deals on half-board.

Auberge de Jeunesse Éthic Étapes
HOSTEL €

(✆02 98 97 03 47; www.ajconcarneau.com; quai de la Croix; dm incl breakfast €15.50) Fall asleep listening to the waves at this welcoming waterfront hostel next to the Marinarium. Extras include a wraparound barbecue terrace, a self-catering kitchen and pastries for breakfast.

Camping Moulin d'Aurore
CAMPGROUND €

(✆02 98 50 53 08; www.moulinaurore.com, in French; 49 rue de Trégunc; site & car for 2 adults €16; ☉Apr-Sep) Facilities at this campground 600m southeast of the harbour and a mere 50m from the sea include a bar/TV room and a laundry. Take bus 1 or 2 to Le Rouz stop from the tourist office or the ferry from Ville Close, then walk southeast along rue Mauduit Duplessis.

Eating

Cafés, pizzerias and crêperies line the waterfront, and there are more inside the walls of Ville Close.

La Porte au Vin
BRETON CUISINE €€

(✆02 98 97 38 11; 9 place St-Guénolé; menus €18-25; ☉Apr-Oct) Highly recommended, this place in the centre of the walled city is a lovely spot in fine weather, with a pretty patio terrace shaded by a red awning. It's consistently strong on traditional cooking (which in Concarneau means fish), as well as its excellent crêpes.

La Verrière
TAPAS €

(✆02 98 60 55 78; 3 rue des Halles; menus €10-25; ☉closed Mon in winter) Barbecued fish is the speciality of Concarneau's hippest hang-out, set around a covered courtyard garden. You can also drop by for tapas or just a drink and take advantage of the free wi-fi.

La Croisiere
SEAFOOD €€

(✆02 98 97 01 87; 11 av du Dr Nicolas; menus €22-34; ☉lunch Tue-Fri & Sun, dinner Tue-Sat, daily in summer) Just back from the boat-filled marina, the lively La Croisiere is a local fave for its seafood straight off the boat.

Self-Catering

There's a **covered market** (☉9am-noon Tue-Sun) on place Jean Jaurès and a busy open-air market in the same square on Monday and Friday mornings.

Enticing *biscuiteries* within Ville Close include **La Torchette** (✆02 98 60 46 87; 9 rue Vauban; ☉10.30am-6.30pm), with chocolate sculptures and Breton biscuits by the bucketful.

🛈 Information

Tourist office (✆02 98 97 01 44; www.tourisme concarneau.fr; quai d'Aiguillon; ☉9am-7pm)

🛈 Getting There & Away

BICYCLE Vedettes Glenn (✆02 98 97 10 31; www.vedettes-glenn.fr; 17 av du Docteur Nicolas; per day €10)

BOAT A small **passenger ferry** (fare €0.80; ☉8am-11pm Jul-Aug, 8am-8.30pm Mon-Sat, 9am-12.30pm & 2-6.30pm Sun Sep-Jun) links Ville Close with place Duquesne on the eastern side of the harbour.

BUS L'Été Évasion (✆02 98 56 82 82; www. autocars-ete.com) runs up to 10 buses daily between Quimper and Quimperlé, calling by Concarneau (€2 from Quimper).

TAXI Call ✆02 98 97 10 93 or ✆02 98 50 70 50.

MORBIHAN COAST

In the crook of Brittany's southern coastline, the Golfe du Morbihan (Morbihan Coast) is a haven of islands, oyster beds and bird life. But the area is perhaps best known for its proliferation of mystifying Celtic megaliths, which are strewn throughout most of the *département*.

Carnac

POP 4580

Predating Stonehenge by around 100 years, Carnac (Garnag in Breton) also tops it with sheer numbers, making this the world's greatest concentration of megalithic sites. There are no fewer than 3000 of these upright stones, most around thigh-high, erected between 5000 and 3500 BC.

Carnac, some 32km west of Vannes, comprises the old stone village Carnac-Ville and the seaside resort of Carnac-Plage, 1.5km south, bordered by the 2km-long sandy

beach. Its megaliths stretch 13km north from Carnac-Ville and east as far as the village of Locmariaquer.

🛏 Sleeping & Eating

Camping des Menhirs CAMPGROUND €
(☑02 97 52 94 67; www.lesmenhirs.com; 7 allée St-Michel, Carnac-Plage; adult/site/electricity €8/29/4; ⊙May-late Sep; 🛜⛵) Carnac and its surrounds have over 15 camping grounds, including this luxury complex of 100-sq-metre sites. Just 300m north of the beach, this is very much the glamorous end of camping with amenities such as a sauna and cocktail bar!

Auberge Le Ratelier B&B €
(☑02 97 52 05 04; www.le-ratelier.com; 4 Chemin du Douet, Carnac-Ville; d €52-62; ⊙Feb-Dec) This vine-clambered former farmhouse, now an eight-room inn with low ceilings and traditional timber furnishings, is in a quiet street one block southwest of place de l'Église. The cheapest rooms have showers only and shared toilets. Lunch and dinner

---

PONT-AVEN

Once the railway was pushed through in the 19th century, the tiny Breton village of Pont-Aven (population 3000), nestled in the 'valley of willows', was discovered by artists. American painters were among the first to uncover it, but things really took off when France's Paul Gaugin and Emile Bernard set up a colony here in the 1850s. Their work, and that of their disciples, morphed into a movement known today as the Pont-Aven School.

There is some debate in artistic and sociological circles as to whether these works folklorised the local Breton people, but they certainly captured the beauty of the little village and the surrounding countryside. For an insight into the town's place in art history, stop by the Musée des Beaux-Arts de Pont-Aven (☑02 98 06 14 43; www.museepontaven.fr; place de l'Hôtel de Ville; adult/child €4.50/2.50; ⊙10.30am-12.30pm & 2pm-6.30pm, closed Jan). And to see the spots where the masters set up their easels, pick up a free walking-trail map from the nearby tourist office (☑02 98 06 04 70; place de l'Hôtel de Ville; ⊙9.30am-7.30pm), which can also help with accommodation if you want to spend the night.

Charming spots for a drink or a meal include the bar-restaurant Auberge de la Fleur d'Ajonc (☑02 98 06 10 65; place de l'Hôtel de Ville; menus €16-23; ⊙lunch Tue-Sun, daily Jul-Aug), in an atmospheric medieval building of sloping stone floors and low ceilings held up by hefty beams; and Le Moulin de Rosmadec (☑02 98 06 00 22; www.moulinderosmadec.com; menus €28-76; ⊙lunch Tue-Wed & Fri-Sun, dinner Mon-Wed, Fri & Sat, closed Feb & Oct), serving gastronomic fare overlooking the town's namesake *pont* (bridge) and *aven* (river in Breton). Le Moulin de Rosmadec also has four delightful guestrooms upstairs (doubles €90, apartment €120).

Since the 1960s Pont-Aven has again become a magnet for artists, with no fewer than 60 galleries here in summer. Even in winter, you'll still find around 20 galleries open on weekends.

Pont-Aven is an easy 18km drive southeast of Concarneau. Buses (⊙02 98 44 46 73; €2) – five Monday to Saturday and two on Sunday – connect Pont-Aven with Quimperlé in the east (30 minutes), Concarneau (30 minutes) and Quimper (one hour).

Morbihan Coast

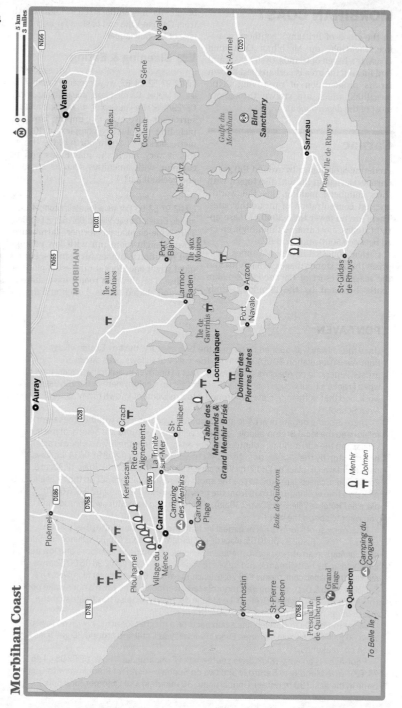

menus (€21 to €46) at its whitewashed, wood-beamed restaurant (closed Wednesday October to December and from February to April) revolve around fresh seafood, particularly lobster.

Crêperie au Pressoir
CRÊPERIE €

(✆02 97 52 01 86; village du Ménec; galettes €3-7; ✆Easter-Sep) Opening hours fluctuate, so we recommend checking ahead, but this artisan crêperie in a traditional long Breton house is a rare opportunity to dine right in the middle of a 70-strong cromlech (circle of menhirs). From Carnac-Ville, take rue St-Cornély northwest and turn right on rue du Ménec and follow it north for about 1km.

Crêperie St-George
CRÊPERIE €

(✆02 97 52 18 34; 8 allée du Parc, Carnac-Plage; menu €10; ✆Apr-Sep) For consistently great-value crêpes close to the beach, try the contemporary Crêperie St-George in the Galeries St-George centre.

ⓘ Information

Tourist office (✆02 97 52 13 52; www.ot-carnac.fr; 74 av des Druides, Carnac-Plage; ✆9am-7pm Mon-Sat & 3-7pm Sun)

ⓘ Getting There & Away

BICYCLE Hire bikes from **Lorcy** (✆02 97 52 09 73; 6 rue de Courdiec, Carnac-Ville; per half-/full day €5.50/9.50) or the pricier **Le Randonneur** (✆02 97 52 02 55; 20 av des Druides, Carnac-Plage; per half-/full day €8/11).

BUS The main bus stops are in Carnac-Ville, outside the police station on rue St-Cornély, and in Carnac-Plage, beside the tourist office. **Keolis Atlantique** (✆02 97 47 29 64; www.keolis-atlantique.com) runs a daily bus to Auray, Vannes and Quiberon (€2).

TAXI Call ✆02 97 52 75 75.

TRAIN The nearest useful train station is in Auray, 12km to the northeast. SNCF has an office in the Carnac-Plage tourist office where you can buy advance tickets.

Quiberon
POP 5200

Quiberon (Kiberen in Breton) sits at the southern tip of a sliver-thin, 14km-long peninsula flanked on the western side by the rocky, wave-lashed Côte Sauvage (Wild Coast). The town fans out around the port where ferries depart for Belle Île, and is wildly popular in summer.

Celtic communities from Ireland, Scotland, Wales, Cornwall, the Isle of Man and Galicia in northwest Spain congregate with Bretons at the Festival Interceltique de Lorient (✆02 97 21 24 29; www.festival-interceltique.com, in French & Breton) over 10 days in early August. Upwards of 600,000 people descend on the city of Lorient, about 30km northwest of Carnac, so book well ahead if you're planning to stay in town for the festival.

⊙ Sights & Activities

FREE Conserverie La Belle-Iloise
SARDINE CANNERY

(✆02 97 50 08 77; www.labelleiloise.fr; rue de Kerné; ✆10-11am & 3-4pm Mon-Fri) North of the train station, guided visits around this former sardine cannery run hourly in summer, with bargain-priced sardines available from the adjacent shop.

La Grande Plage
BEACH

La Grand Plage is a family-friendly beach, with bathing spots towards the peninsula's tip larger and less crowded. The Côte Sauvage on the opposite coast is great for a windy walk, but you'll need a permit for any nautically based activity (such as a diving certificate) or risk a fine – and your safety.

🛏 Sleeping

Camping du Conguel
CAMPGROUND €

(✆02 97 50 19 11; www.campingduconguel.com; bd de la Teignouse; sites €27-44, electricity €4; ✆Apr-Oct; ☀) This splashy option, with an aqua park including water slides, is one of the peninsula's 15 campgrounds. Just 2km east of the town centre, it's beside Plage du Conguel, with four- to six-berth cabins starting at €94 for two nights.

Auberge de Jeunesse – Les Filets Bleus
HOSTEL €

(✆02 97 50 15 54; www.fuaj.org; 45 rue du Roch Priol; dm €11; ✆Apr-Sep) Quiberon's HI-affiliated hostel is in a peaceful part of town, 800m east of the train station and 500m from the beach. There's limited camping (€6) in the grounds; breakfast costs €3.50.

Hôtel L'Océan
HOTEL €

(✆02 97 50 07 58; www.hotel-de-locean.com, in French; 7 quai de l'Océan; d €55-74, tw €71-82;

⊙Easter-Sep; 🗟) Overlooking the harbour and a small beach, this huge white house with multicoloured shutters is something of a local landmark. The cheapest of its 37 rooms don't have TVs, but rooms at the other end of the price scale get you a fabulous harbour view. Parking (very welcome in summer) costs €7.

✕ Eating & Drinking

TOP CHOICE Villa Margot   SEAFOOD €€
(☑02 97 50 33 89; www.villamargot.fr; 7 rue de Port Maria; menus €18-38; ⊙Thu-Mon) The interior of this stunning stone restaurant looks like it'd be at home in a chic Parisian *quartier,* with original art on the walls (painted on adjacent Belle Île), flower-shaped opaque glass light fittings, hot-pink and brown colour schemes, and lobsters clawing in the live tank (caught the night before, along with the fish). That is until you head out onto the timber deck, which has direct access to the beach for a post-repast stroll.

Le Café de Maria   TAPAS BAR €
(☑02 97 50 53 89; 8 rue de Krevozès; mains €12-20) This brand-new, super-slick tapas place, café and wine bar is a marked de-

---

MORBIHAN'S MIGHTY MEGALITHS

Two perplexing questions arise from the Morbihan region's Neolithic menhirs, dolmens, cromlechs, tumuli and cairns. Just *how* did the original constructors hew then haul these blocks (the heaviest weighs 300 tonnes), millennia before the wheel and the mechanical engine reached Brittany? And *why*?

Theories and hypotheses abound, but the vague yet common consensus is that they served some kind of sacred purpose – the same spiritual impulse behind so many monuments built by humankind.

The best way to appreciate the stones' sheer numbers is to walk or bike between the Le Ménec and Kerlescan groups, with menhirs almost continuously in view. Between June and September seven buses a day run between the two sites and both Carnac-Ville and Carnac-Plage.

Sign up for a one-hour guided visit at the Maison des Mégalithes (☑02 97 52 29 81; rte des Alignements; €4; ⊙9am-7pm), running regularly in French year-round and usually in English at 3pm Wednesday, Thursday and Friday from early July to late August. Because of severe erosion, the sites are fenced off to allow the vegetation to regenerate. However, between 10am and 5pm from October to May you can wander freely through parts (ask at the Maison des Mégalithes for updates).

Opposite the Maison des Mégalithes, the largest menhir field – with 1099 stones – is the Alignements du Ménec, 1km north of Carnac-Ville; the eastern section is accessible in winter. From here, the D196 heads northeast for about 1.5km to the equally impressive Alignements de Kermario. Climb the stone observation tower midway along the site to see the alignment from above. Another 500m further on are the Alignements de Kerlescan, a smaller grouping also accessible in winter.

Tumulus St-Michel, at the end of rue du Tumulus and 400m northeast of the Carnac-Ville tourist office, dates back to at least 5000 BC and offers sweeping views.

Between Kermario and Kerlescan, 500m to the south of the D196, deposit your fee in an honour box at Tumulus de Kercado (admission €1), dating from 3800 BC and the burial site of a Neolithic chieftain. From the parking area 300m further along the D196, a 15-minute walk brings you to the Géant du Manio, the highest menhir in the complex.

Near Locmariaquer, 13km southeast of Carnac-Ville, the major monuments are the Table des Marchands, a 30m-long dolmen, and the Grand Menhir Brisé (adult/child €5/free; ⊙10am-6pm), the region's largest menhir, which once stood 20m high but now lies broken on its side. Both are off the D781, just before the village. Just south of Locmariaquer by the sea is the Dolmen des Pierres Plates, a 24m-long chamber with still-visible engravings.

For some background, the Musée de Préhistoire (☑02 97 52 22 04; 10 place de la Chapelle, Carnac-Ville; adult/child €5/2.50; ⊙10am-6pm) chronicles life in and around Carnac from the Palaeolithic and Neolithic eras to the Middle Ages.

parture from the bucket-and-spade eateries along the seafront. It offers a selection of imaginative tapas dishes as well as more substantial mains such as grilled salmon steaks, scallops and sea bream. Add a great wine list, and this is one of Quiberon's best choices.

L'Embarcadère   SEAFOOD €€
(☑02 97 50 17 84; 2 quai de l'Océan; mussels from €8, mains €15-19; ☺7am-9pm Mon-Sat, 10am-9pm Sun) Of the bar-restaurants lined up along the quayfront, L'Embarcadère offers value that's hard to beat. It also serves whopping bowls of *moules frites,* and mixes a great kir.

ℹ Information

Tourist office (☑08 25 13 56 00; www.quiberon .com; 14 rue de Verdun; ☺9am-12.30pm & 2-6pm Mon-Sat) Between the train station and La Grande Plage.

ℹ Getting There & Away

BOAT For ferries between Quiberon and Belle-Île, see p268.

BUS Quiberon is connected by **Keolis Atlantique** (☑02 97 47 29 64; www.keolis -atlantique.com), with one bus per day leaving at 1.45pm and serving Carnac (45 minutes), Auray (1¼ hours) and Vannes (1¾ hours). The flat fare is €2. Buses stop at the train station and at place Hoche near the tourist office and the beach.

CAR High-summer traffic is hellish – consider leaving your vehicle at the 1200-place Sémaphore car park (€3.60 for up to four hours, €12.50 for 24 hours), 1.5km north of the beach, and walking or taking the free shuttle bus into town.

TRAIN In July and August only, a train runs several times a day between Auray and Quiberon (€5.50, 45 minutes). From September to June an SNCF bus service links Quiberon and Auray train stations (€2, 50 minutes) at least seven times a day.

ℹ Getting Around

BICYCLE Cycles Loisirs (☑02 97 50 31 73; www.cyclesloisirs.free.fr; 3 rue Victor Golvan), 200m north of the tourist office, rents touring/ mountain bikes from €11/13 per day. **Cyclomar** (☑02 97 50 26 00; www.cyclomar.fr; 47 place Hoche), around 200m south of the tourist office, rents out bikes for similar prices as well as scooters including helmet from €38 per day plus insurance. It also runs an operation from the train station during July and August.

TAXI Call ☑08 00 85 20 20.

POP 5200

Accessed by ferries from Quiberon, Belle Île (in full, Belle-Île-en-Mer) sees its population swell tenfold in summer thanks to its namesake beauty. But as it's Brittany's largest island (at 20km by 9km), there's room to escape the crowds.

◎ Sights & Activities

Musée Historique   HISTORY MUSEUM
(☑02 97 31 85 54; www.citadellevauban.com; adult/child €6.50/3.50; ☺9am-6pm) The dramatic citadel, strengthened by Vauban in 1682, dominates the little Le Palais port. Inside, the various displays concentrate on the history of the island's defensive system, though there are also interesting sections on the various celebrities who were regular visitors here, the local fish trade and island life.

Grotte de l'Apothicairerie   WALKS
Belle Île's fretted southwestern coast has spectacular rock formations and caves including Grotte de l'Apothicairerie (Cave of the Apothecary's Shop), where waves roll in from two sides.

Beaches & Swimming   BEACHES
Plage de Donnant has awesome surf, though swimming here is dangerous. Sheltered **Port Kérel**, to the southwest, is better for children, as is the 2km-long **Plage des Grands Sables**, the biggest and busiest strand, spanning the calm waters of the island's eastern side.

Walking & Cycling   WALKING & CYCLING
The tourist office sells walking and cycling guides. The ultimate hike is the 95km **coastal path** that follows the island's coastline.

🛏 Sleeping & Eating

Citadelle Vauban Hôtel Musée

                            HISTORIC HOTEL €€
(☑02 97 31 84 17; www.citadellevauban.com; Le Palais; r €145-295, ste €355-500; ☺closed mid-Oct–May; 🛜) Definitely the best hotel on the island, this fantastic conversion within the historic citadel is Belle Île's top address and boasts 53 stunning rooms with antique furniture and stylish trimmings. Note that there's only wi-fi access in the lobby.

Auberge de Jeunesse Haute Boulogne

                                    HOSTEL €
(☑02 97 31 81 33; www.fuaj.org; Haute Boulogne; dm incl sheets & breakfast €13.50; ☺closed Oct;

TREETOP SLEEPING

For the ultimate eco-escape, the only way you can go past Dihan (☑02 97 56 88 27; www.dihan-evasion.org, in French; Kerganiet, Ploëmel; d guestroom/yurt incl breakfast €60/80, d tree house €120-140, table d'hôte from €25; ☎) is in the literal sense, secluded as it is in a leafy dell just outside Ploëmel (follow the black signs from the village).

Run by a fun-loving young couple, Myriam and Arno Le Masle, in its former life the property was Myriam's grandparents' working farm. The farmhouse and barns now house guestrooms, while the grounds shelter two yurts imported from Mongolia and five tree houses, reached by climbing ladders (the highest – at 12m – requires you to strap on a harness to reach it). Should nature call, there are biodegradable dry toilets up here as well as conserved water (you'll find brightly tiled bathrooms and a sauna in the reception building).

Rates include breakfast, which is a combination of organic, fair-trade and local artisan produce, such as a finger-licking *caramel au beurre salé* (Breton caramel spread). Eco-initiatives also include rare-for-France recycling. Fabulous *tables d'hôte* (a combination of Myriam's Breton, Mauritian and Indian heritage; by reservation) take place in the converted *cidrerie*, where pianist Arno hits the keys and bands sometimes drop by. Otherwise, guests can fire up the barbecue and dine beneath a bamboo-sheltered pergola.

All of which would be enough to recommend it heartily, but you can also rent bikes (€10 per day), book a massage (from €80) or even an on-site beauty treatment with biological cosmetics. Both guests and nonguests can saddle up, with horse riding starting at €20 per hour (there are also ponies for kids).

@) This modern 96-bed HI-affiliated hostel with a self-catering kitchen is to the north of the citadel. Its rooms are all twins with bunkbeds and shared toilets.

Hôtel Vauban   HOTEL €
(☑02 97 31 45 42; www.hotelvauban.com, in French; 1 rue des Ramparts, Le Palais; s €50, d €66-85; ⊙Mar–mid-Nov; ☎) This comfy place is perched high on the coastal path, with views of the ferry landing below from many of its 16 spacious rooms. The hotel rents out mountain bikes, there's good wheelchair access and the guest-only restaurant (*menus* from €20) serves seafood from April to September.

La Table du Gouverneur   GASTRONOMIC €€
(☑02 97 31 82 57; www.citadellevauban.com; Le Palais; menus €25-60; ⊙closed mid-Oct–May) You may literally eat off the governor's table here, given that this hugely atmospheric and formal place is housed in his former residence. The gastronomic *menus* are heavily focused on seafood, inventively combining flavours as disparate as lobster, grapefruit and celery to sublime effect.

ⓘ Information

Turn left as you leave the ferry in Le Palais to get to the **tourist office** (☑02 97 31 81 93;

www.belle-ile.com; quai Bonnelle, Le Palais; ⊙8.45am-7pm Mon-Sat, to 1pm Sun). There's a summer-only **information kiosk** (☑02 97 31 69 49; ⊙Easter-Sep) on the quay in Sauzon.

ⓘ Getting There & Away

BOAT Travelling to Belle Île can involve a bit of planning, as taking a car on the ferry is prohibitively expensive for a short trip and needs to be booked well ahead, even outside peak season. On the upside, bikes can be carried free on board ferries.

The shortest crossing to Belle Île is from Quiberon. **Compagnie Océane** (☑08 20 05 61 56; www.compagnie-oceane.fr) operates car/passenger ferries (45 minutes, year-round) and fast passenger ferries to Le Palais and Sauzon in July and August. An adult return passenger fare is €30; transporting a small car costs a hefty €149 return *plus* passenger fares. There are five crossings a day (up to 13 in July and August).

It is also possible to make the trip from Vannes. **Navix** (☑02 97 46 60 29; www.navix. fr, in French with English sections) operates ferries (return €30 to €44) between May and mid-September.

ⓘ Getting Around

BICYCLE Lots of places in Le Palais rent out bicycles/motor scooters for around €12/35 per day.

BUS Seasonal buses run by **Taol Mor** (☏02 97 31 32 32; www.cars-verts.com/taolmor.html) criss-cross the island.

CAR Car-rental rates on the island are expensive and start at about €70 for 24 hours; you'll find outlets at the harbour as you disembark.

Vannes

POP 55,400

Street art, sculptures and intriguing galleries pop up unexpectedly through the half-timbered, cobbled city of Vannes (Gwened in Breton), which has a quirky, creative bent.

The city's integral role in Brittany's history stretches back to pre-Roman times, when it was the capital of the Veneti, a Gaulish tribe of sailors who fortified the town. Conquered by Julius Caesar in the 1st century BC, it became the centre of Breton unity in the 9th century under Breton hero Nominoë, and in 1532 the union of the duchy of Brittany with France was proclaimed here. These days it's a vibrant hub for students attending the city's Université de Bretagne-Sud.

⊙ Sights

Surrounding Vannes' walled old town is a flower-filled moat. Inside, you can weave through the web of narrow alleys ranged around the 13th-century Gothic **Cathédrale St-Pierre**. Tucked away behind rue des Vierges, stairs lead to the accessible section of the **ramparts**. From here, you can see the black-roofed **Vieux Lavoirs** (Old Laundry Houses), though you'll get a better view from the **Tour du Connétable** or from the **Porte Poterne** to the south.

Musée de la Cohue   ART MUSEUM
(☏02 97 01 63 00; 9-15 place St-Pierre; adult/child €4.30/free; ⊙9am-7pm Mon-Sat, 10am-6pm Sun) Since the 14th century, the building now housing the Musée de la Cohue has variously been a produce market, a law court and the seat of the Breton parliament. Today it's a museum of fine arts, displaying mostly 19th-century paintings, sculptures and engravings.

Musée d'Histoire et d'Archélogie
                                  HISTORY MUSEUM
(☏02 97 01 63 00; 2 rue Noë; adult/child €4.30/free; ⊙10am-6pm) In the summer months you can survey Roman and Greek artefacts and study up on megaliths at this museum, housed in the 15th-century Château Gail-

lard. A combined ticket for the two museums costs €6/4 per adult/child.

☞ Tours

Navix   BOAT TOURS
(☏08 25 13 21 00; www.navix.fr, in French) From April to September, Navix runs a range of cruises on the Golfe du Morbihan (Morbihan Coast), departing from the Gare Maritime, 2km south of the tourist office. It's also possible to visit the two largest of the gulf's 40 inhabited islands, Île aux Moines and Île d'Arz.

Compagnie des Îles   BOAT TOURS
(☏08 25 13 41 00; www.compagniedesiles.com, in French) Offers seasonal gulf cruises.

✦ Festivals & Events

Festival de Jazz   JAZZ FESTIVAL
Vannes swings for four days in late July or early August.

Les Musicales du Golfe   MUSIC FESTIVAL
(www.musicalesdugolfe.com) Classical music concerts take place in early August.

Fêtes d'Arvor   CULTURAL FESTIVAL
(www.fetes-arvor.org) This three-day celebration of Breton culture from 13 to 15 August includes parades, concerts and *festoù-noz* (night festivals).

🛏 Sleeping

Hôtel Villa Kerasy   HISTORIC HOTEL €€
(☏02 97 68 36 83; www.villakerasy.com; 20 av Favrel-et-Lincy; d €120-210; ⊙closed mid-Nov–mid-Dec; ☎) Each of the 12 elegant rooms in this grand villa is themed on historic ports of the East India trading route. In summer enjoy the tranquil garden, designed by a Japanese landscape artist. In winter relax in the cosy tearoom, where you can sip Earl Grey from fine Limoges china by the log fire.

Hôtel Le Marina   HOTEL €
(☏02 97 47 22 81; www.hotellemarina.fr; 4 place Gambetta; s €38-57, d €41-61; ☎) By far the best-located place in town, this friendly hotel is run by the same team operating the busy downstairs café. There are 14 simple and rather cramped rooms here in creams and pink, the cheapest of which have facilities in the corridor.

Le Branhoc   FAMILY HOTEL €
(☏02 97 56 41 55; www.hotel-auray.fr; 5 rte du Bono, Auray; s €57, d €47-69; ☎🅿) Situated 17km west of Vannes, just outside the pretty riverside town of Auray (itself well worth a

wander), this peacefully situated, family-run hotel is a handy base for exploring both Vannes and Morbihan's megalithic sites. Rooms are bright, spacious and spotlessly clean.

Hôtel Le Richemont
HOTEL **€**

(☑02 97 47 17 24; www.hotel-richemont-vannes. com; 26 place de la Gare; d €55-65; ⊚) If the heavy wood beams and arched stonework of the mock-medieval breakfast room aren't your cup of tea, you can have a laden tray brought to your very comfortable, sound-proofed and much more contemporary room.

Relais du Golfe
HOTEL **€**

(☑02 97 47 14 74; 10 place du Général de Gaulle; r €40-56) Its name suggests something more flash than these rooms (wedged above a café-bar) actually are, but it's a cheap and central option, and staff are welcoming. The cheapest rooms come with just a sink and share toilets.

✖ Eating & Drinking

Rue des Halles and its offshoots are lined with tempting eateries; classical and contemporary brasseries arc around the port.

Dan Ewen
CRÊPERIE **€**

(☑02 97 42 44 34; 3 place du Général de Gaulle; crêpes €3-8; ⊚Mon-Sat) A near-life-size statue of a sweet, smiling, wrinkled Breton lady bearing a tray greets you at the entrance of this stone and dark-wood crêperie serving fillings such as frangipane, and flambéed options topped with *crème Chantilly*.

Délice Café
BISTRO **€**

(☑02 97 54 23 31; 7 place des Lices; dishes €6-12; ⊚8am-8pm Mon-Sat) Fronted by a timber-decked terrace (warmed by heat lamps in winter), and flowing to a contemporary dining room of gilded mirrors and red velveteen banquettes, this smart place in the centre of the old town has healthy salads and hot dishes like *croques monsieur* (grilled ham-and-cheese sandwiches). Terrace dining costs roughly 10% more.

Côte et Saveurs
MODERN FRENCH **€**

(☑02 97 47 21 94; 8 rue Pierre-René Rogues; mains €8-18; ⊚lunch & dinner Thu-Mon, lunch Tue) A spiral staircase winds through the centre of the ground-floor dining room to the upper level of this airy, contemporary restaurant serving dishes such as *magret de canard* in rhubarb sauce.

Brasserie des Halles et des Arts
BRASSERIE **€€**

(☑02 97 54 08 34; 9 rue des Halles; menus €15-25; ⊚noon-midnight) You can eat at this buzzing brasserie (mains €9.50 to €18), but it's an equally good spot for a drink while browsing the art – such as the Breton images made from tiles that adorn its colourful walls.

A Tribord
DJ BAR

(☑02 97 42 76 94; www.atribord-vannes.com; 28 rue St-Patern; ⊚6pm-2am) Everything from folk music to club nights with DJs hitting the decks takes place at this eclectic venue. You'll find a couple of other bars in the same street.

🛍 Shopping

In keeping with Vannes' artistic spirit, galleries such as Echoppe St-Guénhaël (☑02 97 47 92 37; 29 rue St-Guénhaël) sell innovative (and often amusing) contemporary Breton art.

ℹ Information

Cyber Athalie (4 rue Porte Poterne; per hr €3.50; ⊚10am-12.30pm & 2-7pm Mon-Sat) Internet access.

Post office (2 place de la République)

Tourist office (☑08 25 13 56 10; www. tourisme-vannes.com; ⊚9.30am-12.30pm & 1.30-6pm Mon-Sat) In a smart modern building on the newly developed marina.

ℹ Getting There & Away

BUS The small bus station is opposite the train station. Services include **Keolis Atlantique** (www.keolis-atlantique.com), which runs to Carnac (€7.50, 1¼ hours) and on to Quiberon (€10, a further 45 minutes).

CAR Agencies have offices at the train station:

ADA (☑02 97 42 59 10)

Avis (☑02 97 47 54 54)

Europcar (☑02 97 42 43 43)

TRAIN Frequent trains:

Auray €3.70, 11 minutes

Nantes €22, 1½ hours

Quimper €18, 1½ hours

Rennes €19, 1½ hours

ℹ Getting Around

BICYCLE You can easily use Vannes' Vélib system **Velocea** (www.velocea.fr, in French), which has 16 year-round stations in the city, with more open in the summer months.

BUS **TPV** (www.tpv.fr; tickets €1.30) runs eight city bus lines until 8.15pm. Its Infobus kiosk is on place de la République. Buses 3 and 4 link the train station with place de la République.

TAXI Call ☑02 97 54 34 34.

EASTERN & CENTRAL BRITTANY

The one-time frontier between Brittany and France, fertile eastern Brittany fans out around the region's lively capital, Rennes. Central Brittany conceals the enchanting Forêt de Paimpont, sprinkled with villages and ancient Breton legends.

Josselin

POP 2600

In the shadow of an enormous, witch's-hat-turreted 14th-century castle that was the long-time seat of the counts of Rohan, the story-book village of Josselin lies on the banks of the River Oust, 43km northeast of Vannes. Today, visitors in their thousands continue to fall under its spell. A beautiful square of 16th-century half-timbered houses, place Notre Dame, is the little town's heart. The castle and the tourist office are south, below rue des Trente, the main through street.

◉ Sights & Activities

Château de Josselin   CHÂTEAU
(☑02 97 22 36 45; www.chateaujosselin.com; adult/child €7.50/5; ◷2-5.30pm Apr-Sep) Guarded by its three round towers, the extraordinary town château is an incredible sight that remains the home of the Rohan family today. As such, it can only be visited by guided tour: one English-language tour departs daily from June to September; otherwise you can ask for a leaflet in English. Within the château is the Musée de Poupées (Doll Museum; adult/child €6.50/4.60). A combination ticket for both costs €12.50/8.50 per adult/child.

Basilique Notre Dame du Roncier CHURCH
Parts of the Basilique Notre Dame du Roncier in place Notre Dame date from the 12th century; superb 15th- and 16th-century stained glass illuminates the south aisle.

✲ Festivals & Events

Medieval Festival   MEDIEVAL FESTIVAL
The hulking Château de Josselin makes an evocative backdrop for the village's

two-day Medieval Festival featuring feasting and fireworks, held in mid-July in even-numbered years.

🛏 Sleeping & Eating

Hôtel-Restaurant du Château
                            TRADITIONAL HOTEL €
(☑02 97 22 20 11; www.hotel-chateau.com, in French; 1 rue Général de Gaulle; d €69-75; ☎) This fantastically located hotel is the best choice in town; it's well worth paying the few extra euros for a magnificent view of the château across the Oust River. Its restaurant *menus* range from €10 to €37 and regional specialities abound – bag a table on the delightful terrace overlooking the river and the château if the weather is good.

Camping du Bas de la Lande CAMPGROUND €
(☑02 97 22 22 20; campingbasdelalande@wanadoo.fr; Guégon; sites €6; ◷Apr-Oct) This peaceful spot is 2km west of Josselin, on the south bank of the Oust.

La Table d'O   MODERN FRENCH €
(☑02 97 70 61 39; 9 rue Glatinier; menus €13-46; ◷lunch & dinner Mon & Thu-Sat, lunch Tue) This pleasant family-run place offers an interesting and varied menu of local cooking with a sprinkle of fusion on top, and has become a local favourite. The sweeping views of the town and valley from the terrace are fantastic for a summer lunch. It's a short walk beyond the château.

❶ Information

Tourist office (☑02 97 22 36 43; www.paysdejosselin-tourisme.com; 4 rue Beaumanoir; ◷10am-noon & 2-6pm Mon-Sat, 2-6pm Sun) Located beside the castle entrance. You can use the internet here (up to 15 minutes) for free.

❶ Getting There & Away

Viaoo (www.viaoo29.fr) runs several daily buses to Rennes (€13, 1½ hours).

Forêt de Paimpont

Also known as Brocéliande, the Paimpont Forest is about 40km southwest of Rennes, and legendary as the place where King Arthur received the Excalibur sword (forget that these stories are thought to have been brought to Brittany by Celtic settlers and hence probably took place offshore – it's a magical setting all the same).

BRITTANY JOSSELIN

The best base for exploring the forest is the lakeside village of Paimpont. Some 95% of the forest is private land, but the tourist office (☎02 99 07 84 23; www.tourisme-broceliande.com; ⊙10am-noon & 2-6pm, closed Mon Oct-Mar), beside the 12th-century Église Abbatiale (Abbey Church), has a free brochure outlining a 62km-long driving circuit with numerous short walks along the way that are accessible to the public. It also sells more-detailed walking and cycling guides.

In July and August the tourist office leads guided tours (morning/afternoon/full day €6/10/12) of the forest (the availability of English-speaking guides varies).

Campers can set up their tents at the lakeside Camping Municipal de Paimpont (☎02 99 07 89 16; www.camping-paimpont-broceliande.com; rue du Chevalier Lancelot du Lac; camping €6; ⊙May-Sep), while backpackers will want to head to the Auberge de Jeunesse (☎02 97 22 76 75; www.fuaj.org; dm €11.50; ⊙Jun-Sep), in a lovely old stone farmhouse at Choucan-en-Brocéliande, 5km north of Paimpont.

For more creature comforts, try the Hôtel Le Relais de Brocéliande (☎02 99 07 84 94; www.le-relais-de-broceliande.fr; 5 rue du Forges, Paimpont; r €69-98; 🐾), with rustic rooms and canopied beds. Its on-site restaurant (menus €15 to €36) specialises in local river-caught fish. Illenoo (www.illenoo.fr, in French) runs buses to/from Rennes (€3.20, one hour) from Monday to Saturday.

You can rent mountain bikes from Pays de Merlin (☎02 99 07 80 23; rue Général de Gaulle; per half-/full day €9/12).

Rennes

POP 213,100

A crossroads since Roman times, Brittany's vibrant capital sits at the junction of highways linking northwestern France's major cities. It's a beautifully set-out city, with an elaborate and stately centre and a charming old town that's a joy to get lost in. At night, this student city has no end of lively places to pop in for a pint and its restaurants are also superb.

◉ Sights & Activities

Cathédrale St-Pierre   CATHEDRAL
(⊙9.30am-noon & 3-6pm) Crowning the old city is the 17th-century cathedral, which has an impressive, if rather dark, neoclassical interior. Much of the surrounding old

town was gutted by the great fire of 1720, started by a drunken carpenter who accidentally set alight a pile of shavings. Half-timbered houses that survived line the old city's cobbled streets such as nearby rue St-Michel and rue St-Georges.

Palais du Parlement de Bretagne

LAW COURTS
(place du Parlement de Bretagne) This 17th-century former seat of the rebellious Breton parliament has in more recent times been home to the Palais de Justice. In 1994 this building, too, was destroyed by fire, started by demonstrating fishermen. Now restored, it houses the Court of Appeal. In July and August, guided tours in English (adult/child €7/4; book at the tourist office) take you through the ostentatiously gilded rooms.

Musée des Beaux-Arts

ART MUSEUM
(☎02 23 62 17 45; 20 quai Émile Zola; adult/child €6/free; ⊙10am-noon & 2-6pm Tue-Sun) Rooms devoted to the Pont-Aven school (see p263) are the highlight of the Musée des Beaux-Arts, which also has a 'curiosity gallery' of antiques and illustrations amassed in the 18th century. It also hosts temporary exhibitions, which attract an additional charge.

Champs Libres   CULTURAL CENTRE

(☎02 23 40 66 00; www.leschampslibres.fr; 10 cours des Alliés) Rennes' futuristic cultural centre is home to the Musée de Bretagne (☎02 23 40 66 00; www.musee-bretagne.fr), with displays on Breton history and culture. Under the same roof is Espace des Sciences (☎02 23 40 66 40; www.espace-sciences.org), an interactive science museum, along with a planetarium, a temporary exhibition space and a library. A combined ticket for all sections costs €7/5 per adult/child.

☞ Tours

urbaVag   BOAT TRIPS
(☎02 99 33 16 88; www.urbavag.fr, in French; rue Canal St-Martin; per hr €27-32) Cruise Rennes' waterways on a whisper-quiet electric boat rented from urbaVag. Boats take up to seven passengers; the price drops significantly with each extra hour of rental.

✦✦ Festivals & Events

Les Mercredis du Thabor   CULTURAL FESTIVAL
Traditional Breton dancing and music take place in Rennes' beautiful Parc du Thabor on Wednesdays during June and July (usually from 4pm).

Tombées de la Nuit   CULTURAL FESTIVAL
Rennes' old city comes alive during this music and theatre festival in the first week of July.

Yaouank   NIGHT FESTIVAL
(✆02 99 30 06 87) A huge *fest-noz* of singing, dancing and music played on traditional instruments. Held on the third Saturday in November.

🛏 Sleeping

Angelina Hôtel   HOTEL €
(✆02 99 79 29 66; www.angelina-hotel.com; 1 quai Lamennais; d €58-65; ⊛) It doesn't get more central than this cavernous hotel right next to République, with the old city and shopping district on the doorstep. Reception's on the 3rd floor of this creaking old building (there's a lift), but the wicker-furnished rooms are surprisingly well kept and come with bright modern bathrooms. Book ahead for the two large double corner rooms – possibly the best deal in town.

Hôtel de Nemours   BOUTIQUE HOTEL €
(✆02 99 78 26 26; www.hotelnemours.com; 5 rue de Nemours; r €59-92; ⊛⊛) Lined with historic black-and-white photographs of Rennes, sumptuous Hôtel de Nemours is an understatement in elegance, with cream, chocolate and caramel furnishings, high thread-count white linens, flat-screen TVs and free wi-fi. Slide into a corduroy-upholstered banquette for a breakfast buffet feast (€8.50).

Hôtel des Lices   HOTEL €
(✆02 99 79 14 81; www.hotel-des-lices.com; 7 place des Lices; r €67-83; ⊛⊛) You can peer down from the steel balconies or through the floor-to-ceiling glass doors to see the Saturday-morning market, which snakes right past the front door of this modern six-storey hotel. Inside, rooms are small but sleek with pared-down contemporary furnishings and textured walls. Breakfast (€8) is served in a sunlit ground-floor salon with limed floorboards, white tables and fresh flowers.

Auberge de Jeunesse   HOSTEL €
(✆02 99 33 22 33; www.fuaj.org; 10-12 Canal St-Martin; dm incl breakfast €19; ☺7am-1am) Rennes' well-equipped youth hostel has a self-catering kitchen and a canalside setting 2km north from the centre. Take bus 18 from place de la Mairie.

Vénézia Hôtel   HOTEL €
(✆02 99 30 36 56; 27 rue Dupont des Loges; s €30-42, d €40-48) Named for the Venice-like canals surrounding this small 'island' in the city centre, half of this hotel's 16 rose-toned rooms have pretty views over the canalside garden. The cheapest have a toilet, but share showers. It's something of a Fawlty Towers experience, but the friendliness of the staff wins you over in the end.

Camping des Gayeulles   CAMPGROUND €
(✆02 99 36 91 22; www.camping-rennes.com; rue Professeur Audin; per adult/campervan/tent €3.50/7.20/5.70) Rennes' only campground is in Parc des Bois, 4.5km northeast of the train station. It's open for campervans year-round. Take bus 3 from place de la République to the Gayeulles stop.

🍴 Eating

Rennes has a wide choice of restaurants. Rues St-Malo and St-Georges are the city's two main 'eat streets'; the latter particularly specialises in crêperies.

Léon le Cochon   PORK RESTAURANT €
(✆02 99 79 37 54; 1 rue Maréchal Joffre; menu €25, mains €13-24) Basking in the plaudits of almost every French gastronomic guidebook, but still fun and informal, 'Leon the Pig' specialises not just in pork but porcine products in all their many and varied manifestations.

Café Babylone   MODERN FRENCH €
(✆02 99 85 82 99; 12 rue des Dames; mains €7-18; ☺closed dinner Mon) Despite being virtually built into the walls of Rennes' cathedral, this charming contemporary yet traditional place is a surprisingly tourist-free zone, favoured instead by locals enjoying a plate of oysters or one of the finely produced dishes of rich home cooking on the terrace.

L'Épicerie   CAFÉ €
(✆02 99 38 76 70; 2 rue des Fossés; tartines €4-7; ☺noon-midnight) This fantastic old-town eatery is riotously popular with a studenty crowd who pile in to enjoy the generous *tartines* (open sandwiches) and flasks of beer on the buzzing terrace outside.

Le Café Breton   TRADITIONAL FRENCH €
(✆02 99 30 74 95; 14 rue Nantaise; menus €8-18; ☺closed dinner Mon) Diminutive rue Nantaise has a handful of top restaurants, including this local fave for its tarts, salads and gratins. Definitely book ahead in the evenings.

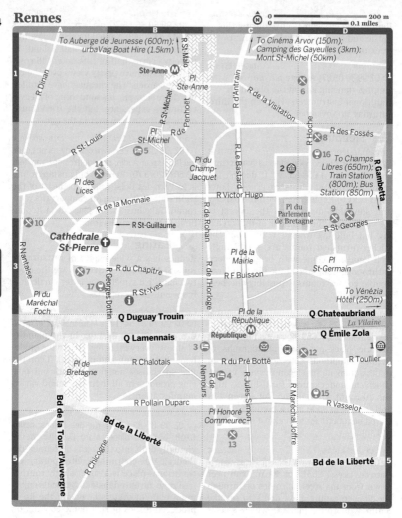

Le Kerlouan CRÊPERIE €

(☎02 99 36 83 02; 17 rue St-Georges; crêpes €2-9.90) This small place manages to punch above its weight with a fantastic selection of imaginative crêpe taste combinations. Service is friendly and fast, and the terrace is always full.

Self-catering

Fresh produce and Breton specialities are available daily at Rennes' covered markets, **Les Halles Centrales** (place Honoré Commeurec; ⏰7am-7pm Mon-Sat, 9.30am-12.30pm Sun). The fabulous **Marché des Lices** (place des Lices, ⏰9am-6pm Sat) sees more than 300 producers converge on Rennes to sell an extraordinary array of fresh produce.

Pick up exquisite pastries and still-warm bread at **Boulangerie Hoche** (☎02 99 63 61 01; 17 rue Hoche, ⏰7am-7.30pm Mon-Sat).

Drinking

Rue St-Michel – nicknamed rue de la Soif (Street of Thirst) for its bars, pubs and cafés – is the best-known drinking strip, but it can get rowdy late at night.

Le Nabuchodonosor WINE BAR

(12 rue Hoche) The favoured haunt of arty and intellectual types in Rennes, this

Rennes

charming wine bar is a great place for an evening drink in buzzing surroundings.

Oan's Pub   PUB
(1 rue Georges Dottin; ☺2pm-1am Mon-Sat) Locals habitually turn up with instruments for impromptu Celtic jam sessions at this cosy cave-like, stone-walled pub with Brittany-brewed Coreff beer on tap.

La Cité d'Ys   PUB
(31 rue Vasselot; ☺noon-1am) If you want to practise your Breton with Breton-speaking locals and bar staff (lubricated by Breton beer), this wooden mezzanine pub is prime. *Yec'hed mat!* (Cheers!)

☆ Entertainment

To find out about upcoming football matches and obtain tickets, check www.staderennais.com (in French).

Cinéma Arvor   CINEMA
(☑02 99 38 72 40; 29 rue d'Antrain) Screens nondubbed films.

❶ Information

NeuroGame (www.neurogame.com; 2 rue Dinan; per 20min €1; ☺10am-midnight Tue-Fri, noon-midnight Mon & Sat, 2-10pm Sun) Internet access.

Peanuts (11 av Janvier; ☺11.30am-6.30pm) Bar offering free wireless.

Post office (place de la République)

Tourist office (☑02 99 67 11 11; www.tourisme-rennes.com; 11 rue St-Yves; ☺9am-7pm Mon-Sat, 11am-1pm & 2-6pm Sun) Offers an audioguide to the city taking you on a walking tour of eight sights for €4.50.Staff can book accommodation for free.

❶ Getting There & Away

BUS Among Rennes' many bus services, **Illenoo** (☑08 10 35 10 35; www.illenoo.fr, in French) runs regular daily services:

Dinan €3.90, 1½ hours

Dinard €3.90, two hours

Mont St-Michel €11, 80 minutes

Paimpont €3.20, one hour

CAR Agencies have offices at the train station:

Avis (☑02 23 42 14 14)

Budget (☑09 64 48 17 96)

Europcar (☑02 23 44 02 72)

Hertz (☑02 23 42 17 01)

National/Citer (☑02 23 44 02 78)

TRAIN Destinations with frequent services:

Brest €32, two hours

Dinan €13.50, one hour including a change

Nantes €23, 1¼ hours

Paris Montparnasse €48, 2¼ hours

Quimper €32, 2½ hours

St-Malo €13, one hour

Vannes €19, 1½ hours

❶ Getting Around

BUS Rennes has an efficient local bus network run by **STAR** (☑08 11 55 55 35; www.star.fr, in French; 12 rue Pré Botté). Bus tickets (single journey €1.20, 10-trip carnet €11, 24-hour pass €3.50) are interchangeable with the metro.

METRO Incredibly for a city its size, Rennes has its own single-line metro system, also run by STAR. The metro line runs northwest to southeast. Main stations include République (place de la République) in the centre, and Ste-Anne (old town).

TAXI Call ☑02 99 30 79 79.

Vitré

POP 17,300

With its narrow cobbled streets, half-timbered houses and colossal castle topped by witch's-hat turrets, Vitré rivals Dinan as

BRETON CRÊPES

Crêpes are Brittany's traditional staple, and ubiquitous throughout the region. Unlike the rolled-up crêpes sold at stalls on Paris' street corners, Breton crêpes are folded envelope-style at the edges, served flat on a plate and eaten using cutlery.

Rennes, as Brittany's capital, has dozens of enticing crêperies, including **La Ville d'Ys** (☎02 99 36 70 28; 5 rue St-Georges; crêpes €2.20-8.40), probably the town's most famous crêperie, named for the fabled Atlantis-style submerged city of Breton legend. Tucked inside a two-storey 15th-century house with a slanted wooden staircase and colourful crockery displayed on the walls, La Ville d'Ys serves up mouth-watering black wheat pancakes with sublime taste combinations.

We spoke to the crêperie's owner-chef, Claudine Thomas, as she cooked in her open kitchen, to find out the secrets behind making Breton crêpes:

What are the essential ingredients in a basic galette?
Blé noir (buckwheat flour) – *sarrasin* in Breton – and salted Breton butter. It's important to keep the Breton tradition; locals take crêpes very seriously. Well, crêpes are crêpes!

What are your favourite traditional toppings?
Andouille (local sausage) and for sweet crêpes, *caramel au beurre salé* (salty caramel sauce) – *salidou* in Breton – which I make here with ingredients from the market.

What's the ideal cooking temperature?
A *galettier* (the hotplate) – *bilig* in Breton – has no temperature dial, only numbers from one to eight. It can't be too hot – the crêpe needs to be brown at the edges; crispy but not burnt.

Do you use a particular recipe?
I use a recipe from Finistère – the crêpes are a finer texture and crispier than other recipes. People always come in because of this recipe; they don't want any other kind. If you want to learn how to create your own crêpes, the **Écoles de Treblec** (☎02 99 34 86 76; www.ecole-maitre-crepier.com, in French with English sections; 66 rue de Guer, Maure-de-Bretagne), 38km southwest of Rennes, runs a variety of courses and classes.

one of Brittany's best-preserved medieval towns – with far fewer tourists and a more laissez-faire village air.

◉ Sights & Activities

Musée du Château　　　　CASTLE MUSEUM
(☎02 99 75 04 54; place du Château; adult/child €4/2.50; ☉10am-6pm) Rising on a rocky outcrop overlooking the River Vilaine, Vitré's medieval castle was built in 1060, and was expanded in the 14th and 15th centuries. A twin-turreted gateway leads you from the cobbled square of place du Château into the triangular inner courtyard, while the museum itself is at the château's southern corner.

⌂ Sleeping

Vitré has a shortage of accommodation, so it's worth booking ahead any time of year.

Hôtel du Château　　　　FAMILY HOTEL €
(☎02 99 74 58 59; www.hotelduchateau35.fr; 5 rue Rallon; s €38-55, d €45-60; ☎🖶) Wake up to the aroma of freshly baked bread and, on upper floors, fantastic vistas of the castle at this family-run hotel at the base of the ramparts. The friendly owners are a fount of local information; there's good wheelchair access, a pleasant courtyard for breakfast and €3 garaged parking.

Mme Faucher　　　　B&B €
(☎02 99 75 08 69; http://bnb.faucher.info; 2 chemin des Tertres Noirs; s/d €44/50; ☎) In a rambling 18th-century stone house looking out over a large leafy garden, this *chambre d'hôte* run by Mme and M Faucher is the kind of familial, down-to-earth place you hoped still existed in France. Their home is filled with family memorabilia, bathrooms are shared, and travellers are welcomed

with open arms. Breakfast is a hearty basketful of brioches and baguettes, along with strong coffee. It's just a short downhill stroll to the town centre, but driving is a bit complicated due to the one-way road system. Check directions online or ask the tourist office for a route map.

 Eating & Drinking

Quaint crêperies and gastronomic restaurants are tucked away throughout the old town.

Le Pichet
TRADITIONAL FRENCH €

(📞02 99 75 24 09; 17 bd de Laval; menus €18-50, mains €12-27; ⊙lunch Mon-Sat, dinner Mon-Tue, Fri & Sat) Classic French cuisine incorporating local fish and regional produce fresh from the market is served on a charming terrace overlooking the garden when the sun's shining, and in front of the crackling open fire in winter.

Le Barabis
MICROBREWERY

(3 rue de la Trémouille; ⊙3pm-3am Mon-Sat, to 10pm Sun) Vitré's funky, laid-back microbrewery creates artisan beers in its gleaming copper boilers, which it serves on tap. In summer try the *blanche,* brewed with citrus zest; in winter, go for the robust *noire* (stout).

ℹ Information

Tourist office (📞02 99 75 04 46; www. ot-vitre.fr; place Général de Gaulle; ⊙9.30am-12.30pm & 2.30-6pm Tue-Sat, 2.30-6pm Mon) Right outside the train station.

ℹ Getting There & Away

Frequent trains travel between Vitré and Rennes (€7, 35 minutes).

Champagne

Includes »

Best Places to Eat

- » Le Foch (p284)
- » La Mignardise (p297)
- » Restaurant Le Théâtre (p292)

Best Places to Stay

- » Le Clos Raymi (p291)
- » Grand Hôtel des Templiers (p284)
- » Hôtel Arlequin (p296)

Why Go?

Champagne arouses all of the senses: the eyes feast on vine-covered hillsides and vertical processions of tiny, sparkling bubbles; the nose is tantalised by the damp soil and the heavenly bouquet of fermentation; the ears rejoice at the clink of glasses and the barely audible fizz; and the palate tingles with every sip. The imagination and the intellect are engaged as Champagne cellar visits reveal the magical processes – governed by the strictest of rules – that transform the world's most pampered pinot noir, pinot meunier and chardonnay grapes into this region's fabled wines. Happily, despite the prestige of their vines, the people of Champagne offer visitors a warm and surprisingly easy-going welcome, both in the stylish cities and along the Champagne Routes, which wend their way through vineyards and villages to family-run cellars where perfectly aged sparklers can be sampled, savoured, compared and purchased.

When to Go

Reims

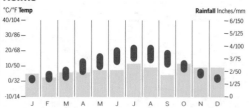

| **March or early April** Fête du Chocolat (chocolate festival) in the Champagne Route village of Äy. | **June (first weekend)** Fêtes Johanniques in Reims celebrate Joan of Arc with medieval re-enactments. | **Late August to September** Champagne harvest is marked by hard work and celebrations. |

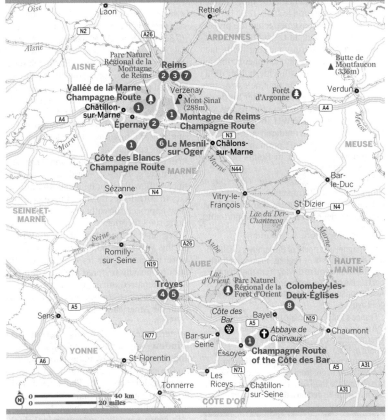

Champagne Highlights

❶ Explore hillside vineyards, picturesque villages and traditional family wineries along the scenic **Champagne Routes** (p286 and p298)

❷ Sip Champagne at the end of a **cellar tour** in Épernay (p290) or Reims (p283)

❸ Climb the tower of **Cathédrale Notre Dame** (p280) in Reims for

360-degree views across France's flattest region

❹ Wander the half-timbered streets of the **old city** (p293) in Troyes

❺ Imagine caressing the sensuous, pre-industrial hand tools at **Maison de l'Outil et de la Pensée Ouvrière** (p295) in Troyes

❻ Marvel at traditional Champagne-making techniques and technology

at the **Musée de la Vigne et du Vin** (p289) in Le Mesnil-sur-Oger

❼ Picture the epoch-defining surrender that ended WWII in Europe at the **Musée de la Reddition** (p281) in Reims

❽ Immerse yourself in mid-20th century France at the new **Mémorial Charles de Gaulle** (p299) in Colombey-les-Églises

History

Champagne's most famous convert to Christianity was the Merovingian warrior-king Clovis I, who founded the Frankish kingdom in the late 5th century and began the tradition of holding royal coronations in Reims. In the Middle Ages, the region – especially Troyes – grew rich from commercial fairs at which merchants from around Europe bought and sold products from as far afield as the Mediterranean.

A 17th-century Benedictine monk named Dom Pierre Pérignon (c 1638–1715) is popularly believed to have perfected the process of using a second, in-the-bottle fermentation to make ho-hum wine sparkle. In fact, while he did make a significant contribution to the production of still wine, bubbly didn't come to dominate Champagne's wine production until over a century after his death.

In more recent history, the region was host to the end of WWII in Europe when Nazi Germany surrendered unconditionally to Allied Supreme Commander General Dwight D Eisenhower in Reims on 7 May 1945 (see p281).

Today, the *paysages du Champagne* (landscapes of Champagne) are being considered for listing as a Unesco World Heritage Site; a decision is expected in mid-2012.

❶ Getting There & Around

Champagne, just north of Burgundy's Châtillonnais and Chablis wine regions, makes a refreshing stopover if you're driving from the Channel ports, Lille or Paris eastward to Lorraine or Alsace, or southeastward towards Dijon, Lyon or Provence.

France's rail lines radiate out from Paris like the spokes of a wheel and, as it happens, Reims, Épernay and Troyes are each on a different spoke (more or less). Although there are pretty good rail connections between Reims and Épernay, the best way to get from Reims to Troyes is by bus. Thanks to the TGV Est Européen line (p981), Reims can be visited on a day trip from Paris.

Reims

POP 187,650

Over the course of a millennium (816 to 1825), some 34 sovereigns – among them two dozen kings – began their reigns in Reims' famed cathedral. Meticulously restored after WWI and again following WWII, the city – whose name is pronounced something like 'rance' and is often anglicised as Rheims – is endowed with handsome pedestrian zones, well-tended parks, lively nightlife and a brand-new tramway. Along with Épernay (just a half-hour away by train), it is the most important centre of Champagne production and makes an excellent base for exploring the Montagne de Reims Champagne Route.

◉ Sights

Around town, dark-brown signs shaped like tine-less forks supply titbits of local history in French and English.

Cathédrale Notre Dame　　CATHEDRAL

(www.cathedrale-reims.culture.fr,www.cathedrale-reims.com, in French; place du Cardinal Luçon; ⊘7.30am-7.30pm, closed during Sun morning Mass) Imagine the egos, extravagance and the over-the-top costumes of a French royal coronation... The focal point of all the bejewelled pomposity was Reims' cathedral, a Gothic edifice begun in 1211 – and mostly completed 100 years later – on a site occupied by churches since the 5th century. The single most famous event to take place here was the coronation of Charles VII, with Joan of Arc at his side, on 17 July 1429. The structure, a Unesco World Heritage Site since 1991, will celebrate its 800th anniversary in 2011. To get the most impressive first view, approach the cathedral from the west, along rue Libergier.

Seriously damaged by artillery and fire during WWI, the 139m-long cathedral is more interesting for its dramatic history than its heavily restored architectural features – repaired during the interwar years, thanks, in part, to significant donations from the American Rockefeller family.

The finest stained-glass windows are the western facade's 12-petalled **great rose window**; its cobalt-blue neighbour below; and the **rose window** in the north transept (to the left as you walk from the entrance to the high altar), above the Flamboyant Gothic **organ case** (15th and 18th centuries) topped with a figure of Christ. Nearby is a 15th-century wooden **astronomical clock**. There are **windows by Chagall** (1974; a sign explains each panel) in the central axial chapel (directly behind the high altar) and, two chapels to the left, you'll find a **statue of Joan of Arc** in full body armour (1901); there's a second statue of her outside on the square, to the right as you exit the cathedral. The tourist office (50m north of the cathedral) rents audioguides (one/two people €5/9) with self-paced tours of the cathedral.

Feeling as strong as Goliath? (Look for his worn figure up on the west facade, held in place with metal straps.) Then consider climbing 250 steps up the **cathedral tower** (adult/under 26yr €7/free, incl the Palais du Tau €9.50; ⊘tours 10am, 11am, 2pm, 3pm & 4pm Tue-Sat & Sun afternoon mid-Mar–Oct, every half-hour 10-11.30am & 2-5pm early May-early Sep) on a one-hour tour. Book at the Palais du Tau.

Palais du Tau
MUSEUM

(☏03 26 47 81 79; www.palais-du-tau.fr; 2 place du Cardinal Luçon; adult/under 26yr €7/free; ☉9.30am-12.30pm & 2-5.30pm, closed Mon) This former archbishop's residence, constructed in 1690, was where French princes stayed before their coronations – and where they hosted sumptuous banquets afterwards. Now a museum, it displays truly exceptional statuary, liturgical objects and tapestries from the cathedral, some in the impressive, Gothic-style Salle de Tau (Great Hall).

Basilique St-Rémi
BASILICA

(place du Chanoine Ladame; ☉8am-nightfall, to 7pm summer) This 121m-long former Benedictine abbey church, a Unesco World Heritage Site, mixes Romanesque elements from the mid-11th century (the worn but stunning nave and transept) with early Gothic features from the latter half of the 12th century (the choir, with a large triforium gallery and, way up top, tiny clerestory windows). It is named in honour of Bishop Remigius, who baptised Clovis and 3000 Frankish warriors in 498. The 12th-century-style chandelier has 96 candles, one for each year of the life of St Rémi, whose tomb (in the choir) is marked by a mausoleum from the mid-1600s. The basilica is situated about 1.5km south-southeast of the tourist office; take the Citadine 1 or 2 or bus A or F to the St-Rémi stop.

Next door, Musée St-Rémi (☏03 26 36 36 90; 53 rue Simon; ☉2-6.30pm Mon-Fri, to 7pm Sat & Sun), in a 17th- and 18th-century abbey, features local Gallo-Roman archaeology, tapestries and 16th- to 19th-century military history.

Place Drouet d'Erlon
SQUARE

Lit up like Las Vegas after dark, Reims' pedestrianised main square draws locals in the mood for a bite, a beer or a bit of shopping. Southeast of the Subé Fountain (built in 1907) – crowned by a gleaming gold statue of Winged Victory – is Galerie d'Erlon, a glass-roofed arcade where you can bask in the shopping vibe of yesteryear. The 12th- to 14th-century Église St-Jacques (rue Marx Dormoy), the city's only remaining medieval parish church, has some 1960s stained glass that's so awful it has to be seen to be believed. The blue and white windows in the nave were added in 2010.

Musée des Beaux-Arts
ART MUSEUM

(Museum of Fine Arts; ☏03 26 35 36 01; 8 rue Chanzy; ☉10am-noon & 2-6pm, closed Tue) This institution's rich collection, housed in an 18th-century abbey, boasts one of only four versions of Jacques-Louis David's world-famous *The Death of Marat* (yes, the bloody corpse in the bathtub), 27 works by Camille Corot (only the Louvre has more), 13 portraits by German Renaissance painters Cranach the Elder and the Younger, lots of Barbizon School landscapes, some art-nouveau creations by Émile Gallé, and two works each by Monet, Gauguin and Pissarro.

Musée Hôtel Le Vergeur
MUSEUM

(☏03 26 47 20 75; 36 place du Forum; adult/child €4/free; ☉2-6pm Tue-Sun) In a 13th- to 16th-century town house, highlights include a series of furnished period rooms (kitchen, smoking room, Napoléon III's bedroom), engravings by Albrecht Dürer and a stunning Renaissance facade facing the interior garden.

Musée de la Reddition
MUSEUM

(Surrender Museum; ☏03 26 47 84 19; 12 rue Franklin Roosevelt; ☉10am-noon & 2-6pm Wed-Mon) The original Allied battle maps are still affixed to the walls of US General Dwight D Eisenhower's headquarters, where Nazi Germany, represented by General Alfred Jodl, surrendered unconditionally at 2.41am on 7 May 1945. Displays include military uniforms and photographs. A 12-minute film is screened in French, English and German.

REIMS DISCOUNTS

The great-value **Discovery Pass** (adult/student €3/free) gets you into Reims' three municipal museums – Musée des Beaux-Arts, Musée St-Rémi and Musée de la Reddition – and Chapelle Foujita. It's sold wherever it's valid.

The **Reims City Card** (€15), available at the tourist office, entitles you to the Champagne house tour of your choice, an audioguide tour of the cathedral and all the benefits of a Discovery Pass.

0 | 200 m
0 | 0.1 miles

CHAMPAGNE

Map labels:

To Neufchâtel
Tram Terminus

R MC Foriaux

R Franklin Roosevelt

Av de Laon

Cimetière
du Nord

R du Champ de Mars

2

13

R Edouard Mignot

8

Pl de la
République

Pl du Boulingrin

24

11

22

27

6

R du Temple

19

Esplanade
du Colonel
Bouchez

Bd Joffre

Bd Lundy

R du Général Sarrail

R de Mars

Bd Foch

Hôtel de
Ville

R Linguet

R St-Hilaire

R des Templiers

14

Bd Louis Roederer

Square
Colbert

R Thiers

23

Bd Général Leclerc

Pl Drouet d'Erlon

R de Talleyrand

Pl de
l'Hôtel
de Ville

Pl Léon
Bourgeois

R Jean-Jacques Rousseau

10

R Pluche

R Courmeaux

30

Pl Aristide
Briand

3

20

R Cadran
St-Pierre

Cours JB Langlet

Pl du
Forum

21

R Cérès

To Taittinger (2km);
Épernay (25km)

25

12

R de l'Étape

R Condorcet

Pl
Royale

R Carnot

15

5

18

R de Thillois

26

Pl Myron-
Herrick

R Guillaume
de Machault

R Buirette

17

28

Pl de
Justice

Cathédrale
Notre Dame

Gardens

29

4

Théâtre

7

Pl du
Cardinal
Luçon

Palais
du Tau

Pl
Carnegie

1

R Jeanne d'Arc

R Théodore
Dubos

9

16

R Libergier

Médiathèque

R de Capucins

To Gare de
Champagne
TGV Tram
Terminus

R de Vesle

R Hincmar

R Chanzy

R Voltaire

To Centre
International
de Séjour (600m)

To Basilique St-Rémi (1.2km)

Roman Reims

ROMAN SITES

For a quick trip back to Roman Gaul, check out the massive **Porte de Mars** (Mars Gate; place de la République), a three-arched triumphal gate built in the 2nd century AD, and the below-street-level **Cryptoportique** (place du Forum; admission free; ☺interior 2-6pm Tue-Sun Jun–mid-Oct), thought to have been used for grain storage in the 3rd century AD. Cultural events are held in the adjacent **amphithea-tre** (place du Forum), inaugurated in 2010.

Art Deco Reims

ARCHITECTURE

The vaulted **Halles du Boulingrin** (rue de Mars) were a symbol of Reims' emergence from the destruction of WWI when they began service as the city's main food market in 1929. Closed in 1988, they will again shelter food stalls – as well as art expositions (on the mezzanine) and cultural events – starting on Valentine's Day 2012. The peculiar name is derived from the English 'bowling green' (as in lawn bowling).

Thanks to a donation from the US-based Carnegie Foundation, the lobby of the **Bibliothèque** (library; 2 place Carnegie) boasts gorgeous 1920s mosaics, stained glass, frescos and an extraordinary chandelier – duck inside for a look!

The tourist office also has a brochure on art deco sites in Reims.

Chapelle Foujita CHAPEL
(Chapelle Notre-Dame de la Paix; 33 rue du Champ de Mars; ☺2-6pm May-Oct, closed Wed) The last great work by the Japanese-born artist Tsuguharu (Léonard) Foujita (1886–1968). Inaugurated in 1966.

👉 Tours

The musty *caves* (cellars) and dusty bottles of eight Reims-area Champagne houses (known as *maisons* – literally, 'houses') can be visited on guided tours. The following places both have fancy websites, cellar temperatures of 10°C to 12°C (bring warm clothes!) and frequent English-language tours that end, *naturellement,* with a tasting session. For details on how Champagne is made, see p932.

Mumm CHAMPAGNE CELLAR
(☑03 26 49 59 70; www.mumm.com; 34 rue du Champ de Mars; tours €10; ☺tours begin 9am-11am & 2-5pm daily Mar-Oct & Sat Nov-Feb) Mumm (pronounced 'moom'), the only *maison* in central Reims, was founded in 1827 and is now the world's third-largest producer (almost eight million bottles a year). Engaging and edifying one-hour tours take you through cellars filled with 25 million bottles of fine bubbly. Tours that include tutored tastings of special vintages cost €15 to €20. Wheelchair accessible. Phone ahead if possible.

Taittinger CHAMPAGNE CELLAR
(☑03 26 85 84 33; www.taittinger.com; 9 place St-Niçaise; tours €10; ☺tours begin 9.30-11.50am & 2pm-4.20pm, closed Sat & Sun mid-Nov–mid-Mar) The headquarters of Taittinger is an excellent place to come for a clear, straightforward presentation on how Champagne is actually made – there's no claptrap about 'the Champagne mystique' here. Parts of the cellars occupy 4th-century Roman stone quarries; other bits were excavated by 13th-century Benedictine monks. No need to reserve. Situated 1.5km southeast of Reims centre; take the Citadine 1 or 2 bus to the St-Niçaise or Salines stops.

🛏 Sleeping

A number of midrange hotels can be found just west of place Drouet d'Erlon along rue

Buirette. The tourist office (by phone or in person) and its website can help with hotel reservations (no charge).

TOP CHOICE / Grand Hôtel des Templiers

HOTEL €€€

(☑03 26 88 55 08; www.grandhoteldestempliers -reims.com; 22 rue des Templiers; r €190-280, ste €350; ❄@🛜🏊) Built in the 1800s as the home of a rich Champagne merchant, this neo-Gothic extravaganza retains its original ceilings, stained glass and furnishings. The imposing wooden staircase gives a certain retro theatricality, but the 18 rooms and suites come with modern marble bathrooms. Bonuses include a basement swimming pool, sauna, *hammam* (Turkish bath) and flowery breakfast room. Wheelchair access available. Situated in a quiet neighbourhood 500m east of the centre.

Hôtel de la Paix

HOTEL €€

(☑03 26 40 04 08; www.bestwestern-lapaix -reims.com; 9 rue Buirette; d €155-205; ❄@🛜🏊) An island of serenity just steps from hopping place Drouet d'Erlon, this modern, Best Western–affiliated hostelry has 169 classy, comfortable rooms; upgrade to 'Deluxe' for lots more space. To mellow out, you can head to the pool, jacuzzi, *hammam* and fitness room – or the calming Japanese garden in the courtyard.

Hôtel de la Cathédrale

HOTEL €

(☑03 26 47 28 46; www.hotel-cathedrale-reims.fr; 20 rue Libergier; s/d/q from €56/59/79; 🛜) Graciousness and a resident Yorkshire terrier greet guests at this hostelry, run by a music-loving couple (she used to teach piano, he ran a music school). The 17 tasteful rooms, spread over four floors (no lift, though), are smallish but pleasingly chintzy, and all have recently been renovated. Corner rooms 14, 23 and 33 are especially bright; room 43 has views of Basilique St-Rémi and the hills to the south.

Latino Hôtel

HOTEL €

(☑03 26 47 48 89; www.latinocafe.fr, in French; 33 place Drouet d'Erlon; d €58-79, ste €130; ❄@🛜) Above a buzzy café with a Latin beat, this almost boutique hotel has a dozen gaily (think fruity) painted guestrooms (cherry, pumpkin and aubergine) over five floors, but no lift. The furnishings are fun, the welcome warm and we love the quotes from the great and the good (Gandhi, Oscar Wilde) sgraffitoed on the hall walls.

Hôtel Cecyl

HOTEL €

(☑03 26 47 57 47; www.hotel-cecyl.fr; 24 rue Buirette; s/d/tr €45/57/77; 🛜) Solid budget value behind a century-old facade. The 27 rooms come with faux parquet floor, flat-screen TV and yellow and orange tones so bright they'll almost give you a tan. Ask for rooms 202, 302 and 402, whose alcoves afford views of place Drouet d'Erlon's Subé Fountain.

Centre International de Séjour

HOSTEL €

(CIS; ☑03 26 40 52 60; www.cis-reims.com; chaussée Bocquaine; bed in s/d/q per person €43/26/20, with shared toilet €33/20/20; ⏱24hr; @) The 85 rooms are institutional and charmless (think showers with timer buttons) but the price is right – and you can cook in the small kitchen *and* there's a washing machine in the basement. Camping cars can park in the lot out back for up to 48 hours. Situated about 1km southwest of the centre and 200m south of the Comédie tram stop.

🍴 Eating

Place Drouet d'Erlon is lined with inexpensive restaurants and pub-cafés (including two that are Irish-style) but, as one local matron put it with arched eyebrows, its eateries are *populaire, ordinaire* and *touristique*. More discerning diners often head to the stretch of rue de Mars facing Halles du Boulingrin and adjacent rue du Temple, and to the restaurants and cafés along the southern side of place du Forum, some of which have seating on the square.

TOP CHOICE / Le Foch

MODERN FRENCH €€

(☑03 26 47 48 22; www.lefoch.com; 37 bd Foch; menus €31-80; ⏱closed Mon, lunch Sat & dinner Sun) Described as 'one of France's best fish restaurants' by the food critic Michael Edwards, elegant Le Foch – holder of one Michelin star – serves up cuisine that's as beautiful as it is delicious.

Brasserie Le Boulingrin

BRASSERIE €€

(☑03 26 40 96 22; www.boulingrin.fr; 48 rue de Mars; menus €18-28; ⏱Mon-Sat) A genuine, old-time brasserie – the decor and zinc bar date back to 1925 – whose ambience and cuisine make it an enduring favourite. From September to June, the culinary focus is on *fruits de mer* (seafood).

Le Bocal

SEAFOOD €

(☑03 26 47 02 51; 27 rue de Mars; mains €13-19; ⏱closed Sun, Mon & dinner Wed) Tastefully decorated in the colours of the North Atlantic, this unpretentious fish and seafood restaurant has just five tables and two hot *plats du jour* (dishes of the day). Enter through the fish shop, where odours of the sea will engulf your senses. Three hot oysters cost €6 and a glass of Champagne is €8.

Côté Cuisine TRADITIONAL FRENCH €
(☑03 26 83 93 68; 43 bd Foch; mains €11.80-22.50, weekday lunch menus €12-15.50, dinner menus €32.50; ⊗closed dinner Sun) A spacious, semiformal place with white tablecloths, modern chandeliers and well-regarded traditional French cuisine. Especially good value at lunchtime.

Self-Catering

Great spots for a picnic include the gardens behind the cathedral and flowery Square Colbert, just southeast of the train station.

Marché du Boulingrin FOOD MARKET €
(place du Boulingrin; ⊗8am-1pm Sat) Under a tent but will move back inside the historic Halles du Boulingrin in 2012.

La Cave aux Fromages CHEESE €
(12 place du Forum; ⊗8am-1pm & 3.30-7.45pm Tue-Sat)

Monoprix SUPERMARKET €
(51 place Drouet d'Erlon) Walk to the back of the Espace d'Erlon shopping mall (Galerie de la Fnac) and take the down escalator.

Drinking

While the focal point of Reims' nightlife is place Drouet d'Erlon, whose perimeter is lined with midrange cafés and pubs, many of the city's more stylish nightspots are elsewhere in town.

TOP CHOICE **Café du Palais** CAFÉ
(www.cafedupalais.fr; 14 place Myron-Herrick; ⊗10am-8.30pm, to midnight or 1am Fri & Sat, closed Sun) Run by the same family since 1930, this old-time café is *the* place to see and be seen, at least if you're a *bon bourgeois* or a theatre type. Decoration includes wall mirrors, an art deco skylight and an extraordinary collection of bric-a-brac that ranges from the tacky to the inspired. The shoes hanging upside down from the dark red ceiling and the life-sized statue of a naked woman with horse's hoofs and elephant tusks – is it art? Is it kitsch?

Hall Place CHAMPAGNE BAR
(☑03 26 46 10 00; www.hallplace.fr; 23bis rue de Mars; wine per glass €4.50-9; ⊗10am-3pm & 6pm-midnight Tue-Fri, 10am-3pm Mon & Sat, closed Sun) Relax, sip bubbly and look fabulous at this trendy wine bar, a huge hit with Reims' young and beautiful set. Streetside,

chest-high butcher-block tables look out on the curves of Halles du Boulingrin, while at the back there's a wine shop. Lunch is served daily except Sunday; dinner is available on Tuesday, Thursday and Friday (€10.50 to €23).

Waïda TEAROOM
(5 place Drouet d'Erlon; ⊗7.30am-7.30pm Tue-Sun) A *salon de thé* (tearoom) and confectioner with old-fashioned mirrors, mosaics and marble. A good place to pick up a box of *biscuits roses* (€3.90), traditionally nibbled with Champagne (€6 to €7.50 a glass). The *religieuses* (cream-filled puff pastries; €2.75) are divine!

☆ Entertainment

Billeterie Fnac BOX OFFICE
(www.fnactickets.com; 51 place Drouet d'Erlon; ⊗10am-7.30pm Mon-Sat) Sells concert and cultural event tickets inside the Espace d'Erlon shopping centre (Galerie de la Fnac), on the lower level (down the escalator).

Cinéma Opéra CINEMA
(☑03 26 47 13 54; www.allocine.fr, in French; 3 rue Théodore Dubois) Screens nondubbed films, some in English.

Shopping

Stylish boutiques line rue de Talleyrand.

TOP CHOICE **Vins CPH** WINE
(www.vinscph.com; 3 place Léon Bourgeois) Shop for wines the way savvy locals do. At the end of the courtyard, head down into the cellar for a huge selection (some 1100 vintages are on offer), including over 200 Champagnes (€14 to €900 – the priciest bottle is a Krug).

Alice Délice KITCHENWARE
(www.alicedelice.com, in French; 53 place Drouet d'Erlon) For a fine selection of kitchen implements and gadgets.

❶ Information

Commercial banks can be found on rue Carnot and at the southern end of place Drouet d'Erlon.

Cyber@Games (52 place Drouet d'Erlon; per hr €4.20; ⊗10am-7pm Mon-Sat) Internet access inside Galerie du Lion d'Or.

Post office (2 rue Cérès) Also exchanges currency.

Tourist office (☑08 92 70 13 51; per minute €0.34; www.reims-tourisme.com; 2 rue Guillaume de Machault; ⊗9am-7pm Mon-Sat, 10am-6pm Sun & holidays)

❶ Getting There & Away

BUS The best way to get to Troyes (€24, 1¾ to 2¼ hours, three to five daily on weekdays, two on Saturday, three on Sunday except school holidays) is to take a bus operated by **TransChampagneArdenne** (☑03 26 65 17 07; www.stdmarne.fr, in French). The stop is out the train station's northern (back) entrance; hours are posted.

CAR Rental agencies:

ADA (☑03 26 82 57 81; www.ada.fr; train station car park)

Avis (☑03 26 47 10 08; train station car park)

Hertz (☑03 26 47 98 78; 26 bd Joffre)

Rent a Car Système (☑03 26 77 87 77; www.rentacar.fr; train station car park)

TRAIN Reims train station, 1km northwest of the cathedral, was renovated in 2010; the bullet marks on the facade date from both world wars. Half the trains to Paris Gare de l'Est (12 to 17 daily) are TGVs (€32 to €41, 45 minutes); the rest are TERs (€24, 1¾ hours). Direct services also go to Épernay (€6, 20 to 36 minutes, 18 daily weekdays, seven to 11 daily weekends), Laon (€9, 35 to 50 minutes, nine daily Monday to Friday, five on Saturday, three on Sunday) and Charles de Gaulle airport (three times a day).

In the city centre, train information and tickets are available at the **Boutique SNCF** (1 cours Jean-Baptiste Langlet; ☉9am-7pm Mon-Fri, 10am-6pm Sat).

❶ Getting Around

BICYCLE ADA (☑03 26 82 57 81; train station parking lot) Rents out bicycles (from €17) and electric bicycles (€24 a day).

BUS & TRAM Starting in April 2011, Reims' first tram line will link the city centre (rue de Vesle and cours JB Langlet) and the train station with Gare de Champagne-Ardenne TGV, on the Paris–Strasbourg TGV Est Européen line.

Two circular bus lines, the clockwise Citadine 1 and the anticlockwise Citadine 2 (single ticket €1, all-day *ticket journée* €3), operated by **TUR** (☑03 26 88 25 38; www.tur.fr, in French; 6 rue Chanzy; ☉7.30am-7.30pm Mon-Fri, 10am-7pm Sat), serve most of the major sights of Reims. Most TUR lines begin their last runs at about 9.50pm; five night lines operate until 12.15am.

TAXI Call ☑03 26 47 05 05.

Champagne Routes of the Marne

The Champagne Routes (Routes Touristiques du Champagne; www.tourisme-en-champagne.com) of the Marne *département* wend their way among neat rows of hillside vines, through hilltop forests and across lowland crop fields. Along the way, they call on winemaking villages and hamlets, some with notable churches or speciality museums, others quite ordinary, most without a centre or even a café. At almost every turn (and there are many), beautiful panoramas unfold and small-scale, family-run Champagne wineries welcome travellers in search of bubbly.

Area tourist offices (eg in Reims, Épernay, Hautvillers and Châtillon-sur-Marne) can supply you with details on B&Bs and on the opening times (and English capabilities) of various Champagne producers – but bear in mind that their map-brochures are far from exhaustive (producers have to pay to be included). Many producers prefer that visitors phone ahead but, if you haven't, don't be shy about knocking on the door. Almost all producers are closed around the *vendange* (grape harvest, ie from very late August into October), when bringing in the crop (picked completely by hand – mechanical harvesters are forbidden here) eclipses all other activities. More and more young *vignerons* (winegrowers) speak English.

The Champagne Routes of the Marne map (p287) shows three serpentine itineraries – Montagne de Reims, Vallée de la Marne and Côte des Blancs. The routes are not designed to be driven in their entirety in a single day so pick and choose segments that suite your mood; we've covered just a few of the villages and highlights you'll find along the way.

The Champagne Routes, which follow secondary and tertiary rural roads, are signposted but there are so many twists and turn-offs that setting off without a map would be as unwise as, well, praising the effervescent liquid marketed – fraudulently and outrageously, as far as locals are concerned – under the name 'California Champagne'. Bookshops and tourist offices sell Michelin's yellow-jacketed, 1:150,000-scale *Aisne, Ardennes, Marne* map (No 306; €4.50).

MONTAGNE DE REIMS CHAMPAGNE ROUTE

Linking Reims with Épernay by skirting the Parc Natural Régional de la Montagne de Reims, a regional park covering the forested Reims Mountain plateau, this meandering, 70km route passes through vineyards planted mainly with pinot noir

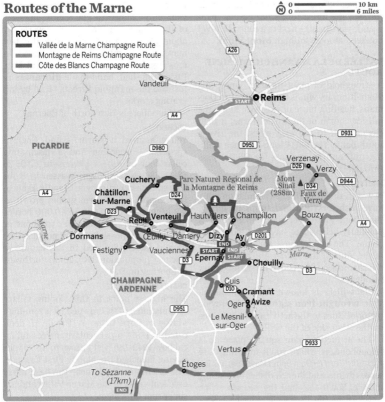

ROUTES

- Vallée de la Marne Champagne Route
- Montagne de Reims Champagne Route
- Côte des Blancs Champagne Route

vines. Villages are listed in the order you'll encounter them if starting out from Reims.

VERZENAY

For the region's best introduction to the art of growing grapes and the cycles of the seasons, head to the Phare de Verzenay (Verzenay Lighthouse; ☎03 26 07 87 87; www.lepharedeverzenay.com, in French; D26; adult incl audioguide €7; ☉10am-6pm Tue-Fri, to 6.30pm Sat & Sun, last entry 1hr earlier, closed Jan-Mar), on a hilltop at the eastern edge of the village. Exactly 101 spiral stairs lead to the top of the lighthouse, constructed as a publicity stunt in 1909, which rewards visitors with unsurpassed 360-degree views of vine, field and forest – and, if you're lucky, a tiny TGV zipping by in the distance. The Sillery sugar mill, visible on the horizon, turns an astounding 16,000 tonnes of beets (a major regional crop) into 2600 tonnes of sugar each day! Stop by the Jardin Panoramique (admission free) to get a look at the four au-

thorised techniques for tying grape vines to horizontal wires (can you make out the differences?). The ticket counter can provide an English translation of the wall texts.

The Moulin de Verzenay (Verzenay Windmill; D26), on the western edge of town, was used as an observation post during WWI and by the US Army during WWII. The interior is closed but the nearby hill offers fine valley views.

PARC NATURAL RÉGIONAL DE LA MONTAGNE DE REIMS

The 500 sq km Montagne de Reims Regional Park is best known for a botanical curiosity, 800 mutant beech trees known as **faux de Verzy** (see http://verzy.verzenay.online.fr for photos). To get a good look at the trees, which have torturously twisted trunks and branches that hang down like an umbrella, take the Balade des Faux **forest walk** from 'Les Faux' parking lot, 2km up D34 from Verzy (situated on D26).

Across D34, a 500m gravel path leads through the forest to a *point de vue* (panoramic viewpoint) – next to a concrete WWI bunker – atop 288m-high **Mont Sinaï**.

VALLÉE DE LA MARNE CHAMPAGNE ROUTE

A stronghold of pinot meunier vines, this 90km itinerary winds from Épernay to Dormans, heading more or less west along the hillsides north of the River Marne; it then circles back to the east along the river's south bank. The GR14 long-distance walking trail and its variants (eg GR141) pass through the area.

HAUTVILLERS

It was in this tidy village (population 800), alive with forsythia and tulips in spring, that Dom Pierre Pérignon (1639–1715) is popularly believed to have created Champagne. The good Dom's tomb is in front of the altar of the Église Abbatiale (abbey church; ☺daily), adorned with 17th-century woodwork.

Hautvillers is known for its medieval-style **wrought-iron signs**, which provide pictorial clues to the activities taking place on the other side of the wall.

The attractive main square, place de la République, is where you'll find the Café d'Hautvillers (☺9am-9pm, closed Tue), which serves drinks and French dishes on a sunny terrace. You'll also find the tourist office (☑03 26 57 06 35; www.tourisme-hautvillers. com; ☺9.30am-1pm & 1.30-6pm Mon-Sat, 10am-5pm Sun Apr–mid-Oct, 10am-noon & 2-5pm Mon-Sat mid-Oct–Mar), where you can pick up excellent free maps for several gorgeous vineyard walks. One-hour guided tours cost €3 (with a Champagne tasting €5).

Astonishing **vineyard views** await a few hundred metres north of the centre along route de Fismes (D386); south along route de Cumières (a road leading to D1); and along the GR14 long-distance walking trail (indicated by red-and-white trail markings) and local vineyard footpaths (yellow markings).

Hautvillers is twinned with the Alsatian town of Eguisheim, which helps explain why two storks (see p321) – Petrus and Leontine (they're named after Dom 'Petrus' Pérignon and Eguisheim-born Pope Leo IX) – live in the Voilière des Cigognes Altavilloises (☑03 26 59 44 58; D386; admission free), an easy 500m walk towards Épernay from place de la République. If

you're not expecting a baby, this may be your only chance to get a close-up view of these majestic birds, each covered by about 15,000 feathers (some day, this fact may prove useful at a cocktail party). In most years, storklings hatch here in May. Inside the shed, hand-made **dioramas** illustrate the manifold threats faced by migrating storks.

Hautvillers is 7km north of Épernay.

CUCHERY

You're assured a warm – and English-speaking – welcome and a fascinating cellar tour at Albert Levasseur (☑03 26 58 11 38; www.champagne-levasseur.fr; 6 rue Sorbier, Cuchery), run by a friendly Franco-Irish couple, which turns grapes grown on 4.2 hectares into 35,000 to 40,000 bottles of Champagne each year. Try to phone or email ahead if possible – but if not just drop by and knock. Situated in the hamlet of Cuchery (population 390), 20km northwest of Épernay on D24.

CHÂTILLON-SUR-MARNE

The highest point in this sloping village (population 840) is crowned by a 25m-high statue of Pope Urban II (Urbain II; dedicated in 1887), a particularly successful local boy (1042–99) best known to history for having launched the bloody First Crusade. The orientation table near the base offers excellent views of the Marne Valley and is a super spot for a picnic.

The tourist office (☑03 26 58 32 86; www. otchatillon51.com, in French; ☺closed morning Mon, Jan & Feb) is very near the partly Romanesque church. A map panel right next to the post office details an 11km, four-hour **vineyard walk**.

Châtillon is 20km west of Épernay, on D23.

ŒUILLY

To get a sense of winegrowing life a century ago, drop by the Écomusée d'Œuilly (☺03 26 57 10 30; adult €6.50; ☺10am-noon & 2-5pm, to 6pm Apr-Oct, closed Sun morning & Tue, closed Mon Nov-Mar), whose three sections include a schoolroom, c 1900. Behind massively built Église St-Memmie (13th century), the churchyard – with panoramic views – is the final resting place of five members of a RAF air crew downed in 1944; each grave bears a moving personal inscription.

Œuilly (population 650) is 15km west of Épernay, just off D3.

CÔTE DES BLANCS CHAMPAGNE ROUTE

This 100km route, planted almost exclusively with white chardonnay grapes (the name means 'hillside of the whites'), begins along Épernay's majestic av du Champagne and then heads south to Sézanne and beyond.

Blanc des Blancs (Champagne made exclusively with chardonnay grapes) is known for its freshness, elegance, clarity, very small bubbles and a bouquet reminiscent of 'yellow fruits' such as pear and plum.

CRAMANT

To appreciate the austere beauty of the Champagne countryside, check out the view from the ridge above this village (population 900), whose northern entrance is adorned by a two-storey-high champagne bottle. Situated on D10 7.5km southeast of Épernay on D10.

AVIZE

Many past, present and future Champagne makers learned, or are learning, their art and science at the Lycée Viticole de la Champagne (Champagne High School of Winemaking; www.les-enfants-de-la-viti.com, in French), run by the Ministry of Agriculture. As part of their studies, students produce quite excellent bubbly, made with grapes from some of Champagne's most prestigious parcels and sold under the label Champagne Sanger (www.sanger.fr). Sanger was established shortly after WWI, which is why the name is pronounced *sans guerre* ('without war'), ie sahn-GHER.

At the Sanger Cellars (☎03 26 57 79 79; 33 rue du Rempart du Midi; ⊗8am-noon & 2-5pm Mon-Fri, closed 1st half Aug), free tours of the high school's impressive production facilities take in both traditional equipment and the latest high-tech machinery, such as a Rube Goldberg gadget that removes sediment from the necks of bottles after *remuage* (riddling) by an automated *gyropalette*. Champagnes are sold at the discounted *prix départ cave* (cellar-door price); profits are reinvested in the school. The entrance is on D19 100m down the hill from D10; if the door is locked, push the intercom button.

Once the abbey church of a Benedictine convent, Église St-Nicolas, on rue de l'Église (D10), mixes Romanesque, Flamboyant Gothic and Renaissance styles. From there, aptly named rue de la Montagne leads up the hill (towards Grauves) – past another oversized Champagne bottle – to

Parc Vix (D19), which affords panoramic vineyard views; a map sign details a 6.5km, two-hour walk through forest and field.

OGER

Oger (population 600) is known for its grand cru fields, prize-winning flower gardens and the Musée du Mariage (Wedding Museum; ☑03 26 57 50 89; www.mariage-et-champagne. com; 1 rue d'Avize/D10; adult €6; ⊗10am-noon & 2-6pm, closed Mon). Featuring colourful and often gaudy objects associated with 19th-century marriage traditions, highlights include a tableau of newlyweds in their nuptial bed – but they're not alone, for they've been woken up early by family and friends bearing Champagne, chocolate and broad smiles. The collection was assembled by the parents of the owner of Champagne Henry de Vaugency (founded 1732), an eighth-generation Champagne grower. An explanatory sheet in English is available.

LE MESNIL-SUR-OGER

TOP CHOICE Musé de la Vigne et du Vin (Vine & Wine Museum; ☑03 26 57 50 15; www. champagne-launois.fr, in French; 2 av Eugène Guillaume, cnr D10; adult incl 3 flutes Champagne €7.50) is so outstanding that it's worth planning your day around a tour – on most days, one begins at 10am. Assembled by a family that has been making Champagne since 1872, this extraordinary collection of century-old Champagne-making equipment includes objects so aesthetically ravishing that you'll want to reach out and touch them. Among the highlights is a massive 16-tonne oak-beam grape press from 1630. Reservations can be made by phone or through their website; tours are not necessarily in English.

Wine and restaurant critic Michael Edwards calls Le Mesnil 'the greatest Chardonnay commune in Champagne'.

For an excellent French meal, head to Le Mesnil (☑03 26 57 95 57; www.restaurantle mesnil.com, in French; 2 rue Pasteur; menus €29-39; ⊗closed Sun, Mon & dinner Tue).

Épernay

POP 25,225

Prosperous Épernay, the self-proclaimed *capitale du champagne* and home to many of the world's most celebrated Champagne houses, is the best place in Champagne for touring cellars and sampling bubbly. The town also makes an excellent base for exploring the Champagne Routes.

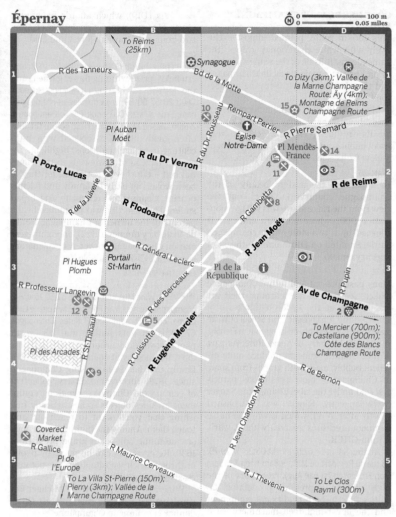

Beneath the streets in 110km of subterranean cellars, more than 200 million bottles of Champagne, just waiting to be popped open on some sparkling occasion, are being aged. In 1950 one such cellar – owned by the irrepressible Mercier family – hosted a car rally without the loss of a single bottle!

Épernay is 25km south of Reims and can be visited by train or car as a day trip from Reims.

◉ Sights & Activities

Many of Épernay's *maisons de champagne* (Champagne houses) are based along the

handsome – and eminently strollable – av de Champagne, lined with elegant town houses that were rebuilt after the devastation of WWI. It stretches eastward from the town's commercial heart, whose liveliest streets are rue Général Leclerc and rue St-Thibault.

Moët & Chandon   CHAMPAGNE HOUSE
(☏03 26 51 20 20; www.moet.com; 20 av de Champagne; adult incl 1/2 glasses €14.50/22, 10-18yr €9; ☺tours 9.30am-noon & 2-4.30pm, closed Sat & Sun mid-Nov–mid-Mar, also closed Jan) This prestigious *maison* offers frequent one-hour tours that are among the region's

Épernay

◎ Sights

◎ Sleeping

◎ Eating

◎ Entertainment

most impressive. At the shop you can pick up a jeroboam (3L bottle) of superpremium Dom Pérignon *millésime* (vintage Champagne) of 1998 for just €2100.

Mercier   CHAMPAGNE HOUSE
(☎03 26 51 22 22; www.champagnemercier.fr; 68-70 av de Champagne; adult incl 1/3 glasses €9/17, 12-17yr €5; ☺tours 9.30-11.30am & 2-4.30pm, closed mid-Dec–mid-Feb) France's most popular brand has thrived on unabashed self-promotion since it was founded in 1847 by Eugène Mercier, a trailblazer in the field of eye-catching publicity stunts and the virtual creator of the cellar tour. Everything here is flashy, including the 160,000L barrel that took two decades to build (for the Universal Exposition of 1889), the lift that transports you 30m underground and the laser-guided touring train.

De Castellane   CHAMPAGNE HOUSE
(☎03 26 51 19 11; www.castellane.com, in French; 64 av de Champagne; adult incl 1 glass €8.50, under 12yr free; ☺tours 10-11am & 2-5pm, closed Christmas–mid-Mar) The 45-minute tours, in French and English, take in an informative bubbly museum dedicated to elucidating the *méthode champenoise* and its diverse technologies. The reward for climbing the 237 steps up the 66m-high tower (built 1905) is a fine panoramic view.

Hôtel de Ville   CITY HALL
(City Hall; 7bis av de Champagne; ☺8.30am-noon & 1.30-6pm Mon-Fri) Next to the tourist office, in the neoclassical Hôtel de Ville, you can take a peek at the ornate, Louis XV–style **Salle de Conseil** (city council room) and **Salle de Mariages** (marriage hall). The adjacent, flowery park is perfect for a picnic.

Théâtre Gabrielle Dorziat   HISTORIC BUILDING
(www.lesalmanazar.fr, in French; place Mendès-France) The north side of Théâtre Gabrielle Dorziat, built in 1902, still shows shell and bullet marks from WWII.

☞ Tours

Champagne Houses   CELLAR TOUR
Several *maisons* offer informative and engaging cellar tours, followed by a *dégustation* (tasting) and a visit to the factory-outlet shop. See the individual Champagne houses on p290.

Champagne Domi Moreau   VINEYARD TOUR
(☎06 30 35 51 07, after 7pm 03 26 59 45 85; www.champagne-domimoreau.com; tours €20; ☺tours 9.30am & 2.30pm except Wed, no tours Christmas & Feb school holidays & 2nd half of Aug) This company runs three-hour minibus tours, in French and English, of nearby vineyards. Pick-up is across the street from the tourist office. They also organise two-hour vineyard tours by bicycle (€10) from Nancy. Call ahead for reservations.

☞ Sleeping

Épernay's hotels fill up fast on weekends from Easter to September and on weekdays, too, in May, June and September.

⬆ TOP CHOICE   Le Clos Raymi   HISTORIC HOTEL €€
(☎03 26 51 00 58; www.closraymi-hotel.com, in French; 3 rue Joseph de Venoge; d from €100, ste €160; ☎) Staying at this atmospheric place is like being a personal guest of Monsieur Chandon of Champagne fame, who occupied this luxurious town house over a century ago. The seven romantic rooms – styles include Provençal, Tuscan and colonial – have giant beds, high ceilings, French windows and parquet floors. In winter there's often a fire in the cosy art deco living room. Perfect for a honeymoon.

La Villa St-Pierre   HOTEL €
(☎03 26 54 40 80; www.villasaintpierre.fr; 14 av Paul Chandon; d €45-50; ☎) In an early-20th-century mansion, this homey place, with 11

MORE BUBBLY FOR EVERYONE

Unlike Cognac, 96% of which is consumed outside France, some 62% of the 400 million bottles of Champagne produced each year are popped open, sipped and savoured in France itself. That doesn't leave much for the rest of us, especially when you consider how many bottles are wasted naming ships and showering victorious football players. But help is at hand. Faced with rising worldwide demand, the government body that regulates where Champagne can be grown has proposed expanding the area – currently 327 sq km – for the first time since 1927. Starting in about 2017, 40 very lucky villages are likely to start planting their very first official Champagne vines. Not surprisingly, the exact delineation of the new vineyards has been hugely controversial, not least because the value of land declared Champagne-worthy will rise by up to 30,000%, to about €1 million per hectare!

Large *maisons* (Champagne houses) with global brand recognition, many of them owned by international luxury-goods conglomerates, send a high percentage of their production to other countries (Moët & Chandon, for example, exports 80% of its bubbly), in part because profit margins are higher. But the region's 4800 small producers (known as *récoltants-manipulants* because they both harvest the grapes and 'manipulate' or 'elaborate' the juice into wine) continue to serve an almost exclusively domestic clientele. About 112 million bottles of Champagne left France in 2009, a drop of 26% compared to 2007 (apparently even Champagne drinkers have been hit by the global recession).

simple rooms, retains some of the charm of yesteryear.

Hôtel de la Cloche
HOTEL €

(03 26 55 15 15; www.hotel-la-cloche.com; 5 place Mendès-France; d €49-63, tr €59-69;) A slightly stiff hotel with 19 rooms decorated in bright, dissonant colours. The 3rd-floor triples, with pitched ceilings, are ideal for kids – but, lest guests be disappointed, they won't rent them out unless you see them first. Some rooms have park or church views. This is a convenient hotel if you're arriving by rail.

Hôtel Les Berceaux
HOTEL €€

(03 26 55 28 84; www.lesberceaux.com; 13 rue des Berceaux; d €95-115;) Founded in 1889, this institution has 28 comfortable, sound-proofed rooms with lots of dark-wood veneer and all-tile bathrooms.

✖ Eating

Épernay's main dining area is along rue Gambetta, whose establishments include three pizzerias and a kebab joint, and around adjacent place de la République.

Restaurant Le Théâtre
TRADTIONAL FRENCH €€

(03 26 58 88 19; www.epernay-rest-letheatre.com, in French; 8 place Mendès-France; lunch menus €17-22, dinner menus €28-46; closed Wed, dinner Tue & dinner Sun) Refined traditional cuisine is served in a classic corner dining room built a century ago as a brasse-

rie, with 4.2m ceilings and floor-to-ceiling windows. The menu changes every three weeks, depending to what's fresh in the markets.

La Cave à Champagne
REGIONAL CUISINE €€

(03 26 55 50 70; www.la-cave-a-champagne.com, in French; 16 rue Gambetta; menus €17-32; closed Wed & dinner Tue) 'The Champagne Cellar' is well regarded by locals for its *champenoise* cuisine, served in a warm, traditional, bourgeois atmosphere. You can sample three different Champagnes for €21.

Bistrot Le 7
MODERN FRENCH €€

(03 26 55 28 84; 13 rue des Berceaux; menus €17-23) One of the restaurants at Hôtel Les Berceaux has earned a Michelin star; the other (this one) serves excellent French cuisine amid semiformal, Mediterranean-chic decor. The escargots in a basil, butter and cream sauce are superior, and the chocolate desserts are to die for.

La Table Kobus
FRENCH €€

(03 26 51 53 53; www.latablekobus.com, in French; 3 rue du Docteur Rousseau; menus €28-39; closed Mon, dinner Sun & dinner Thu) French cuisine in versions traditional and creative, served amid fin-de-siècle Paris bistro decor.

Le Sardaigne
PIZZERIA €

(1 place Mendès-France; pizzas €7-11) Best pizza in town.

Self-catering

Covered market FOOD MARKET €
(Halle St-Thibault; rue Gallice; ⊗7.30am-12.30pm
Wed & Sat)

Open-air market FOOD MARKET €
(place Auban Moët; ⊗Sun morning)

Charcutier-Traiteur GOURMET FOOD €
(9 place Hugues Plomb; ⊗8am-12.45pm &
3-7.30pm, closed Sun & Wed) Scrumptious
prepared dishes.

La Cloche à Fromage CHEESE SHOP €
(19 rue St-Thibault; ⊗8.30am-12.15pm & 3-7pm
Tue-Sat) Has been selling cheeses at this
location for over a century.

Marché Plus SMALL SUPERMARKET €
(13 place Hugues Plomb; ⊗7am-9pm Mon-Sat,
9am-1pm Sun)

☆ Entertainment

Cinéma Le Palace (⊉08 92 68 07 51; www.
le-palace.fr, in French; 33 bd de la Motte) Screens
nondubbed films, some in English.

❶ Information

Cybermania (11 place des Arcades; per hr €3;
⊗10am-10pm Tue-Sat, 2-8pm Sun, 2-10pm
Mon) Internet access.

Post office (place Hugues Plomb) Also exchanges foreign currency.

Tourist office (⊉03 26 53 33 00; www.
ot-epernay.fr; 7 av de Champagne; ⊗9.30am-
12.30pm & 1.30-7pm Mon-Sat, 11am-4pm Sun
& holidays) Has excellent English brochures
and maps on cellar visits, walking and cycling
options and car touring, and rents out a GPS
unit (€7 per day) with self-guided vineyard driving tours in French, English and Dutch.

❶ Getting There & Around

BICYCLE Bicycles can be rented at Épernay's
municipal swimming pool, **Espace Aquatique
Bulléo** (⊉03 26 53 35 60; www.ccepc.fr, in
French; Parc Roger Menu, rue Dom Pérignon;
per half-day/day/week €10/15/70; ⊗10am-
6pm Mon-Fri, to 5.30pm Sat & Sun Apr-Oct),
situated about 700m south of the covered
market.

The tourist office sells cycling maps and map-
cards (€0.50).

CAR Europcar (⊉03 26 54 90 61; 20 rempart
Perrier)

TRAIN The **train station** (place Mendès-France)
has direct services to Reims (€6, 20 to 36 minutes, 18 daily weekdays, seven to 11 daily weekends) and Paris Gare de l'Est (€21, 1¼ hours, five
to 10 daily).

Troyes
POP 63,450

Troyes – like Reims, one of the historic
capitals of Champagne – has a lively centre that's graced with one of France's finest ensembles of half-timbered houses and
Gothic churches. Often overlooked, it's one
of the best places in France to get a sense of
what Europe looked like back when Molière
was penning his finest plays and the *Three
Musketeers* were swashbuckling. Several
unique and very worthwhile museums are
another lure.

Troyes does not have any Champagne
cellars. However, you can shop till you drop
in its scores of outlet stores stuffed with
brand-name clothing and accessories, a legacy of the city's long-time role as France's
knitwear capital.

◉ Sights

Grey panels posted around the old city provide historic background in French and
English.

16th-Century Troyes OLD CITY
Half-timbered houses – some with lurch-
ing walls and floors that aren't quite on-
the-level – line many streets in the old city,
rebuilt after a devastating fire in 1524. The
best place for aimless ambling is the area
bounded by (clockwise from the north)
rue Général de Gaulle, the Hôtel de Ville,
rue Général Saussier and rue de la Pierre;
of special interest are (from southwest to
northeast) **rue de Vauluisant, rue de la
Trinité, rue Champeaux** and **rue Paillot
de Montabert**.

Off rue Champeaux (between No 30 and
32), a stroll along tiny **ruelle des Chats** (Alley of the Cats), as dark and narrow as it
was four centuries ago – the upper floors almost touch – is like stepping back into the
Middle Ages. The stones along the base of
the walls were designed to give pedestrians
a place to stand when horses clattered by.

---

❶ TROYES DISCOUNTS

Le Pass' Troyes (€15), sold at the
tourist offices, gets you free entry to
seven museums, a two-flute Cham-
pagne-tasting session, an old city
tour (with a guide or audioguide) and
discounts at various factory outlet
shops.

CHAMPAGNE

Troyes

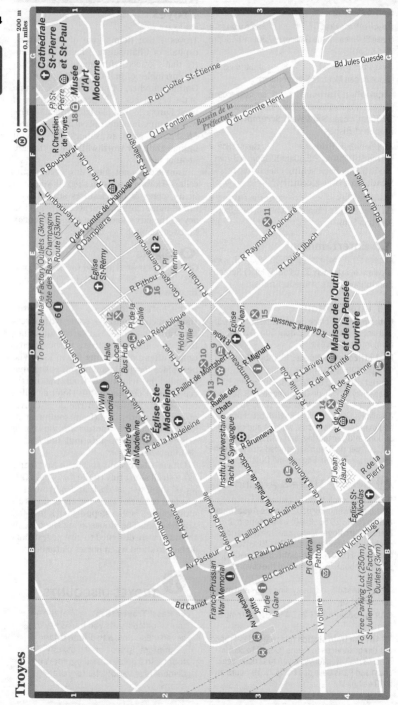

200 m
0.1 miles

Cathédrale
St-Pierre
et St-Paul

Musée
d'Art
Moderne

R du Cloître St-Étienne

Bd Jules Guesde

Pl St-
Pierre
18

R Chrestien
de Troyes

R Boucherat

Bassin de la
Préfecture

Q La Fontaine

Q du Comte Henri

4

R de la Cité

R Salerno

1

Q des Comtes de Champagne

Q Dampierre

R Hennequin

To Pont Ste-Marie Factory Outlets (3km);
Côte des Bars Champagne
Route (53km)

Église
St-Rémy

R Pithou

16

R Georges Clemenceau

Pl
Vernier

2

R Urbain IV

11

R Raymond Poincaré

R Louis Ulbach

Bd du 14 Juillet

Halle
Local
Bus Hub

12

Pl de
la Halle

R de la République

Hôtel de
Ville

R Hennequin

R Mole

Église
St-Jean

15

R Général Saussier

Maison de l'Outil
et de la Pensée
Ouvrière

WWII
Memorial

Bd Gambetta

Théâtre de
la Madeleine

Église Ste-
Madeleine

R de la Madeleine

R Paillot de Montabert

10

R Charbonnet

13

17

Ruelle des
Chats

R Mignard

R Émile Zola

R Larivey

R de la Trinité

R de Turenne

7

3

14

R de Vauluisant

5

Franco-Prussian
War Memorial

R Argence

R Général de Gaulle

Institut Universitaire
Rachi & Synagogue

R Jaillant Deschaînets

R du Palais de Justice

R Brunneval

8

R de la Monnaie

Pl Jean
Jaurès

R de la
Pierre

Église St-
Nicolas

Av Pasteur

R Paul Dubois

Bd Carnot

Pl Général
Patton

Bd Victor Hugo

To Free Parking Lot (250m);
St-Julien-les-Villas Factory
Outlets (3km)

Bd Carnot

Av Maréchal
Joffre

Pl de
la Gare

R Voltaire

Bassin de la...

Troyes

◉ Top Sights

◉ Sights

⬤ Sleeping

◉ Eating

◉ Drinking

◉ Entertainment

◉ Shopping

One of the founders of the Canadian city of Montréal, Paul Chomeday de Maisonneuve (1612–76), once lived in the **Hôtel de Chaudron** (4 rue Chrestien de Troyes).

Cathédrale St-Pierre et St-Paul CATHEDRAL
(place St-Pierre; ⊗9am-noon & 2-7pm, closed Sun morning) Troyes' most important house of worship, 114m long, incorporates elements from every period of *champenois* Gothic architecture. The Flamboyant **west facade**, for instance, dates from the mid-1500s, while the choir and transepts are more than 250 years older. The interior is illuminated by a spectacular series of some 180 **stained-glass windows** (13th to 17th

centuries) that shine like jewels when it's sunny. Also of interest: a fantastical **baroque organ** (1730s) sporting musical putti (cherubs), and a tiny **treasury** (⊗Jul & Aug) with enamels from the Meuse Valley. Back in 1429, Joan of Arc and Charles VII stopped off here on their way to his coronation in Reims.

TOP CHOICE **Maison de l'Outil et de la Pensée Ouvrière** TOOL MUSEUM
(Museum of Tools & Crafts; ☑03 25 73 28 26; www. maison-de-l-outil.com; 7 rue de la Trinité; adult/under 12yr €6.50/free; ⊗10am-6pm, to 8pm Thu, closed Tue Oct-Mar) Worn to a sensuous lustre by generations of skilled hands, the 10,000 hand tools on display here – each designed to perform a single, specialised task with exquisite efficiency – bring to life a world of manual skills made obsolete by the Industrial Revolution. The collection is housed in the magnificent Renaissance-style Hôtel de Mauroy, built in 1556. Videos show how the tools were used and what they were used for. A catalogue in English is available at the reception.

Musée d'Art Moderne ART MUSEUM
(☑03 25 76 26 80; place St-Pierre; adult €5; ⊗10am-noon & 2-5pm Tue-Fri, 11am-6pm Sat & Sun, until 7pm May-Sep) The highlights here are French painting (including lots of fauvist works) created between 1850 and 1950, glass (especially the work of local glassmaker and painter Maurice Marinot) and ceramics. Featured artists include Derain, Dufy, Matisse, Modigliani, Picasso and Soutine. Housed in a 16th- to 18th-century bishop's palace, this place owes its existence to all those crocodile-logo shirts, whose global success allowed Lacoste entrepreneurs Pierre and Denise Lévy to amass this outstanding collection.

Église Ste-Madeleine CHURCH
(rue Général de Gaulle; ⊗2-4.30pm Tue-Sun, until 7pm May-Sep) Troyes' oldest and most interesting neighbourhood church has an early-Gothic nave and transept (early 13th century) and a Renaissance-style choir and tower. The highlights here are the splendid Flamboyant Gothic **rood screen** (early 1500s), dividing the transept from the choir, and the 16th-century **stained glass** in the presbytery portraying scenes from Genesis. In the nave, the statue of a deadly serious **Ste-Marthe** (St Martha), around the pillar from the wooden pulpit, is considered a masterpiece of the 15th-century Troyes School.

Basilique St-Urbain
CHURCH

(place Vernier; ⊙2-4.30pm Tue-Sun, until 7pm May-Sep) Begun in 1262 by the Troyes-born Pope Urban IV, whose father's shoemaker shop once stood on this spot, this church is exuberantly Gothic both inside and out, and has some fine 13th-century stained glass. In the chapel off the south transept arm is **La Vierge au Raisin** (Virgin with Grapes), a graceful, early-15th-century stone statue of Mary and the Christ Child.

Église St-Pantaléon
CHURCH

(rue de Vauluisant; ⊙2-4.30pm Tue-Sun, until 7pm May-Sep) Looking pretty much like it did three centuries years ago, this Renaissance-style church, with its vaulted wood ceiling, is a great place to see the work of the 16th-century Troyes School – check out the sculptures attached to the columns of the nave. The west facade was added in the 18th century. As in many churches, history sheets are available in French, English and German.

Hôtel de Vauluisant
MUSEUM

(☑03 25 43 43 20; 4 rue de Vauluisant; adult €3; ⊙2-7pm Wed-Sun, 11am-1pm Sat & Sun May-Sep, 2-5pm Wed-Sun, 10am-noon Fri-Sun Oct-Apr) This haunted-looking, Renaissance-style mansion houses two unique museums. Plants used to make dyes and oil paints in the Middle Ages grow in the courtyard.

DID YOU KNOW...?

Chances are Troyes has already played at least a cameo role in your life:

» If you've ever read or seen a story about Lancelot or the search for the Holy Grail, you've enjoyed creations of the 12th-century poet and troubadour Chrétien (Chrestien) de Troyes (1135–83), who was, as his name indicates, a local boy.

» If you've ever purchased gold bullion, you've done so using the troy ounce, a unit of measure derived from exchange standards established in Troyes in the 12th and 13th centuries.

» Every time you've admired a Lacoste shirt, Petit Bateau kids clothing or sexy Dim underwear, you've paid homage to a brand name created right here in France's historic knitwear capital.

Musée de l'Art Troyen

Redesigned in 2009, the Museum of Troyes Art features the evocative paintings, stained glass and statuary (stone and wood) of the Troyes School, which flourished here during the economic prosperity and artistic ferment of the early 16th century.

Musée de la Bonneterie

The Hosiery Museum showcases the sock-strewn story of Troyes' 19th-century knitting industry.

Apothicairerie de l'Hôtel-Dieu-le-Comte
MUSEUM

(☑03 25 80 98 97; quai des Comtes de Champagne; adult €2; ⊙10am or 11am-1pm & 2-7pm Thu-Sun & afternoon Wed May-Sep, 10am-noon & 2-5pm Fri-Sun Oct-Apr) If you come down with an old-fashioned malady – scurvy, perhaps, or unbalanced humours – the place to go is this fully outfitted, wood-panelled pharmacy from 1721.

🛏 Sleeping

A number of hotels face the train station.

Hôtel Arlequin
HOTEL €

(☑03 25 83 12 70; www.hotelarlequin.com; 50 rue de Turenne; d €55-58, with shared toilet €43; ⊙reception closed 12.30-2pm Mon-Sat, 12.30-4pm Sun & holidays; ❄🌐) Lovingly kept and efficiently run, this charming and very yellow hostelry shows good taste all round, from the smart custard facade to the lemony breakfast room. The 28 cheerful rooms come with antique furnishings, high ceilings and *commedia dell'arte* playfulness. No lift.

Hôtel Les Comtes de Champagne
HOTEL €

(☑03 25 73 11 70; www.comtesdechampagne.com; 56 rue de la Monnaie; d €53-88, q €71-102, d with washbasin €35; 🌐) The same massive wooden beams have kept this super-welcoming 37-room place more or less vertical since the 16th century. We love the bright courtyard lobby, the flower boxes and the 12th-century cellar. A huge and very romantic double goes for €88. Bicycles are available for rent. No lift.

Le Relais St-Jean
HOTEL €€

(☑03 25 73 89 90; www.relais-st-jean.com; 51 rue Paillot de Montabert; d €95-145; ❄@🌐) On a narrow medieval street in the heart of the old city, this hotel has 25 contemporary rooms, a mini-tropical hothouse, a musical jacuzzi with coloured underwater lights, a small fitness centre and facilities for the

Under the protection of the counts of Champagne, Troyes was home to a small Jewish community during the 11th and 12th centuries. Its most illustrious member was Rabbi Shlomo Yitzhaki (1040–1105), better known as Rashi (Rachi in French).

Rashi's commentaries on the Bible and the Talmud combine literal and nonliteral methods of interpretation and make extensive use of allegories, parables and symbolic meanings. Even a millennium later, they are still vastly important to Jews and have also had an impact on interpretations of the Christian Bible. Rashi's habit of explaining difficult words and passages in the local French vernacular – transliterated into Hebrew characters – has made his writings an important resource for scholars of Old French. In 1475 (a mere three decades after Gutenberg), Rashi's Bible commentary became the first book to be printed in Hebrew.

Troyes' striking Monument Rachi (rue Jules Lebocey), a white-and-black globe that spells out Rashi's acronym in Hebrew letters, stands very near the site of the long-gone Jewish cemetery where he is believed to have been buried.

disabled. There's direct access from the underground car park (€10).

Eating

Troyes has a dynamic and ever-improving cuisine scene. Rue Champeaux, which extends westward from the Hôtel de Ville, has the city's highest concentration of restaurants, cafés and crêperies, though few rise much above the ordinary. Student-oriented eateries can be found just west of the cathedral along rue de la Cité.

Locals are enormously proud of the city's specialities: *andouillettes de Troyes* (sausages made with strips of pigs' intestines) and *tête de veau* (calf's head served without the brain). As far as most non-locals are concerned, they're an acquired taste.

La Mignardise　　TRADITIONAL FRENCH €€
(☑03 25 73 15 30; 1 ruelle des Chats; weekday lunch menu €23, other menus €29-59; ⊗closed Mon & dinner Sun) Traditional French cuisine, fresh and seasonal, is elegantly served beneath ancient wooden beams, 19th-century mouldings and ultramodern halogen lamps. The chef is a particular fan of fish, with plenty of mains from the briny deep.

Au Jardin Gourmand　　TRADITIONAL FRENCH €€
(☑03 25 73 36 13; 31 rue Paillot de Montabert; weekday lunch menu €17, mains €19-23; ⊗closed Sun & lunch Mon) Elegant without being overly formal, this intimate restaurant – with a summer terrace – uses only the freshest ingredients for its classic French and *champenois* dishes; among the latter are no fewer than 11 varieties of *andouillette*. About 20 vintages from the estimable wine list are available by the glass.

L'Ô à la Bouche　　MODERN FRENCH €€
(☑03 25 41 11 09; 14 rue de Turenne; 2-/3-course weekday lunch menus €12.50/15, dinner menus €20-27; ⊗closed Mon, lunch Sat & dinner Sun) Centuries-old wood panelling and sleek table settings harmoniously create the perfect ambience for enjoying dishes described by the chef as *style bistrot amelioré* ('improved' bistro-style French) at midday and semi-*gastronomique* in the evening.

Self-catering

TOP CHOICE / Covered Market　　FOOD MARKET €
(place de la Halle; ⊗8am-12.45pm & 3.30-7pm Mon-Thu, 7am-7pm Fri & Sat, 9am-12.30pm Sun) Fruit, veggies and cheese.

Monoprix　　SUPERMARKET €
(1st fl, 71 rue Émile Zola) Up the escalator in a half-timbered house.

Carrefour Cité　　GROCERIES €
(37 rue Raymond Poincaré; ⊗7am-10pm Mon-Sat, 9am-1pm Sun)

Drinking & Entertainment

La Maison du Boulanger　　BOX OFFICE
(☑03 25 40 15 55; 42 rue Paillot de Montabert; www.maisonduboulanger.com, in French; ⊗closed Sun) Sells tickets to concerts and other cultural events.

Dixi Café　　BAR
(12 rue Pithou; ⊗3pm-3am Tue-Sat) A convivial neighbourhood bar that draws an arty crowd, including students. Among the sipping options: Guinness (€4.50), Champagne (€5.50) and the house speciality, *rhum arrangé* (fruit-infused rum). Has live music – rock, reggae, jazz, French *chansons* – every Friday and Saturday from about 10pm.

Shopping

In the city centre, handsome rue Émile Zola is lined with shops.

Magasins d'Usine FACTORY OUTLETS
(⊘closed Sun) Troyes is famous across France for its factory outlets, a legacy of the now largely *delocalisé* (outsourced-overseas) local knitwear industry. Brand-name sportswear, underwear, baby clothes, shoes and so on – discontinued styles, un-sold stock, returns, prototypes – attract bargain-hunters by the coachload.

Most stores are in two main zones. **St-Julien-les-Villas** is about 3km south of the centre along bd de Dijon (D671 towards Dijon). Here, **Marques Avenue** (www.marquesavenue.com, in French; av de la Maille) boasts 240 name brands. **Pont Ste-Marie** is about 3km northeast of the centre between av Jean Jaurès (D677 towards Châlons-en-Champagne) and av Jules Guesde (D960 towards Nancy). Here, **McArthur Glen Troyes** (www.mcarthurglen.fr) is a wedge-shaped strip mall with over 100 shops, while **Marques City** (www.marquescity.fr) carries scores of brands in nine buildings.

Cellier St-Pierre WINE
(www.celliersaintpierre.fr; 1 place St-Pierre; ⊘closed Sun & Mon) A fine place to purchase bubbly and Aube wines such as *rosé des Riceys*. The cellar has been used since 1840 to distil Prunelle de Troyes (€20 per bottle), a 40 per cent liqueur made with sloe (black-thorn fruit) that's great on ice cream. The modest production facilities, which you can visit, are often fired up on Friday and Saturday mornings.

ℹ Information

Cyber Café Viardin Micro (8 rue Viardin; per hr €2; ⊘2-7pm Mon, 9.30am-noon & 2-7pm Tue-Sat) Internet access half a block west of the Hôtel Arlequin.

Post office (38 rue Louis Ulbach) Also ex-changes currency.

Tourist office (www.tourisme-troyes.com) Has two helpful bureaux: train station (☑03 25 82 62 70; 16 bd Carnot; ⊘9am-12.30pm &

2-6pm Mon-Sat, also 10am-1pm Sun & holidays Nov–early Apr); city centre (☑03 25 73 36 88; rue Mignard; ⊘10am-1pm & 2-6pm Mon-Sat, 10am-noon & 2-5pm Sun & holidays, closed Nov–early Apr). The latter faces the west facade of Église St-Jean.

ℹ Getting There & Away

BUS The best way to get to Reims is by bus (see p286). Departures are from the very last bus berth to the right as you approach the train station; a schedule is posted. The **bus station office** (☑03 25 71 28 42; ⊘8.30am-noon & 2-5.30pm Mon-Fri), run by Courriers de l'Aube, is in the side of the train station.

CAR There's a huge free car park three blocks south of the Hôtel Arlequin – take rue de Turenne, cross the roundabout and turn right. **National Citer** (☑03 25 73 27 37; 10 rue Vol-taire) rents cars. Find it a block south of the train station, near place Général Patton.

TRAIN Troyes is on the rather isolated train line that links Mulhouse (€40, three hours) in Alsace with Paris Gare de l'Est (€24, 1½ hours, 10 to 14 daily). To get to Dijon (€29, 2½ to four hours), change in Chaumont.

ℹ Getting Around

BICYCLE Bicycles can be rented from **Hôtel Les Comtes de Champagne** (☑03 25 73 11 70; www.comtesdechampagne.com; 56 rue de la Monnaie; per half-day/full day/two days/week €8/12/20/60).

TAXI Call ☑03 25 78 30 30.

Champagne Route of the Côte des Bar

Although the Aube *département* (www.aube-champagne.com), of which Troyes is the capital, is a major producer of Cham-pagne (it has about 67 sq km of vineyards, 85% of them pinot noir and 15% chardon-nay), it gets a fraction of the recognition ac-corded to the Marne. Much of the acrimony dates back to 1909, when winemakers of the Aube were excluded from the growing area for Champagne's AOC. Two years later, they were also forbidden to sell their grapes to producers up north, provoking a revolt by local *vignerons,* months of strikes and a situation so chaotic that the army was called in. Only in 1927 were the Aube grow-ers fully certified as producers of genuine Champagne, but by then the Marne had es-tablished market domination.

Today, Champagne production in the southeastern corner of the Aube – just

SELF-GUIDED TOUR

The tourist offices in Troyes can sup-ply you with an **audioguide tour** (€5.50) of the old city in French, Eng-lish, German, Italian or Dutch.

north of Burgundy's Châtillonnais vineyards (see p410) – is relatively modest in scale, though the reputation of the area's wines has been on an upward trajectory in recent years.

The 220km Côte des Bar Champagne Route does curlicues and loop-the-loops through austere fields, neat vineyards and forestland in an area 30km to 50km east and southeast of Troyes. Great for a deliciously leisurely drive, it passes through stone-built villages that are bedecked with flowers in the spring. Tourist offices, including the one in Troyes, can supply map-brochures. The selected highlights that follow are listed from northeast to southwest.

COLOMBEY-LES-DEUX-ÉGLISES
POP 670

Charles de Gaulle lived in this village (www .colombey-les-deux-eglises.com, in French) from 1934 – except, obviously, during WWII – until his death in 1970. It is named after two historic *églises* (churches), one a parish church, the other a Cluniac priory.

Coachloads of (mostly older) French people flock here to visit CDG's home, La Boisserie (www.charles-de-gaulle.org, in French; adult €4; ☺10am-12.30pm & 2-5.30pm Wed-Mon, open daily Apr-Sep, closed mid-Dec–early Feb), its furnishings unchanged since he was laid to rest in the village-centre cimetière (churchyard). Tours (English brochure available) begin at the ticket office, situated across D23 from the house, on the Colombey's southern edge.

The hill just north of town (on D619) is crowned by a 43.5m-high Croix de Lorraine (Lorraine Cross; erected 1972), symbol of France's WWII Resistance. Nearby is the impressive Mémorial Charles de Gaulle (http://memorial-charlesdegaulle.fr, in French; adult €13; ☺10am-5.30pm, until 7pm May-Sep, closed Tue Oct-Apr), opened in 2008, whose graphic, easily digestible exhibits, rich in photos, form an admiring biography of France's greatest modern statesman. Displays help visitors untangle such complicated mid-20th-century events as the Algerian war and the creation of the Fifth Republic, and consider the ways in which De Gaulle's years in power (1958–69) affected French culture, style and economic growth. Audioguides are available. The site affords breathtaking, sublime views of the Haute-Marne countryside.

Colombey-les-Deux-Églises is 72km east of Troyes along D619; taking A5 to exit 23 (88km) is a bit faster.

BAYEL
POP 875

Thanks to the Cristallerie Royale de Champagne (Royal Champagne Glassworks; ☑03 25 92 42 68; www.royaledechampagne. com; place de l'Église), established by a family of glassmakers from Murano, Italy, this quiet village has been a centre of crystal manufacture since 1678. To see the production process, take a factory tour (adult/ student €5/2.30; ☺9.30 & 11am Mon-Fri, closed late Jul-late Aug), which begins at the tourist office (☑03 25 92 42 68; 2 rue Belle Verrière; ☺9.15am-1pm & 2.15-6pm, closed Sunday morning, also closed Sunday afternoon Oct-Mar). Walk through the tourist office to get to the small Musée du Cristal (Crystal Museum; Écomusée; adult €3.80; ☺same as tourist office), which illustrates how crystal is made (ask for a guide sheet in English); the film has soundtracks in French, English and German. For lovely but fragile gifts, head to the Cristalleries de Champagne outlet shop (☺closed Sun), next to the tourist office.

Bayel is 11km southwest of Colombey-les-Deux-Églises.

ABBAYE DE CLAIRVAUX
Bernard de Clairvaux (1090–1153), nemesis of Abelard and preacher of the Second Crusade, founded this hugely influential Cistercian monastery (☑03 25 27 52 55; www.abbayedeclairvaux.com, in French; adult €7; ☺tours begin 11am & 2.30pm or 3pm, additional tours Wed-Sun Mar-Oct, closed Mon & Tue Nov-Feb, may also be closed Wed-Sun mid-Dec–Feb) in 1115. Since the time of Napoléon, the complex has served as one of France's highest-security prisons. Past 'guests' have included Carlos the Jackal; two prisoners who staged a revolt here in 1971 were guillotined.

Several historic abbey buildings have recently been opened to the public. Tours take in some 12th-century structures, built in the austere Cistercian tradition, but more interesting is the half-abandoned, 18th-century Grand Cloître, where you can see collective 'chicken coop' cells (from the 1800s) and individual cells (used until 1971). For security reasons, visitors need to bring ID, mobile phones must be off, and photography is prohibited.

The abbey is on D396 8km south of Bayel and 6km north of A5 exit 23.

ESSOYES
POP 710

It's easy to see why Renoir liked Essoyes (www.essoyes.fr, in French) so much that he spent his last 25 summers – and was buried – here: it's one of the area's prettiest villages, with neat stone houses and a riverfront that glows golden in the late afternoon sun. The great Impressionist's studio, Atelier Renoir (www.renoir-aube-champagne. com), is 150m off D67 at the western edge of town; it was being renovated when we visited, but should have reopened by the time you read this.

On the main street through town (D67), you'll find the tourist office (☏03 25 29 61 34; otee@orange.fr; 12 rue Gambetta) and, behind it, a spiky 19th-century building, known as the Château, that looks like a cross between a castle and a haunted house (it's now a school).

Just northeast of town, up the slope from the Gendarmerie (on D67), the Hôtel des Canotiers (☏03 25 38 61 08; www.hoteldescano tiers.com; d €69-74, q €112; ⊗closed 20 Dec-6 Jan & mid-Feb–mid-Mar; @🕸🌊) has 14 rooms that are modern, upbeat, spacious and practical; each is named after a famous Renoir canvas.

Picnic supplies can be bought on the main square at the Petit Casino grocery (5 rue Gambetta; ⊗7am-12.15pm & 4.30-7.15pm Mon, 7am-12.15pm & 3-7.15pm Tue-Sat, 9am-noon Sun & holidays).

Essoyes is 49km southeast of Troyes.

LES RICEYS
POP 1430

Running along both banks of the picturesque River Laigne, the *commune* of Les Riceys consists of three adjacent villages (Ricey-Bas, Ricey-Haute-Rive and Ricey-Haut) and is famous for its three churches, and for growing wines belonging to three different AOC wines. Its best-known product is *rosé des Riceys*, an exclusive pinot noir rosé that can be made only in particularly sunny years and was a special favourite of Louis XIV. Annual production of this – when there is any – hovers around 65,000 bottles. Lots of Champagne wineries are nestled along and near D70.

For more information, including details on walking circuits through vine and vale, contact the tourist office (☏03 25 29 15 38; www.lesriceys-champagne.com, in French; 14 place des Héros de la Résistance, Ricey-Haut; ⊗9am-noon & 2-5pm, closed Wed, also closed Sat, Sun & holidays Sep-Apr).

Les Riceys is 47km southeast of Troyes and 18km southwest of Essoyes.

Alsace & Lorraine

Includes »

Best Places to Eat

» La Choucrouterie (p311)
» Table du Gourmet (p322)
» La Maison des Têtes (p327)
» Restaurant Thierry (p343)
» Brasserie Excelsior (p337)

Best Places to Stay

» Hôtel de l'Illwald (p320)
» Vignoble Klur (p322)
» Péniche Alclair (p342)
» Hôtel des Prélats (p336)
» Hôtel de la Couronne (p322)

Why Go?

Alsace is a one-off cultural hybrid. With its Germanic dialect and French sense of fashion, love of foie gras and *choucroute* (sauerkraut), fine wine *and* beer, this distinctive region often leaves you wondering quite where you are. Where are you? Why, in the land of living fairy tales of course, where vineyards fade into watercolour distance, hilltop castles send spirits soaring higher than the region's emblematic storks and half-timbered villages look fresh-minted for a Disney film set. If the locals' way with geraniums and pastels seems impossibly twee, take heart – beneath that oh-so-traditional exterior, your average Alsatian is an eccentric just itching to get out.

Lorraine has high culture and effortless grace thanks to its historic roll-call of dukes and art nouveau pioneers, who had an eye for grand designs and good living. Its blessedly underrated cities, cathedrals and art collections leave first-timers spellbound, while its WWI battlefields render visitors speechless time and again with their painful beauty.

When to Go
Strasbourg

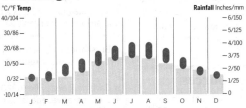

July Strasbourg fireworks, street fun and cathedral illuminations at Les Festiv'Étés.

September Toast the grape harvest with new wine and autumn colour on the Route des Vins.

December Mulled wine, gingerbread and carols galore at Christmas markets throughout Alsace.

Take a guided walk of the WWI battlefields with Jean-Paul de Vries and be touched by the real-life stories of soldiers at Romagne '14–'18 (p348) near Verdun.

Grand Designs

» Strasbourg's sublimely Gothic Cathédrale Notre-Dame (p303)

» The space-age curves of gleaming white Centre Pompidou-Metz (p339)

» Nancy's ever-so-grand neoclassical place Stanislas (p335)

» The light fantastic Cathédrale St-Étienne (p339) in Metz

» Vauban's star-shaped citadel (p326) in Neuf-Brisach

Planning Your Trip

» Book your accommodation at http://hotels.lonelyplanet.com

» Arrange tastings at wineries (p316), route des Vins d'Alsace cycling tours (p328) and tours of Strasbourg's breweries (p309)

» Plan how you're going to get around the region (p333)

Resources

» Northern Alsace Tourism (www.tourisme67.com)

» Southern Alsace Tourism (www.tourisme68.com)

» Lorraine Tourism (www.tourism-lorraine.com)

Glorious Food & Wine

With its chocolate-box villages and lusciously green vineyards, Alsace doesn't only *look* good enough to eat. The Alsatians dine with French finesse and drink with German gusto, and every corner leads to mouth-watering surprises: shops doing a brisk trade in homemade foie gras, gingerbread and macaroons; entire regions dedicated to cheese; mile upon glorious mile of country lanes given over to the life-sweetening pleasures of wine and chocolate. So take the lead of locals: go forth and indulge!

Kick-start your gourmet adventure by visiting www.tourisme-alsace.com and http://gastronomie.vins.tourisme-alsace.com (in French). Local tourist boards can help you fine-tune your visit, be it a stay on a working dairy farm, a chocolate-tasting road trip or a *dégustation* (tasting) of *grand cru* wines.

FOODIE TRAILS

No matter whether you're planning to get behind the wheel for a morning or pedal leisurely through the vineyards for a week, the picture-book Route des Vins d'Alsace (Alsace Wine Route; p316) is a must. Swinging 170km from Marlenheim to Thann, the road is like a 'greatest hits' of Alsace, with its pastoral views, welcoming *caves* (wine cellars) and half-timbered villages. Go to www.alsace-route-des-vins.com to start planning.

Fancy some cheese to go with that wine? Head to Munster (p329) to taste the pungent, creamy *fromage* first made by Benedictine monks. The tourist office (www.la-vallee-de-munster.com) can arrange farmstays and dairy tours.

Having polished off the cheese and wine, it would be rude not to pass the chocolates, not to mention the gingerbread and macarons, on the Route du Chocolat et des Douceurs d'Alsace (p314), 200km of mmmm...

Grape & Grain

» Vignoble Klur (p322) is a friendly, family-run winery producing excellent organic wines. Linger for guided vineyard walks, Alsatian cookery classes and creative workshops.

» Brasseries Heineken (p310) refreshes with informative, free two-hour tours of its brewery. Phone ahead for reservations.

» Cave de Ribeauvillé (p320), France's oldest winegrowers' cooperative, opens its doors for tastings of all seven varieties of Alsatian wine.

» Brasseries Kronenbourg (p310) sells 700 million litres of beer a year in France. Phone ahead for tours that include a, hic..., tasting.

» Cave des Hospices de Strasbourg (p310), deep below Strasbourg's hospital, has been curing all ills with its prized vintages since the 14th century.

ALSACE

History

French influence in Alsace began during the Wars of Religion (1562–98) and increased during the Thirty Years War (1618–48). Most of the region was attached to France in 1648 under the Treaty of Westphalia.

By the time of the French Revolution, Alsatians felt more connected to France than to Germany, but time did little to dampen Germany's appetite for the region they called Elsass. When the Franco-Prussian War ended in 1871, an embittered France was forced to cede Alsace to the Kaiser. The region was returned to France following Germany's defeat in WWI but it was re-annexed by Nazi Germany in 1940.

After WWII Alsace was once again returned to France. Intra-Alsatian tensions ran high, however, as 140,000 Alsatians – as annexed citizens of the Third Reich – had been conscripted into Hitler's armies. These conscripts were known as the 'Malgré-Nous' (literally 'despite ourselves') because the majority went to war against their will. To make Alsace a symbol of hope for future Franco-German (and pan-European) cooperation, Strasbourg was chosen as the seat of the Council of Europe (in 1949) and, later, of the European Parliament.

The Mémorial de l'Alsace-Moselle (www.memorial-alsace-moselle.org, in French & German; adult/child €10/7; ☉10am-6.30pm Tue-Sun), 50km southwest of Strasbourg in Schirmeck, takes an unblinking but reconciliatory look at the region's traumatic modern history, which saw residents change nationality four times in 75 years.

ℹ️ Getting There & Around

Alsace is *almost* in central Europe. It's situated 456km east of Paris, midway between Calais and Prague (about 630km from each), and is slightly closer to Berlin (801km) than to Marseille (814km).

BICYCLE Alsace is interwoven with bike trails (see p328). Bicycles can be taken on virtually all regional TER trains (but not SNCF buses).

CAR & MOTORCYCLE From Strasbourg, the A4 heads northwest towards Metz and Paris, while from Mulhouse the A36 goes southwest towards the Jura and Dijon. The Massif des Vosges gets snowy in winter so winter tyres and/or chains may be required.

TRAIN If you're aged 12 to 25, you can get 50% off on all regional rail travel with an annual Tonus Alsace pass (€15). The great-value Réflexe Alsace ticket, available for those aged 26 and over, costs €25 for a year and gets you a 30% discount on travel on weekdays and a huge 70% reduction at weekends.

Strasbourg

POP 276,000

Strasbourg is the perfect overture to all that is idiosyncratic about Alsace – walking a fine tightrope between France and Germany, a medieval past and a progressive future, it pulls off its act in inimitable Alsatian style.

Tear your gaze away from that mesmerising Gothic cathedral for just a minute and you'll be roaming the old town's twisting alleys lined with crooked half-timbered houses à la Grimm; feasting in the cosiest of *winstubs* (Alsatian taverns) by the canalside in Petite France; and marvelling at how a city that does Christmas markets and gingerbread so well can also be home to the glittering EU Quarter and France's second-largest student population. But that's Strasbourg for you: all the sweeter for its contradictions and cross-cultural quirks.

History

Founded by the Merovingians in the 5th century, Strasbourg was long an important trade centre on the route between northern Europe and the Mediterranean. The city was ruled by democratic guilds in medieval times, when the cathedral, once the highest in Christendom, was built between 1015 and 1439. Johannes Gutenberg developed the first printing press with moveable type here in 1450.

Strasbourg witnessed the Reformation in the 16th century, the founding of its university in 1567 and the debut of *La Marseillaise* (the French national anthem) in 1792. Over ensuing centuries, the city ping-ponged between France and Germany. Strasbourg's prominent place in Europe's heart was confirmed when it became the seat of the Council of Europe in 1949 and of the European Parliament in 1992.

◉ Sights

Cathédrale Notre-Dame   CATHEDRAL
(place de la Cathédrale; ☉7am-7pm; ⌂Langstross) Victor Hugo declared it a 'gigantic and delicate marvel', Goethe professed that its 'loftiness is linked to its beauty' and, no matter the angle or time of day, you too will be captivated by Strasbourg's centrepiece Gothic cathedral. At once immense and

Alsace & Lorraine Highlights

1 Saunter around canal-laced **Petite Venise** (p323) as Colmar starts to twinkle

2 Get a gargoyle's-eye view of Strasbourg from the platform of Gothic **Cathédrale Notre-Dame** (p303)

3 Survey the cross-studded **Verdun Battlefields** (p346) in the early morning silence

4 Be amazed by art nouveau and rococo grace in **Nancy** (p333)

5 Gaze across the vines from the giddy heights of medieval **Château du Haut Kœnigsbourg** (p320)

6 Wish for luck (or lots of babies!) spotting storks in **Hunawihr** (p321)

7 Immerse yourself in modern art at the architecturally innovative **Centre Pompidou-Metz** (p339)

8 Tiptoe through the enchanting forests of the misty **Vosges** (p329) mountains

9 Go dairy-hopping in the verdant **Vallée de Munster** (p329)

10 Save the storybook lanes of half-timbered **Riquewihr** (p321) until dusk

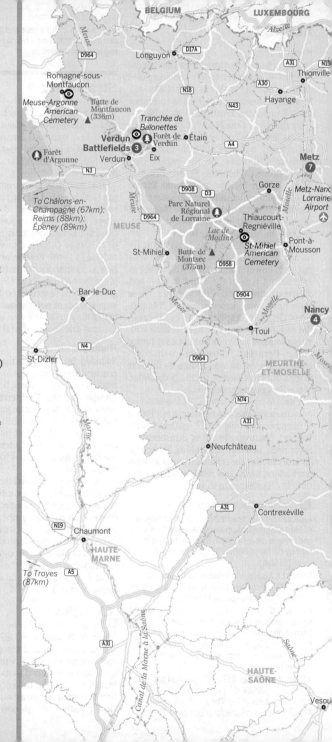

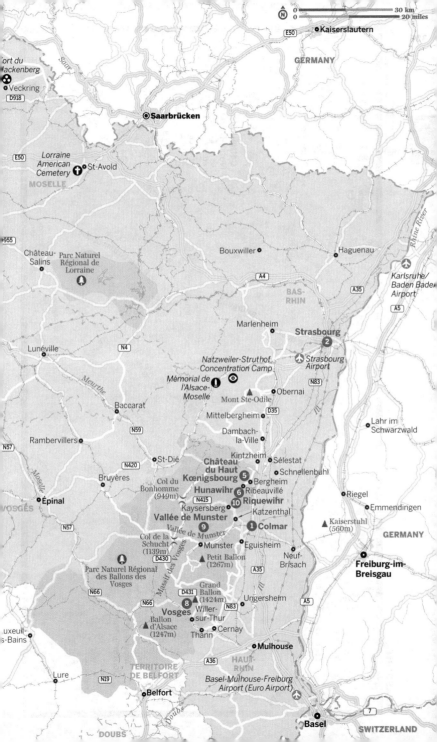

ALSACE & LORRAINE ALSACE

Strasbourg

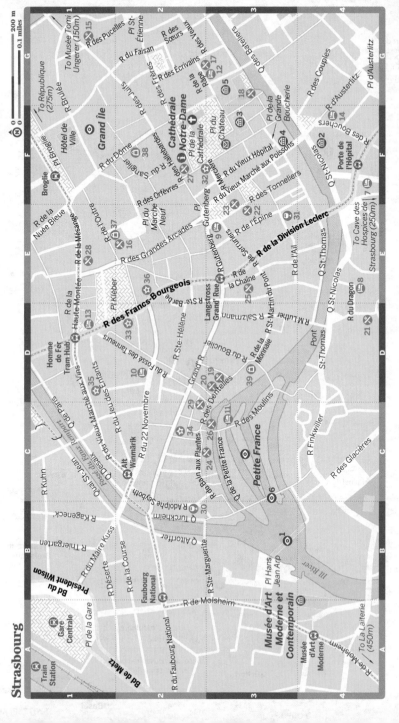

200 m
0.1 miles

Train Station

Gare Centrale

Pl de la Gare

Bd de Metz

Bd du Président Wilson

R du Maire Kuss

R Déserte

R de la Course

R Ste-Marguerite

R de Molsheim

Faubourg National

R du Faubourg National

R de Molsheim

To La Laiterie (450m)

Musée d'Art Moderne et Contemporain

Musée d'Art Moderne

Pl Hans Jean Arp

Ill River

R Thiergarten

R Kuhn

R St-Jean

R Kageneck

Quai St-Jean

Fossé du Faux Rempart

Q Desaix

Q des Bateliers

Alt Winmärik

R du Vieux Marché aux Vins

Q Turckheim

R Adolphe Seyboth

Q Altorffer

Petite France

R de la Petite France

Q de la Petite France

R des Moulins

R Finkwiller

R des Glacières

R du Bain aux Plantes

R des Dentelles

R des Dentelles

Grand' R

R du Bouclier

R Ste-Hélène

R du Fossé des Tanneurs

R du 22 Novembre

R du Jeu des Enfants

Homme de Fer Tram Hub

R de la Haute-Montée

Pl Kléber

R de la Nuée Bleue

R de la Mésange

R de l'Outre

Pl du Marché Neuf

R des Grandes Arcades

R des Orfèvres

Grand Île

R du Dôme

Hôtel de Ville

Pl Broglie

Broglie

R Brûlée

To République (275m)

To Musée Tomi Ungerer (150m)

R des Juifs

R des Pucelles

Pl St-Étienne

R du Faisan

R des Sœurs

R des Frères

R des Veaux

R des Écrivains

Cathédrale Notre-Dame

Pl de la Cathédrale

Pl du Château

R des Hallebardes

R du Sanglier

R Mercière

Pl Gutenberg

R Gutenberg

R du Vieux Marché aux Poissons

R du Vieux Hôpital

R de la Râpe

Pl de la Grande Boucherie

R des Couples

R d'Austerlitz

Pl d'Austerlitz

R des Bouchers

Porte de l'Hôpital

Q St-Nicolas

R des Tonneliers

R de l'Épine

R de Sarmiers

Langstross Grand' Rue

R Ste-Barbe

R Salzmann

R de la Chaîne

R de l'All

Q St-Thomas

R du Dragon

Q St-Nicolas

To Cave des Hospices de Strasbourg (250m)

R St-Martin du Pont

R M Luther

R de la Monnaie

Pont St-Thomas

Petite France

R des Francs-Bourgeois

R de la Division Leclerc

intricate, the cathedral is a riot of filigree stonework and flying buttresses, leering gargoyles and lacy spires.

The west facade, most impressive if approached from rue Mercière, was completed in 1284, but the 142m spire – the tallest of its time – was not in place until 1439; its southern companion was never built.

On a sunny day, the 12th- to 14th-century **stained-glass windows** – especially the rose window over the western portal – shine like jewels. To appreciate the cathedral in peace, visit in the early evening when the crowds have thinned and stay to see its facade glow gold at dusk.

The 30m-high Gothic-meets-Renaissance astronomical clock (adult/child €2/free; ◷tickets sold from 11.50am) strikes solar noon at 12.30pm with a parade of carved wooden figures portraying the different stages of life and Jesus with his apostles.

A spiral staircase twists up to the 66m-high platform (adult/child €4.70/2.30; ◷9am-7.15pm) above the facade, from which the

tower and its Gothic openwork spire soar another 76m. As Hugo put it: 'From the belfry, the view is wonderful. Strasbourg lays at your feet, the old city of tiled triangular roof tops and gable windows, interrupted by towers and churches as picturesque as those of any city in Flanders.'

Grande Île   HISTORIC QUARTER
(🚋Langstross) History seeps through winding lanes dotted with candy-coloured half-timbered houses and vibrant café-rimmed squares in the Unesco World Heritage site of Grande Île, a place made for aimless ambling. These ancient streets cower beneath the soaring magnificence of the cathedral and its sidekick, the gingerbready 15th-century Maison Kammerzell (rue des Hallebardes), with its ornate carvings and leaded windows. The alleys are at their most atmospheric when lantern-lit at night.

Petite France   HISTORIC QUARTER
(🚋Alt Winmärik) Criss-crossed by narrow lanes, canals and locks, impossibly pretty

Petite France is where craftsmen plied their trades in the Middle Ages. The half-timbered houses, sprouting veritable thickets of scarlet geraniums in summer, and the riverside parks attract the masses, but the area still manages to retain its Alsatian atmosphere and charm, especially in the early morning and late evening.

Drink in views of the River Ill and the mighty 17th-century Barrage Vauban (Vauban Dam), undergoing renovation at the time of writing, from the much-photographed Ponts Couverts (Covered Bridges) and their trio of 13th-century towers.

Musée d'Art Moderne et Contemporain
ART MUSEUM

(place Hans Jean Arp; adult/child €6/free; ☺noon-7pm Tue, Wed & Fri, noon-9pm Thu, 10am-6pm Sat & Sun; ⊠Musée d'Art Moderne) This striking glass-and-steel cube showcases an outstanding collection of fine art, graphic art and photography. Kandinsky, Picasso, Magritte and Monet canvases hang out alongside curvaceous works by Strasbourg-born abstract artist Hans Jean Arp. Find details on temporary exhibitions on the website.

Don't leave without enjoying a drink at the glass-fronted Art Café (☺Tue-Sun), graced by bold frescoes by Japanese artist Aki Kuroda. The terrace commands terrific views of the River Ill and Petite France.

Palais Rohan
HISTORIC RESIDENCE

(2 place du Château; adult/child €5/free; ☺noon-6pm Mon & Wed-Fri, 10am-6pm Sat & Sun; ⊠Langstross) Hailed a 'Versailles in

STRASBOURG SAVER

Save on culture with a good-value **Pass des Musées** (1-day/3-day/annual €8/10/25), covering admission to all of Strasbourg's museums, including temporary exhibitions.

The **Strasbourg Pass** (adult/child €12.50/6), a coupon book valid for three consecutive days, includes a visit to one museum, access to the cathedral platform, half a day's bicycle rental and a boat tour, plus hefty discounts on other tours and attractions.

Admission to all of Strasbourg's **museums** (www.musees-strasbourg. org) and the cathedral's platform is free on the first Sunday of the month.

miniature', this opulent 18th-century residence was built for the city's princely bishops, and Louis XV and Marie-Antoinette once slept here.

The basement **Musée Archéologique** takes you from the Palaeolithic period to AD 800. On the ground floor is the **Musée des Arts Décoratifs**, where rooms adorned with Hannong ceramics and gleaming silverware evoke the lavish lifestyle of the nobility in the 18th century. On the 1st floor, the **Musée des Beaux-Arts**' collection of 14th- to 19th-century art reveals El Greco, Botticelli and Flemish Primitive works.

Musée de l'Œuvre Notre-Dame
ECCLESIASTICAL MUSEUM

(3 place du Château; adult/child €4/free; ☺noon-6pm Tue-Fri, 10am-6pm Sat & Sun; ⊠Langstross) Occupying a cluster of sublime 14th- and 16th-century buildings, this museum harbours one of Europe's premier collections of Romanesque, Gothic and Renaissance sculptures (including many originals from the cathedral), plus 15th-century paintings and stained glass. *Christ de Wissembourg* (c 1060; room two) is the oldest work of stained glass in France.

Hollywood gore seems tame compared to the tortures back when Hell really was hell. Sure to scare you into a life of chastity is *Les Amants Trépassés* (the Deceased Lovers; room 23), painted in 1470, showing a grotesque couple being punished for their illicit lust: both of their entrails are being devoured by dragon-headed snakes.

Musée Historique
HISTORY MUSEUM

(2 rue du Vieux Marché aux Poissons; adult/child €5/free; ☺noon-6pm Tue-Fri, 10am-6pm Sat & Sun; ⊠Langstross) Trace Strasbourg's history from its beginnings as a Roman military camp called Argentoratum at this engaging museum housed in a 16th-century slaughterhouse. Highlights include a famous painting of the first-ever performance of *La Marseillaise*, France's stirring national anthem, which – despite its name – was written in Strasbourg in 1792; a 1:600-scale model of the city, created in the 1720s to help Louis XV visualise the city's fortifications; and a Gutenberg Bible from 1485. Kids can try on medieval-style knights' helmets and touch ancient pots and 18th-century cannons.

Musée Alsacien
FOLK MUSEUM

(23 quai St-Nicolas; adult/child €5/free; ☺noon-6pm Mon & Wed-Fri, 10am-6pm Sat & Sun;

Porte de l'Hôpital) Spread across three typical houses from the 1500s and 1600s, this museum affords a fascinating glimpse into Alsatian life over the centuries. Kitchen equipment, children's toys, colourful furniture and even a tiny 18th-century synagogue are on display in the museum's two dozen rooms.

Musée Tomi Ungerer
MUSEUM

(2 av de la Marseillaise; adult/child €5/free; ⊙noon-6pm Mon & Wed-Fri, 10am-6pm Sat & Sun; República) A tribute to one of Strasbourg's most famous sons – award-winning illustrator and cartoonist Tomi Ungerer – this museum is housed in the fetching Villa Greiner. The collection discloses the artist's love of dabbling in many genres, from children's book illustrations to satirical drawings and erotica.

Place de la République
CITY SQUARE

(República) Many of Strasbourg's grandest public buildings, constructed when the city was ruled by the German Reich, huddle northeast of Grande Île around place de la République. The neighbourhood that stretches eastwards to Parc de l'Orangerie is dominated by sturdy stone buildings inspired by late-19th-century Prussian tastes.

Parc de l'Orangerie
PARK

(Droits de l'Homme) Across from the Palais de l'Europe, this flowery park, designed in the 17th century by Le Nôtre of Versailles fame, is a family magnet with its playgrounds and swan-dotted lake. In summer you can rent **row boats** on Lac de l'Orangerie. Kids can get up close to storks and goats at the park's mini **zoo** (admission free).

Le Vaisseau
SCIENCE MUSEUM

(www.levaisseau.com; 1bis rue Philippe Dollinger; adult/child €8/7; ⊙10am-6pm Tue-Sun; Winston Churchill) Science is *never* boring at this interactive science and technology museum, 2.5km southeast of the cathedral. There are plenty of hands-on activities to amuse little minds, from crawling through an ant colony to creating cartoons and broadcasting the news.

Jardin des Deux Rives
GARDEN

(Two-Shores Garden; Aristide Briand) An expression of flourishing Franco-German friendship, Strasbourg and its German neighbour Kehl have turned former customs posts and military installations into this 60-hectare garden, whose play areas, promenades and parkland straddle both

309

BIENVENUE CHEZ LES EUROCRATS

Should the inner workings of the EU intrigue, you can sit in on debates ranging from lively to yawn-a-minute at the **Parlement Européen** (European Parliament; www.europarl.europa.eu; rue Lucien Fèbvre; Parlement Européen); dates are available from the tourist office or on the website. For individuals it's first-come first-served (bring ID).

A futuristic glass crescent, the Council of Europe's **Palais de l'Europe** (Palace of Europe; www.coe.int; Droits de l'Homme) across the Ill can be visited on free one-hour weekday tours; phone ahead for times and reservations.

It's just a hop across the Canal de la Marne to the swirly silver **Palais des Droits de l'Homme** (European Court of Human Rights; www.echr.coe.int; Droits de l'Homme), the most eye-catching of all the EU institutions.

banks of the Rhine. The centrepiece is Marc Mimram's sleek (and hugely expensive) **suspension bridge**, which has proved a big hit with pedestrians and cyclists. From the tram stop, walk east or take bus 21 for three stops.

River Ill
RIVER

(Langstross) The leafy paths that shadow the River Ill and its canalised branch, the Fossé du Faux Rempart, are great for an impromptu picnic or a romantic stroll.

Place Gutenberg
CITY SQUARE

(Langstross) Well worth a peek is for its Renaissance-style Chambre de Commerce (Chamber of Commerce).

☞ Tours

Take a DIY spin of the cathedral and the old city with one of the tourist office's 1½-hour audio guides (adult/child €5.50/3.50), available in five languages.

Batorama
BOAT TRIPS

(www.batorama.fr, in French; adult/child €8.50/4.50; ⊙tours half-hourly 9.30am-9pm; Langstross) This outfit runs scenic 70-minute boat trips, which glide along the storybook canals of Petite France, taking in the Vauban Dam and the glinting EU institutions. Tours depart in front of Palais Rohan.

Brasseries Heineken BREWERY

FREE (☎ 03 88 19 57 55; 4 rue St-Charles; ☺ tours approx hourly 9am-4pm Mon-Fri) In the greatest of keg-rolling traditions, the Heineken brewery promises to refresh the parts that other lagers cannot reach on two-hour tours (some in English; reserve ahead). The brewery is 2.5km north of Grande Île; take bus 4 to the Schiltigheim Mairie stop in Schiltigheim.

Brasseries Kronenbourg BREWERY

(☎ 03 88 27 41 59; 68 rte d'Oberhausbergen; adult/child €6/4; ☺ tours approx hourly 10am-4pm Mon-Sat; ◻ Ducs d'Alsace) Selling 700 million litres of beer in France every year – enough to fill about 250 Olympic swimming pools! – this brewery is in Cronenbourg, 2.5km northwest of Grande Île. Call ahead to join a thirst-quenching 1½-hour tour (some in English), which includes a tasting.

Cave des Hospices de Strasbourg

FREE WINERY

(www.vins-des-hospices-de-strasbourg.fr, in French; 1 place de l'Hôpital; ☺ 8.30am-noon & 1.30-5.30pm Mon-Fri, 9am-12.30pm Sat; ◻ Porte de l'Hôpital) This brick-vaulted wine cellar nestles deep in the bowels of Strasbourg's hospital. A hospice back in the days when wine was considered a cure for all ills, today the cellar bottles first-rate Alsatian wines from rieslings to sweet muscats. One of its historic barrels is filled with a 1472 vintage.

★★ Festivals & Events

Mulled wine, spicy *bredele* (biscuits) and a Santa-loaded children's village are all part and parcel of Strasbourg's sparkly **Marché de Noël** (Christmas Market; www.noel.strasbourg.eu), running from the last Saturday in November until 24 December. Strasbourg slides into summer with fireworks, fairs and striking cathedral illuminations at **Les Fesiv'Étés** in July and August. Raise a glass to Alsatian beer at October's **Mondial de la Bière** (www.mondialbierestrasbourg.com) and wine at the **Riesling du Monde** (www.riesling-du-monde.com) in March.

⌷ Sleeping

It can be tricky to find last-minute accommodation from Monday to Thursday when the European Parliament is in plenary session (see www.europarl.europa.eu for dates). Book ahead for December when beds are at a premium because of the Christmas market. The tourist office can advise about same-night room availability; if you drop by, staff are happy to help reserve a room.

Hôtel Régent Petite France

DESIGN HOTEL €€€

(☎ 03 88 76 43 43; www.regent-hotels.com; 5 rue des Moulins; r €150-445; ✻ @ ☎ ◻ Alt Winmärik) Once an ice factory and now Strasbourg's hottest design hotel, this waterfront pile is quaint on the outside and ubercool on the inside. The sleek rooms dressed in muted colours and plush fabrics sport shiny marble bathrooms. Work your relaxed look in the sauna, chic restaurant and Champagne bar with dreamy River Ill views.

JEWISH ALSACE

Interest in Alsace's rich Jewish heritage (http://judaisme.sdv.fr, in French), spanning 1000 years, has grown tremendously. Indeed, the **European Day of Jewish Culture** (www.jewisheritage.org) in September grew out of an initiative in northern Alsace. Famous people of Alsatian-Jewish origin include Captain Alfred Dreyfus (of the Dreyfus Affair), the Marx Brothers (of *Duck Soup*) and Marcel Marceau (the mime artist).

Today most Alsatian Jews live in Strasbourg, whose vibrant Jewish community – proud of its unique liturgical and musical traditions – numbers about 16,000. Alsace is the only region in France in which the majority of the Jews are Ashkenazim, ie they spoke Yiddish in centuries past.

Towns all over the region, including many along the Route des Vins d'Alsace, have historic synagogues and museums with exhibits related to Alsatian Judaism, such as Strasbourg's Musée de l'Œuvre Notre-Dame and Musée Alsacien, Colmar's Musée Bartholdi and the **Musée Judéo-Alsacien** (62a Grand' Rue; adult/child €6/3; ☺ 10am-noon & 1-6pm Tue-Fri & Sun), housed in a converted synagogue in Bouxwiller, 40km northwest of Strasbourg.

Visit www.tourisme67.com for more background on Judaism in Alsace.

Hôtel du Dragon
SMALL HOTEL €€

(☑03 88 35 79 80; www.dragon.fr; 12 rue du Dragon; s €79-112, d €89-124; @ 🛜 🖫 Porte de l'Hôpital) Step through a tree-shaded courtyard and into the, ahhh...blissful calm of this bijou hotel. The dragon receives glowing reviews for its crisp interiors, attentive service and prime location near Petite France.

Hôtel Gutenberg
HISTORIC HOTEL €€

(☑03 88 32 17 15; www.hotel-gutenberg.com; 31 rue des Serruriers; r €75-135; ❉ @ 🛜 🖫 Langstross) Nestled in the flower-strewn heart of Petite France, this hotel is a harmonious blend of 250 years of history and contemporary design – think clean lines, zesty colours and the occasional antique.

Romantik Hôtel Beaucour
HISTORIC HOTEL €€

(☑03 88 76 72 00; www.hotel-beaucour.com; 5 rue des Bouchers; s €75-110, d €135-165; ❉ @ 🛜 🖫 Porte de l'Hôpital) With its antique flourishes and a cosy salon centred on a fireplace, this place positively oozes half-timbered romance. Rooms are stylishly decked out in warm colours and florals, and most feature (like it!) jacuzzi bathtubs.

Hôtel Hannong
BOUTIQUE HOTEL €€

(☑03 88 32 16 22; www.hotel-hannong.com; 15 rue du 22 Novembre; s €88-108, d €132-197; ❉ 🛜 🖫 Alt Winmärik) Minimalist chic best describes the rooms at this design-focused hotel, kitted out with hardwood floors and colour schemes ranging from space-age silver to chocolate-cream. The skylit lounge bar serves tapas and fine wines.

Royal Lutetia
HOTEL €

(☑03 88 35 20 45; www.royal-lutetia.fr; 2bis rue du Général Rapp; d €62-85; 🛜 🖫 Parc du Contades) A 10-minute stroll north of the centre, this recently revamped hotel has bright and spacious rooms with above-par perks such as flatscreen TVs and free wi-fi.

Le Kléber Hôtel
SMALL HOTEL €€

(☑03 88 32 09 53; www.hotel-kleber.com, in French; 29 place Kléber; s €57-80, d €74-94; 🛜 🖫 Homme de Fer) So what will sweeten your dreams tonight? Pistachio, Pavlova or maybe Meringue? Highly original and super-central, Le Kléber's rooms are named, and decorated, after fruits, spices and other calorific treats – pick one to suit your taste.

Hôtel Suisse
TRADITIONAL HOTEL €€

(☑03 88 35 22 11; www.hotel-suisse.com; 2-4 rue de la Râpe; s €65, d €75-89; @ 🛜 🖫 Langstross) Tucked away in a charming corner of Grand Île, this lemon-fronted hotel exudes Alsa-

tian authenticity with its beams, chandeliers and traditional rooms decorated with solid wood furnishings. Often full.

Camping de la Montagne Verte
CAMPGROUND €

(☑03 88 30 25 46; www.camping-montagne-verte-strasbourg.com; 2 rue Robert Forrer; sites €14-18.50; 🖫 Montagne Verte) Pitch up at this quiet, leafy campground, a 10-minute stroll from Montagne Verte tram stop, 3km west of Petite France. It's right next to the cycling lane that heads into town. Bike hire is available for []10/40 per day/week.

Hôtel Au Cerf d'Or
HISTORIC HOTEL €€

(☑03 88 36 20 05; www.cerf-dor.com, in French; 6 place de l'Hôpital; r €55-110; ❉ ♨ 🖫 Porte de l'Hôpital) A golden *cerf* (stag) hangs proudly out front at this half-timbered Logis de France hotel, with simple, spotless rooms. Best of all it has a jacuzzi, swimming pool, sauna (half-hour €8) and a homely French restaurant.

CIARUS
HOSTEL €

(☑03 88 15 27 88; www.ciarus.com; 7 rue Finkmatt; dm incl breakfast €26, s €46; @) Although the walls are paper-thin and dorms barebones – some smelling of eau de damp socks – this hostel is reasonably central and good value. Light sleepers beware: it's popular among night-active school groups. Take bus 2, 4 or 10 to place de Pierre, north from the city centre.

✖ Eating

Strasbourg dishes up the freshest local ingredients, with a French knack for presentation and a German liking for gut-busting portions. Appetising restaurants abound on Grande Île: try canalside Petite France for Alsatian fare and half-timbered romance; Grand' Rue for curbside kebabs and *tarte flambée* (a thin-crust pizza dough topped with crème fraîche, onions and lardons); and rue des Veaux or rue des Pucelles for hole-in-the-wall eateries serving the world on a plate.

TOP CHOICE La Choucrouterie
ALSATIAN €€

(☑03 88 36 52 87; www.choucrouterie.com, in French; 20 rue St-Louis; choucroute €12-16; ⊙lunch Mon-Fri, dinner daily; 🖫 Porte de l'Hôpital) Naked ladies straddling giant sausages (on the menu, we hasten to add) and eccentric chefs juggling plates of steaming *choucroute garnie* are just the tip of the theatrical iceberg at this inimitable bistro and playhouse double act. Speak a few words of Alsatian and you'll get extra helpings of everything, guaranteed.

Au Crocodile GASTRONOMIC €€€

(☎03 88 32 13 02; www.au-crocodile.com, in French; 10 rue de l'Outre; 3-course lunch menus €35, other menus incl drinks €85/115; ☺Tue-Sat; ☐Broglie) This hushed temple of French gastronomy is named after a stuffed toothy critter (now suspended over the foyer) brought back from Egypt by one of Napoléon's generals. Artistically presented specialities such as smooth foie gras with rhubarb chutney and filet mignon in a mountain-cheese crust have won Au Crocodile a Michelin star. Advance reservations recommended.

La Cloche à Fromage TRADITIONAL FRENCH €€

(☎03 88 23 13 19; www.cheese-gourmet.com; 27 rue des Tonneliers; fondue €21-25; ☺Tue-Sun; ☐Langstross) *Au revoir* diet…loosen a belt notch or three for Strasbourg's gooiest fondues and *raclette* at this temple to *fromage*, saving an inch for the 200-variety cheese board of Guinness Book of World Records fame.

Maison Kammerzell ALSATIAN €€

(☎03 88 32 42 14; www.maison-kammerzell.com; 16 place de la Cathédrale; menus €27-46; ☐Langstross) Slap-bang on Strasbourg's main square, medieval icon Maison Kammerzell serves well-executed Alsatian cuisine like *baeckeoffe* and *choucroute*. A staircase spirals up to frescoed alcoves and the 1st floor where the views – oh the views! – of the floodlit cathedral are sensational.

Bistrot et Chocolat CAFÉ €

(www.bistrotetchocolat.net, in French; 8 rue de la Râpe; snacks €4-8, brunch €10-19; ☺10.30am-7pm Tue-Sun; ☐Langstross) Chocolate fondue, organic hot chocolate with ginger, chocolate soup sprinkled with gingerbread croutons… this boho-chic bistro is an ode to the cocoa bean. Weekend brunches are a treat. Check the website for details on children's cooking classes.

L'Assiette du Vin BISTRO €€

(☎03 88 32 00 92; www.assietteduvin.fr, in French; 5 rue de la Chaîne; lunch menus €19, dinner menus €32-55; ☺closed lunch Mon, Sat & Sun; ☐Langstross) Market-fresh cuisine with a twist, discreet service and an award-winning wine list lure discerning foodies to this rustic-chic bistro in the old town. The *plat du jour* is a snip at €8.50.

Maison des Tanneurs ALSATIAN €€

(☎03 88 32 79 70; 42 rue du Bain aux Plantes; mains €14-22; ☺Tue-Sat; ☐Langstross) Even locals book ahead at this former tannery, creaking under the weight of its 16th-century beams and billowing geraniums. *Choucroute* with fat pork knuckles and garlicky Alsatian-style escargot are matched with top-notch pinots and rieslings. Snag a window table for fine views of Petite France's canals.

La Cambuse SEAFOOD €€

(☎03 88 22 10 22; 1 rue des Dentelles; mains €23-27; ☺Tue-Sat; ☐Langstross) All portholes and polished wood, this shipshape bistro is the closest you'll get to dining on a private yacht in Strasbourg. The experimental chef infuses seafood with Asian spices – think sweet and sour turbot and fish *choucroute* with saffron. Reservations essential.

La Bourse BRASSERIE €€

(☎03 88 36 40 53; 1 place du Maréchal de Lattre de Tassigny; menus €24-32; ☐Étoile) Under a *trompe l'œil* sky, this art deco brasserie serves deliciously crisp *tartes flambées*, flavoursome *baeckeoffe* and meaty Alsatian staples like *fleischnacka*.

La Tinta CAFÉ €

(36 rue du Bain aux Plantes; brunch €9, lunch menus €10; ☺Tue-Sat; ☐Alt Winmärik) Words smother the walls of this boho-flavoured literary café. It's a blissfully relaxed spot for lunch or a cup of organic tea with a slice of homemade tart.

Au Coin des Pucelles ALSATIAN €€

(☎03 88 35 35 14; 12 rue des Pucelles; mains €14-22; ☺Tue-Sat; ☐Broglie) This snug *winstub* has just six tables, a red-checked tablecloth on each, and solid Alsatian fare such as *choucroute au canard*. Perfect for a late dinner.

L' Appart á Tartes CAFÉ €

(9 rue des Dentelles; tarts €5-11; ☐Langstross) Escape the crowds at this laid-back Petite France café, with tasty sweet and savoury tarts, free wi-fi and a kids' play corner.

Poêles de Carottes VEGETARIAN €

(www.poelesdecarottes.com, in French; 2 place des Meuniers; menus €11; ☺Tue-Sat; ☐Langstross) Veggies swear by the organic soups, *tajines* and pasta at this wholesomely hip café, painted in mouth-watering orange and lemon hues.

EAT ALSATIAN

Here's what is probably cooking in the kitchen of that cosy *winstub* (Alsatian tavern):

Baeckeoffe Beef, pork, lamb, vegetable and potato stew, marinated in riesling or pinot blanc and slow-cooked in a ceramic dish.

Choucroute garnie Sauerkraut garnished with salty bacon, ham hock and Alsatian-style sausage. Bring an appetite.

Flammekueche *Tarte flambée* in French. A thin-crust pizza dough topped with crème fraîche, onions and lardons. Fingers are allowed!

Fleischnacka Herby minced beef and egg pasta rolls shaped like *schnacka* (snails).

Kougelhopf Brioche-style raisin cake, baked in its namesake mould, with a hole in the middle and a dusting of icing sugar.

Lewerknepfle Ground liver, shallot and parsley quenelles (dumplings).

Spätzle Thick egg noodles, usually served with onions and/or cheese.

Wädele Pork knuckles, often braised in pinot noir or beer and served with lashings of *choucroute*.

Self-Catering

For picnic supplies:

La Cloche à Fromage boutique
GOURMET FOOD
(32 rue des Tonneliers; Langstross) Sells creamy Tomme, ripe Camembert and other first-rate cheeses.

 Farmers' Market FOOD MARKET
(place du Marché aux Poissons; ⊙7am-1pm Sat; Porte de l'Hôpital) Stalls are piled high with everything from locally produced foie gras to organic fruit and honey.

Monoprix SUPERMARKET
(5 rue des Grandes Arcades; Homme de Fer) Everything under one roof.

Drinking

Strasbourg's 53,000 beer-thirsty students keep the scene lively and the bars and clubs pumping at weekends. Among the city's legions of pubs and bars is a glut of student-oriented places on the small streets east of the cathedral such rue des Juifs, rue des Frères and rue des Sœurs.

Jeannette et les Cycleux BAR
(www.lenetdejeannette.com, in French; 30 rue des Tonneliers; Langstross) Elvis lives on, baby, at this swinging '50s-themed haunt, where classic motorbikes dangle from the chilli-red walls. We dig the good vibes, retro decor and music from rockabilly to Motown.

Académie de la Bière PUB
(www.academiedelabiere.com, in French; 17 rue Adolphe-Seyboth; Alt Winmärik) Get the beers in at this chilled Petite France pub

before a boogie in the cellar disco. There are hundreds of brews on offer, from Kronenbourg to cherry-laced krieks.

Bar Exils BAR
(www.barexils.com, in French; 28 rue de l'Ail; Langstross) This is student central, with darts and billiards, well-worn sofas and plenty of cheap beer on tap.

☆ Entertainment

Cultural event listings appear in the free monthly *Spectacles* (www.spectacles-publications.com, in French), available at the tourist office.

Boutique Culture TICKET OUTLET
(place de la Cathédrale, cnr rue Mercière; ⊙Tue-Sat; Langstross)

Fnac Billetterie TICKET OUTLET
(www.fnacspectacles.com; 2nd fl, 22 place Kléber; ⊙Mon-Sat; Homme de Fer)

La Laiterie LIVE MUSIC
(www.laiterie.artefact.org, in French; 11-13 rue du Hohwald; Laiterie) Reggae, metal, punk, chanson, blues – Strasbourg's premier concert venue covers the entire musical spectrum and stages some 200 gigs a year. Tickets are available at the door and online. La Laiterie is just a five-minute walk (500m) south of Petite France along rue de Molsheim. Trams B and C stop close by.

Théâtre de la CHOUC'routerie THEATRE
(☎03 88 36 07 28; www.theatredelachouc.com, in French; 20 rue St-Louis; Porte de l'Hôpital) In 1984 Roger Siffer, a singer, comedian, actor and producer known for his biting

satire, set up this intimate theatre in a former sauerkraut factory. Performances are fun, experimental and trilingual (Alsatian, French and German). The theatre is a five-minute walk west of Porte de l'Hôpital tram stop, on the opposite side of the river to Grand Île.

L'Artichaut
LIVE MUSIC

(http://lartichaut.fr, in French; 56 Grand' Rue; ☺Tue-Sun; 🚋🚊Langstross) The 'artichoke' is the city's quirkiest arts and culture café, hosting free exhibitions, first-rate jazz concerts and jam sessions. The line-up is posted on the door and on the website.

Le Chalet
CLUB

(www.strasbourg-by-night.com, in French; 376 rte de la Wantzenau; ☺Fri & Sat)
This mammoth entertainment complex, a 15-minute taxi ride north of town, has themed bars and two clubs. DJs crank out everything from techno to retro and club classics.

Le Seven
CLUB

(www.lesevenstrasbourg.com, in French; 25 rue des Tonneliers; ☺Wed-Sat) Hip hop, R&B and house dominate the decks at this central club. Though crowds teeter on prepubescent and drinks are pricey, it still throws a decent party and, as its name suggests, stays open until 7am.

Cinéma Star
CINEMA

(www.cinema-star.com, in French; 27 rue du Jeu des Enfants; 🚊Homme de Fer) Cinema with nondubbed films, some in English.

Odyssée
CINEMA

(www.cinemaodyssee.com, in French; 3 rue des Francs-Bourgeois; 🚊Langstross) An art-house cinema.

Shopping

Strasbourg's swishest shopping street is rue des Hallebardes, whose window displays are real eye candy (**Baccarat** is at No 44). High-street shops punctuate rue des Grandes Arcades and Grand' Rue, while Petite France is crammed with souvenir shops selling stuffed storks and pretzels aplenty. For vintage furniture, hip accessories and works by local creatives, mosey down rue des Veaux.

❶ Information

Linky's Cyber Café (22 rue des Frères; per hr €3; ☺9.30am-9pm Mon-Sat, noon-9pm Sun; 🚊Gallia) Central with a speedy connection.

Main tourist office (☎03 88 52 28 28; www.otstrasbourg.fr; 17 place de la Cathédrale; ☺9am-7pm; 🚊Langstross) A city-centre walking map with English text costs €1; bus/tram and cycling maps are free. *Strolling in Strasbourg* (€4.50) details six architectural walking tours.

Nouvel Hôpital Civil (☎03 88 11 67 68; rue Koeberlé; 🚊Porte de l'Hôpital) 24-hour *urgences* (casualty ward).

Post office (place de la Cathédrale; 🚊Langstross)

Tele SM (3 quai St-Jean; per hr €2; ☺8am-11pm; 🚊Faubourg National) Has 40 PCs and discount calls.

Tourist office annexe (☺9am-7pm; 🚊Gare Centrale) In the train station's southern wing.

DON'T MISS

PASS THE CHOCOLATE

Strasbourg is now 'chocolate box' with good reason, as it's one of the main stops on **La Route du Chocolat et des Douceurs d'Alsace** (Alsace Chocolate and Sweets Road), stretching 80km north to Bad Bergzabern and 125km south to Heimsbrunn near Mulhouse. Pick up a map at the tourist office to pinpoint Alsace's finest patisseries, macaroon shops and confectioners. Here are three sweet-toothed favourites to get you started:

» **Mireille Oster** (www.mireille-oster.com, in French; 14 rue des Dentelles; 🚊Langstross) Cherubs adorn this heavenly shop where Strasbourg's *pain d'épices* (gingerbread) fairy Mireille Oster tempts with handmade varieties with figs, amaretto, cinnamon and chocolate. Have a nibble before you buy.

» **Christian** (www.christian.fr, in French; 12 rue de l'Outre; 🚊Broglie) Sumptuous truffles and pralines, weightless macaroons and edible Strasbourg landmarks – renowned chocolatier Christian's creations are mini works of art.

» **Coco LM** (www.coco-lm.com, in French; 16 rue du Dôme; 🚊Broglie) Bakes scrumptious Alsatian gingerbread, *beerawecka* (Alsatian fruit cake), raisin-stuffed *kougelhopf* and a startlingly spicy ginger biscuit called a *gingerli*.

① Getting There & Away

Air

Strasbourg's international **airport** (www.stras
bourg.aeroport.fr) is 17km southwest of the city
centre (towards Molsheim), near the village of
Entzheim.

Ryanair links London Stansted with **Karlsruhe/
Baden Baden airport** (www.badenairpark
.de), across the Rhine in Germany, 58km northeast of Strasbourg.

Bus

The **Eurolines office** (www.eurolines.com; 6D
place d'Austerlitz; ⓜPorte de l'Hôpital) is a few
blocks southeast of Grande Île; their buses use
a **bus stop** (ⓜLycée Couffignal) 2.5km further
south on rue du Maréchal Lefèbvre (facing the
Citroën garage).

Strasbourg city bus 21 (€1.40) links the Aristide Briand tram terminus with Kehl, the German
town just across the Rhine.

Car & Motorcycle

Rental companies with offices in the south wing
of the train station:

Avis (www.avis.com)

Europcar (www.europcar.com)

National-Citer (www.citer.fr, in French)

Sixt (www.sixt.com)

Train

Built in 1883, the **train station** (ⓜGare Centrale) was given a 120m-long, 23m-high glass
facade and underground galleries in order to
welcome the new TGV Est Européen in grand
style. On the Grande Île, tickets are available
at the **SNCF Boutique** (5 rue des Francs-
Bourgeois; ⓜLangstross).

DOMESTIC Destinations:

Paris Gare de l'Est; €67, 2¼ hours, 17 daily

Lille €94, four hours, 13 daily

Lyon €52, six hours, five daily

Marseille €87, eight hours, five daily

Metz €23, two hours, 20 daily

Nancy €22, 1½ hours, 25 daily

INTERNATIONAL If you take the Eurostar via
Paris or Lille, London is just five hours and 15
minutes away. Cities with direct services include
the following:

Basel SNCF €21, 1¼ hours, 25 daily

Brussels-Nord €70, 5¼ hours, three daily

Karlsruhe €22, 40 minutes, 16 daily

Stuttgart €43, 1¼ hours, four TGVs daily

ROUTE DES VINS From Strasbourg, there are
trains to Route des Vins destinations including
the following:

Colmar €10.50, 30 minutes, 30 daily

Dambach-la-Ville €8, one hour, 12 daily

Obernai €5.50, 30 minutes, 20 daily

Sélestat €7.50, 30 minutes, 46 daily

① Getting Around

To/From the Airport

The speedy new shuttle train links the airport
to the train station (€3.50, nine minutes, four
hourly); the ticket also covers your onward tram
journey into the city centre.

Flight Liner buses (www.flightliner.de) link
Strasbourg with Karlsruhe/Baden Baden airport
(€17, one hour), across the Rhine. Bus times are
coordinated with Ryanair's London services.

Bicycle

A world leader in bicycle-friendly planning,
Strasbourg has an extensive and ever-expanding
réseau cyclable (cycling network). The tourist
office stocks free maps.

The city's **Vélocation** (www.velocation.net)
system can supply you with a well-maintained
one-speed bike (per half-/full day €5/8, Monday
to Friday €13), kid's bike (per day €5) or child
seat (€2). Helmets are not available. A €100 to
€200 deposit is required. Outlets:

City Centre (10 rue des Bouchers; ⓜPorte de
l'Hôpital)

Train Station (ⓜGare Centrale) Situated on
Level -1. Adjacent is an 820-place bicycle parking lot (€1 for 24 hours).

Car & Motorcycle

Virtually the whole city centre is either pedestrianised or a hopeless maze of one-way streets,
so don't even think of getting around Grande Île
by car, or parking there for more than a couple of
hours. For details on city-centre parking garages
see www.parcus.com.

At Strasbourg's nine P+R (park-and-ride) car
parks, all on tram routes, the €2.70 to €3 all-day
fee, payable from 7am to 8pm, gets the driver
and each passenger a free return tram or bus
ride into the city centre. From the autoroute,
follow the signs marked 'P+R Relais Tram'.
The safest picks are north of the city centre at
Rives de l'Aar (ⓜRives de l'Aar), northwest at
Rotonde (ⓜRotonde) and south at **Baggersee**
(ⓜBaggersee).

Public Transport

Five super-efficient tram lines, A through E, form
the backbone of Strasbourg's outstanding public
transport network, run by **CTS** (www.cts-stras
bourg.fr, in French). The main tram hub is Homme
de Fer. Trams generally operate until 12.30am;
buses – few of which pass through Grande Île –
run until about 11pm. Night buses operate from
11.30pm to 5.30am on Fridays and Saturdays,
stopping at nightlife hot spots like La Laiterie.

Tickets, valid on both buses and trams, are sold by bus drivers and ticket machines at tram stops and cost €1.40 (€2.70 return). The 24h Individuel (for one person €4) and Trio (for two to three people €5) tickets, valid for 24 hours from the moment they are stamped, are sold at tourist offices and tram stops.

In the Strasbourg section, the nearest tram stops are indicated with a tram icon 🚊.

Route des Vins d'Alsace

The Route des Vins d'Alsace (Alsace Wine Route) is pure fairy-tale stuff: green vines march up the hillsides to castle-topped crags and the mist-enshrouded Vosges, roadside *caves* (wine cellars) lift spirits and half-timbered villages wait to be unwrapped one by one like Christmas gifts. No wonder it's one of France's most popular drives. Corkscrewing through glorious countryside, the entire route stretches 170km from Marlenheim, 20km west of Strasbourg, southwards to Thann, 35km southwest of Colmar.

Local tourist offices can supply you with the excellent English-language map/brochure, *The Alsace Wine Route* (free), and *Alsace Grand Cru Wines,* detailing Alsace's 50 most prestigious AOC winegrowing micro-regions. More information is available online at www.alsace-route-des-vins.com.

The villages mentioned in the following section, listed from north to south, all have plenty of hotels and restaurants, and some have campgrounds. Tourist offices can provide details on local *chambres d'hôte* (B&Bs), which generally cost €40 to €60 for a double.

☞ Tours

For minibus tours of the Route des Vins (reservations can be made via Colmar's tourist office) try these agencies:

LCA Top Tour   BUS TOUR
(☎03 89 41 90 88; www.alsace-travel.com; 8 place de la Gare, Colmar; half-day €53-56)

Regioscope   BUS TOUR
(☎03 89 44 38 21; www.regioscope.com; morning/afternoon tour €47/55)

❶ Getting There & Around

The Route des Vins comprises several roads (D422, D35, D1B and so on). It is signposted but you might want to pick up a copy of Blay's colour-coded map, *Alsace Touristique* (€5.50). Cyclists have a wide variety of on- and off-road options.

BUS & TRAIN It's entirely possible, if a bit cumbersome, to get around the Route des Vins by public transport, since almost all the towns and villages mentioned here are served by train from Strasbourg or by train and/or bus from Colmar. Bicycles can be taken on virtually all trains.

CAR & MOTORCYCLE Parking can be a nightmare in the high season, especially in Ribeauvillé and Riquewihr; your best bet is to park a bit out of the town centre and walk for a few minutes.

OBERNAI
POP 11,400

Half-timbered houses in sweetshop shades stud the postcard-perfect walled town of Obernai ('nai' rhymes with 'day'), 31km south of Strasbourg. Give the summertime crowds the slip by ducking down cool, flower-bedecked alleyways, such as ruelle des Juifs, next to the tourist office.

◉ Sights & Activities

A number of winegrowers have cellars a short walk from town (the tourist office has a map).

Place du Marché   TOWN SQUARE
Life spirals around this market square, put to use each Thursday morning, where you'll find the 16th-century hôtel de ville (town hall) embellished with baroque *trompe l'œil*; the Renaissance Puits aux Six Seaux (Six Bucket Well) just across rue du Général Gouraud; and the bell-topped, 16th-century Halle aux Blés (Corn Exchange).

Ramparts   RAMPART WALK
Stretch your legs by strolling around Obernai's 13th-century ramparts, accessible from the square in front of twin-spired, neo-Gothic Église St-Pierre et St-Paul.

Sentier Viticole du Schenkenberg
                                      VINEYARD WALK
This 1.5km wine route meanders through vineyards and begins at the hilltop cross north of town – to get there, follow the yellow signs from the cemetery behind Église St-Pierre et St-Paul.

🛏 Sleeping & Eating

La Cloche   HOTEL €
(☎03 88 95 52 89; www.la-cloche.com; 90 rue du Général Gouraud; s/d €50/60, mains €14-18; ✱) Facing the *hôtel de ville*, this hotel has 20 spacious, wood-furnished rooms, some with old-town views. The rustic restaurant rolls out hearty Alsatian fare like *spätzle* oozing Munster cheese.

Halle aux Blés   ALSATIAN €€
(place du Marché; mains €12-19) The old corn exchange does a brisk trade in regional

START **MARLENHEIM**
FINISH **COLMAR**
DISTANCE **87KM**
DURATION **ONE TO TWO DAYS**

Driving Tour
Route des Vins d'Alsace

❯ Weaving through lyrical landscapes, this road trip takes in the best of the vine-strewn Route des Vins d'Alsace.

From the Route des Vins gateway, ❶ **Marlenheim**, a well-marked country lane wriggles through bucolic scenery to medieval ❷ **Molsheim** centred on a picture-perfect square dominated by a carousel and the step-gabled Renaissance *Metzig* (Butcher's Shop). Continue south to ❸ **Rosheim**, where the striking Romanesque Église St-Pierre-St-Paul raises prudish eyebrows with its, ahem, lasciviously copulating gargoyles! Step inside for a moment of cool contemplation before meandering south to pretty, half-timbered ❹ **Obernai** to explore the market square and vineyard trail. Views of the Vosges unfold as you head south to the sleepy hamlet of ❺ **Mittelbergheim**, pausing to taste the local *grand cru* wines at award-winning Domaine Gilg. Even higher peaks slide into view as you cruise south to cellar-studded ❻ **Dambach-la-Ville**, embraced by ancient town walls, and catch your first tantalising glimpse of the turrets of hilltop ❼ **Château du Haut Kœnigsbourg**. After detouring for an astounding panorama from the castle ramparts, slip back in time roaming cobbled streets in half-timbered ❽ **Bergheim** and enchanting tower-speckled ❾ **Ribeauvillé**. Stork lovers' and would-be mothers' hearts are set aflutter at the Centre de Réintroduction Cigognes & Loutres in nearby ❿ **Hunawihr**. Set aside time for serendipitous strolls and medieval towers galore in the storybook half-timbered village of ⓫ **Riquewihr**. Contemplate glass-blowing magic and the house of Nobel Peace Prize winner Albert Schweitzer in riverside ⓬ **Kaysersberg**, then wend your way south to little-known ⓭ **Katzenthal** for organic wine tasting at Vignoble Klur. Wrap up your tour with culture and *winstub* dining in canal-laced ⓮ **Colmar**, Alsatian wine capital and birthplace of Statue of Liberty creator Frédéric Auguste Bartholdi.

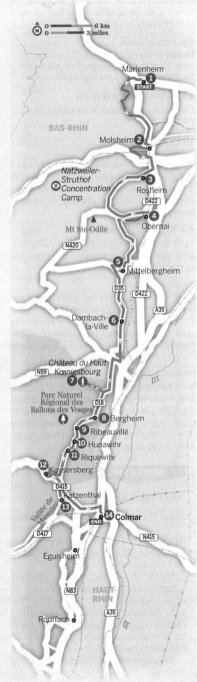

treats such as *tarte flambée* (€10), which are served under stag antlers and hop wreaths in the beamed dining room.

❶ Information

Tourist office (📞 03 88 95 64 13; www.ober nai.fr; place du Beffroi; ⏰9am-noon & 2-6pm Mon-Sun) Tucked behind the *hôtel de ville*.

❶ Getting There & Away

The train station is about 300m east of the old town.

MITTELBERGHEIM
POP 685

Serene, untouristy and set on a hillside, Mittelbergheim sits amid a sea of sylvaner grapevines and seasonal wild tulips, its tiny streets lined with sand-hued, red-roofed houses.

◉ Sights & Activities

Each of Mittelbergheim's *caves* (wine cellars) has an old-fashioned, wrought-iron sign hanging out front.

Sentier Viticole   WALK
From the car park on the D362 at the upper edge of the village next to the cemetery, a paved vineyard trail wriggles across the slopes towards the twin-towered Château du Haut Andlau and the undulating Vosges.

Domaine Gilg   WINERY
(www.domaine-gilg.com, in French; 2 rue Rotland; ⏰8am-noon & 1.30-6pm Mon-Fri, to 5pm Sat, 9.30-11.30am Sun) Nip into this friendly family-run winery to taste award-winning wines, including *grand cru* sylvaners, pinots and rieslings.

🛏 Sleeping & Eating

Private accommodation is good value and easy to come by – you'll see signs in windows all over town. For information, see www.pays-de-barr.com.

Hôtel Gilg   HISTORICAL HOTEL €
(📞03 88 08 91 37; www.hotel-gilg.com; 1 rte du Vin; r €59-89, menus €29-68) For a dose of old-fashioned romance, check into this 17th-century half-timbered pile. A spiral staircase leads up to spacious rooms in pretty pastels, some with wooden beams. The elegantly rustic restaurant serves classic French and Alsatian cuisine.

DAMBACH-LA-VILLE
POP 1970

Ringed by vines and sturdy ramparts, this flowery village has some 60 *caves* (wine cellars) but manages to avoid touristic overload. The renowned Frankstein *grand cru* vineyards cover the southern slopes of four granitic hills west and southwest of Dambach.

◉ Sights & Activities

Some of the eye-catching half-timbered houses, painted in shades like pistachio, caramel and raspberry, date from before 1500.

Ramparts   RAMPART WALK
A gentle stroll takes in the 14th-century, pink-granite ramparts, pierced by four gates, three holding aloft watchtowers and bearing quintessentially Alsatian names: Ebersheim, Blienschwiller and Dieffenthal.

WORTH A TRIP

NATZWEILER-STRUTHOF

About 25km west of Obernai stands Natzweiler-Struthof, the only Nazi concentration camp on French territory. In all, some 22,000 (40% of the total) of the prisoners interned here and at nearby annexe camps died; many were shot or hanged. In early September 1944, as US Army forces approached, the 5517 surviving inmates were sent to Dachau.

Today, the sombre remains of the camp (www.struthof.fr; adult/child €5/2.50; ⏰9am-6.30pm, closed Christmas-Feb) are still surrounded by guard towers and concentric, once-electrified, barbed-wire fences. The four **crématoire** (crematorium ovens), the **salle d'autopsie** (autopsy room) and the **chambre à gaz** (gas chamber), 1.7km from the camp gate, bear grim witness to the atrocities committed here. The nearby Centre Européen du Résistant Déporté (⏰same as camp) pays homage to Europe's Resistance fighters.

To get there from Obernai, take the D426, D214 and D130; follow the signs to 'Le Struthof'.

Sentier Viticole du Frankstein
VINEYARD WALK

It's a pleasant 1½-hour walk through the vineyards on this trail, which begins 70m up the hill from the tourist office on rue du Général de Gaulle. The path meanders among the hallowed vines, passing by hillside Chapelle St-Sébastien (⊙9am-7pm), known for its Romanesque tower and Gothic choir.

🛏 Sleeping

Le Vignoble HOTEL €
(☑03 88 92 43 75; www.hotel-vignoble-alsace. fr; 1 rue de l'Église; s/d €60/68; ⊜) Housed in a beautifully converted 18th-century barn, this hotel has comfortable wood-beamed rooms in fresh lemon and lime hues. It's well situated in the village centre.

❶ Information

Tourist office (☑03 88 92 61 00; www.pays-de -barr.com; place du Marché; ⊙10am-noon & 2-6pm Mon-Fri, 10am-noon Sat) In the Renaissance-style *hôtel de ville*. Hands out walking tour and has details on cycling to Itterwiller.

❶ Getting There & Away

The train station is about 1km east of the old town.

SÉLESTAT
POP 19.650

Wedged between Strasbourg, 50km to the north, and Colmar, 23km to the south, Sélestat is an enticing jumble of colourful half-timbered houses and church spires. The town's claim to cultural fame is its incomparable Humanist Library.

◉ Sights & Activities

Bibliothèque Humaniste LIBRARY
(1 rue de la Bibliothèque; adult/child €4/2.50; ⊙9am-noon & 2-6pm Mon & Wed-Fri, 9am-noon Sat) Founded in 1452, the Humanist Library's stellar collection features a 7th-century book of Merovingian liturgy, a copy of *Cosmographiae Introductio* (printed in 1507), in which the New World was referred to as 'America' for the first time, and – eat your heart out Lapland! – the first written mention of the Christmas tree (1521).

Vieux Sélestat OLD TOWN
Church spires rise gracefully above the red rooftops of the old town, which hugs the left bank of the River Ill. Some of the finest examples of half-timbered and *trompe-l'œil* buildings can be found along the medieval quai des Tanneurs.

Église St-Georges
CHURCH
(place St-Georges; ⊙8am-6pm) One of Alsace's most striking churches, this Gothic giant, built from weighty red sandstone and sporting a colourful mosaic-tile roof, is illuminated by curtains of stained glass in the choir.

Montagne des Singes FAMILY ATTRACTION
(Monkey Mountain; www.montagnedessing-es.com; Kintzheim; adult/child €8.50/5; ⊙10am-noon & 1-6pm, closed Dec-Mar) Kids love to feed the free-roaming Barbary macaques and their cheeky infants popcorn (special monkey popcorn, of course) at this 6-acre woodland park. Take the D35 to Kintzheim, 6km west of Sélestat.

Marché MARKET
(8am-noon Tue) A huge outdoor market, held since 1435, takes over the streets around Romanesque Église St-Foy.

Marché du Terroir MARKET
(place Vanolles; 8am-noon Sat) Local-produce market, on the southern edge of the old town, selling home-grown fruit and veggies.

❶ Information

Tourist office (☑03 88 58 87 20; www.selestat -tourisme.com; bd du Général Leclerc; ⊙9am-noon & 2-5.45pm Mon-Fri, 9am-noon & 2-5pm Sat) On the edge of the town centre, two blocks from the Bibliothèque Humaniste.

❶ Getting There & Around

The tourist office rents out **bicycles** (two hours/ half-day/day €7/9/14; deposit €150) in summer.

The train station is 1km west of the Bibliothèque Humaniste.

BERGHEIM
POP 1890

Enclosed by a sturdy 14th-century ring wall, overflowing with geraniums and enlivened by half-timbered houses in shocking pastels, Bergheim is a joy to behold. But things have not always been so cheerful: overlords, stampeding invaders, women burnt at the stake for witchcraft – this tiny village has seen the lot.

A stroll through the cobbled streets of the well-preserved medieval centre takes in the early Gothic church, the wall-mounted sundial at 44 Grand' Rue dating from 1711, and the imposing, turreted Porte Haute, Bergheim's last remaining town gate. Outside across the park sits the gnarled Herrengarten linden tree, planted around 1300. A 2km path circumnavigates the

DON'T MISS

FOREST FANTASY

What better place to go back to nature than at dreamy Hôtel de l'Illwald (☑03 90 56 11 40; www.illwald.fr; Schnellenbuhl; r €72-85; 🅿), bordering the lushly forested Ill'Wald nature reserve, which harbours France's largest population of wild deer. This half-timbered, red-sandstone hotel keeps the mood intimate in gorgeous rooms, some sleek with hardwood floors and four-poster beds, others rustic with warm pine, antique furnishings and downy bedding. After a day spent walking or cycling, come home to drinks by an open fire and dinner in the frescoed restaurant. The hotel is off the D424 in Schnellenbuhl, 6km south of Sélestat.

town's ramparts. Bergheim's *grands crus* labels are Kanzlerberg and Altenberg de Bergheim.

The tiny tourist office (☑03 89 73 31 98; ◷9.30-noon & 2-6pm Mon-Sat, 10am-1pm Sun) is between the 18th-century hôtel de ville and the deconsecrated Ancienne Synagogue (rue des Juifs), now a cultural centre.

Just inside the Porte Haute, La Cour du Bailli (☑03 89 73 73 46; www.cour-bailli.com; 57 Grand' Rue; r €83-118, menus €20-31; 🅿) is draped around a 16th-century courtyard. The countrified studios and apartments all have kitchenettes. Factor in downtime in the pool and stone-built spa, which pampers with luscious vinotherapy treatments. The atmospheric cellar restaurant serves wine-drenched specialities like *coq au riesling*. There's no lift so be prepared to lug your bags.

HAUT KŒNIGSBOURG

On its fairy-tale perch above vineyards and hills, the turreted red-sandstone Château du Haut Kœnigsbourg (www. haut-koenigsbourg.fr; adult/child €7.50/free; ◷9.15am-5.15pm) is worth the detour for the wraparound panorama from its ramparts, taking in the Vosges, the Black Forest and, on cloud-free days, the Alps. Audioguides delve into the turbulent 800-year history of the castle, which makes a very medieval impression despite having been reconstructed, with German imperial pomposity, by Kaiser Wilhelm II in 1908.

RIBEAUVILLÉ
POP 5100

Nestled snugly in a valley, presided over by a castle, its winding alleys brimming with half-timbered houses – medieval Ribeauvillé is a Route des Vins must. The local *grands crus* are Kirchberg de Ribeauvillé, Osterberg and Geisberg.

👁 Sights & Activities

Vieille Ville OLD TOWN
Along the main street that threads through the old town keep an eye out for the 17th-century Pfifferhüs (Fifers' House; 14 Grand' Rue), which once housed the town's fife-playing minstrels; the hôtel de ville (across from 64 Grand' Rue) and its Renaissance fountain; and the nearby clock-equipped Tour des Bouchers (Butchers' Bell Tower).

Cave de Ribeauvillé WINERY
FREE (www.cave-ribeauville.com; 2 rte de Colmar; ◷8am-noon & 2-6pm Mon-Fri, 10am-noon & 2-6pm Sat & Sun) France's oldest winegrowers' cooperative, founded in 1895, has a viniculture museum, informative brochures and free tastings of its excellent wines, made with all seven of the grape varieties grown in Alsace. On weekends it's staffed by local winegrowers. It's just across two roundabouts north from the tourist office.

Castle Ruins WALK
West and northwest of Ribeauvillé, the ruins of three 12th- and 13th-century hilltop castles – St-Ulrich (530m), Giersberg (530m) and Haut Ribeaupierre (642m) – can be reached on a hike (three hours return) beginning at place de la République (at the northern tip of Grand' Rue).

🛏 Sleeping & Eating

Hôtel de la Tour HOTEL €€
(☑03 89 73 72 73; www.hotel-la-tour.com; 1 rue de la Mairie; s €69-72, d €73-79; 🅿) Ensconced in a stylishly converted winery, this half-timbered hotel has quaint and comfy rooms, some with views of the Tour des Bouchers.

Camping Municipal Pierre de Coubertin
CAMPGROUND €
(☑03 89 73 66 71; 23 rue Landau; sites €16.50; 🅿) This shady campground, with bike and canoe rental and a playground, is 500m east of the town centre.

Zum Pfifferhüs ALSATIAN €€
(☑03 89 73 62 28; 14 Grand' Rue; menus €22; Fri-Tue) Pork cheeks braised in pinot noir, pike dumplings and oxtail are among the forti-

fying specialities on the menu at this convivial wood-beamed *winstub* in the historic Fifers' House.

❶ Information

Tourist office (☎03 89 73 23 23; www.ribeauville-riquewihr.com; 1 Grand' Rue; ☻9.30am-noon & 2-6pm Mon-Sat, 10am-1pm Sun) At the southern end of one-way Grand' Rue.

HUNAWIHR
POP 630

You're absolutely guaranteed to see storks in the quiet walled hamlet of Hunawihr, 1km south of Ribeauvillé. On a hillside just outside the centre, the 16th-century fortified church has been a *simultaneum* – serving both the Catholic and Protestant communities – since 1687.

 **Centre de Réintroduction Cigognes & Loutres**   WILDLIFE CENTRE
(Stork & Otter Reintroduction Centre; www.cigogne-loutre.com, in French; adult/child €8.50/5.50; ☻10am-6pm, closed mid-Nov–Mar) About 500m east of Hunawihr, this delightful centre is home base for 200 free-flying storks; visit in spring to see hatchlings. Cormorants, penguins, otters and sea lions show off their fishing prowess several times each afternoon.

Jardins des Papillons   BUTTERFLY HOUSE
(www.jardinsdespapillons.fr; adult/child €7.50/5; ☻10am-6pm, closed Nov-Easter) Stroll among exotic free-flying butterflies; the butterfly gardens are near to the Centre de Réintroduction Cigognes & Loutres.

RIQUEWIHR
POP 1310

Competition is stiff but Riquewihr is, just maybe, *the* most enchanting town on the Route des Vins. Medieval ramparts enclose its walkable centre, a photogenic maze of twisting lanes, hidden courtyards and half-timbered houses – each brighter and lovelier than the next. Of course, its chocolate-box looks also make it popular, so arrive in the early morning or evening to appreciate the town at its peaceful best.

◉ Sights & Activities

Dolder   CITY GATE
(admission €3, incl Tour des Voleurs €5; ☻10.30am-1pm & 2-6pm) This late 13th-century stone and half-timbered gate, topped by a 25m bell tower, is worth a look for its panoramic views and small local-history museum.

Tour des Voleurs   TOWER
(Thieves' Tower; admission €3, incl Dolder €5; ☻10am-1pm & 2-6pm Easter-1 Nov) From the Dolder, rue des Juifs (site of the former Jewish quarter) leads down the hill to this medieval stone tower. Inside is a gruesome torture chamber with English commentary and an old-style winegrower's kitchen.

Maison de Hansi   MUSEUM
(16 rue du Général de Gaulle; adult/child €2/free; ☻10am-6pm Tue-Sun) Peer into the imagination of celebrated Colmar-born illustrator Jean-Jacques Waltz (1873–1951), aka Hansi, whose idealised images of Alsace are known around the world. On display are the artist's posters, children's books, engravings and even wine labels.

Sentier Viticole des Grands Crus   WALK
A yellow-marked 2km trail takes you out to acclaimed local vineyards, Schœnenbourg (north of town) and Sporen (southeast of town), while a 15km trail with red markers takes you to five nearby villages. Both can be picked up next to Auberge du Schœnenbourg, 100m to the right of the *hôtel de ville*.

☷ Sleeping & Eating

Sugary smells of macaroons, a tradition since coconuts were first brought here in the 1700s, waft through the centre, where you'll find confectioners, *winstubs* and bakeries selling humongous pretzels.

STORKS OF ALSACE

White storks *(cigognes)*, prominent in local folklore, are Alsace's most-beloved symbols. Believed to bring luck (as well as babies), they winter in Africa and then spend summer in Europe, feeding in the marshes and building twig nests on church steeples and rooftops.

In the mid-20th century, environmental changes reduced stork numbers catastrophically. By the early 1980s only two pairs were left in the wild, so research and breeding centres were set up to establish a year-round Alsatian stork population. The program has been a huge success and today Alsace is home to more than 400 pairs – some of which you are bound to spot (or hear bill-clattering) on the Route de Vins.

Hôtel de la Couronne
HOTEL €

(☑03 89 49 03 03; www.hoteldelacouronne.com; 23 rue Landau; s €49-63, d €56-75; @) Worthy of Sleeping Beauty herself with its spiral staircase, 16th-century tower and fragrant wisteria, this hotel has country-style rooms with crisp floral fabrics, low oak beams and period furnishings; many have views over the rooftops to the hills beyond. The only downside: there's no lift.

TOP CHOICE Table du Gourmet
GASTRONOMIC €€€

(☑03 89 49 09 09; www.jlbrendel.com; 5 rue de la Première Armée; menus €39-95; ⊘closed Wed & Thu lunch, Tue) Michelin-starred chef John-Lac Brendel is justly famous for his creative take on seasonal cuisine using organic home-grown produce – from crunchy spring asparagus to plump autumn escargot. The fire-red walls, crisp white linen and contemporary art contrast beautifully with the beams of the original 16th-century structure. Reserve ahead.

❶ Information

Tourist office (☑03 89 73 23 23; www.ribeauville-riquewihr.com; 2 rue de la Première Armée; ⊘9.30am-noon & 2-6pm Mon-Sat, 10am-1pm Sun) In the centre of the old town.

KAYSERSBERG
POP 2770

Kaysersberg, 10km northwest of Colmar, is an instant heart-stealer with its backdrop of gently sloping vines, hilltop castle and 16th-century fortified bridge spanning the gushing River Weiss.

◉ Sights & Activities

Audioguides of the town (1½ to two hours, €5) are available from the tourist office.

Vieille Ville
OLD TOWN

An old-town saunter brings you to the ornate Renaissance hôtel de ville and the red-sandstone Église Ste Croix (⊘9am-4pm), whose altar has 18 painted haut-relief panels of the Passion and the Resurrection. Out front, a Renaissance fountain holds aloft a statue of Emperor Constantine.

Musée Albert Schweitzer
MUSEUM

(126 rue du Général de Gaulle; adult/child €2/1; ⊘9am-noon & 2-6pm) The house where the musicologist, medical doctor and 1952 Nobel Peace Prize winner Albert Schweitzer (1875–1965) was born is now this museum, with exhibits on the good doctor's life in Alsace and Gabon.

Verrerie d'Art
GLASS-BLOWING

(30 rue du Général de Gaulle; ⊘closed Sun & Mon) Many of the colourful half-timbered and baroque houses lining rue du Général de Gaulle harbour art galleries and workshops, such as this one where you can watch master glass-blowers doing their stuff.

Sentiers Viticoles
VINEYARD WALKS

Footpaths lead in all directions through glens and vineyards. A 10-minute walk above town, the remains of the massive, crenulated Château de Kaysersberg stand surrounded by vines; other destinations include Riquewihr (two hours) and Ribeauvillé (four hours). These paths begin through the arch to the right as you face the entrance to the hôtel de ville.

🛏 Sleeping

Hôtel Constantin
HOTEL €

(⊘03 89 47 19 90; www.hotel-constantin.com; 10 rue du Père Kohlmann; d €58-74; ☎) Originally a winegrower's house in the heart of the old town, this hotel has 20 clean and modern rooms with wood furnishings.

❶ Information

Tourist office (☑03 89 71 30 11; www.kaysersberg.com; 37 rue du Général de Gaulle; ⊘9am-12.30pm & 2-6pm Mon-Sat, 10am-12.30pm Sun) Inside the hôtel de ville; supplies walking-tour brochures as well as hiking and cycling maps, and helps with chambres d'hôte reservations; free internet and wi-fi.

KATZENTHAL
POP 550

Close-to-nature Katzenthal, 5km south of Kaysersberg, is great for tiptoeing off the tourist trail for a while. Grand cru vines ensnare the hillside, topped by the medieval ruins of Château du Wineck, where walks through forest and vineyard begin.

TOP CHOICE Vignoble Klur
(☑03 89 80 94 29; www.klur.net; 105 rue des Trois Epis; r €80-110; ☎), an organic family-run winery, has it all – wine tastings, Alsatian cookery classes, herb walks in the vineyards, furniture-making workshops and a tandem to pedal through the vines á deux. Ochre walls and warm wood create a cosy feel in the guesthouse, where you can make yourself at home in a sunny apartment with a kitchenette, read a book by the open fire in the salon, or unwind in the organic sauna. Don't miss Jean-Louis Frick's hilarious mural of hedonistic wine lovers above the entrance – it has raised a few local eyebrows, apparently.

Colmar

POP 67.700

Capital of the Alsace wine region and a happy-ever-after fairy-tale of a city if ever there was one, Colmar is a beguiling maze of higgledy-piggledy lanes, where ginger-bready half-timbered houses and the tranquil canals of Petite Venise elicit little gasps of wonder.

Quaintness aside, Colmar's illustrious past is clearly etched in its magnificent churches and museums, which celebrate local legends from Bartholdi (of Statue of Liberty fame) to the revered Issenheim Altarpiece.

◉ Sights

There's no place like the old town for ditching the map to wander streets like rue des Clefs, Grand' Rue and rue des Marchands, punctuated by impeccably restored half-timbered houses in sugared-almond colours.

Petite Venise   HISTORIC QUARTER

One of Colmar's biggest drawcards is its storybook Little Venice quarter, laced with canals and crammed with half-timbered houses festooned with geraniums. You can almost picture merchants at work in the Middle Ages wandering streets like rue des Tanneurs, with its rooftop verandas for drying hides, and quai de la Poissonnerie, the former fishers' quarter.

Rowboats (€6 per 30 minutes) depart next to **rue de Turenne** bridge and are a relaxed way see Petite Venise from the water. The bridge is also the best spot to see the quarter light up after dark.

Musée d'Unterlinden   ART MUSEUM

(www.musee-unterlinden.com; 1 rue d'Unterlinden; adult/child incl audioguide €7/3; ☺9am-6pm Mon-Sun) Gathered around a Gothic-style Dominican cloister, this museum hides a prized collection of medieval stone statues, late-15th-century prints by Martin Schongauer as well as an ensemble of Upper Rhine Primitives.

The star attraction, though, is the late-Gothic **Rétable d'Issenheim** (Issenheim Altarpiece). Hailed as one of the most profound works of faith ever created and ascribed to the painter Mathias Grünewald and the sculptor Nicolas of Haguenau, the altarpiece realistically depicts scenes from

---

LOCAL KNOWLEDGE

FRANCINE KLUR: VINTNER AT VIGNOBLE KLUR

Wine appreciation is 30% about the wine itself and 70% about the rest – the company, the food, the scenery, the ambience. That's why we take a holistic approach at Vignoble Klur.

Organic Grapes

For me, producing organic, biodynamic wines goes beyond the solar power and natural fertilisers we use – it's about respecting the land and what it can give; doing something out of passion, not profit.

Alsatian Wine

There's an Alsatian wine for every occasion. Try a light, citrusy sylvaner with *tarte flambée* or foie gras, or a crisp, dry riesling with fish or *choucroute*. Gewürztraminer is round and full of exotic fruit and spices, making it the ideal partner for Munster cheese, charcuterie and Asian food. Muscat is aromatic and flowery – great with asparagus or as an aperitif. Pick full-bodied pinot noirs for red meat.

Route des Vins

The Route des Vins is different from France's other wine regions because the villages are small and tight-knit, making it easy for visitors to get acquainted with our wine, food and culture. There are no grand châteaux but there *is* a real neighbourly feel – our doors are always open.

Insider Tips

Take a day to stroll or cycle through the vineyards, stopping for a wine tasting, lunch and to simply enjoy the atmosphere. Visit famous villages like Riquewihr and Ribeauvillé in the evening to have the streets to yourself. My favourite seasons are autumn, when the heady scent of new wine is in the air, and spring, when the cherry trees are in bloom.

the New Testament, from the Nativity to the Resurrection.

The museum's stellar **modern art collection** showcases Monet, Picasso and Renoir originals.

Musée Bartholdi
MUSEUM

(www.musee-bartholdi.com, in French; 30 rue des Marchands; adult/child €4.50/2.50; ☉10am-noon & 2-6pm Wed-Mon) In the house where Frédéric Auguste Bartholdi was born, this museum pays homage to the sculptor who captured the spirit of a nation with his Statue of Liberty. Look out for the full-size plaster model of Lady Liberty's left ear (the lobe

is watermelon-sized!) and the Bartholdi family's sparklingly bourgeois apartment. A ground-floor room shows 18th- and 19th-century Jewish ritual objects.

Église St-Matthieu
CHURCH

(Grand' Rue; ☉10am-noon & 3-5pm) Quintessentially Protestant in its austerity, this church has something of a split personality. From 1715 to 1987, a wall divided the soaring 14th-century Gothic choir from the nave. This arrangement allowed the 14th-century *jubé* (rood screen) to survive the counter-Reformation.

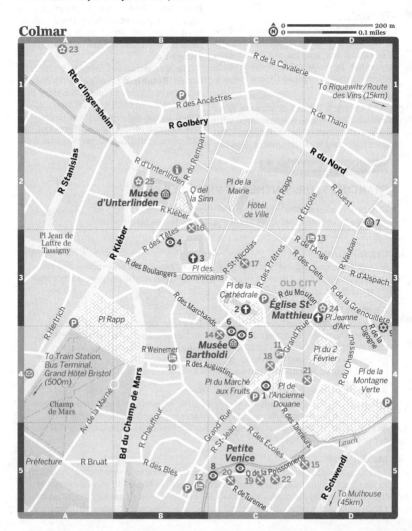

Colmar

0 — 200 m
0 — 0.1 miles

Église des Dominicains   CHURCH
(place des Dominicains; adult/child €1.50/0.50; ☉10am-1pm & 3-6pm mid-Mar–Dec) This de-sanctified Gothic church shelters the celebrated triptych *La Vierge au Buisson de Roses* (The Virgin in the Rose Bush), painted by Martin Schongauer in 1473. The stained glass dates from the 14th and 15th centuries.

Maison des Têtes   HISTORIC HOUSE
(House of the Heads; 19 rue des Têtes) True to its name, this step-gabled house, built in 1609 for a wealthy wine merchant, is festooned with 106 grimacing faces and heads of animals, devils and cherubs.

Ancienne Douane   OLD CUSTOMS
(place de l'Ancienne Douane) At the southern tip of rue des Marchands is this late-medieval old customs house, with its loggia and variegated tile roof, which now hosts temporary exhibitions and concerts.

Collégiale St-Martin   CHURCH
(place de la Cathédrale; ☉8am-7pm) Delicate stonework guides the eye to the mosaic-tiled roof and Mongol-style copper spire (1572) of this Gothic church, where you might spot a stork if you're lucky.

Musée du Jouet   TOY MUSEUM
(www.museejouet.com, in French; 40 rue Vauban; adult/child €4.50/3.50; ☉10am-noon & 2-6pm Wed-Mon) Kids of every age delight at the sight of toys from generations past, from demure 1950s Barbies to Gaultier-clad dolls and, every little boy's dream, Hornby train sets, at this museum.

Maison Pfister   HISTORIC HOUSE
(opposite 36 rue des Marchands) With its delicately painted panels, elaborate oriel window and carved wooden balcony, this 16th-century house is an immediate attention-grabber.

Maison zum Kragen   HISTORIC HOUSE
(9 rue des Marchands) This 15th-century house is identified by its much-photographed sculpture of a *marchand* (merchant).

LADY LIBERTY

Prepare for déjà vu as you approach Colmar on the route de Strasbourg (N83), 3km north of the old town, and spy the spitting image of the Statue of Liberty, albeit on a smaller scale. Bearing her torch aloft, this 12m-high, copper-green replica was erected to mark the centenary of the death of local lad Frédéric Auguste Bartholdi (1834–1904). We wonder how this little lady (four times smaller than her big sister across the Pond) feels about her humble home on a roundabout. New York Harbour it isn't, but she's an icon none the less.

ALSACE & LORRAINE COLMAR

Colmar

Synagogue SYNAGOGUE
(✆03 89 41 38 29; rue de la Cigogne) God only knows why Colmar's classical 19th-century synagogue has its very own tiny belfry (Jews have no tradition of ringing bells). Call ahead to visit the interior.

✷ Festivals & Events

Folksy Soirées Folkloriques (free performances of traditional Alsatian music and dancing) get toes tapping on Tuesday evenings from mid-May to mid-September. Orchestras strike up in historic venues across Colmar, including Musée d'Unterlinden, during July's Festival International de Colmar (www.festival-colmar.com). In summer, villages all over Alsace throw merry Fêtes du Vin (Wine Festivals); the tourist office has details. Colmar's magical Marché de Noël (Christmas Market; www.noel-colmar.com) runs from the last Saturday in November to 31 December.

🛏 Sleeping

Whether you're dreaming of canalside romance or a night in a working winery, Colmar has inexpensive and atmospheric *chambres d'hôte* on almost every corner. Book well ahead for Christmas, Easter and the high summer season.

WORTH A TRIP

THE STAR OF CITADELS

Shaped like an eight-pointed star, Vauban's fortified town of Neuf-Brisach was commissioned by Louis XIV in 1697 to strengthen French defences and prevent the area from falling to the Habsburgs.

A Unesco World Heritage Site since 2008, the citadel has remarkably well-preserved fortifications. The Musée Vauban (7 place de Belfort; adult/child €2.50/1.65; ⊗10am-noon & 2-5pm Wed-Mon May-Sep), below the porte de Belfort gate, tells the history of the citadel through models, documents and building plans. Neuf-Brisach is just 4km from its German twin Breisach am Rhein on the banks of the River Rhine.

To reach Neuf-Brisach, 16km southeast of Colmar, follow the signs on the D415.

Hôtel les Têtes HISTORIC HOTEL €€
(✆03 89 24 43 43; www.maisondestetes.com; 19 rue des Têtes; d €91-146; ✳) Luxurious but never precious, this hotel occupies the magnificent Maison des Têtes. Each of its 21 rooms has rich wood panelling, an elegant sitting area, a marble bathroom and romantic views. Definitely honeymoon material.

Chez Leslie B&B €€
(✆03 89 79 98 99; www.chezleslie.com; 31 rue de Mulhouse; s €57-62, d €74-79; @🛜🛗) Insider tips on Colmar, a high chair for your baby, afternoon tea in the garden – nothing is too much trouble for your kind host Leslie at her attractively restored 1905 town house. Daylight spills into uniquely decorated rooms with hardwood floors and antique beds. It's five minutes' stroll west of the train station.

🍃**Maison Martin Jund** B&B €
(✆03 89 41 58 72; www.martinjund.com; 12 rue de l'Ange; r €30-55, apt €55-85; 🛜) Surrounding a courtyard in the backstreets of the old town, this rosy half-timbered house shelters an organic winery and bright, well-kept studios, many with living rooms and kitchenettes. Breakfast is a treat, with fresh croissants and juice, homemade jams and yoghurt.

Hôtel St-Martin HISTORIC HOTEL €€
(✆03 89 24 11 51; www.hotel-saint-martin.com; 38 Grand' Rue; s €79, d €89-115; ✳@🛗) What a location! Right on the place de l'Ancienne Douane, this 14th-century patrician house captures the elegance of yesteryear in rooms dressed with handcrafted furniture. Choose a top-floor room for rooftop views. Family rooms are available.

Le Maréchal BOUTIQUE HOTEL €€
(✆03 89 41 60 32; www.hotel-le-marechal.com; 46 place des Six Montagnes Noires; s €85-95, d €105-140; @) Peppered with antiques, this 16th-century hotel in Petite Venise cranks up the romance in its cosy (read small) rooms, many with low beams, canopy beds and canal views. Splashing out gets you your own jacuzzi.

Grand Hôtel Bristol TRADITIONAL HOTEL €€
(✆03 89 23 59 59; www.grand-hotel-bristol.com; 7 place de la Gare; r €96-130, menus €44-75; ✳@🛜) Historic meets contemporary at the Bristol. A marble staircase sweeps up to modern rooms and a spa whose sundeck has fabulous city views. In the mood to celebrate? Snag a table at Le Rendez-vous de

THE EPICURE TOUR

Colmar is an exceptional city for all-out indulgence. So go, assemble your gourmet picnic:

» **Fromagerie St-Nicolas** (18 rue St-Nicolas; ⊙closed Sun, Mon morning) Follow your nose to pungent Munster, Tomme and ripe Camembert. BYOB (bring your own baguette) and they'll make you a sandwich.

» **Les Foie Gras de Liesel** (3 rue Turenne; ⊙Tue-Sat) Marco and Marianne Willmann produce the silkiest, most subtly flavoured goose and duck foie gras in town. Check out their tastings to enjoy it with fresh bread, fig chutney and a glass of Gewürztraminer or pinot gris.

» **Choco en Têtes** (7 rue des Têtes; ⊙closed Sun, Mon morning) Edible art describes this chocolatier's seasonally inspired truffles and pralines. Kids love the chocolate stork eggs.

» **Tentations** (quai de la Poissonnerie) Mountains of farm-fresh cheeses and fabulously herby *saucisson* stop you in your tracks for a nibble at this hole-in-the-wall deli.

» **Maison Martin Jund** (www.martinjund.com; 12 rue de l'Ange; ⊙tastings 9am-noon & 2-6.30pm Mon-Sat) Need something to wash it all down? Head to this organic winery to taste home-grown pinots, rieslings and sylvaners.

Chasse restaurant, awarded a Michelin star for Mickaela Peters' imaginative take on regional cuisine.

Hôtel Le Rapp HOTEL €€
(☑03 89 41 62 10; www.rapp-hotel.com; 1-5 rue Weinemer; s €70-80, d €95-115; ✴@🛜✕) On the edge of the old town, this Logis de France hotel has classically elegant rooms as well as a pool, sauna, hammam and fitness room.

✕ Eating

The old town is liberally sprinkled with bistros and *winstubs*, especially place de l'Ancienne Douane, rue des Marchands and Petite Venise.

La Maison des Têtes FRENCH €€
(☑03 89 24 43 43; 19 rue des Têtes; menus €30-65; ⊙closed lunch Tue, dinner Sun & Mon) Behind the leaded windows of the Maison des Têtes awaits a sumptuous dining room, embellished with carved wood, wrought iron and stained glass. Full-bodied wines marry well with refined French-Alsatian dishes such as homemade goose foie gras with riesling, and sea bass with pike mousse and Champagne sauce.

Le Petit Gourmand ALSATIAN €€
(☑03 89 41 09 32; 9 quai de la Poissonnerie; menus €23-26; ⊙Tue-Sun) Just a few lucky, lucky diners can eat at this Lilliputian *winstub*, with a pontoon on the river for warm

nights. The welcome is heartfelt and the *menu* an Alsatian feast that might include fresh duck foie gras with figs and gingerbread and Jean-Pierre's oh-so-smooth *mousse au chocolat*.

Aux Trois Poissons SEAFOOD €€
(☑03 89 41 25 21; 15 quai de la Poissonnerie; menus €21-45; ⊙closed dinner Sun, Tue & Wed) Oil paintings on the walls and Persian carpets on the floor give this fish restaurant a hushed, elegant atmosphere. The chef's signatures include *sandre sur lit de choucroute* (pike-perch on a bed of sauerkraut) and flavoursome bouillabaisse.

Restaurant Le Streusel ALSATIAN €€
(☑03 89 24 98 02; 4 passage de l'Ancienne Douane; mains €11-16) Dig into good old-fashioned Alsatian cooking, from *fleischnacka* to *choucroute* with stubby pork knuckles, at this beamed 16th-century farmhouse-turned-restaurant. Plump for a table in the cobbled courtyard in summer. The €7 *plat du jour* is a bargain.

Au Croissant Doré TEA ROOM €
(28 rue Marchands; tarts €7-8; ⊙Tue-Sun; ☑) Push past the bubblegum-pink art nouveau facade to experience *la vie en rose*. A gramophone and chanson set the tone in this delightfully nostalgic *salon de thé*, rolling out crisp *tarte flambée* and fruit tarts that crumble just so.

Jadis et Gourmande
TEAROOM €

(8 place du Marché aux Fruits; plats du jour €8.50-10.50) A little girl's dream of a *salon de thé*, with an all-wood interior, vintage teddies galore and blankets begging a snuggle. This is a relaxed place for lunch, a glass of wine or a slice of homemade apple strudel.

☆ Entertainment

Fnac Billetterie
TICKET OUTLET

(☏08 92 68 36 22; www.fnacspectacles.com; 1 Grand' Rue; ⏱2-7pm Mon, 10am-7pm Tue-Fri, 9am-7pm Sat)

Théâtre Municipal
THEATRE

(☏03 89 20 29 02; 3 rue Unterlinden) Next to the Musée d'Unterlinden, this is Colmar's biggest stage, hosting concerts, ballet, plays and even the occasional opera.

Comédie de l'Est
THEATRE

(www.atelierdurhin.com, in French; 6 rte d'Ingersheim) Experimental theatre, housed in a former factory, 400m northwest of Colmar.

❶ Information

Cyber Didim (9 rue du Rempart; per hr €2.80; ⏱10am-10pm Mon-Sat, 2-10pm Sun) Upstairs at the doner kebab place.

Hôpital Pasteur (☏03 89 12 40 00; 39 av de la Liberté; ⏱24hr) Situated 700m west of the train station and served by bus lines 1, 3, 10, A, C and S.

Post office (36 av de la République) Has exchange services.

CYCLING THE VINES

Colmar is a great base for slipping into a bicycle saddle to pedal along the Route des Vins and the well-marked Franco-German trails of the nearby Rhine (www.2rives3ponts.eu, in French). Get your two-wheel adventure started by clicking onto www.tourisme68.com and www.tourisme67.com, with detailed information on everything from bicycle hire to luggage-free cycling holidays, itinerary ideas and downloadable route maps.

If you'd rather join a group, Bicyclette Go (06 87 47 44 31; www.bicyclettego.com; 2 impasse du Tokay, Voegtlinshoffen), 12km south of Colmar, arranges all-inclusive half-day to two-week cycling tours in the region.

Tourist office (☏03 89 20 68 92; www.ot-colmar.fr; 4 rue d'Unterlinden; ⏱9am-6pm Mon-Sat, 10am-1pm Sun) Can help find accommodation and supply information on hiking, cycling and bus travel (including schedules) along the Route des Vins and in the Massif des Vosges.

❶ Getting There & Away

AIR Trinational **Basel-Mulhouse-Freiburg airport** (EuroAirport; www.euroairport.com) is 60km south of Colmar.

BUS Public buses are not the quickest way to explore Alsace's Route des Vins but they *are* a viable option; destinations served include Riquewihr, Hunawihr, Ribeauvillé, Kaysersberg and Eguisheim.

The open-air bus terminal is to the right as you exit the train station. Timetables are posted and are also available at the tourist office or online (www.l-k.fr, in French).

Line 1076 goes to Neuf-Brisach (€3.30, 30 minutes), continuing on to the German city of Freiburg (€8, 1¼ hours, seven daily Monday to Friday, four daily weekends).

CAR & MOTORCYCLE Cars can be hired from **ADA** (www.ada.fr, in French; 22bis rue Stanislas). **Avis** (www.avis.com) has an agency in the train station.

TRAIN Colmar has train connections to the following:

Basel SNCF €12, 43 minutes, 25 daily

Mulhouse €7.50, 18 minutes, 38 daily

Paris Gare de l'Est; €74, three hours by direct TGV, 17 daily

Strasbourg €11, 35 minutes, 30 daily

Route des Vins destinations from Colmar include Dambach-la-Ville (€5.50) and Obernai (€7.50), both of which require a change of trains at Sélestat (€4.50, 11 minutes, 30 daily).

About 20 daily autorails or SNCF buses (10 daily on weekends) link Colmar with the Vallée de Munster towns of Munster (€3.50, 37 minutes) and Metzeral (€4.50, 50 minutes); the last run back, by bus, begins a bit after 9pm (7pm at weekends).

❶ Getting Around

TO/FROM THE AIRPORT For Basel-Mulhouse-Freiburg airport (EuroAirport), take one of the frequent trains to St-Louis and catch an airport shuttle bus (€1, eight minutes, every 20 or 30 minutes).

BICYCLE Colmarvélo (place Rapp; per half-/full day €5/6, deposit €50) Municipal city bikes.

Cycles Geiswiller (4-6 bd du Champ de Mars; per half-/full day €6/11) Hybrid bikes for Route des Vins touring; free helmets and cycling maps.

CAR & MOTORCYCLE Free parking can be found on place Scheurer-Kestner just north of Musée d'Unterlinden; a few blocks east of the train station around the German-era, brick-built water tower; and in *part* of the car park at place de la Montagne Verte.

Massif des Vosges

The Vosges range is a little-known region of wooded heights, fragrant pastures, glacial lakes and dairy farms. For added seclusion, head away from the crowds and into the serene Parc Naturel Régional des Ballons des Vosges (www.parc-ballons-vosges. fr), 3000 sq km of pristine greenery in the southern Vosges.

In summer, hang-gliders take to the skies, cyclists roll through pristine countryside and walkers can pick from 10,000km of marked paths, including GRs (*grandes randonnées;* long-distance hiking trails).When the snow settles, three dozen inexpensive skiing areas offer modest downhill and superb cross-country skiing.

VALLÉE DE MUNSTER

This river valley – its cow-nibbled pastures scattered with 16 quaint villages, its upper slopes thickly forested – is one of the loveliest in the Vosges. From the town of Metzeral, you can hike to Schnepfenried, Hohneck, the Petit Ballon and Vallée de la Wormsa, which has a section of the GR5 and a trio of small lakes.

MUNSTER
POP 5080

Spread around gently rolling hills and famous for its notoriously smelly and eponymous cheese, streamside Munster, meaning 'monastery', is a relaxed base for exploring the valley (the GR531 passes by here).

About 20 storks live year-round in the Enclos aux Cigognes (chemin du Dubach; admission free; ⊘24hr), and more hang out on top of it. It's 250m behind the Renaissance *hôtel de ville;* on foot, cross the creek and turn left.

Check out the Cimes et Sentiers (www. sentiersrando.com, in French) website for year-round walking and cycling tours of the Vosges and, in winter, snowshoe hikes.

Based 200m east of the tourist office, Cycle Hop Evasion (5 rue de la République; bike rental per day €14-18; ⊘9.30am-6.30pm Mon-Sat) rents out mountain bikes, arrang-

Rich, white and creamy, with a pungent, earthy aroma when ripe and a mild flavour when fresh, Munster cheese has been made to the time-honoured methods of the Benedictine monks since the 7th century in this valley. Only the milk of the cows that lazily graze the Vosges' highest pastures is good enough for this semisoft cheese, delicious with cumin seeds, rye bread and a glass of spicy Gewürztraminer. See the tourist office website (www.la-vallee-de-munster.com) for details on dairy farms where you can taste, buy and see Munster in the making.

es guides and provides details on cycling routes.

Corinne and Dany extend a warm welcome the lemon-fronted Hôtel Deybach (📞03 89 77 32 71; www.hotel-deybach.com; 4 chemin du Badischhof; s/d €43/56). The fresh, simple rooms have town or country views, and there's a flowery garden for relaxing moments.

Skip dinner and go straight for dessert at Salon de Thé Gilg (11 Grand' Rue; cakes & pastries €2-5; ⊘closed Sun afternoon, Mon), a tea room famous for its delectable *kougelhopf,* petits fours and pastries. Keep an eye out for storks' nests at the food market (place du Marché; ⊘Tue & Sat mornings). Grand' Rue has a handful of restaurants rustling up Alsatian fare and pizza.

🛈 Information
Maison du Parc Naturel Régional des Ballons des Vosges (www.parc-ballons-vosges. fr, in French; 1 cour de l'Abbaye; ⊘10am-noon & 2-6pm Tue-Sun) The regional park's visitors centre has ample information in English. To get there, walk through the arch from place du Marché.

Tourist office (📞03 89 77 31 80; www. la-vallee-de-munster.com; 1 rue du Couvent; ⊘9.30am-12.30pm & 2-6pm Mon-Fri, 10am-noon & 2-6pm Sat) Information on the Munster valley, including visits to cheesemakers. Sells hiking maps and *topoguides* in French. In the same building as the Maison du Parc but downstairs.

ROUTE DES CRÊTES

Partly built during WWI to supply French frontline troops, the Route des Crêtes (Route of the Crests) takes you to the

1. Strasbourg's cathedral (p303)

Cathédrale Notre-Dame is a Gothic marvel of stonework, stained-glass, spires and gargoyles.

2. Petite Venise, Colmar (p323)

Colmar's 'Little Venice' quarter, with its canals and half-timbered houses, is a main attraction.

3. Centre Pompidou-Metz (p339)

The Pompidou-Metz' sleek architecture has created as much buzz as its modern-art exhibits.

4. Place Stanislas, Nancy (p335)

Nancy's neoclassical square is a Unesco World Heritage Site.

Vosges' highest *ballons* (bald, rounded mountain peaks) and to several WWI sites. Mountaintop lookouts afford spectacular views of the Alsace plain, the Black Forest across the Rhine in Germany and – on clear days – the Alps and Mont Blanc.

The route links Col du Bonhomme (949m), about 20km west of Kaysersberg, with Cernay, 15km west of Mulhouse, along the D148, D61, D430 and D431. Sections around Col de la Schlucht (1139m) are closed from the first big snow until about April.

From Col de la Schlucht, home to a small ski station, trails head off in various directions; walking north along the GR5 brings you to three pristine lakes: Lac Vert, Lac Noir and Lac Blanc (Green, Black and White Lakes).

At the dramatic, wind-buffeted summit of 1424m Grand Ballon, the highest point in the Vosges, a short trail takes you to an aircraft-radar ball and a weather station.

BALLON D'ALSACE

Three *régions* (Alsace, Franche-Comté and Lorraine) converge at the rounded 1247m-high summit of Ballon d'Alsace, 20km southwest of Grand Ballon as the crow flies (by road, take the D465 from St-Maurice). Between 1871 and WWI, the frontier between France and Germany passed by here, attracting French tourists eager to glimpse France's 'lost province' of Alsace from the heroic equestrian statue of Joan of Arc and the cast-iron orientation table. During WWI the mountaintop was heavily fortified, but the trenches were never used in battle.

Ballon d'Alsace is a scenic base for walking in summer; the GR5 passes through, as do other trails, including those heading to the bottle-green Lac des Perches (four hours). There's cross-country skiing on well-groomed forest tracks in winter.

Mulhouse

POP 113,130

The dynamic industrial city of Mulhouse (pronounced 'moo-*looze*'), 43km south of Colmar, was allied with nearby Switzerland before voting to join Revolutionary France in 1798. Largely rebuilt after the ravages of WWII, it has little of the quaint Alsatian charm that you find further north, but the city's world-class industrial museums are well worth a stop.

◉ Sights

Cité de l'Automobile   CAR MUSEUM

(www.collection-schlumpf.com; 192 av de Colmar; adult/child €10.50/8; ☉10am-6pm; ⊛) An ode to the automobile, the striking glass-and-steel museum showcases 400 rare and classic motors from old-timers like the Bugatti Royale to Formula 1 dream machines. There's a kiddie corner for would-be mechanics. By car, hop off the A36 at the Mulhouse Centre exit.

Cité du Train   RAILWAY MUSEUM

(www.citedutrain.com; 2 rue Alfred de Glehn; adult/child €10/7.50, incl Cité de l'Automobile €17.50/12.50; ☉10am-6pm) Trainspotters are in their element at Europe's largest railway museum, displaying SNCF's prized collection of locomotives and carriages. Take bus 20 from the train station or, if driving, the Mulhouse-Dornach exit on the A35.

Musée de l'Impression sur Étoffes
FABRIC MUSEUM

(Museum of Textile Printing; www.musee-impression.com; 14 rue Jean-Jacques Henner; adult/child €7/3; ☉10am-noon & 2-6pm Tue-Sun) Once known as the 'French Manchester', Mulhouse is fittingly home to this peerless collection of six million textile samples – from brilliant cashmeres to intricate silk screens – which make it a mecca for fabric designers. It's one long block northeast of the train station.

Musée du Papier Peint   WALLPAPER MUSEUM

(www.museepapierpeint.org; 28 rue Zuber, Rixheim; adult/child €6.50/5; ☉10am-noon & 2-6pm) More stimulating than it sounds, this is a treasure-trove of wallpaper (some of the scenic stuff is as detailed as an oil painting) and the machines used to produce it since the 18th century. To reach it, take bus 18 from the train station to Temple stop, or the Rixheim exit on the A36.

🛏 Sleeping & Eating

Le Strasbourg Hotel   HOTEL €

(☎03 89 36 54 70; www.hotel-le-strasbourg.com; 17 av de Colmar; s/d €50/60) A five-minute stroll north of the main square, this tastefully converted 19th-century town house has large, bright and airy rooms. Free parking is a boon.

Le Petit Zinc   ALSATIAN €€

(☎03 89 46 36 78; 15 rue des Bons Enfants; mains €11-17; ☉closed Sun; ⊛) Old black-and-white snapshots, coffee mills and a polished wooden bar give this art deco bistro a nostalgic air. Pull up a chair for Alsatian classics like *baeckeoffe* and pork cheeks braised in pinot noir.

ℹ️ Information

Tourist office (📞03 89 66 93 13; www.tourism-mulhouse.com; place de la Réunion; ⏰10am-6pm, closed noon-2pm Sun) Located in the 16th-century, *trompe l'œil*–covered former *hôtel de ville*, about 700m northwest of the train station.

ℹ️ Getting There & Around

TRAIN France's second train line, linking Mulhouse with Thann, opened in 1839. The **train station** (10 av du Général Leclerc) is just south of the centre. Trains run at least hourly to the following:

Basel €6.50, 23 minutes

Colmar €7.50, 17 minutes

St-Louis €5, 14 minutes

Strasbourg €15, 52 minutes

Around Mulhouse

Écomusée d'Alsace (www.ecomusee-alsace.fr, in French; Ungersheim; adult/child €13/9; ⏰10am-6pm) is great for keeping little minds active. France's so-called biggest 'living museum' is a fascinating excursion into Alsatian country life and time-honoured crafts. Smiths, cartwrights, potters and coopers do their thing in and among 70 historic Alsatian farmhouses – a veritable village – brought here and meticulously reconstructed for preservation (and so storks can build nests on them). The Écomusée is in Ungersheim, 17km northwest of Mulhouse (off the A35 to Colmar).

Bioscope (www.lebioscope.com, in French; adult/child €13/9; ⏰10am-6pm) makes learning about the environment fun. Tots are kept on their toes at this eco-conscious theme park with hands-on activities, including a virtual journey to the depths of the South Pacific, a recycling-focused labyrinth and the Macroscope garden where everything (roots, apple trees etc) seems larger than life. It's situated 5km by road northeast from the Écomusée.

LORRAINE

Lorraine, between the plains and vines of Champagne and the Massif des Vosges, is fed by the Meurthe, Moselle and Meuse Rivers – hence the names of three of its four *départements* (the fourth is Vosges).

History

Lorraine got its name *Lotharii regnum* (Lothair's kingdom) in the 9th century when it came to be ruled by the Frankish king Lothair II. The area became part of France in 1766 upon the death of Stanisław Leszczyński, the deposed king of Poland who ruled Lorraine as duke in the middle decades of the 18th century. In 1871 the Moselle *département* (along with Alsace) was annexed by Germany and remained part of the Second Reich until 1918, which is why much of Metz feels so imperial while Nancy, which remained French, is so stylishly Gallic. The two cities are rivals to this day.

ℹ️ Getting There & Away

CAR & MOTORCYCLE Metz is on the A4, which links Paris and Reims with Strasbourg. Both Nancy and Metz are on the A31 from Dijon to Luxembourg.

TRAIN The new TGV Est Européen line has significantly reduced travel times from Paris – Metz and Nancy are now just 80 and 90 minutes from the capital, respectively.

Nancy

POP 107,250

Delightful Nancy has an air of refinement found nowhere else in Lorraine. With its resplendent central square, fine museums, formal gardens and shop windows sparkling with Daum and Baccarat crystal, the former capital of the dukes of Lorraine catapults

A ROOM AT THE TOP

Built all in wood in 1922 and run by the Club Vosgien, the region's hiking organisation, the Chalet Hôtel du Grand Ballon (📞03 89 48 77 99; www.chalethotel-grandballon.com, in French; s/d €31/56, menus €15-27; 🍴) sits atop Grand Ballon in splendid isolation, amid a web of hiking and cycling trails. The rooms are spartan but with scenery this breathtaking you won't be spending much time inside. The Alsatian restaurant is perfect for hearty après-hike dining. By car it's 17km up the hill from Willer-sur-Thur (the road is open year-round), northwest of Mulhouse.

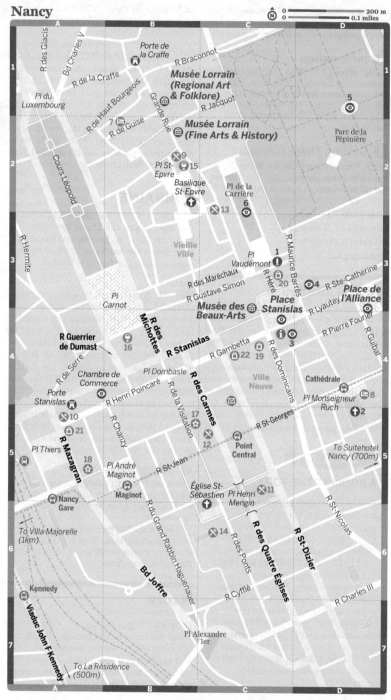

ALSACE & LORRAINE LORRAINE

N 0 ——————— 200 m
0 ——————— 0.1 miles

Nancy

R des Glacis
Bd Charles V
R de la Craffe
R de Haut Bourgeois
Pl du Luxembourg
Cours Léopold
R Hermite
R de Serre

Porte de la Craffe
R Braconnot
Musée Lorrain (Regional Art & Folklore)
R Jacquot
Grande Rue
R de Guise
7
Musée Lorrain (Fine Arts & History)
9
Pl St-Epvre
15
Basilique St-Epvre
Pl de la Carrière
13
6
Vieille Ville
Pl Vaudémont
1
R Maurice Barrès
R Héré
20
R Ste-Catherine
4
R Lyautey
Place de l'Alliance
Pl Carnot
R des Michottes
R des Maréchaux
R Gustave Simon
Musée des Beaux-Arts
Place Stanislas
R Pierre Fourier
5
Parc de la Pépinière

R Guerrier de Dumast
16
R Stanislas
R Gambetta
22
19
3
R des Dominicains
R Guibal
Chambre de Commerce
Pl Dombasle
R Henri Poincaré
R des Carmes
Ville Neuve
Cathédrale
Pl Monseigneur Ruch
8
2
Porte Stanislas
10
R Chanzy
R de la Visitation
17
12
R St-Georges
To Suitehotel Nancy (700m)
21
Pl Thiers
18
Pl André Maginot
R St-Jean
Point Central
Nancy Gare
Maginot
R du Grand Rabbin Haguenauer
Église St-Sébastien
Pl Henri Mengin
11
R St-Nicolas
To Villa Majorelle (1km)
14
R des Quatre Églises
R des Ponts
R St-Dizier
Kennedy
Bd Joffre
R Cyfflé
R Charles III
Viaduc John F Kennedy
Pl Alexandre 1er
To La Résidence (500m)
R Mazagran

you back to the opulence of the 18th century, when much of the city centre was built.

Nancy has long thrived on a combination of innovation and sophistication. The art nouveau movement flourished here (as the Nancy School) thanks to the rebellious spirit of local artists, who set out to prove that everyday objects could be drop-dead gorgeous.

⊙ Sights

Place Stanislas   CITY SQUARE

Laid out in the 1750s, this neoclassical square is one of France's grandest public spaces and a Unesco World Heritage Site. Designed by Emmanuel Héré, it was named after the enlightened, Polish-born Duke of Lorraine who commissioned it, and whose statue stands in the middle. Your gaze will be drawn to a cluster of opulent buildings, including the **hôtel de ville** and the sublime **Opéra National de Lorraine**, as well as gilded wrought-iron gateways by Jean Lamour and rococo fountains by Guibal.

Musée des Beaux-Arts   ART MUSEUM

(3 place Stanislas; adult/child €6/free; ☉10am-6pm Wed-Mon) Daum-made art nouveau glass and a rich selection of paintings from the 14th to 21st centuries are among the star exhibits at this outstanding museum. Caravaggio, Rubens, Picasso and Monet masterpieces hang alongside works by Lorraine-born artists, such as Claude Lorrain's dreamlike baroque landscapes.

Musée de l'École de Nancy   ART MUSEUM

(School of Nancy Museum; www.ecole-de-nancy. com; 36-38 rue du Sergent Blandan; adult/child €6/4; ☉10am-6pm Wed-Sun) A highlight of a visit to Nancy, the Musée de l'École de Nancy brings together an exquisite collection of art nouveau interiors, curvaceous glass and landscaped gardens. It's housed in a 19th-century villa about 2km southwest of the centre; to get there take bus 122 or 123 to the Nancy Thermal or Paul-Painlevé stop.

Musée Lorrain   REGIONAL MUSEUM

(64 & 66 Grande Rue; adult/child for both sections €5.50/3.50; ☉10am-12.30pm & 2-6pm Wed-Mon) Once home to the dukes of Lorraine, the regal Renaissance Palais Ducal now shelters the Musée Lorrain. The rich **fine arts & history collection** spotlights medieval statuary, engravings and lustrous faience (glazed pottery). The **regional art & folklore collection** occupies a 15th-century former Franciscan monastery. Inside, the Gothic **Église des Cordeliers** and the 17th-century **Chapelle Ducale**, modelled on the Medici Chapel in Florence, served as the burial place of the dukes of Lorraine.

Nancy

Place de l'Alliance
CITY SQUARE

A block to the east of place Stanislas, this lime-tree-fringed square, also World Heritage material, is graced by a **baroque fountain** by Bruges-born Louis Cyfflé (1724–1806), inspired by Bernini's *Four Rivers* fountain in Rome's Piazza Navona.

Place de la Carrière
CITY SQUARE

Adjoining place Stanislas – on the other side of Nancy's own Arc de Triomphe, built in the mid-1750s to honour Louis XV – is this quiet square. Once a riding and jousting arena, it is now graced by four rows of linden trees and stately rococo gates in gilded wrought iron.

Vieille Ville
OLD TOWN

A saunter through the charming old town takes in the silver-turreted, 14th-century Porte de la Craffe, Nancy's oldest city gate, and place St-Epvre, dominated by ornate neo-Gothic Basilique St-Epvre.

Parc de la Pépinière
PARK

On a hot summer's day, escape the crowds in this formal garden, with ornamental fountains, a rose garden and a Rodin sculpture of baroque landscape painter Claude Lorrain.

Cathédrale Notre-Dame-de-l'Annonciation
CATHEDRAL

(place Monseigneur Ruch) Crowned by a frescoed dome, Nancy's 18th-century cathedral is a sombre mixture of neoclassical and baroque.

Tours

The tourist office offers multilingual audioguide tours (€6) of the historic centre (two

CULTURE CENT-SAVER

The good-value **Pass Nancy Trois Musées** (€10), valid for three months, gets you into the Musée de l'École de Nancy, the Musée Lorrain and the Musée des Beaux-Arts, and is sold at each museum.

The **City Pass Nancy Culture** (€9), sold at the tourist office, includes an audioguide tour of the city, a bus or tram return trip and a cinema ticket, plus discounts on museums and bike rental. From May to October, the **City Pass Nancy Loisirs** (€13) bestows a few additional benefits.

hours) and the art nouveau quarters (up to three or four hours), or download a free MP3 tour online (www.ot-nancy.fr).

Festivals & Events

Get your groove on to live jazz, blues and Latin at the 10-day Jazz Pulsations (www. nancyjazzpulsations.com) in October. December brings twinkle, carols and handicrafts to the Marché de Nöel (Christmas Market) on place André Maginot.

Sleeping

Characterful midrange hotels are Nancy's forte; budget places tend to be either complete dives or anonymous chains. The tourist office can give you a list of *chambres d'hôte* – expect to pay €60 to €80 for a double.

TOP CHOICE **Hôtel des Prélats** HISTORIC HOTEL €€
(☎03 83 30 20 20; www.hoteldesprelats. com; 56 place Monseigneur Ruch; s & d €69/109; ✳🛜) It's not every day you get to sleep in a former 17th-century bishop's palace right next to the cathedral. This elegant hotel plays up the romance in rooms with stained-glass windows, four-poster beds and shimmery drapes. Service is as polished as the surrounds.

Hôtel de Guise BOUTIQUE HOTEL €€
(☎03 83 32 24 68; www.hoteldeguise.com; 18 rue de Guise; s €63, d €75-100; 🛜) Boutique chic meets 17th-century elegance at this hotel, tucked down an old-town backstreet. A wrought-iron staircase sweeps up to old-fashioned rooms, with antique furnishings, inlaid parquet and heavy drapes. There's a walled garden for quiet moments.

La Résidence TRADITIONAL HOTEL €€
(☎03 83 35 42 34; www.hotel-laresidence-nancy. fr, in French; 30 bd Jean-Jaurès; r €70-85; 🛜🅿 place Centrale) This convivial hotel is one of Nancy's best deals, with an inviting salon and a leafy courtyard for alfresco breakfasts. The snappy new rooms have ultramodern bathrooms and flatscreen TVs.

Suitehotel Nancy APARTHOTEL €€
(☎03 83 32 28 80; www.suitehotel.com; 2 allée du Chanoine Drioton; r €110; @🛜🅿St-George) Prettily set in gardens, this streamlined hotel has spacious, modern apartments with kitchenettes, and a 24-hour gym. Book online at least three weeks ahead for a discount of up to 40%.

In 1900, glassmaker and ceramist Émile Gallé founded the École de Nancy, one of France's leading art nouveau movements, joining creative forces with masters of decorative arts and architecture such as Jacques Gruber, Louis Majorelle and the Daum brothers. Banks, villas, pharmacies, brasseries – wherever you wander in Nancy, you are bound to stumble across their handiwork, from sinuous grillwork to curvaceous stained-glass windows and doorways that are a profusion of naturalistic ornament.

Slip back to this genteel era by picking up the free *Art Nouveau Itineraries* brochure and map at the tourist office, covering four city strolls. Lucien Weissenburger's 1910 **Brasserie Excelsior** and the 1908 **Chambre de Commerce** with wrought-iron by Louis Majorelle, both located on rue Henri Poincaré, are central standouts. Close to the Musée de l'École de Nancy lies the whimsical **Villa Majorelle** (1 rue Louis-Majorelle; adult/child €3.50/2.50; ☉guided tours 2.30pm & 3.45pm Sat & Sun), built by Henri Sauvage in 1901 and bearing the hallmark of Majorelle (furniture) and Gruber (stained glass). The centrepiece is Les Blés dining room with its vinelike stone fireplace.

ALSACE & LORRAINE NANCY

✖ Eating

Foodie rue des Maréchaux, just west of the Arc de Triomphe, dishes up everything from French to Italian, tapas, seafood, Indian and Japanese. Grande Rue is peppered with intimate bistros.

Brasserie Excelsior　　　　　BRASSERIE €€
(☎03 83 35 24 57; 50 rue Henri Poincaré; menus €23-38; ☉8am-12.30am Mon-Sat, 8am-11pm Sun) As opulent as a Fabergé egg with its stucco and stained glass, Excelsior whisks you back to the decadent era of art nouveau. Brusquely efficient waiters bring brasserie classics such as oysters (in the R months), juicy steaks and banquet-like seafood platters to the table.

Chez Tony　　　　　GOURMET FOOD €
(Marché Couvert; plat du jour €6, antipasti €7-11; ☉Tue-Sat) Generously heaped plates of antipasti, freshly made pasta, colourful garden chairs, big smiles all round – it's a Tuscan garden party every lunchtime at Chez Tony in Nancy's covered market. Toast your find with a glass of olive liqueur or Chianti.

Aux Délices du Palais　　　　　BISTRO €
(☎03 83 30 44 19; 69 Grande Rue; starters/mains/desserts €5/9/5; ☉Mon-Fri & dinner Sat) Purple walls and glitter balls, this shabby-chic bistro serves whatever the jovial chef fancies cooking – from flavoursome tagines to fajitas. Great value, so it's no wonder it has an enthusiastic local following.

Chez Tanésy – Le Gastrolâtre　　　BISTRO €€
(☎03 83 35 51 94; 23 Grande Rue; menus €27-44; ☉Tue-Sat) A 16th-century town house has been transformed into this homey, intimate bistro specialising in mouth-watering Lorraine- and Provence-inspired cuisine, including fowl.

La Bouche á L'Oreille　　　　　BISTRO €€
(☎03 83 35 17 17; 42 rue des Carmes; lunch menus/fondues €12/15; ☉lunch Tue-Fri, dinner Mon-Sat) Chandeliers and flowery wallpaper give this bistro the feel of an overgrown doll's house. The menu places an emphasis on cheese, from creative salads to *raclette* and fondues. Service can be slooow.

Self-Catering

Marché Couvert　　　　　FOOD MARKET
(place Henri Mengin; ☉7am-7pm Tue-Sat) A fresh-produce feast for the picnic basket.

Monoprix　　　　　SUPERMARKET
(rue des Ponts) Deep inside the St-Sébastien shopping mall.

🍸 Drinking

Nancy's buoyant nightlife concentrates on bar-dotted Grande Rue, the spectacularly illuminated place Stanislas and laid-back place de St-Epvre in the Vieille Ville, the best spot for sundowners.

Le Ch'timi　　　　　BAR
(17 place St-Epvre; ☉9am-2am Mon-Sat, 9am-8pm Sun) On three brick-and-stone levels, Le Ch'timi is *the* place to go for beer. It's a beloved haunt of students who come for the 150 brewskies, 16 of them on tap.

Le Varadero　　　　　BAR
(27 Grande Rue; ☉Tue-Sat) Cuba it isn't, but this trendy bar still gets the good vibes flowing with live Latin and jazz on the terrace in summer. DJs hit the turntables at the weekend.

Le P'ti K BAR

(7 place Carnot) A slinky interior and prime people-watching terrace on place Carnot make this a great spot for an *apéro* (aperitif).

☆ Entertainment

Details on cultural events appear in French in *Spectacles* (www.spectacles-publications.com) and *Nancy by Night* (www.nancybynight.com). Tickets are available at Fnac Billetterie (www.fnacspectacles.com; 2nd fl, 2 av Foch; ⊙10am-7pm Mon-Sat).

Opéra National de Lorraine OPERA HOUSE

(☑03 83 85 33 11; www.opera-national-lorraine.fr, in French; 1 rue Ste-Catherine) A harmonious blend of neoclassical and art nouveau styles, this is Nancy's lavish stage for opera and classical music. The resident orchestra perform at *concerts apéritifs* (€5), held one Saturday a month.

Café Théâtre le Vertigo THEATRE

(☑03 83 32 71 97; www.levertigo.fr, in French; 29 rue de la Visitation; ⊙Tue-Sat) Go boho at this superb café-theatre, decked out with red velvet banquettes and black-and-white tiles. The eclectic line-up skips from improvised theatre to stand-up comedy and gigs.

🛍 Shopping

Nancy's grand thoroughfares are rue St-Dizier, rue St-Jean and rue St-Georges. Grande Rue is studded with idiosyncratic galleries and antique shops.

TOP CHOICE **Lefèvre-Lemoine** CONFECTIONERY

(47 rue Henri Poincaré; ⊙8.30am-7pm Mon-Sat, 9.30am-12.30pm Sun) Ahhh, they just don't make sweetshops like this 1840s treasure anymore. A bird chirps a welcome as you enter this world of sugar-coated nostalgia. One of the old-fashioned sweet tins made a cameo appearance in the film *Amélie*. Bergamotes de Nancy (boiled sweets made with bergamot, the citrus fruit that flavours Earl Grey tea), caramels, glazed mirabelles (plums) – decisions, decisions...

Maison des Sœurs Macarons MACAROONS

(www.macaron-de-nancy.com; 21 rue Gambetta; ⊙closed Mon morning, Sun) When Nancy's Benedictine nuns hit hard times during the French Revolution, they saw the light in heavenly macaroons. They're still made to the original recipe (egg whites, sugar, Provençal almonds) at this old-world confectioner. A dozen box (€7) makes a great gift.

Baccarat CRYSTAL

(www.baccarat.fr, in French; 2 rue des Dominicains; ⊙closed Mon morning, Sun) Shop like royalty (or window-shop like mere mortals) for exquisite crystal and jewellery here, where the simplest ring – impossibly delicate – goes for €150.

Daum CRYSTAL

(14 place Stanislas; ⊙closed Mon morning, Sun) At Daum's flagship shop you can admire limited-edition crystal knick-knacks and jewellery, often with a naturalistic theme.

ℹ Information

Copycom (3 rue Guerrier de Dumast; per hr €2; ⊙9am-8pm Mon-Sat, 3-8pm Sun) Internet access.

E-café Cyber Café (11 rue des Quatre Églises; per hr €5.50; ⊙11am-9pm Mon & Sat, 9am-9pm Tue-Fri) A proper café whose computers have webcams.

Post office (10 rue St-Dizier) Has currency exchange.

Tourist office (☑03 83 35 22 41; www.ot-nancy.fr; place Stanislas; ⊙9am-7pm Mon-Sat, 10am-5pm Sun) Inside the *hôtel de ville*. Free brochures detailing walking tours of the city centre and art nouveau architecture.

ℹ Getting There & Away

CAR & MOTORCYCLE Rental options:

Europcar (www.europcar.com; 18 rue de Serre)

National-Citer (www.citer.fr, in French; train station departure hall)

TRAIN The **train station** (place Thiers), spruced up for the arrival of the TGV Est Européen, is on the line linking Paris with Strasbourg. Destinations include the following:

Baccarat €9.50, 45 minutes, 15 daily

Metz €9.50, 40 minutes, 48 daily

Paris Gare de l'Est; €54, 1½ hours, 11 daily

Strasbourg €22, 1½ hours, 12 daily

ℹ Getting Around

BICYCLE Nancy is easy to navigate by bicycle. **Vélostan** (www.velostan.com, in French; per half-day/full day/week €3/5/10) has rental sites inside the **train station** (⊙7.30am-7.30pm Mon-Fri, 9am-6pm weekends) and near the Musée de l'École de Nancy in **Espace Thermal** (43bis rue du Sergent Blandan; ⊙10am-1pm & 3-6pm Mon-Fri, 9am-6pm Sat).

CAR & MOTORCYCLE There's free parking along the canalside quai Ste-Catherine, 300m east of place Stanislas, and on some side streets in the working-class neighbourhoods west of the train tracks.

TRAM The local public transport company, **STAN** (www.reseau-stan.com, in French; office 3 rue du Docteur Schmitt; ☉7am-7.30pm Mon-Sat) has its main transfer points at Nancy République and Point Central. One/10 tickets cost €1.30/8.50. The 🚊 icon shows the nearest tram stop for places off the map in this section.

Baccarat

POP 4730

The glitzy Baccarat *cristallerie* (crystal glassworks), founded in 1764, is 60km southeast of Nancy. The Musée Baccarat (www.baccarat.fr, in French; 2 rue des Cristalleries; adult/child €2.50/free; ☉9am-noon & 2-6pm) displays 1100 exquisite pieces of handmade lead crystal. The boutique out front is almost as dazzling as the museum. Nearby crystal shops sell lesser, though more affordable, brands.

On the opposite bank of the park-lined River Meurthe, the dark concrete sanctuary of Église St-Rémy (☉8am-5pm), built in the mid-1950s, is austere on the outside and kaleidoscopic on the inside – dramatically lit by 20,000 Baccarat crystal panels.

The tourist office (☎03 83 75 13 37; www.ot-baccarat.fr; 11 rue Division Leclerc; ☉9am-noon & 2-5pm Mon-Sat), a bit north of the Musée Baccarat, has hiking maps.

Trains run from Baccarat to Nancy (€9.50, 45 minutes, 15 daily). By car, Baccarat makes an easy stop on the way from Nancy to Colmar via the Vosges' Col du Bonhomme.

Metz

POP 125,720

Sitting astride the confluence of the Moselle and Seille rivers, Lorraine's graceful capital Metz (pronounced 'mess') is ready to be fêted. Though the city's Gothic marvel of a cathedral, superlative art collections and Michelin star–studded dining scene long managed to sidestep the world spotlight, that all changed with the show-stopping arrival of Centre Pompidou-Metz. Yet the Pompidou is but the prelude to Metz' other charms: buzzy pavement cafés and shady riverside parks, a beautiful old town built from yellow Jeumont stone and a regal Quartier Impérial up for Unesco World Heritage status. Suddenly, everyone's talking about Metz, and rightly so.

⊙ Sights

Cathédrale St-Étienne CATHEDRAL
(place St-Étienne; ☉8am-6pm) As delicate as Chantilly lace, the golden spires of this Gothic cathedral crown Metz' skyline. Exquisitely lit by kaleidoscopic curtains of 13th- to 20th-century stained glass, the cathedral is nicknamed 'God's lantern'. The **Gothic windows**, on the north transept arm, contrast with the **Renaissance windows** on the south transept arm.

Notice the flamboyant **Chagall windows** in reds, yellows and blues in the ambulatory, which also harbours the treasury (adult/child €2/1; ☉10am-12.30pm & 2-5pm). The sculpture of the **Graoully** ('*grau*-lee'), a dragon said to have terrified pre-Christian Metz, lurks in the 15th-century crypt (adult/child €2/1; ☉10am-12.30pm & 2-5pm). The cathedral looks its most radiant on a bright day and when floodlit in the evening.

Centre Pompidou-Metz GALLERY
(www.centrepompidou-metz.fr; 1 parvis des Droits de l'Homme; adult/child €7/free; ☉11am-6pm Mon, Wed & Sun, 11am-8pm Thu-Sat) Opened in May 2010 to much fanfare, the architecturally innovative Centre Pompidou-Metz is the satellite branch of Paris' Centre Pompidou and the new star of the city's art scene. The gallery draws on Europe's largest collection of modern art to stage ambitious temporary exhibitions, such as the inaugural *Chefs d'oeuvre* (Masterpieces), which presented standouts by Picasso, Matisse and Kandinsky. The dynamic space also hosts top-drawer cultural events.

Musée La Cour d'Or HISTORY MUSEUM
(2 rue du Haut Poirier; adult/child €4.60/free; ☉9am-5pm Mon & Wed-Fri, 10am-5pm Sat & Sun) Delve into the past at this trove of Gallo-Roman antiquities, hiding remnants of the city's Roman baths and a statue of the Egyptian goddess Isis unearthed right here in Metz. Your visit continues with art from the Middle Ages, paintings from the 15th century onwards, and artefacts revealing the history of Metz' ancient Jewish community. A room-by-room brochure in English is available.

Quartier Impérial HISTORIC QUARTER
The stately boulevards and bourgeois villas of the German Imperial Quarter, including rue Gambetta and av Foch, are the brainchild of Kaiser Wilhelm II. Built to trumpet the triumph of Metz' post-1871 status as

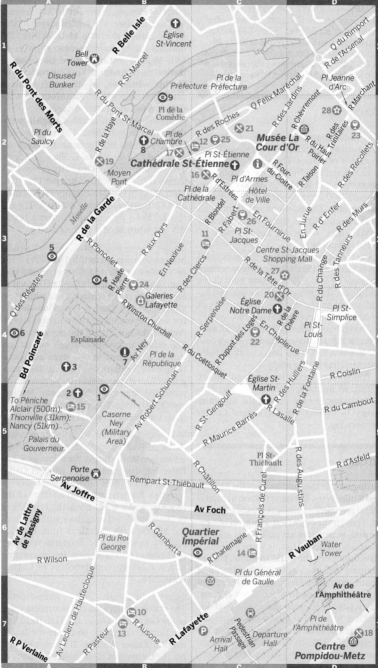

ALSACE & LORRAINE LORRAINE

0 ——— 200 m
0 ——— 0.1 miles

R Belle Isle
Église St-Vincent
Bell Tower
Disused Bunker
R du Pont des Morts
R St-Marcel
Pl de la Préfecture
Préfecture
Q Félix Maréchal
Q du Rimport
Q de l'Arsenal
Pl Jeanne d'Arc
R Marchant
28
R des Trinitaires
23
Pl du Saulcy
R de la Haye
R du Pont St-Marcel
9
Pl de la Comédie
R des Roches
21
Musée La Cour d'Or
R Chèvremont
R du Haut Poirier
R des Recollets
19
Moyen Pont
Pl de Chambre
8
17
12 25
Cathédrale St-Étienne
16
R d'Estrées
Pl St-Étienne
Pl d'Armes
R Four-du-Cloître
R Taison
R d'Enfer
R des Murs
R de la Garde
Moselle
R Poncelet
R aux Ours
R Nexirue
Pl de la Cathédrale
Hôtel de Ville
R Blondel
R Fabert
En Fournirue
En Jurue
R des Tanneurs
5
4
R Haute Pierre
24
Galeries Lafayette
R Winston Churchill
R des Clercs
11
Pl St-Jacques
Centre St-Jacques Shopping Mall
R de la Tête d'Or
27
R du Change
Q des Régates
En Nexirue
R Serpenoise
26
Église Notre Dame
20
R de la Chèvre
Pl St-Simplice
Bd Poincaré
6
Esplanade
7
Av Ney
Pl de la République
R du Coëtlosquet
R Dupont des Loges
22
En Chaplerue
Pl St-Louis
3
2 15
1
Caserne Ney (Military Area)
Av Robert Schuman
R St-Gengoulf
Église St-Martin
R des Huiliers
R de la Fontaine
R Lasalle
R Coislin
R du Cambout
To Péniche Alclair (500m); Thionville (31km); Nancy (51km)
Palais du Gouverneur
R Maurice Barrès
R Châtillon
Pl St-Thiébault
R des Augustins
R d'Asfeld
Porte Serpenoise
Av Joffre
Rempart St-Thiébault
Av Foch
R François de Curel
R Vauban
Water Tower
Av de Lattre de Tassigny
R Wilson
Pl du Roi George
R Gambetta
Quartier Impérial
R Charlemagne
14
Pl du Général de Gaulle
Av de l'Amphithéâtre
Pl de l'Amphithéâtre
18
10
13
R Ausone
R Pasteur
Av Leclerc de Hauteclocque
R Lafayette
Arrival Hall
Pedestrian Passage
Departure Hall
Centre Pompidou-Metz
R P Verlaine

part of the Second Reich, the architecture is a whimsical mix of art deco, neo-Romanesque and neo-Renaissance influences. The area's unique ensemble of Wilhelmian architecture has made it a candidate for Unesco World Heritage status.

Philippe Starck lampposts juxtapose Teutonic sculptures, whose common theme is German imperial might, at the monumental Rhenish neo-Romanesque train station, completed in 1908.

The massive main post office, built in 1911 of red Vosges sandstone, is as solid and heavy as the cathedral is light and lacy.

Place de la Comédie　　　CITY SQUARE
Bounded by one of the channels of the Moselle, this neoclassical square is home to the city's 18th-century Théâtre, France's oldest theatre still in use. During the Revolution, place de l'Égalité (as it was then known) was the site of a guillotine that lopped the heads off 63 'enemies of the people'.

The neo-Romanesque Temple Neuf (Protestant Church; ◎only during services) was constructed under the Germans in 1904.

Esplanade　　　SIGNIFICANT AREA
The formal flowerbeds of the Esplanade – and its statue of a gallant-looking Marshall Ney – are flanked by imposing buildings, including the Arsenal cultural centre and the sober, neoclassical Palais de Justice.

Originally built around 380 as part of a Gallo-Roman spa complex, Église St-Pierre-aux-Nonains (◎1-6pm Tue-Sat & 2-6pm Sun) sidles up to the octagonal, 13th-century Chapelle des Templiers (Chapel of the Knights Templar), the only one of its kind in Lorraine.

Place St-Louis　　　CITY SQUARE
On the eastern edge of the city centre, triangular place St-Louis is surrounded by medieval arcades and merchants' houses dating from the 14th to 16th centuries.

Riverside Park　　　PARK
(quai des Régates) In summer, pedal boats and rowboats can be rented on quai des Régates. The promenade leads through a leafy riverside park, with statues, ponds, swans and a fountain. It's the ideal picnic spot.

☞ Tours

The tourist office's audioguides (€5), available in three languages (English, French and German), cover the city centre (1½ hours) and the Quartier Impérial (45 minutes).

THE RISE AND RISE OF THE POMPIDOU

Finally, it's here. Seven years and €60.7 million in the making, the Centre Pompidou-Metz is redefining the city's up-and-coming Quartier de l'Amphithéâtre and creating a wave of excitement in the art world. It has been likened to Bilbao's Guggenheim and London's Tate Modern, but one look at the tour de force of architects Shigeru Ban (Tokyo) and Jean de Gastines (France) tells you it is nothing of the sort – it is unique.

Unlike its Parisian predecessor, famed for its inside-out scaffolding and multicoloured pipe entrails, Centre Pompidou-Metz is white and sinuous, with trunklike columns that grow towards a roof resembling a gliding manta ray. The translucent membrane allows light to flood exhibition spaces by day and glows ethereally after dark. A dynamic, flexible space for dynamic, flexible exhibitions, Pompidou two has proven that there is life beyond the capital for art lovers in France.

☆ Festivals & Events

Sweet and juicy, the humble mirabelle (plum) has its day at the Fête de la Mirabelle in August. Shop for stocking fillers at the illuminated Marché de Nöel (www.noel-a-metz.com) in December.

🛏 Sleeping

Metz' hotels are fantastic value. Except in summer, they're fullest Monday to Thursday.

TOP CHOICE **Péniche Alclair**   HOUSEBOAT €
(☑06 37 67 16 18; www.chambrespenichemetz.com; allée St-Symphorien; r incl breakfast €65; 🐱) What a clever idea: Cécile and Xavier Bonfils have transformed an old barge into this stylish blue houseboat, where lucky guests can stay in one of two bright rooms, with snazzy bathrooms and watery views. Breakfast is a generous spread of pastries, fresh bread and fruit salad, served in your room or on the sundeck. It's a pleasant 15-minute stroll south of the centre along the river.

Hôtel de la Cathédrale   HISTORIC HOTEL €€
(☑03 87 75 00 02; www.hotelcathedrale-metz.fr; 25 place de Chambre; d €75-110; 🐱) This classy little hotel occupies a 17th-century townhouse opposite the cathedral. Climb the wrought-iron staircase to your classically elegant room, with high ceilings, hardwood floors and antique trappings. Book well ahead for a cathedral view.

La Citadelle   DESIGN HOTEL €€€
(☑03 87 17 17 17; www.citadelle-metz.com; 5 av Ney; d €205-265; ❈@) A 16th-century citadel given a boutique makeover, luxurious La Citadelle blends history with Zen-style sleekness. Monochrome hues and mood lighting define the vast, ultramodern rooms. The hotel's pride and joy is its Mi-chelin-starred Le Magasin aux Vivres restaurant. Free parking is available.

Hôtel Métropole   TRADITIONAL HOTEL €
(☑03 87 66 26 22; www.hotelmetropole-metz.com; 5 place du Général de Gaulle; s €52, d €58-63; 🐱) Beat the crowds to the Centre Pompidou-Metz, five minutes' stroll away, by staying at this German Empire-style townhouse facing the train station. The cheery rooms feature above-par perks like free wifi and flatscreen TVs.

Hôtel Escurial   SMALL HOTEL €€
(☑03 87 66 40 96; www.escurial-hotel.com; 18 rue Pasteur; s €64-76, d €72-84; 🐱) Smooth contours and bold colours lend a modern air to this friendly hotel near the train station. The best of the large, spick-and-span rooms have balconies and city views.

Cécil Hôtel   TRADITIONAL HOTEL €
(☑03 87 66 66 13; www.cecilhotel-metz.com; 14 rue Pasteur; s €62-66, d €69-72; 🐱) Built in 1920, this family-run hotel's smallish rooms are neat, petite and decorated in warm colours. Parking costs €9 per day.

Grand Hôtel de Metz   HISTORIC HOTEL €€
(☑03 87 36 16 33; www.hotel-metz.com; 3 rue des Clercs; d €61-95; 🐱) Not *quite* as grand as its name suggests (but rather nice nonetheless), this 18th-century hotel is just steps from the cathedral. The old-world rooms sport heavy drapes and wood furnishings.

🍴 Eating

Metz has scores of appetising restaurants, many along and near the river. Place St-Jacques becomes one giant open-air café when the sun's out. Cobbled rue Taison and the arcades of place St-Louis shelter moderately priced bistros, pizzerias and cafés.

Restaurant Thierry
FUSION €€

(☑03 87 74 01 23; www.restaurant-thierry.fr; 5 rue des Piques; menus €24-34; ⊘closed Wed & Sun) Walking into this spice-scented, lantern-lit restaurant is like stepping into the glammest of Marrakchi riads. An open fire crackles in the salon, where an aperitif works up an appetite for Asian- and Moroccan-inflected dishes, such as delicate prawn *nems* (spring rolls), seafood tagines and beautifully cooked sole with tempura. Often full, so call ahead if possible.

Le Magasin aux Vivres
GASTRONOMIC €€€

(☑03 87 17 17 17; 5 av Ney; mains €40-70; ⊘closed Sat lunch, Sun & Mon) Conjurer of textures and seasonal flavours, Michelin-starred chef Christophe Dufossé makes creative use of local produce. Moselle wines work well with specialities like plump scallops sliding into a Lorraine beer emulsion and rack of Limousin lamb in spicy jus. Reservations are recommended.

La Voile Blanche
MODERN FRENCH €€

(☑03 87 20 66 66; 1 parvis des Droits de l'Homme; menus €25-35; ⊘closed dinner Sun, Tue; 🖫) Art on a plate is the aim at Centre Pompidou-Metz' kaleidoscope-inspired restaurant, designed by architects Patrick Jouin and Sanjit Manku. The menu is fresh and seasonal – think summery Camargue rice with red mullet and succulent Charolais beef.

Maire
TRADITIONAL FRENCH €€

(☑03 87 32 43 12; www.restaurant-maire.com, in French; 1 rue des Ponts des Morts; menus €37-45; ⊘closed Wed lunch, Tue) This smart riverside restaurant serves up moreish views of the cathedral from its window tables and veranda. With 500 bottles in the cellar, there's bound to be a wine that goes well with market-fresh dishes such as slow-cooked lamb and grilled pike-perch with spiced mirabelles.

La Crêperie
CRÊPES €

(11 rue de Faisan; crêpes €3.50-4, menus €9.50-15.50; ⊘closed Sun, Thu) You can almost smell the briny Atlantic in this eccentric Breton crêperie, stuffed with nautical knick-knacks. Go sweet with crêpes or savoury with galettes topped with *fromage* or escargot. Hosts live Breton music once a week.

La Baraka
NORTH AFRICAN €

(☑03 87 36 33 92; 25 place de Chambre; mains €10-15; ⊘closed Wed) Fancy a change? This unassuming North African place rustles up just-right tagines, meltingly tender lamb and couscous properly infused with saffron.

Pâtisserie Claude Bourguignon
TEAROOM €

(31 rue de la Tête d'Or; snacks €3-8; ⊘Tue-Sat) Sticky éclairs, traditional Quiche Lorraine (with smoked bacon, no cheese) and *tarte aux mirabelles* (sweet plum tart)...wave bye-bye to the waistline and *bonjour* to happiness at this patisserie–tea room.

Drinking

Some 22,000 resident students keep Metz' vibe young and upbeat after dark. For an alfresco sundowner or two, try the open-air cafés on place de Chambre and place St-Jaques.

Café Jehanne d'Arc
CAFÉ

(place Jeanne d'Arc) Dating to the 13th-century, this watering hole oozes history from every fresco and beam. The soundtrack skips from Gainsbourg to classical, and there's often free live jazz. The terrace is a chilled spot for summertime imbibing.

L'Appart
BAR, CLUB

(www.l-endroit.com, in French; 2 rue Haute Pierre; ⊘Wed-Sun) The house in which poet Paul Verlaine was born in 1844 is now a lively, mixed (gay and hetero) bar with a retro 1950s ceiling. Events move from DJ nights to drag shows. Industrial-style club L'Endroit spins house under the same roof.

GO TO MARKET

If only every market were like Metz' grand **Marché Couvert** (Covered Market; place de la Cathédrale; ⊘8am-6.30pm Tue-Sat). Once a bishop's palace, now a temple to fresh local produce, this is the kind of place where you pop in for a baguette and struggle out an hour later with bags overflowing with charcuterie, ripe fruit and five different sorts of *fromage*.

Make a morning of it, stopping for an early, inexpensive lunch and a chat with the market's larger-than-life characters. At **Chez Mauricette** (sandwiches €2-4.50, antipasti plate €5-7), Mauricette tempts with Lorraine goodies from herby *saucisson* to local charcuterie and mirabelle pâté.

Her neighbour is **Soupes á Soups** (soups €2.80-5.50), where Patrick ladles out homemade soups, from mussel to creamy mushroom varieties.

ALSACE & LORRAINE METZ

Pop White   DESIGN BAR

(4 place St-Jacques) Decadently dark and silver-kissed, this voguish lounge is a sundown favourite. Join a pre-clubbing crowd for drinks on the terrace before hitting the dance floor.

Le Strapontin   WINE BAR

(15 place de Chambre; ⊙Tue-Sat) Jazzy beats, a cathedral-facing terrace and a neat selection of wines by the glass draw locals to this stylishly contemporary bar. All-comers are welcome at Thursday evening's salsa class.

Bar Latino   MUSIC BAR

(www.barlatino.fr, in French; 22 rue Dupont des Loges) This party-lovin' Latin bar swings with svelte bodies gyrating to salsa and jiving to rock 'n' roll. Zingy cocktails and Mexican food fuel the dancing.

☆ Entertainment

Details on cultural events appear in free French-language monthlies like *Spectacles* (www.spectacles-publications.com) and *Ce Mois-Ci à Metz,* available at the tourist office.

Fnac Billetterie (www.fnacspectacles.com; Centre St-Jacques shopping mall; ⊙10am-7pm Mon-Fri, 9.30am-7.30pm Sat) sells events tickets.

Les Trinitaires   LIVE MUSIC

(www.lestrinitaires.com, in French; place Jeanne d'Arc) Post-rock, experimental rock and jazz bands take to the stage in the Gothic cellar and, in summer, the illuminated cloister of this soulful arts venue. Enjoy drinks before gigs at the Pop Art bar.

Arsenal   PERFORMING ARTS

(www.arsenal-metz.fr, in French; 3 av Ney; ⊙Tue-Sun) Bearing the hallmark of Catalan post-modernist architect Ricardo Bofill, this striking Jeumont-stone building sits on the site of the former arsenal. It hosts dance, theatre and music performances.

ℹ Information

Bar St-Jacques (10 place St-Jacques; per hr €2; ⊙7am-midnight) This bar has free wi-fi and two internet computers.

Diacom Internet Café (20 rue Gambetta; per hr €3; ⊙9am-8pm Mon-Sat, 11.30am-8pm Sun)

Hospital (1 place Philippe de Vigneulles; ⊙24hr) The casualty ward is in Building F.

Police (10 rue Belle Isle; ⊙24hr)

Post office (9 rue Gambetta) Has currency exchange.

Tourist office (☑03 87 55 53 76; http://tour-isme.mairie-metz.fr; 2 place d'Armes; ⊙9am-7pm Mon-Sat, 10am-5pm Sun) In a one-time guardroom built in the mid-1700s. Free walking-tour and cycling maps, free wi-fi and an internet terminal that works with a phonecard.

ℹ Getting There & Away

CAR & MOTORCYCLE Car rental companies with offices in the train station's arrival hall:

Avis (www.avis.com)

Europcar (www.europcar.com)

National-Citer (www.citer.fr, in French)

TRAIN Metz' ornate early 20th-century **train station** (pl du Général de Gaulle) has a super-sleek TGV linking Paris with Luxembourg. Direct trains include the following:

Luxembourg €14, 50 minutes, at least 15 daily

Paris Gare de l'Est; €53, 80 minutes, 13 daily

Nancy €9.50, 40 minutes, 48 daily

Strasbourg €23, 1¾ hours, 14 daily

Verdun €13, 1½ hours, three daily

ℹ Getting Around

BICYCLE Rent city and mountain bikes cheaply from **Mob Emploi** (www.mobemploi.fr, in French; per half-/full day/week €2/3/8, deposit per bike €100), a nonprofit place. Helmets and locks are free; rental options include kids' bikes, child carriers and even a tandem. There are two bureaus: rue d'Estrées (⊙8am-6pm Mon-Fri, 11am-6pm Sat & Sun) and rue Vauban (⊙5.45am-8pm Mon-Fri) at the base of the water tower just east of the train station.

CAR & MOTORCYCLE There's free parking near the train station on av Foch, northeast of the train station along bd André Maginot; and along bd Paixhans.

Fort du Hackenberg

The largest single Maginot Line bastion in the Metz area was the 1000-man Fort du Hackenberg (www.maginot-hackenberg.com; Veckring; adult/child €8/4; ⊙tours in English 2pm Sat & Sun Apr–mid-Nov, 2pm Sat mid-Nov–March), 30km northeast of Metz, whose 10km of galleries were designed to be self-sufficient for three months and, in battle, to fire four tonnes of shells a minute. An electric trolley takes visitors along 4km of tunnels – always at 12°C – past subterranean installations. Tours last two hours.

Readers have been enthusiastic about the tours (www.maginot-line.com) of Fort du Hackenberg, other Maginot Line sites and Verdun led by Jean-Pascal Speck, an avid amateur historian and owner of the romantic **Hôtel L'Horizon** (☑03 82 88 53 65; www. lhorizon.fr; 5 rte du Crève Coeur; d €98-150) in Thionville. If he's unavailable, he can put you in touch with other English-speaking guides.

Verdun

POP 20,170

They were once men in the prime of their lives, but had fallen for the possession of this hill. This hill, that was partly built on dead bodies already. A battle after which they lay rotting, fraternally united in death...

Georges Blond, Verdun

The unspeakable atrocities that took place in and around Verdun between 21 February and 18 December 1916, the longest battle of WWI, have turned the town's name into a byword for wartime slaughter and futile sacrifice.

Such a dark past means that Verdun always has an air of melancholy, even when the sun bounces brightly off the River Meuse and the town's shuttered houses. Go to the moonscape hills, scarred with trenches and shells; walk through the stony silence of the cemeteries as the morning mist rises, and you will understand why. Time has healed and trees have grown, but the memory of *l'enfer de Verdun* (the hell of Verdun) has survived. And, some say, may it never be forgotten.

History

After the annexation of Lorraine's Moselle *département* and Alsace by Germany in 1871, Verdun became a frontline outpost. Over the next four decades it was turned into the most important and heavily fortified element in France's eastern defence line.

During WWI Verdun itself was never taken by the Germans, but the evacuated town was almost totally destroyed by artillery bombardments. In the hills to the north and east of Verdun, the brutal combat – carried out with artillery, flamethrowers and poison gas – completely wiped out nine villages. During the last two years of WWI, more than 800,000 soldiers (some 400,000 French and almost as many Germans, along with thousands of the Americans who arrived in 1918) lost their lives in this area.

◉ Sights

Citadelle Souterraine CITADEL
(☑03 29 86 62 02; av du 5e RAP; adult/child €6/2.50; ◷9am-7pm, closed Jan) Central Verdun's biggest drawcard is this cavernous subterranean citadel, comprising 7km of underground galleries. Designed by the prolific Vauban in the 17th century and completed in 1838, in 1916 it was turned into an impregnable command centre in which 10,000 *poilus* (French WWI soldiers) lived, many waiting to be dispatched to the front.

About 10% of the galleries have been converted into an imaginative audiovisual re-enactment of the war, making this an excellent introduction to the WWI history of Verdun. Half-hour tours in battery-powered cars, available in six languages, should be booked ahead.

Centre Mondial de la Paix MUSEUM
(World Centre for Peace; www.cmpaix.fr; place Monseigneur Ginisty; adult/child €5/2.50; ◷9.30am-noon & 2-6pm Tue-Sun) Set in Verdun's handsomely classical former bishop's palace, built in 1724, this museum's permanent exhibition touches upon wars, their causes and solutions; human rights; and the fragility of peace.

Cathédrale Notre Dame CATHEDRAL
(place Monseigneur Ginisty; ◷8.45am-7pm) Perched on a hillside, this Romanesque-meets-Gothic cathedral shelters a gilded baroque baldachin, restored after WWI damage. Much of the stained glass is interwar.

FREE **Monument à la Victoire**
VICTORY MONUMENT
(Carrer de la Portella 5) Steep steps lead up to this austere 1920s monument commemorating war victims and survivors. The crypt hides a book listing the soldiers who fought in the Battle of Verdun.

Porte Chaussée CITY GATE
(rue Chaussée) This 14th-century city gate was later used as a prison.

Porte St-Paul CITY GATE
(rue St-Paul) Built in 1877, this city gate is adorned with a marble plaque recalling the 'victorious peace' that inspired a 'cry of joy'.

☞ Tours

The tourist office can book French-language coach tours (€26; ◷2-6pm Mon-Sat May–mid-Sep), which take in the Mémorial de Verdun, Fort de Douaumont, Ossuaire de Douaumont and the Tranchée des Baïonnettes. Private English-speaking guides are available on request.

🛏 Sleeping & Eating

Brasseries and fast-food joints line up along riverside quai de Londres (a plaque on the wall near rue Beaurepaire explains the origin of the name).

Hôtel Montaulbain   SMALL HOTEL €

(☑03 29 86 00 47; 4 rue de la Vieille Prison; d €35-45) It requires very little detective work to pin down this central hotel, which Mr Poirot (true to his name) runs with charm and an eye for detail. The spotless rooms are excellent value.

Auberge de Jeunesse   HOSTEL €

(☑03 29 86 28 28; www.fuaj.org, in French; place Monseigneur Ginisty; dm incl breakfast €17; @) What a view! Next to the cathedral, this well-kept hostel is gathered around a 16th-century cloister and affords far-reaching views of Verdun.

Hôtel Les Orchidées   FAMILY HOTEL €

(☑03 29 86 46 46; www.orchidees-hotel.com, in French; rue d'Etain; d/tr/q €56/75/85; 🛜🛜🐕) Set in quiet gardens, this hotel has light, modern rooms (including spacious family ones), a swimming pool, tennis court and restaurant. It's 2km east of town on the D603.

Épices et Tout   MODERN FRENCH €€

(☑03 29 86 46 88; 35 rue des Gros Degrés; menus €14-23; ⊘closed Wed dinner, Sun) Spice adds variety to the food at this atmospheric cellar bistro. Creative dishes like pork cheeks with caramel and peanuts, and cocoa-laced salmon terrine are well executed and served with panache.

Le Clapier   BISTRO €

(☑03 29 86 20 14; 34 rue des Gros Degrés; menus €14-22; ⊘Tue-Sat) The chef's penchant for Provence's balmy climes shines through on the menu at this cosy bistro. Specialities like crumbly Brie tart and herb-infused leg of lamb are expertly paired with Meuse wines.

Pom'Samba   TRADITIONAL FRENCH €

(☑03 29 83 46 34; 7 av Garibaldi; menus €11; ⊘Mon-Sat) The humble spud is king at this cheerful tiled restaurant, where potatoes are accompanied by everything from escargot to scallops.

ℹ Information

Pass Musées (adult/child €13.50/7.50) Pass covering admission to the Ossuaire de Douaumont, Fort de Douaumont and Mémorial de Verdun, and offering a 20% discount on other sights. Available from the tourist office.

Tourist office (☑03 29 84 55 55; www.tourisme-verdun.fr, in French; Pavillon Japiot, av du Général Mangin; ⊘8.30am-12.30pm & 1.30-6.30pm Mon-Sat, 9am-4pm Sun) Guided tours and free maps of the Verdun Battlefields.

ℹ Getting There & Around

BICYCLE Mountain bikes are an excellent way to tour the Verdun battlefields; you can rent one at **Véloland** (Haudainville; half-day/full day/5 days €10/15/50), 5km south of the centre on the D964.

CAR & MOTORCYCLE You can park free in the car parks south of the tourist office on av du 8 Mai 1945 and rue des Tanneries.

TRAIN Verdun's poorly served train station, built by Eiffel in 1868, has direct services to Metz (€13, 1½ hours, three daily). Three buses a day go to the Gare Meuse TGV station (30 minutes), from where direct TGVs whisk you to Paris' Gare de l'Est (€40, 1¾ hours).

Verdun Battlefields

Much of the Battle of Verdun was fought 5km to 8km (as the crow flies) northeast of Verdun. Today, the forested area – still a jumble of trenches and artillery craters – can be reached by car on the D913 and D112; follow the signs to 'Douamont', 'Vaux' or the 'Champ de Bataille 14–18'. Signposted paths lead to dozens of minor remnants of the war. Site interiors are closed in January.

Mémorial de Verdun   WAR MEMORIAL

(www.memorial-de-verdun.fr; adult/child €7/3.50; ⊘9am-6pm, closed mid-Dec–Jan) The village of Fleury, wiped off the face of the earth in the course of being captured and recaptured 16 times, is now the site of this memorial. It tells the story of '300 days, 300,000 dead, 400,000 wounded', with insightful displays of war artefacts and personal items. Downstairs you'll find a re-creation of the battlefield as it looked on the day the guns finally fell silent.

In the grassy crater-pocked centre of what was once Fleury, a few hundred metres down the road from the memorial, signs among the low ruins indicate the village's former layout.

FREE Ossuaire de Douaumont

WAR MEMORIAL

(www.verdun-douaumont.com; ⊙9am-6pm Mon-Fri, 10am-6pm Sat & Sun) Rising like a gigantic artillery shell above a sea of 15,000 crosses, this sombre, 137m-long ossuary, inaugurated in 1932, is one of France's most important WWI memorials. It contains the bones of about 130,000 unidentified French and German soldiers collected from the Verdun battlefields and buried together in 52 mass graves according to where they fell. Each engraved stone denotes a missing soldier, while a touching display of photographs show Verdun survivors – as they were in WWI and as they are today.

A ticket to the excellent, 20-minute **audiovisual presentation** (adult/child €4/3) on the battle also lets you climb the 46m-high **bell tower**.

Out front, the **French military cemetery** is flanked by memorials to Muslim and Jewish soldiers (to the east and west, respectively) who died fighting for France in WWI. The architecture of the former is evocative of a North African mosque.

Fort de Douaumont

FORT

(adult/child €3/1.50; ⊙10am-6pm) Sitting high on a hill, about 2km northeast of the Douaumont Ossuary, this is the strongest of the 38 fortresses and bastions built along a 45km front to protect Verdun. When the Battle of Verdun began, 400m-long Douaumont – whose 3km network of cold, dripping galleries was built between 1885 and 1913 – had only a skeleton crew. By the fourth day it had been captured easily, a serious blow to French morale; four months later it was retaken by colonial troops from Morocco. It's free to take in the sweeping country views from the fort's crater-pocked roof.

Charles de Gaulle, then a young captain, was wounded and taken prisoner near here in 1916.

FREE Tranchée des Baïonnettes

WAR MEMORIAL

On 12 June 1916 two companies of the 137th Infantry Regiment of the French army were sheltered in their *tranchées* (trenches), *baïonnettes* (bayonets) fixed, waiting for a ferocious artillery bombardment to end. It never did – the incoming shells covered their positions with mud and debris, burying them alive. They weren't found until three years later, when someone spotted several hundred bayonet tips sticking out of the ground. Today the site where they

347

DON'T MISS

MORE SWEET THAN BITTER

Verdun's sweet claim to fame is as the *dragée* (sugared almond) capital of the world. In 1220 a local pharmacist dabbling with almonds, sugar and honey created the tooth-rotting delights that later graced the tables of royalty and nobility – Napoléon and Charles de Gaulle included. **Braquier** (☑03 29 84 30 00; www.dragees-braquier.com; 50 rue du Fort de Vaux; ⊙9am-noon & 2-7pm) has been making Verdun's celebrated *dragées* since 1783 and offers free guided tours of its factory; see the website for times and details.

died is marked by a simple memorial that is always open. The tree-filled valley across the D913 is known as the **Ravin de la Mort** (Ravine of Death).

American Memorials

More than one million American troops participated in the Meuse-Argonne Offensive of late 1918, the last Western Front battle of WWI. The bloody fighting northwest of Verdun, in which more than 26,000 Americans died, convinced the Kaiser's government to cable US President Woodrow Wilson with a request for an armistice. The film *Sergeant York* (1941) is based on events that took place here. The website of the Meuse *département*'s tourism board is www.tourisme-meuse.com (in French).

Apart from Romagne '14–'18, all of the sites mentioned below are managed by the **American Battle Monuments Commission** (www.abmc.gov) and are open from 9am to 5pm daily.

Meuse-Argonne American Cemetery

WAR CEMETERY

The largest US military cemetery in Europe is this WWI ground, where 14,246 soldiers lie buried, in Romagne-sous-Montfaucon, 41km northwest of Verdun along the D38 and D123.

Romagne '14–'18

WAR MUSEUM

(☑03 29 85 10 14; www.romagne14-18.com; 2 rue de l'Andon; guided walks €10, donations welcome; ⊙guided walks 9am-noon, museum noon-6pm, closed Wed) In the same village is this heartwrenching museum, which displays Jean-

ALSACE & LORRAINE AMERICAN MEMORIALS

LOCAL KNOWLEDGE

JEAN-PAUL DE VRIES: GUIDE & MUSEUM OWNER

Ever since I first handled a bayonet aged six, I've been fascinated by WWI. Over the past 35 years I've found some 60,000 artefacts in the surrounding countryside: combs, mess tins, grenades, you name it. That's what Romagne '14–'18 (p348) is all about: life stories, the human being behind the helmet. My museum is basically an old barn showing artefacts in their original state – rust, dirt and all.

My Fascination

Has always been the question: how could it ever happen? Just imagine living in the dirt for four years, far from your family, knowing you would probably die. It is beyond comprehension. I think when I find the answer, I'll stop searching.

Favourite Finds

The shoes that German soldiers, some of them amputees, made for the French kids from their old army boots. I like the things that show human resourcefulness, like coffee filters made from gasmasks and shells transformed into letter openers, ashtrays, even art. Then there is a mess tin with the inscription 'no good for shit' – who knows whether the soldier was referring to the food or the war in general!

Guided Walks

I run guided walks every morning to the trenches and the German lines, so people can picture how it must have been in battle and the cramped conditions of daily life. We nearly always find something, usually ammunition. Walking here alone can be dangerous because of the artillery craters and unexploded ammunition – one third of it is still left in the soil.

When to Visit

In May when the woods are fresh and Memorial Day is held at the Meuse-Argonne and Lorraine American cemeteries. Or in October when the region was liberated; on a cold, rainy autumn day you get a better sense of what happened here, what it must have been like.

Paul de Vries' fascinating private collection of war memorabilia. It's well worth joining Jean-Paul on one of his insightful morning walks of the battlefields.

Lorraine American Cemetery WAR CEMETERY
Verdun also had a significant military presence from the end of WWII until Charles de Gaulle pulled France out of NATO's integrated military command in 1966. Surrounded by woodland and set in landscaped grounds, this is the largest US WWII military cemetery in Europe. It's 45km east of Metz, just outside of St-Avold.

St-Mihiel American Cemetery WAR CEMETERY
In this WWI cemetery, the graves of 4153 American soldiers who died in the 1918 Battle of St-Mihiel radiate towards a central sundial topped by a white American eagle. The cemetery is 40km southeast of Verdun on the outskirts of Thiaucourt-Regniéville.

Butte de Montsec WAR MEMORIAL
This 375m-high mound, site of a US monument with a bronze relief map, is surrounded by a round, neoclassical colonnade. It's a 15km drive southwest of St-Mihiel American Cemetery.

Butte de Montfaucon WAR MEMORIAL
Commemorating the Meuse-Argonne Offensive, this 336m-high mound is topped by a 58m-high Doric column crowned by a statue symbolising liberty. Located about 10km southeast of Romagne-sous-Montfaucon.

The Loire Valley

Best Places to Eat

» Le Pot de Lapin (p381)
» Les Années 30 (p379)
» Le Gambetta (p381)
» Cap Sud (p367)
» Chez Noé (p356)

Best Places to Stay

» Château de Verrières (p381)
» Hôtel Diderot (p378)
» Château Beaulieu (p381)
» Hôtel de l'Abeille (p355)
» La Levraudière (p363)
» Le Pavillon des Lys (p373)
» Hôtel Ronsard (p366)

Why Go?

In centuries past, the River Loire was a key strategic area, one step removed from the French capital and poised on the crucial frontier between northern and southern France. Kings, queens, dukes and nobles established their feudal strongholds and country seats along the Loire, and the broad, flat valley is sprinkled with many of the most extravagant castles and fortresses in France. From sky-topping turrets and glittering banquet halls to slate-crowned cupolas and crenellated towers, the hundreds of châteaux dotted around the Loire Valley – now a Unesco World Heritage Site – comprise 1000 years of astonishingly rich architectural and artistic treasures. If it's aristocratic pomp and architectural splendour you're looking for, the Loire Valley is the place to explore.

When to Go

Tours

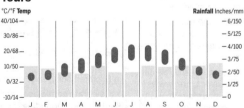

Late April to early May The Fêtes de Jeanne d'Arc in Orléans culminate with parades on 8 May.

June and July Cycle the trails of the Loire Valley from château to château.

September and October Wine tasting during the harvest time.

PLAN AHEAD

Before you go, plan your transport, reserve rooms in hot spots like Saumur, Amboise or Chinon and book castle tours (opposite) or the Cadre Noir equitation presentation (p379).

The Loire's Best Gardens

» Le Clos Lucé (p373)
» Chambord (p361)
» Villandry (p374)
» Cheverny (p362)
» Chenonceau (p369)
» Chaumont (p363)
» Beauregard (p364)

Spring Music Festival

Every Easter over 100,000 music fans converge on Bourges to take in the latest in innovative rock, roots and French music at Le Printemps de Bourges (www.printemps-bourges.com).

Resources

» Loire Valley heritage site: www.valdeloire.org

» Walks and cycling routes in the Loire Valley: www.randonnee-en-val-de-loire.com

» The natural environment of the River Loire: www.observatoireloire.fr, www.cpie-val-de-loire.org, in French

» Regional transport details: www.destineo.fr

Wine in the Loire Valley

Vineyards (www.vinsdeloire.com) dot the fertile Loire Valley and produce some excellent, but relatively little-known red, white and *crémant* (sparkling) wines. Anjou and Saumur alone have 30 AOCs (Appellation d'Origine Contrôlée), and Touraine has nine, including some lively gamays. The most predominant red, though, is the cabernet franc.

Appellations include Saumur-Champigny (try Domaine Clos Rougeard), Bourgueil (try Domaine de la Butte) and Chinon (try the Cuvée des Tireaux from Domaine Olek-Mery).

For whites, Vouvray's chenin blancs are excellent and Sancerre and the appellation across the river, Pouilly-Fumé, produce great sauvignon blancs. The bubbly appellation Crémant de Loire spans many communities.

Maisons des Vins (literally, wine houses) in Blois, Saumur, Cheverny and Angers welcome visitors for tasting and guidance on the region's wine. The Route Touristique des Vignobles is a Loire Valley wine route; before you set out, stop by a tourist office and arm yourself with the *Loire Valley Vineyards* booklet, which lists and maps all the domaines, and *Sur La Route des Vins de Loire,* which maps from Blois to Angers and the coast.

ON THE TRAIL OF ARTISTS & WRITERS

While the fantastical history and high jinks of French royalty gets top billing in the Loire, the valley has also played host to a stream of Europe's greatest artists and thinkers. Mathematician and philosopher René Descartes, poet Pierre de Ronsard and writer and doctor François Rabelais (p378) were all born in the Loire; Leonardo da Vinci (see p373) spent the last years of his life here; and luminaries from sculptor Alexander Calder to novelist Honoré de Balzac (p376) lived and created in this region. Some, like Jean Gênet, were imprisoned here (p383). Then there were those, like Alexandre Dumas (see p383), who were simply inspired here.

Top 5 Activities for Kids

» Be razzle-dazzled by magic and illusion at Maison de la Magie (p359).

» Explore kooky, spooky caves around Saumur (p382).

» Celebrate comic book character Tintin with cracks of lightning and pounding thunder (p362).

» Peer into itsy-bitsy châteaux or play in the parks around a pointy pagoda (p373).

» Hunt for treasure at Château de Montsoreau (p383).

History

The dramas of French history are writ large across the face of the Loire Valley's châteaux. Early on, the Loire was one of Roman Gaul's most important transport arteries and the earliest châteaux were medieval fortresses established in the 9th century to fend off marauding Vikings. By the 11th century massive walls, fortified keeps and moats were all the rage.

During the Hundred Years War (1337–1453) the Loire marked the boundary between French and English forces and the area was ravaged by fierce fighting. After Charles VII regained his crown with the help of Joan of Arc, the Loire emerged as the centre of French court life. Charles took up residence in Loches with his mistress, Agnes Sorèl, and the French nobility and bourgeois elite established their own extravagant châteaux as an expression of wealth and power.

François I (r 1515–47) made his mark by introducing ornate Renaissance palaces to the Loire. François' successor Henri II (r 1547–59), his wife Catherine de Médicis and his mistress Diane de Poitiers played out their interpersonal dramas from castle to castle. While Henri's son, Henri III (r 1573–89) used Blois' castle to assassinate two of his greatest rivals before being assassinated himself eight months later.

ⓘ Getting There & Away

AIR Tours' airport has Ryanair connections to London Stansted, Dublin, Marseille and Porto, and flights to other French cities.

TRAIN The TGV Atlantique connects St-Pierre-des-Corps, near Tours, with Paris' Gare Montparnasse and Charles de Gaulle Airport in around an hour. The Loire's other cities (including Orléans, Blois, Amboise and Angers) are served by high-speed trains to Paris.

ⓘ Getting Around

Most main towns and many châteaux are accessible by train or bus, but if you're working to a timetable, having your own wheels allows significantly more freedom.

BICYCLE The Loire Valley is mostly flat, which makes for excellent cycling country. The **Loire à Vélo** (www.loireavelo.fr) scheme maintains a total of 800km of signposted routes from Cuffy near Nevers all the way to the Atlantic. Pick up a free guide from tourist offices, or download material (including route maps, audioguides and bike-hire details) from the website.

Détours de Loire (⌨02 47 61 22 23; www.locationdevelos.com) has bike-rental shops in Tours, Blois and Saumur and myriad partners; can deliver bikes; and allows you to pick up and drop off bikes along the route for a small surcharge. Prices include a lock, helmet, repair kit and pump. Classic bikes cost €14 per day; weekly hire costs €59 with extra days at €5. Tandems are €45 per day.

Les Châteaux à Vélo (⌨in Blois 02 54 78 62 52; www.chateauxavelo.com; per day €12-14) has a bike rental circuit between Blois, Chambord and Cheverny, 300km of marked trails and can shuttle you by minibus. Get free route maps from the website or tourist offices (also 40 downloadable MP3 guides).

TOURS Hard-core indie travellers might baulk at the idea of a minibus tour of the châteaux, but don't dismiss it out of hand, especially if you don't have your own wheels.

The Blois tourist office and **TLC** (⌨02 54 58 55 44; www.tlcinfo.net, in French) offer a shuttle (€6) from Blois to Chambord and Cheverny, three times per morning from April to August.

Most companies (listed below) offer a choice of well-organised itineraries, taking in various combinations of Azay-le-Rideau, Villandry, Cheverny, Chambord and Chenonceau (plus wine-tasting tours). Half-day trips cost between €18 and €33; full-day trips range from €43 to €50. Entry to the châteaux isn't included, although you'll get a discount on tickets. Reserve via the tourist office in Tours, from where most tours depart.

Acco-Dispo (⌨06 82 00 64 51; www.accodispo-tours.com)

Alienor (⌨06 10 85 35 39; www.alienor.com)

Loire Valley Tours (⌨02 54 33 99 80; www.loire-valley-tours.com) Tours including château admission (€125).

Luxury Tours (⌨06 66 64 20 08; www.luxurytours.fr) Private town cars (€105 to €256).

Quart de Tours (⌨06 30 65 52 01; www.quartdetours.com)

St-Eloi Excursions (⌨02 47 37 08 04; www.saint-eloi.com)

Touraine Evasion (⌨06 07 39 13 31; www.tourevasion.com)

ORLÉANAIS

Taking its name from the historic city of Orléans, famous for its Joan of Arc connections, the Orléanais is the northern gateway to the Loire Valley. In the east are the ecclesiastical treasures of St-Benoît-sur-Loire and Germigny-des-Prés, while to the south lies the marshy Sologne, historically a favourite hunting ground for France's kings and princes.

The Loire Valley Highlights

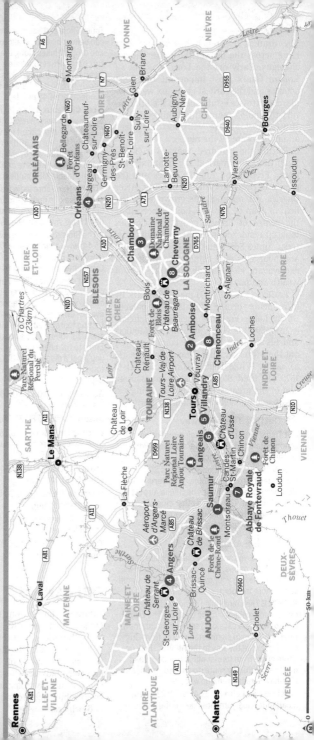

❶ Combine fantastic food, wines and caving with a bit of equestrian history in **Saumur** (p379)

❷ Explore the invention-filled final home of Leonardo da Vinci, at **Clos Lucé** (p373)

❸ Climb to the turret-covered rooftop of **Chambord** (p361), the Loire Valley's most over-the-top château

❹ Sample the Loire Valley's bustling city life in **Tours** (p364), **Angers** (p384) or **Orléans** (p353) for café culture and excellent museums

❺ Admire the meticulous gardens and floral displays of **Villandry** (p374)

❻ Wander back in time at medieval château **Langeais** (p375)

❼ Explore the Loire Valley's greatest ecclesiastical complex, **Abbaye Royale de Fontevraud** (p383)

❽ Peruse the art at **Cheverny** (p362) and **Chenonceau** (p369)

Orléans

POP 116,490

There's a definite big-city buzz around the boulevards, flashy boutiques and elegant buildings of Orléans, 100km south of Paris. It's a city with enduring heritage: already an important settlement by the time of the Romans' arrival, Orléans sealed its place in history in 1429 when a young peasant girl by the name of Jeanne d'Arc (Joan of Arc) rallied the armies of Charles VII and staged a spectacular rout against the besieging English forces, a key turning point in the Hundred Years War. Seven centuries later, the Maid of Orléans still exerts a powerful hold on the French imagination, and you'll discover statues, plaques and museums dedicated to her around town. The city's charming, mostly pedestrianised medieval quarter stretches from the River Loire north to rue Jeanne d'Arc and has an outstanding art museum and fantastical cathedral.

◉ Sights & Activities

The tourist office runs guided **walking tours** (generally in French, but some-

times in English) of Orléans' sights in July and August, and occasionally the rest of the year. Some are combined with a riverboat cruise. The office also sells self-guided walking tour brochures: *Circuit Découverte* (€2) and *9 Balades Entre Ciel et Loire* (€1).

TOP CHOICE **Musée des Beaux-Arts** ART MUSEUM
(☑02 38 79 21 55; 1 rue Fernand Rabier; adult/child incl audio guide €4/2.50; ☺10am-6pm Tue-Sun) Orléans' five-storeyed fine-arts museum is a treat, with an excellent selection of Italian, Flemish and Dutch paintings (including works by Correggio, Velázquez and Bruegel), as well as a huge collection by French artists such as Léon Cogniet (1794–1880) and Orléans-born Alexandre Antigna (1817–78). Among the treasures are an exceedingly rare set of **18th-century pastels** by Maurice Quentin de la Tour and Jean-Baptiste Chardin, and Claude Dervet's *Les Quatre Éléments* (mid-1600s) illustrating air, fire, earth and (frozen) water. The museum's galleries themselves are enormous and spectacular. Free the first Sunday of each month.

CHOOSING YOUR CHÂTEAU

There's no doubt that for dramatic castles, the Loire Valley is definitely the place, but with so many glorious palaces to choose from, how on earth do you go about selecting which one to visit? Here's our whistle-stop guide to help you decide.

For sheer, unadulterated architectural splendour, you can't top the big three: François I's country getaway **Chambord**, Renaissance river-spanning **Chenonceau** and the supremely graceful **Cheverny**. Unsurprisingly, these are also far and away the three most visited châteaux; turn up early or late to dodge the hordes.

If it's the medieval, Monty Python and the Holy Grail kind of castle you're after, head for the imposing fortress of **Langeais**, complete with its original furnishings, battlements and drawbridge; the cylindrical towers of **Chaumont**, once owned by Catherine de Médicis; or the walled stronghold of **Loches**.

For historical significance, top of the list are the royal residences of **Blois**, spanning four distinct periods of French history; stately **Amboise**, home to a succession of French monarchs including Charles VIII and Louis XI; black-stoned **Angers** with its fantastic tapestry; and pastoral **Clos Lucé** in Amboise, where Leonardo da Vinci whiled away his final years.

For literary connections, try the inspiration for *Sleeping Beauty*, **Ussé**; Balzac's residence, **Saché** (see p376); or **Montsoreau**, the setting for a classic Alexandre Dumas novel.

Looking for the picture-perfect setting? Our choices are the moat-ringed **Azay-le-Rideau**, the formal gardens of **Villandry** and the little-visited château of **Beauregard**, famous for its astonishing portrait gallery of medieval celebrities and its peaceful grounds.

And lastly, if you're looking for solitude, visit any of the châteaux we haven't listed here; the chances are the lesser-known places will be much quieter than their bigger, better-known and better-looking cousins elsewhere in the valley.

Cathédrale Ste-Croix CATHEDRAL

(place Ste-Croix; ⊙9.15am-noon & 2.15-5.45pm)
In a country of jaw-dropping churches, the
Cathédrale Ste-Croix still raises a gasp. Towering
above place Ste-Croix, Orléans' Flamboyant
Gothic cathedral was originally built
in the 13th century and then underwent
collective tinkering by successive monarchs,
including Henri IV, who started reconstruction
in 1601, Louis XIII (r 1610–43) who
restored the choir and nave, Louis XIV (r
1643–1715) responsible for the transept, and
Louis XV (r 1715–74) and Louis XVI (r 1774–
92), who rebuilt the western facade, including
its huge arches and wedding-cake towers.
Inside, slender columns soar skywards
towards the vaulted ceiling and 106m spire,
completed in 1895, while a series of vividly
coloured stained-glass windows relate the
life of St Joan, who was canonised in 1920.
Joan came here on 8 May 1429 and was
greeted with a procession of thanks for saving
the town.

FREE **Hôtel Groslot** HISTORIC MANSION

(🖉02 38 79 22 30; place de l'Étape; ⊙9am-
noon & 2-6pm Mon-Fri, 5-7pm Sat, 10am-6pm Sun)
Opposite the fine arts museum, the Renaissance
Hôtel Groslot was built in the 15th
century as a private mansion for Jacques
Groslot, a city bailiff, and later used as
Orléans' town hall during the Revolution.
The neomedieval interior is extravagant,
especially the ornate bedroom in which the
17-year-old King François II died in 1560
(now used as a marriage hall). The gardens
at the rear are lovely.

Maison de Jeanne d'Arc HISTORY MUSEUM

(🖉02 38 52 99 89; www.jeannedarc.com.fr, in
French; 3 place du Général de Gaulle; adult/child
€2/1; ⊙10am-noon & 2-6pm Tue-Sun) This
reconstruction of a 15th-century house
that hosted the Maid between April and
May 1429 (the original was destroyed by
British bombing in 1940, something the
locals politely avoid mentioning) displays
manuscripts, flags and vintage swords,

Orléans

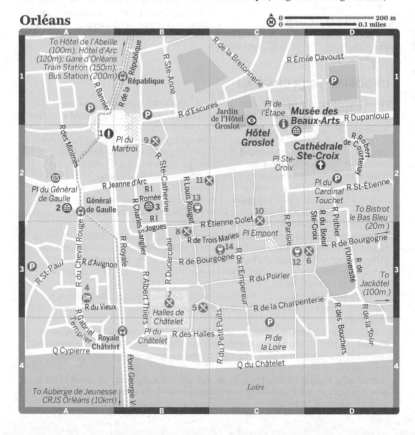

plus a scale model recreating the siege of Orléans.

Musée Historique et Archéologique
ARCHAEOLOGY MUSEUM

(☑02 38 79 25 60; sq Abbé Desnoyers; ☺10am-6pm Tue-Sun) A ticket to Musée des Beaux-Arts also grants entry to this museum, worth visiting for several imaginative representations of the Maid of Orléans, as well as Gallo-Roman sculptures unearthed nearby.

Place du Martroi
CITY SQUARE

Three of Orléans' main boulevards (rue Bannier, rue de la République and rue Royale) converge on place du Martroi, where you'll find a huge bronze **statue** (1855) by Denis Foyatier, the city's most stirring representation of St Joan atop a prancing steed.

★★ Festivals & Events

Since 1430 the Orléanais have celebrated the annual Fêtes de Jeanne d'Arc (www.fetesjeannedarc.com, in French) in late April and early May, commemorating the liberation of the city from the occupying English. A week of street parties, enormous medieval costume parades and concerts ends with a solemn morning Mass at the cathedral on 8 May.

🛏 Sleeping

TOP CHOICE **Hôtel de l'Abeille** HISTORIC HOTEL €€
(☑02 38 53 54 87; www.hoteldelabeille.com; 64 rue Alsace-Lorraine; s €47, d €64-89, 5 people €120; 🚻📶) Bees buzz, floorboards creak and vintage Orléans posters adorn the walls at this gorgeous turn-of-the-century house. It's deliciously old-fashioned, from the scuffed pine floors and wildly floral wall-papers to the hefty dressers and bee-print curtains. For breakfast (€9) there's a choice of coffees, teas, pâtisserie and exotic jams.

Hôtel Archange
BOUTIQUE HOTEL €

(☑02 38 54 42 42; www.hotelarchange.com; 1 bd de Verdun; d €47-57) Gilded mirrors, cherub murals and sofas shaped like giant hands greet you at this station hotel aiming for boutique status. Citrus colour schemes spice up some rooms. Shuttered windows combat daytime tram noise. The hotel is located just around the corner from rue de la République and across from the Centre Commercial Place d'Arc.

Hôtel d'Arc
HOTEL €€

(☑02 38 53 10 94; www.hoteldarc.fr; 37 ter rue de la République; s €90-132, d €104-171; 🚻@📶) Ride the vintage-style lift to swank guestrooms. Rooms vary in size and the Prestige and Deluxe come with plush robes, but all are done up comfortably. Double-glazed windows help with daytime tram noise.

Jackôtel
HOTEL €

(☑02 38 54 48 48; www.jackotel.com; 18 Cloître St-Aignan; d €50-70; 📶) Simple little place tucked in a modernised cloister shaded by chestnut trees. Floral patterns and catalogue furniture fill basic rooms. It's whisper-quiet and has free parking.

Hôtel Marguerite
HOTEL €

(☑02 38 53 74 32; www.hotel-orleans.fr; 14 place du Vieux Marché; s €55-66, d €64-75; 📶) Solid, basic and worth recommending for its central location and wallet-friendly prices. Expect floral-print bedrooms and bright colours; opt for a superior room if you like your bathroom sparkling and your shower powerful.

Auberge de Jeunesse CRJS Orléans
HOSTEL €

(☎02 38 53 60 06; www.creps-crjs-centre.
fr, in French; 7 av de Beaumarchais, La Source;
dm with member's card under 26yr/over 26yr
€10.70/15.25; ⊙reception 8am-7pm Mon-Fri)
For those on a shoestring budget, this is
a bare-bones hostel at the Stade Omnisports (sports stadium), 10km south of Orléans in La Source. Sixty beds in spartan
rooms have cardboard mattresses. Phone
ahead weekends. Jump off the tram or
bus 20 at Université L'Indien.

✗ Eating

Chez Noé
BRASSERIE €€

(☎02 38 53 44 09; 195 rue de Bourgogne; lunch
menus €12, dinner menus €21-32; ⊙lunch Tue-Fri,
dinner Tue-Sat) Characterful – think hardwood floors, checked tablecloths and Louis
Prima on the stereo – cheery and crammed
at lunchtime and on weekends, this lively
brasserie is about uncomplicated food at
fair prices, from garlic snails to salmon
steak.

Au Bon Marché
TRADITIONAL FRENCH €€

(☎02 38 53 04 35; 12 place du Chatelet; lunch
menus €7.50-10, dinner menus €14-27; ☙) An
old-time bar for many years, elegant wood-
en banquets and panelling remain. The
bright, welcoming dining room fills up with
local families out for a nice meal: the kids'
menu (€8) is free with an adult *menu* Sunday to Wednesday. Dig into imaginatively
presented dishes like rosemary duck on a
brochette. Reserve ahead.

Le Brin de Zinc
BISTRO €€

(☎02 38 53 38 77; 62 Rue St-Catherine; lunch
menus €16, dinner menus €22-27) Battered
signs, old telephones and even a vintage
scooter decorate this old-world bistro, serving up lashings of mussels and oysters at
lunchtime and platters of rich bistro food
till late. The daily blackboard *plat du jour*
at €7.80 is an excellent value.

Jin
JAPANESE €€

(☎02 38 53 80 95; 13 rue Louis Roguet; lunch
menus €12, mains €12.50-18) Zingy Japanese restaurant serving authentic sushi,
yakitori and *maki* in a metro setting, all
mauve bucket seats, scarlet lanterns and
shiny chrome, with a sunny terrace.

Le Dariole
TEA HOUSE €€

(☎02 38 77 26 67; 25 rue Étienne Dolet; menus
€17.50-22; ⊙lunch Mon-Fri, dinner Tue-Fri,
salon de thé 2.30-7pm Mon-Sat) This rustic
salon de thé carries loads of teas from
rare Jasmine to Georgian and Chinese
Dragon, as well as homemade cakes and
pâtisserie. After nightfall it transforms
into a smart restaurant specialising in
regional food.

Self-Catering

Covered Market
FOOD MARKET €

(place du Châtelet; ⊙7.30am-7.30pm Tue-Sat,
8am-1pm Sun) Inside the Halles de Châtelet
shopping centre.

Carrefour
SUPERMARKET €

(Centre Commercial Place d'Arc; ⊙8.30am-9pm
Mon-Sat)

Petit Casino
SUPERMARKET €

(15 rue Jeanne d'Arc; ⊙9am-7pm Mon-Sat)

🍷 Drinking & Entertainment

The free *Orléans Poche* (www.orleanspoche.
com, in French) details cultural hot spots
and happenings. Rue de Bourgogne and rue
du Poirier are chock-a-block with drinking
holes.

Bistrot le Bas Bleu
LITERARY CAFÉ

(☎02 38 21 69 24; www.lebasbleu.com; 164
rue de Bourgogne; ⊙3pm-1am Tue-Sat) Lined
with wooden tables and original art, this
intimate bistro fills up for readings and
open mics (Tuesdays from 8pm, with a
free drink for speakers!).

L'Atelier
JAZZ BAR

(☎06 83 02 11 77; www.latelier203.com; 203 rue
de Bourgogne; ⊙5.30pm-2am Mon-Sat, 5-10pm
Sun) Chilled out bar that hosts jazz and
other concerts.

O Lodge
MUSIC BAR

(☎02 38 77 70 15; place de la République;
⊙11am-midnight Mon-Thu, to 1am Fri & Sat)
Bands and DJs provide the tunes while
you tuck into burgers, cocktails and
beers.

Paxton's Head
PUB

(☎02 38 81 23 29; 264-266 rue de Bourgogne;
⊙3pm-3am Tue-Sat) Traditional Brit-style
pub with a murky cellar-bar that hosts
jazz combos and bands on weekends.

ℹ Information

Call Shop (194 rue de Bourgogne; per 15min
€1; ⊙10.30am-8pm Mon-Sat, 5-8pm Sun)
Internet access.

Exagames (5 rue Parisie; per hr €5; ⊙2-7pm
Sun-Tue, 11am-7pm Wed-Thu, 11am-10pm Fri,
2-10pm Sat) Internet access.

Main post office (place du Général de Gaulle) Currency exchange and internet access.

Tourist office (☑02 38 24 05 05; www. tourisme-orleans.com; 2 place de l'Étape; ☺9am-1pm & 2-6pm Mon-Sat)

ⓘ Getting There & Away

BUS Ulys (www.ulys-loiret.com, in French) brings together information for local bus companies serving the Orléanais area. Buy tickets (€2) on board or at the **bus station** (☑02 38 53 94 75; 2 rue Marcel Proust).

Sully-sur-Loire Line 7 via Jargeau, 1¾ hours, three daily Monday to Friday, one Saturday and Sunday

Châteauneuf-sur-Loire Line 3, 40 minutes, five daily Monday to Saturday, two on Sunday

TRAIN The city's two stations, Gare d'Orléans and Gare des Aubrais-Orléans (the latter is 2km to the north), are linked by tram and frequent shuttle trains. Trains usually stop at both stations.

Blois €13 to €20, 45 minutes, hourly

Paris Gare d'Austerlitz €24 to €37, 70 minutes, hourly

Tours €24 to €35, one to 1½ hours, hourly

ⓘ Getting Around

Espace Transport (☑08 00 01 20 00; www.semtao.fr, in French; Gare d'Orléans; ☺6.45am-7.15pm Mon-Fri, 8am-6.30pm Sat) Information and tickets (single/10-ticket *carnet* €1.40/12.30). Trams run until around 12.30am, buses till 8pm or 9pm.

Vélo+ (☑08 00 00 83 56; www.agglo-veloplus. fr, in French; deposit with credit card €3, first 30min free, next 30min €0.50, per subsequent hr €2) On-street bike-hire system, with stations all over town (eg train station, cathedral).

Orléans to Sully-sur-Loire

The 350-sq-km Forêt d'Orléans (one of the few remaining places in France where you can spot wild ospreys) stretches north of Orléans, while east of Orléans lie intriguing churches and little-known châteaux.

Châteauneuf-sur-Loire's Musée de la Marine de Loire (☑02 38 46 84 46; 1 place Aristide Briand; adult/child €3.50/2; ☺10am-6pm Wed-Mon) explores the history of river shipping on the Loire, with a collection of model boats and riverine artefacts displayed in the former stables of the town's château.

TOP CHOICE Oratoire de Germigny-des-Prés (806), another 6km southeast, is one of France's few Carolingian churches,

renowned for its unusual Maltese-cross layout and gilt-and-silver 9th-century mosaic of the Ark of the Covenant.

Twelve kilometres further southeast, St-Benoît-sur-Loire's Romanesque Abbaye de Fleury (☑02 38 35 72 43; www.abbaye-fleury. com; ☺6.30am-10pm) is still home to a practising Benedictine brotherhood, who conduct summertime tours. Look out for the basilica's famous decorated portal and capitals and the relics of St Benedict (480–547) which the monks fetched from Montecassino, Italy in 672.

Nine kilometres southeast of St-Benoît, the Château de Sully-sur-Loire (☑02 38 36 36 86; adult/child €6/3; ☺10am-6pm Tue-Sun, closed noon-2pm Oct-Mar) is a grand example of a fairy-tale castle, with machicolated ramparts and turrets rising from a glassy moat. Built from 1395 to defend one of the Loire's crucial crossings, Louis XIV took refuge here with Anne of Austria. The castle underwent major refurbishment in 2007–08 and has an impressive exposed vaulted roof and historic **tapestries** depicting the story of Psyche. An outdoor music festival (www.festival-sully.com, in French) jams in late May and early June.

La Sologne

For centuries, the boggy wetland and murky woods of La Sologne have been one of France's great hunting grounds, with deer, boars, pheasants and stags roaming the woodland, and eels, carp and pike filling its deep ponds and rivers. François I established it as a royal playground, but years of war and floods turned it into malaria-infested swamp; only in the mid-19th century, after it was drained under Napoléon III, did La Sologne regain its hunting prestige.

In winter it can be a desolate place, with drizzle and thick fog blanketing the landscape, but in summer it's a riot of wildflowers and makes for great country to explore on foot, bike or horseback. Paths and trails criss-cross the area, including the GR31 and the GR3C, but stick to the signposted routes during hunting season to avoid getting buckshot in your backside.

For info on hikes and walks in the Sologne, contact the tourist office (☑02 54 76 43 89; www.tourisme-romorantin.com, in French; ☺9.45am-12.15pm & 1.30-6pm Mon-Sat, also Sun afternoon July & Aug) in Romorantin-Lanthenay, 41km southeast of Blois. Some trails leave from near Saint-Viâtre's **Maison des Étangs** (☑02 54 88 23 00; www.maison-des-etangs.com; 2 rue de la Poste; adult/child €5/2.50; ⊙10am-noon & 2-6pm), a museum exploring La Sologne's 2800 *étangs* (ponds).

On the last weekend in October the annual **Journées Gastronomiques de Sologne** fills the streets of Romorantin with local delicacies like stuffed trout, wild-boar pâté and freshly baked *tarte tatin,* the upside-down apple tart accidentally created in 1888 by two sisters in nearby Lamotte-Beuvron.

Trains run from Romorantin-Lanthenay to Tours (via Gièvres; €19, 1½ hours, six daily). Buses go to Blois (€2, one to four daily).

BLÉSOIS

The countryside around the former royal seat of Blois is surrounded by some of the country's finest châteaux, including graceful Cheverny, little-visited Beauregard and the turret-topped supertanker château to end them all, Chambord.

Blois

POP 40,057

Looming on a rocky escarpment on the northern bank of the Loire, Blois' historic château (formerly the feudal seat of the powerful counts of Blois) provides a whistle-stop tour through the key periods of French history and architecture. Blois suffered heavy bombardment during WWII, and the modern-day town is mostly the result of postwar reconstruction. The twisting streets of the old town give some idea of how Blois might have looked to its medieval inhabitants.

⊙ Sights & Activities

For château tours and bicycling see p357.

Château Royal de Blois   CASTLE
(☑02 54 90 33 32; www.chateaudeblois.fr; place du Château; adult/child €8/4; ⊙9am-6.30pm)
Blois' château and the former royal seat was intended more as an architectural showpiece than a military stronghold, and successive French kings have left their creative mark over the centuries. From the château's huge **central courtyard** you can view four distinct periods of French architecture: the Gothic Salle des États and original medieval castle; François I's Renaissance north wing (1515–24); the classical west wing (1635–38) constructed under Gaston d'Orléans, brother to Louis XIII; and Louis XII's red-brick Flamboyant Gothic east wing (1498–1503).

The impressive **Salle des États Généraux** (Estates General Hall, c 1220) has a soaring double barrel-vaulted roof decorated in royal blues and golden fleurs-de-lis. Blois' medieval lords meted out justice here in the Middle Ages, and Luc Besson used it for the dramatic trial scene in his 1999 biopic *Jeanne d'Arc*.

The most famous feature of the Renaissance wing, the royal apartments of François I and Queen Claude, is the **loggia staircase**, decorated with salamanders and curly 'F's (heraldic symbols of François I). Highlights include the bedchamber in which Catherine de Médicis (Henri II's machiavellian wife) died in 1589. According to Alexandre Dumas, the queen stashed her poisons in secret cupboards behind the elaborately panelled walls of the **studiolo**, one of the few rooms in the castle with its original decor.

The 2nd-floor **king's apartments** were the setting for one of the bloodiest episodes

---

LE PASS' CHÂTEAUX

Many of the châteaux in the Blésois are covered by the **Pass' Châteaux**, which offers savings of between €1.20 and €5.30 depending on which châteaux you visit; contact the tourist offices in Blois, Cheverny and Chambord. Additional formulas include smaller châteaux at Villesavin, Troussay and Talcy.

» Blois–Chambord–Cheverny €20.50
» Blois–Chenonceau–Cheverny–Chambord €30.50
» Chambord–Cheverny–Beauregard €21
» Blois–Chambord–Chaumont €22
» Blois–Chambord–Cheverny–Beauregard €28.50
» Blois–Cheverny–Chaumont–Chambord €28.50

in the château's history: in 1588 Henri III had his arch-rival, Duke Henri I de Guise, murdered by royal bodyguards (the king hid behind a tapestry). He had the Duke's brother, the Cardinal de Guise, killed the next day. Henri III was himself murdered just eight months later by a vengeful monk. Period paintings chronicle the gruesome events.

The brick-and-stone Louis XII wing houses the **Musée des Beaux-Arts**, where the most popular work is a portrait of an alarmingly hairy girl (apparently the result of a rare genetic disease) by the Italian painter Lavinia Fontana.

The château hosts a 45-minute son et lumière (☑02 54 55 26 31; adult/child €7/4; ☉mid-Apr–late Sep) featuring huge projections on the walls (English version Wednesdays).

Maison de la Magie   MAGIC MUSEUM
(House of Magic; ☑02 54 90 33 33; www.maison delamagie.fr, in French; 1 place du Château; adult/child €9/5; ☉10am-12.30pm & 2-6.30pm, closed mornings Mon-Fri Sep) Opposite the château you can't miss the former home of watchmaker, inventor and conjurer Jean Eugène Robert-Houdin (1805–71) when, on the hour, dragons emerge roaring from the windows. It has entertaining live magic shows (three to four daily), exhibits on the history of magic and loads of optical trickery including a mysterious 'Hallucinoscope'. It's goofy, good fun! The great Harry Houdini named himself after Houdin, and there is a short historical film about the American magician.

Musée de l'Objet   ART MUSEUM
(☑02 54 55 37 45; www.museedelobjet.org, in French; 6 rue Franciade; adult/child €4/2; ☉1.30-6.30pm Fri-Sun, closed Dec-Feb) This brilliant modern arts museum is based on the collection of the artist Eric Fabre, and concentrates on artworks made using everyday materials. Among the best pieces are a sculpture of coat-hangers by Man Ray, an *objet scatologique* (involving a large high-heeled shoe) by Salvador Dalí and a *TV Buddha* by Nam June Paik.

Old City   HISTORIC QUARTER
Despite serious damage by German attacks in 1940, Blois' old city is worth exploring, especially around the 17th-century Cathédrale St-Louis (place St-Louis; ☉9am-6pm), with its lovely multistoreyed bell tower, dramatically floodlit after dark. Most of the

COMBO TICKETS

If you're taking in the château, the *son et lumière* and the Maison de la Magie, combination tickets save a bit of cash. Kids under six are free.

» Château & *Son et Lumière* (adult/child €13/6)

» Château & Maison de la Magie (adult/child €14/6.50)

» All three (adult/child €18/10)

stained glass inside was installed by Dutch artist Jan Dibberts in 2000.

Across the square, the facade of Maison des Acrobates (3bis rue Pierre de Blois) is decorated with wooden sculptures taken from medieval farces, and one of the few 15th-century houses to survive. There's another example at No 13 called Hôtel de Villebrême.

Lovely panoramas unfold across town from the peaceful Jardins de l'Évêché and the top of the Escalier Denis Papin.

Tours of Blois   CITY TOURS
The tourist office offers English-language walking tour brochures and guided tours in French. Better yet, château guides run 1½-hour historically oriented city tours (adult/child €5/3), also in French.

Horse-drawn carriage rides (adult/child €6/4; ☉2-6pm) clop around town from the château's main gate. Book at the tourist office, or wait outside the château for the next carriage.

🛏 Sleeping

Côté Loire   HOTEL €
(☑02 54 78 07 86; www.coteloire.com; 2 place de la Grève; d €55-76; ☎) If it's charm and colours you want, head for the centrally located Loire Coast, with rooms decked out in cheery checks, bright pastels and the odd bit of exposed brick. There's a wooden-decked breakfast patio and bustling restaurant (lunch/dinner *menus* €18/28).

Hôtel Anne de Bretagne   HOTEL €
(☑02 54 78 05 38; http://annedebretagne.free. fr; 31 av du Dr Jean Laigret; s €45-51, d €54-56, tr €60-72; ☎🅿) This creeper-covered hotel has friendly staff and a bar full of polished wood and vintage pictures. Modern rooms are finished in flowery wallpaper and stripy bedspreads; some adjoin for families.

Le Monarque HOTEL €
(☑02 54 78 02 35; http://annedebretagne.free.
fr; 61 rue Porte Chartraine; s €38, d €58-59; ❄☀⑤)
Modern, bright and no-nonsense, this hotel
sits at the edge of the old city, and offers
comfort, cleanliness and a restaurant (*menus* €18 to €28). Parking by reservation (€3).

Hôtel Le Savoie HOTEL €
(☑02 54 74 32 21; www.hotel-blois.com, in
French; 6 rue Ducoux; s/d/tr €48/55/79; ⑤)
Handy for train travellers, straightforward, modern chain-style rooms are
cheered up by bright fabrics. Free bike
parking.

RV Parking CAMPGROUND €
Contact the tourist office about their two
RV parking sites, one with waste disposal
and showers near the castle (€5, May to
September) and one on the river (free,
October to April).

✕ Eating

L'Orangerie GASTRONOMIC €€€
(☑02 54 78 05 36; www.orangerie-du-chateau.fr;
1 av du Dr Jean Laigret; menus €33-77) Polish up
those heels and dust off that suit! Tucked
behind wrought-iron gates opposite the
château, the Orangery is cloud nine for connoisseurs of *haute cuisine*. Plates are artfully stacked (duck liver, langoustine, foie
gras) and the sparkling *salon* would make
Louis XIV green with envy. On summer
nights, opt for a courtyard table. The only
warning: desserts sometimes have jarring
flavour combinations.

Les Banquettes Rouges
TRADITIONAL FRENCH €€
(☑02 54 78 74 92; 16 rue des Trois Marchands;
lunch menus €14.50, dinner menus €26-32;
☉Tue-Sat) Handwritten slate menus and
wholesome food distinguish quiet, charming Red Benches: rabbit with marmalade,
duck with lentils, and salmon with apple
vinaigrette, all done with a spicy twist and
a smile.

Au Bouchon Lyonnais LYONNAIS €€
(☑02 54 74 12 87; 25 rue des Violettes; lunch/dinner menus €12.50/20) Classic neighbourhood
bistro with a flavour of bygone days. The
food is straight out of the Lyonnais cookbook: snails and duck steaks. Peasant food
done to perfection.

Le Castelet TRADITIONAL FRENCH €€
(☑02 54 74 66 09; 40 rue St-Lubin; lunch menus
€15, dinner menus €18-32; ☉closed Wed & Sun;

☑⌨) Rusticana and rural frescoes cover
the walls of this country restaurant that
emphasises seasonal ingredients, organics
and vegetarian options.

Self-Catering

Food Market MARKET €
(rue Anne de Bretagne; ☉8am-1pm Tue, Thu &
Sat)

8 à Huit SUPERMARKET €
(11 rue du Commerce; ☉8am-8pm Mon-Sat,
8am-noon Sun)

🍷 Drinking

The best bars are in the old town, particularly in the small alleys off rue Foulerie.

TOP ⧸ CHOICE ⧹ Velvet Jazz Lounge JAZZ BAR
(☑02 54 78 36 32; www.velvetjazz.fr;
15bis rue Haute; ☉3pm-2am Tue-Sat) Lodged
under artful lights, 13th-century vaults
and contemplative Buddhas, Blois' funkiest bar hosts regular jazz acts after dark,
and in winter offers a selection of 30
(count 'em) hot chocolates in its alternative guise as an afternoon *salon de thé*.

Loch Ness Pub SCOTTISH BAR
(☑02 54 56 08 67; cnr rue des Juifs & rue Pierre
de Blois; ☉3pm-3am) The Scottish theme
isn't convincing, but the boozing students
and late-night drinkers don't seem to
mind. Big-screen sports, karaoke and occasional gigs pack 'em in.

❶ Information

Tourist office (☑02 54 90 41 41; www.
bloispaysdechambord.com; 23 place du Château; ☉9am-7pm)

❶ Getting There & Away

BUS TLC (☑02 54 58 55 44; www.tlcinfo.net)
runs a château shuttle as well as buses that
depart from Blois' train station (tickets €2 on
board):

Beaugency Line 16, 55 minutes, four Monday
to Saturday, one Sunday

Chambord Line 3, 40 minutes, four Monday to
Saturday, one Sunday

Cheverny Line 4, 45 minutes, six to eight Monday to Friday, two Saturday, one Sunday

CAR Some rental options:
Avis (☑02 54 45 10 61; train station)
Europcar (☑02 54 43 22 20; 4 rue Gutenberg)
Ligérienne de Location (☑02 54 78 25 45; 96-
100 av de Vendôme)

The Loire offers relatively few opportunities to get out on the water: the currents are often too unpredictable to navigate safely. But it's not completely off-limits.

Croisières de Loire (☑02 47 23 98 64; www.labelandre.com; adult/child €8.50/5.50; ☺Apr-Oct) Offers cruises of Chenonceau, with great views of the château.

Ligérienne de Navigation (☑02 47 52 68 88; www.naviloire.com; adult/child €9/6; ☺Apr-Nov) Runs one of the few cruises on the Loire proper, in a 66-seat boat departing from Rochecorbon to wild islets and nature reserves.

Promenades en Futreau (☑Blois Tourist Office 02 54 90 41 41; adult/child €9/6.50; ☺May-Aug) Sets out from the Blois quayside aboard a traditional *futreau* (flat-bottomed barge).

La Margaretifera, **La Candaise** (☑02 47 95 93 15; adult/child €9/6.50); **L'Hirondelle** (☑02 41 95 14 23) Both use traditional high-cabined Loire vessels known as *toues*, departing from Candes-St-Martin.

TRAIN The train station is at the top of the hill on av Jean Laigret.

Amboise €11, 20 minutes, 10 daily

Orléans €13 to €20, 45 minutes, hourly

Paris Gares d'Austerlitz and Montparnasse €34 to €57, two hours, 26 daily

Tours €13 to €19, 40 minutes, 13 daily

ⓘ Getting Around

BICYCLE The Châteaux à Vélo network (p357) offers 11 waymarked cycling routes in the Blois area.

Detours de Loire (☑02 54 56 07 73; train station; bikes per half-/full day €9/14)

BUS Local buses in Blois and nearby communities, including Cheverny are run by **TUB** (☑02 54 78 15 66; www.tub-blois.fr; 2 place Victor Hugo; ☺1.30-6pm Mon, 8am-noon & 1.30-6pm Tue-Fri, 9am-noon & 1.30-4.30pm Sat). Tickets cost €1.10. Buses run until about 8pm Monday to Saturday, with hardly any on Sunday.

TAXI Available at the train station; cell ☑02 54 78 07 65.

Château de Chambord

For full-blown château splendour, you can't top Chambord (☑02 54 50 50 20; www.chambord.org; adult/under-25yr €9.50/free; ☺9am-7.30pm mid-Jul–mid-Aug, 9am-6.15pm mid-Mar–mid-Jul & mid-Aug–Sep, 9am-5.15pm Jan–mid-Mar & Oct-Dec; ⓟ), one of the crowning examples of French Renaissance architecture, and by far the largest, grandest and most visited château in the Loire Valley. It's worth picking up the multilingual audioguide (adult/child version €4/2), if only to avoid getting lost around the endless rooms and corridors.

Begun in 1519 as a weekend hunting lodge by François I, it quickly snowballed into one of the most ambitious (and expensive) architectural projects ever attempted by any French monarch. Though construction was repeatedly halted by financial problems, design setbacks and military commitments (not to mention the kidnapping of the king's two sons in Spain), by the time Chambord was finally finished 30-odd years later, the castle boasted some 440 rooms, 365 fireplaces and 84 staircases, not to mention a cityscape of turrets, chimneys and lanterns crowning its rooftop, and a famous **double-helix staircase**, reputedly designed by the king's chum, Leonardo da Vinci. Ironically, François ultimately found his elaborate palace too draughty, preferring the royal apartments in Amboise and Blois; he only stayed here for 42 days during his entire reign from 1515 to 1547.

Despite its apparent complexity, Chambord is laid out according to simple mathematical rules. Each section is arranged on a system of symmetrical grid squares around a Maltese cross. At the centre stands the rectangular **keep**, crossed by four great hallways, and at each corner stands one of the castle's four circular bastions. Through the centre of the keep winds the great staircase, with two intertwining flights of stairs leading up to the great **lantern tower** and the castle's rooftop, from where you can gaze out across the landscaped grounds and marvel at the Tolkienesque jumble of cupolas, domes, chimneys and lightning rods.

The most interesting rooms are on the 1st floor, including the **king's and queen's chambers** (complete with interconnecting passages to enable late-night nooky) and a wing devoted to the thwarted attempts of the Comte de Chambord to be crowned Henri V after the fall of the Second Empire. On the 2nd floor the eerie **Museum of Hunting** exhibits a copious display of weapons and hunting trophies. On the ground floor, an interesting multilanguage film relates the history of the castle's construction.

In a place of such ostentatious grandeur, it's often the smallest things that are most interesting: look out for the display of hundreds of cast-iron keys, one for each door in the château.

Several times daily there are 1½-hour guided tours (€4) in English, and during school holidays **costumed tours** entertain the kids. *Son et lumière* shows, known as Chambord, Rêve de Lumières, are projected onto the château's facade nightly from July to mid-September (adult/child €12/10). Outdoor spectacles held throughout summer include a daily equestrian show (☎02 54 20 31 01; www.ecuries-chambord.com, in French; adult/child €9.50/7; ☻May-Sep).

DOMAINE NATIONAL DE CHAMBORD
This huge hunting reserve (the largest in Europe) stretches for 54 sq km around the château, and is reserved solely for the use of high-ranking French government personalities (though somehow it's difficult to imagine Sarkozy astride a galloping stallion). About 10 sq km of the park is publicly accessible, with trails open to walkers, mountain bikers and horse riders.

It's great for **wildlife-spotting**, especially in September and October during the deer mating season. Observation towers dot the park; set out at dawn or dusk to spot stags, boars and red deer.

Hire bikes at a rental kiosk (☎02 54 33 37 54; per hr/half-/full day €6/10/13; ☻Apr-Oct) near the *embarcadère* (jetty) on the River Cosson, where you can also rent boats. Guided bike trips (adult/child €10/6 plus bike hire) depart mid-August to September.

To see the rest of the reserve, jump aboard a Land Rover Safari tour (☎02 54 50 50 06; adult/child €18/10; ☻Apr-Sep), conducted by French-speaking guides with an intimate knowledge of where and when to see the best wildlife.

❶ Getting There & Away

Chambord is 16km east of Blois, 45km southwest of Orléans and 17km northeast of Cheverny. For transport see p360 and p357.

Château de Cheverny

Thought by many to be the most perfectly proportioned château of all, Cheverny (☎02 54 79 96 29; www.chateau-cheverny.fr; adult/child €7.50/3.60; ☻9.15am-6.45pm Jul & Aug, 9.15am-6.15pm Apr-Jun & Sep, 9.45am-5.30pm Oct, 9.45am-5pm Nov-Mar) represents the zenith of French classical architecture, the perfect blend of symmetry, geometry and aesthetic order.

Built from gleaming stone from the nearby Bourré quarries and surrounded by lush parkland, Cheverny is one of the few châteaux whose original architectural vision has survived the centuries practically unscathed. Since its construction between 1625 and 1634 by Jacques Hurault, an intendant to Louis XII, the castle has hardly been altered, and its interior decoration includes some of the most sumptuous furnishings, tapestries and objets d'art anywhere in the Loire Valley. The Hurault

---

WORTH A TRIP

LUNCH BREAK

Need a moment to collect yourself between châteaux? Head to sleepy Bracieux, 7km south of Chambord, for a delicious, light lunch made with fresh seasonal ingredients. Au Fil de Temps (☎02 54 46 03 84; 11 place de la Halle; kids' menus €8, lunch menus €15, mains €18-22; ☻Fri-Wed) beats all the tourist traps into the dust with their simple specialties like tender white asparagus with *beurre blanc* or savoury salmon fillets, all served with vigour and charm. Another diversion? Head over to the nearby Max Vauché chocolate factory (☎02 54 46 07 96; www.maxvauche-chocolatier.com; 22 Les Jardins du Moulin; tour adult/child €3.80/3; ☻10am-12.30pm & 2-7pm, closed Mon & Sun Sep-Jun) for a tour and a taste test!

STAYING OVER

Located at the foot of Cheverny's long driveway, amid 3 hectares of grassland, **La Levraudière** (☑02 54 79 81 99; http://lalevraudiere.free.fr; 1 chemin de la Levraudière; s incl breakfast €55, d €59-65, tr €75-83) is a perfect blend of the farmstyle and the modern. In a peaceful, renovated 19th-century farmhouse, the B&B has a slab-like wooden table for breakfasts featuring fabulous homemade jams. But the crisp linens and meticulously kept house are the opposite of roughing it.

at 5pm April to September and 3pm October to March.

❶ Getting There & Away

Cheverny is 16km southeast of Blois and 17km southwest of Chambord. For transport see p360 and p357.

Château de Chaumont

Set on a defensible bluff behind the Loire, **Chaumont-sur-Loire** (☑02 54 20 99 22; www.domaine-chaumont.fr, in French; adult/child €9/3.50; ☺10am-6.30pm Apr-Sep, to 5pm or 6pm Oct-Mar) presents a resolutely medieval face, with its cylindrical corner turrets and sturdy drawbridge, but the interior mostly dates from the 19th century.

At least two earlier fortresses occupied the site (whose name derives from Chauve Mont, 'Bald Hill'), but the main phase of construction for the present château began sometime around 1465 under Pierre d'Amboise. Originally a strictly defensive fortress, the castle became a short-lived residence for Catherine de Médicis following the death of Henry II in 1560, and later passed into the hands of Diane de Poitiers (Henry II's mistress), who was forced to swap the altogether grander surroundings of Chenonceau for Chaumont by the ruthless Catherine.

The château was thoroughly renovated by Princess de Broglie, heiress to the Say sugar fortune, who bought it in 1875 (and knocked down one entire wing to provide a better view of the river). The most impressive room is the **Council Chamber**, with its original maiolica-tiled floor, plun-

family has owned (and inhabited) the castle for the last six centuries and their fabulous **art collection** includes a portrait of Jeanne of Aragon by Raphael's studio, an 18th-century De la Tour pastel, and a who's who of court painters. Keep your eyes open for the certificate signed by US President George Washington.

The interior was designed by Jean Monier, known for his work on Luxembourg Palace for Queen Marie de Médicis. Highlights include a **formal dining room** with panels depicting the story of Don Quixote, the **king's chamber** with murals relating stories from Greek mythology, a **bridal chamber** and **children's playroom** (complete with Napoléon III-era toys). The **guards' room** is full of pikestaffs, claymores and suits of armour – including a tiny one fit for a kid.

Behind the main château, the 18th-century **Orangerie**, where many priceless artworks, including the *Mona Lisa*, were stashed during WWII, is now a tearoom.

Tintin fans might find the château's facade oddly familiar: Hergé used it as a model (minus the two end towers) for Moulinsart (Marlinspike) Hall, the ancestral home of Tintin's irascible sidekick, Captain Haddock. A dynamic exhibition, **Les Secrets de Moulinsart** (combined ticket with château adult/child €12/7), explores the Tintin connections with re-created scenes, thunder and other special effects.

Near the château's gateway, the **kennels** house pedigreed French pointer/English foxhound hunting dogs still used by the owners of Cheverny: feeding time, known as the **Soupe des Chiens**, takes place daily

ROYAL MENAGERIE

As you visit the Loire's splendiferous châteaux, you may see some surprising zoological emblems etched into the walls, ceilings, towers and floors. See if you can spot:

» Porcupine: Louis XII

» Salamander in flames: François I

» Ermine: Queen Claude

» Stag: Jean II

» Winged stag: Charles V and Charles VII

» Genet (sort of like a spotted civet): Charles VI

dered from a palace in Palermo, but the château's finest architecture is arguably reserved for the **Écuries** (stables), built in 1877 to house the Broglies' horses in truly sumptuous style (the thoroughbreds all had their own personal padded stalls). A collection of vintage carriages is now displayed inside.

Chaumont's English-style park hosts the annual Festival International des Jardins (International Garden Festival; ☑02 54 20 99 22; www.chaumont-jardins.com; adult/child €9.50/7.50; ☺9.30am-sunset) between May and mid-October.

❶ Getting There & Away

Chaumont-sur-Loire is 17km southwest of Blois. Onzain, a 2.5km walk from Chaumont across the Loire, has trains to Blois (€11, 10 minutes, 13 daily) and Tours (€11 to €15, 35 minutes, 10 daily).

Château de Beauregard

Less visited than its sister châteaux, peaceful Beauregard (☑02 54 70 40 05; www.beauregard-loire.com; adult/child €8/6.50; ☺9.30am-6.30pm Jun-Aug, 9.30am-12.30pm & 2-6.30pm Apr-May & Sep-Oct, 9.30am-noon & 2-5pm Nov, Feb & Mar, closed Dec & Jan & Wed Oct-Mar) has special charms all of its own. Built as yet another hunting lodge by François I, the highlight is an amazing **portrait gallery** depicting 327 notables of European royalty, clergy and intelligentsia. Spot famous faces including Christopher Columbus, Sir Francis Drake, Cardinal Richelieu, Catherine de Médicis, Anne de Bretagne, Henry VIII of England and his doomed wife Anne Boleyn, and every French king since Philippe VI. The quiet, 40-hectare grounds encompass numerous **gardens**, including the Garden of Portraits with 12 colour variations.

TOURAINE

Often dubbed the 'Garden of France', the Touraine region is famous for its rich food, tasty cheeses and notoriously pure French accent, as well as a smattering of glorious châteaux: some medieval (Langeais and Loches), others Renaissance (Azay-le-Rideau, Villandry and Chenonceau). The peppy capital, Tours, makes a good base, with castle tours and transportation links.

Tours

POP 139,958

Bustling Tours has a life of its own despite being one of the hubs of castle country. It's a smart, vivacious kind of place, filled with wide 18th-century boulevards, parks and imposing public buildings, as well as a busy university of some 25,000 students. Hovering somewhere between the style of Paris and the conservative sturdiness of central France, Tours makes a useful staging post for exploring the Touraine, with Azay-le-Rideau, Villandry and Langeais all a short drive away.

◉ Sights & Activities

The old city encircles place Plumereau (locally known as place Plum), about 400m west of rue Nationale.

Musée des Beaux-Arts   ART MUSEUM
(☑02 47 05 68 73; 18 place François Sicard; adult/child €4/2; ☺9am-6pm Wed-Mon) Originally the archbishop's gorgeous palace, the Musée des Beaux-Arts is now a fine example of a French provincial arts museum, with grand rooms decorated to reflect the period of the artworks on display. Look out for works by Delacroix, Degas and Monet, as well as a rare Rembrandt miniature and a Rubens *Madonna and Child*. The massive 1804 Lebanese cedar in front of the museum measures a whopping 7.5m around the base. Wheelchair accessible.

Cathédrale St-Gatien   CATHEDRAL
(place de la Cathédrale; ☺9am-7pm) With its twin west towers stretching skyward through a latticework of Gothic decorations, flying buttresses and gargoyles, this cathedral's a show-stopper. It is especially known for its intricate stained glass, particularly the rose windows above the organ. The interior dates from the 13th to 16th centuries, and the domed tops of the two 70m-high towers date from the Renaissance. On the north side, the Cloître de la Psallette (adult/child €2.50/free; ☺9.30am-12.30pm & 2-6pm Mon-Sat, 2-6pm Sun, closed Mon & Tue Oct-Mar) was built from 1442 to 1524.

TOP CHOICE Musée du Compagnonnage
    CRAFT MUSEUM
(☑02 47 21 62 20; 8 rue Nationale, in Cloître St-Julien; adult/child €5/3.30; ☺9am-noon & 2-6pm, closed Tue mid-Sep–mid-Jun) France has long prided itself on the work of its 20,000-odd *compagnons* (craftsmen), whose unique skills have been in demand since the first

Tours

THE LOIRE VALLEY TOURS

0 200 m
0.1 miles

To Rochecorbon (3km);
Amboise (23km)

R François Clouet

R Albert Thomas

22

**Cathédrale
St-Gatien**

1

*Musée des
Beaux-Arts*

Flower
Garden

R des Ursulines

R Jules Simon

Bd Heurteloup
Bd Heurteloup

R du Rempart

To St-Pierre-des-Corps
Train Station (5km)

11

R Édouard Vaillant

Pl de la
Cathédrale

Pl François
Sicard

R Bernard Palissy

R Lavoisier

R de la Barre

R du Cygne

Jardin
de la
Préfecture

Pl du
Général
Leclerc

Av Charles Gilles

R de Bordeaux

13

R Colbert

6

R de Buffon

R Victor Laloux

12

26

R Berthelot

R Pimbert

25

R Corneille

10

R de la Scellerie

Pl de la
Préfecture

7

Pl Jean
Jaurès

5

R Voltaire

*Musée du
Compagnonnage*

R Émile Zola

24

R de la Préfecture

Av de Grammont

To Tour-Val de Loire
Airport (12km)

To Tour de Loire (12km)

Pl Anatole
France

R Nationale

R des Déportés

R des Minimes

18

Pl de la
Résistance

R du Commerce

9

R de Constantine

R de Jérusalem

R Marceau

R Néricault Destouches

R de Clocheville

Bd Béranger
Bd Béranger

To Azay-le-Rideau (26km);
Loches (42km); Chinon (46km)

R des Orfèvres

R des Orfèvres

14

R de la Monnaie

21

R de la Paix

R Briçonnet

R du Milner

Pl
Plumereau

R de l'
Arbalète

R de la Rôtisserie

8

*Basilique
St-Martin*

R Descartes

3

2

R Rapin

R Rabelais

R Léonard
de Vinci

Pl Gaston
Paithou

23

R des Tanneurs

R Bretonneau

R Étienne Marcel

R Eugène Sue

19

R du Grand Marché

16

20

Pl du
Grand
Marché

R des Halles

R Chanoineau

17

Q du Pont Neuf

Pl de la
Victoire

R du Petit
St-Martin

R des Bajais

R de la
Grosse Tour

R de la Victoire

R de la Victoire

To Jardin
Botanique (1km)

15

Tours

showpiece cathedrals started appearing in the early Middle Ages (when the Statue of Liberty was restored in the mid-1980s, French *compagnons* were responsible for the intricate metalwork). In addition to traditional professions such as stonemasonry, carpentry and blacksmithing, the *compagnonnages* (guild organisations) welcome in many metiers, including pastry chefs, coopers and locksmiths. Learn their history and view the masterpieces they create at the end of their apprenticeships (which last

from three to 10 years). Works range from exquisitely carved chests and staircases to handmade tools, booby-trapped locks and enormous cakes (one took 800 hours to make, in the shape of Hospices de Beaune, with 20kg of dough and tiny sheets of gelatin for windows).

Basilique St-Martin   CHURCH
Tours was once an important pilgrimage city thanks to the soldier-turned-evangelist St Martin (c 317–97), bishop of Tours in the 4th century. After his death a Romanesque basilica was constructed above his tomb, but today only the north tower, the **Tour Charlemagne**, remains. A replacement basilica was built in 1862 on a new site a short distance south along rue Descartes to house his relics, while the small Musée St-Martin (✆02 47 64 48 87; 3 rue Rapin; adult/concession €2/1; ⊙9am-12.30pm & 2-5.30pm Wed-Sun) displays artefacts relating to the lost church.

Jardin Botanique   BOTANICAL GARDEN
(bd Tonnelle; ⊙7.45am-sunset) Tours has several public parks, including the 19th-century botanic garden, a 5-hectare landscaped park with a tropical greenhouse, medicinal herb garden and petting zoo. The park is 1.6km west of place Jean Jaurès; bus 4 along bd Béranger stops nearby.

☞ Tours

Walks   WALKING TOURS
The tourist office offers an **audioguide** (€5) for a two-hour self-guided tour or various **guided tours** (adult/child €5.60/4.60) in French.

Train   TRAIN TOUR
(✆04 75 07 45 53; adult/child €6/3) Forty-minute tours leave the tourist office seven times daily.

Carriages   CARRIAGE TOUR
(€1.25; ⊙10am, 11am, 3pm, 4pm & 5pm Tue-Sat, 3pm, 4pm & 5pm Sun May-Sep) Fifty-minute rides depart from place François Sicard near the cathedral. Drivers sell tickets.

⊨ Sleeping

Tours has high-calibre rooms for the prices.

Hôtel Ronsard   BOUTIQUE HOTEL €
(✆02 47 05 25 36; www.hotel-ronsard.com; 2 rue Pimbert; s €53-67, d €59-72; ❋@☎) Completely renovated in 2010 with sleek modern rooms, the Ronsard is centrally located, comfortable and good value. The halls are

lined with colourful photographs and immaculate rooms incorporate muted tones of grey with sparkling white linens. Includes perks like air-con in summer and bike parking.

Hôtel l'Adresse
BOUTIQUE HOTEL €€

(☎02 47 20 85 76; www.hotel-ladresse.com; 12 rue de la Rôtisserie; s €50, d €70-100; ❄️📶) Looking for Parisian style in provincial Tours? Then you're in luck. On a walking street in the old quarter lies a boutique bonanza, with rooms finished in slates, creams and ochres, topped off with flat-screen TVs, designer sinks and reclaimed rafters. Best are the ones with shuttered balconies over the bustling street.

Hôtel de l'Univers
HOTEL €€€

(☎02 47 05 37 12; www.hotel-univers.fr; 5 bd Heurteloup; d €198-270; ❄️@📶) Everyone from Ernest Hemingway to Edith Piaf has bunked at the Universe over its 150-year history, and it's still a prestigious address. Previous guests gaze down from the frescoed balcony above the lobby (find Churchill and Edward VII), and rooms are appropriately glitzy: huge beds, gleaming bathrooms. Wheelchair accessible. Parking €15.

Hôtel Mondial
HOTEL €€

(☎02 47 05 62 68; www.hotelmondialtours.com; 3 place de la Résistance; s €52-72, d €64-87; 📶) This hotel boasts a fantastic city-centre position. The modernised, metropolitan attic rooms in funky greys, browns and scarlets are the nicest, but even the older-style ones are decent. Reception is on the second floor and there is no lift.

Hôtel des Arts
HOTEL €

(☎02 47 05 05 00; www.hoteldesartstours.com; 40 rue de la Préfecture; s €32-45, d €47-50; 📶) A sweet place, with charming management, it has tiny but fastidious and cheery rooms in oranges and siennas. Get one with a balcony for extra light. Public parking across the street.

Hôtel Val de Loire
HOTEL €

(☎02 47 05 37 86; www.hotelvaldeloire.fr; 33 bd Heurteloup; s €45-48, d €50-60; 📶) Higgledy-piggledy rooms with period features including parquet floors and leather chairs, as well as double glazing to dampen road noise. Top-floor rooms are jammed into the rafters; ask for one lower down for more space.

Hôtel du Théâtre
HOTEL €

(☎02 47 05 31 29; www.hotel-du-theatre37.com; 57 rue de la Scellerie; s €59-64, d €64-70; 📶) As its name suggests, this character-ful hotel is down the street from the city theatre. Inside, a spiral staircase reaches up a tiny timber-framed foyer to the 1st-floor lobby; rooms are comfortably old-fashioned with spotless bathrooms.

Auberge de Jeunesse du Vieux Tours
HOSTEL €

(☎02 47 37 81 58; www.ajtours.org; 5 rue Bretonneau; dm €19.50; ⊕reception 8am-noon & 5-11pm; @📶) Friendly, bustling Hostelling International hostel (membership €7 per year; required) with a large foreign-student and young-worker contingent; there are lots of small kitchens and lounges. No en suite bathrooms, and the shared ones are a bit rough. Rents bikes.

🍴 Eating

Place Plumereau is crammed with cheap eats, but the quality can be variable.

TOP CHOICE Cap Sud
GASTRONOMIC BISTRO €€

(☎02 47 05 24 81; 88 rue Colbert; lunch menus €14.50-17, dinner menus €19.50-36; ⊕Tue-Sat) The hot mod red interior combines nicely with the genial service. And the food! The food! Sensitive, refined creations are made from the freshest ingredients presented in style. Dishes are along the lines of tender braised pork with creamy polenta and baby vegetables, or octopus and tuna with a green curry chantilly and cherry tomatoes. Reserve ahead.

Tartines & Co
GOURMET SANDWICHES €

(☎02 47 20 50 60; 6 rue des Fusillés; sandwiches €9-10, lunch menus €13.70; ⊕lunch Tue-Sat, dinner Wed-Fri; ✍️) This snazzy little bistro reinvents the traditional *croque* (toasted sandwich) amid jazz and friendly chatter. Choose your topping (chicken, roasted veg, carpaccio beef) and it's served up quick as a flash on toasted artisanal bread. Or go rich with foie gras with artichokes and honey vinaigrette (€12.90).

Le Zinc
TRADITIONAL FRENCH €€

(☎02 47 20 29 00; 27 place du Grand Marché; menus €19-26; ⊕closed Wed & lunch Sun) One of the new breed of French bistros that's more concerned with simple, classic staples and market-fresh ingredients (sourced direct from the local Halles) than Michelin stars and *haute cuisine* cachet. Country dishes (duck breast, beef fillet, river fish) shine in a buzzy dining room. Attractive and authentic.

L'Atelier Gourmand GASTRONOMIC BISTRO €€
(☎02 47 38 59 87; 37 rue Étienne Marcel; menu €23; ⊙lunch Tue-Fri, dinner Mon-Sat) Another one for the foodies, but you'll need your dark glasses: the fuchsia-and-silver colour scheme is straight out of a Bret Easton Ellis novel. There's no quibbling with the food: hunks of roast lamb, green-pepper duck and authentic bouillabaisse, delivered with a modern spin.

Comme Autre Fouée REGIONAL CUISINE €€
(☎02 47 05 94 78; 11 rue de la Monnaie; lunch menus €10, dinner menus €16-21; ⊙lunch Tue-Thu, Sat & Sun, dinner Tue-Sat) For local flavour, you can't top this place, which churns out the house speciality of *fouées,* a pita-like disc of dough stuffed with pork rillettes, white beans or goat's cheese.

Self-Catering

Les Halles DAILY MARKET
(place Gaston Pailhou; ⊙7am-7pm)

Atac SUPERMARKET
(5 place du Général Leclerc; ⊙7.30am-8pm Mon-Sat)

🍷 Drinking

Place Plumereau and the surrounding streets are plastered with grungy bars and drinking dens, all of which get stuffed to bursting on hot summer nights.

Bistro 64 JAZZ BAR
(☎02 47 38 47 40; 64 rue du Grand Marché; ⊙11am-2am Mon-Sat) One step removed from the place Plum hustle. Scuffed-up decor, jazz combos and plenty of house beers keep the local crowd happy.

La Canteen WINE BAR
(☎02 34 74 10 30; 10 rue de la Grosse Tour; ⊙noon-2.30pm & 7.30-11pm Mon-Sat) For something smoother and sexier, swing by this designer wine bar, where rough stone walls sit alongside leather sofas, razor-sharp tables and a neon-lit bar.

L'Alexandra ENGLISH BAR
(106 rue du Commerce; ⊙noon-2am Mon-Fri, 3pm-2am Sat & Sun; 🛜) Popular Anglo-Saxon bar crammed with students and late-night boozers.

☆ Entertainment

Get the low-down from the free monthly *Tours.infos* (www.tours.fr, in French), available all over town. Buy event tickets at **Fnac billeterie** (☎08 92 68 36 22; 72 rue Nationale).

Le Paradis Vert POOL HALL
(☎02 47 66 00 94; 9 rue Michelet; adult/student pool table per hr €10/8; ⊙10am-2am; 🛜) Fast Eddie eat your heart out! France's biggest pool hall is right here in Tours, with 36 tables and a weekly pool contest open to all comers.

Les Trois Orfèvres MUSIC CLUB
(☎02 47 64 02 73; 6 rue des Orfèvres; admission €3-10; ⊙11pm-5am Wed-Sat) Grungy night-spot in the heart of the medieval quarter, where DJs and bands lean towards alternative and indie, and the students hang out in force.

Excalibur DANCE CLUB
(☎02 47 64 76 78; 35 rue Briçonnet; ⊙11pm-6am Tue-Sat) Hot-and-heavy club lodged in a converted ecclesiastical building. Has varied music, from pop to drum-and-bass, which packs in Tourangeaux (residents of Tours) clubbers.

Grand Théâtre THEATRE
(☎02 47 60 20 20; 34 rue de la Scellerie; ⊙box office 9.30am-12.30pm & 1.30-5.45pm Mon-Sat, also & 30min before performances) Hosts opera (www.operadetours.fr, in French) and symphonic music.

Cinémas Studio CINEMA
(☎08 92 68 37 01; www.studiocine.com, in French; 2 rue des Ursulines)

🛈 Information

Alli@nce Micro (7 rue de la Monnaie; per hr €2; ⊙9.30am-6pm Mon-Sat) Internet access.

Police Station (☎02 47 33 80 69; 70-72 rue Marceau; ⊙24hr)

Post office (1 bd Béranger) Exchanges currency.

SOS Médecins (☎02 47 38 33 33) Phone advice for medical emergencies.

Top Communication (68-70 rue de la Grand Marché; per hr €2; ⊙10.30am-10pm Mon-Sat) Internet access.

Tourist office (☎02 47 70 37 37; www.ligeris. com) main office (78-82 rue Bernard Palissy; ⊙8.30am-7pm Mon-Sat, 10am-12.30pm & 2.30-5pm Sun); place Plumereau (Tout Le Val de Loire; 1 place Plumereau) Buy château tickets at a slight reduction. The annexe at place Plumereau gives info but doesn't sell tickets.

🛈 Getting There & Away

Tours-Val de Loire Airport (☎02 47 49 37 00; www.tours-aeroport.fr), about 5km northeast of town, is linked to London's Stansted, Dublin, Marseille and Porto by Ryanair.

BUS The information desk for **Touraine Fil Vert** (☎02 47 31 14 00; www.touraine-filvert.com, in French; tickets €1.70; ☺information desk 8am-6.30pm Mon-Fri, 8.30am-12.30pm & 1.30-6.30pm Sat) is at the bus station next to the train station. Destinations in the Indre-et-Loire *département*: Line C to Amboise (35 minutes, 12 daily Monday to Saturday) and Chenonceau (1¼ hours, two daily).

CAR Tours' one-way system makes driving a headache, so you'll be glad to park your car. Use an **underground garage** (per 24hrs €10) for stays of more than two hours; check opening hours for the garage you choose, many are reduced on Sundays.

Some car-hire options near the station:

Avis (☎02 47 20 53 27; train station)

Ecoto (☎02 47 66 75 00; www.ecoto.fr; 8 rue Marcel Tribut)

TRAIN Tours is the Loire Valley's main rail hub. The train station is linked to St-Pierre-des-Corps, Tours' TGV train station, by frequent shuttle trains.

Amboise €11, 20 minutes, 12 daily

Angers €23 to €34, one hour, 26 daily

Blois €9.10, 40 minutes, 12 daily

Chenonceau €11, 30 minutes, eight daily

Loches €11, 50 minutes, one or two daily

Orléans €24 to €35, one to 1½ hours, hourly

Paris Gare d'Austerlitz €41 to €62, two to 2¾ hours, five daily (slow trains)

Paris Gare Montparnasse €44 to €83, 1¼ hours, 30 daily (high-speed TGVs)

Saumur €14 to €21, 35 minutes, hourly

TGV trains from Tours also serve Bordeaux (€40 to €62, 2¾ hours), La Rochelle (€35 to €48, 2½ to 3¼ hours) and Nantes (€28 to €55, 1½ hours).

❶ Getting Around

TO/FROM THE AIRPORT A shuttle bus (€5) leaves the bus station 1½ to two hours before and half an hour after each flight.

BICYCLE For hire, try **Détours de Loire** (☎02 47 61 22 23; www.locationdevelos.com; 35 rue Charles Gille; per day/week €14/59), part of the **Loire à Vélo** (www.loireavelo.fr) network, or **Vélomania** (☎02 47 05 10 11; www.velomaniatours.fr, in French; 109 rue Colbert; per day/week €14.50/50.50; ☺10.30am-1.30pm & 3.30-7.30pm Mon-Sat).

BUS Local buses, run by **Fil Bleu** (☎02 47 66 70 70; www.filbleu.fr, in French; information office 9 rue Michelet; ☺7.30am-7pm Mon-Fri, 10am-5pm Sun), stop near place Jean-Jaurès. Tickets cost €1.25. Most lines run until about 8.30pm; several night buses run until about 1am. The informa-tion office is on rue Michelet, off av Charles Gilles (near the train station).

Vouvray

Chenin blanc vineyards carpet the area around Vouvray (population 3161) and Montlouis-sur-Loire, 10km east of Tours, and wine cellars sprinkle the region. Contact the **tourist office** (☎02 47 52 68 73; 12 rue Rabelais; ☺9.30am-1pm & 2-6.30pm, closed Sun & Mon Nov-Apr) for a list of local wine sellers, or stop in to **Cave des Producteurs de Vouvray** (☎02 47 52 75 03; www.cp-vouvray.com; 38 la Vallée Coquette) for a tour and tasting.

Château de Moncontour (☎02 47 52 60 77; www.moncontour.com, in French; Vouvray; ☺10am-1pm & 2-7pm, closed Sun mid-Sep–Mar) also does tastings and has a small wine museum.

Fil Bleu bus 61 links Tours' train station with Vouvray (€1.25, 20 minutes, 10 daily).

Château de Chenonceau

Spanning the languid Cher River via a series of supremely graceful arches, the castle of Chenonceau (☎02 47 23 90 07; www.chenonceau.com; adult/child €10.50/8, audioguide €4.50; ☺9am-8pm Jul & Aug, 9am-7.30pm Jun & Sep, 9am-7pm Apr & May, 9.30am-5pm or 6pm rest of year) is one of the most elegant and unusual in the Loire Valley. You can't help but be swept up in the magical architecture and the glorious surroundings: exquisite formal gardens and landscaped parkland.

This architectural fantasy land is largely the work of several remarkable women (hence its alternative name, Le Château des Dames: 'Ladies' Château'). The initial phase of construction started in 1515 for Thomas Bohier, a court minister of King Charles VIII, although much of the work and design was actually overseen by his wife, Katherine Briçonnet. The château's distinctive arches and one of the formal gardens were added by Diane de Poitiers, mistress of King Henri II. Following Henri's death, Diane was forced to exchange Chenonceau for the rather less grand château of Chaumont by the king's scheming widow, Catherine de Médicis, who completed the construction and added the huge yew-tree **labyrinth** and the western rose garden. Louise of Lorraine's most interesting contribution was her **mourning room**, on the top floor, all

Châteaux of the Loire Valley

French history is written across the landscape of the Loire. Every castle traces a tale: of wars won and lost, romances embarked upon or destroyed, alliances forged and enemies vanquished. From the shockingly grand to the quietly subdued, there should be a castle to match your own mood.

Chambord

1 Château de Chambord gets all the hype for a reason: it's stunning. Visit in the early morning to see it rise, all towers and turrets, from the mist – making it possible to imagine it in the days of François I (p361).

Chenonceau

2 Like an elegant lady, Chenonceau effortlessly occupies its beautiful sur-roundings. The impressive arches that span the calm Cher River draw you in, while the exquisite decor and the fascinating history keep you captivated (p369).

Azay-le-Rideau

3 A cypress-lined drive leads to this com-paratively discreet and certainly romantic castle beautifully reflected in its still, broad moat. Fantastic views of the château from the lush park are lit up at night (p376).

Langeais

4 Over the centuries châteaux change hands, alterations are made... but in the case of Langeais, the details are intact. The 10th-century keep and the intricate medieval interior take you to a time of valiant knights and mysterious ladies (p375).

Angers

5 Whether for its distinctive black stone and watchtowers or for its mind-blowing medieval tapestry, Château d'Angers stands out from the crowd. The forbidding exterior hides a jewel-box of riches (p384).

Clockwise from top left
1. Château de Chambord 2. Château de Chenonceau
3. Château d'Azay-le-Rideau

in black, to which she retreated when her husband, Henri III, was assassinated.

Chenonceau had a heyday under the aristocratic Madame Dupin, who made the château a centre of fashionable 18th-century society and attracted guests including Voltaire and Rousseau (the latter tutored her son). Legend also has it that it was she who single-handedly saved the château from destruction during the Revolution, thanks to her popularity with the local villagers.

The château's interior is crammed with wonderful furniture and tapestries, several stunning original tiled floors and a fabulous **art collection** including works by Tintoretto, Correggio, Rubens, Murillo, Van Dyck and Ribera.

The *pièce de resistance* is the 60m-long window-lined **Grande Gallerie** spanning the Cher, scene of many a wild party hosted by Catherine de Médicis or Madame Dupin. During WWII the Cher also marked the boundary between free and occupied France; local legend has it that the Grand Gallery was used as the escape route for many refugees fleeing the Nazi occupation.

Skip the drab wax museum (€2) and instead visit the **gardens**: it seems as if there's one of every kind imaginable (maze, English, vegetable, playground, flower...). In July and August the illuminated château and grounds are open for the Promenade Nocturne (adult/child €5/free).

Getting There & Away

The château is 34km east of Tours, 10km southeast of Amboise and 40km southwest of Blois. There are trains and buses from all three towns, and you can take boat trips from the château in summer (see p361).

MONTRICHARD

Sitting quietly under a dramatic 12th-century donjon (keep), Montrichard, 9km east of Chenonceau, offers a fizzy pit stop. The 15km-long Caves Monmousseau (☎02 54 32 35 15; www.monmousseau.com; 1 rue du Pont) are carved into the tufa stone under the donjon: a perfect 12°C environment for the local *crémant* (sparkling wine). A 45-minute tour (adult/child €2.75/free) explains the winemaking methods and ends with a copious tasting.

Amboise

POP 12,929

The childhood home of Charles VIII and the final resting place of the great Leonardo da Vinci, elegant Amboise is pleasantly perched on the southern bank of the Loire and overlooked by its fortified 15th-century château. With some seriously posh hotels and a wonderful weekend market, Amboise has become a very popular base for exploring nearby châteaux, and coach tours arrive en masse to visit da Vinci's Clos Lucé.

Sights & Activities

Go to sights early in the day to avoid crowds and buy tickets in advance at the tourist office during high season.

Château Royal d'Amboise   CASTLE
(☎02 47 57 00 98; place Michel Debré; adult/child €10/6.50; ⊙9am-6pm, 9am-5.30pm Mar, 9am-12.30pm & 2-4.45pm Jan-Feb & mid-Nov–Dec) Sprawling across a gorgeously situated rocky escarpment with panoramic views of the river and surrounding countryside, the easily defendable castle presented a formidable prospect to would-be attackers, but in fact saw little military action. It was more often used as a weekend getaway from the official royal seat at nearby Blois. Charles VIII (r 1483–98) was born and brought up here, and was responsible for the château's Italianate remodelling in 1492. François I (r 1515–47), who constructed Chambord, also grew up here alongside his sister Margaret of Angoulême, and later invited da Vinci to work at nearby ClosLucé under his patronage.

Today just a few of the original 15th- and 16th-century structures survive, notably the **Flamboyant Gothic wing** and the **Chapelle St-Hubert**, a small chapel dedicated to the patron saint of hunting (note the carved stag horns and hunting friezes outside) and believed to be the final resting place of da Vinci. The interior highlights include a **guards' room** and a vaulted **Council Chamber** decorated with the initials of Charles VIII and his wife, Anne de Bretagne. Charles died suddenly in 1498 after hitting his head on a lintel while playing *jeu de paume* (an early form of tennis); the widowed Anne was later forced to remarry the new king, Louis XII.

From 1848 to 1852, Abd el-Kader, the leader of the Algerian resistance against French colonialism, was imprisoned here with his family and entourage; a monument in the château's landscaped grounds commemorates the event.

Exit the château through **Tour Hurtault** on an ingenious sloping spiral ramp designed to allow carriages and horses to easily ascend to the château from the town below.

TOP CHOICE **Le Clos Lucé** HISTORIC MANSION
(☑02 47 57 00 73; www.vinci-closluce. com; 2 rue du Clos Lucé; adult/child €12.50/7.50; ☺9am-7pm) Leonardo da Vinci (pronounced van-see in French) took up residence in the grand manor house at Le Clos Lucé in 1516 on the invitation of François I, who was greatly enamoured with the Italian Renaissance. Already 64 by the time he arrived, da Vinci spent his time sketching, tinkering and dreaming up new contraptions: the house is jammed with scale models of many of his inventions. The expansive, beautiful gardens wind through forest and stream and are dotted with full-size replicas of his inventions including a protoautomobile, tank, bridges, hydraulic turbine and even a primitive helicopter. He died here on 2 May 1519.

Pagode de Chanteloup PAGODA
(☑02 47 57 20 97; www.pagode-chanteloup. com, in French; adult/child €8.50/6.50; ☺10am-7pm; ⊕) Two kilometres south of Amboise, the curious Pagode de Chanteloup was built between 1775 and 1778 when the odd blend of classical French architecture and Chinese motifs were all the rage. Clamber to the top for glorious views of the surrounding park and the forested Loire Valley. Picnic hampers (€12 to €26) are sold in summer, and you can while away the afternoon larking about in a rowboat or playing free outdoor games.

Parc de Mini-Châteaux MINI-CASTLES
(☑08 25 08 25 22; www.mini-chateaux.com; adult/child €13.50/9.50; ☺10am-7pm; ⊕) Intricate scale models of 44 of the Loire Valley's most famous châteaux. Squint a bit and it's almost as good as a hot-air balloon trip over the Loire for a fraction of the price.

☞ Tours

Segway SEGWAY TOUR
(per 15min €10) Zip around town on a Segway PT from the tourist office.

Train TRAIN TOUR
(adult/child €6/4.50) Six trains daily depart from the château, with French and English commentary.

🛏 Sleeping

Amboise has some of the smartest places to stay in the Loire Valley, but you'll need deep pockets and to book ahead.

Le Pavillon des Lys BOUTIQUE HOTEL €€
(☑02 47 30 01 01; www.pavillondeslys.com; 9 rue d'Orange; d €98-160; ☺) Beautiful hotel drenched with the kind of chichi style more suited to the Côte d'Azur. Take a cappuccino-coloured 18th-century town house and fill it with designer lamps, just-so furniture, roll-top baths, hi-fis and deep sofas, and you're halfway there; then chuck in a locally renowned restaurant, an elegant patio garden and boutiquey treats. Parking available.

Villa Mary B&B €€
(☑02 47 23 03 31; www.villa-mary.fr; 14 rue de la Concorde; d incl breakfast €90-120) Four tip-top rooms in an impeccably furnished 18th-century town house, crammed with beeswaxed antiques, glittering chandeliers and antique rugs. Choose from Red, Violet, Pink and Blue, all with period pieces and patterned wallpaper; two have separate bathrooms across the corridor. Parking available.

Le Clos d'Amboise HISTORIC HOTEL €€
(☑02 47 30 10 20; www.leclosamboise.com; 27 rue Rabelais; r €97-149; ☒) Another posh pad finished with oodles of style and lashings of luxurious fabrics. Features range from wood panelling to antique beds; some rooms have separate sitting areas, others original fireplaces. The best give views over the manicured grounds and pool. There's even a sauna and gym in the old stables. Parking available.

Hôtel Blason HOTEL €
(☑02 47 23 22 41; www.leblason.fr; 11 place Richelieu; s/d/tr €45/55/70; @) Quirky, creaky budget hotel, on a quiet square in a wood-fronted building. The 25 higgledy-piggledy rooms are wedged in around the corridors: most are titchy, flowery and timber-beamed. Parking available.

Camping Municipal de l'Île d'Or
CAMPGROUND €
(☑02 47 57 23 37; www.camping-amboise.com; Île d'Or; sites per adult/tent €2.50/3.50; ☺Apr-Sep; ☒) Pleasant campground on a peaceful river island. Facilities include tennis courts, ping pong and canoe hire.

Centre Charles Péguy-Auberge de Jeunesse HOSTEL €
(☑02 47 30 60 90; www.mjcamboise.fr; Île d'Or; dm €12; ☺reception 2-8pm Mon-Fri, 5-8pm Sat & Sun; @) Efficient boarding-school-style

hostel on the Île d'Or, with 72 beds mostly in three- or four-bed dorms. Treats include ping pong and bike hire.

Le Manoir Les Minimes   DESIGN HOTEL €€€
(☎02 47 30 40 40; www.manoirlesminimes.com; 34 quai Charles Guinot; d €122-195; ❀) Pricey pamper-palace set around a private courtyard that would put most châteaux to shame. Wheelchair access.

Le Vieux Manoir   B&B €€€
(☎02 47 30 41 27; www.le-vieux-manoir.com; 13 rue Rabelais; r incl breakfast €155-190; ❀) Mansion (run by expat Americans who had an award-winning Boston B&B) stuffed floor to ceiling with period charm.

✗ Eating & Drinking

Chez Bruno   REGIONAL CUISINE €
(☎02 47 57 73 49; place Michel Debré; menus from €12; ☺lunch Tue-Sun, dinner Tue-Sat) Uncork a host of local vintages in a coolly contemporary setting (white tablecloths, big gleaming glasses), accompanied by honest, inexpensive regional cooking. If you're after Loire Valley wine tips, this is the place.

L'Épicerie   TRADITIONAL FRENCH €€
(☎02 47 57 08 94; 46 place Michel Debré; menus €22-34; ☺Wed-Sun) A more time-honoured atmosphere with rich wood and neo-Renaissance decor matched by filling fare like *cuisse de lapin* (rabbit leg) and *tournedos de canard* (duck fillet).

Bigot   TEA HOUSE €
(☎02 47 57 59 32; 2 rue Nationale; ☺9am-7.30pm Tue-Fri, 8.30am-7.30pm Sat & Sun) Since 1913 this award-winning chocolatier and pâtisserie has been whipping up some of the Loire's creamiest cakes and gooiest treats: multicoloured *macarons,* handmade chocolates, éclairs and *petits fours.*

Brasserie de L'Hôtel de Ville   BRASSERIE €€
(☎02 47 57 26 30; 1-3 rue François 1er; lunch menus €9-10, dinner menus €16-25) Straight-up burgers and grills; to give the kids space to run, head to the back terrace in a quiet church square.

Café des Arts   CAFÉ €
(☎02 47 57 25 04; 32 rue Victor Hugo; meals €4-12) Locals' bar, steps from the château's gate. *Chanteurs* occasionally croon while you sip your aperitif.

Self-Catering
Food Market   MARKET €
(☺8am-1pm Fri & Sun) Fills the riverbank west of the tourist office.

Marché Plus   SUPERMARKET €
(5 quai du Général de Gaulle; ☺7am-9pm Mon-Sat, 10am-2pm Sun)

ℹ Information
Playconnect (119 rue Nationale; per hr €3; ☺3-10pm Sun & Mon, 10am-10pm Tue-Sat) Internet access.

Tourist Office (☎02 47 57 09 28; www.amboise-valdeloire.com; ☺9am-7pm Mon-Sat, 10am-1pm & 2-6pm Sun) In a riverside building opposite 7 quai du Général de Gaulle. Sells walking and cycling maps and discount ticket combinations for the château, Clos Lucé and the Pagode de Chanteloup.

ℹ Getting There & Around
Amboise is 34km southwest of Blois and 23km northeast of Tours.

BICYCLE Cycles Richard (☎02 47 57 01 79; 2 rue de Nazelles; per day €15; ☺9am-noon & 2.30-7pm Tue-Sat).

BUS Touraine Fil Vert's (p368) Line C links Amboise's post office with Tours' bus terminal (€1.70, 45 minutes, 12 daily Monday to Saturday). Two go to Chenonceau (€1.70, 15 minutes, Monday to Saturday).

TRAIN The **train station** (bd Gambetta) is across the river from the centre.

Blois €11, 20 minutes, 14 daily

Paris Gare d'Austerlitz €38 to €56, 2¼ hours, 14 daily

Paris Gare Montparnasse €107, 1¼ hours, 10 daily, TGV

Tours €11, 20 minutes, 10 daily

Château de Villandry

Completed in 1756, one of the last major Renaissance châteaux to be built in the Loire Valley, **Villandry** (☎02 47 50 02 09; www.chateauvillandry.com; château & gardens adult/child €9/5, gardens only €6/3.50; ☺château 9am-6pm, to 5.30pm Mar, to 5pm Feb & early Nov, gardens 9am-5pm, to 7.30pm summer) is more famous for what lies outside the château's walls than what lies within. Sheltered with enclosing walls, the château's glorious **landscaped gardens** are some of the finest in France, occupying over 6 hectares filled with completely manicured lime trees, ornamental vines, razor-sharp box hedges and tinkling fountains.

The original gardens and château were built by Jean le Breton, who served François I as finance minister and Italian ambassador (and supervised the construction of Chambord). During his time as ambassador, le Breton became enamoured by the art of Italian Renaissance gardening, and created his own ornamental masterpiece at his newly constructed château at Villandry.

Wandering around the pebbled walkways you'll see formal **water gardens**, a **maze**, **vineyards** and the **Jardin d'Ornement** (Ornamental Garden), which depicts various aspects of love (fickle, passionate, tender and tragic) using geometrically pruned hedges and coloured flowerbeds. The **Sun Garden** is a looser array of gorgeous multicoloured and multiscented perennials. But the highlight is the 16th-century **potager** (kitchen garden), where even the vegetables are laid out in regimental colour-coordinated fashion; plantings change in spring and autumn.

Try to visit when the gardens are in bloom, between April and October; midsummer is most spectacular.

After the gardens, the château's interior is a bit of a let-down compared with others in the region. Nevertheless, highlights include an over-the-top **oriental room**, complete with a gilded ceiling plundered from a 15th-century Moorish palace in Toledo, and a gallery of **Spanish and Flemish art**. Best of all are the bird's-eye views across the gardens and the nearby Loire and Cher rivers from the top of the **donjon** (the only remnant from the original medieval château) and the **belvedere**.

ℹ Getting There & Away

Villandry is 17km southwest of Tours and 11km northeast of Azay-le-Rideau.

BUS Touraine Fil Vert's (p368) bus V travels between Tours and Azay-le-Rideau (€1.70, 50 minutes), stopping at Villandry (30 minutes from Tours), twice daily from June to August.

TRAIN The nearest trains stop in Savonnières, 4km northeast of Villandry, going to Tours (€11, 10 minutes, one daily) and Saumur (€11, 40 minutes, three daily).

Château de Langeais

In contrast to the showy splendour of many châteaux, Langeais (☏02 47 96 72 60; adult/child €8.50/5; ◷9.30am-6.30pm, to 5.30pm Feb & Mar, 9am-7pm Jul & Aug) was constructed first and foremost as a fortress, built in the 1460s to cut off the likely invasion route from Brittany. It is fantastically preserved inside and out, so it remains every inch the medieval stronghold: crenellated ramparts and defensive towers jut out from the jumbled rooftops of the surrounding village.

One of the few châteaux with its original medieval interior, the castle (reached via a creaky drawbridge), has 15th-century furniture throughout its flag-stoned rooms. Among many fine Flemish and Aubusson **tapestries** look out for one from 1530 depicting astrological signs; an intricate *Les Mille Fleurs;* and the famous *Les Neuf Preux* series portraying nine 'worthy' knights who represent the epitome of medieval courtly honour.

In one room, a waxwork display illustrates the marriage of Charles VIII and Anne of Brittany, which was held here on 6 December 1491 and brought about the historic union of France and Brittany.

Up top, stroll the castle's **ramparts** for a soldier's-eye view of the town: gaps underfoot enabled boiling oil, rocks and ordure to be dumped on attackers. Across the château's interior courtyard, climb to the top of the ruined **keep**, constructed by the 10th-century warlord, Count Foulques Nerra. Built in 944, it's the oldest such structure in France.

🛏 Sleeping & Eating

The village of Langeais (population 4031), with its peaceful walking streets, is a fun pit stop in the midst of the mayhem of castle-hunting. The town's market bustles on Sunday mornings.

Reserve ahead to stay at Anne de Bretagne (☏02 47 96 08 52; www.chambresdhotes -langeais.fr, in French; 27 rue Anne de Bretagne; d incl breakfast €60-66) in a town house just down the street from the castle's drawbridge. You can dine at Au Coin des Halles (☏02 47 96 37 25; 9 rue Gambetta; lunch menus €15-18, dinner menus €21-49; ◷lunch Fri-Tue, dinner Thu-Tue) the village's elegant bistro, or grab a quick bite, across from the castle, at the sinfully decadent La Maison de Rabelais (☏02 47 96 82 20; ◷closed Mon Sep-Jun) with its rich pastries and potent coffees.

ℹ Getting There & Away

Langeais is 14km west of Villandry and about 31km southwest of Tours. Its train station, 400m from the château, is on the line linking Tours (€11, 15 minutes, five daily) and Saumur (€11, 25 minutes).

Château d'Azay-le-Rideau

Romantic, moat-ringed Azay-le-Rideau (☎02 47 45 42 04; adult/child €7.50/free; ⏰9.30am-6pm, to 7pm Jul & Aug, 10am-12.30pm & 2-5.30pm Oct-Mar) is wonderfully adorned with slender turrets, geometric windows and decorative stonework, wrapped up within a shady landscaped park. Built in the 1500s on a natural island in middle of the River Indre, the château is one of the Loire's loveliest: Honoré de Balzac called it a 'multifaceted diamond set in the River Indre'.

Its most famous feature is its open **loggia staircase**, in the Italian style, overlooking the central courtyard and decorated with the salamanders and ermines of François I and Queen Claude. The interior is mostly 19th century, remodelled by the Marquis de Biencourt from the original 16th-century château built by Gilles Berthelot, chief treasurer for François I. In July and August, a **son et lumière** (one of the Loire's oldest and best) is projected onto the castle walls nightly. Multilanguage audioguides cost €4.50 and seven daily guided tours in French are free.

ℹ️ Getting There & Away

Château d'Azay-le-Rideau is 26km southwest of Tours. The D84 and D17, on either side of the Indre, are a delight to cycle.

BUS Touraine Fil Vert's (p368) bus V travels from Tours to Azay-le-Rideau (€1.70, 50 minutes) twice daily June to August. An SNCF bus stops near the château.

TRAIN The station is 2.5km from the château. Connections include Tours (€11, 20 to 50 minutes, six daily) and Chinon (€11, 20 minutes).

Château d'Ussé

This main claim to fame of the elaborate Château d'Ussé (☎02 47 95 54 05; www.chateaudusse.fr; adult/child €13/4; ⏰10am-7pm Apr-Aug, to 6pm Sep–mid-Nov & mid-Feb–Mar, closed mid-Nov–mid-Feb) is as the inspiration for Charles Perrault's classic fairy tale, *La Belle au Bois Dormant* (better known to English-speakers as *Sleeping Beauty*).

Ussé's creamy white towers and slate roofs jut out from the edge of the glowering forest of Chinon, offering sweeping views across the flat Loire countryside and the flood-prone River Indre. The castle mainly dates from the 15th and 16th centuries, built on top of a much earlier 11th-century fortress. Its most notable features are the wonderful formal gardens designed by Le Nôtre, architect of Versailles. A popular local rumour claims Ussé was one of Walt Disney's inspirations when he dreamed up his magic kingdom (check out the Disney logo and you might agree).

You may be satisfied just looking at the château from outside, since refurbished rooms are starting to show their age; they include a series of dodgy wax models recounting the tale of *Sleeping Beauty*.

Ussé is on the edge of the small riverside village of Rigny-Ussé, about 14km north of Chinon. There is no public transport.

Loches

POP 7076

The historic town of Loches spirals around the base of its medieval citadel, another forbidding stronghold begun by Foulques Nerra in the 10th century, and later enlarged by Charles VII. Loches earned a last-

---

WORTH A TRIP

MUSÉE BALZAC

Meander down the Indre Valley along the tiny D84, passing mansions, villages and troglodyte caves, and 7km east of Azay-le-Rideau you come to sweet Saché. Once home to American sculptor Alexander Calder (one of his mobiles sits in the town square), it still celebrates the life of long-time inhabitant, Honoré de Balzac (1799–1850), author of *La Comédie Humaine*. The lovely Musée Balzac (☎02 47 26 86 50; www.musee-balzac.fr; adult/child €4.50/3; ⏰10am-6pm Apr-Sep, closed lunchtime & Tue Oct-Mar) inhabits the town's château where Balzac was a habitual guest of his parents' friend, Jean Margonne. On a quiet slope in the lush river valley, the castle features original furnishings, manuscripts, letters and first editions. Feeling the peace, you can easily imagine Balzac escaping his hectic Parisian life and reclining here in his cosy bed, a board on his knees, writing for 12 hours a day – as he did.

ing footnote in the history books in 1429, when Joan of Arc persuaded Charles VII to march north from here to belatedly claim the French crown, but these days the town is a sleepy kind of place, best known for its lively Saturday morning market.

⊙ Sights

From rue de la République, the old gateway **Porte Picois** leads through the cobbled Vieille Ville towards the **Porte Royale** (Royal Gate), flanked by two forbidding 13th-century towers, and the sole entrance to the **Cité Royale de Loches**, aka the citadel.

As you climb uphill you'll pass the **Maison Lansyer** (adult/child €3/2; ⊙10am-noon & 2-6pm Wed-Mon), the former home of the landscape painter Emmanuel Lansyer (1838–93), featuring his paintings alongside works by Canaletto, Millet, Piranese and Delacroix.

Logis Royal   CASTLE
(☑02 47 59 01 32; www.chateau-loches.fr; adult/child €7/4.50; ⊙9am-7pm Apr-Sep, 9.30am-5pm Oct-Mar) At the northern end of the citadel sits the royal residence of Charles VII and his successors, later used as a prison until the 1920s. The basement holds a circular chamber where the unfortunate Cardinal Balue was supposedly kept suspended from the ceiling in a wooden cage for betraying Louis XI. In fact, it was more likely a grain store, although you can see a replica of the cardinal's actual cage elsewhere in the castle, as well as a chilling **Salle des Questions** (otherwise known as a torture chamber). Louis XI also constructed the notorious **Tour Ronde** (Round Tower) and **Tour Martelet** for incarcerating prisoners during the Revolution (read some of their graffiti etched on the walls).

At the southern end of the promontory is the 36m-high **donjon** built in the 11th century by Foulques Nerra. Though the interior floors have fallen away, dizzying catwalks allow you to climb right to the top for fantastic views across town.

Collegiale St-Ours   CHURCH
This church contains the tomb of Agnés Sorel, Charles VII's mistress, who lived in the château during her illicit affair with the king. Notoriously beautiful and fiercely intelligent, Agnés earned many courtly enemies due to her powerful influence over Charles. Having borne three daughters, she died in mysterious circumstances while pregnant with their fourth child. The of-

ficial cause was dysentery, although some scientists have speculated that elevated levels of mercury in her body indicate she may have been poisoned.

🛏 Sleeping & Eating

Le Moulin L'Étang   HISTORIC HOTEL €€
(☑02 47 59 15 10; 1 rue du Moulin, Chanceaux-près-Loches; d €70-80, meals from €30; ☒) This lovingly converted mill, 3.2km west of Loches along the N143, has thick-beamed rooms peeking out through blue shutters onto a private millpond and a 2.8-hectare garden. Home-cooked food is made with local ingredients.

Hôtel de France   HOTEL, RESTAURANT €
(☑02 47 59 00 32; www.hoteldefranceloches. com; 6 rue Picois; d €50-62, menus €18-50) An arched gateway leads into the paved courtyard of this old *relais de poste* (post house), now a trim if rather tired Logis de France. The best rooms are above the restaurant, which serves traditional French standbys.

Food Market   MARKET €
(⊙7am-3pm Wed, 7am-1pm Sat) Fills rue de la République and surrounding streets.

ℹ Information

Éspace Public Numerique (☑02 47 59 49 85; 24 av des Bas-Clos; per hr €2.15; ⊙2-8pm Tue, Thu & Fri, 10am-1pm & 2-7pm Wed, 1-5.30pm Sat May-Sep) Internet access.

Tourist office (☑02 47 91 82 82; www.loches -tourainecotesud.com; place de la Marne; ⊙9am-12.30pm & 2-6.30pm Mon-Sat, from 10am Sun, closed Sun Mar & Apr, Oct-Feb) Beside the river near the end of rue de la République.

ℹ Getting There & Around

Loches is 67km southwest of Blois and 41km southeast of Tours. Trains and SNCF buses link the train station, across the River Indre from the tourist office, with Tours (€11, one hour, six daily).

Chinon

POP 8663

Peacefully placed along the northern bank of the Vienne and dominated by its hulking hillside château, Chinon is best known as one of the Loire's main wine-producing areas. **Chinon AOC** (www.chinon.com) cabernet franc vineyards stretch along both sides of the river. Within the steep muddle of white

WORTH A TRIP

MUSÉE RABELAIS

Follow the signs 9km southwest of Chinon, to the outskirts of Seuilly to find La Devinière, the farm where François Rabelais – doctor, Franciscan friar, theoretician and author – was born (sometime between 1483 and 1494; no one is sure). Set among the fields and vineyards with sweeping views to the private château in Coudray Montpensier, this farm inspired the settings for Rabelais' five satirical, erudite Gargantua and Pantagruel novels. The rambling buildings of the farmstead hold the Musée Rabelais (www.musee-rabelais.fr; adult/child €4.50/3; ☺10am-12.30pm & 2-6pm Wed-Mon), with thoughtful exhibits including early editions of Rabelais' work and a Matisse portrait of the author from 1951. A winding cavern lurks beneath.

tufa houses and black slate rooftops you'll discover an interesting medieval quarter.

◉ Sights

Forteresse Royale de Chinon　　CASTLE
(☎02 47 93 13 45; www.forteresse-chinon.fr; adult/child €7/4.50; ☺9am-7pm) In July 2010 the castle emerged from one of the region's largest restoration projects (at a cost of €14.5 million). It is split into three sections separated by dry moats. The 12th-century **Fort St-Georges** and the **Logis Royal** (Royal Lodgings) remain from the time when the Plantagenet court of Henry II and Eleanor of Aquitaine was held here. The 14th-century **Tour de l'Horloge** (Clock Tower) houses a collection of Joan of Arc memorabilia; she came here in 1429 to meet the future Charles VII. There's a wonderful valley panorama from the top of the 13th-century **Fort du Coudray** and a small historical exhibition in the **Château du Milieu** (the Middle Castle).

Entry to the castle is across from the free lift ascending from the old town.

Old Town　　HISTORIC QUARTER
The author François Rabelais (c 1483–1553), whose works include the Gargantua and Pantagruel series grew up in Chinon; you'll see Rabelais-related names dotted all around the old town, which offers a fine cross-section of medieval architecture, best seen along **rue Haute St-Maurice** and **rue Voltaire**. Look out for the remarkable Hôtel du Gouverneur (rue Haute St-Maurice), an impressive town house with a double-flighted staircase ensconced behind a carved gateway, and the nearby Gothic Palais du Bailliage, the former residence of Chinon's bailiwick (now occupied by the Hostellerie Gargantua). The tourist office has a free walking-tour leaflet and offers guided tours (adult/child €4.70/2.50).

Caves Painctes de Chinon　　WINE CELLAR
(☎02 47 93 30 44; impasse des Caves Painctes; admission €3; ☺guided tours 11am, 3pm, 4.30 & 6pm Tue-Sun) Hidden at the end of a cobbled alleyway off rue Voltaire, these former quarries were converted into wine cellars during the 15th century. The Confrérie des Bons Entonneurs Rabelaisiens, a brotherhood of local winegrowers, runs Tours of the *caves* in July and August.

Musée d'Art et d'Histoire　　MUSEUM
(44 rue Haute St-Maurice; adult/child €3.50/2; ☺2-6pm Thu-Mon, closed mid-Nov–Feb) Art and archaeology exhibits from prehistory to the 19th century relating to Chinon and its environs.

⌂ Sleeping

Hôtel Diderot　　HISTORIC HOTEL €
[TOP CHOICE] (☎02 47 93 18 87; www.hoteldiderot.com; 4 rue de Buffon; s €45-62, d €55-79; ☎) This gorgeous shady town house is tucked amid luscious rose-filled gardens and crammed with polished antiques. The friendly owners impart the kind of glowing charm you'd expect of a hotel twice the price. Rooms are all individually styled, from over-the-top Napoleonic to stripped-back art deco and have large flat-screen TVs. Parking €6.

Hostellerie Gargantua　　HISTORIC HOTEL €€
(☎02 47 93 04 71; www.hotel-gargantua.com; 73 rue Haute St-Maurice; s/d €53/79; ☎) Harry Potter would feel right at home at this turret-topped medieval mansion. The simple, offbeat hotel has spiral staircases, pitch-dark wood and solid stone. Superior rooms are worth the cash, including Grangousier with its fireplace and four-poster, and Badebec with its oak beams and château views. Parking €5.50.

Hôtel Le Plantagenêt
HOTEL €€

(☎02 47 93 36 92; www.hotel-plantagenet.com; 12 place Jeanne d'Arc; s €58-70, d €65-80, tr €90; ❄✿) A basic, dated but perfectly service-able hotel halfway between centre and station, with rooms spread over three buildings. The best is the *maison bourgeoise*. Some air-con. Parking €7.

Eating & Drinking

Reserve ahead on weekends and during high season.

TOP CHOICE Les Années 30 TRADITIONAL FRENCH €€
(☎02 47 93 37 18; 78 rue Voltaire; menus €27-43; ✿lunch Thu-Mon, dinner Thu-Tue) Expect the kind of meal you came to France to eat: exquisite attention to flavours and detail, served up in relaxed intimacy. The interior dining room is golden-lit downstairs and cool blue upstairs; in summer dine under the streetside pergola, in the heart of the old quarter. The menu ranges from traditional coq au vin and duck with cherry coulis to unusual choices such as wild boar.

Restaurant au Chapeau Rouge
TRADITIONAL FRENCH €€

(☎02 47 98 08 08; place du Général de Gaulle; lunch menus €19.50, dinner menus €27-50; ✿lunch Tue-Sun, dinner Tue-Sat) There's an air of a Left Bank brasserie hanging around the Red Hat, sheltered behind red and gold awnings. Chatting families dig into hare fondant, smoked fish and other countrified dishes.

La Treille BISTRO €€
(☎02 47 93 07 71; 4 place Jeanne d'Arc; lunch menus from €16, mains €16; ✿lunch Thu-Tue, dinner Fri-Wed) Descend a couple of stairs into this tiny bistro rife with delicious smells. Specialties include monkfish à l'orange.

Self-Catering

Food Market WEEKLY MARKET €
(place Jeanne d'Arc; ✿Thu morning)

Carrefour SUPERMARKET €
(22 place du Général de Gaulle; ✿7am-10pm Mon-Sat, 9am-1pm Sun)

ⓘ Information

Tourist Office (☎02 47 93 17 85; place Hof-heïm; ✿10am-7pm)

ⓘ Getting There & Away

Chinon is 47km southwest of Tours and 21km southwest of Azay-le-Rideau.

BUS Touraine Fil Vert's bus (p368) **TF** (€1.70) connects Chinon, Azay-le-Rideau and Langeais (one to four Monday to Friday).

TRAIN The train station is 1km east of place du Général de Gaulle. Trains or SNCF buses (12 daily, six on weekends) go to Tours (€11, 45 to 70 minutes) and Azay-le-Rideau (€11, 25 minutes).

ANJOU

In Anjou, Renaissance châteaux give way to chalky white tufa cliffs concealing an astonishing underworld of wine cellars, mushroom farms and art sculptures. Above ground, black slate roofs pepper the vine-rich land from which some of the Loire's best wines are produced.

Angers, the historic capital of Anjou, is famous for its fortified hilltop château and its stunning medieval tapestry. Architectural gems in Anjou's crown include Angers cathedral and, to the southeast, the Romanesque Abbaye de Fontevraud. Europe's highest concentration of troglodyte dwellings dot the banks of the Loire around cosmopolitan Saumur.

The area along the Rivers Loire, Authion and Vienne from Angers southeast to Azay-le-Rideau form the Parc Naturel Régional Loire-Anjou-Touraine.

Saumur
POP 29,587

There's an air of Parisian sophistication around Saumur, but also a sense of laid-back contentment. The food is good, the wine is good, the spot is good – and the Saumurites know it. The town is renowned for its École Nationale d'Équitation, a national cavalry school that's been home to the crack riders of the Cadre Noir since 1828. Soft white tufa cliffs stretch along the riverbanks east and west of town, pock-marked by the unusual man-made caves known as *habitations troglodytes*.

◉ Sights & Activities

Base de Loisirs Millocheau (☎02 41 50 62 72; www.canoe.saumur.free.fr) rents canoes and kayaks by reservation.

TOP CHOICE École Nationale d'Équitation
RIDING SCHOOL

(National Equestrian School; ☎02 41 53 50 60; www.cadrenoir.fr; rte de Marson; adult/child

€7/5) Anchored in France's academic-military riding tradition, Saumur has been an equine centre since 1593. Three kilometres west of town, outside of sleepy St-Hilaire-St-Florent, the École Nationale d'Équitation is one of France's foremost riding academies, responsible for training the country's Olympic teams and members of the elite Cadre Noir, distinguished by their special black jackets, caps, gold spurs and three golden wings on their whips. The Cadre Noir train both the school's instructors and horses (which take around 5½ years to achieve display standard) and are famous for their astonishing discipline and acrobatic manoeuvres (like 'airs above ground'), which are all performed without stirrups.

Advance reservations are essential for the one-hour guided visits (four to 10 per day; enquire about the availability of English-language tours). If you happen to be in town for one of the semi-monthly Cadre Noir presentations (adult/child €16/9) do not miss it: they are like astonishing horse ballets. Check the website for dates.

Le Château de Saumur   CASTLE
(②02 41 40 24 40; adult/child €3/2.50; ☺10am-1pm & 2-5.30pm Tue-Sun Apr-Oct) Lording above the town's rooftops, Saumur's fairytale château was largely built during the 13th century by Louis XI, and has variously served as a dungeon, fortress and country residence, but its defensive heritage took

a hefty knock in 2001 when a large chunk of the western ramparts collapsed without warning, triggering an enormous restoration project that has already lasted 10 years and still shows no sign of completion. Two halls are open with exhibits on equitation and pottery and you can wander the grounds outside.

Musée des Blindés   MILITARY MUSEUM
(②02 41 83 69 95; www.museedesblindes.fr, in French; 1043 rte de Fontevraud; adult/child €7/4; ☺10am-6pm) Want to see more than equine military history? Gearheads love this comprehensive museum of over 200 tanks and military vehicles. Children are allowed to climb on some of them. Examples include many WWI tanks such as the Schneider and dozens of WWII models, such as the Hotchkiss H39, Panzers and an Issoise infantry tractor.

Distillerie Combier   DISTILLERY
(②02 41 40 23 00; www.combier.fr; 48 rue Beaurepaire; adult €3; ☺3-4 guided visits per day, 10am-12.30pm & 2-7pm, closed Mon Oct-May, Sun Nov & Jan-Mar) Though it's existed for 175 years, it is only recently that this distillery has resurrected authentic absinthe (see p388), the famous firewater. Taste it alongside other liqueurs including Royal Combier, Triple Sec and Pastis d'Antan.

FREE Musée de la Cavalerie   CAVALRY MUSEUM
(②02 41 83 69 23; http://museeca valerie.free.fr, in French; place Charles de Fou-

---

STÉPHANE MICHON: CURATOR OF THE MUSHROOM MUSEUM

There are more than 1500km of subterranean caves around Saumur (see also p384), which provide the perfect environment for cultivating mushrooms: a constant year-round temperature (of 13°C to 14°C) and very high humidity (more than 90%). Thanks to Saumur's equestrian connections, we also have ready access to plenty of top-quality fertiliser for our mushroom crops! The caves keep us sheltered from the rain, but they can be quite chilly and damp to work in. I've also nearly lost myself on several occasions – hardly surprising really, since there are dozens of kilometres of caves around Saumur, and no maps!

Varieties

In addition to the *champignon de Paris* (button mushroom), some of our other famous fungi include the *pied bleu* (blue foot), the shiitake and the *pleurote* (oyster mushroom).

How to Eat Them

For me, the best way to eat them is simply either fried with parsley and oil, or in the local speciality, *Galipette*: a large *champignon de Paris*, grilled and then stuffed with goat's cheese, parsley butter or *rillettes*.

cauld; ⊙9am-noon & 2-5pm Mon-Thu, 2-6pm Sat-Sun) Housed in the old military stables of the Cadre Noir, this museum traces the history of the French cavalry from 1445 in the time of Charles VII to modern tanks.

Langlois – Chateau · WINE SCHOOL

(⊠02 41 40 21 40; www.langlois-chateau.fr; 3 rue Léopold Palustre, St-Hilaire-St-Florent; classes adult/child €2/free, extended classes €225; ⊙10am-12.30pm & 2-6pm) Founded in 1912 and specialising in Crémant de Loire sparkling wines, this domaine is open for tours, tasting and a visit to the caves and offers an introduction to winemaking at its wine school. See p350 for more on Loire Valley wines.

☞ Tours

Boat Trip · RIVER TOUR

(⊠06 63 22 87 00; www.bateaux-nantais.fr, in French; adult/child €9/4.50; ⊙2.30-4pm Jun-Sep) The *Saumur-Loire* leaves from across from the town hall on 1¼-hour cruises. Also see p361.

Carriage Rides · CARRIAGE TOUR

(adult/child €7/4; ⊙2-5pm Sat-Thu) Depart from place de la République. Also operate on Fridays in July and August.

⌯ Sleeping

Saumur's accommodation is of a high calibre. Reserve ahead.

TOP CHOICE Château de Verrières · CASTLE HOTEL €€€

(⊠02 41 38 05 15; www.chateau-verrieres.com; 53 rue d'Alsace; r €150-210, ste €260-290; 🅿🕸🖥) Every one of the 10 rooms in this impeccably wonderful 1890 château, ensconced within the woods and ponds of a 1.6-hectare English park, is different. But the feel is universally plush and kingly: antique writing desks, original artwork, wood panelling and fantastic bathrooms. Some, like the top-of-the-line Rising Sun suite (with a dash of modish Japanese minimalism), have views of the sun rising over the Saumur château. Regal with a capital R. Parking free.

Château Beaulieu · CASTLE B&B €€

(⊠02 41 50 83 52; www.chateaudebeaulieu.fr; 98 rte de Montsoreau; d incl breakfast €80-120, ste €140-200; 🕸🖥) Irish expats Mary and Conor welcome you to their sprawling home with a glass of bubbling *crémant*. Rooms are imaginatively and comfortably done up

and the mood among the generally gregarious clientele is one of extended family. Sun yourself by the pool or play billiards in the grand salon. Parking free.

Hôtel Saint-Pierre · HISTORIC HOTEL €€

(⊠02 41 50 33 00; www.saintpierresaumur.com; 8 rue Haute St-Pierre; r €70-155; 🕸🖥) Squeezed down a miniscule alleyway opposite the cathedral, this effortlessly smart hideaway mixes heritage architecture with modern-day comfort: pale stone, thick rugs and vintage lamps sit happily alongside mini-bars and satellite TV. Tiled mosaics line the bathrooms and black-and-white dressage photos enliven the lobby.

Hôtel de Londres · HOTEL €

(⊠02 41 51 23 98; www.lelondres.com; 48 rue d'Orléans; s €40-45, d €48-70; @🖥) Snag one of the refurbished rooms in jolly checks, crisp blues and sunshine yellows, all with gleaming bathrooms and thoughtful spoils including afternoon tea and a well-stocked comic library. Parking €4.

Camping l'Île d'Offard · CAMPGROUND €

(⊠02 41 40 30 00; www.cvtloisirs.com; rue de Verden; sites for 2 people €16-27; ⊙Mar-Sep; 🖥🏊) Well-equipped and very pretty campground on a natural river island, about 1.5km from town.

✘ Eating

Saumur is one of the culinary centres of the Loire; book ahead.

TOP CHOICE Le Pot de Lapin · MODERN FRENCH €€

(⊠02 41 67 12 86; 35 rue Rabelais; tapas €1.50-5, mains €11-19; ⊙Tue-Sat) The jaunty strains of Django Reinhardt's guitar waft from the cheery dining room through the wine bar and onto the streetside terrace. Chef Olivier serves the tables himself, proposing perfect wine pairings, and the food – well, the food is decadent. Spanish meets French in a perfectly seasoned shrimp brochette, and you'll feel sinful but unrepentant if you order the coulis-drizzled foie gras. Somehow the vibe here is, simply put, happiness – happy staff, happy clients.

Le Gambetta · GASTRONOMIC €€

(⊠02 41 67 66 66; www.restaurantlegambetta.com, in French; 12 rue Gambetta; lunch menus €20-27, other menus €27-82; ⊙lunch Thu-Tue, dinner Mon-Tue & Thu-Sat) OK, prepare yourself. This is another place to write home about: a fantastic regional restaurant combining

TROGLODYTE VALLEY

For centuries the creamy white tufa cliffs around Saumur have been a key source of local building materials; in fact, many of the Loire's grandest châteaux were constructed from this soft stone. The rocky bluffs also provided shelter and storage for the local inhabitants, leading to the development of a unique *culture troglodyte* (cave culture), as in the Vézère Valley in the Dordogne. The cool, dank caves were developed into proper houses *(habitations troglodytes)* and perfect natural cellars for everyone from vintners to mushroom farmers (p384). Eat your heart out, Bilbo Baggins!

Find caves lining the Loire east and west of Saumur and radiating from the village of Doué-la-Fontaine; bring a sweater as they remain cool (13°C) year-round.

Rochemenier (☑02 41 59 18 15; www.troglo.info; adult/child €5/2.60; ☺9.30am-7pm Apr-Oct, 2-6pm Sat-Sun Nov, Feb & Mar) Inhabited right up until the 1930s, this abandoned village, 6km north of Doué-la-Fontaine, is one of the best examples of troglodytic culture. Also explore the remains of two farmsteads (complete with houses, stables and an underground chapel).

Les Perrières (☑02 41 59 71 29; www.ville-douelafontaine.fr/perrieres, in French; Doué-la-Fontaine; adult/child €4.50/3; ☺2-6.30pm Tue-Sun, closed Oct-May) Former stone quarries sometimes called the 'cathedral caves' due to their lofty caverns.

Les Maisons Troglodytes (☑02 41 59 00 32; adult/child €5.50/3; ☺9.30am-7pm, closed Nov-Feb) More hobbit-style houses where the only external traces of the underground dwellings are the chimneys poking up from the ground. In Forges, 4km northeast of Doué-la-Fontaine.

Troglodytes et Sarcophages (☑06 77 77 06 94; www.troglo-sarcophages.fr; Doué-la-Fontaine; adult/child €4.50/3; ☺2.30-7pm Jun-Aug, Sat-Sun May) A merovingian mine where sarcophagi were produced from the 6th to the 9th centuries. Atmospheric lantern-lit tours (adult/child €7.50/5.50) are conducted on Tuesday and Friday at 8.30pm in July and August, by reservation.

Troglo des Pommes Tapées (☑02 41 51 48 30; www.letroglodespommestapees.fr; 11 rue des Ducs d'Anjou, Turquant; adult/child €5.50/3.50; ☺10am-12.30pm & 2-6.30pm Wed-Sun, closed mid-Nov–mid-Feb) One of the last places in France to produce the traditional dried apples known as *pommes tapées*. Visit and taste 10km southeast of Saumur.

You'll also find some fantastical pieces of artwork sprinkled around the valley:

Hélice Terrestre de l'Orbière (☑02 41 57 95 92; adult/child €4/2; ☺11am-8pm) Startling piece of rock art sculpted by local artist Jacques Warminski (1946–96). In St-Georges-des-Sept-Voies, 23km northwest of Saumur.

La Cave aux Sculptures (☑02 41 59 15 40; Dénezé-sous-Doué; adult/child €4/2.50; ☺10.30am-1pm & 2-6.30pm Tue-Sun Apr-Oct) Full of leering faces, contorted figures and bestial gargoyles carved sometime between the 16th and 17th century. Six kilometres north of Doué-la-Fontaine.

refined elegance and knock-your-socks-off creative food. The parade of exquisitely presented dishes ranges from roast pork loin in a demi-glace with a strip of perfect polenta to surprisingly delicious wasabi *crème brûlée*. Some menus have bespoke wine pairings (from €25.50) and all are punctuated by surprise treats from the kitchen.

L'Alchimiste　　　MODERN FRENCH **€€**
(☑02 41 67 65 18; 6 rue de Lorraine; menus €15-18; ☺lunch Thu-Tue, dinner Mon-Tue & Thu-Sat)

Simple, clean flavours are the hallmark of this sleek bistro. As a result, the flavours of the fresh ingredients sing out: from tomato gazpacho to fresh fish.

L'Amuse Bouche　　　TRADITIONAL FRENCH **€€**
(☑02 41 67 79 63; 512 rte Montsoreau, Dampierre-sur-Loire; lunch menus €10, dinner menus €21-58; ☺lunch Thu-Tue, dinner Mon & Thu-Sat)

Tuck into delicious, fresh meals prepared with creativity, like *chèvre* with a hint of honey where you don't expect it. The crimson and silver dining room with colourful oil paintings manages to be both cheery and homey and the outside terrace is great in summer. Kids' *menu* €10.

❶ Information

Tourist office (☏02 41 40 20 60; www.saumur-tourisme.com; place de la Bilange; ◷9.15am-12.30pm & 2-6pm)

❶ Getting There & Around

BICYCLE Détours de Loire (☏02 41 53 01 01; 1 rue David d'Angers; ◷9am-12.30pm & 4.30-6.30pm) rents bikes.

BUS See p387 for buses from Angers. **Agglobus** (☏02 41 51 11 87; www.agglobus.fr, in French) runs local buses (tickets €1.35).

TRAIN Services connect Tours (€15 to €23, 50 minutes, 15 daily) and Angers (€11 to €19, 25 minutes, nine daily).

East of Saumur

The tufa bluffs east of Saumur are home to some of the area's main wine producers: you'll see notable vineyards and vintners (www.producteurs-de-saumur-champigny.fr, in French) along the riverside D947, most offering free tasting sessions from around 10am to 6pm from spring to autumn. For example, you'll pass Le Grande Vignolle (☏02 41 38 16 44; www.filliatreau.com; Turquant), a domaine and tasting room in grand tufa caves.

Other sights include mushroom caves (p384).

MONTSOREAU & CANDES-ST-MARTIN

Château de Montsoreau (☏02 41 67 12 60; adult/child €8.50/5.40; ◷10am-7pm, closed mid-Nov-Feb; ⊞), beautifully situated on the edge of the Loire, houses a dynamic museum exploring the castle's history and the river trade that once sustained the Loire Valley (expect sound, lights and drama). Staff provide a treasure hunt for kids. The castle itself, blessed with great views, was built in 1455 by one of Charles VII's advisers, and later became famous thanks to an Alexandre Dumas novel, *La Dame de Monsoreau*.

Maison du Parc (☏02 41 38 38 88; www.parc-loire-anjou-touraine.fr; 15 av de la Loire, Montsoreau; ◷9.30am-7pm) for the Parc Naturel Régional Loire-Anjou-Touraine is a clearinghouse of information on the 2530-sq-km regional park whose mission is to protect both the landscape and the area's extraordinary architectural patrimony.

The nearby village of Candes-St-Martin occupies an idyllic spot at the confluence of the Vienne and the Loire. The 9th- to 15th-century church venerates the spot where St Martin died and was buried in 397 (though his body was later moved to Tours). Candes eventually became a major pilgrimage point and thus bears his name.

Climb the tiny streets and you'll come to inhabited cave dwellings and a view over the rivers. La Brocante Gourmand (20 rue Trochet; sandwich €3; ◷10.30am-8.30pm Tue-Sun), a teahouse and used-book shop, makes for a pastoral, unique hilltop pit stop.

See p361 for boat cruises.

FONTEVRAUD-L'ABBAYE

Abbaye Royale de Fontevraud

HISTORIC ABBEY

(☏02 41 51 71 41; www.abbaye-fontevraud.com; adult/child €8.50/7, tour or audioguide €4; ◷9.30am-6.30pm) Until its closure in 1793 this huge 12th-century complex was one of the largest ecclesiastical centres in Europe. Unusually, both nuns and monks were governed by an abbess (generally a lady of noble birth retiring from public life). The extensive grounds include a **chapter room** with murals of the Passion of Christ by Thomas Pot, dormitories, workrooms and prayer halls, as well as a spooky underground sewer system and a wonderful barrel-vaulted **refectory**, where the monks and nuns would eat in silence while being read the scriptures.

Look out, too, for the multichimneyed, rocket-shaped **kitchen**, built entirely from stone to make it fireproof.

The highlight is undoubtedly the massive, movingly simple **abbey church**, notable for its soaring pillars, Romanesque domes and the polychrome tombs of four illustrious Plantagenets: Henry II, King of England (r 1154–89); his wife Eleanor of Aquitaine (who retired to Fontevraud following Henry's death); their son Richard the Lionheart; and his wife Isabelle of Angoulême.

After the Revolution, the buildings became a prison, in use until 1963. Author Jean Gênet was imprisoned at Fontevraud for stealing, and later wrote *Miracle de la Rose* (1946) based on his experiences.

MUSHROOM MADNESS

Mushroom lovers – or those willing to be seduced by the charms of *champignons* – can learn more, tour caves and taste samples in the Saumar area.

Musée du Champignon (Mushroom Museum; ☏02 41 50 31 55; www.musee-du-champignon.com; rte de Gennes; adult/child €7/4.50; ⊙10am-7pm Feb–mid-Nov) Get acquainted with the fabulous fungus at the museum tucked into a cave at the western edge of St-Hilaire-St-Florent.

La Cave aux Moines (☏02 41 67 95 64; www.cave-aux-moines.com; Chênehutte-Trèves-Cunault; menus €20-23; ⊙lunch Sat-Sun, dinner Fri-Sun) Besides tours of the cave (adult/child €4.50/3), there's a restaurant with all manner of mushrooms, snails and *fouées*, the local fire-baked breads. Kids' *menu* €8. It's 9km northwest of Saumur.

Le Saut aux Loups (☏02 41 51 70 30; www.troglo-sautauxloups.com; Montsoreau; plates €9-15; ⊙lunch Wed-Mon, dinner Fri-Sat) Another chance to explore caves (adult/child €5.90/4.50) and tuck into fresh fungi, 12km southeast of Saumur.

Chez Teresa　　　　　　B&B, TEAROOM €

(☏02 41 51 21 24; www.chezteresa.fr; 6 av Rochechouart; d incl breakfast €49-55, menus €12-15) Keeping up Fontevraud's English connections, this frilly little teashop is run by an expat Englishwoman with a passion for traditional teatime fare: tea for two with sandwiches, scones and cakes is just €8.50, and there are cute upstairs rooms if you fancy staying overnight.

Hôtel Abbaye Royale de Fontevraud

HOTEL, RESTAURANT €€

(☏02 41 51 73 16; www.hotelfp-fontevraud.com; r €78-122, menus €27-40; ⊙lunch Sun, dinner nightly, closed Nov-Mar; ☏) The gastronomic restaurant in the old infirmary at the abbey serves seriously *haute cuisine* (pigeon, duck, lobster, foie gras). Rooms are a bit corporate in comparison to the stellar food, but comfy nonetheless.

Angers

POP 155,700

Often dubbed 'Black Angers' due to the local dark slate used for its roofs, the lively riverside city is famous for its tapestries: the 14th-century *Tenture de l'Apocalypse* in the city's château and the 20th-century *Chant du Monde* at the Jean Lurçat museum. A bustling old town, with many pedestrianised streets and a thriving café culture, makes it a fun eastern gateway to the Loire Valley.

◉ Sights & Activities

A small **tourist train** (☏02 41 23 50 00; adult/child €6/4; ⊙daily May-Sep, weekends Easter-Apr), departing from the château, makes a circuit through the city's highlights.

TOP CHOICE **Château d'Angers**　　　CASTLE

(☏02 41 86 48 77; 2 promenade du Bout du Monde; adult/child €8/free; ⊙9.30am-6.30pm) This impressive black-stone château, formerly the seat of power for the counts of Anjou, looms behind quai de Ligny, ringed by battlements and 17 watchtowers. Unexpectedly, the flower-filled interior is rather cheerful. The star of the show is the stunning **Tenture de l'Apocalypse** (Apocalypse tapestry), a 104m-long series of tapestries commissioned by Louis I, Duke of Anjou around 1375 to illustrate the Book of Revelation. It dramatically recounts the story of the Day of Judgment from start to finish, complete with the Four Horsemen of the Apocalypse, the Battle of Armageddon and the coming of the Beast: look out for graphic depictions of St Michael battling a seven-headed dragon and the fall of Babylon. Audioguides (€4.50) provide useful context, and guided tours are free. That black stone? It's actually called blue schist.

Musée Jean Lurçat et de la Tapisserie Contemporaine　　　TAPESTRY MUSEUM

(☏02 41 05 38 00; 4 bd Arago; adult/child €4/free; ⊙10am-7pm) Providing an interesting counterpoint to Angers' other famous piece of needlework, this museum collects major 20th-century tapestries by Jean Lurçat, Thomas Gleb and others inside the Hôpital St-Jean, a 12th-century hospital founded by Henry Plantagenet. The centrepiece is the *Chant du Monde* (Song of the World), an amazing series depicting the trials and triumphs of modern humanity, from nuclear holocaust and space exploration to the delights of drinking Champagne. Odd and unmissable.

Galerie David d'Angers SCULPTURE MUSEUM
(☏02 41 05 38 90; 33bis rue Toussaint; adult/child €4/free; ☺10am-7pm) Angers' most famous son is the sculptor Pierre-Jean David (1788–1856), often just known as David d'Angers. Renowned for lifelike busts and sculptures, his work adorns public monuments all over France, notably at the Panthéon, the Louvre and Père Lachaise cemetery (where he carved many tombstones, including Honoré de Balzac's). His work

forms the cornerstone of this museum, housed in the converted 12th-century Toussaint Abbey and flooded with light through a striking glass-and-girder ceiling.

Musée des Beaux-Arts ART MUSEUM
(☏02 41 05 38 00; 14 rue du Musée; adult/child €4/free; ☺10am-7pm) The buildings of the sprawling, fantastic fine-arts museum mix plate glass with the fine lines of the typical Angevin aristocratic house. The museum has a section on the history of Angers and an superior 17th- to 20th-century collection: Monet, Ingres, Lorenzo Lippi and Flemish masters including Rogier van der Weyden.

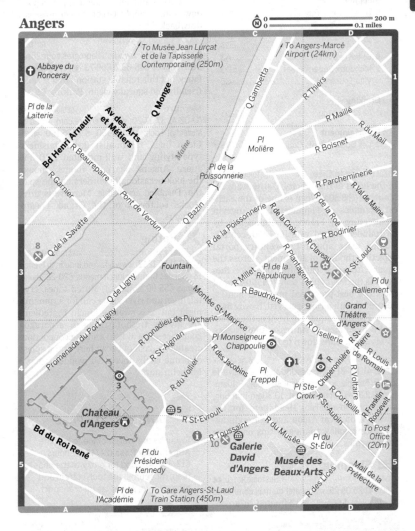

Angers

Quartier de la Cité HISTORIC QUARTER
In the heart of the old city, Cathédrale St-Maurice (⊙8.30am-7pm) is one of the earliest examples of Plantagenet or Angevin architecture in France, distinguished by its rounded ribbed vaulting, 15th-century stained glass and a 12th-century portal depicting the Day of Judgment. Across the square from the cathedral on place Ste-Croix is the Maison d'Adam (c 1500), one of the city's best-preserved medieval houses, decorated with a riot of carved, bawdy figurines. From the square in front of the cathedral a monumental staircase, the Montée St-Maurice, leads down to the river.

Maison du Vin de l'Anjou WINE CENTRE
(☎02 41 88 81 13; mdesvins-angers@vinsvaldeloire.fr; 5bis place du Président Kennedy; ⊙10am-1pm & 2.30-6.30pm Tue-Sat, 10.30am-1pm Sun, closed mid-Jan–mid-Feb) Head here for the lowdown on local Anjou and Loire vintages: tasting, sales, tours and tips on where to buy wines.

🛏 Sleeping

Hôtel du Mail HISTORIC HOTEL €€
(☎02 41 25 05 25; www.hotel-du-mail.com; 8 rue des Ursules; d €65-80; ⊛) Situated in a converted convent around a quiet courtyard, rooms here have a light, airy feel, even if they are a bit worn. The funky lobby, huge buffet breakfast (€10), friendly staff and thoughtful touches (daily newspapers, free umbrellas) make this a peaceful Angers base. Parking €6. Find it just east of the Quartier de la Cité, near the Hôtel de Ville.

Hôtel Continental HOTEL €€
(☎02 41 86 94 94; www.hotellecontinental.com; 14 rue Louis de Romain; s €51-90, d €60-93; ⊛⊛) Wedged into a wafer-shaped building in the city centre, this green-certified, metro-style hotel has 25 rooms decked out in cosy checks and sunny colours, plus a good downstairs café, Le Green. Street noise is a drawback.

Hôtel Le Progrès HOTEL €
(☎02 41 88 10 14; www.hotelleprogres.com; 26 rue Denis Papin; s €45-63, d €59-73; ⊛) It's nothing fancy, but this reliable station hotel is solid, friendly and squeaky clean. Parking €5.

Mercure DESIGN HOTEL €€
(☎02 41 87 37 20; www.mercure.com; 18 bd du Maréchal Foch; s €125-150, d €135-160; ⊛⊛⊛) Clean lines, minimalist decor, business-type styling and wall-mounted LCD TVs adorn Angers' sharpest rooms, though the look occasionally borders on the spartan. Disabled accessible. Mercure is three blocks southeast of the Grand Théâtre d'Angers.

🍴 Eating

Le Favre d'Anne GASTRONOMIC €€€
(☎02 41 36 12 12; www.lefavredanne.fr, in French; 18 quai des Carmes; lunch menus €20-28, dinner menus €55-90; ⊙Tue-Sat) Muted tones, crystal, linen and river views call for a romantic night out or a swanky lunch. Ingredients are always fresh (artichokes, asparagus, goat cheese, local fish) and the concoctions creative: a dash of cacao here and a splash of prune coulis there. No wonder it has a Michelin star.

ANGERS CITY PASS

Swing by the tourist office to buy the **Angers City Pass** (24/48/72 hours €12/19/24), good for entry to the château, museums, the tourist train and other sights, as well as for transport discounts.

THE LOIRE VALLEY ANJOU

Villa Toussaint
FRENCH FUSION €€

(☑02 41 88 15 64; 43 rue Toussaint; mains €16-18; ⊘Tue-Sat) With its chic dining room and decked patio, you know you're in for a treat at this fusion place, combining pan-Asian flavours with classic French ingredients. The *combinaisons* bring together several dishes on one plate, from sushi to Thai chicken and tapas. Reserve ahead.

Chez Toi
BISTRO €€

(☑02 41 87 85 58; 44 rue St-Laud; mains €13-17; ⊘9am-1.30am; ☎☑) Minimalist furniture and technicolour trappings meet head-to-head in this zippy little lounge-bar, much favoured by the trendy Angevin set. All the dishes are named after friends to emphasise the chummy vibe, and the terrace is great for people-watching on a sunny day.

Self-Catering

Food Market
WEEKLY MARKET €

(place Louis Imbach & place Leclerc; ⊘Sat morning)

Monoprix
SUPERMARKET €

(⊘8.30am-9pm Mon-Sat) Across from 59 rue Plantagenêt. Has a food hall.

Drinking & Entertainment

The free *Angers Poche* details local events. Get tickets at Fnac billeterie (☑08 92 68 36 22; 25-29 rue Lenepveu; ⊘10am-7pm Mon-Sat).

Le Kifé du Jour
WINE BAR

(☑02 41 86 80 70; rue St-Laud) Laid-back little wine bar with lots of local wines by the glass or *pichet* (jug; €3).

L'Autrement
MUSIC CLUB

(☑02 41 87 61 95; www.lautrementcafe.com, in French; 90 rue Lionnaise; ⊘Wed-Sat) Jazz troupes, roots bands and local acts grace the stage at Angers' smoothest venue, about 100m west of Abbaye du Ronceray.

Les Quatre-Cents Coups
CINEMA

(☑02 41 88 70 95; www.les400coups.org; 12 rue Claveau) Arts cinema showing nondubbed films.

ℹ Information

Cyber Espace (25 rue de la Roë; per hr €3; ⊘10am-9pm Mon-Thu, 10am-10pm Fri-Sat, 2-6pm Sun) Internet access.

Post office (1 rue Franklin Roosevelt) Exchanges currency.

Tourist office (☑02 41 23 50 00; www.angers loiretourisme.com; 7 place du Président Kennedy; ⊘10am-7pm Mon, 9am-7pm Tue-Sat, 10am-6pm Sun)

ℹ Getting There & Away

Angers is 107km west of Tours and 90km east of Nantes.

AIR At the time of research, **Angers-Marcé Airport** (☑02 41 33 50 00; www.angers.aeroport.fr) had no commercial flights.

BUS Anjou Bus (☑08 20 16 00 49; www.anjou bus.fr, in French) is at the train station.

Brissac-Quincé Bus 9, €4.10, 25 minutes, six daily Monday to Saturday

Doué-La-Fontaine Bus 9, €7.60, one hour

Saumur Buses 5 and 11, €9, 1½ hours, seven daily Monday to Saturday

TRAIN In the centre buy tickets at **Boutique SNCF** (5 rue Chaperonnière; ⊘1.30-7pm Mon, 9.30am-7pm Tue-Fri, 9.30am-6.30pm Sat). From Gare Angers-St-Laud:

Paris Gare Montparnasse €46 to €92, 1¾ hours, hourly

Saumur €11 to €16, 30 minutes, 14 daily

Tours €16, one hour, 13 daily

ℹ Getting Around

At the time of research, work was still continuing on Angers' tram system.

BICYCLE The tourist office rents bikes (half-/full day €9/14) as part of the Détours de Loire network (p357).

BUS Local buses are run by **Keolis Angers** (☑02 41 33 64 64; www.cotra.fr; single/day ticket €1.30/3.50).

CAR Major car-rental companies (including Avis, Hertz, Europcar and National) have desks inside the train station.

TAXI Call ☑02 41 87 65 00, 02 41 34 96 52.

---

24 HOURS OF LE MANS

Every second week of June, race car aficionados converge on Le Mans (population 148,340) to watch this careening, 24-hour endurance race. Corvettes, Porsches, Ferraris and myriad other souped-up speedsters whip around the 13.629km Circuit de la Sarthe track at the world's oldest sports-car race (www.lemans.org), first run in 1923. The rest of the year, visit the museum (☑33 2 43 72 72 24; www.lemusee24h.com), which houses over 150 vehicles from an 1885 De Dion Bouton et Trepardoux steam-driven dog cart to past winners that are just a bit speedier.

ORANGE PEEL & ANISEED LIQUEURS

Some of France's most distinctive liqueurs are distilled in the Loire Valley, including bitter orange Cointreau and the aniseedy (and allegedly hallucinogenic) brew known as absinthe.

Cointreau has its origins in the experiments of two enterprising brothers: Adolphe Cointreau, a sweet-maker, and his brother Édouard-Jean Cointreau, who founded a factory in Angers in 1849 to produce fruit-flavoured liqueurs. In 1875 Édouard-Jean's son (also called Édouard) hit upon the winning concoction of sweet and bitter oranges, flavoured with intensely orangey peel. The liqueur was a massive success; by the early 1900s over 800,000 bottles of Cointreau were being produced to the top-secret recipe, and a century later every one of the 13 million bottles is still distilled to the same formula at the original factory site in Angers.

Carré Cointreau (☏ 02 41 31 50 50; www.cointreau.com; 2 bd des Bretonnières; adult/concession €6/5.40, tasting €3; ☉ by reservation) offers guided tours, which include a visit to the distillery and entry to the Cointreau archive. It is off the ring road east of Angers. From the train station, take bus 7.

By contrast, **absinthe** has had a more chequered history. Brewed from a heady concoction of natural herbs, true absinthe includes three crucial components: green anise, fennel and the foliage of *Artemisia absinthium* (wormwood, used as a remedy since the time of the ancient Egyptians). Legend has it that modern-day absinthe was created by a French doctor (wonderfully called Dr Pierre Ordinaire) in the late 1790s, before being acquired by a father-and-son team who established the first major absinthe factory, Maison Pernod-Fils, in 1805.

The drink's popularity exploded in the 19th century, when it was discovered by bohemian poets and painters (as well as French troops, who were given the drink as an antimalarial drug). Seriously potent, absinthe's traditional green colour and supposedly psychoactive effects led to its popular nickname of 'the green fairy'; everyone from Rimbaud to Vincent van Gogh sang its praises. Ernest Hemingway invented his own absinthe cocktail: ominously dubbed 'Death in the Afternoon'.

But the drink's reputation was ultimately its own downfall: fearing widespread psychic degeneration, governments around the globe banned it in the early 20th century (France in 1915). In the 1990s a group of dedicated *absintheurs* reverse-engineered the liqueur, chemically analysing century-old bottles that had escaped the ban. Try it at Distillerie Combier in Saumur.

Around Angers

South of Angers, the River Maine joins the Loire for the final leg of its journey to the Atlantic. The river banks immediately west of this confluence remain the source of some of the valley's most notable wines, including Savennières and Coteaux du Layon.

CHÂTEAU DE SERRANT

Built from cream-and-fawn tufa stone and topped by bell-shaped, slate-topped towers, the grand Château de Serrant (☏ 02 41 39 13 01; www.chateau-serrant.net; adult/child €9.50/6; ☉ tours 9.45am-5.15pm Jun–mid-Sep, 1.30-5.15pm Wed-Sat, 9.45am-noon & 1.30-5.15pm Sun mid-Mar–May & mid-Sep–mid-Nov) is a wonderful slice of Renaissance style, reminiscent of Cheverny but on a more modest scale. Begun by the aristocrat Charles

de Brie in the 16th century, the château is notable for its 12,000-tome **library**, huge kitchens and an extravagant domed bedroom known as the **Chambre Empire**, designed to host an overnight stay by the Emperor Napoléon (who actually only hung around for about two hours).

The château is near St-Georges-sur-Loire, 15km southwest of Angers on the N23. Anjou bus 18 travels from Angers (€4.10, 40 minutes, two daily, one on Sunday).

CHÂTEAU DE BRISSAC

The tallest castle in France, the Château de Brissac (☏ 02 41 91 22 21; www.chateau-brissac.fr; adult/child incl tour €9/4.50, gardens only €4.50/free; ☉ 10.15am-12.15pm & 2-6pm Wed-Mon) is 15km south of Angers in Brissac-Quincé. Spread over seven storeys and 204 rooms, this chocolate-box mansion was built by the Duke of Brissac in 1502, and is one of the most luxuriously furnished in the valley, with a riot of posh furniture, ornate tapestries, twinkling chandeliers and luxurious bedrooms – even a private theatre. Around the house, 8 sq km of grounds are filled with cedar trees, 19th-century stables and a vineyard, boasting three AOC vintages. Open 10am to 6pm daily in July and August.

Four of the château's bedrooms are offered as ridiculously extravagant **chambres d'hôte** (d incl breakfast €390; ✆), perfect if you've always dreamt of sleeping on an antique four-poster under priceless tapestries and ancestral portraits.

Anjou bus 9 links Angers with Brissac-Quincé (€1.60, 25 minutes, six daily Monday to Saturday).

Burgundy

Includes »

Best Places to Eat

» L'Espérance (p425)

» Loiseau des Vignes (p408)

» La Cimentelle (p421)

» Les Terrasses de Corton (p404)

» Le Chambolle (p404)

» Auberge du Pot d'Etain (p421)

Best Places to Stay

» Villa Louise Hôtel (p404)

» La Cimentelle (p421)

» Maison Sainte-Barbe (p427)

» Le Moulin des Ruats (p421)

» Domaine Dessus Bon Boire (p414)

Why Go?

Burgundy (Bourgogne in French) offers some of France's most gorgeous countryside: rolling green hills dotted with medieval villages, and mustard fields blooming in bright contrast. Two great French passions, wine and food, come together here in a particularly rich and enticing form.

The region's towns and its dashingly handsome capital, Dijon, are heirs to a glorious architectural heritage that goes back to the Renaissance, the Middle Ages and beyond, into the mists of Gallo-Roman and Celtic antiquity.

Burgundy is also a paradise for lovers of the great outdoors. You can hike and cycle through the vineyards of the Côte d'Or, on a network of cycling trails, and in the wild reaches of the Parc Naturel Régional du Morvan (Morvan Regional Park); glide along the waterways of the Yonne in a canal boat; or float above the vineyards in a hot-air balloon.

When to Go

Dijon

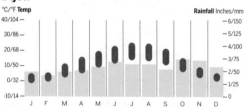

May Mustard blooms in the fields as the vineyards (and the vintners) revive after winter.

July Splendid weather makes summer a perfect time to cycle Burgundy's bike trails.

November Beaune's Trois Glorieuses Festival brims with wine, music and merriment.

Top Wine Regions

Burgundy's red wines and especially those of the Côte d'Or vineyards around Beaune are world-famous. The cellars under the city of Beaune alone comprise millions of bottles of some of the best wines in existence. But don't forget to leave room in your itinerary for a few of the other more laid-back appellations. Charming Irancy is a favourite tasting region for many locals. Chablis, with its unpretentious, crisp white wines, is wonderful on a hot summer day. To really get off the beaten path, head to the Mâconnais and Châtillonais vineyards.

COOKING COURSES

Burgundy's rich, hearty cuisine combines smoky flavours and fresh ingredients. Why not take the opportunity to learn a few of the local techniques? Courses range from the informal to the chic:

Use the refurbished 17th-century kitchen at Château d'Ancy-le-Franc (p418) to learn from Judicäel Ruch of Plaza Athénée in Paris. Classes (€120, once per month, April to November) follow themes like foie gras or *macarons* and include wine with the completed meal.

Le Charlemagne (p404), in the heart of Côte d'Or wine country, has 1½-hour classes (€70) each Saturday, featuring a fresh, seasonal ingredient and accompanied by a wine tasting and dessert.

The proprietress of La Cimentelle (p421), Nathalie, will teach you how to make a *repas gastronomique* in a half-day course (€80) – fun to do with a group of friends.

L'Espérance (p425), Marc Meneau's fabulous restaurant near Vézelay offers two-day cookery classes that include dinner and accommodation at the inn.

The Celts in Burgundy

» Bibracte (p425), the ruins of the capital city of the Aedui people, puts the Celts centre stage at the excellent Museum of Celtic Civilisation. Vercingétorix was proclaimed the chief of the Gauls here before being defeated by Julius Caesar at Alésia, the capital of the Mandubii people.

» Trésor de Vix, a stunning collection of Celtic, Greek and Etruscan objects, is the focus of the Musée du Pays Châtillonnais in Châtillon-sur-Seine (p410).

» The Celtic goddess Sequana is one of the highlights of Dijon's Musée Archéologique (p397): the only existing image of her is this 1st-century-AD bronze depicting her astride a boat.

» Sacred springs and sanctuaries include Fontaines Salées (p425), Fosse Dionne (p417) and Source de la Douix (p411).

WINE TOURS

Although Burgundy is covered in vineyards, not many areas offer organised tours of the wineries. The best hubs for picking up a tour are Dijon, Beaune and Chablis.

Book Ahead

» Wine courses are available at École des Vins de Bourgogne (p419) – plan for anything from three hours to three days.

Burgundy Reading

» *La Maison de Claudine* by Colette (see p415)

» *Jean-Christophe* by Romain Rolland (see p424)

» *The Wines of Burgundy* by Sylvain Pitiot and Jean-Charles Servant

» *Wine and War* by Don and Petie Kladstrupe

Resources

» Biking Burgundy: www. burgundy-by-bike.com

» Train and bus options: www.mobigo-bourgogne. com

» Wines of Burgundy: www.bourgogne-wines. com

» Music and events: www. magma-magazine.fr, in French

History

At its height during the 14th and 15th centuries, the duchy of Burgundy was one of the richest and most powerful states in Europe and encompassed a vast swathe of territory stretching from modern-day Burgundy to Alsace and northwest to Lorraine, Luxembourg, Flanders and Holland. This was a time of bitter rivalry between Burgundy and France; indeed, it was the Burgundians who sold Jeanne d'Arc (Joan of Arc) to the English, and for a while it seemed quite possible that the kingdom of France would be taken over by Burgundy. In the end, though, it worked out the other way around, and in 1477 Burgundy became French.

During the Middle Ages two Burgundy-based monastic orders exerted significant influence across much of Christendom. The ascetic Cistercians were headquartered at Cîteaux, while their bitter rivals, the powerful and worldly Benedictines, were based at Cluny.

ℹ Getting There & Around

By car or rail (including the TGV Sud-Est), Burgundy makes an easy stopover on the way from the English Channel or Paris to the Alps or southern France. See p394 for cycling and walking options.

CAR From Dijon, autoroutes stretch northeast to Alsace (A36), north to Lorraine (A31), north and then west to Champagne (A31, A5 and A26) and south to the Rhône Valley (A6).

BUS & TRAIN The towns and some of the villages mentioned in this chapter are served by trains and buses in high season, though patience and planning are a must as services in many areas are infrequent (especially on Sunday and during school holidays) or have to be booked the day before.

Mobigo (☑08 00 10 20 04; www.mobigo-bourgogne.com) Details of buses and trains around Burgundy.

CÔTE-D'OR

The Côte-d'Or *département* is named after one of the world's foremost winegrowing regions, which stretches from Dijon, bursting with cultural riches, south to the wine town of Beaune and beyond. In the far northwest of the *département*, on the border with Champagne, Châtillon-sur-Seine displays Celtic treasures; in the west you can explore the walled, hilltop town of Semur-en-Auxois.

Dijon

POP 250,000

Dijon is one of France's most appealing cities. Filled with elegant medieval and Renaissance buildings, the lively centre is wonderful for strolling, especially if you like to leaven your cultural enrichment with excellent food, fine wine and shopping.

Dijon wears its long and glorious history with grace, and with a self-confidence that's never smug or off-putting because it's so obviously and richly deserved. The city's 25,000 students keep the nightlife snappy, though people of all ages participate in the city's thriving cultural life.

History

Dijon served as the capital of the duchy of Burgundy from the 11th to 15th centuries, enjoying a golden age during the 14th and 15th centuries under Philippe-le-Hardi (Philip the Bold), Jean-sans-Peur (John the Fearless) and Philippe-le-Bon (Philip the Good). During their reigns, some of the finest painters, sculptors and architects from around the continent were brought to Dijon, turning the city into one of the great centres of European art.

◉ Sights

The Owl's Trail (€2.50), available in 11 languages at the tourist office, details a self-guided city-centre walking tour; the route is marked on the pavement with bronze triangles. All of Dijon's municipal museums are free except, occasionally, for special exhibitions. Major churches are open from 8am to 7pm.

Palais des Ducs et des États de Bourgogne PALACE
(Palace of the Dukes and States of Burgundy) Once home to Burgundy's powerful dukes, this monumental palace is the focal point of old Dijon. Given a neoclassical facade in the 17th and 18th centuries while serving as the seat of the States-General (Parliament) of Burgundy, it overlooks **place de la Libération**, a magnificent semicircular public square designed by Jules Hardouin-Mansart (one of the architects of Versailles) in 1686.

The western wing is occupied by Dijon's **Hôtel de Ville** (City Hall). Inside the arch that's across the street from 92 rue de la Liberté is **Escalier Gabriel** (1730s), a grand marble stairway with gilded railings that's named after its architect.

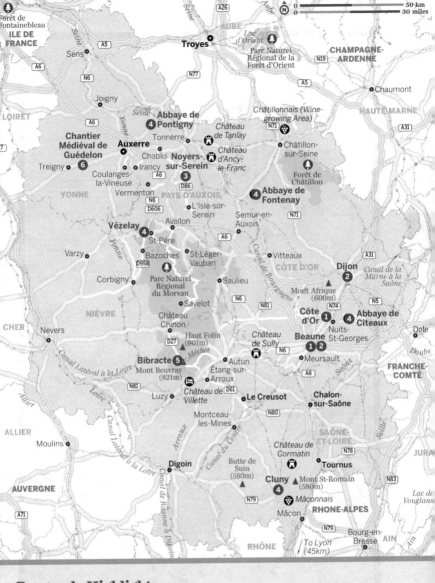

Burgundy Highlights

1 Sample Burgundy's most renowned vintages in **Beaune** (p405) and along the vine-carpeted slopes of the **Côte d'Or** (p403)

2 Marvel at the glories of the late Middle Ages at Dijon's **Musée des Beaux-Arts** (p396) and Beaune's **Hôtel-Dieu** (p405)

3 Explore the quirky village of **Noyers-sur-Serein** (p418) and stroll into the surrounding countryside

4 Conjure up monastic life in the Middle Ages at the abbeys of **Cluny** (p428), **Fontenay** (p410), **Pontigny** (p417), **Cîteaux** (p401) and **Vézelay** (p423)

5 Drop back into the early days of humankind at the ancient Celtic ruins of **Bibracte** (p425) atop Mont Beuvray

6 Watch a château being built with 13th-century technology at the **Chantier Médiéval de Guédelon** (p415)

BURGUNDY CÔTE-D'OR

Dijon

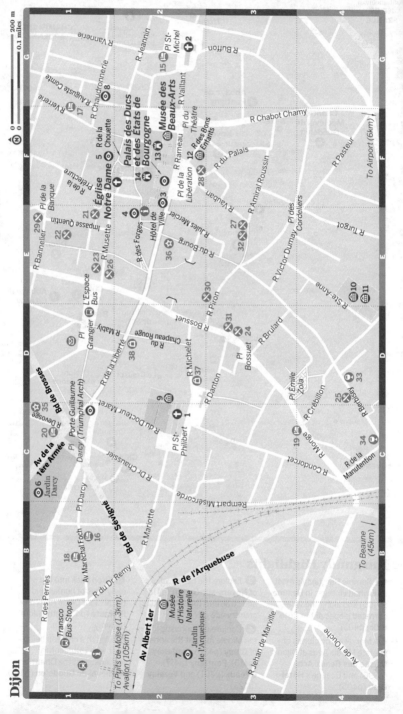

R des Perriés

Transco Bus Stops

To Puits de Moïse (1.3km);
Avallon (105km)

Musée
d'Histoire
Naturelle

R de l'Arquebuse

Av Albert 1er

Jardin
de l'Arquebuse 7

R Jehan de Marville

Av de l'Ouche

To Beaune
(45km)

R du Dr Remy

R Mariotte

Bd de Sévigné

Av Maréchal Foch

Pl Darcy

Av de la
1ère Armée

R Devosge

Bd de Brosses

18 16

R de la Liberté

R Dr Chaussier

Pl Guillaume
Darcy

Porte Guillaume
(Triumphal Arch)

20 35

6 Jardin
Darcy

Pl
Grangier

L'Espace
Bus

R Mably

R du Chapeau Rouge

38

Pl St-
Philibert

R du Docteur Maret

9

1

R Michelet

R Danton

Rempart Miséricorde

Pl St-
Philibert

R Monge

R Condorcet

19

R de la
Manutention

34

Pl Émile
Zola

R Crébillon

Pl
Bossuet

R Brulard

R Rébuffet

25

33

37

24

31

R Bossuet

R Piron

30

R Victor Dumay

R Ste-Anne

Pl des
Cordeliers

10
11

R Turgot

R Banneiler 29

22

Pl de la
Banque

23

26

Impasse Quentin

R Musette

R de la
Préfecture

21

Église
Notre Dame

14

4

R des Forges

Hôtel de
Ville

R Jules Mercier

3

36

R du Bourg

32

27

R Vauban

28

Pl de la
Libération

12 R des Bons
Enfants

R du Palais

R Amiral Roussin

R Victor Dumay

R Émile

R Yverrie

17

R Chaudronnerie

R Auguste Comte

8

5 R de la
Chouette

Palais des
Ducs et des États de
Bourgogne

13

R Rameau

Pl du
Théâtre

R des
Enfants

Musée des
Beaux-Arts

15

R Jeannin

R Vannerie

Pl St-
Michel

2

R Buffon

R Vaillant

R Chabot Charny

R Pasteur

To Airport (6km)

0   200 m
0   0.1 miles

The eastern wing houses the outstanding **Musée des Beaux-Arts**, whose entrance is next to the **Tour de Bar**, a squat 14th-century tower that once served as a prison.

Just off the **Cour d'Honneur**, the 46m-high, mid-15th-century Tour Philippe le Bon (Tower of Philip the Good; ☑03 80 74 52 71; adult/child €2.30/free; ☉accompanied climbs every 45min 9am-noon & 1.45-5.30pm Wed-Sun, closed Thu-Fri late Nov-Easter) affords fantastic views over the city. On a clear day you can see all the way to Mont Blanc.

TOP CHOICE Musée des Beaux-Arts

ART MUSEUM

(☑03 80 74 52 09; audioguide €4, tours adult/child €6/3; ☉9.30am-6pm Wed-Mon) Housed in the eastern wing of the Palais des Ducs, these sprawling galleries make up one of the most outstanding museums in France. The rooms themselves are works of art and a special chance to be inside this monumental building.

The star is the wood-panelled **Salle des Gardes** (Guards' Room), once warmed by a gargantuan Gothic fireplace. It houses the ornate, carved late-medieval sepulchres of dukes John the Fearless and Philip the Bold (by Jean de Marville, Claus Sluter and Claus de Werve), as well as three impossibly intricate gilded Gothic retables from the 1300s. Rogier Van der Weyden's portrait of Philip the Good hangs here as well.

The modern and contemporary art section, with works by Manet and Monet and sculptures by Matisse and Rodin, harbours a particular delight: the **Pompon Room**. Tucked off a back staircase, this room is packed with stylized modern sculptures of animals by François Pompon (1855–1933). Born in Saulieu, Burgundy, Pompon was an assistant to Auguste Rodin; but his own sculptures including the famous *L'Ours Blanc* (White Bear, 1920) and a fantastic orang-utan in black marble, beautifully capture his unique vision of wildlife. Note that the modern and contemporary art galleries close daily from 11.30am to 1.45pm. Schedule your visit accordingly if you want to be sure to see pieces by Rodin, Rouault, Manet and Matisse.

BURGUNDY DIJON

Dijon

Other highlights include a fine collection of **primitives** that give you a good sense of how artistic and aesthetic sensibilities varied between Italy, Switzerland and the Rhineland in the 13th and 14th centuries; a smattering of old masters such as Lorenzo Lotto; and quite a few naturalistic **sculptures** by the Dijon-born artist François Rude (1784–1855).

In the courtyard, the **ducal kitchens** (1433) often host exhibitions of works by local artists.

Église Notre Dame CHURCH

A block north of the Palais des Ducs, Église Notre Dame was built between 1220 and 1240. The extraordinary facade's three tiers are lined with leering gargoyles separated by two rows of pencil-thin columns. The interior has a vast transept and 13th-century stained glass. High atop the church, the 14th-century **Horloge à Jacquemart** (Jacquemart Clock) was transported from Flanders in 1383 by Philip the Bold, who claimed it as a trophy of war. It chimes every quarter-hour.

Hôtels Particuliers HISTORIC MANSIONS

Many of Dijon's finest houses lie north of the Palais des Ducs on and around rue Verrerie, rue Vannerie and rue des Forges, whose names reflect the industries that once thrived there (glassmaking, basket-weaving and metalsmithery, respectively). The early-17th-century Maison des Cariatides (28 rue Chaudronnerie), its facade a riot of stone caryatids, soldiers and vines, is particularly fine. A bit to the west you'll find the 13th-century Hôtel Aubriot (40 rue des Forges) and the Renaissance-style Maison Maillard (38 rue des Forges), all garlands and lions. Go inside the truly splendid 17th-century Hôtel Chambellan (34 rue des Forges; admission free), from whose courtyard a spiral stone staircase leads up to remarkable vaulting.

Behind Église Notre Dame, the 17th-century Hôtel de Vogüé (8 rue de la Chouette) is renowned for the ornate carvings around its exquisitely proportioned Renaissance courtyard. It's worth walking through the pink stone archway for a peek. Figures of an owl and a cat perch high atop the roof of the 15th-century Maison Millière (10 rue de la Chouette), which was a setting in the 1990 film *Cyrano de Bergerac* with Gérard Depardieu.

Cathédrale St-Bénigne CATHEDRAL

(place St-Philibert) Situated above the tomb of St Benignus (who is believed to have brought Christianity to Burgundy in the 2nd century), this Gothic-style church with multicoloured roof tiles was built around 1300 as an abbey church. Some of Burgundy's great figures are buried here. The crypt (admission €2; ☺9.30am-6pm Mon-Fri, to 4pm Sat, 2-6pm Sun) is all that remains of an 11th-century Romanesque basilica and is a maze of arched tunnels, carved capitals and inlaid floors. Guided tours are available.

Musée Magnin ART MUSEUM

(☎03 80 67 11 10; 4 rue des Bon Enfants; adult/child incl audioguide € 3.50/2.50; ☺10am-noon & 2-6pm Tue-Sun) Jeanne and Maurice Magnin turned their historic town house over to the state to display their excellent art collection in perpetuity. Works include fine examples of the Italian Renaissance and Flemish and medieval painting.

FREE Musée Archéologique
ARCHAEOLOGY MUSEUM

(☎03 80 30 88 54; 5 rue du Docteur Maret; ☺9am-12.30pm & 1.30-6pm Wed-Mon, closed Mon Sep–mid-May) Truly surprising Celtic, Roman and Merovingian artefacts are displayed here, including a particularly fine 1st-century-AD bronze of the Celtic goddess Sequana standing on a dual-prowed boat. Upstairs, the early Gothic hall (12th and 13th centuries), with its ogival arches held aloft by two rows of columns, once served as the dormitory of a Benedictine abbey.

FREE Musée de la Vie Bourguignonne
CULTURAL MUSEUM

(☎03 80 48 80 90; 17 rue Ste-Anne; ☺9am-noon & 2-6pm Wed-Mon) Housed in a 17th-century Cistercian convent, this museum explores village and town life in Burgundy in centuries past with evocative tableaux illustrating dress and traditional crafts. Down the alley to the right as you exit the cloister, the Musée d'Art Sacré (15 rue Ste-Anne) displays gleaming Catholic ritual objects from the 12th to 19th centuries inside the convent's copper-domed chapel (1709).

Église St-Michel CHURCH

(place St-Michel) Originally Gothic, this church subsequently underwent a facade-lift operation in which it was given a richly ornamented Renaissance west front. Its two 17th-century towers are topped with cupolas and, higher still, glittering gold spheres.

Tasting fine wines often involves hanging out in dimly lit cellars, but Burgundy is also a paradise for lovers of the great outdoors.

The Comité Régional de Tourisme de Bourgogne (Burgundy Regional Tourist Board; www.burgundy-tourism.com) publishes excellent brochures on outdoors options, including *Burgundy by Bike* and *Boating Holidays in Burgundy,* available at tourist offices.

Hiking & Cycling

Burgundy has thousands of kilometres of walking and cycling trails, including sections of the GR2, GR7 and GR76. Varied local trails take you through some of the most ravishingly beautiful winegrowing areas in France, among them the vineyards of world-renowned Côte d'Or, Chablis and the Mâconnais (in Saône-et-Loire).

Rural footpaths criss-cross the Parc Naturel Régional du Morvan and some depart from the Morvan Visitors Centre, but you can also pick up trails from the Abbaye de Fontenay, Autun, Avallon, Cluny, Noyers-sur-Serein and Vézelay.

You can cycle on or very near the *chemin de halage* (towpath) of the Canal de Bourgogne all the way from Dijon to Migennes (225km). The section from Montbard to Tonnerre (65km) passes by Château d'Ancy-le-Franc; between Montbard and Pouilly-en-Auxois (58km) spurs go to the Abbaye de Fontenay and Semur-en-Auxois.

For details on Burgundy's planned 800km of *véloroutes* (bike paths) and *voies vertes* (green ways), including maps and guides, see www.burgundy-by-bike.com or stop at a tourist office.

Canal & River Boating

Few modes of transport are as relaxing as a houseboat (p975) on Burgundy's 1200km of placid waterways, which include the Rivers Yonne, Saône and Seille and a network of canals, including the Canal de Bourgogne, the Canal du Centre, the Canal du Nivernais and the Canal Latéral à la Loire. Reliable rental companies offering boats from late March to 11 November (canals close for repairs in winter, but rivers don't):

Bateaux de Bourgogne (☑03 86 72 92 10; www.tourisme-yonne.com; 1-2 quai de la République, Auxerre) Reservations centre for four large companies offering 15 points of departure; upstairs from Auxerre's tourist office.

France Afloat (Burgundy Cruisers; ☑03 86 81 67 87, in UK 08700 110 538; www.france afloat.com; 1 quai du Port, Vermenton) Based 23km southeast of Auxerre.

Locaboat Holidays (☑03 86 91 72 72; www.locaboat.com; Port au Bois, Joigny) Rents boats throughout France, including at Joigny (27km northwest of Auxerre).

Hot-Air Ballooning

From about April to October you can take a stunning *montgolfière* (hot-air balloon) ride over Burgundy for around €229 per adult. Book through the Beaune and Dijon tourist offices. Some veteran outfits:

Air Adventures (☑06 08 27 95 39; www.airadventures.fr) Based just outside Pouilly-en-Auxois, 50km west of Dijon.

Air Escargot (☑03 85 87 12 30; www.air-escargot.com) In Remigny, 16km south of Beaune.

Puits de Moïse   MEDIEVAL SCULPTURE
(Well of Moses; Centre Hospitalier Spécialisé, 1 bd Chanoine Kir; admission €3.50; ☺9am-12.30pm & 1.30-6pm) This famous grouping of six Old Testament figures, carved from 1395 to 1405 by court sculptor Claus Sluter and his nephew Claus de Werve, has been open to individual visitors since summer 2010, or

can be seen on a guided tour with the tourist office. It is on the grounds of a psychiatric hospital 1.2km west of the train station; by bus take Line 3 toward Fontaine d'Ouche.

Parks & Gardens   GARDENS
Dijon has plenty of green spaces that are perfect for picnics, including Jardin

Darcy and Jardin de l'Arquebuse, the botanic gardens, with a stream and pond.

Tours

The tourist office has scads of information on tours of the city and the nearby wine regions, and can make bookings.

MP3 Tour   WALKING TOURS
(€6, incl MP3 player with images €12) From the main tourist office.

Walking Tours   HISTORY TOUR
(adult/child €6/3) A slew of different tours depart from the main tourist office. Times vary throughout the year.

Segway Tour   HISTORY TOUR
(adult/child €16/7; ⊙2.30pm & 4pm Mon-Sat) Run by the tourist office, this 1½-hour tour zips around the city centre.

Vineyard Tours   WINE TOURS
Minibus tours in English introduce the Côte d'Or vineyards. Reserve by phone, internet or via the tourist office. Operators include: Alter & Go (☑06 23 37 92 04; www.alterandgo.fr; tours €60-80) with an emphasis on history and winemaking methods, Authentica Tour (☑06 87 01 43 78; www.authentica-tour.com; tours €55-95) and Wine & Voyages (☑03 80 61 15 15; www.wineandvoyages.com; 2/3hr tours €48/58).

Sleeping

Hôtel Le Jacquemart   HOTEL €
(☑03 80 60 09 60; www.hotel-lejacquemart.fr; 32 rue Verrerie; d €49-65; @☎) Right in the heart of old Dijon, this basic hotel has 31 tidy, comfortable rooms; the pricier ones

---

DON'T MISS

THE LUCKY OWL

Around the north side of Notre Dame, rue de la Chouette is named after the small stone *chouette* (owl) carved into the exterior corner of the chapel diagonally across from No 24. Said to grant happiness and wisdom to those who stroke it, it has been worn smooth by generations of fortune-seekers. All sorts of superstitions surround the owl: some insist that walking by the dragon in the lower left corner of the grille of the adjacent window will annul your wish, while others insist that approaching the dragon will actually help make your wish come true.

---

are quite spacious and some come with marble fireplaces. Window boxes make the 18th-century building especially pretty in summer.

Hôtel Le Sauvage   HOTEL €
(Hostellerie du Sauvage; ☑03 80 41 31 21; www.hotellesauvage.com, in French; 64 rue Monge; s €46-55, d €51-61, tr €80; ☎) In a 15th-century *relais de poste* (mail staging post) set around a cobbled, vine-shaded courtyard, this good-value budget hotel is just off lively rue Monge. Some rooms are sparse, others are furnished with antiques. Parking €5.

Hôtel Le Jura   HOTEL €€
(☑03 80 41 61 12; www.oceaniahotels.com; 14 av Maréchal Foch; d €70-92, q €179; ❋☎♨) Near the train station, this straightforward hotel has friendly staff and some rooms overlooking a central courtyard. The 'superior' rooms are really that, with marblesque bathrooms and a sense of luxury. Room prices fluctuate; check online. Parking €9.50.

Hôtel Sofitel La Cloche   HOTEL €€€
(☑03 80 30 12 32; www.hotel-lacloche.com; 14 place Darcy; d €190-240, ste €300-800; ❋@☎) This venerable hostelry, built in 1884, boasts a huge lobby chandelier, an immaculate back garden, a sauna and a small fitness room. Hushed, comfortable rooms mix shiny brass, sleek wood furniture and crisp linen.

Hôtel Chambellan   HOTEL €
(☑03 80 67 12 67; www.hotel-chambellan.com; 92 rue Vannerie; s/d from €45/50; @☎) Built in 1730, and smack in the middle of the old town, this place has a vaguely medieval feel. Most of the rooms, decorated in cheerful tones of red, orange, pink and white, have views of a quiet courtyard.

Ethic Étapes Dijon   HOSTEL €
(Centre De Recontres et de Séjour Internationales, CRISD; ☑03 80 72 95 20; www.cri-dijon.com; 1 av Champollion, Palais de Sports; dm/s/d incl breakfast €21/39/52; @☎) This institutional (though friendly) 219-bed hostel, 2.5km northeast of the centre, was completely renovated in 2006. Most beds are in modern, airy rooms for two. By bus, take Line 4 to the Epirey CRI stop. Disabled accessible. Parking free.

Hôtel Chateaubriand   HOTEL €
(☑03 80 41 42 18; www.hotelchateaubriand.fr, in French; 3 av Maréchal Foch; d €45, with washbasin only €37) An old-fashioned cheapie,

with the air of a well-worn dive but, thanks to the Victorian breakfast room, a bit of character.

✖ Eating

Find loads of restaurants on buzzy rue Berbisey, around place Émile Zola, on rue Amiral Roussin and around the perimeter of the covered market. In warm months, outdoor cafés fill place de la Libération.

Le Pré aux Clercs GASTRONOMIC FRENCH €€€
(☑03 80 38 05 05; www.jeanpierrebilloux.com; 13 place de la Libération; lunch menus €35, dinner menus €50-95; ☺lunch Tue-Sun, dinner Tue-Sat) From the luscious lunch menu (which includes a glass of wine) to the nine-course *dégustation* menu, every detail is cared for at this top-notch restaurant looking out onto the Palais des Ducs. Diners stare in wonderment at concoctions like *flan de foie gras* with pear coulis or an 'opera' of truffles. Save room for the chocolate fondant.

Osteria Enoteca Italiana ITALIAN €€
(☑03 80 50 07 36; 32 rue Amiral Roussin; lunch menus €12.50-16, dinner menus €25-36; ☺lunch Tue-Sun, dinner Tue-Sat; ☑) A lively Italian *ristorante* that's proud of its authentic, heaping plates of pasta (including vegetarian fettuccine), meat and fish dishes, and its scrumptious homemade desserts (think tiramisu). The decor hints at Venice, the chef's hometown, and the wine list is Italian (glass €3.50).

Café Chez Nous CAFÉ €
(☑03 80 50 12 98; impasse Quentin; lunch menus €8; ☺lunch noon-2pm Tue-Sun, bar 10am-2am, 11am-2pm Sun, closed Mon) This quintessentially French *bar du coin* (neighbourhood bar), often crowded, hides down a tiny alleyway near the covered market. Lunches are generally made with organic ingredients. Wine by the glass is a bargain (€1.20 to €2.40). Check the chalkboard for occasional dinners and live music.

La Dame d'Aquitaine BURGUNDIAN €€
(☑03 80 30 45 65; 23 place Bossuet; lunch menus €21, dinner menus €28-43; ☺lunch Tue-Sat, dinner Mon-Sat, closed lunch mid-July–mid-Aug) Excellent Burgundian and southwestern French cuisine is served under the sumptuously lit bays of a 13th-century *cave*. Options include *coq au vin rouge* and *magret de canard aux baies de cassis* (duck's breast with blackcurrant sauce). Classical music filters through the elegant room and the wine list is extensive.

Le Petit Roi de la Lune BISTRO €€
(☑03 80 49 89 93; 28 rue Amiral Roussin; lunch menu €10, mains €15-18; ☺lunch Tue-Sat, dinner Mon-Sat) A hip, younger crowd comes for French cuisine that, explains the chef, has been *revisitée, rearrangée et decalée* (revisited, rearranged and shifted). The hugely popular *Camembert frit avec gelée de mûre* (Camembert wrapped in breadcrumbs, fried, and then served with blackberry jelly) tops the list.

La Mère Folle BURGUNDIAN €€
(☑03 80 50 19 76; 102 rue Berbisey; lunch menus €10, dinner menus €15-23; ☺Tue-Sat) Look past the over-the-top medieval decor and you'll find Burgundian specialities such as *magret de canard au miel, thym et mirabelles* (fillet of duck with honey, thyme and cherry plums). Weekday lunches are a steal and include terrine straight from the crock.

La Petite Marché ORGANIC €
(☑03 80 30 15 10; 27-29 rue Musette; lunch menus €10-14; ☺lunch Mon-Sat; ☑🍴) This organic restaurant serves seven types of salad and quite a few vegetarian options (as well as meat and fish); a good choice if you're tired of heavy Burgundian classics. Upstairs from an organic food shop, it also sells organic wines by the glass (€1.50).

Self-Catering

Covered Market FOOD MARKET €
(Halles du Marché; rue Quentin; ☺7am-1pm Tue & Thu-Sat) A huge market on Friday and Saturday, with a smaller version on Tuesday and Thursday.

Fromagerie CHEESE €
(28 rue Musette; ☺2.30-7pm Mon, 7am-12.30pm & 2.30-7pm Tue-Sat) Friendly, top-quality cheese shop.

Mulot & Petitjean BAKERY €
(13 place Bossuet; ☺2-5pm Mon, 9am-noon & 2-5pm Tue-Sat) Traditional *pain d'épices* (spice bread).

Marché Plus SUPERMARKET €
(2 rue Bannelier; ☺7am-9pm Mon-Sat, 9am-1pm Sun)

Monoprix SUPERMARKET €
(11-13 rue Piron; ☺9am-9.30pm Mon-Sat)

🍷 Drinking

Bars line rue Berbisey.

O Kil BAR
(☑03 80 30 02 48; www.lekil.com, in French; 1 rue Auguste Perdrix) Under stone cellar vaulting,

this cosy pub hosts live music once a month. Fans of English and other languages gather to converse at their 'Café Polyglotte' at 7.30pm on Wednesday.

Le Cappuccino BAR
(☎03 80 41 06 35; 132 rue Berbisey) Coffee isn't even served at this often-packed bar, but wine by the glass and 80 beers are, including Mandubienne, the only beer brewed in Dijon. Occasionally hosts live music.

Café de l'Univers BAR
(☎03 80 30 98 29; 47 rue Berbisey) This ground-floor bar, with walls covered in mirrors and beer ads, has its menu on a chalkboard. In the cellar there's live music from 9pm to 1am on Friday and Saturday. Popular with students but ages are varied.

☆ Entertainment

For the latest on Dijon's and the region's cultural scene, pick up the monthly *Spectacles* (www.spectacles-publications.com, in French) or *Magma* (www.magma-magazine.fr, in French) available free from the tourist office. Event tickets are sold at the Fnac billeterie (☎08 92 68 36 22; www.fnacspectacles.com, in French; 24 rue du Bourg; ⊙10am-7pm Mon-Sat). Dip into classical music and drama at Opera Dijon (☎03 80 48 82 82; www.opera-dijon.fr) and Théâtre Mansart (☎03 80 63 00 00; www.theatre-mansart.com; 94 bd Mansart). Check the Opera website for venues; Théâtre Mansart is located 4km southwest of the Palais des Ducs.

Find nightclubs near the northwest corner of place de la République (eg rue Marceau), 1km north of the Palais des Ducs.

Places listed under Drinking host live music.

Le Cercle Rhumerie Jamaïque MUSIC CLUB
(☎03 80 73 52 19; www.lecerclejamaique.com, in French; 14 place de la République; admission free; ⊙Tue-Sat) Decked out like a bordello, with bold-red walls and gilded mirrors, this club has live music (Cuban, jazz, rock 'n' roll) nightly from 11pm to 3am. The downstairs disco has a blue galactic ceiling and music that's as mixed as the clients' ages (mostly 20 to 40). Located 1km north of the Palais des Ducs.

Cinéma Eldorado CINEMA
(☎03 80 66 51 89, recorded information 08 92 68 01 74; www.cinema-eldorado.fr, in French; 21 rue Alfred de Musset) Art-house cinema, 2km southeast of Palais des Ducs.

Cinéma Devosge CINEMA
(☎03 80 30 74 79, recorded information 08 92 68 73 33; http://cinealpes.allocine.net, in French; 6 rue Devosge) Nondubbed films.

Shopping

The main shopping area is around rue de la Liberté and perpendicular rue du Bourg.

Moutarde Maille MUSTARD
(☎03 80 30 41 02; 32 rue de la Liberté; ⊙10am-7pm Mon-Sat) When you enter the factory boutique of this mustard company, tangy odours assault your nostrils. Thirty-six kinds of mustard, like cassis or truffle and celery, include three on tap that you can sample (from €2.40 per 200ml).

Institut Géographique National MAPS
(IGN; ☎03 80 49 98 58; 2 rue Michelet) Unsurpassed selection of driving, walking and cycling maps.

ⓘ Information

Centre Hospitalier Universitaire (☎03 80 29 30 31; 3 rue du Faubourg Raines; ⊙24hr) Hospital with 24-hour emergency room/casualty ward.

Cyberbisey (☎03 80 30 95 41; 53 rue Berbisey; per hr €3; ⊙10am-8pm Mon-Fri, noon-8pm Sat) Internet access.

Cyberspace 21 (☎03 80 30 57 43; 46 rue Monge; per hr €4; ⊙11am-midnight Mon-Sat, 2pm-midnight Sun) Internet access.

Main post office (place Grangier) Exchanges foreign currency.

Multi-Rezo UnderCity (☎03 80 42 13 89; 55 rue Guillaume Tell; per hr €4; ⊙9am-2am Mon-Fri, 11am-2am Sat, 2pm-midnight Sun) Internet access.

Police station (☎03 80 44 55 00; 2 place Suquet; ⊙24hr) Access on rue du Petit Cîteaux nights, Sundays and holidays.

SOS Médecins (☎03 80 59 80 80) Doctors on call 24 hours.

Tourist office (☎08 92 70 05 58; www.visitdijon.com; ⊙9am-6.30pm Mon-Sat, 10am-6pm Sun) main office (11 rue des Forges); station annexe (train station) The one- to three-day Dijon Côte de Nuits Pass may save you some cash.

ⓘ Getting There & Away

AIR At the time of research, no international flights used **Dijon-Bourgogne Airport** (☎03 80 67 67 67; www.dijon.aeroport.fr).

A single train station **ticket counter** (⊙5.45am-9pm) deals with TER trains, Divia local buses and the *départemental* bus company, Transco.

BUS **Transco** (☑08 00 10 20 04; www.mobigo-bourgogne.com) Buses stop in front of the train station. Free *Guide Horaire* booklet (at the ticket counter) has schedules. Tickets sold on board (€1.50). Bus 60 links Dijon with the northern Côte de Nuits wine villages of Marsannay-la-Côte, Couchey, Fixin and Gevrey-Chambertin (30 minutes). Bus 44 goes to Nuits-St-Georges and Beaune. Bus 43 goes to Abbaye de Cîteaux.

Eurolines (☑03 80 68 20 44; 53 rue Guillaume Tell; ☺Mon-Fri, 10am-3pm Sat) International bus travel.

CAR Avis, Hertz, National-Citer and Europcar have desks in the train-station complex. **ADA** (☑03 80 51 90 90; 109 av Jean Jaurès) 2km south of the station.

TRAIN For destinations within Burgundy, see town listings in this chapter. In Dijon centre, purchase tickets at the **SNCF Boutique** (55 rue du Bourg; ☺12.30-7pm Mon, 10am-7pm Tue-Sat). Trains leave the **train station** (rue du Dr Remy) for the following:

Lyon-Part Dieu €34, two hours, 25 daily

Nice €90, 6¼ hours by TGV, two direct daily

Paris Gare de Lyon €61, 1¾ hours by TGV; €44, three hours non-TGV; 20 daily

Strasbourg €49, 3½ hours by TGV, 4½ hours non-TGV; nine daily

ⓘ Getting Around

A tram system is being built with a planned 2013 launch; as a result, some streets are incredibly torn up, which makes for a maze of diversions.

BICYCLE The **main tourist office** (per half/full-day €12/18) rents bikes with free helmets.

Velodi (☑08 00 20 03 05; www.velodi.net, in French) Dijon's version of Paris' Vélib' automatic rental system; 400 city bikes at 33 sites around town.

BUS Get details of Dijon's bus network, operated by Divia, from **L'Espace Bus** (☑08 00 10 20 04; www.divia.fr, in French; place Grangier; ☺7.30am-6.45pm Mon-Fri, 8.30am-6.30pm Sat). Buses run every 10 to 15 minutes from 5.30am to midnight (from 9am on Sunday).

Forfait Journée ticket €3.40, unlimited trips all day, at tourist office

L'Espace Bus seven-day pass €9.70, valid for one week, from tourist office or L'Espace Bus

Single ticket €1, unlimited use within one hour, sold by drivers

A **free Diviaciti minibus** does a city-centre circuit every six minutes from 7am to 8pm Monday to Saturday.

CAR & MOTORCYCLE All city-centre parking is metered. Free spots are available (clockwise from the train station): northwest of rue Devosge, northeast of bd Thiers, southeast of bd Carnot, south of rue du Transvaal and on the other side of the train tracks from the city centre. There's a free car park at place Suquet, just south of the police station.

TAXI Call ☑03 80 41 41 12.

Côte d'Or Vineyards

Burgundy's most renowned vintages come from the vine-covered Côte d'Or (literally Golden Hillside, but it is actually an abbreviation of Côte d'Orient or Eastern Hillside), the narrow, eastern slopes of a range of hills made of limestone, flint and clay that runs south from Dijon for about 60km. The exquisite terrain with its patchwork of immaculate hand-groomed vines is dotted with peaceful stone villages where every house seems to hold a vintner.

⊙ Sights

Beaune's sights are covered in the city listings.

Abbaye de Cîteaux   ABBEY
(☑03 80 61 32 58; www.citeaux-abbaye.com, in French; D996) In contrast to the showy Benedictines of Cluny, the medieval Cistercian order was known for its austerity, discipline and humility, and for the productive manual labour of its monks, one result of which was groundbreaking wine-producing techniques. The order was named after Cîteaux Abbey (Cistercium in Latin), south of Dijon and 13km east of Nuits-St-Georges, where it was founded in 1098. It enjoyed phenomenal growth in the 12th century under St Bernard (1090–1153), and some 600 Cistercian abbeys soon stretched from Scandinavia to the Near East.

Out in the midst of pastoral mustard fields, Cîteaux was virtually destroyed during the Revolution and the monks didn't return until 1898, but today it is home to about 35 monks. You can visit the monastery on a 1½-hour guided tour (adult/child €7.50/4; ☺tours 10.30am, 11.30am & several times 2-5pm Wed-Sat & Sun afternoon May-Sep, plus Tue Jul & Aug) in French with printed English commentary. It includes an audiovisual presentation on monastic life. Phone ahead or email for reservations.

Visitors may attend daily prayers and Sunday Mass (10.30am). The boutique sells edibles made at monasteries around France, including the abbey's own cheese.

START **GEVREY-CHAM-BERTIN**
FINISH **LA ROCHEPOT**
DISTANCE **47KM**
DURATION **ONE DAY**

Driving Tour
Route des Grands Crus

❯ Burgundy's most famous wine route, the Route des Grands Crus (www.road-of-the-fine-burgundy-wines.com), and its often-narrow variants wend their way between stone-built villages with steeple-topped churches or the turrets of a château peeping above the trees. Vines cascade down the slopes between hamlets – Chambertin, Chambolle, Chassagne, Montrachet. The Côte's lower slopes are seas of vineyards; on the upper slopes, vines give way to forests, cliffs and breathtaking views. Signposted in brown, the Route des Grands Crus generally follows the tertiary roads west of the N74.

Coming from Dijon, the Côte de Nuits begins in earnest just south of Marsannay-la-Côte. Most of the area's *grand cru* vineyards lie between ❶ **Gevrey-Chambertin** (p403) and Vosne-Romanée. In ❷ **Vougeot**, stop at the historic château (p419). ❸ **Vosne-Romanée** (p403) is famed for its Romanée Conti wines, among Burgundy's most prestigious and priciest. Continuing south, visit the Cassissium (p403) in ❹ **Nuits-St-Georges**.

On the Côte de Beaune, the impossibly steep coloured-tile roof of Château Corton-André in ❺ **Aloxe-Corton** is easy to spot, just off the one-lane main street. ❻ **Pernand-Vergelesses** is nestled in a little valley hidden from the N74.

South of Beaune, ❼ **Château de Pommard** (www.chateau-de-pommard.tm.fr), surrounded by a stone wall, is on the D973 on the northeast edge of town. Wander quaint ❽ **Volnay** to its hillside church. Off the main track, ❾ **St-Romain** is a bucolic village situated right where vineyardland meets pastureland, forests and cliffs. Hiking trails from here include the spectacular **Sentier des Roches**, a circuit that follows part of the GR7 and the D17l along the top of the **Falaises de Baubigny** (Baubigny cliffs), 300m above the Saône. Finally, via the hillside hamlet of ❿ **Orches**, which has breathtaking vineyard views, travel to the fantastic 15th-century ⓫ **Château de La Rochepot** (p403).

TOP CHOICE **Château de La Rochepot** CASTLE
(☏03 80 21 71 37; www.larochepot.com; La Rochepot; adult/child €7.50/4; ☺10am-5.30pm Wed-Mon) Conical towers and multicoloured tile roofs rise from thick woods above the ancient village of La Rochepot. Cross the drawbridge and knock three times to gain entry to this marvellous medieval fortress, most famously owned by Knights Régnier and Philippe Pot of the Order of the Golden Fleece. Terraces offer fab views of surrounding countryside and the interiors are a fascinating combination of the utilitarian (weapons) and the luxe (fine paintings). Tours are in French but most guides speak English and an English text is provided.

Cassissium LIQUEUR FACTORY
(☏03 80 62 49 70; www.cassissium.com; Av du Jura, Nuits-St-Georges; adult/child €7.50/5.50; ☺10am-1pm & 2-7pm, last visits 1½hr before closing; ⚐) This museum and factory worships all things liqueur, with a particular focus on the blackcurrant, from which cassis is made. There's fun for the whole family: movies, displays, a 30-minute guided tour and a tasting with non-alcoholic fruit syrups for the kids. Off rue des Frères Montgolfier in the industrial area east of N74. Has a map of the *Route du Cassis,* a nice trip through the countryside.

Château de Savigny MUSEUM CASTLE
(☏03 80 21 55 03; Savigny-les-Beaune; ☺9am-6.30pm) Drop in for wine tasting and stay to see the unexpected collection of race cars, motorcycles, airplanes and fire trucks.

 Activities

Wine Tasting WINE TASTING
The villages of the Côte d'Or offer innumerable places to sample and purchase world-class wines a short walk from where they were made. See Dijon or Beaunefor tours of the vineyards, or drive the Routes des Grands Crus and keep your eyes open for bottles from the listed winemakers in these villages: **Beaune** (Luis Jadot, Joseph Drouhin and Bouchard Père et Fils), **Gevrey-Chambertin** (Denis Bachelet and Domaine Fourrier), **Magny-lès-Villers** (Domaine Cornu), **Meursault** (Comtes Lafon), **Morey-St-Denis** (Domaine Dujac), **Nuits-St-Georges** (Joseph Faiveley), **Savigny-lès-Beaune** (Domaine Chandon de Briailles), **Volnay** (Domaine Hubert de Montille) **Vosne-Romanée** (Domaine de la Romanée Conti).

Fromagerie Delin CHEESE TASTING
(☏03 80 62 87 20; 6 rue des Maizières, Gillyles-Cîteaux; ☺9am-noon & 2-5.30pm Mon-Fri, 8.30am-12.30pm Sat) Try and buy traditional cheeses.

Walking WALKS
The GR7 and its variant, the GR76, run along the Côte d'Or from a bit west of Dijon to the hills west of Beaune, from where they continue southwards. The Beaune tourist office sells an excellent guide, *Walks in the Beaune Countryside* (€3), which details 30 marked routes.

Cycling CYCLING
To get from Dijon to Beaune by bike, follow the quiet (but almost vergeless/shoulderless) D122, which gradually becomes pretty south of Couchey, to Nuits-St-Georges. From there, take either the challenging D8 and the D115C, or the flatter D20, just east of the N74, which offers fine views of the wine slopes. The ride takes three or four hours and covers about 50km. To avoid cycling both ways (or through Dijon's ugly and heavily trafficked urban sprawl, which stretches as far south as Marsannay-la-Côte), you can take your bike along on most Dijon–Beaune trains; look for the bicycle symbol on train schedules.

The 20km **Voie des Vignes** (Vineyard Way), a bike route marked by rectangular green-on-white signs, goes from Beaune's Parc de la Bouzaize via Pommard, Volnay, Meursault, Puligny-Montrachet and Chassagne-Montrachet to Santenay, where you can pick up the **Voie Verte** to Cluny. The Beaune tourist office sells a detailed map, *The Beaune-Santenay Cycle Track* (€2).

Sleeping
Tourist offices have lists of the area's plentiful accommodation, most of which is of a higher calibre than nearby cities.

TOP CHOICE **Villa Louise Hôtel** HOTEL €€
(☏03 80 26 46 70; www.hotel-villa-louise. fr, in French; Aloxe-Corton; d €100-195; ⓐⓡⓢ) Who needs city life when you can stow away in vineyard-side luxury? This tranquil mansion houses elegant, modern rooms, each of them dreamily different. The expansive garden stretches straight to the edge of the vineyard and a separate gazebo shelters the sauna and pool. Genteel Louise Perrin presides, and has a private *cave*, perfect for wine tastings. Reserve ahead as this beauty is often fully booked.

BURGUNDY CÔTE D'OR VINEYARDS

Domaine Corgette
B&B €€

(☑03 80 21 68 08; www.domainecorgette.com; rue de la Perrière, St-Romain; d incl breakfast €80-90; ⓢ) The sun-drenched terrace at this renovated winery looks out on the dramatic cliffs. Tucked in the centre of the quiet village of St-Romain, its rooms are light and airy with crisp linen, and retain classic touches like fireplaces and wood floors.

Maison des Abeilles
B&B €

(☑03 80 62 95 42; http://perso.wanadoo.fr/maison-des-abeilles, in French; Magny-les-Villars; d incl breakfast €58-64, q €90; @ⓜ) Sweet and jolly Jocelyne maintains this impeccably clean *chambre d'hôte* in a small village in the Haute Côte. Rooms have colourful linen and breakfasts are a feast of breads and homemade jams.

La Closerie de Gilly
B&B €€

(☑03 80 62 87 74; www.closerie-gilly.com; av Bouchard, Gilly-lès-Cîteaux; d incl breakfast €75-95, q €120-140, 2-person apt per week €300-425; ⓢⓢⓜ) A homey five-room B&B inside a delightful 18th-century *maison bourgeoise* with a huge, flowery garden. Has bicycles for rent and offers wine-tasting.

Château de Gilly
CASTLE HOTEL €€€

(☑03 80 62 89 98; www.chateau-gilly.com; Gilly-lès-Cîteaux; d €170-326; ste €438-768; @ⓢ) This once-posh hotel occupies the 14th- and 17th-century residence of the abbots of Cîteaux. Spacious rooms look a bit worn, but it's a chance to stay in a castle. Free bicycle use.

✗ Eating

Excellent restaurants are tucked away in the villages of the Côte d'Or. Explore! Château de Gilly offers a deal of a three-course lunch (€19). Reserve ahead in high season.

Les Terrasses de Corton
BURGUNDIAN €€

(☑03 80 26 42 37; 38 rte de Beaune, Ladoix-Serrigny; menus €24-40, s/d €48/60; ⊙noon-1.45pm & 7.30-9pm, closed Wed & lunch Thu, also closed dinner Sun late Oct–early Mar) On the N74 near the southern edge of Ladoix-Serrigny, this place looks like a motel but in fact serves great-value French and Burgundian cuisine. The comfortable dining room fills up with chatting villagers enjoying dishes like home-style *boeuf bourguignon* or glazed duck with sweet potatoes. There are simple rooms upstairs.

Le Chambolle
BURGUNDIAN €€

(☑03 80 62 86 26; 28 rue Basse, Chambolle-Musigny; menus €23-40; ⊙12.15-1.30pm or 2pm & 7.15-8.30pm Fri-Tue) This unpretentious back-roads gem creates traditional Burgundian cuisine with the freshest ingredients. Asparagus in season is a symphony in your mouth. On the D122, a bit east of Vougeot in gorgeous Chambolle-Musigny.

Le Charlemagne
GASTRONOMIC FUSION €€€

(☑03 80 21 51 45; www.lecharlemagne.fr, in French; Pernand-Vergelesses; lunch menus Mon, Thu & Fri €29-35, other menus €50-90; ⊙noon-1.30pm Thu-Mon, 7-9.30pm Wed-Mon, closed dinner Wed Sep-May) Vineyard views are perhaps even more mind-blowing than the imaginatively prepared dishes melding French cuisine with techniques and ingredients from Japan. Attentive service is like a ballet.

La Cabotte
MODERN FRENCH €€

(☑03 80 61 20 77; 24 Grand' Rue, Nuits-St-Georges; menus €28-49; ⊙lunch Tue-Fri, dinner Tue-Sat) This intimate restaurant serves up refined, inventive versions of French dishes. No artifice or posing here, just excellent, if sometimes surprising, food.

❶ Getting There & Around

For details on public transport around Côte d'Or wine villages, see p409 and p401.

Beaune

POP 22,720

Beaune (pronounced similarly to 'bone'), 44km south of Dijon, is the unofficial capital of the Côte d'Or. This thriving town's *raison d'être* and the source of its *joie de vivre* is wine: making it, tasting it, selling it, but most of all, drinking it. Consequently Beaune is one of the best places in all of France for wine tasting.

The jewel of Beaune's old city is the magnificent Hôtel-Dieu, France's most splendiferous medieval charity hospital.

◉ Sights

The amoeba-shaped old city is enclosed by thick stone **ramparts** and a stream which is in turn encircled by a one-way boulevard with seven names. The ramparts, which shelter wine cellars, are lined with overgrown gardens and ringed by a pathway that makes for a lovely stroll.

TOP CHOICE Hôtel-Dieu des Hospices de Beaune
HISTORIC HOSPITAL

(☑03 80 24 45 00; rue de l'Hôtel-Dieu; adult/child €6.50/2.80; ☺9am-6.30pm, interior closes 1hr later) Built in 1443 by Nicolas Rolin, the chancellor to Philippe-le-Bon, and used as a hospital until 1971, this magnificent Gothic hospital building is famously topped by stunning turrets and pitched rooftops covered in multicoloured tiles. Fascinating interior highlights include the barrel-vaulted **Grande Salle** (look for the dragons and peasant heads up on the roof beams); the mural-covered **St-Hughes Room**; an 18th-century **pharmacy** where the nuns made their own medicaments and which is lined with flasks once filled with volatile oils, unguents, elixirs and powders such as *beurre d'antimoine* (antimony butter) and *poudre de cloportes* (woodlouse powder); the huge **kitchens**, with their open hearths; and the 16th-century Flanders **tapestry of St Eloi**. Do not miss the brilliant **Polyptych of the Last Judgement** by the Flemish painter Rogier van der Weyden. Created in the 15th century, this multipanelled masterpiece combines the lush colours of rainbows, the harsh results of the final judgement and a powerful, enigmatic yet serene Archangel Michael.

La Moutarderie
MUSTARD FACTORY

(Mustard Mill; www.fallot.com; 31 rue du Faubourg Bretonnière; adult/child €10/8; ☺tours 10am & 11.30am Mon-Sat, also afternoons summer, closed Nov-Mar 15; ▣) Maison Fallot, Burgundy's last family-run stone-ground mustard company, offers tours of its facilities which include a museum about mustard. Demonstrations include hand-milling mustard seeds – young kids love it! Reserve ahead at the tourist office.

Basilique Collégiale Notre Dame
CHURCH

(place Général Leclerc; ☺8.30am-7pm) Built in the Romanesque and Gothic styles from the 11th to 15th centuries this church was once affiliated with the monastery of Cluny. It's notable for its extra-large porch, and medieval tapestries are displayed inside from Easter till the third weekend in November.

🏃 Activities

Underneath Beaune's buildings, streets and ramparts, millions of dusty bottles of wine are being aged to perfection in cool, dark cellars. Wine-tasting options abound; places below are just a wee sample of what's on offer. Also see p419.

Marché aux Vins
WINE TASTING

(☑03 80 25 08 20; www.marcheauxvins.com, in French; 2 rue Nicolas Rolin; admission €10; ☺9.30-11.45am & 2-5.45pm, no midday closure mid-Jun–Aug) Using a *tastevin*, sample an impressive 15 wines in the candle-lit former Église des Cordeliers and its cellars. Wandering among the vintages takes about an hour. The finest wines are at the end; look for the *premier crus* and the *grand cru*.

Cellier de la Vieille Grange
WINE TASTING

(☑03 80 22 40 06; www.bourgogne-cellier.com, in French; 27 bd Georges Clemenceau; ☺9am-noon & 2-7pm Wed-Sat, by appointment Sun-Tue) This is where locals come to buy Burgundy wines *en vrac* (in bulk) for as little as €1.25 per litre (from €3.40 per litre for AOC). Tasting is done direct from barrels using a pipette. Bring your own jerry can or buy a *cubitainer* (5/20L for €2.75/7.60) or something memorably called a *Vinibag*.

Lycée Viticole
WINE TASTING

(☑03 80 26 35 81; www.lavitibeaune.com, in French; 16 av Charles Jaffelin; ☺8am-noon & 2-5.30pm Mon-Thu, to 5pm Fri, 8am-noon Sat, closed 2 weeks mid-Aug) One of about 20 French secondary schools (at least one in each wine-producing region) that trains young people in every aspect of winemaking. You can visit the cellars and taste the prize-winning wines made by the students, something they're officially not allowed to do till they're 18. (Decades ago wine used to be served with lunch in the school cafeteria!)

Patriarche Père et Fils
WINE TASTING

(☑03 80 24 53 78; www.patriarche.com; 5 rue du Collège; audioguide tour €10; ☺9.30-11.30am & 2-5.30pm) The largest cellars in Burgundy, they are lined with about five million bottles of wine. The oldest is a Beaune Villages AOC from 1904. Visitors sample 13 wines and take the *tastevin* home.

PASS BEAUNE

If you'll be taking in a lot of Beaune and the Côte d'Or's sights and activities, including wine tasting, consider picking up the Pass Beaune at one of the tourist offices. Ticket combos save 5% to 15% depending on the number of sights you plan to visit from Cluny to the Côte d'Or.

BURGUNDY BEAUNE

Hiking & Cycling
WALKS, CYCLING

A number of walking circuits begin at **Parc de la Bouzaize**, just northwest of the Lycée Viticole. **Bourgogne Randonnées** (☑03 80 22 06 03; www.bourgogne-randonnees.com; 7 av du 8 Septembre; bikes per day/week €18/96; ☺9am-noon & 1.30-7pm Mon-Sat, 2-7pm Sun) arranges tailor-made self-guided bike tours, including lodging and meals. ADA (p409) also rents mountain bikes (€13 per day).

🖝 Tours

The small tourist train, **Visiotrain** (☑06 08 07 45 68; adult/child €6.50/4; ☺11am-5.30pm, closed Wed & morning Sat), departs six times

daily from Rue de l'Hôtel-Dieu and tours the old town.

The tourist office handles reservations for **hot-air-balloon rides** (p394), and for **vineyard tours** (per adult/child €38-42/19-21) run by the following companies: **Chemins de Bourgogne** (www.chemins-de-bourgogne. com), **Safari Tours** (www.burgundy-tourism -safaritours.com) and **Vinéatours** (www.vinea tours.com).

★★ Festivals & Events

Trois Glorieuses Festival
WINE FESTIVAL

On the third weekend in November is the grandest of the Côte d'Or's many wine fes-

Beaune

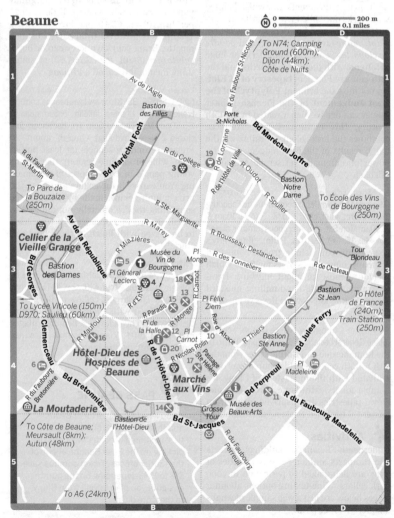

tivals. As part of this three-day extravaganza, the Hospices de Beaune holds a private auction of wines from its endowment, 61 hectares of prime vineyards bequeathed by benefactors; proceeds go to medical facilities and research.

🛏️ Sleeping

Reserve ahead.

Hôtel des Remparts   HISTORIC HOTEL **€€**
(📞03 80 24 94 94; www.hotel-remparts-beaune. com; 48 rue Thiers; d €75-112; ❄️@🛜) Set around two delightful courtyards, this 17th-century town house sits on a quiet street in the old town. Rooms have red tile floors, simple antique furniture and luxurious bathrooms. Friendly staff rent bikes. Parking €8 to €10.

Hôtel Rousseau   HOTEL **€**
(📞03 80 22 13 59; 11 place Madeleine; d incl breakfast €58) An endearingly old-fashioned, 12-room hotel, off the beaten path and run since 1959 by a friendly woman. Reception occasionally shuts for a while without warning so she can go shopping. Parking free.

Hôtel de la Poste   HISTORIC HOTEL **€€€**
(📞03 80 22 08 11; www.hoteldelapostebeaune. com; 1 bd Georges Clemenceau; d €160-220; ❄️🛜) This swank establishment sits on a site that's been home to a hostelry since 1660. The old-time wooden lift carries you to spacious, soothing rooms; no bling here, just impeccable understated elegance. Wheelchair access. Parking €10.

Abbaye de Maizières   HISTORIC HOTEL **€€**
(📞03 80 24 74 64; www.beaune-abbaye-maizieres.com; 19 rue Maizières; d €112; @) An idiosyncratic hotel inside a 12th-century abbey whose 13 tastefully converted rooms, with modern bathrooms, make creative use of the old brickwork and ancient wooden beams. No lift. Parking €8.

Hôtel de France   HOTEL **€**
(📞03 80 24 10 34; www.hoteldefrance-beaune. com; 35 av du 8 Septembre; s/d/tr/q from €38/65/75/85; ❄️@🛜🚗) An unsurprising but comfortable, sound-proofed place with 21 cheery rooms. Near the station, it's ideal if you're arriving by train. Parking €8.50.

Camping Ground   CAMPGROUND **€**
(📞03 80 22 03 91; campinglescentvignes@ mairie-beaune.fr; 10 rue Auguste Dubois; sites per adult/tent €3.80/4.50; ☉mid-Mar–Oct) A flowery, well-equipped campground 700m north of the centre.

Hôtel le Foch   HOTEL **€**
(📞03 80 24 05 65; www.hotelbeaune-lefoch. fr, in French; 24 bd Maréchal Foch; d €43-50) A cheapie, run by a friendly proprietress, whose 10 rooms are basic but clean.

✖️ Eating

Beaune harbours a host of excellent restaurants; you'll find many around place Carnot, place Félix Ziem and place Madeleine. Reserve ahead in high season.

TOP CHOICE **Loiseau des Vignes** GASTRONOMIC **€€€**
(📞03 80 24 12 06; 31 rue Maufoux; lunch menus €20-28, dinner menus €59-75; ☉Tue-Sat) Give yourself up to the splendour of delicate concoctions like an egg poached in

CHEESE, GLORIOUS CHEESE

What else would you pair with your dram of wine but one of the Burgundy or Champagne region's AOC cheeses? There are three, all made with cow's milk.

» Époisses – invented in the 16th century by the monks at Abbaye de Cîteaux, Époisses is a soft, round, orange-skinned white cheese. It takes a month to make, using washes of salt water, rainwater and Marc de Bourgogne (local pomace brandy), resulting in a strong, creamy flavour. Soumaintrain, a milder cheese (but with a spicy burst at the end of a tasting), is similar in appearance.

» Langres – milder than Époisses, but saltier, you'll know the Langres cheese by its unique shape: a depression in the top, perfect for holding a splash of Marc.

» Chaource – these elegant little wheels of soft white cheese can be quite fluid when young. A bit like Camembert, they are ideal with sparkling wines.

white wine with shallots...light as a dream. Could be the best egg you ever eat in your life. Wines are served only by the glass (€3 to €80) from snazzy sleek red degustation contraptions ringing the hushed but relaxed dining room. Service is knowledgeable and attentive, making a meal here a true pleasure.

Caves Madeleine   BURGUNDIAN €€
(☑03 80 22 93 30; 8 rue du Faubourg Madeleine; menus €14-24; ⊙closed Thu, Sun & lunch Fri) A convivial Burgundian restaurant, much appreciated by locals who prize good value; regional classics include *boeuf bourguignon* and *cassolette d'escargots*. Join fellow diners at long communal wooden tables surrounded by wine racks.

Le Bistrot Bourguignon   BURGUNDIAN €€
(☑03 80 22 23 24; 8 rue Monge; lunch menu €12.50, mains €16-19; ⊙Tue-Sat) This lively bistro and wine bar serves hearty cuisine billed as *régionale et originale* and 17 Burgundy wines by the glass (€3 to €9). Hosts live jazz at least once a month.

Le P'tit Paradis   MODERN BURGUNDIAN €€
(☑03 80 24 91 00; 25 rue Paradis; lunch menus €19, dinner menus €28-36; ⊙Tue-Sat) Find this intimate restaurant on a narrow medieval street. An excellent place for *cuisine elaborée* (creatively transformed versions of traditional dishes) made with fresh local products. Has a terrace open in summer.

Le Jardin des Remparts   GASTRONOMIC €€€
(☑03 80 24 79 41; 10 rue de l'Hôtel-Dieu; lunch menus €28, dinner menus €45-70; ⊙Tue-Sat) On the cool terrace under umbrellas or in the refined dining room, dine on treats like foie gras poached with tarragon.

Ma Cuisine   BURGUNDIAN €€
(☑03 80 22 30 22; passage Ste-Hélène; menu €22; ⊙12.15-1.30pm & 7.15-9pm Mon, Tue, Thu & Fri, closed Aug) A low-key place hidden down an alley. Traditional dishes include whole roasted Bresse pigeon (€32). The wine list has 850 vintages (€18 to €830).

Self-Catering

Food Market   MARKET €
(place de la Halle; ⊙until 12.30pm Sat) Elaborate weekly market. There's a much smaller *marché gourmand* (gourmet market) on Wednesday morning.

Alain Hess Fromager   CHEESE SHOP €
(7 place Carnot; ⊙9am-12.15pm & 2.30-7.15pm Mon-Sat, plus 10am-1pm Sun Easter-Dec) Fine cheeses and mustards.

Petit Casino   SUPERMARKET €
(4 rue Carnot; ⊙9am-7.30pm Tue-Sat, 8.30am-12.30pm Sun)

🍷 Drinking

Chatty locals jam **Les Mille et Une Vignes** (61 rue de Lorraine; ⊙Tue-Sat) for drinks at night and quieter coffees during the day.

🛍 Shopping

Athenaeum de la Vigne et du Vin BOOKSHOP
(☑03 80 25 08 30; www.athenaeumfr.com; 7 rue de l'Hôtel-Dieu; ⊙10am-7pm) Stocks thousands of titles on oenology (the art and science of winemaking), including many in English, as well as recipe books and wine-related gifts.

ℹ Information

Get online at the main tourist office (€1.50 per 15 minutes) and at **Le Clos Carnot** (☑03 80 22 73 43; 34 place Carnot; per hr €4; ⊙8am-midnight), a café-brasserie.

Post office (7 bd St-Jacques) Exchanges currency.

Tourist office (☎03 80 26 21 30; www.beaune-tourisme.fr); branch (1 rue de l'Hôtel-Dieu; ⏱10am-1pm & 2-6pm); main office (6 bd Perpreuil; ⏱9am-7pm Mon-Sat, 9am-6pm Sun) Sells Pass Beaune ticket combos.

Getting There & Away

BUS Transco (☎08 00 10 20 04) bus 44 links Beaune with Dijon (€1.50, 1½ hours, two to seven daily), stopping at Côte d'Or villages such as Vougeot, Nuits-St-Georges and Aloxe-Corton. Services reduced in July and August. In Beaune, buses stop along the boulevards around the old city. Timetables at the tourist office.

CAR ADA (☎03 80 22 72 90; 26 av du 8 Septembre) rents cars, scooters (€23 per day) and bikes (€14).

TRAIN Trains connect the following places:

Dijon €11, 25 minutes, 40 daily

Nuits-St-Georges €11, 10 minutes, 40 daily

Paris Gare de Lyon €64 to €118, 2¼ hours by TGV (non-TGV 4½ hours), 20 daily, two direct TGVs daily

Lyon-Part Dieu €31 to €46, 1¾ hours, 16 daily

Mâcon €13, 50 minutes, 16 daily

Getting Around

Parking is free outside the town walls. See p406 for bicycle hire.

Taxi Call ☎06 09 43 21 31 or 06 09 43 12 08.

Pays d'Auxois

West of Dijon, along and around the Canal de Bourgogne, the Pays d'Auxois is verdant and rural. Broad mustard fields, wooded hills and escarpments are dotted with fortified hilltop towns, including Semur-en-Auxois.

SEMUR-EN-AUXOIS

POP 4568

Sights & Activities

Surrounded by a hairpin turn in the River Armançon, this beguiling town is guarded by four massive, 13th- and 14th-century pink-granite bastions. Fear not, the 44m-high **Tour de la Orle d'Or** is not likely to collapse any time soon, those menacing cracks have been there since 1589!

Old City HISTORIC QUARTER

Most of the old city was built when Semur was an important religious centre boasting no fewer than six monasteries. The tourist office (which has a free walking tour brochure) is next to two concentric medieval gates, **Porte Sauvigne** (1417) and fortified **Porte Guillier** (13th century). Through the gates, pedestrianised **rue Buffon** is lined with 17th-century houses. The **confectionary shop** (14 rue Buffon; ⏱Tue-Sun) produces semurettes, delicious dark-chocolate truffles created here a century ago. The **Promenade du Rempart** affords panoramic views from atop the western part of Semur's medieval battlements.

FREE **Musée Municipal** MUSEUM

(☎03 80 97 24 25; rue Jean-Jacques Collenot; ⏱10am-noon & 2-6pm Wed-Mon) Great for the kids, with its extravaganza of stuffed fauna and its enormous fossils. These natural history exhibits are arranged just as they were back in the 19th century. The collection also includes sculpture and paintings.

Collégiale Notre Dame CHURCH

(⏱9am-noon & 2-6.30pm) A stained-glass window (1927) and a plaque commemorating American soldiers who fell in France in WWI are inside this twin-towered, Gothic collegiate church.

Sleeping & Eating

Hôtel de la Côte d'Or HOTEL €€

(☎03 80 97 24 54; www.auxois.fr; 1 rue de la Liberté; d €95-125; ❄@📶) Totally renovated in 2008, contemporary furnishings in the rooms blend beautifully with the old beams and stone fireplaces. Some of the fantastic bathrooms have jacuzzis. Check ahead for discounts.

WORTH A TRIP

GRAND FORGE DE BUFFON

The beautiful **Grand Forge de Buffon** (http://forge.buffon.ifrance.com, in French; adult/child €6/free; ⏱10am-noon & 2.30-6pm Wed-Mon Apr-Sep) sits on the pastoral banks of the Brenne Canal. One of the first fully integrated factories, it was built in 1778 by Georges-Louis Leclerc, the Count of Buffon and a mathematician and naturalist. The forge's existing buildings include a blast furnace that was used for casting molten metals and a supply channel with paddlewheel. The forge sits 8km west of Montbard near the village of Buffon on the D905.

One of France's trademark culinary habits, the consumption of gastropod molluscs – preferably with butter, garlic, parsley and fresh bread – is inextricably linked in the public mind with Burgundy because *Helix pomatia,* though endemic in much of Europe, is best known as *escargot de Bourgogne* (the Burgundy snail). Once a regular, and unwelcome, visitor to the fine-wine vines of Burgundy and a staple on Catholic plates during Lent, the humble hermaphroditic crawler has been decimated by over-harvesting and the use of agricultural chemicals, and is now a protected species. As a result, the vast majority of the critters impaled on French snail forks (the ones with two tongs) are now imported from Turkey, Greece and Eastern Europe.

Hôtel des Cymaises　　　　　　HOTEL €
(☑03 80 97 21 44; www.hotelcymaises.com; 7 rue du Renaudot; s/d/tr €58/63/79; ☎) Set around a quiet courtyard in a grand 18th-century *maison bourgeoise* are comfortable, slightly worn rooms, four apartments and a bright veranda for breakfast.

Carpe Diem　　　　　　　　　BISTRO €
(☑03 80 97 00 35; 4 rue du Vieux Marché; menus €11.50-21; ☺10.30am-2am Tue-Sun; ☎) This friendly neighbourhood bar serves simple meals and hosts occasional live music (jazz, blues) and offers internet access.

Café des Arts　　　　　　　　CAFÉ €
(4 place Gaveau; ☺Tue-Sun) Hosts art exhibitions and serves light meals.

Petit Casino　　　　　SUPERMARKET €
(32 place Notre Dame; ☺8am-12.30pm & 3-7.30pm, closed Sun afternoon & Mon)

ⓘ Information

The **tourist office** (☑03 80 97 05 96; www.ville-semur-en-auxois.fr, in French; 2 place Gaveau; ☺9am-noon & 2-5pm or 6pm Mon-Sat, closed Mon Oct-Apr; ☎) has a free walking-tour brochure in English and a **SNCF train ticket machine**. Carpe Diem bistro offers free **internet** and wi-fi with a drink or meal.

ⓘ Getting There & Away

Transco (☑08 00 10 20 04) bus 49 (two or three daily) goes to Dijon (€1.50, 1¼ hours) and Avallon (40 minutes). Bus 70 goes to Montbard (€1.50, 20 to 60 minutes, three to nine daily) on the Paris–Dijon rail line.

ABBAYE DE FONTENAY
Founded in 1118 and restored to its medieval glory a century ago, Abbaye de Fontenay (Fontenay Abbey; ☑03 80 92 15 00; www.abbayedefontenay.com; adult/child €9.50/5.50; ☺10am-6pm Apr-11 Nov, 10am-noon & 2-5pm 12 Nov-Mar) offers a fascinating glimpse of the austere, serene surroundings in which

Cistercian monks lived lives of contemplation, prayer and manual labour. Set in a bucolic wooded valley along a stream called Ru de Fontenay, the abbey, a Unesco World Heritage Site, includes an unadorned Romanesque church, a barrel-vaulted monks' dormitory, landscaped gardens and the first metallurgical factory in Europe with a forge from 1220. Guided tours (☺hourly 10am-5pm) are in French with printed information in six languages.

From the parking lot, the GR213 trail forms part of two verdant walking circuits: one to Montbard (13km return), the other (11.5km) through Touillon and Le Petit Jailly. Maps and extensive guides to plant life are available in the abbey shop.

Fontenay is 25km north of Semur-en-Auxois. A taxi (☑03 80 92 31 49, 03 80 92 04 79) from the Montbard TGV train station – trains go to Dijon (€16 to €27, 40 minutes) – costs €15 (30% more on Sunday and holidays).

Châtillon-sur-Seine
POP 6257

Châtillon's main claim to fame is the **Trésor de Vix** (Vix Treasure), a collection of Celtic, Etruscan and Greek objects from the 6th century BC on display at the Musée du Pays Châtillonnais (☑03 80 91 24 67; www.musee-vix.fr; 14 rue de la Libération; adult/child €6/3; ☺9am-noon & 2-6pm). The treasure was discovered in 1953 in the tomb of the **Dame de Vix**, a Celtic princess who controlled the trade in Cornish tin in the 6th century. Mined in Cornwall, the tin was brought by boat up the Seine as far as Vix and then carried overland to the Saône and the Rhône, whence river vessels conveyed it south to Marseilles and its most eager consumers, the Greeks, who alloyed it with copper to make bronze. The outstanding collection includes a jaw-droppingly massive bronze Greek *krater* (1.64m high and weighing 208kg!) that can hold 1100L of wine.

The **tourist office** (☑03 80 91 13 19; www.pays-chatillonnais.fr; 9-11 rue de la Libération; ◔9am-noon & 2-6pm Mon-Sat, plus 10am-noon Sun May-Sep) has information on Châtillonnais vineyards. **Au Stand** (☑03 80 91 22 53; 41 rue Maréchal de Lattre; per hr €4; ◔8am-9pm Tue-Sat, 8am-1pm Sun) has internet access.

The town's commercial centre, rebuilt after the war, is bordered by two branches of the Seine, here hardly more than a stream. A short walk east, the idyllic **Source de la Douix** (pronounced 'dwee'), a 600L-a-second artesian spring, flows from a 30m cliff. Perfect for a picnic, it is one of the oldest Celtic religious sites in Europe. Nearby, climb up to crenellated **Tour de Gissey** (c 1500s), for fine views.

Among the wines produced in the **Châtillonnais vineyards**, north of town, is Burgundy's own bubbly, *Crémant de Bourgogne* (www.cremantdebourgogne.fr, in French). Follow the **Route du Crémant**, marked by white-on-brown signs to the vineyards. The Champagne region's Côte des Bar vineyards are just a few kilometres further north.

The pleasant **Hôtel de la Côte d'Or** (☑03 80 91 13 29; www.logishotels.com; 2 rue Charles Ronot; d €60-70) has rooms with antique furnishings and a rustic **restaurant** (menus €20-40).

Bus 50, run by **Transco** (☑08 00 10 20 04), goes to Dijon (€15.50, 1¾ hours, two daily). SNCF buses go to the TGV train station in Montbard (40 minutes, two to five daily).

YONNE

The Yonne *département* (www.tourisme-yonne.com), roughly midway between Dijon and Paris, has long been Burgundy's northern gateway. The verdant countryside harbours the magical hilltop village of Vézelay, in the Parc Natural Régional du Morvan, and the white-wine powerhouse, Chablis. Canal boats cruise from ancient river ports such as Auxerre.

ℹ Getting Around

Bus services in the Yonne are cheap but extremely limited. **Les Rapides de Bourgogne** (☑in Auxerre 03 86 94 95 00, in Avallon 03 86 34 00 00; www.rapidesdebourgogne.com, in French; office 39 rue de Paris, Avallon) bus lines

run only once or twice a day on school days, with two more daily services available on demand; ie you must make a reservation the day before, prior to 5pm, by internet or phone (☑08 00 30 33 09. Tourist offices have timetables.

Line 1 Links Auxerre with Pontigny

Line 4 Links Auxerre to Chablis and Tonnerre

Line 5 Links Avallon's Café de l'Europe taxi stand with Noyers-sur-Serein and Tonnerre

Auxerre

POP 39,756

The alluring riverside town of Auxerre (pronounced 'oh-sair') has been a port since Roman times. The old city clambers up the hillside on the west bank of the River Yonne. Wandering through the maze of its cobbled streets you come upon Roman remains, Gothic churches and timber-framed medieval houses. Views span a jumble of belfries, spires and steep tiled rooftops.

Auxerre makes a good base for exploring northern Burgundy, including Chablis, and is an excellent place to hire a canal boat (see p394).

⊙ Sights & Activities

Get wonderful city views from **Pont Paul Bert** (1857) and the arched footbridge opposite the main tourist office.

Abbaye St-Germain   ABBEY

(☑03 86 18 05 50; place St-Germain; adult/child €6.50/free; ◔10am-noon & 2-6.30pm Wed-Mon) This ancient abbey with its dramatic flying buttresses began as a basilica above the tomb of St Germain, the 5th-century bishop who made Auxerre an important Christian centre. By the Middle Ages it was attracting pilgrims from all over Europe.

The **crypt** (tours €4.80; ◔departures hourly), accessible by tour (in French with printed information in English), contains some of Europe's finest examples of Carolingian architecture. Supported by 1000-year-old oak beams, the walls and vaulted ceiling are decorated with 9th-century frescoes; the far end houses the tomb of St Germain himself. Excavations under the nave reveal sarcophagi from as early as the 6th century.

Housed around the abbey's cloister, the **Musée d'Art et d'Histoire** (admission included in Abbeye ticket) displays rotating contemporary art exhibits, prehistoric artefacts and Gallo-Roman sculptures.

The same ticket also gets you into the Musée Leblanc-Duvernoy.

Cathédrale St-Étienne CATHEDRAL
(place St-Étienne; ☺7.30am-6pm) This vast Gothic cathedral and its stately 68m-high bell tower dominate Auxerre's skyline. The choir, ambulatory and some of the vivid **stained-glass windows** date from the 1200s. The Gothic western front was badly damaged by the Huguenots during the Wars of Religion.

The 11th-century Romanesque crypt (adult/child €3/free; ☺9am-6pm Mon-Sat, 2-6pm Sun, closed Sun Nov-Easter) is ornamented with remarkable frescoes, including a scene of **Christ à Cheval** (Christ on Horseback; late 11th century) unlike any other known in Western art. Upstairs, the treasury (adult/child €1.90/free) has an Entombment painting by Luca Penni (16th century) and illuminated manuscripts. Get tickets in the gift shop off the choir.

From June to September a 70-minute sound-and-light show (€5; ☺9.30pm or 10pm) is held nightly inside the cathedral. In July and August organ concerts (€5; ☺5pm or 6pm) take place every Sunday.

Auxerre

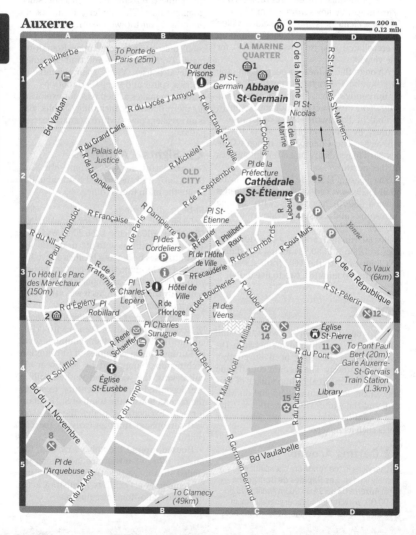

Tour de l'Horloge — CLOCK TOWER

(btwn place de l'Hôtel de Ville & rue de l'Horloge)
In the heart of Auxerre's partly medieval commercial precinct, the golden, spire-topped Tour de l'Horloge was built in 1483 as part of the city's fortifications. On the beautiful 17th-century clock faces (there's one on each side), the sun-hand indicates the time of day; the moon-hand shows the day of the lunar month, making a complete rotation every 29½ days.

Musée Leblanc-Duvernoy — MUSEUM

(9bis rue d'Églény; admission €2.20; ⊘10am-noon & 2-6.30pm Wed-Sun, closed Mon-Fri Oct-Apr) Has a decent collection of faience (pottery) and 18th-century Beauvais tapestries. Admission included with Abbaye ticket.

Cycling — CYCLING

Cycling options include the towpath along the Canal du Nivernais to Clamecy (about 60km), just south of town. See www.la-bourgogne-a-velo.com (in French) for a map.

Boating — BOATS

The main tourist office rents electric boats (per 1hr/half/full day €20/48/85; ⊘Wed-Sun Easter-Sep). It takes at least 1½ hours to get to the locks on the Canal du Nivernais. For longer trips, several boat-hire companies are based in the Auxerre area; see p394.

Tours

The tourist office offers a tour (adult/child €5/3; ⊘Sat & Sun Sep-Jun, daily Jul-Aug) of the town on an electric vehicle with an audio-guide; also group tours in English and the self-guided architectural walking tour brochure, *In the Steps of Cadet Roussel* (€1.50).

Across from the tourist office, **L'Hirondelle** (☑09 75 23 27 89; www.bateaux-auxerrois.com; adult/child €8.50/6; ⊘Tue-Sun) has cruises with commentary.

Sleeping

TOP CHOICE Hôtel Le Parc des Maréchaux

HISTORIC HOTEL €€
(☑03 86 51 43 77; www.hotel-parcmarechaux.com; 6 av Foch; s €84-108, d €95-129; ❄ @ 🛜 ≋) Settle into a mansion of château-like proportions, where everything is treated with the height of gentility. Lounges are luxurious and rooms are decorated with impeccable taste. The two best rooms, great for a romantic getaway, have balconies overlooking the private park. Parking free.

Hôtel Le Commerce — HOTEL €

(☑03 86 52 03 16; hotelducommerceauxerre@wanadoo.fr; 5 rue René Schaeffer; s/d €45/52; 🛜) Simple rooms smack in the centre of town have creative decor inspired by distant sunny lands. Parking €7.50.

Hôtel Normandie — HOTEL €€

(☑03 86 52 57 80; www.hotelnormandie.fr; 41 bd Vauban; d €69-99, q €125; ❄ @ 🛜 🏓) Ivy covers the 19th-century building, and rooms with views make it feel a bit like a country inn. Amenities include a billiard table, workout room and sauna (€6 per person). Wi-fi costs €3.

Eating

La Pause Gourmande — TEA HOUSE €

(☑03 86 33 98 87; 1 rue Fourier; mains €11; ⊘lunch Tue-Sat) Locals cram this *salon de thé* for savoury, inventive salads or home-made foie gras on fresh-baked brioche with garnishes like apricots and shallots. The owner cooks right in front of you and also makes fresh pastries.

Le Flobert — BISTRO €

(☑03 86 51 16 19; 71 rue du Pont; lunch menus €12.50, mains €7.50; ⊘lunch Tue-Sun, dinner Thu-Sun; 🍴) The menu at this sweet little

BURGUNDY AUXERRE

spot, just a simple bar and a few tables in an elegant honey-coloured room, changes every day and always involves seasonal, fresh ingredients. Check the small slates for what's available. Kids' menu €8.

La P'tite Beursaude　　BURGUNDIAN €€
(☑03 86 51 10 21; 55 rue Joubert; lunch menus €18.50-20, dinner menus €25-28; ⊙Thu-Mon) Waitresses wearing traditional Morvan dress serve traditional fish and meat dishes. Specialities include rib steak with Époisses cheese.

Le St-Pèlerin　　BURGUNDIAN €€
(☑03 86 52 77 05; 56 rue St-Pèlerin; menus €25-28; ⊙Tue-Sat) Diners come back satiated from this rustic restaurant, where French and Burgundian dishes are prepared over a wood fire. Specialities include escargots and meats like ham in Chablisienne sauce.

Self-Catering

Food Market　　MARKET €
(place de l'Arquebuse; ⊙7am-1pm Tue & Fri)

Super Monoprix　　SUPERMARKET €
(place Charles Surugue; ⊙8.30am-8pm Mon-Sat)

☆ Entertainment

Find out what's happening throughout the Yonne at www.citedesmusiques.org (in French).

Silex　　ENTERTAINMENT COMPLEX
(☑03 86 40 95 40; www.lesilex.fr, in French; 7 rue de l'Île aux Plaisirs) The city's new

---

WORTH A TRIP

GET AWAY FROM IT ALL...

Domaine Dessus Bon Boire (☑03 86 53 89 99; www.dessusbonboire.com, in French; 19 rue de Vallan; s/d/tr/q incl breakfast €48/58/70/90; 🖥️🅿️), a family-run organic winery, is perfect for a countryside idyll. In sleepy riverside Vaux, 6km south of Auxerre, Catherine and André Donat maintain impeccable rooms with bright floral accents and plenty of peace and quiet. Sample their *aligoté* (a dry white wine) or their Côtes d'Auxerre. Breakfast often includes homebaked goodies.

Pop over the bridge in the evening for authentic, delicious wood-fired pizza at cheery **Pizza-Cotté** (☑03 86 53 33 30; 1 rue de la Poire, Champs-sur-Yonne; pizzas €10-12; ⊙dinner Mon-Sat).

---

theatre complex across the river has a packed slate of drama and concerts, from reggae to rock and jazz (www.jazzclub dauxerre.com, in French), free concerts on Thursday evenings and a Jazz Café.

Mo' Better Blues　　MUSIC BAR
(☑03 86 51 36 64; 36-38 rue du Puits des Dames; admission free; ⊙Wed-Sat) Dynamic jazz bar with live concerts, jam sessions and salsa courses.

Le Théâtre　　THEATRE
(☑03 86 72 24 24; www.auxerreletheatre.com, in French; 54 rue Joubert; ⊙Sep-Jun) Stages music and dance performances.

ⓘ Information

Centre Hospitalier (☑03 86 48 48 48; 2 bd de Verdun) For medical services.

Post office (place Charles Surugue; ⊙noon-6.30pm Mon, 9am-6.30pm Tue-Fri, 9am-12.15pm & 2-5pm Sat) Changes currency.

Speed Informatique 89 (32 rue du Pont; per 10min/1hr €1/5; ⊙2-9pm Mon-Sat) Internet access.

Tourist office (☑03 86 52 06 19; www.ot-aux erre.fr) main office (1-2 quai de la République; ⊙9am-1pm & 2-7pm Mon-Sat, 9.30am-1pm & 3-6.30pm Sun); place de l'Hôtel de Ville annexe (7 place de l'Hôtel de Ville; ⊙10am-noon & 1.30-6pm Tue-Sat, also Sun Jul & Aug) Annexe will change small amounts of money on Sunday and holidays.

ⓘ Getting There & Away

BUS Les Rapides de Bourgogne (☑03 86 94 95 00; www.rapidesdebourgogne.com, in French) Schedules from the tourist office.

CAR ADA (☑03 86 46 01 02; 6bis av Gambetta)

Avis (☑03 86 46 83 47; train station)

Europcar (☑03 86 46 99 08; 9 av Gambetta)

TRAIN Trains run from **Gare Auxerre-St-Gervais** (rue Paul Doumer):

Autun €28, 3¼ hours, one daily

Avallon €13, 1¼ hours, five daily

Dijon €33, two hours, 18 daily

Paris Gare de Lyon or Gare de Bercy €33, 1½ to 2½ hours, 20 daily

Sermizelles-Vézelay €11, one hour, three daily

ⓘ Getting Around

Free parking is available along the river on quais de la Marine and de la République, and on the boulevards that circle the old city: Chainette, Vauban, 11 Novembre and Vaulabelle.

BICYCLE Hire at the main tourist office (three/seven hours €10/18).

BUS Free **shuttle buses** (⊘7.50am-12.10pm & 1.30-7.10pm Mon-Sat) circulate from the parking lot at la Porte de Paris throughout the old town.
TAXI Call ☑03 86 48 17 93 or ☑06 07 80 82 25.

Around Auxerre

Between the River Yonne and the Canal de Bourgogne lie the Auxerrois and the Tonnerrois, rural areas covered with forests, fields, pastures and vineyards. The quiet back roads (like the D124) and many of the walking trails make for excellent cycling.

LA PUISAYE

The countryside west of Auxerre, known as La Puisaye, is a lightly populated landscape of woods, winding creeks and dark hills. The area is best known as the birthplace of Colette (1873–1954), author of *La Maison de Claudine* and *Gigi* (and 50 other novels) and is of particular interest because much of her work explores her rural Burgundian childhood.

Colette lived till the age of 18 in the tiny town of St-Sauveur-en-Puisaye, 40km southwest of Auxerre. The Musée Colette (☑03 86 45 61 95; adult/child €5/2; ⊘10am-6pm Wed-Mon Apr-Oct, 2-6pm Sat & Sun Nov-Mar), in the village château, displays letters, manuscripts, two furnished rooms from her apartment in Paris' Palais Royal and photos featuring her iconic hairdo.

TOP\ Chantier Médiéval de Guédelon CHOICE/ (☑03 86 45 66 66; www.guedelon. fr; D955 near Treigny; adult/child €9/7; ⊘10am-5.30pm or 6pm Thu-Tue, closed Oct-mid-Mar; ⚑) is 45km southwest of Auxerre and 7km southwest of St-Sauveur-en-Puisaye. A team of skilled artisans, aided by archaeologists, has been hard at work building a fortified castle here since 1997 using only 13th-century techniques. No electricity or power tools: stone is quarried on site using iron hand tools forged by a team of blacksmiths, who also produce vital items like door hinges. Clay for tiles is fired for three days using locally cut wood and the mortar, made on site with lime, is transported in freshly woven wicker baskets.

A very worthwhile guided tour, sometimes in English, costs €2 per person. Wear closed shoes, as the site is often a sea of muck. Child-oriented activities include stone carving (using especially soft stone).

The elegant 11th-century Château de Ratilly (☑03 86 74 79 54; www.chateauderatilly.

fr, in French; Treigny; adult/child €4/free; ⊘10am-noon & 2-6pm Mon-Fri, 3-6pm Sat & Sun, no midday closure 15 Jun-15 Sep) sits in the countryside near Treigny and holds a collection of pottery by the Pierlot family and a changing series of excellent contemporary art exhibitions and concerts.

CHABLIS
POP 2580

The well-to-do, picturesque town of Chablis, 19km east of Auxerre, has made its fortune growing, ageing and marketing the dry white wines that have carried its name to the four corners of the earth.

Chablis is made exclusively from chardonnay grapes and originated with the monks of Pontigny. Now it is divided into four AOCs: Petit Chablis, Chablis, Chablis Premier Cru and, most prestigious of all, Chablis Grand Cru. The seven *grands crus* are lovingly grown on just 1 sq km of land on the hillsides northeast of town.

⊙ Sights & Activities

Nearby villages worth exploring include Courgis, which offers great views; Chichée and Chemilly, both on the River Serein; and Chitry-le-Fort, famous for its fortified church. The gorgeous hillside village of Fleys has a number of wineries.

Old Town   HISTORIC CENTRE
The 12th- and 13th-century Gothic Église St-Martin (⊘Jul & Aug), first founded in the 9th century by monks fleeing the Norman attacks on Tours, is two short blocks northwest of place Charles de Gaulle. Southeast along rue Porte Noël are the twin bastions of Porte Noël (1778), which hosts art exhibitions from June to August. Nearby, the enigmatic 16th-century building known as the synagogue (10-14 rue des Juifs) has been restored. The 12th-century cellar of Petit Pontigny (rue de Chichée) was once used by Pontigny's Cistercian monks to ferment wine.

Wine Tasting   WINE TASTING
Local wisdom says it is best to taste in the morning while the palate is fresh. For a vineyard tour, call Chablis Vititours (☑06 11 47 82 98; www.chablis-vititours.fr; 90min/full day €20/45, under 12yr free). Wine can be sampled and purchased at dozens of places (eg along rue des Moulins); the tourist office has a comprehensive list.

La Chablisienne (☑03 86 42 89 98; 8 bd Pasteur; ⊘9am-12.30pm & 2-7pm, no midday

IRANCY WINE COUNTRY

Ask locals where they go to taste western Burgundy's wines and many say: Irancy (www.irancy.org). This relatively new AOC (1999) predominantly uses a pinot noir grape, and the growing villages are extremely picturesque. Set in rolling hills and spring-blooming cherry orchards, Irancy and nearby Coulanges-la-Vineuse lie 13km south of Auxerre. Explore and you'll find many domaines from which to sample. In Irancy you can try Thierry Richoux (☎03 86 42 21 60; 73 rue Soufflot), which is converting to all-organic techniques. In Coulanges-la-Vineuse stop by Clos du Roi (☎03 86 42 25 72; www.closduroi.com, in French; 17 rue André Vilidieu; tasting and tour €3) or, in the heart of the village, Domaine Maltoff (☎03 86 42 32 48; o.maltoff@wanadoo.fr; 20 rue d'Aguesseau; s/d/tr incl breakfast €49/64/79), which is also a B&B.

closure Jul & Aug) A large cooperative cellar founded in 1923, it carries a variety of vintages, including five of Chablis' seven *grands crus*.

Billaud-Simon (☎03 86 42 10 33; 1 quai de Reugny; ⊗by appointment) Get off the beaten path to this unpretentious spot on the verdant edge of the canal. Excellent wines represent each of the appellations.

Laroche (☎03 86 42 89 00; www.larochewines .com; 22 rue Louis Bro)

Jean-Marc Brocard (☎03 86 42 45 76; www.brocard.fr; place Charles de Gaulle)

Walking & Cycling   WALKS, CYCLING
Vineyard walks from Chablis include the Sentier des Grands Crus (8km) and the Sentier des Clos (13km to 24km, depending on your route). The tourist office sells topoguides (€3).

Cycling is a great way to tour the Chablis countryside. One flat, lush option is the 45km Chemin de Serein (www.chemin-serein. com, in French), which follows the old Tacot rail line southeast to Noyers-sur-Serein and L'Isle-sur-Serein. The tourist office hires bikes (per 2hr/half/full day €4/7.50/12) from Easter to September.

🛏 Sleeping

Hôtel du Vieux Moulin   BOUTIQUE HOTEL €€
(☎03 86 42 47 30; www.larochehotel.fr; 18 rue des Moulins; d €125-175, ste €245-270; ❋@⊛) In a one-time mill, the five rooms and two suites, understated and very contemporary, afford luscious views of a branch of the Serein. The breakfast room has *grand cru* views. The swank restaurant, Le Wine Bar, is downstairs (*menus* €22 to €38).

Hôtel Le Bergerand's   HOTEL €€
(☎03 86 18 96 08; www.chablis-france.fr, in French; 4 rue des Moulins; s €58-92, d €68-112; ❋@⊛) This simple rustic hotel with antique wood furniture and cheerful spring colours occupies a one-time coach inn. On weekends breakfast (€7.50) is obligatory.

🍴 Eating

La Cuisine Au Vin   MODERN FRENCH €€
(☎03 86 18 98 52; 16 rue Auxerroise; lunch menus €17, dinner menus €25-39; ⊗lunch Wed-Sun, dinner Wed-Sat) Tuck into exquisitely presented organic meals in a cool 11th-century *cave* highlighted in green neon. An offshoot of the Defaix winery (www.chablisdefaix.com), the restaurant sources its ingredients from its own garden patch. Taste wines upstairs with the very knowledgeable Ken Haney.

Le Bistrot des Grands Crus

                          TRADITIONAL FRENCH €€
(☎03 86 42 19 41; 8-10 rue Jules Rathier; menus €20; ⊗closed mid-Jan–mid-Feb) A block southeast of Porte Noël, this relaxed place serves *cuisine du terroir* (cooking that's deeply connected to the land) made with the freshest local ingredients.

Self-Catering

Food market   MARKET €
(place Charles de Gaulle; ⊗8am-1pm Sun)

Les Jardins Européens   GROCERY €
(11 rue Mar de Lattre De Tassigny; ⊗8am-12.30pm & 3-7pm Mon-Sat, 8am-12.30pm Sun) Local cheeses and exquisite fruit and veggies.

Petit Casino   SUPERMARKET €
(rue du Maréchal Leclerc; ⊗7.30am-1pm & 3-7.30pm Mon-Sat)

ℹ Information

Tourist Office (☎03 86 42 80 80; www.chablis .net; 1 rue du Maréchal de Lattre de Tassigny; ⊗10am-12.30pm & 1.30-7pm, closed Sun Nov-Mar) Has free English walking-tour booklet and maps of vineyards.

❶ Getting There & Away

Chablis is served by bus (www.rapidesdebour gogne.com) between Auxerre and Tonerre (Line 4, €2, one per day, Monday to Saturday). The tourist office has schedules.

ABBAYE DE PONTIGNY

TOP CHOICE Abbaye de Pontigny (☏03 86 47 54 99; www.abbayedepontigny.eu, in French; ⊙9am-7pm), founded in 1114, rises from the lush mustard fields 25km north of Auxerre. The spectacular *abbatiale* (abbey church) is one of the last surviving examples of Cistercian architecture in Burgundy. The simplicity and purity of its white-stone construction reflect the austerity of the Cistercian order (see p401). On summer days sunshine filtering through the high windows creates an amazing sense of peace and tranquillity. *Discovering Pontigny* (€2.50), on sale in the gift shop, points out fascinating architectural details.

The Gothic sanctuary, 108m long and lined with 23 chapels, was built in the mid-12th century; the wooden choir screen, stalls and organ loft were added in the 17th and 18th centuries.

Three archbishops of Canterbury played a role in the history of Pontigny's abbey: Thomas Becket spent the first three years of his exile here (1164–66); Stephen Langton, a refugee from political turmoil in England, lived here for six years (1207–13); and Edmund Rich, who fell ill and died at Soissy in 1240 while on his way to the Vatican, was brought here for burial.

Monks here were the first to perfect the production of Chablis wine. From 1913 to 1922 the church was the site of literary meetings called the Décades de Pontigny involving such luminaries as Gide, Sartre and Malraux. In summer there are concerts.

The tourist office (☏03 86 47 47 03; http://pontigny tourisme.free.fr; 22 rue Paul Desjardins; ⊙10am-12.30pm & 2-5.30pm Mon-Sat or Tue-Sat), across the road, has accommodation information and sells hiking maps.

TONNERRE

POP 5509

The less-than-prosperous town of Tonnerre, on the Canal de Bourgogne, is best known for its Hôtel-Dieu (www.hotel-dieu -tonnerre.com, in French; rue de l'Hôpital; adult/child €4.50/3.50; ⊙9am-noon & 2-6pm Mon-Sat, 10am-1.30pm & 2-4.30pm Sun, closed Sun Nov-Mar), a charity hospital founded in 1293 by

Marguerite de Bourgogne, wife of Charles d'Anjou. At the eastern end of the barrel-vaulted patients' hall, near the chapel and Marguerite's tomb, is an extraordinary 15th-century *Entombment of Christ,* carved from a single block of stone.

About 400m west, 200L of water per second gushes from Fosse Dionne, a natural spring that was sacred to the Celts and whose blue-green tint hints at its great depth. Legend has it that a serpent lurks at the bottom. The pool is surrounded by a mid-18th-century washing house, a semicircle of ancient houses and forested slopes.

If you must overnight in Tonnerre try La Ferme de Fosse Dionne (☏03 86 54 82 62; www.fermefossedionne.com; 11 rue de la Fosse Dionne; d incl breakfast €65). In a late-18th-century farmhouse overlooking Fosse Dionne, this delightful hostelry has a café and antique shop.

The tourist office (☏03 86 55 14 48; www. tonnerre.fr, in French), at the entrance to the Hôtel-Dieu, has a walking-tour brochure and rents bicycles (half-/full day €10/18).

By rail, Tonnerre is linked to Dijon (€16.80, one hour, nine daily) and, via Laroche-Migennes, to Auxerre (€9.70, one hour, eight daily).

CHÂTEAU DE TANLAY

The French Renaissance-style Château de Tanlay (☏03 86 75 86 02; adult/child €8/3.50; ⊙tours 10am, 11.30am, 2.15pm, 3.15pm, 4.15pm & 5.15pm Wed-Mon, closed mid-Nov–Mar), an elegant product of the 17th century, is surrounded by a wide moat and elaborately carved outbuildings. Interior highlights include the **Grande Galerie**, whose walls and ceiling are completely covered with *trompe l'œil*. Find it 10km east of Tonnerre in the village of Tanlay.

CHÂTEAU D'ANCY-LE-FRANC

The Italian Renaissance makes a cameo appearance at Château d'Ancy-le-Franc (☏03 86 75 14 63; www.chateau-ancy.com; adult/child €8/5; ⊙tours 10.30am, 11.30am, 2pm, 3pm, 4pm & 5pm Tue-Sun, closed mid-Nov–Mar), built in the 1540s by the celebrated Italian architect Serlio. The richly painted interior, like the 32m-mural in the **Pharsale Gallery**, is mainly the work of Italian artists brought to Fontainebleau by François I. Tours are in French with written English translations.

The château is located 19km southeast of Tonnerre.

BURGUNDY WINE BASICS

Burgundy's epic vineyards extend approximately 258km from Chablis in the north to the Rhône's Beaujolais in the south and comprise 100 AOCs (Appellation d'Origine Contrôlée). Each region has its own appellations and traits, embodied by a concept called *terroir*, the earth imbuing its produce, like grapes, with unique qualities.

In 1878 the vines of Burgundy came near to extinction due to the phylloxera louse, a sap-sucker related to aphids. The solution was to graft French vine varieties to American root stock which were immune to the insect. Governing bodies throughout the region work in rigorous tandem with vintners to assure that common practices are followed to meet AOC standards. Examples include the use of pesticides and fertilisers, pruning styles and the specific yield allowed in each harvest.

Many aficionados spend a lifetime studying and enjoying the myriad vintages – which depend on *cépage* (grape variety), weather, yield, vinicultural practices and *elévage* (the process for caring for the wine following vinification).

Burgundy's wines are celebrated each year at the Festival Musical des Grands Crus de Bourgogne (☑03 80 34 38 40; www.bourgogne-tourisme.com; ☺Jun-Sep), which features 40 concerts and wine events throughout the region.

For more on wine, see p931.

Here's an ever-so-brief survey of some of Burgundy's major growing regions:

Côte d'Or vineyards The northern section, the **Côte de Nuits**, stretches from Marsannay-la-Côte south to Corgoloin and produces reds known for their robust, full-bodied character. The southern section, the **Côte de Beaune**, lies between Ladoix-Serrigny and Santenay and produces great reds and great whites. Appellations from the area's hilltops are the **Hautes-Côtes de Nuits** and **Hautes-Côtes de Beaune**.

Chablis Four renowned chardonnay white wine appellations from 20 villages around Chablis.

Châtillonnais Approximately 20 villages around Châtillon-sur-Seine producing red and white wines.

Côte Chalonnaise The southernmost continuation of the Côte de Beaune's slopes, the region also produces *Crémant de Bourgogne*, a light sparkling white or rosé.

Irancy Part of the **Auxerrois vineyards**, producing excellent pinot noir reds.

Mâconnais Known for rich or fruity white wines, like the Pouilly-Fuissé chardonnay.

NOYERS-SUR-SEREIN
POP 744

The absolutely picturesque medieval village of Noyers (pronounced 'nwa-yair'), 30km southeast of Auxerre, is surrounded by rolling pastureland, wooded hills and a sharp bend in the River Serein. Stone ramparts and fortified battlements enclose much of the village and, between the two imposing stone gateways, cobbled streets lead past 15th- and 16th-century gabled houses, wood and stone archways and several art galleries.

Lines carved into the facade of the 18th-century mairie (town hall), next to the library, mark the level of historic floods. Diagonally across the street is the tourist office (☑03 86 82 66 06; www.noyers-sur-serein.com; 22 place de l'Hôtel de Ville; ☺10am-1pm & 2-6pm, closed Sun Oct-May).

Noyers is a superb base for walking. Just outside the clock-topped southern gate, Chemin des Fossés leads eastwards to the River Serein and a streamside walk around the village's 13th-century fortifications, 19 of whose original 23 towers are extant. The 9km Balade du Château, trail-marked in red, follows the Serein's right bank past the utterly ruined château just north of Noyers. You can walk or cycle the Chemin de Serein (www.chemin-serein.com, in French) between here and Chablis.

Among the town's quirky galleries is Création Maroquinerie (27 rue de la Petite Étape aux Vins; ☺Tue-Sun), a fantastic leather shop full of chic belts and supple handbags. The proprietors, Yazmhil and Brice, do custom work and make everything on site, sometimes using bison hide. Another inter-

Want to Know More?

Château du Clos de Vougeot (☎03 80 62 86 09; www.tastevin-bourgogne.com; Vougeot; adult/child €3.90/2.90; ☺9am-6.30pm Mon-Fri, to 5pm Sat, closed 25 Dec-Jan) provides a wonderful introduction to Burgundy's winemaking techniques. Originally the property of the Abbaye de Cîteaux, the 16th-century country castle served as a getaway for the abbots. The 12th-century farm buildings were the nexus of the early development of winemaking methods. The Confrérie des Chevaliers du Tastevin (a group dedicated to the promulgation of Burgundian wines and traditions) conducts tours that are choc-full of interesting winemaking facts and offer a chance to discover the workings of enormous ancient wine presses and casks.

Tourist offices provide brochures including *The Burgundy Wine Road* and a useful map, *Roadmap to the Wines of Burgundy* (€0.50). A handy website is www.bourgogne-wines.com.

Lots of books are available at Beaune's Athenaeum de la Vigne et du Vin (p408). Look for these:

» *Burgundy* by Anthony Hanson

» *Côte d'Or: A Celebration of the Great Wines of Burgundy* by Clive Coates

» *The Wines of Burgundy* by Sylvain Pitiot and Jean-Charles Servant (excellent overview)

» *Everything There Is To Know About Burgundy Wines* (concise, easy-to-use introduction to Burgundy's 100 appellations)

» *Wine and War* by Don and Petie Kladstrupe (the tale of France's wine and vintners during WWII)

Or take a class!

École des Vins de Bourgogne
(☎03 80 26 35 10; www.ecoledesvins-bourgogne.com; 6 rue du 16e Chasseurs, Beaune) Offers a variety of courses (from a two-hour fundamentals class for €40 to a full weekend course for €365) to refine your vinicultural vocabulary as well as your palate.

Sensation Vin
(☎03 80 22 17 57; www.sensation-vin.com; 1 rue d'Enfer, Beaune; ☺10am-7pm) Offers introductory tasting sessions (no appointment needed) as well as tailor-made courses.

esting spot is Diane Calvert's **illuminated painting studio** (47 rue de la Petite Étape aux Vins) where she grinds her own pigments from semiprecious stones and uses parchment and quill pens.

Moulin de la Roche (☎03 86 82 68 13; www.bonadresse.com/bourgogne/le-moulin-de-la-roche.htm; rte d'Auxerre; s incl breakfast €58, d €67-75, q €105; ☂) sits on three gorgeous hectares over the River Serein. A renovated mill, it has two beautiful guestrooms and a millwheel in the living room.

La Vieille Tour (☎03 86 82 87 69; fax 03 86 82 66 04; place du Grenier à Sel; d incl breakfast €55-70, q €80-90; ☺Apr-Sep; ☂), in a rambling 17th-century house, has five simply furnished *chambres d'hôte,* loads of local colour and a lovely garden. It is run by a Dutch art historian who promises a warm

welcome but adds, 'I cannot guarantee I have no spiderwebs'.

Noyers has a couple of **grocery shops** and a **weekly market** (☺Wed morning). Four young brothers run the outstanding **Maison Paillot** (☎03 86 82 82 16; www.maison-paillot.com; place de l'Hôtel de Ville; lunch menus €32; ☺shop & wine cellar Tue-Sun, closed Feb, restaurant lunch Tue-Sun, dinner Tue-Sat, closed Jan-Mar) and combine a charcuterie/deli/*cave* with an excellent restaurant, Les Millésimes. Or try the simple, delicious meals at **Restaurant de la Vieille Tour** (☎03 86 82 87 36; rue Porte Peinte; menus €14.50-22; ☺lunch Sat-Wed, dinner Fri-Wed, closed Oct-Mar; ☂☂). Dishes often have an exotic twist and vegetarian options are available.

Avallon

POP 7743

The once-strategic walled town of Avallon, on a picturesque hilltop overlooking the green terraced slopes of two River Cousin tributaries, was in centuries past a stop on the coach road from Paris to Lyon. At its most animated during the Saturday morning market, the city makes a good base for exploring Vézelay and the Parc Naturel Régional du Morvan.

Sights & Activities

The old city is built on a triangular granite hilltop with ravines to the east and west. The main commercial thoroughfares are rue de Paris and rue de Lyon, outside the city walls, and the old city's Grande Rue Aristide Briand, spanned by **Tour de l'Horloge**, a solid, 15th-century clock tower.

TOP CHOICE Musée de l'Avallonnais MUSEUM

(☎03 86 34 03 19; place de la Collégiale; ⏲2-6pm Wed-Mon Jul-Sep) Founded in 1862, this wonderful small museum displays religious art including some fine Romanesque examples. Other highlights include a series of expressionist watercolours by Georges Rouault (1871–1958) and an excellent art deco silver collection by renowned designer and jeweller Jean Després (1889–1980).

Collégiale St-Lazare CHURCH

(rue Bocquillot) Eight centuries ago masses of pilgrims flocked here thanks to a piece of the skull of St Lazarus, believed to provide protection from leprosy. The early-12th-century church once had three portals but one was crushed when the northern belfry came a-tumblin' down in 1633; the two remaining portals are grandly decorated in Romanesque style, though much of the carving has been damaged. Summertime art exhibitions are held next door in Église St-Pierre and across the street in the 18th-century Grenier à Sel (Salt Store).

Walking & Cycling WALKS, CYCLING

A pathway descends from the ancient gateway **Petite Porte**, affording fine views over the Vallée du Cousin. You can walk around the walls, with their 15th- to 18th-century towers, ramparts and bastions.

For a bucolic walk or bike ride in the **Vallée du Cousin**, take the shaded, one-lane D427, which follows the gentle rapids of the River Cousin through dense forests and lush meadows. The tourist office sells hiking maps (eg IGN 2722 ET) and has information on Parc Naturel Régional du Morvan.

Sleeping

AVALLON

Hôtel Les Capucins HOTEL €

(☎03 86 34 06 52; www.avallonlescapucins.com; 6 av Paul Doumer; d €50, 8-person ste €130; ❄@📶) This spotless budget place sits on a quiet, plum-lined sidestreet. Comfortable rooms are decorated with all manner of butterflies.

Hôtel d'Avallon Vauban HOTEL €

(☎03 86 34 36 99; www.avallonvaubanhotel.com; 53 rue de Paris; s/d €55/61, studio €90; ❄@) *Trompe l'œil* trees decorate the facade, real trees fill the private garden, and tidy, spacious rooms and studio apartments have simple furnishings. Parking €2.

VALLÉE DU COUSIN

TOP CHOICE Le Moulin des Ruats HISTORIC HOTEL €€

(☎03 86 34 97 00; www.moulin-des-ruats.com; D427; d €82-154; ⏲closed 15 Nov-20 Feb; 📶) This very romantic former flour mill sits in a gorgeous wooded spot right on the river and has a ravishing waterside terrace. Impeccable rooms come with antique-style furnishings and some have little balconies. Fantastic views from rooms 4 and 12.

DON'T MISS

LA CIMENTELLE

La Cimentelle (☎03 86 31 04 85; http://lacimentelle.com, in French; 2 rue de la Cimentelle, Vassy-lès-Avallon; s incl breakfast €75-90, d €80-95, tr €140; 📶🏊) is a welcoming B&B operated by hosts Stéphane and Nathalie, who retired from life in Lyon to renovate her family estate in the countryside. Situated on shady, extensive grounds 6km north of Avallon, the château houses luxuriously appointed rooms, each one a bit different. One favourite, Hippolyte, has a freestanding claw-foot tub in front of a fireplace. Three-bedroom family apartments (€140 to €210) are fantastic. Do not skip the *repas* (€32 with wine): Nathalie is a gourmet chef and every meal is a sumptuous delight. The swimming pool sits spectacularly atop the ruins of an old cement factory.

Camping Municipal sous Roche
CAMPGROUND €

(☑03 86 34 10 39; campingsousroche@ville-avallon
.fr; sites per adult/tent/car €3.20/2.50/2.50;
☺Apr–mid-Oct) A woody, well-maintained site
2km southeast of the old city on the forested
banks of the Cousin. Has a play structure,
RV hook-ups (€5) and wastewater disposal.

Le Moulin des Templiers
HOTEL €€

(☑03 86 34 10 80; www.hotel-moulin-des-tem
pliers.com; 10 rte de Cousin, D427, Pontaubert; d
€ 69-78; ☺closed Jan) This converted mill's
bedrooms, with country furnishings, are
a bit small but there's a delightful terrace
next to the rushing river.

🍴 Eating & Drinking

Le Gourmillon
BURGUNDIAN €€

(☑03 86 31 62 01; 8 rue de Lyon; lunch menus €11,
dinner menus €15-36; ☺lunch daily, dinner Mon-
Sat; 🖶) This low-key cheerfully colourful
place, popular with locals, serves up French
and Burgundian dishes. Desserts are delicious. Kids' menu €8.

Hôtel Les Capucins
BURGUNDIAN €€

(☑03 86 34 06 52; 6 av Paul Doumer; menus
€14-36) Canvases by local artists adorn the
walls of this elegant restaurant. An excellent place to try *sauce Morvandelle* (made
with shallots, mustard and white wine), for
instance with Charolais beef.

Dame Jeanne
TEA HOUSE €

(☑03 86 34 58 71; 59 Grand rue Aristide Briand;
☺8am-7pm Fri-Wed) Folks come from the
countryside for delicious lunches or special
pastry treats in the garden or 17th-century
salon.

Self-Catering

Saturday Market
MARKET €

(place des Odebert ☺until 1pm Sat) Enormous
weekly market.

Thursday Market
MARKET €

(place du Général de Gaulle; ☺Thu morning)

Auchan
SUPERMARKET €

(rue du Général Leclerc; ☺8.30am-9pm Mon-Sat)

ℹ️ Information

Tourist office (☑03 86 34 14 19; www.avallon
nais-tourisme.com; 6 rue Bocquillot; internet
per 30min €2, wi-fi free) ☺9am-7pm, closed
Sun mid-Sep–mid-Jun) Also has internet access.

ℹ️ Getting There & Away

BUS Transco (☑08 00 10 20 04) buses leave
from the train station to Dijon (€20, two hours,

AUBERGE DU POT D'ETAIN

You wouldn't necessarily expect to
find a gastronomic gem in the modest
village of L'Isle-sur-Sereine, halfway
between Avallon and Noyers-sur-
Serein. But then there is Auberge du
Pot d'Etain (☑03 86 33 88 10; www.
potdetain.com, in French; rue Bouchar-
dot, L'Isle-sur-Sereine; r €60-90, menus
€26-52; ☺noon-1.30pm Wed-Sun, dinner
Mon-Sat, Tue-Sun Jul-Aug), beating all
the odds. Delicacies include a brochette of escargot tempura, pigeon
in chartreuse and foie gras, and other
unlikely surprises. The wine list is epic.

two or three daily), Auxerre and Autun. In July
and August there are sometimes services to
Vézelay.

TRAIN Trains serve the following destinations:

Autun €18, two hours, one daily

Auxerre €13, 1¼ hours, three daily

Dijon €28, two to 2½ hours, two daily

Paris Gare de Lyon or Gare de Bercy €40,
three hours, three daily

Sermizelles-Vézelay €11, 20 minutes, three
daily

ℹ️ Getting Around

Parking in Avallon is free but in places marked
with blue lines you must place a timer *disque*
(disc; €2 at tobacconists) in the window to
demonstrate compliance with the 1½-hour
time limit.

BICYCLE Bikes can be hired from the **tourist office** (per hr/day €4/10) and **Gueneau**
(☑03 86 34 28 11; 26 rue de Paris; half-day/full
day/2 days €8/16/28; ☺8am-noon & 2-6pm
Tue-Sat).

PARC NATUREL RÉGIONAL DU MORVAN

The 2990-sq-km Morvan Regional Park,
bounded more or less by Vézelay, Avallon,
Saulieu and Autun and straddling Burgundy's four *départements* (with the majority in the Nièvre), encompasses 700 sq
km of dense woodland, 13 sq km of lakes
and vast expanses of rolling farmland broken by hedgerows, stone walls and stands
of beech, hornbeam and oak. The sharp-

eyed can observe some of France's largest and most majestic birds of prey perched on trees as they scan for field rodents.

Sights & Activities

The Morvan (a Celtic name meaning 'Black Mountain') offers an abundance of options to fans of outdoor activities. On dry land choose from rambling (the park has over 2500km of marked trails), mountain biking, horse riding, rock climbing, orienteering and fishing. You can raft, canoe and kayak on several lakes and the Chalaux, Cousin, Cure and Yonne Rivers.

In addition to AB Loisirs (p424), the following outfits rent bikes and arrange water sports:

Activital (www.activital.net, in French) Lac de Chaumeçon (☎03 86 22 61 35; St-Martin-du-Puy); Lac des Settons (☎03 86 84 51 98; Montsauche-les-Settons)

Okheanos (☎03 86 84 60 61; www.okheanos. com, in French; Dun-les-Places)

Morvan Visitors Centre PARK CENTRE
(Espace St-Brisson; ☎03 86 78 79 57; www. parcdumorvan.org, in French; ☺tourist office 9.30am-12.30pm & 2-5.30pm Mon-Fri, 10am-12.30pm & 2-5pm Sat, 10am-1pm & 3-5.30pm Sun, closed Sat & Sun mid-Nov–Easter) Surrounded by hills, forests and lakes, Espace St-Brisson is a clearinghouse of park information, including hiking and cycling maps and guides. To get there by car, follow the signs to the 'Maison du Parc' 14km west of Saulieu to St-Brisson. The website has details of local festivals, outdoor activities and lodging.

Guided walks (€4 to €10) of the park, some at night (eg to observe owls), set out from April to October, and there are children's activities in July and August.

Trails passing through St-Brisson include three 5km circuits (Coteaux de St-Brisson, Autour de la Maison du Parc and Autour du Vignan), a 12km circuit to Dolmen Chevresse and a 20km circuit to the village of Gouloux.

The **Verger Conservatoire** (Conservation Orchard) preserves some 200 varieties of legacy fruit trees that are no longer commercially grown; the **Herbularium** features 170 species of Morvan plants.

Other useful (though not always up-to-date) websites include www.morvan-tourisme.org and www.patrimoinedumorvan. org, both in French.

Écomusée du Morvan CULTURAL CENTRES
(☎03 86 78 79 10) Six sites around the park explore traditional Morvan life and customs, including one at Espace St-Brisson. There the **Maison des Hommes et des Paysages** (adult/child €3/2; ☺10am-1pm & 2-6pm, closed 15 Nov-Mar, also Sat morning & Tue except Jul & Aug) has displays in French on the interplay between humans and landscapes. Also, since the Morvan was a major stronghold for the Resistance during WWII, the **Musée de la Résistance en Morvan** (adult/child €4/2.50, audioguide €1) chronicles key events and characters.

Another site, **La Maison Vauban** (☎03 86 32 26 30; www.vaubanecomusee.org; 4 place Vauban; adult/child €5/1; ☺10am-1pm & 2.30-6.30pm Wed-Sun, weekends only Apr-May & Oct-Nov, closed 15 Nov-Mar) in St-Léger-Vauban, is the birthplace of field marshal Sébastien Le Prestre, Marquis of Vauban (1633–1707), and celebrates his life and work. A brilliant military strategist whose methods remained in use for hundreds of years, he is well known for his fortifications, many still extant, and his publications on everything from fair taxes to forest preservation.

Maquis Bernard Résistance Cemetery
HISTORIC CEMETERY
(www.ouroux-en-morvan.com) Seven RAF men (the crew of a bomber shot down near here in 1944) and 21 *résistants* are buried in this neatly tended cemetery surrounded by the dense forests in which British paratroops operated with Free French forces. The nearby drop zone is marked with signs.

The cemetery is about 8km southwest of Montsauche-les-Settons (along the D977) and 5.6km east of Oroux-en-Morvan (along the D12), near the hamlet of Savelot. From the D977, go 2.8km along the narrow dirt road to Savelot.

Vézelay

POP 486

Despite the hordes of tourists who descend on Vézelay, this tiny hilltop village – a Unesco World Heritage Site – is one of France's architectural gems. Perched on a rocky spur crowned by a medieval basilica and surrounded by a sublime patchwork of vineyards, sunflower fields and cows, Vézelay seems to have been lifted from another age.

One of the main pilgrimage routes to Santiago de Compostela in Spain starts here (see www.amis-saint-jacques-de-compostelle.asso.fr, in French).

History
Thanks to the relics of St Mary Magdalene, Vézelay's Benedictine monastery became an important pilgrimage site in the 11th and 12th centuries. St Bernard, leader of the Cistercian order, preached the Second Crusade here in 1146. King Philip Augustus of France and King Richard the Lionheart of England met up here in 1190 before setting out on the Third Crusade.

Vézelay's vineyards, founded in Gallo-Roman times, were wiped out in the late 1800s by phylloxera and were only re-established in 1973.

◉ Sights
Vézelay has long attracted artists and writers. About half a dozen art galleries and several wine and crafts shops line rue St-Pierre and rue St-Étienne. For four days in late July the town gets swept up in exhibitions, craft workshops and theatre during the Vézelay S'Enflamme festival.

Basilique Ste-Madeleine LANDMARK CHURCH
Founded in the 880s AD on a former Roman and then Carolingian site, Basilique Ste-Madeleine has had a turbulent history. Rebuilt between the 11th and 13th centuries, it was trashed by the Huguenots in 1569, desecrated during the Revolution and, to top off the human ravages, repeatedly struck by lightning. By the mid-1800s it was on the point of collapse. In 1840 the architect Viollet-le-Duc undertook the daunting task of rescuing the structure. His work, which included reconstructing the western facade and its doorways, helped Vézelay, previously a ghost town, spring back to life.

On the famous 12th-century **tympanum**, visible from the narthex (enclosed porch), Romanesque carvings show Jesus seated on a throne, radiating his holy spirit to the Apostles. The **nave**, rebuilt following the great fire of 1120, has round arches and detailed capitals, typical features of the Romanesque style; the **transept and choir** (1185) have ogival arches, hallmarks of Gothic architecture. Under the transept a mid-12th-century **crypt** houses a reliquary containing what is believed to be one of Mary Magdalene's bones.

Visitors are welcome to observe prayers or Mass. Concerts of sacred music are held in the nave from June to September; the tourist office and its website have details. Occasional tours of the church are also conducted.

Musée Zervos TOP CHOICE ART MUSEUM
(☎03 86 32 39 26; www.musee-zervos.fr, in French; rue St-Étienne; adult/child €3/free; ☺10am-6pm Wed-Mon mid-Mar–mid-Nov, daily Jul & Aug) This fantastic museum in the exquisite town house of Nobel Prize–winning pacifist writer Romain Rolland (1866–1944) holds the collection of Christian Zervos (1889–1970), the founder of the art journal *Les Cahiers d'Art*. An art critic, gallerist and friend of many modern art luminaries, he and his wife, Yvonne, collected paintings, sculptures and mobiles by Calder, Giacometti, Kandinsky, Léger, Miró and Picasso (for whom he created a pivotal 22-volume catalogue). Many works were gifts or payment from the artists.

Maison Jules Roy FREE HISTORIC HOME
(☎03 86 33 35 10; ☺2-6pm Wed-Sun, 2-5pm Mon, closed Oct-Mar) At the upper end of rue des Écoles, the house of Jules Roy (1907–2000) sits in the shadow of the basilica. Walk around his beautiful gardens and see the Algerian-born writer's study.

⚹ Activities
Walking Trails WALKS
The park behind the basilica affords wonderful views of the Vallée de Cure and nearby villages. A dirt road leads north to the old and new cemeteries. Promenade des

---

BURGUNDY TO THE MOON

In 1971 the astronauts of NASA's Apollo 15 moon mission named one of the lunar craters they found 'St George' in honour of the bottle of Nuits-St-Georges consumed on the way to the moon in Jules Verne's sci-fi epic, *From the Earth to the Moon* (1865):

And lastly, to crown the repast, Ardan had brought out a fine bottle of Nuits, which was found 'by chance' in the provision-box. The three friends drank to the union of the earth and her satellite.

Medieval Art & Architecture

Burgundy, once a powerful duchy and a major ecclesiastical centre, attracted the foremost European artists and builders of the Middle Ages. Now graced with a bounty of excellent museums and monumental architecture, Burgundy offers a trail of human accomplishment through its rolling emerald hills.

Burgundy's clergy established a series of abbeys and churches that remain some of the world's best examples of Romanesque architecture. The austere Cistercian order was founded at the Abbaye de Cîteaux (p401) in 1098 by monks seeking to live St Benedict's teachings: *pax, ora et labora* (peace, pray and work). Their spectacular 1114 Abbaye de Pontigny (p417) is one of the last surviving examples of Cistercian architecture in Burgundy – the purity of its white stone reflects the simplicity of the order.

Cluny's 12th-century Benedictine abbey (p430), now a sprawling ruin woven into the fabric of the town, once held sway over 1100 priories and monasteries stretching from Poland to Portugal.

The 12th-century Cathédrale St-Lazare (p428) is world-renowned for its deceptively austere Gislebertus carvings: a fantastic tympanum of the Last Judgement and extraordinary capitals depicting Bible stories and Greek mythology.

Vézelay's Basilique Ste-Madeleine (p423), a Unesco World Heritage Site, was founded in the 880s. It is adorned with Romanesque carvings and attracts both religious and artistic pilgrims. Abbaye de Fontenay (p410), another Unesco World Heritage Site (founded in 1118), sits in a peaceful forested valley perfect for contemplation.

But let's not forget the royals. Dijon was home to the powerful Dukes of Burgundy (with fabulous names like John the Good,

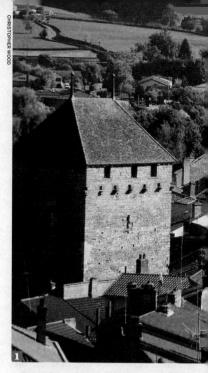

Philip the Bold and John the Fearless), and flourished into one of the art capitals of Europe. Explore the dukes' monumental palace (p392) in central Dijon, home to an excellent fine-arts museum. Or head a bit south to Beaune, where Nicolas Rolin, chancellor to Philip the Good, established a hospital-cum-palace (p405) that houses Rogier van der Weyden's fantastic (and fantastical) *Polyptych of the Last Judgemen*

TOP 5 ARCHITECTURAL & ARTISTIC HOTSPOTS

» Hôtel-Dieu des Hospices de Beaune (p405)
» Abbaye de Pontigny (p417)
» Palais des Ducs et des États de Bourgogne (p392)
» Musée Zervos (p423)
» Cathédrale St-Lazare (p428)

Clockwise from top left
1. The village of Cluny 2. Hôtel-Dieu des Hospices de Beaune 3. Relief in the Cathédrale St-Lazare

Fossés circumnavigates Vézelay's medieval ramparts. A footpath with fine views of the basilica links Porte Neuve, on the northern side of the ramparts, with the village of **Asquins** (pronounced 'ah-kah') and the River Cure. The GR13 trail passes by Vézelay.

AB Loisirs OUTDOOR ACTIVITIES
(☎03 86 33 38 38; www.abloisirs.com, in French; rte du Camping; ☉9.30am-6pm Jul & Aug, phone ahead rest of year) AB Loisirs, whose base is a few kilometres southeast in St-Père, rents bikes (€25 per day) and leads outdoor activities like kayak trips (8/18km from €19/33), rafting (€44), cave exploration (half-day €37) and horse riding (from €17). Bikes can be brought to your hotel. It's best to phone ahead.

🛏 Sleeping
Book ahead.

Les Glycines HISTORIC HOTEL €€
(☎03 86 32 35 30; www.glycines-vezelay.com; rue St-Pierre; s €37, d €69-89; ☉closed mid-Nov–Easter; 🛜) A 1763 bourgeois townhouse built and enveloped in ancient wisteria is now a hotel that's overflowing with old-fashioned character. Hexagonal floor tiles and wooden beams haven't changed in generations. The 11 rooms are all named after famous artists; 'Paul Claudet' is the one to get.

Cabalus HISTORIC HOTEL €
(☎03 86 33 20 66; www.cabalus.com; rue St-Pierre; d €38-58) Upstairs and down the hall from the interesting café, these simple but character-filled rooms are right next to the cathedral, in its ancient *hôtellerie*.

Centre Ste-Madeleine HOSTEL €
(☎03 86 33 22 14; fax 03 86 33 22 14; rue St-Pierre; dm/d €11/40; ☉reception closed lunchtime) Very basic 38-bed hostel, set around an ancient stone courtyard and run by three with-it Franciscan nuns. Sheet hire (€5) and kitchen available.

Hôtel Le Compostelle HOTEL €
(☎03 86 33 28 63; www.lecompostellevezelay.com; 1 place du Champ-de-Foire; d €56-64, tr/q €76/86; ☉closed Jan-mid-Feb; @🛜🛜) Eighteen spotless, practical rooms afford romantic views of either the valley or the village.

Hôtel du Cheval Blanc HOTEL €
(☎03 86 33 22 12; fax 03 86 33 34 29; place du Champ-de-Foire; s/d/tr €38/42/46; ☉closed mid-Jan–mid-Feb, reception closed 3.30-6pm except Jul & Aug) Six neat, no-frills rooms above the restaurant.

🍴 Eating

Le Cheval Blanc TRADITIONAL FRENCH €€
(☎03 86 33 22 12; place du Champ-de-Foire; menus €28-30; ☉closed dinner Wed & Thu except Jul & Aug) It's an understated spot, but the cuisine is delectable, made with fresh seasonal ingredients, mixing traditional recipes and *nouvelle* ideas. Reserve ahead.

Le Bougainville TRADITIONAL FRENCH €€
(☎03 86 33 27 57; 26 rue St-Etienne; menus €22-29; ☉Thu-Mon; 🪑) The smiling owner serves rich French and Burgundian specialties like crispy green salad with hot *chèvre* or escargots. Save room for the fantastic chocolate fondant and homemade pistachio ice cream.

Les Glycines TRADITIONAL FRENCH €€
(☎03 86 32 35 30; rue St-Pierre; menus €19-24; ☉lunch Fri-Wed, dinner varies, closed mid-Nov–Easter) Expect casual, hearty portions of homestyle French food using fresh regional products. Check the chalkboard under the wisteria to see which nights dinner is available.

Cabalus CAFÉ €
(rue St-Pierre; dishes €5; ☉11am-6pm Wed-Sun) Crammed with character under ancient arches, this mellow café displays art and serves quiche and sandwiches.

Vival SUPERMARKET €
(rue St-Étienne; ☉8am-1pm & 3-8pm Mon-Sat, plus 9.30am-1pm Sun mid-Sep–mid-May)

❶ Information
Tourist office (☎03 86 33 23 69; www.vezelaytourisme.com; 12 rue St-Étienne; ☉10am-1pm & 2-6pm, closed Thu Oct-May & Sun Nov-Easter) Sells hiking maps and has internet (€2 per 10 minutes).

❶ Getting There & Away
Vézelay is 15km from Avallon (19km if you take the gorgeous D427 via Pontaubert). There's a free car park 250m from place du Champ-de-Foire (towards Clamecy).

BUS In July and August there are sometimes buses to Avallon. Check with the tourist office.

TRAIN Three trains a day link the Sermizelles-Vézelay train station, about 10km north of Vézelay, with Avallon (€11, 15 minutes) and Auxerre (€11, one hour).

TAXI Call ☎03 86 32 31 88 or 03 86 33 19 06. From Sermizelles-Vézelay train station to

Vézelay costs about €18 (€24 after 7pm and on Sunday).

Around Vézelay

Southeast of Vézelay at the base of the hill, St-Père has a Flamboyant Gothic church.

TOP CHOICE L'Espérance (📞03 86 33 39 10; www.marc-meneau.com; r €120-450; lunch menus €57, dinner menus €150-210; ⊗lunch Thu-Sun, dinner Wed-Mon; 📶🐾), Marc Meneau's legendary French restaurant (and 30-room hotel) with two Michelin stars, however, steals the show. Surrounded by tranquil private gardens, the inn has flawless service and a mood of refined elegance.

Three kilometres south along the D958, the Fontaines Salées (📞03 86 33 26 62; adult/child €4/1.60; ⊗10am-12.30pm & 1.30-6.30pm, closed 11 Nov-Mar) are saltwater springs that were the site of a neolithic development and then a Celtic sanctuary (2nd century BC) and Roman baths (1st century AD). Tickets allow access to Le Musée Arcéhéologique (⊗same as Fontaines Salées) in St-Pére, which holds finds from the site.

About 2km south, the village of Pierre-Perthuis (literally 'pierced stone') is named after a natural stone arch; nearby, a graceful stone bridge (1770) spans the River Cure underneath a modern highway bridge. The neighbouring hamlet of Soeuvres is home to Les Chènevières (📞03 86 32 37 80; www.chenevieres-soeuvres.com; 48 Grand Rue, C5; s incl breakfast €56-77, d €63-84, house per week €430; 🐾) with cosy rooms, extensive grounds along a stream and nearby walking paths.

Le Château de Bazoches (📞03 86 22 10 22; www.chateau-bazoches.com; adult/child €7.50/4; ⊗9.30am-noon & 2.15-6pm, no midday closure Jul & Aug, closed mid-Nov–25 Mar) in Bazoches, sits magnificently on a hillside with views to Vézelay 12km to the north. Built in the 13th century and visited by royalty including Richard the Lionheart, it was acquired by field marshal and military strategist Marquis de Vauban in 1675. It is still owned by his descendants.

Bibracte

TOP CHOICE Bibracte (⊗archaeological sites Jun-Oct), the sprawling archaeological remains of a Celtic city, sits atop beautiful Mont Beuvray, 25km west of Autun. Bibracte was the capital of the Celtic Aedui

people during the 1st and 2nd centuries BC, and it was here, in 52 BC, that Vercingétorix was declared chief of the Gaulish coalition shortly before his defeat by Julius Caesar at Alésia. Caesar also resided here before the city decamped to Augustodunum (Autun). The site is covered with 1000 hectares of forest, blessed with expansive views and criss-crossed by **walking trails**, including the GR13. Stone remnants include ancient ramparts and several complexes of buildings, all in varying states of excavation.

The excellent Museum of Celtic Civilisation (📞03 85 86 52 35; www.bibracte.fr; adult/child incl audioguide €5.75/free; ⊗10am-6pm mid-Mar–mid-Nov, to 7pm Jul & Aug) is housed in an impressive minimalist building designed by Pierre-Louis Faloci. Exhibits explain the technologies, like a sophisticated system of ramparts, and culture of the Celtic Gauls throughout Europe and also display finds from the site. During the high season there are guided tours (in English on Mondays at 2.30pm) and lecture/workshop programs. A Zen-feeling café provides set meals (€16) and picnic baskets (€7 per person).

SAÔNE-ET-LOIRE

In the southern Saône-et-Loire *département* (www.bourgogne-du-sud.com), midway between Dijon and Lyon, highlights include the Gallo-Roman ruins in Autun, Cluny's glorious Romanesque heritage and, around Mâcon, vineyards galore. Several rivers and the Canal du Centre meander among its forests and pastureland.

Autun

POP 16.310

Autun is now a low-key town, but almost two millennia ago (known as Augustodunum) it was one of the most important cities in Roman Gaul, boasting 6km of ramparts, four monumental gates, two theatres, an amphitheatre and a system of aqueducts. Beginning in AD 269, the city was repeatedly sacked by barbarian tribes and its fortunes declined, but things improved considerably in the Middle Ages, making it possible to construct an impressive cathedral. The hilly area around Cathédrale St-Lazare, reached via narrow cobblestone streets, is known as the old city.

If you have a car, Autun is an excellent base for exploring the southern parts of the Parc Naturel Régional du Morvan.

☉ Sights & Activities

Napoléon Bonaparte and his brothers Joseph and Lucien studied in Autun as teenagers. Their old Jesuit college is now a high school called Lycée Joseph Bonaparte, on the west side of Champ de Mars. A small train (adult/child €6/3) offers guided town tours in July and August; contact the tourist office.

TOP CHOICE Cathédrale St-Lazare   CATHEDRAL
(place du Terreau; ☉8am-7pm Sep-Jun, plus 9-11pm Jul & Aug) Originally Romanesque, this cathedral was built in the 12th century to house the sacred relics of St Lazarus. Later additions include the 15th- to 16th-century **bell tower** over the transept and the 19th-century towers over the entrance. Over the main doorway, the famous Romanesque **tympanum** shows the Last Judgement carved in the 1130s by Gislebertus, whose name is inscribed below Jesus' right foot. Look for all manner of symbolism: signs of the zodiac encircling the saved and the damned. Be sure to go upstairs to the **Chapter Room** where the fantastical capitals, many of them by Gislebertus, are displayed.

Musée Rolin   MUSEUM
(☎03 85 52 09 76; 5 rue des Bancs; adult/child €4/free; ☉9.30am-noon & 1.30-6pm Wed-Mon) Explore a worthwhile collection of Gallo-Roman artefacts; 12th-century Romanesque art, including the *Temptation of Eve* by Gislebertus; and 15th-century paintings such as the *Autun Virgin* by the Maître de Moulins. Modern art includes work by Maurice Denis, Jean Dubuffet and Joan Miro.

The adjacent prison (2bis place St-Louis; admission €1; ☉2-6pm Wed-Sun Jul-Sep), a forbidding circular structure built in 1854, was used until 1955.

Gallo-Roman Sites   ANCIENT RUINS
Built during the reign of Constantine, Porte d'Arroux was once one of Augustodunum's four gates. Constructed wholly without mortar, it supports four semicircular arches of the sort that put the 'Roman' in Romanesque: two for vehicles and two for pedestrians. Porte St-André is similar in general design.

Let your imagination run wild at the Théâtre Romain (Roman Theatre; ☉24hr), de-

signed to hold 16,000 people; try picturing the place filled with cheering (or jeering), toga-clad spectators. From the top look southwest to see the Pierre de Couhard (Rock of Couhard), the 27m-high remains of a Gallo-Roman pyramid that was probably a tomb.

Long associated (wrongly) with the Roman god Janus, the 24m-high Temple de Janus (www.temple-de-janus.net, in French), in the middle of farmland 800m north of the train station, is thought to have been a site for Celtic worship. Only two of its massive walls still stand.

Walking & Cycling   WALKS, CYCLING
For a stroll along the city walls (part-Roman but mostly medieval), walk from av du Morvan south to the 12th-century Tour des Ursulines and follow the walls to the northeast. The Chemin des Manies leads out to the Pierre de Couhard, where you can pick up the Circuit des Gorges, three marked forest trails ranging from 4.7km to 11.5km (map IGN 2925 O). Espace Sport et Nature (☎03 85 52 47 09; rte de Chalon) rents bikes (€21 per two hours) and kayaks (€7.50 per hour).

🛏 Sleeping

TOP CHOICE Maison Sainte-Barbe   B&B €
(☎03 85 86 24 77; www.maisonsainte barbe.com, in French; 7 place Sainte-Barbe; s/d incl breakfast €60/65) Smack in the old city in a 15th-century townhouse, around a verdant courtyard, some of the rooms of this colourful, spotless B&B have light-filled views of the cathedral. Friendly, knowledgeable owners prepare delicious breakfasts.

Hôtel de France   HOTEL €
(☎03 85 52 14 00; www.hotel-de-france-autun.fr; 18 av de la République; d €41) A cheery family-run hostelry with 26 basic, clean rooms, across from the train station.

Hôtel St-Louis et de la Poste   HOTEL €€
(☎03 85 52 01 01; www.hotelsaintlouis.net; 6 rue de l'Arbalète; d €99-119; ☎) In a grand 17th-century building that hosted Napoléon no fewer than four times, this 39-room establishment has a lavish 1920s lobby. Book ahead.

Hôtel de la Tête Noire   HOTEL €€
(☎03 85 86 59 99; www.hoteltetenoire.fr; 3 rue de l'Arquebuse; d/tr €74/85; ☉closed Jan; ❋☎) Straightforward rooms, some quite large, and a good restaurant.

CHÂTEAU DE VILLETTE

Set in a 5-sq-km private estate, the delightful 16th- and 18th-century Château de Villette (☎03 86 30 09 13; www.stork-chateau.com; d incl breakfast €135-235, ste €295-365; 🗷) offers the luxurious life of Burgundy's landed aristocracy. After waking up in a ravishingly furnished period room, you can ramble, cycle or hunt escargots in the rolling countryside. Situated 20km southwest of Autun; take the N81, then the D192 for 3km to just beyond Poil, then the C1 for 2km. Call ahead.

Eating

Find restaurants along the north side of Champ de Mars and towards the cathedral, along Grande Rue Chauchien and Petite Rue Chauchien and around place du Terreau.

Restaurant Le Chapitre
TRADITIONAL FRENCH €€
(☎03 85 52 04 01; 11 place du Terreau; menus €28-37; ☺noon-1.30pm Tue-Sun, 7.30-9.30pm Tue-Sat) The intimate dining room in brushed-grey tones fills up with locals out for a quiet, elegant meal. Treats include roasted sole with artichoke mousse. Kids' menu €15. Reserve ahead.

Le Chalet Bleu
MODERN FRENCH €€
(☎03 85 86 27 30; 3 rue Jeannin; menus €16.50-58; ☺lunch Wed-Mon, dinner Wed-Sat) Serves creative French gastronomic cuisine in a light, leafy dining room. Specialities include *meurette d'œufs pochés et escargots* (poached eggs with red-wine reduction and escargots) and thick Charolais steaks. Takeaway plates sold next door.

La Trattoria
PIZZERIA €
(☎03 85 86 10 73; 2 rue des Bancs; pizzas €12; ☺Tue-Sun) Organic pizzas near the cathedral.

Food Market
MARKET €
(Hôtel de Ville; ☺until 12.30pm Wed & Fri)

Petit Casino
SUPERMARKET €
(6 av Charles de Gaulle; ☺7.30am-12.30pm & 3-8pm Tue-Sat, 8.30am-12.30pm & 4-7pm Sun)

Entertainment

Bowling du Lac (☎0385520606; www.bowling-autun.com, in French; rte de Chalon-sur-Saône;

☺11am-2am Tue-Thu, 11am-4am Fri, 3pm-4am Sat, 3pm-2am Sun), 2.5km east of the old city next to the McDonald's, is hugely popular with locals of all ages. It has eight bowling lanes, billiard tables, a bar and a restaurant, and hosts live music once a month.

ℹ Information
Elge Interactive (☎03 85 86 13 07; 6 Grande Rue Chauchien; per hr €4; ☺generally 10.30am-noon & 2-6.30pm Mon-Fri) Internet access.

Tourist office (☎03 85 86 80 38; www.autun-tourisme.com; 13 rue du Général Demetz; ☺9am-1pm & 2-7pm, closed Mon morning & Sun Oct–mid-May) Sells a self-guided walking-tour brochure (€2) and hiking maps. Information on the Parc Naturel Régional du Morvan.

ℹ Getting There & Away
BUS Timetables are posted at the bus shelters next to the train station. **Buscéphale** (☎08 00 07 17 10; www.buscephale.fr) serves Le Creusot and Le Creusot TGV station (Line 5; €1.50, one hour, three daily).

CAR For car hire, try **ADA** (☎03 85 86 37 36; 8 av de la République).

TRAIN The **train station** (av de la République) is on a slow tertiary line that requires a change of train to get almost anywhere except Auxerre (€28, 3½ hours, one daily) and Avallon (€18, two hours, two daily).

Château de Sully

This Renaissance-style château (☎03 85 82 09 86; www.chateaudesully.com, in French; adult/child €7.50/6, gardens only €3.50/2.80; ☺10.30am-4.30pm Apr-11 Nov), on the outskirts of the village of Sully (15km northeast of Autun along the D973), has a beautifully furnished interior and a lovely English-style garden. It was the birthplace of Marshall MacMahon, Duke of Magenta and president of France from 1873 to 1879, whose ancestors fled Ireland several centuries ago and whose descendents still occupy the property.

South of Autun

Thanks to nearby coal deposits and cheap transport via the Canal du Centre (1793), Le Creusot (population 24,350) became a major steel-making centre during the 19th century. The story of the Schneider steelworks, which at one time employed 15,000 workers, is told at Château de la

Verrerie (☎03 85 73 92 00; adult/child/family €6/3.80/15.25; ☺10am-noon & 2-6pm Mon & Wed-Fri, 2-6pm Sat & Sun), a late 18th-century glassworks turned into a private mansion. Its **Musée de l'Homme et de l'Industrie** and **Académie François Bourdon** have models of locomotives, bridges, ships and nuclear powerplants.

The Côte Chalonnaise winegrowing area is just south of the Côte de Beauneandruns from Chagny south to St-Gengoux-le-National.

Tournus (www.tournugeois.fr), on the Saône, is known for its 10th- to 12th-century Romanesque abbey church, Abbatiale St-Philibert (☺8.30am-7pm), whose superb and extremely rare 12th-century **mosaic** of the calendar and the zodiac was discovered by chance in 2002.

The scenic roads that link Tournus with Cluny, including the D14, D15, D82 and D56, pass through lots of tiny villages, many with charming churches. The medieval village of Brancion sits at the base of its château, while Chardonnay is, as one would expect, surrounded by vineyards. There's a panoramic view from 579m Mont St-Romain.

Cormatin, 14km north of Cluny, is home to the Renaissance-style Château de Cormatin (☎03 85 50 16 55; adult/child €9/4; ☺10am-noon & 2-6.30pm, no midday closure mid-Jul–mid-Aug, gardens open till dusk), renowned for its opulent 17th-century, Louis XIII–style interiors and formal gardens.

WORTH A TRIP

CALLING PHOTOGRAPHERS

Musée Nicéphore Niépce (☎03 85 48 41 98; www.museeniepce.com, in French; 28 quai des Messageries, Chalon-sur-Saône; admission free; ☺9.30-11.45am & 2-5.45pm Wed-Mon), named after Chalon-sur-Saône native Joseph Niépce (1765–1833) who is credited with inventing photography in 1816, is chock-full of all things photographic. Peruse thousands of devices and images from the creation of photography through daguerreotypes (Niépce collaborated with Daguerre), calotypes and on up to the modern digital era. Niépce is also credited with inventing an early bicycle-moped and an internal combustion engine.

Cluny

POP 4872

The remains of Cluny's great abbey – Christendom's largest church until the construction of St Peter's Basilica in the Vatican – are fragmentary and scattered, barely discernible among the houses and green spaces of the modern-day town. But with a bit of imagination, it's possible to picture how things looked in the 12th century, when Cluny's Benedictine abbey, renowned for its wealth and power and answerable only to the Pope, held sway over 1100 priories and monasteries stretching from Poland to Portugal.

◉ Sights

Église Abbatiale   LANDMARK CHURCH
(Abbey Church; ☎03 85 59 12 79; adult/child €7/free; ☺9.30am-6.10pm) Cluny's vast abbey church, built between 1088 and 1130, once stretched from the rectangular **map table** in front of the Musée d'Art et d'Archéologie all the way to the trees near the octagonal **Clocher de l'Eau Bénite** (Tower of the Holy Water) and its neighbour, the square **Tour de l'Horloge** – a distance of 187m!

Buy tickets and begin your visit at the Musée d'Art et d'Archéologie. Displays include a model of the Cluny complex, a 10-minute computer-generated 3-D 'virtual tour' of the abbey as it looked in the Middle Ages and some superb Romanesque carvings. It continues on the grounds of the École Nationale Supérieure d'Arts et Métiers (ENSAM; place du 11 Août; ☺same as Église Abbatiale), an institute for training mechanical and industrial engineers that's centred on an 18th-century cloister. You can wander around the grounds at midday and for an hour after the museum closes. Free guided tours in English occur in July and August.

The best place to appreciate the abbey's vastness is from the top of the Tour des Fromages (adult/child €2/free; ☺same as tourist office), once used to ripen cheeses. Access the tower's 120 steps through the tourist office.

Haras National   HORSE STUD
(National Stud Farm; ☎06 22 94 52 69; www.haras-nationaux.fr, in French; 2 rue Porte des Prés; adult/child €5/3; ☺tours 2pm, 3.30pm & 5pm Tue-Sun) Founded by Napoléon in 1806, the Haras National houses some of France's finest thoroughbreds, ponies and draught horses. Visit on a guided tour.

Cluny

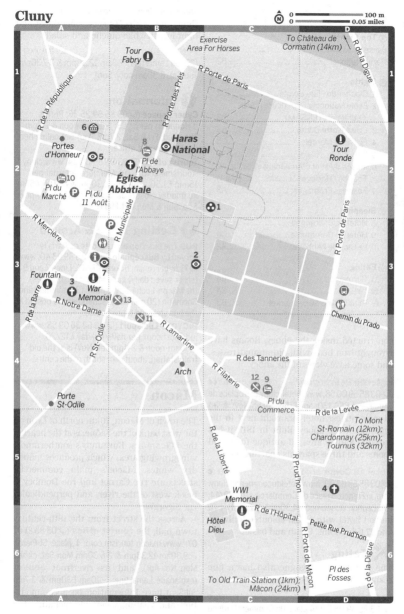

Église St-Marcel CHURCH
(rue Prud'hon; ⊘closed to public) Topped by an octagonal, three-storey belfry.

Église Notre Dame CHURCH
(⊘9am-7pm) A 13th-century church, across from the tourist office.

🛏 Sleeping

Le Clos de l'Abbaye B&B €€
(📞03 85 59 22 06; http://pagesperso-orange.fr/clos.abbaye.cluny, in French; 6 place du Marché; d incl breakfast €85) This cheerful B&B is in the first residential building

Cluny

constructed inside the abbey. Rooms have wrought iron beds with plump mattresses, and some have views of the abbey.

Hôtel de Bourgogne HISTORIC HOTEL €€
(☎03 85 59 00 58; www.hotel-cluny.com; place de l'Abbaye; d €89-130, apt €159; ☻Feb-Nov; ❋⊛) Cluny's ritziest hotel sits right next to the remains of the abbey. Built in 1817, it has a casual lounge area, 13 antique-furnished rooms and three spacious apartments.

Hôtel du Commerce HOTEL €
(☎03 85 59 03 09; www.hotelducommerce-cluny. com, in French; 8 place du Commerce; s/d €29/44; ☻reception closed noon-4.30pm) A family-run budget hotel with peach-coloured hallways and 17 tidy rooms. Clean and basic.

✖ Eating
The Hôtel de Bourgogne also has a fine restaurant.

Le Bistrot BISTRO €
(☎03 85 59 08 07; 14 place du Commerce; menu €12.50; ☻8.30am-1am Wed-Mon) Cool vintage posters jazz up this cheery bistro where old-timers sip bubbly at the bar and families dip into pesto ravioli (€9) out the front.

Germain TEA HOUSE €
(☎03 85 59 11 21; 25 rue Lamartine; ☻7am-8pm) A mouth-watering *pâtisserie-*
chocolaterie whose adjacent *salon de thé* (lunch *menu* €11.50) serves breakfast and light lunches like quiche and salad.

Petit Casino SUPERMARKET €
(29 rue Lamartine; ☻8am-12.30pm & 3-7.30pm Tue-Sat, 8.30am-noon Sun)

❶ Information
Cyber Espace (☎03 85 59 25 36; Portes d'Honneur; per hr €3; ☻10am-noon & 2-7pm Tue, Wed, Fri & Sat, 2-7pm Thu) Get online here or at the tourist office.

Tourist office (☎03 85 59 05 34; www.cluny -tourisme.com; 6 rue Mercière; internet per 15min €1.50; ☻10am-12.30pm & 2.30-6.45pm, no midday closure Jul & Aug, closed Sun Apr & Sep, Sun & Mon Oct-Mar)

❶ Getting There & Around
BUS The bus stop on rue Porte de Paris is served by **Buscéphale** (☎03 85 39 93 40; www. cg71.fr, in French; tickets €1.50). Lines 7 and 9 (six or seven daily) go to Mâcon (45 minutes), the Mâcon-Loché TGV station (30 minutes) and Cormatin (20 minutes). Schedules are posted at the bus stop and tourist office.

BICYCLE Ludisport (☎06 62 36 09 58; www. ludisport.com; per half-/full day €12/20; ☻10am-noon & 2-4pm Feb-Nov) is at the old train station, about 1km south of the centre.

Mâcon
POP 35,040

The town of Mâcon, 70km north of Lyon on the west bank of the Saône, is at the heart of the Mâconnais, Burgundy's southernmost winegrowing area, which produces mainly dry whites. Mâcon's main commercial streets are rue Carnot and rue Dombey, a block west of the river, and perpendicular rue Sigorgne.

Across the street from the 18th-century town hall, the tourist office (☎03 85 21 07 07; www.macon-tourism.com; 1 place St-Pierre; ☻9.30am-12.30pm & 2-6.30pm Mon-Sat, closed Mon Nov-Apr), and its riverfront annexe (esplanade Lamartine; ☻10am-1.30pm & 3-7pm Jul-Sep) have information on accommodation and visiting vineyards including the Beaujolais.

The all-wood Maison de Bois, facing 95 rue Dombey and built around 1500, is decorated with carved wooden figures, some of them very cheeky indeed.

Musée Lamartine (☎03 85 38 96 19; 41 rue Sigorgne; adult/child €2.50/free; ☻10am-noon &

CYCLING THE VOIE VERTE

An old railway line and parts of a former canal towpath have been turned into the Voie Verte (Green Road), a series of paved paths around the Saône-et-Loire *département* that have been designed for walking, cycling and in-line skating. From Cluny, the Voie Verte heads north, via vineyards and valleys, to Givry (42km) and Santenay, where you can pick up the Voie des Vignes (p403) to Beaune. Tourist offices have the free cycling map, *Voies Vertes et Cyclotourisme – Bourgogne du Sud*.

2-6pm Tue-Sat, 2-6pm Sun & Mon) explores the life and times of the Mâcon-born Romantic poet and left-wing politician Alphonse de Lamartine (1790–1869).

Musée des Ursulines (☑03 85 39 90 38; 5 rue des Ursulines; adult/child €2.50/free; ☺10am-noon & 2-6pm Tue-Sat, 2-6pm Sun & Mon), housed in a 17th-century Ursuline convent, features Gallo-Roman archaeology, 16th- to 20th-century paintings and displays about 19th-century Mâconnais life.

The fin de siècle grandeur of the Hôtel d'Europe et d'Angleterre (☑03 85 38 27 94; www.hotel-europeangleterre-macon.com; 92-109 quai Jean Jaurès; d €60-70; ☺reception closed noon-2pm) has faded since Queen Victoria is said to have stayed here, but some of its basic rooms have river views.

L'Ethym' Sel (☑03 85 39 48 84; 10 rue Gambetta; menus €16-32; ☺lunch Thu-Tue, dinner Mon & Thu-Sat), two blocks south of the tourist office, is a modern bistro whose French and Burgundian specialities include locally raised Charolais steak.

About 10km west of Mâcon in the wine country, the Musée de Préhistoire de Solutré (☑03 85 35 85 24; adult/child €3.50/free ☺10am-6pm, closed Dec) displays finds from one of Europe's richest prehistoric sites, occupied from 35,000 to 10,000 BC. A lovely 20-minute walk will get you to the top of the rocky outcrop known as the Roche de Solutré, from where Mont Blanc can sometimes be seen, especially at sunset.

Buscéphale (☑03 85 39 93 40; www.cg71.fr, in French; tickets €1.50) bus lines 7 and 9 serve Cluny. The Mâcon-Ville train station is on the main line (18 daily) linking Dijon (€25, 1¼ hours), Beaune (€18, 50 minutes) and Lyon-Part Dieu (€16, 50 minutes). The Mâcon-Loché TGV station is 5km southwest of town.

Lyon & the Rhône Valley

Best Places to Eat

» Café des Fédérations (p447)

» La Pyramide (p458)

» Restaurant Pic (p459)

» L'Auberge du Pont de Collonges (p451)

» Rue Le Bec (p447)

Best Places to Stay

» Les Roulottes de la Serve (p456)

» Le Royal (p445)

» Hostellerie de Pérouges (p457)

» Lyon Guesthouse (p446)

» Péniche Barnum (p446)

Why Go?

At the crossroads of central Europe and the Atlantic, the Rhineland and the Mediterranean, grand old Lyon is France's third-largest metropolis and its gastronomic capital. Savouring lavish dishes and delicacies in timeless, checked-tableclothed *bouchons* (small bistros) or cutting-edge eating spaces creates unforgettable memories – as do Lyon's majestic Roman amphitheatres, cobbled Unesco-listed old town, romantic parks and rejuvenated riverfront, just for starters.

Beaujolais produces illustrious wines, while the picturesque hilltop village of Pérouges turns out traditional sugar-crusted tarts. Downstream, the Rhône forges past centuries-old Côtes du Rhône vineyards yielding some of France's most respected reds, Valence's *pâtisseries* filled with historic shortbread, and Montélimar's artisan nougat factories to the wild, green Gorges de l'Ardèche, bringing the Ardèche River tumbling to the gates of Languedoc and Provence.

When to Go

Lyon

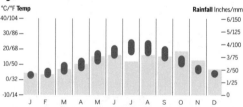

| Late June/early July Swing by Vienne's renowned jazz festival. | Mid-November Celebrate the tapping of the first bottles of Beaujolais *nouveau*, the third Thursday in November. | Early December See Lyon when the Fête des Lumières lights up the city. |

Lyon

POP 480,660

Commercial, industrial and banking power-house for the past 500 years, today Lyon is the focal point of a prosperous area of some 1,748,271 people.

Outstanding museums, a dynamic cultural life, busy clubbing and drinking scene, thriving university and fantastic shopping lend the city a distinctly sophisticated air, while adventurous gourmets can indulge their wildest gastronomic fantasies.

Lyon comprises nine *arrondissements* (neighbourhoods); the *arrondissement* number appears after each street address.

History

The Roman military colony of Lugdunum (Lyon) was founded in 43 BC. It served as the capital of the Roman territories known as the Three Gauls under Augustus, but had to wait for fame and fortune until the arrival of moveable type in 1473 transformed it into one of Europe's foremost publishing centres.

By the mid-18th century the city's influential silk weavers – 40% of Lyon's total workforce – had developed what had already been a textiles centre since the 15th century into the silk-weaving capital of Europe. A century on, Lyon had tripled in size and boasted 100,000 weaving looms.

In 1870 the Lumière family moved to Lyon, and cinema was born when brothers Louis and Auguste shot the world's first moving picture here in 1895.

During WWII some 4000 people (including Resistance leader Jean Moulin) were killed and 7500 others deported to Nazi death camps under Gestapo chief Klaus Barbie (1913–91), the 'butcher of Lyon'. Nazi rule ended in September 1944, when the retreating Germans blew up all but two of Lyon's 28 bridges. Barbie was sentenced to death in absentia in 1952 and again in 1954, but it wasn't until 1987, following his extradition from Bolivia, that he was tried in person in Lyon and sentenced to life imprisonment. He died in prison three years later.

⊙ Sights

VIEUX LYON

Lyon's Unesco-listed old town, with its narrow streets and medieval and Renaissance houses, is divided into three quarters: St-Paul (north), St-Jean (middle) and St-Georges (south). See p441 to find the area's *traboules* (secret passages).

Lyon & the Rhône Valley Highlights

❶ Delve into Lyon's hidden labyrinth of **traboules** (secret passageways; p441)

❷ Bike the vine-ribboned hills of **Beaujolais** (p456)

❸ Marvel at Lyon's basilica and city panoramas at hilltop **Fourvière** (p436)

❹ See crocodiles slumber near **Pierrelatte** (p460)

❺ Learn about Lyon's silk-weaving heritage in **Croix Rousse** (p441)

❻ Canoe beneath the stunning natural stone bridge Pont d'Arc along the **Gorges de l'Ardèche** (p459)

❼ Catch a traditional **puppet show** featuring Lyon's charismatic little raconteur, **Guignol** (p452)

❽ View dramatic Gallo-Roman ruins in **Vienne** (p458)

Cathédrale St-Jean
CATHEDRAL

(place St-Jean, 5e; ⊙8am-noon & 2-7.30pm Mon-Fri, 8am-noon & 2-7pm Sat & Sun; ⓂVieux Lyon) This partly Romanesque cathedral, seat of Lyon's 133rd bishop, was built between the late 11th and early 16th centuries. The portals of its Flamboyant Gothic facade, completed in 1480, are decorated with 280 square stone medallions. Don't miss the **astronomical clock** in the north transept chiming at noon, 2pm, 3pm and 4pm daily.

Medieval & Renaissance Architecture
ARCHITECTURE

Lovely old buildings line rue du Bœuf, rue St-Jean and rue des Trois Maries. Crane your neck upwards to see gargoyles and other cheeky stone characters carved on window ledges along rue Juiverie, home to Lyon's Jewish community in the Middle Ages.

Musées Gadagne
MUSEUMS

(www.museegadagne.com; place du Petit Collège, 5e; 1 museum adult/child €6/free, both museums €8/free; ⊙11am-6.30pm Wed-Sun; ⓂVieux Lyon) Housed in a 16th-century mansion built for two rich Florentine bankers, this newly re-opened museum incorporates an excellent local history museum covering the city's layout as its silk-weaving, cinema and transportation evolved, and an international puppet museum paying homage to Lyon's iconic puppet, Guignol (p452). On the 4th

---

LYON CITY CARD

The Lyon City Card (1/2/3 days adult €20/30/40, child €11/15/20; see www.lyon-france.com) covers admission to every Lyon museum and the roof of Basilique Notre Dame de Fourvière, as well as a guided city tour, a river excursion (April to October) and discounts on Le Grand Tour, the Aquarium du Grand Lyon and other selected attractions, exhibitions and shops.

The card also includes city-wide transport, offering unlimited travel on buses, trams, the funicular and metro (cheaper cards not incorporating transport are available). There are usually discounts if you book online; alternatively buy it from the tourist office or some hotels.

---

floor, a **café** adjoins tranquil, terraced **gardens**, here since the 14th century and laid out two centuries later.

Le Petit Musée Fantastique de Guignol
PUPPET MUSEUM

(www.lamaisondeguignol.fr, in French; 6 rue St-Jean, 5e; adult/child €5/3; ⊙11am-6.30pm Tue-Sun; ⓂVieux Lyon) Guignol is the star of this tiny, two-room museum with cute, sensor-activated exhibits; ask staff to set up the English soundtrack.

Musée des Miniatures et Décors du Cinéma
FILM MUSEUM

(www.mimlyon.com, in French; 60 rue St-Jean, 5e; adult/child €7/5.50; ⊙10am-6.30pm Tue-Fri, to 7pm Sat & Sun; ⓂVieux Lyon) This maze-like museum on tourist-busy rue St-Jean provides an unusual insight into the making of movie sets and special effects achieved with the use of miniatures.

FOURVIÈRE

Over two millennia ago, the Romans built the city of Lugdunum on the slopes of Fourvière. Today it's topped by the Tour Métallique, an Eiffel Tower–like structure (minus its bottom two-thirds) built in 1893 and used as a TV transmitter.

Footpaths wind uphill but the funicular (return ticket €2.40; ⓂVieux Lyon) is the least taxing way up.

Basilique Notre Dame de Fourvière
BASILICA

(☏04 78 25 86 19; www.fourviere.org; ⊙chapel 7am-7pm, basilica 8am-7pm) Crowning the hill – with stunning city panoramas from its terrace – the 66m-long, 19m-wide and 27m-high basilica is lined with intricate mosaics and a superb example of late-19th-century French ecclesiastical architecture. One-hour discovery visits (adult/child €2/1; ⊙several times daily Apr-Nov) take in the main features of the basilica and crypt; rooftop tours (adult/child €5/3; ⊙2.30pm & 4pm daily Apr-Oct, 2.30pm & 3.30pm Wed & Sun Nov) climax on the stone-sculpted roof.

Musée d'Art Religieux
ART MUSEUM

(www.fourviere.org; 8 place de Fourvière, 5e; adult/child €5/free; ⊙10am-12.30pm & 2-5.30pm; ⓂFourvière funicular station) Works of sacred art and worth-the-trip temporary exhibitions are showcased adjacent to the basilica.

Two Days

If your time's tight, begin with an overview of the city on a guided **tour** (unusual options include jogging or roaring around on the back of a Harley) before visiting the magnificent **Musée des Beaux-Arts** and lunching on its terrace. Cycle to expansive **Parc de la Tête d'Or** before dinner at a traditional Lyonnais **bouchon**, and a drink at the bars aboard the Rhône's **péniches** (barges).

Start your second day on what was long known as 'the hill of work', **Croix Rousse**, browsing its outdoor **market** and discovering its **silk-weaving workshops**. Then cross town and ride the funicular to the 'hill of prayer', basilica-crowned **Fourvière**, to uncover Roman Lyon at the fascinating **Musée de la Civilisation Gallo-Romaine** and **Théâtre Romain**. Dine at the panoramic **Le Restaurant de Fourvière**, before making your way downhill to Vieux Lyon's lively **bars**.

Four Days

Spend your third day absorbing more of Lyon's lengthy history at its cache of **museums**, and at a **puppet show** featuring famous little Guignol.

Four days gives you enough time for day trips in the surrounding regions such as wine-rich **Beaujolais**, film-star **Pérouges**, design-driven **St-Étienne** or **downstream along the Rhône**.

Musée de la Civilisation Gallo-Romaine
ARCHAEOLOGICAL MUSEUM

(www.musees-gallo-romains.com; 17 rue Cléberg, 5e; adult/child €4/free, Thu free; ⊙10am-6pm Tue-Sun; Ⓜ Fourvière funicular station) Ancient artefacts found in the Rhône Valley are displayed at the city's Roman museum. Next door, the Théâtre Romain (Ⓜ Fourvière funicular station or Minimes funicular station), built around 15 BC and enlarged in AD 120, sat an audience of 10,000. Romans held poetry readings and musical recitals in the smaller, adjacent odéon.

PRESQU'ÎLE

Lyon's city centre lies on this 500m- to 800m-wide peninsula bounded by the rivers Rhône and Saône.

Musée des Beaux-Arts
[TOP CHOICE] ART MUSEUM

(www.mba-lyon.fr; 20 place des Terreaux, 1er; adult/child €76/free; ⊙10am-6pm Wed, Thu & Sat-Mon, 10.30am-6pm Fri; Ⓜ Hôtel de Ville) This stunning and eminently manageable museum showcases France's finest collection of sculptures and paintings outside Paris from antiquity on. Highlights include works by Rodin, Rubens, Rembrandt, Monet, Matisse and Picasso. Pick up a free audio guide and be sure to stop for a drink or meal on the delightful stone terrace off its **café-restaurant** and take time out in its tranquil **cloister garden**.

Place des Terreaux
CITY SQUARE

(Ⓜ Hôtel de Ville) The centrepiece of the Presqu'île's beautiful central square is a 19th-century fountain made of 21 tonnes of lead and sculpted by Frédéric-Auguste Bartholdi (of Statue of Liberty fame). The four horses pulling the chariot symbolise rivers galloping seawards. The Hôtel de Ville (Town Hall) fronting the square was built in 1655 but given its present ornate facade in 1702. When Daniel Buren's polka-dot 'forest' of 69 granite fountains (embedded in the ground across much of the square) are on, join the kids in a mad dash as the water dances up, down, disappears for a second and gushes back again.

Place Bellecour
CITY SQUARE

(Ⓜ Bellecour) One of Europe's largest public squares, place Bellecour was laid out in the 17th century. In the centre is an equestrian statue of Louis XIV.

Opéra de Lyon
OPERA HOUSE

(Ⓜ Hôtel de Ville) Lyon's neoclassical 1831-built opera house was modernised in 1993 by renowned French architect Jean Nouvel, who added the striking semi-cylindrical glass-domed roof. On its northern side, boarders and bladers buzz around the fountains of place Louis Pradel, surveyed by the Homme de la Liberté (Man of Freedom) on roller skates, sculpted from scrap metal by Marseille-born César.

Lyon

LYON & THE RHÔNE VALLEY

N
0   300 m
0   0.16 miles

To La Dombes
(25km); Pérouges
(27km)

To Rive
Gauche

Pont
Lafayette

Pont
Morand

M Croix
Paquet

Pl Louis
Pradel

R Verdi

52

18

47

55

M Cordeliers

74

R de la Bourse

Pl de la
Bourse

M

R du Griffon

Pl de la
Comédie

30

34

36

Montée St-Sébastien

R Terrailles

70

Hôtel de Ville

31

R Neuve

7

R Francisque Régaud

53

3

60

R de l'Arbre Sec

56

R Gentil

R de la Poulaillerie

Le Village
des Créateurs

Fountain

R du Bât d'Argent

Pl des
Terreaux

Musée
des Beaux
Arts

27

63

69

19

R Dubois

28

R Ste-Catherine

51

R Paul Chenavard

32

29

16

R de la
Fromagerie

37

R Mercière

R des Tables Claudiennes

R René Leynaud

R des Capucins

R Burdeau

1ER

46

R Constantine

R Lanterne

78

Q de la Pêcherie

25

R d'Algérie

R de la Platière

Pont
Alphonse
Juin

To Croix
Rousse

Montée de la
Grande Côte

R Terme

79

62

Jardin des
Plantes

73

Pl
Sathonay

33

40

R Sergent Blandan

75

R de l'Annonciade

R du Jardin des Plantes

66

1

80

Q de Bondy

77

Q Romain Rolland

21

R Pareille

Saône

14

20

65

4

15

Pl St-
Paul

Gare
St-Paul

R Octavio Mey

R Juiverie

R de
Gadagne

Pl du
Gouvernement

ST-PAUL

Montée
St-Barthélemy

Musées
Gadagne

Pl du Petit
Collège

Q Pierre Scize

R Roger Radison

5E

Fourvière
Hill

Tour
Métallique

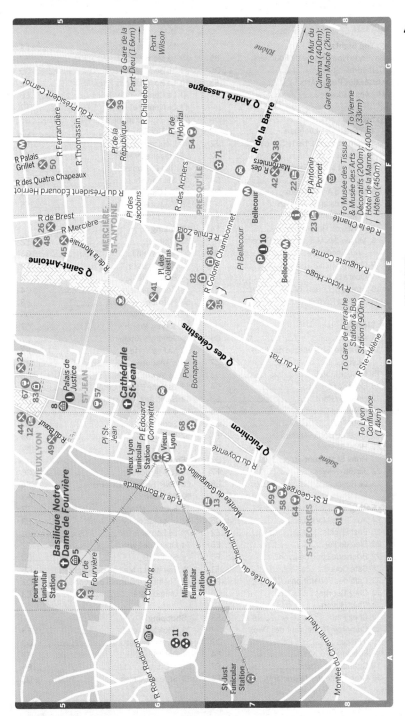

LYON & THE RHÔNE VALLEY LYON

Deep within Vieux Lyon and Croix Rousse, dark, dingy *traboules* (secret passages) wind their way through apartment blocks, under streets and into courtyards. In all, 315 passages link 230 streets, with a combined length of 50km.

A couple of Vieux Lyon's *traboules* date from Roman times, but most were constructed by *canuts* (silk weavers) in the 19th century to transport silk in inclement weather. Resistance fighters found them equally handy during WWII.

Genuine *traboules* (derived from the Latin *trans ambulare*, meaning 'to pass through') cut from one street to another, often wending their way up fabulous spiral staircases en route. Passages that fan out into a courtyard or cul-de-sac aren't *traboules* but *miraboules* (two of the finest examples are at 16 rue Boeuf and 8 rue Juiverie, both in Vieux Lyon).

Vieux Lyon's most celebrated *traboules* include those connecting: 27 rue St-Jean with 6 rue des Trois Maries; 54 rue St-Jean with 27 rue du Bœuf (push the intercom button to buzz open the door); 10 quai Romain Rolland with 2 place du Gouvernement; 17 quai Romain Rolland with 9 rue des Trois Maries; and 31 rue du Bœuf with 14 rue de la Bombarde.

Step into Croix Rousse's underworld at 9 place Colbert, crossing cours des Voraces – renowned for its monumental staircase that zigzags up seven floors – and emerging at 29 rue Imbert Colomès. Others include those linking 1 place Colbert with 10 montée St-Sébastien and 9 place Colbert with 14bis montée St-Sébastien; and the plethora of passages on rue des Capucins – at Nos 3, 6, 13, 22 and 23.

Lyon's tourist office has more information and includes *traboules* on many of its guided walking tours.

Fresque des Lyonnais   MURAL

(cnr rue de la Martinière & quai de la Pêcherie, 1er; MHôtel de Ville) Well-known Lyonnais peer out from this seven-storey mural, including loom inventor Joseph-Marie Jacquard (1752–1834), Renaissance poet Maurice Scève (c 1499–1560), superstar chef Paul Bocuse (b 1926), puppet Guignol, and the yellow-haired Little Prince, created by author/aviator Antoine de St-Exupéry (1900–44).

Musée de l'Imprimerie   PRINTING MUSEUM

(www.imprimerie.lyon.fr, in French; 37 rue de la Poulaillerie, 2e; adult/child/concession €3.80/free/2; ⊙9.30am-noon & 2-6pm Wed-Sun; MCordeliers) Filled with early equipment through to computerised technology, this absorbing museum focuses on the city's extensive printing industry (look for the 1960s airline timetables!).

Musée des Tissus   TEXTILE MUSEUM

(www.musee-des-tissus.com, in French; 34 rue de la Charité, 2e; adult/child €7/4; ⊙10am-5.30pm Tue-Sun; MAmpère) Extraordinary Lyonnais and international silks are showcased here. Ticket includes admission to the adjoining Musée des Arts Décoratifs (10am-noon & 2-5.30pm Tue-Sun), which displays 18th-century furniture, tapestries, wallpaper, ceramics and silver.

Aquarium du Grand Lyon   AQUARIUM

(www.aquariumlyon.fr; 7 rue Stéphane Déchant, La Mulatière; adult/child €14/10; ⊙11am-7pm Wed-Sun, daily during school holidays) Next to the Confluence, Lyon's well-thought-out aquarium is home to some 280 marine species including over 5000 fish. Bus 15 links it with place Bellecour.

CROIX ROUSSE

Independent until it became part of Lyon in 1852, and retaining its own distinct character with its bohemian inhabitants and lush outdoor food market, the hilltop quarter of Croix Rousse slinks north up the steep *pentes* (slopes).

Following the introduction of the mechanical Jacquard loom in 1805, Lyonnais *canuts* (silk weavers) built tens of thousands of workshops in the area, with large windows to let in light and hefty wood-beamed ceilings more than 4m high to accommodate the huge new machines. Weavers spent 14 to 20 hours a day hunched over their looms breathing in silk dust. Two-thirds were illiterate and everyone was paid a pittance; strikes in 1830–31 and 1834 resulted in the death of several hundred weavers.

Most workshops are chic loft apartments today, but a few have been saved (with more in the process of being saved) by the Soierie Vivante association (opposite).

Hidden Croix Rousse gems include place Bertone, a leafy square that doubles as an open-air stage for ad hoc summer entertainment; the Jardin Rosa Mir (enter via 87 Grande Rue, 4e; ⊘3-6pm Sat Apr-Nov; Ⓜ Croix Rousse), a walled garden decorated with thousands of seashells accessed off a narrow laneway; and the panoramic Jardin Publique La Cerisaie (rue Chazière, 4e; Ⓜ Croix Rousse).

Maison des Canuts   SILK MUSEUM
(⊘04 78 28 62 04; www.maisondescanuts.com; 10-12 rue d'Ivry, 4e; adult/child €6/3; ⊘10am-6pm Tue-Sat, guided tours 11am & 3.30pm; Ⓜ Croix Rousse) On a guided tour, learn about weavers' labour-intensive life and the industry's evolution and see manual looms in use, and browse its silk boutique.

Atelier de Passementerie   SILK WORKSHOP
(⊘04 78 27 17 13; www.soierie-vivante.asso.fr; 21 rue Richan, 4e; guided tour adult/child €5/3; ⊘2-6.30pm Tue, 9am-noon & 2-6.30pm Wed-Sat, guided tours & loom demonstrations 2pm & 4pm Tue-Sat; Ⓜ Croix Rousse) Trimmings workshop that functioned until 1979,

weaving braids and intricate pictures. Combination tickets with the Atelier de Tissage cost €8/4 per adult/child.

Atelier de Tissage   SILK WORKSHOP
(cnr rue Godart and rue Lebrun, 4e; guided tour adult/child €5/3; ⊘guided tours and loom demonstrations 3pm & 5pm Thu-Sat; Ⓜ Croix Rousse) Wonderful old workshop with looms that produce larger fabrics.

Mur des Canuts   MURAL
(cnr bd des Canuts & rue Denfert Rochereau, 4e; Ⓜ Hénon) Silk-weaving traditions are illustrated by this fresco.

RIVE GAUCHE
The Rhône's Rive Gauche (left bank) harbours superb parks and museums and day-to-day Lyonnais amenities including its main university and transport hubs.

Parc de la Tête d'Or   PARK
(⊘04 72 69 47 60; www.loisirs-parcdelatetedor. com; bd des Belges, 6e; ⊘6am-11pm; Ⓜ Masséna) Spanning 117 hectares, France's largest urban park was landscaped in the 1860s. It's graced by a lake, botanic garden with greenhouses, rose garden and zoo (admission free; ⊘9am-5pm), with lions, tigers, bears, giraffes and more. In summer hire boats, ride ponies, take a twirl on a fair-

---

RIVERSIDE REJUVENATION

The Rhône's Rive Gauche (left bank), once the domain of high-speed traffic and car parks, has been extensively redeveloped in the past decade to provide Lyon with fabulously landscaped walkway cycling and inline skating tracks, spanning 10 hectares over 5km of riverfront. Known as the Berges du Rhône, a path separates it from traffic along the upper level, while the lower level incorporates riverside woods, grassy fields and paved areas with tiered seating where locals lounge on sunny days. Starting upstream beneath the Winston Churchill bridge, it passes beneath nine more bridges, and past the popular péniches (barges) as it continues downstream to the Lyon Confluence (www.lyon-confluence.fr), where the Rhône and the Saône meet south of Gare de Perrache.

A former industrial wasteland, the Confluence is now the focus of another multi-million-euro rejuvenation project.

Maison de La Confluence (⊘04 78 34 74 00; 28 rue Casimir Perier, 2e; admission free; ⊘2-6.30pm Wed-Sat; ᐅ tramline 1, Montrochet stop), with a bird's-eye view of construction from its rooftop terrace, displays scale models of the area's ongoing development. Already-completed developments include the unique marketplace-like eating space Rue Le Bec (p447), part of Lyonnais chef Nicolas Le Bec's expanding empire.

Prior to the grand opening of the ambitious science-and-humanities museum, the Musée des Confluences (www.museedesconfluences.fr), to be housed in a futuristic steel-and-glass transparent crystal (estimated to open in 2014, about half a decade behind schedule), the Local d'Information du Musée des Confluences (⊘04 78 37 30 00; www.museedesconfluences.fr; 86 quai Perrache, 2e; admission free; ⊘1-6pm Wed-Sat, 10am-noon & 1-6pm Sun) offers sneak previews of its future collection on site. The museum will have its own tram stop once the T1 tramline extension is complete.

LOCAL KNOWLEDGE

HÉLÈNE CARLESCHI

Animatrice de Patrimoine (Heritage Communications), Soierie Vivante

Job? The association formed to save the Atelier de Passementerie (p442) after Mme Letourneau, who wove here for 54 years, donated it and was furious when it was to be turned into private housing. Most of our volunteers are former textile workers; as a full-time employee I do everything from kids' workshops and guided tours to weaving demonstrations and maintaining the looms. **Best thing about working here?** Preserving the area's history – there were once 50,000 silk-weaving workshops in Croix Rousse; I want to help people understand what's behind its architecture and its spirit today. **Life in Croix Rousse?** Like a village, it's very sociable, especially the market (p450) and my favourite restaurant, Le Cinoche (p450). **And the city as a whole?** Lyon's full of culture, it's a really, really living city. Since I was a child, I've visited the crafts market (p454). I like the theatres (p451), drinks at the *péniches* (p453) by the Berges du Rhône and concerts at Transbordeur (p453). I also lead tours at the Musée des Tissus (p441). **Secret spot?** The Jardin Publique La Cerisaie (p441) in Croix Rousse has beautiful views over Lyon.

ground ride or watch a **puppet show** (☑04 78 93 71 75; www.theatre-guignol.com). Buses 41 and 47 link it with metro Part-Dieu.

Musée d'Art Contemporain   ART MUSEUM
(☑04 72 69 17 17; www.moca-lyon.org; 81 quai Charles de Gaulle, 6e; adult/child €8/free; ☺noon-7pm Wed-Fri, 10am-7pm Sat & Sun) Parc de la Tête d'Or's northern realms abut Lyon's contemporary art museum, which mounts edgy temporary exhibitions and the rotating permanent collection of post-1960 art. It closes for up to a couple of months between exhibitions, so check to make sure something's on.

Centre d'Histoire de la Résistance et de la Déportation   MUSEUM
(CHRD; www.chrd.lyon.fr; 14 av Berthelot, 7e; adult/child €4/free; ☺9am-5.30pm Wed-Sun; Ⓜ Perrache or Jean Macé) The 1942–44 WWII headquarters of Gestapo commander Klaus Barbie now evokes Lyon's role as the 'Capital of the Resistance' (as proclaimed by General de Gaulle) through moving multimedia exhibitions. Temporary exhibits cost €4 extra.

TOP CHOICE **Musée Lumière**   FILM MUSEUM
(www.institut-lumiere.org; 25 rue du Premier Film, 8e; adult/child €6/5, audioguide €3; ☺11am-6.30pm Tue-Sun; Ⓜ Monplaisir-Lumière) Cinema's glorious beginnings are showcased at the art nouveau home of Antoine Lumière, who moved to Lyon with sons Auguste and Louis in 1870. The brothers shot the first reels of the world's first motion picture, *La Sortie des Usines Lumières* (Exit of the Lumières Factories) here in one of their father's photographic factories in the grounds on 19 March 1895. Today the former factory houses the Hangar du Premier Film cinema. It's located 3km to the southeast of place Bellecour along cours Gambetta.

Mur du Cinéma   MURAL
(cnr cours Gambetta & Grande Rue de la Guillotière, 7e; Ⓜ Guillotière) Lyon's cinematic story is told in still-image form here in one of the city's many murals.

NORTHERN SUBURBS

Musée Henri Malarte   TRANSPORT MUSEUM
(www.musee-malartre.com, in French; 645 rue du Musée, Rochetaillée-sur-Saône; adult/child €6/free; ☺9am-6pm Tue-Sun) Jean-Paul II's Renault Espace, Hitler's Mercedes, 50-odd motorbikes, bicycles and historical modes of Lyonnais public transport are showcased inside this 15th-century château, 11km north of Lyon along the D433. Take bus number 40 or 70 to the Rochetaillée stop.

 Activities

Rollerbladers (www.generationsroller.asso.fr, in French) hook up on place Bellecour for a mass scoot around town every Friday at 8.30pm (12km, 1¼ hours) for those with less experience (though you'll need to know how to stop!), and 10pm for speed fiends (25km, 1½ hours).

See p455 for bike hire.

GAY & LESBIAN LYON

This gay-friendly city has scads of venues. Free publications listing current hot spots are available from the Forum Gai et Lesbien de Lyon (☑04 78 39 97 72; www.fgllyon. org, in French; 17 rue Romarin, 1er; MCroix Paquet) and ARIS (Accueil Rencontres Informations Service; ☑04 78 27 10 10; www.aris-lyon.org, in French; 19 rue des Capucins, 1er; MCroix Paquet), which both organise social events.

Guys' favourite places to party include gay bar Station B (http://stationb.fr, in French; 21 place Gabriel Rambaud, 1er; ☺Wed-Sun; MHôtel de Ville) and club United Café (www.united-cafe.com, in French; impasse de la Pêcherie, 1er; ☺daily; MHôtel de Ville), while gals congregate at lesbian Le Domaine Bar (http://ledomainebar.fr, in French; 9 rue du Jardin des Plantes, 1er; ☺daily; MHôtel de Ville). Both *filles* and *garçons* (girls and boys – or more specifically *filles* who like *filles* and *garçons* who like *garçons*) enjoy F&G Bar (www.fg-bar.com, in French; 20 rue Terrailles, 1e; ☺Tue-Sat; MHôtel de Ville).

Lyon's Lesbian and Gay Pride (www.fierte.net, in French) march and festivities hit the streets each year in June.

Online, www.lyongay.net (in French) has the lowdown on Lyon's scene.

👉 Tours

Walking Tours WALKING TOUR
(adult/child €9/5) The tourist office organises a variety of English-language tours through Vieux Lyon and Croix Rousse, and several others in French.

Jogg'in City JOGGING TOUR
(☑06 77 793 514; www.joggincity.fr; 1hr tour 1/2/3/4 or more people €70/40/30/25) Fast movers (aged over 18) can take in the sights along a 5km to 6km route.

Harley Davidson tours MOTORCYCLE TOUR
(☑06 19 19 42 43; per person, per hr €80) For a unique way to see the city and beyond, book a guided Harley Davidson tour operated by Le Wine Bar d'à Côté (p451).

Cyclopolitain CYCLE-TAXI
(☑04 78 30 35 90; www.cyclopolitain.com, in French; 30/60min tour 2 people €25/35; ☺10.30am-7pm) Tiny and/or tired feet can rest aboard a cycle-taxi tour.

Navig'inter CRUISES
(☑04 78 42 96 81; www.naviginter.fr, in French; 13bis quai Rambaud, 2e; MBellecour or Vieux Lyon) From April to October, runs river excursions (adult/child €9/6; 1 or 1¼ hr) from its dock (3 quai des Célestins, 2e; MBellecour or Vieux Lyon). Advance bookings are essential for its lunch and dinner cruises (23 quai Claude Bernard, 7e; transport €20-25 plus menus €26-34; MAmpère or Guillotière).

Le Grand Tour BUS TOUR
(☑04 78 56 32 39; www.pariscityrama.com/fr/ visiter_lyon; adult 1-/2-day ticket €17/20, child 1 or 2 days €5; ☺10am-6.30pm) Hop-on, hop-off double-decker bus tours.

🎭 Festivals & Events

Les Nuits de Fourvière MUSIC FESTIVAL
(Fourvière Nights; www.nuitsdefourviere.fr, in French) A diverse program of open-air concerts atmospherically set in Fourvière's Roman amphitheatre from approximately early June to late July.

Biennale de la Danse DANCE FESTIVAL
(www.biennale-de-lyon.org) Month-long dance biennial from around early September to early October in even-numbered years.

Biennale d'Art Contemporain ART FESTIVAL
(www.biennale-de-lyon.org) Huge contemporary art biennial held from around mid-September to early October in odd-numbered years.

Fête des Lumières LIGHT FESTIVAL
(Festival of Lights; www.lumieres.lyon.fr) Over several days around the Feast of the Immaculate Conception (8 December), sound-and-light shows are projected onto key buildings, while locals illuminate window sills with candles.

🛏 Sleeping

Lyon has a wealth of accommodation to suit every taste and budget.

VIEUX LYON

Cour des Loges HOTEL €€€
(☑04 72 77 44 44; www.courdesloges.com; 2-8 rue du Bœuf, 5e; d/ste from €240/505; ❇@🛜🏊; MVieux Lyon) Four 14th- to 17th-century houses wrapped around a *traboule* with preserved features like Italianate loggias make this an exquisite place to stay. Individually designed rooms woo with Philippe

Starck bathroom fittings and a bounty of antiques, while decadent facilities include a spa, an elegant restaurant (menus €60 to €85), swish café (mains €18 to €24) and cross-vaulted bar.

Auberge de Jeunesse du Vieux Lyon

HOSTEL €

(☏04 78 15 05 50; lyon@fuaj.org; 41-45 montée du Chemin Neuf, 5e; dm incl breakfast €18; ⊙reception 7am-1pm, 2-8pm & 9pm-1am; @♠; MMinimes funicular station) Stunning city views unfold from the terrace of Lyon's only hostel, and from many of the (mostly six-bed) dorms. Amenities include a small self-catering kitchen, laundry, 24-hour access and indoor and outdoor bars.

Hôtel St-Paul

HOTEL €

(☏04 78 28 13 29; www.hotelstpaul.fr, in French; 6 rue Lainerie, 5e; d €66-80; @♠; MVieux Lyon) With its classic oyster-grey facade and line-up of large symmetrical windows, this bijou 20-room hotel has enjoyed a renaissance in recent years, and value for money is a cert.

Artelit

B&B €€

(☏04 78 42 84 83; www.dormiralyon.com; 16 rue du Bœuf, 5e; d €100-190, ste €130-250, apt €150-250; MVieux Lyon) Run by Lyonnais photographer Frédéric Jean, the two tower rooms and self-catering apartment of this *chambre d'hôte* (B&B) have centuries of history behind every nook and cranny. If you fall in love with the artworks you can buy them to take home. Breakfast is included in the rate for doubles and suites.

Collège Hotel

HOTEL €€

(☏04 72 10 05 05; www.college-hotel.com; 5 place St-Paul, 5e; d €115-145; ❄@♠; MVieux Lyon) The ultrastark white-on-white minimalism of this hotel's guestrooms is quite startling (which is to say, not everyone will appreciate it). Breakfast on your balcony, in the *salle de classe petit dejeuner*, bedecked like a classroom of yesteryear, or the rooftop garden.

PRESQU'ÎLE

Le Royal

HOTEL €€€

(☏04 78 37 57 31; www.lyonhotelleroyal.com; 20 place Bellecour, 2e; d around €250; ❄@♠; MBellecour) In business since 1895, this timeless visiting card offers Lyon's ultimate in luxury, enveloping you in its stylish *salons* (lounges) and exquisite fabrics and furnishings. Rates vary wildly depending on dates and availability.

Hôtel Le Boulevardier

HOTEL €

(☏04 78 28 48 22; www.leboulevardier.fr; 5 rue de la Fromagerie, 1er; s €49-51, d €51-53; ♠; MHôtel de Ville) Sporting quirky touches like old skis and tennis racquets adorning the hallways, Le Boulevardier is a bargain 11-room hotel with snug, spotless rooms. It's up a steep spiral staircase above a cool little bistro and jazz club of the same name, which doubles as reception.

Hôtel de Paris

HOTEL €€

(☏04 78 28 00 95; www.hoteldeparis-lyon.com; 16 rue de la Platière, 1er; s €49-59, d €65-90; ❄@♠; MHôtel de Ville) At this fantastic-value hotel in a 19th-century bourgeois building, the funkiest rooms' retro '70s decor incorporates a palette of chocolate and turquoise or candyfloss pink. Rooms on the 4th and 5th floors have air conditioning (€2 extra per night).

Jardin d'Hiver

B&B €€

(☏04 78 28 69 34; www.guesthouse-lyon.com; 10 rue des Marronniers, 2e; s/d incl breakfast €110/130, apt per week €500; ❄♠; MBellecour) This chic 3rd-floor B&B (no lift) has just two en-suite rooms – one in understated purple and pistachio, and the other in much more vivid purple and orange – along with a foliage-filled breakfast room and a coffee galley.

Hôtel St-Vincent

HOTEL €

(☏04 78 27 22 56; www.hotel-saintvincent.com, in French; 9 rue Pareille, 1er; s/d €55/70; ♠; MHôtel de Ville) High-beamed ceilings, giant-sized windows, a couple of old stone walls and original wooden floors give this three-floor, 32-room hotel atmosphere to spare.

LYON SLEEPS

The tourist-office-run reservation office (☏04 72 77 72 50; www.lyon-france.com) offers a free booking service and good-value package deals.

Slowly but stylishly, *chambres d'hôte* (B&Bs) are making headway; umbrella organisations include B&B Lyon (☏04 72 32 02 74; www.bb-lyon.com), Chambres Lyon (☏04 72 13 99 35; www.chambreslyon.com) and Gites de France (☏04 72 77 17 50; www.gites-de-france-rhone.com).

Many hotels offer cheaper rates at weekends.

Hôtel des Célestins
HOTEL €€

(☎04 72 56 08 98; www.hotelcelestins.com; 4 rue des Archers, 2e; s €71-121, d €76-126; ❄☎❖; MBellecour) A bouquet's throw from the 18th-century Théâtre des Célestins, this cosy hotel is surrounded by designer boutiques. The priciest rooms face the theatre, the cheaper ones a quiet courtyard.

Hôtel Iris
HOTEL €€

(☎04 78 39 93 80; www.hoteliris.fr; 36 rue de l'Arbre Sec, 1er; s €43-55, d €56-80; MHôtel de Ville) The location of this basic but colourful dame in a centuries-old convent couldn't be better: its street brims with hip places to eat and drink. Ask for a room reached via the open-air staircase.

Hôtel de la Marne
HOTEL €

(☎04 78 37 07 46; www.hoteldelamarne.fr, in French; 78 rue de la Charité, 2e; s €57-63, d €63-69; ☎; MGare de Perrache) Some of the 23 rooms at this stylishly renovated hotel – incorporating smart colour schemes such as chocolate and cherry – open onto a sky-topped courtyard. Wheelchair access is available.

Hotelo
HOTEL €€

(☎04 78 37 39 03; www.hotelo-lyon.com; 37 cours de Verdun, 2e; d from €70; ❄☎❖M Perrache) With a refreshingly contemporary design throughout, one of Hotelo's 17 rooms is equipped for travellers with disabilities, while another sleeps a family of four.

CROIX ROUSSE

 Lyon Guesthouse
B&B €€

(☎04 78 29 62 05; www.lyonguesthouse. com; 6 montée Lieutenant Allouche, 1er; s €60-65, d €85; ☎❖; MCroix Rousse) Perched on the *pentes*, this B&B with prime views of Fourvière is the creation of art collector and gallery owner Françoise Besson. Its three rooms are modern and minimalist, breakfast is a wholly organic affair, and the gallery's collection hangs on the crisp white walls.

RIVE GAUCHE

Péniche Barnum
B&B €€

(☎06 63 64 37 39; www.peniche-barnum. com; 3 Quai du Général Sarrail, 6e; d €120-150; ❄☎❖; MFoch) Moored on the Rhône between Pont Morland and the Passerelle du Collège footbridge, Lyon's most unique B&B is this navy-and-timber barge with two smart en suite guestrooms, a book-filled lounge, and a shaded terrace up on deck. Organic breakfasts cost €10.

NORTHERN SUBURBS

Camping Indigo Lyon
CAMPGROUND €

(☎04 78 35 64 55; www.camping-indigo. com; Porte de Lyon, Dardilly; sites €16.30-18.40, 5-person chalet €39-57, mobile home €60-99; @❖) Open year-round, this leafy campground is founded on strict environmental respect. Wooden chalets beneath the trees sleep five, while mobile homes sleep two to six. Family fun includes outdoor and kids' paddling pools, a playground, ping pong and volleyball.

Eating

A flurry of big-name chefs presides over a sparkling restaurant line-up that embraces all genres: French, fusion, fast and international, as well as traditional Lyonnais *bouchons* (see p448). The website www.lyon resto.com (in French) has reviews, videos and ratings.

Many restaurants offer cheaper lunch *menus* on weekdays only. For self-catering, see p450.

VIEUX LYON

A surfeit of restaurants, most aimed squarely at tourists, jam the streets of Vieux Lyon.

Sol Café
SPANISH €€

(☎04 72 77 66 69; 28 rue du Boeuf, 5e; mains €11.50-21.50; ⊙closed lunch Tue; MVieux Lyon) With a stone interior and sunny terrace, Sol serves up supersized tapas platters, super-fresh salads and sizzling paella, as well as calamari, cured meats and Manchego cheese – washed down with sangria, of course.

Vieux Lyon's most authentic *bouchons*:

Aux Trois Maries
BOUCHON €€

(☎04 78 37 67 28; 1 rue des Trois Maries, 5e; lunch menus €9.50, dinner menus €16.30-40; ⊙lunch Tue-Thu & Sat, dinner Tue-Sat, closed Aug; MVieux Lyon) Opening to a table-filled square, with a wider-than-usual range of seafood.

Le Tire Bouchon
BOUCHON €€

(☎04 78 37 69 95; 16 rue du Boeuf, 5e; menus €19-24; ⊙dinner Tue-Sat; MVieux Lyon) Tucked behind a wine-coloured facade.

FOURVIÈRE

Le Restaurant de Fourvière
LYONNAIS €€

(☎04 78 25 21 15; www.latassee.fr; 9 place de Fourvière, 5e; lunch menus €14.50, dinner menus €26-39; ❖; Mfunicular station Fourvière) The views are so incredible that it'd be easy

LYON & THE RHÔNE VALLEY

for this superbly located restaurant to be a tourist trap, so it's all the more impressive because it's not. Instead it concentrates on well-prepared local specialties including a superb *salade lyonnaise* (greens, bacon, poached egg and croutons).

PRESQU'ÎLE

Cobbled rue Mercière, rue des Marronniers and the northern side of place Antonin Poncet – both in the 2e (metro Bellecour) – are chock-a-block with eating options (of widely varying quality), overflowing with pavement terraces in summer. Near the opera house, rue Verdi, 1er, is likewise table filled.

TOP CHOICE Café des Fédérations   BOUCHON €€
(☑04 78 28 26 00; www.lesfedeslyon.com, in French; 8 rue Major Martin, 1er; lunch menus €19, dinner menus €24-42; ☺Mon-Sat; 🖱; Ⓜ Hôtel de Ville) Black-and-white photos of old Lyon speckle the wood-panelled walls at this treasure of a *bouchon* where nothing has changed for decades – including the heaping portions, the warm service and the convivial atmosphere among diners (and, yes, the Turkish toilet. No matter, this is *bouchon* dining at its best).

Le Bec   FRENCH, FUSION €€€
(☑04 78 42 15 00; www.nicolaslebec.com, 2e; 14 rue Grolée; lunch menus €40, dinner menus €90-135; ☺Tue-Sat, closed 3 weeks August) With two Michelin stars, this is the flagship restaurant of Lyon's hottest chef Nicolas Le Bec, famed for his seasonal, world-influenced cuisine. Le Bec is also the force behind the innovative new concept space Rue Le Bec (☑04 78 92 87 87; 43 quai Rambaud, 2e; mains €9-30, Sunday brunch €45; ☺Tue-Sun; 🚋 tramline 1, Montrochet stop), an airy restaurant set amid a covered-market-like layout of shops and eateries (florist, cheese shop, delicatessen, bakery and more) ranged around a tree-filled central 'street'; and full-service restaurant Espace Le Bec (☑04 72 22 71 86; menus €19.90-25.90; ☺10am-9.30pm Mon-Sat) at St-Exupéry airport.

Le Comptoir des Filles   LYONNAIS €€
(☑04 78 38 03 30; 8 quai des Celestins, 2e; lunch menus €13, mains €15-23; ☺Tue-Sat; 🖱🖊; Ⓜ Bellecour) Elegant in its simplicity; *quenelles* (Lyonnais dumplings) are the specialty of this Saône-side spot. Six varieties are available each day, such as *trois fromages* (three-cheese) or St Jacques (scallops), along with market-prepared *plats* and light, luscious desserts like semolina cake.

Bleu de Toi   SEAFOOD €
(☑04 78 37 24 65;: 51 rue Mercière, 2e; lunch menus €10.90, mains €12.60-14; 🖱; Ⓜ Bellecour) Done out like a rustic fishing shack and opening onto a sunny terrace, this is a diamond find for inexpensive fresh-from-the-ocean seafood followed by crisp-edged crêpes and coffee served with buttery Breton biscuits. Staff are delightful.

Comptoir-Restaurant des Deux Places   BOUCHON €€
(☑04 78 28 95 10; 5 place Fernand Rey, 1er; lunch/dinner menus €13/28; ☺Tue-Sat; Ⓜ Hôtel de Ville) Red-and-white-checked curtains, an antique-crammed interior and handwritten menu contribute to the overwhelmingly traditional neighbourhood feel here. Its quiet pavement terrace beneath trees is idyllic.

Thomas   FRENCH €€
(☑04 72 56 04 76; www.restaurant-thomas.com, in French; 6 rue Laurencin, 2e; lunch/dinner menus €18/41; ☺Mon-Fri; Ⓜ Ampère) Ingenious chef Thomas Ponson gives taste buds the choice between formal dining at his eponymous restaurant, more casual fare in his à la carte wine bar, Comptoir Thomas (3 rue Laurencin; mains €14-25; ☺Mon-Fri), and more casual still at his tapas-inspired Café Thomas (1 rue Laurencin; tapas €1-5; ☺Tue-Sat).

Grand Café des Négociants   BRASSERIE €€
(☑04 78 42 50 05; www.cafe-des-negociants.com, in French; 2 place Francisque Regaud, 2e; lunch menus € 17.90-21.90, mains €17.50-34; ☺7am-3am; Ⓜ Cordeliers) Dubbed Les Négos by locals, this café-style brasserie with mirror-lined walls and a tree-shaded terrace has been a favourite meeting point with Lyonnais since 1864. Don't miss a pot of its deliciously thick hot chocolate (tip: it's cheaper before noon). Look for the gargantuan mulberry flower pots framing the apple-green and cherry-coloured tables out front.

Brasserie Georges   BRASSERIE €€
(☑04 72 56 54 54; www.brasseriegeorges.com; 30 cours de Verdun, 2e; menus €18.50-24; ☺11.30am-11.15pm Sun-Thu, 11am-midnight Fri & Sat; Ⓜ Perrache) Opened as a brewery in 1836 and still in the business (with four brews on tap), Georges' enormous 1924 art deco interior can feed 2000 a day! Famous customers include Rodin, Balzac, Hemingway, Zola, Jules Verne and Piaf; food spans onion soup, sauerkraut, seafood and Lyonnais specialities.

BOUCHONS

A *bouchon* might be a 'bottle stopper' or 'traffic jam' elsewhere in France, but in Lyon it's a small, friendly bistro that cooks up traditional city cuisine using regional produce. *Bouchons* originated in the first half of the 20th century when many large bourgeois families had to let go their in-house cooks, who then set up their own restaurant businesses. The first of these *mères* (mothers) was Mère Guy, followed by Mère Filloux, Mère Brazier (under whom Paul Bocuse trained) and others. Choose carefully – not all *bouchons* are as authentic as they first appear. Many that are have certification with the organisation *Les Authentiques Bouchons Lyonnais* – look for the metal plate on their facades depicting traditional puppet Gnafron (Guignol's mate) with his glass of Beaujolais.

Kick-start a memorable gastronomic experience with a *communard,* an aperitif of red Beaujolais wine and *crème de cassis* (blackcurrant liqueur), named after the supporters of the Paris Commune killed in 1871. Blood red in colour, the mix is considered criminal elsewhere in France. When ordering wine, simply ask for a *pot* – a 46cL glass bottle adorned with an elastic band to prevent wine drips – of local Brouilly, Beaujolais, Côtes du Rhône or Mâcon, costing around €10 to €12; a 25cL version costs around €6 to €7.

Next comes the entrée, perhaps *tablier de sapeur* ('fireman's apron'; actually meaning breaded, fried tripe), *salade de cervelas* (salad of boiled pork sausage sometimes studded with pistachio nuts or black truffle specks), or *caviar de la Croix Rousse* (lentils in creamy sauce). Hearty main dishes include *boudin blanc* (veal sausage), *boudin noir aux pommes* (blood sausage with apples), *quenelles* (feather-light flour, egg and cream dumplings), *quenelles de brochet* (pike dumplings served in a creamy crayfish sauce), *andouillette* (sausage made from pigs' intestines), *gras double* (a type of tripe) and *pieds de mouton/veau/couchon* (sheep/calf/pig trotters).

The cheese course usually comprises a choice of three things: a bowl of *fromage blanc* (a cross between cream cheese and natural yoghurt) with or without thick whipped cream; *cervelle de canut* ('brains of the silk weaver'; *fromage blanc* mixed with chives and garlic, which originated in Croix Rousse and accompanied every meal for 19th-century weavers); or local St Marcellin ripened to gooey perfection.

Desserts are grandma-style: think *tarte aux pommes* (apple tart) or *fromage blanc* (again) with a fruit coulis dribbled on top.

Recently, a new generation of *bouchon*-inspired establishments has started to emerge, putting a lighter, contemporary twist on the traditionally rustic decor and rich cuisine.

Little etiquette is required in *bouchons*. Seldom do you get clean cutlery for each course and mopping your plate with a chunk of bread is fine. Most *bouchons* serve lunch strictly from noon to 2pm (turn up early if you want a full menu) and don't accept diners after 9.30pm; advance reservations are recommended.

Brasserie Léon de Lyon   BRASSERIE €€
(☎04 72 10 11 12; www.leondelyon.com; 1 rue Plény, 1e; menus €19.50-34; ⓜHôtel de Ville) Renowned Lyonnais chef Jean-Paul Lacombe has turned his Michelin-starred gastronomic restaurant into a relaxed brasserie – same 1904 decor, same impeccable service, more affordable prices (the €14.60 *plat du jour* is an excellent deal).

La Mère Jean   BOUCHON €€
(☎04 78 37 81 27; 5 rue des Marronniers, 2e; lunch menus €11.50, other menus €15.50-25; ⓣTue-Sat; ⓜBellecour) Its windows plastered with guidebook plaudits, this thimble-sized *bouchon* dates back to 1923 and rewards booking ahead for its meat-loaded menu.

Chez Georges   BOUCHON €€
(☎04 78 28 30 46; 8 rue du Garet, 1e; lunch menus €16-25, dinner mains €11.50-15; ⓣlunch Mon-Fri, dinner Mon-Sat; ⓜHôtel de Ville) This respected *bouchon*'s decor of lace curtains and sepia-toned lighting retains an intimate ambience. The lunch *menus* and à la carte dinner choices are likewise tried-and-true to local traditions.

Chez Paul

BOUCHON €€

(☎04 78 28 35 83; www.chezpaul.fr, in French; 11 rue Major Martin, 1er; lunch/dinner menus €13.50/25; ☺Mon-Sat; MHôtel de Ville) Self-taught Lyonnaise *mère*, Josiane, takes pride that 'people come to eat as if at home or at their parents' house', and specialises in a creamier-than-usual *tablier de sapeur* (breaded, fried tripe) at this iconic *bouchon*.

Magali et Martin

LYONNAIS €€

(☎04 72 00 88 01; 11 rue Augustins, 1er; lunch/dinner menus €19.50/35; ☺lunch & dinner Mon-Fri, closed 3 weeks Aug & late Dec–mid Jan; MHôtel de Ville) Peep into the third of the trio of large glass windows fronting this fantastic eating space to watch the chefs turning out traditional but lighter, more varied *bouchon*-influenced cuisine.

Le Bouchon des Filles

LYONNAIS €€

(☎04 78 30 40 44; 20 rue Sergent Blandan, 1e; menus €25; ☺dinner Thu-Tue, lunch Sun; MHôtel de Ville) This contemporary ode to Lyon's legendary culinary *mères* is run by two *filles* (daughters), and tablecloths are checked cherry-and-raspberry, rather than classic red-and-white. The atmosphere is especially familial during Sunday lunch.

La Menthe

FRENCH €€

(☎04 78 30 40 44; 15 rue Mercière, 2e; lunch/dinner menus from €12/16; ☺Mon-Sat; MCordeliers) Away from the main pedestrianised drag of this popular eat-street, this pretty, pastel-shaded restaurant serves simple but stylish French fare. Like the food, the service is just right and the value for money top-notch.

Salmon Shop

SEAFOOD €€

(☎04 78 42 97 92; 54 rue Mercière, 2e; lunch menus €12.90, mains €12.60-14.40; ♨; MBelle-cour) Whether smoked, pan-fried, roasted or *tartare* (raw), salmon appears in *every* dish (well, more or less) at this Nordic-style spot. Go for the house specialty *pavé de saumon* – thick-cut, lightly cooked salmon fillet in chive cream sauce accompanied by salads, toast and unlimited fries.

Yinitial G&G

FUSION €€

(☎04 78 42 14 14; 14 rue Palais Grillet, 2e; menus €16.80-32; ☺Tue-Sat, closed Aug; ☑; MCordeliers) At this minimalist space of low-hanging table lights and flickering tea-light candles, the open kitchen throws a pinch of European in the wok alongside Asian spices and herbs to create fragrant world dishes.

Chez Hugon

BOUCHON €€

(☎04 78 28 10 94; 12 rue Pizay, 1er; menus €24; ☺Mon-Fri, closed Aug; MHôtel de Ville) The original 1937 interior is a real blast from the past at Madame Hugon's place, once of the busiest in the city due to its loyal regulars.

Fubuki

JAPANESE €€

(☎04 78 30 41 48; 17 rue Gentil, 2e; lunch menus €10.50-15.50, dinner menus €19-46; ☺Mon-Sat; MCordeliers) Tables are *chauffantes* (heated) at this highly rated Japanese restaurant where traditionally dressed chefs armed with very big knives chop and sizzle up fish before your eyes.

Le Neptune

LYONNAIS €€

(☎04 78 37 08 19; 4 rue des Marronniers, 2e; menus €11-20; MBellecour) Sure, the canteen-style decor is nothing to write home about. But the cooking is surprisingly accomplished given the affordable prices, and good-natured staff are accommodating if you're in a hurry (a rarity in these parts).

Our pick of the Presqu'île's cheapest and tastiest quick eats:

L'épicerie

BISTRO €

(☎04 78 37 70 85; 2 rue de la Monnaie, 2e; tartines €3.80-6.20; ☺noon-midnight; ☑♨; MCordeliers) Done out like an early-20th-century grocer's, with distressed cupboards full of china and old boxes and canisters, serving thick-sliced *tartines* (open-faced sandwiches) with toppings like brie, walnut and honey and delicious desserts like praline tart. There's a handful of other branches in Lyon and beyond.

Giraudet

LUNCH BAR €

(☎04 72 77 98 58; www.giraudet.fr, in French; 2 rue Colonel Chambonnet, 2e; menus €10-13; ☺11am-7pm Mon, 9am-7pm Tue-Sat; ☑; MBellecour) Sleek *quenelle* boutique with seating area to taste the Lyonnais speciality along with homemade soups. There's another branch at Les Halles de Lyon.

Best Bagels

CAFÉ €

(☎04 78 27 65 61; www.bestbagels.fr, in French; 1 place Tobie Robatel, 1er; bagels €4.25-10; ☺11.30am-10pm Mon & Tue, 11.30am-11pm Wed-Fri, 11am-11pm Sat, 11am-3pm Sun; ☑; MHôtel de Ville) Filled bagels and sticky doughnuts to eat in or to go, plus a grocery store selling Jello, Kool Aid et al to a mostly local, student-oriented crowd.

Neo Le Comptoir

CAFÉ €

(☎04 78 30 51 01; www.neolecomptoir.com, in French; 21 rue du Bât d'Argent, 1er; menus

LYON FOOD MARKETS

Food shopping in Lyon is an unmissable part of the city's experience. And with so many urban spaces and parks, there are plenty of picnic spots too.

Lyon's famed indoor food market Les Halles de Lyon (http://halledelyon.free.fr, in French; 102 cours Lafayette, 3e; ⊗8am-7pm Tue-Sat, to noon Sun; ⓜPart-Dieu) has over 60 stalls selling their renowned wares. Pick up a round of impossibly runny St Marcellin from legendary cheesemonger Mère Richard, and a knobbly Jésus de Lyon from pork butcher Collette Sibilia. Or enjoy a sit-down lunch of local produce at the stalls, lip-smacking *coquillages* (shellfish) included. You'll also find tables amid the stalls at the small indoor food market La Halle de Martinière (24 rue de la Martinière, 1er; ⊗Tue-Sun; ⓜHôtel de Ville).

Lyon has two main outdoor food markets: Croix Rousse (bd de la Croix Rousse, 4e; ⊗Tue-Sun morning; ⓜCroix Rousse); Presqu'île (quai St-Antoine, 2e; ⊗Tue-Sun morning; ⓜBellecour or Cordeliers). If you'd rather have it brought to you, fruit-and-veg service Potager City (www.potagercity.fr, in French) shops at markets and delivers by bicycle throughout central Lyon.

€4.50-10; ⊗11am-3pm, closed Sun Jul & Aug; ⓜHôtel de Ville) Pick-and-mix salads in a light-filled bourgeois town house with lime-green and candy-pink walls.

CROIX ROUSSE

From December to April, Croix Rousse café life revolves around oyster-and-white-wine breakfasts, shucked outdoors on crisp sunny mornings.

Mère Brazier LYONNAIS €€€
(☑04 78 23 17 20; 12 rue Royale, 1er; lunch menus €31-35, dinner menus €55-95; ⊗Mon-Fri, closed 3 weeks Aug & 1 week Feb; ⓜCroix Paquet) Chef Mathieu Vianney has reinvented the mythical early-20th-century restaurant that earned Mère (Eugénie) Brazier Lyon's first trio of Michelin stars in 1933 (a copy of the original guidebook takes pride of place). Brazier was also the first-ever chef to earn two sets of three Michelin stars, a feat only equalled decades later by Alain Ducasse. Vianney is doing admirable justice to Brazier's legacy, claiming two Michelin stars himself for his assured cuisine accompanied by an impressive (and impressively well-priced) wine list.

Toutes les Couleurs VEGETARIAN €€
(☑04 72 00 03 95; www.touteslescouleurs. fr, in French; 26 rue Imbert Colomès, 1er; lunch menus €11.50-14.50, dinner menus €19-26; ⊗lunch Tue-Sat, dinner Fri & Sat; ☑; ⓜCroix-Paquet) Lyon's dining scene tends to overlook vegetarians, but its saving grace is this exclusively vegetarian *restaurant bio*, the seasonal menu of which includes *végétalien*

(vegan) and gluten-free options. No cow's milk here – only soy, almond or rice.

Café Cousu CAFÉ €
(☑04 72 98 83 38; www.cafe-cousu.com, in French; Passage Thiaffait, 19 rue René Leynaud, 1er; breakfast €4.50, lunch menus €8.50-11.50, weekend brunch €13; ⊗8.30am-9pm Tue-Fri, 11am-9pm Sat & Sun; ☎☑; ⓜCroix Paquet) Wedged between fashion designers in Le Village des Createurs, this hole in the wall entices an arty crowd with its battery-charging breakfasts, healthy lunches and homemade tarts and cakes, as well as its buzzing weekend brunch from 11am until 5pm.

Le Cinoche CRÊPERIE €
(☑04 72 07 06 99; 7 rue Dumenge, 4e; galettes €9-9.50, crêpes €3.50-6.50; ⊗Tue-Sat; ☑; ⓜCroix Rousse) Reflecting Lyon's cinema heritage with its old projectors, reels, lights, books and posters, savoury galettes and sweet crêpes at this cosy crêperie are named after famous films, such as *Orange Mécanique* (*Clockwork Orange*), with orange, melted chocolate and vodka-infused chantilly.

Le Canut et Les Gones LYONNAIS €€
(☑04 78 29 17 23; 29 rue de Belfort, 4e; plat du jour €9, lunch/dinner menus €16/25; ⊗Tue-Sat; ⓜCroix Rousse) The culinary experience at this retro neighbourhood bistro is as promising as its mustard-yellow facade with mint-green window frames suggests. The crowd is savvy and local, and the creative cuisine utilises produce from Croix Rousse's market.

Gd Kfé de la Soierie
CAFÉ €

(☏04 78 28 11 26; place des Tapis, 4e; breakfast €4.90, mains €10-17; ☺daily; Ⓜ Croix Rousse) Plop down on a Fermob chair outside this time-honoured café when the market is in full swing and you'll love this hilltop quarter forever. The zinc bar is one of its many original features.

RIVE GAUCHE
Le Comptoir
CAFÉ, WINE BAR €€

(☏04 72 60 98 64; 7 rue de la Part-Dieu, 3e; bagel menus €2.90-4.90; ☺lunch Tue-Fri, dinner Wed-Sat; ✐; Ⓜ Place Guichard) In an airy, stylish space filled with fresh flowers and well-chosen antiques just east of the Rhône, savoury tortes, soups and terrines (rabbit, pork, foie gras) are its open kitchen's specialties.

NORTHERN SUBURBS
L'Auberge du Pont de Collonges
FRENCH €€€

(☏04 72 42 90 90; www.bocuse.com; 40 rue de la Plage; menus €115-215; ☺lunch & dinner daily by reservation) Heading some 6.5km north of central Lyon via quai Georges Clemenceau brings you to this triple-Michelin-starred restaurant of the city's most decorated chef, Paul Bocuse. Classics include the likes of sea bass stuffed with lobster mousse in a puff-pastry shell, and thyme-roasted rack of lamb, as well as Bocuse's signature *soupe VGE* (truffle soup created for former French president Valéry Giscard d'Estaing in 1975).

🍷 Drinking & Entertainment

Many establishments start as a relaxed place for a drink (and often food too), morphing into jam-packed bars and/or live-music and dancing venues as the night wears on.

See p452 for details of Lyon's puppet theatres.

VIEUX LYON

If you're still going past closing time, late-night bars open until the *wee* hours are scattered throughout Vieux Lyon – just follow the crowds.

Vieux Lyon British & Irish Pubs
PUBS

Cities the world over have British and Irish pubs, but even by those standards Vieux Lyon has an extraordinary concentration, patronised by expats, visitors and local Lyonnais alike. Firm favourites open daily until at least 1am include the bookshelf-lined Smoking Dog (16 rue Lainerie, 5e; Ⓜ Vieux Lyon) in St Paul; the social James Joyce (68

rue St-Jean, 5e; Ⓜ Vieux Lyon), and home-from-home St-James (19 rue St-Jean, 5e; Ⓜ Vieux Lyon) in St-Jean.

Further south in St-Georges, good bets are Johnny's Kitchen (www.myspace.com/johnnyskitchen; 48 rue St-Georges, 5e; Ⓜ Vieux Lyon), which does decent pub grub; its sister bar (with live music five nights a week) Johnny Walsh's (www.johnnywalshs.com; 56 rue St-Georges, 5e; ☎); and, somewhat off the beaten track, the atmospheric L'Antidote (www.antidote-pub.com; 108 rue St-Georges, 5e; Ⓜ Vieux Lyon).

Saint Just: Caviste pas Pareil
WINE BAR

(☏06 80 47 21 09; www.myspace.com/lesaintjus; 76 rue St-Georges, 5e; ☺vary; Ⓜ Vieux Lyon) This fun, far-from-mainstream wine bar runs relaxed wine-tasting workshops (€18).

(L'A)Kroche
LIVE MUSIC

(☏04 78 37 38 52;; 8 rue Monseigneur Lavarenne, 5e; ☺Tue-Sun; ☎; Ⓜ Vieux Lyon) Hip concert bar/café with DJs spinning electro, soul, funk, disco and live music including rock, pop and indie.

PRESQU'ÎLE
Place des Terreaux
CAFÉS

(12 rue Ste-Catherine, 1er; Ⓜ Hôtel de Ville) The bounty of café terraces on the Presqu'île's central square buzz with drinkers all hours.

Le Wine Bar d'à Côté
WINE BAR

(☏04 78 28 31 46; www.cave-vin-lyon.com, in French; 7 rue Pleney, 1er; ☺Tue-Sat; ☎; Ⓜ Cordeliers) Hidden in a tiny alleyway, this cultured wine bar is furnished like a rustic English gentlemen's club with leather sofa seating and library.

LYON WHAT'S ON

Track new nightclub offerings at www.lyonclubbing.com, www.lyon2night.com and www.night4lyon.com (all in French).

Weekly 'what's on guides include *Lyon Poche* (www.lyonpoche.com, in French; at newsagents €1) and *Le Petit Bulletin* (www.petit-bulletin.fr, in French; free on street corners).

Tickets are sold at **Fnac Billetterie** (www.fnac.com/spectacles; 85 rue de la République, 2e; ☺10am-7pm Mon-Sat; Ⓜ Bellecour).

GUIGNOL: LYON'S HISTORIC PUPPET

The history of Lyon's famous puppet, Guignol, is intertwined with that of the city. In 1797 out-of-work silk-weaver Laurent Mourguet took up dentistry (ie pulling teeth). To attract patients, he set up a puppet show in front of his chair, initially featuring the Italian Polichinelle (who became Punch in England). Success saw Mourguet move into full-time puppetry, creating Guignol in about 1808 and devising shows revolving around working-class issues, the news of the day, social gossip and satire.

Today this little hand-operated glove puppet pops up all over his home town, including on the Fresque des Lyonnais mural (p441) and at puppet museums (p435 and p436).

Guignol's highly visual, slapstick-style antics appeal equally to children and adults (theatres also stage some adult-only evening performances). Shows are in French but also incorporate traditional Lyonnais dialect, such as the words *quinquets* (eyes), *picou* (nose), *bajafler* (talking nonstop) and *gones* (kids, and, by extension, all Lyonnais).

In addition to performances at Parc de la Tête d'Or (p442), Lyon has three dedicated Guignol theatres:

Guignol, un Gone de Lyon (☑04 72 32 11 55; www.guignol-un-gone-de-lyon.com, in French; 65 bd des Canuts, 4e; Ⓜ Hénon) In Croix Rousse.

Théâtre La Maison de Guignol (☑04 72 40 26 61; www.lamaisondeguignol.fr, in French; 2 montée du Gourguillon, 5e; Ⓜ Vieux Lyon) Quaint St-Georges theatre.

Théâtre Le Guignol de Lyon (☑04 78 28 92 57; www.guignol-lyon.com, in French; 2 rue Louis Carrand, 5e; Ⓜ Vieux Lyon) Puppeteers give audiences a behind-the-scenes peek at the props and puppets after certain performances (check ahead for schedules).

More info on Guignol is available at http://amisdeguignol.free.fr.

Albion
PUB

(12 rue Ste-Catherine, 1er; Ⓜ Hôtel de Ville) Rue Ste-Catherine was Lyon's *rue de la soif* (thirst street), but the scene has largely shifted to Vieux Lyon. Bars that are still good for a pint here, however, include this cosy spot.

La Fée Verte
CAFÉ-BAR

(www.myspace.com/lafeevertelyon; 4 rue Pizay, 1er; ⊙vary; ☎; Ⓜ Hôtel de Ville) You guessed it, the green-bedecked Green Fairy specialises in devilish old absinthe. There's usually electro and hip-hop a couple of nights a week.

Harmonie des Vins
WINE BAR

(www.harmoniedesvins.fr, in French; 9 rue Neuve, 1er; ⊙10am-2am Tue-Sat; Ⓜ Hôtel de Ville) Find out all about French wine at this charm-laden wine bar replete with old stone walls, contemporary furnishings, strong coffee and tasty food.

Andy Walha
BAR

(29 rue de l'Arbre Sec, 1er; ⊙daily; Ⓜ Hôtel de Ville) Warhol inspires the pop-art decor at this cocktail bar where a beautiful set quaffs champagne, cocktails and elder-flower cordial.

Hot Club de Lyon
LIVE MUSIC

(www.hotclubjazz.com, in French; 26 rue Lanterne, 1er; admission €5-18; ⊙Tue-Sat; Ⓜ Hôtel de Ville) A stalwart since 1948, this nonprofit venue is Lyon's leading jazz club.

Opéra de Lyon
OPERA HOUSE

(☑08 26 30 53 25; www.opera-lyon.com, in French; place de la Comédie, 1er; ⊙mid-Sep–early Jul; Ⓜ Hôtel de Ville) Lyon's landmark opera house is the premier place to catch opera, ballet and classical concerts.

CNP-Terreaux
CINEMA

(http://ter.cine.allocine.fr, in French; 40 rue du Président Édouard Herriot, 1er; Ⓜ Hôtel de Ville) Screens nondubbed films.

Also recommended:

Barberousse
BAR

(http://lyon.barberousse.com/, in French; 18 rue Terrailles, 1er; ⊙Tue-Sat; Ⓜ Hôtel de Ville) Nautical-styled shooter bar which features over 50 different flavours of rum (including cinnamon, chestnut, violet, rhubarb...).

Soda Bar
BAR

(http://soda-bar.noziris.com, in French; 7 rue de la Martinière, 1er; ⊙Tue-Sat, closed mid-

Jul–mid-Aug; MHôtel de Ville) Spirited bar staff juggle bottles while mixing cocktails (called 'flair bartending', apparently).

Le Voxx
BAR

(1 rue d'Algérie, 1er; ⊙daily; MHôtel de Ville) Minimalist riverside bar packed with a real mix of people, from student to city slicker.

Broc' Café
BAR-CAFÉ

(www.broc-cafe-resto.com, in French; 2 place de l'Hôpital, 2e; MMon-Sat; MBellecour) Second-hand-furnished spot (*'broc'* is short for *brocante* – vintage or jumble) that oozes street cred.

Comptoir de la Bourse
BAR

(www.comptoirdelabourse.fr; 33 rue de la Bourse, 1er; ⊙Mon-Sat; MCordeliers) *Très* trendy.

CROIX ROUSSE

Scout out alternative Croix Rousse to find off-beat bars.

modernartcafé
BAR

(www.modernartcafe.net; 65 bd de la Croix Rousse, 4e; ⊙daily; 🛜; MCroix Rousse) Retro furnishings, changing art on the walls, weekend brunch and various photography-, music- and video-driven events make this art bar a lynchpin of Croix Rousse's creative community.

Le Bec de Jazz
LIVE MUSIC

(19 rue Burdeau; ⊙Wed-Sat; MCroix Paquet) Ubercool late-night jazz club.

La Bistro fait sa Broc'
BAR

(1-3 rue Dumenge, 4e; ⊙Mon-Sat; MCroix Rousse) A lime-green and candyfloss-pink facade greets you at this retro wine bar where no two chairs match. Occasional bands.

RIVE GAUCHE

Péniches
BARGE BARS

Along the Rhône's left bank, a string of *péniches* (barges) with onboard bars rock until around 3am. Depending on the season you'll find upwards of a dozen moored along quai Victor Augagneur between Pont Lafayette (MCordeliers or Guichard) in the north and Pont de la Guillotière (MGuillotière) in the south. Many have DJs and/or live bands. Our favourites include the laid-back Passagère (21 quai Victor Augagneur, 7e; ⊙daily), the classy La Pie (http://lapieresto.com, in French; 2 quai Victor Augagneur, 3e; ⊙Wed-Sat), party-hard Le Sirius (www.lesirius.com, in French; 4 quai Victor Augagneur,

3e; ⊙daily; 🛜), and electro-oriented La Marquise (www.marquise.net, in French; 20 quai Victor Augagneur, 3e; ⊙Tue-Sun).

Ninkasi Gerland
LIVE MUSIC

(www.ninkasi.fr, in French; 267 rue Marcel Mérieux, 7e; ⊙daily; MStade de Gerland) Spilling over with a fun, frenetic crowd, this microbrewery near the stadium is one of several Ninkasi establishments around town, each with their own entertainment programs, ranging from DJs and bands to film projections and more, and sustaining food like fish and chips and build-your-own burgers.

Le Transbordeur
LIVE MUSIC

(www.transbordeur.fr, in French; 3 bd de Stalingrad, Villeurbanne) In an old industrial building, Lyon's prime concert venue draws international acts on the European concert-tour circuit. Take bus 59 from metro Part-Dieu to the Cité Inter Transbordeur stop.

Hangar du Premier Film
CINEMA

(www.institut-lumiere.org; 25 rue du Premier Film, 8e; MMonplaisir-Lumière) Next to the Musée Lumière, this former factory and birthplace of cinema now screens films of all genres and eras in their original languages. From approximately June to September, the big screen moves outside.

Auditorium de Lyon
CLASSICAL MUSIC

(☑04 78 95 95 95; www.auditorium-lyon.com, in French; 82 rue de Bonnel, 3e; ⊙Sep-Jun; MPart-Dieu) Built in 1975, this spaceshiplike auditorium houses the National Orchestra of Lyon, along with workshops, jazz and world-music concerts.

Maison de la Danse
DANCE CLUB

(www.maisondeladanse.com; 8 av Jean Mermoz, 8e) Take bus 23, 24 or 25 to reach Lyon's home of contemporary dance.

In the hip Gare de Brotteaux quarter, start clubbing at ApériKlub (www.aperiklub-first.com, in French; 13-14 place Jules Ferry; MBrotteaux; ⊙Wed-Sat) and end at adjacent First Tendency (13-14 place Jules Ferry; MBrotteaux; ⊙Thu-Sat). Dress sharp for both.

Shopping
VIEUX LYON

Vieux Lyon's narrow streets are dotted with galleries, antiquarian and secondhand bookshops, and quality souvenir shops.

St Jean Délices
SWEETS

(www.saintjeandelices.com; 19 rue St-Jean, 5e; ⊙10am-8pm Tue-Sun; MVieux Lyon) For the sweetest souvenirs, this enticing spot sells all eight varieties of Lyon's specialty sweets made by traditional local confectioners including *les coussins de Lyon* (Curacao-flavoured dark chocolate in sugary almond paste) and *les pralines rouges* (almonds in red vanilla-flavoured caramelised coating, which is a fixture of local desserts and patisseries), as well as handmade chocolates.

Crafts Market CRAFT MARKET
(quai de Bondy, 5e; ⊙9am-noon Sun; ⓂVieux Lyon) Along the Saône, meet artists selling their paintings, sculptures, photography and more.

PRESQU'ÎLE
High-street chains line rue de la République and rue Victor Hugo, while upmarket boutiques and design houses stud rue du Président Édouard Herriot, rue de Brest and the streets between place des Jacobins and place Bellecour. More cluster between art galleries and antique shops around rue Auguste Comte, 2e.

In Cuisine BOOKSHOP
(www.incuisine.fr; 1 place Bellecour, 2e; ⓂBellecour) This foodie haven has an astonishing selection of culinary, gastronomic and wine titles. It also runs cooking courses, demonstrations and tastings, and serves lunch in its *salon de thé*.

Also recommended:
Book Market BOOK MARKET
(quai de la Pêcherie, 1er; ⊙7am-6pm Sat & Sun; ⓂHôtel de Ville) A treasure trove of hard-to-find titles (most in French).

FEVER PITCH

Qui ne saute pas n'est pas Lyonnais! (Whoever doesn't jump isn't Lyonnais!) is the rallying cry for multichampionship-winning football (ie soccer) team **Olympique Lyonnais** (OL; http://olweb.fr), whose home ground is the 1920s-built, 40,000-seater stadium **Stade de Gerland** (353 av Jean Jaurès, 7e; ⓂStade de Gerland). To join the crowds jumping wildly up and down, buy match tickets online or from the club's boutiques: **OL Store** (☑39 69; ⊙10am-7pm Tue-Sat, daily Dec) Gerland (60 av Tony Garnier, 7e; ⓂStade de Gerland); Lyon Centre (cnr rue de Jussieu & rue Grolée, 2e; ⓂCordeliers).

Decitre BOOKSHOP
(www.decitre.fr, in French; 6 place Bellecour, 2e; ⓂBellecour) Stocks foreign-language fiction including English (very limited travel section).

CROIX ROUSSE
Montée de la Grande Côte
GALLERIES, WORKSHOPS
(ⓂCroix Rousse or Croix Paquet) Silk, stained glass and other galleries and workshops come and go the length of this walkway linking Croix Rousse with place des Terreaux, 1er. Several more galleries stud the eastern end of rue Burdeau, 1er.

Le Village des Createurs FASHION
(☑04 78 27 37 21; www.villagedescreateurs.com; Passage Thiaffait, 19 rue René Leynaud, 1e; ⊙2-7pm Wed-Sat; ⓂCroix Paquet) Local, just-known or yet-to-make-their-name designer boutiques.

RIVE GAUCHE
Centre Commercial La Part-Dieu
SHOPPING CENTRE
(www.centrecommercial-partdieu.com, in French; 3e; ⓂPart-Dieu) Adjacent to the Part-Dieu train station, Lyon's vast indoor shopping centre is dominated by a pencil-shaped tower nicknamed *le crayon*.

Au Vieux Campeur OUTDOORS, TRAVEL
(www.auvieuxcampeur.fr, in French; 43 cours de la Liberté, 3e; ⓂGuillotière) Excellent camping store stocking a mammoth range of maps and travel guides (many in English).

ⓘ Information
Emergency
Police station (Commissariat de Police) place Sathonay (☑04 78 28 11 87; 5 place Sathonay, 1er; ⓂHôtel de Ville); rue de la Charité (☑04 78 42 26 56; 47 rue de la Charité, 2e; ⓂPerrache or Ampère)

Internet Access
Planète Net Phone (21 rue Romarin, 1er; ⓂHôtel de Ville; per hr €2; ⊙9.30am-11pm Mon-Sat, noon-11pm Sun; ☎) One of several cheap internet/phone centres on the block.

Raconte-Moi La Terre (www.raconte-moi.com, in French; 14 rue du Plat, 2e; laptop hire per hr €4; ⊙10am-7.30pm Mon-Sat; ☎; ⓂBellecour) Travel bookshop (mainly French-language titles) with free wi-fi; also rents laptops – ask at the café at the back and present some ID.

Medical Services
Hôpital Édouard Herriot (☑08 20 08 20 69; www.chu-lyon.fr, in French; 5 place d'Arsonval,

3e; ☺24hr; Ⓜ Grange Blanche) Has an emergency room.

Pharmacie Blanchet (✆04 78 42 12 42; www.lyon-pharmacie.com, in French; 5 place des Cordeliers, 2e; ☺24hr; Ⓜ Cordeliers)

SOS Médecins (✆04 78 83 51 51; ☺24hr) Medical emergencies.

Money
AOC Exchange (20 rue Gasparin, 2e; ☺9.30am-6.30pm Mon-Sat; Ⓜ Bellecour) Currency exchange.

Post
Post office (10 place Antonin Poncet, 2e; Ⓜ Bellecour) Main post office.

Tourist Information
Tourist office (✆04 72 77 69 69; www.lyon-france.com; place Bellecour, 2e; ☺9am-6pm; Ⓜ Bellecour)

Websites
www.bullesdegones.com (in French) Comprehensive guide on what to do with kids (up to 12 years) in and around Lyon.

www.lyon-blog.fr (in French) One-stop shop for nearly 400 blogs about Lyon.

www.lyon.fr Official city website.

www.petitpaume.com (in French) Savvy city guide written by local university students.

www.rhonealpes-tourisme.com Regional tourist information site.

❶ Getting There & Away
Air
Lyon-St-Exupéry Airport (✆08 26 80 08 26; www.lyon.aeroport.fr; ☎) Located 25km east of the city, serving 120 direct destinations across Europe and beyond, including many budget carriers.

Bus
In the Perrache complex, **Eurolines** (✆04 72 56 95 30; www.eurolines.fr) and Spain-oriented **Linebús** (✆04 72 41 72 27; www.linebus.com, in Spanish) have offices on the bus-station level of the Centre d'Échange (follow the 'Lignes Internationales' signs).

Car
Major car-hire companies have offices at Gare de la Part-Dieu, Gare de Perrache and the airport.

Train
Lyon has two main-line train stations: **Gare de la Part-Dieu** (Ⓜ Part-Dieu), 1.5km east of the Rhône, and **Gare de Perrache** (Ⓜ Perrache). Some local trains stop at **Gare St-Paul** (Ⓜ Vieux Lyon), and **Gare Jean Macé** (Ⓜ Jean Mace). Buy tickets at the stations or at the **SNCF Boutique** (2 place Bellecour, 2e; Ⓜ Bellecour).

Destinations by direct TGV include the following:

Beaune €23.10, 2¼ hours, up to nine daily

Dijon €30.20, two hours, at least 12 daily

Lille-Europe €92, 3¼ hours, nine daily

Marseille €58.60, 1¾ hours, every 30 to 60 minutes

Paris Gare de Lyon €64.30, two hours, every 30 to 60 minutes

Strasbourg €55.90, 4¾ hours, five daily

❶ Getting Around
To/From the Airport
The **Rhonexpress** (✆04 72 68 72 17; www.rhonexpress.fr, in French) tramway links the airport with the Part-Dieu train station in under 30 minutes. Trams depart approximately every 15 minutes between 6am and 9.30pm, and every 30 minutes from 5am to 6am and 9.30pm to midnight. One-way tickets cost €13/free per adult/child (kids over 12 years pay €11).

By taxi, the 30- to 45-minute minute trip between the airport and the city centre costs around €40 during the day and €55 between 7pm and 7am.

Bicycle
Pick up a red-and-silver bike at one of 200-odd bike stations throughout the city and drop it off at another with Lyon's **vélo'v** (www.velov.grandlyon.com) scheme. The first 30 minutes are free, the next hour €1 and subsequent hours €2 with a *carte courte durée* (a short-duration card, costing €3 and valid for seven days), €0.75/1.50 respectively with a *carte longue durée* (long-duration card, costing €15 and valid for one year). Buy either card with a chip-enabled credit card from machines installed at bike stations.

Alternatively, phone for or flag down a chauffeur-driven, soft-roofed tricycle operated by **Cyclopolitain** (✆04 78 30 35 90; www.cyclopolitain.com, in French; per person per km €2; ☺10.30am-7pm).

Public Transport
Buses, trams, a four-line metro and two funiculars linking Vieux Lyon to Fourvière and St-Just are operated by **TCL** (www.tcl.fr), which has

information offices dispensing transport maps adjacent to several metro stations throughout Lyon, including Bellecour, Croix Rousse, Hôtel de Ville, Part-Dieu, Perrache and Vieux Lyon. Public transport runs from around 5am to midnight.

Tickets valid for all forms of public transport cost €1.60 (€13.70 for a *carnet* of 10) and are available from bus and tram drivers and machines at metro entrances. Tickets allowing unlimited travel for two hours after 9am cost €2.40, for all-day travel €4.70, and a Ticket Liberté Soirée allowing unlimited travel after 7pm is €2.40. Bring coins as machines don't accept notes (or some international credit cards). Timestamp tickets on all forms of public transport or risk a fine.

In this chapter, the nearest metro stops are indicated after the street address (Ⓜ).

Taxi

Taxis hover in front of both train stations, on the place Bellecour end of rue de la Barre (2e), at the northern end of rue du Président Édouard Herriot (1er) and along quai Romain Rolland in Vieux Lyon (5e).

Allo Taxi (☑04 78 28 23 23; www.allotaxi.fr, in French)

Taxis Lyonnais (☑04 78 26 81 81; www.taxi lyonnais.com, in French)

North of Lyon

Lush green hills, lakes and vineyards unfold to the north of cosmopolitan Lyon.

BEAUJOLAIS

Hilly Beaujolais, 50km northwest of Lyon, is a land of streams, granite peaks (the highest is 1012m Mont St-Rigaud), pastures and forests.

The region is synonymous with its fruity red wines, especially its 10 premium *crus*, and the Beaujolais Nouveau, drunk at the tender age of just six weeks. Vineyards

stretch south from Mâcon along the right bank of the Saône for some 50km.

At the stroke of midnight on the third Thursday (ie Wednesday night) in November – as soon as French law permits – the *libération* (release) or *mise en perce* (tapping; opening) of the first bottles of cherry-bright Beaujolais Nouveau is celebrated around France and the world. In Beaujeu (population 2023), 64km northwest of Lyon, there's free Beaujolais Nouveau for all as part of the **Sarmentelles de Beaujeu** – a giant street party that kicks off the day before Beaujolais Nouveau for five days of wine tasting, live music and dancing. During the festival a bus runs between Lyon and Beaujeu but otherwise you'll need your own transport.

For details of wine cellars where you can taste and buy wine, contact Beaujeu's tourist office (☑04 74 69 22 88; www.aucoeur dubeaujolais.fr; place de l'Église; ◑9.30am-12.30pm & 2.30-6pm, closed Dec-Feb), which can also help with accommodation. Hotels are practically nonexistent, but there are some charming B&Bs.

TOP CHOICE Les Roulottes de la Serve (☑04 74 04 76 40; www.lesroulottes.com; La Serve, Ouroux; d caravan €60, d €95; ◑Apr-Oct), run by traditional caravan-maker Pascal and his hippie wife, Pascaline, has a trio of romantically furnished 1920s to 1950s gypsy caravans amid the B&B's fields (€3 to €5 extra per night for heating). Bathrooms are provided in the main farmhouse, which has a whimsical en-suite guestroom (with another due by the time you're reading this). Reserve at least two days ahead for food baskets and picnic hampers (€15 per person). Follow the road from Avenas to the Col de Crie for 5km, and at the La Serve crossroads, head to Ouroux; after 100m turn right down the track signposted *chambres d'hôtes en roulottes*.

Exploring Beaujolais' (mostly) gentle hills by **bike** is uplifting. Hire one from Les Sources du Beaujolais (☑04 74 69 20 56; sources.beaujolais@wanadoo.fr; place de l'Hôtel de Ville, Beaujeu; per day €15; ◑Mar-Dec). **Walking** the area's many footpaths is equally invigorating.

To take in the region aboard a Harley Davidson, see p444.

PÉROUGES
POP 1220

French film buffs will recognise photogenic Pérouges. Situated on a hill 30km northeast

---

> ### GREEN BEAUJOLAIS
>
> Billebaudez en Beaujolais Vert (☑04 74 04 77 07; www.billebaudez.com, in French) was formed by local farmers, cheese-makers, oil producers, artists and others to promote sustainability in the region. Through this inspired eco-association you can visit local farms, learn about bee-keeping, fish, horse ride, paint, participate in a fruit harvest and more.

Down-to-business St-Étienne (population 178,530), 62km southwest of Lyon, is drawing on its Industrial Revolution origins and its history of arms, bicycle, textile and ribbon production, to reinvent itself as 'design city'. It's worth a brief stop to visit the exceptional collection of 20th-century and contemporary paintings, sculptures and photographs at the Musée d'Art Moderne (MAM; www.mam-st-etienne.fr; rue Fernard Léger, St-Priest-en-Jarez; adult/child €5/4; 1st Sun of month free; ⊙10am-6pm Wed-Mon), the country's second largest after Paris' Centre Pompidou. Tram 4 (direction Hôpital Nord) links it with the centre.

St-Étienne hosts the forward-looking **Biennale Internationale Design** fair during November in every even-numbered year (2010's theme was 'teleportation'). Find out more and browse exhibitions at the Cité du Design (☑04 77 49 74 70; www.citedu design.com; 3 rue Javelin Pagnon; adult/child €4/2; ⊙10am-6pm Tue-Sun), in a gleaming glass-and-steel building reached by tram 5 (direction La Terrasse).

If you need to stay, the tourist office (☑04 77 49 39 00; www.tourisme-st-etienne. com; 16 av de la Libération; ⊙9.30am-12.30pm & 2pm-6.30pm Mon-Sat), 1km southwest of the train station, has accommodation details.

Hourly-or-better trains link St-Étienne with Lyon Gare Part-Dieu (€9.80, 50 minutes).

of Lyon, this enchanting yellow-stone medieval village has long been used as a set for films like *Les Trois Mousquetaires* (the *Three Musketeers*). It's worth braving the summertime crowds strolling its uneven cobbled alleys, admiring its half-timbered stone houses and 1792-planted liberty tree on place de la Halle and wolfing down *galettes de Pérouges* (warm, thin-pizza-crust-style, sugar-crusted tarts) with cider.

To appreciate Pérouges' charm after the day trippers have left, book a romantic room (try for one with a canopied bed) at the historic Hostellerie de Pérouges (☑04 74 61 00; www.perouges.org; place du Tilleul; s €85-128, d €125-241), which operates a respected restaurant (menus €35-62).

Pérouges' tiny tourist office (☑04 74 46 70 84; www.perouges.org; ⊙10am-noon & 2-5pm Tue-Fri, 2-5pm Sat & Sun) is on the main road opposite the village entrance.

Buses on line 132 run by Cars Philibert (☑04 78 98 56 00; www.philibert-transport.fr, in French) from throughout central Lyon drop you a 15-minute walk from the village.

LA DOMBES

Northwest of Pérouges is La Dombes, a marshy area with hundreds of *étangs* (shallow lakes) that were created from malarial swamps over the past six centuries by farmers. They are used as fish ponds and then drained to grow crops on the fertile lake bed.

La Dombes teems with wildlife, particularly waterfowl. Observe local and exotic birds, including dozens of pairs of storks, at the Parc des Oiseaux (www.parcdesoiseaux. com, in French; adult/child €13/10; ⊙9.30am-7pm, closed Dec-Feb), a landscaped bird park on the edge of Villars-les-Dombes on the N83. The reserve is a 1.6km walk south of Villars-les-Dombes' train station, linked to Lyon's Part-Dieu (€6.80, 40 minutes, at least hourly).

The area is famed for its production of frogs' legs, which you can taste at La Bicyclette Bleue (☑04 74 98 21 48; www.labi cyclettebleue.fr, in French; lunch menus €10, menus €19.50-35.50; ⊙lunch & dinner Thu-Mon; ⊕), 7.5km southeast of Villars-les-Dombes in Joyeux on the D61. Renowned for its *grenouilles fraîches en persillade* (fresh frogs' legs in butter and parsley), this laid-back family affair also runs regular cooking courses (€60) and rents bicycles (per half/full day €12.50/15.50) to explore 11 mapped lakeland circuits, from 12km (one hour) to 59km (four hours).

Downstream along the Rhône

South of Lyon, vineyards meet nuclear power plants. Although it doesn't sound like the most auspicious juxtaposition, there are several worthwhile stops for Lyon-based day trippers or the southbound.

LE CORBUSIER'S CONVENT

It's only for hardened fans of architecture, 'it' being the far-from-pretty futuristic concrete priory Couvent Ste-Marie de la Tourette (☎04 72 19 10 90; www.couvent latourette.com; adult/child €7/5; ☺guided tours 3pm Sun), 30km northwest of Lyon in La Tourette, designed by modern-architecture icon Le Corbusier and inhabited by white-robed Dominican monks. You can book a one-hour guided tour of the working monastery.

From Lyon's Gare de Perrache and Gare St-Paul, frequent trains go to L'Arbresle (€7, 45 minutes), 2km north of La Tourette, from where you can call a taxi (☎04 74 26 90 19) or walk (around 25 minutes). By car, follow the westbound N7 or more scenic D7 from Lyon.

VIENNE
POP 30,409

In a commanding position on the Rhône, 30km south of Lyon, the one-time Gallo-Roman city of Vienne is best known today for its two-week jazz festival (www.jazzavienne.com, in French) in late June/early July.

In the old town, take a look at the superb Corinthian columns of the Temple d'Auguste et de Livie (place Charles de Gaulle), built around 10 BC to honour Emperor Augustus and his wife Livia. Across the river in St-Romain-en-Gal, the excavated remains of the Gallo-Roman city form the Musée Gallo-Romain (www.museesgallo-romains.com, in French; 2 chemin de la Plaine Gal; adult/child €4/free, Thu free; ☺10am-6pm Tue-Sun).

Views over Vienne extend from the Belvédère de Pipet, a balcony with a 6m-tall statue of the Virgin Mary, immediately above the fabulous Théâtre Romain (rue du Cirque; adult/child €2.30/free, 1st Sun of month free; ☺9.30am-1pm & 2-6pm). The vast Roman amphitheatre, built around AD 40–50, is a key jazz-festival venue. Combination tickets (good for six museums and historical sites in the Viennois area) cost €6; the tourist office (☎04 74 53 80 30; www.vienne-tourisme.com; 3 cours Brillier; ☺9am-noon & 1.30-6pm Mon-Sat, 10am-noon & 2-5pm Sun) has details.

TOP　Hôtel de la Pyramide (☎04 74 CHOICE　53 01 96; www.lapyramide.com; 14 bd Fernand-Point; s €190-225, d €200-240, ste from €390; ❋@☎) overlooking La Pyramide de la Cirque (a 15.5m-tall obelisk that in Roman times pierced the centre of a hippodrome), is Vienne's finest address for eating and/or sleeping. This apricot-coloured villa with powder-blue shutters is a haven, especially for foodies. In addition to chef Patrick Henriroux' two-Michelin-star signature restaurant, La Pyramide (lunch menus €61,

dinner menus €99-158; ☺Thu-Mon) serving lobsters, foie gras, black truffles, scallops and other seasonal treats, he also helms the more affordable l'espace PH (mains €13-18; ☺daily), and his Boutique Patrick Henriroux (☺closed Tue & Wed), selling tantalisingly packaged gourmet goodies and chic kitchenware.

Trains link Vienne with Lyon's four stations (€6.10, 20 to 33 minutes, at least hourly) and Valence Centre (€11.70, one hour, at least hourly). All trains to Valence TGV station require changing at Valence Centre.

TOWARDS VALENCE

The Parc Naturel Régional du Pilat spills across 650 sq km southwest of Vienne and offers breathtaking panoramas of the Rhône Valley from its highest peaks, Crêt de l'Œillon (1370m) and Crêt de la Perdrix (1432m). The Montgolfier brothers, who invented the hot-air balloon in 1783 and lent their name to its French term, *montgolfière*, were born and held their first public demonstration on the park's southeastern boundary.

The north section of the Côtes du Rhône winegrowing area stretches from Vienne south to Valence. Two of its most respected appellations, St Joseph and Hermitage, grow around Tain l'Hermitage (population 5933) on the Rhône's left bank.

One or two trains an hour link Tain Gare with Valence Centre (€3.60, 10 minutes) and Lyon Gare Part-Dieu (€13.50, one hour), but exploring really requires your own wheels.

VALENCE
POP 66,567

Several Rhône Valley towns claim to be the gateway to Provence, including Valence, whose quaint old town, Vieux Valence, is crowned by the Cathédrale St-Apollinaire, a late-11th-century pilgrimage church largely destroyed in the Wars of Religion and rebuilt in the 17th century. Allegorical sculpted heads adorn Maison des Têtes (57 Grande Rue), a blend of Flamboyant Gothic and Renaissance from 1530. Get the lowdown from the tourist office (☎08 92 70 70 99; www.tourisme-valence.com; 11 bd Bancel; ⊙9.30am-6.30pm Mon-Sat, 10am-3.30pm Sun), located at the train station.

🛏 Sleeping & Eating

The city is famed for its crunchy, orange-rind-flavoured shortbread shaped like a Vatican Swiss guard to commemorate Pope Pius VI's imprisonment and death in Valence in 1799. Ask for *un suisse* in any *pâtisserie*.

Anne-Sophie Pic, France's only three-Michelin-star female chef, reigns over Valence gastronomy, as her father and grandfather (each triple Michelin star-holders) did before her.

TOP CHOICE Maison Pic (☎04 75 44 15 32; www.pic-valence.com; 285 av Victor Hugo; d €290-400, ste €410-890; ⊙Feb-Dec; ✴@🐾🕸) The Pic family's truffle-coloured, 1889-established inn has ultrachic rooms and public spaces mixing antique, contemporary and kitsch, alongside a couple of stunning restaurants – Restaurant Pic (lunch menus €85, menus €195-320) and Le 7 (menus €19-28). Serious foodies will want to sign up for Pic's cutting-edge cooking school, Scook (☎04 75 44 14 14; www.scook.fr, in French; 243 av Victor Hugo; ⊙Tue-Sat), with 1½-hour courses from €49 through to full-day courses from €240, plus courses for kids aged over six (1½ hours from €37).

ℹ Getting There & Away

From the central train station, Valence Centre (also known as Valence-Ville), there are trains to/from Montélimar (€7.90, 23 minutes, at least five daily), Lyon's Gare Part-Dieu (from €15.80, 1¼ hours, 12 daily), Avignon Centre (€18.70, 1½ hours, five daily), Marseille (€31.90, 2½ hours, five daily) and Grenoble (€14.80, 1¼ hours, nine daily). Many stop at Valence TGV Rhône-Alpes Sud station, 10km east.

MONTÉLIMAR
POP 35.988

In the sunny section of the Drôme *département* known as Drôme Provençale, Montélimar, 46km south of Valence, is an appealing town (once you're through its industrial outskirts), with a shaded, grassy promenade lined by café terraces carving a

C-shape through its centre. The town's biggest claim to fame is its *nougat de Montélimar*, which took off after WWII when motorists travelling to the French Riviera stopped off here to buy the sweeter-than-sweet treat to munch en route.

Authentic Montélimar nougat consists of at least 28% almonds, 25% lavender honey, 2% pistachio nuts, sugar, egg white and vanilla. Texture varies, from *dur* (hard) to *tendre* (light and soft), as does honey strength and crispness of the nuts. Some are coated in chocolate and others have fruit (try the one with figs), but traditional Montélimar nougat is simply off-white.

FREE Nougat factory tours are offered by numerous producers; pick a small (rather than industrial) confectioner, such as Diane-de-Poytiers (☎04 75 01 67 02; www.diane-de-poytiers.fr; 99 av Jean-Jaurès; ⊙8-11am & 2-4pm Tue-Sat), run by the same family for three generations.

The tourist office (☎04 75 01 00 20; www.montelimar-tourisme.com; allées Provençales; ⊙9am-12.15pm & 2-6.30pm Mon-Sat) has a list of nougat and other local producers (lavender, honey and so on), and can help with accommodation in town and throughout the Drôme Provençale.

Montélimar is on the train line linking Valence Centre (€7.90, 20 to 30 minutes, five daily) with Avignon Centre (€12.60, 50 minutes, approximately hourly).

GORGES DE L'ARDÈCHE

The serpentine Ardèche River slithers between towering mauve, yellow and grey limestone cliffs from near Vallon Pont d'Arc (population 2512) to St-Martin de l'Ardèche (population 830), a few kilometres west of the Rhône. En route, it passes beneath the Pont d'Arc, a stunning natural stone bridge created by the river's torrents. Eagles nest in the cliffs and there are numerous caves to explore.

Souvenir-shop-filled Vallon Pont d'Arc is the area's main hub; its tourist office (☎04 75 88 04 01; www.vallon-pont-darc.com; place de la Gare; ⊙9am-12.15pm & 1.30-6pm Mon-Fri, to 5pm Sat) is in the village centre. The scenic D579 from the village out along the gorges is lined by campgrounds and canoeing and kayaking rental outlets. Alternatively, arrange hire through Base Nautique du Pont d'Arc (☎04 75 37 17 79; www.canoe-ardeche.com; rte des Gorges de l'Ardèche; ⊙Apr-Nov). A half-day descent (8km) starts from €13/9 per adult/child; (minimum age

NUCLEAR TOURISM (& CROCODILES)

Nuclear tourism takes on an unlikely twist at the Ferme aux Crocodiles (www.la-fermeauxcrocodiles.com, in French; D59; adult/child €12.50/8; ☺9.30am-7pm), 20km south of Montélimar and just south of Pierrelatte, where 400-odd grouchy Nile crocodiles slumber in exotically landscaped tropical pools heated by the nearby Centre Nucléaire du Tricastin powerplant.

Opposite the plant's reactors, learn about its operations and nuclear energy at its Espace d'Information du Public (public information centre; ☺9am-12.30pm & 2-5.30pm Mon-Fri; admission free).

Take the Montélimar sud or Bollene exit off the A7 and follow the signs.

is seven); longer day and multiday trips are also possible.

SNCF buses link Montélimar's train station with Vallon Pont d'Arc (€10.40, 1¼ hours, four daily).

About 300m above the gorge's waters, the Haute Corniche (D290) has a dizzying series of *belvédères* (panoramic viewpoints) but turns into a chaotic traffic jam in summer. On the plateaux above the gorges, typical Midi villages are surrounded by *garrigue* (aromatic scrub land), lavender fields and vineyards.

The D579 takes cyclists and motorists northwest to Ruoms (population 2263); across the river, the D4 snakes along the Défilé de Ruoms (a narrow rock tunnel) and the Gorges de la Ligne for 8km.

Northwards from the pretty village of Balazuc (population 339), the D579 leads to Aubenas (population 1453), from where scenic roads fan into the countryside. This is **chestnut** land, where the dark-brown fruit is turned into everything from *crème de châtaigne* (sweet purée served with ice cream, crêpes or cake) to *bière aux marrons* (chestnut beer) and *liqueur de châtaigne* (21% alcohol-by-volume liqueur that makes a sweet aperitif when mixed with white wine). In the area's main town, Privas (population 9002), the tourist office (☏04 75 64 33 35; www.paysdeprivas.com; 3 place Général de Gaulle; ☺9am-noon & 2-6pm Mon-Fri, 9am-noon & 2-5.30pm Sat) has a list of regional producers as well as accommodation.

French Alps
& the Jura Mountains

Best Places to Eat

» Les Vieilles Luges (p473)
» Flocons de Sel (p477)
» Chalet la Pricaz (p484)
» La Fruitière (p494)
» Le Saint-Pierre (p510)

Best Places to Stay

» Farmhouse (p478)
» Auberge du Manoir (p471)
» La Ferme du Petit Bonheur (p487)
» Escargot Comtois (p516)
» À la Crécia (p502)

Why Go?

The French Alps are a place of boundless natural beauty. Whether music to your ears is schussing through virgin snow in Chamonix – see our ski trip planning tips on p520 – the rhythm of boots on a lonesome mountain pass, or the silence of a summer's morning as the first rays illuminate Mont Blanc – no lyrics can do these mountains justice. Here a symphony of colossal peaks and glaciers, epic drops and climbs will elevate you, seduce your senses, make your heart pound and leave you crying 'encore!' like few other places on earth.

Now turn your gaze north to the Jura Mountains, like a landscape painting come to life with its vineyards cascading down hillsides, sun-dappled forests and jewel-like lakes. Slip into the picture by visiting dairy farms, tasting fragrant *vin jaune* (yellow wine) in local wineries and cross-country skiing in quiet exhilaration. Unlike the Alps, this region won't leave you breathless, but it will leave you thinking, 'Ahhh, *c'est la vie...*'

When to Go

Grenoble

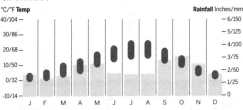

| **March** Grenoble's Jazz Festival and fits of giggles at Méribel's Altitude Festival. | **July to August** The Tour de France, and fireworks light up Annecy at the Fête du Lac. | **December** Championships, freestyle events and fun as the first snow hits the Alps. |

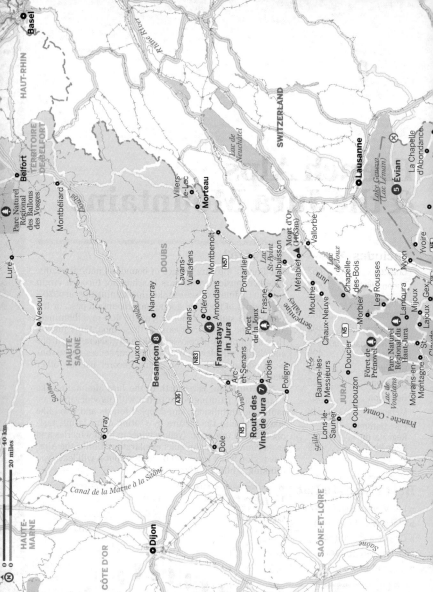

French Alps & the Jura Mountains Highlights

1 Do a Bond, swooshing down the slopes in **Chamonix** (p467) in the distinctive shadow of Mont Blanc

2 Get dizzy on the winding drive to **Briançon** (p505) through the dramatic Parc National des Écrins

3 Delve into castles, medieval lanes and a crystal-clear lake in dreamy **Annecy** (p480)

4 Scamper back to nature at a middle-of-nowhere farm in **Jura** (p514)

5 Bathe like royalty in the mineral-rich waters of **Évian-les-Bains** (p480)

6 Party waaay past your bedtime in Méribel and celebrity-

mad Courchevel in **Les Trois Vallées** (p489)

7 Sip golden *vin jaune* amid the vines on the bucolic **Route des Vins de Jura** (p514)

8 Seek out the Vauban citadel and the stellar Musée des Beaux-Arts in **Besançon** (p507)

9 Grab your walking boots to explore the glaciated grandeur of **Parc National de la Vanoise** (p495)

History

Migrant tribes of Celtic, Gaulish and Teutonic origin arrived in the Alps first; by the time of Christ, communities were well established, especially around the lakes of Geneva and Annecy.

During the Roman conquest the Alps were a strategic stronghold, falling under Roman control during Augustus' reign. The Frankish kings of the Merovingian and Carolingian empires laid the foundations for the modern Alps with their distinctive dialects, traditions and cultures.

The 13th and 14th centuries saw the feudal houses of Savoy, the Dauphiné and Provence fiercely contesting the Alps. The ensuing centuries were marked by successive wars and occupations, a cycle which ended with the union of Savoy with France in 1860.

Michel-Gabriel Paccard and Jacques Balmat made the first successful ascent of Mont Blanc in 1786, and in the late 19th century holidaymakers began to flock to the area.

German and Italian forces occupied the Alps during WWII, while the mountains became one of the main strongholds for the French Resistance. Modern industry, hydroelectric energy and large-scale tourism all contributed to the regeneration of the Alps in the postwar years.

Climate

Snow covers even lower-altitude stations most years from December to April. Weather conditions can change alarmingly quickly in the Alps. Pick up the latest weather report at the tourist office or your hotel reception, or click on www.meteofrance.com (in French).

National & Regional Parks

Wildlife is carefully protected in two national parks, Vanoise (east of Chambéry) and Écrins (southeast of Grenoble), both close to the Italian border, where you may well spot chamois, ibex, marmots and golden eagles. With four regional parks – Queyras (south of Briançon), the Vercors (southwest of Grenoble), Chartreuse (north of the Vercors) and Massif des Bauges (north of the Chartreuse) – the Alps has France's greatest concentration of parks.

The Jura is home to the Parc Naturel Régional du Haut-Jura.

Dangers & Annoyances

Avalanches are a serious danger in snowbound areas and can be fatal. You know the golden rule: never ski, hike or climb alone. Off-piste skiers should never leave home without an avalanche pole, avalanche transceiver, a shovel – and, most importantly, a professional guide. Ski resorts announce the daily risk through signs and coloured flags:

Yellow Low risk

Black and yellow Heightened risk

Black Severe risk

Henry's Avalanche Talk (www.henrysavalanchetalk.com) translates the daily avalanche forecast issued by Météo France into English during the ski season.

At high altitudes, where the UV rays are stronger and intensified by snow glare, wear sunglasses and sunscreen. The air is dry in the Alps, so stay hydrated by drinking plenty of water. Always bring extra layers too: the weather can turn very suddenly.

Skiing & Snowboarding

The 200-plus resorts in the French Alps have carved out their reputation for some of the best – perhaps *the* best – downhill skiing and snowboarding in Europe. The season begins with the first big snow (usually around mid-December) and ends in late April or early May. For fewer crowds and the best deals, avoid skiing in high season, namely Christmas, New Year and French school holidays.

Dependent on snow conditions, summer alpine skiing on glaciers in high-altitude resorts Val d'Isère, Les Deux Alpes and Alpe d'Huez runs for anything from two weeks to two months, June to August.

Skis (alpine, cross-country, telemark), snowboards, boots, poles and helmets can be hired at sport shops in every resort. All-inclusive rental costs around €32/175 per day/six days for alpine equipment and snowboarding gear and €15/65 for cross-country; reserving in advance online typically gets you a 15% discount.

Downhill runs are colour-coded to indicate how kid-easy or killer-hard they are:

Green Beginners

Blue Intermediate

Red Advanced

Black Tough as hell

There's so much more to the mountains than winter skiing and summer hiking. Here are some ideas for an action- and fun-packed holiday.

Winter

Cross-country skiing is cheaper and greener than alpine skiing; not much beats gliding through snow-dusted forests in quiet exhilaration. Try it in the Jura or Savoie Grand Révard.

For wilderness and glorious virgin powder, enlist the help of a guide to go **ski touring** in resorts like Chamonix and Val d'Isère. Or strap on snowshoes to make twinkly tracks away from the crowds; most resorts now have dedicated **snowshoeing** routes and tours.

For a bump-a-minute buzz, *la luge* (**sledging**) on a variety of contraptions is all the rage, and most major resorts have tree-lined runs where you can go whizzing off down the mountains.

Sliding still, you can learn the exhilarating and – phew! – tiring art of **mushing** in Chamonix and Les Trois Vallées.

Summer

Take to the waters or the skies. Wherever there is a river, you'll find **water sports** like white-water rafting, kayaking, canoeing and canyoning; and wherever there is a beautiful breeze and a mountain, there's tandem **paragliding**. Speed-fiends can replace their skis with downhill **mountain bikes** when the snow melts. These activities are available in almost every alpine resort.

Summer glacial skiing is on short greens or blues. Snowboarders are brilliantly catered for in larger resorts with snowparks kitted out with half-pipes, kickers and ramps. Jura excels in scenic rambling cross-country *(ski de fond)* trails.

France's leading ski school, the École du Ski Français (ESF; www.esf.net) – its instructors wear red – teaches snowboarding and skiing. It has a branch in every resort and touts competitive rates; a group lesson typically costs €60 per half-day, €143 for four days and €183 for six days. Private instruction is available on request. Kids can start learning from the age of four; from three years old they can play in the *jardin de neige* (snow garden).

LIFT PASSES

You will need a lift pass *(forfait)* to ride the various *remontées mécaniques* (drag lifts), *télésièges* (chairlifts), *télécabines,* (gondolas), *téléphériques* (cable cars) and *funiculaires* (funicular railways).

Passes – a big chunk out of your budget, €200 or thereabouts for a week – give access to one or more ski sectors. Most lift passes are 'hands-free', with a built-in chip that barriers detect automatically, and can be bought and recharged online. For multi-day/seasonal lift passes, you may need a passport-sized photo.

Children aged under five ski for free but still need a pass; bring along a passport as proof of age.

Cheaper passes – usually around €6 a day – are needed for cross-country ski trails, although these are rarely checked.

INSURANCE

Before you launch yourself like a rocket down that near-vertical black piste, make sure you are properly insured. Accidents happen and expensive (we're talking triple figures here) mountain-rescue costs, medical treatment and repatriation add insult to injury. Rental shops offer insurance for equipment for a small additional charge.

Most packages include insurance or you might have the Carte Neige (www.ffs.fr/site/carteneige, in French), a comprehensive annual policy. It costs €33 to €42 per year (€27 for cross-country skiing only), depending on the level of cover you choose. You can buy it online or through the ESF in most resorts.

Alternatively, buy the Carré Neige (www.carreneige.com) with your lift pass. Every resort offers the all-inclusive insurance scheme, which costs €2.70 a day.

TICKET TO GLIDE

RESORT	ELEVATION (M)	LEVEL	RUNS (KM)	1-DAY LIFT PASS (€)	6-DAY LIFT PASS (€)
Chamonix	1037	intermediate, advanced, off-piste	182	50	240
St-Gervais & Megève	810 & 1113	beginner, intermediate	445	37	176
Les Portes du Soleil	1000-2466	all levels	650	40	205
Les Trois Vallées	1450-2300	all levels, especially advanced	600	47	220
Val d'Isère	1850	intermediate, advanced, off-piste	300	45	219
Les Deux Alpes	1660	intermediate, advanced, snowboarding	225	40	189
Alpe d'Huez	1860	all abilities, snowboarding, Europe's longest black run	245	41	210
La Clusaz	1100	beginner, families	128	30	158
Serre-Chevalier	1200	all levels, off-piste	250	41	195
Le Grand Bornand	1000	beginner, intermediate	90	28	132
Chamrousse	1700	beginner, intermediate	90	17	102
Métabief Mont d'Or	1000	cross-country	210	5.50	30

ⓘ Getting There & Away

AIR The view through the plane window is the best introduction to the Alps: chances are you're landing at **Lyon St-Exupéry Airport** (www.lyon.aeroport.fr), 25km east of Lyon; **Grenoble Airport** (www.grenoble-airport.com), further south; or **Geneva Airport** (www.gva.ch), in neighbouring Switzerland.

BUS From the airports there are buses to numerous ski resorts with Geneva's **Aeroski-Bus** (www.alpski-bus.com) and Lyon's **Satobus-Alpes** (http://satobus-alpes.altibus.com); fares and frequencies are listed under Getting There & Away for destinations in this chapter.

CAR & MOTORCYCLE Traffic on steeply climbing, winding mountain roads can be hellish, especially at weekends. After heavy snowfalls, you may need snow chains. Winter tyres (automatically provided with most hire cars) are a good idea. The Fréjus and Mont Blanc road tunnels connect the French Alps with Italy, as do several mountain passes. Road signs indicate if passes are blocked.

TRAIN Eurostar (www.eurostar.com) ski trains provide a more environment-friendly alternative between London and Moûtiers or Bourg St-Maurice from mid-December to mid-April (return from €150, eight hours, overnight or day service, weekends only). Within France, train services to the Alps are excellent.

SAVOY

'The Alps par excellence' could be the strap line of this northern half of the French Alps, a perfectly executed landscape of wondrous peaks, glassy lakes, dense alpine forests and everlasting snow.

Flanked by Switzerland and Italy, Savoy (Savoie, pronounced sav-wa) rises from the southern shores of Lake Geneva, Europe's largest alpine lake, and culminates at the roof of Europe, mighty 4810m Mont Blanc. In between is a sprinkling of ski resorts such as Chamonix and party-central Val d'Isère, as well as some historical châteaux towns like Chambéry and lakeside Annecy to the southwest.

Rural life, unchanged for centuries, characterises the region's most remote realms like the Bauges massif (so little known it is often mistaken for the northeastern Vosges region), and the wild Parc National de la Vanoise.

Chamonix

POP 9400 / ELEV 1037M

With the pearly white peaks of the Mont Blanc massif as its sensational backdrop, being an icon comes naturally to Chamonix. First 'discovered' by Brits William Windham and Richard Pococke in 1741, this is the mecca of mountaineering, its birthplace, its flag-bearer. It is also a wintertime playground of epic proportions that entices Olympic champions and hard-core skiers to its pistes, and party-mad boarders to its boot-stompin' bars.

Even if you and your karabiner aren't quite ready to scale 'the big one' just yet and your technique doesn't *quite* match that of 007 in his stunt-riddled ski chase in *The World Is Not Enough*, there is no resisting the gravitational pull of those mountains. Whether slaloming La Vallée Blanche like a pro or almost colliding with perpendicular cliffs on the vertigo-inducing Aiguille du Midi cable car, there's a whole lot of adrenalin and, yes, a dash of Bond in every trip to Chamonix.

◎ Sights

Pay for one Chamonix museum and visit the other for free. Discounts also apply for *carte d'hôte* pass-holders.

TOP CHOICE ▸ Aiguille du Midi   VIEWPOINT
A jagged needle of rock rearing above glaciers, snowfields and rocky crags, 8km from the hump of Mont Blanc, the Aiguille du Midi (3842m) is one of Chamonix' most distinctive landmarks. If you can handle the height, the 360-degree views of the French, Swiss and Italian Alps from the summit are (quite literally) breathtaking.

Year-round the vertiginous **Téléphérique de l'Aiguille de Midi** (☑advance reservations 24hr 04 50 53 22 75; place de l'Aiguille du Midi; adult/child return to Aiguille du Midi €41/33, Plan de l'Aiguille €24/19.20; ◉8.30am-4.30pm) cable car links Chamonix with the Aiguille du Midi. Halfway Plan de l'Aiguille (2317m) is a terrific place to start hikes or paraglide. In summer you will need to obtain a boarding card (marked with the number of your departing *and* returning cable car) in addition to a ticket. Advance phone reservations incur a €2 booking fee. Ensure that you bring warm clothes as even in summer the temperature rarely rises above -10°C at the top.

From the Aiguille du Midi, between mid-May and mid-September you can continue for a further 30 minutes of mind-blowing scenery – think suspended glaciers and spurs, seracs and shimmering ice fields – in the smaller bubbles of the **Télécabine Panoramic Mont Blanc** (adult/child return from Chamonix €65/52; ◉8.30am-3.45pm) to Pointe Helbronner (3466m) on the French–Italian border. From here another cable car descends to the Italian ski resort of Courmayeur.

Le Brévent   VIEWPOINT
The highest peak on the western side of the valley, Le Brévent (2525m) has tremendous views of the Mont Blanc massif, myriad hiking trails, ledges to paraglide from and summit restaurant Le Panoramic. Reach it with the **Télécabine du Brévent** (29 rte Henriette d'Angeville; adult/child return €24/19.50; ◉8.50am-4.45pm), from the end of rue de la Mollard, to midstation **Planpraz** (2000m), then continuing to the top.

Mer de Glace   GLACIER
France's largest glacier, the glistening 200m-deep Mer de Glace (Sea of Ice) snakes 7km through mighty rock spires and turrets; it was named by Englishman William Windham, the first foreigner to set eyes on the glacier in 1741. The glacier moves up to 90m a year, and has become a popular attraction thanks to the rack-and-pinion railway line opened in 1908.

Wrap up warm to experience the **Grotte de la Mer de Glace** (◉late Dec-May & mid-Jun–Sep) ice cave, where frozen tunnels and ice sculptures change colour like mood rings.

A quaint red mountain train trundles up from **Gare du Montenvers** (35 place de la Mer de Glace; adult/child €24/19; ◉10am-4.30pm) in Chamonix to Montenvers (1913m), from where a cable car takes you down to the glacier and cave. The ticket covers the 20-minute journey, entry to the caves and the cable car.

The Mer de Glace can be reached on foot via the Grand Balcon Nord trail from Plan de l'Aiguille. The two-hour uphill trail from Chamonix starts near the summer luge track. Traversing the crevassed glacier requires proper equipment and an experienced guide.

Chamonix

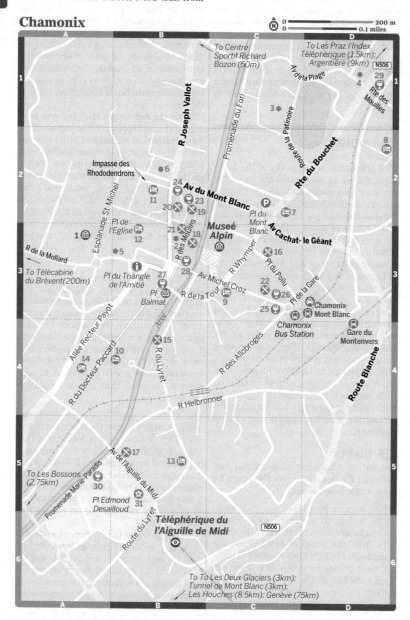

Musée Alpin
ALPINE MUSEUM

(av Michel Croz; adult/child €5.50/free; ☺2-7pm daily, plus 10am-noon during school holidays, closed Oct–mid-Dec) The town's illustrious alpine history zooms into focus at this museum; from the cliffhanging tale of crystal-hunter Jacques Balmat to the first ascent of Mont Blanc in 1786 and the advent of winter tourism.

Musée des Cristaux
CRYSTAL MUSEUM

(Esplanade St-Michel; adult/child €5.50/free; ☺2-7pm daily, plus 10am-noon during school holidays, closed Oct–mid-Dec) As well as cataloguing the region's rich rocks and minerals, this museum hosts intriguing temporary exhibitions such as the history of mountaineering and the impact of climate change on mountains.

🏃 Activities

Winter Activities

Maison de la Montagne
OUTDOOR ACTIVITIES

(190 place de l'Église; ☺8.30am-noon & 3-7pm) Get the Mont Blanc lowdown here, opposite the tourist office. Inside is the highly regarded Compagnie des Guides de Chamonix (☎04 50 53 00 88; www.chamonix-guides.com); the École de Ski Français (ESF; ☎04 50 53 22 57; www.esf-chamonix.com); and the Office de Haute Montagne (OHM; ☎04 50 53 22 08; www.ohm-chamonix.com), which has information on trails, hiking conditions, weather forecasts and *refuges* (mountain huts), and topoguides and maps that are free to consult.

Skiing & Snowboarding

Chamonix skiing is the stuff of legend: glorious off-piste terrain, thrilling descents and unbeatable Mont Blanc views. It's so darn fantastic that skiers don't even mind that accessing the slopes involves lots of transport. Of Chamonix' nine main areas, Le Tour, Les Planards and Les Chosalets are best for beginners. For speed and challenge, it has to be Brévent-Flégère, above Chamonix, and Les Grands Montets, accessible from Argentière, 9km north of Chamonix. Boarders seeking big air zip across to the kickers and rails at Les Grands Montets snowpark and the natural half-pipe in Le Tour.

La Vallée Blanche
OFF-PISTE ROUTE

(per person/group of 4 incl guide €75/283) This mythical descent is *the* off-piste ride of a

Chamonix

lifetime. A veritable obstacle course of a route, La Vallée Blanche takes four to five hours, leading from Aiguille du Midi over the crevasse-riddled Mer de Glace glacier and back through forest to Chamonix, covering 2800m of jaw-dropping vertical. Because of the obvious risks, it must *only* be tackled with a guide (guides can take a maximum of eight people in a group – add an extra €16 per additional person to the price above). Snowboarders require an even better level than skiers. Snow coverage is generally best in February and March.

Haute Route
SKI TOUR

(per person incl guide & full board €880) *Ski de randonnée* (ski touring), at its best between March and May, is big in Chamonix and the range of tours seemingly endless. The backcountry king is this classic six-day route from Chamonix to Zermatt in Switzerland, stopping en route at *refuges*. To tackle it you need to be an experienced off-piste skier and superfit. Shorter two-day trips (about €320 per person) are suitable for advanced skiers but *ski de randonnée* novices.

Compagnie des Guides de Chamonix
SNOWSHOEING

(☑04 50 53 00 88; www.chamonix-guides.com; 190 place de l'Église; half-/full-day/twilight tour per person €32/47/67) A pair of *raquettes* (snowshoes) is all you need to go stomping off through virgin powder and glistening forests. The Compagnie des Guides arranges tours around the Mont Blanc range

from France to Switzerland and Italy, and romantic twilight tours through the forest with dinner. All prices include snowshoe hire and transport.

Huskydalen
MUSHING

(☑04 50 47 77 24; www.huskydalen.com, in French; mushing hr/half-day €55/110, dog walking 2hr €18) Ever fancied trying your hand at mushing? Huskydalen runs introductory courses from December to April. In summer try an old-fashioned version of dog-walking where the dog walks (read: drags) you from a harness.

Summer Activities
When the snow melts, hikers can take their pick of 350km of spectacular high-altitude trails, many reached by cable car. There's enough light to walk until at least 9pm in June and July.

Lac Blanc
WALK

From the top of Les Praz l'Index Télépherique (cable car; one-way/return €18/22) or La Flégère (€11/13), the line's midway point, gentle 1¼- to two-hour trails lead to 2352m Lac Blanc (literally 'White Lake'), a turquoise-coloured lake ensnared by mountains. Stargazers can overnight at the Refuge du Lac Blanc (☑04 50 53 49 14; dm incl half board €49; ◎mid-Jun–Sep), a wooden chalet favoured by photographers for its top-of-Europe Mont Blanc views.

Grand Balcon Sud
WALK

This easygoing trail skirts the western side of the valley, stays at around 2000m and commands a terrific view of Mont Blanc.

DON'T MISS

ADVENTURE KNOW-HOW

These guide companies have got it. So go, create your adventure:

Compagnie des Guides de Chamonix (☑04 50 53 00 88; www.chamonix-guides.com; 190 place de l'Église) Crème de la crème of mountain guides, founded in 1821. Guides for skiing, mountaineering, ice climbing, hiking, mountain biking and every other alpine pastime.

Association Internationale des Guides du Mont Blanc (☑04 50 53 27 05; 98 rue des Moulins) Chamonix-based international guides; extreme skiing, mountaineering, glacier trekking, ice and rock climbing, and paragliding.

Aventure en Tête (☑04 50 54 05 11; www.aventureentete.com; 620 rte du Plagnolet, Argentière) Ski touring and ski-alpinism expeditions; freeride and off-piste courses; mountaineering and climbing in summer. Argentière is 9km north of Chamonix.

Chamonix Experience (☑04 50 54 09 36; www.chamex.com; 141 rue Charlet Straton, Argentière) Courses in off-piste skiing, avalanche awareness, ice climbing and ski touring; in summer, rock and alpine climbing.

PISTES PASS

The **Mont Blanc Unlimited Pass** (1/6 days €50/240) is worth the investment for serious skiers, giving access to 400km of runs, including all ski areas in the Chamonix valley, the Aiguille du Midi cable car and Montenvers train, plus Courmayeur in Italy and Verbier in Switzerland. Cheaper but more limited in scope is the **Chamonix Le Pass** (1/6 days €40/200) with access to most of Chamonix' ski domains. View all options and buy passes online at www.compagniedumontblanc.com.

Reach it on foot from behind Le Brévent's *télécabine* station.

Grand Balcon Nord   WALK
Routes starting from the Plan de l'Aiguille include the challenging Grand Balcon Nord, which takes you to the dazzling Mer de Glace, from where you can walk or take the Montenvers train down to Chamonix.

Mountaineering & High-alpine Tours
MOUNTAIN TOURS
Mountaineers and rock climbers make the pilgrimage to Chamonix in summer, when local guide companies offer exhilarating climbs for those with the necessary skill, experience and stamina, such as five-day rock-climbing courses (€585) and the incomparable Mont Blanc ascent (€785). For hikers, the big draw is the classic 12-day Tour du Mont Blanc (€1240), taking in majestic glaciers and peaks in France, Italy and Switzerland. The price includes half board in *refuges*, picnics, lift tickets and luggage transport.

Cham' Aventure   WATER SPORTS
(04 50 53 55 70; www.cham-aventure.com; Maison de la Montagne, 190 place de l'Église) Thrill-seekers head here for canyoning (half/full day €65/99 per person), rafting (€37/130 for two hours/day) and hydrospeeding (€47/130 for two hours/day) on Chamonix' River Arve and the Dora Baltea in neighbouring Italy. Most activities are unsuitable for young children.

Cycling Trails   CYCLING
Lower-altitude trails like the Petit Balcon Sud (250m) from Argentière to Servoz are perfect for biking. Most outdoor-activity specialists arrange guided mountain-biking expeditions. See p476.

Paragliding   PARAGLIDING
Come summer, the sky above Chamonix is dotted with paragliders wheeling down from the heights. Tandem flights from Planpraz (2000m) cost €100 per person (€220 from the Aiguille du Midi). Paragliding schools include Summits (04 50 53 50 14; www.summits.fr; 27 allée du Savoy) and Les Ailes du Mont Blanc (04 50 53 96 72; www.lesailesdumontblanc.com; 24 av de la Plage).

Festivals & Events

Marathon du Mont Blanc   MARATHON
(www.montblancmarathon.fr) The scenery is as breathtaking as the gruelling climb. Late June.

Fête des Guides   FESTIVAL
Two-day celebrations in mid-August welcoming new members to Chamonix' illustrious Compagnie des Guides with a dramatic *son et lumière,* fireworks, concerts and mountaineering displays.

Sleeping

Book ahead in winter, when hotel beds are at a premium. Many places close from mid-April to May and from November to mid-December. Room rates nosedive in the low season and summer; expect discounts of up to 50% on high-season prices.

Auberge du Manoir   CHALET €€
TOP CHOICE (04 50 53 10 77; http://aubergedumanoir.com, in French; 8 rte du Bouchet; s €94-108, d €104-150, q €165;) Muriel, Frédéric and their friendly golden retriever lift moods at this beautifully converted farmhouse, ablaze with geraniums in summer. Auberge du Manoir ticks all the perfect alpine chalet boxes: pristine mountain views, pine-panelled rooms that are quaint but never cloying and an inviting bar where an open fire keeps things cosy. Breakfast is a treat, with fresh fruit, homemade tarts and DIY boiled eggs.

Hotel Slalom   BOUTIQUE HOTEL €€
(04 50 54 40 60; www.hotelslalom.net; 44 rue de Bellevue, Les Houches; r €158;) Tracy, Heather and Justin are your affable hosts at this gorgeous chalet-style hotel, right at the foot of the slopes in Les Houches (8km west of central Chamonix). Rooms are the epitome of boutique chic – sleek, snowy white

ERIC FAVRET: MOUNTAIN GUIDE

Eric Favret, guide with Compagnie des Guides de Chamonix, was interviewed by Nicola Williams.

Ever since Mont Blanc, the highest peak in the Alps, was first climbed in 1786, Chamonix has attracted travellers worldwide. And there is something really special about it: not only does it sit amid extremely condensed mountaineering potential; it is also a perfectly balanced combination of pure landscape alignment and dramatic mountain views.

Aiguille du Midi

The Aiguille du Midi, with one of the highest cable cars in the world, cannot be missed. Beyond the summit ridge is a world of snow and ice offering some of the greatest intermediate terrain in the Alps.

Off-Piste Thrills

The Vallée Blanche has to be seen. But the Aiguille du Midi also has amazing off-piste runs, such as Envers du Plan, a slightly steeper and more advanced version of Vallée Blanche, offering dramatic views in the heart of the Mont Blanc range. There is also the less frequented run of the 'Virgin' or 'Black Needle'; a striking glacial run, offering different views and a close-up look at the Giant's seracs.

Best-Ever Mont Blanc View

No hesitation: the Traverse from Col des Montets to Lac Blanc. It's as popular as the Eiffel Tower for hikers in summer. I love swimming in mountain lakes, so I like to stop at Lac des Chéserys, just below, where it is quieter: What's better that a swim in pure mountain water, looking at Mont Blanc, the Grandes Jorasses and Aiguille Verte? This is what I call mountain landscape perfection!

and draped with Egyptian cotton linen. A bacon-and-eggs breakfast fires you up for a day's skiing.

Chalet Hotel Hermitage   CHALET €€
(04 50 53 13 87; www.hermitage-paccard.com; 63 chemin du Cé; s/d/tr/q €130/144/213/243; 🖥️🖨️) The trek from the slopes is worth it – Hermitage is a family-run treasure, with an open fire crackling in the bar, a kids' playroom, delicious home cooking and flowery gardens where you can survey Mont Blanc from your sunlounger. Decked out from top to toe in wood, rooms blend traditional alpine style with mod cons and afford mountain views.

Hotel L'Oustalet   FAMILY HOTEL €€
(04 50 55 54 99; www.hotel-oustalet.com; 330 rue du Lyret; d/q €140/180; 🖥️🖨️🖨️) You'll pray for snow at this alpine chalet near Aiguille du Midi cable car, just so you can curl up by the fire with a *chocolat chaud* and unwind in the sauna and whirlpool. The rooms, including family ones, are snugly decorated in solid pine and open onto bal-

conies with Mont Blanc views. There's a pool in the garden for chilling out during the summertime.

Hôtel Faucigny   SMALL HOTEL €€
(04 50 53 01 17; www.hotelfaucigny-chamonix. com; 118 place de l'Église; s/d/tr/q €55/86/98/124; 🖨️🖥️) Jacqueline and Guy Écochard run this bijou hotel, one of the sweetest deals in town. Rooms are comfortable and quiet, and guests can relax by an open fire in winter and on the flower-clad terrace with Mont Blanc views in summer.

Grand Hôtel des Alpes   HISTORIC HOTEL €€€
(04 50 55 37 80; www.grandhoteldesalpes.com; 75 rue du Docteur Paccard; r €330-390, ste €580-750; 🖥️🖨️🖥️🖨️) This grand old dame goes down in the chronicles of Chamonix history as one of the resort's first (built in 1840) and finest. The wood-panelled rooms exude timeless elegance. What distinguishes this hotel, however, is its friendliness: in winter a scrumptious cake buffet greets skiers back from the slopes.

Les Deux Glaciers
CAMPGROUND €

(☎04 50 53 15 84; http://les2glaciers.com; 80 rte des Tissières; sites €14.50; ☒mid-Dec–mid-Nov; ☎) Oh, what a beautiful morning! Draw back your tent flap and be dazzled by Mont Blanc and glaciated peaks at this almost year-round campground in Les Bossons, 3km south of Chamonix. Take the train to Les Bossons, or the Chamonix bus to Tremplin-le-Mont.

Hameau Albert 1er
LUXURY HOTEL €€€

(☎04 50 53 05 09; www.hameaualbert.fr; 38 rte du Bouchet; d €210-540; @☒) Gathered around a hamlet of converted Savoyard farms and chalets, this resort oozes class with its spa, Mont Blanc–facing pool and Michelin-starred restaurant. The rooms harmoniously blend ultramodern and period furniture; those with jacuzzis and fireplaces are definite honeymoon material. Sadly, the service can be snooty.

Hôtel Richemond
SMALL HOTEL €€

(☎04 50 53 08 85; www.richemond.fr; 228 rue du Docteur Paccard; s/d/tr €65/104/133; ☎) This friendly, supercentral hotel has been run by the same family since 1914. OK, corridors have seen better days and the old-fashioned rooms are floral overload, but the Mont Blanc views and fabulous cast-iron bathtubs, a godsend for sore muscles, more than make up for it.

Hôtel El Paso
PARTY HOTEL €

(☎04 50 53 64 20; www.cantina.fr; 37 impasse des Rhododendrons; s/d/tr/q €49/64/75/90) What you'll get is a threadbare mattress and four scuffed walls reminiscent of good times – small sacrifices given that El Paso is cheap, central and *the* place to party, dude. Tex-Mex feasts and DJs downstairs keep the place rocking, so invest in earplugs if sleeping is a priority.

Le Vert Hôtel
PARTY HOTEL €€

(☎04 50 53 13 58; www.verthotel.com; 964 rte des Gaillands; s/d/tr/q € 75/96/120/140) Self-proclaimed 'Chamonix' house of sports and creativity', this party house, 1km south of town, has no-frills rooms, some with microscopically small bathrooms. But what people really come for is the all-happening, ultrahip bar, a regular venue for top DJs and live music. Mnimum three-night stay.

✖ Eating

From postpiste burgers to Michelin-starred finery, Chamonix covers all the bases. Most restaurants open seven days a week in season but have reduced hours out of season. Call ahead to check.

TOP CHOICE Les Vieilles Luges
TRADITIONAL FRENCH €€

(☎06 84 42 37 00; www.lesvieillesluges.com; Les Houches; menus €20-35) Like a scene from a snow globe in winter, this childhood dream of a 250-year-old farmhouse can only be reached by slipping on skis or taking a scenic 20-minute hike from Maison Neuve chairlift. Under low wood beams, Julie and Claude spoil you with their home cooking – dishes such as *grand-mère*'s beef bourguignon and creamy *farçon* (prepared with potatoes, prunes and bacon), all washed down with *vin chaud* (mulled wine) warmed over a wood fire. Magic.

DON'T MISS

CHILD'S PLAY

There's plenty to amuse *les petits* (the little ones) around Chamonix.

Parc de Merlet (www.parcdemerlet.com, in French; admission €6; ☒10am-6pm Tue-Sun) is 5km north of Les Houches. Kids will enjoy getting close to free-roaming chamois, ibex and whistling marmots in this forested park. Or treat them to a fun-packed day on the trampolines, electric cars, forest-adventure obstacle courses and funfair rides at the Parc de Loisirs de Chamonix (www.chamonixparc.com; ☒10am-7.30pm Jul & Aug, hours vary Apr-Oct), near the chairlift in Les Planards. The summer luge (bob run; 1 descent/day pass €6/13) winds through trees at an electrifying speed.

The ice-skating rink (rte de la Patinoire; adult/child €5/4, skate hire €3.50; ☒2-5pm, closed low season) provides amusement when the weather packs up, as do activities at the adjacent Centre Sportif Richard Bozon (214 av de la Plage), a sports complex with indoor and outdoor swimming pools (adult/child €5.50/4; ☒10am-7pm Jul-Aug).

CHAMONIX CLIFFHANGERS

Cliffhanging is an understatement for many of the 18 *refuges* (mountain huts) in the Mont Blanc massif, poised perilously on the mountain edge or teetering precariously over a stomach-churning drop. The **Club Alpin Français** (☎04 50 53 16 03; www.clubalpin-chamonix.com; 136 av Michel Croz; ☺office for enquiries 4.30-7pm Mon-Tue & Thu-Sat) owns eight of the *refuges* and the rest are run privately.

Most *refuges* are staffed by a warden from around mid-June to mid-September and must be reserved in advance by telephone. Snow permitting, many are open – albeit without a warden – for several more months of the year. Expect to pay around €23 for a dorm bed and €40 to €50 for half board. Meals are simple, hearty and prepared by the hut-keeper.

La Petite Kitchen
MODERN EUROPEAN €

(80 place du Poilu; plat du jour €7-13, mains €14-19.50; ☺closed Tue) The little kitchen is just that: a handful of tables for the lucky few who get to indulge in its locally sourced feel-good food. Filling English breakfasts, steaks with homemade *frites* (hot chips) and the stickiest of toffee puddings will send you rolling happily out the door.

Le Bistrot
GASTRONOMIC €€€

(☎04 50 53 57 64; www.lebistrotchamonix.com, in French; 151 av de l'Aiguille du Midi; lunch menus €17, dinner menus €42-65; ✦) Sleek and monochromatic, this is a real foodie's place. Michelin-starred chef Mickey experiments with textures and seasonal flavours to create taste sensations like pan-seared Arctic char with chestnuts, and divine warm chocolate macaroon with raspberry and red pepper coulis.

Le GouThé
TEA ROOM €

(95 rue des Moulins; menus €9; ☺9am-6.30pm Fri-Mon; ✦) Welcome to the sweetest of tea rooms. Philippe's smooth hot chocolates with pistachio and gingerbread infusions, startlingly bright macaroons and crumbly homemade tarts like mirabelle plum with liquorice are just the sugar fix needed for the slopes. He's a dab hand with *galettes* (buckwheat crêpes), too.

Tigre Tigre
INDIAN €€

(☎04 50 55 33 42; 239 av Michel Croz; mains €11-17; ✦) This hip Indian restaurant is all the rage with its slinky bar for nibbling poppadums and sipping Cobra beers before the main event. Nice and spicy tikka, tandoori and biryani dishes get your tastebuds jumping like a Bollywood film set and service comes with – hurrah! – a smile.

Le Chaudron
SAVOYARD CUISINE €€

(☎04 50 53 57 64; 79 rue des Moulins; menus €20-23; ☺dinner) On a cold winter's day, this chic alpine chalet is guaranteed to give you that warm inner glow. Funky cowskin-clad benches are the backdrop for a feast of Savoyard fondues and lamb slow-cooked in red wine to melting perfection.

Munchie
FUSION €€

(☎04 50 53 45 41; www.munchie.eu; 87 rue des Moulins; mains €18-24; ☺dinner) The style of this trendy Swedish-run hangout is pan-Asian fusion: sashimi, sushi, tempura and Malaysian yellow curries are authentic and creatively presented. Sittings go faster than musical chairs, so it's worth a try even if you haven't booked.

Casa Valério
ITALIAN €€

(☎04 50 55 93 40; www.casavalerio.net; 90 rue du Lyret; pizza €8.50-13, mains €20-28; ☺noon-2am) Mona Lisa welcomes you with a wry smile at this buzzy Italian, famous for its delectable pasta, fresh fish and award-winning pizza margherita. Wine lovers are in their element. Sadly, staff with an attitude can let the show down somewhat.

Le Refuge Payot
FOOD MARKET €

(166 rue Joseph Vallot) Stock up on local goodies: cheese, smoked and air-dried meats, sausages, wine, honey etc.

Drinking & Entertainment

Chamonix nightlife rocks. In the centre, quaint old riverside rue des Moulins touts a line-up of drinking holes. Get the lowdown on the slope-side scene at www.lepetitcanardchx.com.

Many of these après-ski joints serve food as well as booze.

Chambre Neuf
BAR

(272 av Michel Croz; ☎) Cover bands, raucous après-ski drinking and Swedish blondes dancing on the tables make Chambre Neuf one of Chamonix' liveliest party haunts. Conversations about epic off-pistes and monster jumps that are, like, totally mental, man, dominate at every table.

MBC
MICROBREWERY

(www.mbchx.com; 350 rte du Bouchet; ☺4pm-2am) This trendy microbrewery run by four Canadians is fab. Be it with their burgers, cheesecake of the week, live music or amazing locally brewed and named beers (Blonde de Chamonix, Stout des Drus, Blanche des Guides etc), MBC delivers.

Monkey Bar
MUSIC BAR

(81 place Edmond Desailloud; ☺1pm-2am; ☎) With a sign touting 'live sports and sexy bar staff', this is one very cheeky monkey. Slightly grungy, very cool, this party hot spot has live gigs and DJs several times a week. There's a mad rush to the bar at 4.45pm when pints are €1.50 for 15 minutes – get 'em in quick!

Bistrot des Sports
PUB

(182 rue Joseph Vallot; ☺7am-2am) An age-old meeting place for muleteers, guides and other men of the mountain, this bolthole has kept a certain charm and authenticity. The street terrace is perfect for a mellow drink.

Elevation 1904
BAR

(259 av Michel Croz; ☺7pm-2am) Alpine paraphernalia lines the walls of this merry bet by the train station, with an all-day snack shack. The suntrap terrace is just right for relaxing over a cold one.

La Terrasse
MUSIC BAR

(www.laterrassechamonix.com; 43 place Balmat; ☺4pm-2am; ☎) Race the clock for cheap drinks (5pm €5, 6pm €6 etc) and take position on the strategically placed terrace on Chamonix' main square. There's live music nightly.

Cantina Club
CLUB

(www.cantina.fr; 37 impasse des Rhododendrons; ☺7pm-3am) DJs spin everything from deep house to Afrobeat and hip hop at this pumping underground club. The street-level restaurant cooks up Tex-Mex food.

Other happening haunts:

Office
BAR

(274 rue Charlet Stratton, Argentière; ☺3pm-2am; ☎) Sunday roast, English footy and a load of Brits, this is Argentière's party headquarters.

Bar'd Up
BAR

(123 rue des Moulins; ☺4pm-2am) Snowboarder fave with themed parties, big-screen sports and cheapish drinks.

Le Privilège
LOUNGE

(52 rue des Moulins; ☺4pm-2am) Rustic-chic lounge with great cocktails and live music.

Le Garage
CLUB

(www.nightclublegarage.com; 200 av de l'Aiguille du Midi; ☺1am-4am) An electro-house club that opens for a short and sweet three hours of pumping beats every night.

ℹ Information

The tourist office has a list of doctors, dentists, pharmacists etc.

DON'T MISS

A LOFTY LUNCH

Feast on fine cuisine and even finer mountain views at these high-altitude favourites.

Crazy as it sounds for a piste restaurant, you might have to book at **La Crémerie du Glacier** (☑04 50 54 07 52; www.lacremerieduglacier.fr, in French; 766 chemin de la Glacière; mains €10-19; ☺closed Wed) to get a chance to bite into its world-famous *croûtes au fromage* (chunky slices of toasted bread topped with melted cheese). Ski to it with the red Pierre à Ric piste in Les Grands Montets.

Le 3842 (☑04 50 55 82 23; Aiguille du Midi; mains €12-21; ☺restaurant mid-Jun–mid-Sep, snack bar all year) offers stylish summit dining and drinking with knockout views at the top of the Aiguille du Midi in what claims to be Europe's highest café.

At **Le Panoramic** (☑04 50 53 44 11; menus from €15; ☺mid-Dec–Apr & late Jun-Sep), views of Mont Blanc are included in the menu of cheeses, cured meats and BBQ fare. For something a little more frugal, a *vin chaud* (hot mulled wine) at the terrace will do just fine. The restaurant is on the summit of Le Brévent (see p467).

GOING GREEN

Chamonix has long battled with air-pollution problems. In a bid to encourage locals and visitors to leave the car at home, the Chamonix valley offers free public transport on the buses in Chamonix and the train between Servoz (14km west) and Vallorcine (15.5km north). All you have to do is get a **carte d'hôte** from your hotel or campground and on you go for free! The card also offers reductions for a number of activities. Details are listed on the card leaflet.

Banque de Savoie (1 place Balmat) Has an exchange bureau.

Enjoy (128 rue des Moulins; internet per min/hr €0.10/5; ⊘9am-7pm) Snack bar with seven PCs. Skype available.

Hospital (☑04 50 53 84 00; 509 rte des Pélerins) In Les Favrands, 2km south of the centre.

Mojo's (21 place Balmat; internet per min/hr €0.10/5; ⊘9am-8pm) Fun sandwich bar with six PCs.

PGHM (☑04 50 53 16 89; 69 rue de la Mollard) Mountain-rescue service for the entire Mont Blanc area.

Police station (☑04 50 53 00 55; 111 rue de la Mollard)

Post office (89 place Balmat)

Tourist office (☑04 50 53 00 24; www.chamonix.com; 85 place du Triangle de l'Amitié; ⊘8.30am-7pm) Accommodation, weather and activity information.

Getting There & Away
Bus

From **Chamonix bus station** (www.sat-montblanc.com; place de la Gare), located next to the train station, two to three buses run daily to/from Geneva airport and bus station (one way/return €33/55, 1½ to two hours) and Courmayeur (one way/return €13/20, 45 minutes). Advanced booking is required for both. See the website for timetables and reservations.

Car & Motorcycle

Approaching Chamonix from Italy, you arrive via the 11.5km-long **Tunnel de Mont Blanc** (www.atmb.net; toll one way/return €35/44), which enters town in the southern suburb of Les Pélerins. From France, the A40 toll motorway – the Autoroute Blanche – hooks up with the Chamonix-bound N205 dual carriageway for the last leg.

Parking in town can be tricky although **Parking du Mont-Blanc** (place du Mont Blanc; 1st hr free, then per hr/day/week €2/8/50) is reliable. If you're lucky enough to get a spot, you can park for free on rue Helbronner and allée du Recteur Payot.

Car-hire companies include **Europcar** (www.europcar.com; 36 place de la Gare).

Train

The Mont Blanc Express narrow-gauge train trundles from St-Gervais–Le Fayet train station, 23km west of Chamonix, to Martigny in Switzerland, stopping en route in Les Houches, Chamonix and Argentière. There are nine to 12 return trips between Chamonix and St-Gervais (€9.50, 40 minutes). Travelling between Servoz and Vallorcine is free if you have the *carte d'hôte*.

From St-Gervais–Le Fayet, there are trains to most major French cities.

Getting Around

BICYCLE You can hire a bike from **Le Grand Bi Cycles** (240 rte du Bouchet; per day €39; ⊘10am-7pm Tue-Sat), which also gives advice on where to go.

BUS Local bus transport is handled by **Chamonix Bus** (www.chamonix-bus.com; 591 promenade Marie-Paradis).From mid-December to the end of April lines to the ski lifts and central car parks depart every 10 minutes or so between 7am and 7pm (town-centre shuttles 8.30am to 6.30pm). All buses are free with the *carte d'hôte* scheme, except the Chamo' Nuit night buses linking Chamonix with Argentière and Les Houches (last departures from Chamonix 11.30pm or midnight; €2).

TAXI For a taxi, call ☑04 50 53 13 94. Taxis pull up in front of the train station.

Megève & St-Gervais

Très chic Megève (population 4050, elevation 1113m) was developed in the 1920s for Baroness de Rothschild of the famous banking family, who found Switzerland's overcrowded St-Moritz frankly rather tiresome. Today the ski village looks almost too perfect to be true: horse-drawn sleighs, exquisitely arranged boutique windows and no fewer than eight Michelin-starred restaurants spill into its cobbled, medieval-style streets. In winter it attracts a moneyed crowd, but the scene is more laid-back in summer.

Sitting snug below Mont Blanc, 24km west of Chamonix, Megève's neighbour is refreshingly authentic St-Gervais-les-Bains (population 5780, elevation 850m), better known as simply St-Gervais. Its postcard-perfect Savoyard village, centred on a baroque church and old-fashioned carousel, is linked to Chamonix by the legendary Mont Blanc Express.

🏃 Activities

A Mont Blanc massif backdrop makes for fabulously scenic skiing in Megève, where downhill is split into three separate areas: Mont d'Arbois-Princesse (linked to St-Gervais), Jaillet-Combloux and Rochebrune-Côte 2000. Skiing in both resorts is mostly for beginners and cruisy intermediates, and there are 445km of well-groomed pistes to play on. Lift passes are sold online at www.skiamegeve.com.

Panoramic hiking trails in the Bettex, Mont d'Arbois and Mont Joly areas head off from both villages. Some of the best mountain-biking terrain is marked between Val d'Arly, Mont Blanc and Beaufortain.

Maison de la Montagne OUTDOOR ACTIVITIES
(176 rue de la Poste, Megève) Based here are Megève's **ESF** (www.megeve-ski.com; ⊙9am-6.30pm Dec-early Apr, 9am-noon & 2-6pm rest of year) and **Compagnie des Guides** (www.guides-megeve.com, in French; ⊙same as ESF), which organise activities such as off-piste skiing, ice climbing, rock climbing, paragliding, canyoning and mountain biking excursions.

Tramway du Mont Blanc FUNICULAR
(rue de la Gare, St-Gervais; return to Bellevue/Nid d'Aigle €25/32; ⊙9am-4.50pm) For spirit-soaring mountain views with zero effort, board France's highest train. Since 1913 it has laboured up to Bellevue (1800m) from St-Gervais–Le Fayet in winter and further up to the 2380m-high Nid d'Aigle (Eagle's Nest) in summer.

🛏 Sleeping & Eating

Tourist offices in Megève (☑04 50 21 29 52) and St-Gervais (☑04 50 47 76 08) run an accommodation service.

Au Coin du Feu BOUTIQUE HOTEL €€€
(☑04 50 21 04 94; www.coindufeu.com; 252 rte de Rochebrune, Megève; d €250-355; ❄☎) This enchanting boutique-chic chalet accentuates its oak-clad interiors with soft lighting and rich fabrics in Christmassy reds and greens. Nurse a *vin chaud* by the fire in the salon, treat yourself to mountain-herb-infused treatments in the spa,

and venture down to cellar restaurant Le Saint Nicholas (mains €22-25) for delicious Savoyard fare.

Le Gai Soleil CHALET €€
(☑04 50 21 00 70; www.le-gai-soleil.fr; 343 rue Crêt du Midi, Megève; d incl breakfast/half board €130/194; @🐕❄🛜) Beth makes you feel right at home in this inviting chalet, harbouring warm, spacious rooms, a jacuzzi and an inviting restaurant. The outdoor pool and sun deck afford sublime mountain views.

Les Dômes de Miage CAMPGROUND €
(☑04 50 93 45 96; www.camping-mont-blanc.com; 197 rte des Contamines, St-Gervais; sites €21; ⊙May–mid-Sep; ☎) Mont Blanc is your wake-up call at this well-equipped campground, beautifully set in wooded hills. The first-rate facilities include a restaurant and playground.

La Chaumière FAMILY HOTEL €
(☑04 50 93 60 10; www.lachaumierehotel.com; 222 av de Genève, St-Gervais-Le Fayet; s/d/tr/q €39/45/55/69; @🐕🛜) This chalet-style hotel is a godsend for cash-strapped skiers, with bright, modern rooms sporting above-par perks like flatscreen TVs and balconies. Family rooms are available. There's free access to the minispa, gym and climbing wall.

TOP CHOICE **Flocons de Sel** GASTRONOMIC €€€
(☑04 50 21 49 99; www.floconsdesel.com; 1775 rte de Leutaz, Megève; lunch menus €35-70, dinner menus €135, cooking classes €60; ⊙cooking classes 4-7pm Mon-Sat)

POTTER'S FANTASY

His name is Monsieur Baranger but he prefers to be called 'the potter behind the church' and that's precisely where you will find his rambling, poster-plastered workshop and gallery in St-Gervais. An eccentric and something of a local legend, M Baranger can often be seen at his wheel, where he throws pots, plates, ornaments and vases, which are then glazed in earthy shades of blue and cream. He's always smiling, he says, because he wakes up every day to do what he loves. And it shows. His workshop is open *quand vous voyez les lumières* (when the lights are on).

Emmanuel Renaut, who trained with Marc Veyrat and at Claridges, mans the stove at this two-Michelin-starred restaurant, housed in a stylishly converted farmhouse. He cooks and artistically presents whatever is fresh that day, be it lake fish or pigeon, rounding out with his signature *flocons de sucre* (sugar snowflakes) dessert. The insightful cooking classes focus on two to three recipes – from simple starters to petits fours.

Le Galeta SAVOYARD CUISINE €€
(☑04 50 93 16 11; 150 impasse des Lupins, St-Gervais; mains €15-25; ☺dinner; ∰) Tucked behind the church, this rustic barn-style restaurant radiates alpine character and warmth. Sylvie and Serge serve up succulent meats grilled over a wood fire and tot up your (rather modest) bill on an antique till.

ℹ Information

Megève tourist office (☑04 50 21 27 28; www.megeve.com; 70 rue de Monseigneur Conseil; ☺9am-7pm)

St-Gervais tourist office (☑04 50 47 76 08; www.st-gervais.net; 43 rue du Mont-Blanc; ☺9am-12.30pm & 2-8pm)

ℹ Getting There & Away

BUS From Megève bus station, there are seven daily services to/from St-Gervais–Le Fayet and Sallanches train stations. In winter, airport shuttles run at least twice daily to/from Geneva airport (one way/return €44/75, 1½ hours) from Megève and St-Gervais.

TRAIN The closest train station to Megève is in Sallanches, 12km north; for information go to the SNCF information desk inside the bus station. St-Gervais is the main train station for Chamonix, linked to the latter by the Mont Blanc Express. Services include several day trains (€86, 5½ hours) and one overnight train (€93, 9½ hours) to Paris, plus frequent trains to Lyon (€32, 3½ hours), Annecy (€13.50, 1½ hours) and Geneva (€12, 1½ hours).

Les Portes du Soleil

Poetically dubbed 'the Gates of the Sun' (elevation 1000m to 2466m; www.portesdusoleil.com), this gargantuan ski area – the world's largest – is formed from a chain of 12 villages strung along the French–Swiss border.

The best known of the villages is Morzine (elevation 1000m), which retains some traditional alpine charm, especially in summer when visits to alpine cheese dairies and traditional slate workshops kick in. Small, trend-conscious Avoriaz (elevation 1800m), a purpose-built ski resort a few kilometres up the valley atop a rock, appeals for its no-cars policy. Horse-drawn sleighs piled high with luggage romantically ferry new arrivals to and from the snowy village centre where wacky 1960s mimetic architecture gets away with an 'avant-garde' tag.

Arriving by road via Cluses you hit smaller Les Gets (elevation 1172m), a family favourite.

🏃 Activities

A mind-blowing 650km of downhill slopes and cross-country trails criss-cross Les Portes de Soleil, served by 202 ski lifts and covered by a single ski pass. Morzine is ideal beginner and intermediate terrain, with scenic tree runs for bad-weather days. The snow-sure slopes of Avoriaz offer more of a challenge. This is freestyle heaven, boarders say, with deep powder, several snowparks to play in and a fantastic superpipe near the top of Prodains cable car.

Mountain bikers can tackle 380km of invigorating trails, such as the 100km-long circular Portes du Soleil tour.

Bureau des Guides OUTDOOR ACTIVITIES
(☑04 50 75 96 65) For local know-how on summer activities – hiking, biking, climbing, canyoning and paragliding – and advice on mountain-bike hire and Morzine's heart-stopping 3300m-long bike descent (free; ☺Jun-Sep) from the top of the Plénéy cable car (1/10 ascents €4.50/35).

🛌 Sleeping & Eating

Bear in mind that most places close in May, October and November. Advance bookings are essential in the high season.

TOP CHOICE **Farmhouse** BOUTIQUE HOTEL €€
(☑04 50 79 08 26; www.thefarmhouse.fr; Le Mas de la Coutettaz, Morzine; d incl half board €169-257, dinner €40) Morzine's oldest pile is this gorgeous 1771 farmhouse run by the charming Dorrien Ricardo. Five rooms (some with Victorian-style bathrooms) are in the main house, and a trio of cottages (including the old *mazot*, a miniature mountain chalet) sit in the lovely grounds. Dining – open to nonguests too – is a lavish affair around one huge banquet table.

Ferme de Montagne
BOUTIQUE HOTEL €€€

(☏04 50 75 36 79; www.fermedemontagne.com, Les Gets; half board per person per week €1500-2250) This glamourpuss of a spa-clad farmhouse has been tipped as one of Europe's hottest boutique ski hotels by glossy-mag critics. The price tag covers every imaginable luxury: personalised ski guides, afternoon tea with homemade cakes by a roaring fire, champagne in the hot tub surrounded by snowy peaks, you name it.

Fleur de Neige
CHALET €€

(☏04 50 79 01 23; www.chalethotelfleurdesneiges.com; Le Mas de la Coutettaz, Morzine; d incl half board €90; ☏⛄) A cheery welcome and solid home cooking await at this family-run chalet, decked out in warm wood. The heated pool and sauna beckon after a day carving the slopes.

Camping Les Marmottes
CAMPGROUND €

(☏04 50 75 74 44; http://campinglesmarmottes.com; Essert-Romand; sites €17) This small, tree-shaded campground nestles in the mountains, 5km north of Morzine. It's open year-round, so those made of hardy stuff can even pitch a tent in the snow (brrrrr...).

La Table du Marché d'Avoriaz
BISTRO €€

(☏04 94 97 91 91; www.christophe-leroy.com; place des Dromonts, Avoriaz; menus €19.50-39) Avoriaz has become so hip that renowned French chef Christophe Leroy has opened a minimalist-chic bistro here, serving market-fresh French flavours like roast beef with shallots and *gratin dauphinois* (finely sliced potatoes oven-baked in cream and a pinch of nutmeg) to a discerning crowd.

ⓘ Information

Avoriaz tourist office (☏04 50 74 02 11; www.avoriaz.com; place Centrale; ☺9am-noon & 2-6pm Mon-Fri) Can book self-catering chalets and studios.

Les Gets tourist office (☏04 50 75 80 80, accommodation service 04 50 75 80 51; www.lesgets.com; place de la Mairie; ☺9am-noon & 2-6pm Mon-Sat)

Morzine tourist office (☏04 50 79 11 57; www.morzine-avoriaz.com; place de la Crusaz; ☺9am-noon & 2-6pm Mon-Sat) Also has an **accommodation service** (☏04 50 79 11 57; www.resa-morzine.com).

ⓘ Getting There & Away

Free shuttle buses serve the lifts of Télécabine Super Morzine, Télécabine du Pléney and Téléphérique Avoriaz.

MULTIPASS MAGIC

Les Portes du Soleil's hottest summer deal is the Multipass, which costs €1 per day for guests and €6 for day trippers. Available from mid-June to mid-September, the pass covers transport from cable cars and chairlifts to shuttle buses; activities including tennis courts, ice rinks and swimming pools; and entry to five cultural sites, from heritage museums to abbeys.

During the ski season, Morzine (one way/return €36/59), Avoriaz (€39/65) and Les Gets (€33/55) are linked by a regular bus service to Geneva airport, about 50km west. From Morzine there are frequent **SAT buses** (www.sat-montblanc.com) to Les Gets and Avoriaz. There are also buses from Morzine to its closest train stations: Thonon-les-Bains and Cluses (one way/return € 11/22).

Thonon-les-Bains

POP 32,850 / ELEV 430M

Just across the water from Lausanne on the French side of Lake Geneva (Lac Léman), Thonon-les-Bains – a fashionable spa town during the belle époque – sits on a bluff above the lake. Winter is deathly dull, but its summer cruises and lakeside strolls appeal.

◉ Sights & Activities

Château de Ripaille
CASTLE

(www.ripaille.fr, in French; 1hr guided tour €6; ☺1-5 tours daily Feb-Oct) This turreted castle, rebuilt in the 19th century on the site of its 15th-century ancestor, is 1km east of town along quai de Ripaille. It has vineyards, a garden for summer dining (mid-April to mid-September) and forested grounds to explore.

Funicular Railway
FUNICULAR

(one way/return €1/1.80; ☺8am-9pm) This nostalgic 230m-long funicular links the upper town with the marina.

Fontaine de la Versoie
FOUNTAIN

(Parc Thermal de Thonon) You can fill your bottle with Thonon mineral water for free at this mosaic-lined fountain.

CGN
LAKE CRUISES

(www.cgn.ch; ☺May-Oct) Regular services from the port in Thonon-les-Bains to destinations around the lake, including

WORTH A TRIP

ÉVIAN, ÉVIAN EVERYWHERE

Trot 9km east from Thonon along the lake and you hit the elegant belle époque spa town of Évian-les-Bains, of mineral-water fame. Discovered in 1790 and bottled since 1826, the water takes 15 years to trickle down through the Chablais Mountains, gathering minerals en route, before emerging at 11.4°C. A favourite country retreat of the dukes of Savoy, Évian was reinvented as a luxury spa resort in the 18th century when wallowing in tubs of mineral water was all the rage. You can wallow yourself in the thermal pools at Les Thermes Évian (www.lesthermesevian.com; place de la Libération; discovery day €55; ⊗9am-6pm Mon-Sat).

Fill your bottle for free at art nouveau spring Buvette Cachat (20 av des sources). For total immersion, call ahead to arrange a tour (☑04 50 84 86 54; admission free, transport €2; ⊗Jun-Sep) of the Évian bottling plant, 5km out of town. The tourist office (www.eviantourism.com; place d'Allinges) can also help.

Geneva (one way/return €28/47), Évian-les-Bains (€12/21) and Yvoire (€14/24). See the website for an up-to-date timetable and other themed cruises.

🛏 Sleeping

La Ferme du Château   B&B **€€**
(☑06 25 06 44 93; www.lafermeduchateau.com, in French; Hameau de Maugny, Draillant; d €85; ▣) Well worth the 10km drive south of town, this renovated 18th-century Savoyard farmhouse is run by dream duo Sophie and Didier. Tranquillity reigns in the country-style rooms clad in wood and stone, the vine-clad garden and by the outdoor pool.

Hôtel à l'Ombre des Marronniers   HOTEL **€**
(☑04 50 71 26 18; www.hotellesmarronniers.com, in French; 17 place de Crète; d €50-62; 🛜▣) Sitting in flowery gardens, this chalet-style hotel is the pick of the in-town options, with modest, well-kept rooms and an outdoor pool.

ℹ Information

Lakeside tourist office (⊗10am-12.30pm & 2-6.30pm Jul & Aug) A chalet where you can also buy boat tickets with CGN (www.cgn.ch).

Tourist office (☑04 50 71 55 55; www.thononlesbains.com; Château de Sonnaz, 2 rue Michaud; ⊗9am-12.15pm & 1.45-6.30pm Mon-Fri, from 10am Sat) In the upper town.

ℹ Getting There & Away

BUS From Thonon bus station (place des Arts), **SAT** (www.sat-leman.com) runs regular buses to/from Évian-les-Bains (€1.50, 20 minutes) and into the Chablais Mountains, including to Morzine (€11, one hour).

TRAIN The train station (place de la Gare) is southwest of place des Arts, the main square. Trains run to/from Geneva (€7, 50 minutes) direct or via Annemasse (€6, 30 minutes).

Yvoire

POP 830 / ELEV 372M

A real sleeping beauty of a medieval village, Yvoire, 16km west of Thonon on the shores of Lake Geneva, makes for a great day trip. The village is a riot of turrets and towers, cob houses and geranium-lined streets. Familiarise yourself with its 700-year history on a 1½-hour guided tour (tour €5.50; ⊗10.45am Tue & Thu, 4.45pm Wed & Fri Jul-Aug).

Slumbering in the shadow of a 14th-century castle and enclosed by walls, the Jardin des Cinq Sens (Garden of Five Senses; www.jardin5sens.net; rue du Lac; adult/child €10/5.50; ⊗10am-7pm) appeals to the senses through touch, sound (gurgling water), scent (fragrant gardens) and taste (edible plants).

The tourist office (☑04 50 72 80 21; www.yvoiretourism.com; place de la Mairie; ⊗9.30am-12.30pm & 1.30-5pm Mon-Sat, noon-4pm Sun) can advise on accommodation.

Annecy

POP 53,000 / ELEV 447M

Annecy paints the prettiest of pictures. Caressed by sapphire Lac d'Annecy, ringed by lushly wooded mountains and spiralling around a medieval old town, it makes visitors – all two million of them a year – stop in wonder and reach for their cameras on every glorious corner.

Come summer, you can sidestep the masses exploring quiet backstreets, strolling flower-strewn promenades and taking a tingly dip in that masterpiece of a lake: one of the world's purest, fed only by rainwater, spring water and mountain streams.

◉ Sights

TOP CHOICE **Palais de l'Isle** MUSEUM

(3 passage de l'Île; adult/child €3.60/1.30; ◔10.30am-6pm) Sitting on a triangular islet in the Canal du Thiou, the whimsically turreted, 12th-century Palais de l'Isle has been a lordly residence, courthouse, mint and prison (lucky inmates!) over the centuries.

Annecy

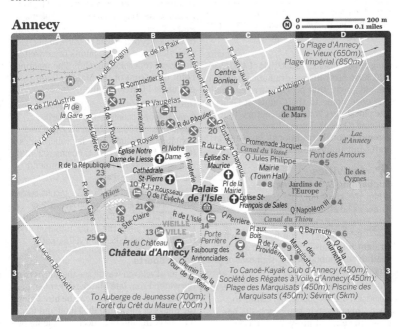

Annecy

Today Annecy's most visible landmark hosts local-history displays.

Vieille Ville & Lakefront   HISTORIC QUARTER
It's a pleasure simply to wander aimlessly around Annecy's medieval old town, a photogenic jumble of narrow streets, turquoise canals and colonnaded passageways. Continue down to the tree-fringed lakefront and the flowery Jardins de l'Europe, linked to the popular picnic spot Champ de Mars by the poetic iron arch of the Pont des Amours (Lovers' Bridge).

Château d'Annecy   CASTLE
(rampe du Château; adult/child €4.90/2.30; 10.30am-6pm) Rising dramatically above the old town, this perkily turreted castle was once home to the Counts of Geneva. The oldest part is the 12th-century Tour de la Reine (Queen's Tower). Its museum takes a romp through traditional Savoyard art, crafts and alpine natural history.

🏃 Activities

Sunbathing & Swimming

When the sun's out, the beaches fringing Annecy's lakefront beckon.

FREE **Plage d'Annecy-le-Vieux**   BEACH
(Jul & Aug) If you feel like diving straight into those crystal-clear waters, head to this public beach, 1km east of Champ de Mars.

Plage Impérial   BEACH
(admission €3.50; Jul & Aug) Closer to town, this privately run beach sits beneath the elegant pre-WWI Impérial Palace.

FREE **Plage des Marquisats**   BEACH
(Jul & Aug) This sand and shingle beach is 1km south of town along rue des Marquisats.

Piscine des Marquisats   SWIMMING POOLS
(29 rue des Marquisats; adult/child €4/3; 10am-7pm May-Aug) Right next door to the beach is this trio of outdoor swimming pools.

Walking

You can amble along the lakefront from the Jardins de l'Europe to the Stade Nautique des Marquisats and beyond. Another scenic stroll begins at Champ de Mars and meanders eastwards towards Annecy-le-Vieux. Forêt du Crêt du Maure, south of Annecy, has myriad walking trails, as do the wildlife-rich wetlands of Bout du Lac, 20km from Annecy on the lake's southern

tip, and Roc de Chère nature reserve, 10km away on the eastern shore.

The tourist office stocks guides and maps, including IGN's *Lac d'Annecy* and *Walks and Treks Lake of Annecy*, listing 15 itineraries in the area (€6.50).

Cycling & Blading

Biking and blading are big, with 46km of cycling tracks encircling the lake. The tourist office and rental outlets have free maps.

Roll'n Cy   BLADING
(www.roll-n-cy.org; 8pm Fri Mar–mid-Dec) Get your skates on for the jaunts organised by this local rollerblading club. The meeting point is in front of the Mairie (Town Hall) on rue de l'Hôtel de Ville.

Roul' ma Poule   CYCLING, BLADING
(www.annecy-location-velo.com; 4 rue des Marquisats; 9.30am-12.30pm & 2-7pm Wed-Mon) Rents per half-/full day rollerblades (€12/18), bikes (€12/18), tandems (€22/33) and scooters (€10/15). Can recommend day trips in the area.

Station Roller   CYCLING, BLADING
(www.roller-golf-annecy.com, in French; 2 av du Petit Port; 9am-10pm) Bike, blade and kayak outlet near the Plage Impérial at the start of the lakeside cycling path.

Water Sports

The most relaxed way to see the lake is from the water. From late March to October, pedal boats and motorboats can be hired along the quays of the Canal du Thiou and Canal du Vassé. In summer check out the following outlets:

Canoë-Kayak Club d'Annecy   KAYAKING
(www.kayak-annecy.com, in French; 33 rue des Marquisats; per hr €7-12) Kayak and canoe hire.

Société des Régates à Voile d'Annecy
    SAILING
(www.srva.info, in French; 31 rue des Marquisats) Rents sailing boats from €30 for two hours.

Annecy Plongée   SAILING
(www.annecyplongee.com; 6 rue des Marquisats) Sells and rents diving gear and arranges two-hour baptism dives (€45).

Adventure Sports

The tourist office has details on a whole host of companies that arrange adrenalin-driven activities on and around Lake Annecy. One of the most central is Takamaka (www.takamaka.fr; 23 faubourg Ste Claire). Introductory course prices start from €85 for tandem paragliding, €33 for waterskiing or wakeboarding, €39 for climbing or freeriding, €49 for canyoning and €55 for bungee jumping.

☞ Tours

Town tours WALKING TOUR
(per person €6; ⊙3pm Thu & Sat) The tourist office organises guided tours of the old town; they are in French but some guides speak a little English. If you would prefer to go it alone, pick up the free *Annecy Town Walks* leaflet.

Compagnie des Bateaux CRUISES
(www.annecy-croisieres.com; 2 place aux Bois; 1/2hr lake cruise €12.50/16; ⊙mid-Mar–Oct) Runs cruises departing from quai Bayreuth. Tickets are sold 15 minutes before departure. From May to September boats also sail across the lake to Menthon-St-Bernard (€5.50), Talloires (€6.50) and other villages.

✦ Festivals & Events

Annecy celebrates the flamboyant **Venetian carnival** in February, the **Fête du Lac** with fireworks over the lake in August, and October's **Le Retour des Alpages**, when the cows come home from the alpine pastures, wreathed in flowers and bells. Street performers wow evening crowds at **Les Noctibules** in July.

⊨ Sleeping

You'll need to book months ahead if you're planning to visit Annecy in July or August when rooms are gold-dust rare. The tourist office has details of campgrounds and *chambres d'hôtes* (B&Bs) scattered around the lake.

Hôtel Alexandra FAMILY HOTEL €
(☑04 50 52 84 33; www.hotelannecy-alexandra. fr; 19 rue Vaugelas; s/d/tr/q €48/59/70/89; 🕸🚻) Nice surprise: Annecy's most charming hotel is also one of its most affordable. The welcome is five-star, rooms are fresh and spotless – a few extra euros get you a balcony and canal view – and breakfast is a generous spread with fresh pastries.

Le Pré Carré BOUTIQUE HOTEL €€€
(☑04 50 52 14 14; www.hotel-annecy.net; 27 rue Sommeiller; s/d €172/202; 🕸@🚻) One of Annecy's chicest hotels, Le Pré Carré keeps things contemporary with Zen colours in rooms with balconies or terraces, a jacuzzi and a business corner. The staff know

Annecy inside out so you're in very good hands.

Hôtel du Château SMALL HOTEL €
(☑04 50 45 27 66; www.annecy-hotel.com; 16 rampe du Château; s/d/tr/q €49/68/75/85; 🚻🕸) Nestled at the foot of the castle, this hotel's trump card is its sun-drenched, panoramic breakfast terrace. Rooms are small but sweet with their pine furniture and pastel tones.

Hôtel des Alpes TRADITIONAL HOTEL €€
(☑04 50 45 04 56; www.hotelannecy.com; 12 rue de la Poste; s/d/tr €67/77/92; 🚻) This bubblegum -pink hotel in Annecy's centre has well-lit rooms with squeaky-clean bathrooms. It's reasonably quiet despite being on a busy street.

Hôtel du Palais de L'Isle HISTORIC HOTEL €€
(☑04 50 45 86 87; www.hoteldupalaisdelisle. com; 13 rue Perrière; s/d €76/108; 🕸🚻) Guests slumber in the heart of old-town action at this 18th-century haunt, where the crisp contemporary decor is soothing after the bustle outside. Rooms sport assorted views of the Palais, the castle or the old town's sea of roofs.

Auberge du Lyonnais TRADITIONAL HOTEL €
(☑04 50 51 26 10; www.auberge-du-lyonnais. com; 9 rue de la République; s €45-60, d €50-75, menus €25-30; 🕸🚻) This canalside contender in the old town has light and comfy (if small) rooms with pine furnishings. The restaurant is renowned for its seafood; the €25 three-course *menu* is worth every cent.

Camping les Rives du Lac CAMPGROUND €
(☑04 50 52 40 14; www.lesrivesdulac-annecy. com; 331 chemin des Communaux; sites €21; ⊙mid-Apr–mid-Oct; 🚻) Pitch your tent near the lakefront at this shady campground, 5km south of town in Sévrier. A cycling track runs into central Annecy from here.

Auberge de Jeunesse HOSTEL €
(☑04 50 45 33 19; www.fuaj.org, in French; 4 rte du Semnoz; dm incl breakfast & sheets €19.50; ⊙mid-Jan–Nov; 🚻) Annecy's smart wood-clad hostel has great facilities (bar, kitchen, barbecue, TV room) and chipper staff. Dorms have en-suite showers. It's a 10-minute walk south of the centre.

✕ Eating

The quays along Canal du Thiou in the Vieille Ville are jam-packed with touristy cafés and pizzerias. Crêpes, kebabs, classic

French cuisine – you'll find it all along pedestrianised rue Carnot, rue de L'Isle and rue Faubourg Ste-Claire.

TOP CHOICE Chalet la Pricaz

TRADITIONAL FRENCH €€

(☑04 50 60 72 61; Col de la Forclaz, mains €18-30; ⏰closed Wed; ☑) On its fairy-tale perch above Lake Annecy, this is prime romantic sunset material. Only locally sourced organic ingredients feature on the menu. Tangy *tartiflettes* (Reblochon cheese with potatoes, crème fraîche, onions and diced bacon) and farm-fresh charcuterie go brilliantly with the first-rate selection of Savoyard wines. The tucked-away restaurant is off the D42, 13km south of Annecy.

L'Estaminet

BISTRO €€

(☑04 50 45 88 83; 8 rue Ste-Claire; mains €15-22; ⏰closed Sun dinner & Mon) With its dark wood and intriguing knick-knacks, this incredibly cosy *estaminet* (Flemish eatery) whisks you to the backstreets of Brussels. Draught Belgian beers pair well with *carbonnade flamande* (rich Flemish beef stew) and *moules* (mussels) with unusual additions like pastis and curry.

La Cuisine des Amis

BISTRO €€

(☑04 50 10 10 80; 9 rue du Pâquier; mains €16.50-25) Walking into this bistro is, at times, like gatecrashing a private party. Here locals and all-comers are treated like one big jolly *famille*. Pull up a chair, *prendre un verre* (have a drink), dine well on regional fare, pat the dog and, finally, see if your snapshot ends up on the wall of merry *amis* (friends).

La Ciboulette

MODERN FRENCH €€

(☑04 50 45 74 57; www.laciboulette-annecy.com; cour du Pré Carré, 10 rue Vaugelas; menus €31-46; ⏰Tue-Sat) Such class! Crisp white linen and gold-kissed walls set the scene at this surprisingly affordable Michelin-starred place, where chef Georges Paccard cooks fresh seasonal specialities, such as slow-roasted Anjou pigeon with Midi asparagus. Reservations are essential.

Contresens

FUSION €€

(☑04 50 32 22 10; 10 rue de la Poste; mains €15; ⏰Tue-Sat; ☑) The menu reads like a mathematical formula but it soon becomes clear: starters are A, mains B, sides C and desserts D. The food is as experimental as the menu – sun-dried tomato, Beaufort cheese and rocket salad burger, mussel ravioli, 'de-

constructed' Snickers – and totally divine. Kid nirvana.

L'Étage

TRADITIONAL FRENCH €€

(☑04 50 51 03 28; 13 rue du Pâquier; mains €14-22, 3-course menus €18) Cheese, glorious cheese... *Fromage* is given pride of place in spot-on fondues and *raclette* (a combination of melting cheese, boiled potatoes, charcuterie and baby gherkins) at L'Étage, where a backdrop of mellow music and cheerful staff keep the ambience relaxed.

Au Fidèle Berger

TEAROOM €

(2 rue Royale; cakes & pastries €2-4; ⏰9.15am-7pm Tue-Sat) Bag a spot on the terrace of this old-English-style tearoom to watch the street entertainers and indulge your sweet tooth on decadent cakes, macaroons and homemade ice creams.

Nature & Saveur

ORGANIC €€

(☑04 50 45 82 29; place des Cordeliers; lunch menus with/without wine €42/32; ⏰lunch Tue-Sat) Laurence Salomon's 100% organic restaurant attracts a boho-chic clientele. Inspired by the seasons, the menu uses wholesome ingredients from local farms, from obscure legumes to locally reared meat.

Food Market

MARKET €

(Vieille Ville; ⏰7am-1am Sun, Tue & Fri) The old-town market is great for picnic fixings.

🍷 Drinking

Annecy needs its beauty sleep, so nights are more about people-watching over relaxed drinks by the canalside than raving it up. For a livelier vibe try try these:

Finn Kelly's

PUB

(10 faubourg des Annonciades; ⏰4.30pm-3am; ☎) Has live sports, darts and billiards, and regular DJ nights and gigs at weekends.

River's Café

BAR

(2 rue de la Gare; ⏰11am-3am) A young and hip crowd linger over expertly mixed caipirinhas and house beats at this voguish lounge bar.

ℹ Information

Hospital (☑04 50 88 33 33; 1 av de Trésum)

Magic Phone (3 rue de l'Industrie; internet per 15min/1hr €1/3; ⏰10am-8pm) High-speed internet access.

Planète Telecom (4 rue Jean Jaurès; internet per hr €3; ⏰9.30am-8pm) Internet access and discount calls.

DON'T MISS

LAKESIDE LEGENDS

Dining and staying *à la* lakeside legend requires a healthy appetite and bank balance. Book at least a week ahead to snag a table.

At the Michelin-starred **La Nouvelle Maison de Marc Veyrat** (☑04 50 09 97 49; www.marcveyrat.fr; 13 vieille rte des Pensières, Veyrier-du-Lac; d €200-300, menus €92; ⊗Thu-Sun late May-Sep) French celebrity chef Marc Veyrat has handed over his stove, culinary flamboyance and signature use of wild herbs to his capable successor Yoann Conte. In Veyrier-du-Lac, 5km southeast of Annecy, the baby-blue house by the lake also has a handful of wonderful rooms.

Whether alfresco on Lake Annecy's shores in summer or in the classically elegant salon in winter, dining at **Auberge du Père Bise** (☑04 50 60 72 01; www.perebise.com; 303 rte du Port, Talloires; d €270-300, menus €76-175; ⊗Thu-Mon) is never less than extraordinary. Female chef Sophie Bise allows the clean flavours and freshness of local produce to shine in signatures like Annecy lake fish with duck foie gras and tart Granny Smith apple. The restaurant is 12km south of Annecy in Talloires.

Police station (☑04 50 52 32 00; 15 rue des Marquisats)

Post office (4bis rue des Glières)

Tourist office (☑04 50 45 00 33; www.lac-annecy.com; 1 rue Jean Jaurès, Centre Bonlieu; ⊗9am-6.30pm Mon-Sat, 10am-1pm Sun) Has a selection of free maps and brochures, and can help with last-minute hotel bookings.

❶ Getting There & Away

BUS From the **bus station** (rue de l'Industrie), adjoining the train station, the **Billetterie Crolard** (www.voyages-crolard.com) sells tickets for roughly hourly buses to lakeside destinations including Menthon-St-Bernard (€2.40, 20 minutes), Veyrier-du-Lac (€2.10, 15 minutes) and Talloires (€2.80, 25 minutes); and for local ski resorts La Clusaz and Le Grand Bornand (one way/return €8.50/16.50, 50 and 60 minutes respectively). It also runs four to five buses daily to/from Lyon St-Exupéry airport (one way/return €33/50, 2¼ hours).

Next door, **Autocars Frossard** (www.frossard.eu) sells tickets for Geneva (€10.50, 1¾ hours, 16 daily), Thonon-les-Bains (€16.50, two hours, twice daily), Évian-les-Bains (€18.50, 2½ hours, twice daily) and Chambéry (€9.20, 1¼ hours).

TRAIN From Annecy's **train station** (place de la Gare), there are frequent trains to/from Aix-les-Bains (€7, 30 minutes), Chambéry (€9, 45 minutes), St-Gervais (€13.50, 1½ hours), Lyon (€23, 2¼ hours) and Paris Gare de Lyon (€75, four hours).

❶ Getting Around

BUS Get info on local buses at **Espace SIBRA** (www.sibra.fr; 21 rue de la Gare), opposite the bus station. Buses run from 6am to 8.30pm

and a single ticket/day pass/*carnet* of 10 costs €1.10/3/9.50.

BICYCLE Bikes can be hired from **Vélonecy** (place de la Gare), situated at the train station, for €15 per day. People with a valid bus or train ticket only pay €5 per day.

Around Annecy

On warm summer days the villages of **Sévrier**, 5km south on Lake Annecy's western shore, and **Menthon-St-Bernard**, 7km south on the lake's eastern shore, make good day trips. South of Menthon, **Talloires** is the most exclusive lakeside spot. All have wonderful beaches.

In winter, ski-keen Annéciens head for the cross-country slopes of **Semnoz** (elevation 1700m; www.semnoz.fr, in French), 18km south; or downhill stations **La Clusaz** (elevation 1100m; www.laclusaz.com), 32km east, and **Le Grand Bornand** (elevation 1000m; www.legrandbornand.com), 34km northeast.

Chambéry

POP 59,100 / ELEV 270M

Chambéry has a lot going for it: strategic location at the crossroads of the main alpine valleys, scenic setting near Lac du Bourget and two regional parks, and a rich heritage of French, Italian and Savoy rules. While the city receives just a trickle of visitors, those who do venture here are rewarded with crowd-free museums and pleasant strolls in its arcaded streets.

KING OF 12 CASTLES

If you love nothing better than a castle, you'll love following in the footsteps of gallant dukes and feudal lords on the Route des Ducs de Savoie (Road of the Dukes of Savoy; www.chateaux-france.com/route-savoie). The route weaves through pristine alpine landscapes from Thonon-les-Bains to Avressieux, 30km west of Chambéry, and ticks off 12 castles, abbeys and historic sites including Château de Ripaille, Château d'Annecy and Château des Ducs de Savoie.

For acting out fairy-tale fantasies, there's little that beats the silver-turreted, high-on-a-hillside Château de Menthon-St-Bernard (www.chateau-de-menthon.com; Menthon-St-Bernard; guided tour adult/child €7.50/4.50; ☺2-6pm Fri-Sun May-Sep), the birthplace of St Bernard (1008). Word has it that the château inspired Walt Disney's *Sleeping Beauty* castle. Tours of the medieval interior, taking in tapestry-adorned salons and a magnificent library, are intriguing, but it's the sparkling Lake Annecy panorama that leaves visitors spellbound.

The city was Savoy's capital from the 13th century until 1563 when the dukes of Savoy shifted their capital to Turin in Italy. The 11th-century castle, which once served as the seat of power for the House of Savoy, now houses the administration for the Savoie *département*.

◉ Sights

For up-to-date information on exhibitions, visit http://musees.chambery.fr (in French). Admission to the city's museums is free on the first Sunday of the month.

Château des Ducs de Savoie　CASTLE
(Castle of the Dukes of Savoy; place du Château; adult/child €2.50/free; ☺tours 2.30pm Tue-Sun) Chambéry's trophy sight is this forbidding medieval castle, once home to the counts and dukes of Savoy. Guided tours leave from the **Accueil des Guides** office, opposite the château, and cover an exhibition tracing Savoy's rich history and the Tour Trésorerie (Treasury Tower). The adjoining **Ste-Chapelle** was built in the 15th century to house the Shroud of Turin and is famous for its 70-bell Grand Carillon, Europe's largest bell chamber. The chapel was closed for renovation at the time of writing and is expected to reopen in 2011.

TOP CHOICE **Les Charmettes**　HISTORIC HOME
(890 chemin des Charmettes; admission free; ☺10am-noon & 2-6pm Wed-Mon) Genevan philosopher, composer and writer Jean-Jacques Rousseau, a key figure of the Enlightenment and French Revolution, lived with his lover, Baronne Louise Éléonore de Warens, at this charming late-17th-century house from 1736 to 1742. Discover Rousseau's passion for botany by taking a stroll in the landscaped garden full of herbs, flowers and vines. Les Charmettes is 1.5km southeast of town.

Fontaine des Éléphants　FOUNTAIN
(place des Éléphants) With its four intricately carved elephants, this fountain could be the model for an Indian postage stamp. It was sculpted in 1838 in honour of Général de Boigne (1751–1830), who made his fortune in the East Indies. When he returned home he bestowed some of his wealth on the town and was honoured posthumously with this monument. The genteel arcaded street that leads from the fountain to Château des Ducs de Savoie is another of his projects.

Cathédrale Métropole St-François de Sales　CATHEDRAL
(place de la Métropole; ☺8am-noon & 2-6.30pm) Built as a Franciscan chapel in the 15th century, Chambéry's cathedral hides unexpected treasures, including Europe's largest collection (some 6,000 sq m) of *trompe l'œil* painting, by artists Sevesi and Vicario, and a 35m-long maze dating from the mid-19th century.

Musée Savoisien　MUSEUM
(sq de Lannoy de Bissy; adult/child €3/free; ☺10am-noon & 2-6pm Wed-Mon) Housed in a Franciscan monastery and linked to the cathedral by cloisters, this museum showcases archaeological finds including a gallery of 13th-century wall paintings. The 2nd floor stages temporary exhibitions concentrating on Savoyard mountain life.

FREE **Musée des Beaux-Arts** ART GALLERY (place du Palais de Justice; ⊘10am-noon & 2-6pm Wed-Mon) Displays a small collection of 14th- to 18th-century Italian works. The gallery was undergoing renovation at the time of writing and is expected to reopen in 2011.

🛏 Sleeping

Chambéry's *chambres d'hôte* and self-catering studios are far more appealing than its nondescript chain hotels. **Gîtes de France** (☑04 79 33 22 56; www.gites-de-france-savoie.com; 24 bd de la Colonne) takes bookings. The nearest hostel is in Aix-les-Bains.

TOP **La Ferme du Petit Bonheur** CHOICE FARMSTAY €€ (☑04 79 85 26 17; www.fermedupetitbonheur. fr; 538 chemin Jean-Jacques; s/d/tr incl breakfast €80/90/110; 🐾) *Bonheur* (happiness) is indeed yours if you stay with Eric (a musician) and Chantal (a painter) at their vine-clad farmhouse in the hills. Their exquisite taste shows in five countrified rooms and personal touches like homemade croissants for breakfast. In summer there is a fragrant garden for enjoying views of the Bauges massif, while in winter you can snuggle by the wood-burning stove in the salon. La Ferme is a 15-minute walk or two-minute drive south of town; follow the signs for Les Charmettes.

Château de Candie HISTORIC HOTEL €€€ (☑04 79 96 63 00; www.chateaudecandie.com; rue du Bois de Candie, Chambéry-le-Vieux; r €160-210; @🛇🗻) Landscaped grounds where ornate fountains trickle, old-world elegance in rooms with period furnishings, a swimming pool with dreamy mountain views and a Michelin-starred restaurant – this sublime 14th-century castle is a taste of the high life for mere mortals. To reach the château by car, take exit 15 on the N201 to Chambéry-le-Vieux.

Les Pervenches FAMILY HOTEL €€ (☑04 79 33 34 26; 600 chemin des Charmettes; r €65-85; 🛇🐾) In a quiet hamlet just 1km from the centre and 200m from Les Charmettes, Les Pervenches has nine cosy rooms with bucolic views of the hills. The restaurant, **Le Clos Normand** (menus €19-32), serves plenty of cheesy goodies but from a different part of France this time (the owners' native Normandy).

Art Hôtel HOTEL € (☑04 79 62 37 26; www.arthotel-chambery.com; 154 rue Sommeiller; s/d/tr €53/63/70; 🛇) There's nothing artistic about this hotel, with its flag-lined concrete facade, drab rooms or the rumble of trains. That said, it *is* well-run, cheap and central, located halfway between the town's centre and the train station.

🍴 Eating

Le Savoyard SAVOYARD CUISINE €€ (☑04 79 33 36 55; 35 place Monge; mains €13-20; ⊘Mon-Sat) The decor is resolutely non-alpine (urban design den rather than Savoyard chalet), but the menu is a wondrous selection of cheesy specialities. One fondue too many? Go for dishes like scallop risotto or steak with homemade *frites*.

Le Modesto Café BISTRO € (☑04 79 68 74 64; 58 rue Ste-Real; menus €12-14; ⊘Mon-Sat; 🛇) A cellar turned snazzy lounge-style bar and bistro, intimate Modesto pairs huge salads, *tartines* (open sandwiches) and tapas with full-bodied wines by the glass. It occasionally hosts events and DJ nights.

La Maniguette FUSION €€ (☑04 79 62 25 28; 103 rue Juiverie; mains €16, 3-course menus €30; ⊘Wed-Sat, lunch only Tue) Everything at this chic bistro goes the extra mile to add a dash of originality: the bread is home baked, the menu changes monthly and always adds a far-away twist to local flavours such as *magret de canard* (duck steaklet) with mango, polenta and Serrano ham.

L'Atelier INTERNATIONAL €€ (☑04 79 70 62 39; 59 rue de la République; menus €20-26) Soft light, tightly packed tables and mellow music set the scene in this contemporary bistro. The market-fresh menu changes daily and reveals Italian inflections in dishes like scallop risotto and veal osso bucco. There's a terrace for alfresco dining.

La Table de Marie TEA ROOM € (193 rue Croix d'Or; mains €10-15; ⊘closed Sun) This pocket-sized *salon de thé*, with prim, flowery decor, does lunchtime Savoyard specialities, but most locals go straight for dessert: scrumptious cakes and tarts, washed down with organic tea or hot chocolate.

Self-Catering

Chambéry's Saturday morning food market (on place du Palais de Justice until 2011 while the covered market on place de Genève gets some much-needed renovation) is a gastronome's rendezvous. Pedestrian rue du Sénat boasts butcher, baker and chocolate-maker shops.

Laiterie des Halles GOURMET FOOD €
(2 place de Genève; ⊙7.30am-12.15pm & 3-7.15pm Tue-Sat) Cheese fiends will go gaga at this dairy shop.

Monoprix SUPERMARKET €
(place du 8 Mai 1945) Stock up on groceries.

 Drinking

The huge square of place St-Léger is the summertime heart of Chambéry's drinking scene.

O'Cardinal's PUB
(5 place de la Métropole; ⊙10am-1.30am Tue-Sat, 5pm-1.30am Sun & Mon) Leather banquette seating, chipper staff and decent pub grub have turned this into Chambéry students' favourite pub. On warm days the cheer spills out onto cathedral-shaded place de la Métropole.

Le Café du Théâtre CAFÉ
(place du Théâtre; ⊙7am-1.30am; ☎) This tiny café, right next to Chambéry's 19th-century theatre, has a buzzy terrace for a cold beer, crêpe or ice cream. Students kick-start their evening here.

ℹ Information

Crédit Agricole (place du Château)

Crédit Lyonnais (26 bd de la Colonne)

Maison des Parcs et de la Montagne (www.maisondesparcsetdelamontagne.fr, in French; 256 rue de la République; ⊙10am-noon & 2-7pm Tue-Sat) Stocks information and exhibitions on the three local parks: national park La Vanoise, and regional parks Les Bauges and La Chartreuse.

Post office (11 place de l'Hôtel de Ville)

Tourist office (☎04 79 33 42 47; www.chambery-tourisme.com; 5bis place du Palais de Justice; ⊙9am-noon & 1.30-6pm Mon-Sat) Arranges guided old-town tours, including night visits, and has information on the local cheese and wine routes.

ℹ Getting There & Away

AIR There are no-frills flights to regional British airports including London Stansted, Manchester and Bristol from **Chambéry-Savoie Airport** (www.chambery-airport.com), 10km north of Chambéry in Viviers-du-Lac.

BUS From the **bus station** (place de la Gare) there are buses to/from local ski resort La Féclaz (€6, 50 minutes, four daily in winter) and Annecy (€6, one hour, seven daily). There are five daily buses to/from Grenoble (€12, 55 minutes).

TRAIN From Chambéry **train station** (place de la Gare) there are frequent trains to/from Paris Gare de Lyon (€93, four hours), Lyon (€16, 1½ hours), Annecy (€9, 50 minutes), Geneva (€15.50, 1½ hours) and Grenoble (€10.50, one hour). Nine daily trains run through the Maurienne Valley to Modane (€15, 1½ hours) and onwards into Italy. In town, buy tickets at the **SNCF Boutique** (21 place St-Léger).

ℹ Getting Around

TO/FROM THE AIRPORT Frustratingly, there are no bus services from Chambéry centre to the airport. The 15-minute journey by taxi costs around €20 – call **Allo Taxi Chambéry** (☎04 79 69 11 12). There are five daily buses to/from Geneva airport (€30, 1½ hours) and Lyon St-Exupéry airport (€22, one hour).

BICYCLE Pick up wheels for €2/10 per hour/day and advice on marked trails and itineraries from Vélo Station at the train station. The greater Chambéry area has 66km of cycling lanes.

BUS City buses run from 6am to around 8pm Monday to Saturday and are operated by **STAC** (www.bus-stac.fr, in French). A single ticket/24-hour pass/carnet of 10 costs €1.10/2.90/7.50. They are sold at tobacconists and the **STAC information kiosk** (23 bd du Musée). Buses 3, 5, 6, 7 and 9 link the train station with Fontaine des Éléphants.

Around Chambéry

PARC NATUREL RÉGIONAL DE CHARTREUSE

The Chartreuse Regional Nature Park (www.parc-chartreuse.net, in French) safeguards the wild forested slopes of the Chartreuse massif, dubbed the 'desert' by the Chartreux monks who settled here more than 1000 years ago. Since 1737 the monks have been producing a herbal liquor from a secret mix of 130 different herbs and plants.

The **park headquarters** (☑04 76 88 75 20; www.chartreuse-tourisme.com) in St-Pierre de Chartreuse, 40km south of Chambéry, has information on visiting the Voiron **distillery** where the liquor is produced, and the **Musée de la Grande Chartreuse** (www.musee-grande-chartreuse.fr; La Correrie, St-Pierre de Chartreuse; adult/child €6/2.50; ☺10am-6.30pm Feb-Oct), which explores the monastery's millennium-long history and the monks' reclusive lifestyle.

PARC NATUREL RÉGIONAL DU MASSIF DES BAUGES

Northeast, outdoor enthusiasts can delve into 800 sq km of hiking and biking opportunities in the little-known **Massif des Bauges Regional Nature Park** (www.parcdesbauges.com) with its endless pastures and plateaux. Several marked trails kick off from the **Maison Faune-Flore** (adult/child €2.50/1.50; ☺10am-12.30pm & 1.30-6.30pm Tue-Sun) in École, where you can learn how to spot some of the 600-odd chamois and plethora of mouflons inhabiting the park.

Chambéry's favourite weekend retreat for a little snow action is nearby **Savoie Grand Révard** (www.savoiegrandrevard.com). Downhill skiing is limited to 50km of pistes, but cross-country skiing is superb with 140km of trails to explore, as is snowshoeing with 60km of marked itineraries.

Tourist offices in **Le Revard** (☑04 79 54 01 60), **La Féclaz** (☑04 79 25 80 49) and **Le Châtelard** (☑04 79 54 84 28; www.lesbauges.com) – the main office in the park – have more information.

AIX-LES-BAINS
POP 27,920 / ELEV 234M

With its leafy shores, grand casino and villas, Aix-les-Bains, a small thermal spa 11km northwest of Chambéry, exudes an air of discreet gentility. Come to sail, swim, pedal-boat, stroll or skate around France's largest natural lake, **Lac du Bourget**.

Contact **Compagnie des Bateaux** (www.gwel.com; 9am-12.30pm & 2-6pm Mon-Fri) at the waterfront Grand Port or the **tourist office** (☑04 79 88 68 00; www.aixlesbains.com; place Maurice Mollard; ☺9am-12.30pm & 2-6.30pm Mon-Sat) in town about lake cruises. A one-hour cruise costs €9.50 and a return trip to the 12th-century **Abbaye d'Hautecombe** on the other side of the lake is €13.

DON'T MISS

TO THE MANOR BORN

What better way to wake up than in the 19th-century manor house **Château des Allues** (☑06 75 38 61 56; www.chateaudesallues.com; Les Allues, St-Pierre d'Albigny; d €120-180, dinner adult/child €42/25), slung high on a hill and proffering sweeping views of the Belledonne range. Painstakingly restored by Stéphane and Didier, the château oozes elegance and originality in five spacious, lavishly furnished rooms, many with four-poster beds, copper fireplaces and antiques.

Served at the family dining table, Stéphane's cooking makes excellent use of the herbs, vegetables and fruit that grow in the garden.

ALBERTVILLE
POP 18,680 / ELEV 328M

The main claim to fame of Albertville, an otherwise uninspiring town 39km east of Chambéry, is that it hosted the 1992 Winter Olympics. The highs and lows are colourfully retold at **Maison des Jeux Olympiques d'Hiver** (11 rue Pargoud; adult/family €3/8; ☺10am-noon & 2-6pm Mon-Sat).

Les Trois Vallées

This is the big one you've heard all about: vast, fast and the largest ski area in the world. The snow has never been hotter than in Les Trois Vallées. Some 600km of pistes and 174 lifts zip across three ritzy resorts: **Val Thorens**, Europe's highest at a heady 2300m; wealthy and ever-so-British **Méribel** (elevation 1450m), founded by Scotsman Colonel Peter Lindsay in 1938; and trendsetting **Courchevel**, which straddles three purpose-built resorts at 1550m, 1650m and 1850m, a fave of Victoria Beckham and the Gucci-shade, Moët-at-five brigade. In between is a sprinkling of lesser-known alpine villages – **Le Praz** (1300m), **St-Martin de Belleville** (1450m) and **La Tania** (1400m), linked by speedy lifts to their big-sister resorts.

🏃 Activities

Winter Activities

Les Trois Vallées appease the feistiest of outdoor-action appetites. Sunny Méribel is intermediate heaven, with 150km of cruisy (mostly blue and red) runs, 57 ski lifts, two snowboarding parks with jumps, pipes and rails, a slalom stadium and two Olympic runs.

In Courchevel there's another 150km of well-groomed pistes, including some knee-trembling black *couloirs* (steep gullies) for the brave, and excellent off-piste terrain. The 2km-long floodlit toboggan run through the forest is an adrenalin-pumping après-ski alternative.

Snow-sure Val Thorens, though smaller, proffers summer skiing on the Glacier de Péclet. The scenery unfolds slowly on 17km of winter walking and snowshoeing tracks and 100km of free cross-country trails. Save time queuing by buying your pass online at www.les3vallees.com.

Courchevel is big on alternative snow action, the key info point being La Croisette (place du Forum; ⊙8.30am-7pm) in Courchevel 1850, where the ESF (www.esfcourchevel.com) resides in winter and the Maison de la Montagne year-round. The latter takes bookings for guided off-piste adventures, snowshoeing and ski mountaineering and ice climbing, and is home to the Bureau des Guides (☑04 79 01 03 66; www.guides-courchevel-meribel.com).

Summer Activities

Summer lures outdoorsy types to Les Trois Vallées for rock climbing, paragliding, and hiking to peaks, wildflower-strewn pastures and topaz lakes in Parc National de la Vanoise. Clip onto vertigo-inducing **via ferrate** (fixed-cable mountain routes) in Méribel and Courchevel to flirt with mountaineering. The resorts are interlaced with hundreds of kilometres of circuits and downhill runs for **mountain bikers**; a trail guide is available at tourist offices.

In July and August Chardon Loisirs (☑04 79 08 39 60; www.chardonloisirs.com; La Croisette) takes you white-water rafting on the Doron de Belleville River for €40.

🎉 Festivals & Events

Altitude Festival COMEDY FESTIVAL
(www.altitudefestival.com) It's a laugh a minute at this Méribel festival in March,

a six-day shindig with stand-up comedy, DJs and concerts, which has previously welcomed the likes of Kate Tunstall and Al Murray.

X-Wing Rally BIKE RALLY
(www.les3vallees.com/xwing) Ride like a pro at Les Trois Vallées' open-slope rally in April.

Boarderweek SNOWBOARD EVENT
(www.boarderweek.com) Freestylers glide over to Val Thorens for competitions and parties in December.

🛏️ Sleeping & Eating

There are accommodation services in Courchevel (☑04 79 08 14 44), Méribel (☑04 79 00 50 00; www.meribel-reservations.com) and Val Thorens (☑04 79 00 01 06). Most hotels and restaurants close from May to mid-June and September through November.

TOP\CHOICE La Bouitte BOUTIQUE HOTEL €€€
(☑04 79 08 96 77; www.la-bouitte.com; St-Marcel; d €265-312; 2-/3-course menus €69/86, mains €50-100; 🖙) One word: wow. This Savoyard farmhouse, in warm wood and stone, invites lingering in its rustic-chic rooms and bubbly hot tub. The spa soothes with treatments like fragrant hay baths. René and Maxime Meilleur's fondness for alpine herbs and seasonal flavours shines through in their Michelin-starred restaurant and terrific cookery classes. La Bouitte is in St-Marcel, 1km south of St-Martin de Belleville.

Hôtel Les Arolles CHALET €€
(☑04 79 00 40 40; www.arolles.com; Méribel-Mottaret; r incl half board per person €130-160; ⛄) This huge mountain chalet gets rave reviews for its perfect ski-in, ski-out location and comfortable, if not fancy, rooms. Classic Savoyard cooking, a log fire burning in the lounge, an indoor pool and games room sweeten the deal.

Hôtel Olympic HOTEL €€
(☑04 79 08 08 24; www.courchevelolympic.com; rue des Tovets, Courchevel 1850; d €138-148; 🖙) You're just a joyous hop from the ski lifts at the Olympic. The bright, colourful rooms sport balconies and big bathtubs, though light sleepers should pack earplugs as noise travels. A generous breakfast fuels a day of slope-bashing fun, and there's a snug bar for après-ski chilling.

Every restaurant in the Alps worth its weight offers *raclette*, *tartiflette* or fondue. To save cents but maximise the cheese, opt for the DIY option; most dairy shops will lend you the required apparatus provided you buy their ingredients. Here's a 'how to' guide for your own cheese fest.

Fondue Savoyarde

Made with three types of cheeses in equal proportions (Emmental, Beaufort and Comté) and dry white wine (about 0.4L of wine for 1kg of cheese). Melt the mix in a cast-iron dish on a hob, then keep it warm with a small burner on the table. Dunk chunks of bread in the cheesy goo.

Our tip: rub or add garlic to the dish – you'll have cheesy breath anyway, so what the hell.

Raclette

Named after the Swiss cheese, *raclette* is a combination of melting cheese, boiled potatoes, charcuterie and baby gherkins. The home *raclette* kit is an oval hotplate with a grill underneath and dishes to melt slices of cheese.

Our tip: avoid a sticky mess by greasing and pre-heating your grill, and go easy on the ingredients (less is more).

Tartiflette

Easy-peasy. Slice a whole Reblochon cheese lengthwise into two rounds. In an ovenproof dish, mix together slices of parboiled potatoes, crème fraîche, onions and lardons (diced bacon). Whack the cheese halves on top, bake for about 40 minutes at 180°C, and ta-da!

Our tip: more crème fraîche and more lardons (a sprinkle of nutmeg is also good).

Le Doron   CHALET €€
(☑04 79 08 60 02; http://hoteldoron.mountain pub.com; rte de la Chaudanne, Méribel-Centre; s/d/tr €121/146/177) It's strictly no frills and set above a rowdy Brit-styled pub, but the crowds still flock to Le Doron for its raucous après-ski and direct access to the pistes. Opposite the tourist office.

Le Farçon   GASTRONOMIC €€
(☑04 79 08 80 34; www.lefarcon.fr; La Tania; lunch menus €25, other menus €36-95) At this forest retreat, Michelin-starred chef Julien Machet puts an imaginative spin on Savoyard dishes, with taste sensations like parmesan-pineapple chestnut soup and organic suckling pig with polenta on the menu. The three-course €25 skiers' lunch would barely buy you a pizza elsewhere.

La Fromagerie   BISTRO €€
(☑04 79 08 55 48; Méribel-Centre; menus €20-30; ☺dinner) Only the tangiest, creamiest alpine cheeses feature at this deli and bistro duo. Try Méribel's tastiest fondues and *raclette* in the rustic cellar. Book ahead.

Evolution   INTERNATIONAL €€
(☑04 79 00 44 26; www.evolutionmeribel.com; Méribel-Centre; mains €16-21, menu incl wine €25; ☜) A funky après-ski bar-cum-restaurant, Evolution is lauded for its monster-sized English breakfasts, Sunday roasts and well-spiced curries. Richard is the man behind the eclectic live music programme and the Altitude Festival in March.

🍸 Drinking & Entertainment

Pace yourself for champagne-sipping, boot-wiggling après-ski in see-and-be-seen Courchevel and party-mad Méribel. Most places are open only when the flakes are falling.

Rond Point   BAR
(www.rondpointmeribel.com; Méribel-Rond Point; ☺9am-7.30pm) Jostle for terrace space during happy hour from 4pm to 5pm, then shimmy in your ski boots to pumping live music between mouthfuls of chips and toffee vodka (hey, don't knock it until you've tried it) at what seasonaires fondly call 'the Ronnie'.

Jack's Bar   BAR
(www.jacksbarmeribel.com; Méribel-Centre; ☺noon-
2am; ☎) Jack's makes for one memorable
hangover, whether you come for the cool
drinks, the chatty staff or the cracking
events line-up – stand-up comedy, air guitar contests, toss-the-bottle Sundays, bring-
your-pants parties, you name it...

Some more favourites:

Le Kalico   BAR
(www.lekalico.com; Le Forum, Courchevel 1850;
☺9am-4am) Courchevel's affordable après-
ski king. Live music and themed parties
fuelled by bubblegum vodkas slide into
clubby nights where DJs play to tireless
revellers.

La Taverne   BAR
(www.tavernemeribel.com; Méribel-Centre;
☺8am-2am; ☎) Ski right up to the terrace, jam-packed with adrenalin junkies
talking legendary descents. Shooters and
lethal Jägermeister bombs complement
live music and big-screen sports.

Dick's Tea Bar   CLUB
(www.dicksteabar.com; rte de Mussillon, Méribel;
☺9pm-4am) Méribel's clubbing main-
stay rocks nightly to a stellar line-up of
DJs, including the Ministry of Sound's
Housexy tribe.

ℹ Information

Courchevel 1850 tourist office (☑04 79
08 00 29; www.courchevel.com; ☺9am-7pm)
Sister offices at 1650m, 1550m and 1300m.

Méribel tourist office (☑04 79 08 60 01;
www.meribel.net; Maison du Tourisme; ☺9am-
7pm)

Val Thorens tourist office (☑04 79 00 08 08;
www.valthorens.com; Maison de Val Thorens;
☺8.30am-7pm)

ℹ Getting There & Away

TO/FROM THE AIRPORT Frequent shuttle
buses link all three resorts with Geneva (€75, 3½
hours) and Lyon St-Exupéry (€68, three to four
hours) airports. There are also regular weekend
buses between Chambéry airport and Moûtiers
(€30, one hour), from where you can catch the
shuttles to the resorts.

BUS There are up to 12 regional buses daily between Moûtiers and Méribel (€10, 45 minutes),
Courchevel (€10, 40 to 60 minutes) and Val
Thorens (€10, one hour) with **Transdev Savoie**
(www.transavoie.com).

CAR & MOTORCYCLE The four-lane A43 links
Chambéry (78km west) with the nearest town,
Moûtiers, 18km north of Méribel. All ski resorts
are signposted as you approach Moûtiers.

TRAIN Moûtiers is the nearest train station,
with trains to/from Chambéry (€12.50, 1¼
hours) and TGVs galore to Paris between late
December and March (€74, 3½ hours). **Eurostar**
(www.eurostar.com) also operates direct trains
to/from London during the winter season (return
from €150, eight hours, overnight or day service,
weekends only).

Val d'Isère

POP 1730 / ELEV 1850M

Ask skiers why they loyally return year after year to Val d'Isère and watch their eyes
light up. For the awesome black runs and
off-piste, say many; for the party vibe and
dancing on the slopes, say some; because
'Val' is a *real* village with a heart and soul,
others tell you. Whatever the reason, they
all have one thing in common: one visit and
they were hooked.

Lac du Chevril looms large on the approach to Val d'Isère, located in the upper
Tarentaise Valley, 32km southeast of Bourg
St-Maurice. The turquoise reservoir lake
and its dam sidle up to Tignes (elevation
2100m), a purpose-built lakeside village
that – together with Val d'Isère – forms
the gargantuan Espace Killy skiing area,
named after home-grown triple Olympic
gold medallist Jean-Claude Killy. In February 2009 it staged the FIS World Alpine Skiing Championships.

🏃 Activities
Winter Activities

Espace Killy has mostly intermediate and
advanced skiing on 300km of pistes between 1550m and 3450m, miles of glorious
off-piste, and summer skiing on the Pissaillas and Grande Motte glaciers. Ski touring is also fabulous, especially in the Parc
National de la Vanoise. The snowboarders'
Snowspace Park in La Daille has a half-
pipe, tables, gaps, quarter-pipes and kicker
ramps, while Tignes' runs attract both
snowboarders and skiers.

Eschew skis in favour of snow-driven
alternatives like ice climbing, snowmo-
biling, mushing and winter paragliding. Floodlit airboarding and snake-gliss
sledging sessions are held four times a

PATRICK ZIMMER: FOUNDER OF TOP SKI

Patrick is an ex-downhill racer and founder of Top Ski, France's oldest independent ski school.

Absolute Beginners

When beginners arrive in Val d'Isère, they think, 'Oh my God, it's too steep', but Espace Killy has some scenic green and blue runs, like the vast, sunny Bellevarde plateau, with Mont Blanc views, and Leissières blue run near Pissaillas glacier. The free nursery slopes in Val Village are great for getting a feel for skiing.

Advanced Skiing

The Face Olympique de Bellevarde, used for World Cup events and the men's Olympic downhill, has fantastic views to Tignes and La Grande Motte [3656m]. It's so steep it's like diving into the village! Ski it first thing to get the morning sunshine. Forêt in Le Fornet is also good for a challenge.

Off-Piste

It all comes down to finding the best and safest snow conditions, so that's where experienced guides come in. Le Fornet to Grand Vallon, the Super L, and the Solaise classic Les Marmottes are just some of my favourites. Bellevarde has incredible off-piste terrain like the Spatule and near-vertical Banane.

When to Go

Between December and February is best for powder snow. The long days and snow crust from March to May make for great telemark ski touring in the stunning Parc National de la Vanoise. Come for summer skiing on the Pissaillas and Grande Motte glaciers.

week on the **Savonette** nursery slope opposite Val Village.

ESF SKI SCHOOL
(☏04 79 06 02 34; carrefour des Dolomites; www.esfvaldisere.com) In slope-side Val Village.

STVI LIFT PASSES
(www.stvi-valdisere.com, in French; ☺8.30am-7pm Mon-Fri & Sun, 8am-8pm Sat) Near ESF, sells lift passes. Unusually, beginner lifts opposite Val Village are free.

Top Ski SKI LESSONS
(☏04 79 06 14 80; www.topskival.com) France's first and highly regarded independent ski school, dating from 1976, arranges one-to-one and group tuition in on- and off-piste skiing, boarding, ski touring and snowshoeing with expert guides.

Summer Activities

The valleys and trails weaving from Val d'Isère into the nearby Parc National de la Vanoise beg outdoor escapades.

Bureau des Guides OUTDOOR ACTIVITIES
(☏06 14 62 90 24; www.guide-montagne-tarentaise.com) Be it hiking, mountain biking, canyoning or rock climbing, this office in the Killy Sport shop can arrange it.

Next door, the tourist office can give you details on family-friendly activities, from donkey trekking to farm visits.

🛏 Sleeping

Find out about availability and make reservations (essential in high season) through the **Centre de Réservation Hôtellerie** (☏04 79 06 18 90). For self-catering accommodation, contact **Val Location** (☏04 79 06 06 60). Prices vary widely, pricey being the common factor.

Hôtel L'Avancher CHALET €€
(☏04 79 06 02 00; http://avancher.com, in French; Val Village; s €90-170, d €170-206; ☏) The kind staff make you feel immediately welcome at this homey chalet, sheltering large pine-clad rooms with downy bedding. There's a small lounge with magazines, board games and a piano.

DON'T MISS

MILKY WAY

Part of Val d'Isère's charm is that it is a village with year-round residents. Claudine is one of them and she runs the delectable La Fermette de Claudine (www.lafermettedeclaudine. com, in French; Val Village), selling unpasteurised milk, wonderful cheeses and yoghurts. Her dairy farm La Ferme de l'Adroit, just 1km down the road in the direction of Col de l'Iseran, is open to the public and you can watch the morning cheese production (Tomme, Avalin, Beaufort) at 8.30am and afternoon milking at 5.30pm. All that dairy goodness lands on your plate in the form of deliciously gooey fondues and *raclette* at the neighbouring L'Étable d'Alain (☑04 79 06 13 02; www.fermedeladroit. com, in French; mains €22-29; ♣), an attractively converted stable where you can feast away while watching cudchewing cows in the adjacent barn. Book well ahead, especially if you want the popular 'cheese vat' table.

Chalet Hôtel Sorbiers   CHALET €€€
(☑04 79 06 23 77; www.hotelsorbiers-valdisere. com; Val Village; s/d/tr/q €190/258/369/388; ☎) A chalet in the traditional alpine mould, this place has a fire crackling in the salon in winter and a sunny garden in summer. The cosy, well-kept rooms have wood trappings, balconies and some even, ahhh..., jacuzzi bathtubs. Breakfast is the works, with fresh pastries, eggs and bacon.

Relais du Ski & La Bailletta   HOTEL €€
(☑04 79 06 02 06; http://lerelaisduski.valdisere.com; rte Fornet, Val Village; s/d/tr/q incl breakfast Relais €90/108/126/160, Bailletta €145/176/216/300; ☎) This hotel double act is a five-minute stroll from the centre. La Bailletta does comfortable midrange rooms while Relais du Ski has nine basic rooms with shared bathrooms. Both places share the buffet breakfast, which is a veritable feast.

✖ Eating
Supermarkets, patisseries and assorted snack stops line Val Village. In winter popular tables fill up fast and reservations

are recommended. Most places open daily from December to April and have limited hours the rest of the year; if in doubt, call ahead.

TOP\ La Fruitière   MODERN FRENCH €€
CHOICE (☑04 79 06 07 17; mains €20-25; ♥lunch) At the top of the La Daille bubble at 2400m, this piste-side oasis of fine dining is legendary. The creative cuisine is prepared with farm-fresh produce, paired with Grand Cru wines and served in a hip dairy setting. Save room for the Savoyard cheese plate. Snuggle under a blanket on the terrace to maximise those incredible mountain views.

L'Atelier d'Edmond   SAVOYARD CUISINE €€€
(☑04 79 00 00 82; Le Fornet; lunch mains €15-25, dinner menus €50-65; ♥closed dinner Sun & Mon) Candlelight bathes the stone walls, low beams and family heirlooms in this gorgeous chalet in Le Fornet, 2km east of Val Village. Locally sourced ingredients go into beautifully presented dishes like lobster and celery ravioli and flavoursome rack of lamb with garlic puree.

Wine Not   BISTRO €€
(☑04 79 00 48 97; Val Village; light meals €10-16) Bold colours, exposed stone and smooth contours make this wine bar Val's sleekest newcomer. Sizzling wok dishes, tapas sharing plates and salads are inspired by the 1st-class wine list, which does a Tour de France from the Rhône to Bordeaux.

Le Salon des Fous   CAFÉ €
(☑04 79 00 17 92; Val Village; sweets & snacks €2.50-10) With its bright-red benches and groovy lighting, this café is hip but never pretentious. Buttery smells waft from the kitchen, which rolls out homemade tarts, quiches, cakes and crêpes, plus an inventive selection of teas, like *la vie en rose* (vanilla, lemon and rose).

Bananas   INTERNATIONAL €€
(☑04 79 06 04 23; www.bananas.fr; Val Village; mains €14-22; ♥11.30am-2am; ☎) This ultracool après-ski shack at the bottom of La Face, behind the Bellevarde Express, dishes up calorie-loaded fare. Join ravenous skiers for Tex-Mex, cheeseburgers with extra cheese and sticky brownies.

♡ Drinking & Entertainment
Après ski in Val d'Isère is way up there with the craziest in the French Alps. Get hold of a copy of the free weekly *Mountain Echo*

magazine or *Valscope*, listing events and other organised fun. Here's our pick of the most happening bars:

La Folie Douce BAR
(www.lafoliedouce.com; Val Village; ⊙noon-5pm) If you can't wait to party until you're back in the village, DJs and live bands big it up every day on this outdoor terrace at the top of La Daille's cable car. Ibiza in the Alps.

Le Petit Danois BAR
(www.lepetitdanois.com; Val Village; ⊙8am-1.30am) Cheap beer, live music and lairy Swedes; thank God they serve full English breakfast the next morning to mop up the mess.

Dick's Tea Bar CLUB
(www.dicksteabar.com; Val Village; ⊙9am-4am) Val d'Isère's party HQ and the fabled home of the *vodka pomme* (apple vodka). Live music starts from 4.30pm; DJs follow later on in the night, all night.

Warm Up BAR
(www.warmupvaldisere.com; Val Village; ⊙11.30am-2am; 🐦) Oh the cosy retro sofas, the gingerbread, hot chocolate and crème brulée shooters, the free wi-fi, the pool table, the fun; it's the perfect après-ski spot..

Moris Pub PUB
(http://morispub.mountainpub.com; Val Village; ⊙4pm-2am) A buzzy British pub with happy hours, big-screen sports and almost nightly gigs – rock 'n' roll band Mullit regularly raises the roof.

ℹ Information

Tourist office (☑04 79 06 06 60; www.valdisere.com; place Jacques Mouflier; ⊙8.30am-7.30pm; 🐦) Internet access here costs €9 per hour or €5 for wi-fi.

ℹ Getting There & Away

TO/FROM THE AIRPORT In Bourg St-Maurice, you can connect to buses for Chambéry airport (one way/return €30/50, 1½ hours, weekend only). Other seasonal bus services include three or four daily to/from Geneva airport (one way/return €57/97, four hours) and two to five daily to/from Lyon St-Exupéry airport (one way/return €58/88, four hours). Advance reservations are essential.

BUS Six daily buses in season link Val d'Isère with Tignes (€3, 25 minutes) and Bourg St-Maurice train station (€10, 40 minutes). Tickets must be reserved 48 hours in advance at the **Boutique Autocars Martin** (☑04 79 06 00

42) on the main street in the resort centre. The SNCF desk here sells train tickets.

TRAIN Eurostar (www.eurostar.com) operates direct winter weekend services between Bourg St-Maurice and London (return from €180, eight hours, overnight or day service).

Parc National de la Vanoise

Rugged snowcapped peaks, mirrorlike lakes and vast glaciers are just the tip of the superlative iceberg in the 530-sq-km Parc National de la Vanoise (www.parcnational-vanoise.fr, in French), which fits neatly between the Tarentaise and Maurienne Valleys. This incredible swathe of wilderness was designated France's first national park in 1963. Five nature reserves and 28 villages border the highly protected core of the park where marmots, chamois and France's largest colony of alpine ibexes graze freely and undisturbed beneath the larch trees. Overhead, 20 pairs of golden eagles and the odd bearded vulture fly in solitary wonder.

A hiker's heaven, yes, although walking trails are only accessible for a fraction of the year – June to late September, usually. The Grand Tour de Haute Maurienne (www.hautemaurienne.com), a hike of five days or more around the upper reaches of the valley, takes in national-park highlights. The GR5 and GR55 cross it, and other trails snake south to the Park National des Écrins and east into Italy's Grand Paradiso National Park.

You can base yourself in Lanslebourg and Bonneval-sur-Arc, two pretty villages along the southern edge of the park. The Maison du Val Cénis (☑04 79 05 23 66; www.valcenis.com; ⊙9am-noon & 3-6pm Mon-Fri) in Lanslebourg, and Bonneval-sur-Arc's tourist office (☑04 79 05 95 95; www.bonneval-sur-arc.com; ⊙9am-noon & 2-6.30pm Mon-Sat) stock practical information on the walking, limited skiing (cross-country and downhill) and other activities in the park. In Termignon-la-Vanoise, 6km southwest of Lanslebourg, the tiny national-park-run Maison de la Vanoise (☑04 79 20 51 67; admission free; ⊙9am-noon & 2-5pm) portrays the park through ethnographical eyes.

ℹ Getting There & Away

CAR & MOTORCYCLE All three mountain passes linking the national park with Italy – the

Col du Petit St-Bernard, Col de l'Iseran and Col du Mont Cénis – are shut in winter.

TRAIN Trains serving the valley leave from Chambéry and run as far as Modane, 23km southwest of Lanslebourg, from where **Transdev Savoie** (www.transavoie.com) runs three to four daily buses to/from Termignon-la-Vanoise (€6, 40 minutes), Val Cénis-Lanslebourg (€10, 50 minutes) and Bonneval-sur-Arc (€10, 1¼ hours).

DAUPHINÉ

Apart from its celebrated *gratin dauphinois,* the Dauphiné's other big legacy to the French lexicon is historical. In 1339 Dauphiné ruler Humbert II established a university in Grenoble. A decade later, lacking money and a successor, he sold Dauphiné to the French king, Charles V, who started the tradition whereby the eldest son of the king of France (the crown prince) ruled Dauphiné and bore the title 'dauphin'.

Today, the Dauphiné refers to territories south and southwest of Savoy, stretching from the River Rhône in the west to the Italian border in the east. It includes the city of Grenoble and the mountainous Parc National des Écrins further east. The gentler terrain of western Dauphiné is typified by the Parc Naturel Régional du Vercors, much loved by cross-country skiers. In the east, the storybook town of Briançon stands sentinel on the Italian frontier.

Grenoble

POP 159,400 / ELEV 215M

With a dress-circle location overlooking the jagged mountains of the Parc Naturel Régional de Chartreuse and the Parc Naturel Régional du Vercors, Grenoble's backdrop is nothing short of extraordinary. That said, the city itself is not an instant heart-stealer with its tower blocks, run-of-the-mill hotels and traffic. Yet despite initial appearances, Grenoble rewards those who make the detour en route to the slopes – fine museums and restaurants, a quaint *quartier des Antiquaires* (Antiques quarter) and effervescent nightlife buoyed by some 60,000 students are all here for the taking.

◉ Sights

Many of Grenoble's museums are free on the first Sunday of the month.

TOP CHOICE **Musée de Grenoble** GALLERY
(Musée des Beaux-Arts; www.musee degrenoble.fr, in French; 5 place de Lavalette; adult/child €5/free; ◷10am-6.30pm Wed-Mon) The glass and steel facade of Grenoble's boldest museum occupies an entire block. Also called the Musée des Beaux-Arts, the museum is renowned for its distinguished modern collection, including star pieces by Chagall, Matisse, Canaletto, Monet and Picasso. The classic collection is equally impressive, spanning works from the 13th to 19th century.

Fort de la Bastille FORTRESS
(www.bastille-grenoble.com) Crowning a hillside above the River Isère, this 19th-century fort is Grenoble's most visible landmark. Built high and mighty to withstand invasions by the dukes of Savoy, the stronghold has long been a focus of military and political action.

Today it lures camera-toting crowds with its far-reaching views over Grenoble and the swiftly flowing River Isère to the peaks of the Vercors and, on cloud-free days, the snowy hump of Mont Blanc. Panels map out trails from gentle family walks to day hikes.

To get to the fort, hop aboard the riverside **Téléphérique Grenoble Bastille** (quai Stéphane Jay; adult/child one way €4.50/2.90, return €6.50/4.05; ◷Feb-Dec). The ascent in glass bubbles, which climb 264m from the quay, is almost more fun than the fort itself. Leave early to beat the queues in summer, or take a pleasant hour's walk uphill (half an hour down).

Magasin Centre National d'Art Contemporain ART GALLERY
(National Centre of Contemporary Art; www. magasin-cnac.org; 155 cours Berriat; adult/child €3.50/2; ◷2-7pm Tue-Sun) Ensconced in a cavernous glass and steel warehouse built by Gustave Eiffel, this is one of Europe's leading centres of contemporary art. A must-see for its architecture alone, the gallery plays host to cutting-edge exhibitions, many designed specifically for the space. Take tram A to Berriat-Le Magasin stop, about 2km west of the town centre.

FREE **Musée Dauphinois** REGIONAL MUSEUM
(www.musee-dauphinois.fr, in French; 30 rue Maurice Gignoux; ◷10am-7pm Wed-Mon) Atmospherically set in a 17th-century convent, this museum spells out alpine

cultures, crafts and traditions, and the region's skiing history. The museum is nestled at the foot of the hill below Fort de la Bastille.

FREE **Musée de l'Ancien Évêché**
HISTORY MUSEUM

(www.ancien-eveche-isere.fr, in French; 2 rue Très Cloîtres; ⏲9am-6pm Wed-Sat & Mon, 10am-7pm Sun, 1.30-6pm Tue) On place Notre Dame, the Italianate **Cathédrale Notre Dame** and adjoining 13th-century **Bishops' Palace** – originally home to Grenoble's bishops – form this museum. The rich collection traces local history from prehistory to the 21st century, and takes visitors beneath the cathedral square to a crypt safeguarding old Roman walls and a baptistery dating from the 4th to 10th centuries.

FREE **Musée de la Résistance et de la Déportation de l'Isère** HISTORY MUSEUM

(www.resistance-en-isere.fr, in French; 14 rue Hébert; ⏲9am-6pm Mon & Wed-Fri, 1.30-6pm Tue, 10am-6pm Sat & Sun) This emotive museum examines the deportation of Jews and other 'undesirables' from Grenoble to Nazi camps during WWII in a cool-headed way. It also zooms in on the role of the Vercors region in the French Resistance.

Activities

To jump lift-pass queues in Grenoble's surrounding ski resorts, buy your pass in advance from the tourist office or the *billetterie* (ticket office) inside **Fnac** (119 Grand Place; ⏲9.30am-8pm Mon-Sat).

Maison de la Montagne MOUNTAIN ACTIVITIES

(www.grenoble-montagne.com; 3 rue Raoul Blanchard; ⏲9.30am-12.30pm & 2-6pm Mon-Fri, 10am-1pm & 2-5pm Sat) Get the scoop on mountain activities around Grenoble – skiing, snowboarding, ice climbing, walking, mountain biking, rock climbing and more – here. The knowledgeable staff can help plan trips and treks with *refuge* stays, or book activities. It sells an excellent range of maps, walking books and topoguides, and runs a library that is free to consult. For walks around Grenoble, ask for the free SIPAVAG maps and itineraries.

Club Alpin Français de l'Isère ALPINE CLUB

(32 av Félix Viallet; www.clubalpin-grenoble. com, in French; ⏲2-6pm Tue & Wed, to 8pm Thu & Fri) Runs most of the *refuges* in the area and posts a list of activities in its window.

(www.guide-grenoble.com, in French; Maison de la Montagne) If it's a guide you're after, this outfit runs the whole gamut of summer and winter activities.

Tours

The tourist office organises imaginative thematic **walking tours** (€6-12.50), in French only, including a two-hour stroll in the footsteps of Grenoble-born novelist Stendhal, museums and various industry-focused tours. Those who'd rather go it alone can hire a two-hour MP3 audioguide (English available; €5) at the tourist office.

Festivals & Events

Grenoble Jazz Festival JAZZ FESTIVAL

(www.jazzgrenoble.com, in French) Jazz greats headline this March festival; MC2 is the venue for many concerts.

Vues d'en Face FILM FESTIVAL

(www.vuesdenface.com, in French) The rainbow flag flies high for this gay and lesbian film fest in April.

Cabaret Frappé MUSIC FESTIVAL

(www.cabaret-frappe.com, in French) Catch poolside concerts in July.

Festival des 38e Rugissants MUSIC FESTIVAL

(www.38rugissants.com) Nomadic beats in November.

Sleeping

Sleeping in Grenoble is a bit of a let-down. Though good value, hotels tend to be soulless and the reluctant preserve of passing business people. The tourist office has a list of *chambres d'hôte* in the area.

Patrick Hôtel MODERN HOTEL €€

(☎04 76 21 26 63; www.patrickhotel-grenoble. com; 116 cours de la Libération; s/d €89/99; ❄🛜) Streamlined and contemporary, the rooms here sport flatscreen TVs and free wi-fi. Rates drop by around 40% at weekends. The hotel is on a busy road 2km south of the centre (just off the A480) and has private parking.

Auberge de Jeunesse HOSTEL €

(☎04 76 09 33 52; www.fuaj.org, in French; 10 av du Grésivaudan; dm incl breakfast €19; @) Green, clean and ultramodern, Grenoble's eco-conscious hostel is set in parkland, 5km from the centre. The top-notch facilities include a bar, kitchen and sun deck. Take

Grenoble

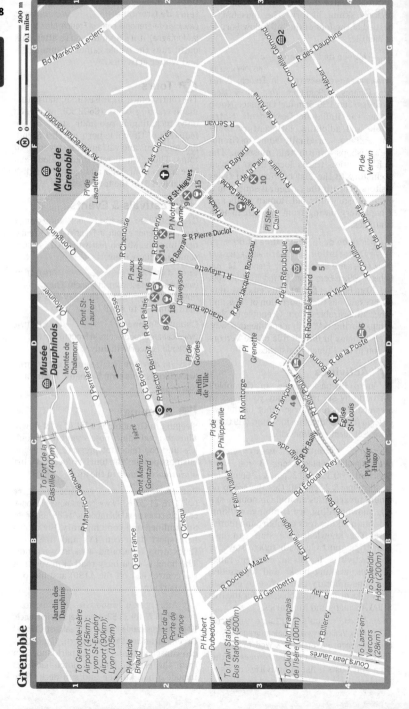

200 m
0.1 miles

bus 1 to La Quinzaine stop, from where the hostel is an easy two-minute walk (follow the signs). Alternatively, take tram A to La Rampe stop and walk east 15 minutes (roughly 1.5km).

Splendid Hôtel   HOTEL €€
(04 76 46 33 12; www.splendid-hotel.com; 22 rue Thiers; s €59, d €75-95; ﹡﹫) Colourful, fresh and jazzed up with funky paintings, this is a welcome break from Grenoble's dreary hotel scene. Some of the simple, cosy rooms have hydromassage showers and all have wi-fi. Take a seat in the leafy courtyard for a copious breakfast with fresh pastries and fruit.

Hôtel de l'Europe   HISTORIC HOTEL €
(04 76 46 16 94; www.hoteleurope.fr; 22 place Grenette; s €31-45, d €41-70) On Grenoble's liveliest square, this 17th-century haunt retains some charm. The snazzy hot-pink breakfast room and grand spiral staircase promise good things, making the rooms something of an anticlimax with their '70s-style wallpaper and postage-stamp bathrooms.

Hôtel de la Poste   SMALL HOTEL €
(04 76 46 67 25; 25 rue de la Poste; s/d/tr €39/47/60; ﹫) Beautifully renovated and oozing old-school charm, these rambling private rooms are a well-kept secret. Some have shared facilities, kept spotlessly clean. Best of all, you get use of the kitchen. Rooms B3 and B5 are top picks.

✗ Eating

Grenoble's most atmospheric bistros huddle down the backstreets of the *quartier des Antiquaires*. As Dauphiné capital, Grenoble is *the* place to sample *gratin dauphinois* (finely sliced potatoes oven-baked in cream and a pinch of nutmeg).

TOP CHOICE Chez Mémé Paulette   CAFÉ €
(04 76 51 38 85; 2 rue St-Hugues; snacks €3-5.50, plat du jour €8; ◔noon-midnight Tue-Sat) Mémé Paulette is an old curiosity shop of a café, crammed with antique books, milk jugs, cuckoo clocks and other eye-catching collectables. It draws a young, arty crowd with its boho vibe and wallet-friendly soul food, from chunky soups to *tartines* and homemade tarts.

Ciao a Te   ITALIAN €€
(04 76 42 54 41; 2 rue de la Paix; mains €15; ◔Tue-Sat, closed Aug) Stylish yet relaxed, Ciao dishes up authentic Italian cuisine: handmade pasta, crispy *panzerotti* (filled pastries), tender veal and the freshest seafood in town. It's a Grenoblois favourite, so book ahead.

L'Épicurien   MODERN FRENCH €€
(04 76 51 96 06; 1 place aux Herbes; menus €25-41) Chandeliers cast flattering light on the leather banquettes, exposed stone and twisting wrought-iron staircase of this chic split-level restaurant. An aperitif at the bar whets your appetite for flavours such as creamy *gratin dauphinois* and herb-crusted lamb.

Le Dix Vins
FUSION €€

(☑04 76 17 14 72; 4 rue de Belgrade; menus €17-38; ☺Mon-Sat; ☝) Pink, black and graced with floral motifs, this diva of a restaurant flaunts a menu as creative as its decor. Try the Dauphiné ravioli filled with gambas (a kind of shrimp) and coriander or the palate-cleansing strawberry and mint soup. There's a €7 kids' menu.

Café de la Table Ronde
BISTRO €€

(☑04 76 44 51 41; 7 place St-André; lunch menus €10, dinner menus €22-30; ☺9am-midnight; ☝) All hail this historic 1739 café, once the beloved haunt of Stendhal and Rousseau. Soak up the atmosphere on the square over regional fare like braised *diots* (mountain sausages) with *gratin dauphinois*, and nutty *tarte aux noix* (walnut tart).

La Peña Andaluza
TAPAS €€

(☑04 76 00 07 77; 3 rue du Palais; tapas €3.50-5.50, mains €17-20; ☺11.30am-1am) Salsa rhythms, moreish tapas and sangria bring southern Spanish pizzazz to Grenoble at this informal, mosaic-tiled bar.

La Fondue
FRENCH €€

(☑04 76 15 20 72; 5 rue Brocherie; fondue €17-20; ☺lunch Tue-Sat, dinner Mon-Sat) Gorge on so-smooth fondues laced with kirsch, Génépi and chartreuse or (double gorge) chocolate. An assortment of *raclettes* and *tartiflettes* completes the mountain cheese feast.

🍷 Drinking & Entertainment

Like every good student city, Grenoble does a mean party. Click onto French-language www.grenews.com and www.petit-bulletin.fr for details on what's happening. Here are a few places to get you started:

Le 365
WINE BAR

(3 rue Bayard; ☺Tue-Sat) If Dionysus (god of wine) had a house, this is surely what it would look like: an irresistible clutter of bottles, oil paintings and candles that create an ultrarelaxed setting for quaffing one of the wines on offer.

Le Tord Boyaux
WINE BAR

(4 rue Auguste Gaché; ☺6pm-2am) More than 30 flavoured wines, some of them quite extravagant (violet, chestnut, Génépi, fig), and a blind test every Tuesday night to see how many your taste buds can recognise.

Le Couche Tard
BAR

(1 rue du Palais) If you're too cool for school, check out the 'go to bed late', a grungy pub

that actively encourages you to graffiti its walls. The merrier you become during happy hour (until 10pm daily), the more imaginative those doodles become...

Styx
BAR

(6 place Claveyson; ☺1pm-2am Mon-Sat) Designer cocktails, DJs, soft red light and attitude by the shakerload. The terrace is a favourite hang-out on warm evenings.

MC2
THEATRE

(☑04 76 00 79 00; www.mc2grenoble.fr, in French; 4 rue Paul Claudel) Grenoble's most dynamic all-rounder for theatre, dance, opera, jazz and other music. It's 2km south of the centre on tram line A, stop MC2.

La Soupe aux Choux
JAZZ CLUB

(☑04 76 87 05 67; http://jazzalasoupe.free.fr, in French; 7 rte de Lyon; ☺Tue-Sat) Going strong for some 25 years, 'cabbage soup' stirs live jazz from swing to blues into Grenoble's after-dark mix. Find it a five-minute walk west of the Musée Dauphinois.

❶ Information

Wi-fi is widely available at hotels, cafés and bars in Grenoble; the tourist office has a list of free hot-spots.

Celsius Café (15 rue Jean-Jacques Rousseau; internet per 30/60min €1.50/2.50; ☺9am-8pm, closed Sat morning, Mon; 🛜) Top location and facilities.

Cyber Phone (2bis rue Très-Cloîtres; internet per 15/60min €0.50/2) Speedy internet and discount calls.

Duty pharmacy (☑04 76 63 42 55)

Grenoble University Hospital (☑04 76 76 75 75) Hôpital Nord La Tronche (av de Marquis du Grésivaudan; La Tronche tram stop); Hôpital Sud (av de Kimberley, Échirolles; bus 11 or 13).

Post office (rue de la République) Next to the tourist office.

Tourist office (☑04 76 42 41 41; www.grenoble-tourisme.com; 14 rue de la République; ☺9am-6.30pm Mon-Sat, 10am-1pm & 2-5pm Sun) Inside the Maison du Tourisme. Sells maps and guides, arranges city tours.

❶ Getting There & Away

AIR A clutch of budget airlines, including Ryanair and easyJet, fly between **Grenoble-Isère Airport** (www.grenoble-airport.com), 45km northwest of Grenoble, and London, Glasgow, Stockholm and Warsaw, among others.

BUS The **bus station** (rue Émile Gueymard), next to the train station, is the main terminus for bus companies, including **VFD** (www.vfd.

fr, in French) and **Transisère** (www.transisere. fr, in French). There are several services daily to Geneva airport (€43, 2½ hours), Lyon St-Exupéry airport (€22, one hour), Chamrousse (€3.20, 1¼ hours), Bourg d'Oisans (€6, 50 minutes), Les Deux Alpes (€5.50, 1¾ hours) and Briançon (€29, 2½ hours). **Eurolines** (www.eurolines.com) handles international destinations.

CAR & MOTORCYCLE Grenoble is well connected to motorways including the A48 (Lyon), A41 (Chambéry, Annecy) and the A51 (Marseille). Major car-hire agencies are in the Europole complex underneath the train station.

TRAIN From the **train station** (rue Émile Gueymard), trains run frequently to/from Paris Gare de Lyon (from €76, 3½ hours), Chambéry (€10.50, one hour) and Lyon (€19, 1½ hours). Train tickets are sold at the station and in town at the **SNCF boutique** (15 rue de la République).

ℹ Getting Around

TO/FROM THE AIRPORT Shuttle buses run by **Grenoble Altitude** (http://grenoble-altitude. com) go to/from Grenoble-Isère Airport and the bus station (one way/return €12.50/22, 45 minutes, twice daily on Tuesday and Saturday).

BICYCLE Underneath the train station, **Métrovélo** (www.metrovelo.fr) rents out bikes for €3/5 per half-/full day. Helmets, child's seat and locks are free. You'll need ID and €50 deposit per bike.

BUS & TRAM Grenoble's four ecofriendly tram lines – A, B, C and D – trundle through the heart of town. A single-trip bus and tram ticket costs €1.40 from ticket machines or drivers. Before boarding, time-stamp your ticket in the blue machines at stops. *Carnets* of 10 tickets (€11.50) and day passes (€3.90) can only be bought at TAG inside the tourist office or next to the train station. Trams run from around 5am to 1am; bus services run until 6pm or 9pm.

CAR & MOTORCYCLE Grenoble is tricky to negotiate because of its bewildering one-way system, disorientating tram network and expensive, limited parking. Your best bet is to head to one of the 13 **P+R** (www.semitag.com, in French) on the outskirts of town, which cost €2 to €3 per day and include a free return tram or bus ride for you and your passengers.

Around Grenoble

Grenoble's high-altitude surrounds lure urbanites craving a weekend snow fix. The vast Vercors plateau is laced with a cool 1000km of cross-country trails, many weaving through snow-dusted forests. Affording sweeping views of the rugged Belledonne massif, Chamrousse (elevation

1700m) attracts families with its beginner-level downhill in winter and gentle hikes through marmot-dotted pastures in summer. The tourist office (☑04 76 89 92 65 www.chamrousse.com; 42 place de Belledonne) has the full lowdown.

Several daily buses link Grenoble with the surrounding resorts (see those sections for details), including Chamrousse (€3.20, 1¼ hours). For day trippers, the Skiligne buses operated by Transisère to 11 different ski resorts in the region are a good deal; rates (from €23 in Chamrousse and Villard de Lans to €37 for Les Deux Alpes and Alpe d'Huez) include a one-day ski pass and return bus fare.

PARC NATUREL RÉGIONAL DU VERCORS

The gently rolling pastures, plateaus and chiselled limestone peaks of this 1750-sq-km nature park, southwest of Grenoble, are great for soft adventure. Quieter and cheaper than neighbouring alpine resorts, the wildlife-rich park is a magnet to families seeking fresh air and activities like cross-country skiing, snowshoeing, caving and hiking.

From pristine, wooded Lans-en-Vercors (elevation 1020m) 28km southwest of Grenoble, buses shuttle downhill skiers 4km east to its 24km Montagnes de Lans ski area. The postcard-perfect village of Villard de Lans (elevation 1050m), 9km up the valley, is linked by ski lifts to Villard-Corrençon for 130km of winter-wonderland downhill pistes at melting prices (€30 for a day). For more snowy fun, the Colline des Bains (1/3hr pass €9/12), in Villard de Lans, comprises six sledging tracks: pick your vehicle (solo sledge, rubber ring or bobsleigh) to whiz down.

Villard de Lans' tourist office (www.villarddelans.com; place Mure Ravaud) has an online service for booking hotels, farmstays and *chambres d'hôte*, and should be your first port of call for activities from canyoning to mountain biking in the Vercors.

Les Accompagnateurs Nature et Patrimoine (☑04 76 95 08 38; www. accompagnateur-vercors.com) allows you to get in tune with nature on half-day (adult/child €15/13) and day walks (adult/child €21/26), with knowledgeable guides who can point out alpine wildflowers and animals from marmots to chamois.

WORTH A TRIP

GREAT ESCAPES

The Vercors has some dreamy chalets and back-to-nature farmhouses. These three are among our favourite escapes; see their websites for maps and details of how to get there.

Les Allières (☎04 76 94 32 32; www.aubergedesallieres.com, in French; Lans-en-Vercors; half board per person €45, mains €16-25). This 1476m-high forest chalet offers no-frills digs (bunk beds, shared toilets) and wondrous mountain food. The wood-fire *raclette* and *tarte aux myrtilles* (blueberry tart) are divine.

À la Crécia (☎04 76 95 46 98; www.gite-en-vercors.com, in French; 436 Chemin des Cléments, Lans-en-Vercors; s/d/tr/q €52/57/72/87, dinners €17; ⊛) Goats, pigs and poultry rule the roost at this 16th-century, solar-powered farm, authentically renovated by Véronique and Pascal. Rooms are stylishly rustic with beams, earthy hues and mosaic bathrooms. Dinner is a feast of farm-fresh produce.

Gîte La Verne (☎04 76 95 21 18; http://gite.laverne.free.fr, in French; La Verne, Méaudre; apt for 4/8 people per week €500/750) Fitted with fully equipped kitchens, this *gîte's* beautiful apartments blend alpine cosiness with mod cons. Whether you opt for self-catering or half board, you'll enjoy the hammam and outdoor Norwegian bath as well as owner Edwige's wonderful hospitality.

❶ Getting There & Away

Up to seven **Transisère** (http://transisere.altibus .com) buses daily link Grenoble with Lans-en-Vercors (€4.30, 45 minutes), Villard de Lans (€4.30, one hour) and Correncon-en-Vercors (€4.30, 1¼ hours).

PARC NATIONAL DES ÉCRINS

No amount of hyperbole about towering peaks, shimmering cirque lakes and wispy falls can quite do justice to the wild Parc National des Écrins (www.les-ecrins-parc -national.fr, in French). Created in 1973, this is France's second-largest national park (918 sq km). Stretching between the towns of Bourg d'Oisans, Briançon and Gap, the area is enclosed by steep, narrow valleys, and sculpted by the Romanche, Durance and Drac rivers and their erstwhile glaciers. It peaks at 4102m with the arrow-shaped Barre des Écrins, a mythical summit for mountaineers.

Bourg d'Oisans, 53km southeast of Grenoble, and Briançon, another 67km in the same direction, are good bases for exploring the park.

BOURG D'OISANS
ELEV 720M

◉ Sights & Activities

Age-old footpaths used by shepherds and smugglers centuries before – 700km in all – criss-cross the national park, making it prime hiking territory. A gateway to several vertiginous mountain passes, Bourg d'Oisans is also a mountain-biking mecca. Check out www.bikes-oisans.com for details on trails, maps and bike hire. Kayaking along the Drac's turquoise waters, rock climbing, *via ferrate* and paragliding are other activities; tourist and park offices have details.

Musée des Minéraux et de la Faune des Alpes MUSEUM
(place de l'Église, Bourg d'Oisans; adult/child €4.60/2; ⊙2-6pm Wed-Mon) Bone up on the national park's fascinating geology, flora and fauna, including ibex and chamois, at this nature-savvy museum.

Chemin de Fer de la Mure TRAIN RIDE
(www.trainlamure.com; adult/child return €19.20 /9.70; ⊙2-4 departures daily Apr-Oct) In summer you can mammal-spot amid spectacular scenery from the window of this pillar-box-red 1920s mountain train. It chugs 30km (1¾ hours) between St-Georges de Commiers and La Mure, burrowing through tunnels, skirting sheer cliffs and traversing viaducts.

🛏 Sleeping & Eating

The tourist office in Bourg d'Oisans knows about *gîtes d'étape* (walkers' guesthouses) open year-round.

Au Fil des Saisons B&B €
(☎04 76 30 07 01; www.chambresdhotes -afs.com, in French; Ferme du Cros, Les Côtes

de Corps; s/d €50/60; 🅿) Dany and Domi extend a heartfelt welcome at this lovingly converted 1731 mountain farm with beamed and vaulted ceilings. Breakfast is a wholesome spread with organic homemade bread and honey, and farm-fresh cheese. Kids love Hôtesse the draft horse. Find the Ferme du Cros 2km from Corps in Les Côtes de Corps; follow the southbound N85 from Grenoble. Advance reservations essential.

La Cascade   CAMPGROUND €
(📷04 76 80 02 42; www.lacascadesarenne.com; rte de l'Alpe d'Huez; sites €14-26; ⊙mid-Dec–Sep; 🅿) A tree-shaded campground 1.5km from the centre of Bourg d'Oisans.

Le Colporteur   CAMPGROUND €
(📷04 76 79 11 44; www.camping-colporteur. com; Le Mas de Plan; sites €18-25; ⊙mid-May–mid-Sep, 🅿🅿) Well-equipped campground with a restaurant-bar, a two-second hop from Bourg d'Oisans.

ℹ Information

Maison du Parc (rue Gambetta, Bourg d'Oisans; ⊙9-11.30am & 2-5pm Mon-Thu, 9-11am Fri) Sells maps and guides.

Oisans (www.tourisme-oisans.com) An excellent source of information on the area, with accommodation and activities listings.

Tourist office (www.bourgdoisans.com, Bourg d'Oisans; quai Girard; ⊙9am-noon & 2-6pm Mon-Sat, 9-11am Sun)

ℹ Getting There & Away

From Bourg d'Oisans **bus station** (av de la Gare), there are two or three buses daily to/from Briançon (€14.50, 1¾ hours), Les Deux Alpes (€2.10, 40 minutes) and Alpe d'Huez (€2.10, 40 minutes), and up to eight daily to/from Grenoble (€6, 50 minutes).

LES DEUX ALPES
ELEV 1600M

Year-round skiing on the 3200m- to 3425m-high Glacier du Mont de Lans, glorious powder for off-piste fans, challenging terrain parks and a party to rival anywhere in the French Alps – Les Deux Alpes, once two humble farming villages, is now a buzzing resort with altitude, located 19km southeast of Bourg d'Oisans.

Freeriders come from far and wide to tackle the breathtaking, near-vertical Vallons de la Meije descent in La Grave (www. la-grave.com), 21km east. The stuff of myth, the run plummets 2150m and is strictly for the crème de la crème of off-piste riders.

⊙ Sights

Grotte de Glace   ICE CAVE
(Ice Cave; admission €4; ⊙10am-3pm) Ice sculptures of metre-tall animals, alpine flowers and shepherds glisten in this ice cave, carved into the Glacier du Mont de Lans at Dôme de Puy Salié (3425m). To reach it, ride the Jandri Express *télécabine* to 3200m and then the Funiculaire Dôme Express to 3400m. Allow an hour to get there. A ticket covering cable cars and cave entry costs €25.

La Croisière Blanche   SCENIC RIDE
(The White Cruise; per ride €7; ⊙10.30am-3pm Sun-Fri) Take a panoramic 50-minute ride on this caterpillar-track minibus. Though undeniably gimmicky, it does allow nonskiers to tickle the summit at 3600m and enjoy 360-degree views. Wrap up for subzero temperatures. Cruise plus cable cars plus ice cave costs €32. You *must* book before you head off.

🏃 Activities

Les Deux Alpes pounds the powder on 225km of pistes and a 2600m-high **snowpark** (www.2alpes-snowpark.com) with an 800m-long axe pipe, 120m-long half-pipe, and numerous jumps as well as technical courses along cornice drops, canyons and corridors in the 'slide' zone. The main skiing domain lies below La Meije (3983m), one of the highest peaks in the Parc National des Écrins. Riders wanting to access La Grave from Les Deux Alpes are pulled by a snowcat from the top of the Dôme Express Funicular (⊙8am-5pm late Nov–Apr, 7am-1pm mid-Jun–Aug). In winter, use of the funicular is included in the cost of your ski pass (see p466); a day pass in summer costs €33.50.

Skiing and boarding aside, snow fiends can dart around the open-air rink (resort centre, rue des Sagnes; €3.50; ⊙3-6.30pm & 8.30-10.30pm mid-Jun–Aug & late Nov–Apr, ice-gliding Thu afternoon & Fri evening winter, Wed evening & Thu afternoon summer) in an ice-glider (dodgems on ice) or go on a snowmobile *(motoneige)* expedition. Contact the Bureau des Guides for organised ice climbing, snowshoeing and off-piste skiing in winter, and rock climbing, canyoning and biking expeditions in summer.

The glacier has Europe's largest **summer skiing** area, set against the majestic backdrop of Mont Blanc, Massif Central and Mont Ventoux; the season runs from mid-June to late August. Otherwise there are 26 nail-biting descents and five cross-country trails for mountain bikers, numerous hiking trails and plenty of opportunities for paragliding.

🛏 Sleeping & Eating

Hotels and restaurants go with the seasons, most opening from December to April and mid-June to August.

Hotel Côte Brune FAMILY HOTEL €€
(☑04 76 80 54 89; www.hotel-cotebrune.com; 6 rue Côte Brune; d incl half board €164-184; 🕿🏠) Ski in and out of this slope-side hotel. The homely pine-panelled rooms radiate alpine charm and come with south-facing balconies; some are geared up for families. Nurse drinks by an open fire or on the terrace before a delicious three-course dinner.

Hotel Serre-Palas CHALET €
(☑04 76 80 56 33; www.hotelserre-palas.fr; 13 place de Venosc; d incl breakfast €70-106) For bright, quiet rooms and marvellous mountain views, you can't beat this spick-and-span chalet. Lionel, your affable host, is a ski instructor and can give you plenty of insider tips.

Le P'tit Polyte GASTRONOMIC €€
(☑04 76 80 56 90; www.chalet-mounier.com; Chalet Mounier, 2 rue de la Chapelle; menus €40-63) The panorama is as every bit as sublime as the food at this refined Michelin-starred restaurant. Inventive specialities, such as gingerbread-encrusted scallops with chicory-arabica remoulade, are presented with flair and married with one of 800 wines. Reservations are essential.

🍷 Drinking

Les Deux Alpes has a well-deserved reputation for raucous après-ski parties. The resort's flurry of bars includes these two favourites:

Smokey Joe's BAR
(www.smokeyjoes.fr; @) Live après-ski music, spicy Tex-Mex food and shot slamming are bound to get you grooving in your snow boots at this postslopes hangout at the base of Jandri gondola. There are guest DJs, big-screen sports and themed parties aplenty.

Smithy's BAR
(www.smithystavern.com; 7 rue de Cairou) Vodka, fajitas and nachos, more vodka – that's the scene at this rocking chalet with a long

bar for lining 'em up. Smithy's hosts gigs, DJ nights and head-spinning parties.

ℹ Information

Maison des Deux Alpes (place des Deux Alpes) is the key source: inside you'll find the **tourist office** (☑04 76 79 22 00; www.les2alpes.com; ⊙8am-7pm), **accommodation service** (☑04 76 79 24 38; www.les2alpesreservation.com), **ESF** (☑04 76 79 21 21; www.esf2alpes.com) and the **Bureau des Guides** (☑04 76 11 36 29; www.guides2alpes.com, in French).

ℹ Getting There & Away

Transisère buses link Grenoble and Les Deux Alpes (€5.50, 1¾ hours, up to 10 daily) via Bourg d'Oisans; return journeys to Grenoble must be booked 72 hours in advance in Les Deux Alpes at **Agence Transisère VFD** (112 av de la Muzelle). There are also services to/from Lyon St-Exupéry airport (one-way/return €32/48, 3½ hours).

ALPE D'HUEZ
ELEV 1860M

Number of hairpin bends: 21. Length: 14km. Average slope gradient: 7.9%. Record time: 37 minutes 35 seconds. Portrait of a mythical *étape* of the Tour de France between Bourg d'Oisans and Alpe d'Huez, a purpose-built resort in the Massif des Grandes Rousses.

🏃 Activities

Apart from legendary cycling, Alpe d'Huez has 245km of groomed pistes that range from dead easy to death-defying; at 16km the breathtakingly sheer **La Sarenne**, accessible from the Pic Blanc cable car, is Europe's longest black run. Experienced skiers can also ski in July and August on glaciers ranging from 2530m to 3330m. Speed is of the essence here and one look at the piste map confirms it's mighty black and hairy out there...

Pic du Lac Blanc (3330m), the highest point accessible year-round by the Tronçons and Pic Blanc **cable cars** (return €14.50; ⊙9am-5pm Jul-Aug & Dec-Apr), commands magical views that reach across the rippling French Alps all the way to neighbouring Italy and Switzerland.

Summer unveils mountains threaded through with marked hiking and biking trails.

🛏 Sleeping & Eating

Le Printemps de Juliette CHALET €€
(☑04 76 11 44 38; www.leprintempsdejuliette.com; av des Jeux; d €125-165; 🕿) View the

world through rose-tinted specs at Juliette's very pretty, very *pink* chalet, where vintage teddies and dolls outnumber the guests. It's pastel and floral overload in the spotlessly clean rooms and the *salon de thé*, where you can sip tea and nibble homemade cakes by the fire.

Le Passe Montagne   TRADITIONAL FRENCH €€
(☑04 76 11 31 53; rte de la Poste; mains €15-25) This stylish wooden chalet has service as smooth as its fondue Savoyarde. An open fire burns in the beamed dining room, the place for a tête-á-tête over a juicy rump steak with morels and Roquefort or oxtail in a rich Madeira wine sauce.

❶ Information

Information hub **Maison de l'Alpe** (place Pagánon) sells ski passes and houses the helpful **tourist office** (☑04 76 11 44 44; www. alpedhuez.com; ☺9am-7pm), **accommodation reservation centre** (☑04 76 80 90 00; www. alpe-vacances.com) and **ESF** (☑04 76 80 31 69; www.esf-alpedhuez.com).

❶ Getting There & Away

Transisère buses link Alpe d'Huez and Grenoble (€5.50, 1¾ hours, up to 10 daily) via Bourg d'Oisans. In winter there is also a frequent ski bus that runs to and from Geneva Airport (€51, 2½ hours).

Briançon

POP 11,950 / ELEV 1320M

No matter whether you come by bus or car, it's a long, long way to Briançon, but it's worth every horn-tooting, head-spinning, glacier-gawping minute. The road from Grenoble is pure drama and not just because of the scenery; the locals adopt a nonchalant attitude to driving, the general consensus being: overtaking on hairpin bends, *pas de problème*! But brave it behind the wheel and you'll be richly rewarded with views of thundering falls, sheer cliffs and jagged peaks razoring above thick larch forests.

All of this is the drum roll to Briançon. Perched high on a hill and straight out of a fairy tale, the walled old town affords views of soaring Vauban fortifications and the snowcapped Écrins peaks on almost every corner. The centre's Italian look and feel is no coincidence – Italy is just another dizzying 20km away.

◉ Sights

TOP CHOICE **Vauban Fortifications** FORTIFICATIONS Briançon's biggest drawcard is its extensive 17th- and early-18th-century Vauban heritage, including the old town's signature star-shaped fortifications, surrounding forts (Fort des Têtes, Fort des Salettes, Fort du Dauphin and Fort du Randouillet) and bridge (Pont d'Asfeld). This architectural ensemble was listed as a Unesco World Heritage Site in 2008, a belated recognition of the pioneering genius of this engineer.

Vieille Ville   HISTORIC QUARTER
Sitting astride a rocky outcrop and surrounded by mighty ramparts, Briançon's old town is a late-medieval time capsule, its winding cobbled lanes punctuated by shuttered town-houses in candy colours and shops selling won't-stop-whistling marmots.

The main street is the steep Grande Rue, also known as **Grande Gargouille** (Great Gargoyle) because of its gushing rivulet. It links the two main gates, **Porte de Pignerol** in the north, just off the Champ de Mars, and **Porte d'Embrun** lower down, at the top of av de la République. The coral-pink **Collégiale Notre Dame et St Nicolas** (place du Temple), another of Vauban's works, is worth a look for its baroque painting.

Fort du Château   FORT
Crowning the old city is the slumbering Fort du Château, affording magnificent mountain views from its battlements. If you can't face the hike up, av Vauban along the town's northern ramparts affords equally spectacular views of the snowy Écrins peaks.

⚡ Activities

Serre Chevalier (www.serre-chevalier-ski.com) ski region, properly called Le Grand Serre Chevalier, links 13 villages and 250km of piste along the Serre Chevalier Valley between Briançon and Le Monêtier-les-Bains, 15km northwest.

The tourist office hands out the excellent booklet *Guide des Itinéraires dans la Vallée de Serre Chevalier* (in French) detailing cultural walks and snowshoeing itineraries for those not so keen on skiing.

Télécabine du Prorel   FUNICULAR
(av René Froger; day pass winter €41.50, adult/ child return summer €11.50/9; ☺9am-5.30pm

DON'T MISS

GREEN HIDEAWAY

Ringed by the majestic peaks of the Écrins National Park, hilltop La Juliane (☑04 92 23 47 49; www.lajuliane.com; Le Martouret, Pelvoux; dm/d €19/52, incl half board €40/91; 🖪) is a sublime chalet built out of larch logs and dry stone. It is also a shining example of responsible tourism, with solar panels, a windmill, a micro-hydroelectric turbine and hemp insulation. Despite this rustic-sounding set-up, rooms are wonderfully cosy and owner Jean-Claude prepares delicious (mostly organic) food.

For energetic types, snowshoeing, skiing, hiking, climbing and mountain biking are available locally. Jean-Claude also runs wild-plant-picking and cooking courses in the spring.

La Juliane is 25km southwest of Briançon in Vallée de la Vallouise: from Pelvoux-le-Saret turn right on rte de l'Eychauda. Drive 500m up the hill until you reach a car park. From there, La Juliane is signposted up a small path. Jean-Claude can pick up luggage and young children by 4WD.

---

mid-Dec–Apr & Jul-Aug) It takes just a few minutes to reach the slopes from the Briançon-Serre Chevalier station at 1200m in Briançon's lower town.

École du Ski Français SKIING
(☑04 92 20 30 57; www.esf-serrechevalier.com, in French; 7 av René Froger; ⊗8.45am-6pm Dec-Apr) ESF runs a seasonal office inside the Prorel cable-car station.

Bureau des Guides et Accompagnateurs OUTDOOR ACTIVITIES
(☑04 92 20 15 73; www.guides-briancon.fr, in French; Central Parc; ⊗10.30am-noon & 4-7pm Jul-Aug, 4-7pm Sep-Jun) Organises the usual off-piste outings alongside treks, paragliding, rafting, cycling, canyoning and *via ferrate* in summer.

Maison du Parc WALKS
(place du Médecin Général Blanchard; ⊗2-6pm Mon-Fri) Nip in here for information and maps on walking in the nearby Écrins national park.

👉 Tours

Service du Patrimoine TOWN WALKS
(☑04 92 20 29 49; Porte de Pignerol; ⊗9.30am-noon & 2-5.30pm Mon-Fri) Tucked away in one of the old town's city gates, this organisation offers guided old-town walks (€5.50 in French, €6.50 in English, 1½ hours).

🛏 Sleeping

The tourist-office-run accommodation service, Briançon Réservation (☑04 92 21 01 01), can help you find a bed. Hotel parking in the pedestrian old town is a headache, so park along the ramparts and walk. Many places close in the shoulder seasons.

Auberge de la Paix HISTORIC HOTEL €€
(☑04 92 21 37 43; www.auberge-de-la-paix.com; 3 rue Porte Méane; s €62-73, d €71-86, menus €26; 🖃) Squirreled away in an old-town backstreet, this is Briançon's oldest hotel, dating from 1845. While the creaky wooden floors remain, the rooms have been totally revamped, the best flaunting groovy pebble bathtubs and flatscreen TVs. The kitsch mock-cave restaurant dishes up regional comfort food.

Hôtel de la Chaussée TRADITIONAL HOTEL €
(☑04 92 21 10 37; www.hotel-de-la-chaussee. com; 4 rue Centrale; r €65-78) The Bonnafoux family has run this place with charm and efficiency since 1892. The renovated rooms fulfil every alpine chalet fantasy: wooden-clad, beautifully furnished, subtly scented and oh so cosy. The restaurant downstairs follows suit and serves a Vauban *menu*.

Auberge de Jeunesse Serre Chevalier HOSTEL €
(☑04 92 24 74 54; www.fuaj.org, in French; Le Bez, Serre Chevalier 1400; dm incl breakfast €13.50; 🖃) Eight kilometres northwest at Serre Chevalier-le-Bez, this hostel is right at the foot of the pistes. It's all very collective (big dorms, big canteen, big parties) and friendly. Take a bus heading to Monêtier-les-Bains, get off at Villeneuve Pré Long and walk 500m.

🍴 Eating

Briançon is milking the Vauban heritage in every possible way, and that includes eating. Five restaurants across town have agreed on a cartel of Vauban menus: no one is allowed to copy the others' recipes of 17th-century fare (think pigeon, rabbit stews and never-heard-of legumes). The tourist office has a list of participating venues.

Le Valentin
REGIONAL CUISINE €€

(📞04 92 21 37 72; www.levalentin.fr; 6 rue de la Mercerie; menus €17.50-32; ⊘dinner Tue-Sun year-round, also lunch Jul–mid-Sep; 🐾) Séverine and Arnaud extend a heartfelt welcome at their softly lit cellar bistro. This is good old-fashioned home cooking along the lines of creamy *tartiflettes*, rosemary-infused lamb with *gratin dauphinois* and calorific desserts. There's a €8.50 kids' menu for *les petits*.

L'Étage
CRÊPES €

(📞04 92 23 09 22; 35 Grand Rue; crêpes €3.50-8) Your saving grace from the crowds on Grand Rue is this alpine-chic crêperie. Loosen your belt for sweet crêpes smothered in whipped cream, and savoury varieties like Normandy-style with Camembert, ham and potatoes.

Le Pied de la Gargouille
REGIONAL CUISINE €€

(📞04 92 20 12 95; 64 Grande Rue; menus €18.50-22; ⊘dinner Wed-Sun) The Gargoyle's Foot is an old-town homage to fondue, *raclette* and *tartiflette*. Call ahead to reserve the speciality, *gigot d'agneau à la ficelle* (whole leg of lamb strung over an open fire), and bring three friends to finish it.

ℹ Information

The **tourist office** (📞04 92 21 08 50; www. ot-briancon.fr, in French; Maison des Templiers, 1 place du Temple; ⊘9am-noon & 2-6pm Mon-Sat, 10.15am-12.15pm & 2.30-5pm Sun) can help book accommodation.

ℹ Getting There & Away

Bus

Grenoble-based **VFD** (www.vfd.fr, in French) runs at least one daily bus to/from Grenoble (€29, 2¾ hours) via Bourg d'Oisans. Tickets must be booked at least 72 hours in advance online.

Other services operated by **SCAL** (www.scal -amv-voyages.com, in French) and leaving from the bus stop on the corner of rue Général Colaud include seven daily buses (except Sunday) to/from Gap (€10, two hours), Marseille (€31, five to six hours) and Aix-en-Provence (€28, five hours). Buses shuttle skiers and boarders to/from Villeneuve-la-Salle every 20 minutes (€4.60, 25 minutes). In winter **Satobus** (http:// satobus-alpes.altibus.com) also runs services to/from Lyon St-Exupéry airport (€58, four

hours, two daily); book at least seven days in advance online.

Car & Motorcycle

The winding Col de Montgenèvre (1850m) mountain pass links Briançon with neighbouring Italy. It stays open year-round, as does the nearby Col du Lautaret (2058m) that links Briançon and Grenoble. Both do occasionally get snow-bogged.

Train

From the **train station** (av du Général de Gaulle), about 1.5km from the Vieille Ville, there are trains to Paris Gare de Lyon (€76, seven hours, five daily). Other destinations include Grenoble (€29, 4½ hours, six daily), Gap (€13, 1½ hours, seven daily) and Marseille (€39, 4½ hours, three daily).

THE JURA MOUNTAINS

The dark wooded hills, rolling dairy country and limestone plateaux of the Jura Mountains, stretching in an arc for 360km along the Franco–Swiss border from the Rhine to the Rhône, comprise one of the least explored pockets in France. Rural, deeply traditional and *un petit peu* eccentric, the Jura is the place, if it is serenity, authentic farmstays and a taste of mountain life you seek.

The Jura – from a Gaulish word meaning 'forest' – is France's premier cross-country skiing area. The range is dotted with ski stations and every year the region hosts the Transjurassienne, one of the world's toughest cross-country skiing events.

The region is not short of culture or history either. From heavy metallurgy to precious-gem cutting, its contribution hasn't gone unnoticed in the country's economy, neither has its historical role as the hotbed of the French Resistance during WWII.

Besançon

POP 121,850 / ELEV 262M

Home to a monumental Vauban citadel and France's first public museum, birthplace of Victor Hugo and the Lumière Brothers – Besançon has an extraordinary background and yet, remarkably, remains something of a secret. Straddling seven hills and hugging the banks of the River Doubs, the cultured capital of Franche-Comté remains refreshingly modest and

FRENCH ALPS & THE JURA MOUNTAINS THE JURA MOUNTAINS

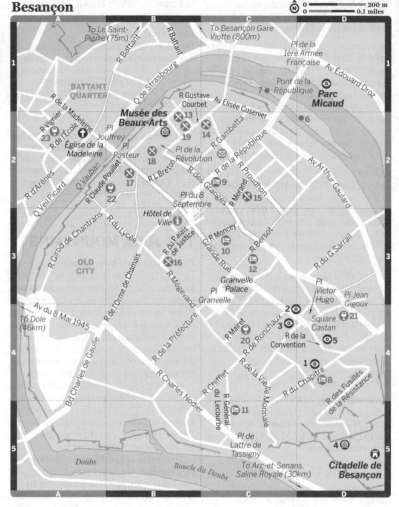

untouristy, despite charms such as its graceful 18th-century old town, first-rate restaurants and happening bars pepped up by the city's students.

It wasn't always that way. In Gallo-Roman times, Besançon was an important stop on the trade routes between Italy, the Alps and the Rhine. This role will come full circle in December 2011 when the new TGV station opens in the village of Auxon, 10km north of the centre. Once again, Besançon will be firmly back on the global map where it belongs.

⊙ Sights

Citadelle de Besançon CITADEL
(www.citadelle.com; rue des Fusillés de la Résistance; adult/child €8/4.60; ⊙9am-6pm) Besançon's crowning glory is this Unesco-listed, formidable feat of engineering, designed by the prolific Vauban for Louis XIV in the late 17th century. Dominating a hill-top and dramatically lit by night, the citadel commands sweeping views of the city's mosaic of red rooftops and the serpentine River Doubs.

The citadel harbours a trio of museums: the **Musée Comtois** zooms in on local tra-

Besançon

ditions, the **Musée d'Histoire Naturelle** covers natural history, and the harrowing **Musée de la Résistance et de la Déportation** takes an in-depth look at the rise of Nazism and fascism, and the French Resistance movement. The latter is unsuitable for young children.

To boost the citadel's family appeal, there's an **insectarium** (home to some meaty tarantulas), an **aquarium**, a pitch-black, ho-hum **noctarium** and an overly cramped **parc zoologique**. Citadel admission covers entry to all museums and attractions.

Musée des Beaux-Arts GALLERY, MUSEUM
(Fine Arts Museum; www.musee-arts-besancon. org, in French; 1 place de la Révolution; adult/child €5/free; ◎9.30am-noon & 2-6pm Wed-Mon) No trip to Besançon is complete without visiting this stately museum. It is France's oldest, founded in 1694 when the Louvre was but a twinkle in Paris' eye. The stellar collection spans archaeology with its Egyptian mummies, Neolithic tools and Gallo-Roman mosaics; a cavernous drawing cabinet with 5500 works including Dürer, Delacroix and Rodin masterpieces; and 14th- to 20th-century painting with standouts by Titian, Rubens, Goya and Matisse.

Parc Micaud PARK
(av Edouard Droz) For that must-have snapshot of the hilltop citadel with the swiftly flowing Doubs in the foreground, take a stroll along this leafy riverside promenade, a great spot for a picnic with a view. A carousel, playground and donkey rides keep kids entertained.

Horloge Astronomique ASTRONOMICAL CLOCK
(rue de la Convention; adult/child €3/free; ◎7 guided tours Wed-Mon) Housed in the 18th-century **Cathédrale St-Jean**, this incredible astronomical clock has 30,000 moving parts, 57 faces, 62 dials and, among other things, tells the time in 16 places around the world, the tides in eight different ports of France, and the time of the local sunrise and sunset.

Porte Noire ROMAN ARCH
(Black Gate; rue de la Convention) A steep 15-minute downhill walk from the citadel, the Porte Noire is a triumphal arch left over from the city's Roman days, dating from the 2nd century AD.

☞ Tours

When the sun's out, a river cruise is a relaxed way to see Besançon. From April to October, vessels dock beneath Pont de la République to take passengers on 1¼-hour cruises along the River Doubs. Both these companies sail along a 375m-long tunnel underneath the citadel:

Bateaux du Saut du Doubs (www.sautdu doubs.fr, in French; adult/child €10.50/8)

Vedettes de Besançon (www.vedettesdebe sancon.com, in French; adult/child €10.50/8).

FRENCH ALPS & THE JURA MOUNTAINS BESANÇON

VISI'PASS

Besançon's top sights and museums, including the citadel and the Musée des Beaux-Arts, can be visited with a good-value **Visi'Pass** (adult/child €8/4.10). You can buy it directly at the sights, online or from the tourist office.

Festivals & Events

Festival de Musique Besançon

MUSIC FESTIVAL

(www.festival-besancon.com) Classical music of the highest calibre resounds in Besançon's historic buildings in September.

Marché de Noël

CHRISTMAS MARKET

In December get into the festive spirit with twinkling carousels, carols and *vin chaud* in the old town.

Sleeping

Charles Quint Hôtel

HISTORIC HOTEL €€

(☑03 81 82 05 49; www.hotel-charlesquint.com; 3 rue du Chapitre; d €89-145; @ ☒) This discreetly grand 18th-century town house turned nine-room boutique hotel is sublime, with period furniture, sumptuous fabrics, a garden with a tiny swimming pool and a wood-panelled dining room. Find it slumbering in the shade of the citadel, behind the cathedral.

Maison de Verre

B&B €€

(☑03 81 81 82 27; http://lamaisondeverre.com, in French; 26 rue Bersot; s/d €75/85, menu €35; ☎) Katherine Bermond has cleverly converted a car factory into this nouveau-chic *chambre d'hôte* with an industrial twist. Clean lines, sculpted furniture and muted colours define the design-oriented rooms and dining room. The food served is inspired by seasonal, locally sourced produce.

Hôtel de Paris

DESIGN HOTEL €€

(☑03 81 81 36 56; www.besanconhoteldeparis. com; 33 rue des Granges; s €60, d €75-105; @☎) Hidden down a side street in the old town, this former 18th-century coaching inn reveals a razor-sharp eye for design. Corridors lit by leaded windows lead to slinky, silver-kissed rooms, a small fitness room and a shady inner courtyard.

Hôtel du Nord

HOTEL €

(☑03 81 81 34 56; www.hotel-du-nord-besancon. com; 8 rue Moncey; d €42-67, q €63-83; ☎) Right in the centre of town, this good-value family pick has spacious and comfortable (if dated) rooms. Free parking is a bonus.

Hôtel Granvelle

TRADITIONAL HOTEL €

(☑03 81 81 33 92; www.hotel-granvelle.fr; 13 rue Lecourbe; s €52-62, d €55-68; @☎) You'll find 30 neat and tidy rooms in this stone building at the back of a courtyard below the citadel. 'Interactive' rooms are equipped with internet-linked computers and flatscreen TVs. Good wheelchair access.

Eating

TOP CHOICE Le Saint-Pierre

MODERN FRENCH €€

(☑03 81 81 20 99; www.restaurant-saintpierre.com, in French; 104 rue Battant; menus €35-60; ☺lunch Mon-Fri, dinner Mon-Sat) This arty restaurant has swiftly become one of Besançon's most coveted. Crisp white linen, exposed stone and subtle lighting are the backdrop for intense flavours, such as lobster fricassee with spinach and herb ravioli, which are expertly paired with regional wines. The three-course *menu marché* including wine and coffee is a steal at €35. The restaurant is 500m (a five-minute walk) north of Grand Rue on the opposite side of the river.

La Table des Halles

MODERN FRENCH €€

(☑03 81 50 62 74; 22 rue Gustave Courbet; menus €15-29; ☺Tue-Sat) The urban loft decor at this fashionable restaurant wouldn't look out of place in New York's Meatpacking District. But what lands on your plate is resolutely French and regional: Lake Geneva fish, fillet of beef with truffle jus, foie gras crumble with tart apple compote. Fabulous.

Mirabelle

CAFÉ €€

(☑03 81 81 40 56; 5 rue Mégevand; mains €11-14; ☺lunch Mon-Fri, dinner Mon-Sat; ☒) Bird boxes dangle from the ceiling and the cheese menu is chalked on a mouse-shaped blackboard at this kinda kitsch, kinda cool café. A boho crowd flocks here for gratins, *croûtes* and scrummy tarts made with seasonal, mostly organic ingredients.

Brasserie du Commerce

BRASSERIE €€

(☑03 81 81 33 11; 31 rue Granges; mains €14-18) Stucco ceilings, gilt mirrors and opulent chandeliers catapult you back to the more glamorous age of belle époque at this buzzy brasserie, rustling up classic fare from fresh fish to beef carpaccio.

MI:AM
BISTRO €€

(☎03 81 82 09 56; 8 rue Morand; mains €15; ⊙Tue-Sun) Upside-down Christmas trees (in midsummer) and popcorn-filled baubles give trendy MI:AM (as in YUM!) quirk factor. Waltz through the heavy velvet curtain or snag a seat on the street terrace for an *apéro dînatoire* (light casual dinner) or an appetising lunchtime *tartine*.

Pum
THAI €

(☎03 81 81 18 47; 1 rue Jean Petit; mains €6.50-7.50; ⊘) Bright-orange Pum is a great place for tight budgets. Take a seat wherever there's space at one of the long wooden tables. Thai staples such as stir-fries and green curries feature prominently. Upstairs, the bar serves cocktails with an Thai twist.

Self-Catering

Self-caterers can bag picnic fixings at the **indoor market** (rue Claude Goudimel; ⊙Tue-Sun morning) and the **outdoor market** (place de la Révolution; ⊙Tue & Fri morning) or the supermarket, **Monoprix** (10 Grande Rue).

Drinking

Students spice up the nightlife in Besançon, concentrated in the old Battant quarter and along the river. With wall-to-wall drinking

holes, lively rue Claude Pouillet is a street made for bar-crawling.

Les Passagers du Zinc
BAR

(5 rue Vignier; ⊙closed Mon) A grungy bar-cum-club with battered leather sofas and multicoloured lights, the regular live bands and music nights keep this place high on the list of best venues in town. Step through the bonnet of an old Citroën DS to reach the cellar.

Bar de l'U
BAR

(5 rue Mairet; ⊙8am-1am Mon-Fri, 11am-2am Sat, 6pm-midnight Sun; ☎) With live music most nights and slamming competitions every second Monday of the month, this is a student mainstay. To attend many events, you'll need a student card.

Le Gibus
BAR

(11 rue Claude Pouillet) A rocking crowd gathers in the 1950s pin-up decor most evenings for live or recorded music and always plenty of good times.

Carpe Diem
CAFÉ

(2 place Jean Gigoux; ⊙9am-1am or 2am Mon-Sat, 9am-8pm Sun) An exemplary French café with a crowd of regulars, on the respectable side of 60 during the day and the carefree side of 30 at night. Regular gigs feature.

ℹ Information

ID PC (28 rue de la République; internet per hr €3; ⊙Tue-Sat) Computer shop with internet terminals.

Post office (23 rue Proudhon) In the old town.

Tourist office (☎03 81 80 92 55; www.besan con-tourisme.com; Hôtel de Ville, place du 8 Septembre; ⊙10am-6pm Mon-Sat, to 1pm Sun) Sells city maps and guides; organises thematic city tours (in French only).

ℹ Getting There & Around

BICYCLE Borrow a bicycle to cruise around town – free with a valid bus ticket – from the local bus company office, **Boutique Ginko** (www.ginkobus.com; 4 place du 8 Septembre). The boutique sells bus tickets costing €1.20/3.60/10 for a single ticket/day ticket/ *carnet* of 10.

BUS There is no bus station in Besançon. Daily services to Ornans (€3, 45 minutes) and Pontarlier (€6, 1¼ hours) stop at the train-station bus stop. You can buy tickets at the **Boutique Mobilignes** (www.mobilignes.com), at the far end of the Besançon Gare Viotte train station.

LIGHTS, CAMERA, HUGO

Victor Hugo, an influential national and political figure and one of France's literary treasures, famous for penning masterpieces such as *Les Misérables* and *Notre-Dame de Paris* (The Hunchback of Notre Dame), was born in 1802 in Besançon. The **House of Victor Hugo** (140 Grande Rue) is identified by a commemorative inscription. Close by on the same street, look out for the plaque marking the **House of the Lumière Brothers**. Born here in 1862 and 1864 respectively, the aptly named Auguste and Louis Lumière (*lumière* means 'light') were among the earliest pioneers of cinema and staged their first screening of motion pictures in 1895.

Mountain Highs

You're tearing down the Alps on your mountain bike, the wind whipping your hair; you're skipping through flowery pastures tinkling with cowbells; you're schussing in Mont Blanc's shadow in Chamonix. Everywhere the scenery makes you feel glad to be alive.

Downhill Skiing

1 Glide to off-piste heaven on the Vallée Blanche (p469), zigzag like an Olympic pro down black pistes in Val d'Isère (p492), or take your pick of Les Portes du Soleil's 650km of runs (p478).

Magical Views

2 Get close-ups of the shimmering Mont Blanc from Aiguille du Midi (p467) or contemplate the ethereal loveliness of the Cascades du Hérisson from the misty water-fall trail (p516). Lake Annecy spreads out like a liquid mirror before the fairest castle of them all: Château de Menthon-St-Bernard (p486).

Sky High

3 The sky is blue, the mountain air sweet – it's a zip-a-dee-doo-dah kind of wonderful day. Just the day to go paragliding or hang-gliding above glistening Lake Annecy (p482).

Alpine Hiking

4 There's nothing like donning a backpack and hitting the trails in the region's national parks. The rugged wilderness of Parc National des Écrins (p502) and the snow-capped majesty of Parc National de la Vanoise (p495) will leave you breathless.

On the Edge

5 For a buzz, little beats racing down Morzine's heart-pumping mountain-bike track (p478). Not enough of a challenge? Take your intrepid self to Chamonix (p471) for adventure among the four-thousanders.

Clockwise from top left
1. Off-piste skiing at the Vallée Blanche **2.** Breathtaking views, Aiguille du Midi **3.** Hang-gliding over Lake Annecy **4.** Hiking in Parc National de la Vanoise.

3

WORTH A TRIP

JURASSIEN HIDEOUTS

Escape civilisation at these more-idyllic-than-idyllic retreats. Advance reservations are essential.

Swiss-run Amondans (☎03 81 86 53 53; www.amondans.com, in French; place du Village, Amondans; s/d/tr incl half board €73/106/147; ⊙May-Oct) is an 18th-century farm, 30km south of Besançon in sleepy Amondans, fusing retro-chic furnishings with centuries-old features. The vast, minimal rooms overlook open fields. Guests are hip, happy, outdoor types who hang out after dinner by an enormous fireplace in a converted barn. Swiss owners George and Geneviève can arrange picnics and all kinds of activities.

Ferme Auberge du Rondeau (☎03 81 59 25 84; http://sebou25.free.fr, in French; Lavans-Vuillafans; s/d €42/53, menus €24-35; ⊙mid-Jan–mid-Dec; 🐾) is 33km south of Besançon off the N57. Coo over goats, boar and dairy cows at this organic farm where the friendly Boudiers keep the snug wood-panelled rooms immaculate and rustle up a fantastic breakfast with homemade yoghurt, jam and fresh-baked bread. Fresh farm specialities like goat's cheese and *sanglier saucisson* (boar sausage) with home-grown veg are served at lunch and dinner. They also sell fleecy mohair jumpers hand-knitted from the wool of their angora goats.

TRAIN From Besançon Gare Viotte, 800m uphill from the city centre, trains run to/from Paris (€41, 2¾ hours, 26 daily), Dijon (€14, 70 minutes, 20 daily), Lyon (€28, 3½ hours, 25 daily), Belfort (€15, 1¼ hours, 20 daily), Arbois (€8.50, 45 minutes, 10 daily) and Arc-et-Senans (€6.50, 30 minutes, 10 daily). Buy tickets at the train station or from the **Boutique SNCF** (44 Grande Rue) in town.

Around Besançon

SALINE ROYALE

Envisaged by its designer, Claude-Nicolas Ledoux, as the 'ideal city', the 18th-century Saline Royale (Royal Saltworks; www.saline royale.com, in French; adult/child €7.50/3.50; ⊙9am-noon & 2-6pm) in Arc-et-Senans, 35km southwest of Besançon, is a showpiece of early Industrial Age town planning. Although its urban dream was never fully realised, Ledoux's semicircular saltworks is now listed as a Unesco World Heritage Site.

Regular trains link Besançon and Arc-et-Senans (€6.50, 30 minutes, 10 daily).

ROUTE PASTEUR

Almost every single town in France has at least one street, square or garden named after Louis Pasteur, the great 19th-century chemist who invented pasteurisation and developed the first rabies vaccine. In the Jura it is even more the case, since the illustrious man was a local lad.

Pasteur was born in the well-preserved medieval town of Dole, former capital of Franche-Comté, 20km west of Arc-et-Senans along the D472. A scenic stroll along the Canal des Tanneurs in the historic tanner's quarter brings you to his childhood home, La Maison Natale de Pasteur (www. musee-pasteur.com; 43 rue Pasteur; adult/child €5/free; ⊙10am-noon & 2-6pm Mon-Sat, 2-6pm Sun), now an atmospheric museum housing exhibits including his cot, first drawings and university cap and gown.

In 1827 the Pasteur family settled in the bucolic village of Arbois (population 3480), 35km east of Dole. His laboratory and workshops here are on display at La Maison de Louis Pasteur (83 rue de Courcelles; adult/child €5.50/2.80; ⊙guided tours hourly 9.45-11.45am & 2-6pm). The house is still decorated with its original 19th-century fixtures and fittings.

ROUTE DES VINS DE JURA

The Route des Vins de Jura (Jura Wine Road; www.laroutedesvinsdujura.com) corkscrews through some 80km of well-tended vines, pretty countryside and stone villages. Plan your route by downloading the winery guide and map from the website.

No visit to Arbois, the Jura wine capital, would be complete without a glass of *vin jaune*. The history of this nutty 'yellow wine' is told in the Musée de la Vigne et du Vin (adult/child €3.50/2.70; ⊙10am-noon & 2-6pm Wed-Mon), housed in the whimsical, turreted Château Pécauld. The 2.5km-long Chemin des Vignes walking trail and the 8km-long Circuit des Vignes mountain-bike route meander through the vines. Both trails (marked with orange signs) begin at the top of the steps next to the Château Pécauld in Arbois; a booklet with more information is available at the tourist office.

La Balance Mets et Vins (☎03 84 37 45 00; 47 rue de Courcelles; menus €23-55; ☺lunch & dinner Thu-Mon, lunch Tue; 🍴), with its lunches favouring local, organic produce, provides the perfect coda to a wine-loving trip. Its signature *coq au vin jaune et aux morilles* casserole and crème brûlée doused in *vin jaune* are must-tastes, as are the wine menus with five glasses of either Jurassienne wine (€15) or *vin jaune* (€25, including a vintage one). Kids can sniff, swirl and sip, too, with three kinds of organic grape juice (€7.50).

High above Arbois is tiny Pupillin, a cute yellow-brick village famous for its wine production. Some 10 different *caves* (wine cellars) are open to visitors.

Arbois tourist office (☎03 84 66 55 50; www.arbois.com; 17 rue de l'Hôtel de Ville; ☺9am-noon & 2-6pm Mon-Sat) has walking and cycling information and a list of *caves* where you can taste and buy the local vintage.

Trains link Arbois and Besançon (€8.50, 45 minutes, 10 daily).

Poligny to Région des Lacs

Comté is indisputable king of the Jura, small-town Poligny (population 4600) serving as the capital of the industry that produces 40 million tonnes of the venerable cheese a year. Learn how 450L is transformed into a 40kg wheel of the tangy cheese, smell some of its 83 different aromas, and have a nibble at the Maison du Comté (www.comte.com; av de la Résistance; adult/child €4/2.50; ☺guided tours 2.30pm, 3.30pm & 4.40pm Tue-Sun). There are dozens of *fruitières* (cheese cooperatives) open to the public. Poligny tourist office (☎03 84 37 24 21; place des Déportés; ☺9am-noon & 2-6pm Mon-Fri, 9am-5pm Sat) stocks an abundance of cheesy info.

Heading south, wiggle along the pretty D68 to Plasne, then continue south to Château-Chalon, a medieval village of yellow stone surrounded by vineyards known for their legendary *vin jaune*. There is a helpful tourist office (☎04 84 44 62 47; www.hauteseille.com; 3 place de la Mairie; ☺9.30am-12.30pm & 2-6pm Mon-Fri) in the nearby village of Voiteur, with plenty of info and maps on surrounding villages, wine and walking in the area.

Nestled at the foot of lushly wooded limestone cliffs and wedged between three glacial valleys, 20km south of Poligny, is Baume-les-Messieurs, a picturesque village of honey-coloured cob houses and red-tiled rooftops. Its abandoned Benedictine

LIQUID GOLD

Legend has it that *vin jaune* (yellow wine) was invented when a winemaker found a forgotten barrel, six years and three months after he'd initially filled it, and discovered its content miraculously transformed into a gold-coloured wine (hence the name).

A long, undisrupted fermentation process gives Jura's signature wine its unique characteristics. Savagnin grapes are harvested late and their sugar-saturated juices left to ferment for a minimum of six years and three months in oak barrels. A thin layer of yeast forms over the wine, which prevents it oxidising, and there are no top-ups to compensate for evaporation (called *la part des anges*, 'the angels' share'). In the end, 100L of grape juice ferments down to 62L of *vin jaune* (lucky angels), which is then bottled in special 0.62L bottles called *clavelin*. *Vin jaune* is actually renowned for its ageing qualities, with prime vintages easily keeping for more than a century. The oldest bottle was a 1774 vintage, a cool 220 years old when sipped by an awestruck committee of experts in 1994.

La Percée du Vin Jaune (www.percee-du-vin-jaune.com) festival takes place annually in early February to celebrate the first tasting of the vintage produced six years and three months earlier. Villages take it in turn to hold the two-day celebrations at which the new vintage is blessed and rated, and street tastings, cooking competitions, cellar visits and auctions keep *vin jaune* aficionados fulfilled.

Abbaye Impériale (Imperial Abbey; adult/child €4.50/2.50; ⊘guided tours 10am-noon & 2-6pm mid-May–Sep) has an exquisite polychrome Flemish altarpiece dating from the 16th century. Nearby, the 30-million-year-old **Grottes de Baume** (Baume Caves; adult/child €5.50/3; ⊘guided tours 10am-5pm Apr-Sep) feature some impressive stalagmites and stalactites.

Immediately east lies Jura's **Région des Lacs** (Lakes District), a region of wild, lonely heights, dark forests, cave-riddled limestone cliffs and gemstone lakes. This family-oriented region is perfect for low-key outdoor pursuits like hiking, fishing and horse riding. You can take in the enchanting **Cascades du Hérisson** waterfalls, including the wispy 65m-high Cascade de l'Éventail, on a walk along the 7km waterfall trail. For details on sights, activities and events, visit www.juralacs.com.

🍴 Sleeping & Eating

In rural areas, most restaurants close on week nights from November to April. The region is sprinkled with atmospheric *chambres d'hôte* and farmstays, but you'll need your own set of wheels.

TOP CHOICE **Escargot Comtois**   B&B €
(☎03 84 24 15 29; www.escargot-comtois.com; 215 rue de Montorient, Courbouzon; s/d/tr/q €48/55/65/80; 🛜🐾) An ode to zee 'umble escargot, Muriel and David Blanchard's carefully restored 1747 stone village house is also one of France's 400 snail farms. The grass-binging activity of the 200,000 gastropods peaks between May and September. The wood-floored rooms are bright and spacious, and there's a sandpit and swings for the kids in the garden. Try the escargots, oozing garlic-herb butter, with a glass of local wine in the dining room. Courbouzon is 16km south of Baume-les-Messieurs.

Hôtel de la Vallée Heureuse   HOTEL €€
(☎03 84 37 12 13; www.hotelvalleeheureuse.com; rte de Genève, Poligny; d €90-120, menus €28-65; 🅿🐾) You will indeed be *heureuse* (happy) to stumble across this beautifully converted 18th-century mill, which sits in riverside parkland and affords gorgeous forest and mountain views. The country retreat has tastefully decorated rooms and a restaurant specialising in Jurassien cuisine, plus a mini spa, and indoor and outdoor pools.

Au Douillet Gourmet   FARMSTAY €
(☎03 84 51 27 24; www.au-douillet-gourmet.com; rue du Château, Montigny-sur-l'Ain; s/d/tr/q incl breakfast €40/52/63/78, incl half board €57/86/108/148; 🐾) If you stay at Pascal and Christelle's welcoming dairy farm, you can learn and even help with milking the cows, bottle-feeding the calves or collecting eggs from the hen hutch. Christelle also does wonderful homemade food and pretty much everything you'll eat comes from the farm. The farm is 16km east of Baume-les-Messieurs and on the northern edge of the Jura lake district.

Le Relais des Abbesses   B&B €€
(☎03 84 44 98 56; www.chambres-hotes-jura.com; rue de la Roche, Château-Chalon; d €72, dinners €25) At this turreted *chambre d'hôte* in hilltop Château-Chalon, Agnès and Gérard have attractively decorated the rooms with hardwood floors, romantic canopy beds and Asian antiques. They are both fine cooks and dinner is an absolute treat, whether it's in the elegant dining room or on the terrace overlooking the countryside.

Le Grand Jardin   B&B €
(☎03 84 44 68 37; www.legrandjardin.fr, in French; rue des Grands Jardins, Baume-les-Messieurs; s/d/tr/q €42/52/63/75, 3-course menus €13.50) Book well ahead in summer to snag one of the three sunny rooms at this delightful *chambre d'hôte,* opposite the abbey in Baume-les-Messieurs. Local cheese, charcuterie and trout appear on the restaurant's appetising menu.

Café Restaurant de l'Abbaye

JURASSIEN CUISINE €
(☎03 84 44 63 44; place Guillaume de Poupet, Baumes-les-Messieurs; menus €21; ⊘lunch daily, dinner Fri, Sat, daily mid-Jun–Sep) Tucked in one of the abbey's old buildings, this stone-walled café-restaurant rolls out a feast of regional fare. Try the *vin jaune* terrine or trout fillet in savagnin wine for a real taste of the Jura.

Belfort

POP 51,350

Squeezed between north and east, France and Germany, art and industry, Belfort has grown into its own distinctive identity (it calls itself a *territoire*, not a *département*). Historically part of Alsace, it only became part of the Franche-Comté region in 1921

HOT BOX, CHRISTMAS ICE & JESUS

It's hot, it's soft and it's packed in a box. Vacherin Mont d'Or is the only French cheese to be eaten with a spoon – hot. Made between 15 August and 15 March with *lait cru* (unpasteurised milk), it derives its unique nutty taste from the spruce bark in which it's wrapped. Connoisseurs top the soft-crusted cheese with chopped onions, garlic and white wine, wrap it in aluminium foil and bake it for 45 minutes to create a *boîte chaude* (hot box). Only 11 factories in the Jura are licensed to produce Vacherin Mont d'Or.

Mouthe, 15km south of Métabief Mont d'Or, is the mother of *liqueur de sapin* (fir-tree liqueur). *Glace de sapin* (fir-tree ice cream) also comes from Mont d'Or, known as the North Pole of France due to its seasonal subzero temperatures (record low: -38°C). Sampling either is rather like ingesting a Christmas tree. Then there's *Jésus* – a small, fat version of *saucisse de Morteau* (Morteau sausage), easily identified by the wooden peg on its end, attached after the sausage is smoked with pinewood sawdust in a traditional *tuyé* (mountain hut).

and is best known today as the manufacturer of the superspeedy TGV train.

◎ Sights & Activities

Citadelle de Belfort CITADEL
(adult/child €7/5.50; ☉10am-6pm Wed-Mon May-Oct) Slung high above the old town, this sturdy citadel, built by the prolific Vauban, is the city's centrepiece. Inside is the Musée d'Histoire, which spells out regional history in artefacts. The citadel stages open-air concerts in summer.

On duty at its foot is a regal 22m-tall lion sculpted in red sandstone by Frédéric-Auguste Bartholdi (of *Statue of Liberty* fame) to commemorate Belfort's resistance to the Prussians in 1870–71. While the rest of Alsace was annexed as part of the greater German Empire, Belfort stubbornly remained part of France.

Musée de l'Aventure Peugeot CAR MUSEUM
(www.musee-peugeot.com; Carrefour de l'Europe; adult/child €7/3.50; ☉10am-6pm) Gleaming old-timers, concept cars and thumb-sized miniatures – it's Peugeots à gogo at this museum, 12km south of Belfort in Sochaux.

Église du Sacré Cœur CHURCH
(Carrer del Palau Reial 27; adult/child €3.50/2.50; ☉10am-6pm Tue-Sun) This modernist church, 4km southeast in Audincourt, is an architecture-buff must.

✈ Festivals & Events

Les Eurockéennes MUSIC FESTIVAL
(www.eurockeennes.fr, in French) Belfort plays host to three-day open-air rock festival in July.

Entre Vues FILM FESTIVAL
(www.festival-entrevues.com) International film festival in late November.

◢ Sleeping & Eating

Don't leave Belfort without biting into a *Belflore*, a scrumptious almond-flavoured pastry filled with raspberries and topped with hazelnuts.

Grand Hôtel du Tonneau d'Or
HISTORIC HOTEL €€
(☏03 84 58 57 56; www.tonneaudor.fr; 1 rue Reiset; d/tr €139/154; ⊞🖀) All stucco, sweeping staircases and art nouveau stained glass, this is a grand hotel with a modest price tag. The large rooms are more modern than the lobby suggests, with creature comforts like minibars and free wi-fi. Rates drop 40% at weekends.

Relais d'Alsace SMALL HOTEL €
(☏03 84 22 15 55; www.arahotel.com; 5 av de la Laurencie; s €40-60, d €60-70; 🖀) The bright, no-frills rooms are spick and span at this good-value guesthouse, on a main road slightly north of the centre. Breakfast is worth the extra €7.

❶ Information

Tourist office (☏03 84 55 90 90; www.ot-belfort.fr; 2bis rue Clémenceau; ☉9am-12.30pm & 2-6.30pm Mon-Sat) Distributes free city maps and has information on accommodation and activities.

❶ Getting There & Away

Connections from Belfort **train station** (av Wilson) include Paris Gare de Lyon via Besançon (€62, four hours, 10 daily), Montbéliard (€3.60,

DON'T MISS

GRANDE TRAVERSÉE DU JURA

Cross-country skiing, mountain biking, walking and snowshoeing, the Grande Traversée du Jura (Grand Jura Crossing; GTJ) cross-country track runs some 200km from Villers-le-Lac (north of Pontarlier) to Hauteville-Lompnes (southwest of Bellegarde). The exact itinerary varies between disciplines but the track peaks at 1500m near the town of Mouthe (south of Métabief) and follows one of France's coldest valleys. To cover the popular, well-groomed track takes 10 days of skiing – a feat even for the ultrafit.

The 76km stretch of the GTJ from Lamoura to Mouthe lures 4000 skiers to the world's second-largest cross-country ski race in February, the Transjurassiene (www.transjurassienne.com), and hundreds of inline skaters to Trans' Roller (www.transroller.com) in September.

For the GTJ lowdown, including maps and accommodation details, visit www.gtj.asso.fr.

15 minutes, 20 daily) and Besançon (€15, 1¼ hours, 14 daily).

Ronchamp

The only reason to rendezvous in Ronchamp, 20km west of Belfort, is to visit Le Corbusier's striking modernist chapel on a hill overlooking the old mining town. Built between 1950 and 1955, the surreal Chapelle de Notre Dame du Haut (Chapel of Our Lady of the Height; www.chapelle deronchamp.fr, in French; adult/child €5/3; ⊙9.30am-7pm), with a sweeping concrete roof, dazzling stained-glass windows and plastic features, is one of the 20th century's architectural masterpieces.

A 15-minute walking trail leads uphill to the chapel from the centre of Ronchamp village; the tourist office (☎03 84 63 50 82; 14 place du 14 Juillet; ⊙9am-12.30pm & 1.30-6pm Tue-Fri, 9am-12.30pm Sat, 1.30-6pm Mon) can guide you.

Trains run from Ronchamp to Belfort (€4.30, 20 minutes, six daily).

Métabief

POP 890 / ELEV 1000M

Métabief, 18km south of Pontarlier on the main road to Lausanne, is the region's leading cross-country ski resort. Year-round lifts take you almost to the top of Mont d'Or (1463m), the highest peak, from where a fantastic 180-degree panorama stretches over the foggy Swiss plain to Lake Geneva (Lac Léman) and all the way from the Matterhorn to Mont Blanc.

Métabief is famed for its unique Vacherin Mont d'Or cheese, which has been produced alongside Comté and Morbier by the Sancey-Richard family at the Fromagerie du Mont d'Or (www.fromageriedumontdor.com, in French; 2 rue Moulin; ⊙9am-12.15pm & 3-7pm Mon-Sat, 9am-noon Sun) since 1953. To see it being made, arrive with the milk lorry around 9am.

The closest tourist office (☎03 81 49 13 81; www.tourisme-metabief.com, in French; 1 place de la Mairie, Les Hôpitaux-Neufs; ⊙9am-12.30pm & 1.30-6pm Mon-Fri) open year-round is in Les Hôpitaux-Neufs, 2.5km northeast of Métabief. The annexe in Métabief is closed October and November, April and May, much like everything else in the village.

Family-run Hôtel Étoile des Neiges (☎03 81 49 11 21; www.hoteletoiledesneiges.fr, in French; 4 rue du Village; s/d/tr/q €54/66/80/94, with half board €70/100/138/168; ⚑🐾) has bright, well-kept rooms, including great mezzanine family rooms. There's an indoor pool and canteen-style restaurant.

You'll need a car to reach Métabief, along the D9 (just off the N57), 58km east of Arbois and 75km south of Besançon.

Around Métabief Mont d'Or

The closest you'll get to the North Pole in these parts is the Christmassy Parc Polaire (www.parcpolaire.com, in French; adult/child €7.50/5.50; ⊙10am-noon & 2-5pm, closed Mon, Sat morning, Nov) in Chaux-Neuve, where Claude and Gilles Malloire will introduce you to huskies, reindeer and some mighty hairy yaks on a 1½-hour guided tour.

A real cliff-hanger of a castle, the medieval Château de Joux (www.chateaudejoux. com, in French; adult/child €6/3.20; ⊘guided tours 10-11.30am & 2-4.30pm Apr–mid-Nov), 10km north of Métabief, used to guard the route between Switzerland and France. Today it houses France's most impressive arms museum, and a 100m-deep well. Guided tours are gripping, full of anecdotes and stories, and available in English (ring ahead). In summer, torch-lit night-time tours are organised for extra spookiness.

Parc Naturel Régional du Haut-Jura

Experience the Jura at its rawest in the Haut-Jura Regional Park, an area of 757 sq km stretching from Chapelle-des-Bois in the north almost to the western tip of Lake Geneva. Forget about exploring the region's lakes, mountains and low-lying valleys without a car.

A great place to start is the Maison du Parc (www.parc-haut-jura.fr; Lajoux; adult/child €5/3; ⊘10am-12.30pm & 2-6.30pm Tue-Fri, 2-6.30pm Sat & Sun), a visitor centre with an interactive sensorial museum that explores the region and its history through sound, touch and smell. The Maison du Parc is in the east of the Haut-Jura Regional Park, 19km east of St-Claude and 5km west of Mijoux on the Swiss border.

There's not much to St-Claude – the largest town in the park – bar its illustrious diamond-cutting industry which, unfortunately, is off limits to visitors.

Les Louvières (☎03 84 42 09 24; www.leslouvieres.com, in French; Pratz; 2-/3-course menus €32/38; ⊘lunch & dinner Wed-Sat, lunch Sun), a solar-powered mountain farmhouse restaurant to rave about, is a 20-minute drive west in Pratz. Philippe's cuisine (foie gras maki-zushi with maple syrup, fish in wasabi sauce etc) is strictly fusion.

Le Clos d'Estelle (☎03 84 42 01 29; www.leclosdestelle.com; Hameau La Marcantine, Charchilla; d €64-82, q €120), 12km north, has four *chambres d'hôte* where you can fall asleep to pin-drop silence. It's run by the lovely Christine and Jean-Pierre Thévenet, Jura locals through and through, who'll enthusiastically share their knowledge of the area with you.

Les Rousses, on the northeastern edge of the park, is the park's prime sports hub, winter (skiing) and summer (walking and mountain biking) alike. The resort comprises four small, predominantly cross-country ski areas: Prémanon, Lamoura, Bois d'Amont and the village Les Rousses. Find out more at the Maison du Tourisme (Fort des Rousses; ⊘9am-noon & 2-6pm Mon-Sat, 9.30am-12.30pm Sun), home to the tourist office (☎03 84 60 02 55; www.lesrousses. com, in French) and the ESF (☎03 84 60 01 61; www.esf-lesrousses.com). You can eat and/or stay the night on the Swiss border at Hôtel Franco-Suisse (below).

The far-reaching vista from the Col de la Faucille mountain pass, 20km south of Les Rousses, reaches across the Jura Mountains to Lake Geneva and the snow-dusted Alps. Savour these incredible views (extra incredible at sunset) from the restaurant terrace, or the poolside in summer, of La Mainaz (☎04 50 41 31 10; www. la-mainaz.com; 5 rte du Col de la Faucille; d €80-120, menus €32-43; ⊘mid-Dec–mid-Oct; ▣), a cosy chalet midway along the mountain pass.

As the N5 wriggles down the Jura Mountains past the small ski resort of Mijoux, the panorama of Lake Geneva embraced by the French Alps and Mont Blanc beyond is stunning. For the best views, ride the Telesiège Val Mijoux (chairlift; adult/child return €6; ⊘10.30am-1pm & 2.15-5.30pm Sat & Sun mid-Jul–mid-Aug) from Mijoux and continue up to 1533m-high Mont Rond.

Heading a further 25km southeast you hit the French–Swiss border, passing

---

WORTH A TRIP

CROSS-BORDER

Sleep soundly with your head in Switzerland and your feet in France at Hôtel Franco-Suisse (☎03 84 60 02 20; www.arbezie-hotel.com; La Cure; s/d/tr/q incl half board €88/127/166/254), a unique bistro inn smack on the Franco–Swiss border. Since 1920 the Arbez family has taken great pride in providing cosy rooms (some are wood-beamed alpine style) and regional cuisine like home-style chicken in *vin jaune*. Find the hotel in the hamlet of La Cure, 2.5km from Les Rousses, wedged between the Col de la Faucille (France) and Col de la Givrine (Switzerland).

through Ferney-Voltaire (www.ferney-volt aire.net), 5km north of Geneva, en route. Following his banishment from Switzerland in 1759, Voltaire lived in Ferney until his return to Paris and death in 1778. Guided tours of his elegant home, Château de Voltaire (allée du Château; adult/child €5/free; ⏱tours in French hourly 10.30am-4.30pm Tue-Sun mid-May–mid-Sep), take in the château, chapel and surrounding 7-hectare park. Past visitors include Auden, Blake and Flaubert, all of whom wrote about the philosopher's home in exile.

PLAN YOUR SKI TRIP

Preplanning your ski trip pays off: sidestep school holidays to stretch your euro further, and book lift passes online to skip past the queues. And with the crème de la crème of instructors at the ubiquitous École du Ski Français, you'll go from bending zee knees to freestyle dancing on skis in no time. Here are some other tips:

» Save by buying a SnowBall Pass (www.snowballpass.com), which offers discounts on ski passes, tuition and equipment hire.

» Contact the Club Alpin Français (www.ffcam.fr) for the lowdown on *refuges* (mountain huts) and book your stay.

» Check out France Montagnes (http://ski-resort-france.co.uk) for Alps resort guides, maps, snow reports and more.

» Surf Piste Hors (http://pistehors.com) if you're planning to head off-piste.

» See p963 for recommended maps.

Massif Central

Best Places to Eat

» Emmanuel Hodencq
(p526)

» François Gagnaire (p543)

» La Table d'Antoine (p531)

» La Parenthèse (p543)

» Jean-Claude Leclerc
(p526)

Best Places to Stay

» Le Chastel Montaigu
(p537)

» Camping Domaine de la
Grande Cascade (p534)

» Hôtel du Parc (p542)

» Villa St-Hubert (p537)

» Aletti Palace Hôtel (p530)

Why Go?

In one of the wildest, emptiest and least-known corners of France, the Massif Central, you can feel nature's heavy machinery at work. Below ground, hot volcanic springs bubble up to supply Vichy and Volvic with their famous mineral waters, while high in the mountains trickling streams join forces to form three of France's mightiest rivers: the Dordogne, the Allier and the Loire.

The Massif Central and surrounding Auvergne region remains deeply traditional. Reliant on agriculture and cattle farming, it shelters the country's largest area of protected landscape with two huge regional parks: the Parc Naturel Régional des Volcans d'Auvergne and its neighbour, the Parc Naturel Régional Livradois-Forez. On-tap outdoor activities include heady hiking trails, plunging ski slopes, paragliding off icy summits, and setting off on an age-old pilgrimage – sustained by some of the halest, heartiest food in France.

When to Go
Clermont-Ferrand

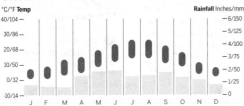

February Catch Clermont-Ferrand's famous short film festival.

15 August See sacred Vierges Noires (Black Madonnas) paraded on Assumption Day.

December to March Swoosh down the ski slopes or rug up for ice-fishing.

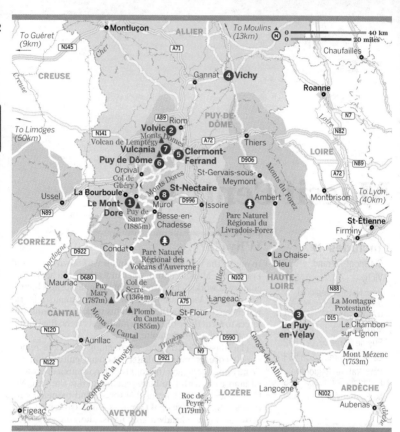

Massif Central Highlights

❶ Snowshoe in fresh powder around **Le Mont-Dore** (p534)

❷ Visit the storybook fortress **Château de Tournoël** (p532) in Volvic

❸ Discover the essence of fiery local liqueur Verveine on a tour of its **distillery** in Le Puy-en-Velay (p542)

❹ Soak up the mineral-rich waters at the spas of belle époque **Vichy** (p528)

❺ Marvel at the Michelin brothers' influence on travel at the inspired new **Michelin museum** (p524) in Clermont-Ferrand

❻ Scale the panoramic summit of **Puy de Dôme** (p532)

❼ Venture inside a booming volcano at the volcanic theme park **Vulcania** (p532)

❽ Drift over picturesque countryside in a hot-air balloon above the famous cheese-producing town of **St-Nectaire** (p537)

History

The historical province of the Auvergne derives its name from a Gallic tribe, the Arverni, who ruled the area until the Romans arrived under Julius Caesar. Arverni chieftain Vercingétorix put up the only real resistance to Caesar's legions. Despite several victories, his armies were finally crushed near Alésia in Burgundy.

The Romans founded a number of settlements including Augustonemetum (later Clermont-Ferrand). Following the fall of the Empire, the Auvergne entered a period of infighting between rival factions of Franks, Aquitanians and Carolingians, before being split into feudal domains during the Middle Ages under the dukes of Auvergne, whose government was in Riom.

With its wide-open pastures and lush green grass, it's not surprising the Auvergne has a long tradition of producing some of France's finest cheeses. The region has five AOC (Appellation d'Origine Contrôlée) and AOP (Appellation d'Origine Protégée, a Europe-wide recognition) cheeses: the semihard, cheddarlike Cantal and premium-quality Salers, both made from the milk of high-pasture cows; St-Nectaire, rich, flat and semi-soft; Fourme d'Ambert, a mild, smooth blue cheese; and Bleu d'Auvergne, a powerful, creamy blue cheese with a Roquefort-like flavour.

To taste them on their home turf, follow the signposted Route des Fromages (www.fromages-aop-auvergne.com) linking local farms and producers. A downloadable map is available on the website.

The area's cheeses figure strongly in many of the Auvergne's traditional dishes, including *aligot* (puréed potato with garlic and Tomme cheese) and *truffade* (sliced potatoes with Cantal cheese), almost always served with a huge helping of *jambon d'Auvergne* (local ham).

For a behind-the-stoves insight into another of the region's AOC specialties, the *lentille verte de Puy* (green Puy lentil), see p544.

After the French Revolution, the capital switched to Clermont-Ferrand, which became a focus of expansion, especially with the Michelin brothers' factories in the late 19th century. Meanwhile aristocrats flocked to the region's fashionable spas, notably in Vichy. During WWII Vichy became the capital of the collaborationist regime under Maréchal Pétain.

ⓘ Getting There & Around

AIR The region's only airport is in Clermont-Ferrand.

BICYCLE For info on cycling in the region, head to shop.lonelyplanet.com to purchase a downloadable PDF of the Massif Central chapter from Lonely Planet's *Cycling in France* guide.

CAR By road, the A75 autoroute (sometimes called La Méridienne) provides high-speed travel to the south of France through the viaducts at Garabit and Millau, while the A89 (La Transeuropéenne) travels west to Bordeaux. Elsewhere the region's roads are twisty, slow and highly scenic: you'll need your own car to reach the more remote spots, as the bus network is almost nonexistent.

TRAIN Though the TGV network hasn't yet arrived, regular trains serve all the main towns including a direct service from Clermont-Ferrand to Paris in 3½ hours.

CLERMONT-FERRAND & AROUND

Clermont-Ferrand

POP 142,948 / ELEV 400M

Sprawled around a long-extinct volcano in the middle of the Massif Central, Clermont-

Ferrand is the capital of the Auvergne and its only metropolis. Home to the Michelin empire and roly-poly Michelin Man (known to the French as Bibendum), the city has been a thumping industrial powerhouse for over a century. Surrounded by smokestack factories and suburban warehouses, the atmospheric old town is crowned by a soaring twin-spired cathedral.

◉ Sights

The narrow lanes of Clermont-Ferrand's old city twist outwards from the cathedral, dotted with mansions dating from the 17th and 18th centuries.

Cathédrale Notre Dame   CATHEDRAL
(place de la Victoire; ⊘8am-noon & 2-6pm Mon-Sat, 9.30am-noon & 3-7.30pm Sun) Carved from the inky volcanic rock from the quarries of Volvic, Clermont's jet-black cathedral, with its massive Gothic facade, was constructed between the 13th and 19th centuries. The interior is a striking contrast of light and shade, brilliantly lit by afternoon sunshine. For fantastic views east to Thiers and west to Puy de Dôme, brave the 250 steps to the top of its only transept tower to have survived the French Revolution, the Tour de la Bayette (admission €1.50; ⊘9am-11.15am & 2-5.15pm Mon-Sat, 3-5.30pm Sun). Two blocks north of the cathedral, the early-16th-century Fontaine d'Amboise also has a panoramic view of the Puy de Dôme and nearby peaks.

Basilique Notre Dame du Port   CHURCH
(⊘8am-7pm) A Unesco World Heritage Site, this 12th-century Romanesque church is

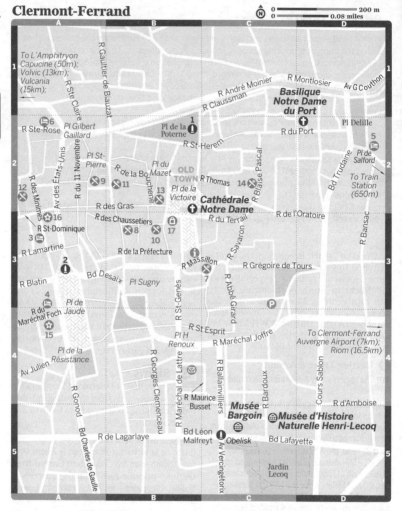

sparkling after recent renovations. Highlights of its simple interior are its raised chorus and fine mosaics.

Place de Jaude   CITY SQUARE

At the southwestern edge of the old city, Clermont's monumental pedestrianised square is overlooked by a statue of heroic Celtic chief Vercingétorix.

TOP CHOICE **L'Aventure Michelin**   MUSEUM

(www.laventuremichelin.com; 32 rue du Clos Four; adult/child €8/5, audioguide €2; ⏰10am-6pm Tue-Sun) Next door to Clermont's mammoth Michelin factory, with a 5300kg tyre

(the world's largest) out front, this gleaming new museum recounts the rubber empire's evolution, of course. But it also sheds light on Michelin's astonishing impact on aviation, rail, maps, travel and restaurant guides, and GPS technology. Hugely entertaining for both adults and kids, there are some great hands-on interactive exhibits and advertising retrospectives. Allow at least a couple of hours; last entry is 90 minutes before closing. Take Tram A to the Stade Marcel Michelin stop. The museum's on-site **gift shop** sells everything from roadmaps to bouncy Bibendum key rings; you can also pick up

Clermont Ferrand

iconic souvenirs at the city-centre Michelin Boutique (2 place de la Victoire).

The following museums can be visited on a three-museum pass (€9) available from the tourist office, or individually (per adult/child €4.50/free).

Musée d'Art Roger Quilliot   ART MUSEUM
(http://museedart.clermont-ferrand.fr; place Louis Deteix; ◎10am-6pm Tue-Fri, 10am-noon & 1-6pm Sat & Sun) In a converted Ursuline convent, with exhibits from the late Middle Ages to the 20th century, including significant works by Delacroix, the Ryckaert family and François Boucher, as well as local artists. Situated northeast of the centre in Montferrand (which joined forces with Clermont in 1630); take Tram A from place de Jaude or Bus 31 from the train station.

Musée Bargoin   MUSEUM
(http://museebargoin.clermont-ferrand.fr; 45 rue Ballainvilliers; ◎10am-noon & 1-5pm Tue-Sat, 2-7pm Sun) Split into an **archaeological** department, displaying excavated Roman coins to neolithic wood carvings, and **textile arts** department, with a dazzling collection of carpets from Tibet, Iran, Syria, China and beyond.

Musée d'Histoire Naturelle Henri-Lecoq
   MUSEUM
(http://museelecoq.clermont-ferrand.fr; 15 rue Bardoux; ◎10am-noon & 2-6pm Mon-Sat, 2-6pm Sun) Named for the celebrated pharmacist and natural scientist who lived in Clermont-Ferrand in the 19th century and amassed rocks, fossils, plants and stuffed animals from the region. Highlights are the gallery of Auvergnat butterflies and over 50 native orchids.

🛏 Sleeping

As a commercial hub, Clermont has plenty of accommodation (though no truly top-end places), with cheaper rates available on weekends.

Hôtel de Lyon   HOTEL €€
(☑04 73 17 60 80; www.hotels-puy-de-dome.com/clermont_ferrand/hoteldelyon; 16 place de Jaude; d €69-98; ❄) You'll glimpse Vercingétorix from your window at this ultra-central pad. Despite its classic exterior, soundproofed rooms are motel-modern (pine furniture, country prints), with the best city views in town. Downstairs, the pub-brasserie (menus €14.50-22), is great for a drink as well as enormous Auvergnat meals.

Hôtel Saint-Joseph   HOTEL €
(☑04 73 92 69 71; www.hotelsaintjoseph.fr, in French; 10 rue de Maringues; s €39-47, d €61; @�❄) Above a corner bar near the Friday morning St-Joseph market, this cheerful little hotel offers the best budget value in Clermont, with decent, double-glazed rooms done out in sunny or stripy colour schemes.

Dav' Hôtel   HOTEL €
(☑04 73 93 31 49; www.davhotel.fr, in French; 10 rue des Minimes; d €55-60; ❄@�❄) Rooms at this central alley hotel are plainer than the strawberry-and-orange-adorned reception area, but they're well equipped and you can kick-start the day on the generous buffet (€10) in the bright lime-and-mulberry-coloured breakfast room.

Volcan Hôtel   HOTEL €€
(☑04 73 19 66 66; www.volcanhotel.fr; 6 rue Sainte-Rose; s/d from €68/78; ❄@�❄) In a

quiet, central street, the Volcan's rooms are a fairly straightforward take on midprice modernism (despite the subtle adherence to the themes of 'volcanoes', 'town', 'sport' and 'nature'), and some have a mezzanine with old-city views.

Hôtel des Puys HOTEL €€
(✆04 73 91 92 06; www.hoteldespuys.fr; 16 place Delille; d €92-184; ❄@🌐👍) The exterior has all the charm of a municipal car park, but inside you'll find cool, minimalist rooms, most with a balcony over trafficky place Delille. More cash buys extra space, separate sitting areas and big bathrooms, but the highlight is the panoramic breakfast room with views over Clermont's rooftops. Parking (€11) and breakfast (€13) are chronically overpriced.

✗ Eating & Drinking

Place de Jaude and the area north around rue St-Dominique are filled with inexpensive eateries. Café terraces ring place de la Victoire, with more on rue Ballainvilliers.

Emmanuel Hodencq GASTRONOMIC €€€
(✆04 73 31 23 23; www.hodencq.com; 6 place St-Pierre; lunch menus €23, other menus incl drinks €37-140; ☉Mon-Sat, closed mid–late Aug; 👍) Langoustines, locally picked wild mushrooms and truffles are among the stars of this elegant Michelin-starred affair, along with chef Emmanuel Hodencq's signature Paris-Brest. Hodencq holds Saturday morning cooking classes (incl breakfast & lunch €130) by reservation.

Les Goûters de Justine TEAROOM €
(11bis rue Blaise Pascal; cakes/lunch €3.90/5.90; ☉noon-7pm Wed-Fri, 2.30-7pm Sat) Sitting amid the jumble of old-fashioned furniture and choosing from homemade cakes on the sideboard feels like settling in at your grandma's place.

Jean-Claude Leclerc GASTRONOMIC €€€
(✆04 73 36 46 30; www.restaurant-leclerc.com, in French; 12 rue Saint Adjutor; lunch menus €30, other menus €40-90; ☉Tue-Sat, closed mid-late Aug; 👍) Egg-yolk-yellow walls and elegant paintings are the backdrop for Jean-Claude Leclerc's Michelin-starred masterpieces, drawn from a palette of France's finest ingredients including snails, fresh goat's cheese and foie gras.

Le St-Vincent REGIONAL CUISINE €€
(✆04 73 90 63 45; www.le-st-vincent.com, in French; 10, rue de la Coifferie; lunch menus €13,

menus €24-49; ☉Tue-Sat) The hotchpotch of haphazard beams, trinkets and wooden furniture at this reassuring spot don't hint at its stellar 'semi-gastronomic' cuisine. Locals are onto it, though, so book ahead.

Ah! St Tropez PROVENÇAL €€
(✆04 73 90 44 64; mains €16-33; 10 rue Massillon; ☉Mon-Sat) Painted with murals and sunbaked colours and stuffed with filling southern dishes such as grilled peppers, fish soup and crunchy figs with lavender, this place is the perfect antidote to a dark, chilly day. There aren't many tables, so booking's essential.

L'Amphitryon Capucine GASTRONOMIC €€€
(✆04 73 31 38 39; www.amphitryoncapucine.com, in French; 50 rue Fontgiève; menus €23-75; ☉Tue-Sat; 👍) Ditch the jeans and dig out your glad rags and you'll be rewarded with splendid seasonal cuisine spread over several courses (including a decadent eight-course *menu gourmand*). Kids' menu available.

Le 1513 CRÊPERIE €€
(3 rue des Chaussetiers; crêpes €2.50-12, menus €19-25; ☉lunch & dinner Mon-Fri, noon-12.20am Sat & Sun; 🚗👍) Through a stone archway inside the vaulted cellars of a 1513-built medieval mansion, local flavours at this cavernous crêperie include its *galette Auvergnate*, with local ham and St-Nectaire cheese.

Bistrot Bancal BISTRO, BAR €€
(✆04 73 14 23 92; 15 rue des Chaussetiers; mains €15-17; ☉lunch Thu-Sun, dinner Tue-Sat) One of Clermont's secret places for hand-picked organic and Auverganat wines accompanied by authentic *saveurs de terroir* (country dishes), charcuterie and cheese.

Self-Catering
Looking like a modern-art experiment gone wrong, the Lego-brick facade of Clermont's covered market (7am-7.30pm Mon-Sat) is on place Saint-Pierre.

☆ Entertainment
Pick up the free monthly what's-on magazine *Zap* (in French) around town, including the tourist office, which also has details of fixtures for Clermont's cherished rugby team.

La Cooperative de Mai LIVE MUSIC
(www.lacoope.org, in French; rue Serge Gainsbourg) Cavernous warehouse gig and concert venue. Catch Tram A to place du 1er Mai.

Le B-Box CLUB
(www.bboxclub.com; av Ernest Cristal, La Pardieu; ☺Thu-Sun) Massive (in every sense), this 4000-capacity multilevel warehouse is France's largest indoor club. DJs spin everything from cheesy chart choons to house, jungle and hardcore. Take bus 6 or 22 to the Cristal stop.

❶ Information

Atlanteam (www.atlanteam.com, in French; 11 av Carnot; per hr €2.50; ☺10am-10pm Mon-Sat, 2-8pm Sun) Internet access.

Main post office (rue Maurice Busset)

Tourist office (☎04 73 98 65 00; www.clermont-fd.com; place de la Victoire; ☺9am-7pm Mon-Fri, 10am-7pm Sat & Sun) Opposite the cathedral, with a free multimedia exhibition on the Auvergne's churches downstairs.

❶ Getting There & Away

AIR Clermont-Ferrand Auvergne airport (www.clermont-aeroport.com), 7km east of the city centre, is an Air France hub. Destinations include Nice, Marseille, Strasbourg and Paris, plus direct international flights to Amsterdam.

CAR The major car-hire companies have branches at the airport and in town.

TRAIN Clermont is the region's main rail hub. You can buy tickets at the two **boutiques SNCF** (☎08 92 35 35 35; 43 rue du 11 Novembre & 80 bd François Mitterand) in the city centre.

Long-haul destinations include Paris Gare de Lyon (€52.40, 3½ hours, six to 10 daily) and Lyon (€30.20, 2½ hours, more than 10 daily), from where there are connections to Nîmes.

Frequent short hauls run to/from Riom (€3, 15 minutes), Vichy (€9.30, 30 minutes), Volvic (€4.10, 30 minutes) and Thiers (€8, 45 minutes), with regular services to Le Mont-Dore (€11.70, 1¼ hours, four or five daily), and Le Puy-en-Velay (€21.30, two hours, three or four daily).

❶ Getting Around

TO/FROM THE AIRPORT Bus 10 or 20 travels to/from the airport four times daily Monday to Saturday, one or two Sunday; a **taxi** (☎04 73 60 06 00) costs around €15.

BUS & TRAM Clermont's public-transport system is handled by **T2C** (www.t2c.fr, in French; 24 bd Charles de Gaulle). A single ticket costs €1.40 and is valid for unlimited onward connections within 70 minutes on either tram or bus; a day ticket costs €3.50. Buses link the city and station, while Tram A connects place de Jaude with Montferrand.

BICYCLE Moovicité (☎08 10 63 00 63; www.moovicite.com, in French; per half-/full day €2/3; ☺7am-7pm Mon-Fri, 8am-7pm Sat); Moovicité Gare (43 av de l'Union Soviétique); Moovicité Renoux (20 place Hippolyte Renoux) hires bikes (with deposit). Hire for up to one hour is free. You can pick up and drop off bikes at either of its two outlets.

Riom

POP 18,745

Capital of the Auvergne region during the Middle Ages, Riom has an old quarter with boulevards lined with mansions and *hôtels particuliers* (historic mansions), mostly built from dark volcanic stone.

The tourist office (☎04 73 38 59 45; www.tourisme-riomlimagne.fr; 27 place de la Fédération; ☺9.30am-12.30pm & 2-5.30pm Tue, Wed, Fri & Sat, 2-5.30pm Mon & Thu) is adjacent to the pretty Romanesque church Église St-Amable (rue St-Amable; ☺9am-7pm).

Climbing 167 steps in Riom's 15th-century Tour de l'Horloge (Clock Tower; rue de l'Horloge; admission €0.50; ☺10am-noon & 2-5pm Tue-Sun Sep-Jun) rewards with wonderful views of the town and mountains.

Customs and traditions of life in the Auvergne are explored at the excellent Musée Régional d'Auvergne (10bis rue Delille; adult/child €3/free; ☺10am-noon & 2-5.30pm Tue-Sun, closed mid-Nov–Mar), while the Musée Francisque Mandet (14 rue de l'Hôtel de Ville; adult/child €3/free; ☺10am-noon & 2-5.30pm Tue-Sun) displays classical finds and 15th- to 19th-century paintings.

FILM CENTRAL

One of the world's foremost festivals of short film, Clermont's Festival International du Court Métrage (www.clermont-filmfest.com; ☺Feb) has three competitions for international and domestic shorts, as well as a touring 'Coup de Cœurs' program visiting cinemas across the Auvergne. Tickets are sold at the tourist office.

Year-round, feature-length flicks screen at the following cinemas:

Ciné Capitole (www.allocine.fr, in French; 32 place de Jaude) Recent nondubbed releases.

Cinéma Les Ambiances (www.cinema-lesambiances.fr, in French; 7 rue St-Dominique) Wonderful art-house venue showing nondubbed films.

THE BLACK MADONNAS OF THE AUVERGNE

The Auvergne has an astonishing number of Vierges Noires (Black Madonnas) in its cathedrals and churches, imbued with considerable sacred significance and miraculous powers.

Usually under 1m tall and carved from cedar or walnut, their origins are a source of constant speculation: some historians believe the tradition began during the Crusades, when Christian soldiers came under the influence of Moorish sculptors. Others believe the figures are part of a much older tradition involving the Egyptian goddess Isis or a pagan Mother Goddess. Still others have suggested that the Black Madonnas are an attempt to depict Mary's original skin colour, which was probably closer to the dark skin of African and Middle Eastern people than the light skin of modern Europeans.

Theories also abound over the figures' colour: that dark woods or varnishes were used to create the dark colouring, or it's caused by natural ageing or even candle soot.

On Assumption Day (15 August) you'll see the statues paraded throughout Auvergne villages, marking the ascension of Mary's spirit to heaven.

The 15th-century Église Notre Dame du Marthuret (rue du Commerce; ⊙9am-6pm) holds Riom's treasured relics: a Vierge Noire (Black Madonna; see above) and delicate Vierge à l'Oiseau, depicting the Virgin and Child accompanied by a fluttering bird.

Riom is 15km north of Clermont on the N9, served by frequent trains (€3, 15 minutes).

Vichy

POP 25,899

Its belle époque heyday may have passed, but there's still an air of understated grandeur about the stately streets and landscaped parks of Vichy, 55km northeast of Clermont-Ferrand. Famous for its volcanic mineral waters since Napoléon III and his entourage sojourned here during the 19th century, and later infamous as the seat of Marshal Pétain's collaborationist regime during WWII, these days Vichy is a well-to-do provincial hub that remains enduringly popular for its therapeutic waters.

⊙ Sights & Activities

Parks   PARKS
The heart of Vichy is the huge Parc des Sources, laid out by Napoléon III in 1812. Filled by chestnut and plane trees, it's encircled by a wrought-iron-canopied colonnade (allowing visitors to perambulate the park without getting wet) and is a beautiful place to stroll.

Other lovely parks include the riverside Parc Kennedy and Parc Napoléon III. Look out for the Swiss-style 19th-century chalet houses along the parks' edge, which once lodged the city's visiting curistes.

Springs   MINERAL SPRINGS
Most sources for drinking the mineral waters (including the elegant glass Hall des Sources and the Source de l'Hôpital, both in the Parc des Sources) require a prescription and are otherwise off limits. If you're keen, the tourist office has a list of local médecins (doctors).

The only place the public can sip is from the **brass taps** of the Source des Célestins (bd du Président Kennedy), where filling up is free (bring your own bottle). The taps are shut in winter to prevent frozen pipes.

Spas   HEALTH SPAS
Book ahead for treatments at Vichy's spas.

Vichy's most luxurious spa, Les Célestins (☑04 70 30 82 82; www.vichy-spa-hotel.com; 111 bd des États-Unis), offers decadent treatments including a douche d'eau de Vichy (four-hand hot-spring massage; from €62 for 12 minutes) and douche au jet (high-powered water jet; from €41 for 10 minutes).

Similar treatments are on offer at Centre Thermal des Dômes (☑04 70 97 39 65; www.destinationvichy.com; 132 bd des États-Unis). This once-lavish complex of Moorish arches and tiled towers is topped by a Byzantine dome, but these days the grand buildings are looking decidedly forsaken.

Vichy

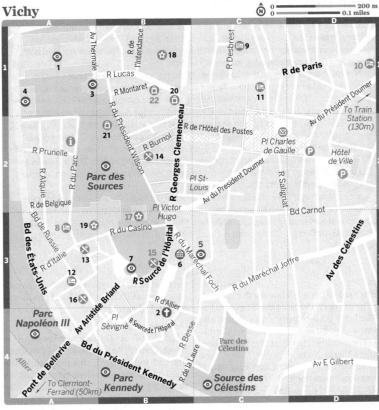

Vichy

VICHY SWEETS

Pastilles de Vichy were first created in 1825 using bicarbonate of soda, but the town's mineral waters later inspired its signature sweets. Since 1875 the bicarbonate has been replaced with salts extracted from the local mineral water, which is mixed with sugar and flavoured with mint, aniseed or lemon.

Not all of these octagonal-shaped sweets are the same, however. Those sold in shops and supermarkets have a different composition to those sold in pharmacies, which contain 10% more mineral salts to enhance their digestive properties. And Vichy is the only place in the world where you can buy the sweets stamped with the 'Vichy Etat' logo and packaged in an iconic metal tin, including at the beautiful glass-paned, rotunda-style kiosk **Maison des Pastilles** (Parc des Sources; ⊙10am-noon & 2-6.30pm Tue-Sun Apr-Oct). To learn more, you can visit the **Pastillerie de Vichy** (⊠04 70 30 94 70; 94 Allée des Ailes; admission free; ⊙9am-noon & 2-5pm Mon-Thu, 9-11am Fri Apr-Oct) plant, 2.5km north of the centre, for an overview of its history and manufacturing process (and free tastings, too).

Vichy also has a trove of exquisite *confiseries* and *chocolateries* selling handmade treats. The pastel-pink-framed windows of **Prunelle** (36 Rue Montaret) entice with a rainbow of translucent lollypops, while **Aux Marocains** (www.auxmarocains.com, in French; 33 rue Georges Clemenceau) is chock-a-block with marzipan, petits fours and caramels.

Old City
HISTORIC CENTRE

Vichy's old city is small but worth exploring.

The art deco 1930s **Église St-Blaise** (rue d'Allier) has 20th-century stained glass and frescos of some of France's famous churches. The original chapel at the rear houses Vichy's Vierge Noire.

The **Musée de l'Opéra de Vichy** (http://opera.vichy.musee.free.fr; 16 rue de Maréchal Foch; adult/child €3.50/2.50; ⊙3-6pm Tue-Sun) houses photographs and other displays documenting Vichy's turn-of-the-20th-century opera house.

FREE **Musée de Vichy** (www.ville-vichy.fr/musee-vichy, in French; 15 rue du Maréchal Foch; ⊙2-6pm Tue-Fri, to 5pm Sat), surprisingly small for such a historic town, has local archaeological artefacts, some Impressionist paintings and letters and coins from the Pétain régime.

🛏 Sleeping

Places to stay are plentiful and well priced. Vichy's spas can also arrange pampering accommodation packages.

Aletti Palace Hôtel
HOTEL €€€

(⊠04 70 30 20 20; www.aletti.fr; 3 place Joseph Aletti; d €125-191; ❄ 🐕 ⎈ 🏊) A billiards room, wood-panelled piano bar and outdoor pool flanked by flowers are among the luxurious amenities at this *grande dame* presiding over the Parc des Sources. Palatial rooms come with marble bathrooms and enor-

mous closets. Its glass-canopied **restaurant** (menus €16-36) utilises local produce in its classical cuisine.

Hotel de Naples
HOTEL €

(⊠04 70 97 91 33; www.hoteldenaples.fr, in French; 22 rue de Paris; d €36-42; @ 🐕) Welcoming and well located, this delightful little hotel has clean, good-sized rooms, split between the main building and a quiet rear annexe overlooking the hotel's car park (free) and terrace garden, where breakfast (€6) is served in summer.

Pavillon d'Enghien
HOTEL €€

(⊠04 70 98 33 30; www.pavillondenghien.com; 32 rue Callou; d €60-81; 🐕 🏊) Soothing white and cream rooms in this converted mansion are livened up with splashes of colour. Ask for a room overlooking the interior courtyard and pool, where you can dine alfresco on market-fresh Auvergnat dishes at its **restaurant** (menus €19-27; ⊙lunch Tue-Sun, dinner Tue-Sat). Located just north of Centre Thermal des Dômes; turn left off av Thermale.

Hôtel Les Nations
HOTEL €€

(⊠04 70 98 21 63; www.lesnations.com; 13 bd de Russie; d €60-105; ⊙Apr–mid-Oct; 🐕) Rooms are individually decorated at this art deco hotel, framed by green-and-white-striped awnings and wrought-iron gates, overlooking tree-filled place Général Leclerc. 'Confort Plus' rooms are worth the extra cash, with their own sitting areas and power showers, and there's an elegantly redecorated traditional **restaurant** (menus €15-23; ✪lunch daily, dinner Mon-Sat).

Hôtel Chambord HOTEL €
(✐04 70 30 16 30; www.hotel-chambord-vichy.com; 82-84 rue de Paris; s €45-54, d €52-64; ❅🛜🖳) The pick of the rooms on the top floors of this typically solid Logis hotel have city views and are a little more removed from the street noise. Some have air conditioning. Snails are a staple of its 1933-established **restaurant** (menus €25-45; ✪lunch Tue-Sun, dinner Tue-Sat).

Hôtel Arverna HOTEL €€
(✐04 70 31 31 19; www.hotels-vichy.com, in French; 12 rue Desbrest; d €50-75; ❅🛜) A seductive hideaway along a quiet side street, Arvena's rooms are filled with warm crimsons, checks and corn yellows. Most come with air-conditioning and some have views over the creeper-covered courtyard garden.

Eating

Many of Vichy's hotels also have good restaurants open to guests and nonguests.

La Table d'Antoine GASTRONOMIC €€€
(✐04 70 98 99 11; www.latabledantoine.com; 8 rue Burnol; lunch menus €20, other menus €32-60; ✪lunch Tue-Sun, dinner Tue-Sat) Abstract portraits and high-backed chairs create a boutique feel at this high-class temple to French fine dining and the food is seriously fancy, from coconut-poached chicken to langoustines and smoked fish. Reserve ahead.

Le Samoa BRASSERIE, CAFÉ €
(13 rue Source de l'Hôpital; dishes €4.50-14; ✪noon-midnight Sun-Wed, noon-2am Thu-Sat; 🛜) With a shaded terrace by the bandstand, this belle époque beauty is perfect for a *plat du jour* (€9), *tartine* or salad, or just a drink.

Brasserie du Casino BRASSERIE €€
(✐04 70 98 23 06; 4 rue du Casino; mains €17.50-24.50; ✪Thu-Mon) All shiny brass, faded wood and squeaky leather, this timeless haunt has a wall of photos featuring the actors and *chanteurs* who've stopped by from the opera house. The food's substantial (duck *confit*, rabbit stew) and the feel unmistakably French.

L'Hippocampe SEAFOOD €€€
(✐04 70 97 68 37; 3 bd de Russie; menus €18-56; ✪lunch Wed-Sun, dinner Wed-Sat) Appropriately enough for a restaurant called the

Sea Horse, scallops, sole and oak-smoked sardines star alongside a truly monumental *assiette de fruits de mer* (seafood platter).

Self-Catering
Vichy's **covered market** is on place PV Léger.

☆ Entertainment

Vichy Mensuel, a free monthly what's-on guide, can be picked up all over town.

Opéra de Vichy OPERA
(✐04 70 30 50 50; www.ville-vichy.fr/opera-vichy, in French; rue du Casino) The Opéra de Vichy stages regular productions. Tickets are sold inside the tourist office.

Casino Vichy Grand Café CASINO
(www.casinovichygrandcafe.com, in French; 7 rue du Casino; ✪noon-3am) Vichy's casino was one of the first-ever opened in France. Today punters can hit the tables in this annex of the now-closed original.

Casino Vichy Les Quatre Chemins CASINO
(www.casino-4chemins.com, in French; 35 rue Lucas; ✪10am-3am) Has orchestra-accompanied tea dances at 3pm Sundays.

❶ Information

At the time of writing there is no internet café in Vichy.

Main post office (place Charles de Gaulle)

Tourist office (✐04 70 98 71 94; www.vichy-tourisme.com; 19 rue du Parc; ✪9am-noon & 2-6pm Mon-Sat, 3-6pm Sun)

❶ Getting There & Around

BICYCLE Near the station, **Cycles Peugeot Gaillardin** (✐04 70 31 52 86; 48 bd Gambetta) rents bikes.

TRAIN Destinations include Paris Gare de Lyon (€47.80, 2½ hours, six to eight daily), with frequent services to Clermont-Ferrand (€9.30, 30 minutes) and Riom (€7.40, 25 minutes).

PARC NATUREL RÉGIONAL DES VOLCANS D'AUVERGNE

A vast tract of cloud-shrouded peaks, snowy uplands and jade-green valleys, the **Parc Naturel Régional des Volcans d'Auvergne** (www.parc-volcans-auvergne.com, in French) occupies most of the western Massif Central, stretching some 3950 sq km and 120km from base to tip. Evidence of its volcanic history abounds – see p532.

FIERY FURNACES

With its peaceful pastures and verdant hills, it's hard to believe that the Massif Central was once one of the most active volcanic areas in Western Europe.

The area consists of three geological bands. The Chaîne des Puys and Monts Dômes, a chain of extinct volcanoes and cinder cones stretching in a 40km north–south line across the northern Massif Central, thrust up around 100,000 years ago. The central Monts Dores are much older, created between 100,000 and three million years ago, while the real grandaddies are the Monts du Cantal, on the Parc Naturel Régional des Volcans d'Auvergne's southern edge, formed by a nine-million-year-old volcano which collapsed inwards, leaving only its caldera (fragmented rim).

Though the volcanoes have been silent for several thousand years (the last serious eruption occurred around 5000 BC), reminders of their turbulent past are dotted across the region – from its mineral waters and geothermal springs to the distinctive black rock often used as a building material across the region.

Unsurprisingly, this is fantastic terrain for outdoor enthusiasts, including skiers, hikers and mountain bikers, as well as paragliders who can often be seen drifting around the region's peaks.

Volvic

POP 4786

Just inside the Parc Naturel Régional des Volcans d'Auvergne's northeastern boundary, 13km north of Clermont-Ferrand, you can get a fascinating overview of the source of Volvic's world-famous mineral water at the company's Espace d'Information (www.volvic.fr, in French; rue des Sources; admission free; ☺9am-noon & 2-6pm Mon-Fri, 2.30-6pm Sat & Sun), and, of course, taste it, too. Outside, **walking trails** (from 30 minutes to three hours) fan into the lush surrounds, linking with the GR441.

FREE Factory tours (☎04 73 64 51 24; ☺by reservation) of its nearby bottling facility, lasting an hour, are available between June and August.

TOP CHOICE Château de Tournoël (www.tournoel.com, in French; adult/child €6/3; ☺2-6pm Wed-Mon), a storybook medieval fortress, is also along the GR441, uphill from the pretty village centre. You can visit the kitchens, kitchen gardens and the castle's 14th-century defensive round tower with its panoramic views.

At the Maison de la Pierre (www.maisondelapierre-volvic.com, in French; 2 route du Pont Jany; adult/child €6.30/4.80; ☺2-6pm), sound-and-light projections illuminate the quarrying of its volcanic stone (wrap up warmly!). Combined tickets with Volcan de Lemptégy (opposite) cost €16.10/13.30 (including the train).

Volvic's tourist office (☎04 73 33 58 73; www.volvic-tourisme.com; ☺9am-noon & 2-6pm Tue-Sat), on the village's central square, has details of accommodation.

Frequent trains link Volvic with Clermont-Ferrand (€4.10, 30 minutes).

Puy de Dôme & Around

The icy summit of Puy de Dôme (1465m) looms 15km west of Clermont-Ferrand. Snowcapped from September to May, the mountain was formed by a volcanic eruption some 10,000 years ago and was later used as a Celtic shrine and Roman temple. You can still see the temple's remains today, along with vistas stretching as far as the Alps.

You can walk to the summit along the scenic 'mule track' – a steep but exhilarating hour's climb from the Col de Ceyssat, 4km off the D941A. The toll road to the top is closed until mid-2012 while a new train to the summit is under construction. Check with Clermont-Ferrand's tourist office for updates.

The Auvergne's long-extinct volcanoes are brought back to life in spectacular style at Vulcania (☎08 20 82 78 28; www.vulcania.com; adult/child €23/15; ☺10am-6pm, closed Mon & Tue Sep) volcanic theme park, 15km west of Clermont on the D941B.

Combining educational museum with thrills and spills, it was dreamt up by French geologists Katia and Maurice Krafft, who were tragically killed in a volcanic eruption on Mt Unzen in Japan a year before its 1992 opening. Entered via a glittering gold dome and simulated crater (with billowing steam and booming eruptions), regularly added attractions keep it cutting edge. Highlights include the 'dynamic 3-D' film **Awakening of the Auvergne Giants**, depicting volcanic eruptions complete with air blasts and water spray; the new **Planet Unveiled**, incorporating satellite imagery that lets you navigate the globe; and a dubious **Dragon Ride** – not very scientific, but good fun all the same.

At Volcan de Lemptégy (04 73 62 23 25; www.auvergne-volcan.com; adult/child €8/6, by train €12/9.50; 10.30am-6.30pm), just across the D941B from Vulcania, you can set off on foot or aboard a little motorised 'train' to discover volcanic landscapes (chimneys, lava flows and more). The intense 'dynamic 3-D' exploding mine film makes a fitting finale, though it's not suitable for littlies. Last entry is two hours before closing; combined tickets are available with Volvic's Maison de la Pierre (opposite).

Orcival

POP 266 / ELEV 870M

Halfway between Puy de Dôme and Le Mont-Dore, the picturesque slate rooftops and tumbledown barns of Orcival huddle around the banks of the Sioulet River. The birthplace of former French president Giscard d'Estaing, this diminutive village centres on the Romanesque Basilique Notre-Dame (8am-12.30pm & 2-7.30pm), renowned for its elegant crypt and 12th-century Virgin of Orcival in the choir. Look too for the rare decorative ironwork depicting apocalyptic scenes on the main door.

If Orcival's tiny tourist office (04 73 21 85 19; www.terresdomes-sancy.com; 2-6pm Tue-Sat), opposite Basilique Notre-Dame, is closed (hours can be unpredictable), the tourist offices in Le Mont-Dore or La Bourboule can suggest **hikes** in the surrounding area including to Lac de Guéry.

Fans of French gardens definitely shouldn't miss the 15th-century Château de Cordès (04 73 65 81 34; www.chateau-cordes-orcival.com, in French; gardens & château adult/child €4/free, gardens only €2.50/free; 10am-noon & 2-6pm Wed-Sun), with rich 18th-century furnishings and magnificent formal grounds laid out by Versailles' garden designer Le Nôtre. It's just north of the village off the D27.

If you're up for paragliding off the area's peaks, you can arrange tandem jumps with Orcival-based Aero Parapente (06 61 24 11 45; www.aeroparapente.fr, in French; per jump incl prep €80; Apr-Oct).

Orcival makes a good day trip but if you want to stay, the simple Hôtel Notre Dame (04 73 65 82 02; s €40, d €45-48; Feb-Dec) has seven snug refurbished rooms, one with its own miniature terrace (plus a built-in alarm clock by way of the Basilique's bells tolling next door). Hearty portions of *chou farci* (pork-stuffed cabbage) and *aligot* (puréed potato with garlic and Tomme cheese) are dished up at its rustic restaurant (menus €13-25).

Orcival is not served by public transport so you'll need your own wheels.

Col de Guéry

South of Orcival, the D27 snakes up to the lofty pass of Col de Guéry, which offers fantastic mountain views on every side. In winter, cross-country skiing is organised by the Foyer Ski de Fond Guéry-Orcival (04 73 65 20 09; www.leguery.fr; day ski pass per adult/child €6.90/2.90).

Beyond the pass is chilly Lac de Guéry – the highest lake in the Massif Central at 1250m and filled with trout and perch. It's a sweet spot for **fishing** (per day €6), even in winter – this is the only lake in France that permits *pêche blanche* (**ice-fishing**; per day €23). Tourist offices in the region have details, or phone Moniteurs de Pêche (04 73 65 61 04). In an unbeatable position right on the shore, the cosy inn Auberge du Lac de Guéry (04 73 65 02 76; www.auberge-lac-guery.fr, in French; d €61;) serves up fresh fish straight from the lake at its fine country restaurant (menus €20-41). Check ahead for seasonal closures.

Le Mont-Dore

POP 1735 / ELEV 1050M

Nestled in a narrow valley 44km southwest of Clermont-Ferrand, and just four kilometres north of Puy de Sancy (1886m), central France's highest peak, Le Mont-Dore is the Massif Central's main wintersports base. Still, it's considerably quieter than the Alps' adrenaline-pumped resorts, making it a haven for hikers and snowsports enthusiasts seeking (relative) peace and quiet.

Sights & Activities

Thermes du Mont-Dore SPA
(☎04 73 65 05 10; 1 place du Panthéon; ☺9am-
noon & 2-5.30pm Mon-Fri, 9am-noon Sat) Long
before anyone thought of hurtling down
the hillsides strapped to a pair of wooden
planks, Le Mont-Dore was frequented for its
hot springs, which bubble out between 37°C
and 40°C. The first bathers were (of course)
the cleanliness-obsessed Romans – you can
still see traces of their original baths. In
addition to treatments, in low season you
can visit the 19th-century neo-Byzantine
building on a 45-minute, French-language
guided tour (adult/child €3.60/2.50; ☺2pm,
3pm & 4pm Mon-Sat).

Funiculaire du Capucin FUNICULAR
(av René Cassin; adult one way/return €3.50/4.40,
child one way/return €2.80/3.50; ☺10am-
12.10pm & 2-5.40pm Wed-Sun, closed Oct–mid-
May) Built in 1898, France's oldest funicular railway (and listed historic monument)
crawls at 1m per second up to the plateau
of Les Capucins, 1270m above town. Various trails lead off the plateau, including the
GR30, which wends southward towards
the Puy de Sancy, continuing to the Pic
du Capucin (1450m; about 45 minutes one
way) or dropping steeply back to town.

Téléphérique du Sancy CABLE CAR
(adult one way/return €5.80/7.50, child one
way/return €5.20/6.80; ☺9am-7pm Jul & Aug,
9am-12.10pm & 1.30-5pm mid-Apr–Jun & Sep,
9am-12.15pm & 1.30-5pm weekends Oct & Easter
holidays) Puy de Sancy's snowcapped summit can be reached by catching the cable
car, followed by a short walk along the
maintained trail and staircase to the top
for fabulous views of the northern *puys* and
the Monts du Cantal.

Snow Sports SNOW SPORTS
Near Le Mont-Dore, the ski and snowboarding fields **Puy de Sancy** and **Super-
Besse** (p536) encompass 85km of downhill
runs (daily joint pass per adult/child
€26.50/18.50) for beginners through to
experienced, plus countless cross-country
trails (day pass adult/child €6.90/2.90).

Snowshoeing is also gaining ground.
Mont-Dore Aventures (☎04 73 65 00 00;
www.montdoreaventures.com; Le Salon du Capucin; call for hire packages), 3km northwest of
Le Mont-Dore signposted off rte de la Tour
d'Auvergne, hires *racquettes* (racquet-style
snowshoes) as well as cross-country gear
and sleds.

There's an abundance of places to hire
snow gear in Le Mont-Dore.

Walking WALKS
Superbly signposted walks around Le
Mont-Dore are marked on good trail maps
such as Chamina's 1:30,000-scale map *Massif du Sancy* (€9.50) or the *Massif du Sancy*
guidebook (€9.50), which outlines 36 hikes
in the area. Both are sold at the tourist
office.

Mont-Dore Aventures OUTDOOR ACTIVITIES
(☎04 73 65 00 00; www.montdoreaventures.com;
Le Salon du Capucin; per 3½ hours adult/
child €21/16; ☺ropes course Apr-Oct)
Operates a fun *parcours acrobatiques
en hauteur* (Tarzan-style treetop ropes
course). Owner/local adventurer Gilles Rio-
creux is a fount of info on off-the-beaten-
track outdoor activities in the area.

Skating Rink SKATING, BOWLING
(☎04 73 65 06 55; allée Georges Lagaye; ice
skating adult/child €6.70/5.30, bowling before/
after 8pm €6/5; ☺Jul-Apr) If the weather's
bad, escape to Le Mont-Dore's rink for a
skate or skittle. Call for session times.

Sleeping

**Camping Domaine de la Grande
Cascade** CAMPGROUND €
(☎04 73 65 06 23; www.camping-grandecascade.
com; rte de Besse; sites from €10; ☺Jun-Sep;
☎⚿) At 1250m up, yes, this campground is
on the chilly side. But it's a stupendous spot
to pitch a tent, near a 30m waterfall, with
wondrous views of the surrounding mountains. Head 3km south of town on the D36.

Hôtel Le Progrès-Dorlotel HOTEL €
(☎04 73 65 05 96; www.hotel-leprogres
-dorlotel.com; 5 & 6 rue Marie-Thérèse; s €40, d
€55-60; ☎) This central family-run hotel has
a rare-for-the-region dedication to eco principles including biodegradable products,
waste management and more. Spruced-up
rooms have clean lines and bright splashes
of colour. Its **restaurant** (menu €13) turns
out regional specialties like stuffed veal.

Hôtel de Russie HOTEL €€
(☎04 73 65 05 97; www.lerussie.com; 3 rue Favart;
d €60-75; @☎⚿) Carefully modernised with
designer style, this town hotel is a treat,
from the scrubbed-up parquet floor and
colour-washed walls to reclaimed wood and
lobby lanterns. The rooms are lovely, finished in cappuccino browns and ice whites,
with brilliant duplex rooms for families,

and its restaurant (menus from €18) has a contemporary countrified elegance.

Grand Hôtel
HOTEL €

(☑04 73 65 02 64; www.hotel-mont-dore.com; 2 rue Meynadier; s/d €54/64; ☺mid-Dec–mid-Nov; ☎⤵) Built in 1850, this Le Mont-Dore landmark has been imaginatively refurbished, providing more comfort and style than its budget prices would imply: deep-red leather sofas, Chagall-style wall murals and designer lighting in the lobby, plus boutiquey bedrooms with thick duvets and deep tubs, including a few with balconies. Breakfast (€7.50) includes handmade jams, freshly squeezed juice and mini-pastries.

Auberge de Jeunesse Le Grand Volcan
HOSTEL €

(☑04 73 65 03 53; le-mont-dore@fuaj.org; rte du Sancy; dm incl breakfast €17.20; ☺mid-Dec–mid-Nov; ☎) Always jammed with skiers and hikers (book way ahead), this excellent hostel is right by the Puy de Sancy cable car, 3.5km south of town. Squeaky-clean two- to six-bed dorms have their own bathrooms, and fun facilities include ping pong, table football and an in-house bar.

Le Buron de Dame Tartine
B&B €€

(☑04 73 65 28 40; www.auberge-dame-tartine. com, in French; rte du Sancy; d €65-80; ☺) This renovated *buron* (shepherd's hut) has rustic rooms with stripped pine furniture, polished floors and to-die-for mountain views. Stout stone, rough brick and hefty rafters fill the restaurant (menus €25), serving mountain recipes including *truffade* (sliced potatoes with Cantal cheese) and *tartiflette* (Savoyard potato, cheese and meat gratin).

✖ Eating

Most of Le Mont-Dore's hotels offer half board, often compulsory during ski season.

La Vieille Étable
CRÊPERIE €€

(☑04 73 65 20 49; rue Maurice Sauvagnat; mains €7.20-16.20; ☺Thu-Mon) A much-loved local favourite (arrive early!). Rich Auvergnat recipes inspire this simple wood-panelled crêperie's wonderful house-special galettes. Try the Montdorienne with Auvergnat ham and *bleu d'Auvergne* cheese.

Le Salon du Capucin
REGIONAL CUISINE €€

(☑04 73 21 89 43; menus €15-35; ☺lunch Wed-Sun, dinner Fri & Sat; ⤵) The heady wooded setting and adventure park (Mont-Dore Aventures) next door fuel your appetite for the filling regional fare at this rural retreat.

Le Bougnat
REGIONAL CUISINE €€

(☑04 73 65 28 19; av Georges Clemenceau; menus €20-28) Hearty mountain dishes are the order of the day at this old farm-style restaurant, with stews and fondues served up at solid wooden tables.

Self-Catering

La Petite Boutique du Bougnat (1 rue Montlosier) sells a smorgasbord of local goodies, including sausages, hams and Auvergnat wine, with cheeses available at its fromagerie (4 rue Montlosier) across the street.

ℹ Information

Post office (place Charles de Gaulle)

s@ncyber (allée Georges Lagaye; per hr €5; ☺2-7pm Mon-Fri) Internet access; extended hours during holidays and the ski season.

Tourist office (☑04 73 65 20 21; www.sancy. com; av de la Libération; ☺9am-12.30pm & 1.30-6pm Mon-Sat, 9am-12.30pm & 1.30-5pm Sun) Posts a daily weather forecast and ski bulletin outside.

TRAIL CENTRAL

The Massif Central is prime walking country, with a network of well-signed trails and as many as 13 GR (long-distance) tracks (including the north–south GR4) criss-crossing the region, supplemented by hundreds of smaller footpaths. Key areas include the Parc des Volcans d'Auvergne and the Monts du Cantal around Murat, and the mountainous area around Le Mont-Dore, Puy de Sancy and the Col de Guéry.

Routes range from day hikes to multiweek epics: hard-core hikers tackle the 290km Traverse of the High Auvergne through the Chaîne des Puys; the Robert Louis Stevenson Trail from Monastier-sur-Gazeille, tracing the author's famous routes through the Cévennes; and the Via Podensis pilgrimage route from Le Puy-en-Velay.

Numerous French-language guidebooks cover walking in the Massif Central, including titles published by Chamina (www.chamina.com, in French).

Online resources abound: www.rando-massifcentral.com (in French) has a database of more than 400 Massif Central walks.

ⓘ Getting There & Around

Direct trains connect Le Mont-Dore with Clermont-Ferrand (€12.40, 1½ hours, two daily), with additional runs by SNCF bus, including some requiring a change at Laqueuille to pick up the train there.

In winter a free skiers' *navette* (shuttle bus) plies regularly between Le Mont-Dore and the Sancy cable car.

Around Le Mont-Dore

LA BOURBOULE
POP 2103 / ELEV 850M

Seven kilometres downriver from Le Mont-Dore, you can experience the spa waters of belle époque La Bourboule at a couple of establishments, including the iconic Les Grands Thermes (☑04 73 81 21 00; www.grandsthermes-bourboule.com, in French; bd Georges Clémenceau; bath/jet shower €14).

Sometimes known as *'la station oxygène'*, La Bourboule is a lovely place to stroll its elegant boulevards and drink in the clear mountain air. From the landscaped Parc Fenestre, filled with giant sequoias, pine trees and open-air games, a télécabine (adult/child return €4.55/2.55) glides up the Plateau de Charlannes (1300m) to summer **hiking trails**.

☷ Sleeping & Eating

Le Pavillon   BOUTIQUE HOTEL €
(☑04 73 65 50 18; www.hotellepavillon.fr, in French; 209 av de l'Angleterre; d €67-87; @❀☊) Rooms at this art deco delight come in softly lit chocolate and caramel tones. Its book-filled lounge is perfect to curl up with coffee, while home-grown herbs and vegetables are used in its restaurant (menus €16-39).

Hôtel Le Parc des Fées   HOTEL €€
(☑04 73 81 01 77; www.parcdesfees.com, in French; 107 quai Maréchal-Fayolle; d €66-71; @❀☊) Definitely ask for a room with Puy de Sancy views at this refined choice mixing belle époque architecture with metro furnishings (leather armchairs, potted plants etc). There's a kids' playroom and a classy restaurant (menus €12-32).

ⓘ Information

La Bourboule's efficient **tourist office** (☑04 73 65 57 71; www.sancy.com; place de la République; ◷9am-noon & 1.30-6pm Mon-Sat) is in the Hôtel de Ville.

ⓘ Getting There & Away

The train to Le Mont-Dore (€1.50, 10 daily) takes just eight minutes.

MUROL & LAC CHAMBON
POP 568 / ELEV 849M

About 10km east of Le Mont-Dore, the 12th-century Château de Murol (☑04 73 26 02 00; www.chateaudemurol.fr, in French; adult/child €9/7; ◷hours vary) squats on a knoll above the surrounding village. Book ahead for medieval guided tours (up to five daily in summer), when costumed guides, scullery maids and jesters re-create daily life in the castle and knights joust beneath the keep.

About 1.5km west of Murol is the **water-sports** playground of Lac Chambon, where you can hire canoes and windsurfing boards from operators along the pretty lakeshore.

🏕 **Camping les Bombes** (☑04 73 88 64 03; www.camping-les-bombes.com; Chemin de Pétary, Chambon-sur-Lac; sites from €13.30 ◷May–mid-Sep; ☷☊), west of the lake, is one of several ecofriendly campgrounds in the Lac Chambon area.

BESSE-EN-CHANDESSE & AROUND
POP 1632 / ELEV 805M

Basalt-brick cottages and cobbled lanes make up the mountain village of Besse-en-Chandesse (also known as Besse-et-Saint-Anastaise), 9.4km south of Murol, where life still ticks along at a laid-back country pace. During the **Transhumance de la Vierge Noire**, local cows are herded to the rich upland pastures on 21 July and back on the first Sunday after 21 September, accompanied by street fairs and fireworks.

Besse is best known for its ski resort Super-Besse (www.sancy.com), less than 7km west of the village, accessible by the D978 or via the GR30 trail in summer (with an optional detour to the 1407m-high summit of Puy de Montchal). Ski passes (p534) are combined with Le Mont-Dore.

In town, skiers will get a kick out of the vintage skis and alpine kit at the Musée du Ski (☑04 73 79 57 30; 11 rue de la Boucherie; admission €4.50; ◷school holidays 9am-noon & 2-7pm). Call to confirm opening times.

ST-NECTAIRE
POP 735 / ELEV 760M

Six kilometres east of Murol, St-Nectaire stretches out along the river beside the D996, and is famed far and wide for its eponymous AOC cheese. The village is split into the newer St-Nectaire-Le-Bas, with a smattering of belle époque buildings remaining from the town's former incarnation as a spa resort; and the much older

St-Nectaire-Le-Haut, reached via a steep switchback lane from the main road.

Sights & Activities

Romanesque church CHURCH
(☉9am-7pm) St-Nectaire's main architectural sight is in the upper village. It has a fine 12th-century statue of the Virgin.

Grottes du Cornadore ROMAN RUINS
(www.grottes-de-cornadore.com; adult/child €6.20/4.70; ☉10am-5pm, closed Nov–mid-Feb) The remains of the town's Roman baths are fascinating.

Site Troglodyte de Jonas CAVES, FRESCOS
(www.grottedejonas.fr; adult/child €6/5; ☉1.30-6pm) Interconnecting caves and medieval frescos, 6km south of town.

La Maison du Fromage CHEESE TASTING
(☎04 73 88 57 97; route de Murol; adult/child €5.50/4.50; ☉10am-noon & 3-7pm) Learn about – and taste – the local cheese.

Auvergne Montgolfière BALLOON RIDES
(☎04 73 88 40 00; www.auvergne-montgolfiere. com; 1/2 adults €240/460) To see St-Nectaire from the air, book a hot-air balloon flight with this outfit. Prices include 4WD transport. Departure points vary according to weather conditions.

Sleeping & Eating
St-Nectaire's hotels include an improbably huge Mercure.

TOP CHOICE **Le Chastel Montaigu** B&B €€€
(☎04 73 96 28 49; www.lechastelmon taigu.com, in French; Montaigut-le-Blanc; d incl breakfast €135-145) Heading 11km east of St-Nectaire on the D996 transports you to this fairytale castle on its own private hilltop. Rebuilt from ruins using authentic medieval materials, the four rooms are filled with heavy stone, rich fabrics and antique wall hangings. One has its own private turret terrace, and all have blindingly good views across the valley. You'll feel like a true *seigneur* wandering around the spiral staircases and medieval terraces. There's a minimum stay of two nights or the full duration of public holiday periods.

Villa St-Hubert B&B €€
(☎04 73 88 41 30; www.villasthubert.com; St-Nectaire-le-Haut; d €50-75; ⊞) Patterned wallpaper, deep, soft beds and a rambling, chestnut-shaded garden make this painstakingly restored 17th-century mansion a treat, as do the *tables d'hôte* (€20; reserve

ahead) served in an opulent dining room lit by chandeliers.

Information
St-Nectaire's **tourist office** (☎04 73 88 50 86; ☉9am-noon & 2-6pm Mon-Fri) is on the main road in St-Nectaire-Le-Bas.

Getting There & Away
A (very) limited one- or two-day-a-week shuttle serves St-Nectaire (check schedules with the tourist office).

Murat & the Monts du Cantal
POP 2154 / ELEV 930M

Tumbling down a steep basalt crag topped by a statue of the Virgin Mary, Murat makes the best base for exploring the Monts du Cantal. With a cluster of dark stone houses huddled beneath the Rocher Bonnevie, it's one of the prettiest towns in the Cantal and a popular hiking and skiing hub.

Sights & Activities
The twisting streets and wonky stone cottages of Murat's old town make an enjoyable afternoon stroll.

To the west are the lofty peaks of Puy Mary (1787m), Plomb du Cantal (1858m) and Puy de Peyre Arse (1806m), the last remnants of an exploded supervolcano that once covered the Cantal Massif.

Église Notre-Dame-des-Oliviers CHURCH
Down in the town, this church is worth a look for its 15th-century bell tower and Vierge Noire.

Maison de la Faune MUSEUM
(www.murat.fr, in French; adult/child €4.50/2.90; ☉10am-noon & 2-5pm Mon-Sat, 2-5pm Sun) Budding entomologists should make a beeline for this spiralling stone tower, opposite place de l'Hôtel de Ville, which houses over 10,000 insects, butterflies and stuffed beasties from the Auvergne to the Amazon.

Rocher Bonnevie WALKING
For the best views you'll need to brave the lung-busting climb up to the top of the Rocher Bonnevie. Local fitness freaks often hold races up to the top, but ordinary mortals reach the summit after about 45 minutes. Follow the red-and-white GR flashes northwestwards out of town, followed by signs for the Rocher.

Le Lioran SKIING
(☑08 25 88 66 00; www.lelioran.com; day ski pass per adult/child €23.50/18.90) Some 14km west of Murat, skiers can hit the slopes here.

🛏 Sleeping & Eating

Auberge de Maître Paul HOTEL €
(☑04 71 20 14 66; www.auberge-paul.fr, in French; 14 place du Planol; s €40, d €50-55, tr €65-70; 🏠) In the middle of Murat, this jovial old favourite has plain, peach-and-yellow rooms spread around the creaky corridors of a 16th-century house. If you're hiking, the owner may even be able to ferry your bags to the next stop. Its reliable Auvergnat restaurant (menus from €9.50) serves planet-sized pizzas for the nippers.

Aux Globe-Trotters HOTEL €
(☑04 71 20 07 22; www.murathotelglobetrotters. com, in French; 22 av du Docteur Mallet; d €34-43; @) Some of the rooms at this cosy spot are jammed up into the top-floor rafters, some overlook the hotel garden, and some face the lively street. All are cute and colourful, with plain pine and a choice of tub or shower.

A la Maison de Justine B&B €
(☑04 71 20 75 72; maurinjc@yahoo.fr; 4 place Gandilhon Gens d'Armes; d €50-65) Right in Murat's medieval heart, this charming three-room B&B is filled with books and antiques.

Camping Municipal Stalapos CAMPGROUND €
(☑04 71 20 01 83; www.camping-murat.com, in French; rue du Stade; sites from €6.20; ⊙Apr-Sep & mid-Dec–mid-Mar; @) Beside the Alagnon River, this pretty campground is 750m south of the train station.

Self-Catering
Near the tourist office, Caldera (3 rue Justin Vigier) sells local cheese, cold cuts, honey, jam and liqueur.

ℹ Information
The tourist office (☑04 71 20 09 47; www. officedetourismepaysdemurat.com; place de l'Hôtel de Ville; ⊙9am-noon & 2-6pm Mon-Sat, 10am-noon Sun) has a wealth of info on walks and activities in the Cantal area.

ℹ Getting There & Around
Buses run by SNCF connect Murat with Clermont-Ferrand (€18.20, 2¼ hours, six daily) and Aurillac (€8.30, one hour).

The countryside makes for splendid, if taxing, cycling. Ô P'tit Montagnard (☑04 71 20 28 40; www.magsport-cantal.com, in French; 8 rue Faubourg Notre Dame) rents reliable machines.

PARC NATUREL RÉGIONAL LIVRADOIS-FOREZ

Blanketed in pine forest, this nature park is one of the largest protected areas in France, stretching from the plains of Limagne in the west to the Monts du Forez in the east. Formerly a centre for logging and agriculture, it's now a haven for nature lovers and weekend walkers.

The Maison du Parc (park information office; ☑04 73 95 57 57; www.parc-livradois-forez. org, in French; ⊙9am-12.30pm & 1.30-5.30pm Mon-Fri, 2-6pm Sat & Sun, closed Sat & Sun early Jun & late Sep) is off the D906 in St-Gervais-sous-Meymont. It's stocked with leaflets detailing local honey shops, lace-makers and perfumers, walking trails and mountain-bike routes.

A lovely (if infrequent) train touristique (☑04 73 82 43 88; www.agrivap.fr, in French) runs through the park from Courpière (15km south of Thiers) via Ambert to La Chaise-Dieu. There are a couple of routes at various times of the year, either aboard a double-decker train panoramique or a vintage steam train.

Thiers
POP 12,559 / ELEV 420M

Precipitously perched above the Gorges de la Durolle, the industrial town of Thiers has been churning out cutlery for centuries and still produces some 70% of the nation's knives.

For an overview head for the Musée de la Coutellerie (Cutlery Museum; www.musee -coutellerie-thiers.com, in French; 23 & 58 rue de la Coutellerie; adult/child €6.90/2.80; ⊙10am-noon & 2-6pm), which is split over two buildings along rue de la Coutellerie. No 23 explores the historical side of cutlery-making, while No 58 houses the museum's unparalleled collection of knives past and present. About 4km upstream from Thiers is the Vallée des Rouets (Valley of the Waterwheels; ⊙noon-6pm), an open-air museum dedicated to the knifemakers who once toiled here in front of water-driven grindstones. The admission price includes a ticket for the shuttle-bus trip from the town museum.

Knife-sellers are dotted round the town's medieval streets lined with half-timbered buildings – ask at the friendly tourist office (☎04 73 80 65 65; www.thiers-tourisme.fr, in French; 1 place du Pirou; ☺9.30am-noon & 2-6pm) for recommended shops.

Thiers isn't worth staying in overnight – it's easily reached by frequent trains from Clermont-Ferrand (€8, 45 minutes).

Ambert

POP 7323 / ELEV 560M

Back in the 16th century, Ambert, 30km north of La Chaise-Dieu, boasted more than 300 water-powered mills supplying the demands of the French paper industry, but the town is better known today for one of the Auvergne's classic cheeses, Fourme d'Ambert.

The tourist office (☎04 73 82 61 90; www.ambert-tourisme.fr; 4 place de l'Hôtel de Ville; ☺9.30am-12.30pm & 1.30-6pm Mon-Sat), opposite the Hôtel de Ville, can help with accommodation.

Around 500 sheets of paper per day are still made using strictly traditional techniques at the restored 14th-century mill Moulin Richard de Bas (www.richarddebas.fr, in French; adult/child €6.50/4.50; ☺9.30am-12.30pm & 2-6pm). It's 4km out of town on the D57.

In Ambert's pedestrianised centre, the Maison de la Fourme d'Ambert (www.maison-fourme-ambert.fr, in French; 29 rue des Chazeaux; adult/child €5/4; ☺10.30am-12.30pm & 1.30-6.30pm Tue-Sat) has displays on the history and manufacture of the town's trademark *fromage*. Three-cheese tastings cost an additional €2.

For local flavour in every sense, grab a table at the busy Brasserie Le Bon Coin (☎04 73 82 03 08; 1 place St-Jean; menus from €29; ♨), where dishes include a bargain €7.90 *plat du jour*. Finish off with its delicious *café gourmand* (coffee accompanied by miniature desserts).

Ambert's Thursday morning **market**, spiralling out around the Hôtel de Ville, is popular with local organic farmers.

SNCF buses connect Ambert with Clermont-Ferrand (€12.90, two hours).

La Chaise-Dieu

POP 885 / ELEV 1082M

The centrepiece of historic La Chaise-Dieu, 42km north of Le Puy-en-Velay, is its monumental Église Abbatiale de St-Robert (☺10am-noon & 2-6pm), built in the 14th century atop an earlier abbey chapel by Pope Clement VI, who served here as a novice monk. Most sights are in the Chœur de l'Église (adult/child €4/1). Highlights include the massive 18th-century **organ**, Clement VI's marble tomb and some fine 16th-century Flemish tapestries, but the most celebrated relic is the chilling fresco **Danse Macabre** in which Death dances a mocking jig around members of 15th-century society.

La Chaise-Dieu's prized organ is also a key part (and the origin) of its prestigious festival of sacred music, held in late August.

Behind the church is the **Salle de l'Echo** – an architectural oddity that allows people on opposite sides of the room to hear each other talking, without being overhead by those in between. It's thought to have been built to enable monks to hear lepers' confessions without contracting the dread disease.

The tourist office (☎04 71 00 01 16; www.la-chaise-dieu.info, in French; place de la Mairie; ☺10am-12.30pm & 2-7pm Tue-Sun) has a free English-language leaflet outlining a walking tour of the village.

Peacefully positioned behind the church, Hotel de l'Echo (☎04 71 00 00 45; hotel delecho@orange.fr; place de l'Echo; d €49-72; ☺Apr–mid-Nov) is a refurbished stone town house with prim rooms and a hearty restaurant (menus from €17) in the old abbey kitchens.

Cute as a button, the frilly rooms at La Jacquerolle (☎04 71 00 07 52; www.lajacquerolle.com, in French; rue Marchédial; d €60-65) B&B are named after flowers and come with plush quilts, antique furniture and wood-panelled walls. Reserve ahead for *tables d'hôte* (€25) using local produce.

Up to three buses per day (€2.50, 45 minutes) link La Chaise-Dieu with Le Puy-en-Velay.

LE PUY-EN-VELAY & AROUND

Le Puy-en-Velay

POP 20,052 / ELEV 630M

Cradled at the base of a broad mountain valley, Le Puy-en-Velay is one of the most striking sights in central France. Three volcanic pillars thrust skywards above the terracotta rooftops, crowned with a trio of ecclesiastical landmarks – a 10th-century church, soaring Romanesque cathedral, and massive cast-iron statue of the Virgin Mary and Child that has stood watch above Le Puy since 1860. Sacred statues and saintly figurines tucked into niches in the medieval and Renaissance houses lining Le Puy's cobbled streets also attest to its role as a focal point for pilgrims for over a millennium, especially those following the Via Podensis from Santiago de Compostela.

Le Puy-en-Velay

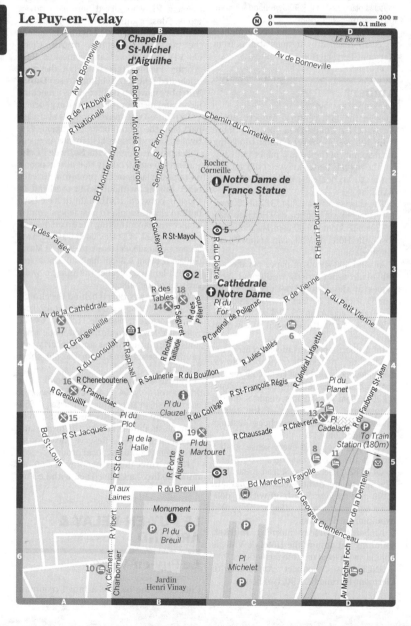

Throughout the lively pedestrianised old town, shops sell the town's trademark exports: lace, lentils, and vivid green liqueur, Verveine.

◉ Sights & Activities

Cathédrale Notre Dame & Cloister
CATHEDRAL, CLOISTER
(www.cathedraledupuy.org; cloister adult/child €5/free; ☺9am-noon & 2-6.30pm) A Unesco-listed wonder, this 11th-century cathedral's multistoreyed facade, soaring pillars, Romanesque archways and Byzantine domes are a celestial sight. The frescoed portal is framed by porphyry columns shipped in from Egypt; inside, it shelters a statue of St Jacques, patron saint of Compostela pilgrims, and one of the Auvergne's most famous Vierges Noires. The 12th-century **cloister** indicates the cathedral's Moorish influences with its multicoloured bricks and columns.

Rocher Corneille & Notre Dame de France
MONUMENT
(adult/child €3/1.50; ☺9am-6pm) Staring out across the rooftops from the tiny portholes inside the rust-red statue of Notre Dame de France (aka the Virgin Mary) that crowns the 757m-high pillar of Rocher Corneille offers dizzying vistas of the town. A creaky spiral staircase winds its way to the top of Le Puy's 22.7m-tall, 835-ton answer to the *Statue of Liberty*, which was fashioned from 213 cannons captured during the Crimean War.

541

PILGRIM'S PASS

Le Puy's four major sights (the cathedral, the Rocher Corneille, the Chapelle St-Michel d'Aiguilhe and the Musée Crozatier) can be visited on a joint **museum pass** (€8.50). Buy it at any of the sights or from the tourist office.

Chapelle St-Michel d'Aiguilhe
CHAPEL
(www.rochersaintmichel.fr, in French; adult/child €3/1.50; ☺9am-6.30pm) Le Puy's oldest chapel (first established in the 10th century, and rebuilt several times since) teeters atop an 85m-high volcanic plug reached by climbing 268 stairs. Stepping inside feels like a lost scene from *Indiana Jones* – the chapel follows the natural contours of the rock, and the unusual carvings and 12th-century frescos create an otherworldly atmosphere.

Centre d'Enseignement de la Dentelle au Fuseau
LACE WORKSHOP
(☎04 71 02 01 68; www.ladentelledupuy.com; 38-40 rue Raphaël; adult/child €3.50/free; ☺9am-noon & 1.30-5.30pm Mon-Fri, 9.30am-4.30pm Sat) As a pilgrimage hub, lace was essential for religious clothing and there were once over 5000 lace workshops hereabouts, though only a handful remain today. At this not-for-profit workshop you can watch bobbin lace-making demonstrations and browse the temporary and permanent exhibits, including intricate patterns, or even

take a **course** (per hour adult/child €16.50/12). The tourist office has details of other workshops that can be visited.

La Distillerie de la Verveine du Velay
VERVEINE DISTILLERY

(☑04 71 03 04 11; www.verveine.com; ⊙10am-noon & 1.30-6.30pm Tue-Sat) Le Puy's fiery green liqueur, Verveine Verte, was invented in 1859 using 32 plants and herbs. Despite its potent 55% alcohol-by-volume strength, it has a refreshingly sweet taste that sees it used in numerous local desserts. Verveine Jaune (yellow) and Verveine Extra (reddish-brown-coloured) varieties are (somewhat) milder at 40% alcohol by volume. During July and August, you can take a 45-minute **guided tour** (€5.90) of its distillery, 6km east along the N88 in St-Germain Laprade. In town, drop into the distillery's new **Espace Pagès Maison Verveine du Velay** (☑04 71 02 46 80; 29 place du Breuil; admission free; ⊙10am-12.30pm & 2.30-7pm); its adjacent bar, **La Distillerie** (⊙Mon-Sat) is the best place in Le Puy for a drink.

Fortresse de Polignac
CASTLE

(www.fondationspolignac.com; adult/child €5/3.50; ⊙10am-12.30pm & 1.30-6.30pm Tue-Sun) Dramatically perched atop a volcanic dome just 5km northwest of Le Puy, this 11th-century château was built by the powerful Polignac family, who once controlled access to the city from the north. It's ringed by a practically continuous wall dotted with lookout towers and a 32m-high rectangular keep.

Musée Crozatier
MUSEUM

(www.mairie-le-puy-en-velay.fr, in French; adult/child €3.20/free; ⊙10am-noon & 2-6pm Wed-Mon Feb-Nov) A hotchpotch of artefacts – from dinosaur bones and Dutch paintings to the first 'praxinoscope', an image-projecting machine that pre-dated modern-day cinema – are on show at Le Puy's museum.

🎉 Festivals & Events

Fête du Roi de l'Oiseau
STREET FESTIVAL

(www.roideloiseau.com, in French) This mid-September four-day street party – complete with outlandish costumes – dates back to 1524, when the title of King *(Roi)* was bestowed on the first archer to shoot down a straw *oiseau* (bird) in return for a year's exemption from taxes.

Latin Music Festival
LATIN MUSIC

A week of tango, flamenco, Cuban, Brazilian and more in mid-July.

Interfolk
FOLK MUSIC

Week-long folk festival in late July.

🛏 Sleeping

The tourist office has a list of *gîtes* and *chambres d'hôte* (B&Bs) in town and the surrounding countryside.

Hôtel du Parc
HOTEL €€

(☑04 71 02 40 40; www.hotel-du-parc-le-puy.com, in French; 4 av Clément Charbonnier; d €75-195; ✳@🅿🛜) Minimalist-chic rooms, adjacent to François Gagnaire's eponymous restaurant, stylishly combine neoretro moulded

---

THE VIA PODENSIS PILGRIMAGE ROUTE

Ever since the 9th century, when a hermit named Pelayo stumbled across the tomb of the apostle James (brother of John the Evangelist), the Spanish town of Santiago de Compostela has been one of the holiest sites in Christendom.

The pilgrimage to Santiago de Compostela is traditionally known as the Camiño de Santiago (Way of St James). There are many different routes from London, Germany and Italy, as well as four that cross the French mainland. But the oldest (and most frequented) French route is the 736km Via Podensis from Le Puy-en-Velay via Figeac, Cahors, Moissac and Rocamadour, established in AD 951 by Le Puy's first bishop.

Early pilgrims were inspired to undertake the arduous journey in exchange for fewer years in purgatory. Today the reward is more tangible: walkers or horse riders who complete the final 100km to Santiago (cyclists the final 200km) qualify for a Compostela Certificate, issued on arrival at the cathedral.

The modern-day **GR36** roughly follows the Via Podensis route, but you'll need good topographic maps if you're going off-road. Plenty of organisations can help you plan your adventure: contact Le Puy's tourist office, or, in Toulouse, the **Association de Coopération Interrégionale: Les Chemins de Saint-Jacques de Compostelle** (☑05 62 27 00 05; www.chemins-compostelle.com, in French). Useful online guides include www.webcompostella.com and www.csj.org.uk.

furniture and enormous bathrooms. The breakfast buffet (€12) includes Gagnaire's lentil yoghurt (see p544).

Hôtel St-Jacques
HOTEL €

(☑04 71 07 20 40; www.hotel-saint-jacques. com; 7 place Cadelade; s €56, d €68-85; ⊙Feb-Dec; ☎📶) It's showing its age, but this intimate little hotel is a great budget base. The pick of the rooms have wood floors, dinky bathrooms and views of the square. Downstairs, the patio café serves knock-out coffee.

Hôtel Le Régina
HOTEL €€

(☑04 71 09 14 71; www.hotelrestregina.com; 34 bd Maréchal Fayolle; s €53-67, d €60-88; ❄☎📶) Topped by a neon-lit art deco turret, the Régina's rooms are individually decorated (our favourite: room 207, with its pop art Chrysler building mural), and some have air-conditioning. Size and style vary considerably depending on price. A grand piano often plays in its refined restaurant (menus €16.50-47).

Hôtel Bristol
HOTEL €€

(☑04 71 09 13 38; www.hotelbristol-lepuy.com; 7-9 av Maréchal Foch; s €52-98, d €62-98; ❄📶) Businessy rooms at this Logis hotel range around its small garden/car park. Rooms in the rear annexe are roomier and smarter (ask for the top floor for rooftop views), while brass fixtures and leather armchairs grace its restaurant (menus €11-28).

Auberge de Jeunesse
HOSTEL €

(☑04 71 05 52 40; auberge.jeunesse@mairie -le-puy-en-velay.fr; 9 rue Jules Vallès; dm €11.20) Inside a former convent, this Hostelling International place has monastic-like dorms and the titchy eat-in kitchen feels cramped when it's busy with hikers, but it's clean and well run, and there's a comfy TV lounge. Phone for info on seasonal openings (and curfews).

Camping Bouthezard
CAMPGROUND €

(☑04 71 09 55 09; chemin de Bouthezard; sites €14.70; ⊙mid-Mar–mid-Oct) Le Puy's campground enjoys an attractive berth beside the River Borne. Bus 6 delivers you outside.

Dyke Hôtel
HOTEL €

(☑04 71 09 05 30; www.dykehotel.fr, in French; 37 bd Maréchal Fayolle; s €39-56, d €46-56; ☎) Named for a volcanic pillar (in case you're wondering), this small hotel is well located if unexciting, with modernish rooms of varying dimensions, some with balconies onto the (very) busy road.

✗ Eating

The local lentille verte du Puy (green Puy lentil; www.lalentilleverttedupuy.com) is the sole pulse with Appellation d'Origine Contrôlée (AOC) classification in mainland France (the only other is the lentille de Cilaos on the French island of Réunion). Rich in protein, vitamin B and iron and gluten-free, Le Puy's lentils are used in dishes ranging from the time-honoured to inventive creations. See also p544.

La Parenthèse
TOP CHOICE · REGIONAL CUISINE €€

(☑04 71 02 83 00; http://laparen-these43.free.fr, in French; 8 av rue de la Cathédrale; menus €18.50-26.50; ⊙Mon-Fri) Rustic farmhouse-style decor fills this cosy spot serving traditional dishes with heart-warming pride. Start with the tartare de saumon et lentilles vertes du Puy (raw salmon with Le Puy lentils); mains are accompanied by a sizzling pot of aligot. Afterwards, don't miss the assiette verveine: verveine ice cream served in a chocolate cup, a moist emerald-coloured macaron and a shot of liqueur.

François Gagnaire
GASTRONOMIC €€€

(☑04 71 02 40 40; www.francois-gagnaire-rest aurant.com, in French; 4 av Clément-Charbonnier; menus €36-97; ⊙by reservation; 📶) Seasonal openings vary, but in any case it's worth booking ahead for a table at the Michelin-starred restaurant of François Gagnaire. Adventurous little tastebuds are catered for with a 'young gastronome' menu (€25).

Comme à la Maison
FRENCH €€

(☑04 71 02 94 73; rue Séguret; menus €23-53; ⊙lunch Tue-Fri & Sun, dinner Tue-Sat) This little restaurant is easy to miss, but if you manage to find it you'll be rewarded with inventive dishes such as fennel-and-mackerel tart or foie gras with dried fruit, served in a funky dining room blending old architecture with bold colours. Excellent and bang up to date, it's where Le Puy's top chefs dine on their days off.

Entrez les Artistes
REGIONAL CUISINE €€

(☑04 71 09 71 78; 29 rue Pannessac; menus €14.50-25; ⊙lunch Tue-Sat, dinner Thu-Sat) Lashings of local lace adorn this cosy place, which dishes up solid local fare – nothing too fancy, but dead filling.

Also recommended:

A Choumas'
REGIONAL CUISINE €€

(☑04 71 03 03 94; 1 place Cadelade; menus €15-30; ⊙Wed-Sun) Cheese dishes galore including steaming fondue.

LOCAL KNOWLEDGE

FRANÇOIS GAGNAIRE: CHEF

Background

I was born in Le Puy-en-Velay and trained under three-star Michelin chefs in Paris and worked all over France and in Japan and Chile, but returned to open my restaurant (p543) for the quality of life and the quality of produce here.

Culinary Philosophy

Using traditional regional products in a modern way; with a forward focus. I keep a notebook and try out different things... the *lentille verte du Puy* can be used for the whole meal.

A Contemporary Lentil-Based Meal?

For the starter, *le caviar du Velay*. Lentils were traditionally known as *caviar du pauvre* (poor man's caviar), which gave me the idea for this dish: first I cook the lentils separately, then in a langoustine bisque, then mix them with the jelly from the bisque and present in a tin – it looks like real caviar! It's spooned onto blinis made with lentil flour and served with lentil soup. For the main course, whole-grain lentils go well with la Noire du Velay (locally bred black lamb). For the cheese course, lentil yoghurt, made from lentil pulp. For dessert, Verveine (local liqueur) soufflé served with lentil confit – cooked with vanilla and sugar – and lentil ice cream.

L'Âme des Poètes　REGIONAL CUISINE　€€
(☑04 71 05 66 57; 16 rue Séguret; menus €22; ⊗mid-Mar–mid-Oct) Lovely umbrella-shaded garden and house-specialty lentil lasagne.

Le Croco　REGIONAL CUISINE　€
(☑04 71 02 40 13; 5 rue Chaussade; menus €8-19; ⊗Mon-Sat; ☑) Simple spot specialising in huge salads and platters featuring Auvergnat ingredients.

Self-Catering

Le Puy's weekly market takes over place du Plot (starting point for the Via Podensis) every Saturday morning. The town's covered market is just off rue Grenouillit. Fromagerie Coulaud (24 rue Grenouillit; ⊗Tue-Sat) has a good selection of local cheeses.

ⓘ Information

Cyb'Aire (17 rue Général Lafayette; per hr before/after 2pm €2.70/3.50; ⊗9am-8pm Mon-Sat, 3-7pm Sun) Welcoming internet café.

Main post office (8 av de la Dentelle)

Tourist office (☑04 71 09 38 41; www.ot-lepuy envelay.fr; 2 place du Clauzel; ⊗8.30am-noon & 1.30-6.15pm;)

ⓘ Getting There & Away

Destinations served by train include Lyon (€20.40, 2½ hours, three to five daily) and Clermont-Ferrand (€21.30, two hours, four to six daily).

ⓘ Getting Around

All five lines of the local TUDIP buses (single ticket/10-trip *carnet* €1.15/8) stop at place Michelet.

For a taxi call ☑04 71 05 42 43.

Gorges de l'Allier

About 30km west of Le Puy, the salmon-filled Allier River – paralleled by the scenic Clermont–Ferrand–Nîmes rail line – weaves between rocky, scrub-covered hills and steep cliffs. Above the river's east bank, the narrow D301 gives fine views as it passes through wild, wide-open countryside and remote, mud-puddle hamlets.

In the sleepy town of Langeac (population 3943), the tourist office (☑04 71 77 05 41; www.haut-allier.com, in French; place Aristide Briand; ⊗9am-noon & 2-6pm Mon-Sat) has details of walking trails crisscrossing the valley walls as well as companies offering canyoning and white-water rafting, such as Tonic Rafting (☑04 71 57 23 90; www.raft-canyon.fr, in French; €54-119).

To explore the area at a gentler pace, book ahead to board the scenic Train des Gorges de l'Allier (☑04 71 77 70 17; www.trainstouristiques-ter.com; adult €10.90-19.90, child €6.90-11.90; ⊗May-Sep), which trundles through the gorges to/from Langeac. Days and itineraries vary.

Plentiful campgrounds in the valley include Langeac's tree-shaded riverside Camping les Gorges de l'Allier (☎04 71 77 05 01; www.campinglangeac.com, in French; sites €12.50; ◷Apr-Oct).

Le Moulin Ferme-Auberge (☎04 71 74 03 09; www.gite-aubergedumoulin.com, in French; St-Arcons-d'Allier; dm €15, with half board €35, d incl breakfast/half board €55/95) has charmingly renovated stone cottages, with dinner served at a big communal table in the 15th-century mill.

La Montagne Protestante

Around 40km east of Le Puy is the sparsely populated highland area, carpeted in rich pastureland and thick fir forest, known as La Montagne Protestante due to its stout Protestant principles. The area's most distinctive landmarks are the peaks of Mont Meygal (1436m), and Mont Mézenc (1753m), the summit of which is accessible via the GR73 and GR7 hiking trails. On a clear day, sweeping views across southeastern France stretch from Mont Blanc, 200km to the northeast, to Mont Ventoux, 140km to the southeast.

Villages are few and far between, but one in particular is worth seeking out – Le Chambon-sur-Lignon (population 2834), 45km east of Le Puy-en-Velay, which played a courageous role in WWII, when the village and surrounding hamlets sheltered over 3000 refugees, including hundreds of Jewish children, from deportation by the Nazis. Info on the town's history is available from the tourist office (☎04 71 59 71 56; www.ot-hautlignon.com; route de Tence; ◷9am-noon & 2-6.30pm Mon-Sat, 10am-noon Sun), which also has details of outdoor activities in the area including horse riding and mountain climbing.

Limousin, the Dordogne & the Lot

Best Places to Eat

» Le Clos St-Front (p566)
» Le Grand Bleu (p572)
» La Ferme de Biorne (p585)
» Auberge de la Truffe (p568)
» Bistro de l'Octroi (p572)

Best Places to Stay

» Château de Castel-Novel (p560)
» Château les Merles (p585)
» Oustal del Barry (p591)
» Camping à la Ferme du Masvidal (p563)
» Domaine des Chapelles (p556)

Why Go?

Together, Limousin, the Dordogne and the Lot are the heart and soul of *la belle France,* an enchanting land of dense oak forests, emerald-green fields and famously rich country cooking. Turreted châteaux and medieval villages line the riverbanks, while wooden-hulled *gabarres* (barges) meander along the waterways.

Of the three adjacent areas, the Limousin *région* – encompassing the Haute-Vienne, Creuse and Corrèze *départements* – is the most traditional, strewn with country farms and sleepy hidden hamlets, as well as a cache of architectural treasures from the Middle Ages in its main hub, Limoges. To the south, the Dordogne *département* has a bevy of *bastides* (fortified towns) and clifftop castles as well as astonishing prehistoric sites including some of Europe's oldest and most spectacular cave paintings. Further south still, the Lot *département* is ribboned with twisting rivers, limestone gorges, subterranean caverns, and vintage vineyards basking in the warm southern French sunshine.

When to Go

Limoges

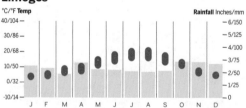

°C/°F Temp — Rainfall Inches/mm

Late February Feast on goose-based specialties as Sarlat-la-Canéda celebrates its feathered mascot.	**Mid-May** See strawberry parades, auctions and more, paint picturesque Beaulieu-sur-Dordogne red.	**December to March** Browse markets selling Périgord black truffles, particularly in 'truffle capital' Sorges.

Regional Parks

This corner of France is renowned for its unspoilt natural beauty, with huge swathes protected in three *parcs naturels régionaux*: **Périgord-Limousin** (www.parc-naturel-perigord-limousin.fr, in French) in the northwest, **Millevaches en Limousin** (www.pnr-millevaches.fr, in French) in the east and **Causses de Quercy** (www.parc-causses-du-quercy.org, in French) in the south. All three regional parks offer a wealth of outdoor activities. Tourist offices throughout the region stock *balades à la journée* (day walk) leaflets and *VTT* (*vélo tout terrain*; mountain bike) guides, while dedicated park topoguides detail major walking routes including the GR (*grands randonées*; long-distance) trails. Numerous trails and bridleways can also be explored on horseback.

RIVER TRIPS

One of the most memorable ways to explore the region is along its scenic waterways. Canoe and kayak operators abound, generally charging under €30 per day including minibus transport, *gilets* (life jackets) and an introduction to basic safety procedures (such as how to survive capsizing!). Or simply sit back and watch the countryside float by aboard a traditional *gabarre* (flat-bottomed boat; see p583).

Unmissable Villages

» **Rocamadour** Clinging to a plunging cliff-face, this ancient pilgrimage spot is one of France's most awe-inspiring sights.

» **St-Cirq Lapopie** Artist studios are tucked throughout the tiny streets of gravity-defying St-Cirq high on a hilltop above the Lot Valley.

» **Brantôme** Pleasure-cruise boats ply the waters of this Venetian-style village criss-crossed by medieval bridges.

» **Collonges-la-Rouge** Red sandstone houses and an 11th-century church huddle in the narrow lanes of France's original 'most beautiful village'.

» **Najac** Nestled beneath a fairy-tale castle in remote rolling countryside.

PRIME HIKING COUNTRY

» Northwest Limousin's mountains

» Along the Lot Valley

» The age-old Santiago de Compostela route, which passes through many of the region's southerly towns

Resources

The area's official tourism sites are a handy way to keep tabs on upcoming festivals, events and exhibitions.

» www.tourismelimousin.com

» www.tourisme-hautevienne.com

» www.tourisme-creuse.com

» www.vacances-en-correze.net

» www.dordogne-perigord-tourisme.fr

» www.tourisme-lot.com

Most Atmospheric Markets

» **Sarlat-La-Canéda** Saturday sees Sarlat's spiderweb of cobbled lanes spill over with stalls laden with local specialties like walnuts, wine and foie gras.

» **Perigueux** Gourmet delicacies galore fill Perigueux's squares on Wednesday and Saturday.

» **Brive-la-Gaillarde** Hectic outdoor markets burst into life every Tuesday and Saturday.

Limousin, the Dordogne & the Lot Highlights

1 Marvel at the prehistoric cave art sheltered in the wooded **Vézère Valley** (p573)

2 Listen to the music of glamorous and eccentric diva Josephine Baker inside her former home, **Château des Milandes** (p582)

3 Tour the stallions' stables, mares' stable and magnificent château of one of France's foremost *haras* (stud farms) at **Arnac-Pompadour** (p559)

4 Taste the local firewater *l'eau de noix* (walnut liqueur) at its 1839-established distillery in **Brive-la-Gaillarde** (p559)

5 Watch craftspeople at work at one of the oldest traditional French accordion-makers in **Tulle** (p561)

6 Stroll the walkways circumnavigating an excavated 1st-century Roman villa in **Périgueux** (p565)

7 Visit the prestigious factories producing France's finest china in **Limoges** (p553)

❶ Getting There & Around

AIR The major transport hub is Limoges, which has regular flights to many French and UK cities. Bergerac also has domestic and international budget flights, as does the new airport at Brive-la-Gaillarde.

BUS The bus network is patchy and frustratingly geared around school timetables; most towns and villages can be reached more quickly and easily by train. A useful rail link runs to Toulouse from Limoges via Brive-la-Gaillarde, Souillac and Cahors; Limoges and Périgueux are both on the southwest main line from Paris.

CAR As always in rural France, having your own wheels is really handy. The A20 motorway heads north from Limoges to Paris and continues south to Toulouse.

LIMOUSIN

With its quiet lanes, flower-filled villages and country markets, Limousin is tailor-made for walkers and cyclists and the perfect place to escape the summertime crowds further south.

The Limousin *région* is made up of three *départements*: Haute-Vienne, in the west, the *préfecture* (capital) of which is the lively city of Limoges; the rural Creuse, in the northeast; and, in the southeast, the Corrèze, home to many of the region's most beautiful villages.

Limoges

POP 141.287

If you're a china connoisseur, you'll already be familiar with the legendary name of Limoges. For over 200 years this elegant city has been the preferred place for the French upper crust to pick up their tableware, and several factories around the city still produce France's finest china. You can see some stunning examples at museums and galleries as well as public spaces around town.

Compact and lively, Limoges is easy to explore on foot. Historic buildings and museums cluster in the medieval Cité quarter and radiate out from the partly pedestrianised Château quarter in the city centre. If you come by train you'll be arriving in style: the city's grand art deco Gare des Bénédictins, completed in 1929, is one of France's most resplendent railway stations, graced by a copper dome, carved frescos and a copper-topped clock tower.

◉ Sights

To discover Limoges' famous enamel and porcelain, see p553.

CHÂTEAU QUARTER

This bustling corner of Limoges is the heart of the old city. Just off place St-Aurélien, the rue de la Boucherie – named after the butchers' shops that lined the street in the Middle Ages – contains many of the city's loveliest timbered houses. The Maison de la Boucherie (36 rue de la Boucherie; admission free; ◉10am-1pm & 2-7pm Jul-Sep) houses a small history museum, and nearby is the tiny Chapelle Saint-Aurélien, dedicated to the patron saint of butchers.

Named for the two granite lions flanking the door, the Église St-Michel des Lions (rue Adrien Dubouché) was built between the 14th and 16th centuries. It contains St-Martial's relics (including his head) and some beautiful 15th-century stained glass, but its most notable feature is the huge copper ball perched atop its 65m-high spire.

Nearby is the Cour du Temple, a tiny enclosed courtyard reached via an alleyway from rue du Temple. The courtyard was formerly a private garden belonging to the nearby *hôtels particulier* (private mansions): look out for various coats-of-arms and the 16th-century stone staircase around the edge of the courtyard.

All that remains of the great pilgrimage abbey of St-Martial, founded in AD 848, is an outline on place de la République. The Crypt of St-Martial contains the tomb of Limoges' first bishop, who converted the population to Christianity. Just to the east is the moody Église St-Pierre du Queyroix (place St-Pierre), which is notable for its characteristic Limousin belfry and stained glass.

Once you've done your cultural duty, chill out at the Aquarium du Limousin (www.aquariumdulimousin.com; 2 bd Gambetta; adult €7, child €4.50-5.50; ◉10.30am-6.30pm), where 2500 fish swim in the subterranean surroundings of Limoges' old water reservoirs.

CITÉ QUARTER

A few steps east of the Château quarter more fine medieval buildings occupy the Cité quarter, where you'll find Limoges' premier museums. Dominating the quarter is the Cathédrale St-Étienne, one of the few Gothic churches south of the Loire. Built

Limoges

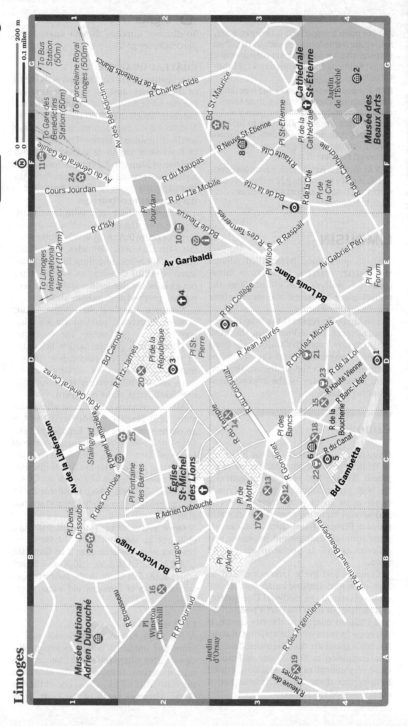

0   200 m
0   0.1 miles

To Bus Station (50m)
To Porcelaine Royal Limoges (500m)
To Gare des Bénédictins Station (50m)
To Limoges International Airport (10.2km)

R de Pénitents Blancs
R Charles Gide
Av des Bénédictins
Av du Général de Gaulle
Cours Jourdan
R d'Isly
R du Maupas
R du 71e Mobile
Pl Jourdan
Bd de Fleurus
R des Tanneries
Av Garibaldi
Bd St-Maurice
R Neuve St-Étienne
Pl St-Étienne
R Haute Cité
R de la Cité
Pl de la Cité
Bd de la cité
R Raspail
Pl Wilson
Bd Louis Blanc
Av Gabriel Péri
Pl du Forum
Cathédrale St-Étienne
Jardin de l'Évêché
Musée des Beaux Arts
R de la Cathédrale

Cathédrale St-Étienne
Av de la Libération
Bd Carnot
R Fitz-James
Pl de la République
Pl St-Pierre
R du Collège
R du Consulat
R Jean Jaurès
R Charles Michels
R de la Loi
R Haute Vienne
R Banc-Léger
R du Temple
Pl des Bancs
R de la Boucherie
R du Canal
Bd Gambetta
R Gondinet
R du Général Cerez
Pl Stalingrad
R Daniel Lamazière
Pl Fontaine des Barres
R des Combes
R Denis Dussoubs
Église St-Michel des Lions
R Adrien Dubouché
Pl de la Motte
Pl d'Aine
Bd Victor Hugo
R Turgot
Av Garibaldi
Musée National Adrien Dubouché
R Brousseau
Pl Winston Churchill
R R Couraud
Jardin d'Orsay
R Neuve des Carmes
R des Argentiers
R Périmenaud Beaupréyat

between 1273 and 1888, the cathedral's highlights include the richly decorated Portail St-Jean, as well as a glorious rose window and a Renaissance rood screen. To the cathedral's south, both medicinal and toxic herbs flourish in the Jardin de l'Évêché, Limoges' botanical garden.

Limoges

The massively refurbished Musée des Beaux Arts (www.museedesbeaux-artsdelimoges.fr; place de la Cathédrale), housed in Limoges' 18th-century bishops palace, is due to have reopened by the time you read this. Its huge decorative-arts collection includes lesser-known paintings by **Pierre Auguste Renoir** (1841–1919), who was born in Limoges and worked in a porcelain factory as a boy, painting designs on fine china.

The Limousin was a stronghold of the Resistance during WWII, and the Musée de la Résistance et de la Déportation is due to reopen at new, expanded premises. The museum's collection ranges from radios to weapons, diaries, letters and even a Free French aeroplane. Ask at the tourist office for updates.

Near the cathedral, the Cité des Métiers et des Arts (www.cma-limoges.com, in French; 5 rue de la Règle; adult/child €5/2.50; ◎2-6pm) showcases work by top members of France's craft guilds.

🛏 Sleeping

Limoges makes a good weekend break, when rates often drop. The majority of the city's hotels are located around the train station.

Nos Rev   HOTEL €
(☑05 55 77 41 43; www.hotelnos-rev.com, in French; 16 rue du Général du Bessol; d €47-72; 🕿) A breath of fresh air, Nos Rev does away with old-fashioned furnishings – its dozen contemporary rooms are decorated in adventurous colours like lime and cherry red, with sharp, stylish bathroom fixtures. For the price, this is the best deal in town. The hotel is just a couple of blocks west of the train station.

Arthôtel Tendance   HOTEL €€
(☑05 55 77 31 72; www.arthoteltendance.com; 37 rue Armand Barbès; s €65-85, d €71-95; @🕿) Decor spans the globe at this quirky 13-room hotel. Its *chambres de thème* include a maple-clad Canadian cabin, a Balinese room with Lombok furniture, and a Grecian room decked out in whites and sea blues. Other overnight destinations include Africa, Egypt, Provence and Morocco. It's around 500m northwest of the train station.

Hôtel de la Paix   HOTEL €
(☑05 55 34 36 00; hoteldelapaix87@hotmail.com; 25 place Jourdan; d €42.50-72; 🕿) This creaky classic is a bit faded but full of charm. The

FROM CATTLE & CLOAKS TO HIGH-CLASS CARS

Limos – stretch or otherwise – may not have originated in Limousin, but the term certainly did. Centuries ago, shepherds who raised Limousin's famed beef cattle wore long cloaks to keep out the cold and rain. Fast-forward to the beginning of the 20th century, when new, luxurious cars were designed with enclosed passenger compartments and open, though roofed, drivers' seats. This open-sided roof resembled the hood of a Limousin cloak, hence the car was named a limousine (the feminine version of *Limousin* in French). The abbreviation limo first appeared in the 1960s. To this day, limo drivers sit in a separate compartment to their passengers (as opposed to other chauffer-driven cars), just like their horse-drawn carriage predecessors.

ground floor is occupied by the owner's Mechanical Music Museum, stuffed with gramophones, rinky-dink record players, barrel organs and other musical oddities, while the upper corridors hide small, clean, serviceable rooms livened up by the odd theatrical knick-knack.

Château Ribagnac   B&B €€

(📞05 55 39 77 91; www.chateauribagnac.com; St Martin-Terressus; d incl breakfast €100-180; 🛜🏊) Heading slightly further afield (19km east of Limoges) brings you to this aristocratic estate owned by two British ex-lawyers, whose struggles to renovate the château were documented in the fly-on-the-wall UK TV series *No Going Back*. It's a real palace, with rooms ranging from a chandelier-lit grand suite to a super-romantic honeymoon suite with its own balcony. You can relax during communal *tables d'hôte* (half board from €200 per double including wine by reservation) as kids dine together earlier.

Hôtel Familia   HOTEL €

(📞05 55 77 51 40; www.hotelfamilia.fr, in French; 18 rue du Général du Bessol; s €48-55, d €53-60) This small family-run hotel is the pick of the budget places near the station. Forget frills – easy-clean fabrics and pastel colours

are the order of the day – but it's good value, especially if you get a room over the flowery back garden.

Hôtel Jeanne d'Arc   HOTEL €€

(📞05 55 77 67 77; www.hoteljeannedarc-limoges. fr; 17 av du Général de Gaulle; s €66-84, d €79-98; 🛜) Originally a *relais de poste* (mail staging post), this smart hotel makes a fine base as long as you're not after anything avant-garde. Classic decor includes richly coloured checked and striped fabrics, heavy drapes and hefty furniture.

🍴 Eating

Les Petits Ventres   REGIONAL CUISINE €€

(📞05 55 34 22 90; www.les-petits-ventres.com; 20 rue de la Boucherie; lunch menus €14.50-25, dinner menus €25-35; ⊘closed Sun & Mon Sep; 🚹) One of several atmospheric restaurants in the old butchers' district, this wood-beamed dining room specialises in meat-heavy classics, from *andouillettes* (tripe sausages) to *fricassée de rognons* (fried kidneys).

Le 27   FRENCH €€

(📞05 55 32 27 27; www.le27.com, in French; 27 rue Haute-Vienne; lunch menus €13.50-14.50, mains €15-23.50; ⊘Mon-Sat) Blending contemporary decor with culinary invention at this cutting-edge restaurant, teardrop lanterns twinkle, neon lights buzz and waistcoated waiters bustle, while the menu takes in everything from gingered guinea-fowl to 'mysterious meringue'. One whole wall is taken up by the wine selection, so you won't be short of a tipple.

Chez Alphonse   REGIONAL CUISINE €€

(📞05 55 34 34 14; 5 place de la Motte; menus €10-25; ⊘Mon-Sat) Hearty ingredients, rich sauces and hard-core French cooking define this unpretentious checked-tablecloth stalwart. The menu's stuffed with regional dishes (including horse steak and veal head), so if you want to try traditional Limousine cuisine, this is definitely the place.

La Parenthèse   RESTAURANT, TEAROOM €

(www.restaurant-tearoom-parenthese-limoges. com; Cour du Temple, 22 rue du Consulat; menus €13.50-16; ⊘11.45am-2.30pm Mon, 10am-6.30pm Tue-Sat; 🅿) Forty teas and 14 coffees are served, in Limoges porcelain of course, at this charming spot, along with salads and traditional menus incorporating regional produce. Save space for the delicious

For over 300 years the name of Limoges has been synonymous with *les arts du feu* (fire arts): *émail* (enamel) and *porcelaine* (porcelain). Limoges had been producing decorative enamel since at least the 12th century, but its fortunes were transformed by the discovery of an extremely pure form of kaolin near St-Yrieix-La-Perche in 1768. This fine white china clay, a vital ingredient in porcelain manufacture (along with quartz and feldspar), had previously been imported at huge expense from the Far East. Its discovery on home soil led to an explosion of hard-paste porcelain production in Limoges in the late-18th and 19th centuries.

Three factors distinguish porcelain from other clay-baked ceramics: it's white, extremely hard and translucent. Porcelain is fired three times, first at about 950°C; again, after being covered by liquid enamel, at about 1450°C, and one last time, at 900°C or so, to ensure the hand-painted or machine-applied decoration adheres to the surface.

Keep your eyes peeled while you wander around the city: many of Limoges' buildings are decorated with porcelain and enamel tiles, such as Pavillon du Verdurier (place St-Pierre), an octagonal, porcelain-faced structure dating from 1900, and the Halles Centrales, with a porcelain fresco depicting the goodies on sale in the market.

Museums and galleries with superb examples of the city's famous fire arts:

Musée National Adrien Dubouché (www.musee-adriendubouche.fr; 8bis place Winston Churchill; adult/child €4.50/free, 1st Sun of month free; ⊙10am-12.25pm & 2-5.40pm Wed-Mon) National museum, with stunning new extensions due to open in 2011, housing one of the two great china collections in France (the other is in Sèvres, near Paris). The 12,000-strong collection features pieces from the golden age of Limoges porcelain as well as from rival factories such as Meissen, Royal Doulton and Worcester, ranging from dinner services and hand-painted vases to porcelain clocks and delicate figurines.

Musée des Beaux Arts (p551) Due to display enamel and porcelain.

Maison de l'Émail (www.enamel-house.com; 18-20 bd de la Cité; admission free; ⊙2-7pm Wed-Sat) Provides a fascinating overview of techniques and hosts exhibitions; serious aficionados should ask about guided visits (in French).

Galerie du Canal (www.galerieducanal.fr, in French; 15 rue du Canal; admission free; ⊙10am-noon & 2-7pm Tue-Sat) Cooperative gallery run by local enamellers displaying contemporary work.

Many of the city's famous factories producing celebrated *marques* (brands) are still in business; the following all have factory shops.

Porcelaine Royal Limoges (☏05 55 33 27 30; www.royal-limoges.fr; 28 rue Donzelot; ⊙shop 10am-6.30pm Mon-Sat) One of the oldest factories, dating from 1797 and housing the Four des Casseaux (www.fourdescasseaux.fr; admission €3; ⊙10.30am-5.30pm Mon-Sat), the only surviving example of the original mighty brick kilns. Standing 19.5m high and capable of reaching the searing temperatures needed to fire porcelain, it certainly puts your microwave into perspective. It's 500m southeast of the train station.

Haviland (www.haviland.fr; av du Président Kennedy; admission free; ⊙10am-1pm & 2-6.30pm Mon-Sat) Screens an informative film and has a little museum. Located 3km southeast of the city centre.

Bernardaud (☏05 55 10 55 91; www.bernardaud.fr; 27 av Albert Thomas; tours adult/child €4.50/free; ⊙9am-11.15am & 1-4pm) Has a small museum and offers guided tours taking you step by step from raw materials to finished pieces – phone ahead for tour times or ask at the tourist office. Bernardaud is situated 1km northwest of the city centre.

homemade desserts like tangy *tarte au citron meringuée* (lemon meringue pie).

Le Bistrot Gourmand
FRENCH €€

(www.bistrotgourmand.fr, in French; 7 place Winston Churchill; menus €10-19.50; ⊙Mon-Sat; ⊛) A lively student crowd fills the wrought-iron and marble tables of this busy bistro lined with vintage advertising posters and paintings. Give yourself plenty of time to deliberate over no fewer than 105 *plats* and 60 different desserts.

Planetalis
ORGANIC €

(www.planetalis.com, in French; place de la République; menus €10-11; ⊙7.30am-8.30pm Mon-Sat; ⊘) If you're a vegetarian and feeling a little unloved about now, drop into Limoges' branch of this *bio* (organic) canteen -style French chain for vitamin-packed sandwiches, salads and hot dishes to eat in or take away.

For the full-flavoured local dining experience, head to the bistros in and around the Halles Centrales, crammed with everyone from office workers to market traders:

Le Bistrot d'Olivier
REGIONAL CUISINE €

(Halles Centrales; menus €12-15; ⊙7am-2pm Mon-Sat) Bistros don't get more Gallic than this rough-and-ready gem.

Chez François
REGIONAL CUISINE €

(Halles Centrales; menus €11-20; ⊙6am-2pm Mon-Sat) If Le Bistrot d'Olivier's full, squeeze in here for authentic local cooking.

Le P'tit Bouchon
REGIONAL CUISINE €

(17 place de la Motte; menus €13; ⊙7am-3pm Tue-Sat) Endearingly scruffy little bistro opposite the market dishing up lunchtime staples to a convivial crowd.

Self-Catering

Halles Centrales (place de la Motte; ⊙to 1pm) covered market is full of local-produce stalls that run the gourmet gamut from local cheese to Limousin beef.

Foodie haven **Paroles de Chef** (☎05 55 32 30 66; www.parolesdechef.com; 15 rue Neuve des Carmes; ⊙épicerie Tue-Sat) has a gourmet *épicerie* (grocer) and runs cooking and wine-tasting courses (from €50), as well as its own restaurant.

Drinking & Entertainment

The large student crowd keeps Limoges' nightspots ticking; you'll find most of the action around rue Charles Michels and place Denis Dussoubs.

Event tickets are sold at **Fnac** (☎08 25 02 00 20; 8 rue des Combes; ⊙2-7pm Mon, 10am-7pm Tue-Sat).

Le Buckingham
BAR, CLUB

(www.lebuckinghamclub.com, in French; 23 bd St-Maurice; ⊙Thu-Sat) Uber-cool late-night bar/disco spinning up-to-the-minute tunes until 7am.

Le Duc Étienne
BAR

(place St-Aurélien; ⊙daily) This long-standing hang-out in the medieval quarter has a hip little bar supplying European beers and late-night coffee to a pre-club crowd. In summer things spill onto the terrace in front of Église St-Aurélien.

La Fourmi
LIVE MUSIC

(www.lafourmi87.net, in French; 3 rue de la Font Pinot) The best place in town for musos, with breaking acts, alternative bands and theatrical spectacles in a twin-floored warehouse-style space. It's about 1km out of town, but worth the trek. Opening times vary so check the website for what's on when.

L'Amicale des Parachutistes Belges
LIVE MUSIC

(www.myspace.com/parachutistes_belges; 17 rue Charles Michels; ⊙Tue-Sun) Belgian beers and a buzzy gig scene are the draws at this boozer where soul, funk, ragga and rock acts regularly grace the stage.

Le Tabernacle
LIVE MUSIC

(http://limoges.limousin.free.fr/tabernacle, in French; 19 rue de la Loi; ⊙Wed-Sat) Part pub, part club, part grungy gig venue. Bare brick and industrial styling conjure up a lived-in vibe at this late-night venue.

Grand Écran (www.grandecran.fr, in French; 9-11 place Denis Dussoubs) Multiplex cinema screening nondubbed films.

Cinéma Lido (www.allocine.fr; 3 av du Général de Gaulle) Artier films.

ℹ Information

Main post office (1 rue Daniel Lamazière) Offers currency-exchange services and has an ATM.

Post office (6 bd de Fleurus) Has an ATM.

TendanceWeb (www.tendanceweb.com, in French; 5 bd Victor Hugo; per hr €3; ⊙10am-2am Mon-Thu, 10am-4am Fri & Sat, 2pm-2am Sun) Internet access.

On the afternoon of 10 June 1944, the little town of Oradour-sur-Glane, 21km northwest of Limoges, witnessed one of the worst Nazi war crimes committed on French soil. German lorries belonging to the SS 'Das Reich' Division surrounded the town and ordered the population on to the market square. The men were divided into groups and forced into *granges* (barns), where they were machine-gunned before the structures were set alight. Several hundred women and children were herded into the church, and the building was set on fire, along with the rest of the town. Only one woman and five men survived the massacre; 642 people, including 193 children, were killed. The same SS Division committed a similarly brutal act in Tulle two days earlier, in which 99 Resistance sympathisers were strung up from the town's balconies as a macabre warning to others.

Since these events, the entire village (☺9am-6pm) has been left untouched, complete with tram tracks, prewar electricity lines, the blackened shells of buildings and the rusting hulks of 1930s automobiles – an evocative memorial to a once-peaceful village caught up in the brutal tide of war. At the centre of the village is an underground memorial inscribed with the victims' names; poignantly, there are also display cases collecting their recovered belongings, including watches, wallets, hairpins and a couple of children's bikes.

Entry is via the Centre de la Mémoire (adult/child €7.70/5.20), which contextualises the massacre using historical exhibitions, video displays and survivors' testimonies. Various theories have been put forward to try to explain the event – perhaps German panic following the Allied landings four days earlier, or reprisal for sabotage raids committed by the Resistance following the invasion – but it may be one of those terrible events that simply defies any rational explanation.

After the war Oradour was rebuilt a few hundred metres west of the ruins. Buses travel from the bus station in Limoges to Oradour-sur-Glane (€2, 30 minutes, several daily except Sundays in winter). By car, take the D9 and follow signs to the *village martyr* (martyred village).

Tourist office (☎05 55 34 46 87; www.tourisme-limoges.com; 12 bd de Fleurus; ☺9am-7pm Mon-Sat, 10am-6pm Sun; ☎)

ℹ Getting There & Away

Air

Just off the A20 10km west of the city, **Limoges International Airport** (☎05 55 43 30 30; www.aeroportlimoges.com) is a major UK gateway, served by budget carriers including Ryanair and Flybe as well as Air France. Domestic destinations include Paris Orly, Lyon, Nice and Figari (Corsica), while UK destinations include London Stansted, London Gatwick, Nottingham, Liverpool, Southampton, Edinburgh, Manchester, Newcastle, Leeds-Bradford and Birmingham. A summertime shuttle (one way €7) between the airport and Limoges' train station operates from mid-June to September; otherwise a taxi takes 15 minutes and costs around €20.

Bus

Limoges' bus station is across the tracks from the train station; tickets anywhere in the Haute-Vienne *département* cost a flat €2.

Bus 12 goes to Oradour-sur-Glane (45 minutes, five daily Monday to Saturday), buses 14 and 21 service Rochechouart (one hour, four to six daily Monday to Saturday), and SNCF line 9 coaches travel to St-Léonard de Noblat (30 minutes, five to eight daily).

Car

Rental companies include **ADA** (☎05 55 79 61 12; 27 av du Général de Gaulle) and **National-Citer** (☎05 55 77 10 10; 3 cours Bugeaud).

Train

Destinations include Paris Gare d'Austerlitz (€52.10, three hours, hourly), Périgueux (€15, one hour, 15 daily), Cahors (€30.50, 2¼ hours, four daily), Brive-la-Gaillarde (€18.20, one hour, 15 daily), Tulle (€18.70, 1¼ hours, five to seven daily) and Arnac-Pompadour (€10.80, 1¼ hours, two to three daily) as well as the nightly train to Barcelona. Tickets can be bought at the station and at the town-centre **SNCF boutique** (4 rue Othon Péconnet).

West of Limoges

ROCHECHOUART & CHASSENON
POP 3930

Meteorites and modern art might be an unlikely combination but they're the twin draws of the walled town of Rochechouart, 45km west of Limoges. Rochechouart witnessed one of the most devastating impacts in Earth's history 200 million years ago when a massive 1.5km-radius lump of intergalactic rock slammed into the Earth at 72,000km/h with the force of 14 million Hiroshima bombs. The impact site, 4km west of town, created a crater 20km wide and 6km deep, but the only visible traces are the unusual rocks, frequently used as local building material, left behind by the massive explosion. The Éspace Météorite Paul Pellas (☎05 55 03 02 70; www.espacemeteorite. com; 16 rue Jean-Parvy; adult/child €4/2; ☉10am-12.30pm & 1.30-6pm Mon-Fri, 2-6pm Sat & Sun) explores this cosmic cataclysm through minerals, models and video displays. Hours are geared around school holidays, so check ahead to make sure it's open.

Housed in the town's refurbished château, highlights of the Musée Départemental d'Art Contemporain (☎05 55 03 77 91; www.musee-rochechouart.com, in French; place du Château; adult/child €4.60/2.30, free 1st Sun of month; ☉10am-12.30pm & 1.30-6pm Wed-Mon) include a collection of works by acclaimed Dadaist Raoul Haussman and an installation of white stones by British artist Richard Long in a room decorated with 16th-century frescoes.

About 5km from Rochechouart are the Gallo-Roman baths of Chassenon (☎05 45 89 32 21; www.cassinomagus.fr; adult/child €5/2.50, audio guide €1, guided tours €1.50; ☉10am-6.30pm Mon-Sun). Rediscovered in 1844 and excavated from 1958 to 1988, this luxurious former way station known to the Romans as Cassinomagnus was an important crossroads on the Via Agrippa, the road that crossed France via Saintes, Périgueux, Limoges, Clermont-Ferrand and Lyon. Much of the complex (including a temple and amphitheatre) were plundered for stone, but you can still make out the baths, plunge pools and hypocausts, the Roman equivalent of underfloor heating. Regular events include live entertainment, Roman sports and exhibitions.

Domaine des Chapelles (☎05 55 78 29 91; www.domainedeschapelles.com; Oradour-sur-Vayres; d €85-140; ☎❄), in open countryside near Oradour-sur-Vayres, is a former shepherd's barn that has been transformed into the ultimate romantic hideaway. Cappuccino-and-cream colour schemes sit alongside exposed stone and rustic tiles in the boutique rooms. Some have private terraces and room 8 even has its own hydromassage bath and sauna. The country restaurant (menus €18-29) is also superb (check out the funky sheep murals!).

For buses to Rochechouart from Limoges see p555.

East of Limoges

GUÉRET & BOURGANEUF
POP GUÉRET 15,089 / BOURGANEUF 3184

The busy town of Guéret grew up around a 12th-century monastery and the 15th-century Château de Moneyroux, now the administrative HQ of the Creuse *départe-*

THE LION OF THE LIMOUSIN

The spectre of Richard Coeur de Lion (Richard the Lionheart) looms over the Haute-Vienne *département*. The crusading king waged several bloody campaigns here in the 12th century before meeting his end at the now-ruined keep of Château de Chalûs-Chabrol, 40km west of Limoges, where he was mortally wounded by a crossbowman in 1199. Legend has it that once the keep was captured, Richard pardoned the crossbowman (actually a young boy), before expiring on 6 April 1199 in the arms of his mother, Eleanor of Aquitaine. Richard's heart was buried in Rouen in Normandy, his brain in the abbey of Charroux in Poitiers and his body in the Loire Valley's Abbaye de Fontevraud beside his father, Henry II; rather unsportingly, the crossbowman was later skinned alive by Richard's captain, Mercadier.

Many other medieval châteaux and monuments nearby share a Lionheart connection, which are signposted along the Route de Richard Coeur de Lion (Richard the Lionheart route; www.routerichardcoeurdelion.fr, in French); pick up the free English-language leaflet from local tourist offices.

ment, of which Guéret is capital. Guéret itself isn't that exciting, but it's a handy base for exploring nearby attractions, including the fascinating wolf sanctuary at Le Parc Animalier des Monts de Guéret (www.loups-chabrieres.com, in French; adult/child €8.50/7; ☉10am-8pm), where black and grey wolves roam free across a 12-hectare park; and the Labyrinthe Géant (www.labyrinthe -gueret.fr, in French; adult/child €6.50/4.50; ☉10am-8pm daily Jul & Aug, 2-8pm Sat & Sun May-Jun & Sep), where you can get well and truly lost among the hedgerows in what's allegedly the world's largest maze.

Bourgeois Bourganeuf is also worth a stop, especially for its atmospheric old town. Its main claim to fame came in 1886, when it became one of the first places in France to be connected to mains electricity. In summer the Musée de l'Électrification, de l'Eau et de la Lumière (☎05 55 64 07 61; rte de la Cascade; admission free; ☉10am-noon & 2-6pm Mon-Sat Jul & Aug) explores this electrifying event.

South of Bourganeuf, the Limousin is at its lushest, especially around Plateau de Millevaches (www.pnr-millevaches.fr, in French) and the glassy Lac de Vassivière (www.vassi viere.com, in French), a popular spot for water sports and afternoon picnics.

🍴 Sleeping & Eating

Abbaye du Palais　　　　　　　B&B €€
(☎05 55 64 02 64; www.abbayedupalais.com; d €90-160; ❄🐾) Between Bourganeuf and Guéret, this cosy B&B is lodged in a former Cistercian-abbey-turned-family home. Cats, dogs, rabbits and kids charge around the grounds, where you'll find the ruins of a chapel, a monks' dorm and a pet farm. Inside the grand house are three doubles and four suites filled with antiques, tapestries and fireplaces. Ask about *tables d'hôte* – and cookery clinics if you fancy polishing up your knife skills.

Le Moulin Noyé　　　　　　　HOTEL €€
(☎05 55 52 81 44; www.moulin-noye.com, in French; route de La Châtre, Glénic; d from €120) With rooms named after composers, in shades like raspberry pink and apple green, this backcountry haven overlooks wooded countryside above the Creuse River 9km northwest of Guéret. Its restaurant (menus €12-62) is a fave of local gourmets for its seasonal local produce, from lake fish to Limousin beef – book ahead.

La Ferme de la Gorce　　　　　FARMSTAY €
(☎05 55 41 11 55; www.gites-de-france-limousin. com, in French; 86 av du Limousin, Guéret; s/d €45/55) Just outside Guéret is this reassuringly rustic base, with plenty of wood and solid stone in the low-ceilinged rooms and friendly hosts who are full of info on the surrounding area.

AUBUSSON
POP 4400

Along with pottery and porcelain, the northern Limousin is famous for its tapestries, which once adorned the walls of aristocratic houses from London to the Loire Valley to insulate against the cold, especially in draughty castles.

The small, very pretty riverside town of Aubusson was the clacking centre of French carpet production during the 19th century (rivalled only by the Gobelins factories in Paris), producing elegant tapestries characterised by their vivid colours, fine detail and exquisite craftsmanship. The industry suffered a steady decline following the French Revolution, before being revived between WWI and WWII by inventive new designers such as Jean Lurçat, Sylvaine Dubuisson and Dom Robert.

⦿ Sights

Tapestry Workshops　　　　WORKSHOPS
Today there are around 20 tapestry workshops in Aubusson and nearby Felletin, 10km south. The tourist office, in Aubusson, arranges visits to local tapestry *ateliers* (workshops), and can supply you with a list of local galleries and showrooms such as Atelier Duché (www.atelier-duche-aubusson. com, in French; 35 Grand Rue; ☉9am-6pm Tue-Sat).

Maison de Tapissier　　　TAPESTRY MUSEUM
(http://mtapissier.lacreuse.com, in French; adult/ child €5/3; ☉9.30am-12.30pm & 2-6pm) Next door to the tourist office in a 16th-century mansion. Exhibits at the Maison de Tapissier re-create the atmosphere of a 17th-century weaver's workshop, with tools, original furniture and (of course) vintage tapestries.

Musée Départemental de la Tapisserie
　　　　　　　　　　　　TAPESTRY MUSEUM
(av des Lissiers; adult/child €5/free; ☉9.30am-noon & 2-6pm Wed-Mon) For a historical overview, head to the Musée Départemental de la Tapisserie, which houses intricate examples of both antique and modern tapestries produced in Aubusson.

ALL ABOARD!

Clamber aboard the carriages pulled by the 1932 steam engine Chemin Touristique Limousin–Périgord (www.trainvapeur.com, in French) to watch the Limousin's gloriously green fields and forests roll by.

The railway runs between mid-July and mid-August. Reservations are essential and can be made through the Limoges tourist office. There are six circuits in all; the following lines run three times a season. Prices are return.

Limoges–Eymoutiers (adult/child €24/10) Follows the old upland railway via St-Leonard-de-Noblat.

Limoges–Pompadour (adult/child €50/45) Includes a visit to the stables of Arnac-Pompadour.

Eymoutiers–Châteauneuf-Bujaleuf (adult/child €13/5) Via the plunging Gorges de la Vienne.

Exposition-Collection Fougerol
TAPESTRY MUSEUM
(34 rue Jules Sandeau; adult/child €3/free; ⊙9.30am-12.30pm & 2-6pm) The Exposition-Collection Fougerol features some 135 tapestries from the 16th to 19th centuries from Aubusson as well as Flanders.

🛏 Sleeping & Eating

Villa Adonis
BOUTIQUE HOTEL €
(📞05 55 66 46 00; www.villa-adonis.com; 14 av de la République; d €55-65; 🛜) From the funky watch-battery keys to the power showers and stripped-back colour schemes, this 19th-century stone villa on Aubusson's outskirts hints at big-city style. All rooms overlook a lovely garden, and the buffet breakfast (€7) includes homemade fresh-fruit jams and proper espresso.

L'Hôtel de France
HOTEL €€
(📞05 55 66 10 22; www.aubussonlefrance.com; 6 rue des Déportés; d €62-95; 🛜) This former post inn-turned-upmarket Logis hotel has 21 plush rooms – some modern, some old-fashioned and frilly, some tucked into the attic with sloping ceilings and roof beams – and a wellness centre including a hammam. Its restaurant (menus €20-36) is the best in town, with a smorgasbord of Limousin dishes served to the tune of a tinkling piano.

❶ Information
Tourist office (📞05 55 66 32 12; rue Vieille; www.ot-aubusson.fr, in French; ⊙9.30am-12.30pm & 2-6pm)

❶ Getting There & Away
Aubusson is 90km east of Limoges. Trains (or SNCF buses) link Aubusson with Limoges (€13.90, 1¾ hours, three daily Monday to Saturday, one on Sunday).

South of Limoges

SOLIGNAC
POP 1497
In the thickly wooded Briance Valley, 10km south of Limoges, the tiny medieval village of Solignac was a major stop on the pilgrimage route to Santiago de Compostela. Its 11th-century church is a Romanesque wonder, renowned for its 14m-wide domed roof. The stalls in the nave are decorated with carved wooden sculptures of human heads, fantastical animals and a monk mooning the world, while the columns depict human figures being devoured by dragons.

Five kilometres southeast are the ruins of the Château de Chalucet, a 12th-century keep occupied by the English during the Hundred Years War. The ruins make a fine picnic spot, with valley views from the tumbledown keep. Nearby in Le Vigen, the Parc Zoologique du Reynou (www.parczoo reynou.com; adult/child €13/9; ⊙10am-8pm, last entry 2hr before closing) is a 35-hectare safari park established on land once owned by the Haviland china dynasty. Its exotic denizens include wolves, giraffes, wildebeest, snowy owls and a pair of breeding tigers.

About the only place to stay nearby is Hôtel Le St-Eloi (📞05 55 00 44 52; www. lesainteloi.fr; 66 av St-Eloi; d €58-85), with 15 sunny rooms inside a shuttered building opposite the church. The ones with jacuzzis and terraces are fantastic value, and half board is available at the restaurant (menus €34-37; ⊙closed dinner Sun).

Three or four buses daily (except Sunday) connect Limoges with Solignac (€2, 25 minutes) and Le Vigen (€2, 35 minutes). The Solignac-Le Vigen train station is linked to

Limoges (€2.70, 10 minutes) and Uzerche (€8.20, 40 minutes) by several trains daily.

ARNAC-POMPADOUR
POP 1279

Actually two contiguous villages, Arnac-Pompadour revolves around its château, rising up in the centre of Pompadour. It's famous (and indeed infamous) for its association with the mistress of Louis XV, Madame de Pompadour (born Jeanne-Antoinette Poisson). Having been presented at the château in 1745, she not only stayed here but also helped develop the area into one of France's foremost *haras* (stud farms). Renowned for its Anglo-Arab pedigrees, this *Cité de Cheval* (horse town) became an Haras National in 1872.

Based at the château, Les Trois Tours (✆05 55 98 51 10; www.les3tours-pompadour.com) arranges one-hour visits of the château (adult/child €7/6), the écuries des étalons (stallions' stables; adult/child €6/5) and the jumenterie de la rivière (mares' stable; adult/child €6/5), and, from July to September, the 80-hectare Chignac (adult/child €6/5) site, where the colts and fillies from the mares' stables reside before starting their training at the age of two. Passes for two/three/four tours cost €11/16.50/22 per adult and €9/13.50/18 per child.

Opposite the château entrance, the tourist office (✆05 55 98 55 47; www.pompadour.net; ◷10.30am-12.30pm & 2-6pm) has details of regular race meetings, as well as a grand horse show on 15 August and a whole day dedicated to the humble *âne* (donkey) on 14 July.

The tourist office also runs tours of the 16th-century Chapelle St-Blaise (adult/child €4/2; ◷up to 6 tours daily Mon-Sat), behind the château, that walls and ceiling of which are graced with a monumental 300-sq-metre **mural** in ethereal blues and greens painted by French artist André Brasilier (b 1929). Tours include entry to the Espace Culturel St-Blaise (place de la Poste), which displays Brasilier's works and screens a film (in French) documenting the mural's creation.

Arnac-Pompadour is about 60km south of Limoges, served by train (€10.80, 1¼ hours, two to three daily).

UZERCHE
POP 3271

On a promontory over the rushing Vézère River, the walled town of Uzerche is one of the Limousin's prettiest hilltop hamlets. Spiky turrets jut out from the walls of the 15th- and 16th-century maisons à tourelles (turret houses) like witches' hats, while the Porte Bécharie, one of the nine original gates that granted access to the village in the 14th century, remains remarkably intact. Uzerche's single street leads uphill to the Église St-Pierre, a fortified church with an 11th-century crypt – one of the oldest crypts in the Limousin. Out the front, there's a fabulous panorama over the river valley from place de la Lunade, which takes its name from a pagan summer solstice (now rejigged as a Christian procession). Nearby, the tourist office (✆05 55 73 15 71; www.pays-uzerche.fr; place de la Libération; ◷10am-noon & 2-6pm Mon-Fri) sells work by local artists, like patchwork teddy bears and handmade pottery, in summer.

Uzerche has just a couple of hotels. Despite the Teyssier's well-worn exterior, inside Hôtel Jean Teyssier (✆05 55 73 10 05; www.hotel-teyssier.com; rue du Pont-Turgot; d €54-68; ✳🖨📶) you'll find a comfortable modern hotel: the 14 rooms are fresh and well furnished, with magnolia walls and checked and striped fabrics. Downstairs, the restaurant (menus €20-26) serves Limousin staples with a Mediterranean twist in a panoramic dining room overlooking the river.

Uzerche's other choice, Hôtel Ambroise (✆05 55 73 28 60; www.hotel-ambroise.com, in French; av Charles de Gaulle; s €46, d €51; ◷closed mid-Nov–Feb; 🖨) has snug, old-fashioned rooms (some with river views) and a gardenside restaurant (menus €13.50-26).

Uzerche is linked to Limoges, 56km to the north, by train (€12.60, 40 minutes, six to eight daily). The train station is 2km north of the old city along the N20.

Brive-la-Gaillarde
POP 51,629

Busy Brive-la-Gaillarde is the main commercial and administrative centre for the Corrèze *département*. Apart from its bustling weekly markets, Brive itself is short on sights, but it's a good base for exploring the Corrèze as well as the upper Lot and northeastern Dordogne.

◉ Sights & Activities

FREE Maison Denoix   DISTILLERY
(✆05 55 74 34 27; www.denoix.fr; 9 bd du Maréchal-Lyautey; ◷9am-noon & 2.30-7pm Tue-Sat Sep-Jun) Since 1839 this traditional

distillery has been producing the favourite firewater of the Corrèze, *l'eau de noix* (walnut liqueur), alongside adventurous concoctions such as chocolate liqueur, quince liqueur and curaçao. You can wander around the old copper cauldrons and stills, or take a (free) guided tour at 2.30pm on Tuesdays and Thursdays in July and August, and sample the wares at its well-stocked shop, including *moutarde violette de Brive* (purple mustard made with grape must).

Musée Labenche   MUSEUM
(www.musee-labenche.com; 26bis, bd Jules-Ferry; adult/child €4.70/2.50; ⊙10am-6.30pm Wed-Mon) Exhibits at the town's main museum explore local history and archaeology, as well as a unique collection of 17th-century English tapestries, accordions dating from the late 19th century to 1939, and a piano that once belonged to Debussy.

Collegiale St-Martin   CHURCH
In the heart of town, the Romanesque Collegiale St-Martin dates from the 11th century, but it's taken a battering over the centuries: the only original parts are the transept and a few decorated columns depicting fabulous beasties and biblical scenes.

🛏 Sleeping & Eating

Brive has no fewer than 150 restaurants, cafés and bars. Limousin beef, goose products, liqueurs, plum brandy and *galette corrézienne* (walnut and chestnut cake) are just some of the specialties at Brive's **markets**, which take over the central place du 14 Juillet every Tuesday and Saturday morning (with a smaller market on Thursday morning).

TOP CHOICE **Château de Castel-Novel**
                                            CASTLE HOTEL €€€
(☎05 55 85 09 03; www.castelnovel.com; Varetz; d €140-390; ❉🅿🍴) Just 10km north of Brive-la-Gaillarde, this beauty of a château was immortalised by the French author Colette, who based herself here while writing *Le Blé en Herbe* and *Chéri*. Topped by turrets, gables and slate tiles, filled with idiosyncratic rooms (including a turret room and Colette's Louis XVI apartment) and surrounded by sweeping lawns and an 18th-century orangery within 10 tree-filled hectares, it's no wonder Madame Colette found it inspiring. Equally inspired is the château's Michelin-starred gastronomic restaurant (menus €26-78).

La Truffe Noire   HOTEL €€
(☎05 55 92 45 00; www.la-truffe-noire.com, in French; 22 bd Anatole-France; d €95-135; ❉🍴) By far the top spot in the town centre, this grand old girl has 27 swish rooms decked out with beige and cream fabrics, big beds and the odd beam or two. The restaurant (menus €25.50-39) is even better, serving rich Limousin fare such as truffle-marinated salmon and Limousin beef with trufflepuréed potatoes.

Hôtel du Chapon Fin   HOTEL €€
(☎05 55 74 23 40; www.chaponfin-brive.com, in French; 1 place de Lattre-de-Tassigny; d €54-84; @🍴🅿) Freshly renovated, spick-and-span rooms in this white-shuttered hotel are smart and contemporary, as is its restaurant (menus €12-40), serving world-influenced cuisine.

Auberge de Jeunesse   HOSTEL €
(☎05 55 24 34 00; brive@fuaj.org; 56 av Maréchal Bugeaud; dm €13.20; 🍴) Well-run and friendly, Brive's hostel is set around a former mansion (housing reception), with squeaky-clean dorms in a newer wing, and a small self-catering kitchen in the 16th-century stables. It's a 1.5km walk from the station; check to make sure someone's around when you arrive.

ℹ Information

The **tourist office** (☎05 55 24 08 80; www.brive-tourisme.com; place du 14 Juillet; ⊙9am-12.30pm & 1.30-6.30pm Mon-Sat) is housed in a former water tower, locally known as the *phare* (lighthouse), overlooking the market square.

ℹ Getting There & Away

Brive is a major rail and bus junction.

AIR Brive-Vallée de la Dordogne Airport (www.aeroport-brive-vallee-dordogne.com), about 10km south of town, has budget flights to Paris-Orly and London City Airport.

BUS The **bus station** (place du 14 Juillet) is next to the tourist office.

TRAIN The **train station** (av Jean Jaurès), 1.3km from the town centre, can be reached via most buses heading south out of town. Regular services include Limoges (€18.20, one hour, 15 to 18 daily), Périgueux (€11.80, one hour, six to eight daily) and Cahors (€18.20, one hour, eight to 10 daily). To get to Sarlat (€8.80, 1½ hours, three to five daily), you'll need to change (usually onto an SNCF bus) at Souillac.

There's nothing more Gallic than the sound of an *accordéon* squeezing out tunes on a street corner. The industrial town of Tulle (population 16,474), 28km northeast of Brive, is renowned as the world's accordion capital. A single accordion consists of between 3500 and 6800 parts and making one requires up to 200 hours' labour, so mass production has never been an option. The very best instruments can fetch upwards of a staggering €9000.

One of the oldest traditional accordion makers, Tulle's celebrated Usine Maugein (☑05 55 20 08 89; rte de Brive; admission free; ☺8am-noon & 2-5.30pm Mon-Thu), runs guided factory tours by reservation, where you can see the craftspeople at work and browse the accordion museum.

The accordion takes centre stage during mid-September's annual four-day street music festival **Nuits de Nacre**; Tulle's tourist office (☑05 55 29 27 74; 2 place Emile Zola; ☺9am-noon & 2-6pm Mon-Sat) has details.

Trains link Tulle with Limoges (€18.70, 1¼ hours, five to seven daily).

East of Brive

GIMEL-LES-CASCADES
POP 703

A huddle of slate roofs, flower-filled balconies and higgledy-piggledy cottages gather along the banks of a rushing brook of this tiny, typically Corrèzien village. It's a place to wander the lanes, drink in the atmosphere, and stroll along the banks of the river. The three crashing cascades, after which the village is named, are reached via a riverside path at the foot of the village. The local church contains a beautiful enamelled reliquary known as the **Châsse de St-Étienne**, made in the 12th century by Limoges craftsmen.

Other nearby sights include the remains of the Cistercian Abbaye d'Aubazine (☑05 55 84 61 12; ☺guided visits 10.30am, 3pm & 4pm Jul & Aug, rest of year by appointment) and the Étang de Ruffaud, a glassy pond that offers a refreshing dip and a shady place for a picnic.

Gimel's teensy tourist office (☑05 55 21 44 32; www.gimellescascades.fr, in French; ☺2-4.30pm Mon-Fri, 10am-noon & 3-6.30pm Sat, 3-6.30pm Sun) shares space with the post office.

The Hostellerie de la Vallée (☑05 55 21 40 60; www.logishotels.com; d €60; ☺Mar-Dec) makes for a sweet stopover, with nine small, pleasant rooms tucked around the corridors of an old stone cottage in the heart of the village. With panoramic valley views, its restaurant (menus from €17) is a down-home treat, with an old-fashioned dining room and hearty dishes like rabbit and beef stew.

South of Brive

Rolling countryside and green pastures unfold south of Brive to the banks of the Dordogne and the border of the northern Lot.

TURENNE
POP 812

Rising up from a solitary spur of rock, the hilltop village of Turenne is an arresting sight: honey-coloured stone cottages and wonky houses are stacked up like dominoes beneath the towering château (☑05 55 85 90 66; www.chateau-turenne.com; adult/child €4/2.60; ☺10am-noon & 2-6pm), built to protect the feudal seat of the Vicomtes de Turenne. The views of the surrounding countryside from the Tour de César, the castle's arrow-straight tower, are so beautiful that you may well find yourself blinking to make sure they're real. Apart from a few ramparts and a 14th-century guard room, the rest of the castle and lordly lodgings have crumbled away, and are now occupied by an ornamental garden.

The tourist office (☑05 55 24 12 95; guided visits adult/child €4/free, fire torch €1; ☺10am-12.30pm & 3-6pm Tue-Sun) is at the base of the village, and runs guided visits as well as torchlit night-time costumed promenades in summer by reservation.

Turenne's only hotel is La Maison des Chanoines (☑05 55 85 93 43; maison-des-chanoines.com, in French; d €56-100; ☺Apr–mid-Oct). Behind its 16th-century Flamboyant Gothic facade you'll find sparingly decorated countrified rooms and a good restaurant (menus €34-49; ☺dinner Thu-Tue) tucked within its stone walls.

LIMOUSIN, THE DORDOGNE & THE LOT EAST OF BRIVE

From Brive, there are usually three daily buses (www.cftaco.fr, in French) from Monday to Saturday (€2; 35 minutes). If you're catching a train (€3.20, 15 minutes), you'll arrive at Turenne Gare, 3km southeast of the village, and will have to make your way on foot.

COLLONGES-LA-ROUGE
POP 475

With its skyline of conical turrets, rickety rooftops and historic buildings built from rust-red sandstone (hence its name), Collonges-la-Rouge is one of the classic postcard villages of the Corrèze. In 1942, thanks to the efforts of villagers, the entire village received classification as a *monument historique*, and in 1982 France's plus beaux villages (most beautiful villages; www.les-plus-beaux-villages-de-france.org) association was established here by Collonges' then mayor, Charles Ceyrac.

Collonges centres on the part-Romanesque church, constructed from the 11th to the 15th centuries on an 8th-century Benedictine priory, which was an important resting place on the pilgrimage to Santiago de Compostela. In a stirring show of ecclesiastical unity, during the late 16th century local Protestants held prayers in the southern nave and their Catholic neighbours prayed in the northern nave. Nearby, the slate roof of the ancient covered market shelters a similarly ancient baker's oven.

Browsing Collonges' artisan shops and pausing at its clutch of traditional cafés and restaurants is an enjoyable way to while away a few hours, but start out early as it steadily fills with tourists as the day wears on.

On the edge of the village, the grandiose B&B Jeanne Maison d'Hôte (☑05 55 25 42 31; www.jeannemaisondhotes.com; d €90; ☎), in a towering 15th-century *maison bourgeoise*, is a real home away from home. The five rooms all have quirky fixtures and antique furniture, from writing desks and decorative screens to chaises longues and latticed windows (our favourite is the chimney room, with its own enormous inglenook fireplace), and the home-cooked *tables d'hôte* (for €35 with wine) are a treat.

A couple of kilometres down the road in the village of Meyssac, Relais du Quercy (☑05 55 25 40 31; www.relaisduquercy.fr; Meyssac; d €55-70; ☎☎) is a jaunty little slate-roofed country hotel with beautiful gardens and comfy and cosy (if unremarkable) rooms. The nicest look out over the rear terrace, but all have spotless bathrooms and soft beds.

The tourist office (☑05 55 25 47 57; www.ot-collonges.fr, in French; ☉10am-noon & 2-6pm) is next to the town hall on the village's 'main' road, off the D38.

Collonges is linked by bus with Brive, 18km to the northwest along the D38 (€3, 30 minutes, four to six daily on weekdays, one on Saturday).

BEAULIEU-SUR-DORDOGNE
POP 1326

On a tranquil bend of the Dordogne hemmed by lush woods and fields, Beaulieu (meaning 'beautiful place') lives up to its name. Once an important stop for Compostela pilgrims, its beautifully preserved medieval quarter is one of the region's finest: a network of curving lanes lined with timber-framed houses and smart mansions, many dating from the 14th and 15th centuries.

Beaulieu's biggest party is the **Fête de la Fraise** (Strawberry Festival), marking the annual harvest on the second Sunday in May. Strawberry-focused events fill the town's streets, including strawberry auctions, strawberry parades and the eating of a gargantuan strawberry tart to close the festival in style.

⊙ Sights & Activities

Abbatiale St-Pierre — ABBEY CHURCH

Beaulieu's most celebrated feature is this 12th-century Romanesque abbey church with a wonderful **tympanum** (c 1130) depicting scenes from the Last Judgment including dancing apostles and resurrected sinners. The nearby Chapelle des Pénitents was built to accommodate pious parishioners – access to the abbey church was strictly reserved for monks and paying pilgrims.

Faubourg de la Chapelle — ARCHITECTURE

A neighbourhood of 17th- and 18th-century houses, near the Abbatiale St-Pierre.

Aventures Dordogne Nature — RIVER CRUISES

(www.adndordogne.org, in French; ☉May-Oct) Runs *gabarre* (flat-bottomed boat – see p583) trips on the picturesque river, ranging from a 1¼-hour spin around Beaulieu (adult/child €6/5) to a 2½-hour gourmet picnic cruise (adult/child €18/13).

Sleeping & Eating

Beaulieu's **market** is on Wednesday and Saturday mornings.

Auberge Les Charmilles HOTEL €€
(☑05 55 91 29 29; www.auberge-charmilles. com, in French; 20 bd Rodolphe de Turenne; d €75-120; 🐾) All eight rooms at this lovely *maison bourgeoise* are named after different types of strawberries. The decor's fresh and fruity, with puffy bedspreads, wooden floors and summery bathrooms. Scrumptious home-cooked dishes are served at its peaceful riverside restaurant (menus €19-48), though vegetarians should note the so-called 'vegetarian *menu*' consists entirely of fish dishes.

Manoir de Beaulieu HOTEL €€
(☑05 55 91 01 34; www.manoirdebeaulieu.com; 4 place du Champ-de-Mars; s €99, d €109-129, ste €169-179; 🐾) Half old-fashioned *auberge*, half modern pamper-pad, this smart village-centre hotel is a find. The rooms mix the best of old and new – stripped wood floors, glass sinks and flat-screen TVs meet solid furniture, velvet armchairs, and the odd cartwheel or reclaimed desk, and the gastronomic courtyard restaurant (menus €16-70) is superb.

Auberge de Jeunesse HOSTEL €
(☑05 55 91 13 82; beaulieu@fuaj.org; place du Monturu; dm €13.50; ☺Apr-Oct) Parts of this quirky 28-bed hostel date from the 15th century, and it certainly looks vintage: latticed windows and a miniature turret decorate the exterior, while inside you'll find a cosy chimney-side lounge, well-stocked kitchen and dinky four-bed rooms, all with private bathrooms.

Camping à la Ferme du Masvidal
CAMPGROUND €
(☑05 55 91 53 14; www.masvidal.fr; bd de Turenne; sites from €6.50, d incl breakfast €55; ☺Apr-Sep; 🐾🏠) In addition to shady sites where you can watch the animals roam at this working farm 7km southwest of Beaulieu, there are also three sloped-ceilinged *chambre d'hôte* (B&B) rooms and hearty home-cooked meals (*menus* €12 to €20) made with produce from the property.

Camping des Îles CAMPGROUND €
(☑05 55 91 02 65; www.camping-des-iles.fr; bd de Turenne; sites €10.90-26.90; ☺Apr-Oct; 🐾📶🏠) Shady camp on an island sandwiched between two branches of the Dordogne.

❶ Information

The **tourist office** (☑05 55 91 09 94; www. beaulieu-tourisme.com; place Marbot; ☺9.30am-12.30pm & 2.30-6pm Mon-Sat, 9.30am-12.30pm Sun) is on the main square.

❶ Getting There & Away

From Monday to Saturday buses link Beaulieu with Brive (€2, one hour, one to three daily).

THE DORDOGNE

With its rich food, heady history and rolling countryside strewn with countless historic castles, the Dordogne has long been a favourite place of escape for second-homing Brits and French families on *les grandes vacances*. But the castle-builders weren't the first to settle on the riverbanks; Cro-Magnon man was here long before, and the Vézère Valley shelters the most spectacular series of prehistoric cave paintings anywhere in Europe.

Better known to the French as the Périgord, the Dordogne *département* is divided into four colour-coded areas for easy navigation: Périgord Blanc (white) after the limestone hills around the capital, Périgueux; Périgord Pourpre (purple) for the wine-growing regions around Bergerac; Périgord Vert (green) for the forested regions of the northwest; and Périgord Noir (black) for the dark oak forests around the Vézère Valley and Sarlat-la-Canéda.

Périgueux
POP 30,808

There's been a settlement on the site of present-day Périgueux for over 2000 years. Initially occupied by Gallic tribes, and later developed by the Romans into the city of Vesunna, Périgueux is still the biggest (and busiest) commercial centre of the Dordogne *département*. But reminders of its lengthy history abound: Roman ruins remain in the Cité quarter, while medieval buildings and Renaissance mansions are dotted around the rabbit-warren old town, Puy St-Front.

❂ Sights
PUY ST-FRONT
Cathédrale St-Front CATHEDRAL
(place de la Clautre; ☺8am-12.30pm & 2.30-7.30pm) Périgueux' most distinctive landmark is most notable for its five Byzantine bump-studded domes (inspired by either

Périgueux

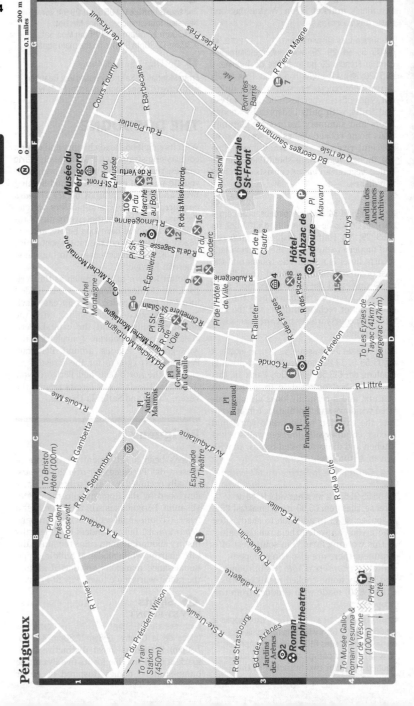

Map labels:

0 100 m
0 0.1 miles

200 m

Cathédrale St-Front

Musée du Périgord

Hôtel d'Abzac de Ladouze

Roman Amphitheatre

Jardins des Arènes

Esplanade du Théâtre

Pl Francheville

Pl du Président Roosevelt

Pl du Président Wilson

Cours Tourny

Cours Michel Montaigne

Bd Michel Montaigne

Pl Michel Montaigne

Pl André Maurois

Pl General du Gaulle

Pl Bugeaud

Pl St Louis

Pl St Silain

Pl du Marché au Bois

Pl de l'Hôtel de Ville

Pl de la Clautre

Pl des Places

Pl Daumesnil

Pl du Coderc

Pl Mauvard

Pl de la Cité

Jardin des Anciennes Archives

R de l'Arsault
R des Prés
R Pierre Magne
R Barbecane
R du Plantier
R de Vertu
R au Musée
R à St-Front
R Limogeanne
R de la Miséricorde
R de la Sagesse
R Éguillerie
R de l'Oie
R Aubergerie
R Taillefer
R des Farges
R Conde
R du Lys
R des Places
R de la Cité
Cours Fénelon
R Littré
R Louis Mie
R Gambetta
R A Gadaud
R du 4 Septembre
R Thiers
R Ste-Ursule
R de Strasbourg
R de Laroette
R Dugueselin
R Guillier
Av d'Aquitaine
Bd des Arènes
Q de l'Isle
Bd Georges Saumande
Cimetière St-Silain

Pont des Barris

Isle

To Bristol Hôtel (100m)
To Train Station (450m)
To Les Eyzies de Tayac (41km); Bergerac (47km)
To Musée Gallo-Romain Vesunna & Tour de Vésone (100m)

Numbered markers: 1, 2, 3, 4, 5, 6, 7, 8, 9, 10, 11, 12, 13, 14, 15, 16, 17

St Mark's Basilica in Venice or the church of the Holy Apostles of Constantinople, depending on whom you ask). Built in the 12th century, and heavily restored by Abadie (the architect of Paris' Sacré Cœur), the interior is laid out in a Greek cross, with the soaring domes supported by svelte arches. The carillon sounds the same on-the-hour chime as Big Ben.

The best views of the cathedral are from **Pont des Barris**, which crosses the River Isle to the east.

Medieval & Renaissance Architecture

ARCHITECTURE

North of the cathedral, Périgueux' broad boulevards give way to a tangle of cobblestone streets lined with haphazard houses: the best examples are along **rue du Plantier**, **rue de la Sagesse** and **rue de la Miséricorde**. **Rue Limogeanne** has graceful Renaissance buildings at Nos 3 and 12, and the elaborately carved **Maison du Pâtissier** is at the end of rue Éguillerie. Most impressive of all is the **Hôtel d'Abzac de Ladouze** (16 rue Aubergerie), which was a fortified mer-chant's house in the 15th century. Of the 28 towers that formed Puy St-Front's medieval fortifications, only the 15th-century Tour Mataguerre, a stout, round bastion next to the tourist office, now remains. The tourist office supplies a street map detailing the city's other architectural sites.

Puy St-Front has a couple of worthwhile museums.

Musée du Périgord   MUSEUM
(22 cours Tourny; adult/child €4.50/2.50; ⊙10.30am-5.30pm Mon & Wed-Fri, 1-6pm Sat & Sun) Archaeological finds include some fine Roman mosaics and unique examples of prehistoric scrimshaw.

Musée Militaire   MILITARY MUSEUM
(32 rue des Farges; adult/child €4/free; ⊙2-6pm Mon-Sat) Eclectic collection of swords, firearms, uniforms and insignia dating from the Middle Ages until WWII, with sections devoted to WWI and the French Resistance.

LA CITÉ

Roman Ruins   ROMAN RUINS
Périgueux (or Vesunna, to give it its Roman name) was among the most important cities in Roman Gaul, but the only remains of this once-thriving outpost are in La Cité, west of the city centre. The **Tour de Vésone**, the last remaining section of a massive Gallo-Roman temple dedicated to the Gaulish goddess Vesunna, is just south of the **Église St-Étienne de la Cité** (place de la Cité), which served as Périgueux' cathedral until 1669.

Roman Amphitheatre   ROMAN RUINS
To the north of the Tour de Vésone are the ruins of the city's Roman amphitheatre, designed to hold over 30,000 baying spectators and one of the largest such structures in Gaul: today only a few creeper-covered arches remain, and its gladiatorial arena is occupied by a peaceful park, the **Jardins des Arènes**.

Musée Gallo-Romain Vesunna   ROMAN VILLA
(www.vesunna.fr, in French; rue Claude Bernard; adult/child €6/4; ⊙9.30am-12.30pm & 1.30-5pm Mon-Fri, 10am-12.30pm & 2.30-6pm Sat & Sun) Just west of the Tour de Vésone is the museum constructed by French architect Jean Nouvel above a 1st-century Roman villa uncovered in 1959. Light floods in through the glass-and-steel structure, and walkways circumnavigate the excavated villa; it's still

LAND OF 1001 CHÂTEAUX

During the Hundred Years War the Dordogne marked the frontier between French and English forces, and the area is sometimes known as the 'Land of 1001 Châteaux' due to its abundance of historic castles. The impervious fortifications of the châteaux of the Dordogne were rarely necessary as frontal assaults were too costly in terms of money and manpower; they were defeated more often through machiavellian intrigue than brute force.

Many of the Dordogne's châteaux can be visited; our favourites include the following:

Château de Biron (p584) South of Monpazier. An eight-century-long evolution incorporating wildly varying architectural styles.

Puymartin (p571) Northwest of Sarlat-la-Canéda. Atmospheric (and allegedly haunted) turret-topped château.

Château de Losse (p580) Southwest of Montignac. Surrounded by an original 15th-century moat.

Château de Beynac (p582) Above the village of Beynac-et-Cazenac, northwest of La Roque Gageac. Mighty fortress with dizzying views along the Dordogne.

Château de Castelnaud (p582) Southwest of La Roque Gageac. Formidable former English stronghold with a museum of medieval warfare.

possible to make out the central fountain, supporting pillars and the underfloor hypo-caust system, as well as original mosaic murals, jewellery, pottery and even a water pump.

Tours

The tourist office runs a range of French-language guided tours (adult/child €6/4.50) around the old city, including a Gallo-Roman tour and a walk around Puy St-Front's medieval and Renaissance buildings.

Sleeping

Château des Reynats   CASTLE HOTEL €€€
(☑05 53 03 53 59; www.chateau-hotel-perigord. com; 15 av des Reynats, Chancelade; d in chateau €190-260, in orangerie €96; ☎❷) Périgueux proper doesn't have any top-end hotels but if you head 3km west you'll find this stately property with flowing guestrooms in the château, as well as simpler rooms in the adjacent orangerie. In addition to lavish dining (lunch *menu* €28, *menus* €39 to €75), Reynats hosts gourmet weekends and other foodie events.

Hôtel des Barris   HOTEL €
(☑05 53 53 04 05; www.hoteldesbarris.com; 2 rue Pierre-Magne; s €47-49, d €53-55; ❊❷❹) Beside the broad River Isle with a cute waterside terrace, this Logis hotel is the best value in Périgueux as long as you can get a river-view room (the ones by the main

road can be hideously noisy). Rooms at the higher end of the modest price scale have air-conditioning.

Hôtel de l'Univers   HOTEL €
(☑05 53 53 34 79; www.hotelrestaurantlunivers. fr; 18 cours Michel Montaigne; s/d from €50/58; ❷) You won't get more central than the Univers, perched above Le Cercle, a swanky little wine bar and brasserie in old Périgueux. Nine fresh, unfussy rooms, most redecorated with soothing shades and the odd rustic curio, are dotted round the upstairs floors; the streetside ones are the quietest.

Bristol Hôtel   HOTEL €€
(☑05 53 08 75 90; www.bristolfrance.com; 37-39 rue Antoine Gadaud; s €60-69, d €66-78; ❊@❷) Look past the Bristol's boxy Lego-brick facade and you'll find traditionally styled rooms with wooden furniture, rich shades of orange, peach and red, and extras including free parking.

Eating

TOP CHOICE **Le Clos St-Front**   GASTRONOMIC €€€
(☑05 53 46 78 58; www.leclossaintfront. com; 12 rue St-Front; menus €20-62; ❹) Set around a lime-shaded garden beside a 16th-century *hôtel particulier,* the city's *grande table* is a delight from start to finish: chef and owner Patrick Feuga has a well-earned reputation for his imaginative versions of

traditional dishes, which range from goose breast with cardamom sauce to sashimi bream and 'hot-and-cold' caramel soufflé. The buzzy courtyard patio is *the* place to eat out in summer, so you'll need military precision to bag a table.

Au Bien Bon   REGIONAL CUISINE €€
(☑05 53 09 69 91; 15 rues des Places; lunch/ dinner menus €10.50/22; ⊘lunch Tue-Fri, dinner Tue-Sat) Checked tablecloths, chalkboard menus and chipped floor tiles set the earthy tone at this rustic place, which makes a fine spot for traditional Périgord cooking: *confit de canard* (duck leg, cured and poached in its own fat), *omelette aux cèpes* (omelette with porcini mushrooms) or full-blown *tête de veau* (vealer's head).

Café de la Place   CAFÉ, BRASSERIE €€
(☑05 53 08 21 11; 7 place du Marché au Bois; mains €14-21) This marvellous streetside café on place du Marché au Bois, with its spinning ceiling fans, shiny brass fittings and smoke-burnished wooden bar is really a place to sit and people-watch over a *petit café*, but there are good brasserie standards if you're peckish, as well as a decadent *café gourmand* (coffee with miniature desserts).

L'Estaminet   REGIONAL CUISINE €€
(☑05 53 06 11 38; 2 Impasse Limogeanne; lunch menus €15-18, dinner menus €18-26; ⊘lunch daily, dinner Tue, Thu & Fri) Secreted in a medieval courtyard, this intimate bistro takes its culinary cue from the daily produce available at the nearby market, so you could find anything from fresh sea bass to rump steak on the menu, all with a Périgordine twist.

Au Petit Chef   BISTRO €€
(☑05 53 53 16 03; 5 place du Coderc; lunch/dinner menus €13.50/24; ⊘Mon-Sat) All the ingredients at this kitsch little bistro come straight from the covered market opposite, so you're guaranteed fresh flavours and authentic *plats régionaux*. It's popular at lunchtime, especially on market days, so pitch up early.

Vegetarians should check out the following:

Le Cocoon   VEGETARIAN €
(☑05 53 53 63 35; 9 place St-Silain; menus €10-15; ⊘lunch Mon-Sat, dinner Mon-Fri; ⎙) The rarest of breeds in the Périgord: an exclusively vegetarian restaurant, with a bohemian dining room spilling onto a sociable umbrella-shaded terrace.

L'Eden   REGIONAL CUISINE €€
(☑05 53 06 31 08; www.leden-restaurant.com, in French; 3 rue Aubergerie; menus €10-15; ⊘lunch Mon-Sat, dinner Mon-Fri; ⎙) Serves beautifully presented dishes like apple-and-foie-gras tart but staff happily cater for vegetarians if you ask.

Self-Catering
Périgueux' chaotic **street markets** explode into action on Wednesday and Saturday, taking over place de la Clautre, place de la Mairie and place du Coderc, where you'll also find the covered market (⊘to 1.30pm). Liveliest of all are the **Marchés de Gras**, when local delicacies such as truffles, wild mushrooms and foie gras are sold on place St-Louis from mid-November to mid-March.

The old city is crammed with shops selling local gourmet goodies; for fabulous cheeses stop by La Ferme Périgourdine (9 rue Limogeanne).

☆ Entertainment
Nightlife is not Périgueux' forte but the 10-screen CAP Cinéma (www.cap-cine.fr, in French; place Francheville) shows mainly new-release films, some in *version originale* (nondubbed).

① Information
Espace Tourisme Périgord (☑05 53 35 50 24; 25 rue du Président Wilson; ⊘8.30am-5.30pm Mon-Fri) Information on the Dordogne *département*.

Post office (1 rue du 4 Septembre)

Tourist office (☑05 53 53 10 63; www.tourisme-perigueux.fr; 26 place Francheville; ⊘9am-7pm Mon-Sat, 10am-1pm & 2-6pm Sun)

① Getting There & Away
BUS The main local operator is **Peribus** (www.peribus.fr, in French); single fares around town cost €1.25.

Further afield, **Trans Périgord** (www.transbus.org, in French) serves destinations including Sarlat (1½ hours, two daily Monday to Friday), Montignac (one hour 40 minutes, one daily Monday to Friday) and Bergerac (70 minutes, six daily Monday to Friday). Tickets cost a flat rate of €2 per adult, €1 child.

CAR The major car-hire agencies are around the train station.

TRAIN The **train station** (rue Denis Papin), 1km northwest of the old city, is served by buses 1, 4 and 5. Direct services run to Bordeaux (€19.10, 1½ hours, 18 daily), Limoges (€15, one hour, 15

TRUFFLE CAPITAL

While the Dordogne is famed for its gourmet goodies, for true culinary connoisseurs there's only one ingredient that matters: the black truffle, often dubbed the *diamant noir* (black diamond) or, hereabouts, the *perle noire du Périgord* (the black pearl of Périgord).

A subterranean fungus that grows naturally in chalky soils (in the Dordogne around the roots of oak trees), this mysterious little mushroom is notoriously capricious; a good truffle spot one year can be inexplicably bare the next, which has made farming them on any kind of serious scale practically impossible. The art of truffle-hunting is a closely guarded secret; it's a matter of luck, judgment and hard-earned experience, with specially trained dogs (and sometimes even pigs) to help in the search. Simple dishes like a plain omelette or sliced onto fresh crusty bread bring out their strong flavour, but they're used by skilful chefs in an infinite array of dishes. It's not simply a matter of culinary perfection; truffles are seriously big business, with a vintage crop fetching as much as €1000 a kilogram at the markets, and infinitely more in shops.

The height of truffle season is between December and March, when special truffle markets are held around the Dordogne, including Périgueux, Sarlat and most notably the small village of Sorges (population 1234), locally championed as the 'world's truffle capital'.

You can discover the secrets of Sorges' truffles at its Ecomusée de la Truffe (☎05 53 05 90 11; www.ecomusee-truffe-sorges.com; Le Bourg, Sorges; adult/child €4/2; ☺10am-noon & 2-5pm, closed Mon Oct-Jan), which has lots of truffle-themed exhibits and may be able to help you hook up with a truffle hunt in season. Alternatively, contact La Truffe Noire de Sorges (☎06 08 45 09 48; www.truffe-sorges.com; 1½hr tours €10; ☺by reservation Dec-Feb & Jun-Sep), which runs tours of *truffières* (the areas where truffles are cultivated), followed by a tasting.

Auberge de la Truffe (☎05 53 05 02 05; www.auberge-de-la-truffe.com, in French; Sorges; s €52-105, d €56-120; ✵✵✵), in the village centre, has stylish rooms in shades such as crimson and sky blue, and is renowned throughout the Dordogne for its restaurant (menus €23-57) serving sensational seasonal cuisine including an all-truffle *menu* (€100) with truffle pastries for dessert.

Sorges is 23km northeast of Perigueux on the N21.

daily) and Brive-la-Gaillarde (€11.80, one hour, six to eight daily). Fewer trains run on Sunday.

Getting to Sarlat-la-Canéda (€13.90, 1¾ hours, three daily) requires a change at Le Buisson.

Brantôme

POP 2169

With its five medieval bridges arcing over the River Dronne, lined by romantic riverfront architecture, Brantôme certainly befits its moniker 'Venice of the Périgord', albeit on a diminutive scale. Surrounded by grassy parks and willow-filled woodland, it's an enchanting spot to while away an afternoon or embark on a boat ride.

◉ Sights & Activities

Brantôme's most illustrious landmark is the former Benedictine Abbey, built and rebuilt from the 11th to 18th centuries and now occupied by the Hôtel de Ville. Next door is the Gothic abbey church and the tourist office.

Behind the modern-day abbey and the tourist office are the remains of Brantôme's original abbey, known as the Parcours Troglodytique (adult/child €4/2; ☺10am-6pm), cut from the rock face by industrious monks in the 8th century. Its most famous feature is a 15th-century rock **frieze** supposedly depicting the Last Judgement. The abbey's 11th-century Romanesque **clocher** (belltower) is allegedly the oldest – and arguably most beautiful – in France.

Pleasure boats depart from the banks of the river in front of the abbey, including Promenade en Bateau (☎05 53 04 74 71; adult/child €7/5) and L'Arche de Noë (adult/child €7/5). Cruises last about 50 minutes, with up to six trips per day from April to mid-October.

🛌 Sleeping & Eating

Hostellerie les Griffons   HOTEL, B&B €€
(☑05 53 45 45 35; www.griffons.fr; Bourdeilles; d €87-110; ☀) River views extend from the blue-shuttered windows of this fantastically atmospheric converted mill. The rooms are an enticing jumble of medieval fireplaces, head-scraping beams and porthole windows – ask for No 6, with its ceiling of muddled crossbeams, or No 2, with stone hearth and town views. There are good deals on half board at its riverside restaurant (menus from €29.50; ☉lunch Sun, dinner daily by reservation), with French doors opening out to the terrace. It's in the nearby town of Bourdeilles, about 9km southwest of Brantôme along the D78.

Maison Fleurie   B&B €€
(☑05 53 35 17 04; www.maison-fleurie.net; 54 rue Gambetta; s €45-50, d €60-90; ☀) Behind the flowering window boxes of this smart stone house are five spick-and-span en-suite rooms (romantics should go for the 'Rose' room, with a four-poster bed) and a sunny interior courtyard filled with geraniums and petunias.

Hostellerie du Périgord Vert   HOTEL €
(☑05 53 05 70 58; www.hotel-hpv.fr; 7 av André Maurois; d €48-55, tr €72; 🐾☀) Creepers cover the outside of this old roadside inn, ranged around a private courtyard set back from the main road and riverfront. The rooms are pleasant in an everyday kind of way, with stout beds, plain bathrooms and a choice of courtyard or pool views. Southwest wines and *cuisine de terroir* (country cuisine) make the restaurant (menus €18-39) especially popular for Sunday lunch.

ℹ Information

Tourist office (☑05 53 05 80 63; www.ville-brantome.fr; ☉10am-6pm)

ℹ Getting There & Away

Brantôme is 27km north of Périgueux along the D939. Three **buses** (www.cftaco.fr, in French) a day (one on Sunday) run to/from Périgueux (€2; 50 minutes). The bus stop is outside the *gendarmerie* (police station) in the village centre.

Sarlat-la-Canéda

POP 9943

A picturesque tangle of honey-coloured buildings, alleyways and secret squares make up Sarlat-la-Canéda. Ringed by forested hilltops, its heart-shaped Cité Médiévale (medieval town) is home to some of the country's best-preserved architecture from the Middle Ages.

The village's photogenic qualities haven't escaped film directors, with more movies shot here than anywhere else in France apart from Paris and Nice. It's a charming launch pad for exploring the Périgord Noir and the Vézère Valley, but it hasn't escaped the attention of tourists, either: as it's one of the region's most popular destinations, you may find it almost impossible to appreciate its charms among the throngs in high summer.

👁 Sights & Activities

Part of the fun of wandering around Sarlat is losing yourself – literally – in its network of twisting alleyways and back streets. **Rue Jean-Jacques Rousseau** or **rue Landry** both make good starting points, but for the grandest buildings and *hôtels particuliers* you'll want to explore **rue des Consuls**. Look out for the medieval fountain, tucked away down steps at the rear of a mossy grotto.

Cathédrale St-Sacerdos   CATHEDRAL
Whichever street you take, sooner or later you'll end up at the cathedral on place du Peyrou, once part of Sarlat's Cluniac abbey. The original abbey church was built in the 1100s, redeveloped in the early 1500s and remodelled again in the 1700s, so it's a real mix of styles. The belfry and western facade are the oldest parts of the building, while the nave, organ and interior chapels are later additions.

Maison de la Boétie   ARCHITECTURE
This 16th-century timber-framed house opposite the cathedral is the birthplace of the writer Étienne de la Boétie (1530–63).

Église Ste-Marie   ARCHITECTURE
A few steps south of place du Marché aux Oies (see p572) is the Église Ste-Marie, ingeniously converted by acclaimed architect Jean Nouvel, whose parents still live in Sarlat. It now not only houses Sarlat's mouthwatering Marché Couvert (covered market), but, by the time you read this, a **panoramic lift** (elevator) will have been installed by Nouvel in its belltower. Check with the tourist office for details.

Historic quarter   ARCHITECTURE
Two medieval courtyards, the Cour des Fontaines and the Cour des Chanoines,

can be reached via an alleyway off rue Tourny. Duck down the passage from Cour des Chanoines to the Chapelle des Pénitents Bleus, a Romanesque chapel that provided the architectural inspiration for the cathedral.

Nearby is the Jardin des Enfeus, Sarlat's first cemetery, and the rocket-shaped Lanterne des Morts (Lantern of the Dead), built to honour a visit by St Bernard, one of the founders of the Cistercian order, in 1147.

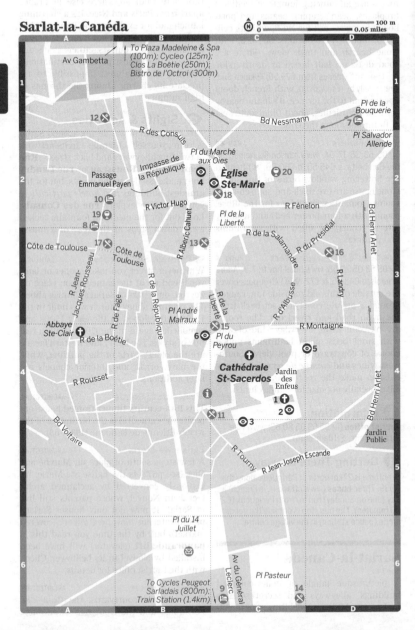

Sarlat-la-Canéda

Ⓝ 0 ▬▬▬▬▬▬ 100 m
0 ▬▬▬▬▬▬ 0.05 miles

To Plaza Madeleine & Spa (100m); Cycleo (125m); Clos La Boëtie (250m); Bistro de l'Octroi (300m)

Av Gambetta

Bd Nessmann

Pl de la Bouquerie
Pl Salvador Allende

R des Consuls

12

Passage Emmanuel Payen

Impasse de la République

Pl du Marché aux Oies

Èglise Ste-Marie
4
18
20

10
19
8

R Victor Hugo

R Fénelon

Côte de Toulouse

17
Côte de Toulouse

R Jean-Jacques Rousseau

R de Fage

R de la République

R Albéric Cahuet

13

Pl de la Liberté

R de la Salamandre

R du Présidial

16

R Landry

Bd Henri Arlet

R de la Liberté

R d'Albusse

Pl André Malraux

6
Pl du Peyrou
15

5

R Montaigne

Abbaye Ste-Clair
R de la Boëtie

R Rousset

Cathédrale St-Sacerdos
Jardin des Enfeus

1
2

Bd Henri Arlet

Bd Voltaire

11
3

R Tourny

Jardin Public

R Jean-Joseph Escande

Pl du 14 Juillet

To Cycles Peugeot Sarladais (800m); Train Station (1.4km)

9

Av du Général Leclerc

Pl Pasteur

14

Puymartin
<small>CHÂTEAU</small>

(www.chateau-de-puymartin.com, in French; adult €7, child €3.50-5; ☉10am-noon & 2-6pm) Heading 8km northwest from town brings you to this turreted château with an elegant partly furnished interior that's best known for the mysterious Dame Blanche, whose restless spirit is said to haunt its corridors.

🛏 Sleeping

Hotel rooms in Sarlat in summer are like gold dust, and budget rooms are thin on the ground at any time; shoestringers should ask at the tourist office about *chambres d'hôte*.

Plaza Madeleine & Spa
<small>SPA HOTEL €€</small>

(☑05 53 59 10 41; www.hoteldelamadeleine -sarlat.com; 1 place de la Petite Rigaudie; d €99-149; ❄🕸🏊) Perfect if you're in need of some pampering, facilities at this statement in luxury include an outdoor jacuzzi, solarium and Finnish sauna. Decorated in autumnal hues, contemporary rooms subtly evoke a bygone era.

Hôtel La Couleuvrine
<small>HOTEL €€</small>

(☑05 53 59 27 80; www.la-couleuvrine.com; 1 place de la Bouquerie; d €56-88; @🌐) Gables, chimneys and red-tile rooftops adorn this rambling hotel, which originally formed part of Sarlat's city wall. It's old, odd and endearingly musty. Strange-shaped rooms are sandwiched between solid stone and wooden rafters, and for maximum quirk factor there are a couple of rooms in the hotel's turret. Dine by the enormous fireplace in the 13th-century hall housing its restaurant (menus €19-32).

Hôtel Les Récollets
<small>HOTEL €</small>

(☑05 53 31 36 00; www.hotel-recollets-sarlat. com; 4 rue Jean-Jacques Rousseau; d €45-69; ❄🕸🌐) Lost in the medieval maze of the old town, the Récollets is a budget beauty. Nineteen topsy-turvy rooms and a charming vaulted breakfast room are rammed in around the medieval *maison*. Our favourites are 305 and 308, with exposed brick and king-size beds.

Clos La Boëtie
<small>BOUTIQUE HOTEL €€€</small>

(☑05 53 29 44 18; www.closlaboetie-sarlat.com; 95-97 av de la Selves; d €210-280, ste €300-340; ❄@🕸🏊) Each of the 11 rooms at this 19th-century mansion is a jewel, right down to the high-thread-count linen and supersoft pillows. Some have terraces and all come with hydromassage showers and balneotherapy (water healing) baths to soothe travel-weary bodies. It's a five-minute walk north of the Cité Médiévale.

Hôtel St-Albert
<small>BOUTIQUE HOTEL €€</small>

(☑05 53 31 55 55; www.hotel-saintalbert.eu; place Pasteur; d from €60; 🕸) At this pared back, stylish hotel with the barest of boutique touches, individually decorated rooms in chocolate-and-cream tones and posh bath goodies make it feel closer to a metropolitan crash pad than an old-town *auberge*.

Villa des Consuls
<small>B&B €€</small>

(☑05 53 31 90 05; www.villaconsuls.fr; 3 rue Jean-Jacques Rousseau; d €87-98, apt €98-175; @🕸) Despite its Renaissance exterior, the four huge rooms and summer-only self-catering apartments here are modern through and through. Some have wood floors, tall windows, sofas and original beams; others are tucked into the attic with split-level staircases, nook-and-cranny windows and lofty ceilings.

WHAT'S GOOD FOR THE GOOSE

A life-size statue of three gold-hued, bronze-sculpted geese in the centre of place du Marché aux Oies (Geese Market) attests to the enduring economic and gastronomic role of the birds in these parts. Sarlat's covered and outdoor markets sell a smorgasbord of goose-based goodies and restaurants serve up all manner of goose dishes including *grillons* (coarse-textured pâté), *magret* (breast), *aiguillettes* (fine slivers of *magret*) and *civet* (stew).

Gaggles of live geese fill the city during the **Fest'Oie** (goose festival) on the third Sunday in February, accompanied by stalls, music and a banquet prepared by Sarlat's top chefs.

Hôtel Le Mas de Castel   BOUTIQUE HOTEL **€€**
(☑05 53 59 02 59; www.hotel-lemasdecastel.
com; route du Sudalissant; d €65-75; @≈⊛) This former farmhouse 3km south of town makes a delightful escape from the hectic hum of central Sarlat. Some of its 14 sunny rooms open to the flower-filled courtyard and pool, and one has self-catering facilities.

Hôtel Altica   HOTEL **€**
(☑05 53 28 18 00; www.altica.fr; av de la Dordogne; d €42-44; ⊛) Situated 1.5km south of Sarlat, this ochre-coloured hotel – part of a small southwestern France chain – definitely isn't big on character. But it is about the cheapest option around, with rooms sleeping up to three people for the same flat rate.

✖ Eating

Sarlat isn't short on restaurants, but many are more concerned with packing in tourists whose loyalty they don't have to earn, rather than tempting tastebuds to return. Choose wisely.

Bistro de l'Octroi   REGIONAL CUISINE **€€**
(☑05 53 30 83 40; www.lebistrodeloctroi.fr, in French; 111 av de Selves; menus €18-26) This locals' tip is a little way out of town, but don't let that dissuade you. Sarladais pack into this cosy town house for the artistically presented, accomplished cooking that doesn't sacrifice substance for style. Top choices are the generous slabs of Limousin beef and sublime seafood; if you can't decide on dessert, go for the *symphonée* with small portions of several.

Le Grand Bleu   GASTRONOMIC **€€€**
(☑05 53 29 82 14; www.legrandbleu.eu, in French; 43 av de la Gare; menus €33-90; ⊗lunch Thu-Sun, dinner Tue-Sat; ⊛) Near the train station, every menu at this Michelin-starred temple to fine dining includes a choice of meat (like

veal sweetbreads with truffles) or seafood (such as lobster risotto with roast eggplant and truffle mousse), with a *'petit gourmet'* menu for little gourmands, and an upcoming program of cooking courses.

Le Présidial   REGIONAL CUISINE **€€**
(☑05 53 28 92 47; 6 rue Landry; menus from €29; ⊗lunch Tue-Sat, dinner Mon-Sat Apr-Nov) Housed in one of Sarlat's most historic buildings (originally a 17th-century courthouse), Le Présidial's stout gates swing back to reveal the city's most romantic terrace, filled with summer flowers and climbing ivy – the perfect place to sit back and enjoy authentic *saveurs de terroir* (country flavours). Goose, duck and foie gras dominate the changing menu, and the wine list is super, especially for Sarlat and Cahors vintages.

Le Bistrot   REGIONAL CUISINE **€€**
(☑05 53 28 28 40; place du Peyrou; menus €18.50-24.50; ⊗Mon-Sat) This diminutive bistro is the best of the bunch on café-clad place du Peyrou. Red-check tablecloths and twinkling fairy lights create an intimate atmosphere, and the menu's heavy on Sarlat classics – especially walnuts, *magret de canard* (duck breast) and *pommes sarlardaises* (potatoes cooked in duck fat).

Le Quatre Saisons   REGIONAL CUISINE **€€**
(☑05 53 29 48 59; www.4saisons-sarlat-perigord.
com, in French; 2 côte de Toulouse; menus from €19; ⊗Thu-Sun; ✐⊛) Tucked off a steep street in the Cité Médiévale. The father-and-son team behind this intimate restaurant use whatever's freshest at the markets to inspire inventive dishes accompanied by a surprisingly international wine list.

Criquettamu's   INTERNATIONAL **€€**
(☑05 53 29 48 59; www.criquettamus.fr, in French; 5 rue des Armes; menus €19-35; ⊗Tue-Sun Mar-Oct; ✐⊛) Searching out this chic little

spot – hidden away in the Cité Médiévale – rewards with 'world platters' including Japanese, island (with banana curry) and Western (gourmet hamburgers), as well as local flavours.

Chez Le Gaulois SAVOYARD €
(☑05 53 59 50 64; 3 rue Tourny; mains €9-13; ◷Tue-Sat) Stonking plates of smoked sausage, cold meats and cheese are served up on wooden platters at this Alpine-style *auberge* as well as authentic *tartiflettes* (cheese, potato and meat gratin).

Self-Catering

Practically every other shop in Sarlat is stocked with local goodies, from *confit de canard* (duck confit) to walnut cake.

Marché Couvert COVERED MARKET €
(◷8.30am-2pm) Inside the converted Église Ste-Marie, this is the best place for supplies from local producers.

Saturday market MARKET €
(place de la Liberté & rue de la République; ◷8.30am-6pm Sat) For the full-blown French market experience, you absolutely mustn't miss Sarlat's chaotic Saturday market, which takes over the streets around the cathedral. Depending on the season, delicacies on offer include local mushrooms, duck- and goose-based products such as foie gras, and even the holy *truffe noir* (black truffle).

Fruit & vegetable market MARKET €
(◷8.30am-1pm Wed) This smaller market is held on place de la Liberté.

Other good shops:

Distillerie du Périgord LIQUEUR €
(place de la Liberté) For local liqueurs.

Julien de Savignac WINE €
(place Pasteur)

Drinking

Sarlat's drinking scene is pretty limited. Closing times vary widely according to the season. Best options:

Le Pub BAR
(1 passage de Gérard du Barry; ◷daily) The enclosed courtyard springs to life with alfresco drinkers in summer.

Café Lébèrou BAR
(5 rue Jean Jacques Rousseau; ◷Tue-Sat) A local hang-out, with great cocktails.

❶ Information

There are several banks along rue de la République, all with ATMs.

Post office (place du 14 Juillet) Currency exchange.

Tourist office (☑05 53 31 45 45; www.sarlat -tourisme.com; rue Tourny; ◷9am-6pm Mon-Sat, 10am-1pm & 2-5pm Sun)

❶ Getting There & Away

Sarlat's train station is 1.3km south of the old city along av de la Gare. Destinations include Périgueux (change at Le Buisson; €13.90, 1¾ hours, three daily), Les Eyzies (change at Le Buisson; €8.60, 50 minutes to 2½ hours depending on connections, three daily) and Bergerac (€11.20, 2½ hours, six daily), as well as a direct service to Bordeaux (€23.90, 2¾ hours, seven daily).

❶ Getting Around

BICYCLE Bikes can be hired for around €12 for half a day from **Cycles Sarladais** (☑05 53 28 50 08; www.cycles-sarladais.com, in French; 16 av Aristide Briande), near the train station, and **Cycleo** (☑05 53 31 90 05; www.cycleo.fr; 44 rue des Cordeliers).

CAR Cars are banned in the Cité Médiévale from June to September, and rue de la République (La Traverse), the main street which bisects the Cité Médiévale, is pedestrianised in July and August. There's no free parking in Sarlat-la-Canéda.

The Vézère Valley

Flanked by limestone cliffs, subterranean caverns and ancient woodland, the Vézère Valley is world famous for its prehistoric sites, notably its incredible collection of cave paintings – the highest concentration of Stone Age art found in Europe. The many underground caves around the Vézère provided shelter for Cro-Magnon people, and the area is littered with tangible reminders of their time here. The otherworldly atmosphere is pretty much shattered by the summer crowds and most of the valley's sites are closed in winter, so spring and autumn are definitely the best times to visit.

Most of the key sites are around the towns of Les Eyzies-de-Tayac-Sireuil and Montignac, which are both well set up for visitors. Nearby Sarlat-la-Canéda, between the Vézère and Dordogne valleys to the west, is also a convenient base for exploring this part of the Dordogne.

ⓘ Getting Around

Public transport is limited, with few trains and even fewer buses. They will get you to most towns but there's usually no transport provided to the caves themselves. Cycling is an option, and hire bikes are often available from campsites, some hotels and rental outlets (ask at tourist offices) but, as always in rural France, having your own car makes things infinitely easier.

LES EYZIES-DE-TAYAC-SIREUIL & AROUND
POP 860

At the heart of the Vézère Valley, Les Eyzies itself makes a fairly uninspiring introduction to the wonders of the Vézère, with postcard sellers and souvenir shops lining the main street. Still, the town has some pleasant hotels and campgrounds and an excellent museum of prehistory, and many major sites are within a short drive.

⊙ Sights

LES EYZIES TOWN
Musée National de Préhistoire

PREHISTORY MUSEUM

(www.musee-prehistoire-eyzies.fr, in French; 1 rue du Musée adult/child €5/free, 1st Sun of month free; ⊙9.30am-6pm Wed-Mon) Inside a marvellous modern building underneath the cliffs, this museum provides a fine prehistory primer (providing your French is good), housing the most comprehensive collection of prehistoric finds in France. Highlights include a huge gallery of Stone Age tools, weapons and jewellery, and skeletons of some of the animals that once roamed the Vézère (including bison, woolly rhinoceros, giant deer and cave bears), as well as a collection of carved reliefs on the 1st floor – look out for an amazing frieze of horses and a bison licking its flank. Much of the jewellery is fashioned from bone, antlers and seashells, and intricately marked with chevrons, dots, dashes and other designs.

Vézère & Dordogne Valleys

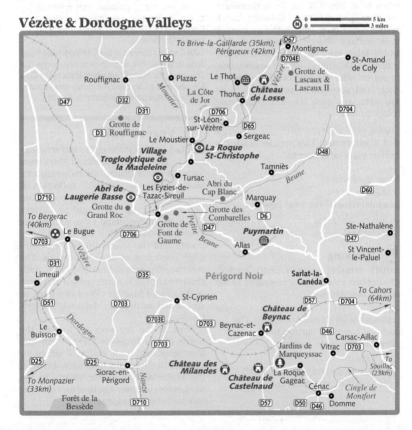

If you're visiting the cave paintings around the Vézère, it helps to know a little about the prehistoric artists who created them. Most of the valley's cave paintings date from the end of the last ice age, between 20,000 BC and 10,000 BC, and were painted by Cro-Magnon people – descendants of the first *Homo erectus* settlers who arrived in Europe from North Africa between 700,000 BC and 100,000 BC. These early humans were an entirely separate species from the shorter, burlier Neanderthals who lived in Europe around the same time and died out suddenly around 35,000 BC.

Until around 20,000 BC much of northern Europe was still covered by vast glaciers and ice sheets: Cro-Magnon people lived a loose hunter-gatherer lifestyle, using natural caves as temporary hunting shelters while they followed the migration routes of their prey (including woolly mammoths, woolly rhinoceros, reindeer and aurochs, an ancestor of the modern cow).

The earliest known cave art in the area is from the so-called Gravettian period, consisting of abstract engravings or paintings of female genitalia or 'Venus' figures and developing into complex animal figures and friezes such as those at Lascaux, Rouffignac and Font de Gaume, which date from around 15,000 BC to 10,000 BC. Curiously, the artwork in more recent caves is often less sophisticated than the ones at Lascaux, suggesting that different tribes had differing traditions and levels of artistry, but also indicating that Lascaux seems to have held an unusual significance for its painters. As well as the paintings, these early artists also created jewellery from shells, bones and antlers, and scrimshaw decorated with animal scenes and geometric patterns.

The paintings seem to have come to an abrupt halt around 10,000 BC, around the same time the last ice sheets disappeared and humans hereabouts settled down to a more fixed lifestyle of farming and agriculture.

Abri Pataud PREHISTORIC SITE
(www.mnhn.fr, in French; 20 rue du Moyen Âge; adult/child €5/3; ⊙10am-noon & 2-6pm Sun-Thu) About 250m north of the Musée National de Préhistoire is this Cro-Magnon *abri* (shelter) inhabited over a period of 15,000 years starting some 37,000 years ago, displaying bones and other excavated artefacts. The ibex carved into the ceiling dates from about 19,000 BC. The admission price includes a one-hour guided tour (some available in English).

EAST OF LES EYZIES

Grotte de Font de Gaume PREHISTORIC SITE
(☑05 53 06 86 00; http://eyzies.monuments -nationaux.fr; adult/child €7/free; ⊙9.30am-12.30pm & 2-5.30pm Sun-Fri) An astounding testament to the breadth and complexity of prehistoric art, this extraordinary cave 1km northeast of Les Eyzies on the D47 contains the only original 'polychrome' (as opposed to single-colour) paintings still open to the public. About 14,000 years ago, the prehistoric artists created the gallery of over 230 figures, including bison, reindeer, horses, mammoths, bears and wolves, although only about 25 are on permanent display. Look out for the famous **Chapelle des Bisons**, a scene of courting reindeer and stunningly realised

horses, several caught in mid-movement. Font de Gaume is such a rare and valuable site that there is ongoing talk of the cave being closed for its own protection. Visitor numbers are already limited to 200 per day: it's worth reserving by phone or through the tourist office a few days ahead, and a week or two in advance from July to September. The 45-minute guided tours are generally in French; ask about the availability of English tours when you book.

Grotte des Combarelles PREHISTORIC SITE
(☑05 53 06 86 00; http://eyzies.monuments -nationaux.fr; adult/child €7/free; ⊙9.30am-12.30pm & 2-5.30pm Sun-Fri) Rediscovered in 1901, this narrow cave 1.5km east of Font de Gaume is renowned for its animal engravings, many of which cleverly use the natural contours of the rock to sculpt the animals' forms: the most impressive examples are delicately drawn mammoths, horses and reindeer, as well as a fantastic mountain lion that seems to leap from the rock face. One wall seems to have been used as a kind of prehistoric sketchpad, with many animals and geometric symbols superimposed on one another. Six- to eight-person group tours last about an hour and can be

Vézère Valley Cave Art

France is renowned for its art – including some of the earliest in European history.

Deep in the Vézère Valley, prehistoric Cro-Magnon artists worked by the light of primitive oil torches, using flint tools for engraving, natural fibre brushes, pads or sponges for painting, and paints derived from minerals like magnesium and charcoal (black), ochre (red/yellow) and iron (red). Usually they painted the animals they hunted, though occasionally left hand-tracings or depicted abstract figures and scenes such as the picture of an injured hunter and bull at Lascaux. But the Cro-Magnon artists' motives remain a mystery.

Some clues come from what they *didn't* draw. There are no landscapes, trees, rivers, skies or rocks in any of the Vézère's caves – only animals, suggesting that the paintings had some kind of ritual or shamanic significance, possibly indicating shrines or sanctuaries. Most mysterious of all are the geometric shapes common to all the caves. Theories range from primitive writing to magic markers, though no one actually knows what they signified.

Head to some of the valley's extraordinary art sites and ponder these theories yourself.

TOP CAVES FOR VIEWING ART

» **Grotte de Lascaux** (p579) Breathtaking re-creations of the Vézère's most ornate cave art

» **Grotte de Rouffignac** (p578) Renowned for its frieze of mammoths, one of the largest cave paintings ever discovered

» **Grotte de Font de Gaume** (p575) The only original polychrome (multicolour) paintings still open

» **Abri du Cap Blanc** (p578) Flint-carved sculptures

Clockwise from top left
1. Painting at the Grotte de Lascaux 2. Mammoths of the Grotte de Rouffignac 3. Detail of bull's head, Grotte de Lascaux.

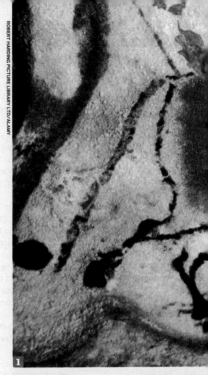

ROBERT HARDING PICTURE LIBRARY LTD/ALAMY

CHRIS HOWES/WILD PLACES PHOTOGRAPHY/ALAMY

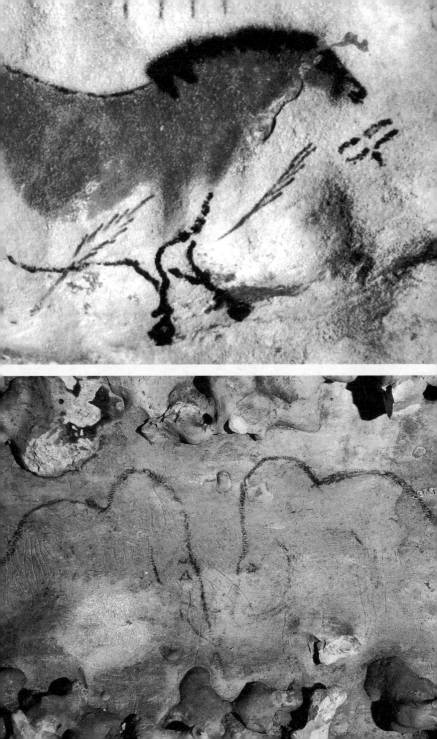

reserved through the Font de Gaume ticket office.

Abri du Cap Blanc PREHISTORIC SITE

(☎05 53 06 86 00; http://eyzies.monuments-nationaux.fr; adult/child €7/free; ⏱9.30am-12.30pm & 2-5.30pm Sun-Fri) While most of the Vézère's caves contain a combination of engravings and paintings, unusually, this rock shelter contains carved sculptures that were hollowed out, shaped and refined using simple flint tools some 14,000 years ago. The **sculpture gallery** of horses, bison and deer occupies about 40m of the natural shelter. It's peacefully situated about 7km east of Les Eyzies.

NORTHWEST OF LES EYZIES

Grotte du Grand Roc PREHISTORIC SITE

(www.semitour.com; adult/child €8.50/4.50; ⏱10am-noon & 2-6 Sun-Fri) Around 3km northwest of Les Eyzies along the D47, this wondrous cave is decorated by a diverse array of glittering stalactites and stalagmites. The admission price includes entry to the adjacent Abris de Laugerie Basse rock shelter originally occupied by Cro-Magnon people and still used as a natural shelter until recent times.

TOP CHOICE Grotte de Rouffignac PREHISTORIC SITE

(www.grottederouffignac.fr; adult/child €6.30/4; tours in French ⏱10-11.30am & 2-5pm) Hidden in woodland 15km north of Les Eyzies, this cave is one of the most complex and rewarding to see in the Dordogne. The massive cavern plunges 10km into the earth through a mind-boggling maze of tunnels and subshafts – luckily, you visit aboard a somewhat ramshackle **electric train**, so there's no chance of getting lost.

Rouffignac is sometimes known as the 'Cave of 100 Mammoths' and you'll see many painted pachyderms on your trip into the underworld, including a frieze of 10 mammoths in procession, one of the largest cave paintings ever discovered. At the end of the tour the train grinds to a halt and you stumble out into a hidden gallery where the entire ceiling is covered in mammoths, ibex, enormous horses, and even a few rhinoceros – some intricately painted, others reduced to simple strokes and lines. Keep your eyes peeled for scratches and hollows on the cave floor, left behind by the long-extinct cave bears who once shared this cave with our prehistoric ancestors. Certainly beats a cat...

Tickets are sold at the cave entrance but can't be reserved in advance so arrive early –

and wrap up warmly as it's chilly below ground.

NORTHEAST OF LES EYZIES

The following sights are situated off the main road linking Les Eyzies with Montignac.

Le Village Troglodytique de la Madeleine PREHISTORIC SITE

(www.village-la-madeleine.com, in French; adult/child €5.50/3.50; ⏱10am-7pm) Cro-Magnons weren't the only ones to use the Vézère's caves for shelter. As in the Loire, many of the area's caves were used for storage, defence or protection as recently as the Middle Ages. In a wooded setting seemingly straight out of a story book, this cave village 8km northeast of Les Eyzies is a prime example. Carved out from the cliff face above the winding Vézère River, the lower level was occupied by prehistoric people 10,000 to 14,000 years ago, while the upper level was used as a fortified village by medieval settlers. Though it's largely ruined, you can still visit the **Ste-Madeleine chapel** (after which the Magdalenian era is named), but most of the archaeological artefacts are at the Musée National de Préhistoire in Les Eyzies.

La Roque St-Christophe PREHISTORIC SITE

(www.roque-st-christophe.com; adult €7.50, child €3.50-4.50; ⏱10am-6.30pm) On a sheer cliff face 80m above the Vézère 9km northeast of Les Eyzies, the commanding position of this 900m-long series of terraces and caves makes a practically unassailable stronghold. No wonder, then, that this troglodytic site has been employed as a natural fortress for almost 50 millennia – initially by Mousterian (Neanderthal) people 50,000 years ago, followed by successive generations until the 16th century. The sweeping views are stunning, though the caverns themselves are largely empty and some of the plastic reconstructions are decidedly lame.

🏃 Activities

For a change from the land-based marvels of the Vézère Valley, Canoës Vallée Vézère (☎05 53 05 10 11; www.canoesvalleevezere.com; 10 promenade de la Vézère, Les Eyzies; trips €12-22; ⏱Apr-Sep) organises canoe and kayak trips from 10km to 26km including minibus transport. A 5km initiation course costs €8; there are also multiday trips staying at campgrounds or hotels.

Sleeping & Eating

Hôtel des Glycines
HOTEL €€

(☑05 53 06 97 07; www.les-glycines-dordogne. com; 4 av de Laugerie; d €112-162, ste 232; ❋☎☲) Les Eyzies' old post house has been converted into this posh pad where Prince Charles once stayed. Plush rooms range from cream-and-check 'Classics' to full-blown private suites, complete with private terrace and garden outlook. (Avoid the 'courtyard rooms' if you can, which overlook the main road out of Les Eyzies.) The hotel's gastronomic restaurant (menus from €39) is a suitably pampering affair.

Hôtel Le Cro-Magnon
HOTEL €€

(☑05 53 06 97 06; www.hostellerie-cro-magnon.com; 54 av de la Préhistoire; d €75-130; ☺mid-Mar–mid-Nov; ☎☲) Though rooms at this 1850-built inn have a modern efficiency (tempered by old-worlde style), if the walls could talk, they'd tell you of the Cro-Magnon discoveries on the site of the property's outbuildings in 1868, which have made it a popular stop for prehistorians. Dining is good value in the beamed-ceilinged restaurant (menus from €17).

Hostellerie du Passeur
HOTEL €€

(☑05 53 06 97 13; www.hostellerie-du-passeur.com; place de la Mairie; d €92-120, ste €180; ☺Feb-Oct; ❋☎) In the middle of Les Eyzies overlooking the meandering Vézère, rooms at this ivy-clad hotel come in 'Charme', 'Elegance' and 'Prestige' categories. The better rooms are worth the cash, with valley views and deep, luxurious beds.

Hôtel des Roches
HOTEL €€

(☑05 53 06 96 59; www.roches-les-eyzies.com; 15 av de la Forge; s €60-80, d €75-98; ☺Apr-Nov; ☎☲♿) For a modern feel, try this smart hotel, chunkily constructed from the area's pale stone and decorated in simple pastoral style. The rear rooms overlook the garden and swimming pool, but you'll have to pay for the privilege.

Les Eyzies has lots of campgrounds, but they get heavily oversubscribed so reserve well ahead.

Camping La Rivière
CAMPGROUND €

(☑05 53 06 97 14; www.lariviereleseyzies.com; site from €15.50; @☎☲♿) The nearest campground to Les Eyzies, a stroll west of town beside the river. Handy facilities include a restaurant, bar, laundry and on-site groceries.

Information

Tourist office (☑05 53 06 97 05; www. tourisme-terredecromagnon.com; ☺9am-noon & 2-6pm Mon-Sat, 10am-noon & 2-5pm Sun) Has a small internet kiosk (per 15 minutes €1.50).

Getting There & Away

Les Eyzies is on the D47, 21km west of Sarlat. The train station is 700m north of town, with connections to Périgueux (€7.20, 30 minutes, 10 daily) and Sarlat (change at Le Buisson; €8.60, 50 minutes to 2½ hours depending on connections, three daily).

MONTIGNAC & AROUND
POP 2946

The riverside town of Montignac is most famous for its proximity to the Grottes de Lascaux, which are hidden away on the densely wooded hilltops just outside the town. Huddled along both banks of the Vézère, Montignac is a peaceful, attractive place and makes a less hectic base than Les Eyzies or Sarlat. The old city and commercial centre is on the river's right bank, but you'll find most of the hotels on the left bank around place Tourny.

To get out onto the river, ask at the tourist office about canoe and kayak rental outlets.

Sights

Grotte de Lascaux & Lascaux II
TOP CHOICE
PREHISTORIC SITE

(☑Lascaux II 05 53 51 95 03; www.semitour. com; adult/child €8.80/6, joint ticket with Le Thot €12.50/8.50; ☺9.30am-6pm) France's most famous prehistoric **cave paintings** are at the Grotte de Lascaux, 2km southeast of Montignac. Discovered in 1940 by four teenage boys who were out searching for their lost dog, Lascaux contains a vast network of chambers and galleries adorned with some of the most extraordinary and complex prehistoric paintings ever found. Far from the comparatively crude etchings of some of the Vézère's other caves, Lascaux' paintings are renowned for their astonishing artistry: the 600-strong menagerie of animal figures are depicted in Technicolor shades of red, black, yellow and brown, and range from reindeer, aurochs, mammoths and horses to a monumental 5.5m-long bull, the largest cave drawing ever found. Lascaux is sometimes referred to as the prehistoric equivalent of the Sistine Chapel, and it's a fitting comparison: after a visit in 1940, Picasso allegedly muttered,

PHILIPPE CAMBA: CAVE GUIDE, LASCAUX II

Job

I'm a teacher by profession but I've always been fascinated by prehistory. I originally studied eco-biology and palaeontology, and combine teaching in the winter with my work as a guide in the summer. In the summer season we can have up to 2000 visitors a day at Lascaux, and take up to six tours each. I do tours in English and French and over the years I've learned the names of the colours, animals and the different body parts in Japanese. It helps a lot!

Impressions of Lascaux

Lascaux is a unique place, with over 2000 of the finest polychrome paintings ever discovered, as well as the largest cave painting ever found. Sadly, I've never been able to see the originals. It's amazing to think that these paintings were all done in one go – they never used sketches or drafts because they couldn't rub out their mistakes. They were real artists, who understood perspective, colour and form. In their own way, Lascaux' paintings are just as complex as those of Picasso or van Gogh.

Best Cave Painting Scenes?

For me, the ones that show the animals in mid-movement. They're like prehistoric movies.

'We have invented nothing'. Carbon dating has shown that the paintings are between 15,000 and 17,000 years old. But despite endless discussion and academic study, no one really knows why the prehistoric painters devoted so much time and effort to their creation, or why this particular site seems to have been so important to them.

The original cave was opened to visitors in 1948, and public interest was unsurprisingly massive. But within a few years it became apparent that human breath and body heat was causing irreparable damage to the paintings, and the cave was closed just 15 years later in 1963. In response to public demand, a replica of the most famous sections of the original cave was meticulously re-created a few hundred metres away – a massive undertaking that required the skills of some 20 artists and took over 11 years. Lascaux II was opened in 1983 and, although the idea sounds rather contrived, the reproductions are enormously moving – especially when the lights are turned off and the paintings seem to spring to life in the light of a flickering torch.

There are several guided tours every hour; ask at the ticket office about the availability of tours in languages including English. From April to October, tickets are sold *only* in Montignac at the ticket office next to Montignac's tourist office.

Le Thot MUSEUM, ANIMAL PARK

(☑05 53 50 70 44; www.semitour.com; adult/child €6.50/4.50, joint ticket with Lascaux €12.50/8.50; ☉10am-6pm) In an effort to bring the prehistoric age to life, Le Thot, 7km southwest of Montignac, places displays about Cro-Magnon life and art alongside real-life animals they depicted, including reindeer, stags, horses, ibex and European bison (plus replicas of now-extinct species like mammoths). Perhaps most interesting, though, are the displays showing the re-creation of the paintings at Lascaux II.

CASTLE, GARDENS

(www.chateaudelosse.com; adult/child €7.50/4; ☉noon-6pm Sun-Fri) An original 15th-century moat and battlements surround this grandly furnished château, 5km southwest of Montignac. Allow time for a fragrant stroll in its ornate gardens.

🛏 Sleeping & Eating

The tourist office has a list of nearby campgrounds and *chambres d'hôte*.

Hostellerie la Roseraie HOTEL €€

(☑05 53 50 53 92; www.laroseraie-hotel.com; 11 place des Armes; d €90-170; ☉Apr-Oct; ☏⊠) As its name implies, the highlight of this mansion in Montignac is the gorgeous rose garden, set around box-edged grounds and a palm-tinged pool. Rococo rooms in various shades of rosy pink and sunflower yellow have solid furniture, sparkling bathrooms and rose garden views. Half board (€100 to €162 per person) is compulsory on weekends in July and August but you'll want to dine here in any case: truffles, chestnuts, pork and guinea fowl find their way on to the seasonal menu, and on warm summer nights the canopy-shaded terrace is the only place to be.

Hôtel de la Grotte   HOTEL €€
(☑05 53 51 80 48; www.hoteldelagrotte.fr; place Tourny; d €56-85; 🐾) This unpretentious country *auberge* in the heart of Montignac makes a charming stop as long as you don't mind frilly bedspreads and floral wallpaper. The gingerbread rooms are a little poky (especially the attic ones, huddled in around the roof beams), but they're reasonably priced and quite comfortable. The garden-set tables at its *restaurant* (menus €12.50-32) are delightful for summertime dining; bike hire is available year-round.

Hotel le Lascaux   HOTEL €
(☑05 53 51 82 81; 109 av Jean-Jaurès; d €46-67; 🐾♿) Candy-cane awnings and climbing ivy decorate the front of this family-owned place on the main road to Lascaux, 300m from Montignac's town centre. It's relaxed and unfussy, with snug, simple rooms, some with striped wallpaper and wooden beds. Bag one with a view on to the tree-shaded back garden if you can.

❶ Information
Tourist office (☑05 53 51 82 60; www.tourisme-lascaux.com; place Bertrand de Born; ⏰9.30am-12.30pm & 2-6pm Mon-Sat) Around 200m west of place Tourny, next to the 14th-century Église St-Georges le Prieuré.

❶ Getting There & Away
The only buses – stopping on place Tourny – are inconveniently geared around school times, so your own wheels are really a must. Montignac is 25km northeast of Les Eyzies on the D706.

The Dordogne Valley

DOMME
POP 1037

Commanding an unparalleled view across the surrounding countryside from a dizzying outcrop above the Dordogne, Domme is one of several of France's official *plus beaux villages* in this area. It's also one of the area's best preserved *bastides*, retaining most of its 13th-century ramparts and three original gateways. Approached via a tortuous switchback road from the valley below, it's the perfect defensive stronghold – a fact not lost on Philippe III of France, who founded the town in 1281 as a bastion against the English. The town's imposing clifftop position is best appreciated from the esplanade du Belvédère and the adjacent promenade de la Barre, which both offer panoramic views across the valley.

◉ Sights
Grottes Naturelles à Concrétions   CAVES
(adult/child incl museum €8/5.50; ⏰tours 10.15am, 11am, noon, 2.15pm, 3pm, 4pm, 5pm & 6pm) Honeycombing the stone underneath the village is a series of large caves decorated with some of the most ornate stalactites and stalagmites in the Dordogne. A lift whisks you back up at the end of the 45-minute tour. Tickets are available from the tourist office, opposite the entrance to the caves.

Musée d'Arts et Traditions Populaires
    HISTORY MUSEUM
(adult/child €4/3, with cave ticket, free; ⏰10.30am-12.30pm & 2.30-6pm Apr-Sep) Across the square from the tourist office, artefacts here include clothing, toys and tools, mainly from the 19th century.

🛏 Sleeping & Eating
La Guérinière   B&B €€
(☑05 53 29 91 97; www.la-gueriniere-dordogne.com; Cénac et St-Julien; d €80-95; 🐾♿) Surrounded by its own 6-hectare grounds complete with a tennis court, rooms at this wonderful *chambre d'hôte* about 5km south of Domme along the D46 are all named after flowers and finished with impeccably good taste: our faves are Mimosa, with its sloping roof and chinoiserie wardrobe, and the supersize Blue room. Book ahead for *tables d'hôte* (€25 including wine) using mostly organic produce.

L'Esplanade   HOTEL €€
(☑05 53 28 31 41; www.esplanade-perigord.com; rue du Pont-Carral; d €85-150; ❋🐾) This place is an absolute spoil from start to finish. Teetering on the edge of the village ramparts, it's a traditional family-owned hotel with a twist of designer chic: four-poster beds, antique desks and upholstered armchairs fill the elegant rooms, some of which have balconies with mind-boggling valley views. Downstairs there's a top-notch *restaurant* (menus €25-45) with a to-die-for terrace overlooking the esplanade du Belvédère.

ℹ Information

Tourist office (☏05 53 31 71 00; www.ot-domme.com; place de la Halle; ☉10am-noon & 2-6pm)

ℹ Getting There & Away

Domme is 18km south of Sarlat along the D46.

LA ROQUE GAGEAC & AROUND
POP 431

La Roque Gageac's jumble of amber buildings crammed into the cliff-face above the Dordogne have earned it recognition as another of France's *plus beaux villages*, with flourishing gardens thanks to its microclimate. It's an idyllic launch for a canoe trip or cruise, while a trio of the region's most famous castles are within a few minutes' drive.

◉ Sights

Fort Troglodyte   FORT

(adult/child €5/2; ☉10am-6pm) A warren of meandering lanes lead up to La Roque's dramatic fort, where a series of defensive positions constructed by medieval engineers have been carved out from the overhanging cliffs.

Jardins de Marqueyssac   GARDENS

(www.marqueyssac.com; adult/child €7.20/3.60; ☉10am-7pm) Signposted walkways wind through Marqueyssac's manicured overhanging gardens, 3km west of La Roque, to a breathtaking *belvédère* (lookout).

Château de Castelnaud   CASTLE

(www.castelnaud.com; adult/child €7.80/3.90; ☉10am-7pm) The massive ramparts and metre-thick walls of this quintessential castle 4.5km southwest of La Roque are topped by crenellations and sturdy towers. From up here you can see right across the Dordogne Valley to Castelnaud's arch-rival, the Château de Beynac. The castle's **museum of medieval warfare** displays daggers, spiked halberds and huge trebuchets. If you fancy seeing them in action, **mock battles** are staged from mid-July to August, as well as one-hour guided **evening tours** by costumed actors (adult/child €9.60/5) – check the events diary on the website.

Château de Beynac   CASTLE

(www.beynac-en-perigord.com; Beynac-et-Cazenac; adult/child €7.50/3.20; ☉10am-6.30pm) Looming ominously from atop a limestone bluff 5km northwest of La Roque, this 12th-century château's panoramic position above the Dordogne made it a key defensive position during the Hundred Years War. Apart from a brief interlude under Richard the Lionheart, Beynac remained fiercely loyal to the French monarchy, often placing it at odds with the English-controlled stronghold of nearby Castelnaud. Protected by 200m cliffs, a double wall and double moat, it presented a formidable proposition for would-be attackers, though it saw little direct action.

Highlights include the château's **Romanesque keep**, a grand **Salle des États** (State Room) and frescoed **chapel**, and the 16th- and 17th-century **apartments** built to lodge the castle barons. From the battlements, there's a vertigo-inducing view along the Dordogne to the château of Marqueyssac.

Below the castle, a steep trail leads to Beynac-et-Cazenac (population 515), another of France's *plus beaux villages*, 150m below on the river bank, where scenes from the Lasse Hallström–directed movie *Chocolat* (2000), starring Johnny Depp and Juliette Binoche, were filmed along rue de l'Ancienne Poste.

Château des Milandes   CASTLE

(www.milandes.com; Castelnaud-la-Chapelle; adult/child €8.50/5.50; ☉10am-7pm) This 15th-century château, 8.5km southwest of La Roque, is less famous for its architecture (impressive though it is) than its former owner: glamorous African-American dancer, singer and music-hall star **Josephine Baker** (1906–75), who took the Parisian cultural scene by storm in the 1920s with her raunchy performances. Her most famous stage outfit consisted of a string of pearls and a skirt of bananas, and she often liked to walk her pet cheetah, Chiquita, on a diamond-studded lead around Paris, terrifying her fellow pedestrians.

Baker purchased the castle in 1936 and lived here until 1958. She was awarded the Croix de Guerre and the Legion of Honour for her work with the French Resistance during WWII. She was later active in the US civil-rights movement and is also remembered for her 'Rainbow Tribe' – 12 children from around the world adopted as 'an experiment in brotherhood' (Brangelina, take note).

The château houses a **museum** documenting the life of the great Ms Baker, and her famous tunes tinkle out from the speaker system as you stroll around. Ask for an English-language leaflet. Between May and

A timeless way to explore the region's scenery is aboard a *gabarre*, a flat-bottomed, wooden boat traditionally used to transport freight up and down the rivers of the Périgord and Lot Valley. *Gabarres* were a common sight in this part of France until the early 20th century, when they were eclipsed by the rise of the railway and the all-conquering automobile.

These days *gabarres* have been reinvented as pleasure vessels offering tranquil cruises departing from several points, from around April until October. Trips generally last about 55 minutes and cost €8.50/6 per adult/child; advance reservations are recommended.

Operators in and around La Roque Gageac include Gabarres Caminade (☑05 53 29 40 95; gabarrescaminade@wanadoo.fr Le Bourg, La Roque Gageac); Gabarres de Beynac (☑05 53 28 51 15; www.gabarre-beynac.com, in French; Le Port, Beynac-et-Cazenac), which does slightly shorter, cheaper trips departing from Beynac (note that kids cruise for free in the mornings); and Gabarres Norbert (☑05 53 29 40 44; www.norbert.fr; Le Bourg, La Roque Gageac).

Bergerac and Beaulieu-sur-Dordogne also have *gabarre* cruises.

October there are also 30-minute-long daily displays by the château's **birds of prey**.

🏃 Activities

Paddling along the river offers a changing panorama of soaring cliffs, castles and picturesque villages. La Roque's quay also serves as a launch point for short **river cruises** aboard a traditional *gabarre* (above). Canoe-trip operators include the following:

Canoë Dordogne   CANOEING
(☑05 53 29 58 50; www.canoe-dordogne.fr, in French; €5-19) Self-guided trips of between one and five hours from various points upriver of La Roque, as well as guided trips in an eight- to 10-person canoe.

Canoë Vacances   CANOEING
(☑05 53 28 17 07; www.canoevacances.com; La Peyssière; canoeing €5-20, canyoning €4-7) Itineraries include La Roque to Les Milandes (9km), from Carsac to La Roque (16km) and Carsac to Les Milandes (25km); adventurous types can try a spot of canyoning. Its base is about 2km northeast of La Roque.

🛏 Sleeping & Eating

Accommodation options are pretty limited, with only a handful of hotels in the area, but the tourist offices in La Roque Gageac and Beynac-et-Cazenac have lists of campgrounds and *chambres d'hôte*.

La Belle Étoile   HOTEL €€
(☑05 53 29 51 44; www.belleetoile.fr; Le Bourg; d €55-75, ste €130; ☺Apr-Oct; ☎) Right on La Roque Gageac's riverfront, this family-run hotel resides in an old stone building with hefty timber beams. Higher-priced rooms come with river views, but those at the cheaper end of the scale look out over the village. Its restaurant (menus from €28; ☺lunch Tue & Thu-Sun, dinner Tue-Sun Apr-Oct) opens to a vine-draped terrace.

❶ Information

Tourist office hours vary seasonally.

Beynac-et-Cazenac tourist office (☑05 53 29 43 08; www.cc-perigord-noir.fr, in French; D703)

La Roque Gageac tourist office (☑05 53 29 17 01; www.cc-perigord-noir.fr, in French; Le Bourg)

❶ Getting There & Away

La Roque Gageac is 15km south of Sarlat, via the D46 and D703; there's no public transport.

Monpazier
POP 539

The best-preserved *bastide* in this corner of France, Monpazier was founded in 1284 by a representative of Edward I (King of England and Duke of Aquitaine). It had a turbulent time during the Wars of Religion and the Peasant Revolts of the 16th century, but despite numerous assaults and campaigns, the town has survived remarkably intact.

◎ Sights

Place des Cornières   TOWN SQUARE
From the town's three gateways, Monpazier's flat, grid-straight streets lead to the arcaded market square (also known as place

Centrale), surrounded by a motley collection of stone houses that reflect centuries of building and rebuilding. In one corner is an old *lavoir* once used for washing clothes. Thursday is **market** day, as it has been since the Middle Ages.

Château de Biron
CASTLE

(www.pays-de-bergerac.com; adult/child €6.50/4.50; ☺10am-12.30pm & 2-6pm Feb-Dec) Some 8km south of Monpazier, this much-filmed château is a glorious mishmash of styles, having been fiddled with by eight centuries of successive heirs. The castle was finally sold in the early 1900s to pay for the extravagant lifestyle of a particularly irresponsible son.

🛏 Sleeping & Eating

Hôtel Edward 1er
HOTEL €€

(☎05 53 22 44 00; www.hoteledward1er.com; 5 rue St-Pierre; d €84-104, ste €132-162; 🛜🗭) Rooms in this tower-topped château/mansion get more luxurious the more you pay: top-of-the-line suites have a choice of jacuzzi or Turkish bath, and views of surrounding hills. It feels slightly dated considering the price tag, but the owners are full of beans, and there's an excellent res-taurant (menus €29-37.50; ☺dinner Thu-Tue Apr-Oct).

Hôtel de France
HOTEL €

(☎05 53 22 60 06; www.hoteldefrancemonpazier. fr; 21 rue Saint Jacques; d €40-70; ☺Apr-Oct) Parts of this epicentral yellow-brick *au-berge* date back centuries (the central staircase was built in the 1400s), so it certainly feels historic. There are wooden furnishings, old rugs and flowery wallpaper in the rooms, small shuttered windows overlooking the town's rooftops and a solid country restaurant (menus from €16). Opening hours (for the hotel and the restaurant) are unpredictable so call ahead.

Bistrot 2
REGIONAL CUISINE €€

(☎05 53 22 60 64; www.bistrot2.fr; Monpazier; menus €24) Opposite the town's medieval gateway, this modern bistro in a square stone-front inn reinvents traditional Périgord staples with minimalist dishes, contemporary flavours and metropolitan style. The wisteria-draped terrace is perfect for Sunday lunch or twilight suppers.

ℹ Information

The **tourist office** (☎05 53 22 68 59; www. pays-des-bastides.com; place des Cornières; ☺10am-12.30pm & 2.30-6pm Tue-Sun) is in the southeastern corner of the square.

ℹ Getting There & Away

Monpazier is 50km southwest of Sarlat and 50km southeast of Bergerac.

Bergerac

POP 28,638

Rich vineyards and flat fields surround Bergerac, capital of the Périgord Pourpre and one of the largest wine-growing areas of the Aquitaine, which centres on its cobbled old town and medieval harbour.

The town's main claim to fame is the dramatist and satirist Savinien Cyrano de Bergerac (1619–55), whose romantic exploits – and oversize nose – have inspired everyone from Molière to Steve Martin. Despite the legend (largely invented by the 19th-century playwright Edmond Rostand), Cyrano's connection with the town is tenuous at best – he's thought to have only stayed here a few nights if at all.

Bergerac's international airport and central location between Périgueux (47km to the northeast) and Bordeaux (93km to the west) makes it a handy gateway to the region.

◉ Sights & Activities

The prettiest parts of Bergerac's old town are place de la Mirpe, with its tree-shaded square and timber houses, and place Pelissière, where a jaunty statue of Cyrano de Bergerac looks up at the nearby church.

Gabarres de Bergerac
RIVER CRUISES

(☎05 53 24 58 80; www.gabarres.fr, in French; quai Salvette; adult/child €8/5; ☺Easter-Oct) Bergerac's wine trade flourished with the river transport provided by *gabarres* (p583), the pivotal role of which is recalled aboard 50-minute cruises.

FREE Maison des Vins
WINE TASTING

(www.vins-bergerac.fr; 1 rue des Récollets; ☺10am-12.30pm & 2-7pm) Sample the area's famous drops or pick up information on touring the local wine country; alternatively maps and info are available from the tourist office.

The town's main museums are dedicated to Bergerac's twin vices:

Musée du Vin et de la Batellerie
WINE MUSEUM

(place de la Mirpe; admission €3; ☺10am-noon & 2-5.30pm Tue-Fri, 10am-noon Sat, 2.30-6.30pm

Sun) Wonderfully musty displays of vintage winemaking equipment and scale models of local river boats.

Musée d'Anthropologie du Tabac
TOBACCO MUSEUM

(10 rue de l'Ancien Port; adult/child €4/free; ⏲10am-noon & 2-6pm Tue-Fri, 10am-noon & 2-5pm Sat, 2.30-6.30pm Sun) Inside the 17th-century Maison Peyrarède, spanning 3000 years including a collection of ornate pipes.

🛏 Sleeping & Eating

If you don't mind travelling a bit further afield, sleeping and eating choices include some superb places in the surrounding countryside.

TOP CHOICE Château les Merles
BOUTIQUE HOTEL €€€

(☑05 53 63 13 42; www.lesmerles.com; Tuilières, Mouleydier; d €165-185, ste €215; @🛜🏊) Behind its 19th-century neoclassical facade, this interior designer's dream is a study in modish minimalism. Monochrome colour schemes including black-and-white sofas, slate-grey throws and artfully chosen antiques run throughout the rooms, most of which would look more at home in Paris than the deep Dordogne, 13km east of Bergerac. It's got wit, style and sexiness in spades: tripod floor lamps, gilt-framed mirrors and just-so objets d'art, along with a nine-hole **golf course** and an utterly ravishing fusion restaurant (menus €36-43).

Château Les Farcies du Pech'
B&B €€

(☑06 30 19 53 20; www.chambre-hote-bergerac. com; Hameau de Péchamant; d €110; ⏲mid-Mar–mid-Nov) Along with its own brace of vintages, this château-winery-B&B 2km north of Bergerac has five rooms all finished in the same scrubbed-up style: patterned rugs, colour-washed walls, hardwood floors and the odd patch of original stonework. The French brekkie, served in the wood-beamed kitchen, is a treat.

Le Colombier de Cyrano et Roxane
B&B €€

(☑05 53 57 96 70; 17 rue du Grand Moulin; www. samedimidi.com, in French; d €68-78; 🛜) One of several sweet *chambres d'hôte* in Bergerac's old town around place de la Mirpe (its alternative address), this 16th-century blue-shuttered stone building has just two colourful rooms with hefty wooden beams

and a flower-filled terrace where you can doze off in the hammock.

Hotel du Commerce
HOTEL €

(☑05 53 27 30 50; www.hotel-du-commerce24. fr; 36 place Gambetta; d €58-62; ❄🛜📶) In a relaxed spot on place Gambetta, this good-value hotel has functional if rather characterless rooms with contemporary furnishings and up-to-date bathrooms (air-conditioned rooms cost a few extra euros).

🍴 La Ferme de Biorne
REGIONAL CUISINE €€

(☑05 53 57 67 26; Lunas; www.biorne. com; menus €19-27; ⏲Tue-Sun Apr-Oct by reservation) Flapping birds at this *ferme auberge* (farm restaurant) in the Périgordine countryside, 13km northwest of Bergerac, feature in dishes like flame-grilled *magret* (breast) and foie gras–stuffed quail.

L'Imparfait
REGIONAL CUISINE €€

(☑05 53 57 47 92; 6-10 rue des Fontaines; www. imparfait.com; menus €21-27) Tucked in a 12th-century cloister. Modest prices belie the artful cooking at this local secret.

ℹ Information

Tourist office (☑05 53 57 03 11; www. bergerac-tourisme.com; 97 rue Neuve d'Argenson; ⏲9.30am-1pm & 2-7pm Mon-Sat; @🛜) Friendly and knowledgeable.

ℹ Getting There & Away

AIR Bergerac's **airport** (www.bergerac.aeroport .fr, in French), 4km southeast of town, is served by several budget carriers. Destinations include Paris Orly, Bristol, Brussels Charleroi, Edinburgh, London Stansted, London Gatwick, East Midlands, Liverpool, Birmingham, Exeter, Leeds-Bradford, Southampton and Rotterdam.

TRAIN Bergerac is on the regional line between Bordeaux (€15, 1½ hours, hourly) and Sarlat (€11.20, 1½ hours, every two hours). For other destinations change at Le Buisson.

THE LOT

Southeast of the Dordogne is the warm, unmistakably southern Lot *département*, which formerly comprised the northern section of the old province of Quercy (along with the northern half of the modern-day *département* of Tarn-et-Garonne). The dry limestone plateau is covered with oak trees, and riddled with canyons carved by the serpentine River Lot. Its *préfecture*, Cahors, is surrounded by celebrated vineyards.

Cahors

POP 21,128

In a U-shape *boucle* (curve) in the River Lot, Cahors has the air of a sunbaked Mediterranean town – a reminder that Languedoc lies just to the south. Pastel-coloured buildings line the shady squares of the old medieval quarter, criss-crossed by a labyrinth of alleyways and cul-de-sacs, which borders the medieval quays.

Slicing through the centre of Cahors, bd Léon Gambetta – named after the French statesman who was born in Cahors in 1838 – neatly divides Vieux Cahors (old Cahors) to the east and the new city to the west.

The city is ringed on three sides by the quays, which once harboured its river-going traffic but are now mostly used by cyclists, rollerbladers and afternoon strollers.

◉ Sights & Activities

Pont Valentré   BRIDGE

The six-span Pont Valentré, on the western side of the city, south of the train station, is one of France's most iconic medieval bridges. Built as part of the town's defences in the 14th century, the parapets projecting from two of its three tall **towers** were designed to allow defenders to drop missiles on attackers below. On the bank opposite the

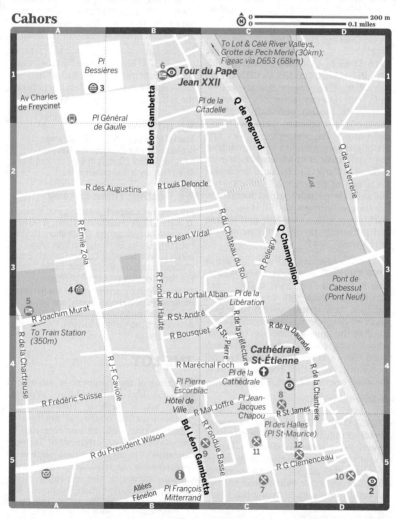

Cahors

bridge, numerous Roman coins have been found at the natural spring known as the Fontaine des Chartreux, dedicated to the city's Gallo-Roman goddess Divona, which still supplies the city's drinking water.

Cathédrale St-Étienne CATHEDRAL

Similar in style to the Cathédrale St-Front in Périgueux, the airy nave of Cahors' Romanesque cathedral, consecrated in 1119, is topped by two cupolas (at 18m wide, the largest in France). Some of the frescos are 14th century, but the side chapels and carvings in the cloître (cloister; ⊙Jun-Sep) mainly date from the Flamboyant Gothic period in the 16th century. On the cathedral's north facade is a carved tympanum depicting Christ surrounded by fluttering angels and pious saints.

Tour du Pape Jean XXII ARCHITECTURE

(3 bd Léon Gambetta) At the top of the old city, the Tour du Pape Jean XXII (closed to the public) is the town's tallest building at 34m high. It was originally part of a 14th-century mansion belonging to Jacques Duèse (later Pope John XXII), who constructed the Pont Valentré and founded Cahors' university.

Old City ARCHITECTURE

In the Middle Ages, Cahors was a prosperous commercial centre, and the old city is densely packed with timber-fronted houses and galleried mansions built by the city's medieval merchants. Many are marked on the *Itinéraires à Travers la Ville* leaflet from the tourist office.

Mechanical clock CLOCK

(place St-Urcisse) Near the cathedral, the 1997-installed clock looks like something out of Tim Burton's sketchbook.

Cahors has just a couple of museums:

Musée Henri Martin MUSEUM

(Musée Municipal; www.mairie-cahors.fr/musee, in French; 792 rue Émile Zola; adult/child €3/1.50; ⊙11am-6pm Mon & Wed-Sat, 2-6pm Sun) Displays include works by the Cahors-born pointillist painter Henri Martin (1893–1972).

FREE Musée de la Résistance MUSEUM

(place Général de Gaulle; ⊙2-6pm) Little museum exploring the city's experiences during WWII.

🛏 Sleeping

Grand Hôtel Terminus HOTEL €€

(☎05 65 53 32 00; www.balandre.com; 5 av Charles de Freycinet; d €70-100, ste €130-160; ❇🐾) Built circa 1920, Cahors' original railway station hotel evokes an air of faded grandeur. Most of the rooms are large and quite comfortable, with hefty radiators, roll-top baths and king-size beds. The decor's starting to look a little dated and the suites are seriously overpriced, but its restaurant, Le Balandre, can't be beat.

Hôtel Jean XXII HOTEL €

(☎05 65 35 07 66; www.hotel-jeanxxii.com, in French; 2 rue Edmond-Albé; s €48, d €58-65; 🐾) Huddled next to the Tour Jean XXII, this excellent little hotel mixes original stone, greenery and well-worn wood with a dash of metropolitan minimalism. Smart rooms have muted colours, and there's a reading area on the 1st floor where you can unwind in leather armchairs.

Auberge de Jeunesse HOSTEL €

(☎05 65 35 64 71; fjt46@wanadoo.fr; 222 rue Joachim Murat; dm €13.20; ⊙9am-12.30pm & 2-7pm; 🐾) In an old convent, Cahors' hostel is basic but friendly and functional, with 50 beds in four- to 10-bed dorms and a rambling garden.

🍴 Eating

Le Balandre GASTRONOMIC €€€

(☎05 65 53 32 00; www.balandre.com; 5 av Charles de Freycinet; menus €42-90; ⊙lunch Tue-Sat, dinner daily) With chandeliers, sparkling glasses and napkins you could cut your finger on, the Grand Hotel Terminus' gourmet restaurant continues to command a devoted following, especially for its foie gras and *confit de canard*. Ask about its program of cooking courses (6hr class €95).

L'O à la Bouche FRENCH €€
(05 65 35 65 69; 134 rue St-Urcisse; menus €19.50-26.50; Tue-Sat) *'Cuisine creative'* are the watchwords at this refined little restaurant where classic ingredients are given a fresh spin, such as cod in a peanut crust and a gorgeous *'tout coco'* chocolate pudding.

Le Marché FUSION €€
(05 65 35 27 27; www.restaurantlemarche.com; 27 place Jean-Jacques Chapou; lunch menus €19, menus €28-50; Tue-Sat) Puce-and-cream armchairs, razor-edge wood and slate walls set the designer tone at the Market, and the menu's just as swish, ranging from roast tarragon beef to lemon-scented sea bass.

Marie Colline VEGETARIAN €
(05 65 35 59 96; 173 rue Georges Clemenceau; mains €8.50; lunch Tue-Fri, closed Aug;) This familial little bistro has such a traditional feel that it comes as something of a surprise that its menu (a handful of daily choices) is entirely meat- and fish-free. Solo diners are seated at a sociable communal table.

Also recommended:

Les 2 Pâtes ITALIAN, BELGIAN €
(81 bd Leon Gambetta; menus €7.50-10; 11am-9pm Mon-Sat;) Pick up a panini, pasta-and-sauce combo or Belgian fries (served with a minifork) to take away or eat on the streetside covered terrace.

Le Lamparo ITALIAN €€
(05 65 35 25 93; www.lelamparo.com; 76 rue Georges Clémenceau; menus €12-23; Mon-Sat;) Decent wood-fired pizzas, pastas and other staples served in a Med-style dining room.

Self-Catering

Cahors' top place for supplies is the Marché Couvert (place des Halles), usually referred to as Les Halles.

The open-air **market** takes place on nearby place Jean-Jacques Chapou on Wednesdays and Saturdays.

☆ Entertainment

Les Docks (05 65 22 36 38; 430 allées des Soupirs; @) is a former warehouse turned cultural centre near the Pont Valentré, with regular gigs, theatre, films and a multimedia café.

Check what's on in Cahors with the tourist office.

ℹ Information

Comité Départemental du Tourisme (05 65 35 07 09; www.tourisme-lot.com; 1st fl, 107 quai Eugène Cavaignac; 8am-12.30pm & 1.30-5.30pm) Information on the Lot *département*.

Cyber Informatique (place Clement Marot; per hr €2; 10am-8pm Mon-Sat, 2-8pm Sun) Internet access.

Post office (257 rue Président Wilson)

Tourist office (05 65 53 20 65; www.tourisme-cahors.com, in French; place François Mitterrand; 9.30am-6.30pm Mon-Sat)

ℹ Getting There & Away

BUS The tourist office has a booklet of bus timetables, *Les Bus du Lot* (www.lot.fr, in French), but most routes are geared around school-term times, making buses of limited use. Services between Cahors and Figeac (€11.70, 1½ hours, four to five daily) stop at Tour-de-Faure, the nearest access to St-Cirq Lapopie.

CAR Major car-hire companies are located at the train station. Parking is free along the river and at place Charles de Gaulle.

TRAIN Cahors is on the main line to Paris Gare d'Austerlitz (€68, five hours, eight to 10 daily), Brive-la-Gaillarde (€18, 1¼ hours), Limoges (€30.50, 2¼ hours) and Souillac (€13, 45 minutes). From Souillac there are SNCF buses to Sarlat (€2, 40 minutes, two daily).

East of Cahors

The narrow, corkscrew D662 (signposted 'Vallée du Lot') tracks the banks of the River Lot eastwards from Cahors towards Figeac. It's a wonderfully scenic, if hairraising, drive, with appealing stops and detours along the way. Figeac can also be reached directly from Cahors by the easier D653.

GROTTE DE PECH MERLE

Discovered in 1922, the 1200m-long Grotte de Pech Merle (05 65 31 27 05; www.pechmerle.com; adult/child €8/4.50; 9.30-noon & 1.30-5pm Apr-Oct) is perched high on the hills above the riverside town of Les Cabrerets, 30km northeast of Cahors. One of the few decorated caves to be discovered around the Lot Valley, Pech Merle makes an intriguing comparison to those in the Vézère, with several wonderful galleries of mammoths, cows, bison and dappled horses, as well as some unique hand tracings, fingerprints and human figures. But the most memorable part of the cave is saved till last – a beautifully preserved adolescent footprint, clearly imprinted into the muddy clay floor.

Entry is by guided tour (usually in French, but some have an English translation) and includes admission to the museum and a 20-minute film (in French and English). Reserve well ahead by phone if you're visiting in peak season as visitor numbers are limited to 700 per day.

ST-CIRQ LAPOPIE
POP 223

Teetering at the crest of a sheer cliff high above the River Lot, miniscule St-Cirq Lapopie's terracotta-roof houses and ramshackle streets tumble down the steep hillside, affording incredible valley views. It's one of the most magical settings in the Lot but be warned: if it's peace and tranquillity you're looking for, you won't find it in high summer.

⊙ Sights

Near the tourist office is the early-16th-century Gothic church and the steep path up to the ruined château at the summit of the village, where you'll be rewarded with a jaw-dropping panorama across the Lot Valley.

Many of the village's houses have been converted into artists studios producing pottery, craftwork and jewellery.

St-Cirque museums:

Maison de la Fourdonne HISTORY MUSEUM
(☑05 65 31 21 51; adult/child €1.50/1; ⊙2.30-7pm) Has a small town museum housing a collection of old postcards, pots and archaeological artefacts.

Musée Rignault ART MUSEUM
(admission €1.50; ⊙10am-12.30pm & 2.30-6pm) Eclectic collection of French furniture and African and Chinese art and a delightful garden.

🛏 Sleeping & Eating

Auberge de Sombral HOTEL €€
(☑05 65 31 26 08; www.lesombral.com; s €50, d €72-80; 🕿) A gorgeous option, with seven cosy doubles and a titchy attic room sparingly decorated with artworks, and up-to-date bathrooms peppered around the

red-roofed house. Local ingredients like foie gras, lamb and trout are cooked up at its delightful restaurant (lunch menus €15-19.50, other menus from €26.50; ⊙lunch daily, dinner Fri & Sat).

Le Gourmet Quercynois REGIONAL CUISINE €€
(☑05 65 31 21 20; www.restaurant-legourmet quercynois.com, in French, menus €20-36) The village's top *table* is a charmingly chaotic place with a menu of biblical proportions ranging from *nougat de porc* to country *cassoulet* (stew). The tables are packed in tight, but you can escape to the little patio to catch the evening rays. The in-house **deli** sells local spoils, including *cèpe* (porcini) mushrooms, gingerbread and chestnut cake.

Good campgrounds near St-Cirq:

La Plage CAMPGROUND €
(☑05 65 30 29 51; www.campingplage. com; sites €15; ⊙Apr–mid-Oct; 🕿🚣) Riverside campground on the left bank of the Lot near a small swimming beach, with a slew of amenities including canoe and kayak rental.

La Truffière CAMPGROUND €
(☑05 65 30 20 22; http://camping-truffiere. com; Le Causse; sites €16; 🏊) Along the D42, 2.5km from St-Cirq in leafy grounds.

❶ Information

The **tourist office** (☑05 65 31 29 06; www.saint-cirqlapopie.com, in French; ⊙10am-7pm) is in the village hall.

❶ Getting There & Away

St-Cirq is 25km east of Cahors and 44km southwest of Figeac.

BUS Buses between Cahors (45 minutes) and Figeac (€11.70, one hour, four to five daily) stop at Tour-de-Faure; from here, it's a lung-busting 3km uphill walk to the village.

CAR The main car park (€3) is at the top of the village. There's also a free one further down, from which a path leads up to St-Cirq's main street.

FIGEAC
POP 10.736

The riverside town of Figeac, 70km northeast of Cahors, has a rough-and-ready charm that comes as a refreshing change after many of the prettified towns in these parts. Traffic buzzes along the river boulevards and the old town has an appealingly lived-in feel, with shady streets lined with ramshackle medieval and Renaissance houses, many with open-air galleries on the top floor (once used for drying leather). Founded by Benedictine monks, the town was later an important medieval trading post and pilgrim's stopover.

◉ Sights

Medieval & Renaissance architecture

ARCHITECTURE

The historic centre of Figeac is place Vival, where the tourist office occupies the ground floor of an arcaded 13th-century building, part of Figeac's lost abbey. Pick up the leaflet *Les Clefs de la Ville* (€0.30) for a guide to the town's medieval and Renaissance architecture. **Rue de Balène** and **rue Caviale** have the best examples of 14th- and 15th-century houses, many with wooden galleries, timber frames and original stone carvings, while **rue de Colomb** has several fine *hôtels particulier* dating from the Renaissance.

Musée du Vieux Figeac   HISTORY MUSEUM

(adult/child €2/1; ⊙10am-12.30pm & 2.30-6pm Mon-Sat, 10am-12.30pm Sun Sep-Jun) Upstairs from the tourist office, the town's historical museum has a collection of antique clocks, coins, fossils and minerals and a propeller blade made by a local aerospace firm.

Musée Champollion   WRITING MUSEUM

(place Champollion; adult/child €4/2; ⊙10.30am -12.30pm & 2-6pm Tue-Sun) Named after the Figeac-born Egyptologist and linguist Jean-François Champollion (1790–1832), whose efforts in deciphering the Rosetta Stone provided the key for cracking Egyptian hieroglyphics, the lavishly restored mansion where he was born is now devoted to the history of writing, with exhibits ranging from illustrated medieval manuscripts to Chinese writing tools. Behind the museum on place des Écritures is a huge replica of the Rosetta tablets, created by artist Joseph Kosuth in 1990.

🛏 Sleeping & Eating

Hostellerie de l'Europe   HOTEL €€

(☏05 65 34 10 16; www.hotel-europe-figeac. com; 51 allée Victor Hugo; s €54-61, d €62-72; ❄🛜🏊🐾) Behind the crimson-shuttered facade, up-to-date rooms at this efficient hotel come with spacious bathrooms, although most are short on character. Its trump card is the gourmet restaurant (menus €14.50-34; ⊙lunch Sun-Thu, dinner Sat-Thu) La Table de Marinette – Figeac's finest for old-fashioned Quercynois dishes. It's

just across the river from the old town on one of the main exit roads.

Hôtel-Café Champollion   HOTEL €

(☏05 65 34 04 37; hotelchampollion@orange. fr; 3 place Champollion; d €45-53; 🛜) Decked out with modern art, the cool café-bar downstairs from this epicentral hotel is as popular for a late-night *bière à la pression* (draught beer) as a morning café. While that means noise can be taxing, surprisingly sleek contemporary rooms are kitted out with mod cons including flat-screen TVs. A couple more caveats: there's no lift and no nearby parking.

Hôtel des Bains   HOTEL €

(☏05 65 34 10 89; www.hoteldesbains.fr; 1 rue Griffoul; d €45-70; ❄🛜🐾) Sailing along by the riverside like a salmon-pink pleasure vessel, this family-owned hotel makes a cheap, cheery stopover in Figeac. Formerly a public bathhouse (hence the name), the hotel's 19 mostly air-conditioned rooms are small and low-key, decked out in crisp whites and sunny pastels; the choicest ones have balconies overlooking the river.

Brasserie 5   BRASSERIE €€

(☏05 65 50 10 81; 5 place Champollion; menus €15-26; ⊙Tue-Sun) Dark wood, plate-glass windows and rich colour schemes give this glossy restaurant a cosmopolitan feel, but while the food offers inventive variations on classic dishes, service operates at a snail's pace.

Self-Catering

Figeac's lively Saturday-morning **market** takes place under the 19th-century cast-iron arcade on place Carnot, with stalls also filling place Champollion and place Vival.

ℹ Information

Post office (8 av Fernand Pezet) Currency exchange.

Tourist office (☏05 65 34 06 25; www. tourisme-figeac.com; place Vival; ⊙10am-12.30pm & 2.30-6pm Mon-Sat, 10am-12.30pm Sun Sep-Jun)

ℹ Getting There & Away

BUS SNCF buses run west to Cahors (€11.70, 1½ hours, four to five daily) via Tour-de-Faure, and south to Villefranche de Rouergue (€6.60, one hour, six to eight daily) and Najac (€8.90, 1¼ hours, six to eight daily).

TRAIN Trains run north to Brive-la-Gaillarde (€13.60, 1¼ hours, six daily).

VILLEFRANCHE DE ROUERGUE
POP 12,673

Villefranche's origins as a *bastide* are barely recognisable beneath the main roads, refurbished buildings and busy shopping streets. But, despite first impressions, it warrants a brief stop. At the centre of the timber-framed old town is the arcaded place Notre Dame – a typical example of a *bastide* square – which still hosts the lively Thursday-morning market. Nearby is the square-pillared 15th-century Collégiale Notre Dame, with its never-completed bell tower and choir stalls, ornamented with a menagerie of comical and cheeky figures.

FREE Musée Urbain Cabrol (☑05 65 45 44 37; place de la Fontaine; ☺10am-noon & 2-6.30pm Tue-Sat Jul & Aug, 2-6pm Tue-Sat Apr-Jun & Sep), a few blocks to the southwest, has an eclectic collection of religious art, local folk art and 19th-century medical equipment. The fountain out the front, decorated with 14th-century carvings, gushes from a natural spring.

The tourist office (☑05 65 45 13 18; www.villefranche.com, in French; promenade du Guiraudet; ☺9am-noon & 2-6pm Mon-Fri, 9am-noon Sat) is next to the town hall.

Villefranche's hotels are patchy; your best bet is Le Relais de Farrou (☑05 65 45 18 11; www.relaisdefarrou.com; rte de Figeac; s €70-95, d €75-106; ⊛⊠), a ruthlessly modernised *relais de poste* in secluded gardens 4km from town. Upmarket facilities include tennis courts, minigolf and even a helipad (just in case you brought your chopper), as well as a glass-paned gastronomic restaurant (menus €22-48).

There are regular buses to Figeac (€6.60, 40 minutes, every two hours) and Najac (€4.60, 15 minutes, every two hours).

NAJAC
POP 774

If you were searching for a film set for Camelot, you've found it. On a hilltop above a hairpin bend in the River Aveyron, the town's castle, the Forteresse Royale de Najac (adult/child €4.50/2.80; ☺10am-12.30pm & 3-5.30pm), looks as if it's fallen from the pages of a fairy tale: slender towers and fluttering flags rise from the crenellated ramparts, surrounded on every side by dizzying *falaises* (cliffs) dropping to the valley floor below. A masterpiece of medieval military planning, and practically unassailable thanks to its position, Najac was a key stronghold during the Middle Ages, and was hotly contested by everyone from English warlords to the powerful counts of Toulouse. Its architecture is beautifully preserved, and the view from the central keep is unsurprisingly superb.

The castle is reached via a steep 1.2km-long cobbled street from place du Faubourg, a beguiling central square surrounded by a hotchpotch of timber-framed houses, some from the 13th century. Beyond the castle is the austere Gothic Église St-Jean, constructed and financed by local villagers on the orders of the Inquisition as punishment for their heretical tendencies.

To take in the glorious surrounding countryside on horseback, contact Centre Équestre de Najac (☑05 65 29 72 90; per hr/day €12.50/59; ☺Apr-Sep).

☷ Sleeping & Eating

TOP CHOICE Oustal del Barry HOTEL €€
(☑05 65 29 74 32; www.oustaldelbarry.com; place du Faubourg; s €49, d €59-77; ☺late Mar–Oct; ⊛⊠) The best place to stay in town is this wonderfully worn and rustic *auberge*, with haphazard rooms filled with trinkets and solid furniture to match its venerable timber-framed facade. Definitely get a room with a balcony if you can. Even if you're not staying here, be sure to stop by its country restaurant (lunch menus €19, menus €25-43.50; ⊠⊠), renowned for miles around for its traditional southwest cuisine, which you can master yourself during a five-day cooking course (incl 4 nights half board €400).

La Salamandre REGIONAL CUISINE €€
(☑05 65 29 74 09; rue du Barriou; menus €18-36) Simple but charming, this little restaurant is a treat for its local dishes and wonderful panoramic terrace overlooking the castle.

❶ Information

Najac's tiny tourist office (☑05 65 29 72 05; www.tourisme-najac.com, in French; 25 place du Faubourg; ☺9.30am-12.30pm & 2.30-6pm Mon-Sat, 10am-1pm Sun) is on the southern side of the main square.

❶ Getting There & Away

Trains link Najac with Figeac (€8.50, 50 minutes, two to four daily).

West of Cahors

Downstream from Cahors, the lower River Lot twists its way through the rich vineyards of the Cahors Appellation d'Origine

Contrôlée region, passing the dams at Luzech, the medieval section of which sits at the base of a donjon, and Castelfranc, with a dramatic suspension bridge. Sights in this region are few and far between – this is working land first and foremost, and the landscape becomes increasingly industrial the further west you travel from Puy l'Évêque. Along the river's right bank, the D9 affords superb views of the vines and the river's many twists and turns.

About 15km west of Puy l'Évêque on the GR36 trail, the imposing feudal Château de Bonaguil (www.bonaguil.org, in French; Fumel; adult/child €7/4; ☉10am-12.30pm & 2-6pm) is a fine example of late-15th-century military architecture, artfully integrating cliffs, outcrops, towers, bastions, loopholes, machicolations and crenellations.

North of Cahors

Some of the Lot's most striking sights lie north of Cahors near Limousin and the Dordogne, including the celebrated pilgrimage site of Rocamadour. Public transport in this area is pretty much nonexistent, so you'll need your own wheels to get around.

ROCAMADOUR
POP 653

The dramatic silhouette of Rocamadour's steeples and pale stone houses clamped to a vertical cliffside beneath the ramparts of a 14th-century château resembles something out of *The Da Vinci Code*. Rocamadour's miraculous Vierge Noire (Black Madonna) drew a steady stream of pilgrims and worshippers from across Europe in the Middle Ages, and tourist traffic is still going strong several centuries on.

Up top, start by exploring the ramparts of Rocamadour's château (admission €2; ☉8am-9pm). From here, either follow the switchback staircase down to the old town (which the pious once climbed on their knees) or take the ascenseur incliné (cable car; one way/return €2.50/4; ☉9am-7pm) halfway down the cliff to the Sanctuaires, a series of 12th- to 14th-century chapels containing the city's most prized relics, including the spooky Vierge Noire in the Chapelle Notre Dame.

More steps, and an ascenseur (elevator; one way/return €2.50/3; ☉9am-9pm) lead from the Sanctuaires further down to the Cité (old city), where you'll find the Cité tourist office (☉10.30am-12.30pm & 1.30-6pm). Its commercial thoroughfare, the Grande Rue, is crammed (just as in the pilgrims' day) with souvenir shops and touristy restaurants. One of the city's original medieval gateways can be seen at the street's far end.

The main tourist office (☑05 65 33 22 00; www.rocamadour.com; ☉10am-12.30pm & 2-6pm Mon-Sat, 1.30-6pm Sun) is on the plateau above the cliff 1.5km from the Cité, in the largely modern and touristy suburb of L'Hospitalet. This area is of limited interest, although kids might enjoy the stalactites and stalagmites of the Grotte des Merveilles (www.grotte-des-merveilles.com, in French; adult/child €6/4; ☉10am-noon & 2-6pm).

You'd be better off giving the overpriced hotels and restaurants around Rocamadour a wide berth – prices for even the dingiest room skyrocket in summer, and most hotels are booked out well in advance by tour bus groups.

Rocamadour is 59km north of Cahors and 51km east of Sarlat; there's parking in L'Hospitalet and by the château.

GOUFFRE DE PADIRAC

TOP CHOICE Gouffre de Padirac (☑05 65 33 64 56; www.gouffre-de-padirac.com; adult/child €9.20/6; ☉10am-7pm) has glittering caverns that are among the most breathtaking in France. Discovered in 1889, the cave's navigable river, 103m below ground level, is reached through a 75m-deep, 33m-wide chasm. Boat pilots ferry visitors along 1km of the subterranean waterway, visiting a series of glorious floodlit caverns en route, including the soaring **Salle de Grand Dôme** and the **Lac des Grands Gours**, a 27m-wide subterranean lake. From Rocamadour, the caverns are 15km to the northeast.

CHÂTEAU DE CASTELNAU-BRETENOUX

Not to be confused with the Château de Castelnaud (p582), Castelnau-Bretenoux (http://castelnau-bretenoux.monuments-nationaux.fr; adult/child €6.50/free; ☉10am-12.30pm & 2-5.30pm, last entry 1hr before closing) was originally constructed in the 12th century and saw heavy action during the Hundred Years War, before being redeveloped with the advent of new forms of artillery. The castle is laid out around a roughly triangular courtyard, with stout towers linked by ramparts and bulwarks. Most of the rooms open to visitors date from the 17th and 18th centuries, when the castle was mainly used as a residential home rather than a defensive fortress. Having fallen into disrepair in the 19th century, the castle was refurbished by Parisian opera singer Jean Mouliérat, before being donated to the state in 1932. It's about 5km south of Beaulieu-sur-Dordogne along the D940.

CARENNAC
POP 401

A cluster of amber houses and brick cottages make up tiny Carennac, secluded on the left bank of the Dordogne. The village's main landmark is the 16th-century Château du Doyen, which now houses a heritage centre/museum, L'Espace Patrimoine (www. pays-vallee-dordogne.com, in French; admission free; ⊙10am-noon & 2-6pm Tue-Fri), showcasing the art and history of the region. Above is the square Tour de Télémaque, named after the hero of Fénelon's *Les Aventures de Télémaque,* written here in 1699.

Just inside the castle gateway is the priory and the Romanesque Église St-Pierre (⊙10am-7pm) with another remarkable Romanesque tympanum of Christ in majesty, similar to those in Cahors and Beaulieu. Off the cloître (adult/child €2.50/0.80), still beautiful despite being heavily damaged in the Revolution, is a remarkable, late-15th-century Mise au Tombeau (Statue of the Entombment).

You'll find the tourist office (☑05 65 10 97 01; www.tourisme-carennac.com, in French; ⊙10am-noon & 2-6pm) next door to the church.

Based in Vayrac, 8km northwest of Carennac, canoe and kayak operator Safaraïd (☑05 65 37 44 87; www.canoe-kayak-dordogne.com; Vayrac; per day €15-28) offers lots of possible routes as well as multiday trips.

With flower-filled hanging baskets and stripy awnings, Hostellerie Fénelon (☑05 65 10 96 46; www.hotel-fenelon.com; s €49-58,

d €54-70; ☒) evokes the feel of an Alsatian summer house. The rooms are fairly unremarkable (think pink-tiled bathrooms, flowery bedspreads and sunflower-coloured walls), but the pricier ones overlook the river and tree-covered Île Calypso. Half board at the downstairs restaurant (menus €24-43) is particularly good value.

MARTEL
POP 1591

Known as *la ville aux sept tours* (the town of seven towers) for its turret-topped skyline, this pale-stone, red-roofed village was the ancient capital of the Vicomte de Turenne, and retains some of the best-preserved medieval architecture in this corner of France.

Buried deep within the pedestrianised centre, the tourist office (☑05 65 37 43 44; www.martel.fr, in French; place des consuls; ⊙9am-noon & 2-6pm Mon-Sat) has maps pointing out architectural and historical highlights and can provide details of the area including working mills that can be visited. It also supplies schedules for the Chemin de Fer Touristique du Haut-Quercy (www.trainduhautquercy.info, in French; ⊙Apr-Sep), which runs one-hour trips from Martel on diesel trains (adult/child €7/4) and steam trains (adult/child €9.50/5.50) east along the precipitous cliff-face to St-Denis.

The pick of places to stay is Relais Sainte-Anne (☑05 65 37 40 56; www.relais-sainte-anne.com; s €50, d €90-145, ste €175-265; ☎☒), with 16 individually decorated rooms that blend country comforts with contemporary flair. Its restaurant (menus €23) utilises produce from Martel's **markets**, which are held in the village centre on Wednesdays and Saturdays. **Truffle markets** also take place in the village during December and January.

Martel is 15km northwest of Carennac and 15km northeast of Souillac.

Atlantic Coast

Best Places to Eat

» La Ribaudière (p615)
» Hostellerie de Plaisance (p627)
» Marché des Capucins (p622)
» La Boîte à Huîtres (p621)
» Le Cheverus Café (p620)

Best Places to Stay

» Maison Flore (p604)
» Hôtel Pommeraye (p599)
» La Baronnie Domaine (p613)
» Ecolodge des Chartrons (p618)
» Un Hôtel en Ville (p608)

Why Go?

With quiet country roads winding through vine-striped hills and wild stretches of coastal sands interspersed with misty islands, the Atlantic coast is where France gets back to nature. Much more laid-back than the Med (but with almost as much sunshine), this is the place to slow the pace right down.

But the Atlantic coast can do cities and culture as well. There's bourgeoise Bordeaux with its wonderful old centre, lively Nantes with its wealth of fascinating museums, and salty La Rochelle with its breathtaking aquarium and beautiful portside setting.

The one thing that unites the people of this area is a love of the finer things in life. The region's exceptional wine is famous worldwide, and to wash it down you'll find fresh-from-the-ocean seafood wherever you go and plenty of regional delicacies including crêpes in the north, snails in the centre and foie gras in the south.

When to Go

Bordeaux

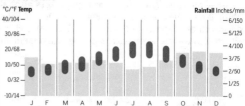

May to June
Ducklings are splashing around the Marais Poitevin and it's prime time to visit La Rochelle.

June and September The beaches are bathed in sunshine but there are no high-season crowds.

September to October Grape-harvesting season around Bordeaux, and oyster and cep mushroom season all over.

Top 5 Museums

» Barbie will eat her heart out when she sees the walking, talking, almost living dolls on display in the Musée des Automates (p605).

» The Musée des Beaux-Arts (p597) in Nantes contains one of the most overpowering collections of fine art in the country.

» At the other end of the art scale are the 'out there' collections found in the CAPC Musée d'Art Contemporain (p617) in Bordeaux.

» Pretend you're Alice in Wonderland in a shrunk-down world at the Musée des Modèles Réduits (p605).

» Enrich yourself with knowledge in the Musée d'Aquitaine (p617) in Bordeaux.

GETTING THERE & AWAY

Bordeaux is the main transport hub for the region, three hours by TGV from Paris. From here, trains can take you pretty much anywhere in France. Nantes, Poitiers and La Rochelle are also well served by TGV, and a good rail service links most of the main attractions within the region. A car gives added freedom for the wine-tasting trail.

The region also has good air services, particularly from the UK, with airports at Bordeaux, Nantes, Poitiers and La Rochelle (all served by low-cost operators Ryanair and EasyJet, among others).

Best for Children

The Atlantic coast has plenty to keep youngsters and teenagers happy.

» While the big boys and girls surf the waves, little 'uns can build sandcastles on the beautiful beaches of **Cap Ferret** (p630).

» From blennies to piranhas and seahorses to giant rays, there's plenty to excite at La Rochelle's high-tech **aquarium** (p605).

» If the kids have square eyes from watching too much TV, show them the future of film at **Futuroscope** (p603).

» There's something about a house-sized mechanical elephant that just cannot fail to impress at **Les Machines de l'Île de Nantes** (p597).

» Spot storks, kingfishers and pond tortoises at **Le Teich Parc Ornithologique** (p630).

TOURING THE WINE COUNTRY

If the Atlantic coast is famous for one thing, it's the pleasure of the grape. The Médoc (p625), St-Émilion, Bordeaux (p619) and Cognac (p614) are names to set a wine connoisseur's heart aflutter. Visit some of the châteaux to learn the secrets of the grape.

Off the Beaten Track

» Arçais p604
» Cap Ferret p630
» Cognac p613
» Île d'Aix p605
» Le Croisic p600

Resources

» Insights into the Loire-Atlantique region: www.ohlaloireatlantique.com

» Inspiration for Poitou-Charentes: www.poitoucharentes.visite.org

» Find out about the Gironde region: www.tourisme-gironde.fr

» Become a wine expert: www.bordeaux.com

» For Cognac aficionados: www.cognac-world.com

Best Birdwatching

» Réserve Naturelle Marais d'Yves (p608)

» Le Teich Parc Ornithologique (p630)

» Marais Poitevin (p604)

Atlantic Coast Highlights

1 Glide through the emerald-green waterways of the **Marais Poitevin** (p604), otherwise known as the 'Green Venice'

2 Dive deep under the waves and come face to face with wobbly jellyfish and jaw-gnashing sharks at La Rochelle's incredible **aquarium** (p605)

3 Cycle the smooth, flat bike paths criss-crossing the sunbaked **Île de Ré** (p613)

4 Ride a three-storey, 60-tonne mechanical elephant in **Nantes** (p597)

5 Tour the dramatically floodlit buildings and monuments making up the world's largest Unesco-listed urban area in central **Bordeaux** (p615)

6 Satisfy your craving for wine in **St-Émilion** (p624), home to some of the world's most famous wines

7 Hang on to your seat for a wild, cinematically simulated ride at the futuristic theme park **Futuroscope** (p603)

UPPER ATLANTIC COAST

This bite of the Loire-Atlantique *département,* where the Loire empties into the ocean, might as easily be termed 'lower Brittany'. Breton in every sense – cultural, architectural and historical – its centrepiece is Brittany's former capital, Nantes.

Nantes

POP 290,950

You can take Nantes out of Brittany (as when regional boundaries were redrawn during WWII), but you can't take Brittany out of its long-time capital, Nantes (Naoned in Breton).

Spirited and innovative, this city on the banks of the Loire, 55km east of the Atlantic, has a long history of reinventing itself. Founded by Celts around 70 BC, in AD 937 Alain Barbe-Torte, the grandson of the last king of Brittany, established the duchy of Brittany here following a series of invasions. The Edict of Nantes, a landmark royal charter guaranteeing civil rights to France's Huguenots (Protestants), was signed in the city by Henri IV in 1598. Its revocation in 1685 led to a Huguenot exodus from the region.

By the 18th century Nantes was France's foremost port, and in the 19th century – following the abolition of slavery – it became a cutting-edge industrial centre; the world's first public-transport service, the omnibus, began here in 1826. Shipbuilding anchored the city's economy until the late 20th century. When the shipyards relocated westwards to St-Nazaire, Nantes transformed itself into a thriving student and cultural hub. The city centre has now nudged past Bordeaux as the country's sixth-largest metropolis, and it's growing, with one in two Nantais today aged under 40.

👁 Sights

TOP CHOICE Les Machines de l'Île de Nantes
GIANT ELEPHANTS

(www.lesmachines-nantes.fr; gallery adult/child €7/5.50, elephant ride €7/5.50; ☉10am-8pm; 🔊) The quirkiest sight in an altogether fairly quirky city has to be Les Machines de l'Île de Nantes. Inside this fantasy world it's perfectly possible to prance around like a Maharajah on the back of a 45-tonne **mechanical elephant** with a

secret lounge inside its belly or voyage on a boat through rough and dangerous oceans where attacks from oversized squid and giant prawns are common. We can only think that Jules Verne would be smiling in his grave if he could see this lot! Gallery tickets are also good for the workshop, where you can watch these fantastical contraptions being built.

Château des Ducs de Bretagne
CASTLE MUSEUM

(www.chateau-nantes.fr; museum adult/child €5/3, museum & exhibition €8/4.80, grounds free; ☉9.30am-8pm) Forget fusty furnishings – the stripped, light-filled interior of the restored Château des Ducs de Bretagne houses new multimedia-rich exhibits detailing the city's history. Computer terminals allow you to tour the old medieval city, juxtaposed with images of today. Other exhibits to look out for include sobering documentation of the slave trade, and vintage scale models of Nantes' evolving cityscape. There's excellent wheelchair access.

Musée des Beaux-Arts
ART MUSEUM

(10 rue Georges Clemenceau; adult/child €3.50/free, 1st Sun of month free; ☉10am-6pm Wed & Fri-Mon, to 8pm Thu) One of the finest collections of French paintings outside Paris hangs in sumptuous galleries linked by grand stone staircases at the Musée des Beaux-Arts, with works by Georges de la Tour, Chagall, Monet, Picasso and Kandinsky among others.

Musée Jules Verne
MUSEUM

(www.julesverne.nantes.fr, in French; 3 rue de l'Hermitage; adult/child €3/1.50; ☉10am-noon & 2-6pm Mon & Wed-Sat, 2-6pm Sun) Overlooking the river, this is a magical museum with 1st-edition books, hand-edited manuscripts and cardboard theatre cut-outs. Child-friendly interactive displays introduce or reintroduce you to the work of Jules Verne,

---

❶ NANTES CITY PASS

The **Pass Nantes** (€18/28/36 for 24/48/72 hours), available from the tourist office, includes unlimited bus and tram transport as well as entry to museums and monuments, and extras like a free guided tour and shopping discounts.

ATLANTIC COAST UPPER ATLANTIC COAST

Nantes

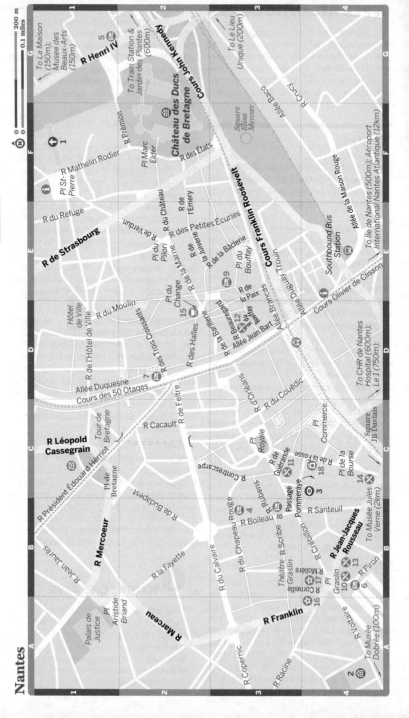

To La Maison (150m); Musee des Beaux-Arts (150m)

R Henri IV

5

To Train Station & Jardin des Plantes (600m)

Cours John Kennedy

To Le Lieu Unique (200m)

R St-Pierre

Pl St-Pierre

R Mathelin Rodier

R Prémion

Château des Ducs de Bretagne

R Marc Elder

R du Refuge

R de Verdun

R du Château

R des États

R de l'Emery

R des Petites Écuries

Cours Franklin Roosevelt

Allée Baco

R Cucy

Square Elisa Mercœur

1

Pl Marc Elder

R de Strasbourg

Pl du Pilori

R de la Marne

R de la Juiverie

R de la Bâclerie

Pl du Bouffay

R de la Paix

9

Allée Chanzy Trouin

Southbound Bus Station

Allée de la Maison Rouge

Hôtel de Ville

R du Moulin

R de l'Hôtel de Ville

Pl du Change

R des Trois Croissants

R de la Baillerie

R des Halles

15

R de Beauregard

R du Bouffay

12

Allée Jean Bart

Allée Brancas

Cours Olivier de Clisson

To Île de Nantes (500m); Aéroport International/Nantes Atlantique (12km)

Tour de Bretagne

R Léopold Cassegrain

R Président Édouard Hérriot

Pl de Bretagne

R de Feltre

7

Allée Duquesne
Cours des 50 Otages

R d'Orléans

R du Couëdic

Pl Commerce

To CHR de Nantes Hospital (600m); Le I (750m)

R Mercoeur

R Jean-Jaurès

R de Budapest

R Cacault

R Contrescarpe

Pl Royale

R de Guérande

R de la Fosse

Pl de la Bourse

Square JB Daviais

R Copernic

Palais de Justice

Pl Aristide Briand

R la Fayette

R du Chapeau Rouge

R du Calvaire

R de Rubens

Passage Pommeraye

R Boileau

11

18

14

3

R Marceau

R Scribe

Théâtre Graslin

R Molière

R Crébillon

R Santeuil

To Musée Jules Verne (2km)

R Franklin

R Corneille

Pl Graslin

16

17

R Jean-Jacques Rousseau

13

10

6

R Piron

R Voltaire

To Musée Dobrée (100m)

R Racine

2

0   200 m
0   0.1 miles

who was born in Nantes in 1828. Signs are in French but Verne's books, such as *Around the World in 80 Days,* are so well known that it's worthwhile visiting regardless. Wheelchair access is good. The museum is a 2km walk down river from the town centre.

Musée d'Histoire Naturelle   MUSEUM
(www.museum.nantes.fr; 12 rue Voltaire; adult/child €3.50/2; ⊙10am-6pm Wed-Mon) The fascinating collection of minerals, fossils and stuffed animals includes a huge whale skeleton and **vivariums** full of beautiful live snakes. There are frequent temporary exhibitions.

Musée Dobrée   MUSEUM
(18 rue Voltaire; adult/child €3/1.50; ⊙1.30-5.30pm Tue-Fri, 2.30-5.30pm Sat & Sun) A wonderful hotchpotch of religious treasures, suits of armour and deadly swords, dazzling jewels and shimmering ceramics – and, in a gold casket, the heart of the Duchess of Brittany, Anne de Bretagne.

Nantes

Jardin des Plantes   PARK
Founded in the early 19th century, the Jardin des Plantes is one of the most exquisite botanical gardens in France, filled with flowerbeds, duck ponds, fountains and towering redwoods (sequoias). There are hothouses and a **children's playground** at the northern end of the gardens, which are opposite the train station.

Cathédrale St-Pierre et St-Paul   CATHEDRAL
(place St-Pierre) Inside the Flamboyant Gothic Cathédrale St-Pierre et St-Paul, the **tomb of François II** (r 1458–88), Duke of Brittany, and his second wife, Marguerite de Foix, is a masterpiece of Renaissance art.

🛏 Sleeping
Nantes makes a good weekend break, when hotel rates often drop. Bookings (including weekend packages with freebies thrown in) can be made through www.resanantes.com.

Hôtel Pommeraye   BOUTIQUE HOTEL €€
TOP CHOICE (02 40 48 78 79; www.hotel-pommeraye.com; 2 rue Boileau; s €54-99, d €59-129;) Sleek and chic, this is more art gallery than hotel. The rooms have shimmering short-pile carpets and textured walls in shades of pale grey, gold, chocolate and violet. The reception and other common areas are adorned in eye-catching art such as inflated pillowcases pierced with cocktail sticks that look like some surreal modernist hedgehog, and where you'd normally find ancient gargoyles you instead discover pop-art faces staring back at you.

Hôtel Graslin   BOUTIQUE HOTEL €€
(02 40 69 72 91; www.hotel-graslin.com; 1 rue Piron; r €75-105;) The unlikely (but very Nantes) marriage of art deco and '70s eras at this refurbished hotel includes details like eggplant-and-orange wing chairs in the lounge. Spiffy rooms feature faux timber and edgy colour combinations like peppermint and bone, plus shag-carpeted rooms in the attic.

Hôtel des Colonies   BOUTIQUE HOTEL €
(02 40 48 79 76; www.hoteldescolonies.fr; 5 rue du Chapeau Rouge; s €58-78, d €65-78;) Local art exhibitions rotate monthly in the lobby of this central spot featuring cherry-red public areas and rooms fitted out with purple, green and orange walls and boxy resin light fittings. The only minus point is that some rooms are a little small.

Pack your bucket and spade for any of these worthwhile coastal excursions from Nantes. The classic seaside town of Le Croisic centres on a pretty, half-timbered fishing harbour adjoining its old town, where shrimps, lobsters, crabs, scallops and sea bass are unloaded. From Nantes, an all-day MétrOcéane (www.metroceane.fr, in French) train ticket to Le Croisic costs €14.50 and includes public transport throughout Nantes. En route to Le Croisic, the same ticket allows you to stop at St-Nazaire, where cruise ships – including the *Queen Mary II* – are built and where Airbus has a factory, which can be toured. Also along this stretch of coast is the glamorous belle-époque resort of La Baule, boasting an enormous beach.

Hôtel La Pérouse   DESIGN HOTEL €€
(☏ 02 40 89 75 00; www.hotel-laperouse.fr; 3 allée Duquesne; r €118; ❋ 🖤 📶) Styled to reflect the city's shipbuilding traditions, a wooden gangway entrance leads to this 46-room design hotel's stone-and-wood lobby, with zigzag chairs, canvas sail-like curtains, and glass bathroom basins and wardrobes. This was the first hotel in Nantes to be awarded an EU Ecolabel thanks to its policy of using Fairtrade and locally grown items at breakfast, soap dispensers that do away with packaging, air-con units that switch off as soon as a window is opened and a number of other green initiatives.

Hôtel du Château   TRADITIONAL HOTEL €
(☏ 02 40 74 17 16; www.hotelduchateau-nantes.fr, in French; 5 place de la Duchesse Anne; s €40-50, d €44-60; 📶) This cosy little establishment opposite the château actually thinks it is a castle. Short histories of various kings and queens grace the doors to the rooms, and the bedrooms themselves have an equally royal flavour with elegant bedspreads and old-fashioned bedside tables. Some rooms have views of the château.

Hôtel St-Daniel   TRADITIONAL HOTEL €
(☏ 02 40 47 41 25; www.hotel-saintdaniel.com, in French; 4 rue du Bouffay; r €38-65; 📶) Peacefully situated overlooking the St-Croix church courtyard in the heart of the old town, this clean, cheery place has a variety of room sizes, including some whoppers, and a friendly Labrador dog is thrown in for free!

Auberge de Jeunesse La Manu   HOSTEL €
(☏ 02 40 29 29 20; www.fuaj.org/Nantes, in French; 2 place de la Manu; dm incl breakfast €18.50; 😊 closed Christmas; 📶) Housed in an old converted factory with good wheelchair access, this well-equipped 123-bed hostel is a 15-minute walk from the centre. Alas, there's a lock-out from noon to 4pm. Take tram 1 to the Manufacture stop.

✗ Eating

For cosmopolitan dining, head to the medieval Bouffay quarter, a couple of blocks west of the château around rue de la Juiverie, rue des Petites Écuries and rue de la Bâclerie. Breton crêperies abound throughout town. West of cours des 50 Otages, rues Jean-Jacques Rousseau and Santeuil are lined with eateries.

See also the listings under Drinking and Entertainment.

TOP CHOICE **Le Bistrot de l'Écrivain**   MODERN FRENCH €€
(☏ 02 51 84 15 15; 15 rue Jean-Jacques Rousseau; menus €14.50-18.50; 😊 closed Sun) Splashed in shades of red, with wine bottles lining the walls, Le Bistrot de l'Écrivain is a relaxed and easygoing place with food that's anything but relaxing and easy to make. There's all the Nantaise standards here, but most have an unexpected twist to them – raspberries in crème brûlée and duck dipped in wonderful sauces being just two examples.

Un Coin en Ville   MODERN FRENCH €€
(☏ 02 40 20 05 97; 2 place de la Bourse; menus from €13; 😊 lunch Tue-Fri, dinner Tue-Sat) Expect flickering tea-light candles, soulful jazz and blues, and cooking that combines local produce with exotic styles, such as red curry with prawns and scallops.

Le 1   GASTRONOMIC €€
(☏ 02 40 08 28 00; 1 rue Olympe de Gouges; lunch/dinner menus €15/23) Legal eagles from Nantes' gleaming 21st-century law court next door lounge in the ultracontemporary bar and dine on fabulous fusion dishes at

this spot overlooking the Loire. The wine cellar is a see-through affair, with over 2000 bottles on stainless-steel racks in a glass cool room.

Crêperie Heb-Ken
BRETON €

(☑02 40 48 79 03; 5 rue de Guérande; crêpes €4.80-18; ☺Mon-Sat; ⓐ) Dozens of varieties of crêpe (such as a delicious trout-and-leek combo, or honey, lemon and almond for dessert) are made with love at this cosy spot. A sure sign of its authenticity: you can order *lait ribot* (thickened milk) by the *bolée* (drinking bowl) or pitcher.

La Table d'Oscar
BISTRO €€

(☑02 40 35 44 33; 13 rue Beauregard; menus €15-25) With its frilly lace curtains and checked tablecloths, this rustic restaurant looks exactly as you'd imagine a classic French bistro should look. The food is as traditional as the decor, making it a good place to experience a slice of old France.

Brasserie La Cigale
BRASSERIE €€

(☑02 51 84 94 94; 4 place Graslin; breakfast €11, brunch €20, mains €12.50-24.50; ☺7.30am-12.30am) No visit to Nantes is complete without joining the old ladies with perfectly manicured hair for a coffee and cake or an all-out feast at 1890s Brasserie La Cigale. Several salons of original gilded tilework and frescoed ceilings are attended by white-aproned waiters.

Drinking

Nantes has no shortage of lively spots for a drink. Two prime areas are the medieval Bouffay quarter and the **Hangar à Bananes** (www.hangarabananes.com, in French; 21 quai des Antilles), a former banana-ripening warehouse on the Île de Nantes. Here you'll find over a dozen restaurants, bars and clubs (and combinations thereof), each hipper than the next. The front terraces of most face onto the Anneaux de Buren, a permanent art installation of metal rings that light up at night.

Café Cult
CAFÉ-BAR

(www.cafe-cult.com, in French; 2 rue des Carmes; ☺2pm-2am Mon & Sat, from noon Tue-Fri) Squeezed inside a darkened half-timbered house and hung with local art, this bohemian place draws a student crowd and sometimes hosts concerts. During the day it serves megacheap but palate-pleasing lunches for around €7.50.

La Maison
BAR

(4 rue Lebrun; ☺3pm-1.30am) You have to see it to believe this trip of a place, decorated room by room like a home furnished in *bad* 1970s taste, playing (what else?) house music.

Entertainment

Good what's-on websites include www.leboost.com (in French).

Le Lieu Unique
PERFORMING ARTS

(☑02 40 12 14 34; www.lelieuunique.com, in French; 2 rue de la Biscuiterie) Within the one-time Lu biscuit factory (crowned by a replica of its original tower, which you can ascend for €2), this industrial-chic space is the venue for dance and theatre performances, eclectic and electronic music, philosophical sessions and contemporary-art exhibitions. Also here is an always-buzzing restaurant, a polished concrete bar, and a decadent *hammam* (Turkish bath) complex in the basement.

Théâtre Graslin
THEATRE, OPERA

(☑02 40 69 77 18; www.angers-nantes-opera.com; place Graslin) Constructed in 1788, the beautifully refurbished Théâtre Graslin is the home of the Nantes Opera.

Cinéma Katorza
CINEMA

(www.katorza.fr; 3 rue Corneille) This six-screen cinema shows nondubbed films.

Shopping

Pedestal statues symbolise traditional Nantais industries inside the ornate three-tiered shopping arcade **Passage Pommeraye**, built in 1843.

Gautier-Debotté
CHOCOLATE

(9 rue de la Fosse; ☺9am-7.15pm Tue-Sat) When Jules Verne was a young boy he too was awed by this beautiful chocolate shop's chandeliers, marble floors and circular velvet banquette, where Nantais have waited while their orders were filled since 1823. Handmade specialities include *mascarons* (finely ground chocolates in a dark-chocolate shell) and a rainbow of hard-boiled sweets.

ⓘ Information

CHR de Nantes hospital (☑02 40 08 33 33; quai Moncousu)

Hôtel de Police (☑02 53 46 70 00; 6 place Waldeck Rousseau) Police Nationale's 24-hour station is 1km northeast of the Monument des 50 Otages. Go to tram stop Motte Rouge.

Main post office (place de Bretagne)

Tourist office (☎08 92 46 40 44; www.
nantes-tourisme.com) Feydeau (3 cours Olivier de Clisson; ⏲10am-6pm, from 10.30am
Thu, closed Sun) St-Pierre (2 place St-Pierre;
⏲10am-1pm & 2-6pm, from 10.30am Thu,
closed Mon)

❶ Getting There & Away

**AIR Aéroport International Nantes-
Atlantique** (☎02 40 84 80 00; www.nantes.
aeroport.fr) The airport is 12km southeast of
town.

BICYCLE Détours de Loire (www.locationde
velos.com; per day/week €14/59; ⏲Apr-Oct)
Lets you pick up and drop off bikes along
the Loire Valley, including Nantes. Check the
website for the current pick-up and drop-off
points.

BUS The Lila bus web covers the entire Loire-
Atlantique *département*. Tickets cost €2/18 per
single ride/10 rides.

Eurolines (☎08 92 89 90 91; www.eurolines.
com; allée de la Maison Rouge; ⏲9.30am-
12.30pm & 1.30-6pm Mon-Sat) Has an office
in town.

CAR Budget, Europcar and Hertz are right outside the train station's southern entrance.

TRAIN The **train station** (27 bd de Stalingrad)
is well connected to most of the country. Destinations include the following:

Paris Gare Montparnasse from €58, two
hours, 15 to 20 daily

Bordeaux €45, four hours, three or four daily

La Rochelle from €24, from 1¾ hours, three or
four daily

Tickets and information are also available at the
SNCF ticket office (La Bourse, 12 place de la
Bourse; ⏲9am-7.20pm Mon-Fri, to 7pm Sat) in
the city centre.

❶ Getting Around

TO/FROM THE AIRPORT A *navette* bus
links the airport with the Gare Centrale bus-
and-tram hub and the train station's southern
entrance (€7, 20 minutes) from about 6.45am
until 11pm.

BICYCLE Nantes' new pick-up, drop-off
bicycle system, **Bicloo** (www.bicloo.nantes
metropole.fr, in French), has stations all over
town, open from 4am to 1am (but you can
keep bikes overnight). Rates are just €1/5 per
24 hours/week.

BUS & TRAM The **TAN network** (www.tan.
fr, in French) includes three modern tram lines
that intersect at the Gare Centrale (Commerce),
the main bus/tram transfer point, and a first-

for-France 'Busway'. Buses run from 6.45am to
10pm. Night services continue until 12.30am.

Bus/tram tickets (€1.50) can be individually
purchased from bus (but not tram) drivers and
at tram-stop ticket machines. They're valid for
one hour after being time-stamped. A *ticket
journalier*, good for 24 hours, costs €4; time-
stamp it only the first time you use it.

TAXI To order a taxi, call ☎02 40 69 22 22.

CENTRAL ATLANTIC COAST

The Poitou-Charentes region, midway
along the Atlantic Coast, scoops up a potpourri of attractions – from the history-rich
capital, Poitiers, to the portside panache of
La Rochelle, the languid beaches of Île de
Ré, and the eponymous home of Cognac.

Poitiers

POP 91,900

Inland from the coast, history-steeped
Poitiers was founded by the Pictones, a
Gaulish tribe. The Romans built up the
city, and there are numerous reminders
still evident, such as extensive ruins uncovered when the large Cordeliers shopping
centre was built in the town centre about
a decade ago. The city rose to prominence
as the former capital of Poitou, the region
governed by the Counts of Poitiers in the
Middle Ages. A pivotal turning point came
in AD 732, when somewhere near Poitiers
(the exact site is not known) the cavalry of
Charles Martel defeated the Muslim forces
of Abd ar-Rahman, governor of Córdoba,
thus ending Muslim attempts to conquer
France. The city's remarkable Romanesque
churches are in part a legacy of Eleanor of
Aquitaine's financial support.

Poitiers has one of the oldest universities in the country, established in 1432 and
today a linchpin of this lively city.

◉ Sights

Poitiers Churches   CHURCHES
Strolling Poitiers' history-trodden streets is
the best way to get a feel for the city's past.
Along the pavements, red, yellow and blue
lines correspond with three **self-guided
walking tours** detailed on a free city map
handed out by the tourist office.

Every evening from 21 June to the third
weekend in September, spectacular colours
are cinematically projected onto the west

facade of the Romanesque Église Notre Dame la Grande (place Charles de Gaulle). The earliest parts of the church date from the 11th century; three of the five choir chapels were added in the 15th century, with the six chapels along the northern wall of the nave added in the 16th century. The only original frescoes are the faint 12th- or 13th-century works that adorn the U-shaped dome above the choir.

The 13th-century stained-glass window illustrating the Crucifixion and the Ascension at the far end of the choir of the Gothic-style Cathédrale St-Pierre (rue de la Cathédrale) is one of the oldest in France.

Constructed in the 4th and 6th centuries on Roman foundations, Baptistère St-Jean (rue Jean Jaurès; adult/child €2/1; ☺10.30am-12.30pm & 3-6pm Wed-Mon, shorter hours Nov-Mar), 100m south of the cathedral, was redecorated in the 10th century and used as a parish church. The octagonal hole under the frescos was used for total-immersion baptisms, practised until the 7th century.

Musée Ste-Croix   MUSEUM

(www.musees-poitiers.org, in French; 3 rue Jean Jaurès; adult/child €4/free, 1st Sun of month free; ☺10am-noon & 1.15-8pm Tue, 10am-noon & 1.15-6pm Wed-Fri, 10am-noon & 2-6pm Sat-Sun) Seven signed statues by Camille Claudel are the highlight of this little museum.

🛏 Sleeping

In addition to chains such as Ibis, Poitiers has a handful of atmospheric, well-located hotels.

Hôtel de l'Europe   HISTORIC HOTEL €

(☎05 49 88 12 00; www.hotel-europe-poitiers.com; 39 rue Carnot; s/d €55/61; 🐾) Behind a dramatically recessed entrance, the main building of this elegant, very un-two-star-like hotel with good wheelchair access dates from 1710, with a sweeping staircase, oversized rooms and refined furnishings. The annexe has modern rooms for the same price.

Le Grand Hôtel   HISTORIC HOTEL €€

(☎05 49 60 90 60; www.grandhotelpoitiers.fr; 28 rue Carnot; s/d from €68/79; ❄🐾) There's nothing fancy about Poitiers' premier hotel. It's just solid, old-fashioned value all the way. Faux art deco furnishings and fittings fill the public areas with character, and rooms are spacious and well equipped.

Hôtel Central   TRADITIONAL HOTEL €

(☎05 49 01 79 79; www.centralhotel86.com, in French; 35 place du Maréchal Leclerc; d €38-65) At the southern edge of a charming pedestrian district of half-timbered houses, this two-star place is a terrific little bargain. It has snug but sunlit rooms with shower or bath, and a lift to save you and your suitcases from scaling its three storeys.

🍴 Eating & Drinking

Prime dining spots tend to be south of place du Maréchal Leclerc.

La Serrurerie   TRADITIONAL FRENCH €

(☎05 49 41 05 14; 28 rue des Grandes Écoles; mains €10-17.50; ☺8am-2am) Showcasing local art, sculpture and a fantastic collection of retro toys, this mosaic-and-steel bistro-bar is Poitiers' communal lounge-dining room. A chalked blackboard menu lists specialities like *tournedos* (thick slices) of salmon, pastas and a crème brûlée you'll be dreaming about until your next visit.

Other good dining bets are the atrium-style bistro La Gazette (☎05 49 61 49 21; 1 rue Gambetta; menus €11-12; ☺Mon-Sat) and the green on the outside, green on the inside La Table du Jardin (☎05 49 41 68 46; 42 rue du Moulin à Vent; menu €21, mains €13-18; ☺Tue-Sat), serving exclusively seasonal market-fresh produce.

ℹ Information

Banks can be found around place du Maréchal Leclerc.

Meissi Cyber (28 rue Carnot; 1hr €2; ☺9.15am-2am) Internet access inside the courtyard of Le Grand Hôtel.

Post office (21 rue des Écossais)

Tourist office (☎05 49 41 21 24; www.ot-poitiers.fr; 45 place Charles de Gaulle; ☺10am-11pm Mon-Sat, 10am-6pm & 7-11pm Sun) Near Église Notre Dame.

ℹ Getting There & Away

The **train station** (☎36 35; bd du Grand Cerf) has direct links to Bordeaux (from €35, 1¾ hours), La Rochelle (€21, 1½ hours), Nantes (from €28, 3¼ hours) and many other cities including Paris' Gare Montparnasse (from €51, 1½ hours, 12 daily).

Around Poitiers

FUTUROSCOPE

Futuristic theme park Futuroscope (☎05 49 49 30 80; www.futuroscope.com; adult/under

16yr €35/26; ☉10am-11.15pm, closed Jan–early Feb) takes you whizzing through space, diving into the deep-blue ocean depths and on a close encounter with creatures of the future among many other space-age cinematic experiences. **Arthur, l'Adventure** goes far beyond the realms of mere 3-D cinema and into the world of 4-D. To keep things cutting edge, one-third of the attractions change annually. Many are motion-seat setups requiring a minimum height of 120cm, but there's a play area for littlies with miniature cars and so on.

Allow at least five hours to see the major attractions; two days to see everything. Futuroscope's numerous hotels are bookable through the website, or directly at the lodging desk.

Futuroscope is 10km north of Poitiers in Jaunay-Clan (take exit 28 off the A10). TGV trains link the park's TGV station with cities including Paris and Bordeaux; times and prices are similar to those to/from Poitiers.

Local **Vitalis** bus 9 and E links Futuroscope (Parc de Loisirs stop) with Poitiers' train station (the stop in front of Avis car rental; €1.30, 30 minutes); there are one to two buses an hour from 6.15am until 7.30pm or 9pm.

MARAIS POITEVIN

TOP CHOICE Parc Naturel Interrégional du Marais Poitevin is a tranquil bird-filled wetland dubbed the Venise Verte (Green Venice) due to the duckweed that turns its maze of waterways emerald green each spring and summer. Covering some 800 sq km of wet and drained marsh, the marshlands are interspersed with villages and woods threaded by canals and bike paths. The whole area is becoming increasingly popular with domestic tourists, and if you want somewhere you can really melt into rural life, the Marais Poitevin waterways are unbeatable. There are two main bases from which to punt out across the waterways: the small honey-coloured town of Coulon and, our favourite, the romantic, and pretty village of **Arçais**.

Boating and cycling are the only way to satisfactorily explore the area and there is no shortage of operators hiring out bikes and flat-bottomed boats or kayaks for watery tours. In Arçais there are three boat operators – Arçais Venise Verte (www.veniseverteloisirs.fr, in French), Au Martin Pecheur (www.aumartinpecheur.com, in French)

and Bardet-Huttiers (www.marais-arcais.com, in French) – all of which offer identical services for the same price: kayak per hour/half-day from €12/30, boat per hour/half-day from €15/38; guided tours are also possible. Coulon has even more operators and rates are identical. Bikes can be hired from several operators in both towns for €6/13 per hour/half-day.

Getting to either Coulon or Arçais is difficult in anything other than your own car.

🛏 Sleeping & Eating

TOP CHOICE **Maison Flore**   BOUTIQUE HOTEL €
(☎05 49 76 27 11; www.maisonflore.com; rue du Grand Port, Arçais; s/d €57/72; ☞) On the Arçais waterfront, this is a wonderfully romantic 10-room guesthouse in which every room is painted and decorated in the colours and style of local marsh plants such as the pale-green angelica or bright, purple iris. But the environmental connection runs much deeper, with solar hot water, geothermal heating and cooling, and an organic breakfast (€9.50) of freshly squeezed OJ, Fairtrade coffee and homemade cakes and yoghurt. The hotel also donates a percentage of profits to projects providing fresh water to villages in the developing world. There's a cosy guest lounge with books and board games, and you can rent boats here.

Hôtel-Restaurant Le Central

TRADITIONAL HOTEL €
(☎05 49 35 90 20; www.hotel-lecentral-coulon.com; 4 rue d'Autremont, Coulon; s/d from €54/64, menus from €19, mains €16-22; ☉lunch Tue-Sun, dinner Tue-Sat, closed 3 weeks Feb; ❄☞) Coulon's best-value accommodation comprises wood-panelled rooms, some overlooking a garden. Sublime dining is to be had at the in-house restaurant, where specialities include crispy eel, sorbet made from angelica, and a mouth-watering cheeseboard.

La Rochelle

POP 79,520

Known as La Ville Blanche (the White City), La Rochelle's luminous limestone facades glow in the bright coastal sunlight. One of France's foremost seaports from the 14th to 17th centuries, the city has arcaded walkways, half-timbered houses (protected from the salt air by slate tiles) and ghoulish gargoyles, rich reminders of its seafaring past.

The early French settlers of Canada, including the founders of Montreal, set sail from here in the 17th century.

This 'white city' is also commendably green, with innovative public transport and open spaces. It's kid-friendly too, with lots of activities for little visitors.

La Rochelle's late-20th-century district of Les Minimes was built on reclaimed land, and now has one of the largest marinas in the country. Unlike the Med with its motor cruisers, the 3500 moorings here are mostly used by yachts, which fill the harbour with billowing spinnakers.

◎ Sights & Activities

TOP CHOICE **Aquarium**   AQUARIUM
(www.aquarium-larochelle.com; quai Louis Prunier; adult/child €13/10, audioguide €3.50; ◎9am-11pm) La Rochelle's number-one tourist attraction is this state-of-the-art family-friendly aquarium. A visit begins by descending in a clunky old 'submarine' to the ocean floor, where you step out into a tunnel of fluoro jellyfish waving their tentacles in time to the classical music that wafts through the aquarium. Other highlights include the huge open ocean aquarium full of UFO-like rays and fearsome sharks, the jungle area with its tree-level walkways and ponds full of teeth-gnashing piranhas, the elegantly dancing seahorses, timid turtles and the bizarre half-newt, total fish mudskippers. The aim is to educate visitors to the wonders of the world's waters and the threats our oceans face. You will learn how sea cucumbers spit their guts out when frightened and then just grow another set, and – here's one that all parents can relate to – how poor mummy octopus becomes so tired at the mere thought of bringing up her precious brood that she dies of exhaustion the moment they hatch out! You should allow a minimum of two hours for a visit.

Toy Museums   MUSEUMS
(www.museeslarochelle.com, in French; 14 rue La Désirée; adult/3-10yr per museum €7.50/5, joint ticket adult/child €11/6.50; ◎9.30am-7pm) A treat for kids (and kids-at-heart) is the **Musée des Automates** (Automation Museum), a small theme-park-style display showing 300 automated dolls from the last two centuries, including a near-life-size re-creation of bygone Montmartre in Paris, right down to the Moulin Rouge and the funicular railway. Trainspotters

will love the equally appealing **Musée des Modèles Réduits** (Scale Model Museum) next door, with miniature cars, computer-automated naval battles and a tootling model railway. Both museums are wheelchair accessible.

Defensive Towers   FAMOUS LANDMARK
(adult/child €8/free; ◎10am-6.30pm) To protect the harbour at night in times of war, an enormous chain was raised between the two 14th-century stone towers at the harbour entrance to La Rochelle, giving rise to the name **Tour de la Chaîne** (Chain Tower). There are superb views from the top and a whizz-bang new permanent exhibit about the Canadian voyagers.

Across the harbour it's also possible to climb the 36m-high, pentagonal **Tour St-Nicolas**.

So named because of its role as the harbour's lighthouse (lit by an enormous candle), and one of the oldest of its kind in the world, the conical 15th-century **Tour de la Lanterne** is also referred to as Tour des Quatre Sergents in memory of four local sergeants, two of whom were held here for plotting to overthrow the newly reinstated monarchy before their execution in Paris in 1822. The English-language graffiti on the walls was carved by English privateers held here during the 18th century.

The most economical way to visit La Rochelle's three defensive towers is with the €8 combined ticket, but there are also combinations if you only want to visit two of the three.

The gateway to the old city, **Tour de la Grosse Horloge** (quai Duperré) is a steadfast Gothic-style clock tower, with a 12th-century base and an 18th-century top. For safety reasons, it's not possible to enter.

Island Hopping   ISLAND EXCURSIONS
Several islands are scattered around La Rochelle, including the nearby Île de Ré (p613), as well as a trio further south.

Accessible only by boat, the tiny crescent-shaped **Île d'Aix** (pronounced 'eel dex'), 16km due south of La Rochelle, has some blissful beaches. Between the Île d'Aix and the larger **Île d'Oléron** (linked to the mainland by a free bridge) is the fortress-island **Fort Boyard**, built during the first half of the 19th century.

Inter-Îles (☑08 25 13 55 00; cours des Dames) has sailings from Easter to early November to Fort Boyard (adult/child €18.50/11.50), Île d'Aix (€27/17.50) and Île

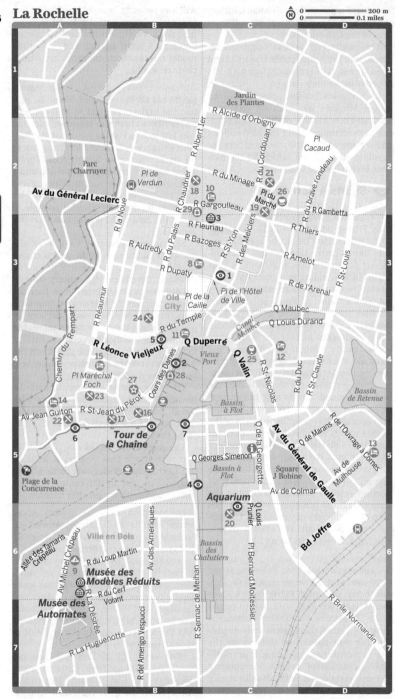

Jardin
des Plantes

R Alcide d'Orbigny

Pl
Cacaud

R Albert 1er

R du Cordeau

Parc
Charruyer

Pl de
Verdun

R du Minage

21

Pl du
Marché

26

19

Av du Général Leclerc

R Chaudrier

18

10

R Gargoulleau

29

3

R du brave rondeau

R Gambetta

R la Noue

R Fleuriau

R Bazoges

R St-Yon

R des Merciers

R Thiers

R Aufredy

R du Palais

8

R Amelot

R St-Louis

R Dupaty

1

R de l'Arenal

**Old
City**

Pl de la
Caille

Pl de l'Hôtel
de Ville

Q Maubec

R Réaumur

24

Q Louis Durand

Canal
Maubec

Chemin du Rempart

5

R du Temple

11

Q Duperré

12

R Léonce Vieljeux

Cours des Dames

2

28

*Vieux
Port*

25

Q Valin

R St-Nicolas

R du Duc

R St-Claude

*Bassin
de Retenue*

15

Pl Maréchal
Foch

27

23

14

22

R St-Jean du Pérot

17

16

7

**Tour de
la Chaîne**

*Bassin
à Flot*

Q de la Georgette

Av du Général de Gaulle

Q de Marans

R de l'Ouvrage à Cornes

13

6

Av de
Mulhouse

*Plage de la
Concurrence*

Q Georges Simenon

*Bassin à
Flot*

Square
J Bobine

Av de Colmar

Bd Joffre

4

Aquarium

20

Q Louis Prunier

Ville en Bois

Av des Amériques

*Bassin
des
Chalutiers*

Pl Bernard Moitessier

Allée des Tamaris Crépeau

Av Michel Crépeau

R du Loup Martin

9

**Musée des
Modèles Réduits**

R du Cerf
Volant

R La Désirée

**Musée des
Automates**

R La Huguenotte

R de Amerigo Vespucci

R Sennac de Melhan

R Brile Normandin

d'Oléron (€27/17.50), plus sailings to Île de Ré (€18.50/11.50) from Easter to September.

La Rochelle's tourist office also has information about reaching the islands by public and private transport.

Musée Maritime　　MARITIME MUSEUM
(Maritime Museum; adult/child €8/5.50; ◎10am-7.30pm) Moored at Bassin à Flot are the meteorological research ship *France 1*, a *chalutier* (fishing boat) and a tug, which together make up the Musée Maritime. If you think your job is tough, just wait until you see what the crew on these sorts of boats have to put up with on the average working day.

Musée du Nouveau Monde　　MUSEUM
(New World Museum; 10 rue Fleuriau; adult/child €4/free; ◎10.30am-12.30pm & 2-6pm Mon & Wed-Sat, 2-6pm Sun) La Rochelle's role as a departure point for North America is interpreted at the 18th-century mansion housing this museum.

☞ Tours

Flanked by a 15th-century Flamboyant Gothic wall and a resplendent 17th-century Renaissance-style courtyard, the **Hôtel de Ville** (Town Hall; place de l'Hôtel de Ville; adult/child €4/1.50) has guided tours in French at 3pm daily in June and September, 3pm and 4pm daily in July and August, and on weekends during the rest of the year.

The tourist office organises a wealth of city tours throughout the summer months (adult/child €9/6), often in French only. Reservations are essential.

✵ Festivals & Events

Festival International du Film　　FILM FESTIVAL
(www.festival-larochelle.org, in French) Silent classics, as well as new nondubbed films, are screened during the 10-day film festival in early July.

Francofolies　　DANCE FESTIVAL
(www.francofolies.fr, in French) A cutting-edge, contemporary music and performing arts festival held over four days in mid-July.

Jazz Festival　　JAZZ FESTIVAL
(www.larochelle-jazz-festival.com) October sees jazz fans jive to La Rochelle's jazz festival.

Sleeping

During the warmer months, dozens of campgrounds open up (and fill up just as quickly) around La Rochelle and Île de Ré. The tourist office has a list of campgrounds

BIRDWATCHING

An easy 15km drive south of La Rochelle, the **Réserve Naturelle Marais d'Yves** (www.marais.yves.reserves-naturelles.org, in French; N137, Yves; ⊙2-6pm Sun & school holidays) has a free nature centre, where you can pop in and peer through telescopes to watch some of the 192-hectare reserve's 250 bird species amid the wetlands. Depending on the season, you might see flocks of over 20,000 birds fill the sky on their migratory path. The website lists various guided walks and cycle rides through the wetlands (available in English), where you'll also learn about the area's 750 species of frogs, flowers and insects.

outside the town. The closest to the city is **Camping du Soleil** (☎05 46 44 42 53; av Michel Crépeau; adult & tent €13.50; ⊙late Jun–late Sep). Take bus 10.

TOP CHOICE **Un Hôtel en Ville** BOUTIQUE HOTEL €€
(☎05 46 41 15 75; 20 place du Maréchal Foch; d €95-135; ☞) Everything about this smart new boutique hotel screams quality – even the pillows and mattresses are in a league above those of most other hotels. The admittedly fairly small rooms are painted in a startling white, offset through the use of dark stone furnishings. Parking's €12.50 and breakfast from €11.

Trianon de la Plage HISTORIC HOTEL €€
(☎05 46 41 21 35; www.hoteltrianon.com; 6 rue de la Monnaie; r from €80; ☞) In a quiet corner of town but only a shipmate's shout from the old town and a mere sandy shuffle from the town beach (with water so polluted bathing is actually forbidden) is this gracefully ageing art deco hotel with stained-glass windows, a curly-whirly staircase, grand dining room and multi-hued rooms.

Hôtel La Marine TRADITIONAL HOTEL €€
(☎05 46 50 51 63; www.hotel-marine.com, in French; 30 quai Duperré; d €70-140; ✳☞⌨) For captivating views of La Rochelle's iconic towers, try for rooms 1, 6, 9 or 13 in this waterfront hotel by the Vieux Port. Each of the 13 rooms is individually decorated with cool, neutral-toned decor and smart designer furniture. Breakfast costs €7.

Masq Hotel DESIGN HOTEL €€
(☎05 46 41 83 83; www.masqhotel.com; 17 rue de l'Ouvrage à Cornes; r €98-138; ✳☞⌨) This designer hotel takes its cue from a chance meeting between owner-creator Michel Dufour and two Balinese brothers, Hindu artists Mantra and Geredeg, whom he commissioned to paint the abstract canvases that hang in all 76 rooms as well as the artistically lit neo-retro foyer.

Other conversation pieces include Philippe Starck Carrara marble tables, and Pierluigi Cerri–designed apple-green leather chairs in the breakfast room. A couple of the ultraspacious suites have terraces. Parking's €7, breakfast €12.

Hôtel St-Nicolas BOUTIQUE HOTEL €€
(☎05 46 41 71 55; www.hotel-saint-nicolas.com; 13 rue Sardinerie et place de la Solette; r from €120; ✳☞⌨) This new hotel offers smart, clean minimalist style and beds so soft and welcoming it'll be a battle to get out of them in the morning. The bathrooms have giant rain showers and the service is excellent. Parking's €7 and breakfast €10.

Hôtel de la Paix HISTORIC HOTEL €
(☎05 46 41 33 44; www.hotelalarochelle.com; 14 rue Gargoulleau; s €63, d €69-79; ☞) In a lovely 18th-century building, the hotel's sweeping staircase of polished wood leads to good-value rooms, some of which have open stone walls and all of which have plenty of splashes of colour and character. Breakfast (€12) is a hearty affair taken in the pleasant next-door café. Reduced-rate parking (€6) can be organised at a nearby car park.

Bar de l'Hôtel de Ville TRADITIONAL HOTEL €
(☎05 46 41 30 25; 5 rue St-Yon; d from €50) This bustling bistro (mains €8) with an attached hotel has just nine recently renovated rooms. The decoration is all rustic Mediterranean with roughly plastered pastel-shaded rooms, some of which come with little lounges and, sadly, blocked-up fireplaces.

Centre International de Séjour-Auberge de Jeunesse HOSTEL €
(☎05 46 44 43 11; www.fuaj.net/homepage/larochelle; av des Minimes; dm €16-18, s/d €27/38; ⊙reception 8am-noon, 2-7pm & 9-10pm, closed Christmas) This popular

HI hostel is 2km southwest of the train station in Les Minimes.

Eating

The port has a plethora of restaurants and cafés, especially on the northern side. In summer, the quays in front of the Vieux Port are closed to traffic from 8pm to midnight Monday to Saturday and 2pm to midnight on Sunday, creating the ambience of a giant street party. Away from the tourist crowds, locals' favoured dining areas are rue St-Jean du Pérot and streets such as rue des Cloutiers surrounding place du Marché.

TOP CHOICE Le Soleil Brille Pour Tout Le Monde INTERNATIONAL, VEGETARIAN €
(☑05 46 41 11 42; 13 rue des Cloutiers; menus/mains from €13/9.50; ⊙closed Sun & Mon; ☑) There's a distinctly bohemian air to this excellent little place, decked out in hippy colours. Some highly original (often vegetarian-based) dishes originate from the kitchen, much of them inspired by the tropical French islands of Réunion and Martinique. As much as possible, all the produce used here comes from the nearby market and you can really tell – plus it's one of those all-too-rare French restaurants not afraid to experiment with spices. Advance reservations are essential.

André SEAFOOD €€
(☑05 46 41 28 24; 8 place de la Chaîne; menus €32-39, mains €17-30; ⊙noon-4pm & 7pm-midnight) Opened in the 1950s as a small seafood café, André grew so popular it began buying adjacent shops. There's now a maze of interconnecting rooms, each with its own individual ambience (like a portholed cabin) but all serving succulent seafood caught the night before. You can choose your fanciful denizens of the deep from the display tables outside: 'Hello, Mr Crab, you look tasty. I'm going to gobble you up,' and with that he'll be thrown in a pan of hot water.

Les Quatre Sergents GASTRONOMIC €€
(☑05 46 41 35 80; 49 rue St-Jean du Pérot; menus & mains from €18) Set inside a beautifully tiled, historic former greenhouse, it's still a jungle in here today with plants scrambling upward to the height of trees. Don't worry though, nothing else about this place is as untamed as the Congo; this is the city's premier address for white-tableclothed elegance and gastronomic French fare such as frogs' legs in a creamy *pineau* (sweet white wine with a Cognac base) sauce.

L'Estamient TRADITIONAL FRENCH
(☑05 46 30 38 74; Échoppe du Marché, rue Gambetta; lunch menu €12; ⊙Mon-Sat) Built into the market walls, this family-run place has a convivial atmosphere and draws plenty of regulars with its tasty and filling lunch menus comprising all the French bistro standards. Book ahead at lunchtime.

Le Café de la Aquarium MODERN FRENCH
(☑05 46 50 17 17; mains €14; ☑) The Aquarium's café serves refined regional cuisine using whatever's in season locally (including a surprising amount of seafood!). There are great harbour views from the dining room and, if that weren't enough, you can also watch giant sharks cruising about – a selling point we're pretty sure nowhere else in La Rochelle can match! The café is open to nonaquarium visitors as well, but sadly you can't leave the aquarium for lunch and re-enter on the same ticket.

Chez Mah Monir MIDDLE EASTERN
(☑05 46 37 50 56; Échoppe du Marché, rue Gambetta; lunch menu/mains from €17/9; ⊙Mon-Sat) Next door to L'Estamient (built into the market walls). Let your taste buds travel a little further afield to the souks of Iran and North Africa at the ever-popular Chez Mah Monir. It's best to book a table at lunchtime.

Lulu MODERN FRENCH €€
(☑05 46 50 69 03; 19ter place de la Préfecture; menus from €16, mains €16) Decorated in striking shades of fuchsia, Lulu is La Rochelle's grooviest restaurant, with a hip young team in the kitchen turning out gourmet fare and a lounge vibe that comes into its own during regular piano soirées.

Café de la Paix BRASSERIE €
(☑05 46 41 39 79; 54 rue Chaudrier; lunch menu €13.50, mains €11-18.50; ⊙7am-10pm Mon-Sat) A visual feast as much as a dining one, this belle-époque brasserie-bar serves up traditional cuisine like beef, duck, foie gras and fish, as well as breakfasts and afternoon teas amid the splendour of soaring frescoed ceilings and gold-edged arched mirrors.

Wine, Glorious Wine

The countryside around the Bordeaux region is full of renowned vineyards and legendary châteaux, many of which can be visited. Venture a little further north and the Cognac region offers a totally different sort of tipple.

Cognac

1 The Atlantic coast's wine attention might fall on Bordeaux, but it isn't the only wine party in town. Cognac (p613) produces a drink so heavenly that even the angels are said to partake.

St-Émilion

2 The quintessential French wine town, St-Émilion (p624), the oldest French wine region, has a honey glow and its robust and generous wines tickle the taste buds. This is the most rewarding of the wine towns to visit.

Bordeaux

3 No wine-tasting tour of the southwest is complete without a course at the École du Vin (p619). Built on the wealth of the grape, Bordeaux (p615) lives up to its bourgeois reputation, but today an army of students has given the city a lighter edge.

The Médoc

4 The Médoc region (p625) encompasses some of the finest wine territory in France, with such grand names as Mouton Rothschild, Latour and Lafite Rothschild hailing from this area.

Secrets of the Vine

5 Learn some of the secrets of a successful bottle on a château, vineyard or cellar tour in Bordeaux (p618 and p619) and St-Émilion (p626), or on a tour of a Cognac house (p614).

Clockwise from top left
1. Barrels of Hennessy Cognac 2. The medieval village of St-Émilion 3. Rooftop view from Tour Pey-Berland, Bordeaux

Aux Table Rondes
TRADITIONAL FRENCH **€€**

(☎05 46 41 31 37; 33 rue St-Jean du Pérot; mains €15-19; ☺lunch Tue & Thu-Sat, dinner Mon-Sat) Those with a tiger in them craving a solid lump of meat should come to this carnivore-friendly institution. As well as steaks, it's also renowned for its *cochon du lait* (pig cooked in milk).

Self-Catering

The lively, 19th-century **covered market** (place du Marché; ☺7am-1pm) seethes with stallholders selling fresh fruit and vegetables, fish splayed on beds of ice, and just-killed meat. On Friday afternoons an **open-air market** sprawls across place Verdun.

In the old city you can pick up staples at **Monoprix supermarket** (30-36 rue du Palais).

Drinking

There's no shortage of places to drink along the main dining strips, but some of the city's best bars (most open to 2am) are sprinkled along the bohemian-feel rue St-Nicolas.

Cave de la Guignette
WINE BAR

(☎05 46 41 05 75; 8 rue St-Nicolas; ☺4-8pm Mon, 10am-1pm & 4-8pm Tue & Wed, 10am-1pm & 3-8pm Thu-Sat) On a hot summer's afternoon, try a glass of Guignette (white wine with tiny bubbles, flavoured with natural fresh fruit) here.

Merling
TEAROOM

(25 rue Gambetta; ☺closed Mon morning & Sun) For fresh-roasted coffee, head to this 1st-floor tearoom, which supplies most cafés in town with their brews.

☆ Entertainment

La Coursive
MUSIC, CINEMA

(☎05 46 51 54 00; 4 rue St-Jean du Pérot; ☺late Aug–mid-Jul) The two auditoriums at La Coursive host regular concerts and non-dubbed art films.

Shopping

Craft market
MARKET

(cours des Dames; ☺daily Jul–mid-Sep, Sat & Sun Easter-Jun) Authentic, handmade leather crafts, jewellery, sand sculptures and more are sold by the artists themselves on the waterfront.

Paul Bossuet
WINE

(21 rue Gargoulleau) Cognac and *pineau* produced by this local vintner make great souvenirs, not least for their decorative bottles.

Information

There are a number of banks on rue du Palais in the old city.

Hospital (☎05 46 45 50 50; rue du Dr Schweitzer)

Hôtel de Police (Police Station; ☎05 46 51 36 36; 2 place de Verdun; ☺24hr)

Post office (6 rue de l'Hôtel de Ville) Changes money.

Tourist office (☎05 46 41 14 68; www.larochelle-tourisme.com, www.ville-larochelle.fr; Le Gabut, 2 quai Georges Simenon; ☺9am-7pm Mon-Sat, 11am-5pm Sun) Sells the **Pass Rochelais**, offering various discounts for public transport, sights and activities.

❶ Getting There & Away

AIR La Rochelle Airport (☎05 46 42 30 26; www.larochelle.aeroport.fr), north of the city centre off the N237, has domestic flights as well as a variety of flights to several UK and Irish airports with Ryanair, EasyJet, Flybe and Jet2. There are also flights to Brussels and Oslo with Ryanair.

BUS From the **bus station** (place de Verdun), **Océcars** (☎05 46 00 95 15) runs services to regional destinations. See p613 for bus services to Île de Ré.

CAR Inexpensive car-rental companies close to the train station include **ADA** (☎05 46 41 02 17; 19 av du Général de Gaulle) and **National/Citer** (☎05 46 29 19 00; 17 av du Général de Gaulle).

TRAIN The **train station** (☎08 36 35 35 35) is linked by TGV to Paris' Gare Montparnasse (from €65, 3¼ hours). Other destinations served by regular direct trains include Nantes (€24.50, 1¾ hours), Poitiers (€21.50, 1½ hours) and Bordeaux (€27, 2¼ hours).

❶ Getting Around

To/From the Airport

Bus 7 (Bus 40A or B on Sundays) runs from the airport to the town centre (€1.20); schedules are available on the airport website. A taxi costs about €10.

Bicycle

The city's distinctive yellow **Yélo Vélo** (place de Verdun; 1st 2hr free, then per hr €1) bikes can be picked up and dropped off from 26 points around the city.

Boat

Le Passeur (tickets €0.70; ☺7.45am-10pm) is a three-minute ferry service linking Tour de la Chaîne with the Avant Port. It runs when there are passengers – press the red button on the board at the top of the gangplank.

The ferry **Bus de Mer** (€1.30, 20 minutes) links Tour de la Chaîne with Les Minimes. It runs daily April to September; at weekends and holidays only from October to March. Boats from the Vieux Port depart every hour on the hour (except at 1pm) from 10am to 7pm (every half-hour and until 11.30pm in July and August).

Bus

Electric buses buzz around town. Local transport system **RTCR/Yélo Bus** (☑05 46 34 02 22) has a main bus hub and **information office** (place de Verdun; ◷7.30am-6.30pm Mon-Fri, 8am-6.30pm Sat). Most lines run until sometime between 7.15pm and 8pm. Tickets cost €1.20.

Bus 1 runs from place de Verdun to the train station, returning via the Vieux Port.

Car & Motorcycle

A free shuttle bus connects the low-cost Park and Ride (P+R) car park off av Jean Moulin.

Taxi

Call ☑05 46 41 55 55.

Île de Ré

POP 16,000

Bathed in the southern sun, drenched in a languid atmosphere and scattered with villages of green-shuttered, whitewashed buildings with red Spanish-tile roofs, Île de Ré is one of the most delightful places on the west coast of France. The island spans just 30km from its most easterly and westerly points, and just 5km at its widest section. But take note, the secret's out and in the high season it can be almost impossible to move around and even harder to find a place to stay.

On the northern coast about 12km from the toll bridge that links the island to La Rochelle is the quaint fishing port of St-Martin-de-Ré (population 2600), the island's main town. Surrounded by 17th-century fortifications (you can stroll along most of the ramparts), the port town is a delightful mesh of streets filled with craft shops, art galleries and salty sea views. St-Martin's **tourist office** (☑05 46 09 20 06; www.iledere.com; av Victor Bouthillier; ◷10am-6pm Mon-Sat, to noon Sun) can provide information for the entire island.

The island's best **beaches** are along the southern edge – including unofficial naturist beaches at Rivedoux Plage and La Couarde-sur-Mer – and around the western tip (northeast and southeast of Phare-des-Baleines). Many beaches are bordered by

dunes that have been fenced off to protect the vegetation.

🏃 Activities

🚲 Cycling
BIKE HIRE

Criss-crossed by an extensive network of well-maintained bicycle paths, the pancake-flat island is ideal for **cycling**. A biking map is available at tourist offices; in summer practically every hamlet has somewhere to hire bikes. Year-round Cycland (www.cycland.fr) can deliver bikes to the bridge.

🛏 Sleeping

Île de Ré is an easy day trip from La Rochelle; however, if you want to spend longer on the island (and you will), each village has a summer tourist office with lists of local accommodation options, including campgrounds and private rooms and houses.

La Baronnie Domaine HISTORIC HOTEL €€€
(☑05 46 09 21 29; www.domainedelabaronnie. com; 21 rue Baron de Chantal, St-Martin de Ré; d from €160) Attention all kings and queens, this place, which oozes history, is so regal you won't be at all surprised to hear that it was once owned by one of your ancestors – Louis XVI.

Hôtel Le Sénéchal BOUTIQUE HOTEL €€
(☑05 46 29 40 42; www.hotel-le-senechal.com; 6 rue Gambetta, Ars en Ré; r €80-200; ❄🕸🐾) Somewhat more down to earth, but no less charming for it, is this place in the centre of the equally charming village of Ars en Ré. When we were visiting, a couple who were checking the rooms commented, 'Oh, isn't it cute.' We couldn't have expressed it better ourselves.

ℹ Getting There & Away

The one-way automobile toll (paid on your way to the island) is €9 (a whopping €16.50 from mid-June to mid-September).

Year-round excruciatingly slow buses link La Rochelle (the train station car park, Tour de la Grosse Horloge and place de Verdun) with all the major towns on the island; the one-hour trip to St-Martin costs €4. There are also intra-island routes.

Cognac

POP 19,850

On the banks of the River Charente amid vine-covered countryside, Cognac is

THE HOME OF COGNAC

According to local lore, divine intervention plays a role in the production of Cognac. Made of grape *eaux-de-vie* (brandies) of various vintages, Cognac is aged in oak barrels and blended by an experienced *maître de chai* (cellar master). Each year some 2% of the casks' volume – *la part des anges* (the angels' share) – evaporates through the pores in the wood, nourishing the tiny black mushrooms that thrive on the walls of Cognac warehouses. That 2% might not sound like much, but it amounts to around 20 million bottles a year – if the angels really are up there knocking back 20 million bottles of Cognac a year, then all we can say is roll on our time behind the pearly gates!

The best-known Cognac houses are open to the public, running tours of their cellars and production facilities, and ending with a tasting session. Opening times vary annually; it's a good idea to reserve in advance.

Camus (☑05 45 32 72 96; www.camus.fr; 29 rue Marguerite de Navarre; adult/child from €7/ free) Located 250m northeast of the Jardin Public.

Hennessey (☑05 45 35 72 68; www.hennessey.com; 8 rue Richonne; adult/12-18yr/ under 12 €9/7/free; ⊘closed Jan & Feb) Situated 100m uphill from quai des Flamands; tours include a film (shown in English) and a boat trip across the Charente to visit the cellars.

Martell (☑05 45 36 33 33; www.martell.com; place Édouard Martell; adult/child €7.50/3) Found 250m northwest of the tourist office; last entry is one hour prior to closing.

Otard (☑05 45 36 88 86; www.otard.com; 127 bd Denfert-Rochereau; adult/child €8.50/4) Housed in the 1494 birthplace of King François I, the Château de Cognac, 650m north of place François 1er.

Rémy Martin (☑05 45 35 76 66; www.visitesremymartin.com) Two locations: the estate (adult/child €15/7; ⊘closed Oct-Apr), 4km southwest of town towards Pons; and, in town, the house (adult/12-18yr/under 12yr €25/14/7; ⊘by appointment), for intimate tastings in groups of eight.

The tourist office has a list of smaller Cognac houses near town; most close between October and mid-March.

---

known worldwide for the double-distilled spirit that bears its name, and on which the local economy thrives. Most visitors head here to visit the famous cognac houses, however, it's a picturesque stop even if you don't happen to be a huge fan of the local firewater.

Cognac's café-ringed central roundabout, place François 1er, is 200m northeast of the tourist office (☑05 45 82 10 71; www.tourism-cognac.com; 16 rue du 14 Juillet; ⊘9.30am-5.30pm Mon-Sat). It's linked to the river by bd Denfert-Rochereau.

◎ Sights & Activities

Half-timbered 15th- to 17th-century houses line the narrow streets of the Vieille Ville (old city), which sits snugly between the partly Romanesque Église St-Léger (rue Aristide Briand) and the river.

Museums   MUSEUMS
(Joint entry adult/child €4.60/free; ⊘10am-6pm) At the southern corner of the leafy Jardin Public is the Musée de Cognac (☑05 45 32 07 25; www.musees-cognac.fr, in French; 48 bd Denfert-Rochereau), showcasing the town's history. The Musée des Arts du Cognac (☑05 45 36 21 10; place de la Salle Verte) takes you step by step through the production of Cognac – from vine to bottle.

La Dame Jeanne   RIVER CRUISE
(☑05 45 82 10 71; adult/child €7/4; ⊘May-Sep; ⬤) You can float with the sticklebacks down the River Charente on *La Dame Jeanne*, a re-creation of one of the flat-bottomed cargo boats known as *gabarres*, that were once the lifeblood of trade along the river. The trip lasts 90 minutes and reservations should be made through the tourist office.

Sleeping & Eating

Hôtel Héritage
BOUTIQUE HOTEL €€

(☎05 45 82 01 26; www.hheritage.com; 25 rue d'Angoulême; d €70-80, mains €10-18; 🛜🍴) Renovated in striking shades of lime green, fuchsia and cherry red, this 17th-century mansion in the heart of town proves period elegance and contemporary style don't have to be mutually exclusive. Oh, and the 'medieval' portraits are like none you've ever seen before. Adjacent to the beautifully restored bar, the hotel's restaurant, La Belle Époque, specialises in reintroducing long-lost regional classics.

Hôtel Le Cheval Blanc
TRADITIONAL HOTEL €

(☎05 45 82 09 55; www.hotel-chevalblanc.fr; 6 place Bayard; d €56; ❄🛜) Miniature bottles of Cognac in the vending machine satiate midnight cravings at this hotel (with good wheelchair access), where rooms are set around a courtyard. Although not vast, the rooms are immaculate.

Bistrot de Claude
BISTRO €€

(☎05 45 82 60 32; 35 rue Grande; menus from €17, mains €12-29; ⏱Mon-Fri) Set in a lovely old wiggly timber building in the heart of the old town, this character-infused restaurant specialises in oysters and both river and sea fish.

ℹ Getting There & Away

Cognac's **train station**, 1km south of the town centre on av du Maréchal Leclerc, has regular trains to/from La Rochelle (from €15, from 1¼ hours).

Around Cognac

Within a short drive of Cognac are some fascinating towns and villages worth seeking out. Just a couple of highlights include the former Gallo-Roman capital of Aquitaine, Saintes (population 26,300), on the River Charente. Dating from the 1st century AD, its Roman legacies include a double arch that served as the town gate, an amazing overgrown amphitheatre built during the reign of Claudius, and an archaeology museum with unearthed statues and even a chariot and harness. Its pedestrianised old town spills over with lively places to shop, eat and drink.

Also straddling the Charente is Jarnac (population 5000), the 1916 birthplace of former president François Mitterrand. The house where he was born has been trans-

formed into a museum; he's now buried in the town's cemetery. The waters around Jarnac are prime for fishing.

Cognac's tourist office has details of these and other areas in its surrounds.

✗ Eating

TOP CHOICE La Ribaudière
GASTRONOMIC €€€

(☎05 45 81 30 54; www.laribaudiere.com; Bourg-Charente; menus from €42; ⏱lunch Wed-Sun, dinner Mon-Sat) This gastronomic haven is set among orchards overlooking the Charente River, in the tiny village of Bourg-Charente (midway between Cognac and Jarnac). Chef Thierry Verrat grows his own vegetables to accompany his seasonally changing, Michelin-starred creations. If the food sends your taste buds into whirls of excitement, you can keep them happy by joining one of the restaurant's **cookery courses** (€110). See the website for details.

LOWER ATLANTIC COAST

At the lower edge of the Atlantic Coast, the expansive Aquitaine region extends to the Dordogne in the east and the Basque Country in the south. The gateway to the region's wealth of attractions, set amid glorious vine-ribbonned countryside, is its capital, Bordeaux.

Bordeaux

POP 238,920

The new millennium was a major turning point for the city long known as La Belle au Bois Dormant (Sleeping Beauty). The mayor, former Prime Minister Alain Juppé, roused Bordeaux, pedestrianising its boulevards, restoring its neoclassical architecture and implementing a high-tech public transport system.

Although Juppé was convicted for abusing public funds in Paris in 2004, it was soon water under the bridge for the Bordelaise, and he was re-elected to the mayorship in 2006 and again in 2008. His efforts paid off: in mid-2007 half of the entire city (18 sq km, from the outer boulevards to the banks of the Garonne) was Unesco-listed, making it the largest urban World Heritage Site.

Bolstered by its high-spirited university-student population (not to mention 2.5 million tourists annually), La Belle Bordeaux now scarcely seems to sleep at all.

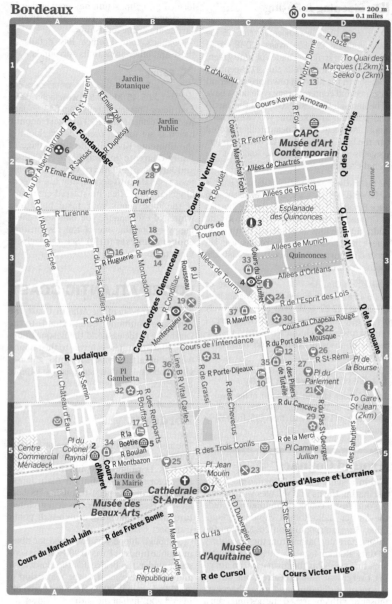

History

Rome colonised the Aquitaine region in 56 BC; the area 100km east of the Atlantic at the lowest bridging point on the River Garonne was named Burdigala. From 1154 to 1453, after Eleanor of Aquitaine married would-be King Henry II of England, the city prospered under the English. Their fondness for the region's red wine (known across the Channel as claret) provided the impetus for Bordeaux' enduring international reputation for quality wines.

◉ Sights & Activities

On the first Sunday of every month, Bordeaux' city centre is closed to cars, and attractions often have extended hours.

Cathédrale St-André   CATHEDRAL

Lording over the city, and a Unesco World Heritage Site prior to the city's classification, the cathedral's oldest section dates from 1096; most of what you see today was built in the 13th and 14th centuries. Exceptional masonry carvings can be seen in the north portal. Even more imposing than the cathedral itself is the gargoyled, 50m-high Gothic belfry, **Tour Pey-Berland** (adult/child €5/free; ⊘10am-1.15pm & 2-6pm), erected between 1440 and 1466. Its spire was added in the 19th century, and in 1863 it was topped off with the statue of Notre Dame de l'Aquitaine (Our Lady of Aquitaine). Scaling the tower's 232 narrow steps rewards you with a spectacular panorama of the city.

Museums   MUSEUMS

(permanent collections/temporary exhibits free/€5 unless stated otherwise below; ⊘11am-6pm Tue-Sun) Bordeaux has a healthy collection of museums and galleries. Gallo-Roman statues and relics dating back 25,000 years are among the highlights at the impressive **Musée d'Aquitaine** (20 cours Pasteur; temporary exhibitions €3). Ask to borrow an English-language catalogue.

Built in 1824 as a warehouse for French colonial produce like coffee, cocoa, peanuts and vanilla, the cavernous Entrepôts Lainé creates a dramatic backdrop for cutting-edge modern art at the **CAPC Musée d'Art Contemporain** (Entrepôt 7, rue Ferrére).

The evolution of Occidental art from the Renaissance to the mid-20th century is on view at Bordeaux' **Musée des Beaux-Arts** (20 cours d'Albret; ⊘Wed-Sun). Occupying two wings of the 1770s-built Hôtel de Ville, either side of the **Jardin de la Mairie** (an elegant public park), the museum was established in 1801; highlights include 17th-century Flemish, Dutch and Italian paintings. Temporary exhibitions are regularly hosted at its nearby annexe, Galerie des Beaux-Arts (place du Colonel Raynal).

Faience pottery, porcelain, gold, iron, glasswork and furniture are displayed at the Musée des Arts Décoratifs (39 rue Bouffard; ⏰2-6pm Wed-Mon, temporary exhibits from 11am Mon-Fri). For your own decorative treasures, browse rue Bouffard's antique and homewares shops.

Parks
PARKS

Landscaping is artistic as well as informative at the Jardin Public (cours de Verdun). Established in 1755 and laid out in the English style a century later, the grounds incorporate the meticulously catalogued Jardin Botanique founded in 1629 and at this site since 1855.

At the vast square esplanade des Quinconces, laid out in 1820, you'll see the fountain Girondins monument, a group of moderate, bourgeois National Assembly deputies during the French Revolution, 22 of whom were executed in 1793 after being convicted of counter-revolutionary activities.

The recently completed facelift of the 4km-long riverfront esplanade incorporates playgrounds, bicycle paths and, everyone's favourite, a wafer thin 'swimming pool' that hot and sticky young Bordelaise roll about in throughout the summer months.

Pretty place Gambetta, a central open area ringed by shaded benches, also has its share of history – during the Reign of Terror that followed the Revolution, a guillotine placed here severed the heads of 300 alleged counter-revolutionaries.

Palais Gallien
ROMAN RUINS

(rue du Docteur Albert Barraud; adult/child €3/2.50; ⏰2-7pm) The only remains of Burdigala today are the crumbling ruins of the 3rd-century amphitheatre, Palais Gallien.

🧭 Tours

The tourist office runs a packed program of bilingual city tours, including a wheelchair-accessible two-hour morning walking tour (adult/child €8/7, plus optional wine tasting €3.50; ⏰tours 10am, plus 3pm mid-Jul–mid-Aug); a night-time walking tour (adult/child €15/10) takes in Bordeaux' floodlit buildings and monuments. Contact the tourist office for details of dozens of other tour options,

including **gourmet** and **wine tours** as well as **river cruises** in the warmer months.

See the boxed text, p619, for highlights of wine-related tours including day trips further afield, as well as wine courses.

All tours take a limited number of participants; reserve ahead.

Courses

If you need some food to go with all that wine, sign up for one of Nicolas Frion's highly regarded half-day cookery courses at the École de Cuisine au Chapon Fin (☎05 56 90 91 92; www.chapon-fin.com; 5 rue Montesquieu, per person €95).

Short **cooking courses** also run periodically and are bookable through the tourist office.

🛌 Sleeping

Accommodation options are plentiful across all categories. The *Découverte* ('Discover Bordeaux') package is a neat little offering from the tourist office that bundles up two nights at your choice of participating hotels along with free public transportation, free access to the city's main monuments and sights, a guided city tour, a vineyard tour including wine tasting (both tours in English and French) and a bottle of wine. Prices start at €200 for a two-night package for two people; kids under 12 stay for free in their parents' room. Book 10 or more days in advance.

TOP CHOICE Ecolodge des Chartrons
B&B €€

(☎05 56 81 49 13; www.ecolodgedeschartrons. com; 23 rue Raze; s/d €98/110) Hidden away in a little side street off the quays in Bordeaux' Chartrons wine merchant district, this *chambre d'hôte* is blazing a trail for ecofriendly sleeping in the city. Owner-hosts Veronique and Yann have added a solar-powered hot-water system, energy-efficient gas heating and hemp-based soundproofing, while preserving the 'soul' of this old wine merchant's house. They've stripped back and limewashed the stone walls, scrubbed the wide floorboards and recycled antique furniture. Each of the five guest rooms has a bathroom built from natural materials such as basalt. You can curl up with a book in the lounge, access the island kitchen, and start the day with an organic breakfast, served at a long timber table.

Thirsty? The 1000-sq-km winegrowing area around the city of Bordeaux is, along with Burgundy, France's most important producer of top-quality wines.

The Bordeaux region is divided into 57 appellations (production areas whose soil and microclimate impart distinctive characteristics to the wine produced there) that are grouped into seven *familles* (families), and then subdivided into a hierarchy of designations (eg *premier grand cru classé*, the most prestigious) that often vary from appellation to appellation. The majority of the Bordeaux region's reds, rosés, sweet and dry whites and sparkling wines have earned the right to include the abbreviation AOC (Appellation d'Origine Contrôlée) on their labels, indicating that the contents have been grown, fermented and aged according to strict regulations that govern such viticultural matters as the number of vines permitted per hectare and acceptable pruning methods.

Bordeaux has over 5000 châteaux (also known as domaines, crus or *clos*), referring not to palatial residences but rather to the properties where grapes are raised, picked, fermented and then matured as wine. The smaller châteaux sometimes accept walk-in visitors, but at many places, especially the better-known ones, you have to make advance reservations. Many close during the *vendange* (grape harvest) in October.

Whet your palate with the tourist office's informal introduction to wine and cheese courses (adult €24), held every Thursday at 4.30pm, where you sip three different wines straight from the cellar and sup on cheese.

Serious students of the grape can enrol at the École du Vin (Wine School; ☎05 56 00 22 66; www.bordeaux.com/Ecole-du-Vin), within the Maison du Vin de Bordeaux (Bordeaux House of Wine; 3 cours du 30 Juillet), across the street from the tourist office. Introductory two-hour courses are held Monday to Saturday from 10am to noon between June and September (adult €25). To really develop your nose (and your dinner-party skills), sign up for one of three progressively more complex two- to three-day courses (€335 to €600) scheduled between May and October, including châteaux visits.

See also p625 and p626 for more on château visits and tastings.

La Maison Bord'eaux HISTORIC HOTEL €€
(☎05 56 44 00 45; www.lamaisonbord-eaux. com; 113 rue du Docteur Albert Barraud; s/d from €130/150; ☎) You'd expect to find a sumptuous 18th-century château with a conifer-flanked courtyard and stable house in the countryside, but this stunning *maison d'hôte* is right in the middle of the city. Public areas include a library with shelves of books and CDs. A *table d'hôte* is available by arrangement (*menus* €30 to €150 including wine).

Une Chambre en Ville BOUTIQUE HOTEL €€
(☎05 56 81 34 53; www.bandb-bx.com; 35 rue Bouffard; s/d €103/115, ste s/d €126/138) On a street full of antique and art shops, this stylish place blends in well because each of the five rooms is an individual work of art in its own right. The decoration ranges from the plush reds and spicy pictures of the Oriental room to the Madame and Monsieur classic style of the suites. Une

Chambre en Ville is gay-friendly (and all-welcoming).

La Maison du Lierre BOUTIQUE HOTEL €€
(☎05 56 51 92 71; www.maisondulierre.com; 57 rue Huguerie; d €68-128; ☎⏏) The delightfully restored 'House of Ivy' has a welcoming *chambre d'hôte* feel. A beautiful Bordelaise stone staircase (no lift) leads to sunlit rooms with polished floorboards, rose-printed fabrics and sparkling bathrooms. The vine-draped garden is a perfect spot to sip fresh orange juice at breakfast (from €8).

Seeko'o DESIGN HOTEL €€€
(☎05 56 39 07 07; www.seekoo-hotel.com; 54 quai de Bacalan; d from €189; ✳☎) The monochrome lobby of this iceberg-shaped hotel leads to 45 retro-futuristic vinyl-and-leather-decorated rooms (some with circular beds), fitted out by Bordeaux designers. Unwind in the free Turkish *hammam,* visit the 1st-floor Champagne bar or just peruse the clever modern art throughout.

Hôtel du Théâtre
BOUTIQUE HOTEL €

(☑05 56 79 05 26; www.hotel-du-theatre.com, in French; 10 rue Maison-Daurade; s/d from €50/75; ☎) The owners of this recently renovated hotel, just off the main shopping street, have done up some rooms in an entirely classic style and some in the sun-burst colours of the Mediterranean. Our favourites are full of flashy sequins and glitter, and look like they just got home from the disco.

Hôtel de la Tour Intendance
BOUTIQUE HOTEL €€

(☑05 56 44 56 56; www.hotel-tour-intendance. com; 14-16 rue de la Vieille Tour; s €78, d €88-148; ✳☎) Wake up to soaring exposed-sandstone walls, stone-laid floors and wood-beamed ceilings at this stylish boutique hotel tucked into a quiet corner of the city. Light-filled rooms have neutral-toned natural fabrics and fibres, limewashed timber panelling and geometric-embossed vinyl, with pebbled bathrooms screened by milky opaque glass.

Adare House
B&B €€

(☑05 56 52 48 45; 8 rue Emile Zola; s/d from €90/110; ☎) Inside a solid old Bordeaux town house, next to the gorgeous Jardin Public, this English-run *chambre d'hôte* has only two rooms, both beautifully presented in modern colours and patterns. One room has a bath to float your duck in and the other a multi-jet shower. Advance reservations essential.

Hôtel de la Presse
TRADITIONAL HOTEL €€

(☑05 56 48 53 88; www.hoteldelapresse.com; 6-8 rue de la Porte Dijeaux; d €78-98; ✳☎) Elegant touches at Hôtel de la Presse, just off the pedestrianised rue Ste-Catherine, include silk and dried flowers, and royal-red bedspreads. Service is polished and professional.

Hôtel Touring
TRADITIONAL HOTEL €

(☑05 56 81 56 73; www.hoteltouring.fr; 16 rue Huguerie; s/d €47-55, with shared bathroom €38/45; ☎) Run with pride by a warm-hearted family, the Touring's rooms are furnished with original 1940s and '50s furniture, like flip-up school-style desks and club chairs. Most have a fridge, TV and telephone.

Hôtel Notre Dame
TRADITIONAL HOTEL €

(☑05 56 52 88 24; 36-38 rue Notre Dame; s/d €47-54; ☎) Location is the key selling point of this clean and simple hotel. It's within an easy stroll of the town centre, just back from the river and in the middle of a lovely villagelike neighbourhood of antique shops and relaxed cafés (although it isn't so lovely at night – be careful!).

Auberge de Jeunesse
HOSTEL €

(☑05 56 33 00 70; www.auberge-jeunesse -bordeaux.com; 22 cours Barbey; dm incl sheets & breakfast €22; ⊙reception 7.30am-1.30pm & 3.30-9.30pm; ☎) Bordeaux' only hostel is housed in an ultramodern building with a self-catering kitchen, good wheelchair access and table football, to boot. From the train station, follow cours de la Marne northwest for 300m and turn left opposite the park; the hostel's about 250m ahead on your left.

✕ Eating

All that fine wine needs fine cuisine to accompany it, and Bordeaux has some excellent restaurants. Place du Parlement, rue du Pas St-Georges and rue des Faussets have a plethora. There are also scads of inexpensive cafés and restaurants around place de la Victoire. The former warehouse district of the Quai des Marques now houses dozens of waterfront restaurants, bars and factory shops. It's a nice place for a sunset meal or drink.

Le Cheverus Café
TOP CHOICE | BRASSERIE €

(☑05 56 48 29 73; 81-83 rue du Loup; menus from €10.50; ⊙closed Sun) In a city full of neighbourhood bistros, this one, smack in the city centre, is one of the most impressive. It's friendly, cosy and chaotically busy (be prepared to wait for a table at lunchtime). The food tastes fresh and home-cooked and it dares to veer slightly away from the bistro standards of steak and chips. The lunch menus, which include wine, are an all-out bargain.

La Tupina
TOP CHOICE | GASTRONOMIC €€

(☑05 56 91 56 37; 6 rue Porte de la Monnaie; menus €16/60, mains €18-40) Filled with the aroma of soup simmering inside an old *tupina* ('kettle' in Basque) over an open fire, this white-tableclothed place is feted far and wide for its seasonal southwestern French specialities such as a minicasserole of foie gras and eggs, milk-fed lamb or goose wings with potatoes and parsley. A €16 lunch *menu* is available on weekdays. La Tupina is a 10-minute walk upriver from the city centre and on a small side street. Any local can point you in the right direction.

BORDELAISE CUISINE – JEAN-PIERRE XIRADAKI

For me the best moment is when I catch the *bonheur* (happiness) in people's eyes, usually as they are eating a particular dish. I was born in Blaye, 50km from Bordeaux, and my cuisine is *paysanne* (country cuisine), rustic; it uses only the best products and traditional recipes from the southwest.

Jean-Pierre Xiradaki's Don't Miss List

Marché des Capucins *Cuisine bordelaise* (Bordeaux cuisine) originates from the south, from Basque-country women who came to work in the great Bordelaise houses. The diversity of produce is enormous. We have river and sea fish, shellfish, oysters, fowl (duck and geese), lamb, beef, mushrooms, vegetables, poultry, truffles... We really have everything, although we miss cheese. I buy my produce from local producers and markets: Marché des Capucins (see p622) in Bordeaux and the twice-weekly market in Blaye (Wednesday and Saturday mornings).

Cassoulet, Macaronade and Eels I love *cassoulet,* typical to the rural southwest and traditionally eaten to celebrate; it's a heart-warming haricot-bean stew with a few giblets, a bit of sausage and some pork thrown in. Then there's *macaronade aux cèpes et au foi gras,* fresh macaroni with local ceps (boletus mushrooms), foie gras and cream. It is very rich, very delicious and demands a healthy appetite! *Lamproie à la bordelaise* (eel-like lamprey), a migratory river fish cooked with wine and leeks, is very typical of our local cuisine.

La Soupe In winter at La Tupina (p620), we always have a cauldron of soup cooking in the fireplace; the fire burns all day just as it did at my grandparents'. We throw in cabbage, carrots, beans, a bit of duck or pork to give it taste and so on, just as peasants did centuries ago. For them it provided all the daily nutrition they needed – water, vegetables and a little meat.

Wine and Oysters Bordelaise essentials! L'Essentiel (☑05 57 24 39 76; 6 rue Guadel) in St-Émilion is *the* place to taste wine, and La Boîte à Huitres (p621), a seafood and shellfish restaurant in Bordeaux, is the *dégustation* (tasting) address for oysters. Favourite wine producers to taste and buy include Château Mayne Lalande (7 route du Mayne) and Château Lestage (www.chateau-lestage.com), both 35km north of Bordeaux in Listrac.

Things You Need To Know

Local markets Every village has a morning food market at least once a week.

Saucy! Anything *à la bordelaise* comes in a wine-based sauce spiced with parsley, shallots and bone marrow.

Cooking lessons With Bordelaise chef Nicolas Frion at the École de Cuisine au Chapon Fin (p618).

Jean-Pierre Xiradaki is a culinary writer and celebrity restaurant owner. He was interviewed by author Nicola Williams.

La Bôite à Huîtres SEAFOOD €
(☑05 56 81 64 97; 36 cours du Chapeau Rouge; menus/mains €18/8) This rickety, wood-panelled little place feels like an Arcachon fisherman's hut. It's a sensation that's quite appropriate because this is by far the best place in Bordeaux to munch on fresh Arcachon oysters. Traditionally they're served with sausage but you can have them in a number of different forms, including with that other southwest delicacy, foie gras. They'll also pack them up so you can take them away for a riverfront picnic.

Baud et Millet CHEESE & WINE €€
(☑05 56 79 05 77; 19 rue Huguerie; menus €23-25, mains €16-18) If you like cheese or wine,

ATLANTIC COAST LOWER ATLANTIC COAST

OYSTERS AT CAPUCINS

A classic Bordeaux experience is a Saturday morning spent slurping oysters and white wine from one of the seafood stands to be found at Marché des Capucins (6 oysters glass of wine €6; ⊘7am-noon). Afterwards you can peruse the stalls while shopping for the freshest ingredients to take on a picnic to one of the city's parks. To get there, head south down cours Pasteur and once at place de la Victoire turn left onto rue Élie Gintrec.

or both of them, then this cute neighbourhood place with over 250 different cheeses served in myriad forms (including a cheese *tagine!*) and almost as many wines is unmissable. Serious *fromage* fans should go for the all-you-can-eat cheese buffet.

L'Estaquade GASTRONOMIC €€€
(☑05 57 54 02 50; quai de Queyries; menu €50, mains €22-26) Set on stilts, this place juts out off the river's eastern bank. The seafood (bass, cod, scampi, scallops etc) and meat dishes (like pigeon with port and blackcurrant sauce) served here even manage to eclipse the magical views of Bordeaux' neoclassical architecture. From place de la Bourse, you'll see the restaurant on the other side of the river.

Karl INTERNATIONAL €€
(☑05 56 81 01 00; place du Parlement; brunch €20; ⊘8.30am-7.30pm; ⓜ) Simply *the* place in town for a morning after the night before brunch. These range from a light continental-style affair to the full works with salmon, cheeses, hams and eggs. It's just as good for a snack at any time of the day and is perpetually packed with a young crowd.

L'Entrecôte BRASSERIE €€
(☑05 56 81 76 10; 4 cours du 30 Juillet; menu €16.50) Opened in 1966, this unpretentious place doesn't take reservations and it has only one menu option. But Bordeaux locals continue to queue for its succulent thin-sliced meat (heated underneath by tea-light candles and topped with a 'secret recipe' sauce made from shallots and bone marrow), salad and unlimited homemade *frites.*

Self-Catering

For a taste of Bordeaux (that for once doesn't involve wine!), head to Baillardran (www.baillardran.com; place des Grands Hommes), which has several branches in town, including one in the Galerie des Grands Hommes shopping centre, where you can watch the chefs make *canelés,* a local vanilla-infused fluted cake. In the shopping centre's basement is a Carrefour supermarket. Nearby, you'll find Jean d'Alos (4 rue Montesquieu), a fine *fromagerie* with over 150 raw-milk and farm cheeses.

Drinking

Considering its synonymy with wine, Bordeaux has surprisingly few bars, meaning restaurants and bistros tend to fill the gap.

Student hang-outs ring place de la Victoire, such as perennial favourite Chez Auguste (3 place de La Victoire).

L'Autre Petit Bois BAR €
(12 place du Parlement) Decorated in an arresting 'modern' baroque and art deco style, this very popular wine bar full of curly-whirly sofas verges on the kitsch but pulls it off with style.

Café Brun JAZZ BAR €
(45 rue St-Rémi) A warm atmosphere and cool jazz make this bar-bistro great for an evening aperitif.

L'Orangerie du Jardin Public CAFÉ €
(Jardin Public; ⊘lunch; ⓜ) Bliss out with a drink, light lunch (menu €9) and the flowers in this colourful glass-fronted building on the edge of the Jardin Public.

Entertainment

Details of events appear in *Clubs & Concerts* (www.clubsetconcerts.com, in French), available for free at the tourist office.

Concert and event tickets can be purchased from the Virgin Megastore billeterie (15-19 place Gambetta).

Nightclubs & Live Music

Trendy pedestrianised streets like rue St-Rémi are good bets to get the evening started. For zoning reasons, many of the city's late-night dance venues are a few blocks northeast of Gare St-Jean along the river, on quai de la Paludate. Clubs also cluster along the river north of the city centre. Bouncers can be selective but there's normally no cover charge.

Le Port de la Lune NIGHTCLUB
(www.leportdelalune.com; 58 quai de la Paludate) Gigs at this dark, atmospheric jazz
club are posted on the website.

Rock School Barbey MUSIC
(☑05 56 33 66 00; www.rockschool-barbey.
com, in French; 18 cours Barbey) Catch regular live bands at the rock school, which
has a regular stream of up-coming
French and international indie bands
playing as well as various exhibitions.
It's almost next door to the Auberge de
Jeunesse.

Bar de l'Hôtel de Ville BAR
(4 rue de l'Hôtel de Ville) A mainly gay crowd
kicks up its heels at this bar, which has
outrageous shows on Sundays.

Theatre & Classical Music

Grand Théâtre OPERA
(☑05 56 00 85 95; www.opera-bordeaux.com,
in French; place de la Comédie) Designed by
Victor Louis (of Chartres Cathedral fame),
the 18th-century Grand Théâtre stages operas, ballets and concerts of orchestral and
chamber music. Guided behind-the-scenes
tours of the building (€3) are possible on
Wednesday and Saturday afternoons at
3pm, 4pm and 5pm.

Théâtre Femina THEATRE
(☑05 56 52 45 19; www.theatrefemina.fr, in
French; 10 rue de Grassi) Plays, dance performances, variety shows and concerts.

Cinemas

Cinéma Utopia CINEMA
(www.cinemas-utopia.org/bordeaux, in French;
3 place Camille Jullian) Screens nondubbed
art-house films.

🛍 Shopping

Europe's longest pedestrian shopping
street, rue Ste-Catherine, is probably the
city's low point. The southern end, towards
place de la Victoire, is the worst half – essentially, an unending shambles of kebab
shops. To give the road its dues though,
things are better at the northern end where
slightly classier chain shops predominate
and you'll find the Galerie Bordelaise (rue
de la Porte Dijeaux & rue Ste-Catherine) 19th-
century shopping arcade.

Luxury-label boutiques concentrate
within *le triangle*, formed by the allées de
Tourny, cours Georges Clemenceau and
cours de l'Intendance.

Antique market MARKET
(place St-Michel) Stalls of antiques fill the
square on Sunday mornings. Located
a 700m walk down river from the city
centre.

Bordeaux Magnum WINE
(3 rue Gobineau) Speciality wine shop.

L'Intendant WINE
(2 allées de Tourny). A central spiral staircase climbing four floors is surrounded
by cylindrical shelves holding 15,000
bottles of regional wine.

Bradley's Bookshop BOOKS
(8 cours d'Albret) Stacks of English-
language books and guides.

Librairie Mollat BOOKS
(15 rue Vital Carles) Books in several different languages.

ℹ Information

Internet Access
Le Cyb (23 cours Pasteur; per hr €2.50;
☺10am-2am Mon-Sat, 2pm-midnight Sun)

Medical Services & Emergency
Hôpital St-André (☑05 56 79 56 79; 1 rue
Jean Burguet)

Police station (☑05 57 85 77 77; 23 rue
François de Sourdis; ☺24hr)

Money
Banks offering currency exchange can be found
near the tourist office on cours de l'Intendance,
rue de l'Esprit des Lois and cours du Chapeau
Rouge.

Post
The post offices at 43 place Gambetta and
place St-Projet are open from 9am to 12.30pm
and 1.30pm to 5pm on Saturday in addition to
weekdays.

DON'T MISS

A TIPPLE WITH THE BEST

When in Rome do like the Romans,
and when in Bordeaux drink wine in
wine's Holy of Holies. The ultrastyl-
ish but very accessible Bar du Vin
(3 cours du 30 Juillet; glass of wine from
€3, with cheese from €5; ☺11am-10pm
Mon-Sat), inside the hallowed halls of
the Maison du Vin de Bordeaux, is the
place to come for a tipple with people
who really know their wine from their
beer.

Main post office (37 rue du Château d'Eau)

Tourist Information

Bordeaux Monumental (☑05 56 48 04 24; 28 rue des Argentiers; ☺9.30am-1pm & 2-6pm Mon-Sat, 10am-1pm & 2-6pm Sun) Specialist tourist office dedicated to the city's history. Hosts free multimedia presentations plus temporary exhibitions with a historical theme.

Main tourist office (☑05 56 00 66 00; www. bordeaux-tourisme.com; 12 cours du 30 Juillet; ☺9am-7pm Mon-Sat, 9.30am-6.30pm Sun) Runs an excellent range of city and regional tours.

Maison du Tourisme de la Gironde (☑05 56 52 61 40; www.tourisme-gironde.fr; 21 cours de l'Intendance; ☺9am-6pm Mon-Fri, 10am-1pm & 2-6.30pm Sat) Information on the Gironde *département*.

Train station tourist office (☺9am-noon & 1-6pm Mon-Sat, 10am-noon & 1-3pm Sun) Small but helpful branch outside the train station building.

Getting There & Away

AIR Bordeaux airport (☑05 56 34 50 00; www. bordeaux.aeroport.fr) is in Mérignac, 10km west of the city centre, with domestic and increasing numbers of international flights to most west European and North African destinations.

BUS Citram Aquitaine (www.citram.fr, in French) runs most buses to destinations in the Gironde.

International bus operator **Eurolines** (32 rue Charles Domercq) faces the train station.

CAR Rental companies have offices in the train-station building and at the airport.

TRAIN Bordeaux is one of France's major rail-transit points. The station, Gare St-Jean, is about 3km from the city centre at the southern terminus of cours de la Marne.

Paris Gare Montparnasse €70, three hours, at least 16 daily

Bayonne €28, two hours

La Rochelle €27, 2¼ hours

Nantes €45, four hours

Poitiers €36, 1¾ hours

Toulouse from €33, 2¼ hours

Getting Around

To/From the Airport

The train station, place Gambetta and the main tourist office are connected to the airport (one way €7) by **Jet'Bus** (☑05 56 34 50 50). The first bus leaves the airport at 7.45am from outside Terminal B (last at 10.45pm daily); the first departure to the airport from the train station is at 6.45am Monday to Friday, and 7.30am Saturday and Sunday (last at 9.45pm daily), with buses at 45-minute intervals throughout the day. The trip takes approximately 45 minutes. A taxi costs around €50.

Bicycle

Le Vélo de la Club (www.vcub.fr; per min €0.15) is Bordeaux' version of the cheap citywide pick-up and drop-off bike hire (€1 for 24 hours). Collection points are on all major squares and elsewhere.

Bus & Tram

Urban buses and trams are run by **TBC** (www. infotbc.com, in French). The company has Espace Bus information-ticket offices at the train station and place Gambetta (4 rue Georges Bonnac) and at esplanade des Quinconces. Tram line C links the train station with the city centre via the riverside.

Single tickets (€1.40) are sold onboard buses, and from machines at tram stops (stamp your ticket onboard). Tickets aren't valid for transfers.

Night buses operate until 1.30am on Thursday, Friday and Saturday nights; line 11 links place de la Victoire with the nightclub zone on quai de la Paludate.

Car

City parking is pricey and hard to find. Look for free spaces in the side streets north of the Musée d'Art Contemporain and west of the Jardin Public.

Taxi

To order a taxi try ☑05 56 96 00 34 or ☑05 56 29 10 25.

St-Émilion

POP 2160

The medieval village of St-Émilion perches above vineyards renowned for producing full-bodied, deeply coloured red wines and is easily the most alluring of all the region's wine towns. Named after Émilion, a miracle-working Benedictine monk who lived in a cave here between 750 and 767, it soon became a stop on pilgrimage routes, and the village and its vineyards are now Unesco-listed. Today, it's well worth venturing 40km east from Bordeaux to experience St-Émilion's magic, particularly when the sun sets over the valley and the

Northwest of Bordeaux, along the western shore of the Gironde Estuary – formed by the confluence of the Garonne and Dordogne Rivers – lie some of Bordeaux' most celebrated vineyards. To their west, fine-sand beaches, bordered by dunes and *étangs* (lagoons), stretch from Pointe de Grave south along the Côte d'Argent (Silver Coast) to the Bassin d'Arcachon and beyond, with some great surf (see the boxed text, p645). On the banks of the muddy Gironde, the port town of Pauillac (population 1300) is at the heart of the wine country, surrounded by the distinguished Haut-Médoc, Margaux and St-Julien appellations. The Pauillac wine appellation encompasses 18 *crus classés* including the world-renowned Mouton Rothschild, Latour and Lafite Rothschild. The town's tourist office houses the Maison du Tourisme et du Vin (☎05 56 59 03 08; www.pauillac-medoc.com; La Verrerie; ☻9.30am-7pm Mon-Sat, 10am-1pm & 2-6pm Sun), which has information on châteaux and how to visit them.

The lack of a public-transport system to most of the châteaux means this area is best explored in your own car or on one of the tours organised by the tourist office in Bordeaux. There are several different types of tour, which get chopped and changed on a regular basis; at the time of research, half-day **Médoc tours** taking in two châteaux and including wine tastings left the Bordeaux tourist office at 1.30pm on Thursdays and Saturdays (tours run to other wine regions the rest of the week) at a cost of €30. On Wednesdays the tourist office runs a day-long Médoc 1855 tour (with lunch €90; ☻tours 9.15am), which takes in three of the best known châteaux (the actual châteaux visited vary). Day-long **La Winery** tours (see below) also depart from Bordeaux' tourist office on Tuesdays and Saturdays at 9.45am. The cost of €45 includes a tasting session and lunch. For any of these tours, advance reservations are essential. Bordeaux Excursions (www.bordeaux-excursions.com) customises private wine-country tours, starting from €190 for one to five people (excluding châteaux fees) for a half-day trip.

If you're travelling under your own steam, the Maison du Vin de Bordeaux supplies free, colour-coded maps of production areas, details on châteaux and the addresses of local *maisons du vin* (tourist offices that mainly deal with winery visits). One of the easiest châteaux to visit is Château Lanessan (☎05 56 58 94 80; www.lanessan.com; Cussac-Fort-Medoc; adult/teenagers €8/2), which offers daily hour-long tours throughout the year including ones tailored to children and hard-to-please teenagers; advance reservations required.

The Médoc is an easy day trip from Bordeaux, but should you have wine-heavy eyes at the end of the day there are numerous *chambres d'hôte* in the area or, in the village of Margaux, try the Le Pavillon de Margaux (☎05 57 88 77 54; www.pavillon margaux.com; 3 rue Georges Mandel, Margaux; d from €95; ☎), a welcoming, family-run place with rooms styled according to famous local châteaux. The same family also runs the highly extravagant Château Marojallia (☎05 57 88 77 54; www.marojallia.com; 2 rue du Général de Gaulle, Margaux; d €175-270; ☎), a truly palatial pad that goes well with the region's wines. Courses in cookery and wine making are also available here.

While you're in the area, don't miss Philippe Raoux' La Winery (☎05 56 39 04 90; www.lawinery.fr, in French; Rond-point des Vendangeurs, D1, Arsac-en-Médoc). A first for France, this vast glass-and-steel wine centre mounts concerts and contemporary-art exhibits alongside various fee-based tastings, including innovative tastings that determine your *signe œnologique* ('wine sign') costing from €16 (booking required), and stocks over 1000 different wines.

limestone buildings glow with halolike golden hues.

Note that the cobbled streets and steep hills of the village make it difficult for travellers with disabilities to get around, but three new trails that allow mobility-impaired visitors to see at least some of the sites are plotted on free maps available from the tourist office.

👁 Sights

Clocher   TOWER

(bell tower; admission €1.25) For captivating views of the hilltop hamlet, collect the key from the tourist office to climb above the church. The entrance is on place des Créneaux.

Collégiale   CHURCH

(Collegiate Church) A domed Romanesque 12th-century nave dominates the former Collégiale, which also boasts an almost-square vaulted choir built between the 14th and 16th centuries. **Cloître de l'Église Collégiale**, the church's tranquil 12th- to 14th-century cloister, is the venue for special events.

Porte de la Cadène   CITY WALLS

(Gate of the Chain) Surviving sections of the town's medieval walls and gates include those running off rue Guadet.

Cloître des Cordeliers   MONASTERY

(rue Porte Brunet; admission free) Within the ruined monastery, the winery Les Corde-liers (guided cellar tours with/without wine tastings €3.50/2) has made sparkling wine for over a century.

Castel daou Rey   CASTLE

(admission €1.25; ⏱11am-7.15pm) The 13th-century donjon known as the Tour du Roi (King's Tower) has exceptional views of the town and the Dordogne Valley.

🏃 Activities

Blind tastings and games (available in English) are a fun and informative introduction to wine tasting at L'École du Vin de St-Émilion (www.vignobleschateaux.fr; 4 rue du Clocher; tasting courses €29; ⏱3pm Apr-Oct, by reservation Nov-Mar). The adjacent Maison du Vin (place Pierre Meyrat; classes €21; ⏱mid-Jul–mid-Sep) also offers bilingual 1½-hour classes starting at 11am.

Eight hiking circuits, from 4km to 14km, loop through the greater World Heritage jurisdiction; the tourist office has maps.

👉 Tours

The only (but highly worthwhile) way to visit the town's most interesting historical sites is with one of the tourist office's guided tours (adult/child €11/free). French-language tours leave from the tourist office daily at 11am, while English tours are at 11am weekends only. The St-Émilion Sou-terrain (Underground St-Émilion; adult/child €7/free) tour takes you beneath the pretty streets and into a fascinating labyrinth of catacombs – highlights are the hermit saint's famous cave, **Grotte de l'Ermitage**, and the 11th-century church, **Église Mono-lithe**, carved out of limestone between the 9th and the 12th centuries. Tours in French depart regularly throughout the day – call ahead to check English tour times (usually 2pm). It's chilly below ground; bring a jumper.

The tourist office organises two-hour afternoon château visits (adult/child €12/free; ⏱tours May-Sep) in French and English. It also runs various events throughout the year, such as La Journée Viticole (Winemakers' Day; minimum 2 people €385; ⏱11am-5pm Jun-Sep) that combines a vineyard visit, lunch, town tour and wine tasting course.

🎉 Festivals & Events

Les Grandes Heures de St-Émilion
MUSIC FESTIVAL

Classical concerts are held at various châteaux between March and December. Tickets (€30) must be booked in advance; the program is posted on the tourist-office website.

Marché du Gout   MARKET

A market selling regional products sets up in the village cloister from 10 to 15 October. The cloister is also the venue for **free concerts** from May to November; the tourist office has the program.

🛏 Sleeping & Eating

The village and its surrounds have some charming, but very expensive boutique hotels. If you're on a budget and don't want to camp, it might be better to visit on a day trip from Bordeaux. Ask the tourist office for a list of nearby, and much cheaper, *chambres d'hôte*. Many of St-Émilion's best restaurants are attached to hotels.

VILLAGE CENTRE
Hôtel-Restaurant du Palais Cardinal
HISTORIC HOTEL €€

(☑05 57 24 72 39; www.palais-cardinal.com; place du 11 Novembre 1918; s/d from €71/88, menus from €28; 🛜⬛🅿) Run by the same family for five generations, this hotel puts a little more thought into its dress sense than the other 'cheap' St-Émilion hotels. The heated pool is set in rambling flower-filled gardens and framed by sections of the original medieval town-wall fortifications, dating from the 13th century. It's well worth partaking in the gastronomic fare served at its restaurant (closed lunch Wednesday and Thursday, and December to March).

Auberge de la Commanderie
TRADITIONAL HOTEL €€

(☑05 57 24 70 19; www.aubergedelacommanderie.com; 2 rue Porte Brunet; r from €76; ⊘mid-Feb–mid-Jan; 🛜🅿) Inside this hotel's 13th-century walls, rooms are modernised with massive murals depicting a Technicolorised pop-art version of an old black-and-white postcard of the village. Larger rooms are in an annexe over the road. Breakfast is €10.

Hostellerie de Plaisance BOUTIQUE HOTEL €€€

(☑05 57 55 07 55; www.hostellerie-plaisance. com; place du Clocher; ste €510-670; ⊘closed Jan; ❄🛜) With a spice-coloured bar opening to a wraparound terrace, this intimate gem in the shadow of the bell tower houses 17 whimsical rooms. (A glass lift concealed in a gazebo whisks you through the rock face down to the new wing.) The rooms are about the size of a castle and look out over a flurry of red terracotta roof tiles and a church tower, but, good as it is, you can't help feeling that it's overpriced. Breakfast is an impressive €28 per person.

Hôtel au Logis des Remparts
TRADITIONAL HOTEL €€

(☑05 57 24 70 43; www.logisdesremparts.com; 18 rue Porte Guadet; r with street/garden view from €98/140; ❄🛜⬛) In a thoughtfully restored town house, the modern rooms are comfortable but lack much sparkle. Much more

exciting is the courtyard garden and swimming pool. Breakfast is €14.

TOP CHOICE / Restaurant Hostellerie de Plaisance
GASTRONOMIC €€€

(☑05 57 55 07 55; www.hostellerie-plaisance. com; place du Clocher; menus €95-130; ⊘closed Sun-Mon) Award-winning chef Philippe Etchebest cooks up food like you've never had before at his double-Michelin-starred restaurant housed in a dining room of eggshell blue and white gold inside the hotel of the same name. The 'discovery menu' allows you to do just that in about eight courses. Advance reservations essential.

L'Huîtres Pie
SEAFOOD €€

(☑05 57 24 69 71; 11 rue de la Porte Bouqueyre; lunch/dinner menus €18/32; ⊘closed Tue & Wed) Arcachon oysters and other seafood feature heavily in the dishes on offer here, but if slippery shellfish don't do it for you, tuck into one of the hearty meat or fish dishes. You can eat inside or outside on the pleasant olive-shaded courtyard.

L'Envers du Décor
REGIONAL CUISINE €€

(☑05 57 74 48 31; http://envers-dudecor.com; 11 rue du Clocher; lunch/dinner menus €19/30) Warmed by a wood fire in the cooler months and with a shady terrace hidden down an alleyway for the warmer ones, this local favourite serves market-fresh dishes.

AROUND ST-ÉMILION
Grand Barrail
HISTORIC HOTEL €€€

(☑05 57 55 37 00; www.grand-barrail.com; rte de Libourne/D243; r from €290, menus from €28; ❄🛜⬛) Grand doesn't even begin to describe this immense 1850-built château, 3km from the village, with its decadent on-site spa, stone-flagged heated swimming pool, free state-of-the-art fitness room, wheelchair access and, if you happen to be arriving by helicopter, its own helipad on the front lawns. Undoubtedly the best seat in its restaurant is the corner table framed by 19th-century stained glass that would make the average church green with envy.

Château de Roques
HISTORIC HOTEL €€

(☑05 57 74 55 69; www.chateau-de-roques.com; Puisseguin; d €71-111, menus from €24; 🛜⬛) If you've dreamed of staying in a romantic countryside château but your budget – or lack thereof – was a rude awakening, you'll be delighted by this affordable 16th-century place in the vineyards, 5km outside St-Émilion. Its restaurant (closed late December to early February) serves foie gras with Cognac and jelly made from locally produced Sauternes white wine. There's good wheelchair access. The best road is the D122 (north from St-Émilion) – the château is just near the junction of the D21.

Camping Domaine de la Barbanne

CAMPGROUND €

(☑05 57 24 75 80; www.camping-saint-emilion. com; rte de Montagne; sites per 2 people, tent & car €30; ☺Apr-Sep; ▣) This family-friendly campground about 2km north of St-Émilion on the D122. There's a five-night minimum for camping in July and August. Cabins, sleeping up to five people, are also available.

Self-catering

Boulangeries (bakeries), such as the one on rue de la Grande Fontaine, open to around 7pm. A **market** fills place de la Porte Bouqueyre every Sunday. Utile Grocery (☺8am-7pm Mon-Sat, to 1pm Sun May–mid-Sep) is a supermarket on the D122, 150m north of town.

Shopping

St-Émilion's sloping streets and squares are lined with about 50 wine shops – one for every eight of the old city's residents. The largest is the Maison du Vin (place Pierre Meyrat; ☺9.30am-12.30pm & 2-6pm), which is owned by the 250 châteaux whose wines it sells at cellar-door prices. It also has a free aromatic exhibit and sells specialist publications. If you think St-Émilion is a good place to get a few bottles of cut-price cheapo wine, then think again. It's all quality only, with price tags to match – a very fast perusal of a few shops showed a top-dollar price of €9200 for a bottle of Petrus 1947. Not the sort of bottle you'd want airport customs confiscating from your hand luggage!

Ursuline nuns brought the recipe for *macarons* (macaroons – almond biscuits) to St-Émilion in the 17th century. Specialist shops around town charge €6 per two dozen.

ℹ Information

The pharmacy and most banks are along rue Guadet.

Post office (rue Guadet) Can exchange currency.

Tourist kiosk (place de l'Église Monolithe) Summertime kiosk with varying hours (usually 10am to noon and 2pm to 6pm Monday to Friday and some weekends).

Tourist office (05 57 55 28 28; www.saint-emilion-tourisme.com; place des Créneaux; ☺9.30am-12.30pm & 1.45-6.30pm) Stacks of brochures in English and details on visiting more than 100 nearby châteaux.

ℹ Getting There & Away

BICYCLE Year-round the tourist office rents out bicycles for €15 per day.

BUS Citram Aquitaine (www.citram.fr, in French) buses to/from Bordeaux' train station run twice daily throughout the summer (single/return €8/13, from Bordeaux 9.20am and 12.25pm, from St-Émilion for Bordeaux 1.35pm and 6pm).

CAR From Bordeaux, follow the signs for Libourne and take the D243.

TAXI To book a taxi call ☑06 77 75 36 64 (www.taxi-st-emilion.com).

TRAIN It's easier to take a train from Bordeaux, with around half a dozen services a day (€8, 35min). St-Émilion station is a kilometre south of town.

Arcachon

POP 11,965

A long-time oyster-harvesting area on the southern side of the tranquil, triangular Bassin d'Arcachon (Arcachon Bay), this seaside town lured bourgeois Bordelaise at the end of the 19th century. Its four little quarters are romantically named for each of the seasons, with villas that evoke the town's golden past amid a scattering of 1950s architecture.

Arcachon seethes with sun-seekers in summer, but you'll find practically deserted beaches a short bike ride away.

◉ Sights

Town & Beaches

TOWN, BEACHES

In the Ville d'Été (Summer Quarter), Arcachon's sandy beach, Plage d'Arcachon, is flanked by two piers. Lively Jetée Thiers is at the western end. In front of the eastern pier, Jetée D'Eyrac, stands the town's turreted Casino de la Plage, built by Adalbert Deganne in 1953 as an exact replica of Château de Boursault in the Marne. Inside, it's a less-grand blinking and bell-ringing riot of poker machines and gaming tables.

On the tree-covered hillside south of the Ville d'Été, the century-old **Ville d'Hiver** (Winter Quarter) has over 300 villas, many decorated with delicate wood tracery, ranging in style from neo-Gothic through to colonial. It's an easy stroll or a short ride up the **art deco public lift** (admission free) in Parc Mauresque.

Aquarium et Musée AQUARIUM
(2 rue du Professeur Jolyet; adult/under 10yr €5/3.50; ☉9.45am-12.15pm & 1.45-7pm) In a wooden shack opposite the casino, this aquarium has a small collection of Atlantic fish in floodlit tanks.

☂ Activities

Ocean Roots SURF COURSES
(☎06 62 26 04 11; www.oceanroots.com; 228 bd de la Côte d'Argent, Le Moulleau; ☝) The exposed ocean beaches to the south of town generally offer good conditions for surfing. Ocean Roots offers lessons and rents out equipment. For more surf spots, see the boxed text, p645.

Cycling
Cycle paths link Arcachon with the Dune du Pilat and Biscarosse (30km to the south), and around the Bassin d'Arcachon to Cap Ferret. From here, a cyclable path parallels the beaches north to Pointe de Grave.

☞ Tours

Les Bateliers Arcachonnais BOAT TOURS
(UBA; ☎05 57 72 28 28; www.bateliers-arcachon. com, in French; ☝) Daily, year-round cruises sail around the **Île aux Oiseaux** (adult/child €14/10), the uninhabited 'bird island' in the middle of the bay. It's a haven for tern, curlew and redshank, so bring your binoculars. In summer there are regular all-day excursions (11am to 5.30pm) to the **Banc d'Arguin** (adult/child €16/11), the sand bank off the Dune du Pilat.

☙ Sleeping

Arcachon has scads of accommodation options. Many are chintzy mid-20th-century time warps, though not without charm.

Hôtel le Dauphin HISTORIC HOTEL €€
(☎05 56 83 02 89; www.dauphin-arcachon.com; 7 av Gounod; s/d from €198/108; ❄☎☔☝)

Don't miss this late-19th-century gingerbread place with patterned red-and-cream brickwork. An icon of its era, it's graced by twin semicircular staircases, magnolias and palms. Plain but spacious rooms are well set up for families. Parking is free.

Park Inn DESIGN HOTEL €€
(☎05 56 83 99 91; www.parkinn.fr; 4 rue du Professeur Jolyet; s/d from €125/135; ❄☎☝) Arcachon's version of this chain is utterly distinctive, thanks to its vivid swirled carpet, candy-striped curtains and primary-coloured modular furniture. It's a bit like bouncing around in a preschoolers' playroom. There are three wheelchair-equipped rooms and the staff are a pleasure to deal with.

☖ Eating

The bay's oysters (served raw and accompanied by the local small, flat sausages, *crepinettes*) appear on *menus* everywhere.

The beachfront promenade between Jetée Thiers and Jetée d'Eyrac is lined with restaurants and places offering pizza and crêpes, plus a couple of standout places serving seafood.

Chez Diego SEAFOOD
(☎05 56 83 84 46; bd Veyrier-Montagnères; menu €36, mains €19-44) One of the standouts among a cluster of tourist traps.

Chez Pierre SEAFOOD
(☎05 56 22 52 94; 1 bd Veyrier Montagnères; menus from €19, seafood platters €20-48) This see-and-be-seen restaurant serves up an ocean of seafood.

Aux Mille Saveurs TRADITIONAL FRENCH €€
(☎05 56 83 40 28; 25 bd du Général Leclerc; menus €19-48; ☉closed dinner Sun &Tue) In a light-filled space of flowing white tablecloths, this genteel restaurant is renowned for its traditional French fare artistically presented on fine china.

❶ Information
Tourist office (☎05 57 52 97 97; www.arca chon.com; Esplanade Georges Pompidou; ☉9am-7pm)

❶ Getting There & Away
There are frequent trains between Bordeaux and Arcachon (€10, 50 minutes).

OYSTER TASTE TEST

Oysters from each of the Bassin d'Arcachon's four oyster-breeding zones hint at subtly different flavours. See if you can detect these:

Banc d'Arguin – milk and sugar

Île aux Oiseaux – minerals

Cap Ferret – citrus

Grand Banc – roasted hazelnuts

Around Arcachon

DUNE DU PILAT

This colossal sand dune (sometimes referred to as the Dune de Pyla because of its location in the resort town of Pyla-sur-Mer), 8km south of Arcachon, stretches from the mouth of the Bassin d'Arcachon southwards for almost 3km. Already the largest in Europe, it's spreading eastwards at 4.5m a year – it has swallowed trees, a road junction and even a hotel.

The view from the top – approximately 114m above sea level – is magnificent. To the west you can see the sandy shoals at the mouth of the Bassin d'Arcachon, including the Banc d'Arguin bird reserve and Cap Ferret. Dense dark-green pine forests stretch from the base of the dune eastwards almost as far as the eye can see.

Take care swimming in this area: powerful currents swirl out to sea from the deceptively tranquil *baïnes* (little bays).

Although just a very quick trip from Arcachon, the area around the dune is an enjoyable place to kick back for a while. Most people choose to camp in one of the swag of seasonal campgrounds. Lists and information on all of these (and more bricks-and-mortar-based accommodation) can be found on www.bassin-arcachon.com.

CAP FERRET
POP 6392

Hidden within a canopy of pine trees at the tip of the Cap Ferret peninsula, the tiny village of Cap Ferret spans a mere 2km between the tranquil bay and the crashing Atlantic waves. It's crowned by its 53m-high, red-and-white lighthouse (adult/child €4.50/3; ⊙10am-7.30pm), with interactive exhibits and stunning views of the surf from the top. If you want to get closer to the surf, the Surf Center (☑05 56 60 61 05; www.surf-center.fr; 22 allées des Goëlands; ⊙Jun-Sep) rents out boards and offers lessons.

Cap Ferret is littered with campgrounds, which can be tracked down on www.bassin-arcachon.com. La Maison du Bassin (☑05 56 60 60 63; www.lamaisondubassin.com; 5 rue des Pionniers; s €120-200, d €140-240, apt €330; ⊙closed Jan) has four dreamy rooms the size of suites tucked away in a separate annexe of this quixotic hideaway, while cosy rooms in the main house have details like a muslin-canopied sleigh bed, or a curtained bathtub in the centre of the room. Its chocolate-toned contemporary restaurant, Le Bistrot du Bassin (menus €25 to €60), will make your taste buds very happy indeed.

Les Bateliers Arcachonnais (UBA; www.bateliers-arcachon.com, in French) runs ferries from Arcachon to Cap Ferret (adult/child return €11.50/8) year-round. In the warmer months, seasonally operating lines include ferries linking Cap Ferret and the Dune du Pilat, and Cap Ferret and Moulleau. Schedules are posted on the website and available from tourist offices.

Cap Ferret is a scenic drive around Bassin d'Arcachon, or to drive here directly from Bordeaux (71.8km) take the D106.

GUJAN MESTRAS
POP 17,680

Picturesque oyster ports are dotted around the town of Gujan Mestras, which sprawls along 9km of coastline.

You'll find the tourist office (☑05 56 66 12 65; www.ville-gujanmestras.fr, in French; 19 av de Lattre de Tassigny; ⊙9.30am-12.30pm & 2-6.30pm Mon-Sat, 9.30am-12.30pm Sun) at the western edge of town in La Hume.

Gujan Mestras' train station is on the train line linking Bordeaux with Arcachon.

⊙ Sights

Le Teich Parc Ornithologique
BIRDWATCHING
(Bird Reserve; ☑05 56 22 80 93; www.parc-ornithologique-du-teich.com; adult/child €7.50/5.10; ⊙10am-sunset; 🏍) A series of trails wind through and around the swamps, lakes and woodlands of the idyllic Parc Ornithologique situated in Le Teich, 5km east of Gujan Mestras. Birds also find the place much to their liking and some 260 species of migratory and

nonmigratory birds call the place home. The stars of the show are the white storks, spoonbills, common cranes, marsh harriers and black kites, all of which can be spied on from a network of well-maintained hides. Away from birds, the park is one of the most reliable places in France to see the now-threatened European pond tortoise. The pool just beyond the ticket office is a real hot spot for it.

Port de Larros   OYSTERS

Flat-bottomed oyster boats moored to weathered wooden shacks line Port de Larros, the largest oyster port around Gujan Mestras. The small **Maison de l'Huître** (adult/child €4.50/2.50; ☺10am-12.30pm & 2.30-6pm Mon-Sat) has a display on oyster farming, including a short film in English. Locally harvested oysters are sold nearby and served at seafood restaurants with waterside terraces.

French Basque Country

Best Places to Eat

» Ithurria (p654)

» Chez Arrambide (p658)

» Chiloa Gurmenta Restaurant (p637)

» Bar Bodega Xurasko (p640)

» Bar Jean (p648)

Best Places to Stay

» La Devinière (p651)

» Zazpi (p651)

» Hôtel Mirano (p644)

» Villa le Goëland (p644)

» Hôtel des Arceaux (p635)

Why Go?

Gently sloping from the foothills of the Pyrenees into the deep-sapphire-blue Bay of Biscay, the Basque Country straddles France and Spain. Yet this feisty, independent land remains profoundly different from either of the nation states that have adopted it.

The Basque Country is famed for the glitzy beach resort of Biarritz, where surfers strut their stuff in the waves, and oiled sun-seekers pack its beaches like glistening sardines. But the region offers so much more than just the pleasures of sun and surf. Nearby Bayonne is a chocolate box of narrow winding streets full of Basque culture, and St-Jean de Luz, further south, is a delightful seaside fishing port.

Inland, up in the lush hills, little one-street villages and green valleys traversed by hiking trails fan out from the walled town of St-Jean Pied de Port, an age-old stop for pilgrims heading over the Spanish border to Santiago de Compostela.

When to Go

Bayonne

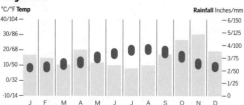

May It's chocolate time in Bayonne and the empty beaches and spring flowers of the mountains are all yours.

August The beaches are alive and kicking, and the Fêtes de Bayonne is loud and messy.

September to October Autumnal colours are glorious in the hills, and surf is as good as it gets.

Bayonne

POP 44,200

Surrounded by sturdy fortifications and splashed in red and white paint, Bayonne (Baiona in Basque), capital of the French Basque Country, is one of the most attractive towns in southwest France. Its perfectly preserved old town (until 1907 it was actually forbidden to build outside the town's fortifications) and shoals of riverside restaurants are an absolute delight to explore.

In addition to its chocolates, which you'll see sold throughout France, Bayonne is famous for its prime cured ham and for the *baïonnette* (bayonet), developed here in 1640 on rue des Faures ('Blacksmiths' Street').

The Rivers Adour and Nive split central Bayonne into three: St-Esprit, the area north of the Adour; Grand Bayonne, the oldest and most attractive part of the city, on the western bank of the Nive; and the very Basque Petit Bayonne quarter on the east.

To the west, Bayonne meets the suburban sprawl of Anglet (famed for its beaches, p641) and the glamorous seaside resort of Biarritz.

⊙ Sights & Activities

Musée Basque et de l'Histoire de Bayonne   MUSEUM
(www.musee-basque.com, in French; 37 quai des Corsaires; adult/child €5.50/free, with Musée Bonnat €9; ⊙10am-6.30pm) The seafaring history, traditions and cultural identity of the Basque people are all explored at this superb museum through exhibits including a reconstructed farm and the interior of a typical *etxe* (home). Labelling is in French, Spanish and Basque only but English information sheets are available. In July and August free 'nocturnal' visits are possible on Wednesday evenings from 6.30pm to 9.30pm.

Musée Bonnat   MUSEUM
(www.museebonnat.bayonne.fr; 5 rue Jacques Lafitte; adult/child €5.50/free, with Musée Basque €9; ⊙10am-6.30pm Wed-Mon) Unexpected treasures are crammed into the Musée Bonnat, including canvases by El Greco, Goya, Ingres and Degas, and a roomful of works by Rubens. Nearby is the Le Carré Musée Bonnat (9 rue Frédéric Bastiat; admission free), which houses the Bonnat museum's ever-changing collection of works by the Basque artists of today.

French Basque Country Highlights

❶ Discover the local chocolate at a factory tour in **Bayonne** (p637)

❷ Tiptoe along the sheer **Iparla Ridge** (p656) in the mist-soaked Pyrenees

❸ Treat yourself to tapas and watch surfers tackle the waves of magisterial **Biarritz** (p641)

❹ Taste traditional Basque seafood dishes at **St-Jean de Luz** (p653)

❺ Browse the farmers market in **St-Jean Pied de Port** (p655)

❻ Explore picturesque villages **Ainhoa** (p654) and **Espelette** (p654), and chug to the summit of **La Rhune** (p654)

❼ Soak up some sun on sands of **Hossegor** or **Moliets** in the region of Les Landes (p644)

Cathédrale Ste-Marie CATHEDRAL
(⏰10-11.45am & 3-5.45pm Mon-Sat, 3.30-6pm Sun) The twin towers of Bayonne's Gothic cathedral soar above the city. Construction began in the 13th century, and was completed in 1451; the mismatched materials in some ways resemble Lego blocks.

Above the north aisle are three lovely stained-glass windows; the oldest, in the Chapelle Saint Jérôme, dates from 1531. The entrance to the stately 13th-century **cloister** (⏰9am-12.30pm & 2-6pm) is on place Louis Pasteur.

Bayonne

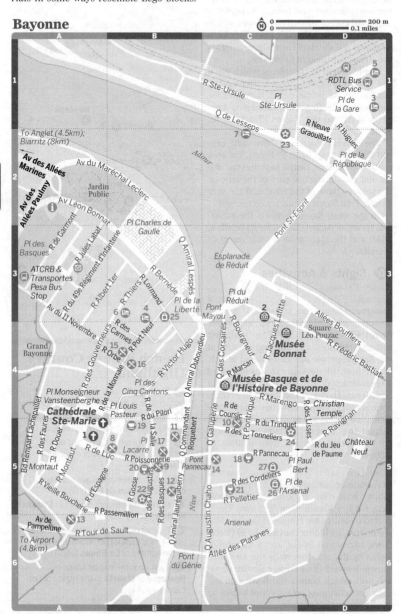

Ramparts

PARKS

Bayonne's 17th-century fortifications are now covered with grass, dotted with trees and enveloped in pretty parks. You can walk the stretches of the old ramparts that rise above bd Rempart Lachepaillet and rue Tour de Sault.

✯✦ Festivals & Events

Ham Fair
FOOD FESTIVAL

During Easter week, the town hosts a Ham Fair, honouring *jambon de Bayonne,* the acclaimed local ham. You may think this is just a recently thought up touristy gimmick to sell ham, but no – this fair in March or April has taken place annually since 1462!

Journées du Chocolat
FOOD FESTIVAL

Master chocolatiers reveal the secrets of chocolate making (with tastings) in May.

Fêtes de Bayonne
CULTURAL FESTIVAL

A five-day extravaganza of food, drink, dance and fireworks in early August.

🛏 Sleeping

Even outside the Fêtes de Bayonne, it's tough to find a bed from mid-July to mid-August.

TOP CHOICE Hôtel des Arceaux BOUTIQUE HOTEL €€
(☎05 59 59 15 53; www.hotel-arceaux.com, in French; 26 rue Port Neuf; d from €79; 🖳)

If this hotel, which is located on one of the prettiest streets in the old town, were a pop star it would surely have to be Lady Gaga or some other flamboyant and over-the-top personality. It easily has more flair and character than all the other hotels in Bayonne put together, and is very well run. All the rooms (some of which can accommodate families) are different, so ask to see a few first.

Péniche Djébelle HOUSEBOAT €€
(☎05 59 25 77 18; www.djebelle.com; face au 17 Quai de Lesseps; d with breakfast €140; ☺closed Oct-Apr) Now here's something really different – can you guess what it is? If you stay here you'll have the best river view in the city, and there's also a chance that you might go to sleep in Bayonne and wake up elsewhere else. Got it yet? Here's a final clue: there's a chance your fellow guests will be mermaids or pirates. Yes, you've guessed it. This unique *chambre d'hôte* is in fact a houseboat floating in the River Ardour! And don't make the mistake of thinking that just because it's a boat it will be uncomfortable, because it's quite the opposite. The two rooms are immaculate and imaginatively decorated; one has a Moroccan theme and the other, which even has the boat's steering wheel built into the bathroom, is full of thoughts of tropical islands. Advance booking essential.

FRENCH BASQUE COUNTRY BAYONNE

FÊTES DE BAYONNE

Beginning on the first Wednesday in August (or occasionally the last in July), the Fêtes de Bayonne attracts up to a million people from across France and Spain for a five-day-long orgy of drinking, dancing, processions, fireworks and bulls. In many ways it's like a less commercialised version of the famous San Fermín festival in Pamplona (Spain) and, just like in Pamplona, Bayonne also indulges in a bit of bull running. However, here the bulls are actually cows – though they still have horns and they still hurt when they mow you down! – and they don't run down the streets, but are instead released on the crowd in front of the Château Neuf. During the *fête,* bullfights take place in the 10,000-seat Les Arènes (tickets from €20; bullfights also take place at other times through the summer; ask at the tourist office for dates and to purchase tickets).

One of the biggest highlights of the *fête* is the opening ceremony, which takes place in front of the Hôtel de Ville at 10pm on the Wednesday night. While the nocturnal activities might be a bit much for children, the daytime processions, marching bands, organised children's picnics and even a children's 'bull' run are tailor-made for the delight of little ones.

If you're planning on attending the *fête,* unless you book at least six to eight months in advance you can give up right now on finding hotel accommodation anywhere in the vicinity of Bayonne. A number of temporary campgrounds (€40 for five days) are erected in and around Bayonne to ease the pressure; otherwise you can just do what most people do and sleep in the back of a car, under a bush or in a pile of vomit (camping outside one of the campgrounds is forbidden). Women would be advised to avoid sleeping rough unless in a group.

Finally, unless you want to stand out like a sore thumb, don't forget to dress all in white with a red sash and neck-scarf. For dates and other *fête* information, see www.fetes.bayonne.fr.

Hôtel Côte Basque TRADITIONAL HOTEL €
(☎05 59 55 10 21; www.hotel-cotebasque.fr; 2 rue Maubec; r from €65; ✳☎) Ride the clanky old-fashioned lift up to your modern room with low-slung beds and colourful art on the walls. Sitting opposite the train station, this recently renovated place offers sizzling value for money. From the end of July to mid-August room rates rise to a minimum of €100.

Hotel Paris-Madrid TRADITIONAL HOTEL €
(☎05 59 55 13 98; sorbois@wanadoo.fr; place de la Gare; r from €38; @) This place, right next to the train station, is a zoo – you'll find crocodiles hanging out behind the reception desk and giraffes sticking their necks into all sorts of unexpected places. It's lively, colourful and oozes character (although the rooms themselves are quite plain and many share bathrooms), and the price is, well, almost unbelievable. For a while now rumours have been floating around that the building is due for demolition to make way for a new high-speed train line (a project that is proving highly unpopular with locals concerned about the environmental damage it's expected to cause). Reservation is by email only.

Le Grand Hôtel HISTORIC HOTEL €€
(☎05 59 59 62 00; www.legrandhotelbayonne.com; 21 rue Thiers; s/d from €106/111; ✳☎♿) This old building was once a convent, but when they ran out of nuns someone turned it into a hotel. Now its cream-toned, wheelchair-accessible rooms and cosy on-site bar (which probably didn't exist when it was a convent) make this friendly business-class hotel a fine place to rest up. Parking's €13.

Auberge de Jeunesse HOSTEL €
(☎05 59 58 70 00; www.hibiarritz.org; 19 rte des Vignes, Anglet; dm incl breakfast €19, camping incl breakfast €12; ☺reception 8.30am-12.30pm & 6-10pm, closed early Nov-Mar; @) In the nearby beach suburb of Anglet, this hostel has reached legendary status for its nonstop international party scene. To keep people well oiled, it comes complete with a basement Scottish pub screening surf films. From the Mairie de Bayonne (Town Hall) bus stop, take bus 7 (C on Sunday and public holidays) to the stop for Les Sables, from where it's a 500m uphill walk. Alternatively, you can catch that bus from Biarritz train station to the Auberge de Jeunesse stop. You

have to be an HI member to stay (you can sign up on arrival).

Eating

Bayonne has some superb places to eat and costs are generally much lower than in nearby Biarritz. Restaurants proliferate around the covered market and nearby quai Amiral Jauréguiberry, as well as quai Galuperie and quai des Corsaires across the River Nive.

TOP CHOICE Chiloa Gurmenta Restaurant

BASQUE €

(7 rue des Tonneliers; menu/mains €12.50/10; 🛗) As Basque as a game of *pelota*, this simple and rustic little restaurant, located inside a former brothel, serves one thing and one thing only: *axoa*. A Basque farmers' dish, *axoa* originates from the nearby village of Espelette and consists of minced veal with Espelette peppers, rice, potato and whatever else is lying around. Anne, your host for the evening, could work in show business.

Al Piccola Ristorante

ITALIAN €€

(☏05 59 59 54 87; 63 rue d'Espagne; mains €12; ⊘lunch Mon-Sat) Every lunchtime a queue of hopefuls forms at the door of this minute restaurant that's essentially just someone's front room. The reward for all that waiting are the beautifully crafted, homemade Italian dishes that'll leave you feeling like you're living *la dolce vita*. If you don't want to join the hopefuls at the door, book ahead.

Bar-Restaurant du Marché

BASQUE €

(☏05 59 59 22 66; 39 rue des Basques; menu/mains €13/7.50; ⊘lunch Mon-Sat) Run by a welcoming Basque-speaking family, this unpretentious place is an absolute institution where everyone knows everyone (and therefore some people may find it slightly intimidating, but don't worry; just dive right in – nobody cares!) and simple but ample home-cooked dishes full of the flavours of the neighbouring market are dished up to all comers.

La Criée Bayonnaise

SEAFOOD €€

(☏05 59 59 56 60; 14 quai Chaho; menus from €15, mains €13-15; ⊘lunch Mon-Sat, dinner Tue-Sat) Decked out in marine colours, this unassuming little find does delicious Basque seafood specialities (such as *les chipirons à l'espagnole* – squid with sweet peppers served with finely ground rice), but you can also get fresh mussels and even fish and chips. For dessert, don't miss the *ardi gasna* (local cheese with cherry jam).

Restaurant Agadir

MOROCCAN €€

(☏05 59 55 66 56; 3 rue Ste-Catherine; menu €15, mains €9-15; ⊘closed lunch Mon) Shimmering with red and gold, this St-Esprit restaurant serves up mountains of Moroccan-style couscous and steaming tagines.

Le Chistera

BASQUE €€

(☏05 59 59 25 93; 42 rue Port Neuf; mains €10-16; ⊘lunch Tue-Sun, dinner Thu-Sun) A local gathering spot, this aromatic, traditional Basque place is named for the *chistera* (basket) that *pelota* players strap to their wrists. It's decorated with motifs from the sport, thanks to two generations of owners who are former professional players.

La Chayote Restaurant Bio

VEGETARIAN €

(9 rue d'Espagne; menu €13; ⊘lunch Mon-Sat; ⏏🛗) A relaxed child-friendly *bio* (organic) café that serves primarily homemade vegetarian fare, although one or two chicken dishes slip in to keep the carnivores happy.

FRENCH BASQUE COUNTRY BAYONNE

BAYONNE CHOCOLATE

Bayonne's long association with chocolate stems from the Spanish Inquisition, when Jews who fled Spain set up their trade in the St-Esprit neighbourhood. By 1870 Bayonne boasted 130 chocolatiers (specialist makers of chocolate), more than in all of Switzerland. Today, 11 are still in business, including **Daranatz** (15 rue Port Neuf) and the 19th-century **Cazenave** (19 rue Port Neuf), which does a sublime *chocolat mousseaux* (rich hot chocolate; €5.50). You can see chocolate being made at **L'Atelier du Chocolat** (www.atelierduchocolat.fr, in French; 1 allée de Gibéléou; adult/child €6/3; ⊘9.30am-6.30pm Mon-Sat), including a historical overview of chocolate in Bayonne and, of course, tastings.

Tastings are also the highlight of the weekend-long **Journées du Chocolat** each May, when master chocolatiers set up the tools of their craft in front of their shops.

For more chocolate heaven, pop by the Planète Musée du Chocolat in Biarritz (p643).

Basque Culture

Call a Basque French or Spanish and it's almost certain you'll receive a glare and a stern 'I'm Basque!' in return. The Basques have over time developed a culture unique in Europe.

The regional game is *pelote Basque (pelota)* and you'll notice every village has its own court – normally backing up against the village church. *Pelota* is actually the generic name for a group of 16 different native Basque ball games, but the most well known has players using a scooplike basket called a *chistera*. Some players are able to throw the ball at speeds of up to 300km/h.

Throughout France the Basques are also famous for their festivals. Some, like La Fête du Thon in St-Jean de Luz (p648), celebrate the region's superlative food. Others, such as the Fêtes de Bayonne (p636), simply celebrate the Basques' sheer joy for life.

Basque festivals are also a good opportunities to see traditional Basque dress. It's said that there are around 400 different Basque dances, many of which require their own special kind of outfit.

But perhaps the most visible symbol of Basque culture is the *lauburu,* also known as the Basque cross and regarded as a symbol of prosperity. It's also used to signify life and death.

TOP BASQUE EATS

» **Piment d'Espelette** This little chilli pepper is an essential accompaniment to many a Basque meal.

» **Fromage des Pyrénées** Cheese – buy it fresh, straight from a shepherd. The best-known cheese is Ossau-Iraty.

» **Jambon de Bayonne** Wafer-thin ham has a fair devoted to it (p635).

» **Axoa** Classic dish – try it at Bayonne's Chiloa Gurmenta Restaurant (p637).

» **Bayonne chocolate** The best chocolate shops in the country (p637).

Clockwise from top left
1. *Pelote Basque* in action 2. Crowds at the Fêtes de Bayonne 3. Gathering at Les Arènes, Bayonne

After eating, slide through the side door to the neighbouring *bio* supermarket.

Self-Catering

The **covered market** (quai Commandant Roquebert) sits on the riverfront. There are a number of tempting food shops and delicatessens along rue Port Neuf and rue d'Espagne. Pick up staples at **Monoprix** (8 rue Orbe).

Drinking

Petit Bayonne is awash with pubs and bars (all generally open from noon to 2am, Monday to Saturday), especially along rue Pannecau, rue des Cordeliers and quai Galuperie.

Chai Ramina   BAR
(11 rue Poissonnerie) In fine weather, rue Poissonnerie is completely blocked by the huge crowds spilling out of Chai Ramina.

Café-Bar Le Patio   BAR
(38 rue Pannecau) Another lively night-time spot.

Massaï Café   BAR
(14 rue des Cordeliers) The place to sip cocktails on rue des Cordeliers.

Cafés Ramuntcho   TEAROOM
(9 rue du Pilori) To sip (or buy to take home) no fewer than 380 different teas (reputedly the most in France), take a seat amid the metal canisters of this café, established in 1920.

Entertainment

Upcoming cultural events are listed in *À l'Affiche* and the trimestrial *Les Saisons de la Culture,* both available free at the tourist office. Every Thursday in July and August, there's traditional **Basque music** (admission free; ⊙9.30pm) in place Charles de Gaulle. Between October and June **Trinquet St-André** (rue des tonneliers; tickets around €9) stages *main nue pelota* matches every Thursday at 4.30pm.

L'Autre Cinéma   CINEMA
(3 quai Sala) Along with its sister cinema, **Cinéma l'Atalante** (www.cinema-atalante. org, in French; 7 rue Denis Etcheverry), L'Autre screens art-house nondubbed films. Both cinemas are in the St-Esprit neighbourhood.

La Luna Negra   MUSIC
(www.lunanegra.fr; in French; rue des Augustins; ⊙7pm-2am Wed-Sat) Catch live jazz, salsa and tango evenings and concerts of world music at this alternative cabaret/theatre venue.

Shopping

For chocolate, head to Daranatz or Cazenave on rue Port Neuf.

Pierre Ibaïalde   FOOD
(41 rue des Cordeliers) To buy Bayonne's famous ham at the lowest prices, visit the covered market or, for the best quality, visit a specialist shop such as Pierre Ibaïalde, where you can taste before you buy.

Elkar   BOOKS
(place de l'Arsenal) Elkar has a wealth of books and films on Basque history and culture, walking in the Basque Country, maps and CDs of Basque music.

Information

There are several internet cafés in the streets around the train station.

Post office (11 rue Jules Labat & 21 bd Alsace-Lorraine)

A TASTE OF SPAIN

You know you're getting close to the border when tapas start cropping up. Bayonne has an increasing number of *pintxo* (tapas in Basque) bars and in some the quality is every bit as good as the legendary *pintxo* bars of San Sebastián, just over the border in Spain. Two of the best are the bar bodegas **Xurasko** (16 rue Poissonnerie; pintxos from €2.50) and **Ibaia** (45 quai Amiral Jauréguiberry; raciones from €8; ⊙closed Sun & Mon Oct-Mar). Tapas start to decorate the bar like little flowers at Xurasko from 7pm and as everyone clocks off work they stop by for a glass of wine and some choice titbits. The golden rule of tapas is to just take one or two (which you pay for when you leave) before moving on to try those elsewhere – only tourists pile their plates up and scoff loads of them! And when you do move on from Xurasko you'd best go straight to Ibaia, which, with hams swinging from hooks in the ceiling and a garlic-heavy atmosphere, is a Bayonne legend. Here the emphasis is more on larger plates of hot tapas such as garlic prawns and spicy chorizo sausages, which you order off a blackboard menu. One plate is often enough for two people.

Tourist office (☑08 20 42 64 64; www. bayonne-tourisme.com; place des Basques; ⊙9am-7pm Mon-Sat, 10am-1pm Sun) Efficient, friendly office providing stacks of informative brochures and free bike rental, plus guided city tours (by appointment only; from €100 for any group of less than 20).

Getting There & Away

Air

Biarritz-Anglet-Bayonne airport (☑05 59 43 83 83; www.biarritz.aeroport.fr) is 5km south-west of central Bayonne and 3km southeast of the centre of Biarritz. It's served by low-cost carriers including EasyJet and Ryanair, as well as Air France, with daily domestic flights and flights to the UK, and regular flights to Ireland, Finland, Switzerland and Holland.

Bus 6 links both Bayonne and Biarritz with the airport (€1.20, buses depart roughly hourly). A taxi from the town centre costs around €15 to €20.

Bus

From place des Basques, **ATCRB buses** follow the coast to the Spanish border. There are nine services daily to St-Jean de Luz (€3, 40 minutes) with connections for Hendaye (€3, one hour). Summer beach traffic can double journey times. **Transportes Pesa** (www.pesa.net) buses leave twice a day Monday to Saturday for Bilbao (€18.50) in Spain, calling by Biarritz, St-Jean de Luz, Irún and San Sebastián (€8.50).

From the train station, **RDTL** (www.rdtl.fr, in French) runs services northwards into Les Landes including Capbreton/Hossegor (€2, 40 minutes, six or seven daily).

Car & Motorcycle

All the big car-rental agencies are represented at the airport; otherwise, close to the train station is **Avis** (www.avis.fr; 1 rue Ste-Ursule).

Train

TGVs run between Bayonne and Paris Gare Montparnasse (€97, five to six hours, eight daily).

There are five trains daily to St-Jean Pied de Port (€9, 1¼ hours) and fairly frequent services to St-Jean de Luz (€4.50, 25 minutes) via Biarritz (€2.50, nine minutes), plus the French and Spanish border towns of Hendaye (€7, 40 minutes) and Irún (from €7, 45 minutes). For travel between Bayonne and Biarritz, however, buses are cheaper and more frequent.

Other services:

Bordeaux from €28, two hours, at least 10 daily

Pau €16, 1¼ hours, nine daily

Toulouse from €40, 3¾ hours, five daily

ⓘ Getting Around

BICYCLE Bayonne's tourist office lends out bikes for free (not overnight); you simply need to leave some ID as a deposit.

BUS STAB buses link Bayonne, Biarritz and Anglet. A single ticket costs €1.20, while *carnets* of five/10 are €5/9.50. Timetables are available from STAB's **information office** (www.bus-stab. com, in French; place du Gaulle). Buses 1 and 2 run between Bayonne and Biarritz about 50 times daily, stopping at the *hôtels de ville* (town halls) and stations of both towns. No 1, which runs every 15 minutes until 8.30pm, is the fastest and most frequent. A free bright-orange *navette* (shuttle bus) loops around the heart of town.

CAR & MOTORCYCLE There's free parking along the southern end of av des Allées Paulmy, within easy walking distance of the tourist office.

TAXI Call **Taxi Bayonne** (☑05 59 59 48 48)

Biarritz

POP 30,700

As ritzy as its name suggests, this stylish coastal town, 8km west of Bayonne, took off as a resort in the mid-19th century when Napoléon III and his Spanish-born wife, Eugénie, visited regularly. Along its rocky coastline are architectural hallmarks of this golden age, and the belle-époque and art deco eras that followed. Although it retains a high glamour quotient (and high prices to match), it's also a magnet for van-loads of surfers, with some of Europe's best waves.

◉ Sights & Activities

Beaches
BEACHES

Biarritz' raison d'être is its fashionable beaches, particularly the two central Grande Plage and Plage Miramar, which are lined end to end with sunbathing bodies on hot summer days. Stripy 1920s-style **beach tents** can be hired for €9.50 per day. The other central Biarritz beach is the tiny cove of Plage du Port Vieux which, thanks to its lack of swell, is the best one for young children to splash about on. North of Pointe St-Martin, the adrenaline-pumping surfing beaches of Anglet (the final 't' is pronounced) continue northwards for more than 4km. Take eastbound bus 9 (line C on Sunday and public holidays) from the bottom of av Verdun (just near av Édouard VII).

To the south, beyond the long, exposed Plage de la Côte des Basques, some 500m

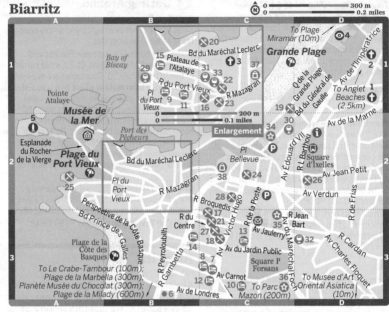

Biarritz

south of Port Vieux, are Plage de Marbella and Plage de la Milady. Take westbound bus 9 from rue Gambetta where it crosses rue Broquedis.

Musée de la Mer   AQUARIUM
(www.museedelamer.com; Esplanade du Rocher de la Vierge; adult/child €8/5.50; ⊙9.30am-midnight) Housed in a wonderful art deco building, Biarritz' Musée de la Mer is seething with underwater life from the Bay of Biscay and beyond, as well as exhibits on fishing recalling Biarritz' whaling past. It's the seals that steal the show though (feeding time, which is always a favourite with children, is at 10.30am and 5pm). In high season it's possible to have the place almost to yourself by visiting late at night.

Arty art deco   ARCHITECTURE
From art deco mansions to Russian Orthodox churches and 1970s tower-block disasters, Biarritz has a fantastic potpourri of architectural styles. If the swell's big, you might get a drenching as you cross the footbridge at the end of Pointe Atalaye to Rocher de la Vierge (Rock of the Virgin), named after its white statue of the Virgin and child. Views from this impressive outcrop extend to the mountains of the Spanish Basque Country.

The tiny fishing port of Port des Pêcheurs is an atmospheric place for a drink or a meal. Above it, the neo-Gothic Église Ste-Eugénie was built in the late 1800s for – who else? – Empress Eugénie.

Dominating the northern end of the Grande Plage is the 19th-century Hôtel du Palais, also built for Empress Eugénie and now a luxury hotel. Opposite is Église Alexandre Newsky (8 av de l'Impératrice), a Russian Orthodox church built by and for the Russian aristocrats who frequented Biarritz until the Soviet Revolution. Eugénie was also the inspiration for the nearby doll's-house-sized Chapelle Impériale (⊙3-7pm Tue, Thu & Sat), constructed in 1864.

Climbing the 258 twisting steps inside the 73m-high Phare de Biarritz (admission €2.50; ⊙10am-12.30pm & 2.30-7pm), the town's 1834 lighthouse, rewards you with sweeping views of the Basque coast.

Musée d'Art Oriental Asiatica   ART MUSEUM
(www.museeasiatica.com; 1 rue Guy Petit; admission €7; ⊙10.30am-6.30pm Mon-Fri, 2-7pm Sat-Sun) Out on the edge of town is this unexpected treasure trove of ancient Indian, Chinese and Tibetan statues, monuments and temple artwork. The layout is a bit haphazard, but the information cards (in several languages) clearly explain the significance of the objects. It's generally considered the finest collection of its type outside Paris.

Surfing   SURF COURSES
Once the almost exclusive haunt of the rich and pampered, Biarritz is now known more as the capital of European surfing (although in truth, the real centre of European surfing is the small town of Hossegor around 25km to the north). Grande Plage itself is good from mid-low tide on a moderate swell, whereas the 4km-long stretch of beaches that make up Anglet are more consistent and generally better.

No fewer than a dozen places around town offer gear and lessons (from €35 per hour); the tourist office keeps a list of most of the surf schools. You should ensure that the school you choose is registered with the Féderation Française de Surf (FFS; www.surfingfrance.com, in French) as some of those not registered with the FFS are slightly fly-by-night operators whose staff may have only a little more surf knowledge than the pupils. Even with the registered schools, the instructors often seem to use the lessons merely as an excuse to go surfing themselves.

Planète Musée du Chocolat
CHOCOLATE MUSEUM
(www.planetemuseeduchocolat.com; 14 av Beau Rivage; adult/child €6/4; ⊙10am-12.30pm & 2.30-6.30pm Mon-Sat) Delve into this real-life *Charlie and the Chocolate Factory* for an indulgent exploration through the world of chocolate, from its earliest beginnings to the mass production of today.

★ Festivals & Events
Major surfing competitions take place year-round.

Biarritz Maider Arosteguy   SURFING
A three-day surfing championship is held at Easter.

Festival des Arts de la Rue   CULTURAL FESTIVAL
Performance artists take to the streets for five days in early May.

Roxy Jam   SURFING
(www.roxyjam.com) A major female longboarding championship on the ASP (Association of Surfing Professionals) circuit, with spin-off events like concerts, held over five days in mid-July.

BEACHES OF LES LANDES

North of Bayonne is the *département* of Les Landes, a vast semiwilderness of pine forests and lakes. This whole area has a special kind of wild beauty, criss-crossed with excellent cycling and walking trails; maps and route suggestions are available from most tourist offices. The trails are broken up by numerous lakes, the best being at Soustons and the small village of Léon, with opportunities for windsurfing, canoeing and other water sports. But for most people, the reason to visit Les Landes is its beaches. From the mouth of the Ardour at Anglet north to Arcachon and beyond to the mouth of the Gironde stretches a ribbon of shimmering golden sand backed by dunes and basking under a deep-blue sky.

Above all else, this is surf country. Towns such as the twin centres of Capbreton and Hossegor now owe their existence to surfing. Capbreton, which still retains some life beyond the waves, is easily the more appealing of the two and its small port supplies the town's numerous seafood restaurants with delicious fresh fish.

Chez Du Camp (☎ 05 58 72 11 33; 4 rue Port d'Albert; menus €28-38, mains €16) is one of the best places in town to indulge. You can sit at a table overlooking ocean-sized tanks swimming with the imminent contents of your dinner. Or, even better, pick from a mix of prawns, mussels, crab, squid and whatever else the boats brought in that morning, get it all cooked up on the spot and then take it away to have as a picnic.

Brash Hossegor, no more than a kilometre north of Capbreton, is renowned for having some of the best beach break waves in the world (see p645), but it has to be said that this reputation has made it the very definition of a 'hey, dude' surf town, where if you're not wearing the right pair of sunglasses or T-shirt you're just not going to be welcome at the party. On the plus side, the beaches here are breathtaking and they only get better the further north towards the village of Seignosse you go. For eating you won't do better than La Tetrade (☎ 05 58 43 51 48; 1187 ave du Touring Club de France; weekday lunch menus €19.40, other times €28-33). Set on the banks of Hossegor's lake, it offers the kind of view to get married to, and a shellfish and seafood menu you'd also marry if you could.

But for the best beach of all, one that's up there with the best in France, you have to continue north another 20 minutes to the tiny seasonal village of Moliets. The vast beach here, which sits at the mouth of a sluggish and inky-coloured river known as the Courant d'Huchet, has sand that sparkles like diamonds and is soft as feathers, while the river itself provides safe bathing for children.

Unfortunately, most of the limited hotel accommodation in this region is seriously poor value and most visitors end up camping at one of the dozens of campgrounds that litter the coast. Local tourist offices can supply details.

Le Temps d'Aimer   DANCE FESTIVAL
A two-week celebration of dance in all its forms is held in mid-September.

🛌 Sleeping

Inexpensive hotels are a rarity in Biarritz, and any kind of room is at a premium in July and August. Outside the high season, however, most prices fall by a good 25%.

TOP CHOICE   Hôtel Mirano   BOUTIQUE HOTEL €€
(☎ 05 59 23 11 63; www.hotelmirano.fr, in French; 11 av Pasteur; d €100-110, ste €140) Squiggly purple, orange and black wallpaper and oversize orange perspex light fittings are some of the rad '70s touches at

this boutique retro hotel, a 10-minute stroll from the town centre. The staff go above and beyond the call of duty in order to please. Oh, and there's a flirty Betty Boop bursting out of her top in the bar! All up, this eccentrically stylish place offers one of the best deals in town. To get there take the D910 southeast out of town, turn left onto av de Grammont and right onto av Pasteur. It's a good 10-minute walk from the centre.

Villa le Goëland   HISTORIC HOTEL €€€
(☎ 05 59 24 25 76; www.villagoeland.com; 12 plateau de l'Atalaye; r from €170; 🐾) This stunning family home with its château-like spires perched high on a plateau above Pointe

Atalaye is one of the most notable buildings in town. Rooms, tastefully furnished with antiques, family photos and mementos, have panoramic views of the town, sea and across to Spain. There are only four rooms (opt for *chambre Goëland* with its huge 35-sq-metre private terrace; €250), so advance booking is essential.

Hôtel Édouard VII   HISTORIC HOTEL €€
(☎05 59 22 39 80; www.hotel-edouardvii.com; 21 av Carnot; d from €118; �✆🖵) From the ornate dining room full of gently tick-tocking clocks to the pots of lavender carefully colour coordinated to match the floral wallpaper, everything about this beautiful and intimate hotel screams 1920s Biarritz chic.

Maison Garnier   BOUTIIQUE HOTEL €€
(☎05 59 01 60 70; www.hotel-biarritz.com; 29 rue Gambetta; r from €115) The seven boutique 'rooms' (suites would be a better description) of this elegant mansion are tastefully decorated and furnished in cool, neutral tones; those up at attic level are especially romantic. A seriously decent breakfast costs an extra €11.

Hôtel les Alizés   BOUTIQUE HOTEL €
(☎05 59 24 11 74; www.alizes-biarritz.com; 13 rue du Port Vieux; s/d/ste €62/90/179; ✆) With its brash and blushing shades clashing brilliantly with the old-fashioned desks and wardrobes, this funky family-run hotel is one of the more memorable cheapies in town. Its position, just back from the cute Plage du Port Vieux, is spot on.

Hôtel Maïtagaria   TRADITIONAL HOTEL €€
(☎05 59 24 26 65; www.hotel-maitagaria.com; 34 av Carnot; s/d €72/83) Overlooking the park, the spotless modern rooms with art deco furniture, leopard-print furnishings and immaculate bathrooms make this friendly place good value. Not least of its charms is its summer terrace opening off the comfy guest lounge, which is warmed in winter by a toasty open fire.

Hôtel St-Julien   TRADITIONAL HOTEL €€
(☎05 59 24 20 39; www.saint-julien-biarritz. com, in French; 20 av Carnot; d €120-130; ✆) A bright shuttered facade graces this attractive late-19th-century villa, with original parquet flooring inside. Third-floor rooms have views of both mountains and sea. Its undoubted quality means it fills quickly. English is spoken.

Hôtel Palym   TRADITIONAL HOTEL €
(☎05 59 24 16 56; 7 rue du Port Vieux; r with toilet €40, r with bathroom €45-58; ⊘mid-Jan–mid-Nov) This welcoming 20-room, family-run place occupies a brightly painted town house on a street packed with hotels. Bedrooms, on the floors above the family's bustling restaurant,

---

TOP SURF SPOTS – BASQUE & ATLANTIC COASTS

France's Basque and Atlantic coasts have some of Europe's best surf. Autumn is prime time, with warm(ish) water temperatures, consistently good conditions and few(er) crowds. The big-name spots are Biarritz and Hossegor (p644), where you can watch Kelly Slater and friends battle it out for crucial world-title points in dredging Gravière barrels during September's ASP (Association of Surfing Professionals; www. aspeurope.com) event. In fact, almost anywhere between St-Jean de Luz in the south and Soulac-sur-Mer up in the north by the mouth of the Gironde River has mighty good surf.

Europe's original big wave spot might have been surpassed by bigger and nastier discoveries, but the reef breaks around Guéthary, just to the south of Biarritz, retain a special sense of magic.

Take a lesson in the mellow waves at Hendaye, just to the south of St-Jean de Luz, where the small, gently breaking waves are tailor-made for learners. The tourist office (☎05 59 20 00 34; www.hendaye-tourisme.fr; 67 bd de la Mer; ⊘9am-7pm Mon-Sat, 10am-1pm & 3.30-6pm Sun) can point you in the right direction. Beginners lessons start at €30 to €35.

Paddle out from the tip of pine-forested Cap Ferret peninsula (p630), or go on surfari to the magnificent beaches around Lacanau, where the surfers of Bordeaux get their kicks.

And for the best waves *away* from the coast, longboarders can attempt the mascaret (http://mascaretgironde.free.fr), a tidal-bore wave travelling inland from the Gironde Estuary. The best place to pick it up is St-Pardon during spring tides

THALASSOTHERAPY

Thalassotherapy ('sea healing'), using the restorative properties of seawater (along with seaweed and mud), has been popular in Biarritz since the late 18th century and continues to serve as an antidote to 21st-century ailments such as stress and insomnia.

In Biarritz, put thalassotherapy's curative powers to the test – or simply bliss out – at the following:

Spa Kémana (☑05 59 22 12 13; www.kemana.fr, in French; 3 carrefour Hélianthe)

Thalassa Biarritz (☑08 25 82 55 28; www.accorthalassa.com; 11 rue Louison-Bobet)

Thermes Marins (☑08 25 12 64 64; www.biarritz-thalasso.com; 80 rue de Madrid)

are colourful, though the bathrooms are a squeeze.

La Maison du Lierre BOUTIQUE HOTEL €€€
(☑05 59 24 06 00; www.maisondulierre.com; 3 av du Jardin Public; r €56-139; ☎) This establishment is a bit of a mixed bag. The cheaper rooms are very small and disappointing, with openly exposed toilets, but for the price you can't complain too much. Go for one of the more expensive ones, though, and you're in for a treat. These rooms are exquisitely decorated with polished floors, gorgeous fabrics and garden views. Sadly, the hotel is let down somewhat by some less-than-welcoming staff.

Hôtel Gardènia TRADITIONAL HOTEL €
(☑05 59 24 10 46; www.hotel-gardenia.com; 19 av Carnot; s €49-66, d €49-76; ☎) One of the cheapest options in Biarritz; the rooms with attached bathrooms are fairly poky but brightly painted. For rugby fans, this is the only place to stay due to the common areas being decked out in memorabilia for Biarritz Olympique, the town's rugby club and one of the top teams in France.

Auberge de Jeunesse de Biarritz HOSTEL €
(☑05 59 41 76 00; www.hibiarritz.org; 8 rue Chiquito de Cambo; dm incl sheets & breakfast €19.50; ⊘reception 8.30-11.30am & 6-9pm, closed mid-Dec–early Jan; @☎) Like Anglet's youth hostel, this popular place offers outdoor activities including surfing. Rooms for two to four hostellers have an en suite. From the train station, follow the railway westwards for 800m.

Biarritz Camping CAMPGROUND €
(☑05 59 23 00 12; www.biarritz-camping.fr; 28 rue d'Harcet; 2 people and tent €24; ⊘mid-May–mid-Sep; ☒) This campground, 2km southwest of the centre, has spacious, shady pitches. Take westbound bus 9 to the Biarritz Camping stop.

🍴 Eating

See-and-be-seen cafés and restaurants line Biarritz' beachfront. Anglet's beaches are also becoming increasingly trendy, with cafés strung along the waterfront.

Casa Juan Pedro SEAFOOD €
(☑05 59 24 00 86; Port des Pêcheurs; mains €5-15) Down by the old port, which is something of a hidden little village of wooden fishing cottages and old-timers, is this cute little fishing-shack restaurant. The gregarious atmosphere ensures that you can wash down your tuna, sardines or squid with plenty of friendly banter from both the staff and other customers. There are several similar neighbouring places.

Le Crabe-Tambour SEAFOOD €€
(☑05 59 23 24 53; 49 rue d'Espagne; lunch menu €13, dinner menus from €18) Named after the famous 1977 film of the same name (the owner was the cook for the film set), this friendly local place, a little way out of the centre, offers great seafood for a price that is hard to fault. The prawns in garlic are particularly good.

Bistrot des Halles BASQUE €€
(☑05 59 24 21 22; 1 rue du Centre; menu €27) One of a cluster of decent restaurants along rue du Centre that get their produce directly from the nearby covered market, this bustling place serves excellent fish and other fresh fare from the blackboard menu in an interior adorned with old metallic advertising posters.

Le Clos Basque BASQUE €€
(☑05 59 24 24 96; 12 rue Louis Barthou; menus €24; ⊘lunch Tue-Sun, dinner Tue-Sat) With its tiles and exposed stonework hung with abstract art, this tiny place could have strayed in from Spain. The cuisine, however, is emphatically Basque, traditional

with a contemporary twist or two, such as sirloin with green mustard, or stuffed eggplant with saffron. Reserve ahead to secure a terrace table.

Bleu Café
LIGHT MEALS €

(✍05 59 22 34 53; Grand Plage; pasta €8-9; ◐9am-midnight) It might be a cliché but nothing really beats plonking yourself down on the beachfront terrace here and watching the waves roll in while sipping a morning coffee, evening sundowner or tucking into one of the light lunches.

Crêperie
CRÊPERIE €

(22 rue Mazagran; galettes €1.80-6; 🚻) The simple name reveals a simple *crêperie*-cum-snack-bar where you can either settle down in one of the stalls and chat away to the lovely owner or take away for a beachside picnic. It's open all day.

Self-Catering

You'll find a picnic hamper of fresh ingredients at the **covered market** and a tempting array of cheeses, wines and pâtés at nearby **Mille et Un Fromages** (8 av Victor Hugo). At sea level, **Épicerie Fine du Port Vieux** (41bis rue Mazagran) is another excellent delicatessen.

There's a good-sized supermarket in the basement of the **Galeries Lafayette** (17 place Clemenceau) department store.

Drinking

There are some great bars on and around rue du Port Vieux, place Clemenceau and the central food-market area. Places generally open from 11am to 2am unless noted otherwise.

TOP CHOICE Miremont
CAFÉ €

(1bis place Georges-Clemenceau; tea & cake €7-9; ◐9am-8pm) Operating since 1880, this grande dame of a place harks back to the time when belle-époque Biarritz was simply the beach resort of choice for the rich and glamorous of Europe. Today it still attracts perfectly coiffured hairdos (and that's just on the poodles) but the somewhat less chic are also now welcome to come and partake of a fine selection of teas, cakes and views over the bay.

Ventilo Caffé
BAR €

(rue du Port Vieux; ◐closed Tue low season) Dressed up like a boudoir, this fun and funky place continues its domination of the Biarritz bar scene.

Arena Café Bar
BAR €

(Plage du Port Vieux; ◐9am-2am, closed Mon & Tue Oct-Mar) Tucked into a tiny cove, this beachfront hang-out combines a style-conscious restaurant (mains €15 to €22) with a fuchsia- and violet-tinged bar with DJs on the turntables.

Milk Bar
BAR €

(17 bd du Géneral-de-Gaulle; ◐closed Mon) If you're on the hunt for a surfer or a surfer at heart, then this place, just back from the beach, provides plenty of opportunities to get your sex wax out.

Red Bar
BAR €

(9 av du Maréchal Foch; ◐Tue-Sun) You mightn't think a rugby bar would attract trendsetters, but this temple to Biarritz Olympique (their colours are red and white – hence the name), with reggae and '70s rock in the background, will make you think again.

☆ Entertainment

Free classical-music concerts take place in high summer at various atmospheric outdoor venues around town; the tourist office has the program.

Cinéma Le Royal
CINEMA

(8 av du Maréchal Foch) Screens a good selection of nondubbed films.

Casino Municipal
CASINO

(1 av Édouard VII) Constructed in 1928, Biarritz' landmark casino has 200-plus fruit machines that whirr and chink until the wee hours.

Fronton Couvert Plaza Berri
SPORT

(42 av du Maréchal Foch) *Pelota* matches are held virtually year-round; ask the tourist office for schedules.

Parc Mazon
SPORT

From July to mid-September, the open-air *fronton* (*pelota* court) has regular *chistera* matches at 9pm on Thursdays.

Euskal-Jaï
SPORT

(av Henri Haget) Regular professional *cesta punta* matches (admission €10 to €20) are held at 9pm at the Parc des Sports d'Aguiléra Complex, 2km east of central Biarritz, between mid-June and mid-September. Bus 1 stops nearby.

Shopping

Pare Gabia
SHOES

(18 rue Mazagran) Vincent Corbun continues his grandfather's business, established in 1935, making and selling espadrilles in a

TAPAS ON THE SEASHORE

Like neighbouring Bayonne, there's a growing number of tapas bars in Biarritz. The area around the covered market, Les Halles, is a real hot spot for character-infused joints with bar tops that are positively loaded with tasty treats. The following spots are our favourites.

Bar Jean (5 rue des Halles; tapas €1-2) The most original, and delicious, selection of tapas in the city is served up with a flamenco soundtrack and a backdrop of blue and white Andalucian tiles. Try the calamari rings wrapped around a stack of lardons and drizzled in olive oil – simply divine. Jean also does *raciones* (plates) for around €6 to €7.

Le Comptoir du Foie Gras/Maison Pujol (1 rue du Centre; tapas €1) This quirky place morphs from a shop selling jars of outstanding foie gras in the day to a tapas bar in the evening. Needless to say the tapas are foie gras heavy, but they also have more vegetarian-suitable options such as those made with guacamole. It's so small that you'll probably end up standing outside shouting your order through the bar window.

Bar Basque (1 rue du Port Vieux; tapas €1.20-7) This rustic-chic newcomer serves bite-size Basque tapas washed down with a fantastic selection of wines.

La Santa María (Plage du Port Vieux; tapas plate €12; ⊘closed Nov-Easter & Wed low season) This place, balanced haphazardly on the rocks at the far end of our favourite Biarritz beach, the cute Plage du Port Vieux, is a fantastic place for a sunset drink and a plate of tapas (€12), but sadly they know the positioning is worth gold and so they charge likewise!

rainbow of colours and styles (customised with ribbons and laces while you wait). A pair starts from €10.

Robert Pariès   CHOCOLATES
(1 place Bellevue) Test your willpower with scrumptious chocolates and Basque sweets.

ℹ Information

Form@tic (15 av de la Marne; per 15min €1.20; ⊘9am-noon & 2-8pm Mon-Fri, 10am-noon & 2-6pm Sat) Bright, stylish internet café with full facilities.

Post office (rue de la Poste)

Tourist office (☎05 59 22 37 00; www.biarritz .fr; square d'Ixelles; ⊘9am-6pm Mon-Sat, 10am-5pm Sun) In July and August there are tourist-office annexes at the airport, train station and at the roundabout just off the Biarritz *sortie* (exit) 4 from the A63.

ℹ Getting There & Away

AIR To reach Biarritz-Anglet-Bayonne airport (p641), take STAB bus 6 or, on Sunday, line C to/ from Biarritz' *hôtel de ville*. Each runs once or twice hourly, from 7am to about 7pm.

BUS Buses run frequently between Bayonne (p641) and Biarritz; they work out much cheaper than taking the train as you'll pay the same to get from Biarritz' train station to its town centre

as you will to get from Bayonne to Biarritz directly on the bus.

Ten daily **ATCRB buses** (www.transdev-atcrb. com) travel down the coast to St-Jean de Luz (€20) from the stop just near the tourist office beside square d'Ixelles. Buses to Spain (p641) also pick up passengers here.

TRAIN Biarritz-La Négresse train station is about 3km south of the town centre; walking to the centre isn't advised due to busy roads without footpaths, so catch buses 2 or 9 (B and C on Sundays). **SNCF** (13 av du Maréchal Foch; ⊘Mon-Fri) has a town-centre office. Times, fares and destinations are much the same as Bayonne's (p641), a nine-minute train journey away.

ℹ Getting Around

BUS Most services stop beside the Hôtel de Ville, from where routes 1 and 2 (€1.20, about 50 daily) go to Bayonne's Hôtel de Ville and station. **STAB** has an information kiosk adjacent to the tourist office.

TAXI Call **Atlantic Taxis** (☎05 59 23 18 18).

St-Jean de Luz & Ciboure

POP 13,600

If you're searching for the quintessential Basque seaside town – with atmospheric narrow streets and a lively fishing port pulling in large catches of sardines, tuna and anchovies that are cooked up at authentic restaurants – you've found it.

St-Jean de Luz, 24km southwest of Bayonne, sits at the mouth of the River Nivelle and is overlooked by the lush Pyrenean foothills. The town and its long beach are on the eastern side of Baie de St-Jean de Luz.

Its sleepy, smaller alter ego, Ciboure, is on the western curve of the bay, separated from St-Jean de Luz by the fishing harbour.

Getting between St-Jean de Luz and Ciboure couldn't be easier. You can cross over the Pont Charles de Gaulle on foot or by car. Or, a more fun alternative, take one of the summer ferries that cross the harbour between the two (see p654).

◉ Sights

A superb panorama of the town unfolds from the promontory of **Pointe Ste-Barbe**, at the northern end of the Baie de St-Jean de Luz and about 1km beyond the town beach. Go to the end of bd Thiers and keep walking.

Beaches   BEACHES

St-Jean de Luz' beautiful banana-shaped sandy beach sprouts stripy bathing tents from June to September. Ciboure has its own modest beach, **Plage de Socoa**, 2km west of Socoa on the corniche (the D912); it's served by ATCRB buses en route to Hendaye and, in the high season, by boats. Both beaches are protected from the wrath of the Atlantic by breakwaters and jetties, and are among the few child-friendly beaches in the Basque Country.

Churches   CHURCHES

The plain facade of France's largest and finest Basque church, **Église St-Jean Baptiste** (rue Gambetta; ⊗8.30am-noon & 2-7pm), conceals a splendid interior with a magnificent baroque altarpiece. It was in front of this very altarpiece that Louis XIV and María Teresa, daughter of King Philip IV of Spain, were married in 1660. After exchanging rings, the couple walked down the aisle and out of the south door, which was then sealed to commemorate peace between the two nations after 24 years of hostilities. You can still see its outline, opposite 20 rue Gambetta.

In Ciboure, the 17th-century **Église St-Vincent** (rue Pocalette) has an octagonal bell tower topped by an unusual three-tiered wooden roof. Inside, the lavish use of wood and tiered galleries is typically Basque. The

church is just off the main seafront road quai Maurice Ravel.

Maison Louis XIV   HISTORICAL BUILDING

(www.maison-louis-xiv.fr, in French; adult/child €5.50/3; ⊗10.30am-12.30pm & 2.30-6.30pm, closed Tue & mid-Oct–Easter) Sitting on a pretty, pedestrianised square is the so-called Maison Louis XIV. Built in 1643 by a wealthy shipowner and furnished in period style, this is where Louis XIV lived out his last days of bachelorhood before marrying María Teresa. See the website for details of half-hour guided tours (with English text).

Alongside, and rather dwarfed by its more imposing neighbour, is St-Jean de Luz' **Hôtel de Ville**, built in 1657.

Socoa   OLD TOWN

The heart of Socoa is about 2.5km west of Ciboure along the continuation of quai Maurice Ravel (named for the *Boléro* composer, who was born in Ciboure in 1875). Its prominent **fort** was built in 1627 and later improved by Vauban (see p944). You can walk out to the Digue de Socoa breakwater or climb to the **lighthouse** via rue du Phare, then out along rue du Sémaphore for fabulous coastal views.

Écomusée Basque   MUSEUM

(adult/child €5.50/2.30; ⊗10am-6.30pm, closed Nov-Mar) Around 2km north of St-Jean de Luz beside the N10, Basque traditions are brought to life on one-hour audioguide tours of this illuminating multimedia museum, which has three entire rooms devoted to Izarra (Basque for 'star'), a liqueur made from 20 different local plants.

Maison de l'Infante   HISTORICAL BUILDING

(quai de l'Infante; adult/child €2.50/free; ⊗11am-12.30pm & 2.30-6.30pm Tue-Sat, closed mid-Oct–May) In the days before her marriage, María Teresa stayed in this mansion (like the temporary home of her husband to be, it was owned by a shipowner), the brick-and-stone Maison Joanoenia, off place Louis XIV, which has fine architectural detail.

⚑ Activities

Opportunities to get out on, in and under the water abound. With a decent swell (rare in the summer), good surf can be found 5.5km north of town at **Plage de Lafitenia**, which have a long but slow right point break.

Odysée Bleue   DIVING SCHOOL

(www.odyssee-bleue.com, in French; hangar 4, chemin des Blocs) Join a diving school in

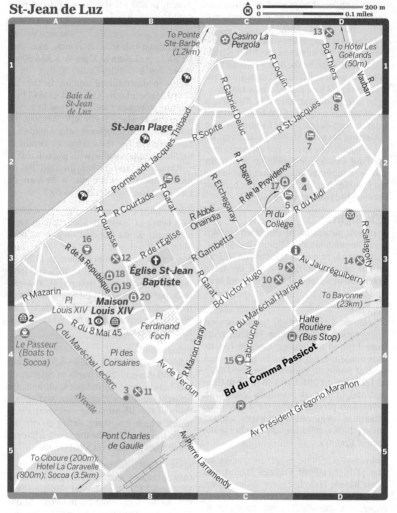

Socoa to dive under the waves to look for
starfish and wrasse.

Tech Ocean   DIVING SCHOOL
(www.tech-ocean.fr, in French; 45 av Commandant
Passicot) Another diving school in Socoa.

Youkoulélé   SURF SCHOOL
(H2O Surf School; ☎05 59 26 81 95; 72 rue
Gambetta) The surf school based inside the
Youkoulélé surf shop in the town centre
can organise surf lessons from €35.

Espace Voile   SURF SCHOOL
(http://espacevoile.free.fr, in French) Windsurfing lessons and yachting courses in Socoa.

École de Voile International   BOATING
(www.ecoledevoileinternationale.fr, in French)
Based in Socoa, this water-sports school
rents out dinghies and motor boats, and
also offers windsurfing lessons and yachting courses.

Nivelle Trois   CRUISES
(www.nivelle3.sextan.com, in French) From
May to mid-September, a boat leaves quai
du Maréchal Leclerc for morning deep-
sea fishing trips (€30) and afternoon
cruises (€15). Despite the name, the boat
currently in use is actually the *Nivelle V*.

★ Festivals & Events

Fêtes de la St-Jean CULTURAL FESTIVAL
Bonfires, music and dancing take place
on the weekend nearest 24 June.

Régates de Traînières BOAT RACES
A weekend of boat races on the first
weekend in July.

La Fête du Thon FOOD FESTIVAL
The Tuna Festival, on another July weekend, fills the streets with brass bands,
Basque music and dancing, while stalls
sell sizzling tuna steaks.

Danses des Sept Provinces Basques
DANCE FESTIVAL
Folk dancers from across the Spanish
and French Basque Country meet in early
summer.

La Nuit de la Sardine CULTURAL FESTIVAL
The Night of the Sardine – a night of
music, folklore and dancing – is held twice
each summer on a Saturday in early July
and the Saturday nearest 15 August.

🛏 Sleeping

July to mid-September are packed and
advance reservations are essential; low-
season prices can drop significantly. There
are a couple of cheap and cheerful places
opposite the train station.

Between St-Jean de Luz and Guéthary,
7km northeast up the coast, are no fewer
than 16 camping grounds. ATCRB's Biarritz and Bayonne buses stop within 1km of
them all.

TOP CHOICE **La Devinière** BOUTIQUE HOTEL €€
(☎05 59 26 05 51; www.hotel-la-deviniere.
com; 5 rue Loquin; r with street/garden view
€120/160; ⊕) You have to love a place that
forsakes TVs for antiquarian books (room
11 even has its own mini-library). Beyond
the living room, with its piano and comfy
armchairs, there's a delightful small patio
equipped with lounges. It's a truly charming place that feels like a little old country
cottage that has somehow been sucked into
the town centre. The rooms are stuffed full
of antique furnishings including old writing desks. It's worth paying the extra for
the garden-facing rooms, which have little
balconies overlooking the riot of vegetation
down below. Breakfast is €12.

Zazpi DESIGN HOTEL €€€
(☎05 59 26 07 77; www.zazpihotel.com; 21 bd
Thiers; r/ste from €205/400; ❋🖥🌊) Seriously
hip, this wonderful old mansion-turned-
designer-hotel is one of the most stylish
hotels in southwest France. Staying here
is like living in a very glamorous interior
design magazine. There's a rooftop terrace
complete with pool and sensational views
over an ocean of terracotta roof tiles to the
fairy-tale green Basque hills. It's fronted by
a snazzy bar with lime and olive modular
sofas and a tearoom (open 11am to 8pm)
serving soups, salads and pastas. Breakfast
is a pricey €16. It's wheelchair accessible.

🏆 **Hôtel Les Goëlands** BOUTIQUE HOTEL €€
(☎05 59 26 10 05; www.hotel-lesgoelands.
com; 4 & 6 av d'Etcheverry; s/d from €60/79;

📶📞) Accommodation devoted to ecological principles is still a rarity in the French Basque Country, but this place goes all out with a forward-looking recycling and energy-saving policy. The owners haven't skimped on the rooms either – they're large, sunny and comfortable, and look down onto the nicest hotel gardens in St-Jean de Luz, where you can eat your breakfast and lounge about in the sun. They also rent electric bikes to guests and cook meals made from fresh local produce (half board is obligatory in July and August).

Hôtel Ohartzia   BOUTIQUE HOTEL **€€**
(📞05 59 26 00 06; www.hotel-ohartzia.com, in French; 28 rue Garat; r with shower/bath €79/89;

📶) Framed by cobalt-blue shutters, this flower-bedecked Basque house is just a few steps from the beach. Immaculate rooms are well furnished and equipped, and the welcome's friendly. The highlight is its hidden foliage-shaded garden full of well-placed tables and chairs. A couple of the rooms are outside in this garden. Breakfast is €7.

Hôtel La Caravelle   BOUTIQUE HOTEL **€€**
(📞05 59 47 18 05; www.hotellacaravelle.com; bd Pierre Benoît; r with street/sea view from €90/110; ❄️📶) In Ciboure, this nautical-themed place was originally two fishermen's cottages. Seven of its 19 light-filled, modernised rooms have beautiful bay views. Parking costs €10. Breakfast is €8.

CROSS-BORDER ENCOUNTERS: A DAY IN SAN SEBASTIÁN

Spain, and the elegant and lively city of San Sebastián, is now so close it could almost be considered rude not to slip over to see for yourself why people make such a fuss about San Sebastián. Put simply, San Sebastián is stunning. The town is set around two sickle-shaped beaches, at least one of which, Playa de la Concha, is the equal of any city beach in Europe. But there's more to the city than just looks. Cool, svelte and flirtatious, San Sebastián really knows how to have a good time: With more bars per square metre than anywhere else on earth, and more Michelin stars per capita than anywhere else in the world, San Sebastián's CV is pretty damn impressive. But it's not just us who think this. A raft of the world's best chefs, including such luminaries as Catalan superstar chef Ferran Adriá, have said that San Sebastián is quite probably the best place on the entire planet in which to eat!

So, how do I get there then? By car it's just a short 20-minute jump down the A64 (and past an awful lot of toll booths!), or you can endure the N10, which has no tolls but gets so clogged up that it will take you a good couple of hours to travel this short distance. Or hop on a bus or a train. Trains run from St-Jean de Luz to Hendaye (and occasionally onto Irun) roughly hourly (€2.90, 12 minutes), from where you can board one of the frequent Eusko Trens for the ride into San Sebastián (€1.30; 30 minutes). Otherwise, PESA buses run twice daily between the two towns (€4.40, one hour 15 minutes).

And about those tapas? The whole of the old town is crammed with tapas (*pintxo* in Basque) bars, all of which, and we truly mean *all*, have a sublime range of bited-size morsels on offer. However, a couple that really stand out are **Astelena** (Calle de Iñigo 1), in the corner of Plaza de la Constitución, and **La Cuchara de San Telmo** (Calle de 31 de Agosto 28), a hidden-away bar serving such delights as *carrílera de ternera al vino tinto* (calf cheeks in red wine), with meat so tender it starts to dissolve almost before it's past your lips.

And if I want to really splash out? With three Michelin stars, **Arzak** (📞943 27 84 65; Avenida Alcalde Jose Elosegui 273; meals €100-160), run by acclaimed Chef Juan Mari Arzak, takes some beating when it comes to *nueva cocina vasca* (new Basque cuisine). Reservations, well in advance, are obligatory.

And if I want to stay the night? **Pensión Amaiur Ostatua** (📞943 42 96 54; www.pensionamaiur.com; Calle de 31 de Agosto 44; s/d from €45/54) and **Pensión Bellas Artes** (📞943 47 49 05; www.pension-bellasartes.com; Calle de Urbieta 64; s/d from €59/79) are our value-for-money hot tips.

And what is there to do there? What? Other than eating, drinking and playing on the beach?! OK, well, there's fantastic shopping, a superb aquarium, a couple of museums and, well, eating, drinking and playing on the beach.

Hôtel Les Almadies
BOUTIQUE HOTEL €€

(☎05 59 85 34 48; www.hotel-les-almadies.com, in French; 58 rue Gambetta; r €110-130; ⊗closed Nov; 🔊) Four of the seven rooms at this family-run gem open to balconies overlooking St-Jean de Luz' pedestrianised shopping street, and all blend restrained countrified fabrics with contemporary furnishings. The timber-decked breakfast (€12) room opens to a sunny terrace. Parking is €10.

✗ Eating

Seafood is the mainstay of restaurant menus and St-Jean de Luz doesn't disappoint in this department – many people come here as much for the food as anything else. Tempting restaurants line rue de la République, rue Tourasse and place Louis XIV.

TOP CHOICE Buvette des Halles
SEAFOOD €

(☎05 59 26 73 59; bd Victor Hugo; dishes €7-14; ⊗6am-2pm & dinner) Tucked into a corner of the covered market, this minuscule restaurant serves goat's cheese, Bayonne ham, grilled sardines, fish soup, mussels and much more, outside beneath the plane trees on the small square between June and September. The rest of the year you can eat tucked up inside, but go early for the best pickings.

Grillerie du Port
SEAFOOD €

(☎05 59 51 18 29; quai du Maréchal Leclerc; ⊗mid-Jun–mid-Sep) In this old shack by the port, join the crowds gorging on fresh sardines, salads and slabs of tuna steak fresh off the boat. It's informal and economical; prices depend on the day's catch but are always reasonable.

Pilpil-Enea
SEAFOOD €

(☎05 59 51 20 80; 3 rue Sallagoity; lunch mains €10-14, lunch menus €9, dinner menus from €25; ⊗closed dinner Tue, Wed & Sun) Strung with fishing nets, this small, simple restaurant decorated in dark timber and blue-and-white checks is set apart from the tourist throng, and is a firm local favourite for its quality cooking based largely on the aquatic world.

Le Peita
SEAFOOD €

(☎05 59 26 86 66; 21 rue Tourasse; mains €14.50-20, menus from €16; ⊗Wed-Sun) Dried Espelette chillies and hams hang from the ceiling at this authentic place with crushed-silk tablecloths and friendly owners. For a taste of the local produce on display, order one of the combination plates accompanied by fresh local cheese. There are several other cosy little places on the same street.

Olatua
BRASSERIE €€

(☎05 59 51 05 22; 30 bd Thiers; menus/mains €30/20) This bright brasserie-style restaurant serves market-fresh fare like *coquilles St-Jacques* (scallops) with risotto and a cloudlike chocolate soufflé with pistachio ice cream for dessert. There's also an outside terrace for sunny days.

Self-Catering

There's a food market every Tuesday and Friday morning inside the covered market (bd Victor Hugo).

🍷 Drinking & Entertainment

La Taverne de Nesle
BAR

(5 av Labrouche; ⊗5pm-2am, closed Tue Oct-Jun) This neighbourhood Irish-style pub has a DJ every Friday year-round (twice a week in July and August).

Pub du Corsaire
BAR

(16 rue de la République; ⊗5pm-2am) Ten of nearly 100 different beers are on draft at this place, which also mixes some mean cocktails.

Sports

In summer frequent *cesta punta* matches take place at Jaï Alaï Compos Berri (rte de Bayonne, N10), 1km northeast of the train station. The tourist office can supply times and prices.

🛍 Shopping

Sandales Concha
SHOES

(2 rue Gambetta) The traditional shoe of the Basque Country is the espadrille and here you can choose from a huge range of locally produced handmade shoes starting from €8.

Macarons Adam
FOOD

(49 rue Gambetta) For something a little more edible, try the wonderful biscuit-like delicacies sold here. Also at 6 rue de la République.

Maison Charles Larre
HOMEWARES

(4 rue de la République) St-Jean de Luz is also a good place to purchase Basque linen.

ℹ Information

Internet World (7 rue Tourasse; per hr €6; ⊗10am-1pm & 2.30-6pm; 10min €1) Friendly internet café with English keyboards (and secondhand English books).

Post office Ciboure (quai Maurice Ravel); St-Jean de Luz (cnr bd Victor Hugo & rue Sallagoity)

Tourist office (☏05 59 26 03 16; www.saint-jean-de-luz.com; 20 bd Victor Hugo; ⏰9am-12.30pm & 2.30-6.30pm Mon-Sat, 10am-1pm Sun, extended hours Jul & Aug) Runs an extensive program of French-language tours around the town and across the Spanish border; ask about English-language tours in summer.

ⓘ Getting There & Away

BUS Buses run by **ATCRB** (www.transdev-atcrb.com, in French) pass the **Halte Routière** bus stop near the train station on their way northeast to Biarritz (€3, 30 minutes, nine daily) and Bayonne (€3, 40 minutes, nine daily). Southwestward, there are around 10 services daily to Hendaye (€1, 35 minutes).

Also passing the Halte Routière is **Transportes Pesa** (p641), serving San Sebastián and Bilbao.

From April to October, **Le Basque Bondissant** (The Leaping Basque; ☏05 59 26 25 87; www.basquebondissant.com, in French) runs buses to La Rhune, including Le Petit Train (adult/child costs €17/12) and the Grottes de Sare (adult/child €10.50/7.50). Buses leave from the Halte Routière.

TRAIN There are frequent trains to Bayonne (€4.50, 25 minutes) via Biarritz (€3, 15 minutes) and to Hendaye (€2.90, 15 minutes), with connections to Spain.

ⓘ Getting Around

BOAT The good ship **Le Passeur** plies between quai de l'Infante and Socoa (€2 one way) every half-hour between June and September.

BUS Between June and September, the Navette Intercommunale, run by ATCRB, provides a local daily bus service, with a skeleton service during the rest of the year. From the Halte Routière, take line 2 for Erromardie and the camping grounds north of town, line 4 for Socoa via Ciboure.

CAR Car-rental companies at the train station include **ADA** (www.ada.fr).

TAXI Call ☏05 59 47 38 38.

Around St-Jean de Luz

LA RHUNE

The first mountain of the Pyrenees, the 905m-high, antenna-topped and border-straddling La Rhune ('Larrun' in Basque), 10km south of St-Jean de Luz, has always been considered sacred among Basques, though today people come for the spectacular views rather than religious or cultural reasons. The mountain is best approached from Col de St-Ignace, 3km northwest of Sare on the D4 (the St-Jean de Luz road). From here, you can take a fairly strenuous five-hour (return) hike, or have all the hikers curse you by hopping on Le Petit Train de la Rhune (www.rhune.com; single/return adult €14/17, child €7/10; ⏰mid-Feb–Nov). This charming little wooden train takes 35 minutes to haul itself up the 4km from col to summit. In July and August departures are every 35 minutes, the rest of the time they leave at 10am and 3pm. Outside high season they knock a few euros off the above prices. Be prepared for a wait of up to an hour in high summer.

GROTTES DE SARE

Who knows what the first inhabitants of the Grottes de Sare (www.grottesdesare.fr; adult/child €7/4; ⏰10am-7pm), some 20,000 years ago, would make of today's whiz-bang technology including lasers and holograms during sound-and-light shows at these caves. Multilingual 45-minute tours take you through a gaping entrance via narrow passages to a huge central cavern. Follow the D306, 6km south of the village of Sare.

AINHOA
POP 599

'*Un des plus jolis villages de la France*', says the sign as you enter this, indeed, very pretty village. Only, this being the Basque Country, someone has painted over '*de la France*'...

Ainhoa's elongated main street is flanked by imposing 17th-century houses, half-timbered and brightly painted. Look for the rectangular stones set above many of the doors, engraved with the date of construction and the name of the family to whom the house belonged. The fortified church has the Basque trademarks of an internal gallery and an embellished altarpiece.

For a memorable Basque meal, stop at the Michelin-starred Ithurria (☏05 59 29 92 11; www.ithurria.com; s €85-105, d €105-120, menus €35-58; ✴🔊✴), established by the Isabal family in an old pilgrims' hostel and now run by Maurice Isabal's two sons (one the sommelier, the other the chef). To make a night of it, Ithurria's rainbow-hued rooms and dreamy swimming pool complement the food perfectly.

ESPELETTE
POP 1879

The whitewashed Basque town of Espelette is famous for its dark-red chillies, an integral ingredient in traditional Basque cuisine. So prized is *le piment d'Espelette* that

LOCAL LINGO

According to linguists, Euskara, the Basque language, is unrelated to any other tongue on earth, and is the only tongue in southwest Europe to have withstood the onslaught of Latin and its derivatives.

Basque is spoken by about a million people in Spain and France, nearly all of whom are bilingual. In the French Basque Country, the language is widely spoken in Bayonne and the hilly hinterland. However, while it is an official language in Spain, it isn't recognised as such in France (although some younger children are educated in Basque at primary-school level). The language also has a higher survival rate on the Spanish side.

But you'll still encounter the language here on Basque-language TV stations, and see the occasional sign reading 'Hemen Euskara emaiten dugu' (Basque spoken here) on shop doors. You'll also see the Basque flag (similar to the UK's but with a red field, a white vertical cross and a green diagonal one) flying throughout the region, as well as another common Basque symbol, the *lauburu* (like a curly four-leaf clover), signifying prosperity, or life and death.

it's been accorded Appellation d'Origine Contrôlée (AOC) status, like fine wine. In autumn you can scarcely see the walls of the houses, strung with rows of chillies drying in the sun. The last weekend in October marks Espelette's Fête du Piment, with processions, a formal blessing of the chilli peppers and the ennoblement of a *chevalier du piment* (a knight of the pimiento).

The tourist office (☑05 59 93 95 02; www.espelette.fr, in French), within a small stone château, shares its premises with the Hôtel de Ville.

Chillies star on the menu at the renowned Hôtel Restaurant Euzkadi (☑05 59 93 91 88; www.hotel-restaurant-euzkadi.com; r from €64, menus €17.50-34; ☎⊗) in dishes such as *axoa* (tender minced veal simmered with onions and fresh chillies). Its comfortable rooms are a true bargain.

St-Jean Pied de Port

POP 1700

At the foot of the Pyrenees, the walled town of St-Jean Pied de Port, 53km southeast of Bayonne, was for centuries the last stop in France for pilgrims heading south over the Spanish border, a mere 8km away, and on to Santiago de Compostela in western Spain. Today it remains a popular departure point for hikers attempting the pilgrim trail, but there are plenty of shorter hikes and opportunities for mountain biking in the area.

If you're the sort of person who thinks God invented cars so we didn't have to walk, then St-Jean Pied de Port, with its attractive old core sliced through by the River Nive, is still well worth a visit.

St-Jean Pied de Port makes an ideal day trip from Bayonne, particularly on Monday when the market is in full swing. Half the reason for coming here is the scenic journey south of Cambo-les-Bains, as both railway and road (the D918) pass through rocky hills, forests and lush meadows dotted with white farmhouses selling *ardi* ('cheese' in Basque).

⊙ Sights & Activities

Old Town   OLD TOWN

The walled old quarter is an attractive place of cobbled streets, geranium-covered balconies and lots of quirky boutiques. Specific sights worth seeking out include the Église Notre Dame du Bout du Pont, with foundations as old as the town itself but thoroughly rebuilt in the 17th century. Beyond Porte de Notre Dame is the photogenic Vieux Pont (Old Bridge), the town's best-known landmark, from where there's a fine view of whitewashed houses with balconies leaning out above the water. Fishing is forbidden where the River Nive passes through town, and the fat, gulping trout seem to know it. A pleasant 500-metre riverbank stroll upstream leads to the steeply arched Pont Romain (meaning Roman Bridge, but in fact dating from the 17th century).

Rue de la Citadelle is edged by substantial, pink-granite 16th- to 18th-century houses. Look for the construction date on door lintels (the oldest we found was 1510). A common motif is the scallop shell, symbol of St Jacques (St James or Santiago) and of the Santiago de Compostela pilgrims. Pilgrims would enter the town through

Rising up above St-Étienne de Baïgorry are wave upon wave of luminous-green mountains, including the sheer-sided ridge of **Iparla** (1056m), which marks the border with Spain. A breathtaking one-day hike (4½ hours without stopping and an elevation gain of 900m) along the edge of this ridge is easily possible for any moderately fit walker. Many experienced Pyrenean walkers describe this as the finest ridge walk in the entire mountain range. Do note, however, that this walk should not be attempted in foggy, snowy or wet conditions. You will need a compass and a *Rando Éditions 1:50,000 Pays Basque Ouest* map wouldn't go amiss either (this can be obtained at any local bookshop as well as many newsagents). Children may need a helping hand on some of the earlier parts of this walk (this author last did it in 30-degree heat with a six-month-old baby strapped to his back) but once on the ridge it'll be plain sailing.

The trail begins from the **Bordazar Berroa**, a traditional Basque farmhouse. To get there, leave St-Étienne de Baïgorry northward on the D9418 and after a couple of kilometres take the narrow turn-off to your left towards Urdos and La Bastide. Continue along this for around 3km, past the second turn-off for Urdos and past the hamlet of La Bastide. Just beyond, you'll reach the farmhouse and a parking area where the walk begins.

Walk in a northwest direction along the track signed to Iparla. Fifteen minutes later, at the fork with the concrete track, head right in a due west direction. Ten minutes later, just after a stream and a shepherd's hut, the trail starts to climb steeply. At the next fork, head right in a northeast direction. You now appear to be heading away from the ridge. After another five minutes the path bends around the top of a low ridge and starts to head downhill. There should be a water trough on your left and a dirt trail heading upwards in a northwest direction, back towards Iparla. Follow this dirt trail for around 10 minutes until you get to another shepherd's hut/barn, where you turn right along a narrow track heading north-northwest.

After a quarter of an hour you come to a scree slope and the path, which is marked by the odd rock cairn, zigzags sharply upwards and onto the Iparla Ridge, crossing over a fence on the way (ignore the more obvious trail that continues along the flank of the hill). This is the hardest part of the walk – poles are useful! Fifteen minutes of huffing and puffing, and you emerge onto the **Iparla Ridge** beside an old BF90 marker stone. You are now on a stretch of the **GR10**, a highly demanding 45-day trek along the entire length of the Pyrenees, but for now things get much easier.

Turn left, following the obvious path and the red and white paint slashes of the GR10 in a westerly, uphill direction, sticking all the time to the ridge edge. Almost straight away you will start to be rewarded with what you might think are spectacular views: they're nothing compared to those you'll get in a few minutes when you finally reach the summit of Iparla, which is indicated with a marker post. It goes without saying that you'll rest a while here admiring the incredible views across half the French and Spanish Basque Country, but while you're soaking it all in keep your eyes peeled for the numerous huge griffon vultures and various eagles and hawks which circle in the thermals here.

It's impossible to get lost now. Just dance along the edge of the ridge for around an hour (at one point the trail dips down slightly before rising back up again), following the red and white GR10 paint slashes all the way. Eventually the path drops sharply downhill, off the ridge, in a southwest direction and reaches a signpost marking the Col d'Harrieta.

Leaving the GR10 behind here (which labours upwards again and onto another ridge), turn left (east) and follow the path downhill through the forest. After around 15 minutes you'll reach a fork and a shepherd's hut. Take the left-hand path (the other one leads to Urdos) in a northwest direction towards the Col de Larrarté. The path turns into a concrete road and, ignoring any turn-offs, descends sharply for half an hour until you arrive back at your car.

the Porte de St-Jacques on the northern side of town, then, refreshed and probably a little poorer, head for Spain through the Porte d'Espagne, south of the river.

Prison des Évêques   MONUMENT
(Bishops' Prison; 41 rue de la Citadelle; adult/under 10yr €3/free; ☉10.30am-9pm) This claustrophobic vaulted cellar gets its history muddled. It served as the town jail from 1795, as a military lock-up in the 19th century, then as a place of internment during WWII for those caught trying to flee to nominally neutral Spain. The lower section dates from the 13th century, when St-Jean Pied de Port was a bishopric of the Avignon papacy; the building above it dates from the 16th century, by which time the bishops were long gone. Inside can be found seasonal exhibitions.

La Citadelle   FORTRESS
From the top of rue de la Citadelle, a rough cobblestone path ascends to the massive citadel itself, from where there's a spectacular panorama of the town and the surrounding hills. Constructed in 1628, the fort was rebuilt around 1680 by military engineers of the Vauban school. Nowadays it serves as a secondary school and is closed to the public.

If you've a head for heights, descend by the steps signed *escalier poterne* (rear stairway). Steep and slippery after rain, they plunge beside the moss-covered ramparts to Porte de l'Échauguette (Watchtower Gate).

Walking & Cycling
Escape the summertime crowds by walking or cycling into the Pyrenean foothills, where the loudest sounds you'll hear are cowbells and the wind. Both the GR10 (the trans-Pyrenean long-distance trail running from the Atlantic to the Mediterranean over the course of 45 days) and the GR65 (the Chemin de St-Jacques pilgrim route) pass through town. Outside the summer season, check with the tourist office or hostels for snow reports and possible rerouting, and plan your accommodation ahead as many places on the Spanish side close.

Pick up a copy of the excellent *Le Guide Rando: Pays Basque* (€17.50) from local bookshops, which maps walking excursions (in French). See also the box text on opposite site for details of what is arguably the best day hike in the region.

To cycle the easy way while enjoying the best of Nive Valley views, load your bicycle onto the train in Bayonne – they're carried free – and roll back down the valley from St-Jean Pied de Port. If you find the ride all the way back to the coast daunting, rejoin the train at Pont-Noblia, for example, or Cambo-les-Bains.

☞ Tours
In July and August, the tourist office organises tours of the old town and visits to the citadel in French and Spanish.

🛏 Sleeping & Eating
Much of the accommodation is geared towards pilgrims on the long hike to Santiago de Compostela in Galicia, Spain. This sort of accommodation is always very basic; normally it consists of just dorm beds, but it's cheap at around €8 to €10 per person. At many places nonpilgrims (or walkers on the GR10) will be turned away. For less active visitors there are also plenty of comfortable and good-value *gîtes* and *chambres d'hôte*.

TOP CHOICE Itzalpea   B&B €
(☏05 59 37 03 66; www.maisondhotes-itzalpea.com; 5 place du Trinquet; s €52-55, d €62-78; ✲🖥🏠) This friendly and cosy *maison d'hôte* has five tastefully renovated rooms (some air-conditioned), all of which differ from one and other and all of which are named after local flowers. It's set above a teashop serving no fewer than 20 different types of teas.

Maison E Bernat   B&B €€
(☏05 59 37 23 10; www.ebernat.com; 20 rue de la Citadelle; d €78-88, extra person €25; 🖥) There are only four bedrooms in this welcoming 17th-century place with thick stone walls, but they're airy, well furnished and meticulously kept, and each has a double and a single bed. There's a great little restaurant on-site, which spills onto a tiny terrace (*menus* start from €19), and the hosts run a program of gourmet-themed weekends (€180).

Central Hôtel   HISTORIC HOTEL €
(☏05 59 37 00 22; 1 place Charles de Gaulle; r €60-71; 🖥) Follow the gleaming polished timber staircase up to 12 old-fashioned but disappointingly dull rooms at this eponymously situated hotel. The owners are welcoming and there's an on-site restaurant (*menus* €19.50 to €45) opening to a riverside terrace.

Hôtel Les Pyrénées   HISTORIC HOTEL €€
(☏05 59 37 01 01; www.hotel-les-pyrenees.com; 19 place Charles de Gaulle; r €100-160, apt €185-250;

⊘mid-Jan–mid-Nov; ✱☎⊠) Some of the large, well-furnished rooms at this one-time coaching inn take in stunning mountain views from balconies, but compared to what's available elsewhere it's a little overpriced.

Camping Municipal Plaza Berri
CAMPGROUND €

(☑05 59 37 11 19; av du Fronton; per adult/tent/car/electricity €2.50/2/2.50; ⊘Apr-Oct) Beside the river, this smallish campground has ample shade.

Chez Arrambide
GOURMET €€€

(menus €40-100, mains €30-48) This twin-Michelin-starred restaurant, the real reason to stop by Hôtel Les Pyrénées, is where chef Firmin Arrambide does wonders with seasonal market produce, such as pan-fried duck breast with ginger and cinnamon or foie-gras-stuffed hare.

Côté Tarte
CAFÉ €

(☑05 59 49 16 78; 5 rue de la Citadelle; menus €14-16; ⊘9am-6pm Mon & Wed-Sat; 🍴) A fresh, contemporary little place – all limed tables and coir carpets – specialising in delicious sweet and savoury tarts, including some unlikely offerings such as a scallop and caviar tart!

Self-Catering

Farmers from the surrounding hills bring fresh produce – chillies and local cheeses and much more – to the town's Monday market (place Charles de Gaulle). In high summer a weekly handicraft and food fair is held most Thursdays in the covered market.

Walkers can stock up at the Champion supermarket (av du Jaï Alaï) near the train station.

☆ Entertainment

Year-round, variants of *pelota* (admission €7 to €10), including a bare-handed *pelota* tournament, are played at the *trinquet*, *fronton* municipal and *jaï alaï* courts. Check schedules at the tourist office.

In high summer traditional Basque music and dancing (think of a very manly group of choir singers crossed with some Morris dancers!) takes place in the *jaï alaï* court or the church. Again, confirm schedules with the tourist office.

ℹ Information

Tourist office (☑05 59 37 03 57; www.pyrenees-basque.com; place Charles de Gaulle; ⊘9am-7pm Mon-Sat, 10am-4pm Sun Jul & Aug, 9am-noon & 2-6pm Mon-Sat Sep-Jun)

ℹ Getting There & Away

Train is the best option to travel to or from Bayonne (€9, 1¼ hours, up to five daily) since the irregular bus service makes a huge detour (and drops you at the station, rather than the centre of town, despite passing right through it – go figure).

St-Étienne de Baïgorry

The village of St-Étienne de Baïgorry and its outlying hamlets straddle the Vallée de Baïgorry. Tranquillity itself after busy St-Jean Pied de Port, the pretty village is stretched thinly along a branch of the Nive. Like so many Basque settlements, the village has two focal points: the church and the *fronton* (*pelota* court). It makes a good base for hikers tackling the **Iparla Ridge** hike (p656). Even if you're not a hiker you can't fail to be impressed by the area's beauty, so an overnight stay is recommended.

🛏 Sleeping & Eating

Hôtel-Restaurant Manechenea HOTEL €

(☑05 59 37 41 68; d €48, menus from €16) A couple of kilometres to the north in the hamlet of Urdos, this rural hotel has butter-yellow rooms which overlook green fields and a bubbling mountain-fed brook. You can eat some of the denizens of said brook, such as delicious trout, for lunch at the in-house restaurant.

Hôtel-Restaurant Arcé HOTEL €€

(☑05 59 37 40 14; www.hotel-arce.com; s/d from €85/105, menus from €29, mains €17; ☎⊠) Back in St-Étienne de Baïgorry, this impressive hotel has a stunning riverside location and spacious rooms with old-style furnishings. To reach the pool you must stroll past the orange trees and cross the river via a little humpback bridge. The in-house restaurant is highly regarded by locals.

The Pyrenees

Best Places to Eat

» Le Viscos (p669)
» Au Fin Gourmet (p662)
» Château de Beauregard
(boxed text, p679)
» Le Sacca (p676)
» Hôtel les Remparts (p679)

Best Places to Stay

» Le Viscos (p669)
» Auberge les Myrtilles
(boxed text, p680)
» Maison des Consuls
(p680)
» Château de Beauregard
(p679)
» Hôtel du Lion d'Or (p675)

Why Go?

They might not be on quite the same lofty scale as the Alps, but the Pyrenees still pack a mighty impressive mountain punch. Crested by snow for much of the year, these high, wild peaks form a natural frontier between southwest France and northern Spain. End to end, they cover a total distance of around 430km, including the 100km strip of protected land known as the Parc National des Pyrénées, created in 1967 and now an important haven for rare wildlife such as eagles, griffon vultures, izards (a type of goat) and some of the last remaining wild brown bears left in France.

Needless to say, if you're a hiker, biker or skier, or if you're simply a sucker for grandstand views, you'll be in seventh heaven in the Pyrenees. From historic ski stations to isolated valleys, from subterranean caves to snow-dusted peaks, there are enough sights to fill a lifetime of visits. Breathe deep: the wilds are calling.

When to Go

Pau

°C/°F Temp   Rainfall Inches/mm

J F M A M J J A S O N D

February Come for Pau's annual carnival. Visit during Easter for the Festival International de Musique Sacrée.

July Shepherds move their flocks in the Transhumance, and the Tour de France races through.

November to March Peak skiing season – book hotels well ahead.

❶ Getting There & Away

The two main towns, Pau and Lourdes, are well served by rail. Both also have airports. Pau is served by Ryanair flights to and from the UK and Belgium, while Air France handles domestic services, and several other budget carriers fly to European cities. Lourdes' airport has scheduled services to Paris.

Outside of the towns there are limited bus services, but to really explore you'll need your own wheels. Drivers needn't worry – the roads are well maintained and nowhere near as hair-raising as other precipitous regions such as the Alps.

Pau

POP 80,600

Palm trees might seem out of place in this mountainous region, but its chief city, Pau (rhymes with 'so'), has long been famed for its mild climate. In the 19th century it was a favourite wintering spot for wealthy Brits and Americans, who left behind grand villas, English-style flower-filled public parks, and promenades with dizzying vistas of the snow-dusted peaks. These days Pau is still an elegant city, and makes an ideal base for exploring the northern reaches of the Pyrenees.

◉ Sights

The town centre sits on a small hill with the Gave de Pau (River Pau) at its base. Along its crest stretches bd des Pyrénées, a wide promenade offering panoramic views of the mountains. A creaky old free funicular railway dating from 1908 clanks down from the bd des Pyrénées to av Napoléon Bonaparte, allowing you to avoid the uphill slog from the train station.

Pau's tiny old centre extends for around 500m around the château, but despite its minuscule dimensions, it's worth a stroll for its much-restored medieval and Renaissance buildings.

Château   CASTLE
(www.musee-chateau-pau.fr, in French; adult/18-25yr €5/3.50; ⊙9.30am-12.30pm & 1.30-6.45pm) Originally the residence of the monarchs of Navarre, Pau's castle was transformed into a Renaissance château amid lavish gardens by Marguerite d'Angoulême in the 16th century. Marguerite's grandson, Henri de Navarre (the future Henri IV), was born here – cradled, so the story goes, in an upturned tortoise shell (still on display in one of the museum's rooms).

Much restored, the château is now mainly worth visiting for its collections of Gobelins tapestries and Sevres porcelain, as well as its fine Renaissance architecture.

Within the brick-and-stone Tour de la Monnaie below the main château, a modern lift (free) hauls you from place de la Monnaie up to the ramparts.

Admission includes an obligatory one-hour guided tour in rapid-fire French (departing every 15 minutes), but you can pick up an English-language guide sheet at the reception desk.

Musée Bernadotte   MUSEUM
(8 rue Tran; adult/student €3/1.50; ⊙10am-noon & 2-6pm Tue-Sun) The Musée Bernadotte has exhibits illustrating the improbable yet true story of how a French general, Jean-Baptiste Bernadotte (nicknamed 'Sergent belle-jambe', apparently on account of his elegant legs), born in this very building, became king of Sweden and Norway in 1810, when the Swedish Riksdag (parliament) reckoned that the only way out of the country's dynastic and political crisis was to stick a foreigner on the throne. The present king of Sweden, Carl Gustaf, is the seventh ruler in the Bernadotte dynasty. You'll spot the museum by the blue-and-yellow Swedish flag fluttering outside.

Musée des Beaux-Arts   ART MUSEUM
(rue Mathieu Lalanne; adult/student €3/1.50; ⊙10am-noon & 2-6pm Wed-Mon) Works by Rubens and El Greco both figure at Pau's fine arts museum, but the museum's prize piece is a famous Degas canvas, *A New Orleans Cotton Office*, painted in 1873.

✦ Festivals & Events

Carnival Week The prelude to Lent brings street parades and a carnival atmosphere to Pau around late February.

Grand Prix Historique (www.grandprixdepauhistorique.com) Vintage-car rally on the streets of Pau, currently held every other year.

L'Été à Pau Lively summer music festival, spanning late July and early August.

⌂ Sleeping

Pau is a popular venue for congresses so it's a good idea to book ahead at any time of year. Rates can spike during festivals and special events.

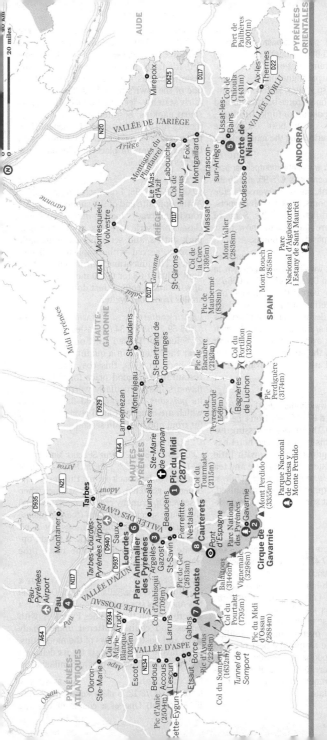

The Pyrenees Highlights

1 Take the funicular to the top of the sky-high **Pic du Midi** (p676)

2 Trek to the face of the breathtaking **Cirque de Gavarnie** (boxed text, p677)

3 See some Pyrenean wildlife at the **Parc Animalier des Pyrénées** (p669)

4 Soak up the rarefied air of **Pau** (p660)

5 Marvel at the prehistoric paintings of the **Grotte de Niaux** (p679)

6 Get spiritual in the holy city of **Lourdes** (p665)

7 Ride the dizzying Artouste mountain train in the **Vallée d'Ossau** (p673)

8 Tackle the trails from the Pont d'Espagne near **Cauterets** (p674)

Hôtel Bristol HOTEL €€

(☎05 59 27 72 98; www.hotelbristol-pau.com; 3 rue Gambetta; s €70-88, d €80-99, f €105-110; ☎) Pau's nicest midrange option, in a heritage building with surprisingly modern rooms, decked out in crisp whites, slates and crimsons, with cool monochrome bathrooms and the odd bit of bespoke art or funky furniture. The upper rooms are the best: ask for one with a balcony overlooking the mountains.

Hôtel Montpensier HOTEL €€

(☎05 59 27 42 72; www.hotel-montpensier-pau. com; 36 rue Montpensier; s €75-95, d €85-95; ✳☎) A pastel-pink, shutter-covered facade conceals smart rooms, all with coir carpets, silk cushions and flat-screen TVs. Some of the bathrooms are starting to show their age, but the free parking's a bonus.

Hôtel Central HOTEL €€

(☎05 59 27 72 75; www.hotelcentralpau.com, in French; 15 rue Léon Daran; s €59-67, d €56-79; ☎) The rambling corridors of this old hotel lead to a selection of higgledy-piggledy rooms, variously decorated in bright stripes and citrus shades, most with tall French windows looking over the street. It's worth asking for one of the larger doubles, as the singles are tiny. Parking's only available on the street outside.

Hôtel Bosquet HOTEL €€

[☎05 59 11 50 11; www.brithotel.fr; 11 rue Valéry Meunier; s €65-75, d €70-80; ☎) Don't be too downhearted by the unprepossessing exterior – inside, this boxy modern hotel has spacious, well-equipped rooms, with little extras such as mineral water, kettle and tea and coffee *(quel luxe!)* It's a bit charmless, but the street's quiet and pedestrianised, and the breakfast spread is great. No parking's a pain.

✗ Eating

TOP CHOICE **Au Fin Gourmet** GASTRONOMIC €€€

(☎05 59 27 47 71; 24 av Gaston Lacoste; menus €28-62; ☺lunch Tue-Sun, dinner Tue-Sat) Run by the much-lauded Ithurriage brothers, Patrick and Laurent, this *restaurant gastronomique* is a real spoil. In a lovely spot near the base of the funicular, with a delightful patio overlooking shrub-filled gardens, it's quite simply the best place to eat in Pau. The food is quintessential gourmet French, where precision of presentation gets just as much attention as the rich flavours on the plate.

Le Majestic TRADITIONAL FRENCH €€€

(☎08 92 68 06 89; 9 place Royale; lunch menu 2/3 courses €15/18, dinner menu €28/38; ☺Mon-Sat) It's fairly new on the scene, but this restaurant has made a name for itself as one of the town's top tables. The setting is fairly starchy – ice-white tablecloths, razor-sharp napkins, besuited waiters – but the menu's full of sophisticated French cuisine: pigeon, turbot, cod steak, local lamb. It's on the leafy square of place Royale, but sadly there's no terrace.

Le Berry BRASSERIE €€

(☎05 59 27 42 95; 4 rue Gachet; mains €13-18) At the opposite end of the snooty scale, this rough-and-ready locals' diner turns out classic brasserie fare: big hunks of steak, pork cutlets and scrumptious homemade desserts, served with simplicity and efficiency. The lunchtime *plat du jour* is brilliant value at €8 (or €9.30 including a glass of wine and a coffee). Just don't expect any smiles from your waiter.

La Michodière TRADITIONAL FRENCH €€

(☎05 59 27 53 85; 34 rue Pasteur; menus €15-27; ☺Tue-Sun) Tucked away on a backstreet near the cinema, in a quaint building dating back to 1609, this cosy little French restaurant is a good place for rich, rustic flavours. It's particularly worth a visit for its *poissons sauvages* (wild fish), most of which are caught in local rivers – look out for trout and bream in season.

L'Entracte BISTRO €

(☎05 59 27 68 31; 2bis rue St-Louis; lunch mains €7-12, menus €19-23; ☺lunch Mon-Sat, dinner Thu-Sat) For laid-back eating, this zesty little diner is a good bet, especially at lunch when it serves up crunchy *croques monsieur* and the house special 'croutons' (toasted cheese in various concoctions). Things get a bit more adventurous after dark. It's right opposite the theatre, hence the name ('the interval').

Royal St-André CAFÉ €

(26 bd des Pyrénées; ☺10am-2am May-Oct, 2-7pm Nov-Apr) This streetside café-glacier sits in a superb spot on the blvd des Pyrénées, with tables and chairs scattered under shady trees and postcard views of the mountains. It's a favourite with locals for its delicious ice-cream sundaes, sorbets and milkshakes.

Le Champagne BRASSERIE €

(☎05 59 27 72 12; 5 place Royale; mains €10-15; ☺Mon-Sat) One of a couple of bustling

Pau

Pau

◉ Top Sights

◉ Sights

⬤ Sleeping

✖ Eating

⬤ Drinking

✪ Entertainment

⬤ Shopping

brasseries on place Royale, ideal for an early-evening beer or a plate of simple *steak-frites*.

Self-Catering

Stock up on picnic goodies at the big **covered market** (place de la République). The smaller **Marché Bio** sells exclusively organic food on place du Foirail every Wednesday and Saturday morning.

 Drinking

Pau has several distinct drinking zones; bars generally open from 10am to 2am.

'Le Triangle', bounded by rue Henri Faisans, rue Émile Garet and rue Castetnau, is the centre of student nightlife. Good bets are **Le Garage** (49 rue Émile Garet) – look for the giant stucco mechanic sitting on the roof – and **Péna Muxu** (35 rue Émile Garet), which sometimes has live music.

A short string of grungy bars (**Galway** and **Australia** among them) extends along bd des Pyrénées.

Congenial wine bars near the château include **Au Grain de Raisin** (11 rue Sully), which also has a good range of draft beers, and **Le Bouchon** (46 rue Maréchal Joffre). Look out for the local Jurançon wines (www.cavedejurancon.com), whose vineyards ribbon the surrounding countryside.

☆ **Entertainment**

For theatre, music, dance and upcoming exhibitions, get hold of *La Culture à Pau*, published every three months and available free from the tourist office.

Exclusively nondubbed films screen at **Cinéma Le Méliès** (☎ 05 59 27 60 52; 6 rue Bargoin), Pau's only cinema.

Rugby fans might want to take in a home game of **Section Paloise** (www.section-paloise.com/accueil.php, in French), one of France's leading club sides, at **Stade du Hameau** (☎ 05 59 02 50 91; bd de l'Aviation).

 Shopping

Pau's renowned chocolatiers include **La Couronne** (place Clemenceau) and **Josuat** (23 rue Serviez). Champion jam-maker **Francis Miot** (48 rue Maréchal Joffre) also makes wonderfully quirky sweets and handmade chocolates.

If you've ever despaired of finding a windproof, soak-proof umbrella, stop by **Au Parapluie des Pyrénées** (12 rue Montpensier); its traditional beech-handled, rattan-ribbed umbrellas are used by Pyrenean shepherds.

 Information

C Cyber Café (20 rue Lamothe; per hr €4.50; ⏰10am-2am Mon-Fri, 2pm-2am Sat & Sun) One of over a dozen internet cafés around town.

Main post office (21 cours Bosquet)

Tourist office (☎ 05 59 27 27 08; www.pau-pyrenees.com; place Royale; ⏰9am-6pm) Closes early Sunday.

 Getting There & Away

AIR The **Aéroport Pau-Pyrénées** (☎ 05 59 33 33 00; www.pau.aeroport.fr) is about 10km northwest of town. Current destinations include London Stansted, Brussels and Paris Beauvais (with Ryanair), plus Paris Orly, Paris Roissy and Lyon with Air France.

BUS Bus services are limited; most regional lines are run by **Citram Pyrénées** (☎ 05 59 27 22 22; http://citrampyrenees.fr). There are four daily buses to Laruns (one hour), plus one daily bus to Agen (3½ hours).

TRAIN As always, trains are the best way of getting around, and there are at least two or three direct TGVs to Paris every day. From Oloron-Ste-Marie, SNCF buses trundle along the Vallée d'Aspe, but the timetables vary greatly depending on the season – ask at the tourist office for details.

Destinations served:

Bayonne €15.50, 1¼ hours

Oloron-Ste-Marie €6.70, 30 minutes

Toulouse €29, 3¼ hours

Paris Montparnasse €84.10, 7½ hours

 Getting Around

TO/FROM THE AIRPORT There are three daily **navettes** (shuttle buses; ☎ 05 59 26 25 87; www.aeroportexpress.com) between Pau and Biarritz airports (to allow people to fly direct from Pau to Orly and Roissy airports in Paris). To get into the city, your only option's a taxi, which costs from €25 to €30 depending on the traffic and time of day. It's a good idea to book on weekends – call ☎ 05 59 02 22 22 or reserve online at http://pau-taxi.com (in French).

BICYCLE Vélo Station (☎ 05 59 02 27 54; 9 bd Alsace Lorraine) rents out all manner of bikes.

CAR & MOTORCYCLE There's extensive free parking on place de Verdun. All the major rental-car companies have branches at both the airport and the train station.

PUBLIC TRANSPORT The local bus company, **STAP** (☎ 05 59 14 15 16; www.bus-stap.com, in French), has a sales and information office on rue Jean Monnet. Single tickets/daily passes/eight-ride *carnets* (books of tickets) cost €1.10/2.50/5.60.

Lourdes

POP 15,700 / ELEVATION 400M

If you've ever wondered what a religious theme park would look like, chances are it'd turn out pretty close to Lourdes. This provincial town, 43km southeast of Pau, has been one of the world's most important pilgrimage sites since 1858, when 14-year-old Bernadette Soubirous (1844–79) saw the Virgin Mary in a series of 18 beatific visions, which came to her in a rocky grotto just outside town. The Vatican confirmed them as bona-fide apparitions, and Bernadette was beatified in 1933; the grotto where she experienced the visions now forms the Sanctuaires Notre Dame de Lourdes, considered to be one of the holiest sites in Christendom.

Despite its spiritual importance, genuine holiness is a little hard to come by in Lourdes these days. Catering to some six million pilgrims every year, the town is awash with neon-signed hotels and countless souvenir shops selling all manner of Christian-themed ephemera, from plastic crucifixes and cut-price rosaries to a huge swathe of Madonna-shaped mementoes (Virgin Mary–shaped plastic bottles are particularly popular – just add holy water at the shrine).

But beyond all the tourist tat, there are constant reminders that many people spend their life savings to come here. Each year, around 70,000 invalids make the spiritual pilgrimage to Lourdes in the hope of finding a cure for all manner of afflictions and ailments, and while the town itself can be a pretty disheartening experience, the sanctuaries themselves are refreshingly free of commercial clutter.

◎ Sights

Sanctuaires Notre Dame de Lourdes
SACRED CAVES

The development of the Sanctuaries of Our Lady of Lourdes began within a decade of Ste Bernadette's apparitions in 1858. The main site is approached via one of two gateways; the Porte St-Michel and Porte St-Joseph (both ⊘5am-midnight) or the Entrée des Lacets (rue Monseigneur Theas; ⊘24hr).

The most dramatic approach is via the Port St-Joseph, from where a broad boulevard sweeps west towards the Byzantine Basilique du Rosaire (Basilica of the Rosary), and the Basilique Supérieure (Upper Basilica), topped by lavishly gilded turrets and tiled frescos depicting Bernadette's visions. Beneath the basilica is Lourdes' most revered site, the Grotte de Massabielle (sometimes known as the Grotte Miraculeuse or the Grotte des Apparitions), where Bernadette allegedly experienced her famous visions.

The Esplanade des Processions, lined with enormous flickering candles left by previous pilgrims, leads along the river to the grotto's entrance, where people line up patiently for the chance to enter the cave itself, or take a chilly dip in one of the sacred baths (⊘9-11am & 2.30-4pm Mon-Sat, 2-4pm Sun & holy days). The baths are open to people of all religious persuasions, but they're definitely not for wallflowers: once behind the curtain, you'll be expected to strip off before being swaddled in a sheet and plunged backwards into the icy water.

From Palm Sunday to mid-October, nightly **torchlight processions** start from the Massabielle Grotto at 9pm, while at 5pm there's the **Procession Eucharistique** (Blessed Sacrament Procession) along the Esplanade des Processions.

Château Fort
CASTLE, MUSEUM

(Fortified Castle; adult/child €5/2.30; ⊘9am-noon & 1.30-6.30pm) On a rocky pinnacle above town squats this imposing castle. There's been some kind of stronghold on this site since Roman times, but the present building is largely medieval, including the stout walls and the central keep. The castle was fortified again in the 17th and 18th centuries, and served as a state prison following the Revolution.

Since the 1920s, the castle has housed the Musée Pyrénéen, which owns one of the region's largest collections of folk art, rural artefacts, tools and other exhibits.

Take the free lift (elevator) from rue Baron Duprat or walk up the ramp at the northern end of rue du Bourg.

Pic du Jer
MOUNTAIN VIEWPOINT

(bd d'Espagne) When the crowds of pilgrims get too much, you can take refuge on the rocky 94m-high pinnacle of the Pic du Jer, which offers panoramic views of Lourdes and the central chain of the Pyrenees.

There are two routes to the top: a punishing three-hour slog along a signed trail, or a speedy six-minute ride on the century-old funicular (bd d'Espagne; adult/child return €9/6; ⊘10am-6pm Mar-Nov & winter holidays,

THE PYRENEES

Lourdes

0 — 300 m
0 — 0.2 miles

Grotte de Massabielle

Av Antoine Béguère

R de Pau

R Pau

Esplanade du Rosaire

Basilique Supérieure

R Monseigneur Theas

Av Monseigneur Schoepfer

Pl de la Merlasse

Chemin de Croix

Esplanade des Processions

Sanctuaires Notre Dame de Lourdes

Basilique Souterraine St-Pie X

R Jean Sempé

Bus for Train Station & Pic du Jer

Pl Mgr Laurence

Av Bernadette Soubirous

R Massabielle

To Citéa St Jean (100m)

Av Peyramale

Pont Vieux

Pau

Av du Paradis

R de l'Egalité

R des Pyrénées

R de la Grotte

Ô St-Jean

R Jacques Fort

Rampe du Fort

R de Bétharram

R Soubirous

Pont St-Michel

Bd de la Grotte

R de la Fontaine

R de Pau

Bd Commandant Célestin Romain

To Relais de Saux (3km);
Tarbes-Lourdes-Pyrénées
Airport (10km); Tarbes (19km)

Av Eugène duViau

Buses to Grotte de Massabielle

Av St-Joseph

Av de la Gare

Bd du Lapacca

R de Langelle

R de Bagnères

Av Joffre

Av du Général Leclerc

Av Maréchal Juin

Pl de l'Église

R Soubies

R Basse

Pl Jeanne d'Arc

Av du Général Baron Maransin

R St-Pierre

Pl Peyra-male

Pl du Marcadal

R Laffite

Av Anselme Lacadé

Chaussée du Bourg

R du Bourg

R des Petits Fossés

R Baron Duprat

R du Fort

R des Pyrénées

To Pic du Jer (600m); Maison de l'Evêque (8km);
Eth Béryè Petit (12km); Hôtel des Rochers;
Le Viscos & St-Savin (15km); Cauterets (30km)

1 2 3 4 5 6 7 8 9 10 11 12 13 14 15 16 17 18 19 20

9am-8pm mid-Jul–Aug). We'll leave it up to you to decide which is the more rewarding.

Either way, the summit makes a superb spot for a picnic. There's a choice of routes back down: a black-run mountain-bike trail, or a more family-friendly option along the Voie Verte des Gaves, a decommissioned railway that finishes up at the lower funicular station.

Take bus 2 from place Monseigneur Laurence.

Chemin de Croix   WALKING TRAIL
The Chemin de Croix (Way of the Cross, sometimes known as the Chemin du Calvaire) leads for 1.5km up the forested hillside from the Basilique Supérieure past 14 Stations of the Cross. Especially devout pilgrims mount to the first station on their knees.

Other Bernadette Sites
On rue Bernadette Soubirous are the Moulin de Boly (Boly Mill; No 12), Bernadette's birthplace; and the Maison Paternelle de

Ste-Bernadette (No 2; admission €1), the house that the town of Lourdes bought for the Soubirous family after Bernadette saw the apparitions. Le Cachot (15 rue des Petits Fossés), a former prison, is where Bernadette lived during the period when she saw the apparitions.

Musée de Lourdes (adult/child €5.50/2.70; ⊙9am-noon & 1.30-6.30pm Apr-Oct) explores the town's history and the life of Ste Bernadette, while the Cinéma Bernadette (6 av Monseigneur Schoepfer; adult/child €6.50/4.50) shows the two-hour feature film *Bernadette*.

★☆ Festivals & Events
Lourdes' renowned week of sacred music, Festival International de Musique Sacrée, is held around Easter.

⌂ Sleeping
Unsurprisingly considering the hordes of pilgrims who descend on the town every year, Lourdes is awash with hotels (it actually has more accommodation than anywhere in France outside Paris). Only a handful in town are worth a second glance, though – book well ahead, especially around religious holidays and from August to October, or better still, base yourself at one of several lovely *chambres d'hôte* instead.

Eth Béryè Petit   B&B €€
(☑05 62 97 90 02; www.beryepetit.com; 15 rte de Vielle, Beaucens; r €58-64) Mountain views unfurl from every window at this idyllic B&B, lodged inside a 17th-century farmhouse. A huge fireplace takes up most of the cosy lounge, while a glorious oak staircase leads up to three country-cosy rooms upstairs. Top of the heap is the Era Galeria room, with its period 19th-century furniture and French windows leading to a private balcony. It's 12km south of Lourdes off the N21 near Beaucens.

Relais de Saux   B&B €€
(☑05 62 94 29 61; www.lourdes-relais.com; Saux; d €90) More period plushness, this time just north of town in a grand ivy-covered mansion. Swags, ruches and half-testers in the olde-worlde rooms, but it's the wonderful surrounds that sell this place: grassy lawns and tree-filled gardens set out against snowy Pyrenean peaks.

Citea St Jean   HOTEL €€
(☑05 62 46 30 07; lourdes@citea.com; 1 av du Paradis; s €48-60, d €68-90; ☎) If you're determined to stay in Lourdes, this town hotel is

just about the best bet, offering plain, modern rooms with nary a Madonna or crucifix in sight. It's part of the Citea chain, so it's businesslike, but even in summer the rates stay reasonable.

Bestwestern Beauséjour HOTEL €€

(☑05 62 94 38 18; 16 av de la Gare; d €78-105; ☎) The attractive heritage facade and glossy lobby promises big things at this Best Western – sadly the rooms are as bland and generic as ever. Still it's businesslike and efficient, handy for the station and it's a lot tidier than many places round town. There's a half-decent bar-brasserie attached to the lobby.

Hôtel Gallia et Londres HOTEL €€€

(☑05 62 94 35 44; www.hotelgallialondres.com; 26 av Bernadette Soubirous; d €120-240; ☺Apr-Oct; ❄@) A fancier option, worth a mention for its lavish chandelier-clad restaurant and wood-panelled lobby, and a lovely garden far removed from the town fizz. The '70s-meets-1700s rooms are considerably less spangly.

Maison de l'Evêque B&B €

(☑05 62 42 02 04; www.maisondeleveque.com; Juncalas; d €50-57) If you've got an aversion to frips and frills, you might want to steer clear of this Juncalas B&B. All four rooms are drowning in flouncy bedspreads, lacy bed canopies and pastel colours, but the whitewashed house has an intriguing history – it was owned by the abbot who confirmed the veracity of Bernadette's early visions. It's in the village of Juncalas, about 8km south of town.

Hôtel des Rochers HOTEL €€

(☑05 62 97 09 52; www.lesrochershotel.com; 1 place du Castillou, St-Savin; d/tr €54/74; ☎) When Lourdes' commercialised clutter gets a bit too much, beat a retreat for this cosy village hideaway in the tiny hamlet of St-Savin, about 16km south of Lourdes (in the same village as Le Viscos). Run by an expat English couple, John and Jane, it's a peaceful place to breathe in the mountain air, offering plain rooms, friendly owners and a decent home-cooking restaurant with outstanding valley views.

✕ Eating

Let's face it – Lourdes' eating options are hardly inspirational. There are plenty of restaurants dotted around the main street, but most are decidedly substandard, so pick very carefully.

Restaurant le Magret TRADITIONAL FRENCH €€

(☑05 62 94 20 55; 10 rue des Quatre Frères Soulas; lunch menu €11.50-14, dinner menu €28; ☺Tue-Sun Feb-Dec) The only place in town worthy of recommendation, a rustic restaurant dotted with sepia-tinted photos of Lourdes. It's strong on regional cuisine – particularly pork, trout, duck and cheese from the Vallée d'Ossau – but the ambience might be a little dingy for some.

Self-Catering

Lourdes' covered market (place du Champ Commun) occupies most of the square. Opposite you'll find a Monoprix supermarket (9 place Champs Commun).

ⓘ Information

Forum information office (☑05 62 42 78 78; www.lourdes-france.com; Esplanade des Processions; ☺8.30am-6.30pm) For information on the Sanctuaires.

Tourist office (☑05 62 42 77 40; www.lourdes-infotourisme.com; place Peyramale; ☺9am-6.30pm)

ⓘ Getting There & Away

AIR Tarbes-Lourdes-Pyrénées airport (www.tlp.aeroport.fr) is 10km north of Lourdes on the N21. There are three daily flights to Paris (Air France), plus a few flights a week to Brussels (JetAir), and London and Manchester (Ryanair). There's no public transport to the airport.

BUS The small **bus station** (place Capdevieille) has services northwards to Pau (though trains are much faster) and is a stop for buses running between Tarbes and Argelès-Gazost (at least eight daily), the gateway to the Pyrenean communities of Cauterets, Luz-St-Sauveur and Gavarnie. SNCF buses to Cauterets (€7, one hour, at least five daily) leave from the train station.

CAR & MOTORCYCLE Lourdes' one-way system changes direction every couple of weeks to keep the souvenir traders happy. Factor in hordes of tourists and you'll be wise to leave your car on the outskirts; there's free parking near the train and bus stations.

TRAIN Lourdes has regular train connections, including TGVs to Pau and Paris Montparnasse. Trains to Toulouse tend to connect through Tarbes.

Destinations served:

Bayonne €21, 1¾ hours

Paris Montparnasse €89.30, 6½ hours

Pau €7.10, 30 minutes

Toulouse €25.10, two hours

Around Lourdes

Grottes de Bétharram
CAVES

(www.betharram.com; adult/child €12.50/7; ☺9am-noon & 1.30-5.30pm mid-Mar–Oct) Along the D937, 14km west of Lourdes, is a series of subterranean caverns carved deep into the limestone rock, and covered with impressive stalactites and stalagmites. Guided visits, by minitrain and barge, last 1½ hours, but be warned: the site gets crushingly busy in high summer.

TOP CHOICE Parc Animalier des Pyrénées
WILDLIFE PARK

(www.parc-animalier-pyrenees.com; adult/child €12/8; ☺9.30am-6pm Apr-Oct) This excellent animal park is home to a menagerie of animals which were once common sights across the Pyrenees, many of which have either been effectively wiped out (such as the wolf) or are teetering on the brink of extinction. Among the residents are marmots, lynxes, giant ravens, squirrels, otters and a few brown bears. It's near the village of Argelès-Gazost.

Parc National des Pyrénées

Sprawling for 100km across the Franco-Spanish border, the Parc National des Pyrénées conceals some of the last pockets of true wilderness left in France. In partnership with the 156-sq-km Parque Nacional de Ordesa y Monte Perdido to the south, this wild mountain landscape is a haven for all kinds of rare flora and fauna, including some of the country's last remaining golden eagles, brown bears and izards (a close relation of the chamois). It's also fiercely proud of its culture and heritage: traditional hill-farming and shepherding are still practised here in much the same way as they were a century ago, although on a much smaller scale.

Within the park's boundaries are shimmering lakes, mountain meadows and the highest peaks in southwest France, including Vignemale (3298m), the Pyrenees' loftiest summit. Unsurprisingly, the park is a popular spot with backcountry hikers and winter skiiers, but even in the high summer you'll still be able to find plenty of quiet trails and pockets of mountain solitude.

The park's boundaries actually cover a tightly defined area that begins at the southern end of the main western valleys of the French Pyrenees and crosses over the border with Spain.

🏃 Activities

Walking

Some 350km of waymarked trails (including the Mediterranean-to-Atlantic GR10)

LE VISCOS

Just 4km south of Argelès-Gazost (16km south of Lourdes) is one of the Pyrenees' jewels, St-Savin. Not only is it officially 'one of France's prettiest villages', but it's home to the wonderful hotel-restaurant **Le Viscos** (☎05 62 97 02 28; www.hotel-leviscos.com; 1 rue Lamarque; d €76-111; ☺closed 2 weeks Jan; ❋🖵).

Run by the seventh generation of the St-Martin family, this country retreat is one of the best gastronomic getaways in the Pyrenees, with cosy rooms stocked with hand-sewn bedspreads and antique furniture, and shuttered windows peeping out onto sublime mountain views.

But it's the **restaurant** (menus €27-89) that keeps people coming from miles around. Run by owner-proprietor and ex-TV chef Jean-Pierre St-Martin, it's one of the most respected tables in southwest France, mixing Basque, Breton and Pyrenean flavours spiced up by the odd flash of fusion inspiration. The house speciality is foie gras served in a variety of creative incarnations, such as a chilled mousse, or on a toasted tartine topped with black truffle. The wine list is full of local cachet, too: Jurançon and Madiran wines both feature heavily. For a real taste adventure, plump for the €89 *menu gastronomique*, which features a belt-busting tour through Jean-Pierre's trademark cuisine, with each dish introduced personally by the chef himself. Be prepared for a long haul and an extra notch on the belt.

Inside the lobby, keep your eyes peeled for some snaps of previous guests (including Paulo Coelho, Michael and Kirk Douglas and the proportionally challenged president himself, Nicolas Sarkozy).

criss-cross the park; some link up with trails in Spain.

Within the park are about 20 *refuges* (mountain huts), primarily run by the Club Alpin Français (CAF). Most are staffed only from July to September but maintain a small wing year-round.

Each of the six park valleys (Vallée d'Aure, Vallée de Luz, Vallée de Cauterets, Val d'Azun, Vallée d'Ossau and Vallée d'Aspe) has a national park folder or booklet in French, *Randonnées dans le Parc National des Pyrénées,* describing 10 to 15 walks. Worthwhile for the route maps alone, they're on sale at local parks and tourist offices.

The park is covered by IGN's 1:25,000 Top 25 maps 1547OT *Ossau,* 1647OT *Vignemale,* 1748OT *Gavarnie* and 1748ET *Néouvielle.*

White-Water Sports

Rivers racing from the Pyrenean heights offer some of France's finest white water, since spring snow melt is supplemented by modest (sometimes not-so-modest) year-round rain, bringing a fairly steady annual flow. Organisations offering rafting and canoeing within or downstream from the national park include A Boste Sport Loisir (☑05 59 38 57 58; www.aboste.com; rue Léon Bérard, 64390 Sauveterre de Béarn) and Centre Nautique de Soeix (☑05 59 39 61 00; http://soeix.free.fr; quartier Soeix, 64400 Oloron-Ste-Marie).

ℹ Information

Park visitor centres can be found at Etsaut, Laruns, Arrens-Marsous, Cauterets, Luz-St-Sauveur, Gavarnie and St-Lary-Soulan. **PNR Pyrenees** (www.parc-pyrenees.com), the park's official tourist site, is packed with useful info.

Vallée d'Aspe

The Vallée d'Aspe has been a transfrontier passage ever since Julius Caesar's Roman legionnaires marched through. South of Pau, the Gave d'Aspe (River Aspe) flows for some 50km from the Col du Somport, which marks the frontier with Spain, down to Oloron-Ste-Marie. Fewer than 3000 people live in the valley's 13 villages.

Its upper reaches are still among the most remote corners of the French Pyrenees and one of the final refuges of their more timid wildlife. But for many people the valley's seclusion is already a thing of the past, especially since the opening of the Tunnel de Somport, an 8km-long road tunnel across the Spanish border, which opened in 2003 despite howls of protest from local residents.

◉ Sights & Activities

FREE Ecomusée de la Vallée d'Aspe

RURAL MUSEUMS

(http://ecomusee.vallee-aspe.com) Life in the Vallée d'Aspe still ticks along at a traditional tilt, and there are four sites around the valley that explore the area's heritage and agricultural traditions, and its connections with the Santiago de Compostela pilgrimage route; they're collectively known as the Écomusée de la Vallée d'Aspe.

There are small folk museums in the villages of Sarrance, Lourdios-Ichère and Borcé, but the most interesting site by far is Les Fermiers Basco-Béarnais (Accous; ☺9.30am-1pm & 2.30-7.30pm), a farmers cooperative and thriving *fromagerie* (cheese shop), where you can sample cheese made from the milk of local local ewes, goats and cows, and stock up with cheesy goodies to take home.

Opening hours at the sites vary widely depending on the time of year; see the website for details.

Outdoor Sports

There are lots of different ways to get out and active in and around the Vallée d'Aspe, with activities from guided walks to white-water rafting and paragliding. The tourist office in Bedous has full lists of accredited operators, along with details of forthcoming guided walks and nature trips around the valley.

One of the best ways to explore the area is from the saddle – Auberge Cavalière (☑05 59 34 72 30; www.auberge-cavaliere.com) in Accous runs multiday horseback trips costing €595/1030 for four/seven days, while La Garbure (☑05 59 34 88 98; www.garbure.net, in French) in Etsaut organises guided hikes and donkey-trekking, with accommodation in local *gîtes* and meals included. Prices start from €110/81 per adult/child for a three-day expedition, or you can even hire your own donkey for the day from €42.

✯ Festivals & Events

The valley holds three annual markets in celebration of its local produce, including an Easter market in Bedous, a summer market in Aydius on the first Sunday of August, and an autumn food fair in Sarrance.

Other events to look out for are Le Transhumance de Lourdios in early June, when the local sheep herds are moved to their summer pastures in early June, and the Fête du Fromage d'Etsaut, a cheese fair on the last Sunday in July.

📖 Sleeping & Eating

Accommodation in the valley is almost entirely geared towards walkers, so hotels and B&Bs are few and far between. There are plenty of campsites and *gîtes d'étapes* dotted around the villages, though – we've listed a few of our favourites below. Most places operate on a *demi-pension* basis.

Auberge Cavalière   B&B, RESTAURANT €€
(📞05 59 34 72 30; www.auberge-cavaliere.com; near Accous; s/d half board €60/101; 🄯🛜) Despite its rustic exterior, this rambling old farm conceals five cute rooms with wood floors, fresh colours and wi-fi, and the owners also run a great country restaurant and offer horse-riding trips round the valley, as well as a self-contained *gîte* overlooking the Cirque de Lescun. The main auberge is about 3km south of Accous and just off the main road.

Au Château d'Arance   B&B €€
(📞05 59 34 75 50; www.hotel-auchateaudarance. com; near Cette-Eygun; r €59-69) From the hamlet of Cette-Eygun, 12km from Lescun, climb eastwards up a narrow, winding lane for 2.25km to reach this impressive 13th-century castle. There are eight rooms, rather old-fashioned, but all with superlative mountain views. The restaurant (*menus* €12 and €31) specialises in *cuisine du terroir* (country cooking).

La Toison d'Or   B&B €€
(📞06 08 70 75 18; www.aubergetoisondor.com; place de l'Église de Cette, Cette-Eygun; s/d/tr/q €40/50/65/75) Also in Cette-Eygun, this homely auberge is another peaceful retreat, offering a couple of doubles and four family rooms, all furnished in (very) rustic style. Luxury it ain't, but the divine hillside position and pleasant restaurant (complete with mountain-view patio, *bien sûr*) merit a special mention.

Le Pic d'Anie   B&B €
(📞05 59 34 71 54; www.hebergement-picdanie. com; Lescun; d/tr €43/58; ⊘Apr-Sep) For Pyrenean atmosphere, this has to be one of the best *chambres d'hôte* in the Pyrenees. In the heart of the mountain village of Lescun,

THE PYRENEAN BROWN BEAR   *MILES RODDIS*

In 2004 in the Vallée d'Aspe, a boar hunter shot the one animal that might (with a great deal of luck) have ensured the genetic survival of the Pyrenean bear. The last surviving native female, known as Cannelle to conservationists, was shot by the hunter, who claimed he was acting in self-defence when the bear charged him. France was in uproar; even then-President Chirac weighed in, declaring it 'a great loss for French and European biodiversity'.

So the Pyrenean brown bear is emphatically dead. But over the past decade-and-a-half, bears have been imported from Slovenia and released, and have now bred successfully. Today, between 15 and 20 brown bears roam the Pyrenees. Tragically, several have been killed in recent years, including one that fell from a cliff and another that was hit by a car on the road between Argèles-Gazost and Lourdes.

The reintroduction of bears is not universally welcomed, though, particularly in the western Pyrenees, where free-roaming sheep are bred for meat (as opposed to fenced sheep producing cheese in the east). It's thought that two to three hundred sheep are killed every year by bears; effective protection requires nightly vigils or the construction of kilometres of fencing to protect flocks.

As bear numbers increase, so too does the controversy. You'll see slogans daubed on rocks, such as '*Non aux ours*' (No to the bears) or '*Pas d'ours*' (No bears); these proliferate throughout the valleys. But the bears still have fans, as evidenced by occasional signs of support such as '*Bonne année et longue vie aux ours!*' (Happy New Year and long life to the bears!).

The government has recently announced that plans to reintroduce more bears to boost the population have been shelved, heralding tough times ahead for this shaggy symbol of French conservation.

WORTH A TRIP

LESCUN

It's worth risking vertigo along the steeply hairpinned, 5.5km detour south of Bedous to the mountain village of Lescun (900m) for jaw-dropping westerly views of the Cirque de Lescun, an amphitheatre of jagged limestone mountains, backed by the 2504m Pic d'Anie.

The village also marks the start of several fantastic day **hikes**. One of the best traces the GR10 northwest via the Refuge de Labérouat and along the base of **Les Orgues de Camplong** (Camplong Organ Pipes). As long as the weather holds, you'll be guaranteed spectacular views back over the Vallée de Lescun and the distinctive Pic du Midi d'Ossau (2884m), but it's a high-altitude hike, so check the weather forecast, wear proper footwear, and pack wet-weather gear just in case.

Another popular route follows the GR10 south from Borce or Etsaut to **Fort du Portalet**, a 19th-century fortress used as a prison in WWII by the Germans and the Vichy government. In summer, two- to three-hour tours (€3) in English can be organised through the Bedous tourist office.

the stout little shuttered house conceals spartan rooms, a beamed dining room and tables covered with red-and-white checked tablecloths. The Carrafancq family also own a couple of self-contained *gîtes* round the village.

La Garbure GÎTE €
(☑05 59 34 88 98; www.garbure.net, in French; per person €12, half board €28) Lovely *gîte d'étape* in Etsaut; also organises donkey treks.

Le Mandragot GÎTE €
(☑05 59 34 59 33; place Sarraillé, Bedous; dm €12) Popular staging post for walkers on the Chemin de St Jacques.

Maison de la Montagne GÎTE €
(☑05 59 34 79 14; http://montagne.randonnee.chez-alice.fr; per person €15, half board €32) *Gîte* accommodation in a converted Lescun barn. The owner runs guided walks.

Camping Municipal de Carole
CAMPGROUND €
(☑05 59 34 59 19; sites €8-12; ☺Mar–mid-Nov) Small and quiet site, off the N134 near Bedous.

Camping Despourrins CAMPGROUND €
(☑05 59 34 71 16; sites €6-8; ☺Mar-Oct) This tiny campsite is just off the N134, tucked behind the Fermiers Basco-Béarnais cheese centre.

❶ Information

Tourist Information

Bedous Tourist Office (☑05 59 34 57 57; www.tourismeaspe.com, in French & Spanish; place Sarraillé, Bedous; ☺9am-12.30pm & 2-5.30pm Mon-Sat) The valley's main tourist office.

Maison du Parc National des Pyrénées
(Park Information Centre; ☑05 59 34 88 30; ☺10.30am-12.30pm & 2-6.30pm May-Oct) The main point of information for the park, housed in Etsaut's old train station

Maps

The 1:50,000-scale *Béarn: Pyrénées Carte No 3*, published by Rando Éditions, is a practical general trekking map of the area. A more detailed option is IGN's 1:25,000-scale Top 25 map 15470T, *Ossau*.

The national park's *Randonnées dans le Parc National des Pyrénées: Aspe* is a pack of information sheets on 11 walks, varying from 1½ hours to eight hours, in and around the valley.

The locally produced *45 Randonnées en Béarn: la Vallée d'Aspe* (€9) offers a great selection of walks in and around the valley.

❶ Getting There & Away

SNCF buses and trains connect Pau and Oloron-Ste-Marie up to 10 times daily. From Oloron there are three to four onward bus connections into the valley via Bedous to Etsaut, the majority continuing to Somport and the Spanish railhead of Canfranc.

Vallée d'Ossau

More scenic splendour awaits in the neighbouring Ossau Valley, which tracks the course of its namesake river for a 60km journey from the watershed at Col du Pourtalet (1794m) to its confluence with the Aspe at Oloron-Ste-Marie. The entrance to the valley as far as Laruns is broad, green and pastoral, but as you travel south the mountains start to stack up in dramatic fashion, before broadening out again near the hamlet of Gabas.

The valley's main village is Laruns (37km from Pau), which has an excellent tourist office and national park centre, both well stocked with information on outdoor activities, including mountain climbing, canyoning, kayaking and horse riding. There are only a couple of hotels and restaurants: the vast majority of visitors tend to stay in one of the many campsites or walking *gîtes*, so the valley is probably best visited as a day trip unless you're packing a tent.

⊙ Sights & Activities

Falaise aux Vautours WILDLIFE RESERVE
(Cliff of the Vultures; www.falaise-aux-vautours.com; adult/child €7/5; ⊙10.30am-12.30pm & 2-6.30pm, closed Jan & Mar) The griffon vulture *(Gyps folvus)* was once a familiar sight over the Pyrenees, but habitat loss, hunting and modern farming methods have all taken their toll on these majestic birds. Now protected by law, over 120 nesting pairs roost around the limestone cliffs of this 82-hectare reserve. Live CCTV images are beamed from their nests to the visitors centre in Aste-Béon. There's also a good display on the vultures' life cycle, with captions in English.

Le Petit Train d'Artouste MOUNTAIN RAILWAY
Six kilometres east of Gabas, the lakeside ski resort of Artouste-Fabrèges (1250m) is hardly the most attractive in the Pyrenees, but it's worth a visit for a quick trip up in the cable car, which soars up the 2032m Pic de la Sagette, and the chance to clamber aboard the open-topped Petit Train d'Artouste (☑reservations 05 59 05 36 99; www.train-artouste.com, in French; adult/child €21.50/17; ⊙half-hourly 8.30am-5pm), a miniature mountain originally built for dam workers in the 1920s.

The train trundles along for 10km from the upper cable-car station to Lac d'Artouste, offering truly heart-stopping views over the valley and the spiky Pic du Midi d'Ossau – don't even think about if you're even vaguely nervy about heights. Unsurprisingly, the train gets busy, carrying over 100,000 passengers in its four months of operation between late May and September. Allow four hours for a visit.

If you're an experienced mountain-biker, you could choose to make the hair-raising BDD *(bicycles de descente)* downhill descent back down the mountain from the Artouste Bike Park. Bikes can be hired for €12/15 for a half/full day: call or ask at the Artouste cable-car stations.

🎎 Festivals & Events

The Vallée d'Ossau is known for its tangy cheese, *fromage d'Ossau,* made here in the high mountains from ewe's milk. You'll see lots of places round the valley selling it in summer, and the valley holds an annual Foire au Fromage (cheese fair) in October.

PYRENEAN PASSES

If you're travelling by road, it's worth remembering that the high-altitude passes around the Vallée d'Ossau, the Vallée d'Aspe and the Vallée de Gaves are often closed due to snow. Many of these mountain passes are infamous among cycling fans as some of the most punishing stages of the Tour de France. Signs are posted along the main roads indicating whether or not they're *ouvert* (open) or *fermé* (closed).

The key ones to look out for are the Col d'Aubisque (1709m) west towards Argelès-Gazost, which is generally only open from May to October. An alternative that's open year-round is the D35 between Louvie-Juzon and Nay.

The narrow D294 between Escot and Bielle corkscrews for 21km over the Col de Marie-Blanque (1035m), providing a useful road link between the Aspe and Ossau valleys. It's generally open from late spring to autumn.

The Col du Pourtalet (1795m) into Spain is usually open for most of the year, as it's an important border crossing, but it also closes regularly during periods of heavy snowfall.

The Col du Tourmalet (2115m) between Barèges and La Mongie is the highest road pass in the Pyrenees. It's only open for a few months of the year, which can be a serious pain if you're thinking about travelling east to the Pic du Midi (for example from Cauterets). When it's closed, you'll have to take an extremely long detour north via Lourdes and Bagnères-de-Bigorre.

ℹ️ Information

La Maison de la Vallée d'Ossau Office de Tourisme (📞05 59 05 31 41; www.valleedossau -tourisme.com; ⏲9am-noon & 2-6pm) On Laruns' main square.

National Park Visitor Centre (📞05 59 05 41 59; ⏲9am-noon & 2-5.30pm) Beside the tourist office in Laruns.

ℹ️ Getting There & Around

Citram Pyrénées (📞05 59 27 22 22) runs buses from Pau to Laruns (one hour, four daily).

SNCF trains from Pau stop at Buzy-en-Béarn from where there are a few onward bus connections as far as Laruns (40 minutes).

Cauterets

POP 1300 / ELEVATION 930M

It might not have the altitude or attitude of its sister ski stations in the Alps, but in many respects Cauterets is a much more pleasant place to hit the slopes. While many of the Alpine resorts have been ruthlessly modernised and crammed to capacity during the winter and summer seasons, Cauterets has clung on to much of its *fin-de-siècle* character, with a stately spa and plenty of grand 19th-century residences dotted round town.

Hemmed in by snowy peaks on every side, Cauterets is a superb summertime base for exploring the forests, meadows, lakes and streams of the Parc National des Pyrénées, and in winter it's doused with snow for at least six months of the year. It's nearly always the first of France's Pyrenean ski stations to open and the last to close.

👁 Sights & Activities

Thermal Spas   HOT BATHS

It wasn't actually the slopes which attracted the first tourists to Cauterets – it was the area's hot springs, which bubble up from deep underground at temperatures between 36°C and 53°C. As always, the waters are rumoured to have numerous healing properties, but miracle cure or not, they're ideal after a long day's hiking.

The **Thermes César** (www.thermesdecau terets.com; rue Docteur Domer; ⏲Feb-Nov) offers lots of different spa packages starting at around €10 for a soak in a hot tub, up to several hundred euros for a multiday spa package.

Pavillon des Abeilles   BEEHIVES

(23bis av du Mamelon Vert; admission free; ⏲3-7pm Wed-Sat) This educational attraction is all about bees, with a glass-sided hive, video and honey of every possible flavour. Longer hours in school holidays.

Pont d'Espagne   WALKING TRAILS

Cauterets is a fantastic summer walking base. Numerous high-altitude trails leave from the viewpoint and giant Puntas car

---

SKIING IN THE FRENCH PYRENEES

Let's be frank: the best Pyrenees skiing lies across the watershed, in Spain's Baqueira-Beret and Andorra's Gran Valira. But the more modest resorts on the French side offer reasonable downhill skiing and snowboarding for beginners and intermediates.

The Pyrenees receive less snow than the much higher Alps and the falls are generally moister and heavier. In addition to downhill skiing, the potential for cross-country skiing, ski touring and, increasingly, snowshoeing is also good.

The French side has over 20 downhill ski stations, and more than 10 cross-country areas.

Ax Trois Domaines Above Ax-les-Thermes are 75km of gentle runs, tracing their way through pine forest and, higher up, the open spaces of Campels.

Barèges-La Mongie This combined resort, on either side of Col du Tourmalet and at the foot of the Pic du Midi de Bigorre, has 69 runs, making it the French Pyrenees' most extensive skiing area.

Cauterets Snow lingers late at this long-established spa town–ski resort; you can still whiz downhill here when other resorts have closed down for the season.

Superbagnères A cabin lift hurtles up from the spa town of Bagnères de Luchon for skiing above the treeline at 1800m.

Val d'Azun The best cross-country skiing in the Pyrenees, about 30km southwest of Lourdes, where you can plough along 110km of trails between 1350m and 1600m.

park at Pont d'Espagne, reached via a four-mile switchbacking D920 from Cauterets (the road is locally known as the Chemin des Cascades thanks to the series of waterfalls which thunder down the valley right beside the road). There's an enormous car park at the top of the road that gets crammed in summer: the first 15 minutes is free, otherwise it's €5 for up to four hours.

Heading south from Pont d'Espagne, there's a choice of two valleys, each slightly different in character. Following the Gave de Gaube upstream through a pine wood brings you to the much-photographed Lac de Gaube and, nearby, Hôtellerie de Gaube, where you can sip a drink or recharge with a snack or midday *menus* (around €15) on the terrace, overlooking a waterfall. Three hours, not counting breaks, is generous for this out-and-back walk. Alternatively, you can cheat by catching the combination télécabine and télésiege (adult/child €8/5) up to the top from the Pont d'Espagne visitor centre, which cuts down walking time to a supremely slack 20 minutes.

A longer trek up the gentler, more open Vallée de Marcadau leads to the high-altitude Refuge Wallon-Marcadau (☑05 62 92 64 28; ⊗Feb–mid-Apr & Jun-Sep) at 1866m. Allow about five hours for the round-trip.

In winter, the Pont d'Espagne is a popular starting point for snowshoe walks and *ski au fond* (cross-country skiing). Ask at the tourist office about local guides.

Shuttle buses (single/return €4/7) between Cauterets bus station and Pont d'Espagne run during the ski season (twice daily) and in summer (six times daily). If you're parking at the Puntas car park, it costs €3 for an hour, €5 for one to six hours, or €7 for more than 12 hours.

Skiing & Mountain Biking

The fast new Télécabine du Lys operates mid-June to mid-September and from December to the end of April. It rises over 900m to the Cirque du Lys, where in summer you can catch the Grand Barbat chairlift up to Crêtes du Lys (2400m). A return trip costs €8/6 per adult/child to Cirque du Lys or €10/7.50 including the chairlift.

During winter, the Cirque du Lys offers around 36km of ski-runs, ranging from 2415m to 1850m, and best suited to beginner and intermediate skiers. Lift passes cost €29.50 per day or €150 for six days. In summer it becomes a great area for

mountain-biking, with a 1500m drop in altitude and plenty of downhill trails.

Ski gear and bike hire are available from several places round town.

🛏 Sleeping

Cauterets has plenty of big hotels, but the vast majority of people choose to stay in *gîtes* or self-catering apartments during the ski season.

⌂ TOP CHOICE Hôtel du Lion d'Or HOTEL €€

(☑05 62 92 52 87; www.liondor.eu; 12 rue Richelieu; d €82-174; ☎) This sweet Alpine-style hotel, under the Logis umbrella, oozes mountain character. The exterior's covered in shutters and window boxes, and inside are lots of charming, old-time rooms decked out in candy-stripe pinks, sunny yellows and duck-egg blues. Knick-knacks and curios are dotted throughout the building – an old gramophone here, a stuffed stag's head there – and the restaurant serves up classic Pyrenean cuisine in cosy surroundings. The owner's a ski instructor, so he's full of tips on things to see and do. Rates tend to fluctuate wildly depending on the season.

Hôtel-Restaurant Astérides-Sacca

HOTEL €€

(☑05 62 92 50 02; www.asterides-sacca.com; 11 bd Latapie-Flurin; r €41-75; ⊗closed early-Oct–early-Dec) On one of the Pyrenees' prettiest streets, lined with 19th-century buildings and often used as a film set, is this venerable, family-run establishment. The checked-fabric rooms have a more contemporary feel than the pastel, floral ones, but all are spacious and appealing. Half- and full-board options let you take full advantage of its splendid restaurant.

Hôtel Christian HOTEL €€

(☑05 62 92 50 04; www.hotel-christian.fr, in French; 10 rue Richelieu; s/d €66/80; ⊗Dec-Sep; ☎) This salmon-pink hotel was originally a posh 19th-century *residence*, and its '80s-style decor could certainly do with a bit of an overhaul. Still, it's clean and very comfortable, and there's a charming rear garden.

Camping Le Péguère CAMPGROUND €€

(☑05 62 92 52 91; www.les-campings.com/peguere; per site €11-13, cabins per week €300-420; ⊗May-Sep) Wonderful mountain-view campsite 1.5km north of town on the D920. Aim for one of the riverside pitches, or plump for a chalet if you're after a bit more comfort.

✗ Eating & Drinking

Le Sacca `TOP CHOICE` TRADITIONAL FRENCH €€
(✆05 62 92 50 02; www.asterides-sacca.
com; 11 bd Latapie-Flurin; menus €17.50-43;
⊙closed 10 Oct–20 Dec) Far and away the
best table in town, the restaurant at the
Asterides-Sacca is a winning blend of classical French fare and artistic presentation.
Mountain produce features heavily – you'll
often see trout, boar and wild game on the
menu – and although it's quite formal inside (starchy napkins, waistcoated waiter),
it's actually a very relaxed affair.

En So de Bedau REGIONAL CUISINE €€
(✆05 62 92 60 21; 11 rue de la Raillère; mains €13-
19, menu €20; ⊙hours vary) A bit rough round
the edges, but for hearty Pyrenean *cuisine
paysanne* you won't find a better place in
town. There's little in the way of decorative
frills – rough stone walls, simple wicker
chairs, scuffed tables – but the rich, traditional dishes are packed with flavour. Look
out for pork dishes made from local black
Bigorre pigs.

La Sierra REGIONAL CUISINE €
(✆05 62 42 68 97; 8 rue Verdun; menus €14-17;
⊙Thu-Tue) Another honest and unpretentious
option, good for local flavours such as grilled
trout, duck and *garbure*, a thick country
soup made with seasonal meat and veg.

La Ferme Basque BAR €
(rte de Cambasque; ⊙hours vary) With a plunging view of Cauterets from its terrace, this
place 4km west of town by road makes a
great spot for a daylight drink.

Self-Catering

Cheese, meats and delicious local sausages
are just some of the things you'll find behind the stalls of Cauterets' covered market (av Leclerc). Other shops worthy of a
mention:

A La Reine Margot SWEET SHOP €
(pl Clemenceau) One of many shops round
town selling the sweet fruit-flavoured pastilles known as 'berlingots', a speciality of
Cauterets. Drop by in the afternoon and
you can often see the sweets being made.

Fromagerie du Saloir GOURMET FOOD €
(av Leclerc) Lots of cheeses, plus meats,
hampers and liqueurs (look out for the
one called Gratte Cul, or 'scratch arse').

Gailhou Durdos GOURMET FOOD €
(rue de Belfort) Local wines and other
specialities.

❶ Information

Maison du Parc National des Pyrénées (✆05
62 92 52 56; place de la Gare; ⊙9.30am-noon
& 3-7pm) Sells walking maps and guidebooks,
and organises guided walks in summer.

Tourist office (✆05 62 92 50 50; www.cauter
ets.com; place Maréchal Foch; ⊙9am-12.30pm
& 2-7pm) The tourist office publishes *Sentiers
du Lavaudon* (in French; €5), outlining seven
easy walks in the area.

❶ Getting There & Away

The last train steamed out of Cauterets' magnificent station in 1947. It now serves as the **bus
station** (✆05 62 92 53 70; place de la Gare),
with SNCF buses running between Cauterets
and Lourdes train station (€7, one hour, at least
five daily).

Vallée des Gaves & Around

Gentle and pastoral, the Vallée des Gaves
(Valley of the Mountain Streams) extends
south from Lourdes to Pierrefitte-Nestalas.
Here the valley forks: the narrow, rugged
eastern tine twists via Gavarnie while the
western prong corkscrews up to Cauterets.

Pic du Midi `TOP CHOICE` VIEWPOINT
(www.picdumidi.com; adult/child €25/15;
⊙daily Feb & Jun–late Sep) The main reason
for venturing along the valley is the chance
to make the unforgettable ascent up to the
Pic du Midi de Bigorre (2877m), one of the
highest points in the Pyrenees. Once the preserve of mountaineers and astronomers, the
Pic du Midi now affords one of the most eye-popping panoramas in the entire Pyrenees.
Several terraces provide 360-degree views all
round the mountain, but needless to say it's
absolutely essential you save it for a nice day –
early morning and late evening are by far the
best times in terms of views.

A cable car climbs right to the top of
the mountain in around 15 minutes from
the ski resort of La Mongie (1800m). Check
the website for opening hours outside of
those given here. If you're travelling east
from the other valleys via the Col du Tourmalet, make doubly sure it's open – see the
boxed text, p673.

Le Donjon des Aigles BIRD PARK
(✆05 62 97 19 59; www.donjon-des-aigles.com;
Beaucens; adult/child €12/7; ⊙10am-noon &
2.30-6.30pm) About 15 minutes' drive south
of Lourdes in the spectacular surroundings
of the 12th-century Château de Beaucens,
you can see one of the world's largest col-

Along with the Pic du Midi, the other absolutely unmissable sight in the Pyrenees is the Cirque de Gavarnie, a breathtaking mountain amphitheatre ringed by icy peaks, several of which top out at over 3000m. With a valley-to-peak height over five times that of the Eiffel Tower, the amphitheatre is impressive enough in its own right, but it's also famous for its huge waterfalls, best seen after periods of heavy rain. In winter, the frozen falls also provide some of the most renowned ice-climbs in the world, frequently used by top mountaineers training for ascents in the Himalayas and other major mountain ascents.

Gavarnie is 52km south of Lourdes at the end of the D921. There are a couple of large car parks in the village, from where it's about a two-hour walk to the base of the amphitheatre. Wear proper shoes, as snow lingers along the trail into early summer. Between Easter and October you can clip-clop along on a horse or donkey (around €25 for a round-trip).

If you still haven't had your scenic thrills, you might feel brave enough to take the detour to another spectacular mountain viewpoint at the little-visited Cirque de Troumouse. It's reached via a hair-raising toll road (€4 per vehicle), which snakes its way precariously up the mountainside to the amphitheatre; there are no road barriers, and the drops are truly stomach-churning, so take things very slowly indeed.

It's about 8km to the top. Snows permitting, the road is open between April and October. Look out for the signposts near Gèdre, 6.5km north of Gavarnie.

---

lections of birds of prey. Among the taloned residents on display are bald eagles, fish eagles, horned owls, vultures and a collection of colourful parrots: you can visit the park throughout the day, but don't miss the daily flying displays at 3.30pm and 5pm (3pm, 4.30pm and 6pm in July and August).

Upper Garonne Valley

ST-BERTRAND DE COMMINGES

On an isolated hillock, St-Bertrand and its Cathédrale Ste-Marie (adult/child incl audioguide in English €4/1.50; ☉9am-7pm Mon-Sat, 2-7pm Sun) loom over the Vallée de Garonne and the much-pillaged remains of the Gallo-Roman town of Lugdunum Convenarum, where you can wander at will for free.

The splendid Renaissance oak choir stalls, carved in 1535 by local artisans, sit below the soaring Gothic east end of the cathedral.

BAGNÈRES DE LUCHON
POP 3032 / ELEVATION 630M

Bagnères de Luchon (or simply Luchon) is a trim little town of gracious 19th-century buildings, expanded to accommodate the *curistes* who came to take the waters at its splendid spa. It's now better known as one of the Pyrenees' most popular ski areas, with the challenging runs of Superbagnères right on its doorstep.

◉ Sights & Activities

For the full range of outdoor possibilities, ask the tourist office for a copy of its free *La Montagne Active* brochure.

Thermes   HOT BATHS
(Health Spa; ☑05 61 79 22 97; www.thermes-luchon.fr; ☉Mar-mid-Nov) Luchon's thermal baths are at the southern end of allée d'Étigny. It's €12 to loll in the scented steam of the 160m-long underground *vaporarium,* then dunk yourself in the caressing 32°C waters of its pool, but there's a huge variety of other packages (from mudpacks to hot stones and nasal douches) if you fancy spoiling yourself for a little longer.

Télécabine   SKI LIFT
(adult/child €7.90/5.90; ☉9am-12.15pm & 2-6pm Jul-Aug, 1.30-6pm weekends May-Jun & Sep, open every day in winter depending on snow conditions) Luchon's ski lift whisks walkers in summer and skiers in winter to Superbagnères (1860m), the starting point for countless walks, ski runs and mountain-bike trails.

Walking

An amazing 250km of marked trails, ranging from gentle valley-bottom strolls to more demanding high-mountain treks, thread their way from Luchon and Superbagnères. The tourist office carries a useful free pamphlet, *Sentiers Balisés du Pays de*

Luchon, and also sells the detailed *Randonnées autour de Luchon* (€10.95).

🛏 Sleeping

Le Castel de la Pique
HOTEL €€

(🖉05 61 88 43 66; www.castel-pique.fr; 31 cours des Quinconces; s €50-60, d €60-70; 🖵) This hotel – formerly one of Luchon's grandest private residences – is chock-full of period charm. The rooms are hardly luxurious, but what they lack in mod-cons they more than compensate for in odd-bod interest. Sanded wood floors, original mantelpieces and tall French windows overlooking the hotel grounds, plus the warmest of family welcomes, make it a really special spot.

Hôtel d'Etigny
HOTEL €€€

(🖉05 61 79 01 42; www.hotel-etigny.com; d €49-138; 🖵) Opposite the thermal baths, this swanky establishment makes the perfect place for some postsoak pampering. The public areas are suitably plush – plenty of upholstered armchairs and chandeliers – but the rooms are quite different, veering from heavy-drape heritage to uncluttered modern. In general, it's worth paying for the more expensive ones. Outside there's a sweet garden where you can breakfast in summer.

Hôtel Panoramic
HOTEL €€

(🖉05 61 79 30 90; www.hotelpanoramic.fr; 6 av Carnot; s €44-75, d €53-75; 🖵) Another spick-and-span option near the centre of town, with corporate-style rooms in standard shades of peach, scarlet and orange. It's not terribly exciting, but the breakfast spread is great and the hotel also offers paragliding packages.

🍴 Eating

Café de la Paix
BRASSERIE €€

(🖉05 61 94 74 70; 19 allée d'Etigny; mains €12-18) Luchon's lively streetside brasserie turns out top-quality fare quick as a flash, especially meat and fish *grillée à la plancha* (grilled Spanish-style on a metal plate).

L'Héptaméron des Gourmets
GASTRONOMIC €€€

(🖉05 61 79 78 55; 2 blvd Charles de Gaulle; menus €25-55; ⊙lunch Sun, dinner Tue-Sun) For a gourmet feed in Luchon, this ubertraditional restaurant gets the local nod, serving up royally rich plates of *filet de jeune cerf* (stag fillet) and *brandade de truite* (trout). It's extremely fussy food, but if you like the formal style, you'll be in for a treat.

L'Arbesquens
REGIONAL CUISINE €€

(🖉05 61 79 33 69; 47 allée d'Étigny; menus €11-25; ⊙closed Wed & dinner Sun) Fondue's definitely the order of the day at this timber-beamed restaurant – there are over 18 varieties on offer, but you'll need at least two people to get through it, and you might feel the need to work off a few calories the next day...

Self-Catering

Luchon's covered market (rue Docteur Germès; ⊙daily Apr-Oct, Wed & Sat Nov-Mar) was established in 1897 and is still going strong.

ℹ Information

Luchon tourist office (🖉05 61 79 21 21; www.luchon.com; 18 allée d'Étigny; ⊙9am-7pm) Shorter hours outside peak season.

ℹ Getting There & Around

SNCF trains and coaches run between Luchon and Montréjeau (€6.60, 50 minutes, seven daily), which has frequent connections to Toulouse (€15.60) and Pau (€17.30).

Vallée de l'Ariège

Deep under the limestone mountains of the sleepy Vallée de l'Ariège, underground rivers have carved out some of Europe's most amazing (and otherworldly) subterranean caverns, many of which many of which are covered with cave paintings left behind by prehistoric people.

◎ Sights & Activities

Lombrives
UNDERGROUND CAVES

(www.grotte-lombrives.fr; standard tour adult/child €7.50/4.50; ⊙May-Sep & school holidays) Europe's largest cave system, with a maze of over 200 stalactite-lined tunnels, grottoes and rock galleries to explore: look out for the sandy expanse known as the Sahara Desert, and several limestone columns variously supposed to resemble a mammoth, a wizard and the Virgin Mary. If you're feeling adventurous, a longer five-hour 'journey to the centre of the earth' (€34.70/25 per adult/child) can be arranged by prior reservation. The cave is 22km north of Ax-les-Thermes on the N20 near the village of Ussat-les-Bains.

Rivière Souterraine de Labouiche
UNDERGROUND RIVER

(🖉05 61 65 04 11; adult/child €8.50/6.50; ⊙9.30am-5.15pm) Beneath Labouiche, 6km northwest of Foix, flows Europe's longest navigable underground river. It's possible to take an amazing 1500m, 75-minute boat trip along part of its length, taking in some of the huge underground caverns and eerie chambers carved out over the course of millions of years.

Château des Comtes de Foix   CASTLE
(www.sesta.fr/chateau-de-foix.html; adult/child €4.50/3.30; ☺9.45am-6.30pm) The triple-towered Château des Comtes de Foix stands guard above the town of Foix. Constructed in the 10th century as a stronghold for the counts of Foix, it served as a prison from the 16th century onwards; look for the graffiti scratched into the stones by some hapless inmate. Today it houses a small archaeological museum. There's usually at least one daily tour of the castle in English. Hours are shorter outside of summer.

Les Forges de Pyrène   MUSEUM
(www.sesta.fr/forges-de-pyrene.html; adult/child €8/6; ☺10am-7pm) In Montgaillard, 4.5km south of Foix, is a living museum of Ariège folk tradition with its own blacksmith, a baker, a cobbler and a basket weaver. Spread over 5 hectares, it illustrates a host of lost or dying trades such as glass-blowing, tanning, thatching and nail-making.

Grotte du Mas d'Azil   CAVE, MUSEUM
(www.sesta.fr/grotte-du-mas-d-azil.html; adult/child €6.30/4; ☺caves 10am-6pm, museum 11am-1pm & 2-7pm) This massive natural rock shelter contains several galleries containing rare prehistoric engravings of bison, horses, fish, deer, a cat and even – most hauntingly of all – a human face. The ticket also includes entry to a small prehistoric museum displaying artefacts discovered in the cave, including flint tools, arrowheads and carvings.

The caves are about 25 northwest of Foix, near the village of Le Mas d'Azil. Opening hours are shorter outside summer.

TOP CHOICE Grotte de Niaux   CAVE ART
(☎05 61 05 88 37; www.sesta.fr/grotte-de-niaux.html; adult/child €9.40/7) The Ariège area has numerous caves used by ancient people. The best known is La Grotte de Niaux, considered to be of similar size and importance as the caves in Lascaux in the Dordogne and Altamira in Spain.

Around the caves' walls are delicate etchings of bison, horses and ibex, but visitor numbers are limited to preserve an even temperature of 12°C inside the cave. Guided tours have to be arranged in advance. There

CHÂTEAU DE BEAUREGARD

If you've always had a secret hankering to play lord of the manor, you won't want to miss this opulent **château complex** (☎05 61 66 66 64; www.chateaubeauregard.net; av de la Résistance, St-Girons; d €80-200; ☎☀) in the little village of **St-Girons**, halfway between St-Gaudens and Foix along the D117. Topped by turrets and surrounded by 2½ hectares of private gardens, it's a bit of an architectural wonder, and the rooms more than live up to the exterior promise: all different, all delightful, all full of quirky touches (such as bathrooms hidden away in the castle's corner towers). Throw in a garden pool, a soothing candlelit spa and an absolutely superb Gascon restaurant (menu €33), and you have one of the best castle hideaways in southwest France. Mum's the word, though...

are hourly tours in summer, dropping to around three a day in winter. From April to September there's usually at least one daily tour in English, but times change regularly, so check in advance with the ticket office.

The caves are near Tarascon-sur-Ariège, abut 12km south of Foix.

Parc de la Préhistoire   MUSEUM
(☎05 61 05 10 10; www.sesta.fr; Tarascon-sur-Ariège; adult/child €9.70/7.20; ☺10am-8pm) This museum-park administers five of the area's key sites, and also houses a fantastic museum exploring the area's ancient history. The centrepiece is the Grand Atelier, in a cutting-edge modern building combining film, projections, cave painting reconstructions, artefacts and exhibits in five separate zones, covering the various stages of the area's artistic and cultural development.

🛏 Sleeping & Eating
Sleeping and eating around Ariège isn't going to set your world on fire, but there are a few half-decent options in and around Foix, and several nice places in the heart-tuggingly pretty village of Mirepoix, about 25 km to the northeast.

TOP CHOICE Hôtel les Remparts   HOTEL €€
(☎05 61 68 12 15; www.hotelremparts.com; 6 cours Pons Tarde, Mirepoix; s €60-80, d €70-90; ☎) If you're driving, you'll be

AUBERGE LES MYRTILLES

Tucked away high in the mountains about 10km to the west of Foix, the Auberge les Myrtilles (☑05 61 65 16 46; www.auberge-les-myrtilles.com; Col des Marrous; r €55-105, half board per person €53.50-65.50; ☒☷) is one of the Pyrenees' secret gems. It feels a bit like stepping into the pages of *Heidi*, with eight contemporary mountain chalet rooms offering truly amazing views across the Ariège countryside. But this is no rustic *auberge*, far from it in fact: there's a jacuzzi, a sauna, and a fantastic pool, all of which offer a different perspective on the surrounding peaks. And as if that's not enough, you can tuck into authentic Ariégeoises home cooking in the excellent restaurant, with dishes such as *cèpes ravioli*, duck stew and the local speciality of *azinat* (sausage, duck and vegetable hotpot). On a sunny summer's day, sitting under trees in the alpine garden, you really won't ever want to leave.

extremely glad you made the detour to this sexy hotel-restaurant in well-to-do Mirepoix. It's an intimate place: just nine rooms, all with their own decorative tics (patches of exposed stone, bundles of twisted willow, stripped-wood floors), plus an absolutely delightful breakfast salon with its original beams and chimney. The restaurant (menus €26 to €48) has made a name for itself, too, thanks to its young chef Nicolas Coutand, and the setting in a brick-vaulted cellar is really one to remember.

Maison des Consuls   HOTEL €€€
(☑05 61 68 81 81; www.maisonsdesconsuls. com; 6 place du Maréchal Leclerc, Mirepoix; d €110-130; ☎) At this elegant hotel, all the rooms have been decorated to echo a historic figure from Mirepoix's history: the nicest are Dame Louise, with its fourposter and fab view over the square, and the Suite de l'Astronome, with a little private terrace overlooking the town's red-tiled rooftops.

Hôtel Restaurant Lons   HOTEL €€
(☑05 34 09 28 00; www.hotel-lons-foix.com; 6 place Dutilh, Foix; d from €53.50) Several of the colourful, good-value rooms at this former coaching inn overlook the river. The attached restaurant (lunch/dinner *menus* from €11.50/14) has similar river views through its picture windows, and offers good-value half board.

Hostellerie la Barbacane du Château
   HOTEL €€
(☑05 61 65 50 44; http://hotelbarbacane.fr; 1 av de Lérida, Foix; d from €50; ☎) Ancient house matched by ancient rooms, all wrapped up in an imposing redbrick *maison bourgeoise* in Foix. It's comfy enough, but it does feel a tad antediluvian.

❶ Information

Foix tourist office (☑05 61 65 12 12; www. tourisme-foix-varilhes.fr; 29 rue Delcassé, Foix; ☺9am-6pm) Shorter hours outside summer.

❶ Getting There & Away

Regular trains connect Toulouse and Foix (€13, 1¼ hours, 10-plus daily).

Toulouse Area

Includes »

Best Places to Eat

» Chez Navarre (p690)
» 7 place St-Sernin (p690)
» L'Esprit du Vin (p696)
» L'Epicurien (p695)
» La Table des Cordeliers (p702)

Best Places to Stay

» Les Bains Douches (p688)
» Château de Pomiro (p703)
» La Lumiane (p703)
» Au Château (p698)
» Domaine de Peyloubère (p700)

Why Go?

Rich food, good wine and slow living: that's what this sun-baked corner of southwest France is all about. Traditionally part of the Languedoc, the redbrick city of Toulouse and the surrounding area has been out on its own since World War II, but scratch beneath the surface and you'll discover the same old southern passions.

The capital city makes the perfect introduction: with its buzzy markets, stately architecture, crackling culture and renowned rugby team, Toulouse is one of France's liveliest provincial cities. Beyond the fringes of La Ville Rose lies a landscape dotted with sturdy *bastides* (fortified towns), soaring cathedrals and traditional country markets, not to mention the historic province of Gascony, famous for its foie gras, fattened ducks and fiery Armagnac. And through it all runs the languid course of the Canal du Midi, the undisputed queen of French canals. Take things slow: life in this corner of France is all about the living.

When to Go

Toulouse

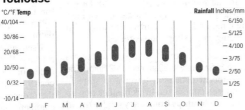

°C/°F **Temp**
40/104 —
30/86 —
20/68 —
10/50 —
0/32 —
-10/14 —

Rainfall Inches/mm
— 6/150
— 5/125
— 4/100
— 3/75
— 2/50
— 1/25
— 0

J F M A M J J A S O N D

February Toulouse celebrates its symbolic flower at the fragrant Festival de la Violette.

March Join the crowds for Albi's annual street carnival.

August Montauban commemorates its martial past at the Legende des Quatre-Cents Coups.

Toulouse

POP 446,200

Elegantly situated at the confluence of the Canal du Midi and the River Garonne, the vibrant southern city of Toulouse is often known as La Ville Rose, a reference to the distinctive hot-pink stone used to build many of its buildings. Busy, buzzy and bustling with students, this grand old riverside dame has a history stretching back over 2000 years, but it's a city with its eyes on the future: it's been an important hub for the aerospace industry since the 1930s, but more recently Toulouse has positioned itself at the forefront of France's drive towards cleaner, greener energies. It's also a city that lives or dies by the fortunes of its rugby team, Stade Toulousain (often known to locals simply as *'les rouges et noirs'*, the reds and blacks), who scooped top honours in the European Cup in 2010.

With a thriving café and cultural scene, a wealth of impressive *hôtels particulier* (private mansions) and an enormously atmospheric old quarter, France's fourth-largest city is a place where you'll definitely want to linger.

◉ Sights

Toulouse's main square is place du Capitole, where Toulousiens turn out en masse on sunny evenings to sip a coffee or an early aperitif. On the square's eastern side is the 128m-long facade of the Capitole, the city hall, built in the 1750s. Inside is the Théâtre du Capitole, one of France's most prestigious opera venues, and the over-the-top, late-19th-century Salle des Illustres (Hall of the Illustrious). Just east of the square is place Wilson, another leafy square ringed with cafés and bistros.

To the south of the square is Toulouse's Vieux Quartier, a tight tangle of meandering lanes and leafy squares brimming with enticing cafés, shops and eateries.

Basilique St-Sernin   CHURCH
(place St-Sernin; ⊙8.30am-noon & 2-6pm) The magnificent octagonal tower and spire of Toulouse's famous red-brick basilica pop up above the rooftops from many angles round the city. This is France's largest and best-preserved example of Romanesque architecture, and it's certainly a sight to behold; inside, the soaring nave and delicate pillars lead towards the ornate tomb of St-Sernin himself, sheltered beneath a sumptuous canopy. The basilica was once an important stop of the Chemin de St-Jacques pilgrimage route.

Cité de l'Éspace   AEROSPACE MUSEUM
(www.cite-espace.com/en; av Jean Gonord; adult/child €22/15.50; ⊙9.30am-7pm, closed Jan) Toulouse's aeronautical history dates back to WWI, and the city was later a hub for pioneering early mail flights to northwest Africa and South America (France's beloved pilot-poet Antoine de St-Exupéry, author of *Le Petit Prince*, often overnighted in Toulouse between sorties). After WWII, Toulouse became the centre for France's burgeoning aerospace industry, and has developed many important aircraft over the last half century including Concorde and the 555-seat Airbus A380, as well as components for many of the world's leading space programs.

On Toulouse's eastern outskirts, the Cité de l'Éspace explores the city's interstellar credentials with a wealth of hands-on exhibits, from space-shuttle simulators and 3D theatres to full-scale replicas of the Mir Space Station and a 53m-high Ariane 5 space rocket. Guided tours (adult/child €4.90/3.90) in French are offered throughout the day, or you can pick up a multilingual audioguide (€4.90/3.90). The best way to get there is by bus; take bus 15 from allée Jean Jaurès to the last stop, from where it's a 500m walk.

Ensemble Conventuel des Jacobins
                                MUSEUM
(www.jacobins.mairie-toulouse.fr; rue Lakanal; ⊙9am-7pm) The church is the centrepiece of this magnificent ensemble. Indeed the extraordinary Gothic structure of Église des Jacobins, flooded by day in multicoloured natural light from the huge stained-glass windows, practically defies gravity. Along the nave, a single row of seven 22m-high columns spread their fanned vaulting like palm trees.

Used as artillery barracks in the 19th century, this is the mother church of the order of Dominican friars. Construction began soon after St Dominic founded the order in 1215, and it took 170 years to complete, including the 45m-tall belfry. Interred beneath the altar are the remains of St Thomas Aquinas (1225–74), early head of the Dominican order.

Equally arresting is a stroll around the Cloître des Jacobins (admission €3), a meditative cloister with boxed-hedge garden and stage for piano recitals in September.

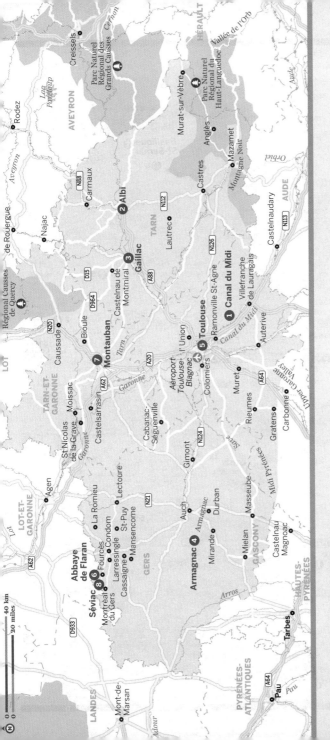

Toulouse Area Highlights

1 Putter down the historic **Canal du Midi** (boxed text p690)

2 Admire the posters, prints and portraits at the **Toulouse-Lautrec Museum** (p693) in Albi

3 Pick up some local vintages around the wine town of **Gaillac** (boxed text p697)

4 Sample some **Armagnac** (p701) straight from the barrel

5 Shop for supplies at Toulouse's bustling covered **markets** (p691)

6 Get spiritual at the **Abbaye de Flaran** (p703), one of southwest France's loveliest Cistercian abbeys

7 Visit the typical *bastide* town of **Montauban** (p696)

8 Marvel at the mosaics at the **Roman villa** (p703) of Séviac near Montréal du Gers

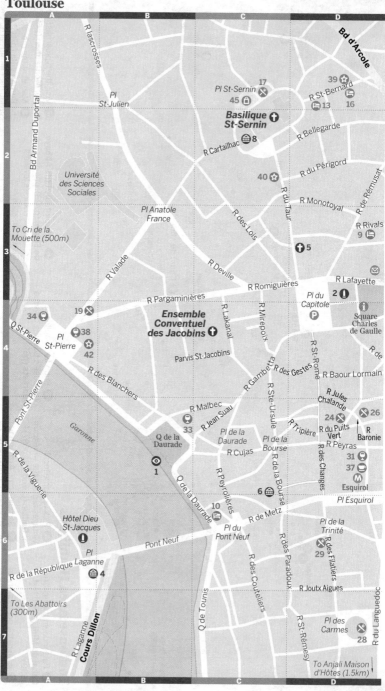

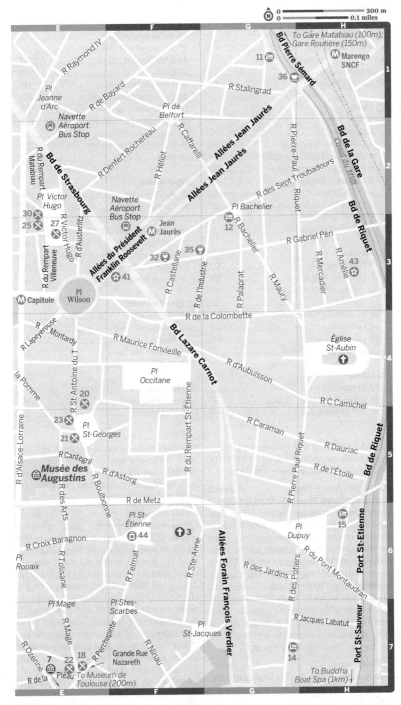

TOULOUSE AREA

Art exhibitions fill the 14th-century refectory, **Les Jacobins** (☏05 61 22 23 82; 69 rue Pargaminières; admission free; ☺9am-7pm).

Musée des Augustins   ART MUSEUM
(www.augustins.org; 21 rue de Metz; adult/child €3/ free, temporary exhibitions €6/free; ☺10am-6pm Thu-Tue, 10am-9pm Wed) Toulouse's fabulous fine arts museum spans the centuries from the Roman era right through to the early 20th century. The highlights are the French rooms, with Delacroix, Ingres and Courbet representing the 18th and 19th centuries, and a few choice works by Toulouse-Lautrec and Monet among the standouts from the 20th-century collection. It's in a former Augustinian monastery, and its two 14th-century cloister gardens are postcard-pretty.

Les Abattoirs   GALLERY
(www.lesabattoirs.org; 76 allée Charles de Fitte; admission €3-10; ☺11am-7pm Sat & Sun, 10am-6pm Wed-Fri) As its name suggests, this red-brick structure was once the city's main abattoir, but it's now been reinvented as a cutting-edge art gallery and venue for concerts and exhibitions.

Hôtel d'Assézat   MUSEUM
(www.fondation-bemberg.fr; place d'Assézat; ☺10am-12.30pm & 1.30-6pm Tue-Sun, to 9pm Thu) Toulouse boasts over fifty *hôtels particulier*, private mansions built for the city's nobles, merchants and aristocrats during the 16th and 17th centuries. One of the finest is the Hôtel d'Assézat, built for a woad merchant in 1555 and now home to the **Fondation Bemberg**, renowned for its fine collection of paintings, sculpture and objets d'art; the 1st floor is mainly devoted to the Renaissance, while impressionism, pointillism and other 20th-century movements occupy the upper floor. Guided tours depart daily at 3.30pm.

Château d'Eau
GALLERY

(www.galeriechateaudeau.org; 1 place Laganne; adult/child €2.50/free; ⊙1-7pm Tue-Sun) Photography exhibitions inside a 19th-century water tower.

Musée St-Raymond
MUSEUM

(www.saintraymond.toulouse.fr; place St-Sernin; adult/child €3/1.50; ⊙10am-7pm) The city's archaeological museum houses Roman sculptures, Christian sarcophagi and Celtic torques.

Musée Paul Dupuy
MUSEUM

(13 rue de la Pléau; adult/child €3/free; ⊙10am-6pm Wed-Mon) Toulouse's decorative arts museum takes in everything from suits of armour to rare clocks.

Museum de Toulouse
MUSEUM

(www.museum.toulouse.fr; 35 allée Jules-Guesde; adult/child €7/5; ⊙10am-6pm) Dinosaur skeletons, ancient fossils and giant reptiles take centre stage at the natural history museum.

Cathédrale de St-Étienne
CATHEDRAL

(Cathedral of St Stephen; place St-Étienne; ⊙8am-7pm Mon-Sat, 9am-7pm Sun) The city cathedral dates mainly from the 12th and 13th centuries, and is worth a visit for its glorious rose window.

Église Notre Dame du Taur
CHURCH

(12 rue du Taur; ⊙2-7pm Mon-Fri, 9am-1pm Sat & Sun) Like the Bastilique St-Sernin, this 14th-century church commemorates the city's patron saint, who was reputedly martyred on this very spot.

Activities

Boat Trips
CRUISES

Toulouse is a river city, and you couldn't possibly leave without venturing out onto the water. From March to November, sev-

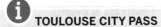

TOULOUSE CITY PASS

The **Toulouse en Liberté card** (per adult/child €10/5) qualifies you for discounts on museum entries, guided tours, sights, accommodation, shopping and lots of other things. Pick it up at the tourist office.

eral operators run scenic boat trips along the Garonne from the quai de la Daurade, and in summer trips also pass through the St-Pierre lock onto the Canal du Midi and Canal de Brienne.

Trips start at around adult/child €8/5 for an hour's scenic cruising. You don't normally need to book; tickets can be purchased on the boat up to 10 minutes before departure. Contact Les Bateaux Toulousains (✆05 61 80 22 26; www.bateaux-toulousains. com), L'Occitania (✆05 61 63 06 06; www.loc citania.fr), which also offers dinner cruises, and Toulouses Croisières (✆05 61 257 257; www.toulouse-croisieres.com).

Tours

The tourist office runs regular walking tours (2hr; adult/child €9/7.50) exploring Toulouse's historic buildings, as well as less frequent ones exploring everything from the city's secret gardens to its metro art. Most tours tend to be in French, although English-language ones are usually available in peak season – ask at the tourist office.

To really get under the city's skin, urban-walk specialist La Gargouille (✆05 34 60 12 75; www.la-gargouille.org; adult/student €6/3) runs guided hikes (in French), departing twice a month from a designated metro station.

TOULOUSE IN...

Two Days

Begin your time in Toulouse by exploring the **Vieux Quartier**, factoring in visits to the **Basilique St-Sernin**, the **Ensemble Conventuel des Jacobins** and some of the city's **hôtels particulier**. Head for lunch at **Au Jardins des Thés** or the restaurants above the **Les Halles Victor-Hugo**, then spend the afternoon exploring the city's modern art institution, **Les Abattoirs**. Book into **Chez Navarre** or **7 place St-Sernin** for supper. Kip at **Les Loges de St-Sernin** or, if you're feeling flush, **Les Bains Douches**.

On day two, spend the morning picking up some picnic supplies at the city's **markets** before blasting off for outer space at the **Cité de l'Éspace**, or taking a leisurely **cruise** along the Canal du Midi and the River Garonne. Sample the gastronomic extravagance at **Anges et Démons** or the more relaxed food at **Au Coin de la Rue** for dinner, perhaps followed by a tipple or two around the bars of **place St-Pierre**.

Festivals & Events

Festival de la Violette FLOWER FESTIVAL
Celebration of Toulouse's favourite flower in early February.

Le Marathon des Mots CULTURAL FESTIVAL
(www.lemarathondesmots.com, in French) 'Word Marathon' revelling in language and literature for four days in June.

Toulouse d'Été MUSIC FESTIVAL
Jazz, classical and other music around town in July and August.

Piano aux Jacobins MUSIC FESTIVAL
(www.pianojacobins.com) Piano recitals in Église des Jacobins in September.

Jazz sur Son 31 JAZZ FESTIVAL
International jazz festival in October.

Sleeping

Toulouse's hotels are strongly geared towards the business crowd, so rates unusually drop at weekends and in July and August. If you're bringing your car, parking can be a real headache. Some hotels offer private garages (usually for an extra charge) or discounted rates at nearby city car parks; otherwise you'll be stuck with expensive street parking.

TOP CHOICE **Anjali Maison d'Hôtes** B&B €€
(☏09 54 22 42 93; www.anjali.fr; 86 grande rue St-Michel; r €80-125; ☎⊞) Taking a 19th-century house with wooden shutters and a secret walled garden as her canvas, Delphine has created four delightful rooms,

---

AIRBUS TOURS

About 10km west of the city in Colomiers is the gargantuan HQ for Airbus, the world-renowned aerospace manufacturer. It's possible to arrange guided tours around the **Jean Luc Lagardère factory** (adult/child €14/11), which mainly builds its A380 aircraft. There's also an optional add-on to see Concorde No 1 (adult/child €4.50/3), one of the first production models of the landmark supersonic aircraft ever to be built (and which later served as the French president's private plane).

Tours must be booked in advance through **Taxiway** (www.taxiway-resa.fr). Cameras are forbidden and you'll need to remember to bring a passport or other form of photo ID.

---

each with its own art-inspired quirk. Hampi is as serene as the journeys to southern India that inspired it; family-friendly Brédoury offers boatlike bunk beds; Tolosa is for wheelchair guests; and black-and-white Cinema Paradiso has its own bedside projector to screen films.

Les Loges de St-Sernin B&B €€
(☏05 61 24 44 44; www.dormiratoulouse.net; 12 rue St-Bernard; r €110-125; ☎⊞) The city's prettiest *chambre d'hôte*, hidden behind an elegant rosy facade just a hop and a skip from the basilica. Owner Sylviane Tatin has polished up her rooms in lively shades of pink, lime and butter-yellow: try St-Sernin, with its exposed stone walls, or Garonne, with its dinky balcony.

Les Bains Douches HOTEL €€€
(☏05 62 72 52 52; www.hotel-bainsdouches.com; 4 & 4bis rue du Pont Guilhemery; d €140-210, ste €280-330; ⊞) If it's style you want, it's style you'll find in abundance at this ubercool establishment, created from scratch by Monsieur and Madame Henriette (motorbike designer and interior designer respectively). They've pulled out all the stops to make this Toulouse's design choice par excellence: shimmering chrome fixtures, sleek surfaces, statement light fittings and a salon-bar that wouldn't look out of place in Paris' more fashionable *arrondissements*.

Hôtel St-Sernin HOTEL €€
(☏05 61 21 73 08; www.hotelstsernin.com; 2 rue St-Bernard; d €111-131; ☎) Another swish little number in the shadow of the Basilique St-Sernin, renovated by a Parisian couple with a sharp eye for interior design. It's beautifully finished – slate-grey walls, crisp white sheets, splashes of zesty colour – but prices have taken an unwelcome hike since the renovations were completed, and you'll need to book well ahead if you want basilica views.

Le Clos des Potiers HOTEL €€
(☏05 61 47 15 15; www.le-clos-des-potiers.com; 12 rue des Potiers; d £100-125, ste €150-225; ☎) This little-known hideaway installed in a *hôtel particulier* near the Cathédrale St-Etienne is one of Toulouse's best-kept secrets – and long may it stay that way. The eight rooms (and two suites) blend the bespoke feel of an upmarket B&B (antique rugs, interesting furniture, original mantelpieces) with the comfort and efficiency of a smart hotel (private garden, lovely lounge, treat tray).

Stretching for 240 languid kilometres between Toulouse and the sultry southern port of Sète, the Canal du Midi is one of the great waterways of southern France. Built in the 17th century and classified as a World Heritage Site since 1996, the canal links the Étang de Thau in the south with the Garonne River in Toulouse. Along with the Canal de Garonne, it forms part of the 'Canal des Deux Mers' (Canal of the Two Seas), which enables boats to enjoy an uninterrupted passage between the Mediterranean and the Atlantic.

The canal was originally commissioned by Louis XIV in 1666 and constructed by the farmer-turned-engineer Pierre-Paul Riquet. It was an enormous engineering enterprise, and took 15 years to complete at enormous expense: in order to overcome the difficult and varied terrain, as well as the ever-present danger of flooding, Riquet had to construct an elaborate system of over 90 locks and 40 aqueducts, as well as a host of dams and bridges, and the first subterranean canal tunnel ever constructed in France.

The canal finally opened in 1681 as the Canal Royal de Languedoc, but it had taken its toll on Riquet: he died several months before the official opening, having racked up enormous personal debts in the hope of recouping costs when the canal finally opened to commercial traffic.

The canal went on to become an important industrial thoroughfare, before it was finally eclipsed by the advent of the railway in the mid-19th century. These days it's mainly used by pleasure-boaters; the tourist office in Toulouse can help with details of local canal hire companies if you feel inspired to explore the canal under your own steam.

Lastly, it's well worth taking a trip upriver to the Musée Canal du Midi (www.musee canaldumidi.fr; blvd Pierre-Paul Riquet, St-Ferréol; adult/child €4/2; ⊙10am-7pm), which explores the history of the canal and the life of Paul Riquet among lovely grounds. It's in the village of St-Ferréol, roughly halfway between Toulouse and Castres along the D2 and D622.

Hôtel des Beaux Arts HOTEL €€€
(☑05 34 45 42 42; www.hoteldesbeauxarts.com; 1 place du Pont Neuf; d €110-250; ※⊛) This handsome heritage hotel sits in a fine spot overlooking the Garonne; unfortunately, it's also on one of the city's busiest commuter routes, so traffic noise can be a problem. But inside you're in for a treat: downstairs, a book-lined lobby stuffed with armchairs and objets d'art and an excellent brasserie; upstairs, individual rooms boasting bespoke wallpaper and snazzy scatter cushions. Breakfast is steep at €14.

Hôtel La Chartreuse HOTEL €
(☑05 61 62 93 39; www.chartreusehotel.com; 4bis bd de Bonrepos; s/d/tr €41/47/57) Station hotels in French cities always tend to be a tad scruffy, and Toulouse is certainly no exception, but this super family-run establishment is a really welcome surprise: clean, friendly and surprisingly quiet, with a lovely little breakfast room and back garden patio. Sure the rooms are a little fusty and small, but for this price, what do you expect?

Hôtel Albert 1er HOTEL €€
(☑05 61 21 17 91; www.hotel-albert1.com; 8 rue Rivals; d €69-89; ※⊛) The city-centre position is the main selling point at this grand old girl, run by the same family for three generations. The rooms are bright and cosy, decked out in colourful checks and cool creams, and the €10 breakfast spread is well worth the outlay.

Hôtel St-Claire HOTEL €€
(☑05 34 405 888; www.stclairehotel.fr; 29 place Bachelier; s €63-69, d €69-129; ⊛) Don't be deterred by the uninspiring exterior: inside this small hotel is a haven of cosiness, with rooms in sunny yellows and creams, spiced up with splashes of feng shui style. Rates at weekends are particularly tempting.

✖ Eating

Bd de Strasbourg, place St-Georges and the western side of place du Capitole are one big café-terrace line-up, perfect for lunch and hot in summer when everything spills outside, but the quality can be very variable when the tables fill up. Rue Pargaminières is the street for kebabs, burgers and other such late-night student grub.

7 Place St-Sernin   REGIONAL CUISINE €€€
(☏05 62 30 05 30; www.7placesaintsernin.com; mains €27-31) For fine French dining, this supremely accomplished restaurant is Toulouse's top address. Head chef Benoît Cantalloube has made a name for himself as one of the city's leading talents; classic southwest ingredients (St-Jacques scallops, Charolais beef, Quercy lamb, Tarbais haricot beans) feature heavily in his cooking, and the setting in a converted church building with views of the basilica is rather lovely. Bookings recommended.

Chez Navarre   GASCON €€
(☏05 62 26 43 06; 49 grande rue Nazareth; lunch/dinner menu €13/20; ☺Mon-Fri) Fancy rubbing shoulders with the locals? Then this wonderful *table d'hôte* is definitely the place, with honest Gascon cuisine served up beneath a creaky beamed ceiling at communal candlelit tables. There's usually only one main meal, supplemented by a soup and a terrine, but its unstarchy atmosphere and unstarry cuisine are hugely convincing.

Au Jardin des Thés   CAFÉ €€
(16 place St-Georges; menus €12.50-15.50) You only have to take one look at the perennially packed-out terrace of this café to know how popular it is with the locals. Salads, *tartes salée* (savoury tarts) and other lunchy treats attract the local office crowd, and it's also a fine spot for afternoon tea, with shady views over one of the city's smartest squares.

Les Halles Victor Hugo   BISTRO €
(place Victor Hugo; menus €10-20; ☺lunch Tue-Sun) For a quintessentially French experience, join the punters at the string of tiny restaurants on the 1st floor of the Victor Hugo food market. They're lunchtime only, and the food is straightforward, simple and unfussy, but they're full of character and the menus are brilliant value.

Faim des Haricots   CAFÉ €
(www.lafaimdesharicots.fr; 3 rue du Puits Vert; ☺Mon-Sat; ☑) A great idea, this – a 100% veggie/wholefood restaurant where everything's served *à volonté* (all you can eat). There are five courses to choose from, usually including a savoury tart, salad, a couple of hot dishes and a pudding; €15.50 buys you the lot with a *pichet* (pitcher) of wine thrown in.

Anges et Démons   CONCEPT DINING €€
(☏05 61 52 66 69; www.restaurant-angesetde mons.com; 1 rue Perchepinte; menus €37-54; ☺dinner Tue-Sat) The city's hot new tip for destination dining, where eating becomes a minor art form. The setting is suitably trendy – moody lighting, exposed brick and minimal furniture, offset by the odd cherub or two – and the menu is a whistle-stop tour of outré ingredients, from yellow chanterelles and mini-asparagus to back of rabbit and veal liver. Superb.

Au Coin de la Rue   BISTRO €€
(2 rue Pargaminières; menu €19-22) This street-corner bistro is a reliable stalwart for simple, unpretentious food, served with the usual dash of French panache. The interior is cute, with a twinkling chandelier and teeny tables, and there's a small pavement patio where you can watch the city spin by.

Emile   FRENCH €€€
(www.restaurant-emile.com; place St-Georges; mains €26-31, menus €36-55; ☺Tue-Sat) Long-standing address for old-school French dining, in business since the 1940s, which

---

CHILLING ON THE CANAL

When the summer sun gets too much in Toulouse, the Canal du Midi makes an ideal place to escape. Here are a few suggestions on ways to unwind on the water...

Buddha Boat Spa (☏05 61 55 54 87; www.buddhaboat.fr; bd Montplaisir; ☺11am-8pm Mon-Fri, 10am-8pm Sat, noon-6pm Sun) Luxuries at this state-of-the-art barge-spa include a Turkish bath, sauna and sun deck. Just the place for escaping the hustle of the city.

La Terrasse aux Violettes (☏05 61 99 01 30; www.lamaisondelaviolette.fr; cakes €3-8; ☺2-6.30pm Mon-Sat) Opposite the train station, this button-cute barge serves up dainty cakes, afternoon teas and ice-creams flavoured with Toulouse's trademark flower, the violet.

regularly graces the pages of the top foodie guides. It's especially known for its *cassoulet*, touted as the city's best.

Self-Catering

Toulouse has two fantastic covered food markets, **Les Halles Victor Hugo** (place Victor Hugo; ⏰7am-1pm Tue-Sun) and **Marché des Carmes** (place des Carmes; ⏰7am-1pm Tue-Sun), as well as lots of intriguing delis and specialist suppliers. A few of our favourites:

Boulangerie St-Georges   BAKERY €
(6 place St-Georges; ⏰9am-5pm Mon-Sat) Great sandwich shop; the €7.50 *formule déjeuner* includes a sandwich, drink and dessert.

Papillotes et Berlingots   SWEET SHOP €
(www.papillotes-berlingots.fr; 49 rue des Filatiers; ⏰noon-7pm Mon, 10am-2pm & 3-7pm Tue-Sat) Candy fans will be in seventh heaven at this olde-worlde sweet shop: look out for chocolate and sweets flavoured with Toulouse's trademark violet.

Le Fournil de Victor Hugo   BAKERY €
(place Victor Hugo; ⏰10am-5pm Mon-Sat) Artisan breads and freshly made sandwiches.

Le Paradis Gourmand   GOURMET FOOD €
(65 rue des Tourneurs; ⏰10am-noon & 2-7pm Mon-Sat) Biscuits, sweeties and other gastronomic goodies.

Xavier   CHEESE SHOP €
(place Victor Hugo; ⏰9.30am-1.15pm & 2.30-7.15pm, closed Mon) The city's best cheese shop.

🍷 Drinking

Almost every square in the Vieux Quartier has at least one café, busy day and night. Other busy after-dark streets include rue Castellane, rue Gabriel Péri and near the river around place St-Pierre.

Au Père Louis   BAR
(45 rue des Tourneurs; ⏰8.30am-3pm & 5-10.30pm Mon-Sat) This gorgeous streetside bar has been slaking the city's thirst since 1889, and it's crammed with interesting nooks and crannies. Lots of wines and beers, and a rather nice line in afternoon tea.

Le Bar Basque   BAR
(7 place St-Pierre; ⏰11am-2am Mon-Fri, 1pm-5am Sat, 1pm-2am Sun) Lively sports bar with a huge outside terrace where Toulousiens like to congregate when the rugby's on.

L'Autre Salon de Thé   CAFÉ
(✆05 61 22 11 63; 45 rue des Tourneurs; lunch menu €12-14, Sun brunch €17; ⏰noon-7pm) An old-world tearoom wedged onto Toulouse's oldest bar, **Au Père Louis**, this sweet spot is perfect for a tart-and-salad lunch or a cuppa poured from a flowery old-fashioned china teapot. Its cakes are particularly irresistible.

Bodega Bodega   BAR
(1 rue Gabriel Péri; tapas €4.50-10; ⏰7pm-2am) All the fun of the *féria* in a historic building where the tax authority once lived. It heaves at weekends with live music, and the tapas is tip-top.

Café des Artistes   CAFÉ
(13 place de la Daurade; ⏰11am-2am) A popular café with the city's artsy set, who come to sip cappuccinos and aperitifs with views of the Garonne.

La Couleur de la Culotte   CLUB
(14 place St-Pierre; ⏰9am-2pm) Funky café-club decked out in zesty shades of pink, orange and blue, offset by plenty of exposed brick and retro styling. Coffees and light bites by day, with DJs spinning electro and ambient after dark.

La Maison   BAR
(✆05 61 62 87 22; 9 rue Gabriel Péri; ⏰5pm-2am) 'The House' is a hip, shabby-chic hang-out for students and trendy types, with plenty of scruffy sofas and second-hand chairs dotted round the old townhouse, and house cocktails and imported beers behind the bar.

Opus Café   CLUB
(24 rue Bachelier; ⏰11pm-6am) Dance until dawn at this much-loved venue for seasoned clubbers who flock here late for that quintessential French *l'after*.

⭐ Entertainment

Cinemas

The city's top places to watch films in *v.o.* (*version originale,* ie not dubbed) are the cinephile **Cinéma ABC** (www.abc-toulouse.fr; 13 rue St-Bernard) and art-house **Cinémathèque de Toulouse** (www.lacinematheque detoulouse.com; 69 rue du Taur).

Live Music

Toulouse has a crackling live-music and clubbing scene. Pick up free listings guides at the *billetterie spectacles* (box office) in **Fnac** (16 allée Franklin Roosevelt), or check http://toulouse.sortir.eu for the latest events.

Le Cri de la Mouette　　　MUSIC, CLUB
(www.lecridelamouette.com; 78 allée de Barce-
lone) Club-bar and gig venue on a converted canal boat.

Le Bikini　　　ROCK
(www.lebikini.com; rue Hermès, Ramonville
St-Agne) Legendary music club which has
been rocking for nigh on a quarter-
century. At the end of metro line B (Ramonville metro stop).

Le Saint des Seins　　　JAZZ, LIVE MUSIC
(www.lesaintdesseins.com; 5 place St-Pierre)
Hip corner club on place St-Pierre, with
regular jam sessions and gigs.

Le Zénith　　　CONCERTS
(11 av Raymond Badiou) The city's big stadium concert venue. Near Arènes and
Patte d'Oie metro stops.

Rest'ô Jazz　　　JAZZ
(www.restojazz.com; 8 rue Amélie; ⊙closed Sun)
Dark, atmospheric and jazzy.

🛍 Shopping
Mainstream shopping embraces rue du
Taur, rue d'Alsace-Lorraine, rue de la
Pomme, rue des Arts and nearby streets.
The place St-Georges area is boutique-
fashionable.

　　Markets include a bit-of-everything **market** (place du Capitole; ⊙Wed), a **flea market**
(place St-Sernin; ⊙Sat & Sun) and an antiquarian **book market** (place St-Étienne; ⊙Sat).

ℹ Information
Laverie des Lois (19 rue des Lois; http://laverie
deslois.spaces.live.com; per hr €4; ⊙cybercafé
9.30am-9pm, laundrette 8am-9pm) Surf the net
while your smocks wash.

Le Ch@t de la Voisine (25 rue des Sept Troubadours; per hr €2; ⊙10am-midnight) Internet
access.

Tourist office (☎05 61 11 02 22; www.toulouse
-tourisme.com; square Charles de Gaulle; ⊙9am-
7pm) Shorter hours outside of summer.

ℹ Getting There & Away
AIR Toulouse-Blagnac Airport (www.toulouse.
aeroport.fr/en) Eight kilometres northwest of
the centre, Toulouse's main airport has frequent
flights to Paris and other large French cities, plus
major hubs in the UK (including London Gatwick
and Stansted, Bristol, Leeds and Manchester),
Spain (Barcelona, Madrid, Seville), Italy (Milan,
Naples, Rome, Venice) and Germany (Frankfurt,
Hamburg, Munich, Breme). Budget carriers
serving the airport include Easyjet, BMIBaby,
Ryanair, KLM, Flybe and Germanwings.

BUS As always in France, you'll find it much simpler to use the train to get around; bus services
are provided by a number of different operators
and mainly operate according to the school
timetable. All buses and coaches stop at the
Gare Routière (bus station; bd Pierre Sémard).

TRAIN Buy tickets at the **SNCF boutique** (5
rue Peyras) in town or at Toulouse's main train
station, **Gare Matabiau** (bd Pierre Sémard), 1km
northeast of the centre. Toulouse is served by
frequent fast TGVs, which run west to Montauban, Agen and Bordeaux (which has connections
to Bayonne and the southwest, plus Paris), and
east to Carcassonne, Narbonne, Montpellier
and beyond. Most smaller towns are served by
slower Corail trains.

Destinations:

Albi €12.00, one hour

Auch €13.60, 1½ hours

Bayonne €39.90, 3¼ hours

Bordeaux €36.90, two hours

Carcassonne €12, one hour

Castres €13.40, 1¼ hours

Lourdes €25.10, 1¾ hours

Montauban €8.50, 30 minutes

Pau €29.00, 2¼ hours

ℹ Getting Around
To/from the Airport
The **Navette Aéroport Flybus** (airport shuttle;
☎05 61 41 70 70; www.tisseo.fr) links the airport
with town (single €5, 20 minutes, every 20 minutes from 5am to 8.20pm from town and 7.35am
to midnight from the airport). Catch the bus in
front of the bus station, outside the Jean Jaurès
metro station or at place Jeanne d'Arc. The trip
takes between 20 and 40 minutes depending
on traffic.

　　A **taxi** (☎05 61 30 02 54) to/from town costs
€25 to €35. Taxis can be booked through one
central reservation number.

Bicycle
The city's bike-hire scheme **Vélô Toulouse**
(www.velo.toulouse.fr) has pick-up/drop-off stations dotted every 300m or so round the city. A
day/week ticket costs €1/5, plus a €150 credit-
card deposit (you'll need a chip and pin card to
work the automated machines).

　　If you'd rather let someone else do the work,
Toulouse's bike-taxi scheme **Cycloville** (www.
cycloville.com; ⊙11am-7pm Mon-Sat) has stations on place Esquirol, place Jeanne d'Arc and
allée Jean-Jaurès. It costs €1 minimum fare plus
€1 per person per kilometre.

Bus & Metro
Local buses and the two-line metro are run by
Tisséo (www.tisseo.fr), which has ticket kiosks

located on place Jeanne d'Arc and cours Dillon. A one-way/return ticket for either costs €1.40/2.50, a 10-ticket carnet is €11.70 and a one-/two-day pass is €4.20/7.

Most bus lines run daily until at least 8pm (night bus lines 10pm to midnight).

Albi

POP 48,600

Looming up from the centre of Albi is one of southwest France's most monumental structures, the enormous Gothic Cathédrale Ste-Cécile. It's more castle than cathedral, with soaring fortified walls built to provide sanctuary from the religious conflicts that plagued the city throughout much of the Middle Ages.

Cathedral aside, Albi's main claim to fame is as the birthplace of one of France's most beloved painters, Henri Toulouse-Lautrec, whose artistic exploits in the bars and brothels of turn-of-the-century Paris are evocatively explored at the town's fantastic Musée Toulouse-Lautrec.

⊙ Sights & Activities

Cathédrale Ste-Cécile   CATHEDRAL
(place Ste-Cécile; ⊙9am-6.30pm) Right at the heart of Albi is the mighty Cathédrale Ste-Cécile, which was begun in 1282 but took well over a century to complete. Attractive isn't the word – what strikes you most is its sheer mass rising over town like some Tolkienesque tower rather than a place of Christian worship.

Step inside and the contrast with that brutal exterior is astonishing. No surface was left untouched by the Italian artists who, in the early 16th century, painted their way, chapel by chapel, the length of its vast nave. An intricately carved, lacy rood screen, many of its statues smashed in the Revolution, spans the sanctuary. The stained-glass windows in the apse and choir date from the 14th to 16th centuries.

On no account miss the **grand chœur** (great choir; adult/child €2/free) with its frescos, chapels and 30 biblical polychrome figures, finely carved in stone.

At the western end, behind today's main altar, is *Le Jugement Dernier* (The Last Judgement; 1490), a vivid doomsday horror show of the damned being boiled in oil, beheaded or tortured by demons and monsters.

Look out for organ concerts in July and August (5pm Wednesday, 4pm Sunday).

Musée Toulouse-Lautrec   MUSEUM
(www.museetoulouselautrec.net; place Ste-Cécile; adult/student €5/2.50; ⊙9am-6pm, closed Tue Oct-Mar) Lodged inside another of Albi's impressive red-brick landmarks, the Palais de la Berbie (built in the early Middle Ages for the town's archbishop), this wonderful museum offers a comprehensive overview of the life and career of Albi's most celebrated son. The museum owns over 500 original works by Toulouse-Lautrec (the largest collection in France outside the Musée d'Orsay), spanning the artist's development from his early impressionist influences en

ALBI CITY PASS

This **card** (€6.50), sold at the tourist office, gives free admission to the Musée Toulouse-Lautrec and cathedral choir and offers other concessions around town.

TOULOUSE-LAUTREC

Henri de Toulouse-Lautrec (1864–1901), Albi's most famous son, was famously short. As a teenager he broke both legs in separate accidents, stunting his growth and leaving him unable to walk without his trademark canes.

He spent his early 20s studying painting in Paris, where he mixed with other artists including Van Gogh. In 1890, at the height of the belle époque, he abandoned impressionism and took to observing and sketching Paris' colourful nightlife. His favourite subjects included cabaret singer Aristide Bruant, cancan dancers from the Moulin Rouge and prostitutes from the rue des Moulins, sketched to capture movement and expression in a few simple lines.

With sure, fast strokes he would sketch on whatever was at hand – a scrap of paper or a tablecloth, tracing paper or buff-coloured cardboard. He also became a skilled and sought-after lithographer and poster designer until drinking and general overindulgence in the heady nightlife scene led to his premature death in 1901.

route to his celebrated poster art and Parisian brothel scenes.

Pride of place goes to two versions of the *Au Salon de la rue des Moulins*, hung side-by-side to illustrate the artist's subtly different technique. Elsewhere around the museum, look out for a fascinating collection of Toulouse-Lautrec portraits and works by artists of the period (including Degas, Matisse and Rodin) on the top floor.

A short stroll away is the privately owned **Maison Natale de Toulouse-Lautrec** (14 rue Henri de Toulouse-Lautrec) where the artist was born. Next-door neighbour is **La Maison de Lapérouse** (14 rue Henri de Toulouse-Lautrec), where the Albi-born explorer lived before sailing around the Pacific in 1785; guided visits can be arranged for groups via the tourist office.

Old Town   ARCHITECTURE

Vieil Alby is an attractive muddle of winding streets and half-timbered houses, one of which, the **Maison du Vieil Alby** (1 rue de la Croix Blanche; ⏰3-7pm Mon, 10.30-12.30 & 3-7pm Tue-Sat) houses a small exhibition on the city's history and its connections with Toulouse-Lautrec.

Boat Trips   CRUISES

From June to September, **Albi Croisières** (www.albi-croisieres.com) runs half-hour **boat trips** (adult/child €6/4; ⏰11am, 11.45am & every 40min 2-6pm) aboard a *gabarre,* a flat-bottomed sailing barge of the kind used to haul goods down the Garonne to Bordeaux. Boats depart from the Berges du Tarn landing stage.

For a longer spell on the river, the company also offers **full-day trips** (single/return €15/23) between the village of Aiguelèze, near Gaillac, and Albi. Trips depart at 10am and include an afternoon in Albi, with the return journey arriving back in Aiguelèze around 7pm.

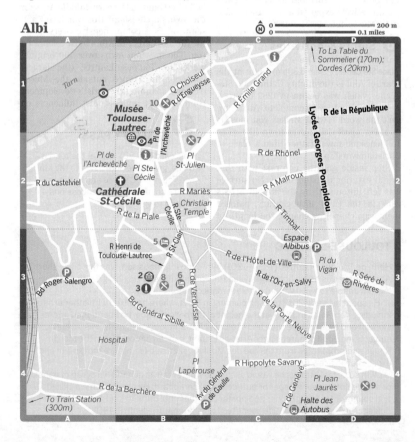

Albi

Festivals & Events

Carnaval CARNIVAL

Albi celebrates Carnaval at the beginning of Lent (February or March) with gusto and confetti.

Voix-là MUSIC FESTIVAL

In May, Voix-là (it's a pun) celebrates vocal music in all its richness.

Pause Guitare MUSIC FESTIVAL

Guitar concerts and traditional vocals in the sumptuous space of place Ste-Cécile. Held in July.

Sleeping

Hôtel St-Clair HOTEL €

(☎05 63 54 25 66; http://andrieu.michele.free.fr; 8 rue St-Clair; s €40-48, d €48-75; ❋🐾) You couldn't ask for a more central position; this higgledy-piggledy hotel is slap-bang in the centre of town, lodged inside a pretty medieval building. It's a real rabbit's warren inside – wonky floors, hefty beams and low ceilings galore – but it's quaint and charming, and on sunny days breakfast is served on a lovely enclosed terrace. Private parking is available (some distance away) for €8.

Le Vieil Alby HOTEL €

(☎05 63 54 14 69; http://pagesperso-orange.fr/le-vieil-alby; 25 rue Henri de Toulouse-Lautrec; s/d €44/53; ⊘closed Jan) Now part of the Logis group, this is another great old-fashioned French hotel perched on the fringes of the old city. The rooms are plain but very pleasant, but the real draw here is the excellent terroir **restaurant**.

Les Buis de St-Martin B&B €€

(☎05 63 55 41 23; http://pagesperso-orange.fr/les-buis-de-saint-martin; 11 rue St-Martin, Marssac sur Tarn; d €110; 🐾) It's a bit of a drive west of town (10km, in fact), but if you've got your own wheels this divine château *chambre d'hôte* in a 19th-century residence is well worth investigating. The two bedrooms (Sophie and Julie) are elegantly done in soft shades of beige, and there's a self-contained *gîte* (cottage) for longer stays. Breakfast is served in the lovely country kitchen.

Eating

Albi has loads of places to eat, including a whole string of places on rue Henri de Toulouse-Lautrec, just downhill from the cathedral.

Le Lautrec RESTAURANT €€

(☎05 63 54 86 55; 13-15 rue Henri de Toulouse-Lautrec; lunch menus €15-17, dinner menus €16-38; ⊘lunch Tue-Sun, dinner Tue-Sat) This excellent restaurant is right opposite the Toulouse-Lautrec family home (in its former life it served as the carriage house and horse stables). It's now one our favourite food finds in Albi, offering a market-driven menu brimming with Gascon goodness and Gaillac wines, and a choice of tempting settings: a knick knack–packed interior or an outside patio shaded by fragrant wisteria.

L'Epicurien RESTAURANT €€€

(☎05 63 53 10 70; www.restaurantlepicurien.com; 42 place Jean Jaurès; menus €26-68; ⊘Tue-Sat) The steely grey and glass facade says it all: this establishment is a temple to cutting-edge contemporary French cuisine, run by Swedish chef Rikard Hult and his wife Patricia. The presentation is so arty you'll almost feel guilty tucking into the dishes: delicate towers of roast monkfish or lamb noisettes, accompanied by an arty slash of sauce or a just-so sprig of herb. An utter spoil.

La Table du Sommelier BISTRO €€

(☎05 63 46 20 10; 20 rue Porta; lunch menus €13-16, dinner menus €25; ⊘Tue-Sat) Across the 11th-century Pont Vieux is this bright, friendly bistro where the food almost takes a back seat to the wines: the owner's a qualified sommelier, and he's passionately knowledgeable about local vintages.

Albi

L'Esprit du Vin GASTRONOMIC €€€
(☎05 63 54 60 44; 11 quai Choiseul; menus €60-98; ☉Tue-Sat) David Enjalran's gastronomic restaurant is a gutbuster, renowned for lavish spreads of fine French food with a sky-high price tag to match. Menus are divided into five 'ateliers' (levels), and take their culinary cue from the changing seasons: the approach is very much Michelin-style, so it might be a bit stuffy for some. The lunchtime 'Pause Gourmande' is marginally more affordable at €23/27 for one/two courses. Reservations recommended.

Le Vieil Alby GASCON €€
(☎05 63 54 14 69; 25 rue Henri de Toulouse-Lautrec; menus from €17.50; ☉closed Jan) For authentic southwest flavours, this hotel restaurant is hard to better – it's a specialist in rich, traditional Gascon fare, heavy on the beef, duck and tarbais beans. House specials include homemade melsat sausages, dried pork stuffed with radishes and (of course) piping hot *cassoulet*.

Self-catering

Albi's landmark turn-of-the-century **covered market** (place St-Julien; ☉8am-2pm plus 5-8pm Fri & Sat) is (as usual) a foodie delight. You can even fill up your water bottle with wine (€1.10 a litre).

Information

Post office (place du Vigan)

Tourist office (www.albi-tourisme.fr; place Ste-Cécile; ☉9am-7pm) Ask for one of the themed walking leaflets around old Albi. Staff make hotel reservations (free by phone or email, €2 in situ). Shorter hours outside summer.

ⓘ Getting There & Away

Pick up information on local bus services at **Espace Albibus** (14 rue de l'Hôtel de Ville; ☉2-5pm Mon, 10am-5pm Tue-Fri). From the main bus stop on place Jean Jaurès, buses serve Castres (€2, 50 minutes, up to 10 daily).

From the **train station** (place Stalingrad) there are trains to/from Rodez (€13, 1½ hours, seven daily), Millau (€21.50, 2¾ hours, two daily) and Toulouse (€12, one hour, at least hourly).

Castres

POP 42,900

Founded by the Romans as a *castrum* (settlement), this sleepy town is best-known as the birthplace of Jean Jaurès, the founding father of French socialism, but it's mainly worth visiting for the Musée Goya (goya@ville-castres.fr; Hôtel de Ville, rue de l'Hôtel de Ville; adult/child €3/free; ☉10am-6pm), which houses a renowned collection of Spanish art, including works by Goya, Murillo, Ribera and Picasso. The museum's gardens were laid out by Le Nôtre, architect of Versailles' parkland.

La Terrasse de Lautrec B&B €
(☎05 63 75 84 22; rue de l'Eglise; d €75-105; Lautrec; ✉) In the quiet village of Lautrec, a few miles drive north of Castres, this excellent *chambre d'hôte* offers spacious rooms with an air of bygone elegance: lofty ceilings, original cornicing, mantelpieces, upholstered furniture and an amazing salon with its own painted rococo fresco. Parking available.

Montauban

POP 53,200

Bastides (fortified towns) litter the landscape of southwest France, and there's no finer example than Montauban, nestled on the banks of the River Tarn. Founded in 1144, Montauban is southern France's second-oldest *bastide* (the oldest is Mont-de-Marsan). All roads lead to its characteristic central square, place Nationale, hemmed in on every side by arcaded walkways and tall pink buildings. Many of the streets around the square would originally have marked the town's fortified walls; the town was badly battered during both the Hundred Years War and the Wars of Religion, and famously withstood an 86-day siege imposed by Louis XIII in 1621 during which the defenders resorted to eating horses, rats and dogs to survive.

◉ Sights

Musée Ingres ART MUSEUM
(13 rue de l'Hôtel de Ville; adult/child €4/free; ☉10am-6pm) Apart from the pleasure of wandering round Montauban's shady streets, the main focus of a visit is this fine arts museum, which centres on the work of the neoclassical painter (and accomplished violinist) Jean Auguste Dominique Ingres, who was born in Montauban in 1780. Inspired by Poussin and David, Ingres became one of the most celebrated portrait painters of his day, and the museum houses many of his key works alongside old masters such as Tintoretto, Van Dyck and Gustave Courbet. The entry ticket also admits you to the

Eat out at any restaurant in this corner of France and you're pretty much guaranteed to stumble across the name of Gaillac somewhere on the menu. This little village is one of the area's top wine producers, particularly known for its rosés, light whites and rich, summery reds.

The vineyards around Gaillac are among the oldest winegrowing areas in France, first planted by the Romans, and benefiting from a kind of crossroads climate halfway between the balmy summer temperatures of the Mediterranean and the cooling rains of the Atlantic.

There are several AOCs (Appellation d'Origines Controlées) covering the Gaillac area, including Gaillac Rouge, Gaillac Blanc Sec and Gaillac Rosé, as well as more unusual ones such as AOC Gaillac Perle (for the area's sparkling or *petillant* white wine) and AOC Mousseux Methode Gaillacacoise (for a special type of Champagne-style sparkling wine made by only a few of the area's vineyards).

There are lots of châteaux dotted around the area offering *dégustation* (tasting) and cellar visits, connected by a signposted Route des Vins (Wine Route).

Have a look at the useful site www.vins-gaillac.com for more information, or contact the Gaillac Tourist Office (☎05 63 57 14 65; tourisme@ville-gaillac.fr; pl St-Michel), which can help you arrange local vineyard visits.

nearby Histoire Naturelle (natural history), Terroir (local costumes and traditions) and Résistance et Déportation (with mementos of WWII) museums.

Another Ingres masterpiece, *Le Vœu de Louis XIII*, depicting the king pledging France to the Virgin, hangs in Montauban's 18th-century Cathédrale Notre Dame de l'Assomption (place Franklin Roosevelt; ◷10am-noon & 2-6pm Mon-Sat).

★ Festivals & Events

Alors Chante   SONG FESTIVAL
A festival of French song in May.

Jazz à Montauban   JAZZ FESTIVAL
A week-long jam in July.

Légende des Quatre-Cent Coups
     STREET FESTIVAL
(400 Blows) This weekend street festival at the end of August commemorates the moment when, says local lore, a fortune-teller told Louis XIII, besieging Montauban, to blast off 400 cannons simultaneously against the town, which still failed to fall.

⌂ Sleeping

Mas des Anges   B&B €€
(☎05 63 24 27 05; www.lemasdesanges.com; 🗢) Five miles south of Montauban is this idyllic rural retreat, a working vineyard surrounded by 4.5 hectares of old vines. It's run by Sophie and Juan Kervyn, a friendly couple who've made winemaking into a life-

long passion. The three ground-floor rooms each have a slightly different theme (African, Latin, Marine). Tree-filled grounds, a fine pool and guest barbecues are the icing on the cake.

Hôtel du Commerce   HOTEL €€
(☎05 63 66 31 32; www.hotel-commerce-montauban.com; 9 place Franklin Roosevelt; s €58, d €59-77; ❊🌐🗢) Hardly spectacular, but this smart family-run hotel is just about the city's best place to stay. Pleasant, floral rooms have shutters overlooking the cathedral square, and there's an impressive breakfast salon that still boasts its original 1930s floor tiles.

Château de Seguenville   B&B €€
(☎05 62 13 42 67; www.chateau-de-seguenville.com; Cabanac Séguenville; d €100-130, tr €140-180, f €180-195; 🗢) Roughly equidistant from Toulouse, Montauban and Auch (and ideal for exploring all three), this spiky-roofed château *chambre d'hôte* makes a grand base for exploring the Toulouse area. A massive central staircase opens onto a 1st-floor gallery and five boho rooms, each named after aristocratic nobles and each with a different view over the gorgeous grounds.

✕ Eating

Morning farmers markets are on Saturday (place Prax-Paris) and Wednesday (place Lalaque), in addition to a smaller daily one (place Nationale).

Le Meilleur Restaurant de la Rue BISTRO €€
(☎05 63 63 18 07; 52 rue de la Palisse; lunch menu
€15, mains €16-21) The 'best restaurant on
the street', eh? Well, who are we to argue?
This sassy restaurant specialises in classic
dishes with a quirky twist ('cuisine inventive', they like to call it): duck breast stuffed
with goat's cheese, or herby langoustines
with Turkish *kadaïf* pastry. The decor's
similarly eclectic: puce chairs, starburst
chandeliers, bric-a-brac, nauticalia, and a
heart-meltingly pretty patio.

Au Fil de l'Eau GASTRONOMIC €€
(☎05 63 66 11 85; www.aufildeleau82.com; 14
quai du Dr Lafforgue; menus €35-50; ☺Tue-
Sat, lunch Sun) Ask someone in Montauban
where to go for a treat, and they'll probably
point you straight to this riverside restaurant, where the modern art and quirky
fixtures are mirrored by the classy *cuisine
gastronomique*. There's an €18 lunch *menu*
Tuesday to Friday.

Les Boissières REGIONAL CUISINE €€
(☎05 63 24 50 02; www.lesboissieres.com; Bioule; menus €22-51) If you don't mind driving,
this much-recommended restaurant in the
little village of Bioule serves some of the
best *cuisine régionale* for miles around.
There are several *menus*: plump for the
market *menu* and sit back to enjoy fresh
French food in garden surroundings. The
hotel rooms aren't bad, either.

ℹ Information

Tourist office (☎05 63 63 60 60; www.montau
ban-tourisme.com; 4 rue du Collège; ☺9.30am-
6.30pm Mon-Sat, 9.30am-12.30pm Sun)

ℹ Getting There & Away

From the **train station** (av Mayenne), about 1km
from place Nationale across the Tarn, trains
serve Toulouse (€8.50, 30 minutes, frequent),
Bordeaux (€27.30, two hours, frequent) and
Moissac (€5.60, 20 minutes, five daily).

Moissac

POP 12,300

Riverside Moissac has been an important
stop-off on the Santiago de Compostela
trail since the 12th century thanks to the
glorious **Abbaye St-Pierre** (place Durand de Bredon), resplendent with some of
France's finest Romanesque architecture.
It's particularly known for its **tympanum**, the crescent-shaped frieze above its

south portal. Completed in 1130, it depicts
St John's vision of the Apocalypse, with
Christ in majesty flanked by the apostles,
angels and 24 awestruck elders. If you've
got time, it's well worth comparing it with
the one in Beaulieu-sur-Dordogne, which
is thought to have been carved around
the same time, very possibly by the same
stonemasons.

Outside, the wonderful **cloister** (adult/
child €5/3.50; ☺9am-7pm) is encircled by
delicate marble columns, topped by carved
capitals depicting foliage, figures or biblical
scenes. Sadly, the Revolution took its toll –
nearly every face is smashed.

Entry to the abbey is via the **tourist office** (www.moissac.fr; 6 place Durand de Bredon;
☺9am-7pm). Hours here and at the cloister
are shorter outside summer.

🛌 Sleeping & Eating

Le Pont Napoléon HOTEL €
(☎05 63 04 01 55; www.le-pont-napoleon.com; 2
allée Montebello; s €43, d €50-70; ☏) This riverside hotel is beautifully situated next to
the bridge built by Napoleon after his visit
to Moissac in 1808. It's definitely worth
splashing out on a room with a view over
the Tarn; if you can, ask for the Napoléon
Suite, which has a touch of designer flair
with its retro-flock wallpaper and zingy
colours. The hotel restaurant, **Le Table de
Nos Fils** (menus €28-42; ☺Fri-Tue) is run by
talented chef Patrick Delaroux, who also
runs weekend cooking courses.

Le Moulin de Moissac HOTEL €€
(☎05 63 32 88 88; www.lemoulindemoissac.com,
in French; esplanade du Moulin; d €80-152; ☏)
Housed in a 15th-century grain mill overlooking the Tarn, this is another treat. In
the rooms, distressed wallpaper, wicker
chairs and tall French windows opening
onto river-view balconies; elsewhere, a super waterside **restaurant** (mains €18 to €55),
a smart sauna-spa and a spiffy jacuzzi sheltered under a brick vaulted roof.

Au Château B&B €€
(☎05 63 95 96 82; www.au-chateau-stn.com; St
Nicolas de la Grave; r €52-103; ✴☏☒) Despite
its historic facade, this supremely swish
B&B in a 19th-century mansion conceals a
contemporary heart. The rooms are all designated as suites, and quite rightly: they're
all huge, and the shiny wood floors, luxurious fabrics and big flatscreen TVs contrast
gracefully with the house's heritage architecture. The Madeleine suite even has its

own lounge and attic bedroom. It's about 10km south of Moissac.

❶ Getting There & Away

A few local buses serve Moissac, but it's much more convenient to catch a **train**. There are frequent connections to Montauban (€5.40, 20 minutes), which has onward services to Toulouse (€12.50).

Auch

POP 23,500

Auch has been a key crossroads since Roman times, when it became the capital of the Roman province of Novempopulana, but the town's heyday was in the Middle Ages, when the counts of Armagnac and their archbishops jointly ran the city and built its cathedral. Its second flowering was in the late 18th century, as new roads were pushed southwards to Toulouse and into the Pyrenees, and in the 20th century it became the capital of the Gers *département*.

The centre of old Auch is perched on the top of a hill, from where a jumble of lanes, steps and courtyards leads down to the banks of the River Gers and the newer quarters of town. In truth, the town's been a little down-at-heel in recent years, but a major investment program has started to clean up many of its buildings, including its famous Renaissance staircase.

❍ Sights

Cathédrale Ste-Marie   CATHEDRAL
(☺8.30am-noon & 2-5pm) Even by French standards, Auch's cathedral is a real eye-opener: Napoleon II was so bowled over he's said to have proclaimed 'A cathedral like this should be put in a museum!'. Started in 1489 and constructed over the course of two centuries, the cathedral spans a range of architectural styles from classic Gothic to showy Renaissance. It's particularly known for its ornately carved choir, a series of stunning 16th-century stained glass windows designed by the artisan Arnaud de Moles, and a gargantuan 17th-century pipe organ, one of the largest in France, built by Jean de Joyeuse.

Little wonder that the whole building's been classed a World Heritage Site by Unesco: to appreciate it at its best, you really need to visit during a service or for one of the chamber concerts held throughout the summer. Ask at the tourist office for forthcoming events.

Behind the cathedral, the 14th-century, 40m-high Tour d'Armagnac was built to house the archive of Auch's archbishops, and briefly served as a prison during the Revolution.

Musée des Jacobins   MUSEUM
(4 place Louis Blanc; adult/child €4/2; ☺10am-noon & 2-6pm) This eclectic museum is one of the oldest in France, founded in 1793 inside a former Dominican monastery. Its eclectic collection came from property seized during the Revolution and includes early Gallo-Roman villa frescos, pre-Columbian artefacts from the Americas and a rich collection of 19th-century Gascon costumes. Show your ticket to the cathedral's choir to get half-price admission to the museum, and vice versa.

Escalier Monumental   ARCHITECTURE
Auch's huge Escalier Monumental (Monumental Staircase) drops down to the river from place Salinis. Built in 1863, it consists of either 275 steps or 370 steps depending on whether you count the double-flighted section at the top. Either way, it's one of the grandest staircases you could ever hope to see, and halfway up you can see a stature of d'Artagnan, the fictional swashbuckling Gascon hero immortalised by Alexandre Dumas in his classic tale *Les Trois Mousquetaires (The Three Musketeers)*. Dumas actually based the character on a real figure, Charles de Batz, a nobleman born in the town of Lupiac (about 35km southwest of Auch) around 1610.

Near the top of the staircase is **The Observatory of Time**, an abstract artwork by the Catalan artist J Plensa, commissioned to commemorate the devastating floods that swept through Auch in 1976.

The Escalier Monumental is currently the focus of a major restoration project, so at least some sections are likely to be shrouded in scaffold until 2011 at the earliest.

🛌 Sleeping

Auch is a bit short on hotels, so you might find it more convenient to visit as a day trip.

Hôtel de France   HOTEL €€€
(☏05 62 61 71 71; www.hoteldefrance-auch.com; 2 place de la Libération; s €67-87, d €72-92, ste €150-220; ❋) Under new owners since 2009, this hotel in the heart of Auch is still the best place to stay in town. A steady refurbishment program is slowly enlivening its rooms: most offer a pleasant blend of old-

fashioned style and modern fixtures, and if you can splash on the *chambres prestige*, you'll be a very happy bunny indeed.

Domaine de Peyloubère   B&B, COTTAGES €€
(✆05 62 05 74 97; www.peyloubere.com; Pavie, Le Gers; 1-night stay s/d €95/125, longer €80/110, cottages per week €480-1850; 🕲🐾🌢) This regal estate 10 minutes south of Auch is an utter treat for longer stays. Set around a listed manor house dating from the 17th century, the estate was owned by the Italian artist Mario Caviglieri until the late 1960s, and many of the gorgeous B&B rooms still sport painted frescos and cupboards designed by the artist's own hand. There's a sauna, spa and heated pool, plus five self-catering cottages that are perfect for longer stays.

Eating & Drinking

A stroll along rue Dessoles uncovers several informal, friendly bars-cum-bistros.

La Table d'Oste   BISTRO €€
(www.table-oste-restaurant.com; 7 rue Lamartine; lunch/dinner menu €16/24; ☉lunch Tue-Sat, dinner Mon-Fri) Fine dining it certainly ain't, but for no-nonsense Gascon grub, this little streetside bistro is well worth a look. Copper pans, rickety furniture and rural bric-a-brac covers the interior, and the menu's heavy on hale and hearty portions of duck, chicken, beef and foie gras.

Au Café Gascon   RESTAURANT €€
(✆05 62 61 88 08; 5 rue Lamartine; ☉closed Sun & dinner Mon & Tue) Next-door neighbour Georges Nosella offers slightly more sophisticated food, but it's still shot through with southwest flavours and ingredients. *Menus* must be booked in advance; otherwise the only choice is the fixed €22 meal. There's often live music while you dine.

ℹ Information

Tourist office (www.auch-tourisme.com; 1 rue Dessoles; ☉9.30am-6.30pm) Inside the 15th-century Maison Fedel; shorter hours outside summer.

ℹ Getting There & Away

From the **bus station** (✆05 62 05 76 37; av Pierre Mendès-France) buses serve Condom (€7, 50 minutes, three daily) and Agen (€12, 1½ hours, five to seven daily). Hourly trains or SNCF buses link Auch with Toulouse (€13.60, 1½ hours) from the neighbouring **train station** (av Pierre Mendès-France).

Condom

POP 7250

Poor Condom, whose name has made it the butt of so many nudge-snigger, English-language jokes (the French don't even use the word, preferring *préservatif* or, more familiarly, *capote anglaise,* meaning 'English hood'). Condom's name is actually a derivation of its old Gallo-Roman name, Condatomagus, and like many Gers towns, it later became an important waypoint for Compostela pilgrims: you'll still probably see plenty of them trudging into town.

These days Condom is a mellow, sleepy town, spanning both banks of the River Baïse. The surrounding area is largely dominated by agriculture and vineyards, and it's also a centre of production of Armagnac, the feisty firewater that's often used to flavour the local Gascon cuisine.

☉ Sights & Activities

There's not all that much to keep you occupied in Condom itself, although the **Cathédrale St-Pierre** (place St-Pierre) is worth a peek. With its lofty nave and elaborate chancel, it's a rich example of Flamboy-

---

LES LINOTTES

For a slice of the good life, eco-chic **Les Linottes** (✆05 62 61 04 79; www.leslinottes. com; Porteteny, Durban; d incl breakfast €59-65), 17km south of Auch, offers country living mixed with admirably green credentials. The creative owners, Laurence and Patrice, have made it a personal mission to restore their three-room *chambre d'hôte* using traditional eco-friendly methods: walls are built from hay-bales plastered with earth and straw, timbers are formed from reclaimed wood, bathrooms are finished in natural stone.

But despite the rustic construction methods, the rooms are utterly contemporary: each has its own little patio terrace overlooking the garden. Best of all, the creative couple behind the project have recently added an ecological swimming pool, filtered naturally by aquatic plants and reeds.

Ask any Gascon: Armagnac slips down just as smoothly as the more heavily produced and marketed Cognac to the north. Produced from white grapes that ripen in the sandy soils hereabouts and aged in barrels of local black oak, it was originally taken for medicinal reasons but is drunk with gusto today, often as a digestive. In local restaurants, Floc de Gascogne – a liqueur wine made from Armagnac and red or white grape juice – is the traditional aperitif.

A couple of major distillers are headquartered in Condom, and driving or cycling among the vineyards, you'll stumble upon one siren-call notice after another, signalling you to taste and buy direct from a small-scale farmer-distiller in his *chais* (traditional wine cellar).

Two dreamy addresses oozing history are 13th-century Château de Cassaigne (☑05 62 28 04 02; www.chateaudecassaigne.com; Cassaigne; ☉10am-7pm Jul & Aug, 9am-noon & 2-6pm Tue-Sun Sep-Jun), 6.5km southwest of Condom, just off the D931 to Eauze, where you can visit the cellars and sample the Armagnac from its 18th-century distillery; and 17th-century Château du Busca Maniban (☑05 62 28 40 38; www.buscamaniban.com; Mansencome; ☉2-6pm Mon-Sat Apr-Nov), the stuff of dreams 5.5km further south along the scenic D229 in Mansencome.

ant Gothic architecture, while on the northern side is a 16th-century **cloister**, topped with a tent-like structure built to provide shelter for Compostela pilgrims.

Musée de l'Armagnac   MUSEUM

(2 rue Jules Ferry; adult/child €2.20/1.10; ☉10am-noon & 3-6pm, closed Jan) For the lowdown on Armagnac, Gascony's traditional cockle-warming tipple, this little museum makes the ideal place to start. It offers a good overview of the history of Armagnac-making, and collects together various bits and bobs of Armagnac-related ephemera including vintage bottles, agricultural tools and a huge 18-ton press dating from the 19th century.

The only thing the museum doesn't offer is the chance to try some of the stuff for yourself. For that, you'll need to head to Armagnac Ryst-Dupeyron (36 rue Jean Jaurès; ☉10am-noon & 2-6.30pm Mon-Fri), one of several Armagnac producers around town offering free sampling. Alternatively, you could try the Cave Cooperative (☑05 62 28 12 16) on the D931.

Musée du Preservatif   MUSEUM

(Condom Museum; ☑05 62 68 25 69; 2 rue Jules Ferry; adult/child €3/1.50; ☉10am-noon & 3-7pm summer) Condom's seasonal Musée du Preservatif has a small exhibition relating to the contraceptive's history from its birth in 1665 to the present day. Some of the exhibits will make you very, very thankful for the invention of latex.

River Trips   CRUISES

From April to October, Gascogne Navigation (☑05 62 28 46 46; www.gascogne-navigation.com; La Capitainerie, 3 av d'Aquitaine) runs 1½-hour river cruises (adult/child €8/6) and 2½-hour lunch cruises (€33/19) along the Baïse River, departing from quai Bouquerie. They also rent small motorboats (hour/half day/full day €30/65/150) for up to six people.

🛏 Sleeping

Le Logis des Cordeliers   HOTEL €€

(☑05 62 28 03 68; www.logisdescordeliers.com; rue de la Paix; d €53-75; ☉Feb-Dec; 🛜🏊) The modern shoebox building isn't much to look at, but this family-run hotel makes a great Condom base, set back from the main town in its own private gardens with a lovely pool. Rooms at the back are cheaper and overlook a street.

Hôtel Continental   HÔTEL €€

(☑05 62 68 37 00; www.lecontinental.net; 20 rue Maréchal Foch; d €43-68; 🛜) Efficient waterfront hotel near the quay, with clean, spick-and-span rooms and an excellent in-house restaurant. Ask for a room overlooking the garden, as the road out front is very busy.

Le Relais de la Ténarèze   HOTEL €€

(☑05 62 28 02 54; 22 av d'Aquitaine; d/tr €51/74) This welcoming *étape pèlerin* (pilgrim stop) run by pinny-clad Madame for the past 15 years gets packed with groups of Spain-bound cyclists and walkers of Chemin de St-Jacques. For hearty home cooking, invest in the evening *menu du terroir*

(€19) of gigantic dimensions. From April to October reservations are essential.

Les Trois Lys
HOTEL €€€

(☎05 62 28 33 33; www.lestroislys.com; 38 rue Gambetta; d €130-170; ❀❀❀) It's by far the most expensive place to stay in town, but if it's heritage, antiques and aristocratic cachet that float your boat, this is definitely the choice. The 10 rooms are set around an amber-stoned 18th-century mansion, and some look over the sweet interior courtyard.

Camping Caravaning Municipal de l'Argenté
CAMPGROUND €

(☎05 62 28 17 32; campingmunicipal@condom. org; chemin de l'Argenté; tent/adult/under 7yr €4/2/1.50; ☉Apr-Sep, reception 1.30-8pm) Condom's town campsite is about 2.5km southwest of town along the D931. The facilities are fairly basic, but it's a pleasant place to pitch your tent, right on the banks of the river with kayak and canoe hire in summer.

✖ Eating

There are a few cheap-and-cheerful restaurants dotted round Condom, but for proper food you're better off going *demi-pension* at Hôtel Continental or the Relais de la Tenarèze, or splashing out at the town's Michelin-starred wonder.

La Table des Cordeliers
RESTAURANT €€€

(☎05 62 68 43 82; www.latabledescordeliers.fr; 1 rue des Cordeliers; menus €25-67; ☉Tue-Sat) Michelin-starred and mightily impressive. Condom's stunning *table gastronomique* is ensconced beneath the vaulted arches of a former chapel. Head man Eric Sampietro is one of the region's big culinary names, and his menu is well stocked with complex Gascon goodies. Top billing goes to the 'Tout Canard' (all duck) starter menu followed by the 'Assiette des Cordeliers', incorporating duck steak, duck liver and a duck pie.

Librairie Gourmande
CAFÉ €

(3 place Bossuet; plat du jour €7; ☉10am-12.30pm & 3.30-7pm Tue-Fri, 10am-12.30pm Sat) Browse for books while tucking into crumbly fruitcake and afternoon tea at this delightful little café, on a quiet square near the cathedral.

Self-catering

The weekly Marché au Gras held Wednesday and Saturday morning in the covered market (place Sapian Dupleix) is more experience than shopping trip.

Churchill's: The British Grocer in Gers (place Sapian Dupleix; ☉10am-12.30pm & 2-5.30pm Tue-Sat) is the place for homesick Brits, with shelves full of Marmite, English teabags and Kellogg's cereal.

Information

Tourist office (☎05 62 28 00 80; www. tourisme-tenareze.com; 50 bd de la Libération; ☉9am-noon & 2-6pm Mon-Sat) The tourist office occupies new premises on the outskirts of town following a fire.

❶ Getting There & Around

Condom's pretty poorly served on the public-transport front. About the only option are the three daily **buses** to/from Auch (€7, 50 minutes). Depending on the season, there's usually one bus which runs on to Toulouse (€17, 2½ hours), and another to Bordeaux (€20.50, 2¾ hours, Monday to Saturday).

Around Condom

This corner of the ancient province of Gascon was in its time wild frontier country, caught between the French, entrenched in Toulouse, and the English with their power base in Bordeaux. The better endowed of the hapless villages caught in the crossfire between opposing forces fortified themselves against attack, creating the distinctive *bastide* towns that now litter the area.

There are several within easy reach of Condom, all of which can be covered in a leisurely morning's drive or, better still, a gorgeous day's bike ride.

◉ Sights

Fourcès
BASTIDE

Some 13km northwest of Condom, Fourcès (the 's' is pronounced) is a picturesque *bastide* on the River Auzoue, worth a visit for its unusual shape – unlike most *bastides*, it's circular rather than square-shaped. The village bursts into colour during the last weekend of April as thousands pour in for its Marché aux Fleurs, more a flower festival than a market.

Cité des Machines du Moyen Age
MUSEUM

(www.larressingle.free.fr; adult/child €8/5; ☉10am-7pm) Sometimes known locally as 'little Carcassonne', the textbook bastion of Larressingle, 5km west of Condom, must be France's cutest fortified village. Just outside town, this outdoor museum (closed in winter) collects together an assortment of replica trebuchets, catapults and siege machines arranged as if they're about to assault the town. You can see several of the machines in action, and kids can clamber around a miniature fort.

Villa Gallo-Romaine ROMAN VILLA
(☑05 62 29 48 57; adult/child €4/free; ☻10am-7pm, closed winter) About 1.5km southwest of the *bastide* town of Montréal du Gers are the excavated remains of a luxurious 4th-century Gallo-Roman villa, once part of the agricultural estate of a Roman aristocrat. Archaeologists so far have revealed the villa's baths, outbuildings and huge areas of spectacular mosaic floors, still boasting dazzlingly bright colours despite centuries of being buried underground.

Admission includes entry to the small museum within Montréal's tourist office (☑05 62 29 42 85; place Hôtel de Ville; ☻9.30am-12.30pm & 2-6pm Tue-Sat) displaying artefacts from Séviac.

Abbaye de Flaran ABBEY
(☑05 62 28 50 19; http://www.fources.fr/abbayeflaran.html; Valence sur Baïse; adult/student €4/2; ☻9.30am-7pm Jul & Aug, closed 2 weeks Jan) Founded in 1151 by Pyrenees monks from Escaladieu, and guarded by a 14th-century fortress door turned pigeon loft, this abbey is the loveliest in southwest France. Built in a remote green spot, it was occupied until the French Revolution, by which point no more than a handful of monks remained. Its vaulted chapter hall propped up by coloured marble columns, refectory with 15th-century triple arch window and decorative moulding (spot the phoenix and pelican), and renovated monks' cells, are particularly fine. Watch for art exhibitions and classical-music concerts in its grounds.

Collegiale St-Pierre CHURCH
(adult/child €4.80/free; ☻9.30am-7pm Mon-Sat, 2-7pm Sun) Towering over the little village of La Romieu, 11km northeast of Condom, this enormous 14th-century collegiale is famous for its twin 33m towers and a fine Gothic cloister. Left of the altar is the sacristy where original medieval frescos include arcane biblical characters, black angels and esoteric symbols. Climb the 136 steps of the double-helix stairway to the top of the octagonal tower for a memorable countryside panorama.

Tickets and access are via the helpful tourist office (☑05 62 28 86 33; www.la-romieu.com).

Les Jardins de Coursiana GARDENS
(☑05 62 68 22 80; www.jardinsdecoursiana.com, in French; adult/child €6.50/4; ☻10am-8pm Mon-Sat mid-Apr–Oct) Also in La Romieu, these landscaped gardens are the handiwork of a local agricultural engineer. Over 700 trees and rare plants, each clearly labelled, flourish in the arboretum English garden, aromatic herb garden and *potager familial* (family vegetable patch). A ticket covering the church and gardens costs €9.30.

Musée Archéologique ARCHEOLOGY MUSEUM
(☑05 62 68 70 22; place du Général de Gaulle; adult/child €4/free; ☻10am-noon & 2-6pm Mar-Sep, Wed-Mon Oct-Feb) Lectoure's archaeology museum displays various finds from local Gallo-Roman sites (including 20 bull- or ram-head pagan altars, used for sacrifice), Roman jewellery and mosaics.

🛏 Sleeping & Eating

La Lumiane B&B €
[TOP CHOICE]
(☑05 62 28 95 95; www.lalumiane.com; grande rue, St-Puy; s €42-52, d €51-61; 🖥🏊) Halfway between Condom and Auch in the gorgeous little village of St-Puy, this is quite simply one of our favourite *chambres d'hôte* in southwest France. It's delightfully simple and heart-warmingly homely, lodged inside a lemon-stoned house graced with china-blue shutters and a sweet garden and enormous tree-fringed pool. Inside, a magnificent stone staircase leads up to two spacious suites, each with their own fireplace and rustic overhead beams, or three cosy rooms on the top floor. Downstairs, owners Alain and Gisele serve up super regional food in the stone-walled kitchen. You really won't ever want to leave.

Château de Pomiro B&B €
(☑05 62 69 57 99; www.chateaupomiro.com; Montréal du Gers; d €150; 🏊) You'll really feel like the king of the castle at this turreted mansion near Montréal. Once a hunting lodge belonging to the Marquis and Marquise de Noë, the château now offers some wonderful period bedrooms, full of intriguing antiques and features: the Grande Chambre even has its own huge open fireplace. Meals available (four-course meal €40).

Languedoc-Roussillon

Best Places to Eat

» Terroirs (p714)
» Carré d'Art (p705)
» La Girafe (p719)
» La Péniche (p725)
» Octopus (p726)

Best Places to Stay

» Hôtel Restaurant du Général d'Entraigues (p713)
» Hôtel Le Guilhem (p718)
» Hôtel des Arcades (p747)
» L'Orque Bleue (p724)
» Hôtel des Poètes (p726)

Why Go?

Languedoc-Roussillon comes in three distinct flavours. Bas-Languedoc (Lower Languedoc), land of bullfighting, rugby and robust red wines, thumbs its nose at more genteel Provence to its east. Here on the plain are the region's major towns: Montpellier, the vibrant capital; sun-baked Nîmes with its fine Roman amphitheatre; and fairy-tale Carcassonne, with its witches'-hat turrets.

Haut-Languedoc (Upper Languedoc) is a sparsely populated terrain. Its limestone hills, great for walking or huffing-puffing cycling, are covered with sparse grasses or cloaked in chestnut trees. Riddled with caves, the hills are split by deep gorges.

Roussillon gives more than a glance over the frontier to Spanish Catalonia, with which it shares a language and culture. Alongside its rocky coastline lies pretty Collioure, which drew the likes of Matisse and Picasso, while the Pyrenees, their foothills capped by stark, lonely Cathar fortresses, stretch westwards, culminating in mighty Mont Canigou, symbol of Catalan identity.

When to Go

Montpellier

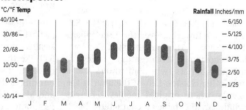

April and May
Springtime walking or cycling in Haut-Languedoc.

Third weekend in September
Grape harvest and partying at Nîmes' Féria des Vendanges.

September and October
Explore magical, still-warm Carcassonne after the summer crowds have left.

BAS-LANGUEDOC

Languedoc takes its name from *langue d'oc* (Occitan), a language closely related to Catalan and distinct from *langue d'oïl*, the forerunner of modern French spoken to the north (the words *oc* and *oïl* meant 'yes' in their respective languages). The plains of Bas-Languedoc boast all Languedoc's towns of consequence, its beaches, rich Roman heritage and France's largest wine-producing area.

Phoenicians, Greeks, Romans, Visigoths, Moors and Franks all passed through Languedoc. Around the 12th century, when Occitan was the language of the troubadours and the cultured speech of southern France, Occitania (today's Languedoc) reached its zenith. However, the Albigensian Crusade, launched in 1208 to suppress the 'heresy' of Catharism, led to Languedoc's annexation by the French kingdom. The treaty of Villers-Cotterêts (1539) made *langue d'oïl* the realm's official language, downgrading Occitan. Continuing to be spoken in the south, it enjoyed a literary revival in the 19th century, spearheaded by the poet Frédéric Mistral, who wrote in the Provençal variety of the language.

Nîmes

POP 146,500

Plough your way through the bleak, traffic-clogged outskirts of Nîmes to reach its true heart, still beating where the Romans established their town more than two millennia ago. Here you'll find some of France's best-preserved classical buildings, together with a few stunning modern constructions as the city continues its centuries-old rivalry with Montpellier, just along the autoroute.

The city's other, less obvious claim to fame is sartorial. During the 1849 Californian gold rush, one Levi Strauss was making trousers for miners. Looking for a tough, hard-wearing fabric, he began importing the traditionally blue *serge de Nîmes*, nowadays known as denim.

◉ Sights

Les Arènes   ROMAN ARENA
(adult/child incl audioguide €7.80/4.50; ⊙9am-6.30pm) Nîmes' magnificent Roman amphitheatre, the best preserved in the whole of the Roman Empire, was built around AD 100 to seat 24,000 spectators. It's easy to forget, as one marvels at the architectural accomplishments of the Romans, what a nasty streak they had too. The arena hosted animal fights to the death, stag hunts, man against lion or bear confrontations and, of course, gladiatorial combats. In the contemporary arena, it's only the bulls that get killed. An advance of a kind, you might say.

There's a mock-up of the gladiators' quarters and, if you time it right, you'll see a couple of actors in full combat gear slugging it out in the arena.

Buy your ticket at the reception point, tucked into the northern walls.

Maison Carrée   ROMAN TEMPLE
(Square House; place de la Maison Carrée; adult/child €4.50/3.70; ⊙10am-6.30pm) The Maison Carrée is a remarkably well preserved rectangular Roman temple, constructed around AD 5 to honour Emperor Augustus' two adopted sons. Within, a 22-minute 3D film, *Héros de Nîmes,* is screened every half-hour. An epic piece of flummery subtitled in English and French, it calls up characters from the city's history.

Carré d'Art   CONTEMPORARY ARCHITECTURE
The striking glass and steel building facing the Maison Carrée and completed in 1993, is the Carré d'Art (Art Square). Within are the municipal library and **Musée d'Art Contemporain**. The work of British architect Sir Norman Foster, it's a wonderful, airy building with a great top-floor **restaurant** and terrace.

Jardins de la Fontaine   ROMAN REMAINS
Nîmes' other major Roman monuments enrich the elegant Jardins de la Fontaine (Fountain Gardens). The Source de la Fontaine was the site of a spring, temple and baths in Roman times. The remains of the Temple de Diane are in the lower northwest corner ('it is strictly forbidden to escalade this monument', says the quaint sign).

BILLET NÎMES ROMAINE

You can make something of a saving by purchasing a **combination ticket** (adult/child €9.90/7.60), valid for three days, that admits you to Les Arènes, Maison Carrée and Tour Magne. Pick one up at the first site you visit.

Languedoc-Roussillon Highlights

1 Gasp at your first glimpse of La Cité's witches'-hat turrets above **Carcassonne** (p730)

2 Spend a morning and more exploring the delights of Montpellier's **Musée Fabre** (p717)

3 Spot vultures looping and swooping high above **Gorges de la Jonte** (p739)

4 Swim under the bridge for an original perspective of the **Pont du Gard** (p712)

5 Drift lazily down the **Gorges du Tarn** (p737) in a canoe

6 Walk a stage or two of Robert Louis Stevenson's **donkey trek** (p735) in Parc National des Cévennes

7 Enjoy spectacular Pyrenean scenery

Mediterranean
Sea

HERAULT

La Grande
Motte

Palavas-
les-Flots

Sète

Le Cap
d'Agde

Agde

Canal du Midi ⑧

Béziers

Vallée de l'Orb

Vallée de l'Orb

Parc Naturel
Régional de
Camargue ⑬

Parc Naturel
Régional du
Haut-Languedoc ④

Mazamet

Montagne Noir

Orbiel

Carcassonne ①

Preixan

Canal du Midi

Narbonne

Réserve
Africaine
de Sigean ⑭

AUDE

Orbieu

To Château de
Puilaurens (12km);
Château de
Montségur (63km)

Château
d'Aguilar ⑯

Château de
Peyrepertuse ⑮

Château de
Quéribus ⑯

Tautavel

Vérdouble

Vérdouble

**PYRÉNÉES-
ORIENTALES**

Prades

**Villefranche-
de-Conflent** ⑦

Vernet-
les-Bains

Pic du Canigou
(2784m) ▲

Massif du Canigou

Vallée de la Têt

Têt

Perpignan

Canet-
Plage

Tech

D900

Collioure

Port-Vendres

Côte Vermeille

Pauilles

Banyuls

Cerbère

Vallée du Tech

Céret

PYRÉNÉES

La Catalane

SPAIN

from the trundling
Train Jaune (Yellow
Train; p749), near
Villefranche-de-
Conflent

⑧ Take a slow boat
along the **Canal du
Midi** (p727)

A 10-minute uphill walk brings you to the crumbling shell of the 30m-high Tour Magne (adult/child €2.70/2.30; ☺9.30am-6.30pm), raised around 15 BC. Built as a display of imperial power, it's the largest of a chain of towers that once punctuated the city's 7km-long Roman ramparts. At the top of its 140 steps, there's an orientation table to help you interpret the magnificent panorama of Nîmes.

FREE **Musée d'Art Contemporain**
CONTEMPORARY ART
(place de la Maison Carrée; ☺10am-6pm, closed Monday) Within the Carré d'Art, the museum houses both permanent and rotating exhibitions of modern art. It merits a visit in its own right and to prowl the innards of this striking building.

Each of Nîmes' other museums follows a common timetable (open 10am to 6pm, closed Monday). Most are in sore need of a new broom.

FREE **Musée du Vieux Nîmes**   MUSEUM
(place aux Herbes) In the 17th-century episcopal palace, this small museum has, in addition to the usual period costumes and furniture, a whole room showcasing denim, with smiling pin-ups of Elvis, James Dean and Marilyn Monroe.

FREE **Musée Archéologique**
ARCHAEOLOGICAL MUSEUM
(13 bd Amiral Courbet) Nîmes' archaeological museum brings together Roman and pre-Roman tombs, mosaics, inscriptions and artefacts unearthed in and around the city. It also houses a hotchpotch of artefacts from Africa, piled high and tagged with yellowing captions such as 'Abyssinia' and 'Dahomey'.

FREE **Musée d'Histoire Naturelle** MUSEUM
Sharing the same building as the Musée Archéologique, this museum has a musty collection of stuffed animals gazing bleakly out. Only the custodians, protected from visitors inside their own glass case, have life.

Musée des Beaux-Arts   ART MUSEUM
(Fine Arts Museum; rue de la Cité Foulc; adult/child €5/3.70) The city's fine-arts museum has a wonderfully preserved Roman mosaic (look down upon it from the 1st floor). This apart, it houses a fairly pedestrian collection of Flemish, Italian and French works.

✪ Festivals & Events

In July and August there's an abundance of dance, theatre, rock, pop and jazz events. Year-round, the tourist office regularly updates its list of events, *Les Rendez-Vous de Nîmes*.

Les Grands Jeux Romains ROMAN RE-CREATION
For two days in mid-April, Romans again take over town with an encampment, bread and circuses in Les Arènes and a triumphal street parade.

Féria de Pentecôte & Féria des Vendanges   WINE, BULLS
Nîmes becomes more Spanish than French during its two *férias* (bullfighting festivals): the five-day Féria de Pentecôte (Whitsuntide Festival) in June, and the three-day Féria des Vendanges celebrating the grape harvest on the third weekend in September. Each is marked by daily *corridas* (bullfights). The Billeterie des Arènes (☎04 66 02 80 90; www.arenesdenimes.com; 2 rue de la Violette) sells tickets both to callers-in and via its website.

Jeudis de Nîmes   FOOD, MUSIC
Between 6pm and 10.30pm every Thursday in July and August, artists, artisans and vendors of local food specialities take over the main squares of central Nîmes, where there are also free concerts of music in all its many genres.

🛏 Sleeping

Royal Hôtel   HOTEL €€
(☎04 66 58 28 27; www.royalhotel-nimes.com, in French; 3 bd Alphonse Daudet; r €60-80; ✱🖥) You can't squeeze this 21-room hotel, popular with visiting artists and raffishly bohemian, into a standard mould. Rooms, some with ceiling fans, others with air-con and nearly all with bathtubs, are furnished with flair. Most overlook pedestrian place d'Assas, a work of modern art in its own right – fine for the view, though the noise might be intrusive on summer nights.

Hôtel Amphithéâtre   HOTEL €
(☎04 66 67 28 51; http://perso.wanadoo.fr/hotel-amphitheatre; 4 rue des Arènes; s €41-45, d €53-70; ✱) The welcoming, family-run Amphithéâtre is just up the road from its namesake. Once a pair of 18th-century mansions, it has 15 rooms decorated in warm, woody colours, each named after a writer or painter. We suggest dipping into Montesquieu or Arrabal, both large and with a balcony

Nîmes

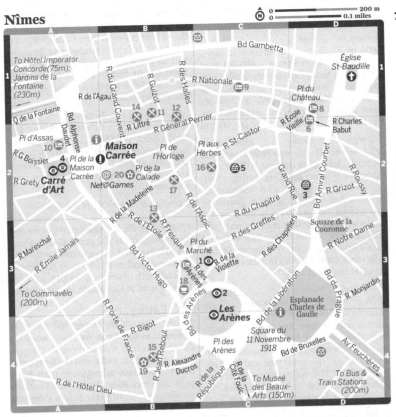

Nîmes

◎ Top Sights

◎ Sights

⊜ Sleeping

⊗ Eating

⊜ Drinking

◉ Entertainment

overlooking pedestrian place du Marché. Rooms on the 3rd floor enjoy air-con.

Maison de l'Octroi
B&B €€

(☑04 66 27 15 95; www.bed-breakfast-nimes. com; 209 chemin de Russan; r €80-85) Host Nicole Crès keeps her two *chambre d'hôte* rooms spick and span and serves delicious breakfasts. Rooms overlook a 5000-sq-metre garden shaded by oak and lime trees. Her house is 1.5km north of the city centre.

Auberge de Jeunesse
YOUTH HOSTEL €

(☑04 66 68 03 20; www.hinimes.com; 257 chemin de l'Auberge de Jeunesse, la Cigale; dm/d €13.50/34; ⊙closed Jan) This sterling, well-equipped youth hostel with self-catering facilities has everything from dorms to cute houses for two to six in its extensive grounds, 3.5km northwest of the train station. It rents out bikes (per day €14) and there's limited camping (per person €6.65). Take bus I, direction Alès or Villeverte, and get off at the Stade stop.

New Hôtel La Baume
HOTEL €€

(☑04 66 76 28 42; www.new-hotel.com; 21 rue Nationale; s/d €110/140; ✵@☎) In an unfashionable part of town and in fact far from new, this 34-room hotel occupies an attractive 17th-century town mansion with a glorious interior courtyard and twisting stairway. The bedrooms, decorated in sensuous ochre, beige and cream, blend the traditional and strictly contemporary.

Hôtel Central
HOTEL €

(☑04 66 67 27 75; www.hotel-central.org; 2 place du Château; s/d €45/50; ☎) With its creaky floorboards and bunches of wildflowers painted on each bedroom door, this friendly hotel is full of character. Room 20, on the 5th floor, has great rooftop views.

Hôtel Imperator Concorde
HOTEL €€€

(☑04 66 21 90 30; http://nimes.concorde-hotels. com; quai de la Fontaine; r €175-243; ✵☎) This *grande dame* of Nîmes hotels is a favourite

---

THE CROCODILE OF NÎMES

Around town and in tourist literature, you'll see the city's shield: a crocodile chained to a palm tree. It recalls the city's foundation, when retiring Roman legionnaires who had sweated with Caesar during his River Nile campaign, were granted land to cultivate hereabouts.

---

of visiting matadors. Its bar, the 'Hemingway', commemorates the swaggering author's brief presence here in room 310. The 62 rooms are richly draped and furnished and there's a large garden with a playing fountain. Its highly regarded restaurant, L'Enclos de la Fontaine, is equally grand and distinguished.

Hôtel Acanthe du Temple
HOTEL €

(☑04 66 67 54 61; www.hotel-temple.com; 1 rue Charles Babut; s €42-50, d €54-65; ✵☎) At this long-established hotel, every room is neat and clean and has its own individual decor. Five rooms have air-con and the rest come with fans.

Camping Domaine de la Bastide
CAMPGROUND €

(☑04 66 62 05 82; www.camping-nimes.com; rte de Générac; site & 2 people €14.90; ⊙year-round) This shady campground with bar/restaurant and small children's playground is 4km south of town on the D13. Take bus D and get off at La Bastide, the terminus.

✗ Eating

Nîmes' gastronomy owes as much to Provence as to Languedoc. Tasty southern delights, such as aïoli and *rouille* (mayonnaise of olive oil, garlic and chilli peppers), are as abundant as *cassoulet* (rich bean, pork and duck stew). Sample the Costières de Nîmes wines from the pebbly vineyards to the south.

TOP CHOICE Carré d'Art
CLASSIC FRENCH €€

(☑04 66 67 52 40; www.restaurant -lecarredart.com, in French; 2 rue Gaston Boissier; 1-/2-/3-course menus €19/24/29; ⊙closed Sun) This is a place to enjoy exceptional cuisine in sublimely tasteful surroundings. The classical decor with its gilded mirrors and moulded ceilings blends harmoniously with fresh flowers, bright, contemporary artwork, cascading, feather-light chandeliers and *sotto voce* canned jazz.

Le Marché sur la Table
MODERN FRENCH €€

(☑04 66 67 22 50; 10 rue Littré; mains €17-19; ⊙Wed-Sun) You *could* just pop in for a glass of wine at this friendly spot, run by up-and-coming young chef Éric Vidal (see his impressive culinary credentials on the toilet wall, no less) and his partner, Caroline. But you'd be missing a lot. Éric buys fresh and organic from the nearby food market, his fish is never farmed and Caroline maintains a large selection of local wines. Eat in the attractively furnished interior or quiet, green rear courtyard.

Au Plaisir des Halles MEDITERRANEAN €€
(☎04 66 36 01 02; 4 rue Littré; mains €24-30; ☺Tue-Sat) Ingredients here are the freshest and the lunchtime three-course *menu* (€20) is excellent value. The photo portraits around the walls are of the winegrowers whose produce features on its impressive list of Languedoc vintages. Located just along the road from the covered market.

Le 9 BAR, RESTAURANT €€
(☎04 66 21 80 77; 9 rue de l'Étoile; mains €15-18, lunch menu €15; ☺Mon-Sat & lunch Sun May-Sep) Have a meal or simply drop in for a drink at this mildly eccentric place, tucked away behind high green doors with just a sign swinging outside. Eat in the vast, arched former stables or in the leafy, vine-clad courtyard. Everything except the lunch *menu* is à la carte.

Les Olivades RESTAURANT, WINE €€
(☎04 66 21 71 78; 18 rue Jean Reboul; mains around €13, lunch/dinner menus €12/22; ☺Tue-Fri & dinner Sat) To the rear of this excellent wine shop, which alone justifies a visit, there's an intimate dining area, where Madame in the kitchen and her husband as maître will treat you royally.

Self-Catering
There are colourful Thursday markets in the old city in July and August. Year-round, Nîmes' covered food market (rue Général Perrier) offers riches for the picnic hamper.

Maison Villaret BAKERY
(13 rue de la Madeleine) This family bakery makes 25 different kinds of bread, cakes, biscuits and local specialities such as *caladons* (honey and almond-studded biscuits).

L'Oustaù Nadal GOURMET FOOD
(place aux Herbes; ☺closed Mon) Packed with goodies such as brandade, tapenade, honey from the hills and virgin olive oil, including three kinds on draught.

🍷 Drinking
Place aux Herbes and place du Marché become bustling, communal outdoor cafés in summer. For somewhere more tranquil, sip a drink on place d'Assas, the creation of quirky French artist Martial Raysse.

Le Ciel de Nîmes ROOFTOP BAR
(☎04 66 36 71 70; place de la Maison Carrée; ☺10am-6pm Tue-Sun year-round, to 10.30pm Fri & Sat May-Sep) On the rooftop terrace of the Carré d'Art, this is the perfect place for a relaxing drink, lording it over the hubbub in the square below. It also does tasty, filling and delightfully presented **lunches** (€16 to €28).

Grand Café de la Bourse et du Commerce CAFÉ
(bd des Arènes) This vast, flamboyant café, right opposite Les Arènes, is a great spot for breakfast, a quick coffee or a sundowner, either on the terrace or inside.

La Bodeguita BAR
(place d'Assas; ☺Mon-Sat) With a Spanish click of the heels and attached to the Royal Hôtel, this is a popular venue for the local intelligentsia. On summer evenings, there's often live music.

☆ Entertainment
Les Arènes is the major venue for outdoor spectacles such as concerts, pageants and bullfights.

Ciné Sémaphore CINEMA
(☎04 66 67 83 11; www.semaphore.free.fr, in French; 25 rue Porte de France) Has five screens and shows nondubbed films.

Théâtre de Nîmes THEATRE
(☎04 66 36 02 04; www.theatredenimes.com, in French; place de la Calade) The major venue for drama and music.

ℹ️ Information
Net@Games (place de la Maison Carrée; per hr €2; ☺9am-1am Mon-Fri, noon-1am Sat & Sun) Internet access.

Tourist office (☎04 66 58 38 00; www.ot-nimes .fr; 6 rue Auguste; ☺8.30am-6.30pm Mon-Fri, 9am-6.30pm Sat, 10am-5pm Sun) Rents out audioguides to central Nîmes (one/two terminals €8/10).

ℹ️ Getting There & Away
AIR Nîmes' **airport** (☎04 66 70 49 49), 10km southeast of the city on the A54, is served only by Ryanair, which flies to/from London (Luton) and Liverpool in the UK.

BUS The **bus station** (☎04 66 38 59 43; rue Ste-Félicité) connects with the train station. International operators **Eurolines** (☎08 92 89 90 91) and **Line Bus** (☎04 66 29 50 62) both have kiosks there.

A single journey anywhere within in the Gard *département* costs only €1.50. Among the regional destinations:

Pont du Gard 30 minutes, two to seven daily

Uzès 45 minutes, four to 10 daily

CAR & MOTORCYCLE Avis, Europcar and Hertz have kiosks at both the airport and the train station.

TRAIN More than 12 TGVs daily run to/from Paris Gare de Lyon (€52 to €99.70, three hours). Frequent trains serve the following:

Alès €8.50, 40 minutes

Arles €7.50, 30 minutes

Avignon €8.50, 30 minutes

Marseille €19, 1¼ hours

Montpellier €8.60, 30 minutes

Sète €12.20, one hour

 Getting Around

TO/FROM THE AIRPORT An **airport bus** (€5, 30 minutes) meets and greets Ryanair flights, leaving from the train station. To confirm times, call ☎04 66 29 27 29.

BICYCLE Commavélo (☎06 07 41 80 61; www.commavelo.com; 28 rue Émile Jamais; ◷9.30am-1pm & 2-7pm) rents out town bikes (per half-day/full day/three days €7/12/30) and mountain bikes (per half-day/full day/three days €9/15/37.50).

Drivers who leave their vehicles in the car parks of Les Arènes or place d'Assas can borrow a town bike for free. Present your parking ticket at the pay desk.

TAXI Call ☎04 66 29 40 11.

Around Nîmes

PERRIER PLANT

Ever wondered how they get the bubbles into a bottle of Perrier water? Or why it's that stubby shape? Take the one-hour tour in French of **Perrier's bottling plant** (☎04 66 87 61 01; adult/child €5/2; ◷tours approx hourly 10am-4pm Mon-Fri). In Vergèze, on the RN113, 13km southwest of Nîmes, it fills around 400 million bottles of mineral water each year. We trust their tongue is firmly in their cheek when they advertise *dégustation gratuité* (free tasting)! Call to reserve.

PONT DU GARD

Pont du Gard   ROMAN AQUEDUCT

A Unesco World Heritage Site, this exceptionally well-preserved, three-tiered Roman aqueduct was once part of a 50km-long system of water channels built around 19 BC to bring water from nearby Uzès to Nîmes. The scale is huge: the 35 arches of its 275m-long upper tier, running 50m above the River Gard, contain a water-course designed to carry 20,000 cu metres

of water per day. Each and every construction block (the largest weigh over five tonnes) was hauled from quarries near and far by cart or raft.

It's about a 400m walk, with excellent wheelchair access, from car parks on both left and right banks of the River Gard to the bridge itself. The road bridge, built in 1743, runs parallel with the aqueduct's lower tier. The best, least encumbered view is from upstream, where you can swim on hot days.

Its **visitors centre** (☎04 66 37 50 99; www.pontdugard.fr; ◷9.30-7pm May-Sep; to 5pm or 6pm Oct-Apr) on the left, northern bank, rents out multilingual **audioguides** (€6).

Museo de la Romanité   INTERPRETIVE CENTRE

Do take in this vast, hugely informative and innovative, high-tech Museum of the Roman World, which has captions and signs in English. Within the complex's cinema, a 25-minute large-screen **film** (screenings in English at noon and 3pm) shows the bridge from land and air. Though there's little danger of boredom hereabouts, children can have a fun learning experience at **Ludo**, an adjacent activity play area for five- to 12-year olds.

Mémoires de Garrigue   WALK

To leave the crowds behind, walk, for free, this 1.4km trail with interpretive signs as it winds through typical Mediterranean bush and scrubland. You'll need to borrow or buy the explanatory booklet in English (€4) to get the most out of it.

ⓘ Getting There & Away

The Pont du Gard is 21km northeast of Nîmes and 26km west of Avignon. Buses normally stop on the D981, 500m north of the visitors centre. In summer, some buses make a diversion to the Pont du Gard car park.

Edgard (www.edgard-transport.fr, in French) bus B21 runs three to seven times daily to/from Nîmes, while bus A15 leaves Avignon three to six times daily.

Parking in the extensive car parks on each bank of the river costs €5.

RIVER GARD

The wild, unpredictable River Gard descends from the Cévennes mountains. Torrential rains can raise the water level by as much as five metres in a flash. During long dry spells, by contrast, sections may disappear completely, as the water continues to trickle through an underground channel.

The river has sliced itself a meandering gorge (Les Gorges du Gardon) through the hills from Russan to the village of Collias, about 6km upstream from the Pont du Gard. The GR6 long-distance hiking trail runs beside it most of the way.

In Collias, 4km west of the D981, Le Tourbillon (04 66 22 85 54; www.canoe-le-tourbillon.com), Kayak Vert (04 66 22 80 76; www.canoefrance.com/gardon) and Canoë Collias (04 66 22 87 20; www.canoe-collias. com, in French) rent out kayaks and canoes. Kayak Vert also offers mountain-bike hire.

You can paddle 8km down to the Pont du Gard (€20 per person, two hours), or arrange to be dropped upstream at Russan, from where a great 23km descent leads back to Collias through Gorges du Gardon (€30, full day). The latter's usually possible only between March and mid-June, when the river is high enough.

UZÈS
POP 8450

Uzès, 25km northeast of Nîmes, once derived wealth from silk, linen and, bizarrely, liquorice. When all three industries collapsed, it went through hard times. But it's again on the upsurge thanks to tourism, as visitors come to enjoy its faithfully restored Renaissance facades, impressive Duché (Ducal Palace) and splendid place aux Herbes, the shady, arcaded central square, all odd angles and off-kilter.

SUMMER SPECIAL

Think of an evening return to see the **Pont du Gard** in a very special light. Every night from sunset to midnight, it's spectacularly illuminated. There's free parking from 7pm.

Farmers from all around sell their produce at the market, held each Wednesday and Saturday on place aux Herbes.

◎ Sights & Activities

The tourist office's free multilingual pamphlet, *Uzès: Premier Duché de France,* describes a walking tour of the historic centre's highlights.

Jardin Médiéval   GARDEN

(Medieval Garden; adult/child €4/2; ⊙10.30am-12.30pm & 2-6pm Apr-Oct) This delightful garden, set back from rue Port Royal, basks in the shadow of the Duché's keep. It's bright with medieval plants and flowers, impressively researched and documented (with English translation too).

Musée du Bonbon   SWEET MUSEUM

(Pont des Charrettes; adult/child €6/4; ⊙10am-1pm & 2-6pm Tue-Sun, daily Jul-Sep, closed Jan) Here's a place for a little indulgence. A plaque at the entrance declares 'This museum is dedicated to all who have devoted their lives to a slightly guilty passion – greed'. All signs at this candy museum belonging to manufacturers Haribo are multilingual. Parents will be pestered to purchase kilos of goodies at wholesale prices.

Duché   CHÂTEAU

(www.duche-uzes.fr; ⊙10am-noon & 2-6pm) This fortified château belonged to the Dukes of Uzès for more than 1000 years. Altered almost continuously from the 11th to 18th century, it has fine period furniture, tapestries and paintings. You can take the French-language one-hour **guided tour** (€16/12 per adult/child) or wander at will around the keep (admission €11).

☆☆ Festivals & Events

Foire aux Truffes   TRUFFLE FAIR

A full-blown truffle fair, the third Sunday in January.

Foire à l'Ail   GARLIC FAIR

Uzès positively reeks during its garlic fair on 24 June.

Nuits Musicales d'Uzès   MUSIC FESTIVAL

An international festival of baroque music and jazz in the second half of July.

⊨ Sleeping & Eating

TOP CHOICE **Hôtel Restaurant du Général d'Entraigues**   HOTEL, RESTAURANT €€

(04 66 22 32 68; www.hoteldentraigues.com, in French; place de l'Évêché; r €90-130; ❄️ 🛜 ⊠) Trace your way through history as you

explore this hotel, an amalgamation of four private houses dating from the 15th to 18th centuries. It's an agreeable mix of odd angles, low beams, arches, crannies, corridors and staircases that may or may not lead somewhere. Modern touches include aircon in the majority of its 36 rooms and a small elevated pool where breakfast diners can watch early morning swimmers – from below. The hotel restaurant, **Les Jardins de Castille** (menus €15-21), offers contemporary cuisine in an equally traditional setting.

TOP CHOICE **Terroirs** CAFÉ-GOURMET FOOD € (www.enviedeterroirs.com; 5 place aux Herbes; snacks around €4.50, mixed platters €10-14; ◎9am-10.30pm, to 6pm Oct-Mar) Snack copiously under the deep arcades or on the cobbled square at this restaurant and delicatessen, where Tom and Corinne Graisse source nearly all their goods locally. Their mixed platters and toasted open sandwiches are filled with delights, described explicitly in the English version of the menu.

🛍 Shopping
Maison de la Truffe TRUFFLES
(27 place aux Herbes) At the splendid Maison de la Truffe, it's truffles with everything – adding aroma to chocolate, steeped in oil, bagged with rice and much more.

ℹ Information
The **tourist office** (☏04 66 22 68 88; www.uzes -tourisme.com; ◎10am-6pm or 7pm Mon-Fri, 10am-1pm Sat & Sun, closed Sat afternoon & Sun Oct-May) is on place Albert I, just outside the old quarter. It rents out **audioguides** (€5) for a self-guided walking tour.

ℹ Getting There & Away
The bus station – grandly named and in fact merely a bus stop – is on av de la Libération, beside Banque Populaire. Buses running between Avignon (one hour) and Alès (50 minutes) call by three to five times daily. There are also at least five daily services to/from Nîmes (45 minutes). All journeys cost only €1.50.

Alès & Around
POP 41,100

Alès, 45km from Nîmes and 70km from Montpellier, snuggles against the River Gard. Gateway to the Cévennes, it's the Gard *département*'s second-largest town. Coal was mined here from the 13th century, when monks first dug into the surrounding hills, until the last pit closed in 1986.

The pedestrianised heart of town, which long ago shed its sooty past, is bright with flowers in summer.

👁 Sights & Activities
Train à Vapeur des Cévennes STEAM TRAIN
(www.trainavapeur.com; adult/child one-way €10/6.50, return €13/8; ◎Apr-Oct) This authentic steam train takes 40 minutes to chug the 13km between St-Jean du Gard and Anduze, calling at the Bambouseraie and making three to four return trips each day.

Mine Témoin COALMINE MUSEUM
(www.mine-temoin.fr, in French; chemin de la Cité Ste-Marie; adult/child €7/4.50; ◎9.30am-12.30pm & 2-6pm Mar–mid-Nov) Don a safety helmet, arm yourself with the guide booklet in English and take the cage down to explore an actual mine in Alès that was used to train apprentice colliers. Preceded by a 20-minute video (in French), the one-hour guided tour (in French) leads you along 700m of underground galleries. Slip on a sweater since the temperature underground rarely reaches 16°C.

Musée du Désert HUGUENOT MUSEUM
(Museum of the Wilderness; www.museedudesert. com; adult/child €5/4; ◎9.30am-noon & 2-6pm Mar-Nov) The Musée du Désert portrays the way of life of the Huguenots (see boxed text, p715), their persecution, clandestine resistance for more than a century and emigration of up to half a million to more tolerant lands. It's in the charming hamlet of Le Mas Soubeyran, 5.5km north of the Bambouseraie.

Bambouseraie de Prafrance
TROPICAL GARDENS
(www.bambouseraie.com; adult/child €8/4.50; ◎9.30am-dusk Mar–mid-Nov) It's over 150 years since the first shoots of this rambling, mature bamboo grove were planted by a spice merchant returning from the tropics. Here in Générargues, 12km southwest of Alès, 150 bamboo species sprout amid aquatic gardens, a Laotian village and a Japanese garden. The Cévennes steam train stops right beside the reception.

La Caracole SNAIL FARM
(☏04 66 25 65 70; www.lacaracole.fr; adult/child €6/4; ◎tours 4.30pm & 6.30pm Jul & Aug, 3pm & 4.30pm Wed & Sun Apr-Jun & Sep) Here's one to make the kids squirm. La Caracole, with a cast of over 250,000, presents 'the astonishing, exciting world of the snail'. In this snail

THE CAMISARD REVOLT

Early in the 18th century, a guerrilla war raged through the Cévennes as Protestants took on Louis XIV's army. The revocation of the Edict of Nantes in 1685 removed rights that the Protestant Huguenots had enjoyed since 1598. Many emigrated, while others fled deep into the wild Cévennes, from where a local leader, Roland Laporte, only 22 at the time, led the resistance against the French army sent to crush them.

Poorly equipped, the outlaws resisted for two years. They fought in their shirts (*camiso* in *langue d'oc*); hence their popular name, Camisards. Once the royal army gained the upper hand, the local population was either massacred or forced to flee. Their leader was killed and most villages were destroyed.

On the first Sunday of September, thousands of French Protestants meet at Roland's birthplace in Le Mas Soubeyran. It's now the Musée du Désert (p714), which details the persecution of Protestants in the Cévennes between 1685 and the 1787 Edict of Tolerance, which marked the reintroduction of religious freedom.

farm's appropriately small museum, there's information on – oh yes – the snail in religion, the snail in art and the snail through the centuries. After the tour (in simultaneous English and French), there's free sampling and the chance to buy a tin or two of former farm members embalmed in a variety of tempting sauces. It's in St-Florent sur Auzonnet, 12km from Alés. Take the D904 northwards (towards Aubenas), then turn left onto the D59.

🛌 Sleeping & Eating

Mas de Rochebelle　B&B **€€**
(🖉04 66 30 57 03; www.masderochebelle.fr; 44 chemin de la Cité Ste-Marie; s €55-70, d €70-90;🕸) Near the Mine Témoin, this welcoming *chambre d'hôte* in Alès was once the mine director's residence. It has five attractive rooms and a vast garden, where you can wander, swim or simply relax under its magnificent yew tree. No credit cards.

Hôtel Restaurant Le Riche　HOTEL **€**
(🖉04 66 86 00 33; www.leriche.fr, in French; 42 place Pierre Sémard; s/d €52/68; ⊙closed Aug; 🕸🛜)Opposite the train station in Alès, this great-value hotel is highly recommended as much for its 19 pleasant, modern rooms as for the fine cuisine of its restaurant (menus €21-50) with its attentive service and wonderful stucco mouldings.

Camping la Croix Clémentine
　　　　　CAMPGROUND **€**
(🖉04 66 86 52 69; www.clementine.fr, in French; site & 2 people according to season €14-26.60; ⊙Apr-Sep; 🕸) This campground is in Cendras, 5km northwest of Alès. Sites, within or on the fringes of an oak wood, are shady

and there are plenty of activities to keep the children occupied.

ℹ️ Information

The Alès **tourist office** (🖉04 66 52 32 15; www.ville-ales.fr, in French; place Hôtel de Ville; ⊙9am-noon & 1.30-5.30pm Mon-Sat, also 9.30am-12.30pm Sun Jul & Aug) occupies a modern building set into the shell of a baroque chapel.

ℹ️ Getting There & Away

BUS From the **Gare Routière** (🖉04 66 52 31 31; place Pierre Sémard), beside the train station, one bus heads into the Cévennes to Florac (€13, 1¼ hours, Monday to Saturday mid-April to mid-September, Wednesday and Saturday only rest of the year), and three to five serve Uzès (€1.50, 50 minutes), most continuing to Avignon (€1.50, 1¾ hours).

TRAIN There are up to 10 trains daily to/from Montpellier (€15, 1½ hours), some requiring a change in Nîmes (€8.45, 40 minutes).

Montpellier

POP 257,100

The 17th-century philosopher John Locke may have had one glass of Minervois wine too many when he wrote: 'I find it much better to go twise (sic) to Montpellier than once to the other world'. It stops short of paradise, but Montpellier, where students make up around a third of the population, is innovative, fast-growing, self-confident and a worthy rival to Toulouse for the title of southern France's most vital city. Two high-speed tram routes – with a third under construction – cut across this most pedestrian-friendly of cities, where more

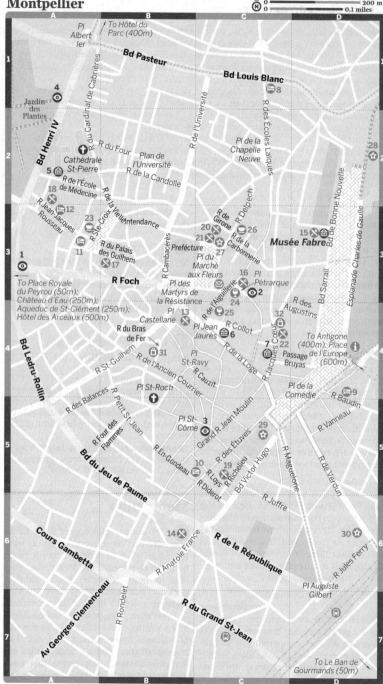

than 12,000 parking spaces, over 1000 bikes for borrowing and around 150km of cycling paths encourage motorists to leave their cars behind.

One of the few cities in southern France without a Roman heritage, Montpellier started late-ish. Founded by the Counts of Toulouse, it's first mentioned in a written document in 985. By medieval times, it had become a prosperous city with trading links all over the Mediterranean. Its scholastic tradition is a long one: Europe's first medical school was founded here in the 12th century. The population swelled dramatically in the 1960s when many French settlers left independent Algeria and settled here.

Montpellier owes much of its contemporary syle and swagger (such as the mammoth 1980s neoclassical housing project of Antigone) to Georges Frêche. Constantly controversial and locally revered, he ruled as mayor from 1977 until 2004.

⊙ Sights

Musée Fabre ART GALLERY
(www.museefabre.fr; 39 bd Bonne Nouvelle; adult/child €6/4, with Département des Art Décoratifs €7/5; ⏰10am-6pm Tue & Thu-Sun, 1-9pm Wed) A delightfully spacious, superbly lit venue

with one of France's richest collections of European works from the 16th century onwards, plus seven galleries of bright, dynamic 20th-century art. Its annexe, the recently opened Département des Arts Décoratifs displays in context elegant 18th- and 19th-century furniture, ceramics and jewellery.

Serre Amazonienne RAINFOREST SIMULATION
(www.zoo.montpellier.fr, in French; 50 av Agropolis; adult/child €6/2.50, audioguide €2; ⏰9am-5pm or 7pm) A 10-minute walk from Agropolis, this is a spectacular appendix to Montpellier's zoo. A humid hothouse replicates the Amazonian rainforest. Piranha and alligators swim in the first two tanks but it gets friendlier as you progress. Stars include a pair of bright-eyed young leopards, a family of Bolivian squirrel monkeys and flitting bats. Afterwards, you can explore the rest of the zoo, France's second-largest, for free.

Agropolis INTERPRETIVE CENTRE
(www.museum.agropolis.fr; 951 av Agropolis; adult/child €5/free; ⏰10am-12.30pm & 2-6pm Mon-Fri & some weekends) Agropolis, 4km north of the centre, is all about food and how people around the world grow it. Historically, it follows our progression from

Montpellier

hunter-gatherer to supermarket shopper. Fascinating stuff, it's instructive, enjoyable and pitched at both children and adults. For this and Serre Amazonienne, take tram 1 to the St-Eloi stop, from where a regular shuttle bus does a circular route.

Odysseum
LEISURE COMPLEX

At the end of tram line 1 and 3.5km east of the centre, this leisure complex has an ice rink, planetarium, multiscreen cinema and, in particular, **Aquarium Mare Nostrum** (adult/child €12.50/9; ⊙10am-7pm, 8pm or 10pm), which takes you through 15 different aquatic environments, from polar waters to tropical forests.

Hôtels Particulier
HISTORIC MANSIONS

During the 17th and 18th centuries, Montpellier's wealthier merchants built grand private mansions, often externally quite sober but with resplendent inner courtyards (mostly, alas, closed to the public). Fine examples are **Hôtel de Varennes** (2 place Pétrarque), a harmonious 18th-century makeover of an originally medieval structure, and **Hôtel St-Côme** (Grand Rue Jean Moulin), nowadays the city's Chamber of Commerce. The 17th-century **Hôtel des Trésoriers de France** (7 rue Jacques Cœur) today houses the Musée Languedocien. Within the old quarter are several other such mansions, each marked by a descriptive plaque in French.

Place Royale du Peyrou & Around
ESPLANADE, GARDENS

At the eastern end of this wide, tree-lined esplanade is the **Arc de Triomphe** (1692). From the **Château d'Eau**, an elaborate hexagonal water tower at its western limit, stretches the **Aqueduc de St-Clément**, spectacularly illuminated at night. North of the esplanade is the **Jardin des Plantes** (⊙noon-6pm or 8pm Tue-Sun; entry on bd Henri IV), France's oldest botanical garden, laid

CITY CARD

The **Montpellier City Card** (per 1/2/3 days €12/19/25, children half-price), sold at the tourist office, allows free or reduced admission to several sites and spectacles, plus unlimited bus and tram travel and a place on a guided walking tour. Ask at the tourist office for the latest offers.

out in 1593 and still used as a research resource by the University of Montpellier.

Montpellier has several stimulating museums that catalogue its rich history:

Musée Languedocien
ARCHAEOLOGY MUSEUM

(7 rue Jacques Cœur; adult/student €6/3; ⊙3-6pm Mon-Sat) Displays the area's rich archaeological finds from its earliest days as well as 16th- to 19th-century objets d'art.

FREE Musée du Vieux Montpellier
HISTORY MUSEUM

(2 place Pétrarque; ⊙9.30am-noon & 1.30-5pm Tue-Sat) A storehouse of the city's memorabilia from the Middle Ages to the Revolution.

Musée de l'Histoire de Montpellier
HISTORY MUSEUM

(place Jean Jaurès; admission incl audioguide €1.60; ⊙10.30-11.45am & 1.30-5.15pm Tue-Sat) Down among the remains of the crypt of the church of Notre Dame des Tables, this museum offers a rather plodding 35-minute version of the city's history enlivened by the high-tech presentation.

FREE Musée Atger
ART MUSEUM

(2 rue de l'École de Médecine; ⊙1.30-5.45pm Mon, Wed & Fri Sep-Jul) Within the medical faculty, this museum displays a striking collection of French, Italian and Flemish drawings.

Festivals & Events

Printemps des Comédiens
ARTS FESTIVAL

(www.printempsdescomediens.com) A music, dance and theatre festival in June.

Montpellier Danse
DANCE FESTIVAL

(www.montpellierdanse.com, in French) A two-week international dance festival in June or July.

Festival de Radio France et Montpellier
MUSIC FESTIVAL

(www.festivalradiofrancemontpellier.com, in French) Top-notch classical music and opera, plus a parallel program of free concerts of all musical genres, in the second half of July.

Sleeping

TOP CHOICE Hôtel Le Guilhem
HOTEL €€

(☎04 67 52 90 90; www.hotel-le-guilhem. com; 18 rue Jean-Jacques Rousseau; s €85, d €96-192; ❄@🖃) Occupying a couple of interconnecting 16th-century buildings, Hôtel Le Guilhem's 35 rooms are exquisitely and individually furnished. Nearly all overlook the tranquil garden of nearby Restaurant Le Petit Jardin. Room 100 (€158) has its own little terrace and garden. It's wise to reserve at any time of year; Le Guilhem has faithful clientele who return again and again. Free wi-fi.

Hôtel du Parc HOTEL €€
(☑04 67 41 16 49; www.hotelduparc-montpellier. com, in French; 8 rue Achille-Bégé; s €68-75, d €83-90, s/d with shower €46/53; ❋ ☏) At this 18th-century former *hôtel particulier* with its grand curling wrought-iron staircase, bibelots and knick-knacks add an at-home touch to each of the 19 individually decorated rooms (ask for room 7, bedchamber of the previous owner, Comte Vivier de Châtelard). Those on the ground floor have a small balcony. To get here, head north from place Albert I along av Faubourg Boutonnet.

Hôtel des Arceaux HOTEL €
(☑04 67 92 03 03; www.hoteldesarceaux.com; 33-35 bd des Arceaux; s €54-65, d €65-70; ❋ ☏) This delightful town house, tucked beneath an aqueduct, is in a village-like cranny of Montpellier that's a mere 10-minute walk from the centre. Enjoy breakfast, brunch or dinner in the tranquil garden.

Hôtel du Palais HOTEL €€
(☑04 67 60 47 38; www.hoteldupalais-mont pellier.fr; 3 rue du Palais des Guilhem; s €66, d €72-85; ❋ ☏) All 26 rooms of this delightful hotel are decorated by a local artist and tastefully and individually furnished. With its wrought-iron balconies, oyster-grey shutters and flower boxes overlooking a quiet square, it will seduce you instantly.

Hôtel des Étuves HOTEL €
(☑04 67 60 78 19; www.hoteldesetuves.fr; 24 rue des Étuves; s €31-42, d €39-49; ☏) This welcoming, 13-room family hotel, creeping around a spiral staircase like a vine, offers exceptional value. Rooms are simple but functional and the six overlooking the quiet pedestrian street are beautifully sunlit. Does not take credit cards.

Hôtel de la Comédie HOTEL €
(☑04 67 58 43 64; hoteldelacomedie@cegetel. net; 1bis rue Baudin; s €42-49, d €52-69; ❋ ☏) This friendly, family-run place, just off place de la Comédie, is a favourite with visiting musicians and theatre troupes. All 20 rooms have air-con, heating and double-glazing.

Auberge de Jeunesse YOUTH HOSTEL €
(☑04 67 60 32 22; montpellier@fuaj.org; 2 impasse de la Petite Corraterie; €16.70 incl breakfast; ☒closed Dec; @) Montpellier's HI-affiliated youth hostel is just off rue des Écoles Laïques. Rooms sleep two to 10 and there's a small, shaded garden. Take the tram to the Louis Blanc stop.

Camping Oasis Palavasienne CAMPGROUND €
(☑04 67 15 11 61; www.oasis-palavasienne.com; rte de Palavas; site according to season €16-33; ☒mid-Apr–mid-Sep; ☒) This shady campground has a large heated pool with waterslide, sauna, children's playground, bar and restaurant. Take bus 17 from the bus station. The campground runs a free shuttle bus to the beach resort of Palavas, 4km away.

✕ Eating

You'll find plenty of cheap and cheerful eateries on rue de l'Université, rue des Écoles Laïques and the streets interlinking them.

La Girafe FUSION €€
(☑04 67 54 48 89; 14 rue du Palais des Guilhem; mains €15-18; ☒Tue-Sat) You're indeed greeted by a tall model giraffe as you enter. Dine in the intimate downstairs area with its ox-blood-red decor and original artwork, or upstairs beneath the cross arches of this former chapel. Chef Pascal Schmitt gets his ingredients fresh from the market and nothing but nothing comes from the freezer. Try the heavenly breast of chicken rolled around prawns with fresh coriander and satay sauce.

Le Petit Jardin MODERN FRENCH €€
(☑04 67 60 78 78; www.petit-jardin.com, in French; 20 rue Jean-Jacques Rousseau; mains €22-29, lunch menus €17-33; ☒mid-May–mid-Oct, closed Mon rest of year) The Little Garden is just that: a restaurant offering imaginative cuisine, its big bay windows overlooking a shady, fairy-tale greenness at the rear. The menu, with its hints of Asian fusion, is short, simple yet with plenty of variety.

TOP CHOICE Tamarillos FRUIT & FLOWERS €€
(☑04 67 60 06 00; http://tamarillos. biz; 2 place du Marché aux Fleurs; mains €24-34, menus €38-88) 'A cuisine of fruit and flowers' is Tamarillos' motto and, indeed, all dishes, sweet or savoury, have fruit as an ingredient or main element. Chef Philippe Chapon is *double champion de France de dessert* and taught a young Gordon Ramsay his pastry cooking. Go for a full meal or

nibble on a lunchtime salad (€14 to €19) or special (€15).

Mesdames Messieurs MODERN FRENCH €€
(☑04 67 63 49 53; www.mesdamesmessieurs.com, in French; 5 rue de Girone; mains €13-19; ☺7pm-1am Tue-Sat, 11am-4pm Sun; ☑) As much wine bar as restaurant, this hip new venue serves mainly organic produce and has a selection of at least 15 wines by the glass. Its copious Sunday brunch (€23) will set you up for the whole day.

Les Bains de Montpellier FISH, FRENCH €€
(☑04 67 60 70 87; www.les-bains-de-montpellier.com; 6 rue Richelieu; mains €21-25, menu €24; ☺Tue-Sat) This former public bathhouse is now a highly recommended restaurant. Tables are set around the old perimeter bathrooms where you can almost hear the gurgle and slurp of long-emptied tubs. For something light, try the *assiette des Bains,* a platter with salads, pasta, garnishes, vegetables and a hint of meat. If you're hungrier, select from its prime quality fish dishes.

Insensé MUSEUM RESTAURANT €€
(☑04 67 58 97 78; Musée Fabre; mains around €15, 2-/3-course lunch €21/28; ☺Tue-Sat, lunch Sun) Restaurant of Musée Fabre, Insensé is just as contemporary and tasteful as you'd expect from such a venue. The dominant shade is black: tables, chairs, floor tiles – even the pepper pots. The innovative cuisine is altogether more colourful.

Le Ban des Gourmands TRADITIONAL FRENCH €€
(☑04 67 65 00 85; www.bandesgourmands.com, in French; 5 place Carnot; mains €16-27, menu €28; ☺Tue-Sat) Jacques and Catherine Delépine serve delicious classic cuisine at this appealing restaurant, a favourite of locals in the know, tucked away south of the train station.

La Diligence TRADITIONAL FRENCH €€
(☑04 67 66 12 21; 2 place Pétrarque; lunch menus €15-20, dinner menus €26-63; ☺Tue-Fri, dinner Sat & Mon) Dine beneath attractive vaults and arches at this former cloth warehouse. Savour the creative cuisine, impressive wine cellar and elegant rear patio overlooked by a gallery of the Hôtel de Varennes.

Tripti Kulai VEGETARIAN FUSION €
(☑04 67 66 30 51; 20 rue Jacques Cœur; salads €9.50, menus €12-16.50; ☺noon-9.30pm Mon-Sat; ☑) Barrel-vaulted and cosy, this popular vegetarian restaurant and tea house stands out for its juices and the originality

of many of its dishes, culled from world cuisine.

Self-Catering

The city's food markets include Halles Castellane (rue de la Loge), which is the biggest, and Halles Laissac (rue Anatole France).

There's a Saturday organic food market under the arches of Aqueduc de St-Clément and a farmers market every Sunday morning on av Samuel de Champlain in the Antigone complex, just east of the town centre.

☕ Drinking

With nearly 80,000 students, Montpellier has a multitude of places to drink and dance. You'll find dense concentrations around rue En-Gondeau, off Grand Rue Jean Moulin, around place Jean Jaurès and around the intersection of rue de l'Université and rue de la Candolle.

Place de la Comédie (known to locals as *l'œuf,* the egg, for its ovoid shape) is alive with cafés where you can drink, grab a quick bite and watch street entertainers strut their stuff. Another popular venue is smaller, more intimate place St-Ravy, to its northwest.

Chez Boris WINE BAR
(20 rue de l'Aiguillerie; ☺Mon-Sat, lunch Sun) This friendly wine bar (tapas €4 to €11, mains €13 to €20), with its regularly changing dishes and wines to match, could just as easily feature as a recommended place to eat. Early evening punters slip in for an aperitif and perhaps a snack. Later, once diners have departed, Chez Boris is also a splendid spot for a last drink.

Café Latitude CAFÉ
(1 rue Ste-Croix; ☺7.30am-8pm Tue-Sat) Sink back into the comfiest of seats at this relaxed café with its faintly colonial decor and watch the little life that passes by on place Canourgue, one of Montpellier's most peaceful squares.

L'Heure Bleue TEA HOUSE
(1 rue de la Carbonnerie; ☺Tue-Sun) At this tearoom, sip an exotic blend to a background of classical music, enjoy a light lunch (around €15), with plenty of choice for vegetarians, or relax over an aperitif.

Le Huit MUSIC BAR
(☑04 67 66 14 18; 8 rue de l'Aiguillerie) Local bands play at this trendy hideout, where Wednesdays are for indie rock.

☆ Entertainment

To find out what's on where, pick up the free weekly *Sortir à Montpellier,* available around town and at the tourist office. To tune into the active gay and lesbian scene, call by Café de la Mer (5 place du Marché aux Fleurs); the friendly staff will arm you with a map of gay venues.

L'Amigo, a night bus, does a circuit of Espace Latipolia and other dance venues on the periphery of town, leaving the train station at midnight and 1am, returning at 2.30am, 3.30am and (yawn!) 5am, Thursday to Saturday.

Opéra-Comédie   BOX OFFICE
(☎04 67 60 19 80; place de la Comédie) Tickets for Montpellier's theatres are sold at the box office of the Opéra-Comédie.

Rockstore   CLUB, DISCO
(☎04 67 06 80 00; www.rockstore.fr, in French; 20 rue de Verdun) In the heart of town, this long-standing discotheque and club is recognisable by the rear of a classic '70s Cadillac jutting out above the entrance. Opening days and times vary.

Espace Latipolia   DISCOS
There's a critical mass of discos outside town in Espace Latipolia, about 10km from Montpellier on route de Palavas heading towards the coast. Major players include La Nitro (☎04 67 22 45 82; www. lanitro.com, in French), which thumps out techno and house, and Le Matchico (☎04 67 64 19 20; www.matchico.fr, in French), good for retro music.

Le Corum   VENUE
(☎04 67 61 67 61; esplanade Charles de Gaulle) The city's prime concert venue.

Le Heaven   GAY & LESBIAN
(1 rue Delpech) Just around the corner from Café de la Mer, this bar for gay guys and gals gets busy from 8pm.

🛍 Shopping

Le Bookshop   BOOKSHOP
(www.lebookshop.com; 8 rue du Bras de Fer) As much social centre as bookshop, it carries a large stock of new and secondhand books in English and runs conversation exchanges and cultural events.

Les Cinq Continents   TRAVEL BOOKSHOP
(20 rue Jacques Cœur) A specialist travel bookshop with an excellent selection of maps and travel literature.

ℹ Information

Dimension 4 Cybercafé (11 rue des Balances; per hr €3; ☉10am-midnight) Internet access.
Tourist office (☎04 67 60 60 60; www. ot-montpellier.fr; esplanade Charles de Gaulle; ☉9am-6.30pm Mon-Fri, 10am-6pm Sat, 10am-1pm & 2-5pm Sun)

ℹ Getting There & Away

AIR Montpellier's **airport** (☎04 67 20 85 00; www.montpellier.aeroport.fr) is 8km southeast of town. EasyJet flies to/from London (Gatwick) and Ryanair to/from Leeds-Bradford.

BUS The **bus station** (☎04 67 92 01 43; rue du Grand St-Jean) is an easy walk from the train station. **Hérault Transport** (☎04 34 88 89 99; www.herault-transport.fr) runs buses approximately hourly to La Grande Motte (bus 106, €4, 35 minutes) via Carnon from Odysseum at the end of tram line 1. Up to four daily services continue to Aigues Mortes (€8.60, one hour).

Eurolines (☎08 92 89 90 91; 8 rue de Verdun) has buses to Barcelona (€18, five hours) and most European destinations.

TRAIN Destinations from Montpellier's two-storey train station include the following:
Carcassonne (€22.70, 1½ hours, up to 10 daily)
Millau (€26.10, 1¾ hours, three daily)
Narbonne (€14.80, one hour, frequent)
Nîmes (€8.60, 30 minutes, frequent)
Paris Gare de Lyon (€100 to €119.50, 3½ hours, at least 10 daily)
Perpignan (€23.10, 1¾ hours, frequent)

ℹ Getting Around

TO/FROM THE AIRPORT A frequent **shuttle bus** (☎08 25 34 01 34; €1.50; ☉every 15 min) runs between the airport and the place de l'Europe tram stop.

BICYCLE Montpellier is hugely bicycle-friendly. To rent a bike (per half-/full day €1/2), call by the tourist office or VéloMagg (27 rue Maguelone; ☉8am-8pm), which is handy for the train station, with your passport or ID card.

CAR & MOTORCYCLE The easiest and most ecofriendly option is to leave your vehicle in one of the vast car parks beside major tram stops such as Odysseum. Just €4 gets you all-day parking and return tram tickets to the heart of town for up to five people.

TAXI Ring **Taxis Bleu** (☎04 67 03 20 00) or **Taxis Tram** (☎04 67 58 10 10).

TRAM & BUS Savour Montpellier's high-tech, high-speed, leave-your-car-at-home trams. Like city buses, they're run by **TaM** (☎04 67 22 87 87; www.tam-way.com, in French).

1. **Château Royal, Collioure (p750)**
Artistic Collioure provided inspiration for
Matisse, Derain, Picasso and Braque.

2. **Pont du Gard (p712)**
Built around 19 BC, the huge Roman aqueduct
Pont du Gard is a Unesco World Heritage Site.

3. **Notre Dame de Anges, Collioure (p750)**
The medieval church, once also used as a
lighthouse, is home to an excellent alterpiece.

4. **Puilaurens fortress (p748)**
The Cathars took refuge in clifftop fortresses
during the 13th-century Albigensian Crusade.

JOHN ELK III

Single-journey bus and tram tickets cost €1.40. A one-day pass/10-ticket *carnet* cost €3.40/11.50. Pick them up from newsagents or any tram station.

Around Montpellier

The closest beaches are at Palavas-les-Flots, 12km south of the city and a veritable Montpellier-on-Sea in summer. Take TaM bus 131 from the Port Marianne tram stop. Heading north on the coastal road towards Carnon, you stand a chance of seeing flamingos hoovering the shallows of the lagoons either side of the D21.

Carnon itself comes out fairly low in the charm stakes despite its huge marina. Better to continue hugging the coast along the D59 (Le Petit Travers) alongside several kilometres of white-sand beach, uncrowded and without a kiosk or café in sight.

About 10km northeast of Carnon is La Grande Motte, purpose-built on a grand scale back in the 1960s to plug the tourist drain southwards into Spain. Its architecture, considered revolutionary at the time, now comes over as fairly heavy and leaden, contrasting with the more organic growth of adjacent Grau du Roi, deeper rooted and still an active fishing port.

Aigues-Mortes (p786), on the western edge of the Camargue, is another 11km eastwards.

Sète

POP 43,600

Sète is France's largest Mediterranean fishing port and biggest commercial entrepôt after Marseille. Established by Louis XIV in the 17th century, it prospered as the harbours of Aigues-Mortes and Narbonne, to north and south respectively, were cut off from the sea by silt deposits.

Huddled beneath Mont St-Clair, Sète has lots in its favour: waterways and canals, beaches, shoals of fish and seafood restaurants.

◉ Sights & Activities

Musée International des Arts Modestes QUIRKY MUSEUM

(MIAM; www.miam.org, in French; 23 quai Maréchal de Lattre de Tassigny; adult/child €5/free; ◷10am-noon & 2-6pm Jul & Aug, closed Tue Sep-Jun) Local artists Hervé di Rosa and Bernard Belluc have assembled an eccen-

tric, wholly delightful collection of simple, everyday objects, lots that will be familiar to any visitor, others more exotic.

Cimetière Marin CEMETERY

Sète was the birthplace of the symbolist poet Paul Valéry (1871–1945), whose remains lie in this cemetery by the sea, the inspiration for his most famous poem. You'll understand why when you gaze at the view.

Espace Georges Brassens MUSIC MUSEUM

(67 bd Camille Blanc; adult/child €5/free; ◷10am-noon & 2-6pm Jun-Sep, closed Mon Oct-May) The town was the childhood home of singer and infinitely more accessible poet Georges Brassens (1921–81), whose mellow voice still speaks at this multimedia space.

Azur Croisières & Sète Croisières BOAT TOURS

Between April and November boats of Azur Croisières and Sète Croisières nudge into the canals, port and inland Bassin de Thau, leaving from Pont de la Savonnerie. Both also do half-day **fishing trips** in July and August.

✪ Festivals & Events

Fête de la St-Pierre TRADITIONAL FESTIVAL

Over a long weekend in the first half of July. Also called Fête des Pêcheurs (Fisherfolks' Festival).

Fête de la St-Louis TRADITIONAL FESTIVAL

Six frantic days around 25 August with *joutes nautiques,* where participants in competing boats try to topple each other into the water.

⛏ Sleeping & Eating

Tempting fish restaurants line quai Durand and quai Maximin Licciardi all the way from Pont de la Savonnerie to the wholesale fish market.

Auberge de Jeunesse YOUTH HOSTEL €

(☏04 67 53 46 68; sete@fuaj.org; rue Général Revest; incl breakfast €17.20, d €38.50; ◷Feb–mid-Dec) Scarcely 1km northwest of the tourist office, it enjoys a lovely wooded site with great views over town and harbour.

L'Orque Bleue QUAYSIDE HOTEL €€

(☏04 67 74 72 13; www.hotel-orquebleue-sete.com; 10 quai Aspirant Herber; r interior €89-93, canalside €115-125; ◷closed Jan; ✴❋) Right on the quayside and prominent among its dowdier neighbours, this hotel occupies a former shipping magnate's mansion, clad throughout in marble. To truly sense Sète as a living port, go for one of the more expensive nine rooms overlooking the canal, unless you're a light sleeper.

TOP CHOICE **La Péniche** FLOATING RESTAURANT €€
(☎04 67 48 64 13; 1 quai des Moulins; mains €13-15, menus €10-22; ☺Mon-Fri, dinner Sat & lunch Sun) The service is brisk and friendly and the clientele a mix of local workers, suits and sweaters on this converted barge. For the *menu du matelot* (sailor's menu; €15), two pots of pâté, into which you dig at will, are slapped before you, followed by a significant dollop of Russian salad and half a lettuce. For the main course, it has to be the house speciality, *rouille sétoise* – whole baby octopuses smothered in a peppery *rouille* sauce (mayonnaise of olive oil, garlic and chilli peppers). Then comes dessert...

Les Demoiselles Dupuy SEAFOOD €€
(☎04 67 74 03 46; 4 quai Maximin Licciardi; mains €10-18.50; ☺Thu-Tue) This tiny place, crowded and rough and ready, serves up the freshest of seafood at economical prices in unpretentious surroundings. The oysters, shucked before you, come straight from Les Demoiselles Dupuy's own offshore beds.

ℹ Information

The **tourist office** (☎04 99 04 71 71; www.tourisme-sete.com; 60 Grand' Rue Mario Roustan; ☺9.30am-6pm, to 7.30pm Jul & Aug) rents out **audioguides** (per route €5) covering six walks (two with English commentary) in and around town.

Agde
POP 21,600

There are really three Agdes: old Agde, the original settlement beside the River Hérault; Grau d'Agde, a small, modern fishing port; and Le Cap d'Agde, a vast summertime playground, famed for its long beaches and large nudist colony.

Of these, old Agde, originally a Phoenician then a Greek settlement, is significantly the most interesting. It's named after Agatha Tyche, the Greek goddess, and its inhabitants are still called Agathois.

The dark grey basalt of its imposing hotels particulier (private mansions) and the fortresslike, mainly 12th-century Cathédrale St-Étienne motivated Marco Polo to describe the town as the 'black pearl of the Mediterranean'.

Musée Agathois (5 rue de la Fraternité; adult/child €4.70/1.80; ☺9.30am-6.30pm daily Jul & Aug, 9am-noon & 2-6pm, Wed-Mon Sep-Jun), within an attractive 17th-century mansion, is a wonderful cornucopia of local treasures, including rooms furnished in period style with mannequins in period dress, a couple of kitchens, model boats, stuffed birds, swords and sextants, ex-votos, an unparalleled collection of bedpans and so much more.

Once a convent then a coaching inn, **Hôtel le Donjon** (☎04 67 94 12 32; www.hotel agde.com; place Jean Jaurès; r €55-74; ☎) is full of character and decidedly on the up. The dynamic new owner, a dab hand at DIY, has himself undertaken long-needed renovations. While the furniture, though smart, speaks of the mid-20th century, rooms are spruce and freshly painted.

TOP CHOICE **Lou Pescadou** (☎04 67 21 17 10; 18 rue Chassefière; menu €15) has been serving the same take-it-or-leave-it five-course *menu* since 1965. First, a rich, fishy broth. After a steaming plate of mussels, piled high, comes a big bowl of pâté. Then it's a giant grilled fish or slab of steak followed by an equally gut-busting dessert. Come back tomorrow, next week, next year and repeat the experience; Lou Pescadou is one of life's few constants.

Plenty of fish restaurants with terraces and pontoons splay along the quayside.

Agde's **tourist office** (☎04 67 62 91 99; www.capdagde.com; ☺10am-noon & 2-6pm daily Jul & Aug, Tue-Sat Sep-Jun) is on rue Jean Roger. Ask for *Capital City*, the walking-tour leaflet in English. The office sells tickets for three companies that run short and very agreeable **boat trips** along the Canal du Midi, which joins the River Hérault just upstream from old Agde.

Buses run at least hourly along the 6km route to the modern tourist resort of Le Cap d'Agde.

Béziers
POP 74,200

Béziers, first settled by the Phoenicians, became an important military post in Roman times. It was almost completely destroyed in 1209 during the Albigensian Crusade, when some 20,000 'heretics', many seeking refuge in the cathedral, were slaughtered. In happier times, the local tax collector Paul Riquet (1604–80) directed the digging of the Unesco World Heritage Site Canal du Midi, a 240km-long marvel of engineering (see p689) that runs from Toulouse to Sète. There's a fine statue to Béziers' most famous son on allées Paul Riquet, a wide, leafy esplanade at the heart of the town that's enlivened by a splendid flower market every Friday.

Fortified Cathédrale St-Nazaire (⊙9am-noon & 2.30-5.30pm), surrounded by narrow alleys, is typical of the area, with massive towers, an imposing facade and a huge 14th-century rose window.

Musée du Biterrois (place des Casernes; adult/child €2.80/1.40; ⊙9am-noon & 2-6pm Tue-Sun) is a well-lit, well-organised museum of the town's history, its largest sections devoted to Roman artefacts and wine-making.

Pont-Canal, an easy walk from the heart of Béziers, is a grand aqueduct, slung across the shallow valley of the river Orb in the mid-19th century to iron out a kink in the Canal du Midi. Just upstream, at Écluses de Fontseranes, a tight stepladder of nine locks, you can hire **bikes** and electric **boats**.

Popular annual events include the week-long Festa d'Oc, a celebration of Mediterranean music and dance in late July; and the féria, a five-day celebration with bullfights, when the town becomes more Spanish than Languedocien, held around 15 August.

TOP CHOICE Hôtel des Poètes (✆04 67 76 38 66; www.hoteldespoetes.net; 80 allées Paul Riquet; s/d from €45/55; ☏) is a spruce, delightfully quiet, 14-room hotel with fresh flowers, gay floral pattern bedheads and stylish furnishings – the feminine touch is everywhere. The two friendly owners speak excellent English, will collect your car from the nearby private garage, lend a bike for free and even reserve you a restaurant table.

TOP CHOICE Octopus (✆04 67 49 90 00; www.restaurant-octopus.com, in French; 12 rue Boïeldieu; mains €26-28, menus €29-75; ⊙Tue-Sat) is a tasteful venue where each tempting dish is a work of visual as well as gastronomic art. The lunchtime deal (starter, main, coffee and wine for €21 – or €29 if you can squeeze in a dessert) is superb value.

Béziers' tourist office (✆04 67 76 84 00; www.beziers-tourisme.fr; 29 av St-Saëns; ⊙9am-noon & 2-5pm or 6pm Mon-Sat) is in the Palais des Congrès.

Narbonne

POP 52,500

Once a coastal port but now a whole 13km inland because of silting up, Narbonne in its time was capital of Gallia Narbonensis and one of the principal Roman cities in Gaul.

The splendid Cathédrale St-Just (entry on rue Armand Gauthier; ⊙9am-noon & 2-6pm or 7pm) is, in fact, no more than its towers and a soaring choir, construction having stopped in the early 14th century. The ambulatory chapel directly behind the main altar has a haunting alabaster *Virgin and Child* and fine, much knocked-about polychrome stone carving. Its treasury (admission €2.20; ⊙11am-6pm Jul-Sep, 2-5pm Oct-Jun) has a beautiful Flemish tapestry of the Creation, while grotesque gargoyles leer down upon the 16th-century cloister.

The elaborate mock-Renaissance 19th-century facade of the Hôtel de Ville (place de la Hôtel de Ville) was designed by Viollet-le-Duc.

Facing the same square (below which you can see a stretch of the Via Domitia Roman highway), the fortified Palais des Archevêques (Archbishops' Palace; ⊙9.30am-12.15pm & 2-6pm Apr-Sep, 10am-noon & 2-5pm Tue-Sun Oct-Mar) houses Narbonne's Musée d'Art et d'Histoire and Musée Archéologique, the latter with an impressive collection of Roman mosaics and paintings on stucco. Nearby are the Horreum, an underground gallery of Gallo-Roman shops and the Musée Lapidaire, notable for its catchy 30-minute **sound-and-light show** (every hour on the hour) projected onto walls, ceiling and vast hunks of original Roman masonry. Opening hours for the above sites are the same as Palais des Archevêques.

Also take in Les Halles (⊙Mon-Sat), Narbonne's imposing art nouveau covered market, a colourful place to stock up on food and itself an architectural jewel.

COMBINATION TICKET

Unless you're planning to visit only one site in Narbonne, it's cheaper to invest in a **four-museum pass** (€5.20), valid for three days, covering entry to Palais des Archevêques, Musée Archéologique, the Horreum and Musée Lapidaire.

Just off the A9, 15km south of Narbonne, is the **Réserve Africaine de Sigean** (www.reserveafricainesigean.fr; adult/child €26/20; ◉9am-6.30pm), where lions, tigers and other 'safari' animals live in semi-liberty. If you arrive by bike or on foot, there's free transport around the reserve.

Narbonne's **tourist office** (☑04 68 65 15 60; www.narbonne-tourisme.com; 31 rue Jean Jaurès; ◉9am-7pm Apr–mid-Sep, closed Sun afternoons mid-Sep–Mar) occupies smart premises beside Canal de la Robine.

Carcassonne

POP 49,100

From afar, Carcassonne looks like some fairy-tale medieval city. Bathed in late-afternoon sunshine and highlighted by dark clouds, La Cité, as the old walled city is known, is truly breathtaking. But once you're inside, La Cité loses its magic and mystery. Luring almost four million visitors annually, it can be a tourist hell in high summer. This said, you'll have to be fairly stone-hearted not to be moved.

But Carcassonne is more than La Cité. The Ville Basse (Lower Town), altogether more tranquil and established in the 13th century, is a more modest stepsister to camp Cinderella up the hill and also merits more than a browse.

The hill on which La Cité stands has been fortified across the centuries – by Gauls, Romans, Visigoths, Moors and Franks. In the 13th century, the walls protected one of the major Cathar strongholds (see boxed text, p748). Once Roussillon was annexed to France in 1659, Carcassonne, no longer a frontier town, sank into slow decline. By the 19th century La Cité was simply crumbling away. It was rescued by the elaborate intervention of Viollet-le-Duc, who also set his controversial stamp upon, for example, the cathedrals of Notre Dame in Paris and Vézelay in Burgundy.

◉ Sights & Activities

La Cité   WALLED CITY
La Cité (Map p730), dramatically illuminated at night, is enclosed by two rampart walls and punctuated by 52 stone towers. But only the lower sections of the walls are original; the rest, including the anachronistic witches'-hat roofs (the originals were altogether flatter and weren't covered with slate), were stuck on by Viollet-le-Duc in the 19th century.

If you enter via the main entrance, before you rears a massive bastion, the **Porte Narbonnaise** and, just inside, the tourist office annexe. Rue Cros Mayrevieille, suffocating in kitschy souvenir shops, leads up to place du Château, heart of La Cité.

Through another archway and across a second dry moat is the 12th-century **Château Comtal** (adult/child €8.50/free; ◉10am-6.30pm). The entrance fee lets you look around the castle itself, enjoy an 11-minute film and join an optional 30- to 40-minute guided tour of the ramparts (tours in English, July and August). Descriptive panels around the castle, in both French and English, are explicit. For more detail, invest in an **audioguide** (1/2 people €4/6).

South of place du Château is **Basilique St-Nazaire** (◉9am-11.45am & 1.45-5pm or 5.30pm). Highlights are the graceful Gothic transept arms with a pair of superb 13th- and 14th-century rose windows at each end.

The **Petit Train de la Cité** (adult/child €7/3; ◉May-Sep), with multilingual commentary, beats the bounds of the ramparts. Alternatively, a **horse-drawn carriage** (www.carcassonne-caleches.com; adult/child €7/4; ◉Jul, Aug & school holidays), hauled by a pair of magnificent dray horses, does a similar 20-minute trip.

Canal du Midi   BOAT RIDES
(Map p728) **Lou Gabaret**, **L'Hélios** and **Solal** (adult €8-10.50, child €6.50-7.50; ◉Apr-Oct) chug along the Canal du Midi, departing from the bridge beside the train station. Sailings with commentary last from 1¾ to 2½ hours and prices vary accordingly.

Génération VTT   CYCLING
(Map p728; ☑06 09 59 30 85; www.generation-vtt.com/carcassonne, in French; ◉9am-1pm & 2-7pm Apr-Oct) Here, beside the Canal du Midi, you can rent a bike (per two hours/half-/full day €10/12/18) for a spin along its banks or around town. The young team also lead two- and three-hour cultural and gastronomic **cycle tours** (per 2/3 hours €20/30).

✦ Festivals & Events

Embrasement de la Cité   BASTILLE DAY
(Setting La Cité Ablaze) Carcassonne knows how to party. On 14 July at 10.30pm, it celebrates Bastille Day with a fireworks display rivalled only by Paris' pyrotechnics.

Festival de Carcassonne   CULTURAL FESTIVAL
(www.festivaldecarcassonne.fr) Brings music, dance and theatre to town for three weeks in July. Of the more than 100

LANGUEDOC-ROUSSILLON BAS-LANGUEDOC

spectacles, around 70 are free and enliven Carcassonne's squares and public spaces.

🛏 Sleeping

Chambres d'Hôte Nicole Cordonnnier
B&B €€

(Map p730; ☑04 68 25 16 67; http://legrandpuits. free.fr, in French; 8 place du Grand Puits; d incl breakfast €50-70) In the heart of La Cité, two of Madame Cordonnier's warmly recommended three rooms are particularly large, have a kitchenette for self-caterers, private terrace and can accommodate up to six (€10 per extra person).

Sidsmums
B&B €

(☑04 68 26 94 49; www.sidsmums.com; 11 chemin de la Croix d'Achille; dm €21.50, d with corridor bathroom €42-48) In Preixan, 10km south of Carcassonne, this is a splendid budget option. You can hire a bike, take a guided walk with Georges and Jim, the dogs, and cook for yourself in the self-contained kitchen. In

the garden are four chalets (€46 to €51.50), each sleeping up to four. Take the Quillan bus (four daily).

Hôtel Le Donjon
HOTEL €€

(Map p730; ☑04 68 11 23 00; www.hotel-donjon. fr; 2 rue du Comte Roger; d €105-153; 🕸@🛜) Low-beamed, thick-walled, venerable and cosy, 15th-century Le Donjon was originally an orphanage. Rooms overlook either its shady garden or the ramparts. Of its two equally comfortable annexes, Les Remparts is more contemporary, if shorter on period charm, while Maison du Comte Roger, with its striking medieval staircase, has superior standard rooms.

Hôtel du Pont Vieux
HOTEL €€

(Map p730; ☑04 68 25 24 99; www.lacitedecar cassonne.fr; 32 rue Trivalle; r €56-90; 🕸@🛜) Bedrooms, most with a bathtub, have attractively rough-hewn walls. On the 3rd floor, rooms 18 and 19 have unsurpassed

Carcassonne

views of the Cité. The buffet breakfast (€7) is truly gargantuan, and there's a large garden with olive and fig trees and flowering shrubs.

Hôtel de la Cité
HOTEL €€€

(Map p730; ☎04 68 71 98 71; www.hoteldelacite. orient-express.com; place Auguste Pont; r from €425; ❄️✳️🛜🏊) Neo-Gothic Hôtel de la Cité has rooms fit for royalty (literally so: 'A favourite hideaway for Europe's crowned heads, film stars, writers and intellectuals', proclaims its glossy brochure), should you fancy a retreat in such august company.

Hôtel des Trois Couronnes
HOTEL €€

(Map p728; ☎04 68 25 36 10; www.hotel-destrois couronnes.com; 2 rue des Trois Couronnes; r from €90; ✳️🛜🏊) Both rooms and reception area have been recently renovated at this attractive modern hotel beside the River Aude. There are uninterrupted views of La Cité from east-facing rooms (€20 extra). Up on the 4th floor, there's a a heated indoor pool and a particularly good **restaurant**.

Hôtel Astoria
HOTEL €

(Map p728; ☎04 68 25 31 38; www.astoria carcassonne.com, in French; 18 rue Tourtel; d/ tr/q €52/64/79, r with shared bathroom €34; ❄️closed Feb; ✳️🛜) Rooms (a few have aircon) are fresh and pleasant at this hotel and its equally agreeable annexe. Bathrooms are a bit poky but all in all it's a welcom-

ing place that offers very good value. Free parking.

Auberge de Jeunesse
YOUTH HOSTEL €

(Map p730; ☎04 68 25 23 16; carcassonne@fuaj. org; rue Vicomte Trencavel; incl breakfast €20.80; ❄️Feb–mid-Dec; @🛜) Carcassonne's cheery HI-affiliated youth hostel, in the heart of La Cité, has rooms sleeping four to six. It has a members' kitchen, a summertime snack bar, great outside terrace and an internet station. It rents out bikes (€10 per day) to hostellers. Although it has 120 beds, it's smart to reserve year-round.

Camping de la Cité
CAMPGROUND €

(☎04 68 25 11 77; www.campeole.com; sites €16-28.40; ❄️mid-Mar–mid-Oct;🏊) A walking and cycling trail leads from this site to both La Cité and the Ville Basse. From mid-June to mid-September, a shuttle bus connects the campsite with La Cité and the train station every 20 minutes.

Eating

Even if it's a boiling summer's day, don't leave town without trying *cassoulet,* a piping-hot dish blending white beans, juicy pork cubes, even bigger cylinders of meaty sausage and, in the most popular local variant, a hunk of duck.

VILLE BASSE

Cantine Robert Rodriguez
RETRO RESTAURANT €€

(Map p728; ☎04 68 47 37 80; www.restauran trobertrodriguez.com; 39 rue Coste Reboulh; mains around €25; ❄️closed Wed dinner & Sun; 🛜) Chef Robert Rodriguez works with exclusively organic raw materials and considers himself as much artisan as chef. *Fraicheur, saison, tradition, créativité* (fresh, seasonal, traditional and creative) is the leitmotif at his *cantine*. It's all consciously retro with marble-topped tables, bentwood chairs and early Edith Piaf and Charles Trenet warbling in the background. Walls are bedecked with his many diplomas and awards, plus photos of your heavily moustachioed host with famous guests.

Restaurant des Trois Couronnes
RESTAURANT €€

(Map p728; ☎04 68 25 36 10; mains €15-16, menu €21; ❄️Tue-Sat) This fine restaurant, on the 4th floor of Hôtel des Trois Couronnes, offers great cuisine with a magnificent panorama of La Cité thrown in.

LANGUEDOC-ROUSSILLON CARCASSONNE

L'Écurie
RESTAURANT €€

(Map p728; ☎04 68 72 04 04; www.restaurant-lecurie.fr; 43 bd Barbès; mains €12-23, lunch menu €15, menus €24.50-34; ⊙Mon-Sat & lunch Sun) Enjoy fine fare either within this attractively renovated 18th-century stable, all polished woodwork, brass and leather, or in the large, shaded garden. Pick from its long and choice selection of local wines.

Chez Fred
RESTAURANT €€

(Map p728; ☎04 68 72 02 23; www.chez-fred.fr; 31 bd Omer Sarraut; menus €25-30; ⊙lunch Tue-Fri & dinner daily) With a large window pierced in one of the walls of the ox-blood-red interior, you can peek at what Fred's chefs are rustling up; it's sure to be something creative. Alternatively, dine on its shaded tunnel of a terrace. The weekday *menu bistro* (lunch €17, dinner €21) is superb value.

LA CITÉ

Place Marcou is hemmed in on three sides by eateries. Indeed, throughout La Cité every second building seems to be a café or restaurant. It's wise to reserve, particularly for lunch.

Carcassonne – La Cité

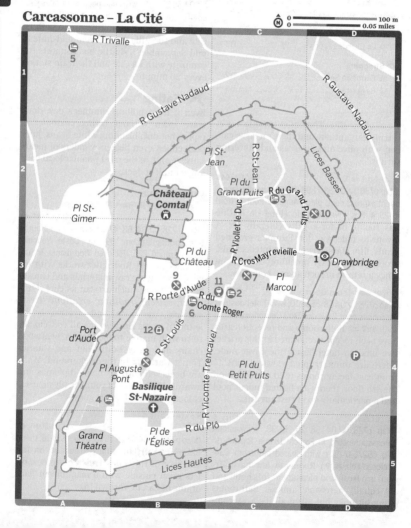

LA CITÉ AT ITS BEST

Linger after the crowds have left. Then, La Cité belongs only to its 100 or so inhabitants and the few visitors staying at hotels within its ramparts.

Chez Saskia
BRASSERIE €€

(Map p730; ☑04 68 71 98 71; place Auguste Pont; mains €18-23, menus €23-45; ☺Mar-Jan) This brasserie, which offers tasty, great-value dishes and a particularly rich range of desserts, belongs to Hôtel de la Cité. All around its walls are photos of the great and good who have stayed at the hotel: Jacques Chirac, Winston Churchill, Yves Montand and many more, recognisable and less so.

Auberge de Dame Carcas
TRADITIONAL FRENCH €€

(Map p730; ☑04 68 71 23 23; 3 place du Château; mains €12-15, menus €15-26; ☺Thu-Tue) This casual restaurant specialises in suckling pig (spot the model porkers all around) and carries a fine selection of well-priced local wines (including a delightfully smooth house red at €11). The ground floor is cosy and agreeably rustic, and you can see the chefs at work. The larger upstairs room offers more light, and there's a summer terrace too.

L'Écu d'Or
REGIONAL CUISINE €€

(Map p730; ☑04 68 25 49 03; 7-9 rue Porte d'Aude; mains €14-20, lunch menu €18, menus €25-33) Step down to semi-basement level to dine in style within the thick stone walls of this friendly spot. It serves, among many other delightful dishes, five varieties of *cassoulet* and a delicious range of creative desserts.

Auberge des Musées
RESTAURANT €€

(Map p730; ☑06 17 05 24 90; 17 rue du Grand Puits; menus €14.50-28) This unpretentious place has three rear terraces with views of the ramparts. It bakes its own organic bread and offers excellent-value meals. It doesn't take credit cards.

Self-Catering

Try the covered market (Map p728; rue Aimé Ramond; ☺Mon-Sat) or the open-air market (Map p728; place Carnot; ☺Tue, Thu & Sat). See also Shopping.

 Drinking

Cafés overlooking place Carnot in the Ville Basse spill onto the square in summer. In La Cité, place Marcou is one big outside café.

Comptoir des Vins et Terroirs
WINE BAR

(Map p730; 3 rue du Comte Roger; dishes €6.50-15; ☺Easter–mid-October) Run by a couple of qualified sommeliers, this wine bar carries a carefully selected range of mainly Languedoc-Roussillon wines, mostly from small-scale producers and many available by the glass. Indulge in their sampling of three wines, described to you in excellent English, and nibble at their cheese and charcuterie snacks, also predominantly local.

La Cité des Arômes
CAFÉ

(Map p728; 14 place Carnot) In the northwestern corner of place Carnot, this café wafts out scents of rich arabica and carries a huge selection of coffees.

 Shopping

La Ferme
GOURMET FOOD

(Map p728; 26 rue Chartran) A particularly well-stocked delicatessen, piled high with

731

LANGUEDOC-ROUSSILLON CARCASSONNE

vintage cheeses, wines, sausages and lots of other *gourmandises,* including homemade crème Chantilly.

Esprit de Sel
BRIC-A-BRAC

(Map p728; 10 rue de la République; ⊙Tue-Sat) This wonderful emporium is a place to browse and squeal with pleasure as you discover some unexpected treasure that you never knew you wanted or needed until now. Jocelyne Feller has an eye for quirky, off-centre items, ranging from the seriously retro to up-to-the-minute contemporary. Penetrate deep into the three galleries to explore the wares, culled from suppliers both large and small, and local producers – umbrellas, suitcases, boots, soaps and lotions, ornaments large to tiny, lampstands, ceramics, clothing and much more.

L'Art Gourmand
CHOCOLATE

(Map p730; 13 rue St-Louis) Chocolate fiends should definitely descend upon this place, which sells a huge range of goodies. The ice cream is pretty great too – all 31 varieties of it.

ⓘ Information

Alerte Rouge (73 rue de Verdun; per hr €3; ⊙9.30am-10pm Mon-Sat) Buy a drink and you can wi-fi for free for an hour. And here's a rare internet café that actually does great coffee.

Main tourist office (☏04 68 10 24 30; www. carcassonne-tourisme.com; 28 rue de Verdun; ⊙9am-6pm or 7pm Mon-Sat, 9am-noon or 1pm Sun) Borrow an **audioguide** to the Ville Basse (€3 for two hours).

Tourist office annexes La Cité (Porte Narbonnaise; ⊙year-round); Ville Basse (av Joffre; ⊙mid-Apr–Oct)

ⓘ Getting There & Away

AIR Ryanair is the only airline to fly in and out of Carcassonne's **airport** (☏04 68 71 96 46),

APPROACHING LA CITÉ

When approaching La Cité you could, like most visitors, leave your vehicle in one of the vast car parks beside the main entrance. But for a wonderful perspective of the ramparts, growing larger as you ascend, approach La Cité from the Ville Basse, on foot. Cross narrow Pont Vieux, walk along rue de la Barbacane, then up and in through Porte d'Aude.

5.5km from town. It serves several UK destinations, plus Cork and Dublin in Ireland.

TRAIN Carcassonne is on the busy main line linking Toulouse (€14, 50 minutes) with Narbonne (€9.80, 30 minutes) and Montpellier (€22.70, 1½ hours). For Perpignan (€18.30, 1½ hours), change in Narbonne.

ⓘ Getting Around

TO/FROM THE AIRPORT The **Navette Aéroport** runs to and from the airport (€5, 25 minutes), leaving the train station approximately two hours before each Ryanair departure. By car, take the Carcassonne Ouest A61 motorway exit.

BICYCLE Génération VTT (see Sights & Activities) rents both touring and mountain bikes, plus child seats and trailers.

CAR & MOTORCYCLE For La Cité, leave your vehicle in the huge car park (€5 for up to five hours) just east of the main entrance.

PUBLIC TRANSPORT Buses run only until about 7pm, Monday to Saturday.

Bus 4 runs roughly every 45 minutes from the train station and Ville Basse to La Cité's main entrance.

Between July and September, a dinky **motorised train** (single/return €2/3; ⊙10am-12.45pm & 2.15-7.30pm Mon-Sat) links La Cité, the town centre and train station every 20 minutes via Pont Vieux.

TAXI Call ☏04 68 71 50 50 for a taxi.

HAUT-LANGUEDOC

Haut-Languedoc is a world away from the towns, vineyards and beaches of the broad coastal plain. More sparsely populated, it's a land of deeply incised gorges, high windswept plateaux and dense forest, ideal for those who love being out in the open air.

Mende
POP 13,200

Mende, a quiet little place straddling the River Lot, is the capital of Lozère, France's least populous *département.* Its oval-shaped centre is ringed by a one-way road that acts as something of a *cordon sanitaire,* leaving the old quarter almost traffic-free.

⊙ Sights & Activities

The tourist office's brochure, *Listen to the Story of Mende,* highlights the town's main historical features.

Cathédrale Notre Dame
CATHEDRAL

(place Urbain V) The dark interior of the 14th-century, twin-towered cathedral makes the pincushion panes of the 17th-century rose window at the west end positively glow. But you'll have to peer hard to make out detail on the eight 18th-century Aubusson tapestries, hung high above the nave, that illustrate the life of the Virgin.

Mimat Adventures
ADVENTURE PARK

(☑04 66 45 00 24; adult/child €19/16; ☉9.30am-7.30pm Jul & Aug, 2-7pm Sat & Sun Apr-Jun & Sep) High upon Causse de Mende, which looms above town to the south, this treetop adventure park has 76 different aerial activities for all ages. You can also rent mountain bikes here and take off along the heights.

🛏 Sleeping & Eating

TOP CHOICE | Hôtel de France
HOTEL €€

(☑04 66 65 00 04; www.hoteldefrance -mende.com, in French; 9 bd Lucien Arnault; d €58-95; ❋@🐾) Most rooms at this one-time coaching inn (whose owner speaks excellent English) have sweeping views over the valley and gardens below. All 19 rooms are particularly large, with separate toilet and gleaming bathroom. For families, there are two duplexes (€98) and a pair of rooms with small roof terrace (also €98). On the inner ring road, it runs a first-class *restaurant* (menus €28 to €32).

Hôtel le Commerce
HOTEL €

(☑04 66 65 13 73; www.lecommerce-mende.com; 2 bd Henri Bourrillon; s/d €43/53; 🐾) Opposite place du Foirail on the busy ring road, this agreeably labyrinthine hotel, run by the same family for three generations, has 10 impeccable rooms. The owner is an ale fanatic and his popular bar carries a great range of beers.

Restaurant Les Voûtes
GRILLS, PIZZAS €€

(☑04 66 49 00 05; 13 rue d'Aigues-Passes; menus €25; ☉Mon-Sat) The Vaults enjoys a splendid setting, deep within an ex-convent. Run by three brothers, it offers salads big enough to fill a fruit bowl, plus pizzas and grills. It also does great all-on-one-plate lunchtime specials (€13.50).

Le Mazel
REGIONAL CUISINE €€

(☑04 66 65 05 33; 25 rue du Collège; mains €19-26, lunch menu €16; ☉closed Wed & dinner Sun) This restaurant with its stylish decor offers mainly local cuisine, imaginatively prepared (start, for example, with the *pigeon ramier crème de foie gras*, wood pigeon

with cream of foie gras). A recognised gourmet venue, it provides exceptional value.

Self-Catering

Saturday is market day, when a farmers market takes over place Urbain V. La Fromagerie (30bis rue Soubeyran), overlooked by the buttresses of the cathedral's east end, has an impressive range of cheeses, regional meats and pâtés.

❶ Information

Tourist office (☑04 66 94 00 23; www.ot-mende.fr; place du Foirail; ☉9am-noon & 2-6pm Mon-Fri, 9am-noon Sat, also open Sun Jul & Aug; 🐾) Free wi-fi, which extends to the café terrace nearby.

❶ Getting There & Away

BUS Buses leave from the train station, most passing by place du Foirail, beside the tourist office. On weekdays, there's one bus daily to Le Puy-en-Velay (€26, two hours). Two SNCF buses run daily to/from Clermont-Ferrand in the Massif Central (€31, three hours).

TRAIN The train station is 1km north of town across the River Lot. There are two trains daily to Alès (€17.20, 2½ hours).

Around Mende

Parc du Gévaudan
WOLF PARK

(www.loupsdugevaudan.com, in French; adult/child €7/4; ☉10am-6pm or 7pm) Wolves once prowled freely through the Lozère forests but today you'll see them only in this sanctuary, in Ste-Lucie, 7km north of Marvejols. The park sustains around 100 Mongolian, Canadian, Siberian and Polish wolves living in semi-freedom.

Réserve de Bisons d'Europe
BISON PARK

(☑04 66 31 40 40; www.bisoneurope.com, in French; ☉10am-5pm or 6pm) Near the small village of Ste-Eulalie-en-Margeride, around 40 bison roam freely. Visitors, on the other hand, must follow a 50-minute guided tour, either by horse-drawn carriage (per adult/child €12.50/7) or, in winter, by sledge (€14.50/8). From mid-June to September, you can follow a self-guided 1km walking path (per adult/child €6/4) around the periphery.

Parc National des Cévennes

Drier, hotter and in general leafier than the Auvergne to their north, the Cévennes have more in common with Mediterranean lands. Dotted with isolated hamlets, they harbour a huge diversity of fauna and flora (an astounding 2250 plant species have been logged). Creatures such as red deer, beavers and vultures, long gone from these lands, have been successfully reintroduced. The park covers four main areas: Mont Lozère, much of the Causse Méjean, the Vallées Cévenoles (Cévennes Valleys) and Mont Aigoual.

The best map of the park is the IGN's *Parc National des Cévennes* (€6.20) at 1:100,000.

History

The 910-sq-km park was created in 1970 to bring ecological stability to an area that, because of religious and later economic upheavals, has long had a destabilising human presence. Population influxes, which saw the destruction of forests for logging and pasture, were followed by mass desertions as people gave up the fight against the inhospitable climate and terrain. Emigration led to the abandonment of hamlets and farms, many of which have been snapped up by wealthy Parisians and foreigners.

◉ Sights

MONT LOZÈRE

This 1699m-high lump of granite in the north of the park is shrouded in cloud and ice in winter and covered with heather and blueberries, peat bogs and flowing streams in summer. The Musée du Mont Lozère (adult/child incl audioguide €3.50/2.50; ◷2.30-6.30pm Apr-Oct, also 10.30am-12.30pm Jun-Sep), within a hideous concrete hulk at Pont de Montvert, 20km northeast of Florac, is a fascinating introduction to the region and its traditional rural crafts. Alas, the English audio commentary is a disaster; you're better off reading the French text.

VALLÉES CÉVENOLES

First planted in the Middle Ages, *châtaigniers* (sweet-chestnut trees) carpet the Vallées Cévenoles, the park's central area of plunging ravines and jagged ridges. Along one of these ridges runs the breathtaking Corniche des Cévennes, linking St-Jean du Gard and Florac.

MONT AIGOUAL

Mont Aigoual (1567m) and neighbouring Montagne du Lingas are renowned for their searing winds and heavy snowfall. The area is dense with beech trees, thanks to a refor-

estation program that counteracts years of uncontrolled logging. The observatory atop the summit has an exhibition (www.aigoual. asso.fr; admission free; ◷10am-1pm & 2-6pm May-Sep), where you can learn about weather prediction (and even take part in preparing the next day's forecast), cloud formation and lots more. Captions are in French but much of the exhibition is highly visual.

🏃 Activities

In winter there's **cross-country skiing** (more than 100km of marked trails) on Mont Aigoual and Mont Lozère, while **donkey treks** are popular in the park in warmer months. There are 600km of donkey- and horse-riding trails and 200km marked out for mountain-bike enthusiasts.

An equally well-developed network of trails makes the park a walking paradise year-round. It's criss-crossed by a dozen GR (*grande randonnée*; hiking) trails and there are over 20 shorter signposted walks lasting between two and seven hours.

❶ Getting There & Away

By car, the most spectacular route from the east is the Corniche des Cévennes, a ridge road that winds along the mountain crests of the Cévennes for 56km from St-Jean du Gard to Florac.

If you're approaching Florac from Mende and the north, leave the N106 (itself a scenic run) at Balsièges and drive the much quieter, even prettier D31. This crosses the wild, upland Causse de Sauveterre, then descends to Ispagnac, where you turn left to rejoin the main N106.

Florac

POP 2000

Florac, 79km northwest of Alès and 38km southeast of Mende, makes a great base for exploring the Parc National des Cévennes and the upper reaches of the Gorges du Tarn. Lively in summer and moribund for most of the rest of the year, it's draped along the west bank of River Tarnon, one of the tributaries of the Tarn, while the sheer cliffs of the Causse Méjean loom 1000m overhead.

🏃 Activities

The tourist office's *Guide Touristique* has page upon page detailing a whole summer's worth of outdoor activities, from short walks to caving and paragliding.

Walking

For detailed information on the park's rich walking potential, contact Maison du Parc National des Cévennes (☎04 66 49 53 01; www.cevennes-parcnational.fr, in French; ☺9am-6.30pm Jul & Aug, 9.30am-12.15pm & 1.30-5.30pm Mon-Fri Oct-Apr). It occupies the handsome, restored 17th-century Château de Florac. Resources include a dozen excellent information kits (€5 each) describing circular walks from various starting points within the park and also an English version of its guidebook *Parc National des Cévennes* (€15). There's a splendidly informative interactive exhibition (admission free), *Passagers du Paysage*, with captions, a recorded commentary in English (delivered, alas, by a couple of glum, monotone native speakers) and a 15-minute slide show. Ask about **Festival Nature**, the park's summertime mix of outdoor activities, lectures and field trips.

Donkey Treks

Why not follow the lead of Robert Louis Stevenson and hire a pack animal? Several companies around Florac are in the donkey business. They include Gentiâne (☎04 66 41 04 16; http://anegenti.free.fr) in Castagnols and Tramontane (☎04 66 45 92 44; chantal.tramontane@nomade.fr) in St-Martin de Lansuscle.

Typical prices are €45 to €50 per day and €225 to €245 per week. Each outfit can reserve accommodation along the route. Though each is outside Florac, they'll transport the donkeys to town or a place of your choosing for a fee (around €1 per kilometre).

Other Activities

Cévennes Évasion (www.cevennes-evasion .com, in French; 5 place Boyer) rents out **mountain bikes** for €13/19 per half-/full day and furnishes riders with handy colour route maps. In summer it will take you for free (minimum five persons) up to the Causse Méjean, from where you can whiz effortlessly back down. It also arranges **caving**, **canyon-clambering** and **rock-climbing** expeditions (trust these guys; for the 2010 opening ceremony of Dubai's Burj Khalifa, the world's tallest building, they hung fireworks all the way up its 828m facade). It also runs guided and independent **walking** and **cycling** holidays, where your accommodation is booked ahead and your luggage transported onwards daily.

TRAVELS WITH A DONKEY

The Cévennes were even wilder and more untamed back in October 1878, when Scottish writer Robert Louis Stevenson crossed them with only a donkey, Modestine, for company.

'I was looked upon with contempt, like a man who should project a journey to the moon, but yet with a respectful interest, like one setting forth for the inclement Pole,' Stevenson wrote in his *Travels with a Donkey in the Cévennes*.

Accompanied by the wayward Modestine, bought for 65 francs and a glass of brandy, Stevenson took a respectable 12 days to travel the 232km on foot (Modestine carried his gear) from Le Monastier-sur-Gazelle, southeast of Le Puy-en-Velay, to St-Jean du Gard, west of Alès.

The Stevenson trail, first retraced and marked with the cross of St Andrew by a Scottish woman in 1978, is nowadays designated the GR70 and extends from Le Puy to Alès.

Whether you're swaying on a donkey or simply walking, you'll find *The Robert Louis Stevenson Trail* by Alan Castle an excellent, practical, well-informed companion. Consult also www.chemin-stevenson.org and www.gr70-stevenson.com, and pick up the free pamphlet *Sur Le Chemin de Robert Louis Stevenson* (On the Robert Louis Stevenson Trail). Stocked by tourist offices, it has a comprehensive list of accommodation en route. For the lightest of travel, these organisations will haul your baggage from stage to stage:

La Malle Postale (☎06 67 79 38 16; www.lamallepostale.com, in French)

Stevenson Bagages (☎06 07 29 01 23; www.stevenson-bagages.com, in French)

Transbagages (☎04 66 65 27 75)

🛏 Sleeping

La Carline   WALKERS' ACCOMMODATION €

(☎04 66 45 24 54; www.gite-florac.fr, in French; 18 rue du Pêcher; per person €13; ☺Easter-Oct) This welcoming trekkers' favourite occupies an 18th-century house and has self-catering facilities. All rooms have corridor bathrooms and there's a pair of cosy doubles on the top floor.

Grand Hôtel du Parc   HOTEL €

(☎04 66 45 03 05; www.grandhotelduparc.fr; 47 av Jean Monestier; r €50-70; ☺mid-Mar–mid-Nov; 🛜🞉) This venerable building has 55 spacious rooms. It sits on extensive grounds with a pool, terrace and delightful, well-tended gardens shaded by mature cedars.

Hôtel Les Gorges du Tarn   HOTEL €

(☎04 66 45 00 63; www.hotel-gorgesdutarn.com; 48 rue du Pêcher; d €46-62; ☺Easter-Oct; 🛜🞉) Rooms in both the main building and annexe of this 26-room Logis de France are bright as a new pin. This said, it's worth paying the higher rate for a double in the designer-cool annexe. A pair of studios (€82) sleep up to four and have cooking facilities. Its restaurant, **Adonis** (mains €17-22, menus €16-47; ☺closed Wed) merits a visit whether or not you're staying here.

Camping Le Pont du Tarn   CAMPGROUND €

(☎04 66 45 18 26; www.camping-florac.com; site & 2 persons €16; ☺Apr-Sep;🞉) At this large, attractive, shaded campsite, 2km from Florac beside the D998, you can swim either in the heated pool or river Tarn, which runs right by.

🍴 Eating

In summer L'Esplanade, a shady, pedestrianised avenue, becomes one long dining area where you can eat both well and economically.

La Source du Pêcher   MEDITERRANEAN €€

(☎04 66 45 03 01; 1 rue de Remuret; menus €16-38; ☺Easter-Oct) Dine on the enchanting open-air terrace, perched above a pool where trout glide. The cuisine, enhanced by an extensive choice of wines, teas and coffees, is as impressive as the site at this much garlanded restaurant. On the downside, service can be very slow and they don't take reservations – so do arrive early.

🌿**Chez les Paysans**   LOCAL CUISINE €

(☎04 66 31 22 07; 3 rue Théophile Roussel; mains €10-13, menus €12-15; ☺May-Oct, lunch Tue-Sat Nov-Apr) At this restaurant you can sample fresh, very reasonably priced local fare either inside or on its vine-shaded terrace. Its **shop** has a great selection of produce from small farmers in the area.

🛍 Shopping

Maison du Pays Cévenol   GOURMET FOOD

(3 rue du Pêcher) This gastronomic treasure trove sells local specialities – liqueurs, jams, Pélardon cheeses and chestnuts in all their guises.

Biojour   ORGANIC GROCER

(5 rue du Pêcher) Just along the street from Maison du Pays Cévenol and altogether smaller, Biojour sells a range of organic produce.

THE FARM EXPERIENCE

A couple of splendid working farms, both accessible from Florac, will welcome you for a night or longer stay.

La Ferme de Vimbouches (☎04 66 31 56 55; www.causses-cevennes.com/ferme-vimbouches; r incl breakfast €50, half board per person €45; ☺Mar-Nov), where Philip trains his horses and Cathy is your welcoming hostess, is a friendly getaway superb for an overnight stop or a stay of several days, especially for families. Borrow a donkey for a day's walking, visit the pig pen and chicken run and commune with their pedigree horses, plebeian pigs, rabbits and goats. To get there from Florac, continue along the N106 towards Alès and, after 27km (it's well worth it), turn left onto the D29, following signs for Vimbouches, reached after a further 6km.

La Ferme de la Borie (☎04 66 45 10 90; www.encevennes.com, in French; incl breakfast s €23-29, d €36-44; ☺Mar-Nov) will see you bowled over by the sheer enthusiasm and *joie de vivre* of host Jean-Christophe Barthes. And you'll groan contentedly as you head to bed after a blow-out dinner of produce from his organic farm, accompanied by as much wine as you wish. Be sure to reserve – by phone or email (ferme-auberge-la-borie@orange.fr), since there's no link from the website. To get there, turn right onto the narrow C4, signed La Borie, barely a kilometre southeast of Florac on the N106.

ℹ Information

Tourist office (☎04 66 45 01 14; www.
mescevennes.com, in French; 33 av Jean Monestier; ⊙9am-noon & 2-5pm or 6pm Mon-Sat)

ℹ Getting There & Away

It's a pain without your own vehicle. From mid-
April to mid-September, one **Transports Reilhes**
(☎04 66 45 00 18, 06 60 58 58 10) minibus
runs to/from Alès (€13, 1¼ hours), Monday to
Saturday, leaving from the old railway station at
9am. During the rest of the year, it leaves at 8am
only on Wednesday and Saturday.

Gorges du Tarn

The Tarn gushes down from the flanks
of Mont Lozère. Over millennia, the river
and its few tributaries have carved and
weathered the deep, spectacular Gorges du
Tarn. Winding southwest for about 50km
from the village of Ispagnac, 9km northwest of Florac, this deep ravine marks the
boundary between the Causse Méjean and
its south and the Causse de Sauveterre to
the north. Until the construction of the riverside road in 1905, the only way to move
through the gorges was by boat. On a summer's day, when over 2500 vehicles grind
through Ste-Énimie each day, this road
(the D907bis) is often jammed with traffic.
For much of the rest of the year, it's lightly
trafficked.

STE-ÉNIMIE
POP 550

It's worth lingering a while in Ste-Énimie,
where you'll find its features well signed
in both French and English. Twenty-seven
kilometres from Florac, 56km from Millau
and midway along the gorges, it tumbles
like an avalanche of grey-brown stone.
Long isolated, it's now a favoured starting
or finishing point for canoe or kayak descents of the Tarn.

The tiny Écomusée Le Vieux Logis
(adult/child €2/1.50; ⊙Sun, Mon & Wed-Fri
mid-Jun–mid-Sep) has one vaulted room,
crammed with antique local furniture,
lamps, tableware and costumes.

Highlights of the small, cobbled old
quarter, where most houses have been re-
painted and restored, are the 12th-century
Romanesque Église de Ste-Énimie, and
the Halle aux Blés, where cereal crops
from the high Causses were bartered for
wine, fresh fruit and walnut oil.

☂ Activities

Riding the River Tarn is at its best in high
summer, when the river is usually low and
the descent a lazy trip over mostly calm
water. You can canoe as far as the impassable Pas de Soucy, a barrier of boulders
about 9km downriver from La Malène.
Downstream from here, there are further
possibilities.

The Ste-Énimie tourist office carries information on the veritable flotilla of companies offering **canoe** and **kayak descents**
between April and September. These include Au Moulin de la Malène (☎04 66 48 51
14; www.canoeblanc.com) in La Malène, Canoë
2000 (☎04 66 48 57 71; www.canoe2000.fr) in
Ste-Énimie and La Malène, Locanoë (☎04
66 48 55 57; www.gorges-du-tarn.fr, in French) in
Castelbouc and Ste-Énimie, and Le Cano-
phile (☎04 66 48 57 60; www.canoe-tarn.com, in
French) in Ste-Énimie.

Typical trips and tariffs for canoe and
kayak descents: Castelbouc to Ste-Énimie
(€13, 7km, two hours), Ste-Énimie to La
Malène (€18, 13km, 3½ hours), Castelbouc
to La Malène (€21, 20km, one day), Ste-
Énimie to Les Baumes Basses (€22, 22km,
one day).

If you'd rather someone else did the
hard work, spend an effortless hour with
Les Bateliers de la Malène (www.gorges
dutarn.com; ⊙Apr-Oct), who, for €20.50 per
person, will punt you down an 8km stretch
of the gorge from La Malène, then drive
you back.

🛏 Sleeping

All along the gorges, there are plenty of
campgrounds to choose from.

Two splendid *chambres d'hôte* lie at each
end of the Gorges du Tarn.

La Pause   B&B €
(☎05 65 62 63 06; www.hebergement-gorges
dutarn.com; rte de Caplac, Le Rozier; s/d €40/50;
▣) At the gorges' southern end, in the
village of Le Rozier, La Pause has three
tastefully furnished rooms decorated in
attractive colours, plus a couple of suites.
At breakfast, jams – fig, quince, cherry
and more – are all made by your hostess,
Pierrette Espinasse. To get there, turn left
(signed Capluc), after the village church.

Maison de Marius   B&B €
(☎04 66 44 25 05; www.maisondemarius.fr, in
French; 8 rue Pontet, Quézac; r €40-80; ⊙Mar-
Oct) In Quézac, at the northern limit of

the gorges near Ispagnac, each of Dany Méjean's delightful rooms has its own character, and you've never tasted sweeter water, drawn from the nearby mineral springs. To get there, skirt the village (its main street is unidirectional against you) and follow signs from the church.

Manoir de Montesquiou HOTEL €€
(☎04 66 48 51 12; www.manoir-montesquiou. com; r €77-111; ⊙Apr-Oct; 🐾) This 16th-century mansion with its broad terrace overlooks the bridge in La Malène. Install yourself in one of its comfortable, traditional rooms, then reserve a table at its reputed **restaurant** (menus €28-49) For something lighter, sample one of its range of chocolate drinks or order a large slice of squishy chocolate cake.

❶ Information

The Ste-Énimie **tourist office** (☎04 66 48 53 44; www.gorgesdutarn.net; ⊙9.30am-12.30pm & 2-5.30pm or 6pm Mon-Sat, also Sun Jul & Aug) covers all of the ravine. It stocks maps and walking guides, including the walker-friendly IGN Top 25 map No 2640OT *Gorges du Tarn*. There's also a small seasonal **annexe** (⊙mid-May–Aug) in La Malène.

Parc Naturel Régional des Grands Causses

The Grands Causses, the Massif Central's most southerly expression, are mainly harsh limestone plateau. Scorched in summer and windswept in winter, the stony surface holds little moisture as water filters through the limestone to form an underground world, ideal for cavers.

The Rivers Tarn, Jonte and Dourbie have sliced deep gorges through the 5000-sq-km plateau, creating four *causses* ('plateaux' in the local lingo): Sauveterre, Méjean, Noir and Larzac, each different in its delicate geological forms. One resembles a dark lunar surface, another's like a Scottish moor covered with the thinnest layer of grass, while the next is gentler and more fertile. But all are eerie and empty except for the occasional shepherd and his flock – and all offer magnificent walking and mountain biking.

Millau, at the heart of the park, is a good base for venturing into this wild area. The Gorges de la Jonte, where birds of prey wheel and swoop, skim the park's eastern boundary, rivalling in their rugged splendour the neighbouring, more famous Gorges du Tarn.

◉ Sights

CAUSSE DE SAUVETERRE
This, the northernmost of the *causses* is a gentle, hilly plateau dotted with a few compact and isolated farms. Every possible patch of fertile earth is cultivated, creating irregular, intricately patterned wheat fields.

CAUSSE MÉJEAN
Causse Méjean, the highest, is also the most barren and isolated. Defined to the north by the Gorges du Tarn and, southwards, by the Gorges de la Jonte, it looms over Florac on its eastern flank. It's a land of poor pasture enriched by occasional fertile depressions, where streams gurgle down into limestone through sinkholes, funnels and fissures.

CHESTNUT: THE ALL-PURPOSE TREE

In the Cévennes, the chestnut tree (known as *l'arbre à pain*, or bread tree) provided the staple food of many families. The nuts were eaten raw, roasted and dried, or ground into flour. Blended with milk or wine, chestnuts were the essence of *bajanat*, a nourishing soup. Part of the harvest would feed the pigs while the leaves of pruned twigs and branches provided fodder for sheep and goats.

Harvested at ground level with small forks – of chestnut wood, of course – the prickly husks (called *hérissons*, or hedgehogs) were removed by being trampled upon in spiky boots. Nowadays, chestnuts are the favourite food of the Cévennes' wild boars and still feature in a number of local sauces and desserts.

Nothing was wasted. Sections of hollowed-out trunk would serve as beehives, smaller branches would be woven into baskets, while larger ones were whittled into stakes for fencing or used to build trellises. The wood, hard and resistant to parasites, was used for rafters, rakes and household furniture – everything from, quite literally, the cradle to the coffin.

This combination of water and limestone has created some spectacular underground scenery. Within the cavern of Aven Armand (www.aven-armand.com; adult/child €9.10/6.20; ☺10am-noon & 1.30-5pm Apr-Oct), reached by a funicular railway that drops 60 vertical metres, bristles the world's greatest concentration of stalagmites. Guided visits, lasting about 45 minutes (there's an accompanying information sheet in English) head underground about every 20 minutes. A **combination ticket** (per adult/child €12.80/8.25) also includes admission to the Chaos de Montpellier-le-Vieux.

CAUSSE NOIR

Rising immediately east of Millau, the 'Black Causse' is best known for the Chaos de Montpellier-le-Vieux (www.montpellier levieux.com; adult/child €5.70/4.05; ☺9.30am-5.30pm Apr-Oct), 18km northeast of Millau, overlooking the Gorges de la Dourbie. Water erosion has created more than 120 hectares of tortured limestone formations with fanciful names such as the Sphinx and the Elephant. Three trails, lasting one to three hours, cover the site, as does a tourist train (adult/child €3.65/2.70).

If you're here outside official opening times, there's nothing to stop you wandering around freely.

CAUSSE DU LARZAC

The Causse du Larzac is the largest of the four *causses*. An endless sweep of distant horizons and rocky steppes broken by medieval villages, it's known as the 'French Desert'.

You'll stumble across venerable, fortified villages such as Ste-Eulalie de Cernon, long the capital of the Larzac region, and La Cavalerie, both built by the Knights Templar, a religious military order that distinguished itself during the Crusades.

GORGES DE LA JONTE

The Gorges de la Jonte, 15km long, cleave east–west from Meyrueis to Le Rozier, separating in dramatic fashion the Causse Noir from Causse Méjean.

Just south of the gorge, Dargilan (www. grotte-dargilan.com; adult/child €8.50/5.80; ☺10am-5.30pm or 6.30pm Apr-Oct) is known as La Grotte Rose (the pink cave) for its dominant natural colouring. The most arresting moment of the one-hour, 1km tour through this vast chasm is a sudden, dazzling exit onto a ledge with a dizzying view of the Gorges de la Jonte way below.

Belvédère des Vautours (Vulture Viewing Point; ☎05 65 62 69 69; www.vautours -lozere.com; adult/child €6.50/3; ☺10am-5pm or 6pm Apr-Oct) is just west of Le Truel on the D996. Reintroduced after having all but disappeared locally, the vultures now freely wheel and plane in the *causses* skies and nest high in the sheer cliffs on the opposite side of the valley. The viewing point has an impressive multimedia exhibition, including live video transmission from the nesting sites. It also organises three varied half-day birding walks (adult/child €7/3.50; reservation essential).

ⓘ Information

Parc Naturel Régional des Grands Causses office (☎05 65 61 35 50; www.parc-grands-causses.fr, in French; 71 bd de l'Ayrolle, Millau; ☺9am-noon or 12.30pm & 2-5pm or 6pm Mon-Fri)

Millau

POP 22,900

Millau (pronounced 'mee-yo') squeezes between the Causse Noir and Causse du Larzac at the confluence of the Rivers Tarn and Dourbie. Though falling just over the border into the Midi-Pyrénées *département* of Aveyron, it's tied to Languedoc historically and culturally. Famous within France for glove-making, it's also the main centre for the Parc Naturel Régional des Grands Causses and a taking-off point for hiking and other outdoor activities – particularly hang-gliding and paragliding, exploiting the uplifting thermals.

⊙ Sights

FREE Causse Gantier   GLOVE MUSEUM
(bd des Gantières; ☺9.30am-12.30pm & 2-7pm Mon-Sat) Causse Gantier is the only company that still make gloves in Millau (all the rest import their leather goods and trade on their past reputations). Within this architecturally pleasing building, both workshop and display, you can watch craftspeople at work. Buy here and you can be certain your gloves were made on the spot.

Musée de Millau   MUSEUM
(place Maréchal Foch; adult/chlld €5.10/free; ☺10am-noon & 2-6pm Sep-Jun, closed Sun Oct-Apr) Millau's museum has a rich collection

of fossils, including a 4m-long, almost intact skeleton of a prehistoric marine reptile from the Causse du Larzac. In the basement is a huge array of plates and vases from **La Graufesenque**, in its time the largest pottery workshop in the western Roman Empire. The 1st-floor leather and glove section illustrates Millau's tanneries and their products through the ages. A **combined ticket** (€6) includes admission to La Graufesenque archaeological site, at the confluence of the Rivers Tarn and Dourbie.

Le Beffroi
BELFRY

(rue Droite; adult/child €3/free; ☺10am-noon & 2-6pm mid-Jun–Sep) Clamber up this 42m-tall belfry for a great overview of town. From its square base dating from the 12th century, you ascend as it tapers into a 17th-century octagonal tower.

🏃 Activities

Hang-gliding & Paragliding

Several outfits run introductory courses (around €350 for five days) and beginner flights with an instructor (€55 to €70). Two long-established players:

Horizon
HANG-GLIDING, PARAGLIDING

(www.horizon-millau.com, in French; 6 place Lucien Grégoire) Also offers caving, canyon descents, rock climbing and Naturaventure, a multi-adventure trail.

Roc et Canyon
HANG-GLIDING, PARAGLIDING

(www.roc-et-canyon.com, in French; 55 av Jean Jaurès) In summer it has a base beside Pont de Cureplat. Also offers caving, rock climbing, canyon descents, rafting and bungee jumping.

Rock Climbing

The high cliffs of the Gorges de la Jonte are an internationally renowned venue for climbers. Both Horizon and Roc et Canyon (p740) offer monitored climbs and can put you in touch with local climbers.

Walking & Cycling

The tourist office sells a handy box of 15 folders (€8; €1 per folder) of clearly described walks in the region, varying from one to 4½ hours. Alternatively, *Les Belles Balades de l'Aveyron* (€8) describes 22 walks in the area and also details 10 mountain-bike and 10 tourer routes.

✨ Festivals & Events

Natural Games
SPORTS FESTIVAL

(www.naturalgames.fr) An international festival of outdoor sports such as climbing, canoeing and extreme mountain biking. Four days, end-June.

Millau Jazz Festival
JAZZ FESTIVAL

A week-long wail in mid-July.

Mondial de Pétanque
PÉTANQUE FESTIVAL

(Pétanque world series; www.millau-petanque. com, in French) Six days in mid-August. Attracts more than 10,000 players and more than twice as many spectators.

🛏 Sleeping

There are several huge riverside campgrounds along both banks of the River Tarn.

Château de Creissels
CASTLE HOTEL €€

(☎05 65 60 16 59; www.chateau-de-creissels. com; Creissels; r new wing €71-85, old wing €108; ☺Mar-Dec) In the village of Creissels, 2km southwest of Millau on the D992 and well signed, this castle has a split personality. Rooms in the old 12th-century tower breathe history while those in the 20th-century wings (most of them extensively renovated in 2010), have balconies overlooking the large garden. There's an excellent **restaurant**.

Hôtel La Capelle
HOTEL €

(☎05 65 60 14 72; www.hotel-millau-capelle.com; 7 place de la Capelle; r €48-61, with shared bathroom €30-45; ✳☻) In the converted wing of a one-time leather factory, La Capelle is a great budget choice. Rooms are large with separate bathroom and toilet and the large terrace with views towards the Causse Noir makes for a perfect breakfast spot. Some rooms have air-con (€5 supplement).

🍴 Eating

La Mangeoire
REGIONAL CUISINE €€

(☎05 65 60 13 16; 8 bd de la Capelle; lunch menu €14.50, menus €19.50-46; ☺Tue-Sun) Millau's oldest restaurant, in the vaults beneath the former city walls, serves delightful, mainly regional dishes. Its pride is the open wood-fire barbecue. In winter, spits pierce wild game such as hare and partridge. Year-round, meat and fish (€14 to €22) are sizzled to perfection.

La Marmite du Pêcheur
CREATIVE CONTEMPORARY €€

(☎05 65 61 20 44; 14-16 bd de la Capelle; lunch menu €14.50, mains €17-19, menus €19.50-55; ☺closed Mon & lunch Tue Jul-Sep, Tue & Wed Oct-Jun) A few doors from La Mangeoire and

PONT DE MILLAU

This toll bridge, slung across the wide Tarn Valley and bearing the A75 motorway, is a true 21st-century icon. Designed by the British architect Sir Norman Foster, it carries more than 4.5 million vehicles each year. It's a work of industrial art and an amazing feat of engineering. Only seven pylons, hollow and seemingly slim as needles, support 2.5km of four-lane motorway. Rising to 343m above the valley bottom, it ranks among the tallest road bridges in the world.

Construction cost 400 million euros, and gobbled up 127,000 cu metres of concrete, 19,000 tonnes of reinforcing steel and 5000 tonnes of cables and stays. Yet despite these heavyweight superlatives, it still looks like a gossamer thread.

Viaduc Espace (☺10am-5pm, to 7pm Apr-Oct), at ground level beneath the viaduct, has a 10-minute film that tells the story of the bridge's construction and there are 45-minute **guided visits** (in English on request; per adult/child €6/3.50).

You don't have to have a vehicle to visit the Pont de Millau. An open-top, canary-yellow **bus** (per adult/child €10/6) leaves Millau's place de la Capelle five times daily for a 1¾-hour guided tour. For a leisurely glide along the Tarn Valley and an original, crane-your-neck perspective of the bridge from below, take a 1½-hour boat trip with **Bateliers du Viaduc** (www.bateliersduviaduc.com; Creissels; adult/child €22/12.50; ☺every 45 minutes from 9.45am).

run by an engaging young couple, this place too is attractively vaulted and has hearty regional *menus* within much the same price range. Try the chef's *marmite du pêcheur à ma façon* of salmon, perch and red mullet, gambas and scallops gratin (€24).

Le Capion   TRADITIONAL FRENCH **€€**
(☎05 65 60 00 91; 3 rue J-F Alméras; mains €15.50-19.50, lunch menu €14.50, menus €16-39; ☺Thu-Mon & lunch Tue) Peer into the kitchen to see the team at work as you walk past on the way to the larger of its two dining rooms. Portions are tasty and plentiful – none more so than the trolley of tempting homemade desserts and rich cheese platter (where, of course, Roquefort stars).

Château de Creissels restaurant
GOURMET CUISINE **€€**
(☎05 65 60 16 59; mains €16-22, menus €23-53; ☺Tue-Sat & lunch Sun) The castle's restaurant offers classic French cuisine, where meat lovers will savour the *menu autour de l'agneau des Grands Causses* (€34) with its two main courses of tender local lamb and ewe's-milk cheese. Enjoy great views from the terrace.

Self-catering
There are markets each Wednesday and Friday morning in place Maréchal Foch, place Emma Calvé and the covered market at place des Halles. In July and August, an evening market spreads over place Mancharous.

🛍 Shopping

L'Atelier du Gantier (21 rue Droite) is a wonderful little shop that sells gloves and only gloves of the softest leather. Hit the right moment and you can see staff sewing away at a trio of vintage Singer machines.

Les Vitrines du Terroir (17 bd de l'Ayrolle) and **Le Buron** (18 rue Droite) are a pair of delightfully rich, pungent cheese and gourmet food shops.

ℹ Information

ABCD PC (cnr rue Droite & rue Solignac; per hr €3; ☺9.30am-12.30pm & 4.30-7.30pm Mon-Fri, 2.30-7.30pm Sat) Internet access.

Tourist office (☎05 65 60 02 42; www.ot-millau .fr; 1 place du Beffroi; ☺9.30am-12.30pm & 2-6.30pm, closed Sun Oct-Easter)

ℹ Getting There & Around

BICYCLE Cycles Arturi (☎05 65 60 28 23; 2 rue du Barry; ☺closed Sun Jul & Aug, Sun & Mon Sep-Jun) rents out city bikes for €9/12 per half-/full day and mountain bikes for €11/15.

BUS Millau's **bus station** (www.gareroutierede millau.com, in French) is beside the train station; its **information office** (☎05 65 59 89 33) is inside. There are two buses daily to Albi (€17.80, 2¼ hours), one continuing to Toulouse (€26.80, four hours) and at least six daily services to/from Montpellier (€18, 2¼ hours).

TRAIN Train or SNCF bus connections from Millau include Montpellier (€22.10, 1¾ hours, one daily) and Rodez (€11.80, 1½ hours, five daily).

Around Millau

ROQUEFORT

POP 700

In the heart of Parc Naturel Régional des Grands Causses and 25km southwest of Millau, the village of Roquefort turns ewe's milk into France's most famous blue cheese. Its steep streets lead to the cool natural caves, where seven producers ripen 21,000 tonnes of Roquefort cheese every year.

Four producers offer visits.

La Société (www.roquefort-societe.com), established in 1842, is the largest Roquefort producer, churning out 70% of the world's supply, over 30% of which is exported. One-hour guided tours (adult/child €3.50/ free; ☺9.30am-noon & 1.30-5pm) of the caves include a fairly feeble sound-and-light show and sampling of the three varieties the company makes.

FREE Le Papillon (www.roquefort-papillon. com; ☺9.30-noon & 1-5pm or 6.30pm) has tours of its equally pungent caves, lasting around 45 minutes and including a 15-minute film.

FREE Le Vieux Berger (www.le-vieux -berger.com, in French; ☺8.30am- noon & 1.30-6.30pm Mon-Fri) is the smallest of the major Roquefort producers, and the only place where you can watch staff at work. Its 18-minute promotional film is the most professional. Take the first turning right after the tourist office and follow av du Combalou for 0.5km.

FREE Gabriel Coulet (www.gabriel-coulet. fr; ☺9.30-11.50am & 1.30-4.50pm or 5.50pm) sales outlet is good for a more rapid appreciation of the Roquefort making process. You can descend into the vaulted, penicillin-streaked caves below the shop, wander at your own pace and take in the 10-minute film.

Parking in Roquefort is a nightmare. Leave your vehicle beside Roquefort's tourist office (☎05 65 58 56 00; www.roquefort.fr; ☺9am-5pm or 6pm Mon-Sat, to 7pm daily Jul & Aug), at the western entry to the village.

MICROPOLIS

Ever felt small? The mind-boggling high-tech experience of Micropolis (☎05 65 58 50 50; www.micropolis.biz; adult/child €11.20/7.60, audioguide €2; ☺10am-5pm, closed Mon Sep, closed Mon-Fri Oct & Mar, closed mid-Nov-Jan) happens in a building where 6m-high grass dwarfs the visitor. The swarms of facts about insect life, all compellingly present-ed, seem equally tall but all are true. There's a 20-minute 3D film and captions are in French and English. Allow a good two hours (don't bypass its quirky, imaginative Outdoor Trail), perhaps rounding off with a snack or local speciality at the bright, reasonably priced **restaurant**. 'La Cité des Insectes' (Insect City) is off the D911, 19km northwest of Millau.

PASTORALIA

Pastoralia (☎05 65 98 10 23; www.pastoralia. com, in French; adult/child €4.80/3.50, 2 adults & 2 children €15; ☺10am-noon & 2-6pm Easter-Oct), 3km west of St-Affrique, tells the story of the 800,000 ewes who graze the high plateaus, producing nearly 200 million litres of milk annually, over half of which is turned into Roquefort and other regional cheeses. There are interactive panels with English translation, a 10-minute film, and in summer children can feed the sheep.

ROUSSILLON

Roussillon, sometimes known as French Catalonia, sits on Spain's doorstep at the eastern end of the Pyrenees. It's the land of the Tramontane, a violent wind that howls down from the mountains, chilling to the bone in winter and in summer strong enough to overturn a caravan. Roussillon's only city is Perpignan, capital of the Pyrénées-Orientales *département*.

History

Roussillon's history was for a long time closely bound with events over the Pyrenees in present-day Spain. After flourishing for a time in its own right as the capital of the kingdom of Mallorca, it fell under Aragonese rule for much of the late Middle Ages. In 1640 the Catalans on both sides of the Pyrenees revolted against the rule of distant Madrid. Peace came in 1659 with the Treaty of the Pyrenees, defining the border between Spain and France once and for all and ceding Roussillon (until then the northern section of Catalonia) to the French, much to the indignation of the locals.

Long part of Catalonia (the name which nowadays officially designates only the semi-autonomous region over the border in northeast Spain), Roussillon retains many symbols of Catalan identity. The *sardane* folk dance is still performed, and the Cata-

THE KING OF CHEESES

The mouldy blue-green veins that run through Roquefort are, in fact, the spores of microscopic mushrooms, cultivated on leavened bread.

As the cheeses are ripened in natural caves, enlarged and gouged from the mountainside, draughts of air called *fleurines* flow through, encouraging the blue *Penicillium roqueforti* to eat its way through the white cheese curds.

Roquefort ranks as one of France's most noble cheeses. In 1407 Charles VI granted exclusive Roquefort cheesemaking rights to the villagers, while in the 17th century the Sovereign Court of the Parliament of Toulouse imposed severe penalties against fraudulent cheesemakers trading under the Roquefort name.

lan language, closely related to Provençal, is fairly widely spoken.

ℹ Getting Around

Abandon your car and jump aboard the **bus**. Year round, you can travel the length and breadth of Roussillon for no more than €1 per journey, thanks to the region's ecofriendly transport policy. Pick up a leaflet from any tourist office or phone 📞04 68 80 80 80 for route details and numbers.

Perpignan

POP 118,200

Back in the 13th and 14th centuries, Perpignan (Perpinyà in Catalan) was capital of the kingdom of Mallorca, a Mediterranean power that stretched northwards as far as Montpellier and included all the Balearic Islands. The town later became an important commercial centre and remains the third-largest Catalan city after Barcelona and Lleida (Lérida) in Spain.

Still as much Catalan as French, it's far from being a 'villainous ugly town' – the sour judgement of 18th-century traveller Henry Swinburne. Today's population is a mixed one. Iberian blood flows in the veins of the descendants of the thousands of refugees who fled over the mountains at the end of the Spanish Civil War. Many other families, Arab and displaced French

settlers alike, have their recent origins in north Africa.

At the foothills of the Pyrenees and with the Côte Vermeille to its southeast, Perpignan is a good base for day trips along the coast or to the mountains and Cathar castles of the interior. It's commendably well documented; outside every major historical building is a free-standing sign with information in French, Catalan and English.

◎ Sights

Le Castillet & Casa Païral FOLK MUSEUM
(place de Verdun; adult/child €4/free; ⊙9.30am-noon & 1.30-6pm Wed-Mon) Once a prison, the 14th-century red-brick town gate of Le Castillet is the only vestige of Vauban's fortified town walls. Inside, Casa Pairal, a folklore museum, houses bits and pieces of everything Catalan – from traditional bonnets and lace mantillas to an entire 17th-century kitchen.

Place de la Loge SQUARE
Place de la Loge has three fine stone structures. Fourteenth-century Le Loge de Mer, rebuilt during the Renaissance, was once Perpignan's stock exchange, then maritime tribunal. Between it and the Palais de la Députation, formerly seat of the local parliament, is the Hôtel de Ville with its typically Roussillon red-brick and pebble facade.

Palais des Rois de Majorque PALACE
(Palace of the Kings of Mallorca; entrance on rue des Archers; adult/child €4/free; ⊙10am-6pm) The Palais des Rois de Majorque sits on a small hill. Symbol of Perpignan's late-medieval splendour but now echoing and sparsely furnished, the palace was built in 1276 for the ruler of the newly founded kingdom. It was once surrounded by extensive fig and olive groves and a hunting reserve, both lost once Vauban's formidable citadel walls enclosed the palace. Pick up a guide sheet as you enter and climb the 70 steps of Tour de l'Hommage for a sweeping panorama of the Pyrenees and Mediterranean.

Cathédrale St-Jean CATHEDRAL
(place Gambetta; ⊙7.30am-6pm) Topped by a typically Provençal wrought-iron bell cage, Cathédrale St-Jean, begun in 1324 and not completed until 1509, has a flat facade of red brick and smooth, zigzagging river stones. The cavernous single nave is

marked by the fine carving and relative sobriety of its Catalan altarpiece. For centuries, Perpignan believers have venerated the engagingly naive statue of the Virgin and child in the chapel of Nostra Senyora dels Correchs in the north aisle.

⭐ Festivals & Events

As befits a town so close to the Spanish border, Perpignan is strong on fiestas.

Jeudis de Perpignan STREET FUN
The streets come alive with stalls, theatre and music of all genres. Thursday evenings, mid-July to mid-August.

Procession de la Sanch EASTER PROCESSION
Barefoot penitents wearing the *caperutxa* (traditional hooded robes) parade silently through the old city. Good Friday.

Fête de la Sant Joan RELIGIOUS FESTIVAL
A 'sacred' flame is brought down from Mont Canigou. Around 23 June.

Fête du Vin WINE FESTIVAL
To mark this wine festival, a barrel of the year's new production is ceremonially borne to Cathédrale St-Jean to be blessed. Third weekend in October.

Perpignan

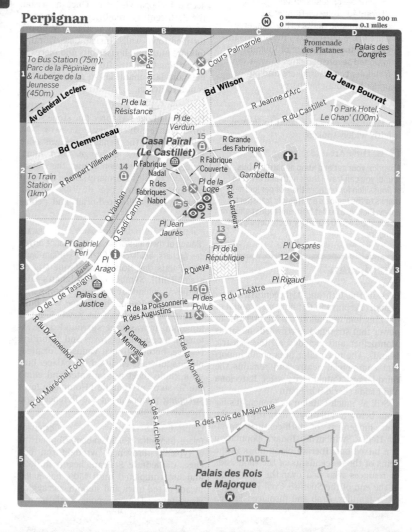

🛏 Sleeping

Hôtel de La Loge
HOTEL €

(📞04 68 34 41 02; www.hoteldelaloge.fr; 1 rue des Fabriques Nabot; s/d from €47/55; ❄🌐) Mireille and Hervé Barraud, who took over this increasingly threadbare hotel in 2010, have already stamped their personality on their new home, redecorating and refreshing while preserving the best of the attractive Catalan polished wood furniture. Of the more expensive rooms, 106 and 206 overlook place de la Loge.

Park Hotel
HOTEL €€

(📞04 68 35 14 14; www.parkhotel-fr.com; 18 bd Jean Bourrat; r from €80;❄@🌐) Each of this pleasant hotel's soundproofed rooms is individually and engagingly furnished and decorated. The *supérieure* rooms (from €100), with separate bathroom, shower cubicle and toilet, are a cut above the already attractive rest. The largest (numbers ending in 04 and 05) overlook the park. Reputed chef Alexandre Klimenko runs the hotel's Michelin one-star Le Chap' restaurant.

Hôtel New Christina
HOTEL €€

(📞04 68 35 12 21; www.hotel-newchristina.com, in French; 51 cours Lassus; r €93; ❄🌐🏊) Rooms are attractively decorated in blue and beige and bathrooms, all with bathtubs, are separate from toilets. Rooms at the front overlook a public park. The open-air pool, up on the roof, has central Perpignan's only jacuzzi.

Auberge de Jeunesse
YOUTH HOSTEL €

(📞04 68 34 63 32; perpignan@fuaj.org; allée Marc Pierre; incl breakfast €16.70; ⊙Mar–mid-Nov) Perpignan's HI-affiliated youth hostel, just north of Parc de la Pépinière, is a welcoming place with a kitchen for self-caterers.

Camping La Garrigole
CAMPGROUND €

(📞04 68 54 66 10; 2 rue Maurice Lévy; site & 2 persons €12; ⊙year-round) Take bus 2 and get off at the Garrigole stop to reach this small campsite, 1.5km west of the train station.

🍴 Eating

La Galinette
GOURMET CUISINE €€€

(📞04 68 35 00 90; 23 rue Jean Payra; mains €28-30, lunch menu €19; ⊙Tue-Sat) In an elegant setting, La Galinette offers refined cuisine, delicately confectioned desserts and an ample selection of regional wines. For a frisson of the unexpected, go for the *menu confiance* fish menu (€55) and let the chef select the best that the sea can offer that day.

La Passerelle
FISH €€

(📞04 68 51 30 65; 1 cours Palmarole; mains €19-28, lunch menu €22; ⊙Tue-Sat & dinner Mon) The attractive marine decor hints at the riches within the kitchen. La Passerelle is *the* restaurant in Perpignan for Mediterranean fish, guaranteed fresh and without a hint of freezer or fish farm.

Al Trés
MODERN MEDITERRANEAN €€

(📞04 68 34 88 39; 3 rue de la Poissonnerie; mains €19-25, lunch menu €14, menu €25; ⊙Tue-Sun) At this stylish place with its roughly plastered ox-blood-coloured walls and vast, carved wooden bar that could double up as an altar, you'll appreciate the freshness of the ingredients and innovative cuisine.

Laurens'O
MEDITERRANEAN FUSION €€

(📞04 68 34 66 66; 5 place des Poilus; mains €17-23, lunch menu €17; ⊙Tue-Sat) This cheerful

Perpignan

modern locale with its striped tablecloths and orange and black decor offers innovative Mediterranean cooking. Its distinctly Italian flavour is garnished with a creative French twist and a little Thai touch here and there.

Au Vrai Chic Parisien FRENCH €
(☑04 68 35 19 16; www.auvraichicparisien.com, in French; 14 rue Grande la Monnaie; dinner mains around €18, lunch menus €10-11.50; ☺lunch Mon-Fri, dinner Fri & Sat) No, not some snobby Parisian implant but a friendly, popular place in a popular quarter. Furniture is simple, rustic and brightly painted and walls are a clutter of posters, old menus, newspaper clippings and bric-a-brac. The midday choice is limited but tasty (try the piping-hot potato-based *tartiflette*). Weekend dinners offer Savoyard fondues and barbecued meats. And the toilets are particularly exciting (we leave you to discover why).

Les Antiquaires TRADITIONAL FRENCH €€
(☑04 68 34 06 58; place Desprès; mains €14-23, menus €24-43; ☺Tue-Sat & lunch Sun) The cuisine is as traditional, reliable and mature as both the clientele and the splendid line of vintage bottles displayed above the fireplace. Portions, such as the two huge dollops of chocolate mousse for dessert, are mightily generous.

Casa Sansa CATALAN €€
(☑04 68 34 21 84; entrances 2 rue Fabrique Nadal & rue Fabrique Couverte; mains €15-39, menus €14-32) Here's another highly popular spot – or rather two adjacent places. Choose the older, more southerly one, its walls scarcely visible beneath photos of the famous and less famous who have enjoyed its fine Catalan cuisine.

Le France MEDITERRANEAN €€
(☑04 68 51 61 71; place de la Loge; pizzas €10-15, mains €14-26; ☺noon-10pm) Le France manages to insert harmoniously the ultramodern – right down to the all-glass handbasins in the toilets – within the historical setting of what was once Perpignan's stock exchange. Mains are smallish but attractively presented and there's a good selection of tapas and pizzas.

Self-catering

There's a morning fresh fruit and vegetable market on place de la République daily except Monday. Saturday is organic day. See also Shopping.

Drinking

Républic Café CAFÉ
(2 place de la République) Down your first coffee of the day on the busy terrace of Républic Café and return later to sip an aperitif and linger in its Gaudí-inspired interior, all sinuous shapes and white ceramic fragments.

☆ Entertainment

The tourist office publishes *L'Agenda,* a comprehensive, free monthly guide to exhibitions and cultural events. *Catacult,* published monthly, and *Le Bizz,* out every two months, are what's-on tap-ins to the club scene and nightlife.

🛍 Shopping

Maison Sala GOURMET FOOD
(1 rue Paratilla; ☺Tue-Sat & Sun morning) Along short, scented rue Paratilla, known popularly to locals as rue des Épices (Spice St), shops sell dried fruits, herbs, jams, hams, cheeses and more. Most famous is Maison Sala, run by the same family for nearly a century.

Maison Quinta BRIC-A-BRAC
(3 rue Grande des Fabriques; ☺Tue-Sat) Take time to browse this Aladdin's cave of wares, tasteful, kitsch, utilitarian or unashamedly frivolous. They're piled high and higgledy-piggledy on three floors of this former noble mansion.

Espi CHOCOLATES, CAKES
(43bis quai Vauban) Gorge yourself on Espi's homemade chocolates, multicoloured macaroons and tempting ice creams. They'll even, given notice, knock you up a multi-storeyed birthday cake. It's also a pleasant **café** serving good coffee.

ℹ Information

Net & Games (45bis av Général Leclerc; per hr €3; ☺8am or 1pm-1am Mon-Sat, 1-8pm Sun) Internet access.

Tourist office (☑04 68 66 30 30; www.perpignantourisme.com; ☺9am-6pm or 7pm Mon-Sat, 10am-1pm or 4pm Sun) In the Palais des Congrès, off promenade des Platanes.

Tourist office annexe (Espace Palmarium, place Arago; ☺10am-6pm or 7pm; closed Sun)

ℹ Getting There & Away

AIR Perpignan's **airport** (☑04 68 52 60 70) is 5km northwest of the town centre. Perpignan has these flights to/from the UK:

Ryanair London (Stansted)

Flybe Southampton and Birmingham (summer only)

BMI Baby Manchester

BUS A bus ride anywhere within the Pyrénées-Orientales *département* cost only €1.

From the **bus station** (av Général Leclerc), **Courriers Catalans** (www.courrierscatalans.com, in French) buses run to the following destinations:

Côte Vermeille Nine daily to/from Collioure and Port-Vendres, six continuing to Banyuls (1¼ hours)

Têt Valley Nine daily to Prades (one hour), Villefranche-de-Conflent (1¼ hours) and Vernet-les-Bains (1½ hours)

Tech Valley Frequent service to Céret (50 minutes)

CAR Rental companies include **Avis** (☑airport 04 68 61 58 97) and **Budget** (☑airport 04 68 61 38 85).

TRAIN Trains cross the Pyrenees to Barcelona (€37 direct, three hours, twice daily; €18.50 changing at Cerbère/Portbou, 4½ hours, at least four daily). There are frequent services to Montpellier (€23.10, 1¾ hours) via Narbonne (€10.40, 45 minutes) and Béziers (€13.70, one hour). For Carcassonne (€18.30, 1½ hours), change in Narbonne. Up to nine TGVs daily run to Paris Gare de Lyon (€108.50, five hours).

Closer to home is Cerbère/Portbou on the Spanish border (€7.50, 40 minutes, around 15 daily) via Collioure (€5.20), Port-Vendres (€5.80) and Banyuls (€6.60).

❶ Getting Around

TO/FROM THE AIRPORT The **Navette Aéroport** bus runs from the train station via place de Catalogne and the bus station.

BICYCLE At **Vélostation** (☑04 68 35 45 82), on the 1st floor beneath street level of Parking Arago, hire a bike at the rock-bottom rate of €1.50/3 per half/full day.

BUS A ticket costs €1.10, a one-day pass is €4.10 and a 10-ticket *carnet* €7.80. **Le P'tit Bus** is a free hop-on, hop-off minibus that plies a circular route around the town centre.

TAXI **Accueil Perpignan Taxis** (☑04 68 35 15 15)

Around Perpignan

CÉRET
POP 7850

It's mainly the Musée d'Art Moderne (www.musee-ceret.com, in French; 8 bd Maréchal Joffre; adult/child €5.50/free; ⊙10am-6pm or 7pm, closed Tue Oct-Apr) that draws visitors

to Céret, settled snugly in the Pyrenean foothills just off the Tech Valley. Superbly endowed, the gallery's collection owes much to an earlier generation of visitors and residents, including Picasso, Braque, Chagall, Matisse, Miró and Dalí, all of whom donated their works (53 from Picasso alone).

Firmly Catalan and famous for its juicy cherries (the first pickings of the season are packed off to the French president), Céret is also a party town. First comes the Fête de la Cerise (Cherry Festival) in late May. Summer celebrations include La Féria, time of bullfights and general fun; Fête de la Sardane, celebrating the *sardane*, Catalan folk dance par excellence; and Les Méennes, primarily a festival of classical music.

TOP CHOICE Hôtel des Arcades (☑04 68 87 12 30; www.hotel-arcades-ceret.com; r €44-60;❋) is a friendly hotel overlooking place Picasso with its monumental plane trees and a sizeable hunk of the old town ramparts. Run with panache by a dynamic brother and sister duo, it's a gallery in its own right, where just about every square centimetre of wall space has a poster, photo or print.

Céret's tourist office (☑04 68 87 00 53; www.ot-ceret.fr, in French; 1 av Clemenceau; ⊙9am-noon & 2-6pm Mon-Fri, 9am-12.30pm Sat) is just around the corner from the gallery.

Hourly buses run to/from Perpignan (50 minutes). If you're driving, aim for the well-signed Musée d'Art Moderne car park.

TAUTAVEL
The Arago Cave, on the slopes above the village of Tautavel, 27km northwest of Perpignan along the D117, has yielded a human skull, estimated to be 450,000 years old, along with a host of other prehistoric finds. The Musée de Préhistoire (Prehistory Museum; www.tautavel.com, in French; av Jean Jaurès; adult/child incl audioguide €8/4; ⊙10am-12.30pm & 2-5pm or 6pm) has a full-size reproduction of the cave (in season, cameras show in real time archaeologists excavating the real cave), together with holograms, dioramas, TVs dispensing knowledge from every corner and lots of fossilised bones and stone tools. The ticket includes entry to a secondary exhibition, at Musée des Premiers Habitants d'Europe, a signed 300m away. Allow a good 1½ hours to take in both venues.

LANGUEDOC-ROUSSILLON AROUND PERPIGNAN

THE CATHARS

The term *le Pays Cathare* (Cathar Land) recalls the cruel Albigensian Crusade – the hounding and extermination of a religious sect called the Cathars.

The Cathars were the fundamentalists of their day: people of extreme beliefs, warily regarded by the mainstream yet convinced that they alone knew the one true way to salvation. Cathars (from the Greek word *katharos* meaning 'pure') believed that God's kingdom was locked in battle with Satan's evil world and that humans were base at heart. But, they reckoned, a pure life followed by several reincarnations could free the spirit. Reacting against worldly Rome and preaching in *langue d'oc*, the local tongue, the sect gained many followers. Their most extreme followers were the ascetic *parfaits* (perfects), who followed strict vegetarian diets and abstained from sex.

In 1208 Pope Innocent III preached a crusade against the Cathars. The Albigensian Crusade had a political as much as spiritual dimension, giving northern rulers the chance to expand their domains by ingesting Languedoc.

After long sieges, the major Cathar centres in Béziers, Carcassonne, Minerve and the dramatically sited fortresses of Montségur, Quéribus and Peyrepertuse were taken and hundreds of 'perfects' were burned as heretics. In Béziers as many as 20,000 faithful were slaughtered. Montségur witnessed another cruel massacre in 1244, when 200 Cathars, refusing to renounce their faith, were burned alive in a mass funerary pyre. In 1321 the burning of the last 'perfect', Guillaume Bélibaste, marked the end of Catharism in Languedoc.

CATHAR FORTRESSES

You can visit the four major Cathar fortresses in a day's drive from Perpignan or, with an earlier start, from Carcassonne.

When the Albigensian Crusade forced the Cathars into the mountains that once marked the frontier between France and Aragon, they sought refuge in these inaccessible strongholds that had long protected the border. Each clings to a clifftop, offers a dramatic wraparound panorama and requires a short, stiff climb from its car park. This is wild country, hot as hell in summer, so be sure to pack extra water.

Puilaurens (adult/child €3.50/1.50; ⊗10am-dusk Feb–mid-Nov) last saw action as a prison. Peyrepertuse (☑04 68 45 40 55; adult/child €5/3, audioguide €4; ⊗9am-8.30pm Jun-Aug, 10am-5pm or 7pm Sep-May) is the largest, with a drop of several hundred metres on all sides. Quéribus (☑04 68 45 03 69; adult/child €5/3, audioguide €2; ⊗9am-8pm Jul & Aug, 9.30am-7pm Apr-Jun & Sep, 10am-5pm or 6.30pm Oct-Mar) was the site of the Cathars' last stand in 1255, and Aguilar (☑04 68 45 51 00; adult/child €3.50/1.50; ⊗10am-7pm mid-Jun–Sep, 10.30am-5.30pm Apr–mid-Jun, 11am-5pm Oct–mid-Nov) is the smallest and sadly in need of care and attention.

For more on Catharism, call up www.payscathare.org. You might want to invest €3 in a *Passeport des Sites du Pays Ca-*thare, which gives reductions to 20 sites, major and minor.

Têt Valley

Fruit orchards carpet the lower reaches of the Têt Valley. Beyond the strategic fortress town of Villefranche-de-Conflent, the scenery becomes wilder, more open and undulating as the valley climbs towards Spanish Catalonia and Andorra.

PRADES
POP 6750

Prades is an attractive town with houses of river stone and brick, liberally adorned with pink marble from nearby quarries. At the heart of the Têt Valley and 44km from Perpignan, it's internationally famed for its annual classical music festival.

The bell tower of Église St-Pierre (⊗9am-noon & 2-6.30pm) is all that remains of the original Romanesque church, rebuilt in the 17th century. The wonderfully expressive, ill-lit 17th-century *Entombment of Christ* at its western end is by the Catalan sculptor Josep Sunyer, who also carved the exuberant main altarpiece, a *chef-d'œuvre* of Catalan baroque.

FREE Musée Pablo Casals (☑04 68 96 28 55; 33 rue de L'Hospice; ⊗10am-noon & 2-5pm Tue-Fri) commemorates the world-renowned Spanish cellist, who settled in Prades after fleeing Franco's Spain. **Festival Pablo Casals** (www.prades-festival-casals.com), held over two weeks in late July or early August, brings top-flight classical musicians to this small town.

Hiking & Walking Around Prades details 20 easy to moderate **walks** lasting from 1¼ to 3½ hours. *Six Grandes Randonnées en Conflent* (in French) describes six more challenging day walks, including the classic ascent of Mont Canigou (2784m), an emotive symbol for Catalans on both sides of the border. The tourist office sells both (€3 each).

Prades' **tourist office** (☑04 68 05 41 02; www.prades-tourisme.fr; 10 place de la République; ☺9am-noon & 2-6pm Mon-Sat, 10am-noon Sun) is on the main square.

Cycles Flament (8 rue Arago; ☺Tue-Sat), just off place de la République, rents bikes (per half-/full day €10/13).

There's a robust general **market** on place de la République every Tuesday and a **farmers market** each Saturday.

VILLEFRANCHE-DE-CONFLENT
POP 240

Villefranche, hemmed in by tall cliffs, sits at the strategic confluence of the valley of the Rivers Têt and Cady (hence the 'de Conflent' in its name). It's encircled by thick fortifications built in the 17th century to augment the original 11th-century defences, which have survived intact.

The fortress high above town, built by Vauban and strengthened under Napoléon III, is the heavily promoted **Château-Fort Liberia** (www.fort-liberia.com, in French; adult/

RIDING THE CANARY

Carrying nearly half a million passengers during the three peak months of high summer, **Le Train Jaune** (Yellow Train; 4 daily Jun-Sep, 2 daily Oct-May), nicknamed The Canary, runs from Villefranche-de-Conflent (427m) to Latour de Carol (1231m) through spectacular Pyrenean scenery. For the most spectacular stretch, jump aboard for **Mont Louis** (return adult/child €18.20/9.20) or **Font Romeu** (return adult/child €22.20/11.20). You can't make reservations, and it's wise to arrive a good hour before departure in high summer.

---

child €6/3.50; ☺10am-6pm), offering spectacular views.

Villefranche's **tourist information point** (☑04 68 96 22 96; www.villefranchedeconflent.fr, in French; 2 rue St-Jean; ☺10.30am-12.30pm & 2-6pm) abuts the entrance to the spectacular **ramparts** (adult/child €4/free; ☺10am-7pm or 8pm Jun-Sep, variable rest of year), beside the western Porte d'Espagne.

Leave your vehicle in one of the car parks outside each of the two main town gates.

VERNET-LES-BAINS
POP 1550

Busy in summer and a ghost town for the rest of the year, this charming little spa was much frequented by the British aristocracy in the late 19th century. Vernet has the status of *village arboretum* in recognition of more than 300 varieties of trees that flourish on its slopes, many brought in as seeds by overseas visitors (the tourist office carries pamphlets describing in French four 1km to 2km walks beneath their canopy).

Vernet is a great base for **mountain biking** and **hiking** – particularly for attacking **Mont Canigou** (2784m). The tourist office has a pamphlet in English detailing walking routes from the village. To bag the summit an easier way, bounce up in a 4WD (€25 per person return) with **Garage Villacèque** (☑04 68 05 51 14; rue du Conflent) or **Jeeps de Canigou** (☑04 68 05 99 89; 17 bd des Pyrénées) as far as Les Cortalets (2175m), from where the summit is a three-hour return hike.

Randonnées dans la Vallée de Cady et le Massif du Canigou (€6), in French and with detailed maps, describes a holiday's worth of less demanding treks. The free pamphlet *Espace VTT-FFC Le Canigou*, in French, describes 12 signed mountain-bike trails that snake out from the village.

The **tourist office** (☑04 68 05 55 35; www.ot-vernet-les-bains.fr; ☺9am-noon & 2-6pm Mon-Fri, also open Sat May-Sep) is on place de la République, the main square. Upstairs, there's a well-mounted free exhibition recounting Vernet's past.

Côte Vermeille

The Côte Vermeille (Vermilion Coast) runs south from Collioure to Cerbère on the Spanish border, where the Pyrenees foothills dip to the sea. Against a backdrop of vineyards and pinched between the Mediterranean and the mountains, it's riddled with small, rocky bays and little ports.

If you're driving from Perpignan, leave the N114 at exit 13 and follow the lovely coastal road all the way to Banyuls.

COLLIOURE
POP 3000

Collioure, where boats bob against a backdrop of houses washed in soft pastel colours, is the smallest and most picturesque of the Côte Vermeille resorts. Once Perpignan's port, it found fame in the early 20th century when it inspired the fauvist artists Henri Matisse and André Derain and later both Picasso and Braque.

In summer Collioure is almost overwhelmed by visitors, drawn by its artistic reputation (there are over 30 galleries and workshops), its wine and the chance to buy the famed Collioure anchovies at source.

Across the creek is the Château Royal (adult/child €4/2; ⊙10am-4.15pm or 5.15pm), which enjoyed its greatest splendour as the summer residence of the kings of Mallorca. Vauban added its towering defensive walls in the 17th century.

The medieval church tower of Notre Dame des Anges (⊙9am-noon & 2-6pm), at the northern end of the harbour, once doubled as a lighthouse. Inside is a superb altarpiece, crafted by the Catalan master Josep Sunyer.

Collioure's Musée d'Art Moderne (rte de Port-Vendres; adult/child €2/free; ⊙10am-noon & 2-6pm Jul & Aug, closed Tue Sep-Jun) has a good collection of 20th-century and contemporary canvases.

Just beside the museum's entrance gate, the Cellier des Dominicains (☑04 68 82 05 63; ⊙9am-noon & 2-6pm or 7pm Apr-Sep, closed Sun Oct-Mar) is the showcase for more than 150 local wine producers.

FREE Moulin de la Cortina (⊙10am-noon Wed & Sat Apr-Sep) is an easy 20-minute round-trip ascent through olive and almond groves. From the terrace of this restored 14th-century windmill there are sweeping views of the bay.

For a different but equally compelling lower-level perspective of Collioure and its castle, dine on the terrace of La Voile de Neptune (☑04 68 82 02 27; www.leneptune-collioure.com, in French; salads €11-13, mains €19-30; ⊙Apr-Oct), it's rigid sails poking across the bay, or sample the exquisite food of its Michelin-starred parent restaurant Neptune (menus €38-79, mains €19-30; closed Tue Apr-Sep, Tue & Wed rest of year), just above.

The tourist office (☑04 68 82 15 47; www.collioure.com; ⊙9am-8pm Mon-Sat, 10am-6pm Sun Jul & Aug, 9am-noon & 2-6pm or 7pm Mon-Sat Sep-Jun) is on place 18 Juin.

Between May and September, leave your car in Parking Cap Dourats, at the top of the hill that plunges down to the village, and take the shuttle bus that runs to the village every 10 minutes. Year-round, there's a large car park behind the castle.

PORT-VENDRES
POP 4500

Three kilometres south of Collioure, Port-Vendres, Roussillon's only natural harbour and deep-water port, has been exploited ever since Greek mariners roamed the rocky coastline. Until the independence of France's North African territories in the 1960s, it was an important port linking them with the mainland. It's still a significant cargo and fishing harbour with everything from small coastal chuggers to giant deep-sea vessels bristling with radar. There's also a large leisure marina.

The tourist office (☑04 68 82 07 54; www.port-vendres.com; 1 quai François Joly; ⊙9am-12.30pm & 2-5pm or 6pm Mon-Sat) is in the port's northwest corner.

PAULILLES

Part industrial relic, part nature walk, this 35-hectare coastal site is between Port-

THE HIGH ROAD

This 15km alternative drive between Port-Vendres and Banyuls is a wonderful way to escape the summer coastal crawl and get the wind whistling through your hair. On the D914 southeast of Port-Vendres, turn right at a sharp bend, just beyond the Cave Tambour wine producer's booth (don't call by; you'll need to keep your faculties sharp!). Signed Medaloc, and Circuit du Vignoble, the D86 winds inland, tight and single lane for most of its length. Views are breathtaking as, scarcely more than a track, it climbs above vineyards, almond and fig groves, through scrub and past bare schist outcrops.

Vendres and Banyuls. Remote, as befits a one-time dynamite factory, it was set up by the Swede Alfred Nobel, founder of the Nobel prize, and subsequently abandoned for over a quarter of a century. Haunting photos and text (in English too) inside the former director's house (admission free; ☺9am-1pm & 2-7pm, closed Tue Oct-Apr) tell of the hard lives and close community of workers, whose explosives helped to blast the Panama Canal, Trans-Siberian Railway and Mont Blanc Tunnel.

Banyuls, 7km south of Port-Vendres, is noted for its wines – particularly robust reds and dessert varieties.

Aquarium du Laboratoire Arago (☎04 68 88 73 39; adult/child €4.80/2.40; ☺9am-noon & 2-6.30pm, to 8.30pm summer) is at the promenade's southern limit. This aquarium, which displays local Mediterranean marine life (and a collection of more than 250 stuffed sea and mountain birds), is also the oceanographic research station of Paris' Université Pierre et Marie Curie.

More strenuously aquatic but well worth the effort is **snorkelling** for free around the *sentier soumarin*, a 500m **underwater trail**. Just off Plage de Peyrefite, midway between Banyuls and Cerbère and within a protected marine area, it has five underwater information points. You can hire fins and masks (€7; from noon to 5pm in July and August). If you have your own gear, you can swim the trail at any time during these two months.

FREE Cellier des Templiers (www.banyuls.com; rte du Mas Reig; ☺10am-7.30pm), 1.75km inland, gives you the chance to sample the robust red and rosé wines of Banyuls and Collioure. Tours are preceded by a 15-minute video (you'll probably loathe its posturing chef), subtitled in English, and followed by a tasting.

Banyuls' tourist office (☎04 68 88 31 58; www.banyuls-sur-mer.com, in French; av de la République; ☺9am-noon & 2-6pm or 7pm Mon-Sat) overlooks the pebbly beach.

Provence

Best Places to Eat

» Véranda (p811)

» L'Epuisette (p767)

» La Ferme Ste-Cécile (p814)

» L'Oustau de Baumanière (p795)

» La Bastide de Moustiers (p814)

Best Places to Stay

» Domaine des Andéols (p809)

» Le Mas Julien (p796)

» Hôtel La Mirande (p791)

» Le Mas de la Beaume (p808)

» L'Hôtel Particulier (p782)

Why Go?

Provence conjures images of lavender fields, blooming sunflowers, gorgeous stone villages, wonderful food and superb wine – most people's idea of a perfect holiday. It certainly delivers on all those fronts, but what many visitors don't expect is Provence's incredible diversity. The Vaucluse and Luberon regions epitomise the Provençal cliché. But, near the mouth of the Rhône, craggy limestone yields to salt marshes, where pink flamingos replace purple lavender. In the south, the light, which captivated Van Gogh and Cézanne, begins to change, a prelude to Camargue's bleached landscapes. Amid Haute-Provence's soaring peaks and raw wilderness, half-mile-high granite walls lord over a serpentine river at the Gorges du Verdon. The region's other surprises are its cities, like sultry Marseille, the 2013 European Capital of Culture.

One thing remains constant everywhere: the food – clean, bright flavours as simple as sweet tomatoes drizzled with olive oil and sprinkled with fleur de sel from the Camargue.

When to Go

Marseille

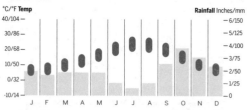

Easter Kick off the bullfighting season with Arles' Feria Pascale.

July and August Wade through blooming lavender, and see performing artists at Festival d'Avignon.

September and October Wait for cooling temperatures and the grape harvest to bike the back roads of the Luberon.

Embrace the Arts

Dull holiday snaps? Improve your photography skills with a tailor-made two-day course (from €250) at Les Ateliers de L'Image Photography Workshops (☑04 90 92 51 50; www.hotelphoto.com; 36 bd Victor Hugo, St-Rémy de Provence), in a design hotel.

Or try your hand at Jean-Claude Lorber's painting and drawing workshops at L'Atelier Doré (☑04 90 06 29 60; www.mas-des-amandiers.com, in French; 48 chemin des Puits Neufs, Cavaillon; 2hr session adult/child €21/17, 20hrs €195/140) in an 18th-century farmhouse.

Brush up on your French at Le Mas Perréal (☑04 90 75 46 31; www.masperreal.com; Lieu-dit la Fortune, St-Saturnin-lès-Apt), where Elisabeth, a long-time French teacher, offers lessons to guests (€30 per hour) at her gorgeous *chambre d'hôte* (B&B).

Top Cooking Courses

» Auberge La Fenière (p811) Cooking classes and lunch with Michelin-starred chef Reine Sammut (€145) or her staff (€75 to €95) include baking for children.

» La Chassagnette (p783) Pick your ingredients from the garden of Alain Ducasse–prodigy Armand Arnal, then work with him to prepare an unforgettable lunch (€90).

» Le Marmiton (p791) At Avignon's Hôtel la Mirande, create a fabulous lunch (€110) or dinner (€135) with the region's best chefs; or put the kids to work (€46).

» La Table de Pablo (p809) Join up-and-coming chef Thomas Gallardo on Saturday morning to learn the tricks of the trade (€70).

Bike Hire

Many companies deliver bikes to your door for free; book ahead if you want to pedal part of your journey. Check www.provence-a-velo.fr or town information sections in this chapter for more information.

Planning Ahead

If you're around for the region's biggest festivals, booking tickets and accommodation in advance is essential:

» Arles Feria Pascale (bull-fighting festival; p781)
» Festival d'Avignon (p791)
» Festival de Lacoste (p810)

Resources

» Farm visits (www.bien venue-a-la-ferme.com)
» La Route Napoléon (www.route-napoleon.com)
» Provence-Alpes-Côte d'Azur information, including eco-travel (www.decouverte-paca.fr)
» Current events (www.visitprovence.com)
» Vaucluse guide (www.provenceguide.com)
» Bus information (www.vaucluse.fr)

Provence Highlights

1 Soak up seething, heady **Marseille** (p756)

2 Trail **Van Gogh** (p780) around Arles, visiting spots where he painted some of his best-known canvases

3 Spot pink flamingos while riding white horses in the **Camargue** (p784)

4 Canoe, canyon, raft or float down the vertigo-inducing **Gorges du Verdon** (p814)

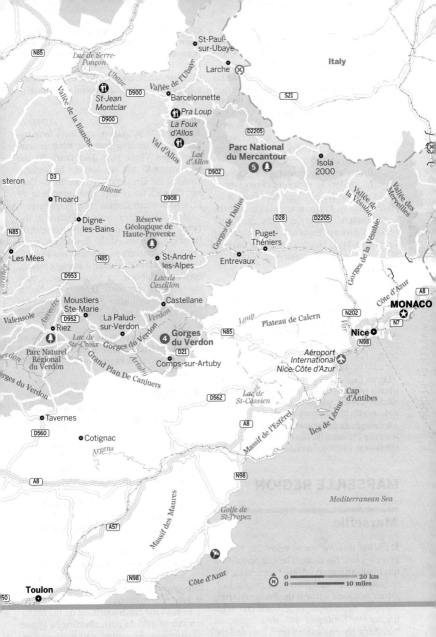

5 Take a walk on the wild side in the stunning, remote valleys of the **Parc National du Mercantour** (p815)

6 Watch an opera at Orange's exceptional **Roman theatre** (Théâtre Antique; p780) on a balmy summer night

7 Explore winding roads and stone villages like **Roussillon** (p809) amid Luberon's cherry orchards and sunflower fields

History

Settled over the centuries variously by the Ligurians, the Celts and the Greeks, the area between the Alps, the sea and the Rhône River flourished following Julius Caesar's conquest in the mid-1st century BC. The Romans called the area Provincia Romana, which evolved into the name Provence. After the collapse of the Roman Empire in the late 5th century, Provence was invaded several times, by the Visigoths, Burgundians and Ostrogoths.

During the 14th century the Catholic Church, under a series of French-born popes, moved its headquarters from feud-riven Rome to Avignon, thus beginning the most resplendent period in the city's (and region's) history. Provence became part of France in 1481, but Avignon and Carpentras remained under papal control until the Revolution.

ℹ Getting There & Away

The TGV (Train à Grande Vitesse, ie 'high-speed train') zips from Paris to Aix-en-Provence (three hours), Arles (four hours), Avignon (2¾ hours) and Marseille (three hours). On Saturdays in July and August, there's direct Eurostar service from London to Avignon (from €135 return, six hours; see p973 for more details on Eurostar Travel).

Lignes Express Régional (LER; www.info-ler. fr) runs regional buses. For buses to the Alps of Haute-Provence, see www.cg04.fr (in French), and navigate to 'transport'.

A smorgasbord of airlines serve Aéroport Marseille-Provence (p770). Ferries sail from Marseille to Sardinia, Tunisia and Corsica (p770).

MARSEILLE REGION

Marseille

POP 860,363

Marseille was for many years the butt of French jokes. No more. The *cité phocéenne* has made an unprecedented comeback, undergoing a vast makeover. The results look rather fabulous: witness the Panier quarter, the new République neighbourhood with its swanky boutiques and Haussmannian buildings, the city's shiny tram line, and the brand new docks and marina around the famous striped Cathédrale de la Major.

Marseillais will tell you that the city's rough-and-tumble edginess is part of its charm and that, for all its flaws, it is a very endearing place. They're right: Marseille

grows on you with its history, fusion of cultures, *souq*-like markets, millennia-old port and *corniches* (coastal roads) along rocky inlets and sun-baked beaches. Their ultimate vindication came with Marseille's selection as European Capital of Culture in 2013.

History

Around 600 BC, Greek mariners founded Massilia, a trading post, at what is now Marseille's Vieux Port (Old Port). In the 1st century BC the city lost out by backing Pompey the Great rather than Julius Caesar: Caesar's forces captured Massilia in 49 BC and directed Roman trade elsewhere.

Marseille became part of France in the 1480s, but retained its rebellious streak. Its citizens embraced the Revolution, sending 500 volunteers to defend Paris in 1792. Heading north, they sang a rousing march, ever after dubbed 'La Marseillaise' – now the national anthem. Trade with North Africa escalated after France occupied Algeria in 1830, and the Suez Canal opened in 1869.

After the World Wars, a steady flow of migration from North Africa began and with it the rapid expansion of Marseille's periphery.

◉ Sights

Vieux Port　　　HISTORIC NEIGHBOURHOOD
(Map p762) Ships have docked for more than 26 centuries at Marseille's colourful Vieux Port. Although the main commercial docks were transferred to the Joliette area on the coast north of here in the 1840s, it still overflows with fishing craft, yachts and local ferries.

FREE **Cross-Port Ferry** (⊗8am-12.30pm & 1-5pm) runs between the town hall (north side) and place aux Huiles (south side).

Guarding the harbour are Bas Fort St-Nicolas on the southern side and, across the water, Fort St-Jean, founded in the 13th century by the Knights Hospitaller of St John of Jerusalem.

In 1943 the neighbourhood on the northern side of quai du Port, abutting Le Panier quarter, was dynamited, and much of it rebuilt afterward.

Standing guard between the old and the 'new' port is the striking Byzantine-style Cathédrale de la Major. Its 'stripy' facade is made of local Cassis stone and green Florentine marble. Amazingly this unique monument stood for years in a wasteland, but now it's the center of the dynamic dockland redevelopment around La Joliette.

On the Vieux Port's southern side, late-night restaurants and cafés pack place Thiars and cours Honoré d'Estienne d'Orves pedestrian zone.

Northeast of La Canebière and cours Belsunce, the run-down Belsunce area is slowly being rehabilitated.

For chic, street-smart shopping, stroll west to the fashionable 6th arrondissement, especially pedestrianised rue St-Ferréol. The once-deserted, newly rehabilitated rue de la République resembles a Parisian boulevard, and is lined with major chains.

Heading west of the Vieux Port brings you to Abbaye St-Victor, birthplace of Christianity in Marseille, built on a 3rd-century BC necropolis. Perched at the peninsula's edge, the Jardin du Pharo is a perfect picnic spot and ideal for watching sunsets.

Le Panier   HISTORIC NEIGHBOURHOOD

(Map p762) North of the Vieux Port, Marseille's old city, Le Panier quarter (2e), translates to 'the basket', and was the site of the Greek *agora* (marketplace). Today its winding, narrow streets are a jumble of artisans shops and washing lines strung outside candy-coloured houses. Expect to get lost (even locals get turned around); that's part of the fun. On warm evenings, cafés at place de Lenche provide great people-watching.

Marseille architect and sculptor Pierre Puget (1620–94) was born in the house opposite 10 rue du Petit Puits, and designed the arcaded courtyard of the Centre de la Vieille Charité (Old Charity Cultural Centre; 2 rue de la Charité, 2e; M Joliette) Initially built as a charity shelter for the town's poor, the stunning arched pink-stone courtyard now houses Marseille's beautiful Musée d'Archéologie Méditerranéenne (Museum of Mediterranean Archeology) and Musée d'Arts Africains, Océaniens & Amérindiens (Museum of African, Oceanic & American Indian Art). The latter contains a striking collection of masks from the Americas, Africa and the Pacific.

Château d'If   ISLAND CHÂTEAU

(http://if.monuments-nationaux.fr/en/; adult/child €5/free; ⊙9.30am-6.30pm, closed Mon winter) Immortalised in Alexandre Dumas' classic 1840s novel Le Comte de Monte Cris-to (The Count of Monte Cristo), the 16th-century fortress-turned-prison Château d'If sits on a 3-hectare island 3.5km west of the Vieux Port. Political prisoners were incarcerated here, along with hundreds of Protestants (many of whom perished in the dungeons), the Revolutionary hero Mirabeau (who didn't fare so badly, once he'd seduced the cook) and the Communards of 1871.

Frioul If Express (Map p762; ☑04 91 46 54 65; www.frioul-if-express.com; 1 quai des Belges, 1er) boats leave for Château d'If from the Vieux Port at the corner of quai de la Fraternité and quai de Rive Neuve. There are over 15 daily departures in summer, fewer in winter (€10 return, 20 minutes).

Basilique Notre Dame de la Garde   CHURCH

(Map p758; montée de la Bonne Mère; ⊙basilica & crypt 7am-7pm, longer hrs in summer) The opulent, domed 19th-century Romano-Byzantine basilica occupies Marseille's highest point, lording it over the city skyline. Built from 1853 to 1864, it's ornamented with coloured marble, murals depicting the safe passage of sailing vessels and intricate gold-laid mosaics superbly restored in 2006. Crowning the bell tower, a 9.7m-tall gilded statue of the Virgin Mary stands atop a 12m-high pedestal. Bullet marks and shrapnel scars on the northern facade evidence the fierce fighting of Marseille's Battle of Liberation (15–25 August 1944).

Bus 60 links the Vieux Port with the basilica. Or, the 'little train' (p761) departs from the port and remains for 20 minutes before returning downhill. By foot, plan 30 minutes (expect steep hills) each way from the Vieux Port.

Îles du Frioul   HISTORIC ISLANDS

A few hundred metres west of the Château d'If are the Ratonneau and Pomègues. The tiny islands (each about 2.5km long) were linked by a dyke in the 1820s. From the 17th to 19th centuries they were used to quarantine those suspected of carrying plague or cholera: the city was ravaged by plague in 1720, when a merchant vessel carrying the disease broke quarantine to avoid losing its shipment. The resultant epidemics killed around 50,000 of the city's 90,000 inhabitants. The island of Ratonneau has ruins of the old yellow-fever quarantine hospital. Seabirds and rare plants thrive on the islands, which also have uncrowded beaches.

PROVENCE MARSEILLE

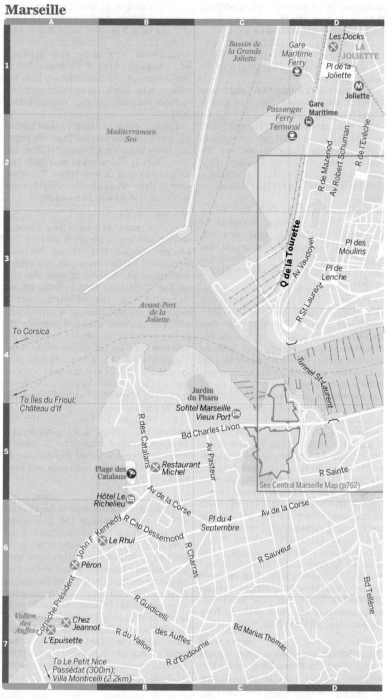

See Central Marseille Map (p762)

PROVENCE MARSEILLE REGION

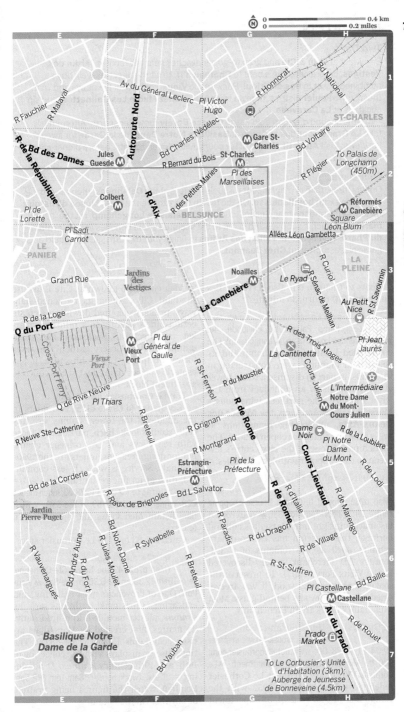

0.4 km
0.2 miles

N

E **F** **G** **H**

R Fauchier
R Malaval
Av du Général Leclerc
Pl Victor Hugo
R Honnorat
Bd National

R de la République
Bd des Dames

Autoroute Nord
Bd Charles Nédélec
R Bernard du Bois

Jules Guesde
St-Charles
Gare St-Charles
Bd Voltaire

To Palais de Longchamp (450m)

ST-CHARLES

R Flégier

Colbert
R d'Aix
R des Petites Maries
Pl des Marseillaises

BELSUNCE

Réformés Canebière
Square Léon Blum

Pl de Lorette

Pl Sadi Carnot

Allées Léon Gambetta

LE PANIER

Grand Rue

Jardins des Véstiges

Noailles
Le Ryad
R Curiol
P Sénac de Melhan

LA PLEINE

Au Petit Nice

R St-Savournin

R de la Loge

Q du Port

La Canebière

Vieux Port

Pl du Général de Gaulle

R des Trois Mages

La Cantinetta

Pl Jean Jaurès

Cross-Port ferry

Vieux Port

Q de Rive Neuve
Pl Thiars

R St-Ferréol
R du Moustier

Cours Julien

L'Intermédiaire
Notre Dame du Mont-Cours Julien

R Neuve Ste-Catherine

R Breteuil

R de Rome

R Grignan

R Montgrand

Dame Noir
R de la Loubière
Pl Notre Dame du Mont
R de Lodi

Estrangin-Préfecture
Pl de la Préfecture

Cours Lieutaud

R de Rome
R d'Italie
R de Marengo

Bd de la Corderie

R Roux de Brignoles
Bd L Salvator

Jardin Pierre Puget

R Vauvenargues
Bd André Aune
R du Fort
R Jules Moulet
Bd Notre Dame
R Sylvabelle
R Breteuil
R Paradis
R du Dragon
R de Village

R St-Suffren

Pl Castellane
Bd Baille
Castellane

Basilique Notre Dame de la Garde

Bd Vauban

Av du Prado

Prado Market
R de Rouet

To Le Corbusier's Unité d'Habitation (3km);
Auberge de Jeunesse de Bonneveine (4.5km)

1 **2** **3** **4** **5** **6** **7**

E **F** **G** **H**

MARSEILLE IN...

Two Days

Breakfast at **Pain & Cie** and grab to-go sandwiches near the ferry at **Jardin des Vestiges**, before catching a boat to **Château d'If**; to hit the beach as well, buy a combined ticket to **îles du Frioul**. Back on the **Vieux Port**, stroll the quays and visit the historic **Panier** district. Dine on fresh fish at **Chez Madie Les Galinettes**, and sip cocktails at **La Caravelle**.

On the second day, hop on bikes to **Espace Borély** for water sports. Alternatively, take **Le Grand Tour** bus and stop at **Basilique Notre Dame de la Garde** for sweeping views. Visit **Au Petit Nice** in artsy cours Julien for an aperitif, before dinner at **La Cantinetta**.

Four Days

On day three, take in magnificent turquoise waters at the **Calanques**, then reward your hiking with **bouillabaisse**. On the fourth day, explore the great **Musée d'Histoire de Marseille** and the magnificent fountains at **Palais de Longchamp**. Hit the **markets** for picnic supplies and climb to the sculpted stone benches at the **Jardin du Pharo**. Visit beautiful **Vallon des Auffes** to finish your trip with sautéed squid and garlic pizza, rooftop at **Chez Jeannot**.

Boats to Château d'If also serve the Îles du Frioul (€10 return, 35 minutes).

FREE **Palais de Longchamp**   PALACE, PARK
(Longchamp Palace; bd Philippon, 4e; MCinq Avenues Longchamp, Longchamp) The colonnaded Palais de Longchamp and its spectacular fountains were constructed in the 1860s, in part to disguise a water tower at the terminus of an aqueduct from the River Durance. The northern wing houses Marseille's oldest museum, the **Musée des Beaux-Arts**, undergoing renovations at press time and slated to reopen in 2012. The shaded park is one of the city centre's few green spaces, popular with local families.

Musée d'Histoire de Marseille

HISTORY MUSEUM
(Map p762; ground fl, Centre Bourse shopping centre, 1er; ◎noon-7pm Mon-Sat; MVieux Port) A fascinating insight into Marseille's cultural heritage, this museum has extraordinary exhibits, such as the remains of a 3rd-century AD merchant vessel, discovered in the Vieux Port in 1974. To preserve the soaked and decaying wood, it was freeze-dried where it now sits behind glass. Most explanatory notes are in French only.

Le Corbusier's Unité d'Habitation

MODERNIST ARCHITECTURE
(04 91 16 78 00; www.hotellecorbusier.com; 280 bd Michelet, 8e; ◎by appointment; MLe Corbusier) Visionary architect Le Corbusier redefined urban living in 1952 with the completion of this vertical, 337-apartment 'garden city', also known as Cité Radieuse (Radiant City). Along its darkened hallways, primary-coloured downlights create eerie tunnels leading to a minisupermarket, architectural bookshop and panoramic rooftop 'desert garden'. However forward-thinking the architecture, it has esoteric appeal: many just see a concrete apartment block.

For Le Courbusier lovers, stay at Hôtel Le Corbusier (d €95 to €125), two floors in the middle of the tower. 'Cabins' are tiny cells; studios look sharp, particularly those with sea views and Le Corbusier chairs, but for design reasons, toilets are the 1950s originals. Service is weak. If less committed, dine at its fine restaurant, Le Ventre de l'Architecte (04 91 16 78 00; lunch menus €28, dinner menus €59-69; ◎Tue-Sat), which has distant Med views and specialises in foie gras.

Catch bus 83 or 21 to Le Corbusier stop.

FREE **Musée du Santon**   DOLL MUSEUM
(Map p762; 49 rue Neuve Ste-Catherine, 7e; ◎10am-12.30pm & 2-6.30pm Tue-Sat; MVieux Port) One of Provence's most enduring, and endearing, Christmas traditions are its *santons,* plaster-moulded, kiln-fired nativity figures, first created by Marseillais artisan Jean-Louis Lagnel (1764–1822). The tiny museum displays a private collection of 18th- and 19th-century *santons.* At adjoining ateliers (workshops; ◎8am-1pm & 2-5pm Mon-Thu), watch the figures being crafted, or buy them at the boutique.

Activities

Cycling
BIKE RIDES

Hop on *le vélo* (p771) rental bikes and pedal towards the Pharo area, then south along the corniche to take in the seascape. Stop at cute little fishing port **Vallon des Auffes** before pressing on towards the beaches and leisure areas of **Espace Borély**, where cycle lanes start. The trip is about 6km. For the energetic, it's 10km round trip from Borély to the charming hamlet of **Les Goudes**, where it used to be all the rage to own a fishing cabin.

Beaches
BEACHES

On hot days, locals crowd easy-to-reach **Plage des Catalans** (Map p758; 3 rue des Catalans; ☺8.30am-6.30pm) and, further south, the **Prado Beaches** (end of av Prado). Or visit the peaceful, rocky shores of Îles du Frioul.

La Bastide des Bains
SPA

(Map p762; ☑04 91 33 39 13; www.bastide-des-bains.com, in French; 19 rue Sainte; entrance €30; ☺10am-8pm Mon-Sat, to 6pm Sun) A beautiful *hammam* with mixed and women-only opening hours. Treatments available.

Tours

Le Grand Tour
BUS TOUR

(Map p762; ☑04 91 91 05 82; www.marseillele grandtour.com; adult/child €18/8; ☺10am-7pm) Hop-on, hop-off, open-topped double-decker bus travels between the main sights, starting at Vieux Port, and including the Corniche and Basilique Notre Dame de la Garde. Buy tickets from the tourist office or on board.

Little Train
TRAIN TOUR

(Map p762; www.petit-train-marseille.com; adult/child €7/4; ☺10am-6pm) Tootles around Le Panier's hilly streets.

Guided Tour
WALKING TOUR

(per person €6.50; ☺tours 10am Sat Jul & Aug, 2pm every other Sat Sep-Jun) From the tourist office.

FREE Marseille Provence Greeters
WALKING TOUR

(www.marseilleprovencegreeters.com) Free walking tours by locals; advance website registration required.

Croisières Marseille Calanques
BOAT TOUR

(☑08 25 13 68 00; www.croisieres-marseille -calanques.com, in French; 74 quai du Port, 2e) Boat trips (in French) from the Vieux Port to Cassis (€25). Trips pass the Calanques.

Festivals & Events

Carnaval de Marseille
STREET CARNIVAL

Mad festival with decorated floats; March.

Beach Volleyball World Championships
SPORTS

Hosted by Plage du Prado; July.

Festival de Marseille
PERFORMING ARTS

(www.festivaldemarseille.com, in French) Three weeks of contemporary international dance, theatre, music and art; July.

Five Continents Jazz Festival
JAZZ

(www.festival-jazz-cinq-continents.com, in French) Acid jazz, funk and folk music fest; July.

Fiesta des Suds
WORLD MUSIC

(www.dock-des-suds.org) World music at Dock des Suds; October.

Foire aux Santonniers
CHRISTMAS FIGURINES

Since 1803 traditional *santon* makers have flocked to Marseille for this annual fair; December.

Sleeping

Marseille's hotels have been upgraded in preparation for 2013 festivities, with reliable midrange options and some top-end stand-outs. The hostel scene is underdeveloped.

TOP CHOICE Casa Honoré
BOUTIQUE B&B €€€

(Map p762; ☑04 96 11 01 62, 06 09 50 38 52; www.casahonore.com; 123 rue Sainte, 7e; d €150-200; ☀☎❄; MVieux Port) Los Angeles meets Marseille at this four-room *maison d'hôte*, built around a central courtyard with lap pool shaded by banana trees. The fashion-forward style reflects the owner's love for contemporary interior design (she has a shop down the block), using disparate elements like black wicker and the occasional cow skull, which come together in one sexy package. One complaint: bathrooms are partitioned by curtains, not doors.

Villa Monticelli
B&B €€

(☑04 91 22 15 20; www.villamonticelli.com; 96 rue du Commandant Rolland, 8e; d €90-110; ☀☎) Colette and Jean are passionate about their city and share their favourite addresses with guests. The five exquisite *chambre d'hôte* rooms in their stunning villa are worth the slightly outer-city location. Breakfast of homemade everything (jams, yoghurts, crêpes, etc) is served on the panoramic-view terrace. Best value for this class of accommodation.

Central Marseille

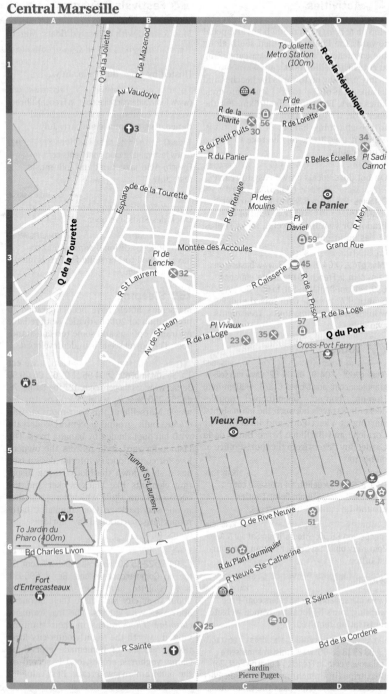

To Joliette
Metro Station
(100m)

R de la République

Q de la Joliette

R de Mazenod

Av. Vaudoyer

4

Pl de
Lorette 41

R de la
Charité 56

R de Lorette

30

34

R du Petit Puits

R du Panier

R Belles Écuelles

Pl Sadi
Carnot

3

Esplanade de la Tourette

R du Refuge

Pl des
Moulins

Le Panier

R Mery

Pl
Daviel

59

Q de la Tourette

Pl de
Lenche

Montée des Accoules

Grand Rue

R St Laurent

32

R Caisserie

45

R de la Prison

R de la Loge

Av de St-Jean

Pl Vivaux
R de la Loge

23 35

57

Q du Port

Cross-Port Ferry

5

Vieux Port

Tunnel St-Laurent

29

47 54

Q de Rive Neuve

51

2

To Jardin du
Pharo (400m)

Bd Charles Livon

50

R du Plan Fourmiguier

R Neuve Ste-Catherine

Fort
d'Entrecasteaux

6

R Sainte

R Sainte

25

10

Bd de la Corderie

R Sainte

1

Jardin
Pierre Puget

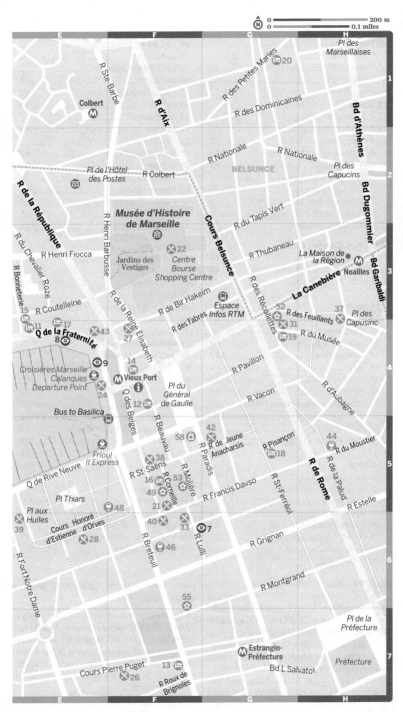

Central Marseille

Hôtel Résidence du Vieux Port

VIEW HOTEL €€€

(Map p762; ☑04 91 91 91 22; www.hotelmarseille.com; 18 quai du Port, 2e; d €180-200, apt €260; ❄@🛜🚇; MVieux Port) Marseille's top view hotel got a makeover in 2010 in vaguely Jetsons-meets-Mondrian style, with swoop-backed furniture and bold primary colours. Every room looks sharp, and has a balcony with knockout views of the old port and Notre Dame. Save €20 by booking a lower floor.

Le Petit Nice-Passédat

LUXURY INN €€€

(☑04 91 59 25 92; www.passedat.fr; Anse de Maldormé, 7e; d from €370; ❄@🛜🏊) Marseille's very best small luxury hotel is home to virtuositic Gerald Passédat (menus €85-250; ◔Tue-Sat), Marseille's only three-Michelin-star restaurant.

Sofitel Marseille Vieux Port

LUXURY HOTEL €€€

(Map p758; ☑04 91 15 59 55; www.sofitel-mar seille-vieuxport.com; 36 bd Charles Livon, 7e; d from €205; ✳@🅿🛜🏊) Marseille's top full-service hotel commands spectacular views of the sea and the old port. Rooms have all requisite bells and whistles, from iPod docks to feather beds; some have double-size soaking tubs. Great spa.

Hôtel Saint-Ferréol

SMALL HOTEL €€

(Map p762; ☑04 91 33 12 21; www.hotelsaint ferreol.com; 19 rue Pisançon, 1er; d €99-120; ✳@🛜; ⓂVieux Port) On the corner of the city's pretti-est pedestrianised street, this plush hotel has individually decorated rooms, many inspired by artists like Van Gogh and Cézanne, with thick carpeting and spotless bathrooms. Exceptional service.

Hôtel Belle-Vue

VIEW HOTEL €€

(Map p762; ☑04 96 17 05 40; 34 quai du Port, 2e; d €84-135; ✳@🛜; ⓂVieux Port) Rooms at this old-fashioned hotel are tastefully deco-rated with midbudget simplicity, but have million-dollar portside views. Bathrooms have occasional mildew spots, but nothing egregious. No lift and steep stairs, but La Caravelle, one of Marseille's coolest bars, is downstairs.

Hôtel Le Richelieu

SMALL HOTEL €€

(Map p758; ☑04 91 31 01 92; www.lerichelieu -marseille.com; 52 corniche Président John F Ken-nedy, 7e; d €53-88, tr €91-110; ✳@🛜) An eco-nomical seaside choice with odd-shaped rooms, but the owners keep them look-ing fresh. The best face the sea, lending a beach-house feel. There's an adjacent beach and shared water-view terrace, but no lift.

Hôtel Hermès

HOTEL €€

(Map p762; ☑04 96 11 63 63; www.hotelmar seille.com; 2 rue Bonneterie, 2e; s €50, d €70-90; ✳@🛜; ⓂVieux Port) Rooms are small and need new paint and wallpaper, but they're otherwise clean and well kept. A rooftop ter-race, for breakfast or evening drinks, adds value. The nuptial suite (€100), up a rooftop ladder, has knockout panoramic views.

Le Ryad

BOUTIQUE HOTEL €€

(Map p758; ☑04 91 47 74 54; www.leryad.fr; 16 rue Sénac de Meilhan, 1er; s €80-125, d €95-140; ⓂNoailles, 🚋Canebière Garibaldi) With arched alcoves, warm colours and minimalist de-cor, Le Ryad draws influence from Morocco. Despite the four-storey walk-up, it's worth booking the top-floor room (Mogador) for

ℹ️ MAX-OUT MARSEILLE

765

The **Marseille City Pass** (€22/29 for a 1-/2-day pass) gives you access to the city's museums, guided tours of the town and unlimited travel on all public transport (including the little train to Notre Dame). It also includes the boat trip and entrance to the Châ-teau d'If, and offers discounts, such as on Le Grand Tour tourist bus. It's not necessary for children under 12, as many attractions are greatly reduced or free. Buy it at the tourist office.

its tiny rooftop terrace. Great service makes up for the sometimes-sketchy neighbour-hood.

Hôtel Escale Oceania

HOTEL €€

(Map p762; ☑04 91 90 61 61; www.oceaniaho tels.com; 5 La Canebière, 1er; d €100-160; ✳🛜; ⓂVieux Port) Though rooms run small – you're buying the Vieux Port location – they're fresh and clean, following a 2009 renovation. Spotless bathrooms have big walk-in showers. Rooms on the Canebière side have wrought-iron port-view balconies.

🔺TOP CHOICE Hôtel Vertigo

HOSTEL, HOTEL €

(Map p762; ☑04 91 91 07 11; www.ho telvertigo.fr; 42 rue des Petites Maries, 1er; dm €25-27, d €60-70; @🛜; ⓂGare St-Charles SNCF) This snappy boutique hostel kisses goodbye to dodgy bunks and hospital-like decor. Here it's 'hello' to vintage posters, designer chrome kitchen, groovy communal spaces and polite multilingual staff. Double rooms are particularly good, some with private terrace. No curfew (or lift, alas). A second, all-dorm facility is closer to the Vieux Port.

Hôtel du Palais

SMALL HOTEL €€

(Map p758; ☑04 91 37 78 86; www.hotelmarseille. com; 26 rue Breteuil, 6e; d €98-130; ✳🛜; ⓂEs-trangin Préfecture) Ten of the 22 rooms at this small hotel have king-sized beds, a rarity in France. If you're a light sleeper, book a courtyard-facing room. Fourth-floor rooms have the most charm, with sloping, beamed ceilings.

Hôtel Carré du Vieux Port

HOTEL €€

(Map p762; ☑04 91 33 02 33; www.hvpm.fr; 6 rue Beauveau, 1er; s €86-92, d €92-98, tr €110; ✳@🛜; ⓂVieux Port) The look is generic – think stucco walls and low-pile carpeting – but the location is central, rooms fresh and

PROVENCE MARSEILLE

baths spotless. Double-pane windows block noise.

Hôtel Relax
SMALL HOTEL €

(Map p762; ☑04 91 33 15 87; http://relax hotel. free.fr, in French; 4 rue Corneille, 1er; d €60-70; ❄☎; MVieux Port) Overlooking Marseille's Opera House, this family-run 20-room hotel lacks good noise insulation and space, but given the location, cleanliness and extras like fridges and hairdryers, it's a bargain. No lift.

Hôtel St-Louis
BUDGET HOTEL €

(Map p762; ☑04 91 54 02 74; www.hotel-st -louis.com; 2 rue des Récollettes, 1er; d €67-72, tr €90; ❄@☎; MNoailles, ⬜Canebière Garib- aldi) Though we like the vintage-1800s facade, good mattresses, wooden furni- ture, central location and friendly service, some find rooms shabby and noisy (rooms 11 and 12 are loudest).

Auberge de Jeunesse de Bonneveine
HOSTEL €

(☑04 91 17 63 30; www.fuaj.org, in French; im- passe du Docteur Bonfils, 8e; dm €18.60, d incl sheets & breakfast €44; ⊙Feb-Dec; @) Rooms are spartan and it's far out of town, *but* is close to the beach, and organises activi- ties like kayaking and kitesurfing. Take bus 44 (stop Bonnefon).

✖ Eating

Marseille is known for bouillabaisse and *supions* (pan-sautéed squid with garlic, parsley and lemon).

The Vieux Port is packed with restau- rants, but choose carefully. The cours Ju- lien and surrounding streets have world cuisine. For pizza and couscous under €10, nose around near Marché des Capucins. In summer, find €2 fresh-squeezed juices at the seasonal stand near the little train, at Vieux Port. New eateries are popping up at Les Docks (Map p758; 10 place de la Joliette, 2e; MJoliette), in the developing Joliette neigh- bourhood.

Cafés crowd quai de Rive Neuve and cours Honoré d'Estienne d'Orves (1e), a large, long, open square two blocks south of the quay. Another cluster overlooks place de la Préfecture, at the southern end of rue St-Ferréol (1er).

Péron
CONTEMPORARY €€€

(Map p758; ☑04 91 52 15 22; www.restaurant -peron.com, in French; 56 corniche Président John F Kennedy, 7e; mains €35; ⊙lunch Tue-Sun, dinner Tue-Sat) Perched on the edge of the corniche, with magnificent views of the Château d'If, Péron is one of Marseille's top tables. The seafood-heavy menu (think marinated tuna, scallops with lemon po- lenta) is phenomenal; book before dark to watch the sunset.

La Cantinetta
ITALIAN €€

(Map p758; ☑04 91 48 10 48; 24 cours Julien; mains €9-19; ⊙Tue-Sat; MNotre Dame du Mont- Cours Julien) The top table at cours Julien serves perfectly al dente housemade pasta, paper-thin prosciutto, marinated vegeta- bles, *bresaola* (air-dried beef) and risotto. Tables in the convivial dining room are cheek by jowl; we prefer the sun-dappled, tiled-patio garden. Reservations essential.

Chez Madie Les Galinettes
PROVENÇAL €€

(Map p762; ☑04 91 90 40 87; 138 quai du Port, 2e; menus €25-35; ⊙lunch & dinner Mon-Sat, closed Sat lunch in summer; ♿MVieux Port) The port- side terrace is perfect on long summer eve- nings, but if weather isn't cooperating, the interior's modern art brings consolation. The Provençal-rooted menu features lots of fish and good bouillabaisse you'll need to order 48 hours ahead.

Jardin des Vestiges
ARMENIAN-MEDITERRANEAN €

(Map p762; 15 rue Reine Elizabeth, 1er; mains €7- 13; ⊙9am-6pm Mon-Sat; MVieux Port) Our fa- vourite budget choice draws on Armenian, Greek and Lebanese in dishes like kebabs, stuffed eggplant, moussaka and tabouleh. It's ideal for to-go sandwiches (€4 to €6) be- fore boarding ferries to the islands.

La Cantine
FRENCH-CORSICAN €€

(Map p762; ☑04 91 33 37 09; 27 cours Honoré d'Estienne d'Orves, 1er; mains 15-18; ⊙lunch Mon- Sat, dinner nightly; MVieux Port) Down-tempo beats, low lighting and wood-beamed ceil- ings set a sexy backdrop for Corsican spe- cialities, including *figatelli* (coarse-ground robustly seasoned sausage); and earthy French dishes like sautéed veal liver *en persillade* (parsley, garlic and herbs) and grilled fish. Reservations advised.

Pizzaria Chez Étienne
ITALIAN €€

(Map p762; 43 rue de Lorette, 2e; mains €12-15; ⊙Mon-Sat; MColbert) This classic family- style neighbourhood haunt serves the best wood-fired pizza in Marseille, succu- lent beef steak and scrumptious pan-fried squid. Pop in beforehand to reserve in per- son (there's no phone). Skip the nothing- special pastas. No credit cards.

BOUILLABAISSE

Originally cooked by fishermen from the scraps of their catch, bouillabaisse is Marseille's classic signature dish. True bouillabaisse includes at least four different kinds of fish, sometimes shellfish, which is why it's served to a minimum of two people. Don't trust tourist-trap restaurants that promise cheap bouillabaisse. The real McCoy costs about €55 per person and should be reserved 48 hours ahead, enough time to procure the correct ingredients. It's served in two parts: the broth (*soupe de poisson*), rich with tomato, saffron and fennel; and the cooked fish, deboned tableside and presented on a platter. On the side are croutons and *rouille* (a bread-thickened garlic-chilli pepper mayonnaise) and grated cheese, usually gruyère. Spread *rouille* on the crouton, top with cheese, and float it in the soup. Be prepared for a huge meal (over 200g of protein per person) and tons of garlic.

The most reliably consistent spots for real bouillabaisse include:

Le Rhul (Map p758; ☎04 91 52 01 77; www.lerhul.fr, in French; 269 corniche John F Kennedy; €50) This long-standing classic has atmosphere (however kitschy): a 1940s seaside hotel with Mediterranean views.

L'Epuisette (Map p758; ☎04 91 52 17 82; www.l-epuisette.com; Vallon des Auffes; €55; ⏱Tue-Sat) The swankest (by far) has a Michelin star and knockout water-level views from an elegantly austere dining room. First courses cost €34 to €45 and desserts €20, though you'll likely not have room.

Restaurant Michel (Map p758; Chez Michel; ☎04 91 52 30 63; http://restaurant-michel-13.fr, in French; 6 rue des Catalans; €60; ⏱dinner) Tops since 1946. Alas, the overly bright dining room lacks romance.

Chez Jeannot   MARSEILLAIS €€
(Map p758; ☎04 91 52 11 28; 129 rue du Vallon des Auffes; mains €12-25; ⏱Tue-Sat, lunch Sun) An institution among Marseillais, the jovial rooftop terrace overlooking the port of Vallon des Auffes books days ahead (but you can usually score an inside table). Stick to thin-crust pizzas and *supions,* called 'chippirons' on the menu; seafood and meats are overpriced.

Le Mas   CLASSIC FRENCH €€
(Map p762; ☎04 91 33 25 90; 4 rue Lulli; mains €18-26; ⏱noon-4pm & 8pm-6am Mon-Sat; MEstrangin Préfecture) Celebrities' photos line the walls at Marseille's only late-night restaurant, ideal when you've lingered too long over cocktails. Portions are hearty, flavours rich. Standouts include *steak au poivre* and spaghetti with clams, but you really can't go wrong.

Le Clan des Cigales   PROVENÇAL €
(Map p762; www.leclandescigales.com; 8 rue du Petit Puits, 2e; mains €9-11; ⏱9am-7pm Mon-Sat; MJoliette, ⬛Sadi-Carnot) On Fridays this little café serves classic homemade aïoli (a traditional Provençal garlic mayonnaise) with cod, winkles, poached vegetables and hard-boiled eggs. Savoury tarts are great when wandering the Panier.

Le Moment   CONTEMPORARY €€€
(Map p762; ☎04 91 52 47 49; www.lemoment-marseille.com; 5 place Sadi Carnot, 2e; lunch menus €19-25, dinner menus €46-64; ⏱Tue-Sat, Mon lunch; MColbert, ⬛Sadi-Carnot) Marseille's new gastronomic hotshot, Christian Ernst, also gives cooking classes (€59) at his sophisticated restaurant.

Une Table au Sud
    CONTEMPORARY MEDITERRANEAN €€€
(Map p762; ☎04 91 90 63 53; www.unetableausud.com; 2 quai du Port, 2e; lunch menus €33-47, dinner menus €68-125; ⏱Tue-Sat; MVieux Port) It was the *milkshake de bouilleabaisse* that clinched it for us; Vieux Port's top table has one Michelin star.

Le Femina   ALGERIAN €€
(Map p762; ☎04 91 54 03 56; 1 rue de Musée, 1er; menus €16; ⏱Tue-Sat; MNoailles, ⬛Canebière Garibaldi) Succulent couscous since 1921.

Le Souk   MOROCCAN €€
(Map p762; ☎04 91 91 29 29; 100 quai du Port, 2e; menus €20-30; ⏱Tue-Sat, lunch Sun; MVieux Port) Standout Moroccan, with great *tagines* (slow-cooked stews) and honey-nut pastries.

La Nautique   FRENCH €€
(Map p762; ☎04 91 33 01 78; opposite 20 quai de Rive Neuve, 7e; mains €13-18) Grilled fish

and steaks with a view; ideal on Sundays, when others close.

Simply Food
ORGANIC FOOD €

(Map p762; 16 rue du jeune Anacharsis, 1er; mains €4-6; ⏰9am-7pm Mon-Sat; Ⓜ Vieux Port) Organic salads, smoothies, wraps, sandwiches and soups.

Pain & Cie
CAFÉ €

(Map p762; place aux Huiles, 1er; brunch €21; ⏰Tue-Sat 8am-10.30pm, to 6pm Sun & Mon; Ⓜ Vieux Port) Trendy spot for weekend brunch, quick sandwiches, cake or coffee.

O'Stop
SNACK STAND €

(Map p762; 15 rue St-Saëns, 1er; menus€10; ⏰24hr; Ⓜ Vieux Port) Order the *boulettes de viandes* (meatball) sandwich with fries: deelish.

Café Debout
CAFÉ €

(Map p762; 46 rue Francis Davso, 1er; ⏰8.30am-7pm Mon-Sat; Ⓜ Vieux Port) Good for people-watching as you recharge on espresso, chocolates and cake.

Self-Catering

See p769 for more markets. Find supermarkets in the concrete Centre Bourse shopping centre (Map p762).

Marché des Capucins
MARKET €

(Map p762; place des Capucins, 1er; ⏰8am-7pm Mon-Sat; Ⓜ Noailles, 🚋 Canebière Garibaldi) One block south of La Canebière.

Fruit & Vegetable Market
MARKET €

(Map p762; cours Pierre Puget, 6e; ⏰8am-1pm Mon-Fri; Ⓜ Estrangin Préfecture)

Fish Market
FISH MARKET €

(Map p762; quai des Belges; ⏰8am-1pm; Ⓜ Vieux Port) Small but picturesque fixture at the Vieux Port.

Four des Navettes
BAKERY €

(Map p758; 136 rue Sainte, 7e) Marseille's iconic boat-shaped, orange-flower Navette biscuits.

Pain de l'Opéra
BAKERY €

(Map p762; 61 rue Francis Davso, 1er; Ⓜ Vieux Port) The best pastries near the Vieux Port; also has to-go savoury foods.

Le Glacier du Roi
ICE CREAMERY €

(Map p762; 4 place de Lenche, 2e) Fantastic homemade Italian ice cream.

Drinking

Cafés and bars surround the Vieux Port. Students and artists congregate near cours Julien and its surrounding streets. Sundays are dead.

TOP CHOICE La Caravelle
CAFÉ, BAR

(Map p762; 34 quai du Port, 2e; ⏰7am-2am; Ⓜ Vieux Port) Look up or miss this standout, upstairs hideaway, styled with rich wood and leather, zinc bar and yellowing vintage murals. If it's warm, snag a coveted spot on the portside terrace. On Friday, live jazz plays 9pm to midnight.

La Part des Anges
WINE BAR

(Map p762; 33 rue Sainte; mains €15; ⏰lunch Mon-Sat, dinner nightly) The wine list at this happening wine bar and restaurant is an oenologist's dream. Great cheese and charcuterie plates.

Dame Noir
BAR

(Map p758; 30 place Notre Dame de Mont, 6e; ⏰5pm-2am Tue-Sat; Ⓜ Notre Dame du Mont-Cours Julien) A crowd of hip cats spills onto the sidewalk from this neighbourhood bar. DJs spin Thursday to Saturday. No sign; look for the red lights by the door.

Au Petit Nice
CAFÉ, BAR

(Map p758; 28 place Jean Jaurès, 6e; ⏰10am-2am; Ⓜ Notre Dame du Mont-Cours Julien) Cheap and cheerful: €2 beers in a happening courtyard café with a youthful, diverse crowd. (NB: If you're taking a taxi, this is *not* the hotel of the same name.)

Le Bar de la Marine
BAR

(Map p762; 15 quai de Rive Neuve, 7e; ⏰7am-1am; Ⓜ Vieux Port) Marcel Pagnol filmed the card-party scenes in *Marius* at this Marseille institution, which draws folks from every walk of life.

Cup of Tea
TEA SALON €

(Map p762; 1 rue Caisserie, 2e; ⏰8.30am-7pm Mon-Sat; 🚋 Sadi-Carnot) Cute café with 55 tea varieties, and good Corsican beer.

☆ Entertainment

Cultural events are covered in *L'Hebdo* (in French; €1.20), available around town, or www.marseillebynight.com (in French).

Tickets for most events are sold at *billetteries* (ticket counters) including Fnac (Map p762; Centre Bourse shopping centre; Ⓜ Vieux Port) and the tourist office.

Olympique de Marseille
FOOTBALL

Marseille's cherished football team plays at Stade Vélodrome (3 bd Michelet, 8e; Ⓜ Rond Point du Prado). Buy tickets at OM's Boutique Officielle (Map p762; ☎04 91 33 20 01; 44 La Canebière, 1er; ⏰10am-7pm Mon-Sat; Ⓜ Noailles, 🚋 Canebière Garibaldi) for as little as €20.

Opéra Municipal de Marseille
OPERA

(Map p762; ☑04 91 55 11 10; http://opera.
mairie-marseille.fr; 2 rue Molière, 1er; Ⓜ Vieux
Port) Season runs September to June.

Live Music & Nightclubs

Pelle Mêle
JAZZ CLUB

(Map p762; 8 place aux Huiles, 1er; ⊘6pm-1am,
closed Sun Oct-Apr; Ⓜ Vieux Port) A thirty-
something crowd jives to good jazz at this
lively portside bistro.

L'Intermédiaire
DIVE CLUB

(Map p758; 63 place Jean Jaurès, 6e; ⊘7pm-2am;
Ⓜ Notre Dame du Mont-Cours Julien) Grungy
venue with graffitied walls is one of the
best for live bands or DJs (usually techno or
alternative).

La Noche
NIGHTCLUB

(Map p762; www.lanocheclub.com; 40 rue plan
Fourmiguier, 7e; ⊘Fri & Sat) Downstairs, bands
play; upstairs, DJs spin everything from
electro to salsa.

Le Trolleybus
DANCE CLUB

(Map p762; 24 quai de Rive Neuve, 7e; ⊘Wed-Sat;
Ⓜ Vieux Port) Shake it to techno, funk and
indie at this tunnel-like harbourside club.

Au Son des Guitars
NIGHTCLUB

(Map p762; 18 rue Corneille, 1er; ⊘Thu-Sun;
Ⓜ Vieux Port) Popular with Corsican locals,
this small club has limited dancing, lots
of drinking, and occasionally a Corsican
singer. Look sharp to get in.

Ma Demoiselle
NIGHTCLUB

(Map p762; 8 rue Corneille, 1er; Ⓜ Vieux Port) Visiting DJs sometimes play this tiny downstairs girly-girl club.

Gay & Lesbian Venues

The website www.gaymapmarseille.com
has general coverage of Marseille's and
Aix-en-Provence's gay life. Marseille's small
scene is a moving target, and only coalesces
weekends. Gay nights happen at various
bars, which are generally straight or mixed
other nights.

Caffè Noir (Map p762; 3 rue Moustier, 1er)
and Polikarpov (Map p762; 24 cours Honoré
d'Estienne d'Orves, 1er Ⓜ Vieux Port) are reliable addresses for a young, mixed, hard-
drinking crowd. Skip Cargo, Caffe' Noir's
adjoining sauna, whose steam room has
an exposed steam vent, on which a number
of people have reported burning their legs.
The better *hammam* is XY Le Club (Map
p762; www.xy-leclub.com; 66 rue Montgrand, 6e;
⊘1.30pm-midnight Mon, Tue, Thu, 1.30pm-2am

Wed, Fri-Sun; Ⓜ Estrangin-Préfecture), which
only gets busy Sunday afternoons; sometimes it throws mixed parties. Friendly
door staff are an excellent resource for
what's happening now. Catch-as-catch-can
bar Le Trash (www.trash-bar.com; 28 rue du
Berceau, 5e; ⊘Fri-Wed; Ⓜ Baille) is as its name
suggests.

🛍 Shopping

You'll find artisan specialities in streets
surrounding the Vieux Port, especially in
Le Panier.

La Maison du Pastis
DISTILLERY

(Map p762; ☑04 91 90 86 77; 108 quai du Port)
Sample over 90 varieties of the region's
speciality, pastis (an aniseed-flavoured
aperitif), or try absinthe.

Librairie de la Bourse
BOOKS

(Map p762; 8 rue Paradis, 1er; Ⓜ Vieux Port)
Range of maps and Lonely Planet guides.

Prado Market
MARKET

(Map p758; ⊘8am-1pm; Ⓜ Castellane or Périer)
This daily market stretches from the Castellane metro station along av du Prado
to the Périer metro station, with a staggering array of clothes, fruit and speciality items. Flower market Friday morning.

Markets
MARKETS

(Map p758; cours Julien; ⊘8am-7pm; Ⓜ Notre
Dame du Mont-Cours Julien) Wednesday-
morning organic fruit and vegetable
market and an Aladdin's cave bric-a-
brac market every second Sunday of the
month.

ℹ Information

Dangers & Annoyances

Marseille isn't a hotbed of violent crime, but
petty crimes and muggings are commonplace.
Play it cool. Don't get visibly drunk and stumble
home alone at 4am; you may as well wear a
target. The tourist office advice is to take taxis
at night.

If you're nervous, avoid the Belsunce area
(southwest of the train station, bounded by La
Canebière, cours Belsunce and rue d'Aix, rue
Bernard du Bois and bd d'Athènes). Walking the
Canebiére is annoying, but generally not danger-
ous; expect to encounter kids peddling hash.

Solo women travellers should be warned that
they will get catcalls from passing strangers.

Emergency

Préfecture de Police (☑04 91 39 80 00; place
de la Préfecture, 1er; ⊘24hr; Ⓜ Estrangin
Préfecture)

PROVENCE MARSEILLE

The Panier is home to many of the city's artisans and craftspeople, and by far the most fun for stocking up on gifts. Pick up the essential *savon de Marseille* (locally made olive-oil soap) at La Compagnie de Provence (1 rue Caisserie) or gorgeous AOC (Appellation d'Origine Contrôlée; a guarantee that products originate from a specific region) Provençal olive oils, and jars of tapenade and aïoli at Place aux Huiles (2 place Daviel). Brilliantly scented olive soaps, some with chocolate and tomato leaf, and lip-smacking preserves fill 72% Pétanque (10 rue du Petit Puits). Nearby a clutch of ceramic ateliers have shops attached; wander in and say bonjour.

Internet Access

Info Café (☑04 91 33 74 98; 1 quai de Rive Neuve, 1er; per hr €3; ☺9am-10pm Mon-Sat, 2.30-7.30pm Sun; Ⓜ Vieux Port) Also fax.

Medical Services

Hôpital de la Timone (☑04 91 38 60 00; 264 rue St-Pierre, 5e; Ⓜ La Timone) East of city centre.

Money

Canebière Change (39 La Canebière, 1er; ☺8am-6pm Mon-Fri, 8.30am-noon & 2-4.30pm Sat; Ⓜ Vieux Port)

Post

Main post office (1 place de l'Hôtel des Postes, 1er; Ⓜ Colbert) Currency exchange.

Tourist Information

Maison de la Région (61 La Canebière, 1er; 11am-6pm Mon-Sat; Ⓜ Vieux Port)

Tourist office (☑04 91 13 89 00; www.marseille-tourisme.com; 4 La Canebière, 1er; ☺9am-7pm Mon-Sat, 10am-5pm Sun; Ⓜ Vieux Port)

Websites

2013 European Capital of Culture (www.marseille-provence2013.fr)

🅘 Getting There & Away

Air

Aéroport Marseille-Provence (MRS; ☑04 42 14 14 14; www.marseille.aeroport.fr) Also called Aéroport Marseille-Marignane; 25km northwest of town in Marignane.

Boat

The **passenger-ferry terminal** (www.marseille-port.fr; Ⓜ Ⓕ Joliette) is 250m south of place de la Joliette (1er).

Algérie Ferries (☑04 91 90 89 28; 58 bd des Dames, 2e; ☺9am-noon & 1-5pm Mon-Fri; Ⓜ Colbert)

Société Nationale Maritime Corse-Méditerranée (www.sncm.fr; 61 bd des Dames, 2e; ☺8am-6pm Mon-Fri, 8.30am-noon & 2-5.30pm Sat; Ⓜ Ⓕ Joliette) Links Marseille with Corsica, Sardinia, Algeria and Tunisia.

Bus

The **bus station** (3 rue Honnorat, 3e; Ⓜ Gare St-Charles SNCF) is at the back of the train station. Purchase tickets from the information desk inside the train station or from the driver.

Aix-en-Provence €4.90, 35 to 60 minutes, every five to 10 minutes

Avignon €18.50, two hours, one daily

Cannes €25, two hours, up to three daily

Carpentras €14, two hours, three daily

Nice €27, three hours, up to three daily

Services to some destinations, including Cassis, use the stop on **place Castellane** (6e; Ⓜ Castellane), south of the centre. Drivers sell tickets.

Eurolines (www.eurolines.com; 3 allées Léon Gambetta; ☺9am-6pm Tue-Fri, 9am-noon & 2-6pm Mon & Sat) has international services (p971).

Car

At the train station:

Avis (☑08 20 61 16 36; www.avis.com)

Europcar (☑08 25 82 56 80; www.europcar.com)

Train

Gare St-Charles (Map p758; ☺information 9am-8pm Mon-Sat, tickets 5.15am-10pm) is served by both metro lines. The **left-luggage office** (from €3.50; ☺7.30am-10pm) is next to platform A.

In town, buy tickets at the SNCF Boutique inside the Centre Bourse shopping centre.

From Marseille trains, including TGVs, go all over France and Europe.

Avignon €23, 35 minutes, 27 daily

Lyon €47, 1¾ hours, 16 daily

Nice €30, 2½ hours, 21 daily

Paris Gare de Lyon €84, three hours, 21 daily

❶ Getting Around

For transport information in English: www.lepilote.com.

To/From the Airport

Navette (☑Marseille 04 91 50 59 34, airport 04 42 14 31 27; www.lepilote.com) shuttles link to Marseille's train station (€8.50, 25 minutes, every 20 minutes, 5am-11.30pm).

Bicycle

Pick up/drop off a bike from 100-plus bike stations across the city using le vélo (www.levelo-mpm.fr) system; it's free the first 30 minutes, costs €1 for the next 30, and then €1 per hour thereafter. You'll need a credit card to register; instructions are in French. Stations dot the corniche to Anse de la Pointe Rouge (8km south of the Vieux Port) and the centre. NB: for deposit, expect a hold on your credit/ATM account card.

Public Transport

Marseille has two metro lines (Métro 1 and Métro 2), two tram lines (yellow and green) and an extensive bus network, run by the Régie des Transports Marseillais (RTM).

Bus services stop around 9.30pm, when night buses take over until 12.30am. Most start in front of the **Espace Infos RTM** (6 rue des Fabres, 1er; ⊙8.30am-6pm Mon-Fri, 9am-12.30pm & 2-5.30pm Sat; Ⓜ Vieux Port), where you can obtain information and transport tickets.

The metro runs 5am to 10.30pm Monday to Thursday, until 12.30am Friday to Sunday; the tram runs between 5am and 1am daily.

Bus, metro or tram tickets (€1.50) can be used on all public transportation for one hour after they've been time-stamped. A pass for one/three days costs €5/10.50.

WORTH A TRIP

THE CALANQUES: FRANCE'S NEWEST NATIONAL PARK

Marseille abuts the wild and spectacular Calanques, a 20km stretch of high, rocky promontories, rising from brilliant-turquoise Mediterranean waters. The sheer cliffs are occasionally interrupted by small idyllic beaches, some impossible to reach without a kayak. The Marseillais cherish the Calanques, and come to soak up sun or take a long day's hike. The promontories have been protected since 1975, and should be a national park by the time you read this (www.gipcalanques.fr, in French).

The best way to see the Calanques, October to June, is to hike the many maquis-lined trails. During summer trails close because of fire danger: take a boat tour (p761), but be forewarned, they don't stop to let you swim; or try negotiating with a fisherman to take you from the Vieux Port. Otherwise, drive or take public transport.

Calanque de Sormiou is the largest rocky inlet. Two seasonal restaurants serve lunch with fabulous views, and require reservations. Le Château (☑04 91 25 08 69; mains €18-24; ⊙Apr–mid-Oct) has the best food and Le Lunch (☑04 91 25 05 39/37; http://wp.resto.fr/lelunch; mains €16-28; ⊙Apr–mid-Oct), the better view. By bus, take the 23 from the Rond Point du Prado metro stop to La Cayolle stop, from where it's a 3km walk. (NB: Diners with reservations are allowed to drive through; otherwise, the road is open to cars weekdays only, September to June.)

Nearer by, head east along Marseille's corniche (waterfront road) to its end, Callelongue, an idyllic fishing port where you can fuel up on crispy-crust pizzas or a proper fish lunch at Restaurant La Grotte (www.lagrotte-13.com; 1 Ave des Pébrons; menus €12-22) before hitting the trail. By bus: from Rond Point du Prado metro stop, take Bus 19 to the route's end, then transfer to Bus 20.

Marseille's tourist office leads guided walks (no kids under eight) of the Calanques, and has information about trail closures. Wear sturdy shoes. A coastal walk from Cassis to Morgiou, embracing the main six calanques (about 15km), takes 5½ to 6½ hours.

If you have a car, the nearby village of Cassis makes a postcard-perfect day trip. After a glorious morning driving above aquamarine coves, plan to lunch, with an obligatory bottle of crisp Cassis white, at one of the portside restaurants. Cassis' tourist office (www.ot-cassis.com; quai des Moulins; ⊙9am-12.30pm & 2-6pm Tue-Sat) supplies free maps of cellars open for tastings.

Taxi

Drivers don't speak much English, but they're supposed to learn by 2013: *bon courage* (good luck). There's a taxi stand at the train station.

Taxi Radio Marseille (☎04 91 02 20 20)

Aix-en-Provence

POP 146,700

Aix-en-Provence is to Provence what the Left Bank is to Paris: an enclave of bourgeois-bohemian chic. It's hard to believe Aix (pronounced 'ex') is just 25km from chaotic, exotic Marseille, and it's no surprise the two remain at odds. Some

30,000 students from the Université de Provence Aix-Marseille, many from overseas, set the mood on the street: bars, cafés and affordable restaurants. The city is rich in culture (two of Aix's most famous sons are Paul Cézanne and Émile Zola) and oh-so respectable, with plane-tree-shaded boulevards and fancy-pants boutiques. Were it not for all those kids, Aix would be stuffy.

◉ Sights & Activities

Vieil Aix   HISTORIC QUARTER
Art, culture and architecture abound in Aix and is a stroller's paradise, especially the mostly pedestrian old city, Vieil Aix.

Aix-en-Provence

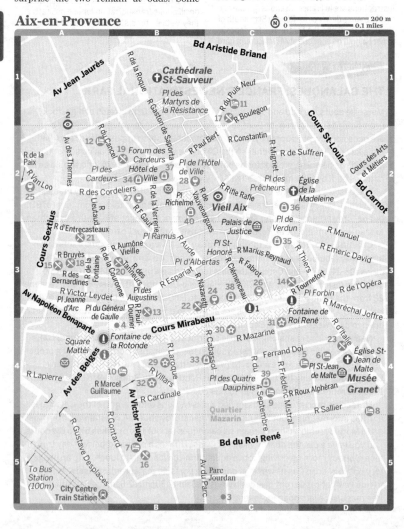

The graceful **cours Mirabeau** is the heart of Aix. Cafés spill onto the sidewalks on the sunny northern side. The southern side shelters a string of elegant Renaissance *hôtels particuliers* (private mansions). The mossy **fontaine d'Eau Thermale**, at the intersection of cours Mirabeau and rue du 4 Septembre, spouts 34°C water, a pleasant hint of what awaits at the **Thermes Sextius** (thermal spa; ☑04 42 23 81 82; www.thermes-sextius.com; 55 av des Thermes; day pass €40).

South of cours Mirabeau, **Quartier Mazarin** was laid out in the 17th century, and is home to some of Aix' finest buildings. Further south still is the peaceful **parc Jourdan**, dominated by Aix' largest fountain and home to the town's **Boulodrome Municipal**, where locals gather beneath plane trees to play *pétanque*.

For more greenery (dry maquis, actually), the nearby **Montagne Ste-Victoire** offers dozens of walking and cycling tracks. The tourist office sells the excellent *Montagne Ste-Victoire* map (€4.50), with 24 detailed itineraries.

Musée Granet ART MUSEUM
(www.museegranet-aixenprovence.fr, in French; place St-Jean de Malte; adult/child €4/free; ⊘11am-7pm Tue-Sun) Housed in a 17th-century Knights of Malta priory, the museum's pride and joy are its nine Cézanne paintings. The unique De Cézanne à Giacometti collection features works by Picasso, Léger, Matisse, Tal Coat and Giacometti, among others. There are also extensive 16th- to 20th-century Italian, Flemish and French collections and rotating exhibitions.

[TOP CHOICE] **Fondation Victor Vasarely**
CONTEMPORARY ART
(www.fondationvasarely.fr; 1 av Marcel Pagnol; adult/child €9/6; ⊘10am-1pm & 2-6pm Tue-Sun) This thrilling centre, 4km west of the city, was designed by the optical art innovator himself, in a series of repeating triangles and hexagons, right down to the honeycomb ceiling glass. Though in need of

Aix-en-Provence

AIX-CELLENT

Brilliant savings come in the form of the **Aix City Pass**, which costs €15, lasts five days and includes admission to Atelier Paul Cézanne, Bastide du Jas de Bouffan and Musée Granet, as well as a trip on the mini-tram and one of the tourist office's guided walks. Buy it at the tourist office or the two Cézanne sights.

repairs, the building is a masterpiece: 16 interconnecting six-walled galleries, purpose-built to display and reflect the patterning of the artist's acid-trip-ready, floor-to-ceiling geometric artworks. Take bus 4 or 6 to the Vasarely stop.

Cathédrale St-Sauveur   CATHEDRAL
(rue Laroque; ⊙8am-noon & 2-6pm) Built between 1285 and 1350 in a potpourri of styles, the cathedral includes a Romanesque 12th-century nave in its southern aisle; chapels from the 14th and 15th centuries; and a 5th-century sarcophagus in the apse. More recent additions include the 18th-century gilt baroque organ. The acoustics make Gregorian chants (4.30pm Sunday) unforgettable.

Cézanne Sights   ART APPRECIATION
His star may have reached its greatest heights after his death, but the life of local lad Paul Cézanne (1839–1906) is treasured in Aix. To see where he ate, drank, studied and painted, follow the Circuit de Cézanne (Cézanne Trail), marked by footpath-embedded bronze plaques inscribed with the letter C. An informative English-language guide to the plaques, *Cézanne's Footsteps,* is available free from the tourist office.

Though none of his works hang here, Cézanne's last studio, Atelier Paul Cézanne (www.atelier-cezanne.com; 9 av Paul Cézanne; adult/student €5.50/2; ⊙10am-noon & 2-6pm, closed Sun winter), 1.5km north of the tourist office on a hilltop, is a must for any Cézanne fan. It's painstakingly preserved as it was at the time of his death, strewn with his tools and still-life models; his admirers claim this is where Cézanne is most present. Take bus 1 or 20 to the Atelier Cézanne stop, or walk (20 minutes) from the centre.

The other two main Cézanne sights in Aix are the Bastide du Jas de Bouffan (on the western fringes of the city), the former family home where Cézanne started painting as a young man, and the Bibémus quarries, where he did most of his Montagne Ste-Victoire paintings. Head to the tourist office for bookings (required) and information.

Tours

Tourist Office   TOURS
The tourist office has DIY **walking itineraries** and runs a packed schedule of **guided walking** (€8) or **bus tours** (from €28) in English, like Retracing Cézanne's Steps. Bus tours include Luberon and Alpilles.

Mini-Tram   TRAM
(☎06 11 54 27 73; www.cpts.fr, in French; €6) Leaves from place du Général de Gaulle and winds its way through the Quartier Mazarin, along cours Mirabeau, and around Vieil Aix. Multilingual.

Festivals & Events

The tourist office has a list of Aix's seemingly continuous festivals.

Rencontres du 9ème Art   ANIMATION
(www.bd-aix.com, in French) Comic books, animation and cartoons; March.

Festival International d'Art Lyrique d'Aix-en-Provence   PERFORMING ARTS
(International Festival of Lyrical Art; www.festival-aix.com) The highlight of Aix's sumptuous cultural calendar. This month-long festival brings classical music, opera and buskers; July.

Festival de le Roque d'Anthéron
    PIANO MUSIC
(www.festival-piano.com) From Aix to the Luberon; mid-July to mid-August.

Sleeping

The tourist office lists *chambres d'hôte* and *gîtes ruraux* (self-contained holiday cottages). Bookings are coordinated through the Centrale de Réservation (☎04 42 16 11 84; www.aixenprovencetourism.com).

TOP CHOICE **Hôtel Cardinal**   SMALL HOTEL €
(☎04 42 38 32 30; www.hotel-cardinal -aix.com; 24 rue Cardinale; s/d/ste €60/70/110, self-catering ste €110) Beneath stratospheric ceilings, Hôtel Cardinal's 29 romantic rooms are beautifully furnished with antiques, tasselled curtains and newly tiled bathrooms. The choice picks are the six gigantic suites located in the annexe (about

100m further up the street), each with a kitchenette and dining room, ideal for longer stays.

Hôtel Cézanne
BOUTIQUE HOTEL €€€

(☎04 42 91 11 11; http://cezanne.hotelaix.com; 40 av Victor Hugo; d €179-249; ❀@☎) Aix's hippest hotel is a study in clean lines, with sharp-edged built-in desks and love seats that feel a touch Ikea. We actually prefer the less expensive 'luxe' rooms, which have the same top-end linens, but more charm, with Provençal-style painted furniture; alas, you'll sacrifice the deep soaking tub. Best is breakfast (€19), which includes smoked salmon and Champagne. Free parking.

Hôtel Saint-Christophe
FULL-SERVICE HOTEL €€

(☎04 42 26 01 24; www.hotel-saintchristophe. com; 2 av Victor Hugo; s €82-108, d €89-117, ste €128-152; ❀☎❀) The Saint-Christophe is a proper hotel, with a big lobby and helpful staff. Rooms nod to Art Deco in their styling, and have the standard midbudget amenities, including good bathrooms; some have terraces, some can sleep four. Parking (€12) by reservation. On-site Brasserie Léopold (mains €15-20) is a sure bet for *steak-frites*.

L'Épicerie
B&B €€

(☎06 08 85 38 68; www.unechambreenville.eu; 12 rue du Cancel; s €80-120, d €100-130; ☎❀) This intimate B&B is the fabulous creation of born-and-bred Aixois lad, Luc. His breakfast room re-creates a 1950s grocery store, and the flowery garden out back is perfect for evening dining (book ahead). Morning meals are veritable feasts. Two rooms accommodate families of four.

Hôtel les Quatre Dauphins
SMALL HOTEL €€

(☎04 42 38 16 39; www.lesquatredauphins.fr; 54 rue Roux Alphéran; s €55-60, d €70-85; ❀☎) Close to cours Mirabeau, this sweet 13-room hotel, a former private mansion, was redone in 2010 and looks fresh and clean, with new bathrooms and rainfall shower-heads. The tall terracotta-tiled staircase (no lift) leads to four attic rooms, with sloped beamed ceilings.

La Petite Maison de Carla
B&B €€

(☎04 42 21 20 73, 06 74 18 60 98; www.la-petite -maison-de-carla.com; 7 rue du Puits Neuf; s €60-75, d €75-90, ste €130-150; ☎) Better known as Chez Carla or Chez Maria (they're sisters), this five-room B&B occupies an 18th-century town house, painted in earthy colours, with flowers throughout. Each room

is different; best is the Manuela suite, with jacuzzi, open kitchen and roof terrace.

Auberge de Jeunesse du Jas de Bouffan
HOSTEL €

(☎04 42 20 15 99; www.auberge-jeunesse-aix. fr; 3 av Marcel Pagnol; dm incl breakfast & sheets €19-22; ⊘reception 7am-2.30pm & 4.30pm-midnight, closed mid-Dec–Jan; ☎) Shiny new with bar, tennis, secure bike shed and massive summer barbecues, this HI hostel is 2km west of the centre. Too bad the motorway is just below... Take Bus 4 from La Rotonde to the Vasarely stop.

Camping Arc-en-Ciel
CAMPGROUND €

(☎04 42 26 14 28; www.campingarcenciel.com; rte de Nice; site for 2 plus car €19; ⊘Apr-Sep; ☎❀) Tranquil wooded hills out back, but a busy motorway in front. It's 2km southeast of town, at Pont des Trois Sautets. Take Bus 3 to Les Trois Sautets stop.

Hôtel Concorde
MIDSIZE HOTEL €

(☎04 42 26 03 95; 68 bd du Roi René; d without bath €52, with bath €62-90; ❀☎) Ask for a room in the back ('sur jardin') to avoid being roared to sleep by incessant traffic. Rooms are functional and basic; 10 have small balconies, and higher-priced rooms come with air-con. Parking €8.

✖ Eating

Aix's culinary scene reflects the city itself: classic, not too risky. Restaurants on cours Mirabeau are overpriced.

Le Poivre d'Ane
CONTEMPORARY €€

(☎04 42 21 32 66; www.restaurantlepoivredane. com; 40 place des Cardeurs; menus €28-45; ⊘dinner Thu-Tue) Poivre d'Ane isn't afraid to break ranks with culinary norms: fancy a haddock milkshake, duck sushi, or thyme-and-cinnamon apple tart with Baileys whipped cream? The 10-table dining room's decor is austere, save for splashes of bold colour, reflecting the chef's playfulness. In summer outdoor tables are smack dab on one of Aix's loveliest pedestrian squares. Reservations essential.

Amphitryon
PROVENÇAL FRENCH €€

(☎04 42 26 54 10; www.restaurant-amphitryon. fr; 2-4 rue Paul Doumer; lunch menus €25, dinner menus €30-40; ⊘Tue-Sat) Run by fiery duo maître d' Patrice Lesné and chef Bruno Ungaro, Amphitryon enjoys a solid reputation among Aix's bourgeoisie, particularly in summer for its market-driven cooking and alfresco dining in the cloister-garden. The

CULINARY DETOUR: VENTABREN

A lesser-known hilltop village, Ventabren (population 5000), 16km west of Aix, provides the perfect lazy-day detour. Meander sun-dappled cobbled lanes; peep inside a 17th-century church; and take in panoramic views of Provence from the ruins of Château de la Reine Jeanne before a superb lunch or dinner at La Table de Ventabren (☎04 42 28 79 33; www.latabledeventabren.com; 1 rue Cézanne; menus €41-50; ☺lunch Wed-Sun, dinner Tue-Sun), reason enough to visit. The terrace looks out to distant mountains, magical on starry summer evenings. Chef Dan Bessoudo, who recently received a coveted Michelin star, creates inventive, wholly modern French dishes and knockout desserts. Get here before the prices double. Reservations essential.

attached **Comptoir de l'Amphi** (mains €12-17) is a less expensive alternative.

La Tomate Verte   CONTEMPORARY PROVENÇAL €€
(☎04 42 60 04 58; www.latomateverte.com; in French; 15 rue des Tanneurs; lunch/dinner menus €19/29; ☺Tue-Sat) The house speciality at this apple-green bistro is green-tomato tart, a tangy-delicious lead to the Provençal comfort food, simple as roast lamb with rosemary and garlic. Tile floors mean noise; if that matters, choose a table in the side dining room.

Le Petit Verdot   PROVINCIAL FRENCH €€
(☎04 42 27 30 12; www.lepetitverdot.fr; 7 rue Entrecasteaux; mains €15-25; ☺dinner Mon-Sat, lunch Sat) Wine is the primary focus at this earthy restaurant, where tabletops are made of cast-off wine crates. The meat-heavy menu is designed to marry with the wines, not the other way round. It's fun when you're feeling festive, but decibel levels are too high for a romantic night out.

Charlotte   NEIGHBOURHOOD BISTRO €€
(☎04 42 26 77 56; 32 rue des Bernardines; 2-/3-course menus €15/18; ☺Tue-Sat) Townspeople congregate like extended family at this bustling, cheek-by-jowl neighbourhood restaurant, which turns out simple home cooking, including terrines, homemade

soups, grilled meat and savoury tarts, from its open kitchen. In summer, feast in the garden.

La Chimère Café   SUPPER CLUB €€
(☎04 42 38 30 00; www.lachimerecafe.com; 15 rue Bruyes; menus €28-32) Aix's party crowd laps up the cabaret atmosphere of this former nightclub: starry-night vaulted ceiling in the underground room; grand chandeliers with crimson, velvety furnishings on the main floor. On the plate, the food is good, classic French. Come when you feel like donning heels and making a night of it.

Self-Catering

Aix is blessed with bountiful markets (p777).

La Boulangerie du Coin   BAKERY €
(4 rue Boulegon; ☺Tue-Sun) Bakes on Sunday.

Boulangerie   BAKERY €
(5 rue Tournefort; ☺24hr)

Monoprix   SUPERMARKET €
(24 cours Mirabeau; ☺8.30am-9pm Mon-Sat)

Petit Casino   SUPERMARKET €
(rue d'Italie; ☺9am-7pm Mon-Sat)

🍷 Drinking

The scene is fun, but fickle. The areas around rue de la Verrerie and place Richelme are prime for nightlife. Listings on the website www.marseillebynight.com (in French) also cover Aix. Open-air cafés crowd the city's squares, especially place des Cardeurs, place de Verdun and place de l'Hôtel de Ville.

La Belle Époque   BAR
(29 cours Mirabeau; ☺7am-2am) Swanky, purple and fluoro-lit, it's a favourite of happening DJs and students. It's 'appy 'our between 7pm and 9pm, with two-for-one drinks.

L'Unic   BAR, CAFÉ
(40 rue de Vauvenargues; ☺6am-2am) On one of the town's most charming squares, timeless and reliable, it serves anything from breakfast to aperitifs. Pensioners love it for the postmarket slot; students crowd it to kick-start their evening.

Le Med Boy   GAY BAR
(www.med-boy.com; 6 rue de la Paix; ☺9.30pm-2am) Aix's only gay bar packs in stand-and-drink twenty-somethings.

Les Deux Garçons   CAFÉ
(53 cours Mirabeau; ☺7am-2am) Cézanne and Zola once lingered in this classic

brasserie/café, but it rests on its laurels: best for a drink or small bite.

L'Orienthé LOUNGE
(5 rue de Félibre Gaut; ⊘1pm-1am) A *Thousand and One Nights* soft-lit den ideal for lounge music, *sheeshas* (water pipes) and teas.

☆ Entertainment

Le Mois à Aix (free from the tourist office) reports what's on.

Nightclubs

Le Mistral NIGHTCLUB
(3 rue Fréderic Mistral; ⊘midnight-6am Tue-Sat) If anyone's awake past midnight, chances are they'll wind up at this happening basement club, with three bars and a dance floor. DJs spin house, R&B, techno and rap. For a table, buy a bottle.

Cinemas

Aix's student population ensures great cinema, from Oscar contenders to cult flicks, often in English. Consult www.lescinema saixois.com (in French). Cinemas: Ciné Mazarin (6 rue Laroque), Cinéma Renoir (24 cours Mirabeau), Le Cézanne (1 rue Marcel Guillaume).

Theatre

Grand Théâtre de Provence THEATRE
(☑04 42 91 69 70; www.legrandtheatre.net; 380 Av Max Juvénal) State-of-the-art, 1380-seat theatre; presents musical performances and opera.

Le Ballet Preljocaj BALLET
(☑04 42 93 48 00; www.preljocaj.org; 530 Av Mozart) Performs at the 650-seat Pavillon Noir.

🔒 Shopping

Aix's most chic shops cluster along pedestrian rue Marius Reynaud and cours Mirabeau. The newly developed Allées de Provence (bordered by av Guisseppe Verdi, av Mozart and av Max Juvénal) has chain stores like Fnac, H&M and Sephora.

Cave du Félibrige WINE
(www.aix-en-provence.com/cave-felibrige; 18 rue des Cordeliers) Splendid array of wines, some *very* expensive.

Book in Bar ENGLISH BOOKS
(4 rue Cabassol) Best selection of English-language books; has a great café.

Librairie Goulard BOOKS
(37 cours Mirabeau) Best selection of Lonely Planet guides.

Paradox Librairie Internationale
BOOKS, GROCERY
(15 rue du 4 Septembre) English-language fiction and British grocery (Heinz tomato soup, Quavers and digestive biscuits, it's all here!).

Produce Market MARKET
(place Richelme) Each morning, tables display olives, lavender, honey, melons and other sun-kissed products.

Food Market FOOD MARKET
(place des Prêcheurs) Tuesday, Thursday and Saturday mornings.

Flower Market FLOWER MARKETS
Rainbows of flowers fill place des Prêcheurs on Sunday mornings and place de l'Hôtel de Ville on Tuesday, Thursday and Saturday mornings.

Flea Market FLEA MARKET
(place de Verdun; ⊘Tue, Thu & Sat mornings) Quirky vintage items.

ℹ Information

Centre Hospitalier du Pays d'Aix (☑04 42 33 50 00; www.ch-aix.fr, in French; av des Tamaris) Medical services.

Change Nazareth (7 rue Nazareth; ⊘9am-6.30pm Mon-Sat, open Sun Jun-Sep) Changes money. Inside a jewellery shop.

Netgames (52 rue Aumône Vieille; per hr €3; ⊘10am-midnight) Internet access.

Police station (☑04 42 93 97 00; 10 av de l'Europe)

Post office (place de l'Hôtel de Ville)

SOS Médecins (☑04 42 26 24 00) Medical advice.

SWEET TREAT

Aix's sweetest treat since King René's wedding banquet in 1473 is the marzipan-like local speciality, *calisson d'Aix*, a small, diamond-shaped, chewy delicacy made on a wafer base with ground almonds and fruit syrup, glazed with icing sugar. Traditional *calissonniers* still make them, including Confisserie Léonard Parli (☑04 42 26 05 71; www.leonard-parli.com; 35 av Victor Hugo), which also offers free guided tours at its onsite factory; call ahead for details.

Tourist office (www.aixenprovencetourism. com; 2 place du Général de Gaulle; ⏰8.30am-7pm Mon-Sat, 10am-1pm & 2-6pm Sun) Longer hours in summer; very proactive and helpful.

ℹ️ Getting There & Away

AIR Aéroport Marseille-Provence (www. marseille.aeroport.fr), aka Aéroport Marseille-Marignane, is 25km from Aix-en-Provence and is served by regular shuttle buses.

BUS Aix' **bus station** (av de l'Europe) is a 10-minute walk southwest from La Rotonde. Sunday service is limited. Services include Marseille (€4.90, 35 minutes via the autoroute or one hour via the D8), Arles (€9, 1½ hours), Avignon (€15, 1¼ hours) and Toulon (€10.50, one hour).

CAR & MOTORCYCLE Circumnavigating the one-way, three-lane orbital system circling the old town is a nightmare. Street parking spaces are like hen's teeth, but secure, pricier covered parking is plentiful.

TRAIN Aix' tiny **city centre train station** (⏰7am-7pm) is at the southern end of av Victor Hugo. It serves Marseille (€7, 50 minutes).

Aix' **TGV station**, 15km from the city centre and accessible by shuttle bus, has many more services. From there it's only 12 minutes to Marseille (€7), with about 20 services a day.

ℹ️ Getting Around

TO/FROM THE AIRPORT & TGV STATION Aix's bus station is linked to both the TGV station (15km outside town; €3.70) and the airport (€8) from 4.40am to 10.30pm, by half-hourly Navette shuttles.

BUS La Rotonde is the main bus hub. Most services run until 8pm. A single/10 tickets costs €1/7; a three-day pass €5.

Aix en Bus (www.aixenbus.com, in French) Information desk inside the tourist office.

Train station Minibus 2 serves La Rotonde and cours Mirabeau.

Vieil Aix Diabline electric shuttles cost €0.50.

TAXI Outside the bus station.
Taxi Mirabeau (☎04 42 21 61 61)
Taxi Radio Aixois (☎04 42 27 71 11)

ARLES & THE CAMARGUE

Arles

POP 52,400

Arles' poster boy is the celebrated impressionist painter Vincent van Gogh. If you're familiar with his work, you'll be familiar with Arles: the light, the colours, the landmarks, the atmosphere, all faithfully captured.

But long before Van Gogh captured this grand Rhône River locale on canvas, the Romans valued its worth. In 49 BC Arles' prosperity and political standing rose meteorically when it backed a winner in Julius Caesar (who would never meet defeat in his entire career). After Caesar plundered Marseille, which had supported his rival Pompey the Great, Arles eclipsed Marseille as the region's major port. Within a century and a half, it boasted a 12,000-seat theatre and a 20,000-seat amphitheatre to entertain its citizens with gruesome gladiatorial spectacles and chariot races.

Still impressively intact, the two structures now stage events including Arles' famous *ferias* (bull-running festivals), with their controversial lethal bullfights and three-day street parties.

◉ Sights & Activities

Unless otherwise noted, the last entry to sights is 30 minutes prior to closing. Winter hours are shorter than those listed below; places that close at 7pm in summer usually close at 5pm in winter. The Museon Arlaten is closed for renovations until 2013.

Roman Monuments

If you're keen to dig into Arles' Roman past, the 'Circuit Romain' combined ticket (€9/7 per adult/child) gives access to the four following sites. The Pass Monument (€13.50/12) accesses all Arles' museums and sites. Buy tickets at the tourist office or any of the sites.

Les Arènes   ROMAN AMPHITEATRE
(adult/student incl Théâtre Antique €6/4.50; ⏰9am-7pm) Arles' remarkable Roman amphitheatre, Les Arènes, was built around the late 1st or early 2nd century. It was the venue for chariot races, and gladiatorial displays where slaves and criminals met their demise before jubilant crowds.

During the Arab invasions of early medieval times, the amphitheatre became a fortress. When it was decided in the 1820s to finally return it to its original state, there were still 212 houses and two churches on the site. The amphitheatre is now undergoing restoration, but the polished finish of the renovated walls isn't popular with everyone. Debate is ongoing about what should be done to the metallic structure inside that seats 12,000 during Arles' bullfighting season.

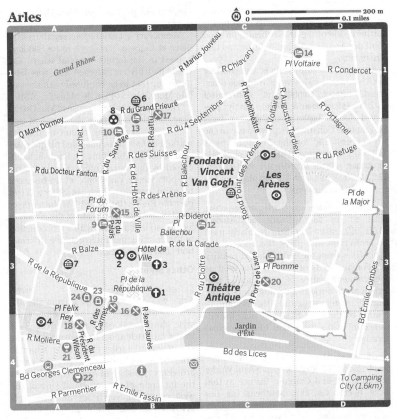

The Bureau de Location (ticket office; ☎08 91 70 03 70; www.arenes-arles.com), on the northern side of the amphitheatre on rond point des Arènes, sells bullfighting and theatre tickets.

Amphitheatre admission is also good for the Thermes de Constantin (rue du Grand Prieuré; without amphitheatre adult/student €3/2.20; ☉9am-noon & 2-7pm), partly preserved Roman baths near the river, built for Emperor Constantin's private use in the 4th century; and for the Cryptoporticus du Forum (entrance via Hôtel de Ville, place de la République; without amphitheatre adult/student €3.50/2.60; ☉9am-noon & 2-7pm May-Sep) 1st-century BC storerooms.

Théâtre Antique   ROMAN THEATRE
(enter on rue de la Calade; adult/student €3.50/2.60; ☉9am-7pm) Still regularly used for projections and plays, the Théâtre Antique dates from the end of the 1st century BC. For hundreds of years it was used as a convenient source of construction materials, with workers chipping away at the 102m-diameter structure (the remaining column on the right-hand side near the entrance indicates the height of the original arcade).

Les Alyscamps   NECROPOLIS
(adult/student €3.50/2.60; ☉9am-7pm) Works of Van Gogh and Gauguin feature in this large necropolis, 1km southeast of Les Arènes. Founded by the Romans and taken over by Christians in the 4th century, it became a coveted resting place because of the tombs of martyr St Genest and Arles' first bishops.

Van Gogh Sights

Although Van Gogh painted around 200 canvases in Arles, not a single one remains here today. There's a certain poetic justice, considering that following his altercation with housemate Paul Gauguin in place Victor Hugo (see boxed text, opposite), a petition was raised by fearful neighbours, and Van Gogh was committed for one month on the mayor's orders.

But Arles has admirably made up for it. Fitting tributes to Van Gogh's art include Fondation Vincent Van Gogh (24bis Rond Point des Arènes; adult/student €6/4; ☉10am-7pm), where important modern-day artists, including David Hockney, Francis Bacon and Fernando Botero, pay homage to the artist's distinctive style. The collection and its diversity show just how widely Van Gogh's influence has been felt in the artistic world.

Temporary art exhibitions regularly take place at Espace Van Gogh (place Félix Rey), housed in the former hospital where Van Gogh had his ear stitched and was later locked up (not to be confused with the asylum Monastère St-Paul de Mausole, p781).

The best way to get a sense of Van Gogh's time in Arles is to take the excellent Van Gogh Trail, a walking circuit of the city marked by footpath-embedded plaques. Accompanied by a brochure (in English) handed out by the tourist office, the trail takes in spots where Van Gogh set up his easel to paint canvases such as *Starry Night over the Rhône* (1888) and *The Amphitheatre* (1888). At each stop along the circuit, a lectern-style signboard with a reproduction of the painting has interpretative information (also in English).

Other Sights

Église St-Trophime   CHURCH
Arles was an archbishopric from the 4th century until 1790, and this Romanesque-style church was once a cathedral. Built in the late 11th and 12th centuries on the site of several earlier churches, it's named after St Trophime, a late-2nd- or early-3rd-century bishop of Arles. If you look on the far right of the left-hand side of the western portal, you'll see an intricately **sculpted façade** of biblical scenes (more spectacular than the interior), with St Trophime holding a spiral staff in his right hand. Inside the austere church, the most fascinating feature is the **treasury**, containing bone fragments of Arles' bishops who were later canonised. Many of the statues inside were decapitated during the French Revolution.

Across the courtyard, the 12th- and 14th-century Cloître St-Trophime (St-Trophime Cloister; adult/student €3.50/2.60; ☉9am-7pm) was built to accommodate the monks' daily lives. It comprises a reading room, dormitory and dining room.

Musée de l'Arles et de la Provence Antiques   MUSEUM
(av de la 1ère Division Française; adult/child €5.50/free; ☉9am-7pm Wed-Mon) This museum's striking, state-of-the-art cobalt-blue building perches on the edge of what used to be the Roman chariot racing track (circus), 1.5km southwest of the tourist office. The rich collection of pagan and Christian

It's easy to forget that Vincent van Gogh was only 37 when he died, as he appears much older in his self-portraits. Born in 1853, the Dutch painter arrived in Arles in 1888 after living in Paris with his younger brother Theo, an art dealer who financially supported Vincent from his own modest income. In Paris he had become acquainted with seminal artists Edgar Degas, Camille Pissarro, Henri de Toulouse-Lautrec and Paul Gauguin.

Revelling in Arles' intense light and bright colours, Van Gogh painted with a burning fervour, unfazed by howling mistrals. During a mistral he would kneel on his canvases and paint horizontally, or lash his easel to iron stakes driven deep into the ground. He sent paintings to Theo for him to try to sell, and dreamed of founding an artists' colony here, but only Gauguin followed up his invitation. Their differing artistic approaches (Gauguin believed in painting from imagination, Van Gogh painting what he saw) and their artistic temperaments came to a head with the argument in December 1888 that led to Van Gogh lopping off part of his own ear.

In May 1889 Van Gogh voluntarily entered an asylum, Monastère St-Paul de Mausole (☑04 90 92 77 00; www.cloitresaintpaul-valetudo.com, in French; adult/child €4/3; ☺9.30am-7pm Apr-Sep, 10.15am-5.15pm Oct-Mar) in St-Rémy de Provence, 25km northeast of Arles over the Alpilles. During his one year, one week, and one day's confinement he painted 150-odd canvases, including masterpieces like *Starry Night* (not to be confused with *Starry Night over the Rhône,* painted in Arles).

In February 1890 his 1888 Arles-painted work *The Red Vines* was bought by Anne Boch, sister of his friend Eugene Boch, for 400 francs (around €50 today) – the only painting he sold in his lifetime. It now hangs in the Pushkin State Museum of Fine Arts.

On 16 May 1890 Van Gogh moved to Auvers-sur-Oise, just outside Paris, to be closer to Theo. But on 27 July that year he shot himself, possibly to avoid further financial burden for his brother. He died two days later with Theo at his side. Theo subsequently had a breakdown, was committed and died, aged 33, just six months after Vincent. Less than a decade later, Van Gogh's talent started to achieve recognition, with major museums acquiring his work.

PROVENCE ARLES

art includes stunning mosaics. The museum is also a leading mosaic restoration centre; watch the work in progress.

Musée Réattu   MUSEUM, GALLERY
(10 rue du Grand Prieuré; adult/child €7/5; ☺10am-12.30pm & 2-6.30pm Tue-Sun) Housed in a former 15th-century priory, this splendid museum has two Picasso paintings, and 57 sketches from the early 1970s. It also contains works by 18th- and 19th-century Provençal artists, but it's best known for its cutting-edge photographic displays.

☞ Tours

In addition to the Van Gogh Trail, other self-guided walks with a brochure (Roman, medieval, Renaissance and classical) are marked along Arles' footpaths.

From July to September the tourist office runs guided tours (€6), with the Vieil Arles tour in English on Saturday at 5pm, and the Van Gogh tour on Tuesday at 5pm.

✸ Festivals & Events

Feria Pascale   BULLFIGHTING
Around Easter, Arles heralds the beginning of the bullfighting season.

Fête des Gardians   CAMARGUE CULTURE
May 1 brings the crowning of the Queen of Arles, Camargue cowboys parading through the streets, and Camargue games in the amphitheatre.

Fêtes d'Arles   PERFORMING ARTS
For two weeks starting around the end of June, enjoy dance, theatre, music and poetry.

Les Rencontres Internationales de la Photographie   PHOTOGRAPHY
(International Photography Festival; www.rencontres-arles.com) In early July, photographers from around the world display works until September.

⏹ Sleeping

Except during festivals, bullfights and July and August, Arles has plenty of reasonably priced accommodation. Most hotels shut during January, or the entire low season; check ahead. **Gîtes ruraux** (☎04 90 59 49 40) dot the surrounding countryside; ask the tourist office for a list.

TOP CHOICE L'Hôtel Particulier
BOUTIQUE HOTEL €€€

(☎04 90 52 51 40; www.hotel-particulier.com; 4 rue de la Monnaie; d €239-259; ❃@☞❋) A hidden spot, this exclusive boutique hotel with restaurant, spa and *hammam* oozes chic charm. From the big black door with heavy knocker to the crisp white linens and minimalist decor, everything about this 18th-century private mansion enchants. Find it two blocks west of Espace Van Gogh.

Hôtel de l'Amphithéâtre
HISTORIC HOTEL €€

(☎04 90 96 10 30; www.hotelamphitheatre.fr; 5-7 rue Diderot; d €55-95; ❃@☞) Crimson, chocolate, terracotta and other rich earthy colours dress the 17th-century stone bones of this stylish hotel, with narrow staircases, roaring fire and alfresco breakfasts in a courtyard. The romantic suite (€155), with dreamy lilac-walled terrace overlooks rooftops. Wheelchair access.

Hôtel Arlatan
HISTORIC HOTEL €€

(☎04 90 93 56 66; www.hotel-arlatan.fr; 26 rue du Sauvage; d €85-155; ❃@☞❋) The heated swimming pool, pretty garden and plush rooms decorated with antique furniture are just some of the things going for this hotel. Add to that a setting steeped in history, with Roman foundations visible through a glass floor in the lobby and 15th-century paintings on one of the lounges' ceilings. Wheelchair access.

Grand Hôtel Nord Pinus
LUXURY HOTEL €€€

(☎04 90 93 44 44; www.nord-pinus.com; place du Forum; d €170-310; ❋) Drawing on the town's Roma and Spanish heritage, this intimate hotel is lined with vintage *feria* posters and antiques. Stunning room 10 is a favourite for many famous matadors. Amazing B&W Peter Beard photographs adorn the downstairs.

Hôtel du Musée
BOUTIQUE HOTEL €

(☎04 90 93 88 88; www.hoteldumusee.com; 11 rue du Grand Prieuré; d €60-70, tr/q €80/95; ❃☞❋) In a fine 17th- to 18th-century building, this impeccable hotel has 28 comfortable rooms, a checkerboard-tiled breakfast room and a sugar-sweet patio garden brimming with pretty blossoms.

Le Bélvédère Hôtel
BOUTIQUE HOTEL €€

(☎04 90 91 45 94; www.hotellebelvedere-arles.fr; 5 place Voltaire; d €70-90; ❃☞) This sleek 17-room hotel is one of the best Arlésian pads. A red-glass chandelier adorns the lobby-lounge and the rooms are fitted out in stylish red, chocolate brown, grey and beige colour schemes.

Hôtel Calendal
HOTEL €€

(☎04 90 96 11 89; www.lecalendal.com; 5 rue Porte de Laure; d €109-159; ❃@☞) Next to the amphitheatre and overlooking the Théâtre Antique, rooms have beamed ceilings and bright Provençal fabrics. There's a peaceful garden terrace with a giant chessboard, and a spa. Wheelchair access.

Auberge de Jeunesse
HOSTEL €

(☎04 90 96 18 25; www.fuaj.org, in French; 20 av Maréchal Foch; dm incl breakfast & sheets €17; ⏱reception closed 10am-5pm; ☞) This

---

A BULLISH AFFAIR

Animal lovers fear not: not all types of bullfights end with blood. The local Camargue variation, the *course Camarguaise*, sees amateur *razeteurs* (from the word 'shave'), wearing skin-tight white shirts and trousers, get as close as they dare to the *taureau* (bull) to try to snatch rosettes and ribbons tied to the bull's horns, using a *crochet* (a razor-sharp comb) held between their fingers – leaping over the arena's barrier as the bull charges, making spectators' hearts lurch.

Bulls are bred on a *manade* (bull farm) by *manadiers*, who are helped in their daily chores by *gardians* (Camargue cattle-herding cowboys). These mounted herdsmen parade through town during the Fête des Gardians in Arles in May.

Many *manades* also breed the creamy white *cheval de Camargue* (Camargue horse) and some welcome visitors; ask at tourist offices in Arles and Stes-Maries de la Mer.

A calendar of *courses Camarguaises* is online at the Fédération Française de la Course Camarguaise (French Federation of Camargue Bullfights; ☎04 66 26 05 35; www.ffcc.info, in French). *Recortadores* (a type of bull-baiting with lots of bull-jumping) also happens during the bullfighting season (Easter to September).

sunlit place, made up of eight-bed dorms, is just 10 minutes' walk from the centre. Its bar closes at 11pm, just like its gates (except during *ferias*).

Camping City CAMPGROUND €
(☑04 90 93 08 86; www.camping-city.com; 67 rte de Crau; sites €18; ☺Apr-Sep; ☒) This campground is the closest to town, 1.5km southeast on the road to Marseille, and has bike hire and laundry. Supermarkets nearby. Take Bus 2 to the Hermite stop.

✖ Eating

The Roman place du Forum, shaded by outstretched plane trees, turns into a giant dining table during summer and it's home to **Café la Nuit**, thought to be captured by Van Gogh in his *Café Terrace at Night* (1888); now mostly a tourist trap.

L'Atelier GASTRONOMIC €€€
(☑04 90 91 07 69; www.rabanel.com; 7 rue des Carmes; lunch/dinner menus from €45/85; ☺lunch & dinner Wed-Sun) A beautiful and modern gastronomic experience. Opt for a series of seven or 13 edible works of art, then sit back and revel in Jean-Luc Rabanel's superbly crafted symphony of fresh organic tastes. No wonder this green-fingered urban chef with his own veggie patch has two Michelin stars.

Le Cilantro PROVENÇAL €€
(☑04 90 18 25 05; www.restaurantcilantro.com, in French; 31 rue Porte de Laure; mains €35; ☺lunch Tue-Fri, dinner Tue-Sat) Chef Jêrome Laurant, a born-and-bred local lad, runs this hot spot and combines local ingredients with world spices to create accomplished dishes like lamb in almond oil.

La Mule Blanche BISTRO €€
(☑04 90 93 98 54; www.restaurant-mule-blanche.com, in French; 8 rue du Président Wilson; mains €12-20; ☺lunch Tue-Sun, dinner Wed-Sun, closed Sun winter) Jazz piano tinkles in the White Mule's domed interior, but the hottest tables at this soulful bistro are aboard the pavement terrace, easily the town's prettiest with its violet awning, Saturday-morning market view and lazy mood.

Comptoir du Sud CAFÉ €
(☑04 90 96 22 17; 2 rue Jean Jaurès) Wonderful gourmet sandwiches (tasty chutneys, succulent meat, foie gras) and divine little salads, all at rock-bottom prices, served at a counter.

La Chassagnette GASTRONOMIC €€€
(☑04 90 97 26 96; http://lachassagnette-uk.blogspirit.com; rte du Sambuc, Le Sambuc; lunch/dinner menus €34/54; ☺lunch & dinner Thu-Mon) Ultimate Camargue dine: Alain Ducasse prodigy Armand Arnal cooks up 100% organics 12km southeast of Arles on the D36.

Corazón ECLECTIC EUROPEAN €€
(☑04 90 96 32 53; 1bis rue Réattu; mains €18-25; ☺lunch & dinner Tue-Sat) Combines a contemporary art gallery with a modern restaurant serving imaginative fare: rabbit ravioli with pumpkin sauce.

Au Jardin du Calendal TRADITIONAL FRENCH €€
(☑04 90 96 11 89; 5 rue Porte de Laure; mains €15; ☺noon-7pm Tue-Sun; ☎) Gourmet salads or tea and cake in the leafy courtyard garden.

Self-Catering

Food Markets MARKETS €
(bd Georges Clemenceau & bd des Lices; ☺Sat) Stretches the length of the main boulevard selling strong cheese, Camargue salt, olive oil and bull sausages. On Wednesday, market stalls set up along bd Émile Combes (east of Les Arènes).

Monoprix SUPERMARKET €
(place Lamartine; ☺8.30am-7.30pm Mon-Sat) Near the northern end of bd Émile Combes.

⚓ Drinking

Oli Pan CAFÉ
(☑04 90 96 11 89; 5 rue Porte de Laure; dishes €3-10; ☺9am-7pm; ☎) Le Calendal's crowd-pleaser serves organic sandwiches and Mövenpick ice creams on a sunset-facing terrace.

L'Australian Café Walla Beer BAR
(☑04 90 97 22 17; 7 rue Molière) Arles is pretty quiet at night outside of *ferias*, but this place is popular for an evening drink on the terrace overlooking bd Georges Clemenceau.

Paddy Mullins BAR, MUSI
(☑04 90 49 67 25; 5 bd Georges Clemenceau; ☺10am-2am) Irish-style pub featuring regular live music.

🛍 Shopping

Next door to the first-ever boutique of home-grown fashion designer **Christian Lacroix** (52 rue de la République) is **Puyricard**

(54 rue de la République), purveying exquisite Provençal chocolates.

ℹ Information

Cyber Saladelle (☎04 90 93 13 56; www.cyber saladelle.com; 17 rue de la République; per hr €3.50; ☺10am-7pm Tue-Sat) Internet access.

Post office (5 bd des Lices)

Tourist office main office (☎04 90 18 41 20; www.tourisme.ville-arles.fr; esplanade Charles de Gaulle; ☺9am-6.45pm Apr-Sep, 9am-4.45pm Mon-Sat, 10am-12.45pm Sun Oct-Mar); train station (☎04 90 43 33 57; ☺9am-1.30pm & 2.30-4.45pm Mon-Fri Apr-Sep)

ℹ Getting There & Away

AIR Nîmes Airport (p711), 20km northwest of Arles, via the A54. No public transport between the airport and Arles.

BUS Telleschi (☎04 42 28 40 22) runs services to/from the following:

Aix-en-Provence €9, 1½ hours

Les Stes-Maries-de-la-Mer €2.50, one hour

Nîmes €1.50, 1 hour

TRAIN Trains go to the following:

Avignon €7, 20 minutes

Marseille €13, 55 minutes

Nîmes €7.50, 30 minutes

ℹ Getting Around

BUS Star (☎08 10 00 08 16; information office 24 bd Georges Clemenceau; ☺8.30am-noon & 2-5.30pm Mon-Fri) operates local buses from 6.30am to 7.30pm Monday to Saturday, and 9.30am to 5.30pm Sunday. The office is the main hub, although most buses also stop at place Lamartine, just south of the train station. Tickets cost €0.80. Free minibuses called Starlets circle most of the old city every 20 to 25 minutes from 7.10am to 7.15pm Monday to Saturday.

TAXI Call ☎04 90 96 90 03.

The Camargue

Just south of Arles, Provence's rolling landscapes yield to the flat, marshy wilds of the Camargue, famous for its teeming birdlife, roughly 500 species. King of all is the pink flamingo, which enjoys the expansive wetlands' mild winters. Equally famous are the Camargue's small white horses; their mellow disposition makes horse riding the ideal way to explore the region's patchwork of salt pans and rice fields, and meadows dotted with grazing bulls. Bring binoculars – and mosquito repellent.

Enclosed by the Petit Rhône and Grand Rhône Rivers, most of the Camargue wetlands fall within the 850-sq-km Parc Naturel Régional de Camargue, established in 1970 to preserve the area's fragile ecosystems while sustaining local agriculture. On the periphery, the Étang de Vaccarès and nearby peninsulas and islands form the Réserve Nationale de Camargue, a 135-sq-km nature reserve.

The Camargue's two largest towns are the seaside pilgrim's outpost Les Stes-Maries-de-la-Mer and, to the northwest, the walled town of Aigues Mortes.

◉ Sights

Musée Camarguais MUSEUM
(☎04 90 97 10 82; Mas du Pont de Rousty; adult/child €4.50/free; ☺9am-6pm Wed-Mon) Inside an 1812-built sheep shed, the Camargue Museum gives a fantastic introduction to this unique area, covering history and ecosystems, as well as the traditional lifestyle of the *gardian,* Camargue's cowboys. A 3.5km nature trail leads to an observation tower with bird's-eye views. Find it 10km southwest of Arles on the D570 to Les Stes-Maries-de-la-Mer.

Le Parc Ornithologique du Pont de Gau NATURE RESERVE
(☎04 90 97 82 62; adult/child €7/4; ☺9am-sunset) Get up close and personal with some 2000 pink flamingos at this wonderful semiwild nature reserve 4km north of Les Stes-Maries on the D570. Dozens more bird species live on the reserve; watch them from 7km of beautiful trails meandering the site.

🏃 Activities

WALKING

Walking paths and trails wend through the Parc Naturel Régional and the Réserve Nationale, on the embankments and along the coast. Bookshops sell detailed walking maps (*IGN Série Bleue 2943ET* and *2944OT*) and tourist offices have good free maps.

BOATING & WATER SPORTS

The marshy Camargue lends itself to exploration by boat. All charge around €10/5 per adult/child per 1½-hour trip. Find **Camargue Bateau de Promenade** (☎04 90

DID YOU KNOW?

The Camargue's animals change colours. Pink flamingos turn white in winter because of the lack of carotene-rich brine shrimp. And the famous white horses are born brown, turning white only at maturity.

97 84 72; http://bateau-camargue.com; 5 rue des Launes) and Quatre Maries (☑04 90 97 70 10; www.bateaux-4maries.camargue.fr; 36 av Théodore Aubanel) in Les Stes-Maries. Le Tiki III (☑04 90 97 81 68; www.tiki3.fr) is a beat-up old paddle boat at the mouth of the Petit Rhône 1.5km west of Les Stes-Maries.

For canoeing and kayaking on the Petit Rhône, contact Kayak Vert Camargue (☑04 66 73 57 17; www.kayakvert-camargue.fr; Mas de Sylvéréal), 14km north of Les Stes-Maries off the D38.

HORSE RIDING

Farms along rte d'Arles (D570) offer *promenades à cheval* (horse riding) astride white Camargue horses, but some are tacky. Les Cabanes de Cacharel (☑04 90 97 84 10, 06 11 57 74 75; www.cabanesdecacharel.com, in French; rte de Cacharel/D85A) charges the same as other stables (€15/26/38 per one-/two-/three-hour trek in the marshes) and offers horse-and-carriage rides.

For kids' pony rides, head to ranch theme-park Domaine Paul Ricard (☑04 90 97 10 62; www.mejanes.camargue.fr; ☺year-round, by reservation mid-Oct–Easter), on the northwestern bank of Étang de Vaccarès, in Méjanes. Drive 14km south along D570 from Arles, turn left along eastbound D37, then right toward Méjanes.

ℹ Information

Réserve Nationale de Camargue Office (☑04 90 97 00 97; www.reserve-camargue.org; La Capelière; ☺9am-6pm, closed Tue Oct-Mar) Along the D36B, on the eastern side of Étang de Vaccarès, with exhibits on the Camargue's ecosystems. Many trails and paths originate here.

ℹ Getting There & Away

Two buses daily in July and August go from Les Stes-Maries to Montpellier (€10.50, two hours) via Aigues Mortes.

ℹ Getting Around

Bicycles are ideal on the Camargue's flat (if windy) terrain. East of Les Stes-Maries, the seafront and inland areas are reserved for walkers and cyclists.

Le Vélo Saintois (19 rue de la République, Les Stes-Maries) English-language list of cycling routes. Rents mountain bikes (€15/34 per day/three days).

Le Vélociste (☑04 90 97 83 26; place Mireille, Les Stes-Maries) Rents bikes, organises cycling-horseback (€36) or cycling-canoeing (€30) packages.

LES STES-MARIES DE LA MER
POP 2500

You could be forgiven for thinking you'd crossed into Spain at this remote seaside outpost where whitewashed buildings line dusty streets and dancers in bright dresses spin flamenco. During its Roma pilgrimages, street-cooked pans of paella fuel chaotic crowds of carnivalesque guitarists, dancers and mounted cowboys.

Away from the small village, 30km of uninterrupted sandy beach bask in hot midday sun and narrow roads beg to be biked: the northbound D85A and the D38 are particularly scenic cycling routes.

◉ Sights

Tickets for bullfights at Les Stes-Maries' Arènes are sold at the arena. The 30km of uninterrupted fine-sand beaches include the area around the lighthouse Phare de la Gacholle (for bathing without a suit), 11km east of town.

Église des Stes-Maries   HISTORIC CHURCH
(place de l'Église) During their pilgrimages, legions of Roma pour into this 12th- to 15th-century church to venerate the statue of black Sara, their highly revered patron saint. The relics of Sara along with those of Marie-Salomé and Sainte Marie-Jacobé, all found in the crypt by King René in 1448, are enshrined in a painted wooden chest, stashed in the stone wall above the choir. From the church's rooftop terrace (adult/child €2/1.50; ☺10am-12.30pm & 2-6.30pm Mon-Fri, 10am-7pm Sat & Sun, only Wed, Sat & Sun Nov-Feb), a great panorama unfolds.

🛏 Sleeping

Low-rise hotels line the D570 heading into Les Stes-Maries. Old farmhouses surrounding town often let rooms.

TOP CHOICE   **L'Auberge Cavalière**
       HISTORIC FARMHOUSE   €€
(☑04 90 97 88 88; www.aubergecavaliere.com; D570; d €140-195; ✻@☲) Approximately

THE STORY OF THE MARYS & GITAN PILGRIMAGES

Catholicism first reached European shores in what's now tiny Les Stes-Maries. So the stories go, Stes Marie-Salomé and Marie-Jacobé (and some say Mary Magdalene) fled the Holy Land in a little boat and were caught in a storm, drifting at sea until washing ashore here.

Provençal and Catholic lore diverge at this point: Catholicism relates that Sara, patron saint of the *gitans* (Roma Gitano people, also known as gypsies), travelled with the two Marys on the boat; Provençal legend says Sara was already here and was the first person to recognise their holiness. In 1448, skeletal remains said to belong to Sara and the two Marys were found in a crypt in Les Stes-Maries.

Gitans continue to make pilgrimages (Pèlerinage des Gitans) here on 24 and 25 May (often staying for up to three weeks), dancing and playing music in the streets, and parading a statue of Sara through town. The Sunday in October closest to the 22nd sees a second pilgrimage dedicated to the two Stes Maries; *courses Camarguaises* (nonlethal bullfights) are also held at this time.

1.5km north of Les Stes-Maries, this salt-of-the-earth hotel spreads out over a typical Camargue landscape of wetlands and meadows. Rooms 340 to 345 look over a pond teeming with birdlife; the thatched cabins offer cosy independent quarters. Horse-riding trips and great regional restaurant (menus €18-42).

Hôtel Méditerranée   HOTEL €
(☑04 90 97 82 09; www.mediterraneehotel.com, in French; 4 av Frédéric Mistral; d €46-60; ✳) Handily located in the centre of town, one of the cheapest and most charming options. Simple rooms seconds from the sea.

Le Mas de Peint   HISTORIC FARMHOUSE €€€
(☑04 90 97 20 62; www.masdepeint.com; Le Sambuc; d/ste from €235/375; ☺mid-Mar–mid-Nov & mid-Dec–mid-Jan; ✳ ✿) Camargue's most upmarket *mas* (farmhouse): think chic, gentrified country quarters right out of the pages of design mag *Côte Sud*. Horses and bikes to ride, and a tasty **restaurant** to boot.

Camping La Brise   CAMPGROUND €
(☑04 90 97 84 67; fax 04 90 97 72 01; av Marcel Carrière; per site €19-22; ☺closed mid-Nov–mid-Dec; ✿) Right on the beach, with two swimming pools. Good option for families. Can be very windy; pick somewhere sheltered.

Auberge de Jeunesse   HOSTEL €
(☑04 90 97 51 72; www.auberge-de-jeunesse. camargue.fr, in French; Pioch Badet; dm incl breakfast, dinner & sheets €30; ☺reception 7.30-10.30am & 5-11pm Sep-Jun) Half board is part of the package at this rural hostel, 8km north of Les Stes-Maries on the

D570 to Arles. Buses from Arles drop you at the door.

✗ Eating

TOP CHOICE La Cabane aux Coquillages
    SEAFOOD €
(rue Théodore Aubanel) As the day's blazing heat fades, join the crowds at this pocket-sized fish shop on the seafront with crates of crustaceans piled high inside and a gaggle of sea-blue chairs outside. Buy shellfish to savour at home, relax on the packed pavement terrace with a seafood platter or indulge in a glass of dry white and half-a-dozen oysters (€6).

ℹ Information

Tourist office (☑04 90 97 82 55; www.saint esmaries.com; 5 av Van Gogh; ☺9am-7pm) Excellent website, information on activities including maps for walking and cycling, and guided walking tours (€7).

AIGUES-MORTES
POP 7705

Actually located over the border from Provence in the Gard *département*, the town of Aigues-Mortes is 28km northwest of Les Stes-Maries at the western extremity of the Camargue. Aigues-Mortes is set in flat marshland and encircled by walls. The town was established in the mid-13th century by Louis IX to give the French crown a Mediterranean port under its direct control, and in 1248 Louis IX's flotilla of 1500 ships massed here before setting sail to the Holy Land for the Seventh Crusade.

The cobbled streets inside the city walls are lined with restaurants, cafés and bars, giving it a festive atmosphere. It's definitely a charming option from which to explore the area.

Sights & Activities

Scaling the ramparts rewards you with sweeping views. Head to the top of the tower, **Tour de Constance** (adult/child €6.50/free; ⊙10am-7pm). The 1.6km wall-top walk takes about one hour.

The southern ramparts afford views of the stretching salt-pans (the Salins du Midi), which you can travel through aboard the **salt train** (☑04 66 73 40 24; www.salins.fr; adult/child €8/6; ⊙Mar-Oct), accompanied by commentary in English. Book tickets at the office at Porte de la Gardette, from where you will catch a bus to the salt-pan site.

Sleeping & Eating

Parking within the town walls is practically impossible but there are plenty of car parks outside.

L'Hermitage de St-Antoine B&B €€
(☑06 03 04 34 05; www.hermitagesa.com; 9 bd Intérieur Nord; r €79; ❀) Inside the walled town, this pocket-sized *chambre d'hôte* has three exquisitely appointed rooms, one with a small private terrace, and all with fresh, crisp decor. The continental breakfast takes on new dimensions in the sun-filled patio. Only children aged over 12.

Hôtel L'Escale HOTEL €
(☑04 66 53 71 14; http://hotel.escale.free.fr; 3 av Tour de Constance; r €32-40, 4-5-person r €65-75; ❀) L'Escale caters fantastically to budget travellers. Basic rooms are immaculate, as are the shared bathrooms and toilets of the cheaper rooms. Bigger rooms in the annexe are good value for families. The **restaurant** (mains €7 to €10) has a flower-lined terrace.

Le Café de Bouzigues MODERN FRENCH €€
(☑04 66 53 73 95; 7 rue Pasteur; menus €30) This unexpected find is trendy, fun and unconventional. Both the interior and the seasonally changing food have slightly wacky tendencies (hot and cold oysters with figs and an onion and ginger puree), but both ways it is a resounding success.

Information

Tourist office (☑04 66 53 73 00; www.ot-aiguesmortes.fr; place St-Louis; ⊙9am-noon & 1-6pm) Inside the walled city.

The Vaucluse is like every Provençal cliché rolled into one: lavender fields, scenic hills, rows upon rows of vineyards, enchanting villages and picturesque markets, traditional stone houses, beating summer sun and howling winter mistral. At the heart of Vaucluse, which means 'closed valley', is the exquisite town of Avignon.

A car is the ideal way to cover the Vaucluse, but it's possible (if not expedient) to get around by bus.

Avignon

POP 93.566

Hooped by 4.3km of superbly preserved stone ramparts, this graceful city is the belle of Provence's ball. Its turn as the papal seat of power has bestowed Avignon with a treasury of magnificent art and architecture, none grander than the massive medieval fortress and papal palace, the Palais des Papes.

Famed for its annual performing arts festival, these days Avignon is also an animated student city and an ideal spot from which to step out into the surrounding region. Avignon is also known for its fabled bridge, the Pont St-Bénézet, aka the Pont d'Avignon.

History

Avignon first gained its ramparts and its reputation as a city of art and culture during the 14th century, when Pope Clement V and his court fled political turmoil in Rome for Avignon. From 1309 to 1377 the seven French-born popes invested huge sums of money in building and decorating the papal palace. Under the popes' rule, Jews and political dissidents took shelter here. Pope

PASSION PASS

The nifty **Avignon Passion Pass** entitles you to discounts on museum visits, trips and tours in Avignon and Villeneuve-lès-Avignon. The first place you use the pass costs the full amount, but after that there's a 10% to 50% reduction. It's valid for 15 days, and covers a family of five. Pick up your pass from the tourist office, or any of the tourist sites.

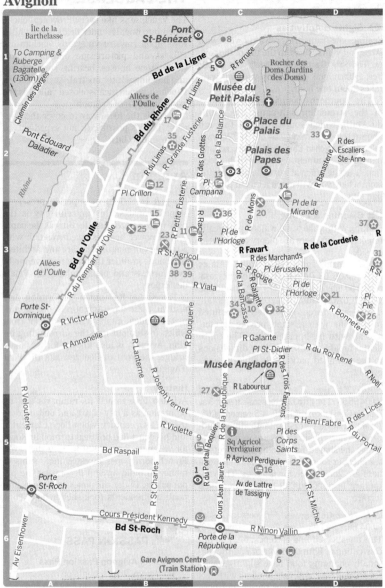

Gregory XI left Avignon in 1376, but his death two years later led to the Great Schism (1378–1417), during which rival popes (up to three at one time) resided at Rome and Avignon, denouncing and excommunicating one another. Even after the schism was set-tled and an impartial pope, Martin V, established himself in Rome, Avignon remained under papal rule. The city and Comtat Venaissin (now the Vaucluse *département*) were ruled by papal legates until 1791, when they were annexed to France.

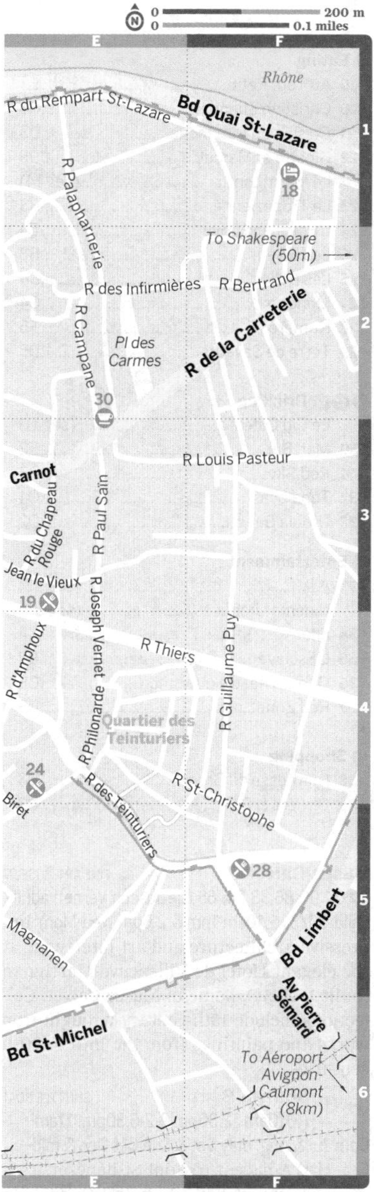

Sights & Activities

Wrapping around the city, Avignon's ramparts, built between 1359 and 1370, were restored during the 19th century, minus their original moats. One of the city's chief joys is to wander aimlessly, peeking into its hidden corners. Ticket offices for most sights close up to one hour before overall closing times.

Palais des Papes HISTORIC PALACE

(Palace of the Popes; ☎04 90 27 50 00; www.palais-des-papes.com; place du Palais; adult/child incl audioguide €6/3; ⏲9am-7pm) This Unesco World Heritage Site, the world's largest Gothic palace, was built when Pope Clement V abandoned Rome in 1309 and settled in Avignon. The immense scale of the palace, with its cavernous stone halls and vast courtyards, testifies to the wealth of the popes; the 3m-thick walls, portcullises and watchtowers emphasise their need for defence.

Today it takes some imagination to picture the former luxury of these vast bare rooms. You can catch whispering glimpses in the wonderful 14th-century **chapel frescos** painted by Matteo Giovannetti; in the dark-blue walls of the **Pope's apartment**, threaded with dusky red flowers; and in the superb **Chambre du Cerf**, alive with medieval hunting scenes. Visit at lunchtime to avoid group tours.

Place du Palais LANDMARK SQUARE

A golden statue of the Virgin Mary (weighing a portly 4.5 tons) stands on the dome of the Romanesque Cathédrale Notre Dame des Doms (built 1671–72), outstretched arms protecting the city. Admire fine views from Rocher des Doms gardens. Opposite the palace, the building dripping with outsized carvings of fruit and heraldic beasts is the former 17th-century mint, Hôtel des Monnaies.

Pont St-Bénézet LANDMARK BRIDGE

(St Bénézet's Bridge; adult/child €4.50/3.50; ⏲9am-8pm, 9.30am-5.45pm Nov-Mar) According to legend, pastor Bénézet had three saintly visions urging him to build a bridge across the Rhône. Known to countless kids as the Pont d'Avignon from the chirpy French rhyme, it was completed in 1185 and linked Avignon with Villeneuve-lès-Avignon, controlling trade at this vital crossroads. It was rebuilt several times before all but four of its spans were washed away in the mid-1600s. If you don't feel like paying to visit the bridge, you can see it for free from the Rocher des Doms park, Pont Édouard Daladier or from across the river on the Île de la Barthelasse's chemin des Berges.

Musée Anglabon ART MUSEUM

(📞04 90 82 29 03; www.anglabon.com; 5 rue La-boureur; adult/child €6/4; ⊙1-6pm Tue-Sun Apr-Nov, 1-6pm Wed-Sun Jan-Mar, closed Dec) Born out of the private collection of couturier Jacques Doucet (1853–1929), this charming museum harbours Impressionist treasures, including the only Van Gogh painting in Provence (*Railway Wagons*), and works by Cézanne, Manet, Degas and Picasso. Upstairs is a collection of antique furniture and 16th- and 17th-century paintings.

Musée du Petit Palais RELIGIOUS ART MUSEUM

(📞04 90 86 44 58; www.petit-palais.org; place du Palais; adult/child €6/free; ⊙10am-1pm & 2-6pm Wed-Mon) The bishops' and archbishops' palace during the 14th and 15th centuries is now home to an outstanding collection of lavish 13th- to 16th-century Italian religious paintings created by artists including Botticelli, Carpaccio and Giovanni di Paolo.

Musée Calvet FINE ART MUSEUM

(📞04 90 86 33 84; 65 rue Joseph Vernet; adult/child €6/3; ⊙10am-1pm & 2-6pm Wed-Mon) Impressive architecture and art intertwine at the elegant Hôtel de Villeneuve-Martignan (built 1741–54), home of Musée Calvet. Collections include 15th-century wrought-iron works and paintings from the 16th to 20th centuries.

FREE **Shuttle Boat** SHUTTLE BOAT

(⊙10am-12.30pm & 2-6.30pm, 11am-9pm Jul & Aug, only Sat & Sun Oct-Dec & mid-Feb–Mar) Adjacent to Pont St-Bénézet; connects the walled city with the Île de la Barthelasse.

👉 Tours

The tourist office has a map in English which has four walking tours around the old town.

Les Grands Bateaux de Provence
BOAT TOUR

(☏04 90 85 62 25; www.mireio.net, in French; allées de l'Oulle) April to September loop under the bridge and to Villeneuve-lès-Avignon (€8). Year-round travel the Rhône to Arles or the vineyard area of Châteauneuf-du-Pape on a restaurant-boat (€48, including a meal).

Guided Tours
WALKING TOURS

(adult/child €17/7; ⊙10am daily, Sat only Nov-Mar) Two-hour tours of Avignon in English and French depart from the tourist office.

Autocars Lieutaud
BUS TOURS

(☏04 90 86 36 75; 36 bd Saint-Roch; www.cars-lieutaud.fr) Half- and full-day tours visit nearby vineyards, the Pont du Gars or the Luberon (€45). For a vintage experience, do it in the archetypal Citroën 2CV (€145 for a three-hour chauffeured trip in the Alpilles).

★ Festivals & Events

Festival d'Avignon
PERFORMING ARTS

(☏04 90 27 66 50; www.festival-avignon.com; Espace St-Louis, 20 rue du Portail Boquier; tickets €16-50) Hundreds of artists take to the stage and streets during this world-famous festival, founded in 1946 and held every year from early July to early August.

Festival Off
PERFORMING ARTS

(☏04 90 85 13 08; www.avignonleoff.com, in French; 5 rue Ninon Vallin) Paralleling the official Avignon festival, this fringe event has an eclectic, cheaper program of experimental performances. La Carte Off (€13) discount card gets 30% off all performances.

🛏 Sleeping

Avignon is one of the few places in Provence that caters well for budget-conscious travellers. Book many months ahead for a room during the festival, when prices soar.

TOP CHOICE Hôtel La Mirande
LUXURY HOTEL €€€

(☏04 90 14 20 20; www.la-mirande.fr; 4 place de la Mirande; d €390-540; ❋ @ 🛜) Avignon's top hotel (by far) occupies a converted 16th-century cardinal's palace with dramatic high-ceilinged spaces decked out in oriental rugs, gold-threaded tapestries, marble staircases and dizzying over-the-top Gallic style. Low-end rooms are smallish, but still conjure the feeling of being a guest in someone's private château. The on-

site formal restaurant, Le Marmiton (mains from €35), offers cooking classes (from €80) and a twice-weekly chef's table (€92, reservations essential); afternoon tea is served (albeit slowly) in the glittering lobby.

Le Limas
B&B €€

(☏04 90 14 67 19; www.le-limas-avignon.com; 51 rue du Limas; d/tr from €120/200; ❋ @) Behind its discreet lavender door, this chic B&B in an 18th-century town house is like something out of *Vogue Living*. It's everything interior designers strive for when mixing old and new: from the state-of-the-art kitchen and minimalist white decor to antique fireplaces and 18th-century spiral staircase. Breakfast by the fireplace or on the sun-drenched terrace is a treat, as is bubbly Marion.

Hôtel Boquier
HOTEL €

(☏04 90 82 34 43; www.hotel-boquier.com, in French; 6 rue du Portail Boquier; d €50-70; ❋ 🛜) The infectious enthusiasm of owners Sylvie and Pascal Sendra sweeps through this central little place. It's bright, airy and spacious; try for the themed rooms Morocco or Lavender.

Lumani
B&B €€

(☏04 90 82 94 11; www.avignon-lumani.com; 37 rue du Rempart St-Lazare; d €100-170; ❋ 🛜) This fabulous *maison d'hôte* run by Elisabeth, whose art is hung throughout the stunning house, is a fount of inspiration for artists. Rooms include two suites and there's a fountained garden.

Hôtel de l'Horloge
HOTEL €€

(☏04 90 16 42 00; www.hotels-ocre-azur.com; place de l'Horloge; r €95-180; ❋ 🛜) Most rooms at this supercentral hotel are straightforward (comfortable, all mod cons), but the five terrace rooms have the edge with sophisticated furnishings and views: ask for 505 with its incredible view of the Palais des Papes. Wheelchair access.

Hôtel de Garlande
HISTORIC HOTEL €€

(☏04 90 80 08 85; www.hoteldegarlande.com; 20 rue Galante; d €80-108; ❋ 🛜) Central for just about everything, the sweet, cheerily coloured rooms in a historic *hôtel particulier* overlook a narrow street. Rooms are elegantly decorated, bathrooms sparkling new, but the stairway's steep.

Hôtel du Palais des Papes
HISTORIC HOTEL €€

(☏04 90 86 04 13; www.hotel-avignon.com; 3 place du Palais; d €75-85, ste €120) This old-fashioned abode has wrought-iron furniture, frescoed ceilings and exposed stone walls. Pricier rooms do indeed sport views of the Palais des Papes. There's also a wonderfully authentic restaurant, Le Lutrin (menus €25-35).

Hôtel Mignon
HOTEL €

(☑04 90 82 17 30; www.hotel-mignon.com; 12 rue Joseph Vernet; r incl breakfast €45-80; ✳@) Cute and comfy, this 16-room place within the walled city is a favourite for its small rooms in pretty shades (and tiny bathrooms), and its friendly staff.

Hôtel Splendid
HOTEL €

(☑04 90 86 14 46; www.avignon-splendid-hotel.com; 17 rue Agricol Perdiguier; s €40, d €57-70, apt €75-95; ✳) This cyclist-friendly place has charming rooms, half of them overlooking the pretty neighbouring park. Ground-floor flat has its own patio. Environmentally minded owners use only natural cleaning products.

Hôtel d'Europe
LUXURY HOTEL €€€

(☑04 90 14 76 76; www.heurope.com; 12 place Crillon; d €195-480; ✳🕙) Though guests once included everyone from Napoleon to Jaqueline Kennedy-Onasis, now the famous address rests on its laurels and needs new fabrics and better lighting.

YMCA-UCJG
HOSTEL €

(☑04 90 25 46 20; www.ymca-avignon.com; 7bis chemin de la Justice; dm without/with bathroom €25/36; ⊘reception 8.30am-6pm, closed Dec-early Jan; 🕙🏊) This spotless hostel across the river, just outside Villeneuve-lès-Avignon, has some private rooms and a swimming pool and terrace with panoramic views of the city. Sheets included. Wheelchair access. Take bus 10 to the Monteau stop.

Camping & Auberge Bagatelle
CAMPGROUND, HOSTEL €

(☑04 90 86 30 39; www.campingbagatelle.com; Île de la Barthelasse; tent only per person €6, car per person €13, dm incl breakfast €18; ⊘reception 8am-9pm) Shaded and only 20 minutes' walk from the centre on Île de la Barthelasse. Also, basic serviceable two-to eight-bed dorms; sheets are €2.50.

🍴 Eating

Place de l'Horloge's touristy cafés only have so-so food. Restaurants open seven days during summer-festival season, when reservations become essential. *Papaline d'Avignon* is a pink chocolate ball filled with potent Mont Ventoux herbal liqueur.

TOP CHOICE Cuisine du Dimanche
PROVINCIAL FRENCH €€

(☑04 90 82 99 10; www.lacuisinedudimanche.com, in French; 31 rue Bonneterie; mains €15-25; ⊘closed Sun & Mon Oct-May) Spitfire chef Marie shops every morning at Les Halles to find the freshest ingredients for her earthy flavour-packed cooking, and takes no culinary short cuts. The market-driven menu changes daily, but specialities include scallops and a simple roast chicken with pan gravy. The narrow stone-walled dining room is a mishmash of textures, from contemporary resin chairs to antique crystal goblets, befitting the chef's eclecticism. Make reservations.

Les 5 Sens
GASTRONOMIC €€

(☑04 90 85 26 51; www.restaurantles5sens.com; 18 rue Joseph Vernet; lunch menus €20, lunch mains €13-17, dinner mains €22-30; ⊘Tue-Sat) Chef Thierry Baucher, one of France's *meilleurs ouvriers* (top chefs), reveals his southwestern origins in specialities including cassoulet and foie gras, but goes contemporary-Mediterranean in his gastronomic dishes, such as butternut-squash ravioli with escargots. The dining room is refreshingly unfussy, vaguely French Colonial with rattan and carved wood, and service impeccable.

Au Tout Petit
CONTEMPORARY FRENCH €€

(☑04 90 82 38 86; 4 rue d'Amphoux; lunch menus €11, dinner menus €16-24; ⊘Tue-Sat) The 'Teeny Tiny' packs big flavours into every imaginative dish, such as tuna carpaccio with vanilla, or apricot *tarte Tatin* with rosemary ice cream; simple, smart cooking, maximizing the use of spice. Wines by the glass cost a mere €2.50, and lunch is a steal. Only eight tables make reservations essential.

L'Epice and Love
HOMESTYLE FRENCH €

(☑04 90 82 45 96, 30 rue des Lices; mains €11-12; ⊘dinner Mon-Sat) Tables are cheek by jowl at this tiny bohemian restaurant, decorated with antique kitchenware and mismatched chairs. There's nothing fancy, just straightforward bistro fare, stews, roasts and other homestyle French dishes. No credit cards.

Numéro 75
CONTEMPORARY FRENCH €€

(☑04 90 27 16 00; 75 rue Guillaume Puy; menus €26-32; ⊘Mon-Sat) The stately dining room of absinthe inventor Jules Pernod's former mansion is a fitting backdrop for stylized Med cooking. The menu changes nightly, and may only include three mains, but brevity guarantees freshness. On balmy nights book a table in the courtyard garden.

Christian Etienne
GASTRONOMIC €€€
(☑04 90 86 16 50; 10 rue de Mons; mains €28-45; ⊙Tue-Sat) Avignon's top table rests on its laurels and could stand some redecorating, but the refined Provençal cuisine remains exceptional, most notably the summertime-only starter-to-dessert tomato menu. Reservations essential.

Ginette et Marcel
SANDWICHES €
(27 place des Corps Saints; dishes €4-6; ⊙11am-midnight) Snacks or a light meal of *tartines* (open-faced sandwiches) and fruit tarts.

Terre de Saveurs
VEGETARIAN €€
(☑04 90 86 68 72; rue Saint Michel, off place des Corps Saints; mains €14.50; ⊙lunch Tue-Sat, dinner Fri & Sat; ☑) Half the menu is all-organic vegetarian, the other half veg-heavy meat dishes.

Self-Catering
Take a picnic to Rocher des Doms, a bluff-top park with views spanning the Rhône, Pont St-Bénézet, Villeneuve-lès-Avignon and Mont Ventoux.

Les Halles
FOOD MARKET €
(place Pie; ⊙7am-1pm Tue-Sun)

Monoprix
SUPERMARKET €
(24 rue de la République; ⊙8am-9pm Mon-Sat)

La Tropézienne
PATISSERIE €
(22 rue St-Agricol; ⊙8.30am-7.30pm Mon-Fri, to 2pm Sat) St-Tropez's famous cream-and-cake concoction, *tarte tropézienne,* and other Avignon treats.

Drinking

Mon Bar
CAFÉ
(17 rue Portail-Matheron; ⊙8am-8pm) This Parisian-looking bistro has been going for 70 years and looks set to go for another 70. It's a neighbourhood institution; don't expect more than a scowl if you try to order your coffee in English.

Tapalocas
TAPAS BAR
(15 rue Galante; tapas from €3; ⊙noon-1am) In the pedestrian area, tuck into a seemingly endless array of traditional Spanish tapas over a sangria or two.

Utopia Bar
BAR
(4 rue des escaliers Ste-Anne; ⊙noon-midnight) At the foot of the imposing Palais des Papes walls, l'Utopia has something of a thespian bent with its red velvet benches, beautiful glass verandah and great mirrors throughout. Perfect for a glass of wine.

Le Cid Café
MUSIC BAR
(☑04 90 82 30 28; 11 place de l'Horloge; ⊙11am-late) DJs keep the beats coming at this fluoro-lit, happening joint on Place de l'Horloge. Locals love it and so do visitors keen for a piece of the action.

Red Sky
ENGLISH PUB
(☑04 90 85 93 23; rue St-Jean le Vieux; ⊙10am-1am) Looking as though someone picked it up in central London and plonked it in Avignon, this cherry-red English pub has gigs, theme nights and plenty of sport on TV.

⭐ Entertainment
Avignon's nightlife revolves around live music and theatre, rather than wild bars and clubs. The free *César* weekly magazine and the tourist office's fortnightly newsletter, *Rendez-vous d'Avignon,* (both in French) carry listings. Tickets are sold at Fnac (☑08 25 02 00 20; 19 rue de la République; ⊙10am-7pm Mon-Sat) or the tourist office.

Opéra Théâtre d'Avignon
PERFORMING ARTS
(☑04 90 82 81 40; www.operatheatredavignon. fr; place de l'Horloge; ⊙box office 11am-6pm Tue-Sat) Housed in an imposing structure built in 1847, Opéra d'Avignon stages everything from operas to ballets, October to June.

AJMI
JAZZ CLUB
(Association pour Le Jazz & La Musique Improvisée; ☑04 90 86 08 61; www.jazzalajmi.com, in French; 4 rue des Escaliers Ste-Anne) This 30-year-old jazz club is inside the arts centre, La Manutention.

Cinéma Utopia
MOVIE THEATRE
(☑04 90 82 65 36; www.cinemas-utopia.org, in French; 4 rue des Escaliers Ste-Anne) Screens films in original languages; inside the arts centre.

Red Zone
NIGHTCLUB
(☑04 90 27 02 44; 25 rue Carnot) A studenty crowd gathers here for its regular gigs, boogying and always-buzzing bar.

L'Esclave
GAY CLUB
(☑04 90 85 14 91; www.esclavebar.com, in French; 12 rue du Limas) Avignon's inner-city gay hot spot rocks most nights starting at 11:30pm.

🛍 Shopping

Comtesse du Barry
GOURMET FOOD
(25 rue St-Agricol) Stock up on gourmet goodies like fine wine and foie gras.

Oliviers & Co OLIVE PRODUCTS

(19 rue St-Agricol) Fine olive oil and olive oil–based products such as soap, creams and biscuits.

Shakespeare BOOKS

(☑04 90 27 38 50; 155 rue de la Carreterie; ☺Tue-Sat) Enjoy homemade scones with your tomes at this English bookshop and *salon de thé*.

ℹ️ Information

Note that it's hard to change money on weekends in Avignon. Internet cafés dot place Pie.

CIC (13 rue de la République) Has an ATM.

La Cabine (☑04 90 14 18 20; 15 rue Florence; per 30min €1; ☺9am-midnight Mon-Sat) Internet access.

Post office (cours Président Kennedy) Changes currency.

Provence Guide (www.provenceguide.com) Vaucluse region information, including B&Bs.

Tourist office (www.avignon-tourisme.com; 41 cours Jean Jaurès; ☺9am-5pm Mon-Sat, 9.45am-5pm Sun)

ℹ️ Getting There & Away

Air

Aéroport Avignon-Caumont (☑04 90 81 51 51; www.avignon.aeroport.fr) Eight kilometres southeast of Avignon. Flights from Britain and Ireland, April to October.

Bus

The **bus station** (bd St-Roch; ☺information window 8am-7pm Mon-Fri, to 1pm Sat) is in the basement of the building that's down the ramp to the right as you exit the train station. Tickets sold on board. On Sunday most lines have reduced frequency.

Aix-en-Provence €14, 1¼ hour

Arles €8, 1½ hours

Carpentras €2, 35 minutes

Marseille €20, two hours

Nîmes €8, 1¼ hours

Orange €3, 45 minutes

Linebús (☑04 90 85 30 48; www.linebus.com), with direct service to Barcelona, and **Eurolines** (☑04 90 85 27 60; www.eurolines.com) have offices at the far end of the platforms.

Car & Motorcycle

Car-hire agencies are either inside the main train station or nearby.

To reduce traffic within the walls, the city has over 900 free, monitored parking spaces at Parking de L'Île Piot and Parking des Italiens, both served by a free shuttle bus. There's also free parking just outside the walls, along the city's southern and eastern ramparts.

Train

Avignon has two stations: **Gare Avignon TGV**, 4km southwest in Courtine; and central **Gare Avignon Centre** (42 bd St-Roch) with service to/from:

Arles €6.50, 20 minutes

Nîmes €8.50, 30 minutes

Orange €5.50, 20 minutes

Some TGVs to/from Paris stop at Gare Avignon Centre, but TGVs for Marseille (€23, 35 minutes) and Nice (€54, three hours) only use Gare Avignon TGV.

In July and August there's a direct **Eurostar** (www.eurostar.com) service on Saturday from London (from €135 return, six hours) to Gare Avignon Centre. See p973 for more details.

Left luggage (per bag from €4; ☺7am-7pm winter, to 10pm summer) is inside the station.

ℹ️ Getting Around

To/From the Airport

No public transport to the airport. Taxis cost around €20.

Bicycle & Motorcycle

Provence Bike (www.provence-bike.com, in French; 52 bd St-Roch) Also rents scooters and motorbikes.

Vélopop (☑08 10 45 64 56; www.velopop.fr, in French) Shared-bicycle service, with 19 stations around town. Pick up at one, return at another. The first 30 minutes are free. One day/week costs €1/3, plus a refundable deposit of €150 guaranteed to your credit card. Sign up by phone, or use the credit-card machines at stations.

Bus

Local **TCRA** (Transports en Commun de la Région d'Avignon; www.tcra.fr, in French) bus tickets cost €1.20 each, purchased on board. Buses run from 7am to about 7.40pm (less frequently on Sunday, from 8am to 6pm). The two most important bus transfer points are the Poste stop at the main post office and place Pie.

Agence Commerciale TCRA (av de Lattre de Tassigny; ☺8.30am-12.30pm & 1.30-6pm Mon-Fri) or its TGV station branch have free maps and sell *carnets* of 10 tickets (€9.50).

Villeneuve-lès-Avignon Bus 11 stops in front of the main post office and on the western side of the walled city near Porte de l'Oulle.

Navette shuttle buses link Gare Avignon TGV with the centre (€1.20, 10 to 13 minutes, half-hourly between 6.15am and 11.30pm), at the post office on cours Président Kennedy.

Pont St-Bénézet, for awesome views of the walled city.

Around Avignon

VILLENEUVE-LÈS-AVIGNON
POP 13,084

Thirteenth-century Villeneuve-lès-Avignon gazes across the Rhône at Avignon like a wistful little sister. Entranced by the bigger city's charm, most visitors barely glance at Villeneuve; but frankly, it's our preferred sibling, with monuments to rival Avignon's and none of the crowds.

Just 3km from Avignon, Villeneuve is easily reached by foot or Bus 11 from Avignon's main post office. Sights are included in the Avignon Passion pass.

Chartreuse du Val de Bénédiction
MONASTERY

(☎04 90 15 24 24; www.chartreuse.org; 58 rue de la République; adult/child €6.50/free; ◷9.30am-6.30pm) Three cloisters, 40 cells, church and chapels, washhouse, and nook-and-cranny gardens make up the biggest Carthusian monastery in France. Pope Innocent VI founded it in 1352...and was buried here 10 years later in an elaborate mausoleum.

Musée Pierre de Luxembourg RELIGIOUS ART

(☎04 90 27 49 66; 3 rue de la République; admission €3.10; ◷10am-12.30pm & 2-6.30pm). If you're remotely interested in religious art, see Enguerrand Quarton's lavish and dramatic 1453 painting *The Crowning of the Virgin* (accompanying notes give insight into its commissioning and meaning) and the rare 14th-century *Ivory Virgin*.

Fort St-André FORT

(☎04 90 25 45 35; adult/child €5/free; ◷10am-1pm & 2-5.30pm). Walk a section of the majestic 14th-century ramparts, and admire the 360-degree views from the top of the **Tour des Masques** (Mask Tower) and **Tour Jumelles** (Twin Towers). Meandering pathways at one of France's top 100 gardens, Jardins de l'Abbaye (admission €5), cross a rose garden, duck under wisteria-covered pergolas and thread by three ancient ruined churches.

Tour Philippe-le-Bel MONUMENTAL TOWER

(☎04 32 70 08 57; admission €2; ◷10am-12.30pm & 2-6.30pm Tue-Sun, closed noon-2pm Oct, Nov & Mar). Take the spiral steps to the top of this 14th-century defensive tower, built at what was the northwestern end of

LES BAUX DE PROVENCE
POP 380

At the heart of the Alpilles and spectacularly perched above picture-perfect rolling hills of vineyards, olive groves and orchards is one of the most visited villages in France: Les Baux de Provence, 30km south of Avignon towards Arles. Les Baux was vividly immortalised by Van Gogh during his time in nearby St-Rémy de Provence (see boxed text, p781). Visit in the early evening after the caterpillar of tourist coaches has crawled back downhill.

Château des Baux (☎04 90 54 55 56; www.chateau-baux-provence.com; adult/child €7.50/5.50; ◷9am-6pm, to 8pm Jul & Aug) perches on a 245m-high grey limestone *baou* (Provençal for rocky spur) at the top of the village and dominates the surrounding countryside. Thought to date to the 10th century, the castle was largely destroyed in 1633 during the reign of Louis XIII. Explore its 7 hectares of mazelike ruins with the free audioguide, or just run wild through deep dungeons and up crumbling towers (from where there are out-of-this-world views). Demonstrations of medieval warfare occur in summer.

Large-scale sound-and-light projections at Cathédrale d'Images (www.cathedrale-images.com; adult/child €7.50/3.50) flicker against the backdrop of a former quarry cave, a few minutes' stroll north of the village. The show, which changes each year, is quite unique; wear warm clothes.

Legendary L'Oustau de Baumanière (☎04 90 54 33 07; www.oustaudebaumaniere.com; menus €95-150; ☎) serves rarefied cuisine, including a (trés gourmet) vegetarian menu, with ingredients plucked from its own organic garden. There is also fine accommodation (doubles from €290). Head chef and owner Jean-André Charial's kingdom also includes the Michelin-star restaurant and luxury rooms of La Cabro d'Or (☎04 90 54 33 21; www.lacabrodor.com; d from €245), also in Les Baux. Reservations are imperative for both.

The tourist office (☎04 90 54 34 39; www.lesbauxdeprovence.com; ◷9.30am-5pm Mon-Fri, 10am-5.30pm Sat & Sun) has information on accommodation. Parking within 800m of the village costs €3 to €5 or park for free at Cathédrale d'Images.

DETOUR: CHÂTEAUNEUF-DU-PAPE WINES

Carpets of vineyards unfurl around the tiny medieval village of Châteauneuf-du-Pape, epicentre of one of the world's great winegrowing regions. Only a small ruin remains of the château – a lone wall, high on a hilltop – once the summer residence of Avignon's popes, later bombed by Germans in WWII. Now it belongs to picnickers and day hikers who ascend the hill to scout their lines with a 360-degree panorama.

Thank geology for these luscious wines: when glaciers receded, they left *galets* scattered atop the red-clay soil; these large pebbles trap the Provençal sun, releasing heat after sunset, helping grapes ripen with steady warmth. Most Châteauneuf-du-Pape wines are red; only 6% are white (rosé is forbidden). Strict regulations (which formed the basis for the entire *appellation contrôlée* system) govern production. Reds come from 13 different grape varieties – grenache is the biggie – and should age at least five years. The full-bodied whites drink well young (except for all-rousanne varieties) and make an excellent, mineral-y aperitif wine, hard to find anywhere else (but taste before you buy, as some may lack acidity).

Sample them at over two dozen wine shops with free tastings (*dégustations gratuites*), or at the Musée du Vin (www.brotte.com; rte d'Avignon; admission free; ⊙9am-1pm & 2-7pm), which has extensive exhibits on winemaking. The tourist office (www.pays provence.fr, in French; place du Portail; ⊙9.30am-6pm Mon-Sat Jun-Sep, closed Wed & Sun Oct-May) has a brochure of estates, showing which ones allow cellar visits, have English tours, allow drop-in visitors and offer free tastings.

Perched beneath the ruined château, Le Verger des Papes (⊡04 90 83 50 40; 4 rue du Château; menus €20-30; ⊙variable, call ahead) has knockout vistas from its leafy terrace, and serves town's best traditional French cooking, with bread from a wood-fired oven – but call ahead: sometimes it closes without warning. Park at the chateau's ruins, and walk down the steps.

Make a weekend of it by staying in a 17th-century farmhouse, surrounded by vineyards. Each room at Le Mas Julien (⊡04 90 34 99 49; www.mas-julien.com; 704 chemin de Saint Jean, Orange; r/apt with kitchen incl breakfast €110/130; ❋ @ ⍫ ⛢) artfully blends contemporary and Provençal style, and there's a studio apartment, with kitchen, that sleeps three (add €30 for third person). After a day exploring, nothing beats sprawling by the big pool, glass of wine in hand.

Orange

POP 29,000

Considering how exceptional Orange's Roman theatre is (if you see only one Roman site in France, make it this one), the ultra-conservative town is surprisingly untouristy, and dead in winter. Accommodation is good value, compared with swankier towns like Avignon, but it's nearly impossible to find an open restaurant on Sunday or Monday night.

The House of Orange, the princely dynasty that had ruled Orange since the 12th century, made its mark on the history of the Netherlands through a 16th-century marriage with the German House of Nassau, and then English history through William of Orange. Orange was ceded to France in 1713 by the Treaty of Utrecht. To this day, many members of the royal house of the Netherlands are known as the princes and princesses of Orange-Nassau.

◉ Sights

TOP CHOICE Théâtre Antique   ROMAN THEATRE
(www.theatre-antique.com; adult/child €8/6, 2nd child free; ⊙9am-6pm, to 4.30pm Nov-Feb) Orange's Roman theatre is by far the most impressive Roman sight in France. Its sheer size and age are awe-inspiring: designed to seat 10,000 spectators, it's thought to have been built during Augustus Caesar's rule (27 BC–AD 14). The 103m-wide, 37m-high stage wall is one of only three in the world still standing in its entirety (the others are in Syria and Turkey) minus a few mosaics and with a new roof. Admission includes a seven-language audioguide.

The theatre still regularly stages theatrical and musical performances (see opposite). Balmy summer nights in this millennia-old venue are truly magical.

Admission to the theatre includes entry to the museum (museum only adult/child €4.60/3.60) across the road, which has unassuming treasures. These include segments of the Roman survey registers (a precursor to the tax department) and the friezes that formed part of the theatre's scenery.

Follow montée Philbert de Chalons or montée Lambert to the top of Colline St-Eutrope (St Eutrope Hill; elevation 97m) for a bird's-eye view of the theatre, and for phenomenal views of the Mont Ventoux and the Dentelles de Montmirail. En route you pass the ruins of a 12th-century château, the former residence of the princes of Orange.

Arc de Triomphe ROMAN MONUMENT
Orange's 1st-century AD triumphal arch was restored in 2009, revealing exquisite detail: ornate sculptures commemorate the Romans' victories over the Gauls in 49 BC. The 19m-high arch stands at the northern end of tree-lined av de l'Arc de Triomphe, 450m northwest of the town centre.

✴ Festivals & Events

Jazz Festival MUSIC
Swings into town in the last week of June.

Les Chorégies d'Orange PERFORMING ARTS
(www.choregies.asso.fr) July and August, the Théâtre Antique comes alive with all-night concerts, weekend operas, and choral performances. Reserve tickets (€25 to €240) months ahead.

⏽ Sleeping

Hôtel Arène HOTEL €€
(☏04 90 11 40 40; www.bestwestern.fr; place de Langes; d €78-180; ✳@⚹✈🐾) With by far the best and biggest bathrooms in town, the Arène is the closest you'll find to business class in Orange. Despite being part of a chain, it still manages to retain some individuality, and has an entire floor of hypo-allergenic rooms. Kids love the two heated pools (one indoors, one out); parents appreciate the family-size rooms. Request a remodelled room, though the older ones remain very comfortable.

Le Glacier SMALL HOTEL €€
(☏04 90 34 02 01; www.le-glacier.com; 46 cours Aristide Briand; d €49-130; ✳@⚹) All 28 rooms are individually decorated with fresh fabrics, and impeccably maintained by charming owners, who pay attention to detail and keep the place spotless. They also rent bikes (per half-/full day €12/16). Equidistant to the theatre, tourist office and town centre.

Hôtel Saint Jean SMALL HOTEL €
(☏04 90 51 15 56; www.hotelsaint-jean.com; 1 Cours Pourtoules; s €60-70, d €70-85, tr/q €95/110; ✳@⚹🐾) We like the rooms' comfortable proportions and colourful Provençal fabrics at this simple, spiffy hotel, next to the theatre. Extras like free bike storage, soundproof windows and flat-screen TVs add value.

Hôtel l'Herbier d'Orange SMALL HOTEL €
(☏04 90 34 09 23; www.lherbierdorange.com, in French; 8 place aux Herbes; s/d/tr incl breakfast €55/60/70; ✳@⚹🐾) New, friendly owners took over in 2009, installing double-pane windows and new bathrooms in this clean, basic hotel with central location. Evening aperitif included.

Camping Le Jonquier CAMPGROUND €
(☏04 90 34 49 48; www.campinglejonquier.com, in French; 1321 rue Alexis Carrel; 2 people €20-26; ☼Easter-Sep; ⚹✈) Perfect for activity junkies, with pool, minigolf, tennis, ping pong and hot tub. From the Arc de Triomphe walk 100m north, turn left onto rue du Bourbonnais and right again at the second roundabout onto rue Alexis Carrel. Find it 300m on your left.

✗ Eating
Stalls fill the town centre every Thursday for the weekly market. For self-catering, there's a Petit Casino (35 rue St-Martin).

À la Maison BISTRO €
(☏04 90 60 98 83; 4 place des Cordeliers; mains €10-16; ☼Mon-Sat) There's no better spot on a warm night than the leafy fountain courtyard at this simple bistro, which serves consistently good homestyle cooking like grilled fish and steaks, pastas and composed salads.

Le Forum CLASSIC FRENCH €€
(☏04 90 34 01 09; 3 rue Mazeau; menus €19-39; ☼lunch & dinner Tue-Fri & Sun, dinner Sat) The classical dishes, such as beef filet with morel sauce, are well executed, and service is warm and welcoming. Good for a quiet date.

Le Parvis GASTRONOMIC €€
(☏04 90 34 82 00; 55 cours Pourtoules; 2-/3-course menus €23/26; ☼lunch & dinner Tue-Sat, lunch Sun) Nobody speaks above a whisper at Orange's top table, which, despite being a bit stiff, serves excellent food at good value.

Vieux Port

AN ITINERARY

Bold and busy and open-armed to the sea, Marseille is France's oldest city. Standing on the quai des Belges it's hard to get a sense of the extent of the old port, a kilometre long on either side, running down to the great bastions of St-Jean and St-Nicolas, which once had their guns trained on the rebellious population rather than out to sea. Immerse yourself in the city's history with this full-day itinerary.

Go early to experience the fish market **1**, where you'll swap tall tales with the gregarious vendors. Hungry? Grab a balcony seat at La Caravelle, where views of the Basilique Notre Dame de la Garde accompany your morning coffee. Afterwards, take a boat trip **2** to Château d'If, made famous by the Dumas novel, *The Count of Monte Cristo*. Alternatively, stay landside and explore the apricot-coloured alleys of Le Panier **3**, browsing the exhibits at the Centre de la Vieille Charité **4**.

In the afternoon, hop on the free cross-port ferry to the port's south side and wander into the Abbaye St-Victor **5** to see the bones of martyrs enshrined in gold. You can then catch the sunset from the stone benches in the Jardin du Pharo **6**. As the warm southern evening sets in, join the throngs on cours Honoré d'Estienne d'Orves, where you can drink pastis beneath a giant statue of a lion devouring a man – the *Milo de Croton* **7**.

GLENN BEANLAND

Le Panier
The site of the Greek town of Massilia, Le Panier woos walkers with its sloping streets. Grand Rue follows the ancient road and opens out into place de Lenche, the location of the Greek market. It is still the place to shop for artisan products.

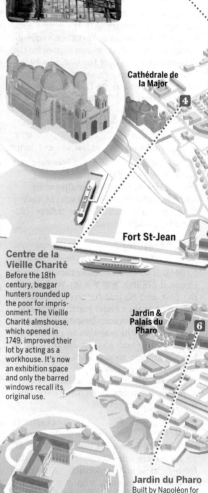

Cathédrale de la Major

4

Fort St-Jean

Centre de la Vieille Charité
Before the 18th century, beggar hunters rounded up the poor for imprisonment. The Vieille Charité almshouse, which opened in 1749, improved their lot by acting as a workhouse. It's now an exhibition space and only the barred windows recall its original use.

Jardin & Palais du Pharo

6

Jardin du Pharo
Built by Napoléon for the Empress Eugénie, the Pharo Palace was designed with its 'feet in the water'. Today it is a private centre, but the gardens with their magnificent view are open all day.

CAPITAL OF CULTURE 2013

The largest urban renewal project in Europe, the Euroméditerranée project aims to rehabilitate the commercial Joliette docks along the same lines as London's Docklands. The city's green-and-white striped Cathédrale de la Major, for years abandoned in an area of urban wasteland, will form its centrepiece.

Fish Market

Marseille's small fish market still sets up each morning to hawk the daily catch. Take a lesson in local seafood, spotting sea squirts, scorpion fish, sea urchins and conger eels. Get there before 9am if you're buying.

Milo de Croton

Subversive local artist Pierre Puget carved the savage *Milo de Croton* for Louis XIV. The statue, whose original is in the Louvre, is a meditation on man's pride and shows the Greek Olympian being devoured by a lion, his Olympic cup cast down.

Frioul If Express

Catch the Frioul If Express to Château d'If, France's equivalent to Alcatraz. Prisoners were housed according to class: the poorest at the bottom in windowless dungeons, the wealthiest in paid-for private cells, with windows and a fireplace.

Rue de la République

La Caravelle →

Quai des Belges

1

2

3

7

Quai du Port

Cross-Port Ferry →

Quai de Rive Neuve

Cours Honoré d'Estienne d'Orves ↑

Bas Fort St-Nicolas

5

Lunch Break

Pick up sandwiches from Jardin des Vestiges, enjoy portside chic at Une Table au Sud, or go for earthy French-Corsican specials at La Cantine.

Abbaye St-Victor

St-Victor was built (420–30) to house the remains of tortured Christian martyrs. On Candlemas (2 February) the black Madonna is brought up from the crypt and the arch-bishop blesses the city and the sea.

TOP EDGE AND/ALAMY

DAN HERRICK

La Roselière
BISTRO €

(3 rue Mazeau; mains €12-15; ⊙Tue-Sat) Bric-a-brac crowds the ceiling while the chef-owner shouts jokes from the kitchen, often at other tables' expense. By your second glass of wine you'll be laughing along, unless you're shy, in which case don't come. Food is simple classics like lentils and sausages. Cash only.

Brasserie Le Palace
BRASSERIE €

(7 rue de la République; mains €10-14; ⊙8am-7.30pm Mon-Sat) Outdoor leather sofas crowd the terrace good for coffee or a *plat du jour*.

ⓘ Information

Post office (679 bd Édouard Daladier) The only place in Orange that changes money.

Tourist office (☑04 90 34 70 88; www.otorange.fr; 5 cours Aristide Briand; ⊙10am-6.30pm, closed Sun Oct-Mar) Hotel bookings.

ⓘ Getting There & Away

BUS Trans Vaucluse (www.cars-lieutaud.fr) buses stop on bd Édouard Daladier, southwest of the post office.

Avignon €3, 45 minutes

Carpentras €2, 45 minutes

Vaison-la-Romaine €3, 45 minutes

TRAIN Train station (www.voyages-sncf.com; av Frédéric Mistral)

Avignon €5.50, 15 minutes

Lyon €27, two hours

Marseille €22, 1½ hours

Vaison-la-Romaine

POP 6392

Nestled in a valley at the crossroads of seven hills, Vaison-la-Romaine has long been a traditional exchange centre: this endures at its thriving Tuesday market. The village's rich Roman legacy is evident: 20th-century buildings jostle for space with the ruins of France's largest archaeological site. A Roman bridge crosses the glinting River Ouvèze, which divides a delightful pedestrianised centre and the walled, cobbled-street Cité Médiévale on the hilltop. Vaison is a good base for jaunts into the Dentelles' villages or an excursion on Mont Ventoux.

⊙ Sights

Gallo-Roman Ruins
ARCHAEOLOGICAL SITE

(adult/child €8/3.50; ⊙closed Jan-early Feb) The ruined remains of Vasio Vocontiorum, the Roman city that flourished here from the 6th to 2nd centuries BC, fill two sites. The Pass, valid for two days, includes an audio-guide and admission to all Roman sites and the cathedral's cloister. From April to September there are free French-only **guided tours** of the sites, as well as thematic tours such as Roman gastronomy. Check the tourist office for schedules.

At Puymin (av du Général de Gaulle; ⊙9.30am-6pm, closed noon-2pm Oct-Mar) see noblemen's houses, mosaics, the still-functioning **Théâtre Antique** (built around AD 20 for an audience of 6000) and an **archaeological museum** with a swag of fine statues, including likenesses of Hadrian and his wife Sabina.

Colonnaded shops, public baths' foundations and a limestone-paved street with an underground sewer are visible at La Villasse (⊙10am-noon & 2.30-6pm), to the west of the same road. **Maison au Dauphin** has splendid marble-lined fish ponds.

Your ticket also includes entry to the peaceful 12th-century Romanesque cloister at Cathédrale Notre-Dame de Nazareth (cloister €1.50; ⊙10am-12.30pm & 2-6pm, closed Jan & Feb), a five-minute walk west of La Villasse. This is also a great spot to take refuge from the summer heat.

Cité Médiévale
MEDIEVAL CITY

Across the pretty Pont Romain (Roman Bridge), cobblestone alleyways known as *calades* carve through the stone walls up to an imposing 12th-century château (guided tours in French €2; ⊙check with tourist office) built by the counts of Toulouse, from where there are bird's-eye views.

🛌 Sleeping

The tourist office has lists of *chambres d'hôte* and self-catering accommodation.

Hôtel Le Burrhus
DESIGN HOTEL €

(☑04 90 36 00 11; www.burrhus.com; 1 place de Montfort; d €55-87, apt €140; 🕾) Right on Vaison's vibrant central square, this might look like a quaint old place from the outside, but inside, its 38 rooms have ultra-modern decor with cutting-edge designer fittings, original artwork and hip mosaic bathrooms. Parking €7.

Hostellerie Le Beffroi
HISTORIC HOTEL €€

(☑04 90 36 04 71; www.le-beffroi.com; rue de l'Évêché; d €90-144; ⊙Apr-Jan; 🕱) Within the medieval city's walls, this 1554-built *hostellerie* fills two buildings (the 'newer' one was built in 1690). A fairy-tale hideaway, its 22 rough-hewn stone-and-wood-beamed rooms are romantically furnished, and its restaurant (menus €28 to €45) tumbles onto a rambling rose-and-herb garden with kids' swings. Parking €10.

L'Évêché   B&B €€

(✆04 90 36 13 46; http://eveche.free.fr; rue de l'Évêché, Cité Médiévale; d €80-135) With its groaning bookshelves, vaulted ceilings, higgledy-piggledy staircase, intimate lounges and exquisite art, this five-room *chambre d'hôte* is absolutely divine. Knowledgeable owners Jean-Loup and Aude lend bikes to explore the area.

Le Moulin de César   FAMILY RESORT €

(✆04 90 36 00 78; www.escapade-vacances. com/vaison; av César Geoffray; d half board per person €43; ☺Mar-Nov) Around 500m southeast of town, this modern family resort is set over peaceful, sprawling grounds on the edge of the river, with views of Mont Ventoux. This being France, half board (obligatory) includes wine. Parking free.

Camping du Théâtre Romain

      CAMPGROUND €

(✆04 90 28 78 66; www.camping-theatre.com; chemin de Brusquet; camping per 2 people €21; ☺mid-Mar–mid-Nov; 🛜🏊) Opposite Théâtre Antique, the site is a little exposed to the Provençal sun but you can cool off in the pool.

✗ Eating

TOP CHOICE **Moulin à Huile**   GASTRONOMIC €€€

(✆04 90 36 20 67; www.moulin-huile. com; quai Maréchal Foch; lunch menu €40, dinner menus €60-75; ☺Tue-Sat, lunch Sun) Michelin-starred Chef Robert Bardot showcases his gastronomic prowess in a former olive-oil mill in the shadow of the Cité Médievale. Sample a cross-section of his creations with the €75 tasting menu, or pick and choose from the handwritten *carte* (bring your eyeglasses). In summer, dine riverside on the outdoor terrace. Make a night of it by booking one of the three handsome guestrooms (€130-150; ❄).

La Lyriste   BISTRO €€

(✆04 90 36 04 67; 45 cours Taulignan; menus €18-36; ☺Wed-Sun) The contemporary Provençal menu at this charming bistro emphasizes seasonal-regional ingredients in dishes ranging from *bourride* (fish stew) to a foie gras tasting *menu* (€36).

Good-value three-course *menu* for €18. In summer book a table on the terrace.

Self-Catering

Wines, honey and nougat are local specialities, but nothing compares to the area's delectable black truffles. They don't come cheap (€500 to €1000 per kg depending on season and rainfall) but a few shavings transform any dish.

A magnificent market, an attraction in its own right, snakes through the central streets Tuesday until 1pm.

ⓘ Information

You can change money at hotels.

Tourist office (✆04 90 36 02 11; www.vaison -la-romaine.com; place du Chanoine Sautel; ☺9am-noon & 2-5.45pm Mon-Sat, 9am-noon Sun, closed Sun mid-Oct–Mar) Inside the Maison du Tourisme et des Vins, just off av du Général de Gaulle.

ⓘ Getting There & Away

The bus station is 400m east of the town centre on ave des Choralies, where **Autocars Lieutaud/Trans Vaucluse** (www.cars-lieutaud. fr) has an office.

Avignon via Orange; €6, 1½ hours

Carpentras €3, 45 minutes

Orange €3, 45 minutes

Mont Ventoux

Visible from miles around, Mont Ventoux (1909m), nicknamed *le géant de Provence* (Provence's giant), stands like a sentinel over northern Provence. From its summit, accessible by road between May and October, vistas extend to the Alps and, on a clear day, the Camargue.

Because of the mountain's dimensions, every European climate type is present on its slopes, from Mediterranean on its lower southern reaches to Arctic on its exposed northern ridge. As you ascend the relentless gradients (which regularly feature in the Tour de France), temperatures can plummet by 20°C, and there's twice as much precipitation as on the plains below. The relentless mistral wind blows 130 days a year, sometimes at a speed of 250km/h. So bring warm clothes and rain gear, even in summer.

This unique and unusual climatic patchwork is reflected in the mountain's hugely diverse fauna and flora, which is now actively protected by Unesco Biosphere Reserve status.

In winter, visitors can take in the joys of snow at the Mont Serein (1445m) ski resort (☎04 90 63 42 02; www.stationdumont serein.com), 5km from Mont Ventoux' summit on the D974. Snow generally melts by April, so the white glimmering stuff you see in summer are *lauzes:* broken white stones.

Piercing the sky to the west of Mont Ventoux are the spectacular limestone pinnacles of another walker's paradise, Dentelles de Montmirail. On the other side of the Dentelles sits the snug village of Beaumes de Venise, home to Frances's finest muscat.

The most common starting point for forays into the Ventoux area is the town of Malaucène, a former summer residence of the Avignon popes.

🏃 Activities

Walking

Running from the River Ardèche east, the GR4 crosses the Dentelles de Montmirail before scaling the northern face of Mont Ventoux, where it meets the GR9. Both trails traverse the ridge before the GR4 branches eastwards to the Gorges du Verdon. Continuing on the GR9 takes you across the Monts du Vaucluse and the Luberon Range. Lonely Planet's *Walking in France* has information on walking in Luberon.

MAPS

Didier-Richard's 1:50,000 map *Massif du Ventoux* includes Mont Ventoux, the Monts du Vaucluse and the Dentelles de Montmirail. More detailed are IGN's Série Bleue 1:25,000 *Mont Ventoux* (ref 3140ET) and *Carpentras/Vaison-la-Romaine/Dentelles de Montmirail* (ref 3040ET).

Area tourist offices also provide dozens of walking itineraries, including the excellent *Randonnées dans les Dentelles* (15 detailed, detachable itineraries in French, English and German; €5).

Cycling

The Mont Ventoux is on par with Alpe d'Huez when it comes to epic, leg-breaking cycling ascents. So before you gingerly hop on your bicycle to tackle an ascent from Bédoin, Malaucène or Sault, know that a 1½ to two-hour trip makes you Tour de France potential, and even cycling half an hour uphill requires serious pedal power. There are plenty of less-demanding options in the area.

Tourist offices distribute *Massif du Mont Ventoux: 9 Itinéraires VTT,* a free booklet detailing nine mountain-bike itineraries ranging from 3.9km (one hour) to a gruelling 56.7km (seven to eight hours). See www.lemontventoux.net/ventoux-anglais. htm for 16 cycling routes around Ventoux.

Rent road bikes/mountain bikes/tandems from €25/15/30 per half-day from Vélo France Locations (☎04 90 67 07 40; www.larouteduventoux.com; rte du Ventoux, Bédoin), Ventoux Bikes (☎04 90 62 58 19; www. ventoux-bikes.fr; 1 ave de Verdun, Malaucène) or Albion Cycles (☎04 90 64 09 32; www.albion cycles.com; rte de St-Trinit, Sault).

ℹ Information

TOURIST INFORMATION

Beaumes de Venise (☎04 90 62 94 39; www. ot-beaumesdevenise.com; place du Marché; ◷9am-noon & 2-7pm Mon-Sat, to 5pm winter) Excellent info on nearby Dentelles and vineyards that sell the region's famous muscat.

Malaucène (☎04 90 65 22 59; place de la Mairie; ◷10am-noon & 3-5pm Mon-Fri, 10am-noon Sat) Info for walkers and cyclists.

Sault (☎04 90 64 01 21; www.saultenprovence .com; av de la Promenade; ◷9am-noon & 2-6pm Mon-Sat)

WEBSITES

Destination Ventoux (www.destination-ventoux.com)

Provence Cycling (www.provence-cycling.com)

Provence des Papes (www.hautvaucluse.com)

ℹ Getting There & Around

Reach Mont Ventoux by car from Sault via the D164; or (summer only) from Malaucène or St-Estève via the D974, often snow-blocked until April.

Carpentras

POP 29,601

Try to visit Carpentras on a Friday morning, when the streets spill over with more than 350 stalls laden with breads, honeys, cheeses, olives, fruit and a rainbow of *berlingots,* Carpentras' striped, pillow-shaped hard-boiled sweets. During winter the pungent truffle market murmurs with hushed-tones transactions. The season is kicked off by Carpentras' biggest fair, held during the Fête de St-Siffrein on 27 November, when more than 1000 stalls spill across town.

Markets aside, this slightly rundown agricultural town has a handful of architectural treats. A Greek trading centre and later a Gallo-Roman city, it became papal territory in 1229, and was also shaped by a strong Jewish presence, as Jews who had been expelled from French crown territory took refuge here. The 14th-century synagogue is the oldest still in use in France.

⊙ Sights

Hidden behind the cathedral, the Arc Romain, built under Augustus in the 1st century AD, is decorated with worn carvings of enslaved Gauls. Carpentras' museums are only open from April to September, from 10am to noon and 2pm to 6pm Wednesday to Monday. Admission is €2.

Synagogue
HISTORIC SYNAGOGUE

(☑04 90 63 39 97; place Juiverie; ⊙10am-noon & 3-5pm Mon-Thu, 10am-noon & 3-4pm Fri) The centre of Jewish life for centuries and still a place of worship today, Carpentras' moving synagogue bears witness to the centuries of persecution that Jewish people have endured. Although Jews were initially welcomed into papal territory, by the 17th century they were forced to live in ghettos established in Avignon, Carpentras, Cavaillon and L'Isle-sur-la-Sorgue. Founded in 1367, the synagogue was rebuilt between 1741 and 1743 and restored in 1929 and 1954. The wood-panelled **prayer hall** holds 18th-century liturgical objects, while the ground floor houses older features such as the ablution basin and bakeries. The tourist office runs **tours** (Tuesday, Wednesday and Thursday, April to September).

Cathédrale St-Siffrein
CATHEDRAL

(⊙7.30am-noon & 2-5pm, no visits during services) Église St-Siffrein, once Carpentras' cathedral, was built in the Méridional (southern French) Gothic style between 1405 and 1519 and is topped by a distinctive contemporary bell tower. Sadly, due to theft, its **Trésor d'Art Sacré** (Treasury of Religious Art), which holds precious 14th- to 19th-century religious relics, is now only available for public viewing during the Fête de St-Siffrein on 27 November.

Musée Comtadin
CULTURAL MUSEUM

(243 bd Albin Durand) Artefacts relating to local history and folklore.

Musée Duplessis
ART MUSEUM

(243 bd Albin Durand) Paintings spanning nine centuries.

Musée Sobirats
DECOR MUSEUM

(112 rue du Collège) Ornate 18th-century residence filled with furniture and objets d'art in the Louis XV and Louis XVI styles.

Hôtel Dieu
HISTORIC HOSPITAL

(place Aristide Briand) The former 18th-century hospital has a well-preserved old-fashioned **pharmacy** and a **chapel**.

🛏 Sleeping & Eating

Hôtel du Fiacre
HOTEL €€

(☑04 90 63 03 15; www.hotel-du-fiacre.com; 153 rue Vigne; d €68-110; ⊙reception 8am-9pm; 🛜) The faded grandeur of this endearing 18th-century mansion grows on you the minute you walk in: everything from the beautiful patio to the canopied beds, grand interior and genuine warmth of its owners will want to make you stay longer. Parking €5.

Hôtel La Lavande
HOTEL €

(☑04 90 63 13 49; 282 bd Alfred Rogier; r €32-70) Well, you sure won't miss the nearly luminescent purple cladding, but thankfully the interior is not as brash, with basic, clean rooms. The restaurant downstairs (mains €7 to €15) serves North African fare as well as traditional, quick lunchtime fixes.

Les Palmiers
BRASSERIE €

(☑04 90 63 12 31; 77 place du Général de Gaulle; mains from €9; ⊙7am-10pm) This cheap and cheerful brasserie is packed to the rafters at lunchtime with colleagues tucking into the €9 *plat du jour* and lapping up their *café gourmand* (an espresso served with miniature desserts) before heading back to work.

La Ciboulette
PROVENÇAL €€

(☑04 90 60 75 00; 30 place de l'Horloge; lunch/dinner menus from €18/24; ⊙Tue-Sun) Fresh local ingredients taste all the better when eaten in the sunshine on the flowered patio. Cinnamon-coloured walls, well-spaced tables and a warm welcome create an easy air. In season, there's a gourmet truffle *menu*; year-round, old favourites are given new life – try the lavender crème brûlée.

Chez Serge
PROVENÇAL €€

(☑04 90 63 21 24; www.chez-serge.com; 90 rue Cottier; lunch/dinner menus €17/35; ⊙lunch Sun-Fri, dinner Mon-Sat) Paris meets Provence when Serge serves up his culinary creations in a charming atmosphere. Good selection of truffle-flavoured dishes.

🛍 Shopping

Friday Market
MARKET

Carpentras' fantastic Friday morning market fills Rue d'Inguimbert and most of av Jean Jaurès (and many side streets).

Truffle Market   MARKET
(place Aristide Briand; ⊘9-10am Fri late Nov-early Mar) In winter brokers, merchants and wholesalers from all over France trade 'black diamonds'.

Chocolats Clavel   SWEETS
(30 Porte d'Orange) Spectacularly sculptured and delicious sweets.

ℹ Information

Tourist office (www.carpentras-ventoux.com; 97 place du 25 Août 1944; ⊘9.30am-12.30pm & 2-6pm Mon-Sat) Excellent website; multilingual guided **tours** (adult/child €4/2.50; ⊘Apr-Sep). Free English-language *Discovery Circuit* brochure explains a *berlingot*-marked walking circuit.

ℹ Getting There & Away

There's no passenger-train service. The **bus station** (place Terradou) is 150m southwest of the tourist office. Schedules are available across the square at **Cars Comtadins** (192 av Clemenceau) and from **Cars Arnaud** (www.voyages-arnaud -carpentras.com, in French; 8 av Victor Hugo).

Avignon €2, 40 minutes

Cavaillon €3, 45 minutes

L'Isle-sur-Sorgue €2, 25 minutes

Marseille €14.50, 2 hours, 2 daily

Vaison-la-Romaine €3, 45 minutes (via **Malaucène**, at the southwest foot of Mont Ventoux. €2, 35 minutes)

Fontaine de Vaucluse

POP 694

France's most powerful spring surges out of nowhere above the pretty little village of Fontaine de Vaucluse. All the rain that falls within 1200 sq km gushes out here as the River Sorgue. The miraculous appearance of this crystal-clear flood draws 1.5 million tourists each year; aim to arrive early in the morning before the trickle of visitors becomes a deluge. It's at its most dazzling after heavy rain, but in drought times the normally surging hole looks like something out of a Harry Potter book, with eerily calm emerald water.

◉ Sights

Most visitors come to see the spring.

Musée d'Histoire 1939-1945   WWII MUSEUM
(☑04 90 20 24 00; chemin de la Fontaine; adult/child €3.50/1.50; ⊘10am-6pm Wed-Mon, Sat & Sun only Mar, Nov & Dec) Excellent examination of life in occupied France during WWII.

Musée Pétrarque   LITERARY MUSEUM
(☑04 90 20 37 20; rive Gauche de la Sorgue; adult/child €3.50/1.50; ⊘10am-12.30pm & 1.30-6pm Wed-Mon, closed Nov-Mar) Devoted to the Italian Renaissance poet Francesco Petrarch, who lived in Fontaine de Vaucluse from 1337 to 1353. He expressed in heartbreaking verse his futile love for Laura, wife of Hugues de Sade.

Ecomusée du Gouffre   CAVING MUSEUM
(☑04 90 20 34 13; chemin de la Fontaine; adult/child €5.50/4; ⊘10am-noon & 2-6pm, closed mid-Nov–Jan) Follow a caving expert along underground tunnels to learn more about Fontaine's spring and the history of caves and caving.

🍴 Sleeping & Eating

Hôtel du Poète   HISTORIC HOTE €€
(☑04 90 20 34 05; www.hoteldupoete.com; r €90-240; ⊘closed Dec–mid-Feb; ❋🤚🏊) Fall asleep to the relaxing sound of rushing water in elegant rooms in a restored mill, stretch out by the pool and ponds, or chill in a jacuzzi that straddles a stream. Find this stunner by the river as you enter the village.

La Figuière   PROVENÇAL €€
(☑04 90 20 37 41; www.la-figuiere.com; chemin de la Grangette; menus €20-28) Savour Provençal dishes (rabbit, sea bass etc) in the lovely front garden, or stay in one of the *chambres d'hôte* in the beautiful stone house.

Auberge de Jeunesse   HOSTEL €
(☑04 90 20 31 65; www.fuaj.org; chemin de la Vignasse; dm incl breakfast & sheets €17.50; ⊘reception 7.30-10am & 5.30-9pm, closed mid-Nov–Jan; 🚲) In a lovely old farmhouse, about 800m

---

WORTH A TRIP

L'ISLE-SUR-LA-SORGUE

A moat of flowing water encircles the ancient and prosperous town of L'Isle-sur-la-Sorgue, 7km west of Fontaine. This 'Venice of Provence' is stuffed to bursting with antique shops: disused mills and factories along the main road contain seven **antiques villages** (⊘10am-6pm Sat-Mon) which house around 300 dealers. For bargains, the giant four-day antiques fairs held in mid-August and over Easter are the best bet.

south of town, this peaceful hostel with a kitchen is popular with families and hikers (it's on the GR6 trail). In summer you can pitch your tent in the garden.

Information

Tourist office (www.oti-delasorgue.fr; place de la Colonne; ◷10am-1pm & 2-6pm)

Getting There & Away

Fontaine de Vaucluse is 21km southeast of Carpentras and 30km west of Apt. **Trans Vaucluse/Voyages Raoux** (www.voyages-raoux.fr, in French) buses operate from Avignon (€3, one hour) via L'Isle-sur-Sorgue.

Parking costs €3.

THE LUBERON

The picture-perfect area that makes up the Luberon takes the shape of a rectangle on a map. But navigating its bucolic rolling hills, golden-hued perched villages and hidden valleys is a bit like fitting together a jigsaw puzzle. The Luberon is named after its main mountain range, which is split in the centre by the Combe de Lourmarin, a beautiful narrow river valley. Luberon's hues, fragrances and flavours subtly transform in tune with the seasons.

The region's capital, Apt, is a central hub for practicalities, but the heart of the Luberon is in the tiny stone villages fanning out across the countryside, which encompasses a 1200-sq-km regional park, the Abbaye de Sénanque and ancient, stone *bories* (dry-walled huts). Luberon is best seen with your own wheels (motorised or leg-powered). **Le Luberon en Vélo** (www.veloloisirluberon.com) trails has a network of 236km signposted routes.

Apt

POP 11,450

Sleepy little Apt comes alive during its Saturday morning market brimming with local specialities, otherwise it's primarily a hub for shopping or practicalities.

Sights

FREE **Confiserie Kerry Aptunion**

SWEETS FACTORY

(☑04 90 76 31 43; rte Nationale 100, quartier Salignan; hshop 9am-12.30pm & 1.30-6.30pm Mon-Sat, tours by reservation) The world's larg-

ℹ️ **COULEUR PASS**

Sold at local tourist offices, the handy Couleur Pass Luberon (€5) gives a discount of up to 50% on entry fees for 16 major tourist sights and activities in the region.

est crystallised-fruits factory: it candies 30 tonnes of cherries a day. It offers a free film, tastings and tours. The factory is 2.5km west of town.

FREE **Fondation Blachère** ART GALLERY
(☑04 32 52 06 15; 384 av des Argiles; ◷2-6.30pm Tue-Sun) Runs a series of interesting art exhibitions.

🛏️ Sleeping

TOP CHOICE **Le Couvent** B&B €€
(☑04 90 04 55 36; www.loucouvent.com, in French; 36 rue Louis Rousset; d €95-120; @ ⊠) Hidden behind a high stone wall and flowering gardens in the town centre, this stunning *maison d'hôte* occupies a 17th-century convent and offers exceptional value: get one of just five sumptuous rooms and breakfast in a vaulted stone dining room.

Hôtel l'Aptois HOTEL €
(☑04 90 74 02 02; www.aptois.fr, in French; 289 cours Lauze de Perret; d €40-66) Cyclist-friendly stylish hotel with good wheelchair access.

Camping Municipal Les Cèdres
CAMPGROUND €
(☑/fax 04 90 74 14 61; www.camping-les-cedres.fr, in French; rte de Rustrel; tent €4.30; ◷mid-Feb–mid-Nov) Back-to-basics riverside campground just out of town.

🍴 Eating

L'Intramuros PROVENÇAL €€
(☑04 90 06 18 87; 120 rue de la République; menus €24-30; ◷Tue-Sat) Beloved by locals for its 'instinctive Provençal' cooking in a 19th-century grocery shop filled with nostalgic bric-a-brac. On Saturday a fresh-as-it-gets market soup bubbles aromatically in its open kitchen.

Les Délices de Léa BISTRO €
(☑04 90 74 32 77; 87 rue de la République; mains €10; ◷Tue-Sat) Aptois frequent this place for Léa's tender green salads and inventive *plats du jour*.

Lavender Trail

Pilgrims come from all over to follow the Routes de la Lavande (www.routes-lavande.com), tracking Provence's aromatic purple bloom. In flower from June to August, it usually hits peak splendour in late July. Cruise the fields, visit mountainside distilleries or scoop up all things lavender at abundant local markets.

Abbaye Notre-Dame de Sénanque

1 Follow the winding D177 north of Gordes to this idyllic 12th-century Cistercian abbey (p808), tucked between hills and surrounded by brilliant fields of lavender. Resident monks tend the crops and stock their shop with monk-made goodies.

Château du Bois

2 Provence is dotted with distilleries, but if you make it to tiny Lagarde d'Apt (p809) you're in for a treat: 80 hectares of Lavande des Alpes de Haute Provence, 'true lavender' (*Lavandula angustifolia*).

Sault

3 The slopes of Mont Ventoux (p801), north of Lagarde d'Apt, make for prime high-altitude lavender. Aim to visit during the Fête de la Lavande (www.saultenprovence.com), usually on 15 August.

Forcalquier

4 Folks come from throughout the region for the booming Monday-morning market in Forcalquier (p812). An embarrassment of riches, the market has venders selling lavender everything, plus mountain honeys, creamy cheeses and handmade sausages.

Plateau de Valensole

5 For sheer heady expansiveness, you can't beat the Plateau de Valensole's carpets of lavender, stretching, dreamlike, as far as the eye can see. Cruise across it on the D6 or D8 east of Manosque, and the A51.

Clockwise from top left
Rows of lavender, Sault; Bunches of lavender for sale at a local market; A carpet of purple blooms, Plateau de Valensole

Thym, te Voilà
BISTRO €

(☑04 90 74 28 25; 59 rue St-Martin; mains €10; ⊙11.30am-6pm Tue-Sat) For a sit-down meal in the town centre.

Sylla
WINE & CHEESE €

(☑04 90 74 95 80; N100; ⊙9am-7pm Mon-Sat) West of Apt, this local winery serves cheese and light meals with its wine.

Le Fournil du Luberon
BAKERY €

(☑04 90 74 20 52; place de la Bouquerie; ⊙7am-7pm Tue-Sat, to 1pm Sun) Apt's best bakery, directly across from the tourist office.

ℹ Information

Maison du Parc (www.parcduluberon.fr, in French; 60 place Jean Jaurès; ⊙8.30am-noon & 1-6pm Mon-Fri, 9am-noon Sat, closed Sat & Sun Oct-Mar) Information on Parc Naturel Régional du Luberon and area history.

Tourist office (☑04 90 74 03 18; www.luberon-apt.fr; 20 av Philippe de Girard; ⊙9.30am-noon & 2.30-6.30pm Mon-Sat, 9.30am-12.30pm Sun) Excellent source for activities, excursions and walks; makes hotel bookings. Sells maps like 1:25,000 IGN (3242OT) Apt/Parc Naturel Régional du Luberon (€9.50).

ℹ Getting There & Away

The **bus station** (250 av de la Libération) is east of the city centre. **Trans Vaucluse** (www.vaucluse.fr, in French) buses go to Aix-en-Provence (€5, two hours), Avignon (€5, 1½ hours), and Cavaillon (€3, 45 minutes, four daily).

North of Apt

GORDES

Forming an amphitheatre over the Rivers Sorgue and Calavon, the tiered village of Gordes sits spectacularly on the white rock face of the Vaucluse plateau. In the early evenings the village is theatrically lit by the setting sun, turning the stone buildings a shimmering gold. Gordes has top billing on many tourists' must-see lists (particularly those of high-profile Parisians) so high season sees a cavalcade of coaches.

⊙ Sights

Village des Bories
STONE HUTS

(☑04 90 72 03 48; adult/child €6/4; ⊙9am-sunset) You'll spot beehive-shaped *bories* while you're buzzing around Provence (1610 have been counted to date), but the Village des Bories, 4km southwest of

Gordes, has loads of them. Reminiscent of Ireland's clochàn, these dry-walled huts constructed from slivers of limestone were first built in the area in the Bronze Age. Their original purpose isn't known, but over time they've been used as homes, workshops, wine cellars and silkworm huts. This 'village' contains about 20 *bories*, best visited early in the morning or just before sunset for the interplay of light and shadow.

Abbaye Notre-Dame de Sénanque
ABBEY

(☑04 90 72 05 72; guided tour in French adult/child €7/3; ⊙tours by reservation) Framed by fields of lavender in July, this picture-postcard Cistercian abbey, 4km northwest of Gordes off the D177, sits in a magical valley. The abbey was founded in 1148 and is inhabited by a few monks who celebrate mass at noon, Tuesday to Saturday, and 10am Sunday. A 1½-hour walk will get you to or from Gordes.

🛏 Sleeping & Eating

TOP CHOICE **Le Mas de la Beaume**
B&B €€

(☑04 90 72 02 96; www.labeaume.com; at entrance Gordes village; d €125-150; 🖳) Behind a stone wall, this impeccable five-room *maison d'hôte* is the pride and joy of hosts Wendy and Miguel. The 'blue room' has views of Gordes' château and bell tower from the bed. Home-grown produce from the garden arrives on your plate at breakfast.

Le Mas Regalade
B&B €€

(☑04 90 76 90 79; www.masregalade-luberon.com; D2, quartier de la Sénancole, Les Imberts; d from €110; 🗑🖳) Conscientious owner Stefane has artfully decorated rooms with both modern touches and charming antiques. The artefacts spread poolside too, where a vintage Citroën peeks out from hedgerows of lavender and rosemary. Located 3.5km south of Gordes.

Le Mas Tourteron
GASTRONOMIC €€€

(☑04 90 72 00 16; chemin de St-Blaise, Les Imberts; www.mastourteron.com; menus from €45) Dining at the lilac-clothed tables in the stone dining room or amid the flourishing gardens of chef Elisabeth Bourgeois-Baique and her sommelier husband Philippe's welcoming farmhouse is like eating at the home of friends. Elisabeth's seasonally changing menus and her legendary desserts marry with wines hand-picked by Philippe from over 200 vintages. Find it

3.5km south of Gordes, signposted off the D2. Check website for hours.

ℹ Information

Tourist office (☑04 90 72 02 75; www.gordes -village.com; place du Château; ☺9am-noon & 2-6pm)

ROUSSILLON

Some two millennia ago, the Romans used the ochreous earth around the spectacular village of Roussillon, set in the valley between the Plateau de Vaucluse and the Luberon range, for producing pottery glazes. These days the whole village, even gravestones in the cemetery, is built of the reddish stone.

From the town, take a 45-minute walk along the Sentier des Ocres (Ochre Trail; adult/child €2.50/free; ☺9am-7.30pm Jul & Aug, to 5pm Mar-11 Nov). Within fairy-tale groves of chestnuts, maritime pines and scrub, the trail leads you through a stunning sunset-coloured paint palette of ochre formations.

Conservatoire des Ocres et de la Couleur (Ochre & Colour Conservatory; ☑04 90 05 66 69; www.okhra.com, in French; rte d'Apt; guided tours adult/child €6/4; ☺9am-7pm, Wed-Sun only Sep-Jun) is a unique nonprofit organisation celebrating everything about colour, in a conscientious, sustainable way. Located in an old ochre factory on the D104 east towards Apt, it holds workshops (some in English), explores the properties of ochre, and has a fantastic shop.

In Gargas, 7km east of Roussillon, Europe's last remaining ochre quarry Les Mines d'Ocre de Broux (☑04 90 06 22 59; admission €7.50; ☺10am-7pm) produces around 1000 tonnes a year, 45% of which is exported. The parts of the 45km of mines that are open to the public seem like a serene mineral church of spires.

The friendly owner of Les Passiflores (☑04 90 71 43 08; www.passiflores.fr; Hameau des Huguets; d incl breakfast from €70; ✸) welcomes you into this quiet *chambre d'hôte*, tucked into a back square in the tiny hamlet of Huguets, south of Roussillon. Tidy rooms have king-sized beds with floral quilts. The pool is a natural one, with plants in it.

Eat under the willow trees at unpretentious working *ferme auberge* Les Grands Camps (☑04 90 74 67 33; Le Chêne; menus adult/child incl wine & coffee €26/13; ☺lunch Sun, dinner Mon, Wed, Fri & Sat Jul & Aug, lunch Sun, dinner Fri & Sat Sep-Jun). Not far from Gargas' ochre quarry, it serves up heaping feasts of

farm-fresh duck, lamb and the like. Take the signposted dirt road north from the hamlet Le Chêne.

For more information about the area, visit the **Tourist office** (☑04 90 05 60 25; www. roussillon-provence.com, in French; place de la Poste; ☺10am-noon & 1.30-5pm Mon-Sat)

ST-SATURNIN-LÈS-APT & AROUND

Enjoy rooftop views of St-Saturnin-lès-Apt, 9km north of Apt, and the surrounding Vaucluse hilltops by climbing to the ruins atop the village or from the 17th-century windmill, 1km north of the village off the D943 to Sault. Lunch at the welcoming Le Restaurant L'Estrade (☑04 90 71 15 75; 6 av Victor Hugo; menus from €13; ☺lunch), run by friendly women who prepare a seasonal menu.

In Lagarde d'Apt, 20km northeast of Apt, volunteers at the Observatoire Sirene (☑04 90 75 04 17; www.obs-sirene.com, in French; day/night/child €10/40/free; ☺by reservation) teach you about astronomy amid the lavender fields by day; but the best time to visit is during an all-night star-gazing session.

Lagarde d'Apt is also home to a 800,000-sq-metre lavender farm, Château du Bois (☑04 90 76 91 23; www.lechateaudu bois.com), where a 2km-long lavender trail blazes from late June until mid-July when the sweet-smelling flower is harvested.

TOP CHOICE Domaine des Andéols (☑04 90 75 50 63; www.domainedesandeols. com; D2, 2km west of St-Saturnin-lès-Apt; ste €260-770; ☺Apr-Nov; ✸@✸), Alain Ducasse's ode to design, sits in a velvet-green valley with views from the infinity pool to russet promontories. Individual houses are decorated down to the last cutting-edge detail. Or head to the restaurant (menus €39 to €59): on summer nights candlelit tables cluster beneath stars.

TOP CHOICE Colorado Provençal (☑04 32 52 09 75; ☺9am-dusk), on the eastern side of the Luberon, is a savage landscape of red-ochre sand with extraordinary rock formations like the fiery upright Cheminée de Fée (Fairy Chimney).

Near Rustrel, deep within the Colorado, and bordered by forest, La Forge (☑04 90 04 92 22; www.laforge.com.fr; Notre-Dame des Anges; d incl breakfast €86-199; ☺✸) is an 1840-built former iron foundry that has been transformed into an incredible *maison d'hôte*. No credit cards.

TOP CHOICE La Table de Pablo (☑04 90 75 45 18; www.latabledepablo.com; Hameau

Les Petits Cléments; lunch/dinner menus from €16/28; ⊘closed Wed, lunch Thu & Sat), near Villars, is home to young chef Thomas Gallardo. On the heels of his first Michelin mention, he wows with inventive gastronomic creations such as a delectable maize soup with chestnuts and tasso, or a frappé of soft, white cheese. He has created a comfortable, modern dining room decorated with local art and it is well worth the excursion through the rolling cherry orchards. Gallardo also offers cooking courses.

South of Apt

South of the N100, the deep Combe de Lourmarin carves a north–south divide through the Luberon massif. Le Petit Luberon (Little Luberon) sits on the western side and its rocky landscape is sprinkled with cake-decoration-like villages *perchés* (perched villages) overlooking thick cedar forests and Côtes du Luberon vineyards. To its east, Le Grand Luberon takes in dramatic gorges, grand fortresses and lavender fields.

◉ Sights & Activities

Highlights include Bonnieux, which burst onto cinema screens in *A Good Year* (2006) as the village where Russell Crowe's character Max Skinner, a British financier, finds *joie de vivre* in the vineyards of Provence.

Lacoste harbours the 9th-century Château de Lacoste, where the notorious Marquis de Sade (1740–1814) retreated when his writings became too scandalous for Paris. The erotic novels penned by the marquis (who gave rise to the term 'sadism') were only freely published after WWII. The 45-room palace remained an eerie ruin until transformed by couturier Pierre Cardin into a 1000-seat theatre and opera stage hosting July's month-long Festival de Lacoste (www.festivaldelacoste.com).

Scaling the steep streets to Ménerbes, moored on a hilltop, rewards you with uninterrupted views. The maze of streets conceals a 12th-century village church and the fabulous Maison de la Truffe et du Vin (☑04 90 72 52 10; www.vin-truffe-luberon.com; place de l'Horloge; ⊘10am-12.30pm & 2-5pm Thu-Sat, daily Jul & Aug), where the Brotherhood of Truffles and Wine of Luberon represents 60 domaines and sells their wines at rock-bottom prices. In July and August it organises two-hour wine-tasting sessions (€20) and truffle workshops (€95).

Ménerbes captured the attention of millions when it was memorably rendered by British author Peter Mayle. The lavishly detailed books *A Year in Provence* and *Toujours Provence* recount renovating a *mas* just outside the village in the late 1980s. Mayle subsequently sold up and moved abroad, though the Luberon's charm has lured him back to Lourmarin. His former home, 2km southeast of Ménerbes on the D3 to Bonnieux, is the second house on the right after the football pitch.

Oppède-le-Vieux, a medieval hilltop village 6km southwest of Ménerbes, was abandoned in 1910 by villagers who moved down the valley to the cultivated plains to earn their living. Today, a handful of artists (population 20) lives here among the cool ruins. The Sentier Vigneron d'Oppède, a 1½-hour winegrowers' trail, winds through olive groves, cherry orchards and vineyards.

Purple lavender carpets the Plateau de Claparèdes area between Buoux (west), Sivergues (south), Auribeau (east) and picture-postcard Saignon (north). Cycle, walk or motor through the lavender fields and along the northern slopes of Mourre Nègre (1125m). Stop for views of gorgeous Saignon before you wander its streets.

At the base of the Combe de Lourmarin and, unlike many of the Luberon's precarious hilltop townships, easily accessed, the alluring village of Lourmarin makes for a lovely stroll with its charming streets, cafés and a lively Friday morning market.

🛏 Sleeping

Le Clos du Buis   HOTEL B&B €€

(☑04 90 75 88 48; www.leclosdubuis.fr; rue Victor Hugo, Bonnieux; d €84-112, cottages per week from €300; ⊘mid-Feb–mid-Nov; ✳🏤🐶) Smack-dab in the village, this stone town house spills out to a vast garden. The dining room serves up panoramic views along with *tables d'hôtes* (set menus at a fixed price; by reservation), and there's a self-catering kitchen. One room is wheelchair accessible.

TOP CHOICE Auberge de Presbytère

     HISTORIC HOTEL €€

(☑04 90 74 11 50; www.auberge-presbytere.com; place de la Fontaine, Saignon; d €85-145; ⊘closed mid-Jan–mid-Feb) In the 11th and 12th centuries it was three presbyteries. Now it is a village inn with beautiful wood-beamed rooms and an enticing terrace restaurant (menus €26 to €35) overlooking the village fountain. Try to get a room with views of the ruins and valley in the rear.

La Magnanerie
B&B €€

(☎04 90 72 42 88; www.magnanerie.com; rte de Bonnieux, Lieu-dit le Roucas, Ménerbes; d €95; ⊗mid-Mar–mid-Nov & mid-Dec–early Jan; 🖥🗷) At this welcoming *maison d'hôte* in the serene, misty hills enjoy one of six stylish rooms and homemade jams and cobblers at breakfast. Guests can barbecue in the summer kitchen. Find it 200m down a lane, signposted off the D103. No credit cards.

Le Mas de Foncaudette
B&B €€

(☎04 90 08 42 51; www.foncaudette.com; signposted off the D27 btwn Lourmarin & Puyvert; d €110; 🖥🗷🖶) Perfect colourful rooms, and some suites ideal for families, surround a fig-tree-shaded central courtyard. Sweeping grounds enjoy views of the valley.

Chambre de Séjour avec Vue
B&B €€

(☎04 90 04 85 01; www.chambreavecvue.com, in French; Saignon; d/studio €80/100) Husband and wife artists Kamila Regent and Pierre Jaccaud are the creative force behind this amazing 16th-century village house turned *chambre d'hôte*–art studio.

✕ Eating

TOP CHOICE Véranda
MODERN FRENCH €€

(☎04 90 72 33 33; 104 av Marcellin Poncet, Ménerbes; lunch mains €10-13, dinner menus €38; ⊗lunch Tue-Sun, dinner Tue-Sat) Well-travelled chef Laurent Jouin is doing impressive things in the kitchen of his excellent establishment high up in the village, with views overlooking the valley. Effortlessly elegant, the magnificent meals are built from seasonal fresh fruit and vegetables. The smoked salmon ravioli is to die for.

TOP CHOICE Ferme Auberge Le Castelas
FARM MEAL €€

(Chez Gianni; ☎04 90 74 60 89; Sivergues; menus incl wine €25-30; ⊗by reservation only Mar-Dec) Well off any track, beaten or not, this farm welcomes celebs such as Catherine Deneuve, who drop in via helicopter to pass around heaping platters at long, shared timber tables. Fresh-from-the-farm feasts include bite-sized toast topped with *tomme* (a mild cows'-milk cheese) and whole, roasted pigs.

Auberge La Fenière
GASTRONOMIC, HOTEL €€€

(☎04 90 68 11 79; www.reinesammut.com; rte de Cadenet; 🖥🗷) Visit this restored old post office, 3km south of Lourmarin, for an excellent meal or an idyllic night's stay (single/double from €150/180). This is the exquisite domain of Michelin-starred Reine Sammut, who tends her own kitchen garden to supply her outstanding restaurant (lunch/dinner menus from €46/80) and her simpler, but equally wonderful bistro (menus from €35).

La Bastide de Capelongue
GASTRONOMIC, HOTEL €€€

(☎04 90 75 89 78; www.capelongue.com; lunch/dinner menus from €70/120; ⊗closed mid-Nov–mid-Mar) High above Bonnieux sits the bastion of wunderkind chef Édouard Loubet, who moved here with his two Michelin stars from Le Moulin de Lourmarin. The hotel (doubles from €160) is impeccably decorated by Édouard's mother, and his grandmother is the inspiration for many of his renowned recipes.

Café du Progrès
CAFÉ €

(☎04 90 72 22 09; place Albert Roure, Ménerbes; menus €13-16; ⊗lunch, bar 6am-midnight) This tobacconist-newsagent-bar, run by good-humoured Patrick, hasn't changed much since it opened a century ago. This utterly authentic spot is great for a lunch stop and taking in a spectacular sweep of the countryside.

Auberge de l'Aiguebrun
INN, BISTRO €€€

(☎04 90 04 47 00; www.aubergedelaiguebrun. fr; d €175-205; 🖶🗷) Dine at stone tables on a cobbled terrace with riverside views (lunch/dinner *menu* €27/45), and stroll through gardens graced with peacocks, a greenhouse and dovecote. The inn is hidden in the dramatic heart of the Combe de Lourmarin, 6km southeast of Bonnieux off the D943.

L'Art Glacier
ICE CREAMERY €

(☎04 90 77 75 72; Les Hautes Terres hamlet; ⊗vary) Go further afield to find ice cream that's an art. Michel and Sigrid Perrière handcraft mind-boggling varieties of the sweet stuff: from lavender to sesame to cassis. The ice-creamery sits between Ansouis and La Tour d'Aigues on a hilltop off the D9 (look for the signs posted on roundabouts) and has views all around.

NORTHEASTERN PROVENCE

Haute-Provence's heady mountain ranges arc across the top of the Côte d'Azur to the Italian border, creating a far-flung crown of snowy peaks and precipitous valleys.

To the west, a string of sweet, untouristy hilltop villages and lavender fields drape the Vallée de la Durance. Magical Moustiers Ste-Marie is a gateway to the plunging white waters of Europe's largest canyon, the Gorges du Verdon. In the east, the 'valley of wonders' wows with 36,000 Bronze Age rock carvings. In the far north are the winter ski slopes and summer mountain retreats of the Ubaye and Blanche Valleys. Outside of ski areas, many establishments close in winter.

Vallée de la Durance

At the western edge of Haute-Provence, the winding waters of the 324km-long River Durance, an affluent of the Rhône, follow the Via Domitia, the road from Italy that allowed the Romans to infiltrate the whole of France.

◉ Sights & Activities

Highlights of the region include Pays de Forcalquier, delightfully off mass-tourism's radar, which shelters sweet hilltop villages and wildflower-strewn countryside. At its heart, the eponymous town, Forcalquier, sits atop a rocky perch and its fantastic Monday market draws locals from throughout the region. Steep steps lead to its gold-topped citadel and octagonal chapel, where carillon concerts are held most Sundays from 11.30am to 12.30pm. On the way up, peruse the local artists' workshops packed with pottery and furniture.

There are few more peaceful places in Provence than the 13th-century Prieuré de Salagon (☑04 92 75 70 50; www.musee -de-salagon.com, in French; adult/child €6/3.60; ☺10am-7.30pm, 2-5pm Oct & Feb-Apr, 2-5pm Sun Nov & Dec, closed Jan), 4km south of Forcalquier outside the walled city of Mane. Tour excellent gardens or see concerts and exhibitions in the restored priory.

In St-Michel l'Observatoire, a stroll up to the hilltop overlook passes along winding walkways and tiny ateliers. After the 12th-century Église Haute, arrive at a 360-degree view from the Luberon to the Alps. Or visit the nearby Observatoire de Haute-Provence (☑04 92 70 64 00; www. obs-hp.fr, in French; adult/child €2.50/1.50), a national research centre. Buy tickets for the 30-minute guided tour from the ticket office in St-Michel's village square.

TOP CHOICE Prieuré de Ganagobie (☑04 92 68 00 04; ☺3-5pm Tue-Sun), 10km south of Les Mées, offers the chance to stroll the quiet hilltop grounds and soak up the ethereal magic of this 10th-century working Benedictine monastery. The chapel is the only enclosed section of the monastery open to visitors. Its exquisite 12th-century floor mosaic is the largest of its kind in France. The shop stocks handmade soaps, honeys and the like, all made by the monks, and houses a small collection of artefacts found on-site.

The stunner in Sisteron is its spectacular citadel, an imposing 3rd- to 16th-century fortress perched on a rock above a transverse valley. The town itself has a lived-in feeling and there's not a whiff of the tourist trap. The tourist office conducts 1¼-hour walking tours (€1) and open-air classical-music concerts are held during the Festival des Nuits de la Citadelle from mid-July to mid-August.

🛏 Sleeping & Eating

TOP CHOICE **Le Vieil Aiglun** B&B €€
(☑04 92 34 67 00; www.vieil-aiglun.com; outside Aiglun; s/d €65/85; ▨) Retreat to a magical hilltop enclave in a painstakingly restored Celtic village. An old church, dating from 1555, still sits behind this one-of-a-kind gorgeous *chambre d'hôte,* where every detail is looked after. Located 11km southwest of Digne-les-Bains.

Mas Saint-Joseph B&B €€
(☑04 92 62 47 54; www.lemassaintjoseph.com; Châteauneuf-Val-St-Donat; d/q from €54/92; ☺Apr-Oct; ▨ ▥) Location, location, location: this converted farmhouse overlooks a sweeping valley, and is surrounded by layers of terraces and flower beds. Historic wood accents stand in beautiful contrast to serene whitewashed rooms. Amenities include jacuzzi and shared kitchen space. On the D951 to Sisteron.

Auberge La Bannette
B&B, TRADITIONAL FRENCH €
(☑04 92 34 68 88; www.aubergelabannette.com, in French; s/d from €48/53) The friendly Wisner family runs this farmstead overlooking Thoard village. Rustic cabins sit beneath star-strewn skies, and the nightly meal is like a feast from the middle ages (*menu* for guests €20).

La Magnanerie HOTEL, GASTRONOMIC €€
(☎04 92 62 60 11; www.la-magnanerie.net; N85; menus €17-50; ☺lunch & dinner) Relax in the understatedly elegant dining room of this recent Logis de France award-winner, 1km north of Château-Arnoux St-Auban. Magnificently presented dishes include duck cooked to perfection with a drizzle of raspberry reduction. Stylish rooms start at €59.

Restaurant La Marmite du Pêcheur

GASTRONOMIC €€
(☎04 92 34 35 56; Les Mées; menus €20-56; ☺lunch & dinner Thu-Mon) Chef Christophe Roldan prepares decadent multicourse menus rich in foie gras and tender, slow-cooked lamb.

❶ Information

Forcalquier tourist office (☎04 92 75 10 02; www.forcalquier.com; 13 place du Bourguet; ☺9am-noon & 2-6pm Mon-Sat)

Gorges du Verdon

Under the protection of the Parc Naturel Régional du Verdon since 1997, Europe's largest canyon, the plunging Gorges du Verdon, slices a 25km swathe through Provence's limestone plateau.

The main gorge begins at Rougon near the confluence of the Verdon and the Jabron Rivers, and then winds westwards until the Verdon's green waters flow into Lac de Ste-Croix. At a dizzying 250m to 700m deep, the gorge's floors are just 8m to 90m wide, and its overhanging rims are from 200m to 1500m apart. The two main jumping-off points for exploring the gorges are the villages of Moustiers Ste-Marie in the west and Castellane, east of Rougon.

◉ Sights

The deep floors are only accessible by foot or raft. Motorists, horse riders and cyclists take in staggering panoramas from two vertigo-inducing cliffside roads. In Castellane, Chapelle Notre Dame du Roc is perched spectacularly above town on a needlelike rock.

Dubbed the Etoile de Provence (Star of Provence), the charming little village Moustiers Ste-Marie (population 635, elevation 634m) makes a fair claim to the title. Tucked between two limestone cliffs, it overlooks open fields and far-off mountains. A 227m-long gold chain bearing a shining star is suspended over the town, so legend claims, by the Knight of Blacas, grateful to have returned safely from the Crusades. Beneath the star, clinging to a cliff ledge, 14th-century Chapelle Notre Dame de Beauvoir (tours adult/child €3/free; ☺tours 10am Tue & Thu Jul-Aug) is built on the site of an AD 470 temple. Moustiers is also known for its decorative **faience** (earthenware pottery); 15 ateliers display their own styles.

✦ Activities

Cycling & Driving

The Route des Crêtes (D952 & D23; ☺closed Nov-Feb) corkscrews along the northern rim, past Point Sublime, which offers a fisheye-lens view of serrated rock formations falling away to the river below. The best view from the northern side is from Belvédère de l'Escalès.

Also heart-palpitating, La Corniche Sublime (the D955 to the D71 to the D19) twists along the southern rim, taking in landmarks such as the Balcons de la Mescla (Mescla Terraces) and Pont de l'Artuby (Artuby Bridge), the highest bridge in Europe.

A complete circuit of the Gorges du Verdon via Moustiers Ste-Marie involves about 140km of relentless hairpin-turn driving. Tourist offices have driving itineraries. The only village en route is La Palud-sur-Verdon (930m). In winter, roads get icy or snowy; watch for falling rocks year-round; and heaven forbid that you get stuck behind a caravan in summer – opportunities to pass are rare.

Walking

You can walk most of the canyon along the often-difficult GR4, a route covered by IGN map 3442OT, 1:25,000 *Gorges du Verdon*. The full route takes two days, though short descents into the canyon are possible. Bring a torch (flashlight) and drinking water. Camping on gravel beaches is illegal; waters rise quickly and sweep things away. Check with tourist offices before embarking.

In addition to canyon descents, dozens of blazed trails fan out from Castellane and Moustiers through untamed countryside. The excellent English-language *Canyon du Verdon* (€4.20), available at the tourist offices, lists 28 walks in the gorges and the *Canyon du Verdon* map shows five.

Outdoor Sports

Castellane's and Moustiers' tourist offices have complete lists of companies offering rafting, canyoning, horse riding, mountaineering, biking and more. The newest thrill-seeking pursuit is **floating**: river-running with only a buoyancy bag strapped to your back.

Castellane is the main base for watersports companies; all offer similarly priced trips (April to September, by reservation). Families should bear in mind that many activities are unsuitable for children under eight.

Guides Aventure   OUTDOOR SPORTS
(☎06 85 94 46 61; www.guidesaventure.com) Canyoning (€45/70 per half-/full day), rock climbing, rafting (€55/75) and 'floating' (€50/90).

Latitude Challenge   BUNGEE JUMPING
(☎04 91 09 04 10; www.latitude-challenge.fr, in French; €105) Adrenaline-seekers throw themselves off the 182m Artuby Bridge.

Aboard Rafting   WATER SPORTS
(☎/fax 04 92 83 76 11; www.aboard-rafting.com; place de l'Église, Castellane) White-water rafting and canyoning trips.

🛏 Sleeping & Eating
CASTELLANE & AROUND
The nearby river is lined with seasonal camping areas. Hotels and restaurants cluster around the central square, place Marcel Sauvaire and place de l'Église.

Gîte de Chasteuil   B&B €
(☎04 92 83 72 45; www.gitedechasteuil.com; Hameau de Chasteuil; s/d/tr from €56/66/84) This irresistible *chambre d'hôte* in an old schoolhouse in the 16th-century hamlet of Chasteuil has fantastic views to the mountains 12km west of Castellane. Impeccable rooms with crisp linens are a perfect stop for walkers on the GR4, which passes right outside.

Domaine de Chasteuil Provence
CAMPGROUND €
(☎04 92 83 61 21; www.chasteuil-provence.com; camping per site €14.50-25; ☺May-Sep; 🐾🏊) Lovely, leafy grounds, optional powered sites, and timber chalets (from €105 for two nights for four people). Just south of Castellane.

Nouvel Hôtel Restaurant du Commerce
HOTEL, PROVENÇAL €€
(☎04 92 83 61 00; www.hotel-fradet.com; place de l'Église; s/d €75/95; ☺Mar-Oct; 🕸@🛜)

Exceptionally friendly spot opens to a large garden. Best known for its 'rustic-gastronomic' restaurant (menus €22-28), serving Provençal favourites.

Auberge du Teillon   PROVENÇAL €€
(☎04 92 83 60 88; D4805 to Grasse; menus €22-34; ☺lunch Tue-Sun, dinner Tue-Sat, closed mid-Nov–mid-Mar) Locals flock 5km east of Castellane to La Garde for the area's best eats: housemade pâté or tender-roasted pigeon.

MOUSTIERS & AROUND

TOP CHOICE Le Petit Ségriès   B&B €
(☎04 92 74 68 83; www.gite-segries.fr; s/d from €50/60) Friendly hosts Sylvie and Noël maintain six French-washed rooms and have lively *tables d'hôte* (€21 including wine) at a massive chestnut table with farm-fresh lamb, rabbit and mountain honey. Rent bikes (per half-day €19) or sign up for a bike tour (from €65).

La Bastide de Moustiers
LUXURY HOTEL, GASTRONOMIC €€€
(☎04 92 70 47 47; www.bastide-moustiers.com; d from €240, menus €55-75; 🕸🏊) This exquisite Provençal nest belonging to legendary chef Alain Ducasse is known up and down the country for its very fine cuisine – hence the helicopter pad in the garden. Rooms are equally sophisticated and breakfast is served on a shaded terrace while baby deer scamper on the grounds.

La Ferme Rose   COUNTRY HOTEL €€
(☎04 92 75 75 75; www.lafermerose.com; chemin de Quinson; d €78-148; 🕸🛜) This fabulous converted farmhouse contains quirky collections including a Wurlitzer jukebox and a display case of coffee grinders. Its dozen boutique rooms draped with embroidered canopies are named for the colour dramatising each chic sleeping area. Off the D952, 1km from Moustiers.

Le Petit Lac   CAMPGROUND €
(☎04 92 74 67 11; www.lepetitlac.com; rte du lac de Ste-Croix; tent per 2 people €14-22, eco-cabins per week from €229; ☺camping mid-Jun–Sep, cabins Apr–mid-Oct; 🏊) In a peaceful lakeside spot, this activity-oriented campground has great eco-cabins (two-night minimum) with hemp walls, solar hot water and low-output electricity.

TOP CHOICE La Ferme Ste-Cécile GASTRONOMIC €€
(☎04 92 74 64 18; D952, quartier St-Michel; menus €26-35; ☺lunch & dinner Tue-Sun,

closed mid-Nov–Dec) Seek out one of Haute-Provence's best meals. Among the delicious culinary surprises served on the terrace of this authentic *ferme auberge* find the thinnest slice of Roquefort and pear warmed in filo pastry, or foie gras wrapped in sweet quince. Everything on the menu is seasonal, such as the exquisite crème brûlée with fresh truffles!

Les Comtes   ECLECTIC CONTINENTAL **€€**
(☑04 92 74 63 88; rue de la Bourgade; mains €16-28; ⊙lunch Tue-Sun, dinner Tue-Sat, closed Nov-Feb) Laidback meals start with a mountain fruit aperitif. Follow up with dishes like squid-ink tagliatelle with saffron. In summer dine in the sunshine, in winter the mosaic-covered dining room.

ⓘ Information

TOURIST INFORMATION

Castellane (www.castellane.org; rue Nationale; ⊙9am-1pm & 2-7pm Jul & Aug, 9.15am-noon & 2-6pm Mon-Fri Sep-Jun)
Moustiers Ste-Marie (☑04 92 74 67 84; www.moustiers.fr; ⊙daily, hr vary) Tip-top tourist office with resourceful staff and excellent documentation for exploring the area.

ⓘ Getting There & Around

Public transport to, from and around the Gorges du Verdon is limited. The Moustiers tourist-office website provides current schedules.

Daily in July and August, and at weekends from April to September, the Navettes des Gorges shuttlebuses (€7) link Castellane with Point Sublime, La Palud, La Maline and Moustiers. Tourist offices have schedules and bike-hire information.

Parc National du Mercantour

Deeply isolated and breathtakingly beautiful, the Parc National du Mercantour (www.mercantour.eu) is one of the last bastions of true wilderness in France. The terrain is mountainous but the sunshine (in excess of 300 days a year) is definitely Provençal. The park spreads across six valleys (Ubaye, Haut Verdon, Haut Var, Tinée, Vésubie and Roya-Béréva).

VALLÉE DE L'UBAYE

Vallée de l'Ubaye is ringed by a rollercoaster of rugged mountains. The valley's only town, Barcelonnette (elevation 1135m), has a fascinating Mexican heritage, resulting in some exceptional, very un-Alpine architecture. From the 18th century until WWII, some 5000 Barcelonnettais emigrated to Mexico to seek their fortunes in the silk- and wool-weaving industries, building mansions throughout the town upon their return.

Rising 8.5km southwest, the twin ski resorts of Pra Loup 1500 (sometimes called Les Molanes) and Pra Loup 1600 (which has more infrastructure and nightlife) are connected by a lift system with the ski resort La Foux d'Allos. Pra Loup's 50 lifts are between 1600m and 2600m, with 180km of runs and a vertical drop of almost 1000m. In summer it's a hiker's and mountain biker's heaven. Outfitters in Le Martinet rent mountain bikes and arrange guided rides.

PROVENCE PARC NATIONAL DU MERCANTOUR

WORTH A TRIP

VALLÉE DE LA BLANCHE & LAC DE SERRE-PONÇON

Remote and sparsely populated, the beautiful Vallée de la Blanche (www.valleedelablanche.com) is an unspoilt haven. The main 'resort' (although it's so tiny that it seems funny to call it a resort) is the 1350m St-Jean Montclar. It's particularly great for families, with skiing in winter and trekking galore in summer. The tourist office (☑04 92 30 92 01; www.montclar.com) has plenty of info.

Straddling the Haute-Provence–Hautes-Alpes border, Europe's largest manmade lake, Lac de Serre-Ponçon, sits high in the mountains and flows into Ubaye Valley. The lake district's main town, Embrun (elevation 870m), was the Roman capital of the Alps and later a bishopric. Its enchanting tangle of cobblestone streets lead to the dramatic black-and-white stone cathedral. In town, pack a lakeside picnic from the farm produce at La Ferme Embrunaise (☑04 92 43 01 98; place Barthelon) and the chocolatier-pâtisserie of Luc Eyriey (☑04 92 43 01 37; place Barthelon).

Hidden deep in the forest, 3km uphill from the lake's eastern bank, is the beautiful 12th-century Abbaye de Boscodon (☑04 92 43 14 45; Crots; admission €3.50; ⊙8.30am-7pm Mon-Sat, 12.15-7pm Sun).

Pra Loup's tourist office (☑04 92 84 10 04; www.praloup.com; ☺9am-noon & 2-5pm May-Nov, 9am-7pm Dec-Apr) has lists of accommodation. Free shuttles operate between Barcelonnette and Pra Loup.

VALLÉE DE LA VÉSUBIE

A dead-end valley accessed from the south, Vésubie is often referred to as 'Nice's Switzerland' due to its proximity to the Côte d'Azur. In St-Martin-Vésubie, Escapade Bureau des Guides (☑04 93 03 31 32; www.guidescapade.com; place du Marché; ☺Jul & Aug) organises guided walks, climbs (€35) and canyoning (€30 to €60) and leads walks into the Vallée des Merveilles.

The tourist office (☑04 93 03 21 28; www.saintmartinvesubie.fr, in French; place Félix Faure; ☺9am-noon & 2-6pm Mon-Sat, 9am-noon Sun) and the Parc National du Mercantour Visitors' Centre St-Martin-Vésubie (☑04 93 03 23 15; ☺9am-noon & 2-6pm) have loads of information.

Sustained hunting over 1000 years led to the eventual disappearance of the wolf (Canis lupus) from France in 1930. But in 1992 two 'funny-looking dogs' were spotted near Utelle. Since then wolves have been making a natural return, loping across the Alps from Italy. Set high in the mountains of Le Boréon, Wolf Watch at Alpha (☑04 93 02 33 69; www.alpha-loup.com; Le Boréon; adult/child €10/8) allows visitors to find out how man is learning to live with the wolf and watch wolves roam wild. Visit year-round, but opening hours vary; call ahead or visit its website for details.

Magical mountain views unfold from the timber terrace of secluded Le Boréon (☑04 93 03 20 35; www.hotel-boreon.com, in French; d/tr €67/96, half board per person €64), the quintessential chalet. Cosy up in one of its dozen rooms and watch the snowflakes fall outside while dining on Alpine specialities (menu from €22).

In nearby La Colmiane, 7km west of St-Martin-Vésubie, the Bureau des Guides (☑04 93 02 88 30) leads outdoor activities and Colmiane Sports (☑04 93 02 87 00) and Ferrata Sport (☑04 93 02 80 56) lead walks and hire mountain bikes. The small ski station has one chairlift to Pic de la Colmiane (1795m) and 30km of ski slopes and walking and mountain-bike trails.

Public transport is minimal in the area but TRAM (☑04 93 85 92 60) operates two daily buses between Nice and St-Martin.

VALLÉE DES MERVEILLES

The 'Valley of Wonders' contains one of the world's most stupendous collections of Bronze Age petroglyphs. They date from between 1800 and 1500 BC and are thought to have been made by a Ligurian cult. Effectively an open-air art gallery, wedged between the Vésubie and Roya Valleys, it shelters more than 36,000 rock engravings of human figures, bulls and other animals spread over 30 sq km around Mont Bégo (2870m).

The main access route into the valley is the eastbound D91 running from St-Dalmas de Tende in the Vallée de la Roya to Castérino, where the Parc National du Mercantour has a summertime-only park office (☑04 93 04 89 79). Alternatively, go via the dead-end D171, which leads north to the valley from Roquebillière in the Vallée de la Vésubie. As the area is snow-covered much of the year, the best time to visit, unless you are snow-shoeing, is July to September.

Access is restricted to protect the precious artworks: walkers should only visit with an official guide; contact a Parc National du Mercantour Visitors Centre (Castérino ☑04 93 04 89 79, Tende 04 93 04 67 00) or one of the private outfitters like Bureau des Guides (☑04 93 04 67 88; www.berengeraventures.com, in French; 6bis rue Grandis, Tende).

The French Riviera & Monaco

Best Places to Eat

» Auberge de l'Oumède (p851)

» Luc Salsedo (p829)

» Mantel (p843)

» Les Charavins (p848)

» Les Deux Frères (p857)

Best Places to Stay

» Château Eza (p857)

» Pastis (p849)

» Villa Rivoli (p827)

» Hôtel 7e Art (p842)

» La Colombe d'Or (p838)

Why Go?

With its glistening seas, idyllic beaches and fabulous weather, the Riviera encapsulates many people's idea of the good life. The beauty is that there is so much more to do than just going to the beach – although the Riviera does take beach-going *very* seriously: from nudist beach to secluded cove or exclusive club, there is something for everyone.

Culture vultures will revel in the region's thriving art scene: the Riviera has some fine museums, including world-class modern art, and a rich history to explore in Roman ruins, WWII memorials and excellent museums.

Foodies for their part will rejoice at the prospect of lingering in fruit and veg markets, touring vineyards and feasting on some of France's best cuisines, whilst outdoor enthusiasts will be spoilt for choice with coastal paths to explore, and snorkelling and swimming galore.

When to Go
Monaco

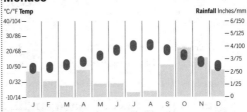

February Carnival season, with two weeks of festivities in Nice and Menton.

May Jet-setters descend on the Riviera for the Grand Prix and the Cannes Film Festival.

July Fireworks on 14 July, outdoor clubbing in Cannes and jazz in Antibes.

The French Riviera & Monaco Highlights

1 Try your luck at Monaco's opulent **casino** (p859)

2 Catch a ferry to **Île de Port-Cros** (p853) for pristine Mediterranean seascapes

3 Enjoy a fabulous day at a **St-Tropez beach club** (p849)

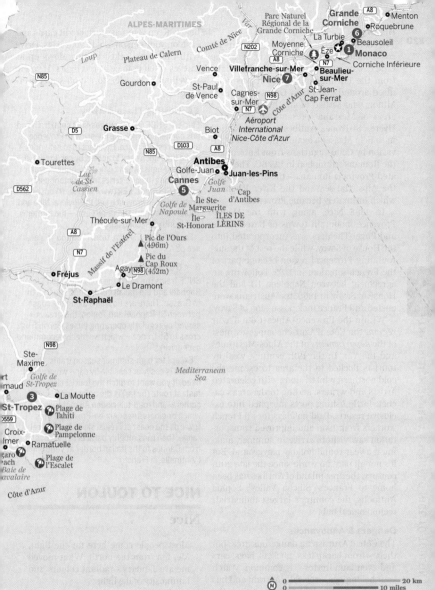

ALPES-MARITIMES

Loup

Plateau de Calern

Comté de Nice

N85

Gourdon

St-Paul
de Vence

Vence

Tourettes

D5

Grasse

N85

D103

A8

Biot

D562

Lac
de St-
Cassien

Golfe-Juan

Antibes

Cannes

Juan-les-Pins

Golfe
Juan

Cap
d'Antibes

Théoule-sur-Mer

Golfe de
Napoule

Île Ste-
Marguerite

Île
St-Honorat

ÎLES DE
LÉRINS

A8

N7

Massif de l'Estérel

Pic de l'Ours
(496m)

Pic du
Cap Roux
(452m)

Fréjus

Agay

N98

Le Dramont

St-Raphaël

Var

Parc Naturel
Régional de la
Grande Corniche

Grande
Corniche

A8

Menton

Roquebrune

La Turbie

Moyenne
Corniche

Éze

Beausoleil

Monaco

Corniche Inférieure

N202

Villefranche-sur-Mer

Nice

A8

N7

Beaulieu-
sur-Mer

Cagnes-
sur-Mer

N98

N7

Côte d'Azur

St-Jean-
Cap Ferrat

Aéroport
International
Nice-Côte d'Azur

N98

Ste-
Maxime

Golfe de
St-Tropez

rt

maud

St-Tropez

Plage de
Tahiti

Plage de
Pampelonne

Croix-
lmer

559

Ramatuelle

caro
ach

Baie de
avalaire

Plage de
l'Escalet

Côte d'Azur

Mediterranean
Sea

Ⓝ   0   20 km
     0   10 miles

4 Wind your way through
Bandol's vineyards and try
some of the area's famed
wines at **Maison des Vins**
(p855)

5 Dress to impress and party
the night away in **Cannes**
(p844)

6 Take a scenic drive along
the **Grande Corniche** (p857)
for jaw-dropping views of the
Med

7 Retrace Matisse's steps in
and around **Nice** (p825)

History

The eastern part of France's Mediterranean coast, including the area now known as the Côte d'Azur, was occupied by the Ligurians from the 1st millennium BC. It was colonised around 600 BC by Greeks from Asia Minor, who settled along the coast in the areas of Massalia (present-day Marseille), Hyères, St-Tropez, Antibes and Nice. Called in to help Massalia against the threat of invasion by Celto-Ligurians from Entremont, the Romans triumphed in 125 BC. They created Provincia Romana – the area between the Alps, the sea and the River Rhône – which ultimately became Provence.

In 1388 Nice, along with the Haute-Provence mountain towns of Barcelonette and Puget-Théniers, was incorporated into the House of Savoy, while the rest of the surrounding Provençal region became part of the French kingdom in 1482. Following an agreement between Napoléon III and the House of Savoy in 1860, the Austrians were ousted and France took possession of Savoy.

Within the Provence–Alpes–Côte d'Azur *région*, the Côte d'Azur encompasses most of the *départements* of the Alpes-Maritimes and the Var. In the 19th century, wealthy tourists flocked to the area to escape the cold northern winter, along with celebrated artists and writers, adding to the area's cachet. Little fishing ports morphed into exclusive resorts. Paid holidays for all French workers from 1936 and improved transportation saw visitors arrive in summer, making it a year-round holiday playground. But it's not all play, no work: since the late 20th century, the area inland of Antibes has been home to France's 'Silicon Valley', Sophia Antipolis, the country's largest industrial/technological hub.

Dangers & Annoyances

The Côte d'Azur isn't a dangerous area, but theft – from backpacks, pockets, bags, cars and even laundrettes – is common. Watch your belongings, especially at train and bus stations, on overnight trains, and on the beach. Keep your passport, credit cards and cash on your person, not in your bags. Drive with the doors locked and windows up as thieves often pounce at red lights. If you're travelling by bicycle, store it off-street overnight.

❶ Getting There & Away

Efficient **SNCF** (www.voyages-sncf.com) train and bus connections link the Riviera with Provence and the rest of France. Excellent road networks make the region easy to access by car, except in July and August when bumper-to-bumper traffic snarls along major arteries, most notoriously around St-Tropez. **LER** (www.info-ler.fr) buses operate between Provence and the Riviera. Nice and Toulon have international airports – the former is the country's second busiest.

For ferries to Corsica, from Nice and Toulon, see p873.

8 Getting Around

SNCF trains run along the coast between St-Raphaël and the Italian border, and spur north to Grasse. There are no trains along the coast between St-Raphaël and Toulon; this area is served by regularly operating buses. Ferries cross to St-Tropez – which we highly recommend over driving.

Except for high-summer season traffic, the Riviera is easily accessible by car – which you'll need, if you want to ditch the tourist circuit. The fastest route (by far) is the uninspiring, speed-camera- and road-toll-ridden A8 motorway, which originates near Aix-en-Provence, dips towards the coast at Fréjus, skirts the Estérel range, then runs roughly parallel to the coast, from Cannes to the Italian border at Ventimiglia (Vintimille, in French).

NICE TO TOULON

Nice

POP 352,400

> Most people come here for the light. Me, I'm from the north. What moved me are January's radiant colours and luminosity of daylight.
>
> *Henri Matisse*

ACCOMMODATION WARNING

Accommodation can be impossible to find, not to mention prohibitively expensive, during the Cannes Film Festival and the Monaco Grand Prix (both held in May). This applies to the coast between Menton and Cannes but doesn't affect areas beyond Massif de l'Estérel (St-Raphaël, St-Tropez etc).

July and August are busy everywhere, so if you have your heart set on staying at a particular hotel, make sure you book well in advance to avoid disappointment.

The words are Matisse's but they could be those of any painter, or, in fact, of any visitor who comes to Nice, for it's true: the light here is magical. The city also offers exceptional quality of life: shimmering Mediterranean shores, the very best of Mediterranean food, a unique historical heritage and Alpine wilderness within an hour's drive. No wonder so many young French people aspire to live here and tourists keep flooding in.

History

Nice was founded around 350 BC by the Greek seafarers who had settled Marseille. They named the colony Nikaia, apparently to commemorate a nearby victory (*nike* in Greek). In 154 BC the Greeks were followed by the Romans, who settled further uphill around what is now Cimiez, where there are still Roman ruins.

By the 10th century, Nice was ruled by the counts of Provence but turned to Amadeus VII of the House of Savoy in 1388. In the 18th and 19th centuries it was occupied several times by the French, but didn't definitively become part of France until 1860, when Napoléon III struck a deal (known as the Treaty of Turin) with the House of Savoy.

During the Victorian period, the English aristocracy and European royalty enjoyed Nice's mild winter climate. Throughout the 20th century, the city's exceptional art scene spanned every movement from Impressionism to new realism. The new tram line (customised by local and international artists) and the decision to open all museums for free in 2008 show that art is still very much a part of city life.

◉ Sights

Nice has a number of world-class sights but the star attraction is probably the city itself: atmospheric, beautiful and photogenic, it's a wonderful place to stroll or watch the world go by, so make sure you leave yourself plenty of time to soak it all in.

VIEUX NICE

Vieux Nice   OLD TOWN

Leave your maps and books behind and embrace Nice's labyrinthine baroque old town. There is something unique about this tangle of alleyways and backstreets bursting with local life and history. The northern end of this historical centre, running against bd Jean Jaurès, is packed with shops and holes in the wall, all claiming to sell *spécialités niçoises* more genuine than their neighbours'. Further south, atmospheric squares are filled with cafés, street artists and delighted *flâneurs* (strollers). Cours Saleya, running parallel to the seafront at the southern end of Vieux Nice, is the venue for one of the most vibrant, vividly hued local markets in the south of France.

Jutting above the rooflines are the spires of some historic churches, including the baroque Cathédrale Ste-Réparate (place Rossetti) and its stunning glazed terracotta

THE FRENCH RIVIERA & MONACO NICE

NICE IN...

Two Days
Kick-start the day with an invigorating walk or in-line skate along **Promenade des Anglais**. Browse the fragrant flower and produce **markets** for picnic supplies to take up to the **Colline du Château**. Amble the little alleys of **Vieux Nice**, then laze away the afternoon on the beach, or sail the **Baie des Anges** on a catamaran. Settle down for dinner at the fabulous **Luc Salsedo** and round off the night in your favourite **bar**. The following day, trace Matisse's artistic evolution at the **Musée Matisse**. Grab some Nice-style tapas at **Chez René Socca** for lunch before immersing yourself in Nice's belle époque history at the beautiful **Musée Masséna**. Finish your day with a long aperitif at **Les Distilleries Idéales** and a flamboyant dinner of Italian fare at **Luna Rossa**.

Four Days
Traverse the twisting cliff-side **corniches** (coastal roads) to the medieval village of **Èze**. Walk down **Nietzsche's path** to Èze-sur-Mer and catch the train to **Monaco** for a punt at the **Casino de Monte Carlo**, a tour of the aquarium at the **Musée Océanographique de Monaco** and a taste of the principality's culinary delights at **Bar Nautique**. On the fourth day, go inland to **Grasse** to tour its **perfumeries** and, in season, flower-filled fields, or venture west to tackle one of the 100-odd hiking trails criss-crossing the jagged red crags of the **Massif de l'Estérel**.

THE FRENCH RIVIERA & MONACO NICE TO TOULON

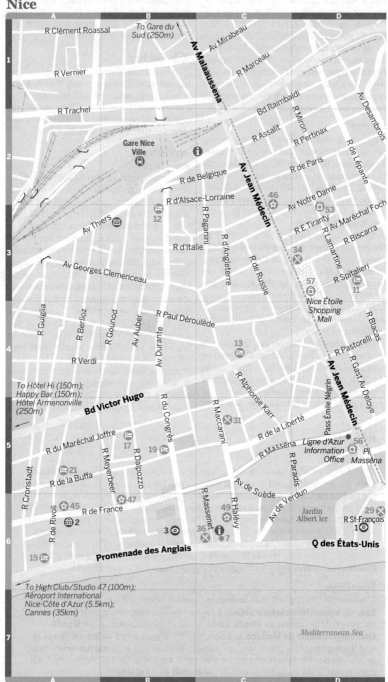

R Clément Roassal

To Gare du Sud (250m)

R Vernier

R Trachel

Av Malaussena

Av Mirabeau

R Marceau

Bd Raïmbaldi

R Assalit

R Miron

R Pertinax

Av Desambrois

R de Lépante

Gare Nice Ville

R de Belgique

R de Paris

R d'Alsace-Lorraine

Av Jean Médecin

Av Notre Dame

46

53

R E Tiranty

Av Thiers

12

R Paganini

R d'Italie

R d'Angleterre

R de Russie

34

R Lamartine

Av Maréchal Foch

R Biscarra

57

R Spitalieri

11

Av Georges Clemenceau

Nice Étoile Shopping Mall

R Blacas

R Guiglia

R Berlioz

R Gounod

R Auber

Av Durante

R Paul Déroulède

13

R Pastorelli

R Gast Av Delove

R Verdi

R Alphonse Karr

Av Jean Médecin

Pass Émile Négrin

To Hôtel Hi (150m);
Happy Bar (150m);
Hôtel Armenonville (250m)

Bd Victor Hugo

R du Congrès

R Maccarani

31

R de la Liberté

R Massena

R du Maréchal Joffre

17

R Meyerbeer

R Dalpozzo

19

Ligne d'Azur Information Office

56

Pl Masséna

21

R de la Buffa

R Paradis

R Cronstadt

45

R de Rivoli

2

R de France

47

Av de Suède

R Massénet

36

3

7

49

R Halévy

Av de Verdun

Jardin Albert 1er

29

R St-François

1

Q des États-Unis

15

Promenade des Anglais

To High Club/Studio 47 (100m);
Aéroport International
Nice-Côte d'Azur (5.5km);
Cannes (35km)

Mediterranean Sea

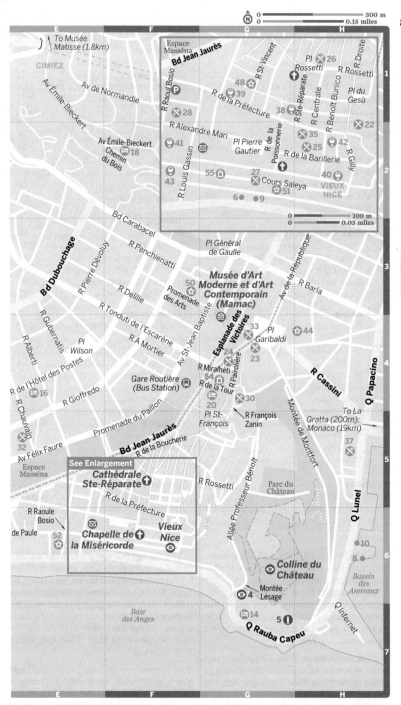

0 ————— 300 m
0 ————— 0.15 miles

E

To Musée Matisse (1.8km)

CIMIEZ

Av de Normandie

Av Émile-Bieckert

Av Émile-Bieckert
Chemin du Bois

Bd Carabacel

Bd Dubouchage

R Penchienatti

R Pierre Devoluy

R Delille

R Tonduti de l'Escarène

R A Mortier

Pl Wilson

R Gubernatis

R de l'Hôtel des Postes

R Alberti

R Gioffredo

R Chauvain

Promenade du Paillon

Av Félix Faure

Espace Masséna

Bd Jean Jaurès

See Enlargement

R Raoule Bosio

de Paule

F

Espace Masséna

Bd Jean Jaurès

R Raoul Bosio

R St-Vincent

R de la Préfecture

R Alexandre Mari

Pl Pierre Gautier

R Louis Gassin

55

27

6

9

G

Pl
Rossetti

Ste-Réparate

R de la Poissonnerie

Cours Saleya

51

Pl Général de Gaulle

Musée d'Art Moderne et d'Art Contemporain (Mamac)

Promenade des Arts

50

Esplanade des Victoires

33

Pl Garibaldi

23

24

R Miralhéti

R Pavlovie

R de la Tour

30

Pl St-François

R François Zanin

R de la Boucherie

Cathédrale Ste-Réparate

R de la Préfecture

Chapelle de la Miséricorde

R Rossetti

Vieux Nice

Allée Professeur Bénoit

Montée de Montfort

Parc du Château

Colline du Château

Montée Lesage

4

14

5

Q Rauba Capeu

Baie des Anges

H

Pl
Rossetti

R Rossetti

R Droite

26

Pl du Gesù

R Ste-Réparate

R Centrale

R Benoît Bunico

22

35

25

42

R de la Barillerie

40

VIEUX NICE

Av de la République

R Barla

44

R Cassini

Q Papacino

To La Gratta (200m); Monaco (19km)

37

Q Lunel

Bassin des Amiraux

10

8

Q Internet

0 ————— 100 m
0 ————— 0.05 miles

THE FRENCH RIVIERA & MONACO NICE

dome, built around 1650, and the exuberantly mid-18th-century **Chapelle de la Miséricorde** (cours Saleya).

Perpendicular to rue Rossetti is the notorious **rue Benoît Bunico**, Nice's old Jewish ghetto, where a 1430 law ordered Jews to be locked in by gates at each end of the street from sunset to dawn.

Colline du Château   PARK
From this 92m hilltop park, the glittering views of the Vieux Nice spires and Baie des Anges are mesmerising.

The shaded hill and park, at the eastern end of quai des États-Unis, are named after a 12th-century château that was razed by Louis XIV in a fit of pique in 1706 and never rebuilt. To reach the park you can walk up montée Lesage, climb the steps at the eastern end of rue Rossetti or take the **ascenseur** (lift; per person €1.10; ⊙9am-7pm) under Tour Bellanda.

Port Lympia   PORT
Nice's port, with its beautiful Venetian-coloured buildings, is often overlooked, but

a stroll along its quays is lovely, as is the walk to get here: come down through the Colline du Château or follow quai Rauba Capeu, the atmospheric headland at the end of the promenade where a massive **memorial** hewn from the rock commemorates the 4000 Niçois who died in both world wars.

CIMIEZ

Cimiez used to be the playground of European aristocrats wintering on the Riviera. These days, it's Nice's affluent residents who live in the area's beautiful Victorian villas.

FREE **Musée Matisse** ART MUSEUM
(www.musee-matisse-nice.org; 164 av des Arènes de Cimiez; ☺10am-6pm Wed-Mon) Housed in a 17th-century Genoese mansion, this small museum reveals Matisse's evolution as an artist rather than wowing the crowds with masterpieces. There are some well-known works such as the blue paper cut-outs *Blue Nude IV* and *Woman with Amphora,* but you'll also see a number of lesser-known sculptures and experimental pieces using cloth, paper, oils, ink etc.

Take bus 17 from the bus station or bus 22 from place Masséna to the Arènes stop.

Musée National Message Biblique Marc Chagall ART MUSEUM
(Marc Chagall Biblical Message Museum; www.musee-chagall.fr, in French; 4 av Dr Ménard; adult/child €7.50/5.50; ☺10am-6pm Wed-Mon) This small museum houses the largest public collection of the Russian-born artist's seminal paintings of *Old Testament* scenes. Be sure to peek through the plate-glass window across a reflecting pond to view a mosaic of the rose window at Metz Cathedral. Take bus 22 from place Masséna (Masséna/Guitry stop) to the front of the museum or walk. The same bus goes to the Musée Matisse. Chagall (1887–1985) is buried in St-Paul de Vence.

FREE **Musée et Site Archéologiques** ARCHAEOLOGY MUSEUM
(Archaeological Museum & Site; 160 av des Arènes de Cimiez; ☺10am-6pm Wed-Mon) Nice's little-spoken but lingering language, Nissart, derives most of its vocabulary from the Roman city of Cemenelum, founded by Augustus in 14 BC. Its ruins lie behind the Musée Matisse, on the eastern side of the Parc des Arènes, and are the focus of the Musée et Site Archéologiques. You'll need a little imagination to picture the public baths, amphitheatre and original paved streets signposted across the site, but the relics inside the museum such as ceramics, glass, coins and tools bring it to life.

CENTRAL NICE

Promenade des Anglais PROMENADE
Established by English expats in 1822, this wide, palm-lined promenade is a timelessly elegant place for a beachfront stroll. The Promenade des Anglais is lined with grand buildings, chief amongst them the

---

MAGICAL MATISSE TOUR

If you're mad about Matisse, you can cherry-pick a Côte d'Azur itinerary that takes in some of the major sites of his life.

Born on New Year's Eve in 1869, Henri Matisse arrived in Nice from Paris in 1917 to recover from bronchitis. He remained here until his death in 1954 at his home and studio in the mansion-lined suburb, Cimiez.

Checking into the **Hôtel Beau Rivage**, he went on to rent a flat on quai des États-Unis, then moved to what is now the **Palais de la Méditerranée**, a luxury hotel on the Promenade des Anglais, where he also exhibited. Many of the works he painted in Nice are housed in the city's **Musée Matisse**.

Matisse's visits to **Renoir's villa** (see p836) in Cagnes-sur-Mer provided further inspiration for paintings, including the 1917 *Oliviers, Jardin de Renoir à Cagnes* (Olive Trees, Renoir's Garden in Cagnes).

During WWII Matisse rented **Villa Le Rêve** (www.villalerevevence.com; 261 av Henri Matisse, Vence), where he was visited by Picasso and Aragon, among others. It was during his stay in Vence that he designed the **Chapelle du Rosaire** (p838). Villa Le Rêve now hosts regular painting workshops.

Matisse is buried at the **Monastère Notre Dame de Cimiez** (Cimiez Notre Dame Monastery; ☺8.30am-12.30pm & 2.30-6.30pm), near the Musée Matisse; signs lead to his grave.

Tourist offices throughout the Riviera have an info-packed brochure (available in English) about tracing Matisse's footsteps.

WORTH A TRIP

THE PINE CONE TRAIN

Chugging between the mountains and the sea, the narrow-gauge railway Train des Pignes (Pine Cone Train; www.trainprovence.com) is one of Provence's most picturesque rides. Rising to 1000m, with breathtaking views, the 151km track between Nice and Digne-les-Bains passes through Haute Provence's scarcely populated back country.

The service runs five times a day and is ideal for a day trip inland. The beautiful medieval village of Entrevaux is just 1½ hours from Nice (return €18), perfect for a picnic and a wander through its historic centre and citadel.

1912 pink-domed Hôtel Negresco. Another landmark is art deco Palais de la Méditerranée, saved from demolition in the 1980s and now part of a luxury hotel.

It's generally warm enough to swim from April to October, when beaches teem with sun seekers. If you're not much of a water babe, there are dedicated cycling and skating lanes on the promenade.

FREE **Musée Masséna**   CITY MUSEUM
(65 rue de France; ⊙10am-6pm Wed-Mon) Housed in a marvellous Italianate neoclassical villa (1898), this museum explores the city and Riviera's history from the early 19th century to WWII. It's a fascinating journey, with a roll call of monarchs, a succession of nationalities (British, Russians, Americans), the advent of tourism, the prominence of the carnival and much more. History is told through an excellent mix of furniture, objects, art deco posters, early photographs and paintings and the lovely setting – the city of Nice still uses the ground floor rooms for official occasions.

FREE **Musée d'Art Moderne et d'Art Contemporain (Mamac)**   ART MUSEUM
(Museum of Modern & Contemporary Art; www.mamac-nice.org; Promenade des Arts; ⊙10am-6pm Tue-Sun) Designed by Yves Bayard and Henri Vidal, Mamac is worth a visit for its stunning architecture alone, but it also houses some fantastic avant-garde art from the 1960s to the present. Exhibits include iconic pop art from Roy Lichtenstein and

Andy Warhol's 1965 *Campbell's Soup Can*. The marbled towers' glass walkways lead to highlights Niki de St-Phalle's papiermâché sculptures and a shopping trolley wrapped by Christo. An awesome panorama of Vieux Nice unfolds from the rooftop garden/gallery, which features works by Nice-born Yves Klein (1928–62).

Cathédrale Orthodoxe Russe St-Nicolas   CATHEDRAL
(Russian Orthodox Cathedral of St-Nicolas; Av Nicolas II; admission €3; ⊙9am-noon & 2.30-5pm Mon-Sat, 2.30-5pm Sun) Crowned by six multicoloured onion domes, the Cathédrale Orthodoxe Russe St-Nicolas is the largest cathedral outside Russia. It was built between 1902 and 1912 for Nice's growing Russian community. Shorts, miniskirts and sleeveless shirts are forbidden.

🏃 Activities

In-line skating

Smooth and flat, with great views to boot, Nice's seafront provides 7km of perfect skating ground between the port and the airport.

Roller Station   IN-LINE SKATING
(www.roller-station.fr, in French; 49 quai des États-Unis) Rents out skates for €7 a day and bikes for €15 a day. Some ID is required as a deposit.

Beaches & Water Sports

You'll need at least a beach mat to cushion your tush from Nice's pebbled beaches. On the beach, operators hire out catamarans, paddleboats and jet skis; you can also parascend, waterski or paraglide. There are showers and toilets on every beach.

Plages privées   BEACHES
(private beaches; www.pagesdenice.com, in French; ⊙May-Sep) Free sections of beach alternate with 15 sun lounge-lined private beaches, for which you have to pay by renting a chair (around €15 a day) or mattress (around €10).

Le Poséidon   DIVING
(☎04 92 00 43 86; www.poseidon-nice.com; quai Lunel; introductory dives €45) Offers PADI courses and runs diving expeditions in English.

Nice Diving   DIVING
(☎04 93 89 42 44; www.nicediving.com; 14 quai des Docks) Runs PADI courses and diving expeditions in English. An introductory dive costs around €45, with equipment.

☞ Tours

WALKING TOURS

Guided walking tours
WALKING TOURS

The tourist office runs 2½-hour walking tours (adult/child €12/6; ☺9.30am Sat) of Vieux Nice, in English, departing from the main office on the promenade des Anglais. The Centre du Patrimoine (☎04 92 00 41 90; www.nice.fr, in French) also runs 11 thematic two-hour walking tours (adult/child €5/2.50). English-language tours must be booked two days in advance. The tourist office has a full listing.

Trans Côte d'Azur
BOAT TOURS

(www.trans-cote-azur.com, in French; quai Lunel; ☺Apr-Oct) Runs scenic one-hour coastal cruises (adult/child €15/9) as well as day trips to the Îles de Lérins (adult/child €34/24), St-Tropez (adult/child €55/41) and Monaco (adult/child €32/23).

✵ Festivals & Events

Carnaval de Nice
CARNIVAL

(www.nicecarnaval.com) This two-week carnival, held in February, is particularly famous for its battles of flowers, where thousands of blooms are tossed into the crowds from passing floats, as well as its fantastic fireworks display.

Nice Jazz Festival
MUSIC FESTIVAL

(www.nicejazzfestival.fr) In July Nice swings to the week-long jazz festival at the Arènes de Cimiez, amid the Roman ruins.

🛏 Sleeping

Nice has a suite of places to sleep, from stellar independent backpacker hostels to international art-filled icons. Prices jump during summer and also for regional festivals such as Monaco's Grand Prix or the Cannes Film Festival.

[TOP CHOICE] Villa Rivoli
BOUTIQUE HOTEL €€

(☎04 93 88 80 25; www.villa-rivoli.com; 10 rue de Rivoli; s €85-155, d €99-175, q €210; ❄️🛜) Built in 1890, this stately villa feels like your own pied-à-terre in the heart of Nice. A marble staircase leads to spotlessly clean character-rich rooms, some with fabric-covered walls, gilt-edged mirrors and marble mantelpieces. Take breakfast in the garden's sun-dappled shade, or in the grand belle époque salon. Eight of the 26 rooms face the street and (until 2011) have single-pane glass; light-sleepers, book a room by the garden.

RIVIERA PASS
827

If you're planning on making many visits and taking many tours in and around Nice, the **Nice Riviera Pass** (see www.frenchrivierapass.com) is a good option for saving a few bob. Available for one, two or three days, it costs €24/36/54 and gives you free entry to Nice's paying sites – the Marc Chagall museum and the Cathédrale Orthodoxe Russe St-Nicolas. It also includes guided tours organised by Nice's tourist office and the Centre du Patrimoine, as well as a number of regional attractions such as the Jardin Exotique and the Musée Océanographique in Monaco, the Musée Renoir in Cagnes-sur-Mer and the Musée Picasso in Antibes. The pass also offers reductions in a number of shops and restaurants. Check the website for full listings.

Hôtel Windsor
BOUTIQUE HOTEL €€

(☎04 93 88 59 35; www.hotelwindsornice.com; 11 rue Dalpozzo; d €120-175; ❄️@🛜🏊) Though owned by the same family since 1942, there's nothing traditional about the Windsor. Underground graffiti artists decorated several of the oversize rooms, with aggressive splashes of colour. Traditional rooms are more soothing yet still nod to the arts with hand-painted wall murals. Rooms facing the backyard tropical garden have single-pane glass but a lush view; choose these over street-side, unless you're a light sleeper. Warm service compensates for the unheated pool.

Hôtel La Pérouse
LUXURY HOTEL €€€

(☎04 93 62 34 63; www.hotel-la-perouse.com; 11 quai Rauba Capeu; d €260-510; ❄️@🛜🏊) Built into the rock cliff next to Tour Bellanda, La Pérouse captures the vibe of a genteel villa. Lower-floor rooms face the lemon-tree-shaded courtyard and infinity pool; upper-floor rooms have magnificent vistas of the promenade and sea. Smart accent colours add flair to otherwise traditional decor; big marble bathroom vanities provide space to unpack. Excellent service. Private beach.

Nice Garden Hôtel
BOUTIQUE HOTEL €€

(☎04 93 87 35 63; www.nicegardenhotel.com; 11 rue du Congrès; s/d €75/100; ❄️🛜) Behind heavy iron gates hides this little gem of a hotel: the nine beautifully appointed rooms, the work of the exquisite Marion, are a subtle blend of old and new and overlook a delightful garden with a glorious orange tree. Amazingly, all this charm and peacefulness is just two blocks from the promenade.

Villa Saint-Exupéry
HOSTEL €

(☑04 93 84 42 83; www.villahostels.com; 22 av Gravier; dm €25-30, s/d €45/90; @🌐📶) Why can't all hostels be like this? Set in a lovely converted monastery in the north of the city, this is a great place to put down your bags for a few days. Chill out in the 24-hour common room housed in the old stained-glass chapel, sip a €1 beer on the barbecue terrace, cook in the state-of-the-art self-catering kitchen, and stock up on travel tips. The villa staff will come and pick you up from the nearby Comte de Falicon tram stop or St-Maurice stop for Bus 23 (direct from the airport) when you first arrive. Rates include breakfast.

Hôtel Wilson
BOUTIQUE HOTEL €

(☑04 93 85 47 79; www.hotel-wilson-nice.com; 39 rue de l'Hôtel des Postes; s/d €50/55; 🌐) Many years of travelling, an experimental nature and exquisite taste have turned Jean-Marie's rambling flat into a compelling place to stay. The 16 rooms have individual, carefully crafted decor, and share the eclectic dining room. Mind the two resident tortoises as you sit down for a breakfast of fresh bread and croissants (served until a very civilised noon). The hotel is on the third floor and there's no elevator.

Le Petit Palais
HOTEL €€

(☑04 93 62 19 11; www.petitpalaisnice.fr, in French; 17 av Émile-Bieckert; d €150; ❄🌐) Near Cimiez' breezy heights, this yellow neoclassical mansion offers breathtaking views of Nice – the views get better with every floor you climb (three in total). Ground-floor rooms are deprived of vistas but make up for it with private gardens. Decor is elegant throughout. The only downside is the *steep* 10 minutes' walk from bd Carabacel.

Villa la Tour
BOUTIQUE HOTEL €€

(☑04 93 80 08 15; www.villa-la-tour.com; 4 rue de la Tour; s/d €78/89; ❄@) Small but perfectly formed, the Villa la Tour is delightful, with warm, romantic Provençal rooms, a location at the heart of Vieux Nice, and a diminutive flower-decked roof terrace with views of the Colline du Château and surrounding rooftops.

Hôtel Armenonville
HOTEL €€

(☑04 93 96 86 00; www.hotel-armenonville.com; 20 av des Fleurs; d €86-105; @🌐📶) Tucked away at the back of an alleyway and shielded by its large garden, this grand early-20th-century mansion has sober rooms, three of them (rooms 12, 13 and 14) with a huge terrace overlooking the garden. Some of the rooms have air-con but there is no elevator.

Hôtel Hi
HOTEL €€€

(☑04 97 07 26 26; www.hi-hotel.net; 3 av des Fleurs; s/d from €249/269; ❄@🌐🏊) Think of what the most techno-funk, whacky, futuristic designer place would look like in your wildest dreams – now quadruple that, and you have Hôtel Hi. Designed by Matali Crasset, a student of Philippe Starck, Hi won't be for everyone and some of the designs already look tired, but the hotel is big in sustainability and the rooftop pool, spa and funky bar are good perks. Tariffs include an organic buffet breakfast. The hotel has an elevator.

Also recommended:

Hôtel Negresco
HOTEL €€€

(☑04 93 16 64 00; www.hotel-negresco-nice. com; 37 promenade des Anglais; d from €400; ❄@) Nice's most extravagant palace is indulging in a two-year renovation project to look its best for its centenary in 2012. If you don't stay there, make sure you still pop in to have a look at the magnificent halls.

Belle Meunière
HOSTEL €

(☑04 93 88 66 15; www.bellemeuniere.com; 21 av Durante; dm €18-24, d €55-62; 🌐📶) Great for unfussy families, but the street outside is loud and there's only single-pane glass.

Auberge de Jeunesse – Les Camélias
HOSTEL €

(☑04 93 62 15 54; www.fuaj.org, in French; 3 rue Spitaleri; dm incl breakfast & sheets €23; @🌐) This hostel has clean, spacious dorms, a bar, a self-catering kitchen and a laundry. There is a midday lockout (11am to 3pm) but no night curfew.

Exedra
DESIGN HOTEL €€€

(☑04 97 03 89 89; www.boscolohotels.com; 12 av Victor Hugo; d €240-460; @) Totally gutted in 2008, the belle époque shell now houses one of Nice's most aggressively sexy hotels. Alas, service is weak for this price.

✕ Eating

Restaurants in Vieux Nice are a mixed bag of tourist traps and genuine good finds. Follow your instincts, or our recommendations.

Luc Salsedo   MODERN FRENCH €€€
(☎04 93 82 24 12; www.restaurant-salsedo.com, in French; 14 rue Maccarani; lunch/dinner menu €26/44, mains €26; ⊙lunch Fri & Sun-Tue, dinner Thu-Tue, dinner only Jul-Aug; ✐) The cuisine of Salsedo, a young chef who's built a fine reputation, is local and seasonal. His menu (which, unusually, caters well for vegetarians) changes every 10 days to reflect the mood of the market stalls. The food is delightful and served without pomp on plates, rustic boards or authentic cast-iron pots. The wine list is another hit, with an all-French cast from white to red and rosé.

Luna Rossa   ITALIAN €€
(☎04 93 85 55 66; www.lelunarossa.com; 3 rue Chauvain; mains €15-25; ⊙lunch & dinner Tue-Fri, dinner Sat) Luna Rossa is like your dream Mediterranean dinner come true: fresh pasta, exquisitely cooked seafood (pan-fried John Dory, grilled sea bass, sautéed king prawns, sun-kissed vegetables (artichoke hearts, sun-dried tomatoes, asparagus tips) and divine meats (beef carpaccio with truffle and parmesan shavings). Wash it down with one of the excellent bottles of red or rosé from the cellar.

La Merenda   NIÇOIS CUISINE €€
(4 rue Raoul Bosio; mains €12-15; ⊙Mon-Fri) Closed at weekends, with no phone number or credit card machine, La Merenda is one of a kind. This tiny restaurant serves some of the most unusual fare in town: stockfish (dried cod soaked in running water for a few days and then simmered with onions, tomatoes, garlic, olives and potatoes) is the house speciality, as is tripe. La Merenda also serves Bellet wines, a rare local vintage.

La Petite Maison   NIÇOIS CUISINE €€€
(☎04 93 92 59 59; www.lapetitemaison-nice.com; 11 rue St-François de Paule; mains €20-40; ⊙Mon-Sat) Nice's hottest table draws celebs and politicians for its happening scene and elegantly executed Niçois specialities. We love the drama of the noisy, high-ceilinged room, aglow with flickering candlelight, and the contemporary spins of local classics, but waiters putter (unless you're famous), portions run small and tables are packed together. Still, it's tops for a splashy night out. Reservations essential.

Fenocchio   ICE CREAM €
(2 place Rossetti; ice cream from €2; ⊙9am-midnight, closed Nov-Jan) The best place to beat Nice's heat is this *glacier*, serving 50 flavours of ice cream – eschew predictable favourites and indulge in a new taste sensation: black olive, tomato-basil, rhubarb, avocado, rosemary, *calisson* (almond biscuit frosted with icing sugar), lavender, ginger or liquorice.

Chez René Socca   BISTRO €
(2 rue Miralhéti; dishes from €2; ⊙9am-9pm Tue-Sun, closed Nov) Forget about presentation and manners; here, it's all about taste. Grab a portion of *socca* (chickpea-flour pancake) or a plate of *petits farcis* (stuffed vegetables) and head across the street to the bar for a *grand pointu* (glass) of red, white or rosé.

Zucca Magica   VEGETARIAN €€
(☎04 93 56 25 27; www.lazuccamagica.com; 4bis quai Papacino; menus €30; ⊙Tue-Sat; ✐ ❦) The 'Magic Pumpkin' is a rare thing in France: a vegetarian restaurant that nonvegetarians actually like to go to. Bring an appetite: *menus* comprise four set dishes (five for dinner) plus dessert, depending on what green giant and chef Marco Folicaldi finds at the markets.

Le Safari   NIÇOIS CUISINE €€
(☎04 93 80 18 44; restaurantsafari.fr; 1 cours Saleya; mains €12-27; ⊙noon–11.30pm) The only restaurant on touristy Cours Saleya that merits your attention, Le Safari serves Niçois specialities – *daube de boeuf* (beef stew), *petite friture* (fried small fish) and *petits farcis* – on a bustling heated terrace and a more romantic (smoke-free) wood-beamed dining room lined with jars of olives.

La Table Alziari   NIÇOIS CUISINE €€
(☎04 93 80 34 03; 4 rue François Zanin; mains €9-15; ⊙Tue-Sat) Run by the grandson of the famous Alziari olive oil family, this citrus-coloured restaurant off the busy rue Pairolière is not here to brag about anything. The day's menu is chalked on a blackboard, with local specialities such as *morue à la niçoise* (cod served with potatoes, olives and a tomato sauce) or grilled goat's cheese washed down with regional wines.

Sarao   SPANISH €€
(☎04 92 00 50 90; www.sarao-restaurant.com; 7 promenade des Anglais; 2-/3-course menu €14/18; ⊙8am-11pm) Good-value cooking blending Spanish and French, with live

bossa nova on Saturday nights and brunch on Sunday. Many wines under €30.

Pasta Basta
ITALIAN €

(04 93 80 03 57; 18 rue de la Préfecture; 3-course menu €14.50, mains €13) Choose a pasta, pick a sauce and – hey presto! – a plate of amazing pasta made on the premises. Best enjoyed on the street-side terrace.

Acchiardo
BISTRO €

(04 93 85 51 16; 38 rue Droite; mains €14-20; ⊙Mon-Fri) Going strong since 1927, locals flock to Acchiardo for the *plat du jour* (daily special), a glass of wine and a load of gossip served straight up on the counter.

Café de Turin
SEAFOOD €€

(04 93 62 29 52; www.cafedeturin.fr; 5 place Garibaldi; seafood platters from €20; ⊙8am-10pm) Nice's best oysters and *plateaux de fruits de mer* (cold seafood platters).

Delhi Belhi
INDIAN €€

(04 93 92 51 87; www.delhibelhi.com; 22 rue de la Barillerie; mains €13, menus from €22; ⊙dinner;) An excellent Indian restaurant, ideal if you've overdosed on Mediterranean flavours.

Self-Catering

Pack the ultimate picnic hamper from cours Saleya's magnificent fruit and vegetable market (⊙6am-1.30pm Tue-Sun), where long trestle tables groan with shiny fruit and veg, pastries, *fruits confits* (glazed or candied fruits such as figs, ginger, pears etc) and more.

Supermarkets and minimarkets abound: Monoprix av Jean Médecin (42 av Jean Médecin; ⊙8.30am-9pm Mon-Sat); place Garibaldi (place Garibaldi; ⊙8.30am-8.45pm Mon-Sat).

 Drinking

Vieux Nice's little streets runneth over with local bars and cafés: from a morning espresso to a lunchtime *pastis* (the tipple of choice in the south of France), a chilled evening beer or a midnight cocktail, the choice is yours.

Les Distilleries Idéales
CAFÉ

(24 rue de la Préfecture; ⊙9am-12.30am) Whether you're after an espresso on your way to cours Saleya or a sundowner, the atmosphere in this brilliant bistro is infectious: you're bound to leave with a skip in your step.

Ma Nolan's
PUB

(www.ma-nolans.com; 2 rue St-François de Paule; ⊙noon-2am Mon-Fri, 11pm-2am Sat & Sun) Irish pub Ma Nolan's is a backpacker favourite with its Monday-night pub quiz, televised sport, nightly live music and full-English brekkie.

Le Six
GAY BAR

(www.le6.fr; 6 rue Raoul Bosio; ⊙Tue-Sun 10pm-4.30am) Primped and pretty A-gays crowd shoulder to shoulder at Nice's compact, perennially popular 'mo bar. The thing to do: climb the ladder to the mezzanine (watch your head!).

La Civette du Cours
CAFÉ

(1 cours Saleya; ⊙8am-1am) Nurse a hangover with a cappuccino in the morning sun, or join the locals for a prelunch pastis at this cheerful café.

Happy Bar
BAR

(www.hi-hotel.net; 3 av des Fleurs; ⊙7pm-midnight Tue-Sat) This once-trendy bar now looks a touch dated, but the garden remains a fun spot for a drink; DJs spin monthly.

Chez Wayne's
BAR

(www.waynes.fr; 15 rue de la Préfecture; ⊙2.30pm-12.30am) Raucous watering hole Chez Wayne's also has live bands every night.

☆ **Entertainment**

The tourist office has info on Nice's cultural activities listed in its free publications –

FAST FOOD: PAN BAGNAT

When locals want a quick bite, they hunt down a *pan bagnat* – loosely translated as sopped bread – the local version of a tuna sandwich, made with crusty bread, chunks of cold tuna, lettuce, tomatoes, onions, radish and egg, all drizzled with local olive oil. You'll see versions all over town, but the best come from the port-side snack-bar La Gratta (2 bd Franck Pilatte; sandwiches €4.50; ⊙lunch), which uses excellent ingredients including tender-crusted fresh bread and fruity green olive oil. Find a spot along the port where you can dangle your feet over the quai, and watch masts bob in the harbour while you drip olive oil down your chin.

Nice Rendez-vous (monthly) and Côte d'Azur en Fêtes (quarterly) – or consult the weekly Semaine des Spectacles (€1), available from newsstands on Wednesday. All are in French. Buy event tickets at Fnac (44 av Jean Médecin).

Cinemas

Catch nondubbed flicks at Cinéma Nouveau Mercury (16 place Garibaldi) and Cinéma Rialto (4 rue de Rivoli).

Live Music

Le Bar des Oiseaux   CABARET
(www.bardesoiseaux.com, in French; 5 rue St-Vincent; ☺to midnight weekdays, to 1am or 2am Fri & Sat) Artists dig this bohemian bar (and adjoining theatre) for live jazz, chanson française (French songs) and cabaret nights. Cover costs around €5 when there's entertainment; you can also dine here (menus around €20; lunch Monday to Saturday, dinner Tuesday to Saturday).

La Havane   LATINO
(32 rue de France; ☺2pm-2.30am) For sultry Latin vibes, this bar-restaurant alternates live salsa and Latino jazz with merengue and bachata Tuesday to Saturday nights. Musicians play three sets of 45 minutes, starting at 9.30pm.

Opéra de Nice   OPERA
(www.opera-nice.org; 4-6 rue St-François de Paule; ☺box office 9am-5.45pm Tue-Sat, to 7.45pm Fri, closed mid-Jun–Sep) The vintage 1885 grande dame hosts operas, ballets and orchestral concerts. Tickets cost €7 to €85.

Nightclubs

 Le Smarties   LOUNGE BAR
(http://nicesmarties.free.fr; 10 rue Defly; ☺6pm-2am Tue-Sat) We love Smarties' sexy '70s swirly orange style, which draws a hot-looking straight-gay crowd. On weekends, the tiny dance floor fills when DJs spin deep house, electro, techno and occasionally disco; weekdays are mellower. Free buffet with happy hour (nightly 6pm to 9pm).

High Club/Studio 47   NIGHTCLUB
(www.highclub.fr, in French; 45 Promenade des Anglais; ☺Fri-Sun 11.30pm-5am) The High Club's mega sound system draws the occasional big-name DJ and throngs of 20-somethings every weekend. Over-30s hang out in the adjoining Studio 47, a secondary bar in the room behind the vast dance floor. Doormen are fussy; look sharp or don't get in. Every second Sunday is gay night.

Bliss Bar   LOUNGE BAR
(www.myspace.com/blissbar06; cnr rue de l'Abbaye & rue Colonna d'Istria; ☺Wed-Sat 10pm-2am) Trendy Bliss is a favourite of happening 20-somethings. If you can't decide whether to wait, peer inside the windows to get a taste of who's inside. You'll know right away if it's a yes or no.

Les Trois Diables   NIGHTCLUB
(2 cours Saleya; ☺5pm-2.15am) Music is a mix of trip-hop, house and electro at this small local club. Thursday is student night (show your ID); Wednesday is karaoke.

Le Klub   GAY NIGHTCLUB
(www.leklub.net; 6 rue Halévy; ☺Thurs-Sun 11.30pm-5am) Nice's hit-or-miss gay club occupies two floors – dance floor down, bar up. Friday through Sunday, expect a €10 to €15 cover, one drink included.

🔒 Shopping

Designer names abound in the fashionable, part-pedestrian area defined by rue Paradis, av de Suède, rue Alphonse Karr and rue du Maréchal Joffre (all west of av Jean Médecin).

Cours Saleya markets   MARKETS
(☺6am-5.30pm Tue-Sat, to 1.30pm Sun) Split between its beautiful **flower market** and rightly famous **food market**. On Mondays from 6am to 6pm, flowers and food make way for an **antiques market**.

Cave de la Tour (3 rue de la Tour)   WINE
The best-value place for tasting and buying wine.

Cat's Whiskers (30 rue Lamartine)   BOOKSHOP
Linda and her four-legged assistant Vodka will help you pick new and second-hand English-language books.

Maison de la Presse (1 place Masséna)   BOOKSHOP
Maps and guides, plus books and magazines in English.

Nice Étoile (av Jean Médecin)   SHOPPING MALL
This enormous shopping mall spans a city block and hosts the usual fashion franchises.

ℹ️ Information

Barclays Bank (2 rue Alphonse Karr) Has a change counter.

Police station (☎04 92 17 22 22, Foreign Tourist Department 04 92 17 20 31; 1 av Maréchal Foch)

1. St-Paul de Vence (p837)
Cobblestoned St-Paul de Vence has been home to many 20th-century artists, including Chagall.

2. Èze (p857)
Medieval Èze sits atop a 427m-high peak, with magnificent views across the Mediterranean.

3. Musée Picasso, Antibes (p835)
In 1946, Picasso made his studio in the Château Grimaldi. Today it houses a museum of his work.

4. Beach at Cannes (p839)
Cannes has glitz and glamour year-round, not only during its famous film festival.

BILL WASSMAN

Post office Main post office (23 av Thiers); Vieux Nice (2 rue Louis Gassin)

Tourist office Airport tourist information desk (Terminal 1; ⊘8am-9pm, closed Sun Oct-May); main tourist office (www.nicetourisme.com; 5 promenade des Anglais; ⊘8am-8pm Mon-Sat, 9am-7pm Sun); train station (av Thiers; ⊘8am-8pm Mon-Sat, 9am-7pm Sun)

Travelex (13 av Thiers; ⊘8am-8pm Mon-Fri, 9am-5.30pm Sat & Sun) Opposite the station.

Getting There & Away

A second tram line is planned that will connect Nice's centre with the airport. The bus station is also slated to be demolished and rebuilt at another location. Check with the tourist office or call ☎08 00 06 01 06 for updates.

Air

Aéroport International Nice-Côte d'Azur (www.nice.aeroport.fr) lies 6km west of the city centre. A free **shuttle** (⊘every 10min 4.30am-midnight) connects its two terminals. Carriers include low-cost **BMIBaby** (www.bmibaby.com) and **EasyJet** (www.easyjet.com).

Heli Air Monaco (www.heliairmonaco.com) helicopters connect Nice airport and Monaco in seven minutes; one-way adult/child fares cost €120/80.

Boat

The fastest, least-expensive ferries from France to Corsica depart from Nice (see p873). To go to the port, take Buses 9 or 10 off av Jean Médecin (stop Médecin/Pastorelli) to the Port stop. Ferry companies:

Corsica Ferries (www.corsicaferries.com; quai Lunel)

SNCM (www.sncm.fr; ferry terminal, quai du Commerce)

Bus

Ligne d'Azur (www.lignedazur.com) buses leave from the **bus station** (gare routière; 5 bd Jean Jaurès). A single €1 fare takes you anywhere in the Alpes-Maritimes *département* (with a few exceptions, such as the airport) and includes one connection, within 74 minutes. Buses run daily to Antibes (one hour), Cannes (1½ hours), Grasse (1½ hours), Menton (1½ hours), Monaco

(45 minutes), St-Paul de Vence (55 minutes) and Vence (one hour).

Eurolines (www.eurolines.com) Operates from the bus station and serves long-haul European destinations.

Train

From July to September the SNCF's Carte Isabelle (€14, available from train stations) lets you make unlimited trips in a single day (except TGV trains) from Fréjus to Ventimiglia in Italy, and from Nice to Tende.

Gare Nice Ville (av Thiers) is 1.2km north of the beach. There are frequent services to coastal towns, including Antibes (€4, 30 minutes), Cannes (€6.50, 40 minutes), Menton (€4.50, 35 minutes), Monaco (€3.40, 20 minutes) and St-Raphaël (€11, 50 minutes). Direct TGV trains link Nice with Paris' Gare de Lyon (€115, 5½ hours).

SOS Voyageurs (☎04 93 16 02 61; ⊘9am-noon & 3-6pm Mon-Fri) Handles lost luggage and other problems.

Getting Around

Regional network **Ligne d'Azur** (www.lignedazur.com; 3 place Masséna; ⊘7.45am-6.30pm Mon-Fri, 8.30am-6pm Sat) operates local and intercity buses, and the tram. Fares cost €1 per trip (except to the airport), including one connection. Buy tickets from the driver or ticket machines at tram stops. An unlimited-travel day pass costs €4.

To/From the Airport

Ligne d'Azur operates two airport buses; the €4 ticket is then valid on other buses for the entire day. Route 99 departs Gare Nice Ville and goes directly to the airport every half-hour from 8am to 9pm daily. Route 98 departs from the bus station every 20 minutes (every 30 minutes on Sunday), making stops en route along the Promenade des Anglais, from 6am to 9pm.

Taxis from the airport to the city centre cost €25 to €30, depending on the time of day.

Bus

Walking or riding the tram is the best way to get around the city centre, but for anywhere beyond the station–Masséna–Vieux Nice triangle, buses are the way to go. Four night buses (N1,

---

RESOURCES

» **Côte d'Azur Tourisme** (www.cotedazur-tourisme.com) Comprehensive online resource to the Riviera

» **PACA** (www.crt-paca.fr) Umbrella site for all of Provence and the Riviera

» **Riviera Guide** (www.guideriviera.com) Covers the eastern Riviera

» **Var Destination** (www.vardestination.com) Info on the Riviera's western Var region

N2, N3 and N4) run north, east and west from place Masséna every half-hour from 9.10pm until 2am.

Car, Motorcycle & Bicycle

Major car-rental companies (Avis, Budget, Europcar, Hertz etc) have offices at the train station. The best rates are generally via their websites; the earlier you book, the better.

To go native, go for two wheels (and be prepared for hefty safety deposits):

Elite Rent-a-Bike (www.elite-rentabike.com; 21 rue de Rivoli) Near the station.

Holiday Bikes (www.holiday-bikes.com; 23 rue de Belgique; ⊘closed 12.30-2pm & Sun Oct-May) Rents bicycles/50cc scooters/125cc motorcycles for €14/26/57. Enquire for rates on bigger motorcycles.

Vélo Bleu (✆04 93 72 06 06, in English; www.velobleu.org, in French) A shared-bicycle service with over 100 stations around the city – pick up at one, return at another. One-day/week subscriptions costs €1/5, plus usage: free the first 30 minutes, €1 the next 30, then €2 per hour thereafter. You'll need a mobile phone to sign up and operate the system, which can be done in English. Beware the week-to-10-days' return time of your €200 deposit, which they charge you each time you resubscribe; it's better to subscribe once for the week than for five individual days in a row, lest you temporarily max out your credit card.

Taxi

Only out-of-towners take taxis, and drivers know it – the tourist office constantly gets complaints. Ensure your driver uses the meter and charges the correct fare, which is clearly printed on a laminated card that drivers are required to display. Find taxi stands outside the Gare Nice Ville and on av Félix Faure close to place Masséna; otherwise, call ✆04 93 13 78 78.

Tram

Nice's sleek new trams are ideal for getting around. Line 1 runs a V-shaped northwest-south-northeast itinerary from 4.30am to 1.30am, serving convenient areas such as the train station, old town and the Acropolis in the centre.

Antibes & Juan-les-Pins

POP 76,800

Antibes is a concentrate of Mediterranean history. The town's sea walls bear witness to a defensive past (neighbouring Nice had switched allegiance to rival Savoy). Golfe Juan staged Napoléon Bonaparte's triumphant return from exile in Elba. Picasso painted in the Château Grimaldi and F

TRAM TRIVIA

Thirteen international artists contributed to customising the trams' snazzy look, from original soundbites at each stop to local artist Ben's stop-name calligraphy and futuristic art installations along the tram's itinerary. The most visible work is *The Conversation* by Catalan artist Jaume Plensa, overhead on av Jean Jaurès near place Masséna. Most people mistake the seven glowing figures for Buddhas. In fact, they represent the earth's continents and change colours in time with each other to signify world dialogue.

Scott Fitzgerald wrote his seminal novel *Tender is the Night* based on life in Antibes.

Nowadays, Antibes sports the second biggest marina in Europe and attracts throngs of 'yachties' in search of seafaring adventures. The town itself is relatively small and low-key, however, with Cap d'Antibes being a favourite of millionaires. It's a perfect day trip from Nice or Cannes, or a lovely Riviera base if you're after something quieter than the coast's cities.

◉ Sights & Activities

Musée Picasso ART MUSEUM

(www.antibes-juanlespins.com; Château Grimaldi, 4 rue des Cordiers, Antibes; adult/child €6/3; ⊘10am-6pm Tue-Sun) Spectacularly positioned overlooking the sea, 14th-century Château Grimaldi served as Picasso's studio from July to December 1946. The museum, which underwent substantial renovation, now houses an excellent collection of the master's paintings, lithographs, drawings and ceramics, as well as a photographic record of the artist at work.

Vieil Antibes OLD TOWN

Vieil Antibes is a pleasant mix of food shops, boutiques and restaurants. Mornings are a good time to meander along the little alleyways, when the marché (market; Cours Masséna) is in full swing. Check out the views from the sea walls, from the urban sprawl of Nice to the snowy peaks of the Alps and nearby Cap d'Antibes. The area has always been a magnet for artists and celebrities; to find out more, join the Accueil Touristique du Vieil Antibes (✆04 93 34 65 65; 32 bd d'Aguillon; ⊘10am-noon & 1-6pm Mon-Sat) on one of its two-hour guided tours (adult/child €7/free). Check for exact dates and bookings.

Cap d'Antibes — WALKING

Cap d'Antibes' 4.8km of wooded shores are the perfect setting for a walk-swim-walk-swim afternoon. Paths are well marked. The tourist office maps show itineraries.

Musée Peynet — ART MUSEUM

(www.antibes-juanlespins.com; place Nationale, Antibes; adult/child €3/free; ☉10am-noon & 2-6pm Tue-Sun) More than 300 humorous pictures, cartoons and costumes by Antibes-born cartoonist Raymond Peynet, as well as brilliant temporary exhibitions.

Beaches — BEACHES

Antibes' small sandy beach, Plage de la Gravette, gets packed; you'll find the best beaches in Juan-les-Pins, including some free beaches on bd Littoral and bd Charles Guillaumont. Plage de la Salis, on the road between Vieil Antibes and Cap d'Antibes, has the most incredible view of the Alps.

⚜ Festivals & Events

Jazz à Juan — MUSIC FESTIVAL

(www.jazzajuan.fr) All jazz greats, from Sidney Bechet and Miles Davis to John

---

WORTH A TRIP

MUSÉE RENOIR

The city of Cagnes-sur-Mer is nothing to write home about. What is, however, is the exquisite Musée Renoir (www.cagnes-tourisme.com; Chemin des Collettes, Cagnes-sur-Mer; adult/child €4/free; ☉10am-noon & 2-5pm Wed-Mon). Le Domaine des Collettes (as the property was known) was home and studio to an arthritis-crippled Renoir (1841–1919) from 1907 until his death. He lived there with his wife and three children, and the house is wonderfully evocative.

Works on display include *Les Grandes Baigneuses* (The Women Bathers; 1892), a reworking of the 1887 original, and rooms are dotted with photographs and personal possessions. The beautiful olive and citrus groves are as much an attraction as the museum itself. Many visitors set up their own easel to paint.

Coltrane and Keith Jarrett, have played at this summer festival held in mid-July in Antibes' La Pinède park, next to the casino.

🛏 Sleeping

TOP CHOICE Hôtel La Jabotte — B&B €€

(☎04 93 61 45 89; www.jabotte.com; 13 av Max Maurey, Cap d'Antibes; s/d incl breakfast from €108/118; ❄ 🕏) A hotel with *chambre d'hôte* (B&B) feel, La Jabotte is Antibes' hidden gem. Just 50m from the sea (and 20 minutes' walk from Vieil Antibes), its 10 Provençal rooms all look out onto an exquisite patio where breakfast is served from spring to autumn. Much of the decor is the work of Yves, whose work you'll also be able to buy.

Villa Val des Roses — BOUTIQUE B&B €€€

(☎06 85 06 06 29; www.val-des-roses.com; 6 chemin des Lauriers; d incl breakfast low/high season from €140/250; ❄ @ 🕏 ⛱) This beautiful 19th-century bourgeois villa with marble floors, laptop and jacuzzi bath in each room is a 20-minute stroll from the old town. But it's a mere moment from sandy Plage de la Salis and its walled garden is an oasis of peace, best enjoyed in the morning whilst tucking into the grand breakfast buffet.

Relais International de la Jeunesse — HOSTEL €

(☎04 93 61 34 40; www.clajsud.fr; 272 bd de la Garoupe, Cap d'Antibes; dm incl breakfast & sheets €18) In the most perfect of Mediterranean locations, with sea views the envy of neighbouring millionaires, this friendly hostel is particularly popular with 'yachties' looking for their next job in Antibes' port.

Le Relais du Postillon — HOTEL €

(☎04 93 34 20 77; www.relaisdupostillon.com; 8 rue Championnet, Antibes; s/d €49/73; 🕏) Housed in a 17th-century coach house, the great-value Postillon is in the heart of the old town.

🍴 Eating

TOP CHOICE Le Broc en Bouche — MODERN FRENCH €€

(☎04 93 34 75 60; 8 rue des Palmiers, Antibes; mains €15-30; ☉closed Tue dinner & Wed) You'll melt for Flo and Fred's gourmet bistro, their *foie gras,* their *magret de canard* (duck breast) and whatever daily special they'll come up with. And if you like what you see in the fantastic bric-a-brac decor, you could be going home with it: it's all for sale.

La Taverne du Safranier — SEAFOOD €€

(☎04 93 34 80 50; place Safranier, Antibes; mains €10-20, 2-course menu €25; ☉lunch Wed-

Sun, dinner Tue-Sat) Specialities at this casual side-street restaurant include mussels, *petite friture* (fried tiny fish) and *soupe de poisson* (fish soup), served on paper-topped tables surrounded by plastic picnic chairs – tops for an honest seafood dinner with zero fuss.

Le Jardin MODERN FRENCH €€
(✆04 93 34 64 74; www.restaurant-lejardin.fr; 5 rue Sade, Antibes; menus €19.50-33, mains €20) Le Jardin has a delightful garden for alfresco dining, the perfect setting for the restaurant's sunny cuisine. The menu changes with the seasons but is always imaginative and the dishes are beautifully presented.

Auberge Provençale SEAFOOD €€
(✆04 93 34 13 24; www.aubergeprovencale. com; 61 place Nationale, Antibes; menus €17.50-60; ☺Tue-Sat) The auberge is famed for its fabulous seafood. In winter, make sure you get a table in the Vieux Couvent; in summer, opt for the courtyard.

La Ferme au Foie Gras SANDWICH SHOP €
(www.vente-foie-gras.net; 35 rue Aubernon, Antibes; sandwiches €3.50-8; ☺7am-7pm Tue-Sun) Now this is our idea of what a good sandwich should be like: filled with foie gras and delicious chutneys. The adjoining shop also sells excellent foie gras.

Self-catering

Marché Provençal MARKET €
(cours Masséna, Antibes; ☺closed Mon Sep-May) The morning market is perfect for picking up picnic supplies.

🍴 Drinking & Entertainment

Balade en Provence ABSINTHE BAR
(25 cours Masséna, Antibes; ☺6pm-2am) Flirt with the green fairy at this dedicated absinthe bar, complete with original 1860 zinc bar, round tables and accessories (four-tapped water fountain, sugar cubes etc). Make sure you strike up conversation with the hugely knowledgeable staff.

Pearl La Siesta NIGHTCLUB
(rte du Bord de Mer, Antibes; cover €15-20; ☺7pm-5am Thu-Sat) This legendary establishment is famous up and down the coast for its beachside nightclub (Le Pearl) and all-night dancing under the stars. Open from early June to mid-September only, you can still party at the indoor bar-lounge (Le Flamingo) during the rest of the year.

ⓘ Information

Eurochange (4 rue Georges Clémenceau, Antibes; ☺9am-6pm Mon-Sat)

Post office (2 av Paul Doumer, Antibes)

Tourist office (www.antibesjuanlespins.com; ☺9am-12.30pm & 1.30-6pm Mon-Fri, 9am-noon & 2-6pm Sat, 10am-12.30pm & 2.30-5pm Sun) Antibes (11 place du Général de Gaulle); Juan-les-Pins (55 bd Charles Guillaumont)

Workstation Cyber Café (1 av St-Roch, Antibes; per hr €4.50; ☺9am-7pm Mon-Fri, 10am-6pm Sat & Sun)

ⓘ Getting There & Away

Antibes is an easy day trip by train from Nice (€4, 30 minutes) or Cannes (€2.60, 15 minutes).

The **bus station** (gare routière, place Guynemer) has services to surrounding towns, including Biot; buses also depart next to the tourist office.

Biot

POP 9200

From the 16th to 18th centuries, the little hillside village of Biot was famous across the Med for the exceptional quality of its olive-oil jars. Very little remains of that pottery hegemony, but Biot is now famous for another much prettier, but far less pragmatic, art form: bubbled glass.

The famous bubbles are produced by rolling molten glass in baking soda to create a chemical reaction, then trapping the bubbles with a second layer of glass; the latest frosted look uses acid dips.

You can watch work under way at the factory La Verrerie de Biot (Glassworks of Biot; www.verreriebiot.com; Chemin des Combes; admission free, 45min guided tour in English €6; ☺9.30am-6pm Mon-Sat, 10.30am-1.30pm & 2.30-6.30pm Sun), at the foot of the village.

Biot's tourist office (✆04 93 65 78 00; www.biot.fr; 46 rue St-Sébastien; ☺9am-noon & 2-6pm Mon-Fri, 2-6pm Sat & Sun) is located in the village itself, another hilltop warren full of century-old buildings.

Bus 10 (€1, 10 minutes) links the village and the Biot train station half-hourly. In summer, a free shuttle takes in the train station, the *verrerie* and the village.

St-Paul de Vence & Around

POP 3400

What's distinguished the medieval hilltop village of St-Paul de Vence from every other medieval hilltop village around is its phenomenal art legacy. St-Paul attracted many seminal 20th-century artists who lived and worked in the village, such as Russian painter Marc Chagall, who is now buried in St-Paul's interdenominational cemetery.

St-Paul de Vence's cobblestone streets and 16th-century fortifications, dramatically floodlit at night, are an attraction in their own right, one that draws 2.5 million visitors a year.

◉ Sights

Fondation Maeght   GALLERY
(www.fondation-maeght.com; 623 chemin des Gardettes, St-Paul de Vence; adult/child €14/9; ⊙10am-7pm) Browsing the gallery-lined village streets (64 galleries in total!) is a fine entrée for art lovers, but the pièce de résistance is this private gallery, about 500m from the old village. It was designed by architect Josep Luis Sert in conjunction with contemporary artists such as Chagall, who created an exterior mosaic. With an outdoor sculpture 'labyrinth' by Spanish surrealist Joan Miró, interspersed with reflecting pools and mosaics, it was inaugurated in 1964. Its extraordinary permanent collection of 40,000 works is exhibited on a rotating basis.

Chapelle du Rosaire   CHAPEL
(Rosary Chapel; www.vence.fr/the-rosaire-chapel.html; 466 av Henri Matisse, Vence; admission €3; ⊙2-5.30pm Mon, Wed & Sat, 10-11.30am & 2-5.30pm Tue & Thu, closed mid-Nov–mid-Dec) While living in Vence, Matisse's friendship

DON'T MISS

LES ARCADES

The enchanting hotel-restaurant Les Arcades (☑04 93 65 01 04; www.hotel-restaurant-les-arcades.com, in French; 16 place des Arcades, Biot; d €55-100, menus €28-32; ⊙closed Mon & dinner Sun) has become an institution in Biot: the 15th-century building is now home to a prestigious modern art collection, the result of 50 years of friendship between André and Mimi Brothier (the owners) and the many artists living in Biot in the postwar years, such as César, Novaro, Vasarely and Léger. The more-expensive rooms, with their unique works of art, heavy oak furniture, monumental fireplaces and palatial bathrooms, are worth every penny.

① GOING TO FONDATION MAEGHT

Most tourists take the main road to go to the Fondation, but Chemin Ste-Claire is much more inspirational. It was Chagall's route to the village, and along the way you'll pass three chapels, a convent and two Chagall reproductions, placed roughly on the spot where he created the originals. The views en route are truly magnificent, and it's not as hilly as the main road.

with his former model-turned-Dominican Sister Jacques-Marie inspired him to design what he called his masterwork, completed when he was 81. The light from the chapel's stained-glass windows is particularly beautiful in the morning. The artistic blueprints for the chapel, including 42 drawings, 21 paper cuttings, two stained-glass windows, two ceramic pieces and a sculpture, are on display in the Musée Matisse in Nice.

🛏 Sleeping & Eating

La Colombe d'Or   BOUTIQUE HOTEL €€€
(☑04 93 32 80 02; www.la-colombe-dor.com; St-Paul de Vence; r from €250-430, lunch mains €20-60, dinner mains €60-70; ⊙closed Nov-Christmas; ☞⊠) This world-famous inn could double as the Fondation Maeght's annexe: La Colombe d'Or (located outside the walls, at the entrance of the village) was the party HQ of many 20th-century artists (Chagall, Braque, Matisse, Picasso etc) who often paid for their meals in kind, resulting in an incredible private art collection. Don't expect to get a table (or a room) unless you book well in advance, but it will be worth the wait: every room houses unique art and vintage furniture, as do the dining room and garden.

① Information

Tourist office (☑04 93 32 86 95; www.saint-pauldevence.com; 2 rue Grande; ⊙10am-7pm)

① Getting There & Away

From Nice, the frequent bus 400 stops in St-Paul de Vence (€1, 55 minutes) and Vence (€1, one hour).

Cannes

POP 71,800

Most people have heard of Cannes and its eponymous film festival. The latter only lasts for two weeks in May, but the buzz and glitz are there year-round – unlike neighbouring St-Tropez, which shuts down in winter – mostly thanks to regular visits from celebrities enjoying the creature comforts of bd de la Croisette's palaces.

However, what people may not know is that, for all its glamour, Cannes retains a genuine small-town feel: just like anywhere in the south, you'll witness pensioners hotly debating who won the last round of *pétanque* (a game not unlike lawn bowls) under the main square's plane trees (in this case, at Sq Lord Brougham). You'll also get a chance to escape to the unspoilt Îles de Lérins, and to become familiar with more than 2000 years of history – from Ligurian fishing communities in 200 BC to one of Europe's oldest religious communities (5th century AD), to the enigmatic Man in the Iron Mask and a stardom born out of anti-fascist efforts.

◉ Sights & Activities

CANNES

Le Suquet   OLD TOWN

Predating the glitz and glam of the town's festival days, Cannes' historic quarter has retained a quaint village feel with its steep, meandering alleyways. There are wonderful views of the Baie de Cannes from the top of the hill, and the fascinating Musée de la Castre (place de la Castre; adult/child €3.20/free; ◎10am-7pm, closed Mon Sep-Jun). The museum has beautifully presented ethnographic collections.

Palais des Festivals   LANDMARK

(Festival Palace; bd de la Croisette) At the western end of La Croisette, this concrete bunker is the unlikely host of the world's most glamorous film festival. The tourist office runs 1½-hour guided tours (adult/child €3/free; ◎2.30pm), where as well as climbing the red carpet you'll walk down the auditorium, tread the stage and hear many anecdotes about the festival. The tours take place several times a month, except in May. Check with the tourist office for dates and book, as the tours are extremely popular.

STARRING AT CANNES

For 12 days in May, Cannes becomes the centre of the cinematic universe. Over 30,000 producers, distributors, directors, publicists, stars and hangers-on descend on Cannes each year to buy, sell or promote more than 2000 films.

At the centre of the whirlwind is the surprisingly ugly **Palais des Festivals et des Congrès** (Festival Palace; dubbed 'the bunker' by locals), where the official selection is screened. Celebrities usually get their big moment climbing its stairs in an electric storm of flashes (for your own red-carpet moment, said carpet is there most of the year).

The first Cannes Film Festival, on 1 September 1939, was organised as a response to Mussolini's fascist propaganda film festival in Venice. Hitler's invasion of Poland abruptly halted the festival but it restarted in 1946. Over the years the festival split into 'in competition' and 'out of competition' selections. The ultimate prize for 'in competition' films is the prestigious Palme d'Or, awarded by the jury and its president to the film that best 'serves the evolution of cinematic art'. Notable winners include Federico Fellini's *La Dolce Vita* (1960), Francis Ford Coppola's *Apocalypse Now* (1979), Quentin Tarantino's *Pulp Fiction* (1994), documentary-maker Michael Moore's anti-Bush-administration polemic *Fahrenheit 9/11* (2004) and 2008 winner *The Class* by Laurent Cantet, a chronicle of life in a tough Paris school.

Tickets to the festival are generally restricted to film-industry high fliers, but you may get free tickets to selected individual films, usually after their first screening. Invitations must be picked up on the day at Espace Cannes Cinéphiles (La Pantiéro; ◎9am-5.30pm) and are limited. Alternatively, take a tour of the Palais des Festivals to find out what goes on behind and on the scene. For the film-festival programme, consult the official website: www.festival-cannes.com.

Cannes

N

0   200 m
0   0.1 miles

Bd d'Alsace

Bd de la République

R Marceau

R d'Antibes

R Molière

R du Batéguier

29

22

Pl Gambetta

R des Alliés

R Teisseire

R d'Antibes

R Florian

R Chabaud

18

8

R Pradignac

R Commandant André

10

R des Frères

27

25

R Macé

R du Dr Gérard Monod

28

R H Vagliano

R des États-Unis

24

R Jean Jaurès

R Hoche

R des Serbes

Baie de Cannes

Esplanade George Pompidou

R 24 Août

13

R Notre Dame

11

R des Belges

9

R Maréchal Foch

21

R Buttura

R d'Antibes

R Bivouac Napoléon

Bd de la Croisette

30

Pl du 18 Juin

R Venizelos

15

R Jean de Riouffe

R Maréchal Joffre

Pl Général de Gaulle

Pl Mérimée

Palais des Festivals et des Congrès

Jetée Albert Édouard

4

16

R Rouguière

26

12

2

1

R Émile Négrin

6

Square Lord Brougham

La Pantiéro

23

Vieux Port

To Boats to Îles de Lérins (30m); Trans Côte d'Azur (30m)

R Louis Blanc

17

Hôtel de Ville

Pl Bernard Cornut Gentille

Q St-Pierre

Q Max Laubeuf

R du Port

Square du Général Leclerc

R du Marché Forville

20

R Meynadier

R Félix Faure

R du Dr Gazagnaire

15

R St-Antoine

14

R Forville

19

R du Suquet

R St-Dizier

R Louis Perissol

1

R de la Castre

R du Pré

Le Suquet

R Georges Clemenceau

Bd Jean Hibert

To Plages du Midi (50m); Plages de la Bocca (500m)

Bd Victor Tuby

Av des Anciens Combattants d'Afrique du Nord

R des Suisses

R des Orangers

7

To JKL (250m); Z Plage (500m); Hôtel Martinez (500m); Le Bâoli (2.2km)

3

The central, sandy beaches along bd de la Croisette are sectioned off for hotel patrons. Many accept day guests: rates range from €19 per day for a mattress and yellow-and-white parasol on **Plage du Gray d'Albion** (◷10am-5pm Mar-Oct) – it has a waterskiing school – to €51 for the pearl-white lounges on the pier of the super-stylish **Z Plage** (◷9.30am-6pm May-Sep), the beach of Hôtel Martinez.

A microscopic strip of sand near the Palais des Festivals is free, but you'll find better free sand on **Plages du Midi** and **Plages de la Bocca**, west from the Vieux Port along bd Jean Hibert and bd du Midi.

ÎLES DE LÉRINS

Although just 20 minutes away by boat, the tranquil Îles de Lérins feel far from the madding crowd.

The closest of these two tiny islands is the 3.25km by 1km **Île Ste-Marguerite**, where the mysterious Man in the Iron Mask was incarcerated during the late 17th century. Its shores are an endless succession of perfect castaway beaches and fishing spots, and its eucalyptus and pine forest makes for a heavenly refuge from the Riviera heat.

As you get off the boat, a map indicates a handful of rustic restaurants as well as trails and paths across the island. It also directs you to Fort Royal, built in the 17th century, and now harbouring the **Musée de la Mer** (Museum of the Sea; adult/child €3.20/free; ◷10am-5.45pm). The door to the left as you enter leads to the old state prisons, built under Louis XIV. Exhibits interpret the fort's history, with displays on shipwrecks found off the island's coast.

Smaller still, at just 1.5km long by 400m wide, **Île St-Honorat** has been a monastery since the 5th century. Its Cistercian monks welcome visitors all year-round: you can visit the church and small chapels scattered around the island and stroll among the vineyards and forests. Camping and cycling are forbidden. The monks run a restaurant, **La Tonnelle** (☑04 92 99 18 07; mains €25; ◷lunch), which has lovely views of the sea and serves wine from the abbey's own vineyards (bottles are expensive but glasses are available). It's also a stellar spot for afternoon tea.

Boats for the islands leave Cannes from quai des Îles (along from quai Max Laubeuf) on the western side of the harbour. **Riviera Lines** (www.riviera-lines.com) runs ferries to Île Ste-Marguerite (return adult/child €11.50/6), while **Compagnie Planaria** (www.cannes-ilesdelerins.com) operates boats to Île St-Honorat (return adult/child €12/6).

Cannes

☞ Tours

Trans Côte d'Azur   BOAT TOUR

(☎04 92 98 71 30; www.trans-cote-azur.com; quai Max Laubeuf) The most serene way to see the coast. There are day trips to the stunning red cliffs of the Massif de l'Estérel (adult/child €25/15), St-Tropez (adult/child €41/28) and Monaco (adult/child €46/28).

☆ Festivals & Events

Festival de Cannes   FILM FESTIVAL

You won't get in, but it's fun because you see all the celebs walking around. And unlike the Oscars, you can get close to the red carpet without tickets. Held in May.

Les Plages Électroniques   DANCE FESTIVAL

(www.plages-electroniques.com; €5; ⊙7.30pm-12.30am) DJs spin on the sand at the Plage du Palais des Festivals during this relaxed festival. Anyone is welcome, just come with beach wear. Held July to August.

Festival Pantiero   MUSIC FESTIVAL

(www.festivalpantiero.com; €20) Electronic music festival on the rooftop terrace of the Palais des Festivals; very cool. Mid-August.

Festival d'Art Pyrotechnique   FIREWORKS

(www.festival-pyrotechnique-cannes.com) Around 200,000 people cram onto the Croisette every summer to admire the outstanding fireworks display over the Bay of Cannes. Magical. Held on six nights from July to August.

TOP BEACHES

» **Plage de Pampelonne, St Tropez** (p849) Sea, sand and celebrity.

» **Z Plage, Cannes** (p841) For glamour and creature comforts, nothing beats the beach of Hôtel Martinez.

» **Plage de Gigaro, La Croix-Valmer** (p852) Not too big, along wooded shores. Beautiful.

» **Calanques, Massif de l'Estérel** (p846) Take your pick from the dozen coves with crystal-clear waters.

» **Île de Port-Cros** (p853) Most beaches on this beautiful island will make you feel like a castaway.

🛏 Sleeping

Hotel prices in Cannes fluctuate wildly according to the season, and soar during the film festival when you'll need to book months in advance. Many places only accept 12-day bookings during this time. There is no hostel in Cannes.

⟦TOP CHOICE⟧ Hôtel 7e Art   BOUTIQUE HOTEL

(☎04 93 68 66 66; www.7arthotel.com; 23 rue Maréchal Joffre; s €68, d €60-98; ✻☜) Hôtel 7e Art opened in 2010, putting boutique style within reach of budgeters. The owners schooled in Switzerland and got the basics right, with great beds, sparkling-clean baths and excellent soundproofing. The snappy design of putty-coloured walls, padded headboards and pop art far exceeds what you'd expect at this price.

Hôtel Le Mistral   BOUTIQUE HOTEL €€

(☎04 93 39 91 46; www.mistral-hotel.com; 13 rue des Belges; d from €89; ✻☜) This small hotel wins the Palme d'Or for best value in town: rooms are decked out in flattering red and plum tones, bathrooms feature lovely designer fittings, there are sea views from the top floor and the hotel is a mere 50m from La Croisette. No elevator.

Hotel Le Romanesque   BOUTIQUE HOTEL €€

(☎04 93 68 04 20; www.hotelleromanesque.com; 10 rue Batéguier; r €90-150; ✻☜) Every room is individually decorated at this eight-room boutique charmer in the heart of the Carré d'Or nightlife district (book a back room if you're a light sleeper). Favourite rooms include Charlotte, with its sun-drenched bath; and Elizabeth, the former maid's quarters, with low, sloping beamed ceilings. Gay-friendly. Great service.

La Villa Tosca   HOTEL €€

(☎04 93 38 34 40; www.villa-tosca.com; 11 rue Hoche; s/d €80/100; ✻☜⌨) This elegant bourgeois townhouse is a great choice in the heart of Cannes' shopping area. Rue Hoche is semipedestrianised so you won't be bothered by the noise. Rooms, a palette of beige and brown, are comfortable and those with balcony are perfect for a spot of people watching. The hotel has a lift.

Hôtel Alnéa   HOTEL €€

(☎04 93 68 77 77; www.hotel-alnea.com; 20 rue Jean de Riouffe; s/d €68/88; ✻☜) You'll be won over by this wonderfully friendly place. A breath of fresh air in a town of stars, Noémi and Cédric have put their heart and soul into their hotel, with bright, colourful rooms, original paintings and numerous little details such as the afternoon coffee break, the self-service minibar and the bike or *boules* (to play *pétanque*) loans. No elevator.

Hôtel Splendid
BOUTIQUE HOTEL €€
(☑04 97 06 22 22; www.splendid-hotel-cannes. com; 4-6 rue Félix Faure; s/d from €160/190; ❄) This elaborate 1871 building has everything it takes to rival the nearby palaces: beautifully decorated rooms, fabulous location, stunning views. But what the owners have also added is a touch of pragmatism: 15 of the 62 rooms are equipped with kitchenettes, your chance to make the very best of those balconies and sea views! The hotel is equipped with an elevator.

Hôtel Majestic Barrière
LUXURY HOTEL €€€
(☑04 92 98 77 00; www.lucienbarriere.com; 10 bd de la Croisette; r from €300; ❄@🕾≋) Cannes' most magnificent luxury hotel reopened in 2010, following an €80 million renovation. This is where the stars stay during the film festival. Top choice for a devil-may-care weekend.

Hôtel 3.14
BOUTIQUE HOTEL €€€
(☑04 92 99 72 00; www.3-14hotel.com; 5 rue François Einesy; d from €200; ❄🕾≋) The themed 'world' decoration, profusion of velvet and low lighting are all starting to look a little tired. But the Zen spa, vertigo-inducing rooftop jacuzzi and weeknight DJ parties still draw many of Cannes' beautiful people. Rue François Einesy runs off bd de la Croisette, east of Park 45 restaurant.

Also recommended:

Hôtel des Orangers
HOTEL €€
(☑04 93 39 99 92; www.hotel-orangers.com; 1 rue des Orangers; s/d €90/100; ❄@) With a Provençal decor, Les Orangers is ideally located for the restaurants galore on rue du Suquet. Has an elevator.

Hôtel Martinez
LUXURY HOTEL €€€
(☑04 92 98 73 00; www.hotel-martinez.com; 73 bd de la Croisette; d from €270; ❄@🕾≋) Live the high life in fabulous art deco style.

Parc Bellevue
CAMPGROUND €
(☑04 93 47 28 97; www.parcbellevue.com; 67 av Maurice Chevalier, Cannes-la-Bocca; 2 adults, tent & car €20; ⊙Apr-Sep; ≋) About 5.5km west of the city, the closest campsite to Cannes, with facilities galore.

Hôtel Le Florian
HOTEL €€
(☑04 93 39 24 82; www.hotel-leflorian.com; 8 rue Commandant André; s/d from €66/74; ❄@) Clean, great location and affable owners.

Hôtel des Allées
HOTEL €€
(☑04 93 39 53 90; www.hotel-des-allees.com; 6 rue Émile Négrin; s/d €55/80; ❄@🕾) A spotless, Swiss family-run establishment located on a vibrant pedestrian street.

✖ Eating

Generally, you'll find the least expensive restaurants on and around rue du Marché Forville. Hipper and pricier establishments can be found in Le Suquet and in the Carré d'Or (the streets between La Croisette and rue d'Antibes). Many restaurants have tables on the street. Square Lord Brougham, next to the Vieux Port, is a great place for a picnic.

TOP CHOICE Mantel
MODERN EUROPEAN €€
(☑04 93 39 13 10; www.restaurantmantel.com; 22 rue St-Antoine; lunch/dinner menus €25/28; ⊙closed Wed & lunch Tue & Thu) The Italian maître d' will make you feel like a million dollars and you'll melt for Noël Mantel's divine cuisine and great-value prices. Best of all, you get not one but two desserts with your menu (oh, the panna cotta...). Never mind the Croisette's palaces, you'll definitely have a regal night at Mantel.

Coquillages Brun
SEAFOOD €€
(☑04 93 39 21 87; www.astouxbrun.com; 27 rue Félix Faure; menus from €28; ⊙noon-1am) Cannes' most famous seafood brasserie, this is *the* place to indulge in oysters, mussels, prawns, crayfish and other delightfully fresh shellfish with a glass of crisp white wine. The restaurant is full every night, so make sure you book.

Aux Bons Enfants
TRADITIONAL FRENCH €€
(80 rue Meynadier; menu €23; ⊙Tue-Sat) This familial little place doesn't have a phone, and there are no plans to get one any time soon: it's always full. The lucky ones who get a table (get there early or late) can feast on regional dishes made from ingredients picked up at the adjacent market.

Le Riad
MOROCCAN €€
(☑04 93 38 60 95; www.restaurant-le-riad.fr; 6 impasse Florian; mains €13-26; ⊙noon-midnight Tue-Sat) At the end of an alley in the Carré d'Or nightlife district, Le Riad imports Moroccan hospitality and authentic cooking, with classics such as *tagine* (stews cooked in conical-covered earthenware), *méchoui* (spit-roasted lamb) and a real *pastilla* (pigeon pie) – rare even in Morocco. On

weekend nights a belly dancer sets a party mood. Excellent service.

Also recommended:

Auberge Provençale PROVENÇAL €€
(☏04 92 99 27 17; www.auberge-provencale. com; 10 rue St-Antoine; mains €24-55) Cuisine served in sun-drenched, rustic decor at Cannes' oldest restaurant.

PhilCat SNACK BAR €
(La Pantiéro; sandwiches or salads €5; ☺8.30am-5pm) An unassuming prefab cabin which churns out freshly prepared sandwiches, salads and homemade cakes.

Volupté CAFÉ €
(www.volupte-cannes.com; 32 rue Hoche; snacks €4.50, mains €13-15; ☺9am-8pm Mon-Sat) An elegant, trendy café ideal for a sophisticated break or a light lunch.

Park 45 GASTRONOMIC €€€
(☏04 93 38 15 45; www.grand-hotel-cannes. com; 45 bd de la Croisette; menus €40-80, mains €30-36) Perfect for a lingering lunch or swank romantic dinner, Park 45 holds one Michelin star for its imaginative cooking.

Self-Catering

Marché Forville MARKET
(rue du Marché Forville; ☺mornings Tue-Sun) Where many of the city's restaurants shop and where you should get your picnic supplies.

Carrefour SUPERMARKET
(6 rue Meynadier; ☺8.30am-7.30pm Mon-Sat)

Monoprix SUPERMARKET
(9 rue Maréchal Foch; ☺8.30am-8pm Mon-Sat)

🍷 Drinking

The party bloc in town is located around the intersection of rue des Frères Pradignac and rue du Commandant André.

To mingle with the rich and famous, Cannes' hotel palaces all have drop-dead-posh bars. Mere mortals head to the following places.

TOP CHOICE Le Sun 7 COCKTAIL BAR
(5 rue du Dr Gérard Monod; ☺9pm-2.30am; 🛜) The cocktail list is an arm long (literally), and it doesn't even include the 350 whiskies and many draught beers also served at this happening bar. The crowd is young on weekend nights when DJs spin their stuff, but it's much more eclectic during the week. There is no cover charge and the door policy is pretty relaxed.

For You DANCE BAR
(www.sparklingforyou.com; 6-8 rue des Frères Pradignac; ☺6pm-4am) An easy-going bar where you can shake your stuff whilst sipping on a beer or cocktail. Door policy and dress codes are relaxed.

Zanzibar GAY BAR
(www.lezanzibar.com, in French; 85 rue Félix Faure; ☺6pm-4am) Cannes' longest-running gay bar is often dead, but we dig the fabulous mahogany panelling and half-century-old sailor murals. Ideal for quiet cocktails. Ask for a postcard.

☆ Entertainment

Ask the tourist office for a copy of the free monthly *Le Mois à Cannes,* which lists what's on, where.

Dress up or you won't get in, and warm up your credit card: Cannes' nightlife ain't cheap.

Le Palais NIGHTCLUB
(www.palais-club.com; Palais des Festivals, bd de la Croisette; ☺midnight-dawn Jul-Aug) This ephemeral nightclub (it's open only for 50 nights each year) has become the hottest ticket in DJ land, a combination of the most happening names in music and its spectacular setting at the heart of the Palais des Festivals. It's the VIPs' favourite spot so door policy is pretty tight: no guys without girls, only fabulous-looking people and €25 minimum (€60 on big nights).

Le Bâoli NIGHTCLUB
(☏04 93 43 03 43; www.lebaoli.com; Port Pierre Canto, bd de la Croisette; ☺8pm-6am Thu-Sat) This is Cannes' coolest, trendiest and most selective night spot. So selective in fact that your entire posse may not get in unless you're dressed to the nines. The Bâoli is part-club part-restaurant so the only way to ensure you'll get in is to book a table for dinner (mains €60) and make a night of it. Unlike the Palais it's open year-round, and in summer the two compete.

Le Night GAY CLUB
(www.nightlife06.fr; 52 rue Jean Jaurès; ☺9.30pm-5am) Cannes' happening, young gay bar hosts theme nights, from poppers parties to singing contests. Arrive around midnight.

Da Da Da Club NIGHTCLUB
(☏04 93 39 62 70; www.dadadaclub.com; 15 rue Frères Pradignac; ☺11pm-5am) DJs spin electro to house to French pop at this black-on-

black thump-thump disco, which sometimes hosts international acts like Boy George. Look sharp or don't get in.

Information

You'll find half a dozen banks along rue d'Antibes.

Cap Cyber (12 rue 24 Août; per hr €3; ☺10am-9pm Mon-Sat) Has Qwerty keyboards and Asian language software.

Post office (22 rue Bivouac Napoléon; ☺9am-7pm Mon-Fri, 9am-noon Sat) Has an ATM.

Tourist office (☑04 92 99 84 22; www.cannes.travel; bd de la Croisette; ☺9am-7pm Mon-Sat) On the ground floor of the Palais des Festivals.

Tourist office annexe (☑04 93 99 19 77; ☺9am-7pm Mon-Sat) Next to the train station.

ℹ Getting There & Away

BUS Regular bus services to Nice (bus 200, €1, 1½ hours), Nice airport (Bus 210, €15, 50 minutes, half-hourly from 8am to 6pm) and other destinations leave from the bus station on place Bernard Cornut Gentille.

TRAIN There's an information desk and left-luggage facility at the train station.

Destinations within easy reach include Nice (€6.50, 40 minutes), Grasse (€3.80, 30 minutes) and Marseille (€22, two hours), as well as St-Raphaël (€6.50, 25 minutes), from where you can get buses to St-Tropez and Toulon.

ℹ Getting Around

BUS Serving Cannes and destinations up to 7km away is **Bus Azur** (www.busazur.com; place Bernard Cornut Gentille; tickets €1). Bus 8 runs along the coast to the port and Palm Beach Casino on Pointe de la Croisette.

For €0.60 per day you can hop on the electric **Élo Bus**. It has no set stops, so just flag it down as it passes. Its itinerary is marked by a blue line on the road and includes useful locations such as the bus hub at Hôtel de Ville, the Croisette, rue d'Antibes and the train station. It's free if you show a parking-lot claim ticket.

CAR, MOTORCYCLE & BICYCLE There are plenty of paying car parks, including the Palais underground car park (per hour/day €2.60/20) next to the tourist office, which lends out free bicycles if you park here. Parking is free on Pointe de la Croisette.

Elite Rent-a-Bike (www.elite-rentabike.com; 32 av Maréchal Juin) Rents bicycles/scooters/motorcycles from €16/25/100, and also has Harleys from €130; talk to Thiéry.

JKL (www.jkl-forrent.com; 59 angle de la Croisette) Rents luxury and speciality cars fit for celebs.

Mistral Location (www.mistral-location.com; 4 rue Georges Clemenceau) Rents scooters from €26 a day, bicycles from €16.

TAXI Find taxi stands around town, notably outside the train station and Palais des Festivals. Call ☑08 90 71 22 27.

Grasse

POP 51,300

Grasse is not the most picturesque spot on the Riviera. The town is an important administrative centre, with a huge suburban sprawl and neglected historical centre. It's also a leading international perfume centre. For visitors, this means that unless you have an interest in the perfume industry, Grasse has little to justify a visit. If, however, you entertain the slightest curiosity about scents, we'd definitely recommend a trip to the perfumeries or even a flower field nearby.

◉ Sights & Activities

Perfumeries PERFUMERIES

Grasse has more than 30 perfumeries, creating essences sold primarily to factories (for aromatically enhanced foodstuffs and soaps) as well as to prestigious couture houses. Several perfumeries offer free tours, taking you stage by stage through the perfume production process, from extraction and distillation to the work of the 'noses' (perfume creators).

Situated at the foot of the old town, **Fragonard** (www.fragonard.com; 20 bd Fragonard; ☺9am-6pm) is the easiest perfumery to

ROUTE NAPOLÉON

In 1814 French emperor Napoléon Bonaparte abdicated following his defeat at the Battle of Leipzig. He was exiled to the island of Elba in the Mediterranean but a year later, hearing rumours that he was about to be sent to the Atlantic island of St Helena, he decided to attempt to seize back power. Bonaparte escaped Elba and landed in Golfe-Juan; his plan was to reach Lyon via the Alps, to avoid royalist opposition, and he made it to Grenoble via Grasse, Dignes and Gap.

The road from Grasse to Grenoble is now the scenic N85 or Route Napoléon (www.route-napoleon.com), a favourite of road-trippers and bikers.

reach on foot; the tourist office can provide information about other perfumeries.

PERFUME MUSEUM

(International Perfumery Museum; www.musees degrasse.com; 2 bd du Jeu de Ballon; adult/child €3/free; ⊙10am-7pm, closed Tue Oct-Apr) A great interactive museum about the history and art of perfumery.

Domaine de Manon   FARM

(☑04 93 60 12 76; admission €6) You can visit this family-run farm at harvest time to learn more about flower cultivation. Roses are picked mid-May to mid-June, and jasmine from July to late October.

ℹ Information

Banks line bd du Jeu de Ballon, but none changes currency.

Tourist office (☑04 93 36 66 66; www.grasse. fr; 22 cours Honoré Cresp; ⊙9am-7pm Mon-Sat, 9am-1pm & 2-6pm Sun) Has information on accommodation.

ℹ Getting There & Away

BUS The **bus station** (place de la Buanderie) is north of the city centre. Bus 600 goes to Cannes (€1, 50 minutes, every 20 minutes) and Bus 500 goes to Nice (€1, 1½ hours, hourly).

TRAIN The train station is 2km south of the city centre and linked to the old town and bus station by a free shuttle (6.40am to 8pm). Trains regularly serve Cannes (€3.80, 25 minutes) and Nice (€9, one hour).

Massif de l'Estérel

Punctuated by pine, oak and eucalyptus trees, the rugged red mountain range Massif de l'Estérel contrasts dramatically with the brilliant blue sea.

Extending east from St-Raphaël to Mandelieu-La Napoule (near Cannes), the famous Corniche de l'Estérel (also known as the Corniche d'Or and the N98) coastal road passes through summer villages and inlets that are ideal for swimming. Many of the coves (called calanques) are only big enough for a few families; access is generally by a small path, signposted from the road. These include Le Dramont, where the 36th US Division landed on 15 August 1944, and Agay, a sheltered bay with an excellent beach.

More than 100 hiking trails criss-cross the Massif de l'Estérel's interior. Many of the most popular walks, such as those up to Pic de l'Ours (496m) and Pic du Cap Roux (452m), are signposted. Views from the top are breathtaking. Trails are open from 9am to 7pm – therefore, camping is not possible – and access to the range is generally prohibited on windy or particularly hot days because of fire risks, so check with the tourist office before setting off.

Fréjus & St-Raphaël

The twin towns of Fréjus (population 53,300) and St-Raphaël (population 35,000) bear the hallmarks of the area's history over the millennia.

The site of some great Roman ruins, Fréjus was settled by Massiliots (the Greeks who founded Marseille) and colonised by Julius Caesar around 49 BC as Forum Julii. It was settled thanks to the extension of the Roman road Via Aurelia, which linked Italy with Arles. The town's commercial activity largely ceased after its harbour silted up in the 16th century (Fréjus' town centre is 3km from the sea). The Roman ruins are scattered in and around the lively pedestrianised town centre.

St-Raphaël is better known for its natural wonders. Sitting snug at the foot of the Massif de l'Estérel, it became a fashionable hang-out in the 1920s, when F Scott Fitzgerald wrote *Tender is the Night* here. With the development of diving activities, St-Raphaël's fate as an adventure-prone destination was sealed.

St-Raphaël's centre is 2km southeast of Fréjus' historical centre, but the towns' suburbs have become so intertwined that they essentially form a single town.

◎ Sights

Roman Ruins   ROMAN SITES

(⊙9.30am-12.30pm & 2-6pm Tue-Sun) Fréjus' Roman-times population is calculated at 10,000, based on the capacity of its 1st- and 2nd-century arènes (amphitheatre; rue Henri Vadon, Fréjus). It was once one of Gaul's largest amphitheatres, and it's hoped a comprehensive renovation programme (the site has played host to numerous archaeological digs) will breathe new life back into it.

The Roman theatre (rue du Théâtre Romain, Fréjus), north of the old town, is also a shadow of its former self. Much more gratifying is the small but fascinating Musée Archéologique (Archaeological Museum; place

Calvini, Fréjus), whose unearthed treasures include a double-faced marble statue of Hermes, a head of Jupiter and a stunning 3rd-century mosaic depicting a leopard.

Le Groupe Épiscopal — CATHEDRAL

(58 rue de Fleury, Fréjus; adult/child €5/3.50; ☺9am-6.30pm, closed Mon Oct-May) The jewel in the crown of the dramatic Episcopal ensemble is the series of rare, intricate 14th-century painted cornices of the cloister ceiling, depicting fabled as well as real animals and characters.

Built on the site of a Roman temple, the ensemble includes the 11th- and 12th-century cathedral and a unique 5th-century octagonal baptistry. The 12th- and 13th-century cloister acted as the antichamber of the cathedral. Some of its columns come from the podium of the Roman theatre. Admission includes a 10-minute film in multiple languages.

Activities

Sentier du Littoral — WALKING TRAIL

This clearly marked coastal trail (yellow markers) follows the stunning coastline for 11km. Starting at Port Santa Lucia, southeast of St-Raphaël's city centre, and finishing at the Beaumette lighthouse, you can cut short at any stage by heading back up to the coastal road and catching Bus 8 home (there are bus stops every 500m). The whole path takes about 4½ hours to complete.

Diving & Snorkelling — DIVING TOURS

St-Raphaël is a leading dive centre, with numerous WWII shipwrecks off the coast. Euro Plongée (☎04 94 19 03 26; www.europlongee.fr, in French; Port de Boulouris, St-Raphaël; ☺Mar-Nov) offers introductory dives and courses as well as great two-hour snorkelling tours (€25). They're fantastic for families: kids will love spotting starfish,

sea anemones, urchins and other colourful Mediterranean residents.

Beaches — SWIMMING

With its 36km of coastline, St-Raphaël and the Corniche de l'Estérel claim no fewer than 30 beaches, running the gamut of beach possibilities: sandy, pebbly, rocky, long, covelike, nudist...you name it, St-Raph has it.

☞ Tours

Guided tour — WALKING TOUR

A guided tour (€5, two hours), run by the Fréjus tourist office and available in English on request, is the best way to get the most out of Fréjus' rich Roman heritage.

Les Bateaux de St-Raphaël — BOAT TOURS

(www.bateauxsaintraphael.com, in French; Gare Maritime, St-Raphaël) Les Bateaux organises boat excursions from St-Raphaël to Île Ste-Marguerite (adult/child €18/10) and the nearby Estérel mountains (adult/child €15/9). It also runs boats to St-Tropez (single/return adult €14/23, child €9/13) between April and October; check for seasonal schedules.

🛏 Sleeping

L'Aréna — HOTEL €€

(☎04 94 17 09 40; www.hotel-frejus-arena.com; 145 rue du Général de Gaulle, Fréjus; d €95-170; ✳@🛜❄🐾) This elegant hotel with its sienna-coloured walls and lush garden is delightful and ideally located to explore Fréjus' Roman ruins. The 39 comfortable rooms are decked out in warm Provençal prints. Those in the Jasmine annexe are more spacious but there is no lift in that building.

Hôtel Cyrnos — HOTEL €

(☎04 94 95 17 13; www.hotel-cyrnos.com; 840 bd Alphonse Juin, St-Raphaël; d €40-80) This beautiful 1883 mansion has kept much of its early-20th-century Riviera charm, with its grand staircase, terracotta-tiled floors, spacious balconies and wonderfully cool garden. The rooms are simple but comfortable, and Hélène and Patrick are charming hosts. A mere 300m from the beach, it's also ideally located for the *sentier du littoral* walks.

Auberge de Jeunesse Fréjus-St-Raphaël — HOSTEL €

(☎04 94 53 18 75; www.fuaj.org, in French; chemin du Counillier, Fréjus; dm incl breakfast & sheets

---

🛈 CENT SAVER

A seven-day **Fréjus Pass** (€4.60/3.10 per adult/child) covers admission to the Roman amphitheatre, theatre and archaeological museum (otherwise, it's €2 per sight). To visit the Groupe Épiscopal as well, buy a seven-day **Fréjus Pass Intégral** (€6.50) instead. Participating sights sell passes, except the Groupe Épiscopal.

€15.50; ⊙closed mid-Nov–Feb; ☺) A rambling HI-affiliated hostel set in 10 hectares of pine trees, where you can also pitch your tent. Take Bus 7 from St-Raphaël or Fréjus train stations to stop Les Chênes, then cross the roundabout and take chemin du Counillier on your left; the hostel is 600m ahead. There is a daily lock-out between noon and 5.30pm.

✖ Eating

TOP CHOICE **Les Charavins** TRADITIONAL FRENCH €€
(☎04 94 95 03 76; 36 rue Charabois; mains €18-26; ⊙dinner Thu-Tue, lunch Thu, Fri, Mon & Tue) Dining at this jolly wine bar, run by the formidable Philippe Furnémont, a former Michelin-starred chef and wine connoisseur, is all about enjoying the finer pleasures of life. The cuisine is resolutely French, traditional and cooked to perfection: try the homemade foie gras with shallot jam or the oversized macaroni with sausages and sea urchin, and don't even think about turning down Philippe's wine suggestion, it would be akin to lese-majesty!

Le Poivrier FUSION €€
(☎04 94 52 28 50; 52 place Paul Albert Février; lunch/dinner menu €16/30; ⊙Tue-Sat) Tucked away on one of Fréjus' pretty market squares, you'd never guess from the cute alfresco set-up that downstairs is a grandiose vaulted dining room with a monumental fireplace. A Templar's cross on the wall suggests this was a garrison room many centuries ago. Nowadays, Le Poivrier is a wonderful address serving exquisitely fresh dishes inspired by local traditions and faraway climes (the owner is an avid traveller).

L'Arbousier GASTRONOMIC €€
(☎04 94 95 25 00; www.arbousier.net; 6 av de Valescure; lunch/dinner menu €30/44, mains €35; ⊙closed Mon & Tue in winter) One of St-Raphaël's best-known restaurants, the cuisine is a subtle blend of French *gastronomie* and world influences best enjoyed under the shade of the *arbousiers* (strawberry trees).

ℹ Information

BNP (232 rue Jean Jaurès, Fréjus) Just west of the tourist office; there's an ATM.

Post office Fréjus (av Aristide Briand); St-Raphaël (av Victor Hugo)

Tourist office Fréjus (☎04 94 51 83 83; www.frejus.fr; 249 rue Jean Jaurès; ⊙9am-6pm Mon-Fri, 9.30am-12.30pm & 2-6pm Sat, also open Sun Jul & Aug); St-Raphaël (☎04 94 19 52 52; www.saint-raphael.com; 99 quai Albert 1er; ⊙9am-12.30pm & 2-6.30pm Mon-Sat; @☎)

ℹ Getting There & Away

BUS Bus 5, part of the **AggloBus** (www.agglo-frejus-saintraphael.fr, in French) network, links Fréjus train station and place Paul Vernet (also in Fréjus) with St-Raphaël.

TRAIN Fréjus and St-Raphaël are on the train line from Nice to Marseille. There's a frequent service (€11, 50 minutes) from Nice to St-Raphaël Valescure train station, with breathtaking views of the Med and red slopes of the Estérel.

St-Tropez

POP 5700

In the soft autumn or winter light, it's hard to believe that the pretty terracotta fishing village of St-Tropez is yet another stop on the Riviera celebrity circuit. It seems far removed from its glitzy siblings further up the coast, but come spring or summer, it's a different world: the town's population increases tenfold, prices triple and funseekers come in droves to party till dawn, strut their stuff and enjoy the creature comforts of an exclusive beach.

If you can at all avoid visiting in July and August, do. But if not, take heart: it's always fun to play 'I spy...' (a celebrity).

History

St-Tropez acquired its name in AD 68 when a Roman officer named Torpes was beheaded on Nero's orders in Pisa, and packed into a boat with a dog and a rooster to devour his remains. His headless corpse washed up here intact, leading the villagers to adopt him as their patron saint.

For centuries St-Tropez remained a peaceful little fishing village, attracting painters like pointillist Paul Signac, but few tourists. That changed dramatically in 1956 when *Et Dieu Créa la Femme* (And God Created Woman) was shot here starring Brigitte Bardot (aka BB), catapulting the village into the international limelight.

◎ Sights

Musée de l'Annonciade ART MUSEUM
(place Grammont, Vieux Port; adult/child €6/4; ⊙10am-noon & 3-7pm Wed-Mon, closed Nov) Displayed in a disused chapel, the Musée de l'Annonciade displays an impressive collection of artworks by Matisse, Bonnard, Dufy

and especially Signac, who set up his home and studio in St-Tropez.

Citadelle de St-Tropez
MONUMENT

(admission €2.50; ⊙10am-6.30pm) The panoramas of St-Tropez' bay from the elevated 17th-century Citadelle de St-Tropez are worth the climb.

🏃 Activities

Beaches
BEACHES

The glistening sandy Plage de Tahiti, 4km southeast of town, morphs into the celebrity-studded Plage de Pampelonne, which in summer incorporates a sequence of exclusive restaurant/clubs. The bus to Ramatuelle stops at various points along a road that runs about 1km inland from the beach. Beach mats can be rented for around €15 per day.

Sentier du Littoral
WALKING TRAIL

Marked by yellow ('easy') blazes, a 35km **coastal trail** starts from St-Tropez' old fishing quarter La Ponche, and arcs around the Presqu'Île de St-Tropez to Cavalaire-sur-Mer along a spectacular series of rocky outcrops and hidden bays. Allow 2½ hours to Plage des Salins and 3½ hours to Plage de Tahiti. The tourist office has a free easy-to-follow map showing distances and average walking times.

🛏 Sleeping

St-Tropez is no shoestring destination, but there are plenty of camping grounds to the southeast along Plage de Pampelonne. Most hotels close at some stage in winter; the tourist office keeps a list. Also, if you're planning to drive, find out if your hotel has parking and how much it costs.

TOP CHOICE Lou Cagnard
HOTEL €€

(☑04 94 97 04 24; www.hotel-lou-cagnard.com; 18 av Paul-Roussel; d €69-140, tr €160; ❄️🛜) Book well ahead for this great-value courtyard charmer, shaded by lemon and fig trees, and owned by schooled hoteliers. Rooms inside the former home are spotlessly kept, decorated with painted Provençal furniture. Five have ground-floor garden terraces. Top-end extras include lighted makeup mirrors and in-room safes; 15 of the 19 rooms have air-con; ask when booking.

Pastis
BOUTIQUE HOTEL €€€

(☑04 98 12 56 50; www.pastis-st-tropez.com; 61 av du Général Leclerc; d from €200-350; ❄️🌊) This stunning hotel is the brainchild of an

---

ST-TROPEZ BEACH RESTAURANTS

Despite a new push to limit how much space beach restaurants can occupy on Plage de Pampelonne (St-Tropez' main beach), they currently take up the lion's share of sand. Yes, there are occasional public beaches, but St-Tropez' seaside scene is defined by its restaurants – and they're all wildly different. Mattresses (€15 to €20) and parking (€5) are extra. Most are open May to September (call ahead); all are marked on the tourist office map. Book lunch (well ahead) at one of the following.

Club 55 (☑04 94 55 55 55; www.leclub55.fr; 43 bd Path; mains €28-43) The oldest-running club dates to the 1950s, and was originally the crew canteen during the filming of *And God Created Woman*. Now it caters to celebs who do *not* want to be seen. The food is – remarkably – nothing special.

Nikki Beach (☑04 94 79 82 04; www.nikkibeach.com/sttropez; rte de l'Epi; mains €15-30) Favoured by dance-on-the-bar celebs (ie Paris Hilton and Pamela Anderson) who *want* to be seen. The deafening scene ends at midnight.

Plage des Jumeaux (☑04 94 55 21 80; rte de l'Epi; mains €22-30; 👶) First choice for families, with playground equipment and beach toys; tops for seafood. Open year-round.

Aqua Club (☑04 94 79 84 35; www.aqua-club-plage.fr; rte de l'Epi; mains €22-29) Friendly mixed gay-straight crowd – the most diverse by far.

Moorea Plage (☑04 94 97 18 17; www.moorea-plage-st-tropez.com; rte des Plages, Ramatuelle; mains €15-29) Moorea Plage is ideal for conversation and backgammon; tops for steak.

Liberty Plage (☑04 94 79 80 62; www.plageleliberty.com; chemin des Tamaris; mains €16-29) Clothing optional – eat naked. Open year-round.

English couple besotted with Provence and passionate about modern art. If it doesn't sound like an obvious combination, one look at Pastis will dispel any doubt: you'll die for the pop-art-inspired interior, and long for a swim in the emerald-green pool and a snooze under the centenarian palm trees.

La Mistralée
BOUTIQUE HOTEL €€€

(☎04 98 12 91 12; www.hotel-mistralee.com; 1 av du Général Leclerc; d from €330; ❄❄❄❄) The flamboyant former home of hairdresser to the stars Alexandre (famously *sans* surname), this totally over-the-top 1960s-decorated hotel includes, for example, fabric presented to Alexandre by the king of Morocco. At night the restaurant (*menus* €50 to €60), tucked at the back of the luxurious garden by the mosaic-lined pool, feels like a palace from the 1001 Nights.

Hôtel Le Colombier
HOTEL €€

(☎04 94 97 05 31; impasse des Conquettes; r without bath €76, with bath €84-158; ❄) An immaculately clean converted house, five minutes' walk from place des Lices, the Colombier's fresh, summery decor is feminine and uncluttered, with pale pink bedrooms, bright white Provençal *boutis* bedspreads and handmade lace atop vintage wood furniture. Not all rooms have air-con. Rooms without baths share a toilet, but have bidet, sink and shower, open to the bedroom; rooms with baths may only have a partial wall separating them from the bedroom. Enquire when booking.

Hôtel Ermitage
BOUTIQUE HOTEL €€€

(☎04 94 27 52 33; www.ermitagehotel.fr; av Paul Signac; r €180-300; ❄❄❄) Kate Moss and Lenny Kravitz favour St-Trop's latest rocker crash pad, which draws inspiration from St-Trop in the '50s through '70s – disco meets midcentury modern. Ermitage plays off thrift-shop cool, all velour and lacquer, with rooms designed by celebs including Chloë Sevigny and Lapo Elkann. Its off-the-beaten-path residential, hillside location ups the exclusivity factor, and yields knock-out views over town. Swimming pool slated for 2011.

Kube Hôtel
DESIGNER HOTEL €€€

(☎04 94 97 20 00; www.kubehotel.com; 13 chemin de Rogon de la Valette, Gassin; r from €390; ❄❄❄❄) Why go to a nightclub when you can sleep at one? The hotel houses several bars, and neon-black-lit corridors (carry a flashlight) lead to chichi guest-rooms with glitter wallpaper. All you need bring is an attitude.

Les Palmiers
HOTEL €€

(☎04 94 97 01 61; www.hotel-les-palmiers.com; 26 bd Vasserot; d €89-189; ❄) Opposite place des Lices, in an old villa, Les Palmiers has friendly service and simple rooms. Choose one in the main building rather than the annexe.

La Maison Blanche
DESIGNER HOTEL €€€

(☎04 94 97 52 66; www.hotellamaisonblanche.com; place des Lices; d from €220; ☺closed Feb; ❄) An ode to minimalist design, La Maison Blanche has spared no expense in its pursuit of comfort and elegance.

🍴 Eating

Quai Jean Jaurès on the old port is littered with restaurants and cafés – they have mediocre menus, but strategic views of the opulent wealth of nearby yachts. Many establishments close during the winter so your choice may be drastically reduced.

Auberge des Maures
PROVENÇAL €€

(☎04 94 97 01 50; 4 rue du Docteur Boutin; menu €49, mains €31-39; ☺dinner) The town's oldest restaurant remains the locals' choice for always-good, copious portions of earthy Provençal cooking, like *daube* or tapenade-stuffed lamb shoulder. Book a table (essential) on the leafy courtyard.

Le Sporting
BRASSERIE €€

(☎04 94 97 00 65; place des Lices; mains €14-24; ☺8am-1am) There's a bit of everything on the menu at always-packed Le Sporting, but the speciality is hamburger topped with foie gras and morel cream sauce (surprisingly great, if gut-busting). The Brittany-born owner also serves perfect buckwheat crêpes, honest lunch deals, and a simple salad and *croque monsieur* (open-faced grilled cheese with béchamel sauce). Drawback: cigarette smoke, especially near the open storefront. Reservations essential.

Brasserie des Arts
MODERN FRENCH €€

(☎04 94 40 27 37; www.brasseriedesarts.com; 5 place des Lices; mains/menu €20/29) Wedged in a line-up of eating/drinking terraces jockeying for attention on St-Tropez' people-watching square, BA, as it is known, is where the locals go. Out of season ask for a table at the back to experience the real vibe. Unless you're feeling flush, skip à la carte: the fixed three-course menu is gourmet and excellent value.

Auberge de l'Oumède PROVENÇAL €€€
(☎04 94 44 11 11; www.aubergedeloumede.com; Chemin de l'Oumède, Ramatuelle; mains €39-59; ☺dinner, closed Sun & Mon Apr-Jun, Sep & Oct) Epicureans come from far and wide to savour Jean-Pierre Frezia's divine Provençal cuisine in the idyllic setting of his hilltop *mas* (traditional Provençal stone building). With red mullet and spinach cannelloni, grilled catch of the day and sensational desserts, all accompanied by some *very* fine wines, dining at l'Oumède is a once-in-a-lifetime treat.

La Tarte Tropézienne CAFÉ €
(☎04 94 97 71 42; www.tarte-tropezienne.com; 36 rue Georges Clémenceau; ☺7am-7.30pm) A must-try is the local speciality, *tarte Tropézienne,* an orange-blossom-flavoured double sponge cake filled with thick cream, created by a Polish baker and christened by BB in the 1950s. This bakery, the original creator, is the best place to buy one. For an informal sit-down lunch, head to the café of the same name on place des Lices, where you can undo the goodness of the salads (€10 to €15) with a piece of *tarte.*

Self-Catering

Place des Lices market MARKET
(☺mornings Tue & Sat) A highlight of local life: people come for the gossip as much as the colourful stalls.

Monoprix SUPERMARKET
(9 av du Général Leclerc; ☺8am-8pm Mon-Sat) For groceries.

🍸 Drinking & Entertainment

Looks – and deep pockets – are an essential accessory for a night out in St-Tropez. Don't bother turning up in shorts and trainers, it's bling, heels and hairspray that does it for doormen.

In winter most bars only open on weekends, but in summer it's party central seven days a week.

Ice Bar THEME BAR
(☎04 94 97 20 00; www.kubehotel.com; 13 chemin de Rogon de la Valette, Gassin; admission €30; ☺6.30pm-1am) Reservations are essential at this bar made of ice, where admission gets you four Grey Goose vodka cocktails, which you must consume within 30 minutes. Then you leave. Parka, gloves and hat included. Best between 11pm and 1am.

L'Esquinade NIGHTCLUB
(rue du Four; ☺11pm to 5am, closed Mon-Fri Oct-May) Where the party winds up when you want to dance till dawn. The only club open year-round is also the Tropéziens' top choice.

L'Octave Café NIGHTCLUB
(☎04 94 97 22 56; place de la Garonne; ☺8pm-5am, closed Nov-Mar) Twirl in a cocktail dress at this intimate club with live band that plays standards and pop – ideal on date night. Dress to impress.

Bar at l'Ermitage LOUNGE BAR
(www.ermitagehotel.fr; av Paul Signac; ☺5pm-midnight) Escape the crowds at the laid-back Ermitage, kitted out in distressed '50s-modern furniture, worn floor tiles and wobbly antique café tables. Knockout views.

Bar du Port BAR
(www.barduport.com; quai Suffren; ☺7am-3am) A young, happening bar for beautiful people, with a chichi decor in shades of white and silver.

Les Caves du Roy NIGHTCLUB
(www.byblos.com; Hôtel Byblos, av Paul Signac) The star-studded bar of the infamous Hôtel Byblos. The music is better on the top floor. Come dressed to the nines.

Café de Paris CAFÉ
(www.saint-tropez.com/cafe-de-paris; Hotel Sube, quai Suffren; ☺8am-2am) The outdoor terrace is *the* place to sport your new strappy sandals over aperitifs at five. Or come in the morning for the €13 continental breakfast – a good deal in St-Tropez.

🛍 Shopping

Atelier Rondini SANDALS
(www.rondini.fr; 16 rue Georges Clémenceau) When Colette returned to St-Tropez from Greece, she brought back a pair of sandals, which she took to her cobbler to replicate. That cobbler was Atelier Rondini, open since 1927 and still making the same sandals for about €120. You can only get them in town, and they can't be shipped. If you don't find any that fit they can be made to order, but it takes a week and you must come in person for the final fitting and pickup.

K Jacques SANDALS
(www.kjacques.com; 25 rue Allard & 16 rue Seillon) St-Tropez' other sandal-maker supplies

more celebrities because but it exports and does internet business.

Information

The English-language brochure *Out and About* is available in tourist offices in the area.

Bay of St-Tropez (www.bay-of-saint-tropez. com) A good information source for the surrounding towns and beaches.

Crédit Lyonnais (21 quai Suffren) At the port.

Kreatik Café (www.kreatik.com; 19 av Général Leclerc; per hr €7; ☺9.30am-9pm Mon-Sat, 2-8pm Sun) Even the internet café looks fit for celebrities.

Master Change (18 rue du Général Allard) The town's only currency exchange.

Post office (place Celli)

Tourist office (☑04 94 97 45 21; www.ot-saint-tropez.com; quai Jean Jaurès; ☺9.30am-12.30pm & 2-7pm) Keeps a useful list of hotels and restaurants open in the low season.

Getting There & Away

BOAT Les Bateaux de St-Raphaël (www. bateauxsaintraphael.com, in French) runs boats between St-Raphaël and St-Tropez (single/ return adult €14/23, child €9/13) from April to October.

Trans Côte d'Azur (www.trans-cote-azur.com) runs day trips from Nice (adult/child €55/41) and Cannes (adult/child €41/28) between April and September.

Les Bateaux Verts (www.bateauxverts.com; Ste-Maxime) operates a shuttle boat between Ste-Maxime and St-Tropez (one way adult/child €7/3.75, 20 minutes), and Port Grimaud (adult/child €6.50/3.50, 15 minutes) from February to October and for a couple of weeks around Christmas and New Year.

BUS St-Tropez' **bus station** (av Général de Gaulle), on the southwestern edge of town on the main road, also has an **information office** (☺8.30am-noon & 2-4.30pm Mon-Fri, 8.30am-noon Sat).

VarLib (www.varlib.fr, in French) tickets cost just €2 for anywhere within the Var *département* (except Toulon-Hyères airport), including Ramatuelle (35 minutes), St-Raphaël (1¼ hours) via Grimaud and Port Grimaud, and Fréjus (€9, one hour). Buses to Toulon (two hours, seven daily, less in summer) stop at Le Lavandou (one hour) and Hyères (1½ hours). There are four daily buses to Toulon-Hyères airport (€15; 1½ hours).

CAR & MOTORCYCLE To avoid the worst of the high-season traffic, approach from the A8 motorway and exit at Le Muy (exit 35). Take the D558 road across the Massif des Maures, via La Garde Freinet to Port Grimaud, then park here

and take the shuttle boat that runs to St-Tropez from Easter to October.

 Getting Around

If you'd like to retain some sort of inner peace while in St-Tropez, you're strongly advised to opt for two wheels rather than four: traffic here is infamous. To find parking in summer, arrive in town by 7am; leave after 8pm to avoid outbound traffic jams. Overnight public parking costs over €40, and lots fill early in the day.

Car hire companies can be found on av du Général Leclerc.

Marine Service (☑06 09 57 31 22; Le Pilon) Taxi boat.

Rolling Bikes (www.rolling-bikes.com, in French; 14 av du Général Leclerc) Rents bikes/ scooters/motorcycles from €15/40/120 per day, plus a hefty deposit.

Taxi ☑04 94 97 05 27

St-Tropez to Toulon

MASSIF DES MAURES

Shrouded by a forest of pine, chestnut and cork oak trees, the Massif des Maures arcs inland between Hyères and Fréjus. Roamed by wild boars, its near-black vegetation gives rise to its name, derived from the Provençal word *mauro* (dark pine wood).

Contact the Conservatoire du Patrimoine (☑04 94 43 08 57; www.conservatoiredu freinet.org; Chapelle St-Jean, place de la Mairie) in La Garde Freinet for various workshops, horse and donkey treks and weekly forest walks to see cork being harvested. Hiking and cycling opportunities abound, especially around La Sauvette (779m), the massif's highest peak. The village of Collobrières is the largest town in the massif and renowned for its wonderful chestnut purée and *marrons glacés* (candied chestnuts).The tourist office (☑04 94 48 08 00; www.collobrieres-tourisme.com; bd Charles Caminat, Collobrières; ☺10am-12.30pm & 3-6.30pm Mon-Sat, closed Sun & Mon Sep-Jun) has maps, information on guided walks and plenty of tips to make the best of the area.

CORNICHE DES MAURES

This coastal road snakes from La Croix-Valmer to Le Lavandou along the D559. In addition to stunning views, there are some superb spots for swimming, sunbathing and walking.

La Croix-Valmer's Gigaro beach is one not to miss, as is the walking path towards

Cap Lardier, which is one of the most beautiful, least-trodden bits of the coast.

TOP CHOICE Domaine du Rayol (☑04 94 04 44 00; www.domainedurayol.org; av des Belges, Le Rayol-Canadel; adult/child €9/6; ⊙9.30am-6.30pm) is a wonderful spot. A former seaside estate rescued from ruin, it has been transformed into a stunning 20-hectare botanical garden, with plants from Mediterranean climates around the world. Paths meander down to the sea. In summer, call ahead for snorkelling tours (adult/child €18/14) of the underwater marine garden and botanist-guided walks. One of only a few sights open at lunchtime, there's an on-site café.

Le Lavandou (www.ot-lelavandou.fr) is famous for its 12km of fine beaches and 12 types of sand. The town has retained a pretty historical centre, and its 1000-boat marina is a prime evening-stroll venue.

Up in the hills, you'll find the quintessential Provençal village of Bormes-les-Mimosas. The vieux (old) village is spectacularly flowered year-round, with the eponymous mimosas in winter and deep-fuchsia bougainvilleas in summer. Old cobbled streets are lined with artists' galleries and boutiques selling traditional Provençal products, natural soap and essential oils. Hostellerie du Cigallou (☑04 94 41 51 27; www.hostellerieducigallou.com; place Gambetta, Bormes-les-Mimosas; d €136-173; ❋➷❄) is a plush hotel with fantastic views and dreamy pool. Cheaper and utterly charming, also with sensational views, is Hôtel Bellevue (☑04 94 71 15 15; www.bellevuebormes.com; place Gambetta, Bormes-les-Mimosas; d €42-74; ❋➷❄). Both are in the centre of the village.

For breathtaking views of the islands, the Route des Crêtes winds its way through maquis-covered hills some 400m above the sea. Take the D41 as you head out of Bormes-les-Mimosas past the Chapelle St-François; 1.5km up the hill, turn immediately right after the sign for Col de Caguo-Ven to follow 13km of tight bends and spectacular views. The light is truly exquisite in the late afternoon or early evening.

TOP CHOICE Relais du Vieux Sauvaire (☑04 94 05 84 22; rte des Crêtes; mains €18-30; ⊙closed Oct-May; ❄) is the hidden gem of these hills. With 180-degree views you could only dream of, this restaurant and pool (most people come here for lunch and then stay all afternoon) is one of a kind. Owner Roland Gallo has been here since 1960 and clearly has no intention of ever going anywhere else (you'll understand why when you get there). The food is as sunny as the views: pizzas, melon and Parma ham, or whole sea bass in salt crust. The rte des Crêtes goes back down towards Le Rayol-Canadel on the coastal D559 after the restaurant.

You'll need a car to travel to Bormes and along the rte des Crêtes, but the coastal road is on the itinerary of the Toulon to St-Tropez VarLib (www.varlib.fr, in French; ticket €2) bus, which stops in most towns, including Le Lavandou.

HYÈRES

Despite its profusion of palm trees, the small town of Hyères is rather underwhelming. Much more interesting is the nearby Presqu'Île de Giens (Giens Peninsula), a protected wetland harbouring amazing birdlife, including pink flamingos, herons, terns, egrets and cormorants. The Maison du Tourisme (☑04 94 38 50 91), housed in the same building as the tourist office (☑04 94 01 84 50; www.hyeres-tourisme.com; 3 av Ambroise Thomas; ⊙9am-6pm Mon-Fri, 10am-4pm Sat), runs two-hour guided walks (per person €5) to the wetlands and salt marshes. Call ahead for dates and bookings.

ÎLES D'HYÈRES

For some inexplicable reason, these paradisiacal islands (also known as Îles d'Or – Golden Islands – for their shimmering mica rock) have remained mostly unknown to foreign crowds.

The easternmost and largest of this trio of islands is the little-visited Île du Levant, split into an odd combination of army land and nudist colony. Île de Port-Cros, the middle and smallest island, is the jewel in the islands' crown. France's first marine national park (www.portcrosparcnational.fr, in French), it boasts exceptional marine fauna and flora, which makes it a snorkelling paradise. The island is also covered with 30km of marked trails through thick forest, ragged cliff tops and deserted beaches.

The largest and westernmost island is Île de Porquerolles (www.porquerolles.com). Run as a hacienda in the early 20th century, it has kept many of its sprawling plantation features. There are plenty of walking trails, but the best way to get around is by cycling. There are several bicycle-rental places, as well as a few restaurants and hotels.

ℹ Getting There & Away

Boats to the Îles d'Hyères leave from various towns along the coast. **Vedettes Îles d'Or** (www. vedettesilesdor.fr) operates boats to all three islands from Le Lavandou, and between Port-Cros and Porquerolles in summer.

Le Levant return adult/child €25/21, 35 minutes or one hour (depending on which island the boat goes to first)

Porquerolles return adult/child €33/26, 40 minutes

Port-Cros return adult/child €25/21, 35 minutes

TLV-TVM (www.tlv-tvm.com) runs services to Porquerolles (return adult/child €17/15, 10 minutes) from the La Tour Fondue port at the bottom of the Giens Peninsula. It also runs services to Port-Cros (return adult/child €25/22, one hour) and Le Levant (adult/child €25/22, 1½ hours) from Hyères' port.

Toulon

POP 168,800

Toulon is no Riviera highlight. As a major port and naval base, it's nothing to write home about, unless you're a keen WWII history buff. It was here in 1942 that the entire French fleet was scuttled in the *rade* (sheltered bay lined with quays) to escape German forces. The city was practically razed following the 1944 Allied landing.

The main reason why you might find yourself in Toulon is that it is an important transport hub, with good train connections, ferries to Corsica and an expanding international airport.

◉ Sights & Activities

Le Batelier de la Rade   BOAT TOUR

(quai de la Sinse; per person €10) From the port you can take a spin around the *rade*, with a commentary (in French only) on the local events of WWII.

Plages du Mourillon   BEACHES

Good beaches for soaking up some rays are 2km southeast at Mourillon. Take Bus 3 and get off at the Michelet stop.

Mont Faron   WAR MEMORIAL

Towering over the old city to the north is Mont Faron (580m), offering a fantastic panorama of the bay. Near the summit is the **Mémorial du Débarquement** (adult/child €3.90/1.70; ⊙10am-noon & 2-5.30pm Tue-Sun), a WWII museum commemorating the Allied landings that took place along the coast in August 1944. A **téléphérique** (cable car; www.telepherique-faron.com, in French; return adult/child €6.50/4.60; ⊙9.30am-7pm) ascends the mountain from bd de Vence. Take Bus 40 from place de la Liberté and get off at the téléphérique stop. A combined bus and cable car ticket costs €6.

🛏 Sleeping & Eating

Hôtel Little Palace   HOTEL €

(☏04 94 92 26 62; www.hotel-littlepalace.com; 6-8 rue Berthelot; s/d €54/64; ✳@📶) The over-the-top Italian-inspired decor lacks authenticity but Little Palace is well run. Request a room on the ground floor if you have heavy bags as there is no elevator.

Grand Hôtel Dauphiné   HOTEL €

(☏04 94 92 20 28; www.grandhoteldauphine. com; 10 rue Berthelot; s/d from €60/66; ✳📶) A clean, functional hotel, with newly refurbished bathrooms and efficient staff. The hotel has an elevator.

Le Chantilly   BRASSERIE €

(☏04 94 92 24 37; place Puget; mains €10-25; ⊙6.30am-11pm) Going strong since 1907, Le Chantilly will sort you out for food, whatever the time of day.

AU NATUREL

Not a fan of tan lines? This coastal stretch of the Riviera is well endowed with *naturiste* (nudist) beaches. **Plage de Tahiti**, the northern stretch of Plage de Pampelonne in St-Tropez, is probably the best known. More secluded is **Plage de l'Escalet**, on the southern side of Cap Camarat on the Presqu'île de St-Tropez, a beautiful but hard to reach spot.

Most isolated is the oldest and largest *naturiste* colony in the region, which occupies half of the 8km-long island **Île du Levant**.

The coast's laid-back, let-it-all-hang-out attitude was the premise of Jean Girault's cult 1964 farce film *Le Gendarme de St-Tropez*, in which Louis de Funès starred as the policeman of the title, who attempted to crack down on local nudists.

ℹ️ Information

Find banks along bd de Strasbourg.

Change du Port (15 quai Cronstadt; ⊙8.30am-noon & 1.30-4.45pm Mon-Fri) Currency exchange.

Post office (rue Dr Jean Bertholet)

Tourist office (www.toulontourisme.com; 12 place Louis Blanc; ⊙9am-6pm Mon-Sat, 9am-1pm Sun) Distributes a useful monthly agenda summarising museum hours and events.

ℹ️ Getting There & Around

AIR The small international **Toulon-Hyères Airport** (www.toulon-hyeres.aeroport.fr) is 23km east of Toulon, on the edge of the Giens Peninsula. Bus 102 (five daily) links the airport with Toulon's bus and train station (€1.40, 40 minutes).

BOAT Ferries operated by **Corsica Ferries** (www.corsica-ferries.co.uk; Port de Commerce) run to Corsica and Sardinia.

BUS VarLib buses (www.varlib.fr, in French) operate from the bus station, next to the train station. Travel within the Var département costs €2. Bus 103 to St-Tropez (eight buses daily) runs east along the coast via Hyères (35 minutes) and Le Lavandou (one hour).

The tourist office sells a **one-day pass** (www.reseaumistral.com; €6) that includes unlimited travel on local buses and commuter boats, and a return ticket for the Mont Faron Téléphérique. Single fare on local buses is €1.40.

TRAIN Frequent train connections include Marseille (€11.50, 40 minutes), St-Raphaël (€15, 50 minutes), Cannes (€19.50, 1¼ hours), Monaco (€26, 2¼ hours) and Nice (€23.50, 1¾ hours).

West of Toulon

BANDOL
POP 8800

To many, the name Bandol conjures up images of rosés chilled to perfection and noble reds elevating meat dishes to new heights. The seaside resort town of Bandol itself is lesser known, but with its 1600-boat marina, pretty beaches and steep hills proffering uninterrupted sea views, it's a long-standing favourite of French holiday-home owners.

⊙ Sights & Activities

Maison des Vins   WINE TASTING
(www.maisondesvins-bandol.com, in French; place Artaud; ⊙10am-1pm & 3-7pm Mon-Sat, 10am-1pm Sun) Bandol's 49 vineyards carefully manage their prized production (collectively held under the Appellation d'Origine Con-

trôlée Vins de Bandol label) of red, rosé and white. The Maison des Vins is the best place to find out more: manager Pascal Perier, a living Bandol encyclopaedia, organises tastings and keeps a well-supplied shop.

Sentier du Littoral   WALKING TRAIL
This yellow-marked coastal trail runs 12km (allow 3½ to four hours) from Bandol's port to La Madrague in St-Cyr-Les-Lecques, with the beautiful **Calanque de Port d'Alon** roughly halfway. The easiest way is to take the bus from Bandol to Les-Lecques (the tourist office has timetables) and walk back to Bandol at your own pace.

🛏️ Sleeping & Eating

Key Largo   HOTEL €€
(☑04 94 29 46 93; www.hotel-key-largo.com; 19 corniche Bonaparte; d €75-105; ❄️) Strategically located halfway between the port and the pretty beach of Renécros, the eight rooms with sea views (and private terrace for three of them) are an absolute steal. The remaining 10 still enjoy the same simple but stylish decor and look out on neighbouring gardens. And there are homemade cakes for breakfast no matter where you sleep.

L'Assiette des Saveurs   FUSION €€
(☑04 94 29 80 08; 1 rue Louis Marçon; mains €10) One street back from the busy marina, with its pretty street-side terrace, L'Assiette prepares classic recipes with a cheeky fusion twist – such as monkfish in orange sauce or satay lamb chops. It gets our vote for best value in town.

KV&B   MODERN FRENCH €€
(☑04 94 74 25 77; 5 rue de la Paroisse; lunch/dinner menu €15/28; ⊙lunch & dinner Mon, Tue & Thu-Sat, lunch Sun) The address to enjoy local wine over tapas in a crisp contemporary bar à vin setting (we love the Haribo sweets on the bar).

ℹ️ Information

Banque Populaire (31 quai de Gaulle) On the marina; exchanges currency.

Tourist office (www.bandol.fr, in French; Allées Vivien; ⊙9am-noon & 2-6pm Mon-Sat) Has a comprehensive guide in English.

ℹ️ Getting There & Away

BUS VarLib (www.varlib.fr, in French) bus 8804 connects Bandol with Toulon, bus 8806 with Sanary. Tickets cost €2.

TRAIN Bandol is on the line between Toulon (€3.40, 15 minutes) and Marseille (€9, 45 minutes).

AROUND BANDOL

Bandol's 1500 hectares of vineyards spread inland across scenic rolling landscapes and stunning villages (you'll need wheels to get around). The most famous village of all is the hilltop Le Castellet, a medieval wonder culminating in a 12th-century castle. Its steep, boutique-lined pedestrian streets are chock-a-block in summer.

TOP CHOICE Les Quatre Saisons (☎04 94 25 24 90; www.lesquatresaisons.org; 370 montée des Oliviers, rte du Brûlat, Le Castellet; d incl breakfast €90-130; ❋ ☀) is a wonderful B&B sitting snug below Le Castellet. In their gorgeous *mas* (traditional Provençal stone house), Patrice and Didier have decorated five exquisite rooms in the purest Provençal style. All rooms open onto a central swimming pool; some also offer breathtaking views of the area. Patrice's *tables d'hôte* (set menu; €40 including drinks) is worth every penny. For a share of Patrice's culinary secrets, try his half-day cooking course (€40 per person).

Back on the coast, the pretty-as-a-picture seaside town of Sanary-sur-Mer is a stroller's dream. Watch the fishermen unload their catch on the quay (in winter you can regale in *oursinade,* fresh sea urchin served with a squeeze of lemon juice and a slice of buttered bread), or admire the traditional fishing boats from one of the seafront cafés. Wednesday's colourful grand marché (market; ◷7.30am-1pm) is the area's main market, drawing crowds from miles around.

NICE TO MENTON

The Corniches

Some of the Riviera's most spectacular scenery stretches between Nice and Menton. A trio of corniches (coastal roads) hugs the cliffs between Nice and Monaco, each higher up the hill than the last. The middle corniche ends in Monaco; the upper and lower continue to Menton.

Grace Kelly, Princess of Monaco, is strongly associated with this part of the world. The Grande Corniche appears in Hitchcock's *To Catch a Thief,* as does the bridge to Èze on the Moyenne Corniche, and Kelly herself died in a car crash on the D53, a road linking the Grande and Moyenne corniches.

CORNICHE INFÉRIEURE

Skimming the villa-lined waterfront, the Corniche Inférieure (also known as the Basse Corniche, the Lower Corniche or the N98) sticks pretty close to the train line, passing (west to east) through Villefranche-sur-Mer, St-Jean-Cap Ferrat, Beaulieu-sur-Mer, Èze-sur-Mer and Cap d'Ail.

VILLEFRANCHE-SUR-MER
POP 6700

This picturesque pastel-coloured, terracotta-roofed fishing port overlooking the Cap Ferrat peninsula was a favourite with Jean Cocteau, who painted the frescos in the 17th-century Chapelle St-Pierre. Steps split the steep cobblestone streets that weave through the old town, including the oldest, rue Obscure, an eerie vaulted passageway built in 1295. Looking down on the township is the 16th-century citadel. Beyond the port is a sandy beach offering picture-perfect views of the town.

ST-JEAN-CAP FERRAT
POP 2100

On the Cap Ferrat peninsula, this fishing-village-turned-playground-for-the-wealthy conceals an enclave of millionaires' villas, with illustrious residents both present and past. On the narrow isthmus of the town, the extravagant Villa Ephrussi de Rothschild (www.villa-ephrussi.com; adult/child €10/7.50; ◷10am-6pm) gives you an appreci-

TOP RIVIERA GARDENS

» **Jardin d'Èze** Thousands of cacti, the history of Èze and the most enthralling, sweeping views of the Mediterranean.

» **Jardin Exotique de Monaco** Stroll among century-old cacti and thousands of succulent plants, with stunning views of the principality.

» **Jardin Botanique Exotique du Val Rahmeh, Menton** The original botanical garden, beautifully maintained, and home to one of the last Easter Island trees (extinct on the island).

» **Villa Ephrussi de Rothschild, St-Jean-Cap Ferrat** Nine different gardens, all exquisite, in the grounds of this early 20th-century folly.

» **Domaine du Rayol** Mediterranean wonder and a unique marine garden.

ation of the area's wealth. Housed in a 1912 Tuscan-style villa built for the Baroness de Rothschild, it's full of 18th-century furniture, paintings, tapestries and porcelain. A combined ticket with the Villa Grecque Kérylos in Beaulieu costs €15/10.50 for adults/children.

The peninsula also has three walking trails with glimmering seascapes, and secluded coves for swimming.

BEAULIEU-SUR-MER
POP 3700

Some of the best-preserved belle époque architecture along the coast is in the seaside holiday town of Beaulieu-sur-Mer, including its elaborate 1904 rotunda with Corinthian columns capped by a cupola. Another belle époque beauty is the Villa Grecque Kérylos (www.villa-kerylos.com; av Gustave Eiffel; adult/student €8.50/6.50; ⊙10am-6pm), a reproduction of an Athenian villa built by archaeologist Théodore Reinach in 1902.

MOYENNE CORNICHE

The Moyenne Corniche – the middle coastal road (N7) – clings to the hillside. If you want to enjoy the views, the bus to Monaco takes this road, so bag a seat on the right from Nice to Monaco (on the left in the opposite direction). From Nice, the Moyenne Corniche travels past Col de Villefranche, through Èze and to Beausoleil, the French town bordering Monte Carlo.

ÈZE
POP 3000

On the pinnacle of a 427m peak is the medieval stone village of Èze. Once occupied by Ligurians and Phoenicians, today it's home to one-off galleries and artisan boutiques within its enclosed walls (there's only one doorway in or out of the village). The high point is the Jardin Èze (admission €5; ⊙9am-sunset), a slanting cliff-side garden of exotic cacti with views of the Med all the way to Corsica (on a good day).

To explore the village's nooks and crannies after the tour buses have left, stay at the magnificent Château Eza (☑04 93 41 12 24; www.chateaueza.com; rue de la Pise; d from €180; ❋🛜), which also has a lofty gastronomic restaurant and terrace (lunch menus €49 to €59, dinner mains €50), with views of the Med on a plate.

On the seaside below is the village's coastal and very belle époque counterpart, Èze-sur-Mer (where U2's Bono has a villa). Èze-sur-Mer and Èze village are connected

by a spectacular (and steep!) walking path, where German philosopher Friedrich Nietzsche (1844–1900) mused about the theories that formed the basis of his work *Thus Spoke Zarathustra*. Now labelled Chemin de Nietzsche, the rocky path takes about an hour, and in winter it's the only link between the two villages if you don't have a car. In summer a shuttle bus meets every train at Èze-sur-Mer (on the train line between Nice and Ventimiglia, which also stops at Monaco and Menton) and takes visitors to Èze village.

Year-round, Buses 82 and 112 run direct to Èze village from Nice (€1, 20 minutes). There's a helpful tourist office (☑04 93 41 26 00; www.eze-riviera.com; place du Général de Gaulle) at the base of the village.

GRANDE CORNICHE

The Grande Corniche, whose panoramas are the most dramatic of all, leaves Nice as the D2564. It passes La Turbie, which sits on a promontory directly above Monaco and offers vertigo-inducing views of the principality. The best views are from the town's Trophée des Alps (cours Albert 1; adult/child €5/3.50; ⊙9.30am-1pm & 2.30-6.30pm Tue-Sun), one of only two Roman trophy monuments in the world (the other's in Romania), built by Augustus in 6 BC.

On a breezy spot in the village, Restaurant La Terrasse (☑04 93 41 21 84; www.restaurant-la-terrasse-laturbie.com; 17 place Neuve; 3-course menu €19.50, mains €9-20; 🛜) serves a great-value three-course *menu*. Monégaques often come here for dinner when it gets too hot on the coast. The restaurant owners used to live in the US and will let American visitors ring their mother back in the US for nostalgia's sake!

The corniche continues to Roquebrune, a hilltop village where architect Le Corbusier is buried. Les Deux Frères (☑04 93 28 99 00; www.lesdeuxfreres.com; place des Deux Frères; lunch/dinner menu €28/48; ⊙lunch & dinner Wed-Sat, lunch Sun, dinner Tue) is the choice restaurant in the village. Dramatically perched on a panoramic terrace, it has jaw-dropping views of the Med. Waiters wear formal black, and mains (traditional French cuisine) come hidden beneath silver domed platters. In winter, guests lunch or dine in the minimalist dining room with its contemporary fireplace. The lunch *menu*, including a half-bottle of wine, is good value.

Menton

POP 29,100

To the east of Monaco, the pastel-shaded, palm-lined seaside town of Menton is within walking distance of the Italian border.

Protected by the surrounding mountains, Menton enjoys a warm, near-subtropical climate that has made its good fortune: 19th-century European royals moved their winter residences to its shores, and Menton was Europe's biggest lemon producer until the 1930s. Production is much smaller these days but the sun-coloured fruit is celebrated every year during the February Fête du Citron.

For visitors, Menton's appeal is limited, with little in the way of sights or nightlife. It does have one excellent restaurant, however, which would make it an ideal lunch stop on a Nice to Italy journey.

⊙ Sights & Activities

Jardin Botanique Exotique du Val Rahmeh
GARDEN

(www.jardins-menton.fr; Av St-Jacques; adult/child €6/3.50; ◷10am-12.30pm & 3.30-6.30pm Wed-Mon) This wonderful garden was laid out in 1905 for Lord Radcliffe, then governor of Malta. The terraces overflow with exotic fruit-tree collections and subtropical plants, including the only European specimen of the Easter Island tree *Sophora toromiro*, now extinct on the island.

Musée Jean Cocteau
ART MUSEUM

(quai Napoléon III; admission €3; ◷10am-noon & 2-6pm Wed-Mon) Displays drawings, tapestries and mosaics by the multitalented poet, dramatist, artist and film director. In 2005, avid Cocteau collector Séverin Wunderman donated some 1500 Cocteau works to Menton, which will be displayed in a new museum scheduled to open in 2011.

Plage de Menton
BEACH

With more than 300 days of sunshine per year, it's very likely you'll want to spend some time on Menton's free pebble beaches or private sandy ones.

🛏 Sleeping & Eating

Le Paris-Rome
HOTEL €€

(✆04 93 35 73 45; www.paris-rome.com; 79 av Porte-de-France; s/d €52/90, lunch/dinner menu €34/55; ◷lunch & dinner Wed-Sun, dinner Tue; ❋🐾🛜) By far the best place to stay in Menton, Le Paris-Rome sits right on the border with Italy. The 20-odd rooms are all individually and tastefully decorated, with styles ranging from contemporary Zen to Louis XVI. As for the restaurant, Menton finally has a gastronomic (Michelin) star. Chef Yannick Fauries prepares modern and creative cuisine, and has embraced the concept of informal eating with gastronomic picnic hampers (to order, €35) and a nibble menu (€19).

A Braïjade Méridiounale
PROVENÇAL €€

(✆04 93 35 65 65; 66 rue longue; menu €28, mains €18-25; ◷Thu-Tue) In a beautiful stone-walled dining room framed by heavy wooden beams, A Braïjade's speciality is flambé skewers (think orange-marinated chicken and pesto-marinated prawns flambéed with Cognac). Not only does it taste good, it also looks fabulous (the kebab is flambéed at your table). The menu, which includes an aperitif, glass of local wine and digestive, is excellent value.

Sucre & Salés
CAFÉ €

(8 promenade Maréchal Leclerc; cakes/sandwiches €3/5; ◷7.30am-8pm Mon-Sat) Opposite the bus station, a contemporary spot to enjoy a coffee, cake or sandwich. The desserts are a work of art. The pâtisserie also serves breakfast (€5).

FRUITY FÊTE

Since the 1930s, Menton's lemon cultivation has been embraced during its Fête du Citron (Lemon Festival; www.feteducitron.com). Every February, kitsch lemon-adorned floats weave processions along the seafront, accompanied by marching bands and dancers in skimpy outfits, and the Jardins Biovès fill with giant wire-framed sculptures bearing thousands of lemons.

Five metric tonnes of the total 150 are used to replace fruit that rots during the course of the festival. Undamaged fruit is sold off at bargain prices outside the Palais de l'Europe once sculptures have been dismantled. Ironically, the lemons used for the festival come from Spain because Menton's lemons are too irregularly shaped to fit neatly on the floats.

ℹ️ Information

There are plenty of banks with exchange facilities along rue Partouneaux.

Banque Populaire Côte d'Azur (31 av Félix Faure) Has an automated exchange machine outside.

Post office (cours George V)

Tourist office (☎04 92 41 76 76; www.menton. fr; 8 av Boyer; ⊙9am-7pm) Makes same-day room reservations. Has a list of internet cafés.

ℹ️ Getting There & Away

BUS Bus RCA (www.rca.tm.fr, in French) operates from the bus station on promenade Maréchal Leclerc, the northern continuation of av Boyer. There are buses to Monaco (30 minutes), Nice (1¼ hours) and Nice's airport (1½ hours). Fares cost €1, except to the airport, which costs €18.

TUM (Transports Urbains de Menton) operates local bus routes. Lines 1 and 2 link the train station with the old town (€1).

TRAIN There are regular services to Monaco (€1.90, 15 minutes) and Nice (€4.50, one hour).

MONACO (PRINCIPAUTÉ DE MONACO)

POP 32,000 / ☑377

Your first glimpse of this pocket-sized principality will probably make your heart sink: after all the gorgeous medieval hilltop villages, glittering beaches and secluded peninsulas of the surrounding area, Monaco's concrete high-rises, reclaimed land and astronomic prices might come as a shock.

But Monaco is beguiling. The world's second-smallest state (a smidgen bigger than the Vatican), it is as famous for its tax haven status as it is for its glittering casino, thriving performing art and sport scene (Formula One, world-famous circus festival and tennis open), and eventful royal family (its members regularly feature in gossip magazines).

For visitors, it just means an exciting trip: from an evening at the stunning casino and a visit to the excellent Musée Océanographique to a spot of celebrity/royalty spotting, Monaco is a fun day out on the Riviera.

In terms of practicalities, Monaco is a sovereign state but there is no border control. It has its own flag (red and white), national holiday (19 November), postal system (good for the card home to grandma) and

telephone country code (377), but the official language is French and the country uses the euro even though it is not part of the European Union.

History

Originally from the nearby Genoa region of Italy (hence the Monégasque language's similarity with the Genoese dialect), the Grimaldi family has ruled Monaco for most of the period since 1297, except for its occupation during the French Revolution and its loss of territories in 1848. Its independence was again recognised by France in 1860. Five years later, a monetary agreement with France and the opening of the Monte Carlo casino revived the country's fortunes. Today there are just 7800 Monégasque citizens, by either parentage or marriage, out of a total population of 32,000 (and 107 nationalities); they live an idyllic tax-free life of cradle-to-grave security. Alas, all other residents and businesses pay tax.

Ever since the marriage of Prince Rainier III of Monaco (r 1949–2005) to Hollywood actress Grace Kelly in 1956, Monaco's ruling family has regularly featured in gossip magazines. Albert II, prince since his father's death in 2005, hasn't escaped media scrutiny (he has no legitimate heirs but two illegitimate children), but his achievements as an athlete (he played for the Monaco football team and is a black belt in judo), his charity work and promotion of the arts have earned him favourable press. Engaged to South African Olympic swimmer and former model Charlene Wittstock in June 2010, Prince Albert was due to marry in July 2011 as this book went to press.

⊙ Sights & Activities

Casino de Monte Carlo   CASINO
(www.casinomontecarlo.com; place du Casino; admission to European/Private Rooms €10/20; ⊙European Rooms from noon Sat & Sun, from 2pm Mon-Fri) Living out your James Bond fantasies just doesn't get any better than at Monte Carlo's monumental, richly decorated showpiece, the 1910-built casino. The European Rooms have poker/slot machines, French roulette and *trente et quarante* (a card game), while the Private Rooms offer baccarat, blackjack, craps and American roulette. The jacket-and-tie dress code kicks in after 8pm. Minimum entry age for both rooms is 18; bring photo ID.

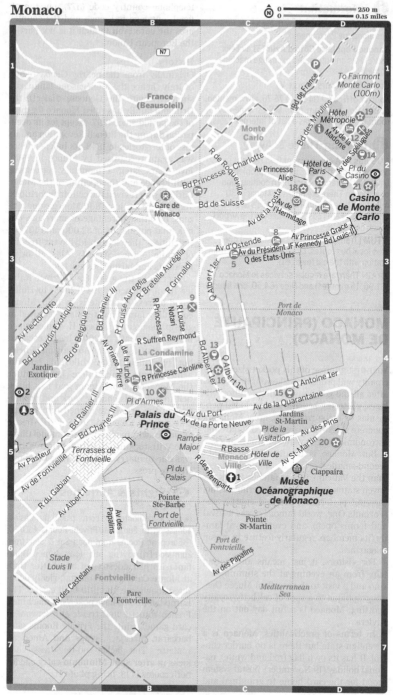

N7

France
(Beausoleil)

To Fairmont
Monte Carlo
(100m)

Monte
Carlo

Hôtel
Métropole   19

Av de la
Madone   12
Av des Spélugués   14

Bd de France
Bd des Moulins

R de Roqueville

Av Princesse
Alice
Hôtel de
Paris

Pl du
Casino   21

Charlotte
Bd Princesse   7
Bd de Suisse
Gare de
Monaco

18   17

4   **Casino
de Monte
Carlo**

Av de la Costa
Av de
l'Hermitage

Av d'Ostende   8   Av Princesse Grace
Av du Président JF Kennedy   Bd Louis-II
5   Q des États-Unis

R Bretelle Auréglia
R Grimaldi
R Louise Auréglia

*Port de
Monaco*

R Princesse
R Louise
Notari
9

R Suffren Reymond

La Condamine
13
Q Albert 1er

11   R Princesse Caroline
6   16

Jardin
Exotique

Bd Rainier III
Bd de Belgique
Bd du Jardin Exotique
Av Prince Pierre
R de la Turbie
Av Hector Otto

10   15   Q Antoine 1er
Pl d'Armes   Av de la Quarantaine

2
3

Bd Rainier III

Bd Charles III
Av Pasteur
Av de Fontvieille
Terrasses de
Fontvieille

**Palais du
Prince**

Av du Port
Av de la Porte Neuve

Jardins
St-Martin
Pl de la
Visitation   Av des Pins

Rampe
Major
R Basse
Monaco
Ville   Hôtel de
Ville   Av St-Martin   20

Ciappaira

R des Remparts

R du Gabian
Av Albert II

Pl du
Palais
Pointe
Ste-Barbe
Port de
Fontvieille

R des Remparts   1

**Musée
Océanographique
de Monaco**

Pointe
St-Martin

Av des Papalins

*Port de
Fontvieille*

*Mediterranean
Sea*

Stade
Louis II

Fontvieille

Av des Castelans
Av des Papalins
Parc
Fontvieille

TOP CHOICE Musée Océanographique de Monaco

AQUARIUM

(www.oceano.org; Av St-Martin; adult/child €13/6.50; ⊙9.30am-7pm) Propped on a sheer cliff-face, the graceful Musée Océanographique de Monaco, built in 1910, houses a fantastic aquarium. There are eerie sharks and bemusing tropical fish, a tactile basin where you can touch a variety of sea creatures, and daily sessions with the aquarium's technicians to find out more about the ins and outs of running an aquarium. All signs are translated into English, Italian and German. One vast, columned floor explores the evolution of oceanography with amazing fossils and ship replicas. And don't miss the spectacular views from the rooftop terrace.

Palais du Prince

PALACE

(www.palais.mc; Monaco Ville; adult/child €8/3.50; ⊙9.30am-6.30pm, closed Nov-Mar) For a glimpse into royal life, you can tour the state apartments with an 11-language audioguide. The palace is what you would expect of any aristocratic abode: lavish furnishings and expensive 18th- and 19th-century art. Guards are changed outside the palace at 11.55am every day.

Cathédrale de Monaco

CATHEDRAL

(4 rue Colonel) An adoring crowd continually shuffles past Prince Rainier's and Princess Grace's graves, located inside the cathedral choir of the 1875 Romanesque-Byzantine Cathédrale de Monaco. The Monaco's boys' choir, Les Petits Chanteurs de Monaco, sings Sunday Mass at 10am between September and June.

Jardin Exotique

GARDEN

(www.jardin-exotique.mc; 62 bd du Jardin Exotique; adult/child €7/3.70; ⊙9am-7pm) Flowering year-round, over 1000 species of cacti and succulents tumble down the slopes of the Jardin Exotique. For nongardeners, the main draw is undoubtedly the spectacular vistas over the principality and shimmering Mediterranean. Admission also includes a half-hour guided visit of the stalactites and stalagmites in the Observatory Caves. Access to the gardens is from bd du Jardin Exotique only. From the tourist office, take Bus 2 to the Jardin Exotique terminus.

Beaches

Monaco's beaches are in the neighbourhood of Larvotto, east of Monte Carlo. There are paying as well as free beaches.

⭐ Festivals & Events

International Circus Festival of Monaco

PERFORMING ARTS FESTIVAL

(www.montecarlofestivals.com) The International Circus Festival of Monaco, held each year in late January, showcases heart-stopping acts from around the globe.

Formula One Grand Prix

MOTOR RACING

(Automobile Club de Monaco; www.formula1 monaco.com) Brazilian triple-world champion Nelson Piquet famously likened driv-

---

Monaco

Monte Carlo Casino

A TIMELINE

1863 Charles III inaugurates the first Casino on the Plateau des Spélugues. The atrium **1** is a small room with a wooden platform from which an orchestra 'enlivens' the gambling.

1864 Hôtel de Paris opens and the area becomes known as the 'Golden Square'.

1865 Construction of Salon Europe **2**. Cathedral-like, it is lined with onyx columns and lit by eight Bohemian crystal chandeliers weighing 150kg each.

1868 The steam train arrives in Monaco and Café de Paris **3** is completed.

1878–79 Gambling moves to Hôtel de Paris while Charles Garnier is charged with building a new casino with a miniature replica of the Paris Opera House, Salle Garnier **4**.

1890 The advent of electricity casts a glow on architect Jules Touzet's newly added gaming rooms **5** for high rollers.

1903 Inspired by female gamblers, Henri Schmit decorates Salle Blanche **6** with caryatids and the painting *Les Grâces Florentines*.

1904 Smoking is banned in the gaming rooms and Salon Rose **7**, a new smoking room, is added.

1910 Salle Médecin **8**, immense and grand, hosts the high-spending Private Circle.

1966 Celebrations mark 100 years of uninterrupted gambling despite two World Wars.

JOHN VLAHIDES

Salle Blanche
Look up, away from the jarring wall-to-wall slot machines, to admire Schmit's caryatids, wings spread for flight. They illustrate the emerging emancipation of women, modelled on fashionable courtesans like La Belle Otero, who placed her first bet here age 18.

Salon Rose
Smoking was banned in the gaming rooms after a fraud involving a croupier letting his ash fall on the floor. The gaze of Gallelli's famous cigarillo-smoking nudes are said to follow you around the room.

Hôtel de Paris
Notice the horse's shiny nose (and testicles) on the lobby's statue of Louis XIV on horseback. Legend has it, rubbing them brings good luck in the casino.

Hôtel de Paris

Salle Garnier
Taking eight months to build and two years to restore (2004–06), the opera's original statuary is rehabilitated using original moulds saved by the creator's grandson. Individual air-con and heating vents are installed beneath each of the 525 seats.

JOHN VLAHIDES

TOP TIPS

» Bring photo ID

» Jackets are required in the private gaming rooms, and after 8pm

» The cashier will exchange any currency

» In the main room, the minimum bet is €10, the maximum €2000

» In the Salons Privés, the minimum bet is €500, with no maximum

Atrium

The casino's 'lobby', so to speak, is paved in marble and lined with 28 Ionic columns, which support a balustraded gallery canopied with an engraved glass ceiling.

Salon Europe

The oldest part of the casino, where they continue to play *trente-et-quarante* and European roulette, which have been played here since 1863. Tip: the bull's-eye windows around the room originally served as security observation points.

Café de Paris

With the arrival of Diaghilev as director of the Monte Carlo Opera in 1911, Café de Paris becomes the go-to address for artists and gamblers. It retains the same high-glamour ambience today. Tip: snag a seat on the terrace and people-watch.

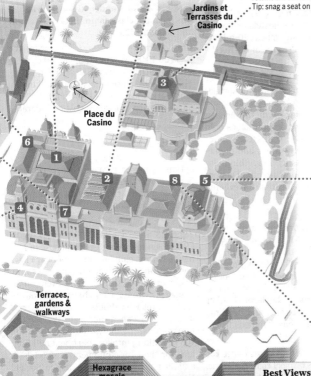

Jardins et Terrasses du Casino

Place du Casino

6 1 2 8 5 3 7 4

Terraces, gardens & walkways

Salles Touzet

This vast partitioned hall, 21m by 24m, is decorated in the most lavish style: oak, Tonkin mahogany and oriental jasper panelling are offset by vast canvases, Marseille bronzes, Italian mosaics, sculptural reliefs and stained-glass windows.

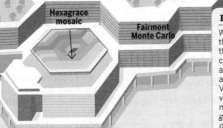

Hexagrace mosaic

Fairmont Monte Carlo

Best Views

Wander behind the casino through manicured gardens and gaze across Victor Vasarely's vibrant op-art mosaic, *Hexagrace*, to views of the harbour and the sea.

Salle Médecin

Also known as Salle Empire because of its extravagant Empire-style decor, Monégasque architect François Médecin's gaming room was originally intended for the casino's biggest gamblers. Nowadays, three adjoining Super Privés rooms keep them hidden from prying eyes.

ing Monaco's Formula One Grand Prix, held in May, with 'riding a bicycle around your living room'. Monaco's cachet means it's the most coveted trophy nonetheless, and the narrow lanes, tortuous road layout and hairpin bends along Monaco's streets mean spectators can get closer to the action than at most circuits. Trackside tickets (from about €70 standing, €270 seated) for the event can be purchased from the Automobile Club de Monaco, but get in early as demand is steeper than the near-vertical streets. If you're dead keen, you can walk the 3.2km circuit; the tourist office has maps.

🛏 Sleeping

If your budget's fraying, consider basing yourself at one of Nice's hostels or budget hotels and taking the quick 20-minute train trip to Monaco. Prices soar during the Grand Prix.

Ni Hôtel　　　　BOUTIQUE HOTEL €€
(🏠97 97 51 51; www.nihotel.com; 1bis rue Grimaldi; s/d from €120/150; 🅿🛜) This uberhip and modern hotel is the new kid on the block in Monaco. Its distinctive design makes bold use of flashy primary colours (the shower walls, chairs and stairs are made of see-through coloured plastic). Everything else is a sobering black and white mix. The roof terrace is in a prime location for evening drinks.

Hôtel Miramar　　　　HOTEL €€
(🏠93 30 86 48; http://miramar.monaco-hotel. com; 1 av du Président JF Kennedy; d €145; 🅿🛜) This 1950s seaside hotel with rooftop terrace bar for those lazy breakfasts, lunches and evening drinks is a fabulous option right by the port. Except for the polka-dotted or stripy carpets, the decor is rather minimalist with plain walls and bedding. Seven of the 11 rooms have fabulous balconies overlooking the yachts.

Fairmont Monte Carlo　　LUXURY HOTEL €€€
(🏠93 50 65 00; www.fairmont.com/montecarlo; 12 av des Spélugues; r from €350; 🅿🛜🏊) The venerable North American luxury chain has that rarest of treats in France: king-size beds. Best rooms have sea-view balconies; our favourites also overlook *Hexagrace,* the giant Vasarely mosaic behind the casino.

Port Palace　　　　BOUTIQUE HOTEL €€€
(🏠97 97 90 00; www.portpalace.com; 7 av du Président JF Kennedy; r from €365; 🅿🛜) Built into the hillside overlooking the yacht

harbor, this discreetly sexy boutique hotel was styled by Hermès' artistic director, who used fine silks, Carrara marble and (of course) stitched buttery-soft leather, but eschewed the colour black. All rooms have water views; the best are up high.

Relais International de la Jeunesse Thalassa　　　　HOSTEL €
(🏠04 93 81 27 63; www.clajsud.fr; 2 av Gramaglia, Cap d'Ail; dm incl sheets & breakfast €18; ⊗closed Nov-Mar) The closest hostel to Monaco, in a beautiful spot right by the sea in Cap d'Ail.

Novotel　　　　CHAIN HOTEL €€€
(🏠99 99 83 00; www.novotel.com/5275; 16 bd Princesse Charlotte; r incl breakfast €180; 🅿📶🛜🏊🐾) Kids under 16 stay free at this business-class chain. Book way ahead and score a €129 rate.

Hôtel Hermitage　　　　HOTEL €€€
(🏠98 06 40 00; www.montecarloresort.com; sq Beaumarchais; d from €385; 🅿📶🛜🏊) This opulent, fresco-cloistered, Italianate landmark hotel is well known for its plush interior. Sea views cost considerably more.

🍴 Eating

For those on a budget, a picnic is the best option. There are plenty of parks and benches to sit and take in the atmosphere, and you'll find a raft of sandwich bars and cheap eateries along quai Albert 1er.

TOP CHOICE **Le Nautique**　　　CAFÉ €
(3 av du Président JF Kennedy; mains €9-13; ⊗lunch Mon-Sat) The clubhouse of Monaco's rowing club has million-dollar views and €10 lunches, served upstairs in a sunny linoleum-floored dining room overseen by manager Erminia, who's like your favourite Italian aunt who shouts *mangia, mangia!* until you've cleaned your plate. It's tricky to find, and ascending the stairs you'll think you're walking into an apartment building; look for the gym equipment at street level and the inconspicuous sign marked 'Société Nautique Fédération Monégasque Sport Avion Snack Bar'. Hurry: it's slated for demolition in 2013.

Mandarine　　　　GASTRONOMIC €€€
(🏠97 97 90 00; www.portpalace.com; 7 av du Président JF Kennedy; mains €32-37) The casually sophisticated, glass-walled dining room at the Port Palace hotel has mesmerising views over the yacht harbour, and gained a Michelin star in 2010 for its seamless mar-

riage of earthy cooking, artistic presentations and thoughtful service. Monday to Friday there's a €36 lunch *menu*.

Tip Top
PIZZERIA €

(11 rue Spélugues; mains €12-24; ⊘24hr) Tip Top is where local Monégasques gather all night long for pizza, pasta and gossip. Snag a booth by the bar to spy on the scene. At lunch there's a good-value €13 *menu*.

Cosmopolitan
MODERN EUROPEAN €€

(☑93 25 78 68; www.cosmopolitan.mc; 7 rue du Portier; lunch menu €19.50, mains €16-31) Cosmopolitan serves timeless international classics with gusto: say hello to fish and chips, three-cheese gnocchi or veal cutlets in Béarnaise sauce, all revisited by Cosmo's talented chefs. The result is refreshingly good and unpretentious, and tastes even better with one of the many wines on offer (including a dozen available by the glass).

Huit & Demi
ITALIAN €€

(☑93 50 97 02; www.huit-et-demi.com; rue Princesse Caroline; mains €13-27; ⊘lunch & dinner Mon-Fri, dinner Sat) Very chic and very popular. You can savour your Italian fare indoors amid crimson-coloured walls lined with celebrity B&W portraits, or on the street-side terrace.

Self-catering

Casino Supermarket
SUPERMARKET

(17 quai Albert 1er; pizza slices & sandwiches from €3; ⊘8.30am-10pm Mon-Sat) Has an excellent sandwich shop and takeaway pizza bar, both amazing value for Monaco.

Food market
MARKET

(place d'Armes; ⊘7am-1pm) For juicy fruit and veg.

Drinking

Brasserie de Monaco
MICROBREWERY

(www.brasseriedemonaco.com; 36 rte de la Piscine; ⊘11am-1am Sun-Thu, 11am-3am Fri & Sat) Tourists and locals rub shoulders at Monaco's only microbrewery, which crafts rich organic ales and lager, and serves tasty (if pricy) antipasti plates. Happy hour runs from 5pm to 9pm.

Stars 'n' Bars
BAR

(www.starsnbars.com; 6 quai Antoine 1er; ⊘noon-2.30am, closed Mon Oct-May;) Any star worth his or her reputation has partied at this American western saloon: check out the gazillion pictures of in-situ celebrities and admire the Grand Prix paraphernalia while you prop up the bar with a bottled beer or heavy-duty cocktail. Stars 'n' Bars also serves monstrous burgers.

Café de Paris
CAFÉ

(www.montecarloresort.com; place du Casino; mains €17-53; ⊘7am-2am) Adjacent to the opulent Monte Carlo Casino, this is a fabulous spot for a decadent – if grossly overpriced – coffee or aperitif whilst limo-spotting from the sprawling 300-seat terrace.

☆ Entertainment

Pack your evening wear for concerts, opera and ballet, which are held at various venues. The tourist office has a schedule of local events. Tickets for most cultural events are sold at fnac (Centre Commercial le Métropole).

Black Legend
NIGHTCLUB

(www.black-legend.com; 20 rte de la Piscine; ⊘restaurant noon-11.30pm, nightclub 12.30am-5am) The over-30 yachting set swills cocktails at retro-'70s-fashioned Black Legend, with all-black velour snugs and a light-up dance floor copied from *Saturday Night Fever*. Before midnight it's a supper club (reservations essential, mains €25 to €40); after midnight DJs spin house. Drinks cost €20. Look sharp. No sneakers.

Flashman's
BAR

(7 av Princesse Alice; ⊘8am-5am Mon & Wed-Fri, 7pm-5am Sat & Sun) The retro American diner-style decor with fluoro lights and chrome counter is rather funky at night. Happy hour is between 5.30pm and 8pm on weeknights. DJs start playing around 10pm.

Cinéma Le Sporting
CINEMA

(place du Casino) Often has movies in their original language.

Open-air Cinema
CINEMA

(parking des Pêcheurs) Has nightly shows from June to September, specialising in crowd-pleasing blockbusters, mostly in English.

Opéra de Monte-Carlo
OPERA

(www.opera.mc) Adjacent to the casino, the magnificent Opera de Monte-Carlo generally stages productions from October to May.

❶ Information

INTERNET ACCESS Téléphone Européen
(30 bd des Moulins; per 15min/hr €2/5; ⊘Mon-Sat)

ART ON THE RIVIERA

Every influential 20th-century artist seems to have come to the French Riviera for inspiration and left a little something behind: a chapel here (Matisse, see p838), a museum there (Picasso, p835), a few seminal novels (F Scott Fitzgerald, JG Ballard) or a masterpiece or two in lieu of payment at a friendly restaurant (check in or dine at Les Arcades p838 or La Colombe d'Or p838).

Many of these artists lived in the region: you can visit Renoir's rambling house and studio (p836) or retrace Matisse's steps from Nice to Vence (p825).

The region is also home to the world-class Fondation Maeght (p838), an outstanding modern art gallery where you'll be able to admire works by Miró and Giacometti, and other excellent art museums such as Mamac (p826) in Nice or the small Musée de l'Annonciade (p848) in St-Tropez.

MEDICAL SERVICES Centre Hospitalier Princesse Grace (☑emergency 97 98 97 69, switchboard 97 98 99 00; av Pasteur)

MONEY Monaco-imprinted euro coins are rarely spotted in circulation, and are quickly pocketed by collectors.

There are (naturally!) numerous banks near the casino. In La Condamine, you'll find banks on bd Albert 1er.

POST Monégasque stamps must be used to post mail within Monaco and to countries beyond; rates are the same as for France. There are post office branches in each of Monaco's districts.

Post office (1 av Henri Dunant)

TELEPHONE Calls between Monaco and France are international calls. Dial 00 followed by Monaco's country code (377) when calling Monaco from France or elsewhere abroad. To phone France from Monaco, dial 00 and France's country code (33), even if you're only calling from the eastern side of bd de France (in Monaco) to its western side (in France)!

TOURIST INFORMATION Monaco's **tourist office** (www.visitmonaco.com; 2a bd des Moulins; ☺9am-7pm Mon-Sat, 11am-1pm Sun) is across the public gardens from the casino. From mid-June to late-September, additional tourist information kiosks open around the harbour and the train station.

❶ Getting There & Away

BUS Bus 100 is the main intercity bus linking Nice to Menton via Monaco. It stops at various places around the city; the tourist office has schedules and maps. Fares are €1.

CAR & MOTORCYCLE Some 25 official paying car parks are scattered around the principality. One of the most convenient is the Parking des Boulingrins under the casino. The first hour is

free; the next six hours costs €2.40 per hour, and it's €0.80 per hour beyond that.

If you're driving (not really necessary in this compact little country), note that you can't take your car into Monaco Ville unless you have either a Monaco or 06 (Alpes-Maritimes) licence plate.

HELICOPTER Heli Air Monaco (www.heliair monaco.com; one way adult/child €120/80) helicopters connect Nice airport and Monaco in seven minutes.

TRAIN Trains to and from Monaco's **train station** (av Prince Pierre) are run by the French SNCF. There are three exits that go in very different directions: Fontvielle leads you to Av Prince Pierre; Le Port/La Condamine leads you to the harbour and bd Albert 1er; and Monte Carlo/Jardin Exotique leads you to bd Princesse Charlotte. To reach the tourist office, take the Monte Carlo/Jardin Exotique exit from the station, cross the street and take Bus 2 (direction Monaco Ville) or Bus 4 (direction La Condamine–Place des Moulins).

A train trip along the coast offers mesmerising views of the Mediterranean Sea and the mountains. There are frequent trains to Nice (€3.40, 20 minutes), and east to Menton (€1.90, 10 minutes) and the first town across the border in Italy, Ventimiglia (€3.80, 20 minutes).

❶ Getting Around

BUS Several urban bus lines traverse Monaco; Bus 4 links the train station with the tourist office and also with the casino. Tickets cost €1.

LIFTS About 15 *ascenseurs publics* (public lifts) whisk you up and down the hillsides. Most operate 24 hours; others run between 6am and midnight or 1am.

TAXI Minimum fare is €10. Expect to pay around €14 for a 10-minute taxi ride. To order, call ☑04 93 15 01 01.

Corsica

Best Places to Eat

» Auberge Santa Barbara (p888)

» Pasquale Paoli (p876)

» L'Altru Versu (p886)

» Pâtisserie Casanova (p895)

» Emile's (p878)

Best Places to Stay

» A Pignata (p894)

» Hôtel Demeure Castel Brando (p874)

» Hôtel Kallisté (p885)

» Hôtel La Villa (p878)

» Chambre d'hôte Osteria di l'Orta (p893)

Why Go?

Corsica is for (beach) lovers. And culture buffs. And hikers. And divers. It combines vast stretches of shoreline with the beauty of the mountains, plenty of activities for your body and some rich history to engage your mind. Jutting out of the Med like an impregnable fortress, Corsica resembles a miniature continent, with astounding geographical diversity. Within half an hour, the landscape morphs from glittering bays, glitzy coastal cities and fabulous beaches to sawtooth peaks, breathtaking valleys, dense forests and enigmatic hilltop villages. The scenery that unfurls along the island's crooked roads will have you constantly stopping to whip out your camera.

Though Corsica's been officially part of France for over 200 years, it feels different from the mainland in everything from customs to cuisine, language and character, and that's part of its appeal.

When to Go
Ajaccio

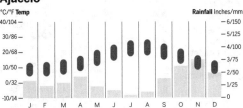

| **March/April (Easter)** Easter is marked by solemn procession and colourful Passion plays. | **May and June** The maquis is in full blossom, the scents are memorable and the vivid hues unforgettable. | **July to September** Get your tan on glistening beaches or explore the island's rugged heart. |

Corsica Highlights

1 Cruise the sapphire waters of the **Réserve Naturelle de Scandola** (p880)

2 Explore the remote peninsula of **Cap Corse** (p874) by way of winding coastal roads

3 Mosey around the cobbled alleyways of mysterious **Sartène** (p887), preferably at Easter

4 Work your suntan and slip into turquoise waters at **Plage de Palombaggia** and **Plage de Santa Giulia** (p891)

5 Step back in time and wander amid enigmatic dolmens and menhirs at **Filitosa** or **Cauria** (p888)

6 Get active in grandiose scenery at **Col de Bavella** (p894)

7 Ride the **Tramway de la Balagne** (p879) for an unforgettable coastal journey

8 Discover your own pocket-sized island paradise for a day on the **Îles Lavezzi** (p889)

9 Wander the backstreets of **Bonifacio's citadel** (p888) for stunning seascapes as well as for the history

10 Bone up on your Bonaparte around Napoléon's hometown, **Ajaccio** (p882)

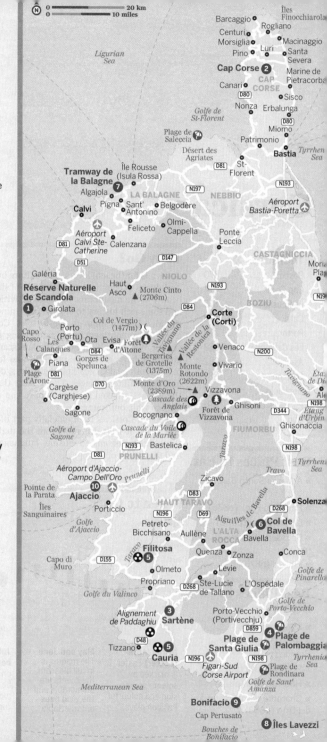

CORSICAN TEMPTATIONS

Cheese

Gourmands will delight in all the flavours and textures of Corsican cheeses, from hard, tangy Tomme Corse (semihard ewe's-milk cheese) to the king of the island's cheeses, Brocciu (a crumbly white ewe's- or goat's-milk cheese).

Charcuterie

Prisuttu (dry ham), *lonzu* (tender smoked fillet), *coppa* (shoulder), *figatellu* (liver sausage), *salamu* (salami-style sausage), *terrine de sanglier* (wild-boar pâté) – wherever you go, you'll find a wide array of cured meats on offer, made from free-range pigs that feed on chestnuts. Just make sure you buy it in speciality shops.

Sweet Treats

From *canistrelli* (biscuits made with almonds, walnuts, lemon or aniseed) and *frappe* (little fritters made from chestnut flour) to *fiadone* (a light flan made with cheese, lemon and egg) and *falculelli* (frittered Brocciu cheese served on a chestnut leaf), Corsica's dessert menu is sure to torment the sweet tooth. Oh, and there are devilish ice creams, too, with original flavours such as myrtle, Brocciu or chestnut.

Wine & Liqueurs

Corsica has nine AOC-labelled wines and countless fruit liqueurs, including Cap Corse Mattei. Areas to watch out for are Patrimonio, Cap Corse, Ajaccio, Sartène and Porto-Vecchio.

Olive Oil

La Balagne and L'Alta Rocca produce extremely aromatic olive oils, available direct from the producer.

Seafood

Fish lovers will be in heaven. Lobster, oysters, mussels, squid, sea bass… Corsica has them all, but stick to reputable fish restaurants.

History

From the 11th to 13th centuries Corsica was ruled by the Italian city-state of Pisa, superseded in 1284 by its arch-rival, Genoa. To prevent seaborne raids, a massive system of coastal citadels and watchtowers was constructed, many of which still ring the coastline.

In 1755, after 25 years of sporadic warfare against the Genoese, Corsicans declared their independence, led by Pascal Paoli (1725–1807). Under Paoli's rule they established a National Assembly and founded the most democratic constitution in Europe.

Corsicans made the inland town of Corte their capital, but the island's independence was short-lived. In 1768 the Genoese ceded Corsica to Louis XV, whose troops crushed Paoli's army in 1769. The island has since been part of France, except for 1794–96, when it was briefly under English domination.

A movement for Corsican autonomy was formed in the 1960s to combat what some perceived as France's 'colonialist' policy towards the island. In 1976, the Front de Libération Nationale de la Corse (FLNC) was created, and talk of autonomy increasingly turned to claims for full independence. By the 1990s the FLNC has broken into multiple splinter groups, most armed and mostly violent. This said, relatively few Corsicans support the separatist movements. In 2003 a long-awaited referendum, which would have granted the island greater autonomy, was rejected despite a nail-biting electoral race. Nevertheless, the nationalist issue remains a burning topic, but tourists are always made welcome.

ⓘ Getting There & Away

AIR

Corsica has four airports: Ajaccio, Bastia, Calvi and Figari (north of Bonifacio). There are frequent flights to/from various French mainland airports, including Paris, Marseille, Lyon and Nice, operated year-round by **Air France** (www.airfrance.com) and the Corsican home-grown **CCM Airlines**, also known as Air Corsica. There are also seasonal flights from Paris to Ajaccio and from Lyon and Paris to Bastia with **EasyJet** (www.easyjet.com), while **XL Airways** (www.xl.com) operates flights to Figari out of Paris.

From May to September, direct international flights are also available from a number of European countries, including the UK. EasyJet serves Ajaccio and Bastia from London Gatwick, while Ryanair flies to Figari. **Titan Airways** (www.titan-airways.co.uk) flies to Calvi from London Stansted. Outside the summer months, you'll have to look at flying via a French mainland airport.

BOAT

MAINLAND FRANCE Corsica has six ferry ports (Ajaccio, Bastia, Calvi, Île Rousse, Porto-Vecchio and Propriano) and can be reached from the ports of Nice, Marseille and Toulon. Contact the following companies:

Corsica Ferries (www.corsicaferries.com) Year-round from Nice to Ajaccio, Bastia, Calvi and Île Rousse, and from Toulon to Ajaccio, Bastia and Île Rousse. The crossing lasts from 5½ hours to 6¼ hours.

La Méridionale (www.lameridionale.fr) Has year-round overnight sailings from Marseille to Ajaccio, Bastia and Propriano (all 12 hours).

Moby Lines (www.moby.it) Started a service from Toulon to Bastia in 2010.

SNCM (www.sncm.fr) From April to September, it operates speedy *navires à grande vitesse* (NGVs) from Nice to Île Rousse (3½ hours), Ajaccio (five hours) and Bastia (4½ hours). Normal ferries run from Marseille to Ajaccio (9¾ hours), Bastia (10 hours), Île Rousse (10 hours), Porto-Vecchio (13 hours) and Propriano (9¼ hours).

There can be as many as 10 boats a day in the high season, dropping to a single daily sailing in winter: reservations are essential in summer. The fare structure varies depending on your route, the crossing time, the class of comfort and the brand of your vehicle. Fares start at around €40 and rise to around €90 per person (one way), with various discounts offered throughout the year. Expect to pay up to €400 return for a car and two passengers via NGV from Nice to Ajaccio in July or August.

ITALY Between April and September or October, ferries operated by Corsica Ferries and Moby Lines link Corsica with the Italian ports of Genoa, Livorno and Savona, and Porto Torres on Sardinia. Fares from Italy are lower than from mainland France. They vary depending on the crossing time and route, with one-way trips starting as low as €10 per adult. It costs from around €50 to transport a small car.

Operators include the following:

Corsica Ferries (www.corsicaferries.com) Livorno, Piombino and Savona to Bastia. Also serves Calvi and Île Rousse from Savona (June to August).

La Méridionale (www.lameridionale.fr) Ferries year-round between Porto Torres (Sardinia) and Propriano.

Moby Lines (www.moby.it) Runs seasonal ferry services to Bastia from Genoa and Livorno. Also serves Bonifacio from Santa Teresa di Gallura (Sardinia).

Saremar (www.saremar.it) Runs seasonal ferry services between Santa Teresa di Gallura (Sardinia) and Bonifacio.

ⓘ Getting Around

By far the best way to get around Corsica is by car, whether hired or brought from home, but navigating the island's narrow, twisting roads is not easy. A good road map is indispensable. The two IGN *Carte de Promenade* maps (No 73 for the north and No 74 for the south) at a scale of 1:100,000 are excellent. Bus services are lean and not very convenient. The train is an attractive, though limited, option, running through stunning countryside between Bastia and Ajaccio, with a branch route to Calvi.

BASTIA & CAP CORSE

Bastia

POP 44,000

Filled with heart, soul and character, the bustling old port of Bastia is a good surprise. Sure, it might not measure up to the sexy style of Ajaccio or the architectural appeal of Bonifacio, but it has an irresistible magnetism. Don't be put off by its hectic traffic, peeling paintwork and ramshackle tenement blocks. Bastia is a more authentic snapshot of modern-day Corsica, a lived-in city that's resisted the urge to polish up its image just to please the tourists. Allow yourself at least a day to take in the city's seething old port, compelling museum (re-opened in 2010) and dramatic citadel.

⊙ Sights

Place St-Nicolas   TOWN SQUARE

Bastia's buzzing focal point is the 19th-century square of place St-Nicolas, which sprawls along the seafront between the ferry port and the harbour. Named after the

MONEY MATTERS

Be warned: surprisingly, many restaurants and hotels in Corsica don't accept plastic, and it's very rare for *chambres d'hôte* to take credit cards. Some places refuse cards for small amounts (typically under €15). And it's common to come across a reputable restaurant where the credit-card machine has been *en panne* (out of order) for several weeks. Always inquire first. Also note that ATMs are scarce in rural areas, especially in Cap Corse, which has only two ATMs, and the Alta Rocca (only one, in San Gavino di Carbini). It's wise to stock up with euros beforehand.

patron saint of sailors – a nod to Corsica's seagoing heritage – the square is lined with plane trees and a string of attractive terrace cafés along its western edge, as well as a **statue of Napoléon Bonaparte**.

Terra Vecchia   HISTORIC QUARTER

A network of narrow lanes leads south towards the old port and the neighbourhood of Terra Vecchia, a muddle of crumbling apartments and balconied blocks. The shady **place de l'Hôtel de Ville** hosts Bastia's lively morning market from Tuesday to Saturday. One block to the west, don't miss the baroque **Chapelle de l'Immaculée Conception** (rue des Terrasses), with its elaborately painted barrel-vaulted ceiling; it briefly served as the seat of the short-lived Anglo-Corsican parliament in 1795. Further north is **Chapelle St-Roch** (rue Napoléon), known for its 18th-century organ and *trompe l'œil* roof.

Vieux Port   HARBOUR

Immediately south of Terra Vecchia is the Vieux Port (Old Port), Bastia's most picturesque area, ringed by pastel-coloured tenements and buzzy brasseries, as well as the twin-towered **Église St-Jean Baptiste**. The best views of the harbour are from the hillside park of **Jardin Romieu**, reached via a twisting staircase from the waterfront.

Citadel   HISTORIC DISTRICT

Behind Jardin Romieu looms Bastia's citadel, built from the 15th to 17th centuries as a stronghold for the city's Genoese masters. One of the citadel's landmarks, the **Palais des Gouverneurs** (Governors' Palace;

place du Donjon) houses **Musée d'Histoire de Bastia** (04 95 31 09 12; admission €5; Tue-Sun 10am-6pm), which provides an overview of the history of the city. A few streets to the south, don't miss the majestic **Église Ste-Marie** (rue de l'Évêché) and the nearby **Église Ste-Croix** (rue de l'Évêché), featuring gilded ceilings and a mysterious black-oak crucifix, which was found in the sea in 1428.

Sleeping

Hôtel Central   HOTEL €€

(04 95 31 71 12; www.centralhotel.fr; 3 rue Miot; d €85-100, ste €120-140;) This family-run number set in a stately 19th-century building is very well priced for such a central location and offers 21 rooms wrapped with a retro feel (parquet or terracotta-tiled floors, period furnishings). Minuses: there's no lift and rooms aren't air-conditioned (the suites are, though).

Hôtel Les Voyageurs   HOTEL €€

(04 95 34 90 80; www.hotel-lesvoyageurs.com; 9 av Maréchal Sébastiani; s €75-95, d €90-115;) A good bet for picky travellers. What sets it apart are the buttermilk walls, modern-art prints and blindingly white bathrooms that contrast sharply with the more austere facade. There's covered parking (€7).

Hôtel Pietracap   HOTEL €€

(04 95 31 64 63; rte de San Martino, Pietranera; d €92-215;) Life feels less hurried in this oasis of calm, about 3km north of Bastia. The rooms are nothing too out of the ordinary, but it's the leafy park, the hush, the sea views and the huge swimming pool that make this place special. It's also handy to the port.

Eating

You'll find endless restaurants around the old port and quai des Martyrs.

A Casarella   MODERN CORSICAN €€

(04 95 32 02 32; 6 rue Ste-Croix; mains €15-28; Tue-Sun) Poised above the old port in the heart of the citadel, this restaurant boasts the loveliest terrace in Bastia. Tuck into innovative dishes based on organic Corsican produce – caramelised local pork, roasted cuttlefish with parsley – with the twinkling lights of the harbour below.

Raugi   ICE-CREAM PARLOUR €

(2 rue du Chanoine Colombani; scoops €1.50, ice-cream cups €4-19; 9am-12.30pm & 2-11pm

Bastia

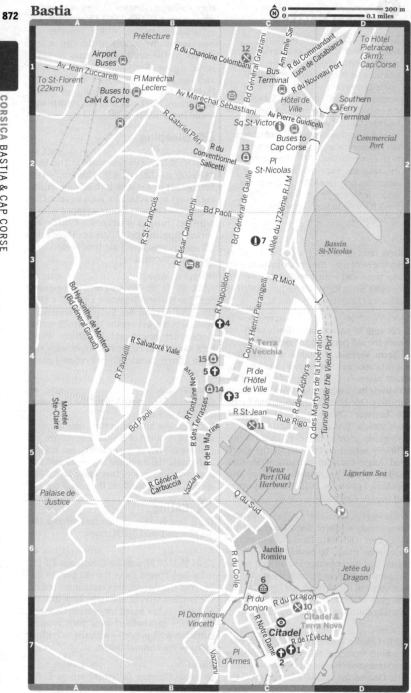

0   200 m
0   0.1 miles

Préfecture

Airport Buses

Av Jean Zuccarelli

To St-Florent (22km)

Pl Maréchal Leclerc

Buses to Calvi & Corte

R du Chanoine Colombani

R Gabriel Péri

Av Maréchal Sébastiani

R du Conventionnel Salicetti

R St-François

R César Campinchi

Bd Paoli

Bd Général de Gaulle

Bd Général Graziani

Av Emile Sar

R du Commandant Luce de Casabianca

R du Nouveau Port

Bus Terminal

Hôtel de Ville

Av Pierre Guidicelli

Sq St-Victor

Buses to Cap Corse

Pl St-Nicolas

Southern Ferry Terminal

Commercial Port

12

9

13

To Hôtel Pietracap (3km); Cap Corse

Bassin St-Nicolas

Allée du 173ème R.I.M.

R Napoléon

R Miot

Cours Henri Pierangelli

Terra Vecchia

Bd Hyacinthe de Montera (Bd Général Giraud)

R Salvatoré Viale

R Favalelli

Montée Ste-Claire

Bd Paoli

R Fontaine Neuve

R des Terrasses

R de la Marine

R Général Carbuccia

Vazzani

Q du Sud

Pl de l'Hôtel de Ville

R St-Jean

Rue Rigo

R des Zéphyrs

Q des Martyrs de la Libération

Tunnel Under the Vieux Port

Vieux Port (Old Harbour)

Ligurian Sea

Palaise de Justice

Jardin Romieu

R du Colle

Pl du Donjon

Pl Dominique Vincetti

Vazzani

Pl d'Armes

R du Dragon

Citadel & Terra Nova

R Notre Dame

R de l'Évêché

Citadel

Jetée du Dragon

7

4

15

5

14

3

11

8

6

10

1

2

Tue-Sat) You say you're itching for an ice-cream fix? Good, because it's hard to resist the giant-sized ice-cream cups served at this longstanding venture.

Chez Vincent CORSICAN €€
(☏04 95 31 62 50; 12 rue St-Michel; mains €9-22, menu €25; ☉lunch & dinner Mon-Fri, dinner Sat) A Casarella's neighbour, Chez Vincent offers Corsican staples and wood-fired pizzas. The *assiette du bandit Corse* (€18.50) features a smorgasbord of local nosh, including stewed veal chestnuts, cured meats, ewe's-milk cheese, wild boar pâté and roast *figatellu* (liver sausage).

Le Bouchon BISTRO €€
(☏04 95 58 14 22; 4bis rue St-Jean; mains €16-29, menu €25; ☉closed Wed & Sun Sep-Jun) This reputable restaurant-cum-wine-bar over-looking the Vieux Port will tempt the gour-mand in you with dishes such as organic Corsican veal or *tartare de liche* (raw leer-fish). Since wines also feature highly here, let things rip with the list of well-chosen Corsican tipples (from €3.10).

Drinking
Place St-Nicolas and the backstreets around the Vieux Port are the places to head to when it comes to sampling a cold Pietra (locally brewed amber beer, whose ingredients include chestnut flour from the Castagniccia region).

Shopping
Bastia has a smattering of tempting shops selling quality local delicacies. Drop by the iconic LN Mattei (www.capcorsemattei.com; 15 bd Général de Gaulle), which is housed in a gloriously retro building, U Paese (www.

u-paese.com; 4 rue Napoléon) and Santa Catalina (8 rue des Terrasses).

ℹ Information
Tourist office (www.bastia-tourisme.com; place St-Nicolas; ☉8.30am-8pm Apr-Sep) Multilingual tourist office.

ℹ Getting There & Away
AIR Aéroport Bastia-Poretta (www.bastia.aeroport.fr) is 24km south of the city. Buses (€8.50, 30 minutes, 10 daily) depart from outside the Préfecture building. Timetables are posted at the bus stop and are available at the tourist office. A taxi will set you back €40/55 during the day/night with **Taxis Bleus** (☏04 95 32 70 70).

BOAT Bastia has two ferry terminals. All the ferry companies have information offices in the southern terminal, which usually opens for same-day ticket sales a couple of hours before each sailing. Ferry services head to/from Marseille, Toulon and Nice on mainland France, and Livorno, Savona, Piombino and Genoa in Italy, see p873 for more. Corsica Ferries, Moby Lines and La Méridionale have offices nearby.

Corsica Ferries (www.corsicaferries.com; 15bis rue Chanoine Leschi) Opposite the northern terminal.

La Méridionale (www.lameridionale.fr)

Moby Lines (www.moby.it; 4 rue du Commandant Luce de Casabianca)

SNCM (www.sncm.fr; inside southern terminal)

BUS As well as the 'bus station' (actually a car park) north of place St-Nicolas, there are several bus stops scattered among the centre. For buses to Cap Corse, see p876.

Autocars Cortenais (☏04 95 46 02 12) Travels to Corte (€11, two hours) once daily on Monday, Wednesday and Friday. Buses leave from the train station.

Bastia

Beaux Voyages (04 95 65 11 35) Buses to Île Rousse (€13, 90 minutes) and Calvi (€16, 2½ hours) run daily except Sunday. Buses leave from the train station.

Eurocorse (04 95 31 73 76) Buses to Ajaccio (€21, three hours) via Corte (€11.50, two hours) twice daily except on Sunday from Bastia's 'bus station'.

Les Rapides Bleus (04 95 31 03 79; 1 av Maréchal Sébastiani) Buses leave from in front the post office to Porto-Vecchio (€22, three hours) twice daily except Sundays and holidays.

TRAIN The **train station** (av Maréchal Sébastiani) is beside the large roundabout on place Maréchal Leclerc. Main destinations include Ajaccio (€25, 3¾ hours, four daily) via Corte (1¾ hours), and Calvi (three hours, three or four daily) via Île Rousse.

Cap Corse

Often described as 'an island within an island', Corsica's spiny northeastern peninsula, Cap Corse, stands out from the rest of Corsica. About 40km long and 10km wide, it resembles a giant geographical finger poked towards mainland France. What does it have on its menu? For starters, you can choose from a smattering of beguiling coastal fishing villages and small settlements perched precariously up in the hills. For main course, adjust your camera setting to 'panoramic' and shoot lovely images of enigmatic Genoese watchtowers dotted around the coastline. And for dessert there's an array of jagged coves and rocky cliffs. Be prepared for some adventurous driving; although the peninsula is only 40km long, the narrow road that rounds its coast crams in 120km of switchback curves and breathtaking drops into the sea, especially along the west coast.

ⓘ Getting There & Away

The main road around Cap Corse is the D80. **Société des Transports Interurbains Bastiais** runs several daily buses to Cap Corse from Bastia, with destinations including Erbalunga and Pietracorbara. **Transports Miguelli** runs to Macinaggio (€7, two daily Monday to Saturday). Buses leave from outside the Bastia tourist office.

ERBALUNGA

From Bastia, the coast unfolds through seaside resorts and small beaches towards the quaint harbour of Erbalunga, 9km north. Wander down to the tiny village square and quayside, which has a cluster of cute cafés and restaurants. Narrow alleys lead through shady courtyards to the tower. Each August, the Festival d'Erbalunga promotes open-air concerts in the village's central square.

The stylish and welcoming Hôtel Demeure Castel Brando (04 95 30 10 30; www.castelbrando.com; rte Principale; d €115-225; 꿈꿈꿈꿈) is set in a mid-19th-century mansion surrounded by palm-shaded gardens and three modern annexes that house even more luxurious accommodation. Reason itself to visit Erbalunga is Le Pirate (04 95 33 24 20; harbour; menus €35-90; ⏰Mar-Dec, closed Mon & Tue low season), an award-winning restaurant with a lovely terrace overlooking the harbour – magical on starry summer evenings. Its contemporary cuisine is creative and refined.

MACINAGGIO

The hub of the eastern cape, Macinaggio has a pleasant little harbour that offers the island's best moorings. It also has the cape's sole tourist office (www.ot-rogliano-macinaggio.com; port de Plaisance; ⏰9am-noon & 2.30-6pm Mon-Sat).

With a range of activities, the town makes a good base for exploring the northern reaches of the promontory. In summer, the San Paulu (04 95 35 07 09; www.sanpaulu.com; port de Plaisance; 🚤) which docks opposite the tourist office, cruises along the stunning coastline to the remote village of Barcaggio and back (round trip €23, two hours). The return trip takes a turn around the nature reserve of the Îles Finocchiarola, an important breeding site for seabirds.

Hikers will love the Sentiers des Douaniers (Customs Officers' Trail), a rugged coastal path that leads to Barcaggio, passing two Genoese towers.

Macinaggio is not bereft of accommodation options, but if you're after a charming B&B, it's worth taking a detour inland to the village of Rogliano, about 4km from Macinaggio, where you'll find U Sant'Agnellu (04 95 35 40 59; www.hotel-usantagnellu.com; d incl breakfast €90-160; ⏰May–mid-Oct; 🔊). This beautifully restored villa is located opposite the church in the centre of the village. Be sure to book one of the seven rooms that face the sea.

CENTURI

Crayfish, anyone? The tiny, boat-crammed harbour of Centuri is not only the most picturesque in Cap Corse, it's also home to the most important crayfish fleet on the island. Now's your chance to savour a seafood feast in one of the numerous eateries on the quayside. The *pâtes a la langouste* (crayfish with pasta) served at Au Vieux Moulin (☎04 95 35 60 15; mains €17-45, menus €15-60; ⊙May-Oct) will linger long on the palate. A Macciotta (☎04 95 35 64 12; mains €13-35; ⊙May-Oct) is another well-regarded option specialising in seafood.

If you're after a good-value hotel in the heart of Centuri, you won't do better than L'Auberge du Pêcheur (☎04 95 35 60 14; d €60-75; ⊙Apr-Oct), which has only five doubles. They're simple but fresh and trim. For serious cosseting, head to Au Vieux Moulin (doubles €110 to €220).

NONZA

Clinging to the flanks of a rocky pinnacle topped with a stone tower and overlooking a black-sand beach, the village of Nonza is easily the most attractive on the cape's western coast. With its jumble of schist-roofed stone houses looking ready to tumble down the steep hillside, it fits the picture-postcard ideal. Make a beeline for the red-and-yellow 16th-century Église Ste-Julie, with a polychrom marble altar created in Florence in 1693, and the massive Tour de Nonza (Nonza Watchtower).

Sleeping & Eating

Chambre d'hôte Le Relais du Cap B&B €

(☎04 95 37 86 53; www.relaisducap.com; Marine de Negru; d with shared bathroom €60-80; ⊙Apr-Oct; 📶) For the ultimate seaside escape, this is hard to beat. Tucked improbably between a towering cliff and a pocket-sized pebble beach, this pert little B&B features four unpretentious yet neat doubles, all offering staggering sunset-facing sea views. No air-con here – but who needs it with the sea breezes puffing in? The copious breakfast served on a terrace overlooking the sea is another draw. It's 4km south of Nonza.

Chambre d'hôte Casa Maria B&B €€

(☎04 95 37 80 95; www.casamaria.fr; d €75-95; ❄📶) A bewitching little hideaway in the heart of the village, this B&B occupies a coolly refurbished 18th-century mansion. Four of its five rooms have sea views, and three sit harmoniously beneath the sloping roof.

A Sassa RESTAURANT €

(☎06 11 99 49 03; mains €12-24; ⊙lunch May-Oct, dinner Jul-Aug) Feeling peckish? A Sassa, nestled among the rock outcrops below the tower, is a wonderful option, with a scatter of rickety tables and benches on a clifftop terrace. It majors on grilled meat, pasta and salads.

LA BALAGNE

If you could visit only one region after the sensational Golfe de Porto, it would have to be La Balagne. This region has a blend of history, culture and beach all rolled into one, with a dash of Mediterranean glam sealing the deal. Refine your art of sampling *la dolce vita* in Calvi and Île Rousse before venturing inland in search of that picture-postcard perfect village.

Île Rousse (Isula Rossa)

POP 3000

Sun-worshippers, celebrities and holidaying yachties all buzz around the busy beach town of Île Rousse, straddling a long, sandy curve of land backed by maquis-cloaked mountains and a sparkling beach. Originally founded by Pascal Paoli in 1758 as a rival port to pro-Genoese Calvi, the town was later renamed after the russet-coloured rock of Île de la Pietra offshore (now home to the town's ferry port and lighthouse).

Sights

Old Town HISTORIC QUARTER

Delve into the alleyways of the town centre and soak up the atmosphere. Surprise: constructed around 1850, the covered food market (place Paoli; ⊙8am-1pm), with its 21 classical columns, resembles a Greek temple. It abuts the tree-shaded place Paoli, Île-Rousse's central square, where you can watch nightly boules contests courtesy of the local gents while you sip an apéritif on the terrace of venerable Café des Platanes – it can't get more Île Rousse than that.

Promenade a Marinella SEAFRONT & BEACHES

Île Rousse's sandy beaches stretch along the seafront, known as Promenade a Marinella, for 3km east of town. It's not a bad idea, though, to head to less crowded beaches around Île Rousse, including plage de Bodri, immediately southwest of town, Algajola, 7km to the west, or the magnificent plage de Lozari, about 6km to the east. They're accessible via the clanking Tramway de la Balagne.

Île de la Pietra
PROMONTORY

For an easy stroll, head over the short umbilical causeway that links rocky Île de la Pietra to the mainland, past a small Genoese watchtower and up to the lighthouse, from where there's a spectacular seascape. Club Nautique d'Île Rousse (www.cnir.org; rte du Port) organises gentle two-hour sea-kayak trips (€30) around the promontory and its offshore islets.

Parc de Saleccia
BOTANICAL GARDENS

(☏04 95 36 88 83; www.parc-saleccia.fr; rte de Bastia; adult/child €7/5; ☺10am-8pm) Wander the 7 hectares of these landscaped gardens to explore the flora of Corsica – the tough plants of the maquis, pines, myrtles, fig trees and over 100 varieties of olive trees. The gardens are 4.5km from town on the Bastia road; hours are shorter outside summer.

🛏 Sleeping & Eating

Hotel Cala di L'Oru
HOTEL €€

(☏04 95 60 14 75; www.hotel-caladiloru.com; bd Pierre Pasquini; s €74-114, d €78-166; ☺Mar-Oct; ❉❉☎) This peaceful option sporting 26 rooms is run by a family of artists, and it shows: paintings and photos in the public areas are by the owners' sons. The flowery garden is a good place to mooch around and soak up the tranquil charm, or you can relax in the stress-melting pool.

Hôtel-Restaurant Le Grillon
HOTEL €

(☏04 95 60 00 49; www.hotel-grillon.net; 10 av Paul Doumer; d €52-62; ☺Apr-Oct; ❉☎) The most obvious choice if you're counting the pennies, Le Grillon has well-kept, space-efficient rooms with straightforward decor and neat bathrooms, as well as a popular ground-floor restaurant.

Hôtel Perla Rossa
BOUTIQUE HOTEL €€€

(☏04 95 48 45 30; www.hotelperlarossa.com; 30 rue Notre-Dame; ste from €260; ☺Mar-Oct; ❉☎♿) This refined cocoon smack dab in the centre adds a touch of glam to the local hotel scene, with artfully designed and sensitively furnished rooms.

Restaurant Pasquale Paoli
GASTRONOMIC CORSICAN €€€

(☏04 95 47 67 70; 2 place Paoli; mains €15-39, menus €45-80; ☺dinner daily Jul-Aug, lunch & dinner Mon, Tue, Thu-Sat, lunch Sun Sep-Jun) Île Rousse's choicest restaurant has been awarded one Michelin star, and you'll certainly enjoy a sophisticated dining experience inside the whitewashed, vaulted dining room. Expect innovative fare made from the island's best ingredients. There's also a terrace overlooking place Paoli, from where you can see the town's nightly boules contests.

U Spuntinu
CORSICAN €€

(☏04 95 60 00 05; 1 rue Napoléon; mains €15-22, menus €22-26; ☺lunch daily, dinner Mon-Sat) This venue right in the centre boasts a happy buzz at lunchtime and whips up lip-smacking Corsican meals. Try the *assiette Corse* (Corsican platter; €21.50) which features a selection of island favourites.

U Libecciu
SEAFOOD €€

(☏04 95 60 13 82; rue Notre-Dame; mains €12-32; ☺Apr-Oct) A short hop from the market, this restaurant serves up the town's best seafood, including steaming mussels prepared in different ways (try them with the house Cap Corse sauce).

❶ Information

Tourist office (www.balagne-corsica.com; place Paoli; ☺9am-7pm Mon-Sat, 10am-1pm Sun) Shorter hours outside summer.

❶ Getting There & Away

BOAT Ferries run to/from Nice, Marseille and Toulon (France) and Savona (Italy). For more, see p873

BUS Les Beaux Voyages (☏04 95 65 11 35) runs buses between Calvi and Bastia that pass through Île Rousse. The service runs from Monday to Saturday year-round.

TRAIN There are two departures daily to Bastia (2½ hours) and Ajaccio (four hours), each requiring a change in Ponte Leccia.

Calvi
POP 5600

Basking between the fiery orange bastions of its 15th-century citadel and the glittering waters of a moon-shaped bay, Calvi feels closer to the chi-chi sophistication of a Côte d'Azur resort than a historic Corsican port. Palatial yachts and private cruisers jostle for space along its harbourside, lined with upmarket brasseries and cafés, while high above the quay the watchtowers and battlements of the town's Genoese stronghold stand guard, proffering sweeping views inland to Monte Cinto (2706m). Unsurprisingly, Calvi is one of Corsica's most popular tourist spots and in summer it's crammed to bursting – pitch up in the shoulder sea-

LA BALAGNE INTERIOR

What a difference a few miles can make! If you need an escape from the hullaballo of the coastal fleshpots, grab the steering wheel, jump on a serpentine country road and explore inland Balagne. In the countless valleys and spurs that slice up the spectacular scenery are scattered cute-as-can-be hilltop villages, Romanesque chapels, olive groves and lush vineyards. The Balagne hinterland is also a source of inspiration for many artisans. A signposted route, the Strada di L'Artiagni (rte des Artisans; www.routedesartisans.fr), links up the region's most attractive villages, and details local workshops. You can pick up a route map from the tourist offices in Calvi and Île Rousse. Of particular interest is the craft centre of Pigna, 7km from Île Rousse (follow the D151), where dotted around the cobbled streets you'll find makers of everything from candles to lutes and music boxes. South of Pigna (continue along the D151), the ubercute village of Sant'Antonino, precariously perched on a rocky outcrop (views!), is well worth a gander, as is Feliceto, famous for its great AOC (Appellation d'Origine Contrôlée) wines. The D71 (and then the D63) will take you to Olmi-Cappella, from which you can head to Belgodère, another adorable village.

Should you fall in love with the area, you'll find a smattering of atmospheric options. In Pigna, Casa Musicale (☎04 95 61 77 31; www.casa-musicale.org; d €70-110, mains €11-24) has quirky rooms finished with painted frescos and fabulous valley views, while Hôtel U Palazzu (☎04 95 47 32 78; www.hotel-corse-palazzu.com; d from €140, ste from €240; ⊙Apr-Oct) offers plush rooms in an 18th-century mansion. In Olmi-Cappella, Chambre d'hôte U Chiosu di a Pietra (☎04 95 61 91 01; d €70-82) is a bucolic retreat with four oh-so-inviting rooms.

---

sons, when you'll be able to stroll the citadel's cobbled alleys in relative peace and quiet.

◉ Sights & Activities

Citadel   HISTORIC NEIGHBOURHOOD
Set atop a lofty promontory, Calvi's massive fortified citadel offers superb wraparound views of the town and the bay at almost every turn. Built by the town's Genoese governors, Calvi's citadel has seen off several major assaults down the centuries, fending off everyone from Franco-Turkish raiders to Anglo-Corsican armies. Inside the battlements, don't miss the well-proportioned Caserne Sampiero (place d'Armes), which was the seat of power for the Genoese administration, and the 13th-century cathédrale St-Jean Baptiste; its most celebrated relic is the ebony *Christ des Miracles,* credited with saving the town from Saracen invasion in 1553.

The citadel has five bastions, each offering wonderful seascapes.

Pointe de la Revellata   WALK
A two-hour (round-trip) walk along a well-defined track brings you to the nearest Corsican point to the French mainland, home to a lighthouse and a gorgeous view of Calvi and the spiky mountains of La Balagne. It's 4km west of Calvi.

Water Sports
Sunworshippers don't have far to stroll – Calvi's stellar 4km beach begins at the marina and runs east around the Golfe de Calvi. If you fancy something more strenuous than pressing a beach towel, you can rent out **kayaks** and **windsurfers** from the Calvi Nautique Club (www.calvinc.org; Base Nautique, port de Plaisance; ⊙May-Oct). There are also excellent diving and snorkelling options near the Pointe de la Revellata. Reputable dive centres include Calvi Plongée Citadelle (www.calviplongee2b.com; quai Landry) and EPIC (http://perso.orange.fr/epiccalvi/plongee; quai Landry; 📶), both at the harbour.

★★ Festivals & Events

La Semaine Sainte   EASTER FESTIVAL
Easter festival, culminating in street processions on Good Friday.

Calvi Jazz festival   JAZZ FESTIVAL
Corsica's biggest jazz festival, in late June.

Rencontres Polyphoniques   MUSIC FESTIVAL
Traditional Corsican chants can be heard at this five-day music festival in September.

Festiventu   WIND FESTIVAL
Held in late October, this festival celebrates the role of wind with hundreds of kites on the beach.

🛏 Sleeping

Hôtel La Villa   HOTEL €€€
(☎04 95 65 10 10; www.hotel-lavilla.com; d from €400; ⊘Apr-Jan; ❄✦⊛🌐) If you want to do Calvi in style, head straight for this lavish hilltop hideaway, brimming with boutique trappings. Clean lines, cappuccino-and-chocolate colour schemes, designer fabrics and minimalist motifs distinguish the rooms, while the exterior facilities include spas, tennis courts, a Michelin-starred restaurant and one of the most fabulous infinity pools you could ever hope to see.

Hôtel Belvedere   HOTEL €€
(☎04 95 65 01 25; www.resa-hotels-calvi.com; place Christophe Colomb; d €70-120; ❄🌐) With a top-of-the-town position striking distance from the citadel and 24 comfortable yet smallish rooms, the Belvedere won't disappoint. The rooms on the 3rd floor boast top-notch views of the Golfe de Calvi.

Hôtel du Centre   HOTEL €
(☎04 95 65 02 01; 14 rue Alsace Lorraine; d with shared bathroom €32-47; ⊘Jun-Sep) Not the most charming choice – furnishings are seriously dated – but at this price and in such a brilliant location it would be churlish to quibble. The most expensive rooms have a shower.

Other options:

Camping La Pinède   CAMPGROUND €
(☎04 95 65 17 80; www.camping-calvi.com; rte de la Pinède; adult/tent/car €9/5/3.50; ⊘Apr-Oct; ❄🐾) Handy for Calvi town and the beach.

Hôtel Christophe Colomb   HOTEL €€
(☎04 95 65 06 04; www.hotelchristophecolomb. com; place Bel Ombra; d €85-120; ❄🌐) A reasonably priced option within striking distance of the citadel. Mediterranean colourwashes keep things jolly in the rooms.

Hôtel Le Magnolia   HOTEL €€
(☎04 95 65 19 16; www.hotel-le-magnolia.com; rue Alsace Lorraine; d €95-140; ❄🌐) An oasis from the harbourside fizz, set behind a walled courtyard and a handsome magnolia tree.

🍴 Eating

Calvi's quayside is chock-a-bloc with restaurants, but many focus more on the ocean ambience than on the quality of the food.

Emile's   GASTRONOMIC €€€
(☎04 95 65 09 60; quai Landry; mains €38-46, menu €50; ⊘Apr-Oct) Yes, the set *menu* has the potential to flag a red alert to Amex, but it's the top-end darling of central Calvi. From the scenic 1st-floor terrace overlooking the quayside, it provides a memorable dining experience with unobtrusive service and fabulous food. If you've never had the chance to try grilled lobster, this is *the* place to do it, washed down with an ice-cold bottle of white.

U Fornu   MODERN CORSICAN €€
(☎04 95 65 27 60; www.ufornu.com; bd Wilson; mains €18-25, menu €18; ⊘Apr-Oct) A surprisingly hip restaurant inside a restored stately house, this cool culinary outpost specialises in creative dishes that stray off the familiar Corsican path. Dishes are elegantly presented and filled with subtle flavours, and the *menu Corse* is excellent value. Eat in the sassy grey and red interior, or on the shady terrace. U Fornu is smack dab in the centre, but tucked away in a quiet cul-de-sac off the main thoroughfare.

Le Tire-Bouchon   BISTRO €€
(☎04 95 65 24 41; rue Clémenceau; mains €12-20, menu €19; ⊘April-Oct, closed Wed Apr, May & Oct) This buzzy option, as much wine bar as restaurant, is a gourmand's playground. Perch yourself on the balcony overlooking the crowds milling on rue Clémenceau, then order from the dishes of the day, posted on a chalkboard. Be good to yourself with veal stew, tagliatelle with Brocciu (fresh ewe's or goat's cheese), a cheese platter and luscious local tipples.

A Scola   TEA HOUSE €
(☎04 95 65 07 09; Citadel; mains €10-18, menu €18; ⊘Mar-Oct, 10am-7pm summer) If you think life is unbearable without a homemade pastry (mmm, the melt-in-the-mouth chocolate cake), bookmark this little tea house opposite the cathedral door. It's also ideal for a refreshing cup or a quick and affordable sit-down lunch as you explore the citadel. The tables at the back have jaw-dropping views of the bay.

U Callelu   SEAFOOD €€
(☎04 95 65 22 18; quai Landry; mains €16-29, menu €24; ⊘Mar-Oct, closed Mon except Jul-Aug) The *menu* chases the changing seasons at this homespun eatery, run with passion and flair by a born-and-bred islander who tracks down the best local ingredients for his dishes: meat and veg from the mar-

ket, wine direct from the vineyards, fish straight off the boats. It's on the quayside.

La Voûte TRADITIONAL CORSICAN €
(☎06 22 14 40 87; 2 rue St-Antoine, Citadel; mains €10-20; ⊗closed Sun in winter) This simple eatery set in a vaulted room cooks up robust Corsican classics such as lasagne with wild boar, pasta with Brocciu and veal stew.

Drinking

There are plenty of places around town at which to whet your whistle. The best buzz can be found on the quayside.

Chez Tao MUSIC BAR
(rue St-Antoine; ⊗Jun-Sep) Within the citadel, Chez Tao is an institution. This super-smooth piano bar occupying a lavishly decorated vaulted room was founded in 1935 by Tao Kanbey de Kerekoff, a White Russian émigré, and it still attracts hedonistic hipsters seven decades later.

Le Havanita COCKTAIL BAR
(quai Landry; ⊗Apr-Sep) Kick off the night with a few mojitos at this cheerful den on the quayside.

A Cantina WINE BAR
(10 rue Joffre; ⊗Apr-Oct) Treat yourself to a taste of the finest Calvi AOC wine at this supercool tapas and wine bar on the quayside.

❶ Information

Tourist office (☎04 95 65 16 67; www.balagne-corsica.com; Port de Plaisance; ⊗9am-noon & 3-6.30pm daily Jul & Aug, closed Sun May, Jun, Sep & Oct, closed Sat & Sun Nov-Apr)

❶ Getting There & Away

AIR Seven kilometres southeast of town is **Aéroport Calvi Ste-Catherine** (www.calvi.aeroport.fr). There's no airport bus: a **taxi** (☎04 95 65 03 10) to and from town costs €20. See p892 for more information.

BOAT Calvi's ferry terminal is at the northeastern end of quai Landry, with regular ferries to/from Nice (France) and Savona (Italy); see p873 for details. Ferry tickets can be bought from **CCR/Tramar** (☎04 95 65 01 38, 04 95 65 00 63; quai Landry) at the harbour.

BUS Les Beaux Voyages (☎04 95 65 11 35; place de la Porteuse d'Eau) runs one bus, Monday to Saturday year-round, from Calvi to Bastia (€16, 2½ hours) via Île Rousse. **Transports Ceccaldi** (☎04 95 22 41 99) runs a daily bus to Porto (€16, 2¾ hours) leaving from opposite the

❶

BALAGNE TRAMWAY

The best way to access the numerous hidden coves and beaches that are sprinkled along the Balagne coastline is to take the Tramway de la Balagne. Not only is this dinky little train very convenient (no traffic jams!), but it also makes for an unforgettable journey beside getaway beaches. The *trinighellu* (trembler), as it's affectionately dubbed, trundles between Calvi and Île Rousse up to eight times daily between Easter and September, calling at 15 stations en route, all of which are request only. Hop off at an intermediate rocky cove or, for sand, leave the train at Algajola or Plage de Bodri, the last stop before Île Rousse. It costs €5.40 one way.

Super U supermarket in Calvi and the main road opposite the pharmacy in Porto. There's one bus daily from July to mid-September. From mid-May to June, and late September to May, there's no bus on Sunday.

TRAIN Calvi's train station is south of the harbour, near the tourist office. There are at least two departures daily to Bastia (three hours) and Ajaccio (five hours), each requiring a change in Ponte Leccia. From April to October, the Tramway de la Balagne clatters along the coast between Calvi and Île Rousse (€5.50, 45 minutes).

PORTO TO AJACCIO

Porto (Portu)

POP 250

The setting couldn't be more grandiose. The crowning glory of the west coast, the seaside town of Porto sprawls at the base of a thickly forested valley trammelled on either side by crimson peaks. Buzzing in season and practically deserted in winter, it's a fantastic spot for exploring the shimmering seas around the Réserve Naturelle de Scandola, a Unesco-protected marine reservation, Les Calanques and the rugged interior.

The village is split by a promontory, topped by a restored Genoese square tower, erected in the 16th century to protect the gulf from Barbary incursions.

◉ Sights

Porto's main sights are all dotted around the harbour. Once you've climbed the russet-coloured rocks up to the Genoese tower (€2.50; ⊘9am-9pm Jul & Aug, 11am-7pm Sep-Jun), you can stroll round to the bustling marina, from where an arched footbridge crosses the estuary to a eucalyptus grove and Porto's pebbly patch of beach. Fish fanatics can drop by the Aquarium de la Poudrière (☑04 95 26 19 24; €5.50, joint ticket with Genoese Tower €6.50), which houses fishy specimens from around the Golfe de Porto.

🏃 Activities

Boat Trips

There's no vehicle access or footpath that leads into the magnificent, protected Réserve Naturelle de Scandola, so the only way to get up close is by sea. Between April and October, several companies based around Porto's marina sail to the base of its cliffs, often taking in Les Calanques and Girolata.

Expect to pay around €25 for trips to Les Calanques, or €40 for trips including Réserve Naturelle de Scandola and Girolata. Most offer informative commentaries (usually in French).

Diving & Snorkelling

Do you see the exceptional coastal wilderness of Golfe de Porto and the crags and cliffs that fret the skyline? It's more or less the same story below the waterline. This gulf boasts an exceptional diversity of underwater wonders, with a jaw-dropping topography – just as on land – and masses of fish due to the proximity of the Réserve Naturelle de Scandola.

Porto's three diving outfits, all based at the quay, offer introductory dives (from €45) and courses for beginners, as well as snorkelling trips (€15) to choice spots including the fringe of the Réserve Naturelle de Scandola.

Centre de Plongée du Golfe de Porto (www.plongeeporto.com; marina; ⊘Easter-Oct)

Génération Bleue (www.generation-bleue. com; marina; ⊘May-Oct)

Méditerranée Porto Sub (www.plongeecose .fr; marina; ⊘mid-Apr–Sep)

Hiking

The Porto area is a haven for hikers. The *Hikes & Walks in the Area of Porto* brochure from the tourist office details 28 signed walks at all levels of difficulty. Hidden in the hills inland from Porto (follow the D124), the quintessentially Corsican villages of Ota and Evisa offer the best opportunities, within striking distance of Gorges de Spelunca, one of the deepest natural canyons on the island. A path runs along the steep sides of the Spelunca canyon beneath huge, humbling cliffs.

🛏 Sleeping

Le Colombo   HOTEL €€

(☑04 95 26 10 14; www.hotellecolombo.com; rte de Calvi; d incl breakfast €67-110; ⊘Apr-Oct; ❋)
A smart place to rest your head, Le Colombo is built on three levels following the steep slope of the hillside. Most rooms are a soothing sky-blue with views of garden, sea and mountain, and corridors are adorned with striking images by local photographer Robert Candela. Mooch around the lovely small garden, shaded by a giant palm and overflowing with bougainvillea.

Le Maquis   HOTEL €

(☑04 95 26 12 19; www.hotel-lemaquis.com; cnr D214 & D81; d €48-110; ⊘Apr–mid-Nov; 🛜)
Removed from the harbour hustle, the well-managed Le Maquis won't get you writing home but the rooms are discreetly decorated and comfortable, with quality mattresses and prim bathrooms (cheaper rooms have outside bathrooms). The plunging valley views are super, and another draw is the on-site restaurant.

Le Belvédère   HOTEL €

(☑04 95 26 12 01; www.hotel-le-belvedere.com; marina; d €55-125; ⊘Apr-Oct; ❋🛜♿) With a regal setting overlooking the marina, the Belvédère offers modernised rooms with shiny bathrooms. For the full Porto experience, be sure to fork out for a room facing the bay – the other ones have obstructed views. The only downside is that there's no private car park.

Camping Les Oliviers   CAMPGROUND €

(☑04 95 26 14 49; www.camping-oliviers-porto. com; per person €7.50-10, tent €3-3.50; ⊘late Mar-early Nov; 🏊♿) Idyllically set among overhanging olive trees, this campsite's deluxe facilities include a gym, pizzeria and rock-surround swimming pool. It also rents wooden chalets (by the week).

Eating

Le Sud
MODERN CORSICAN €€

(☑04 95 26 14 11; marina; mains €16-27, menu €29; ⊘Apr-Oct) Reasons for making your way here are threefold: to admire the views of the marina and the watchtower from the delightful vine-covered veranda; to sample the lip-smacking fish and meat dishes that grace the menu (what about veal with banana?); and to enjoy the relaxing atmosphere and lovely Mediterranean decor. For a little midday indulgence, tuck into its brimming *assiette repas*.

La Mer
SEAFOOD €€

(☑04 95 26 11 27; marina; mains €13-38, menus €19-29; ⊘Apr-Oct) An oasis from the harbourside fizz, La Mer has the finest views of all from its terrace overlooking the gulf and the Genoese tower. The fish on offer is determined by what's in the nets of the previous day's catch. Meat dishes also feature on the menu.

Le Maquis
TRADITIONAL CORSICAN €€

(☑04 95 26 12 19; cnr D214 & D81; mains €21-29, menus €22-34; ⊘Apr-Oct) This character-filled eatery set in a granite house is held in high regard by locals and tourists alike. The food's a delight, with a tempting menu based on traditional Corsican cooking. There's a cosy all-wood interior but, for preference, reserve a table on the balcony, which has great views.

Information

Tourist office (www.porto-tourisme.com; place de la Marine; ⊘9am-7pm, closed Sat & Sun Oct-Mar) Just behind the marina's upper car park.

Getting There & Around

Autocars Ceccaldi (☑04 95 22 41 99) operates buses from Porto to Ajaccio (€12, 2½ hours, two daily, no Sunday buses except from July to mid-September), stopping at Piana and Cargèse en route. For buses from Porto to Calvi, see p879).

Transports Mordiconi (☑04 95 48 00 44) bus company links Porto with Corte (€20, 2¾ hours) once daily except on Sunday from July to mid-September.

Piana
POP 500

Teetering above the Golfe de Porto and surrounded by the scarlet pillars of Les Calanques, Piana makes for a less frenzied base than nearby Porto in the high season, and is a useful launching pad for exploring the idyllic beaches of Ficajola (4km from Piana) and Arone (11km southwest on the D824). The town's main landmark is the Église Ste-Marie, which is the focus for the annual Good Friday procession of La Granitola.

Sleeping & Eating

Hôtel Scandola
HOTEL €€

(☑04 95 27 80 07; www.hotelscandola.com; d €82-120; ✸🐾) Don't be put off by the pinkish facade of this place, located uphill from the village on the left-hand side of the D81 as you drive towards Cargèse. It's a good port of call, with renovated rooms, professional service and million-dollar views of the coast.

Les Roches Rouges
HOTEL €€

(☑04 95 27 81 81; www.lesrochesrouges.com; D81; d incl breakfast €114-135; ⊘mid-Mar–mid-Nov; 🐾) Corsica's original luxury hotel, built in 1912, is still one of the quirkiest places to stay on the island. It's on the right-hand side of the D81 as you drive from Porto, just before Piana. The rambling corridors and musty rooms are full of early-20th-century ambience, despite en suites, wi-fi and phone lines – you half expect Hercule Poirot to wander round the corner twiddling his moustache. Don't even consider cutting costs by not taking a sea-view room – you'll regret it. Even if you don't stay here, stop in for a drink or, even better, a meal at its superb gourmet restaurant (mains €21 to €34, *menus* €37 to €44) and savour the vista.

U Spuntinu
REGIONAL CUISINE €€

(☑04 95 27 80 02; mains €8-16, menu €19; ⊘lunch & dinner summer, lunch low season) The fare at U Spuntinu, located just near Hôtel Scandola, is not gourmet but has a temptingly pronounced regional flavour. Among the winners are the *omelette au Brocciu* (omelette with Brocciu) and lamb rib.

Information

Tourist office (www.otpiana.com; place Mairie; ⊘9am-6pm Mon-Fri) Next to the post office.

Getting There & Around

Buses between Porto and Ajaccio stop near the church and the post office.

Les Calanques

A trip to Les Calanques is an iconic Corsica experience. No amount of hyperbole could communicate the astonishing beauty of these sheer cliffs that rear up above the sea in teetering columns, towers and irregularly shaped boulders of pink, ochre and ginger. Flaming fiery red in the sunlight, the Calanques are one of Corsica's most photogenic sights. As you sway around switchback after switchback on the D81 between Porto and Piana, one breathtaking vista follows another. For the full technicolour experience, savour Les Calanques on foot. Several trails wind their way around these dramatic rock formations, many of which start near the Pont de Mezzanu, a road bridge about 3km from Piana along the D81. At the Piana tourist office, pick up the leaflet *Piana: Sentiers de Randonnée*, which details six walks within the area.

Cargèse (Carghjese)

POP 900

Surprise: with its whitewashed houses and sunbaked streets, Cargèse feels more like a Greek hilltop village than a Corsican harbour – this is hardly surprising, since the village was founded by refugee Greeks fleeing their Ottoman-controlled homeland in the 19th century.

◉ Sights & Activities

The town is known for its twin churches – one Eastern (Orthodox), the other Western (Catholic) – that eye each other across vegetable plots, like boxers squaring up for a bout. The interior of the 19th-century Greek church contains original relics carried across by settlers from their Peloponnese homeland.

Boat trips sail to Scandola, Girolata and Les Calanques in summer.

One kilometre north of Cargèse is the small strip of Plage de Pero, overlooked by a couple of Genoese watchtowers, but for more space you'll need to push on south towards the popular bay of Sagone, about 10km further along the coastal D81.

🛏 Sleeping & Eating

Hôtel Cyrnos HOTEL €

(☑04 95 26 49 47; www.torraccia.com; rue de la République; d €38-68; 🐾) The friendly Hôtel Cyrnos, a lemon-yellow town house in the heart of Cargèse, has nine sun-filled, good-value rooms. The pick have dinky balconies teetering over the town's rooftops.

Motel Ta Kladia MOTEL €€

(☑04 95 26 40 73; www.motel-takladia.com; Plage de Pero; d €70-120; ⊙Apr-Oct; 🐾) If you want to be within earshot of the sea, opt for this place on Pero beach. Rooms are comfortable but hardly fuel the imagination. Never mind. Not even the hardest of hearts can deny the location is perfect – this place is *les pieds dans l'eau* (right by the water).

A Volta RESTAURANT €€

(☑06 19 55 11 84; mains €14-25; ⊙summer) With a magical setting overlooking the Med, snazzy A Volta has fresh-as-it-gets salads, inventive pastas and well-prepared meat and fish dishes, as well as a long, tantalising list of ice creams and sorbets.

❶ Information

Tourist office (www.cargese.net; rue du Docteur Dragacci; ⊙9am-7pm, closed Sun Oct-May) A little way north of the churches.

❶ Getting There & Around

Two daily buses from Ota (1½ hours) via Porto (one hour) to Ajaccio (one hour) stop in front of the post office. There are no buses on Sunday except in July and August.

Ajaccio (Aiacciu)

POP 52,880

Ajaccio is all class – and seduction. Commanding a lovely sweep of bay, the city breathes confidence and has more than a whiff of the Côte d'Azur. Everyone from solo travellers to romance-seeking couples and families will love moseying around the centre, replete with mellow-toned buildings and buzzing cafés – not to mention its large marina and the trendy rte des Sanguinaires area, a few kilometres to the west.

The spectre of Corsica's general looms over Ajaccio. Napoléon Bonaparte was born here in 1769, and the city is dotted with sites relating to the diminutive dictator, from his childhood home to seafront statues, museums and countless street names.

◉ Sights

Musée National de la Maison Bonaparte
MUSEUM

(☑04 95 21 43 89; rue St-Charles; adult/concession €5/3.50; ⊙9-11.30am & 2-5.30pm) Napoléon spent his first nine years in this house. Ransacked by Corsican nationalists in 1793, requisitioned by English troops from 1794 to 1796, and eventually rebuilt by Napoléon's mother, the house became a place of pilgrimage for French revolutionaries, and visitors are still encouraged to observe suitably hushed tones. It hosts memorabilia of the emperor and his siblings, including a glass medallion containing a lock of his hair. It's closed Monday mornings.

Palais Fesch – Musée des Beaux-Arts

MUSEUM

(☏04 95 21 48 17; www.musee-fesch.com; 50-52 rue du Cardinal Fesch; adult/child €8/5;

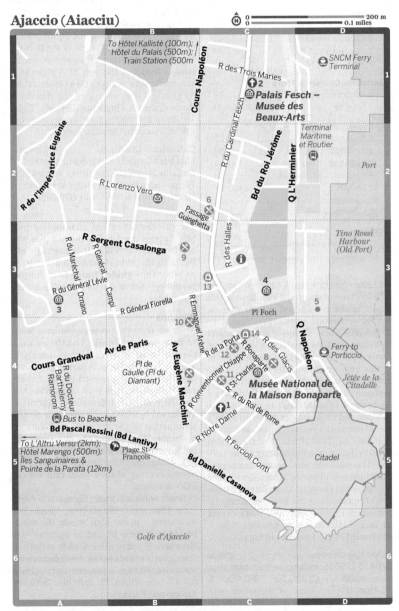

Ajaccio (Aiacciu)

◎10.30am-5pm Mon, Wed & Sat, noon-5pm Thu, Fri & Sun) One of the island's must-sees, this superb museum reopened in 2010 after extensive renovation works. Established by Napoléon's uncle, it has France's largest collection of Italian paintings outside the Louvre. Mostly the works of minor or anonymous 14th- to 19th-century artists, there are also canvases by Titian, Fra Bartolomeo, Veronese, Botticelli and Bellini. Look out for *La Vierge à l'Enfant Soutenu par un Ange* (Mother and Child Supported by an Angel), one of Botticelli's masterpieces. *Portrait de l'Homme au Gant* (Portrait of the Gloved Man) by Titian matches another in the Louvre. The museum also houses temporary exhibitions. Within the Chapelle Impériale (Imperial Chapel), constructed in 1860, several members of the imperial family lie entombed in the crypt. But don't expect to find Napoleon's own remains here – he's buried in Les Invalides in Paris.

Salon Napoléonien   MUSEUM

(☑04 95 21 90 15; www.musee-fesch.com; place Foch; adult/child €2.30/1.50; ◎9-11.45am & 2-5.45pm Mon-Fri) Fans of Napoléon will make a beeline for this museum on the 1st floor of the Hôtel de Ville. It exhibits Napoléonic medals, portraits and busts, as well as a fabulously frescoed ceiling of Napoléon and entourage.

Musée a Bandera   MUSEUM

(☑04 95 51 07 34; 1 rue du Général Lévie; admission €4; ◎9am-7pm Mon-Sat, 9am-noon Sun) Tucked away on a little side street, this quirky little museum explores Corsican history up to WWII. Among the highlights are a diorama of the 1769 battle of Ponte Novo that confirmed French conquest of the island, a model of the port of Ajaccio as it was in the same period, and a proclamation by Gilbert Elliot, viceroy of the shortlived Anglo-Corsican kingdom (1794–96). There are also a few worthy panels describing the role of women in Corsican society.

Cathédrale Ste-Marie   CATHEDRAL

(rue Forcioli Conti) The 16th-century cathedral contains Napoléon's baptismal font and the *Vierge au Sacré-Cœur* (Virgin of the Sacred Heart) by Eugène Delacroix (1798–1863).

Citadel   FORTRESS

The 15th-century citadel, an imposing military fortress overlooking the sea that was a prison during WWII. It is normally off-limits to the general public, but the tourist office runs **guided tours** from June to September. Ask at the tourist office for the exact dates.

Beaches

After all that sightseeing, you may want to flake out on a beach. The town's most popular beach, Plage de Ricanto, popularly known as Tahiti Plage, is 5km east of town towards the airport, served by Bus 1. A series of small beaches west of Ajaccio (Ariane, Neptune, Palm Beach and Marinella) are served by Bus 5 from the town centre, terminating at the car park on Pointe de la Parata, 12km west of the city. From the point you'll have a grandstand view of the Îles Sanguinaires (Bloody Islands), so named because of their vivid crimson colours at sunset.

Beach bums will prefer the sands of Porticcio, 17km across the bay from Ajaccio, but be warned – in the high season the windbreaks pack them in sardine-tight, so look elsewhere if you're after seaside seclusion. Découvertes Naturelles (www.decouvertes -naturelles.net) runs a summer ferry service (€5/8 single/return, 20 minutes) between Ajaccio and Porticcio.

NAPOLÉON, SON OF CORSICA?

Despite Ajaccio's endless Napoléonic connections, *le petit caporal's* attitude to his home island was rather ambivalent. Born to an Italian father and a Corsican mother, and largely educated in France (where he was mercilessly mocked for his provincial Corsican accent), Napoléon actually spent relatively little time on the island, and never returned following his coronation as Emperor of France in 1804. But there's no doubt that Napoléon's Corsican roots exerted a powerful hold on his imagination – famously, while exiled on Elba, he is said to have claimed he could recognise his homeland purely from the scent of the maquis.

Activities

Boat Trips

Two companies run boat trips around the Golfe d'Ajaccio and the Îles Sanguinaires (€27), and excursions to the Réserve Naturelle de Scandola (adult/child €50/35), departing daily from the quayside opposite place Foch.

Découvertes Naturelles (www.decouvertes-naturelles.net; ⊙May-Sep; 🚢) Also offers a sunset cruise to the Îles Sanguinaires (€27).

Nave Va (www.naveva.com; ⊙May-Sep; 🚢) Also offers a cultural tour (adult/child €28/20) and a voyage down to Bonifacio (€58/40), including a four-hour stop on shore.

Walking

The **Pointe de la Parata**, about 12km west of Ajaccio, is a magnet for walkers and photographers alike. From the car park, you'll find a short, much-trodden walking trail that leads around the promontory. A stroll along here rewards you with great sea views and tantalising close-ups of the four islets of the Îles Sanguinaires. Come here at sunset – the scenery is awesome.

Festivals & Events

Like many of Corsica's towns, Ajaccio has a line-up of annual festivities that adds some extra spice to the town's streets.

Festival de la St-Érasme   FESTIVAL
Fishy festival in honour of the patron saint of *pêcheurs* (fishermen), held around 2 June.

Fêtes Napoléoniennes   NAPOLÉON'S BIRTHDAY
Ajaccio's biggest bash celebrates Napoléon's birthday on 15 August, with military-themed parades, street spectacles and a huge fireworks display.

La relève de la Garde Impériale   CEREMONY
Every Thursday at 7pm in summer, you can watch the pomp and ceremony of the changing of the guard on place Foch in front of the town hall.

Sleeping

Hôtel Kallisté   HOTEL €€
(☏04 95 51 34 45; www.hotel-kalliste-ajaccio.com; 51 cours Napoléon; s €67-77, d €85-105; ❄🌐⚐) Exposed brick, neutral tones, terracotta tiles and a funky glass lift conjure a neo-boutique feel at the Kallisté, which occupies a typical 19th-century Ajaccio town house. Double-glazing keeps out the traffic hum from nearby cours Napoléon, and the facilities are fab – wi-fi, satellite TV and a copious buffet breakfast served in a spacious room. Unfortunately, the secret's out, so book ahead.

Hôtel Marengo   HOTEL €
(☏04 95 21 43 66; www.hotel-marengo.com; 2 rue Marengo; d €61-83; ⊙Apr-Oct; ❄) For something more personal, try this charmingly eccentric small hotel down a cul de sac off bd Madame Mère. Its 17 rooms all have a balcony, there's a quiet flower-filled courtyard and reception is an agreeable clutter of tasteful prints and personal objects. Oh, and it's just a stroll from the beach.

Hôtel du Palais   HOTEL €€
(☏04 95 22 73 68; www.hoteldupalaisajaccio.com; 5 av Beverini Vico; s incl breakfast €70-75, d €80-85; ❄🌐) Handy for the port, this venture is good value. Ignore the somewhat scruffy façade – inside the decor is embellished with contemporary colour schemes. The eight rooms won't win any design awards but they get the job done.

Eating

Tiny streetside restaurants cram the old quarter, and eating out there on a sultry summer night is an experience not to be missed.

Le Grand Café Napoléon MEDITERRANEAN €€
(✆04 95 21 42 54; 10-12 cours Napoléon; mains €23-30, menus €17-45) This one-of-a-kind Ajaccio institution scores a perfect 10 on our 'charm-meter' for its mind-blowing decor and refined cuisine. Push beyond the streetside terrace (itself rich in atmosphere) to the august belle époque former ballroom, with its tall mirrors, high ceilings, black-and-white terrazzo floors and soaring cream arches. Despite the classical surroundings, the menu is surprisingly modern, featuring elegantly presented fish and meat dishes. The weekday lunchtime *menu du marché* represents excellent value.

L'Altru Versu GASTRONOMIC €€
(✆04 95 50 05 22; rte des Sanguinaires, Les Sept Chapelles; mains €22-30, menus €32-40; ⊗closed Mon Oct-May) Ajaccio's top-notch restaurant belongs to the Mezzacqui brothers (Jean-Pierre front of house, Pierre powering the kitchen), who are passionate gastronomes and excellent singers – they hitch on their guitars and serenade guests each Friday and Saturday night. Their creative cuisine sings in the mouth – what about pork with honey and clementine zests?

U Pampasgiolu TRADITIONAL CORSICAN €€
(✆06 09 39 26 92; 15 rue de la Porta; mains €14-28; ⊗dinner Mon-Sat) The rustic arch-vaulted dining room of this Ajaccio institution is packed with punters nearly every night of the week. They come for the first-rate Corsican food made from carefully chosen ingredients. Go à la carte, or choose from the *planche spuntinu* (snack selection) or *planche de la mer* (fish and seafood selection) for a great assortment of Corsican specialities served on wooden platters.

Le 20123 TRADITIONAL CORSICA €€
(✆04 95 21 50 05; www.20123.fr; 2 rue du Roi de Rome; menus €32; ⊗dinner Tue-Sun) This one-of-a-kind place started life in the village of Pila Canale (postcode 20123 – get it?), and when the owner upped sticks to Ajaccio he decided to take the old village with him – water pump, washing line, life-sized dolls in traditional dress, central square et al. It all sounds a bit tacky, and it is (see the website) – but you won't find any more character-filled places in Corsica. Needless to say, the food is 100% authentic, too. There's just a single menu, presented orally.

Le Bilboq – Chez Jean Jean SEAFOOD €€€
(✆04 95 51 35 40; 1 rue du des Glacis; mains around €50; ⊗dinner) In business for decades, this Ajaccio icon is famous for one thing and one thing only: *langouste* (lobster), best enjoyed on the oh-so-cute little terrace in a pedestrian street. Knock it all down with a well-chosen Corsican wine, and you'll be in seventh heaven.

Da Mamma TRADITIONAL CORSICAN €
(✆04 95 21 39 44; 3 passage Guinghetta; mains €12-25, menus €12-21; ⊗lunch & dinner Tue-Sat, dinner Mon) Staunchly Corsican cuisine aside, the main draw of this unfussy eatery is its location – it's tucked away down a steep alley and shaded by a magnificent rubber tree.

Other temptations:

Le Spago FUSION €
(✆04 95 21 15 71; rue Emmanuel Arène; mains €12-20; ⊗lunch & dinner Mon-Fri, dinner Sat) No Corsican speciality at this cool designer restaurant decked out in lime green – just salads and innovative dishes such as pork with apricots.

L'Estaminet MEDITERRANEAN €€
(✆04 95 50 10 42; 5 rue du Roi de Rome; mains €17-25, menus €19-25; ⊗dinner Jun-Sep, dinner Mon, Sat & Sun, lunch Tue, lunch & dinner Thu & Fri Oct-May) An old-style brasserie decked out with shiny wood and polished brass, plus plenty of flavoursome dishes.

🔒 Shopping

For Corsican goodies, there's only one address that matters: **U Stazzu** (1 rue Bonaparte; ⊗9am-12.30pm & 2.30-7pm), famous for its handmade charcuterie. It also sells the usual range of Corsican delicacies from other small producers. Sweet-lovers will lose all self-control at **Boulangerie Galeani** (3 rue du Cardinal Fesch; ⊗7am-8pm Tue-Sat, 7am-1pm Sun) – see if you can resist the devilish *beignet de Brocciu* (Brocciu fritters) and *canistrelli* (biscuits made with almond, walnuts, lemon or aniseed) served at this longstanding bakery.

🍷 Drinking

Most of Ajaccio's action is along bd Lantivy, which has a good selection of atmospheric bars. Look around the chi-chi port Charles-Ornano, at the marina, too. In summer, the centre of pleasurable gravity shifts to the rte des Sanguinaires, which is lined with trendy *paillotes* (beachside venues) and discos.

ℹ️ Information

Tourist office (www.ajaccio-tourisme.com; 3 bd du Roi Jérôme; ⊕9am-6pm Mon-Sat, 9am-1pm Sun Jun-Sep, Mon-Fri Oct-May)

ℹ️ Getting There & Away

AIR Aéroport d'Ajaccio-Campo dell'Oro (www.ajaccio.aeroport.fr) is 8km east of the city centre. Town Bus 8 (€4.50, 20 minutes) runs frequently between the airport and Ajaccio's bus station. A taxi costs around €25.

BOAT Boats depart from **Terminal Maritime et Routier** (quai l'Herminier), the combined bus/ferry terminal. Ferry services head to/from Toulon, Nice and Marseille on mainland France. See p873 for more.

Corsica Ferries (www.corsicaferries.com) Inside the terminal.

La Méridionale (www.lameridionale.fr; bd Sampiero) Located inside the terminal.

SNCM (www.sncm.fr) The main office is on quai L'Herminier, and there's a ticket and information kiosk inside the terminal, which opens before most sailings.

BUS Lots of local bus companies have kiosks inside the terminal building. As always in Corsica, expect reduced services on Sunday and during the winter months. The bus-station information desk can supply timetables.

Autocars Ceccaldi (☑04 95 22 41 99) Travels to Porto (2½ hours, two daily, no Sunday buses except from July to mid-September) via Cargèse (one hour) and Piana (1½ hours).

Eurocorse (☑04 95 21 06 30) Travels to Bastia (three hours, two daily) via Corte (two hours). There's also a route to Bonifacio (four hours, two daily from Monday to Saturday, one on Sunday) via Sartène (two hours).

TRAIN From the **train station** (place de la Gare), services include Bastia (four hours, three to four daily), Corte (two hours, three to four daily) and Calvi (five hours, two daily; change at Ponte Leccia).

THE SOUTH

Sartène (Sartè)

POP 3500

With its grey granite houses, secretive culs-de-sac and slightly sombre, introspective air, Sartène has long been said to encapsulate Corsica's rugged spirit (French novelist Prosper Mérimée dubbed it the 'most Corsican of Corsican towns'). There's no doubt that Sartène feels a long way from the glitter of the Corsican coast; the hillside houses are endearingly ramshackle, the streets are shady and scruffy, and life still crawls along at a traditional tilt. But it offers a much more convincing glimpse of how life was once lived in rural Corsica than do any of the island's more well-heeled towns. Notorious for its banditry and bloody vendettas in the 19th century, Sartène has more recently found fame thanks to the annual Procession du Catenacciu, a re-enactment of the Passion that takes place in the town every Good Friday.

⊙ Sights & Activities

The only way to explore Sartène is on foot, and the town's corkscrew alleyways and shady staircases make an agreeable stroll on a blazing summer's afternoon. An archway through the town hall (formerly the Governors' Palace) leads to the residential Santa Anna quarter, where you'll find the town's most atmospheric streets.

Near the WWI memorial on place Porta is the granite Église Ste-Marie, which houses the 35kg cross and 17kg chain used in the annual Procession du Catenacciu. Since the Middle Ages, every Good Friday the Catenacciu ('chained one') has lugged this massive hunk of wood through town in a re-enactment of Christ's journey to Calvary. Barefoot, red-robed and cowled (to preserve his anonymity), the penitent is chosen by the parish priest to atone for a grave sin – in times gone by, legend has it that notorious bandits descended from the maquis to expiate their crimes.

Feel like seeing the area around Sartène from horseback instead of a car seat? Domaine de Croccano (www.corsenature.com; D148, rte de Granace) offers various horse-riding programs starting from €23 per hour. The *Promenade-Découverte du Sartenais* (three hours) is a lovely ramble amid the maquis, with special views over Sartène and the sea. It's 3.5km out of town on the road to Granace.

🛏️ Sleeping & Eating

Hôtel San Damianu HOTEL €€
(☑04 95 70 55 41; www.sandamianu.fr; d €95-167; ⊕Apr-Oct; ❋🛜🌊) The San Damianu has everything in spades: a perfect location just staggering distance from the *vieille ville* (old town), sleek rooms with all mod cons, a soothing yellow colour scheme, million-dollar views over the Rizzanese valley and the mandatory sparkling swimming pool.

Hôtel-Restaurant des Roches HOTEL €€
(☑04 95 77 07 61; www.sartenehotel.fr; rue Jean
Jaurès; s €60-91, d €70-105; ❉❄) The only
venture in the centre of town, which means
it's in high demand in summer. With a regal setting overlooking the valley and the
Golfe du Valinco, it offers 60 modernised
rooms with spotless bathrooms and air-
conditioning. Nab a room with a view –
the other ones look onto the parking lot.
There's an attached restaurant.

Auberge Santa Barbara MODERN CORSICAN €€
(☑04 95 77 09 06; www.santabarbara.fr; mains
€12-38, menu €36; ⊙Tue-Sun Apr-Oct) Send
your tastebuds into a tailspin at this iconic
restaurant serving authentic dishes with a
creative twist. Award-winning chef Giséle
Lovichi is a true alchemist, with such delectable concoctions as pigeon with myrtle
sauce or veal stew with tagliatelle. Another
draw is the bucolic setting, with elegant
tables set around a well-manicured flower
garden. A respectable wine list completes
the perfect picture. It's about 1.3km from
the centre on the road to Propriano; follow
the signs.

❶ Information

Tourist office (www.oti-sartenaisvalinco.com;
cours Sœur Amélie; ⊙9am-7pm)

❶ Getting There & Away

Sartène is on the twice-daily (on one Sunday)
Eurocorse (☑04 95 21 06 30) bus line linking
Ajaccio with Bonifacio.

Bonifacio (Bunifaziu) & Around

POP 2700

With its glittering harbour, creamy white
cliffs and stout citadel teetering above the
cornflower-blue waters of the Bouches de
Bonifacio, this dazzling port is an essential
stop on everyone's Corsican itinerary. Just
a short hop from Sardinia, Bonifacio has
a distinctly Italianate feel: sun-bleached
townhouses, dangling washing lines and
murky chapels cram the web of alleyways of the old citadel, while down below
on the harbourside, brasseries and boat
kiosks tout their wares to the droves of
day-trippers. Bonifacio's also perfectly positioned for exploring the island's southerly
beaches and the Îles Lavezzi.

◉ Sights

Citadel (Haute Ville) HISTORIC NEIGHBOURHOOD
Much of Bonifacio's charm comes from
strolling the citadel's shady streets, soaking
up the architecture and the atmosphere.

PREHISTORIC CORSICA

Southern Corsica boasts the island's most astonishing prehistoric sites, which are
must-sees for anyone with an interest in Corsica's ancient civilisations. Some time
around 4000 BC to 3000 BC, Corsica developed its own megalithic faith (possibly
imported by seafaring settlers from mainland Europe); most of the island's standing
stones and menhirs date from this period. The most important site is Filitosa (☑04
95 74 00 91; www.filitosa.fr; admission €6; ⊙8am-8pm Apr-Oct), northwest of Sartène,
where a collection of extraordinary carved menhirs were discovered in 1946. The
Filitosa menhirs are highly unusual: several have detailed faces, anatomical features
(such as ribcages) and even swords and armour, suggesting that they may commemorate specific warriors or chieftains.

About 15km south of Sartène, the desolate and beautiful Cauria plateau is home to
three megalithic curiosities: the *alignements* (lines) of Stantari and Renaju – several
of which show similar anatomical details and weaponry to those of Filitosa – and the
Fontanaccia dolmen, one of Corsica's few burial chambers, with its supporting pillars and capstones. Look out for the turn-off about 8km along the D48 towards Tiz-
zano. What did these strange sites signify for their megalithic architects? Were they
ritual temples? Sacred graveyards? Mythical armies? Or even celestial timepieces?
Despite countless theories, no one has the foggiest idea.

Inland from Porto-Vecchio, the Alta Rocca region also musters up a handful of well-
preserved megalithic remains. About 7km to the north of Levie, Pianu di Levie (adult/
child €5.50/3; ⊙9am-7pm) comprises two archaeological sites, the *castelli* (castles) of
Cucuruzzu and Capula, connected by an interpretive trail. Archaeologists believe they
were erected during the Bronze Age, around 1200 BC.

From the marina, the paved montée Rastello and montée St-Roch bring you to the citadel's old gateway, the Porte de Gênes, complete with its original 16th-century drawbridge. Inside the gateway is the 13th-century Bastion de l'Étendard (admission €2.50; ⊘9am-7pm Apr-Oct), which houses a small historical museum exploring Bonifacio's past. Stroll the ramparts to place du Marché and place de la Manichella, which both offer jaw-dropping views over the Bouches de Bonifacio.

Several streets are spanned by arched aqueducts, which originally collected rainwater to fill the communal cistern opposite Église Ste-Marie Majeure. Look out for the wooden loggia outside the church: though heavily restored, it's one of the best examples of medieval carpentry in Corsica.

From the citadel, the Escalier du Roi d'Aragon (King of Aragon's stairway; admission €2.50; ⊘9am-7pm Apr-Oct) cuts down the southern cliff-face. Its 187 steps were supposedly carved in a single night by Aragonese troops during the siege of 1420, although the troops were rebuffed by retaliating Bonifacio residents once they reached the top.

West along the limestone headland is the Église Ste-Dominique (admission €2.50; ⊘9.30am-12.30pm & 3-6pm Mon-Sat mid-Jun–mid-Sep), one of Corsica's few Gothic churches. It has reliquaries carried in processions through the town during a number of religious festivals.

Further to the west, you'll pass by a few windmills before reaching the eerily quiet marine cemetery, with its immaculate lines of tombs and imposing mausoleums, and the adjoining Église St-François. At the western tip of the peninsula, an underground passage dug by hand during WWII leads to the Gouvernail de la Corse (Rudder of Corsica; admission €2.50; ⊘9am-6pm), a rock about a dozen metres from the shore with a shape reminiscent of the rudder of a ship.

Îles Lavezzi   ARCHIPELAGO
Paradise! Part of a protected area (known as La Réserve Naturelle des Bouches de Bonifacio), the Îles Lavezzi is a clutch of uninhabited islets that are made for those who love nothing better than splashing in tranquil lapis lazuli waters.

The 65-hectare Île Lavezzi, which gives its name to the whole archipelago, is the most accessible of the islands and the southernmost point of Corsica. The island's savage beauty aside, its superb natural pools and scenic stretches of sand invite long sunbathing and swimming sessions. The island also has a cemetery for the victims who perished on board the *Sémillante*, a three-mast frigate that ran aground on Île Lavezzi in February 1855.

In summer, various companies organise **boat excursions** to the island; you can book at the ticket booths located on Bonifacio's marina. Boats are operated on a shuttle fashion, which allows you to linger on Île Lavezzi. You will need to bring your own lunch and drinks, as there is nowhere on the islands to buy anything. Trips to the Îles Lavezzi are also available from Porto-Vecchio.

Beaches
Bonifacio's town beaches are a little underwhelming. Plage de Sotta Rocca is a small pebbly cove below the citadel, reached by steps from av Charles de Gaulle, while plage de la Catena and plage de l'Arinella are sandy inlets on the northern side of Bouches de Bonifacio. On foot, follow the trail from av Sylvère Bohn, near the Esso petrol station.

For finer stretches of sand you'll need to head east along the D58 to the little cove of Spérone, opposite the islets of Cavallo and Lavezzi. Nearby Piantarella is popular with windsurfers, while further east is shingly Calalonga. There are several other lovely beaches around the Golfe de Sant'Amanza, 8km east of Bonifacio, including Plage de Maora.

🏃 Activities

Phare de Pertusato   WALK
If you're after that perfect picture, don't miss this fantastic, easy walk along the cliffs to Phare de Pertusato (Pertusato Lighthouse), from where the seamless views of the cliffs, the Îles Lavezzi, Bonifacio and Sardinia are memorable. The signposted starting point is just to the left of the sharp bend on the hill up to Bonifacio's citadel. Count on three hours (round trip).

Mérouville   DIVE SITE
The waters off Bonifacio offer plenty of scope for diving. The Îles Lavezzi (left) – the most popular diving area – feature a variety of sites for all levels. At Mérouville, Bonifacio's signature dive site, divers are guaranteed to get up close and personal with big groupers. Sign up with Corsica

Diving (www.corsicadiving.fr: quai Sennola), which is a well-established dive operator. A single dive starts at around €40.

Boat Trips

Don't leave Bonifacio without taking a boat trip around its extraordinary coastline, where you'll get the best perspective of the town's precarious position on top of the magnificent chalky cliffs. The one-hour itinerary (€19) includes the Goulet de Bonifacio, several *calanques* (deep rocky inlets) with clear aquamarine waters, a lighthouse, the Escalier du Roi d'Aragon and the Grotte du Sdragonato (Little Dragon Cave), a vast watery cave with a natural rooftop skylight.

Numerous companies vie for customers in summer; ticket booths are located on the marina. They all offer pretty much the same deal.

🛏 Sleeping

Hôtel des Étrangers   HOTEL €
(☑04 95 73 01 09; hoteldesetrangers.ifrance. com; av Sylvère Bohn; d €46-65; ⊙Apr–mid-Oct; ❋🐕) The Foreigners' Hotel is unspectacular, but it provides excellent value. Look at the rates! It's a solid, unfussy place offering spick-and-span rooms, all with tiled floors, clean bathrooms and simple colour schemes (more expensive ones have aircon). Yes, the main road outside's a bother, but for this price nobody's complaining. It's north of the harbour.

Hôtel Le Colomba   HOTEL €€
(☑04 95 73 73 44; www.hotel-bonifacio-corse.fr; rue Simon Varsi; d €100-160; ⊙Mar-Nov; ❋🐕) Occupying a tastefully renovated 14th-century building, this beautiful hotel is a delightful address in a picturesque street, bang in the heart of the old town. Rooms are simple and smallish but fresh and pleasantly individual – wrought-iron bedsteads and country fabrics in some, carved bedheads and chequerboard tiles in others. Breakfast in a vaulted room is another highlight.

Domaine de Licetto   HOTEL €€
(☑04 95 73 03 59, 04 95 73 19 48; www.licetto. com; rte du Phare; d €65-100; ❋🏊) Located just a couple of kilometres east of Bonifacio yet light years away from the hustle and bustle of the coast, this is a very nice surprise. The seven rooms sport well-chosen tiles and modern furnishings, and feel fresh and comfortable. There's a well-regarded on-site restaurant.

Hotel Genovese   HOTEL €€
(☑04 95 73 12 34; www.hotel-genovese.com; rte de Bonifacio; d €130-185; ⊙Oct-Mar; ❋🏊🐕) A breath of fresh air, this tasteful hotel is built on the ramparts. With its lovely swimming pool, stylish furniture and soothing tones, it's hard to resist. Try to score an outside-facing room, rather than a darker courtyard-facing one.

Camping l'Araguina   CAMPGROUND €
(☑04 95 73 02 96; www.camping-araguina-bonifacio.com; av Sylvère Bohn; per person/tent/car €6.60/2.70/2.70; ⊙Mar-Oct) Bonifacio's main campsite is near the Hôtel des Étrangers, with plenty of tent sites and rental chalets, but the roadside location can be less than soothing.

🍴 Eating

Swish terrace restaurants pack the quayside, but the food isn't always as fancy as the ambience suggests.

Kissing Pigs   MODERN CORSICAN €€
(☑04 95 73 56 09; quai Banda del Ferro; mains €10-19, menus €13-20; ⊙closed Wed & Sun low season) Soothingly positioned by the harbour, this widely acclaimed restaurant and wine bar serves savoury fare in a seductively cosy interior, complete with wooden fixtures and swinging sausages. It's famed for its cheese and charcuterie platters. For the indecisive, the *moitié-moitié* (half and half), which is a combination of the two, is the perfect answer. The wine list is another hit, with a good selection of Corsican tipples, available by the glass.

Cantina Doria   CORSICAN €
(☑04 95 73 50 49; 27 rue Doria; mains €10-14; ⊙Mon-Sat Apr-Sep) A Bonifacio institution, this cavernous little joint has a tantalising menu showcasing all the classics of Corsican cuisine, served in snug surrounds complete with wooden benches, copper pots, rustic tools and dented signs. Tuck into perennial favourites such as *lasagnes au fromage Corse* (lasagne with Corsican cheese) and *soupe Corse, aubergines à la bonifacienne* (aubergines stuffed with breadcrumbs and cheese), and you'll leave patting your tummy contentedly.

Domaine de Licetto   TRADITIONAL CORSICAN €€
(☑04 95 73 03 59; rte du Phare; menu €36; ⊙dinner daily Aug, Mon-Sat Apr-Jul & Sep–mid-Oct.) If you're after an authentic Corsican experience, this place is hard to beat. Bring an empty tum: the five-course menu

is a culinary feast based on local ingredients that come directly from small-scale farmers. Menu stalwarts include suckling lamb and *aubergines à la bonifacienne*. It's right in the maquis, on the way to Phare de Pertusato.

Le Gregale SEAFOOD €€
(☑04 95 73 51 46; Plage de Maora; fish €7 per 100g, lobster from €14 per 100g; ☺dinner Jun-Sep) On Plage de Maora, Le Gregale is well worth the detour. This is the place towards which all heads turn when it comes to tasting the freshest of fish. Depending on the daily catch, the menu may feature John Dory, sea bream, sea bass... and lobster. It's a family affair, with Mum, Dad (the cooks) and two sons (fishermen and waiters). Another draw is the rustic-chic setting, with blond-wood furniture and beams.

L'Archivolto MODERN CORSICAN €€
(☑04 95 73 17 58; rue de l'Archivolto; mains €13-21; ☺dinner Jul-Aug, lunch Mon-Sat Apr-Jun & Sep,) Steps from the Église Ste-Marie Majeure, this gloriously offbeat bistro feels like an antique shop, with an onslaught of quirky collectables from floor to ceiling. The chalked-up menu is just as eclectic, with an assortment of fish and meat dishes, as well as frondy salads. In summer the tables spill out onto the lovely piazza outside.

❶ Information

There are only two ATMs in Bonifacio: at the post office (within the citadel) and at the Société Générale bank (at the marina).

Tourist office (www.bonifacio.fr; 2 rue Fred Scamaroni; ☺9am-8pm)

❶ Getting There & Away

AIR Figari-Sud Corse airport (www.figari. aeroport.fr) is about 21km north of Bonifacio. See p892 for further information. There's no public transport to/from the airport. A taxi costs about €40.

BOAT Sardinia's main ferry operators, **Saremar** (www.saremar.it) and **Moby Lines** (www.moby. it), offer services between Bonifacio and Santa Teresa di Gallura in summer. Costs vary according to the time and day of sailing, but range from around €10 to €19 one way plus taxes; the crossing lasts about an hour.

BUS Eurocorse (☑04 95 70 13 83) has two daily services (one on Sunday) between Bonifacio and Porto-Vecchio, Sartène, Propriano and Ajaccio in July and August. From September to June, it runs one daily service from Monday to Saturday. For Bastia, you'll have to change in Porto-Vecchio.

Porto-Vecchio (Portivecchju) & Around

POP 10,600

Shamelessly seductive and fashionable, Porto-Vecchio is usually dubbed the Corsican St-Tropez, and it's no wonder. Sitting in a marvellous bay, it's the kind of place that lures French A-listers and wealthy tourists. The city has also a well-established party reputation during the season. Although there is no beach by the town proper, some of the island's best, and most famous, beaches are close by.

◉ Sights & Activities

Porto-Vecchio is fairly short on sights but the Haute Ville, with its picturesque backstreets lined with restaurant terraces and designer shops, has charm in spades. The atmospheric rue Borgo gives a glimpse of what the city was like in earlier days. The ruins of the old Genoese citadel are well worth a peek – you can't miss the **Porte Génoise** and the **Bastion de France** (closed to the public; you can admire from the outside).

Boat Trips

Various operators offer boat excursions to Îles Lavezzi (p889) and Bonifacio. The full-day excursion passes along the Réserve Naturelle des Îles Cerbicale and the beaches to the south of Porto-Vecchio. It costs €60/30 for adults/children and includes lunch.

Monte Cristo (www.croisieres-montecristo. com; ☺May-Sep; 👪) and Ruscana (www. amour-des-iles.com; ☺May-Sep; 👪) both have a booth at the marina.

Beaches

You didn't think we would forget beach lovers? When it comes to wishing for the archetypal 'idyllic beach', it's impossible to think past the immense Plage de Palombaggia. This is the Corsican paradise you've been daydreaming about: sparkling turquoise waters, long stretches of sand edged with pine trees and splendiferous views over the Îles Cerbicale. South of Plage de Palombaggia, Plage de la Folacca (also known as Plage de Tamaricciu) is no less impressive. Continue a few kilometres further south over a pass called Bocca di L'Oru and you'll come across another gem of a beach, the gently curving Plage de Santa Giulia. From Porto-Vecchio, follow the N198 to the south and turn left onto rte de Palombaggia (it's signposted), which winds around the coast.

To the north, the coast is also sprinkled with scenic expanses of sand. The gorgeous, lucent depths of the beaches at Cala Rossa and Baie de San Ciprianu are sure to set your heart aflutter. Further to the north is the stunning Golfe de Pinarello with its Genoese tower and yet more beautiful expanses of sand lapped by shallow waters.

🛌 Sleeping

TOP CHOICE Chambre d'hôte A Littariccia

B&B €€

(☎04 95 70 41 33; www.littariccia.com; rte de Palombaggia; d €90-200; ☀) Find bucolic bliss at this attractive B&B that boasts a *faaabulous* location, in the hills overlooking Plage de Palombaggia. Your heart will lift at the dreamy views over the Med; your soul will find peace in the six button-cute rooms; and your body will relax in the small pool. Not all rooms come with a sea view, though.

Hôtel-Restaurant Le Goéland   HOTEL €€

(☎04 95 70 14 15; www.hotelgoeland.com; La Marine; d incl half board €180-360; ☺Mar-Nov; ❄🛜📶) Right on the seashore near the marina, this venture is all dolled up with a stylish lobby and crisp rooms (think soft sandy yellow and pastel tones, terracotta floors and dark furniture). After a day of turf pounding, plop into a sun-lounger and forget your hardships in the well-manicured garden complete with oleanders, pines and eucalypts. Be sure to ask for the *'vue mer'* (room with a sea view). There's an on-site restaurant.

Hôtel San Giovanni   HOTEL €€

(☎04 95 70 22 25; www.hotel-san-giovanni.com; rte d'Arca; d €90-140; ☺Mar-Oct; ❄🛜📶) San Giovanni's main draw? The 1.25-hectare landscaped gardens, with lots of flowers, ponds and palm trees, not to mention a lovely pool. Other perks include bike hire, jacuzzi and tennis court. By comparison, the rooms are a bit disappointing, with simple furnishings.

🍴 Eating

Tamaricciu   MODERN CORSICAN €€

(☎04 95 70 49 89; www.tamaricciu.com; rte de Palombaggia; mains €15-32; ☺lunch May, Jun & Sep, lunch & dinner Jul-Aug) Among the various *pail-*

lottes (beach restaurants) that are scattered along the beaches south of Porto-Vecchio, Tamaricciu has that special hip touch that makes it stand out. It specialises in the greats of Mediterranean cuisine: grilled fish (seabass, John Dory), meat dishes (lamb, beef) and pasta, all beautifully presented. The lunchtime menu also includes pizza served bubbling hot from the oven. It's at the southern tip of Plage de Palombaggia.

A Cantina di L'Orriu   CORSICAN €

(☎04 95 70 26 21; cours Napoléon; mains €10-28; ☺May-Sep) This is the gourmet choice in Porto-Vecchio, with excellent meat dishes, cheese and charcuterie platters, homemade ravioli with Brocciu cheese and great salads. Wine enthusiasts will love the selection of local wines.

Sous La Tonnelle   MODERN CORSICAN €€

(☎04 95 70 02 17; rue Abbatucci; mains €13-25; ☺closed Sun & Mon low season) Alfresco on a little vine-clad pavement terrace or inside the pretty dining room decorated with earthy tones, dining at this cosy eatery is a treat – you'll be delighted with a fine selection of fish and meat renditions of Corsican staples that sing in the mouth.

🍷 Drinking & Entertainment

Night owls will be pleased to know that the city has a well-established party reputation during the season. There's no shortage of hip cafés around place de la République, in the Upper Town, as well as along the seafront. For something more authentic, make a beeline for La Taverne du Roi (☺from 10pm), an intimate place tucked into the Porte Génoise, which features Corsican singing with guitar accompaniment.

On the southern outskirts of Porto-Vecchio, Via Notte (www.vianotte.com; rte de Porra; ☺daily in season) is the hottest club in Corsica, and one of the most famous in the Med. With up to 5000 revellers and superstar DJs most nights in summer, it has to be seen to be believed.

ℹ Information

Tourist office (www.destination-sudcorse. com; rue Camille de Rocca Serra; ☺9am-8pm Mon-Sat, 9am-1pm Sun) Closed Sunday out of season.

ℹ Getting There & Away

AIR Figari-Sud Corse airport (www.figari. aeroport.fr) is about 25km from Porto-Vecchio, near the village of Figari. Daily flights from mainland France, plus charter flights in summer from other European countries, serve both Porto-Vecchio and Bonifacio. See also p971.

BOAT Ferries run to/from Marseille to Porto-Vecchio. For more, see p873.

BUS Les Rapides Bleus (☑04 95 70 10 36; rue Jean Jaurès) operates a service (daily except Sunday and public holidays in winter) to Bastia (three hours). It also operates a shuttle service to Plage de Palombaggia and Plage de Santa Giulia in summer (€7 return, four shuttles daily). **Balési Évasion** (☑04 95 70 15 55; rte de Bastia) has buses to Ajaccio via the Alta Rocca. Buses depart daily in July and August, and on Monday and Friday only in winter. **Eurocorse** (☑04 95 71 24 64; rue Pasteur) operates a service to Ajaccio (3½ hours) via Sartène. In summer there are four departures daily Monday to Saturday (two on Sunday and public holidays). In the other direction, buses run twice daily to Bonifacio (30 minutes).

CORTE AREA

Corte (Corti)

POP 5700 / ELEVATION 400M

Secretive. Inward looking. Staunchly Corsican. In many ways, the mountain town of Corte feels different to other Corsican cities. This is the heart and soul of Corsica. It has been at the centre of the island's fortunes since Pascal Paoli made it the capital of his short-lived Corsican republic in 1755, and it remains a nationalist stronghold.

Beautifully positioned at the confluence of several rivers, Corte is blessed with an awesome setting. The fairytale sight of the citadel atop a craggy mount that bursts forth from the valley is sensational. Despite its isolation, the town is also full of atmosphere. Its sizeable student population gives it a special buzz during term time. In summer, it's mainly tourists who make their base here, eager to explore the Restonica and Tavignano Valleys just on the outskirts of town.

◉ Sights & Activities

Citadel   HISTORIC NEIGHBOURHOOD

Of Corsica's six citadels, Corte's is the only one not on the coast. Jutting out above the Rivers Tavignanu and Restonica and the cobbled alleyways of the Haute Ville, the citadel's highest point is the château (known as the Nid d'Aigle – the Eagle's Nest), built in 1419.

The town's finest views are from the belvédère (viewing platform), reached via a steep staircase just outside the citadel's ramparts. Inside the walls are the former barracks and administrative buildings, which previously served as a WWII prison and a French Foreign Legion base. They now house the tourist office and the Museu di a Corsica (Museum of Corsica; ☑04 95 45 25 45; admission €5.50; ⏰10am-8pm summer, closed Mon shoulder seasons, closed Sun & Mon winter), a definite must-see for anyone interested in Corsica's culture. It houses an outstanding exhibition on Corsican traditions, crafts, agriculture and anthropology. The building has two main galleries, with a third space allocated to temporary exhibitions.

Cours Paoli   STREET

A gentle wander along the main strip makes a pleasant prelude to an aperitif or a fine meal at one of the town's good restaurants. Start from place Paoli, Corte's focal point, which is dominated by a statue of Pascal Paoli, and stroll down the cours. It's a short walk, but allow plenty of time as there are lots of temptations along the way.

Place Gaffory   SQUARE

At the foot of the citadel is place Gaffory, a lively square lined with restaurants and cafés and dominated by the Église de l'Annonciation, built in the mid-15th century. The walls of nearby houses are pock-marked with bullet holes, reputedly from Corsica's war of independence.

Outdoor Activities

The Corte area is a mecca for the skittish. Canyoning, walking, rock climbing and mountain biking are all available in the nearby valleys. Contact outfitters Altipiani (www.altipiani-corse.com; 5 rue du Pr Santiaggi) for details.

🛏 Sleeping

Chambre d'hôte Osteria di l'Orta – Casa Guelfucci   B&B €€

(☑04 95 61 06 41; www.osteria-di-l-orta.com; d €85; ❋🎧🐾) Inside a powder-blue townhouse on the N193, this peach of a B&B is run by a charming couple with a keen designer's eye. The four rooms (named after local notables) are lovely, with polished wood floors, gleaming walls and great showers, but for real luxury, go for the massive Pascal Paoli suite. At the end of the day, make sure you treat yourself to a copious dinner (€26) taken in the dining room, below the main building, with its vast bay windows; the delicious Corsican specialities are made using the finest local produce.

Hôtel du Nord HOTEL **€€**
(☎04 95 46 00 68; www.hoteldunord-corte. com; 22 cours Paoli; d incl breakfast €80-100; ✳🖤) Never mind the busy thoroughfare in summer and the somewhat-peeling fa-

L'ALTA ROCCA

If you've had a temporary surfeit of superb seascapes, take a couple of days to explore the Alta Rocca, north of Porto-Vecchio. Here you can really feel a sense of wilderness, a world away from the bling and bustle of the coast. At the south of the long spine that traverses the island, it's a bewildering combination of dense, mixed evergreen-deciduous forests and granite villages strung over rocky ledges.

Leave Porto-Vecchio by the winding D368 that will take you to the calm surroundings of L'Ospédale, at an altitude of about 1000m. The village is close to the Forêt de L'Ospédale, which offers excellent walking opportunities and tranquil picnic spots. Follow signs to Zonza, a quintessential village mountain with the soaring Aiguilles de Bavella as a backdrop. Zonza is a perfect base for exploring the Alta Rocca, with a good range of restaurants and accommodation options. L'Aiglon (☎04 95 78 67 79; mains €16-23, menu €23; ⏱Apr-Oct) is the best place around to sample a refined Corsican meal. About 2km from Zonza, Chambre d'hôte de Cavanello (☎04 95 78 66 82; www.locationzonza.com; d €60-70; 🖤🛒) features nine cosy rooms and several hectares of meadows and forests.

Another little charmer is the nearby village of Quenza. It's cradled by thickly wooded mountains and the Aiguilles de Bavella loom on the horizon. If you're after a typically Corsican atmosphere and the most tranquil location imaginable, at an altitude of about 1200m, bookmark Chez Pierrot (☎04 95 78 63 21; Ghjallicu; d incl half board €110), southern Corsica's most idiosyncratic venture. This multifaceted place – *gîte*, B&B, restaurant (meals €23) and equestrian centre – is run by charismatic Pierrot, a local character who's been living here since his early childhood. It's on Plateau de Ghjallicu, about 5km uphill from Quenza (it's signposted).

From Zonza or Quenza, it's a short drive to the Col de Bavella (Bavella Pass; 1218m), from where you can marvel at the iconic Aiguilles de Bavella (Bavella Needles). Jabbing the skyline at an altitude of more than 1600m, these granite pinnacles resemble giant shark's jaws and are, unsurprisingly, an all-time photographic favourite. The Bavella area is also a fantastic playground. Walking, rock-climbing, canyoning or simply picnicking... it can all be done in the vicinity of the col. You can recharge the batteries at the Auberge du col de Bavella (☎04 95 72 09 87; www. auberge-bavella.com; mains €10-25; ⏱Apr-Oct), a typical Corsican inn that serves excellent meat dishes.

For culture vultures, Levie is a definite must-see, with an interesting museum and a lovely archaeological site amid superb scenery. The well-organised Musée de l'Alta Rocca (admission €4; ⏱9am-6pm daily May-Oct, 10am-5pm Tue-Sat Nov-Apr) does a good job of elucidating Corsican geology, climate, flora and fauna. It also features ethnology and archaeology sections. After a visit to the museum, head to the archaeological site of Pianu di Levie (see boxed text p888), about 7km to the north (it's signposted). Here you can get a feel for what life was like in ancient times in Corsica. Levie has one of Corsica's most attractive accommodation options, A Pignata (☎04 95 78 41 90; www.apignata.com; rte du Pianu; d €110-260; ⏱Apr-Oct; 🖤🛒). This boutique-style inn offers superb rooms and splendid suites, and the on-site restaurant (*menu* €38) rates as one of the best in southern Corsica.

From Levie, drive to Ste-Lucie de Tallano, which has a few monuments worthy of interest, including the well-proportioned Église Ste-Lucie and the Renaissance-style Couvent St-François, an imposing building scenically positioned at the edge of the village.

cade – the grande dame of Corte's sleeping scene is kept shipshape. It has a cache of cheerful and spacious rooms with contemporary colour schemes and all the creature comfort.

Hôtel Duc de Padoue HOTEL €€
(☑04 95 46 01 37; www.ducdepadoue.com; place Padoue; d €92-123; ❄️📶) Don't be deterred by the scruffy facade of this professionally run abode. Renovated throughout a few years ago, the hotel has an inviting interior that offers well-equipped rooms, flat-screen TVs, plump bedding, muted tones and squeaky-clean bathrooms.

Camping Saint-Pancrace CAMPGROUND €
(☑04 95 46 09 22; per tent/person/car €6/3/3; ☺Jun-Sep) The pick of Corte's campsites, with lots of pleasant sites sheltering under olive trees and green oak. It's a 20-minute walk north of town, in a peaceful neighbourhood. The owners run a small dairy farm – if you're after local cheese, this place is hard to beat.

✖️ Eating

Pâtisserie Casanova PASTRY SHOP €
(☑04 95 46 00 79; 6 cours Paoli; pastries from €2; ☺7am-7pm Mon-Sat) Gourmands, you'll be in seventh heaven! Back home, don't tell your dietetician that you couldn't resist the *falculella* (a Corsican dessert made with Brocciu and chestnut flour) at this longstanding pastry shop (it's been around since 1887). It also doubles as a coffee lounge – perfect for a gourmet coffee break after exploring central Corte.

Le 24 MODERN CORSICAN €€
(☑04 95 46 02 90; 24 cours Paoli; mains €13-24, menus €18-25; ☺closed Sun lunch Sep-Jun) After something upmarket? Then swing by this snazzy spot on the main drag. It boasts contemporary furnishings, a sexy atmosphere and an innovative menu that uses top-quality ingredients and changes with the season. The house desserts, chalked up on the blackboard, hit the right spot.

A Scudella MODERN CORSICAN €€
(☑04 95 46 25 31; 2 place Paoli; mains €10-17, menus €13-23; ☺Mon-Sat) This snug place on Corte's liveliest square owes its reputation to a carefully composed menu, based solidly on good-quality local produce. The decor in the dining room won't win any prizes, but the outdoor seating is pleasant enough.

🍷 Drinking

There's a lively bar scene along cours Paoli. The unfussy Café du Cours (22 cours Paoli) is a great place to watch the world go by, while the sleek Le Rex Lounge (1 cours Paoli) serves excellent cocktails.

ℹ️ Information

Tourist office (www.centru-corsica.com; citadelle; ☺10am-5pm Mon, Wed & Sat, 9am-7pm Tue, Thu & Fri Jul & Aug, closed Sat & Sun Sep-Jun)

ℹ️ Getting There & Away

BUS The most useful bus service is run by **Eurocorse** (☑04 95 31 73 76) from Ajaccio to Bastia stopping at Corte en route (two hours). There are two daily buses except on Sunday. **Transports Mordiconi** (☑04 95 48 00 44) links Corte with Porto (2¾ hours) once daily except on Sunday from July to mid-September, leaving from outside the train station.

TRAIN The train station is east of the city centre. Destinations include Bastia (two hours, three to four daily) and Ajaccio (two hours, three to four daily).

Around Corte

Here in the mountainous area around Corte you'll find fresh mountain air, deep forests, picturesque valleys and abundant hiking trails. You come here to enjoy the scenery and rejuvenate mind and body in a pristine environment.

VALLÉE DE LA RESTONICA
The Vallée de la Restonica is one of the prettiest spots in all Corsica. The river, rising in the grey-green mountains, has scoured little basins in the rock, offering sheltered pinewood settings for bathing and sunbathing alike. From Corte, the D623 winds its way through the valley for 15km to the Bergeries de Grotelle (1375m), where a car park (€5) and a huddle of shepherds' huts (three of which offer drinks, local cheeses and snacks) mark the end of the road. From them, a path leads to a pair of picture-pretty glacial lakes, Lac de Melu (1711m), reached after about one hour, and Lac de Capitellu (1930m), 45 minutes' walk further on.

There are a couple of tempting sleeping choices in the early reaches of the valley, including Les Jardins de la Glacière (☑04 95 45 27 00; www.lesjardinsdelaglaciere.com; d €85-100; ☺Apr–mid-Nov; ❄️📶🏊), which has clean, fresh rooms, impeccable communal areas and a fantastic location by the river (avoid the rooms facing the road, though).

VALLÉE DU TAVIGNANO

If you have a day to spare, do not miss the opportunity to hike into the car-free (and much quieter than Restonica) Vallée du Tavignano. Corsica's deepest gorge is only accessible on foot and remains well off the beaten track, despite being on Corte's doorstep. From Corte, the signposted track leads to the Passerelle de Rossolino footbridge, reached after about 2½ hours. It's an idyllic spot for a picnic, and there's plenty of transparent green natural pools in which you can dunk yourself. The valley can also be explored on horseback; contact L'Albadu (www.

hebergement-albadu.fr; ancienne rte d'Ajaccio, Corte) for more information.

VIZZAVONA

South of Corte, the N193 climbs steeply in the shadow of Monte d'Oro (2389m) before arriving at the cool mountain hamlet of Vizzavona. A mere cluster of houses and hotels around a train station, Vizzavona is an ideal base to explore the Forêt de Vizzavona, where the 1633 hectares are covered mainly by beech and laricio pines. A magnet for walkers, it features lots of excellent hikes. Look for the signpost indicating a short, gentle path that meanders down through a superb forest to Cascades des Anglais, a sequence of gleaming waterfalls.

Understand France

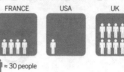
France Today

A New Breed of President

Presidential elections in 2007 ushered out old-school Jacques Chirac (in his 70s with two terms under his belt) and brought in Nicolas Sarkozy (b 1955). Dynamic, ambitious and far from media-shy, the former interior minister and chairman of centre-right party UMP *(Union pour un Mouvement Populaire)* wooed voters with big talk about job creation, lower taxes, crime crackdown and help for France's substantial immigrant population – something that had particular pulling power coming from the son of a Hungarian immigrant father and Greek Jewish-French mother. Female Socialist Party candidate Ségolène Royal (b 1953) put up a grand fight. But the majority of French, fed up with an economically stagnant, socially discontented France, appeared to be looking for change. And this personality-driven, silky-tongued politician seemed to be the man to do it. A new breed of French president was born.

Yet rather than the work of knuckling down to implement his rigorous economic reform platform, it was Sarkozy's personal affairs that got the attention in his first months in office – falling out of love with wife Cecilia, divorcing, falling in love with Italian multimillionaire singer Carla Bruni and remarrying, all in a few hasty months. His popularity plummeted and it seemed the honeymoon was over.

Economic Woes

Sarkozy pledged to reduce unemployment and income tax (between 5.5% and 40%), create jobs and boost growth in a economy that nonetheless ranks as the world's eighth largest. Unemployment frog-leaped from 8.7% in 2007, to 7.6% during the global banking crisis in 2008 (when the government injected €10.5 billion into France's six major banks), to 9.1% in 2010 – all to the horror of the French, who traditionally

---

» Population: 64.4 million

» Area: 551,000 sq km

» GDP: US$2.10 trillion

» GDP growth: -2.2%

» Inflation: 0.1%

» Unemployment: 9.1%

Faux Pas

» Splitting the bill is deemed the height of unsophistication. The person who invites pays, although close friends often go Dutch.

» Fondle fruit, veg, flowers or clothing in shops and you'll be greeted with a killer glare from the shop assistant

» Take flowers (not chrysanthemums, which are only brought to cemeteries) or Champagne when invited to someone's home

» Never ever discuss money over dinner

Top Books

The Death of French Culture (Donald Morrison) Thought-provoking look at France's past and present

Me Talk Pretty One Day (David Sedaris) Caustic take on moving to France and learning the lingo

belief systems
(% of population)

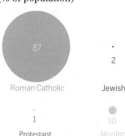

87 Roman Catholic

2 Jewish

1 Protestant

10 Muslim

if France were 100 people

77 would live in cities
23 would live in rural areas

have great expectations of their economy: France is a country accustomed to receiving free education and health care (employees pay 8% of their salary in social-security contributions, deducted at source), state-subsidised child care, travel concessions for families, ample leisure time and a 35-hour working week. In June 2009 economic growth shrank by 1.3% and for a few fleeting months France joined much of the rest of Europe in recession.

Hard-line attempts to reform a pension system, unchanged since 1982, which entitles 1.6 million workers in the rail, metro, energy-supply and fishing industries to draw a full state pension after 37.5 working years (and everyone else after 40), only provoked widespread dismay and a series of national strikes and protests. So too have suggestions that the retirement age, currently 60, should be extended to at least 62 (it is much higher in almost every other European country). In June 2010 when the French government unveiled concrete plans to push the retirement age back to 62 by 2018, much of the country went on strike.

Helter-Skelter Downhill

If the results of the 2010 regional elections are anything to go by, Sarkozy could be out of a job after the next presidential elections in 2012. His party got a real battering, the left scooping 54% of votes and control of 21 out of 22 regions on mainland France and Corsica – Alsace in northeast France was the only region the centre-right UMP held on to.

By spring 2010 unemployment was hovering at a disconcerting 10% and government popularity at an all-time low. Inciting further disillusionment with the government, scandal erupted in July over allegations by investigative news service Mediapart that France's richest woman and L'Oréal heir, 87-year-old Liliane Bettencourt, had made illegal cash

France maintains a rigid distinction between Church and State. Indeed, the country is a secular republic, meaning no mention of religion – any religion – on national school syllabuses.

Top Surfs

Paris by Mouth (http://parisbymouth.com) Resource for capital dining and drinking
Wine Travel Guide (www.winetravelguides.com)
France 24 (www.france24.com/en/france) French news in English

Top Albums

Histoire de Melody Nelson (Serge Gainsbourg, 1971) France's most-loved crooner
Moon Safari (AIR; 1998) Electronic
Made in Medina (Rachid Taha, 2002) *Rai*
Dante (Abd al Malik, 2008) Rap

Top Films

Code Inconnu (Code Unknown; 2001) Art-house film
Les Choristes (The Chorus; 2004) Stunning soundtrack!
La Môme (La Vie en Rose; 2007) Story of singer Edith Piaf
Lucky Luke (2009) France's most famous cowboy

donations of €150,000 to Sarkozy's 2007 presidential election campaign. By law, nonparty members can donate up to €7500 (maximum €150 in cash). French prosecutors are investigating.

What was seen as a measurement of just how volatile the country had become came the same month – riots ripped through the Alpine town of Grenoble after a 27-year-old man was shot dead by police while allegedly trying to rob a casino. The burning cars and street clashes with riot police echoed the violence that had bloodied a Parisian suburb in 2005 – and spread like wildfire countrywide creating a state of emergency – following the death of two teenage boys, electrocuted after hiding in an electrical substation while on the run from the police.

The two boys were of North African origin, an ethnic minority in a country long known for its multiculturalism. Several thousand burnt cars and buildings later, after peace was restored, then-president Jacques Chirac had assured France there would be no more urban violence and steps would be taken to create equal opportunities for immigrants.

> France has always drawn immigrants: 4.3 million from Europe between 1850 and WWI, and another three million between the world wars. Post-WWII, several million unskilled workers followed from North Africa and French-speaking sub-Saharan Africa.

Banning the Burqa

The wearing of crucifixes, the Islamic headscarf and other overtly religious symbols in state schools has been banned in France since 2004, and in September 2010 a controversial law banning face-covering veils in public was approved by the Senate – by 246 votes to one. Intended to place school children on an equal footing in the classroom, the law is seen by many Muslims in particular as intolerant and evidence that the French State is not prepared to truly integrate them into French society. Women caught wearing a burqa will be fined €150 and be required to attend 'citizenship classes'.

Greeting People

» 'Monsieur' for men; 'Madame' for 'Mrs'; 'Mademoiselle' for unmarried women – to be used upon entering a shop, restaurant etc

» 'S'il vous plaît' – never 'garçon' (meaning 'boy') – is the only way to summon a waiter

Cheese Etiquette

» Cut small circular cheeses into pie wedges

» Larger cheeses already sliced into a wedge must be cut tip to rind – don't slice off the tip

» Chop semihard cheeses horizontally

Tap Water

» Safe to drink, as is water spouting from fountains flagged 'eau potable'

» If the sign says 'eau non potable', don't drink it!

» Save money by ordering une carafe d'eau (a jug of free tap water)

History

The history of France could be said to be a microcosm of the history of much of Europe. As elsewhere, the beginnings involved the mass migration of a nomadic people (the peripatetic Celts), the subjugation by and – dare we say? – the civilising influence of the Romans, and the rise of a local nobility. Christianity would bring a degree of unity, but perhaps nowhere else would such a strongly independent church continue to coexist under a powerful central authority. From Charles 'The Hammer' Martel and Louis XIV's claim to be the state itself, to the present government's ambitious president dealing with '60 million different opinions', this dichotomy is the basis of France's story.

The following is just a broad introduction to the history of France. If you would like to know more about this extensive and very complex subject – either in general or on a specific topic – see p902 for some recommended titles.

Roman Gaul

What is now France was settled by several different groups of people in the Iron Age, but the largest and most organised were the Celtic Gauls. The subjugation of these people and their territory by Rome was gradual, and within a few centuries Rome had imposed its government, roads, trade, culture and even language. A Gallo-Roman culture emerged and Gaul was increasingly integrated into the Roman Empire.

It began in the 1st millennium BC as the Greeks and Romans established colonies on the Mediterranean coast, including Massilia (Marseille). Centuries of conflict between the Gauls and the Romans ended in 52 BC when Caesar's legions crushed a revolt by many Gallic tribes led by Celtic Arverni tribe chief Vercingétorix at Gergovia near present-day Clermont-Ferrand. For the next couple of years, during the so-called Gallic Wars, the Gauls hounded the Romans with guerrilla warfare and stood up to them in several match-drawn pitched

TIMELINE

c 30,000 BC	c 7000 BC	1500–500 BC
During the Middle Palaeolithic Period, Cro-Magnon people start decorating their homes in the Vézère Valley of the Dordogne with colourful scenes of animals, human figures and geometric shapes.	Neolithic man turns his hand to monumental menhirs and dolmen during the New Stone Age, creating a fine collection in Brittany that continues to baffle historians.	Celtic Gauls move into the region and establish trading links with the Greeks, whose colonies included Massilia (Marseille) on the Mediterranean coast; the latter bring grapes and olives.

battles. But gradually Gallic resistance collapsed and Roman rule in Gaul reigned supreme.

The stone architecture left by the occupiers was impressive and Roman France is magnificent, climaxing with the mighty Pont du Gard aqueduct, built to bring water to the city of Nîmes in southern France, and splendid theatres and amphitheatres dating from this period are still extant in that city as well as at Autun, Arles and Orange. Some Roman remains became part of something else. In an early form of recycling, the 1st-century Roman amphitheatre at Périgueux in the Dordogne was dismantled in the 3rd century and its stones were used to build the city walls.

Romans' intangible legacy to what would become a new culture was equally great. Sophisticated urban centres with markets and baths of hot and cold running water began to emerge. The Romans planted vineyards, notably in Burgundy and Bordeaux, and introduced techniques to process wine. Most importantly, they introduced the newfangled faith of Christianity, which would eventually beat out the not-dissimilar worship of Mithra in the popularity sweepstakes.

Later the Franks would adopt these important elements of Gallo-Roman civilisation (including Christianity), and their eventual assimilation resulted in a fusion of Germanic culture with that of the Celts and the Romans.

HISTORICAL READS

» **Is Paris Burning?** (Larry Collins & Dominique Lapierre; 1965) A tense and very intelligent reportage of the last days of the Nazi occupation of Paris.

» **The French** (Theodore Zeldin; 1997) Stimulating social history in the guise of a 'how-to' book by the British scholar who was appointed to a committee advising the Sarkozy government on labour-market reforms in 2007.

» **Citizens: A Chronicle of the French Revolution** (Simon Schama; 1990) Highly acclaimed and truly monumental work that looks at the first few years of the revolutionary government after 1789.

» **The Sun King** (Nancy Mitford; 1966) Classic work on Louis XIV and the country he ruled by acclaimed author and biographer who lived and died in Versailles.

» **The Discovery of France: A Historical Geography** (Graham Robb; 2008) Winner of the 2008 Ondaatje Prize, this much-lauded work is an anecdotal account of France's formation based on 20,000km of research by bicycle around rural France.

» **The Shameful Peace: How French Artists and Intellectuals Survived the Nazi Occupation** (Frederic Spotts; 2010) This is the book that separates the wheat from the chaff, the saints from the sinners, the 'no' and the 'yes' men.

3rd century BC	121 BC	55–52 BC	c AD 100–300
The Celtic Parisii tribe builds a handful of wattle-and-daub huts on what is now the Île de la Cité in Paris; the capital city is christened Lutetia by the Romans.	The Romans begin taking Gallic territory, annexing southern Gaul as the province of Gallia Narbonensis (in modern Provence and Languedoc), with its capital at the present-day town of Narbonne.	Julius Caesar launches his invasion of Britain from the Côte d'Opale in far northern France; the Gauls defeat the Romans at Gergovia near present-day Clermont-Ferrand.	The Romans go on a building spree throughout France, erecting magnificent baths, temples and aqueducts of almighty proportions such as the Pont du Gard near Nîmes in southern France.

The Agony & the Ecstasy: Medieval France

The collapse of the Roman Empire opened the gates to a wave of Franks and other Germanic tribes under Merovius from the north and northeast who overran the territory. Merovius' grandson, Clovis I, converted to Christianity, giving him greater legitimacy and power over his Christian subjects, and made Paris his seat; his successors founded the abbey of St-Germain des Prés in Paris and later the one at St-Denis to the north, which would become the richest, most important monastery in France and the final resting place of its kings.

The Frankish tradition, by which the king was succeeded by all of his sons, led to power struggles and the eventual disintegration of the kingdom into a collection of small feudal states. The dominant house to emerge was that of the Carolingians.

Carolingian power reached apogee under Charlemagne, who extended the boundaries of the kingdom and was crowned Holy Roman Emperor (Emperor of the West) in 800. But during the 9th century Scandinavian Vikings (also called Norsemen, thus Normans) raided France's western coast, settling in the lower Seine Valley and forming the duchy of Normandy a century later. This would be a century of disunity in France, marked politically by the rise of Norman power and religiously by the foundation of influential abbeys like the Benedictine one at Cluny. By the time Hugh Capet ascended the throne in 987, heralding the arrival of the Capetian dynasty, the king's domain was a humble parcel of land around Paris and Orléans.

The exciting tale of how William the Conqueror and his forces mounted a successful invasion of England from their base in Normandy in 1066 is told on the Bayeux Tapestry, showcased inside Bayeux' Musée de la Tapisserie de Bayeux. To complicate matters further, in 1152 Eleanor of Aquitaine wed Henry of Anjou, bringing a further third of France under the control of the English crown. The subsequent rivalry between France and England for control of Aquitaine and the vast English territories in France lasted three centuries.

> The French invented the first digital calculator, the hot-air balloon, Braille and margarine, not to mention Grand Prix racing and the first public interactive computer network. Find out what else at http://inventors.about.com/od/frenchinventors.

Hundred Years War

In 1337 the hostility between the Capetians and the Anglo-Normans degenerated into the Hundred Years War, which would be fought on and off until the middle of the 15th century. The Black Death, which broke out a decade after the hostilities began and lasted more than two years, killed more than a third (an estimated 80,000 souls) of Paris' population alone but only briefly interrupted the fighting.

The French suffered particularly nasty defeats at Crécy and Agincourt. Abbey-studded Mont St-Michel in present-day Normandy was the only place in northern and western France not to fall into English

c 455–70	732	800–900	987
France remains under Roman rule until the 5th century, when the Franks (hence the name 'France') and the Alemanii invade and overrun the country from the east.	Somewhere near Poitiers Charles Martel and his cavalry repel the Muslim Moors. His grandson, Charlemagne, extends the boundaries of the kingdom and is crowned Holy Roman Emperor.	Scandinavian Vikings (also called Norsemen, thus Normans) raid France's western coast and settle in the lower Seine Valley where they later form the Duchy of Normandy.	Five centuries of Merovingian and Carolingian rule ends with the crowning of Hugh Capet; a dynasty that will rule one of Europe's most powerful countries for the next eight centuries is born.

hands. The dukes of Burgundy (allied with the English) occupied Paris and in 1422 John Plantagenet, duke of Bedford, was made regent of France for England's King Henry VI, then an infant. Less than a decade later he was crowned king of France.

Luckily for the French, a 17-year-old girl called Jeanne d'Arc (Joan of Arc) came along with the outlandish tale that she had a divine mission from God to expel the English from France and bring about the coronation of French legitimist Charles VII in Reims.

The Virgin Warrior

Many stories surround the origins of Jeanne d'Arc (Joan of Arc), the legendary *pucelle* (virgin) warrior burned at the stake by the English, and France's patron saint. Some say she was the bastard child of Louis d'Orléans, King Charles VI's brother. The less glamorous but more accurate account pinpoints Domrémy in northeastern France (Domrémy-la-Pucelle today) as the place where she was born to a simple peasant family in 1412.

Revelations delivered by the Archangel Michael prompted Jeanne d'Arc to flee the fold in 1428. Her mission: to raise a siege against the city of Orléans and see the dauphin (the future Charles VII) crowned king of France. An enquiry conducted by clergy and university clerks in Poitiers tried to establish if Jeanne d'Arc was a fraud or a gift, as she claimed, from the king of Heaven to the king of France. Her virginity was likewise certified. Following the six-week interrogation Jeanne was

PRIMITIVE ART

The Cro-Magnons, a *Homo sapiens* variety who arrived in what is now France about 35,000 years ago, had larger brains than their ancestors, the Neanderthals, long and narrow skulls, and short, wide faces. Their hands were nimble, and with the aid of improved tools they hunted reindeer, bison, horses and mammoths to eat. They played music, danced and had fairly complex social patterns.

Those agile hands were not just used to make tools and hunt; Cro-Magnons were also artists. A tour of Grotte de Lascaux II – a replica of the Lascaux cave where one of the world's best examples of Cro-Magnon drawings was found in 1940 – demonstrates how initial simplistic drawings and engravings of animals gradually became more detailed and realistic. Dubbed 'Périgord's Sistine Chapel', the Lascaux cave contains some 2000 paintings of human figures and abstract signs as well as animals and is one of 25 known decorated caves in Dordogne's Vézère Valley (see also p573).

The Neolithic Period produced France's incredible collection of menhirs and dolmens: Brittany's Morbihan Coast is awash in megalithic monuments.

1066	1095	1152	1253
Duke of Normandy William the Conqueror and his Norman forces occupy England, making Normandy and, later, Plantagenet-ruled England formidable rivals of the kingdom of France.	Pope Urban II preaches the First Crusade in Clermont-Ferrand, prompting France to take a leading role and giving rise to some splendid cathedrals, eg at Reims, Strasbourg, Metz and Chartres.	Eleanor of Aquitaine weds Henry of Anjou, bringing a further third of France under the control of the English crown and sparking a French-English rivalry that will last three centuries.	La Sorbonne is founded by Robert de Sorbon, confessor of Louis IX, as a theological college for impoverished students in the area of the Left Bank known as the Latin Quarter.

sent by Charles VII to Tours, where she was equipped with intendants, a horse, a sword and her own standard featuring God sitting in judgment on a cloud. In Blois the divine warrior collected her army, drummed up by Charles VII from his Royal Army Headquarters there. In April 1429 Jeanne d'Arc started her attack on Orléans, besieged by the English from October of the previous year. Defiant to their defences she entered the city, rallying its inhabitants and gaining their support. On 5 and 6 May respectively the French gained control of the Bastille St-Loup and the Bastille des Augustins, followed the next day by the legendary Fort des Tourelles – a fort guarding the only access to the city from the left bank. This last shattering defeat prompted the English to lay down the siege on 8 May and was a decisive turning point in the Hundred Years War.

From Orléans Jeanne d'Arc went on to defeat the English at Jargeau, Beaugency and Patay. Charles VII stayed at châteaux in Loches and Sully-sur-Loire at this time and prayed to St Benedict with his protégé at Abbaye de St-Benoît in St-Benoît-sur-Loire. Despite Charles' promised coronation in July 1429, battles between the English and the French waged until 1453, by which time the virginal warrior responsible for turning the war around had long been dead. Jeanne d'Arc was captured by the Burgundians, sold to the English, convicted of witchcraft and heresy by a tribunal of French ecclesiastics in Rouen in 1431 and burned at the stake. She was canonised in 1920.

Track France in the news, learn about its history and catch up on stacks more background info with www.discov erfrance.net.

NEWS

The Rise of the French Court

With the arrival of Italian Renaissance culture during the reign of François I (r 1515–47), the focus shifted to the Loire Valley. Italian artists decorated royal castles at Amboise, Azay-le-Rideau, Blois, Chambord and Chaumont, with Leonardo da Vinci making Le Clos Lucé in Amboise his home for three years until his death in 1519.

Renaissance ideas of scientific and geographic scholarship and discovery assumed a new importance, as did the value of secular matters over religious life. Writers such as Rabelais, Marot and Ronsard of La Pléiade were influential as were artist and architect disciples of Michelangelo and Raphael. Evidence of this architectural influence can be seen in François I's château at Fontainebleau – where superb artisans, many of them brought over from Italy, blended Italian and French styles to create what is known as the First School of Fontainebleau – and the Petit Château at Chantilly, both near Paris. This new architecture was meant to reflect the splendour of the monarchy, which was fast moving towards absolutism. But all this grandeur and show of strength was not enough to stem the tide of Protestantism that was flowing into France.

The Reformation swept through Europe in the 1530s, spearheaded by the ideas of Jean (John) Calvin, a Frenchman born in Picardy but

1309	1337	1358	1422
French-born Pope Clément V moves papal headquarters from Rome to Avignon, where the Holy Seat remains until 1377; 'home' is the resplendent Palais des Papes built under Benoît XII (1334–42).	Incessant struggles between the Capetians and England's King Edward III, a Plantagenet, over the powerful French throne degenerate into the Hundred Years War, which will last until 1453.	The war between France and England and the devastation and poverty caused by the plague lead to the ill-fated peasants' revolt led by Étienne Marcel.	John Plantagenet, duke of Bedford, is made regent of France for England's King Henry VI, then an infant; in less than a decade he is crowned king of France at Paris' Notre Dame.

exiled to Geneva. Following the Edict of January 1562, which afforded the Protestants certain rights, the Wars of Religion broke out between the Huguenots (French Protestants who received help from the English), the Catholic League (led by the House of Guise) and the Catholic monarchy, and lasting three dozen years.

Henri IV, founder of the Bourbon dynasty, issued the controversial Edict of Nantes in 1598, guaranteeing the Huguenots many civil and political rights, notably freedom of conscience. Ultra-Catholic Paris refused to allow the new Protestant king to enter the city, and a siege of the capital continued for almost five years. Only when Henri IV embraced Catholicism at the cathedral in St-Denis did the capital submit to him.

Arguably France's most famous king of this or any other century, Louis XIV (r 1643–1715), called Le Roi Soleil (the Sun King), ascended the throne at the tender age of five. Bolstered by claims of divine right – indeed, he was yet another Louis named after France's patron saint, and paintings in the Royal Chapel at Versailles evoke the idea that the French king was chosen by God and is thus his lieutenant on earth – he involved the kingdom in a series of costly, almost continuous wars with Holland, Austria and England, which gained France territory but nearly bankrupted the treasury. State taxation to refill the coffers caused widespread poverty and vagrancy, especially in the cities. In Versailles, Louis XIV built an extravagant palace and made his courtiers compete with each other for royal favour, thereby quashing the ambitious, feuding aristocracy and creating the first centralised French state. In 1685 he revoked the Edict of Nantes.

The Seven Years War (1756–63), known as the French and Indian War in North America, was one of a series of ruinous military engagements pursued by Louis XV, the Sun King's grandson. It led to the loss of France's flourishing colonies in Canada, the West Indies and India. It was in part to avenge these losses that his successor Louis XVI sided with the colonists in the American War of Independence a dozen years later. But the Seven Years War cost France a fortune and, more disastrously for the monarchy, it helped to disseminate at home the radical democratic ideas that were thrust upon the world stage by the American Revolution.

From Revolution to Republic

As the 18th century progressed, new economic and social circumstances rendered the *ancien régime* (old order) dangerously out of step with the needs of the country. The regime was further weakened by the antiestablishment and anticlerical ideas of the Enlightenment, whose leading lights included Voltaire, Rousseau and Diderot. But entrenched

1431	1491
Jeanne d'Arc (Joan of Arc) is burned at the stake in Rouen for heresy; the English are not driven out of France until 1453.	Charles VIII weds Anne de Bretagne at Château de Langeais in the castle-studded Loire Valley, marking the unification of independent Brittany with France.

» Statue of Joan of Arc, Paris

vested interests, a cumbersome power structure and royal lassitude prevented change from starting until the 1770s, by which time the monarchy's moment had passed.

By the late 1780s, the indecisive Louis XVI and his dominating consort, Marie-Antoinette, had managed to alienate virtually every segment of society, and the king became increasingly isolated as unrest and dissatisfaction reached boiling point. When he tried to neutralise the power of the more reform-minded delegates at a meeting of the États-Généraux (States-General) at the Jeu de Paume in Versailles in May and June 1789, the masses took to the streets of Paris. On 14 July, a mob raided the armoury at the Hôtel des Invalides for rifles, seizing 32,000 muskets, then stormed the prison at Bastille – the ultimate symbol of the despotic *ancien régime*. The French Revolution had begun.

At first, the Revolution was in the hands of moderate republicans called the Girondins. France was declared a constitutional monarchy and various reforms were introduced, including the adoption of the Déclaration des Droits de l'Homme et du Citoyen (Declaration of the Rights of Man and of the Citizen) modelled on the American Declaration of Independence. But as the masses armed themselves against the external threat to the new government – posed by Austria, Prussia and the exiled French nobles – patriotism and nationalism mixed with extreme fervour, popularising and radicalising the Revolution. It was not long before the Girondins lost out to the extremist Jacobins, who abolished the monarchy and declared the First Republic after Louis XVI proved unreliable as a constitutional monarch. The Assemblée Nationale (National Assembly) was replaced by an elected Revolutionary Convention.

In January 1793 Louis XVI, who had tried to flee the country with his family but only got as far as Lorraine, was convicted of 'conspiring against the liberty of the nation' and guillotined at place de la Révolution, today's place de la Concorde, in Paris. Two months later the Jacobins set up the notorious Committee of Public Safety to deal with national defence and to apprehend and try 'traitors'. This body had dictatorial control over the country during the so-called Reign of Terror (September 1793 to July 1794), which saw most religious freedoms revoked and churches closed to worship and desecrated, cathedrals turned into 'Temples of Reason', and thousands incarcerated in dungeons in Paris' Conciergerie on Île de la Cité before being beheaded.

After the Reign of Terror faded, a five-man delegation of moderate republicans set itself up to rule the republic as the Directoire (Directory).

NATIONAL ASSEMBLY

Keep tabs on the moves and motions of France's National Assembly at www.assemblee-nat.fr.

1515	1530s	1572	1588
With the reign of François I the royal court moves to the Loire Valley, where a rash of stunning Renaissance châteaux and hunting lodges is built.	The Reformation, spurred by the writings of French Jean (John) Calvin, sweeps through France, pitting Catholics against Protestants and eventually leading to the Wars of Religion (1562–98).	Some 3000 Huguenots visiting Paris to celebrate the wedding of the Protestant Henri of Navarre (the future Henri IV) are slaughtered on 23–24 August, in the so-called St Bartholomew's Day Massacre.	The Catholic League forces Henri III (r 1574–89), the last of the Valois kings, to flee the royal court at the Louvre; the next year he is assassinated by a fanatical Dominican friar.

Napoléon & Empire

It was true happenstance that brought a dashing young Corsican general named Napoléon Bonaparte to the attention of France. In October 1795 a group of royalist youths bent on overthrowing the Directory were intercepted on rue St-Honoré in Paris by forces under Bonaparte, who fired into the crowd. For this 'whiff of grapeshot' he was put in command of the French forces in Italy, where he was particularly successful in the campaign against Austria. His victories would soon turn him into an independent political force.

In 1799 Napoléon overthrew the Directory and assumed power as First Consul, chosen by popular vote. A referendum three years later declared him 'Consul for Life' and his birthday became a national holiday. In 1804, when he crowned himself 'Emperor of the French' in the presence of Pope Pius VII at Notre Dame in Paris, the scope and nature of Napoléon's ambitions were obvious to all.

To consolidate and legitimise his authority, Napoléon needed more victories on the battlefield. So began a seemingly endless series of wars and victories by which France would come to control most of Europe. In 1812 his troops captured Moscow, only to be killed off by the brutal Russian winter. Two years later Allied armies entered Paris, exiled Napoléon to Elba and restored the House of Bourbon to the French throne at the Congress of Vienna.

In early 1815 Napoléon escaped from the Mediterranean island, landed in southern France and gathered a large army as he marched towards Paris. On 1 June he reclaimed the throne at celebrations held at the Champ de Mars. But his reign came to an end just three weeks later

---

THE KINDEST CUT

Hanging, then drawing and quartering – roping the victim's limbs to four oxen, which then ran in four different directions – was once the favoured method of publicly executing commoners. In a bid to make public executions more humane, French physician Joseph Ignace Guillotin (1738–1814) came up with the guillotine.

Several tests on dead bodies down the line, highwayman Nicolas Jacques Pelletie was the first in France to have his head sliced off by the 2m-odd falling blade on 25 April 1792 on place de Grève (today's place de l'Hôtel de Ville) in Paris. During the Reign of Terror, at least 17,000 met their death by guillotine.

By the time the last person in France to be guillotined (murderer Hamida Djandoubi in Marseille) was given the chop in 1977 (behind closed doors – the last public execution was in 1939), the lethal contraption had been sufficiently refined to slice off a head in 2/100 of a second. France abolished capital punishment in 1981.

1589	1598	1635	1643
Henri IV, the first Bourbon king, ascends the throne after renouncing Protestantism; *'Paris vaut bien une messe'* (Paris is well worth a Mass), he is reputed to have said upon taking communion.	Henri IV gives French Protestants freedom of conscience with the Edict of Nantes – much to the horror of staunchly Catholic Paris, where many refuse to acknowledge the forward-thinking document.	Cardinal Richelieu, de facto ruler during the reign of Henri IV's son, Louis XIII, founds the Académie Française, the first and best known of France's five institutes of arts and sciences.	The Roi Soleil (Sun King), Louis XIV, all of five years old, assumes the French throne. In 1682 he moves his court lock, stock and satin slipper – from Paris' Palais des Tuileries to Versailles.

when his forces were defeated at Waterloo in Belgium. Napoléon was exiled again, this time to the island of St Helena in the South Atlantic, where he died in 1821. In 1840 his remains were moved to Paris' Église du Dôme.

Although reactionary in some ways – he re-established slavery in France's colonies in 1802, for example – Napoléon instituted a number of important reforms, including a reorganisation of the judicial system; the promulgation of a new legal code, the Code Napoléon (or civil code), which forms the basis of the French legal system to this day; and the establishment of a new educational system. More importantly, he preserved the essence of the changes brought about by the Revolution.

A struggle between extreme monarchists seeking a return to the *ancien régime,* people who saw the changes wrought by the Revolution as irreversible, and the radicals of the poor working-class neighbourhoods of Paris dominated the reign of Louis XVIII (r 1815–24). His successor Charles X responded to the conflict with ineptitude and was overthrown in the so-called July Revolution of 1830. Those who were killed in the accompanying Paris street battles are buried in vaults under the Colonne de Juillet in the centre of place de la Bastille. Louis-Philippe, a constitutional monarch of bourgeois sympathies who followed him, was subsequently chosen as ruler by parliament, only to be ousted by the 1848 Revolution.

The Second Republic was established and elections brought in Napoléon's inept nephew, the German-reared (and accented) Louis Napoléon Bonaparte, as president. In 1851 he staged a coup d'état and proclaimed himself Emperor Napoléon III of the Second Empire, which lasted until 1870.

France enjoyed significant economic growth at this time. Paris was transformed under urban planner Baron Haussmann (1809–91), who created the 12 huge boulevards radiating from the Arc de Triomphe. Napoléon III threw glittering parties at the royal palace in Compiègne, and breathed in fashionable sea air at Biarritz and Deauville.

Like his uncle before him, Napoléon III embroiled France in a number of costly conflicts, including the disastrous Crimean War (1854–56). In 1870 Otto von Bismarck goaded Napoléon III into declaring war on Prussia. Within months the thoroughly unprepared French army was defeated and the emperor taken prisoner.

The Belle Époque

Although it would usher in the glittering belle époque (beautiful age), there was nothing very attractive about the start of the Third Republic. Born as a provisional government of national defence in September 1870, it was quickly besieged by the Prussians, who laid siege to Paris

1756–63	1789	1793	1795
The Seven Years War against Britain and Prussia is one of a series of ruinous wars pursued by Louis XV, leading to the loss of France's colonies in Canada, the West Indies and India.	The French Revolution begins when a mob arms itself with weapons taken from the Hôtel des Invalides and storms the prison at Bastille, freeing a total of just seven prisoners.	Louis XVI is tried and convicted as citizen 'Louis Capet' (as all kings since Hugh Capet were declared to have ruled illegally) and executed; Marie-Antoinette's turn comes nine months later.	A five-man delegation of moderate republicans led by Paul Barras sets itself up as the *Directoire* (Directory) and rules the First Republic for five years.

and demanded National Assembly elections be held. Unfortunately, the first move made by the resultant monarchist-controlled assembly was to ratify the Treaty of Frankfurt. The harsh terms of the treaty – a huge war indemnity and surrender of the provinces of Alsace and Lorraine – prompted immediate revolt (known as the Paris Commune), during which several thousand Communards were killed and another 20,000 executed. The Wall of the Federalists in Paris' Cimetière du Père Lachaise serves as a deathly reminder of the bloodshed.

The belle époque launched art nouveau architecture, a whole field of artistic 'isms' from Impressionism onwards, and advances in science and engineering, including the construction of the first metro line in Paris. World Exhibitions were held in the capital in 1889 (showcased by the Eiffel Tower) and again in 1901 in the purpose-built Petit Palais.

But all was not well in the republic. France was consumed with a desire for revenge after its defeat by Germany, and looking for scapegoats. The so-called Dreyfus Affair began in 1894 when a Jewish army captain named Alfred Dreyfus was accused of betraying military secrets to Germany; he was then court-martialled and sentenced to life imprisonment on Devil's Island in French Guiana. Liberal politicians and writers succeeded in having the case reopened despite bitter opposition from

A DATE WITH THE REVOLUTION

Along with standardising France's system of weights and measures with the almost universal metric system, the revolutionary government adopted a new, 'more rational' calendar from which all 'superstitious' associations (ie saints' days and mythology) were removed. Year 1 began on 22 September 1792, the day the First Republic was proclaimed.

The names of the 12 months – Vendémaire, Brumaire, Frimaire, Nivôse, Pluviôse, Ventôse, Germinal, Floréal, Prairial, Messidor, Thermidor and Fructidor – were chosen according to the seasons. The autumn months, for instance, were Vendémaire (derived from *vendange*, grape harvest), Brumaire (from *brume*, mist or fog) and Frimaire (from *frimas*, wintry weather). In turn, each month was divided into three 10-day 'weeks' called *décades*, the last day of which was a rest day. The five remaining days of the year were used to celebrate Virtue, Genius, Labour, Opinion and Rewards. These festivals were initially called *sans-culottides* in honour of the *sans-culottes*, the extreme revolutionaries who wore pantaloons rather than the short breeches favoured by the upper classes.

While the republican calendar worked well in theory, it caused no end of confusion for France in its communications and trade abroad because the months and days kept changing in relation to those of the Gregorian calendar. The revolutionary calendar was abandoned and the old system restored in 1806 by Napoléon Bonaparte.

1799

Napoléon Bonaparte overthrows the Directory and seizes control of the government in a *coup d'état*, opening the doors to 16 years of despotic rule, victory and then defeat on the battlefield.

1815

British and Prussian forces under the Duke of Wellington defeat Napoléon at Waterloo; he is again sent into exile, to a remote island in the South Atlantic where he dies six years later.

» Napoléon and family in wax, Musée Grévin, Paris

the army command, right-wing politicians and many Catholic groups – and Dreyfus was vindicated in 1900. This resulted in more rigorous civilian control of the military and, in 1905, the legal separation of Church and State.

The Two World Wars

Central to France's entry into war against Austria-Hungary and Germany had been its desire to regain Alsace and Lorraine, lost to Germany in the Franco-Prussian War – but it would prove to be a costly piece of real estate in terms of human life. By the time the armistice was signed in November 1918, some 1.3 million French soldiers had been killed and almost one million crippled. At the Battle of Verdun alone, the French (under the command of General Philippe Pétain) and the Germans each lost about 400,000 men.

The 1920s and '30s saw Paris as a centre of the avant-garde, with painters pushing into new fields of art such as cubism and surrealism, Le Corbusier rewriting the textbook for architecture, foreign writers such as Ernest Hemingway and James Joyce drawn by the city's liberal atmosphere (and cheap booze), and nightlife establishing a cutting-edge reputation for everything from jazz clubs to striptease.

The naming of Adolf Hitler as Germany's chancellor in 1933 signalled the end of a decade of compromise between France and Germany over border guarantees. Initially the French tried to appease Hitler, but two days after Germany invaded Poland in 1939 France joined Britain in declaring war on Germany. By June 1940 France had capitulated. The Maginot Line (see p912) had proved useless, with German armoured divisions outflanking it by going through Belgium.

The Germans divided France into a zone under direct German rule (along the western coast and the north, including Paris), and a puppet-state based in the spa town of Vichy and led by General Pétain, the ageing WWI hero of the Battle of Verdun. The Vichy regime was viciously anti-Semitic, and local police proved very helpful to the Nazis in rounding up French Jews and others for deportation to Auschwitz and other death camps.

The underground movement known as the Résistance (Resistance), or Maquis, whose active members never amounted to more than about 5% of the French population, engaged in such activities as sabotaging railways, collecting intelligence for the Allies, helping Allied airmen who had been shot down, and publishing anti-German leaflets. The vast majority of the rest of the population did little or nothing to resist the occupiers or assist their victims, or collaborated.

An 80km-long stretch of beach (see the boxed text, p211) was the site of the D-Day landings on 6 June 1944, when more than 100,000 Allied

A full 20% of all Frenchmen – one out of every five males – between 20 and 45 years of age were killed in WWI.

WWI

1851	1858	1871	1889
Louis Napoléon leads a coup d'état and proclaims himself Emperor Napoléon III of the Second Empire (1852–70), a period of significant economic growth and building under Baron Haussmann.	A 14-year-old peasant girl in Lourdes sees the Virgin Mary in 18 visions that come to her in a grotto; the sleepy market town in the Pyrenees later becomes a world pilgrimage site.	The Treaty of Frankfurt is signed, the harsh terms of which (a 5-billion-franc war indemnity, surrender of the provinces of Alsace and Lorraine) prompt immediate revolt.	The Eiffel Tower is completed in time for the opening of the Exposition Universelle (World Exhibition) but is vilified in the press and on the street as the 'metal asparagus'.

Published posthumously in 2004, the award-winning *Suite Française* by Ukrainian-born author Irène Némirovsky, who was murdered at Auschwitz in 1942, evokes the horror of Nazi-occupied Paris from June 1940 until July 1941.

troops stormed the coastline to liberate most of Normandy and Brittany. Paris was liberated on 25 August by a force spearheaded by Free French units, sent in ahead of the Americans so the French would have the honour of liberating their own capital.

The war ruined France. More than one-third of industrial production fed the German war machine during WWII, the occupiers requisitioning practically everything that wasn't (and was) nailed down: ferrous and nonferrous metals, statues, iron grills, zinc bar tops, coal, leather, textiles and chemicals. Agriculture, strangled by the lack of raw materials, fell by 25%.

In their retreat, the Germans burned bridges (2600 destroyed) and the Allied bombardments tore up railroad tracks (40,000km). The roadways hadn't been maintained since 1939, ports were damaged, and nearly half a million buildings and 60,000 factories were destroyed. The French had to pay for the needs of the occupying soldiers to the tune of 400 million francs a day, prompting an inflation rip tide.

Rebuilding & the Loss of the Colonies

The magnitude of France's postwar economic devastation required a strong central government with broad powers to rebuild the country's

THE MAGINOT LINE

The Ligne Maginot, named after France's minister of war from 1929 to 1932, was one of the most spectacular blunders of WWII. This elaborate, mostly subterranean defence network, built between 1930 and 1940 (and, in the history of military architecture, second only to the Great Wall of China in sheer size), was the pride of prewar France. It included everything France's finest military architects thought would be needed to defend the nation in a 'modern war' of poison gas, tanks and aeroplanes: reinforced concrete bunkers, subterranean lines of supply and communication, minefields, antitank canals, floodable basins and even artillery emplacements that popped out of the ground to fire and then disappeared. The only things visible above ground were firing posts and lookout towers. The line stretched along the Franco-German frontier from the Swiss border all the way to Belgium where, for political and budgetary reasons, it stopped. The Maginot Line even had a slogan: *'Ils ne passeront pas'* (They won't get through).

'They' – the Germans – never did. Rather than attack the Maginot Line straight on, Hitler's armoured divisions simply circled around through Belgium and invaded France across its unprotected northern frontier. They then attacked the Maginot Line from the rear.

industrial and commercial base. Soon after liberation most banks, insurance companies, car manufacturers and energy-producing companies fell under government control. Other businesses remained in private hands, the objective being to combine the efficiency of state planning with the dynamism of private initiative. But progress was slow. By 1947 rationing remained in effect and France had to turn to the USA for loans as part of the Marshall Plan to rebuild Europe.

One of the aims of the plan was to stabilise postwar Europe financially and politically, thus thwarting the expansion of Soviet power. As the Iron Curtain fell over Eastern Europe, the pro-Stalinist bent of France's Communist Party put it in a politically untenable position. Seeking at once to exercise power within the government and at the same time oppose its measures as insufficiently Marxist, the communists found themselves on the losing end of disputes involving the colonies, workers' demands and American aid. In 1947 they were booted out of government.

The economy gathered steam in the 1950s. The French government invested in hydroelectric and nuclear-power plants, oil and gas exploration, petrochemical refineries, steel production, naval construction, auto factories and building construction to accommodate a baby boom and consumer goods. The future at home was looking brighter; the situation of *la France d'outre-mer* (overseas France) was another story altogether.

France's humiliation at the hands of the Germans had not been lost on its restive colonies. As the war economy tightened its grip, native-born people, poorer to begin with, noticed that they were bearing the brunt of the pain. In North Africa the Algerians coalesced around a movement for greater autonomy, which blossomed into a full-scale independence movement by the end of the war. The Japanese moved into strategically important Indochina in 1940. The Vietnamese resistance movement that developed quickly took on an anti-French, nationalistic tone, setting the stage for Vietnam's eventual independence.

The 1950s spelled the end of French colonialism. When Japan surrendered to the Allies in 1945, nationalist Ho Chi Minh launched a push for an autonomous Vietnam that became a drive for independence. Under the brilliant General Giap, the Vietnamese perfected a form of guerrilla warfare that proved highly effective against the French army. After their defeat at Dien Bien Phu in 1954, the French withdrew from Indochina.

The struggle for Algerian independence was nastier. Technically a French *département*, Algeria was in effect ruled by a million or so French settlers who wished at all costs to protect their privileges. Heads stuck firmly in the Saharan sands (especially in the south, where the

WWII

Since the end of WWII France has been one of the five permanent members of the UN Security Council. Follow its movements at www.un.org/docs/sc.

1918	1920s
The armistice ending WWI signed at Fôret de Compiègne near Paris sees the return of lost territories (Alsace and Lorraine), but the war brought about the loss of more than a million French soldiers.	Paris sparkles as the centre of the avant-garde. The luxurious Train Bleu (Blue Train) makes its first run, and Sylvia Beach of the Shakespeare & Company bookshop publishes James Joyce's *Ulysses*.

» WWI cemetery, Verdun

NEIL SETCHFIELD

oil was), the colonial community and its supporters in the army and the right wing refused all Algerian demands for political and economic equality.

The Algerian War of Independence (1954–62) was brutal. Nationalist rebel attacks were met with summary executions, inquisitions, torture and massacres, which only made Algerians more determined to gain their independence. The government responded with half-hearted reform and reorganisation programs that failed to address the fact that most people didn't want to be part of France.

International pressure on France to pull out of Algeria came from the UN, the USSR and the USA, while *pieds noirs* (literally 'black feet', as Algerian-born French people are known in France), elements of the military and extreme right-wingers became increasingly enraged at what they saw as defeatism in dealing with the problem. A plot to overthrow the French government and replace it with a military-style regime was narrowly avoided when General Charles de Gaulle, France's undersecretary of war who had fled Paris for London in 1940 after France capitulated and had spent more than a dozen years in opposition to the postwar Fourth Republic, agreed to assume the presidency in 1958.

De Gaulle's initial attempts at reform – according the Algerians political equality and recognising their right in principle to self-determination – only infuriated right-wingers without quenching the Algerian thirst for independence. Following a failed coup attempt by military officers in 1961, the Organisation de l'Armée Secrète (OAS; a group of French settlers and sympathisers opposed to Algerian independence) resorted to terrorism. It tried to assassinate de Gaulle several times and in 1961 violence broke out on the streets of Paris. Police attacked Algerian demonstrators, killing more than 100 people. Algeria was granted independence the following year.

The Road to Prosperity & Europe

By the late 1960s de Gaulle, president of the Fifth Republic for almost a decade by then, was appearing more and more like yesterday's man. Loss of the colonies, a surge in immigration and the rise in unemployment had weakened his government. De Gaulle's government by decree was starting to gall the anti-authoritarian baby-boomer generation, now at university and agitating for change. Students reading Herbert Marcuse and Wilhelm Reich found much to admire in Fidel Castro, Che Guevara and the black struggle for civil rights in America, and vociferously denounced the war in Vietnam.

Student protests of 1968 climaxed with a brutal overreaction by police to a protest meeting at the Sorbonne, Paris' most renowned

1939	1944	1949	1951
Nazi Germany occupies France and divides it into a zone under direct German occupation (along the north and western coasts) and a puppet state led by General Pétain and based in the spa town of Vichy.	Normandy and Brittany are the first to be liberated by Allied troops following the D-Day landings in June, followed by Paris on 25 August by a force spearheaded by Free French units.	France signs the Atlantic Pact uniting North America and Western Europe in a mutual defence alliance (NATO); the Council of Europe, of which France is part, is born.	The fear of communism and a resurgent Germany prompts the first steps towards European integration with the European Coal and Steel Community and military accords three years later.

university. Overnight, public opinion turned in favour of the students, while the students themselves occupied the Sorbonne and erected barricades in the Latin Quarter. Within days a general strike by 10 million workers countrywide paralysed France.

But such comradeship between workers and students did not last long. While the former wanted a greater share of the consumer market, the latter wanted to destroy it. After much hesitancy de Gaulle took advantage of this division by appealing to people's fear of anarchy. Just as the country seemed on the brink of revolution and an overthrow of the Fifth Republic, stability returned. The government immediately decentralised the higher-education system and followed through in the 1970s with a wave of other reforms (lowering the voting age to 18, instituting legalised abortion and so on). De Gaulle meanwhile resigned from office in 1969 after losing an important referendum on regionalisation, and suffered a fatal heart attack the following year.

Georges Pompidou, prime minister under de Gaulle, stepped onto the presidential podium in 1969. Despite embarking on an ambitious modernisation program, investing in aerospace, telecommunications and nuclear power, he failed to stave off inflation and social unrest following the global oil crisis of 1973 and died the following year.

In 1974 Valéry Giscard d'Estaing inherited a deteriorating economic climate and sharp divisions between the left and the right. Hampered by a lack of media savvy and what was perceived as an arrogant demeanour, d'Estaing proved unpopular. His friendship with emperor and alleged cannibal Jean-Bédel Bokassa of the Central African Republic did little to win him friends, and in 1981 he was ousted by long-time head of the Parti Socialiste (PS; Socialist Party), François Mitterrand.

Despite France's first socialist president instantly alienating the business community by setting out to nationalise 36 privately owned banks,

Peep into the presidential palace and have a good old nose around at www.elysee.fr.

THE BIRTH OF THE BIKINI

Almost called *atome* (atom) rather than bikini, after its pinprick size, the scanty little two-piece bathing suit was the 1946 creation of Cannes fashion designer Jacques Heim and automotive engineer Louis Réard.

Top-and-bottom swimsuits had existed for centuries, but it was the French duo who both made them briefer than brief and plumped for the name 'bikini' – after Bikini, an atoll in the Marshall Islands chosen by the USA in the same year as the testing ground for atomic bombs.

Once wrapped top and bottom around the curvaceous 1950s sex-bomb Brigitte Bardot on St-Tropez' Plage de Pampelonne, there was no looking back. The bikini was here to stay.

1946–62	1966	1968	1977
French colonialism ends with war in Indochina (1946–54) followed by the Algerian War of Independence (1954–62), brought to a close with the signing of the Accord d'Évian (Evian Accord) in Évian-les-Bains.	France withdraws from NATO's joint military command in 1966; it has maintained an independent arsenal of nuclear weapons since 1960. A year later NATO moves out of its headquarters near Paris.	Large-scale anti-authoritarian student protests (known since as 'May 1968') aimed at de Gaulle's style of government by decree escalate into a countrywide protest that eventually brings down the president.	The Centre Pompidou, the first of a string of *grands projets* – huge public edifices through which French leaders seek to immortalise themselves – opens to great controversy near Les Halles in Paris.

industrial groups and other parts of the economy, Mitterrand did give France something of a sparkle. Potent symbols of France's advanced technological savvy – the Minitel, a proto-personal computer in everyone's home, and high-speed TGV train service between Paris and Lyon – were launched in 1980 and 1981 respectively; a clutch of *grands projets* (p945) were embarked upon in the French capital; and the biggest commercial centre in Europe (at the time), Les Quatre Temps, opened in 1981 at La Défense, the futuristic skyscraper district 3km west of Paris. The death penalty was abolished, homosexuality was legalised, a 39-hour work week was instituted, annual holiday time was upped from four to five weeks and the right to retire at 60 was guaranteed.

However, by 1986 the economy was weakening and in parliamentary elections that year the right-wing opposition, led by Jacques Chirac (mayor of Paris since 1977), won a majority in the National Assembly. For the next two years Mitterrand worked with a prime minister and cabinet from the opposition, an unprecedented arrangement known as *cohabitation*. The extreme-right Front National (FN; National Front) meanwhile quietly gained ground by loudly blaming France's economic woes on immigration.

Presidential elections in 1995 ushered Chirac (an ailing Mitterrand did not run and died the following year) into the Élysée Palace. Whiz-kid foreign minister Alain Juppé was appointed prime minister and several women were placed in top cabinet positions. However, Chirac's attempts to reform France's colossal public sector in order to meet the criteria of European Monetary Union (EMU) were met with the largest protests since 1968, and his decision to resume nuclear testing on the Polynesian island of Mururoa and a nearby atoll was the focus of worldwide outrage. Always the maverick, Chirac called

GAULLISH FACTS

» Charles de Gaulle was a record breaker: according to the *Guinness Book of Records* he survived more assassination attempts – 32, to be precise – than anyone else in the world.

» The present constitution, known as the Fifth Republic and the 11th since 1789, was instituted by good old de Gaulle in 1958.

» He really did say that thing about cheese, opinion and his compatriots: *'On ne peut pas rassembler à froid un pays qui compte 265 spécialités de fromages.'* (You cannot easily bring together a country that counts 265 types of cheese.)

Find out what else he said and did at www.charles-de-gaulle.org.

1981	1989	1994	1995
The superspeedy TGV makes its first commercial journey from Paris to Lyon, breaking all speed records to complete the train journey in two hours instead of six.	President Mitterrand's *grand projet*, Opéra Bastille, opens to mark the bicentennial of the French Revolution; IM Pei's love-it-or-leave-it Grande Pyramide is unveiled at the Louvre.	The 50km-long Channel Tunnel linking France with Britain opens after seven years of hard graft by 10,000 workers; a year later the first land link since the last ice age announces a £925-million loss.	After twice serving as prime minister, Jacques Chirac becomes president of France, winning popular acclaim for his direct words and actions in matters relating to the EU and the war in Bosnia.

early parliamentary elections in 1997 – only for his party, the Rassemblement pour la République (RPR; Rally for the Republic), to lose out to a coalition of socialists, communists and greens. Another period of *cohabitation* ensued (this time with Chirac on the other side) that would last well into the new millennium.

The presidential elections in 2002 surprised everybody. Not only did the first round of voting see left-wing PS leader Lionel Jospin eliminated, it also saw the FN's racist demagogue Jean-Marie Le Pen – legendary for his dismissal of the Holocaust as a 'mere detail of history' in the 1980s and his 'inequality of races' jargon in the late 1990s – scoop 17% of the national vote. In the fortnight preceding the subsequent run-off ballot, demonstrators took to the streets with cries of 'Vote for the crook, not the fascist' ('crook' referring to the various party financing scandals floating around Chirac). On the big day itself, left-wing voters – without a candidate of their own – hedged their bets with 'lesser-of-two-evils' Chirac to give him 82% of votes. Chirac's landslide victory was echoed in parliamentary elections a month later when the president-backed coalition UMP (Union pour un Mouvement Populaire) won 354 of the 577 parliamentary seats, leaving Le Pen's FN without a single seat in parliament and ending years of *cohabitation*.

The same year France, one of the six founding members of the European Economic Community (precursor of the European Union) in 1958, adopted the euro as its currency in place of the franc, once again assuring its central position in Europe.

1998	2000	2001	2002
After resuming nuclear testing in the South Pacific in the early 1990s, France signs the worldwide test-ban treaty, bringing an end to French nuclear testing once and for all.	An Air France Concorde bound for New York bursts into flames just after take-off at Roissy Charles de Gaulle airport and crashes, killing all 109 people on board and four on the ground.	Socialist Bertrand Delanoë becomes the first openly gay mayor of Paris (and of any European capital); he is wounded in a knife attack by a homophobic assailant the following year.	The French franc, first minted in 1360, is thrown onto the scrap heap of history as the country adopts the euro as its official currency along with 14 other EU member-states.

The French

Superchic, stylish, sexy, charming, arrogant, rude, bureaucratic, sexist, chauvinistic... France is a country whose people have attracted more stubborn myths and stereotypes than any other in Europe, and, over the centuries, dozens of tags, true or otherwise, have been pinned on the garlic -eating, beret-wearing, *sacrebleu*-swearing French. (The French, by the way, don't wear berets or use old chestnuts such as '*sacrebleu*' anymore.) Sit in a café some afternoon and you'll soon hear the gentle expressions of surprise favoured by Parisians these days as they slip on dog droppings (a frequent sight on most pavements). '*Merde*' (shit) is quite popular.

Suckers for tradition, the French are slow to embrace new ideas and technologies: it took the country an age to embrace the internet, clinging on for dear life to their own at-the-time-innovative Minitel system for eons. Yet the French are also incredibly innovative – a dichotomy reflected in every facet of French life: they drink and smoke more than anyone else, yet live longer. They eat like kings, but are not fat... how so very enviable.

Sixty Million Frenchmen Can't Be Wrong: What Makes the French so French ask Jean-Benoît Nadeau and Julie Barlow in their witty, well-written and at times downright comical musings on the French.

Superiority Complex

Most people are extremely proud to be French and are staunchly nationalistic to boot, a result of the country's republican stance that places nationality – rather than religion, for example – at the top of the self-identity list. This has created an overwhelmingly self-confident nation, both culturally and intellectually, that invariably comes across as a French superiority complex.

Contrary to popular belief, many French speak a foreign language fairly well, travel and are happy to use their language skills should the need arise. Of course, if monolingual English-speakers don't at least try to speak French, there is no way proud French linguists will let on they speak fluent English! French men, incidentally, deem an English gal's heavily accented French as irresistibly sexy as many people deem a Frenchman speaking English. Hard to believe, but true.

Naturally Sexy

On the subject of sex, not all French men ooze romance or light Gitane cigarettes all day. Nor are they as civilised about adultery as French cinema would have you believe. Adultery, illegal in France until 1975, was actually grounds for automatic divorce until as late as mid-2004.

Kissing is an integral part of French life. (The expression 'French kissing' doesn't exist in French, incidentally.) That said, put a Parisian in Provence and there's no saying they will know when to stop. Countrywide, people who know each other reasonably well, really well, a tad or barely at all greet each other with a glancing peck on each cheek. Southern France aside (where everyone kisses everyone), two men rarely kiss (unless they are related or artists) but always shake hands. Boys and girls start kissing as soon as they're out of nappies, or so it seems.

Kissing French-style is not completely straightforward, 'how many' and 'which side first' potentially being problematic. In Paris it is definitely two: unless parties are related, *very* close friends or haven't seen each other in an age, anything more is deemed affected. That said, in certain trendy 20-something circles, friends swap three or four cheek-skimming kisses, as do many young teenagers at school.

Travel south and the *bisous* (kisses) multiply, three or four being the norm in Provence. The bits of France neighbouring Switzerland around Lake Geneva tend to be three-kiss country (in keeping with Swiss habits); and in the Loire Valley it is four. Corsicans, bizarrely, stick to two but kiss left cheek first – which can lead to locked lips given that everyone else in France starts with the right cheek.

Lifestyle

Be a fly on the wall in the 5th-floor bourgeois apartment of Monsieur et Madame Tout le Monde and you'll see them dunking croissants in bowls of *café au lait* for breakfast, buying a baguette every day from the bakery (Monsieur nibbles the top off on his way home) and recycling nothing bar a few glass bottles.

They go to the movies once a month, work precisely 35 hours a week (many French still toil 39 hours or more a week – employers can enforce a 39-hour work week for a negotiable extra cost), and enjoy five weeks' holiday and five bank (public) holidays a year. The couple view the web-radio production company their 24-year-old son set up and heads in Paris with a mix of pride, amusement and pure scepticism. Their 20-year-old daughter is a student: France's overcrowded state-run universities are free and open to anyone who passes the *baccalauréat,* although Sarkozy had a stab at changing this by giving universities the autonomy to select students and seek outside funding.

Madame buys a load of hot-gossip weekly magazines, Monsieur meets his mates to play boules, and August is the *only* month to summer holiday (with the rest of France). Dodging dog poo on pavements is a sport practised from birth and everything goes on the *carte bleue* (credit or debit card) when shopping. This *is* the society, after all, that microchipped credit cards long before anyone else even dreamt of scrapping the swipe-and-sign system. The couple have a landlord: with a tradition of renting rather than buying, home ownership is low (57% of households own their own home; the rest rent).

Les Femmes

Women were granted suffrage in 1945, but until 1964 a woman needed her husband's permission to open a bank account or get a passport. Younger French women in particular are quite outspoken and emancipated. But this self-confidence has yet to translate into equality in the workplace, where women hold few senior and management positions. Sexual harassment is addressed with a law imposing financial penalties on the offender. A great achievement in the last decade has been *Parité,* the law requiring political parties to fill 50% of their slates in all elections with female candidates.

Abortion is legal during the first 12 weeks of pregnancy, girls under 16 not needing parental consent provided they are accompanied by an adult of their choice: 30 abortions take place in France for every 100 live births.

Above all else French women are known for their natural chic, style and class. And there's no doubt that contemporary French women are sassier than ever. Take the Rykiel women: in the 1970s, legendary Parisian knitwear designer Sonia Rykiel designed the skin-tight, boob-hugging sweater worn with no bra beneath. In the new millennium, daughter Nathalie created Rykiel Woman, a sensual label embracing everything from lingerie to sex toys and aimed squarely at women who know what they want. The up-to-the-minute duo blogs under the pseudonym Dita du Flore (www.rykielles.com), has an e-shop (www.soniarykiel.com) and is on Facebook.

Linguistic Patriotism

Speaking a language other than their own is an emotional affair for the French, memorably illustrated a few years back when the then French president Jacques Chirac walked out of an EU summit session after a

FRANCE'S NORTH–SOUTH DIVIDE

No film better illustrates what southerners think of those from 'the sticks' in the far north than Dany Boon's Bienvenue chez les Ch'tis (Welcome to the Sticks; 2008). With gags a minute, the warm-hearted comedy is a poignant commentary on France's north–south divide – eagerly lapped up by the French, curious to see if Boon's cinematic portrayal of regional prejudices matched up to reality.

For starters, the weather in the cold rainy north is revolting ('1°C in summer and down to -40°C in winter'): the north for a southerner is pretty much anything north of Lyon. So no surprise that post-office chief Philippe, upon setting off north from his native Salon-de-Provence on the sun-drenched Côte d'Azur, dons several jumpers, puffer jacket and scarf as he bids a dramatic farewell to bronzed wife Julie. Bizarrely, the weather doesn't change until he passes the 'Nord-Pas de Calais' sign – at which point it doesn't just rain but slashes down beyond windscreen-wiper control. Even the gendarme on the autoroute, upon stopping him for driving too slowly, lets him off with a sympathetic smile and his deepest condolences when he hears where he's heading: Bergues, a dumpy ex-mining town of 4300 inhabitants, 9km from Dunkirk. (The place exists, is not dumpy, nor as grey and grim as southerners suppose, and is suddenly all the rage as visitors flock to see its post office, its municipal bell tower, the central square with its chip van and so on.) Bienvenue chez les Ch'tis is a kaleidoscope of comic scenes that slowly chip away at the deeply entrenched prejudices surrounding this northern land of redundant coal mines and its unemployed, impoverished, pale, unhealthy and 'uncultured' inhabitants who drink too much beer and speak like this – Ej t'ermerci inne banes (that means Merci beaucoup).

Yes, their thick Ch'timi dialect (old Picard peppered with Flemish) is incomprehensible to outsiders. Yes, they dunk stinky Maroilles cheese and bread in chicorée café (chicory-flavoured instant coffee) for breakfast. Yes, they skip the traditional French three-course lunch for an alfresco round of frites fricadelle, sauce picadilly (chips 'n' meatballs; never ask what's in the balls) from the local baraque à frites (chip van) – eaten with their fingers. Yes, their long, sandy and windy beaches are brilliant for le char à voile (sand yachting). And yes, their very nickname – les Ch'tis – was borne out of prejudice during WWI when French soldiers mocked the thickly accented way their northern comrades spoke – 'ch'est ti, ch'est mi' (c'est toi, c'est moi – it's you, it's me), hence 'Ch'ti'.

The north and its regional characteristics are no mystery to director Boon, a born-and-bred northerner who grew up in Armentières, near Lille, on bread-and-butter dishes like tarte au Maroilles, chicons au gratin (oven-baked chicory, chicons being the Ch'ti word for 'chicories') and carbonnade flamande (beef stew). His father was an Algerian-born bus driver, his mother a cleaner and he is one of France's best-known stand-up comics and directors and, since the film, best-paid actors – he plays the buffoonish postal worker, Antoine. Indeed, if anyone is best placed to speak of les Ch'tis and their homeland, it's Boon, whose lovable, huge-hearted character in the film says it all: 'An outsider who comes to the north cries twice, once when he arrives, and once when he leaves.'

'About time too', a feminist anywhere else on the planet would argue. Indeed, it is only now that French women have decided no more 'Mademoiselle', meaning 'Miss', 'not married', 'virgin', 'sexually available' and so on, says Paris-based feminist group Les Chiennes de Garde (meaning 'guard dogs', or rather, 'guard bitches'). The group has launched a petition for the term 'Mademoiselle' to be eradicated from the administrative and political arena. It also wants the standard 'maiden name' box struck off official forms and documents.

'Mademoiselle' originates from the medieval word *'damoiselle'*, meaning a young upper-class girl (male equivalents were called *'damoisel'*). Later merged with *'ma'* to denote an unmarried woman, the term was tantamount to 'sad old spinster who can't find a husband' in the 17th and 18th centuries. In the 19th century, novelist Adolphe Belot borrowed the term to depict a frigid wife in *Mademoiselle Giraud, ma Femme*.

So the fight is on to become a Madame from birth. Already a Madame, I, for one, not to mention practically all my 30-something-with-kids girlfriends, am delighted if someone dares call me 'Mademoiselle'. Despite the kids in tow, dirty washing and first wrinkle, it means I still look young.

fellow countryman had the audacity to address the meeting in English. 'Don't speak English!' was *Le Monde*'s headline the next day, while the French blogosphere seethed with debate on linguistic patriotism: 'Open your eyes, Mr President, you are on another planet', 'it is a long time since French was the language of the international arena' taunted modern-day French bloggers, most of whom write in English.

Current president Nicolas Sarkozy is faring marginally better than his monolingual predecessor. Yet the bottom line is Sarkozy sticks to what he knows best in public, so much so that the couple of lines he has uttered in English were instantly plastered over the internet as a video link and swiftly went viral.

With English words like 'weekend', 'jogging', 'stop' and 'OK' firmly entrenched in daily French usage, language purists might just have lost the battle. One look at the many Anglo-American shop and restaurant signs featured in the online Musée des Horreurs (Museum of Horrors) on the website of the Paris-based Défense de la Langue Française (DLF; Defence of the French Language; www.langue-francaise.org, in French) says it all.

French was the main language of the EU until 1995 when Sweden and Finland came into the EU fold. French broadcasting laws restrict the amount of air time radio and TV stations can devote to non-French music, but little can be done to restrict who airs what on the internet.

Multiculturalism

The face of France is multicultural (immigrants make up 7.4% of the population), yet its republican code, while inclusive and nondiscriminatory, has been criticised for doing little to accommodate a multicultural society (and, interestingly, none of the members of France's National Assembly represents the immigrant population, first or second generation). Nothing reflects this dichotomy better than the law, in place since 2004, banning the Islamic headscarf, Jewish skullcap, crucifix and other religious symbols in French schools (see p900).

Some 90% of the French Muslim community – Europe's largest – are noncitizens. Most are illegal immigrants living in poverty-stricken *bidonvilles* (tinpot towns) around Paris, Lyon and other metropolitan centres. Many are unemployed (youth unemployment in many suburbs is 40%) and face little prospect of getting a job.

Fewer French couples are marrying (3% less each year). Those that do marry are doing so later (women at the age of 29, men at 31) and waiting longer to have an average of two children. Like everywhere else in Europe, divorce is rising (49% of marriages end in divorce compared to 30% in 1985).

Multiculturalism is a dominant feature of French football, with more than half of the 23 players in the 2010 World Cup being of African, West Indian, Algerian or other non-French origin. The country's golden boy of football, Marseille-born midfielder ace Zinedine Zidane (b 1972), now retired, is a classic example. The son of Algerian immigrants, he wooed the nation with a sparkling career of goal-scoring headers and extraordinary footwork that unfortunately ended with him head-butting an Italian player during the 2006 World Cup final. But such was the power of his humble Marseillais grin (since used to advertise Adidas sports gear, Volvic mineral water and Christian Dior fashion) that the French nation instantly forgave him.

Good Sports

Most French wouldn't be seen dead walking down the street in trainers and tracksuits. But contrary to appearances, they love sport. Shaved-leg cyclists toil up Mont Ventoux, football fans fill stadiums and anyone who can flits off for the weekend to ski or snowboard.

Les 24 Heures du Mans and the F1 Grand Prix in Monte Carlo are the world's raciest dates in motor sports; the French Open in Paris in late May to early June is the second of the year's four grand-slam tennis tournaments; and the Tour de France is – indisputably – the world's most prestigious bicycle race. Bringing together 189 of the world's top male cyclists (21 teams of nine) and 15 million spectators in July each year for a spectacular 3000-plus-kilometre cycle around the country, the three-week race always labours through the Alps and Pyrenees and finishes on Paris' Champs-Élysées. The route in between changes each year but wherever it goes, the French systematically turn out in their droves – armed with table, chairs and picnic hamper – to make a day of it. The serpentine publicity caravan preceding the cyclists showers roadside spectators with coffee samples, logo-emblazoned balloons, pens and other free junk-advertising gifts and is easily as much fun as watching the cyclists themselves speed through – in 10 seconds flat.

France's greatest moment in football history came at the 1998 World Cup, which the country hosted and won. But the game has produced no stars since, losing to Italy in the final of the 2006 World Cup. There was also no luck for *les Bleus* in South Africa in 2010, which saw the French team eliminated in the first round – but not before striker Nicolas Anelka was sent home to Paris for arguing with the referee, prompting

PÉTANQUE

France's traditional ball games include *pétanque* and the more formal boules, which has a 70-page rule book. Both are played by men on a gravel pitch. In the Basque Country, *pelote Basque* (*pelota*) is the thing to do with French balls.

TOP FIVE: FROGS VS ROSBIFS

In the finest of traditions, rivalry between the English (*rosbifs*) and the French (*frogs*) sells like hotcakes. Our favourites:

» *That Sweet Enemy: the French and the British from the Sun King to the Present,* by Robert and Isabelle Tombs – cross-Channel rivalry in a historical context, light-hearted nonetheless.

» *Help, the English Are Invading Us!* by José-Alain Fralon – they're everywhere. Slowly but surely the English are invading us...

» *Cross Channel,* by Julian Barnes – a selection of classic short stories zooming in on everything both sides of the English Channel, from sex, art and love to literature, the Channel tunnel and the Eurostar.

» *More France Please! We're British!* by Helen Frith-Powell – France from the perspective of Brits who choose to live there permanently.

» *A Year in the Merde* and *Merde Actually,* by Stephen Clarke – dog poo everywhere, unnecessary bureaucracy, transport; Clarke spouts on about it all. You'll love it or hate it.

TOUR TRIVIA

» French journalist and cyclist Henri Desgrange came up with the Tour de France in 1903 as a means of promoting his sports newspaper *L'Auto* (now called *L'Équipe*).

» With the exception of two world-war-induced intervals, the Tour de France has not missed a year since its inception.

» The 1998 race was the 'tour of shame': fewer than 100 riders crossed the finish line after several teams were disqualified for doping.

» *Le Blaireau* (the Badger), Brittany-born biking legend Bernard Hinault (b 1954), won the Tour de France five times before retiring in 1986.

» American sports icon Lance Armstrong (b 1971) is the indisputable Tour de France king. He overcame testicular cancer, won seven consecutive times (1999 to 2005), retired, and returned to competitive cycling in 2009 (finishing third that year in the Tour).

the rest of the side to 'strike' in protest during a training session. Back home, deep shame at a team that had clearly not been good sports was what most French felt.

Losing out to London in its bid to host the 2012 Summer Olympics was a major loss of face for Paris. The French capital last hosted the gargantuan event in 1924.

Bon Appétit

Eating well is of prime importance to most French people, who spend an inordinate amount of time thinking about, discussing and enjoying food and wine – with gusto. Yet dining out doesn't have to be a ceremonious occasion or one riddled with pitfalls for the uninitiated. Approach food with half the enthusiasm *les français* do, and you will be welcomed, encouraged and exceedingly well fed.

Two natural factors determine what you eat on your French travels. Season and geography sees the hot south favour olive oil, garlic and tomatoes; the cooler, pastoral regions of northern France turn to cream and butter; and coastal areas are awash with mussels, oysters, saltwater fish and other seafood.

Borders are far from firmly drawn and while each region courts a handful of distinctly local dishes, you might well encounter influences of Gascon cuisine in the Atlantic region, an Alsatian-style *choucroute* (sauerkraut with sausage and other prepared meats) in seafaring Marseille or *andouillette* (Lyonnais pig-intestine sausage) in Paris.

Dining Diary

What the French call *petit déjeuner* is not every foreigner's cup of tea. The French just don't go all out at breakfast, kick-starting the day with a humble *tartine* (bit of baguette smeared with unsalted butter and jam) washed down with *un café* (espresso), long milky *café au lait* or – especially kids – hot chocolate. In hotels you get a cup but in French homes, the latter two are drunk from a cereal bowl – perfect bread-dunking terrain.

Urbanites might grab a coffee and croissant on the way to work, but otherwise croissants (eaten straight, never with butter or jam) are a weekend treat alongside brioches (sweet bread buns), *pains au chocolat* (chocolate-filled croissant), pains aux raisins (raisin-studded croissant swirl), *chaussons aux pommes* (apple-filled croissant) and other *viennoiserie* (baked goods), often still oven-warm, from the local bakery.

Next up is *déjeuner* (lunch), a meal no French would miss and one that is far more than, horror of horrors, a quick sandwich eaten at the desk. The traditional main meal of the day, it translates – at the very least – as a starter and main course with wine, followed by a short sharp *café*. (Never end a meal with a cappuccino, *café au lait* or cup of tea, which, incidentally, never comes with milk in France). Irrespective of time of day, a premeal aperitif is sacred to many.

Sunday lunch is a long, languid affair in many French families, when several hours are devoted to enjoying the many courses it entails. Indeed, a fully fledged, traditional French meal – lunch or *dîner* – is an awesome event, often comprising six distinct *plats* (courses), each accompanied by a wine to complement the cuisine. As in many top-end restaurants, this might mean an *amuse-bouche* (hors d'oeuvre) between the starter and main course; a sweet equivalent before dessert, plus petit fours with coffee.

LA CUISINE FRANÇAISE

The Food of France by Waverley Root, first published in 1958, remains the seminal work in English on *la cuisine française*, with a focus on historical development, by a long-time Paris-based American foreign correspondent.

Dining Lexicon

» **Auberge** Country inn serving traditional country fare, often attached to a rural B&B or small hotel

» **Ferme auberge** Working farm that cooks up meals built squarely from local farm products; usually served *table d'hôte* (literally 'host's table'), meaning in set courses with little or no choice

» **Bistro** (also spelled *bistrot*) Anything from a pub or bar with snacks and light meals to a small, fully fledged restaurant

» **Brasserie** Very much like a café except it serves full meals, drinks and coffee from morning until 11pm or even later. Typical fare includes *choucroute* (sauerkraut) and *moules frites* (mussels and fries).

» **Restaurant** Born in Paris in 1765 when Monsieur A Boulanger opened a small business on rue Bailleul in the 1er *arrondissement* selling soups, broths and other restaurants ('restoratives'); most today serve lunch and dinner five or six days; for standard opening hours see p958

» **Buffet** (or *buvette*) Kiosk, usually at train stations and airports, selling drinks, filled baguettes and snacks

» **Café** Serves basic food as well as drinks, most commonly a chunk of baguette filled with Camembert or pâté and *cornichons* (miniature gherkins), a *croque monsieur* (grilled ham and toasted cheese sandwich) or a *croque madame* (a toasted cheese sandwich topped with a fried egg)

» **Crêperie** (also *galetteries*) Casual address specialising in sweet crêpes and savoury galettes (buckwheat crêpes)

» **Salon de Thé** Trendy tearoom often serving light lunches (quiche, salads, cakes, tarts, pies and pastries) as well as black and herbal teas

Bread

The nuts-and-bolts of French cuisine is *pain* (bread), typically eaten at every meal. Order in a restaurant and within minutes a basket should be on your table. Except in a handful of top-end gastronomic restaurants, butter (unsalted in the main) is never an accompaniment.

Bread comes in infinite shapes, sizes and variety. Plain old *pain* is a 400g, traditional-shaped loaf, soft inside and crusty out. The iconic classic is *une baguette*, a long thin crusty loaf weighing 250g. Anything fatter and it becomes *une flûte*, thinner *une ficelle*. When buying bread in a *boulangerie* (bakery), ask for a *demi-baguette* or a *demi-pain* if you only need a half-baguette or -loaf. (Bear in mind, while French baguettes are impossibly good, they turn unpleasantly dry within four hours, rock-hard within 12.)

Many bakeries carry heavier breads made with all sorts of grains and cereals, nuts, raisins, herbs, cheese and so on. These generally keep much longer than baguettes and standard white-flour breads.

THE MENU

In any anglophone country the menu is the menu (called the *carte* in French) – that is, the list of what's cooking in the order you'd eat it: entrée (starter), *plat* (main course), *fromage* (cheese) then dessert (pudding).

In France, however, *le menu* is a two- or three-course meal at a fixed price. It's by far the best-value dining there is and most bistros and restaurants chalk one on the board. Lunch *menus* occasionally include a glass of wine and/or coffee, and dinner *menus* in top-end gastronomic restaurants sometimes pair each course with a perfectly matched glass of wine.

Not to be confused with a *menu* is *une formule*, a cheaper lunchtime option comprising a main – often the *plat du jour* (dish of the day) plus starter or dessert.

Cheese

France is cheese land and the local *fromagerie* (cheese shop) is the pongiest shop in town. With more than 500 varieties – which can be raw, pasteurised or *petit-lait* ('little-milk', the whey left over after the fats and solids have been curdled with rennet) – buying cheese can be an overwhelming affair. Any self-respecting *fromager* (cheese merchant) will let you taste before you buy – just ask. Say when you intend eating it to ensure the cheese is *fait* (ripe) to a perfect degree.

Contrary to opinion, the French don't eat cheese with every meal – just every fine meal, which rolls out the cheeseboard before dessert (much to the surprise of those used to eating it after dessert back home). It is always served with baguette, never crackers, and no butter.

Wine and cheese can be a match made in heaven. In general, strong pungent cheeses require a young, full-bodied red or a sweet wine, while soft cheeses with a refined flavour call for more quality and age. Classic pairings include Alsatian Gewürztraminer and Munster; Côtes du Rhone with Roquefort; Côte d'Or (Burgundy) and Brie or Camembert; and mature Bordeaux with emmental or Cantal. Even Champagne can get in on the act; drink it with mushroom-like Chaource.

> Strict vegetarians note: most French cheeses are made with rennet, an enzyme derived from the stomach of a calf or young goat, and some red wines (especially Bordeaux) are clarified with the albumin of egg whites.

Charcuterie

Charcuterie is the backbone of any self-respecting picnic made in almost every French region. Alsace, Lyon and the Auvergne in the Massif Cen-

---

THE PERFECT CHEESEBOARD

Treat your taste buds to the perfect balance of cheese by taking at least one of each type from the cheeseboard:

» **Goat's cheese** (*fromage de chèvre*) Made from goat's milk, this cheese is creamy, sweet and faintly salty when fresh, but hardens and gets saltier as it matures. Among the best are Ste-Maure de Touraine, a mild creamy cheese from the Loire Valley; the classic but saltier Crottin de Chavignol from Burgundy; Cabécou de Rocamadour from Midi-Pyrénées, often served warm with salad or marinated in oil and rosemary; and Lyon's St-Marcellin, a soft white cheese that should be served nothing other than impossibly runny.

» **Blue cheese** (*fromage à pâté persillée*) 'Marbled' or with veins that resemble *persil* (parsley). Don't miss king of French cheese Roquefort, a ewe's-milk veined cheese from Languedoc; the very mild cow's-milk cheese Fourme d'Ambert from the Rhône Valley; or Bleu du Haut Jura (also called Bleu de Gex), a mild blue-veined mountain cheese from the Jura.

» **Soft cheese** (*fromage à pâté molle*) Moulded or rind-washed, the classic soft cheese that everyone knows is Camembert from Normandy and the refined Brie de Meaux; both are made from unpasteurised cow's milk. Munster from Alsace and the strong and seriously smelly Époisses de Bourgogne are fine-textured, rind-washed cheeses.

» **Semihard cheese** (*fromage à pâté demi-dure*) Among the finest uncooked, pressed cheese is Tomme de Savoie, made from either pasteurised or unpasteurised cow's milk not far from the Alps; cantal, a cow's-milk cheese from Auvergne that bears a faint resemblance to English cheddar; St-Nectaire, a strong-smelling pressed cheese that has a complex taste; and Ossau-Iraty, a ewe's-milk cheese made in the Basque Country.

» **Hard cheese** (*fromage à pâté dure*) Absolute must-taste cooked and pressed cheeses are Beaufort, a grainy cow's-milk cheese with a slightly fruity taste from Rhône-Alpes; Comté, a cheese made with raw cow's milk in Franche-Comté; emmental, a cow's-milk cheese made all over France; and Mimolette, an Edam-like bright-orange cheese from Lille that can be aged for as long as 36 months.

tral produce the best salami and sausages; and the Dordogne and northern France the best pâtés and terrines.

Traditionally charcuterie is made only from pork, though other meats (beef, veal, chicken or goose) are used in making sausages, salamis, blood puddings and other cured and salted meats. Pâtés, terrines and rillettes (coarsely shredded potted meat) are also considered types of charcuterie. The difference between a pâté and a terrine is academic: a pâté is removed from its container and sliced before it is served, while a terrine is sliced from the container itself. Rillettes, on the other hand, is potted meat or even fish that has not been ground or chopped but shredded with two forks, seasoned, and mixed with fat. It is spread cold over bread or toast.

Popular types of charcuterie include *andouillette* (soft raw sausage made from the pig's small intestines that is grilled and eaten with onions and potatoes – Lyon is famed for them); *boudin noir* (blood sausage or pudding made with pig's blood, onions and spices); *jambon* (ham, smoked or salt-cured); *saucisse* (small fresh sausage, boiled or grilled before eating); *saucisson* (large salami eaten cold); and *saucisson sec* (air-dried salami).

Regional Specialities

Diverse as it is, French cuisine is typified by certain regions, notably Normandy, Burgundy, the Dordogne, Lyon and, to a lesser extent, the Loire Valley, Alsace and Provence. Others – Brittany, Languedoc, the Basque Country and Corsica – have made incalculable contributions to what can generically be called French food.

NORMANDY

Cream, apples and cider are the essentials of Norman cuisine, which sees mussels simmered in cream and a splash of cider to make *moules à la crème normande* and tripe thrown in the slow pot with cider and vegetables to make, several hours later, *tripes á la mode de Caen.* Creamy Camembert cheese made from local cow's milk is the only *fromage* to have as cheese course or on a picnic, and on the coast it is *coquilles St-Jacques* (sublime pan-fried scallop) and *huîtres* (oysters) that rule the seafood roost. Apples are the essence of the region's main tipples: tangy cider (p192) and the potent apple-brandy *calvados,* exquisite straight or splashed on apple sorbet.

BURGUNDY

A region particularly popular for cooking courses (p391), vine-wealthy Burgundy honours a culinary trinity of beef, red wine and Dijon mustard. Savour an authentic *bœuf bourguignon* (beef marinated and cooked in young red wine with mushrooms, onions, carrots and bacon) or beef with sauce Morvandelle (shallot, mustard and white wine sauce), followed by the pick of Burgundy AOC (Appellation d'Origine Contrôlée) cheeses (p408).

January

Black truffles abound in Provence and the Dordogne. Lemons are picked on the French Riviera and skiers in the French Alps dip into cheese fondue.

February

On the Mediterranean, sea urchins are caught and eaten west of Marseille. Inland, the Dordogne exalts the goose's contribution to French cooking with festive foie gras.

March

Asparagus appears at markets in southern France and it's almost the end of black truffles. This is the last chance in Provence to buy the year's olive oil and in the Alps, to dip into fondue.

April

Spring means fresh goat's cheese, artichokes, Pâques (Easter), *œufs au chocolat* (chocolate eggs) filled with candy, fish and chickens to hunt with the kids, and a traditional lamb for lunch.

May

During the traditional transhumance, shepherds move their cows and flocks of sheep up to higher pastures to graze. Heading south, the first strawberries turn market stalls red.

June

Fresh garlic is harvested and piled high in woven garlands alongside melons and cherries at Provençal markets. In Brittany shallots are hand-harvested.

Foodie Towns

» **Le Puy-en-Velay** for lentils

» **Dijon** for mustard

» **Privas** for chestnuts

» **Cancale** for oysters

» **Espelette** for red chillies

» **Colmar** for chocolate stork eggs

» **Lyon** for piggy-part cuisine

Or eat a snail (p410), traditionally served by the dozen and oven-baked in their shells with butter, garlic and parsley to a gooey delicious-ness – mop the juices up with bread.

THE DORDOGNE

Known as Périgord by the French, this southwest region is fabulously famous for its black truffles (p568) and poultry, especially ducks and geese, whose fattened livers are turned into *pâté de foie gras* (duck- or goose-liver pâté), which, somewhat predictably, comes straight or fla-voured with Cognac and truffles. *Confit de canard* and *confit d'oie* are duck or goose joints cooked very slowly in their own fat. The preserved fowl is then left to stand for some months before being eaten. The es-cargot (snail) is the Dordogne's other tasty treat – savour one stuffed with foie gras.

LYON

All too often it is dubbed France's gastronomic capital. And while it hardly competes with France's real capital when it comes to sheer vari-ety of international cuisine, it certainly holds its own when it comes to titillating taste buds with the unusual and inventive. Take the age-old repertoire of feisty, often pork-driven dishes served in the city's legend-ary *bouchons* (small bistros): breaded fried tripe, big fat *andouillettes* (put bluntly, sausage made from the intestine of a pig – or perhaps you prefer his trotters?), silk-weaver's brains – there is no way you can ever say Lyonnais cuisine is run-of-the-mill.

A perfect picnic companion is wafer-thin slices of *saucisson de Lyon* (dried pork sausage) and *cornichons* (miniature gherkins). A lighter, less meaty speciality is *quenelle de brochet*, a poached dumpling made of freshwater fish (usually pike) and served with sauce Nantua (a cream and freshwater-crayfish sauce).

For a complete rundown of what's on the Lyonnais menu see p448.

THE LOIRE VALLEY

Rabelais' phrase *'le jardin de France'* (the garden of France) has been ex-ploited nationwide since he coined it in the 16th century to describe his native Touraine. Yet it is the Loire that remains most true to his image of a green and succulent, well-watered landscape laden with lush fruit, flowers, nuts and vegetables: *pruneaux de Tours* (prunes dried from lus-cious damson plums) are justifiably famous, and mushrooms polka-dot the forests. In the Loire's unique troglodyte caves *champignons de Paris* (button mushrooms) are cultivated (see p384).

Appropriately, it was the cooking refined in the kitchens of the re-gion's châteaux in the 16th century that became what most today con-sider to be 'quintessentially French': coq au vin (chicken in red wine), *cuisses de grenouilles* (frogs legs) and *tarte tatin* (upside-down apple tart) all originate from this riverside region. Poultry and game dishes were the pride and joy of the medieval kitchen, and once or twice a year

---

A CAKE FOR KINGS

One tradition very much alive is *Jour des Rois* (Day of the Kings), or Epiphany, on 6 January when the Three Wise Men paid homage to the infant Jesus. A *galette des rois* (literally 'kings' cake'; a puff-pastry tart with frangipane cream) is placed in the centre of the table and sliced while the youngest person ducks under the table, call-ing out who gets each slice. The excitement lies in who gets *la fève* (literally 'bean', which translates these days as a miniature porcelain figurine) hidden inside the tart; whoever does is crowned king with a gold paper crown that's sold with the galette.

a fattened pig was slaughtered and meat from its neck minced up and fried to make rillettes, a cold paste ranked as the region's signature dish.

Fresh fish from the River Loire and Atlantic Ocean has been served with *beurre blanc* (white sauce) since the 19th century and goat's cheeses from the valley – Crottins de Chavignol, Ste-Maure de Touraine, Pouligny St-Pierre and black ash-dusted Selles-sur-Cher are among France's best.

ALSACE

With its close cultural ties to Germany, Alsace enjoys a cuisine quite distinct from the rest of France (see also p313). Meaty, Teutonic and served in *winstubs* (traditional Alsatian taverns), no dish is more classic than *choucroute alsacienne* (also called *choucroute garnie*) – sauerkraut flavoured with juniper berries and served hot with sausages, bacon, pork and/or ham knuckle. *Wädele braisé au pinot noir* (ham knuckles braised in wine) also come with sauerkraut. Crack open a bottle of chilled riesling or Alsatian pinot noir to accompany either and round off the filling feast with a *tarte alsacienne,* a scrumptious custard tart made with local fruit like mirabelles (sweet yellow plums) or *quetsches* (a variety of purple plum). Beer is big in Alsace but a big no-no when it comes to sauerkraut.

The quintessential lighter meal is Flammekueche or *tarte flambée.* The Alsatian interpretation of a pizza, it sees onions, *lardons* (bacon bits) and crème fraiche (sour cream) loaded on top of a wafer-thin dough base and oven-baked until crisp – great finger-licking, lip-smacking stuff.

Picnic idea: bread and holy Munster cheese (see p329).

PROVENCE & THE RIVIERA

Cuisine in this sun-baked land is laden with tomatoes, melons, cherries, peaches, olives, Mediterranean fish and Alpine cheese and has not changed for centuries. Farmers still gather at the weekly market to sell their fruit and vegetables, olives, woven garlic plaits and dried herbs displayed in stubby coarse sacks. *À la Provençal* still means anything with a generous dose of garlic-seasoned tomatoes; while a simple filet mignon sprinkled with olive oil and rosemary fresh from the garden makes the same magnificent Sunday lunch it did a generation ago.

Yet there are exciting culinary contrasts in this region, which see fishermen return with the catch of the day in seafaring Marseille; grazing bulls and paddy fields in the Camargue; lambs in the Alpilles; black truffles in the Vaucluse; cheese made from cow's milk in Alpine pastures and an Italianate accent to cooking in seaside Nice.

Bouillabaisse is Provence's most famous contribution to French cuisine. The chowder must contain at least three kinds of fresh saltwater fish, cooked for about 10 minutes in a broth containing onions,

Tomatoes every shade of red, apricots, fresh figs, peaches, melons and cherries jam-pack markets.

August

July's fruit-and-veg bonanza continues and harvested lavender appears. The Atlantic and Mediterranean coasts revel in their rich year-round bounty of seafood and shellfish – mussels and oysters are everywhere.

September

The Camargue's nutty red rice is harvested. The boletus-mushroom season begins around wine-rich Bordeaux and elsewhere. In higher areas, flocks are shepherded back down the mountain for winter.

October

Normandy apples fall from trees to make France's finest cider. Espelette chilli peppers are hung out to dry and the chestnut harvest starts in the Ardèche, Cévennes and Corsica.

November

Nets are strung beneath silvery groves in Provence and Corsica to catch black and green olives, later pressed for their oil. In damp woods everywhere mushrooming is now in earnest.

December

Pungent markets in the Dordogne and Provence sell black truffles. In the Alps the first skiers dip into cheese fondue. Christmas means Champagne and oysters, chestnut-stuffed turkey and yule logs.

tomatoes, saffron and various herbs, and eaten as a main course with toasted bread and *rouille,* a spicy red mayonnaise of olive oil, garlic and chilli peppers.

BRITTANY

Brittany is a paradise for seafood-lovers (think lobster, scallops, sea bass, turbot, mussels etc), and kids, thanks to the humble crêpe and galette, an ancient culinary tradition that has long ruled Breton cuisine. Pair a sweet wheat-flour pancake or savoury buckwheat galette with *une bolée* (a stubby terracotta goblet) of apple-rich Breton cider and taste buds enter gourmet heaven. Then learn to cook your authentic own (p276).

Cheese is not big in Brittany, but *la beurre de Bretagne* (Breton butter) is. Traditionally sea-salted and exceedingly creamy, a knob of it naturally goes into crêpes, galettes and the most outrageously butteriest cake you're likely to ever taste in your life – *kouig amann* (Breton butter cake). Imagine dough loaded with butter and sugar and baked into a salty-sweet caramelised bliss. Bretons, unlike the rest of the French, even butter their bread. Butter handmade by Jean-Yves Bourdier – you can buy it at his shop in St-Malo (p239) – ends up on tables of top restaurants around the world.

Seaweed and 80% of French shallots are other Breton culinary curiosities.

LANGUEDOC-ROUSSILLON

No dish better evokes Languedoc than *cassoulet,* an earthy cockle-warming stew of white beans and meat that fires passionate debate (and yes, people do eat it in summer too). Everyone knows best which type of bean and meat hunk should be thrown in the *cassole,* the traditional earthenware dish it is cooked and brought to the table in. The version made in Toulouse adds *saucisse de Toulouse,* a fat, mild-tasting pork sausage.

Otherwise this region's overtly cuisine *campagnarde* (country cooking) sees fishermen tend lagoon oyster beds on the coast, olives pressed in gentle hills inland, blue-veined 'king of cheeses' ripening in caves in Roquefort (p743), fattened geese and gaggles of ducks around Toulouse, sheep in salty marsh meadows around Montpellier, and mushrooms in its forests.

A Spanish accent gives cuisine in neighbouring Roussillon a fiery twist of Catalan exuberance.

BASQUE COUNTRY

Among the essential ingredients of Basque cooking are the deep-red Espelette chillies that add an extra bite to many of the region's dishes, including the dusting on the signature *jambon de Bayonne,* the locally prepared Bayonne ham. Eating out in this Catalan neck of the woods is a real charm thanks to its many casual *pintxo* bars serving garlic prawns, spicy chorizo sausages and other local dishes tapas-style (see p640).

Basques love cakes, especially *gâteau basque* (layer cake filled with cream or cherry jam). Then there's Bayonne chocolate (p637).

CORSICA

The hills and mountains of the island of Corsica have always been ideal for raising stock, and the dense Corsican underbrush called the *maquis* is made up of shrubs mixed with wild herbs. These raw materials come together to create aromatic trademark Corsican dishes like *stufatu* (fragrant mutton stew), *premonata* (beef braised with juniper berries) and *lonzo* (Corsican sausage cooked with white beans, white wine and herbs). For more on Corsican cuisine, see p869.

French Wine

French wines might not be the world's most venerated, but making them is an ancient art and tradition that bears its own unique trademark. *Dégustation* (tasting), moreover, is an essential part of any French travel experience: quaff Champagne with friends in a Lille wine bar designed in 1892 by Gustave Eiffel's architectural firm; hike between Alsatian vines with an organic wine producer; trail walking itineraries in St-Émilion's Unesco World Heritage vineyards; taste with one of the world's top sommeliers to determine your star sign of wine... experiences such as these are the essence of French wine culture.

There are dozens of wine-producing regions throughout France, but the seven principal ones are Burgundy, Bordeaux, the Rhône and Loire valleys, Champagne, Languedoc, Provence and Alsace. Wines are generally named after the location of the vineyard rather than the grape varietal. Organic and biodynamic wines are becoming increasingly popular.

The best French wines are Appellation d'Origine Contrôlée (AOC), meaning they meet stringent regulations governing where, how and under what conditions they are grown, fermented and bottled. Some regions, such as Alsace, only have a single AOC; others, like Burgundy, have scores. About a third of all French wine carries that AOC hallmark of guarantee.

Some viticulturists have honed their skills and techniques to such a degree that their wine is known as a *grand cru* (literally 'great growth'). If this wine has been produced in a year of optimum climatic conditions, it becomes a *millésime* (vintage) wine. *Grands crus* are aged in small oak barrels then bottles, sometimes for 20 years or more, to create those memorable bottles with price tags to match that wine experts enthuse about with such passion.

Burgundy

During the reign of Charlemagne, monks began making the wine that gave Burgundy (Bourgogne in French) its sterling reputation for viticulture. Burgundy's *vignerons* (winegrowers) only have small vineyards, rarely more than 10 hectares, and they produce small quantities of very good wine. Burgundy reds are made with pinot noir grapes and the best vintages demand 10 to 20 years to age; whites are made with chardonnay. See p419 for tasting addresses and so on.

Burgundy's most famed winegrowing areas are Côte d'Or, Chablis, Châtillon and Mâcon. Lesser known Irancy (p416) is a charming, local wine-tasting favourite.

Bordeaux

Britons have had a taste for Bordeaux' full-bodied wines, known as clarets in the UK, since the mid-12th century when King Henry II, who controlled the region through marriage, tried to gain the favour of the

---

Top Wine Schools

» **Langlois-Château** Saumur, Loire Valley

» **École des Vins de Bourgogne & Sensation Vin** Beaune, Burgundy

» **École du Vin** Bordeaux

» **Château Marojallia** The Médoc

» **École du Vin de St-Émilion** St-Émilion

» **Centre de Dégustation Jacques Vivet** Paris

The French day might no longer start with a shot of red wine followed by a black coffee to *tuer le ver* (kill the worm), but lunch without *une verre du vin* is unimaginable.

locals by granting them tax-free trade status with England. Thus began a roaring business in wine exporting.

Bordeaux has the perfect climate for producing wine; as a result its 1100 sq km of vineyards produce more fine wine than any other region in the world. Bordeaux reds are often described as well balanced, a quality achieved by blending several grape varieties. The grapes predominantly used are merlot, cabernet sauvignon and cabernet franc.

Bordeaux' foremost winegrowing areas are the Médoc, Pomerol, St-Émilion and Graves. The nectarlike sweet whites of the Sauternes area are the world's finest dessert wines.

Côtes du Rhône

Dramatically different soil, climate, topography and grapes in the Rhône Valley region means very different wines in this vast appellation – France's second largest – covering 771 sq km. The most renowned is Châteauneuf du Pape, a full-bodied wine bequeathed to Provence by the Avignon popes who planted the distinctive stone-covered vineyards, 10km south of Orange.

Châteauneuf du Pape reds are strong (minimum alcohol content 12.5%) and well structured. Winegrowers, obliged to pick their grapes by hand, say it is the *galets* (large smooth, yellowish stones) covering their vineyards that distinguish their wines from others. Both whites and reds can be drunk young (two to three years) or old (plus seven years).

Another popular Rhône Valley *grand cru* is red and rosé Gigondas. The medieval golden-stone village with its ruined castle, Provençal campanile and stunning vistas is a delight to meander and its reds are among Provence's most sought after. In nearby Beames de Venise it is the sweet dessert wine, Muscat de Beaumes de Venise, that delights, enjoyed in equal measure as an aperitif or poured inside half a Cavaillon melon as dessert.

The Loire

The Loire's 700 sq km of vineyards rank it as France's third-largest area for the production of quality wines. Although sunny, the climate is humid, meaning not all grape varieties thrive. Still, the Loire produces the greatest variety of wines of any region in the country. The most common grapes are the muscadet, cabernet franc and chenin blanc varieties. Wines tend to be light and delicate. Be sure to sample wines from Pouilly-Fumé, Vouvray, Sancerre, Bourgueil, Chinon and Saumur.

Champagne

Champagne, northeast of Paris, has been the centre France's best-known wine since the 17th century, when innovative monk Dom Pierre Pérignon perfected a technique for making sparkling wine.

Champagne is made from the red pinot noir, the black pinot meunier or the white chardonnay grape. Each vine is vigorously pruned and trained to produce a small quantity of high-quality grapes. Indeed, to

TASTING & BUYING WINE

Wine can be bought direct from the *producteur* (wine producer) or *vigneron* (wine-grower), most of whom offer a *dégustation* (tasting), allowing you to sample two or three vintages with no obligation to buy. For cheap plonk *(vin de table)* costing €2 or so per litre, fill up your own container at the local wine cooperative; every wine-producing village has one. Lists of estates, *caves* (wine cellars) and cooperatives are available from tourist offices and *maisons des vins* (wine houses) in main towns in wine-producing areas.

Making Champagne is a complex procedure. There are two fermentation processes, the first in casks and the second after the wine has been bottled and had sugar and yeast added. Bottles are then aged in cellars for two to five years, depending on the *cuvée* (vintage).

During the two months in early spring that the bottles are aged in cellars kept at 12°C, the wine turns effervescent. The sediment that forms in the bottle is removed by *remuage*, a painstakingly slow process in which each bottle – stored horizontally – is rotated slightly every day for weeks until the sludge works its way to the cork. Next comes *dégorgement:* the neck of the bottle is frozen, creating a blob of solidified Champagne and sediment, then removed.

maintain exclusivity (and price), the designated areas where grapes used for Champagne can be grown and the amount of wine produced each year are limited. In 2008 the borders that confine the Champagne AOC label were extended to include another 40 villages, increasing the value of their vineyards and its produce by tens of millions of euros (and making partygoers around the world forever grateful). Yet the bulk of Champagne is consumed in France.

If the final product is labelled *brut,* it is extra dry, with only 1.5% sugar content. *Extra-sec* means very dry (but not as dry as *brut*), *sec* is dry and *demi-sec* slightly sweet. The sweetest Champagne is labelled *doux.* Whatever the label, it is sacrilege to drink it out of anything other than a traditional Champagne *flûte,* narrow at the bottom to help the bubbles develop, wider in the middle to promote the diffusion of aromas, and narrower at the top again to concentrate those precious aromas.

Most of the famous Champagne *maisons* (houses) can be visited. See p286 for details.

Languedoc

Winemaking here is enjoying a renaissance. Following violent protests over Italian imports in the mid-1970s, farmers were subsidised to cut down their vines and replant with better quality AOC grapes, hence Languedoc's splendid wine and gargantuan production today: up to 40% of France's wine is produced in this vast sea of vines (just over a third of France's total).

Of increasing interest are the thoroughly modern table wines made under the Vin de Pays d'Oc (www.vindepaysdoc.com) label. Free of AOC restriction, these wines fly in the face of viticulture tradition as they experiment with new grape blends. The result: creative, affordable wines with funky names, designer etiquettes (and pink neocorks in the case of rosés) to reflect a contemporary lifestyle. Try a Mas de Daumas Gassac (www.daumas-gassac.com) or one of the 'chicken wines' of pioneering viticulturist Sacha Lichine (www.sachalichine.com).

Languedoc's best-known AOC wines are Minervois (drink its white with local sardines!) and Corbières, both known for well-structured reds. An island of six villages in the Minervois produces Minervois La Livinière, a red *vin de garde* (wine suitable for ageing) par excellence. Fitou, the granddad of Languedoc appellations (1948), is another red, easy to keep for four or five years.

Provence

There is no more quintessential image of daily life in this hot part of southern France than lounging beneath a vine-laced pergola, glass of chilled pink rosé in hand.

Top Self-Drive Wine Itineraries

» **Marne & Côte des Bar Champagne routes** Champagne

» **Route des Vins d'Alsace** Alsace

» **Route Touristique des Vignobles** Loire Valley

Meals in France are preceded by an *apéritif* such as a *kir* (white wine sweetened with black-currant syrup), *kir royale* (Champagne with black-currant syrup), *pineau* (cognac and grape juice) or a glass of sweet white Coteaux du Layon from the Loire Valley. In southern France aniseed-flavoured pastis, clear in the bottle, cloudy when mixed with water, is the aperitif to drink alfresco; in the southwest, go local with a Floc de Gascogne, a liqueur wine made from Armagnac and red or white grape juice.

After-dinner drinks accompany coffee. France's most famous brandies are Cognac and Armagnac, both made from grapes in the regions of those names. *Eaux de vie*, literally 'waters of life', can be made with grape skins and the pulp left over after being pressed for wine (Marc de Champagne, Marc de Bourgogne), apples (Calvados) and pears (Poire William), as well as such fruits as plums *(eau de vie de prune)* and even raspberries *(eau de vie de framboise)*. In the Loire Valley a shot of orange (aka a glass of local Cointreau liqueur) ends the meal.

When in Normandy, do as the festive Normans do: refresh the palate between courses with a *trou normand* (literally 'Norman hole') – traditionally a shot of *calva* (Calvados) or a contemporary scoop of apple sorbet doused in the local apple brandy.

Dating from 1977, Côtes de Provence is the region's largest appellation and France's sixth largest, producing 75% of Provençal wine. Its vineyards carpet 20 hectares between Nice and Aix-en-Provence, and its *terroir* (land) is astonishingly varied; few other appellations support such a variety of grape varieties – at least a dozen. Drunk young and served at 8°C to 10°C, it is among the world's oldest wines. Vines were planted by the Greeks in Massilia (Marseille) around 600 BC.

Smaller appellations include Coteaux d'Aix-en-Provence and Palette around Aix-en-Provence; Côtes du Ventoux (light and fruity reds drunk young); Côtes du Luberon (young reds made trendy by rich foreigners and media stars buying up its vineyards); and Coteaux Varois of Angelina Jolie and Brad Pitt fame (in 2008 the celeb pair rented Château de Miraval, a gold-stone château on a prestigious organic wine-producing estate in Correns, where Pink Floyd recorded part of *The Wall* in 1979).

The real star of the Provence show though is Bandol, with its own AOC since 1941. Its deep-flavoured reds are produced from dark-berried *mourvèdre* grapes grown on the coast near Toulon and ripened by oodles of sun, hence its rarity. In Roman times these wines were famous across Gaul, and their ability to mature at sea meant they travelled far beyond their home shores in the 16th and 17th centuries.

A little west along the same coast is Cassis, known for its crisp whites, the dream companion for the bijou port's bounty of shellfish and seafood.

Don't bring wine if you're invited into a French home, unless it's a bottle of chilled Champagne. The wine your host has chosen will be an expression of their tastes, but Champagne is welcomed by all.

Alsace

Alsace produces almost exclusively white wines – mostly varieties produced nowhere else in France – that are known for their clean, fresh taste and compatibility with the often heavy local cuisine. Unusually, some of the fruity Alsatian whites also go well with red meat. The vineyards closest to Strasbourg produce light red wines from pinot noir that are similar to rosé and are best served chilled.

Alsace's four most important varietal wines are riesling (known for its subtlety), Gewürztraminer (pungent and highly regarded), pinot gris (robust and high in alcohol) and muscat d'Alsace (less sweet than muscats from southern France).

The Arts

Literature

Courtly Love to Symbolism

Troubadours' lyric poems of courtly love dominated medieval French literature, while the *roman* (literally 'romance', now meaning 'novel') drew on old Celtic tales. With the *Roman de la Rose,* a 22,000-line poem by Guillaume de Lorris and Jean de Meung, allegorical figures like Pleasure, Shame and Fear appeared.

French Renaissance literature was great: La Pléiade was a group of lyrical poets active in the 1550s and 1560s. The exuberant narrative of Loire Valley-born François Rabelais (1494–1553) blends coarse humour with encyclopaedic erudition in a vast panorama of subjects that includes every existent kind of person, occupation and jargon in 16th-century France. Michel de Montaigne (1533–92) covered cannibals, war horses, drunkenness and the resemblance of children to their fathers and other themes.

The *grand siècle* (golden age) ushered in classical lofty odes to tragedy. François de Malherbe (1555–1628) brought a new rigour to rhythm in poetry; and Marie de La Fayette (1634–93) penned the first French novel, *La Princesse de Clèves* (1678).

The philosophical Voltaire (1694–1778) dominated the 18th century. A century on, Besançon gave birth to French romantic Victor Hugo. The breadth of interest and technical innovations exhibited in his poems and novels – *Les Misérables* and *The Hunchback of Notre Dame* among them – was phenomenal: after his death, his coffin was laid beneath the Arc de Triomphe for an all-night vigil.

In 1857 literary landmarks *Madame Bovary* by Gustave Flaubert (1821–80), and Charles Baudelaire's (1821–67) poems *Les Fleurs du Mal* (The Flowers of Evil), were published. Émile Zola (1840–1902) saw novel-writing as a science in his powerful series, *Les Rougon-Macquart.*

Evoking mental states was the dream of symbolists Paul Verlaine (1844–96) and Stéphane Mallarmé (1842-98). Verlaine shared a tempestuous homosexual relationship with poet Arthur Rimbaud (1854–91): enter French literature's first modern poems.

Modern Literature

The world's longest novel – a seven-volume 9,609,000-character giant by Marcel Proust (1871–1922) – dominated the early 20th century. *À la Recherche du Temps Perdu* (Remembrance of Things Past) explores in evocative detail the true meaning of past experience recovered from the unconscious by 'involuntary memory'.

Surrealism proved a vital force until WWII. André Breton (1896–1966) captured the spirit of surrealism – a fascination with dreams, divination and all manifestations of 'the marvellous' – in his autobiographical narratives. In Paris the bohemian Colette (1873–1954) captivated and

---

Literary Sights

» Colette's Paris: St-Germain cafés

» Sartre and Simone de Beauvoir graves, Cimetière du Montparnasse, Paris

» Oscar Wilde grave, Cimetière du Père Lachaise, Paris

» Musée Colette, Burgundy

» Musée Jules Verne, Nantes

shocked with her titillating novels detailing the amorous exploits of heroines such as schoolgirl Claudine.

After WWII, existentialism developed around the lively debates of Jean-Paul Sartre (1905–80), Simone de Beauvoir (1908–86) and Albert Camus (1913–60) in Paris' Left Bank cafés.

The *nouveau roman* of the 1950s saw experimental young writers seek new ways of organising narratives, with Nathalie Sarraute slashing identifiable characters and plot in *Les Fruits d'Or* (The Golden Fruits). *Histoire d'O* (Story of O), an erotic sadomasochistic novel written by Dominique Aury under a pseudonym in 1954, sold more copies outside France than any other contemporary French novel. In the 1960s, novelist Philippe Sollers raised eyebrows.

Contemporary Literature

Contemporary authors include Françoise Sagan, Pascal Quignard, Anna Gavalda, Emmanuel Carrère and Stéphane Bourguignon. No French writer better delves into the mind, mood and politics of the country's ethnic population than Faïza Guène (b 1985), sensation of the French literary scene. Born and bred on a ghetto housing estate outside Paris, she stunned critics with her debut novel, *Kiffe Kiffe Demain* (2004), sold in 27 countries and published in English as *Just Like Tomorrow* (2006). Like the parents of most of her friends and neighbours, Faïza Guène's father moved from a village in western Algeria to northern France in 1952, aged 17, to work in the mines. Only in the 1980s could he return to Algeria. There he met his wife, whom he brought back to France – to Les Courtillières housing estate in Seine-St-Denis, where 6000-odd immigrants live like sardines in five-storey high-rise blocks stretching for 1.5km. Such is the setting for Guène's first book and her second semi-autobiographical novel, *Du Rêve pour les Oeufs* (2006), published in English as *Dreams from the Endz* (2008). Watch for the English translation of her equally successful third novel, *Les Gens du Balto* (www.faiza-guene-lesgensdubalto.fr, in French).

A LITERARY FELLOW: THE FRENCH JAMES BOND

Secret agent OSS 117, aka France's James Bond, was a literary fellow – created four years before Ian Fleming's 007 by French novelist Jean Bruce (1921–63). Making his debut in 1949 with *Tu Parles d'une Ingénue* (You Speak of an Ingénue), Hubert Bonisseur de La Bath, colonel in the Office of Strategic Service (OSS), starred in 87 novels (selling 24 million copies) before his creator died in a car accident in 1963.

But the silky-smooth, dark-haired action man with a penchant for beautiful women, fancy gadgets and dicing with death was not dead. Three years after Bruce's death, his widow Josette took over, penning another incredible 143 adventures between 1966 and 1985. Josette died in 1996.

Next up, the couple's children, François and Martine Bruce, turned their hand to story writing, picking up the family tradition in 1987 with *OSS 117 est Mort* (OSS 117 is Dead) and churning out 24 more adventures in all. By the time *OSS 117 Prend le Large* (OSS 117 Takes Off) – the last to be published – hit the streets in 1992, the best-selling French series had been translated into 17 languages and sold 75 million copies.

As with 007, OSS 117 became a silver-screen idol too. French film director Jean Sacha brought the suave, womanising secret agent to life in his film adaptation of *OSS 117 n'est Pas Mort* (OSS 117 is Not Dead) in 1957. But it is the more recent, laugh-a-second parody starring France's best comic actor Jean Dujardin (b 1972) as the sexist, racist, macho, uncultured and cringingly outdated 1950s 'Bond...James Bond', or rather, 'Bonisseur de la Bath...Hubert Bonisseur de la Bath' in *OSS 117: Le Caire, Nid d'Espions* (OSS 117: Cairo, Nest of Spies; 2006) that gets the biggest curtain call.

One way of ensuring your beach reading is right up to the minute is to plump for the latest winner of the **Prix Goncourt**, France's most prestigious literary prize. Marcel Proust won it in 1919 for *À l'Ombre des Jeunes Filles en Fleurs* (Within a Budding Grove, 1924); Simon de Beauvoir in 1954 for *Les Mandarins* (The Mandarins, 1957); and, more recently, French-Afghan writer/film-maker Atiq Rahimi (b 1956) with *Syngué Sabour* (The Stone of Patience, 2008), and French-Senegalese novelist/playwright Marie NDiaye with *Trois Femmes Puissantes* (2009). Aged 21, the latter stunned the literary world with *Comédie Classique* (1988), a 200-page novel comprising just one single sentence. The 2010 winner was *La Carte et le Territoire* by Michel Houellebecq (b 1958). Winning works are generally translated pretty swiftly into English.

Add to your reading list the proud laureate of France's other big literary award, the **Grand Prix du Roman de l'Académie Française**, and your holiday reading list is sorted. The 2009 winner, *Les Onze,* by French novelist Pierre Michon (b 1945) hadn't been published in English at the time of research but given several of his other works are – *Small Lives* (2008) and *Master & Servants* (1997) included – it's not likely to be long before it is. *Nagasaki* by Eric Faye (b 1963) was the prize getter of 2010.

Music

Classical

French baroque music influenced European musical output in the 17th and 18th centuries. French musical luminaries – Charles Gounod (1818–93), César Franck (1822–90) and *Carmen* creator Georges Bizet (1838–75) among them – were a dime a dozen in the 19th century. Modern orchestration was founded by French romantic Hector Berlioz (1803–69). He demanded gargantuan forces: his ideal orchestra included 240 stringed instruments, 30 grand pianos and 30 harps.

Claude Debussy (1862–1918) revolutionised classical music with *Prélude à l'Après-Midi d'un Faune* (Prelude to the Afternoon of a Fawn), creating a light, almost Asian musical Impressionism. Impressionist comrade Maurice Ravel (1875–1937) peppered his work, including *Boléro,* with sensuousness and tonal colour. Contemporary composer Olivier Messiaen (1908–92) combined modern, almost mystical music with natural sounds such as birdsong. Unsurprisingly, his student Pierre Boulez (b 1925) works with computer-generated sound.

Jazz & French Chansons

Jazz hit 1920s Paris in the banana-clad form of Josephine Baker, an African-American cabaret dancer. Post-WWII ushered in a much-appreciated bunch of musicians – Sidney Bechet, Kenny Clarke, Bud Powell and Dexter Gordon among them. In 1934 a chance meeting between Parisian jazz guitarist Stéphane Grappelli and three-fingered Roma guitarist Django Reinhardt (whose birth centenary was celebrated nationwide in 2010) in a Montparnasse nightclub led to the formation of the Hot Club of France quintet. Claude Luter and his Dixieland band were hot in the 1950s.

The *chanson française,* a French folk-song tradition dating from the troubadours of the Middle Ages, was eclipsed by the music halls and burlesque of the early 20th century, but was revived in the 1930s by Piaf and Charles Trenet. In the 1950s, Paris' Left Bank cabarets nurtured *chansonniers* (cabaret singers) such as Léo Ferré, Georges Brassens, Claude Nougaro, Jacques Brel and the very charming, very sexy, very French Serge Gainsbourg. A biopic celebrating his life, *Serge Gainsbourg: Une Vie Héroïque* (Serge Gainsbourg: A Heroic Life) was released in 2009 to wide acclaim.

Musical Pilgrimages

» Serge Gainsbourg grave, Cimetière du Montparnasse, Paris

» Jim Morrison grave, Cimetière du Père Lachaise, Paris

» La Cigale, Paris

» Château des Millandes, the Dordogne

» Le Lieu Unique, Nantes

» Espace Georges Brassens, Sète

In the 1980s irresistible crooners Jean-Pierre Lang and Pierre Bachelet revived the *chanson* tradition with classics such as *Les Corons* (1982), a passionate ode to northern France's miners. Exciting contemporary performers of a genre clearly here to stay include Vincent Delerm, Bénabar, Jeanne Cherhal, Camille, Soha and a group called Les Têtes Raides. The next hip crooner on the scene, on Facebook and Youtube, is Arnaud Fleurent-Didier (www.arnaudfleurent didier.com).

Rap

For contemporary younger folk, France is probably best known for its rap, an original 1990s sound spearheaded by Senegal-born, Paris-reared rapper MC Solaar and Suprême NTM (NTM being an acronym for a French expression far too offensive to print). Most big-name rappers are French 20-somethings of Arabic or African origin whose prime preoccupation is the frustrations and fury of fed-up immigrants in the French *banlieues* (suburbs). Take 20-something, hot-shot rapper Disiz La Peste, born in Amiens to a Senegalese father and French mother: his third album *Histoires Extra-Ordinaires d'un Jeune de Banlieue* (The Extraordinary Stories of a Youth in the Suburbs; 2005) did just what its title suggested, as did his 'last' album *Disiz the End* (2009), following which he morphed into Peter Punk (www.disizpeterpunk.com) and created a very different rock-punk-electro sound with *Dans La Ventre du Crocodile* (In the Crocodile's Stomach; 2010).

Other rappers to listen out for include Monsieur R of Congolese origin, known for his hardcore, antiestablishment 'fuck everything' lyrics, which have landed him in court in the past; Parisian heavyweight Booba of Senegalese origin; ghetto kid Rohff (www.roh2f.com, in French) and the trio Malekal Morte.

One of France's few female rappers, Cyprus-born Diam's (short for '*diamant*' meaning 'diamond'; www.diams-lesite.com), who arrived in Paris aged seven, was voted MTV's French Artist of the Year in 2007. Rap bands include Marseille's hugely successful home-grown IAM (www.iam.tm.fr, in French), five-piece band KDD from Toulouse and Brittany's Manau trio (www.manau.com, in French), who fuse hip hop with traditional Celtic sounds.

No artist has cemented France's reputation in world music more than Paris-born, Franco-Congolese rapper, slam poet and three-time Victoire de la Musique award winner, Abd al Malik (www.abdalmalik. fr). His albums *Gibraltar* (2006) and *Dante* (2008) are classics, and his latest album *Château Rouge* (2010) will undoubtedly follow suit.

Rock & Pop

One could be forgiven for thinking that French pop is becoming dynastic. The very distinctive M (for Mathieu) is the son of singer Louis Chédid; Arthur H is the progeny of pop-rock musician Jacques Higelin; and Thomas Dutronc is the offspring of 1960s idols Jacques and Françoise Hardy. And the Gainsbourg dynasty doesn't look like ending any time soon. Serge's daughter with Jane Birkin, Charlotte, released her third album at the end of 2009.

Noir Désir was *the* sound of French rock until its lead singer, Bertrand Cantat, was imprisoned for the murder of his girlfriend and it disbanded. Worth noting are Louise Attack, Mickey 3D and Nosfell, who sings in his very own invented language. The hottest group to emerge in recent years, Pony Pony Run Run (www.ponyponyrunrun.net), sing in English.

Cinematic Experiences

» Musée Lumière, Lyon

» Hangar du Premier Film, Lyon

» Cannes Film Festival, Cannes

» Musée Jean Cocteau, Menton

» American Film Festival, Deauville

World

With styles from Algerian *rai* to other North African music (artists include Cheb Khaled, Natacha Atlas, Jamel, Cheb Mami) and Senegalese *mbalax* (Youssou N'Dour), West Indian zouk (Kassav', Zouk Machine) and Cuban salsa, France's world beat is strong. One musician who uses world elements to stunning effect is Manu Chao (www.manuchao.net), the Paris-born son of Spanish parents, whose albums are international best sellers.

In the late 1980s, bands Mano Negra and Les Négresses Vertes combined many of these elements with brilliant results. Magic System from Côte d'Ivoire popularised *zouglou* (a kind of West African rap and dance music) with its album *Premier Gaou,* and Congolese Koffi Olomide still packs the halls. Watch for the blind singing couple, Amadou and Mariam, and Rokia Traoré from Mali.

Another hot musical export is Parisian electrodance duo Daft Punk (www.daftalive.com), whose debut album *Homework* (1997) fused disco, house, funk and techno. Electronica duo Air (an acronym for 'Amour, Imagination, Rêve' meaning 'Love, Imagination, Dream') bagged a massive loyal following with its sensational album *Moon Safari* (1998) and didn't disappoint with its fifth, *Pocket Symphony* (2007). Then there is Rachid Taha, a Franco-Algerian DJ-turned-singer whose fifth album *Made in Medina* (2002) mixes Arab and Western musical styles to create an extraordinarily rich fusion of rock, punk, afro-pop, Algerian *rai,* salsa and pretty much you-name-it-it's-there. To add extra appeal there are song lyrics in English and Berber as well as French.

Painting

Prehistoric to Landscape

France's oldest known prehistoric cave paintings (created 31,000 years ago) adorn the Grotte Chauvet-Pont-d'Arc in the Rhône Valley and the underwater Grotte Cosquer near Marseille; neither can be visited.

According to Voltaire, French painting proper began with baroque painter Nicolas Poussin (1594–1665), known for his classical mythological and biblical scenes bathed in golden light. Wind forward a couple of centuries and modern still life popped up with Jean-Baptiste Chardin (1699–1779). A century later, neoclassical artist Jacques Louis David (1748–1825) wooed the public with his vast portraits.

While Romantics such as Eugène Delacroix (find his grave in Paris' Cimetière du Père Lachaise) revamped the subject picture, the Barbizon School effected a parallel transformation of landscape painting. Barbizons included landscape artist Jean-Baptiste Camille Corot (1796–1875) and Jean-François Millet (1814–75). The son of a peasant farmer from Normandy, Millet took many of his subjects from

1920s

French film flourishes. Sound ushers in René Clair's (1898–1981) world of fantasy and satirical surrealism. **Watch** Abel Gance's antiwar blockbuster *J'Accuse!* (I Accuse!; 1919), filmed on actual WWI battlefields.

1930s

WWI inspires a new realism: portraits of ordinary lives dominate film. **Watch** *La Grande Illusion* (The Great Illusion; 1937), a devastating evocation of war's folly based on the trench warfare experience of director Jean Renoir.

1940s

Surrealists eschew realism. **Watch** Jean Cocteau's *La Belle et la Bête* (Beauty and the Beast; 1945) and *Orphée* (Orpheus; 1950). WWII saps the film industry of both talent and money.

1950s

Nouvelle Vague (New Wave) sees small budgets, no stars and real-life subject matter. **Watch** poverty and alcoholism in *Le Beau Serge* (Bitter Reunion; 1958), time and memory in *Hiroshima, Mon Amour* (1959).

1960s

France as the land of romance. **Watch** Claude Lelouch's *Un Homme et une Femme* (A Man and a Woman; 1966) and Jacques Demy's bittersweet *Les Parapluies de Cherbourg* (The Umbrellas of Cherbourg; 1964).

peasant life, and reproductions of his *L'Angélus* (The Angelus; 1857) – the best-known painting in France after the *Mona Lisa* – are strung above mantelpieces all over rural France. The original hangs in Paris' Musée d'Orsay.

Realism & Impressionism

The Realists were all about social comment: Édouard Manet (1832–83) zoomed in on Parisian middle-class life and Gustave Courbet (1819–77) depicted the drudgery of the working class.

It was in a flower-filled garden in a Normandy village that Claude Monet (1840–1926) expounded Impressionism, a term of derision taken from the title of his experimental painting *Impression: Soleil Levant* (Impression: Sunrise; 1874). A trip to the Musée d'Orsay unveils a rash of other members of the school – Boudin, Sisley, Pissarro, Renoir, Degas and so on.

An arthritis-crippled Renoir painted out his last Impressionist days in a villa on the French Riviera. With a warmth and astonishing intensity of light hard to equal, the Riviera inspired dozens of artists post-Renoir: Paul Cézanne (1839–1906) is particularly celebrated for his post-Impressionist still lifes and landscapes done in Aix-en-Provence, where he was born and worked; Paul Gauguin (1848–1903) worked in Arles; while Dutch artist Vincent van Gogh (1853–90) painted Arles and St-Rémy-de-Provence. In St-Tropez pointillism took off: Georges Seurat (1859–91) was the first to apply paint in small dots or uniform brush strokes of unmixed colour, producing fine mosaics of warm and cool tones, but it was his pupil Paul Signac (1863–1935) who is best known for his pointillist works.

20th Century

Twentieth-century French painting is characterised by a bewildering diversity of styles, including cubism, and fauvism, which was named after the slur of a critic who compared the exhibitors at the 1906 autumn Salon in Paris with *fauves* (wild animals) because of their radical use of intensely bright colours. Spanish prodigy Pablo Picasso (1881–1973) was the man behind the former, and Henri Matisse (1869–1954) the latter. Both chose southern France to set up studio, Matisse living in Nice and Picasso opting for a 12th-century château (now the Musée Picasso) in Antibes. Cubism, as developed by Picasso and Georges Braque

Modern Art Meccas

» Monet's garden, Giverny

» Renoir's studio, French Riviera

» Picasso's château studio, Antibes

» Musée Matisse, Nice

» Cézanne's pad, Aix-en-Provence

» Chemin du Fauvisme (Fauvism Trail), Collioure

» La Piscine Musée d'Art et d'Industrie, Lille

» Les Abattoirs, Toulouse

LE 7ÈME ART: CINEMA CLASSICS

» **La Règle du Jeu** (The Rules of the Game; 1939) Shunned by the public and censored, Jean Renoir's story of a 1930s bourgeois hunting party in the Loire Valley is dark and satirical.

» **Et Dieu Créa la Femme** (And God Created Woman; 1956) Roger Vadim's tale of the amorality of modern youth made a star out of Brigitte Bardot and St-Tropez.

» **Les Quatre Cents Coups** (The 400 Blows; 1959) Partly based on the rebellious adolescence of New Wave director François Truffaut (1932–84).

» **Diva** (1981) and **37°2 le Matin** (Betty Blue; 1986) Two visually compelling films by Jean-Jacques Beineix. *Diva* stars French icon Richard Bohringer.

» **Jean de Florette** (1986) Claude Berri's famous portrait of prewar Provence in southern France.

» **Shoah** (1985) Claude Lanzmann's 9½-hour-long B&W documentary of interviews with Holocaust survivors worldwide took 11 years to make.

» **Subway** (1985), **Le Grand Bleu** (The Big Blue; 1988), **Nikita** (1990) and **Jeanne d'Arc** (Joan of Arc; 1999) The pick of Luc Besson box-office hits.

(1882–1963), deconstructed the subject into a system of intersecting planes and presented various aspects of it simultaneously.

The early 20th century also saw the rise of the Dada movement, and no piece of French art better captures its rebellious spirit than Marcel Duchamp's *Mona Lisa,* complete with moustache and goatee. In 1922 German Dadaist Max Ernst moved to Paris and worked on surrealism, a Dada offshoot that drew on the theories of Freud to reunite the conscious and unconscious realms and permeate daily life with fantasies and dreams.

With the close of WWII, Paris' role as the artistic capital of the world ended, leaving critics ever since wondering where all the artists have gone. The focus shifted back to southern France in the 1960s with new realists such as Arman (1928–2005) and Yves Klein (1928–62), both from Nice. In 1960 Klein famously produced *Anthropométrie de l'Époque Bleue,* a series of imprints made by naked women (covered from head to toe in blue paint) rolling around on a white canvas – in front of an orchestra of violins and an audience in evening dress. A decade on the Supports/Surfaces movement deconstructed the concept of a painting, transforming one of its structural components (such as the frame or canvas) into a work of art instead.

Artists in the 1990s turned to the minutiae of everyday urban life to express social and political angst, using media other than paint to let rip. Conceptual artist Daniel Buren (b 1938) reduced his painting to a signature series of vertical 8.7cm-wide stripes that he applies to every surface imaginable – white marble columns in the courtyard of Paris' Palais Royal included. The painter (who in 1967, as part of the radical *groupe BMPT,* signed a manifesto declaring he was not a painter) was the *enfant terrible* of French art in the 1980s. Partner-in-crime Michel Parmentier (1938–2000) insisted on monochrome painting – blue in 1966, grey in 1967 and red in 1968.

Paris-born conceptual artist Sophie Calle (b 1953) brazenly exposes her private life in public with her eye-catching installations, which most recently involved 107 women – including Carla Bruni before she became First Lady – reading and interpreting an email she received from her French lover, dumping her. The resultant work of art – compelling and addictive – is published in the artist's book *Take Care of Yourself.*

Some contemporary art trendsetters worth a look: Palais de Tokyo, in Paris, Fondation Maeght, in St-Paul de Vence, Centre Pompidou-Metz, in Metz.

1970s

The limelight baton goes to lesser-known directors like Éric Rohmer (b 1920), who make beautiful but uneventful films in which the characters endlessly analyse their feelings.

1980s

Big-name stars, slick production values and nostalgia: generous state subsidies see film-makers switch to costume dramas and comedies in the face of growing competition from the USA.

1990s & New Millennium

Box-office hits starring France's best-known, biggest-nosed actor, Gérard Depardieu, win over huge audiences in France and abroad. **Watch** *Cyrano de Bergerac* (1990) and *Astérix et Obélix: Mission Cléopâtre* (2002).

Architecture

From prehistoric megaliths around Carnac in Brittany to Vauban's 33 star-shaped citadels dotted around France to defend its 17th-century frontiers, French architecture has always been of *grand-projet* proportions.

Prehistoric to Roman

No part of France better demonstrates the work of the country's earliest architects than Brittany, which has more megalithic menhirs (monumental upright stones), tombs, cairns and burial chambers than anywhere else on earth. Many date from around 3500 BC and the most frequent structure is the dolmen, a covered burial chamber consisting of vertical menhirs topped by a flat capstone. Bizarrely, Brittany's ancient architects had different architectural tastes from their European neighbours – rather than the cromlechs (stone circles) commonly found in Britain, Ireland, Germany and Spain, they were much keener on building arrow-straight rows of menhirs known as *alignements*. And indeed, Carnac's monumental Alignements de Carnac is the world's largest known prehistoric structure.

The Romans left behind a colossal architectural legacy in Provence and the French Riviera. Thousands of men took three to five years to haul the 21,000 cu metres of local stone needed to build the Pont du Gard near Nîmes. Other fine pieces of Roman architecture, still operational, include amphitheatres in Nîmes and Arles, open-air theatres in Orange and Fréjus, and Nîmes' Maison Carrée.

Romanesque

A religious revival in the 11th century led to the construction of Romanesque churches, so-called because their architects adopted many architectural elements (eg vaulting) from Gallo-Roman buildings still standing at the time. Romanesque buildings typically have round arches, heavy walls, few windows and a lack of ornamentation that borders on the austere.

Romanesque masterpieces include Toulouse's Basilique St-Sernin, Poitiers' Église Notre Dame la Grande, the exquisitely haunting Basilique St-Rémi in Reims, Caen's twinset of famous Romanesque abbeys and Provence's trio in the Luberon (Sénanque, Le Thoronet and Silvacane). In Normandy the nave and south transept of the abbey-church on Mont St-Michel are beautiful examples of Norman Romanesque.

Then there is Burgundy's astonishing portfolio of Romanesque abbeys, among the world's finest.

Gothic

Avignon's pontifical palace is Gothic architecture on a gargantuan scale. The Gothic style originated in the mid-12th century in northern France, where the region's great wealth attracted the finest architects,

Big-Name Buildings

» **Frank Gehry** Cinémathèque Française (Paris), Cité de la Vigne (Gruissan)

» **Jean Nouvel** Institut du Monde Arabe and Fondation d'Art pour l'Art Contemporain (Paris), Les Docks Vauban (Le Havre)

» **Sir Norman Foster** Carrée d'Art (Nîmes), Pont de Millau (Languedoc), Musée de la Préhistoire des Gorges du Verdon (Quinson)

engineers and artisans. Gothic structures are characterised by ribbed vaults carved with great precision, pointed arches, slender verticals, chapels (often built or endowed by the wealthy or by guilds), galleries and arcades along the nave and chancel, refined decoration and large stained-glass windows. If you look closely at certain Gothic buildings, however, you'll notice minor asymmetrical elements introduced to avoid monotony.

The world's first Gothic building was the Basilique de St-Denis near Paris, which combined various late-Romanesque elements to create a new kind of structural support in which each arch counteracted and complemented the next. The basilica served as a model for many other 12th-century French cathedrals, including Notre Dame de Paris and Chartres cathedral – both known for their soaring flying buttresses. No Gothic belfry is finer to scale than that of Bordeaux' Cathédrale St-André.

In the 14th century, the Radiant Gothic style developed, named after the radiating tracery of the rose windows, with interiors becoming even lighter thanks to broader windows and more translucent stained glass. One of the most influential Rayonnant buildings was Paris' Ste-Chapelle, whose stained glass forms a curtain of glazing on the 1st floor.

Catch up with southern France's prehistoric architects at Marseille's Centre de la Vieille Charité, Quinson's Musée de la Préhistoire des Gorges du Verdon and the beehive-shaped huts called *bories* near Gordes in the Luberon.

Renaissance

The Renaissance, which began in Italy in the early 15th century, set out to realise a 'rebirth' of classical Greek and Roman culture. It had its first impact on France at the end of that century, when Charles VIII began a series of invasions of Italy, returning with some new ideas.

To trace the shift from late Gothic to Renaissance, travel along the Loire Valley: typical of early Renaissance architecture, Château de Chambord illustrates the mix of classical components and decorative motifs (columns, tunnel vaults, round arches, domes etc) with the rich decoration of Flamboyant Gothic. See p370 for a pictorial look at this valley's astonishing architecture.

BORIES

Mannerism, which followed Early Renaissance, was introduced by Italian architects and artists brought to France around 1530 by François I, whose royal château at Fontainebleau was designed by Italian architects. Over the following decades, French architects who had studied in Italy took over from their Italian colleagues. In 1635 early-baroque architect François Mansart (1598–1666) designed the classical wing of Château de Blois, while his younger rival, Louis Le Vau (1612–70), started work on Louis XIV's palace at Versailles.

The Mannerist style lasted until the early 17th century, when it was subsumed by the baroque style.

Baroque

During the baroque period (the tail end of the 16th to the late 18th centuries), painting, sculpture and classical architecture were integrated

---

FRANCE'S MOST BEAUTIFUL VILLAGES

One of French architecture's signature structures popped up in rural France from the 13th century, 'up' being the operative word for these *bastides* or *villages perchés* (fortified hilltop villages) built high on a hill to afford maximum protection for previously scattered populations. Provence in the south of France and the Dordogne are key regions to hike up, down and around one medieval hilltop village after another, but you can find them in almost every French region. The most dramatic and stunning appear on France's list of *plus beaux villages* (most beautiful villages; www.les-plus-beaux-villages-de-france.org).

ARCHITECTURE

VAUBAN'S CITADELS

From the mid-17th century to the mid-19th century, the design of defensive fortifications around the world was dominated by the work of one man: Sébastien le Prestre de Vauban (1633–1707).

Born to a relatively poor family of the petty nobility, Vauban worked as a military engineer during almost the entire reign of Louis XIV, revolutionising both the design of fortresses and siege techniques. To defend France's frontiers, he built 33 immense citadels, many of them shaped like stars and surrounded by moats, and he rebuilt or refined more than 100. Vauban's most famous citadel is situated at Lille, but his work can also be seen at Antibes, Belfort, Belle Île, Besançon, Concarneau, Neuf-Brisach (Alsace), Perpignan, St-Jean Pied de Port and St-Malo. The Vauban citadel in Verdun comprises 7km of underground galleries. Since 2008, 13 sites (www.sites-vauban. org) star on Unesco's World Heritage list under a 'Vauban Fortifications' banner.

to create structures and interiors of great subtlety, refinement and elegance. Architecture became more pictorial, with the painted ceilings in churches illustrating the Passion of Christ to the faithful, and palaces invoking the power and order of the state.

Salomon de Brosse, who designed Paris' Palais du Luxembourg in 1615, set the stage for two of France's most prominent early-baroque architects: François Mansart (1598–1666), who designed the classical wing of Château de Blois, and his younger rival Louis Le Vau (1612–70), who worked on France's grandest palace at Versailles.

Neoclassicism

Nancy's place Stanislas in northern France is the country's loveliest neoclassical square. Neoclassical architecture, which emerged in about 1740 and remained popular until well into the 19th century, had its roots in the renewed interest in the classical forms and conventions of Graeco-Roman antiquity: columns, simple geometric forms and traditional ornamentation.

Among the earliest examples of this style is the Italianate facade of Paris' Église St-Sulpice, designed in 1733 by Giovanni Servandoni, which took inspiration from Christopher Wren's St Paul's Cathedral in London; and the Petit Trianon at Versailles, designed by Jacques-Ange Gabriel for Louis XV in 1761. France's greatest neoclassical architect of the 18th century was Jacques-Germain Soufflot, the man behind the Panthéon in Left Bank Paris.

Neoclassicism peaked under Napoleon III, who used it extensively for monumental architecture intended to embody the grandeur of imperial France and its capital: the Arc de Triomphe, La Madeleine, the Arc du Carrousel at the Louvre, the Assemblée Nationale building and the Palais Garnier.

The true showcase of this era though is Monte Carlo Casino in Monaco, created by French architect Charles Garnier (1825–98) in 1878. See p859 for details.

Art Nouveau

Art nouveau (1850–1910) combined iron, brick, glass and ceramics in ways never before seen. The style emerged in Europe and the USA under various names (Jugendstil, Sezessionstil, Stile Liberty) and caught on quickly in Paris. The style was characterised by sinuous curves and flowing, asymmetrical forms reminiscent of creeping vines, water lilies, the patterns on insect wings and the flowering boughs of trees. Influenced by the arrival of exotic *objets d'art* from Japan, its French

---

Architect-Buff Sleeps

» BLC Design Hôtel, L'Apostrophe, Cadran Hôtel & Kube Hôtel, Paris

» Les Bains Douches, Toulouse

» Hôtel Le Corbusier, Marseille

» Hôtel Negresco, Nice

» Hôtel 3.14, Cannes

» Zazpi, St-Jean de Luz

» L'Hermitage Gantois, Lille

name came from a Paris gallery that featured works in the 'new art' style. True buffs should make a beeline for the art nouveau tourist trail in Nancy (see p337).

A Beautiful Age

The glittering belle époque, hot on the heels of art nouveau, heralded an eclecticism of decorative stucco friezes, *trompe l'œil* paintings, glittering wall mosaics, brightly coloured Moorish minarets and Turkish towers. Immerse yourself in its fabulous and whimsical designs with a stroll along Promenade des Anglais in Nice, where the pink-domed Hôtel Negresco (1912) is the icing on the cake, or, up north, around the colourful Imperial Quarter of Metz. Or flop in a beautiful belle époque spa like Vichy.

Modern

The Fondation Vasarely by the 'father of op art' Victor Vasarely (1908–97) was an architectural coup when unveiled in Aix-en-Provence in 1976. Its 14 giant monumental hexagons reflected what Vasarely had already achieved in art: the creation of optical illusion and changing perspective through the juxtaposition of geometrical shapes and colours.

France's best-known 20th-century architect, Charles-Édouard Jeanneret (better known as Le Corbusier; 1887–1965), was born in Switzerland but settled in Paris in 1917 at the age of 30. A radical modernist, he tried to adapt buildings to their functions in industrialised society without ignoring the human element, thus rewriting the architectural style book with his sweeping lines and functionalised forms adapted to fit the human form. Chapelle de Notre-Dame du Haut in the Jura and Couvent Ste-Marie de la Tourette near Lyon are 20th-century architectural icons.

Until 1968, French architects were still being trained almost exclusively at the conformist École de Beaux-Arts, which certainly shows in most of the early structures erected in the Parisian skyscraper district of La Défense and Montparnasse's ungainly 210m-tall Tour Montparnasse (1973).

Contemporary

French political leaders have long sought to immortalise themselves through the erection of huge public edifices aka *grands projects*. Georges Pompidou commissioned the Centre Pompidou (1977) in which the architects – in order to keep the exhibition halls as uncluttered as possible – put the building's insides out; Valéry Giscard d'Estaing transformed a derelict train station into the glorious Musée d'Orsay; and François Mitterrand commissioned the capital's best-known contemporary architectural landmarks (taxpayers' bill: a whopping €4.6 billion), including IM Pei's glass pyramid at the Louvre, the Opéra Bastille, the Grande Arche in La Défense and the four glass towers of the national

ARCHITECTURE

Art Nouveau in Paris

» Hector Guimard's noodle-like metro entrances

» Interior of the Musée d'Orsay

» Department stores Le Bon Marché & Galeries Lafayette

» Glass roof over the Grand Palais

France's biggest **architectural scandals-turned-successes**: Renzo Piano and Richard Rogers' Centre Pompidou, and IM Pei's glass pyramid at the Louvre, both in Paris.

BUILDING GREEN

A signature architectural feature of the French capital that has since been exported to other European cities is the vertical garden – *mur végétal* (vegetation wall) – especially that of Patrick Blanc (www.verticalgardenpatrickblanc.com). His most famous work is at the Musée du Quai Branly. Seeming to defy the very laws of gravity, the museum's vertical garden consists of some 15,000 low-light foliage plants from Central Europe, the USA, Japan and China planted on a surface of 800 sq metres and held in place by a frame of metal, PVC and nonbiodegradable felt – but no soil.

library. Jacques Chirac's only *grand projet* was Jean Nouvel's iconic riverside museum, the Musée du Quai Branly.

In the provinces, notable buildings include Strasbourg's European Parliament, Dutch architect Rem Koolhaas's Euralille, Jean Nouvel's glass-and-steel Vesunna Musée Gallo-Romain in Périgueux, a 1920s art deco swimming pool-turned-art museum in Lille and the fantastic Louvre II in little Lens, 37km south of Lille. Also noteworthy are an 11th-century abbey-turned-monumental sculpture gallery in Angers and Le Havre's rejuvenated 19th-century docks.

Architecture et Musique (www.architecmusique.com) is a fine concept: enjoy a classical-music concert amid an architectural masterpiece; the annual program is online.

Then, of course, there's one of the world's tallest bridges, the stunning Pont de Millau in Languedoc, designed by Sir Norman Foster. Other bridges worth noting for their architectural ingenuity are Normandy's Pont de Normandie (1995) near Le Havre and Paris' striking Passerelle Simone de Beauvoir (2006). Both cross the Seine.

One of the most beautiful and successful of France's contemporary buildings is the Institut du Monde Arabe (1987), a highly praised structure in Paris that successfully mixes modern and traditional Arab and Western elements. It was designed by Jean Nouvel, France's leading and arguably most talented architect. His current project, the ambitious Philharmonie de Paris (2014), will have an auditorium of 2400 'terrace' seats surrounding the orchestra. Daring duo Shigeru Ban (Tokyo) and Jean de Gastines (Paris) are the *tour de force* behind the very white, bright Centre Pompidou-Metz (2010).

Looking south, Frank Gehry is the big-name architect behind Arles' innovative new cultural centre: all ashimmer in the bright southern sun, rocklike Fondation Luma (2013) evokes the nearby Alpilles mountain range with its two linked towers topped with aluminium. Sir Norman Foster is busy designing a new yacht club for Monaco (2012) and in Lyon, a shimmering glass-and-steel cloud will rise out of the wasteland at the confluence of the Rhône and Saône Rivers.

Lyrical Landscapes

The Land

France is a land of art. Fantastic portraits and paintings adorn the walls of galleries big and small, villages throughout the land look like oil paintings of a bygone rural age and the people, with their natural sense of style, could be called works of art themselves. But as gorgeous as the manmade art of France is, it fades when compared to the sheer beauty of the countryside itself.

Hexagon-shaped France, the largest country in Europe after Russia and the Ukraine, is encircled by water or mountains along every side except in the northeast.

The country's 3200km-long coastline is incredibly diverse, ranging from white-chalk cliffs (Normandy) and treacherous promontories (Brittany) to broad expanses of fine sand (Atlantic coast) and pebbly beaches (the Mediterranean coast).

Western Europe's highest peak, Mont Blanc (4810m), spectacularly crowns the French Alps, which stagger along France's eastern border. North of Lake Geneva, the gentle limestone Jura Mountains run along the Swiss frontier to reach heights of around 1700m, while the rugged Pyrenees define France's 450km-long border with Spain and Andorra, peaking at 3404m.

Five major river systems criss-cross the country: the Garonne (which includes the Tarn, the Lot and the Dordogne) empties into the Atlantic; the Rhône links Lake Geneva and the Alps with the Mediterranean; Paris is licked in poetic verse by the Seine, which slithers through the

WILDLIFE

Travellers Nature Guides: France by Bob Gibbons is the definitive guide to where to watch wildlife in France.

HIGH-FACTOR PROTECTION

Over 10% of the coastline of mainland France and Corsica is managed by the **Conservatoire du Littoral** (www.conservatoire-du-littoral.fr), a public coastal-protection body that acquires – sometimes by expropriation – threatened natural areas by the sea in order to restore, rejuvenate and protect them.

Among the *conservatoire*'s rich pageant of *espaces naturels protégés* (protected natural areas) are the rare-orchid-dotted sand dunes east of Dunkirk, the Baie de Somme with its ornithological park, several wet and watery pockets of the horse-studded Camargue, and a Corsican desert. (The Désert des Agriates covers 16,000 hectres of wilderness between the towns of St-Florent and La Balagne – not so long ago a highly fertile area but today a barren landscape due to severe soil erosion resulting from human activities).

For a list of France's 24 **Ramsar Convention wetland sites**, see www.wetlands. org/rsis.

city en route from Burgundy to the English Channel; and tributaries of the North Sea–bound Rhine drain much of the area north and east of the capital. Then there's France's longest river, the château-studded Loire, which meanders through history from the Massif Central to the Atlantic.

Wildlife

France is blessed with a rich variety of flora and fauna, although few habitats have escaped human-induced impacts: intensive agriculture, wetland draining, urbanisation, hunting and the encroachment of industry and tourism infrastructure menace dozens of species.

Animals

France has more mammal species (around 135 including marine mammals and some introduced species) than any other country in Europe. Couple this with around 500 bird species (depending on which rare migrants are included), 40 types of amphibian, 36 varieties of reptile and 72 kinds of fish, and wildlife-watchers are in paradise. Of France's 40,000 identified insect species, 10,000 creep and crawl in the Parc National du Mercantour in the Alps.

High-altitude plains in the Alps and the Pyrenees shelter the marmot, which hibernates from October to April and has a shrill and distinctive whistle; the nimble chamois (mountain antelope), with its dark-striped head; and the *bouquetin* (Alpine ibex; see p952), which can be seen in large numbers in the Parc National de la Vanoise. Mouflons (wild mountain sheep), introduced in the 1950s, clamber over stony sunlit scree slopes in the mountains; while red and roe deer and wild boar are common in lower-altitude forested areas. The Alpine hare welcomes winter with its white coat, while 19 of Europe's 29 bat species hang out in the dark in the Alpine national parks.

The *loup* (wolf), which disappeared from France in the 1930s, returned to the Parc National du Mercantour in 1992 – much to the horror of the mouflon (on which it preys) and local sheep farmers. Dogs, corrals and sound machines have been used as an effective, nonlethal way of keeping the growing free-roaming wolf population of the Mercantour and other Alpine areas from feasting on domesticated sheep herds.

FERUS

Follow the progress of France's precious wolf, bear and lynx populations with FERUS, France's conservation group for the wellbeing of these protected predators, online at www.ferus.org, in French.

WHERE TO WATCH WILDLIFE

The national parks and their regional siblings offer all sorts of options to visitors who are keen to observe animals in their natural habitat, including nature walks with an expert guide. Details are in the regional chapters. The following (at non-national parks) are also worth a gander:

» Ten thousand flamingos in the Camargue, the best-known wetland site in France, as well as over 400 bird species including rollers and glossy ibis.

» Vultures in the Pyrenees at Falaise aux Vautours (Cliff of the Vultures) in the Vallée d'Ossau and in Languedoc at the Belvédère des Vautours in the Parc Naturel Régional des Grands Causses.

» Storks in Alsace at the Centre de Réintroduction des Cigognes, in Hunawihr, and the Enclos aux Cigognes in Munster; on the Atlantic coast at Le Teich Parc Ornithologique and the Parc Ornithologique du Marquenterre; and at the Parc des Oiseaux outside Villars-les-Dombes near Lyon.

Other easy-to-reach and highly rewarding areas for wildlife include the Forêt de Fontainebleau outside Paris, the Marais Poitevin on the Atlantic coast, the stunning underwater life between Cerbére and Banyuls, and the central mountains of Corsica, around Corte.

The brown bear disappeared from the Alps in the mid-1930s. The 150-odd native bears living in the Pyrenees a century ago had dwindled to one orphaned cub following the controversial shooting of its mother – the last female bear of Pyrenean stock – by a hunter in 2004. However another 12 to 18 bears of Slovenian origin also call the French and Spanish Pyrenees home, though the reintroduction program has faced fierce opposition from sheep herders (see the boxed text, p671).

A rare but wonderful treat is the sighting of an *aigle royal* (golden eagle): 40 pairs nest in the Parc National du Mercantour, 20 pairs nest in the Vanoise, 30-odd in the Écrins and some 50 in the Pyrenees. Other birds of prey include the peregrine falcon, the kestrel, the buzzard and the bearded vulture, with its bone-breaking habits. The last – Europe's largest bird of prey, with an awe-inspiring wingspan of 2.8m – was extinct in the Alps from the 19th century until the 1980s, when it was reintroduced. More recently, the small, pale-coloured Egyptian vulture (once worshipped by the Egyptians, hence its name) has been spreading throughout the Alps and Pyrenees.

Even the eagle-eyed will have difficulty spotting the ptarmigan, a chickenlike species that moults three times a year to ensure a foolproof camouflage for every season (brown in summer, white in winter). It lives on rocky slopes and in Alpine meadows above 2000m. The nutcracker, with its loud and buoyant singsong and larch-forest habitat, the black grouse, rock partridge, the very rare eagle owl and the three-toed woodpecker are among the other 120-odd species to keep birdwatchers on their toes in highland realms.

Elsewhere on the French watch-the-birdie front, there are now 12,000 pairs of white storks – up from seven breeding pairs in 1974; 10% of the world's flamingo population hangs out in the Camargue; giant black cormorants – some with a wingspan of 170cm – on an island off Pointe du Grouin on the north coast of Brittany; and unique seagull and fishing-eagle populations in the Réserve Naturelle de Scandola on Corsica. The *balbuzard pêcheur* (osprey), a migratory hunter that winters in Africa and returns to France in February or March, today only inhabits two regions of France: Corsica and the Loire Valley area.

Plants

About 140,000 sq km of forest – beech, oak and pine in the main – covers 20% of France, while 4900 different species of native flowering plant countrywide (2250 alone grow in the Parc National des Cévennes). In forests in the Champagne region, mutant beech trees grow in a bizarrely stunted, malformed shape in Parc Natural Régional de la Montagne de Reims.

The Alpine and Pyrenean regions nurture fir, spruce and beech forests on north-facing slopes between 800m and 1500m. Larch trees, mountain and arolla pines, rhododendrons and junipers stud shrubby subalpine zones between 1500m and 2000m; and a brilliant riot of spring and summertime wildflowers carpets grassy meadows above the treeline in the alpine zone (up to 3000m).

Alpine blooms include the single golden-yellow flower of the arnica, which has long been used in herbal and homeopathic bruise-relieving remedies; the flame-coloured fire lily; and the hardy Alpine columbine, with its delicate blue petals. The protected 'queen of the Alps' (aka the Alpine eryngo) bears an uncanny resemblance to a purple thistle but is, in fact, a member of the parsley family (to which the carrot also belongs).

The rare twinflower only grows in the Parc National de la Vanoise. Of France's 150 orchids, the black vanilla orchid is one to look out for – its small red-brown flowers exude a sweet vanilla fragrance.

Find out what to spot, where and when with the Ligue de Protection des Oiseaux (LPO; League for the Protection of Birds; www.lpo.fr, in French) and its regional *délégations* (on the website under 'Nos sites web').

Spotted a bearded vulture? Lucky you! Note down when, where, any distinguishing marks and the bird's behaviour patterns and send the details to the Beared Vulture Reintroduction into the Alps project at www.wild.unizh.ch/bg.

Corsica and the Massif des Maures, west of St-Tropez on the Côte d'Azur, are closely related botanically: both have chestnut and cork-oak trees (the bark of which gets stuffed in bottles) and are thickly carpeted with *garrigues* and *maquis* – heavily scented scrubland, where dozens of fragrant shrubs and herbs find shelter.

National Parks

The proportion of protected land in France is surprisingly low, relative to the size of the country. Six small *parcs nationaux* (national parks; www.parcsnationaux-fr.com) fully protect just 0.8% of the country. Another 13% (70,000 sq km) in metropolitan France and its overseas territories, with three million inhabitants, is protected to a substantially lesser degree by 45 *parcs naturels régionaux* (regional nature parks; www.parcs-naturels-regionaux.tm.fr, in French), and a further few per cent by 320 smaller *réserves naturelles* (nature reserves; www.reserves-naturelles.org), some of them under the eagle eye of the Conservatoire du Littoral.

While the central zones of national parks are uninhabited and fully protected by legislation (dogs, vehicles and hunting are banned and camping is restricted), their delicate ecosystems spill over into populated peripheral zones in which economic activities, some of them environmentally unfriendly, are permitted and even encouraged.

Most regional nature parks and reserves were established not only to improve (or at least maintain) local ecosystems, but also to encourage economic development and tourism in areas suffering from economic hardship and diminishing populations (such as the Massif Central and Corsica).

Select pockets of nature – the Pyrenees, Mont St-Michel and its bay, part of the Loire Valley and a clutch of capes on Corsica – have been declared Unesco World Heritage Sites.

Environmental Issues

The threats to France's environment are many and varied.

As elsewhere in the world, wetlands – incredibly productive ecosystems that are essential for the survival of birds, reptiles, fish and amphibians – are shrinking. More than 20,000 sq km (3% of French territory) are considered important wetlands but only 4% of this land is currently protected.

Great tracts of forest land burn each summer, often because of careless day-trippers but occasionally, as is sometimes reported in the Maures and Estérel ranges on the Côte d'Azur, because they're intentionally torched by people hoping to get licences to build on the damaged lands. Since the mid-1970s, between 31 sq km and 615 sq km of land has been reduced to a black stubble each year by an average of 540 fires – although overall, as prevention and fire-fighting improve, the number of fires is falling, according to the Office National des Forêts (www.onf.fr, in French), the national forestry commission responsible for public forests in France.

Dogs and guns also pose a threat to French animal life, brown bears included (see also p671). While the number of hunters has fallen by more than 20% in the last decade, there are still a lot more hunters in France (1.3 million) than in any other Western European country.

Despite the 1979 Brussels Directive for the protection of wild birds, their eggs, nests and habitats in the EU, the French government has been very slow to make its provisions part of French law, meaning birds that can fly safely over other countries can still be hunted as they cross France. A good handful of birds – estimated at at least 1000 birds of prey a year – are found to be electrocuted by high-voltage power lines.

Guide de la Nature en France by Michel Viard is an excellent field guide to the most commonly seen plants, birds and animals of France. It's in French but the glossy photos are universal.

Check out the wildlife-watching holidays in France offered by UK-based tour company Nature Trek (www.naturetrek.co.uk). These range from butterfly-spotting in Normandy to explorations of the wetlands of the Carmargue.

LYRICAL LANDSCAPES ENVIRONMENTAL ISSUES

PARK	FEATURES	ACTIVITIES	WHEN TO GO
Parc National des Cévennes (p733)	wild peat bogs, granite peaks, ravines & ridges bordering the Massif Central & Languedoc (910 sq km); red deer, beavers, vultures, wolves, bison	walking, donkey trekking, mountain biking, horse riding, cross-country skiing, caving, canoeing, botany (2250 plant species)	spring & winter
Parc National des Écrins (p502)	glaciers, glacial lakes & mountaintops soaring up to 4102m in the French Alps (1770 sq km); marmots, lynx, ibex, chamois, bearded vultures	walking, climbing, hang-gliding & para-gliding; kayaking	spring & summer
Parc National du Mer-cantour (p815)	Provence at its most majes-tic with 3000m-plus peaks & dead-end valleys along the Italian border; marmots, mouflons, chamois, ibex, wolves, golden & short-toed eagles, bearded vultures; Bronze Age petroglyphs	alpine skiing, white-water sports, moun-tain biking, walking, donkey trekking	spring, summer & winter
Parc National de Port-Cros (p853)	island marine park off the Côte d'Azur forming France's smallest national park & Eu-rope's first marine park (700 hectares & 1288 hectares of water); puffins, shearwaters, migratory birds	snorkelling, bird-watching, swimming, gentle strolling	summer & autumn (for birdwatching)
Parc National des Pyré-nées (p669)	100km of mountains along the Spanish border (457 sq km); marmots, izards, brown bears, golden eagles, vultures, buzzards	alpine & cross-coun-try skiing, walking, mountaineering, rock-climbing, white-water sports, canoeing, kayaking, mountain biking	spring, summer & winter
Parc National de la Vanoise (p495)	postglacial mountain landscape of Alpine peaks, beech-fir forests & 80 sq km of glaciers forming France's first national park (530 sq km); chamois, ibex, mar-mots, golden eagles; bearded vultures	alpine & cross-country skiing, walk-ing, mountaineering, mountain biking	spring, summer & winter

The state-owned electricity company, Electricité de France, has an enviable record on minimising greenhouse-gas emissions – fossil-fuel-fired power plants account for just 4.6% of its production. Clean, renewable hydropower, generated by 220 dams, comprises 8.8% of the company's generating capacity but this does affect animal habitats.

LIFE & DEATH OF THE IBEX

The nippy *bouquetin des Alpes* (Alpine ibex), with its imposingly large, curly-wurly horns (we're talking 1m long and a good 5kg in weight) and a penchant for hanging out on sickeningly high crags and ledges, is the animal most synonymous with the French Alps. In the 16th century, higher altitudes were loaded with the handsome beast, the males spraying themselves with urine and sporting a strong body odour. Three centuries on, however, its extravagant and unusual horns had become a must-have item in any self-respecting gentleman's trophy cabinet, and within a few years the Alpine ibex had been hunted to the brink of extinction.

In 1963 the Parc National de la Vanoise was created in the Alps to stop hunters in the Vanoise massif from shooting the few Alpine ibex that remained. The creation of similar nature reserves and the pursuit of rigorous conservation campaigns to protect the animal have seen populations surely and steadily recover – to the point where today the Alpine ibex is thriving. Not that you're likely to encounter one: the canny old ibex has realised that some mammals are best avoided.

On a less positive note, ibex also used to thrive in the Pyrenees but in a pattern that mirrored that of the Alpine populations, ibex numbers tumbled until, by 1900, only around 100 of them remained. Unlike in the Alps, though, protection measures never worked here and, in January 2000, the Pyrenean Ibex finally became extinct when the last surviving female was killed by a falling tree. Or did they become extinct? Nine years after the wiping out of the species the Pyrenean ibex became, for seven minutes, the first species in history to become 'un-extinct' when a cloned female was born alive before dying of breathing difficulties.

And no less than 75% (the highest in the world) of France's electricity comes from another controversial carbon-zero source: nuclear power, generated by 59 nuclear reactors at 20 sites.

The world's most ambitious nuclear-power program will soon have a new reactor, Flamanville 3 on Normandy's west coast near Cherbourg, due for completion in 2012.

As energy demands increase and global warming looms ever larger in the public energy debate, France's continuing commitment to nuclear power – a position that looked risky and retrograde after Chernobyl, whose fallout raised radiation levels in Alsace, the Lyon and Nice regions and Corsica – now seems possibly prescient. In July 2008 radioactive leaks occurred at two French nuclear-power stations and, perhaps because of this, for the first time French public opinion is now more anti (57%) than pro nuclear power. What is certain, though, is that nuclear energy has helped France meet its Kyoto targets without having to make many inconvenient cuts in its energy use. Learn the official version of how spent nuclear fuel is reprocessed by visiting France's La Hague Reprocessing plant (www.lahague.areva-nc.com), 25km west of Cherbourg on the Cotentin Peninsula in Normandy.

Europe's largest solar-powered electricity-generating station is being built on a 1000m-high, south-facing slope near the tiny Provence village of Curbans. The 300-hectare array of photovoltaic cells, which will eventually produce 33 megawatts, is supposed to generate its first commercial watt in 2011. This will remove 120,000 metric tonnes of carbon dioxide annually from the French energy bill.

Survival Guide

Directory A–Z

Accommodation

Be it a fairy-tale château, a boutique hideaway or a mountain refuge, France has accommodation to suit every taste and pocket. In this guide we've listed reviews by author preference.

Categories

As a rule of thumb, budget covers everything from bare-bones hostels to simple family-run places; midrange means a few extra creature comforts such as satellite TV and free wi-fi; while top end places stretch from luxury five-star chains with air conditioning, swimming pools and restaurants to boutique-chic chalets in the Alps.

Costs

Accommodation costs vary wildly between regions: what will buy you a night in a romantic *chambre d'hôte* (B&B) in the countryside may only get you a dorm bed in major cities and ski resorts; see individual chapters to gauge costs.

Price Icons

The price indicators in this book refer to the cost of a double room, including private bathroom (any combination of toilet, bathtub, shower and washbasin) and excluding breakfast unless otherwise noted. Breakfast is assumed to be included at a B&B. Where half board (breakfast and dinner) and full board (breakfast, lunch and dinner) is included, this is mentioned in the price.

CATEGORY	COST
€ budget	< €70 (< €80 in Paris)
€€ midrange	€70–175 (€80–180)
€€€ top end	> €175 (> €180 in Paris)

Reservations

Some tourist offices make room reservations, often for a fee of €5, but many only do so if you stop by in person. In the Alps, many tourist offices for ski resorts run a central reservation service for booking accommodation.

Seasons

» Rates in this guide are high season.

» In ski resorts, high season is Christmas and New Year, and the February–March school holidays.

» On the coast, high season is summer, particularly August.

» Hotels in inland cities charge low-season rates in summer.

» Rates often drop outside the high season – in some cases by as much as 50%.

» In business-oriented hotels in cities, rooms are most expensive from Monday to Thursday and cheaper over the weekend.

» In the Alps, hotels usually close between seasons, from around May to mid-June and from mid-September to early December.

B&Bs

For charm, a heartfelt *bienvenue* (welcome) and solid home cooking, it's hard to beat France's privately run *chambres d'hôte* (B&Bs), which are urban rarities but are plentiful in rural areas. Many hosts prepare an evening meal *(table d'hôte)* for an extra charge of around €20 to €30. Pick up lists of *chambres d'hôte* at local tourist offices, or find one to suit your style on the following websites:

Bienvenue à la Ferme (www.bienvenue-a-la-ferme. com) Escape to the country at a *chambre d'hôte* on a farm. You can search online or order a catalogue.

Chambres d'Hôtes France (www.chambresdhotesfrance. com) Great choice of B&Bs, all searchable by region.

en France (www.bbfrance. com) A selection of B&Bs and *gîtes* (cottages) from Bordeaux to Brittany.

Fleurs de Soleil (http:// fleursdesoleil.fr, in French) Has a click-happy map of France showing *chambres d'hôte* by region.

Gîtes de France (www. gites-de-france.fr) Acts as an umbrella organisation for B&Bs. Check out their catalogue *Gîtes de Charme* (www.gites-de-france -charme.com), or ask at local tourist offices about Gîtes de France brochures.

CAMPING CHIC

Farewell clammy canvas, adieu inflatable mattress... In recent years, camping in France has gone cool and creative, with *écolo chic* (eco-chic) and adventurous alternatives springing up all the time. If you fancy doing a Robinson Crusoe by staying in a tree house with an incredible view over the treetops, check out **Les Cabanes de France** (www.cabanes-de-france.com, in French), which covers leafy options all over France. Prefer to keep your feet firmly on the ground? Keep an eye out for eco-conscious campsites where you can snooze in a *tipi* (tepee) or in a giant hammock.

Samedi Midi Éditions (www.samedimidi.com) Country, mountain, seaside... choose your *chambre d'hôte* by location.

Camping

Camping in France is still very much in vogue, with thousands of well-equipped campgrounds across the country, many scenically located near rivers, lakes and the sea. Gîtes de France and Bienvenue à la Ferme coordinate camping on farms.

» Most campgrounds open from March or April to October; popular spots fill up fast in summer when it is wise to call ahead.

» In this book, 'sites' refer to fixed-price deals for two people including a tent and a car. Otherwise the price is broken down per adult/tent/car. Factor in a few extra euro per night for *taxe de séjour* (holiday tax) and electricity.

» Euro-economisers should look out for the good-value but no-frills *campings municipaux* (municipal campgrounds).

» If tents leave you cold, some campgrounds offer mobile homes with mod cons from heating to satellite TV.

» Camping in nondesignated spots (*camping sauvage*) is illegal in France.

» Campsite offices often close during the day, but a growing number have a PIN

code system so you can enter and leave when you choose.

» Getting to and from many campgrounds without your own transport can be slow and costly.

» Easy-to-navigate websites with campsites searchable by location, theme and facilities:

Camping en France (www.camping.fr)

Camping France (www.campingfrance.com)

Guide du Camping (www.guideducamping.com)

HPA Guide (http://camping.hpaguide.com)

Homestays

One of the best way to brush up your *français* and immerse yourself in local life is by staying with a French family under an arrangement known as *hôtes payants* or *hébergement chez l'habitant*. Popular among students and young people, this set up means you rent a room and usually have access (sometimes limited) to the bathroom and the kitchen; meals may also be available. If you are sensitive

to smoke or pets make sure you mention this. The following organisations arrange homestays:

Accueil Familial des Jeunes Étrangers (www.afje-paris.org) Homestays in or near Paris from €555 a month with breakfast.

France Lodge (www.apartments-in-paris.com) Accommodation in private Parisian homes; €30 to €55 a night for one person, €40 to €80 for two.

Homestay France (www.homestaybooking.com/homestay-france) Homestays in major French cities from €105 per week.

Hostels

Hostels in France range from funky to threadbare; some are little more than a few spartan rooms set aside in a hostel for young workers (*foyer de jeunes travailleurs/travailleuses*), while others are hip hang-outs with perks a-plenty.

» In university towns, *foyers d'étudiant* (student dormitories) are sometimes converted for use by travellers during summer.

» A dorm bed in an *auberge de jeunesse* (youth hostel) costs about €25 in Paris, and anything from €10.50 to €28 in the provinces, depending on location, amenities and facilities; sheets and breakfast are often included.

» To prevent outbreaks of bed bugs, sleeping bags are no longer permitted.

» Hostels by the sea or in the mountains sometimes offer seasonal outdoor activities.

» All hostels are totally nonsmoking.

BOOK YOUR STAY ONLINE

For more accommodation reviews by Lonely Planet authors, check out hotels.lonelyplanet.com/France. You'll find independent reviews, as well as recommendations on the best places to stay. Best of all, you can book online.

HOSTELLING CARD

You'll need to purchase an annual Hostelling International card (€11/16 for under/over 26s) or a nightly Welcome Stamp (€1.80 to €2.90, up to a maximum of six) to stay at the two major French hostelling associations: **Fédération Unie des Auberges de Jeunesse** (www.fuaj.org, in French) and **Ligue Française pour les Auberges de la Jeunesse** (www.auberges-de-jeunesse. com).

Hotels

In this book we have tried to feature well-situated, independent hotels that offer good value, a warm welcome, at least a bit of charm and a palpable sense of place.

Hotels in France are rated with one to five stars, although the ratings are based on highly objective criteria (eg the size of the entry hall), not the quality of the service, the decor or cleanliness. For this reason star ratings are not quoted in the reviews in this book.

» French hotels almost never include breakfast in their rates. Unless specified otherwise, prices quoted in this guide don't include breakfast, which costs around €7/10/20 in a budget/midrange/top-end hotel.

» When you book, hotels usually ask for a credit-card number and, occasionally, written (faxed) confirmation; some require a deposit.

» A double room generally has one double bed (often two pushed-together singles!); a room with twin beds (*deux lits*) is usually more expensive, as is a room with a bathtub instead of a shower.

» Feather pillows are practically nonexistent in France, even in top-end hotels.

» All hotel restaurant terraces allow smoking; if you are sensitive to smoke sit inside or carry a respirator.

CHAIN HOTELS

France's chain hotels stretch from nondescript establishments near the autoroute to central four-star hotels with character. Most conform to certain standards of decor, service and facilities (air conditioning, free wi-fi, 24-hour check-in etc), and offer competitive rates and last-minute and/or weekend deals. The countrywide biggies include the following:

B&B Hôtels (www.hotel-bb. com) Cheap motel-style digs.

Best Western (www.best western.com) Independent two- to four-star hotels, each with its own local character.

WHICH FLOOR?

In France, as elsewhere in Europe, 'ground floor' refers to the floor at street level; the 1st floor – what would be called the 2nd floor in the US – is the floor above that. This book follows local usage of the terms.

PRACTICALITIES

» **Classifieds** Pick up the free *FUSAC* (France USA Contacts; www.fusac.fr) in Anglophone haunts in Paris for classified ads about housing, babysitting, jobs and language exchanges.

» **Laundry** Virtually all French cities and towns have at least one *laverie libre-service* (self-service laundrette). The machines runs on coins – bring plenty in various denominations in case the change-maker is on the fritz.

» **Newspapers & Magazines** Locals read their news in centre-left, highly intellectual *Le Monde* (www.lemonde.fr), right-leaning *Le Figaro* (www.lefigaro.fr) or left-leaning *Libération* (www.liberation.fr).

» **Radio** For news, tune in to the French-language France Info (105.5MHz), the multilanguage RFI (738kHz or 89MHz in Paris) or, in northern France, the BBC World Service (648kHz) and BBC Radio 4 (198kHz). Popular national FM music stations include NRJ (www.nrj.fr, in French), Skyrock (www.skyrock.fm, in French) and Nostalgie (www.nostalgie.fr, in French).

» **Smoking** Smoking is illegal in all indoor public spaces, including restaurants and pubs (though, of course, smokers still light up on the terraces outside) – and, to the surprise of some, the law is actually obeyed!

» **Travel Conditions** In many areas, Autoroute Info (107.7MHz) has round-the-clock traffic information.

» **TV & Video** TV is Secam; videos work on the PAL system.

» **Weights & Measures** France uses the metric system.

Campanile (www.campanile.com) Good value hotels geared up for families.

Citôtel (www.citotel.com) Independent two- and three-star hotels.

Contact Hôtel (www.contact-hotel.com) Inexpensive two- and three-star hotels.

Etap (www.etaphotel.com) Ubiquitous chain.

Formule 1 (www.hotelformule1.com) Nondescript roadside cheapie.

Ibis (www.ibishotel.com) Midrange pick.

Inter-Hotel (www.inter-hotel.fr) Two- and three-star hotels, some quite charming.

Kyriad (www.kyriad.com) Comfortable midrange choices.

Novotel (www.novotel.com) Family-friendly chain.

Première Classe (www.premiereclasse.com) Motel-style accommodation.

Sofitel (www.sofitel.com) Range of top-end hotels in major French cities.

Refuges & Gîtes d'Étape

» *Refuges* (mountain huts or shelters) are bog-basic cabins established along trails in uninhabited mountainous areas and operated by national-park authorities, the **Club Alpin Français** (www.ffcam.fr, in French) or other private organisations.

» *Refuges* are marked on hiking and climbing maps.

ONLINE DEALS

Try these websites for deals on last-minute accommodation in France:

» alpharooms.com

» lastminute.com

» laterooms.com

» priceline.com

» quickrooms.com

» A bunk in the dorm generally costs €10 to €20. Hot meals are sometimes available and, in a few cases, mandatory, pushing the price up to €30 or beyond.

» Advance reservations and a weather check are essential before setting out.

» *Gîtes d'étape*, better equipped and more comfortable than *refuges* (some even have showers), are situated along walking trails in less remote areas, often villages.

» Your first port of call should be **Gîtes d'Étape et Refuges** (www.gites-refuges.com), covering 4,000 *gîtes d'étape* and *refuges*.

Rental Accommodation

If you are planning on staying put for more than a few days or are travelling in a group, renting a furnished studio, apartment or villa can be an economical alternative. You will have the chance to live like a local, with trips to the farmers market and the *boulangerie*.

Finding an apartment for long-term rental can be gruelling. Landlords, many of whom prefer locals to foreigners, usually require substantial proof of financial responsibility and sufficient funds in France; many ask for a *caution* (guarantee) and a hefty deposit.

» Gîtes de France handles some of the most charming *gîtes ruraux* (self-contained holiday cottages) in rural areas.

» Cleaning, linen rental and electricity fees usually cost extra.

» Classified ads appear in *De Particulier à Particulier* (www.pap.fr, in French), published on Thursday and sold at newsstands.

» For apartments outside Paris it's best to search at your destination.

» Check places like bars and *tabacs* (tobacconists) for free local newspapers (often named after the number of the *département*) with classifieds listings.

Activities

From the glaciers, rivers and canyons of the Alps to the volcanic peaks of the Massif Central – not to mention 3200km of coastline stretching from Italy to Spain and from the Basque country to the Straits of Dover – France's spirit-lifting landscapes beg exhilarating outdoor escapes.

For details on regional activities, courses, equipment hire, clubs and companies, see this book's On the Road chapters and get in contact with local tourist offices.

Organisations

Whether you are a peak bagger, a surfer dude or a thrill-seeking mountain biker, the following organisations can help you plan your *petit* adventure:

CYCLING

Fédération Française de Cyclisme (www.ffc.fr, in French) Founded in 1881, the French Cycling Federation is *the* authority on competitive cycling in France and mountain biking (VTT), including freeriding, cross-country and downhill.

Fédération Française de Cyclotourisme (www.ffct.org, in French) This organisation promotes bicycle touring and mountain biking.

Union Touristique Les Amis de la Nature (http://troisv.amis-nature.org, in French) Has details on local, regional and long-distance *véloroutes* (cycling routes) around France.

Véloroutes et Voies Vertes (www.af3v.org) A database of 250 signposted *véloroutes* (bike paths) and

WALK THE WALK

The French countryside is criss-crossed by a staggering 120,000km of **sentiers balisés** (marked walking paths), which pass through every imaginable terrain in every region of the country. No permit is needed to hike. Probably the best-known walking trails are the **sentiers de grande randonnée (GR)**, long-distance paths marked by red-and-white-striped track indicators.

See p963 for recommended maps and *topoguides* (walking guides).

voies vertes (greenways) for cycling and in-line skating.

GLIDING

Fédération Française de Vol à Voile (FFVV; www.ffvv.org, in French) Provides details of *vol à voile* (gliding) clubs countrywide.

Fédération Française de Vol Libre (http://federation.ffvl.fr, in French) Groups regional clubs specialising in *deltaplane* (hang-gliding), *parapente* (paragliding) and *le kite-surf* (kitesurfing).

MOUNTAIN & SNOW SPORTS

Club Alpin Français (French Alpine Club; www.ffcam.fr, in French) This highly regarded organisation groups 280 local mountain sports clubs and arranges professional

guides for escapades in *alpinisme* (mountaineering), *escalade* (rock climbing), *escalade de glace* (ice climbing) and other highland activities. They also run many of the *refuges* (mountain huts) in the French Alps.

École du Ski Français (ESF; French Ski School; www.esf.net) The largest ski school in the world, operating everywhere in France big enough to have a ski lift and high enough to be snow-sure. The tuition is first rate.

WALKING

Parcs Nationaux (http://federation.ffvl.fr, in French) First port of call if you are planning a visit to one of France's six national parks.

Parcs Naturels Régionaux (www.parcs-naturels-region

aux.tm.fr, in French) Has the low-down on activities, accommodation and events in France's 46 regional nature parks.

Grande Randonnée (www.grande-randonnee.fr, in French) A good source of information on France's long-distance footpaths. The website www.gr-infos.com also has details on specific walks in English.

Business Hours

French business hours are regulated by a maze of government regulations, including the 35-hour working week.

» The midday break is uncommon in Paris but, in general, gets longer the further south you go.

» French law requires that most businesses close on Sunday; exceptions include grocery stores, *boulangeries*, florists and businesses catering to the tourist trade.

» In some places shops close on Monday.

» Many service stations open 24 hours a day and stock basic groceries.

» Restaurants generally close one or two days of the week, chosen according to the owner's whim. In this

THE ART OF SLEEPING

A château, a country manor, five-star opulence at the foot of the Eiffel Tower – whether you want to live like a lord, sleep like a log or blow the budget, there's a room with your name on it.

Alistair Sawday's (www.sawdays.co.uk) Boutique retreats and *chambres d'hôte*, placing the accent on originality and authentic hospitality.

Hôtels de Charme (www.hotelsdecharme.com, in French) Abbeys, manors, châteaux – this is a mixed bag of (as the name says) charming hotels.

Grandes Étapes Françaises (www.grandesetapes.fr) Beautiful chateaux-hotels and four-star residences.

Logis de France (www.logis-de-france.fr) Small, often family-run hotels with charm and a warm welcome.

Relais & Châteaux (www.relaischateaux.com) Seductive selection of villas, châteaux and historic hotels.

Relais du Silence (www.relaisdusilence.com) Fall asleep to complete silence in a gorgeous château, spa-clad auberge, vineyard hotel...

Small Luxury Hotels of the World (www.slh.com) Super-luxurious boutique hotels, chalets and resorts.

STANDARD HOURS

We've only listed business hours where they differ from the following standards.

BUSINESS	OPENING HOURS
Bank	9 or 9.30am-1pm & 2-5pm Mon-Fri or Tue-Sat
Bar	7pm to 1am Mon-Sat
Café	7 or 8am-10 or 11pm Mon-Sat
Nightclub	10pm-3, 4 or 5am Thu-Sat
Post office	8.30am or 9am to 5pm or 6pm Mon-Fri, 8am-noon Sat
Restaurant	lunch noon-2.30 or 3pm, dinner 7-10 or 11pm
Shop	9 or 10am-noon & 2-6 or 7pm Mon-Sat
Supermarket	9am to 7pm or 8pm Mon-Sat

book, opening days/hours are only specified if the restaurant isn't open for both lunch and dinner daily.

» Most (but not all) national museums are closed on Tuesday, while most local museums are closed on Monday, though in summer some open daily. Many museums close at lunchtime.

» In this book we give high-season hours for sights and attractions; hours are generally reduced during low season.

Customs Regulations

Goods brought in and out of countries within the EU incur no additional taxes provided duty has been paid somewhere within the EU and the goods are for personal consumption. Duty-free shopping is available only if you are leaving the EU.

Duty-free allowances (for adults) coming from non-EU countries (including the Channel Islands):

» 200 cigarettes
» 50 cigars
» 1L spirits

» 2L wine
» 50ml perfume
» 250ml eau de toilette
» other goods up to the value of €175 (€90 for under 15s)

Higher limits apply if you are coming from Andorra; anything over these limits must be declared. For further details, see www.douane.gouv.fr (partly in English).

Discount Cards

Discount cards yield fantastic benefits and easily pay for themselves. As well as the card fee, you'll often need a passport-sized photo and some form of ID with proof of age (eg passport or birth certificate).

People over 60 or 65 are entitled to discounts on things like public transport, museum admission fees and theatres. For details of the SNCF's Carte Sénior, see p982.

Discount card options:

Camping Card International (CCI; www.camping cardinternational.com; €51 per family) Use as ID for checking into campsites;

includes 3rd-party liability insurance; usually yields 5-20% discount. Available at automobile associations, camping federations, camping grounds

European Youth Card (Euro<26 card; www.euro26. org; €14) Wide range of discounts for under-26s. Available online.

International Student Identity Card (ISIC; www. isic.org; €12) Discounts on travel, shopping, attractions and entertainment for full-time students. Available at ISIC points (see website).

International Teacher Identity Card (ITIC; www. isic.org; €12) Similar benefits to ISIC, for full-time teachers. Available at ISIC points (see website).

International Youth Travel Card (IYTC; www.isic.org; €12) Similar benefits to ISIC, for under-26s. Available at ISIC points (see website).

SnowBall Pass (www.snow ballpass.com; €18) Discounts on lift passes, equipment hire, ski tuition, restaurants and accommodation in French Alps resorts. Available online.

Electricity

230V/50Hz

European two-pin plugs are standard. France has 230V at 50Hz AC (you may need a transformer for 110V electrical appliances).

Embassies & Consulates

» All foreign embassies are in Paris.

» Many countries – including Canada, Japan, the UK, USA and most Euro-pean countries – also have consulates in other major cities such as Bordeaux, Lyon, Nice, Marseille and Strasbourg.

» To find a consulate or an embassy not listed here, visit www.embassiesabroad.com or look up 'ambassade' in the super user-friendly **Pages Jaunes** (Yellow Pages; www.pagesjaunes.fr, in French).

Gay & Lesbian Travellers

Gay mayors (including Paris' very own Bertrand Delanoë), artists and film directors, camper-than-camp fashion designers – the rainbow flag flies high in France, a country that left its closet long before many of its European neighbours. *Laissez-faire* perfectly sums up France's liberal attitude towards

EMBASSIES & CONSULATES IN FRANCE

COUNTRY	TELEPHONE	WEBSITE	ADDRESS	NEAREST METRO
Australia	01 40 59 33 00	www.france.embassy.gov.au	4 rue Jean Rey	Ⓜ Bir Hakeim
Belgium	01 44 09 39 39	www.diplomatie.be/paris, in French & Flemish	9 rue de Tilsitt	Ⓜ Charles de Gaulle-Étoile
Canada	01 44 43 29 00	www.amb-canada.fr	35 av Montaigne	Ⓜ Franklin D Roosevelt
Germany	01 53 83 45 00	www.paris.diplo.de, in French & German	13 av Franklin D Roosevelt	Ⓜ Franklin D Roosevelt
Ireland	01 44 17 67 00	www.embassyofireland.fr	12 av Foch	Ⓜ Argentine
Italy	01 49 54 03 00	www.ambparigi.esteri.it, in French & Italian	51 rue de Varenne	Ⓜ Rue du Bac
Japan	01 48 88 62 00	www.amb-japon.fr, in French & Japanese	7 av Hoche	Ⓜ Courcelles
Netherlands	01 40 62 33 00	www.amb-pays-bas.fr, in French & Dutch	7 rue Eblé	Ⓜ St-François Xavier
New Zealand	01 45 01 43 43	www.nzembassy.com	7ter rue Léonard de Vinci	Ⓜ Victor Hugo
South Africa	01 53 59 23 23	www.afriquesud.net	59 quai d'Orsay	Ⓜ Invalides
Spain	01 44 43 18 00	www.amb-espagne.fr, in French & Spanish	22 av Marceau	Ⓜ Alma-Marceau
Switzerland	01 49 55 67 00	www.eda.admin.ch, in French	142 rue de Grenelle	Ⓜ Varenne
UK	01 44 51 31 00	http://ukinfrance.fco.gov.uk	35 rue du Faubourg St-Honoré	Ⓜ Concorde
USA	01 43 12 22 22	http://france.usembassy.gov	4 av Gabriel	Ⓜ Concorde

homosexuality and people's private lives in general; in part because of a long tradition of public tolerance towards unconventional lifestyles.

» Paris has been a thriving gay and lesbian centre since the late 1970s, and most major organisations are based there today.

» Bordeaux, Lille, Lyon, Montpellier, Toulouse and many other towns also have an active queer scene.

» Attitudes towards homosexuality tend to be more conservative in the countryside and villages.

» France's lesbian scene is less public than its gay male counterpart and is centred mainly on women's cafés and bars.

» Introduced in 1999, PACS (civil solidarity pacts) afford same-sex couples most of the rights, legal protections and responsibilities as their married counterparts.

» Gay Pride marches are held in major French cities from mid-May to early July.

Publications

Damron (www.damron.com) Publishes English-language travel guides, including the *Damron Women's Traveller* for lesbians and the *Damron Men's Travel Guide* for gays.

Lesbia French-language lesbian monthly.

Spartacus International Gay Guide (www.spartacusworld.com) Annual English-language travel guide for men.

Têtu (www.tetu.com, in French) A glossy monthly that bills itself as *le magazine des gais et des lesbiennes*. Has a France-wide directory of bars, clubs and hotels.

Websites

Cité Gay (www.citegay.fr, in French) Has the low-down on gay and lesbian events.

French Government Tourist Office (http://us.franceguide.com/special-interests/gay-friendly) Information about 'the gay-friendly destination par excellence'.

France Queer Resources Directory (www.france.qrd.org, in French) Gay and lesbian directory.

Gay France (www.gay-france.net, in French) Insider tips on gay life in France.

Gay Travel France (www.gaytravelfrance.com) Gay and lesbian hotels, apartment rentals and *chambres d'hôte* in France.

Gayscape (www.gayscape.com) Hundreds of links to gay- and lesbian-related sites.

Gayvox (www.gayvox.com/guide3, in French) Online travel guide to France, with listings by region.

Paris Gay (www.paris-gay.com) All you need to know about gay Paris.

Tasse de Thé (www.tassedethe.com, in French) A *webzine lesbien* with lots of useful links.

Health

France is a healthy place so your main risks are likely to be sunburn, foot blisters, insect bites and mild stomach problems from eating and drinking with too much gusto.

Before You Go

» Bring your medications in their original, clearly labelled, containers.

» A signed and dated letter from your physician describing your medical conditions and medications, including generic names (French medicine names are often completely different to those in other countries), is also a good idea.

» Dental care in France is usually good; however, it is sensible to have a dental check-up before a long trip.

» No vaccinations are required to travel to France but the World Health Organization (WHO) recommends that all travellers be covered for diphtheria, tetanus, measles, mumps, rubella and polio, regardless of their destination.

EUROPEAN HEALTH INSURANCE CARD

Citizens of the EU, Switzerland, Iceland, Norway or Liechtenstein receive free or reduced-cost state-provided health-care cover with the European Health Insurance Card (EHIC) for medical treatment that becomes necessary while in France. (The EHIC replaced the E111 in 2006.) Each family member will need a separate card. UK residents can get application forms from post offices, or download them from the Department of Health website (www.dh.gov.uk), which has comprehensive information about the card's coverage.

The EHIC does not cover private healthcare, so make sure that you are treated by a state healthcare provider (*conventionné*). You will need to pay directly and fill in a treatment form (*feuille de soins*); keep the form to claim any refunds. In general, you can claim back around 70% of the standard treatment cost.

Citizens of other countries need to check if there is a reciprocal arrangement for free medical care between their country and France.

Availability & Cost of Health Care

» Visitors to France can get excellent health care from hospital (*hôpital*) emergency rooms/casualty wards (*salles des urgences*) and at a doctors' office (*cabinet médical*).

» For minor illnesses, trained staff in pharmacies – in every village and town with a green-cross sign outside that flashes when open – give valuable advice, sell medications, can tell you when more specialised help is needed and will point you in the right direction.

» You will need to pay upfront for any health care you receive, be it at a doctor's surgery, pharmacy or hospital, unless your insurance plan makes payments directly to providers.

» The standard rate for a consultation with a GP/specialist is around €22 to €25.

» Emergency contraception is available with a doctor's prescription. Condoms (*les préservatifs*) are readily available.

Insurance

» Comprehensive travel insurance to cover theft, loss and medical problems is highly recommended.

» Some policies specifically exclude dangerous activities such as scuba diving, motorcycling, skiing and even trekking: read the fine print.

» Check that the policy covers ambulances or an emergency flight home.

» Find out in advance if your insurance plan will

make payments directly to providers or reimburse you later for overseas health expenditures.

» If you have to claim later, make sure you keep all documentation.

» Paying for your airline ticket with a credit card often provides limited travel accident insurance – ask your credit-card company what it is prepared to cover.

» Worldwide travel insurance is available at www.lonelyplanet.com/travel_services. You can buy, extend and claim online anytime – even if you are already on the road.

Internet Access

» Wireless (wi-fi) access points can now be found at major airports, in many (if not most) hotels and at most cafés.

» Some tourist offices and numerous cafés and bars tout wi-fi hot spots that let laptop owners hook up for free.

» To search for free wi-fi hot spots in France, visit www.hotspot-locations.co.uk or www.free-hotspot.com.

» Internet cafés can be found in towns and cities countrywide; some are listed under Information in this book's On the Road chapters. Prices range from €2 to €6 per hour.

» Public libraries (*bibliothèques or médiathèques*) often have free or inexpensive internet access, though hours are limited and you may have to fill in some forms.

» If you'll be accessing dial-up ISPs with your laptop, you will need a telephone-plug adaptor, available at large supermarkets.

Language Courses

» www.studyabroadlinks.com can help you find specific courses and summer programs, while www.edufrance.fr/en has information about university study.

» All manner of French language courses are available in Paris and provincial towns and cities; many also arrange accommodation.

» Prices and courses vary greatly and the content can often be tailored to your specific needs (for a fee).

» The government site www.diplomatie.gouv.fr (under 'Francophony') and www.europa-pages.com/france list language schools in France.

» Some schools you might consider:

Alliance Française (☑01 42 84 90 00; www.alliancefr.org; 101 bd Raspail, 6e, Paris; ⓂSt-Placide) Venerable institution for the worldwide promotion of French language and civilisation, with intensive and extensive classes, including literature and business French.

Centre de Linguistique Appliquée de Besançon (☑03 81 66 52 00; http://cla.univ-fcomte.fr; 6 rue Gabriel Plançon, Besançon) One of France's largest language schools, in a beautiful city, with a variety of language and culture classes.

Centre Méditerranéen d'Études Françaises (☑04 93 78 21 59; www.monte-carlo.mc/centremed; chemin des Oliviers, Cap d'Ail) Côte d'Azur school dating from 1952, with an open-air amphitheatre designed by Jean Cocteau overlooking the sparkling blue Med.

Eurocentre d'Amboise (☑02 47 23 10 60; www.

WHAT THE ICON MEANS

Throughout this guide, only accommodation providers that have an actual computer that guests can use to access the internet are flagged with a computer icon (@). The 🛜icon indicates anywhere with wi-fi access. Where this icon appears, assume the wi-fi is free unless otherwise specified.

eurocentres.com; 9 mail St-Thomas, Amboise) Small, well-organised school in the charming Loire Valley. Eurocentre has branches in La Rochelle and Paris.

Université de Provence (☎04 42 95 32 17; http://sites.univ-provence.fr/wscefee; 29 av Robert Schumann, Aix-en-Provence) A hot choice in lovely Aix: semester-long language courses as well as shorter summer classes.

Legal Matters

Police

» French police have wide powers of search and seizure and can ask you to prove your identity at any time – whether or not there is 'probable cause'.

» Foreigners must be able to prove their legal status in France (eg passport, visa, residency permit) without delay.

» If the police stop you for any reason, be polite and remain calm. Verbally (and of course physically) abusing a police officer can lead to a hefty fine, and even imprisonment.

» You may refuse to sign a police statement, and have the right to ask for a copy.

» People who are arrested are considered innocent until proven guilty, but can be held in custody until trial.

» Because of the threat of terrorism, French police are very strict about security. Do not leave baggage unattended, especially at airports or train stations: suspicious objects may be summarily blown up.

Maps

Countrywide, road and city maps are available at Maisons de la Presse (large newsagencies), bookshops, airports, tourist offices and newspaper kiosks. Local organisations also produce

topoguides that supply details on trail conditions, flora, fauna and mountain shelters. Visit http://fr.mappy.com (in French) for online maps and a journey planner.

Blay (www.blayfoldex.com, in French) Produces over 180 orange-jacketed street maps of French cities and towns.

FFRP (www.ffrandonnee.fr, in French) Publishes around 120 *topoguides* – map-equipped booklets about major trails (eg GRs) – in French.

Institut Géographique National (IGN; www.ign.fr) One of France's major map publishers, with regional fold-out maps as well as an all-France volume, *France – Routes, Autoroutes*. Has a great variety of *topoguides* and 1:50,000-scale maps that are ideal for hiking or walking. Its specialised *cyclocartes* (cycle maps) show dozens of suggested bicycle tours around France. The IGN also has themed maps showing wine regions, museums and so on.

Michelin (http://boutique cartesetguides.michelin.fr, in French, www.viamichelin. com for online maps) Has excellent city maps of Paris and Lyon. Michelin's green-jacketed *Environs de*

963

LEGAL AGE

Age of majority 18
Buying alcohol 18
Driving 18
Minor under anti-pornography & prostitution laws under 18
Sexual consent 15 (for everyone)
Voting 18

Paris and *Banlieue de Paris* maps (€4.50) help with the confusing drive into and out of Paris. The yellow-orange 1:200,000-scale regional maps (€6.50) are perfect for cross-country driving. If you are covering more than a few regions, the national *Atlas Routier France* (€16) is better value.

Money

A guide to costs and exchange rates (at time of publication) can be found on p15.

ATMs

Automated Teller Machines (ATMs) – known as *distributeurs automatiques de billets* (DAB) or *points d'argent*

DRUGS & ALCOHOL

» French law does not distinguish between 'hard' and 'soft' drugs.

» The penalty for any personal use of *stupéfiants* (including cannabis, amphetamines, ecstasy and heroin) can be a one-year jail sentence and a €3750 fine but, depending on the circumstances, it might be anything from a stern word to a compulsory rehab program.

» Importing, possessing, selling or buying drugs can get you up to 10 years' prison and a fine of up to €500,000.

» Police have been known to search chartered coaches, cars and train passengers for drugs just because they're coming from Amsterdam.

» *Ivresse* (drunkeness) in public is punishable by a €150 fine.

in French – are the cheapest and most convenient way to get money. ATMs connected to international networks are situated in all cities and towns and usually offer an excellent exchange rate.

Cash

You always get a better exchange rate in-country but it is a good idea to arrive in France with enough euros to take a taxi to a hotel if you have to.

Credit & Debit Cards

» Credit and debit cards, accepted almost everywhere in France, are convenient, relatively secure and usually offer a better exchange rate than travellers cheques or cash exchanges.

» Credit cards issued in France have embedded chips – you have to type in a PIN to make a purchase.

» Visa, MasterCard and Amex can be used in shops and supermarkets and for train travel, car hire and motorway tolls, though some places (eg 24-hour petrol stations, some autoroute toll machines) only take French-style credit cards with chips and PINs.

» Don't assume that you can pay for a meal or a budget hotel with a credit card – enquire first.

» Cash advances are a supremely convenient way to stay stocked up with euros but getting cash with a credit card involves both fees (sometimes US$10 or more) and interest – ask your credit-card issuer for details. Debit-card fees are usually much less.

LOST CARDS

For lost cards, these numbers operate 24 hours:
Amex (☑01 47 77 72 00)
Diners Club (☑08 10 31 41 59)
MasterCard (☑08 00 90 13 87)
Visa (Carte Bleue; ☑08 00 90 11 79)

Moneychangers

» Commercial banks usually charge a stiff €3 to €5 fee per foreign-currency transaction – if they even bother to offer exchange services any more.

» In Paris and major cities, bureaux de change (exchange bureaux) are faster and easier, open longer hours and often give better rates than banks.

» Some post-office branches exchange travellers cheques and banknotes in a variety of currencies but charge €5 commission for cash; most won't take US$100 bills.

TIPPING

By law, restaurant and bar prices are service compris (include a 15% service charge), so there is no need to leave a pourboire (tip). If you were extremely satisfied with the service, however, you can – as many locals do – show your appreciation by leaving a small 'extra' tip for your waiter or waitress.

WHERE/WHO	CUSTOMARY TIP
bar	round to nearest euro
hotel cleaning staff	€1-1.50 per day
hotel porter	€1-1.50 per bag
restaurant	5-10%
taxi	10-15%
toilet attendant	€0.20-0.50
tour guide	€ 1-2 per person

Travellers Cheques

Travellers cheques, a relic of the 19th and 20th centuries, cannot be used to pay most French merchants directly and so have to be changed into euro banknotes at banks, exchange bureaux or post offices.

Public Holidays

The following jours fériés (public holidays) are observed in France:

New Year's Day (Jour de l'An) 1 January – parties in larger cities; fireworks are subdued by international standards

Easter Sunday & Monday (Pâques & lundi de Pâques) Late March/April

May Day (Fête du Travail) 1 May – traditional parades

Victoire 1945 8 May – commemorates the Allied victory in Europe that ended WWII

Ascension Thursday (Ascension) May – celebrated on the 40th day after Easter

Pentecost/Whit Sunday & Whit Monday (Pentecôte & lundi de Pentecôte) Mid-May to mid-June – celebrated on the seventh Sunday after Easter

Bastille Day/National Day (Fête Nationale) 14 July – the national holiday

Assumption Day (Assomption) 15 August

All Saints' Day (Toussaint) 1 November

Remembrance Day (L'onze novembre) 11 November – marks the WWI armistice

Christmas (Noël) 25 December

The following are not public holidays in France: Shrove Tuesday (Mardi Gras; the first day of Lent); Maundy (or Holy) Thursday and Good Friday, just before Easter; and Boxing Day (26 December).

Note: Good Friday and Boxing Day are public holidays in Alsace.

Safe Travel

France is generally a safe place in which to live and travel but crime has risen dramatically in the last few years. Although property crime is a major problem, it is extremely unlikely that you will be physically assaulted while walking down the street. Always check your government's travel advisory warnings.

The France hunting season runs from September to February. If you see signs reading 'chasseurs' or 'chasse gardée' strung up or tacked to trees, think twice about wandering into the area. As well as millions of wild animals, 25 French hunters die each year after being shot by other hunters. Hunting is traditional and commonplace in all rural areas in France, especially the Vosges, the Sologne, the southwest and the Baie de Somme.

Natural Dangers

» There are powerful tides and strong undertows at many places along the Atlantic Coast, from the Spanish border north to Brittany and Normandy.

» Only swim in *zones de baignade surveillée* (beaches monitored by life guards).

» Be aware of tide times and the high-tide mark if walking or sleeping on a beach.

» Thunderstorms in the mountains and the hot southern plains can be extremely sudden and violent.

» Check the weather report before setting out on a long walk and be prepared for sudden storms and temperature drops if you are heading into the high country of the Alps or Pyrenees.

» Avalanches pose a significant danger in the French Alps.

Theft

Pickpocketing and bag snatching (eg in dense crowds and public places) are prevalent in big cities, particularly Paris, Marseille and Nice. There's no need whatsoever to travel in fear. A few simple precautions will minimise your chances of being ripped off.

» On trains, keep bags as close to you as possible: luggage racks at the ends of carriage are easy prey for thieves; in sleeping compartments, lock the door carefully at night.

» Be especially vigilant for bag-snatchers at train stations, airports, fast-food outlets, outdoor cafés, beaches and on public transport.

» Break-ins to parked cars are a widespread problem. Never, ever leave anything valuable – or not valuable – inside your car, even in the boot (trunk).

» Aggressive theft from cars stopped at red lights is occasionally a problem, especially in Marseille and Nice. As a precaution, lock your car doors and roll up the windows.

Telephone
Mobile Phones

» French mobile phone numbers begin with ☐06 or ☐07.

» France uses GSM 900/1800, which is compatible with the rest of Europe and Australia but not with the North American GSM 1900 or the totally different system in Japan (though some North Americans have tri-band phones that work here).

» Check with your service provider about roaming charges – dialling a mobile phone from a fixed-line phone or another mobile can be incredibly expensive.

» It may be cheaper to buy your own French SIM card – and locals you meet are much more likely to ring you if your number is French.

» If you already have a compatible phone, you can slip in a SIM card (€20 to €30) and rev it up with prepaid credit, though this is likely to run out fast as domestic prepaid calls cost about €0.50 per minute.

» Recharge cards are sold at most *tabacs* and newsagents.

» SIMs are available at the ubiquitous outlets run by France's three mobile phone companies, **Bouygues** (www.bouyguestelecom.fr), France Telecom's **Orange** (www.orange.com) and **SFR** (www.sfr.com, in French).

Phone Codes

Calling France from abroad Dial your country's international access code, then ☐33 (France's country code), then the 10-digit local number *without* the initial zero.

Calling internationally from France Dial ☐00 (the international access code), the *indicatif* (country code), the area code (without the initial zero if there is one) and the local number. Some country codes are posted in public telephones.

Directory inquiries For France Telecom's *service des renseignements* (directory inquiries) dial ☑11 87 12. Not all operators speak English. For help in English with all France Telecom's services, see www.france telecom.com or call ☑09 69 36 39 00.

Emergency numbers Can be dialled from public phones without a phonecard. See p15 for important numbers.

Hotel calls Hotels, *gîtes*, hostels and *chambres d'hôte* are free to meter their calls as they like. The surcharge is usually around €0.30 per minute but can be higher.

International directory inquiries For numbers outside France, dial ☑11 87 00.

Phonecards

» For explanations in English and other languages on how to use a public telephone, push the button engraved with a two-flags icon.

» For both international and domestic calling, most public phones operate using either a credit card or two kinds of *télécartes* (phonecards): *cartes à puce* (cards with a magnetic chip) issued by France Télécom and sold at post offices for €8 or €15; and *cartes à code* (cards where you dial a free access number and then the card's scratch-off code), sold at *tabacs*, newsagents and post offices.

» Phonecards with codes offer *much* better international rates than France Télécom chip cards or Country Direct services (for which you are billed at home by your long-distance carrier).

» The shop you buy a phonecard from should be able to tell you which type is best for the country you want to call. Using phonecards from a home phone is much

cheaper that using them from public phones or mobile phones.

Tariffs

Additional charges may apply when calling from a hotel phone or mobile (cell) phone.

NUMBER	PER MINUTE
☑08 00	free
☑08 05	free
☑08 10	same as a local call
☑08 20	€0.12
☑08 21	€0.12
☑08 25	€0.15
☑08 26	€0.15
☑08 92	€0.34
☑11 87 12 (directory inquiries)	€1 per call, then €0.23 per minute
☑11 87 00 (international directory inquiries)	€2-3

Time

France uses the 24-hour clock and is on Central European Time, which is one hour ahead of GMT/UTC. During daylight-saving time, which runs from the last Sunday in March to the last Sunday in October, France is two hours ahead of GMT/UTC.

The following times do not take daylight saving into account.

CITY	NOON IN PARIS
Auckland	11pm
Berlin	noon
Cape Town	noon
London	11am
New York	6am
San Francisco	3am
Sydney	9pm
Tokyo	8pm

Toilets

Public toilets, signposted WC or *toilettes*, are not always plentiful in France, especially outside of the big cities.

Love them (as a sci-fi geek) or loathe them (as a claustrophobe), France's 24-hour self-cleaning toilets are here to stay. Outside of Paris – where they are free – these mechanical WCs cost around €0.50 a go. Don't even think about nipping in after someone else to avoid paying unless you fancy a *douche* (shower) with disinfectant. There is no time for dawdling either: you have precisely 15 minutes before being (ooh-la-la!) exposed to passers-by. Green means *libre* (vacant) and red means *occupé* (occupied).

Some older establishments and motorway stops still have the hole-in-the-floor *toilettes à la turque* (squat toilets). Provided you hover, these are actually very hygienic, but take care not to get soaked by the flush.

Keep some loose change handy for tipping toilet attendants, who keep a hawk-like eye on many of France's public toilets.

The French are more blasé about unisex toilets than elsewhere, so save your blushes when tiptoeing past the urinals to reach the ladies' loo.

Tourist Information

Almost every city, town, village and hamlet has an *office de tourisme* (a tourist office run by some unit of local government) or *syndicat d'initiative* (a tourist office run by an organisation of local merchants). Both are excellent resources and can supply you with local maps as well as details on accommodation, restaurants and activities. If you have a special interest such as walking,

ALSACE
67 Bas-Rhin
68 Haut-Rhin

AQUITAINE
24 Dordogne
33 Gironde
40 Landes
47 Lot-et-Garonne
64 Pyrénées-Atlantiques

AUVERGNE
03 Allier
15 Cantal
43 Haute-Loire
63 Puy-de-Dôme

BASSE-NORMANDIE
14 Calvados
50 Manche
61 Orne

BOURGOGNE
21 Côte-d'Or
58 Nièvre
71 Saône-et-Loire
89 Yonne

BRETAGNE
22 Côte-d'Armor
29 Finistère
35 Ille-et-Vilaine
56 Morbihan

CENTRE
18 Cher
28 Eure-et-Loir
36 Indre
37 Indre-et-Loire
45 Loiret
41 Loir-et-Cher

CHAMPAGNE-ARDENNE
08 Ardennes
10 Aube
51 Marne
52 Haute-Marne

CORSE
2A Corse-du-Sud
2B Haute-Corse

FRANCHE-COMTÉ
25 Doubs
39 Jura
70 Haute-Saône
90 Territoire de Belfort

HAUTE-NORMANDIE
27 Eure
76 Seine-Maritime

ÎLE-DE-FRANCE
91 Essonne
92 Haut-de-Seine
75 Paris
78 Seine-et-Marne
93 Seine-St-Denis
94 Val-de-Marne
95 Val-d'Oise
77 Yvelines

LANGUEDOC-ROUSSILLON
11 Aude
30 Gard
34 Hérault
48 Lozère
66 Pyrénées-Orientales

LIMOUSIN
19 Corrèze
23 Creuse
87 Haute-Vienne

LORRAINE
54 Meurthe-et-Moselle
55 Meuse
57 Moselle
88 Vosges

MIDI-PYRÉNÉES
09 Ariège
12 Aveyron
32 Gers
31 Haute-Garonne
65 Hautes-Pyrénées
46 Lot
81 Tarn
82 Tarn-et-Garonne

NORD-PAS-DE-CALAIS
59 Nord
62 Pas-de-Calais

PAYS DE LA LOIRE
44 Loire-Atlantique
49 Maine-et-Loire
53 Mayenne
72 Sarthe
85 Vendée

PICARDIE
02 Aisne
60 Oise
80 Somme

POITOU-CHARENTES
16 Charente
17 Charente-Maritime
79 Deux-Sèvres
86 Vienne

PROVENCE-ALPES-CÔTE D'AZUR
04 Alpes-de-Haute-Provence
06 Alpes-Maritimes
13 Bouches-du-Rhône
05 Hautes-Alpes
83 Var
84 Vaucluse

RHÔNE-ALPES
01 Ain
07 Ardèche
26 Drôme
74 Haute-Savoie
38 Isère
42 Loire
69 Rhône
73 Savoie

International Boundary
Région Boundary
Département Boundary

0 — 200 km
0 — 120 miles

UNITED KINGDOM

English Channel (La Manche)

62 NORD-PAS-DE-CALAIS

BELGIUM

GERMANY

LUXEMBOURG

76 HAUTE-NORMANDIE
80 PICARDIE
60
Paris
02
08

50
14
Rouen
75

BASSE-NORMANDIE
27
92 95 93
94
LORRAINE
55
57
67
Strasbourg
ALSACE

29 22 BRETAGNE
35
72
77 ÎLE-DE-FRANCE 78
CHAMPAGNE-ARDENNE
10
52
88
68

56
PAYS DE LA LOIRE
41
45
89
21
70 90
FRANCHE-COMTÉ

44 49
37
CENTRE
18
58
BOURGOGNE
Dijon
25

Nantes
85
79
86
36
71
39
SWITZERLAND

POITOU-CHARENTES
03
01
74

17
16
87 23
LIMOUSIN
42 69 Lyon
RHÔNE-ALPES
73

19
AUVERGNE
15
43
38
ITALY

33
Bordeaux
AQUITAINE
24
07
26
05

47
46
48
04
06
Nice

40
82
12
30
84
PROVENCE-ALPES-CÔTE D'AZUR
13
83
MONACO

Bay of Biscay

CORSE (Corsica)
2B
2A

MIDI-PYRÉNÉES
32
81
34
Toulouse
LANGUEDOC-ROUSSILLON
Marseille

64
31
11
65
09
66
Mediterranean Sea

SPAIN

ANDORRA

cycling, architecture or wine sampling, ask about it.

In this book tourist office details appear under Information at the end of each city, town or area listing.

» Many tourist offices make local hotel and B&B reservations, sometimes for a nominal fee. Some have limited currency-exchange services.

» *Comités régionaux de tourisme* (CRTs; regional tourist boards), their *départemental* analogues (CDTs), and their websites are a superb source of information and hyperlinks.

» French government tourist offices (usually called Maisons de la France) provide every imaginable sort of tourist information on France.

» Useful websites:

French Government Tourist Office (www.franceguide.com) The low-down on sights, activities, transport and special interest holidays in all of France's regions. Brochures can be downloaded online. There are links to country-specific websites.

Réseau National des Destinations Départementales (www.fncdt.net, in French) Find CRT (regional

tourist board) websites here.

Travellers with Disabilities

While France presents evident challenges for *handicapés* (people with disabilities) – namely cobblestone, café-lined streets that are a nightmare to navigate in a wheelchair, a lack of kerb ramps, older public facilities and many budget hotels without lifts – don't let that stop you from visiting. With a little careful planning, you can enjoy a hassle-free accessible stay.

The Paris metro, most of it built decades ago, is hopeless, but you will be pleased to know that taxi drivers are obliged by law to assist and accept passengers with disabilities (and their guide dogs, where relevant). Choose central accommodation to avoid spending a small fortune on taxi fares.

Whether you are looking for wheelchair-friendly accommodation, sights, attractions or restaurants, these associations and agencies should be able to point you in the right direction:

Accès Plus Transilien (☑08 10 64 64 64; www.

infomobi.com, in French) Has comprehensive information on accessible travel in Paris.

Access Travel (☑in UK 01942-888 844; www.access-travel.co.uk) Specialised UK-based agency for accessible travel.

Association des Paralysés de France (APF; www.apf.asso.fr, in French) National organisation for people with disabilities, with offices in every region in France.

Centre du Service Accès Plus (☑08 90 64 06 50; www.accessibilite.sncf.fr, in French) Can advise on station accessibility and arrange a *fauteuil roulant* (wheelchair) or help getting on or off a train.

Mobile en Ville (www.mobile-en-ville.asso.fr, in French) Works to make Paris wheelchair accessible and publishes *Paris Comme sur les Roulettes,* which showcases 20 tours of the city.

Paris Convention & Visitors Bureau (http://en.parisinfo.com) Has information and brochures on accessible Paris.

Tourisme et Handicaps (www.tourisme-handicaps.org, in French) Issues the 'Tourisme et Handicap' label to tourist sites, restaurants and hotels that comply with

---

ACCESSIBILITY INFORMATION

» SNCF's French-language booklet *Guide des Voyageurs Handicapés et à Mobilité Réduite,* available at train stations, gives details of rail access for people with disabilities.

» Michelin's *Guide Rouge* uses icons to indicate hotels with lifts (elevators) and facilities that make them at least partly accessible to people with disabilities.

» *Handitourisme* (€16), a national guide in French, is published by **Petit Futé** (www.petitfute.fr, in French).

» www.jaccede.com (in French) has loads of information and reviews.

» *Access in Paris* is a useful guide published by **Access Project** (www.accessproject-phsp.org) and can be downloaded as PDF files.

» **Gîtes de France** (www.gites-de-france.com) can provide details of accessible *gîtes ruraux* and *chambres d'hôte* (search the website with the term 'disabled access').

» **France Guide** (www.franceguide.com) has a dedicated 'special needs' area with lots of info for travellers with disabilities.

strict accessibility and usability standards. Different symbols indicate the sort of access afforded to people with physical, mental, hearing and/or visual disabilities.

Tourism for All (☑in UK 0845-124 9971; www.tourismforall.info) A UK-based group that provides tips and information for travellers with disabilities.

Visas

For up-to-date details on visa requirements, see the website of the **French Foreign Affairs Ministry** (www.diplomatie.gouv.fr) and click 'Going to France'. Tourist visas *cannot* be extended except in emergencies (such as medical problems). When your visa expires you'll need to leave and reapply from outside France.

Visa Requirements

» EU nationals and citizens of Iceland, Norway and Switzerland need only a passport or a national identity card in order to enter France and stay in the country, even for stays of over 90 days. However, citizens of new EU member states may be subject to various limitations on living and working in France.

» Citizens of Australia, the USA, Canada, Hong Kong, Israel, Japan, Malaysia, New Zealand, Singapore, South Korea and many Latin American countries do not need visas to visit France as tourists for up to 90 days. For long stays of over 90 days, contact your nearest French embassy or consulate and begin your application well in advance as it can take months.

» Other people wishing to come to France as tourists have to apply for a **Schengen Visa**, named after the agreements that abolished passport controls between 15 European countries. It allows unlimited travel throughout the entire zone

for a 90-day period. Apply to the consulate of the country you are entering first, or your main destination. Among other things, you will need travel and repatriation insurance and be able to show that you have sufficient funds to support yourself.

» Tourist visas cannot be changed into student visas after arrival. However, short-term visas are available for students sitting university-entrance exams in France.

Carte de Séjour

» EU passport-holders and citizens of Switzerland, Iceland and Norway do not need a *carte de séjour* (residence permit) to reside or work in France.

» Nationals of other countries with long-stay visas must contact the local *mairie* (city hall) or *préfecture* (prefecture) to apply for a *carte de séjour*. Usually, you are required to do so within eight days of arrival in France. Make sure you have all the necessary documents before you arrive.

» Students of all nationalities studying in Paris must apply for a *carte de séjour* either through their university (if the option exists) or at the Centre des Étudiants Étrangers in Paris; see the website of Paris' **Préfecture de Police** (www.prefecture-police-paris.interieur.gouv.fr, in French) for more information.

Working Holiday Visa

Citizens of Australia, Canada, Japan and New Zealand aged between 18 and 30 are eligible for a 12-month, multiple-entry Working Holiday Visa (*Permis Vacances Travail*), allowing combined tourism and employment in France.

» Apply to the embassy or consulate in your home country. Do this early as there are annual quotas.

» You must be applying for a Working Holiday Visa for France for the first time.

» You will need comprehensive travel insurance for the duration of your stay.

» You must meet all health and character requirements.

» You will need a return plane ticket and proof of sufficient funds (usually around (€2100) to get you through the start of your stay.

» Once you have arrived in France and have found a job, you must apply for an *autorisation provisoire de travail* (temporary work permit), which will only be valid for the duration of the employment offered. The permit can be renewed under the same conditions up to the limit of the authorised length of stay.

» You can also study or do training programs but the visa cannot be extended, nor can it turned into a student visa.

» After one year you *must* go home.

» Once in France, the **Centre d'Information et Documentation Jeunesse** (CIDJ; www.cidj.com) can help with information.

Volunteering

Websites like **www.volunteerabroad.com** and **www.transitionsabroad.com** throw up a colourful selection of volunteering opportunities in France: helping out on a family farm in the Alps, restoring an historic monument in Provence or participating in a summertime archaeological excavation are but some of the golden opportunities awaiting those keen to volunteer their skills and services.

Interesting volunteer organisations:

Club du Vieux Manoir (http://clubduvieuxmanoir.asso.fr, in French) Restore a medieval fortress, an abbey or a historic château at a summer work camp.

Conservation Corps (www.geovisions.org) Volunteer 15 hours a week to teach a French family English in exchange for room and board.

Rempart (www.rempart. com) Brings together 170 organisations countrywide committed to preserving France's religious, military, civil, industrial and natural heritage.

Volunteers for Peace (www.vfp.org) USA-based nonprofit organisation. Can link you up with a voluntary service project dealing with social work, the environment, education or the arts.

World Wide Opportunities on Organic Farms (WWOOF; www.wwoof.org & www.wwoof. fr) Work on a small farm or other organic venture (harvesting chestnuts, renovating an abandoned olive farm near Nice etc).

Work

» EU nationals have an automatic right to work in France.

» Most others will need a hard-to-get work permit, issued at the request of your employer, who will have to show that no one in France – or the entire European Economic Area – can do your job.

» Exceptions may be made for artists, computer engineers and translation specialists.

» Working 'in the black' (that is, without documents) is difficult and risky for non-EU nationals.

» The only instance in which the government might turn a blind eye to workers without documents is during fruit harvests (mid-May to November) and the *vendange* (grape harvest; mid-September to mid- or late October). Though, of course, undocumented workers harvest at their own risk.

» Au-pair work is also very popular and can be done legally even by non-EU citizens. To apply, contact a placement agency at least three months in advance.

Finding Work

EU nationals with the right to work in France can find seasonal and casual work in restaurants, bars and hotels (particularly in the Alps during the winter skiing season). Teaching English is another option, either for a company or through private lessons. Useful websites for finding your dream job include the following:

AJF (www.afj-aupair.org/ apfrance.htm) A reputable source for finding au-pair work in France.

Centre d'Information et de Documentation Jeunesse (CIDJ; www.cidj.com, in French) Provides young people with information on jobs (including seasonal summer jobs), housing, education and more. It has offices all over France.

French Entrée (www.french entree.com) Handy tips on working in France, from preparing a CV to finding a job.

FUSAC (France USA Contacts; www.fusac.fr) Paris-based mag. Advertises jobs for English speakers, including au-pair work, babysitting and language teaching.

Job d'Été (www.jobdete. com, in French) Search for France's hottest summer jobs by region.

Mountain Pub (www.moun tainpub.com) Worth checking for bar and hotel work in the French Alps.

Natives (www.natives.co.uk) *Seasonaire* central for winter and summer seasonal work.

Pôle Emploi (www.pole -emploi.fr, in French) France's national employment service has offices throughout France; the website has job listings.

Season Workers (www.sea sonworkers.com) Search for summer and winter jobs.

Transport

GETTING THERE & AWAY

Flights, tours and rail tickets can be booked online at lonelyplanet.com/bookings.

Entering the Country

Entering France from other parts of the EU is usually a breeze – no border checkpoints and no customs – thanks to the Schengen agreement, signed by all of France's neighbours except the UK, the Channel Islands and Andorra. For these three entities, old-fashioned document and customs checks are still the norm, at least when exiting France (when entering France in the case of Andorra).

Air

Paris' Charles de Gaulle airport is the second-busiest in Europe, after London's Heathrow.

Smaller provincial airports with international flights, mainly to/from the UK, continental Europe and North Africa, include Angoulême, Paris-Beauvais (Beauvais-

Tillé), Bergerac, Béziers, Biarritz, Brest, Brive-Vallée de la Dordogne, Caen, Carcassonne, Deauville, Dinard, Grenoble, La Rochelle, Le Touquet, Limoges, Montpellier, Nîmes, Pau, Perpignan, Poitiers, Rennes, Rodez, St-Étienne, Toulon and Tours. Relevant local airports, including those on Corsica, are listed in destination chapters.

International Airports

Charles de Gaulle (Roissy) (www.aeroportsdeparis.fr)

Orly (www.aeroportsde paris.fr)

Bordeaux (www.bordeaux. aeroport.fr)

Lille (www.lille.aeroport.fr)

Lyon (www.lyon.aeroport.fr)

Marseille (www.mrsairport. com)

Mulhouse-Basel-Freiburg (EuroAirport) (www.euro airport.com, www.fly-euroair port.com)

Nantes (www.nantes.aero port.fr)

Nice (www.nice.aeroport.fr)

Strasbourg (www.stras bourg.aeroport.fr)

Toulouse (www.toulouse. aeroport.fr)

Bicycle

Getting a bicycle to France is a breeze.

On **Eurotunnel shuttle trains** (☑for bicycle reservations Mon-Fri 01303-282 201 in the UK; www.eurotunnel. com) through the Channel Tunnel, the fee for a bicycle, including its rider, is UK£16 one-way.

A bike that's been dismantled so it's the size of a suitcase can be carried on board a **Eurostar train** (☑reservations in UK 0844-822 5822; www.eurostar.com) from London or Brussels just like any other luggage. Otherwise, there's a UK£20 charge and you'll need advance reservations. For links relevant to taking your bike on other international trains to France, see www.railpas senger.info.

On ferries, foot passengers – where allowed – can usually (but not always) bring along a bicycle for no charge.

European Bike Express (☑in UK 01430-422 111; www. bike-express.co.uk) transports cyclists and their bikes from the UK to places around France.

Bus

Eurolines (☑08 92 89 90 91; www.eurolines.eu), a grouping of 32 long-haul coach operators (including the UK's National Express), links France with cities all across Europe and in Morocco and Russia. Discounts are available to people under 26 and over 60. It's a good idea to make advance reservations, especially in July and August.

The standard Paris–London fare is €46 (€57 including high-season supplements) but the trip – including a Channel crossing either by ferry or the Chunnel – can cost as little as €15 if you book 45 days ahead.

Car & Motorcycle

A right-hand-drive vehicle brought to France from the UK or Ireland must have deflectors affixed to the headlights to avoid dazzling oncoming traffic. In the UK, information on driving in France is available from the **RAC** (www.rac.co.uk/driving -abroad/france) and the **AA** (www.theaa.com/motoring _advice/overseas).

Police searches are not uncommon for vehicles entering France, particularly from Spain and Belgium (via which drugs from Morocco or the Netherlands can enter France). See p977 for details about driving in France.

A foreign motor vehicle entering France must display a sticker or licence plate identifying its country of registration.

EUROTUNNEL

The Channel Tunnel (Chunnel), inaugurated in 1994, is the first dry-land link between England and France since the last ice age.

High-speed **Eurotunnel shuttle trains** (✆ in UK 08443-35 35 35, in France 08 10 63 03 04; www.eurotunnel. com) whisk bicycles, motorcycles, cars and coaches from Folkestone through the Channel Tunnel to Coquelles, 5km southwest of Calais, in air-conditioned and soundproofed comfort in just 35 minutes. Shuttles run 24 hours a day, every day of the year, with up to three departures an hour during peak periods. LPG and CNG tanks are not permitted, so gas-powered cars and many campers and caravans have to travel by ferry.

Eurotunnel sets its fares the way budget airlines do: the further in advance you book and the lower the demand for a particular crossing, the less you pay; same-day fares can cost a small fortune. Standard fares for a car, including up to nine passengers, start at UK£53.

SAMPLE TRAIN FARES

ROUTE	FULL FARE (€)	DURATION (HR)
Amsterdam-Paris	79	3¼
Barcelona-Montpellier	57	4½
Berlin-Paris	238	8
Brussels-Paris	44-64	1½
Frankfurt-Paris	106	4
Geneva-Lyon	25	2
Geneva-Marseille	65	3½
Vienna-Strasbourg	149	9

Train

Rail services – including a dwindling number of overnight services to/from Spain, Italy and Germany – link France with virtually every country in Europe. For details on train travel within France, see p980.

You can book tickets and get train information from **Rail Europe** (www.raileurope. com). In France ticketing is handled by **SNCF** (✆ in France 36 35, from abroad +33-8 92 35 35 35; www.sncf. com); telephone and internet bookings are possible but they won't post tickets outside France.

For details on Europe's 200,000km rail network, see www.railpassenger. info, set up by a grouping of European rail companies. Information on 'seamless high-speed rail travel' between France and the UK, Belgium, the Netherlands, Germany and Austria is available from www.rail team.co.uk and www.tgv -europe.com.

Certain rail services between France and its continental neighbours are marketed under a number of peculiar brand names:
Artésia (www.artesia.eu) Serves Italian cities such as Milan and, overnight, Venice, Florence and Rome.

Elipsos (www.elipsos.com) Luxurious 'train-hotel' services to Spain.
TGV Lyria (www.tgv-lyria.fr) To Switzerland.
Thalys (www.thalys.com) Links Paris Gare du Nord with destinations such as Bruxelles-Midi (82 minutes), Amsterdam CS (three hours and 20 minutes) and Cologne's Hauptbahnhof (3¼ hours).

A very useful train-travel resource is the information-packed website **The Man in Seat 61** (www.seat61.com).

EURAIL PASS

In general, rail passes are worthwhile only if you plan to really clock up the kilometres.

Available only to people who don't live in Europe, the **Eurail Pass** (www.eurail.com) is valid in up to 21 countries, including France. People 25 and under get the best deals. Other benefits include a 'passholder' discount on the London–Paris Eurostar (one-way/return €89/150 or UK£57/100) and 30% off the adult pedestrian fare for Irish Ferries crossings between Ireland and France (make sure you book ahead). Passes must be validated at a train-station ticket window before you begin your first journey.

EUROSTAR

The highly civilised **Eurostar** (☑in UK 08432-186 186, in France 08 92 35 35 39; www.eurostar.com) whisks you from London to Paris in an incredible 2¼ hours, with easy onward connections to destinations all over France.

Except late at night, trains link London (St Pancras International) with Paris (Gare du Nord; hourly), Calais (Calais-Fréthun; one hour, three daily), Lille (Gare Lille-Europe; 1½ hours, eight daily) and Disneyland Resort Paris (2½ hours, one direct daily), with less frequent services departing from Ebbsfleet and Ashford, both in Kent. Ski trains connect England with the French Alps on weekends from mid-December to mid-April.

Eurostar offers a bewildering array of fares. A fully flexible 2nd-class one-way/return ticket from London to Paris costs a whopping UK£179/309 (€245/435), but super-discount returns go for as little as UK£69.

You'll get the best deals if you buy a return ticket, stay over a Saturday night, book well (ie up to 120 days) in advance – the cheapest fares sell out early – and don't mind nonexchangeability and nonrefundability. Discount fares are available if you're under 26 or over 60 on your departure date. Credit-card purchases (but not debit) incur a fee of UK£3. Student travel agencies may offer youth fares not available directly from Eurostar.

Sea

For a map of ferry routes across the English Channel and the Mediterranean, see the Trains & Ferries map, p976.

Some ferry companies have started setting fares the way budget airlines do: the longer in advance you book and the lower the demand for a particular sailing, the less you pay, with the cheapest tickets costing just a third of the priciest ones. Last-minute tickets are the most expensive. Seasonal demand is a crucial factor (Christmas, Easter, UK and French school holidays, July and August are especially busy), as is the time of day (an early evening ferry can cost much more than one at 4am). People under 25 and over 60 may qualify for discounts.

To get the best fares, you might want to check out the booking service offered by **Ferry Savers** (☑in UK 0844-371 8021; www.ferrysavers .com); booking by phone incurs a fee.

INTERNATIONAL FERRY COMPANIES

COMPANY	CONNECTION	WEBSITE
Brittany Ferries	England-Normandy, England-Brittany, Ireland-Brittany	www.brittany-ferries.co.uk; www.brittany ferries.ie
Celtic Link Ferries	Ireland-Normandy	www.celticlinkferries.com
Comanav & Comarit	Morocco-France	www.aferry.to/comanav.htm; www.aferry.to/comarit.htm
Condor Ferries	England-Normandy, England-Brittany, Channel Islands-Brittany	www.condorferries.co.uk
CTN	Tunisia-France	www.ctn.com.tn
Irish Ferries	Ireland-Normandy, Ireland-Brittany	www.irishferries.ie; www.shamrock-irlande.com, in French
LD Lines	England-Channel Ports, England-Normandy	www.ldlines.co.uk
Manche Îles Express	Channel Islands-Normandy	www.manche-iles-express.com
Norfolk Line	England-Channel Ports	www.norfolkline.com
P&O Ferries	England-Channel Ports	www.poferries.com
SeaFrance	England-Channel Ports	www.seafrance.com
SNCM	Algeria-France, Sardinia-France, Tunisia-France	www.sncm.fr
Transmanche Ferries	England-Normandy	www.transmancheferries.com

Foot passengers are not allowed on any Dover–Boulogne, Dover–Dunkirk or Dover–Calais car ferries except for daytime (and, from Calais to Dover, evening) crossings run by P&O Ferries. On ferries that do allow foot passengers, taking a bicycle is often (but not always) free.

Several ferry companies ply the waters between Corsica and Italy. For details, see p870.

GETTING AROUND

Driving is the simplest way to get around France but a car is a liability in traffic-plagued, parking-starved city centres, and those petrol bills and *autoroute* (dual carriageway/divided highway) tolls can really add up.

France is famous for its truly excellent public-transport network, which serves every corner of the land except some rural areas. In addition to its environmental benefits, travelling by train, metro, tram and bus lets you experience France the way many ordinary French people do, taking in the sights, encountering the unexpected, and meeting locals at a pace set by the rhythm of day-to-day life.

The state-owned Société Nationale des Chemins de Fer Français (SNCF) takes care of almost all land transport between *départements* (administrative divisions of

France). Transport within *départements* is handled by a combination of short-haul trains, SNCF buses and local bus companies that are either government owned or government contracted.

Domestic air travel has been partly deregulated but smaller carriers still struggle.

Air

France's vaunted high-speed train network has made rail travel between some cities (eg from Paris to Lyon and Marseille) faster and easier than flying.

Airlines in France

Air France (☑36 54; www.airfrance.com) and its subsidiaries **Brit Air** (☑36 54; www.britair.fr) and **Régional** (☑36 54; www.regional.com) continue to control the lion's share of France's long-protected domestic airline industry.

Significant discounts are available to:

» people aged 12 to 24 (26 and under for students)

» people over 60

» couples who are married or can prove they live together

» parents or grandparents travelling with at least one child or grandchild aged 12 to 25 (27 in the case of students).

Good deals can also be had if:

» you buy your ticket well in advance (at least 42 days ahead for the very best deals)

» stay over a Saturday night

» don't mind tickets that can't be changed or reimbursed.

The Air France website posts special last-minute offers.

Budget carriers offering flights within France include **EasyJet** (www.easyjet.com), **Airlinair** (www.airlinair.com), **Twin Jet** (www.twinjet.net) and **CCM** (www.aircorsica.com).

For more information on flights to Corsica, see p869.

Bicycle

France is generally a great place to cycle. Not only is much of the countryside drop-dead gorgeous, but the country has a growing number of urban and rural *pistes cyclables* (bike paths and lanes; see www.voiesvertes.com, in French) and an extensive network of secondary and tertiary roads with relatively light traffic. One pitfall: back roads rarely have proper shoulders so consulting local cyclists (eg at bike shops) when choosing your route, and wearing a fluorescent reflective vest, is highly recommended.

French law requires that bicycles must have two functioning brakes, a bell, a red reflector on the back and yellow reflectors on the pedals. After sunset and when vis-

---

CLIMATE CHANGE & TRAVEL

Every form of transport that relies on carbon-based fuel generates CO_2, the main cause of human-induced climate change. Modern travel is dependent on aeroplanes, which might use less fuel per kilometre per person than most cars but travel much greater distances. The altitude at which aircraft emit gases (including CO_2) and particles also contributes to their climate change impact. Many websites offer 'carbon calculators' that allow people to estimate the carbon emissions generated by their journey and, for those who wish to do so, to offset the impact of the greenhouse gases emitted with contributions to portfolios of climate-friendly initiatives throughout the world. Lonely Planet offsets the carbon footprint of all staff and author travel.

ibility is poor, cyclists must turn on a white headlamp and a red tail lamp. When being overtaken by a vehicle, cyclists are required to ride in single file. Towing children in a bike trailer is permitted.

Never leave your bicycle locked up outside overnight if you want to see it – or at least most of its parts – again. Some hotels offer enclosed bicycle parking.

See p957 for cycling organisations.

Transportation

The SNCF does its best to make travelling with a bicycle easy and even has a special website for cyclists, www. velo.sncf.com (in French).

Bicycles (not disassembled) can be taken along on virtually all intraregional TER trains and most long-distance intercity trains, subject to space availability. There's no charge on TER and Corail Intercité trains but TGV, Téoz and Lunéa trains require a €10 reservation fee that must be made when you purchase your passenger ticket. Bike reservations can be made by phone (☎36 35) or at an SNCF ticket office but not via the internet.

Bicycles that have been partly disassembled and put in a box (housse), with maximum dimensions of 120cm by 90cm, can be taken along for no charge in the baggage compartments of TGV, Téoz, Lunéa and Corail Intercité trains.

In the Paris area, bicycles are allowed aboard Transilien and RER trains except Monday to Friday in the following times:

» 6.30am to 9am for trains heading into Paris
» 4.30pm to 7pm for trains travelling out of Paris
» 6am to 9am and 4.30pm to 7pm on RER lines A and B

With precious few exceptions, bicycles are not allowed on metros, trams and local, intra-département

and SNCF buses (the latter replace trains on some runs).

Bike Rental

Most French cities and towns have at least one bike shop or municipal sports complex that rents out vélos tout terrains (mountain bikes; generally €10 to €20 a day), popularly known as VTTs, as well as more road-oriented vélos tout chemin (VTCs), or cheaper city bikes. You usually have to leave ID and/or a deposit (often a credit-card slip) that you forfeit if the bike is damaged or stolen. Some cities, such as Strasbourg and La Rochelle, have inexpensive rental agencies run by the municipality. For details on rental options, see Getting Around under city and town listings throughout this book.

A growing number of cities – most famously Paris and Lyon, but also Aix-en-Provence, Amiens, Besançon, Caen, Dijon, La Rochelle, Marseille, Montpellier, Mulhouse, Nancy, Nantes, Orléans, Perpignan, Rennes, Rouen and Toulouse – have automatic bike-rental systems, intended to encourage cycling as a form of urban transport, with computerised pick-up and drop-off sites all over town. In general, you have to sign up either short term or long term, providing credit-card details, and can then use the bikes for no charge for the first half-hour; after that, hourly charges rise quickly. For details on Paris' Vélib' system, see p131.

If you'll be doing lots of cycling but don't want to bring your bike from home, it may be worthwhile to buy a VTT (prices start at around €250) and resell it at the end of your trip for around two-thirds of its purchase price, something that's possible at certain bike shops.

Boat

For information on boat services along France's coasts

and to offshore islands, see individual town and city sections.

Canal Boating

Transportation and tranquillity are usually mutually exclusive – but not if you rent a houseboat and cruise along France's canals and navigable rivers, stopping at whim to pick up supplies, dine at a village restaurant or check out a local château by bicycle. Changes in altitude are taken care of by a system of écluses (locks).

Boats generally accommodate from two to 12 passengers and are fully outfitted with bedding and cooking facilities. Anyone over 18 can pilot a riverboat but first-time skippers are given a short instruction session so they qualify for a carte de plaisance (a temporary cruising permit). The speed limit is 6km/h on canals and 8km/h on rivers.

Prices start at around €450 a week for a small boat and can top €3000 a week for a large, luxurious craft. Except in July and August, you can often rent over a weekend (Friday to Monday; from €280) or from Monday to Friday.

Advance reservations are essential for holiday periods, over long weekends and in July and August, especially for larger boats.

Online rental agencies:

Canal Boat Holidays (www.canalboatholidays.com)
H2olidays (Barging in France; www.barginginfrance.com)
Worldwide River Cruise (www.worldwide-river-cruise.com)

See also destination chapters for more information on canal boating in individual regions.

Bus

Buses are widely used for short-distance travel within départements, especially in

NON-TGV PARIS DEPARTURE STATIONS

Gare du Nord
Gare de l'Est
Gare de Lyon
Gare d'Austerlitz
Gare Montparnasse
Gare St-Lazare

TGV LINES & DEPARTURE STATIONS

TGV Fast Track	TGV Non-Fast Track	
		TGV Nord, Thalys & Eurostar – departure from Gare du Nord
		TGV Atlantique Sud-Ouest & TGV Atlantique Ouest – departure from Gare Montparnasse
		TGV Sud-Est & TGV Midi-Mediterranée – departure from Gare de Lyon
		TGV Est Européen – departure from Gare de l'Est
		Normal SNCF track

rural areas with relatively few train lines (eg Brittany and Normandy). Unfortunately, services in some regions are infrequent and slow, in part because they were designed to get children to their schools in the towns rather than transport visitors around the countryside.

Over the years, certain uneconomical train lines have been replaced by SNCF buses, which, unlike regional buses, are free if you've got a rail pass.

Eurolines may soon be permitted to transport passengers between cities within France.

Car & Motorcycle

Having your own wheels gives you exceptional freedom and makes it easy to visit more remote parts of France. Unfortunately driving can be expensive. For example, by autoroute, the 925km drive from Paris to Nice (nine hours of driving) in a small car costs about €70 for petrol and €69 for tolls – by comparison, a one-way, 2nd-class TGV ticket for the 5½-hour Paris to Nice run costs €41 to €165 per person. Also, in the cities, traffic and finding a place to park are frequently a major headache. During holiday periods and over long weekends, roads throughout France also get backed up with traffic jams (bouchons).

Motorcyclists will find France great for touring, with winding roads of good quality and lots of stunning scenery. Just make sure your wet-weather gear is up to scratch.

France (along with Belgium) has the densest highway network in Europe. There are four types of inter-city roads:

Autoroutes (highway names beginning with A) Multilane divided highways, usually (except near Calais and Lille) with tolls (péages). Generously outfitted with rest stops.

Routes Nationales (N, RN) National highways. Some sections have divider strips.

Routes Départementales (D) Local highways and roads.

Routes Communales (C, V) Minor rural roads.

Information on autoroute tolls, rest areas, traffic and weather is available from www.autoroutes.fr. Bison Futé (www.bison-fute.equipement.gouv.fr) is also a good source of information about traffic conditions. The websites www.viamichelin.com and www.mappy.fr (in French) plot itineraries between your departure and arrival points.

Note that theft from cars is a major problem in France, especially in the south – see p965.

Car Hire

To hire a car in France, you'll generally need to be over 21 years old, have had a driving licence for at least a year, and have an international credit card. Drivers under 25 usually have to pay a surcharge (frais jeune conducteur) of €25 to €35 per day.

Car-hire companies provide mandatory third-party liability insurance but things such as collision-damage waivers (CDW, or assurance tous risques) vary greatly from company to company. When comparing rates and conditions (ie the fine print), the most important thing to check is the franchise (deductible/excess), which for a small car is usually around €600 for damage and €800 for theft. With many companies, you can reduce the excess by half, and perhaps to zero, by paying a daily insurance supplement of €10 to €16. Your credit card may cover CDW if you use it to pay for the rental but the car-hire company won't know anything about this – verify conditions and details with your credit-card issuer to be sure.

Arranging your car hire or fly/drive package before you leave home is usually considerably cheaper than a walk-in rental, but beware of website offers that don't include a CDW or you may be liable for up to 100% of the car's value.

International car-hire companies:

Avis (☎08 21 23 07 60; www.avis.com)

Budget (☎08 25 00 35 64; www.budget.com or www.budget.fr, in French)

Easycar (☎in UK 08710 500 444; www.easycar.com)

Europcar (☎08 25 35 83 58; www.europcar.com or www.europcar.fr, in French)

Hertz (www.hertz.com or www.hertz.fr, in French)

National-Citer (www.nationalcar.com or www.citer.fr)

Sixt (☎08 20 00 74 98; www.sixt.fr, in French)

French car-hire companies:

ADA (www.ada.fr, in French)

DLM (www.dlm.fr, in French)

France Cars (www.francecars.fr, in French)

Locauto (www.locauto.fr)

Renault Rent (☎08 25 10 11 12; www.renault-rent.com, in French)

Rent-a-Car Système (☎08 91 70 02 00; www.rentacar.fr)

Deals can be found on the internet and through companies such as the following:

Auto Europe (☎in USA 1-888-223-5555; www.autoeurope.com)

DriveAway Holidays (☎in Australia 1300 723 972; www.driveaway.com.au)

Holiday Autos (☎in UK 0871-472 5229; www.holidayautos.co.uk)

In this book, car-hire addresses are listed under large cities and towns.

Note that rental cars with automatic transmission are very much the exception in France and will usually need to ordered well in advance.

For insurance reasons, it is usually forbidden to take rental cars on ferries, eg to Corsica.

All rental cars registered in France have a distinctive number on the licence plate, making them easily identifiable – including to thieves, so never leave anything of value in a parked car, even in the boot.

TRANSPORT GETTING AROUND

	Bayonne	Bordeaux	Brest	Caen	Cahors	Calais	Chambéry	Cherbourg	Clermont-Ferrand	Dijon	Grenoble	Lille	Lyon	Marseille	Nantes	Nice	Paris	Perpignan	Strasbourg	Toulouse
Bordeaux	184																			
Brest	811	623																		
Caen	764	568	376																	
Cahors	307	218	788	661																
Calais	164	876	710	339	875															
Chambéry	860	651	120	800	523	834														
Cherbourg	835	647	399	124	743	461	923													
Clermont-Ferrand	564	358	805	566	269	717	295	689												
Dijon	807	619	867	548	378	572	273	671	279											
Grenoble	827	657	1126	806	501	863	56	929	300	302										
Lille	997	809	725	353	808	112	767	476	650	505	798									
Lyon	831	528	1018	698	439	755	103	820	171	194	110	687								
Marseille	700	651	1271	1010	521	1067	344	1132	477	506	273	999	314							
Nantes	513	326	298	292	491	593	780	317	462	656	787	609	618	975						
Nice	858	810	1429	1168	679	1225	410	1291	636	664	337	1157	473	190	1131					
Paris	771	583	596	232	582	289	565	355	424	313	571	222	462	775	384	932				
Perpignan	499	451	1070	998	320	1149	478	1094	441	640	445	1081	448	319	773	476	857			
Strasbourg	1254	1066	1079	730	847	621	496	853	584	335	551	522	488	803	867	804	490	935		
Toulouse	300	247	866	865	116	991	565	890	890	727	533	923	536	407	568	564	699	205	1022	
Tours	536	348	490	246	413	531	611	369	369	418	618	463	449	795	197	952	238	795	721	593

Purchase-Repurchase Plans

If you don't live in the EU and will need a car in France (or Europe) for one to six months (up to one year if you'll be studying), by far the cheapest option is to 'purchase' a new one and then 'sell' it back at the end of your trip. In reality, you pay only for the number of days you have the vehicle but the 'temporary transit' (TT) paperwork means that the car is registered under your name – and that the whole deal is exempt from all sorts of taxes. Lonely Planet authors love these plans!

Companies offering purchase-repurchase (achat-rachat) plans:

Peugeot (Open Europe; www.peugeot-openeurope.com)

Renault (Eurodrive; www.eurodrive.renault.com)

Citroën (Eurocar TT, DriveEurope or EuroPass; www.eurocartt.com, www.citroendriveeurope.com.au or www.citroentt.com)

Eligibility is restricted to people who are not residents of the EU (citizens of EU countries are eligible if they live outside the EU); the minimum age is 18 (in some cases 21). Pricing and special offers depend on your home country. All the plans include unlimited kilometres, 24-hour towing and breakdown service, and comprehensive insurance with absolutely no deductible/excess, so returning the car is hassle-free, even if it's damaged.

Extending your contract (up to a maximum of 165 days) after you start using the car is possible but you'll end up paying about double the prepaid per-day rate.

Purchase-repurchase cars, which have special red licence plates, can be picked up at about three-dozen cities and airports all over France and dropped off at the agency of your choosing. For a fee, you can also pick up or return your car in certain cities outside France.

Driving Licence & Documents

An International Driving Permit (IDP), valid only if accompanied by your original licence, is good for a year and can be issued by your local automobile association before you leave home.

Drivers must carry the following at all times:

» passport or an EU national ID card

» valid driving licence (*permis de conduire;* most foreign licences can be used in France for up to a year)

» car-ownership papers, known as a *carte grise* (grey card)

» proof of third-party liability *assurance* (insurance)

Fuel

Essence (petrol), also known as *carburant* (fuel), costs around €1.40/L (US$7 per US gallon) for 95 unleaded (Sans Plomb 95 or SP95, usually available from a green pump) and €1.30 for diesel (*diesel, gazole* or *gasoil,* usually available from a yellow pump). Filling up *(faire le plein)* is most expensive at autoroute rest stops and often cheapest at hypermarkets.

Many small petrol stations close on Sunday afternoons and, even in cities, it can be hard to find a staffed station open late at night. In general, after-hours purchases (eg at hypermarkets' fully automatic, 24-hour stations) can only be made with a credit card that has an embedded PIN chip, so if all you've got is cash or a magnetic-strip credit card, you could be stuck.

Insurance

Third-party liability insurance *(assurance au tiers)* is compulsory for all vehicles in France, including cars brought in from abroad. Normally, cars registered and insured in other European countries can circulate freely in France, but it's a good idea to contact your insurance company before you leave home to make sure you've got coverage – and to check whom to contact in case of a breakdown or accident.

If you get into a minor accident with no injuries, the easiest way for drivers to sort things out with their insurance companies is to fill out a Constat Aimable d'Accident Automobile (European Accident Statement), a standardised way of recording important details about what happened. In rental cars it's usually in the packet of documents in the glove compartment. Make sure the report includes any information that will help you prove that the accident was not your fault. Remember, if it *was* your fault you may be liable for a hefty insurance deductible/excess. Don't sign anything you don't fully understand. If problems crop up, call the police (☏17).

French-registered cars have details on their insurance company printed on a little green square affixed to the windscreen.

Parking

In city centres, most on-the-street parking places are *payant* (metered) from about 9am to 7pm (sometimes with a break from noon to 2pm) from Monday to Saturday, except bank holidays. Details on places near city centres where parking is free – and without the usual two-hour time limits – appear in the Getting Around sections of many city listings in this book.

Road Rules

Enforcement of French traffic laws (see www.securiteroutiere.gouv.fr, in French) has been stepped up considerably in recent years. Speed cameras are becoming ever more common, as are radar traps, unmarked police vehicles and saliva drug tests. Fines for many infractions are given on the spot, and serious violations can lead to the confiscation of your driving licence and car.

Speed limits outside built-up areas (except where signposted otherwise):

Undivided N and D highways 90km/h (80km/h when raining)

Non-autoroute divided highways 110km/h (100km/h when raining)

PRIORITY TO THE RIGHT

Under the *priorité à droite* ('priority to the right') rule, any car entering an intersection (including a T-junction) from a road (including a tiny village backstreet) on your right has the right-of-way. Locals assume every driver knows this, so don't be surprised if they courteously cede the right-of-way when you're about to turn from an alley onto a highway – and boldly assert their rights when you're the one zipping down a main road.

Priorité à droite is suspended (eg on arterial roads) when you pass a sign showing an upended yellow square with a black square in the middle. The same sign with a horizontal bar through the square lozenge reinstates the *priorité à droite* rule.

When you arrive at a roundabout at which you do not have the right-of-way (ie the cars already in the roundabout do), you'll often see signs reading *vous n'avez pas la priorité* (you do not have right of way) or *cédez le passage* (give way).

Autoroutes 130km/h (110km/h when raining, 60km/h in icy conditions)

To reduce carbon emissions, autoroute speed limits have recently been reduced to 110km/h in some areas.

Unless otherwise sign-posted, a limit of 50km/h applies in *all* areas designated as built up, no matter how rural they may appear. You must slow to 50km/h the moment you come to a white sign with a red border and a place name written on it; the speed limit applies until you pass an identical sign with a horizontal bar through it.

Most of the speed-limit signs you'll see in cities, towns and villages merely remind you of something you're already supposed to know – that's why they begin with the word *rappel* ('remember'). You can be fined for going as little as 10km over the speed limit.

Other important driving rules:

» Blood-alcohol limit is 0.05% (0.5g per litre of blood) – the equivalent of two glasses of wine for a 75kg adult. Police often conduct random breatha-lyser tests and penalties can be severe, including imprisonment.

» All passengers, including those in the back seat, must wear seat belts.

» Mobile phones may be used only if they are equipped with a hands-free kit or speakerphone.

» Turning right on a red light is illegal.

» Cars from the UK and Ireland must have deflectors affixed to their headlights to avoid dazzling oncoming motorists.

» Radar detectors, even if they're switched off, are illegal; fines are hefty.

Child-seat rules:

» Children under 10 are not permitted to ride in the front seat (unless the back is already occupied by other children under 10).

» A child under 13kg must travel in a backward-facing child seat (permitted in the front seat only for babies under 9kg and if the airbag is deactivated).

» Up to age 10, children must use a size-appropriate type of front-facing child seat or booster.

All vehicles driven in France must carry a high-visibility reflective safety vest (stored inside the vehicle, not in the trunk/boot), and a reflective triangle. The fine for not car-rying one/both is €90/135.

If you'll be driving on snowy roads, make sure you've got snow chains *(chaînes neige)*, required by law whenever and wherever the police post signs.

Riders of any type of two-wheeled vehicle with a motor (except motor-assisted bi-cycles) must wear a helmet. No special licence is required to ride a motorbike whose engine is smaller than 50cc, which is why rental scooters are often rated at 49.9cc.

Hitching

Hitching is never entirely safe in any country in the world, and we don't recommend it. Travellers who decide to hitch should under-stand that they are taking a small but potentially serious risk. Remember that it's safer to travel in pairs and be sure to inform someone of your intended destination. Hitching is not really part of French culture and is not recommended for women in France, even in pairs.

Hitching from city centres is pretty much hopeless, so your best bet is to take pub-lic transport to the outskirts. It is illegal to hitch on auto-routes but you can stand near an entrance ramp as long as you don't block traf-fic. Hitching in remote rural areas is better, but once you get off the *routes nationales* traffic can be light and local. If your itinerary includes a ferry crossing, it's worth trying to score a ride before the ferry since vehicle tickets usually include a number of passengers free of charge. At dusk, give up and think about finding somewhere to stay.

Ride Share

A number of organisations around France arrange *co-voiturage* (car sharing), ie putting people looking for rides in touch with drivers going to the same destina-tion. The best known is Paris-based **Allostop** (☎01 53 20 42 42; www.allostop.net, in French; ☺phone staffed 10am-1pm & 2-4pm Mon-Fri, 10am-1pm Sat), where you pay a per-kilometre fee to the driver (€15/27 for 300/700km) plus an administrative charge (€3 to €8, depending on the distance). You might also try www.covoiturage.fr (in French) or, for international journeys, www.karzoo.eu.

Local Transport

France's cities and larger towns have world-class public-transport systems. There are *métros* (under-ground subway systems) in Paris, Lyon, Marseille, Lille and Toulouse and ultramod-ern light-rail lines *(tramways)* in cities such as Bordeaux, Grenoble, Lille, Lyon, Nancy, Nantes, Nice, Reims, Rouen and Strasbourg, as well as parts of greater Paris.

In addition to a *billet à l'unité* (single ticket), you can purchase a *carnet* (booklet or bunch) of 10 tickets or a *pass journée* (all-day pass).

For details, see Getting Around sections under city and town listings.

Taxi

All medium and large train stations – and many small ones – have a taxi stand out front. For details on the tariffs and regulations applicable in major cities, see p133. In small cities and towns, where taxi drivers are unlikely to find another fare anywhere near where they let you off, one-way and return trips often cost the same. Tariffs are about 30% higher at night and on Sundays and holidays. Having a cab wait for you while you visit something costs about €19 an hour (about €30 in Paris). There may be a surcharge to get picked up at a train station or airport and a small additional fee for a fourth passenger and/or for suitcases.

Train

Travelling by train in France is a comfortable, classy and environmentally sustainable way to see the country. Since many train stations have car-hire agencies, it's easy to combine rail travel with rural exploration by car.

The jewel in the crown of France's public-transport system – alongside the Paris métro – is its extensive rail network, almost all of it run by the state-owned **SNCF** (☑ 36 35; www.sncf.com). Although it employs the most advanced rail technology, the network's layout reflects the country's centuries-old Paris-centric nature: most of the principal rail lines radiate out from Paris like the spokes of a wheel, the result being that services between provincial towns situated on different spokes can be infrequent and slow. For a map of France's rail system, see p976. Up-to-the-minute information on *perturbations* (service disruptions), eg because of strikes, can be found on www.infolignes. com (in French).

Since its inauguration in the 1980s, the pride and joy of SNCF – and the French – is the renowned **TGV** (Train à Grande Vitesse; www.tgv.com), pronounced 'teh zheh veh',

LEFT-LUGGAGE FACILITIES

Because of security concerns, few French train stations still have *consignes automatiques* (left-luggage lockers), but in some larger stations you can leave your bags in a *consigne manuelle* (staffed left-luggage facility) – usually in an out-of-the-way corner of the station – where items are handed over in person and x-rayed before being stowed. Charges are €5 for up to 10 hours and €8 for 24 hours; payment must be made in cash. To find out which stations let you leave your bags and when their *consignes* are open (they're often closed on Sunday and after 7pm or 8pm), go to www. gares-en-mouvement.com, select a station, click 'Practical Information' ('Services en gare') and then the 'Services' tab.

which zips passengers along at speeds of up to 320km/h (198mph). In 2007, a specially modified TGV achieved a new speed record for non-maglev (magnetic levitation) trains: 574.8km/h.

The four main TGV lines (or LGVs, short for *lignes à grande vitesse*, ie high-speed rail lines) head north, east, southeast and southwest from Paris (trains use slower local tracks to get to destinations off the main line):

TGV Nord, Thalys & Eurostar Link Paris Gare du Nord with Arras, Lille, Calais, Brussels (Bruxelles-Midi), Amsterdam, Cologne and, via the Channel Tunnel, Ashford, Ebbsfleet and London St Pancras.

TGV Est Européen Connects Paris Gare de l'Est with Reims, Nancy, Metz, Strasbourg, Zurich and Germany, including Frankfurt and Stuttgart. At present, the super-high-speed track stretches only as far east as Lorraine but it's supposed to reach Strasbourg in 2016.

TGV Sud-Est & TGV Midi-Méditerranée Link Paris Gare de Lyon with the southeast, including Dijon, Lyon, Geneva, the Alps, Avignon, Marseille, Nice and Montpellier.

TGV Atlantique Sud-Ouest & TGV Atlantique

Ouest Link Paris Gare Montparnasse with western and southwestern France, including Brittany (Rennes, Brest, Quimper), Tours, Nantes, Poitiers, La Rochelle, Bordeaux, Biarritz and Toulouse.

The TGV tracks are interconnected, making it possible to go directly from, say, Lyon to Nantes or Bordeaux to Lille without switching trains in Paris – or, like in the old days, having to transfer from one of Paris' six main train stations to another. Stops on the link-up, which runs east and south of Paris, include Charles de Gaulle airport and Disneyland Resort Paris.

A train that is not a TGV is often referred to as a *corail*, a *classique* or, for intraregional services, a **TER** (Train Express Régional; www. ter-sncf.com, in French). Certain non-TGV services have been given peculiar names:

Corail Intercités Medium-haul routes.

Lunéa (www.coraillunea.fr, in French) Overnight trains with couchettes for cross-country travel – getting rarer in the age of the TGV.

Téoz (www.corailteoz.com, in French) Especially comfortable trains that run southward from Paris Gare d'Austerlitz to Clermont-Ferrand, Limoges, Cahors,

SNCF FARES & DISCOUNTS

Full-fare tickets can be quite expensive. Fortunately, a dizzying array of discounts are available and station staff are very good about helping travellers find the very best fare. But first, the basics:

» 1st-class travel, where available, costs 20% to 30% extra.

» Ticket prices for some trains, including most TGVs, are pricier during peak periods.

» The further in advance you reserve, the lower the fares.

» Children under four travel for free (€8.50 to any destination if they need a seat).

» Children aged four to 11 travel for half price.

Discount Tickets

The SNCF's most heavily discounted tickets are known as **Prem's**. They can be booked on the internet, by phone, at ticket windows and from ticket machines a maximum of 90 days and a minimum of 14 days before your travel date. Once you buy a Prem's ticket, it's use it or lose it – getting your money back or changing the time is not allowed.

Bons Plans fares, a grab bag of really cheap options on a changing array of routes and dates, are advertised on www.voyages-sncf.com under the title 'Dernière Minute' (last minute).

In an effort to make train travel both affordable and hip for the iPod generation, the SNCF's youthful subsidiary **iDTGV** (www.idtgv.com) sells tickets (online only) for as little as €19 for advance-purchase TGV travel between about 30 cities.

On regional trains, discount fares requiring neither a discount card nor advance purchase:

Loisir Week-End rates Good for return travel that includes a Saturday night at your destination or involves travel on a Saturday or Sunday.

Découverte fares Available for low-demand 'blue-period' trains to people aged 12 to 25, seniors and the adult travel companions of children under 12.

Mini-Groupe tickets In some regions, these bring big savings for three to six people travelling together, provided you spend a Saturday night at your destination.

Certain French *régions* (eg Basse-Normandie and Alsace) offer great deals on intra-regional TER transport for day trips or weekend travel.

Discount Cards

Reductions of at least 25% (for last-minute bookings), and of 40%, 50% or even 60% (if you reserve well ahead or travel during low-volume 'blue' periods), are available with several discount cards (valid for one year):

Carte 12-25 (www.12-25-sncf.com in, French; €49) Available to travellers aged 12 to 25.

Carte Enfant Plus (www.enfantplus-sncf.com, in French; €70) For one to four adults travelling with a child aged four to 11.

Carte Escapades (www.escapades-sncf.com, in French; €85) For people aged 26 to 59. Gets you discounts on return journeys of at least 200km that either include a Saturday night away or only involve travel on a Saturday or Sunday.

Carte Sénior (www.senior-sncf.com, in French; €56) For travellers over 60.

Rail Passes

Residents of Europe who do not live in France can purchase an **InterRail One Country Pass** (www.interrailnet.com; 3/4/6/8 days €194/209/269/299, 12-25 yr €126/136/175/194), which entitles its bearer to unlimited travel on SNCF trains for three to eight days over the course of a month.

For non-European residents, **Rail Europe** (www.raileurope.com, www.raileurope.com.au) offers the **France Rail Pass** (www.francerailpass.com; 3/6/9 days over 1 month US$186/268/341).

You need to really rack up the kilometres to make these passes worthwhile.

Toulouse, Montpellier, Perpignan, Marseille and Nice.

Transilien (www.transilien.com) SNCF services in the Île de France (the Paris region).

For details on especially scenic train routes all around France, see www.trainstouristiques-ter.com.

Information on train accessibility for people with disabilities can be found at www.accessibilite.sncf.fr (in French) and, for greater Paris, www.infomobi.com (in French).

Long-distance trains sometimes split at a station – that is, each half of the train heads off for a different destination. Check the destination panel on your car as you board or you could wind up very, very far from wherever it was you intended to go.

Tickets & Reservations

Large stations often have separate ticket windows for *international, grandes lignes* (long-haul) and *banlieue* (suburban) lines, and for people whose train is about to leave *(départ immédiat* or *départ dans l'heure)*. Nearly every SNCF station has at least one *borne libre-service* (self-service terminal) or *billeterie automatique* (automatic ticket machine) that accepts both cash and PIN-chip credit cards. Select the Union Jack for instructions in English.

Using a credit card, you can buy a ticket by phone or via the SNCF internet booking site (www.voyages-sncf.com, in French) and either have it sent to you by post (if you have an address in France) or collect it from any SNCF ticket office or from train-station ticket machines.

Before boarding the train, you must validate *(composter)* your ticket by time-stamping it in a *composteur,* one of those yellow posts located on the way to the platform. If you forget (or don't have a ticket for some other reason), find a conductor on the train before they find you – otherwise you can be fined.

CHANGES & REIMBURSEMENTS

For trains that do not assign reserved seats (eg TER and Corail Intercités trains), full-fare tickets are useable whenever you like for 61 days from the date they were purchased. Like all SNCF tickets, they cannot be replaced if lost or stolen.

If you've got a full-fare Loisir Week-End ticket, you can change your reservation by phone, internet or at train stations for no charge until the day before your departure; changes made on the day of your reserved trip incur a charge of €10 (€3 for tickets bought with a discount card).

Pro tickets (eg TGV Pro, Téoz Pro) allow full reimbursement up to 30 minutes *after* the time of departure (eg by calling ✆36 35). If you turn up at your departure station up to two hours after your original travel time, you can reschedule your trip on a later train.

Very cheap promotional tickets (eg Prem's) cannot be modified and are non-reimbursable.

Language

WANT MORE?

For in-depth language information and handy phrases, check out Lonely Planet's *French Phrasebook*. You'll find it at **shop .lonelyplanet.com**, or you can buy Lonely Planet's iPhone phrasebooks at the Apple App Store.

Standard French is taught and spoken throughout France. Regional accents and dialects are an important part of identity in certain regions, but you'll have no trouble being understood anywhere if you stick to standard French, which we've also used in the phrases below.

The sounds used in spoken French can almost all be found in English. There are a couple of exceptions: nasal vowels (represented in our pronunciation guides by o or u followed by an almost inaudible nasal consonant sound m, n or ng), the 'funny' *u* (ew in our guides) and the deep-in-the-throat *r*. Bearing these few points in mind and reading our pronunciation guides below as if they were English, you'll be understood just fine.

BASICS

French has two words for 'you' – use the polite form *vous* unless you're talking to close friends, children or animals in which case you'd use the informal *tu*. You can also use *tu* when a person invites you to use *tu*.

All nouns in French are either masculine or feminine, and so are the adjectives, articles *le/la* (the) and *un/une* (a), and possessives *mon/ma* (my), *ton/ta* (your) and *son/sa* (his, her) that go with the nouns. In this chapter we have included masculine and femine forms where necessary, separated by a slash and indicated with 'm/f'.

Hello.	*Bonjour.*	bon·zhoor
Goodbye.	*Au revoir.*	o·rer·vwa
Excuse me.	*Excusez-moi.*	ek·skew·zay·mwa
Sorry.	*Pardon.*	par·don
Yes./No.	*Oui./Non.*	wee/non
Please.	*S'il vous plaît.*	seel voo play
Thank you.	*Merci.*	mair·see

How are you?
Comment allez-vous?   ko·mon ta·lay·voo

Fine, and you?
Bien, merci. Et vous?   byun mair·see ay voo

You're welcome.
De rien.   der ree·en

My name is ...
Je m'appelle ...   zher ma·pel ...

What's your name?
Comment vous appelez-vous?   ko·mon voo· za·play voo

Do you speak English?
Parlez-vous anglais?   par·lay·voo ong·glay

I don't understand.
Je ne comprends pas.   zher ner kom·pron pa

How much is it?
C'est combien?   say kom·byun

ACCOMMODATION

Do you have any rooms available?
Est-ce que vous avez des chambres libres?   es·ker voo za·vay day shom·brer lee·brer

How much is it per night/person?
Quel est le prix par nuit/personne?   kel ay ler pree par nwee/per·son

Is breakfast included?
Est-ce que le petit déjeuner est inclus?   es·ker ler per·tee day·zher·nay ayt en·klew

campsite	*camping*	kom·peeng
dorm	*dortoir*	dor·twar
guest house	*pension*	pon·syon
hotel	*hôtel*	o·tel
youth hostel	*auberge de jeunesse*	o·berzh der zher·nes
a ... room	*une chambre ...*	ewn shom·brer ...
single	*à un lit*	a un lee
double	*avec un grand lit*	a·vek un gron lee
twin	*avec des lits jumeaux*	a·vek day lee zhew·mo
with (a)...	*avec ...*	a·vek ...
air-con	*climatiseur*	klee·ma·tee·zer
bathroom	*une salle de bains*	ewn sal der bun
window	*fenêtre*	fer·nay·trer

DIRECTIONS

Where's ...?
Où est ...?   oo ay ...

What's the address?
Quelle est l'adresse?   kel ay la·dres

Could you write the address, please?
Est-ce que vous pourriez   es·ker voo poo·ryay
écrire l'adresse,   ay·kreer la·dres
s'il vous plaît?   seel voo play

Can you show me (on the map)?
Pouvez-vous m'indiquer   poo·vay·voo mun·dee·kay
(sur la carte)?   (sewr la kart)

at the corner	*au coin*	o kwun
at the traffic lights	*aux feux*	o fer
behind	*derrière*	dair·ryair
in front of	*devant*	der·von
far (from)	*loin (de)*	lwun (der)
left	*gauche*	gosh
near (to)	*près (de)*	pray (der)
next to ...	*à côté de ...*	a ko·tay der...
opposite ...	*en face de ...*	on fas der ...
right	*droite*	drwat
straight ahead	*tout droit*	too drwa

EATING & DRINKING

What would you recommend?
Qu'est-ce que vous   kes·ker voo
conseillez?   kon·say·yay

What's in that dish?
Quels sont les   kel son lay
ingrédients?   zun·gray·dyon

To get by in French, mix and match these simple patterns with words of your choice:

Where's (the entry)?
Où est (l'entrée)?   oo ay (lon·tray)

Where can I (buy a ticket)?
Où est-ce que je peux   oo es·ker zher per
(acheter un billet)?   (ash·tay un bee·yay)

When's (the next train)?
Quand est   kon ay
(le prochain train)?   (ler pro·shun trun)

How much is (a room)?
C'est combien pour   say kom·buyn poor
(une chambre)?   (ewn shom·brer)

Do you have (a map)?
Avez-vous (une carte)?   a·vay voo (ewn kart)

Is there (a toilet)?
Y a-t-il (des toilettes)?   ee a teel (day twa·let)

I'd like (to book a room).
Je voudrais   zher voo·dray
(réserver   (ray·ser·vay
une chambre).   ewn shom·brer)

Can I (enter)?
Puis-je (entrer)?   pweezh (on·tray)

Could you please (help)?
Pouvez-vous   poo·vay voo
(m'aider),   (may·day)
s'il vous plaît?   seel voo play

Do I have to (book a seat)?
Faut-il (réserver   fo·teel (ray·ser·vay
une place)?   ewn plas)

I'm a vegetarian.
Je suis végétarien/   zher swee vay·zhay·ta·ryun/
végétarienne.   vay·zhay·ta·ryen (m/f)

I don't eat ...
Je ne mange pas ...   zher ner monzh pa ...

Cheers!
Santé!   son·tay

That was delicious.
C'était délicieux!   say·tay day·lee·syer

Please bring the bill.
Apportez-moi   a·por·tay·mwa
l'addition,   la·dee·syon
s'il vous plaît.   seel voo play

I'd like to reserve a table for ...	*Je voudrais réserver une table pour ...*	zher voo·dray ray·zair·vay ewn ta·bler poor ...
(eight) o'clock	*(vingt) heures*	(vungt) er
(two) people	*(deux) personnes*	(der) pair·son

Signs

Entrée	Entrance
Femmes	Women
Fermé	Closed
Hommes	Men
Interdit	Prohibited
Ouvert	Open
Renseignements	Information
Sortie	Exit
Toilettes/WC	Toilets

Key Words

appetiser	*entrée*	on·tray
bottle	*bouteille*	boo·tay
breakfast	*petit déjeuner*	per·tee day·zher·nay
children's menu	*menu pour enfants*	mer·new poor on·fon
cold	*froid*	frwa
delicatessen	*traiteur*	tray·ter
dinner	*dîner*	dee·nay
dish	*plat*	pla
food	*nourriture*	noo·ree·tewr
fork	*fourchette*	foor·shet
glass	*verre*	vair
grocery store	*épicerie*	ay·pees·ree
highchair	*chaise haute*	shay zot
hot	*chaud*	sho
knife	*couteau*	koo·to
local speciality	*spécialité locale*	spay·sya·lee·tay lo·kal
lunch	*déjeuner*	day·zher·nay
main course	*plat principal*	pla prun·see·pal
market	*marché*	mar·shay
menu (in English)	*carte (en anglais)*	kart (on ong·glay)
plate	*assiette*	a·syet
spoon	*cuillère*	kwee·yair
wine list	*carte des vins*	kart day vun
with/without	*avec/sans*	a·vek/son

Meat & Fish

beef	*bœuf*	berf
chicken	*poulet*	poo·lay
lamb	*agneau*	a·nyo
pork	*porc*	por
turkey	*dinde*	dund
veal	*veau*	vo

Fruit & Vegetables

apple	*pomme*	pom
apricot	*abricot*	ab·ree·ko
asparagus	*asperge*	a·spairzh
beans	*haricots*	a·ree·ko
beetroot	*betterave*	be·trav
cabbage	*chou*	shoo
celery	*céleri*	sel·ree
cherry	*cerise*	ser·reez
corn	*maïs*	ma·ees
cucumber	*concombre*	kong·kom·brer
gherkin (pickle)	*cornichon*	kor·nee·shon
grape	*raisin*	ray·zun
leek	*poireau*	pwa·ro
lemon	*citron*	see·tron
lettuce	*laitue*	lay·tew
mushroom	*champignon*	shom·pee·nyon
peach	*pêche*	pesh
peas	*petit pois*	per·tee pwa
(red/green) pepper	*poivron (rouge/vert)*	pwa·vron (roozh/vair)
pineapple	*ananas*	a·na·nas
plum	*prune*	prewn
potato	*pomme de terre*	pom der tair
prune	*pruneau*	prew·no
pumpkin	*citrouille*	see·troo·yer
shallot	*échalote*	eh·sha·lot
spinach	*épinards*	eh·pee·nar
strawberry	*fraise*	frez
tomato	*tomate*	to·mat
turnip	*navet*	na·vay
vegetable	*légume*	lay·gewm

Other

bread	*pain*	pun
butter	*beurre*	ber
cheese	*fromage*	fro·mazh
egg	*œuf*	erf
honey	*miel*	myel
jam	*confiture*	kon·fee·tewr
lentils	*lentilles*	lon·tee·yer
oil	*huile*	weel
pasta/noodles	*pâtes*	pat
pepper	*poivre*	pwa·vrer
rice	*riz*	ree
salt	*sel*	sel
sugar	*sucre*	sew·krer
vinegar	*vinaigre*	vee·nay·grer

Drinks

beer	*bière*	bee·yair
coffee	*café*	ka·fay
(orange) juice	*jus (d'orange)*	zhew (do·ronzh)
milk	*lait*	lay
tea	*thé*	tay
(mineral) water	*eau (minérale)*	o (mee·nay·ral)
(red) wine	*vin (rouge)*	vun (roozh)
(white) wine	*vin (blanc)*	vun (blong)

EMERGENCIES

Help!
Au secours!   o skoor

I'm lost.
Je suis perdu/perdue.   zhe swee·pair·dew (m/f)

Leave me alone!
Fichez-moi la paix!   fee·shay·mwa la pay

There's been an accident.
Il y a eu un accident.   eel ya ew un ak·see·don

Call a doctor.
Appelez un médecin.   a·play un mayd·sun

Call the police.
Appelez la police.   a·play la po·lees

I'm ill.
Je suis malade.   zher swee ma·lad

It hurts here.
J'ai une douleur ici.   zhay ewn doo·ler ee·see

I'm allergic to ...
Je suis allergique ... zher swee za·lair·zheek ...

SHOPPING & SERVICES

I'd like to buy ...
Je voudrais acheter ...   zher voo·dray ash·tay ...

May I look at it?
Est-ce que je   es·ker zher
peux le voir?   per ler vwar

I'm just looking.
Je regarde.   zher rer·gard

I don't like it.
Cela ne me plaît pas.   ser·la ner mer play pa

How much is it?
C'est combien?   say kom·byun

It's too expensive.
C'est trop cher.   say tro shair

Question Words

How?	*Comment?*	ko·mon
What?	*Quoi?*	kwa
When?	*Quand?*	kon
Where?	*Où?*	oo
Who?	*Qui?*	kee
Why?	*Pourquoi?*	poor·kwa

Can you lower the price?
Vous pouvez baisser   voo poo·vay bay·say
le prix?   ler pree

There's a mistake in the bill.
Il y a une erreur dans   eel ya ewn ay·rer don
la note.   la not

ATM	*guichet automatique de banque*	gee·shay o·to·ma·teek der bonk
credit card	*carte de crédit*	kart der kray·dee
internet café	*cybercafé*	see·bair·ka·fay
post office	*bureau de poste*	bew·ro der post
tourist office	*office de tourisme*	o·fees der too·rees·mer

TIME & DATES

What time is it?
Quelle heure est-il?   kel er ay til

It's (eight) o'clock.
Il est (huit) heures.   il ay (weet) er

It's half past (10).
Il est (dix) heures   il ay (deez) er
et demie.   ay day·mee

morning	*matin*	ma·tun
afternoon	*après-midi*	a·pray·mee·dee
evening	*soir*	swar
yesterday	*hier*	yair
today	*aujourd'hui*	o·zhoor·dwee
tomorrow	*demain*	der·mun

Monday	*lundi*	lun·dee
Tuesday	*mardi*	mar·dee
Wednesday	*mercredi*	mair·krer·dee
Thursday	*jeudi*	zher·dee
Friday	*vendredi*	von·drer·dee
Saturday	*samedi*	sam·dee
Sunday	*dimanche*	dee·monsh

January	*janvier*	zhon·vyay
February	*février*	fayv·ryay
March	*mars*	mars
April	*avril*	a·vreel
May	*mai*	may
June	*juin*	zhwun
July	*juillet*	zhwee·yay
August	*août*	oot
September	*septembre*	sep·tom·brer
October	*octobre*	ok·to·brer
November	*novembre*	no·vom·brer
December	*décembre*	day·som·brer

Numbers

1	*un*	un
2	*deux*	der
3	*trois*	trwa
4	*quatre*	ka·trer
5	*cinq*	sungk
6	*six*	sees
7	*sept*	set
8	*huit*	weet
9	*neuf*	nerf
10	*dix*	dees
20	*vingt*	vung
30	*trente*	tront
40	*quarante*	ka·ront
50	*cinquante*	sung·kont
60	*soixante*	swa·sont
70	*soixante-dix*	swa·son·dees
80	*quatre-vingts*	ka·trer·vung
90	*quatre-vingt-dix*	ka·trer·vung·dees
100	*cent*	son
1000	*mille*	meel

TRANSPORT

Public Transport

boat	*bateau*	ba·to
bus	*bus*	bews
plane	*avion*	a·vyon
train	*train*	trun

I want to go to ...
Je voudrais aller à ... zher voo·dray a·lay a ...

Does it stop at (Amboise)?
Est-ce qu'il s'arrête à es·kil sa·ret a
(Amboise)? (om·bwaz)

At what time does it leave/arrive?
À quelle heure est-ce a kel er es
qu'il part/arrive? kil par/a·reev

Can you tell me when we get to ...?
Pouvez-vous me poo·vay·voo mer
dire quand deer kon
nous arrivons à ...? noo za·ree·von a ...

I want to get off here.
Je veux descendre zher ver day·son·drer
ici. ee·see

first	*premier*	prer·myay
last	*dernier*	dair·nyay
next	*prochain*	pro·shun

a ... ticket	*un billet ...*	un bee·yay ...
1st-class	*de première classe*	der prem·yair klas
2nd-class	*de deuxième classe*	der der·zyem las
one-way	*simple*	sum·pler
return	*aller et retour*	a·lay ay rer·toor

aisle seat	*côté couloir*	ko·tay kool·war
delayed	*en retard*	on rer·tar
cancelled	*annulé*	a·new·lay
platform	*quai*	kay
ticket office	*guichet*	gee·shay
timetable	*horaire*	o·rair
train station	*gare*	gar
window seat	*côté fenêtre*	ko·tay fe·ne·trer

Driving & Cycling

I'd like to hire a ...	*Je voudrais louer ...*	zher voo·dray loo·way ...
4WD	*un quatre-quatre*	un kat·kat
car	*une voiture*	ewn vwa·tewr
bicycle	*un vélo*	un vay·lo
motorcycle	*une moto*	ewn mo·to

child seat	*siège-enfant*	syezh·on·fon
diesel	*diesel*	dyay·zel
helmet	*casque*	kask
mechanic	*mécanicien*	may·ka·nee·syun
petrol/gas	*essence*	ay·sons
service station	*station-service*	sta·syon·ser·vees

Is this the road to ...?
C'est la route pour ...? say la root poor ...

(How long) Can I park here?
(Combien de temps) (kom·byun der tom)
Est-ce que je peux es·ker zher per
stationner ici? sta·syo·nay ee·see

The car/motorbike has broken down (at ...).
La voiture/moto est la vwa·tewr/mo·to ay
tombée en panne (à ...). tom·bay on pan (a ...)

I have a flat tyre.
Mon pneu est à plat. mom pner ay ta pla

I've run out of petrol.
Je suis en panne zher swee zon pan
d'essence. day·sons

I've lost my car keys.
J'ai perdu les clés de zhay per·dew lay klay der
ma voiture. ma vwa·tewr

GLOSSARY

(m) indicates masculine gender, (f) feminine gender and (pl) plural

accueil (m) – reception

alignements (m pl) – a series of standing stones, or menhirs, in straight lines

AOC – Appellation d'Origine Contrôlée; system of French wine and olive oil classification showing that items have met government regulations as to where and how they are produced

AOP – Appellation d'Origine Protégée; Europe-wide equivalent to the *AOC*

arrondissement (m) – administrative division of large city; abbreviated on signs as 1er (1st arrondissement), 2e (2nd) etc

atelier (m) – workshop or studio

auberge – inn

auberge de jeunesse (f) – youth hostel

baie (f) – bay

bassin (m) – bay or basin

bastide (f) – medieval settlement in southwestern France, usually built on a grid plan and surrounding an arcaded square; fortified town; also a country house in Provence

belle époque (f) – literally 'beautiful age'; era of elegance and gaiety characterising fashionable Parisian life in the period preceding WWI

billet (m) – ticket

billet jumelé (m) – combination ticket, good for more than one site, museum etc

billetterie (f) – ticket office or counter

bouchon – Lyonnais bistro

boulangerie (f) – bakery or bread shop

boules (f pl) – a game similar to lawn bowls played with heavy metal balls on a sandy pitch; also called *pétanque*

BP – *boîte postale*; post office box

brasserie (f) – restaurant similar to a *café* but usually serving full meals all day (original meaning: brewery)

bureau de change (m) – exchange bureau

bureau de poste (m) – post office

carnet (m) – a book of five or 10 bus, tram or metro tickets sold at a reduced rate

carrefour (m) – crossroad

carte (f) – card; menu; map

cave (f) – wine cellar

chambre (f) – room

chambre d'hôte (f) – B&B

charcuterie (f) – butcher's shop and delicatessen; the prepared meats it sells

cimetière (f) – cemetery

col (m) – mountain pass

consigne or **consigne manuelle** (f) – left-luggage office

consigne automatique (f) – left-luggage locker

correspondance (f) – linking tunnel or walkway, eg in the metro; rail or bus connection

couchette (f) – sleeping berth on a train or ferry

cour (f) – courtyard

crémerie (f) – dairy or cheese shop

dégustation (f) – tasting

demi (m) – 330mL glass of beer

demi-pension (f) – half board (B&B with either lunch or dinner)

département (m) – administrative division of France

donjon (m) – castle keep

église (f) – church

épicerie (f) – small grocery store

ESF – École de Ski Français; France's leading ski school

fest-noz or **festoù-noz** (pl) – night festival

fête (f) – festival

Fnac – retail chain selling entertainment goods, electronics and tickets

forêt (f) – forest

formule or **formule rapide** (f) – lunchtime set similar to a *menu* but with two of three courses on offer (eg starter and main or main and dessert)

fromagerie (f) – cheese shop

FUAJ – Fédération Unie des Auberges de Jeunesse; France's major hostel association

funiculaire (m) – funicular railway

galerie (f) – covered shopping centre or arcade

gare or **gare SNCF** (f) – railway station

gare maritime (f) – ferry terminal

gare routière (f) – bus station

gendarmerie (f) – police station; police force

gîte d'étape (m) – hikers accommodation, usually in a village

gîte rural (m) – country cottage

golfe (m) – gulf

GR – *grande randonnée*; long-distance hiking trail

grand cru (m) – wine of exceptional quality

halles (f pl) – covered market; central food market

halte routière (f) – bus stop

horaire (m) – timetable or schedule

hostellerie – hostelry

hôtel de ville (m) – city or town hall

hôtel particulier (m) – private mansion

intra-muros – old city (literally 'within the walls')

jardin (m) – garden

jardin botanique (m) – botanic garden

laverie (f) or **lavomatique** (m) – laundrette

mairie (f) – city or town hall

maison du parc (f) – a national park's headquarters and/or visitors centre

marché (m) – market

marché aux puces (m) – flea market

marché couvert (m) – covered market

mas (m) – farmhouse in southern France

menu (m) – fixed-price meal with two or more courses

mistral (m) – strong north or northwest wind in southern France

musée (m) – museum

navette (f) – shuttle bus, train or boat

palais de justice (m) – law courts

parapente – paragliding

parlement (m) – parliament

parvis (m) – square

pâtisserie (f) – cake and pastry shop

pétanque (f) – a game similar to lawn bowls played with heavy metal balls on a sandy pitch; also called *boules*

place (f) – square or plaza

plage (f) – beach

plan (m) – city map

plan du quartier (m) – map of nearby streets (hung on the wall near metro exits)

plat du jour (m) – daily special in a restaurant

pont (m) – bridge

porte (f) – gate in a city wall

poste (f) – post office

préfecture (f) – prefecture (capital of a *département*)

presqu'île (f) – peninsula

pression (f) – draught beer

puy (m) – volcanic cone or peak

quai (m) – quay or railway platform

quartier (m) – quarter or district

refuge (m) – mountain hut, basic shelter for hikers

région (f) – administrative division of France

rive (f) – bank of a river

rond point (m) – roundabout

sentier (m) – trail

service des urgences (f) – casualty ward

ski de fond – cross-country skiing

SNCF – Société Nationale des Chemins de Fer; state-owned railway company

SNCM – Société Nationale Maritime Corse-Méditerranée; state-owned ferry company linking Corsica and mainland France

sortie (f) – exit

square (m) – public garden

tabac (m) – tobacconist (also selling bus tickets, phonecards etc)

table d'hôte – set menu at a fixed price

taxe de séjour (f) – municipal tourist tax

télécarte (f) – phonecard

téléphérique (m) – cableway or cable car

télésiège (m) – chairlift

téléski (m) – ski lift or tow

TGV – *Train à Grande Vitesse*; high-speed train or bullet train

tour (f) – tower

vallée (f) – valley

v.f. (f) – *version française*; a film dubbed in French

vieille ville (f) – old town or old city

ville neuve (f) – new town or new city

v.o. (f) – *version originale*; a nondubbed film with French subtitles

voie (f) – train platform

VTT – *vélo tout terrain;* mountain bike

winstub – traditional Alsatian eatery

behind the scenes

SEND US YOUR FEEDBACK

We love to hear from travellers – your comments keep us on our toes and help make our books better. Our well-travelled team reads every word on what you loved or loathed about this book. Although we cannot reply individually to postal submissions, we always guarantee that your feedback goes straight to the appropriate authors, in time for the next edition. Each person who sends us information is thanked in the next edition – and the most useful submissions are rewarded with a free book.

Visit **lonelyplanet.com/contact** to submit your updates and suggestions or to ask for help. Our award-winning website also features inspirational travel stories, news and discussions.

Note: We may edit, reproduce and incorporate your comments in Lonely Planet products such as guidebooks, websites and digital products, so let us know if you don't want your comments reproduced or your name acknowledged. For a copy of our privacy policy visit lonelyplanet.com/privacy.

OUR READERS

Many thanks to the travellers who used the last edition and wrote to us with helpful hints, useful advice and interesting anecdotes:
Patrik Åqvist, Stephen Bannon, Paul Beach, Tim Bennett, Jules Black, Rowan Blackmore, Elma Blokker, Nora Buur, Natalie Caputo, Alex Cimbleris, John Craven, Catherine Davis, Wouter De Sutter, Nick Dillen, Zver Domonkos, Michael Eisenring, Gaetan, Elizabeth Glascoe, Yehuda Goldberg, Martin Gottwald, Susan Greenwood, Christophe Guerin, Kate Harrison, Nicola Keen, Janez Kompan, Henrik Ladegaard, David Leaney, Kim Lockwood, Anne Manning, George Mckenna, Catherine Murphy, Bente Pedersen, Artemis Preeshl, Michael Preston, George Reid, Bronwyn Roe, Martin Schilling, Katja Schmidt, Stefanie Schout, Sara Siegel, Ian Slaughter, Michael Stavy, John Van Bavel, Rebecca Wiles

AUTHOR THANKS
Nicola Williams

What can I say? This book was a gargantuan project and its authors went above and beyond the call of duty to deliver one great guidebook. Kudos to commissioning editor Paula Hardy whose exceptional vision and creativity made this guide, and to John Vlahides for his courage. *Merci* to Parisians Tariq Krim (www.jolicloud.com), Patricia Wells (www.patriciawells.com), Laure Chouillou and Sophie Maisonnier. At home *bisous* to travel companion Matthias and our three wonderfully travel-happy kids, Niko (eight), Mischa (six) and Kaya (six months).

Alexis Averbuck

Life on the road wouldn't be nearly so pleasant without the kindness of strangers. Thanks to Virginie Fournier for making the Côte d'Or a home away from home and Ken Haney for his expert instruction on Chablis wines. I owe Freddie Grimwood the beverage of his choice for his tips on Romanesque art and architecture. Life wouldn't be nearly as fun without Amy, Rod, Lola and Romy in Marseille. Special thanks to Paula Hardy and Nicola Williams for pulling it all together in style.

Oliver Berry

Big thanks to everyone for keeping the home fires burning and the cups of tea coming, but biggest thanks as always to Susie Berry and Molly Berry. Big thanks also to helpful people I met along the way or who helped during research, including Sandrine Cofflard, Emmanuelle Bouvet, Claire Thomas-Chenard and Jean-François Carille. Lastly thanks to Paula Hardy for the gig, Nicola Williams for steering the ship, and of course all my co-authors, along with the Hobo for keeping me company when all other lights went out.

Stuart Butler

Twenty-five years ago I first visited the small Landes coastal village of Moliets and so now it's only right that I should thank Moliets and its people for introducing me to three of my favourite things – my wife, surfing and a love of France itself. Talking of my wife I want to thank Heather once again for everything she does and, most of all, for the gift of our Franglais son, Jake, just as I started research for this book. I would also like to thank Rosie Warren in Bordeaux and Nicky Worth and Benoît Crespy for La Rochelle advice.

Jean-Bernard Carillet

A huge thanks to everyone who helped out and made this trip an enlightenment, including Marie and Paul-André, as well as all the wonderfully Corsican people who helped along the way. At Lonely Planet, Laura Stansfeld deserves huge thanks for her support throughout the project. I'm also grateful to Paula (you'll be missed) and Nicola, coordinating author extraordinaire, for her help and sense of organisation. As always, a phenomenal *gros bisou* to my daughter Eva.

Kerry Christiani

First up, a big *merci* to my husband Andy for being with me every step of the way. Thank you to my brilliant interviewees: Eric Favret (Chamonix), Patrick Zimmer (Val d'Isère), Francine Klur (Route des Vins d'Alsace) and Jean-Paul de Vries (Romagne-sous-Montfaucon). Huge thanks to Leonora Parry for the fondue and invaluable tips on Les Trois Vallées; and to all the tourism professionals I met on the road, especially Marlene Heinrich (Alsace), Sophie Martin (Val d'Isère) and the Chamonix team.

Steve Fallon

A number of people helped me in the updating of my bits of *France* but first and foremost stands Paris resident Brenda Turnnidge, ever helpful, always knowledgeable. Thanks, too, to Zahia Hafs, Olivier Cirendini, Caroline Guilleminot, Daniel Meyers, Patricia Ribault and Chew Terrière for assistance, ideas, hospitality and/or a few laughs during what was a very cold, very snowy, very dark winter in and around the City of Light. A very special *merci* to France coordinator, Nicola Williams, a true professional. As always, I'd like to dedicate my share of the book to my partner Michael Rothschild, a veritable walking Larousse Gastronomique.

Emilie Filou

A huge thank you to fellow author John Vlahides for sharing my enthusiasm for the region and being great fun to work with. Thanks also to coordinating author Nicola Williams and editors Annelies Mertens and Laura Crawford for their support on the formatting, and to everyone else who pulled together to make this unusual gig happen.

Catherine Le Nevez

Un grand merci to all of the locals, tourism professionals and fellow travellers who provided insights, inspiration and great times during my journey. As ever, there are way too many people to list individually, but thanks in particular to Hélène Carleschi and François Gagnaire for the interviews and the Lyon crew (you know who you are!), as well as everyone at Lonely Planet. And, as ever, *merci surtout* to my family, especially my brother and *belle-sœur*, for their support and understanding.

Tom Masters

Many thanks to my parents Rosemary and Paul Masters for their help, advice and hospitality during my research trip to Brittany and Normandy. Thanks too to Jocelyne, Fabien, Darryl, Drew, Stoyan, Camille, and David. A huge thanks to all the hard-working tourist office employees, too numerous to name, throughout my regions – you often went well beyond the call of duty. A special thanks also to coordinating author Nicola Williams, commissioning editor Paula Hardy and all the team in-house at Lonely Planet.

Daniel Robinson

Tous mes remerciements à (in chronological order) my wife Rachel and our eagerly awaited *premier-né*, Yohan Stern and Barbara Burtin, David Saliamonas, Pauline Bebe and Tom Cohen, my cousins Natasha, Pascal, Alyosha and Timur, Madame Sadou, Michael Ewing-Chow, Dalia Hierro, David Levasseur and Andrea Levasseur-Flanagan, Marie-Claude Mobuchon, Françoise Gauthier, Pascal Henry, Severine Launois, Isabelle Pierot, Raquel, Elie and Claude Margen, Samuel and Galit Vacrate, Thierry Chayo, Guy, Claudine and Marian Zarka, Craig and Lorna Rahanian, Lucien Dayan, Anny Monet and my virtuoso Lonely Planet colleagues Nicola Williams, Paula Hardy, Jo Potts and Annelies Mertens.

Miles Roddis

Huge thanks, as always, ever, to Ingrid: chauffeur, proofer, dining companion and restaurant critique, stalwart supporter and first lady. Thanks too to so many cheerful and informed tourist office staff: Marie-Pierre (Perpignan), Pascale (Prades), Audrey (Collioure), Renée (Vernet-les-Bains), Monika (Nîmes), Loïc Falcher (Uzès), Isabelle Vidal (Pont du Gard), Carole (Florac), Laetitia and Miriam (Millau), Delphine Atché (Roquefort) and both Muriel and Françoise (Carcassonne). You made my task so much easier.

John A Vlahides

I owe tremendous gratitude to Paula Hardy, Caroline Sieg, Nicola Williams, Laura Crawford and Annelies Mertens. For holding my hand when I most needed it, I'm forever indebted to Brandon Presser, Brice Gosnell, Marg Toohey, Alexis Averbuck, and Emilie Filou. Doors in France opened because of the generosity of spirit of Louis-Paul Astraud, Valère Carlin, Elodie Rothan, Claude Benard, Rabiha Benaissa, Greg Joye, Audrey Parot, and Anne-Marie Rohm. For their help with details, thanks to Michel Caraisco, Florence Lecointre, Myriam Chokairy, Frédérique Tamet, Audric Jaubert, Guillaume Jahan de Lestang, and Jean-François Gourdon. *Merci mille fois à tous!*

ACKNOWLEDGMENTS

Climate map data adapted from Peel MC, Finlayson BL & McMahon TA (2007) 'Updated World Map of the Köppen-Geiger Climate Classification', *Hydrology and Earth System Sciences*, 11, 163344.

Illustrations p48-9, p62-3, p140-1, p228-9, p798-9 and p862-3 by Javier Zarracina.

Cover photograph: Lavender field, Provence, Bethune Carmichael, Many of the images in this guide are available for licensing from Lonely Planet Images: www.lonelyplanetimages.com.

This Book

For this 9th edition of France, Nicola Williams coordinated a skilled team of authors composed of Alexis Averbuck, Oliver Berry, Stuart Butler, Jean-Bernard Carillet, Kerry Christiani, Steve Fallon, Emilie Filou, Catherine Le Nevez, Tom Masters, Daniel Robinson, Miles Roddis and John A Vlahides. Nicola, Oliver, Steve, Emilie, Catherine, Daniel and Miles also made major contributions to previous editions, as did Teresa Fisher, Jeremy Gray, Annabel Hart, Paul Hellander, Jonathan Knight, Leanne Logan, Oda O'Carroll, Jeanne Oliver and Andrew Stone. This guidebook was commissioned in Lonely Planet's London office, and produced by the following:

Commissioning Editors
Paula Hardy, Joanna Potts

Coordinating Editor Laura Crawford
Coordinating Cartographer Valentina Kremenchutskaya
Coordinating Layout Designer Jim Hsu
Managing Editor Annelies Mertens
Managing Cartographer Herman So
Managing Layout Designers Laura Jane, Celia Wood
Assisting Editors Holly Alexander, Janet Austin, Janice Bird, Michala Green, Jocelyn Harewood, Kate James, Jackey Coyle, Peter Cruttenden, Katie O'Connell, Charlotte Orr, Alison Ridgway, Branislava Vladisavljevic
Assisting Cartographers Enes Basic, Hunor Csutoros, Julie Dodkins, Mark Griffiths, Amanda Sierp

Assisting Layout Designers Kerrianne Southway
Cover Research Naomi Parker
Internal Image Research Aude Vauconsant

Thanks to Mark Adams, Jane Atkin, Judith Bamber, Imogen Bannister, David Connolly, Melanie Dankel, Stefanie Di Trocchio, Janine Eberle, Ryan Evans,Joshua Geoghegan, Mark Germanchis, Michelle Glynn, Lauren Hunt, Laura Jane, David Kemp, Indra Kilfoyle, Yvonne Kirk, Lisa Knights, Nic Lehman, Katie Lynch, John Mazzocchi, Dan Moore, Wayne Murphy, Darren O'Connell, Trent Paton, Adrian Persoglia, Piers Pickard, Averil Robertson, Lachlan Ross, Michael Ruff, Julie Sheridan, Lyahna Spencer, Laura Stansfeld, John Taufa, Sam Trafford, Gina Tsarouhas, Juan Winata, Emily Wolman, Nick Wood

BEHIND THE SCENES

index

Map Pages **p000**
Image Pages **p000**

how to use this book

These symbols will help you find the listings you want:

- ⊙ Sights
- 🏃 Activities
- 🐢 Courses
- 👉 Tours
- 🎊 Festivals & Events
- 🛏 Sleeping
- 🍴 Eating
- 🍷 Drinking
- ☆ Entertainment
- 🔒 Shopping
- ℹ Information/Transport

Look out for these icons:

TOP CHOICE	Our author's recommendation
FREE	No payment required
🌿	A green or sustainable option

Our authors have nominated these places as demonstrating a strong commitment to sustainability – for example by supporting local communities and producers, operating in an environmentally friendly way, or supporting conservation projects.

These symbols give you the vital information for each listing:

- 🎵 Telephone Numbers
- ⊙ Opening Hours
- P Parking
- ⊖ Nonsmoking
- ❄ Air-Conditioning
- @ Internet Access
- 🛜 Wi-Fi Access
- 🏊 Swimming Pool
- 🥗 Vegetarian Selection
- 📖 English-Language Menu
- 👪 Family-Friendly
- 🐾 Pet-Friendly
- 🚌 Bus
- ⛴ Ferry
- Ⓜ Metro
- Ⓢ Subway
- ⊖ London Tube
- 🚊 Tram
- 🚆 Train

Reviews are organised by author preference.

Map Legend

Sights
- ⊙ Beach
- ⊙ Buddhist
- ⊙ Castle
- ⊙ Christian
- ⊙ Hindu
- ⊙ Islamic
- ⊙ Jewish
- ⊙ Monument
- ⊙ Museum/Gallery
- ⊙ Ruin
- ⊙ Winery/Vineyard
- ⊙ Zoo
- ⊙ Other Sight

Activities, Courses & Tours
- ⊙ Diving/Snorkelling
- ⊙ Canoeing/Kayaking
- ⊙ Skiing
- ⊙ Surfing
- ⊙ Swimming/Pool
- ⊙ Walking
- ⊙ Windsurfing
- • Other Activity/Course/Tour

Sleeping
- ⊙ Sleeping
- ⊙ Camping

Eating
- ⊙ Eating

Drinking
- ⊙ Drinking
- ⊙ Cafe

Entertainment
- ⊙ Entertainment

Shopping
- ⊙ Shopping

Information
- ⊙ Post Office
- ⊙ Tourist Information

Transport
- ⊙ Airport
- ⊗ Border Crossing
- ⊙ Bus
- ⊕ Cable Car/Funicular
- ⊙ Cycling
- ⊙ Ferry
- Ⓜ Metro
- ⊙ Monorail
- P Parking
- Ⓢ S-Bahn
- ⊙ Taxi
- ⊙ Train/Railway
- ⊙ Tram
- ⊙ Tube Station
- Ⓤ U-Bahn
- • Other Transport

Routes
- Tollway
- Freeway
- Primary
- Secondary
- Tertiary
- Lane
- Unsealed Road
- Plaza/Mall
- Steps
-)≡(Tunnel
- Pedestrian Overpass
- Walking Tour
- Walking Tour Detour
- Path

Boundaries
- — — — International
- State/Province
- — — Disputed
- Regional/Suburb
- Marine Park
- Cliff
- Wall

Population
- ● Capital (National)
- ◉ Capital (State/Province)
- ● City/Large Town
- • Town/Village

Geographic
- ⊕ Hut/Shelter
- ⊙ Lighthouse
- ⊙ Lookout
- ▲ Mountain/Volcano
- ⊙ Oasis
- ⊙ Park
-)(Pass
- ⊙ Picnic Area
- ⊙ Waterfall

Hydrography
- River/Creek
- Intermittent River
- Swamp/Mangrove
- Reef
- Canal
- Water
- Dry/Salt/Intermittent Lake
- Glacier

Areas
- Beach/Desert
- Cemetery (Christian)
- Cemetery (Other)
- Park/Forest
- Sportsground
- Sight (Building)
- Top Sight (Building)

Miles Roddis

Languedoc-Roussillon Living over the Pyrenees in Valencia (Spain) Miles and his wife, Ingrid, visit France for work or simply for fun at least once a year. Among more than 50 Lonely Planet titles that he has written or contributed to are six editions of this guide plus regional guidebooks to Languedoc-Roussillon, Corsica, Brittany and Normandy and – most satisfyingly of all – *Walking in France*.

John A Vlahides

Provence, The French Riviera & Monaco John A Vlahides co-hosts the TV series *Lonely Planet: Roads Less Travelled*, screening on National Geographic Channels International. John worked as a French-English interpreter in Paris, where he also studied cooking with the same chefs who trained Julia Child. He's a former luxury-hotel concierge and member of *Les Clefs d'Or*, the international union of the world's elite concierges. John lives in northern California, and looks forward to returning to Provence during tomato season. For more, see johnvlahides.com and twitter.com/johnvlahides.

Kerry Christiani

Alsace & Lorraine, French Alps & the Jura Mountains, Directory A-Z Kerry has been travelling to France since her school days to brush up her *français*, which she studied to MA level. On clear days, she can just about spy the Vosges from her home in the Black Forest, an hour's drive from the French border. For this edition, Kerry overindulged in Alsace, experienced whiteout in Chamonix and was among the first to step foot in the new Centre Pompidou-Metz. Kerry is also the author of Lonely Planet guides to Germany, Switzerland and Austria.

Jean-Bernard Carillet

Corsica Paris-based (and Metz-born) journalist and photographer, Jean-Bernard was delighted to research his own turf – it proved to be an exhilarating experience. He has clocked up countless trips to all French regions and written extensively about Provence, the Basque Country, Brittany, Alsace and, of course, Corsica. As an incorrigible Frenchman and foodie, he confesses a pronounced penchant for the robust Corsican cuisine, but regularly burns off the calories by meandering along hiking trails in central Corsica or diving the Gulf of Porto.

Steve Fallon

Around Paris, History Steve, who has worked on every edition of *France* except the first, visited Paris for the first time at age 16 to drink *vin ordinaire* from plastic bottles and learn swear words, but returned five years later to complete a degree at the Sorbonne in proper French (and drink proper wine). Now based in East London, Steve gets over to the 'City of Light' frequently and will be just one Underground stop away when Eurostar trains finally start departing from Stratford.

Read more about Steve at:
lonelyplanet.com/members/stevefallon

Emilie Filou

The French Riviera & Monaco Emilie was born in Paris but spent most of her childhood holidays roaming the south of France and the Alps. She left France to travel when she was 18 and never quite made it back. She studied geography at Oxford and took a grand total of three gap years to see more of Africa, Asia and the Pacific. She is now settled in London, where she works as a journalist. She still goes to the Riviera every summer.

Read more about Emily at:
lonelyplanet.com/members/emiliefilou

Catherine Le Nevez

Lyon & the Rhône Valley; Massif Central; Limousin, the Dordogne & the Lot Catherine's wanderlust kicked in when she road-tripped throughout France from her Parisian base, aged four, and she's been road-tripping across the country at every opportunity since, completing her Doctorate of Creative Arts in Writing, Masters in Professional Writing, and qualifications in Editing and Publishing along the way. Catherine has authored or co-authored over two dozen guidebooks worldwide, including previous editions of this book, Lonely Planet's *Paris Encounter* and *Provence & the Côte d'Azur*, as well as newspaper and magazine articles.

Tom Masters

Normandy, Brittany Tom grew up in England and France to francophone parents who inculcated a love of all things French from childhood. With his parents now residing in Paris and rural Brittany, France's northwestern chunk seemed to be the natural place for Tom to research between obsessive-compulsive crêpe stops. His best experience while researching this guide was getting caught up in a local wedding in Roscoff and partying with the locals until dawn. You can read more of his work at www.tommasters.net.

Read more about Tom at:
lonelyplanet.com/members/tommasters

Daniel Robinson

Lille, Flanders & the Somme; Champagne; Transport Over the past two decades, Daniel's articles and guidebooks – published in 10 languages – have covered every region of France, but he is particularly fond of the creativity and panache – and foresighted public-transport initiatives – of dynamic northern cities such as Lille and Reims. Brought up in the US and Israel, Daniel holds degrees from Princeton University and Tel Aviv University. His travel writing appears in the *New York Times* and various magazines.

OUR STORY

A beat-up old car, a few dollars in the pocket and a sense of adventure. In 1972 that's all Tony and Maureen Wheeler needed for the trip of a lifetime – across Europe and Asia overland to Australia. It took several months, and at the end – broke but inspired – they sat at their kitchen table writing and stapling together their first travel guide, *Across Asia on the Cheap*. Within a week they'd sold 1500 copies. Lonely Planet was born.

Today, Lonely Planet has offices in Melbourne, London and Oakland, with more than 600 staff and writers. We share Tony's belief that 'a great guidebook should do three things: inform, educate and amuse'.

OUR WRITERS

Nicola Williams

Coordinating Author, Plan Your Trip, Paris, France Today, The French, Bon Appétit, French Wine, The Arts, Architecture Independent travel writer and editorial consultant Nicola Williams has lived in France and written about it for more than a decade. From her hillside house on the southern shore of Lake Geneva, it's a quick and easy hop to the French Alps (call her a ski fiend...), Paris (...art buff), southern France (...foodie). Paris this time around meant stylish apartment living in the heart of St-Germain des Prés. Nicola has worked on numerous Lonely Planet titles, including *France, Discover France, Paris, Provence & the Côte d'Azur* and *The Loire*. She blogs at tripalong. wordpress.com and tweets @Tripalong.

Read more about Nicola at:
lonelyplanet.com/members/nicolawilliams

Alexis Averbuck

The Loire Valley, Burgundy, Provence Alexis Averbuck first came to France when she was four and now visits every chance she gets. Whether sipping wines in Burgundy, château-hopping in the Loire or careening through hilltop villages in Provence (she also contributes to Lonely Planet's *Provence & the Côte d'Azur*), she immerses herself in all things French. A travel writer for two decades, Alexis has lived in Antarctica for a year, crossed the Pacific by sailboat and is also a painter – see her work at www.alexisaverbuck.com.

Read more about Alexis at:
lonelyplanet.com/members/alexisaverbuck

Oliver Berry

The Pyrenees, Toulouse Area Oliver's French love affair began at the age of two, and he's since travelled practically every inch of the country while contributing to several editions of Lonely Planet's *France* guide, among other books. Research highlights for this edition included tackling the trails of the Pyrenees, cruising the Canal du Midi, and seeing the sun rise over the Cirque du Troumouse. He currently lives in Cornwall and works as a writer and photographer. You can see his latest work at www.oliverberry.com.

Read more about Oliver at:
lonelyplanet.com/members/oliverberry

Stuart Butler

Atlantic Coast, French Basque Country, Lyrical Landscapes Stuart's first encounters with southwest France came on family holidays. When he was older he spent every summer surfing off the beaches of the southwest until one day he found himself so hooked on the region that he was unable to leave – he has been there ever since. When not writing for Lonely Planet he hunts for uncharted surf on remote coastlines. The results of these trips appear frequently in international surf media. His website is www.oceansurfpublications.co.uk.

OVER PAGE | MORE WRITERS

Published by Lonely Planet Publications Pty Ltd
ABN 36 005 607 983
9th edition – Mar 2011
ISBN 978 1 74179 594 3
© Lonely Planet 2011   Photographs © as indicated 2011
10 9 8 7 6 5 4 3 2 1
Printed in China